Y0-BUT-260

TRANSACTIONS

OF THE

AMERICAN SOCIETY

OF

CIVIL ENGINEERS

(INSTITUTED 1852)

VOLUME 92

1928

Edited by the Secretary, under the direction of the Committee on Meetings and Publications.

NEW YORK
PUBLISHED BY THE SOCIETY

1928

NOTE.—This Society is not responsible for any statement made or opinion expressed in its publications.

CONTENTS

PAPERS

MEMOIRS OF DECEASED MEMBERS

ERRATA

Transactions Vol. 88 (1925)

Page 1194, Lines 1 and 3 from bottom, for "p_5", read "P_5".
Page 1204, Fig. 27(*b*), for "c_y", read "e_y".

Transactions Vol. 90 (1927)

Page 486, Equation (29*a*), last term in first bracket, for "$\frac{\sin 2\,\phi_1}{\phi_1}$", read "$\frac{\sin^2 \phi_1}{\phi_1}$".

Page 541, Equation (109), last term, for "$(\phi_1 + \sin 2\,\phi_2)$", read "$(\phi_1 + \sin \phi_1)$".

Transactions Vol. 91 (1927)

Page 519, "Fig. 6" should read "Fig. 7" and "Fig. 7" should read "Fig. 6".

Page 524, Line 27 from top, for "$\frac{12}{17}$-in. outlet pipe", read "12-in. outlet pipe".

Page 716, Line 27 from top, statements in second and third sentences of discussion by W. H. R. Nimmo, Assoc. M. Am. Soc. C. E., are in error owing to the fact that the effect of the value of Poisson's ratio was not taken into account.

PAPERS AND REPORTS OF SPECIAL COMMITTEES PUBLISHED IN PROCEEDINGS, AM. SOC. C. E., AUGUST, 1927, TO MAY, 1928, INCLUSIVE, NOT PUBLISHED IN TRANSACTIONS, VOL. 92.

* Published in *Proceedings* only.

AMERICAN SOCIETY OF CIVIL ENGINEERS
INSTITUTED 1852

TRANSACTIONS

Paper No. 1656

AUTOMOBILE HAZARD IN CITIES AND ITS REDUCTION*

By William J. Cox,† Jun. Am. Soc. C. E.‡

With Discussion by Messrs. William T. Lyle, M. O. Eldridge, C. W. Stark, L. G. Holleran, S. Johannesson, W. Graham Cole, Harold M. Lewis, J. K. Finch, G. G. Kelcey, Raymond A. O'Hara, John A. Miller, Jr., T. Kennard Thomson, W. W. Crosby, Theodore T. McCrosky, R. S. Kirby, Lee S. Trainor, Sidney J. Williams, A. B. Barber, and William J. Cox.

Synopsis

This paper directs attention to the great variations in the hazard of automobile operation in the larger cities of the United States; shows what this variation is; derives a theoretical formula to account for it; shows the applicability of this formula to cities of the United States; and discusses conclusions resulting from the investigation, which show the great extent to which street hazard is controllable by proper city planning and zoning measures.

Introduction

In taking first place among the causes of accidental deaths in this country the automobile has created a serious accident problem. Its solution has been attempted almost wholly by the use of police or regulatory measures, rather than by the application of engineering principles. State highway engineers, it is true, study highway safety and, sometimes, give it an important place in their design. City engineers have given some attention to safe road surfaces, to the improvement of especially dangerous corners, and other such details; but from the broader standpoint of city planning, the problem of traffic accidents has received little attention.

* Presented at the meeting of May 4, 1927.

† Asst. Prof., Dept. of Eng. Mechanics, Sheffield Scientific School, Yale Univ., New Haven, Conn.

‡ Now Assoc. M. Am. Soc. C. E.

Yet street safety is certainly one of the problems of the city planner. It is just as important that streets be safe as that they be convenient. This is realized in an abstract way, and the principle is applied in such obvious matters as grade separation at extra hazardous intersections; but street safety has held so little place in the minds of city planners that no fundamental analysis has been made of the automobile hazard with the object of determining the extent to which it is controlled by the physical characteristics of a city, and by what characteristics.

Failure to attempt such analysis has no doubt resulted from a general impression that personal factors, such as effectiveness of police control of traffic, carefulness of pedestrians, and average driving skill, together with variations in the ratio of automobiles to population, account for such differences as may exist in the hazard of automobile operation in different cities. This erroneous idea, in turn, no doubt rests on a general lack of knowledge of the tremendous variation in that hazard between cities of the same size, a variation so great and of such nature as to be accounted for only on the basis of controlling physical differences in the cities themselves rather than by personal differences in their inhabitants.

The hazard variation being what it is, discovery of its underlying cause is important because of the light it may throw on means of hazard reduction. The primary purpose of this paper, therefore, is to find this cause.

Accident Frequencies in Various Cities

The average driver of a private passenger automobile in New York, N. Y., will probably injure (or possibly kill) some one with his automobile about once in six years. If an operator goes eight years without such an accident either he drives less than the average, or he is an unusually good driver, or is exceptionally lucky. In Indianapolis, Ind., however, on the basis of present conditions, the driver of a private passenger car who is responsible for more than one personal injury accident in his entire lifetime of driving, is below par in driving skill, or drives more than the average, or is attended with worse luck.

This is not a random assertion, but a statement based on accurate records of the casualty insurance companies. For every 100 automobile public liability insurance policies (covering personal injury accidents) written in 1922 on private passenger cars by a large group of insurance carriers in New York City, 16.6 accidents involving personal injury claims resulted. For every 100 such policies written in Indianapolis, Ind., in 1922, only 2.7 such accidents resulted. Most other large cities fall between these two extremes. In Buffalo, N. Y., there were 9.6 accidents; in Chicago, Ill., 6.6; and in Detroit, Mich., 4.0, per 100 policies.*

It will be shown subsequently that the rate charged for this insurance in any large city is so established that it may be accepted as a fair criterion of the personal injury hazard of operation of a private passenger automobile. Consequently, the variation in rates from city to city measures the variation

* 1922 policy year experience, National Bureau of Casualty and Surety Underwriters, New York City.

in driving hazard. Table 1 shows this variation in rates (and in hazard) for a few representative cities.

Throughout this paper the expressions, "automobile hazard" and "hazard of automobile operation", unless otherwise specifically noted, mean the hazard to which an individual automobile operator is subject, of inflicting injury on some one with his automobile. It does not mean the hazard of injury to which the operator himself or a pedestrian is subject. It is the hazard involved in driving an automobile.

Importance of Differences in Hazard

Few people realize that these great differences in driving hazard exist. The automobile accident situation has become so serious in practically every city as to obscure this fact. These differences, however, are of tremendous importance; the annual cost of public liability insurance for all the automobiles in New York City would be in excess of $75 000 000. This may be taken as less rather than more than the economic loss from personal injuries from automobile accidents, as the administrative cost of handling this business, which of course is included in the rates charged, is offset by the facts that, in a collision between two automobiles, this insurance covers the injuries sustained by only one of the parties to the accident, and that in a collision between an automobile and a pedestrian (if contributory negligence on the part of the pedestrian is shown) the pedestrian is likely to receive little or no indemnification for his injuries. Therefore, accepting the cost of insurance as the economic loss (from personal injuries only) the annual cost of these in New York City is at least $75 000 000. If the hazard in New York were the same as that in Chicago, the resulting injury cost would be reduced to about $28 000 000 per year, and the resulting saving would be about $47 000 000.

TABLE 1.—Automobile Public Liability Insurance Rates, in Percentages of the Rate for New York City.*

Place.	Percentage.	Place.	Percentage.
New York, N. Y.	100	Detroit, Mich.	27
Buffalo, N. Y.	52	Atlanta, Ga.	24
Philadelphia, Pa.	50	Washington, D. C.	22
Cleveland, Ohio	46	New Orleans, La.	22
Providence, R. I.	40	Los Angeles, Calif.	22
Chicago, Ill.	37	Indianapolis, Ind.	20

* Based on 1924 Manual of Automobile Insurance, National Bureau of Casualty and Surety Underwriters, New York City.

Investigation of this hazard variation with a view of determining why it exists and whether it must necessarily exist is, therefore, worth while. A superficial examination of rates shows no necessary reason for its existence. It can be noted that rates are generally higher in large than in small cities; higher in the East and North than in the West and South; and higher in old than in new cities.

There are so many exceptions, however, to each of these rules as to make it apparent that none of them controls the hazard. If the hazard is greater in large, old, Eastern cities, it is not because of their size, age, or geographical location, but rather because of some other factor which usually, but far from invariably, accompanies size, age, and certain geographical locations. The problem, then, is to discover this unknown controlling factor.

Measure of Hazard Variation

Before attempting the solution, however, the validity of the standard selected for measuring hazard variation will be explained briefly. In discussions of the automobile problem the automobile death rate in terms of population is usually invoked to show the seriousness of the situation; and, properly, because this seriousness bears a relationship to the proportion of the population killed, rather than to the number of automobiles which did the killing. In discussing why the death rate is what it is, however, the ratio of automobiles to population cannot be neglected. The City of Los Angeles, Calif., for example, with one car to each three persons, would be expected to have more automobile fatalities in proportion to population than the City of New York, with one car to each fifteen persons. What is not necessarily expected is that New York, instead of having one-fifth or one-sixth as many fatalities in proportion to population as Los Angeles, should have one-half as many; in other words, that the death rate per automobile should be three times as great in New York as in Los Angeles.

This is a significant fact in the problem. Automobile use will continue and doubtless will increase. Improvement will not come about by reduction of the number of automobiles in use, but by reduction of the damage attributable to each automobile. Anything that decreases the hazard created by each automobile will decrease the total automobile hazard. Hence, the individual automobile and the hazard created by the individual automobile are the starting points, and hazard variation must be correlated with registration of automobiles rather than with population.

On this basis, the first measure of hazard which comes to mind is the ratio of automobile fatalities to automobile registrations; but the proportion of accidents that result fatally is small, and is not uniform between cities. Data from some localities indicate as many as four or five fatalities per hundred personal injury automobile accidents, whereas other localities apparently have only two or three fatalities from a hundred such accidents.* Also, for all but the very largest cities, automobile fatalities are not so numerous as to furnish fatality rates comparatively unaffected by chance, and in consequence wide variations occur from year to year. Further still, reliable figures for automobile registrations in cities are largely lacking. For these reasons, fatality rates are not available as a satisfactory measure of the hazard of automobile operation.

Insurance Rates as Measure

Automobile liability insurance rates, however, do furnish a reasonably accurate index, and practically the only index, as the larger insurance com-

* Report of Committee on Statistics, First National Conference on Street and Highway Safety, p. 11. The great deviations between the ratios given for different cities (from slightly more than one fatality per hundred injuries to six fatalities per hundred injuries) are no doubt, as noted in the report, largely due to differences as between cities in definitions of an "injury" and in methods of reporting accidents, but must also reflect considerable differences in the true ratios.

panies are the only agencies which deal with automobile accidents, both fatal and non-fatal, on a nation-wide basis. This index is not wholly satisfactory, first because not all automobiles carry insurance, and, secondly, because no one insurance policy covers the entire hazard. It is, however, the best index available. There is no reason to believe that the hazard created by an insured car is materially different from that created by an uninsured car; or at least that the difference in hazard created by the two classes of cars varies materially between cities. Although separate policies are written to cover the personal injuries and the property damage resulting from automobile accidents, if automobile public liability rates are accepted as the index, they will broaden the scope to include the hazard of all personal injuries of any moment, whether fatal or not. Such injuries constitute the bulk of the automobile problem. These rates, as applied to private passenger cars, were used in Table 1.

Rate-Making

"Public liability" insurance is an automobile owner's insurance against legal liability for personal injuries which may result from operation of his insured car. From a somewhat haphazard system in the early days of the automobile, rate-making has reached a high degree of accuracy, so that now the public liability insurance rate of a large city may be considered a satisfactory measure of the legal liability hazard which automobile operation in that city entails. Subsequently it will be shown that the total chance of inflicting personal injury (whether the injury results in legal liability or not) is proportional to the legal liability hazard. Therefore, the variation in public liability insurance rates (Table 1) also measures the variation in the chance of injuring some one while driving an automobile.

Rates for this insurance are promulgated annually by a bureau maintained for this purpose by about thirty of the leading stock casualty insurance companies. Each member company furnishes this bureau with its loss experience, and in this way a sufficient body of experience to serve as a reliable guide is accumulated. Practically all automobile liability insurance written in the United States is based on rates established by this bureau.

For establishment of these rates, the country is divided into 251 territories (consisting each of a large city and its closest suburbs) or territorial groups (consisting each of several small cities or several counties). For each of these territories or groups separate loss experience is secured. In some cases the volume of exposure of a territory or group is not sufficiently large to be fairly indicative, and further combination is necessitated. However, for each community that develops a sufficient exposure (and this includes most of the larger cities, say, of 200 000 population and more) rates are calculated from the community's individual data and are in consequence a reflection of that community's traffic hazard.

The method of establishing the rates on private cars is as follows:* The number of cars insured in the community during each of the three preceding years is ascertained, and also the losses incurred in each of these years as indem-

* For a full discussion of this subject see "Automobile Rate-Making," by H. P. Stellwagen, *Proceedings*, Casualty Actuarial Soc., Vol. XI, Pt. 2.

nities for accidents attributable to the insured cars. Dividing the losses for each year by the number of cars insured, and averaging the three resulting quotients, gives the average loss per car or "pure premium". This average "pure premium" is weighted by a fixed percentage to cover the administrative cost of the business and the average rate is thus determined for each community or group. For purposes of business administration these groups are then combined into a much smaller number of "rate territories", in each of which the rate is the average of the rates of the groups included in that "rate territory". The units comprising any given territory may be widely scattered over the country, but the average rate assessed against all localities which are placed in any one rate territory is within a very few per cent. of the rate determined individually for each group placed in that territory. Sixteen (in 1924 and 1925) average public liability rates for private passenger cars are thus established, some one of which will apply to any locality in the United States. Finally, by another set of calculations differentials are obtained which are applied to the average rate to give the actual listed rate for different makes of cars.

Thus, the variation in liability rates for private passenger cars, considering only cities large enough to be individually rated, is an accurate reflection of the public liability hazard for insured cars. There is no reason to believe that the hazard of operation of uninsured cars is materially different from that of insured cars; the variation of rates from city to city for commercial cars and public vehicles is nearly the same as for private passenger cars; and private passenger cars very largely predominate in every city. For these reasons the variation of rates for private passenger cars (Table 1) may be taken to indicate the variation in public liability hazard of all automobile operation in such cities.

What, then, is the reason for this great variation, and what is the determinant of a hazard that varies so widely from one city to another?

Theoretical Derivation of Formula for Hazard Variation

For purposes of analysis, imagine a city in which traffic, both vehicular and pedestrian, is distributed uniformly over the entire street mileage, all paved; in which no automobile accidents occur except collisions of automobiles with other automobiles and with pedestrians; in which all automobiles are of the same type, and are the only vehicles in use; and in which the percentage of automobiles in use at any given time is the same as the percentage of the population using the streets as pedestrians at that same time.

Let H = the hazard that results from the annual use in this city of the average automobile (average in respect to total annual mileage, maintenance, and driving skill).

h = the hazard that results from operation of this automobile through a unit distance.

h_a and h_p = the components of this hazard that relate to collisions with other automobiles and with pedestrians, respectively.

Then,

$$h = h_a + h_p$$

Let M = the street mileage of the city.
P = the population of the city.
R = the number of automobiles registered in the city.
a = the average number of occupants of each automobile in use.
p and r = the number of pedestrians and of automobiles, respectively, that the average automobile passes from any direction in traveling a unit distance.

As pedestrians and automobiles are uniformly distributed over the streets of the city, $p \propto \frac{P - a R}{M}$ and $r \propto \frac{R}{M}$.

As every time an automobile passes a pedestrian or another automobile, there is danger of a collision, obviously, $h_p \propto p$ and $h_a \propto r$.

Then,

$$h_p \propto \frac{P - a R}{M}, \text{ or } h_p = k_1 \frac{P - a R}{M}$$

and,

$$h_a \propto \frac{R}{M}, \text{ or } h_a = k_2 \frac{R}{M}$$

k_1 and k_2 being constants.

And,

$$h = k_1 \frac{P - a R}{M} + k_2 \frac{R}{M}$$

Let,

$$\frac{k_2}{k_1} = w$$

then,

$$h = k_1 \frac{P - a R}{M} + k_1 \frac{w R}{M}$$

or,

$$h \propto \frac{P - a R + w R}{M}$$

or,

$$h \propto \frac{P + (w - a) R}{M}$$

If $w = a$, (and it will be shown that from a public liability standpoint for cities of the United States this is approximately true), the expression becomes,

$$h \propto \frac{P}{M}$$

Also,

$$H \propto h;$$

then,

$$H \propto \frac{P}{M}$$

giving the basic relation of automobile hazard to physical surroundings.

This variation is rationally deduced and should express accurately (assuming that $a = w$) the elements of the public liability hazard of automobile operation in the hypothetical city. It does not necessarily follow that it accurately expresses the elements determining the hazard of operation in cities of the United States, because assumptions were made in the derivation of the formula which do not hold true, and the effect of these untrue assumptions on the applicability of the formula is problematical.

Test of Validity of the Formula

There is, however, the means of testing what this effect is, to what extent it invalidates applicability of the formula to American cities. The actual variation in hazard from one city to another is known from insurance rates. It has been shown that this variation covers a very wide range and that it is independent of the size, age, or geographical location of cities. The variation is also not caused by automobile congestion or by differences in the effectiveness of traffic control.

These possible causes of the variation can be quickly eliminated. If automobile congestion determined hazard, New York City, with a hazard four and one-half times that of Los Angeles, would have to have a vehicular congestion four and one-half times as great, not only in the center of the city, but in residential districts as well. This is not true. In fact, some cities in which automobile use is most extensive are those in which the hazard is least.

As to the variation being caused by differences in efficiency of traffic control, any such idea is disproved by study of the variation itself (see Fig. 3). The cities having the most advanced traffic regulation, as, for example, those in States embraced in the Eastern Conference of Motor Vehicle Administrators, often show the highest, not the lowest, hazards. If excellence of traffic regulation determined hazard, the variation would be in many respects just the reverse of what it is now. This is true because good traffic regulation is usually the outgrowth of high hazard—of conditions so intolerable that they force improvement.

On the other hand, if this hazard variation can be accounted for on the basis of the formula, $H \propto \frac{P}{M}$, very strong evidence will be furnished that this formula does correctly set forth the determinants of public liability hazard. If comparison of the variation calculated from the formula with the actual variation as known from insurance rates, reveals discrepancies, these discrepancies may serve to define the limitations of the formula or to indicate modifications that must be made before it will be applicable to cities of the United States.

Modification for Unpaved Streets

One such modification of the formula is necessary before this comparison of the calculated and actual variations can be attempted. In deriving the formula it was assumed that all streets of the hypothetical city were paved. In actual cities this is not true—the ratio of unpaved to paved mileage varies between wide limits. In applying the formula it is not fair wholly to disregard this unpaved mileage, nor should it be included at its face value. In a typical city in which the unpaved mileage makes up 25 or 30% of the total, the unpaved streets are largely on the outskirts of the city, where perhaps the majority of lots are vacant and the streets do not carry the traffic that would warrant their being paved. Hence, in including them with paved mileage, they should be weighted at much less than unity to indicate their much lower mile-for-mile value in distributing traffic and population.

Considering a city, however, in which there are several miles of unpaved streets for each mile of paved streets, a large portion of unpaved streets will be in outlying, partly developed areas, but a part will also be in built-up districts and will carry almost as much local traffic as they would carry if paved. These latter streets should be included with paved streets at not much less than their face value, or if both these classes of unpaved streets be lumped together (as must be done, practically) a higher coefficient should be used to express their average weighted value than was used for the typical city in which paved mileage exceeds the unpaved. This principle can be expressed as follows:

In determining the value of M in the expression, $H \propto \frac{P}{M}$, paved street mileage should be counted at its full face value, whereas unpaved street mileage should be multiplied by a coefficient less than one, this coefficient increasing, at a slowly decreasing rate, with the increase in the ratio of unpaved streets to total street mileage.

The values to be assigned this coefficient are wholly matters of judgment. It seems impossible to express exactly the relative importance of the two classes of streets in all cities by a single graph, but as an approximation sufficiently close for present purposes, the writer suggests Fig. 1.

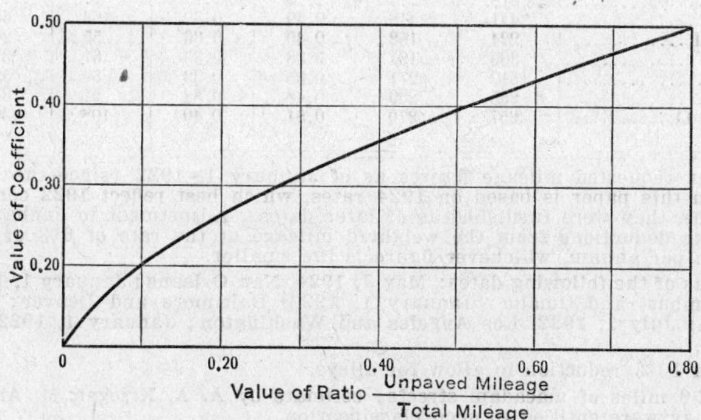

FIG. 1.—COEFFICIENTS TO BE USED IN WEIGHTING MILEAGES OF UNPAVED STREETS.

HANDLING OF WATER-BOUND MACADAM STREETS

In applying the principle of weighting unpaved mileage at less than a normal value, gravel and water-bound macadam streets present a problem. In most cities they could be classified as unpaved streets in that the surfacing is temporary, pending sufficient development to warrant improved paving.

In a few instances, however, the mileage of water-bound macadam streets is so great as to lead to a belief that it is continued in use on streets which have reached their full (usually residential) development. In this paper, therefore, the term, "paved streets", is restricted to include only types of paving better than water-bound macadam, except where the mileage of water-bound macadam exceeds that of the better types. In such cities (Providence, R. I., Denver, Colo., Worcester, Mass., and Hartford, Conn., for example) the excess of water-bound macadam over higher types of paving is considered as "paved".

TABLE 2.—STREET MILEAGES OF CITIES OF 200 000 POPULATION AND MORE.

City.	Paved mileage.†	Unpaved mileage.†	Ratio, unpaved / Total	Unpaved mileage coefficient.	Weighted unpaved mileage.	Weighted total mileage.	Adjusted weighted mileage,* M.
(1)	(2)	(3)	(4)	(5)	(6)	(7)	(8)
Akron, Ohio	143	257	0.64	0.44	113	256	256
Baltimore, Md.	657	173	0.21	0.27	47	704	694
¶Boston, Mass.	762	294	0.28	0.31	91	853	853
Buffalo, N. Y.	456	189	0.29	0.32	60	516	516
Chicago, Ill.	2 756	600	0.18	0.25	150	2 906	2 834
Cincinnati, Ohio	306	646	0.68	0.45	291‡	597‡	537‡
Cleveland, Ohio	657	293	0.31	0.33	97‡	754‡	678‡
Columbus, Ohio	340	110	0.24	0.29	32	372	359
Denver, Colo.	241	659	0.73	0.47	309	550	536
Detroit, Mich.	826	600	0.42	0.37	222	1 048	1 048
Indianapolis, Ind.	558	135	0.19	0.26	35	593	593
Los Angeles, Calif.	557	1 599	0.74	0.47	751‡	1 308‡	1 163‡
Louisville, Ky.	245§	99	0.29	0.32	32	277	273
Milwaukee, Wis.	446	58	0.12	0.22	13	459	459
‖Minneapolis and St. Paul, Minn.	334	1 116	0.77	0.48	536	870	870
New Orleans, La.	203	890	0.81	0.50	445	648	618
**New York, N. Y.	1 829	1 505	0.45	0.38	571	2 400	2 400
Omaha, Nebr.	290	380	0.56	0.42	159	449	414
Philadelphia, Pa.	1 177	.....	....	....	...	.....	1 413
Pittsburgh, Pa.	518	.....	....	....	...	.....	622
Portland, Ore.	441	418	0.49	0.39	163	604	504
††Providence, R. I.	224	152	0.40	0.36	55	279	279
Rochester, N. Y.	309	191	0.38	0.35	67	376	353
Seattle, Wash.	510	271	0.35	0.33	89	599	599
Toledo, Ohio	255	239	0.48	0.38	91	346	346
Washington, D. C.	257	270	0.51	0.40	108	365	357

* The writer requested mileage figures as of January 1, 1922 (since the hazard variation discussed in this paper is based on 1924 rates, which best reflect 1922 conditions), but, in some instances, they were furnished as of later dates. Adjustment to January 1, 1922, is as follows: Make deductions from the weighted mileage at the rate of 6% of the paved or unpaved mileage per annum, whichever figure is the smaller.

† Mileages as of the following dates: May 7, 1924, New Orleans; January 1, 1924, Chicago, Rochester, Columbus, and Omaha; January 1, 1923, Baltimore and Denver; September 1, 1922, Louisville; July 1, 1922, Los Angeles and Washington; January 1, 1922, in all other cases.

‡ Includes a 10% reduction to allow for alleys.

§ Includes 56 miles of macadam streets; estimate by A. A. Krieger, M. Am. Soc. C. E., indicated that they were entitled to such classification.

‖ Includes the Cities of Brookline, Cambridge, Chelsea, Everett, Malden, and Somerville which are included in Boston insurance territory.

¶ Minneapolis and St. Paul form one insurance territory.

** Excludes Staten Island, which is not included in New York City insurance territory.

†† Includes the City of Pawtucket, R. I., which is included in Providence insurance territory.

Table 2 shows mileages weighted in accordance with these principles for all cities in the United States of 200 000 population and more (except Newark and Jersey City, N. J., which will be discussed later) for which the writer has been able to secure the necessary data. These mileages will be used for the quantity, M, in the formula, $H \propto \frac{P}{M}$.

The data in Columns (1) and (2) of Table 2 (except for Philadelphia and Pittsburgh) were secured, if possible, from engineering departments; failing this, from municipal reference libraries, or other official sources. Paved mileages shown for Philadelphia and Pittsburgh are based on *Circular No. 9,* of the Asphalt Association, New York City, and are stated to come from official sources; figures include only paved mileage as defined in this paper, and are as of January 1, 1923; to convert these figures to weighted mileage as of January 1, 1922, they are arbitrarily increased by one-fifth their value.

VALUES OF a AND OF w

It remains, however, to justify the assumption made in deriving the formula—that the quantities, a and w, are approximately equal in cities of the United States. The symbol, a, represents the average number of occupants of each automobile in use. A traffic census taken by the writer in San Diego, Calif., in 1925, showed the average number of occupants of all types of cars, Sundays and week-days, to be 2.06. A similar census taken at the same time in Washington, showed an average of 2.0. Apparently, it can be assumed with little error that in any city the average number of occupants is not far from 2, and this value will be used for a.

The symbol, w, represents the ratio, $\frac{k_2}{k_1}$, these constants being used in the equation,

$$h = k_1 \frac{P - a\,R}{M} + k_2 \frac{R}{M}$$

As,

$$h_a = k_2 \frac{R}{M}$$

and,

$$h_p = k_1 \frac{P - a\,R}{M}$$

$$\frac{h_a}{h_p} = \frac{k_2\,R}{k_1\,P'}$$

in which, $P' = P - a\,R$.

Now the relative importance, $\frac{h_a}{h_p}$, of the hazard of collisions between two automobiles as compared with the hazard of collisions of an automobile with a pedestrian depends jointly on the relative severity and the relative frequency of these two types of collision. Investigation of about 1 500 accidents shows practically the same public liability resulting from a collision between two automobiles as from a collision between an automobile and a pedestrian. This number of accidents was not sufficiently large to serve as an entirely reliable guide, but in the absence of more complete data equal severity may be assumed for the two types of collisions. Therefore, their relative importance depends on their relative frequency, or,

$$\frac{h_a}{h_p} = \frac{f_a}{f_p}$$

in which, f_a and f_p represent the two frequencies. Equating the two values of $\frac{h_a}{h_p}$,

$$\frac{k_2 R}{k_1 P'} = \frac{f_a}{f_p}$$

or,

$$\frac{k_2}{k_1} = \frac{f_a}{f_p} \times \frac{P'}{R} = w$$

The next step is to consider the relative frequency, $\frac{f_a}{f_p}$, of collisions between two automobiles and collisions of an automobile with a pedestrian. For a city in which all travel was by automobile, obviously all accidents would be collisions between two automobiles (assuming only the two types of collisions here dealt with) and the ratio, $\frac{f_a}{f_p}$, would be infinity. In a city with very few automobiles in proportion to the population, practically all accidents would be collisions with pedestrians, and the value of the ratio would approach zero. Hence, if the abscissas of a set of co-ordinates represent values of $\frac{P'}{R}$ and the ordinates represent values of the ratio, $\frac{f_a}{f_p}$, this ratio will be expressed by a graph tangent to the Y-axis at plus infinity, and to the X-axis at plus infinity. Reliable data for the determination of intermediate points are lacking, as such data involve not only complete reports of both fatal and non-fatal personal injury accidents over a considerable period to establish the ratio, $\frac{f_a}{f_p}$, but also accurate figures for automobile registrations to establish the ratio, $\frac{P'}{R}$*. It is difficult to obtain trustworthy figures covering all these quantities in any one city. The writer has secured what appear to be fairly reliable figures for $\frac{f_a}{f_p}$, however, for ratios of $\frac{P'}{R}$, which are probably about 3.0, 6.2, and 14.0. These points are plotted on Fig. 2, on which is drawn also a hyperbolic curve such that any ordinate multiplied by its corresponding abscissa (that is, $\frac{f_a}{f_p} \times \frac{P'}{R}$, the product being the quantity, w), gives a value of 2. This curve fits the three plotted points (both co-ordinates to which, it

* These registrations, moreover, must be accurately divided into private passenger, commercial, and public passenger vehicles, since these latter two classes carry higher average rates than the first. Since P is much greater than R and since the ratio of "equivalent private passenger cars" to "actual private passenger cars" is about the same for most cities, this refinement can be neglected in the main formula without introducing errors greater than 1 or 2 per cent. It cannot, however, be omitted in the determination of w without introducing prohibitive errors.

will be recalled, are of somewhat doubtful accuracy) with sufficient exactness to permit the acceptance of 2 as the approximate value of w. This is especially true as the quantity, R, in the expression,

$$H \propto \frac{P + (w - a) R}{M}$$

is so much smaller than P for most cities that a considerable error in the value of the coefficient of R has a comparatively small effect on the value of H. Within the limits of exactness attempted in this paper, then, it may be assumed that $w = 2$, and, hence, that $a = w$. The expression,

$$H \propto \frac{P + (w - a) R}{M}$$

thus reduces to $H \propto \frac{P}{M}$.

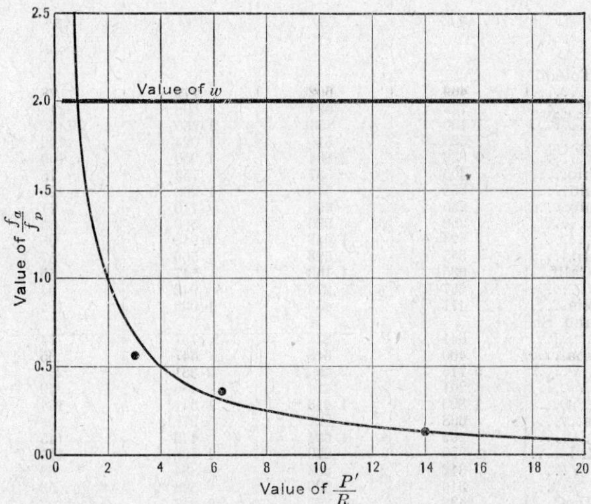

FIG. 2.—VALUES OF $\frac{f_a}{f_p}$ (RELATIVE FREQUENCIES OF ACCIDENTS TO AUTOMOBILES AND PEDESTRIANS) AND OF $\frac{f_a}{f_p} \times \frac{P'}{R}$ (OR w) FOR VARIOUS RATIOS OF $\frac{P'}{R}$ (PEDESTRIANS TO AUTOMOBILES).

"ACTUAL" AND "CALCULATED" HAZARD VARIATIONS

Proceeding with the comparison of the variation in public liability hazard as calculated from the formula with the actual variation shown by insurance rates, Table 3 shows these variations for all the cities included in Table 2. The Chicago rate is taken as the base, as percentages of which the other rates are shown. The population, P (Column (2)), is from the Census Bureau estimates of 1922.

The variation shown by insurance rates (Column (6) in Table 3) will hereafter be referred to as the "actual variation" in hazard, and the rate of any city (expressed as a percentage of the Chicago rate) will be termed its actual hazard. The hazard variation as determined from $H \propto \frac{P}{M}$ (Column (5) in

Table 3) will hereafter be referred to as the "calculated variation" and the hazard it shows for any city (expressed as a percentage of the Chicago hazard) will be termed the "calculated hazard" of that city.

Fig. 3 is a graphic comparison of the actual and calculated variations shown in Columns (5) and (6) of Table 3. To show the diversity in size of the cities entering into the comparison, the two variations are projected against a background proportional in width to the populations of the respective cities.

TABLE 3.—CALCULATED AND ACTUAL VARIATIONS IN HAZARD.

City.	Population, (P), in thousands.	Weighted street mileage, (M).	$\frac{P}{M}$	Calculated variation.*	Actual variation.*
(1)	(2)	(3)	(4)	(5)	(6)
†Akron and Toledo, Ohio	469	602	779	78	78
Baltimore, Md.	762	694	1 098	110	80
‡Boston, Mass.	1 150	853	1 350	135	125
Buffalo, N. Y.	528	516	1 024	102	142
Chicago, Ill.	2 833	2 834	1 000	100	100
Cincinnati, Ohio	405	537	753	75	75
Cleveland, Ohio	855	678	1 262	126	125
Columbus, Ohio	255	359	710	71	64**
Denver, Colo.	268	536	500	50	54
Detroit, Mich.	994	1 048	948	95	75
Indianapolis, Ind.	335	593	566	57	54**
Los Angeles, Calif.	635	1 163	547	55	59
Louisville, Ky.	257	273	942	94	80**
Milwaukee, Wis.	477	459	1 039	104	64
§Minneapolis and St. Paul, Minn.	641	870	737	74	80
New Orleans, La.	400	618	647	65	59
‖New York, N. Y.	5 715	2 400	2 381	238	273
Omaha, Nebr.	201	414	486	49	54**
Philadelphia, Pa.	1 895	1 413	1 341	134	137
Pittsburgh, Pa.	608	622	978	98	100
Portland, Ore.	269	604	446	45	59
¶Providence, R. I.	309	279	1 108	111	109
Rochester, N. Y.	312	353	884	88	92
Seattle, Wash.	316	599	528	53	59**
Washington, D. C.	438	357	1 227	123	59

* As percentages of the value for Chicago.

† Loss experience for these two cities is combined to get an indicative exposure for determination of their insurance rate (the calculated hazard for Akron alone would be 81 and for Toledo alone would be 75).

‡ Includes the Cities of Brookline, Cambridge, Chelsea, Everett, Malden, and Somerville.

§ Minneapolis and St. Paul form one insurance territory.

‖ Exclusive of Staten Island, which is not included in New York City insurance territory.

¶ Includes the City of Pawtucket.

** Determined from local loss experience combined with similar experience in smaller cities near-by, owing to insufficient volume of local loss experience.

AGREEMENT OF VARIATIONS—CITIES OF GROUP 1

The cities included in Fig. 3 have been divided into two groups. In Group 1, consisting of twenty-one cities in nineteen rate-making units, the average discrepancy between actual and calculated hazards is 6 per cent. Considering the seventeen cities (fifteen units) of the group for which the insurance rate is based on individual experience (and for which it is certain that the insurance rate is the true, rather than the approximate, actual hazard), the mean deviation is only 5 per cent. No one of these latter cities has a deviation of more than 10%, except New York City which shows a deviation of 13%, in the direction which would be anticipated from topographical and other peculiarities of that city and that insurance territory.

Any inaccuracies in the mileage figures used will hardly increase the mean deviation by more than 1 or 2%, if at all. As the expression, $H \propto \frac{P}{M}$, accounts for the hazard variation in three-fourths of the cities investigated, its applicability to the average city of the United States under 1922 conditions seems evident.

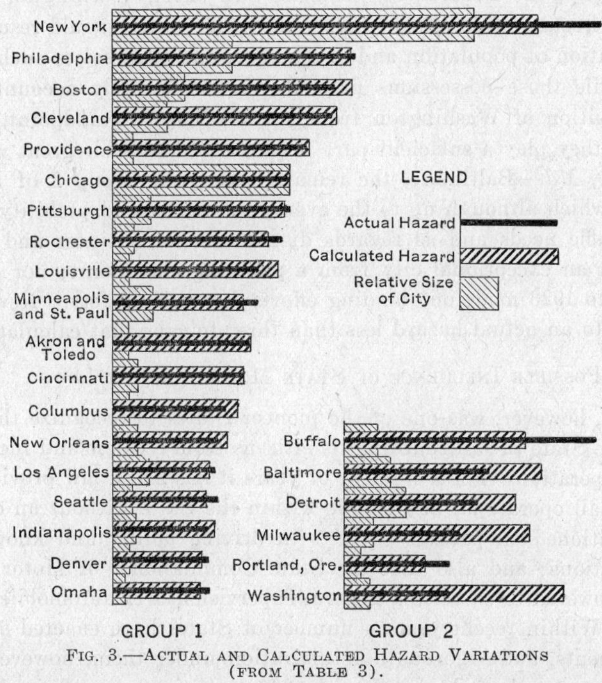

FIG. 3.—ACTUAL AND CALCULATED HAZARD VARIATIONS (FROM TABLE 3).

DISCREPANCIES IN VARIATIONS—CITIES OF GROUP 2

Referring to Group 2 of six cities, these show discrepancies between actual and calculated hazards ranging from 24% of the actual hazard for Portland, Ore., to 109% for Washington. A full discussion of the reasons underlying these discrepancies is beyond the scope of this paper. The formula, $H \propto \frac{P}{M}$, is applicable to actual cities only because the large number of factors which it fails to take into consideration seem usually to compensate for one another. Where the formula fails to apply, these factors fail to compensate, perhaps because of some one outstanding deviation from the average or of a number of minor variations all chancing to fall in the same direction. The deviations in the cases of Washington and Baltimore, however, suggest important conclusions.

Washington, D. C.—Washington shows the greatest discrepancy between actual and calculated hazards of any city of Fig. 3, the actual hazard being less than one-half the calculated. One explanation that immediately presents itself is the superior planning of the city. This includes the street layout, with its liberal widths of pavement, its set-back building lines, with consequent good sight distances at intersections, and its straight, continuous thoroughfares, almost free from "bottle-necks" and well distributed to carry the traffic of all sections of the city. In addition, it includes the satisfactory distribution of population which results from the absence of slums and crowded tenements and the satisfactory geographical distribution of the principal business of the city, the Federal Government. In short, Washington possesses a system of streets well designed to carry the traffic which should result from a good distribution of population and of business, and it possesses such a distribution. While these possessions probably do not entirely account for the favorable position of Washington from a traffic hazard standpoint, it seems certain that they play a sufficient part to make evident their great value.

Baltimore, Md.—Baltimore, the remaining city in Group 2 of Fig. 3, is an old city, which although up to the average as regards adaptability of street layout to traffic needs and as regards distribution of business and of population, is not an exceptional city from a planning standpoint; nor had it as a city prior to 1923 made outstanding efforts for traffic safety. Nevertheless, it is subject to an actual hazard less than three-fourths that calculated for it.

Possible Influence of State Motor Vehicle Laws

Maryland, however, was one of the pioneer States to recognize the responsibility of the State in safeguarding its citizens from reckless and incompetent automobile operation. For a number of years it has had a law providing that no citizen shall operate an automobile within the State without an operator's license conditioned on passage of tests in driving ability and knowledge of traffic regulations; and also that the State Commissioner of Motor Vehicles shall be empowered to exercise a general supervision over automobile accident conditions. Within recent years a number of States have enacted such laws. Such enactments, and vigorous administration under them, however, do not date back far enough to have affected 1922 conditions, except in Maryland, Connecticut, Massachusetts, and New Jersey. Hazard conditions in these States may serve to show whether there is support for the suggestion which Baltimore conditions make that such laws are effective in reducing the hazard of automobile operation below what it otherwise would be; and the extent to which the expression, $H \propto \frac{P}{M}$, which seems to hold good generally as between cities without this special type of legislation, applies between cities in States with this type of legislation.

Few cities in these States have populations of 200 000 or more for comparison with those already studied. Connecticut has no cities of this size, but has three cities with populations of 100 000, or more—Bridgeport, Hartford, and New Haven. These cities have the same insurance rate, derived from their combined loss experience (compare Akron and Toledo in Table 3). Since their actual hazard is the same, the three cities may be combined in this paper for comparison of both their calculated and actual hazards.

Similarly, eight cities in Massachusetts with populations of less than 200 000 are combined into one or more groups for determination of their insurance rate. The writer is not advised whether this hazard is determined from one grouping or several, but as all the cities have the same rate, it will be proper to consider them in one group for comparison of their actual and calculated hazards. These cities are Fall River, Haverhill, Lawrence, Lowell, Lynn, New Bedford, Springfield, and Worcester. The City of Boston, of course, will be considered separately, as its actual hazard is different from that of the grouped cities.

Baltimore is the only city in Maryland of sufficient size to warrant investigation in this connection.

New Jersey has two cities—Newark and Jersey City—with populations of more than 200 000. These cities were not included in Tables 2 and 3, nor in Fig. 3 because they are not their own metropolitan centers, but form part of the Metropolitan Area of New York City (U. S. Census Bureau classification) and this has a disturbing influence on their street hazard, which is thus somewhat indeterminate. This effect results principally from the fact that, owing to the suburban location of these cities, the ratio of daytime population to resident population differs from that of the average city. In the average city there is an influx from surrounding suburban and rural areas every morning, which flows out again at night, so that the daytime (and hazard-producing) population is greater than the resident population. It is assumed that this influx is proportional to the population of a city, in which case it has no effect on the expression $H \propto \frac{P}{M}$. This assumption apparently holds true for cities which are their own metropolitan centers, but in suburban insurance territories like Newark and Jersey City, the flow of population is outward in the morning and back again at night, so that in them there is a smaller, instead of a larger, daytime than resident population. This causes less congestion on the streets and lower hazard than there would be if the cities were isolated.

This effect is heightened in such cities, and particularly in Newark, by the fact that all the suburban area about New York City is divided into sections, each of which constitutes one insurance territory, although it may contain several cities. Thus, Jersey City territory contains Bayonne and several smaller cities and towns of Hudson County, and Newark territory contains Montclair, Summit, the Oranges, and other commuting centers.

A contrary effect to that just described results from through traffic, bound in and out of New York City and traversing these suburban areas. This adds to street congestion in these areas, and partly compensates for the outflow of commuters. The compensation is more complete in Jersey City territory than in Newark territory, as the former is less of a commuting area, and, also, being closer to New York, is traversed by more through traffic.

The net effect of these suburban conditions is indeterminate, but that there is such an effect, and that it is greater in the Newark territory than in the Jersey City territory should be kept in mind.

Table 4 shows populations, weighted street mileages, the ratio, $\frac{P}{M}$, and calculated and actual hazard variations (based on Chicago) for the cities which have been mentioned as being in States which in 1922 had the better type of motor-vehicle legislation.

The street mileages shown are paved and unpaved mileages weighted and combined in accordance with principles set forth previously. The figures for the larger cities are from local sources, usually engineer departments; those for the smaller cities are usually from local sources, but are supplemented in some instances by data from The Asphalt Association, with estimates of the mileage of unsurfaced streets. The error in the mileage figures should in all cases be less than 10 per cent. Hoboken, in Jersey City territory, and Irvington and Bloomfield, in Newark territory, are omitted from Table 4 because of lack of mileage data. The population figures are from 1922 Census estimates.

TABLE 4.—CALCULATED AND ACTUAL HAZARD VARIATIONS FOR CITIES IN CONNECTICUT, MARYLAND, MASSACHUSETTS, AND NEW JERSEY.

Cities.	Population, P, in thousands.	Weighted street mileage, M.	$\frac{P}{M}$.	Calculated variation.*	Actual variation.*
Connecticut:					
Bridgeport, Hartford, New Haven	452	420	1 075	108	78
Massachusetts:					
†Boston	1 150	853	1 350	135	125
Fall River, Haverhill, Lawrence, Lowell, Lynn, New Bedford, Springfield, Worcester	945	818	1 154	115	78
Maryland:					
Baltimore	762	694	1 098	110	80
New Jersey:					
‡Jersey City	463	255	1 818	182	125
§Newark	580	476	1 220	122	80

* As percentages of the value for Chicago.

† Includes Cities of Brookline, Cambridge, Chelsea, Everett, Malden, and Somerville.

‡ Includes Bayonne, West Hoboken, and West York, which are included in Jersey City insurance territory.

§ Includes Montclair, East Orange, Orange, West Orange, and Summit, which are included in Newark insurance territory.

INDICATED BENEFITS OF STATE CONTROL

Table 4 shows calculated hazards considerably greater than the actual hazards in all cases. For the Connecticut cities, for Baltimore, and for the smaller Massachusetts cities, the discrepancies between the two hazards are 28, 27, and 32%, respectively, of the calculated hazards. The discrepancy for

Boston is 7% of the calculated hazard, for Jersey City, 31%, and for Newark, 34 per cent.

As already noted the suburban location of Jersey City and Newark gives them unusual advantages in regard to the hazard of automobile operation, which have the effect of making actual hazards perhaps 5% lower in Jersey City and 10% lower in Newark than they would be if these cities were isolated. Making this allowance, the remaining discrepancies between their calculated and actual hazards become 28% of the calculated hazards in both cases. Then, for all the cities or groups in Table 4, except Boston, approximately the same discrepancy—about 28% of the respective calculated hazards—can be accounted for on the basis of a beneficent influence exercised by their motor-vehicle laws. As this discrepancy is so nearly the same in all cases, the following conclusions would be justified (except for Boston):

1.—As between themselves, the variation in public liability hazard of automobile operation is given by the expression, $H \propto \frac{P}{M}$.

2.—In comparison with other municipalities, cities in States having the better laws show this hazard to be from 25 to 30% lower in proportion to population congestion.

The fact that Boston has a calculated hazard only 7% in excess of the actual hazard still must be explained. As already noted, Washington benefits tremendously from a well-planned street layout. Boston, by reason of topography, age, and random growth many decades ago, suffers from street conditions which in many of the older parts of the city are more or less the antithesis of those from which Washington benefits. It would seem logical, therefore, that Boston should have an actual hazard larger than its calculated hazard by perhaps 20 per cent. Instead it is 7% smaller. This discrepancy of 27% is attributable to the State motor-vehicle law. Hence, Boston tends to confirm rather than to upset the conclusions just stated.

The first conclusion supports what the first group of cities in Fig. 3 indicated, namely, that the great determinant of the public liability hazard resulting from automobile operation is population density. Of the two conclusions just stated, this is the more important from an engineering standpoint—perhaps from any standpoint.

The second conclusion—that a well-drawn and well-administered motor-vehicle law is capable of greatly reducing this hazard—is of great importance, to every motorist and to every citizen. It is of particular importance to city or State officials concerned with accidents on streets and highways.

It is interesting to note what this decrease in hazard means in terms of money. According to the National Automobile Chamber of Commerce, the registration of automobiles in Massachusetts in 1924 was 486 952 private passenger cars and 83 626 commercial and public automobiles, the increase in registrations from 1922 to 1924 being 48 per cent. If it is conservatively estimated that the increase in registrations from 1924 to 1926 was only 25%, the 1926 figures will be 618 000 private passenger cars and 105 000 commercial and public vehicles. The average private passenger car public liability insurance rate in Massachusetts is about \$30. The average commercial or public vehicle rate is more than twice this, or at least \$65. The cost of public liability insurance in standard amounts for every automobile in the State for 1926 would thus be about \$25 000 000. As has been pointed out this is less rather than more than the economic loss from automobile personal injuries, which will approximate \$25 000 000 for the year. The automobile hazard level in Massachusetts cities has been shown to be only about 0.7 as high as the level which would be anticipated for them. If this difference between actual and anticipated levels prevails throughout the State, the anticipated personal injury loss for the year would be about \$36 000 000, \$11 000 000 more than it actually is. This \$11 000 000 represents a saving from decrease in personal injuries only, and, of course, is accompanied by a saving from decrease in property damage from automobile accidents. Placing this latter saving at less than half as much, or \$5 000 000, which seems conservative, the annual automobile accident loss in the State is \$16 000 000 less than would be expected.

The annual cost of administration of this law is about \$1 000 000 (\$648 725.90 for 1922, fiscal year).

"Natural" Variation in Hazard

It may be said that $\frac{P}{M}$ is the determinant of the "natural" level of public liability hazard resulting from operation of an automobile, and that the variation as between cities given by the expression, $H \propto \frac{P}{M}$, is the "natural" variation in this hazard, that is, the variation that would obtain if all cities were on a par as regards street layout and methods of traffic regulation.

Transition from Public Liability to Total Personal Injury Basis

Up to this point discussion has been limited to public liability hazard, because of the lack of any reliable check on the applicability of a theoretical formula to actual hazard conditions except the variation from city to city of automobile public liability rates. As has been shown these rates vary closely with the public liability hazard of automobile operation, which, consequently, is accounted for by the expression, $H \propto \frac{P}{M}$. This same variation, however, holds good not only as regards public liability hazard, but also for the hazard of all personal injuries which automobile operation may entail.

The expression, $H \propto \frac{P}{M}$, was related to public liability hazard; when in determining the value of w it was stated that as regards public liability the average collision between two automobiles is of the same severity as the average collision between an automobile and a pedestrian.

Since when two automobiles collide the total personal injuries inflicted by each, the car responsible for the accident and the car not responsible, upon occupants of the other, tend to be equal, the total personal injury from a collision between two automobiles tends to be twice the public liability. In a collision between an automobile and a pedestrian, public liability means legal liability of the motorist for injuries to the pedestrian. If the accident resulted wholly from some fault of the pedestrian, legal liability of the motorist does not exist; if it resulted from joint carelessness of both parties, the motorist's liability is at least curtailed.

It is impossible to determine the proportion of collisions between automobiles and pedestrians for which pedestrians are responsible. The smallest degree of responsibility is given by the Massachusetts Registry of Motor Vehicles, which reports pedestrian liability as from 35 to 40% of all automobile accidents involving pedestrians. Similar reports from New York State indicate about 50% responsibility; and from New York City (Police Department) and the State of Connecticut, somewhat more than 50 per cent.

Probably one-half, or a little less, of the personal injury to pedestrians by insured automobiles is indemnified. In other words, the total personal injury damage from such accidents tends, as in collisions between two automobiles, to be about twice the public liability. Assuming this, it follows that from either a public liability or a total personal injury standpoint, the two types of collision are of the same average severity, and the expression, $H \propto \frac{P}{M}$, holds good for both.

There are other automobile accidents in cities, such as collisions of automobiles with trains and electric cars, with fixed objects, etc. The total is small, however, compared with the two great classes, collisions between automobiles and of automobiles with pedestrians. Moreover, this small disturbing influence is doubtless in such direction as to be counteracted by any excess (of which there is probably a little) of liability of pedestrians for accidents involving them above what has been assumed for them.

It may be safely stated that the determinant of the total personal injury hazard which results from operation of an automobile in any city is given by the expression, $H \propto \frac{P \pm n R}{M}$, in which, n is a fraction probably varying a little as between cities, but always so small that the quantity, nR, is of negligible importance in comparison with P. In other words, from the standpoint either of public liability or of all personal injuries, the natural determinant of hazard of automobile operation is simply the density of population, it being practically immaterial to a motorist from a personal injury hazard standpoint, whether this population, or the proportion of it using the streets at any given time, is encountered as pedestrians or in automobiles.

Automobile Fatalities

As regards automobile fatality hazard, however, this is not true. Under unvarying methods and efficiency of traffic control and of public education in traffic safety, and with no change in the ratio, $\frac{P}{M}$, of a city during a period of years, there should be no change in the personal injury hazard of automobile operation. If, however, during this period the ratio of automobiles to population is increasing, the ratio of automobile fatalities to automobile registrations should steadily decrease; that is, the fatality hazard of automobile operation normally decreases with an increase in the number of automobiles.

Death Rate per One Thousand Automobiles Registered

To demonstrate this: The expression for personal injury hazard of automobile operation, $H \propto \frac{P}{M}$, is derived from,

$$H \propto \frac{P - (a\,R - w\,R)}{M}$$

in which, $a = 2$ and $w = \frac{f_a}{f_p} \times \frac{P - a\,R}{R}$, which product is also approximately equal to 2 for all ratios of $\frac{P - a\,R}{R}$. In other words, whatever the degree of motorization of the city, the second term of the numerator cancels, leaving the population density, $\frac{P}{M}$, as the determinant of personal injury hazard.

Considering the fatality hazard, which may be termed, H_F, the expression may be derived,

$$H_F \propto \frac{P - (a\,R - w_F\,R)}{M}$$

in which,

$$w_F = \frac{F_a}{F_P} \times \frac{P - a\,R}{R}$$

F_a and F_p representing the numbers of motorists and pedestrians killed in automobile accidents, respectively. Then,

$$H_F \propto \frac{P - a\,R + \left(\frac{F_a}{F_p} \times \frac{P - a\,R}{R}\right) R}{M}$$

or,

$$H_F \propto \frac{\left(1 + \frac{F_a}{F_p}\right)(P - a\,R)}{M}$$

For the average city, a may be taken as 2, the expression thus becoming,

$$H_F \propto \frac{\left(1 + \frac{F_a}{F_p}\right)(P - 2\,R)}{M}$$

The expression for the variation of personal injury hazard could have been written in similar form, namely,

$$H \propto \frac{\left(1 + \frac{f_a}{f_p}\right)(P - 2\,R)}{M}$$

Here, however, as the importance of R relative to P increases, the increase of $\frac{f_a}{f_p}$ (Fig. 2) tends to neutralize it, giving the simpler form, $H \propto \frac{P}{M}$.

However, the ratio of fatalities of the two types, that is, $\frac{F_a}{F_p}$, for a given ratio of population to automobiles, has not the same value as has the collision ratio, $\frac{f_a}{f_p}$ (Fig. 2). Thus, in 1922, the ratio of collisions between automobiles to collisions with pedestrians, $\frac{f_a}{f_p}$, was apparently greater than 1.0 in Los Angeles, whereas the ratio of motorists killed to pedestrians killed, $\frac{F_a}{F_p}$, appears to have been as low as 0.33 or 0.25. Similarly, in New York City, the ratio, $\frac{f_a}{f_p}$, was about 0.12 in 1922, and the ratio, $\frac{F_a}{F_p}$, was 0.07. The ratio, $\frac{F_a}{F_p}$, always has lower values than $\frac{f_a}{f_p}$, and its values increase much less rapidly than those of $\frac{f_a}{f_p}$ from less highly to more highly motorized cities. The increase in the first factor of the numerator of the expression,

$$\frac{\left(1 + \frac{F_a}{F_p}\right)(P - 2R)}{M}$$

is insufficient to counterbalance the decrease in the second factor as the motorization increases; consequently, the fatality hazard decreases with increase in motorization, the population density, $\frac{P}{M}$, remaining constant.

The formula for H_F is entirely theoretical and neglects the effects of chance and other possible factors. The importance of these effects is indeterminate, as it is impossible to make a satisfactory check of the fatality hazard formula against the automobile death rate (as the personal injury hazard formula, $H \propto \frac{P}{M}$, was checked against the insurance rate). This is true because (*a*) the automobile fatality figures available through the Census Bureau are for deaths occurring in the respective cities, irrespective of the place of occurrence of accident, and a high automobile fatality rate in a city may indicate good hospital facilities (attracting persons injured outside) as much as bad traffic conditions; (*b*) there are apparently no figures for automobile registrations available for some cities, and, in other cities, the registration figures appear to be of doubtful accuracy; and (*c*) figures are almost wholly lacking for the ratios of motorists killed to pedestrians killed, in the several cities.

The great fluctuation in the automobile fatality rate from year to year in most cities indicates that chance plays a considerable part, as would be expected. This part may be even so great as to make it not permissible to speak of a "probable" fatality hazard. As attempts have been made, however, to account for the variation in automobile fatality rates between cities by means of formulas, the writer suggests the formula for H_F as being apparently more applicable than any other that has come to his attention.

Empirical Formula

The principle that increase in motorization lowers the fatality hazard of operation of each automobile, may be clearly expressed by the empirical formula,

$$H_F \propto \frac{P}{M}\left(\frac{P}{R}\right)^{\frac{3}{8}}$$

This formula appears to give almost as satisfactory results as the more rationally deduced expression,

$$H_F \propto \frac{\left(1 + \frac{F_a}{F_p}\right)(P - 2\,R)}{M}$$

Such application of both these formulas as can be made in the light of present information reveals discrepancies for several cities due to some other unknown factor, probably the average speed of traffic. Cities with unusually slow average speeds seem to have fatality rates lower than would be anticipated from the formulas, and *vice versa.*

It may be noted that the average speed of traffic should have much less influence on personal injury hazard than on fatality hazard; low speeds lead to carelessness and many accidents of minor severity, whereas high speeds cause fewer accidents, but of higher individual severity, the total severity being much the same in both cases. This applies primarily to cities in which low speeds are caused by extreme congestion, especially of pedestrians, and in which high speeds are made possible through special traffic regulations, such as the "boulevard" stop plan.

Automobile Death Rate per 100 000 Population

The formulas for fatality hazard relate to the operation of the individual automobile; that is, to the hazard as expressed by the automobile death rate per thousand automobiles registered. To express the variation in the automobile death rate per 100 000 population, these formulas can be written:

$$H_{FP} \propto \frac{\left(1 + \frac{F_a}{F_p}\right)(P - 2\,R)}{M} \times \frac{R}{P}$$

and,

$$H_{FP} \propto \frac{P}{M}\left(\frac{P}{R}\right)^{\frac{3}{8}}\left(\frac{R}{P}\right)$$

or,

$$H_{FP} \propto \frac{P^{\frac{3}{8}}\,R^{\frac{5}{8}}}{M}$$

in which, H_{FP} represents the automobile death rate per 100 000 population. In these formulas, strictly speaking, R, except in the term, $(P - 2R)$, should denote "equivalent private passenger cars"; that is, the actual registration of private passenger cars plus the registrations of commercial and public vehicles weighted in such a manner as to reflect the excess of hazard which the latter create over that of the average private car. This is a refinement difficult to apply and one that may be neglected without invalidating the principle of the formulas.

Conclusions

From city planning and engineering standpoints three conclusions may be based on this study of street hazard.

Zoning to Prevent Congestion.—The variation expressing the personal injury hazard of automobile operation as proportional to population density, $\frac{P}{M}$, adds a warning against such degrees of congestion of population as prevail in almost all older large cities. This congestion will occur in newer cities and grow still worse in old cities unless the tendency is checked by zoning regulations.

Since the desirability of such zoning measures is evident from other considerations than that of street safety, it might be said that this warning is unnecessary. This is hardly a sound argument, however, because anything which may serve to show the danger of population congestion is worth while from the standpoint of its influence on public opinion, on which zoning measures must ultimately rest.

To change the population density of a city is a slow process, however. It attacks the hazard problem from a preventive standpoint, but offers little cure for existing bad conditions. The second conclusion relates to such a cure.

Traffic Segregation.—From the derivation of $H \propto \frac{P}{M}$, it is seen that this expression holds good as the determinant of hazard because the ratio, $\frac{P}{M}$, measures, for the average city, the frequency of crossings of the path of an automobile by other automobiles and by pedestrians. In other words, diffusion of population leads to a decrease in the number of possible collisions per unit distance of travel, and thereby reduces hazard. Any other measures which do the same should likewise reduce hazard. Such measures are to be found in a proper segregation of street traffic.

"Traffic segregation" is no new term, but is ordinarily used in a very limited sense to mean separation of slow-moving from fast-moving vehicular traffic. As regards safety, this is the least important of three forms of traffic segregation.

The second form is the segregation of right-angled streams of vehicular traffic from one another at intersections. This may be a space segregation, resulting from a separation of grades, or a time segregation. One of these forms is always present except when an accident occurs. Space segregation being usually out of the question, the reduction of collisions between automobiles rests largely on a more certain time segregation. As the majority of collisions between automobiles in the average city occur at a comparatively small number of intersections, proper time-segregation measures may be quite effective in reducing the hazard of collision between automobiles. The situation in almost any city is susceptible of improvement through such means.

The third and most important form of traffic segregation, however, is given least attention. This form is the segregation of pedestrian from vehicular street use, and its importance in any community as compared with vehicular segregation at intersections is measured by the ratio of collisions with pedestrians to collisions between automobiles. Thus, in New York City, the prevention of collisions with pedestrians is, from a personal injury standpoint, at least five times as important as the prevention of collisions between automobiles, and as regards fatalities it is seven or eight times as important.

At present, about the only special effort made to reduce accidents involving pedestrians is through "jay-walking" campaigns and educational work. Such campaigns are meeting with considerable success, but the problem is sufficiently serious to merit supplementing them by careful studies to see whether a better segregation of pedestrian and vehicular street use and travel may not be accomplished. Although improved methods of handling traffic at street intersections may greatly reduce the hazard of collisions between vehicles, they will have little effect on collisions between automobiles and pedestrians, only a small proportion of which occur at street intersections.

A complete segregation of pedestrian and vehicular traffic is not possible, and would be undesirable because of the restrictions it would place on street use, or the great expense it would entail. In practically any city, however, a much safer distribution of pedestrian and vehicular travel might be realized at small expense and with facilitation rather than restriction of traffic.

To go into detailed methods of doing this is beyond the scope of this paper, but many applications of the principle may be discovered in any city. As most automobile collisions with pedestrians occur in residential districts, particular attention should be given to the segregation of pedestrian from automobile traffic in those districts, as far as possible through measures which will naturally drain the greatest possible proportion of automobile traffic into arterial ways.

A study of the high hazard areas shown on the automobile fatality map maintained by the Police Department of New York City illustrates very strikingly the great hazard from intermittent vehicular traffic through tenement streets filled with playing children. Under such conditions, even elaborate measures to bring about a better segregation of vehicles from pedestrians are justified. The roping off of "play streets" barred to vehicle use, in such areas, is the first step. The logical supplement to this is the provision of some means through which other near-by streets may be kept clear, between curb lines, of pedestrians (particularly of children at play) so that vehicles may pass through them at good rates of speed and without high hazards.

Extreme conditions may even justify the erection of fences along the curb lines of certain main traffic arteries through congested tenement districts. Such fenced streets would have to be provided with tunnels or bridges for cross traffic at intervals. These would be of great value from a safety standpoint and might prove of little inconvenience if traffic were heavy in two directions and light at right angles. They should always be the supplement of "play streets" or other adequate play areas.

In many cities where automobile hazard conditions are very bad, the regulation of traffic by police and motor-vehicle departments seems to be approaching the limits of its effectiveness. Further improvement must apparently come largely from engineering measures to insure a safer distribution of pedestrians and automobiles over the street system. Such measures imply better traffic segregation, particularly of vehicles from pedestrians, and secondarily of conflicting streams of vehicles at street intersections. These measures are apt to be expensive and so should always be based on careful determination of the benefits that may be expected. A case in point is furnished by the railroad grade crossing, which for some reason attracts excessive attention as a highway hazard, with a consequence that sums of money out of proportion to the resulting benefits have been devoted to this elimination.

It seems not to be generally realized that the sore spot in the traffic accident situation is the crowded residential or tenement district, that for every person killed or injured at a grade crossing, in the more urban States at least, ten are killed or injured in the slums and near slums.

Street Plan.—The third conclusion, of particular importance to the future growth of cities, results primarily from the deviation from anticipated hazard which the City of Washington presents. The conclusion is that a well-planned street layout with adequate provision of long, straight, broad, and well located traffic thoroughfares, particularly if supplemented by measures that will bring about a good distribution of homes and business, will reduce street hazard far below its anticipated $\frac{P}{M}$-level.

Motor Vehicle Legislation.—These three conclusions as to zoning and other engineering means of street hazard reduction are supplemented by a fourth, equally important not only to engineers, but to all citizens—that street traffic hazard is responsive to proper efforts for increase in carefulness in street use by pedestrians and motorists. The enactment and efficient administration of the type of State motor-vehicle law outlined in this paper may, and as experience has proved does, reduce street and highway hazards 25 to 30 per cent.

DISCUSSION

William T. Lyle,* M. Am. Soc. C. E. (by letter).—This paper commands attention not only for its originality, but also for its suggestiveness. It may be classed as a contribution to the literature of city planning. The end sought is the reduction of automobile hazard. The investigations made and conclusions reached are beyond the frontiers of present knowledge.

The analysis is clear and reasonable. The author is careful to define the term, "automobile hazard", at the outset of his paper and this definition must be borne in mind throughout. The hazard resulting from the use of a single automobile varies as $\frac{P}{M}$, the population density; therefore, the variation in the automobile accident rate per unit of population no doubt would be obtained as $\frac{P}{M} \times \frac{R}{P} = \frac{R}{M}$, the automobile density. It is necessary to appreciate these two values in order to grasp the argument for zoning, traffic segregation, street plan, and motor vehicle legislation. Fig. 3 is not only interesting, but provocative also of many questions. It demonstrates conclusively the value of motor vehicle legislation and of a city plan.

Since the variation in the automobile accident rate per unit of population is expressed by the automobile density, uniform traffic distribution and traffic control have added to the carrying capacity of streets, the safety of pedestrians, and the efficiency of the police and fire departments. Without traffic control, modern street movement would be impossible. Since, however, the effectiveness of traffic control decreases with increasing congestion, there is a point beyond which it fails.

As the solution of the traffic problem, traffic control has demonstrated its inadequacy; and traffic regulation, as made possible by physical improvements, is necessary to afford permanent relief. The traffic problem, therefore, is being transferred from the domain of municipal administration to the field of municipal design and construction. In other words, it is becoming the problem of the city planner. Whereas, in the past, its solution has been sought in the control of the traffic stream, in the future, it will be secured by improving the container. Temporary makeshifts will not answer; a radical treatment is required. This is to be found in street widening and in the general improvement of the street plan; nor in these alone, because they are piecemeal methods and, therefore, will not fully satisfy. The traffic problem (including the problem of hazards) affects, and is affected by, all the elements of the city plan. Therefore, it should form a part of a comprehensive plan in which all the physical elements of the city are treated in their mutual relationships.

The conclusions drawn by the author might be enlarged in scope to include practically the whole subject of city and regional planning. The doctrines of centralization and decentralization might be discussed from this new viewpoint, from which also the merits of a well-proportioned radial and

* Prof. of Civ. Eng., Washington and Lee Univ., Lexington, Va.

circumferential street plan, of a simplified railroad plan with grade crossings eliminated, and of parks and playgrounds as substitutes for the high-hazard residential and tenement areas, might be presented in a new light.

M. O. ELDRIDGE,* ASSOC. M. AM. SOC. C. E. (by letter).—In his paper, Mr. Cox shows that the automobile public liability insurance rates are lower in some cities than in others. On the ordinary \$5 000 and \$10 000 policy, the rates for 1927 are, as follows:

New York, N. Y.	\$107	Detroit, Mich.	\$23
Buffalo, N. Y.	57	Atlanta, Ga.	26
Philadelphia, Pa.	59	Washington, D. C.	20
Providence, R. I.	45	New Orleans, La.	20
Cleveland, Ohio	40	Los Angeles, Calif.	20
Chicago, Ill.	32	Indianapolis, Ind.	18

The rate in Milwaukee, Wis., which has about the same population as Washington, D. C., is \$29.

In discussing the relations between actual and calculated hazards, Mr. Cox shows that there are discrepancies between such hazards ranging from 24% of the actual hazards for Portland, Ore., to 109% for Washington. Noting that for Washington the actual hazard is less than one-half the calculated, he attributes this, to a large extent, to superior planning of the city.

While the avenues in Washington, of which there is one for each State, are wide, the paved portions of the numbered streets running north and south, and the lettered streets running east and west, are narrow when compared with other cities. The average width of the pavement on these streets is from 30 to 32 ft., leaving barely sufficient space for two lines of traffic when automobiles are parked at the curb.

Many other streets in Washington are so narrow as to leave only one traffic lane between parked automobiles. The writer, therefore, cannot agree that these streets are well designed to carry the traffic.

The wide avenues radiating from the Capitol and White House and numerous circles at an angle of 45° to the narrow lettered and numbered streets only tend to complicate this situation from a traffic standpoint. In fact, it is said that this system of street layout was designed by L'Enfant more as a means of internal defense than as a method of handling traffic. As many as ten streets and avenues converge into some of the larger circles in Washington, and this tends to increase the traffic hazards.

Since 1924 the City of Washington has made considerable progress in reducing the number of traffic fatalities and accidents. The fatality and accident records for the District of Columbia, which is co-extensive with Washington, are as follows:

Year.	Traffic Fatalities.	Year.	Traffic Accidents.
1923	91	1923	8 491
1924	91	1924	9 131
1925	84	1925	9 331
1926	76	1926	6 485

* Director of Traffic, Washington, D. C.

These reductions have been made in spite of the fact that the population has increased considerably during this period and that the registration of automobiles and the number of new drivers has practically doubled.

It cannot be said, therefore, that this improvement has been brought about by the city planners, by the favorable street layout, or by the width of streets, etc. In reality, these reductions are attributable to the following causes:

1.—The establishment of a well laid-out system of boulevard highways at which motorists are required to stop before entering or crossing, thus speeding up traffic on these highways and making the intersections with adjacent streets much safer.

2.—The elimination of parking on the flow sides of boulevard highways during the morning and afternoon rush hours. This not only facilitates the movement of traffic, but adds an additional traffic lane during the rush hours and reduces the possibility of accidents to pedestrians who may walk out into rapidly moving traffic from between parked automobiles.

3.—The establishment of traffic control on some of the main thoroughfares by means of electric traffic signal lights which operate from 7:00 A. M. until midnight, under a plan of co-ordinated control developed in Washington.

4.—The establishment of a uniform speed limit throughout the District of 22 miles per hour, except on certain sections of boulevard and other highways in the outlying districts, where a speed of 30 miles an hour is permitted as indicated by signs.

5.—The elimination of bad drivers by the cancellation of permits for first offense in leaving after colliding or in driving while intoxicated, for second offense in reckless driving, and for third offense in speeding. Permits are also suspended or canceled for other causes, such as mental and physical defects of drivers. All new drivers are examined on the regulations and are required to demonstrate their ability to operate a motor vehicle safely in congested traffic. An eyesight test is also required.

6.—The adoption of a modern traffic code based on the principles laid down by the Hoover Conference on Street and Highway Safety. This code is being enforced without "fear or favor" by the Police Department and by a Traffic Court which holds sessions every week-day, including holidays, from 9:00 A. M. until 11:00 P. M.

C. W. STARK,* ASSOC. M. AM. SOC. C. E. (by letter).—The author has made a very valuable and unusual contribution to Society publications. It is to be hoped that such discussions will not be so unusual in the future, for the best efforts of the engineer are needed to help solve the traffic problem, to reduce the annual accident toll, the tremendous economic waste due to inadequacy of street and highway facilities, and the unscientific use of existing facilities.

From the viewpoint of the insurance companies and also of the individual motorist it is reassuring to know, as Mr. Cox has demonstrated, that the hazard of the individual automobile does not increase with the number of

* Transportation and Communication Dept., Chamber of Commerce of the United States, Washington, D. C.

automobiles. From the viewpoint of the man on the street this is not so cheering, because it confirms his belief that the hazard to himself, be he afoot or in a motor car, is the sum of the hazards to himself from each motor vehicle and, therefore, increases with the number of motor vehicles. Since this number is constantly and rapidly increasing, it behooves each one to bestir himself in every way to reduce the unit hazards for self-protection.

Although Mr. Cox proves mathematically that $w = a$ and, therefore, that the hazard to the pedestrian is the same as that to the occupant of the other motor car, those who do much walking will still feel that there must be some flaw in the reasoning. Perhaps the seeming discrepancy between formula and experience can largely be explained by the author's statement that in a collision between an automobile and a pedestrian, if contributory negligence on the part of the pedestrian is shown, the pedestrian is likely to receive little or no indemnification for his injuries. Since the pedestrian is alleged to be at fault in about one-half the cases, evidently this half does not enter into the formula. Of course, many automobile collisions also do not enter.

It might be added that injuries to persons are seldom averted by such persons leaping to safety from automobiles about to suffer collision, whereas pedestrians are constantly avoiding accidents by jumping and dodging. Only by their own agility, exercised in many cases where they clearly have the right of way, do they avert many accidents, and thereby greatly reduce h_p.

Mr. Cox quotes several agencies to derive an average conclusion that pedestrians are at fault in about one-half the pedestrian accidents. Obviously, it is much easier to get testimony from a living motorist than from a dead pedestrian. Obviously, also, if a pedestrian is found injured or dead in a roadway in the middle of a block, it is reasonably certain that he was not crossing the street on a cross-walk. But there may be no witnesses or other proof of the fact that the motor vehicle was going at double the legal speed, or was on the left-hand side; that the pedestrian saw the vehicle and would have had ample time to get out of its way, but that the driver wilfully or heedlessly ran him down. On the other hand, if the pedestrian is hit on a cross-walk there is always the chance to prove that he wavered or darted forward suddenly, or did something else that the oncoming motorist could not foresee and, therefore, he was at fault. Pedestrians jumping for their lives from the paths of reckless, unidentified drivers, have darted into the paths of law-abiding drivers. Cause of accident—confusion of pedestrian.

Thinking further along these lines, those who live and walk in Washington, D. C., will not be lulled into a false sense of security by the fact that the "actual" hazard is less than one-half the calculated hazard, because there comes into the problem another element, which could not very well be calculated by Mr. Cox, namely, the indifference of the Washington police and apparently the prosecuting authorities to the welfare of the pedestrian. The great majority of Washington traffic officers operate their signals as if pedestrians were non-existent, shifting traffic without regard to persons on foot marooned in the middle of the street, giving no interval for the clearing of intersections, and permitting vehicles to crowd and obstruct the cross-walks and make illegal right turns with little interference. Naturally, such officers are of little help in proving the responsibility of motorists when pedestrians are injured. The writer's personal experience has been that in Washington the interest of the public authorities in the welfare of the pedestrian approaches zero. For this reason the likelihood of insurance companies having to pay claims resulting from pedestrian accidents approaches zero, and, therefore, h_p approaches zero.

The wide streets of Washington certainly provide an opportunity for safety not enjoyed by many cities. They make it possible for vehicles to operate with a minimum of interference with each other; but they also make possible higher speeds and more rapid rounding of corners, more lanes of traffic, and greater distances for the pedestrian to negotiate, creating additional hazards for the pedestrian and calling for special effort on the part of the regulatory authorities to overcome those hazards. Because such special effort is not in evidence, the writer has heard more than one man, coming from the hurly burly of New York City, with its abnormally high value of H, to work with committees of the National Conference on Street and Highway Safety, express fear of walking on Washington's streets, and a desire to get back quickly to the comparative safety of the metropolis.

From the author's opinion that improved methods of handling traffic at street intersections will have little effect on collisions between automobiles and pedestrians, the writer emphatically dissents. Is there not a very positive relationship between the treatment accorded the pedestrian at intersections and his general attitude toward traffic? If he has no guaranty of protection when he proceeds on a "Go" sign—if he has to wait intolerably long periods for the signal to go, because there is little wheel traffic going his way, and when he does get the signal has to detour around cars stopped on the cross-walk and dodge other cars making all manner of turns, and then, perhaps, be left in the middle of the swirl by a sudden shifting of the signals—and if at unofficered intersections he has to weave his way through solid lines of vehicles that completely obliterate the cross-walks, and have the motorists blow their horns and crowd up to close the gaps so that he cannot get through—in short, if the whole scheme of traffic control makes him a mere incident, he is, of course, going to cast rules and regulations to the winds and cross the streets whenever, wherever, and however his judgment, faulty and inconsiderate though it be, determines. Give him a decent chance at the cross-walks. Mark them conspicuously and keep standing motor vehicles off them. Instil in motorists a wholesome respect for these intersections of sidewalk and roadway, and show pedestrians that regulation of pedestrians does not mean merely restriction for the convenience of motorists—and see whether this does not bring about changes in walking and in motoring habits that will cut pedestrian fatalities in half.

This dissertation on the pedestrian may seem a far cry from engineering, and unscientific. Surely, however, the engineering mind must see that, with pedestrian fatalities constituting about two-thirds of all fatalities in which the motor vehicle is involved, the pedestrian problem is the most serious phase of the traffic problem; and it is about the most neglected.

Mr. Cox's figure of $15 000 000 annual saving to the State of Massachusetts (after cost of administering the laws is deducted), because of its advanced motor-vehicle laws, should be brought to the attention of all those who believe that the cost of administering such laws would be prohibitive.

Reasonable, enforceable rules of the road are one of the essentials of advanced motor-vehicle laws. Another essential on which Mr. Cox might well have laid more emphasis is the licensing of drivers. All four of the States which he cites as having advanced legislation in 1922 require and did require in 1922 that all operators and chauffeurs be licensed; and it is important to note that in none of these States is this licensing a mere perfunctory registration of drivers. The applicant for a license must prove by an examination that he has the qualifications for a safe driver. Such examinations permanently eliminate a small percentage of hopeless incompetents and compel a much larger number of applicants to familiarize themselves with the laws and regulations and really to learn to drive safely before they are turned loose on the highways. This system costs the State some money, but very little in comparison with such savings as Mr. Cox's figures show. No State having tried the licensing and examination system has discarded it.

The skeptics should not overlook the significant statement in the paper that "good traffic regulation is usually the outgrowth of high hazard—of conditions so intolerable that they force improvement." Experience is a costly school, but perhaps the only possible school for the dozen States that have suffered most and gone farthest in working out sound legislation. While these States are grappling with the problems still unsolved—and the relation of pedestrian and motorist is one of the gravest of these—the remaining three dozen States have an opportunity to profit by the experience of the dozen.

Engineers do not need to be told the advantages of intelligent zoning and traffic segregation or of well-planned street layouts. What they do need to realize is that the engineering problems are being handled to a large extent by others than engineers, and that they should hasten to take over that part of the traffic problem for which they are peculiarly fitted, so that mistakes already made, can be corrected as promptly as possible, and new and costly mistakes can be avoided.

L. G. Holleran,* M. Am. Soc. C. E.—This paper is both timely and interesting. Its only defect is that it does not go far enough. It gives an outlook on this problem from a new angle and arrives at a solution in a novel way; but it is regrettable that more ground could not be covered in the study of methods for reducing the automobile hazard.

This hazard is only one phase, although a most important one, of the large problem of taking care of automobile traffic with the inadequate street systems and facilities which exist in practically all American cities. As some one has aptly put it "we are building 40-story cities around street

* Deputy Chf. Engr., Westchester County Park Comm., Bronxville, N. Y.

systems designed for 3-story towns"; he might have added "and we are suffering the consequences".

It is enlightening to examine Mr. Cox's formula and to see what application it has to existing conditions. He found that this formula, $H \propto \frac{P}{M}$, did not hold good for a number of cities and came to the conclusion that several factors might serve to modify it. These factors will be discussed later.

On considering the formula, it is apparent that the hazard can be reduced in two ways, first, by decreasing the population, P, and, second, by increasing the street mileage, M. It is obvious that the population is decreasing in few cities of the United States, and, in fact, is increasing in most of them, so there is no hope for immediate relief in that direction. Accepting the formula, therefore, the only manner in which relief is possible is by increasing the mileage of streets and roads in such a way as better to distribute automobile traffic throughout the area under consideration.

That is the method by which the Westchester County Park Commission is attacking the problem. The County has an area of about 450 sq. miles and a population of about 500 000. It is in reality an urban district subject to the limitations inferred in the paper. It is the front dooryard of the City of New York; in addition to traffic originating in the County, its roads and streets must carry a tremendous through traffic going to or coming from the city. This through traffic has been carried almost wholly on two routes: The Albany Post Road and the Boston Post Road. Each of these routes leads through the business center of every city and village it traverses, thus greatly aggravating local traffic conditions and increasing the automobile hazard until a point was reached a few years ago where it was realized that remedies must be found or the development of the County would be seriously retarded.

The result was the appointment of the Commission which, after investigation, came to the conclusion that the only practicable way to relieve conditions was to lay out new routes, parallel to the over-taxed existing routes, to be located away from the business centers of the cities and villages, and as far as possible in undeveloped territory for reasons of economy as well as to provide for a better distribution of the population. Of such new routes 140 miles have been laid out, and the Board of Supervisors has appropriated nearly $40 000 000 for the acquisition of the real estate and the construction of these new routes, in addition to the land and construction work necessary for the development of recreational facilities throughout the County.

In order to facilitate the passage of traffic, as well as to reduce the automobile hazard, the new driveways are being constructed with a pavement width of from 40 to 80 ft. Truck traffic will be segregated on driveways other than those carrying passenger traffic. Grade crossings at all the principal street intersections are being eliminated, curves super-elevated, non-skid pavement used, modern lighting installed, and traffic regulated in accordance with approved methods.

Working along similar lines, the State of New Jersey is building a 50-ft. driveway, 13 miles long, from the westerly end of the Holland Tunnel to a point near Elizabeth, at an estimated cost of more than $30 000 000. New York City is to build an elevated roadway on its west side from the easterly end of the Holland Tunnel to connect with the southerly end of the Riverside Drive at 72d Street. The City of Chicago, Ill., has recently widened Western Avenue from 60 to 100 ft., for a distance of more than 20 miles, and is cutting through additional streets at great expense. Detroit, Mich., is building boulevards, 204 ft. or more in width, and Wayne County is carrying the boulevards from the city line for many miles out into the country. Philadelphia cut a wide diagonal street leading out from the heart of the city for a distance of about 1¼ miles a few years ago. Other cities are attempting to solve the problem by similar methods.

Such a program for Westchester County is possible largely because the County happens to be a very wealthy community. It, also, fortunately had within its borders leaders and officials possessed of those qualities of imagination and foresight which insured support of the comprehensive program proposed by the Commission. If men of vision and courage could be found to lead, most communities could discover the way to finance the program of improvements in its street system necessary to remedy unsafe, uneconomical, and unsatisfactory conditions.

If the losses due to fatal and non-fatal accidents, loss of business, loss of the time of drivers of private and commercial cars, and the general inconvenience of traffic congestion, could be evaluated and credit allowed for the increase in real estate values resulting from the improvement, it would be found, in most if not all cases, that the actual return in dollars and cents more than justified the expenditures necessary to attack the problem in the comprehensive way it deserves. It is a fact, however, that due to lack of proper leadership and other causes, a great many communities will decide that they cannot finance the large costs required to effect a relatively complete cure. It is necessary, therefore, to consider what means can be found to alleviate conditions with the funds which can usually be made available.

Mr. Cox concludes that the automobile hazard may be reduced in four general ways. These methods are of equal effect in solving the problem of automobile traffic as a whole. In addition, there are a number of others which, in the absence of funds to attack the problem in a comprehensive way, will tend to better distribute the traffic; facilitate the passage of automobiles through the streets; and, at the same time, reduce the hazard:

1.—Uniform traffic regulations throughout the United States. As it is now, even adjacent municipalities have different regulations which lead to the confusion of strangers who often constitute a relatively large proportion of the total number of drivers on through traffic routes.

2.—Widening of existing streets parallel to those for which the records show the greatest hazard, with this end in view, to attract a part of the traffic away from dangerous localities. One additional lane of traffic can often be secured by narrowing the sidewalks. Where this is insufficient or impracticable, streets can often be selected for widening where the damages to existing structures are at a minimum. It is of little avail, however, to widen streets in the congested district, as such widening merely serves to attract traffic from adjacent parallel streets and the congestion soon becomes worse instead of better.

3.—Connecting up segments of existing streets to form new thoroughfares, where, due to improper control of real estate layouts, or other reasons, the streets in adjacent developments do not connect. Increased mileage of through streets and better distribution of traffic may often be secured in this way at comparatively small cost.

4.—Re-routing of trolley cars from congested streets to less used parallel streets. A few years ago when Chicago had a strike of street railroad employees and the surface cars ceased to operate for several days, traffic counts at a number of street intersections made during the strike and compared with counts taken afterward showed that the capacity of the streets decreased about 50% when the trolley cars were in operation.

5.—Paving through streets in the outlying districts to a width of not less than 30 ft. to provide a third lane of traffic so that one automobile may pass another in safety. Statistics show that a considerable proportion of automobile accidents occur while one car is trying to pass another.

6.—Providing sidewalks or paths along streets and roads in the outlying sections and along through traffic routes.

7.—Preventing the parking of automobiles in congested districts, leaving the streets free for the passage of traffic.

8.—Restricting the number of taxicabs and forbidding the practice of "cruising" for business.

9.—Removal of obstructions and encroachments, both public and private, from sidewalks and streets wherever possible.

10.—Preventing the practice of storing building materials and conducting building operations on parts of streets or sidewalks.

11.—Preventing the use of the sidewalk and a part of the street for considerable periods of time for the purpose of loading and unloading merchandise. This practice often forces pedestrians to make use of the streets and increases the possibility of accidents.

12.—Reducing the number of street openings for sewers, water, gas, or other public utilities, to a minimum, and making it a provision of the permit that the work of making and closing these openings shall be done in the shortest possible time. The repair of the pavement should always be done by the municipality at the expense of the person to whom the permit is granted.

13.—The use of the proper types of pavement for different traffic conditions.

14.—The prompt and efficient repair of the street surface when it begins to deteriorate.

15.—Increasing the radii of curbs at street intersections, not to invite an increase of speed in turning the corners, but to prevent cars with a long wheel base from encroaching on the wrong side of the street at turns and thus increasing the possibility of collisions with other cars as well as with pedestrians.

16.—Where it is impracticable to eliminate grade crossings at important intersecting streets, it is often possible to locate a circular island at the center of the intersection, requiring a rotary movement of traffic. This is relatively ineffective, however, unless the island has a rather large diameter, probably not less than 60 ft.

17.—Loading platforms raised about 6 in. above the street have been provided in some cities for the safety of passengers boarding or alighting from trolley cars. Safety isles for the same purposes have also been provided by marking off parts of the pavement with temporary posts connected with rope.

18.—The establishment of more playgrounds in or near the congested districts for the purpose of keeping children off the streets.

19.—Last, but not least, educating the public as to safety measures, beginning with the children in the schools.

It must be admitted that many of these suggestions are palliatives and not cures, but they will continue to be necessary until the street systems can be made over and a rational and uniform method of procedure for handling automobile traffic can be worked out and put in operation.

S. JOHANNESSON,* M. AM. SOC. C. E.—In his excellent paper the author comes to the conclusion that generally the personal injury hazard of automobile operation is proportional to the population density. It appears, however, that other factors may be involved, as may be illustrated by the following example. Traffic counts have been made by the State Highway Department of New Jersey at Rahway on July 4 every year since 1921, except 1925. The counts have been as follows:

Year.	Number of Vehicles.	Year	Number of Vehicles.
1921	12 153	1924	26 573
1922	16 610	1925	....
1923	18 314	1926	43 735

These counts indicate an increase of traffic during the 5-year period of 259 per cent. The exact population increase during the same period is not available, but it is probably not more than 20 per cent.

In this case the traffic increase is exaggerated by the traffic in transit from New York to the New Jersey coast resorts; nevertheless, it is a fact that the traveling habit is steadily on the increase. Not only does the ratio of number of cars to total population increase, but the average distance each car travels is increasing. The rate of increase of the traveling habit may decrease when the congestion of traffic on existing streets becomes excessive; but whenever new roads are built or present roads are improved the traveling habit will increase.

Consequently, it would seem as if the traffic density (which presumably is proportional to the personal injury hazard) cannot be taken to be proportional to the population density, unless the comparison is made at a definite time. It is possible to imagine, for example, a community in which the expression, $\frac{R}{M}$, might be the same in 1921 and 1926; but it seems probable that the personal injury hazard in 1926 would have increased materially over that in 1921 on account of the materially greater density of traffic.

In his "Conclusions", the author suggests traffic segregation at intersections as a means of reducing the hazard. At present, the New Jersey State Highway Commission is constructing a new highway leading from the Holland Tunnel Plaza in Jersey City through Newark and Elizabeth, where connections are made to existing traffic routes leading west and to the New Jersey coast resorts. On this highway, "space segregation" of traffic is being pro-

* Designing Engr., State Highway Comm., Jersey City, N. J.

vided by building it so that there will be no grade crossings with either railroads or existing streets. This space segregation is being provided largely on account of economic considerations. Investigations have been made which indicate that on this road, which is expected to carry about 18 000 000 vehicles per year, the cost of time segregation, or in other words, the loss in cost of operation of the vehicles on account of the delays at crossings, would exceed the additional cost of construction on account of the space segregation.

The results of these investigations indicate that, where the traffic is heavy, it may be worth while to consider the comparative economics of time segregation and space segregation.

W. GRAHAM COLE,* ESQ.—The author applies a strict mathematical formula to a problem that involves a consideration of engineering principles and human psychology. These principles are so inter-related that only an incomplete and inaccurate picture of the problem is obtainable from a purely mathematical viewpoint. Thus, if the formula, $h = \frac{P}{M}$, is carried to the nth degree of reasoning, namely, if M is sufficiently large in comparison with P, the value of h will approach zero as a limit.

It is obvious, however, that if pedestrians can be eliminated entirely from thoroughfares used by vehicular traffic no accidents between the two will be possible. Before this limit is reached a zone will be found in which the intermittent and unexpected appearance of a pedestrian on a thoroughfare, otherwise frequented by vehicles, will produce a greater hazard to the individual pedestrian than he now encounters at heavily congested intersections, where his presence is anticipated by the motorist. This is borne out by the experience of many cities, which shows that the majority of traffic accidents do not occur in congested sections, but rather in outlying sections, where lack of congestion permits of speeding and reckless practice.

The theoretical solution of the pedestrian-motor accident problem is the complete and permanent segregation of these two types of street users. Such steps, however, would not affect, to any great degree, the problem of vehicular collisions with each other or with stationary obstructions.

The segregation of vehicular traffic by direction so as to make impossible the intersection of one line of moving vehicles with another would prevent the intersection accident, but would leave unaffected many other types. Such segregations are impractical from a cost standpoint, if from no other, except at a few unusual locations in the most congested communities. As a general solution to the traffic problem, they are beyond the realm of practical consideration. The traffic problem is a serious one, dealing with the deaths of about 24 000 persons per year, a number that is increasing at an approximate rate of 1 death per 1 000 added motor vehicles. On account of this increasing toll, methods of dealing with the problem that are within the scope of practical application by the average community are not only highly desirable, but absolutely essential to the public welfare.

* Safety Engr., Metropolitan Life Insurance Co., New York, N. Y.

The Engineering Profession can render a great service to humanity by giving to this problem the same practical consideration and study that it has given to other problems. It can assist the Nation, the State, and the individual community to devise and take definite steps leading to the correction of existing conditions.

Mr. Cox has pointed out that the actual hazard, as he has developed it, is greater than the calculated hazard in many cities where traffic control has been practiced. Granting that the basis of his calculations is correct, this fact indicates that traffic control has been applied in the places most needing it; but it may also indicate that the most effective methods of traffic control have not been devised. The fact does not condemn the practice of traffic control, but rather emphasizes the need for greater and more intensive study of this important branch of engineering.

Accidents are largely the result of the inability of the human race to modify its habits of life quickly to conform with the tremendous changes of environment brought about by engineering advancement and commercial development. The average pedestrian still wishes to amble across a busy thoroughfare carrying thousands of powerful machines, in much the same way that his ancestors sauntered across a village street between a few slow-moving, horse-drawn vehicles. Engineering devices can be developed to alter certain environments so that they will conform more closely with the unchanged habits of the public. On the other hand, educational methods must be applied, in order to alter habits to satisfy changed conditions.

Accident prevention work in industry has demonstrated that only a small reduction of accidents can be effected by mechanical guards and engineering revision. This work must be supplemented by definite and organized educational activities. Likewise in the matter of public accidents only a small reduction will be made if the educational phase of the problem is overlooked. Through this educational work the individual citizen must be reached, his interest appealed to, and he, as an integral part of the community, must be taught new responsibilities.

In a number of communities, organizations have been perfected for the purpose of conducting continuous safety educational activities. The gratifying results obtained have proven beyond doubt that a community can be organized for the prevention of accidents, very much as industrial plants have been organized.

Of the list of cities given on Fig. 3, nine have been conducting organized educational work for some time. Of these nine, seven have an actual hazard below the calculated hazard.

Harold M. Lewis,* M. Am. Soc. C. E.—The author has presented a strong case for the formula he has set up—that automobile accident hazard within a city is directly proportional to the population and inversely proportional to the street mileage. Such a formula implies that the most practical way of reducing such hazards is by decreasing the density of population along a typical street within a community. This points directly to some form of decentralization

* Executive Engr., Regional Plan of New York and Its Environs, New York, N. Y.

that will bring about a better distribution of population and activities within cities. The need for such a re-arrangement has been much discussed in recent years, and it seems desirable for many reasons.

Mr. Cox assumes that motor-vehicle density is not the controlling factor, because he has developed from other factors an equation which fits his accident statistics. This is not proof. It is quite possible that by starting with motor-vehicle densities and applying necessary corrections, such as he has applied to street mileages, automobile density may also be proved to be an important controlling factor. Although fatality records vary too greatly in small areas to yield any general principles, they should indicate actual trends in large areas, such as States. They do have advantage in being more complete than accident records.

The National Conference on Street and Highway Safety presented very complete fatality statistics for 1923, 1924, and 1925. These were tabulated for total State areas and also for the total rural districts and total cities within each State of the United States. An analysis of the 1923 statistics showed that there was a larger variation in the fatality rates in the rural districts than in the cities, as might be expected because of the greater variation in conditions. The maximum rate in the groups of rural districts was 38.6 per 100 000 of population in California, and was greater than the rates for any of the various groups of cities. The average of the rural district rates, however, was only 11.1 fatalities per 100 000, and the fatalities in the total rural districts listed amounted to only 10.4 per 100 000. In contrast with these figures, the statistics for fatalities in the different groups of cities showed an average rate of about 20 fatalities per 100 000, or almost twice as great. Data for the later years showed approximately the same conditions.

One of the most striking features in the tables was the small variation for the different groups of cities, which indicated that the motor-vehicle hazard in any place was primarily a result of urban conditions and quite independent of the size of the city. Comparing the fatality rates of the different States with the automobile density in terms of cars per capita, it appeared that communities with the least number of cars per capita had the lowest fatality rates and *vice versa*. California, which had by far the greatest number of vehicles per capita, had the largest fatality rate. The States with more or less average fatality rates showed no such direct relation, and other factors apparently obtained.

It is hardly enough to know that one must have better motor-vehicle legislation, or a street system like Washington, D. C., in order to reduce motor-vehicle hazard. Other cities cannot afford to duplicate Washington in its rather extravagant provision of street areas. Proper planning must be based on analysis of the more specific causes of accidents, such as has been made by the National Conference on Street and Highway Safety, and by Connecticut, Wisconsin, and other States. The Connecticut analysis indicates that the ratio of accidents to registration increased fourfold from 1918 to 1925, while the automobile density increased only two and one-half times. These data must be discounted to a certain extent to allow for more complete returns in the later years, due to improved methods of reporting accidents.

On the other hand, the statistics of the National Conference on Street and Highway Safety show that the ratio of fatalities to registration decreased steadily from 1917 to 1924. The same trend was indicated by an analysis of fatality figures for New York City, New York State, and the entire United States, from 1917 to 1923, made by the Regional Plan of New York and Its Environs. It appeared that, in general, the number of fatalities in each of these widely different areas had been increasing as the three-quarters power of the motor-vehicle registration. During the four years ending with 1926, there was a decided change in this relationship in New York City when motor-vehicle fatalities increased as only about the one-third power of the registration.

TABLE 5.—AUTOMOBILE FATALITIES IN NEW YORK AND LONDON.

Year.	New York City.	London Metropolitan District.
1917	441	471
1918	503	440
1919	696	533
1920	730	512
1921	851	460
1922	846	560
1923	934	569
1924	936	720
1925	1 002	742
1926	1 023	895

It may be of interest to compare motor-vehicle fatality figures for New York City with those for the London Metropolitan District. New York City has less than one-half the area of the London Metropolitan District, but has an automobile density three or four times as great. Table 5 gives the information from 1917 to 1926, inclusive.

It is estimated that in the entire New York Region—defined as all the area within approximately 50 miles of the City Hall—there were about 1 870 motor-vehicle fatalities during 1925. This enormous loss of life indicates very forcibly the seriousness of present conditions. The London figures show that the problem also exists in the large metropolitan areas in other countries.

J. K. FINCH,* ASSOC. M. AM. SOC. C. E.—The author has taken up a problem of the first magnitude—think of New York City alone spending $75 000 000 annually on automobile accidents. He has pointed out clearly certain laws of automobile hazard—that these laws must be taken into account in city planning if the hazard is to be kept down to a minimum. Unfortunately, the problem is generally the reverse, namely, to reduce the hazard in cities, in the planning and growth of which no attention has been given to this Twentieth Century problem.

About ten years ago, under Police Commissioner Woods, the speaker served on a special committee of three to study the street accident problem of New York. Fairly reliable data had been secured by the Police Department which showed about 22 000 street accidents of all kinds in 1916. More than 25% of

* Prof., Civ. Eng., Columbia Univ., New York, N. Y.

these accidents were due to "collisions" between pedestrians and automobiles, and, therefore, it was clearly indicated that the problem, already alarming, would continue and grow with the rapid increase in automobile use. In 1926 there were more than 50 000 street accidents in New York.

Unfortunately, little time was available for this study, as the Committee was appointed just at the close of Mr. Woods' administration. Such studies as were made, however, established two fundamental laws of street accidents. The principal type of accident being due to a collision between a pedestrian and an automobile, these laws have to do first with the population characteristics which affect the accident rate; and, second, with the traffic characteristics, which tend to increase the number of accidents.

The first of these laws was the relation of population density to the number of accidents, which has been so clearly brought out by Mr. Cox's studies of insurance rates in cities of different population densities. He has also suggested a unit—population per mile of street—that reduces this hazard element to comparable figures. This unit applies equally well to entire cities or to parts of cities. For example, the Committee went so far as to compare a map showing the location of street accidents in New York with one showing the density of population. The coincidence was striking. The reason for this law appeared to be simple—the great bulk of the accidents was due to collisions of vehicles and pedestrians. This means, in general, the greater the number of pedestrians, the more accidents.

In continuing this line of thought, however, and arguing the more vehicles, the more accidents, the conclusion fails. Statistics showed that the maximum number of accidents did not occur, for example, on Fifth Avenue where there was a constant and almost solid stream of vehicles and where the sidewalks were crowded with people. On the contrary, they proved that the second law, which applies to vehicles, was different, that is, the number of street accidents was greatest on streets used by a variety of vehicles, such as trucks, passenger automobiles, and trolley cars, and where there was not sufficient congestion to prevent a fairly high speed with open spaces between vehicles. Eighth and Tenth Avenues below 59th Street, for example, and First Avenue throughout its length, are streets of this type with especially high accident rates.

One fundamental law in reference to city planning or to the design of new traffic lines is clear from this, namely, that new traffic routes, such as new streets, or bridge or tunnel outlets, should be kept away from centers of high population density. Thus, in attacking the street accident problem as it now exists in any city it is important to diffuse population and to concentrate traffic.

The chances of diffusing the population, or, to be more exact, of reducing the population density in heavy traffic sections, seem very small. Mr. Cox has mentioned zoning laws. It is also clear that the development of low-priced homes in suburban sections with adequate rapid transit facilities, may aid in this direction. In general, however, the population densities of great cities is increasing and is certain to continue to increase with the construction of the skyscraper apartments, offices, and hotels. It seems clear that little can be done through attempting to secure a diffusion of population.

are subject to moderation. In any event, it is believed that hazard will tend to approach, as a limit, the base values which depend on the mass factors of population, registrations, and street mileage, and which may be considered as the inevitable and unavoidable price of progress.

If, as in the paper, "hazard" refers to all classes of vehicles and if it may be measured by insurance rates, then such insurance rates must be the average charge for insurance per car for the various hazards insured. This average charge for insurance must then be the total insurance paid by cars of all classes, divided by the number of cars. If this is the case, it does not seem proper to predicate conclusions with respect to hazard in general on insurance experience and rates, for the following reasons:

(1) It is generally understood, although not definitely confirmed, that less than one-half the motor vehicles in an average community are insured and that the percentage varies.

(2) The lower the rates, the greater are the number of insured and the less is the average individual risk.

(3) As the rates are increased, the preferred class of risk drops out until, as in New York City, the rate is so high that there is an undue percentage of bad risks.

(4) The majority of cars insured in cities, such as Indianapolis, Ind., are private, and may be expected to cover less than 10 000 miles per year; whereas the majority of cars insured in a city like New York are commercial and have a mileage range from 25 000 to 100 000 miles per year in the case of many taxicabs. Hence, if the degree of hazard is to be established, all vehicles involved must be included in the calculation.

If it is true that higher rates do cause the preferred risk to drop out, leaving the costly risk, and so on in a vicious circle, and if many drivers who are greater risks cover many times the average mileage of a lesser risk, is it not reasonable to assume that insurance experience is not an exact measure of a hazard of the city as a whole, but reflects instead an unbalanced situation?

This brings in the matter of automobile club insurance competition in such cities as Chicago, Los Angeles, San Francisco, and Detroit. These clubs have the advantage of a membership fee, and sell their insurance to members at a very low sales cost and, it is assumed, without profit. In all these cities insurance rates are exceedingly low. For example, in Detroit the Automobile Club began selling insurance in March, 1922. Conference rates, to which Mr. Cox refers, continued without change through 1923, but, in 1924, public liability insurance on a Ford dropped 30%, on Buicks, 32%, and on Cadillacs, 31 per cent. The other cities referred to are understood to have had a similar experience.

It seems reasonable to conclude that the insurance companies are subject, not only to variations in risk, but that their rates are subject to the same competitive conditions which cause price variations in gasoline. If this is so, insurance rates cannot be taken as an accurate basis for measuring automobile accident hazard.

As a general conclusion, the paper suggests that: "The variation expressing the personal injury hazard * * * as population divided by street mileage, adds a warning against such degrees of congestion of population as prevail in almost all older large cities." Again, "the diffusion of population leads to a decrease in the number of possible collisions per unit distance of travel and thereby reduces hazard". And, finally, "most automobile collisions with pedestrians occur in residential districts." These statements seem to be contradictory since, for the most part, residential districts are areas in which the population is diffused.

Recently, some one asked the head of a large insurance company to state where, in his opinion, was the safest place. His answer was, first, on a railroad train; and, second, at the crossing of 42d Street and Fifth Avenue, New York, when it is carrying a maximum load of traffic.

It seems reasonable to suggest that, under conditions either of congested movements of vehicles or pedestrians, the hazard per unit vehicle or pedestrian is reduced, although the total reported accidents may be increased. In general support of this conclusion, Fig. 4 has been prepared from 1926 figures furnished through the courtesy of W. A. Van Duzer, M. Am. Soc. C. E., Deputy Engineering Executive of the Pennsylvania State Highway Department. This diagram shows the volume of traffic and the number of accidents for each hour of the day. From this information the degree of hazard (accidents, in terms of traffic) is determined. The curve indicates a rising hazard as the density of traffic decreases. It is reasonable to suppose that the declining density of traffic is, in part, responsible for this increase in hazard.

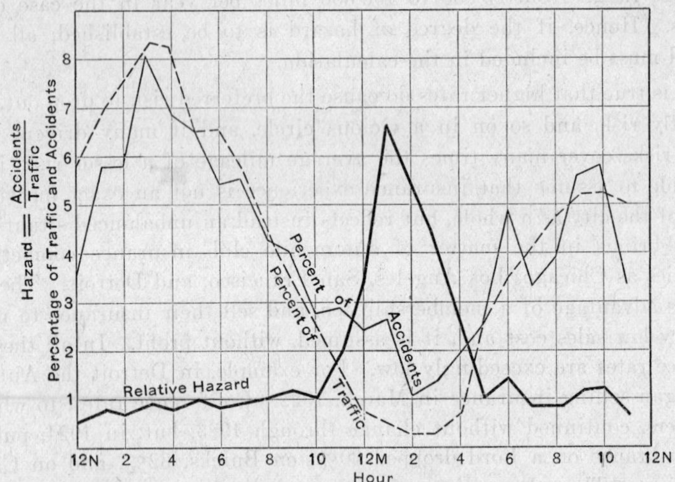

FIG. 4.—ACCIDENT HAZARD BY HOURS, PENNSYLVANIA STATE HIGHWAYS.

Mr. Cox is to be commended on his effort to clarify a subject which is shrouded in the fog of confusion, misinformation, and opinion. It is the speaker's conclusion, however, that he has not included all the factors necessary, in his formula, and that, although insurance rates and experiences are an index to the hazard experiences of selected classes and groups of cars, they are of doubtful value in measuring the hazard of a whole community.

Raymond A. O'Hara,* Assoc. M. Am. Soc. C. E.—That automobile hazard may be reduced by proper planning, is recognized if not appreciated. Roads on which intersecting highway grades have been separated minimize the chance of accident. Good examples of this type of highway are the Bronx River Parkway, extending from the northerly end of Bronx Park in New York City to the Kensico Dam in Westchester County, New York, and the highway being constructed by the New Jersey State Highway Department to connect with the Holland Vehicular Tunnels. The proposed West Side Elevated Roadway in Manhattan is another example.

There is a relationship between building bulk and automobile traffic. Replacing buildings of low heights with higher buildings brings additional traffic into the district. Further congestion and increasing hazards may be expected with increasing building bulk. Traffic control signals have played a part in the reduction of accidents and fatalities.

John A. Miller, Jr.,† Assoc. M. Am. Soc. C. E.—Where comprehensive traffic regulations have been adopted, as Mr. Cox points out, the accident hazard often is worse than in other cities. This suggests that the method of regulation is not always well suited to the needs of the situation. In New York City, for example, an elaborate system of traffic signals has been installed. Unfortunately, however, they are so operated that many of the beneficial results which might easily be obtained, are lost.

Several shortcomings stand out prominently. Signals all flash simultaneously over long stretches of important thoroughfares. Thus, all traffic on these streets starts and stops at regular intervals. There is no speed at which the driver of the vehicle may go and be assured of making continuous progress. Naturally, he tries to cover as much ground as possible while the signal is clear. This leads to excessive speed and many dangerous attempts to "beat" the lights.

In other cities this difficulty has been overcome by the installation of lights operated on a progressive or wave plan. In essence this is nothing more than alternation of the lights in groups of two or more, so that a vehicle starting when the light changes to green can proceed at a regular moderate pace throughout the entire area controlled without stopping, successive groups of lights changing to green as the vehicle approaches them. Under this system traffic as a whole moves faster than under the system used in New York, but excessive speed is penalized. From the point of view of reducing the accident hazard, it has marked advantages over the synchronized signal system.

Another glaring defect of the New York traffic signal arrangement is its failure to adjust the time intervals to suit conditions at the individual intersections. Traffic is held up very frequently when there is no cross traffic on the intersecting street. This constitutes an altogether unnecessary delay and slows up vehicular movement. The detrimental effect of synchronized signals was practically admitted by the Police Commissioner when he asked for an appropriation to extend the system. He said that the installation of lights

* Prin. Asst. Engr., Regional Plan of New York and Its Environs, New York, N. Y.

† Editor, *Area;* Associate Editor, *Electric Railway Journal,* New York, N. Y.

on any street caused the drivers of vehicles to avoid that street and use a parallel thoroughfare. This he wished to discourage by equipping the parallel street with similar signals. Such lack of adjustment of the system to meet actual needs causes disgust with the whole arrangement and frequent disregard of it.

This leads directly to the third weakness of the system now in vogue in New York City—its slipshod enforcement by the police. Where traffic officers are present, they sometimes enforce immediate compliance with the signals, sometimes allow vehicles to "steal" a little on the light, and not infrequently make no attempt at all to see that the signals are obeyed. Where no traffic officers are present, a majority of the drivers of vehicles obey the lights, but a large minority ignore them. From an accident standpoint this creates a hazard at least as great as, if not greater than, that which would exist without the signals.

Thus, it appears that two things are urgently needed to improve traffic control in New York City: First, an engineering study to determine the most efficient type of signal system, and how it should be operated; and, second, more careful enforcement of traffic regulations.

T. Kennard Thomson,* M. Am. Soc. C. E.—For more than sixteen years the speaker has done some work nearly every day on a plan which, it is hoped, will not merely reduce, but almost eliminate, the automobile hazard.

It is almost needless to point out the intolerable condition of New York streets—where one can often walk a mile quicker than he can ride—to say nothing of the accidents. There is no reason why the city should not have buildings as high as it wants, as many people as can occupy the buildings without congestion of the sidewalks, streets, or transit lines, and without the enormous cost of subways, which now is about $9 000 000 per mile.

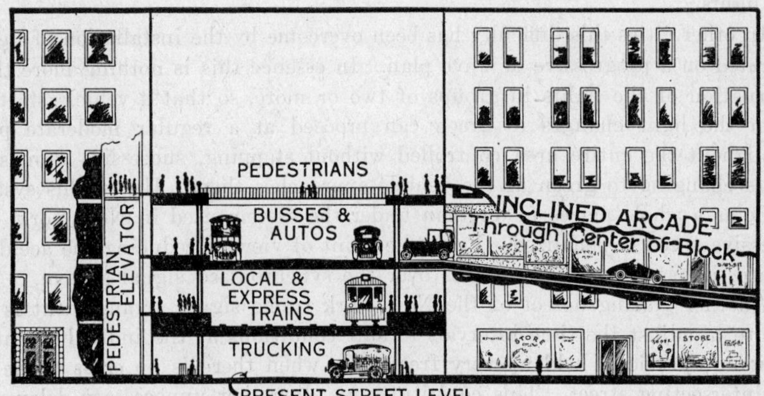

Fig. 5.—Proposed Rapid Transit Plan.

The city cannot raise money to build enough subways to eliminate the congestion. The remedy which the speaker has been advocating for many

* Cons. Engr., New York, N. Y.

years is multiple streets (one over the other) with separation of different kinds of traffic and the ultimate elimination of subways for passengers. Subways never should have been built, for five streets above ground can be built for the cost of one subway.

Fig. 5 shows a plan for three elevated streets (not viaducts) above the present grade. The ground or present street level of the avenues is to be reserved for trucking; the next level for transit lines, with the local cars running close to the sidewalks, allowing the passengers to observe well-lighted shop windows all the way. This level, as well as the one above it, will have elevated sidewalks so that one cannot step in front of automobiles or transit lines.

Access from the third or automobile level to the present ground line will be by inclined arcades through the centers of the blocks, giving four sidewalks where two now exist. At first, these inclined arcades should be placed a mile or two apart. Later, they may be installed wherever the property owners are willing to beg or pay for such accommodation, which means, eventually, every block.

The most valuable floor of a building is the ground floor—this plan gives four ground floors. By leaving the present cross streets as they are, there would be natural ventilation every 200 ft. on the two lower levels of the improved avenues. These levels would have perfect artificial lighting. The third, or automobile, level, and the fourth (sidewalks only), would have sunlight.

When first the speaker started these plans most people laughed at him. Later, there were various attempts to appropriate his plans bodily.

The speaker is always interested, although sometimes skeptical, in discussions on zoning. To advocate, as some very prominent men have done, that areas within New York City be laid out with very narrow streets, which will never permit thoroughfare traffic, would result in the value of the land being restricted to that for a two or three-story building—would be confiscation.

Even the multi-millionaires scrap their marble mansions when the value of the land becomes high enough. One man built what was then the highest building in New York, and at once tried to convince people that no one else should be allowed to put up a high building. When zoning becomes confiscation it is time to pause.

W. W. Crosby,* M. Am. Soc. C. E. (by letter).—The proper location of highways, the writer has long contended, is fundamental to reducing or relieving many highway difficulties, including those of highway safety. Location shares with zoning in a recognition and understanding of the kinds of traffic to be provided for; it comprehends, as does planning, the automatic segregation of traffic; the avoidance of congestion when and where necessary; the question of speeds; and the widths of highways, as well as alignment of the roadway.

As to "hazards" and "safety", at this time when such a highly scientific consideration of a common public matter is being carried on, a note of warning

* Cons. Engr., Coronado, Calif.

should be sounded. People should remain unemotional in considering this matter, strongly as they may be impelled for a while to personalize "safety", in order to bring home to the Nation, through the individual, the need for action to attain a lasting public benefit.

"Safety first" does not seem to convey the meaning elsewhere that it has in the United States. In America, highway safety began with the "watch-your-step" injunction of the New York subways and surface railways. That this had as a basis the safeguarding of the financial interests of these corporations against liability for personal damages can hardly be denied. There followed the somewhat broader "safety first" with its personal and individual appeal.

The Parisian practice of arresting the pedestrian run down by a vehicle in the streets of that city, and charging the unfortunate with "disturbing traffic,"* may sufficiently exemplify the basis on which European ideas of safety on the public roads seem to rest and from which foundation the present attitude has been developed in the European capitals, where most highway problems are older and, in some ways at least, better understood.

A study of the reports of the Fifth International Road Congress (Milan, September, 1926) impresses one with the recognition, apparent in the minds of the higher road authorities, of the public interest in the secure (safe) and steady (economic) flow or circulation of all traffic over the highways. The thought and effort seem to be toward "the efficient utilization of the highways with the greatest possible integrity of the most rapid circulation practicable"; first, by means of engineering expedients, and, second, when necessary, by supplementary general regulation. As long as it is consistent with the ends in view, the public is left unhampered in the choice of its means of highway use. Interruption of the personal choice of transportation, or other use of the highway by the individual, is imposed only where reliance on the individual responsibility, for his own and the general welfare, cannot longer be satisfactory to the community.

Mr. Cox has given a scientific treatment of what is so often regarded as a psychological or sociological problem. He brings out with astonishing clarity the functions of the engineer and proves his theories with intelligible mathematics. The elimination of some of the indefinite factors in these problems and the resolution of others into mathematical equivalents strike the writer as both logical and ingenious—well worth imitation and development.

THEODORE T. MCCROSKY,† JUN. AM. SOC. C. E. (by letter).—In reducing the complex problem of automobile accident hazard to mathematical terms, the author has found a formula which gives a gratifying agreement with the "actual hazard", as determined by insurance companies for rate-making purposes.

The author deduces that, from a public liability standpoint, the hazard is proportional to $\frac{P}{M}$, for any given city, and hence is independent of the number

* Highway Code, Article 55.

† Asst. Engr., E. P. Goodrich, New York, N. Y.

of automobiles in the city. Some cities have a large concentrated population, but very few automobiles. The value of the hazard, H, would be high, as given by the formula, $H \alpha \frac{P}{M}$. There are many such cities in Europe, in which, automobiles being scarce, the accident hazard is necessarily low.

Mr. Cox has proved that, for 1922, street width, good motor vehicle laws, and efficient handling of traffic are quantities which appear as mutually compensating in the majority of American cities of more than 200 000 population; and, consequently, need not be taken into consideration as variables in the problem. In the case of the other cities, he has taken up these three auxiliary factors as accounting for discrepancies between calculated and actual hazards. In the practical application of his formula, it would be hard to predict when these variables would compensate.

The writer believes that these three variables, as well as the registered number of automobiles, should appear in the formula, because all four of these considerations have changed greatly since 1922, and are becoming increasingly important.

Streets are being widened in the congested parts of cities where sidewalk widths permit. There are rigid motor vehicle laws in many more States than the four listed in 1922. The scientific regulation of traffic has increased enormously, but it is far more efficient in some cities than in others. Since 1922, the automobile registration in the United States has increased more than 80 per cent.

The writer fears that the author, in his praiseworthy attempt to reduce the problem to simple terms, has somewhat overshot his mark by omitting from his analysis these unknowns which, unfortunately, should no longer be neglected.

R. S. Kirby,* M. Am. Soc. C. E. (by letter).—The author has made a keen analysis of a pressing and intricate problem, from an actuarial standpoint, using a type of mathematical reasoning not so familiar to the average engineer, and the result comes out as a formula. Engineers delight in formulas, but are chary about using them unless they are reasonably familiar both with their antecedents and with their consequences.

Concerning the author's basic formula, $H = \frac{P}{M}$, a number of facts should be kept clearly in mind:

First.—The whole discussion has to do with fairly large centers of population, where less than one-half the automobile accidents occur. In less thickly settled localities this problem assumes quite a different aspect; there are fewer street intersections, and a much smaller proportion of pedestrians to cars.

Second.—The author centers his discussion about automobile accidents in which pedestrians and automobilists are injured or killed. An accident in which both cars were hopelessly wrecked, if providentially no one was injured,

* Associate Prof., Eng. Drawing, Yale Univ., New Haven, Conn.

would not figure in his analysis at all. Neither, apparently, would an accident in which the driver was killed, or any of the occupants of his car. This is, of course, confining the argument within narrow limits and excluding a large percentage of what are commonly thought of as automobile accidents. For example, in 1926, in the entire State of Connecticut, out of every 100 accidents reported to the Motor Vehicle Commissioner, 65 involved damage to property only and 35 resulted in injury to a person, either in a car or on the street. Of all the accidents reported, only about 15% were collisions with pedestrians. Of the persons killed in Connecticut in 4 years, 55% were pedestrians. The percentage of pedestrians among the injured was about 45. Of course, in large cities, all these percentages are quite different.

Third.—Dealing with the problem as one of insurance, the author entirely neglects the large number (about 50%) of uninsured cars, dismissing them with the statement that "there is no reason to believe that the hazard created by an insured car is materially different from that created by an uninsured car; * * *". Of course, it is yet too early to draw any certain conclusions from experience with compulsory insurance.

Fourth. Concerning the natural deductions from the $\frac{P}{M}$ formula, it is, of course, not logical to assume that the expression holds true for all possible values of the variables. If P were zero, as in remote country districts, there might still be automobile accidents, from cars passing through. Accidents caused by out-of-town and out-of-State cars form nearly one-half the total each year in Connecticut towns. The writer understands that another implication, and a justifiable one, is that if P were doubled, the hazard per car would be doubled, but the total number of accidents would be quadrupled. If the miles of improved road could be doubled over night, the number of accidents to-morrow would not, necessarily, be altered at all. This is partly because, as the author states, "a majority of collisions between automobiles in the average city occur at a comparatively small number of intersections." What effect, then, could a sudden increase in mileage in outlying sections have on traffic hazards in crowded tenement districts?

From his own experience the writer can thoroughly appreciate the author's difficulties in securing, from different localities, accident statistics which are exactly comparable. For example, the author's discussion considers only the number of injury accidents. The number of persons injured may be considerably greater and is more usually recorded.

What is a motor vehicle accident? The various States are not uniform in their definitions. Connecticut, for example, requires the reporting of all accidents which result either in any personal injury or in property damage to an apparent extent of more than $10. Other States neglect property damage accidents entirely. This illustrates only one phase of the difficulties in securing comparable statistics from various cities. Uniformity in this matter is a long way off, and some of the statistics that the author needs in order to substantiate his reasoning are available only in a very few cities, if at all. Engineers are natural born statisticians and can help in keeping such facts before the public.

The author states emphatically that the variation in hazard between different cities is not caused by differences in automobile congestion or in the effectiveness of traffic control. However, in the case of Boston, Mass., may it not perhaps be that both these factors contribute, each in its own way, to reduce the local hazard?

The latter portion of the paper, in which certain methods of reducing accidents are most concisely outlined, should have been expanded. For example, the main motor-vehicle arteries of the future will not pass through the centers of any towns. This involves intelligent engineering, and is vastly more important than much of the minor puttering and patching which is being done. A decided reduction in accidents can be brought about by intensive local public campaigns designed to crystallize public sentiment against three practices. Of these, the first is speeding, or driving too fast for conditions. The second is unnecessary driving in congested areas, or using the public highways for trivial errands. The third is a lack of consideration for the other fellow, be he on wheels or on foot. While these three practices are not engineering matters, nevertheless, the engineer, as a private citizen, can do much in his quiet methodical way to better conditions.

All the author's suggestions concerning the use of streets as playgrounds, particularly in tenement districts, are reasonable. Autoists of the future must, perforce, give up many more of their "rights" for the common good.

Drivers are responsible for three-quarters of all automobile accidents (including collisions between cars), at least that is the conclusion of the Connecticut Motor Vehicle Department which has had long experience in determining primary causes. When drivers are trained to concentrate their attention on their driving, to have a decent regard for ordinary rules of the road, and to drive so carefully that their cars need never skid, two-thirds of the automobile accidents will have disappeared.

The State of Connecticut held pedestrians to have been at fault in 74% of the pedestrian collisions last year. The 1926 percentage in Massachusetts was estimated at 37 for non-fatal collisions and 25 for fatal, a wide divergence, due probably in large part to varying methods of analysis.

LEE S. TRAINOR,* ASSOC. M. AM. SOC. C. E. (by letter).—This paper is most valuable and presents clearly the existing automobile hazards in cities and the major points of traffic control affecting these hazards. The writer wishes to call attention to a few factors of particular importance to municipal engineers.

In a paper before the Society of Automotive Engineers, T. R. Agg, M. Am. Soc. C. E.,† emphasized the fact that whereas vehicles were formerly designed to fit the road, to-day pavements are built to suit the vehicle. Several points in the relationship of pavements to the vehicles operating on them, should be given consideration.

The type of street pavement and its condition has an important bearing on the safety with which traffic moves. A street can hardly be considered as

* Mgr., Highways and Municipal Bureau, Portland Cement Association, Chicago, Ill.

† "The Design and Construction of Highway Systems," *Journal*, Soc. of Automotive Engrs., Vol. XXI (August, 1927), p. 200.

giving efficient transportation service unless the pavement on the street is in such a condition, from curb to curb, that vehicles are given the uninterrupted use of the entire width of the thoroughfare. A poor street pavement, the surface of which is irregular, or spotted with holes, offers a hazard to passing vehicles which is often difficult to surmount. Bad holes or rough places cause vehicles to deflect from their line of travel into another line, creating a hazard for oncoming vehicles. It is important, therefore, that heavily traveled thoroughfares be provided with pavements that retain smoothness of surface and that can be maintained with minimum expense and the least interference to the normal flow of traffic. The Keystone Automobile Club, of Philadelphia, Pa., reports that the City of Philadelphia expends $500 000 per year in damages for accidents caused by defective pavements.

Congestion of traffic in large centers of population is mounting more rapidly each year. Unfortunately, the majority of the larger cities in the United States were laid out and developed long before traffic congestion had become a problem. The unprecedented growth of the motor industry and its allied industries, which has produced the present-day volume of traffic, could not have been imagined at that time. Consequently, the street systems of the larger cities have become antiquated and do not render full transportation service.

Because of the lack of proper street width, congestion presents a traffic hazard that is most difficult to overcome. American cities have grown at such a rapid rate that street widening in densely populated areas has become an expensive operation. Congestion is truly a sufficient cause for providing main arteries of traffic with such pavements that the maximum service of the existing width can be obtained. Many American cities are spending millions of dollars annually for street widening in order to reduce the hazard of congestion.

Blind corners, short-radius street intersections, and poor visibility, especially at night, are other hazards encountered by traffic in metropolitan areas. Even the color of a pavement affects the safety of moving vehicles, especially at night. A dark pavement has a tendency to absorb the rays of headlights to such an extent that the limits of the thoroughfare are but dimly defined. It is also more difficult to see pedestrians and parked vehicles at a safe distance. The same is true concerning the amount of light perceived from vehicles approaching from the right or left at street intersections. A light-colored pavement reflects the rays of the head lamps, thus outlining the course for a greater distance ahead. A light-colored pavement also creates enough contrast to give a clear outline of parked vehicles or other hazards that may be placed at the curb. During wet weather, such a pavement is especially conducive to safety because of the contrast in color with surrounding objects.

Heavily traveled arteries should be provided with pavements that are reliable under all conditions. Skidding and sliding with locked wheels are the causes of many accidents on congested thoroughfares. Safety on the boulevard has become more than a matter of good tires and good brakes.

The characteristics of pavement surfaces must be considered. Any pavement that becomes slippery when it is wet is a source of danger often beyond the control of the driver. A rough and bumpy street often induces skidding as tires lose contact with the surface.

Starting and stopping must be accomplished rapidly, and the pavement must do its part perfectly if the hazards are to be reduced. The surface should be such that it will not be slippery and cause skidding on sudden application of the brakes. It should be sufficiently gritty to provide a grip for the tires, and bring the vehicle to a stop as quickly as possible. A pavement surface of this character is especially beneficial during wet weather. On steep grades it provides enough traction to make ascent easy and safe, and on descent provides sufficient tractive resistance to prevent skidding or side sliding. Such a surface automatically provides hazard elimination for the motorist. The construction of streets and pavements suited to present-day traffic is of material assistance in reducing automobile hazard in cities.

Sidney J. Williams,* M. Am. Soc. C. E. (by letter).—This paper by Mr. Cox is the first real attempt to develop a scientific formula for the occurrence of automobile accidents in cities. Like any other pioneer job, this method is doubtless open to refinement at the hands of the author or some one else. Further information may correct some of the assumptions that Mr. Cox was compelled to make; but he has at least given all students of the subject something to "shoot at", and his careful and intelligent analysis constitutes a real contribution to the safety movement in the United States.

It would be very desirable to check the formula against data later than 1922 and to check the application of it to the changing experience of one or more cities from year to year.

Many things have happened since 1922 to affect accident causation and accident prevention on the highways. In various cities, there has been opportunity to observe the effect, on the accident record, of various changes in the traffic control situation and in the state of public opinion. It has been found that, in fact as well as in theory, the accident record of a city can be vitally affected by factors other than those stated in the basic formula developed by Mr. Cox; for example, by better traffic regulation and by the right kind of public education. Cities are beginning to accumulate statistical evidence, covering a period of years, to show that continuous and properly organized educational campaigns can be depended on to reduce the accidents in a community just as they do in a factory.

Aside from definite safety educational campaigns, there is the element of the general public attitude toward law enforcement. As a native of the State of Wisconsin, the writer feels able to say with some assurance that the attitude toward law observance in that State and in the City of Milwaukee is very different, and much better, than in the State of Illinois and the City of Chicago, for example. This is probably one reason for the accident record in Milwaukee being better than anticipated, as shown in Mr. Cox's paper. In

* Director, Public Safety Div., National Safety Council, Chicago, Ill.

fact, the writer feels that the general public attitude toward law observance and accident prevention will be found to have an even greater effect on the accident experience of the community, than the street mileage or any other engineering factor. The statisticians and engineers of the National Safety Council, for example, are just beginning to obtain data on which to make quantitative studies of these complicated and important factors. These remarks are in extension and not in criticism of Mr. Cox's excellent paper.

A. B. BARBER,* M. AM. SOC. C. E. (by letter).—This paper is a distinctly original contribution to the study of the automobile accident and traffic problem and is of special value because of its method of approach. It establishes, in mathematical form, facts that have heretofore generally been supported only by opinion. It is teeming with suggestion, both in and between the lines.

No one who has seriously studied the traffic problem will be surprised at the deduction that, H, the hazard from the operation of the individual automobile, varies directly with population, P. Unfortunately, motor traffic is still generally so poorly organized and pedestrians still roam so freely over the street surface that the assumption of uniform distribution of both these elements is not a material departure from the fact.

The expression, $H \propto \frac{P}{M}$, suggests that H can be lowered by reducing P, or by increasing M. To reduce P signifies relieving a portion of the population (including those in cars as well as those on foot) from the hazard of individually threading their way among moving automobiles. This can be done in a variety of ways. The policeman at the corner with his stop-and-go signal; the school-boy patrol holding up traffic to let the children pass; the automatic traffic signal system; all these are means for decreasing the aggregate amount of the population subject to the hazard indicated in Mr. Cox's initial assumption. That they are successful is shown by the practical elimination of accidents on streets where traffic control is well established and enforced, by officers or by automatic signals. This, as Mr. Cox points out, is one form of traffic "segregation."

Pedestrian control also reduces the amount of the population, P, exposed to the automobile danger. Control, however, is objected to by some pedestrians as a violation of "inalienable rights", just as some motorists regard licensing of drivers as violation of their rights. Both are safety measures, the importance of which is just beginning to be realized.

Under Mr. Cox's formula, H may also be reduced by increasing M. While this holds for the purpose of this paper it may not be true as a permanent measure of accident reduction, for it is natural to suppose that any great increase of street mileage through decentralization or a general spreading out of the population would lead to such an increase of distance traveled per automobile as to require that new element to be taken into account. Proper city planning and zoning measures, however, would serve to offset this tendency. The modern conception of a city or metropolitan region contem-

* Mgr. Transportation and Communications Dept., Chamber of Commerce of the United States, and Director, National Conference on Street and Highway Safety, Washington, D. C.

plates the location of commercial, industrial, and other centers at appropriate widely distributed points, with housing and community facilites for employees in close proximity to each center. The working out of this conception should economize, not only time and expense of travel, but should also tend to reduce the accident hazard.

WILLIAM J. COX,* JUN. AM. SOC. C. E. (by letter).†—The writer's purpose in the presentation of this paper was not to create a finished document, nor to state a final word. Rather it was to open a new line of thought on the problem of automobile accidents, and to encourage thinking along more fundamental lines as to the basic factors in their occurrence. He feels gratified that the paper has aroused so much discussion.

The writer did not intend to suggest that the automobile accident problem cannot be influenced by other factors than the density of population. He did wish to show that density of population is the basic factor in determining the personal injury hazard of operating an automobile in a city. Other factors, some susceptible to statistical treatment, perhaps, and some not, may exert a modifying influence and should, of course, be given careful consideration in traffic control and accident prevention work; but, basically, the hazard level is a function of the density of population. The writer is satisfied in his own mind that this is the case, and has been pleased to note that most of the commentators on the paper agreed on this point. It was suggested by several of the discussors that more stress should have been placed on conclusions to be drawn from the principle that the paper set forth. It is the writer's feeling that to have done that would have enlarged the scope of the paper unwisely. The aim was, as stated, to call attention to the principle in the hope that it might encourage further work and thought on the part of others as to its applications and implications.

Among the many points brought to light was the particularly interesting discussion of traffic conditions in Washington, D. C., by Messrs. Stark and Eldridge. Mr. Eldridge is in a position to know the difficulties of traffic administration in Washington, but the writer is unable to agree with him that Washington streets are not well designed to carry the traffic. It is true that many of the streets in the city are narrow, but there is no reason why all the streets of a city, or even a majority of them, should be wide. Provided there is a sufficient network of arterial ways to carry through traffic, it is advantageous for several reasons that intermediate streets should not be too wide. Like all cities, designed before the invention of the automobile, Washington has an inadequate street system, but its streets are more nearly adequate for their traffic needs than those of any other large American city, and the distribution of business and population through the city is also unusually good.

Mr. Eldridge speaks of the hazard introduced by the convergence of a number of streets at certain points in Washington; as, for example, at Thomas and Scott Circles. The writer is not in possession of accident

* Asst. Prof., Dept. of Eng. Mechanics, Sheffield Scientific School, Yale Univ., New Haven, Conn.

† Now Assoc. M. Am. Soc. C. E.

statistics for these two localities, and they may be more dangerous than they appear, but he has repeatedly watched the streams of traffic converging on them and diverging, and has been impressed with the smoothness and safety with which they move. He finds it difficult to believe that such circles add to the street hazards of Washington.

Mr. Eldridge calls attention to the decrease in automobile fatalities and accidents in Washington from 1923 to 1926, and suggests certain causes, denying that the improvement was brought about by the planning of the city, etc. This is true. From 1923 to 1926 there was no marked shift in the planning of the city. The writer's paper was based on 1922 conditions; and the improvement subsequent to that time, which no doubt is due to the causes enumerated by Mr. Eldridge, is outside the scope of the paper. The planning of the city and perhaps the superior administration of traffic in Washington, even before Mr. Eldridge took charge, made it possible for the improvement to which he refers to be based on hazard conditions that were apparently already surprisingly good.

Mr. Stark, in vigorously dissenting from the views set forth by Mr. Eldridge as to the excellence of police regulation of traffic in Washington in recent times, makes a well-reasoned plea for a greater consideration of the pedestrian in traffic. He has convinced the writer of the error in stating that improved methods of handling traffic at intersections will have little effect on collisions between automobiles and pedestrians. He advances a sound argument that the effect, although indirect, is nevertheless present.

Mr. Williams also stresses the indirect connection between traffic hazards and "the general public attitude toward law observance and accident prevention". The writer recognizes the weight of Mr. Williams' judgment in this matter and the very great importance of the relationship he mentions. The writer does not believe, however, that any differences in this attitude of the public could exist sufficiently great to overbalance entirely the physical advantage of low population density. That is, he doubts if such an improvement in the attitude of citizens toward traffic rules in New York, coupled with such a retrogression in Indianapolis, could occur as to overbalance the differences in population congestion and place those cities on a par from an automobile-operation hazard standpoint.

Mr. Lewis is apparently confusing the fatality rate per unit of population and the fatality rate per automobile. All the data to which he refers are based on the automobile-fatality rate per population unit, while the writer's paper was a discussion of the hazard per car—the hazard of operating an automobile. This was found to be $\frac{P}{M}$. As Professor Lyle points out, the hazard per unit of population derived from this formula is $\frac{R}{M}$, which would seem to accord with Mr. Lewis' views.

Among those who discussed the paper, Mr. Kelcey was the only one to express marked distrust of the use of automobile liability insurance rates to measure hazards. There were probably other readers who felt about this as Mr. Kelcey did, since there is a general disposition on the part of the public to suspect that insurance rates are established wholly competitively and are based on what the traffic will bear.

Mr. Kelcey's objections to the insurance rate as a measure were along three lines. He states that the proportion of taxicabs and commercial vehicles among the total number of cars insured in New York is much greater than in smaller cities, such as Indianapolis; that these public and commercial vehicles have much greater annual mileages than the average private passenger car, and, therefore, a greater annual hazard; and that, consequently, they distort the insurance rate of New York, making it unduly high in comparison with those of other cities where the proportion of relatively safe private passenger cars insured is greater. Mr. Kelcey's argument would be sound, granting his premises, if the insurance rate were established, as he assumes, by totaling the premiums paid by cars of all classes, and dividing it by the total number of insured cars of all classes in the city. Insurance rates are not made this way, however, but separately for cars of each type, private passenger, public passenger, and commercial. As stated by the writer, the private passenger car rate, being by far the most important and the most accurately determined, is the one selected as a means of comparison. The variation from city to city of commercial and public passenger car rates does not differ greatly from that of private passenger car rates, and no material error is introduced by selecting the latter as a standard. The fact that the ratio of insured taxicabs to insured private passenger cars is greater in New York than elsewhere, if true, is without force as regards this discussion.

A second question raised by Mr. Kelcey may be more pertinent. He suggests that, as insurance rates increase from cities of low hazard to cities of high hazard, the better class of risks drop out, leaving a higher proportion of "bad risks" in cities with high rates, thus continually raising the rates still higher. This is a view held by many people, but by no means universally; and among those who hold that there is such a tendency, opinion differs as to how marked and how important it is. Light will be shed on this question when the Massachusetts law, providing that every automobile must carry liability insurance, has been in effect longer. So far as the writer is able to learn during the few months of its existence there has been no decided indication that the addition of the large number of those formerly uninsured to those already carrying insurance, either in Boston, with its high rates, or in small cities in the State, where rates are much lower, has either raised or lowered the loss ratio; that is, the newly insured cars, taken as a whole, seem to be neither worse nor better risks, in any decided degree, than those formerly insured.

The most serious objection Mr. Kelcey raises is that insurance rates are established, in considerable part, by business competition. In substantiation of this, he instances that the Detroit Automobile Club began in 1922 to sell insurance to its members at a lower rate than that of the stock insurance companies, and that within the next two years the stock companies' rate was reduced 30 per cent. He states that the Cities of Los Angeles, San Francisco, and Chicago "are understood" to have had a similar experience following the sale of automobile insurance by local automobile clubs to their members.

The loss experience sheets of the National Bureau of Casualty and Surety Underwriters show that on policies written in Detroit in 1922 the claim frequency was 4.0; that is, for every hundred policies written that year, 4.0 claims resulted. In 1923, this frequency dropped to 3.7, and, in 1924, to 3.0. Correspondingly, the insurance rate dropped 25% from 1922 to 1926. Thus, the rate trend followed the claim frequency trend, and no competitive influence of the automobile club is apparent.

In Los Angeles, claim frequency dropped from 4.4 in 1922 to 2.6 in 1924. The 1922 claim frequency was abnormally high, so that the improvement trend has not been so great as appears from these two figures alone. Since 1922, insurance rates have declined 20 per cent. Here, again, while a decline in rates has occurred, as Mr. Kelcey states, it is less than the decline in the frequency of claims. If the Automobile Club of Southern California has played a part in rate reduction, that part has consisted in its valuable hazard-reducing work in the traffic education field.

In San Francisco, despite the existence of the automobile club to which Mr. Kelcey refers, there has been a slight increase in automobile liability insurance rates since 1922. In 1926, they stood 5% above the 1922 level. There has been no sustained trend in the claim frequency. It was 4.0 in 1922 and, again, in 1923. In 1924, it dropped to 3.0, but, in 1925, rose to 3.7. The average severity of accidents also appears to have been abnormally high in 1924 and 1925.

In Chicago, claim frequency dropped from 6.6 in 1922 to 6.5 in 1923 and 4.8 in 1924. The insurance rate declined 22% from 1922 to 1926. In none of these instances does the competition envisioned by Mr. Kelcey appear to have played a part in affecting the insurance rate level.

It is not the writer's view that public liability insurance rates make a perfect yard-stick for measuring hazard variations, but he does believe that they are decidedly the best measure available. He emphatically does not believe (and the figures support him) that insurance rates fluctuate competitively in the sense that gasoline prices do. Rates are not an immediate reflection of hazard fluctuations because they are damped (by the use of mathematical formulas, of country-wide application) to smooth out extreme peaks and hollows and, therefore, show only established, not accidental, trends. However, there is no question but that they are determined by such trends, rather than by business competition.

Mr. Kelcey apparently takes issue with the whole conclusion of the writer's paper that diffusion of population decreases the hazard of operating an automobile. He instances the infrequency of traffic accidents in the dense vehicular and pedestrian traffic at Fifth Avenue and 42d Street, New York City. He finds a contradiction in the writer's statements that, "diffusion of population leads to a decrease in the number of possible collisions per unit distance of travel and thereby reduces hazard" and "most automobile collisions with pedestrians occur in residential districts." Residential districts, he states, are areas in which the population is diffused; hence, the contradiction.

The fallacy in Mr. Kelcey's reasoning is that sometimes population is diffused in residential areas and sometimes it is not. Who would say that the Lower East Side of New York was not a residential area and who would say that it was an area of diffused population? The fact of the matter is that most pedestrian accidents occur in residential areas, and that, as a rule, these areas are the congested, tenement districts of the residential part of the city as a whole. The writer mentioned this in his "Conclusions". Data since collected enable him now to illustrate the point numerically.

In New Haven, the highest class (single-family) residential area, where population is most diffused, is traversed by approximately 16 miles of streets. In this region, records of the Department of Motor Vehicles of Connecticut show that not a single pedestrian accident occurred during 1926. Approximately, 100 miles of streets traverse areas outside the central business district which are unrestricted for residential use. On these 100 miles of streets there were in excess of 200 pedestrian accidents in 1926.

Mr. Kelcey presents a diagram (Fig. 4), based on data from the State Highway Department of Pennsylvania, which, to his mind, shows that the more diffused vehicular traffic becomes, the more hazardous automobile operation becomes. His data relate to rural, not urban, conditions, and it is questionable whether they do not indicate the reckless character of the traffic on the highways at 2:00 A. M., as much as anything else. He is correct, however, in thinking that decreasing the density of vehicular traffic may add to the hazard of automobile operation. The explanation is obvious. A very dense vehicular traffic must be controlled; and a controlled traffic is a safe traffic. A diffused vehicular traffic becomes an unregulated traffic, and often becomes a high-speed traffic, which is correspondingly dangerous.

The writer has not urged that vehicular traffic be diffused. He has urged that population be diffused, and that in passing through areas of diffused population, vehicular traffic be concentrated in arterial ways into streams of sufficient density that their continuity may bring safety.

Professor Finch expressed the idea much more effectively than the writer. "* * * in attacking the street accident problem as it now exists in any city," he states, "it is important to diffuse population and to concentrate [vehicular] traffic." In other words, spread out population until the smallest possible proportion is encountered in a given street, and then put the largest possible proportion of the vehicular traffic through that street, regulating it as may be necessary. As Professor Finch points out, diffusion of population is often impracticable. Concentration of traffic is much less often impracticable; it is obviously good sense, but is often not done.

As an instance of this in the neighborhood of the writer's home, traffic on a "through" route traversing the city, has intentionally been routed over several parallel streets, although the volume of it is not so great that one street could not handle it all. As a result, sparse streams of out-of-town vehicular traffic pass through an apparently quiet residential section at fairly high speeds and, without warning, come to a cross street carrying a fairly high speed and fairly heavy, but often intermittent, city traffic. Some of the worst accident corners in the city are the result. The through traffic should be gathered into a condensed stream on one street, freeing the parallel residential streets of it; and this stream should be controlled by lights or otherwise where it crosses other traffic arteries. Almost every city can show examples of the same failure to appreciate this law of safe street use.

A number of other worth-while points were brought out in the discussion. Mr. Cole called attention to the fact that nine of the cities shown on the writer's Fig. 3 have been doing organized street safety work for some years, and that seven of these nine cities had "actual hazards" lower than their "calculated hazards." This is very significant as an indication of the possibility of modifying the "natural" hazard level.

Professor Kirby calls attention to the very great need of more adequate and better organized statistics relating to street and highway accidents. Mr. Holleran and Mr. Johannesson deal interestingly with measures developed in their sphere of highway work to make highways safer. Space is lacking to comment adequately here on other points of interest.

Colonel Barber's discussion emphasizes, in words that will bear repetition, the fundamental importance of more satisfactory planning of cities, as follows:

"The modern conception of a city or metropolitan region contemplates the location of commercial, industrial, and other centers at appropriate widely distributed points, with housing and community facilities for employees in close proximity to each center. The working out of this conception should economize not only time and expense of travel, but should also tend to reduce the accident hazard."

As suggested, the street safety problem is tied up closely with the matter of the economical use of city streets; that is, with the basic economics of city life.

The problem of automobile accidents confronts the city as an existing condition. This fact has been often pointed out, and, unfortunately, people have already suffered enormously from the too great emphasis placed on it. In the last 20 years the population of most large cities in the United States has increased from 50 to 600, or more, per cent. There is reason to believe that such increases of urban population will continue to be typical. There is, therefore, every reason to give more constructive thought than has yet been generally given to the probability of such increases and to their street-traffic implications. By all means, cities should avail themselves of the expedients that Mr. Holleran's discussion enumerates and describes as palliatives rather than cures. However, with them they must give (and progressive cities are giving) increasing consideration to a more far-sighted view of future traffic needs and to the provision of the proper facilities to meet them.

AMERICAN SOCIETY OF CIVIL ENGINEERS
INSTITUTED 1852

TRANSACTIONS

This Society is not responsible for any statement made or opinion expressed in its publications.

Paper No. 1657

CONSTRUCTION METHODS ON THE MOFFAT TUNNEL*

By R. H. Keays,† M. Am. Soc. C. E.

With Discussion by Messrs. T. Kennard Thomson, H. F. Dunham, and Lazarus White.

Synopsis

This paper describes in detail the interesting methods used in the excavation of the Moffat Tunnel in Colorado. This work is really two parallel headings constructed at the same time, one a single-track railroad tunnel and the other a pressure tunnel for water.

There is also included a brief statement of the location and purpose for which the tunnels are built, as well as some notes on the financing of the work by the Moffat Tunnel Commission representing the Moffat Tunnel Improvement District, the form of contract for the construction, and the workmen's bonus plan.

The Moffat Tunnel is the longest railway tunnel in America, and the methods used in its construction are believed to represent the best present-day practice.

This paper was written before the completion of the project and describes methods used only up to August 1, 1925, at which date the headings were approximately 62% completed.

Selection of Site

For many years the general location selected for the Moffat Tunnel has been considered the best place, in fact, the only practicable location in Northern Colorado for building a railroad through the Continental Divide. At this point the approaches on both east and west sides are most favorable.

* Presented at the meeting of March 2, 1927.

† Chf. Engr., Ulen & Co., Athens, Greece.

At various times tunnels have been laid out at different elevations and of different lengths, the higher ones of course being shorter and having the merit only of relative cheapness. The Moffat Tunnel is at the lowest practicable elevation. Any further lowering would require a much longer tunnel and would not improve the alignment or grades of the railroad on either side of the Divide. The work is at an elevation of approximately 9 200 ft. and is 32 250 ft. long.

Physical and General Conditions

The tunnel is to be used by the Denver and Salt Lake Railroad—usually known as the Moffat Road—which has been in operation for twenty years. The original builders always had in mind that ultimately a tunnel would be built at this location, but were induced to locate a line "over the hill" as a temporary expedient. The gradient of the railroad from the East Portal to Denver, Colo., 50 miles east, is 2%, down-hill practically all the way. On the west side the grade from the West Portal to Tabernash, Colo., 9 miles beyond, is 2% down-hill and thence 1% down-hill to State Bridge, 60 miles farther on. As shown on Fig. 1, it is intended eventually to build a connection between the Moffat Road and the Denver and Rio Grande Western Railway, the so-called Dotsero cut-off. By developing the line between Tabernash and the West Portal (Fig. 2), it is feasible to build all the way from the Denver and Rio Grande Western Railway to the West Portal on a 1% ruling grade against the traffic. There is also a project on foot to build a connection between Salt Lake City, Utah, and Craig, Colo., the western terminus of the Moffat Railroad.

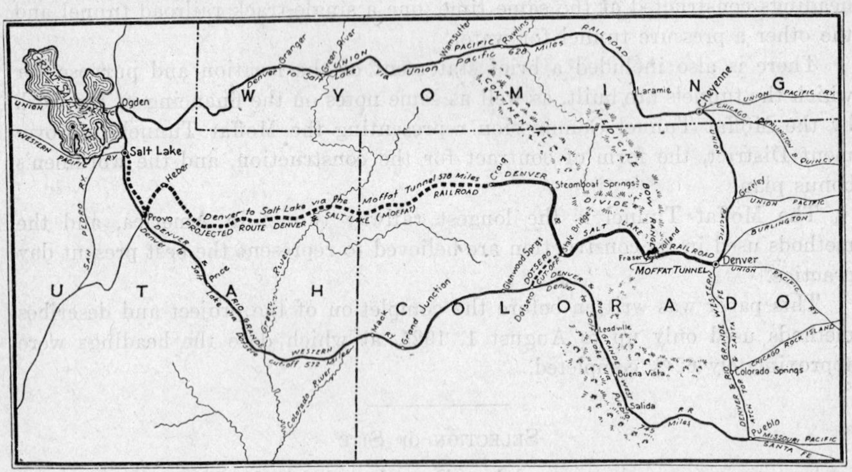

FIG. 1.—MOFFAT TUNNEL AND ITS RELATION TO WESTERN RAILROADS.

The line "over the hill", however, is built on a 4% grade from a short distance above the tunnel elevation to the summit at Corona, Colo., an elevation of 11 660 ft. Snow, ice, and wind conditions are not serious matters up as far as the elevation of the tunnel, but above this point the conditions

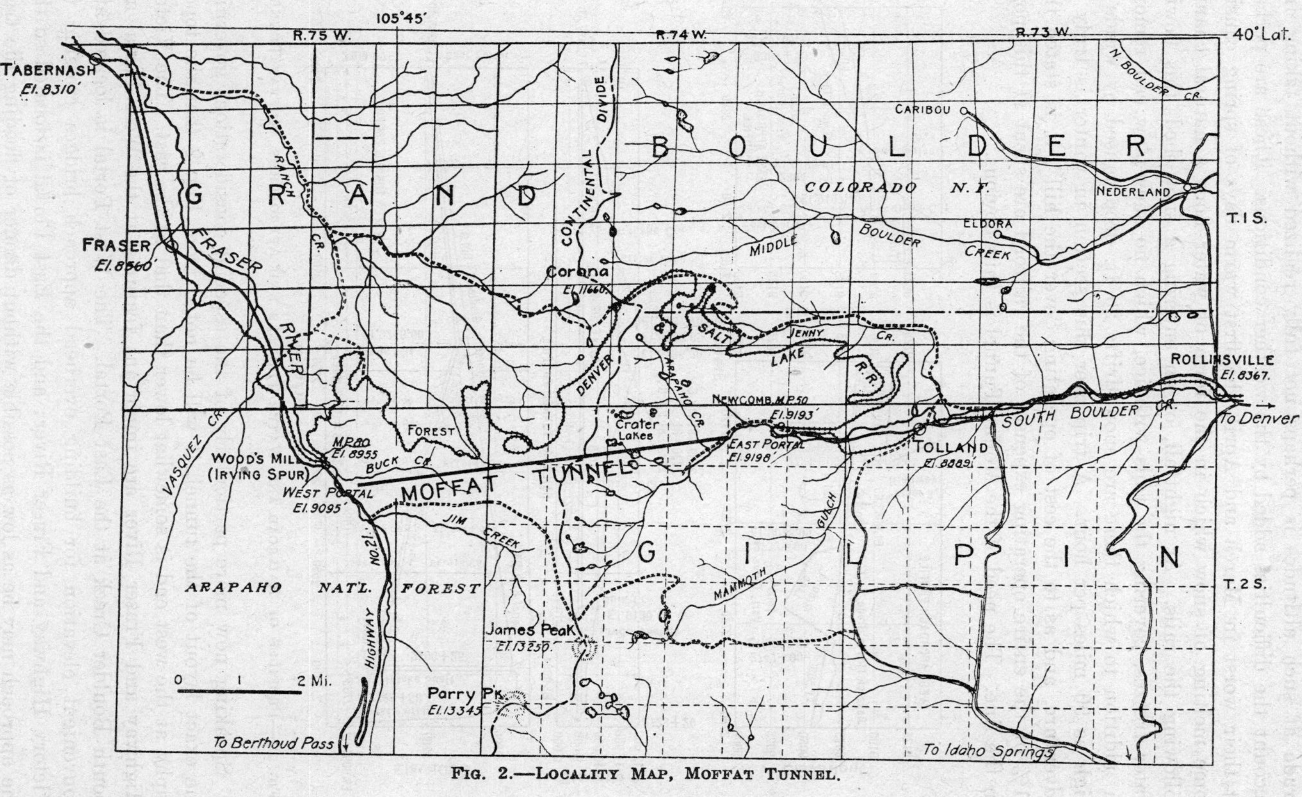

Fig. 2.—Locality Map, Moffat Tunnel.

become much worse up to the top of the range. The significance of a 4% grade at such altitudes is perhaps not fully realized without taking into account the difficulties added by the weather conditions. These are perhaps at their worst in March and April, the first warm days of spring causing some melting of snow which in the form of water finds a natural channel following the rails. At nightfall, or on entering a snow-shed, this flowing water freezes, covering the rails with ice, which no snow-plow can remove; in addition to which there are snow drifts 20 ft. deep caused by winds as high as 90 miles per hour. A trip over this section in winter is truly an adventure, and as to the cost of operating "over the hill", it is stated that 41% of the entire operating expenses of the railroad are spent at this point on the line. The need of the Moffat Tunnel is thus obvious.

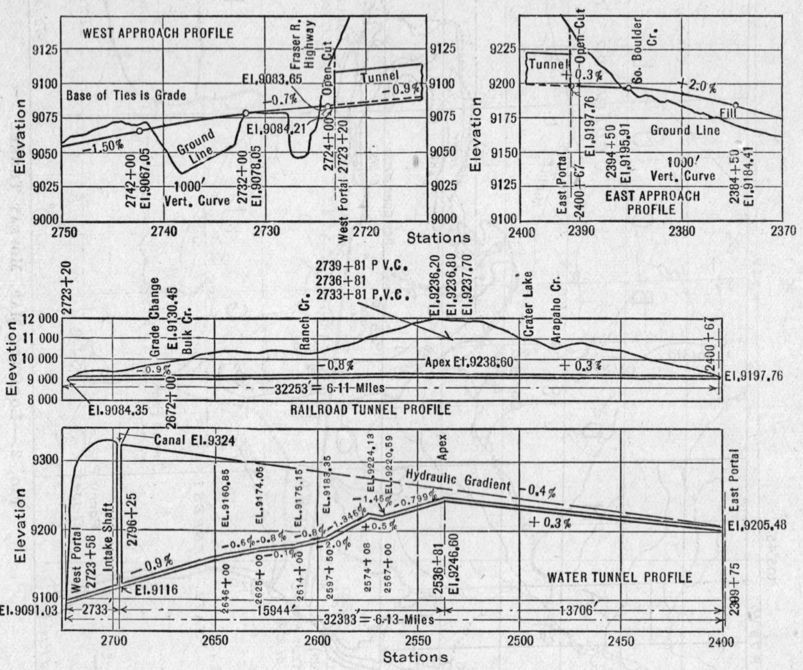

FIG. 3.—PROFILES OF RAILROAD AND WATER TUNNELS AND APPROACHES, MOFFAT TUNNEL.

Speaking now more particularly of the especial considerations governing the exact layout of the tunnel, it will be noted from Fig. 2 that the topography at the west end is somewhat lower than that at the east. The Victory Highway and Fraser River are important features at the West Portal and South Boulder Creek at the East Portal. The West Portal is located at a convenient elevation for building overhead approach bridges crossing the Victory Highway and Fraser River; and the East Portal is located so that the approach may be as low as possible without danger of flooding the track by the waters of South Boulder Creek, and so that the disposal of muck would interfere as little as possible with the outflow from the water tunnel.

The grades in the tunnel itself (Fig. 3) were fixed with the idea of running to an apex near the middle to provide drainage during construction. This worked out as a 0.3% grade on the east end (the minimum required for drainage), and a 0.9% grade on the west end. At the request of the officials of the Denver and Salt Lake Railroad, the upper part of the 0.9% grade was later changed to 0.8 per cent. This threw the apex farther east, which, together with the fact that the work at the East Portal had advanced much faster than that at the West Portal, made it necessary to drive part of the tunnel down-hill.

The Moffat Tunnel is being built out of the proceeds of the sale of bond issues by the Moffat Tunnel Improvement District, a political sub-division of the State created for the especial purpose of building the Moffat Tunnel and leasing it for railroad purposes. This District is composed of the City of Denver and the whole northwestern part of the State. It was required by the law creating the District that provision should be made in building the tunnel for the conveyance of water from the western to the eastern slope of the Divide, as a prospective domestic water supply for the City of Denver, to the amount of 100 000 acre-ft. per year. It was decided by the Board of Consulting Engineers for the Moffat Tunnel Commission that this object could be best obtained by constructing a separate parallel and smaller tunnel for the conveyance of water only. Such a plan would incidentally enable both tunnels to be advanced simultaneously by the so-called pioneer, or better, the twin-heading method, a plan similar to those used on the Simplon and Rogers Pass Tunnels. Such a plan is very desirable for purposes of ventilation, if for no other reason.

The water tunnel was located 75 ft. south of the center line of the railroad tunnel (Fig. 3). In grade the center line of the water tunnel follows approximately the center line of the railroad tunnel. This design requires the west end of the water tunnel to be under pressure. The hydraulic grade originally designed to be 0.3% was later changed to 0.4 per cent. The necessary pressure at the west end will be obtained by constructing a shaft about 265 ft. deep (Fig. 3) to connect with collection ditches on the western slope. The shaft is located about 2 500 ft. in from the end. The water tunnel will be closed by a concrete plug west of the shaft, thus abandoning the west end of the tunnel which will have served no purpose except to facilitate the construction of the remainder of the water tunnel and of the whole railroad tunnel.

Geology of the Region and Its Effect

Briefly, the whole region is part of the great uplift of the Continental Divide. Practically all the rock in the immediate neighborhood of the tunnel is biotite granite gneiss. There are some pegmatite intrusions, particularly one directly at the West Portal, which determined the exact location of the portal as it was the only rock outcrop in this vicinity. In a long stretch of tunnel from the West Portal eastward the rock has been profoundly disturbed by geologic action probably incident to the mountain-making movements.

The pegmatite which extended in about 500 ft. from the West Portal turned out to be somewhat weathered. Thence, for 1 100 ft. the material almost resembled the output of a crusher, dust and all, containing enough water to form a cohering mass. There was some semblance of bedding planes, however, and practically all the fragments showed slicken-sided faces. For a further distance of 6 400 ft. the formation is different in that the faulting is more localized. The material in some of these faults was dry and crushed so fine that when exposed by blasting it would run into the tunnel like dry sand. Several of these faults, however, carried water in addition to the crushed material which complicated matters. As to soundness, however, the rock condition averaged considerably better the farther the headings advanced. To illustrate the irregular faulting in this formation, it was observed that the conditions at opposite points in the two tunnels only 75 ft. distant were invariably quite different.

As to the limit to which this faulted zone extended, it is interesting to note that east of the point where the abrupt western slope of the range near the summit intersects the tunnel grade the rock formation is relatively sound, which would indicate that the strata forming this slope extend to the tunnel grade. The eastward extension of these strata, all biotite granite gneiss, is terminated by a vertical fault at the crest of the range forming an eastward facing escarpment several hundred feet high. The escarpment is not continuous in this vicinity, however, being broken at intervals by several narrow granite formations extending eastward for various distances from several hundred feet to ½ mile. The eastern slope of these granite formations is gradual enough to form a path for access to the top of the range, which at the tunnel line is 12 000 ft. in altitude.

The eastern slope of the range, as may be seen from Fig. 3, is much more precipitous than the western. An interesting feature of the topography of the eastern slope is the so-called Crater lakes (Fig. 2) formed by glacier action, the water being dammed up by moraines of glacial till. It was rumored that some of these Crater lakes were bottomless which would mean water all the way down to the tunnel level. In reality all these lakes appear to be shallow. In one case, however, there was doubtless a connection between one of the lakes and the tunnel by means of a faulted zone. This was demonstrated in the latter part of February, 1925, when in blasting a round in the water tunnel at the East Portal a sudden flow of water was encountered, amounting approximately to 1 800 gal. per min. This water flowed down the ditch alongside the track in the water tunnel and was diverted at one of the cross-cuts to the railroad tunnel.

Unfortunately, however, the large quantity of silt carried by this water filled up the ditches, as a result of which the track in the water tunnel was flooded. As any flows previously met were trivial in quantity, the Crater lakes were suspected as being the source of this water. One of these lakes was directly above the leak, at a level about 1 400 ft. above the tunnel. Although it was during the middle of winter, men were sent up to investigate conditions but found the lake covered by several feet of ice. Digging a hole in the ice at a convenient point near the middle of the lake, which was 10 acres in extent and about 10 ft. deep, they dumped in a package of chloride of lime on the remote chance that some might be carried into the tunnel by way of the "leak". Strange to say tests of water two hours later in the tunnel showed the presence of the chloride of lime. After a few days the flow rapidly diminished to less than 100 gal. per min. This apparently was due to the silting up of the fissure, as a subsequent inspection of the lake showed no material lowering of the water level, and a further test with chloride of lime showed that the connection still existed between the Crater lake and the tunnel, the chemical coming through in 20 min.

At the East Portal the rock was granite gneiss and schist, and the bedding nearly vertical, the strike of the beds being at an angle of about 15° with the axis of the tunnel. This rock has been faulted somewhat, the faults following the bedding approximately. It is curious that at the fault where the flow of water was encountered in the water tunnel practically none was found in the railroad tunnel heading only 75 ft. away.

No minerals have been found in the excavations. The problem of high rock temperatures as in some of the Alpine tunnels, notably the Simplon, seems to be non-existent at the Moffat Tunnel. Therefore, not much attention has been paid to temperature measurements, but it is interesting to note that near the East Portal the rock temperature as measured in drilled holes was about 60° Fahr. 1 000 ft. in from the East Portal and 68° at a point 8 000 ft. from the portal where the cover was 1 400 ft. At the West Portal there was little increase of temperature with the greater cover, which was probably due to the cooling effect of descending ground-waters.

Overlying the unsound rock section near the West Portal for about 2 500 ft. from the portal the surface of the ground averages 250 ft. above the tunnel level. Over the greater part of this area the depth to rock is not known, although attempts were made before the tunnel was started to determine it. One test pit was sunk by hand in the overlying glacial drift to a depth of 75 ft. Progress was then so slow and expensive that a well drill contractor was employed to start a hole in the bottom of the test pit with a well drill outfit of the percussion type. Curiously enough, within 1 ft. of the bottom of the test pit, rock was struck—hard red granite—and after drilling a hole for 10 ft. into the formation it was claimed that this was ledge rock. To test this theory another hole was started near-by drilling from the surface through the glacial drift. Practically no progress could be made, however, and the hole was soon abandoned. By this time the tunnel was being excavated from the portal and no further investigation by borings was made. Other test pits in the meantime had been abandoned on account of water. The uncertainty of the position of rock at the West Portal was the cause of moving the tunnel at the west end 400 ft. south from the previously accepted location. This lengthened the tunnel slightly but gave considerably more cover with the likelihood of a greater depth of rock overhead.

This change in alignment was adopted in August, 1923, at which time the final layout was approved. This fixed the grades, the location of the water tunnel 75 ft. to the south of the railroad tunnel, and the shifting of the East Portal 75 ft. north of the previously accepted location, which last change allowed more room on the south side of the canyon to take care of the waters of South Boulder Creek and the water from the water tunnel.

Form of Contract

On account of the hazardous nature of the work it was considered doubtful whether bids could be obtained from reputable contractors for constructing the tunnel on a unit price basis. Therefore, the law creating the Moffat Tunnel Improvement District and providing for the appointment of a Commission to go on with the work permitted the Commission to construct the tunnel with its own forces, or to make a contract for the construction on some other basis than the usual unit price method.

Specifications and plans were prepared, however, on the assumption of constructing the tunnel by contract on the unit price basis. Proposals were asked from reputable contractors on this basis, the bids to be submitted September 12, 1923.

However, no bids were submitted except one to which had been added qualifying conditions making it irregular. This bid was held temporarily for investigation and it was stated informally by the Moffat Tunnel Commission that the work would have to be done in some other way than by the straight contract unit price method. On this announcement about eight more informal bids were submitted made up in eight different ways, all being variations of the straight percentage contract or "cost plus".

These proposals were not solicited by the Commission and created considerable confusion as to their relative merits so that it was decided by the Board of Consulting Engineers, in consultation with the Moffat Tunnel Commission, to prepare a proposed form of contract on the cost plus basis and to ask bids thereon from only four of those who had previously submitted informal bids.

The governing features of this form of contract were as follows: Plans and specifications as already prepared were to be closely followed with the single notable exception that the work involved in handling "free flowing mud or sand or the influx of water in such volumes or temperatures as to render the work impractical without special drainage or cooling devices", was to be considered as extra work to be paid for in addition to the regular items of the contract. Ordinarily a contractor is required to assume such risks and in transferring the entire risk to the Moffat Tunnel District it was expected that contractors would be more inclined to submit bids.

Otherwise the form of a contract devised by the Board of Consulting Engineers can be described as a "cost plus a maximum and minimum fee" contract. The maximum fee was to be paid to the contractor in the event of the cost of the work being less than a certain assumed total upset price and the minimum fee in the event of the cost of the work being more than the upset price. The form of contract also contained a profit-sharing clause, namely, in the event that the cost of the work was less than the upset price one-half the saving was to be paid to the contractor as additional compensation. There was also provided a time bonus and penalty on a daily basis for finishing the work before or later than a certain fixed date. All the extra work and all work not susceptible of classification under the regular items of the specifications were to be paid for at cost plus a percentage.

In asking for bids under this form of contract the total upset price was fixed at $5 250 000 on the assumption that the final estimated quantities would be the same as those proposed for the comparison of bids on the unit price basis. As the final quantities would no doubt differ from those in the preliminary estimate it was considered necessary to vary the upset price as the quantities varied. The bidders therefore were requested to submit a schedule of prices, which, multiplied by the estimated quantities, would amount to the upset price. The bidder was expected to make these prices reasonable in respect to one another, so that his proposition should not be rejected as being unbalanced.

Bonus, Fees, and Penalties

The time for the completion of the work was fixed at forty-six months from September 20, 1923. This would bring the contract date for finishing the work to July 20, 1927. The time bonus and penalty at the rate of $1 000 per day were to be calculated from this date.

It was further provided that all the work done and methods used were subject to the approval of the Chief Engineer of the Moffat Tunnel Commission, and that if the work were not prosecuted satisfactorily by the contractors the contract could be annulled by the Moffat Tunnel Commission.

For extra work the contractor was to be paid 5% of the cost thereof independently of all other provisions of the contract. All funds for every purpose were to be provided by the Moffat Tunnel Commission.

On these general terms the bidder was asked to state a maximum and minimum fee for which he would agree to supervise the work. F. C. Hitchcock, M. Am. Soc. C. E., and Mr. C. C. Tinkler jointly submitted a bid naming a minimum fee of $140 000 and made their maximum fee the same. This was lower than that of any of the other contestants and as their bid was satisfactory in other respects it was decided to award them the contract.

This form of contract has some novel features. In order to make these entirely clear several examples of total payments under various assumptions of cost and time required for completion are given.

1.—Presume that the final upset price is $5 200 000; that the actual cost including fee is $4 640 000; that the percentage work is $200 000; and that the contract is completed 100 days ahead of time. The contractors will receive:

One-half of savings in cost	$280 000
Fee (maximum)	140 000
Time bonus	100 000
5% of $200 000	10 000
	$530 000

2.—Presume the same final upset price, the cost as $5 500 000, the percentage work as previously, and the contract completed 100 days ahead of time. The contractors will receive:

No savings	......
Fee (minimum)	$140 000
Time bonus	100 000
5% on $200 000.....................	10 000
	$250 000

3.—Presume the same conditions as in Example 1, except that the work is finished 100 days behind time. The contractors will receive:

One-half of saving..................	$280 000
Fee (maximum)	140 000
5% on $200 000......................	10 000
	$430 000
Time penalty	100 000
	$330 000

Time penalties, however, cannot operate to reduce the payment to the contractor, not including percentage work, below the minimum fee of $140 000. The large time bonus or penalty, $1 000 per day, represented at the time the contract was let approximately the cost of carrying the investment. On account of an additional bond issue sold to provide for an unlooked for increase in the cost of the work and also to defray the cost of supplementary work not included in the original contract, the value of speed of completion later became worth considerably more than $1 000 per day. Under these circumstances obviously a policy of energetic and rapid prosecution of the work was the only course. It is probably true that this policy was also the most economical in other respects.

To this end the contractors who, on being awarded the contract, organized the corporation of Hitchcock and Tinkler, Inc., to take over the work, decided to install the most modern and complete plant and equipment in all departments, to build, equip, and maintain high-class camps, and to pay wages and salaries high enough to attract the best class of workmen.

Construction Begun by Commission

On account of the urgency in getting the work under way the Moffat Tunnel Commission several months before the actual letting of the contract for the tunnel construction, had contracted with the Colorado Power Company for the erection of a transmission line from its power-house on Boulder Creek to the East Portal of the tunnel and thence over the Divide to the West Portal, and also for the furnishing by the same company at both portals of electric power at 44 000-volt, three-phase, 60-cycle, alternating current. The Commission had also authorized the beginning of camp construction and opening up the portals of the tunnels by hand, which work had been started as early as the middle of July, 1923. Some of the heavy machinery had also been ordered to insure delivery before winter.

General Plan of Operations at the East Portal

The details of the water and railroad tunnels, both unlined, are shown in Figs. 4 and 5. A view inside the water tunnel is shown in Fig. 6. The work of preparation of the water tunnel for the actual carrying of water was not included in this contract.

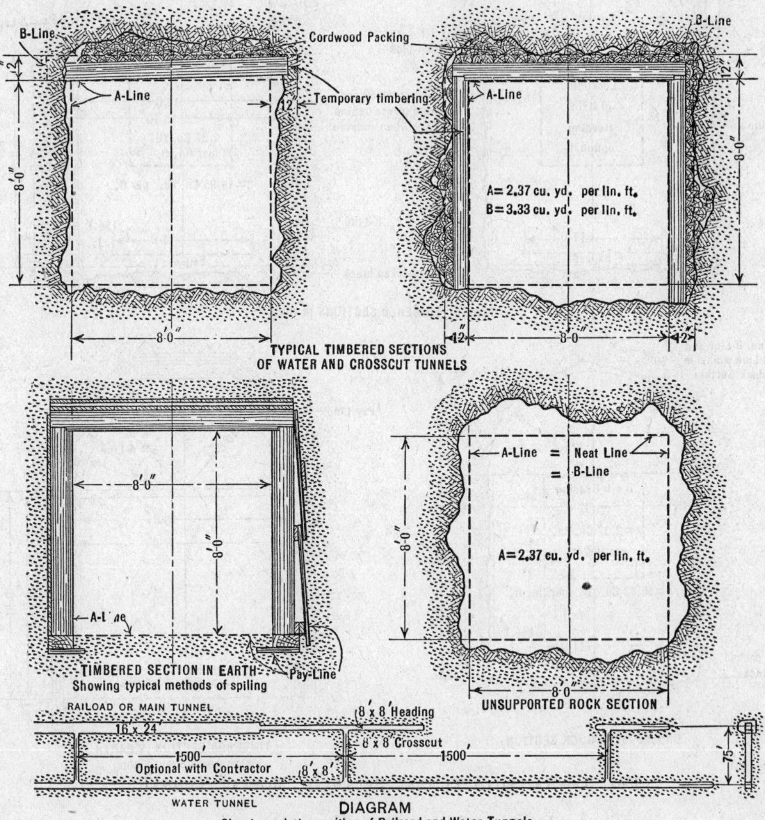

Fig. 4.—Water Tunnel Sections, Moffat Tunnel.

It had been recommended by the Board of Consulting Engineers that the grade of the water tunnel should be at mid-height of the railroad tunnel, on the assumption that the water tunnel would always be in advance of the railroad tunnel, and that cross-cuts could be driven at convenient intervals from the water tunnel to the center line of the railroad tunnel from which point another heading was to be driven, called the main heading of the railroad tunnel, and located on its center line both for line and grade (Fig. 5). This main heading of the railroad tunnel was to be of the same dimensions as the water tunnel, was to be driven both ways from each cross-cut, and all operations in the main headings were to be carried out by obtaining access through the cross-cuts (Fig. 4). At a convenient distance back of the face of the main headings ring-drilling operations were to be carried on for the enlargement of the main heading to a full-sized railroad tunnel.

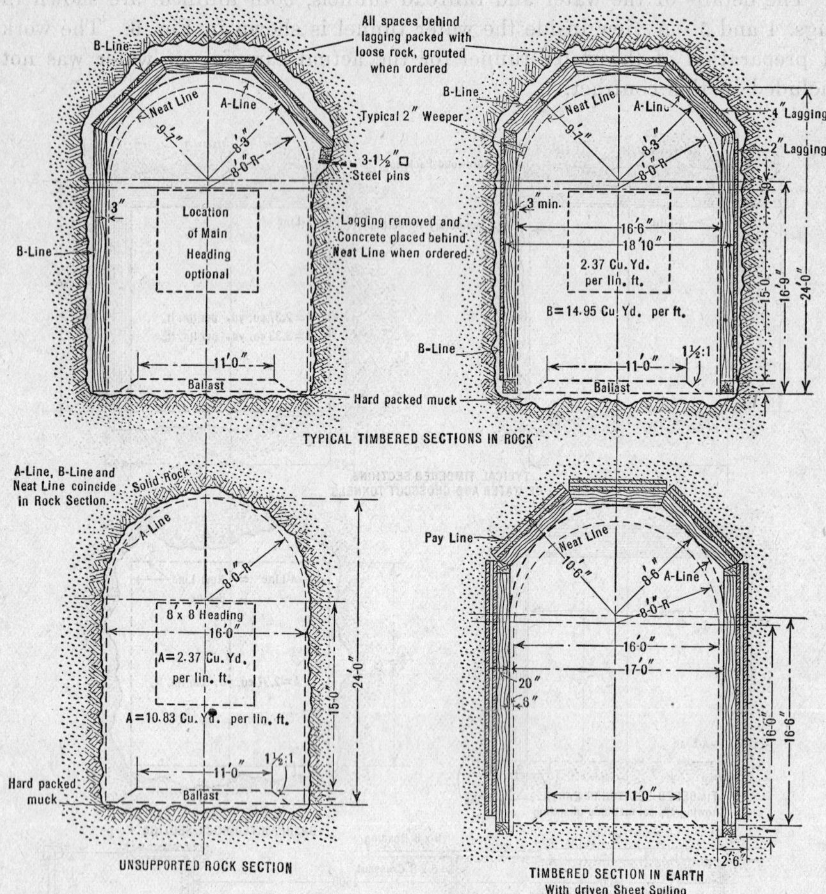

Fig. 5.—Railroad Tunnel Sections, Moffat Tunnel.

Driving Headings, East Portal

Some doubt was expressed that this was really the best way. It was not considered a proved fact that the small water tunnel could really be driven faster than the railroad tunnel, for at this time hand-mucking operation in the water tunnel was the only method proven to be entirely feasible. Hand-mucking, as a matter of fact, was the only method used for several months, and the writer finds in his notes a statement to the effect that an average progress of 15 ft. per day was probably all that could be expected under the circumstances. However, at this time there had been developed in the lead mines of the Flat River, Missouri, District, the so-called Conway loader.

After investigation several of these loaders were purchased and proved to be a great improvement over hand methods of mucking. By the use of these machines an average progress of 24 ft. per day could readily be obtained. This result fully determined that the water tunnel could be driven faster than the railroad tunnel. Nor was this the only good feature connected with the use of the loaders. It was soon evident that a mucking crew could load out all the broken rock from a heading in about the same time that a drill crew operating four drifter drills could set up, drill, and blast a standard round, nominally 8 ft. long. This led immediately to the adoption of the so-called "alternating method" of excavation wherein the main heading was driven only one way from a cross-cut, and the drilling and mucking crews alternated between the water tunnel and the single main heading. In this manner each crew had the field to itself for a period of approximately four hours, and great economies in labor were possible because none of the men in one crew found it necessary to wait on the other operation. Then, too, a spirit of competition was introduced between the two crews as to which could finish first.

Where each heading is driven independently both crews are in the heading at the same time and there is more or less interference. To minimize the interference the method of drilling is entirely different—only two drills are used, working from a single horizontal bar instead of four drills from two columns; and a different layout of the drill holes is necessary for the reason that to save time as few holes as possible are drilled in the lower half of the tunnel.

After shooting, the heading is full of muck about two-thirds of the way to the roof. The drill foreman assigns one of his men to scale the roof and the remainder of the drill gang level off the top of the muck pile so that a horizontal bar may be set up about 3 ft. from the roof. On this bar two drills are mounted and drilling is commenced immediately. In the meantime the mucking crew starts work and loads out the broken rock until the men get close to the bar when it is necessary to stop so as not to interfere with the drillers. The drillers continue drilling from the upper position of the bar until all the holes accessible from this position are finished. A horizontal V-cut or pyramid cut at the bottom of the heading is used.

The drill crew then removes its equipment and the mucking crew resumes work, cleaning up the heading. The drill crew then sets up its bar at what is called the lower position and drills 4 or more holes at the bottom of the heading, thus completing its work.

In the alternating method, with four drills working from columns in a heading free from muck, about 26 holes are drilled, making a regular vertical V-cut. The adoption of this method, giving each drill crew a clean heading in which to start work immediately, provided an ideal condition for using a drill carriage on which all the equipment could be mounted. With the older method all the equipment was moved by hand. Fig. 7 shows how the drill carriage operates. The horizontal bar, when in operating position, is jacked against the walls of the tunnel. The bar carries four arms, on each of which a drill is mounted. These arms are long enough for the drills to be placed in any position in the heading. When drilling is finished, the bar is turned on a vertical axis mounted on the end of a long cantilever extending forward from a small truck. In this turned position the drill equipment will clear the walls of the tunnel. For transportation to and from the heading, the drill equipment is drawn back by a sprocket chain and sheaves to a position immediately over the truck.

With such a mounting the bar and column arms are made much heavier than in the case of equipment intended to be worked by hand. This arrangement diminishes vibration and increases drilling speed. An automatic oiler and drill manifold are mounted on this same truck.

By the use of this carriage the average elapsed time from the arrival of the drill crew in the heading until the air was turned on the drills was 15 min. as against 40 min. in the case of hand-operated equipment.

The Conway loader (Fig. 8) is probably better adapted on the whole to the particular problem of loading muck in these headings than any other machine. In considering the choice of a shoveling machine the speed with which a car can be loaded is perhaps the least important qualification. The method of placing empty cars in position to be loaded is perhaps the most important. In the operation at the Moffat Tunnel a muck car with a capacity of 50 cu. ft. could be loaded under favorable circumstances in less than 1½ min., while it took about twice as long to remove the full car and place an empty one in position. This situation could be improved somewhat by using cars of larger capacity, which, in turn, since the car is attached to the loader while being loaded, would probably require that the back and forth motion of the Conway loader on the track be geared lower to diminish the strains incident to the rapid reversal of direction. All the cars were equipped with spring couplings.

The Conway loader is particularly good at loading scattered or so-called "fly" rock, which is really quite important. It is a rugged simple machine. Among its disadvantages are its limited range of operation on either side of the track and its ability to load only on a practically straight track.

Transportation to Headings

The transportation equipment used in the headings included storage battery locomotives, having a 3-ton chassis with Edison batteries, and 4-ton General Electric trolley locomotives. The muck cars were of 50 ft. capacity, having steel bodies dumping to one side only with an angle of dump of 37° and roller-bearing wheels. The track was of 2-ft. gauge and the rail 40 lb. to the yard. Special flat cars were used for other purposes, particularly for transporting drill steel and men. These locomotives also served the ring drilling and other operations in the main heading but were used mainly only as gathering locomotives. All the long-haul work was done by 4-ton trolley locomotives operating in the water tunnel from the portal to the last cross-cut, at which point switching arrangements were such that transfers were readily made. All the trolley locomotives operated on 250-volt direct current.

Fig. 6.—View of Water Tunnel.

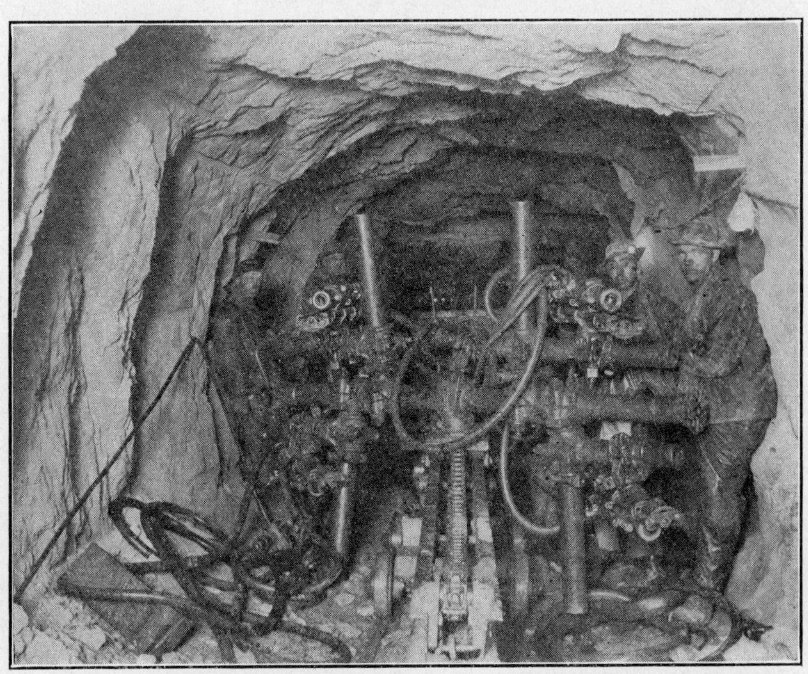

Fig. 7.—View Showing Drill Carriage, East Portal, Moffat Tunnel.

Fig. 8.—Moffat Tunnel, East Portal, Showing Conway Mucker in Water Tunnel During Flood.

Fig. 9.—View of "Jumbo" Set, Moffat Tunnel.

Power for all operations in the tunnel was brought in on a 2 300-volt, three-wire, lead-covered cable. This voltage was used directly to operate 65-kw. motor generator sets generating 250-volt direct current for the trolley service and also for the Conway loaders and for low-pressure fans forming part of the ventilating system. It was also used directly to operate 100-h.p. motors direct-connected to pressure blowers forming part of the ventilating system. For lighting purposes the 2 300-volt current was transformed to low-voltage alternating current. The use of high-voltage current in this way in the West is very general and quite successful.

Auxiliary Heading Method

An auxiliary tunnel to facilitate excavation has been used on a larger scale on two other tunnels—the Simplon Tunnel and Rogers Pass Tunnel—while in an incidental way it has been used no doubt in many other cases.

In the Simplon Tunnel the auxiliary heading, which was later to be enlarged to a single-track railroad tunnel, was at the grade of the bottom of the main tunnel, which was driven by the bottom-heading method, and the functions of the auxiliary heading were entirely devoted to ventilation and transportation. In view of the tremendous difficulties encountered, due to excessive heat and hot water, its use as such was indispensable. No attempt was made to keep the face of the auxiliary heading at a point opposite the main heading.

In the Rogers Pass Tunnel the purposes of the pioneer tunnel were the same as in the Moffat Tunnel—to facilitate transportation and ventilation and at the same time to afford a means of access to the ring-drilling operations (which were first used on the Rogers Pass Tunnel). No mucking machines were used, however, all mucking being by hand, and the headings were driven independently of each other.

In driving the Moffat Tunnel the auxiliary heading proved particularly useful in avoiding inevitable delays, due to encountering areas of unsound rock usually crossing the tunnel at a small angle. If the railroad tunnel had been excavated without the aid of the water tunnel, these unsound areas would have caused great delay and expense due to the time necessary to place the timber. These areas were found in no less than fifteen different places, requiring timbering in lengths varying from a few feet to 500 ft.

Handling Unsound Rock

All this unsound rock was readily excavated and timbered far in advance of the regular enlargement operations. Access to the work was obtained through one of the cross-cuts, thus interfering in no way with the ring-drilling or steam shovel work of the regular enlargement operations.

The method of excavating and timbering these areas was to build in the main heading throughout the unsound area a so-called "jumbo" (Figs. 9 and 10), which was merely a succession of heavy timber square-sets covered on top with heavy lagging. Under the protection of these timbers, transportation could be carried on without interference. The rock overhead was then stoped down and loaded by trapping methods into muck cars standing under the protection of the "jumbo". Timbering closely followed the excavation. Five-piece segmental sets of 12 by 12-in. timber supported on 12 by 12-in. wall-plates were used here. The wall-plates were set 19 ft. apart on a rock bench. This distance is 1 ft. more than standard—to facilitate setting the posts under the wall-plates in the subsequent operations. Wall-plates were set about level with the top of the main center heading. After all the over-head timber was placed and all broken rock taken out, down to the level of the top of the main heading, the "jumbo" was removed and the material at the sides then excavated and loaded into cars by hand. This excavation was carried down only to the level of the bottom of the main heading, leaving an 8-ft. bench of rock which was excavated as part of the ring-drilling and excavation operations.

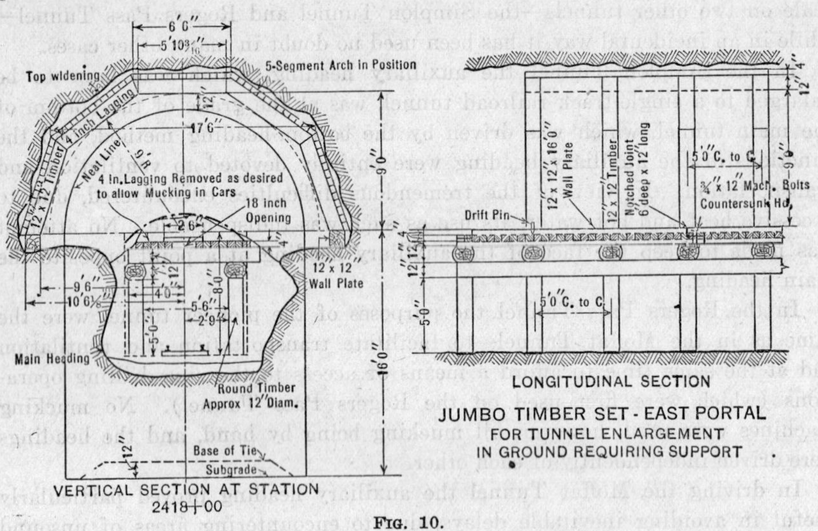

Fig. 10.

Enlargement Operations, East Portal

The standard method of enlarging the tunnel to full size at the East Portal was by the ring-drilling and shooting method. The broken rock was loaded into side-dump cars of nominal 4-yd. capacity, by a special railroad-type, Osgood, compressed-air shovel with a ¾-yd. dipper. Both cars and shovel ran on tracks of 3-ft. gauge. The dimensions of the shovel and cars were such that in a tunnel 16 ft. wide there was just clearance enough for the shovel to load a car alongside on a parallel track.

In the railroad tunnel 8-ton trolley locomotives were used. As in the water tunnel the trolley voltage was 250-volt direct current. The trolley wire was about 17 ft. above the top of rail, clearing the shovel, which was 16 ft. 7 in. high. For service close to the bench beyond the end of the trolley wire a reel was provided on the locomotive carrying several hundred feet of cable. Later, it was found more satisfactory to erect a temporary trolley wire along the sides of the tunnel on brackets at a low elevation, using an auxiliary trolley pole.

The Osgood shovel was operated by compressed air and was equipped with a compressed-air receiver. Otherwise, it was similar in design to a steam shovel of the railroad type, the dimensions being made as small as possible, particularly as to the boom and dipper arm. The shovel ran on a track made up in 5-ft. sections, a section being added as soon as enough broken rock had been removed. A small derrick was mounted on the rear end of the shovel for lifting empty cars spotted directly behind the shovel, to the loading track.

One locomotive ordinarily kept empty cars under the derrick while another hauled out the full cars and pushed the empty ones into the loading position. This second locomotive also hauled the loaded trains to the portal and returned with empty ones. Meanwhile, the switching locomotive took its place in serving the steam shovel, but before doing so it assembled a long train of empty cars behind the steam shovel, which were hauled under the derrick, as needed, by a small air hoist mounted on the back end of the steam shovel.

Ring Drilling and Shooting

One of the advantages of using an auxiliary tunnel in conjunction with a main heading is that it facilitates drilling and shooting for the enlargement of the railroad tunnel in parallel transverse rings (ring drilling [illegible] Moffat Tunnel, drills were set up in the main heading [illegible] in a radial direction perpendicular (or with a sligh [illegible] tunnel. The depth of these holes was such that thei [illegible] outside the periphery of the completed tunnel. The [illegible] (or rather two half rings) at a time, furnishing mu [illegible] to load.

In this method all drilling is done without interf [illegible] shovel operations. Drilling may be carried on hun [illegible] of the other work without interruptions. Access [illegible] heading through one of the cross-cuts, serving for piping, wiring and transportation of workmen, equipment, and supplies. The ring-drilling method contemplates the use of a main heading of minimum size (this being expensive work) and the enlargement to full size in only one more operation, giving a maximum amount of excavation to be handled by the economical air-shovel method. These advantages are important and outweigh the many disadvantages, to be mentioned later.

As a modification of this method it has been proposed to drive the heading at one side of the railroad tunnel instead of on the center line. This would facilitate drilling, in that there would be less holes, and blasting, in that the holes would be of more uniform depth.

It was also proposed to introduce another operation—widening out the heading to full width before the ring-drilling operation was carried on. The object of this was to minimize over-breakage on the sides of the railroad tunnel; to facilitate the drilling of the lower holes in the ring-drilling operation; to diminish the amount of rock to be blasted by the ring method (there being a tendency to have operations blocked by the large quantity of muck to be handled); to separate the bench from the roof, making it easy to shoot the bench and roof separately; to enable a more rational distribution of holes to be drilled in the ring drilling; and to save in the use of dynamite.

However, the only change actually carried out was to drive the main heading 1 ft. lower than previously planned. This made the nominal bottom line of the heading 7 instead of 8 ft. above the sub-grade of the railroad tunnel, which had the effect of reducing the drilling of "down" holes mainly by making them shorter (there was little trouble drilling the upper ones) and of facilitating the breakage of the rock in the bench in the blasting operations. There was enough over-break in driving the main heading to furnish the necessary clearance for handling drill steels. The blasting of the roof was always comparatively easy, everything being in plain view with no muck in the way.

A great deal of experimenting was done by the contractors' organization in bringing this method to its final state of satisfactory operation. At the outset it was apparent that the shooting could not be done in complete rings. If there were no muck pile in the way, "fly" rock would [illegible] thrown far down the tunnel, making an endless task for the shovel [illegible] ng it up. On the [illegible] hand if a muck pile were allowed [illegible] gh enough to stop [illegible] which was absolu[illegible]). In the [illegible] would fall down [illegible] ve[illegible] and holes were drilled [illegible] ed. [illegible] t lift) to the axis of the [illegible] ring in advance [illegible] bottoms were 6 to 12 in. [illegible] introduced a bad [illegible] holes were shot one ring [illegible] s were short and [illegible] ck for the Osgood shovel [illegible] e was a tendency [illegible] osite side. There [illegible] ering in any way with the [illegible] lower bench in [illegible] ndreds of feet in advance [illegible] the lower bench [illegible] is obtained to the main [illegible] ould be thr[illegible] piping [illegible] blasting. This was especially true where the rock was relatively soft; frequently it became necessary to shovel away by hand a quantity of muck lying on the bench in order to load and blast the bottom holes.

It was customary to blast two rings at a time, that is, two upper half rings and two lower half rings. All the holes in the upper half rings were blasted in succession by the use of delay exploders. In the lower rings or bench the first row was shot with instantaneous or "no-delay" exploders and the second row with delay exploders. In order to throw the muck away from the bench as much as possible it was important to use instantaneous exploders for the first row, so that the explosion of all the holes would be simultaneous. Under these circumstances it was the usual program to have such an accumulation of muck in front of the bench at the end of a week or ten days that it was necessary to stop blasting additional rock and allow the shovel to clean up as closely as possible to the bench and then start all over again. Instances of missed holes and consequent "high bottom" of course would necessitate an immediate cleaning up. The bottom holes were loaded heavily, while the top holes were loaded with little dynamite.

FIG. 11.—RING DRILLING, MOFFAT TUNNEL, EAST PORTAL.

FIG. 12.—RING DRILLING, MOFFAT TUNNEL, EAST PORTAL.

The successful drilling of the rings was quite a problem particularly the drilling of "down" holes. It is absolutely necessary in drilling to have all the holes in the adjacent rings parallel and to have the holes in any one ring uniformly spaced and drilled to a depth at least 6 in. outside the periphery of the tunnel. The bottom holes are drilled at least 1 ft. outside.

In drilling "down" holes, heavy two-man drills of the jack-hammer type were first tried. These drills were so heavy to handle that it was impracticable to drill a hole in any other direction than approximately straight down, and although a mounting for them was considered, it was never tried. Standard drifter drills mounted on an arm on a column were then tried, but were not at all successful at first because the steel became jammed in the holes. This was remedied by arranging the water needle so that a large amount of air was forced through the drill steel in addition to the water, thus by the use of a home-made air siphon removing the water and rock cuttings from around the hole.

To remedy the difficulty in pointing the holes it was decided that the drills should be mounted on a column arm carried on a transverse horizontal bar (Fig. 11). Mounted on the column arm with the drill was an apparatus consisting essentially of two round disks about 4 in. apart, concentric about the column arm and at right angles to the axis of the tunnel. In these disks were pairs of holes drilled in such a way that a steel pin could be inserted in the two holes of a pair until the pin came in contact with the shell of the drill. The proper spacing of these holes gave the drill runner a ready means of pointing the drill. Spacing of rings about 4 ft. apart seemed to give the best results. For this spacing, the horizontal bars were set up 8 ft. apart and, by drilling on a column arm of such a length that the drill could be set up 2 ft. from the bar on either side, all the bottom holes could be drilled.

As shown on Fig. 13, two settings for the column arm were used to drill a complete set of bottom holes. This spacing was necessary in order to obtain clearance for handling the drill steels, and convenient in that it minimized the work of shifting the drills from one hole to the next and also the amount of mucking necessary to get a clear surface of rock in which to start the drill. This latter requirement was quite a problem, for, although the heading had been previously mucked carefully by hand, there was always further accumulation of rock débris, rock cuttings, and rubbish, and necessarily all depressions were always filled with water. In fact, this is one of the great disadvantages of the ring-drilling system, as the cost of this hand-mucking per foot of tunnel is more than one-half the cost of the air-shovel work. After the holes were drilled, they were plugged with a big wooden plug until ready for use.

The upper holes of the rings were always drilled with stoper drills. Air-feed stopers proved very satisfactory. As shown on Figs. 12 and 13, all these holes were drilled from one setting of the stoper on the center line. The stoper was mounted on a bar as in the case of the drifter drills. At first, the drills were mounted directly on a bar, which was of lighter weight than that used for the drifter drills. This required a bar to be set for each ring. Later, however, the same bar was used as for the drifter drills, and the stoper was mounted on a column arm on the center line of the tunnel. In this way a bar set every 8 ft. sufficed. The pointing of the holes drilled by the stopers was facilitated by placing another bar several feet above the drill bar and parallel to it, on which were marks to show the alignment for each hole. Even with all these aids for the drill runners in the matter of pointing holes it was soon found necessary to have an inspector on each drill shift to check up and supervise the setting of the drills and drilling of the holes.

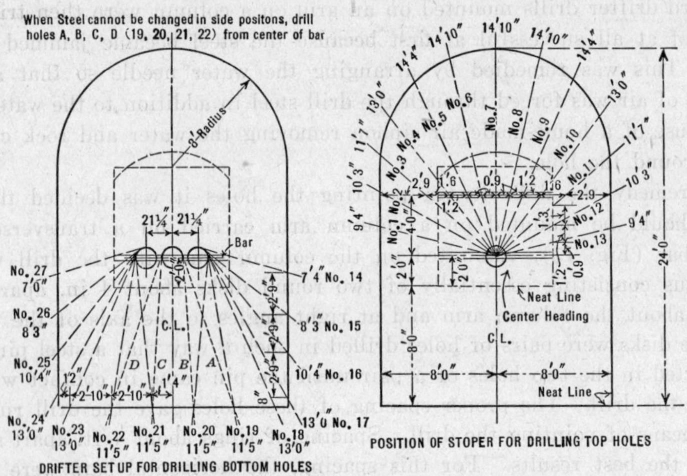

FIG. 13.—RING-DRILLING DIAGRAMS, RAILROAD TUNNEL, MOFFAT TUNNEL.

After all the experimenting the final methods for the enlargement work were very satisfactory. After lowering the heading 1 ft., and probably also due to the harder and better breaking rock, the blasting operations became quite successful in that it was no longer necessary to stop blasting operations at intervals of a week or more to clean up. Unless there were missed holes the blasting was continuous. The muck-pile was maintained just high enough so that there was no "fly" rock. The drilling and blasting were done so accurately that there was a minimum of over-break and trimming.

BLASTING OPERATIONS IN GENERAL

The headings were drilled as shown on Fig. 14. In blasting, 60% low freezing gelatin dynamite was used exclusively. "No-delay" and about four periods of electric-delay exploders were used. The "no-delay" exploders were used in the V-cut. The holes were connected in multiple, attachment being made directly from the lead wires to two copper bus wires, stretched across the face of the heading and supported on wooden pins. All the primers were prepared at the portal in the primer house and brought in with the dynamite. The drill gangs loaded and fired their own headings, although if the required time extended beyond the end of any shift the work ordinarily was completed by the succeeding shift. In the alternating system of driving these headings the 8-hour period for each shift was rigidly maintained. Uncompleted tasks were immediately taken up by the succeeding shift. The air pressure was not even taken off the drills for a moment, operators remaining at their posts until relieved by the incoming shift.

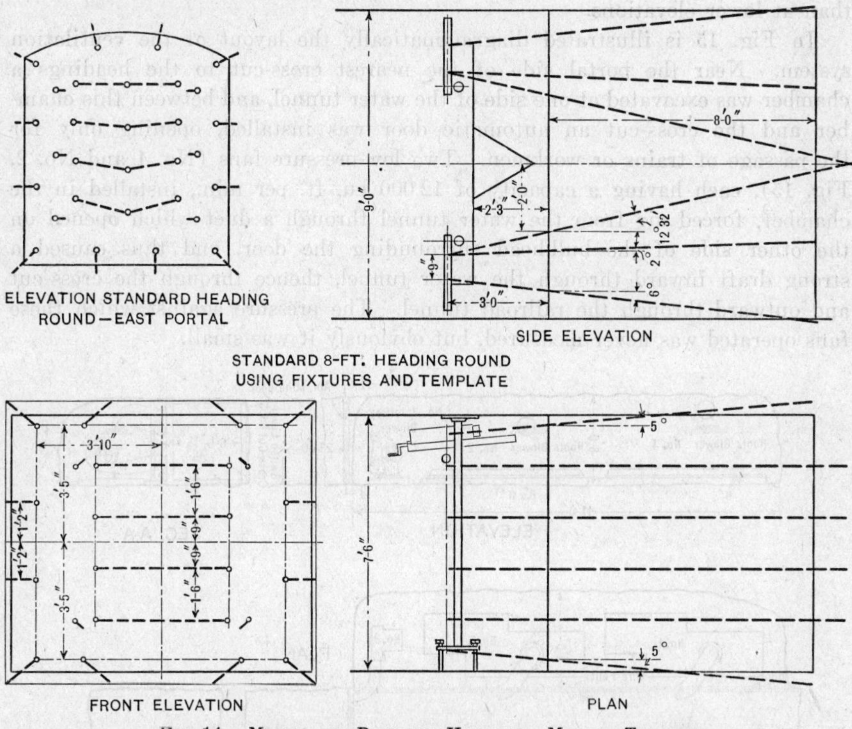

FIG. 14.—METHOD OF DRILLING HEADINGS, MOFFAT TUNNEL.

In the enlargement operations a special blasting crew was on duty most of the time. While two shifts were working on the shovel operation, this crew loaded and blasted as opportunity offered during meal hours and between shifts. Seldom was it necessary to interfere with the shovel. This crew also drilled and blasted any "tight" rock or "high bottom", and "scaled" the roof. It was necessary, however, to have a special trimming crew follow up at a convenient distance behind the shovel. In enlarging, 60% gelatin dynamite was used ordinarily in the bottom holes and 60% and 40% in the roof holes. These holes were connected in series. Two rings were usually shot at the same time by using no-delay exploders on the first ring and delay exploders on the second. It would be desirable to devise a system of shooting wherein the second ring or a third and fourth also could be shot simultaneously, so that the advantage of the greater effect of such shooting could be obtained.

VENTILATION OF EAST PORTAL

Perhaps the greatest advantage derived from the use of the auxiliary tunnel was its solution of the ventilation problem. Without it the products of combustion of so much dynamite and the heat and bad air caused by the presence of so many workmen could hardly be disposed of satisfactorily. At this altitude the oxygen in 1 cu. ft. of air is only about two-thirds of that at sea level, and men seem to be much more easily overcome by dynamite fumes than at lower elevations.

In Fig. 15 is illustrated diagrammatically the layout of the ventilation system. Near the portal side of the nearest cross-cut to the headings a chamber was excavated at one side of the water tunnel, and between this chamber and the cross-cut an automatic door was installed, opening only for the passage of trains or workmen. Two low-pressure fans (No. 1 and No. 2, Fig. 15), each having a capacity of 12 000 cu. ft. per min., installed in the chamber, forced air from the water tunnel through a duct which opened on the other side of the bulkhead surrounding the door, and thus caused a strong draft inward through the water tunnel, thence through the cross-cut and outward through the railroad tunnel. The pressure against which these fans operated was never measured, but obviously it was small.

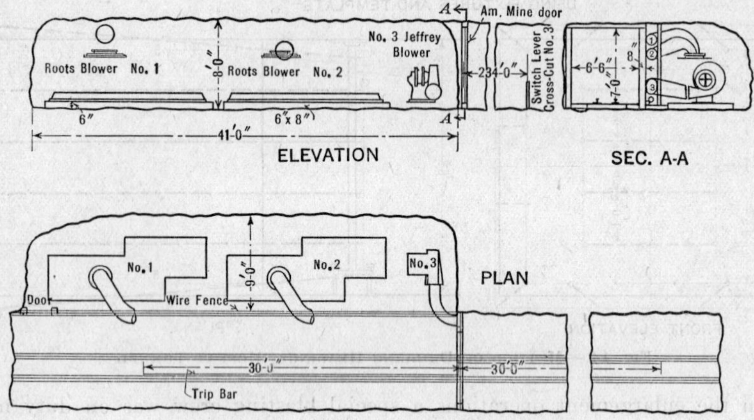

FIG. 15.—VENTILATION LAYOUT, MOFFAT TUNNEL.

Also in the same chamber was installed a blower (No. 3) with a capacity of 4 000 cu. ft. per min., designed for a pressure of 4 lb. This blower, working on the plenum system, took air from the water tunnel at this point and delivered it through a 12-in. pipe to a point near the headings of the water and railroad tunnels. By means of valves at the cross-cut the full capacity of the blower could be directed to either heading at will. This blower was operated usually only after blasting in the headings, to force the foul air back only as far as the first cross-cut from the heading, at which point it could be caught up by the strong current of air from the fans and forced out through the railroad tunnel.

The headings advanced so rapidly and the pipe was so liable to injury by flying rock that the end of the pipe was usually kept several hundred feet back from the heading. Under these circumstances, after blasting, high-pressure air was blown in from the drill line directly at the heading, which expedient forced the foul air back far enough so that the 12-in. ventilator line could effectively dispose of it.

The bank of smoke emitted from the heading was so rapidly diluted as it came within the influence of the jet of air from the 12-in. ventilator line, vanishing into thin air as it were, that it was the firm conviction of all the workmen that the jet held the smoke in the heading. They, therefore, considered it bad practice to operate the blower until the smoke had passed the end of the 12-in. pipe. This is only one of the numerous superstitions prevalent among tunnel men particularly in regard to ventilation systems.

All other cross-cuts except the one next the heading, as long as they were in use, were provided with doors, after which they were sealed up tight. This insured against "short circuits" in the ventilation. In some instances the headings were allowed to advance a distance of two cross-cuts before it was necessary to move the ventilation system. In this the controlling factor was the capacity of the blower to force the requisite amount of air through the pipe. This blower was supposed to be able to supply 4 000 cu. ft. of air through about 1 mile of pipe, but leakage made it advisable to move oftener. The pipe was 12 in. in diameter, 20-gauge, with slip-joints. Extreme care was taken to make the joints tight, even by going so far as to put reinforcing rings on the inside in order that a joint of the Dresser type could be used. These connections were effective, but on the other hand it was found that even at the light pressure (4 lb.) all the riveted joints leaked also. In addition, the pipe was noisy, apparently because of the pulsating discharge of the blowers.

Even with this large amount of air for ventilation the condition was not entirely satisfactory in that the completed railroad tunnel between the bench and the portal remained so smoky as to interfere seriously with trimming operations and transportation.

Workmen's Bonus

The principal requirement in all this work was speed. To this end a bonus program for the workmen was early considered. In tunnel work it is very hard to devise a plan that will obtain results and at the same time be fair. On the adoption of the alternating system of working the two headings it was apparent that operations would become so systematized and methods so standardized that a bonus plan could safely be tried. After considerable discussion the following plan was adopted applicable only to the heading crews at the East Portal.* Quoting from the statement announcing the bonus plan, which was started on May 1, 1924:

"The number of crews employed and their organization are to remain as they are at present. No changes are to be made in the distances required due to changes in the character of the rock or for other reasons. The base rate above which the bonus is to be paid is for an average of 17 ft. per day in both the water tunnel and main headings or 34 ft. total. Should the above crews, as they will at times, do work in the cross-cuts, credit will be allowed for work done there but for no other reason such as enlargements for plant.

* Later this was used at the West Portal when ground permitted the alternating method.

"The bonus will be paid at semi-monthly periods corresponding to the pay roll periods on the total footage accomplished in these periods, which means that in a 15-day period at 17 ft. per day per heading, the total footage above which a bonus will be paid is 510 ft. and in a 16-day period 544 ft. Furthermore the bonus will be paid only to men who work every shift during the period except when excused by the superintendent on account of injury in which case a bonus will be paid proportional to the number of shifts worked.*

"In case a man is promoted from a lower to a higher group or *vice versa,* as shown below, his bonus will be based on the number of shifts worked in each group.

"The bonus will be a fixed amount to be paid to each man in proportion to the number of feet excavated in excess of the minimum as stated above. The fixed amount, however, is not the same for all men in the crews but varies according to the importance of their duties. For this purpose the men are divided into three groups.

"Group No. 1 will consist of: Assistant Superintendents, Shifters (Foremen), Scalers, Miners (Drill Runners), Helpers (Drill Helpers or Chuck Tenders), and Nippers.

"Group No. 2 will consist of: Mucking Machine Operators and the Muckers in the crew of the Mucking Machine.

"Group No. 3 will consist of: Tunnel Motormen and Brakemen, engaged in hauling from headings only.

"There will be no others than those stated above to be entitled to a bonus.

"The bonus to be paid to members of the different groups for each additional foot of advance will also vary in that it increases with the distance gained as stated below, it being understood that for a 16-day period all distances given below are increased by 34 ft.

"For members of Group No. 1 there will be paid:

"For every foot advance above 510 ft. up to and including 600 ft. the amount of 15 cents per ft., which we will call rate 'A'.

"For every foot advance above 600 ft. up to and including 675 ft. the amount of 20 cents per ft., which we will call rate 'B'.

"For every foot advance above 675 ft., the amount of 30 cents per ft. which we will call rate 'C'.

"For the members of Group No. 2, the distances are the same but the bonus paid is 10 cents, 12 cents, and 18 cents, respectively.

"For Group No. 3, the bonus paid is 5 cents, 7 cents, and 10 cents, respectively."

Judged by the high rates of progress later attained, these rates appear too high.

No attempt was made to apply a bonus to the other operations at the East Portal. The enlargement operation could easily progress faster than the headings by working two shifts per day, and as for the other work, extra progress required only the addition of more men or equipment.

Disposal of Spoil

The matter of disposal of the material excavated from the tunnel was not very serious. The muck cars from the water tunnel were dumped into chutes leading to 4-yd. cars standing in the approach cut to the railroad tunnel. A whole train was dumped without shifting the cars. These cars were hauled out on the spoil bank by an 8-ton trolley locomotive which also served the

* Soon afterward the superintendent also was authorized to issue excuses on account of illness.

railroad tunnel. The spoil bank was located as to line and grade to form a convenient permanent railroad approach to the tunnel.

Mechanical Equipment

The compressor equipment at the East Portal consisted of one compressor with a capacity of 450 cu. ft. of free air per min., two of 1 150 ft., one of 1 245 ft., and one of 1 300 ft. At times, all these machines were in use. It is to be remembered that at this altitude a large allowance in extra capacity had to be provided. The main high-pressure air line was 7⅝-in. well-casing, with Dayton joints for about 1½ miles and 6¼-in. for the remainder. Three of the large compressors were driven by 200-h.p. synchronous motors which served to maintain the power factor. The monthly maximum demand average of three 3-min. peaks up to August 1, 1925, was about 1 100 h.p. This, however, did not include one of the large compressors, which was put in operation later.

All drill steels were used only once, requiring the sharpening of about 1 500 bits per day. Two sharpening machines were used. The steels were heated in oil furnaces, and another furnace was used for tempering. All the furnaces were served by special low-pressure blowers to avoid the waste of high-pressure air.

Four-point bits were used, with extra wing thickness to avoid rifling of the holes. Later, the so-called McClellan bit, a modification of the standard four-point bit, was adopted with satisfactory results.

Storage battery locomotives were provided with extra batteries so that they might always be ready for service. A motor generator set supplying 250-volt direct current and located in the power house was used for charging the batteries and also for trolley service, supplemented as heretofore described by motor generator sets under ground.

Three 400-kv-a., single-phase, 44 000-2 300-volt transformers occupied the East Portal Sub-Station.

Plan of Operations at the West Portal

On account of the great amount of "heavy ground" at the West Portal the operations there were much different from those at the East Portal. On beginning the work little was known of the amount of this unsound rock and it was assumed to extend less than 1 800 ft., so that the plant and equipment provided was practically the same as at the East Portal.

The portal cuts were entirely in earth at the West Portal, likewise the water and railroad tunnels for a short distance. The water tunnel was given the same relative location with respect to the railroad tunnel as at the East Portal. It was started first and was a long way underground before the portal of the railroad tunnel was turned. Work on the portal cut of the railroad tunnel was slow on account of difficulties with the shovel, with frozen ground, and with disposal of the excavated material. Realizing this situation, the first cross-cut from the water tunnel to the railroad tunnel was excavated as near the portal as possible. Although every one continued optimistic as to the kind of material about to be encountered, no really sound rock was found for many thousand feet. Under these circumstances the use of the water tunnel as an auxiliary heading was a tremendous advantage in expediting the work by providing access to the railroad tunnel through several cross-cuts at the same time. In this way it was possible to carry on excavation work in the railroad tunnel in as many as eight different places at one time.

Water Tunnel in Heavy Ground, West Portal

While the idea of "bad ground" immediately conjures up ideas of high cost and small progress in tunnel work, this is not strictly true in the case of a tunnel as small as the water tunnel and in rock of the particular character encountered at the West Portal. These troubles are primarily due to the necessity of timbering close to the working face and of taking precautions to avoid knocking down the timber in blasting operations. In the water tunnel at the West Portal, however, where timbering had to be carried close to the working face, the rock was uniformly so soft as to need little drilling, thus saving labor, and little dynamite in blasting, thus saving this large expense. The cost of timbering, however, was a large item. Much of this tunnel was excavated without the necessity of timbering close to the heading. Heavy ground pressures ordinarily did not become evident until some time after the face was exposed.

Where necessary, the water tunnel was timbered with square sets. Usually the caps and posts were of native lodgepole pine about 10 to 12 in. in diameter. In much of this tunnel it was necessary to drive ahead for a new set by driving spiling or poling-boards of 4-in. native timber. After the poling-boards had been driven, a cap was set under the front ends to support them, the cap in turn being supported by two cantilever beams extending from the under sides of the last caps in position. Under the protection thus afforded mucking operations were carried on so that posts could be set in position under the ends of the advanced caps.

A swinging false set for this operation was suggested but never used. No doubt it would have been an improvement for the worst of this work as it would have facilitated greatly the driving of the poling-boards. In part of this tunnel it was also necessary to drive poling-boards on the sides. In some favorable places the timber could be erected at a distance back from the heading so as not to interfere with the excavation. Then, again, much of the water tunnel did not require timbering at all. The uncertain nature of this rock is illustrated by the fact that from Cross-Cut No. 3 for 3 433 ft. eastward there were twenty places needing timber, aggregating only 1 167 ft. in all. The peculiar feature of the heavy ground at this end of the water tunnel was the relatively high pressure developed on the sides of the tunnel. Because of this pressure there was always a tendency for the posts to be forced into the tunnel. Many of them were broken and it became necessary to place reinforcing sets, frequently of 12 by 12-in. Oregon pine.

At first the posts were set vertically, a spreader of 3 by 8-in. native timber being used at the bottom between opposite posts. Settlement of the posts frequently broke these spreaders. Afterward it was decided to set the posts battering outward so that their bottoms were 12 in. farther apart than their tops. After this, no more trouble was experienced from posts "kicking in"; but by this time the worst of the "heavy ground" was past. Many caps also were broken and were replaced with Oregon fir sets. In addition, many of the posts settled, bringing the caps down with them and thus decreasing the clearance overhead to a point requiring the replacement of the timber at a higher elevation. These serious troubles only extended about to Cross-Cut No. 3 and beyond that point, generally speaking, the timber stood very well. Cross-Cut No. 2 itself was so bad that it was necessary finally to reinforce the timber by using steel I-beams for caps. Even then the clearances were cut down to such an extent by these I-beams and other reinforcing timbers as to interfere seriously with its use.

Although much of the first 8 000 ft. of the water tunnel did not require any timbering, the adjacent railroad tunnel required it all the way. Beyond Cross-Cut No. 3 the average character of the rock in the water tunnel improved greatly, containing considerable stretches of fairly good material, but, at intervals, decidedly crushed zones that were the occasion for very serious cave-ins.

The use of native timber in the water tunnel was unsatisfactory in another important respect in that it was peculiarly subject to fungus attack and rapid decay. With the improved ventilation resulting from the use of the water tunnel as an intake, as at the East Portal, this condition was greatly relieved.

At first the water tunnel at the West Portal was driven independently of any other headings. The shifts of men assigned to this heading were selected by promotion from other work, the object being to expedite this part so that the ground could be quickly explored and more cross-cuts opened up for access to the railroad tunnel and thus the work "holed through" as soon as possible. In most of this work hand-mucking methods were used and the drill shift not only did its regular work of drilling and blasting but also all the timber work with the help of the muckers. Later, a Conway loader was used in this heading but it was of doubtful advantage in passing through bad ground as there was much lost time anyway.

The drilling and blasting followed the method as used in independent headings already described, namely, with two drills only, mounted on a horizontal bar. After July 1, 1925, however, the rock then being of much better quality, the heading was driven by the alternating method as at the East Portal, in turn with the main heading, then being driven from Cross-Cut No. 6. Thereafter progress in these headings became almost as good as at the East Portal.

Timbering Railroad Tunnel in Heavy Ground, West Portal

By far the most interesting of the operations on the Moffat Tunnel was the excavation and timbering of the railroad tunnel. The decision to try to hold this heavy ground permanently with timber only was a bold one. There is no record in engineering literature of any one having ever seriously considered such a thing as practicable, nor is it likely that it will ever be attempted again.

The ideas in regard to the weights and pressures that a timber or masonry tunnel lining will have to sustain as evolved by various theorists, seem to be in no way in accord with any reasonable assumptions and quite impractical in their applications. There is also the question of so-called "swelling ground" *versus* just ordinary "heavy ground". What, if anything, is there in the theory current in mining districts that the weight on the timbering can be relieved by "bleeding" the timber, that is, raking out some of the loose rock behind it? Or what in the theory that as time goes on weight on timber grows less instead of greater, due to the fact that the loose ground outside the tunnel tends to adjust itself into the form of an arch? Are vertical posts less likely to be pushed in at the bottom if set straight, or battered out, or battered in; and will setting the posts on foot-blocks or wedges inclined outward prevent them from "kicking" in? Is it better practice to pack the spaces outside the timber with cordwood or with rock fragments? Which is the better method in a single-track railroad tunnel, to use 3-piece, 4-piece, or 5-piece segmental arches; and what should be the particular design of these arches? How about wall-plates? Is it feasible to build a tunnel in heavy ground without them? Should lagging be made thick enough to resist decay as long as the heavy timbers or should it be made so thin that it will be the first thing to break under load? Is there anything in the old theory that the first requirement in tunneling in bad ground is to hold everything absolutely in place?

The contract for the construction of the Moffat Tunnel showed as a typical section of timbered tunnel a 3-piece set of 12 by 12-in. timber, a 12 by 12-in. wall-plate, and 12 by 12-in. posts. Timbering was not considered at that time as a serious difficulty and there were elastic provisions in the specifications for a change in design if that became necessary. All timbering operations described in the specifications contemplated the use of side-drifts in which the wall-plates were to be set in place ahead of the face of the heading. This method involves the use of a top heading and the removal of the remaining bench in one or more lifts. To work in well with this plan, the location of the water tunnel at an elevation 8 ft. below the top heading, is rather awkward. As it turned out the best method was to drive the cross-cut on a level grade and then ascend in the railroad tunnel as rapidly as possible.

However, for other reasons it turned out that practically none of the wall-plate drifts was driven. This method was tried in the earth part of the upper heading at the portal but was soon abandoned on account of its slowness. At about the same time, Cross-Cut No. 1 having been finished, a so-called timbered main heading on a rapidly ascending grade was started each way from this cross-cut, and after two or three wall-plates had been set at the portal and the heading permanently timbered to the end of them, a similar main heading was started to meet that coming from Cross-Cut No. 1. This was only a short distance, as Cross-Cut No. 1 was close to the portal.

This timbered main heading was similar to the timbered heading driven in the water tunnel except that the posts were much longer. The dimensions of the heading as to height were governed by the fact that the under side of the cap of the square-set as it was to be left in place must clear the cap of the permanent timber, a nominal clearance of 1 ft. being allowed. The bottom of the heading was low enough to facilitate the placing of wall-plates. The operations of widening the heading and setting permanent segmental timbering followed the driving of the main heading at a convenient distance behind, sometimes not for months afterward.

The first experiment in the way of setting wall-plates from this main heading was to drive them, as it were, laterally rather than longitudinally. To this end cantilevered poling-boards were driven out laterally from the main heading to clear the tops of the wall-plates. This was not successful and was soon abandoned in favor of a method, the so-called "winging out" method (Fig. 16), wherein, working longitudinally of the tunnel, complete 5-piece sets of temporary timber (false sets) were placed outside the prospective position of the permanent timber, ample clearance being left for the placing of the permanent timber. When 3-piece permanent sets were used, these false sets were practically 3-piece sets themselves, the lower segment being quite short and vertical. When the permanent timber was changed to 5-piece sets, the lower leg of the false sets was lengthened but was still left vertical. These false sets were largely used throughout the timbered portion of the railroad tunnel. Sometimes the ground was so stable that the wing sets could be left out if the permanent timber were placed immediately after the excavation of the rock; and sometimes the rock was so bad that only by the most careful work and the extensive use of poling-boards on the top and sides could the widening be accomplished.

At the cross-cuts the main headings were driven at a steep up-grade until they were high enough for the caps to clear the permanent timber. In widening out there remained a considerable length of tunnel in the vicinity of the cross-cuts that could not be enlarged, and it was the custom to leave this part to the last and work toward the cross-cuts from the completed top headings, driving practically a new main heading on top of the old. This was ticklish work on account of the amount of ground that had to be opened up at one time and was the cause of two bad cave-ins.

The false sets (Fig. 16) were not very well framed but were good enough for the purpose. The upper inclined segment was merely beveled on the end and rested against the end of the cap of the square-set and the short vertical leg was supported by a small foot block.

The setting of the permanent arch timber—wall-plates and segmental sets—immediately followed the widening-out process. The wall-plates were first placed, carefully blocked up in position, and checked for alignment and grade; then the segments were erected, the lagging was placed, the weight of the false sets transferred to the permanent sets by blocking, the original posts of the temporary square-sets were removed, and cordwood or rock packing was carefully placed between the permanent timber and the false sets.

This system was pretty consistently followed throughout. Its disadvantages lay in the large amount of extra excavation and timber and cordwood required and the extra weight that will be applied later when the temporary timber

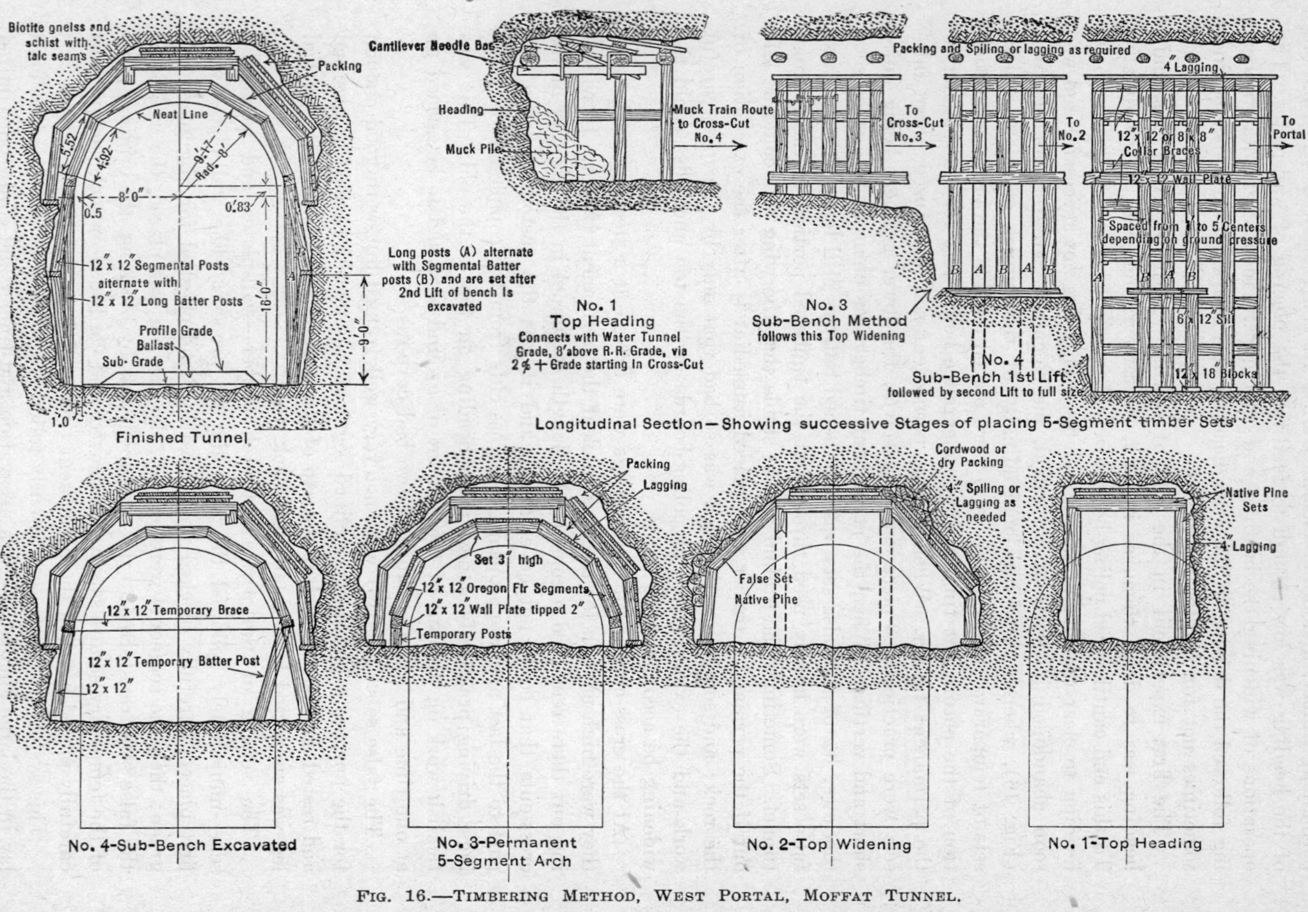

FIG. 16.—TIMBERING METHOD, WEST PORTAL, MOFFAT TUNNEL.

and cordwood compress and decay. Its advantage was its speed and the excellent appearance of the permanent timber (Fig. 19).

Many plans were proposed for placing the permanent timber directly against the rock, but none of them was tried. The permanent timber as first placed followed closely the design shown in the contract drawings, a 3-piece set with wall-plate and posts (Fig. 5). Modifications adopted shortly afterward to facilitate excavation, when it was realized that the weights to be held would be considerable, were the omission of the notch cut in the wall-plate for a bearing for the segments. This was to strengthen the wall-plate as a beam. A steel plate bent in the form of a Z-bar was used as a bearing instead. This was not successful in holding the segments in place, and it was also soon apparent that no reliance could be placed on blocking the timber away from the rock as a means of holding it in place. Instead, the wall-plate was tilted to obtain a better bearing for the segments and at the same time a five-segment arch in place of the three-segment design was adopted.

The main elements governing the design of the five-segment arch were that space should be left for 12 in. of concrete overhead, for 9 in. on the haunches, and for 6 in. at the wall-plates. This was the same as for the three-segment arches. The lower segment of the 5-piece set was inclined at an angle of 25½° from the vertical the segments were identical, and the wall-plate was about 2½ ft. lower than in the 3-piece design.

Later, in better ground, the 5-piece arch design was modified in that all the angles between the segments were made 30°, and a steel wall-plate was used instead of 12 by 12-in. timber. The steel wall-plate was an I-beam laid on its side. Its advantage is that it does not compress, holds the posts and segments in position, and practically puts the segments and posts in contact.

Details of Operations, West Portal

The excavation of the main headings advanced much more slowly than that of the water tunnel. This was due largely to their greater height. At times several of these headings were being excavated simultaneously, access being obtained from the various cross-cuts. Usually only the most advanced heading was equipped with a Conway loader. Access for the heading-widening operations was also obtained from the various cross-cuts. The headings were always driven through from one cross-cut to the other before widening was started in order that circulation of air could be established as soon as possible.

The transportation system in the water tunnel operated in the same way as at the East Portal. The trolley, however, served only the water-tunnel heading and the work in the railroad tunnel, which was carried on from the next cross-cut to the heading. Necessary haulage from other cross-cuts was handled all the way to the spoil bank by storage battery locomotives. The trolley was always given the right of way.

Water from the headings drained out through the water tunnel all the way to Cross-Cut No. 1, where it was discharged into the railroad tunnel. The quantity of water handled probably never exceeded 200 gal. per min.

On the assumption that there was to be but little unsound rock at the West Portal, the same equipment for the enlargement operation to full size was ordered as at the East Portal, an Osgood air shovel, dump cars of nominal 4-yd. capacity, 3-ft. gauge track, 40-lb. rail, and 8-ton trolley locomotives.

In order to have enough head-room for the shovel it was necessary to take out the full bench, nominally 16 ft. high, in one operation and also to keep a clear space 16 ft. wide at all times. In a timbered tunnel this introduced quite a problem as to the temporary support of the overhead timber while excavating. All kinds of travelers were proposed for this work, all supported on tracks at invert grade. The excavation, however, was started at the portal by removing only a small part of the bench at a time, batter posts close to the bench being set to support the wall-plates until permanent posts could be placed.

The rock at this point was comparatively good, a partly disintegrated pegmatite extending in for about 500 ft. from the portal. In attempting to use the shovel it was found to be a very poor piece of apparatus for mucking out short rounds. On account of the small radius of the dipper arm anything in the nature of a corner could not be reached at all. This necessitated much mucking by hand—and into high cars at that. The bench being so high and there being so little head-room above, most of the holes drilled were "lifters".

Needle-Bar Method for Bench Excavation

In any kind of industrial work the first concern is so to organize the work that all men are fully employed for the entire shift, that they do not interfere with one another, and that, if there is a regular cycle of operations each step of which has to be done in regular rotation, the cycle may be completed at regular intervals of 24 hours each so that the various shifts can go to work at the same time each day. The use of a "call" shift should be avoided on account of the ensuing extra expense, irregular sleep and meals for the workmen, and the consequent demoralization. Particularly should this be avoided where highly trained workmen, such as steam-shovel operatives, are employed.

Under the conditions at the West Portal it will readily be seen that the bench excavation by this method was very unsatisfactory as, among other things, the shovel crew could clean up all the muck from one round in about two hours. This constituted a day's work for them and, furthermore, this work had to be arranged to come during the day shift.

To remedy this situation it was imperative that some better method for supporting the wall-plates be found so that a longer round could be taken out. The solution of this difficulty for the time being was found in the use of two 24-in. by 25-ft. I-beams as so-called needle-beams.

As shown in Figs. 17 and 18, these beams were disposed longitudinally of the tunnel, one on either side. They were supported on transverse cross-beams one of which was in turn supported on the wall-plates at a point to the rear of the permanent posts, and the other on the wall-plates at a point where these plates in turn were supported by the bench not yet excavated. Another set of three or four cross-beams was hung by heavy bolts from the needle-beams. Being placed under the opposite wall-plates, this set served as their only support for 10 or 15 ft., or more. Later, 40-ft. instead of 25-ft. beams were used.

With this system a much longer round could be excavated, although even then it was not possible to employ the shovel crew for its full time. It was also apparent that the needle-beam apparatus should be improved, especially as to the arrangements for moving ahead. Of course it would not be possible to use such a system if heading work was going on at the same time, as the heading would be blocked. In the Moffat Tunnel, however, as all the heading work was done from the water tunnel and cross-cuts, this objection did not hold.

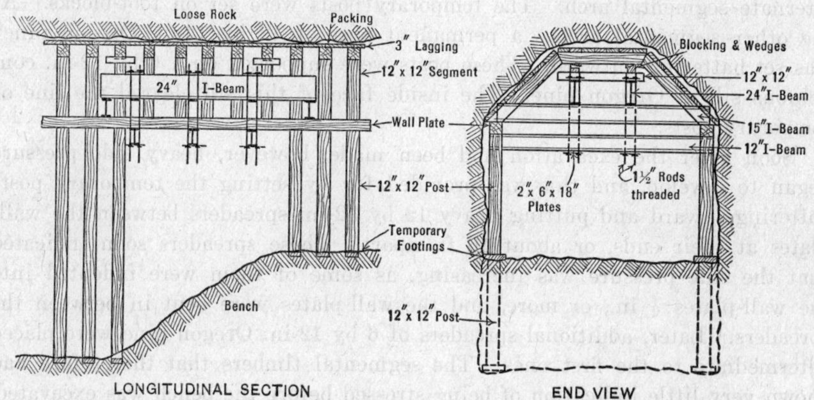

FIG. 17.—NEEDLE BARS FOR SUPPORT OF ARCHES, MOFFAT TUNNEL.

SUB-BENCH METHOD FOR EXTRA HEAVY GROUND

The excavation of the bench went on as described to the end of the pegmatite formation. This point was also the beginning of the worst section of tunnel. In entering this formation the same system was continued but on blasting the first round there was a bad cave-in from behind the wall-plate on one side. The wall-plate settled also and there were indications of careless work in supporting these plates.

It was decided that it was unsafe to attempt to take out such a high bench in such unstable material. The next decision was to take out the bench in two lifts, the so-called sub-bench method. It was also apparent at this time that a concrete lining should be placed in such stretches of unsound rock and that any attempt to depend on timber as a permanent lining would be a mistake.

The method adopted for prosecuting the work as far as it was necessary to use the sub-bench method was first to take out the top lift or upper sub-bench as far as Cross-Cut No. 2, the work being handled from the railroad tunnel portal. After passing Cross-Cut No. 2 the upper sub-bench would be handled from that cross-cut and the lower sub-bench started and handled in turn from the portal. On account of the lack of room in camp for more men and the desire to push the heading work there was no attempt to work both sub-benches at the same time, although this could have been done.

The method of excavation was to be by hand, although to cheapen the mucking operation a plan was contemplated of excavating first through the upper sub-bench a trench about 10 ft. wide and 8 ft. deep, the mucking to be done with a Conway loader. There being no loader available, however, this method was not tried.

In timbering the upper sub-bench it was necessary then to design a system of timbering that would enable the lower sub-bench to be excavated readily, and at the same time to provide for a stronger concrete lining than had heretofore been contemplated, one adapted to resist side pressure on the tunnel. At first the idea was to set vertical round posts under the wall-plate at every alternate segmental arch. The temporary posts were set on foot-blocks. At the other segmental arches a permanent post of 12 by 12-in. Oregon pine* was set battering outward. These posts were supported on a 6 by 12-in. continuous sill of Oregon pine. The inside face of this sill cleared the line of temporary posts.

Soon after the excavation had been made, however, heavy side pressure began to develop, and this was provided for by setting the temporary posts battering inward and putting heavy 12 by 12-in. spreaders between the wall-plates at their ends, or about 16 ft. apart. These spreaders soon indicated that the side pressure was increasing, as some of them were indented into the wall-plates ½ in., or more, and the wall-plates were bent in between the spreaders. Later, additional spreaders of 6 by 12-in. Oregon pine were placed intermediate to the first ones. The segmental timbers that theretofore had shown very little indication of being stressed before the bench was excavated, also began to take weight, not so much however as the posts under the wall-plates. The sudden increase in vertical weight is easily explained by noting that the weight previously had been taken by the false sets but that now, the foundation having been taken away from under the false sets, all the weight was transferred to the permanent timber. The peculiar design of the false sets is probably responsible for the development of excessive side pressure. With evidence of such tremendous lateral pressure it was quite evident that no ordinary system of segmental timber arches could withstand the strain and that the problem required a heavy concrete lining as its solution.

Meanwhile the completed timber work near the portal began to show evidence of much strain. This was in the pegmatite formation. All the timber here was of 3-piece, segmental arch design. Some of the posts were broken and all of them were bent quite visibly; in two places the wall-plate was broken, rotated over backward, the lower legs of the arches were pushed outward on top of the wall-plates, and the wall-plates forced into the tunnel. To meet this condition reinforcing timber was placed inside the regular sets. This was intended to be removed and a concrete lining placed later.

In November, 1924, the upper bench having passed Cross-Cut No. 2, preparations were made to start work taking out the lower sub-bench. The ground beyond Cross-Cut No. 2 having become more stable as the work advanced, it was decided to drop down to the bottom grade and take out the

* This timber has been replaced by separate sets of 12 by 18-in. Oregon fir (p. 104).

full bench, using hand-mucking methods. At Cross-Cut No. 4 also, work was started taking out the full bench, working west from the cross-cut and using hand methods. At both Cross-Cut No. 2 and Cross-Cut No. 4 the method was changed somewhat, as soon as a sufficient height of bench was reached, in that the bench was taken out in two lifts, the upper one being 20 ft. or more ahead of the lower. This was because more men thus could be put to work advantageously.

By means of wheel-barrows on a runway the muck was carried out and dumped into cars standing on the lower level exactly as is done in mucking out by hand a tunnel driven by the top-heading and bench method. Wall-plates were held successfully in place by the use of 10-ton single-screw pipe-jacks extending transversely of the tunnel and tightly jacked against opposite wall-plates. It is only necessary to use a sufficient number of such jacks, placed with judgment, to hold any overhead weight.

On the lower sub-bench no progress had been made since the previous July (1924). Slow progress was anticipated here and to expedite the mucking operation a so-called St. Joe loader was obtained on trial. It was operated entirely by electricity and would load into the high 4-yd. muck cars. After a trial extending over a week or more it was decided that this machine offered little advantage over hand-mucking methods mainly on account of the lack of clearance for its quick operation. As great hopes had been held out for the successful operation of this machine no other adequate method of mucking was available and it was necessary to return to hand-mucking methods.

The first timbering in the excavation of the lower sub-bench consisted in removing the temporary round posts placed at the time the upper sub-bench was removed, and replacing them by full length 12 by 12-in. posts extending to sub-grade and set on foot-blocks. Also, under the 6 by 12-in. sill was placed a short post battering in so that at the bottom it was in line with the long posts. This short post was set under the permanent batter posts placed with the upper bench and in connection with them was intended to form an arch that would help to resist side pressure. However, mainly on account of the compressibility of the 6 by 12-in. sill in resisting compression across the grain, they were of little value in this respect.

Immediately on excavating the lower sub-bench, the side pressures increased greatly. It was necessary to place spreaders lower down than the wall-plates and directly against the posts, which showed signs of breaking. A trussed design for the long posts adapted to take side strain was adopted and it was decided to replace the segmental posts by trussed posts also.

Traveling Cantilever Needle Bar

At this time a policy was adopted of attempting to hold all the tunnel by permanent timber, there being little realization of the tremendous pressures to be withstood and the inadequacy of timber for such a purpose. It was also determined to try out the Osgood shovel again. For this purpose it was necessary to return to the needle-beam method. A modification of the original needle-beam method for supporting the wall-plates was adopted (Fig. 19), using the cantilever principle. Two heavy 42-in. girders, 60 ft. long, cantilevered out from the high bench on which they were supported, were the main feature of the design. These girders were framed together in one unit and were pulled ahead on a track by a small air hoist. Improved cross-beams and a wedge arrangement for raising them to a bearing on the under side of the wall-plates were also features of the method. These cantilevers were designed for use on the full bench, which being at this time east of Cross-Cut No. 2 could not be reached by the Osgood shovel because the lower sub-bench was not yet excavated.

It was then determined to use the cantilevers and the Osgood shovel on the lower sub-bench. This necessitated the erection of the girders on cribbing about 8 ft. high above the sub-bench (Fig. 20) and the removal of the spreaders between the wall-plates. It was hoped that it would be safe to take out the spreaders and use instead 3-piece arches placed alternately between the 5-piece arches already in place. These 3-piece sets were intended to maintain the wall-plates against lateral pressure as did the spreaders and it was necessary to make the substitution in advance of the progress of the girders. The clearance under these 3-piece sets was less than under the 5-piece sets, and it became necessary to lower the girders which, in turn, made it necessary to lower the sub-grade of the tunnel 9 in. to provide clearance for the shovel in loading cars.

Original Timber Lining Replaced by Separate Sets

Through the worst of this heavy ground section trussed posts were placed on close centers and for part of the way they were placed practically "skin tight". All this work turned out to be inadequate for shortly after the timber was finished tremendous pressures began to develop. Again the wall-plates were the main source of trouble. Even with the thorough bracing against side pressure provided by the 3-piece reinforcing sets the wall-plates were gradually forced into the tunnel. In so doing they were crushed and sheared in places almost to shreds (Fig. 21). The trussed posts were also inadequate to withstand the pressures and spreaders were again placed in part of the tunnel. An attempt was made after Cross-Cut No. 2 was reached to turn the drainage of the water tunnel into the main tunnel. Immediately some of the posts on the south side of the tunnel "kicked" in at the bottom, owing to the softening of material around the foot-blocks by the water.

It was now realized that the timber already placed was inadequate and would have to be replaced by something much stronger and particularly that the wall-plates must be eliminated.

The design adopted which is about the last word in timbering consists of a 3-piece arch set of 12 by 12-in. timber, the inclined legs being placed somewhat more vertical than usual. These sets rest directly on 12 by 18-in. posts. To erect this timber it was necessary to remove all the old timber and much of the cordwood packing behind it, just enough ground being exposed at any one time to enable one new set to be erected. This reconstruction work will probably extend over at least 2 000 ft. of tunnel much of the timber being set "skin tight". Later, it was decided to make the inclined legs of the arches of 12 by 18-in. instead of 12 by 12-in. timber, the 18-in.

FIG. 18.—MOFFAT TUNNEL, WEST PORTAL, SHOWING I-BEAM NEEDLE-BAR AS SEEN FROM HEADING.

FIG. 19.—MOFFAT TUNNEL, WEST PORTAL, SHOWING LEWIS TRAVELING CANTILEVER NEEDLE-BAR, LOOKING TOWARD HEADING.

FIG. 20.—VIEW OF CANTILEVER NEEDLE-BAR ON SUB-BENCH, MOFFAT TUNNEL, WEST PORTAL.

FIG. 21.—VIEW OF 12 BY 12-INCH WALL-PLATE FAILURE, MOFFAT TUNNEL, WEST PORTAL.

dimension, as with the posts, being transverse of the tunnel. Meanwhile the bench excavation had been making progress and east of Cross-Cut No. 2 the full height of bench was attacked. This stretch of tunnel, although consisting of rock much better than that where the sub-bench method was used, had to be excavated with great care to avoid cave-ins due to the great height of the unsupported bench. As further progress was made, however, the rock became more self-supporting.

Ventilation of West Portal

The ventilation system installed at the West Portal was the same as that at the East Portal. It did not work so satisfactorily, however, due to the main headings being late in "holing through" and to smoke sifting through from the railroad tunnel to the water tunnel through some of the cross-cuts which could not be made air-tight on account of being timbered. The other apparatus used at the West Portal was much like that already described for the East Portal. There was not, however, as much air-compressor capacity required as at the East Portal because less drilling was required.

Disposal

At the West Portal all muck trains from the water tunnel went directly to the dump, descending on a 2% grade to the lower level.

Timber Framing and Treating

The large amount of timbering to be done at the West Portal led to the installation of a plant for framing and notching these timbers. The dapping machine designed on the job for this purpose was a great success.

It was also considered advisable to creosote the foot-blocks. This was done by the open-tank process. Because of indications of attack by fungus growths, the advisability of treating with preservatives all the timber was seriously considered, but after a thorough study of creosoting and other processes ordinarily used, it did not appear that any of them was adapted to the particular requirements of timbering for the Moffat Tunnel.

Papers on the same subject and treating various phases of the subject are listed as follows:

Municipal Facts, Denver, Colo., August-September, 1923; September-October, 1924; March-April, 1925; September-October, 1925.

Railway Age, November 15, 1923.

The Explosives Engineer, February, 1925.

Compressed Air Magazine, February, March, and April, 1925.

Successful Methods, June, 1925.

Engineering News-Record, December 13, 1923; March 6, 1924; May, 1925; June 11, 1925; February 18, 1926.

"Engineering Features of the Moffat Tunnel", by David W. Brunton, Colorado Scientific Society, October, 1923.

Mining and Metallurgy, November, 1925.

Mining Congress Journal, March, 1926.

DISCUSSION

T. Kennard Thomson,* M. Am. Soc. C. E.—The two things that make engineering really worth while are the contacts with fine men and interesting problems. This paper brings up recollections of forty-four years ago, and it would be a pleasure to tell about many of the then young men who have since made international reputations. However, only one who has passed on will be mentioned, the late Albert Brainerd Rogers, M. Am. Soc. C. E., the only engineer to discover two passes through the Rocky Mountains, one of which was mentioned by the author. Hundreds of interesting stories are told about this engineer, who discovered "Rogers Pass" (now called "Connaught"), which gave a short cut of 67 miles instead of 163 miles around the Columbia River. The discovery resulted in the Canadian Pacific Railroad awarding to Major Rogers a bonus of $5 000. Later, Mr. William C. Van Horne asked him why the check had not been cashed and was told that never before, in nearly sixty years, had any one paid him a cent more than obliged to—so he had framed the check. Mr. Van Horne again sent for Major Rogers and showed him a gold watch which was to be given him when the check was cashed. This overcame his reluctance.

On the Canadian Pacific Railroad through the Rockies some of the tunnel problems were similar to those at the Moffat Tunnel, but with very different working conditions. The timber lining and sections were similar. One of the earlier tunnels was distorted several times and finally collapsed, due to shifting clay, although the timber lining before the final collapse was a solid 12 by 14-in. wall. It was then abandoned and a temporary line (requiring a 23° curve) was used, until years afterward, a longer tunnel was built in a much safer location.

The earlier tunnel work suffered from the lack of high-grade tools, electric current, and even coal, all supplies except wood and water coming through Winnipeg, a thousand miles away, much of it from Chicago and Ontario. Nor were there any blueprints, ready made India ink, or typewriters. The labor problems likewise were radically different as all labor had to come from the East, and the men could not quit, although the payrolls were sometimes very late in arriving. Even bathing was difficult.

Only those who know the Rockies can realize how fortunate it was that, in crossing the Continental Divide, the Canadian Pacific Railroad did not have to reach any such elevations as the 11 660 ft. of the Denver and Rio Grande Western Railroad in Colorado, nor even the 9 200 ft. of the Moffat Tunnel. The highest point of the Canadian Pacific base of rail is 5 300 ft. at the summit, in British Columbia, not very far west of Banff. Elevations such as those in Colorado would probably have been prohibitive in British Columbia. The Canadian National Railway, much farther north, is still more fortunate with a maximum elevation of 3 717 ft.—a kind dispensation of Nature.

The author mentions exploders. In the East River (New York City) it was necessary to do some submarine blasting by drilling a number of holes

* Cons. Engr., New York, N. Y.

under the bed of the river from a coffer-dam, and exploding all the charges at one operation. The makers of the exploders sent an expert to supervise the loading and wiring, but, unfortunately, only a few of the charges were detonated. On connecting about twenty-five similar exploders in the same manner, but without the dynamite, and sending the current through them, only four or five went off. Several efforts were necessary to get all the exploders detonated, which illustrates the improvements that have been made in explosives.

It is interesting to note that the same kind of gneiss rock as extends under New York City was encountered in the Moffat Tunnel and that it was decomposed 100 ft. or more below the surface. In New York, so far, this "rotten" rock has been found only near the surface, although as much as 50 ft. (in depth) of this soft rock has been removed.

H. F. Dunham,* M. Am. Soc. C. E. (by letter).—In the Ohio Valley District there is a tradition—possibly unwarranted—that oak timbers as large as 12 by 12 in. decay far more rapidly than timbers 6 by 12 in., spaced ½ in. apart for air circulation, where "heavy ground" requires a continuous 12-in. oak lining.

Every tunnel engineer knows that the integrity of his work depends largely on maintaining the exact position of the wall-plates. Years ago when in charge of such heavy ground construction for double-track steam railway in West Virginia, the writer found that carefully placed wall-plates were continually being disturbed in removing the bench. The contractor was ordered to secure and use 60-ton jacks in the re-alignment of the wall-plates. After the first few days the hydraulic jacks acted by catalysis only.

The instrument work for alignment and grade in long tunnels offers a chance for improvement over earlier conditions by using electricity. If one "bright spot" of known position could be shown when desired, on the face of a heading, or maintained all the time, the use of a light template would ensure a correct outline for the whole heading, tending to save needless rock removal and replacement.

The line of probable least disturbance in the average tunnel would presumably be near the wall-plate line, say, 1 ft. inside and 1 ft. above that line. In most rock tunnels there is firm rock along the side walls within distances of 500 or 1 000 ft. At such points a vertical piece of timber could be anchor-bolted to the wall holding a bracket strong enough to support a wye-level on a base similar to that used by an instrument maker in adjustments between artificial, infinite-distant points. The level supported on such a bracket and brought into line by means of proper back-sights should then be reversed in its wyes, thus carrying both grade and alignment with great accuracy to the heading. A small platform for the operator would be required and a fender guard might possibly be needed, but there should be several hundred feet between the last bracket and the heading.

The next step should be to require of the instrument maker a light cylinder of the exact size of the level barrel, to be equipped with a light bulb and with

* Civ. and Hydr. Engr., New York, N. Y.

suitable lenses to converge the rays and take the place of the level barrel in projecting the desired bright spot. A simple correction of 2 in. for every ½ mile would provide for earth curvature.

LAZARUS WHITE,* M. AM. SOC. C. E.—A project such as the Moffat Tunnel has three aspects: (1) Economic; (2) engineering; and (3) contract relationship. It is difficult to understand its economic aspects, particularly as it is being built previous to an agreement with the only railroad that can operate it. Although this is quite the usual practice, it often leads to a poor bargain on the part of the community that originally finances such a project. Of course, the building of this tunnel is a fine thing for the railroad, which secures a great bulk of valuable freight during its construction and, later, will be in a position to drive a good bargain. Perhaps the community takes its profit in the opening of a new district west of the Rocky Mountains.

For building the Moffat Tunnel a new method of contracting was devised; the contractor is compensated at a small fixed fee set by himself, the main incentive of profit coming from completion ahead of time, thereby securing a bonus. Because of the difficulty in driving the tunnel, it appears that the bonus will be hard to realize and that the contractors, despite their very excellent work, experience, and abilities, will not receive much compensation, unless it is through sources not apparent in the original contract. This form of contract is, in fact, a method of hiring superintendence. In the long run, it would practically eliminate contractors, as ordinarily understood, and would substitute for them professional men in a sort of dual capacity of engineers and superintendents, operating on a salary with an incentive of a bonus, but lacking the element of profit, which is the principal attraction for the type of man who usually makes a successful contractor.

The engineering problems are those which have repeatedly arisen in connection with the driving of other long mountain tunnels of Alpine character, such as that at Rogers Pass. The difference between these two tunnels, however, is due to the presence of, or freedom from, heavy ground. The methods of overcoming heavy pressures are interesting and ingenious. Apparently, the construction was hampered by the difficulty of securing steel, cement, and concrete materials so that resource was had largely to heavy timbering. In the writer's opinion such problems could better be met by steel and concrete.

In such cases timber is not a reliable material and cannot be trusted to hold heavy pressures permanently. The failures noted in this paper are similar to those historic examples in Drinker's "Tunneling". Nowadays, because steel is readily available and methods of placing concrete by compressed air have been developed to a high degree, bad ground can be more readily supported by steel and permanent concrete lining in the writer's opinion.

This paper is valuable inasmuch as Mr. Keays very frankly states his problems and expresses doubts that the solutions reached were the best. Such an attitude leads to progress. In describing a completed construction, there is a tendency to give the impression that the methods used were the best, thus leading others to copy examples that are questionable.

* Pres., Spencer, White & Prentis, Inc., New York, N. Y.

AMERICAN SOCIETY OF CIVIL ENGINEERS

INSTITUTED 1852

TRANSACTIONS

This Society is not responsible for any statement made or opinion expressed in its publications.

Paper No. 1658

CIVIL ENGINEERING FEATURES OF THE HELL GATE STATION*

By Ernest M. Van Norden,† and George A. Hughes,‡
Members, Am. Soc. C. E.

With Discussion by Messrs. George A. Orrok, A. Streiff, and Ernest M. Van Norden.

The Hell Gate Station of The United Electric Light and Power Company, located on the East River between 132d and 134th Streets, New York, N. Y., has been well described in the technical press and also in publications issued from time to time by its owners. It is very natural in such publicity for the author to confine himself to a description of the mechanical and electrical equipment and to neglect much of the detail pertaining to the structure. The problems involving civil engineering, within the commonly accepted meaning of this term, are usually lightly touched upon, although these problems may be difficult of solution, intricate in design, and expensive in execution.

The Hell Gate Station involved many problems in this class, some of which are not found in other power station designs; and for their successful solution much credit is due the designers and contractors. It is the purpose of this paper to describe the more important civil engineering features of this station, introducing only such mechanical and electrical details as may be required to make a complete picture.

Three factors controlled the selection of the site:

First.—Proximity to the center of gravity of the load.

Second.—Real estate values.

Third.—Water-front facilities for receiving coal and supplying circulating water for the condensers.

---

* Presented at the meeting of the Power Division, New York, N. Y., January 21, 1926.

† Civ. Engr., New York Edison Co., New York, N. Y.

‡ Civ. Engr., Thomas E. Murray, Inc., New York, N. Y.

The station was designed to supply electric energy to Queens Borough and Westchester County, as well as to the Boroughs of Manhattan and The Bronx, and from the standpoint of center of gravity of the load the site was well chosen. Even with considerable increase in the load the center of gravity would still remain about the same.

From the standpoint of real estate values the Company was fortunate in being able to secure this property at a reasonable price. The number of water-front properties available in the City of New York that could be used for power-station development are few, and the question of cost might be regarded as unimportant, although in this particular case the relatively low cost tended to make a quicker decision as to location.

The Company succeeded in securing from the city the exclusive privilege of mooring at the foot of 134th Street. The entire length of water-front, therefore, ran from the north side of 132d Street to the north side of 134th Street, a distance of about 500 ft. It was planned to receive coal at this station in ocean-going ships capable of carrying 10 000 tons with a draft of 28 ft., but the capacity of the boats which so far have entered this service rarely exceeds 6 000 tons, with a draft of 24 ft. To accommodate the large ships safely it was necessary to obtain 35 ft. of water alongside the wharf.

An aeroplane photograph looking toward the northeast (Fig. 1) illustrates the excellent water-front advantages enjoyed by this station. The area immediately south of 132d Street, shown in the foreground, is to be developed as a freight yard for the New York, New Haven and Hartford Railroad Company which plans to build a bulkhead at the easterly end for transferring water and railroad freight. At the time this photograph was taken the station was not entirely completed, the view showing only three stacks of a total of four.

The survey to determine the elevations of the surface and the bedrock had to be carried beyond the low-water mark. The wash borings that were made, partly on land and partly from floats, proved to be very accurate, making it possible to contract on a lump-sum basis for the removal of the over-burden and the rock down to the levels required.

As shown in the topographical survey of the rock surface (Fig. 3), the contour lines, assuming the over-burden to be removed, indicate that the rock slopes rapidly down offshore. On this map is indicated the main outline of the station structure.

The turbo-generator room was located parallel with the water-front so that the water for the condensers could be pumped directly from the river, thereby avoiding the construction of a long intake tunnel. The discharge tunnel for the condensing water was also located parallel with the water-front and as close to the river wall of the station as possible. The absence of an intake tunnel for the condensing water renders this station unique among power stations in the City of New York.

The entire rock excavation, therefore, was confined to an area very close to the water-front and was done by under-water blasting. It was necessary to go to certain depths for the discharge tunnel and for the suction pipes and screens. It was also necessary to provide sufficient depth of water for ocean-going ships along the entire length of the wharf.

FIG. 1.—AEROPLANE VIEW, SHOWING WATER-FRONT ADVANTAGES OF THE HELL GATE STATION.

FIG. 2.—VIEW OF DRILL BOAT IN POSITION AND DREDGE IN OPERATION, HELL GATE STATION.

Fig. 4 is a cross-section of the station showing the cut required in the rock and also the relative position of the sea-wall supporting the easterly wall of the station and the discharge tunnel and wharf.

The contractor first dredged the site to remove the over-burden and then used two drill boats especially constructed for submarine drilling. The size of the drill bits was 4¾ in., making holes approximately 5 in. in diameter. These holes were drilled on 5-ft. centers in both directions over the entire area and were carried down to 5 or 6 ft. below the finished rock grade.

The operation of drilling was as follows: The drill boat was located by shore rangers and held in position by lines run out to anchors, by lines to the shore, and also by spuds on the boat resting on the river bed. A drill pipe was dropped down until it rested on the bottom, and the drill rod was dropped through the pipe. The drill was operated by steam and was fed down as the rock was drilled. After the hole was finished it was loaded with dynamite through the drill pipe and the wire brought up and attached to the boat. Every day all the wires were connected, the boat pulled out into the stream beyond danger, and these holes were fired. The boat then took up a new position and commenced drilling again. After the area had been drilled over it was dredged off and if soundings indicated high spots, these were re-drilled and the same procedure was repeated.

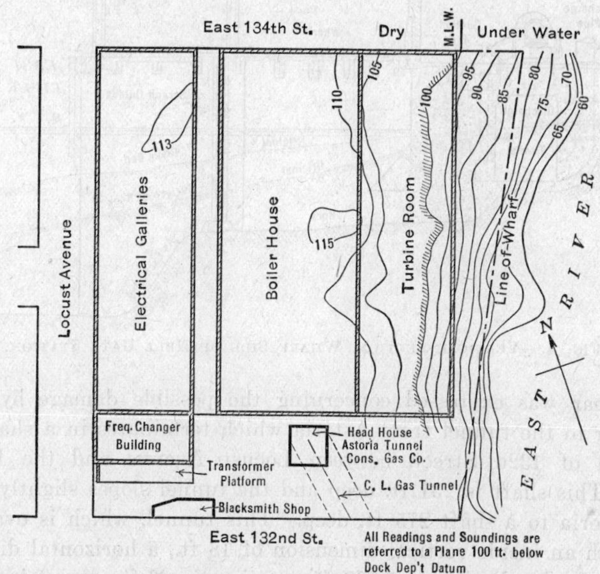

FIG. 3.—MAP SHOWING TOPOGRAPHIC SURVEY OF ROCK SURFACE AND MAIN OUTLINE OF THE HELL GATE STATION STRUCTURE.

The length of the holes ranged from 6 to 20 ft., with an average of 11 ft. A total of 1 776 holes were drilled. The average rate of drilling was about 60 ft. per day. This under-water work was started in March, 1920, and was completed in September, 1921.

Before drilling of rock was started, 2 000 cu. yd. of over-burden were dredged. In all, 23 600 cu. yd. of rock were removed by the dredge and 13 400 cu. yd. in the dry, both place measurement. An attempt was made to have the work in shallow water done by a shot drill. This was started about opposite 133d Street. A total of ten holes about 20 ft. deep were drilled when this method was abandoned because the soft strata of rock would cause the core to break and wedge the drills and also caused them to lose their shot. These holes were 6 in. in diameter. The contractor then tried a wagon drill near 134th Street in shallow water, but progress was so slow that it was abandoned. It was the custom to bring the drill boat in at high tide and work offshore at low tide. Fig. 2 looking south shows the drill boat in position at the south end of the site and also the dredge in operation. The temporary pier shown in the center of the photograph was constructed to accommodate the shot drilling.

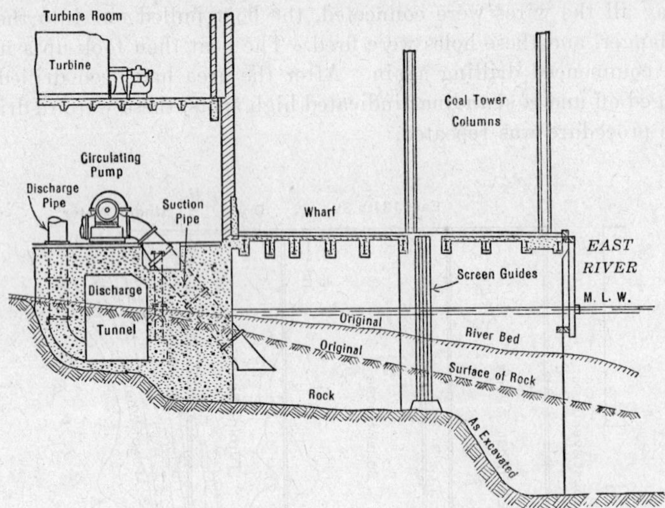

FIG. 4.—VERTICAL SECTION, WHARF SIDE OF HELL GATE STATION.

Some fear was expressed concerning the possible damage by reason of the blasting to the tunnel from Astoria which terminates in a shaft immediately north of 132d Street, between Locust Avenue and the East River (Fig. 3). This shaft is 231 ft. deep and the tunnel slopes slightly downward toward Astoria to a shaft 275 ft. deep. This tunnel, which is oval in cross-section, with an inside vertical dimension of 18 ft., a horizontal dimension of 16 ft. 9 in., and a length of 5 168 ft., carries two 6-ft. gas mains and some smaller pipes and conduits. During the blasting an inspector was stationed in the tunnel for purposes of observation and as a precaution the charges were made lighter at the south end of the excavation near the tunnel. The blasts were barely perceptible in the tunnel and no damage occurred.

To save the cost and delay of a coffer-dam the construction of the river-wall footing down to bed-rock at a depth of approximately 16 ft. below mean low water was started immediately on the completion of the rock excavation. This footing was designed with returns inshore so as to take the part of a coffer-dam and permit the construction of a discharge tunnel in the open. The foundation of the river wall was made of concrete deposited by tremie. For convenience in construction it was divided into sections about 14 ft. long, alternate sections being constructed in the first operation. The second operation filled in between the alternate sections thus completing the continuous wall with its return.

The concrete sea-wall is trapezoidal in cross-section with an average depth of 28.5 ft. and a base 12 ft. wide. Alternate sections about 14 ft. long were first poured, with keys formed in the ends. The forms, built on the ground in advance, in the shape of an open box, were of 2 by 10-in. planks laid in a horizontal direction on all four sides. On the ends these were reinforced with 6 by 6-in. timbers and tie-rods 1 in. in diameter and on the sides the reinforcement consisted of 12 and 15-in. steel channels with similar tie-rods. The rods were run through pipe sleeves so that they could be easily removed after the concrete had set. After the forms were lowered into place by weighting them with reinforcing bars, the voids between the bottom of the box and the rock were filled in with sand bags placed by divers. Then the bottom was sealed with concrete poured by the tremie method, the sea water pumped out, and the remainder of the wall poured in the dry.

Fig. 5 shows one section of the concrete wall in place with the forms stripped and an adjacent form being lowered into place. This view is taken looking north along the line of the sea-wall, showing the movable plant of the contractor at the left. After the forms were placed in position divers sealed the spaces between the bottom of the form and irregular rock surfaces.

The view, Fig. 6, was taken from the south end of the rock showing the opening for the discharge tunnel through the sea-wall in the foreground and also the operation of shooting concrete into the tremie funnel.

Provision was made in the wall to receive the cast-iron suction pipes which run from the condenser pumps in the basement of the turbo-generator room at a slope of 45° through the concrete wall to a point 5 ft. below mean low water.

After the completion of the concrete footing of the river wall of the station the water back of the wall was pumped out and work was started on the discharge tunnel and the basement floor of the turbo-generator room, the finished elevation of which is 11 ft. above mean low water. The sea-wall proved to be exceptionally water-tight and the bed-rock was free from any open veins. To keep the excavation back of the sea-wall free from water a single 8-in. centrifugal pump was found to be adequate. Fig. 7 shows the rear of the sea-wall after it had been unwatered. The 52-in. cast-iron suction pipes are shown concreted in place and the concrete bottom of the discharge tunnel is also shown resting directly on the bed-rock. In the foreground the strike of the rock is seen to run parallel with the sea-wall.

Owing to experience at other stations in the disintegration of concrete in discharge tunnels special care was taken to make the inside surfaces of the Hell Gate discharge tunnel of a smooth, hard, and impervious concrete. To use a similar high-grade concrete for back-filling under the entire basement would have been unnecessary waste and, therefore, a method was devised to place high-grade concrete at least 12 in. thick next to the discharge tunnel form and at the same time, lean concrete for the large mass. Fig. 8 shows the tunnel in an advanced state of construction. In addition to the suction pipes shown in the other photographs it also shows on the left-hand side the 42-in. cast-iron discharge pipes which were embedded in the concrete fill in the basement of the turbo-generator room terminating in an elbow at the bottom of the discharge tunnel. This tunnel is 11½ ft. wide by 15½ ft. high, running the full length of the turbo-generator room, the bottom elevation being 10 ft. below mean low water.

The "mixed aggregate" of sand and gravel used on this work was delivered in barge load lots and unloaded with a clam-shell bucket. In depositing this material in the storage piles the separation of the sand and gravel, particularly when the piling was done in cones, was so marked that re-apportioning of the ingredients was necessary to insure uniformity of the mixture for the special high-grade concrete used in the lining of the discharge tunnel and the reinforced concrete work.

The wharf is constructed of reinforced concrete slabs spanning between deep Bethlehem I-beams protected with a 4½-in. covering of concrete. The steel framing is supported by rectangular concrete piers, 6 ft. wide and 31 ft. long, reinforced with vertical rods and spaced 30 ft. 3 in. on centers. In several places cylindrical piers were used, 6 ft. in diameter and 46 ft. deep, and reinforced with thirty-two vertical rods, 1⅛ in. in diameter, and hoops, 12 in. on centers. The bottom of the pier is bonded into the rock with three dowels, 3½ in. in diameter. The deck of the wharf is finished with 4½-in. paving brick laid in a 1½-in. sand cushion.

The river water passes through steel screens before entering the intake basins. Each basin has an opening 24 ft. wide and 20 ft. high and is protected by four removable screens set in vertical bars spaced about 1 in. on centers and mounted in 4-in. channel frames. All the concrete below the water line was deposited through tremie pipes in forms sealed at the bottom as in the case of the sea-wall. Fig. 9 shows the wharf construction with the forms for the girder covering and deck slabs started. Fig. 10 is a "close-up" of the screen construction, showing the opening in the deck of the wharf to give access to the screens and also the base of the steel work for the coal trestle.

To provide for the ashes, which are discharged hydraulically through pipes to the water-front, a concrete bin was constructed within the lines of the wharf into which the ashes are deposited and from which they are removed by a clam-shell bucket. The hoisting apparatus (Fig. 11) is arranged so that the ashes may be deposited in barges alongside or in trucks.

The steel trestle on the wharf, which is 107 ft. high and supports two traveling coal towers also appears in Fig. 11. In this trestle construction is shown the crane beams for removing the ashes from the ash-pit so arranged as to permit ashes to be deposited in barges or in motor trucks.

Fig. 5.—Hell Gate Station: View Showing Section of Concrete Wall in Place, with Forms Stripped and Adjacent Form Being Lowered.

Fig. 6.—Hell Gate Station: View Showing Opening for Discharge Tunnel Through the Sea-Wall, and Operation of Shooting Concrete Into Tremie Funnel.

Fig. 7.—View of Rear of Sea-Wall After Unwatering, Hell Gate Station.

Fig. 8.—Discharge Tunnel in Advanced State of Construction, Hell Gate Station.

FIG. 9.—VIEW OF WHARF CONSTRUCTION, WITH FORMS FOR GIRDER COVERING AND DECK SLABS STARTED, HELL GATE STATION.

FIG. 10.—"CLOSE-UP" OF SCREEN CONSTRUCTION, HELL GATE STATION.

FIG. 11.—VIEW OF HOISTING APPARATUS, HELL GATE STATION.

On top of this trestle is carried a system of double tracks which parallel the bulkhead about at the level of the roof of the station. The tracks continue across bridges connecting the trestle with the turbine room, and another bridge spans the court between the boiler-house and control galleries. Where the cars cross the turbine room, the tracks are supported on the bottom chord of the roof trusses which have a span of 98 ft. West of the control galleries, the tracks are again carried on a steel trestle spanning Locust Avenue and extending 175 ft. to the center of the two city blocks used for coal storage (Figs. 12 and 13). This structure has an expansion joint at the control galleries and another at the rigid tower construction, and the three intermediate truss spans are supported by two flexible towers. The wind pressure on this trestle was assumed at 24 lb. per sq. ft., and the customary fiber stresses for static loads were used in designing the steel work. The cars deliver the coal to receiving hoppers suspended from the track floor and from there it is carried through steel chutes, 65 ft. long, and piled 35 ft. high in the storage yard for distribution by a drag scraper.

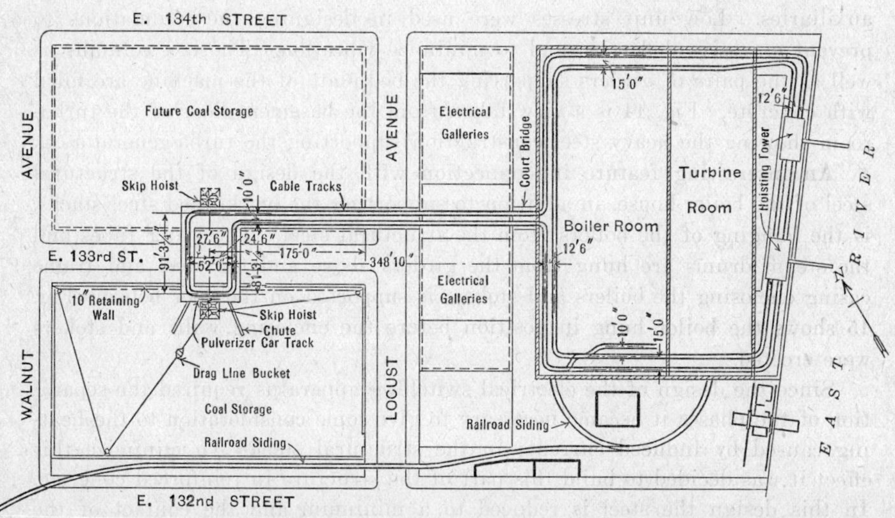

Fig. 12.—Plan of Station and Coal Storage Yard, Hell Gate Station.

In Fig. 12 are shown the coal tracks from the bulkhead trestle into the storage yard in the rear, crossing Locust Avenue and also East 133d Street; also the track siding from the New York, New Haven and Hartford Railroad, which serves as an auxiliary means of supplying coal.

Four self-supporting steel stacks are carried on the roof framing of the boiler-house. Each stack has a diameter of 22 ft. and a top elevation of 258 ft. above the boiler-room floor, with provision for a possible future extension of 50 ft. A wind pressure of 25 lb. per sq. ft. of projected area was assumed on the stack and a maximum compression of 10 000 lb. per sq. in. was used in designing the steel plates. The base of the stack is anchored to the supporting girders by thirty-two bolts 2¼ in. in diameter. The wind shear on the stack is carried down to the foundation through a system of wind bracing between the boiler-house columns.

The turbine room is served by two electric traveling cranes having a span of 96 ft., one with a capacity of 110 tons and the other of 90 tons. Each bridge girder of the heavy crane has two $\frac{7}{16}$-in. web-plates, 8 ft. 8 in. deep at the center and 3 ft. 8 in. deep at the trucks. The weight of one bridge girder is 75 000 lb.

The end walls of the turbine room are braced by horizontal wind trusses 6 ft. deep, spanning 98 ft. These trusses are located about midway between the basement floor and the bottom chord of the roof trusses, a distance of 108 ft. Between the basement and the wind truss and again between the wind truss and the bottom chord bracing, three vertical columns are framed which are covered with brick pilasters to stiffen the wall.

The main turbo-generators in the turbine room have a capacity ranging from 35 000 to 50 000 kw. The machines are supported on steel foundations in order to provide sufficient space in the basement for the condensers and auxiliaries. Low unit stresses were used in designing the foundations to prevent excessive deflection and to minimize vibration. The box columns as well as the pairs of girders supporting the bed-plate of the machine are filled with concrete. Fig. 14 is a view taken from the basement floor of the turbo-room showing the heavy steel construction supporting the turbo-generators.

An interesting feature in connection with the design of the structural steel of the boiler-house, in addition to supporting the brick-lined steel stacks, is the hanging of the boilers from the structural steel. The water tubes and the steam drums are hung from the girders above and the steel and frame casing enclosing the boilers and stokers is supported on the floor below. Fig. 15 shows the boiler hung in position before the enclosing walls and stokers were erected.

Since the design of the electrical switching apparatus required the separation of the phases it became necessary to give some consideration to the heating caused by induced currents in the structural steel. To minimize this effect it was decided to build this part of the structure in reinforced concrete. In this design the steel is reduced to a minimum and the contact of the various parts of the reinforcement forming loops around the single-phase conductors is too poor to permit any appreciable rise in temperature. The electrical switching apparatus is housed in concrete compartments producing very heavy floor loads and requiring a reinforced concrete construction of rather an exceptional weight.

The first section of the switching galleries which take care of approximately one-half the total capacity of the station is 120 by 105 ft. and seven stories high. The concrete mixing plant used for this part of the work was located on the west side of Locust Avenue. The concrete was shot from a lifting tower, 220 ft. high, to a distributing tower across the street, 200 ft. high. The mixer was of ¾-cu. yd. capacity. The work on this first section of the electrical galleries, involving 6 600 cu. yd. of concrete and 574 tons of

Fig. 13.—View of Steel Trestle Carrying Tracks Across Locust Avenue, Hell Gate Station.

Fig. 14.—View from Basement Floor of Turbo-Generator Room, Showing Heavy Steel Construction Supporting Turbo-Generators, Hell Gate Station.

FIG. 15.—BOILER HUNG IN POSITION BEFORE WALLS AND STOKERS WERE ERECTED, HELL GATE STATION.

FIG. 16.—FIRST SECTION OF REINFORCED CONCRETE SWITCHING GALLERIES UNDER CONSTRUCTION, HELL GATE STATION.

Fig. 17.—Forms Used in Concreting in Construction of High-Tension Switch Compartments, Hell Gate Station.

Fig. 18.—View Showing High-Tension Switch Compartments, Hell Gate Station.

reinforcing bars, was started on February 2, and completed on March 29, 1921. Fig. 16 shows the first section of the reinforced concrete switching galleries under construction. This work is independent of the boiler-house, the structural steel framework of which is also shown.

The separation of the phases is effected by continuous walls running through all the floors designed so that it was possible to introduce ventilating shafts communicating with the various floors and arranged so that in addition to the continuous ventilation required it would be possible to remove the smoke quickly from burning oil or insulation should any short circuit to ground take place within any one of the sections.

While the high-tension switch compartments might be considered a part of the electrical switching equipment it is equally true that they are part of the structure of the building and the problems involved in their design and construction belong to the structural engineer's field. The switching equipment is probably the most interesting part of this station and to describe it properly would require a volume in itself. Those who are interested will find many excellent descriptions in the technical press.* In view of the duplication of detail in the construction of the compartments, of which there are about 3 000, a special effort was made to produce a form for concreting which could be used many times and which was readily demountable. Estimates were prepared comparing wooden with metal forms and economy seemed to point to the metal forms. These forms (Fig. 17) were constructed and assembled in the shop of the manufacturer and bolt holes and blocking were introduced where necessary to hold the inserts, which formed a part of the electrical construction, within the concrete of the compartment. The forms proved satisfactory except that in special places the sheet metal used was too light and it became necessary to introduce wooden struts. This, however, was inexpensive and successful.

The actual experience in construction again opened the question of the relative cost of metal *versus* wooden forms and in the second section of the electrical galleries, built about two years after the first ones, wooden forms were used throughout. One of the advantages of wooden forms as compared with metal forms is the flexibility of introducing and changing the inserts which could be very readily attached to wooden forms in any desired position. The inserts, numbering more than 30 000, form an important part of the detail of construction.

The compartments in general are about 4½ ft. wide by the full height of the floor, with 4-in. concrete side-walls and 6-in. rear wall (Fig. 18). The side-walls are rabbeted to receive doors which are hung in position and made readily removable.

A detail which proved most satisfactory was designed in connection with the acid-proofing of the storage-battery floors. It was absolutely essential that the sulfuric acid from the storage batteries be prevented from coming into contact with the reinforcing rods and structural steel members of the building, and the double acid-proofing method was introduced. Between the first

* Particularly in the *Electrical World* and the publications of the United Electric Light & Power Co.

layer of acid-proofing and the surface layer there was a layer of concrete about 3 in. thick. The effect of the acid on the concrete is to increase appreciably the volume and if the acid penetrates the top layer it would be evident by the swelling of the acid-proof surface, permitting a repair to be made and the defective concrete to be removed before the acid could penetrate the second layer.

The drain from this floor is a lead pipe terminating in a non-corrosive metal drain box. Fig. 19 is a cross-section of the acid-proof floor construction through the drain box.

The quantity of water pumped through the condensers has often been referred to on account of the very large volume required. When the station is completed there will be eight condensers (Fig. 20) ranging in size from 50 000 to 65 000 sq. ft. The quantity of water varies from 70 000 to 90 000 gal. per min. On the assumption that all pumps are operating, the quantity of water pumped through the condensers would be 640 000 gal. per min., or 940 000 000 gal. per day. On a 40% load factor the quantity pumped would be 376 000 000 gal. per day. A better idea of what these figures mean is obtained by comparing this quantity of water with that delivered each day to the entire City of New York, which is about 850 000 000 gal.

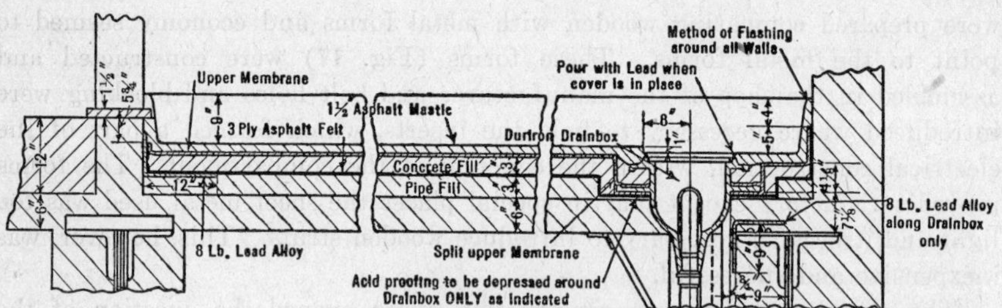

FIG. 19.—CROSS-SECTION OF THE ACID-PROOF FLOOR CONSTRUCTION, THROUGH DRAIN BOX, HELL GATE STATION.

The energy for pumping this enormous quantity of water is relatively small, since the only work required is to overcome the friction in the pipes and condensers. The whole system is operated as a siphon and the height to which the water is raised (approximately 30 ft.) does not materially affect the amount of energy required to produce circulation. Fig. 21 shows the two 54-in. suction pipes and the two 35 000-gal., motor-driven centrifugal pumps.

To insure against the possibility of the fresh-water supply (feed water) being cut off from this station arrangements were made with the city to receive water from three independent sources. The first taps the water supply at 138th Street and Southern Boulevard; the second, on a different main, from 133d Street and Southern Boulevard; and the third from the local water main immediately adjacent to the station.

The proximity of the New York, New Haven and Hartford Yard, immediately south of 132d Street, made it possible to install at this station a railroad siding (Fig. 12) which is frequently used for receiving equipment. The possibility of receiving coal on this siding was considered but it is not

Fig. 20.—Section of Type of Water Condensers Used at Hell Gate Station.

Fig. 21.—View of Suction Pipes and Centrifugal Pumps, Hell Gate Station.

used to any extent since the cheapest coal that could be received in the harbor naturally comes by boat. As an emergency measure, however, coal might be received by rail.

The exterior finish of the building is a red face brick with precast imitation granite base and trim. The reinforced concrete electrical galleries are veneered with the same brick secured to the concrete by metal clips which gives an outward appearance of continuous steel and brick construction. The exterior window frames and sashes are of metal, the size of the openings being designed to use standard frames of a stock pattern.

The Hell Gate Station was put into service in the fall of 1921. At present (1927) there are seven turbo-generator units in operation with an aggregate capacity of 275 000 kw., of which 105 000 kw. has a frequency of 25 cycles and 170 000 kw. a frequency of 60 cycles. There is also a frequency changer of 35 000 kw. capacity. The eighth and last generator of 160 000 kw. capacity has been ordered and will be in service in 1928.

DISCUSSION

George A. Orrok,* M. Am. Soc. C. E.—The Waterside Station of The New York Edison Company was designed and built in 1899. Although the machinery in this station has been enlarged three and one-half times since then, most of the original steel work is in place. An extra expenditure at the time of building (possibly $150 000) has saved several millions of dollars in these reconstructions.

The quantity of condensing water involves two questions—the summer water temperature and the water-rate curve of the turbine with respect to vacuum. If the designer is satisfied with 26 in. of vacuum in the summer, increasing the water rate of the turbine ½ lb. or more, then a 30 to 1 ratio may be used; but if the water rates are to be kept at the guaranteed quantities and the best efficiency secured, then the ratio should be between 60 and 90 to 1, depending on the summer temperature. If the temperature of intake water rises to 90° Fahr., the ratio should be more than 100 to 1.

A. Streiff,† M. Am. Soc. C. E. (by letter).—Apparently, there is still a great deal of difference among engineers as to how the modern large steam turbine should be supported. The usual specification issued by the Turbine Departments of the Westinghouse and General Electric Companies prescribes that the turbine foundation shall be detached from the building structure. On the other hand, the Allis-Chalmers Company favors the opposite practice of a monolithic building.

Detached foundations are made for seismographs and equatorials of astronomical observatories, but to require such a foundation for the steam turbine seems unwarranted. The modern steam turbine is marvelously well balanced, and fear of damage to the structure by reason of undue vibrations seems illusory. The large mass of the building naturally diminishes the amplitude of the vibrations and if these are objectionable, they surely would be excessive for a separate turbine support.

In a shop test on running balance the practice of the Allis Chalmers Company is to remove the foundation bolts one by one until the machine is entirely free from its temporary foundations. Such a machine would hardly need to be entirely detached from the remaining building.

The Hell Gate Station shows the turbine supports interconnected with the main structure, whereas in other very large stations as at Kearny, N. J., the turbine supports are separate. The former practice results in a roomy and simple supporting structure and is greatly to be preferred if both systems are equally satisfactory under running conditions.

Again, the requirement of applying a horizontal thrust equal to 25% of the vertical weight on the supporting frames of the turbine, as given by the Westinghouse and General Electric Companies, seems absurd. Such a thrust does not occur under any circumstance. In the direction of the shaft the largest thrust is the one possibly exerted by the steam main, which should be

* Cons. Engr., New York, N. Y.

† Cons. Engr., Jackson, Mich.

kept small. At right angles to the shaft the largest impact occurs during a short circuit, but this is an internal stress affecting only the supporting beams of the stator frames and does not introduce a horizontal thrust. Such a requirement causes heavy bracing and this interferes more or less with air coolers, condensers, bleeder connections, heaters, etc. The Allis Chalmers Company does not require such a horizontal thrust to be applied to the frame.

The arrangement of the turbine support followed at the Hell Gate Station seems to the writer the correct form. A statement as to its behavior under operating conditions would be of interest.

ERNEST M. VAN NORDEN,* M. AM. SOC. C. E. (by letter).—The writer appreciates the interest shown by Mr. Streiff and agrees with him that it is not essential to isolate the foundations of the turbo-generators from the structural steel framework of the building. Owing to the nature of the design, however, the steel foundations are not as rigidly connected to that framework as would be the case if a floor had to be designed to carry the loads to the main columns of the building. All the columns carrying the turbo-generator loads are independent of the building columns and the connections to the main structure are only useful in carrying a floor load for operating purposes.

It would be difficult to determine a formula for calculating the sections of the steel members, because the necessity for rigidity requires a factor of safety so high that erroneous conclusions are drawn as to the reason for using what appears to be extremely low unit stresses. The allowance of 25% of the vertical load for the horizontal thrust may seem excessive, and this may be a poor way of determining the sections, but it is quite likely that the usual design for this class of construction carries with it sufficient rigidity to take care of such stresses and perhaps greater ones in the horizontal direction.

The design that has given excellent results was made during the period when the turbine manufacturers believed that only concrete could be used for this purpose. The doubt concerning the rigidity of a steel structure was so strong that the steel designers were undoubtedly influenced by the fear shown by the turbine manufacturers and, therefore, very low unit stresses were used, care being taken to introduce rivets in shear only. It is fortunate, perhaps, that the steel design was started in this way, because it has been demonstrated beyond question that the low unit stresses, which cannot be well determined by any formula, and which were the result of extreme caution, have proved safe and economic.

The results of several years' operation at the Hell Gate Station indicate that the steel framework was well designed and can be recommended without hesitation for any other turbine foundation. The vibration from unbalanced machines, which occurred on several occasions due to accidents, was taken up by the steel foundations without transferring any perceptible vibration to the building structure.

* Civ. Engr., New York Edison Co., New York, N. Y.

AMERICAN SOCIETY OF CIVIL ENGINEERS
INSTITUTED 1852

TRANSACTIONS

This Society is not responsible for any statement made or opinion expressed in its publications.

Paper No. 1659

THE CIVIL ENGINEERING FEATURES OF THE KEARNY POWER STATION*

By Roman von Fabrice,† Assoc. M. Am. Soc. C. E.

With Discussion by George A. Orrok, M. Am. Soc. C. E.

Synopsis

The object of this paper is to set forth the problems that the civil engineer is called upon to solve in order to make "super-power" a possibility. To this end the civil engineering features of the design and construction of the Kearny Power Station are treated, each phase of the work separately.

The Kearny Power Station is situated on the west bank of the Hackensack River in the Town of Kearny, N. J., about midway between Newark and Jersey City, and is interconnected with the Essex and Marion Stations by a 132 000-volt transmission line supported on steel towers. It is the largest electric generating station in the State of New Jersey and will have a capacity of more than 400 000 kv-a. when completed.

"Super-power" means the production of electrical energy in great magnitudes and its distribution over long distances. Among the public, as well as among the Engineering Profession in general, the impression has been created that developments for this purpose primarily concern electrical engineers. This is erroneous, and although it is true that electrial engineers are responsible for the electrical features, the mechanical engineers and civil engineers are entitled to equal recognition in the problem of making super-power a possibility.

This paper will show the importance of the problems which the civil engineer was called upon to solve in this station, such as foundations and superstructures, high-tension sub-stations, transmission lines, coal and ash-handling structures, cooling water systems, etc. To provide, in co-operation

---

* Presented at the meeting of the Power Division, New York, N. Y., January 21, 1926.

† Designing Engr., Public Service Production Co., Newark, N. J.

with the architect, the proper structures for the accommodation of the equipment selected by the electrical and mechanical engineers, constitutes the chief problem of the civil engineer in such undertakings.

In order to accomplish these results properly he must be familiar, not only with the construction and requirements of the various types of electrical and mechanical equipment, but also with their operation, so as to be able to produce suitable and economical structures both for the support and housing of such apparatus.

General Description of Plant and Property

The Kearny Power Station, New Jersey's largest and newest generating station, built by the Public Service Production Company for the Public Service Electric Power Company, is situated on the west bank of the Hackensack River in the Town of Kearny, N. J. (Fig. 1). The site selected is near the load center, has adequate condensing-water facilities, and offers both rail and water transportation for the fuel required for the continuous and commercial operation of the station. The property on which the station is located comprises 78.9 acres of salt-water meadow land, partly submerged at high tide and requiring piling for the support of the structures.

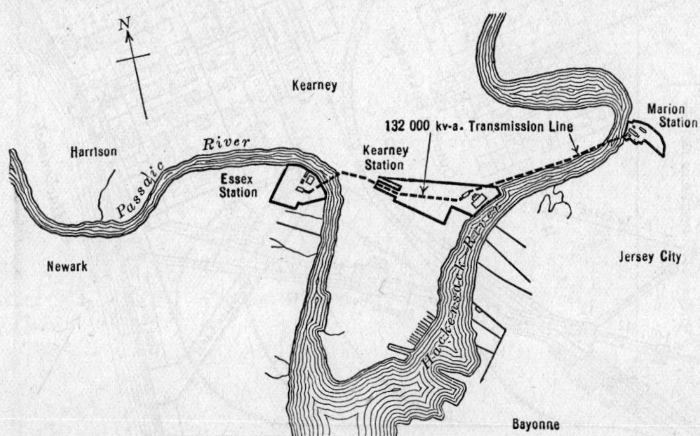

Fig. 1.—Map Showing Relative Locations of Kearny, Essex, and Marion Power Stations.

The initial capacity of the station is 205 100 kv-a., this being the largest ever installed at one time. The ultimate capacity, after the completion of the second half, will be more than 400 000 kv-a.

Beginning at the river the various buildings and structures are arranged in the following sequence (Figs. 2 and 3): Coal-bunker, boiler-house, turbine room, switch-house, service building, high-voltage outdoor sub-station, and transmission towers, the coal and ash-handling system and coal storage being to the west of the other structures. This arrangement was determined after most careful consideration as to the cost of fuel delivery, utilization of real estate, railroad sidings, fuel-handling and storage, cooling water supply, electrical distribution, and economy of design.

Architectural Features

All buildings have been designed to act as parts of a single unit, the central axis of the plant passing through the center of each building. The service building and switch-house form the central motif of the whole group. The main elevation of the turbine room consists of a series of typical bays, the end bays being paneled. The buildings are classical in style, the Corinthian order being utilized where enrichment occurs. As far as was consistent with power-house architecture, projections were held flat and details were refined. A striking feature is a cast-iron Palladian window, 70 ft. high, at the end of the turbine room and a similar but somewhat smaller one in the center of the front of the switch-house (both are seen in Fig. 4).

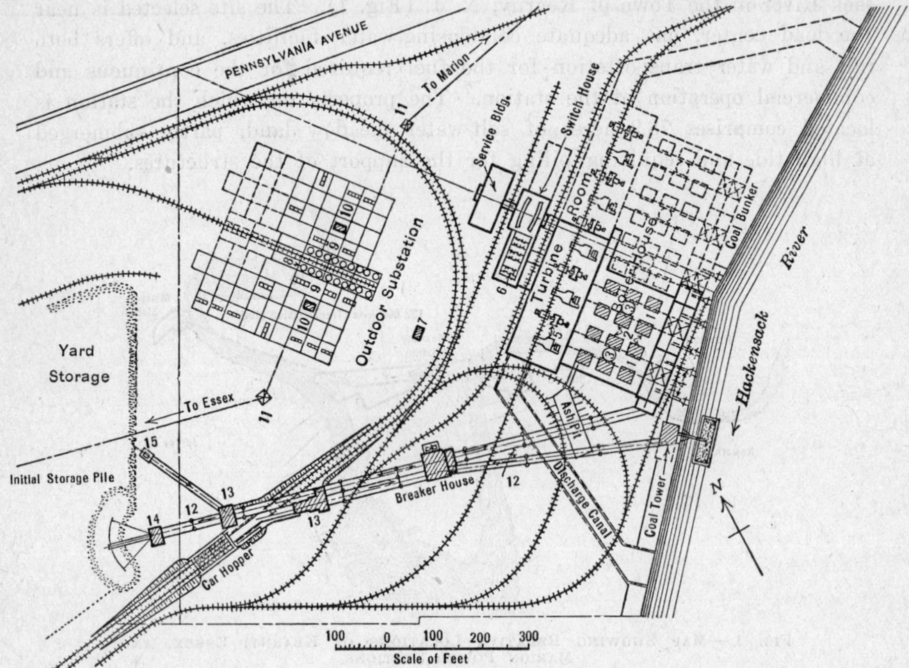

Fig. 2.—Plan of Kearny Power Station: (1) Firing Aisle; (2) Boilers; (3) Stacks; (4) Intake Tunnels; (5) Turbo-Generator; (6) Cell Structures for Isolated Switching Equipment; (7) Oil Purifying Plant; (8) 132-kv-a. Transmission Transformers; (9) Oil-Circuit Breaker; (10) Relay House; (11) Transmission Towers; (12) Conveyors for Fuel-Handling System; (13) Drive House for Conveyors; (14) Swinging Boom Tower; and (15) Reclaiming Pit and Hopper.

The interior of all buildings is severely utilitarian with the exception of the turbine room (Fig. 5), which is finished with gray face-brick panels and pilasters and a red tile floor. The control room in the switch-house has plastered walls and ceiling, a plaster cornice, and a rubber tile flooring.

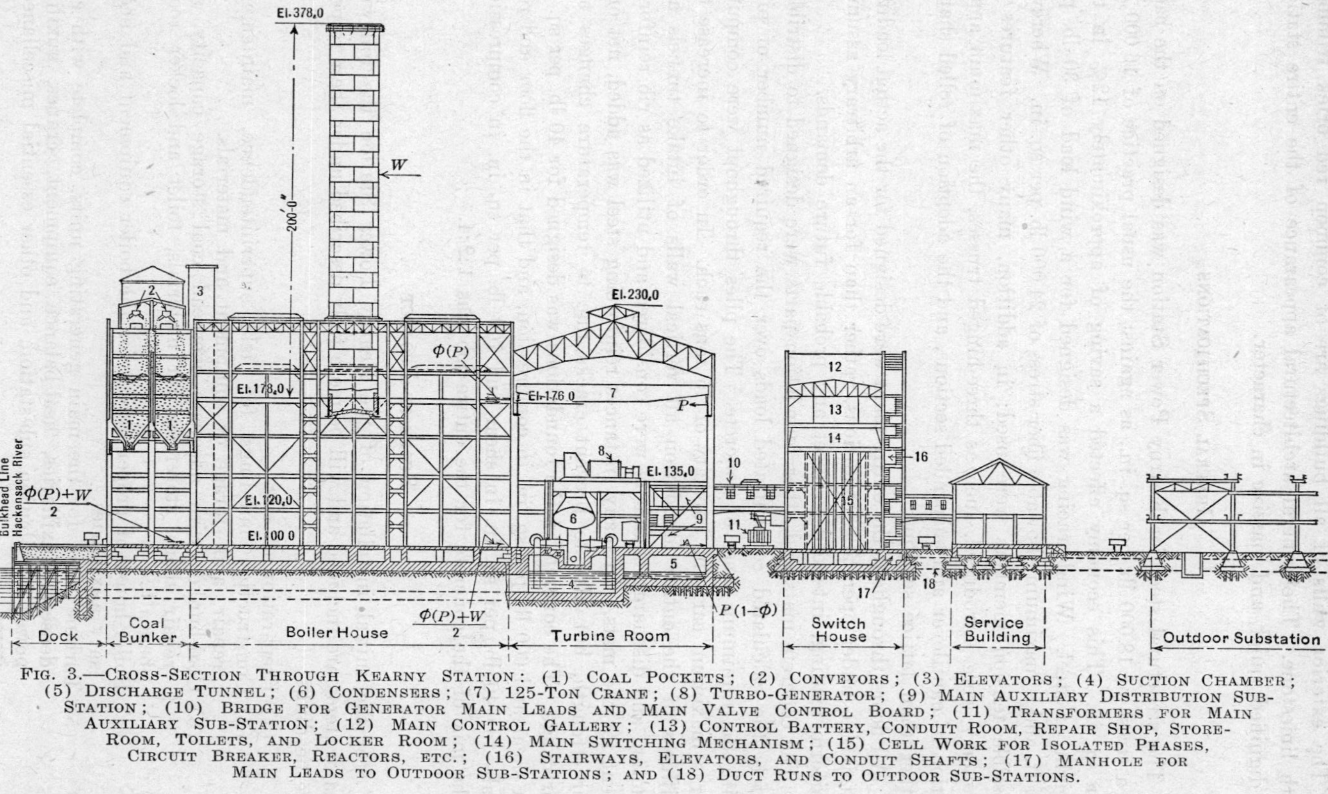

FIG. 3.—CROSS-SECTION THROUGH KEARNY STATION: (1) COAL POCKETS; (2) CONVEYORS; (3) ELEVATORS; (4) SUCTION CHAMBER; (5) DISCHARGE TUNNEL; (6) CONDENSERS; (7) 125-TON CRANE; (8) TURBO-GENERATOR; (9) MAIN AUXILIARY DISTRIBUTION SUB-STATION; (10) BRIDGE FOR GENERATOR MAIN LEADS AND MAIN VALVE CONTROL BOARD; (11) TRANSFORMERS FOR MAIN AUXILIARY SUB-STATION; (12) MAIN CONTROL GALLERY; (13) CONTROL BATTERY, CONDUIT ROOM, REPAIR SHOP, STORE-ROOM, TOILETS, AND LOCKER ROOM; (14) MAIN SWITCHING MECHANISM; (15) CELL WORK FOR ISOLATED PHASES, CIRCUIT BREAKER, REACTORS, ETC.; (16) STAIRWAYS, ELEVATORS, AND CONDUIT SHAFTS; (17) MANHOLE FOR MAIN LEADS TO OUTDOOR SUB-STATIONS; AND (18) DUCT RUNS TO OUTDOOR SUB-STATIONS.

The exterior walls of all buildings are of common red brick trimmed with limestone. The general architectural appearance of the entire station is dignified, quiet, and massive in character.

General Specifications

The structural steel for Kearny Power Station was designed on the basis of a stress of 18 000 lb. per sq. in., as against the usual practice of 16 000 lb. per sq. in. This economy effected a saving of approximately 12% in the weight of steel. Wind-bracing was designed for a wind load of 30 lb. per sq. ft. and a maximum allowable fiber stress of 24 000 lb. per sq. in. Wherever possible tension members were used; in addition, many other features of economy were introduced, such as three-hinged trusses, the maximum application of cantilever and suspended sections, and the adoption of rolled shapes rather than lattice sections.

All floors throughout the entire plant were designed for the actual loadings obtainable under operating conditions, rather than for an arbitrary assumed uniform loading, intended to meet any probable future demands.

The concrete mats and other foundation parts were designed to distribute safely the calculated concentrated loads over the required number of piles with the minimum mass of concrete. The piles throughout were computed for a maximum carrying capacity of 15 tons each. In order to increase the stiffness of the entire foundation all vertical walls of intake tunnels and suction and discharge chambers were considered and utilized as rib reinforcement for the mats. In many instances reinforcing steel was added, not only for strength, but also to prevent cracks due to temperature changes and shrinkage. The concrete in the foundations was designed for 40 lb. per sq. in. in shear and 600 lb. per sq. in. in compression, and that in the floor and roof slabs for 40 lb. per sq. in. in shear and 700 lb. per sq. in. in compression. The mix of the concrete for the entire job was 1:2:4.

Scope of Project

For the initial installation of the Kearny Power Station the following major items are included and will be more fully described under their respective headings:

(1) Preparation of site.
(2) Construction buildings for field superintendence, maintenance, repair, and storage of equipment and materials.
(3) Coal-bunker with adequate overhead coal storage capacity, and repair shops, storeroom for materials, toilet and locker rooms beneath.
(4) Boiler-house of proper design for the boiler equipment and necessary auxiliaries.
(5) Turbine room for the main generating units, complete with condensers, auxiliaries, heat-balance equipment, cranes, auxiliary power distribution sub-station, and other essential miscellaneous items.
(6) Canals and tunnels for supplying water required for service and condenser equipment.

FIG. 4.—GENERAL VIEW, KEARNY POWER STATION; (1) SERVICE BUILDING; (2) SWITCH-HOUSE; (3) TURBINE ROOM; (4) BOILER-HOUSE; (5) COAL BUNKER; AND (6) HEAD TOWER OF CONVEYOR TRESTLE.

FIG. 5.—INTERIOR VIEW OF TURBINE ROOM, KEARNY POWER STATION.

(7) Switch-house to accommodate the necessary switching equipment, busses, conduits, switchboards, storage batteries, and other miscellaneous items.
(8) Service building for offices, restaurant, hospital, and other administrative facilities.
(9) Coal-handling system with storage and reclaiming system, yard trackage, unloading equipment from barges and railroad cars, bridges, towers, conveyors, and miscellaneous apparatus.
(10) Ash-handling system with pits, hoppers, bridges, and other disposal facilities.
(11) Sewerage and drainage system.
(12) Supply of fresh water, with sufficient storage facilities to insure against interruption of service.
(13) Dock, railroad sidings, and roadways.
(14) Outdoor step-up sub-station, including superstructures and foundations for transformers, switching equipment, duct runs and overhead busses, and transmission lines to sub-stations at Marion and Essex Stations.
(15) Transformer stations at Essex and Marion Stations.

The materials required for the initial construction at the Kearny Power Station are as follows:

Bricks	7 500 000
Wooden piles, 30 to 70 ft. in length (Fig. 14)	29 000
Structural steel, in tons	16 000
Concrete for foundations, canals, and substructures, in cubic yards	72 000
Reinforced concrete floors, requiring 5 000 cu. yd. of concrete, in square feet	235 000
Reinforced concrete roof slabs, requiring 1 900 cu. yd. of concrete, in square feet	92 000
Heavy type steel sash, in square feet	35 500
Excavation for foundations and canals, in cubic yards	125 000
Dredging in front of the dock, in cubic yards	120 000
Iron conduit, in miles	68
Fiber conduit, in miles	10
Electrical wire (in cables), in miles	585
Boiler tubes, 4 in. in outside diameter, in miles	46
Admiralty condenser tubes, 1 in. in outside diameter by 16 gauge, in miles	184
Lumber for dock, in board-feet	1 300 000
Cinders for fill, in cubic yards	700 000

These items do not include the lumber used for forms, steel required for reinforcement for canals, foundations, floor and roof slabs, and steel for flues, ducts, and galleries, nor brickwork for boiler settings. The volume of all buildings, exclusive of those for the coal-handling system, is 10 500 000 cu. ft.

Preparation of Site

Careful consideration had to be given, when laying out the construction program, to the proper location of the various final structures and of the temporary construction sheds, office buildings, railroad tracks, storage space, etc. (Fig. 6), in order not to interfere with the permanent buildings. The swampy nature of the land (Fig. 7) made it necessary to build embankments for railroad tracks and to improve and extend the present roads across the marshes linking them to the existing main highways for access of heavy trucks to the site (Fig. 7).

About 700 000 cu. yd. of ashes hauled to the site by motor trucks were used in filling the land on which the various construction buildings (Fig. 8), roadways, and railroad tracks were located and to provide space for storage of materials. Office buildings for the field force, wash and locker rooms for the workmen, a hospital, storage houses for material and smaller apparatus, a compressor plant, a distribution sub-station, and various work and repair shops were also erected to prepare for actual construction of the project.

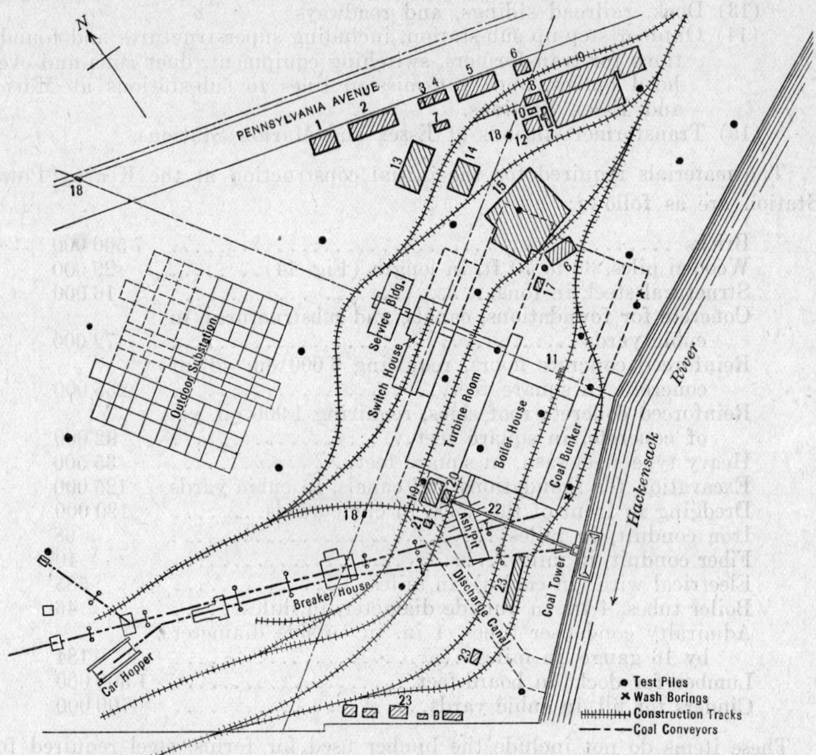

Fig. 6.—Plan Showing Construction Sheds and Tracks, Kearny Power Station: (1) Mess Hall; (2) Offices; (3) Gate-House; (4) Emergency Hospital; (5) Locker and Wash House; (6) Sub-Station; (7) Boiler House; (8) House for Locomotive Cranes; (9) Storage and Shops; (10) Garage; (11) Core Boring; (12) Air Compressor; (13) Store House No. 1; (14) Store House No. 2; (15) Brick Shed; (16) Cement Shed; (17) Shed for Lumber Saw; (18) Monuments on Base Line; (19) Cement Store; (20) Mixing Plant and Concrete Tower; (21) Boiler House for Concrete Plant; (22) Material Conveyor Trestle for Concrete Mixing Plant; and (23) Sub-Contractors' Offices.

The tracks (Fig. 6) were laid in positions to give easy access for the storage of the various materials and to handle them effectively when required during construction, and not to interfere with permanent structure.

FIG. 7.—BUILDING SITE SHOWING MARION POWER STATION IN BACKGROUND: (1) MARION STATION; (2) WEST END GAS PLANT; (3) SEABOARD BY-PRODUCTS COMPANY; (4) HACKENSACK RIVER; AND (5) PILE-DRIVER DRIVING TEST PILES.

FIG. 8.—CONSTRUCTION SHEDS, KEARNY POWER STATION.

FIG. 9.—VIEW SHOWING TEMPORARY BULKHEAD AT HACKENSACK RIVER.

A fresh-water supply for operating the final station as well as for construction purposes had to be laid across the meadows from the city mains. Similar provisions were made for sanitation.

An unloading station for sand, rock, and gravel was erected at the river and connected by a trestle to the concrete mixing plant and distribution tower, the position of which had been selected so as to give uninterrupted service during the construction of the first half of the ultimate station.

A series of test piles (Fig. 6) were driven to determine the length and carrying capacity of the piling; wash and core borings were also made to ascertain the nature of the subsoil. These borings showed that the strata under the station site were composed of a layer several feet in thickness of vegetable matter underlaid by a mixture of clay and sand with vegetable matter, then layers of sand, becoming coarser as the depth increased, and, finally, shale and rock. In some places strata of quicksand were also found.

In order to keep the site from being flooded by the tides a temporary timber bulkhead (Fig. 9) was constructed along the water-front, and earthen dikes along the sides of the excavation. The excavation was kept dry by pumping.

Coal-Bunker

The coal-bunker (Figs. 2, 3, and 10) is on the water-front of the station. In order to insure the continuous operation of the plant, an ultimate bunker capacity of 19 000 tons was required. The grouping of the boilers around five stacks and firing aisles also necessitated the planning of five individual bunkers, each longitudinally divided by a center wall into two pockets. The initial installment has two bunkers of a total capacity of 7 600 tons, serving twelve boilers.

The coal is conveyed from the bunkers to the boilers by a traveling weigh-larry having a capacity of 25 tons. The bottom elevation of the bunkers was determined by the height of the stoker hoppers, and the head-room needed for the coal larry. The resulting space below the bottom of the coal-bunker was utilized to house the machine and repair shops, stores for material for station equipment maintenance, wash and locker rooms, toilets, and other minor facilities (Fig. 10). The bunker building is of steel frame construction with concrete slabs for floors and coal-pockets. The vertical bunker walls are of concrete, while the walls for the store-rooms are of brick. The longitudinal center wall, dividing each bunker into two pockets, is of hollow construction and designed to withstand the horizontal thrust due to the coal with either pocket full. The bunker walls have smooth surfaces to prevent the coal from arching and are tied together by I-beams protected by concrete (Fig. 10).

The bunker building is 43 ft. 9 in. wide, and 236 ft. 5 in. long for the initial installation and 501 ft. 6 in. for the final station. The conveyor gallery is 114 ft. long and its roof is 131 ft. above grade. The cut-off gates at the bottom of the hoppers are 51 ft. above grade and the maximum height of coal stored in the bunkers is 60 ft.

The inclined bottom of the coal-bunkers forms the roof of the store-room buildings beneath. The heavy vertical loads in the bottom of the pockets were

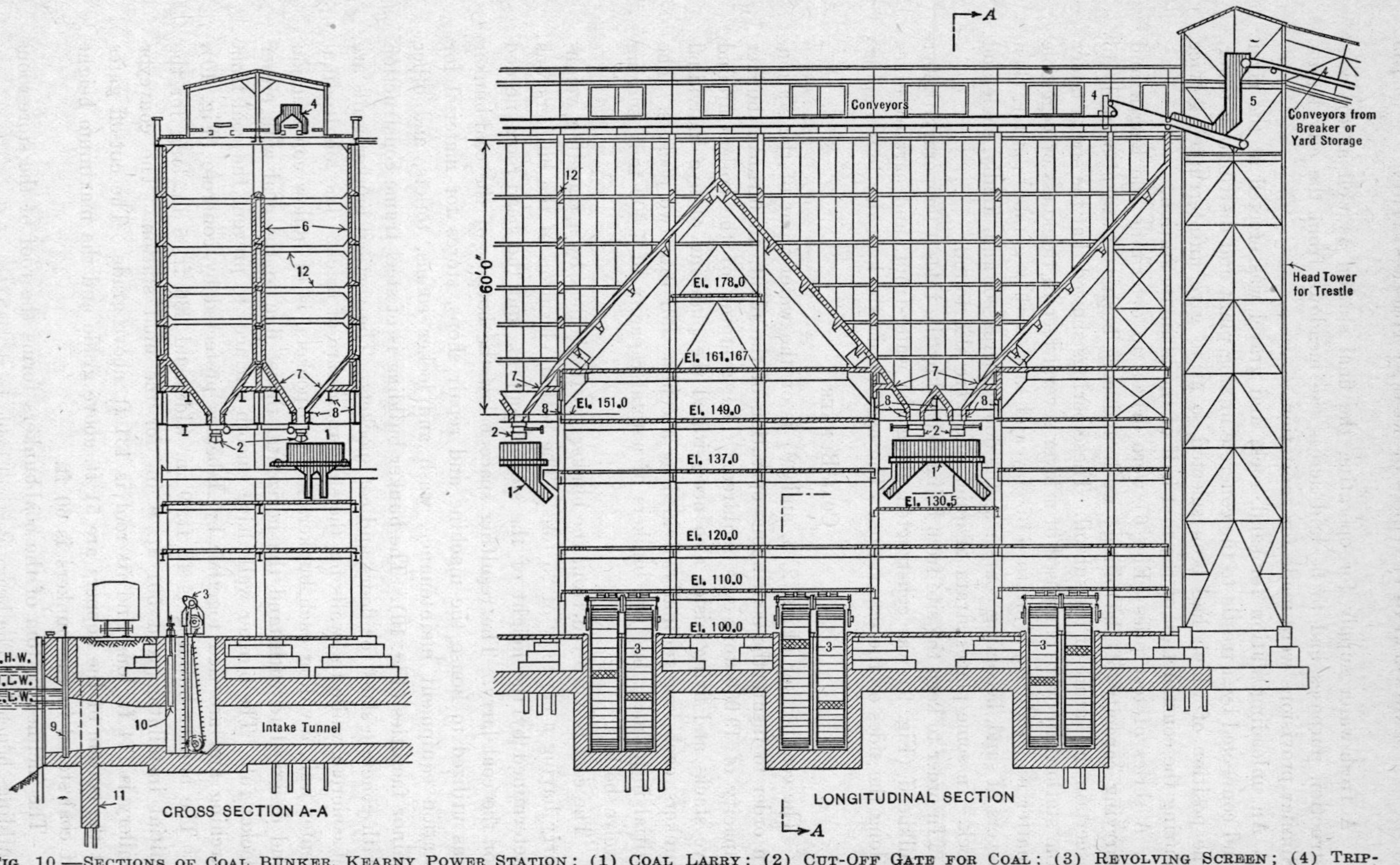

FIG. 10.—SECTIONS OF COAL BUNKER, KEARNY POWER STATION: (1) COAL LARRY; (2) CUT-OFF GATE FOR COAL; (3) REVOLVING SCREEN; (4) TRIPPER; (5) TRANSFER SPOUT; (6) CONCRETE WALLS, SMOOTH FACE; (7) CONCRETE HOPPER BOTTOM; (8) SUPPORTING GIRDERS; (9) TRASH RACK; (10) CUT-OFF GATE; (11) CUT-OFF WALL; (12) TIE-BEAMS PROTECTED BY CONCRETE.

taken by steel plate girders, while the hopper shape itself was obtained by the use of concrete, reinforced to take the horizontal components of the loads (Fig. 11). This proved more economical than a suspended hip-and-valley steel construction which would have been necessary to form this lower portion.

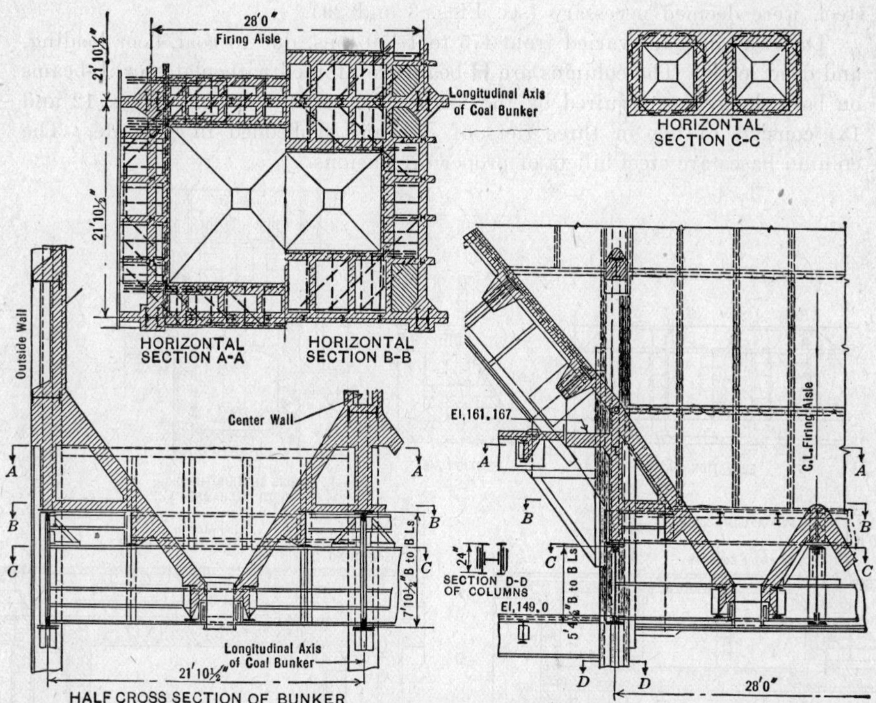

FIG. 11.—DETAILS OF STEEL AND CONCRETE IN BOTTOM OF COAL BUNKERS, KEARNY STATION.

All calculations for the coal-bunker were based on a weight, w, of 50 lb. per cu. ft. of coal. The horizontal pressure, P, for a depth, h, of coal, and an angle of repose, ϕ, was defined by the well-known formula,

$$P = \frac{1}{2} w h^2 \frac{1 - \sin \phi}{1 + \sin \phi}$$

The bunker foundations are supported on piles. The design of the foundations took advantage of the vertical walls of the intake tunnels under the foundation mat, also utilizing the outside building wall foundation as reinforcing ribs for the comparatively thin mat. A satisfactory distribution of the heavy concentrated column loads was thus obtained. The foundation problem was further complicated by the large wells for the revolving screens installed inside the bunker-house in the intake canals (Fig. 13).

In front of the coal-bunker house was a cut-off wall extending below the line of deepest dredging; this concrete wall was reinforced and tied to the intake tunnels and foundation mat. Its purpose was, first, to prevent the subsoil from being washed out from under the foundation due to dredging; and, second, to form a seal against the possible entrance of marine borers in case they should infest these waters at some later date.

The bunker building is held laterally by the main bracing system of the boiler-house; no other special provisions, except tying to the boiler-house steel, were deemed necessary (see Figs. 3 and 29).

The column loads varied from 475 to 1 450 tons, due to coal, floor loading, and dead loads. The columns are H-beams reinforced with plates or I-beams on both flanges as required by the load. The grillage system (Figs. 12 and 13) consists of two or three tiers of I-beams embedded in concrete. The column bases are steel billets of proper dimensions.

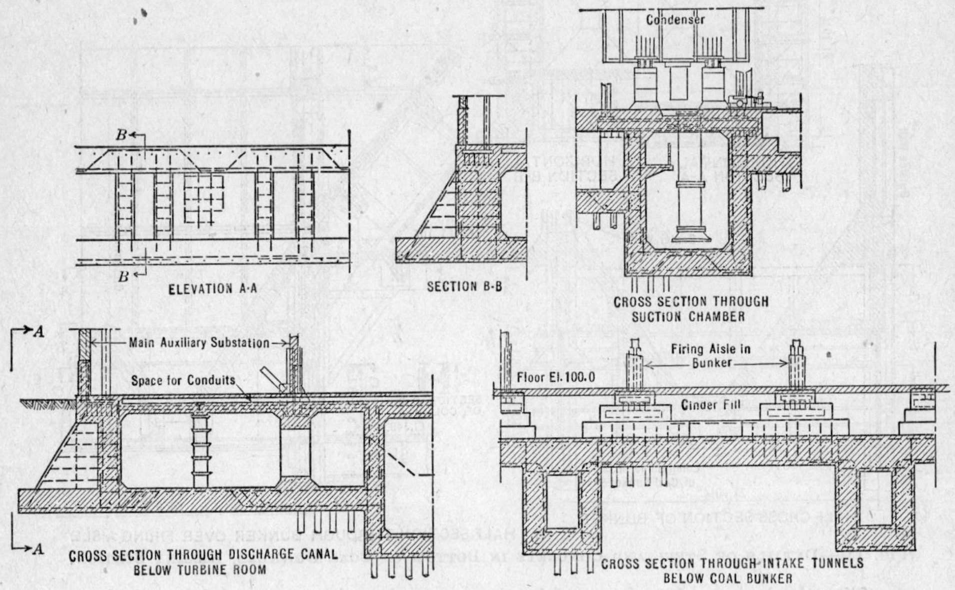

Fig. 12.—Details of Foundations and Reinforcing in Coal Bunker and Turbine Room, Kearny Power Station.

Boiler-House

The design of the boiler-house steel and foundations (Fig. 14) was governed primarily by the equipment to be installed. Briefly, this equipment consists of twelve Babcock and Wilcox Company 3-pass, water-tube, cross-drum boilers, each having 23 600 sq. ft. of heating surface and 4 130 sq. ft. of superheating surface, designed for a maximum steam pressure in the tubes of 385 lb. (gauge) and 720° Fahr. at 200% of rating and capable of operating at a maximum rating of 350 per cent.

The general layout of the boiler-house is shown in Figs. 15 and 16 and the steel work in Fig. 17. The boiler settings are 22 ft. high and arranged in single units with solid walls and steel jackets. Provisions are made for ventilating and cooling the settings. The brickwork is clear of the building columns and supported on heavy girders designed for the loading imposed and the special requirements for stokers and their mechanism.

Fig. 13.—Foundations for Coal Bunker, Kearny Power Station: (1) Concrete Tower; (2) Bulkhead; (3) Intake; and (4) Screen Well.

Fig. 14.—Piling Under Boiler-House, Kearny Power Station: (1) Intake Tunnels; and (2) Temporary Bulkhead.

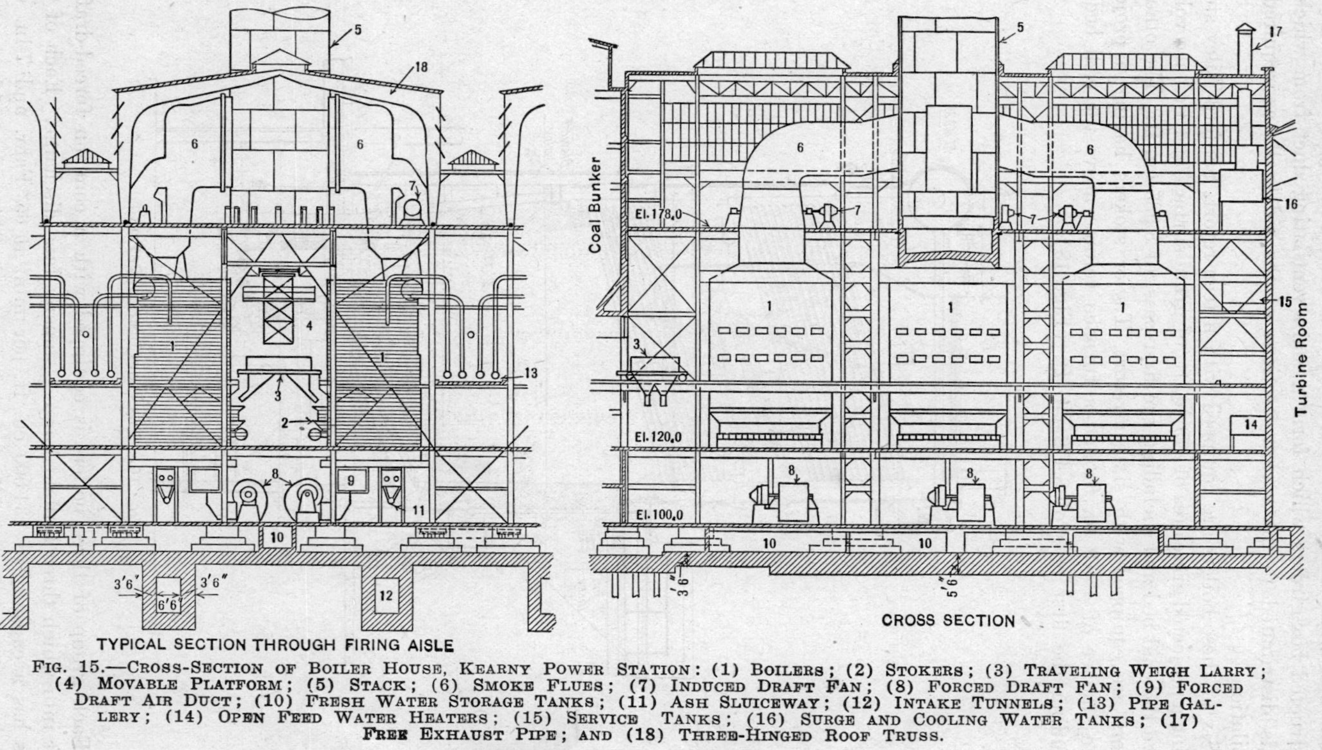

FIG. 15.—CROSS-SECTION OF BOILER HOUSE, KEARNY POWER STATION: (1) BOILERS; (2) STOKERS; (3) TRAVELING WEIGH LARRY; (4) MOVABLE PLATFORM; (5) STACK; (6) SMOKE FLUES; (7) INDUCED DRAFT FAN; (8) FORCED DRAFT FAN; (9) FORCED DRAFT AIR DUCT; (10) FRESH WATER STORAGE TANKS; (11) ASH SLUICEWAY; (12) INTAKE TUNNELS; (13) PIPE GALLERY; (14) OPEN FEED WATER HEATERS; (15) SERVICE TANKS; (16) SURGE AND COOLING WATER TANKS; (17) FREE EXHAUST PIPE; AND (18) THREE-HINGED ROOF TRUSS.

The side-walls above the combustion chambers are supported on specially constructed box-girders which form a main ventilating duct from which the air is distributed to the various sections of the side-walls as required for ventilation.

Six of these boilers are equipped with fifteen-retort, Sanford Riley stokers having a projected grate area of 479 sq. ft. of grate surface and furnace volume, above the coal bed and including the first pass, of 8 985 cu. ft. The other six boilers are equipped with sixteen-retort, Taylor stokers having a projected grate surface of 459.9 sq. ft. and a furnace volume above the coal bed and including the first pass of 8 472 cu. ft. (Fig. 18).

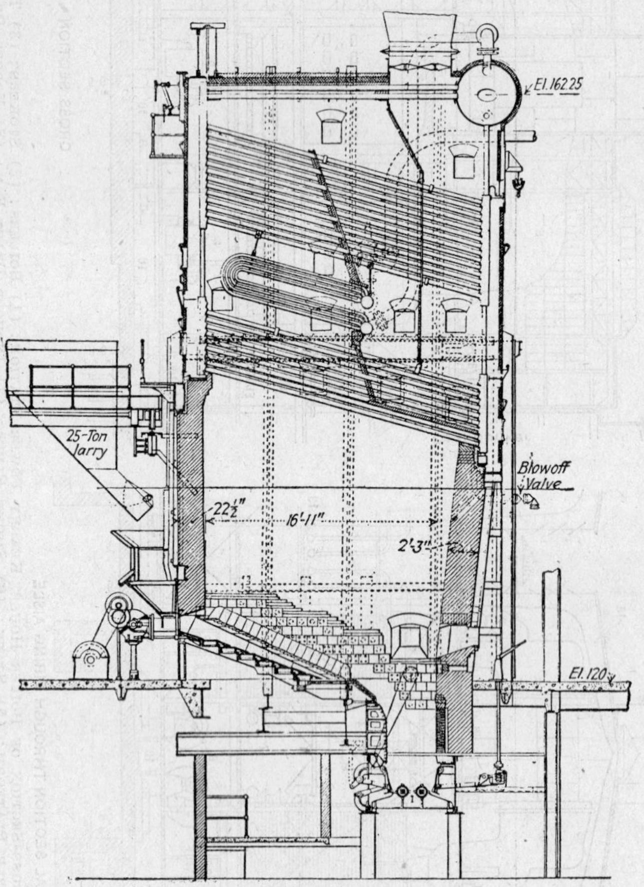

Fig. 16.—Plan of Boiler Setting.

Each group of three boilers is equipped with a common forced-draft air duct into which three Buffalo Forge Company fans discharge. Each of these fans has a capacity of 134 000 cu. ft. per min. at 65° Fahr. and 7-in. water pressure. The fans are driven by a two-speed, 2 300-volt, 225-h. p. General Electric motor. Two of these fans will supply all the air necessary for com-

FIG. 17.—KEARNY POWER STATION DURING ERECTION OF STEEL: (1) COAL BUNKER; (2) THREE-HINGED BOILER-HOUSE ROOF TRUSS; (3) STACK; (4) TURBINE ROOM; AND (5) CONCRETE TOWER AND MIXING PLANT.

FIG. 18.—FIRING AISLE AND STOKERS, WEIGH LARRY IN BACKGROUND: (1) STOKERS; AND (2) EXTENSION HOPPERS.

bustion under normal operating conditions for three boilers, leaving one fan as a spare unit.

The forced-draft air duct is constructed of brick and concrete, utilizing the main floor as the top and the wall between the ash cellar and the forced-draft fan room as one side. This arrangement (Fig. 16) proved to be more economical in design and operation than the conventional steel ducts.

Each boiler has one double width, double inlet, multi-vane Sturtevant induced draft fan, having a capacity of 275 000 cu. ft. per min., at 650° Fahr., and 3.5 in. of water suction, driven by a two-speed, 300-h. p., 2 300-volt General Electric motor. Each fan inlet is directly connected to the breeching of the boiler and the fan discharges into the flues leading to the stacks. Arrangements are also made to by-pass the fans, so that the products of combustion may go directly from the boilers to the stacks under normal rating. (See Fig. 15.)

Five de-aerating and metering water heaters with jet heater open feed and with a capacity of 400 000 to 1 000 000 lb. of water per hour, which were furnished by the Cochrane Corporation, are installed in the bay adjoining the turbine room.

Additional equipment, such as boiler feed pumps, service pumps, air compressors, sluiceways and sluice pumps, ash-disposal piping, feed-water heaters, fresh-water storage tanks, service tanks, storage battery, elevators, oil-purification system, power-distribution sub-stations, and other incidental equipment (Fig. 15) were provided in the design of the building.

Each group of six boilers is arranged to discharge the products of combustion into one stack. For the ultimate station it is planned that five stacks will be installed, two being furnished in the initial section. The stacks have an exterior diameter of 26 ft. 0 in. and are brick-lined throughout, the internal diameter being 24 ft. 7 in. The stacks are 200 ft. high, and supported on steelwork 78 ft. above grade; they are designed to withstand the wind pressure of a gale blowing 120 miles per hour. This wind velocity striking the cylindrical surface of the stack produces a horizontal wind load equivalent to 33.3 lb. acting upon a vertical plane area. The stacks are built of overlapping steel plates having a thickness of $\frac{3}{8}$ in. at the top and $\frac{3}{4}$ in. at the bottom. These plates are stiffened by vertical angle stiffeners and by horizontal rings made of angles and plates. The horizontal stiffeners are closer together at the bottom than at the top and serve to support and keep the brick lining in position.

The lining was grouted to the steel shell and a space was left between the top of the brickwork and the underside of the next ring or support for the following section. The vertical plate of the horizontal stiffeners was bolted to the angle ring after the lower brick lining was in place and before the following section of brickwork was built.

The stacks are supported on a heavy steel plate-girder platform at the level of the blower floor; the simple arrangement of this platform is shown in Fig. 19. Oblique girders have been avoided as much as possible to simplify fabrication and erection. The anchorage of the steel stack to the supporting structure is also shown. A graphical solution for the determination of the zero line (neutral axis) of the horizontal cross-section at the anchorage is shown on Fig. 19. Since the directions of the wind causing the most unfavorable stresses in the various girders could not be determined offhand, the bending moments, etc., have been found for several conditions, varying with the direction of the wind. The envelope line enclosing these various moment curves (Fig. 19) was taken as the maximum moment curve and the girders were proportioned accordingly.

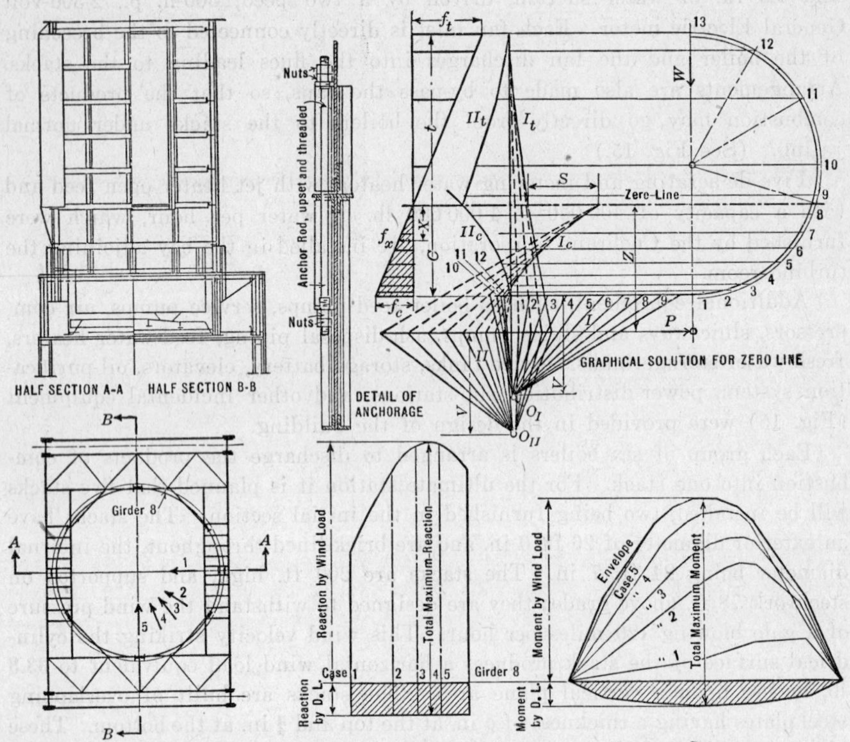

Fig. 19.—Details of Stack Support and Anchorage, Kearny Station.

The following stresses were used in the design for the shell of the stack:

Axial tension	10 000 lb. per sq. in.
Axial compression	9 000 " " " "
Rivet shear	10 000 " " " "
Rivet bearing	20 000 " " " "

Rivets in horizontal and vertical seams were computed at 70% efficiency. The opening in the stack for the flue has been heavily reinforced by angles and plates to compensate for the reduction in area.

To obtain the zero line (Fig. 19), Compression Areas 1 to 9 and Tension Areas 10 to 13 are laid off to a convenient scale and any pole distance, V, is taken. Draw the funicular polygons, I_c and I_t. The sides of these polygons are prolonged until they intersect the resultant, P. With these intercepts and the pole distance, V, the funicular polygons, $I\,I_c$ and $I\,I_t$, are drawn. Their intersection point will locate the zero line.

With $f_x = b\,x$,

$$Z = \frac{\int x^2\,d\,I}{\int x\,d\,A}$$

The maximum compression in rim is,

$$f_c' = \frac{P\,c}{2\,S\,V}$$

The maximum tension in anchors is,

$$f_t = f_c\,\frac{t}{c}$$

Each group of six boilers is provided with one double-hopper, 25-ton, coal-weighing larry (Figs. 15 and 18), traveling along the firing aisle, receiving coal from the bottom of the bunkers, and delivering it to the stokers under the boilers. In addition to the weigh larry a movable platform (Fig. 15), which serves a group of six boilers, has also been provided. This platform is designed to travel the entire length of the firing aisle and is adjustable in height to suit the requirement of the work at hand on the boilers. The runways for this platform are bracketed from the overhead steel above the firing aisle. The ashes from the boilers after passing through the clinker grinders on the stokers are dropped into a sluiceway and then delivered into a settling pit whence they are removed as will be described subsequently.

Since adequate bracing for the stacks was necessary, it was made the nucleus of the entire bracing system for the station, as may be seen from Fig. 3.

The turbine room and bunker building have no major bracing; they obtain their stability from the boiler-house. Due to boilers and stokers projecting into the firing aisle, the transverse bracing had to be brought into the vertical plane of the rear boiler columns. This necessitated the arrangement of a horizontal bracing system at the level of the stack support, in order that the wind loads acting on the stack might be transmitted into the transverse bracing system.

The boiler-house roof is carried by three-hinged trusses (Figs. 15 and 17). This three-hinged system above the induced draft blower floor was adopted after making careful studies to determine the most economical solution of this problem, and also to simplify the installation of the flues and induced draft equipment. This design is lighter than conventional straight bottom chord roof trusses, showing a net ultimate saving of 110 800 lb. of steel for this portion of the work. Three-hinged arches are statically determined in regard to outer forces. Reactions and stresses are easily found, and the latter are not affected by changes of temperature. The arches provided an open space, free from obstructions, and resulted in obtaining a spacious room for the equipment at a reduction in the height of the building of more than 4 ft. and in the cubic contents of the buildings by 27 690 cu. ft. per section, or an ultimate total reduction of 138 450 cu. ft. of building volume.

The boiler-house building is 167 ft. 6 in. wide, 206 ft. 3 in. long for the initial installation, and 495 ft. 2 in. for the ultimate station, which will consist of five units each containing six boilers, one stack, and auxiliary equipment.

Turbine Room

The turbine-room building (Figs. 15 and 20) was designed to take the following equipment:

(*a*) Three General Electric Company, 39 200-kv-a. turbo-generators, 1800 rev. per min., designed to operate at a steam pressure of 325 lb. gauge and superheat of 271° Fahr. at the throttles; and

(*b*) Two Westinghouse Electric and Manufacturing Company, 43 750-kv-a., turbo-generators operating under the same conditions.

These turbo-generators are supported on structural steel foundations. Each is equipped with one surface condenser having 50 000 sq. ft. of tube surface, the water-boxes having vertical diaphragms so that one-half the condenser can be cleaned while the other half is in operation. The condensers weigh 700 000 lb. (full) and are supported on springs. Special rubber expansion joints are inserted in the water inlet and discharge pipes.

For each condenser two circulating pumps (Fig. 21) are installed, each having a capacity of 38 000 gal. per min., and being driven by one 500-h. p., 2 300-volt motor. In addition to these pumps, two motor-driven 1 000 gal. per min. condensate pumps and two twin two-stage steam-jet air pumps are installed for each condenser.

Each generator is equipped with one Griscom-Russell, two-pass, "U-Fin" cooler for cooling the air for the generators. The coolers for the General Electric units have a tube surface of 1 820 sq. ft. and a fin surface of 18 240 sq. ft., while the Westinghouse units are provided with air coolers having a tube surface of 2 280 sq. ft. and a fin surface of 22 800 sq. ft. each. The larger size of the latter coolers is due to the greater generator capacity of the Westinghouse machines.

To secure the greatest economy, motor-driven auxiliaries are used throughout, except the minimum spare equipment. For feed-water heating purposes a four-stage bleeding system from the main units has been installed. All possible precautions have been taken for the proper operation of the heat balance system including the bleeding of steam from the main units. To accomplish the desired results, one high-pressure, one intermediate-pressure, and one low-pressure, closed, feed-water heater complete with all necessary valves, piping, controls, etc., were installed for each unit.

For the erection and operation of the turbine room equipment two 125-ton Cleveland Crane and Engineering Company cranes were installed (Figs. 3 and 20). The runway girders supporting the crane were designed for the two cranes in closest position with a vertical live load impact of 25% and a horizontal impact of 10% acting along the longitudinal axis of the crane. The impact in the direction of travel of the crane, due to sudden stops, was assumed at 14% of the maximum total reaction of the crane, governing the design of the longitudinal bracing in the side-walls of the turbine room. This

Fig. 20.—Turbine Room Interior During Installation of Equipment: (1) Surge and Cooling Water Tanks; (2) Service Tanks; (3) Boiler-House Piping; and (4) Conduits for Turbine Instrument Board.

Fig. 21.—Circulating Pump Condenser and Piping: (1) Condenser; (2) Circulating Pump; (3) Condenser Overflow Pipe; (4) Turbine Foundation Steel; and (5) Support for Enclosed Generator Air Coolers.

Fig. 22.—Suspension of Floors in Main Auxiliary Sub-Station: (1) Suspension Truss; (2) Hanger; and (3) Conduits in Floor and Wall.

Fig. 23.—Conduits in Floor of Main Auxiliary Sub-Station.

bracing of the initial portion was placed in only three bays for structural economy and in order not to detract from the architectural appearance. Wherever possible the bracing was placed in the panel bays. Architectural demands also governed the shape of the roof trusses, which were designed with arched bottom chords (Fig. 3), thus lending to the gracefulness of the turbine-room interior.

The dimensions of the turbine room were governed by the space required for the installation and operation of the main equipment. The building is 106 ft. 8 in. wide, 283 ft. 8 in. long for the initial installation, and will be 543 ft. 0 in. long after the ultimate ten generating units are installed. The main operating floor is 35 ft. 0 in. above grade, or basement, level, while the turbine-room cranes are supported on girders 41 ft. above the main floor, or 76 ft. above the basement.

The structure of the turbine room receives its stability from the bracing system of the boiler-house. The columns of the turbine room do not line up with those of the boiler-house and the transmission of the horizontal forces was accomplished at the blower-floor elevation (or 78 ft. 0 in. above the basement) by a horizontal plate girder, riveted to the beams of the blower floor, and in part by the roof trusses (Fig. 3).

The turbo-generators are supported on individual structural steel foundations 35 ft. in height; these foundations are entirely isolated from the main building steel (Fig. 21). The design of the turbine-supporting structures was based principally on deflections, care being taken that the deflection along the longitudinal axis of the foundations was uniform under each bearing. All connections and web sections were properly proportioned for impact. The horizontal bracing was designed by assuming 30% of the vertical loads as acting horizontally.

The entire upper platform of these turbine foundations was reinforced against vibration by the addition of diaphragms and concrete fill between parallel members. The design of the foundation steel was complicated by the space requirements of the condensers, pumps, air coolers for the generator, piping, generator leads, etc., thereby limiting the space available for bracing.

In addition to the turbo-generator equipment, the turbine-room building contains the main auxiliary distribution sub-station, situated under the main floor of the turbine room and consisting of three-phase, 2 300-volt, and 440-volt busses, which are supplied from the main tie bus in the switch-house through 5% reactors, and of three 7 500-kv-a. transformer banks. Two boiler-house and three coal-handling sub-stations are at present supplied from the main auxiliary sub-station, which ultimately will supply four boiler-house and four coal-handling sub-stations. All auxiliaries have duplicate feeds and panels of the truck type. The equipment of this main auxiliary sub-station is located on three floors, the upper one carrying also the leads from the generators to the switch-house on separate supports. All sub-station floors are suspended from a triangular truss (Figs. 3 and 22) which also serves to brace the lower portion of the outside turbine-room columns. An idea of the work of conduits in the floor of this sub-station may be gained from Fig. 23.

The system of intake and discharge tunnels, suction chambers, discharge chambers, etc., complicated the foundation design both for the building and equipment. The designs, however, were developed so that the walls of the various chambers were utilized to stiffen the entire structure and consequently operated to reduce the thickness of the mat (see Fig. 12).

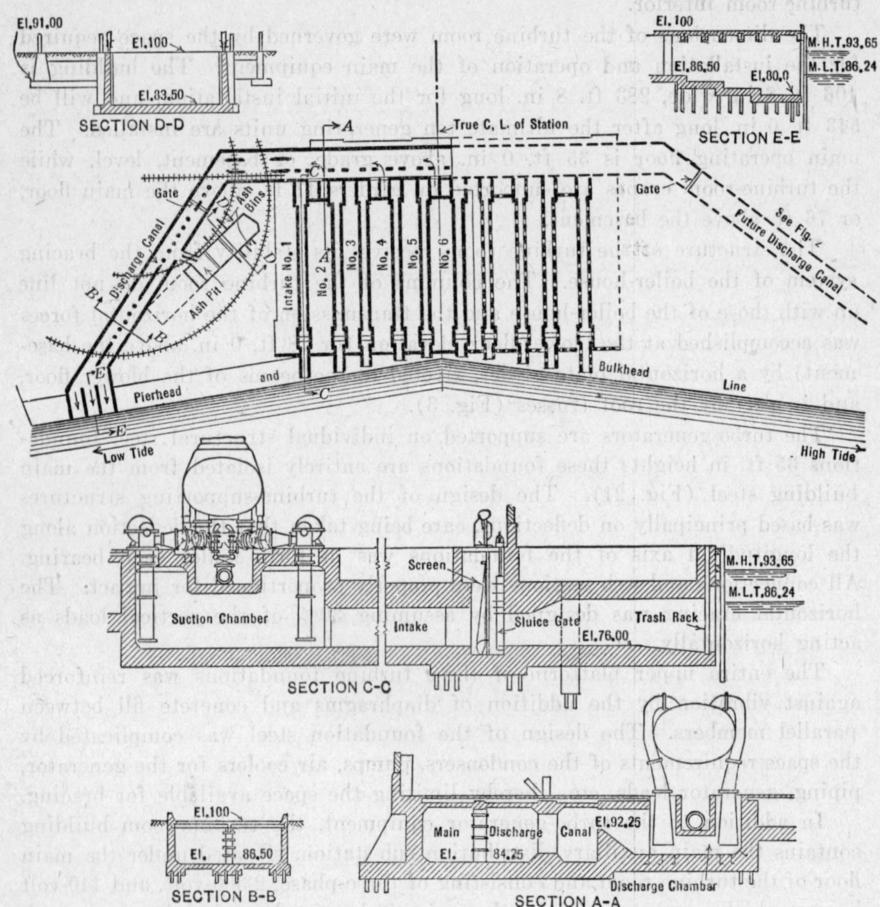

FIG. 24.—DETAILS OF CIRCULATING WATER SYSTEM, KEARNY STATION.

INTAKE TUNNELS AND DISCHARGE CANAL

The location of the station on the Hackensack River gives it an unlimited supply of condensing water. This water enters the intake tunnels through trash racks, is cleaned by revolving screens installed in the bunker-house, and then passes to the suction chambers and through circulating pumps into the condensers. From the condensers the water goes into the discharge chambers and then overflows into the common discharge canal, which delivers the warm water to the river. An individual intake tunnel, suction chamber, and discharge chamber are provided for each turbine unit (Fig. 24).

Each intake tunnel was designed to furnish 78 000 gal. of water per min. for condensing purposes and 10 000 gal. per min. for miscellaneous other station requirements, at a velocity of 3.2 ft. per sec. The discharge tunnel is designed to take care of the entire condensing water from ten units, or 780 000 gal. per min., at a velocity of 3.8 to 7.5 ft. per sec., depending on the tide.

The Hackensack River is subjected to variations of flow and of tide. To insure a continuous water supply irrespective of the tidal stage, the underside of the roof of the intake tunnels was fixed at 2 ft. below lowest tide (Fig. 10). The ultimate arrangement is to return the water to the river at two points, one up stream and the other down stream from the intake tunnels (Figs. 2 and 24), so that the danger of re-circulation may be eliminated. Ultimately it is planned to discharge the water into the river corresponding to the direction of the tide. This is accomplished by the introduction of balanced segmental gates as shown in Fig. 24. The discharge canal terminates at the face of the dock in a forebay, which was designed to reduce the velocity of the water emerging from the tunnel, thereby facilitating the handling of barges along the dock front. The forebay was roofed over to support loadings due to 10-ton trucks over the area along the dock.

The intake tunnels are built of reinforced concrete and extend from the front of the dock under the bunker and boiler-house to the suction chamber under the turbine foundations. The face of the intake tunnels was brought inward about 4 ft. from the edge of the dock to prevent obstruction to the flow by barges tied to the wharf. The rectangular cross-section of the intake tunnels is 6 ft. 6 in. wide and 8 ft. 6 in. high.

The position of the tunnels below the foundation mat was utilized to make them an integral part of the foundations of the turbine room, boiler-house, and bunkers. The vertical walls were designed to act as ribs, reinforcing the mat and allowing a safe distribution of the heavy concentrated loads over the proper number of piles. The tunnels are provided with trash racks at the entrance and revolving screens inside the bunker basement (Fig. 10). The screen wells can be shut off for cleaning and necessary repairs by a motor-operated sluice-gate.

The discharge chambers spill the water into the main discharge canal over a weir (Fig. 24, Section *A-A*). This was necessary to insure that the over-flow, or tail-pipes, from the condensers should always be submerged to main-tain the siphon effect, irrespective of the water level in the discharge canal, due either to the quantity of water handled or the condition of the tides. The opening above the weir was made of sufficient size to reduce the velocity of the water and to minimize the effect of erosion.

The bottoms of the discharge chambers directly below the condenser over-flow as well as the top of the weir were protected against possible erosion from the condenser discharge water by heavy cast-iron plates set in place. Cast-iron plates were also inserted under the pump suction.

The discharge canal is of rectangular cross-section and extends along the entire northern side of the turbine room. The foundation walls for the main building as well as the foundations for the turbo-generators, were utilized as side-walls for the discharge canal, requiring only a slight increase in depth for obtaining the required area. To distribute the heavy turbine-room loads over the piles, the floor of the discharge canal was heavily reinforced. The roof is a concrete slab supported between heavy steel girders and carrying railroad tracks and sub-station equipment (see Fig. 12.)

Beyond the turbine room the bottom of the discharge canal was raised and the rectangular cross-section was changed to maintain the net area required. This proved more economical, since it reduced the depth of excavation and also the height of the outside walls. The construction of the discharge canal outside the turbine room is similar to that inside, including a concrete roof supported on steel beams, reinforced to take care of railroad and truck loading, whenever they occur. The roof structure, except for railroad crossings, was supported in the center of the canals by concrete piers cast inside vertical 30-in. tile-pipe spaced 15 ft. centers (Figs. 24 and 25). The pipe was used as a form for pouring the concrete and was left in place to protect the piers against erosion. At railroad crossings regular concrete piers are used (Fig. 24).

Switch-House

The switch-house structure and foundation were designed to accommodate vertically isolated phases on the three lower floors, and complete separation of oil-immersed apparatus; also manual gang-operated disconnecting switches, and solenoid-operated oil circuit breakers with a rupturing capacity of 1 500 000 kv-a., all mechanically and electrically interlocked. The operating mechanism is on the fourth floor, and the main control room on the sixth floor, with the conduit room below.

The requirements imposed many complications in regard to obtaining a stable and suitable structure. This can readily be seen in Fig. 26. The entire central portion of the first four floors of the building is occupied by the cell structures for busses, circuit breakers, reactors, mechanism, etc. One rigid requirement was that no steel should be used which would cross through the floors from one side of the building to the other; this was to insure the greatest effect of the electrical isolation of phases.

The lowest main steel crossing the building is on the fifth floor, which carries the main storage batteries for control purposes, motor generator sets, machine and repair shops, storerooms, toilets, and conduit room. The total loading of this floor, due to these items and to the large number of conduits embedded in concrete, amounted to 375 lb. per sq. ft. This floor is suspended by hangers from the roof truss, except in those bays containing the control and conduit room. The suspended floor girders are connected by brackets to the outside columns for stiffeners (see Figs. 3 and 26).

The entire building is designed as a shell surrounding the inner cell structures for electrical equipment, and is independent of these structures for stability. For the three lower floors the stability of the building was obtained by the introduction of secondary columns opposite every second outer main column, and by the use of a horizontal bracing system at each floor

Fig. 25.—Boiler-House, Turbine Room, and Switch-House Foundation: (1) Discharge Canal; (2) Piers for Building and Turbine Foundation Columns; (3) Suction Chamber; (4) Intake Tunnel; and (5) Construction Offices, Etc.

Fig. 26.—Switch-House Steel: (1) Roof Truss; (2) Suspended Fifth Floor; (3) Temporary Tie; (4) Vertical Portal Bracing; and (5) Horizontal Brace.

FIG. 27.—INTERIOR OF SWITCH-HOUSE DURING CONSTRUCTION: (1) VERTICAL PORTAL BRACING; (2) HORIZONTAL BRACING; (3) SECTION WALLS, STRUCTURAL. NOTE ABSENCE OF CROSS-TIES.

FIG. 28.—CONDUIT ROOM IN SWITCH-HOUSE UNDER MAIN CONTROL FLOOR: (1) CONTROL ROOM FLOOR; AND (2) DIAGONALS OF TRUSS CARRYING BOTH FLOORS.

Fig. 29.—Kearny Power Station, General View: (1) Coal Bunker; (2) Boiler-House; (3) Turbine Room; (4) Switch-House; (5) Control Room; (6) Conduit Room; (7) Service Building; (8) Outdoor Sub-Station; and (9) Transmission Tower.

level (Fig. 27). This also reduced the amount of steel required and facilitated erection.

The control of all apparatus and the operation of the generators are supervised from the main control room on the sixth floor in the center of the future complete building. The complexity of the main control system necessitated thousands of conduits, and made it essential to include provisions for terminating the conduits at or near the switchboard. Therefore, a conduit room, or vault, was built under the main switchboard for properly manipulating the conduits (Fig. 28). The control room floor is carried by the top chords of the trusses spanning across the width of the building, while the conduit floor beneath is carried on the bottom chords of the same trusses (Figs. 28 and 29).

The foundation for the building consists of a reinforced concrete mat proportioned to distribute the weight over the piling. The cell structures are supported on transverse walls, which also allowed a simple and economical installation of conduits and cables. All floors were reinforced with a minimum amount of steel; great care was exercised to isolate this reinforcement in order to prevent undesired magnetic fields. All precautions were taken to isolate the phases as perfectly as possible and to minimize all disturbances, thus assuring a safe, continuous operation of the plant.

The generator leads were brought over from the turbo-generators in concrete compartments cast integrally with the roof slabs of the bridges between the turbine room and switch-house. The leads were carried in inverted concrete troughs supported on separate steel work through the auxiliary substation in the turbine room.

Service Building

The service building is designed as the central architectural feature of the ultimate station (see Fig. 4). It was planned to house all the administrative offices required for the operation of the station, as well as a restaurant, assembly room, hospital, paymasters' offices, and other minor facilities.

The building is a two-story, steel-frame structure with exterior walls of common brick, trimmed with limestone. It is carried on a pile foundation designed to meet the requirements imposed by the structure itself as well as the conditions due to various conduit and duct lines (Fig. 35) leading from the switch-house to the outdoor sub-station. These duct lines are separated from the foundations of the building, to avoid possible damage by unexpected settlement. Special features were provided to bridge the foundation walls over these conduits.

Coal Handling

The location of the Kearny Station on the Hackensack River permits the receipt of coal by water as well as by rail. A yard storage of 125 000 tons was provided. The pockets in the coal-bunker have a capacity of 3 800 tons for each group of six boilers, or a total of 19 000 tons for the ultimate station. This bunker capacity constitutes an insurance for continuity of service in case of break-down of any part of the coal-handling machinery.

The entire coal-handling system, as installed, is shown in plan on Fig. 2 and in elevation on Fig. 30. It is designed for the use of belt conveyors throughout, which gives the most satisfactory and economical service both as to construction and operation.

Coal arriving by water is hoisted from the barges by a Mead-Morrison, motor-driven, grab-bucket hoist having a capacity of 350 tons per hour; and delivered by an inclined conveyor to a Bradford breaker in the breaker-house. Thence, it may either be conveyed to the yard storage or to the bunkers. Coal arriving by rail is unloaded in the car-hopper house and dumped on the inclined conveyors leading to the breaker-house, passing through the Bradford breaker, etc., as before.

All coal designated for yard storage is carried by the conveyors to a swinging boom 90 ft. long itself having a conveyor, which builds up an initial pile from which the coal is dragged to storage by a drag scraper. The tower for the swinging boom is designed to take the loads of the boom and to provide for the support of the conveyor trestle (Fig. 30). It is tied to the drive-house through the conveyor bridge trusses, thereby stiffening the tower against overturning due to boom loads and consequently reducing the cost of both foundations and steel.

The drag scraper also reclaims the coal and delivers it to a pit, from which it is elevated by a conveyor to the horizontal reversible conveyors between the breaker-house and the yard storage (Fig. 30). These, in turn, transfer the coal to the breaker-house and thence to the inclined conveyors leading up to the bunkers, where it is distributed to the various pockets as required.

The entire conveyor-storage and reclaiming system is designed to handle 400 tons of coal per hour, duplicate belts in the initial installation being provided over the bunkers and from the breaker-house to the bunkers. Provisions are made throughout for duplicate conveyors for the ultimate installation, except the conveyor from the coal tower to the breakers, the conveyor on the swinging boom, the belt feeder in the reclaiming pit, and the conveyor from the pit to the reversible conveyors.

The drag-scraper equipment, furnished by the Maine Electric Company, has a maximum capacity of 400 tons per hour, and is driven by a 200-h.p., General Electric motor, working on a maximum haul of 600 ft. and giving a yard storage of 125 000 tons for a pile 15 ft. deep. Future extensions to the coal-storage system will provide for an ultimate capacity of 275 000 tons, while an additional 90 000 tons of coal can be stored and reclaimed by locomotive cranes.

The design of the trestles, bents, and other structures was governed to a great extent by tunnels, railroad clearances, ash-handling equipment, roadways etc. These conditions made it necessary to utilize long spans for the trusses. In order to decrease the weight of steel and reduce deflection, these long spans were built with cantilever arms, 20 to 25 ft. in length, and with suspended spans 100 ft. in length (Fig. 30). The main trusses were built up of "star" web sections and channel or angle chords. The flooring consists of $3\frac{1}{2}$-in. reinforced concrete, and the roof and siding of asbestos-protected metal.

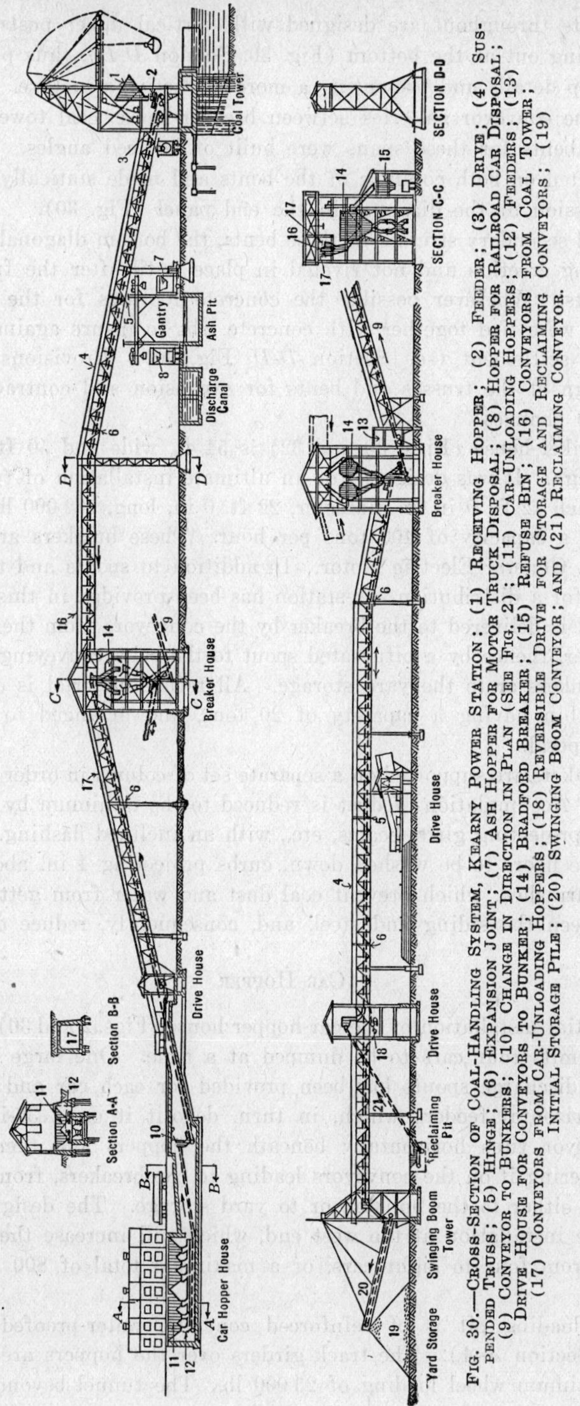

Fig. 30.—Cross-Section of Coal-Handling System, Kearny Power Station: (1) Receiving Hopper; (2) Feeder; (3) Drive; (4) Suspended Truss; (5) Hinge; (6) Expansion Joint; (7) Ash Hopper for Motor Truck Disposal; (8) Hopper for Railroad Car Disposal; (9) Conveyor to Bunkers; (10) Change in Direction in Plan (See Fig. 2); (11) Car-Unloading Hoppers; (12) Feeders; (13) Drive House for Conveyors to Bunker; (14) Bradford Breaker; (15) Refuse Bin; (16) Conveyors from Coal Tower; (17) Conveyors from Car-Unloading Hoppers; (18) Reversible Drive for Storage and Reclaiming Conveyors; (19) Initial Storage Pile; (20) Swinging Boom Conveyor; and (21) Reclaiming Conveyor.

The bents throughout are designed with vertical upper posts, and tower legs spreading out at the bottom (Fig. 30, Section *D-D*), thus providing for simpler shop details and presenting a more attractive structure. Due to the height of the conveyor galleries between breaker-house, coal tower, and coal-bunker the bents for these spans were built of latticed angles. The trusses were supported on both columns of the bents and made statically determined by the omission of the diagonal in the end panel (Fig. 30).

To avoid secondary stresses in these bents, the bottom diagonal was merely bolted during erection and not riveted in place until after the full load was on the bents. Wherever possible the concrete footings for the columns of these bents were tied together with concrete ribs to insure against spreading or unequal settlement (see Section *D-D,* Fig. 30). Provisions were made in the design of the trusses and bents for expansion and contraction due to temperature changes.

The breaker-house (Figs. 30 and 32) is 54 ft. wide and 50 ft. 6 in. long by 90 ft. high. It was designed for an ultimate installation of two Bradford breakers, each 12 ft. 0 in. in diameter, 22 ft. 0 in. long, 102 000 lb. in weight, and having a capacity of 400 tons per hour. These breakers are driven by one 150-h.p. General Electric motor. In addition to spouts and transfers for coal, space for a distribution sub-station has been provided in this building.

The coal is delivered to the breaker by the conveyors from the car hoppers or coal tower, thence by a bifurcated spout to the belts conveying it either to the coal-bunkers or to the yard storage. All refuse material is dumped into bins, each bin having a capacity of 20 tons, and arranged to empty into cars for disposal.

The breakers are supported on a separate set of colums in order to minimize vibrations. Accumulation of dust is reduced to the minimum by covering all horizontal projecting girts, beams, etc., with an inclined flashing. To permit the concrete floors to be washed down, curbs projecting 4 in. above the floor level are furnished, which prevent coal dust and water from getting into the joints between the siding and steel, and, consequently, reduce corrosion.

Car Hopper

The initial installation of the car-hopper house (Figs. 2 and 30) and unloading pit permits four cars to be dumped at a time. One large steel hopper with three discharge spouts has been provided for each car and delivers the coal to horizontal feeders which, in turn, deposit it on a 36-in. conveyor. This conveyor runs horizontally beneath the hoppers and then rises to a spout delivering it on the conveyors leading to the breakers, from which it is transferred either to the bunkers or to yard storage. The design allows for a duplicate installation at the west end, which will increase the capacity of this unit from four to eight cars, or a maximum total of 800 tons of coal per hour.

The unloading pit is of reinforced concrete, water-proofed throughout (Fig. 30, Section *A-A*). The track girders over the hoppers are designed to take a maximum wheel loading of 25 000 lb. The tunnel beyond the hopper building is also water-proofed and its roof is of sufficient strength to take the maximum railroad loading and fill.

Coal Tower

The coal tower on the river-front was designed for the initial installation of one hoisting unit. Foundations, however, have been built for the ultimate installation of two units.

Each tower unit consists of one 350-ton per hour, Mead-Morrison, hoisting machine, with one 5 500-lb. bucket having a capacity of 5 000 lb. of coal, driven by a 300-h.p., General Electric Company, 2 300-volt motor, and designed to make a round trip in 26 sec. In addition to one motor-driven air compressor, receiving hopper, feeder, chute, conveyor drives, and other miscellaneous equipment, the coal tower also contains one distribution sub-station.

The height of the tower was governed by railroad clearances under the conveyor trestle leading to the breakers. The boom, 60 ft. long, is arranged to swing clear of the dock line. The entire lower portion of the tower is enclosed with asbestos-protected, corrugated sheet metal. The foundations were designed for the maximum stresses due to snow, wind, bucket-loading, dead loads, and loads due to equipment and inclined conveyor trestle.

The piling was driven in two coffer-dams, which were excavated to 30 ft. below mean tide and filled with concrete, as shown on Fig. 30. The coffer-dams under both the front and the rear columns were tied together at the top by a concrete mat and also anchored back to "dead men". This was deemed advisable owing to the soil conditions at this point. The encasement of the piles by concrete also protects them against an eventual attack by marine borers, which are known to be in the vicinity of New York Harbor.

Ash Handling

The ashes from the boilers are washed through sluice-ways to a settling pit at the west of the building (Figs. 2 and 31).

The sluice-ways are arranged so that each group of three boilers deposits into one short continuous trough, or sluice, which leads into the main sluice-way carrying the ashes to the settling pit. An electrically operated Cleveland gantry crane, equipped with a grab-bucket, travels along the entire length of the settling pit and hoists the ashes into overhead hoppers from which they can be dumped either into trucks or railroad cars (Fig. 31). A large overhead hopper capacity was provided to make the operation of the gantry crane independent of cars or trucks for ash disposal. The pits have a storage capacity of 600 cu. yd. of ashes, which will take care of somewhat more than a maximum day's use of the ultimate station. Extensions to the pit can be made without impairing the operation, if later demands should require.

The two interior partition walls in the settling pit are made of timbers for easy removal if required for pit extensions. Overflow openings in the partitions and end walls are installed, with skimmers to prevent floating cinders from being carried into the discharge canal. The settling pit was designed to withstand hydrostatic head on the bottom, and car and truck loading on the sides. The hopper foundations were combined with the pit structure (Fig. 31).

Docks

In order to receive coal and materials shipped by water, it was necessary to build a dock along a part of the river-front of the property. With the exception of those sections in front of the bunker-house and the coal tower, the dock has been constructed of wooden piles and timber deck supporting a 9-ft. cinder fill, with a reinforced concrete retaining wall 9 ft. high. along the face. The concrete face is protected against injuries from boats, etc., by timbers and fender piles (Fig. 3).

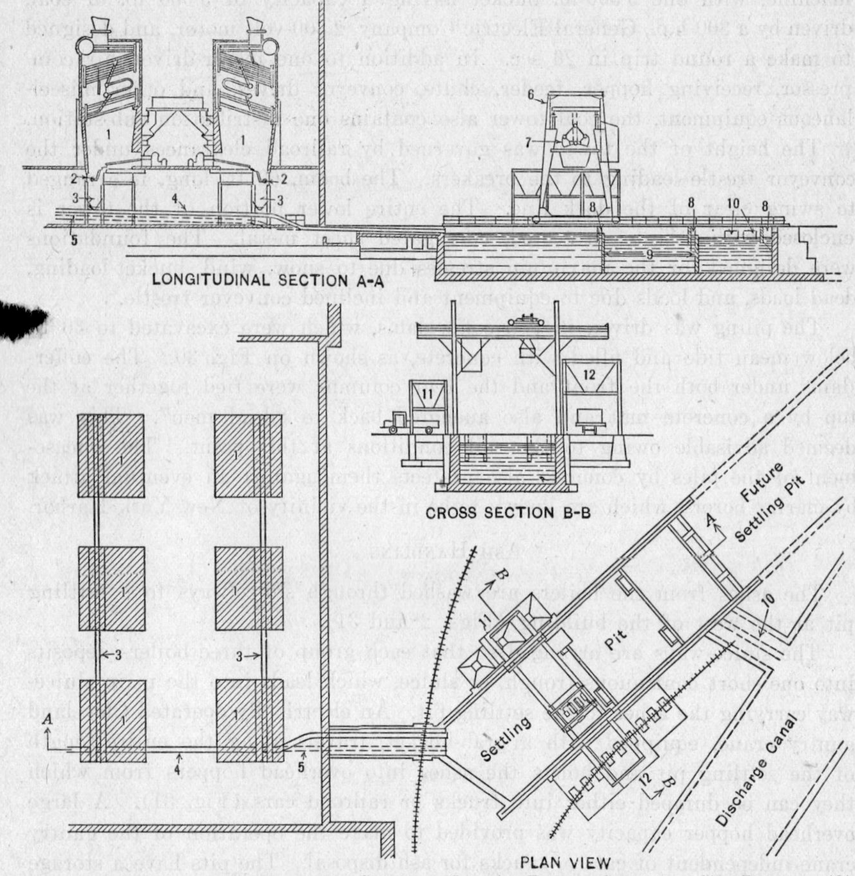

Fig. 31.—Plan of Ash-Handling System, Kearny Power Station: (1) Boiler; (2) Clinker Grinder; (3) Branch Sluice; (4) Main Sluice; (5) Future Main Sluice; (6) Traveling Gantry; (7) Bucket; (8) Skimmer; (9) Temporary Walls; (10) Overflow to Discharge Canal; (11) Ash Hopper for Motor Truck Disposal; (12) Ash Hopper for Railroad Car Disposal.

The design of the dock was based on a dead load of 500 lb. per sq. ft., a uniformly distributed, superimposed live load of 500 lb. per sq. ft., for storage purposes, equivalent to a Cooper E-50 railroad load.

At the rear of the dock, sheet-piling was driven to prevent the earth from sliding and being washed out. To resist the resulting horizontal earth pressure a number of batter piles were provided (Fig. 3).

FIG. 32.—COAL-HANDLING SYSTEM: (1) CONVEYOR FROM CAR-UNLOADING HOPPER; (2) BREAKER HOUSE; (3) CONVEYOR TO BUNKER; (4) BUNKER; (5) CONVEYOR TO AND FROM YARD STORAGE; AND (6) DRIVE HOUSE.

FIG. 33.—END VIEW SHOWING TRANSFORMER BAY OF SUB-STATION: (1) TRANSFORMERS; (2) DISCONNECTING SWITCHES; (3) SUSPENSION INSULATORS; (4) RELAY HOUSE; AND (5) PORTAL TRUSS OVER TRANSFORMER BAY.

The Outdoor Sub-Station

The outdoor sub-station (Figs. 2 and 33) was designed to step-up the entire electrical output of the generators from 13 200 to 132 000 volts for transmission purposes.

The initial installation is: Fifteen 15 000-kv-a., Allis-Chalmers, single-phase, oil-insulated, self-cooled transformers; four 90 000-kv-a., 132 000-volt, three-phase, sixty-cycle, outgoing feeders; thirteen General Electric (type "FHKO-39"), 132 000-volt, oil circuit breakers, with remote control, having a rupturing capacity of 1 500 000 kv-a.; fifty-five Westinghouse (Type 800 A), 154 000-volt, motor-operated, remote-control, disconnecting switches; thirty-three transformers; ten feeders; thirty-three oil circuit breakers; and one hundred and twenty-five disconnecting switches, of the types just mentioned.

The design of the sub-station includes two relay houses with vaults, oil purification house, and oil storage system, together with all the mechanical equipment and piping for treating and handling the oil.

The axis of the sub-station was determined by the direction of the outgoing feeders, property limitations, and coal storage and handling system for the operation of the station. The transformers, therefore, were arranged in two parallel rows along the center line of the sub-station and the oil circuit breakers in the adjoining bays as shown in Figs. 2, 34, and 35.

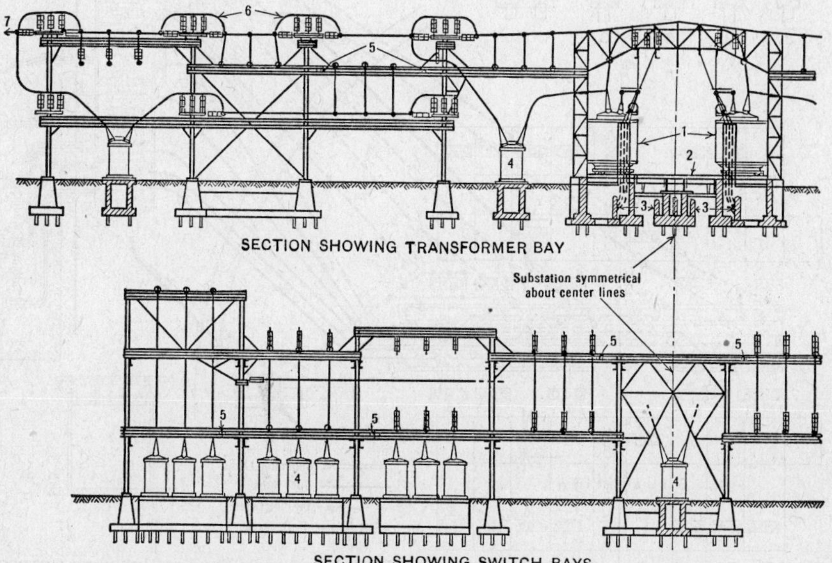

Fig. 34.—Sections of Outdoor Sub-Station, Kearny Power Station: (1) 132 Kv-a. Transformers; (2) Transfer Car; (3) Duct Runs; (4) Oil Circuit Breakers; (5) Splice; (6) Disconnecting Switches; and (7) To Transmission Line.

The electrical requirements as to clearances were determined at 8 ft. 0 in. between phases and 6 ft. 0 in. to ground, thereby establishing the general dimensions of the sub-station. The steelwork involved a departure from general practice by replacing latticed sections with solid shapes. H-sections were used for columns and channels for overhead supporting steel, except in the transformer aisle (Fig. 34), where the columns consist of four angles latticed, supporting an arched truss which carries the busses and the necessary apparatus for the overhead transformer connections.

The stability of the entire structure is obtained by diagonal bracing in the center or end bays (Fig. 34). The horizontal members supporting the busses and disconnecting switches consist of two 15-in. channels, braced laterally and designed as continuous beams over two or more supports with splices at the points of contraflexure. This arrangement was found to be considerably more economical than the usual lattice sections and simplified the shop details and erection, as well as the maintenance of the structure.

The foundations for the steel and equipment are carried on piling throughout. The transformers weigh 170 000 lb. each, and their transfer for repair makes it necessary that the tracks supporting the transfer car be on a solid footing so that they can be handled (Fig. 33).

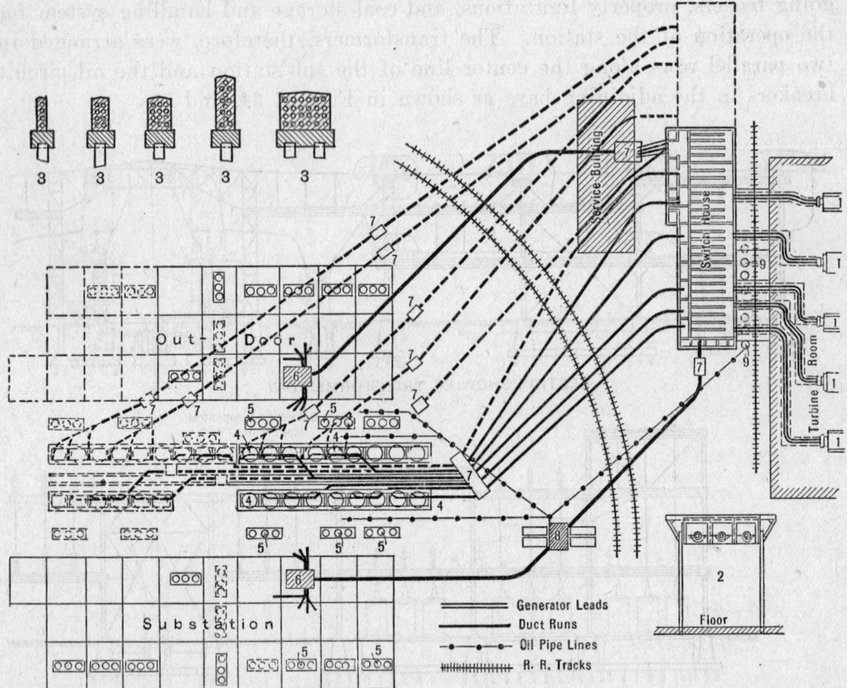

FIG. 35.—PLAN SHOWING GENERATOR LEADS AND DUCT RUNS FROM SWITCH-HOUSE TO OUTDOOR SUB-STATION, KEARNY STATION: (1) GENERATORS; (2) SUSPENDER GENERATOR LEAD COMPARTMENTS IN AUXILIARY SUB-STATION; (3) CROSS-SECTION, DUCT RUNS; (4) 132 KV-A. TRANSFORMERS; (5) OIL CIRCUIT BREAKERS; (6) RELAY HOUSE; (7) MANHOLES; (8) OIL STORAGE AND PURIFYING PLANT; AND (9) TRANSFORMERS FOR AUXILIARY SUB-STATION.

The duct runs, feeding each transformer, consist of 5-in. fiber ducts encased in concrete; one 5-in. fiber duct was provided as a spare for emergency use. These ducts are carried to the top of the transformers in con-

FIG. 36.—OUTDOOR SUB-STATION, MARION: (1) OUTGOING LINES TO TOWER; (2) DEAD END FOR OUTGOING LINES; (3) DISCONNECTING SWITCHES; (4) TRANSFORMERS; (5) OIL CIRCUIT BREAKERS; (6) OIL STORAGE TANKS; (7) BRIDGE FOR LEADS TO SWITCH HOUSE; AND (8) CENTER OF ULTIMATE STATION.

FIG. 37.—OUTDOOR SUB-STATION, ESSEX: (1) DEAD ENDS FOR LINES FROM TOWER; (2) DISCONNECTING SWITCHES; (3) TRANSMISSION TOWER; (4) BRIDGE FOR LEADS TO SWITCH HOUSE; (5) BENT FOR BRIDGE; (6) OIL-CIRCUIT BREAKERS; (7) RELAY HOUSE; AND (8) OIL STORAGE TANKS.

crete piers (Figs. 34 and 35). Between the sub-station and the switch-house the duct runs are supported on piles, care being taken to leave sufficient space between adjacent lines for heat radiation, and also to pitch the ducts toward the manholes for drainage. Several specially supported duct groups or conduit lines for control cable were installed.

The transmission lines from Kearny to Marion and Essex Stations consist of a high-tension bus suspended from steel towers connecting the three stations. The tower line uses a private right of way over the "Meadows" and is designed to meet railroad and harbor regulations at railroad and river crossings. The towers are designed to carry two lines and a ground. The transmission wires are 500 000 cir. mils copper strand supported from the cross-arms by suspension insulators. The energy is transformed at the Marion and Essex Stations to lower voltages as desired and distributed over the 26 400 and 13 200-volt system of the Company.

Eighteen towers were installed on the line between Essex, Kearny, and Marion, varying in height from 116 ft. 0 in. to 231 ft. 6 in. and having spans from 600 ft. 0 in. to 1 136 ft. 0 in. Along the entire right of way a roadway was built to facilitate construction and maintenance. All the steel was galvanized and all field connections were bolted with galvanized bolts and nuts.

The corner piers of all tower foundations were tied together to insure stability. The foundations on the river banks where no docks are installed, are protected against damage from ice by wooden sheet-pile coffer-dams. The entire space inside these coffer-dams was filled with cinders. The foundations for all towers are supported on piles, designed to sustain the loading from wind, snow, ice, wires, and pull due to angularity in the transmission line.

The tower footings for the terminal tower at Marion Station were complicated by space limitations, an angle in the line, dock construction, and the great depth to which piles had to be driven to get proper bearing. Due to these conditions it was found necessary to anchor the foundation against overturning; this was accomplished by the introduction of ties, utilizing the foundations of the building for anchorages. The gas and oil lines governed the location of these ties.

The 13 200-volt feeders from the outdoor sub-station at Marion to the switch-house were carried on steel bridges on account of existing conduit lines, and gas and water mains, which made it practically impossible to use an underground cable system. The design for the steel and foundations for this structure (Fig. 36) is similar to that for the Kearny Station, that is, H-sections were used for columns and rolled sections for supporting the miscellaneous electrical apparatus.

The present installation consists of: Seven 15 000-kv-a., single-phase, oil-insulated, self-cooled transformers; five 132 000-volt, oil circuit breakers, with remote control, having a rupturing capacity of 1 500 000 kv-a.; and fourteen 154 000-volt, motor-operated, remote-control disconnecting switches. The ultimate sub-station will have thirteen transformers, ten oil circuit breakers, and twenty-eight disconnecting switches.

The general design of the outdoor sub-station at Essex (Fig. 37) follows that of Marion and Kearny. At Essex, as at Marion, the 13 200-volt feeds for the outdoor sub-stations to the switch-house were carried on a light overhead trestle. Difficulty in spacing of bents, due to railroad tracks and other local obstructions, made it necessary to select long spans. In order to reduce the weight of the steel to the minimum, cantilevers and suspended spans were used. The length of this bridge is 508 ft. Expansion joints are provided as well as pivot bearings at the base of the bents to allow for movement due to temperature changes.

The present installation at the outdoor sub-station at Essex consists of: Seven 15 000-kv-a., single-phase, oil-insulated, self-cooled transformers; five 132 000-volt, oil circuit breakers with remote control, having a rupturing capacity of 1 500 000 kv-a.; and fourteen 154 000-volt, motor-operated, remote-control disconnecting switches.

Future Developments

The completion of the present portion of the new Kearny Power Station, together with the outdoor sub-stations at the Kearny, Marion, and Essex Stations and the 132 000-volt interconnecting transmission lines, will form the first link of the ultimate State-wide high-tension transmission system as planned by the Public Service Electric and Gas Company. This ultimate high-tension transmission system will consist of more than 100 miles of 132 000-volt transmission lines, together with not less than nine 132 000-volt distribution sub-stations.

This high-tension transmission project will eventually spread across the entire State of New Jersey and will take the form of an immense letter, P. It will provide carrying capacity for practically the entire load of the system not radially distributed from the main generating stations. The upper portion of the loop of this transmission system will include about 50% of the system's load and the tail will extend at least as far as Trenton and possibly will include Camden. This transmission system when completed will provide facilities for the location of new super-power stations at any point of the loop or system that may be determined by geographical considerations, and will make it possible to feed the entire output of these new super-power stations directly into this high-tension distribution system.

The design and the construction of the Kearny Power Station, of the Marion, Essex, and Kearny Outdoor Sub-Stations, as well as of the high-tension transmission line connecting these sub-stations, was done by the Public Service Production Company.

Acknowledgment is due to E. Rothenburg, Structural Designer with the Public Service Production Company and associated with the writer on the design of the steel and foundations of the Kearny Power Station, for valuable suggestions and assistance in the preparation of this paper.

DISCUSSION

George A. Orrok,* M. Am. Soc. C. E.—A distinction should be drawn between the two types of foundations—the Hell Gate type,† on New York shale, and the Kearny type on the mud and silt of the Jersey meadows. In both cases the proportioning appears to be well done. When the foundation is sufficient, nothing more can be said.

As to the use of 18 000 lb. as the fiber stress in the steel design, this policy might be correct when the weights to be carried by the structure are well known or when the static load is many times greater than the moving load. Where, however, constant improvements are to be made in the machinery in both power and weight, it appears wiser to use both lower fiber stress and an excessive loading. Within less than two years structures designed for 30 000 kw. may be used for 60 000 kw., or possibly 100 000 kw. This is true of boilers and auxiliaries as well as of generating machinery.

It makes little difference what is spent on the steel work since this rarely exceeds 10 to 12% of the station cost, usually much less. Ordinarily, it is better to allow for future developments than to consider rebuilding the station within a few years. In a certain station, several years ago, a load of 600 lb. per sq. ft. of floor was used in the design of the steel work. Before the steel was erected two of the floors had to be increased to 1 000 lb. per sq. ft. and within five years one of these floors was carrying 2 000 lb. per sq. ft. Such a difference would vitally affect the use of 18 000 lb. as the fiber stress.

* Cons. Engr., New York, N. Y.

† Described in paper by Ernest M. Van Norden and George A. Hughes, Members, Am. Soc. C. E., entitled "Civil Engineering Features of the Hell Gate Station," p. 113.

AMERICAN SOCIETY OF CIVIL ENGINEERS
INSTITUTED 1852

TRANSACTIONS

Paper No. 1660

WATER SUPPLY FOR ARMY RAILWAYS IN FRANCE*

By Paul M. LaBach,† M. Am. Soc. C. E.

With Discussion by Messrs. Charles H. Lee, William G. Atwood, and Paul M. LaBach.

Synopsis

This history of water supply development, principally for United States Army railway transportation in France during the World War, 1917-19, outlines briefly the factors ordinarily taken into consideration in problems of supply and distribution of boiler water for commercial railway purposes.

Then follows a discussion of the difficulties encountered in changing the water supply and distributing systems of several light traffic commercial railways into suitable installations for a unified military railway with very dense traffic.

In conclusion, an outline of the organization of forces used in the work, is given, together with a discussion of recommendations for an organization which would aid in simplifying and expediting similar operations.

Introduction

One of the fundamental requirements for railroad operation is water for boiler use. All division points where engines are turned or stored must have small power plants and facilities for washing out boilers. In addition, there must also be roadside stations between terminals so located that the locomotive tenders may be filled at suitable intervals, the intervals or spacing being largely governed by the nature of the traffic as well as its density. Where through

* Published in April, 1927, *Proceedings*.

† Engr., Water Service, Rock Island Lines, Chicago, Ill.

traffic only is handled the spacing may be longer than on lines carrying a large proportion of local freight which requires frequent train stops and much switching. The design of the locomotive also enters into the problem. Where superheaters are used with large tenders, as in modern practice, considerably longer intervals may be economical for through traffic than was formerly allowable.

On most of the world's steam railways the development of equipment for furnishing water to locomotives has been gradual. When railways are first built the traffic is usually light and the coal and water problem is not a very serious one in the aggregate, although neither can be neglected. As traffic increases, however, the size of both coal and water stations must also expand in proportion to the ton-miles per hour per mile of single track. Whether the interval between water stations must increase or decrease with the increase in traffic depends on local conditions and, as mentioned, the design of the power used. The intervals for freight traffic are also different from those required for passenger service. The problem at terminals is based on considerations which have little in common with road service.

In most countries heavy traffic railways have grown up gradually and there has been time to adjust coal and water facilities to the needs of the moment. These needs are seldom static and frequent changes are taking place under ordinary operating conditions. The general term, "operating conditions", covers a multitude of factors. Without some actual practical knowledge of daily train movements over a considerable period of time little can be told as to the practicability of any specific scheme of improvement. Other factors besides those stated enter into the subject of spacing, such as proximity of passenger stops, telegraph offices, signal blocks, passing sidings, grade crossing, and adverse grades.

The fuel problem, although serious, is not as exacting as that of water; coaling stations can be placed farther apart and coal can be stored for use at a future time. It is seldom practicable to store water for a longer period than one day on account of the bulk and resultant tankage required. The weight of the coal used is only about one-fifth that of the water. Coal can be stored in large quantities, hauled in ordinary cars, and put at convenient location for use without regard to its place of origin.

Coal Handling

In France, during the period of American participation in the World War, all coal was unloaded at the base ports by the different colliers, shipped to the points required, and unloaded in piles on platforms from which it was shoveled into the tenders. Although this is not the best economic method according to American standards it was effective. This has always been a common practice in Europe where labor is cheap.

Rainfall and Water Supply

In a well-watered country, such as the States of New York and Pennsylvania, water can be found, as a rule, within a reasonable distance of stations, which may be located to conform to operating conditions. The problem of finding a suitable supply is largely an economic one, unless the quality of the water is objectionable. In the Western United States one railroad company has to go more than 100 miles for water that is usable. Therefore, in using the term, "water", the word, "pure", should be also added when it is to be used for locomotive boiler purposes. "Pure" in this sense has a special meaning, best defined by the use of negatives. Pure water will not cause pitting, corrosion, boiler scale, or foaming in switch engines.

It would be difficult to persuade a soldier of the American Expeditionary Force that water was not always easily available in large quantities in France, but such was the case. The exclamation of a returned soldier at a movie of some event over there, taken in the rain, a year or two after his return, was "Good Lord, it ain't stopped raining yet!" In many minds this was and still is the popular idea of the French climate. Then there is the expression "sunny France". A sunny country is usually an arid country. Which statement is true? Both are true in a sense, depending on the season. There is a wet season and a dry season. For agricultural purposes the country is all well watered, but that is largely due to humidity. The average annual rainfall varies from 600 mm. (24 in.) to 1 500 mm. (59 in.) within the area of railroad operations. Within the space of 100 km. (62 miles) the variation is from 700 to 1 000 mm., etc.

Each water station was dependent on an entirely separate source of supply. The quantity available was always governed by local conditions. The climate also had to be considered, that is, the ratio of wet to dry seasons. The basis of computation had to be the dry-weather yield, as that was the period of maximum effort anticipated. The geology and topography in the vicinity of any proposed station also frequently added their share of difficulties to the problem.

All roadside water stations of the kind contemplated are practically of equal importance unless they are close enough together for a train to skip one. In this case there was so little material available for construction that it was impossible to make the more extensive installations.

The coal and water needed for the proposed traffic scheme were in direct proportion to the tonnage to be hauled. This statement seems axiomatic, but the lack of appreciation of this fact was the cause of much of the failure of those not familiar with such matters to understand what would happen when a double-track line was given the maximum tonnage it could carry without slowing down train movement to take water. This meant that the station spacing had to be as far apart as practicable and the supply adequate at all times. The channel ports and the railroads north and east of Paris were reserved for the use of the British and French Armies. This left the Port of Brest and the ports on the Bay of Biscay for the American Army. The Ports of Marseilles and Cette in the Mediterranean were in use for transportation to Africa and the Orient. As the route from America was through Gibraltar where the submarine hazard was very great, and also the distance much greater, these ports were not much used except in special cases, until the western ports had become crowded.

Railways of the American Army Area

At the beginning, the so-called American Sector centered on Toul although the American Army operated subsequently in many other sections and had divisions as far west as Flanders on the British front. To bring the necessary supplies into the Toul Sector by rail was the object of the railroads herein discussed.

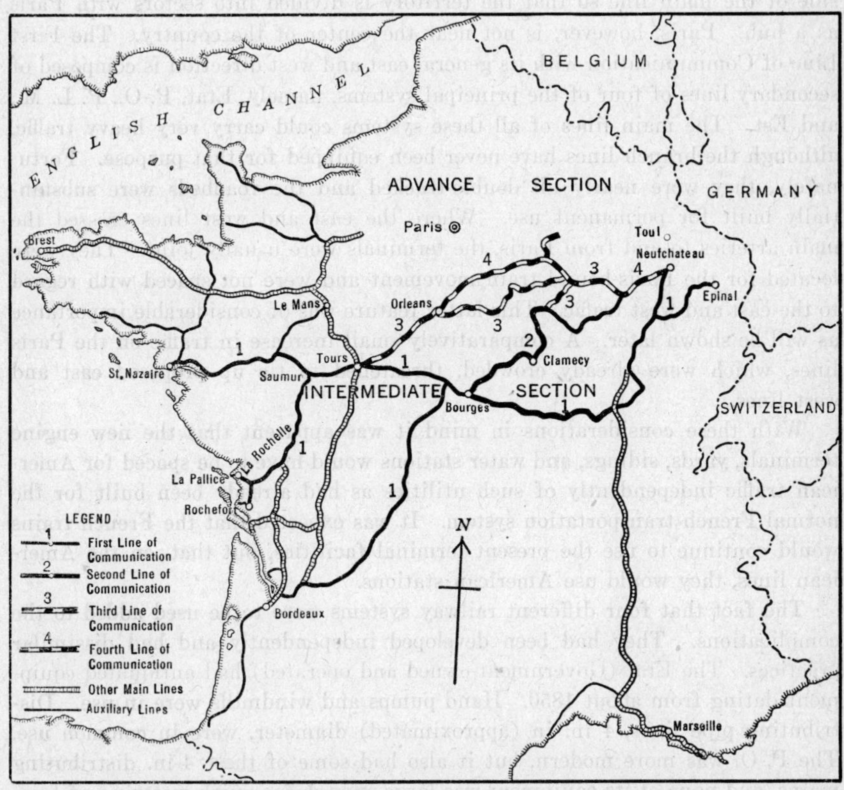

Fig. 1.—Lines of Communication, A. E. F., November, 1918.

The First Line of Communication planned (Fig. 1) started at the base port of St. Nazaire and extended to Neufchateau and Epinal in the Toul Area. In addition, it included the line from the Ports of La Pallice and Rochefort which connected at Saumur with the first line, and also the line from Bordeaux to Bourges. It will be noted (Fig. 1) that if the lines at the base ports were congested there would be a greater density in the line east of Bourges. For this reason the Second Line of Communication, extending from Bourges to Neufchateau by way of Clamecy, was adopted. The Third Line of Communication started at Tours and reached Neufchateau by way of Orleans. Other main lines leading eastwardly from Brest and northwardly from Marseilles will be noted.

The First, Second, and Third Lines of Communication, shown as continuous in Fig. 1, are in reality composed of parts of secondary lines (except east from Brest and north from Marseilles) of the four great systems of French railways, the Etat, Paris-Orleans, Paris-Lyons-Mediterranean, and Est. The six railway systems of France are the Nord, Est, P.-O., Etat, P. L. M., and Midi. With the exception of the Midi, which runs east and west in the south of France, all the systems radiate from Paris. The branches lie on either side of the main line so that the territory is divided into sectors with Paris as a hub. Paris, however, is not near the center of the country. The First Line of Communication with its general east and west direction is composed of secondary lines of four of the principal systems, namely, Etat, P.-O., P. L. M., and Est. The main lines of all these systems could carry very heavy traffic, although the branch lines have never been equipped for that purpose. Fortunately, they were nearly all double-tracked and the roadbeds were substantially built for permanent use. Where the east and west lines crossed the main arteries to and from Paris, the terminals were usually joint. They were located for the Paris-bound train movement and were not spaced with regard to the east and west traffic. This latter feature was of considerable importance as will be shown later. A comparatively small increase in traffic on the Paris lines, which were already crowded, threatened to tie up proposed east and west lines.

With these considerations in mind it was apparent that the new engine terminals, yards, sidings, and water stations would have to be spaced for American traffic independently of such utilities as had already been built for the normal French transportation system. It was expected that the French trains would continue to use the present terminal facilities, but that, on the American lines, they would use American stations.

The fact that four different railway systems were to be used added to the complications. They had been developed independently and had dissimilar practices. The Etat (Government-owned and operated) had antiquated equipment dating from about 1850. Hand pumps and windmills were in use. Distributing pipe lines, 4 in. in (approximated) diameter, were in common use. The P.-O. was more modern, but it also had some of these 4-in. distributing mains, and none of its equipment was large enough for quick watering of locomotives. The P. L. M. was quite modern, and the Est probably came second. The water crane in use everywhere was of old design, whatever its size. The engineer would stop the engine while the fireman adjusted the spout at the tender manhole. The engineer would then climb down to the ground level and turn on the water by opening a gate-valve with a wheel. Altogether the process was slow and the time necessary to fill the tender was from 10 to 30 min.

Each of the four systems naturally had its own method of handling all all questions concerning any changes in its property. Their consent was necessary for matters of large or small importance. After permission had been given, the companies also desired to be kept informed as to the progress of the work. This involved a large number of conferences with their officials. Usually a number of their men were present to pass on such points as might arise. A knowledge of colloquial French was indispensable; to this had to be added the technical equivalents for engineering terms and special apparatus to be used, little of which could be found in any published dictionary. The way to learn a proper name was usually to point out the object to a Frenchman and inquire its name and gender. The desire of the French officials to help was generally manifest.

Methods of Computation

At the beginning the only basis of calculation for water supply had to be made from a more or less hasty inspection. This showed, beginning at the west, a coastal plain, then river valleys, and, finally, territory that was mountainous. Adjacent streams would drain areas, ranging from a few, to hundreds of square miles, which might be anything from a swamp or permeable sands to steep slopes with impervious soil. The rainfall might range from 600 to 1 500 mm. As time progressed another variable was found; rain falls 150 days per year on the west coast of France, whereas the average is only 55 days at Marseilles. The change is not uniform throughout the intervening territory.

At first, there was considerable difficulty in estimating the tonnage to be hauled and the number of trains to be watered at each point. The quantity, 60 lb. per soldier per day, landing at the base ports, was used. One-third of this would be unloaded before the advance section was reached. From this beginning, the freight to be moved was calculated. The evaporation curves and horse-power curves were then used to get a tonnage rating of the American locomotives on the French tracks. The French profiles were in the metric units and the other figures in English units. A tentative tonnage rating was made and, fortunately, a trial was possible. The actual tonnage was only 3% less than the theoretical rating made by the Engineer Water Supply. The number of French trains was known, so on each line trains were added, to the point of saturation, which was assumed as being 1 train each way for each 15 min.

The accelerated growth of American participation in the war was another variable in the problem, as to quantities of water for transportation at different points. The problem would usually be presented to the Engineer Water Supply in this guise: How much water will be needed at a number of points (probably 25) when there are 500 000 soldiers in France? How much for 1 000 000? How much for 1 500 000? These questions had the advantage of being easier to ask than to answer. There were more unknown quantities than equations.

The record shows that the basis of 500 000 men in France was still being used as late as May 6, 1918. This can be explained by the fact that many of those in high command had doubts whether a large army would ever get across the Atlantic. Published diaries of some of these officers show this very clearly; naturally the same view was reflected by subordinates.

The "get-together" spirit evolved by Ludendorf's drive in March, 1918, resulted in an expansion of American ideas on the subject, and larger figures than hitherto used were common. In July, 1918, the Engineer Water Supply used as a basis an estimated total force of 4 000 000 men in France by July, 1919. In November, 1918, 2 000 000 men were already there.

The rate of increase in the Army was never officially announced. It had to be assumed by the person making the estimate. It was necessary to keep pace with these changing conditions until at the last the assumption was made that the Army would advance as far as the Rhine. (Fig. 2.) The rapid retreat of the German Army in October, 1918, indicated that it would be necessary to move the former broad-gauge rail-heads from the places they had occupied for several years to new locations across the devastated areas evacuated by the enemy.

Inquiries were made to determine which railroad lines would be available for the movement of supplies for the American Army in an advance to the Rhine. This program was supplemented with estimates of material and locations for water stations which would be needed to replace those destroyed by the retreating enemy. These locations are shown on Fig. 2. Every effort was made to procure all this material well in advance of the necessity for its use.

At this time also, much information was collected and assembled, from which plans were made for water stations on the advanced lines. The studies of available sources were well advanced when the signing of the Armistice put an end to the big army program. A few installations were made in order to carry out the terms of that agreement.

Previous Preparation

Not until one year after the United States entered the war was a department organized that was responsible for all water supplies to be used in the Transportation Service. In April, 1918, the Department of Engineer of Water Service, under the Engineer of Construction, Transportation Service, was formed with the writer (then Major), and H. Malcolm Pirnie, M. Am. Soc. C. E. (then Captain), as Engineer and Assistant Engineer of Water Supply, respectively.*

The new Department was a good many laps behind the other departments which were fortunate in being able to make some preliminary strides before the rush began. However, the need for water for transportation had not been omitted in calculations for future needs.

Engineer Stores Requisition No. 6, prepared July 14, 1917, stands as the keystone in the arch of important steps absolutely needed to carry out the Transportation Service program in France. This requisition ordered material needed immediately for an army of 500 000 men. A monthly supply to be added to this without further requisition was also provided. In addition, this requisition was to be increased in proportion to any additions to the Army above 500 000 men. During the seventeen months from the time this requisition was made until the Armistice, when the proposed strength of the Army

* The Department was afterward augmented by the addition of F. D. Nash, M. Am. Soc. C. E. (then Lieutenant). During the entire period, Sergt. J. T. Brinkley maintained a corner in a barracks called an office, with the aid (part of the time) of Private Thompson. Five was the maximum force on this work while due to illness and other causes the average was about three.

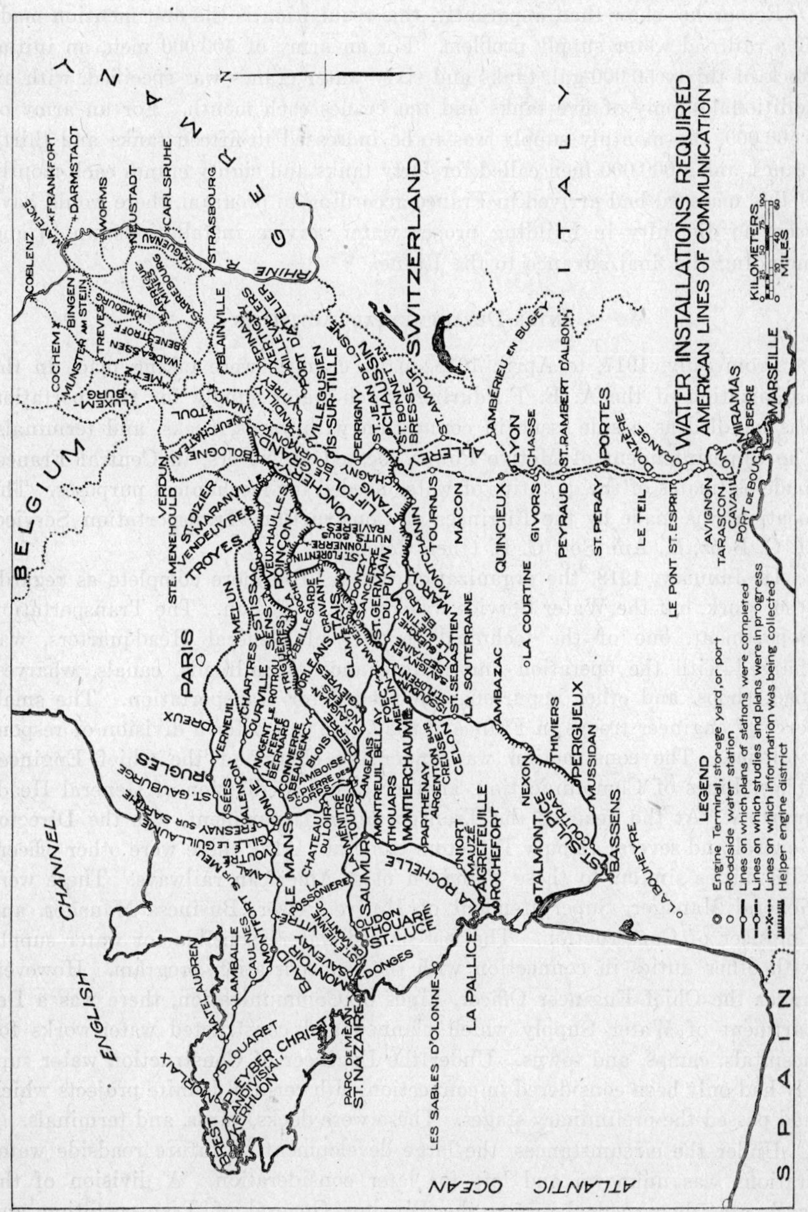
WATER INSTALLATIONS REQUIRED
AMERICAN LINES OF COMMUNICATION
LEGEND
Engine Terminal, storage yard, or port
Roadside water station
Lines on which plans of stations were completed
Lines on which studies and plans were in progress
Lines on which information was being collected
Helper engine district
KILOMETERS
MILES
BELGIUM
GERMANY
SWITZERLAND
ITALY
SPAIN
ENGLISH CHANNEL
ATLANTIC OCEAN
PARIS
LYON
MARSEILLE
RHINE R.

Fig. 2.

had been increased eight times, this requisition demonstrated the remarkable accuracy of its details.* This was true of large items as well as the smaller ones which included railroad water supply material.

Researches show that, apparently, this requisition is the first mention made of a railroad water supply problem. For an army of 500 000 men, an initial stock of thirty 50 000-gal. tanks and sixty water cranes was specified, with an additional supply of five tanks and ten cranes each month. For an army of 1 500 000, the monthly supply was to be increased to fifteen tanks and thirty cranes, and 4 000 000 men called for forty tanks and eighty cranes each month. If this material had arrived in France according to program, there would have been no difficulty in building proper water service installations up to and including the final advance to the Rhine.

Inter-Departmental Activities

From July, 1917, to April, 1918, many changes were taking place in the organization of the A. E. F., during which water supply for transportation was handled as a side issue in connection with yards, docks, and terminals. The Superintendent of Motive Power, located at Nevers, in Central France, made estimates of the quantity of water needed for mechanical purposes. The location was made by the Engineer of Construction, Transportation Service, H. C. Booz, M. Am. Soc. C. E. (then Colonel).

In January, 1918, the organization was a little more complete as regards other work, but the Water Service was still in confusion. The Transportation Department, one of the technical services of General Headquarters, was charged with the operation and maintenance of railroads, canals, wharves, road, shops, and other appurtenances needed for transportation. The small force of engineer troops in France at that time called for a division of responsibilities. The construction was under the charge of the Chief Engineer Office, Lines of Communication, another technical division of General Headquarters. At the head of the Transportation Department, was the Director General and several Deputy Directors General. Also, there were other officers with duties similar to those found on most American railways. These were General Manager, Superintendent of Motive Power, Business Manager, and Engineer of Construction. The last named was responsible for water supply with other duties in connection with the transportation program. However, under the Chief Engineer Officer, Lines of Communication, there was a Department of Water Supply which planned and constructed water-works for hospitals, camps, and towns. Under the Engineer of Construction water supply had only been considered in connection with certain definite projects which had passed the preliminary stages. These were docks, yards, and terminals.

Under the circumstances, the large development of future roadside water stations was unknown and left for later consideration. A division of the work was then made between the Director General of Transportation and the Chief Engineer Officer, Lines of Communication, in which the responsi-

* This requisition was made under the direction of W. J. Wilgus, M. Am. Soc. C. E. (then Colonel).

bility for the design and construction of supply works for transportation was given to the Chief Engineer Officer.

Under this ruling the Director General of Transportation wrote a letter to the Chief Engineer Officer, Lines of Communication, January 5, 1918, submitting plans of eight yards and terminal projects prepared by the Engineer of Construction. This letter included estimates by the Superintendent of Motive Power, as to the quantity of water desired. In this letter is found a statement that had a great influence on future inter-department relations.

"3.—We would suggest for your approval that your Water Supply Department furnish all water requirements, piping same to the connection to the water tanks, and that we erect the tanks and provide all the piping from the tanks to the service outlets, such as water columns, ash-pits, round-houses, etc. Such an arrangement will allow the one Water Supply Department to consider our requirements in connection with those of other branches of the service, and to equate the existing or new sources of supplies to the total needs."

This was immediately agreed to and left the Engineer of Construction with authority over the design of distributing systems only. As it turned out, more than 75% of the railroad water supply systems planned were at points at which there were no camps, hospitals, or other army activities; hence, the reason for the division of authority did not hold except for the projects then considered. However, this idea was expanded to include various other matters and resulted in the duplication of investigations and calculations by two departments.

Organization of Water Supply Department for Transportation

The Department of Engineer of Water Supply was organized April 4, 1918. The organizers and re-organizers had gotten to work and on March 12, 1918, had given all the old authority of the Director General of Transportation to a Chief of Utilities who reported to the Commanding General, Services of Supply, who, in turn, reported to the Commander-in-Chief. The Department of Construction and Forestry was created, which took over all construction matters and the procurement of material required for construction purposes. The Engineer of Construction, Transportation Department, however, still retained the power to design, but had no control over construction. Thus, at the outset, the Engineer Water Supply* could design only the distributing systems while the Department of Construction and Forestry had the authority to investigate and design the supply systems for which it was to procure the material and construct the complete water stations.

In July, 1918, another radical change was made by General Order No. 114, G. H. Q. The Service of Utilities was abolished and the Transportation Service established in much the same position it formerly occupied with respect to design, but construction was vested in the Department of Construction and Forestry. General Order No. 29, S. O. S., July 12, 1918, announced the re-organization of the Office of the Chief Engineer Officer, A. E. F., giving the Department of Construction and Forestry as one of three sub-

* The term, "Engineer Water Supply", and the pronouns used as equivalents refer throughout to the entire Department as a whole and not to the head in person.

divisions. The Director of Construction and Forestry then proceeded to reorganize. The area was divided into sections each in charge of a section engineer officer who handled all construction matters, together with requisitions for materials. The Water Supply Section of the Department of Construction and Forestry only passed upon its requisitions and helped expedite the procurement of materials. The organization was decentralized. The Transportation Department on the contrary had its authority highly centralized, as transportation was a continuous process from the sea coast to the front. (Fig. 3.)

The New Transportation Corps Water Department found itself in a peculiar position as far as its authority and responsibility were concerned. The following is quoted from an official report:

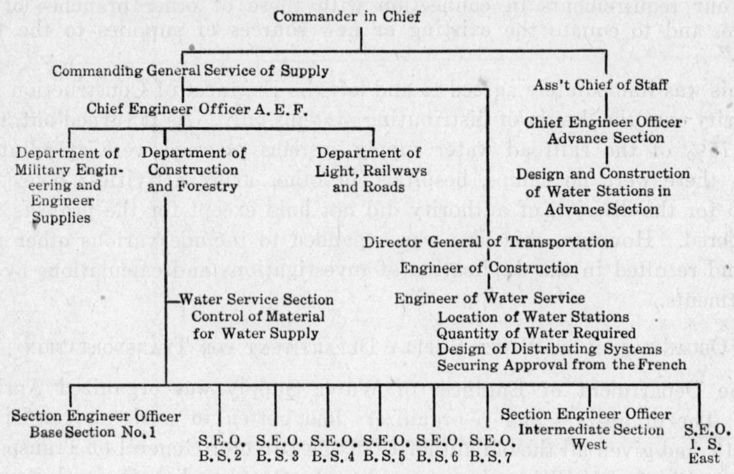

Example of Procedure According to Organization.

1.—Engineer of Water Supply prepares letter from Director General of Transportation to Department of Construction and Forestry stating 200 000 gal. of water per day required at Lothiers. Letter signed by Engineer of Construction by direction of Director General of Transportation.

2.—Received by Department of Construction and Forestry.

3.—Referred to Water Supply Section for action.

4.—Indorsed over to Section Engineer Officer, Intermediate Section West.

5.—Section Engineer Officer sends engineer on ground to investigate.

6.—Engineer reports development is not practicable.

7.—Section Engineer Officer indorses report back to Department of Construction and Forestry.

8.—Referred to Water Supply Section for preparation of indorsement to Director General of Transportation.

9.—Indorsed letter received by Director General of Transportation and referred to Engineer of Construction.

10.—Engineer of Construction refers letter to Engineer of Water Supply showing development of Lothiers impracticable.

The result is that a new spacing of water stations must be devised planning to skip Lothiers; and the above procedure resorted to again.

FIG. 3.—DIAGRAM OF ORGANIZATION AFFECTING RAILROAD WATER STATIONS.

"It had authority to state when and in what quantities water would be required for railroad purposes and to design the distributing systems from the points of delivery of the supply to and including the railroad service, but it did not have authority to select the sources of supply, to specify what kind of supply equipment should be installed, or to superintend the construction in any part of the water stations. However, it was responsible for the selection of adequate sources, installation of ample supply equipment and the proper and timely construction of all water stations to insure the train operation incident to the carrying out of the transportation program for which the Director General of Transportation was responsible. In other words, the Engineer of Water Supply was responsible not only for the correct locations and proper capacities of railroad water services, but also for providing for the services an adequate supply of good water at all times, but he could not determine the source of supply, the kind and size of supply equipment, procure the material or direct the construction of any part of the installation."

Method of Authorizing Work

Before work could be begun on either new or supplemental water stations, authority had to be had from the Commanding General, Service of Supply, G-4, U. S. A., and the French railroad on which the facility was located. A blanket approval was given by the Commanding General, Service of Supply, G-4, for all railroad water stations. The French railway companies had to be approached in either one of two methods—by official channels with consequent delays or by conferences with the French railway officials.

The official method was a roundabout course, involving complete working plans before anything could be started. The Engineer Water Supply would submit his plans to the Deputy Director General of Transportation at Paris. It then went to the Franco-American Mission for its approval, and thence to the French railway officials. With any suggested alterations, it was then returned to the point of origin through the same channels. The Engineer Water Supply through the Director General of Transportation then directed the Department of Construction and Forestry to begin construction. With this procedure, which might take a month, practically no progress could be made for obvious reasons. Knowledge of the available sources of supply and the details of the existing equipment were absolutely necessary before the spacing of the proposed water stations could be made. Detailed descriptions of the proposed equipment and method of placing it were demanded by the French railway officials before their consent could be given. Designs of distributing systems were required by the Department of Construction and Forestry in order that it might investigate the source of water and make requisitions for material for the supply works to be subsequently built by the Section Engineer.

In more ways than one this was getting "the cart before the horse". The Engineer of Water Supply was obliged to investigate sources of supply and all available materials before he could turn a wheel if he wished to provide for the train operation required. The elements involved would be:

1.—Inspection of existing water stations with their sources of supply.

2.—Inspection of proposed sites with their sources of supply. (The geology and contour of the country were important items.)

3.—Procurement of detail plans and other information for all French water stations on the different French railways included in the Lines of Communication.

4.—Translation from the French and tabulation of the results.

5.—Studies of these and other available water sources; computation of the drainage areas to determine whether the supply would be adequate. These were to be made after inspection on the ground with the help of such records of stream flow as were available.

6.—Determination of the best spacing of water stations to meet the proposed American operations and still to conform to locations where adequate sources of supply were available within reasonable distance.

7.—Determination of the quantities required at each water station for the constantly increasing transportation problem.

8.—Submission of this information to the Department of Construction and Forestry for its investigation. (French tanks were to be used where available.)

9.—Preparation of plans for both new and reinforced water stations.*

10.—Submission of these designs to the different French railways with all available information as to the probable mechanical equipment.

11.—Transmission of the approved plans to the Department of Construction and Forestry for construction.

12.—Following up all schemes of every nature not entirely completed.

13.—Special investigation of doubtful sources of supply.

14.—Preparation of priority construction programs in order to use the small amount of material available to the best advantage.

15.—Inspections to aid in expediting construction and procurement of construction material from America.

Inspections and Surveys

Inspections made during April and May, 1918, showed that on the First Line of Communication the intermediate water stations had several months' reserve capacity for the transportation program of 1 500 000 men. Therefore, the supplies for the new yards and terminals were given the priority for immediate study. The facilities to suit each scheme were then indicated on the large scale maps prepared by the Engineer of Construction and forwarded to the Department of Construction and Forestry for action.

Plans and detailed information for all existing water stations on the First, Second, and Third Lines of Communication (Fig. 2) were requested May 1, 1918, from the P.-O., P. L. M., and Est Railways. These data were translated and compiled, together with computed drainage areas from contour maps and estimates of capacities per minute of local pipe lines.

These studies revealed the fact that several points which would have been suitable as to spacing, did not have sufficient supplies for future requirements. The deficient stations were pointed out in conference with the Water Supply Section of the Department of Construction and Forestry, with requests for stream measurements in July, August, and September. The Water Supply Engineer of the Department of Military Engineering and Engineering Supplies was asked to furnish data on rainfall and run-off in France for estimating probable yields.

* The term, "reinforced water station", was applied to French water stations which did not have adequate velocity of flow at the water crane and had to be augmented to secure 2 500 gal. per min., usually by the addition of crane lines and water cranes.

Up to this time, nothing had been done to determine dry-weather flow. Where water was required for railroad use such information was of the greatest importance, as the maximum traffic was expected to coincide with the dry season. The following statement taken from a report of the Assistant Engineer of Water Supply very ably illustrated some of the difficulties:

"The line from Perigueux to Argenton-sur-Creuse may be taken as a typical section of the lines of communication on which doubtful sources of supply existed [see Fig. 2]. The drainage areas of streams adjacent to the French roadside water stations were drawn and studied in connection with the existing supplies and the locations of stations to be used as water stops for American trains were determined to use the best existing facilities as far as possible and conform to the desired spacing of from 20 to 25 miles. The water stations chosen were Perigueux, Thiviers, Nexon, Ambazac, La Souterraine, and water station for heavy south-bound trains climbing the grade from Argenton to La Souterraine. The average annual precipitation at these different water stations varied from 750 mm. at Celon to over 1 000 mm. at Ambazac, and Thiviers. La Souterraine, between Celon and Ambazac, and Nexon, half way between Ambazac and Thiviers, had annual rainfalls at 850 mm. Figures on the distribution of the rainfalls throughout the year were not obtained, but observation through the summer demonstrated that the rainfall during the dry period was much greater in the mountainous region of Ambazac than it was in the less mountainous areas near the other stations.

"Storage or new sources were, therefore, necessary to supply deficiencies at La Souterraine, Nexon and Celon, although the drainage areas at these points were nearly as large as that giving an ample supply at Ambazac. Accordingly, it was planned to build a dam on the stream below Celon to store water for the dry period of 1919, and to lay a pipe line to the existing dam of Etang du Chi, near La Souterraine, which had sufficient capacity and elevation to furnish the additional water requirements by gravity."

Water supply problems similar to the foregoing were found on all points of the line, and attention has been drawn to this one simply for the purpose of illustrating conditions, rather than to convey the impression that it was a particularly bad territory.

Number of Stations Projected

On the First Line of Communication (Fig. 1) from St. Nazaire and Bordeaux to the rail-heads there were ninety-two French water stations. All these stations were studied carefully and the results tabulated on data sheets similar to those already described. (See Fig. 2.)

The necessity for an early start being apparent, a preliminary list of forty-one water stations was sent to the Department of Construction and Forestry on April 19, 1918 (see Tables 1 and 2). This was some time before it was possible to secure and work out any detailed information, and after only one inspection trip had been made. Later studies caused only minor changes in six of these preliminary locations. The estimated quantities also varied but slightly.

The lines from Brest to Tours *via* Le Mans; from Rochefort and La Rochelle to Saumur and the so-called Second and Third Lines of Communication had ninety-two stations which were also tabulated and studied on receipt of the necessary information. (See Figs. 1 and 2.) Thus, there were

184 water stations covering 1 760 miles, which were studied in connection with the program in effect as early as April, 1918.

TABLE 1.—WATER FACILITIES REQUIRED BETWEEN ST. NAZAIRE AND NEUFCHATEAU (*via* CERCY LA TOUR), FRANCE.

Stations and intervals (miles).	Mile posts.	Gallons per day.
St. Nazaire (6)	0	Some facilities
Montoir (14)	6	427 000
St. Etienne de Montluc	20	135 000
Nantes	39.7	......
St. Luce	..	160 000
Oudon (30)	49	180 000
La Possonniere (24)	79	180 000
La Menitre (16)	103	180 000
Saumur (24)	119	587 000
Langeais (28)	143	260 000
Dierre (22)	171	260 000
St. Aignan-Noyers (13)	193	260 000
Gievres (26)	206	817 000
Foecy (24)	232	300 000
Savigny en Septaine (26)	256	370 000
Le Guetin	282	370 000
Cercy la Tour (19)	321	1 173 000
Luzy (24)	340	700 000
Marmagne sur Creusot (33)	364	700 000
Santenay (29)	397	700 000
Vougeot (12)	426	700 000
Is sur Tille (19)	438	1 561 000
Villeguisien (23)	457	760 000
Avrecourt (Chal.-Neuf) (19)	480	360 000
Bourmont (13)	499	360 000
Neufchateau	512	427 000
Vitrey-Vernoise (Chal.-Epinal) (21)	481	360 000
Conflans-Varigney (23)	502	360 000
Xertigny (12)	525	360 000
Epinal	537	427 000

By November 11, 1918, 260 stations had been tabulated and studied in detail as to their availability for American transportation. Of these, 105 were selected for reserve or entirely new stations to fit the transportation program. By that time plans had been prepared for all the distributing systems, most of which had been approved by the French and transmitted to the Department of Construction and Forestry, while the remainder were in the hands of the Franco-American Mission (Fig. 2).

TABLE 2.—WATER FACILITIES REQUIRED BETWEEN BASSENS AND PONT VERTE, FRANCE.

Stations and intervals (miles).	Mile posts (from Bordeaux).	Gallons per day.
Bassens (10)	2	470 000
St. Sulpice (18)	12	150 000
Coutras (26)	30	250 000
Mussidan (24)	56	250 000
Perigueux (23)	80	570 000
Thiviers (25)	103	390 000
Nexon (25)	128	390 000
Ambazac (25)	153	390 000
La Souterraine (23)	178	260 000
Celon (25)	201	260 000
Chateauroux (32)	226	390 000
St. Florent	258	260 000

Thus, at the time of the Armistice, 105 plans had been completed for 1 900 miles of railroad; studies were well under way for 1 000 miles more; and data had been assembled and plans made for 100 water stations on the 1 500 miles of railroad which would have been required to advance the rail-heads to the Rhine.

Spacing of Water Stations

A number of factors must be considered in spacing railroad water stations: First, the rate of evaporation at different locomotive speeds must be known; second, the capacity of the tenders; third, the profile to be traversed; and, fourth, the method or scheme of operating trains. The last factor can only be anticipated in view of many years of past experience.

The tanks of the American locomotives held 4 900 to 5 300 gal. of water. The rate of consumption was 70 to 120 gal. per mile with a locomotive having its full tonnage rating. The variation was caused by the rise and fall in the grade line. A locomotive running on a level track uses more water per mile than one with the same load on a profile having many changes from adverse to favoring grades, where the engine works at full throttle ascending, but can coast down the favoring grades without using steam. The maximum rate of consumption takes place on an adverse maximum grade involving possible engine delays, so that it would not be safe to have less than 1 000 gal. of water in the tender. For these reasons, a maximum span of 30 miles was adopted with an average of 20 to 25 miles. The small French water stations were located between these points and could be used in an emergency.

American Locomotive Used

The principal American locomotive was similar to one class of French locomotives. The statistics of the engine were about as follows:

Cylinders	21 by 28 in.
Steam pressure	190 lb.
Diameter of driving wheels	56 in.
Wheel-base of driving wheels	15 ft. 6 in.
Grate area	32.7 sq. ft.
Tractive power	35 600 lb.
Weight, in working order	166 400 lb.

A total of 3 490 standard-gauge Consolidation locomotives were purchased for overseas use. This is more than twice the total number operated by the Chicago and Northwestern Railway Company with 8 500 miles of line. Not all of them were delivered, however.

In all, 1 303 Consolidation locomotives were shipped for use by the A. E. F. In addition, 332 locomotives were en route to France or on docks in the United States awaiting shipment at the time of the Armistice. Also, 30 saddle-back switching locomotives were in use. Hence the undertaking to supply them with water was not a small one. On 1% grade, an engine would haul about 1 450 tons at the speed required under the circumstances.

General Plans

The roadside water stations having been selected, the French station plans were copied and the new facilities shown on them. These stations were of two general types (Fig. 4), one for trains with single engines, the other for helper engine districts.

The standard distributing equipment consisted of a 50 000-gal. wooden tank on a wooden tower located as close to a No. 11 Sheffield, 10-in. water crane as possible. The pipe line from the tank to the crane was of 10-in. threaded pipe with couplings. Existing French pipe lines were used, when available, by the addition of other lines to increase the capacity to that of the 10-in. line. Water cranes were placed, when possible, between the main track and passing sidings so that engines could take water without blocking the main line. They were designed to furnish water to American locomotives during 5-min. stops (Fig. 4).

At a few points, such as the Perigueux Engine Terminal, high ground was available for the concrete reservoirs, but this was rare. The prime requisites for watering a locomotive quickly are pipe lines of large volume and water at comparatively low heads, to avoid valve and pipe-line troubles from water ram due to sudden closing of large valves.

The quantity of water needed at each of these stations was calculated from the average daily tonnages necessary to supply the Army. It is obvious that military situations might have changed the whole conception of the matter and have required any one of the lines to be used at its full capacity. This was taken as 3 to 4 trains per hour in each direction for a 24-hour day.

At engine terminals, 5 000 gal. per engine entering was used. As the terminal spacings were the same as for the roadside stations, it was assumed that each engine would take 3 500 gal. of water when entering and 1 500 gal. would be needed for losses while standing idle. An allowance of 10 000 gal. per day was made for each switch engine and from 30 000 to 90 000 gal. per day for power plants, boiler washing, and miscellaneous uses.

Fortunately, the quality of water did not complicate the situation to any extent. Most of the water from the coast to the northeast part of France is what is called "light". It is not very hard until the Vosges territory is reached. At the sea coast, in 1918, considerable trouble was experienced with foaming. During the summer months, the reservoirs were pumped down so that seepage changed from the landward side to the seaward side. The salt water caused the trouble.

Organization Difficulties

The actual working history of an organization is usually dry reading. However, as similar situations may occur in any campaign, it seems advisable to give a brief outline of organization troubles that added immensely to the work without in themselves producing any water stations; and it was water stations that were required.

On January 5, 1918, preliminary plans, including water requirements at several engine terminals, were sent to the Chief Engineer Officer, Lines of

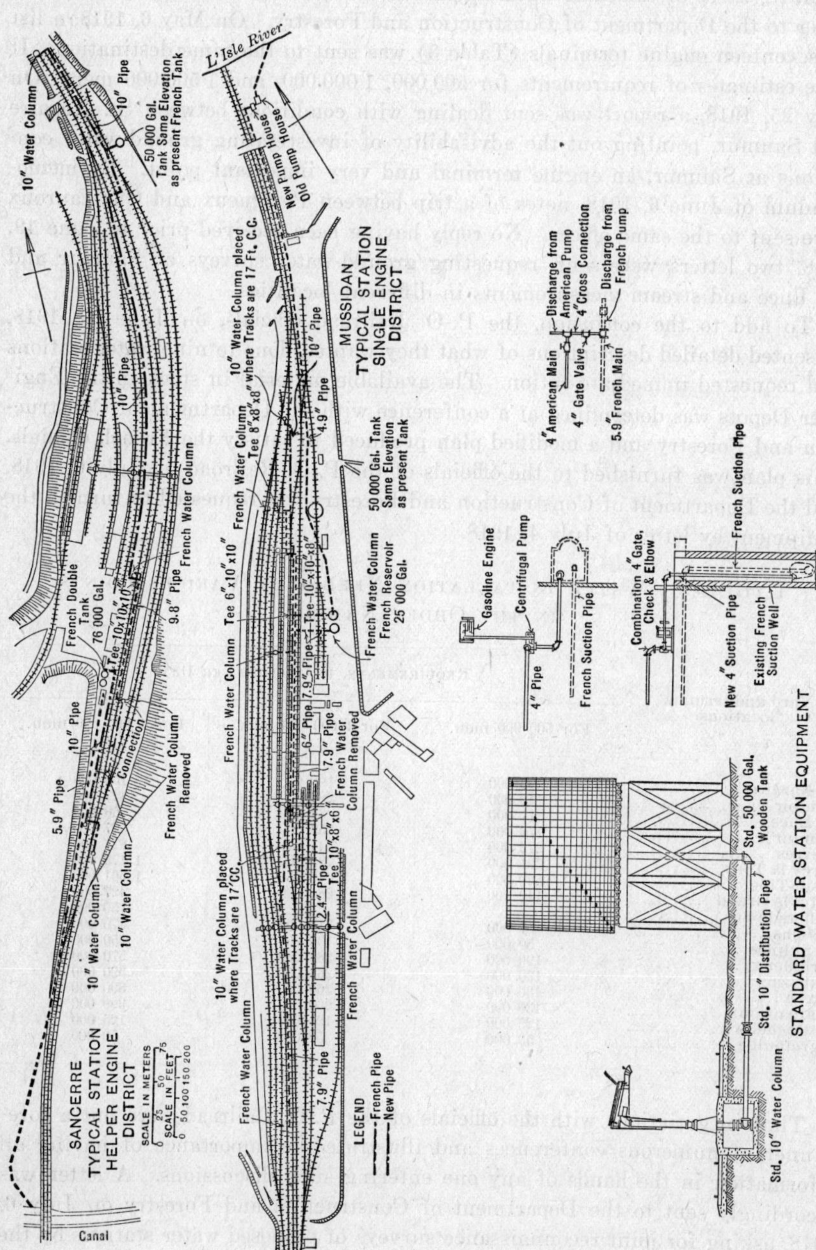

FIG. 4.—TYPICAL REINFORCED ROADSIDE WATER STATIONS AND STANDARD EQUIPMENT, TRANSPORTATION CORPS, A. E. F.

Communication (later Department of Construction and Forestry). On April 19, 1918, a set of tables of water requirements (Tables 1 and 2) was sent by letter to the Department of Construction and Forestry. On May 6, 1918, a list of seventeen engine terminals (Table 3) was sent to the same destination. It gave estimates of requirements for 500 000, 1 000 000, and 1 500 000 men. On May 25, 1918, a report was sent dealing with conditions between St. Nazaire and Saumur, pointing out the advisability of investigating ground-water conditions at Saumur, an engine terminal and very important point. By memorandum of June 6, 1918, notes of a trip between Perigueux and Chateauroux were sent to the same officer. No reply having been received prior to June 19, 1918, two letters were sent, requesting ground-water surveys at Saumur and St. Luce and stream measurements in different localities.

To add to the confusion, the P.-O. Railroad officials, on June 30, 1918, presented detailed descriptions of what they wanted done to nine water stations and requested immediate action. The available material in stock in the Engineer Depots was determined at a conference with the Department of Construction and Forestry and a modified plan produced to satisfy the French officials. This plan was furnished to the officials of the P.-O. Railroad on July 6, 1918, and the Department of Construction and Forestry was requested to furnish the equipment by letter of July 4, 1918.

TABLE 3.—WATER INSTALLATION NEEDED AT VARIOUS POINTS IN THE ORDER NAMED.

Yard and terminal locations.	Requirements, in Gallons per Day.		
	For 500 000 men.	For 1 000 000 men.	For 1 500 000 men.
St. Nazaire	50 000	100 000	150 000
Montoir	142 000	284 000	427 000
St. Luce	17 000	34 000	50 000
Saumur	176 000	352 000	527 000
Gievres	272 000	544 000	817 000
Cercy la Tour	391 000	782 000	1 173 000
Is sur Tille	520 000	1 040 000	1 561 000
Liffol le Grand	142 000	284 000	427 000
Villiers le Sec	....	....	750 000
Bassens	157 000	314 000	470 000
St. Sulpice	50 000	100 000	150 000
Perigueux	190 000	380 000	570 000
Ambazac	130 000	260 000	390 000
Nexon	130 000	260 000	390 000
Chateauroux	130 000	260 000	390 000
La Rochelle	125 000	125 000	125 000
Aigrefeuille	50 000	50 000	50 000

These negotiations with the officials of the P.-O. Railroad were but a forerunner of numerous conferences and illustrate the importance of having all information in the hands of any one entering such discussions. A letter was accordingly sent to the Department of Construction and Forestry on July 6, 1918, asking for joint reconnaissance surveys of proposed water stations by the representatives of the Engineer of Water Supply of the Transportation Service and Section Engineers of the Department of Construction and Forestry, with authority to agree on methods, etc. This letter was unanswered, and telephone inquiry only resulted in the information that the Section Engineers were too busy to pay any attention to these details.

The next move (July 17, 1918) was to appeal to the Commanding General, Service of Supply, for an adjudication. His decision is found in a memorandum of July 23, 1918, forwarded to the Department of Construction and Forestry, stating in part:

"It would appear that there can be no objection to permitting representatives of the Transportation Department working jointly with the Construction and Forestry Departments in investigating sources of water supply at various water stations. However, the responsibility for supplying an ample supply of water where needed, rests squarely on the D. C. & F. Any information of sources of water which the T. D. has, should be turned over to the D. C. & F. The importance of this matter is so great that immediate attention must be given to this problem." (See Fig. 3.)

No one was able to explain just how much of this information was to be turned over. It consisted in part of mental conceptions resulting from many years of experience in similar matters, and could not be made into a neat package for delivery.

During the negotiations, the Water Supply Section of the Department of Construction and Forestry secured a geologist to go over the line from Perigueux to Celon. He was accompanied by a representative of Engineer Water Supply of the Transportation Department. This was the beginning, and by September 10, 1918, the first complete reports of the proposed methods of developing doubtful sources of supply were received.

Engineers are prone to make curves to illustrate their meaning with the idea that busy men will get the point without effort. This was tried in order to relieve the busy Section Engineers of labor. It worked like the well-known Australian boomerang; the information was used by the Section Engineer of the Department of Construction and Forestry as an argument against the reinforcement of certain stations. The small French stations had to be used between engine terminals until all the reinforced stations in the district had been completed. Hence the small actual consumption at the selected roadside water stations was compared with the requirements for any day taken from the curves and used as an argument against the immediate necessity of proceeding with construction.

Difficulties in Securing Material

The rapid increase in the size of the Army and the military activities due to the St. Mihiel Drive in September, 1918, produced such a density of traffic as to bring out forcibly the weak points. The roadside water stations had not been reinforced to deliver water rapidly, and all trains were stopping at the small French water stations to take water. Sometimes they obstructed the main track for 20 min., thus automatically limiting train movement to 2 trains per hour. Such conditions finally brought the problem of railroad water supply into the spotlight, and this resulted in accelerated construction which thereafter advanced as fast as material was received.

Lack of suitable material was the most serious factor in delaying construction. Requisitions had been made for material, but the shipping tonnage allotted the Transportation Department was so small that it was deemed necessary at first to utilize all of it for locomotives, cars, rails, etc. When the new Department of Engineer of Water Supply was formed, in April, 1918, it was discovered that no material for water service had arrived and none had been called for by the Department of Construction and Forestry during the previous two months, when the work had been under its jurisdiction. Consequently, the first shipment was requested on April 18, 1918, as a part of the tonnage quota of the Director General of Transportation. The same was true of May and June.

The Engineer Water Supply explored every possible channel for procuring tanks in Europe, but without success. The only ones found were several 25 000-gal. wooden tanks made by the construction forces at Gievres. These were excellent, but construction of them had been discontinued. Thus, it was necessary to depend entirely on shipments from the United States. When notice of the first shipment of tanks was received, a list of the points where they were most urgently needed was given to the Department of Construction and Forestry. This was done from time to time, but by October 17, 1918, it became apparent that only the tanks on the original requisition had arrived. (For that matter these were all that ever did reach France.) A hurry-up movement was then instituted to get shipments of tanks for the proposed drive to the Rhine, but this was stopped by the Armistice.

In conference with the officials of the P. L. M. Railway, it was found that they could use German war prisoners to build reinforced concrete tanks for American transportation by contract. This scheme was carried into effect at three different points before the cessation of hostilities, but, even then, American water cranes had to be used, for not even one was obtainable in France.

Paper Work and Construction

Quoting again from an official report:

"However, as the organization stood, a great deal of the work was only done on paper with a comparatively small accomplishment in actual construction. An excellent example of this may be seen in the case of the roadside water station reinforcement proposed at Thiviers. In all there were 46 letters, telegrams, and conferences extending over a period of six months, with which the Engineer of Water Supply was concerned, on this one project. And at the time the Armistice was signed, the construction had not started, although a shipment of 6-in. supply pipe had arrived a short time before." (See Fig. 3.)

By the careful assignment of available material to the new engine terminals, yards, and weakest roadside stations, it was possible for the American Lines of Communication to carry one-third of the total tonnage needed to supply 4 000 000 men. In November, 1918, water facilities had been installed sufficient for 1 300 000 men, which was nearly the size of the Army contemplated in July, 1918, for the campaign in 1919.

When the Armistice was signed, eighty of the projects were canceled, the remainder being used for the different movements needed for the return of troops to the base ports, the maximum traffic being reached about the middle of December, 1918.

In addition to the principal duties in connection with train movement the Engineer of Water Supply, Transportation Department, was called on for various other odd jobs. Among these were fire protection at Bassens docks, water facilities on forestry sidings, supplying drinking water to train crews and to troops in transit, aid in the rehabilitation of the Lines of Communication through the fighting area into Germany after the Armistice was signed, and aid in operating the lines taken over after the St. Mihiel Drive. His advice and assistance in securing all kinds of approvals from the French were necessary before they could be carried out.

One of the problems that was carried to a conclusion was that of mending the damaged water supply at Couflans-Jarny (on the front north of Toul) on the section of railroad near the Luxembourg border, operated by the Americans. This terminal had been badly damaged by American artillery fire. The large distributing mains had been broken in six different places and the pumping machinery carried away by the Germans. The mending of the breaks and the installation of a steam pumping plant was carried out under the direction of the Department of Engineer of Water Supply and a report submitted recommending what was needed at other water stations on the section under American control.

At the time the Armistice was signed, the writer was investigating a very mysterious cause of foaming on the lines of the Woevre (near Thiaucourt). This was on a line that had been taken over after the St. Mihiel Drive. Engines foamed on Wednesdays and Thursdays. A voyage of inspection of several miles up the creek from which the water was taken disclosed a village with a large public laundry. The inhabitants washed their lingerie on Mondays and Tuesdays, the soda and soap reached the engines on Wednesdays and Thursdays; hence, the disturbance. It is the only case on record during years of experience, in which engine foaming conformed to the calendar. As it was impossible, with due regard to the *entente cordiale,* to sentence the population to wearing soiled shirts, nothing was done about it, except to protest.

Conclusions

The lessons to be drawn from all these experiences may be summarized briefly as follows:

The Engineer of Water Supply, Transportation Department, should have primary control of certain fundamentals with sufficient personnel to carry matters to a conclusion:

1.—All investigations necessary to determine the sources of water supply for transportation.

2.—Design of supply systems to the extent of specifying capacities of pipe lines to be installed and general location plans.

3.—Control of essentially railroad water service material, such as tanks, water cranes, valves, piping, engines, and pumps.

4.—Installation of water tanks, water cranes, and connections for roadside water stations.

5.—Control of a maintenance force for their upkeep. When accidents happen, the enginemen must report it by wire to the dispatcher so that he can change his train movements accordingly. The repair forces should be within easy reach of this source of information.

There is no essential difference between engines, cars, coal, and water as parts of a transportation scheme, and they should be under the same general head. To assemble engines and cars is not far different from erecting water stations. It is believed that the supply of equipment for indefinite problems is best handled from one large depot and is, therefore, rightly under the Department of Construction and Forestry. This includes pumps and engines which can more readily be selected from a large stock.

The main object in work of this kind is to preserve the continuity of all operation. This has been accomplished under civilian control by the organization of "all line gangs". These are under the control of one official who can move them about into different divisional jurisdictions. Similar forces, completely equipped, could have simplified matters in France. The chief obstacle to be avoided in transportation is delay. As a chain is only as strong as its weakest link, so local delays may interfere with train movements perhaps hundreds of miles away.

It would not seem difficult under military organization to accomplish this by the creation of a separate unit. This unit would have absolute control over its own activities from the starting point, or investigation, to the conclusion—a completely equipped water station with sufficient supply to enable it to deliver water to locomotives at points best suited to the expediting of traffic.

DISCUSSION

Charles H. Lee,* M. Am. Soc. C. E. (by letter).—The author has vividly described the difficulties faced by the engineer officer in specialized service during the World War. His experience had its duplicate in all the combatant armies, but with the A. E. F. it was possibly intensified because of general unpreparedness for overseas duty and the speed with which organization and expansion were undertaken. To those who shared with the author in his experience there remain two lasting impressions: First, the display of ingenuity and energy on the part of officers drawn from civilian life in accomplishing results without the accustomed facilities; and, second, the tremendous loss of time and effort due to the lack of information, material, and appropriate equipment for specialized military engineering operations. The lesson to be learned is the need of a greater degree of preparedness in order that lost motion may be reduced to a minimum.

The writer was assigned to the Water Supply Service of the A. E. F. late in 1917, and during the following eighteen months was attached at various times to the Water Supply Sections of the Office of Chief Engineer, A. E. F., Office of Chief Engineer, First Corps, the Department of Military Engineering and Engineering Supplies, and the Office of Chief Engineer, First Army. His duties (as Captain) were related to the selection and development of water sources and the control of specialized equipment used in water development and transmission.

The organization diagram, Fig. 3, pertains entirely to the Service of Supply and the Advance Section. It does not include the Zone of the Armies, which is the field of operation of the combatant forces. The latter might be indicated on the diagram by extending the top line to the right and adding below it, "Commanding General First Army", "Commanding General Second Army", etc. Each Army had its Water Supply Service and Water Supply Officer, nominally consisting of one engineer regiment of water supply troops and its commanding officer.

The diagram might also be made more complete by the addition of "Water Supply Section", under the Chief Engineer Officer, A. E. F., Department of Military Engineering and Engineering Supplies. This office had technical supervision of all the water supply activities of the A. E. F., including the Water Supply Services of the First and Second Armies, the Service of Supply, Department of Construction and Forestry, and the Advance Section. F. F. Longley, M. Am. Soc. C. E., was placed in charge of this office in September, 1917, and continued throughout the war.

A quotation from Paragraph 2, General Orders No. 131, A. E. F., dated August 7, 1918, indicates the status of the Water Supply Service as a branch of the A. E. F.:

"I.—1. Section VI, G. O. No. 34, G. H. Q., 1918, is hereby revoked and the following substituted therefor.

"2. The responsibility for water supply work for the A. E. F. is divided as follows:

* Cons. Hydr. Engr., San Francisco, Calif.

"(*a*) In the army zones special engineer troops (Water Supply) assigned to armies shall be responsible for the supply of adequate quantities of water at 'water points' located as conveniently for the troops as service conditions will permit. This water will, if necessary, be purified by filtration or disinfection, or both, in such a manner as to insure the delivery of water of the best quality practicably obtainable under the conditions.

"(*b*) In all areas occupied by the American troops outside of army zones the Engineer Department will be responsible for the development, as required, of water supplies for the use of American troops and for American activities of every kind. This water will be given such treatment as the conditions demand and permit."

Its character and functions are also well shown by the following quotation:*

"A.—ORGANIZATION OF WATER SUPPLY SERVICE

"I.—The Water Supply Service of the American E. F. is organized as a branch of the Engineer Department. It consists of certain officers and special engineer troops experienced in water supply work, including examinations, design and construction. Its duties are defined by Sec. I, G. O. No. 131, G. H. Q. A. E. F., 1918.

"For each army the water supply service will consist of Army Engineer troops (not to exceed one regimental headquarters and six companies), especially trained and equipped for water supply work and such additional officers as conditions may require.

"In general, the functions of the Army water supply organization will include the investigation of water resources, the development of water supply, and the construction and operation of such works as may be necessary to make water available at 'water points', including conveniences for watering animals, filling water carts, water-tank trains, buckets, canteens, and other containers. Tactical units will make provision for the transportation of water from 'water points' to the final point of consumption."

The Water Supply Service, as thus established, was modeled somewhat after that of the French and British Armies with modifications that experience had shown desirable. One water supply regiment, the 26th Engineers, was organized and functioned in scattered units in the Service of Supply, the Advance Section, and the Zone of the Armies. A number of detached officers with qualifying civilian experience were also assigned to water supply duty. Water supply systems were designed and built for all purposes throughout the area embraced within the American Lines of Communication. These scattered units and officers were attached to the various base sections and functioned under the direction of base section engineer officers. Companies of the 26th Engineers also saw active service in the Zone of the Armies supplying water to combatant troops. Watering stations for light railways were also established at many points in the Army Zone. In addition to design and construction, much work was done by specially qualified officers attached to the Water Supply Section, Department of Military Engineers and Engineer Supplies, in compiling general water resource and water requirement information

* *Bulletin No. 55*, A. E. F., dated August 8, 1918.

and recommending specific sources of supply for various hospitals, aviation fields, depots, base ports, railway points, etc.

The office of Engineer of Water Service under the Engineer of Construction, Transportation Service, was apparently not established as a part of the general Water Supply Service of the A. E. F., but as an independent unit within the Transportation Department. Its functions, as shown in Fig. 3, were limited, and were in conformity with the suggestion of the Director General of Transportation in his letter of January 5, 1918, quoted on page 207. The inter-departmental difficulties described by the author were incident to the building up of a utility organization under tremendous pressure for results, but without precedent and without previous information of requirements or of physical resources. Time would undoubtedly have dissolved these difficulties and proved the worth of the type of organizations as formed.

The relation of water resources to railway water supply is of great importance. Much depends on the choice of an adequate, dependable, and pure source of water supply. For military purposes, the time required for development and the type and amount of material required are also of greatest importance. The experience of the A. E. F. in France emphasizes the need of carefully compiled and analyzed water resource data as an element of preparedness both to aid in the choice of sources of water supply and in ordering equipment and material. The sources of data are so diverse and so scattered in the various countries of the world, that it is only in times of peace that they can be assembled and reduced to a condition of usefulness.

As a nucleus for the study of water resources of any region there should be available, as complete as possible, a collection of published data relating to the region; together with topographic and geologic maps, geologic sections, and maps showing forests, streams, lakes, and, if possible, springs and wells. With the A. E. F., in France, the Geologic Section, Office of Chief Engineer, and Meteorologic Division of the Signal Corps, co-operated with the Water Supply Section, Office of Chief Engineer, both in obtaining maps and data from French sources and in making mutually available all data secured. This procedure proved valuable to all concerned.

The precipitation and hydrologic data were obtained from time to time as the pressure of current work permitted, and, although available for reference, it was not possible to analyze and compile them for general use until just before the Armistice. The following summary is of more than passing interest, as it illustrates the general features of a water resource compilation for any country.

There are three distinct hydrologic types in France which serve to divide the country into districts useful in the selection of sources of water supply, study of water supply characteristics, determination of methods for development, and choice of construction material and equipment.

The first type is represented by elevated igneous rock masses flanked or partly overlaid by metamorphic rocks constituting much of the mountainous area of France, and receiving an average annual precipitation of from 35 to 60 in. Falling within this type are the following hydrologic provinces (see Fig. 5 for location): (1) The Brittany Peninsula; (2) the assembly of ranges in Central France, known as the "Central Massif"; (3) the Ardenne; (4) the Vosges Mountains; (5) the Pyrenees Mountains; and (6) the main chain of the Alps. The igneous and metamorphic rocks are dense and unfissured except superficially, and have no stratification of porous and impervious formations characteristic of the more recent sedimentary formations. The principal source of water in these areas is direct run-off from precipitation. In the Brittany Peninsula and Central Massif the rainfall is relatively light and the run-off rapid. In the higher mountain districts (Areas Nos. 3 to 6), the stream flow is more regular due to the heavier precipitation with snow storage and forest litter. Important railway lines operated by the American forces traversed the Brittany Peninsula and Central Massif (Figs. 1, 2, and 5), and it was necessary to resort to artificial storage in these areas. Springs afforded minor supplies, which were of little value for railway purposes in any areas of the first type.

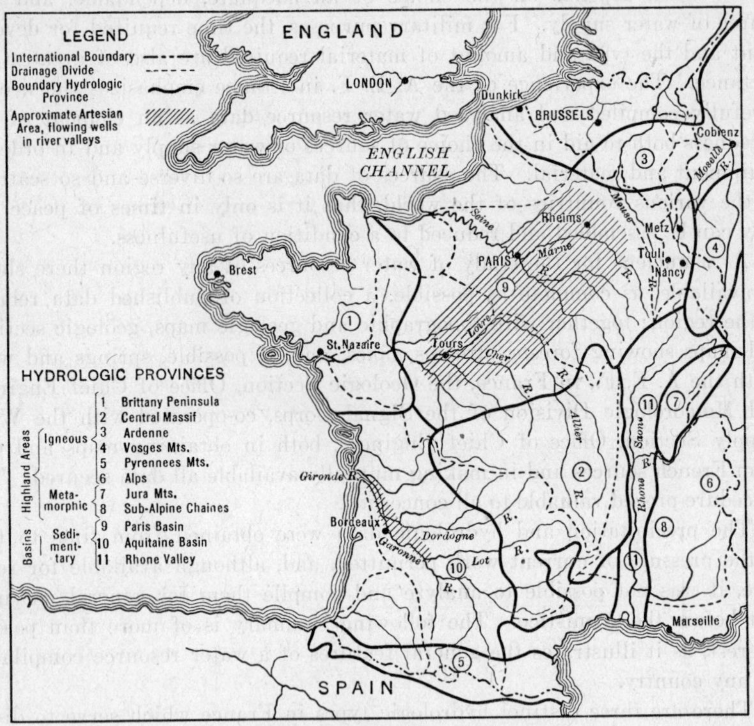

FIG. 5.—HYDROLOGIC MAP OF FRANCE.

The second type of hydrologic province is composed of elevated and highly tilted and folded sedimentary rocks receiving an annual precipitation of from 35 to 60 in. This type includes (7) the Jura Mountains, and (8) the Sub-Alpine Mountain chains bordering the Rhone Valley on the east. Rock formations in these areas are more or less fissured and sometimes cavernous, but seldom porous. The principal sources of water supply are flowing streams fed by melting snow and ice. Some very large cavern springs occur in the limestone regions. The southern end of the railway, terminating at Marseilles, lay in the Sub-Alpine Province (Figs. 2 and 5).

The third type of hydrologic province comprises the great "structural basins" embracing the valley and plateau areas of France. The precipitation varies from 24 to 35 in. per year over these areas. Included in this type are: (9) The Paris Basin; (10) the Aquitaine Basin; and (11) the Rhone Valley. These basins are filled to a great depth with comparatively soft, regularly stratified, sedimentary rocks of the Secondary and Tertiary Series, and are bordered by the upturned and exposed edges of the various underlying strata. They contain the most highly developed agricultural and industrial areas of France, and are the regions of densest population. Local Quaternary deposits of unconsolidated gravel, sand, and silt occur in the various river valleys. This area also includes most of the territory traversed by the American Lines of Communication from base ports to rail-head (Figs. 1, 2, and 5), as well as the Zone of the Armies.

The sources of water supply are more varied than in the highland provinces. Numerous rivers with dependable flow have their sources in the mountain areas and traverse the basins, affording ample supply for railway purposes, except in the elevated limestone plateau districts and the flat clay and shale areas, such as the Woevre District in the Toul Sector and northward to Stenay. In the latter occur many shallow lakes ("etangs"), in which the water is more or less stagnant and often colored from vegetation, but can be easily clarified for use. Springs are common in the limestone districts, many with large and reasonably dependable flow. The "contact" type of spring is especially important in the northeastern part of the Paris Basin. These springs issue from fissured limestone, interbedded with layers of shale or clay, the latter serving as an impervious base on which the water absorbed from precipitation may accumulate in the fissures and crevices of the overlying rock. Such springs were the most generally used sources of water supply in the Argonne-Meuse Offensive, and also for small hospital and camp supplies in the Advance Section. They were occasionally of sufficient size for railway supply.

Water-bearing river deposits, consisting of porous sand and gravel transported from the highland areas, were deposited in shallow beds along river bottoms. These form an important source of supply where the stream traversing the valley has a permanent flow accessible to the gravels. The method of developing for military purposes was by use of small dug, driven, or drilled wells.

Shattered limestone at the margins of river valleys and in ravine bottoms with shallow water planes, sometimes yielded large quantities of water from shallow dug wells. The success of such a well is a matter of chance, however, due to the local occurrence of fissures. One of these wells at Sorcy Gare, the rail-head for the Tour Sector, produced considerable water.

Deep, water-bearing formations were also an important source in the basin provinces. These consist of porous water-bearing strata lying at various depths below the surface, exceeding 100 ft., from which water may be obtained in considerable quantity from drilled cased wells, either by pumping or by artesian flow. The water-bearing formations have an outcrop along the margins of the basins and are fed by streams flowing from the adjacent highland areas. Water is encountered in drilling at depths of from 200 to 1 000 ft. The yield of a single well is often ample for extensive railway use. The time required for drilling wells precluded their use in the Army Zone, but they were practical for railway purposes. Several flowing artesian wells were drilled by the Water Supply Service at Bassens, the American rail terminal near Bordeaux, and gave an ample supply for railway, ship, and camp use.

These wells were drilled to recognized water-bearing strata. In other locations where wells were drilled without consideration of the geology and in unfavorable locations, either dry holes, or very poor yields, were obtained. The author expresses the opinion that the supply of equipment for indefinite problems is best handled from one large depot, and includes pumps and engines. The writer would also include well-drilling equipment. Obviously, the supply of such equipment must be limited in overseas military operations. The idea is quite commonly held among officers responsible for the location of camps, hospitals, aviation fields, depots, etc., that a water supply can be obtained anywhere by drilling, if sufficient depth is reached. Acting on this concept, requisitions for well-drilling rigs and tools received at Headquarters, soon far exceeded the supply. Investigation of the local geological formations by a trained representative of the Water Service or Geological Section often showed the utter impossibility of securing water by drilling, due to the local geological formation. With such information available, and a system of material control in effect, requisitions for well-drilling equipment could be filled in the order of probability of securing a water supply.

The writer does not agree with the author's first "Conclusion," as he believes that this work could be done more readily and with less duplication by a general office. The same is true of the second "Conclusion," although full co-operation should be maintained, and when only railway requirements are involved, the latter should be given the preference.

The writer wishes to emphasize the desirability of compiling and digesting complete geologic and water resource data for the various countries of the world as a peace-time activity of the General Staff.

William G. Atwood,* M. Am. Soc. C. E. (by letter).—This paper is a valuable addition to the record of the engineering activities of the American Expeditionary Forces and illustrates, as all thoughtful papers must, the woeful waste caused by unpreparedness. The lack of any plans for army organization, which included the engineering and transportation phases of the operations of an overseas army, made necessary the continual re-organization mentioned, until a satisfactory one was developed. The delays and losses of time resulting can be imagined, but must have been experienced to be fully appreciated. They were unavoidable under the conditions. Papers like this will put on record the experiences and needs of the multitudinous services

* Cons. Engr., New York, N. Y.

of a large army in such a way that similar experimenting will not have to be done in the face of an active enemy in the next emergency.

If it had not been for the inspired foresight of Col. Wilgus when he prepared the famous Requisition No. 6 only a short time after the 1st Division landed in France, conditions would have been much worse than they were. That a requisition could be prepared providing for automatic shipment of the enormous number of items required for the construction, operation, and maintenance of the army transportation net based on the number of men in the field was a wonderful piece of work. To have that requisition so complete that it was successfully made the basis for the supply of the transportation needs of the Army during the entire period of hostilities was still more wonderful.

It was unfortunate that the Water Supply Service of the Transportation Corps could not have been organized sooner, since it would have been very helpful had the Section Engineers known what would be needed in the way of roadside water stations; but this condition was no different from those pertaining to the facilities of any other branch of the Army.

The general water supply problem was one of the most serious among the many that had to be solved. There was always apparently water enough to make mud, but little for any other purpose. When the original plans for the development of the St. Nazaire-Montoir Area were submitted by the 17th Engineers (Railway) in October, 1917, the doubtful factor was the water supply.

The Montoir Yard, according to Table 1, would require a new supply of 427 000 gal. per day, but the city, camps, hospitals, and ships were estimated to require 2 500 000 gal. more, with an existing plant in the city furnishing a maximum of 375 000 gal. It was necessary to construct a number of reservoirs, some of them 25 miles away, to secure sufficient storage; and when the water had been impounded the problem of getting it to the point of use was still more serious in view of the lack of pipe and pumps. About 5 miles of 24-in., and 2 or 3 miles of 12-in., pipe were all that could be secured. The final pumping capacity, including boosters, was about 10 000 000 gal. per day. The railroad consumption at the Port of St. Nazaire and Montoir was roughly one-fifth of the total, and while the railroad use was of equal importance with the others it would have been "putting the cart before the horse" to have placed the design and construction of this plant in the hands of the Railroad Water Service, had it been organized at that time.

In the Montoir Area, roughly 2 by 6 miles, where all the construction was in virgin territory, the six railroad water tanks and engine house were supplied from the same mains that served the camps and the new wharf. In the other terminals in Base Section No. 1, Nantes-St. Luce, La Rochelle, La Pallice (later Base Section No. 5), and Saumur, the latter was the only point at which the railroad and other activities were so separated as to make the railroad water supply an individual problem and in that case the solution was simple.

All the roadside water stations were relatively small, but some of them were hard problems because of the difficulty of developing adequate supplies with available equipment and material. Aside from the tanks and water columns they required no material or equipment not common to other water supply installations, and a number of railroad water tanks were used for other purposes.

The theory of army organization does not differ from that of any other well-organized activity. There is complete centralization of authority as to policy and complete decentralization as to execution, but always there is a clear line of authority and responsibility.

The author would change this procedure so far as the water supply organization is concerned, and in this the writer believes he is wrong. The purpose of all activities of an army is to defeat the enemy and the duty of each part of the organization is to carry out the plans of headquarters to this end; for that reason the line of authority and consequent responsibility must be clear. One of the greatest steps for the improvement of conditions relating to construction in the A. E. F. was made when the General Purchasing Board under General Dawes placed the different items of supply in the hands of some one branch of the Army and made it responsible.

The writer believes that the final organization of the construction and operating activities of the A. E. F. was good. The Transportation Corps, Medical Corps, Quartermaster Corps, Air Corps, and others presented their approved plans to the Director of Construction and Forestry, and they were passed along for execution to the Section Engineers, each in his respective Section. The Section Engineer controlled all available labor and supplies in his Section and allocated them in conformity with the priority schedules furnished him. Any other plan is bound to be wasteful of both material and labor, neither of which were or ever will be adequate.

The Engineer of Water Supply, Transportation Corps, should be a specialist and should have adequate assistance, but he, as well as most other specialists, should be Staff Officers. The Section Engineers should have, and did have as far as Base Section No. 1 was concerned, such corresponding staff specialists as were needed. The section organization knows local conditions and, with proper information as to requirements and general design, should be able to construct adequate facilities much more efficiently and with much less waste of labor and material than a number of small independent organizations.

No units were organized for base section work in the A. E. F., but the two most important Base Sections, Nos. 1 and 2, were continually supervised from August, 1917, to the Armistice by the 17th and 18th Engineers (Railway), respectively. The writer believes as a result of his experience as Section Engineer of Base Section No. 1 that organizations of this type are fully competent to supervise installations for all branches of the service once they are informed of the requirements, and that independent individual organizations of specialists are out of place, except as designers or, in Army parlance, staff departments. The use of separate construction organizations and sources of supply for various branches of the Service was tried in the A. E. F. and found wanting.

The writer, therefore, finds himself in disagreement with the author on most of his conclusions. He believes that the Engineer of Water Supply, Transportation Corps, should furnish a statement of the requirements in as much detail as possible. This will reach the Section Engineer with an indication of the desired priority and from that time on the Section Engineer is responsible for furnishing the necessary facilities at the proper time. He knows what labor and material he has or can make available, and it is his business to follow as closely as possible the plans furnished him. At the proper time he must furnish an operating unit that will perform the required service whether or not it conforms to the plans in all respects.

The writer agrees with the author's Conclusion 5, regarding the maintenance and operation of the water stations once they are completed.

The delays on account of the necessity of sending formal communications through channels are very real, but many of them can be avoided by informal conference and agreement. In the A. E. F., work was delayed on account of the necessity for securing approval from the French; but this was not an unreasonable requirement on their part, although it was very trying at times. The writer remembers one case when approval of the plans for an arch dam for a very badly needed hospital water supply was long delayed because of doubt in the minds of the French engineers as to the adequacy of the structure. When they finally authorized the work to go ahead it was with the expressed hope that the Americans would never find it necessary to fill the reservoir. At that very moment there was 10 ft. of water behind the dam and it was rapidly filling.

The matter of army engineering organization is one which all civilian engineers should study because it will be the case in the next war as in the last one that the Reserve Officers will have to furnish the largest proportion of the personnel, and they should have as complete a picture as possible of the requirements and difficulties. Railway water supply is an extremely important item, and this paper very fully and correctly shows its difficulties.

Paul M. LaBach,* M. Am. Soc. C. E. (by letter).—Mr. Lee's discussion contains much information, particularly with reference to a variety of activities concerning water supply for the A. E. F. in France. As he states, the water supply for railways was a special branch. However, he is mistaken in the idea that its activities extended only over the areas of the Service of Supply and Advance Sections. The last railway line taken over by the Transportation Corps before the Armistice, was above Sorcy in the Woevre (Second Army Area). Fig. 2 shows very clearly the areas finally covered. In warfare, rail transportation will always be extended just as far as possible into the combat areas, and, at times, facilities are destroyed. These facilities are linked with others farther back in a manner not always appreciated. The idea that the whole problem is a chain is not generally apparent except as regards track.

One of the plans followed by the writer was to consult French hydraulic engineers, located in Paris (as a rule), and much general information was

* Engr., Water Service, Rock Island Lines, Chicago, Ill.

acquired in that manner. Also, the writer made an extensive trip with a French Major in that line of work in civil life. By this method the Water Supply Department for Transportation kept itself sometimes several months ahead of the information furnished by other Departments in the A. E. F. This was due to the fact that they had nothing in common at many points, and no reason to make any investigations.

The situation as to the numerous different water supply bodies described by Mr. Lee, has no real application to this specific case. It is too general. There is the same situation in peace times. The United States is fairly well covered with hydraulic engineers and State organizations. Much work has been done along these lines, which is available in print or otherwise.

However, practically every large railway system has an engineer of water service and water service organizations on every division. In making investigations, the railway engineer of water service usually has all the published data and much information acquired in years of practice. He uses these just as one should do in an army if there is time to acquire it from co-related departments. In the end, however, he must make his own investigations and decisions, which are based on considerations of railroad operation.

A railway water service engineer does not have to go to the State Engineer of a given area to obtain help either in making investigations or in the construction of facilities. The State Engineer would nearly correspond to the Section Engineer as outlined in the A. E. F. No industry like a railway would dream of such a procedure, on account of the delay, even in time of peace when delay is less important than in time of war.

Organization diagrams are only an index of offices or utilities in their relation to each other. When once made they should not become sacrosanct. Mr. Lee's idea is that "time would undoubtedly have dissolved these difficulties and proved the worth of the type of organizations as formed". That may be true, but the time came only after all the work was finished and nothing was left of urgent importance. The war was over. The object of organization is to aid, particularly when things are beginning and time is of major importance. If, then, it is found that the organization hampers the work the thing to do is to change the former, if the work is efficiently managed.

Mr. Lee's discussion is interesting, but the Water Department of the Transportation Corps probably had a greater collection of general data than any other single organization. However, general information is only an index showing the probable direction for investigation. The writer has refrained from touching on such matters, as it is desired to confine the paper strictly to the subject assigned. The writer heartily concurs in Mr. Lee's statement in regard to wells. The idea is only too prevalent that a well can be put down anywhere.

Judging from his discussion, Mr. Atwood seems to have gained the impression that the writer wishes to change the entire structure of Army organization. The real purpose of the paper was to give a short account of successes and failures under a given set of circumstances. The suggestion of changes in organization was not directed at any other activities than those in his own department.

The Construction Division was decentralized, that is, the Section Engineers were in charge of construction in a given area. This was a territorial subdivision and each sub-division was independent of its neighbor. The water supply for Army railways was under central control, as it could not be handled otherwise. It covered a small area in width, but extended from the Base Ports to the Rhine. In this area, construction, maintenance, and operation were being handled at the same time without a clear line of demarcation between them. To use a railway term, they were "interlocked". To open one line, another had to be closed. The writer's proposal is to put such an area in the same basis as a "Section". This would not change any fundamentals of organization in any manner, but would bring correlated and interlocked activities under one head. This would be similar to actual civil practice so successful for many years.

Armies are organized for combat service, and the attempt is usually made to adapt the same organization to constructive activities. Its very virtues in combat sometimes are hindrances under other circumstances. The question of rank and the authority which goes with it have some bearing. When a new military unit is invented, or borrowed from civil life, it is usual to put somebody, perhaps an expert, in a staff position to take charge of its activities. If it is a large staff, and he desires to get anything done, he must devote much of his energy to getting priorities. Having had many years' experience, the chief of staff will naturally lean toward and favor activities with which he has had personal knowledge. New schemes from civil life, while old subjects to the proponent, are new to him, and so the new staff officer starts with a handicap. In the A. E. F., these debates were called the "Battles of Chaumont, Paris, Tours, Toul", etc.

For this the writer would wish to substitute direct action in the case under discussion. Make the responsibility for results and the authority necessary to secure them co-extensive. It was practically impossible to hold meetings with a scattered organization except at wide intervals. To convince those present of the importance of the work under debate was not always possible. Everybody told a similar tale of woe to the Section Engineers.

As an illustration of the workings of the system the writer recalls two communications of the same day about three weeks before the Armistice. One stated that, because of the failure of a small French water station and the fact that the new station had not been completed, 5 miles of trains loaded with ammunition and other supplies were unable to proceed. The other was from a Section Engineer and contained an argument against doing any work on the reinforcement of a water station because the work would never be needed. The benefit of the experience of one was lost in so far as the other was concerned, although both water stations were integral parts of the same machine.

Observation in two wars and several revolutions makes the writer somewhat skeptical on the subject of staff jobs as a cure for troubles. In the World

War practically every peace-time staff had to be re-organized after hostilities had begun. The French General Staff, while it had wide control of the railways, did not interfere with actual operation, which was conducted by the railway organization from start to finish. These organizations could not expand to help the American Army as they were already short of both men and material. Most of the personnel had had Army service before the war. When it came to a critical situation at one time it was found that results on the P.-L.-M. Railway could be obtained more quickly through its organization and the use of German war prisoners than through any military channels. This was due to the centralized organization in direct contact with daily operations.

Decentralized organizations were much more useful in former times than at present. They grew up out of necessity due to slow methods of communication. At present, with the telegraph, telephone, radio, and aeroplane, the same reason does not exist.

In water supply for military railways, the writer's plea, in railroad parlance, is for grade separation as distinguished from interlocking.

AMERICAN SOCIETY OF CIVIL ENGINEERS
INSTITUTED 1852

TRANSACTIONS

This Society is not responsible for any statement made or opinion expressed in its publications.

Paper No. 1661

THE SHANDAKEN TUNNEL*

By R. W. Gausmann,† M. Am. Soc. C. E.

With Discussion by Messrs. W. W. Brush and Charles Goodman.

Synopsis

The Shandaken Tunnel, extending between Prattsville and Shandaken (mostly in Greene County), N. Y., is about 18 miles in length, the longest yet built. It connects two water-sheds, making the run-off of Schoharie Creek as impounded by the Gilboa Dam on the north available to the Esopus water-shed on the south, already serving the City of New York.

The paper recounts the development of this project and the geology of the region. The actual construction work is covered in detail, both construction shafts and tunnel proper. Drilling, dynamiting, mucking, timbering, and concrete lining operations are described; also mechanical equipment, progress, and costs.

Some special features, such as the use of the concrete gun, organization problems for efficient progress, and transportation, are treated incidentally. Actually, the construction was under way from November, 1917, to October, 1924.

General

The Shandaken Tunnel forms a part of the Catskill Water Supply System of New York City. Its function is to carry water from Schoharie Creek to Esopus Creek, from which the flow is to the Ashokan Reservoir (Fig. 1). The tunnel is 18.1 miles long, being the longest continuous tunnel in the world for any purpose. It is horseshoe-shaped and concrete-lined, with inside dimen-

* Presented at the meeting of June 1, 1927.

† Gen. Mgr., Ulen & Co., Athens, Greece.

sions of 11 ft. 6 in. in height by 10 ft. 3 in. width, and has a uniform slope of 4.4 ft. per mile, except for the northerly 3½ miles which is depressed, making that portion a pressure tunnel. Its capacity, computed as a grade tunnel, is 650 000 000 gal. daily.

The intake is located about 3½ miles north of Prattsville, N. Y. From this point the tunnel extends in a general southeasterly direction to just south of Allaben, N. Y., where it discharges into Esopus Creek. An intake shaft and seven intermediate shafts are provided, the aggregate depth of the shafts being 3 238 lin. ft., the maximum depth of a single shaft being 630 ft. The minimum distance between shafts is 1.3 miles, and the maximum, 2.7 miles. All shafts are circular with a diameter of 14 ft. inside the concrete lining. The upper portion of the intake shaft is so constructed that it will act as a Venturi meter, the building over this shaft containing the control gates and keeper's residence; discussion of the intake and outlet structures is not included in this paper.

Historical

Apparently, the first mention of a tunnel carrying water from Schoharie Creek to Esopus Creek was made in a paper published in the *Scientific American,* of September 4, 1886. Years later, in 1903, a survey was made for such a tunnel by the Commission on Additional Water Supply for New York City (William H. Burr, M. Am. Soc. C. E., the late Rudolph Hering, M. Am. Soc. C. E., and John R. Freeman, Past-President, Am. Soc. C. E.). The first engineering work on this project by the Board of Water Supply of New York City was done in 1907 when a line of levels was run. The surveys from which the final alignment of the tunnel was made, were run in 1916. The contract for construction was let on November 10, 1917, to the Degnon Contracting Company, and all work was completed on October 22, 1924. Thus, a period of 38 years elapsed from the time of the original published proposal to the final completion of the work.

Geology

In the region penetrated by the tunnel the rock was gray sandstone and red and gray shale (red predominating) lying in nearly horizontal layers, the dip being from 2½ to 2° in a southerly direction. The shales drilled easily, broke well to line, and would sometimes stand for a limited time, but they had a marked tendency to disintegrate when exposed to the atmosphere. Of slightly coarser texture, but often difficult to distinguish from the shales, were the red sandstones. Almost invariably the two were more or less mixed, and, when penetrated in the roof of the tunnel, needed support. The gray and blue sandstones, being the hardest and coarsest grained rocks in the vicinity, were more difficult to drill and shoot, but had an advantage in that they required little sealing and generally stood well without support when not too thinly bedded.

During driving the temperature in different parts of the tunnel remained almost constant at 59° Fahr. despite the variation in cover from 200 to 2 200 ft. This constant temperature may have been due to the system of ventila-

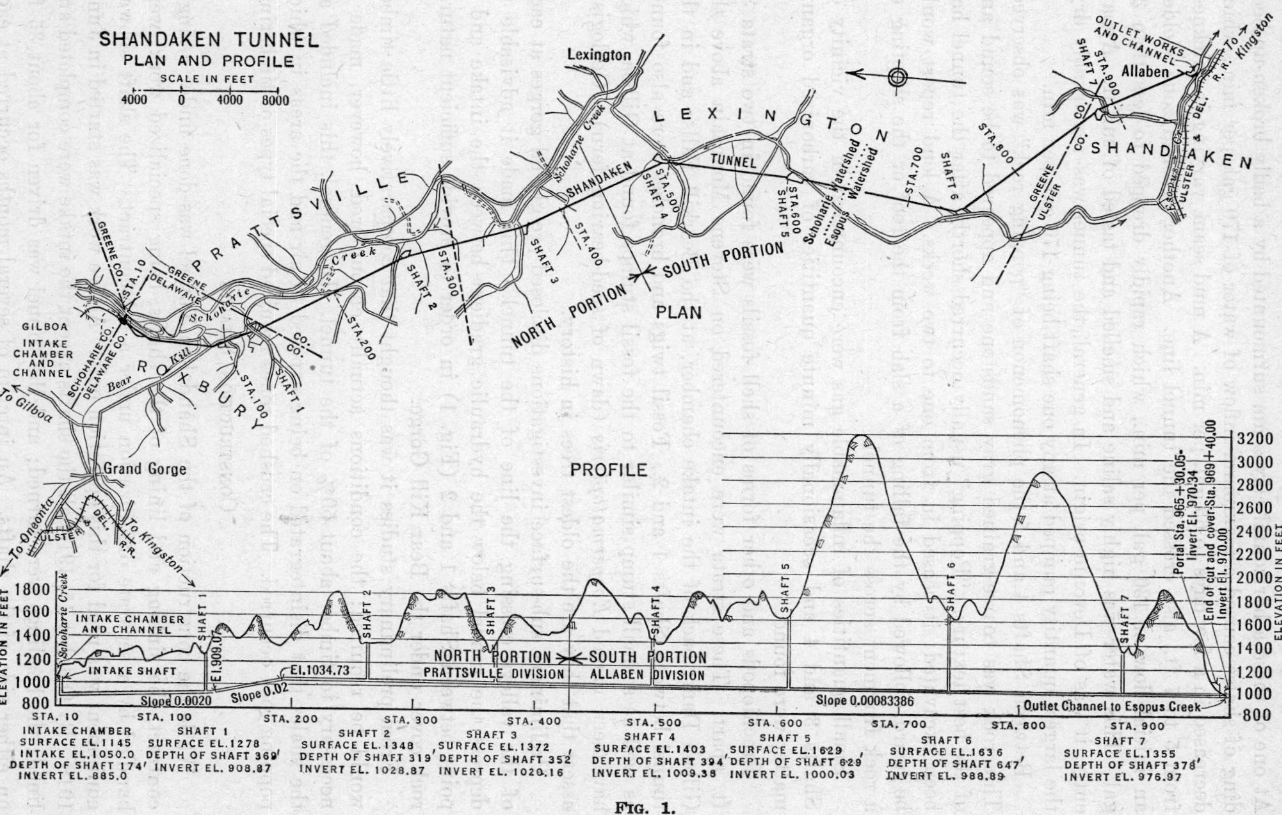
SHANDAKEN TUNNEL
PLAN AND PROFILE
SCALE IN FEET
4000 0 4000 8000
PLAN
PROFILE
GILBOA
INTAKE CHAMBER AND CHANNEL
To Gilboa
Grand Gorge
To Oneonta
To Kingston
ULSTER
DEL. R.R.
Bear Kill
ROXBURY
PRATTSVILLE
LEXINGTON
SHANDAKEN
Lexington
Schoharie Creek
GREENE CO.
SCHOHARIE CO.
DELAWARE CO.
GREENE
DELAWARE
ULSTER
CO.
SHANDAKEN TUNNEL
NORTH PORTION
SOUTH PORTION
Schoharie Watershed
Esopus Watershed
Allaben
OUTLET WORKS AND CHANNEL
To Kingston
R.R.
DEL. & ULSTER
Esopus Cr.
STA. 10
STA. 100
STA. 200
STA. 300
STA. 400
STA. 500
STA. 600
STA. 700
STA. 800
STA. 900
SHAFT 1
SHAFT 2
SHAFT 3
SHAFT 4
SHAFT 5
SHAFT 6
SHAFT 7
ELEVATION IN FEET
INTAKE CHAMBER AND CHANNEL
INTAKE SHAFT
El. 909.07
El. 1034.73
Slope 0.0020
Slope 0.02
Slope 0.00083386
NORTH PORTION
PRATTSVILLE DIVISION
SOUTH PORTION
ALLABEN DIVISION
Outlet Channel to Esopus Creek
Portal Sta. 965+30.05
Invert El. 970.34
End of cut and cover-Sta. 969+40.00
Invert El. 970.00
STA. 10 INTAKE CHAMBER SURFACE EL. 1145 INTAKE EL. 1050.0 DEPTH OF SHAFT 174' INVERT EL. 885.0
SHAFT 1 SURFACE EL. 1278 DEPTH OF SHAFT 369' INVERT EL. 908.87
SHAFT 2 SURFACE EL. 1348 DEPTH OF SHAFT 319' INVERT EL. 1028.87
SHAFT 3 SURFACE EL. 1372 DEPTH OF SHAFT 352' INVERT EL. 1020.16
SHAFT 4 SURFACE EL. 1403 DEPTH OF SHAFT 394' INVERT EL. 1009.38
SHAFT 5 SURFACE EL. 1629 DEPTH OF SHAFT 629 INVERT EL. 1000.03
SHAFT 6 SURFACE EL. 1636 DEPTH OF SHAFT 647' INVERT EL. 988.89
SHAFT 7 SURFACE EL. 1355 DEPTH OF SHAFT 378' INVERT EL. 976.97
800
1000
1200
1400
1600
1800
2000
2200
2400
2600
2800
3000
3200

FIG. 1.

tion. Several crush zones were encountered between Shafts 3 and 4 (Fig. 1). At one of these a horizontal clay seam surmounted by a badly broken-up bedding of shales caused a maximum inflow of water of 170 gal. per min., which decreased in a few days to 65 gal. per min. A mud seam, varying in thickness from 5 to 7 ft., also crossed the tunnel line. Another crushed zone yielded an initial flow of 130 gal. per min., which rapidly dropped to less than 30 gal. This water was highly saline and smelled and tasted of sulfur. Apparently, it was of Devonic origin. In general, the tunnel was remarkably dry, the largest quantity pumped at any one shaft being 170 gal. per min.

Between Shafts 4 and 5 the phenomenon of "popping rock" was observed. This rock was coarse-grained gray sandstone and appeared to be sound and of the best texture. "Popping" usually occurred shortly after the tunnel had been excavated; it ceased in from one to two weeks. A loud report would be heard, followed by the falling of a slab from the roof or the shooting of a rock fragment across the tunnel.

Small quantities of inflammable gas were encountered in the vicinity of Shafts 3 and 4 and occasionally minute quantities of carbonized organic matter were found.

Brachiopods and other forms of shell fossils were found in two strata 30 ft. apart. These strata were encountered on Stevens Mountain above the Gilboa Dam; back of the intake chamber, at the Bearkill Falls; and in the tunnel between Shafts 1 and 2. Fossil twigs and branches were also found, as well as a small stump similar to the fossil stumps found at Gilboa, which have been named *Eospermatopteris* (dawn of seed-bearing fern). Geologists assert that they are the oldest trees in history.

Preliminary sub-surface investigations disclosed pre-glacial gorges at each of the valleys crossing the line of the tunnel. This made it advisable to depress the tunnel below the hydraulic gradient between the intake and a point between Shafts 1 and 2 (Fig. 1) in order to provide sufficient natural rock cover under the Bear Kill Gorge.

From preliminary studies it was thought that comparatively little timber would be required; the conditions actually encountered, however, made it necessary to timber about 50% of the tunnel. In general, this included all the shales that disintegrated on being exposed to air and the areas in which popping rock occurred. The crushed zones required special types of timbering.

Construction Shafts

While the construction of the Shandaken Tunnel was done under a single contract, the sinking and lining of the shafts, being specialized work, were handled by a separate organization under a sub-contract. The shaft subway equipment was used for this operation only. Active work was started in June, 1918. By October 15, 1919, all the shafts except the intake were completed and lined; the headings were turned; and the tunnel was driven for about 35 ft. on either side of the shafts. An interim of several months occurred at each shaft before tunnel driving, using regular tunnel equipment, was started.

In general, the method of sinking the shafts was to excavate the earth cover by hand, using a derrick. When this part had been timbered (in some cases, concreted), a light temporary head-frame was set up and the remainder of the shaft was sunk and lined.

In all, 24 521 cu. yd. of rock and 1 066 cu. yd. of earth were excavated for shafts. The actual volume of excavation in rock per linear foot of shaft was 7.65 cu. yd.; and the payment volume, 8.01 cu. yd.

The general method of drilling and shooting is shown in Fig. 2 and Tables 1 and 2. At some of the shafts the relief holes were omitted; this reduced the amount of drilling, also of powder, and gave equally good results.

There was a considerable variation at the different shafts in the number of holes drilled per round, in the depth of holes, and in the quantity of powder used. These variations were frequently due more to the superintendent than to the character of the rock. In general, the number of holes varied from 30 to 38, the linear foot of hole per cubic yard of excavation from 5.3 to 6.5, and the powder from 1.3 to 3.2 lb. per cu. yd. The "pull" per round was between 5 and 8 ft.

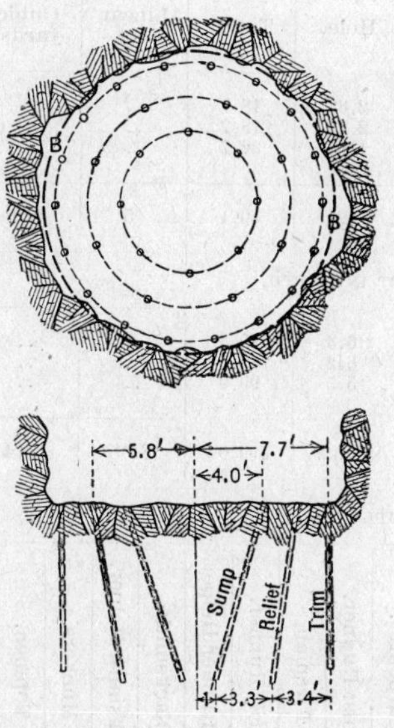

DRILLS USED

MAKE	DIAM. OF STEEL	DIAM. OF BIT	LENGTH	REMARKS
Ingersoll Jack Hammer Drills	7/8"	1 3/4"	2' to 3'	Starters
	7/8"	1 1/2"	5'	
	7/8"	1 1/4"	8' to 10"	

Note:- 60% dynamite was used in sticks 8" x 1" diam., weighing ½ lb.

All holes drilled before any shooting or mucking done.

See Tables 1, 2 and 3 for added data.

SHANDAKEN TUNNEL
SHAFT EXCAVATION IN ROCK
METHOD OF DRILLING & SHOOTING

Fig. 2.

Supplementing the other data, Table 3 gives a more detailed analysis of excavation at Shafts 4 and 5. The variable in these two shafts was the percentage of shale. The shale drilled more easily and broke better, otherwise conditions at both shafts were about the same, and the difference in progress may be attributed to the difference in plant, that at Shaft 5 being much better than that at Shaft 4.

When any appreciable quantity of water was encountered in sinking the shafts, holes were drilled and grouted to shut off the flow. For example, while drilling a round of holes between Elevation 1 254 and 1 247 at Shaft 4, the flow of water, which had been no greater than 3 gal. per min., suddenly increased to 18 gal. per min. The sump was thoroughly cleaned and eleven equally spaced holes, as near the outer side of the excavation as possible, were drilled 9 ft. deep, pointing outward so that the lower ends were 3 ft. outside the ordinary limits of excavation. Pipes were wedged tightly into the holes and 68 cu. ft. of liquid grout, in the proportion of 9 gal. of water to 1 bag of cement, was forced in by means of a Canniff tank under a pressure of 70 lb. The flow practically stopped for the time being, but it broke out after mucking had reached Elevation 1 236. Five horizontal holes were then drilled 3 ft. deep in a seam at Elevation 1 244. Through these, 14 cu. ft. of grout was forced at 70 lb. pressure. This effectually stopped the leak.

TABLE 1.—PRATTSVILLE DIVISION—DRILLING AND SHOOTING DATA.

Description.	Order of shooting.	Number of holes.	Depth, in feet.	Linear feet of holes.	Powder Used, in Pounds.		Average Pull per Round.		Powder used, in pounds, per cubic yard of excavation.
					Hole.	Total.	Linear feet.	Cubic yards.	
Holes, 7 Feet in Depth.									
Sump....	1	8	7	56	2.33	18.7	..	..	..
Relief....	2	8	7	56	2.33	18.7	..	..	..
Trim.....	3	18	6	108	1.82	32.7	..	..	..
Totals..	..	34	..	220	..	70.1	5	39.6	1.77
Holes, 10 Feet in Depth.									
Sump....	1	8	10	80	6.3	50.4	..	..	..
Relief....	2	8	10	80	6.2	49.6	..	..	..
Trim.....	3	18	9	162	5.5	99.0	..	..	..
Totals..	..	34	..	322	..	199.0	8.0*	63.4	3.15

FORCE EMPLOYED.

Shift.	Class of work.	Superintendent.	Shift Boss.	Mechanic.	Carpenter.	Hoist Runner.	Fireman.	Drill Runner.	Drill Runner Helper.	Blacksmith.	Blacksmith Helper.	Muckers.	Topmen.	Laborers.	Timekeeper.	Total.
12:00 M. to 8:00 A. M....	Drilling†...	..	1	..	..	1	1	3	3	..	..	..	1	2	..	12
8:00 A. M. to 4:00 P. M..	Mucking...	1	1	1	1	1	1	..	..	1	1	5	1	4	1	19
4:00 P. M. to 12:00 M....	Drilling†...	1	1	..	..	1	1	3	3	..	..	..	1	2	..	13
Totals..............	....	2	3	1	1	3	3	6	6	1	1	5	3	8	1	44

* Not obtained at first shooting, it generally being necessary to blow out butts, reload, and fire a second time. This accounts for excessive use of powder.

† When drilling is finished before end of shift, drillers complete shift as muckers.

After the shaft had been excavated to a depth of from 100 to 300 ft., depending on the character of the rock, it was lined with concrete starting from the bottom and working up. Simple, metal-covered, wooden forms were used, 5 ft. high in four 90° sections, with a key. Concrete was mixed at the top of the shaft, lowered in a bucket, and dumped on a platform from which it was shoveled into the forms.

This mix was in the proportion 1:2.33:4.67, a bag of cement being estimated as 0.905 cu. ft., and no correction being made for swell in the aggregate due to moisture. The cement factor for concrete placed in the shafts averaged 1.57 bbl. per cu. yd. Fine aggregate came from local pits or crusher screenings; coarse aggregate was either crushed sandstone from the excavation or crushed field stone from neighboring stone walls. Grout was forced behind the lining at all water-bearing seams, by the method already explained.

TABLE 2.—ALLABEN DIVISION—DRILLING AND SHOOTING DATA.
(Compiled by averaging data from Shafts 4, 5, 6, and 7.)

Description.	Order of shooting.	Number of holes.	Depth, in feet.	Linear feet of holes.	Powder Used, in Pounds.		Average Pull per Round.		Powder used, in pounds, per cubic yard of excavation.
					Hole.	Total.	Linear feet.	Cubic yards.	
Sump	1	9	8½	76½	5—	43	....	....	....
Relief	2	9	8	72	5—	42	....	....	....
Trim	3	17	8	136	4+	70	....	....	....
Totals	....	35	....	284½	....	155	6.4	51±	3.04

FORCE EMPLOYED.

Shift.	Class of work.	Superintendent.	Shift Boss.	Mechanic.	Carpenter.	Hoist Runner.	Fireman.	Drill Runner.	Drill Runner Helper.	Blacksmith.	Blacksmith Helper.	Muckers.	Topmen.	Laborers.	Timekeeper.	Total.
12:00 M. to 8:00 A. M.	Drilling*	..	1	..	..	1	1	2	..	..	..	4	3	..	..	12
8:00 A. M. to 4:00 P. M.	Mucking	1	1	1	..	1	1	2	..	1	1	4	3	..	1	17
4:00 P. M. to 12:00 M.	Drilling*	1	1	..	..	1	1	2	..	..	..	4	3	..	..	13
Totals	....	2	3	1	..	3	3	6	..	1	1	12	9	..	1	42

* When drilling is finished before end of shift, drillers complete shift as muckers.

The average progress for all shafts was 1.1 ft. per shift; and for lining, 6.1 ft. The average progress for sinking and lining was 8.3 ft. per week.

The plant at each shaft included a compressor with a capacity of from 275 to 528 cu. ft. of free air per min.; three to six jack-hammer drills; a hoisting engine; a crushing and screening plant; a boiler or boilers aggregating from 50 to 100 h.p.; a ½-yd. concrete mixer; a generator of from 2 to 3¾ kw.; and trucks and teams.

Small camps were built at each shaft and enlarged before tunnel driving started; these will be described later.

TABLE 3.—Details of Work at Shafts 4 and 5.

Item.	Shaft 4.	Shaft 5.
Character of rock:		
Percentage of shale	25	52
Percentage of sandstone	75	48
Progress:		
Date started	October 21	January 2
Date finished	February 4	February 18
Time consumed, in days	107	48
Dimensions:		
Elevation, top, in feet	1 389	1 418
Elevation, bottom, in feet	1 140	1 236
Depth, in feet	249	182
Quantities:		
Payment, in cubic yards	±2 023	±1 441
Actual, in cubic yards	±1 915	±1 283
Percentage, excess of actual	6	12
Excavation per day:		
In linear feet	2.3	3.8
In cubic yards	18	27
Sump:		
Number of holes	± 10	± 11
Depth, in feet	± 8.5	9.5
Radius, in feet	5	6
Charge, in sticks of dynamite	85	113
Relief:		
Number of holes	± 10	*
Depth, in feet	± 8.5	......
Radius, in feet	6.33	......
Charge, in sticks of dynamite	85	......
Trimming:		
Number of holes	± 18	± 18
Depth, in feet	± 8	8
Radius, in feet	7.58	7.67
Charge, in sticks of dynamite	144	133
Round:		
Number of holes	± 38	30
Depth of excavation, in feet	6 to 7	7
Charge, in sticks of dynamite	314	246

* Only one set of relief holes was drilled. This round consisted of 8 holes, each 8 ft. deep; 80 sticks of dynamite were used.

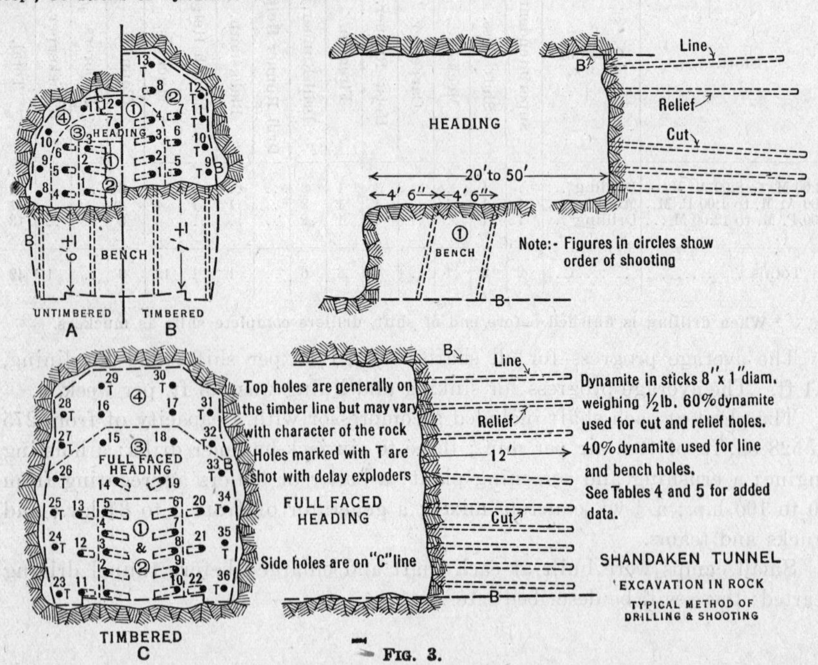

Fig. 3.

Tunnel Construction

The tunnel was driven both ways from all shafts except Shaft 2 (Fig. 1). A short length of tunnel was driven from the outlet, in earth, but none from the intake.

In general, three methods of driving were used: The top heading, the full-face heading, and the bottom heading. In sound rock most of the tunnel was driven with a top heading with a bench from 40 to 50 ft. long. In the earlier stages of the work the bottom heading was used, but this was abandoned later, when the work encountered unsound rock, which seemed better adapted to the full-face heading. In unsound rock, where support was required up to the face, the full-face heading, combined with a mechanical mucker, permitted the most satisfactory progress.

Details of the average methods used in these two types of driving are shown on Fig. 3 and in Tables 4 and 5. Vertical columns for supporting the drills were used in both methods.

Drills.—In the headings Ingersoll-Rand water Leyner drills No. 248 were used, and on the bench, Jap drills, B. C. R. No. 430. After numerous tests the six-point, or rose, bit was adopted. This bit has a flat taper for a short distance back from the face, which prevents the points from breaking. After each round the drill steel was sharpened with a special machine. The drills were carried back from the heading, taken apart, cleaned and greased, and made ready for the next round. As it was found difficult to make the drillers keep their machines oiled, a 1-gal. oil cup was placed on the air-line and regulated in such a manner that a predetermined quantity of oil would be fed to the drills with the air. An expert drill man spent his entire time going from shaft to shaft, inspecting and repairing the drills so that they might be kept at maximum efficiency.

Scaling was done after each shot and at regular intervals throughout the length of the untimbered tunnel. Except for that done immediately after blasting, little was necessary.

Trimming.—Once a week the trimming was determined and marked. In general, the tunnel was kept trimmed at all times well toward the heading and down to 1 ft. above the invert grade.

Muck.—In the top-heading method, muck was shoveled into wheel-barrows, wheeled along a runway supported on pipes extending across the tunnel, and dumped into muck cars—Sanford end dumpers—holding about 1 cu. yd. of solid rock. Trains of six or seven cars were hauled to the shaft; cars were taken up singly to the tipple and dumped into Western 4-yd. dump cars, which were pushed to the dump by electric locomotives. Each shaft was equipped with two cages so that when a full car was going up an empty one was going down.

The tunnel locomotives were of the storage battery type, the greater number being General Electric, 4-ton capacity, 30-in. gauge, with a drawbar pull of 1 000 lb., a speed of 5 to 6 miles per hour, and a voltage of 85 to 125. The batteries were readily detachable, extra ones being kept in the tunnel, where they were charged.

TABLE 4.—DRILLING AND SHOOTING DATA, ROCK TUNNEL (SEE FIG. 3).

	Description.	Location.			Number of Holes.			Depth of Holes, in Feet.			Linear Feet of Holes.			Number of columns.	Number of Drills.			Average Time to Drill, in Hours.			Feet Drilled per Hour.			Pounds of Powder Used. Hole.			Pounds of Powder Used. Total.			Average Pull per Round. Linear feet			Average Pull per Round. Cubic yards.			Pounds of powder used per cubic yard of excavation.		
		A.	B.	C.	A.	B.	C.	A.	B.	C.	A.	B.	C.		A.	B.	C.	A.	B.	C.	A.	B.	C.	A.	B.	C.	A.	B.	C.	A.	B.	C.	A.	B.	C.	A.	B.	C.
Heading.	Cut...	1 to 3	1 to 4	5 to 10	6	8	10	13	12	12	78	96	120	2	....	....	....	....	....	....	....	....	....	14.9	11.4	8.1	80	91	81	....	....	....	....	....	....	....	....	....
Heading.	Relief.	4 to 7	5 to 8	11 to 22	7	8	12	12	11	12	84	88	144	2	....	....	....	....	....	....	....	....	....	6.3	7.6	6.3	44	61	88	....	....	....	....	....	....	....	....	....
Heading.	Line..	8 to 12	9 to 13	23 to 35	9	10	14	12	10	12	108	100	168	2	....	....	....	....	....	....	....	....	....	7.2	7.7	6.0	65	77	84	....	....	....	....	....	....	....	....	....
Heading.	Total....	....	....	....	22	26	36	....	....	....	270	284	432	2	4	4	6	3.0	3.1	3.1	22.5	22.9	23.2	....	....	....	198	229	253	10.2	8.7	9.8	33.3	32.5	65.3	5.9	7.0	3.9
Bench	Untimbered, A....				8			7½			60			....	2			4			7.5			5.9			47.2			8.6			22.7			2.1		
Bench	Timbered, B......				8			9			72			....	2			4.2			8.6			6.1			48.8			8.5			24.6			2.0		

TABLE 5.—TYPICAL FORCE EMPLOYED FOR ONE SHIFT, ROCK TUNNEL.

Class of work.	Superintendent.	Walker.	Timekeeper.	Janitor.	Electrician.	Mechanic.	Pipeman.	Hoist Runner.	Compressor Engineer.	Motorman.	Brakeman.	Signal Man.	Dumpman.	Blacksmith.	Blacksmith, Helper.	Muck Boss.	Muckers.	Muck Machine Operator.	Heading Boss.	Drill Runner.	Drill Runner, Helper.	Powder Man.	Nipper.	Track Boss.	Track Man.	Timber Boss.	Timber Man.	Timber Helper.	Top Man.	Total.	Location.
General.........	1	1	1	1	1	1	2	1	1	1	..	2	1	1	1	..	..	..	..	..	..	..	..	..	..	..	..	..	2	18	Two headings
Mucking.........	..	..	..	..	..	..	..	..	..	2	1	2	..	..	..	1	25	*	..	..	..	..	..	..	..	..	..	..	..	31	One heading
Drilling.........	..	..	..	..	..	..	..	..	..	..	..	..	..	..	..	..	..	..	1	6	6	1	1	..	..	..	..	..	..	15	One heading
Timbering......	..	..	..	..	..	..	..	..	..	..	..	..	..	..	..	..	..	..	..	..	..	..	..	..	..	1	3	2	..	6	One heading
Track gang.....	..	..	..	..	..	..	..	..	..	..	..	..	..	..	..	..	..	..	..	..	..	..	..	1	6	..	..	..	..	7	Two headings

* Where mucking machine is in operation only two muckers and one mucker machine operator are employed.

For the full-face heading a Myers-Whaley mucking machine was used to load the cars. This lifted the muck on to a traveling belt which emptied into the muck car. As each car was loaded it was placed on a near-by siding until the whole train was loaded.

Support.—It was a difficult matter to decide, in advance of excavation, the type of timbering that would best suit the conditions. In general, the ground did not develop heavy pressure, as evidenced by the rather wide (7½-ft.) spacing of arch ribs; yet when allowed to stand for a considerable period, the rock frequently disintegrated and "reeded". The use of temporary timber at such a place would have necessitated considerable additional excavation preparatory to placing concrete. This work is slow and expensive; and interferes greatly with lining operations. It was the rule to place permanent timber wherever the roof was in soft red shale, or in thinly bedded sandstones, or where "popping rock" occurred. Where support was needed merely to protect men from the small thin slabs that fell, temporary timber was placed. About 570 cu. yd. of rock, or an average of 0.1 cu. yd. per lin. ft., was removed with the temporary timber. This was not evenly distributed; where the temporary support was replaced with a permanent one the amount was greatly in excess of this average.

The usual type of support was a three-piece arch rib of 10 by 10-in. timbers, spaced 7½ ft., center to center, with 3 or 4-in. lagging. It was supported on each side on a short 3-in. plate resting on three 1¼-in. steel pins, 24 in. long, set 18 in. in the rock. From four to seven 2 by 10-in. planks (known as "lacing") were spiked to the under side of the arch ribs to provide lateral support. Extra lacing was placed near the heading to protect the timber.

The same type of construction was used for both temporary and permanent timber (Fig. 4), the permanent timber being placed above the normal concrete lining while the temporary timber was lower. The space between the permanent timber and the roof of the tunnel was packed with rock. Ordinarily, temporary timber was left without packing, but in case of high breakage cordwood was used.

Lumber for crown pieces, lagging, and lacing was cut to dimensions in the Allaben Yard. A special device made it possible to measure the length of legs accurately in the tunnel and then cut them on top, thus saving labor and transportation. The timber used was miscellaneous hard and soft woods. All varieties showed a marked tendency to decay; and much of it that had been in place for two or three years was punky and lifeless. Due to this, some bents fell and others had to have supplementary supports for the lagging. At other places the lagging failed. In all, thirty-one bents were replaced or supplemented. While this is a very minute percentage of the total number of bents, it certainly shows that it is not safe to rely on timber support for too long a time.

Progress of Timbering.—Approximately 3 083 000 ft. B. M. of lumber was placed in the permanent support and 363 000 ft. B. M. in the temporary support. About 6 700 lin. ft., or 7% of the length of the tunnel, was driven with the temporary support. Approximately 1 000 lin. ft. of this was later replaced with permanent timber; this, with the 38 950 lin. ft. driven as a permanently supported type, gave a total length of 45 650 lin. ft. of timbered tunnel, or 47.7% of the total length.

The force on the timbering included 1 carpenter and 2 laborers cutting on top of the shaft; and 1 foreman, 3 carpenters, and 4 laborers erecting in the tunnel. This gang could make an average progress of 20 lin. ft. completely erected and dry-packed in 8 hours.

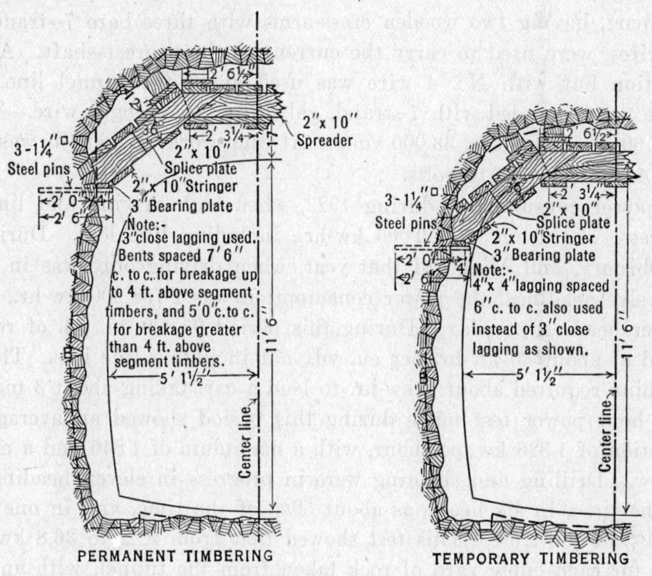

Fig. 4.—Standard Timber Roof Support, Shandaken Tunnel.

Explosives.—Various well-known brands of explosives were tried. Finally, Dupont gelatine low-freezing dynamite was adopted, as this appeared to give the smallest amount of objectionable fumes. A special wrapper, developed by the powder manufacturer for use on this job, was very effective in reducing objectionable fumes. A saving was effected by using 60% dynamite for cut holes and 40% for all others. A slight saving was also effected by having the size of the sticks slightly reduced, as the loader measured his charge by the number of sticks and not by weight. In general, cut holes had to be fired more than once and occasionally three times on account of the depth.

Dupont electric blasting caps (No. 8) fired from a switch on the electric circuit, were used for exploders. First delay exploders were used for line holes. Some second delay exploders were tried, but for various reasons were finally discarded. A small amount of shooting was done with a fuse, using No. 6 fuse caps for exploders. This burned at the rate of 1 ft. per min. Two men lit the fuse, one on each side of the face. Two reasons for not using fuse more generally were the lack of experienced men and the improvement of delay exploders.

Tamping material consisted of crusher screenings or natural sand put up in paper bags 12 in. long and $\frac{1}{14}$ in. in diameter. Brass or copper pipe was used to blow out holes that had once been loaded.

Storage for 400 to 10 000 lb. of explosives was provided at each shaft in specially constructed magazines, built to conform to the rules of the State Industrial Code. There was also a small magazine near the shaft head for storage between loading periods.

Power.—Electric power was purchased from outside sources. This involved the construction of 48 miles of line. Wooden poles, 35 to 50 ft. long, spaced 150 ft. apart, having two wooden cross-arms with three bare 7-strand, No. 1 copper wires, were used to carry the current to the nearest shaft. A similar construction but with No. 4 wire was used along the tunnel line. Every fifth pole was grounded with 7-strand, galvanized, messenger wire. The current was 60-cycle, 3-phase, 33 000 volts. At each working point it was stepped down to 440, 220, and 110 volts.

The power consumption during 1922, when both driving and lining was in progress, was about 11 700 000 kw-hr., including line loss. During January, February, and March of that year, when driving only was in progress in all twelve headings, the power consumption was 2 758 000 kw-hr., or 2 554 kw-hr. per heading per day. During this period 95 000 cu. yd. of rock were excavated at about 30 kw-hr. per cu. yd., not including line loss. The mucking machine required about 1 kw-hr. to load a car, taking about 3 min.

A 71-hour power test made during this period showed an average power consumption of 1 328 kw. per hour, with a maximum of 1 840 and a minimum of 960 kw. Drilling and shooting were in progress in eleven headings about 5% of the time, in six headings about 50% of the time, and in one heading about 90% of the time. This test showed that from 22.2 to 36.8 kw-hr. was required for each cubic yard of rock taken from the tunnel, with an average of 27.3 kw-hr.

Ventilation.—The plenum process was used. A Connersville blower with a capacity of 2.77 cu. ft. of free air per rev., was driven by an electric motor at speeds sufficient to supply from 900 to 1 200 cu. ft. of compressed air at from 7 to 10 lb. pressure. The air was conveyed down the shaft by an 8-in. pipe and through the tunnel in a 6-in. steel well-casing about $\frac{1}{8}$ in. thick, weighing 11.65 lb. per ft. and supported on rods driven into the sides of the tunnel about 5 ft. above the invert.

The pipe was made with Dresser joints. This joint is flexible, requires no threading, and permits the use of comparatively thin pipe; it is quickly and easily repaired or replaced. During the shooting period, and for a short time afterward, the 4-in. air-line used for drilling, was opened at the heading. This helped to clear the heading rapidly and drive the smoke cloud toward the shaft. Generally speaking, the ventilation was satisfactory except that smoke clouds occasionally interfered with alignment work in the longer headings.

Compressed Air.—Two compressors, each rated at 750 cu. ft. of free air per min., and electric-driven, furnished air for the drills. A 4-in. steel well-casing, weighing 6.06 lb. per ft., and suspended on rods driven in the side of the tunnel, carried the air to the heading. This pipe was also made with Dresser joints. Air was furnished to the drills at about 90 lb., varying with the length of the tunnel. A manifold at the end of the line served the drills. There was always sufficient compressed air.

Pumpage.—Water was either drained by gravity or was pumped by air or electricity to a sump at the foot of the shaft, whence it was pumped to the surface. A typical installation for this was a Gould triplex, 5 by 8-in. pump, rated at 120 gal. per min., driven by an electric motor delivering water to the sump; and a Cameron pump with a 5-in. water cylinder, 10-in. air cylinder by 13-in. stroke, rated at 125 gal. per min., raising it to the surface. At the top of the shaft the water was measured over a V-notch weir equipped with an automatic recording gauge. The inflow of water was never great enough to influence progress, the maximum in any heading being 170 gal., and the minimum, 7 gal., per min. The total pay pumpage was 162 545 000 000 ft.-gal.

Illumination.—A 220-volt current was used for lighting the shaft and tunnel, the spoil area, and parts of the camp. The current was carried into the tunnel by three No. 0000-gauge cables supported on pins driven in the side of the tunnel about 8 ft. above the track. Attached to these cables from 40 to 50 ft. apart were 50-watt lamps. Within a few hundred feet of the heading the voltage was reduced to 110 by a small portable transformer; a portable cable, No. 12 gauge, carried current for lights in the heading.

Progress.—In general, some work was in progress throughout the 24 hours. Two methods were used. In one, the drilling and mucking shifts overlapped four hours and two advances were made in a heading each day; in the other, known as the swing shift, two advances were made in the north heading and one in the south on one day, and one advance was made in the north heading and two in the south on the next day. A law preventing men from working more than 8 hours per day was in force until May 25, 1923.

In all, 613 668 cu. yd. of rock were excavated in the tunnel. The quantities of excavation, in cubic yards per linear foot, for the two principal types of tunnel, were, as given in Table 6.

TABLE 6.

Quantities.	Unsupported.	Supported.
Theoretical	5.71	6.61
Actual	6.09	6.91

The unsettled condition affecting the country generally, as a result of the World War, had its effect on the progress of the work and the cost to the contractor. On November 11, 1920, the Degnon Contracting Company made an assignment to the Shandaken Tunnel Corporation for which the active agent was the Ulen Contracting Corporation. At the time the contract was assigned the work was approximately a year behind schedule. The job, however, had been well equipped by the Degnon Contracting Company.

With new capital and efficient management the new organization succeeded in overcoming the time handicap and completed the underground work four months ahead of schedule. This is shown effectively on Fig. 5, which indicates the rates of progress for the principal items. The excavation by years is given in Table 7.

The average monthly progress of excavation per heading, including the time when, for various reasons, work was not in progress, was 280 ft. In headings, where work was more nearly continuous, the average progress with two drilling and two mucking shifts was about 417 ft. per month, with a maximum of 612 ft. The average "pull" per round in the various headings varied from 7.5 to 10 ft.

Bonus.—During 1921 the contractor worked out a bonus system which was successful in reducing costs and increasing progress. A bonus was given the superintendent and walking bosses at each shaft, provided the costs per cubic yard of excavation were decreased below a fixed figure. Likewise for each shaft, the drilling foreman whose gang made the highest average "pull" per shot for the week received a bonus, while a similar bonus was distributed to the gang in proportion to their pay.

TABLE 7.—PROGRESS IN EXCAVATING SHANDAKEN TUNNEL.

Year.	Progress, in linear feet.	Remarks.
1919........	1 095	Shaft sinking completed and tunnel excavation started October 27 at one point.
1920........	12 041	Contract assigned November 11.
1921........	47 363	Steady acceleration of progress.
1922........	33 435	All but one heading "holed through" during year.
1923........	1 134	Finished excavation February 13.

The effect of this bonus on progress was very marked. Before installing the system the average "pull" was 7.5 ft. Three weeks after the bonus had gone into effect the average "pull" had increased to 8.18 ft. and within five months it had reached 9.34 lin. ft.

Earth Tunnel.—At the south end the roof of the tunnel for 534 lin. ft. was in earth. At the junction with the rock the earth was a compact mass of clay, sand, and boulders, with little or no water. No difficulty was experienced in driving this part of the tunnel.

The support for the earth part of the tunnel driven from Shaft 7 was a 5-bar arch, 5 ft. on centers, supported on wall-plates. The methods of excavation were similar to those used in rock including, to some extent, the use of light charges of explosives. The advance was made with a top heading kept from 10 to 70 ft. ahead of the bench. About 240 ft. was successfully driven in this manner. However, as the heading advanced pockets of blue clay were encountered and, later, the material changed to a saturated mixture of clay, sand, and gravel of the consistency of wet concrete. Driving became difficult and the full heading was abandoned; wall-plate drifts, or a center drift, or a combination of both, were substituted. The spacing of bents was

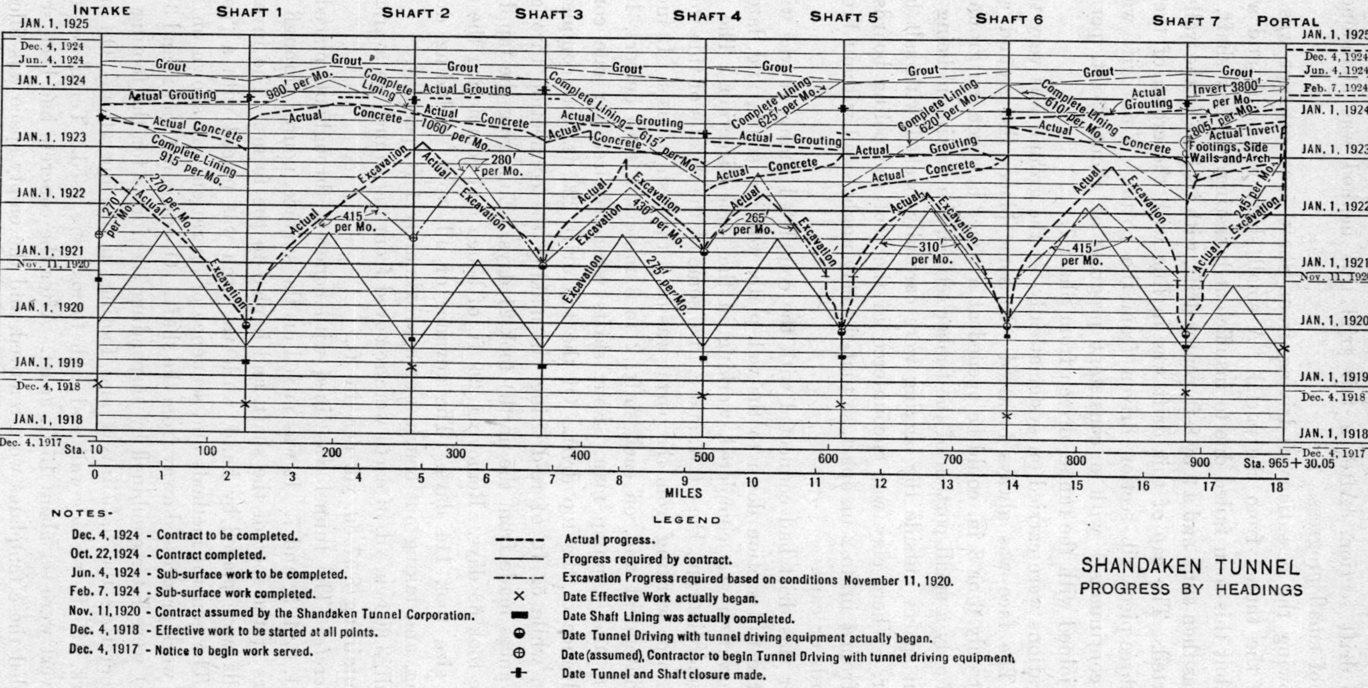
SHANDAKEN TUNNEL
PROGRESS BY HEADINGS
INTAKE
SHAFT 1
SHAFT 2
SHAFT 3
SHAFT 4
SHAFT 5
SHAFT 6
SHAFT 7
PORTAL
MILES
Sta. 10
Sta. 965+30.05
JAN. 1, 1925
Dec. 4, 1924
Jun. 4, 1924
Feb. 7, 1924
JAN. 1, 1924
JAN. 1, 1923
JAN. 1, 1922
JAN. 1, 1921
Nov. 11, 1920
JAN. 1, 1920
JAN. 1, 1919
Dec. 4, 1918
JAN. 1, 1918
Dec. 4, 1917
NOTES-
Dec. 4, 1924 - Contract to be completed.
Oct. 22,1924 - Contract completed.
Jun. 4, 1924 - Sub-surface work to be completed.
Feb. 7, 1924 - Sub-surface work completed.
Nov. 11,1920 - Contract assumed by the Shandaken Tunnel Corporation.
Dec. 4, 1918 - Effective work to be started at all points.
Dec. 4, 1917 - Notice to begin work served.
LEGEND
Actual progress.
Progress required by contract.
Excavation Progress required based on conditions November 11, 1920.
Date Effective Work actually began.
Date Shaft Lining was actually oompleted.
Date Tunnel Driving with tunnel driving equipment actually began.
Date (assumed), Contractor to begin Tunnel Driving with tunnel driving equipment.
Date Tunnel and Shaft closure made.

Fig. 5.

reduced to 3 ft. and then to 2 and 1½ ft. Breasting was necessary for the full drift section. After a fair trial this method was abandoned on account of small progress.

Following the cessation of driving from Shaft 7 an attempt was made to drive the tunnel from the portal. A small shaft was sunk and a drift started, but this soon failed due to insufficient breasting. A new shaft, 16 by 16 ft., was then sunk and a 9 by 8-ft. center drift, with its base at the wall-plate, was started. The cap of this drift was in line with the crown of the completed three-piece rib section driven from the portal. This drift was advanced continuously with a consistent progress of about 25 ft. per week until it joined with the tunnel driven from Shaft 7.

Operations were carried on systematically, as the ground was very treacherous. The face was always breasted. In some places the ground was so bad that only 6 or 8 in. could be opened at a time; however, no ground was lost and only a small portion of the timber settled, the maximum being 4½ in. All open spaces outside the lagging were carefully packed with salt hay or excelsior. Where clay was encountered in the roof the poling boards were spaced from ¼ in. to 2 in. apart, so that the clay might swell without breaking the boards or caps.

After this drift had connected with the completed tunnel it was widened out to the full section down to the wall-plate, working south, and, later, the full excavation was completed, working in the same direction. The photographs and diagram, Figs. 6, 7, and 8, give some of the details of this work.

The force working from the portal was on a three-shift basis. It included a superintendent and, on each shift, 2 to 3 miners, 2 to 3 helpers, 1 hoist engineer, and 1 pump man. Four shifts were required for one complete 5-ft. advance of the top drift. Of the top drift 220 ft. was completed in 65 days, while 52 ft. of re-drifting (in making the connection through the last advances made from the north) took 21 days. Enlarging the top drift to full size took 68 days. Removing 299 ft. of bench and completing the tunnel to full size took 114 days. The advance of all work, including drifting, widening, and taking out bench, was approximately 1 ft. per day.

In all, 3 669 cu. yd. of earth were removed from the tunnel, an average section containing 8.57 cu. yd. per lin. ft.

Concrete.—The tunnel was lined with concrete throughout, placed from Shafts 1, 3, 4, 5, and 7. It was mixed on the surface, poured through a pipe into cars at the foot of the shaft, and hauled to the forms. The invert and side-walls were placed by hand, while the arch was placed with a "concrete gun". The general methods and sequence of operations are shown on Fig. 9.

The work progressed away from the shaft. Operations 1 and 2, and 3 and 4, (Fig. 9) were later combined by suspending the forms for the footing course and concreting the half invert and footing in one operation. On part of the work, 150 ft. of side-wall and arch forms were used. Templates for the half invert were set about 15 ft. apart. After the concrete had been screeded and rolled these templates were removed, and the empty space was filled with

Fig. 6.—Earth Tunnel, 9 by 8-Foot Center Drift, Three-Bar Type.

Fig. 7.—Earth Tunnel, Completed Timber Lining, Five-Bar Type.

concrete. Pipes were set in the invert about 50 ft. apart to provide a vent for the relief of any pressures that might accumulate.

The fine aggregate consisted entirely of particles of crushed rock, as there was no acceptable natural sand in the vicinity. Part of this material came from the crusher, but most of it was made with sand rolls. The material proved satisfactory except that it caused difficulty in securing a smooth invert. The average fineness modulus was about 3.2. The amount passing the 100 sieve varied from 5 to 11 per cent. The coarse aggregate came from sandstone taken from the tunnel and from quarries opened up near the shafts. Shale was not used.

The concrete mix was 1 : $2\frac{1}{3}$: $4\frac{2}{3}$ by volume, 1 bag of cement being assumed as 0.905 cu. ft. Measurement was made in pyramid-shaped hoppers, all materials being measured loose without correction for moisture. During cold weather the sand and stone were thawed out by placing steam pipes in the bins, approximately 100 sq. ft. of radiation being supplied to each bin. The water was heated with live steam. The cement factor was 1.48 bbl. per cu. yd. of concrete. Empty cement bags were shaken by machine, with a recovery of 1 bag of cement to every 170 bags shaken. In general, sufficient water was added to make a plastic mix. The average compressive strength determined from twenty-eight representative cylinders was 1 484 lb. per sq. in. at the age of 28 days.

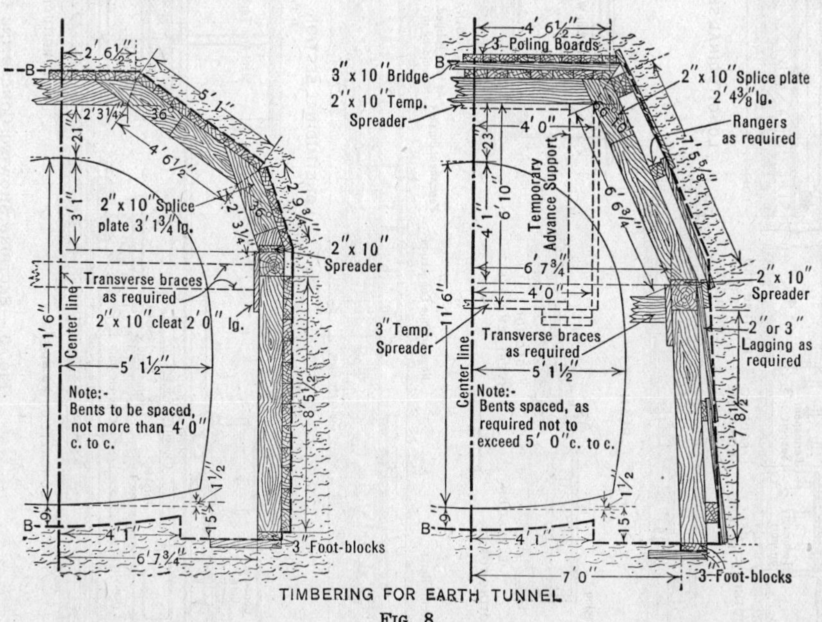

FIG. 8.

The concrete gun (Fig. 9) proved an efficient tool for placing concrete in the arch. A short section of arch was placed by hand; later, holes were drilled through the crown, and the depth was tested. By comparison it was found that 76% of the depth was filled by the hand method while 89% was

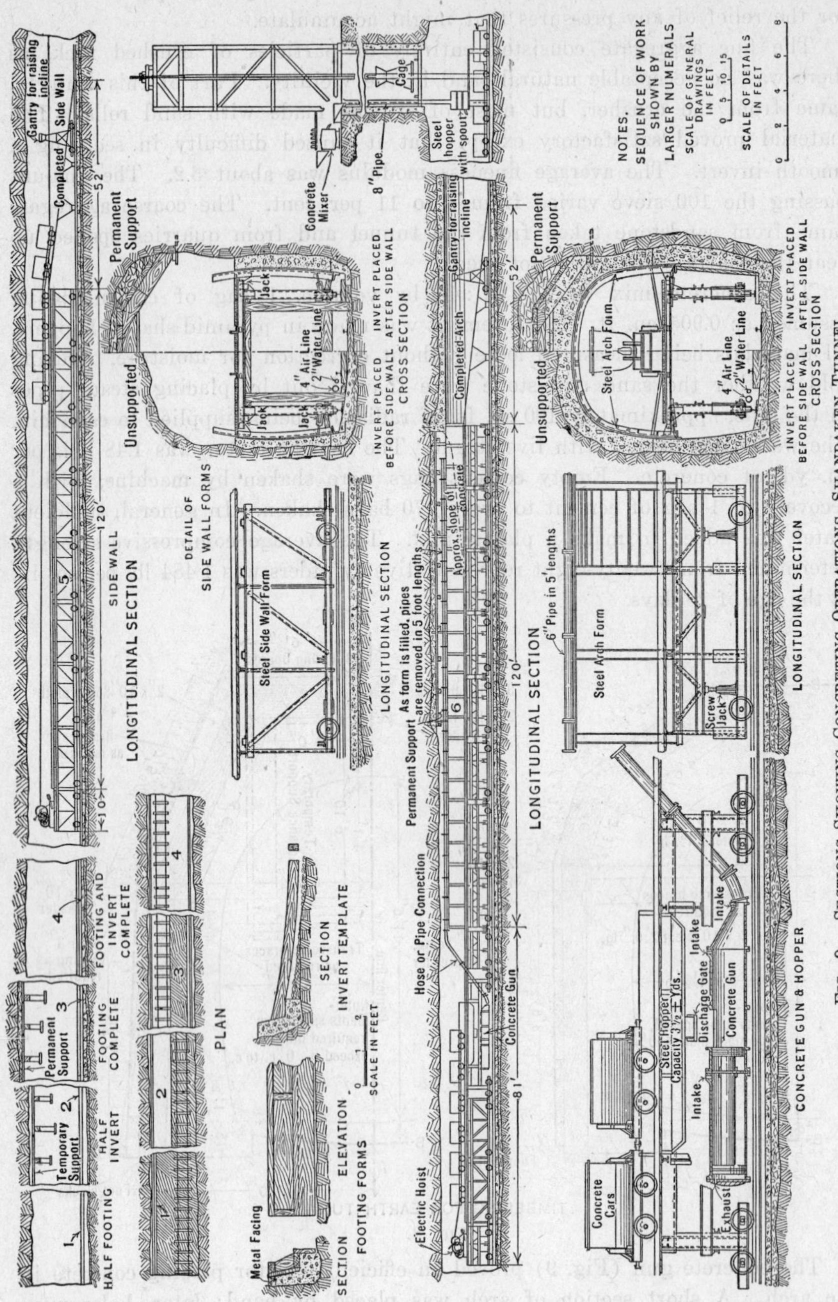

FIG. 9.—SECTIONS SHOWING CONCRETING OPERATIONS, SHANDAKEN TUNNEL.

filled with the gun. The latter product was of good quality, with few honeycomb spots and a dense, smooth surface. It flowed on an average slope of 1 on 13. When working at a distance from the shaft the gun required about 1 200 to 1 500 cu. ft. of air to operate it. It was possible to shoot a 6-car load, or 5½ cu. yd. of concrete, in 10 min.

The force placing concrete included:

7 men transporting materials on the surface;
1 foreman and 7 men operating mixer;
4 motormen and 1 signalman in tunnel transporting concrete;
1 foreman and 10 men placing concrete invert or footings*;
1 foreman and 11 men placing concrete side-wall *;
1 foreman and 9 men placing concrete arch *; and
1 foreman and 4 to 6 laborers on forms.

Using two side-wall forms and two arch forms in the tunnel between Shafts 5 and 6, 120 ft. of lining was completed in 24 hours with three shifts. The average progress from Shaft 4 to Shaft 5 was 58.7 lin. ft. per day; and from Shaft 5 to Shaft 6, 59.4 lin. ft. This is a fair average for the entire job. In general, the rate of progress was limited by transportation.

In the lining, 212 677 cu. yd. of concrete were placed. The quantity per linear foot varied from 2.109 to 3.378 cu. yd. The quantity of pay concrete was only 183 564 cu. yd., because the contractor preferred driving a slightly enlarged tunnel to trimming. He was paid a nominal sum for the excess concrete plus the cost of the extra cement.

Grouting.—Liquid grout under low pressure was placed between the lining and the rock throughout the supported tunnel, and in all but 21 942 lin. ft. of the unsupported tunnel. The purpose of the grout was to bind the lining solidly to the rock, all voids being filled. The lining thus forms an air-tight cover around the permanent timber to arrest decay.

During the placing of the permanent timber, 2-in. pipes were set, extending through the lagging approximately to the roof of the tunnel. These pipes were near the center line, approximately 50 ft. apart. Before placing the concrete, 1½-in. pipes, extending down to the forms, were telescoped inside these pipes, and securely wedged. In addition, grout pipes were placed aproximately 50 ft. apart on either side of the tunnel extended through the lagging near the lower limits of the dry packing. The lower end of each pipe was fitted with a coupling that was kept about ½ in. from the forms, by means of a screw-plug, or what was more successful, by means of a bit of oily waste, which aided in locating the hole after the removal of the forms.

In the untimbered part of the tunnel pipes were placed along the axis at intervals of about 40 ft. and also at points of especially high breakage. These pipes were held in place by being screwed to a special flange attached to the key-plate. In special types of timber with tight lagging behind the plumb-posts, grout pipes were placed through the lagging.

Where water was encountered the leaks were caulked, or, if they extended over a considerable area, they were covered with tin. In either case the

* Only one of these three operations was carried on at a time.

water was collected and led into the tunnel through a pipe usually placed on top of the side-wall. No attempt was made to shut off this leakage as the water was of good quality; but, in general, most of the leakage was stopped by grouting.

Grout was placed either with Canniff machines or with the concrete gun. After a sufficient trial it was found that the gun was not sufficiently mobile, and it was abandoned. In the early operations materials were mixed inside the tunnel with the Canniff machine. As grout could not be made in the gun it was mixed on the surface and transported to the gun. Although the gun was abandoned, the practice of mixing on the surface was continued, either 5 or 10-bag batches being made in the Ransome mixer in the proportions of 1 bag of cement, 1 bag of sand (90 lb. net), and from 5.5 to 7 gal. of water, with an average liquid volume of 1.92 cu. ft. per bag.

The mixture was poured down an 8-in. pipe into concrete cars at the foot of the shaft. The cars were hauled in trains of from three to six cars to the Canniff machines. The grout was then pumped to a small tank from which it flowed by gravity into the Canniff tanks. During the pumping, the material in the cars was agitated continuously. The tanks forced the grout out at a pressure of from 30 to 75 lb. in rock; and at less than 20 lb. in earth. The grout traveled a maximum distance of 700 ft. in the timbered tunnel with an average of 200 ft. In the untimbered tunnel, the maximum travel was 470 ft., and the average, 50 ft. Connection was usually made to a low hole, and when a good flow of grout appeared in an adjacent high hole, that hole was plugged.

A natural fine sand, obtained from local pits, was used for grouting. When screened to remove the coarse particles this sand had a fineness modulus of about 1.6. Only about 18% was coarser than the No. 30 sieve, and 60% coarser than the No. 50. It was all finer than the No. 8 sieve.

Contraction cracks were found in the tunnel from 15 to 30 ft. apart, extending across the arch and down the side-wall. They were very noticeable when grouting was in progress, as were the horizontal and vertical construction joints. It is thought that all these cracks were effectually closed by grouting.

The force for a single shift was 12 men on the surface and from 9 to 12 men inside the tunnel. At some shafts the outside force mixed grout for two headings. Grouting was done on a 1, 2, and 3-shift basis. A single shift placed on an average thirty-five 10-bag batches per 12 hours in unsupported tunnel. In supported tunnel a single shift averaged about ninety 10-bag batches in 10 hours. In the Allaben Division, where most of the grout was placed, the maximum linear feet of tunnel grouted per week was 4 000 in unsupported tunnel and 2 400 in supported tunnel; the average was 1 500 and 1 000. An average of 13.4 cu. ft. of liquid grout per linear foot of tunnel was placed in the supported, and 2.8 cu. ft. in the unsupported, type. The maximum quantity of liquid grout placed from one connection was 9 650 cu. ft. A total of 23 449 cu. yd. of grout was placed, at 3.5 bbl. of cement per cu. yd.

Cleaning

After grouting was completed the tunnel was cleaned. The first operation, working against the flow, was to remove the lumber, forms, clay, and muck that had accumulated on the invert. This allowed a fairly free passage for the flow of water. The side-walls were then scraped, using long-handled chisels with a 3-in. blade. Lips formed by the junction of forms were removed and the very few places that were honeycombed were cut out and patched.

The arch was then scraped from a high platform placed on a flat car, with the same tool used for the side-walls. Plugs were removed from grout pipes and the ends of the pipes were packed with mortar. Finally, the rails and ties were removed, and the invert was given a final scraping and brooming, working with the flow. The pipes left at 50-ft. intervals in the invert were cleaned out, or, when these could not be found, holes were drilled through the invert.

In the shafts all cage timbers, pipes, etc., were removed, all bolt holes plugged with mortar, and the sides scraped, after which the head-frame was removed. A concrete cover with a metal grating was then placed over the shaft.

Two shifts of about 10 men each, working 10 hours per day, made an average progress of 125 lin. ft. of finished cleaning in the tunnel (including all operations) per day.

Intake and Outlet

The intake is an open channel through rock to a down-take shaft equipped with gates for controlling the flow, and a vertical Venturi meter. The outlet is through short lengths of standard and pressure aqueduct to a water-seal, thence through an open channel to Esopus Creek. Both are specialized structures, beyond the scope of this paper.

Force and Housing

A maximum force of nearly 1 500 men was employed on this work; for a year and seven months the number exceeded 1 000. Except for a small percentage of local labor, this force had to be imported and housed near the various shafts. Generally, men were housed in 28-man barracks, two men to a room, heated with stoves and lighted by electricity. The men were furnished with iron spring cots, mattresses, and blankets, which were regularly cleaned. They were fed in large mess halls, the food being ample and good.

Dry houses were built at each shaft, but, in general, were not used, probably owing to the dryness of the tunnels. Wash-houses were equipped with hot and cold water, shower baths, and facilities for washing clothes. Toilet facilities consisted of Kaustine units in buildings on the surface and portable Kaustine closets in the tunnel. An ample supply of wholesome water was piped from near-by springs or pumps. This supply was analyzed from time to time and was carefully guarded. Smaller houses were supplied for married men, and bungalows for superintendents and executives.

Due to the general unrest, the isolated location of the camps, and other conditions, the labor turn-over was high, frequently as much as 700% in a year.

Supplies and Transportation

Materials were brought by railroad to the Allaben Yard, or to a siding at Grand Gorge, and taken to the shafts by motor truck. The road from Shandaken to Lexington was of dirt—at some times fairly good, but, at others, nearly impassable. The contractor did considerable work on this road to keep it usable. In the winter, he kept the entire road along the tunnel line open, using snow plows attached to trucks or tractors. At times, it became necessary to shovel parts of the roads to keep them open. As an example of the amount of material handled, 609 carloads of cement and 387 carloads of other freight were hauled from the Allaben Yard alone in 1922.

Costs

The following are the contract costs to the city: The entire tunnel, including the Venturi meter and sluice-gates, cost $12 292 411, at the rate of about $128 per ft., or $679 000 per mile. The surface work at the intake, including the superstructure and sluice-gates, cost $382 444. The sub-surface work, including the Venturi meter, cost $99 868. The outlet cost $132 448.

The shafts, excluding the intake, cost $367.52 per lin. ft., as follows:

Surface work	9%	=	$33.08—
Sinking	79.97%	=	293.91—
Lining	10.87%	=	39.95—
Grouting	0.16%	=	0.59+
Total		=	$367.52

The entire length of tunnel alone cost $109.21 per lin. ft., made up as follows:

Driving	65.71%	=	$71.76+
Timbering	2.51%	=	2.74+
Dry packing	0.47%	=	0.51+
Concrete lining	28.15%	=	30.74+
Grouting	3.16%	=	3.45+
Total		=	$109.21

The normal unsupported type of tunnel cost per linear foot:

To drive	$66.91
With temporary timber	72.63
To drive and line with concrete	96.30
With temporary timber	102.02
To drive and line with concrete and grout	98.09
With temporary timber	103.81

The normal supported type of tunnel cost per linear foot:

To drive	$77.05
With permanent timber	82.55
With permanent timber and concrete lining	115.31
With permanent timber, concrete lining, and grout	122.22

Conclusions

From the experience gained on this work, it seems desirable that in tunnels of this size the shafts should be much farther apart. As will be noted from Fig. 5, consistent progress was maintained from Shaft 1 toward Shaft 3, even when the distance was greater than 2½ miles. This would indicate that shafts might be placed from 5 to 6 miles apart.

Progress in tunnel driving was limited by the removal of muck from the heading. A somewhat larger section permitting the use of an air-operated shovel might have been constructed more quickly and cheaply. To a considerable extent the progress of driving and concreting depended on the condition of the single track. Derailed trains caused by poor track retarded progress greatly. Well-kept double track might be economically sound for a long tunnel.

DISCUSSION

W. W. Brush,* M. Am. Soc. C. E.—The speaker cannot add any information as to the construction work for the Shandaken Tunnel. For the last twenty-two years the City of New York has carried on its water supply work under two separate organizations. The Board of Water Supply has designed and constructed the works for additional water supply, and the Department of Water Supply, Gas, and Electricity has taken over the completed works and maintained and operated them.

The tunnel was indirectly responsible in part for the Ashokan Reservoir being at a very low level on two separate occasions. This statement is not a charge against the tunnel because some of the men in the Department of Water Supply, Gas, and Electricity were directly responsible. The first low level was in 1923, when, to avoid unnecessary pumping, the Department tried to utilize the maximum quantity of water that might be drawn from the Catskill System, with enough left over to take care of the needs of the City until the supply came from the Schoharie through the Shandaken Tunnel. The run-off was low during that year, so that in the fall of 1923 the Ashokan Reservoir was down to about 16 000 000 000 gal. capacity as against 130 000 000 000 gal. when full.

By June, 1924, with the aid of the tunnel, the reservoir was nearly full. In 1926 a low level was again recorded due, once more, to the engineering desire to avoid the expense of unnecessary pumping. This low level resulted in a very sensational newspaper story about leakage from the Ashokan Reservoir. It was stated that the water was going out through the bottom as fast as it came in, and that was the reason why the reservoir was low in the fall of 1926. At present (June, 1927) it is nearly full, containing more water than at any time since the spring of 1917, and no evidence of a leak has ever been found.

From an engineering viewpoint the story of the leak was absurd, but from the viewpoint of the consumer in the city, who pays very little attention to his or her water supply, except when that supply is interrupted for any cause, it made an unfortunate impression which remains in the minds of many to-day.

It is not an engineering question, but a very human one, whether it was wise to try to save hundreds of thousands of dollars by avoiding unnecessary pumping through lowering the level of the water in the Ashokan Reservoir, thus unintentionally creating in the minds of many a feeling that the system had not been functioning successfully, or whether it would have been wise to spend the money to pump the water and let it go over the dam in the spring of 1927. Apparently, the people of New York would be perfectly satisfied to pay the bill and not save hundreds of thousands of dollars, simply so that they could see plenty of water in the reservoir.

The probabilities are that, with the tunnel and the reservoir completed, and with the consumption in the city increased, it will not be safe to take the reservoir level down to as low a point as it was taken in the fall of 1926.

* Chf. Engr., Bureau of Water Supply, Dept. of Water Supply, Gas and Electricity, New York, N. Y.

The speaker believes that the people in the city would rather pay the cost of pumping some water that would go over the dam rather than save their money, have a low reservoir level, and be asked to conserve water. Although the Department only requested care in use of water, the public thought the Department was trying to develop a water famine for the purpose of accelerating action on an additional water supply system for the city. With water flowing over the Croton Dam yearly, it is impossible to convey to the average citizen of New York the idea that the city needs to go farther afield to get additional water supply. That seems to be a thought that cannot be brought home.

It would manifestly appeal to engineers that if several sources of water supply are available, the obvious thing to do is to operate the system so as to minimize the cost; and, yet, when an engineer tries to serve the several million people in New York City, and to utilize the water-works in the most efficient and economical manner, it seems almost impossible to obtain the public support. When the people are told that they will need additional sources of supply made available ten years hence, many think that this is an exaggerated statement made for the purpose of enabling the engineer to plan and carry out additional works at the cost of the tax-payer.

The people of New York are very proud of their water supply system, and justly so, but they seem to be very suspicious of the need of developing additional sources of supply. The Shandaken Tunnel, prior to the completion of the Schoharie Reservoir in the fall of 1926, furnished an average of 170 000 000 gal. per day for about two and one-half years. It was a great aid in enabling the Department to meet the requirements of the city without installing additional pumping equipment to raise the Croton water to a higher level.

With the completion of the tunnel, the normal available yield of the Catskill System will be about 600 000 000 gal. per day. Just what the maximum dependable yield will be is necessarily uncertain. The stream-flow record in the Catskills is only for twenty odd years, and that is not long enough to determine what water supply is available; but water supply operations will be on the basis of 600 000 000 per day.

The Catskill Aqueduct will deliver about 630 000 000 gal. per day. It did deliver about 660 000 000 gal. per day in 1925, but with the higher water level now maintained and with the resultant growths on the sides, which have interfered with the flow, the daily capacity is now about 630 000 000 gal. The present delivery capacity is being raised by the use of chlorine to destroy the growths on the inside surface of the aqueduct.

The maximum delivery of the tunnel has been practically 650 000 000 gal. per day (the figure set by the designer), and the normal dependable supply that will be obtained by the combined use of the tunnel and the reservoir will be about 300 000 000 gal. per day.

The Schoharie Reservoir has once been virtually full and then emptied since the fall of 1926, and it is now (June, 1927) about half full. It will probably be emptied rather rapidly later in the year. Usually, the Schoharie Reservoir will be at a low level for the purpose of holding the flood flows, because the reservoir is small compared with the capacity of the water-shed. The reservoir has a capacity of only 20 000 000 000 gal.

The work that the Board of Water Supply has done on the Catskill System has been designed and carried out in such a manner that it has met every promise made for it, and all the parts have functioned, from the operating viewpoint, in an exceptionally efficient manner.

CHARLES GOODMAN,* M. AM. SOC. C. E.—The trimming of a rock tunnel is made necessary where a minimum dimensioned cross-section is called for; usually it is needed for a timber or concrete structure. This trimming is best done immediately back of the heading before the track, the pump, the air-pipe lines, and the electric light and power lines are laid; otherwise, these must be moved out of the way of the blasting for trimming, thereby incurring additional expense and a loss of time.

Careful setting of line and grade plugs for directing tunnel alignment results in saving rock-trimming work. One plug set to correct line every 50 ft. is better than incorrect plugs every 25 ft.

In driving a heading, the rim line to guide in locating drill holes has to be painted. The question arises as to whether this line shall be painted at the minimum section or 3 to 6 in. wider than the minimum section, in order to avoid subsequent trimming work. If the rock is hard, usually it will blast out in an approximate straight line between the drill holes; and in softer rock, back of the drill holes. The deviation of a straight line between drill holes 30 in. apart from a curved rim of 5 ft. radius is more than 2 in.

In pointing a drill hole, a driller must have some leeway and allowance for the space occupied by the drill; thus, where a tight roof exists, the drill hole must be started possibly 3 in. inside the rim line, and the hole must be pointed carefully to insure that the bottom will not be wide. Experience shows that considerable trimming has to be done when drill holes are placed on the neat line. If they are placed 6 in. wider than the neat line, the additional cost per square foot of tunnel surface for the extra ½ cu. ft. of rock removed, would be about 5 cents; and for the ½ cu. ft. of excess concrete, about 20 cents; or a total of about 25 cents per sq. ft. The speaker believes that trimming costs would be much more than this and, therefore, recommends that drill holes be located 6 in. back of the neat lines.

The next step is to arrange carefully, so that drilling can be properly done to line. Place the column, whether horizontal or vertical, at a certain regular distance from the rock face to be drilled. The column arms supporting the drills should also be placed at studied locations. Thus, the drill can be easily brought to its correct position from which the hole will be bored in its intended location. Drill holes located straight in or straight down aid in speeding up work and simplify the alignment. Downward bench holes should end at the proper heights, measurements being taken from the column and column arms.

The spacing, depth of holes, and quantity of dynamite charge needed in each hole to break the rock can be best ascertained by results which, in turn, will indicate how the holes should be drilled to eliminate trimming. It is

* Gen. Contr. (Heyman & Goodman Co.), New York, N. Y.

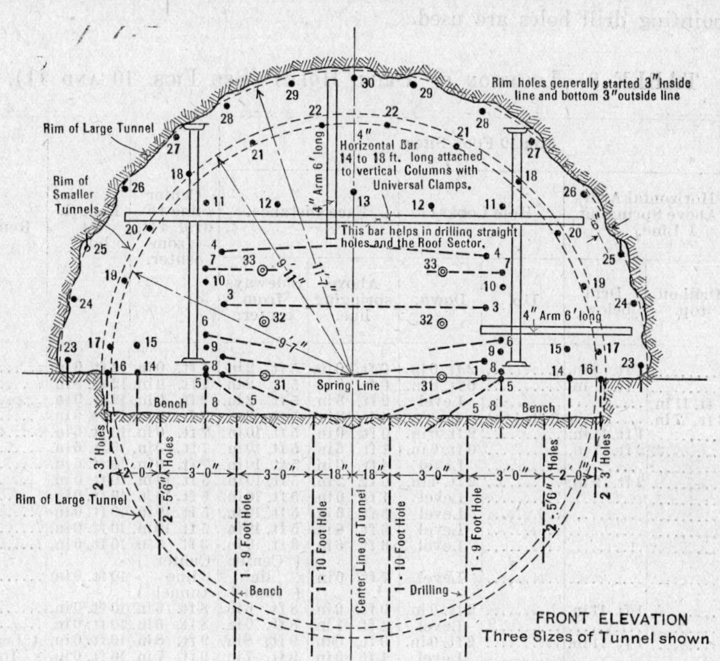

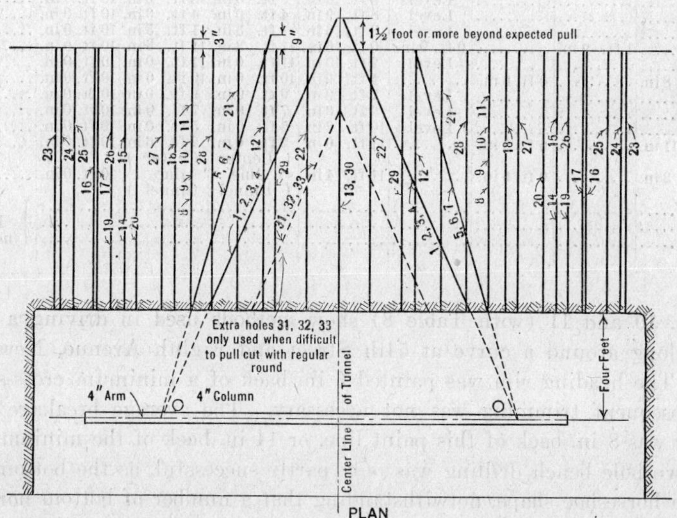

FIG. 10.—TUNNEL AT 54TH STREET AND EIGHTH AVENUE, NEW YORK, N. Y. PLAN AND SECTION SHOWING LOCATION OF DRILL HOLES.

believed that rock miners will not object to using methods which would result in eliminating subsequent trimming, especially if simple mechanical devices for pointing drill holes are used.

TABLE 8.—Location of Drill Holes (See Figs. 10 and 11).

No. of drill hole.	For 10-Foot Shot.						Center line to drill, 4 ft. from center.	Length of hole.	Remarks.
	Horizontal Arm Above Springing Line.		Hole Looks:		Face Distance.				
	Drill on top.	Drill below.	Up.	Down.	Above springing line.	Sideways from center.			
1	....	1 ft. 8 in.	....	2 ft. 0 in.	0 ft. 0 in.	5 ft. 2 in.	7 ft. 0 in.	12 ft. 9 in.	....
2	....	1 ft. 11 in.	....	0 ft. 8 in.	0 ft. 8 in.	5 ft. 2 in.	7 ft. 0 in.	12 ft. 9 in.	....
3	1 ft. 11 in.	....	....	Level	2 ft. 8 in.	5 ft. 2 in.	7 ft. 0 in.	12 ft. 9 in.	....
4	3 ft. 7 in.	....	0 ft. 4 in.	....	4 ft. 8 in.	5 ft. 2 in.	7 ft. 0 in.	12 ft. 9 in.	....
5	....	1 ft. 11 in.	....	2 ft. 0 in.	0 ft. 0 in.	5 ft. 10 in.	7 ft. 0 in.	10 ft. 6 in.	....
6	....	2 ft. 7 in.	....	0 ft. 6 in.	1 ft. 6 in.	5 ft. 10 in.	7 ft. 0 in.	10 ft. 6 in.	....
7	....	....	....	Level	4 ft. 0 in.	5 ft. 10 in.	7 ft. 0 in.	10 ft. 6 in.	....
8	....	2 ft. 2 in.	....	2 ft. 4 in.	0 ft. 2 in.	5 ft. 10 in.	5 ft. 10 in.	10 ft. 0 in.	....
9	....	....	....	Level	1 ft. 0 in.	5 ft. 10 in.	5 ft. 10 in.	10 ft. 0 in.	....
10	....	....	....	Level	3 ft. 6 in.	5 ft. 10 in.	5 ft. 10 in.	10 ft. 0 in-	....
11	....	....	....	Level	6 ft. 6 in.	5 ft. 10 in.	5 ft. 10 in.	10 ft. 0 in.	....
12	....	....	....	Level	6 ft. 6 in.	3 ft. 0 in.	3 ft. 0 in.	10 ft. 0 in.	....
13	....	....	....	Level	7 ft. 0 in.	Center line tunnel	Center line tunnel	10 ft. 0 in.	....
14	....	1 ft. 11 in.	....	2 ft. 0 in.	0 ft. 0 in.	8 ft. 6 in.	8 ft. 6 in.	10 ft. 0 in.	....
15	....	....	....	Level	1 ft. 1 in.	8 ft. 6 in.	8 ft. 6 in.	10 ft. 0 in.	....
16	....	1 ft. 11 in.	....	2 ft. 0 in.	0 ft. 0 in.	9 ft. 8 in.	9 ft. 8 in.	10 ft. 0 in.	Leave out
17	....	....	....	Level	1 ft. 0 in,	9 ft. 7 in.	9 ft. 7 in.	10 ft. 0 in.	for 11 ft.
18	....	....	....	Level	7 ft. 6 in.	6 ft. 6 in.	6 ft. 6 in.	10 ft. 0 in.	7 in. tunnel
19	....	....	....	Level	3 ft. 6 in	9 ft. 0 in.	9 ft. 0 in.	10 ft. 0 in.	....
20	....	....	....	Level	5 ft. 6 in.	8 ft. 0 in.	8 ft. 0 in.	10 ft. 0 in.	....
21	....	....	....	Level	8 ft. 9 in.	4 ft. 0 in.	4 ft. 0 in.	10 ft. 0 in.	....
22	....	....	....	Level	9 ft. 6 in.	1 ft. 3 in.	1 ft. 3 in.	10 ft. 0 in.	....
23	....	1 ft. 9 in.	....	0 ft. 9 in.	0 ft. 6 in.	11 ft. 3 in.	11 ft. 3 in.	10 ft. 0 in.	....
24	....	....	....	Level	2 ft. 10 in	11 ft. 0 in.	11 ft. 0 in.	10 ft. 0 in.	....
25	3 ft. 8 in.	....	0 ft. 6 in.	....	4 ft. 9 in.	10 ft. 6 in.	10 ft. 6 in.	10 ft. 0 in.	....
26	....	....	....	Level	7 ft. 0 in.	9 ft. 0 in.	9 ft. 0 in.	10 ft. 0 in.	....
27	....	....	....	Level	9 ft. 0 in.	7 ft. 0 in.	7 ft. 0 in.	10 ft. 0 in.	....
28	....	....	....	Level	10 ft. 2 in.	5 ft. 0 in.	5 ft. 0 in.	10 ft. 0 in.	....
29	9 ft. 11 in.	....	0 ft. 6 in.	....	11 ft. 0 in.	2 ft. 6 in.	2 ft. 6 in.	10 ft. 0 in.	....
30	10 ft. 2 in.	....	0 ft. 6 in.	....	11 ft. 4 in.	Center line tunnel	Center line tunnel	10 ft. 0 in.	....
31	....	....	....	....	....	....	....	....	Extra
32	....	....	....	....	....	....	....	....	holes if
33	....	....	....	....	....	....	....	....	necessary

Figs. 10 and 11 (with Table 8) show methods used in driving a tunnel 250 ft. long around a curve at 54th Street and Eighth Avenue, New York, N. Y. The heading rim was painted 6 in. back of a minimum cross-section, and subsequent trimming was not necessary. The average breakage of the heading was 8 in. back of this paint line, or 14 in. back of the minimum line. The down-hole bench drilling was only partly successful, as the bottom broke out in a horseshoe shape, notwithstanding that a number of bottom horizontal holes were used. However, subsequent trimming of the bottom half was not necessary. The average bottom breakage was 17 in. back of the neat line.

Straight holes, nearly perpendicular to the face, were used for driving the heading of the last half of this tunnel. The cut holes extended at least 1 ft.

beyond the expected advance of the round. This cut was placed at the top of the bench. A long 4-in. horizontal bar was attached to two 4-in. vertical columns; 6-ft. arms attached to the columns and to the horizontal bar enabled

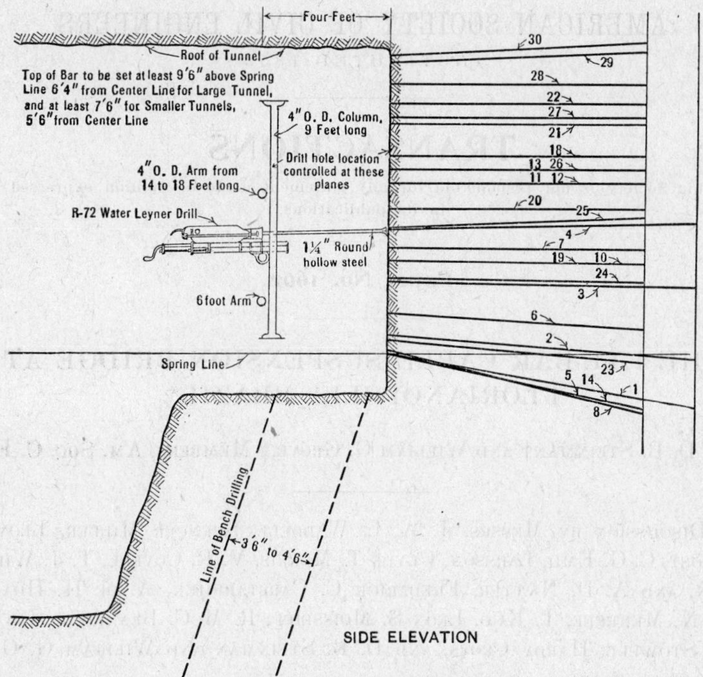

FIG. 11.—TUNNEL AT 54TH STREET AND EIGHTH AVENUE, NEW YORK, N. Y. ELEVATIONS SHOWING DRILL HOLES.

the drills to be placed close to the rim, so that a straight, almost perpendicular, hole could be drilled. This supporting system made a rigid frame on which six or eight drills could be mounted.

AMERICAN SOCIETY OF CIVIL ENGINEERS

INSTITUTED 1852

TRANSACTIONS

This Society is not responsible for any statement made or opinion expressed in its publications.

Paper No. 1662

THE EYE-BAR CABLE SUSPENSION BRIDGE AT FLORIANOPOLIS, BRAZIL*

By D. B. Steinman† and William G. Grove,‡ Members, Am. Soc. C. E.

With Discussion by Messrs. J. A. L. Waddell, Spencer Miller, Lloyd G. Frost, C. G. Emil Larsson, Clyde T. Morris, V. R. Covell, T. J. Wilkerson, and A. D. Nutter, Frederick C. Carstarphen, A. de H. Hoadley, F. N. Menefee, T. Kuo, Leon S. Moisseiff, R. McC. Beanfield, Charles F. Stowell, Hardy Cross, and D. B. Steinman and William G. Grove.

Synopsis

The recently completed Florianopolis Suspension Bridge, with a main span of 1 113 ft. 9 in., is the longest span bridge in South America and the longest eye-bar suspension span in the world. The bridge was constructed for the Brazilian State of Santa Catharina, and spans the waters of a strait of the Atlantic Ocean. It is to carry a highway, electric railway, and water-supply main to Florianopolis, the island capital of that State.

The structure is of interest to bridge engineers as the first executed example of a new form of suspension stiffening construction, whereby greatly increased rigidity and economy of material are secured simultaneously. The distinctive feature of this construction is the utilization of the cable to replace a part of the top chord of the stiffening truss, and the consequent change from the conventional parallel chord truss to a stiffening truss of more effective outline.

Another departure from customary practice is the use of rocker towers, yielding advantages in economy of material. The Florianopolis Bridge is the first suspension bridge in the Americas to be built with rocker towers.

* Presented at the Meeting of the Structural Division, New York, N. Y., January 21, 1926.

† Cons. Engr. (Robinson & Steinman), New York, N. Y.

‡ Asst. Engr., Am. Bridge Co., New York, N. Y.

The bridge is of further interest to engineers as the first application of an important new structural material. Instead of wire for the cables, eye-bars are used; and these are made of the newly developed, high-tension, heat-treated carbon steel, having a yield point exceeding 75 000 lb. per sq. in., and intended to be used with a working stress of 50 000 lb. per sq. in. The bid price for this type reduced the total cost to the lowest estimated cost with wire cables.

Originally the suspension type, of conventional design, was adopted for this bridge in economic competition with cantilever designs. Subsequent modifications yielded further economies in favor of the suspension type.

In the foundation work for the main piers, novel construction methods were devised to overcome unusual difficulties. The concrete anchorages are of special design, U-form in plan, for maximum efficiency. One anchorage is founded on rock, the other on piles.

Finally, an entirely new method was developed for the erection of the eye-bar cable and suspension span stiffening trusses, using an overhead trolley, thus eliminating wooden falsework and working platforms. The entire field operations extending over a period of one year were conducted without loss of human life.

This paper describes the methods by which the bridge was designed, fabricated, transported, and successfully erected.

History of the Project

The City of Florianopolis is the capital of Santa Catharina (Fig. 1), one of the twenty-one States of Brazil. The site is on the Island of Santa Catharina, separated from the mainland by a narrow strait. The city lies on the strait side of the island about midway from the ends. There, because of peninsulas extending out from both the mainland and island, the strait is only about 1 500 ft. wide. The water is too shallow for large vessels so that most ocean-going ships anchor at the northern end of the island, passengers and cargo being transferred to the city by tugs and lighters.

A few years ago the late Governor of Santa Catharina, Señor Hercilio Luz, conceived the idea of developing the Port of Florianopolis and the whole east central portion of the State of Santa Catharina in order to provide a means of outlet for the products of the interior part of the State direct to ocean-going steamships for shipment to the United States and Europe. The entire project had a fourfold objective:

First.—To improve the harbor at the northern end of the island.

Second.—To build an electric car line about 12 miles long from the new port to the City of Florianopolis.

Third.—To construct a bridge connecting the island with the mainland.

Fourth.—To build about 100 miles of railroad direct into the interior connecting with the railroad extending from São Paulo, Brazil, to Montevideo, Uruguay.

Prior to 1920, various competitive designs had been submitted by American and European contractors and engineers for the proposed bridge at Florianopolis. Finally, the general contract was awarded to Byington and Sundstrom, Contracting Engineers, of São Paulo, Brazil, on the basis of a cantilever design. The bids on this design exceeded the appropriation and the general contractors wrote to H. D. Robinson, M. Am. Soc. C. E., about the advisability of preparing an alternative suspension design. Mr. Robinson in collaboration with one of the writers, Mr. Steinman, prepared a preliminary wire cable design.

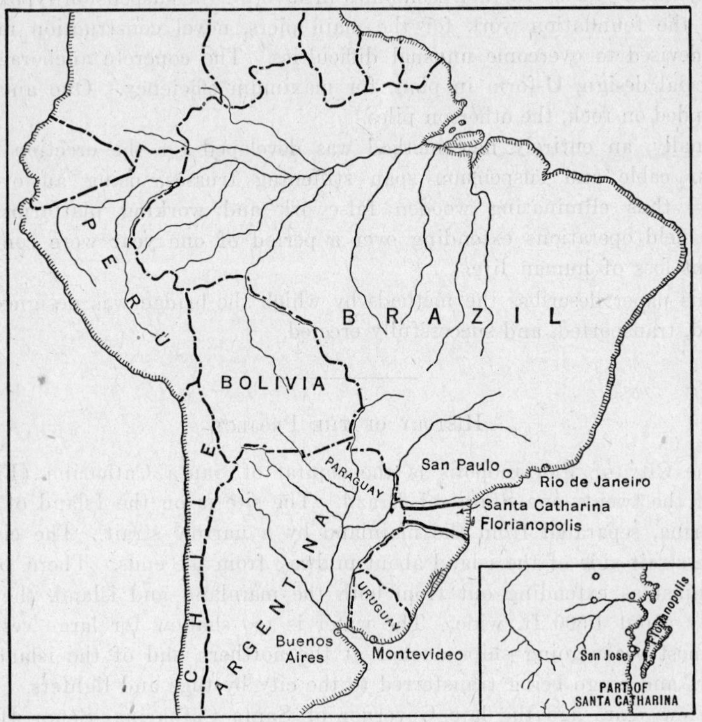

FIG. 1.—MAP OF SOUTH AMERICA, SHOWING POSITION OF FLORIANOPOLIS.

In 1920, A. Y. Sundstrom, M. Am. Soc. C. E., came to New York, N. Y., and, acting for his firm, engaged Messrs. Robinson and Steinman to develop the suspension design for the Florianopolis Bridge. At the same time, he arranged with the American Bridge Company, through the United States Steel Products Company, to revise the cantilever design, and to submit price quotations on both types. On the basis of the respective unit prices quoted by the Steel Company, the suspension design lost out by a small margin. Consequently, when they secured from the State of Santa Catharina the general contract for the construction of the bridge, Byington and Sundstrom adopted the revised cantilever design, Fig. 2 (*c*). Before any work was commenced, the entire project was suspended by the failure of the

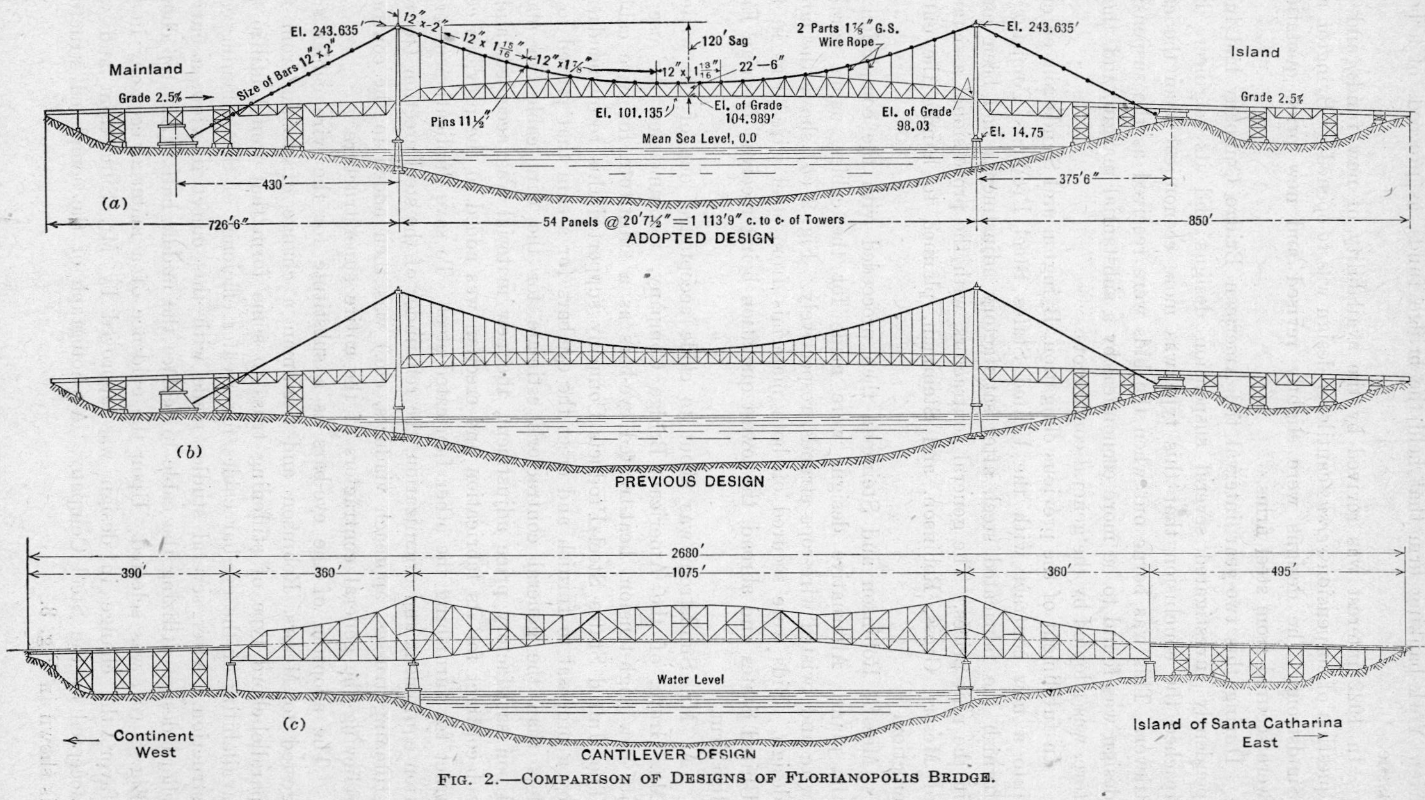

FIG. 2.—COMPARISON OF DESIGNS OF FLORIANOPOLIS BRIDGE.

New York banking firm that held the bridge funds, as proceeds of a bond issue.

In 1922 interest was revived by the availability of new funds, and the question of suspension *versus* cantilever design was re-opened by Byington and Sundstrom. The designs were slightly revised and new price quotations were secured from steel firms.

During this two-year interval the American Bridge Company had independently investigated several suspension designs and its engineers had reached the conclusion that this type was more economical than the cantilever. This was borne out when the bids were received as the suspension design was found to be more economical by a substantial margin, and, therefore, was adopted by the general contractors.

In fulfillment of the previous obligation, Byington and Sundstrom entered into a new contract with the United States Steel Products Company to furnish the fabricated steel, after satisfactory adjustments had been made in the unit prices. The general contractors, with the professional assistance of Messrs. Gross, Robinson, and Steinman, planned to handle the entire erection.

Messrs. Robinson and Steinman then proceeded with the completion of the plans. Alternative designs were made for the cables, using parallel wire and twisted wire-rope strands, respectively. Fig. 2 (*b*) shows the latter design. Bids were secured on both materials from steel wire firms in the United States and abroad, the lowest quotation being received from an English firm.

As Mr. Sundstrom was about to cable acceptance, one of the writers, Mr. Grove, of the American Bridge Company, recommended the use of its new high-tension, heat-treated eye-bars as a substitute for wire cables. The United States Steel Products Company supported this recommendation by a proposal to furnish and erect the eye-bars for a sum that proved to be less than the general contractor's estimate for the wire cables in place. Upon satisfactory price adjustment, the new material was accepted, and a sub-contract for its fabrication and erection was added to the previous contract for furnishing the other fabricated steel. To save duplication of erection equipment and organization, the remainder of the steel erection (towers, stiffening trusses, approach viaducts, etc.) was then added to the contract, relieving the general contractors of the entire superstructure.

The adoption of the eye-bars as a substitute for the wire cables suggested to Messrs. Robinson and Steinman a change of design from the parallel-chord type of stiffening truss to some form that would utilize the availability of the eye-bar cables for greater efficiency of the stiffening construction. After several studies made with this object in view, a curved chord design utilizing the cable to replace the middle half of the top chord, Fig. 2 (*a*), was selected. Upon the evidence of a material economy in its favor, the change in design was approved by Mr. Sundstrom and was accepted by the Steel Company. A photograph of the completed structure is shown in **Fig. 3.**

FIG. 3.—VIEW OF FLORIANOPOLIS BRIDGE, COMPLETED, 1926.

FIG. 4.—VIEW OF CROSSING DURING CONSTRUCTION OF MAIN PIERS, FLORIANOPOLIS BRIDGE.

Location of the Bridge

The location of the crossing is shown in Figs. 4 and 5. The east, or island, end of the bridge (background, Fig. 4) was determined by a rocky promontory pointing toward the continent, and by a high rocky knoll a short distance back affording an ideal anchorage site. The west, or continent, end of the bridge (foreground, Fig. 4) was at a point where soundings indicated shallow depth for main pier foundations, and where the steep abutting topography provided a practical approach for the electric railway connection. To facilitate this connection, a curve was introduced in the west end of the approach viaduct.

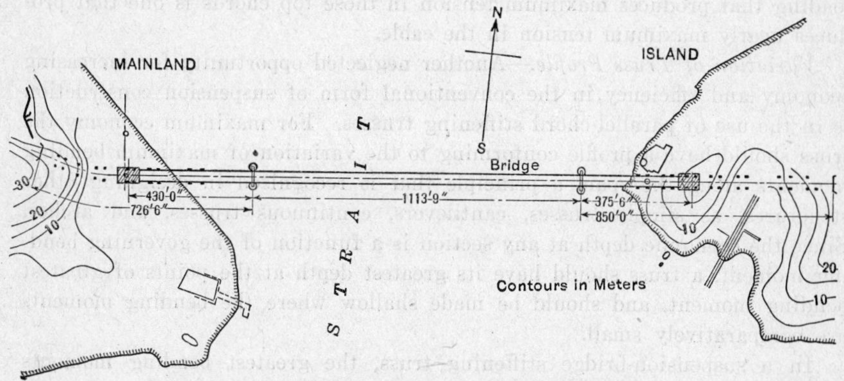

Fig. 5.—Location Plan of the Florianopolis Bridge.

The Government contract specified a main span of 340 m. for either a cantilever or a suspension bridge. This span length was based on the preliminary soundings and layouts, and was retained (with slight changes for English units and uniform panel lengths) in the final design.

Considerations of the profile, anchorage sites, highway crossings, and duplication of spans determined the span lengths and arrangement of the towers and spans of the two viaduct approaches.

New Type of Stiffening Truss

The form of stiffening construction adopted for the Florianopolis Bridge is an innovation. A comparison of the adopted design with other conventional layouts which it superseded (Fig. 2), shows the distinctive characteristics of the new type.

Utilization of the Cable as Truss Chord.—In the central portion of the conventional form of suspension construction, the cable, sustaining the dominant tensile stress, closely follows the upper chord of the stiffening truss, which has compression for its governing stress. Such juxtaposition of two principal members carrying opposing stresses represents a waste of material or, rather, a neglected opportunity for economizing. By combining the two opposing structural elements, one member is made to take the place of two;

the result is a subtraction of stresses instead of an addition of sections. This effects a partial neutralization of the maximum tension in the middle portion of the cable, and the omission of a corresponding portion of the upper chord of the truss.

This utilization of the cable as the upper chord of the stiffening truss should preferably be limited to the central half of the span. To extend this construction to the ends of the span would not be economical, because the saving of the top chord in the outer quarters would be offset by the increase in the length of the web members in a region where the stiffening truss has its maximum shears. Moreover, beyond the quarter-points there would be an addition instead of a subtraction of stresses, since the condition of loading that produces maximum tension in those top chords is one that produces nearly maximum tension in the cable.

Variation of Truss Profile.—Another neglected opportunity for increasing economy and efficiency in the conventional form of suspension construction is in the use of parallel-chord stiffening trusses. For maximum economy the truss should have a profile conforming to the variation of maximum bending moments along the span, a principle that is recognized in designing other structures, as simple trusses, cantilevers, continuous trusses, and arches. Since the economic depth at any section is a function of the governing bending moment, a truss should have its greatest depth at the points of greatest bending moment, and should be made shallow where the bending moments are comparatively small.

In a suspension-bridge stiffening truss, the greatest bending moments occur near the quarter-points of the span; consequently, the economic profile of a stiffening truss is one having maximum depth near the quarter-points and mimimum depth at mid-span and at the ends. This conclusion is strengthened by the fact that the shears in a stiffening truss are a minimum near the quarter-points and attain maximum values at the middle and ends of the span. Thus, a truss profile with maximum depth near the quarter-points also gives economy in web members since it provides the shallowest depth in the regions where the web stresses are greatest. Such a profile yields the additional advantage of greater uniformity of required chord sections throughout the span as a wide range of variation usually involves a waste of material in those chord members requiring minimum sections.

Another consideration governing truss depth is that of efficiency in reducing deflections. The most serious deflection of a stiffening truss, as measured by the resulting deflection gradients, is produced under the condition of live load covering approximately one-half the span. Half-span loading produces a downward deflection of the loaded segment and a smaller upward deflection of the unloaded segment, with a maximum deflection gradient at the loaded end. The magnitude of this deformation depends on the truss depth at and near the quarter-points. Calculations show that to limit the deflection gradient to 1%, a truss depth of about one-forty-fifth of the span is required. A parallel chord stiffening truss of such depth (as illustrated by the Williamsburgh Bridge, New York, N. Y.) would render the structure unsightly. To secure the requisite stiffness without resorting to a stiffening truss of clumsy proportions, it is necessary to depart from the parallel-chord type and to adopt an outline providing the extreme depth only where it is needed, namely, in the vicinity of the quarter-points of the span.

Two Features Combined.—From the foregoing considerations the two logical means for improving conventional suspension design for increased economy and efficiency are:

1.—Utilization of the cable to replace a portion of the top chord of the stiffening truss (preferably limited to the middle half of the span).

2.—Variation of the truss profile to give maximum depth near the quarter-points of the span.

Fortunately, compliance with the first of these requirements automatically helps with the second. The result is the form of suspension construction adopted for the Florianopolis Bridge.

Originality of the Type

Although the Florianopolis Bridge is the first executed example of this new type of suspension construction, the idea appears to have been anticipated by others. The following prior proposals of designs embody the same or similar ideas.

In 1895, Landsberg described a similar design proposed for a bridge over the Rhine, at Bonn, Germany.* L. S. Moisseiff, M. Am. Soc. C. E., reported† a design embodying similar features which he had prepared in 1907 for a proposed 1 200-ft. span, with 600-ft. side spans. In 1911, R. Sontag published‡ a paper suggesting similar ideas for suspension designs.

The Revision of Design

The bridge had already been designed along conventional lines, when the decision to substitute eye-bar cables for wire cables prompted consideration of the revised truss design and facilitated its application. In the parallel-chord design, the stiffening truss was 25 ft. deep throughout; the revised lay-out, utilizing part of the chain as the top chord, provides a truss with depth varying from 22.5 to 42.5 ft.

In the first plans for the new design, the upper chord in the outer quarters of the span was made curved so as to produce an effect of symmetry about the quarter-points. Straight chords were substituted, however, at the decision of the purchaser, in order to minimize fabrication costs. Minimum cost was the outstanding requirement governing the entire design. The question of relative appearance of straight and curved chords in the outer quarters of the span is a matter of individual preference.

Although the revision from the conventional design was prompted and facilitated by the adoption of eye-bar cables for the principal suspension elements, the new form of stiffening construction can also be used in con-

* Described in *Zentralblatt der Bauverwaltung* and proposed by the Maschinenfabrik Esslingen; see discussion in *Die Bautechnik,* March 13, 1925; also *Der Bauingenieur,* No. 35, December, 1925.

† *Engineering News-Record,* November 27, 1924.

‡ *Eisenbau,* July, 1911.

junction with wire cables.* Approved details of the necessary connections between truss members and wire cables have been developed by Messrs. Robinson and Steinman for designs of this type.†

Economy of the Adopted Design

Comparative cost estimates of the two designs shown in Fig. 1 (*a*) and (*b*) demonstrate a material saving in favor of the adopted design. In addition to the major elements of economy inherent in the salient features of the new form of construction, a number of incidental savings arise from the change in design:

1.—Saving the material represented by the middle half of the top chord of each stiffening truss.

2.—A general saving in the remaining chord material resulting from the use of an economic truss profile conforming to the variation of bending moments along the span; and, in particular, a material reduction in the maximum chord sections near the quarter-points.

3.—A saving in details and in minimum sections resulting from the greater uniformity of required chord sections throughout the span.

4.—A saving in web material on account of the reduced truss depth in the regions of maximum shear.

5.—The omission, in the middle half of the span, of the sub-verticals previously required to shorten the compression chord members, now replaced by tension members.

6.—The omission of the intermediate top laterals previously required to stay these shortened compression chord members in a horizontal plane.

7.—As a result of these savings, a reduction of about one-third in the total weight of the stiffening truss, and a consequent further saving in all parts affected by the dead load of the truss.

8.—A saving in cable sections resulting from the reduced dead load of the truss and from the consequent reduced dead load of the cable.

9.—The omission of the suspenders in the middle half of the span and a reduction in length of the remaining suspenders.

10.—A combined saving in the towers resulting in part from the reduction (6.5 ft. in the case of the Florianopolis Bridge) in the total height in consequence of the reduced distance between the cable and lower chord at the center.

11.—A material saving in the anchorages resulting from the reduced dead load of the truss and cable and the reduced elevation of the back-stays.

In the case of the Florianopolis Bridge, much of this economy was not capitalized but was turned back into the structure in the form of a general reduction of unit stresses to provide a greater margin of safety for future load increases. Thus, the design stress for the stiffening truss was lowered from 20 000 to 18 500 lb. per sq. in. (actually 14 500 lb. as calculated by the

* Used in the suspension design by Messrs. Robinson and Steinman for the Sydney Harbor Bridge.

† *Engineering and Contracting*, June 24, 1925, pp. 1377–1386; *Die Bautechnik*, 1925, No. 33, pp. 451–452, and 1925, No. 44, p. 630.

exact method); and the unit stress in the cable was reduced from 50 000 to 46 500 lb. per sq. in.

Designs have been proposed, in the past, in which the cable would be utilized as the top chord of an overhead bracing system. G. Lindenthal, M. Am. Soc. C. E., advocated for the Manhattan Bridge and for the Quebec Bridge, eye-bar cable designs with bracing systems having the maximum depth near the quarter-points of the span. In those designs, however, the stiffening system would have to leave the roadway level to follow the line of the cable in the outer quarters of the span.

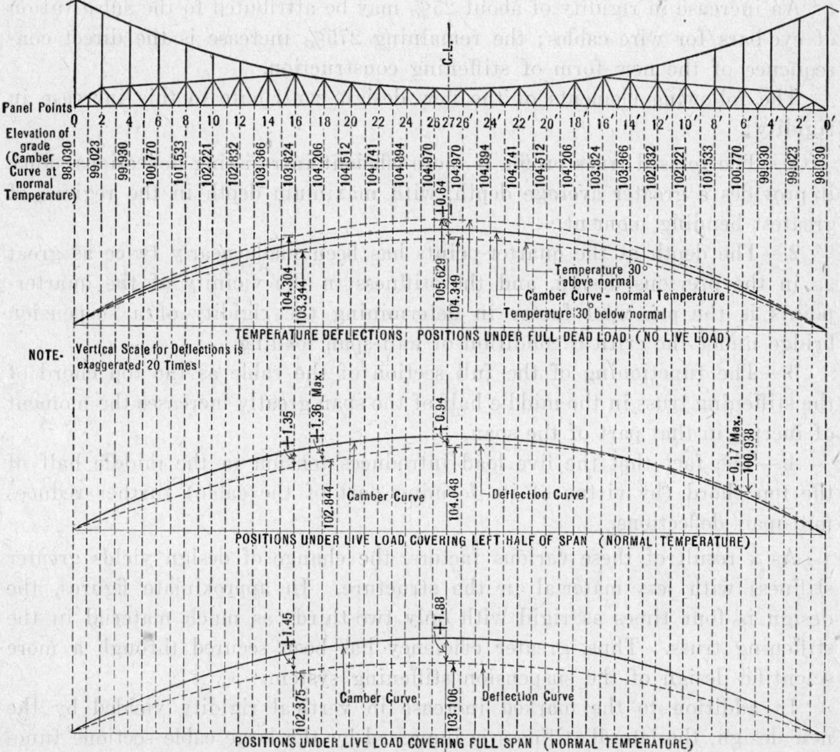

FIG. 6.—CALCULATED DEFLECTION GRAPHS FOR THE FLORIANOPOLIS BRIDGE.

The design of the Florianopolis Bridge secures the desired advantages while retaining a stiffening truss at the roadway level from tower to tower. The use of an overhead trussing system (departing from the roadway level) would necessitate separate wind chords for lateral stiffening.

GAIN IN RIGIDITY

Although the governing consideration in the change of design was that of economy, the change yielded greatly increased rigidity (300%) as an incidental advantage.

According to the deflection graphs calculated for the adopted design (Fig. 6), the maximum deflection under full-span loading is only 1.88 ft., or

$\frac{1}{592}$ of the span; and the maximum deflection under half-span loading is only 1.36 ft., or $\frac{1}{820}$ of the span, with uplift in the unloaded half practically eliminated. The actual deflections will be about 30% less than these calculated values, since the deflection calculations were based on the elastic, or "approximate", method and since no allowance was made for the stiffening effect of details. These deflections are approximately one-fourth of the corresponding values for the previous (conventional) design. As the Florianopolis Bridge is designed to carry a railway as its principal element of live load, this reduction of the governing deflections is of practical significance.

An increase in rigidity of about 25% may be attributed to the substitution of eye-bars for wire cables; the remaining 275% increase is the direct consequence of the new form of stiffening construction.

The following elements of the new design contribute to this increase in rigidity:

1.—The revised truss profile is more efficient in resisting deflections, since it provides a greater average depth, with maximum depth in the regions of greatest bending moment.

2.—The depth at the quarter-points has been made nearly twice as great as in the previous design, and the stiffness in the vicinity of the quarter-points is the principal factor in determining the rigidity of a suspension bridge under the critical condition of half-span loading.

3.—The functioning of the full section of the cable as the top chord of the stiffening truss in the middle half of the span greatly increases the moment of inertia in that part of the span.

4.—The fact that the live load introduces tension in the middle half of the top chord (by virtue of its forming part of the cable) further reduces mid-span deflections.

As a result of these various factors, the change of design yields greater stiffness with less material in the structure. In approximate figures, the design is four times as rigid with only two-thirds as much material in the stiffening truss. Thus, greater efficiency has been secured through a more scientific design of the suspension stiffening system.

In addition to the marked increase in vertical rigidity yielded by the new design, the lateral stiffness is improved by the large cable sections functioning as wind chords in the middle half of the span; and ideal longitudinal rigidity is secured by the direct connection of the truss to the cables. Longitudinal or braking forces are carried directly into the cable.

The net result of the change in design as applied to the Florianopolis Bridge is a reduction in cost (through actual saving in material), an increase in safety and longevity (through lowered unit stresses), and an increase in efficiency (as measured by resistance to deflections).

Rigidity in Suspension Bridge Design

There are differences of opinion among bridge engineers as to the desirability of rigidity in suspension designs. Those who advocate maximum stiffness as a desideratum are applying to suspension systems considerations borrowed from other types of bridge construction. In those other types, rigidity, strength, safety, and longevity are intimately related.

In the suspension type, on the other hand, strength, safety, and longevity are not dependent on the degree of rigidity. A suspension bridge has greater safety and longevity than other types, even when its deflections are many times greater; and its strength is not measured by its rigidity.

Long-span suspension bridges of recent design or construction have been intentionally proportioned to permit maximum deflections of as much as 15 or 20 ft., without impairing the safety or permanence of the structure. A certain amount of flexibility is an advantage in a structure, providing, as it does, resilience to resist the effects of impact and shock. Nevertheless, for practical reasons, proper methods must be available for restricting or minimizing suspension-bridge deflections. One of these reasons is the requirements of railway traffic. For such loading, the permissible deflection gradients are limited; and the "traveling wave", involving the upward deflection of the unloaded part of the span, is cited as an objection. A design of the Florianopolis type permits the deflection gradients to be restricted adequately, and the "traveling wave" to be eliminated.

Another reason is a prejudice among laymen and others, against the suspension type on the score of its flexibility. Adverse impressions derived from flimsy, improperly designed, suspension spans are that the suspension type is necessarily light and shaky. To meet these conditions, it is most desirable to be able to limit and control the deflections of suspension designs.

Suspension Bridges Can Be Designed to Have Any Desired Degree of Rigidity

In the Sydney, Australia, Harbor Bridge competition, the suspension type was officially excluded on the score of alleged excessive flexibility; the engineer in charge declared that the deflection of the 1 600-ft. span under the heavy railroad traffic would amount to 11 ft. in a suspension design. As a challenge to this objection, a design submitted by Messrs. Robinson and Steinman embodied an extension of the principles of the Florianopolis type, the stiffening trusses being extended as a continuous structure through the towers to the anchorages. The calculated maximum deflection under the full live load of 12 000 lb. per lin. ft. was only 1.28 ft.; and the calculated maximum deflection under half-span loading was only 0.83 ft., or $\frac{1}{1930}$ of the span, with only an imperceptible uplift (a fraction of an inch) in the unloaded half of the span.

The Florianopolis type, by supplying great depth and stiffness at the quarter-points, minimizes the critical half-span deflections. The tendency toward upward deflection in the unloaded half-span is thus reduced and its value just about balances the downward tendency from the deflection of the span as a whole; consequently, there is no upward movement, or practically none, of the unloaded half of the span. In this manner, the "traveling wave" under an advancing train load may be completely eliminated with such design.

With the parallel-chord stiffening truss, flexibility is reducible by deepening the stiffening truss, usually at a sacrifice of both economy and appearance. With the Florianopolis type of construction, greatly increased rigidity may be secured without resorting to clumsy proportions and with a reduction, instead of an increase, in the weight of steel required.

Esthetic Considerations

Discussions of comparative æsthetic values in structural design are generally unsatisfying on account of the existing differences of individual taste. Any attempt to compare the Florianopolis design with the conventional suspension design must suffer from that limitation. At first comparison with the conventional type, the new design is under a certain disadvantage on account of the subconscious prejudice against novelty of form in favor of that which is familiar through custom.

Nevertheless, the new outline has certain æsthetic values to commend it:

1.—It produces an impression of sturdiness and strength in contrast with the apparent lightness and inadequacy of the usual suspension design.

2.—It relieves the effect of a long straight stiffening truss by introducing a curvilinear variation in depth of truss; this variation is particularly pleasing when the top chord in the outer quarters of the span is also made curved in symmetry.

3.—It contributes certain pleasing values through the more harmonious adjustment of chord outline to curve of cable.

4.—It produces a sense of a stronger functional relationship between truss and cable.

5.—The reduction of lines and members to a minimum enhances the effect of sturdy simplicity.

Finally, the new design has a certain æsthetic value on account of its obvious efficiency. Conflicting and redundant lines have been eliminated, and adjustment of form to function has been emphasized. The harmonious expression of efficiency and strength is, after all, the essence of structural æsthetics.

Heat-Treated Eye-Bars

In the Florianopolis Bridge a new material, in the form of high-tension, heat-treated, carbon-steel eye-bars, found its first application. This material, intended to be used with a working stress of 50 000 lb. per sq. in., was developed through experimental research by the American Bridge Company. It is furnished under guaranty of minimum elastic limit of 75 000 and minimum ultimate strength of 105 000 lb. per sq. in., and minimum elongation of 5% in 18 ft.

Heat treatment of steel has been known and used for some time, but it is only within the last decade that its application has been made to structural steel bridges. Carbon steel is the material used, but the amount of carbon is higher than in the ordinary structural grade with an ultimate strength of 55 000 to 65 000 lb. per sq. in.

After the steel is manufactured and rolled in the eye-bar sizes, the eye-bars are upset in the usual manner, except that the heads are made ⅛ in. thicker than the body of the bar. The bars are then placed in the heat-treating or annealing furnaces and subjected to temperatures necessary to produce elastic limits and ultimate strengths of the desired amounts. After quenching, the bars are re-heated and then cooled slowly. Each bar is treated separately.

On account of the nature of the work of heat-treating, the Steel Company felt obliged to place restrictions around the inspection. There were more than 400 bars on the bridge to be heat-treated separately, each operation taking from 4 to 5 hours. All bars were 12 in. wide and varied from 1⅜ to 2 in. in thickness. The 12 by 1⅜-in. bars were about 20 ft. long, all others being 40 ft., or more. Thus, all bars except the 20-ft. bars exceeded in length the limits for the testing machine. Cutting and re-heading of test pieces selected from bars exceeding 40 ft. in length meant that these bars would have to be re-treated as the heating necessary for re-heading the bars would destroy the effect of the previous heat treatment. It was decided therefore to test two short and ten long bars. The two additional short bars were added to the thirty-two short bars needed and the entire group of thirty-four were headed and heat-treated. The inspector then selected two of the finished bars for Test Pieces Nos. 1 and 2.

Enough additional material was ordered from the mill for two bars, 12 by 1 13/16 in.; two bars, 12 by 1⅞ in.; two bars, 12 by 1 15/16 in.; and four bars, 12 by 2 in. Before the remainder of the bars were made, the inspector selected from the mill material ten bars of the sizes mentioned. These ten pieces were cut to lengths to fit the testing machine, headed, and heat-treated for Test Bars Nos. 3 to 12, inclusive.

The policy of secrecy covering the material and processes of heat-treatment was unsatisfactory to the consulting engineers, but the Steel Company took the position that its contractual obligation was to furnish bars with stated properties, and that if the full-sized test bars satisfied these requirements, the processes giving these results were not open to the inspector but were to be considered as private. Under those circumstances, the consulting engineers declined to assume any responsibility for the strength and safety of the eye-bars furnished for the structure; and the matter was left with the understanding that the Steel Company assumed sole responsibility for that material.

In nine full-sized tests made during the period of experimental development, prior to the offering of the material for the Florianopolis Bridge, the physical properties ranged as shown in Table 1.

Of the twelve full-sized tests made during the fabrication of the eye-bars for Florianopolis, only one eye-bar, No. 12, failed to meet all the specified requirements, passing the elastic limit and ultimate strength requirements, but having an elongation of only 3.8 instead of 5 per cent. A new eye-bar, No. 13, was made up for "re-test" and passed the requirements with an elongation of 8.1 per cent. The complete physical properties for the thirteen test bars are given in Table 2.

It is possible to check the uniformity and reliability of this material by Brinell tests supplementing the strength tests. A comparison of the Brinell hardness numbers secured at different points of the finished eye-bar furnishes an index of the uniformity of treatment and physical qualities over the length of the bar.

TABLE 1.—PROPERTIES OF HEAT-TREATED STEEL.

	Maximum.	Minimum.	Average.
Elastic limit, in pounds per square inch	89 000	78 500	83 920
Ultimate strength, in pounds per square inch	132 600	113 900	123 200
Percentage of elongation (in 10 ft.)	9.2	6.1	7.2
Percentage of contraction of area	39.2	16.5	24.6

USE OF ROCKER TOWERS

The Florianopolis Bridge is believed to be the first American suspension bridge built with rocker towers. The only large bridges previously built with this feature are the Elizabeth Bridge at Budapest, Hungary (1903), and the bridge over the Rhine at Cologne, Germany (1915).

TABLE 2.—PHYSICAL PROPERTIES OF FULL-SIZED TEST EYE-BARS, FLORIANOPOLIS BRIDGE.

TESTS MADE DURING MAY, 1924, AND JANUARY, 1925.

No.	Nominal section, in inches.	LENGTH. Feet.	LENGTH. Inches.	Elastic limit, in pounds per square inch.	Ultimate strength, in pounds per square inch.	Percentage of elongation.	Fracture.
1	12 by 1⅜	17	6	88 000	126 450	8.08 in 13 ft.	40% silky cup, 60% silky square
2	12 by 1⅜	17	6	96 830	137 900	6.43 in 13 ft.	Silky square
3	12 by 1 13/16	39	0	90 100	132 600	6.86 in 18 ft.	100% silky square
4	12 by 1 13/16	40	0	82 810	122 820	7.7 in 18 ft.	30% cup, 70% silky square
5	12 by 1⅞	40	0	85 710	124 600	7.4 in 18 ft.	Silky square
6	12 by 1⅞	40	0	86 740	127 160	6.5 in 18 ft.	Silky square
7	12 by 1 15/16	40	0	83 340	120 300	7.2 in 18 ft.	Silky square
8	12 by 1 15/16	40	0	78 180	115 970	7.6 in 18 ft.	Silky square
9	12 by 2	40	0	83 470	122 500	6.3 in 18 ft.	Silky square
10	12 by 2	40	0	79 440	114 660	6.6 in 18 ft.	Silky square
11	12 by 2	40	0	81 190	116 820	5.7 in 18 ft.	Silky square
12	12 by 2	40	0	82 780	116 720	3.8 in 18 ft.	Silky square
13	12 by 2	40	0	79 960	120 350	8.1 in 18 ft.	Silky square
Average				84 500	123 000	6.8 in 18 ft.	
Minimum requirements				75 000	105 000	5.0 in 18 ft.	

The evolution of suspension-bridge tower design has been marked by three successive types. First came the rigid form of tower, typified by the masonry towers of the Brooklyn Bridge. The principle of rigid-tower construction persisted for some time after steel replaced masonry, as illustrated in the towers of the Williamsburgh Bridge (New York City). When engineers realized that the rollers on the tower tops were usually inoperative and could not be relied on to provide the necessary movement of the cable saddles, the flexible type of tower was introduced. In that type, the saddles are fixed on the tops of the towers, and the horizontal movement necessitated by unbalanced cable pull is provided by flexure of the slender, fixed-base towers. First used in the Manhattan Bridge (also in New York City), the flexible type of tower has been applied in the more recent structures, such as the Rondout (at Kingston, N. Y.), Bear Mountain (over the Hudson River), and Philadelphia-Camden Bridges. As a further step toward the reduction and simplification of tower stresses, the rocker type of tower has been developed.

The rocker type offers the most economical and scientific design for suspension bridge towers. It eliminates the bending stresses from unbalanced cable pull, thereby yielding a saving in tower material, and it obviates the difficulties of the necessary erection operation of pulling back the tops of the towers prior to stringing the cables.

In the case of the Florianopolis Bridge, the change was made from fixed bases after comparative estimates showed a net saving of about 20% in the weight of the towers in favor of the rocker type. There is a substantial reduction in the main sections by the elimination of the bending stresses. Another important advantage is the elimination of bending stress from the piers, permitting their size and reinforcement to be reduced.

Details of the Tower Design

As shown in Fig. 7, the towers are approximately 230 ft. high. The legs are battered, from a top width of 33 ft. 6 in. to a width of 55 ft. 6 in. at the base. The width at the top corresponds to the spacing, center to center, of trusses, the cables hanging in vertical planes. This form of tower design, introduced into suspension bridge construction by Mr. Robinson, has for its chief advantage the facility of running the truss and roadway construction through the tower portal without interference from the tower legs; an additional advantage is the increased transverse stability, of particular importance for narrow bridges.

The two legs of the Florianopolis tower design are braced together with rigid diagonal and transverse bracing members, the latter including a transverse distributing girder at the tower top, a transverse reaction girder (Fig. 8) supporting the stiffening truss and approach truss bearings, and a transverse portal girder (Fig. 9) immediately above the stiffening truss portal.

The reaction girder (Fig. 8) has a box section and supports the roller expansion bearings of the approach span and the pin-connected rocker supports of the main span stiffening truss. These rockers take care of the vertical reactions (both positive and negative) while permitting the necessary longitudinal expansion movements.

Each tower leg or column is made up of a double box section (Fig. 7), having a maximum longitudinal width of 8 ft. and a constant transverse width of 3 ft. 6½ in. The 8-ft. width tapers to 4 ft. 6 in. at the top, and to 5 ft. 0 in. at the base. Transverse stiffening diaphragms are provided at intervals, two in each column section.

The tower is designed for a maximum horizontal component of 3 860 000 lb. in each cable, resulting in a maximum vertical reaction of 3 790 000 lb. per column; this is supplemented by the vertical reactions of the stiffening

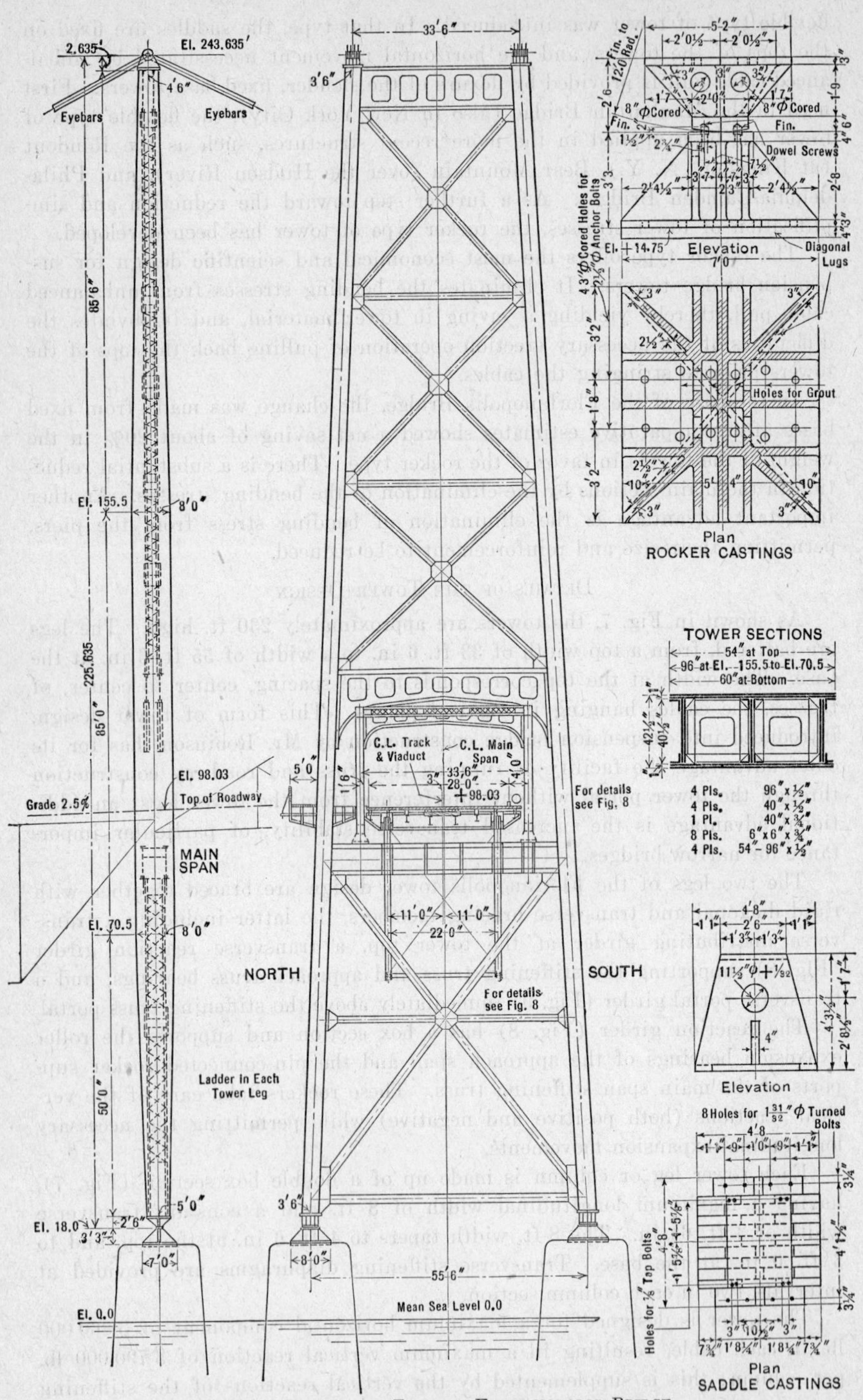

FIG. 7.—DETAILS OF TOWERS, FLORIANOPOLIS BRIDGE.

truss (240 000 lb.) and approach span (300 000 lb.), which reactions, however, affect only the lower sections of the tower. In addition, the tower top is subjected to a maximum lateral pull of 75 000 lb. per tower from wind forces transmitted through the cables; and, at the lower level, the tower receives the lateral reactions (190 000 lb.) from the trusses. All these forces are taken into account in proportioning the tower columns and the transverse bracing. Unbalanced cable pull at the top of the towers, which would otherwise materially affect the column sections, is eliminated by the rocker feature.

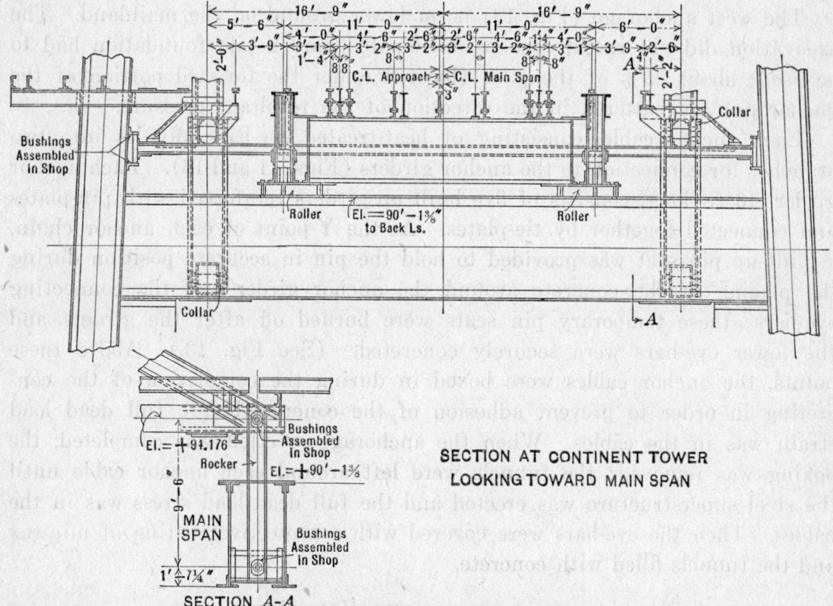

Fig. 8.—Assembly Diagram of Transverse Reaction Girder in Towers of Florianopolis Bridge.

The tower column has a maximum cross-section of 370 sq. in., tapering to a minimum of 285.5 sq. in. at the top and 297.5 sq. in. at the base. This variation in cross-section (and in moment of inertia), similar to that provided in derrick booms, is calculated to take care of the varying flexural stress produced by the long column action.

The rocker base details are shown in Figs. 7 and 10. The pedestal or base casting, which rests on the concrete piers, is finished to a plane top surface, 27 by 45 in. The rocker casting, which is affixed to the column base, is finished on its lower or bearing surface to a radius of 12 ft. The line of contact is 45 in. long. For security against any possibility of creeping displacement, four screw dowels, 3 in. in diameter, are provided (Fig. 7). The rocking of the upper casting on the lower was tested in the shop with the dowels temporarily in place. In the bottom face of the pedestal casting are two full-length diagonal lugs which engage corresponding grooves in the masonry to prevent any possible sliding of the casting. The maximum vertical reaction on each rocker bearing is 2 420 tons. Details of the saddle casting are also shown in Figs. 7 and 10.

Design and Construction of the Anchorages

The design of the island anchorage is shown in Fig. 11. Both anchorages are U-form in plan, for maximum efficiency.

The east anchorage (Fig. 11) is on rock. The anchor cables and reaction girders are embedded in concrete in two stepped trenches excavated in the solid rock; the sides of these trenches were given a negative batter to increase the vertical resistance. On this construction is superimposed the buttressed concrete anchorage structure.

The west anchorage (Fig. 12) is on lower ground on the mainland. The excavation did not reveal rock as anticipated, and a pile foundation had to be used; about 25% of the piles (located under the forward portion of the anchorage) are battered in the direction of the resultant pressure.

Each anchor cable, consisting of heat-treated eye-bars, divides into two branches for connection to the anchor girders (Figs. 11 and 13). Each anchor girder, 16 ft. long, consists of five built-up girders reinforced with pin-plates and connected together by tie-plates. At the Y-point of each anchor chain, a built-up pin seat was provided to hold the pin in accurate position during the placing of the concrete around the anchor girder and the connecting eye-bars; these temporary pin seats were burned off after the girders and the lower eye-bars were securely concreted. (See Fig. 13.) Above these points, the anchor cables were boxed in during the completion of the concreting in order to prevent adhesion of the concrete before full dead load strain was in the cables. When the anchorage erection was completed, the boxing was removed; the tunnels were left around each anchor cable until the steel superstructure was erected and the full dead load stress was in the cables. Then the eye-bars were covered with a protective coating of minwax and the tunnels filled with concrete.

Construction of the Main Piers

The four main piers of the Florianopolis Bridge are cylindrical concrete shafts, 16 ft. in diameter, with coping 17 ft. in diameter. (See Fig. 16.) The base of each pier is 30 ft. square. The unusually small size of the pier shafts was made possible by the adoption of rocker towers, eliminating the pier bending stresses due to tower flexure. A separate pier cylinder is provided under each tower leg.

Construction was commenced in the spring of 1923. Huge, irregular boulders in the ocean bed were found to make the rock soundings quite misleading, the presence of these boulders and the slope of the bed-rock surface complicating the foundation work.

An open square coffer-dam of steel sheet-piles was driven for each of the four main pier foundations. The sheet-piles, ordered to the length found from previous soundings, went down to a maximum of 38 ft. below mean water level, while the rock lay at depths from 30 to 60 ft. below water.

A novel procedure was adopted in the case of the north mainland pier. After excavation within the 30-ft. square coffer-dam was carried down nearly to the bottom of the sheet-piles, a central test pit, 8 by 8 ft., was sunk within

Fig. 9.—Transverse Portal Girder in Tower, Florianopolis Bridge.

Fig. 10.—Rocker Castings at Base of Tower Leg, Florianopolis Bridge.

the coffer-dam to bed-rock at Elevation —59. This test pit was concreted, and then adjoining sections were similarly excavated and concreted, in succession, until the entire area within the coffer-dam had thus been underpinned down to bed-rock. On the concrete footing thus obtained, the square pier was built up, and stepped off at different levels, terminating in the cylindrical shaft.

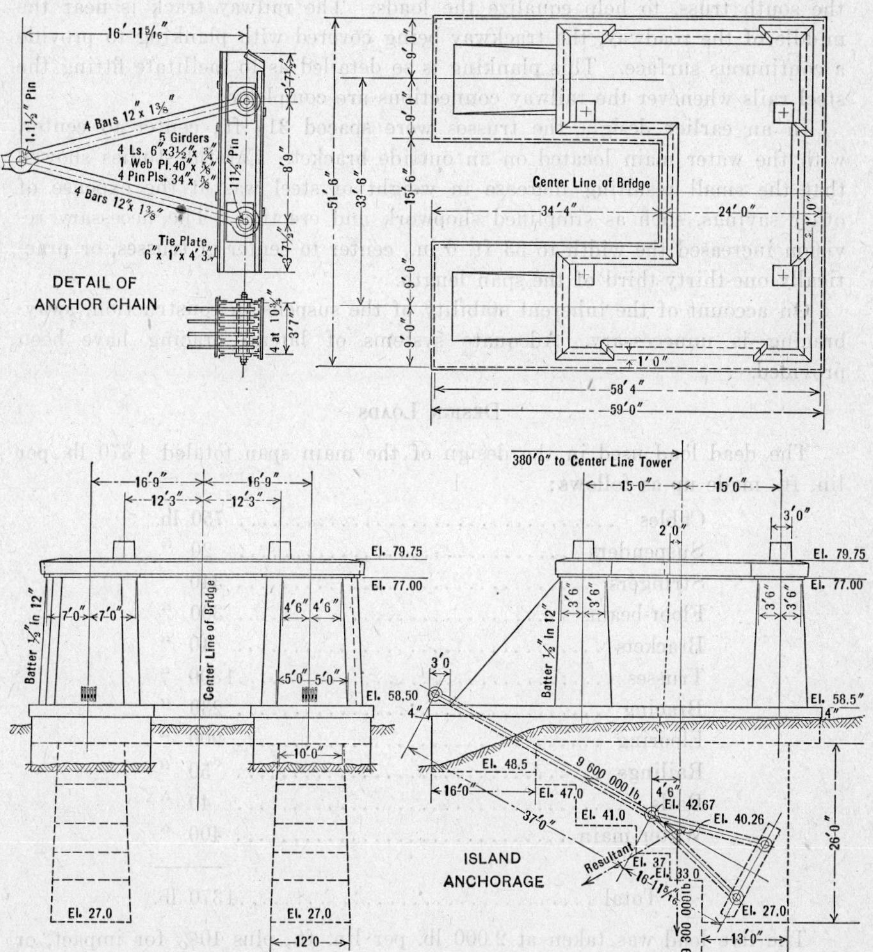

FIG. 11.—FINAL DESIGN FOR ANCHORAGES OF FLORIANOPOLIS BRIDGE.

In the adjacent (south) coffer-dam, rock was found at Elevation —32 over the greater part of the area, falling off sharply to Elevation —60 at one corner. Only this corner had to be sheeted down below the coffer-dam piling. The two island main piers reached rock at Elevations —37 and —50, respectively. The entire substructure work, including the concrete piers and anchorages, was completed in June, 1924.

Cross-Section of the Bridge

The Florianopolis Bridge was specified to carry a 28-ft. roadway, a meter-gauge electric railway, a 24-in. water main, and a 9-ft. sidewalk. The arrangement of cross-section finally adopted is shown in Fig. 14 (*a*); that of the approach viaducts is given in Fig. 14 (*b*). The sidewalk is carried on an outside bracket along the north truss; and the water main is located just inside the south truss, to help equalize the loads. The railway track is near the middle of the roadway, the trackway being covered with planking to provide a continuous surface. This planking is so detailed as to facilitate fitting the steel rails whenever the railway connections are completed.

In an earlier design, the trusses were spaced 31½ ft., center to center, with the water main located on an outside bracket. Careful studies showed that the small resulting increase in weight of steel was at the expense of other savings, such as simplified shopwork and erection. The necessary revision increased the width to 33 ft. 6 in., center to center of trusses, or practically one-thirty-third of the span length.

On account of the inherent stability of the suspension construction, sway-bracing is unnecessary. Adequate systems of lateral bracing have been provided.

Design Loads

The dead load used in the design of the main span totaled 4 370 lb. per lin. ft., made up as follows:

Cables	750 lb.
Suspenders	20 "
Stringers	340 "
Floor-beams	300 "
Brackets	40 "
Trusses	1300 "
Bracing	230 "
Flooring	900 "
Railings	50 "
Rails	40 "
Water main	400 "
Total	4370 lb.

The live load was taken at 2 000 lb. per lin. ft., plus 10% for impact, or a total of 2 200 lb. per lin. ft., for the design of the stiffening trusses. For the design of the cables, which require full-span loading (and extreme temperature) for maximum stress, the live load was taken at 1 850 lb. per lin. ft.

The floor was proportioned for the following moving loads:

Railway Loading.—A 50-ton electric locomotive followed by 2 000 lb. per lin. ft., plus 50% impact (Fig. 14).

Highway Loading.—A 6-ton motor truck, or 60 lb. per sq. ft., with 25% impact (Fig. 14).

Sidewalk Loading.—60 lb. per sq. ft.

Fig. 12.—Continent Anchorage, Completed, Florianopolis Bridge.

Fig. 13.—Anchor Girders and Eye-Bars in Place Before Concreting, Florianopolis Bridge.

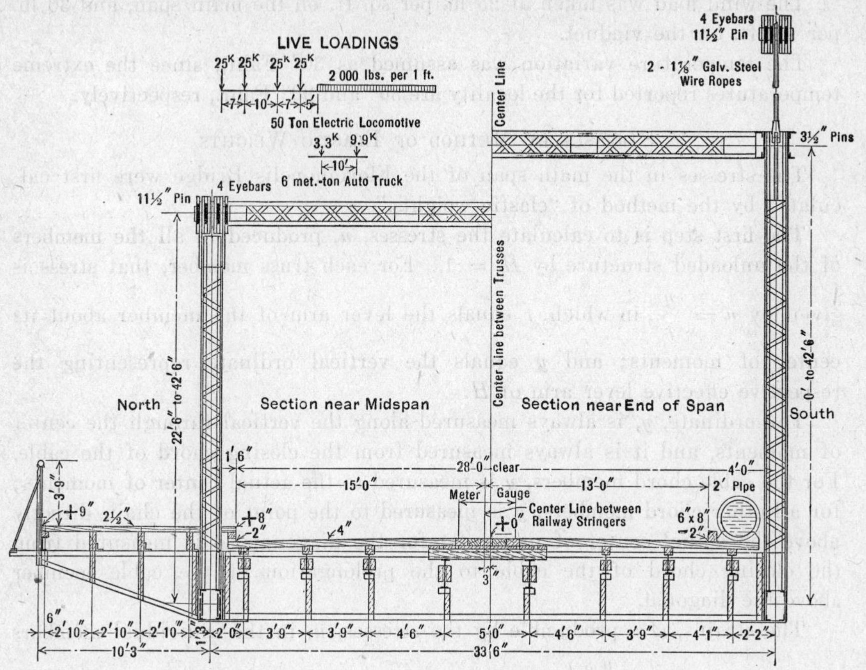

(*a*) Cross-Section of Main Span, Florianopolis Bridge.

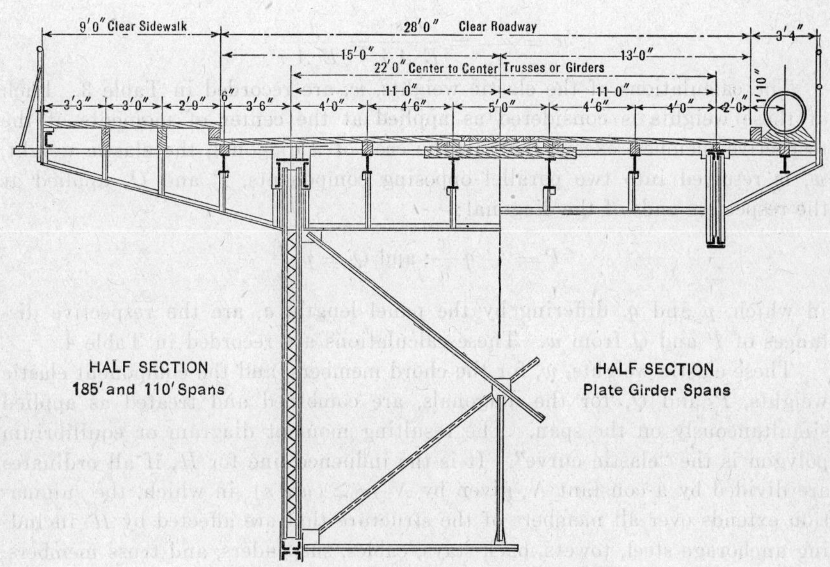

(*b*) Cross-Section of Approach Viaducts.

Fig. 14.

The wind load was taken at 25 lb. per sq. ft. on the main span, and 30 lb. per sq. ft. on the viaduct.

The temperature variation was assumed as 30° Fahr., since the extreme temperatures reported for the locality are 30° and 90° Fahr., respectively.

Stresses by Method of Elastic Weights

The stresses in the main span of the Florianopolis Bridge were first calculated by the method of "elastic weights."

The first step is to calculate the stresses, u, produced in all the members of the unloaded structure by $H = 1$. For each truss member, that stress is given by $u = \frac{y}{r}$, in which, r equals the lever arm of the member about its center of moments; and y equals the vertical ordinate representing the respective effective lever arm of H.

The ordinate, y, is always measured along the vertical through the center of moments, and it is always measured from the closing chord of the cable. For the cable chord members, y is measured to the actual center of moments; for all other chord members, y is measured to the point of the chain directly above the actual center of moments; for the diagonals, y is measured from the closing chord of the cable to the prolongation of the cable member above the diagonal.

The strains, Δs, producible by the stresses, u, in the individual members are given by $\Delta s = \frac{u\,s}{E\,A}$, in which, s and A are the length and gross section of the member.

The next step is to calculate, for each truss member, the elastic weight, w, given by,

$$w = \frac{\Delta s}{r} = \frac{u\,s}{E\,A\,r} = \frac{y\,s}{E\,A\,r^2}$$

The calculations of the elastic weights, w, are recorded in Table 3. Each of these weights is considered as applied at the center of moments of the respective member, except that, in the case of a diagonal, the elastic weight, w, is resolved into two parallel opposing components, P and Q, applied at the respective ends of the diagonal:

$$P = -q\,\frac{w}{a};\text{ and } Q = p\,\frac{w}{a}$$

in which, p and q, differing by the panel length, a, are the respective distances of P and Q from w. These calculations are recorded in Table 4.

These elastic weights, w, for the chord members, and the component elastic weights, P and Q, for the diagonals, are combined and treated as applied simultaneously on the span. The resulting moment diagram or equilibrium polygon is the "elastic curve". It is the influence line for H, if all ordinates are divided by a constant N, given by $N = \Sigma\,(u\,\Delta s)$, in which, the summation extends over all members of the structure that are affected by H, including anchorage steel, towers, back-stays, cables, suspenders, and truss members. This calculation is recorded in Table 5.

TABLE 3.—Calculation of Elastic Weights for Chord Members.

Member.	Length, s, in feet.	Gross area, A, in square inches.	Modulus, E, in pounds per square inch.	Center of Moments.		Lever arm, r, in feet.	For H = Unity = 1 Lb.			
				Panel point.	Cable ordinate, y, in feet.		Stress, $u = \frac{y}{r}$, in pounds.	Stretch, $\Delta S = \frac{u\,s}{E\,A}$, in feet.	Elastic weight, $w = \Delta a = \frac{\Delta s}{r}$, in pounds.	$\Delta l = y\,\Delta a$, in foot-pounds.
(1)	(2)	(3)	(4)	(5)	(6)	(7)	(8)	(9)	(10)	(11)
				Lower Chord.						
0–2	41.262	31.4	29 000 000	1	8.691	—11.247	—0.7727	-0.3502×10^{-7}	0.3113×10^{-8}	2.7057×10^{-8}
2–3	20.630	31.4	29 000 000	2	17.382	—22.495	—0.7727	—0.1751 "	0.0778 "	1.3527 "
3–5	41.260	41.4	29 000 000	4	33.471	—25.133	—1.3318	—0.4577 "	0.1821 "	6.0950 "
5–7	41.258	61.4	29 000 000	6	48.269	—27.839	—1.7339	—0.4018 "	0.1443 "	6.9658 "
7–9	41.256	61.4	29 000 000	8	61.716	—30.623	—2.0154	—0.4670 "	0.1525 "	9.4106 "
9–11	41.256	70.1	29 000 000	10	73.761	—33.480	—2.2031	—0.4471 "	0.1335 "	9.8504 "
11–13	41.254	70.1	29 000 000	12	84.358	—36.415	—2.3166	—0.4701 "	0.1291 "	10.8904 "
13–15	41.252	70.1	29 000 000	14	93.488	—39.428	—2.3711	—0.4812 "	0.1220 "	11.4086 "
15–17	41.252	70.1	29 000 000	16	101.147	—42.516	—2.3790	—0.4828 "	0.1136 "	11.4863 "
17–19	41.252	79.1	29 000 000	18	107.440	—35.841	—2.9977	—0.5391 "	0.1504 "	16.1601 "
19–21	41.250	86.6	29 000 000	20	112.472	—30.505	—3.6870	—0.6056 "	0.1985 "	22.3279 "
21–23	41.250	100.1	29 000 000	22	116.243	—26.505	—4.3857	—0.6232 "	0.2351 "	27.3322 "
23–25	41.250	100.1	29 000 000	24	118.751	—23.844	—4.9803	—0.7077 "	0.2968 "	35.2453 "
25–27	41.250	100.1	29 000 000	26	120.000	—22.519	—5.3288	—0.7572 "	0.3362 "	40.3500 "

TABLE 3.—(*Continued*).

Member.	Length, s, in feet.	Gross area, A, in square inches.	Modulus, E, in pounds per square inch.	Center of Moments.		Lever arm, r, in feet.	For H = Unity = 1 Lb.			
				Panel point.	Cable ordinate, y, in feet.		Stress, $u = \frac{y}{r}$, in pounds.	Stretch, $\Delta S = \frac{u\,s}{E\,A}$, in feet.	Elastic weight, $w = \Delta a = \frac{\Delta s}{r}$, in pounds.	$\Delta l = y \Delta a$, in foot-pounds.
(1)	(2)	(3)	(4)	(5)	(6)	(7)	(8)	(9)	(10)	(11)
					Upper Chord.					
0–1	23.735	74.7	29 000 000	1	8.691	+ 9.776	+0.8890	+0.0974 × 10^{-7}	0.0996 × 10^{-8}	0.8659 × 10^{-8}
1–2	23.735	74.7	29 000 000	2	17.382	19.552	0.8890	0.0974 "	0.0498 "	0.8659 "
2–4	41.402	41.4	29 000 000	3	25.427	23.718	1.0720	0.3697 "	0.1559 "	3.9633 "
4–6	41.402	51.8	29 000 000	5	40.870	26.375	1.5496	0.4271 "	0.1619 "	6.6179 "
6–8	41.402	63.8	29 000 000	7	54.993	29.109	1.8892	0.4228 "	0.1452 "	7.9866 "
8–10	41.402	71.8	29 000 000	9	67.739	31.919	2.1222	0.4220 "	0.1322 "	8.9553 "
10–12	41.402	75.8	29 000 000	11	79.060	34.805	2.2715	0.4278 "	0.1229 "	9.7182 "
12–14	41.402	75.8	29 000 000	13	88.923	37.766	2.3546	0.4435 "	0.1174 "	10.4418 "
14–16	41.402	75.8	29 000 000	15	97.318	40.805	2.3850	0.4492 "	0.1101 "	10.7130 "
16–18 (*CH*)*	41.727	93.0	27 000 000	17	143.455	38.714	3.7055	0.6158 "	0.1591 "	22.8174 "
18–20 "	41.556	93.0	27 000 000	19	143.111	32.911	4.3484	0.7197 "	0.2187 "	31.2931 "
20–22 "	41.422	90.0	27 000 000	21	142.844	28.369	5.0352	0.8583 "	0.3026 "	43.2177 "
22–24 "	41.326	90.0	27 000 000	23	142.653	25.110	5.6811	0.9662 "	0.3848 "	54.8896 "
24–26 "	41.269	87.0	27 000 000	25	142.538	23.151	6.1569	1.0817 "	0.4672 "	66.5983 "
26–27 "	20.625	87.0	27 000 000	27	142.500	22.500	6.3333	0.5561 "	0.2472 "	35.2190 "
For chord members (½ truss), Σ Δ l = ...										525.7443 "

* *C H* = Eye-bar chain.

TABLE 4.—CALCULATION OF ELASTIC WEIGHTS FOR DIAGONALS.

Diagonal.	Length, s, in feet.	Modulus, E, in pounds per square inch.	Gross area, A, in square inches.	CENTER OF MOMENTS.		Lever arm, r, in feet.	FOR $H = 1$ LB.	
				x, in feet.	y, in feet.		Stress, $u = \frac{y}{r}$, in pounds.	Stretch, $\Delta s = \frac{u \cdot s}{E A}$, in feet.
(1)	(2)	(3)	(4)	(5)	(6)	(7)	(8)	(9)
1– 2	23.260	29 000 000	14.7	0	0	+ 19.444	0	0
2– 3	30.179	29 000 000	14.7	− 314.346	−121.313	+ 280.500	−0.4325	−0.3062 × 10^{-7}
3– 4	32.858	29 000 000	14.7	− 306.178	−118.128	− 281.593	+0.4195	+0.3233 "
4– 5	32.179	29 000 000	14.7	− 306.178	−105.963	+ 319.749	−0.3314	−0.2501 "
5– 6	34.974	29 000 000	14.7	− 295.123	−101.997	− 317.068	+0.3217	+0.2639 "
6– 7	34.329	29 000 000	14.7	− 294.834	− 88.184	+ 356.235	−0.2475	−0.1993 "
7– 8	37.225	29 000 000	14.7	− 282.686	− 84.224	− 351.368	+0.2397	+0.2093 "
8– 9	36.624	29 000 000	14.7	− 282.996	− 69.099	+ 391.896	−0.1763	−0.1515 "
9–10	39.604	29 000 000	19.8	− 271.013	− 65.600	− 386.079	+0.1699	+0.1172 "
10–11	39.051	29 000 000	19.8	− 270.353	− 48.677	+ 426.339	−0.1142	−0.0776 "
11–12	42.104	29 000 000	19.8	− 257.978	− 45.498	− 419.389	+0.1085	+0.0796 "
12–13	41.605	29 000 000	19.8	− 257.648	− 27.448	+ 460.226	−0.0596	−0.0432 "
13–14	44.718	29 000 000	19.8	− 244.880	− 24.622	− 452.348	+0.0544	+0.0424 "
14–15	44.279	29 000 000	19.8	− 244.530	− 5.527	+ 493.247	−0.0112	−0.0086 "
15–16	47.445	29 000 000	19.8	− 231.062	− 3.027	− 484.316	+0.0063	+0.0052 "
16–17	47.068	29 000 000	19.8	+ 591.298	+141.010	− 217.408	−0.6486	−0.5317 "
17–18	41.503	29 000 000	19.8	+ 593.979	+141.419	+ 210.169	+0.6729	+0.4864 "
18–19	41.205	29 000 000	19.8	+ 646.264	+140.988	− 221.261	−0.6372	−0.4573 "
19–20	36.934	29 000 000	19.8	+ 649.914	+141.434	+ 213.118	+0.6636	+0.4269 "
20–21	36.713	29 000 000	14.7	+ 724.268	+140.973	− 241.911	−0.5828	−0.5019 "
21–22	33.660	29 000 000	19.8	+ 729.568	+141.458	+ 233.434	+0.6060	+0.3552 "
22–23	33.509	29 000 000	14.7	+ 858 990	+140.882	− 304.219	−0.4631	−0.3640 "
23–24	31.570	29 000 000	19.8	+ 869.839	+141.541	+ 298.691	+0.4739	+0.2605 "
24–25	31.484	29 000 000	14.7	+1 217.143	+140.617	− 531.279	−0.2647	−0.1955 "
25–26	30.551	29 000 000	19.8	+1 257.444	+141.837	+ 546.789	+0.2594	+0.1380 "
26–27	30.523	29 000 000	14.7	+24 981.206	+120.000	−18 019.568	−0.0067	−0.0048 "

TABLE 4.—(*Continued.*)

Elastic weight, $w = \frac{\Delta s}{r}$, in pounds.	*P* at Panel Point No.	Distance from *c*, *p*, in feet.	Elastic weight, $P = q. \frac{w}{a}$, in pounds.	*Q* at Panel Point No,	Distance from *c*. *q*, in feet.	Elastic weight, $Q = p. \frac{w}{a}$, in pounds.	$\Delta l = u \Delta s$, in foot-pounds.
(10)	(11)	(12)	(13)	(14)	(15)	(16)	(17)
0	1	20.625	0	2	41.250	0	0
—10.9152 × 10^{-11}	2	355.596	—0.1991 × 10^{-8}	3	376.221	0.1882 × 10^{-8}	1.3242 × 10^{-8}
—11.4825 "	3	368.053	—0.2164 "	4	388.678	0.2094 "	1.3564 "
— 7.8233 "	4	388.678	—0.1553 "	5	409.303	0.1474 "	0.8290 "
— 8.3237 "	5	398.248	—0.1690 "	6	418.878	0.1607 "	0.8490 "
— 5.5957 "	6	418.584	—0.1192 "	7	430.209	0.1136 "	0.4934 "
— 5.9570 "	7	427.061	—0.1293 "	8	447.686	0.1223 "	0.5017 "
— 3.8653 "	8	447.996	—0.0878 "	9	468.621	0.0840 "	0.2671 "
— 3.0354 "	9	456.638	—0.0702 "	10	477.263	0.0672 "	0.1991 "
— 1.8212 "	10	476.603	—0.0439 "	11	497.228	0.0421 "	0.0886 "
— 1.8968 "	11	484.853	—0.0465 "	12	505.478	0.0446 "	0.0863 "
— 0.9390 "	12	505.148	—0.0239 "	13	525.773	0.0230 "	0.0258 "
— 0.9371 "	13	513.005	—0.0242 "	14	533.630	0.0233 "	0.0231 "
— 0.1753 "	14	533.280	—0.0047 "	15	553.905	0.0045 "	0.0010 "
— 0.1066 "	15	540.437	— 0.0029 "	16	561.062	0.0028 "	0.0003 "
+24.4548 "	16	261.282	—0.2853 "	17	240.656	0.3008 "	3.4484 "
+23.1412 "	17	243.354	—0.2499 "	18	222.729	0.2730 "	3.2726 "
+20.6661 "	18	275.014	—0.2549 "	19	254.389	0.2756 "	2.9137 "
+20.0298 "	19	258.039	—0.2306 "	20	237.414	0.2506 "	2.8329 "
+20.7459 "	20	311.768	—0.2628 "	21	291.143	0.3136 "	2.9246 "
+15.2176 "	21	296.443	—0.2035 "	22	275.818	0.2187 "	2.1527 "
+11.9655 "	22	405.240	—0.2231 "	23	384.615	0.2351 "	1.6857 "
+ 8.7227 "	23	395.464	—0.1585 "	24	374.839	0.1672 "	1.2346 "
+ 3.6793 "	24	722.143	—0.1251 "	25	701.518	0.1288 "	0.5174 "
+ 2.5241 "	25	741.819	—0.0883 "	26	721.194	0.6908 "	0.3580 "
+ 0.0026 "	26	24 414.956	—0.0031 "	27	24 424.331	0.0031 "	0.0003 "
For diagonals (½ truss), $\Sigma \Delta l =$							27.3859 × 10^{-8}

TABLE 5.—CALCULATION OF Δl FOR ANCHORAGE STEEL, CABLE, SUSPENDERS, BACK-STAYS, AND TOWERS.

Member.		Length, s, in feet.	Modulus, E, in pounds per square inch.	Gross area A, in square inches.	For $H = 1$ Lb.			
					Stress, u, in pounds.	Stretch, $\Delta s = \frac{u\,s}{E\,A}$, in feet.	$\Delta l = u\,\Delta s$ in foot-pounds, for one-half truss.	Δl, for one truss.
(1)		(2)	(3)	(4)	(5)	(6)	(7)	(8)
Cable	0–2	44.763	27 000 000	96	1.0852	1.8740×10^{-8}	2.0336×10^{-8}	....
	2–4	44.277	27 000 000	96	1.0734	1.8336 "	1.9681	....
	4–6	43.824	27 000 000	93	1.0624	1.8542 "	1.9699	....
	6–8	43.386	27 000 000	93	1.0518	1.8173 "	1.9114	....
	8–10	42.973	27 000 000	93	1.0418	1.7829 "	1.8573	....
	10–12	42.589	27 000 000	93	1.0325	1.7512 "	1.8080	....
	12–14	42.248	27 000 000	90	1.0242	1.7807 "	1.8237	....
	14–16	41.955	27 000 000	90	1.0171	1.7560 "	1.7861	....
$\Sigma\,\Delta l =$							15.1581	30.3162×10^{-8}
Suspenders	2	108.584	20 000 000	3.4706	0.0313	4.9035×10^{-8}	0.1537	....
	4	88.949	20 000 000	3.4706	0.0313	4.0106 "	0.1255	....
	6	70.606	20 000 000	3.4706	0.0328	3.3315 "	0.1091	....
	8	53.613	20 000 000	3.4706	0.0340	2.6252 "	0.0892	....
	10	38.023	20 000 000	3.4706	0.0351	1.9229 "	0.0675	....
	12	23.880	20 000 000	3.4706	0.0356	1.2235 "	0.0435	....
	14	11.205	20 000 000	3.4706	0.0357	0.5757 "	0.0205	....
$\Sigma\,\Delta l =$							0.6090	1.2180×10^{-8}

TABLE 5.—(*Continued*).

Member.		Length, s, in feet.	Modulus E, in pounds per square inch.	Gross area, A, in square inches.	For H = 1 Lb.			
					Stress, u, in pounds.	Stretch, $\Delta s = \frac{u s}{A E}$, in feet.	$\Delta l = u \Delta s$ in foot-pounds, for one-half truss.	Δl, for one truss.
(1)		(2)	(3)	(4)	(5)	(6)	(7)	(8)
Mainland tower........	El. 20.5–El. 88.0	67.584	29 000 000	342.8	—0.5764	—0.3919 × 10^{-8}	....	0.2259 × 10^{-8}
	El. 88.0–El. 241.0	153.190	29 000 000	346.0	—0.9983	—1.5241 "	....	1.5215 "
Island tower ..	El. 20.5–El. 88.0	67.584	29 000 000	342.8	—0.5614	—0.3816 "	....	0.2143 "
	El. 88.0–El. 241.0	153.190	29 000 000	346.0	—0.9833	—1.5012 "	....	1.4761 "
Mainland back-stay..................		490.144	27 000 000	96.0	....	....	....	24.5734 "
Island back-stay..................		425.930	27 000 000	96.0	....	....	....	21.1445 "
Mainland anchorage steel.........		....	27 000 000	......	....	....	....	0.8802 "
Island anchorage steel............		....	27 000 000	......	....	....	....	0.8758 "
For diagonals, $\Sigma \Delta l$ = ...								54.7718 × 10^{-8}
For chords, $\Sigma \Delta l$ = ...								1 051.4886 × 10^{-8}
Total, δ = ...								1 188.7069 × 10^{-8}

It is to be noted that the foregoing procedure is equivalent to constructing the H-curve to satisfy the influence-line equation,

$$H = \frac{\Sigma\,(Z\,\Delta\,s)}{\Sigma\,(u\,\Delta\,s)}$$

in which, Z equals the stress producible in each truss member by a unit concentrated load traversing the span, if the span were a simple truss without a cable. The elastic weight, w, for any member can be defined as that imaginary concentrated weight which must be placed on the span to yield a simple-beam moment diagram identical with the influence line for $Z\,\Delta\,s$ for that member. The equilibrium polygon for all the elastic weights, w, combined is the summation of the individual influence lines for $Z\,\Delta\,s$ and is, therefore, the influence line for $\Sigma\,(Z\,\Delta\,s)$, the numerator of the H-equation.

On the elastic curve, or H-curve, constructed as described (see Table 6), the simple-span straight-line influence diagrams for the various truss members (drawn to corresponding scale) are superimposed, and the intercepted areas are the required influence areas for the respective members.

TABLE 6.—CALCULATION OF ORDINATES TO H-CURVE.

Panel point.	Elastic weight for chord members, L-lower, U-upper, in pounds.	ELASTIC WEIGHTS FOR DIAGONALS.		Total elastic weight, in pounds.	Shear, in pounds.	Moment, in foot-pounds.	H, ordinates.
		P, in pounds.	Q, in pounds.				
(1)	(2)	(3)	(4)	(5)	(6)	(7)	(8)
1	L 0.3113 × 10^{-8} U 0.0996 "	....	....	0.4109 × 10^{-8}	5.5462 × 10^{-8}	114.39 × 10^{-8}	0.0962
2	L 0.0778 " U 0.0498 "	—0.1991 × 10^{-8}	....	—0.0715 "	5.1353 "	220.31 "	0.1853
3	U 0.1559 "	—0.2164 "	0.1882 × 10^{-8}	0.1277 "	5.2068 "	327.70 "	0.2757
4	L 0.1821 "	—0.1553 "	0.2049 "	0.2317 "	5.0791 "	432.45 "	0.3638
5	U 0.1619 "	—0.1690 "	0.1474 "	0.1403 "	4.8474 "	532.43 "	0.4479
6	L 0.1443 "	—0.1192 "	0.1607 "	0.1858 "	4.7071 "	629.51 "	0.5296
7	U 0.1452 "	—0.1293 "	0.1136 "	0.1295 "	4.5213 "	722.77 "	0.6080
8	L 0.1525 "	—0.0878 "	0.1233 "	0.1880 "	4.3918 "	813.35 "	0.6842
9	U 0.1322 "	—0.0702 "	0.0840 "	0.1460 "	4.2038 "	900.05 "	0.7572
10	L 0.1335 "	—0.0439 "	0.0672 "	0.1568 "	4.0578 "	983.74 "	0.8276
11	U 0.1229 "	—0.0465 "	0.0421 "	0.1185 "	3.9010 "	1064.20 "	0.8953
12	L 0.1291 "	—0.0239 "	0.0446 "	0.1498 "	3.7825 "	1142.21 "	0.9609
13	U 0.1174 "	—0.0242 "	0.0230 "	0.1162 "	3.6327 "	1217.14 "	1.0239
14	L 0.1220 "	—0.0047 "	0.0233 "	0.1406 "	3.5165 "	1289.67 "	1.0849
15	U 0.1101 "	—0.0029 "	0.0045 "	0.1117 "	3.3759 "	1359.29 "	1.1435
16	L 0.1136 "	—0.2853 "	0.0028 "	—0.1689 "	3.2642 "	1426.62 "	1.2001
17	U 0.1591 "	—0.2499 "	0.3098 "	0.2190 "	3.4331 "	1497.43 "	1.2597
18	L 0.1504 "	—0.2549 "	0.2730 "	0.1685 "	3.2141 "	1563.72 "	1.3155
19	U 0.2187 "	—0.2306 "	0.2756 "	0.2637 "	3.0456 "	1626.53 "	1.3683
20	L 0.1985 "	—0.2928 "	0.2506 "	0.1563 "	2.7819 "	1383.91 "	1.4166
21	U 0.3026 "	—0.2035 "	0.3136 "	0.4127 "	2.6256 "	1738.06 "	1.4621
22	L 0.2351 "	—0.2231 "	0.2187 "	0.2307 "	2.2129 "	1783.70 "	1.5005
23	U 0.3848 "	—0.1585 "	0.2351 "	0.4614 "	1.9822 "	1824.59 "	1.5349
24	L 0.2968 "	—0.1251 "	0.1672 "	0.3389 "	1.5208 "	1855.95 "	1.5613
25	U 0.4672 "	—0.0883 "	0.1288 "	0.5077 "	1.1819 "	1880.33 "	1.5818
26	L 0.3362 "	—0.0031 "	0.0908 "	0.4239 "	0.6742 "	1894.24 "	1.5935
27	U 0.2472 "	....	0.0031 "	0.2503 "	0.2503 "	1899.40 "	1.5979

The influence diagrams obtained in this manner for the chord members are reproduced in Fig. 15. Similar influence diagrams for the diagonals were drawn, but are not reproduced here. The influence diagrams for the upper chord members in the middle part of the span clearly show the stresses reduced as a result of the cable combination.

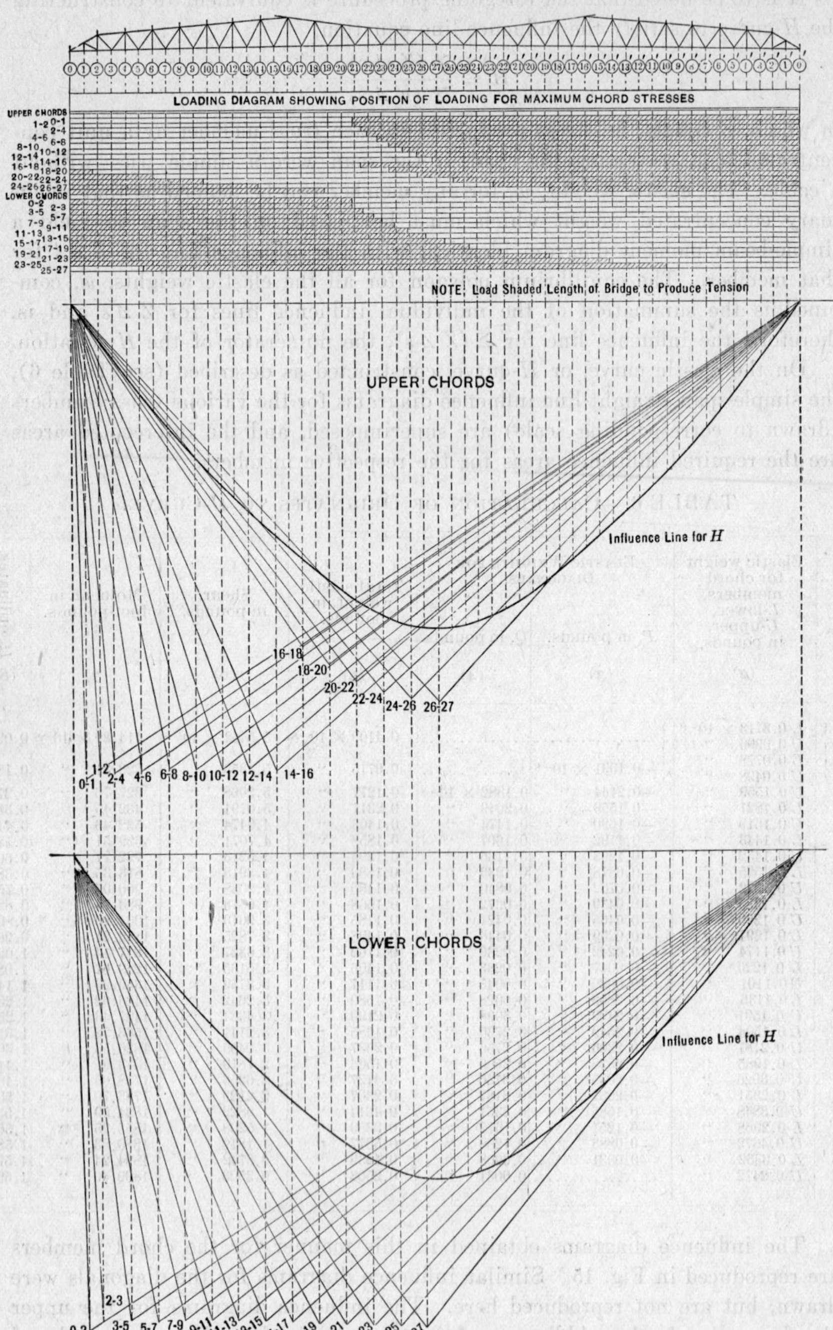

FIG. 15.—INFLUENCE DIAGRAMS FOR CHORD MEMBERS, FLORIANOPOLIS BRIDGE.

Stresses by the Deflection Theory

Following the calculation of the stiffening truss stresses by the Method of Elastic Weights, a re-calculation was made by the "More Exact" Method, or Deflection Theory.* The methods of analysis that do not make correction for the deformed configuration of the suspension system are only approximate; the resulting values of the stresses are too high, satisfying safety but not economy. The application of the deflection theory to the Florianopolis Bridge yielded a material reduction in the values of the stresses previously calculated by the less exact method.

Thus, for the quarter-points of the span, the deflection theory showed a maximum bending moment of 24 367 000 ft-lb. (with load extending from one end over 0.450 of the span), as compared with a bending moment of 30 300 000 ft-lb. obtained by the approximate method—a reduction of 20 per cent. For the middle or half-point of the span, the corresponding moments were 16 929 000 ft-lb. (with load covering the middle 0.460 of the span), as compared with 26 800 000 ft-lb. obtained by the approximate method—a reduction of 37 per cent.

In more flexible suspension spans, greater reductions of calculated stress are found by application of the "more exact" method. In the Philadelphia-Camden Bridge, these were 34 and 38%, respectively.

The final values of the maximum stresses in the Florianopolis stiffening truss, by the "more exact" theory, are about 14 500 lb. per sq. in. for the assumed loading. Since a working stress of 18 500 lb., or even 20 000 lb., is amply safe for stiffening truss members, the Florianopolis Bridge has a capacity for concentrated loads considerably in excess of that specified.

Unit Stresses Used in Design

In consideration of the comparatively generous assumptions of loading and impact, the unit stresses used in the design were as given in Table 7.

TABLE 7.—Assumed Unit Stresses.

Floor system	Tension	17 000 lb. per sq. in.
	Compression	$17\,000 - 80 \frac{l}{r}$
Stiffening truss, towers, etc.	Tension	18 500 lb. per sq. in.
	Compression	$18\,500 - 85 \frac{l}{r}$
	For combination of $D + L + I$ and $T + W$, increase, unit stresses, 25%.	
Suspenders	Tension	55 000 lb. per sq. in.
Chains	Tension	46 500 lb. per sq. in.

The towers and trusses, originally designed for a unit stress of 20 000 lb. per sq. in., were revised to reduce the maximum stress to 18 500 lb. per sq. in. (14 500 lb. by the "more exact" method). These unit stresses are increased 25% in computing any additional section required for temperature (T), and wind load (W), Table 8.

* See Melan-Steinman, "Theory of Arches and Suspension Bridges," pp. 76–86; Johnson, Bryan, and Turneaure, "Modern Framed Structures," Part II, pp. 276–318; and W. H. Burr; "Suspension Bridges," pp. 212–247.

TABLE 8.—Design of Stiffening Trusses.

Chords.

Member.	Max. stress: D.	L + I (+)	L + I (−)	T.	W. (+)	W. (−)	Total (+)	Total (−)	Two web-plates.	Four outside angles.	Two inside plates.	Two outside plates.	Area, Gross.	Area, Net.
U0– 2	0	+ 224	−414	± 27	......	......	+ 251	− 441	24 by ¾	4 by 4 by ¾	(Cover, 27 by ⅝)		74.7	61.2
2– 4	0	+ 260	−492	± 32	......	− 81	+ 292	− 605	24 by ⅝	4 by 4 by ⅜	....	....	41.4	34.0
4– 6	0	+ 343	−678	± 46	+ 81	−115	+ 470	− 839	24 by ⅝	4 by 4 by ¾	....	....	51.8	42.5
6– 8	0	+ 372	−776	± 57	+155	−223	+ 584	−1 056	24 by ⅝	4 by 4 by ¾	....	16 by ⅜	63.8	52.3
8–10	0	+ 365	−823	± 63	+223	−284	+ 651	−1 170	24 by ⅝	4 by 4 by ¾	....	16 by ⅜	71.8	59.7
10–12	0	+ 341	−828	± 67	+284	−338	+ 692	−1 233	24 by ⅝	4 by 4 by ¾	....	16 by ¾	75.8	62.2
12–14	0	+ 297	−796	± 70	+338	−385	+ 705	−1 251	24 by ⅝	4 by 4 by ¾	....	16 by ¾	75.8	62.2
14–16	0	+ 244	−755	± 71	+385	−425	+ 700	−1 251	24 by ⅝	4 by 4 by ¾	....	16 by ¾	75.8	62.2
16–18	+2 863	+ 771	−281	±112	+425	−460	+4 171	....	....	....	....	....	93.0	93.0
18–20	+2 849	+ 686	−322	±133	+460	−486	+4 128	....	....	....	....	....	93.0	93.0
20–22	+2 837	+ 577	−356	±155	+486	−507	+4 055	....	....	....	....	....	90.0	90.0
22–24	+2 832	+ 455	−375	±176	+507	−520	+3 970	....	....	....	....	....	90.0	90.0
24–26	+2 830	+ 356	−357	±191	+520	−527	+3 897	....	....	....	....	....	87.0	87.0
26–26′	+2 823	+ 318	−332	±196	+527	−527	+3 864	....	....	....	....	....	87.0	87.0
										Four inside angles.	....	....	......	....
L0– 2	0	+ 378	−210	± 23	0	− 88	+ 401	− 321	20 by ½	4 by 4 by ⅜	....	....	31.4	25.9
2– 3	0	+ 362	−197	± 23	+ 88	−169	+ 473	− 389	20 by ½	4 by 4 by ⅜	....	....	31.4	25.9
3– 5	0	+ 592	−308	± 40	+169	−244	+ 801	− 592	20 by ¾	4 by 4 by ⅜	....	....	41.4	33.9
5– 7	0	+ 730	−364	± 52	+244	−311	+1 026	− 727	20 by ¾	4 by 4 by ⅜	....	20 by ½	61.4	49.9
7– 9	0	+ 800	−375	± 60	+311	−372	+1 171	− 807	20 by ¾	4 by 4 by ⅜	....	20 by ½	61.4	49.9
9–11	0	+ 818	−360	± 65	+372	−425	+1 255	− 850	20 by ¾	4 by 4 by 11/16	....	20 by ½	70.1	57.4
11–13	0	+ 811	−325	± 68	+425	−474	+1 304	− 867	20 by ¾	4 by 4 by 11/16	....	20 by ½	70.1	57.4
13–15	0	+ 773	−275	± 70	+474	−514	+1 317	− 859	20 by ¾	4 by 4 by 11/16	....	20 by ½	70.1	57.4
15–17	0	+ 717	−220	± 71	+514	−548	+1 302	− 839	20 by ¾	4 by 4 by 11/16	....	20 by ½	70.1	57.4
17–19	0	+ 846	−207	± 91	+548	−575	+1 485	− 873	20 by ¾	4 by 4 by 11/16	12 by ⅜	20 by ½	79.1	64.9
19–21	0	+ 962	−174	±110	+575	−595	+1 647	− 879	20 by ¾	4 by 4 by 11/16	12 by 11/16	20 by ½	86.6	71.2
21–23	0	+1 058	−120	±136	+595	−608	+1 789	− 864	20 by ¾	4 by 4 by 11/16	12 by 11/16 18 by ⅜	20 by ½	100.1	81.7
23–25	0	+1 140	− 73	±154	+608	−615	+1 902	− 842	20 by ¾	4 by 4 by 11/16	12 by 11/16 18 by ⅜	20 by ½	100.1	81.7
25–27	0	+1 180	− 33	±165	+615	−615	+1 960	− 813	20 by ¾	4 by 4 by 11/16	12 by 11/16 18 by ⅜	20 by ½	100.1	81.7

Maximum stress in suspenders, in 1 000 lb. $\left\{\begin{array}{l} D = 85 \\ L = 74 \\ I = 31 \end{array}\right\}$, total, 190.

Maximum stress in verticals, in 1 000 lb.......... $\left\{\begin{array}{l} D = +30 \\ L = +44 \\ I = +19 \end{array}\right\}$, total + 93.

Diagonals.

Member.	D + L + I (+)	D + L + I (−)	T.	Two channels.	Gross area, in feet.	Net area, in feet.
D1-2	......	− 95	0	....	....	....
2–3	+198	−100	±13	....	....	....
3–4	+102	−172	±12	....	....	....
4–5	+153	− 72	±10	....	....	....
5–6	+ 82	−131	±10	12-in. by 25-lb.	14.7	12.1
6–7	+126	− 61	± 7	....	....	....
7–8	+ 76	−109	± 7	....	....	....
8–9	+114	− 67	± 5	....	....	....
9–10	+ 86	−103	± 5	....	....	....
10–11	+120	− 86	± 3	....	....	....
11–12	+103	−111	± 3	....	....	....
12–13	+131	−105	± 2	....	....	....
13–14	+123	−121	± 2	....	....	....
14–15	+140	−123	± 1	15-in. by 33-lb.	19.8	16.2
15–16	+198	−186	± 1	....	....	....
16–17	+195	− 35	±21	....	....	....
17–18	+ 41	−177	±22	....	....	....
18–19	+207	− 39	±20	....	....	....
19–20	+ 51	−193	±21	....	....	....
20–21	+220	− 69	±19	12-in. by 25-lb.	14.7	12.1
21–22	+ 82	−210	±20	15 in. by 33-lb.	19.8	16.2
22–23	+231	−111	±15	12-in. by 25-lb.	14.7	12.1
23–24	+128	−220	±15	15-in. by 33-lb.	19.8	16.2
24–25	+235	−155	± 8	12-in. by 25-lb.	14.7	12.1
25–26	+172	−221	± 8	15-in. by 33-lb.	19.8	16.2
26–27	+218	−192	0	12-in. by 25 lb.	14.7	12.1

Sections of Truss Members

The sections used for the members of the stiffening trusses are shown in Table 8.

The top chord sections are composed of two built-up channels, 24½ in. high and 17¼ in. apart, with flanges turned out. The bottom chord sections are composed of two built-up channels, 20½ in. high by 16¼ in. wide, with flanges turned in. The diagonals are made up of two 12 or 15-in. channels, with flanges turned in. All verticals (functioning only as hangers) are four-angled sections, with single plane of lacing, providing a net section of 8.8 sq. in. to carry a maximum tension of 93 000 lb.

The details of one of the top chord members (*U*-14-*U*-16 which connects to the chain at *U*-16) are shown in Fig. 17.

Sections of Eye-Bars

Each eye-bar cable consisted of four similar members of 12-in. depth and of widths varying from 2 to 1⅞ in. The methods of compilation have already been described. For convenience, the details of stresses and sections have been listed in Table 9.

TABLE 9.—Design of Chains.

Member.	Maximum stress, in thousands of pounds.	Four eye-bars, size, in inches.	Section, in square inches.
Back-stays	+4 381	12 by 2	96
0–2	+4 179	12 by 2	96
2–4	+4 133	12 by 2	96
4–6	+4 094	12 by 1^15/16	93
6–8	+4 059	12 by 1^15/16	93
8–10	+4 024	12 by 1^15/16	93
10–12	+3 990	12 by 1^15/16	93
12–14	+3 959	12 by 1⅞	90
14–16	+3 932	12 by 1⅞	90
16–18	+4 171	12 by 1^15/16	93
18–20	+4 128	12 by 1^15/16	93
20–22	+4 055	12 by 1⅞	90
22–24	+3 970	12 by 1⅞	90
24–26	+3 897	12 by 1^13/16	87
26–26′	+3 864	12 by 1^13/16	87

The Approach Viaducts

The cross-section of the two viaduct approaches is shown in Fig. 14 (*b*). Immediately flanking the main suspension span are 185-ft. deck trusses, spanning from each main tower to the near-by shore. These deck spans were used for tying in and holding the main rocker towers during erection. Symmetry terminates with the 30-ft. tower spans flanking the 185-ft. deck spans. Each approach also contains a 110-ft. deck-truss span, over existing highways.

The remainder of each viaduct is made up, as far as practicable, of 60-ft. girder spans and 30-ft. tower spans; each anchorage serves to support one of the latter. An odd 45-ft. girder span also occurs in each viaduct, adjoining the anchorage on the island side and adjoining a bent on the continent side.

A length of 135 ft. near the east end of the continent viaduct is laid out to a curved center line of 150-m. radius (Fig. 5), for easement of the electric railway connections.

The total length of viaduct construction is 850 ft. on the island approach and 726 ft. 6 in. on the continent approach. Adding the main-span length of 1 113 ft. 9 in., the total length of structure from abutment to abutment is 2 690 ft. 3 in.

The grade is $2\frac{1}{2}\%$ on each approach, the main span being cambered to a parabolic curve between these tangent gradients.

Development of Design of Viaducts and Towers

The design of the viaducts was normal for that class of work and no special problems developed in the preparation of the detail plans except where the tower columns were tied in to the adjoining 185-ft. spans during the erection of the towers.

On account of the hinged bases the main columns had to be supported during erection until such time as they were held definitely in position by the eye-bar cables. On account of shipping and erection requirements the weight of each column section was limited to about 15 gross tons, or 34 000 lb. There were, therefore, ten column sections ranging in length from 20 to 25 ft., with an average length of 22 ft. for each of the four main columns, the elevation of the top of the fourth section being somewhat higher than the viaduct floor level. Provision was made to connect the top of the second column section back to the end bottom chord, Point *L*-1, of the 185-ft. span, with a temporary strut until the third and fourth column sections were placed; then to connect the top of the fourth column section back to the corresponding *U*-1 point with a second temporary strut and to remove the first. Several of the permanent bottom laterals of the suspension span were used for these temporary struts. The second or upper temporary struts were to be removed after the eye-bar chains were swung.

Rivets 1 in. in diameter for both shop and field work were used in the main columns. To insure the tower members fitting together easily in the field, each tower was assembled complete in the yards of the Elmira Plant and the field connections were reamed and match-marked.

Development of Design of Eye-Bars and Pins

The suspension span was designed so that the entire dead load was carried by the eye-bar cables. This dead load was not uniform either along the cable or along the horizontal so that the pins connecting the eye-bars lay neither in a catenary nor in a parabola. The position of the eye-bar cable in space was an equilibrium polygon passing through three fixed points, the top of each tower and a point at the center of the span having a sag of 120 ft.

Fig. 16.—View of One of the Main Piers, Completed, Florianopolis Bridge.

Fig. 17.—Top Chord Detail at *U*-16, Florianopolis Bridge.

Given the distance of 1 113 ft. 9 in., center to center of towers, a sag of 120 ft., twenty-seven equi-distant panels of 41 ft. 3 in. each, and twenty-six panel loads, of amounts varying from 85 000 to 98 400 lb., but symmetrical about the center line of span, it was possible to calculate the ordinates of the equilibrium polygon and the lengths of its rays. These lengths represented the lengths of the eye-bars under full dead load stress. The horizontal component of the eye-bar cable stress, which was constant from anchorage to anchorage, was calculated by the usual method and from this the stresses in the other eye-bar panels were computed. The elongation of each panel of eye-bars was computed from the formula, $\lambda = \frac{P\,l}{a\,E}$, using a value of 27 000 000 for E. The lengths of the eye-bars under dead load were shortened by the amounts of these elongations and the eye-bars were fabricated to these shortened lengths, center to center of pin-holes, making due allowance for the small amount of pin play. Table 10 gives the panel loads.

TABLE 10.—DEAD LOAD PANEL CONCENTRATIONS FOR EYE-BAR CABLE, IN POUNDS.

Item.	Panel Point.												
	2	4	6	8	10	12	14	16	18	20	22	24	26
Cable	17 790	17 400	16 950	16 890	16 700	16 390	15 980	16 170	16 390	16 060	15 710	15 450	15 240
Suspenders	2 220	2 000	1 780	1 570	1 400	1 220	1 060	......	......	......	......	......	......
Truss	22 360	22 460	27 130	29 750	33 160	34 290	34 890	30 820	23 030	23 040	24 360	24 350	23 990
Bracing	6 030	4 840	4 640	4 390	4 240	4 000	3 770	3 710	3 680	3 600	3 530	3 500	3 470
Floor steel	15 500	15 500	15 500	15 500	15 500	15 500	15 500	15 500	15 500	15 500	15 500	15 500	15 500
Floor timber	16 400	16 400	16 400	16 400	16 400	16 400	16 400	16 400	16 400	16 400	16 400	16 400	16 400
Railing	1 000	1 000	1 000	1 000	1 000	1 000	1 000	1 000	1 000	1 000	1 000	1 000	1 000
Water main	9 000	9 000	9 000	9 000	9 000	9 000	9 000	9 000	9 000	9 000	9 000	9 000	9 000
Rails	800	800	800	800	800	800	800	800	800	800	800	800	800
Total load per cable	91 100	89 400	93 200	95 300	98 200	98 600	98 400	93 400	85 800	85 400	86 300	86 000	85 400

For connecting the 12-in. eye-bars of the cables, pins, 11½ in. in diameter, were used; consequently, with eye-bar heads the same thickness as the body of the bar, the bearing pressure on these pins would have exceeded the working tension in the eye-bars. To reduce this high unit bearing pressure the heads were made ⅛ in. thicker than the remainder of the bars, thus reducing the unit pressure from 6 to 9%, depending on the bar thickness. To resist the high unit stress the pins were made of special heat-treated steel with a yield point ranging between 60 000 and 65 000 lb. per sq. in., and a tensile strength ranging between 100 000 and 105 000 lb. per sq. in. A few of the pins are of chrome-nickel steel having the same range of strength.

To facilitate the entry of the pins during erection, a novel detail in the form of oval pin-holes was developed. (See Fig. 18.) The hole is made somewhat elongated axially and enlarged on the inside, to provide more clearance for the insertion of the pin or for slipping the bar over the pin, while retaining a close fit in the segment in contact. The outer or bearing semicircle exceeds the diameter of the pin by only 0.005 in., while the inner semicircle is bored to the diameter of the pin plus $\frac{1}{32}$ in., and the two centers are separated $\frac{1}{8}$ in. along the axis of the eye-bar. The unusually close fit thus secured along the bearing surface reduces the secondary stresses in the eye-bar head. This detail is patented* by the American Bridge Company.

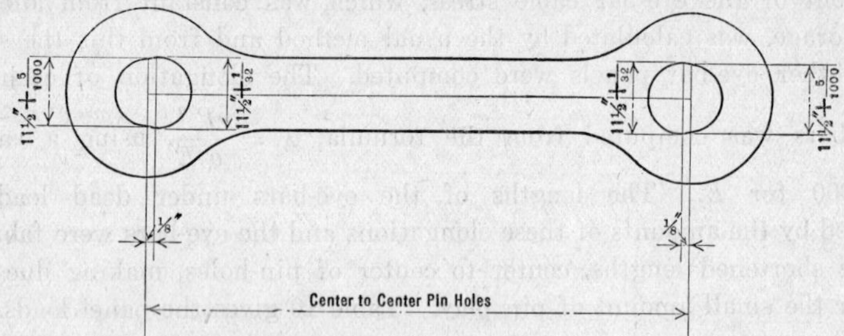

FIG. 18.—NOVEL PIN-HOLE DETAIL FOR EYE-BARS OF FLORIANOPOLIS BRIDGE.

DEVELOPMENT OF DESIGN OF SUSPENSION SPAN TRUSSES

The decision to make the central part of the top chord integral with the eye-bar cable presented some interesting studies in fabrication and erection. According to the design the eye-bar cable was to support the entire dead weight of the bridge; and the stiffening truss was designed for live load, wind, and temperature. This meant that when the entire dead load was suspended from the eye-bar cables they would occupy a definite fixed position in space at a given normal temperature and with no wind blowing. Top chord Points 2 to 14, inclusive, at each end of the truss, are supported from the cables by rope hangers, while top chord Points 16 to 16 are parts of the eye-bar cables.

The rope hangers are made with provision for permanent adjustment whereas between Points 16 and 16 there are no means of adjustment. For this reason all diagonal members of the truss between Points 16 were shipped with rivet holes in both ends of the diagonals; but the gusset-plates of the bottom chords to which these diagonals connected, were shipped blank. After the entire dead load was supported from the eye-bar cables the rivet holes could be drilled in these gusset-plates using the holes in the diagonals as templets and thus insuring the erection of the truss members under zero dead load stress.

This meant the drilling of 1 728 field holes; but as the material was in every case the $\frac{1}{2}$-in. gusset-plates, it was considered safer to do the field drilling than to run the risk of poorly matched holes which would involve either drifting and the introduction of dead load stress in the truss members or the necessity of excessive reaming.

The truss and bracing members were of normal sizes for heavy highway work and presented no special difficulties in the shop. In fact, the entire structure was fabricated without unusual difficulties.

* Patent No. 1,600,233, filed July 2, 1924, Serial No. 723,761.

Development of Method for Erecting Cables

The success of the construction was dependent on the successful erection of the eye-bars forming the main cables. When the entire dead load was carried by the cables the sag at the center should be 120 ft. with the main towers vertical. At that time the dead load of the main span, including the cables, was about 4 400 lb. per lin. ft. of bridge, and the dead load of the back-stay portion of the cable, which consisted of eye-bars and pins only, was 900 lb. per lin. ft. of bridge. The weight of the eye-bars and pins of the main span was about 850 lb. per lin. ft. of bridge. Therefore, under dead load the total weight per linear foot of the main span was about five times as much as for the cables themselves. When the eye-bar cables were swung under their own weight only, the main span portions weighed less per linear foot than the back-stay portions, and the calculated sag at the center of the main span was about 116 ft., based on the towers being tilted back so that the distance, center to center of column tops, was 1 115 ft. 7 in.

To make the erection of the eye-bars as simple and cheap as possible it was decided to hang them by hand-operated chain hoists which in turn were suspended from flexible ropes; then, after all the eye-bars and pins were placed and supported by the ropes, to swing the eye-bar cables by paying out the chain hoists. To make this vertical release movement of the eye-bars as small as possible, the ropes were made of such length that when all the bars were supported, the sag of the ropes (and, hence, of the bars) should be 115 ft., just 1 ft. less than the sag of the bars swinging under their own weight. The ropes had to support themselves as well as the bars. The weight on the main span portion of the ropes, consisting of the eye-bars, pins, ropes, chain hoists, clamps, and connections, was about 500 lb. per lin. ft of each cable.

To save as much erection material as possible flexible hoisting ropes, 1 in. in diameter, were used, so that after having served their purpose in the erection of the two eye-bar cables they could be cut up and used for ordinary hoisting rope in the Erecting Department. The grade selected had an approximate ultimate strength of 90 000 lb. per rope; a factor of safety of three was used for erection. Based on a sag of 115 ft. and a span of 1 115 ft. 7 in., the horizontal component of the stress in the ropes when they supported all the eye-bars was 660 000 lb. and the maximum stress that occurred in the anchorage portion of the ropes was 770 000 lb. At 32 000 lb. per rope, twenty-four 1-in. ropes were required.

After their completion the main towers will rock on their pedestals (see Fig. 10) under various conditions of loading in such manner as to make the horizontal components of the cable stresses constant from anchorage to anchorage and so give resultant vertical loads only. Therefore, the saddles (Fig. 7) were fixed to the tops of the columns. During the erection of the eye-bars, however, the main tower columns were locked into the 185-ft. spans. To insure that the horizontal components of the stresses in the erection rope would be taken entirely by the anchorages, temporary I-beam grillages were provided, bearing on rollers which in turn rested on top of the column castings (Fig. 29).

Wire rope is much more elastic than ordinary structural steel. It was necessary to ascertain either the modulus of elasticity of the ropes or their elongation under a stress of 32 000 lb. per rope. The lengths of the erection ropes, under full load, had then to be shortened by the amount of this elongation so that when they supported all the eye-bars, the sag at the center would not exceed 115 ft. Ordinarily, the rope used for suspension bridge cables, consisting of 6 strands with a wire center, has a modulus of elasticity of from 12 000 000 to 20 000 000, depending upon the lay of the rope and the stress it carries. Ordinary flexible hoisting rope consisting of 6 strands with a hemp center has a modulus of elasticity of from 5 000 000 to 10 000 000.

The method adopted for the erection of the eye-bars was to attach them and their pins to the lower ends of the hand-operated chain hoists, the upper ends of which were held by clamps around the ropes. The load at each panel point was 19 000 lb., so that hoists with capacities of 20 000 lb. were selected. When all bars were suspended, the chain hoists could be played out and the eye-bars lowered from a sag of 115 ft. until they were carrying their own weight under a sag of 116 ft. As the loads on the hoists were released, the erection ropes were relieved of their stress, and shortened to a length corresponding to their own weight but not to their original length because of the permanent set they had acquired. The sag meanwhile decreased from 115 ft. until it reached an amount dependent on the new length of the ropes. This decrease had to be determined in order to provide the proper amount of chain for the operation of the chain hoists. The greatest vertical movement was of course at the center of the span, the amount decreasing toward the towers at which points there was none. The center of the ropes was 6 ft. above the center of the main pins on top of the towers. The chain hoists were to be originally set so that the eye-bar pins would be a uniform distance of 6 ft. below the ropes when the eye-bars were first lifted into position. The problem therefore was twofold:

First.—To make the ropes short enough at the start so that when they had elongated under the weight of all the bars, the sag at the center would be such as to permit all the eye-bars to be placed. If the sag reached 116 ft. before all the eye-bars were placed it would be difficult to slip the remaining ones over the pins.

Second.—To make the ropes long enough at the start so that when they again supported their own weight only (after they had been relieved of the weight of the eye-bars and had received their permanent set), the sag would still come within the limits of the amount of chain provided for the operation of the chain hoists. Otherwise, it would be impossible to swing the eye-bar cables by the chain hoists alone.

Tests of Erection Rope

The success of the operation therefore depended on the movements and behavior of the erection ropes. As this method of erection of eye-bars was a new departure in bridge construction it was decided to make a series of tests on the actual ropes used. In conferences with the engineers of the

American Steel and Wire Company which fabricated the ropes, the following procedure was adopted. The distance, center to center of the girders that served to anchor the ropes, was about 1 700 ft., and to provide for proper end fastening each of the twenty-four ropes was made 1 800 ft. long. It was very desirable to have the ropes stretch uniformly so that as far as possible each should carry its share of the load. Hence, the rope fabricators decided to spin four ropes in lengths of 10 800 ft. each, using extra precautions in the spinning, and then to cut each of these four pieces into six equal parts of 1 800 ft. each, thus making the twenty-four ropes.

One test piece was cut from each end of each of the four 10 800-ft. ropes. The twenty-four ropes were to be lettered from *A* to *X* so that the test pieces were cut from Ropes *A, F, G, K, M, R, S,* and *X*. The second long length of rope was spun only to about 9 000 ft., so that an additional 1 800-ft. piece had to be made. This became Rope *L,* from which a test piece was cut so that there were actually nine test pieces. These were fitted with sockets at each end, the distance between sockets being the standard testing length of about 36 in. The tests were made on the Emery hydraulic testing machine at the Worcester Plant of the American Steel and Wire Company, the measurements being taken by an extensometer reading to 0.0001 in. in a gauge length of 10 in.

The ropes were to be used twice in the field during the erection of the bars. They were first to be put up over the north columns. Supporting its own weight, each rope would be stressed to about 3 000 lb. The eye-bars for the north cable were then to be supported from the ropes, the average stress per rope under this condition being about 30 000 lb. The north cable would then be swung and the ropes again would support their own weight only, under a stress of 3 000 lb. per rope. Next the ropes were to be transferred to the tops of the south columns and the operation repeated.

To approximate erection conditions as far as possible each of the test pieces was stressed twice to an amount exceeding 30 000 lb. After taking a zero reading at 200 lb., loads were applied in 200-lb. increments up to 3 000 lb., and then by 1 000-lb. increments up to 35 000 lb. The load was then released and the tests repeated to 50 000 lb. This method applied for test pieces from Ropes *A, F, G,* and *K*.

For the remaining five ropes (*L, M, R, S,* and *X*), the following method which more closely approximated service conditions was adopted. After an initial load of 200 lb., increments of 200 lb. were applied up to 3 000 lb., and from there in increments of 1 000 lb., up to 35 000 lb. Instead of releasing the load entirely it was lessened gradually to 3 000 lb. and then increased a second time by 1 000-lb. increments to 50 000 lb. These test loads corresponded to the excessive stresses during the erection. They were carried to 35 000 lb. and to 50 000 lb. merely to have information in case the loads exceeded 30 000 lb. per rope. Actually, the stress in the back-stay portions was about 32 000 lb.

Readings of the elongations at each increment were plotted, making it possible to compute the moduli of elasticity for any stresses. From these moduli could be determined the proper lengths for the ropes and the movements that would take place during the erection of the cables. These tests were made in August and September, 1924. Table 11 shows a representative set of gauge readings of elongations and Figs. 19 and 20 show the corresponding plots of these readings.

TABLE 11.—DISTANCES USING DIFFERENT, E, FOR VARIOUS PARTS OF ROPE.

Conditions of load.	Stress, in Pounds per Rope.		Values of E, in Millions.		Sag, in feet.	Distances, in Feet, Along Rope.			
	Main span.	Approach.	Main span.	Approach.		AB.	BD.	DE.	Total.
Ropes on ground	200	200	....	....	....	272.9	1 136.5	292.6	1 702.0
Ropes supporting themselves	3 100	3 500	5.3	5.5	87	273.3	1 138.3	293.1	1 704.7
Ropes supporting half bars first time	18 600	21 000	7.3	7.5	107	274.7	1 143.9	294.6	1 713.2
Ropes supporting all bars first time	28 500	32 000	8.0	8.3	115	275.4	1 146.4	295.3	1 717.1
Ropes after first eye-bar cable released	2 700	3 000	1.5	1.7	99	274.1	1 141.7	293.9	1 709.7
Ropes supporting half bars second time	18 300	20 500	6.4	6.8	109	274.9	1 144.5	294.7	1 714.1
Ropes supporting all bars second time	28 500	32 000	8.0	8.4	115	275.4	1 146.4	295.3	1 717.1

LOCATION OF ERECTION ROPES

In order to save in the length of ropes required and to facilitate their transfer from the north to the south side, the rope girders for fastening the ends of the ropes were placed at Points A and E (Fig. 21) above the viaduct floor level. The permanent eye-bars from Points X to CA-6 on the continent side and from Points IA-6 to Y on the island side were erected on falsework bents near the pins at their permanent elevations. The rope girder pins were long and rested on the permanent eye-bar heads at Points A and E; two temporary eye-bars extended from the rope girder pins back to the permanent pins at Points CA-7 and IA-7. After the permanent eye-bars were placed from Points X to CA-6 and from Points Y to IA-6, the temporary eye-bars, temporary pins, and rope girders were erected on the north side of the bridge. The horizontal and vertical locations of the rope girder pins were thus known with respect to the pedestals in the anchorages and also to the bases of the main tower columns.

When the sag of the erection ropes was 115 ft. (when they held all the eye-bars, Fig. 22 (c)), the calculated distance, center to center of rope shoes, on the tops of the tower columns was 1 115 ft. 7 in. and the rope shoes were assumed to be exactly over the center of the tops of the main tower columns. Under this condition the length of Rope AE was 1 717.1 ft., made up of AB = 275.4 ft., BD = 1 146.4 ft., and DE = 295.3 ft., measured

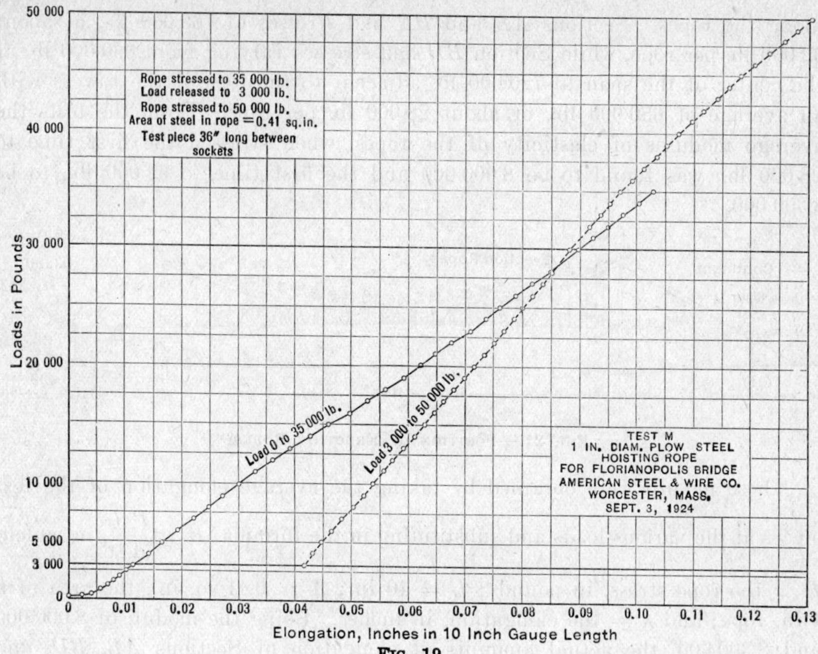
Rope stressed to 35 000 lb.
Load released to 3 000 lb.
Rope stressed to 50 000 lb.
Area of steel in rope = 0.41 sq.in.
Test piece 36″ long between sockets
Load 0 to 35 000 lb.
Load 3 000 to 50 000 lb.
TEST M
1 IN. DIAM. PLOW STEEL HOISTING ROPE
FOR FLORIANOPOLIS BRIDGE
AMERICAN STEEL & WIRE CO.
WORCESTER, MASS.
SEPT. 3, 1924
Loads in Pounds
Elongation, Inches in 10 Inch Gauge Length
0
3 000
5 000
10 000
20 000
30 000
40 000
50 000
0 0.01 0.02 0.03 0.04 0.05 0.06 0.07 0.08 0.09 0.10 0.11 0.12 0.13

FIG. 19.

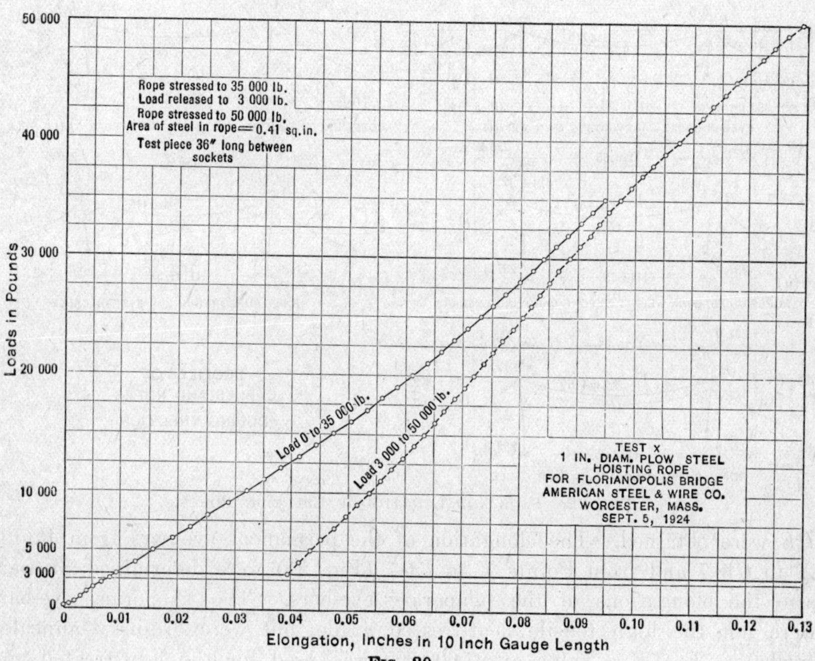
Rope stressed to 35 000 lb.
Load released to 3 000 lb.
Rope stressed to 50 000 lb.
Area of steel in rope = 0.41 sq.in.
Test piece 36″ long between sockets
Load 0 to 35 000 lb.
Load 3 000 to 50 000 lb.
TEST X
1 IN. DIAM. PLOW STEEL HOISTING ROPE
FOR FLORIANOPOLIS BRIDGE
AMERICAN STEEL & WIRE CO.
WORCESTER, MASS.
SEPT. 5, 1924
Loads in Pounds
Elongation, Inches in 10 Inch Gauge Length
0
3 000
5 000
10 000
20 000
30 000
40 000
50 000
0 0.01 0.02 0.03 0.04 0.05 0.06 0.07 0.08 0.09 0.10 0.11 0.12 0.13

FIG. 20.

along the ropes. Sections AB and DE had stresses of 768 000 lb., or about 32 000 lb. per rope, while Section BD had stresses varying from 660 000 lb. at the center of the span to 720 000 lb. adjacent to the tops of the towers with an average of 680 000 lb., or about 28 000 lb. per rope. From the tests the average modulus of elasticity of the ropes, when stressed the first time to 28 000 lb., was found to be 8 000 000 and the first time to 32 000 lb., to be 8 300 000.

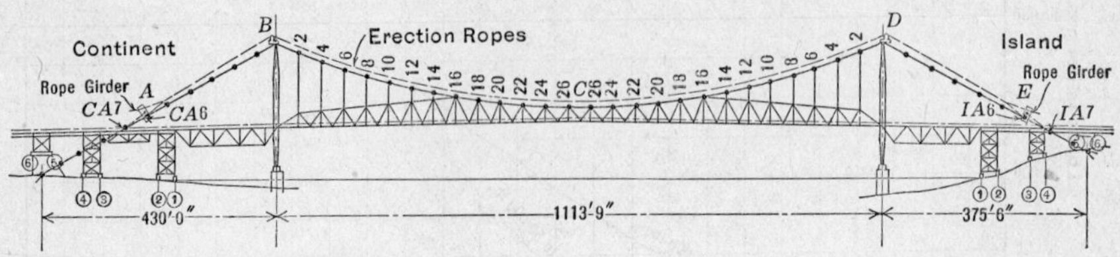

FIG. 21.—POSITION OF ERECTION ROPES.

These moduli were obtained by taking the average elongation of the test pieces at the various loads and substituting in the formula, $E = \frac{P\,L}{A\,\lambda}$, in which, P = the rope stress, in pounds; L = 10 in.; A = 0.41 sq. in., the area of a 1-in. rope; and λ = the elongation, in inches. Using the moduli of 8 000 000 and 8 300 000, the actual amounts of elongation of Sections AB, BD, and

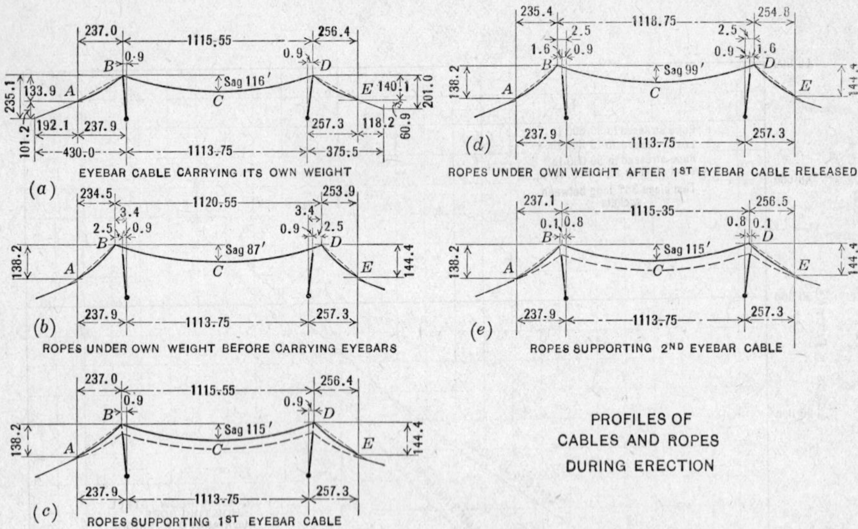

FIG. 22.—SAGS AND LENGTHS OF ERECTION ROPES.

DE were obtained. The elongation of the permanent eye-bars from Points X to CA-7 and from Points Y to IA-7 (Fig. 21) were determined, as were also the elongations of the temporary eye-bars. The temporary eye-bars were not the high tensile heat-treated grade, but were ordinary annealed eye-bars. For E a value of 27 000 000 was used for the heat-treated and

29 000 000 for the ordinary eye-bars. From these values and the known lengths the elongations of both the permanent and temporary eye-bars were ascertained.

Variation in Position of Ropes During Erection of Eye-Bars

When the main span part of the ropes had a sag of 115 ft., the continent and island portions of the back-stays had sags of 5.4 ft. and 6.3 ft., respectively. These sags were determined from the formula, $f_1 = f \frac{w_1}{w} \left(\frac{l_1}{l} \right)^2$, in which, f = main span sag; l = length of main span; l_1 = horizontal projection of back-stay; w = weight per linear foot of load on main span; and w_1 = weight per linear foot of load on back-stay, both lengths and loads being measured along the horizontal.

While the ropes had the same sections from A to E (Fig. 21), the loads of the eye-bars were applied at points approximately 40 ft. apart along the ropes. These loads were not equal so that the ropes hung in an equilibrium polygon such that the horizontal components of the rope stress were constant from anchorage to anchorage. The general shape of the curve, however, approximated a parabola and the lengths of the rope sections were computed on that basis. These rope lengths under full load being AB = 275.4 ft., BD = 1146.4 ft., and DE = 293.3 ft., and the elongations being 2.6 ft., 9.8 ft., and 2.7 ft., the lengths of the three sections under a stress of 200 lb. per rope were, therefore, 272.8 ft., 1 136.6 ft., and 292.6 ft., respectively, making a total length of rope between rope girders of 1 702 ft. The fabricating plant marked Pilot Rope M with wires at Points A, B, C, D, and E, such that AB, BD, and DE were 273 ft., 1 137 ft., and 293 ft., totaling 1 703 ft. The mark, C, was placed midway between Points B and D, and the distances from Points A and E to the two ends of the rope were about 48 ft. 6 in. The information for marking the pilot rope was given to the plant before the final calculations were made, which accounts for the difference between the computed distances of 1 702 and 1 703 ft.

Having fixed the distance between the marks under 200 lb. stress it was necessary to determine the stretch under the weight of the ropes themselves so as to place the rope shoes in proper position on top of the tower columns. Trial positions and a trial sag were assumed and the horizontal component of the stress then computed. From this the actual stress of the back-stay portions and the average stress of the main span portion were calculated and the elongations of the several parts determined. Adding these elongations to the lengths of AB, BD, and DE, under a stress of 200 lb. per rope, gave the three respective lengths when the ropes carried their own weights only (Fig. 22(b)).

Assuming the ropes to follow the parabolic form, the lengths of these distances, AB, BD, and DE, were calculated and the parabolic lengths compared with the lengths previously found by adding the elongations to the original fabricated lengths. Corrections were then made and new trial sags, or trial positions of the rope shoes on top of the towers, or both, were assumed and the process was repeated until the two sets checked within small amounts. It was found that the second or third trial gave the desired results sufficiently close. These figures: AB = 273.3 ft., BD = 1 138.3 ft., and DE = 293.1 ft., totaling 1 704.7 ft., with a sag of 87 ft., gave the length and sag of the ropes when stretched between the towers for the first time.

The same procedure was followed for the determination of the lengths and sags of the ropes after the north eye-bar cable was swung and the ropes were again supporting their own weight only (Fig. 22 (*d*)). This corresponded to the condition of Test Ropes *L, M, R, S,* and *X,* after they had been stressed up to 35 000 lb. and then released to 3 000 lb. These lengths were AB = 274.1 ft., BD = 1 141.7 ft., and DE = 293.9 ft., totaling 1 709.7 ft., with a sag of 99 ft.

The sags and lengths of the ropes when supporting the eye-bars a second time (Fig. 22 (*e*)) were then computed as previously. This corresponded to the condition of the test ropes when stressed a second time to 30 000 lb. per rope. For comparison the various sags under the several conditions are shown together in Fig. 22. Table 12 gives a summary of these sags, the moduli of elasticity, the stresses in the ropes, and the lengths of the ropes under the different conditions of loading.

When the ropes had been returned to the United States after having been used in the successful erection of the span, two pieces were cut from the pilot rope, *M,* one from the back-stay portion near *A* and the other from the main span portion near *B.* These were tested in February, 1926, at Worcester.

Shipment of Material

The steelwork was shipped in four sections. The advance shipment, consisting of the eye-bars, pins, and girders that were to be embedded in the masonry, was shipped in 1923. This material was placed by the general contractors during the construction of the anchorages. The three remaining shipments, comprising the remainder of the material, were made during the period from June to October, 1924; in the first was included both viaduct approaches and parts of the main towers; in the second the remainder of the towers, the eye-bars, pins, and parts of the main span; in the third and last, the remainder of the main span, the railing, erection ropes, and miscellaneous material. The eye-bars were shipped in nests of three bars each, making shipping pieces with over-all dimensions about 28 in. by 12 in. by 50 ft. long and weighing about 6 tons.

All the material arrived at the site in excellent condition, the eye-bars particularly standing the 6 000-mile ocean voyage without any damage other than slight rust in some spots where the shop coat of paint had worn off in transit.

Field Organization

On account of the special nature of the erection, the field organization was selected with the greatest care. It was considered to be better equipped for foreign work than any other ever assembled by the United States Steel Products Company.

TABLE 12.—Gauge Readings for Test Ropes *M* and *X*.

Load, in pounds.	Rope *M*.				Rope *X*.			
	First Test.		Second Test.		First Test.		Second Test.	
	Gauge reading, in inches.	Value of *E*.	Gauge reading, in inches.	Value of *E*.	Gauge reading, in inches.	Value of *E*.	Gauge reading, in inches.	Value of *E*.
200	0	...	...	...	0	...	...	...
400	0.0027	...	...	...	0.0010	...	...	...
600	0.0042	...	...	...	0.0017	...	...	...
800	0.0051	...	...	...	0.0023	...	...	...
1 000	0.0059	4 140 000	...	...	0.0029	8 400 000	...	...
1 200	0.0066	...	...	...	0.0035	...	...	...
1 400	0.0071	...	...	...	0.0040	...	...	...
1 600	0.0077	...	...	...	0.0047	...	...	...
1 800	0.0083	...	...	...	0.0053	...	...	...
2 000	0.0088	5 550 000	...	...	0.0060	8 120 000	...	...
2 200	0.0094	...	...	...	0.0067	...	...	...
2 400	0.0099	...	...	...	0.073	...	...	...
2 600	0.0104	...	...	...	0.081	...	...	...
2 800	0.0110	...	...	...	0.088	...	...	...
3 000	0.0115	6 360 000	0.0418	1 750 000	0.0094	7 780 000	0.0395	1 850 000
4 000	0.0141	6 930 000	0.0431	2 260 000	0.0125	7 820 000	0.0414	2 360 000
5 000	0.0166	7 350 000	0.0448	2 720 000	0.0157	7 780 000	0.0433	2 820 000
6 000	0.0193	...	0.0466	...	0.0191	...	0.0454	...
7 000	0.0222	...	0.0483	...	0.0224	...	0.0475	...
8 000	0.0247	...	0.0503	...	0.0254	...	0.0496	...
9 000	0.0272	...	0.0521	...	0.0288	...	0.0518	...
10 000	0.0301	8 100 000	0.0539	4 530 000	0.0321	7 600 000	0.0537	4 550 000
11 000	0.0331	...	0.0556	...	0.0351	...	0.0556	...
12 000	0.0361	...	0.0573	...	0.0384	...	0.0576	...
13 000	0.0391	...	0.0592	...	0.0415	...	0.0596	...
14 000	0.0427	...	0.0611	...	0.0445	...	0.0615	...
15 000	0.0462	7 920 000	0.0629	5 830 000	0.0475	7 700 000	0.0633	5 800 000
16 000	0.0499	...	0.0646	...	0.0505	...	0.0650	...
17 000	0.0527	...	0.0662	...	0.0532	...	0.0668	...
18 000	0.0560	...	0.0680	...	0.0560	...	0.0686	...
19 000	0.0594	...	0.0698	...	0.0585	...	0.0705	...
20 000	0.0621	7 860 000	0.0716	6 820 000	0.0613	7 950 000	0.0720	6 690 000
21 000	0.0646	...	0.0735	...	0.0639	...	0.0737	...
22 000	0.0675	...	0.0753	...	0.0662	...	0.0754	...
23 000	0.0710	...	0.0770	...	0.0686	...	0.0770	...
24 000	0.0737	...	0.0786	...	0.0710	...	0.0788	...
25 000	0.0762	8 000 000	0.0803	7 600 000	0.0732	8 350 000	0.0805	7 580 000
26 000	0.0790	...	0.0820	...	0.0753	...	0.0820	...
27 000	0.0817	...	0.0838	...	0.0775	...	0.0835	...
28 000	0.0849	...	0.0852	...	0.0797	...	0.0852	...
29 000	0.0870	...	0.0868	...	0.0821	...	0.0868	...
30 000	...	8 160 000	0.0884	8 280 000	0.0841	8 720 000	0.0886	8 260 000
31 000	0.0923	...	0.0901	...	0.0861	...	0.0903	...
32 000	0.0950	...	0.0918	...	0.0884	...	0.0921	...
33 000	0.0977	...	0.0937	...	0.0905	...	0.0938	...
34 000	0.1004	...	0.0954	...	0.0926	...	0.0954	...
35 000	0.1030	8 280 000	0.0971	8 800 000	0.0947	9 040 000	0.0972	8 800 000
36 000	...	...	0.0992	...	...	...	0.0991	...
37 000	...	...	0.1014	...	...	...	0.1013	...
38 000	...	...	0.1036	...	...	...	0.1032	...
39 000	...	...	0.1053	...	...	...	0.1051	...
40 000	...	...	0.1073	9 080 000	...	...	0.1076	9 080 000
41 000	...	...	0.1096	...	...	...	0.1096	...
42 000	...	...	0.1119	...	...	...	0.1118	...
43 000	...	...	0.1141	...	...	...	0.1136	...
44 000	...	...	0.1162	...	...	...	0.1156	...
45 000	...	...	0.1183	9 260 000	...	...	0.1178	9 320 000
46 000	...	...	0.1208	...	...	...	0.1199	...
47 000	...	...	0.1233	...	...	...	0.1222	...
48 000	...	...	0.1257	...	...	...	0.1245	...
49 000	...	...	0.1282	...	...	...	0.1266	...
50 000	...	...	0.1307	9 350 000	...	...	0.1293	9 430 000

The whole scheme was a departure from the conventional method of suspension bridge erection, in the nature of an experiment 6 000 miles from office and plant, so that every precaution was taken to provide against possible contingencies. The superintendent was assisted by two foremen, seventeen American bridge men, and a time-keeper. Two field engineers were assigned to the field organization. In addition to the American nuclei of twenty-two men, the field force was augmented by local labor. This Brazilian labor did most of the work in the material yard while the Americans attended to the actual raising of the steel.

Several of the natives, however, developed into fairly good bridge men and were used on the erection of the main span. The Company was fortunate in obtaining the local services of two Italians who were familiar with steel erection and who were put in charge of the native labor in the material yard.

Unloading of Material

The first contingent of the erection organization left New York, on July 5, 1924, and arrived at Florianopolis about July 25. This part of the organization distributed the steel over the material yard, which was located at the mainland end of the bridge, as the several steel shipments arrived. The large, ocean-going freight boats could not enter the shallow strait between the Island of Santa Catharina and the mainland, and it was necessary, therefore, to discharge the cargo from the ships into lighters and tow the lighters about 10 miles from the ships to the landing dock.

The locomotive crane in the yard unloaded the lighter during the day and distributed the material over the yard. Usually, during the night the lighter was towed back to the ship, reloaded with another batch of material, and towed back to the dock, ready for unloading the following morning, although the barges were often unloaded also at night.

Erection of Approach Viaducts

Erection of steel was started on the continent end of the bridge by erecting Towers 1-2 and 3-4 (Fig. 21), using a locomotive crane. A "jinniwink" derrick was then raised to the top of Tower 3-4. The two trusses of the 110-ft. span, Tower 2-3, were riveted up on the ground and then raised into position. In the meantime falsework had been driven under the 185-ft. span (adjoining the tower), which was erected on the falsework by the jinniwink. The erection of the remainder of the continent viaduct was completed by the jinniwink, working back toward the west abutment. Using a track laid in the material yard parallel to the continent viaduct on the south side, the locomotive crane carried the viaduct steel to its proper location, from which it was raised to the viaduct floor level by the jinniwink.

The east or island viaduct was erected in the same general manner except that the steel had to be lightered over to the island from the material yard, and that there was no locomotive crane on the island side.

No special difficulties were encountered in the erection of the viaducts except that the rate of progress was somewhat slow owing to the large number of pieces to be handled.

The continent viaduct was completed about November 8, 1924, taking 3 months; and the island viaduct was completed about January 5, 1925, taking 2½ months.

Erection of Main Towers

The shoes of the continent tower were set in the center of the continent piers using the jinniwink derrick on top of the viaduct. The first sections of the continent tower columns (Fig. 23) were placed tilted back toward the viaduct so that the tops of the columns would come about 1 ft. back of their final position making the distance, center to center of column tops, 1 115 ft. 7 in. (for reasons already explained). The temporary struts attaching the tower to the 185 ft. span, during erection, are shown in Fig. 24. The lower bracing and the main cross-girder were placed as the column sections were erected. This much of the tower was erected using the jinniwink on the deck of the viaduct.

A special climbing traveler (Fig. 25) was then built around the tower and the remaining six column sections were placed by this creeper traveler, which climbed up the tower as the sections were added. The remainder of the tower bracing was placed as the column sections were added.

As a preliminary measurement across the channel had indicated that the distance, center to center of piers, might be 6 in. in error, these island piers were made 2 ft. larger in diameter than the continent piers. When the island piers were completed sufficiently to enable a more accurate measurement to be taken, it was found that the centers of the continent and island piers were 3 in. farther apart than the proper distance of 1 113 ft. 9 in. The island tower shoes, therefore, were set 3 in. off the center of the island piers in accordance with the triangulation measurements so that the steel towers would be the proper distance, center to center. With the island piers 2 ft. larger in diameter than the continent piers, the minimum distance from the main shoes to the edge of the island piers was at least as great as the same distance on the continent piers.

The island main tower was then erected in a manner similar to the continent tower (Fig. 26). The material for both towers was loaded on the lighter and brought to the foot of the towers. The creeper traveler performed its part of the work in a very satisfactory manner. The continent tower was completed about December 27, 1924, taking 6 weeks; and the island tower was completed about February 1, 1925, taking 5 weeks.

Erection of Ropes, Trolleys, Clamps, and Chain Hoists

The steel towers were erected by February 1, 1925. The beam grillages, temporary rollers, and rope shoes were then placed on top of the two north columns. All the eye-bars from the anchorages up to the viaduct floor level had been placed previously, and the temporary eye-bars and the rope girders on the north side of the bridge followed during the first week of February. A continuous ¾-in. rope was then run across the main channel, lifted to the top of each tower, and placed on the top transverse tower strut adjacent to the north eye-bar shoes.

Twelve of the twenty-four reels containing the erection ropes had been transferred from the continent to the island side and on February 10, 1925, everything was ready for the placing of the pilot rope. The free end of this pilot rope was unwound from its reel on the continent side and lifted to the floor level of the viaduct. It was then fastened to the continuous ⅞-in. rope, hauled up to the top of the tower, across the strait, and over the top of the island tower, using the hoisting engine on the island viaduct. The two ends were then wound one and one-half times around the rope girders and clamped into position so that Marks *A* and *E* came at the proper position on the rope girders.

The centers of the rope shoes had been placed 2½ ft. back from the center of the eye-bar shoes on the tops of the main columns in accordance with the calculations. (Fig. 22 (*b*)). The pilot rope was then lifted into the grooves on the rope shoes, Marks *B* and *D* being placed in the center of these shoes. An observation taken on Mark *C* midway between Marks *B* and *D* showed the sag to be between 86 and 87 ft., or within 1 ft. of the calculated distance. During the next three days the remaining twenty-three erection ropes were placed in a similar manner and fastened to the rope girders so that the sags were the same as the sag of the pilot rope. The rope ends were fastened together in pairs, the free end of one rope after one and one-half complete turns around the rope girder being clamped to its adjacent neighbor by 6-rope clamps (Fig. 27).

After the main span and back-stay trolleys had been placed in position on the ropes, the main span trolley was moved across from the island to the continent side placing the clamps which bound the twenty-four ropes into one cable unit. These clamps were placed at variable distances along the erection ropes in such positions that the chain hoists would hang approximately vertical when all the eye-bars were supported by the ropes. After the twenty-six clamps were in position the main-span trolley moved back to the island side attaching the twenty-six Harrington chain hoists to the clamps. These two operations took about a week. In the meantime, the back-stay trolleys had been placing the clamps on the continent and island back-stay portions of the erection ropes, starting at the top of the towers and working down toward the rope girders.

Erection of North Eye-Bar Cable

By February 23 all the clamps and chain hoists were in place and everything was ready for the erection of the eye-bars. To eliminate the driving of pins up in the air, the two inner eye-bars of alternate panels were assembled in the yard and the two pins inserted in the holes (Fig. 28). In this manner all pins except those at the tops of the tower columns were inserted in the material yard.

The eye-bars were loaded on a lighter which was towed out to position under the ropes and anchored. The main-span trolley moved to a position over the lighter, picked up the two inner eye-bars with pins for Panel 24-26,

FIG. 23.—VIEW SHOWING ERECTION OF FIRST SECTION OF CONTINENT COLUMNS, FLORIANOPOLIS BRIDGE.

FIG. 24.—VIEW OF LOWER PART OF CONTINENT TOWER, FLORIANOPOLIS BRIDGE, SHOWING TEMPORARY STRUT CONNECTIONS.

Fig. 25.—View Showing Erection of Eighth Section of Continent Tower Column, Florianopolis Bridge.

Fig. 26.—Creeper Traveler on Island for Tower Erection, Florianopolis Bridge.

Island Side, raised them up into position at the proper chain hoists where they were fastened to the lower ends of the chain hoists approximately 6 ft. below the erection ropes. The trolley then lifted the eye-bars, 24-26, Continent Side, into position. Fig. 28 is a near view of a pair of eye-bars leaving the barge, while Fig. 31 shows the trolley lifting the second pair of eye-bars, the first pair having already been attached to the chain hoists.

On the main span the ropes were actually about 16 ft. longer than the chord between the tops of the columns while on the back-stays the arc was only about 2 in. longer than the chord. It was impossible, therefore, to pull the shoes off the towers by loading the main span; but it was possible for them to slip off backward if the back-stay eye-bars had been placed with few or no eye-bars weighting the main span.

At the start, therefore, the eye-bars were grouped toward the center of the span. The object was to put as much weight as possible on the central part of the main-span erection ropes so as to bring the rope shoes from 2½ ft. back of the center of the columns (Fig. 29) to a position over the center of the columns (Fig. 30) as quickly as possible. By the time twenty-six eye-bars had been supported on the erection ropes, the rope shoes had moved from a position 2½ ft. away from the column center to 1 ft. from the column center. It was then felt safe to commence the erection of the eye-bars on the two back-stays.

When all the eye-bars had been placed the temporary rope shoes had moved from the original position of 2 ft. 6 in. back of the saddle-casting to a position practically over the center of the saddle (Fig. 30). The entire erection of the 156 bars took 2 weeks.

By Saturday noon, March 7, all the eye-bars were erected, the entire eye-bar cable hanging from the erection ropes. The day being clear and calm, it was decided to swing the eye-bar cable that afternoon. The actual sag at that time when the erection ropes carried all the eye-bars was 113 instead of 115 ft., the difference being partly due to not placing the gusset-plates and hangers as was originally contemplated when the calculations were made. The eye-bars had been slipped over the pins without difficulty, thanks to the elongated pin-holes and also to the use of short pilot nuts on each pin. (See Fig. 28.)

Men took positions on the eye-bars at the chain hoists and at 2:30 P. M. the signal was given for the men to slacken off the chain hoists; and in a few minutes the normal 6-ft. gap between the erection ropes and eye-bars began to increase. Some of the men operated the chain hoists faster than others and to keep the eye-bar cable in a smooth curve it was necessary to have them wait until the slower ones could catch up. By 3:15 P. M. all the chain hoists were slack, showing that the eye-bar cable was swinging free of the ropes under its own weight and the erection ropes were carrying their own weight under a sag of between 99 and 100 ft. instead of the calculated sag of 99 ft. The entire operation of swinging took 45 min. and was a complete success in every respect.

Transfer of Ropes

As the next operation, the main-span trolley, starting from the continent tower, moved across the ropes removing the chain hoists and clamps and placing the rope hangers and steel hangers (Fig. 34). In the meantime the back-stay trolleys were removing the clamps and eye-bar supports from the back-stay parts of the ropes. These operations took about a week. The main-span and back-stay trolleys were taken down and the twenty-four ropes were moved from the north to the south of the towers.

The ropes were first lifted out of the rope shoes one at a time and spread out across the top transverse struts of the main towers. The ends were then unclamped, slipped off the rope girders, and fastened temporarily to the viaduct floor-beams. The rope shoes, rollers, and I-beam grillages were transferred to the tops of the south columns, and the rope girders and temporary eye-bars were transferred to the south sides of the viaducts. The rope ends were then fastened to the rope girders in a manner similar to that used for the north cable, and the ropes were lifted into the grooves on the rope shoes on top of the tower columns. The three trolleys were then re-erected on the ropes and the rope clamps and chain hoists placed. These several operations took about two weeks.

Erection of South Eye-Bar Cable

On March 26, erection of the south eye-bar cable was commenced. The method used here was the same as that used for the north cable and the entire 156 eye-bars were placed in one week, just one-half the time that it took for the north cable.

By April 2 all the eye-bars were hanging from the erection ropes. At 3:30 P. M. the signal was given for the men at the hoists to slacken off (Fig. 32); by 4:00 P. M. all the hoists were loose and the south eye-bar cable was self-supporting (Fig. 33). Clamps and chain hoists were then removed; rope hangers and steel hangers were erected; and the three rope trolleys were taken down. These operations took about four days.

Erection of Trusses

The first two truss panels at each end of the bridge were erected by jinniwinks standing on the viaducts, the remainder of the main span being erected by the overhead trolley method.

Two erection ropes were lifted from the rope shoe and placed on the wheels on top of the transverse struts adjacent to the cast-steel shoes. The ends of these ropes were then loosened from the rope girders and fastened around the rope-girder pins, each end being shortened 5 ft. so that when fastened to the pins the length of the ropes from pin to pin was 1 691 instead of 1 701 ft. This change was made so that when the center bottom chord section weighing 18 000 lb. was lifted into position the member would be above its proper elevation and could be easily slipped into position and connected to the bottom of the steel hangers.

By this time the verticals of the trusses had already been placed (Fig. 34). Before any other permanent member was erected a test load of 18 000 lb. was

Fig. 27.—Clamping of Twenty-Four Erection Ropes Around Rope Girder, Florianopolis Bridge.

Fig. 28.—View Showing Raising of Eye-Bars with Pins, Florianopolis Bridge.

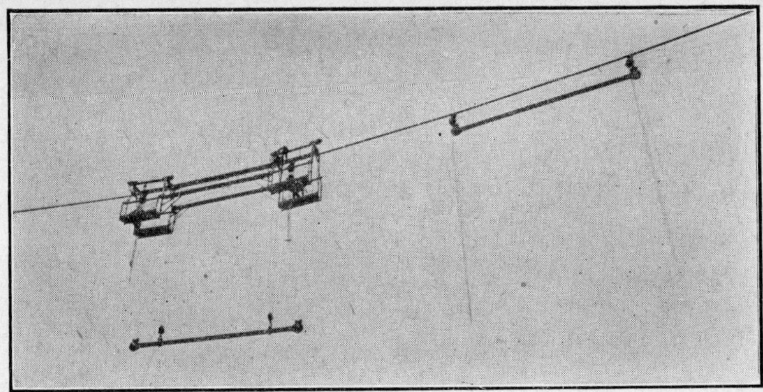

Fig. 31.—Trolley Lifting Second Pair of Eye-Bars, Florianopolis Bridge.

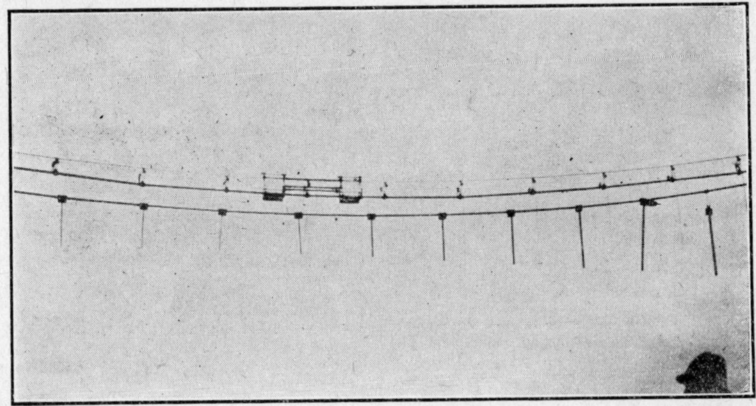

Fig. 32.—South Eye-Bar Cable Supported from Ropes, 3:30 p. m., April 2, 1925, Florianopolis Bridge.

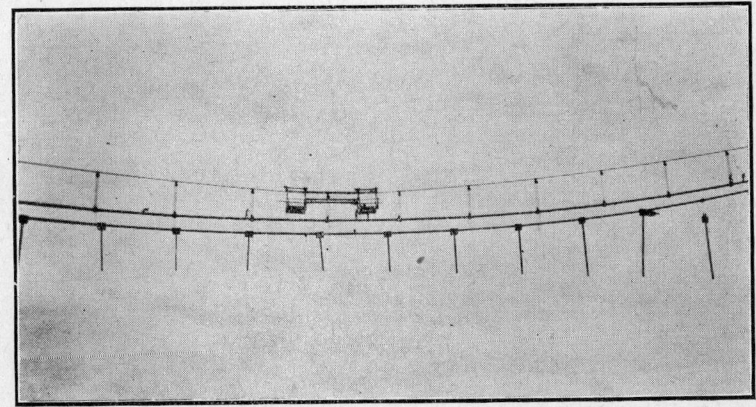

Fig. 33.—South Eye-Bar Cable, Self-Supporting and Free of Ropes, 4:00 p. m., April 2, 1925, Florianopolis Bridge.

placed on the small rope trolley that had been erected on the two 1-in. ropes, and the trolley was pulled out to the center of the span. This test checked the calculations and proved that it was possible to erect the bottom chords by this method. It would have been a simple matter to have made the ropes shorter; then the trolley would have been high enough to attach the truss member, but the stress per rope would have exceeded the 32 000 lb., and it was undesirable to use three ropes as the trolley equipment had been designed for support on two ropes only.

The south bottom chords were the first truss members erected by the overhead method. These were placed starting from the continent and working toward the island. When the continent half of the bottom chords was suspended from the hangers the weight distorted the eye-bar cable. As the remainder of the south bottom chord was placed the eye-bar cable gradually came back to its symmetrical form (Fig. 35); and when the last section of bottom chord was placed there was a gap of about 6 in., due to the camber being high under the partial dead load. The south truss diagonals were then erected, using the same trolley. The bottom chords were erected in 14 hours and the diagonals in an equal period.

Another trolley was then erected on two more of the erection ropes placed adjacent to the cast-steel shoes on the north columns and the north bottom chords and diagonals were erected in a similar manner. The bottom chords of this truss were placed in 10 hours and the diagonals also in 10 hours.

The north and south top chords were then erected, first on the continent side and then on the island side. This operation took about 18 hours. Fig. 36 shows a top chord being lifted into position. Erection of the floor-beams, stringers, and bottom laterals then took place, followed by the top laterals, top struts, and portals. The total time consumed in the main span erection was 45 working days for the erection of about 1 000 members. Fig. 37 shows a view from the continent tower looking toward the island during the erection of the trusses.

Placing Temporary Counterweight and Drilling Holes in Web Members

When all the steel was erected the total dead load was only 3 000 lb. per lin. ft. so that the sag had not reached 120 ft. Under this condition it was impossible to connect the web members and top chords because the fabricated lengths of these members were based on the geometric lengths they would occupy under a sag of 120 ft.

The delivery date of the floor lumber was uncertain so that some temporary load had to be placed upon the main span to bring the eye-bar cable to the correct dead load position, in order that the holes in the blank gusset-plates could be drilled and the diagonals outside Panel Points 16 could be connected under zero stress. As there was considerable sand on the beach along the continent shore it was decided to make use of this material. A sand load equivalent to 1 400 lb. per lin. ft. of bridge was placed on the steel floor system, and this brought the diagonals from Points 0 to 16 at each end of the bridge to such position that connections could be made with practically no drifting. The 1 728 holes in the bottom chord gusset-plates between Points 16 were then drilled and the diagonals connected under this condition. One of the erectors set a record by drilling 240 holes (in ½-in. material) in 1 day of 8 working hours.

Riveting and Painting

There were more than 50 000 field rivets to be driven on the main span and this work was completed during July, 1925. The temporary sand counterweight was then removed and the structure given two coats of field paint.

The last contingent of the erection organization arrived in the United States on August 31, so that a few days less than fourteen months elapsed from the time that the first section of field forces left the country until the last section returned; the actual time of field erection was just about one year.

Summary of Erection

The successful design, fabrication, transportation, and erection of the Florianopolis Bridge has demonstrated the fact that suspension bridges with eye-bar cables are practical and that falsework of the ordinary kind, or, on the other hand, elaborate staging to support the eye-bars during erection, is unnecessary.

A particularly gratifying feature of the bridge from an engineering standpoint was the manner in which the actual movements both of the erection ropes and of the permanent steel towers and main span agreed with the designed movements. It was possible from the calculations to predict the movements or positions under various conditions of erection with a very small error.

The placing of the wooden floor was done by the general contractors, Byington and Sundstrom, and completed during March, 1926. The official opening of the bridge took place on May 3, 1926.

During the entire work in the field extending over a whole year from about August 1, 1924, to August 1, 1925, there was no loss of life. Furthermore, the actual cost of the entire steel superstructure was within the estimate. The Florianopolis type of suspension bridge, therefore, has shown itself to be a practical, a safe, and an economical type of structure.

Total Weights, Quantities, and Costs

The weight of steel in the Florianopolis Bridge, including the approaches, is approximately 4 400 tons, made up as follows:

Chains:	
Eye-bars and pins	780 tons
Main Span:	
Trusses and bracing	840 "
Floor system	420 "
Main Towers:	
Columns and bracing	830 "
Castings	90 "
Carried forward	2 960 tons

FIG. 34.—FLORIANOPOLIS BRIDGE: TROLLEY REMOVING CLAMPS AND HOISTS AND PLACING OF HANGERS.

FIG. 35.—FLORIANOPOLIS BRIDGE: VIEW OF SOUTH BOTTOM CHORD ERECTED.

Fig. 36.—View Showing Erection of Top Chord, Florianopolis Bridge.

Fig. 37.—View from Top of Continent Tower Looking East Toward the Island, Florianopolis Bridge.

Brought forward	2 960 tons
Anchorages:	
Eye-bars and girders	110 "
Approaches:	
Spans (including floor and bracing)	960 "
Towers and bracing	290 "
Miscellaneous:	
Railings, etc.	80 "
Total	4 400 tons

The total quantity of concrete in the anchorages and piers is approximately 14 500 cu. yd., made up as follows:

Island anchorage	3 500 cu. yd.
Continent anchorage	6 000 " "
Piers and abutments	5 000 " "
Total	14 500 cu. yd.

The total cost of the Florianopolis Bridge, including the contractor's profit, as represented by the amount of the general contract, was upward of $1 400 000 (the exact amount is difficult to state on account of the fluctuating value of the Brazilian currency at the time). Of this total amount, the cost of the superstructure, as represented by the amount of that sub-contract, was approximately one-half.

Acknowledgments

The Florianopolis Bridge was built for the Brazilian State of Santa Catharina under a general contract awarded to Byington and Sundstrom, of São Paulo. That firm handled the substructure work, including the foundations, piers, anchorages, and abutments.

The principal contractors retained Messrs. Robinson and Steinman, of New York, as Consulting and Designing Engineers, and L. N. Gross as Associated Consulting Engineer on construction, plant, and equipment. G. A. Brinkerhoff, Assoc. M. Am. Soc. C. E., went to Florianopolis to superintend the carrying out of the Consulting Engineers' plans for the foundations and masonry. W. E. Joyce, Assoc. M. Am. Soc. C. E., was in charge of the office organization of Robinson and Steinman during the preparation of the final design. Mr. J. Gunnar and A. Johnson, J. London and R. Boblow, Juniors, Am. Soc. C. E., assisted in the preparation of the design.

The steel superstructure was fabricated by the American Bridge Company, the late C. W. Bryan, M. Am. Soc. C. E., Chief Engineer, and erected by the United States Steel Products Company, W. H. Stratton, Manager, Bridge Department. The development of the design was done in the Eastern Division of the American Bridge Company, J. E. Wadsworth, M. Am. Soc. C. E., Division Engineer, S. J. Ott, M. Am. Soc. C. E., Assistant Engineer. The detail drawings were made at the Trenton Plant, J. E. Elliot, M. Am. Soc. C. E., Engineer. The eye-bars, pins, and large castings were fabricated at the Ambridge Plant and the remainder of the material at the Elmira Plant.

The wire rope was manufactured at the Worcester Plant of the American Steel and Wire Company, J. F. Howe, Engineer, the railing by the Somerville Company, and the hand-operated chain hoists by the Harrington Hoist Company. The shop paint was Dixon's red lead graphite primer and the field paint was Dixon's silica graphite.

The field work was carried out under the direction of R. Khuen, Jr., M. Am. Soc. C. E., General Manager of Erection, and C. S. Garner, Manager of Foreign Erection. Messrs. E. G. Amesbury was Resident Engineer and T. S. Melton was Field Superintendent.

Mr. Sundstrom, of the contracting firm, dividing his time between New York and Brazil, gave his personal attention to the preliminary surveys and studies, final designs, construction of the substructure, and the superstructure contract. Acknowledgment is due him for his good offices in the various negotiations with the local officials, which smoothed over many difficulties usually encountered in foreign work due to lack of familiarity with local customs and procedure.

The success of the structure was made possible by the experimental work on the method of heat-treating eye-bars, to get an elastic limit of 75 000 lb. per sq. in., developed by the late C. W. Bryan, Chief Engineer, and by C. G. E. Larsson, M. Am. Soc. C. E., Assistant Chief Engineer (now Chief Consulting Engineer), of the American Bridge Company. One of the writers, Mr. Grove, Assistant Engineer, was in charge of the engineering features of the steel superstructure and spent several months at Florianopolis during the erection of the eye-bar cables and of the stiffening trusses.

DISCUSSION

J. A. L. Waddell,* M. Am. Soc. C. E. (by letter).—This bridge marks a forward step in the development of economics in suspension-bridge designing. All those concerned in its evolution are entitled to the hearty thanks of the Engineering Profession for their valuable contribution to the science and art of bridge building.

The structure contains a number of important innovations in bridgework, the principal ones of which are the utilization of the cables for forming a portion of the top chords of the stiffening trusses, the employment of rocker towers, the use of eye-bar cables, and the heat-treatment of carbon-steel eye-bars. It is true that these features of design and construction are not absolutely new; but they are unusual—especially in the United States—hence the designers and builders deserve much credit for their courage and enterprise in departing from the beaten paths.

The authors have pointed out many economies in making the cables serve as a portion of the top chords of the stiffening trusses; and the summation of these constitutes a saving in cost that must be of considerable magnitude. The authors state that "this utilization of the cable as the upper chord of the stiffening truss should preferably be limited to the central half of the span." From Fig. 2 it appears that this limit has not been utilized, because there are eleven double panels in the central portion and eight in each side portion. By adding two double panels to the center and taking one from each side, the central portion would be made almost the half-span length; and, in the writer's opinion, the appearance would be improved, especially as the side portions could be made to appear almost identical with the halves of the central portion of the stiffening trusses. In Fig. 38 this suggested layout is shown beneath the layout adopted.

Possibly the designer of the structure had some good and sufficient reason for using the short central portion; and it would be interesting to learn what it was. It is evident (page 280) that he recognizes the improvement in appearance that could be effected by curving the outer portions of the top chords of the trusses. The writer, however, is of the opinion that if that had been done, the variation from parallelism of chords would not have been sufficiently pronounced in the adopted layout.

The writer is in agreement with the authors' claims of "esthetic values" for their structure, Fig. 2 (*a*), as compared with the previous design, Fig. 2 (*b*). The latter would have had a better appearance had one-half the suspenders been omitted, and had the truss been made a little deeper.

The esthetics of the cantilever design, Fig. 2 (*c*), could have been improved somewhat by accentuating the apices and the points of suspension, for the truss depths are too nearly uniform from anchorage to anchorage.

Rocker towers, compared with those fixed at the bottom, are both more scientific and more economical of metal; but it must be remembered that they will have to be guyed, or otherwise held in correct position, during erection.

* Cons. Engr. (Waddell & Hardesty), New York, N. Y.

Whatever method may be adopted, some extra expense will be involved. The writer is of the opinion, however, that ultimately the hinging of the tower feet would prove to be economical.

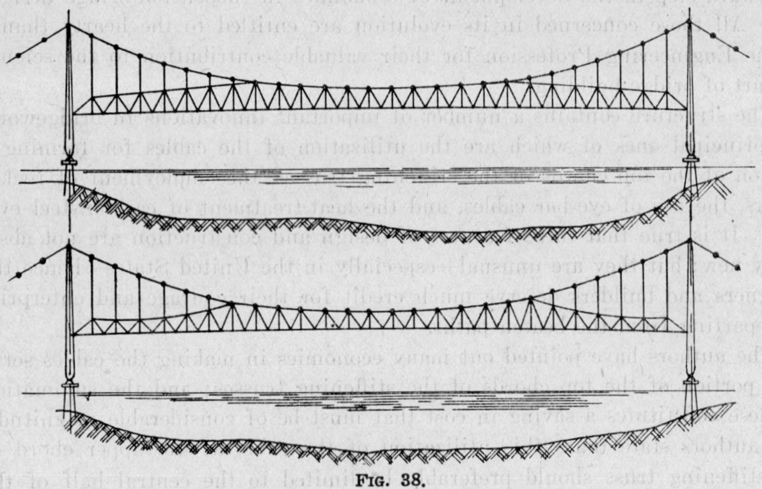

FIG. 38.

In May, 1920, the writer stated* that, under the then ruling prices, heat-treated, carbon-steel eye-bars having an elastic limit of 50 000 lb. per sq. in., could not compete with wire cables, even for spans as short as 1 000 ft., although the difference in costs was not great. Since then, however, the elastic limit of such eye-bars has been raised to 75 000 lb. per sq. in. This would reverse the conclusion for comparatively short spans; but, on the other hand, the cost of wire has been reduced about 25%, consequently it is still a mooted point as to whether wire cables or heat-treated, carbon-steel, eye-bar cables are the cheaper. A good test of this question for long spans will soon appear in the competitive bidding on the superstructure of the proposed Hudson River Bridge to be built for the Port of New York Authority.† The competition in the case of the Florianopolis Bridge does not afford any conclusive comparison, because the manufacturers of the new type of eye-bars were greatly desirous of introducing them on the market.

The manufacture of eye-bars, so common in the United States three or four decades ago, is now a monopoly, hence low prices for heat-treated bars need not be anticipated, unless some rival company should start making them. In the old days, eye-bars were generally considered to be the cheapest part of the metal work of any pin-connected bridge, but nowadays the reverse seems to be the case.

As for the heat treatment of eye-bars, that question appears to have been settled by the American Bridge Company to its own satisfaction; but facilities for the inspection of the manufacture and the testing of full-length

* *Proceedings,* Engrs. Soc. of Western Pennsylvania, Vol. 36, 1920–21, p. 418.

† As a result of this bidding, a contract was awarded for the wire cable type.—EDITOR.

bars will have to be furnished before consulting bridge engineers in general will be willing to utilize the new product. It seems to the writer that a working intensity of 50 000 lb. is rather high for an elastic limit of 75 000 lb., and that, for a time at least, it would be more judicious and conservative to limit the stress to 45 000 lb. per sq. in.

The claims for greater rigidity in the new type of stiffening truss appear to the writer to be well founded, but he would like to ask whether any deflection tests have been made on the finished structure, and, if so, with what results. Incidentally, the "novel" pin-hole detail "patented by the American Bridge Company," was evolved by the writer* about 1912.

SPENCER MILLER,† M. AM. SOC. C. E.—The authors have made a notable contribution to engineering art in the design of the cableways for the erection of this bridge. It was a brilliant thought to use a large number of small cables grouped together, to act as a trackway, which afterward were available as hoist ropes. It would be interesting to know how many cables were really in contact with the main sheave pulleys in the traveling carriage itself, and how an equality of stress was provided on the part of the individual cables? Perhaps a cross-section of the cables as they actually appeared in practice, showing the dimensions and the character of the pulleys and their grooving, would be instructive.

Another question concerns the method of applying power for lifting loads from the barge. A diagrammatic view illustrating how the ropes were led from hoisting drums to the traveling carriage and fall-block, together with all leading sheave pulleys, would further add to the value of the paper.

LLOYD G. FROST,‡ ASSOC. M. AM. SOC. C. E. (by letter).—In departing from conventional practice in suspension bridge design and construction, the authors have met the conditions peculiar to this problem in a signally efficacious manner. Further, they have rendered a distinct service to the Engineering Profession in establishing the practicability and economy of certain innovations in design and erection.

Most engineers specializing in bridge work find little occasion to investigate or design a long-span suspension bridge. In the light of conventional practice, with the massive towers, foundations, and expensive erection methods required, the use of the suspension bridge has been necessarily restricted to certain exceptional cases.

In the design and execution of the Florianopolis Bridge the authors have laid a basis for revising accepted practice in this regard. The exceptional economy of foundations, secured by the use of rocker towers, together with the generally improved conditions of rigidity and economy, point to a possibility of widening the range of use of suspension bridges to include many cases to which the conventional type of structure could not be adapted. Particularly does this seem possible in the case of highway structures with light loads and comparatively short spans, where the difficult and expensive foundations

* "Bridge Engineering," pp. 611–612.

† Cons. Engr., South Orange, N. J.

‡ Cons. Engr., Shreveport, La.

required in other types of bridges might be largely or wholly obviated by an adaptation of this variety of suspension bridge.

A study of this paper in connection with a projected structure has led the writer to make an estimate of the cost of a similar design in comparison with arch and cantilever types previously considered. Until the results of this and similar studies have been secured and thoroughly digested, no definite idea can be had of the effect of the Florianopolis project on suspension bridge design; but it is not improbable that the noteworthy economies attained will largely affect the design of suspension bridges in the future.

C. G. Emil Larsson,* M. Am. Soc. C. E. (by letter).—As the design for the Florianopolis Bridge was made possible by the use of high-tension, heat-treated eye-bars, it may be of interest to note the development of the eye-bar industry.

About 1880 the first non-welded steel eye-bars were made. These bars had a minimum elastic limit of 28 000 lb. per sq. in., a minimum ultimate strength of 55 000 lb. per sq. in., and a minimum elongation of 15% in 10 ft. They fulfilled the construction requirements until in 1904 New York City undertook to build the Queensborough Bridge. As this long-span structure carried a heavy load, it was felt that a material reduction in cost could be accomplished if eye-bars could be made to have higher physical qualities than standard bars. After considerable discussion nickel steel was adopted as the material. Full-sized tests showed a minimum elastic limit of 47 000 lb. per sq. in., a minimum ultimate strength of 80 000 lb. per sq. in., and a minimum elongation of 10% in 18 ft. This type of bar was found to be quite expensive, and considerable study was devoted to the possibility of making a cheaper bar having about the same physical properties.

By 1914 study had led to the consideration of heat-treated carbon steel. Experiments were undertaken and after various difficulties were solved it was considered safe to state that heat-treated eye-bars could be produced of such quality that tests on full-sized bars would show a minimum elastic limit of 50 000 lb. per sq. in., a minimum ultimate strength of 80 000 lb. per sq. in., and a minimum elongation of 8% in 18 ft. Since 1914 full-sized bars to the number of 134 have been tested under the supervision of the purchaser's engineers. These tests indicate an average elastic limit of 57 800 lb. per sq. in., an ultimate strength of 86 200 lb. per sq. in., and a minimum elongation of 10.7% in 18 ft., showing that the specification proposed by the manufacturer was rather conservative. Of the 134 bars tested only one proved to be unsatisfactory to the purchaser, due to too small elongation, although even this item was considerably larger than that obtained on riveted tension members.

On account of the good results from this type of bar, it was considered practicable to produce eye-bars having still higher physical qualities. Therefore, a second series of experiments on full-sized bars was undertaken in 1921, with the result that eye-bars can now be made which are guaranteed to show a minimum elastic limit of 75 000 lb. per sq. in., a minimum ulti-

*Chf. Cons. Engr., Am. Bridge Co., New York, N. Y.

mate strength of 105 000 lb. per sq. in., and a minimum elongation of 5% in 18 ft. (See Table 2.) Almost always full-sized eye-bar tests have been made during the construction of a structure of any magnitude, while it has been quite unusual to make full-sized tests of riveted work. The knowledge of the strength of eye-bars is, therefore, much greater than that of riveted work.

Concern is expressed in the paper regarding the policy of secrecy covering the manufacture of these bars. One reason for this policy was that the manufacturer, being responsible for the quality of the bars, wanted to be free to adopt any variation in method that would improve them. The art of making heat-treated eye-bars has advanced so far, and the process is so well established, that the policy of secrecy has been discontinued.

Clyde T. Morris,* M. Am. Soc. C. E. (by letter).—A number of important long-span bridges have recently been constructed or proposed. Three unusual features of the Florianopolis Bridge make this design a notable one: (*a*) Eye-bar cables; (*b*) hinged towers; and (*c*) the combination of the stiffening truss with the central portion of the cables. The marked economies possible with the new type of stiffening truss and its increased efficiency seem evident; for these the authors deserve great credit.

They state that "the Florianopolis Bridge is the first suspension bridge in the Americas to be built with rocker towers." In 1914-15, a suspension bridge 700 ft. long was built over the Muskingum River at Dresden, Ohio, in which rocker towers were used (Fig. 39). The design was made by the writer, and the bridge was built under the supervision of Ralph H. Strait, County Engineer of Muskingum County, Ohio. This bridge also had eye-bar cables and an unusual stiffening truss. A brief description of it may be of interest here.

The first bridge over the Muskingum River at Dresden, was begun in 1851, and completed and opened to traffic in 1853. It was a private enterprise, constructed under a charter from the State of Ohio granted in 1848, and operated as a toll bridge until July, 1868, when it was purchased by Muskingum County and became a free bridge.

This old bridge was a suspension structure supported on four stone towers, with a central span of about 450 ft. Each of the four cables carrying the roadway was composed of 200 wires, No. 10 gauge, and was about 3 in. in diameter. It had wooden stiffening trusses and a wooden floor with a 17-ft. roadway, and was designed and constructed under the supervision of Mr. George Copeland.

The flood of March, 1913, rose above the tops of the stiffening trusses, and the current pulled the cables off the towers, thus wrecking the bridge. Local residents were strongly against changing the type of bridge. For years it had been the only suspension bridge in the State, and as the U. S. War Department objected to locating piers in the river, it was decided to use the suspension type for the new bridge.

The abrupt bank on the east side of the river in contrast with the wide flood plain on the west side, made an unsymmetrical bridge desirable. The

* Prof. of Structural Eng., Ohio State Univ., Columbus, Ohio.

river span was made 450 ft., with an approach span of 200 ft., suspended from the cable on the west side and a short 50-ft. simple span on the east. The east cables run directly from the tower to the anchorage.

Considerable study was given to the relative merits and costs of eye-bar and wire cables, and bids were asked for the two kinds, but both the preliminary estimates and the bids received showed the eye-bar cables to be the more economical. The material was open-hearth structural steel of 60 000 to 70 000 lb. ultimate tensile strength.

The erection was carried on during the winter when there was no river traffic (there is very little river traffic at any time of the year). This permitted falsework to be used for the entire length of the bridge. Probably the possibility of erection from falsework is partly responsible for the low cost of the eye-bar cable bridge.

Three-hinged stiffening trusses with parallel chords were used. According to the usual assumptions of constant shape of cable curve and equal hanger loads, such trusses are statically determinate, and their deflections are only slightly greater than those of a two-hinged truss. One objection to the three-hinged truss is the localization of the bending at the center hinge, thus causing a cusp in the camber curve at this point under extremes of temperature. This is quite noticeable at mid-summer when the maximum temperature deflection occurs. It may be rendered unnoticeable by adjusting the hangers so that the curve is smooth at mid-summer, allowing the center to rise in winter.

The stiffening trusses are suspended from the cables by square hanger rods with turn-buckles. The ends of the trusses are supported at the piers on independent rocker bents instead of on the main towers. (See Fig. 40.)

The 20-ft. roadway is paved with creosoted wood block on 3-in. creosoted plank. The bridge has been in service now for twelve years, and has proven entirely satisfactory. It is very rigid under traffic.

V. R. COVELL* AND T. J. WILKERSON,† MEMBERS, AM. SOC. C. E., AND A. D. NUTTER,‡ ESQ. (by letter).—From the standpoint of economy, rigidity, and general structural efficiency, the Florianopolis Suspension Bridge is a splendid type, having advantages that cannot be questioned. The authors' claim for its esthetic value is not so easily established. They state very truthfully, that "æsthetic values in structural designs are generally unsatisfying on account of the existing differences of individual taste." Very rarely, in fact, have those who are considered competent to judge, been in agreement.

The design of L. S. Moisseiff, M. Am. Soc. C. E., for a bridge across the Kill van Kull (see Fig. 42) gives a more satisfactory outline, in that the side spans are supported by the back-stays and the same type of stiffening truss carried from end to end of anchorages. This gives a desirable continuity to the structure, which is lacking in the Florianopolis Bridge, with its straight back-stays and separate deck viaduct construction for the side spans.

* Chf. Engr., Bureau of Bridges, Dept. of Public Works, Allegheny County, Pittsburgh, Pa.

† Cons. Engr., Beaver Falls, Pa.

‡ Chf. Design Engr., Bureau of Bridges, Dept. of Public Works, Allegheny County, Pittsburgh, Pa.

Fig. 39.—General View, New Suspension Bridge, Dresden, Ohio, Built in 1915.

Fig. 40.—Detail of West Main Tower, Dresden Bridge.

Both bridges are more pleasing in an outline drawing than in the finished structure because the actual widths of members influence the appearance so greatly. As viewed in the field, the wide built members stand out boldly (particularly the top chord of the stiffening truss), while the eye-bar chain and wire rope hangers seem to be much more faint and tend to disappear entirely when viewed from a distance. This results in an outline profile which every one except the members of the Engineering Profession finds rather difficult to understand and reconcile with such a long span. The appearance of this type of suspension bridge would be greatly improved with a slight sacrifice in economy, by using a light false member to maintain the full width of the top chord of the stiffening truss over the part where it is combined with the eye-bar chain.

The weight of steel in the Florianopolis Bridge, given as approximately 4 400 tons, is surprisingly low for a structure with a main span of more than 1 100 ft. and a total length of about 2 700 ft. This is an average of less than 3 300 lb. per ft. of bridge and approaches. The following factors account mainly for the lightness of the structure: (1) The use of a timber floor with the consequent saving of dead load; (2) the use of high-tension, heat-treated carbon steel eye-bars for the chain; and, (3) the economy of metal in the type of span used.

The first factor makes impossible a direct comparison with highway bridges, as built in the larger centers of population in the United States. The practice of using timber floors is fast becoming obsolete, especially on bridges in highly congested centers; but where the traffic is rather light, causing relatively little mechanical wear, and where a minimum cost is the outstanding requirement governing the design, a timber floor is undoubtedly the most satisfactory type to adopt.

During the past few years there has been a great increase in the loads passing over highways and these must, necessarily, pass over some of the bridges. While floor systems are being designed for 18-ton trucks, very frequently electrical equipment and road machines, weighing from 26 to 35 tons, must be accommodated. The legal weight for trucks using highways in Pennsylvania is 13 tons. It would be interesting to know whether the 6-ton truck used for the highway loading of the Florianopolis Bridge is the maximum load anticipated. The use of 4-in. plank on a stringer spacing varying from 3 ft. 9 in. to 4 ft. 6 in., apparently contemplates no increase and no exceptional loads.

A question arises as to the advisability of using high-tension, heat-treated carbon steel for bridge members. On the Florianopolis Bridge it was specified that this material should meet the following requirements:

Ultimate strength....................	105 000 lb. per sq. in.
Elastic limit	75 000 "
Minimum elongation in 18 ft..........	5 per cent.

Both the elastic limit and ultimate strength are easily controlled by the carbon content and heat treatment, but with a sacrifice of ductility; and a favorable combination of the first two characteristics gives no positive information as to what may be expected in the third. For ordinary carbon steel, annealed eye-bars, the minimum elongation in 18 ft. is generally specified as 12% and for heat-treated eye-bars having an elastic limit of 50 000 and an ultimate strength of 80 000, as 8 per cent. While most of the test bars give an elongation of more than 6%, one gave the very low value of 3.8%, and it is quite possible that a number of bars used in the chain, if tested, might run below 5 per cent.

Nickel, manganese, and silicon alloy steels combine the desirable qualities of high tensile strength and ductility and should undoubtedly be given careful consideration in conjunction with high-strength, heat-treated bars for any particular condition, where high ductility is necessary.

The designers of the Florianopolis Bridge have used the proper material for the eye-bar chain, the only question being, what is a satisfactory minimum value for ductility? It seems as if 5% were sufficient, but that the higher values should be used for truss members.

Following a suggestion of the American Bridge Company, the use of heat-treated eye-bars was adopted by Allegheny County, Pennsylvania, in the design of all large county bridges constructed since 1924, or under construction, with unit stresses somewhat lower than those used in the bridge under discussion, all such eye-bars being tested by the Brinell hardness test to insure uniformity of treatment. By taking lower unit stresses, it is possible to use bars without thickened heads, and, in many cases, to use ordinary carbon steel for pins. These heat-treated eye-bars have been used in three bridges of the suspension type, in three of the cantilever type, and in two of the simple truss type.

The hinged tower for the suspension bridge is a step in the right direction, and this design was adopted in the 6th, 7th, and 9th Street Suspension Bridges over the Allegheny River at Pittsburgh, Pa.

The elongated pin-hole in the eye-bar heads leaves an opening in front of the pin. Was it considered necessary to fill this space to exclude water and prevent corrosion at these points?

The authors have met all the limiting conditions imposed on them in the development of the design of this structure, and it is an outstanding example of a large project consummated in a satisfactory manner with a limited amount of material and funds.

Frederick C. Carstarphen,* M. Am. Soc. C. E. (by letter).—This paper is a worthy contribution to engineering literature. It is complete. It gives the primary premise, the analysis, and the conclusions drawn from the structure in place. Engineers who are interested in suspension bridges, are glad to know that, in design, another milestone has been passed, and they feel that the authors should be complimented on their boldness in using the mid-portion of the cable for the upper chord of the stiffening truss, thus securing in practice, an economy of material that others have contemplated but have not attained.

It is possible that engineers have hesitated to adopt an obvious economy because extreme accuracy must be secured in design and fabrication to attain

* Cons. Engr., Denver, Colo.

a satisfactory deck position without excessive use of shims beneath the girders. One-half of the Florianopolis Bridge is without suspender adjustment. The completed structure is a testimonial to the accuracy of the calculations, the care of fabrication, and the competency of erection.

This bridge is noteworthy for the use of eye-bars under tensions of 50 000 lb. per sq. in. Those who have been interested in heat-treated and alloy steels knew that their use under high tensile stresses could not be long deferred. The supremacy of wire cables for suspension bridges having a span of 2 000 ft. and less is now challenged by high-tension eye-bars. The use of overhead or messenger cable in the erection of the eye-bar spans is also a forward step.

From the data presented it might be inferred that the calculation of the initial position of the messenger cable can best be made by trial methods, but such is not the case. It is important to the contractor that the problem be correctly solved, so that the eye-bars may be joined and the chain-blocks released; although the latter could be accomplished (with additional expense), by the aid of auxiliary tackle.

The writer has been interested in this problem ever since anchored spans for the track cables of aerial tramways became the vogue. The problem is to determine the position of the empty cable so that, when it is loaded, the resulting tension will not exceed a predetermined value. The cable positions recorded during the erection of the Florianopolis Bridge will serve as an excellent control of the method of calculation.

If a wire cable did not stretch or possess elasticity, an increase in symmetrical loading would not cause it to change its position, but it would increase the tension. The supports are assumed to be rigid. Unfortunately, for simplicity of analysis, this is not the case.

When they are first placed in tension, cables become longer because of the compression of the core and other adjustments of the component wires. This set is noted in all wire ropes, but its magnitude differs somewhat with the use of hemp or wire centers, or lock-coil construction. Reference is here made to the accompanying stress-strain graphs (Fig. 41). They show the effect of progressive and retrogressive loadings applied successively to a 2½-in., 6 by 37 monitor plow-steel cable.

The permanent set of the rope was not fully developed until after the third application of the load. It will be noted that the graphs do not coincide, but after the third alternation they form a closed curve. They are foot-pound diagrams, similar to those secured with an indicator, and may be used to determine the magnitude of the internal friction, or resistance to stretching. They might be called frictional hysteresis graphs.

Up to a certain point the modulus of elasticity varies with the tension. As the loads increase the elongations become proportional to the stress, and the value of the elastic modulus is nearly constant. This is so when the internal friction is sufficient to cause the rope to behave as a homogeneous bar, although the value of the modulus of elasticity of the rope is never equal, numerically, to that of the steel from which it is made.

Two applications of a load are not sufficient to determine the true value of the modulus of elasticity (see Fig. 41 (*a*) and (*b*)). To this extent the values given by the authors for 1-in. ropes are open for scrutiny. It will be shown from the behavior of the ropes in service that the modulus of elasticity was nearer 12 000 000 than the 8 300 000 lb. per sq. in. reported to have been used in the calculations. If Fig. 19 is a correct plotting of the stress-strain curve of Specimen *M*, under successive loading, then the crossing of these graphs is difficult to understand. It implies a recapture of the permanent set of the rope, which is not in accord with experience, and leaves the accuracy of the test in doubt.

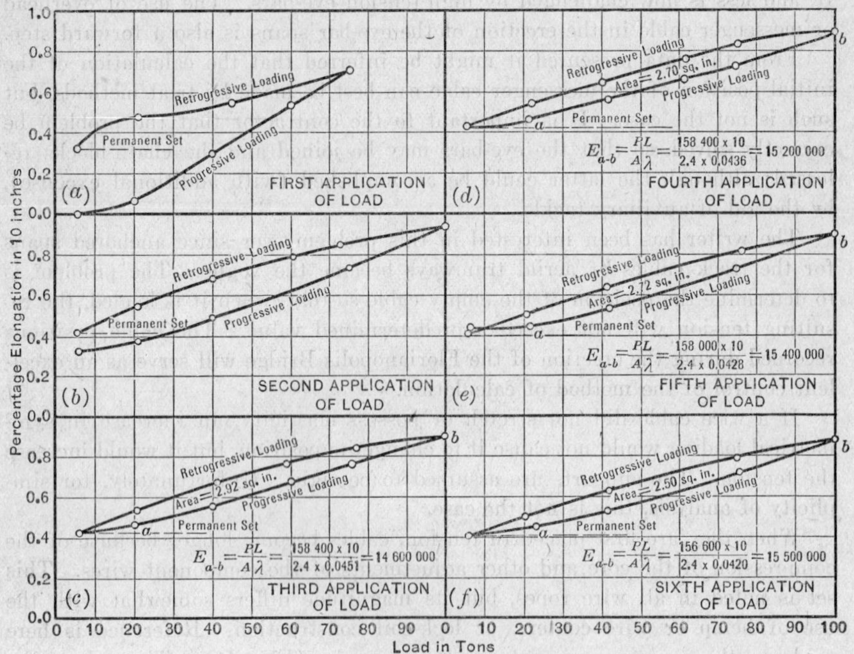

Fig. 41.—Results of Cable Tests.

To secure a factor of safety of 3, ropes having an ultimate strength of 90 000 lb. (monitor plow grade) were selected to sustain the eye-bar chains. The increase in tension per rope from 27 500 lb. in the horizontal portion of the main span to 32 000 lb. in the back-stays is discussed, but the authors seem to be silent as to the additional stress in the cables due to bending them around the tower and anchorage shoes. Was the factor of safety in the ropes approximately 3, or was it less than 2?

A few years ago the inquiry would have proceeded along these lines: What is the direct stress? 32 000 lb. What is the minimum radius of curvature of the shoes? 7½ in. What is the resulting bending stress?* 17 920 lb. What is the total stress? 49 920 lb. If the ultimate strength of the rope is 90 000 lb., what is the factor of safety? 1.8. By the Hewitt and Rankine formulas the factor of safety vanishes. However, these views concerning the magnitude of bending stress in wire ropes could not be reconciled with the

* See "American Wire Rope," 1913 Edition, p. 38.

experience of the rigger who knows that the ropes do not fall apart when bent around the small sheaves of the usual rope-block, but on the contrary lift loads weighing tons. When a $\frac{3}{4}$-in. 6 by 19 plow-steel cable is bent around a sheave having a 3-in. radius, its ultimate strength is reduced only 3 000 lb.

The reduction in the strength of 1-in. ropes due to bending them around a $7\frac{1}{2}$-in. radius would be about 600 lb. so that this factor need not be considered further.

Wrapping the rope $1\frac{1}{2}$ times around the anchor post prevented the equalizing of tensions in the two parts of the bight, but relieved the rope clips of the greater part of their load. The method of using a nest of sheaves for the anchorage results in low tensions when the ropes are looped around the sheaves and clipped. The present method is a departure from the usual one.

Since the eye-bar chain does not hang as a parabola, due to the variation in the loading, a determination of its position is in order, so that its departure from this curve may be known. (See Table 13.) The case is illustrated in Fig. 22 (*a*), the eye-bars carrying only their own weight, the span, 1 115.55 ft., the center deflection, 116 ft., and the loading as given in Table 10.

The panel length (41.25 ft.) is based on a span of 1 113.75 ft. and must be adjusted to the new length of 1 115.55 ft. The same purpose will be served if the 1.80-ft. difference is divided (0.07 ft. in each of 26 panels) so that the new spacing is 41.32 ft.

The reaction at each support is one-half the sum of the span loads, or 213 120 lb. With a center deflection of 116 ft., the span is in equilibrium when the horizontal component of the tension amounts to 519 527.8 lb. To find the deflections of a parabolic span having the same tension and center deflection, the value of the panel-point loads must be decided. The natural tendency would be to average the tabulated values to 16 393 lb., but if these loads are used with a 116-ft. center deflection, the tension will be more than that developed by the actual loading. The equal loading may be easily found by the formula:*

$$y = \frac{g\,s\,n}{4\,t}\left(1 - \frac{n}{2}\,q\right) + \frac{w\,s^2}{8\,t} \pm \frac{h}{2} \quad \text{(1)}$$

in which,

y = center deflection.
g = load.
n = number of loads.
t = horizontal tension.
q = ratio, load spacing to span.
s = span.
h = difference in elevation between the supports.

Solving:

$$116 = \frac{g \times 26 \times 1\,115.55}{4 \times 519\,527.8}\left(1 - 13\,\frac{41.32}{1\,115.55}\right)$$

$$g = \frac{116}{0.0072345} = 16\,034.3 \text{ lb.}$$

* *Transactions*, Am. Soc. C. E., Vol. LXXXIII (1919-20), p. 1388, Case III.

Notice that the last two terms drop out of this equation because w and h are zero.

Having discovered the loading, the deflections can now be found most easily by the sum of the first and second differences.* These differences are numerically equal and are found from the expression:

$$-\frac{a\,g}{t} = -\frac{41.32 \times 16\,034.3}{519\,527.8} = 1.27527.$$

The deflections of a series of equal loads on a parabolic arc as compared with those at Florianopolis, both with a tension of 519 527.8 lb., are as given in Table 13.

TABLE 13.—Comparison of Deflections in Florianopolis Cable and True Parabola.

Panel points.	0.	2.	4.	6.	8.	10.	12.	14.	16.	18.	20.	22.	24.	26.
Parabolic curve deflections, in feet.	0.00	16.53	31.83	45.86	58.61	70.09	80.29	89.22	96.87	103.25	108.35	112.74	114.73	116.00
Florianopolis deflections, in feet.........	0.00	16.95	32.48	46.64	59.44	70.91	81.03	89.86	97.41	103.68	108.65	112.34	114.78	116.00

The differences in these deflections illustrate the influence of small changes in loads on the position of the equilibrium polygon. With a center deflection of 115 ft., the tension becomes,

$$\frac{116}{115} \times 519\,527.8 = 524\,045.1 \text{ lb.}$$

This is the horizontal component of the tension required to support the eye-bars with a center deflection of 115 ft. The number of ropes required to support the chain and their own weight may next be approximated. One-inch monitor plow, 6 by 19 hoisting ropes have a tabulated breaking strength of 90 000 lb. With a factor safety of 3, the working tension can be 30 000 lb. The useful load tension is three-fourths of the working tension, or 22 500 lb.; $\frac{524\,045.1}{22\,500} = 25$ ropes, thus checking nearly the 24 ropes used. The actual tensions are less than 30 000 lb. so that checks the use of 24 ropes.

The manner of erection now must be considered. If the eye-bar chain is joined in the center of the span, the messenger cables must support all loads as well as a 20 000-lb. traveler, causing an increase in the tension of the cables that cannot be ignored. This method will be the easier for the erection crew because it insures the proper position of the eye-bars along the span. However, if the eye-bars are started at the center of the span, the tower connections can be made without the traveler being at the center. The contractor is to be complimented on the successful manner in which the eye-bars were handled, using the last method.

* *Transactions*, Am. Soc. C. E., Vol. LXXXIII (1919–20), p. 1388.

The panel loading of the messenger cables may be taken as 16 034.3 + 510 (chain-blocks) + 106 lb. for clips, or a total of 16 650 lb. The weight per foot of cable is 24 by 1.58 = 37.92 lb. The horizontal component of the tension of the assembly, may be found by the formula * extended to include the cables, thus:

$$t = \frac{g\,s\,n}{4\,y}\left(1 - \frac{n}{2}\,q\right) + \frac{w\,s^2}{8\,y} \qquad (2)$$

$$= \frac{16\,650 \times 1\,115.55 \times 26}{4 \times 115}\left(1 + \frac{13 \times 41.32}{1\,115.55}\right) + \frac{37.92 \times 1\,115.55^2}{8 \times 115}$$

$$= 544\,335.84 + 51\,291.72 = 595\,627.56 \text{ lb.}$$

The slope of the tangent at the support is easily found as follows:†

$$\tan \beta = \frac{n\,g}{t}\left(1 - \frac{(n+1)\,a}{2\,s}\right) + \frac{w\,s}{2\,t} \qquad (3)$$

$$= \frac{26 \times 16\,650}{595\,627.56}\left(1 - \frac{13.5 \times 41.32}{1\,115.55}\right) + \frac{37.92 \times 1\,115.55}{2 \times 595\,627.56}$$

$$= 0.36335 + 0.03551 = 0.39886 = \tan 21^\circ\,45'$$

The tension of the ropes at the tower of the long span is:

$$595\,627.56 \text{ lb.} \times \sec 21^\circ\,45' = 641\,282.41 \text{ lb.}$$

It will be noted that the horizontal tension of the messenger cables (when supporting the eye-bars at a 115-ft. center deflection, span 1 115.55 ft.) is 595 627.56 lb. instead of 660 000 lb. as mentioned on page 311. The tension of the abutment cable is:

$$595\,627.56 \text{ lb.} \times \sec 30^\circ = 687\,770 \text{ lb.}$$

compared with the 770 000 lb. reported.

These tensions may be reduced to stresses in the single ropes, as: Abutment span, 28 657 lb.; main slope, 26 720 lb.; and horizontal tension, 24 817.8 lb. The factor of safety is 3.14, a figure well within that desired by the contractor.

The length of the loaded span may be approximated by the formula:‡

$$L = s + \frac{8}{3}\,\frac{y^2}{s} \qquad (4)$$

$$= 1\,115.55 + \frac{2.6667 \times 115^2}{1\,115.55}$$

$$= 1\,146.15 \text{ ft.}$$

The approximate nature of this formula, when the deflection exceeds one-twentieth of the span, is well known.

It is easy to ascertain the change in slope at the panel points from the relation of $\frac{g}{t}$ to the load intersection angle, and $\frac{w\,a}{t}$ to the cable angle. The sum of these tangents is 0.03059 = tan 1° 45′.

* *Transactions,* Am. Soc. C. E., Vol. LXXXIII (1919–20), p. 1388.

† *Loc. cit.,* p. 1387.

‡ *Loc. cit.,* p. 1393.

The length of the loaded span may be determined for an odd number of links by taking the summation of the hypotenuse of triangles composing the equilibrium polygon of the deflection, as follows:

$$L = a\,[2\,\Sigma \sec \alpha + 1] \quad \ldots\ldots (5)$$

$$L = 2 \times 41.32 \times 13.35156 + 41.32 = 1\,144.689 \text{ ft.}$$

Having found the length of the loaded span (Table 14), the next step is to find the length of these cables, or the tension, when hanging as an empty span, so that when carrying the given loads, the tension will not exceed 595 627.56 lb.

For convenience, a single rope will be used in making this calculation; weight, 1.58 lb. per ft.; and tension, when loaded, 24 817.8 lb., say, 24 820 lb.

It is obvious that the loading of the empty span increases its length and increases the tension to the limiting amount, hence the loaded span length, L, is the sum of the length of the empty span and the stretch, and so the expression takes the following form*:

$$L = s + \frac{w^2\,s^3}{24\,t^2} + \lambda\,(T - t)\,s \quad \ldots\ldots (6)$$

TABLE 14.—Tabulated Computations for Σ sec α.

Member.	Angle.	Secant a.	Deflection, in feet.
26-26	0	....	115.00
24	1° 45′	1.00009	113.74
22	3° 30′	1.00187	111.21
20	5° 15′	1.00425	107.41
18	6° 00′	1.00551	102.36
16	7° 45′	1.00922	96.04
14	9° 30′	1.01391	88.45
12	11° 15′	1.01960	79.60
10	13° 00′	1.02630	70.29
8	14° 45′	1.03408	58.11
6	16° 30′	1.04295	45.47
4	18° 15′	1.05296	31.56
2	20° 00′	1.06418	16.39
0	21° 45′	1.07664	0
Σ sec. a = ...	....	13.35156	....

The position of the cable, will be ascertained by using both 8 500 000 and 12 000 000 lb. per sq. in. for the value of the modulus of elasticity in tension. The value of the elongation per 1 000 lb. per ft. is:

$$\lambda = \frac{1\,000}{0.41 \times 8\,500\,000} = 0.000287 \text{ ft.}$$

$$\lambda = \frac{1\,000}{0.41 \times 12\,000\,000} = 0.000203 \text{ ft.}$$

Substituting in Equation (6):

$$1\,144.69 = 1\,115.55 + \frac{1.58^2 \times 1\,115.55^3}{24\,t^2} + 0.000287\,(24\,820 - t)\,1.11555$$

* *Transactions*, Am. Soc. C. E., Vol. LXXXIII (1919-20), p. 1387.

Reducing:

$$21.19 = \frac{144\,400\,000}{t^2} - 0.00032\,t$$

This is a cubic equation, having one real root and is in a form that admits of easy solution by means of a slide-rule, thus:

$b = \dfrac{t}{1\,000}$	$\dfrac{144.4}{b^2}$	$-\,0.32\,b$	21.19
2.56	22.05	0.82	21.23
2.57	21.90	0.82	21.08
2.565	22.00	0.81	21.19

Therefore, 2 565 lb. would be the erection tension if there were no adjoining spans or back-stays. The amount of run of rope from these spans must be found when the tension changes from 2 960 to 28 659 lb. actual, or 25 700 lb. The chord lengths of the spans are 272.23 and 292.16 ft.; sag, 0.26 and 0.27 ft.; stretch, 2.02 and 2.16 ft.; and run, 2.28 and 2.43 ft. The total run is 4.71 ft. Allowing for the increase in length of the temporary eye-bars when under tension, the allowance of 5 ft. for run (made during erection), was correct. The span of the empty cable, therefore, would be increased to 1 115.55 + 5.00 = 1 120.55 ft., and the equation for tension becomes:

$$1\,144.69 = 1\,120.55 + \frac{1.58^2 \times 1\,120.55^3}{24\,t^2} + 0.000287\,(24\,820 - t)\,1.12055$$

$$16.16 = \frac{146\,300\,000}{t^2} - 0.000287\,t$$

$b = \dfrac{t}{1\,000}$	$\dfrac{146.3}{b^2}$	$-\,0.3216\,b$	16.16
2.92	17.1	0.94	16.16

Therefore, if the main cables are to have a center deflection of 115 ft. when loaded, and their modulus of elasticity is 8 500 000 lb. per sq. in., the pilot cable should be erected with a horizontal tension of 2 920 lb., or a center deflection of 84.12 ft.

Instead of 84 ft., a deflection of 87 ft. was used, and it will be noted that the loaded cables deflected to 113, and not 115 ft. This loading of the messenger cable may be regarded as a method of determining the modulus of elasticity. The cables, when erected with a deflection of 87 ft., were under a horizontal tension of 2 820 lb. each; at 99 ft., the tension was 2 480 lb. Loaded to a deflection of 113 ft., the tension was 25 476 lb. The difference in the length of the cable between a deflection of 113 ft. and 87 ft. is 7.54 ft.; the difference in tension is 22 656 lb.; from which the modulus of elasticity in tension may be computed:

$$E = \frac{22\,656 \times 1\,703}{0.41 \times 7.54} = 12\,400\,000 \text{ lb. per sq. in.}$$

It has been stated* that 12 000 000 lb. per sq. in. was adopted for wire ropes with hemp centers, after making numerous and careful tests, and, therefore, it appears that these ropes were not exceptional in this regard.

* "American Wire Rope," p. 33.

The tension equation, using elongation based on a modulus of 12 000 000 lb. per sq. in., becomes:

$$1\,144.69 = 1\,120.55 + \frac{1.58^2 \times 1\,120.55^3}{t^2} + 0.000203\ (24\,820 - t)\ 1.12055$$

$$18.44 = \frac{146\,300\,000}{t^2} - 0.000229\ t$$

The value of t is 2 760 lb. and the corresponding deflection is 89 ft. It is known from experience that if these empty cables were so placed they would sag to the desired 115 ft. when loaded. Fortune favored the contractor, for the excess of cable length, resulting from approximate methods of calculation offset the effect of using 8 300 000 lb. per sq. in. for the modulus of elasticity.

The messenger system of erecting eye-bar spans has proved to be a meritorious one, and it has been a pleasure to study its application to the Florianopolis Bridge.

A. DE H. HOADLEY,* JUN. AM. SOC. C. E. (by letter).—The writer's interest in the Florianopolis Bridge began in 1925 when Charles M. Spofford, M. Am. Soc. C. E., suggested that he make a stress analysis of this bridge for thesis work. The writer presents a brief account of the method used and shows that it is merely another form of expressing the influence line equation given by Mr. Steinman for the method of elastic weights.

Castigliano showed that if the stress in each member of a structure which is indeterminate to the first degree, as is the bridge in question, is expressed in terms of a single unknown internal stress, the derivative of the internal work with respect to the unknown stress will be equal to zero, thus giving an equation from which the unknown can be found. Here the panel load, x, due to a unit load at some point on the bridge, was taken as the unknown. This load was assumed to be equal at all points because the truss deflection was neglected. The stress, U, in each member was then expressed in terms of x, and the unit load and the value of the derivative of the internal work with respect to x, were found and equated to zero. It was decided to neglect the effect of shear, so that the internal work of the truss could be expressed in terms of the bending moment, M, and the moment of inertia of the truss. This gave the equation:

$$\frac{d\,w}{d\,x} = 0 = \sum \frac{U s}{A E}\frac{d U}{d x} + \frac{E}{E c}\sum \frac{U s}{A E}\frac{d U}{d x} + \frac{A}{A_1 A_2}\sum \int \frac{M}{\delta^2}\frac{d M}{d x}\,d y$$

in which,

U = total stress in member.
s = length of member.
A_1 = area of top chord.
A_2 = area of bottom chord.
$A = A_1 + A_2$.
δ^2 = depth of truss at any point.
$I = \dfrac{A_1 A_2 \delta^2}{A}$

* Asst. Prof., Civ. Eng., Union Coll., Schenectady, N. Y.

Solving this equation for a unit load, successively placed at different points on the span, gave the influence line for x from which the H-influence line was readily obtained.

The first term deals with the work in the towers, the second with that in the cable and back-stays, and the third with that in the stiffening truss.

In order to bring the last term of the writer's equation into an integrable form, δ had to be expressed as a function of the horizontal distance, y. For the end thirds, δ varied directly with y. In the middle third it was found that a parabola through U-16 and U-27 nearly coincided with the cable curve, so that δ was the distance from that parabola to the one on which the lower chord was laid.

The following results were obtained.

Panel Point.	Ordinate to H-Influence line.	Panel Point.	Ordinate to H-Influence line.
2	0.2012	16	1.2831
4	0.3705	18	1.3926
6	0.5445	20	1.4896
8	0.7104	22	1.5773
10	0.8684	24	1.6367
12	1.0108	26	1.6774
14	1.1516		

This shows the elastic weight value to be 5% less than the least work value at Panel Point 26. If the elastic weights for the diagonals are omitted, the writer found, on the basis of the other elastic weights given by Mr. Steinman, the H-influence line ordinate at Panel Point 26 to be 1.5621. This is 7% less than the least work value in which the diagonals were neglected and shows the omission of diagonals to reduce the elastic weight values 2 per cent.

The effect of the top chord members in the middle third of the truss appears in both the second and third members of the least work equation. In the second term there is positive work due to cable tension and in the third term also positive work usually due to compression from bending in the truss. The actual internal work is not the sum of that caused by the forces acting separately (as here taken), but is that due to the algebraic sum of the forces. This may account for a part of the discrepancy between the least work and elastic weight values.

The least work equation readily lends itself to a study of the effect of varying the chord sections on the H-influence line. Once having evaluated the integrals for the different positions of the unit load, it is a simple matter to substitute different values of $\frac{A}{A_1 A_2}$ for each section and compare the results obtained. The third term of the equation, which is that involving the chord members, has much greater weight than either of the other two terms. Consequently, the factor, $\frac{A}{A_1 A_2}$, is an important one. This is shown in the summation of $u \Delta s$ (the denominator of the H-equation) given by Mr. Steinman in Table 5. Here, $u \Delta s$ is given as $1\,188.7069 \times 10^{-8}$ ft-lb., to which the chord members alone contribute $1\,051.4886 \times 10^{-8}$ ft-lb.

The influence line equation given by Mr. Steinman can be obtained by assuming H as the unknown, expressing the internal work of each member in terms of H and of the unit load, and equating the derivative of the internal work with respect to H to zero.

S = length of member.
u = stress in member due to $H = 1$.
Z = stress in member of a simple span truss with same dimensions as the stiffening truss due to unit load.
U = total stress in member = $Z + uH$.

The total internal work is,

$$W = \frac{U^2 S}{2 A E}$$

$$\frac{d W}{d H} = 0 = \sum \frac{U S}{A E} \frac{d U}{d h} = \sum \frac{Z u S}{A E} + \sum \frac{u^2 H S}{A E}$$

$$H = \frac{-\sum \frac{Z u S}{A E}}{\sum \frac{u^2 S}{A E}} = \frac{-\Sigma Z \Delta s}{\Sigma u \Delta s}$$

as

$$\Delta s = \frac{u S}{A E}$$

If only one or two points on the H-influence line were desired, they could be found more rapidly on the basis of this equation than by the method of elastic weights. However, if all the ordinates were desired, the method of elastic weights will be much shorter, because $\Sigma Z \Delta s$ has to be evaluated for every ordinate to the influence line. Taking the value of $\Sigma u \Delta s$ given in Table 5 and the values for Δs given in Tables 3, 4, and 5, the writer computed $\Sigma Z \Delta s$ for a unit load at the center of the bridge and found the corresponding value of H to agree (as it should) with that found by the method of elastic weights.

F. N. Menefee,* M. Am. Soc. C. E. (by letter).—The use of heat-treated carbon steel in bridge construction is very interesting. Readers of the *Transactions* of the Society will recall the studies by J. A. L. Waddell, M. Am. Soc. C. E., of alloy steels a few years ago.† At that time, however, heat-treating was confined almost entirely to smaller units than those usually found in bridges, and was only economical when a large number of small parts were being produced.

* Prof., Eng. Mechanics, Univ. of Michigan, Ann Arbor, Mich.

† "The Possibilities in Bridge Construction by the Use of High Alloy Steels," *Transactions,* Am. Soc. C. E., Vol. LXXVIII (1915), p. 1.

The secrecy of the heat-treatment process need not cause any general concern among engineers. There is no longer any real mystery about heat-treatment, and it will soon be found that all the large companies will produce heat-treated bridge members as wanted.

The Brinell test will form a fairly reliable check on the uniformity of the treatment and of the tensile strength. Comparisons may be made against a standard by Brinelling a few full-sized members throughout their length and then testing them to destruction to determine their physical properties.

Considering the fact that stresses in a pin-connected structure, such as a suspension bridge made up of eye-bars, are more accurately determinable than those in a stiff-jointed structure, and that impact, as it is generally understood, on railroad bridges has little or no effect on a bridge the joints of which will yield, as in the case of the suspension type, it would seem that the working stress of 46 500 lb. per sq. in. is well within the limits of safety on steel the elastic limit of which is 80 000 lb. per sq. in.

Secondary stresses due to uneven settlement of piers do not enter into the stress conditions of the cable portion of the suspension bridge. Axial loading reduces the amount of members which otherwise might have bending moment and shear, and this at once introduces some heavy material in a neutral zone where it does little or no work.

Eye-bars, instead of cable, in the upper chord, will serve two purposes: (*a*) By adding stiffness in vertical and horizontal planes, and (*b*) by decreasing deflection. For the same total area of steel, a cable will elongate under load more than a solid piece of steel.

T. Kuo,* Esq. (by letter).—In considering the question of rigidity of suspension bridges, one must recognize at the start the characteristic features of two different types of construction with special regard to the make-up of their principal carrying member, the cable. The degree of rigidity attainable in each design depends to a large extent on the question whether the cable is free or braced.

Theoretically, a flexible free cable may be viewed as a structural polygon with an infinite number of hinges connecting bars of infinitesimal lengths. Such a polygon will never constitute a rigid system. While an inverted three-hinged arch would be just sufficient to be stable, the free cable alone, as a structural system, is extremely defective.

Such a flexible cable not only possesses the characteristic property of altering its position of equilibrium with new distribution of loading, but this change of shape, causing excessive deflections in an actual bridge system, has nothing whatever to do with the question of stress and strain. Until the final position of equilibrium is reached, the cable will never be stressed.

Therefore, a free cable suspension bridge is by nature a flexible structure. Even with the stiffening truss, which is designed only to prevent undue deflection, it still retains these basic characteristics to a greater or less extent, depending on the rigidity of the stiffening truss used and the relative magnitude of the live load over the dead load.

---

* Structural Draftsman, with Ralph Modjeski, Cons. Engr., New York, N. Y.

When the cable is combined into a rigid system of triangles (braced-cable construction), the result is a stable trussed structure, radically different from a purely free cable suspension bridge made adequate for practical requirements by a secondary stiffening truss. Although this braced cable construction retains much of the general nature of a suspension bridge, it lacks the flexible character of an unstable system. All deflections are directly due to the internal deformation of its component members and not to a mere unrestrained movement of a loose system to satisfy a new set of loadings.

One, therefore, must look on the greater flexibility of a free cable suspension bridge somewhat as an inherent characteristic of a certain type of construction and tolerate it as a necessary disadvantage, because of the superior qualities in its other features.

By adopting an unusually heavy and deep stiffening truss, it is possible to design even a free cable suspension bridge to any desired degree of rigidity. Nevertheless, this departure from the usual proportions set by the best modern practice results in a very uneconomical and clumsy design.

Moreover, there are other ways of limiting and controlling the deflection of suspension bridges. In the Florianopolis Bridge, the designer has accomplished this in a very scientific and economical manner. The structure belongs to the partly braced type.

On the other hand, deflection is certainly not desirable if it is excessive. Besides the good reasons relating to practical requirements, as set forth in the paper, there is another of more than technical interest for controlling and limiting the deflections in suspension bridges. As the stiffening truss deflects, the floor system deflects with it. This forced deformation on stringers rigidly connected to the girder (except expansion ends), produces secondary stresses that are not taken care of in the stringer design.

Knowing the deflection of the truss, and assuming the curve to be parabolic, the change of end slopes of the stringer and the movement of one end relative to the other, can be readily computed. Then, using the general slope-deflection formula involving these factors, the actual stresses are not difficult to ascertain. The writer has found them to be so extremely high, that they cannot be rightly regarded as being of secondary importance.

While the writer does not doubt the wisdom of using rocker towers in this design for that particular location, he is of the opinion that the use of such towers, like that of pin-connected trusses in ordinary bridge construction, should in general be discouraged.

In time of earthquake, the fixed ended towers are in a much better position to resist the forces produced, and it is quite possible that objectionable displacement between the rocker and the foundation is likely to occur. A rocker tower, due to its construction, is not in integral connection with its supporting pier. When destructive horizontal ground movements are taking place, the inertia of the tower acts against them. Unless the movements are extremely slow, which is hardly the case with an earthquake, the tower cannot be expected to move back and forth along with the pier.

Severe earthquakes are usually infrequent at any one place, and, therefore, elaborate and expensive precautions against them are not to be recommended in all locations. However, in view of the existence of a potential earthquake, even in regions that are generally considered dependably quiet, it seems to be good engineering policy to utilize the superior advantage of fixed ended towers against possible hazard of this kind. Moreover, they involve only a little extra cost.

The new departure of the stiffening truss from parallel chords and the union of the cable with the middle portion of the top chord into a single member are two of the most admirable features of the design. Striving for a more scientific proportion in the height of the stiffening truss and for a more economical structural combination in the make-up of the whole bridge, the designers of the Florianopolis Bridge have established a distinct development in the art of suspension bridge construction. The remarkable results achieved in regard to rigidity and economy of material from this seemingly theoretical complication has been already comprehensively treated in the paper.

That the height of the truss should vary with the magnitude of the maximum bending moment seems to be one of the broad and fundamental principles of good design. Compliance with it always results in a better design. It is in perfect accord with structural requirement: A longer arm for a bigger moment.

It also converts the outline of the bridge into a more expressive form, which is virtually a modified maximum moment diagram. While it may not be possible for one to write into the structure the story of its conception so that "all who run may read", nevertheless it can be at least plainly felt in the minds of designers that structural fitness could not be more strikingly expressed in other ways.

Leon S. Moisseiff,* M. Am. Soc. C. E.—This paper is of much interest. It tells of the design of a new type of suspension bridge and how it has been successfully erected and put in use in a foreign country. It also tells of a novel material that has been used in bridge building. The engineers who have planned, designed, erected, and managed the enterprise and now report on it deserve much credit.

The form used for the stiffening truss of the Florianopolis Bridge has undergone a long evolution and has been discussed at various times in engineering offices and publications before it took its present shape. It may be well to sketch here briefly the development of the stiffened cable bridge.

Since the time when suspension bridges, stiffened by a railing, had been found to be too limber, it has been the aim of many engineers to stiffen the cable directly by making it serve either wholly or partly as a stiff member. The simplest form that this idea took was that of splitting the cable in two parallel chords placed vertically apart and bracing them to each other so as to form an inverted arch. This form has been realized in several smaller bridges, and several decades ago it was proposed by Gustav Lindenthal, M. Am. Soc. C. E., for a bridge over the Hudson River. In 1874, the late James B. Eads, F. Am. Soc. C. E., patented a design of a braced cable in the form of

* Cons. Engr., New York, N. Y.

an inverted three-hinged arch made of two bi-convex halves. The same idea found a simpler expression later in the bowstring type of which the Old Point Bridge, built at Pittsburgh, Pa., in 1878, by Hemberle, offered an excellent example. In 1875, Fidler, in England, proposed a modified type of bridge consisting of two intersecting cables tied together by web bracing. Each cable was to take the form of an equilibrium curve with one half span uniformly loaded. The upper branches of these curves then become straight lines and constitute the upper chords of the stiffening truss. When the bridge is fully and uniformly loaded the equilibrium curve of the system will coincide with the neutral curve of the braced arch. The stress in the chords will always remain in tension. They can be built, therefore, as tension members exclusively. This, of course, offers a substantial advantage in economy.

It appears that Fidler's braced arch is but a special case of a general type of a suspension bridge formed of two curves intersecting at mid-span and braced to each other and possessing the characteristic mentioned, of tensile stresses in the chords exclusively. Résal, in France, published in 1893 a sketch, and, in the same year, Max am Ende, in England, published the general analysis, of this type of truss. Ende shows that, by selecting a depth of truss at the quarter-points that is a function of the ratio of the live load to the dead load, two curves can always be adapted that will form the chords of two crescents hinged together. These curves will remain in tension under all positions of the specified intensity of live load. In other words, the axial stress, due to the weight of the bridge and the live load on it, will never be exceeded by the stress caused by the flexure of the truss.

In 1895, the speaker, under the guidance of William H. Burr, M. Am. Soc. C. E., selected as a thesis the then much discussed bridge over the Hudson River, with a span of 3 000 ft., and developed a design on this type. In 1910, the Pennsylvania Steel Company submitted several designs for the second Quebec Bridge. One of them was the design proposed by Mr. Lindenthal for a suspension bridge. It consisted in the center span of two intersecting curves forming two braced crescents hinged together at mid-span. The side spans consisted of braced segments formed of a lower curve and an upper straight line chord. In 1924, the McClintic-Marshall Company, among other designs for the Sydney Harbor Bridge, also proposed a 1 600-ft. span on practically the same lines.

German engineers have been always much interested in these forms of stiffened suspension bridges and since the Nineties many and various forms of this kind have been discussed in German engineering literature.

In 1903, Mr. Lindenthal, while Commissioner of Bridges of New York City, proposed an eye-bar bridge for what is at present the Manhattan Bridge. The main feature of his plan was a chain of eye-bars that would sustain the dead load of the bridge and form an equilibrium polygon. To the chain a truss was attached which consisted of a lower chord capable of resisting tension, and also a compression and a web system. The lower chord, beginning from the hinged support of the chain on the tower, descended to the roadway level at about the quarter-points and continued parallel with the roadway grade so that the middle half of the span was practically horizontal. The live load and temperature that would come on the bridge, would be jointly sustained by the chain and the lower chord forming an inverted braced arch.

In designing this bridge it soon became apparent that an additional wind chord would be required for the outer quarters of the span, or for about one-half the bridge. The speaker, who was in charge of the design, then arrived at the conclusion that the form now adopted for the Florianopolis Bridge would prove more suitable, as it does not require an additional wind chord and presents a more pleasing appearance.

In 1907, the speaker made a design for a bridge across the Kill van Kull between Staten Island, New York, and New Jersey, in which he proposed a stiffened suspension bridge of exactly the type adopted subsequently for the Florianopolis Bridge. An outline of its elevation and cross-section is shown in Fig. 42.

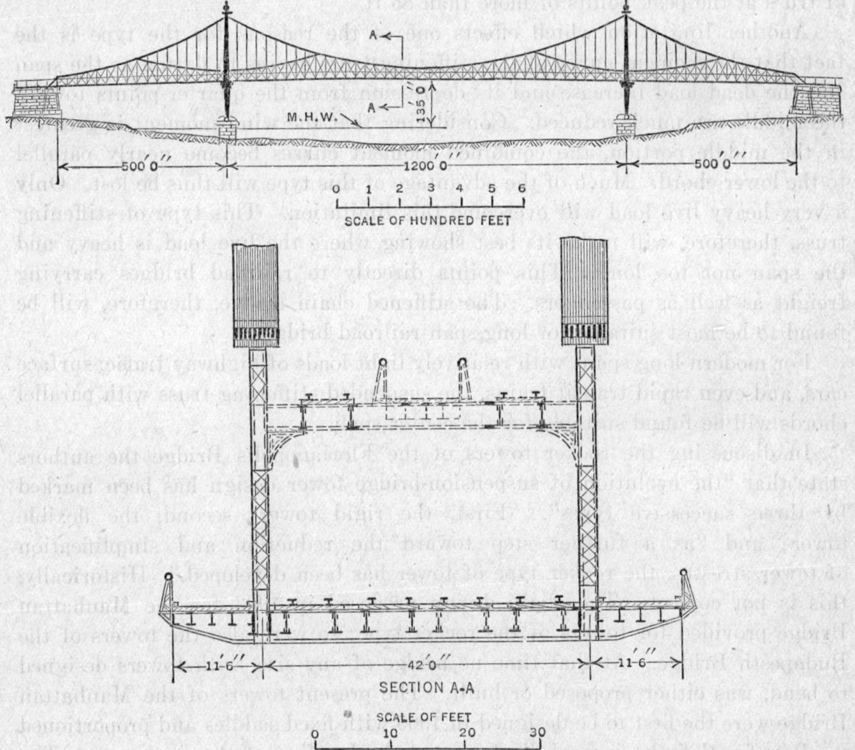

Fig. 42.—Section of Proposed Bridge Over the Kill van Kull.

The bridge was planned as a combination railroad and highway bridge. It was proposed to provide for four railroad tracks, two surface-car tracks, two narrow roadways, and a footwalk. With the heavy live load, amounting to 22 000 lb. per lin. ft. of bridge, and the greater stiffness required for railroad traffic, a deep stiffening truss became a necessity. The design shown was the more suitable because the comparatively short span of 1 200 ft., which was slightly longer than that of the Florianopolis Bridge, lent itself to the economic use of nickel-steel eye-bars. At that time these bars were the strongest structural steel bars available. The arrangement of the eye-bars is shown on the cross-section. The lower chord was utilized as the chord of the horizontal wind truss. For better appearance, the truss ends at the towers show the line of the upper chords continued.

The type of the stiffening truss of the Florianopolis Bridge, however, has its limitations. As the span grows longer the depth at the peaks of the truss becomes greater, with the result that the web members become excessively long and limber. This is still more accentuated by the fact that to obtain the most economy with this type of truss the versine of the chain should be relatively large and with it the depth of the truss at the peaks increases in proportion. Thus, for example, a span of 2 000 ft. would well result in a depth of truss at the peak points of more than 85 ft.

Another limitation which effects one of the reasons for the type is the fact that the moment curve of the stiffening truss begins to flatten as the span and the dead load increase and its depression from the quarter-points toward the middle are much reduced. Considering that the wind moment is greatest in the middle portion, the combined moment curves become nearly parallel to the lower chord. Much of the advantage of this type will thus be lost. Only a very heavy live load will overcome this limitation. This type of stiffening truss, therefore, will make its best showing where the live load is heavy and the span not too long. This points directly to railroad bridges carrying freight as well as passengers. The stiffened chain bridge, therefore, will be found to be most suitable for long-span railroad bridges.

For modern long spans with relatively light loads of highway traffic, surface cars, and even rapid transit trains, the suspended stiffening truss with parallel chords will be found suitable for the center span.

In discussing the rocker towers of the Florianopolis Bridge the authors state that "the evolution of suspension-bridge tower design has been marked by three successive types". First, the rigid tower; second, the flexible tower; and "as a further step toward the reduction and simplification of tower stresses, the rocker type of tower has been developed." Historically, this is not correct. The chain design proposed in 1903 for the Manhattan Bridge provided for towers of the rocker type; so were also the towers of the Budapesth Bridge. At that time no bridge of any size, with towers designed to bend, was either proposed or built. The present towers of the Manhattan Bridge were the first to be designed in 1905 with fixed saddles and proportioned to allow for their horizontal displacements by bending of the steel posts. The fixed-tower design was then chosen for its better appearance as well as easier erection. The Budapesth and the Cologne Bridges are low-level bridges and of comparatively short spans, their towers are not high, and to deflect them horizontally was impracticable. For these bridges rocking towers were considered best. However, where the towers attain great heights, their resistance to the horizontal displacement of the top becomes very small, and the bending stresses caused by it become light for slender towers. One needs only to recollect that the unit stress for bending is inversely proportional to the square of the tower height. This is the guiding principle in the technical selection of the tower. Correctly designed and proportioned, a tall tower with a fixed base should hardly require more material than a rocker tower.

It may be of interest to state that the McClintic-Marshall Company, that is building the Detroit River Bridge with a span of 1 850 ft., has adopted towers of the fixed-base type.

R. McC. BEANFIELD,* ASSOC. M. AM. SOC. C. E. (by letter).—This paper presents much information of great value and considerable interest, especially from an economic standpoint, in the design and erection of long-span bridges. The novel features in the design and installation of this large structure have demonstrated some economical advantages that will doubtless have considerable influence in the planning of future long-span bridge projects.

The writer has had occasion to check the stresses in a structure containing several groups of eye-bar members. Extensometer readings were made with considerable care (with a Berry 8-in. machine) and temperature changes checked with a standard try-bar. Considerable variation in stress was found in the individual eye-bars that were grouped to form a member of the truss. While the cause of this variation in stress in each eye-bar is not definitely known, it is the writer's opinion that the pin clearance, minor differences between pin-hole distances that require extreme care in shop measurements, and secondary stresses and deformations in the eye-bar heads, were the underlying reasons.

It would be interesting to know if extensometer readings were taken on the eye-bar chains to ascertain if there was any great variation in stress in the individual eye-bars that were grouped to form a unit or link of the chain. By comparison, it would be of further interest to know if there is much variation in stress in the wire strands in some of the large suspension bridge cables.

One of the most important structural units in a suspension bridge is the tower castings supporting the cable. Maximum intensity of stresses in these castings should be comparatively low. In this connection, there may be some question as to the amount and intensity of the secondary stresses induced in the casting and connecting eye-bars due to fixity or lack of rotation in the pin joint. If the primary stresses in the eye-bars are not sufficient to overcome the frictional resistance of the pin, rotation will not occur, and the joint may be considered as fixed. According to experiments of Föppl, the coefficients of friction for steel pins on steel may vary from 0.25 to 0.29, which would indicate that the pin friction would permit stresses of about 50% in excess of the primary stress prior to rotation on the pin.

Data on the frictional resistance of pins are very meager. Any assumption made relative to the coefficient of pin friction is more or less a matter of guesswork which, in turn, reduces the reliability of secondary stress analysis relative to pin joints.

* Structural and Mech. Engr., Los Angeles, Calif.

The design of the rocker casting details at the base of the tower (Fig. 7) presents some very interesting features that raise some questions, as follows:

(*a*) Security against displacement by earthquake shock, particularly by horizontal shear.

(*b*) The extreme high bearing stress on the contact surface of the rocker castings extending over a line of contact 45 in. long, on which 4 840 000 lb. must be supported.

The action of the horizontal component, or wave of an earthquake, sets up a violent movement of the earth's crust which, in turn, is transmitted to the lower supporting medium of the structure. The upper part of the structure, due to its inertia, tends to remain in its original position. Therefore, the hinged or flexible tower castings, together with the four 3-in. screwed dowels and columns, must resist violent successive forces (shears) before they can move the superstructure in the direction of the vibration.

Furthermore, the effect of the period of seismic vibrations on the induced stresses in the structure, combined with the period of elastic vibration of the structure itself, is a matter of considerable importance, especially in the tower frames, where nearly all the load of the suspended spans is supported on the top of the towers. This condition tends to intensify the oscillatory movement, thus increasing the destructive forces induced in the structure. For this reason, it would indicate that suspension bridges, in general, are not adaptable for locations known to have (active) seismic disturbances.

In general, more serious consideration should be given to the resistance to seismic forces in structures, particularly those projects involving millions of dollars in cost. It is a fact that there are no white spots on the earth that are free from seismic disturbances. There are ample records showing that the eastern slopes of the Western Hemisphere have had a fair number of very destructive earthquakes, such as a series of violent earthquakes in the St. Lawrence region in 1633, the Boston earthquake in 1755, the Missouri earthquake in 1811, and the Charleston earthquake in 1886.

Engineers on the Pacific Coast are giving serious consideration to the subject of seismic analysis of structures, probably more than ever, due to the influence of the recent Japanese earthquake. Also, since the Pacific Coast earthquake, the insurance rates have been unduly increased, the same applying alike to properly and poorly designed structures.

In the design and construction of the Carquinez Strait Bridge, in California, one of the largest cantilever type bridges in the world, resistance to seismic forces was considered by the installation of hydraulic buffers to absorb some of the shock and automatically bind the structure together, to increase its rigidity.

The cost of providing proper resistance to minimize damage from earthquake shocks is a very small percentage of the total cost of most structures; therefore, from an economic standpoint, it would be a wise policy.

Relative to the rocker bearing, which is virtually a linear contact 45 in. long, supporting about 4 800 000 lb., there must be considerable deformation of the contact surfaces with a unit bearing stress of high intensity. It would be interesting and instructive to know the basis of design for this important detail.

Charles F. Stowell,* M. Am. Soc. C. E. (by letter).—The Florianopolis Bridge marks an epoch in suspension bridge construction and although it is of comparatively moderate dimensions for a bridge of that character, in design and construction it so typifies, in nearly all its elements, the most advanced ideas and research that it is likely to serve for a long time as an example to be followed by those who seek perfection in the building of such bridges. While many of the distinctive elements have been previously suggested, it remained for the designers of this bridge to put them into practical use for the first time; and the designers' clear and complete explanation of the steps and processes leading to their results make this paper a classic of its kind.

The one discordant note in the otherwise harmonious whole is the unfortunate predominance of the single element of cost, which prevented the use of wire instead of eye-bars for cables "by a small margin". The superiority of wire over eye-bars for cables is so great that a difference in cost "by a small margin" should not be a controlling factor in deciding between them.

In any long-span bridge of whatever type the dead load is always the chief part of the weight to be supported, and various devices are adopted to reduce this weight to its lowest terms. This is accomplished both by skillful designing and by the use of various kinds of alloy steel of greater strength than ordinary structural steel, thus permitting a smaller quantity to be used; or, as in this case, by special heat treatment of steel normally of less strength, to increase its strength and thus reduce the dead weight of the structure.

The cables of the Florianopolis Bridge are made of eye-bars, each cable composed of four bars 12 in. wide and approximately 41 ft. long and of a thickness varying from $1\frac{13}{16}$ to 2 in., proportionate to the varying maximum stress in the different panel lengths. The chemical composition of the steel used for these eye-bars is not given, so that its approximate normal strength before heat treatment cannot be estimated; but, after treatment, the thirteen bars used for full-sized tests gave an elastic limit (yield point) varying from 78 180 to 96 830 lb. per sq. in. and an ultimate strength of 115 970 to 137 900 lb. per sq. in., the specified requirements being a minimum of 75 000 lb. and 105 000 lb., respectively. The capacity of the machine on which full-sized tests were to be made, was limited to lengths of 40 ft., or less than the lengths generally to be used for the cables; so that of the twelve bars originally decided upon for such tests, only two were actually selected from those made and intended for use in the bridge, while the other ten were bars made expressly for testing purposes and not actually representative of those to be used in the bridge. It is contrary to the experience of human nature not to assume that, knowing that these ten bars were the ones made expressly for test purposes, extraordinary care would have been taken to make them in every particular as nearly perfect as was humanly possible; and yet one of them failed signally in that it did not give nearly the percentage of elongation expected and specified; and so another test bar was made, which fortunately did fill all the

* Civ. Engr., Albany, N. Y.

requirements. How many of the other bars, which were not tested, might show similar results there is no possible means of determining. All the bars made, including the one that failed, were subjected to delicate and ingenious tests to determine their degree of hardness and the uniformity of their texture; but, unfortunately, no one can tell how much a bar is going to stretch without stretching it.

It may be interesting to consider what may be the result if even one of these were to have as low a percentage of elongation as the test bar that failed. This bar measured 12 by 2 in. and showed a percentage of elongation of 3.8 on a measured length of 18 ft., while the other ten bars tested showed an average percentage of 6.996, or, say, 7 for the same length. The bars of this size are mostly used in the back-stays (176 in all) and in each panel length there are four such bars, bearing a total maximum stress of 4 381 000 lb., or 45 635 lb. per sq. in., if all four pull equally. When placed under stress all these four bars must elongate to an equal amount and if any one of them is abnormal in respect of having a lower elongation ratio than the other three then that bar must bear more than its normal proportion of the total stress and the others will be correspondingly relieved. With one bar in a group of four having an elongation percentage of 3.8, while the percentage of the others is 7.0, means that, in order to stretch all of them to an equal amount, the abnormal bar will have to carry 35.2% of the total load and each of the others 21.6% thereof; that is, for a maximum total stress of 4 381 000 lb., the abnormal bar will carry 1 542 112 lb., or 64 250 lb. per sq. in., while the three normal bars carry 2 838 888 lb., or 39 429 lb. per sq. in., instead of the intended maximum of 45 635 lb. per sq. in. which all were designed to carry.

This, of course, is pure hypothesis and is only offered as an illustration of the uncertainty necessarily incidental to the use of chains of this type and against which there is no positive insurance.

With every kind of forged or riveted structural members, full-sized tests are destructive to the members tested and, at best, knowledge of the actual strength of the members used in the structure is based inferentially on the behavior of similar members tested to destruction; but with cable wire two full-sized tests on every individual wire in the cable can be made; and these tests, moreover, are always made on parts of the wire known from experience to be the poorest, namely, near the ends. The process of wire-drawing itself is a good criterion of quality and uniformity. Occasionally, but not very often, a wire will break in drawing, which indicates some undiscovered flaw or inequality in the metal, and, of course, causes the rejection of that particular wire. There is no kind of steel construction about which there is such absolute and accurate knowledge of qualities and strength as modern wire bridge cable.

Another advantage of wire over eye-bar cables is the very much less weight of metal used for splicing purposes. In the Florianopolis Bridge the cable bars are connected at intervals of about 41 ft. and the amount of metal used for connection purposes only, consisting of eye-bar heads, pins, nuts, etc., is obviously large, but the given data are not sufficient to estimate it accurately. In a wire cable the wires are ordinarily about 3 300 ft. long and weigh approximately 330 lb., each wire being spliced to the next one by a sleeve-nut. In the Manhattan Bridge these sleeve-nuts are $1\frac{3}{8}$ in. long and weigh about $\frac{1}{2}$ oz. On the Delaware River Bridge they are 2 in. long and weigh about $\frac{7}{8}$ oz.

In an eye-bar cable, moreover, there are many places accessible to moisture, which cannot be reached by a paint brush or even by a spray, such as the spaces between eye-bar heads and, in the case of elongated eyes, as in the Florianopolis Bridge, the vacant part of the eye. In a wire cable, the entire interior is saturated with a rust-resisting mixture, tightly squeezed under powerful pressure, tightly wrapped with galvanized wire, and, finally, painted, making every part of the cable as nearly proof against rust as it possibly can be.

The strength of ordinary cable wire, moreover, is such that it may safely be used for a maximum unit stress of 80 000 to 100 000 lb. per sq. in., as against 46 500 lb. for heat-treated eye-bars, thus effecting a further saving in the important item of dead weight.

There is, apparently, among some steel manufacturers a fascination for secrecy in parts of their work, which is amusing even if rather silly. In olden times metal workers ascribed their success in producing some particular results to conjuring, and apparently the idea or something like it seems still to persist. One of the largest manufacturers of wire used to, and perhaps still pretends to, claim that there is a mystery about the bath of molten lead through which the wire is drawn for the purpose of so-called "galvanizing", and the receptacle for this bath is carefully locked and guarded throughout the process. A large manufacturer of steel plates for rust-resisting floor-treads declines to furnish any analysis of his product on the ground that it is a secret that he prefers not to make public, apparently oblivious to the fact that any one who wants such an analysis can very easily make it. As a matter of fact, these plates are made of an ordinary grade of steel with the addition of as much copper as can be used without making it "red short". It is a good mixture and well adapted for its purpose, but the pretense of secrecy about its composition is amusing. In the case of the eye-bars for the Florianopolis Bridge the manufacturers adopted a policy of secrecy and refused to permit any investigation of their proceedings; whereupon the engineers wisely declined any responsibility for such bars. Heat treatment of steel for the purpose of increasing its strength is not a new idea, but its application on a considerable scale has not been practiced until recently, and, although the manufacturers of these bars deemed it necessary to clothe their operations in a smoke-screen of mystery, there is no reason to believe that any skillful eye-bar maker could not duplicate their results after very little experimenting and without any pretense of conjuring. Apparently, however, the makers of these bars did not foresee that their secret operations would necessarily lead to the result that engineers in charge of work would decline responsibility for any manufactured article produced by pretended secret processes. It is gratifying to learn that the manufacturers of the eye-bars have accordingly decided to discard the element of secrecy, under the somewhat tenuous pretext that the process is now so far perfected that resort to secret operation is no longer necessary.

HARDY CROSS,* M. AM. SOC. C. E. (by letter).—That this paper represents a valuable contribution to the art of bridge design and construction is at once recognized. The writer's comments are restricted to only one aspect of the design.

The authors indicate doubt as to the propriety of applying to suspension bridges criteria for stiffness borrowed from other types of bridge construction. In this they are probably correct. The question is of importance in considering the economics of continuous and other structures. Live-load deflection is often only the obvious and measurable phenomenon which accompanies other phenomena of greater importance.

Large deflection of bridges may be objectionable because:

(*a*) It produces unsightly distortions. This can almost always be corrected by camber.

(*b*) Distortion produces grades in the roadway which interfere with traffic operation. This is a definite limit on deflection; so far as the writer knows, it occurs only in suspension bridges.

(*c*) Vibration accompanies deflection, and vibration is to be avoided because: (1) It wears out the structure; and (2) it may be psychologically objectionable, producing a sense of fear in the pedestrian or passenger.

In most bridges the objections to deflection are associated with vibration. It is clearly recognized that vibration wears out—or tends to wear out—a structure; it loosens rivets in steel work and probably destroys bond in reinforced concrete. It may also produce what is usually called fatigue. While this is clearly recognized qualitatively, a quantitative measure seems impossible in the present state of the structural art. Structural mechanics commonly ignores entirely those phenomena which occur while parts of the structure are in motion and restricts itself to conditions existing when the structure has come to rest. Vaguely, designers treat the effects of deflection by the application of an "impact" coefficient.

It is probably true that a large deflection is an indication of high "impact" effects; but that it is a satisfactory measure, or that the durability or the freedom from shock is a function chiefly of deflection, independent of the type of structure, there seems to be no evidence at all.

As regards the objectionable psychological effect of vibration, it is probable that deflection is no fair measure at all. Objectionable movement probably means high acceleration; passengers apparently are not conscious of uniform movement.

It is possible to establish certain relations between the acceleration produced at any point by a unit load at any other point and the velocity of the load, but this does not help the problem very much.

The whole subject becomes of great importance in many cases. The limitations on deflection borrowed from practice in the design of simple spans affect the economy of continuous girders and trusses adversely. There

* Prof. of Structural Eng., Univ. of Illinois, Urbana, Ill.

is not much basis for a comparison of the types. The writer would appreciate any information as to who first established the existing rules in this regard, and why they were established.

D. B. STEINMAN* AND WILLIAM G. GROVE,† MEMBERS, AM. SOC. C. E. (by letter).—The economic advantages of the Florianopolis type of suspension bridge has received commercial recognition and confirmation in the proposal and adoption of this form of construction in two successive bidding competitions. These are the 700-ft. spans over the Ohio River at Point Pleasant, W. Va., and St. Mary's, W. Va., respectively. In each case, the Florianopolis type was proposed by the American Bridge Company as an alternative bid, at a price sufficiently below the tenders on the conventional suspension designs to win the respective competitions. The bids showed that, for a span length of 700 ft. and for the relative unit stresses specified, heat-treated eye-bars are more economical than wire cables at present prices; and that the combination of the eye-bars with the Florianopolis type offers a further saving in the cost of the structure.

It is true, as stated in some of the discussions, that the relative economy of eye-bars and wire cables was not conclusively demonstrated by the case of the Florianopolis Bridge. The relative unit stresses specified for the two materials and the length of the span are governing factors. In the wire cable design for Florianopolis, the specified working stress was 70 000 lb. per sq. in., and the heat-treated eye-bars were offered (at equal total cost) to be used with a working stress of 50 000 lb. per sq. in. Had a higher stress been specified for the wire or a lower stress for the eye-bars, so as to provide equal factors of safety for the two materials, it would have been more difficult for the eye-bars to be offered at equal cost. In the opinion of the designers of the Florianopolis Bridge, the fair stress ratio to use is 2 to 1, since that is approximately the ratio of the respective specified yield points or ultimate strengths of the two materials. This suggested ratio of working stresses has not yet become established because of the difficulty of overcoming the conventions of past conservative practice in wire cable design—a handicap from which the newer material of heat-treated eye-bars does not suffer.

There is, however, a marked present trend toward the adoption of higher unit stresses for cable wire. For the Ohio River Bridge, at Portsmouth, Ohio, the adopted design stress for the wire cables was 80 000 lb. per sq. in. In the recent bidding competition for the Hudson River Bridge, at New York, N. Y., the respective specified unit stresses were 50 000 lb. per sq. in. (with the secondary stresses included) for the heat-treated eye-bars, and 82 000 lb. per sq. in. (with secondary stresses not included) for the wire cables. During the past few months, heat-treated cable wire has been developed, offering a minimum yield point of 190 000 and a minimum ultimate strength of 220 000 lb. per sq. in. This wire has been adopted for the international bridge at Detroit, Mich. (span, 1 850 ft.) and for the Mount Hope Bay Bridge, in Rhode Island (span, 1 200 ft.), with a working stress of 84 000 lb. per sq. in.

* Cons. Engr. (Robinson & Steinman), New York, N. Y.

† Asst. Engr., Am. Bridge Co., New York, N. Y.

for the former and 88 000 lb. per sq. in. for the latter. Heat-treated bright wire is now offered with a yield point of 200 000 and an ultimate strength of 240 000 lb. per sq. in., for which still higher unit stresses would be specified.

In the bidding on the Hudson River Bridge, the wire design won by a margin of $2 000 000, indicating that the eye-bars cannot compete with wire cables for extremely long spans. The awards on the Point Pleasant and St. Mary's Bridges indicate that heat-treated eye-bars, at present relative prices and working stresses, are more economical than wire cables for spans as short as 700 ft. It is difficult to predict the relative economy of the two materials for span lengths between these limits (700 ft. and 3 500 ft.) without further bidding competitions. Any conclusions are subject to revision with changes in relative working stresses and with fluctuations in unit prices.

Although the manufacture of eye-bars is now a monopoly, the prices for heat-treated eye-bars are affected by the economic competition offered by wire cables. This competition, which came into play with the bidding on the Florianopolis Bridge following the development of the heat-treated eye-bars, has had a wholesome effect in stimulating improvements in the materials for higher physical properties and improvements in economic production toward reduced unit prices; also in prompting engineers to scrutinize established conventions with a view toward securing a more consistent basis for the specification of working stresses.

The writers fully appreciate the generous discussions that have been contributed to this paper, and will refer to them in the order of their presentation.

Mr. Waddell raises some questions in regard to details of proportions and form for designs of the Florianopolis type. The writers' statement that the utilization of the cable as the upper chord of the stiffening truss "should preferably be limited to the central half of the span", referred only to the loss of economy if the construction were extended to the ends of the span; it was not intended to specify any definite proportion as most economical. A variation of a few panels on either side of the quarter-points would produce a negligible difference in economy of material; practical considerations govern instead. In the case of the Florianopolis Bridge, after several variations of the design were studied, the outline shown in Fig. 2 (*a*) was adopted, with somewhat less than one-half the span (11 double panels out of 27) utilizing the cable as the top chord; this was done to avoid excessive height, and excessive variation in height, of the truss. In the design adopted for the Ohio River Bridges at Point Pleasant and St. Mary's, the central construction also extends over less than the half-span (12 panels out of 28), on the basis of similar practical considerations.

The proportions and outlines suggested by Mr. Waddell were included among those studied for the Florianopolis Bridge and were abandoned in favor of the adopted layout. The question of the comparative appearance of the design used and that suggested by Mr. Waddell in his Fig. 38 is one of individual taste; this also applies to his remark that the conventional design, Fig. 2 (*b*), would have had a better appearance with a deeper truss and with fewer suspenders; on both these points there are many who would take the opposing view. In the adopted design, the top chords in the outer quarters of the span were made straight, rather than curved, for the advantages of economy and simplicity in detailing and fabrication, as well as for structural efficiency. It is questionable whether curved top chords in the outer quarters (Fig. 38) really offer improved appearance, except where the construction is carried symmetrically into the side spans as in Fig. 42.

Mr. Waddell, while recognizing the justification of the claims for greater rigidity of the new type of stiffening truss, inquires in regard to confirmatory deflection tests on the finished structure. Such tests cannot be made without great difficulty until the railroad, which was intended to traverse the bridge, is built; and it is doubtful whether the local governmental authorities would be sufficiently interested in the scientific value of the results to authorize the expense of deflection tests. The designers are confident of the confirmation that would be yielded by such tests, for it is invariably found that the actual measured deflections of a suspension bridge are less than the calculated amounts. Although no live load deflection tests have been recorded for the Florianopolis Bridge, a close verification of the computed dead load deflections was afforded by the official test to determine whether the required vertical under-clearance from water level had been realized.

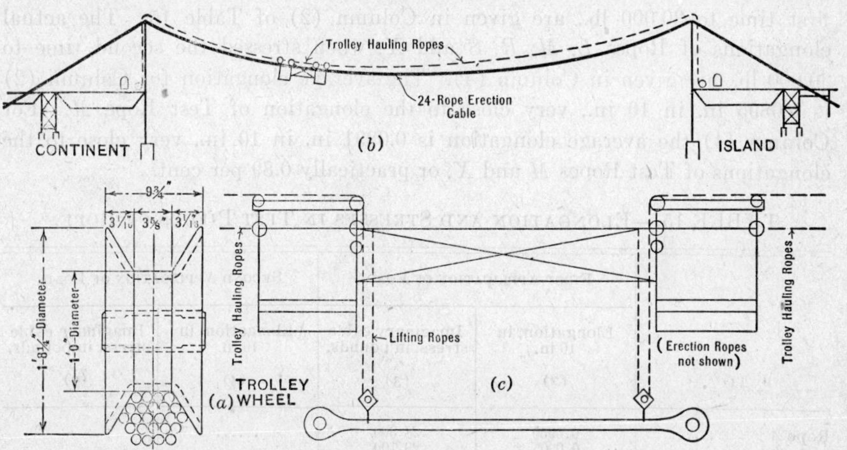

FIG. 43.—MAIN SPAN EYE-BAR TROLLEY OPERATION.

The problem of supporting the rocker towers during their construction and during the erection of the eye-bar cables was given considerable study. A solution was found whereby the actual amount of erection material required was very small, consisting merely of some plates and angles at the ends of the temporary struts which tied the tower columns to the *U*-1 and *L*-1 points of the adjoining 185-ft. spans. The struts themselves consisted of material later used for the suspension-span bracing in the finished structure.

The principle of the double-bored pin-hole in the eye-bar heads was used by the American Bridge Company in 1912 in the connecting links joining the spans of the Kenova Bridge* during cantilever erection, in order to facilitate the swinging of the spans. To the writers' best knowledge, this principle had never actually been incorporated in holes in the heads of eye-bars, prior to its use on the Florianopolis Bridge.

The writers appreciate the complimentary remarks of Mr. Miller, relative to the use of 1-in. ropes to form the temporary cable from which the eye-bars were erected.

The twenty-four erection ropes were grouped together in the form of an elongated hexagon shown in Fig. 43 (*a*). The wheels of the main-span trolley used to erect the eye-bar cables were made to fit this hexagon, so that eight ropes were actually in contact with the wheels. They were closely compacted to the remaining sixteen ropes by the weight of the trolleys and by the loads of eye-bars applied to the ropes by the chain hoists.

After the pilot rope was erected, the remaining twenty-three ropes were placed and adjusted to the same sag as the pilot rope. Each rope under its own weight then had a stress of approximately 3 000 lb. and had stretched about 2.7 ft. in 1 700 ft. Later, when the entire weight of the eye-bars was supported by the ropes, each rope had an average stress of approximately 30 000 lb. and had stretched about 15.1 ft. in 1 700 ft.

The actual elongations of the nine test pieces of rope, when stressed the first time to 30 000 lb., are given in Column (2) of Table 15. The actual elongations of Ropes *L, M, R, S* and *X,* when stressed the second time to 30 000 lb., are given in Column (4). The average elongation for Column (2) is 0.0895 in. in 10 in., very close to the elongation of Test Rope *M*. For Column (4) the average elongation is 0.0891 in. in 10 in., very close to the elongations of Test Ropes *M* and *X,* or practically 0.89 per cent.

TABLE 15.—ELONGATION AND STRESSES IN TEST PIECES OF ROPE.

	FIRST APPLICATION OF LOAD.		SECOND APPLICATION OF LOAD.	
	Elongation, in 10 in.	Imaginary cable stress, in pounds.	Elongation, in 10 in.	Imaginary cable stress, in pounds.
(1)	(2)	(3)	(4)	(5)
Rope *A*	0.0950	28 300	......	......
" *F*	0.0905	29 700	.....	......
" *G*	0.0997	27 000	......	......
" *K*	0.0976	27 500	......	......
" *L*	0.0984	27 300	0.1042	25 600
" *M*	0.0897	30 000	0.0884	30 200
" *R*	0.0657	41 000	0.0712	37 600
" *S*	0.0850	31 600	0.0929	28 800
" *X*	0.0841	32 000	0.0886	30 200
Average	0.0895	30 500	0.0891	30 500

Assuming a composite cable made up of the nine test ropes to carry an average of 30 000 lb. per rope when elongated 0.89%, it is found that Test

* See "Reconstruction of the Norfolk and Western Railway Company's Bridge Over the Ohio River at Kenova, West Virginia," by William G. Grove, M. Am. Soc. C. E., and Henry Taylor, Esq., *Transactions,* Am. Soc. C. E., Vol. LXXIX (1915), p. 411.

Rope *R* would carry more, and Test Rope *L* less, than 30 000 lb. The actual stress that each test rope would carry when the 9-rope cable is stressed to 30 000 lb. the first time is given in Column (3) of Table 15 and the actual stress that each of Test Ropes, *L, M, R, S,* and *X* would carry when this rope cable is stressed to 30 000 lb. the second time is given in Column (5). It is seen that the actual stress in the nine test ropes would vary from 27 300 to 41 000 lb. when the 9-rope cable is stressed to 30 000 lb. the first time, and the actual stress in the five test ropes would vary from 25 600 to 37 600 lb. when the 5-rope cable is stressed to 30 000 lb. the second time. From this analysis it may be reasonable to assume that the actual stress in the twenty-four ropes used in the cable varied from 25 000 to 40 000 lb., when the entire 24-rope cable carried an average stress of 30 000 lb. per rope.

In reference to the operating ropes for the main-span trolley used to erect the eye-bars, Fig. 43 (*b*) is a diagrammatic view of the operating lines running to the tops of the towers and thence down to engines on the viaduct floor. Fig. 43 (*c*) shows, to enlarged scale, both the operating and the load lines. When the continent engine pulled the trolley westward, the island engine played out the operating rope. When the trolley had been properly spotted, both engines were used to raise the eye-bars. Either end of the eye-bars could be raised or lowered slightly by operating the particular engine controlling that end of the bar without operating the other engine.

Fig. 44 shows diagrammatically the trolley used for the erection of the suspended span. In the upper view (Fig. 44 (*a*)) are seen the operating lines to the two engines which controlled the movements of this trolley in a manner similar to that in which the movements of the main-span eye-bar trolley were controlled. The lower view (Fig. 44 (*b*)) shows both operating and load lines. In the case of the load line, there was only one set of falls and the line ran continuous from engine to engine. When the lift was near the continent, the continent engine was operated; when near the island, the control was by the island engine. When the trolley itself was moved, the lifting line ran idle through the block.

Mr. Frost states that the Florianopolis design and its method of erection may extend the range of use of structures of the suspension type. In this connection, it may be noted that the past few years have marked a period of renewed activity all over the United States in the design and construction of suspension bridges, especially for spans ranging in length from 600 to 1 200 ft. Contributing factors have been improvements in economical design and erection, the development of higher strength eye-bars and wire, and the competitive reduction of unit prices on the two materials. Erroneous notions of the relative expensiveness of suspension construction have been partly dispelled, and the advantages of the type have become more widely recognized. It is difficult, at this stage, to appraise the influence of the Florianopolis design and method of erection on this development. Nevertheless, it may be significant to note that four Ohio River bridges (Portsmouth, Steubenville, Point Pleasant, and St. Mary's) commenced in 1926-27, are suspension structures, where cantilever construction previously prevailed; and that only two of these bridges are wire cable designs, the other two being eye-bar designs of the Florianopolis type.

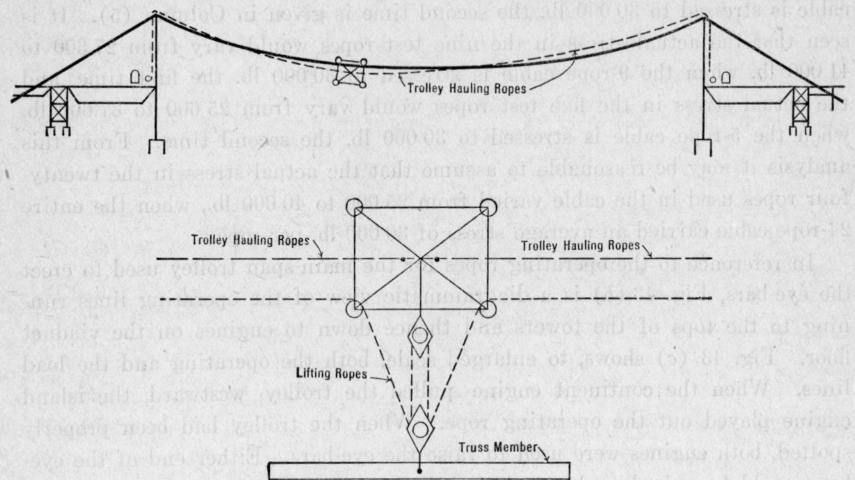

Fig. 44.—Trolley Used for Suspended Span Erection.

Mr. Larsson presents an interesting historical outline of the development of the eye-bar industry. As is generally well known in the profession, Mr. Larsson with the late C. W. Bryan, M. Am. Soc. C. E., Chief Engineer of the American Bridge Company, deserves full credit for the development of the heat-treated eye-bars, first in the medium grade (elastic limit, 50 000 lb. per sq. in.) developed in 1914, and, subsequently, in the high-tension grade (elastic limit, 75 000 lb. per sq. in.) developed in 1921 and receiving its first practical application in the Florianopolis Bridge. It was this high-tension grade of heat-treated eye-bars that made it possible for an eye-bar design to be proposed for competitive bidding as one of the two alternative official designs for the 3 500-ft. Hudson River Bridge.

A deterrent to the more ready acceptance of the new material has been the policy of secrecy covering its manufacture. Structural engineers hesitate to accept a material without full privileges of inspection and chemical analysis. Mr. Larsson's announcement that the policy of secrecy has been discontinued, will be welcomed by the profession. The remaining deterrent, namely, the difficulty of making full-sized tests, should next be removed by the provision of a testing machine large enough to take the longest bars furnished for any structure.

Professor Morris reports an eye-bar suspension bridge of 450-ft. span built in 1914-15 over the Muskingum River, at Dresden, Ohio. The writers regret that they did not know of this structure and that Professor Morris had therein preceded them in the adoption of rocker towers. It is also of interest to note that for this span of 450 ft., constructed in 1914-15, eye-bars of structural steel grade (ultimate strength, 60 000 to 70 000 lb. per sq. in.) won over wire cables in the bidding competition.

An instructive joint discussion has been submitted by Messrs. Covell, Wilkerson, and Nutter. They commend the Florianopolis Bridge as "a splendid type" from the standpoint of economy, rigidity, and general structural efficiency. On the question of its esthetic value, they express a preference for a curved side-span design with symmetrical contruction, like Fig. 42; but such design would not have suited the local conditions at Florianopolis. On the question of economy, they point out that the total weight of steel in the Florianopolis Bridge is surprisingly low for a structure with a main span of more than 1 100 ft. and a total length of about 2 700 ft.; and the credit for this showing of economy they rightly ascribe to the type of span and the use of high-tension heat-treated eye-bars and a timber floor. On the last point, it may be stated that advantage was taken of the availability of South American hardwood to provide a floor material of great strength and longevity.

The maximum loadings of 50-ton locomotives for the railway and 6-ton trucks for the highway were the official Government specifications for the design; and the local authorities regard as extremely remote any possibility of these loadings ever being exceeded in that locality.

Messrs. Covell, Wilkerson, and Nutter agree that the high-tension heat-treated eye-bars are a proper material for an eye-bar chain (as in the Florianopolis Bridge), but they question whether the ductility of 5% would be sufficient for the use of this material for truss members. To the writers' knowledge, the high-tension eye-bars have not thus far been used in any truss structures; only the medium grade heat-treated eye-bars (8% elongation) have been so used, as in the Carquinez Cantilever Bridge, with two spans of 1 100 ft., and in the Oil City simple spans of 260 and 350 ft.

The three engineers also agree with the writers that the hinged tower for the suspension bridge is a step in the right direction, and they cite their adoption of the rocker-tower design for the Sixth, Seventh, and Ninth Street Suspension Bridges over the Allegheny River at Pittsburgh, Pa.

With respect to appearance, it is impossible to get a real profile view of the Florianopolis structure except when crossing the Strait. From any point on either shore, the bridge is viewed obliquely, and the eye-bar cable seems larger due to seeing all four eye-bars of each cable. The photograph, Fig. 3, does not do justice to the appearance of the structure as ordinarily viewed.

The writers desire to thank Mr. Carstarphen for his comprehensive discussion of the erection problem with reference to the behavior of the wire ropes used to erect the eye-bar cables.

They agree with him that two applications of the load are not sufficient to determine the true value of the modulus of elasticity of wire rope. In the use of the ropes at Florianopolis, however, the modulus of elasticity was not of direct interest, except as a means for determining the actual elongations of the ropes under certain conditions of loading during the erection. There were only two eye-bar cables to erect so that there was an actual condition in the field corresponding to Mr. Carstarphen's Tests (*a*) and (*b*) of Fig. 41. For these requirements, it was necessary to compute the elongations starting from the original length of the rope, and not from a permanent set value determined from a previous stress in the rope. Referring to Fig. 41, if the modulus was based upon an elongation starting not from the permanent set points, but from the zero points, the result would be as shown in Table 16. The resulting average value of the modulus is fairly close to 8 300 000 lb. per sq. in., the value used at Florianopolis.

As Mr. Carstarphen states, it is known from actual practice that hemp center ropes do not fall apart when bent around sheaves. In fact, the American Bridge Company uses 16-in. sheaves as standard sheaves with 1-in. rope.

In Mr. Carstarphen's discussion, he arrives at a horizontal component in the erection ropes (messenger cables), when these ropes supported all the eye-bars, of 595 627 lb. instead of 660 000 lb. mentioned in the paper. To obtain the horizontal component of 519 527 lb. in the eye-bar cable under its own weight, with a sag of 116 ft., he used the dead load panel concentrations for the eye-bar cable only, as given in Table 10. It was the original intention to erect not only the eye-bar cable, but also the permanent rope hangers (at the ends) and the top chord gusset-plates (at the central portion of the span) from the erection ropes; and the 116-ft. sag was based on the eye-bar cable plus this additional weight. Considering these additional loads, the horizontal component in the eye-bar cable would be 569 000 lb. instead of 519 527 lb. He also assumes 616 lb. for the weight of the chain hoists and their connections; this latter figure was actually very close to 1 000 lb. These additional weights on the erection ropes account for the difference between the two calculated values of 660 000 lb. and 595 627 lb. for the horizontal component in the ropes.

TABLE 16.—ELONGATIONS IN TEST SPECIMENS.

Reference.	Load, in pounds.	Percentage of elongation in 10 in.
Fig. 41 (*c*)	158 400	0.451
" (*d*)	158 400	0.436
" (*e*)	158 000	0.428
" (*f*)	156 600	0.420
Average	157 850	0.434

$$E = \frac{157\ 850 \times 10}{2.4\ [0.0434 + 0.0410]} = 7\ 800\ 000$$

The length of the erection rope cable was based on the assumption of a parabolic curve, but the formula was extended to include the third term in the series,

$$L = l + \frac{8}{3}\frac{y^2}{l} - \frac{32}{5}\frac{y^4}{l^3} + \cdots$$

it having been found that this last term had an appreciable influence on the length.

Mr. Hoadley reports an independent stress analysis which he made of the Florianopolis Bridge for thesis work. He presents an outline of his method, using the "least work" equation based on Castigliano's principle, and he shows that it is merely another form of expressing the influence line equation for the method of elastic weights as used by the designers of the bridge. The values derived by Mr. Hoadley for the H-influence line are somewhat higher than those of Messrs. Robinson and Steinman (5% higher at mid-span), and he volunteers the explanation that this may be due to an inherent error in his method. His treatment of the top chord members in the middle part of the span requires him to add the contributions of the opposing tension and compression components arithmetically, whereas they should be added algebraically. A review of Mr. Hoadley's thesis shows that his resultant values for the governing stresses in the stiffening truss are lower than the values obtained by Messrs. Robinson and Steinman and used by them in proportioning the structure, affording a welcome independent check on the safety of the design analysis. Mr. Hoadley also derives the H-influence line equation by a modified method, and computes therefrom a value of H agreeing with that found by Messrs. Robinson and Steinman by the method of elastic weights.

Professor Menefee states that there is no longer any real mystery about heat treatment, and he predicts that all the large companies will soon be producing heat-treated bridge members as wanted. He approves the use of the Brinell test as a check on the uniformity of the heat treatment and of the tensile strength. Referring to the absence of the usual secondary and impact stresses, he considers 46 500 lb. per sq. in. (as used in the Florianopolis eye-bar cables) a safe working stress for steel with an elastic limit of 80 000 lb. per sq. in.

The writers agree with Professor Menefee that the substitution of eye-bars for wire cables adds stiffness and reduces deflections. His statement that a cable of equal sectional area will elongate under load more than a solid piece of steel requires clarification. For the same load and the same area of cross-section, a parallel wire cable and a chain of heat-treated eye-bars should show substantially the same elongation, since the respective values of the modulus of elasticity are substantially equal (about 27 000 000 lb. per sq. in.). The more recently developed heat-treated cable wire has a higher value of E (29 000 000 lb. per sq. in.), and, therefore, would elongate about 7% less than heat-treated eye-bars. The reason an eye-bar chain as applied in an actual design would yield smaller elastic elongation and resulting deflection than a parallel wire cable is because the eye-bar chain would be designed with a lower working stress and, therefore, would be provided with a proportionally larger sectional area. With the incorporation of the Florianopolis type, this increase in rigidity is further augmented (very materially) by the effect of the modified form of stiffening truss.

Mr. Kuo presents a valuable discussion of the inherent problem of providing rigidity in suspension bridges. He distinguishes between free cable bridges (with suspended truss) and braced (triangulated) cable types; and he points out that to secure high rigidity in a free cable suspension bridge requires an unusually heavy stiffening truss, resulting in an uneconomical design of clumsy appearance. He considers the Florianopolis Bridge (which he classifies as a partly braced type) a very scientific and economical solution of the problem.

To the practical reasons given in the paper for seeking rigidity, Mr. Kuo adds another of more technical nature, namely, the reduction of forced deformations in the floor system. He reports having calculated extremely high secondary stresses in stringers resulting from stiffening truss deflections.

In regard to the use of rocker towers, Mr. Kuo points out a possible objection, in some locations, on the score of reduced security against severe earthquake effects. The dowels provided in the base castings of the Florianopolis towers are intended to provide resistance to displacement by such forces; and the writers believe that, with proper design of the base details, rocker towers can be given the same security as fixed base towers against earthquake forces.

Mr. Kuo commends the new departure of the stiffening truss from parallel chords and the unification of the cable with the middle portion of the top chord as the two most admirable features of the Florianopolis design, representing a distinct development in the art of suspension bridge construction. He also points out the visible structural fitness of a design in which the truss depth varies with the magnitude of the bending moments.

Mr. Moisseiff recounts the evolution of stiffening truss forms to that used at Florianopolis. On this subject, to facilitate a review of structural and chronological relationship, the writers have prepared Fig. 45, showing successive developments of suspension bridge forms, illustrated as far as possible with actual applications and their dates. The development of braced cable types embraces the form with full trussing between cable and roadway (like the bridge at Frankfort-on-Main, Germany, 1869-1921, Fig. 45(*c*)); the three-hinged form (Fig. 45(*d*)), with parabolic lower chord and straight top chords (represented by Hemberle's Point Bridge at Pittsburgh, 1877-1927); the forms with parallel chords (like the Seventh Street Bridge, at Pittsburgh, 1884-1926, Fig. 45(*e*), designed by Gustav Lindenthal, M. Am. Soc. C. E., and his more recent design for a Hudson River Bridge at 59th Street, New York); the Fidler truss and other three-hinged forms (Fig. 45(*f*)), using intersecting cable curves (like the bridge built in 1889 over the Tiber at Rome; also Mr. Lindenthal's 1910 design for the Quebec Bridge and his design in 1923 for the Sydney Harbor Bridge); and the two-hinged type (Fig. 45 (*g*)) with parabolic upper chord and polygonal bottom chord (like Mr. Lindenthal's 1899 design for the Quebec Bridge and his 1903 design for the Manhattan Bridge). In comparison with the last type, Mr. Moisseiff arrived at the same conclusion as the writers, namely, that the form now adopted for the Florianopolis Bridge (Fig. 45(*h*)) would be more advantageous, as it dispenses with the necessity of additional wind chords and presents a more pleasing appearance.

Mr. Moisseiff's contribution of an illustrated description of his design in 1907 for a proposed bridge of 1 200-ft. span over the Kill van Kull (Fig. 42), anticipating the Florianopolis design, helps to make the record complete.

Mr. Moisseiff would limit the economic applicability of the Florianopolis type to bridges where the live load is heavy and the span not too long. These

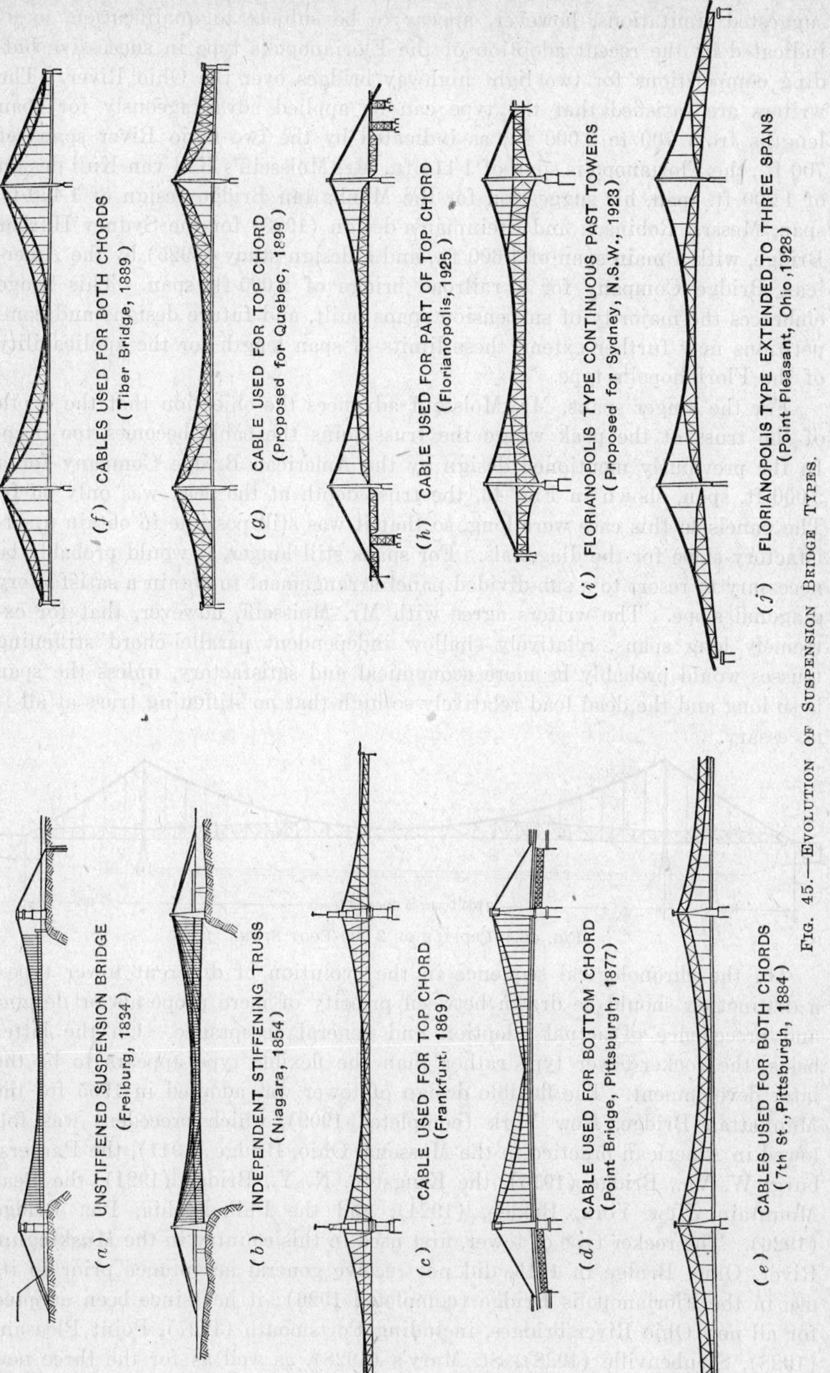

FIG. 45.—EVOLUTION OF SUSPENSION BRIDGE TYPES.

suggested limitations, however, appear to be subject to qualification, as is indicated by the recent adoption of the Florianopolis type in successive bidding competitions for two light highway bridges over the Ohio River. The writers are satisfied that the type can be applied advantageously for span lengths from 700 to 2 000 ft., as indicated by the two Ohio River spans of 700 ft., the Florianopolis span of 1 114 ft., Mr. Moisseiff's Kill van Kull design of 1 200 ft. span, his suggestion for the Manhattan Bridge design of 1 470-ft. span, Messrs. Robinson and Steinman's design (1923) for the Sydney Harbor Bridge, with a main span of 1 600 ft., and a design study (1925) by the American Bridge Company for a railroad bridge of 2 000-ft. span. This range embraces the majority of suspension spans built, and future designs and competitions may further extend these limits of span length for the applicability of the Florianopolis type.

For the longer spans, Mr. Moisseiff advances the objection that the depth of the truss at the peak where the truss joins the cable becomes too deep. In the previously mentioned design by the American Bridge Company for a 2 000-ft. span, shown in Fig. 46, the truss depth at the peak was only 65 ft. The panels in this case were long, so that it was still possible to obtain a satisfactory slope for the diagonals. For spans still longer, it would probably be necessary to resort to a sub-divided panel arrangement to obtain a satisfactory diagonal slope. The writers agree with Mr. Moisseiff, however, that for extremely long spans, relatively shallow independent parallel-chord stiffening trusses would probably be more economical and satisfactory, unless the span is so long and the dead load relatively so high that no stiffening truss at all is necessary.

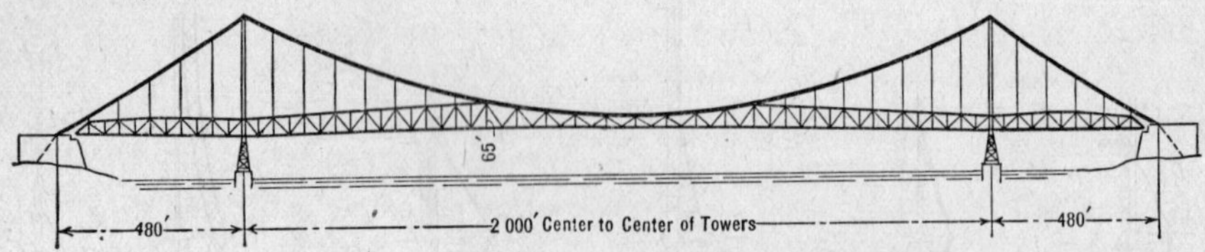

Fig. 46.—Profile of 2 000-Foot Span.

On the chronological sequence in the evolution of different tower types, a distinction should be drawn between priority of mere proposals or designs and precedence of actual adoption and general acceptance. On the latter basis, the rocker-tower type rather than the flexible type appears to be the later development. The flexible design of tower was adopted in 1905 for the Manhattan Bridge, New York (completed 1909), which precedent was followed in American practice in the Massena, Ohio, Bridge (1911), the Parkersburg, W. Va., Bridge (1916), the Kingston, N. Y., Bridge (1921), the Bear Mountain, New York, Bridge, (1924), and the Philadelphia, Pa., Bridge (1926). The rocker type of tower, first used in this country in the Muskingum River, Ohio, Bridge in 1915, did not receive general acceptance prior to its use in the Florianopolis Bridge (completed 1926); it has since been adopted for all new Ohio River bridges, including Portsmouth (1927), Point Pleasant (1928), Steubenville (1928), St. Mary's (1928), as well as for the three new Pittsburgh suspension bridges at Ninth Street (1926), Seventh Street (1927), and Sixth Street (1928). For two decades (1905-25) the flexible type of tower prevailed, almost without exception; then, commencing with the Florianopolis Bridge, the rocker tower design was generally accepted, with eight bridges of this type built in three years as against only three of the fixed base type undertaken in the same period. This succession of types in actual practice is what the writers had in mind in their remarks on the evolution of suspension-bridge tower design.

Mr. Moisseiff suggests that the choice between rocker and flexible types would depend on the height of the tower, since "a tall tower with a fixed base should hardly require more material than a rocker tower". There are other considerations, besides economy of material, that affect the choice, such as the difficulties and expense of cable erection adjustments with fixed base towers on the one hand, and the availability or lack of convenient means for holding the rocker towers during erection on the other. That the erection advantages of the rocker type are recognized by experienced erectors is indicated by the request of the American Bridge Company, during 1927, for permission to change the towers of the Mid-Hudson Bridge at Poughkeepsie, N. Y. (1 500-ft. span) from the flexible type to the rocker type under its contract.

The use of rocker towers greatly facilitates the necessary erection adjustments. Such towers are easily tilted back shoreward any amount as required for the connection of the back-stays to the saddle castings in bridges with eye-bar cables, or for the balancing of the catenaries during cable construction in bridges with wire cables. To hold the rocker towers in the required position during erection generally requires only a small amount of temporary material at the tower bases. With the use of fixed base towers, the necessary tower-top adjustments for cable erection are made more difficult.

Mr. Moisseiff cites the fact that the designers of the Detroit River Bridge (of 1 850-ft. span) have adopted towers of the fixed base type. Calculations recently made by Messrs. Robinson and Steinman, in the course of their erection studies for the cable contractors on this bridge, reveal the fact that the tower tops have to be moved shoreward the unprecedented amounts of 7.34 ft. on the American side and 5.04 ft. on the Canadian side, in order to balance the cable catenaries during erection. Pulling the towers back these indicated amounts would be a difficult and expensive operation, and methods for obviating this necessity also involve unanticipated difficulties and expense. If these results had been foreseen, it is doubtful whether fixed base towers would have been selected, since the adoption of rocker towers would have eliminated these difficulties.

The required tower movements during cable erection are most serious in designs with "straight" (unloaded) back-stays as in the Florianopolis, Bear Mountain, and Detroit Bridges. In such layouts, the rocker type of tower has especial advantages.

In addition to the advantages of economy of material in the towers and the elimination of expensive tower or saddle adjustments during erection, another advantage of rocker towers must not be overlooked; namely, the reduction of stresses (and consequent possible reduction of dimensions) in the masonry piers from the elimination of tower bending stresses.

Mr. Beanfield refers to extensometer readings made on bridge members composed of groups of eye-bars and reports that he found considerable variation of stress in the individual eye-bars of a group. He attributes this to pin clearance, minor differences between pin-hole distances, and deformations in the eye-bar heads. The writers regret that no extensometer readings were taken on the eye-bar cables of the Florianopolis Bridge to ascertain, as suggested, if there is any great variation in stress in the individual eye-bars of each link. Neither, to their knowledge, have such measurements ever been made on the wire strands of large suspension bridge cables. In the case of a wire cable, the method of stringing (to equal sags) practically assures uniform tension of all the wires; and any local slackness of a wire is not material since it is only one of thousands of wires composing the cable and, therefore, represents only a very small fraction of 1% of the total section. Moreover, the compacting of a wire cable after stringing is such as to assure unified stress action; even if a wire is cut at any point, it will be found to have full stress again (transmitted by the frictional bond) a short distance away from the section.

Referring to the details of the top castings on the towers, Mr. Beanfield raises the question of secondary stresses arising from the frictional resistance to rotation of the eye-bars on the pins. In the case of the Florianopolis Bridge, the anticipated deflection movements under live load are so small that the resulting angle changes at the ends of the eye-bar cables would not produce any serious secondary stresses.

That the eye-bars rotated about the pins to take care of angle changes during erection was visibly demonstrated just after the first two panels of truss members at the continent end were erected by the "jinniwink" standing on the 185-ft. span. When the jinniwink was moved out to Panel Point 2 in order to erect truss members in Panels 2-4, there was a heavy local concentration on Point *C*2 of the eye-bar cable. This heavy load distorted the equilibrium polygon of the eye-bar cable so much—causing the eye-bars, *C*0-2 and *C*2-4, to rotate about Pin *C*2—that it was impossible to place the top chord, *C*2-4. The distance between Points 2 and 4 at the top chord was about 4 ft. too short for that chord to enter. The frictional resistance of the eye-bar stress on the pins was certainly overcome in this instance.

Mr. Beanfield, like Mr. Kuo, expresses concern as to the security of the tower base castings against earthquake forces. Although provision against earthquake effects was not definitely specified or allowed for in the design of the Florianopolis Bridge, a few minutes with the slide-rule are sufficient to show that the tower base details are amply proportioned to resist displacement under the most severe seismic disturbances thus far recorded. These sixteen 3-in. dowels provide a total resisting section of 112 sq. in., or a safe shearing resistance (at 15 000 lb. per sq. in.) of 1 680 000 lb. The total weight of the suspension bridge (including towers, cables, back-stays, and suspended structure) is approximately 3 000 tons. This total weight would have to be subjected to a horizontal acceleration of 28% of gravity, or 9 ft. per sec. per sec., before the safe shearing resistance of the steel dowels would be exceeded. This acceleration (representing earthquake intensity) is seven times as high as that assumed in the design of the Carquinez Strait Bridge which, as cited by Mr.

Beanfield, was designed with especial consideration to possible earthquake forces. Moreover, the foregoing comparison assumes the Florianopolis Bridge to be a free structure, with its entire inertia resisted solely at the tower bases. Actually, the structure has safe additional restraint in the fact that the tops of the towers are securely tied back to the massive concrete anchorages.

Mr. Beanfield voices a common misconception when he states that suspension bridges, in general, are not adaptable for locations subject to earthquake disturbances. Consideration of the functional characteristics of the suspension type should show that it is pre-eminently the bridge type best adapted to resist seismic forces. The longitudinal continuity of the principal element, the positive anchorage at each end, the comparative lightness of weight, the low center of gravity, and the characteristic resilience of the structure—all combine to give the highest security against earthquake effects. The contrary misconception is perhaps prompted by the thought of the relative flexibility of a suspension span; but this very flexibility gives safety against seismic shock or any suddenly applied force. A suspension bridge functions like an anchored steel spring, whereas other bridge types would act like stacks of blocks. Resilience is a valuable factor of safety against seismic effects. The Eiffel Tower would obviously be safer than Cleopatra's Needle in an earthquake; and the Florianopolis Bridge is likewise many times safer than the Carquinez Bridge against seismic effects. Where the suspension type is at all suitable, the writers would choose it every time in preference to a cantilever bridge in earthquake country.

On the question of the proportioning of the rocker bearings, the following notes may be of interest: For the base castings with a radius of contact of 12 ft., the designers adopted an allowable working pressure of 108 000 lb. per lin. in., equal to $750r$, or $375d$. This is five-eighths of the linear bearing pressure ($600d$) allowed by the specifications for steel rollers adopted by the Society's Special Committee on Specifications for Bridge Design and Construction.* Specifications of this form are based on theoretical derivations which take into account the anticipated elastic deformation of the line of contact into a narrow strip of contact area. They also take into account the supporting and relieving effect of the unloaded metal adjacent to the strip of contact. Actual tests on large steel roller or rocker bearings are needed in order to verify the theoretical deductions and to fix the coefficients more definitely.

Mr. Stowell remarks that the element of cost is the "discordant note in the harmonious whole" of the Florianopolis Bridge project. This phase, however, may be viewed from a different angle. Had there been plenty of money available, a cantilever bridge of the type shown in Fig. 2 (*c*) would have been adopted. While this cantilever span would have held the record for monumental bridges in South America, still, no new features in bridge design and erection would have been introduced. Necessity is the mother of invention, and the scant supply of money taxed the ingenuity of the engineers connected with the development and execution of the project, and resulted in the production of the suspension type of structure with all its novel features.

* *Transactions*, Am. Soc. C. E., Vol. LXXXVII (1924), p. 1281.

Mr. Stowell expresses his conviction that the superiority of wire over eye-bars for cables is so great that the question of relative cost should not be a controlling factor in deciding between them. On this point, there will be legitimate differences of opinion. Each type has its advocates and, apparently, a field for its appropriate utilization.

Mr. Stowell questions the reliability of the heat-treated eye-bars, on the score that the limitations of the testing machine necessitated the use of bars especially made for test instead of permitting selections from the finished lot to be used for testing. He cites the low elongation (3%) of one of the test bars as compared with the 7% average of the others, and he directs attention to the hazard of using eye-bars of different elongation in the same cable member. In justice to the eye-bars, however, it is only fair to note that the varying elongations shown in the test reports relate to the ultimate load and not to the working stresses below the elastic limit.

In further reference to the results of the full-sized tests on the eye-bars, the following explanatory notes are submitted: The American Bridge Company was under contractual obligation to have the test bars pass the minimum requirements of 75 000 lb. per sq. in. elastic limit, 105 000 lb. per sq. in. ultimate strength, and 5% elongation in 18 ft. As long as these requirements were met, the Company felt that here was an opportunity to experiment and ascertain whether eye-bars with 100 000 lb. per sq. in. elastic limit could be produced. This accounts for the variations in the elastic limit values, since the Company was not trying to produce uniform results. As a matter of fact, an elastic limit of 100 000 lb. per sq. in. was not quite attained, the nearest approach being 96 830 lb. per sq. in. While it is true that one bar failed in the elongation requirement, that same bar had an elastic limit of 82 780 lb. per sq. in., 10% higher than the guaranteed minimum, and an ultimate strength of 116 720 lb. per sq. in., 11% higher than the guaranteed minimum. On the additional bar which was tested, the elongation was 8.1%, or well above the guaranteed minimum.

Mr. Stowell appears to have misinterpreted the results of the eye-bar tests in his reasoning with respect to the variation of stress in the several eye-bars in any one panel. The entire theory of elastic structures is based on Hooke's law that, within the elastic limit of the material, unit stress is proportional to unit strain or distortion, the constant ratio between them being the modulus of elasticity. While it is true that the value of this modulus may vary slightly in different specimens of the same material, there is no such variation as would cause the distribution of stress among four eye-bars in one panel to be, as Mr. Stowell suggests, 35.2% in one bar and 21.6% in each of the other three bars. Before testing, each bar was marked with points 1 ft. apart for a distance of 13 ft. on two bars and from 34 to 38 ft. on the remaining eleven bars. After failure, the distances between these points were measured and the results were as plotted in Fig. 47. These curves show a very uniform elongation at all points on the bar except at the point of failure.

Mr. Stowell points out the exceptional reliability of wire for cables, in that two full-sized tests are made on each individual wire in addition

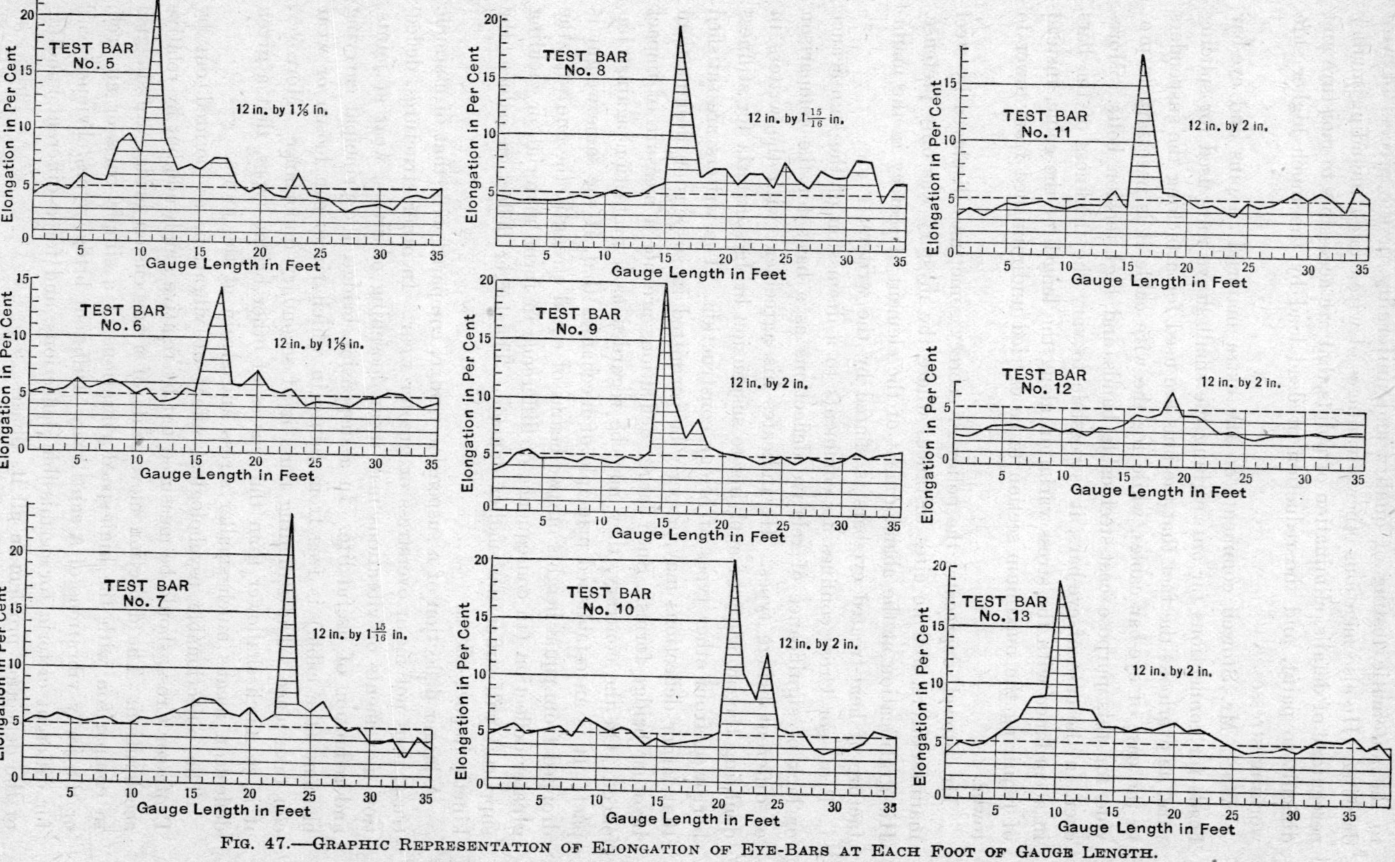

Fig. 47.—Graphic Representation of Elongation of Eye-Bars at Each Foot of Gauge Length.

to the automatic testing of quality and uniformity in the process of wire drawing. He also mentions other advantages of wire cables, including smaller percentage of details, elimination of points that are accessible to moisture and difficult to paint, and the reduction of dead load by the much higher safe working stresses.

When Mr. Stowell comments on the extra material in pins and eye-bar heads for connections far outweighing the small sleeve nuts used for splicing wire, he overlooks the fact that the pins are used for attaching the suspenders in the case of eye-bar cables, while for the wire cable it is necessary to provide for this purpose cast-steel cable bands and high-tension bolts. Moreover, in the case of eye-bars, it is possible to vary the thickness of the bars in accordance with the stress variation along the length of the cable, instead of requiring the maximum section to be carried undiminished from tower to tower.

Mr. Stowell deprecates the policy of secrecy sometimes displayed by steel manufacturers, and he cites instances where the mystery was only pretense. His gratification at the abandonment of the element of secrecy in the manufacture of heat-treated eye-bars is shared by the writers.

Professor Cross confines his comments to a discussion of the significance or lack of significance of relative deflections as a basis for the comparison of different bridge types. He indicates his agreement with the writers in doubting the propriety of applying to suspension bridges criteria for stiffness borrowed from other types of bridge construction. The writers are satisfied that larger deflections may properly be permitted in suspension designs than in other bridge forms. Such larger deflections are not a measure of impact effect. On the contrary, they may be regarded as a protection against impact. It is an established principle of mechanics that, if the same weight is dropped from equal heights on two beams of equal strength, the one with the greater deflection (in consequence of difference in form, material, or yielding supports) will suffer the smaller damage. The larger deflection reduces the kinetic impact effect.

A larger deflection of a suspension bridge, compared with that of a simple truss, does not mean overstress or greater wear. In other structures, deflection movements or vibrations may mean loosening of rivets, wear at joints, and reduction of useful life. In a suspension bridge, the principal carrying element (the cable) is free from joints in which rivets can loosen or wear can take place. The stiffening truss is of secondary importance. Moreover, it is so much shallower than the trusses of other bridge types, that a given deflection means much smaller stress and strain at the joints.

The objectionable psychological effect of vibration, as pointed out by Professor Cross, should be measured not by relative amplitude but by relative acceleration. The deflection movements of a suspension bridge are sluggish in comparison with the high-speed vibrations of a simple truss or an arch, or the jerky vibrations of a cantilever. Different bridge types obviously call for different criteria for permissible deflections, and for a different handling of the deflection problem in all its phases.

Concluding Remarks.—An interesting confirmation of the economy of material in the Florianopolis Bridge as compared with other suspension structures is found in a paper by Mr. W. H. Thorpe on "Steel Bridge Weights".* Mr. Thorpe has analyzed the weights of steel per unit of live load for a large range of bridges and, after making corrections for differences in relative floor weight, has plotted the results as a function of span length to establish a mean curve for each respective type of bridge. In the graph of plotted points for suspension bridges, one point stands out prominently as the lowest one relative to the mean curve, and that is the point representing the steel weight factor of the Florianopolis Bridge. In comparison with the neighboring points in the plotted graph, the respective steel weight factors (per unit of live load) are:

Bridge.	Steel weight factor.
Elizabeth Bridge (951-ft. span, eye-bars)...............	2.4
Florianopolis Bridge (1 114-ft. span, eye-bars)..........	1.6
Manhattan Bridge (1 470-ft. span, wire)................	2.5

The low weight factor recorded for the Florianopolis Bridge cannot be ascribed to the use of a timber floor, since correction for relative floor weight has been made in Mr. Thorpe's analysis; nor is the use of high-tension eye-bars a governing factor, since bridges with wire cables of higher unit tension are included in the comparison. The form of the structure, therefore, must be the principal reason for the low value of the weight factor. This is a gratifying independent verification of the steel-weight economy of the Florianopolis type of suspension structure.

Since this paper was written, the Florianopolis Bridge has been thrown open to highway traffic. A. Y. Sundstrom, M. Am. Soc. C. E., reports that the traffic amounts to approximately 1 000 vehicles and 10 000 pedestrians per day. The tolls charged are 100 reis (about 1 cent) per pedestrian and 1 milreis (about 10 cents) per vehicle, and thus amount to about $200 per day. A local firm, Corsini Brothers, has the contract, on a fixed annual basis, for the maintenance of the bridge and the collection of tolls, the surplus receipts being turned over to the Treasury of the State.

In conclusion, the writers wish to thank all those who have so generously enhanced the usefulness of the paper by the contribution of their discussions. If, as predicted in some of the discussions, the novel features in the design and construction of the Florianopolis Bridge will serve to enlarge the field of usefulness of suspension structures, the writers will feel fully repaid for their efforts.

Any departure from precedent in structural form, materials, or erection methods, is offered, not to replace, but to supplement those previously developed. The availability of alternative forms, materials, and methods should serve to increase the resources and to stimulate the resourcefulness of the bridge engineer. The healthiest condition in a profession is not the blind following of standardized precedent, but the open-minded evaluation and selection of the best of various possible solutions for a given problem.

---

* *Engineering* (London), October 30, 1925.

AMERICAN SOCIETY OF CIVIL ENGINEERS

INSTITUTED 1852

TRANSACTIONS

This Society is not responsible for any statement made or opinion expressed in its publications.

Paper No. 1663

THE RELATION OF HIGHWAY TRANSPORTATION TO THE RAILWAY*

By Ralph Budd,† M. Am. Soc. C. E.

With Discussion by Messrs. John V. Hanna, E. A. Hadley, F. G. Jonah, W. W. Crosby, William T. Lyle, M. H. Gerry, Jr., and Ralph Budd.

In the past twenty-five years (since 1900) the American public has increased the investment in its transportation plant from $10 500 000 000 to $50 000 000 000, and its annual expenditure for transportation of property and persons from $1 500 000 000 to between $18 000 000 000 and $20 000 000 000. The change has been most rapid in the last five years (since 1920), during which the investment has increased from $36 000 000 000 to $50 000 000 000, and the annual transportation charge from about $12 000 000 000 to more than $18 000 000 000. This increase in the annual transportation charge in five years has been due entirely to the increased expenditure on highway travel, which has more than doubled in that time, while the charge for railway transportation has actually declined.

The public is supporting two transportation plants, in each of which is invested upward of $25 000 000 000. The property owned by the railway companies is reasonably permanent, while the equipment used on the highways is of more transient character. The annual cost of transportation furnished by the railways is about one-half that produced on the highways.

An inventory of the nation's transportation system at the beginning of 1926 would have disclosed something like the following:

* Presented at the Spring Meeting, Kansas City, Mo., April 14, 1926.

† Pres., G. N. Ry., St. Paul, Minn.

Railways and Equipment.		Improved Highways and Motor Vehicles.	
Miles	251 000	Miles	495 000
Locomotives	70 000	Motor trucks....	2 500 000
Freight cars	2 440 000	Automobiles	17 430 000
Passenger cars ..	56 500	Motor buses	70 000
Rail motor cars.	500		
Total units	2 567 000	Total units	20 000 000
Investment	$25 000 000 000	Investment	$25 000 000 000
Annual cost	$6 310 000 000	Annual cost	$12 125 000 000

Five years ago it would have been like this:

Railways and Equipment.		Improved Highways and Motor Vehicles.	
Miles	253 000	Miles	370 000
Locomotives	70 600	Motor trucks ..	1 000 000
Freight cars	2 400 000	Automobiles	8 220 000
Passenger cars ..	56 150	Motor buses	5 000
Rail motor cars..	50		
Total units	2 526 800	Total units	9 225 000
Investment	$22 000 000 000	Investment	$13 800 000 000
Annual cost	$6 360 000 000	Annual cost	$6 000 000 000

Twenty-five years ago the inventory would have been blank so far as modern highway transportation is concerned; railway investment would have been about $10 500 000 000, and the annual cost of railway transportation about $1 500 000 000, or only one-twelfth as much as the country's present annual transportation bill.

Influence of Transportation

Means of communication always have been a controlling factor in the life of every country. Until the Nineteenth Century, water transportation was so much cheaper and more efficient than any other, that population and industry concentrated only where it was available.

The most important single factor which influenced the character of settlement in the interior parts of America was the substitution of overland transportation by rail for that by canal, river, and highway. The railway eliminated the backwoods and caused cities to be built at what had been the frontier. It is not too much to say that the political unity of the United States was preserved largely by the railways, which alone made communication between parts of so vast a Commonwealth practicable and convenient. Without them, people in some sections of the country might have found it more advantageous to trade with foreigners than at home; and in a continent where National lines were forming, allegiance well might have followed the course of commerce.

George Washington was much concerned about the remoteness and inaccessibility of the country lying west of the Allegheny Mountains, and to overcome the physical difficulties of communicating with the Atlantic seaboard he investigated the trade routes by which the Great Lakes and the Ohio and Mississippi Rivers could be reached most easily from the East. These routes were to be developed by improving the rivers, making them navigable as far up stream as possible, and then connecting the heads of navigation on the opposite sides of the mountains by highways. He mapped routes by way of the Hudson and Mohawk Valleys, and by the passes at the head-waters of the Potomac, the James, and the Juniata Fork of the Susquehanna. Each of these routes was occupied by an important railway line soon after the supremacy of the railway over other forms of transportation became recognized.

The anxiety of the Father of his Country would have been greatly relieved could he have known of the revolutionary changes in inland transportation to come within fifty years after his death, and that the railroads not only would carry the commerce between the western valleys and the Atlantic seaboard, but would be extended 2 000 miles beyond the westerly outposts of his time, crossing three major mountain ranges, knitting the political and commercial life of the nation from Atlantic to Pacific, and providing incidentally the long sought route to India over, rather than around or through, the continent.

Railways Essential

The railways to-day are as essential to the National and commercial life of the United States as ever, and anything that would jeopardize their success or efficiency should be avoided as a public menace. Other forms of transportation, however, are factors too, and it is well to consider them in their relationship to the railways and to the general transportation scheme.

In the development of transportation one form has succeeded another with astonishing rapidity, but not without a struggle; thus, we find operators of pack trains contesting with Conestoga wagon drivers, canal companies resisting railway projects, the graceful, yacht-like clipper ships yielding reluctantly to steamships, and steam railways competing with interurban electric lines for local passenger travel. Now, steam and electric lines, which had surpassed all others in the field of transportation, have encountered something that excels them both in certain particulars and under certain conditions. They find local traffic is taken from them by the most universal of all carriers, the motor car on the highway. As in former competitions between old and new means of transport, that which gives most of what the public wants will win. There must be speed, safety, dependability, comfort, convenience, and, in the case of public carriers, economy.

Automobile Industry

That most phenomenal of all industrial developments, the automobile industry, is the youngest, and now is said to be the largest, in the United

States. It is barely twenty-five years old. Its importance is so great, taken as a whole, that the railways gain much more from the freight traffic it gives them than they lose from the freight and passenger business it takes away.

Like all great developments, that of motor travel has been the result of a combination of favorable circumstances. Most important were the perfection of the gasoline engine and the paved highway, which latter depended largely on good, cheap cement. Added to these is the fact that in America there is a standard of living so high that luxuries are not beyond the reach of the many. Each of these conditions is partly the cause and partly the consequence of the others. Of all the automobiles in the world 83% are in this country, which has about 7% of the world's population. Even more are produced in the United States than are used, but it is a mistake to think that the automobile originated here, or that it always has been peculiarly American. Before the manufacture of automobiles was of any importance in the United States, they were in more or less common use in England and on the Continent, and had reached a much higher state of perfection there than here. It was not until about 1905 that the number of cars in the United States exceeded the number in Great Britain. There was comparatively little improved highway in this country then, but there were magnificent distances which afforded an opportunity for the automobile to attain its fullest capabilities. Moreover, the great individual purchasing power of the population constituted a potential demand which required only the encouragement of reasonably priced, reliable cars and better highways to burst into actuality. The volume of this demand made quantity production possible and brought the low priced car, together with a program of general highway improvement throughout the country. The almost universal ownership of the automobile which has resulted demonstrates the fact that when the public finds something it approves of and desires, its response is quick and emphatic. The new contenders for local freight and passenger traffic—the motor truck and bus—are outgrowths of the automobile.

WHY THE MOTOR BUS?

Probably the questions most commonly asked by railway men concerning the motor bus, are "What can its attraction be?" and "Is it not a fad which soon will lose its novelty and disappear?" Let us consider these questions. In many localities the bus does have some advantages over the railway train for local travel. Two of these are the greater frequency and the flexibility of its service. Compared with the railway train, the bus can give service at more frequent intervals, because each unit of service is small and may be operated cheaply in comparison with the cost of operating a train.

The ratio of cost of highway bus to steam train operation is about 1 to 5, which means that for the cost of one train in each direction, say, morning and evening, a bus can be run every 2 hours in each direction from 8.00 A. M. to 4.00 P. M., and this more frequent service better suits the needs of the average rural community. Owing to the extensive use of the private automobile there is scarcely enough travel even morning and evening on the average local run to justify one train, much less several trains, during the day; but the smaller and less expensive motor bus operating on the highway may pick up sufficient traffic to make it profitable. Besides greater frequency, there is the advantage of more convenient starting and stopping places. The motor bus is able to take on and discharge passengers at any street corner or at any house along the road. In other words, the motor bus is able to give a more flexible service than the train. People in the country can hardly use the railway for travel between neighboring stations, because, in proportion to the whole journey, the trips to and from the stations are so long. Not so with the bus. It gives continuous service all along the highway, while the railway gives it only at points 4 to 6 miles apart. Now, the amount of this strictly local business which railways cannot handle is considerable, and may be enough to insure the success of bus transportation.

Rail motor cars are being used rather extensively in lieu of steam passenger trains. They provide a unit of more suitable size, and economize by substituting the internal combustion engine for the steam locomotive, as well as in other ways. About five hundred such cars of various types are in service, and the cost per mile for operation is about one-third that of a passenger train. They are successful, therefore, to that extent, but are subject to the inherent limitations of any vehicle operating on railroad right of way. They cannot get as much "pick-up" business as buses, which run along the highways and streets, and stop at houses, stores, offices, hotels, and any other desired place. The special field for the rail motor car is to take the place of the steam train on light traffic runs, such as branches and local and suburban districts where, for various reasons, service must be provided.

At recent hearings before the Minnesota Railroad and Warehouse Commission, Edgar Zelle, President of the Jefferson Highway Transportation Company, presented an analysis of the train and bus schedules in the territory served by his line south of St. Paul and Minneapolis. The substance of what he said in respect to one community is quoted here:

"Owatonna is a town 77 miles from Minneapolis on two lines of railway. Seven daily trains give direct service to and from Minneapolis, but the schedules are such that service is concentrated morning and evening, without any trains during long intervening periods. For example, of the seven north-bound trains, three leave within one hour and seventeen minutes of each other, with a fourth trailing just an hour later, all four of these trains leaving before 7:30 A. M. After this there is no more morning train service, and only three more trains left for the balance of the day. One of these, a limited, leaves at 1:10 P. M., and then the other two locals keep each other company, both of them leaving around 4:00 P. M. within thirty-eight minutes of each other. Thus, six-sevenths, or 86%, of the north-bound rail passenger service at Owatonna is used to give service at but two periods of the day.

"South-bound service shows another abundance of rail service at two particular periods. A train arrives at 10:23 A. M. with another close behind at 11:30 A. M. Then everything is quiet until 5:20 P. M., when the first train arrives, with another at 6:43 P. M., followed immediately at 6:59 P. M., with still another. On south-bound service the railroads thus concentrate five-sevenths of their passenger service at two periods of the day.

"The Jefferson Company, on the other hand, because it uses a type of equipment that can economically be distributed for local passenger service, gives Owatonna service from the north every two hours from eleven o'clock in the morning to eleven at night.

"That the public appreciates a frequency of service that is spread over the day at regular intervals is illustrated by the traffic records of the Jefferson Company. Over the twelve-month period ending August 31, 1925, there is a surprising uniformity of patronage, ranging from 27 to 38 passengers handled daily on each of these two hour scheduled south-bound runs. The north-bound records show a similar uniformity beginning with the first through run out of Mason City, leaving at 7:15 A.M., which carried 13 323 passengers, to the 5:15 P. M. run, which carried 15 123 over a period of twelve months, ranging from 31 to 41 passengers handled daily on each of these north-bound runs.

"The same uniformity is illustrated in the 19 831 passengers who used the outbound service at Owatonna. The pleasant month of June, with 1 342 outbound passengers, was the lightest month, while the cold month of January was the heaviest month, when 1 959 outbound passengers were taken out of Owatonna, averaging 45 per day in June to 63 per day in January.

"Owatonna, credited in the last census with a population of 7 252, furnished the Jefferson buses with a total of 37 928 in and out bound passengers in the twelve-month period.

"This two-hour bus service is not only patronized at small stations where the railroads restrict their service, but also at any point between stations. The cross-roads or any point on the highway is the stopping place of the bus."

While inapplicable to the territory adjacent to the largest cities or to sparsely settled regions, the condition described by Mr. Zelle is fairly typical of a great part of the United States.

The radius of travel of an individual multiplies many times when he becomes the owner of an automobile. His sense of independence and freedom, and his ability to give himself and his family enjoyment not otherwise obtainable, are sufficient reasons for sacrifices, if necessary, in other directions in order to have a car. For short-distance travel the most ideal way yet devised is by the private automobile. This is an important truth, because it accounts for most of the development in motor-bus transportation and most of the railways' loss of passenger traffic. For those who do not have their own automobiles, or having them, prefer occasionally not to drive, the motor bus affords a substitute.

The congestion of city streets has become a serious problem for the automobile user. In all cities, during the busiest hours of the day, much of the advantage of the automobile is lost for lack of parking space on the streets. This problem is having attention, and doubtless, to some extent, it will be solved by providing convenient places for parking cars near business centers. The cost of such parking, however, will influence some private car users to avoid the congested centers. In very large cities the bulk of commutation travel probably can be handled only by railway trains, subways, and elevated lines, but there seem to be many cities where the street congestion is not too great for motor buses, yet is too great for private cars to operate conveniently, comfortably, and economically. In such places the motor bus has positive advantages.

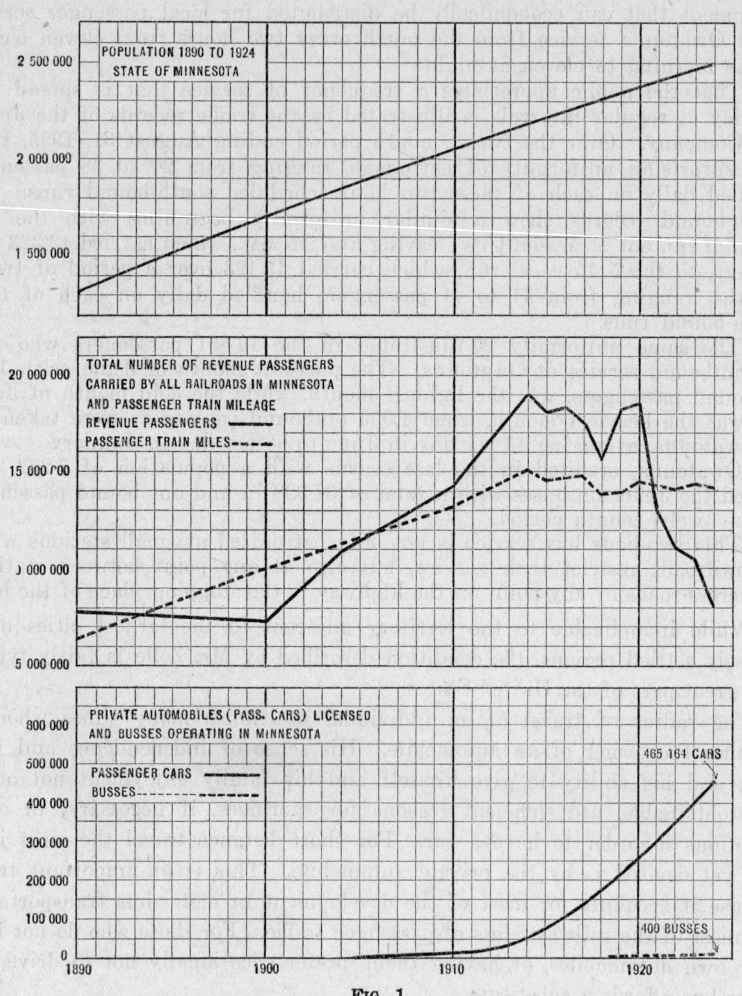

FIG. 1.

THE AUTOMOBILE AND LOCAL TRAVEL

In connection with these questions of frequency and flexibility of service, which are the main advantages of local highway over local railway passenger service, consider whether the railways really lost their business to motor buses or to private automobiles. Statements submitted to the Minnesota Railroad and Warehouse Commission recently indicate that the railways in Minnesota had lost a substantial part of their local passenger traffic before motor buses began operating to any extent, and that the number of automobiles continued to increase as the number of passengers carried by railways declined; also that at stations where motor buses have been operating for some time, the loss of passenger business has not been materially greater than at stations where they never have operated.

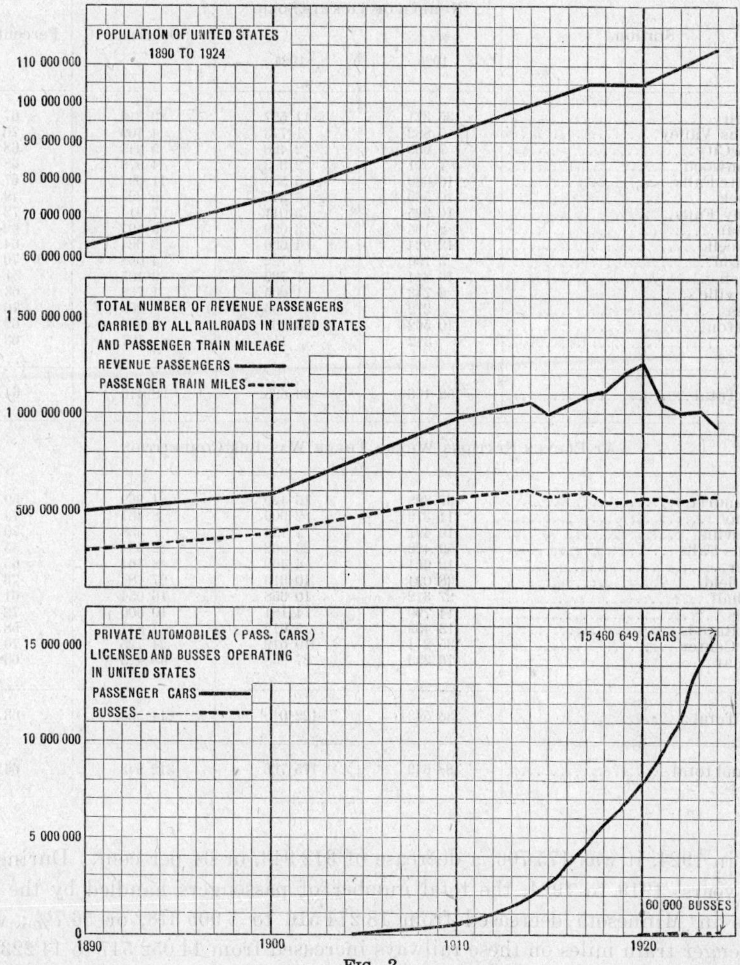

Fig. 2.

Fig. 1 shows the number of passengers handled by the railways in Minnesota since 1890, passenger-train miles, automobiles, and buses in Minnesota, and population; Fig. 2 gives similar information for the United States; and Table 1 shows the ticket sales at twenty-six railway stations in Minnesota. At fifteen stations, where there was no bus competition, the decrease in passenger tickets sold in 1924 as compared with 1920, was 49 to 76%, with an average of 64.6 per cent. At eleven others, where there was bus competition, the decrease was 55 to 74%, with an average of 63.7 per cent. The total number of tickets sold at the twenty-six stations in 1920 was 488 649,

TABLE 1.—RECORD OF TICKETS SOLD IN 1920 AND 1924, IN MINNESOTA.

AT FIFTEEN STATIONS WHERE THERE WAS NO BUS COMPETITION.

Station.	Number of Tickets Sold.		Decrease.	Percentage.
	1920.	1924.		
Benson	35 371	11 557	23 814	67
Browns Valley	5 882	1 773	4 109	70
Clara City	7 665	2 420	5 245	68
Cottonwood	7 371	2 393	4 978	68
Granite Falls	16 680	5 583	11 097	67
Hallock	10 569	5 345	5 224	49
Hanley Falls	10 925	3 011	7 914	72
Herman	8 196	3 099	5 097	62
Monticello	12 924	4 600	8 324	64
Ruthton	5 790	1 722	4 068	70
Warren	16 844	7 739	9 105	54
Ortonville	2 743	1 005	1 738	63
Odessa	272	66	206	76
Appleton	10 562	3 268	7 294	69
Milan	312	115	197	63
Total	152 106	53 696	98 410	64.6

AT ELEVEN STATIONS WHERE THERE WAS BUS COMPETITION.

Station.	1920.	1924.	Decrease.	Percentage.
Alexandria	37 398	15 429	21 969	59
Delano	11 376	2 909	8 467	74
Evansville	10 491	3 153	7 338	70
Fergus Falls	59 422	26 868	32 554	55
Jasper	12 624	4 460	8 164	65
Litchfield	38 094	10 310	27 784	73
Marshall	27 312	10 658	16 654	61
Osakis	14 790	4 184	10 606	72
Park Rapids	13 459	5 612	7 847	58
Sauk Center	35 244	10 519	24 725	70
Willmar	76 333	27 908	48 425	63
Total	336 543	122 010	214 533	63.7
Grand total	488 649	175 706	312 943	64.0

and in 1924, it was 175 706, a decrease of 312 943, or 64 per cent. During the five years, 1919 to 1924, the total number of passengers handled by the railways in Minnesota decreased from 18 274 516 to 7 905 378, or 56.7%; while passenger-train miles on these railways increased from 14 052 547 to 14 223 456, or 1.2%; and the number of motor vehicles in the State increased from 259 741 to 503 437, or 93.8 per cent. Compared with 1919, the year 1921 shows a decrease of 4 902 444, or 26.8% in railway passengers; an increase of 535 584, or 3.8% in passenger-train miles; and an increase of about 60 000, or 25%, in automobiles, while buses had not yet become a factor. These and other data point to the conclusion that the private automobile has had a great deal more to do with the loss of railway passenger business in Minnesota than the motor bus. They also suggest, and railway statistics support, the suspicion that before bus operation began, the local passenger traffic of the railways in Minnesota had decreased to a point where much of it was being done at a loss, largely because passenger-train miles had not been correspondingly reduced. Manifestly, the taking off of passenger trains in such instances is justified. Every train that is removed, however, serves to increase the advantage of the competitor on the highways; but if the business disappeared while the railway service was maintained, there is hardly reason for continuing such trains. Whatever may be the various reasons, local travel, to a very large extent, has left the railway train for the automobile and bus. This patronage of buses seems to establish beyond any doubt that they will continue, and probably will increase in number. From the foregoing it seems clear that the railways must recognize that public necessity and convenience require the development of transportation on the highways; that they should not attempt by arbitrary means to eliminate motor-vehicle competition, and should only insist that such competition be subject to proper public control; and, further, that they should seriously consider whether or not this new form of transportation, from the public as well as from their own point of view, cannot be more advantageously conducted under railway direction than otherwise.

Regulation

The rapid development of the common carrier motor vehicle, especially as embodied in the bus, has resulted in the enactment of regulatory measures by thirty-seven States. Similar measures are under consideration by legislative bodies of other States. The important and main provisions of these regulatory acts grant to the State the power to determine whether or not common carrier motor vehicles should be permitted to operate. If the State regulatory body is of the opinion that the public interests demand the operation of such motor-vehicle service, it issues a certificate therefor which is commonly called a "certificate of public convenience and necessity." No operation of common carrier motor vehicles can be carried on in these States without obtaining such a certificate. These laws,

1.—Require an adequate bond to protect the traveling public.
2.—Require State control of rates charged.
3.—Require State control of schedules of operation.
4.—Prohibit discrimination between individuals and communities.
5.—Require safety of operation with reference to the type of vehicle, and in other details affecting the safety of the traveling public.

These acts grant to the State regulatory boards the same control in general which these boards exercise over railway carriers. The regulatory board is required to give consideration to the effect the proposed service may have on other carriers, whether those carriers be railways or other motor-vehicle carriers.

These regulatory acts are wholesome and were necessary. Without such regulation the public had no protection from so-called "fly-by-night" operators, who had no capital and who were unable to furnish adequate service. These irresponsible operators would come and go as the seasonal business might permit. That made it impossible for the legitimate operator to make reasonable profits and maintain adequate service. Sound regulation is building up in the several States a fixed and dependable service, and one which, in co-ordination with the railway service, gives to the public the best conceivable local transportation. The rates which the bus companies are permitted to charge in general bear a fair relation to the railway rates, and are generally only a fraction of a cent per passenger mile less than railway fares.*

The States have no power to forbid the operation of interstate carriers and have very little regulatory power over them. The Supreme Court of the United States has held that a State law which prohibits common carriers for hire from using the highways by motor vehicles between fixed termini or over regular routes without having obtained from the Director of Public Works a certificate declaring that public convenience and necessity require such operation, is primarily not a regulation to secure safety on highways, or to conserve them, but a prohibition of competition; and, as applied to one desirous of using the highways as a common carrier of passengers and express purely in interstate commerce, is a violation of the commerce clause, besides defeating the purposes expressed in Acts of Congress giving Federal aid for the construction of interstate highways. Prior to this decision, many of the States were regulating interstate carriers.

Truck and bus operators engaged in interstate commerce recognize that Federal regulation sooner or later is inevitable. The Federal Government, however, in regulating the interstate motor carriers, should leave that regulation, so far as the Constitution will permit, to the Commissions of the interested States. About 75% of the railway business is interstate, and, therefore, the regulatory power of the railways is properly vested in the Federal Government. The truck and bus business, by its nature, always will remain largely a local problem. Perhaps as much as 90% of the truck and bus transportation of the country always will be intrastate. Those vehicles travel highways which were built by the State, and are policed and maintained by the State. It is, therefore, most proper that the power that regulates be delegated to the several States as far as practicable.

Congress has under consideration a bill regulating interstate motor-vehicle transportation. Its main features are as follows:

No common carrier truck or bus can be operated in interstate commerce without obtaining a certificate of public convenience and necessity therefor.

This certificate is to be obtained from a Joint Board composed of representatives from the several States in which the applicant proposes to operate. An appeal from the decision of the Joint Board so created, lies to the Interstate Commerce Commission.

The Joint Board has complete power to regulate the service and rates and safety of operation of such motor vehicles. The bill as drawn is intended not to hinder or hamper the development of common carrier transportation upon the highways, but to protect the legitimate operator thereon. It recognizes as a fundamental principle that common carrier transportation service must be in the hands of a responsible operator and that he should be protected from the irresponsible and casual operator.

* A tabulation of the State Laws in force as of January 1, 1926, has been made by the National Automobile Chamber of Commerce.

The necessity of Federal regulation in the large States is not acute for the reason that nearly all such carriers are engaged in intrastate transportation and are subject to the regulation of the State. However, where these transportation companies are operating in the smaller States and it is possible to cross State lines in a normal day's operation, the necessity of Federal regulation is apparent. The public cannot be adequately protected unless the Federal Government enacts legislation that will require the operating company to furnish security for damage to persons or property, and unless the service and rates of such operators are fixed and determined through public authority.

The proponents of the bill have agreed that it should provide that operating companies, which were in operation on March 1, 1925, should, as a matter of course, without further proof of public convenience and necessity, receive a certificate.

Taxation

Every user of facilities furnished by the State should pay reasonable compensation for the use thereof, especially when such facilities are used for private gain. Common carrier motor vehicles should pay a fair and reasonable tax for the use of the highways, but regulation should not be attempted through taxation; that is, taxes should not influence the granting of permission to operate, and they should not be burdensome to the point of preventing low fares.

A highway is constructed for the benefit of society as a whole. Society, in the aggregate, benefits whether or not each individual may or may not use the highway. It has never been the policy of a State to charge the entire cost of upkeep of the highway to the users thereof. The highways are used by private individuals in the transaction of their private business for profit. They are used also by those who travel for pleasure, and they are used by common carrier transportation companies. Those individuals who choose not to drive their own cars, but to ride in common carrier motor vehicles, should not be asked to bear an unfair share of the burden of upkeep of the highways, nor should they be deprived of the advantage of cheap transport as inevitably must happen if public motor vehicles are taxed unduly, resulting in higher fares.

There are about as many different methods of taxing common carrier motor vehicles as there are States in the Union. Some States tax these vehicles solely on the basis of value or cost, some on a percentage of the gross revenue received, some on weight plus a fraction of a cent per passenger mile, and some on the seating capacity of the vehicle, or on the horse-power, or so much per hundred pounds of weight, or a combination of all. In addition to these forms of taxation, nearly every State has a per gallon gasoline tax. This tax amounts to about one-third of a cent per mile for the common carrier motor vehicle. Speaking generally, the taxes paid by buses are fair and just. In Minnesota, the tax is based on the value of the vehicle. The parlor-car type of bus in common use in Minnesota costs from $10 000 to $12 000. The annual tax paid on each vehicle is 10% on the cost for the first year, decreasing 10% per annum to a minimum of $350. The average for the modern bus is about $750. The average annual tax paid on a Ford car is $12. It thus appears that the annual tax on a bus is about sixty times that on a Ford car. In addition, a tax of 2 cents is paid upon each gallon of gasoline used. The writer is advised that the tax paid by the bus companies in Minnesota is between 6 and 7% of the gross earnings of the operating companies. The tax on gross railway revenue in that State is 5 per cent.

The annual tax on a standard parlor car bus of a seating capacity of 30 passengers, weighing approximately 10 000 lb., and costing $10 000, would vary in the different States from $150 per bus per year to $1 000 per bus per year.

Commercial highway users themselves have taken an active part in forming an enlightened public opinion on the questions of regulation and taxation. In January, 1926, the Motor Vehicle Conference Committee published, among other articles, the following:

1.—Sound and Equitable Principles for Intra-State Regulation,

2.—Recommended Restrictions on Motor Vehicle Sizes, Weights, and Speeds,

3.—Sound and Equitable Principles to Control Special Taxation for Motor Vehicles.

These are attached as Appendices A, B, and C, respectively.*

One may not agree with the details of these recommendations, but it must be conceded that the free and unrestricted use of the highways by commercial vehicles in competition with the railways is a thing of the past, and that the operators themselves recognize the desirability of having their use of the highways controlled by appropriate laws rationally administered.

Whether a railway company itself should own and manage buses may depend on its willingness or unwillingness to take on additional obligations and responsibilities; but if no prejudice exists against bus operation, the deciding question probably will be whether, by such control, wasteful duplication can be eliminated and the service improved. There have been instances where, by co-ordinating the schedules, bus service has supplemented train service, to the end that for a lesser total expenditure a more complete and satisfactory service has been rendered. Each case is one for individual consideration. In many places throughout the United States electric lines have abandoned all or part of their tracks, and substituted bus service. In other cases, notably in New England, steam roads have substituted buses and trucks for branch lines.

The National Automobile Chamber of Commerce has compiled a census of bus operation as of January 1, 1926. Of 28 145 common carrier buses reported, 5 462, or 19.4%, were owned by steam or electric railways. The number of non-common carrier buses reported was 29 605. They are used by

* Pamphlets containing digest of State laws governing motor vehicles may be obtained without charge from the National Automobile Chamber of Commerce, 366 Madison Avenue, New York, N. Y.

hotels, industries, schools, and for sight-seeing and depot transfer. The geographical distribution of the buses reported is general. Of common carriers, the largest number in any State was 2 672 in New York, while Wyoming reported only 58. Ohio, with 2 454, had the most non-common carriers, while 11 for Rhode Island was the least reported.

Cost of Bus Operation

The question of cost of operating buses is vital for the future of that form of transportation, but reliable records have not been kept long enough to establish what might be called normal costs for certain routes or localities, as is the case with transportation costs on the different divisions of railway systems.

An article entitled "What Does it Cost to Operate Buses and Trucks?" has been published,* in which detailed estimates of the cost of operating a city type bus in New York are given. These costs vary from 23.6 to 30.6 cents per bus-mile, depending on whether the bus averages 200 or 100 miles per day. The details of these estimates have been compared with cost data, with which the writer is familiar, and he believes they are as reliable as can be made at this time, taking into account the fact that local conditions will determine several of the items in any such estimate. The cost of bus operation, however, should be at least 15% less than it is, and unless it is reduced that much, the business will not grow to its full possibilities.

The bus has come a long way from its origin in the motor truck, but it is not perfected yet. Lists of the different makes and types of motor-bus chassis designed exclusively for passenger transportation have also been published.† In this list are shown 96 types put out by 46 manufacturers. Standardization should result in substantial reduction in first cost, and the lessening of obsolescence would reduce the amortization or depreciation charges. The items of oil and gasoline and tires, of course, automatically would decrease if a car weighing 9 000 lb. could be substituted for one weighing 12 000 lb. Cost of insurance also will be less as the business is stabilized. With lower costs, rates can be reduced and travel increased. Many people living along bus routes would take buses to town instead of driving their own cars, especially if the fare was low enough. Here is an opportunity to render a service to rural communities, and it is a logical development in rural transportation for the bus to take the place of the private car on many occasions.

The Motor Truck

There are about 2 500 000 motor trucks in the United States. About 95% of them are non-common carriers, and are not subject to regulation as to rates or service. They are the successors of the horse-drawn warehouse, transfer, and delivery vehicles, and of the farm wagon, but the motor has given them radii of operation many times those of their predecessors. In freight, as in passenger, business the railway is supreme in the long-distance field.

* *The Railway Age*, March 27, 1926.

† *The Commercial Car Journal*, March 15, 1926.

It is also supreme in the handling of the great volume of bulk commodities, such as coal, ore, and grain. Indeed, there is nothing in the records of truck transportation to indicate that trucks are or can be contenders for any railway freight, except where the convenience of direct door-to-door delivery, together with the saving of terminal trucking and handling, outweigh the extra ton-mile cost of moving freight by truck on the highway over the ton-mile cost of railway line haul.

The principles governing the regulation and taxation of commercial freight carriers on highways are similar to those governing buses, but the handling of freight is so different from the handling of passengers that the truck bears a relationship to railroad freight service different from that of the bus to railroad passenger service. Freight shippers are interested solely in dependable, prompt, and cheap transport, whether the shipment be over a long or a short distance. The charge for freight service is important, but the question of economy does not enter into the vast bulk of local passenger travel which moves by private automobile. The flexibility and elasticity of truck operation, that is, its ability to make door-to-door delivery and to give radial service to both rural and urban communities, gives it a large field of activity. The elimination of one or two handlings and the consequent saving in time amounts to more than the excess cost of road haul by truck over that by rail up to some undetermined distance beyond the terminal. What that distance is no one knows. So many variables enter into the problem, such as the freight available on a given route, the character of the commodities, the relative importance of direct delivery to store doors, the extent to which return loading is obtainable, climatic conditions, the condition of the highways, etc., that only actual experience can determine how far beyond the city in each instance the truck can take the place of the box car. The horse-drawn truck excels the motor truck only for such freight as involves short movement and long delay in loading and unloading; the motor truck similarly excels the railway only where the distance involved is short enough so that the saving and convenience in terminal cost and handling offset the higher cost of transit by highway over railway, and only for comparatively small units of freight.

Common carrier trucks should not be permitted to operate in competition with railways except where there is a real public convenience or necessity. The convenience of a few in obtaining a quick delivery of property should not be controlling. It is most important that regulatory bodies, before granting a certificate for the operation of trucks, should carefully analyze what effect that operation will have on the essential rail carrier. The public cannot maintain two freight-transportation agencies without paying for both; and unless each performs a service which the other cannot do economically and efficiently, both should not be supported.

Railways are using trucks to assemble freight in cities in lieu of switch engines, and in some cases operate lines of trucks in lieu of local freight trains. Especially in large and congested terminals the use of trucks, whether by the railways or by others, is economical because local freight trains, due to the light tonnage, station work, and heavy switching cost incident thereto, may be and often are unprofitable. Unlike the case of passenger traffic, freight train mileage may be reduced approximately in proportion when freight traffic declines.

Summary

The situation may be summarized as follows: The superiority of the railway for long-distance and bulk freight and passenger traffic is well established; motor-truck and bus competition is not a factor in those fields. Commercial users of highways should be subjected to reasonable regulation and taxation. Existing and proposed State and Federal legislation, generally speaking, will provide for this. The extensive ownership of automobiles and the large mileage of improved highways have resulted in the loss of most of the local passenger travel of the railways, except in the vicinity of the largest cities. The removal of local trains has left many communities with comparatively little railway passenger service. The small amount of local travel in many such instances does not warrant more railway service, but does warrant the operation of buses at comparatively frequent intervals. The station to station, and even shorter travel, which would not go by rail, makes up a considerable portion of the bus traffic. The bus business promises to increase if better service can be given and if the cost of operation can be reduced. The additional business which buses may expect will come largely from automobile users rather than from rail patrons. Buses may serve to supplement railway transportation more effectively in some localities, if managed by railways, than if operated independently. Street railway and interurban electric lines are making extensive use of buses. The field of the private carrier motor truck is wide, taking the place, as it does, of the horse-drawn vehicle both in the city and in the country. The common carrier truck has a much narrower field, because of the competition with the private truck on the one hand, and the common carrier railway on the other hand, the latter unquestionably being more economical for any but comparatively small lots and comparatively short haul. Motor trucks relieve railway terminal congestion by moving freight direct from door of consignor to door of consignee. In many cases, this does not represent a loss to the railway because at large centers, where trucks are most used, the terminal costs may absorb the profit of rail haul on local freight.

In considering public convenience and necessity—the *sine qua non* for any permit to operate a commercial vehicle on public streets or highways—due regard should be had for the existing modes and means of transport. When essential carriers are able to give service that is measurably similar to that proposed, or when the success or efficiency of the existing essential carrier would be seriously impaired without definite and distinct improvement in service to the public, then public necessity does not warrant the new facility, and it is in the true public interest to deny the application. The public must support whatever transportation agencies are maintained and should not undertake two where one will suffice. On the other hand, where such additional facility is in the public interest and, therefore, is permitted, it should not be hampered by undue restriction or unfair taxation, but should be encouraged to operate as efficiently and cheaply as possible. Under the accepted plan of providing public transportation in this country, the service is rendered at cost; including in cost, however, a fair return on the value of the property used for transportation purposes. So long as this principle obtains, and for practical purposes that is so long as transportation is furnished by private rather than by Government agencies, it is in the true public interest to avoid unnecessary duplication of capital, and in every other reasonable way to help both old and new carriers keep down the cost of producing transportation. Cheap transportation of the highest quality is the key to much of the past and possibly more of the future prosperity.

APPENDIX A

Sound and Equitable Principles for Intrastate Regulation

(Recommended by the Motor Vehicle Conference Committee)

1.—Control over intrastate transportation of persons and property for hire, over regular routes or between fixed points, if adopted, should be exclusively in the hands of some agency of the State. No power, whatever, in the premises should be vested in the governing bodies of any political subdivision of the State.

2.—Such State control over motor vehicle common carriers should be placed in existing commissions, such as the Public Utility Commissions or other appropriate State regulatory bodies, of the various States.

3.—As a pre-requisite to the operation of the motor vehicle common carrier, the owner thereof should be obliged:

(*a*) To receive a Certificate of Public Convenience and Necessity, provided that lines in *bona fide* operation on the first calendar day of the legislative session at which the law is passed shall be presumed to be necessary to public convenience and necessity and such lines in the absence of evidence overcoming such presumption, shall receive a certificate for routes established by them.

(*b*) To take out liability insurance adequate to indemnify injuries to persons or damage to property resulting from negligent operation.

4.—The State regulatory bodies having control over motor vehicle common carriers should be vested with the powers they exercise in controlling other forms of public utilities.

5.—Taxes on motor vehicle common carriers should consist of:

(*a*) Those imposed in the particular State upon motor vehicles, the proceeds from such taxes being first applied to the maintenance, and any surplus thereof to all other costs of highways of general motor use.

(*b*) Proper and equitable taxes in exchange for franchise rights, provided that if such taxes are adopted, an amount equivalent to those paid under (*a*) should be deducted.

6.—Legislation should be enacted enabling steam railroads, trolleys, shipping companies, and other public utilities to acquire, own, and operate motor vehicles in conjunction with the regular lines of business.

APPENDIX B

Recommended Restrictions on Motor Vehicle Sizes, Weights, and Speeds

(Recommended by the Motor Vehicle Conference Committee)

Size Restrictions

1.—Width, including load, 96 in. (Traction engines 108 in.)
2.—Height, including load, 12 ft. 6 in.
3.—Length, including load:

(*a*) Single vehicle, 30 ft.
(*b*) Combination of vehicles, 85 ft.

Note.—From the foregoing it is apparent that in order to admit of the safe passage of two vehicles each of which with its load is 96 in. wide, a highway at least 20 ft. in width is desirable.

Weight Restrictions

1.—Single vehicular unit of four wheels or less (tractors and semi-trailers to be regarded as separate units), 28 000 lb.

2.—Any one axle of the vehicle or any additional axles of semi-trailers or trailers, 22 400 lb.

3.—Per inch width of tire measured between flanges of the rim in case of solid rubber tires:

Size of Tire	Load per Inch (Maximum)
3 in.	400 lb.
3½ "	400 "
4 "	500 "
5 "	600 "
6 "	700 "
7 "	750 "
8 "	800 "
10 "	800 "
12 "	800 "
14 "	800 "

4.—Minimum thickness of rubber for solid rubber tires:

3; 3½; 4; 5-in. tires	⅞ in.
6; 7; 8-in. tires	1 "
10; 12; 14-in. tires	1⅛ "

Speed Restrictions

In the matter of speed restrictions no motor vehicle should be operated upon a public highway at a rate of speed greater than is reasonable and proper, having regard to the traffic and use of the highway, or so as to endanger the life or limb of any person or the safety of any property, and should not in any event, while upon an urban street, run at a rate of speed greater than 15 miles per hour; upon a suburban street at a rate of speed greater than 20 miles per hour; or upon any other street or highway at a speed greater than 30 miles per hour.

Note.—The laws of many States prescribe for the three types of thoroughfares indicated a graduated schedule of speed limits based on the kind of tire equipment of the vehicle and its gross weight. Such elaborate and detailed schedules, however, are very difficult to enforce.

Special Permits to Raise Restrictions

There are, of course, times when it is imperative on certain highways or portions thereof that the movement of vehicles bigger and heavier than those allowed by law be permitted.

To meet such situations—which should be the rare exception rather than the rule—the State, county, or municipality exercising jurisdiction over roads and bridges should be empowered under definite limitations to grant written permits for the movement of restricted vehicles to meet emergency conditions.

Special Permits to Lower Restrictions

To deal with bad frost or other similar conditions where it is essential to lower the weight or speed restrictions ordinarily enforced, the power of the State, as centralized in its highway departments or the county or local highway authorities, after consultation with and permission from the State highway department, should have power to reduce the weight or speed restrictions to points deemed essential to the preservation of highways or the safeguarding of travel.

In all such cases, however, there should be public hearings on the subject; due notice of the reduced restrictions should be given to the traveling public and the highways or portions thereof affected should be properly posted.

From the nature of the case, size restrictions on the vehicle, of course, can never be reduced.

Local Powers

Except as indicated, the subordinate political sub-divisions of the State, such as counties, cities, towns, boroughs, townships, etc., should have absolutely no power to prescribe size, weight, or speed restrictions at variance with those allowed for the State as a whole. The need for such limitations on local governing bodies is too obvious to require discussion.

APPENDIX C

Sound and Equitable Principles to Control Special Taxation for Motor Vehicles

(Recommended by the Motor Vehicle Conference Committee)

1.—The State should be the sole special taxing agency—Federal, County, and Municipal Governments should be excluded from the field.

2.—The motor vehicle tax should be simple in form and distributed in equitable and just proportion between the different types of motor vehicles.

3.—No highway should be improved by expenditure of public funds in excess of its earning capacity. The return to the public in the form of economic transportation is the sole measure of the justification for the degree of improvement.

4.—All money raised by such special taxes should be placed in the State Motor Vehicle Highway Fund and to secure the best results should be expended under the direction of the State Highway Department.

5.—The cost of building and maintaining adequate systems of highways should be distributed in an equitable relation to the benefits derived. These may be summarized as follows:

(*a*) Benefits to society in general, such as influence on education, recreation, health, fire prevention, police protection, the National defense, the postal service, living and distribution costs.

(*b*) Benefits to definite groups, such as agriculture, manufacture, labor, railroads, mining, forestry, and waterways.

(*c*) Benefits to property served.

(*d*) Benefits to the road user.

6.—For the purpose of apportioning costs in relation to benefits received, all highways may be divided into two classes: First, those used by the general motoring public; and, second, those which perform a purely local service function.

7.—Special motor vehicle taxes should be levied and used only for the improvement and maintenance of highways used by the general public, *i. e.*, for general highway traffic flow lines.

8.—The wide variance in valuations, tax burdens, number of motor vehicles in use, and the status of highway development in the several States prevent the adoption of any fixed formula as to the proportion of the total cost of highways of general use which should be paid for from motor vehicle funds. Generally speaking, however, these principles may be set forth:

(*a*) In States where the income from motor vehicles is insufficient to meet all of the maintenance costs of highways of general motor use without undue burden to the individual motorist, such funds should be applied first to the maintenance of interstate and State highway systems.

(*b*) In States where the income from motor vehicles is sufficient to meet all maintenance costs of highways of general motor use without undue burden to the individual motorist, any surplus should be used for this class of highway reconstruction and administration costs.

(*c*) In States where the number of motor vehicles will bring in large sums in excess of maintenance without placing undue burdens upon the individual motorist, such surplus should be used to defray all the costs of maintenance and a substantial share of all of the other costs of highways of general motor use.

(*d*) In those States where the motor vehicle income is more than sufficient to meet maintenance costs of highways of general motor use without undue burden to the individual motorist, it may be found advisable to use such surplus for the purpose of defraying all or part of the costs of bond issues to expedite construction of economically desirable motor highways.

9.—Roads of a purely local interest, serving only local needs, should be financed out of local revenues obtained from local general taxes. Special assessments on adjoining land to defray a portion of the costs of such roads may be justified.

10.—Where extraordinary improvements are undertaken in the vicinity of or serving congested areas of population the increment, if any, in property valuation following the improvement should be drawn upon to defray an equitable portion of the cost.

11.—Irrespective of the particular form of special tax of the motor vehicle, whether registration fees or motor fuel taxes, the aggregate amount of these taxes in any one year should not be so great as to impose an undue burden on the individual motorist.

DISCUSSION

JOHN V. HANNA,* M. AM. SOC. C. E.—It may be said, as a matter of economics, that the traveling and shipping public is going to make use of any new instrument of transportation which offers better service than it has had heretofore. Consequently, when motor cars, buses, and trucks can perform service economically they will enter the field, driving out less attractive or less economical agencies. Efforts to do away with this form of competition, by characterizing it as unfair, and attempting to prevent the issuance of certificates of necessity and convenience, are not likely to meet with success as long as the traveling public shows a preference for such service.

The passenger motor car, it is generally agreed, has caused loss of business to the steam railroads. If it does not always afford cheaper transportation than the railroad, it offers an attractive form of touring, unrestricted by schedules dictated by considerations other than the wishes or convenience of a particular traveler. The motor car has also a distinctly business application, as in the case of the traveling salesman, who can make his trips to suit his convenience, avoiding considerable loss of time waiting for scheduled trains. Many other instances might be cited.

As far as the tourist is concerned, most railroad officers regard the loss from this cause as permanent. The same is true of short business trips. Bus transportation is in a somewhat different category. The bus usually offers to the man who formerly used the railroad train a trip in greater comfort, more frequent schedules, and greater convenience in beginning and ending his journey. It would appear that this is a field, heretofore occupied by the steam and electric interurban railroads, which such roads might legitimately consider their own and continue to occupy, abandoning the old equipment and route for the new.

It does not appear likely that the bus will take any considerable part of the railroad's long-distance travel. The item of comfort disappears in long journeys, particularly those extending over night, and the frequent stops by buses for local passengers slow up their average speed to a point below that of the express train. There appears to be a logical place for the bus for short daylight runs, and these are more likely than not to parallel the line of the railroad.

There is little doubt that the service now rendered by the accommodation train, traveling 75 to 150 miles, and made up entirely of day coaches, would, for most passengers, be more acceptably rendered by a line of buses with more frequent service, but carrying smaller numbers in each unit. There is a proper use of the bus as a feeder for a line of railroad, also for branch-line service, now given by train. Such cases can only be determined by thorough examination. This has been done by a number of the steam roads and bus service has been inaugurated.

One feature of such service that should appeal to the public is the existence of regulation, both State and National. Bus transportation to-day is

* Chf. Engr., Kansas City Terminal Ry., Kansas City, Mo.

frequently in the hands of men with small financial resources. The sentiment that all public transportation agencies or common carriers should be held responsible for their acts of omission and commission has taken firm root. The responsibility of steam railroads for personal injuries, and loss and damage to property is well established, and it seems reasonable that the traveling public should expect and demand the same responsibility on the part of all general transportation agencies. While public demand will undoubtedly call for regulation of bus transportation, whether in the hands of steam railroads or independent agencies, the machinery of regulation of steam railroads is already in existence, is well understood, and can readily be extended to any other means of transportation the railroad may use.

An important consideration in bus and truck transportation, one that appeals particularly to all users of the public roads, is the question of taxes for the construction and maintenance of those roads. Instances have been known of electric interurban lines, the business of which has been seriously injured, if not destroyed, by motor travel on parallel public roads, having been highly taxed for the construction of those same roads. The public road not infrequently has been parallel with and adjacent to the interurban line. The injustice of a tax on the interurban's right of way is apparent and needs no argument. It is not clear, however, that there is an application of this argument to the case of the steam railroad which uses the bus as a feeder, to replace an accommodation train, a self-propelled unit, or in branch-line service. Where train service is replaced by bus service on public roads paralleling the railroads, it may be said that the permanent way is provided for the railroad at public expense in the same manner and to the same extent as it is furnished to other users; and it is equitable that the property of the railroad should be taxed in the same manner as the property of others. There is danger, however, in a direct property tax, such as some States apply, of an assessment out of proportion to the benefit the railroad receives.

The improved country road is often the means of affording readier access to the railroad on the part of the people along its lines who receive their supplies and ship their crops or merchandise over the railroad. Improved roads, offering encouragement to development of the country and the increase of its population, may prove to be a source of revenue to the rail line. To the extent that improved highways promote the growth and prosperity of the country, they promote the prosperity of the railroad serving that country.

Construction of the State Road System of Missouri is being carried out with funds obtained from the sale of bonds, together with portions of the motor vehicle and gasoline taxes. Where the motor vehicle license is proportional, or roughly so, to the horse-power of the vehicle, there is no gross inequity in that license or the gas tax. It is not true that damage to public roads is directly proportional to weight of vehicle and consumption of gasoline; but on the whole there is some approach to fairness in this general proposition, and its simplicity commends it for use in the place of more complicated methods, which attempt to take into account the destructive effects of particular types of vehicles.

The present policy of Missouri is to construct and maintain State roads without a direct property tax or benefit assessment. The motor vehicle and gasoline taxes, it is now estimated by the State Highway Commission, will yield an amount large enough to supply a sinking fund for retirement of road bonds, to pay maintenance costs, and, later, to provide money for new construction. By this means it is expected that the entire system of State highways, more than 7 000 miles, will be completed without a bond issue other than that of $60 000 000 now authorized.

The use of trucks in making a part of the complete movement of merchandise, from shipper to consignee, has obtained for many years, first, in the shape of the horse-drawn vehicle and, later, the motor truck. The movement between the freight house has not been handled by the rail company until a comparatively recent date and even now is not commonly so handled. The cost of the trucking part of the complete movement has always been paid ultimately by the consignee or consumer as a necessary part of the whole transportation charge. Except for the reluctance of railroad managements to add to their machinery for the transaction of business, there appears to be no sound reason why the rail company should not handle the entire goods movement from origin to destination.

The truck movement, particularly in large cities, has been handled by the shipper or consignee himself, or by trucking companies organized for that purpose, or by individuals. It would be manifestly a convenience, both to the shipper and consignee, if store-door pick-up and delivery were the general practice; the entire movement made under one bill of lading and the collection of charges made by one agency. There should be no increase in total costs. There might be a slight decrease in cost if all trucking to and from the freight house were performed by one agency instead of a number of unrelated concerns. It is evident, upon a little reflection, that once this trucking unit is organized, its operation can be extended to road haul, as long as the distance traveled is kept within economical limits.

A less than car load movement of, say, 30 miles by rail requires that (1) the merchandise be loaded into a truck; (2) be taken to the freight house; (3) be unloaded and placed in a car; (4) the car switched into a local freight train; (5) be hauled the 30 miles; (6) be set at the freight house or unloaded by the crew of a local freight train; (7) the goods be loaded into a truck; (8) the truck be drawn to the place of business of the consignee; and (9) the goods be unloaded. If this movement were made entirely by truck, six of these operations would be eliminated. The movement in the truck would undoubtedly mean a higher ton-mile cost than the rail haul considered alone; but a point must exist where the total of all costs for the combined rail and truck movement would exceed the total cost of the truck movement. Beyond this point the transfer from truck to car and *vice versa* would be justified by the lower cost of the rail haul. Short of this point the all-truck haul would be cheaper. Without analysis of cost, the length of profitable truck haul cannot be determined—it will vary with local conditions and type of equipment used.

As in the case of buses for passenger movement, convenience to the public is a feature likely to meet favorable reception. There appears to be no good reason why tariffs should not be fixed to give appropriate rates for points within limits of economical truck haul. Again, it is feasible to handle the truck movement by contract with independent agencies, or by the rail company under its own ownership and direction with a separate department. The advantages to the public would be in eliminating some of the agencies with which the shipper and consignee must now deal and in placing the entire movement in the hands of a financially responsible concern subject to regulation by existing State and National bodies.

E. A. Hadley,* M. Am. Soc. C. E.—The author has well stated that transportation always has been a controlling factor in the commercial expansion of a country. One of the highest types of ancient civilization was that of the Roman Empire. Its road construction and maintenance was such that certain of its highways have survived to the present time and have set an example of what constitutes permanent highway construction.

When and how a line of highway should depart from its general course to pass through a small city or town, or to give service to an agricultural or industrial community, is a problem which cannot be settled by any predetermined rule, nor is it likely to be settled to the satisfaction of all parties concerned. The question of deciding locations for highways where only natural physical conditions are involved, causes less trouble to the engineer than where features of ultimate development of the territory must also be considered. A highway located so that it serves as a direct feeder to other transportation lines is a distinct asset to the community as a whole. In the construction of such highways the railroad company finds itself most favorably interested.

During the early periods of American history, the Government, by means of Congressional appropriations, from time to time aided in the construction of certain toll roads and canals, as well as inland waterway projects and railroads. These appropriations were spasmodic and followed no definite plan, nor were they equalized among the several States. Probably they were governed largely by immediate military necessity or political influence rather than for any definite purpose of development of the country as a whole.

Norway has records of legislation more than 1 000 years old, providing for the building and upkeep of roads and bridges. In 1274 a rather complete code of highway laws was enacted, which was replaced by a new code in 1604. In 1824 there was another revision and from that time dates Norway's modern road system. Highway legislation in England also dates back many hundreds of years.

In the United States, the interest of the Federal Government began to take definite form when a small department was originated in Washington, D. C., in 1893, called the "Office of Road Survey", the function of which was to collect data on highway conditions. This department was later designated as the "Office of Public Roads", and the scope and volume of its work and

* Chf. Engr., Mo. Pac. R. R., St. Louis, Mo.

its personnel was largely increased until it finally developed into that branch of the Department of Agriculture, now known as the "Bureau of Public Roads."

The Bureau has played an important part in the development of the highway movement, although prior to 1916 it took little active part in local or State affairs, other than in research and investigation work. Largely through its recommendations a provision was inserted in the original Federal Aid Road Act requiring that as a condition prior to receipt of Federal Aid, an adequate State Highway Department must be created and maintained. Beginning with 1916 when the Federal Government appropriated $75 000 000 to be allotted to the States annually over a 5-year period, on a graduated scale, the Government has increased such appropriations from time to time so that the total made for the years 1917 to 1926, inclusive, has amounted to $615 000 000.

It is to be presumed that these funds of the Federal Government have been accumulated by taxation under which the railroad companies have at least paid their proper proportion. As property owners and taxpayers in the several States, they are, therefore, entitled to their proper share in the distribution of Federal Aid to the States in highway construction. Unfortunately, this view does not seem to prevail in certain States, and those in authority fail to consider the railroad company's interests in the application of such Federal aid as is secured.

In other words, Federal aid has been applied to projects which have not involved separation of grades from the tracks of a railroad company, and the cost of such separations has been divided between the State and the railroad, eliminating any consideration of Federal aid funds allotted to the State for highway work. This is not entirely fair to the railroads. They are setting up the claim that Federal aid should be prorated in such manner that the railroad companies will benefit in the same proportion as other property owners and taxpayers in the community.

The theory of highway taxes for maintenance of roadways is quite ancient. As early as 1661, during the reign of King Charles II in England, four hundred hacks were licensed for operation in London, Westminster, and vicinity, and within a radius of six miles. The revenues from these licenses were used for paving the roadways.

The gasoline tax, as mentioned by Mr. Budd, is an efficient device for making those using the highways pay for such use in somewhat the same manner as toll-gates once required such payments. Thirty-nine States and the District of Columbia now tax gasoline sales, revenue from which is used for the benefit of the highways of those States. According to report the Republic of Mexico has imposed a gasoline tax for the purpose of raising funds for improving highways.

It has been estimated that in 1925 about 20 000 gal. of gasoline were consumed in the United States during every minute. The domestic consumption of gasoline has increased from 4 474 000 000 gal. in 1921 to 8 950 000 000 gal. in 1925, or almost exactly 100% in 5 years. Records indicate that there are in excess of 20 000 000 motor vehicles in the United States, or 1 for every 6 people (which exceeds the number of telephones). Under such conditions the gasoline tax is widely distributed and seems to be the most logical method of raising funds for the construction and maintenance of highways.

A uniform bill for motor vehicle regulation by the several States has been proposed by the American Electrical Railway Association (it also has the support of the American Short Line Railroad Association). The Association has gone so far as to prepare a complete bill which it recommends be passed, vesting authority in the Railroad Commission of the State for the regulation of highway traffic. This bill proposed a tax of 1 cent per ton-mile for pneumatic tired vehicles, and 1½ cents per ton-mile for hard tired vehicles, which figures were arrived at by a committee of the Association after extensive studies. The Committee admits that the information on which the amount of the taxes was based was incomplete, but believes that any change which may be necessary in the future will be in the form of an upward, rather than a downward, revision.

The railway companies have complained because of the general and special taxes they are obliged to pay to help construct and maintain highways, on which motor vehicles compete with them. Spokesmen of the motor industry have replied by showing that the total taxes paid on motor vehicles are larger than on railroads and by referring to the large amount of freight business that the motor manufacturing industries give the railways.

The fact, however, must not be lost sight of that part of the taxes collected from the railways are used to pay for the highways on which motor vehicles operate, whereas none of the taxes paid on motor vehicles is used to help provide highways for the railroad trains. Many taxes assessed against motor vehicles are against private passenger automobiles; therefore, the total amount paid is no indication as to whether or not the taxes now being levied on motor buses and trucks are adequate. The railways operate on roadways which they themselves construct and maintain, while buses and trucks operate over highways which the public has constructed and maintains. Eventually, they must pay in some form their *pro rata* of this cost if an equal balance is to prevail.

Regulation of buses and trucks operating as common carriers appears to have the unanimous approval of virtually all interests. The principle of taxation has similar approval; however, the amount of the taxes which would be fair and just is a point on which there is sharp controversy. It appears to be generally agreed that taxation should not be adopted for the purpose of strangling highway transportation, and the conservative elements on both sides of the question advocate a tax schedule that would impose a fair share of the cost of construction and maintenance of highways on trucks and buses without unduly burdening them or restricting the development of this form of transportation.

F. G. Jonah,* M. Am. Soc. C. E.—Transportation is one of the distinguishing characteristics of civilization. Savages and barbarians had none,

* Chf. Engr., St. L. & S. F. Ry., St. Louis, Mo.

or, at best, very crude methods. Primitive man traveled very little. The first migrations that he made were probably in following game and for spoliation or conquest of neighboring tribes. In the earliest forms of transportation man himself was the vehicle, burdens being carried by women and slaves. After a time he learned to domesticate and harness animals, and thereupon transferred the burden of transportation from his own shoulders to the backs of four-footed creatures.

All transportation is founded on the use of the wheel, also much of the industrial development. At a very early age when the wheel was invented, transportation took an immeasurable stride forward. The first development of the vehicle on wheels was the chariot of the ancients, harnessed to horses, and used largely in military operations. The necessity of furnishing some path on which these vehicles could travel gave birth to the good roads idea.

The Romans built the great roads of antiquity as a basis for military, rather than commercial, operations. However, they substantially formed the basis of the vast network of highways which became of great use in the development of Central Europe.

There was little change in transportation methods for a period of almost 2 000 years, the only difference being that vehicles became more ornate, more commodious and more substantial, and that the roads on which they traveled became better. It was not until 100 years ago that anything was evolved that could be termed "rapid transportation" and that possibly only after mechanical means were utilized for propulsion.

In 1925 England celebrated the one-hundredth anniversary of the founding of the steam railway. Railway development in the United States began about 90 years ago. It was far more rapid, efficient, and economical than anything the world had previously enjoyed, so it is not surprising that on its introduction all other forms of transportation quickly fell into disuse. The stage coach, pony express, river steamer, and canal-boat became almost obsolete in the United States, and the fact that railway transportation was developed so quickly and so efficiently led for a time to the neglect of the highways. In this respect America was entirely different from the European countries because their highways had been established and well developed before the steam locomotive was invented.

In the Eighties, electricity was introduced as a motive power for transportation. At once the interurban car became exceedingly popular for the simple reason that it could traverse the streets of cities and villages, could be boarded at almost any street corner, and made frequent trips between various parts of the cities and adjacent country districts. Then the railroad companies were faced with a new competitive factor, one with which they could not wholly compete for short-line hauls.

A few years later, or about 1900, the automobile became a reality, and its use, with the motor trucks, has become so general that an entirely new situation has developed in transportation. About the first important result of the widespread ownership of automobiles was an insistent demand for the construction of good roads, and the various States undertook to supply this deficiency with characteristic American hasté and waste.

Good roads have been, and are now being, developed along previously established routes of communication; that is, generally they are parallel with the trunk lines of the railway companies. It is not at all improbable that many expenditures thus made were unnecessary, and that more good would result to the country eventually if the roads had been built into remote districts, making them accessible and tributary to the existing railways.

The centers of population were built along the railroad lines, which usually represented the shortest distance from one flourishing community to the next. As the object of the highway systems was to link up important towns, it was natural that the railroads would be paralleled to a great extent.

On the completion of these highways, bus lines were introduced, in close competition with the railways—in some instances, with the electric lines. Being more flexible and mobile in their movements, they have become a highly competitive instrument in transportation, so that in many cases railway companies have been obliged to curtail their local passenger service. To the present time they have not entered the field of freight carrying to any great extent, although that is coming. Certain companies in the East have put on freight-carrying buses to handle their local freight traffic within certain territories. This has one distinct advantage—it makes store-door delivery possible within a certain radius.

In the early days of railroad development it was regarded as very essential to have freight and passenger stations as near the heart of the city as possible. This was in the days of the horse-drawn vehicle when the haul was of particular moment; but nowadays, with well-paved streets and quick-moving motor vehicles, it is not so essential, and cheaper sites on the outskirts of the cities can be obtained. The moving of these freight terminals probably will lessen congestion on the business streets of the city to a great extent, so that eventually the railroad companies may be able to make substantial savings. In many instances the railroad companies own extremely valuable properties in the hearts of cities, which may be dismantled and the ground sold for more than enough to erect modern and commodious terminals on the outskirts.

The question arises as to what is the railroad company to do to meet the bus competition? To some extent it can, and does, put motor-driven cars on its rails, as for local passenger service; but this does not fully meet the situation because the car is still confined to the rails, and is not as mobile as the bus, which can gather up its passengers around the street corners of the cities.

As to less than carload freight, the time is undoubtedly coming when manufacturers in cities will distribute goods from their factory doors to their customers within a radius of many miles by their own motor trucks; or the service may be performed by truck companies, the goods being only handled twice—once from the factory into the truck, and again from the truck to the store. Evidently, there is some economy in this handling as compared with methods pursued in the past. Just as the railroad companies performed a more efficient service than had hitherto been enjoyed, so the motor bus and motor truck, with the possibility of cheaper transportation, will undoubtedly secure a part of the business, and the railroad companies will have to adjust their operations accordingly.

There is a widespread movement for American railroads to enter into motor-bus and motor-truck transportation.* Railroad companies are applying to the Interstate Commerce Commission for permission to publish joint through-passenger fares covering transportation partly by train and partly by motor bus. Several companies are adding greatly to the buses already in service.

The Chicago and Alton Railroad Company has announced that it will put on motor buses to travel the highways between certain important points on its lines. On no other railroad in the Middle West could this experiment be tried with as good prospects of success, nor would the experiment be so well justified. Situated as it is across the populous State of Illinois, extending from Chicago to St. Louis, Mo., and having many large and important towns only a few miles apart over its entire distance, and paralleled practically the entire way with an electric line on one side and a concrete highway on the other, this railroad seems to be ideally fitted to try out a system of motor transportation under railroad management. One result of the developments of the last few years has been that local passenger trains have become much less generally used, and the chances are that in the next few years many local freight trains also will disappear.

The good roads have been and are being established, and the motor bus and motor truck are being more efficiently developed from year to year. All three are fixed parts of the transportation plan, and the railroad company will have to utilize these and add them to its established facilities as another arm of its service.

It is not at all unlikely that the railroad companies, with their skilled shop forces, whereby repairs to motor equipment can be maintained more cheaply than by private companies, will be in a position to render this service perhaps cheaper than any other agency. It can be set down as a certainty that the cheapest and quickest method of transportation will, in the end, be the most used. There is no possibility that for long hauls any method can supplant the railroad for the movement of either passengers or freight.

The increasing use of the automobile, motor bus, and motor truck is having a pronounced effect on rural life. The growth of small country towns as business centers has been arrested. The country store, country school, country church, country doctor, and country newspaper are passing, and business activities and population are being centralized. The local business of the railroad companies is being affected by this tendency.

Years ago, when railways were first built, and in the days of horse-drawn vehicles when highways were generally in bad condition, it was thought necessary to have stations about seven miles apart. Now, when communica-

* *The Railway Age*, March 27, 1926.

tion is so much more rapid and easy, business will seek better markets, and there is a strong likelihood that in many instances the local stations of the railways can be abandoned, and possibly the railway companies may be able to effect some savings by reducing service where it is no longer needed.

The railroad companies have not always been treated fairly by State Commissions in respect to the curtailment of their passenger service. It has been clearly shown in many hearings that the introduction of bus lines has taken away the necessity for the operation of local passenger trains and yet the Commissions refuse to allow the companies to change their schedules. The time is at hand when a comprehensive plan of regulation must be worked out, governing the operation of buses and trucks engaged for hire on the public highways; and the interests of the railroad companies must be taken into account by the regulatory bodies. The aim should be adequate service without wasteful duplication.

W. W. Crosby,* M. Am. Soc. C. E. (by letter).—"The Relation of Highway Transportation to the Railway", as set forth by Mr. Budd, seems to be the fairest statement of fact that has been printed on this subject. It seems refreshingly frank, lacking in prejudice, thoughtful, and even prophetic; with a calmly judicial atmosphere permeating it which adds to its convincing quality.

Perhaps one might wish that brevity had been sacrificed for the sake of greater clarity in some cases. For instance, in his "Inventory", it is not apparent just how the "investment" figures are reached. Do they include land or right-of-way values in any or all cases? "Cost" figures always suggest detailed explanation and scrutiny before acceptance. Just what is meant by the statement that "twenty-five years ago the inventory would have been blank so far as modern highway transportation is concerned"? Were not the rights of way existent and valuable? And are not some of the important highways of to-day in the main the same highways of twenty-five years ago?

The essentiality of the railways is well set forth by Mr. Budd, and the writer is glad to see it emphasized contemporaneously with the recognition accorded by the author to the importance and supplemental abilities of the newer means and forms of transportation. In these days of "consumptionism" there is certainly a need of brakes on the apparently growing tendency to throw away the old for the sake of something new. The arguments for economy in transportation for the sake of public welfare seem soundly, if briefly, stated.

Mr. Budd points out correctly that the automobile is not of American origin, but there may be some argument—of the "hen or the egg" variety—with his statements as to the relation of automobiles and highway improvement. From his own observation and experience, the writer would be inclined to put the highway before the automobile.

Arguing most convincingly in the matter of motor-bus competition with, or in addition to, railway transportation, the author reaches conclusions that, with perhaps one exception, appeal strongly. As to the conclusion that, "the

* Cons. Engr., Coronado, Calif.

public must support whatever transportation agencies are maintained and should not undertake two where one will suffice", he may be correct theoretically, but at the same time give a wrong impression.

Is not a reasonable amount of competition needed in transportation now, as well as in trade, to insure the proper economic "life"? If railway officials were always able to act as calmly and fairly as Mr. Budd has written, there might be less need for competition; but even with the belief that,

"—the days are hastening on
By Prophet-Bards foretold,"

it still seems advisable to allow reasonable competition in many lines of activity, including transportation; not putting into the "one basket" of "railway direction" all the "eggs" of the "new form of transportation"; nor, indeed, in that basket until that railway direction shall have substantially recovered from its past handicaps of "public damnation", Government control, etc. Mr. Budd's last sentence is a mildly expressed, pithy summary of the whole matter.

WILLIAM T. LYLE,* M. AM. SOC. C. E. (by letter).—The fundamental economic principle governing the relations between railway and highway transportation should be co-ordination. The public cannot afford superfluous and overlapping service, but requires, and should demand, a smooth-running and efficient transportation system. Without it the National commercial and industrial structure will disintegrate.

The following information, collected by the Interstate Commerce Commission, is based on replies received from 164 out of 176, Class I line-haul steam railways, including all the larger companies; 377 out of 635 Class II and Class III steam railways; and 118 out of 260 unclassified electric railways.†

Steam Railways.—Buses.—No buses are operated by subsidiaries in terminal service as compared to 506 in line service. Leading Class I railroads have reported subsidiary bus lines operating buses for service in connection with their own operations, as follows: The New York, New Haven and Hartford, 118; the New York Central, 81; and the Union Pacific System, 39; all in line service. In addition, the Great Northern reported 74 in competition with its own operations and 83 in competition with other railroads. The railroads of Class I owned 225 of the buses in operation and those in Class II and Class III, owned 23.

Motor transport companies and individuals operate 1 511 buses in terminal service to Class I railways and 19 in terminal service to Class II and Class III railways. Only one of these is engaged in interstate traffic. The buses operated by motor transport companies and individuals in line service competing with Class II and Class III railways, number nearly 600.

The New York Central reports 473 buses; the Chicago and Eastern Illinois, 246; the "Big Four", 349; the Pennsylvania, 292; and others, 170; to a total of 1 530 buses operated by motor transportation companies and private individuals in competition with Class I railroads in terminal service. On line

* Prof. of Civ. Eng., Washington and Lee Univ., Lexington, Va.

† Docket No. 18 300.

service the Pennsylvania reports 2 463 buses competing; the Baltimore and Ohio, 838; Chicago, Milwaukee, and St. Paul, 1 234; Atchison, Topeka, and Santa Fé, 1 079; the Southern Pacific lines 1 891; and other Class I roads, 11 594; making a total of 19 099 competing buses. There are also 1 253 independently operated buses that do not compete, but supplement the service of the steam roads. Of the combined total of 20 352, 2 848 are engaged in interstate traffic, 14 193 in intrastate traffic, and 3 311 in traffic of both kinds.

Steam Railways.—Motor Trucks.—Steam railways of all classes report somewhat similar conditions with respect to motor trucks. Only 27 trucks are operated directly by first, second, and third-class railroads in terminal and line service and only 57 trucks by subsidiaries.

The railroads own 56 of the motor trucks in operation, and the motor transportation companies subsidized by them do not own any. The New York Central declares that 526 trucks are operated by motor transportation companies and private individuals in terminal service along their lines; the Pennsylvania, 603; the "Big Four", 381; and all others, 407; making a total of 1 917 trucks. Of this number only 13 affect the service of Class II and Class III railroads, the remainder being reported by Class I roads.

In line service, the reports are: New York, New Haven and Hartford, 2 229; New York Central, 2 648; Pennsylvania, 6 564; Chicago, Milwaukee, and St. Paul, 1 978; Atchison, Topeka, and Santa Fé, 3 662; the Union Pacific System, 3 531; and all other Class I roads, 22 595; or a total of 43 207 trucks in competitive service. These roads report, likewise, that there are 225 privately owned trucks operating in connection with their own lines.

In line service, Class II and Class III railroads are affected by only 545 private motor trucks, while railroads in Class I have 43 207 competing against them. Of this last number, about one-half are engaged in intrastate traffic and the remainder in interstate traffic, or a combination of both kinds.

A similar analysis of tabulated data obtained from operators of electric railways reveals the following facts.

Electric Railways.—Buses.—There are 401 buses in terminal service, practically all in intrastate traffic. In line service, working within State lines, there are 350 buses; 751 in all. Of this total, 300 are competing with the railroad reporting; 100 are competing with other roads; and 351 are not competing with any railroad.

Subsidiaries operate 190 buses in terminal service, chiefly in intrastate traffic; and 406 in line service of which 59 are engaged in interstate traffic, 178 in intrastate traffic, and 169 in traffic otherwise unclassified. Subdividing further, 339 of the total operate in connection with the electric roads reporting; 226 compete with them; and 31 compete with other railroads.

There are 955 buses owned by electric railway companies from the eight National regions, with the Southern region listing none. There are only 75 buses owned by subsidiaries.

Motor transport companies and individuals operate 75 buses in terminal traffic, all of an intrastate character; and 1 356 in line service, of which 170 are distinctly in interstate service, 586 in intrastate service, and 600 not classified. In the line service, only 1 040 buses compete with electric lines.

Electric Railways.—Motor Trucks.—Railroad companies report that they operate 30 trucks and their subsidiaries 19, both being of negligible significance. They state that they own 36 of the trucks, the subsidiaries owning none.

Motor transport companies and individuals operate 27 trucks in terminal service and 2 394 trucks in line service. Of the 2 394 trucks in line service, 77 operate in interstate service; 1 297 in intrastate service; and 1 020 in service common to both.

Of these same 2 394 trucks, 43 are run in connection with electric railway operations and 2 351 in competition with them. Of the 2 351 trucks, the large number of 1 340 are operated by the Pacific Electric.

Comment.—This investigation shows that a comparatively small percentage of buses and a large but undetermined percentage of motor trucks are operated in interstate traffic.

The information presented reveals a very large degree of competition in transportation service, which should be closely investigated in each individual case. The principle laid down by the author that common carrier motor trucks should not be permitted to operate in competition with railways, except when they are a real public convenience or necessity, appears to be thoroughly sound. His view that the railways must recognize that public convenience and necessity require the development of transportation on the highways, and that they should not attempt to eliminate motor-vehicle competition by arbitrary means, appears to be liberal. Such competition should be subject to proper control. Consideration should be given to the question whether or not highway passenger transportation can be conducted more advantageously under railway direction. The importance of National, State, and joint board regulation is apparent and, for the present, each case should be carefully determined on its own individual merits.

M. H. Gerry, Jr.,* M. Am. Soc. C. E. (by letter).—American railway transportation is undoubtedly the best and cheapest in the world, nevertheless, it has reached a point where it is too slow, too inflexible, and too costly to meet the requirements of expanding business in this country. The motorized highways have very greatly relieved the situation, and to an increasing extent will continue to do so; but a satisfactory general solution is not likely of attainment save through a re-organization of the railways, and their operation in combination with other facilities now available for public transportation. Perhaps the most important matter confronting industry to-day is that of providing quicker and cheaper means of moving freight and passengers over the great distances separating sections of this country.

The United States presents the largest and the most diversified market for goods and products, and it has also an abundant supply of raw materials, power, and virgin soil. Foreign competition at home can develop only as permitted by insufficient means of domestic distribution.

* Cons. Engr., San Francisco, Calif.

There is no known limit to the amount of transportation that may ultimately be utilized if made sufficiently rapid and proportionately cheap. The tremendous development of the highways has demonstrated this fact, and furthermore it has shown that speed and convenience both draw and create traffic and that the public appreciates the saving in time and will pay accordingly.

It must be quite apparent to any one who has given the matter serious thought, that there must be continual improvement, betterment, and much new construction in connection with the railroads, or National transportation will be seriously impaired within the next decade. For a considerable period there has been no general expansion of the railways, at a time when highway development has been the greatest in history. Nevertheless, the rails are still the back-bone of public transportation and are likely to remain so, as no other facilities on land, when properly operated, are their equal for moving dense passenger or freight traffic over material distances.

In recent times the railways have represented about the only great business in the United States that has not shown material expansion. This can be illustrated by Mr. Budd's figures on equipment in use, invested capital, and annual cost of transportation during the past five years (1900-1925). However, there has been substantial progress in other directions. The railroads have handled more freight than ever before and have reduced the time in transit; operating conditions have been bettered and efficiency has been increased; their financial position has been improved, and their securities are now relatively attractive as investments. On the other hand they have added but little to their facilities or their capital.

Since 1922 the electric and gas public utilities of the United States have placed about $8 000 000 000 of new securities, while the industrials gained about $10 000 000 000. For the same period the railways issued only about $3 000 000 000. There is a reason for this situation, and it can hardly be found in a lack of public demand for the kind of transportation which the railways can best provide; nor can it be found in the impossibility of financing any well-considered development. It may have arisen in part from conservatism in railroad management, or it may be due to Government restrictions; but it is probably the result, in no small degree, of reliance on the fallacy that the total amount of traffic was a fixed entity, controlled only by population and industrial conditions, and not susceptible of material increase by betterment of its own characteristics of speed, convenience, and cost. It has now been proved, however, by experience with motorized highways that traffic, like the demand for electrical power or for merchandise, responds in volume to improved service at lower cost.

There are large sections in the interior of the United States that would profit immensely by quicker and less expensive transportation, and if this can be attained in any way, a great increase in the volume of traffic may be expected, with profit alike to the region served and to the carrier companies. It is probable, therefore, that very soon "public convenience and necessity" will demand much more expeditious and efficient mass-distance transportation, coupled with some form of collection and delivery system operating under one contract. To accomplish these results, new facilities must be used and new methods employed. Thus, the problems involved, to a material degree are those of engineering and a discussion by the profession is, therefore, opportune.

Time in Transportation.—Of all the elements of transportation, except costs, time is the most important. It bears directly on the value of the service and it enters materially into the cost. Most things of importance in the business world run with time: Interest, depreciation, taxes, labor costs, life itself, are measured in its terms. Every advance in transportation has been based primarily on time. The quickest movement at equal cost will always win, be it for a letter, a passenger, or 1 000 000 tons of coal. The public will pay more for fast service because it is of greater value.

The motorized highways have provided a very much quicker movement of passengers and freight under a great variety of conditions, and, therefore, they have not only taken over from the railways their slow-moving local traffic, but they have created a fast volume of business not heretofore existing. Time enters, not only as speed in transit, but as the full interval required, from readiness to move to arrival at final destination. Therefore, frequent service, regular schedules, convenient terminals, and expeditious gathering and delivery of merchandise, all accelerate transportation and increase its value.

In the movement of passengers, comfort and safety are important factors, but they control the volume of business only when co-ordinated with time. The railroads now provide a high degree of safety and reasonable comfort on most of their trains. It is true, of course, that some "locals" hardly compare in comfort with the best motor coaches, but it is doubtful whether much traffic has been lost on that score alone. The automobile and the motor-bus have diverted traffic from the railroads because they take the passenger over more territory, where he wants to go, with less expenditure of his time, when he is ready to move; and for him this is cheaper transportation. Mr. Budd points out that the buses gain traffic by making frequent stops along the highways, but after all this is only another way of providing a quicker movement of the passenger from the point of origin to destination. Moreover, in California, there are fast bus lines that operate only from depots, make fewer stops than the trains, and better time in transit. With frequent schedules, this service has created for itself a very large volume of business without materially affecting railway traffic in the same territory.

The question is frequently asked, to what extent can the rails compete with the highways for passenger business? The answer is that they can compete wherever the volume of traffic is sufficient to justify a faster over-all service than that possible on the highways, at substantially the same fare. For every distance, there is a certain volume that meets this condition, modified, of course, by local situations.

The motor truck has succeeded also largely because it saves time. Shippers realize that there is value in time and will pay for it. The truck is faster than the rails for short hauls, and in many cases for hauls of considerable distance, due to saving in time otherwise required in transferring to and from terminals and in waiting for train movements. For example, a certain freight shipment in California required 2 days, including the terminal transfers and loadings. The same movement is made by truck in 5 hours, with one loading and one unloading. The truck haul costs more, but it is worth more to the shippers. For short hauls the truck is not only a time-saver, but it is less expensive to operate. However, as in the case of passengers, if the volume of freight be increased sufficiently, a point is finally reached for every distance, except the very shortest, where the rails can move the traffic in less time and at smaller cost than is possible with trucks on the highways.

In the last analysis, time is the controlling factor in transportation. To industry, speedy delivery of materials and products means a reduction of waste in large measure, due to the lesser amount of equipment and capital required in the business. To the carrier companies, faster movements mean greater volume of traffic handled with substantially the same facilities and labor.

It is said that, by good management since the World War, the railways have accelerated the movement of freight on an average by 25 per cent. This is an excellent showing, but it is not enough to meet the future requirements of American business. However, with equipment and facilities which can now be made available, it is believed feasible to further reduce the time required for completed movements of freight and passengers by at least 50% for average conditions in the United States. This improvement, nevertheless, is not possible without a change of motive power and a re-arrangement of the main railway lines, co-ordinated with motorized facilities on the highways.

Arterial Railways.—Highway development is producing great arterial thoroughfares extending from the Atlantic to the Pacific and from Canada to Mexico and the Gulf. These main traffic lanes are contributing largely to the extent and popularity of highway transportation.

The railways, on the other hand, have provided no such arterial ways, although in their case the need is more urgent. This situation has been caused, in part, by diversity of ownership, by competition for business, or by Governmental restrictions, but, in a larger sense, it is the result of lack of vision in connection with the requirements of continental transportation.

All the principal railway companies are operating main-line through services over their own rails and in various combinations with others, but these arrangements do not qualify as arterial trafficways in the sense here intended. To be truly "arterial" they should drain the territory served and fully utilize other rails, buses, trucks, and all available means, as gathering, forwarding, and distributing agencies. The routes followed of course should be the most direct, regardless of present ownership, and, in the end, the rail companies will find a way, by merger or otherwise, to accomplish this result with full protection to all vested interests.

The arterial railways must be equipped, of necessity, for rapid and expeditious movement of passengers and freight over long distances, leaving to the other rails and the highways the task of collecting and distributing the traffic.

Such a service would meet with public favor, and it should reduce the time as well as the cost of long-distance transportation.

Electric Traction.—This subject is introduced here because of its material bearing on the future relation of highway to rail transportation. As previously stressed in this discussion, it is believed that speed is a far greater factor in controlling the volume of traffic than the carriers or the public have ever fully realized. For a long period the railways were supreme in this direction, but now, under many conditions, they provide slower transportation than that furnished by the highways, or even in some cases by the waterways.

It is well known that there are many existing limitations to speed on rails, but their removal does not involve difficulties, either physical or financial, as great as those which have been overcome in the development of motorized highways since 1900. Some will say that the track and roadbed cannot be further improved economically, and that this will limit speed. However, only a few engineers will agree with this view. Others will cite many real or supposed obstacles, but most men will agree that improved motive power and train control are essential if any great increase in speed is attained.

The application of electric traction to trunk railroads has been discussed from many angles for a number of years, but mainly from the one of cost of operation under existing railway conditions. The general conclusion among railway men has been that a change in motive power was not justified, and, viewed solely from the standpoint of arrested development, they are probably right. For special reasons, however, electric power has been applied to heavy railroading in a number of cases, under a wide variety of conditions, and the results obtained are ample to establish its possibilities in connection with any great increase of speed in railway operation. The modern steam locomotive is a wonderful power plant, considering its limitations of space and weight, but it is fundamentally unsuited for supplying mechanical energy at the rate necessary for moving trains at materially higher speeds.

It is recognized that there must soon be further material improvements in long-distance transportation. The basic requirements are more speed with less cost, and electric traction offers greater promise of aiding in these directions than any other known agency. There are sound engineering reasons for this statement, based on the highest technical authorities, and fully substantiated by wide experience in both the electrical power and railway fields.

The thought is therefore expressed that the main rail lines should be electrified and highly improved so as to adapt them for very fast and heavy traffic; that the less important rail routes and branch lines should be equipped with rail-motor cars, or Diesel electric locomotives; and, finally, that all gathering, transfer, delivery, and short-haul business should be handled by fleets of trucks and buses operating on the highways.

Summary.—Ample, fast, and cheap public transportation is the most essential of all factors in establishing and maintaining American prosperity.

The movement of freight and passengers is inherently a universal public service and ought to be conducted by corporations or other agencies of National character, functioning under one form of Governmental supervision.

The railroad corporations should extend the scope of their operations to include the highways, the waterways, and the airways.

Arterial railways, electrified and fully equipped for heavy traffic at high speeds, are an essential part of any continental transportation system adequate for future industrial needs.

With improved and unified methods of operation, by utilizing facilities now available, it is commercially feasible to reduce materially the cost of conducting transportation and to expedite the movement of traffic in the United States.

RALPH BUDD,* M. AM. SOC. C. E. (by letter).—Mr. Crosby properly questions the writer's "Inventory". Values for highway right of way were not included and to that extent the figures given for investment in highway transportation were too low.

He also questions whether competition should not be permitted between different carriers even though such competition would add to the total cost of producing the transportation by the competing carriers. The writer does not believe in eliminating all competition, but, in the case of commercial highway transportation, the theory of regulated monopoly has much to commend it. Just how far this can go in practice is, of course, a question of judgment to be determined by the circumstances in each instance.

Mr. Gerry's plea for quicker and cheaper transportation is in line with the ever-increasing need for efficiency. As far as passenger travel is concerned, the operation of through sleeping cars from the East to the West Coast, and *vice versa*, is practically all that the writer can think of that would eliminate delay and inconvenience in long-distance railway travel on the present-day fine, through trains. It is true that freight movement by rail can be expedited still more than it has been during the years since the World War, but most of the saving in time will come from avoiding terminal delays rather than from operating freight trains at higher speeds.

By some further consolidation of railways, transfer of cars and the incident inspection will be unnecessary, and the cars may be kept moving more of the time.

The problem of taxation was discussed by Messrs. Hanna and Hadley. It seems a most difficult one to solve. The principles stated in the paper still seem to be correct.

The obvious injustice of taxing the railways to provide highways for competitors should be removed, but not by imposing an unjust tax on other transportation agencies. The fairer method is to transfer the burden of taxation from the users of the railways to the users of the highways and to tax each of the latter on the basis of the proportion that its use bears to the total use made of the highways.

The trend of local passenger travel from the railways to the highways of the country, due to the increasing number of automobiles and highway motor buses and the improvement of roads, has continued uninterruptedly through 1926 and 1927. The decrease in railway passenger revenue in 1927

* Pres., G. N. Ry., St. Paul, Minn.

compared with 1925 was $78 800 000, and the decrease in the number of passengers handled was 51 000 000, or 5.8 per cent.

The astonishing thing is that many railway men thought and said in 1925 that the bottom had been reached in the decline of railway passenger travel. The conclusion seems inescapable that the railways have lost irretrievably the short-haul passenger business. The common sense course open to them is to substitute smaller, lower cost, gas or oil-electric units for steam-operated passenger trains, where trains are essential, and to eliminate unprofitable trains wherever they are not necessary. The latter process may be advanced by the operation of high-class, convenient motor-bus service on highways adjacent to and often parallel with the railways.

Probably the most striking statistics concerning the operation of the railways of the United States for recent years are those which show a decline in passenger revenues from $1 290 000 000 in 1920 to $980 000 000 in 1927, with practically no reduction in passenger train-miles during that period. The effect of this loss in passenger revenue is, therefore, a loss in net railway operating income of approximately $310 000 000 in 1927 compared with 1920, or the equivalent of 1% on $31 000 000 000. This is more than the total investment in the railways of the United States.

It is the 20 600 000 private automobiles, and not the 90 000 highway buses, that are responsible for this continuing decline in railway passenger revenue, although the total travel by bus is increasing, as is also the average length of ride per passenger. No one can say how much more railway travel will decline, but it is evident that the long-haul passenger business is going to remain with the railways just as the long-haul bulk freight will. To keep as much travel on railway trains as possible, the railways are justified in providing extra fine through trains and small economical units for short runs and branch-line operation. In many places highway buses can be substituted for unprofitable trains by co-operating with bus operators, or by the railways controlling the bus companies themselves.

Regulation of buses by the same commissions that regulate railway operation seems essential for complete correlation of rail and highway service. There is pending in Congress a bill to provide some Federal control of common carriers on highways and that bill very wisely leaves most of such regulation to the State authorities. Beyond the issuance of certificates of public convenience and necessity authorizing interstate operation, there does not seem to be any real need for Federal jurisdiction.

During the last two years there has been substantial improvement in bus transportation. The capacity of buses has been enlarged, until the newest types carry thirty-eight passengers. Luxuries have been added in the way of air-cushioned seats, interior baggage racks, hot-water heaters, storm windows, and ventilators. Chassis also have been improved in riding qualities and motors of greater reliability and economy have been produced. The interiors of the latest buses are painted in pleasing colors giving a decorative effect comparable with the treatment of the fine transcontinental trains. Now, the use of aluminum alloy is proposed to lessen their weight by 3 000 lb., or more.

There is in active progress a series of consolidations of small bus companies into a lesser number of stronger and more efficient systems. In this respect, the bus situation, to-day, resembles the railway situation in the Fifties when amalgamation of many short lines into systems like the New York Central; New York, New Haven and Hartford; Pennsylvania; Baltimore and Ohio; and others was beginning. There is no doubt that larger and stronger bus companies will be able to improve upon the service of the small weak companies and to operate much more economically, just as the larger railway systems were able to improve upon the service of the many small railway lines operating independently. How far consolidation of bus lines will enable highway buses to compete more effectively with the railways for long-haul travel, is one of the most important transportation problems of the day.

AMERICAN SOCIETY OF CIVIL ENGINEERS

INSTITUTED 1852

TRANSACTIONS

Paper No. 1664

URBAN AND INTERURBAN BUSES*

By Britton I. Budd,† Esq.

With Discussion by Messrs. Robert P. Woods, Fred G. Buffe, B. H. Piepmeier, C. E. Smith, Winters Haydock, John W. Reid, Lucius S. Storrs, Anson Marston, and Britton I. Budd.

Rapid development of the bus, or as some prefer—the motor coach—in urban and interurban transportation, has given railway operators a new problem; that is, to find the best and most economical use to which the motor coach can be put, and then to fit it into its proper place in the transportation system.

The demand for motor-coach service in recent years has come directly from the traveling public. We have been living in an era of great prosperity in which the number of private automobiles averages almost one for every family in the country. The comfort and convenience of the automobile has created a demand for de luxe travel, and the motor coach has appeared to meet that demand, regardless of economic law which, under less prosperous conditions, would be a determining factor.

It is the business of transportation companies to supply the public with the character of service it demands. If the public prefers to ride on rubber tires at increased cost, the transportation company must supply that service, even if it may not be the most economical.

Co-ordination of all transportation facilities so that each may be assigned to the kind of work it is best fitted to perform is the problem which must be solved before the future of the motor coach can be forecast with any degree of accuracy. The public must look to the operators of the steam and electric

* Presented at the Spring Meeting, Kansas City, Mo., April 14, 1926.

† Pres., Chic., North Shore & Milwaukee R. R., Chicago, Ill.

railways for the solution. They are the men who by training and experience are qualified to perform this service.

That rapid strides are being made in the co-ordination of facilities is seen in the manner in which steam and electric railway companies have adopted the motor coach.

A survey made by the National Automobile Chamber of Commerce shows about 20 steam railroads operating motor coaches as a part of their regular passenger service at the end of 1925 and that 18 others are now (1926) considering similar service. The same survey shows that 51 steam railroads in the United States and Canada are using motor trucks to supplement their freight service.

The adoption of the motor coach by the electric railways of the country is much more marked. In 1920 there were only 16 such companies using motor coaches as a part of their service, whereas, at the end of 1925, 280 companies were using them.

This great increase has come in the last two years. In January, 1924, only 14% of the electric railway companies of the country were operating motor coaches. In January, 1926, the percentage had risen to 35. These companies are operating 13 000 miles of motor-coach routes.

That most of this traffic is new business is seen in the fact that electric railways in the same period carried more passengers than ever before in their history. The steam railroads carried more freight in 1925 than in any previous year and materially reduced the time lost in transit.

As the adoption of the motor coach and the motor truck by the electric and steam railroads goes on, it is probable that in the near future the existing transportation agencies will handle all this traffic as a properly co-ordinated part of their systems. The problem is one of adjustment.

Some of the electric railway companies of the country have gone into the motor-coach business on an extensive scale. The largest is the Public Service Company of New Jersey which is operating more than 800 motor coaches in connection with its rail lines. Many other companies on a less extensive scale have fleets of 50 to 100 motor coaches in service, while some operate only a few from the end of their rail lines.

This extensive use of the motor coach and the motor truck by the railway companies is only a small phase of the industry. The number of independent motor-coach operators has increased until there is a network of routes all over the United States. On January 1, 1926, 6 455 companies were operating motor coaches over routes aggregating 232 341 miles. The latest figures indicate an increase of 15% in the number of coaches and 8% in miles of route. It it probable that by the end of 1926 the miles of route will be in excess of 250 000, a mileage almost equal to that of Class I steam railroads, and the number of motor coaches will exceed 75 000.

Although the experience of the last few years has demonstrated the usefulness of the motor coach as a transportation agent, it has shown as clearly that it has certain definite limitations. The experience in some instances has been a costly one to the public and to private investors. The public suffered because of inadequate service and the independent motor-coach operator lost all or part of his investment.

In the urban field it has been shown by the experience of Akron, Ohio, and Des Moines, Iowa (to mention only two of the number of cities which tried the experiment) that the motor coach is not suited for mass transportation. It cannot substitute for the electric railway.

In the interurban field the experience of Indiana is a strong argument for co-ordination of the motor coach with the electric railway.

Comparison of the relative speeds and carrying capacity of the motor coach, the street car, and the rapid transit line (elevated or subway) under heavy traffic conditions, tends to place each agency in its proper place in urban transportation.

Under average conditions in the large city during the hours of heaviest travel, the speed of the motor coach is 8 to 9 miles per hour and the utmost capacity of double-deck buses in a one-way movement under the most favorable conditions is from 5 000 to 6 000 passengers.

The average speed of the surface electric car is 9 to 11 miles per hour and its carrying capacity from 14 000 to 16 000 passengers.

The rapid transit lines (subway or elevated), operating trains instead of single cars, have an average speed per hour of 14 to 15 miles in local service and 18 to 25 miles in express service. The maximum capacity is from 35 000 to 50 000 passengers per hour.

In a city like Chicago, Ill., where the rapid transit elevated lines are called on to carry 80 000 to 90 000 passengers into the "Loop" each morning in the space of an hour and an almost equal number out in the same time in the evening, it will be seen at once that this service could not be rendered by gasoline-driven vehicles which occupy relatively much greater space per passenger carried.

What has been said of Chicago applies in degree to every large city in the country in the traffic peak hours. There has been considerable loose talk that the motor coach is destined to supplant the electric railway in city and interurban transportation, but there is no substantial basis on which to rest such claims. Neither are such claims made by those qualified to speak on transportation subjects.

Reference was made to the experience in Indiana. Probably no State can furnish a better example of the results of competition between motor-coach and interurban railroad routes. The fact that the motor-coach company controlling the larger number of bus routes is now in a receivership does not prove that the motor coach is not a useful medium of transportation. It proves that in Indiana it was used in the wrong way; that is, in competition with the interurban railroads for long-haul traffic. Both the rail and motor-coach lines suffered while the competitive war was on. The motor-coach lines could not compete successfully with the interurban lines on long hauls, and the electric lines could not compete with the motor coach in local traffic.

In a recent public statement Fred I. Jones, Receiver for the motor-coach lines, was quoted as follows:

"It is becoming apparent, it seems to me, that the operation of motor buses be co-ordinated with existent steam and electric forms of transportation. This is particularly true in Indiana, which is covered by such a network of steam and interurban railways serving the population fairly satisfactorily. The buses find it impossible to stand alone, but are logically indispensable in rounding out a complete and unified transportation system".

Certain definite conclusions may be drawn from the Indiana experience. It proves that competition between two transportation systems serving the same communities, prevents either system from giving the public the best service. It proves that rates of fare that do not provide a reasonable rate of return on the capital investment lead to bankruptcy.

The Indiana experience has shown that the motor coach is neither more popular nor more economical than the electric railroad for long-distance travel. It has shown that the motor coach is not a medium around which any great system of interconnecting transportation can be built, but that there is a profitable field for its operation co-ordinate with other agencies.

Courts and regulatory commissions are now generally agreed that competition between utilities giving the same kind of service is not to the best interest of the public. In a rate-cutting "war" what the public gains temporarily in lower rates it loses in quality of service; in the long run it pays higher rates when the competing companies combine or one is forced out of business. The company that remains must recoup its losses sustained during the "war".

Many motor-coach operators made the mistake of establishing rates of fare on a competitive basis with electric railways. Motor-coach service costs more to produce than electric railway service and it probably always will; but the public demands this special service which more nearly approaches the comfort and convenience of the private automobile. That the public has shown its willingness to pay a higher rate of fare, is seen in the patronage given the motor coach in New York, N. Y., Chicago, St. Louis, Mo., and other large cities, where higher fares are charged than on the electric railways.

Although no general rule can be laid down for every situation, either with respect to motor-coach operation or the rate of fare to be charged, experience indicates that in city service the rate necessary to maintain motor-coach service should be approximately twice that paid on electric railways. In interurban service, the rate should be from 30% to 50% more than the railroad rate. The future of motor-coach industry depends on its being made self-supporting.

California was one of the first States to adopt the motor coach on an extensive scale. At first, the industry was entirely unregulated, but afterward the motor bus was brought under the regulation of the State Railroad Commission which prescribes the system of keeping accounts. An incomplete report issued by the Commission covering motor-coach operation for the year 1924 brings up the question whether the rate structure is sound.

An analysis of the report made by the Chief Statistician of the American Electric Railway Association shows that, although the California motor-bus operators carried 1.5% more passengers in 1924 than they did in 1923 and that their total revenues increased 8%, their net revenue from operations showed a decrease of 7.6 per cent. Operating expenses, exclusive of taxes, increased 10% over the previous year. Taxes were increased 165% during the year, and when they are deducted the net income showed a decrease of 42.5 per cent.

The motor vehicle operators of California have had more experience than those of any other State. Nearly all of them operate independently of electric railways. If, as the report shows, they are finding it necessary to increase their operating ratio in spite of an increase in business, it indicates that the rate structure is not on a sound economic basis.

Electric railway companies which have gone into the motor-coach business have generally adapted a rate structure from their railway practice. Experience so far tends to show that railway rates applied to motor-coach transportation will not cover the cost of operation.

The largest item of expense in the upkeep of the private automobile is depreciation, an item that escapes the attention of many users. That item alone exceeds all other expenses of upkeep, including gasoline and tires, garage rent, insurance, and repairs. One large manufacturer of automobiles who has made a study of depreciation finds that the average automobile is traded in for a new model after being run 16 000 miles. The constant demand for the latest model runs depreciation charges up to a high figure.

In a measure the same applies to the motor coach. Manufacturers are constantly making improvements in motor coaches as they learn by experience. The public must have the latest or patronage will decrease. Just as the owner of the private automobile will exchange his car long before it is worn out to obtain a newer model, so must the motor-coach operator keep up with the latest styles.

With greater experience no doubt the depreciation costs on the motor coach will be materially reduced. Not enough attention has been paid to this phase of operation. Railway companies which exercise the utmost care in seeing that their railway equipment is maintained at the highest efficiency, provide few facilities for maintaining their motor coaches in the same way. They will employ only the most highly skilled workmen to inspect and repair their railway equipment, yet they will entrust their motor coaches to the care of inexperienced and unskilled men. There is no doubt that operating costs are often made higher than necessary from this cause.

If motor-coach operation is to be made successful more attention must be given to garage facilities and to proper maintenance. Careful studies must be made of tire costs and gas consumption. The motor coach must now be considered as much a part of a transportation system as the electric car, and the costs of operation must be studied as closely.

City motor-coach operation and interurban or inter-city operation are separate and distinct propositions. The type of equipment that might prove satisfactory in city operation where the haul is comparatively short, would not meet the requirements in inter-city service. Motor coaches engaged in long-haul operation must be attractive in type and comfortable. Where they are in constant service on regular routes, it may not be necessary that they should be quite as luxurious in furnishings as the types used for special tours, but they must be greatly superior to the ordinary type used in city service.

In interurban and inter-city service motor-coach schedules must be arranged with great care. They must provide for convenient rest stops and public comfort facilities. These conveniences must be counted in the capital investment and in the cost of operation and maintenance, items which many independent operators do not consider.

One phase of motor-coach operation that is proving attractive to the traveling public and profitable to the operators is the chartered coach business. To a large extent this is pleasure riding. A small organization plans an outing. It may be for a single day, for a week, or a month. The motor coach is the convenient agent for such travel because of its flexibility. The time spent on the road is not a factor as in the ordinary business trip. More opportunities are afforded the traveler to see the country through which he passes. The rate which such parties are willing to pay makes the operation profitable for the carrier as the travelers are more interested in getting the kind of service they wish than in what it costs them. If the parties are of sufficient numbers to equal the number of seats, or nearly so, the rate charge can be made quite reasonable and still give the carrier a fair profit. The writer knows of instances where such chartered motor-coach operation has proved sufficiently profitable to offset the losses sustained in operating non-paying regular routes, so that the business of a company as a whole showed a margin of profit.

In summing up the motor-coach situation in the urban and interurban service, some fairly definite conclusions may be drawn:

1.—In city service the motor coach has its greatest economic value when operated in conjunction with electric railways. It is a most convenient agent to give transportation service along boulevards and parks and to serve as a feeder to electric lines in territory not otherwise served.

2.—In the suburban and interurban fields the motor coach is most useful for comparatively short hauls of 20 miles or less. In long-haul traffic it is not as useful nor as economical as the high-speed electric railroad and should not be operated in territory served by rail. As an auxiliary to the railroad the motor coach has its greatest usefulness in the interurban service, as it can be used to serve territory contiguous to the railroad for a distance of 25 miles or more.

3.—The cost of operating motor-coach service is greater than that of rail service and is always likely to be so.

4.—Railway operators with their special training and experience are best qualified to operate motor coaches and co-ordinate them with the railways.

5.—In the near future, under a properly co-ordinated transportation system, the motor-coach business will be placed on a sound economic basis. Where motor coaches can be operated economically they will be run, and where it is found that the public will be better and more economically served by rail lines, the latter will carry the traffic.

DISCUSSION

Robert P. Woods,* M. Am. Soc. C. E.—Motor coach operation between cities and towns as a unit of transportation has grown rapidly since 1924. Included in this interurban service are the necessary and the unnecessary, the desirable and the undesirable. Vehicles ranging from the luxurious 30-passenger, high-powered, $12 000 coach to the well-worn touring car are in use. Here and there the business is standardized to a certain extent, but, on the whole, the situation, due to the quick growth and misapplication to existing necessities, is far from being stabilized. The character of equipment, amount of service, rates of fare, and ownership of lines and companies are changing rapidly and new routes are opening. The lines of the routes vary from a few miles to several hundred, and the rates of fare from 1.5 to 5 cents or more per mile. The higher rates apply more particularly where infrequent service with light patronage is given. The average rate is low. The schedules range from one or two trips per day to regular hourly and half-hourly service.

Thirty-eight States have passed laws controlling interurban coach service, but not Missouri. A number of the States made changes in their laws at the Legislative Sessions of 1925-26. An intensive move is under way for inter-state regulation by the Federal Government.

The motor-coach service is welcome and popular with many people. Helpful in this direction has been the development and great use of the automobile, of which there are now (1926) 20 000 000 in the United States, a sufficient number to enable practically the entire population to ride at the same time. Few, therefore, are immune to its pleasures, its readiness to serve, its speed, and its accessibility. The number justifies the statement that the people have formed the riding habit.

Another help has been the extension of improved hard-surfaced roads. Motor-coach manufacturers have developed a high-grade equipment and this, in contrast with the present character of many interurban electric railways, has been favorable to the motor-coach patronage. Interurban electric railways, however, generally have been handicapped financially because they suffered a loss in net earnings, due to the low rates of fare and the increased operating expenses. Motor-coach carriers may encounter the same handicap. The tremendous use of the private automobile has created a restless spirit that will brook no delays, and it is to this more than to any other factor that the growth of motor coaches may be attributed.

The motor coach as a carrier is expensive in initial cost, operation, and maintenance, more so than the public realizes—in fact, more so than many of the newer operators believe, because the maintenance and renewal expenses will come as a future revelation.

The cost of owning, operating, and maintaining a private automobile is no small item, but when a person rides or drives in the family car the feeling of pleasure and personal interest discounts the expenses, and if a similar spirit is felt in riding in the public motor coaches, sufficient revenues may be

* Pres. and Gen. Mgr., Kansas City, Clay County & St. Joseph Ry., Kansas City, Mo.

expected to sustain good service. It should be remembered, however, that the present status as a carrier has been built up during a period of low fares.

Motor coaches are in operation where formerly there was no transportation. They are used as feeders to steam and electric railways, and for special trips, both long and short; also, where the service was deemed inadequate, as along steam railroads with only one round-trip train each day, the stations of which are somewhat remote from the center of the retail business districts.

Opinions as to the future of interurban motor-coach transportation will be varied, depending on familiarity, knowledge, experience, and personal interest. In part, at least, it will hinge upon "whose ox is gored". Among those looking at the subject from this angle will be the coach manufacturer, the coach owner, steam and electric railway officials, the coach salesman, the accessories representative, those receiving special benefits from its operation, and, lastly, the public.

The speaker will try to be as free of bias as possible. As an independent unit of transportation in the interurban field the success of the motor coach as a carrier will be spotted. In progressing it will meet the same measure of regulation as that given to the regular transportation carriers as soon as it emerges from the swaddling clothes of newness. If the volume of traffic becomes heavy, it, like the electric interurban roads, will probably be forced to secure private right of way in such sections. This the coach line would require for safety and to maintain its speed; and the authorities would require it on account of traffic congestion and extra wear and tear on highways. The steam and electric railways are getting into the field more and more and, in time, will probably control the greater number of parallel coach lines.

Much has been said of the "co-ordination" of coaches with other carriers, but the word seems not to have the meaning given in the dictionary. The intent in many places is rather to parallel and "cut under" the regular carriers. Proper co-ordination, however, is needful for the public good. In time, it will prevail, but when it does the operation of the motor coaches will be on a different basis from that prevailing to-day. Duplication of service is an economic loss, first, underwritten by the interests involved, and, later, paid for by the public, whose portion is not always earmarked, but who finally settles for it in one way or another. Excess service, especially when unprofitable, produces bad after effects; the equipment deteriorates and then recovery brings higher rates for the public to pay—in short, the public pays "going and coming".

It must not be inferred that the interurban motor coach carrier will be banished—far from it; it will fit into the transportation picture nicely, but not as operated at present. Its development has been remarkable and in these days of enterprise and keen competition it may be that the industry could not have attained the wide recognition it has by any other introductory means than have been used. The justice of the means in some instances, however, is at least questionable.

A tabulation of the various coach lines throughout the country, showing the complete character of service, local conditions, volume of traffic, competition, and other pertinent facts, would disclose interesting information from which a reliable estimate, rather than a guess, could be made of the future tendency of the industry; but such a summary would be voluminous and hardly worth the effort, for before it could be compiled and studied the situation would be changed. However, a short review of the interurban motor-coach service in and out of Kansas City, Mo., will supply definite knowledge that is applicable to the conditions found in a large part of the industry as a whole.

Interurban motor coaches are operated between Kansas City and seventeen other terminals. Twenty separate coach lines are operated and competition extends over three, and a part of a fourth, of these seventeen routes. Three of the routes practically parallel electric railways and all cover territory served by steam railroads. The total length of highways traversed (not doubling where competing lines exist) is 1 773 lin. miles. The twenty coach lines run 250 total trips daily into and out of Kansas City, covering, all told, 12 419 coach-miles, or a distance equal to half way around the earth. On sixteen of the twenty coach lines the vehicles seat twelve or more persons, and, on the remaining four lines, touring cars are used. These various routes with their length are given in Table 1.

TABLE 1.—VARIOUS MOTOR COACH ROUTES AND THEIR DISTANCES INTO AND OUT OF KANSAS CITY, MISSOURI.

Place.	Miles.	Place.	Miles.
Topeka, Kans	75	Higginsville, Mo	58
Leavenworth, Kans	33	Sweet Springs, Mo	62
Excelsior Springs, Mo	32*	Warrensburg, Mo	60
St. Joseph, Mo	60†	Harrisonville, Mo	41
Parkville, Mo	10	Lees Summit, Mo	20
Plattsburg, Mo	38	Osawatomie, Mo	62
Lexington, Mo	47	Denver, Colo	677*
Booneville, Mo	104	St. Louis, Mo	267*
Columbia, Mo	130		

* Two separate companies.
† Part-way competition.

The rates of fare vary from 1 to 0.7 cent per coach-mile, as in the case of the two lines to Denver, to 3.9 cents per mile. The rate from Kansas City to St. Louis, on both lines, is 2.6 cents per mile on a single-trip basis, or 2.3 cents on a round-trip basis. The numerical average rate of fare for all routes is 3 cents per mile one way and 2.9 cents per mile on a round-trip basis.

The net earnings of these lines are not known, but as they are dependent on volume of business, kind and amount of service given, depreciation provisions, and rates of fare, it is believed that, taken as a whole, there has been no profit. Recently,* much to the surprise of many, seven or eight of the large interurban motor coach lines operating out from Indianapolis, Ind., have failed. Time is bringing adjustments to the coach industry throughout the country, and the Kansas City field will show modifications from time to time

* Between March and April, 1926.

due to the foregoing factors and such regulation as may be added by legislation.

An example of operation in competition with long-established steam and electric transportation is the line along the Kansas City, Clay County and St. Joseph Railway. This railway, situated entirely in Missouri and one of the outstanding interurban electric railways of America, has been in continuous operation since early in 1913. It is a high-speed, heavy-type, electric road, with a 1 200-volt catenary trolley, all steel passenger cars, automatic block signals, and all on private right of way, with a dozen or more grade separations. The train service is hourly, with half-hourly service at rush periods. Many of the trains are of two cars. The rate of fare is 2.5 cents per mile.

On February 15, 1924, the new, hard-surfaced highway between Kansas City and Excelsior Springs was opened to traffic, at which time a motor coach company (Yellow Line) began operation between the two terminals, paralleling the Electric Railway with large high-type motor coaches on a 2-hour service, which by June 1 was increased to hourly service. At rush-hour periods it was necessary for the company to send out two coaches seating twenty-six persons each. The Yellow Line is still operating and as a competitor of the Electric Railway.

On August 7, 1924, the Kansas City, Clay County and St. Joseph Auto Transit Company (Blue Line) owned by stockholders of the Electric Railway and managed by the latter's officers and heads of departments, inaugurated a 2-hour service between Kansas City and Excelsior Springs, with large de luxe motor coaches, thus paralleling the Electric Railway and the Yellow Line. This service being too infrequent to draw patronage, it was changed to hourly service, with extras during the rush-hour movement. The combined heavy service of both coach companies, amounting much of the time to about ninety coach trips per day, continued until May, 1925. During this period the passenger cars of Electric Railway showed a heavy decrease of patronage, yet it maintained and still maintains its former schedule of hourly service, with a half-hourly rush-period schedule. Beginning with May, 1925, by agreement, each coach company reduced its service to an hourly schedule, thereby eliminating the extra service that had developed.

Three reasons may be given for the attitude of the Electric Railway Company: One was a spirit to give to the public coach service to the extent it desired; another was to protect ultimately the $5 125 000 invested in the property; and the other was to indicate to those contemplating further paralleling of the line that they would have competition in kind. For considerably more than a year the Blue Coach Line (ally of the Electric Railway Company) has operated from Kansas City to St. Joseph, 60 miles, and from Kansas City to Parkville, 10 miles. It has no bus competition between the terminals at Kansas City and St. Joseph. The line to Parkville has no competition; it partly parallels the Electric Railway, but also acts as a feeder.

Notwithstanding the frequent and high-grade motor-coach service given by the two companies between Kansas City and Excelsior Springs, patronage has been steadily falling off recently (1925-26) on both and that on the Electric

Railway has been increasing. Previously, the combined coach service was twice that of the Electric Railway. From March 31 to April 6, 1926, there was no motor-coach service on the coach lines, due to a heavy fall of snow. Upon resumption, the Yellow and Blue Lines, on account of the falling off in business, agreed to operate coaches every two hours instead of hourly, with some modifications, such as an extra coach for the short haul at 6:00 P. M. and the partial elimination of the last or theatre run. A few figures will show the change in the flow of patronage from the coaches to the Electric Railway between Kansas City and Excelsior Springs.

During the calendar year 1925 the railway, with about one-third the combined service of the Electric Railway and two coach lines, carried twice as many passengers as both the coach lines and during the last five months of 1925 it carried two and one-third times as many, showing the increasing tendency to switch to the Electric Railway.

For the first three months of 1926 the number of coach passengers on both coach lines has decreased about 32%, and the number of passengers on the Electric Railway has increased about 33%, to a number 2.94 times as large as both motor coach lines. During this period the coaches curtailed their mileage, while that of the Electric Railway was increased, the railway supplying 38% of the total mileage.

Therefore, with rates of fare practically the same on all lines, the combined motor-coach patronage with its extensive service decreased, as compared with the year previous, with the rate of decrease greater during the last three months. Whether or not this tendency will hold is problematical. The motor coach is here to stay. Adjustments and modifications will be made from time to time and gradually there will be a real co-ordination with the other long-established and more reliable transportation carriers.

FRED G. BUFFE,* ESQ.—It seems indicative of a better era in business to find thinking men actively engaged in constructive work in their communities, seriously studying transportation, and by so doing helping those in the business to solve their problems.

The bus has been, and still is, a problem. To the unthinking it may not seem so. It is easy to say, "We like this new method of riding—the smell of gasoline and a ride on rubber—and if the street railways, the interurbans, and the railroads will not furnish such rides, three cheers for the fellow who will." Such was the attitude that existed when competing street railways were built; when competing railroads were invited; when gas and electric franchises were had for the asking, on the theory that competition is the life of trade, and "the more the merrier." It took many years of loss and efficiency before this mistake was generally recognized and before the public accepted *in toto* the theory that certain services, chief of which is transportation, are natural monopolies, and that regulation and not competition is the proper check against abuse.

Therefore, the bus must be considered not only as a vehicle capable of carrying people, but in its relation to the transportation situation as a

* Vice-Pres. in Chg. of Operations, Kansas City Public Service Co., Kansas City, Mo.

whole. In the last analysis the problem and its proper solution becomes that of the public. There is danger of magnifying the importance of the motor coach and of giving it a disproportionate place in transportation. This is natural with a new development, especially one that has enjoyed the advertising and propaganda given to the bus. People are prone to like new toys.

A bus system is a valuable agency in urban transportation when it can be built carefully and properly, with due regard to other facilities. If, because of too much propaganda or threatened competition, or without due regard to its effect on transportation, it is used improperly, it will in the end work a real public harm where there is an apparent public gain. It is valuable because of its flexibility. It can be used anywhere—routes can be changed, detours made, and delays avoided. It requires a lower investment per seat furnished. It affords an easy and less costly method of making extensions, of serving undeveloped territory, and of instituting cross-town lines. It readily lends itself to park and boulevard service that have grown away from car lines. It fills a gap between the street car and the taxicab, and gives the street railway operator a vehicle that appeals to his former patrons who have deserted his service for the private automobile.

The bus is not, and very evidently never can be, a substitute for the electric railway in moving large numbers of persons during the rush hours. The street railway is here to stay, and its usefulness will increase as the vehicle for mass transportation at the lowest possible fare. The street car is more reliable; its rides can be furnished at less cost; it takes up less pavement space per passenger moved; it moves on a fixed track and congests traffic the least, considering the number carried. The street car is the backbone of urban transportation, the great servant of the masses, the foundation on which rests the superstructure of real estate and business prosperity, furnishing the maximum service for the minimum fare. The bus is primarily a "seat-for-every-passenger" vehicle offering a preferential service at a higher fare.

As confirmation of this statement, it is only necessary to call attention to the present-day electric railway activity. There is a great awakening in every city; new equipment is being bought; tracks are being rebuilt; higher standards of service are being maintained; the more important street railway securities are no longer a drug in financial centers. These things are not by chance. Bankers of long experience would not advise or permit such programs if these properties were going out of business over night.

The competing bus is a pirate in its very nature. Instead of rendering a public service as it seems, it is in reality working a great public injury. It is a backward step in urban transportation, and at some future date the bill must be paid. It will be paid in lack of capital for improvements, in impaired service—often in forced consolidation by which the promoters collect their profit and the street railway as a public agent pays the loss, which, in turn, becomes that of the public. Such competition exists only because it is permitted to serve a preferred territory having great traffic density and a high load factor. It does not assume the burden and the obligation of city-wide service, of undeveloped lines and districts, but leaves these to the street railway while it takes the business the railway must have to support its service obligations. With its system of flat fares and universal transfers, city-wide transportation is properly a municipal problem, and certain sections can be served only because the better lines support the entire structure. Unwise bus competition has often been most unfair, in not being given the advantage of short hauls and profitable territory, but rather in being relieved of paving, street cleaning, and tax burdens, with which its older competitor has been laden.

The proper place for the bus is as an integral part of the co-ordinated transportation plan. Webster says, "to co-ordinate" is "to adjust, to harmonize". With this adjustment, this harmony, transportation may be developed along proper and natural lines. Co-ordinated transportation contemplates a complete service, using both bus and street car, not making one subordinate to the other, but fitting each vehicle to its proper field to avoid duplication and to render a more efficient and desirable public service.

The bus when used as a feeder, as a server of undeveloped territories, such as cross-town facilities and on lines where track must be rebuilt and where there is no rush-hour problem, plainly meets a real need. It can also be used as a main or through-line carrier, serving districts heavily built up away from car lines and along boulevards and parks where car lines would not be permitted.

On the other hand the bus should not be used half-heartedly and confined to the outskirts. The public desires bus transportation, and transportation agencies must meet this public desire. The down-town bus can be used to advantage. It offers a different service, makes an appeal to a certain class of riders who are willing to pay a higher fare on a "seat-for-every-passenger" basis. There is also in many cities opportunity for a limited-stop express service from distant residential districts at a 25-cent fare.

Kansas City, Mo., operates 69 buses on four down-town routes, one express route, one cross-town route, and four feeder routes, a total of 44 route-miles. The fare is 10 cents without transfer except on feeder and cross-town routes, where transfers are given from bus to street car and from street car to bus on payment of a 3-cent differential. The express fare is 25 cents. In all, 200 000 bus-miles per month are run and 540 000 passengers carried.

This bus installation is a good example of co-ordination and of a proper public attitude. Kansas City desired buses. There was an extended investigation by merchants' associations and others, and the general public opinion was that such service should be available. A franchise was submitted by promoters financially able to carry out their commitments. Had this competition been successful in Kansas City, it would have wrecked The Kansas City Railways and postponed the lifting of the receivership indefinitely. Incidentally, it may be said that jitney competition in 1918 and 1919, taking $3 000 per day in revenue, was a large contributing factor to the receivership.

The public, the press, and the city authorities took the position that in providing the desired bus service, the first opportunity should be given The Railways, and that competition should not be permitted. As a result, after careful analysis and planning, The Railways have co-ordinated bus transportation so as to furnish a maximum of service and not compete directly with existing facilities.

The bus, properly developed and co-ordinated, has a future as a transportation agency. It will be further perfected and refined. New uses for it will be found. It will develop its own clientele. It will do its part to solve the traffic and parking problems. It offers new opportunities to serve as well as new problems to solve, and in the end its proper development will mean a distinct public gain.

B. H. PIEPMEIER,* M. AM. SOC. C. E.—Urban and interurban transportation in its various stages of development has been confronting civilization since the beginning of time. The rapid development of different kinds of transportation has been watched with interest. Many have predicted that the truck and bus could not compete with the electrical car and train, but since their inception, the truck and urban and interurban buses have continued to increase in size, speed, and number. The growth of this form of transportation shows that it is increasing in public favor.

The flexibility and convenience of motor-bus transportation have made it very popular. In the congested centers it is being more extensively used, as it provides a means of transportation at a faster rate of speed and with less congestion than perhaps any other form that has been developed to date. The business man who in the past has been driving his private car to the office and parking it at or near his place of business, is now forced off the street by congestion and parking regulations, and has substituted the use of urban buses.

Every one will concede that the motor car and bus have afforded a means for rapid growth and development of suburban communities. It would be difficult for any one, at this time, to predict the future development of this form of transportation, or just what effect it may have on the future growth of suburban communities. At present, in nearly all parts of the United States, urban and interurban bus traffic is developing by leaps and bounds. During the last five years the vehicles themselves have become almost the last word in convenience and pleasure. Some may raise the question that they are developing faster than they should, or beyond the point of economic transportation.

The maintenance of the road-bed for both steam and electric railroads has been one of the chief expenses imposed on transportation companies, and the public is just beginning to realize that it is shouldering this tremendous upkeep due to urban and interurban bus transportation. It is perhaps impossible, at this time, to estimate just how much of this expense should be assigned to the companies. Modern highways and streets are being designed to withstand the present-day motor bus. It is evident, however, that roads built ten years ago (1916) were not, as a general rule, designed to meet the requirements of modern use. One of the big problems, therefore, confronting the engineer and business man of to-day, is to work out an equitable tax which

* Care, Diversified Investments, Incorporated, Kansas City, Mo.

should be charged against urban and interurban buses, so that they may pay their share toward road construction and maintenance costs.

If the public were entirely dependent on buses for transportation, the question of taxing commercial vehicles would not be so serious; but public highways are designed, built, and maintained primarily for individual use. The commercial use, therefore, presents a problem of taxation that has not yet been solved. The public should not pay an indirect obligation from which it will receive no benefit, and yet the bus should be able to continue to serve and aid in the development of community life.

It is a matter of experience that all roads wear out or deteriorate with use, thereby impairing their function in the transportation system. To overcome this, constant maintenance must be provided and replacements must be made at intervals. The traffic is responsible for the deterioration, and, hence, should pay sufficient fees and taxes to meet the annual cost of maintenance and of periodic replacements. In Missouri, all motor vehicles pay a part of this obligation through license fees, based on the horse-power of the engine, and through a gasoline tax, based on the number of gallons used. There is, however, another condition peculiar to motor buses operating for profit—they are using a roadway built at the expense of the motor-vehicle owners at large, and are making a profit out of such use; they are getting a benefit from investments in roadways out of proportion to their contribution to such investments. In addition to the regular license fees and gas tax, they should pay such proportion of the interest charge as the motor-bus traffic bears to the total traffic.

To illustrate this principle, consider as an assumed case—a road 20 miles long, costing \$35 000 per mile, and carrying 1 500 tons of traffic per day; over this road motor buses having a gross weight of 4 tons make 14 trips per day, or an equivalent of 56 tons of traffic. The motor buses, therefore, produce $\frac{56}{1\,500}$ of the traffic, and should pay interest at $4\frac{1}{2}\%$ on $\frac{56}{1\,500}$ of the cost of constructing the road, or about \$1 200 per annum.

Motor buses may be able to pay such fees if properly regulated. If they are allowed to operate promiscuously on the streets or highways, they may cause unnecessary damage and encounter such competition that they will not be able to pay their proportionate part of the construction and maintenance expenses. All motor buses, therefore, should be granted permits on the basis of a public necessity and be regulated and controlled by public service commissions.

Engineers should also give more time and study to the design of highways with reference to the economical movement of traffic. Railroads and electric lines have, in general, received much more study than the highway. The outstanding reason is that they have developed gradually over a period of years and this has given engineers a chance to study their needs and to establish economic principles, whereas the motor vehicle has developed so rapidly that engineers have been forced to overlook, in many instances, the economic location and design of roads, in order to keep traffic out of the mud.

Much has been done during the past few years in developing a type of pavement that more nearly meets the requirements of modern transportation. The heavy bus and the speed with which it is driven over the highways has done untold damage. This condition, however, is no cause for complaint against the bus or the engineer who has been directing the work of building roads. The bus has developed so rapidly that time or money would not permit the building or rebuilding of roads to meet the new requirements. It is encouraging to know, however, that the newer types of roads will withstand this modern type of transportation.

There must be developed, however, a sentiment for more uniform regulation of all modern traffic to insure economy in the design of pavements and the proper development of urban and interurban buses. The carelessness of the operator, in many instances, has developed a sentiment against the bus. While it is generally admitted that this form of transportation will continue to develop, it is also agreed that it must be regulated and properly controlled to insure its greatest usefulness.

The question of additional width of highways should be considered very seriously, especially since buses travel at a rate of 45 to 50 miles per hour. It is apparent that either the buses must be narrowed; the main roads widened; or additional routes built to meet all the requirements of modern traffic.

The answer is to build additional routes in the suburban territory rather than wider routes. The highway between Kansas City and St. Louis, which is known as the air-line route, is 26 miles shorter than the shortest railroad between these two points; it is, however, only 18 ft. in width on a 60-ft. right of way. When the system is completed these two main terminal cities will be joined by two or three other routes across the State, which will serve not only the two main terminals but all intermediate points. It is very evident, therefore, that additional routes render greater service to the public than the building of wider roads or super-highways. This does not generally apply to congested districts such as exist around Kansas City, St. Louis, and Detroit.

C. E. Smith,* M. Am. Soc. C. E.—The extent to which the local urban and interurban motor-bus and electric-railway situation has been misunderstood is well illustrated by the statement of L. F. Loree, M. Am. Soc. C. E., before the St. Louis Chamber of Commerce to the effect that an investment of about $6 000 000 000 in street and electric railways in the United States should be written off the books because the automobile has thrown these systems into the discard just as clearly as the steam railroad has superseded the stage coach of olden days. His words created quite a sensation; but few transportation experts will agree with him. They are true of some street railway tracks in the congested centers of large cities where the transportation is furnished by rapid transit lines on upper and lower levels, and of many interurban lines; but the street railway will remain the backbone of the transportation system in all other large cities.

* Vice-Pres., N. Y., N. H. & H. R. R., New Haven, Conn.

There is a big field for the motor bus. Its principal use will be for service beyond the ends of steam railroad and interurban lines into territories where it has not been economical in the past, and would not be in the future, to build and operate rail lines. This is particularly true of the suburban districts surrounding large cities.

In the past the radii of residential areas were pretty well-defined and limited by rail lines because there was no other means of mass transportation; but with the coming of the automobile those limits have been extended. With cities spread over much larger areas the density of population has been reduced. Whereas railway lines have been serving districts in which the population has been more dense, outlying residence areas to-day have from 2 to 6 people per acre. Yet these people need transportation. It will not pay to build rail lines for them, because the density of population will not support such lines.

In city service, there is need for motor-bus transportation only in coordination with established rail routes; in competition it would mean duplication of service, costing more in the long run. It is uneconomical to operate cars and trailers during the crowded hour, carrying 250 people on each train, for local service in an intermediate area; each time the car and trailer stop for one passenger the whole train is delayed. This has been necessary in the past because it has not been feasible to provide both local and express service on street car lines, but now it is possible to supplement the rail service by motor buses which will take care of the local traffic—the street to street traffic within the intermediate area—while the street cars run express, stopping only at cross-town streets.

On the whole street car traffic appears to give indications that it is "coming back"; as a matter of fact it never got very far away except in particular instances. Statistics issued by the American Electric Railway Association show that street cars to-day, and for several years past, have carried about 17 000 000 000 cash-fare passengers each year. That has not increased very much, but it has not decreased to any appreciable extent. Automobiles and motor buses have taken away the normal increase that would otherwise have used the rail lines. The future is yet uncertain. In Greater New York the rapid transit lines carry about 1 500 000 000 cash passengers per year, the street cars about 1 000 000 000, and the motor buses only about 100 000 000.

St. Louis, Mo., gives a good example of competitive systems. Its large street railway system is laid out with radial and circumferential lines on good engineering principles. There is also a motor-bus system that the promoters tried to lay out as a radial system with cross-town lines, to compete with the street railways. The street cars carry 90% of the riding public, the motor buses, 10 per cent. First the buses were put on the principal streets and took the "cream" of the traffic. They were quite profitable. Later, the bus company secured permits to operate on additional streets into territory where the street car company could not afford to put lines. With this additional service the motor buses are not paying, although the fare is 10 cents. The car fare is 7 cents, but by reason of motor-bus competition and diversion of business to automobiles the car company is taking steps to increase its fares. It is paying about 11% of its gross revenues in all sorts of public charges; the motor-bus company pays about 4%, which does not reimburse the city for the pavements the motor buses wear out. The buses do not carry their share of the peak load. The peak load on the street railway is six to eight times the base load during the day, whereas the buses provide very little more service during the peak than during the day, when there are sufficient empty seats on the cars to carry all the passengers using the buses.

The failure of the motor buses to provide peak-load service increases the peak load on the street railway line. In bad weather the uncovered double-deck motor buses have their loads cut in two, the half lost being thrown on the street railway—a bad condition during rush hours. This is being corrected gradually by the enclosure of the upper decks of the motor buses.

Street railway fares in St. Louis amount to about $1 500 000 per month. If it were possible to take off all street cars and put on enough motor buses to carry the whole load, the transportation bill would increase another $1 000 000 per month. It may be that the psychology of gas and rubber has led to the point where the public is willing to pay that much more for motor-bus transportation, but it does seem that eventually when money is not so plentiful people will look a little closer at this material difference. The same relation applies to other large cities.

One reason why the public has welcomed competitive motor-bus transportation even at higher cost, is the dissatisfaction with street railway service and strap-hanging. People have been educated by the automobile to get around more quickly. All other means of transportation have improved, while the street car, which, in St. Louis carries nearly 1 500 000 cash and transfer passengers per day—about 75% of the traveling public—does not move any faster than it did before.

Motor buses performing local service in large cities have proved a disappointment as far as speed of transit is concerned, but many people prefer them, when standing passengers are not carried and for other reasons, real or fancied. In large cities, street cars run at an average speed of about 10 miles per hour. The motor buses run about 1 mile per hour slower than the street cars in St. Louis; unless some means are found for speeding up street car and motor-bus service, people will find ways of getting around faster, and the value of street railway property will decrease as traffic is deflected.

Before it becomes necessary to provide rapid transit on other levels than the surface, frequently street car service may be accelerated. In many cities streets are being widened from 50 to 60 ft. to 100 ft. At the time a street is widened, it does not cost much more to make the width 120 or 150 ft. In streets more than 100 ft. wide cars can be operated at much higher speeds notwithstanding the crossing of other streets at grade.

A 100-ft. highway, paved the full width, is dangerous for people to cross; but if it is made wider and is divided into three parts, a roadway for traffic in each direction and a reservation in the center for street-car tracks, the danger is largely eliminated. On the other hand, where the track reservations are in streets only 100 ft. wide the side roadways—less than 30 ft.—are so narrow that other users, particularly the Fire Department, object.

The motor bus will be useful as a feeder and distributor of traffic for rapid transit lines. This combined service can be furnished in some instances at greater speed than by street cars, and unless street railway fares are kept low, the cost of rapid transit, motor-bus service will not exceed street railway service in the larger cities and, of course, will be more satisfactory in congested districts.

WINTERS HAYDOCK,* M. AM. SOC. C. E.—There is a very direct relationship between the rapidly increasing importance of bus transportation on highways and the design of those highways as traffic carriers. The large size of the bus and the high speed which it must maintain in order to fulfill its proper mission bring into prominence this relationship between inter-city bus transportation and the capacity and efficiency of the highways which the buses must use.

It is probably true that the most urgent duty of State highway departments at the present time is to obtain the greatest possible mileage of well-paved highways for the money available. However, it is obvious to any one who observes the present trend of traffic conditions on important trunk highways, and even on some of less importance, that within a short time the most important work of the engineer will be the improvement of these highways as to their traffic-carrying efficiency.

A fundamental principle of highway design, to which sufficient attention perhaps has not been given, is that no highway can be an efficient carrier of traffic in large volume if there is provision for only one lane of moving traffic in each direction. This is true because the various vehicles using any highway will necessarily and properly operate at various speeds, and if there is only one lane the slowest vehicle will set the pace or compel the faster vehicles to pass it only through the dangerous expedient of dodging into the lane of traffic moving in the opposite direction. If, however, there are two or more lanes for traffic in each direction, all vehicles may be required to keep to the right-hand lane except when passing slower vehicles. Thus, each vehicle may travel at the speed which is individually appropriate for it and the flow of traffic is made flexible and fluid through the constant ability of vehicles to weave in and out from one lane to another without ever trespassing on the part of the roadway assigned to traffic in the opposite direction.

Evidently to insure two unobstructed lanes for moving traffic on a heavily loaded highway there must be provision for stationary vehicles off the traveled section. It is not possible to prevent the stopping of vehicles. Property owners also have rights to the use of their frontage, and this often means that space along this frontage must be available for standing vehicles. Therefore, the minimum requirement for efficiency as a traffic carrier is that a highway should have not less than two lanes for unobstructed moving traffic

* Directing Engr., Dept. of City Transit, Pittsburgh, Pa.

in each direction, with provision for standing vehicles on each side and pedestrian ways.

This principle of highway design for traffic-carrying efficiency is so simple and obvious that it would scarcely seem necessary to dwell on it were it not that its importance is insufficiently realized. Highway engineers are giving only scant attention to the problem of securing sufficient right of way for trunk-line highways to permit their proper amplification at such time in the future as it becomes financially possible. They are even building long stretches of new highway on newly acquired rights of way which are too narrow for this future amplification, although they pass through open country where the increased width could be obtained at only a moderate additional expense. Along these new highways, and also along the now open parts of the old highways, new improvements and new villages will be built, which will make the future acquisition of right of way exceedingly expensive. The sooner it is realized by highway engineers that the biggest problem they will have to face in the future will be the amplification of present highways, and the sooner they undertake intensive study of the means of meeting this problem, the less will be the inevitably enormous expense involved.

John W. Reid,* M. Am. Soc. C. E.—The City of Detroit, Mich., is one of the very few of the major cities which own and operate street railway systems serving their entire cities. The Detroit City Charter, adopted in June, 1918, authorized the ownership and operation of a street railway system and the creation of a commission for that purpose.

In 1920 and 1921, the Department of Street Railways built a system consisting of 61 miles of track and 30 miles of trackage, and operated it privately under a "day to day" permit. In accordance with the terms and conditions of this permit, the Commission has taken over this system and has built some new trackage in territories annexed to the city subsequent to the city's purchase in 1922 of the properties, power plant, car houses, yards, and 273 miles of track of the privately owned street railway company. The total trackage is 400 miles with 1 590 cars operating. The fare is 6 cents with a 1-cent transfer charge.

Supplementing this service is a privately and very largely locally owned bus company, operating eight routes, with a total of 350 buses, of which 145 are of a double, and 205 of a single-deck type. The company operates on a day to day permit from the city. A 10-cent fare is charged. Many of the company's lines parallel important street railway lines. This condition has brought rather sharply to the fore the question, "Since the City is in the transportation business, should it not control and operate all types and thus eliminate competition?"

As a partial answer to this question, and also as a practical means of meeting demands for some degree of transportation in newly developed and rapidly developing areas, the Street Railway Department has established a number of bus lines. Several lines have been placed in streets having street railway service. These are operated in an effort to furnish both express and

* Commr., Dept. of Public Works, Detroit, Mich.

local service and to eliminate the "jitney." The buses are well patronized, but the "jitney" persists and in increased numbers. The question of the city's right to effect its order of more than a year ago, banishing the "jitney" from its streets, is now (1926) before the Supreme Court of the United States.

The matter of adequate highways has been very carefully worked out in connection with the Rapid Transit Commission's studies for a complete rapid transportation system. The Commission's plans contemplate subways within the 6-mile circle from the center of the city. Outside this area a system of super-highways, having a width of 204 ft. is projected, the center 84 ft. being reserved for 4-track rapid transit on the surface. On each side is 60 ft. for pedestrian and vehicle traffic. The intersecting highways, at approximately ½-mile intervals, will pass under the super-highway, thus allowing uninterrupted movement to high-speed through-traffic vehicles. Woodward Avenue, from the north city limit of Detroit to the City of Pontiac, a distance of approximately 18 miles, has been developed in this fashion during the past three years, except that intersecting highways are not separated.

Super-highways are proposed every 3 miles at right angles to one another. Intermediate 120-ft. highways will be located on each mile line and 86-ft. highways on each half mile, local service streets (so-called) being 60 ft. wide. This general plan has been adopted by the Common Council of the City of Detroit and the Wayne County Board of Supervisors as the plan toward which to work. At its 1925 session, the Michigan Legislature passed a law authorizing adjoining counties, through their Boards of Supervisors and Road Commissions, to join for the purpose of securing rights of way by dedication, purchase, or condemnation. The Counties of Wayne, Oakland and Macomb have, under this authority, acquired a very considerable mileage of such right of way by dedications.

In connection with its subway route studies, within the Six Mile Circle, the Rapid Transit Commission also developed an interior thoroughfare plan, so-called, which is a very valuable contribution to the solution of Detroit's street problem in the older and densely settled areas of the city. The older part of the city is laid out over old ribbon-like French farms, which extended back from the Detroit River from 1 to 3 miles. Uncontrolled platting of these by the original and successive owners accounts in large measure for many of the street openings, widenings, and straightenings necessary to afford a reasonably good arterial system for both transportation and traffic.

The problem of the parking of automobiles, particularly that falling in the "storage" classification, in the streets of the city, is a most serious one. It is a matter of tremendous import to both trade and traffic. The city is spending approximately $3 000 000 annually in widening existing street pavements to provide greater freedom and safety in traffic movements, but the new pavement areas thus obtained are quickly seized upon as "storage" space for automobiles. Notwithstanding this, the traffic capacity has been materially increased; but the "parking" problem is yet to be solved in Detroit, the center of the automobile industry.

Lucius S. Storrs,* Esq. (by letter).—The status of the automotive vehicle in public transportation service has been thoroughly and convincingly presented by Mr. Budd. Its true economic position will not be determined until a full realization is had of the fundamentals expressed in his conclusions.

The rapid expansion of American cities has been primarily because public transportation is available to every resident of the community. Maximum convenience and efficiency of such public transportation can be accomplished only when all such agencies are under the direct control of one able transportation group whereby the maximum efficiency of each unit can be planned with direct relation to all other such units.

The automotive vehicle presents an exceedingly valuable aid in expanding public transportation throughout an entire urban area. It performs a higher grade of service than is rendered by rail units—a kind that will attract a large portion of the public accustomed to using private means of transportation. In this way the motor bus or motor coach will serve the communities themselves by making possible a reduction in the number of private automobiles utilizing the public ways.

Anson Marston,† M. Am. Soc. C. E.—The speaker began his professional life in railway location and construction, and his memory extends back to a period when "wild cat" railways were still being promoted and sometimes constructed. Those who have never worked on a "wild cat" railway, uncertain of ever getting their pay, have missed a wonderful experience.

The railway system of the United States was not laid out originally as a National system, carefully planned. It was developed by a method of "trial and error". Roads were built in numerous instances because localities could be found that would offer attractive bonuses. Later, many such lines, or parts of lines, have had to be abandoned.

The speaker has been a member of the State Highway Commission of Iowa for 22 years and wishes to discuss motor truck and bus transportation from the standpoint of the State Highway Commission. The highways of the United States are passing through a period similar in some respects to the early stage of railway development, referred to previously. No sufficiently scientific study has yet been made of the proper design of an adequate National highway transportation system for the United States. Development of highways and of highway transportation has been, and still is, proceeding to a considerable extent by a method of trial and error. The speaker does not feel that such a method is wholly objectionable. Scientific research should, in general, proceed by a method that permits variation of technique, and even of immediate objective, from time to time, as the facts developed in the investigation may indicate to be wise.

From the standpoint of State highway departments, the present situation as to the development of motor-truck and bus transportation on the highways

* Managing Director, Am. Elec. Ry. Assoc., New York, N. Y.

† Dean of Eng., Iowa State Coll., Ames, Iowa.

is unsatisfactory. Such traffic has developed unsought, and its present chaotic condition constitutes an almost impossible situation, very much as if the electric or steam railways had to build bridges and roadbeds without knowing the kind of rolling stock or the amount of traffic to be anticipated. Even in States that have adequate legal restrictions on motor-truck and bus transportation, there is in most cases little effective enforcement of the law.

Nevertheless, the speaker adheres to the general belief that motor-truck and bus transportation is here to stay. State highway departments are intensely interested in the early development of adequate regulatory measures. Immense sums of money are being spent on the construction of permanent highways. The interests of the public require the early adoption of measures by which these costly structures can be protected against excessive damage by what, after all, constitutes only a small percentage of total highway traffic.

A study of transportation needs in Iowa indicates that there are important sections that are likely to be entirely dependent on truck and motor-bus transportation for passenger and freight traffic. Some railway branch lines have already been abandoned. In fact, in more than one instance, a State highway has been built in part upon the abandoned roadbed of a former railroad. The speaker believes that the railroads are finding it unprofitable to operate several other branch lines not yet abandoned. The longest interurban railway in Iowa is already operating motor buses for passenger transportation between different points on its line. The speaker believes that this practice is likely to extend to the steam railways in some instances.

Nevertheless, there may be a reaction in favor of street cars and railway cars, showing that they are preferred from the standpoint of convenience and safety. It may be that the present preference for motor-bus transportation is to some extent a temporary fad.

The speaker has had the opportunity, as a bystander, to observe two interesting instances of experience with motor-bus transportation as a substitute for street railway service. The first was in the case of a town of 10 000 population, where for a time a motor-bus system operated in competition with the street railways. The bus operation continued until the buses were worn out, when the company went into bankruptcy. A serious accident occurred shortly before the bankruptcy in which, by a gasoline explosion during the filling of the tank, some people were injured, and one injured passenger died. The bus company was so irresponsible that no damage suit was filed against it, but suit was brought against the gasoline filling station. After the bankruptcy of this system the street railway company secured a franchise and is operating a bus system of its own, and the combination is giving satisfaction to date.

The second instance was in the case of the City of Des Moines, which had a population of 141 441 in 1925. On account of a controversy between the electric railway company and the citizens over a franchise, the street railway entirely suspended operation, and the city was left entirely dependent on motor buses. After a comparatively short period of this experience, the franchise was voted as demanded by the street car company.

BRITTON I. BUDD,* ESQ. (by letter).—The discussion emphasizes the chief points brought out by the paper, namely, the necessity of co-ordinating motor-coach with rail service, placing the operation of buses in the hands of skilled bus transportation men, and eliminating wasteful and uneconomic duplication of service.

Developments since the paper was written have increased, rather than diminished, the evil effects of unrestricted competition and unregulated motor-coach operation. This is particularly true in interstate traffic which at this time is wholly unregulated. Regulation of a sort obtains in most States in intrastate business, but irresponsible bus operators can easily escape such regulation by laying out routes that cross State lines.

This condition presents the most serious problem to-day in interurban and interstate motor-coach transportation. Eventually, irresponsible bus companies will be forced to the wall, thus relieving a situation here and there, but others will arise to enter into competition with responsible transportation companies that are giving the public dependable service, unless regulative measures are adopted.

Several of the discussors have pointed to the damage being done to highways by buses, which do not pay their proportionate share of taxes. That is unquestionably true and is a condition likely to continue until a sane and uniform system of regulation is adopted.

* Pres., Chic., North Shore & Milwaukee R. R., Chicago, Ill.

AMERICAN SOCIETY OF CIVIL ENGINEERS
INSTITUTED 1852

TRANSACTIONS

Paper No. 1665

THE LOGGING AND LUMBERING INTERESTS OF THE PACIFIC NORTHWEST

A SYMPOSIUM*

With Discussion by Messrs. Roland H. Stock, Hugo Winkenwerder, C. S. Chapman, and Wesley Vandercook.

* Presented at the Summer Meeting, Seattle, Wash., July 14, 1926.

THE ENGINEER IN THE LUMBER INDUSTRY

By J. J. Donovan,* M. Am. Soc. C. E.

Sawing boards seems a simple task. It was in the old days of the single circular saw which replaced the primitive whip-saw and when the market was usually within the radius of one day's journey by horse from the mill. Those days are gone. Now turbines generate electricity which drives the great band-saws and the many varieties of special machines with a speed and accuracy unknown a few years ago. With the old machines went the long hours, and the mills and camps of the Northwest have had the eight-hour day for more than eight years.

Problems of Production

Lumbering is the great industry of the Pacific Northwest. The forests of Washington will last for fifty years and those of Oregon for one hundred years at the present rate of cutting, allowing nothing for new growth. The industry is here to stay—if the common sense of the engineer is applied to the problems before it is too late. What are the problems?

First.—Cutting the trees, hauling them to the mills, and sawing them into lumber without unnecessary expense or waste.

Second.—Explaining to distant markets the special value and practical use of different species and grades of lumber.

Third.—Shipping and delivering lumber from the mill to the ultimate distributor with the utmost economy.

Fourth.—Protecting the young forests in order that future generations may have fuel, implements, shelter, and clothing, such as have served man from the earliest ages.

There are many subdivisions of these four major theses, but only a few will be discussed in this paper.

Modern lumbering requires the trained mind of the civil, mechanical, electrical, and steam engineer, with skilled mechanics of many kinds, with salesmanship that grasps the need of both buyer and seller, with knowledge of the strength and life of materials. Finally, future foresters must have knowledge of silviculture and some ability to deal with the ever-present political factor.

Methods—Old and New

Until 1890 the logging on Puget Sound and along the Columbia River was almost entirely over skid-roads made by embedding maple, alder, or hemlock logs, 8 ft. long, spaced 8 ft. or less, from the shore to the forest. The logs to be hauled were barked to give a smooth riding surface; the "greaser" swabbed his skids; and six to ten pair of oxen with much straining and a wealth of picturesque language on the driver's part moved the log to the water.

* Vice-Pres., Bloedel Donovan Lumber Mills, Bellingham, Wash.

Two miles was the ordinary limit for such roads. Horses occasionally replaced the patient ox (Fig. 1), but were less reliable in mud and swamp.

Following the use of horses in logging came the small single-drum donkey engines with a "line horse" struggling through the brush from the skid-road to the log. The "line horse" hauled the line from the engine drum through an almost impassable tangle to the log that was to be hauled in. The maximum range was 300 ft. The adoption of double drums and the increased use of railways (Fig. 2) came thirty years ago (1896); but it is only ten years since a revolutionary change occurred in the handling of logs. This was the use of trees as masts (Fig. 3) with great blocks, some weighing 1 200 lb. and hung 180 ft. from the ground. The engine is run up against the tree, the main line runs through the roof to the block, and thence off to the logs. The tree or mast itself is guyed with ten or more heavy steel cables and the whole trimmed, rigged, and made ready for work with phenomenal speed by a small crew of highly skilled men.

The most picturesque figure in the woods is the "high rigger" who, with life-belt, spurs, and axe, climbs a tree to a point nearly 200 ft. from the ground, trims it, cuts off the top, hauls up blocks and lines, and ultimately rigs the tree as shown in Fig. 2. This method, used with a radius of 600 ft., immediately brought a lifting strain on the end of the log, and it came in at twice the speed of the old ground-yarding method.

Steam Is Main Power

The modern unit consists of an oil-burning boiler mounted on a heavy steel railroad car supplying steam for a duplex loading engine and a yarding engine with one main and three auxiliary drums. Each engine is arranged to run independently, yarding and loading going on simultaneously.

A good logging outfit thirty years ago cost \$25 000; to-day, it costs \$500 000. Most camps use steam generated by oil as their main power. A few use electricity. Diesel engines are in the experimental stage. Many auxiliaries are gasoline or gasoline and electric.

The latest development in logging is the heavy skidder (Fig. 4) with an articulated steel mast 100 ft. high, which, with yarding and loading engines, blocks, and lines, complete on three cars, represents an investment of \$75 000.

Such a unit can be installed with remarkable speed, the steel mast replacing the tree of the high-lead system. A tail tree, carrying the outer end of the trolley line at a distance of 1 500 to 2 000 ft., marks the radius of action. In rough ground a unit of this kind will effect a saving of about \$1 per 1 000 board-ft. over the high-lead system. This saving is due to a reduction of about 50% in railroad branches and the ability to reach into and across gulches at higher speed. This skidder system lifts the log by one end to a trolley line and then drags it to the railway.

Railway Development

Logging railways were scarce thirty years ago, and such as existed were poorly built, with 30 to 35-lb. rail. Locomotives weighed 30 to 40 tons.

To-day, the railway is the most necessary and usually the most expensive factor in logging operations. The weight of steel rail has more than doubled and that of equipment, tripled. The modern logging railway has 60 to 70-lb. steel rails, heavy geared and compound Mallet locomotives, and high-class special cars with all modern safety appliances. Special types of locomotives and cars have been developed to carry the increasing loads over the longer distances with economy and safety. On no trans-continental railway is more care used on grades and curves than on the logging railways. Fig. 5 shows a Baldwin Mallet locomotive for main-line work, which handles 24 loaded cars up a 1.5% grade. Its weight on the drivers is 90 tons.

Another type is the Climax geared locomotive (see Fig. 2) which works successfully on grades up to 8 per cent. Both engines have superheaters, which reduce the fuel consumption one-third. A typical development of a mountain side is a main line using a 6% sustained grade from the valley, a distance of more than 6 miles. Branch lines are extended from the main line on approximately parallel lines 1 200 ft. apart horizontally and from 200 to 300 ft. vertically. Thirty-six spar-trees were used on this development of 1 200 acres. Two high-lead machines and one skidder worked on this location with an average monthly output of 7 000 000 board-ft. and a cost exclusive of stumpage, taxes, overhead, and depreciation of $8 per 1 000 ft. of logs.

Primitive Bridges

To illustrate the work of the engineer in logging operations a view of the Cavanaugh Creek Bridge is submitted (Fig. 6). This structure is notable for three things:

(*a*) It is built almost entirely of timber cut on the site.

(*b*) The piling is all single length, and in some of the falsework it is 140 ft. long.

(*c*) The Howe truss is made of four single fir trees, 108 ft. long, braced properly, and was swung into place with an ordinary pile-driver. The height from rail to the water is 130 ft. The span was constructed to insure against slides up the canyon and sudden rushes of water, such as wrecked a locomotive and cost four lives only 10 miles away. The length is 1 000 ft., and the cost was $30 000.

The civil engineer has made his mark in the woods and his mechanical brother has kept pace at the mills and docks. Labor-saving devices of many kinds—package handling, conveyors, steam and electric cranes—all do their share to give the men of the Northwest the best pay and the shortest hours of any lumbermen in the world.

The necessity for application of engineering principles to the proper utilization of wood was never greater. Obsolete and expensive specifications are still used on many contracts. Much progress has been made in the standardization of certain sizes, varieties, and grades under the lead of the U. S. Department of Commerce.

With it all is the effort to eliminate waste and to use the right size and the right grade of lumber in the proper place. The testing laboratories at

Fig. 1.—Horse Logging.

Fig. 2.—Logging Railway.

Fig. 3.—Typical High Lead.

Fig. 4.—View of Modern Skidder.

Fig. 5.—Mallet Main Line Locomotive for Logging Railway.

Fig. 6.—View of Cavanaugh Creek Bridge.

Madison, Wis., under Government engineers, have rendered service of great value in proving strength, fire-resisting power, and other qualities under varying conditions. Likewise, the National Committee on Wood Utilization has done notable work in bringing together the various interests and agencies dealing with wood.

There is much ill-informed talk of a timber famine. There is more of fire dangers in wood construction which do not exist and a determined, well financed, and specious propaganda for wood substitutes. The fact remains that there is plenty of wood at prices which make it the building material for nine-tenths of the homes, and for most of the granaries, warehouses, and miscellaneous buildings of the country.

All the railway ties, a considerable amount of car, bridge, and building material of the railways, is wood and will continue to be, because it gives the best service for the money. There is no substitute for wooden ties. Close and intelligent studies of methods of logging, milling, selling, shipping, and using are being made.

Reforestation

Reforestation is largely a matter of protecting Nature in its work. The National Government set aside great areas thirty years ago. It owns more forest area in Washington than is in private hands, and nearly as much stumpage. The State also has great forest areas in trust for the schools and about $20 000 000 has been realized from sales that have been made. Washington is slowly developing a forest policy, but it still has far to go. It has more logged-off lands than any other owner. It cannot sell them because of the minimum price of $10 per acre fixed by law. These lands are usually Sections 16 and 36 in each township. They are often surrounded by private logged-off lands, some of which are reverting to the State for taxes.

Private reforestation is impossible economically under the existing law. Even with better laws the inducement is small. The State should survey and grade its logged-off lands, sell all that will bring the minimum price of $10 per acre for agriculture and grazing, and buy adjacent lands more suitable for forests for a maximum price of, say $5 per acre, and develop and protect the young forests which fifty years hence will have value. Some exchanges with private owners may be possible as has already been effected by the State with the National Government.

Co-Operate for Forest Protection

There is need of close co-operation between National, State, and private owners of timber for fire protection and reforestation. There is better understanding to-day than ever before and fire protection is especially good. The proper building up of State forests has only begun, not only in Washington, but in many other States. Private forests cannot survive in many States under the existing laws and are capable of giving financial return at present only as pulp producers in conjunction with paper mills.

It is well to remember that in 1907 the country produced and used 45 000 000 000 board-ft. of lumber; that in 1925 this fell to 35 000 000 000, and that per capita consumption fell from more than 500 to 300 board-ft. Further, it is significant that all the soft woods exist in great abundance and at low prices, and that engineers who produce and sell these woods ask their brethren in the Engineering Profession to remember that wood is economically available for many classes of construction and often has special advantages worthy of careful consideration.

LOGGING RAILROADS

By Walter J. Ryan,* M. Am. Soc. C. E.

This paper gives a brief description of the location, construction, and operation of logging railroads, in comparison with standard railway practice, and shows the relationship between the railroad and the logging operation that it serves. It tells of the work of the engineer in connection with logging railroads and points out a field for further usefulness.

The primary function of a logging railroad is the transportation of logs from woods to saw-mill. This service was originally performed by teams of oxen that dragged the logs over poles laid across the roads as shown in Fig. 7. The modern logging railroad has progressed a long way toward standard railway practice, but it still bears some of the characteristics of this ancestor, the "skid-road".

Logging Engineering

The first logging railroads were built without any technical engineering. This is well illustrated by Fig. 8, which shows an early type of crib bridge. It was part of the duty of the logging superintendent to locate his railroads, and he had little time or opportunity to plan further ahead than the section in which he was working. These roads were extended from year to year, until the easy country was logged off or some serious obstacle to further progress was encountered. About this time, locating engineers were called in to solve the difficulties, and the original lines had to be abandoned and new lines built to reach the tracts of timber farther back. These engineers were given no opportunity to learn the requirements of the logger and many times the results were not satisfactory. There finally came a realization of the fact that an engineer was required who understood logging. The Pacific Logging Congress, in 1912, began an active campaign for "the creation of the profession of Logging Engineering as a distinct branch of mechanical science". As a result of this effort, the Western universities have established courses and are graduating classes each year with a degree in Logging Engineering.

The larger companies now maintain Engineering Departments, and there are a number of engineering firms that do all such work for their clients, usually the smaller operators who do not feel justified in maintaining an engineer in continuous employment. There are many parts of the logging operation in which an engineer is called upon to assist, but the principal part of his duty consists in the location of railroads.

Relationship of Railroads to Logging

The object of logging railroad location is not to provide a route through a territory or to connect two definite points, but to serve a given area with a

* Civ. Engr., Weyerhaeuser Timber Co., Tacoma, Wash.

network of rails. Any part of a tract of timber that is not within "yarding distance" of a railroad is in the same position as a piece of land above the ditch on an irrigation project. This "yarding distance" is the distance that it is economical to bring logs from the stump to the "landing" where they are loaded on cars. It varies from 600 to 3 000 ft. with different types of logging equipment in use. Thus, the spacing of the railroads will vary from ¼ mile to 1 mile.

It is the relationship between the cost of logging by different methods and the cost of the railroad, that determines the type of logging equipment best suited to each situation. As railroad construction becomes more difficult, more expense is justified for logging equipment and labor to give longer yarding.

Every phase of railroad construction and operation is intimately connected with the logging which it is to serve, and a reconnaissance for a railroad is incomplete unless it covers a study of the area from the point of view of logging as well as of railroading. The modern timber cruiser, after examining a tract of timber land, makes a detailed report of the timber that he finds, by species and grade, and prepares a contour map of the area. These cruisers' maps are made by pacing distances and by measuring elevations with an aneroid barometer. The maps are usually on a scale of about 6 in. to the mile, with contour intervals of from 25 to 100 ft. The U. S. Geological Survey has mapped part of the timbered area of the Western States, but there are some districts of which there are no maps worthy of the name.

The maps available are made the basis of preliminary study, but most operators recognize the value of an accurate contour map so that the reconnaissance survey usually takes the form of a mapping party. Well made maps, with accurate cruises of the timber, allow the operation to be planned so that the railroads can be built in the proper location for economical logging, with the minimum of cost.

Logging Railroad Location

When the logging railroad leaves the timber and is built for some distance to a log dump at the mill or rafting ground, the selection of a route does not differ from that for standard railway or highway practice, except that controlling rates of grade and curvature may have been determined by conditions in the timber (Fig. 9). This route to the timber and one or more lines through the tract make up the main line over which full trains are handled. Grades as high as 4% and curves as sharp as 24° are used on these main lines, and the construction cost runs as high as $50 000 per mile.

Branches and spurs serve the logging, and from these the loaded cars are switched by lighter locomotives. Geared locomotives permit the use of curvature as sharp as 40° and grades of 6% on these spurs. Where timber is still out of reach, inclines are used.

The field work of location is usually done with small parties of from three to six men. A transit or compass preliminary line is run, often with an axeman, a chainman, and an instrumentman, using a 500-ft. tape and setting

Fig. 7.—Oxen Dragging Fir Log, 14 Feet in Diameter, on a Skid-Road.

Fig. 8.—Early Type of Crib Bridge, for Logging Railroad.

Fig. 9.—View Showing Logging Railroad Near Foot of Mt. Baker, Washington.

Fig. 10.—Frame Trestle of Logging Railroad Erected by "Sky Line."

stakes at 100-ft. stations. The same party runs levels and takes topography. A center line projected from this preliminary line may be run in the field or simply staked by offsets. A small party can do the locating and look after the construction of 10 or 15 miles of road per year. This proves more satisfactory than employing a larger party on intermittent work.

Logging Railroad Construction

Clearing the right of way is often the most expensive part of the railroad construction. Much road has been built with no other power than dynamite, where stumps and logs up to 10 ft. in diameter were to be removed. Horses and steam-logging "donkey" engines have been used for the clearing. Recently, gasoline "donkeys" and tractors have come into use. If power shovels or drag-lines are used for the grading, the same machine often does the "chunking out".

Culverts are usually built of logs. Where long life is required, Western red cedar or redwood is used, as these woods resist decay almost completely under the conditions found in most culverts.

Until recently, the grading was done largely by hand. The only power commonly used was a drag scraper pulled by a logging engine. A limited use is made of large steam shovels. Nowadays, the small revolving power shovel or dragline, on crawler treads, is doing a large portion of the work. If the range of the machine is sufficient it is common practice to waste the material from the cuts and to borrow for the fills. The shovel runner and his helper may constitute the entire grading crew and the finishing may be left for the crew that lays the track. Where it is necessary to haul the excavated material, it is customary to use car and track, although auto-trucks are used to some extent.

The construction of bridges has shown more variation from standard railway practice than any other feature of logging railroads. The bridges that were built on the skid-roads of "bull-team" days were cribs of logs with a solid deck. The first railroads were laid over this same type of bridge (Fig. 8) with ballast under the ties. The logs in these bridges were seldom salvaged; this fact made the cost excessive when timber became of greater value. Framed trestles (Fig. 10) and pile trestles, as now used, show wide variations in design.

Pile trestles 100 ft. or more in height are frequently built. Where the ground allows little or no penetration for piling, the sticks are set, butt down, on the rock or hardpan and held in place by the driver until capped and braced. Piling as long as 100 ft., with a top diameter of 14 in., has been used in this manner.

The trestle over Cedar River Canyon (Fig. 11) is a good example of a high pile structure. This was built in two decks with Douglas fir timbers of 120 ft. and 80 ft. in length. In all, more than 500 pieces of piling and 400 000 board-ft. of sawed lumber were used, all obtained near-by. The height of 203 ft. is claimed to be the record for high timber trestles.

Pile trestles are built of material cut at the site, when it is available in suitable sizes; the caps and stringers are hewn to size and small poles are used for bracing. Fig. 12 shows such a trestle, with a log span near the center. In many stands of timber, there are no trees suitable for bridge material, and it is necessary to haul timber in by rail from the saw-mill or another part of the operation. Pile trestles are very cheaply constructed when suitable material is available on the ground. For many years, some companies built spurs entirely on trestle as they found it to cost less than grading and ballast.

Sawn timbers with depths of as much as 48 in. are available and are suitable for spans up to 40 ft. Logs are used as girders for spans as long as 50 ft., without any form of truss. Spans of 100 ft. have been built by placing a solid deck of logs on falsework and laying ties about 20 ft. in length on top of this deck. Two additional large logs are placed on top of the ties, one on each side of the bridge. The cap of the falsework is bolted through the logs above and below the ties to act as a floor-beam, and the whole structure is laced together with wire cable. On high trestles, these log spans may be used to give channel clearance and to support frame bents (Fig. 10) to carry the deck.

An overhead cableway is often used in the erection of high trestles as shown in Fig. 10. The cable is stretched above the site of the structure and on or near the center line. The cableway is used to deliver material and, in case of a framed structure, to raise the bents. Wire rope up to 2 in. in diameter is usually available around a logging operation. With the use of a logging "donkey" for power, it is possible to design such a cableway for very heavy loads. Wooden Howe trusses, steel girders, and steel trusses are in use. Their design and construction conform to standard railroad practice.

Tunnels have been built on some logging railroads and are usually timber-lined. The only variation from standard practice has been the wider section sometimes adopted to provide clearance for wide loads, due to knots or limbs on the logs. Some standard roads have refused to accept logs for haul over lines with tunnels, but there have been few accidents reported from this cause.

Track

Track laying is usually done from a push-car or from cars handled by a locomotive. A car is arranged so that the rails may be placed on the floor or bunks and the ties piled on the same car, on timbers, to hold them clear of the rail. The ties are rolled off the end of the car and the rail pulled out and placed by hand. Track-laying machines are used by some companies. These are built with an overhead trolley supported on a truss and extending about 20 ft. in front and 50 ft. behind the car on which the machine is built. The rails are piled on the floor under the machine, and two cars of ties follow behind. The ties are handled in bundles and delivered in the center of the grade ahead of the machine. When they are in place, the

FIG. 11.—TRESTLE OVER CEDAR RIVER CANYON BUILT OF OLD GROWTH DOUGLAS FIR.

Fig. 12.—View Showing Pile Trestle with Log Span, for Logging Railroad.

Fig. 13.—Logging Railroad: View Showing Skeleton Log Cars Loaded with Fir Timber.

rail is delivered and held by tongs until swung into position. The rails are held by bridles until the train has gone ahead. Spiking is done by a crew in the rear.

The ties are usually from local timber, hewn in the woods to the thickness of 6 in. If the work is directly connected with a saw-mill, sawn ties are frequently used in sections from 6 by 8 in. to 7 by 9 in.

Good ballast is almost an essential along the west slope of the Cascades. Gravel is used where available. Sometimes it is purchased on cars and delivered by the standard railroads. Most companies have ballast pits at one or more places on their properties and load into center-dump cars. The cars are loaded by shovels, draglines, scrapers, grab buckets, and other devices.

The most common weight of rail is 60 lb. per yd.; some of lighter section is in use and a few roads are adopting a heavier type. Re-lay rail, purchased from the standard railroads, has been used almost entirely, although some foreign rail and a little American-rolled new rail have been laid.

The sharp curves usually make necessary some lateral support for the track. Rail-braces are used for this purpose, and, on some roads, tie-plates alone hold the rail. When it is necessary to put locomotives with unflanged drivers around the very sharp curves, five rails are used, two inner guard-rails and a rail outside the track rail on the inside of the curve.

Creeping rail presents a serious problem to logging railroads. The loaded traffic is all in one direction, usually down grade. The common practice has been to allow the rail to creep and to place "points" in the track to prevent buckling. The gaps that occur are filled with "Dutchmen", and the broken angle-bars replaced. Some effort has been made to hold the track by driving piling in front of long ties and by tying the track to stumps with pieces of cable. Rail anchors have proved successful in some instances and are coming into more general use.

Train Equipment

The cars originally used for hauling logs were separate trucks equipped with log bunks. The ends of the log are placed on a pair of these disconnected trucks and these loads connected into trains. With light logs, the load is sometimes fastened to the bunk with chains, but in the fir district there is seldom anything to hold the trucks together except the weight of the logs on the bunk. Hand brakes are provided on each truck.

In order to allow the use of the air brakes, these trucks are connected into skeleton cars (Fig. 13) by means of a center sill that carries the air cylinder and brake equipment. These skeleton cars are built in lengths up to 70 ft. The standard railroads are building some skeleton cars, although most of the logs that they haul are loaded on standard "flats", provided with log bunks on the deck.

All the Western States have safety requirements governing the construction and operation of logging railroads, but these requirements are not as stringent as those for common carrier roads and allow the operation of trains without air on the cars. A skeleton car for common carrier roads is built with platforms on the ends and a wider walkway from end to end.

A geared locomotive is commonly used for short hauls and switching. These machines are built in weights of 40 to 90 tons, all on the drivers. For longer haul, a direct-connected locomotive is used, the most popular type being the Mikado 2-8-2. For service on heavy grades, these locomotives are built with tanks for oil and water on the locomotive. The Mallet type is becoming popular and gives the advantage of a heavier unit with light wheel loads (see Fig. 5). The Mallet type locomotives in use in the woods are much lighter than those built for standard service and are frequently built with saddle tanks.

Train Operation

Oil is the fuel most favored. The fire risk is much less with an oil-burning locomotive and this, with the saving in time and labor in handling, justifies its use, although the cost is higher than for coal or wood. Gasoline locomotives are built for light service, but are seldom used for hauling logs. Some logs are being handled by electric lines, and one logging railroad has adopted Diesel electric power.

The train length is usually limited to about 30 cars. The speed seldom exceeds 20 miles per hour with loads; but due to the short hauls and the facility with which cars are loaded and unloaded, it is not unusual to have a record of daily car loading in excess of the number of cars in use. The service is very severe on cars. Logs often drop from the tongs on to the cars, and rough track and frequent derailments make car repairs a large element in the cost of operation. This cost is much less with the log trucks and skeleton cars than it is with standard flat cars.

Train despatching is conducted by telephone and is usually very simple. Most companies have a man who gives all, or part of, his time to keeping the position of trains and directing their movements. Train crews are smaller than on common carrier roads and the labor cost of hauling is less.

All these factors combine to make the operation of the logging railroads cheaper than that of common carriers. The rates on common carrier roads have recently been increased in the State of Washington to a point where many of the loggers feel that they can build and operate their own roads more cheaply than they can pay freight. This is resulting in the extension of some roads to the mills or to tide-water. The logging roads are always being extended into more remote territory as the timber is cut. Of the track of a logging railroad, from 20 to 60%, is laid on temporary spurs that are in use only a few months and then removed.

The Field for Logging Engineering

In the Pacific Coast District, there are more than 6 000 miles of logging railroad in operation. The total is increasing about 5% per year. The annual replacement of spurs probably amounts to more than 25% of the total mileage. This makes the total length of railroad built annually about 2 000 miles, which is about one-half as much as the average annual construction of all the Class I railroads for additional main lines, yards, and sidings, during the decade, 1915-25.

The railroad cost is often as much as 40% of the total logging cost and probably totals more than $30 000 000 per year in the Pacific Coast District, yet there is very little either in construction, operation, or maintenance that can be called standard practice.

The economics of railroad location, as applied to logging railroads, has received no study that is entitled to be called scientific. The problem is difficult, but the increasing magnitude of the industry would justify the expenditure of a large amount of effort in its solution. Accurate cost data on every part of the cost of logging, as well as of railroading, are the first requisite of such a study.

The wide variation in natural conditions and operating methods makes it difficult to formulate rules, and the rapid progress in the development of new equipment and logging methods soon renders old data obsolete. The principles that will cover all conditions must be basic and will require time studies of many features of the work.

Conclusion

The practice that now prevails is remarkably efficient. It has been the survival of the fittest and is a result of the good judgment and experience of a group of men who are typical of the best that American industry has produced. With such a background, there is every incentive for the engineer to carry on, and the next few years should see Logging Engineering entitled to a high rank in the profession.

SKYLINE METHODS USED FOR LOGGING

By K. Berger,* Esq.

The logging industry as a whole, not only employs a great number of engineers, but develops men faster along engineering lines than any other business. It does not necessarily follow that all engineers may become successful loggers or that all loggers are engineers, but it is necessary for the logger, in order to be successful, to develop quick and sound judgment along engineering lines, whether trained in the Engineering Profession or not. It is interesting to note the ingenious ways and means devised, in order to get results with the least amount of equipment which is always inaccessible and often inadequate, except wire rope, which is one of the most important requirements. The ever-present wire rope in the woods is no doubt responsible for the varied methods utilized for the transportation of logs, the most important of which are briefly explained.

North Bend System

Of the various skyline systems now used for logging purposes, the North Bend system is the best known. The chief reason for its extensive use even up to the present is its simplicity (both as regards rigging and machinery for operation), and its usefulness for yarding, as well as for swing, that is, hauling loads of logs between two definite points.

With this system any double-drum machine may be used, as there are only two operating lines, the main or hauling line and the haulback line. A tight skyline is used, that is, a track cable is put up permanently for that particular setting. The simple carriage is equipped with double-track sheaves and a sheave in the bottom of the carriage. The hauling line is fastened and a fall-block is used to run on it. The chokers are fastened to the lower part of the carriage to this block, as is also the haulback line which runs out and through the haulback block. The haulback block is placed where the turn (the load of logs brought in) is to to be hooked on, then in and on to the haulback drum. The main or hauling line leads from the carriage through the fall-block and on to the hauling drum on the engine. The idea of the skyline is to lift the end of the turn to clear all obstructions or to carry the turn entirely suspended in the air while it is being hauled in, as well as to guide it and make inhaul easier.

The North Bend system is suitable only on even up-hill ground, as the lifting of the turn is dependent on the retarding strain on the haulback line, which, of course, must be paid out as fast as the turn is hauled in (Fig. 14). On a down-hill setting, the retarding strain on the haulback line would generate too much heat on the brake in order to lift the turn sufficiently to clear obstructions (Fig. 15). For that reason, in yarding down hill, the hauling line is fastened in the block and is led over the lower sheave in the carriage

* Chf. Engr., Washington Iron Works, Seattle, Wash.

and then through the fall-block, thus giving block purchase for lifting the load and correspondingly decreasing the strain on the haulback brake.

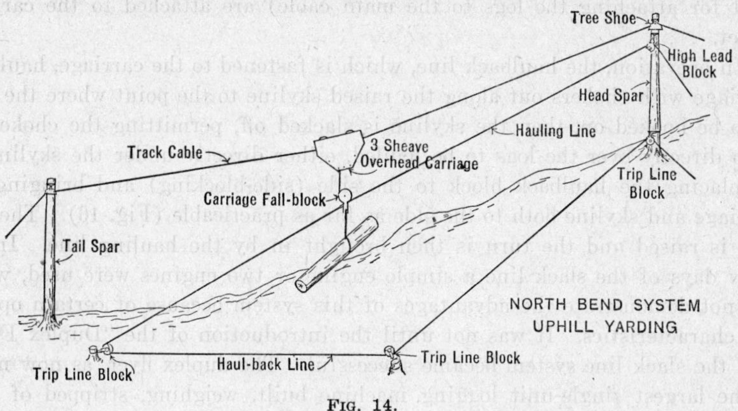

FIG. 14.

Modifications of rigging include fastening the end of the hauling line in the carriage, then leading it through the fall-block and through the lower sheave in the carriage. To keep the carriage in position while unloading, some sort of latch is utilized which serves to engage the carriage and hold it in place while slack is paid out for releasing the load.

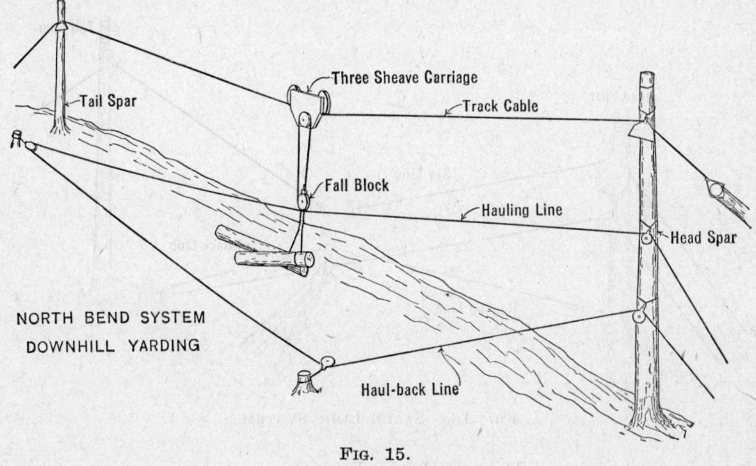

FIG. 15.

SLACK LINE SYSTEM

Until recently this system, first developed and operated in 1908, has not been used as extensively as the North Bend system. Although it is quite simple, as regards the number of lines used, it requires a somewhat larger and more complete special engine. With present-day machinery, it is one of the fastest logging systems in use, both for yarding and swinging. The skyline, instead of being permanently tightened, as in the North Bend system, is raised and lowered with each turn by a separate engine. Hauling and haulback lines control the travel of the carriage with its load. The chokers (pieces of wire rope with eye-splices on one end and hooks on the other end which are used for attaching the logs to the main cable) are attached to the carriage direct.

In operation, the haulback line, which is fastened to the carriage, hauls the carriage with chokers out along the raised skyline to the point where the turn is to be hooked on, then the skyline is slacked off, permitting the chokers to drop directly over the logs to be hauled, either directly under the skyline, or by placing the haulback block to the side (side-blocking) and bringing the carriage and skyline both to the side as far as practicable (Fig. 16). The skyline is raised and the turn is then brought in by the hauling line. In the early days of the slack line a simple engine or two engines were used, which did not demonstrate the advantages of this system because of certain operating characteristics. It was not until the introduction of the "Duplex Flyer" that the slack line system became successful. The duplex flyer, as now made, is the largest single-unit logging machine built, weighing, stripped of lines and water, as much as 130 000 lb. Two sets of engines take steam from a common boiler and are built on a common base. One set is used for operating the skyline, the other set for hauling, haulback, straw line, that is, a light line used for handling changes of haulback line block, and sometimes a transfer line, a heavy line for handling changes of track cable or hauling line. The engines as built are controlled entirely by air.

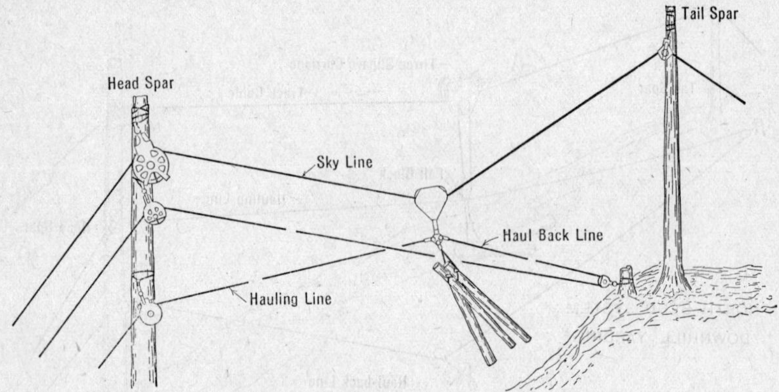

FIG. 16.—SLACK-LINE SYSTEM.

DOUBLE SLACK-LINE SYSTEM

This method (Fig. 17), in operation and rigging, is similar to the single slack-line system, only as regards hauling and haulback lines. The skyline, instead of being fastened at the tail spar-tree, used at the outer end of the track cable, as in the single slack-line system, is led through a block at the tail spar-tree, and each end is wound on a separate drum on the engine. This permits the use of a lighter skyline and gives two speeds on the skyline inhaul. One drum may be held under brake while the other is engaged for winding in the line. This gives one speed. If both skyline drums are engaged at the same time, the speed will be doubled and, consequently, the pull halved. This system has been used successfully for spans more than a mile in length.

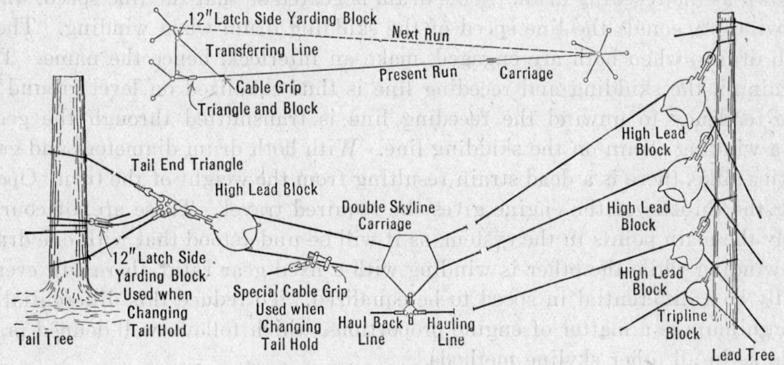

FIG. 17.—DOUBLE SLACK-LINE SYSTEM.

INTERLOCKING SKIDDER SYSTEM

This is one of the oldest systems. A tight skyline and a carriage equipped with two track sheaves, one slack-puller sheave, and a block known as the depending block (fall-block), are used (Fig. 18). The skidding line leading from the skidding drum on the engine is run through a block in the spar-tree and then through the depending block on the carriage. Another line, the

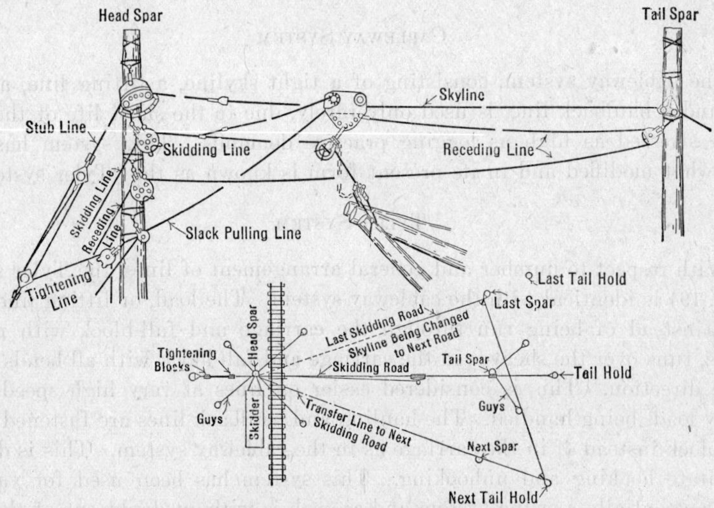

FIG. 18.—INTERLOCKING SKIDDER SYSTEM.

slack puller, is fastened to the skidding line some distance back from the block and runs through the slack-puller sheave on the carriage and in through another block on the spar-tree and on to a drum, the slack puller. The part of the skidding line from the point where the slack puller is attached to the end where the chokers are fastened, is called the tong line. The haulback or receding line, as it is called, on the skidder is fastened in the carriage and runs out to or near the tail spar-tree and returns to the drum on the engine, known as the receding drum. This drum is geared so that the line speed, when unwinding, equals the line speed of the skidding drum when winding. These two drums, when both are engaged, make an interlock, hence the name. The strain on the skidding and receding line is thus equalized on level ground as the tendency to unwind the receding line is transmitted through the gears to a winding strain on the skidding line. With both drum diameters and gear ratios alike, there is a dead strain resulting from the weight of the turn. Opening the throttle of the engine gives the required travel. These are, of course, only the main points in the system, as it will be understood that with one drum unwinding while the other is winding with a fixed gear ratio, there will eventually be a differential in speed to be equalized. To reduce this differential to a minimum is a matter of engine proportions, which follows well-defined practice as in all other skyline methods.

Another way of obtaining an equalized interlock line speed is to use two gypsy spools of the same diameter and arranged to be interlocked for handling skidding and receding lines, which are wound in opposite directions around the spools. These spools are independent of the skidding and receding drums, which are not geared for interlock. The line pull is imparted from whichever drum happens to be winding. The other drum is left to unwind with just sufficient strain on the brake to keep the line from sliding on the spool. Interlocking skidders are used both for yarding and swinging.

Cableway System

The cableway system, consisting of a tight skyline, a lifting line, a hauling and a haulback line, is used only rarely, due to the short life of the lines when stressed as high as logging practice demands. This system has been somewhat modified and in its present form is known as the "Tyler system."

Tyler System

With respect to number and general arrangement of lines, the Tyler system (Fig. 19) is identical with the cableway system. The load, or lifting line, however, instead of being run through the carriage and fall-block with reverse bends, runs over the sheaves in the carriage and fall-block with all bends in the same direction. This is considered easier on lines at very high speeds with heavy loads being handled. The hauling and haulback lines are fastened in the fall-block instead of in the carriage as in the cableway system. This is done to facilitate hooking and unhooking. This system has been used for yarding, but is essentially a swing system and as such is without doubt one of the most efficient for this purpose.

Dunham System

This new yarding method has only been in use a few years and has proved its worth in short yarding settings. The engine for operating need not be specially built for the purpose, although with such an engine, the usefulness

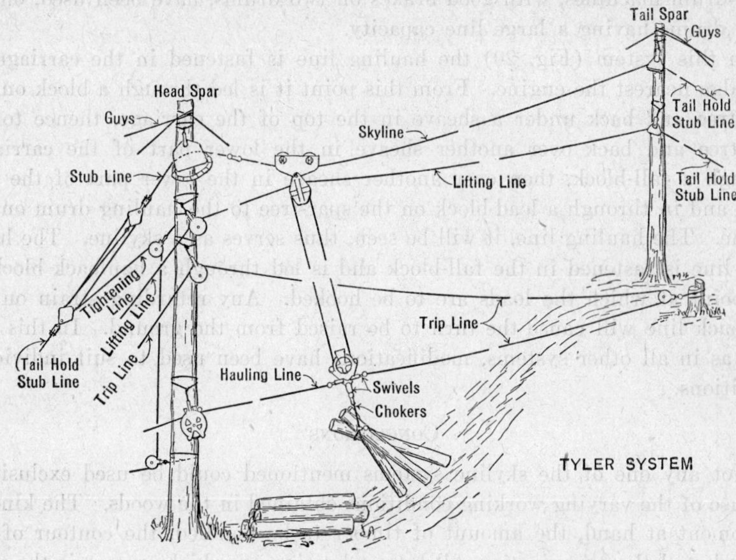

FIG. 19.

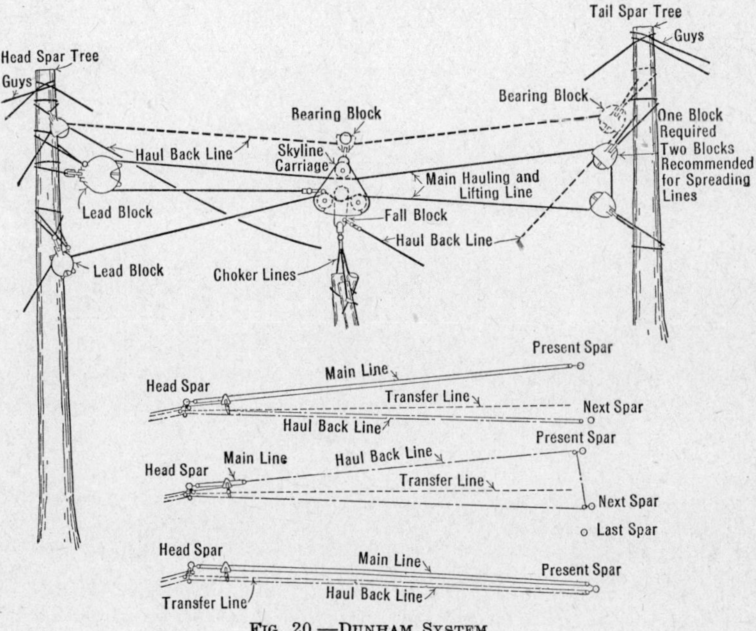

FIG. 20.—DUNHAM SYSTEM.

of the system would be extended considerably. To the present only simple three-drum machines, with good brakes on two drums, have been used, one of these drums having a large line capacity.

In this system (Fig. 20) the hauling line is fastened in the carriage on the edge nearest the engine. From this point it is led through a block on the spar-tree and back under a sheave in the top of the carriage, thence to the tail tree and back over another sheave in the lower part of the carriage; through a fall-block, then over another sheave in the lower part of the carriage and in through a lead-block on the spar-tree to the hauling drum on the engine. The hauling line, it will be seen, thus serves as a skyline. The haulback line is fastened in the fall-block and is led through a haulback block at the point at which the loads are to be hooked. Any retarding strain on the haulback line will cause the turn to be raised from the ground. In this system, as in all other systems, modifications have been used to suit individual conditions.

Conclusions

Not any one of the skyline systems mentioned could be used exclusively because of the varying working conditions obtained in the woods. The kind of equipment at hand, the amount of timber to be handled, the contour of the ground, and the organization, all have a bearing on which system is the most economical to use. Radical improvements in the equipment for handling any one system may eliminate others, but there would still be conditions justifying the use of most systems.

LOGGING FLUMES

By Ulysses B. Hough,* Esq.

For some years the writer has been interested in the transporting of white pine logs, mining timber, and cedar poles from their place of production in Idaho, Washington, and British Columbia, to the place of manufacture and shipment to Eastern markets. Two methods have been used for transporting where such distances as 20 to 100 miles are necessary: First by the use of natural streams having sufficient water to float timber at all seasons of the year; and, second, by railroads, the former being much cheaper but not always available.

Methods of Transportation.—In using either method of transportation—by water or by rail—the products must be gathered to some central point of loading. Various means are used for this, such as hauling by sleighs in winter, the use of trucks in summer, V-shaped flumes, and sliding or trailing chutes in which two logs are placed side by side and the top hewn to form a flat V, the logs sliding by gravity on the heavy grades and being hauled over the lighter grades by horses, caterpillar tractors, or donkey engines.

Water Supply.—The writer early saw the value of the V-shaped flumes, as much of the country is rough and rolling and well supplied with small streams. Some streams afford an abundant supply of water at all seasons of the year for transporting timber, whereas others have so small a flow that impounding dams are necessary to store water for flood periods. A very insignificant stream affording only 2 to 5 sec-ft., if impounded for 2 to 12 hours, will afford an abundant supply of water to transport 100 000 to 200 000 ft. of timber many miles each day. Although the initial cost of the flumes is great, the cost of upkeep and operation is so low that it becomes a very attractive means of transporting timber.

Construction Methods.—The usual method of constructing these flumes is shown in Fig. 21. The sides are placed 45° from the vertical, forming a V, with an opening of 90 degrees. Various angles have been tried for this opening, but 90° requires the least water for floating the timber and affords a ready relief in event of jams, by increasing the quantity of water, thereby affording a greater carrying surface. A three-cornered piece, formed by splitting a 6 by 6-in. timber cornerwise, is placed at the bottom of the V to economize in the use of water and afford strengthening as well. The yokes or ribs of the flume are spaced 4 ft. on centers, and these, in turn, are supported by stringers 16 ft. long. A walk is usually provided to afford easy inspection of the inside of the flumes and access to any jam that may occur. Fig. 21 shows by circles up to 36 in., how little water is required to move the timber. Advantage of this is taken in branch flumes where only 4 000 000 to 10 000 000 ft. of timber is to be removed to the main line. Although the logs may drag heavily, causing excessive wear, the flume will last through the operation which is all that is desired.

* Cons. Engr., Spokane, Wash.

Hugus Creek Flume.—To show more fully the use of these flumes and afford a basis of costs the writer will describe the flume built by him on Hugus Creek, near St. Joe, Idaho, for the Winton Lumber Company. This flume, known as the main-line flume, is 7 miles long, with three branches, 1, 1½, and 1¾ miles long, respectively. The main Hugus Creek has a flow of only 8 sec-ft. at low stage, making impounding dams necessary. This dam is large enough to hold water for a 1-hour flood. As much as 100 000 ft. of timber is removed in 40 min. to the St. Joe River, where it floats to the mill at St. Joe, about 9 miles below.

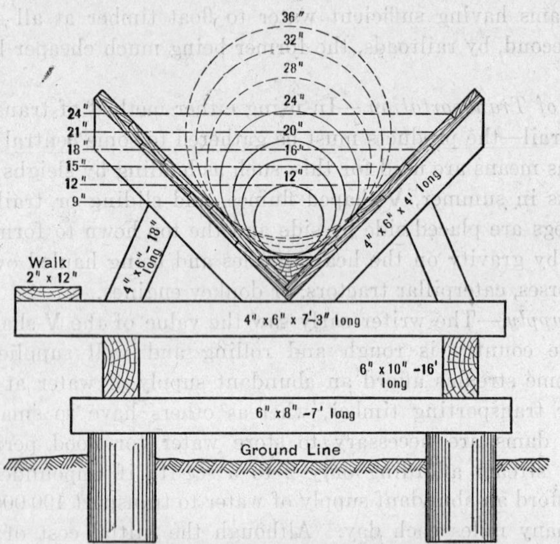

FIG. 21.—SECTION SHOWING METHOD OF CONSTRUCTING LOGGING FLUMES.

Use of Flume in Dry Gulches.—The three branch flumes were built in nearly dry gulches so that the rains in the fall and the melting snow and rain in the spring had to be relied upon for removing the crop. Dams were built at the head of each flume, by the same method as that used on the main-line flume. The 1-mile flume had about 14 000 000 ft. of timber tributary to it and 7 000 cedar poles, all of which were removed in two seasons with no trouble. The 1½-mile flume had no water that would resemble a creek in the summer season, but 4 000 000 ft. of timber and 4 000 cedar poles were removed in one season. The logs were decked along the flume during the fall and winter and were removed the following spring in a few days. The 1¾-mile flume had 7 000 000 ft. of logs and 4 000 poles which were removed in two seasons. This gulch had a set of logging camps and the water supply was not enough to supply the camps the entire season, yet, 7 000 000 ft. of timber were removed at a cost far below any other method that could have been used.

Size of Flume.—The timber of this part of the country is generally small, 10 to 11 logs to 1 000 board-ft., although some logs in the upper part of the main line were 4 ft. in diameter. A flume with 4-ft. sides was selected for

Fig. 22.—Logging Flume from 30% to 9% Grade.

Fig. 23.—Long Radius Curve in Logging Flume.

the main line, 3½-ft. for the 1-mile line, and 3-ft. for the other two. All flumes are lined with 1-in., rough material doubled. Small saw-mills of capacities of 10 000 to 15 000 ft. per day were located along the main line, 2 and 2½ miles apart, for cutting the material. The flume was started at each mill and the water of the stream diverted into it, the construction material being floated to place from day to day as the work advanced, no material however, being allowed to get on the ground after leaving the mill. Only such timber as spruce, red and white fir, and tamarack were used in the construction. The average progress per day was 320 ft., the greatest in one month being 8 000 ft. The branch flumes being smaller, greater progress was made; as much as 640 ft. was placed in 1 day and 400 ft. was an ordinary day's work.

Power.—Steam was used for power in some of the small saw-mills and in others gasoline engines were used, with the result that gas has proved the cheaper, although the gasoline was brought in on muleback or pack train and cost on the ground $0.30 per gal. Two elements entered into the use of gasoline: First, the fire risk which is almost negligible; and, second, the inaccessibility of the territory in which such flumes are used. As these flumes are often built in countries that have no wagon roads, simply pack trails, the mill and engine can be taken apart, loaded on muleback, packed to the place, and re-assembled. The writer has built one flume in which the plant has been moved 20 miles in this way. The gasoline used was 2¼ gal. per 1 000 ft. of lumber cut.

Allowable Grades.—The grades of flumes vary, being 1% at the discharge end and as high as 16% in some parts of the main line. One of the branches has a 22% grade for 800 ft. As a rule, 3 to 6% grades are used. What the limiting grades of a flume should be is a question; the writer has used as high as 40% with satisfactory results. Care should be taken in the transition from one grade to the other to use long vertical curves. Although it is desirable to use as little change in grade as possible, this particular flume was intended to receive timber nearly its entire length and, therefore, had to be located on the lowest ground and near to the ground, in order that the object for which it was being built might not be defeated, namely, moving timber cheaply. Too much money should not be expended in getting timber into it.

Curvature.—Curves should be of as long radius as possible to prevent wear on the sides of the flume, 10° being the maximum used in this construction. Poles 60 to 70 ft. long pass these curves with no trouble. Fig. 22 shows a change in grade from 30% to 9% in a V-type flume and Fig. 23 illustrates the use of long radius curves in such flume.

Heavy Grades.—These flumes on heavy grades are often spoken of as "wet chutes", but the timber, traveling faster than the water by 10 to 12%, plows the water out of the flume to some extent, and, at the same time, piles it up and rides on top of it, preventing the heavy wear that occurs in wet chutes or slides.

Handling Timber to Flume.—It is often desirable to place timber in the pond formed by the impounding dam. Part of these logs can be sluiced through when the water has flowed out so that the flume will not overflow at full-gate opening. A bear-trap gate placed in the sluiceway up stream from the sluice-gate is more convenient, and enables the sluicing of logs during the entire flood. The shorter leg of the bear-trap is placed up stream so as to control the flow of water at full head, the longer leg forming a guiding apron for the passage of logs and water to the floor of the sluice below. This trap is hinged at its upper end to the sluiceway floor and the cables attached to the apex hinge-pin pass to a winch on the top of the dam. It is better practice, however, to place the timber in the flume below the dam, and if a constant flow of water is available to dispose of it as fast as received. Otherwise, the timbers are decked alongside so that advantage may be taken of periodical floods or splashes.

Fig. 24 shows the number of logs that will pass through the flume per hour for various depths of water and grades.

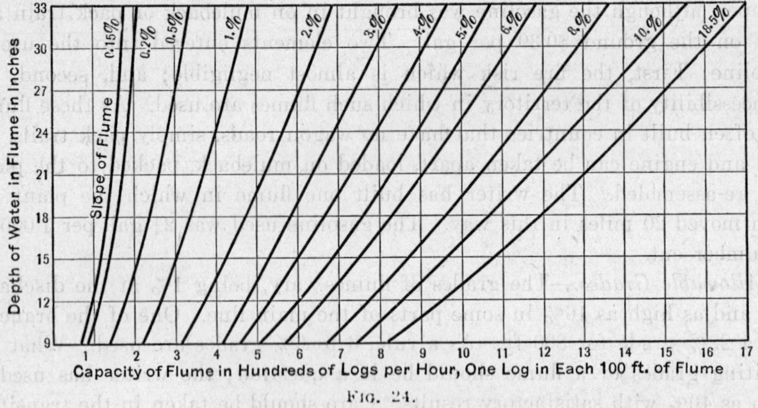

Fig. 24.

Cost of Flume.—The cost of this flume has been as follows: The 4-ft. flume mentioned cost $9 183 per mile, or $1.74 per ft. With the impounding dams, the cost was $9 733 per mile, or $1.84 per ft. of flume. The main flume has two dams, one at the head and the other 2 miles below. The wages paid were $6.00 for flume carpenters and $4.50 for common laborers for an 8-hour day.

The $1\frac{3}{4}$ miles of 3-ft. flume cost $6 466 per mile, or $1.22 per ft. of flume, the dam and flume costing $7 379 per mile, or $1.40 per ft. of flume. The wages paid were $5.00 per day for flume carpenters and $4.00 for common laborers for an 8-hour day.

The entire flume, dams and branches, cost $106 899. The timber to be removed was 60 000 000 ft. of logs, thus making a cost of $1.78 per 1 000 ft. b. m. for the flume. The cost of upkeep of the flume for 1925 was $0.03 per 1 000 ft. of logs flumed and the cost of fluming has been $0.49 per 1 000 ft. b. m. Only the flume walker was employed for the entire length of the flume, with an occasional day of extra help for repairs.

Future Possibilities.—These flumes have been used successfully for transporting cord wood, posts, poles, mining timber, lumber, and logs over long as well as short distances, and as knowledge of their reliability becomes more general, their uses will be extended.

LOGGING INCLINES

By H. G. Cowling,* Esq.

The logging incline may be defined as the connecting link between two separate and distinct units of logging.

Modern logging operations of any magnitude cover stands of timber ranging in elevation from the main watercourses to the natural timber line. This difference of elevation may be 3 000 ft., or more, depending on the topography of the country in the timber holdings.

The logging industry, like any other, has developed with the demands made upon it. The early operations were naturally along the coast line and as the timber line moved slowly away from the coast up the natural waterways to the higher levels, the method of logging necessarily changed, not only to take care of the rougher ground but to supply the increased demand. Having passed through the era of "bulls and cant-hooks", horses, road engines with horse yarding, and road engines with ground-lead yarding engines, lumbermen now use the high lead, slack skyline, and skidders. With these more modern methods of yarding and by the aid of the switchback method of railroading, the higher timber of lower unit is successfully logged.

Change of Method

As early as 1906 it became apparent that some plan had to be devised for removing timber from places that for physical or financial reasons were inaccessible to the logging railroad. Such conditions brought about the first spur-tracks too steep for geared locomotives. Thus, with an old yarding donkey or road donkey engine used as a snubber the first single-line incline was devised.

The empty car was "snubbed down", and without unhooking, was "spotted" at the landing. When loaded the car was pulled up the incline by the donkey to the top of the hill and another empty car sent down. No money was spent for additional equipment, and under the conditions at the time it probably served its purpose well in comparison with other equipment and camp output.

It is evident that such an appliance could not keep pace with the strides in logging during the past twenty years (1906-26). The single line ("load down one trip and empty up the next trip") type of incline is still used in the logging of isolated settings, and in some instances this type has been refined by the use of a special snubbing engine, special line, and the necessary side and track rollers.

The first snubber of this kind was installed near Ranier, Ore., about 1906, and replaced a log chute 3 300 ft. long, with an average grade of 25 per cent. The operation of the log chute was discontinued because of the large loss in breakage. The first snubber was equipped with hydraulic cylinders to control the load in its descent but proved impractical and was soon discontinued. It was used long enough to demonstrate that the general plan of handling cars in this manner was feasible, provided the right kind of equipment was built to serve it.

* Chf. Engr., St. Paul & Tacoma Lumber Co., Tacoma, Wash.

First Snubber Built

For this purpose the Willamette Iron and Steel Works, of Portland, Ore., constructed a direct-geared engine with 16 by 20-in. cylinders and a single drum. Steam was furnished by a horizontal tubular boiler. This engine was in successful operation for many years, and probably was the first hoisting and lowering engine used in the logging industry.

The forerunner of the modern lowering engine designed particularly for the job, was the "gypsy"* type, counterbalance machine, built for the Yosemite Lumber Company, of El Portal, Calif., in which an empty car ascended as a loaded car descended. The next important counterbalance was Incline No. 1 of the Manley-Moore Lumber Company's operation at Fairfax, Wash., in 1914. Later, the writer had the opportunity of operating this incline, and studying that operation technically.

About 1913, Mr. Hugh E. Sessoms, of the Ebey Logging Company, at Arlington, Wash., conceived the idea of putting a block purchase in the line, using a pilot car carrying three 36-in. sheaves around which the lowering line passed in going from the "snubber" to the tail hold. This, with the counterbalance type of incline, will be elaborated later.

Since 1916 the development of the "snubber" or lowering engine has reached a very high order. Extensive investigations and tests have been made to determine the power consumed, the proper dissipation of the heat generated, and the economical distribution of materials. The design of the brake has been a great study as well as the character and cross-section of the brake flange. The cross-sectional design of the "gypsy" has come in for its share of study to eliminate rope wear through the side and end slipping of the rope during one operating run, and there is still room for improvement. Brakes are operated by steam, air, and hand levers, with the most recent installations using air almost exclusively.

The steam requirements of a lowering engine of the counterbalance type are usually very small, and the size of the steam plant is determined by the loads to be hoisted. In the single-line system, steam requirements are much greater. Electricity lends itself admirably to the incline problem and where available should be used. Advantage can be taken of the generating feature of the motor to assist in braking or retarding the loads in their descent.

The importance of the development of the lowering engine can be gauged from the fact that the simple early machines of twenty years ago sold for \$3 000 to \$4 000, whereas recent self-contained machines sell for as much as \$20 000 and, in one instance, an electric machine was installed at a cost of about \$60 000.

The Yosemite Incline

The first counterbalance incline of the Yosemite Lumber Company, at El Portal, measured 8 000 ft. on the slope of the track, with a difference of elevation of 3 100 ft., starting at Elevation 1 900. The foot of the incline is 54 miles up the Merced River from the mill at Merced Falls. From the top of the

* Large drum built like a spool, which carries 3½ wraps of line.

incline all timber was reached from a main line using 4% grade with a maximum curve of 40 degrees. The incline is located from the highest point of the ridge, without horizontal curves, to the center of the railroad yards at El Portal, and has gravity switching tracks at the top and bottom. The Merced River is crossed with a 76-ft. span and there are two other trestles over ravines and a bent trestle at a point where one side is over a cliff. The grades range from 10 to 78% maximum. The 10% grade is in a saddle in the ridge, and comes at the foot of 700 ft. of 78% grade. At this point on the double track, towers were erected, anchored with rock and concrete to prevent the cable from lifting 250 ft. in the air. A system of ten sheaves for each cable, set in the arc of a circle 16 ft. above the track holds the line in place and the cars pass under as they would enter the portal of a tunnel.

The flat cars used are the steel under-frame type especially designed. A bulkhead is built at one end 5 ft. above the bunk line, and riveted to the car. The cable is attached to a cast-steel draw-bar riveted to the car above the draft gear.

The first car was lowered on this incline on July 27, 1912, seventeen cars being lowered that day. The success of the operation having been proved with an initial line speed of 500 ft. per min., this was increased to 960 ft. per min. the following year, and with a few changes in vertical curves the ultimate result was the safe delivery of a car in 7 min. with 1 min. for switching and hooking on another car. This Company is now operating its second incline, 9 000 ft. long, with a maximum grade of 68%, in conjunction with a third incline about 2 miles back, 1 500 ft. long, with a 30% maximum grade.

The first incline of the counterbalance type in the State of Washington was built by the Manley-Moore Lumber Company, at Fairfax, Wash. This incline is 4 900 ft. long horizontal measurement, with a difference of elevation of 1 600 ft., beginning at Elevation 1 500. It has a maximum grade of 59 per cent.

After a careful study of this incline the writer was asked to select the proper site and build Incline No. 2 across the Carbon River from the mill of the Company. This incline is 3 323 ft. in horizontal measurement, with a difference of elevation of 815 ft. Of rock, 5 000 cu. yd. were moved, and a log bulkhead, 400 ft. long and 14 ft. high, was built near the top. The "snubber" is designed to handle 40 loads of logs per day of 8 hours. About 280 000 000 board-ft. are to be moved. There must be gravity switching tracks at the top and bottom; single track on the lower half and double track on the upper half, the cars passing in the clear above the half-way switch. A contour map was made of the strip of ground selected for the site, and a center line projected, which would place the 50-ft. contours as nearly an equal distance apart horizontally as practical, thus insuring a minimum of excavation with the most uniform grade possible.

It is the curve of the uncounterbalanced load rather than the actual ground profile that is the measure by which the operation of an incline can be judged. The "snubber" at the top of the hill absorbs the energy not otherwise consumed in friction and in bringing up the empty car. This is evident in the form of heat at the brake drum. Points on the load curve were calculated for each 40 ft. from "hook-on" to "hook-on" and plotted as on Fig. 25, showing a profile of the incline on which has been drawn the curves for two different conditions of loading. The lower curve is for a 32-ton loaded car and a 14-ton empty, and the upper curve is for a 45-ton loaded car and a 13-ton empty.

The ascending (heavy) portions of the curve represent brake applications; the nearly horizontal portions represent a period of holding the brakes applied and the descending portions represent periods of brake releases. For example, following the descending load, note that, while the load is passing over the 200-ft. vertical curve from 11 to 45% at Station 65, the brake application increases from 3 250 to 29 800 lb., at which point there is a slight release as the load comes on the 45% grade. This release is necessary for the reason that, while the load continues on the 45% grade, the ascending empty car is changing from a 28% grade to a 34% grade on the upper end of the 160-ft. vertical curve at Station 49 + 50 (Fig. 25). Note, also, that of the two calculated braking curves, the lower one shows five brake applications, whereas the upper shows seven applications. This difference was caused by the change in grade shown at the foot of the hill from 9 to 10 and 13%, and the shortening of the vertical curve from 200 ft. to 160 ft.

Time is also a factor in the operation. For instance, on the vertical curve from the 11% to the 45% grade at Station 65, 14.3 sec. are required with a line speed of 840 ft. per min. During this time the uncounterbalanced load increases 26 550 lb., or 1 856 lb. per sec., and the strain on the load end of the rope increases 27 090 lb., or 1 894 lb. per sec. If the vertical curve were only 100 ft. long these changes would take place in one-half the time. This illustrates the advisability of long vertical curves.

To keep the engine man advised at all times as to the exact position of the cars the profile and brake-power curve is before him on a vertical cylinder with an indicator wire.

Experience has developed the fact that the construction of the rope used is very important. Various kinds of track rollers and side rollers have been made to protect the line on vertical and horizontal curves, and it has proved economical to use well constructed roller-bearing journals.

A tower is constructed at the head of the incline between the hook-on point and the "snubber". The cars, in switching, pass under this tower while the ropes pass over the top. Beginning at the upper hook-on point and following through to the lower hook-on point, the cable passes over six 20-in. tower sheaves set on a uniform radius of 30.46 ft.; thence it passes over the top of the tower to the 5½-ft. gypsy around which there are 3½ turns, thence over six 20-in. sheaves on the tower set on a radius of 33.84 ft.; thence down over the numerous track rollers to the foot of the hill. These changes in direction of the rope in running its course are necessary to the operation, and rope manufacturers are bending every effort to evolve a product to satisfy the variable conditions under which these ropes must work. The ropes used on a counterbalance are from 1½ in. to 1¾ in. in diameter.

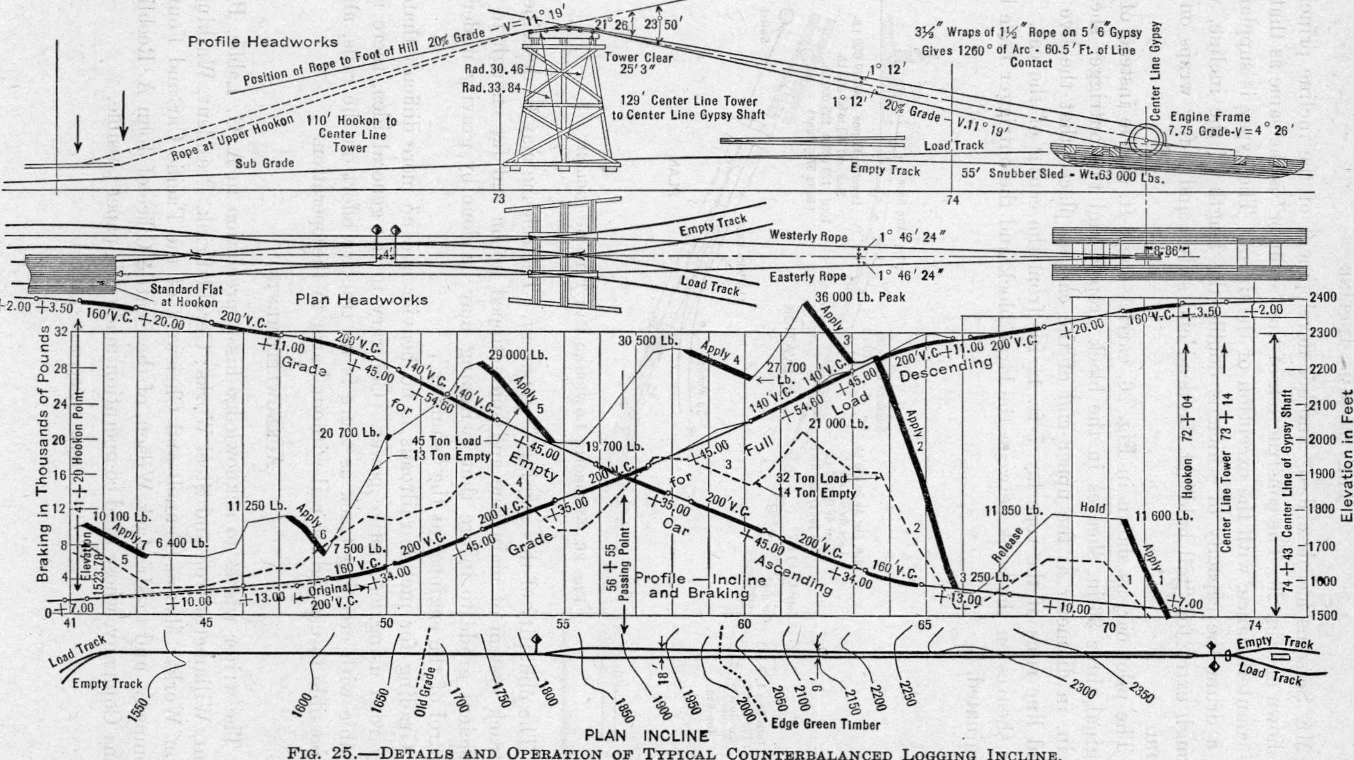

FIG. 25.—DETAILS AND OPERATION OF TYPICAL COUNTERBALANCED LOGGING INCLINE.

The Sessoms Incline

Mr. Sessoms has described* another development of the incline principle, as shown on Fig. 26. The construction of the "snubber" is the same as that for the counterbalance, with the exception of the drum. The gypsy is supplanted by a drum the capacity of which is double the length of the incline, with enough extra for "tail hold" at the dead end swivel and a few wraps on the drum.

The pilot car, as shown in Fig. 26, carries one 6-ft. sheave instead of the original three 36-in. sheaves in the block proper, and two outrigger sheaves 19 in. in diameter at the upper end of the car, so placed that the live and dead line runs of the rope lay 7 ft. 1⅛ in. from the center of the car. The two sheaves on the bunk between the large block and the outrigger have been eliminated.

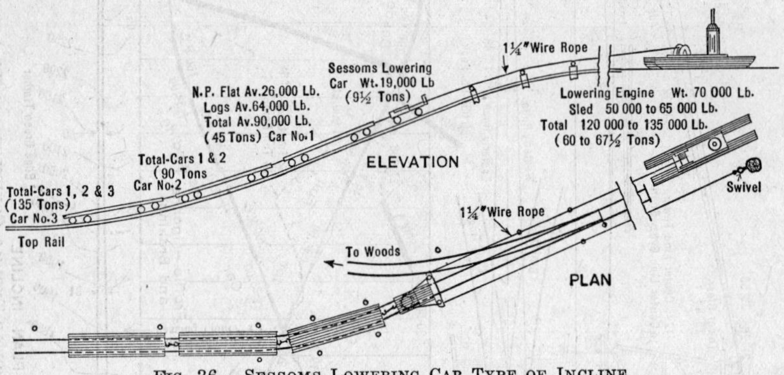

Fig. 26.—Sessoms Lowering Car Type of Incline.

The pliability of this rigging is apparent. The scheme may be described as a track system of main line and spurs tipped up on end far enough to give sufficient grade to insure that switching may be done by gravity under the control of the engineer at the "snubber".

Grading for incline railroads is no heavier and no more difficult than for any road using locomotive power. Contrary to the general idea, there is no trouble with creeping track as there is no tractive effort on the rails, and it is possible to use lighter rail without harm to the operation.

Acknowledgments

The writer wishes to acknowledge his appreciation to A. G. Labbe, President, Willamette Iron and Steel Works; Gerald Frink, President, Washington Iron Works; Messrs. Fennell and Chriswell, of the Pacific Car and Foundry Company, and to Mr. Jack Wilson, of the Seattle Office of John A. Roebling's Sons Company, whose kind co-operation made this paper possible.

* *The Timberman*, 1913.

OCEAN LOG RAFTS

By W. T. Evenson,* Esq.

The subject of "Lumber Rafts" is so broad that this paper has been limited to "Ocean Log Rafts". The Davis raft and the Benson raft are the only two types of ocean-going rafts now in practical use. The Davis raft is built by various loggers and operators under patents held by Captain G. T. Davis. The Benson raft is now used only by the Benson Timber Company, and the Benson Lumber Company, affiliated corporations.

The Davis Raft

The Davis raft is built without the aid of a cradle, and as constructed by the Multnomah Lumber and Box Company, of Portland, Ore., contains from 600 000 to 900 000 ft. of logs. It is much in demand for short trips across rough water, and because of the economy of building. It is practical for use in salt water because it requires no cradle for its construction as does the Benson raft.

The Davis raft is built by first laying a floor of long logs, held together by interlacing cables over and under the logs of the floor which are properly fastened to keep the floor intact until the raft is broken up at its destination. When the floor is completed, logs are rolled upon it, submerging it gradually. At intervals wires are run across the raft to strengthen and bind it together. When the floor is submerged to the proper depth, the cables are fastened across the top and the raft is ready for towing.

The loss on this type of raft has not been large, and the distance of the tow in no instance has been very far. At present (1926), a new Davis raft is in course of development which will take logs of all lengths and which, it is estimated, will carry in excess of 3 000 000 ft. of logs on long tows.

The Benson Raft

In 1906, Messrs. S. Benson and O. J. Evenson started in the ocean-rafting business at Wallace Slough, Ore., on the Columbia River, engaging Mr. J. A. Festabend to superintend the construction of a cradle and raft. Previous to this time Mr. Festabend had constructed rafts for Captain Robertson, the originator of the ocean log raft. Messrs. Festabend and Evenson constructed a simple cradle with an improved center-locking device, and improved on the towing gear and system used by Captain Robertson.

The first raft built was small as compared with present-day rafts and contained not only piling and saw-logs of all sizes and lengths, but several hundred thousand feet of sawn timbers and lumber for a complete saw-mill which was to be constructed in San Diego, Calif. The towing distance was 1 100 miles and was twice that ever before attempted with an ocean raft. The

* Asst. Mgr., Benson Timber Co., Clatskanie, Ore.

safe arrival and excellent condition of the raft caused considerable comment in San Diego. These rafts produce from 4 000 000 to 5 000 000 ft. of lumber. Of these rafts, seventy-two have been landed safely in San Diego Harbor, only two meeting with misfortune. More than 50% of these rafts have carried deck loads. Cedar poles, spars, shingles, lath, and fence posts have been successfully "decked-loaded" and delivered in good order.

The towing season is from June 15 to September 15. The average towing time is about 15 days from bar to bar. For safety, the rafts are equipped with two lights which will burn for 21 days without any attention from the tugboat.

The Benson raft, which is cigar-shaped (Fig. 27), is built in a floating cradle, or form, which is constructed in sections so that on the completion of the raft the sections can be removed from one side and the raft "kicked out" of the other half of the cradle which is moored to piling. When the completed raft is launched the sections are towed back into place, the center locks are set, and the cradle is ready for the next raft. The Benson raft is not feasible in bacteria infested waters because the cradle will not last more than two years. On the side of the cradle moored to the piling, a derrick moves back and forth on a running line, pushing and pulling the river raft with it as the logs are placed throughout the raft, course upon course, over the length of the cradle. All sizes and lengths of logs are used, but the strength of the raft is dependent on a large portion of tree-length material. The long logs give the necessary strength to resist the action of the ocean waves and ground-swells.

The cradle keeps sinking in the water as the logs are loaded, and when one-half the raft is completed, a 2½-in. anchor chain is run along the center from end to end. This chain is the back-bone of the raft. Herring-bone chains shackled to the center chain are attached to the five chains that circle the raft at each end. A tow chain, 180 ft. in length, is attached under the raft to the third circle chain from each end, which furnishes an emergency tow chain to be used if the one in service becomes unshackled or breaks from any cause. The raft tows equally well from either end. When pull is exerted the 180 ft. of chain acts as an equalizer, taking care of the surges of the tug, the pull being transmitted by the tow chain through the herring-bone chains to the circle chains on the opposite end of the raft, and the slack created is taken up by the working of the raft in the sea which always tends to lengthen the raft. After the tow chain is in place the process of piling on logs continues until a draft of 26 to 28 ft. is reached. Then the circle chains are fastened around the raft and cinched with the aid of a donkey engine and a set of six sheave-blocks and grab-shackles. The circle chains are of 1⅞-in. anchor chain and are placed at 12-ft. intervals. The total weight of the chain on one of these rafts is about 175 tons. The raft dimensions are 55 ft. wide, about 35 ft. deep, and 835 ft. long, with a draft of 26 to 28 ft.

The great advantage of the Benson type of raft is that it is self-tightening, and there is no tendency to loosen the mass. When the raft is being towed and, in fact, as soon as it is out of the cradle, it tends to flatten and tighten the circle chains, and as it is towed it tends to lengthen and tighten itself.

Fig. 27.—View of Logging Raft.

THE ENGINEERING ASPECTS OF SAW-MILL CONSTRUCTION AND OPERATION

By Bror L. Grondal,* Esq.

This paper refers mainly to saw-mills of the Douglas fir region, and to saw-mills that may be classed as of fair size, for it is in these that engineering problems become more real.

Douglas Fir Logs Are Long and Large

The logs in the Douglas fir region are often very large and heavy. Many reach very great dimensions, both in diameter and in length. The tallest Douglas fir on record was 380 ft. high—which is also the maximum height recorded for redwood. The largest tree ever found had a diameter, at breast height, of 15 ft., and individual trees have yielded as much as 60 000 board-ft. of lumber.

Such trees are of course exceptional specimens, but this will serve to emphasize the fact that Douglas fir is often a very large tree. It is customary to cut logs in long lengths—usually about 40 ft.—to build full flat-car loads, and as these logs often scale as much as 5 000 ft., b. m., with a consequent dead weight of 16 tons, or more, the necessity for a log pond, in which the logs may be dumped from the cars and sorted, becomes apparent.

Log Ponds Offer Problems

Here is one of the engineering problems that confronts the mill designer. A site must be chosen where level land for the mill itself and the yard may be obtained. Moreover, this site must have good transportation facilities, not only to permit logs to be hauled to the mill, but in order that the finished lumber may be shipped; and more, this site must be where a log pond large enough to store a sufficient number of logs to run the mill at least three weeks or a month can be provided. A fairly large Douglas fir mill, cutting 300 000 board-ft. per day, operating on a double shift, will require, therefore, a pond at least 15 acres in extent, preferably larger. This pond must be reasonably deep, so that it will not fill up quickly with débris. A good water supply, to replenish the loss by evaporation and to keep the pond from fouling, is also necessary.

No great stretch of the imagination is required, therefore, to assume that dams must often be built, reliable dams, but cheap, for the margin of profit in the sawing of logs is very small, and the overhead cost of the mill must be held to a reasonable figure.

From the pond the logs may be lifted into the mill with the aid of a sling hoist, by which the logs are parbuckled to the deck; or they may be carried up on an endless chain, known as a log jacker, log haul, or log chain.

* Associate Prof., Forest Products, Coll. of Forestry, Univ. of Washington, Seattle, Wash.

Heavy Logs Demand Power Devices for Handling

As the log deck, which must be heavily built, is inclined toward the carriage, a log-stop must be provided to prevent the log from rolling forward when not wanted. This, as well as a log kicker, to kick the logs out of the haul-up, when such a device is used to bring the logs into the mill, must be actuated by a steam cylinder. A log turner, to load the logs on the carriage, and to turn them as occasion demands during the sawing, must also be provided. A "Simondson" turner is usually provided for larger logs, a "nigger" for smaller logs, and an overhead canting gear for emergencies and to handle extremely large logs.

Automatic Log Carriage Equipment Saves Sawing Time

The carriage must be large enough, and sufficiently strong, to accommodate the largest logs that are likely to be sawed. The carriage is usually operated by a reversible twin steam engine geared to a drum, around which is wrapped a cable. This passes through sheaves at both ends of the track, and both ends are attached to the carriage. In one of the most modern mills, an electrically driven motor carriage feed is provided. In still another modern mill a huge steam "shot-gun" feed has been installed. This feed, consisting of a 48-ft. steam cylinder, piston, and piston rod, dwarfs the familiar "shot-guns" of mills in other regions. On the carriage itself are skids of steel or "blocks" on which the log rests. On these skids are also "knees" against which the logs are held by power or hand-operated "dogs". Two types of quick-acting, automatic, power, dogging devices have been developed—one a compressed air apparatus, and the other an electrically controlled mechanism. Both types are good and save valuable time.

Set Works Are Electrically Operated

The log is moved out into the line of cut with the aid of the "set works", which is now usually electrically driven, and which moves the knees forward on the blocks an equal distance, when the log has been squared, but which must also be built in such a manner that one knee can be moved at a faster rate than the others on the carriage.

Taper of Giant Logs Complicates Sawing Methods

Here, again, is an engineering problem in operation. Although many logs are approximately round, all of them taper. The most valuable material in the log is in the outer part, which is free from knots. If the taper of the log is disregarded in sawing, expensive waste occurs. The scope of this paper does not permit extended discussion of the proper sawing of logs, and the so-called taper-sawing, but engineers who are interested in mathematics as an abstract science will find some very interesting problems in it. A "head sawyer" can almost make or break a mill, and it is obvious that he must be, intuitively, a good engineer. It may be of interest that one of the best head sawyers the writer has ever known was a graduate civil engineer who liked his "job".

Band-saws are now almost exclusively used in Douglas fir mills; for large logs, the single-cutting type, and, for smaller logs, the double-cutting type. Band-saws produce less saw-dust than circular saws and have other marked superiorities in producing a high grade of lumber. Band head-saws with 10-ft. wheels are very common, and larger saws are in use in many plants.

Head Saws Do Not Govern Mill Capacity

In other regions most of the sawing is done on the head-saw, and, in the Baltic pine region of Europe, gang head-saws are commonly used. In Douglas fir mills the head-saws are used primarily to break the logs into large cants, and to square up timbers from the interior of the log. A mill of comparatively small capacity may be provided with just as complete deck equipment and as large a head-saw as one of large capacity. The capacity of a mill depends to a great extent on the type of equipment after the head-saw has been passed. Two head-saws, one single cutting and one double cutting, represent the "head end" of one of the largest mills ever built.

A band head-saw of the type commonly used demands a motor of approximately 400 h.p., and larger motors have been used. These motors usually drive through belts, although at least one machinery manufacturer is now successfully building such a saw with a direct-connected motor suspended from the massive extended base of the machine. Roller and ball-bearings, which reduce the starting demand and the average input of power materially, are now often used in mounting the wheels of band mills.

As the cants drop from the carriage, they are carried away on "live rolls", of steel, and are picked off by means of "jump chains" to the chains on which they are conveyed to the edger-feed table. Mechanical liners are used for lining up the cants before they go through the edger, for they are often too heavy to be moved by hand.

Heavy Edgers Require Mechanical Saw Shifters

The edgers are large, to accommodate wide and thick cants—often as large as 14 by 72 in.—and are usually provided with mechanical saw shifters to move the large and heavy saws. The largest edgers require as much as 400 h.p., and are often equipped with direct-connected motors. At the rear of the edger is a series of live rolls carried on a truss extending over the chains which carry the edgings and slabs to the "slasher". The boards coming from the edger are dumped over the end of these rolls on chains leading to the automatic trimmer.

Edgers in Douglas fir mills often serve a dual purpose. Heavy boards and cants are edged, to free them from bark and wane. In this respect, the edger is operated in the manner that its name implies it should be. On the other hand, the edger is commonly used to re-saw cants into thick boards, which, in turn, are re-sawed later. In this process of re-sawing, the heavy kerf of the circular saws used in the edger causes a great waste of valuable wood, for the teeth of the saw are often swaged to a width of almost $\frac{1}{3}$ in.

Timbers cut on the head-saw go out to the timber dock on live rolls, passing right through the mill. Slabs are kicked off by means of jump chains to the slasher chains below. Edgings and slabs pass under a battery of ten saws, spaced 4 ft. apart, all on the same arbor, driven by a direct-connected motor of approximately 50 h.p.

Mechanical Automatic Trimmers an Innovation

The boards that have passed through the edger go to the trimmer which, in all modern mills, is of the automatic type, with twenty-one saws that can be dropped at the will of the trimmerman so that the boards passing under the saw on chains can be trimmed to proper length and in such a manner that a proper grade of lumber will be produced. Three types of automatic trimmers are in use. In the most common type the saws are lifted by compressed air acting on pistons in cylinders. In extremely cold weather, the air lines may become frozen, but this can be prevented by introducing alcohol into them. On another type the saws are lifted by means of electric solenoids. Several modern mills have such installations. A new and vastly improved type is purely mechanical and as it is free from complications it bids fair to become the standard type of trimmer. In every case, the trimmerman operates the saws by remote control from a cage facing the bank of saws, a keyboard being provided for his convenience. The saws in the trimmer are belted to a series of pulleys on a single shaft, driven by a direct-connected motor of about 50 h.p. After the lumber passes through the trimmer, it is discharged on a sorting table, from which it is pulled for re-sawing, re-edging, or re-trimming.

Pony and Gang Saws Simplify Cutting of Vertical Grain Material

As has been indicated previously, the capacity of a mill in this region depends on the amount and nature of machinery after the lumber has passed the head-saw. So-called "pony rigs", for re-sawing cants produced on the head-saw, may be included in the design of the mill. A pony rig must have a cant deck with chains, turners (usually of the "nigger" type), and a carriage similar to that used at the head rig. Means must be provided for conveying the cants from the head rig to the pony rig, and, therefore, the pony rig is usually the first piece of re-sawing equipment in the mill. As the pony rig usually consists of a band-saw cutting a narrow kerf, its use is advantageous.

Another machine, which is achieving deserved popularity in the mills of the Douglas fir region, is the vertical reciprocating gang saw. These saws are often built to accommodate cants 12 in. thick, and sometimes have a width of 4 ft. They require extremely heavy foundations, as the vibration caused by the reciprocating parts is very great, although, recently, so-called "balanced" gangs have been introduced. The gang saw is always belt-driven, and requires, in the larger sizes, a 100-h.p. motor.

The pony head rig and the vertical gang saw save much lumber and greatly simplify the cutting of vertical grain material. They also greatly increase the cost of mill construction and complicate the work of the mill designer, but are almost indispensable in large mills.

In the re-sawing room of the mill, the layout must be such that lumber may be pulled from the sorting chains for re-sawing, re-edging, or re-trimming, and returned to the same chains in such a manner that it may be re-worked over and over again. At the same time, sufficient storage room must be provided at each machine, so that the mill can be kept running at the highest efficiency in every department.

A vertical gang saw will usually produce enough lumber in 1 or 2-in. thicknesses to keep a trimmer busy. Plenty of storage space for cants must be provided in front of the gang, so that it may be kept supplied with proper material.

Two types of band re-saws are commonly used. The most popular is the vertical roller band mill with 6, 7, or 8-ft. wheels. In this device the boards to be re-sawed are fed to the saw on edge between rollers, and, therefore, the stock to be re-sawed must have at least one straight edge. A horizontal band re-saw, in which the lumber is re-sawed while flat, does not demand square-edged stock, and, therefore, has advantages that are quite apparent. On the other hand, horizontal band re-saws require more skillful filing, because if the saws are not properly fitted, very poor lumber may be produced. Horizontal band re-saws are sometimes used for re-sawing slabs, and are useful for this purpose.

After the lumber leaves the re-sawing room it passes out on the sorting chains, where it is graded and sorted, being pulled from the chains by hand and placed on trucks.

Various types of automatic drop sorters have been installed in the largest Douglas fir mills, but these are expensive and are not as practical in this as in other regions, for the multiplicity of sizes, grades, and length produced greatly complicates the problem of automatic sorting.

Kiln-Drying of Entire Output of Mill a Recent Development

A recent development, and a logical one, has been the kiln-drying of the complete output of the mill, with the exception of timbers. Air-drying on the Pacific Coast is very slow and expensive, for the relative humidity is comparatively high, except during the summer months. The cost of shipping green lumber is enormous, for almost one-half its weight is due to moisture. All this water cannot, of course, be removed, but a large proportion can be eliminated by proper kiln-drying. As the freight charges paid to the railroad companies sometimes exceed the value of the lumber at the mill, the desirability of kiln-drying becomes apparent.

Edge stacking for the dry kilns is common practice at most of the larger mills, and is very desirable, as it reduces the cost of stacking and unstacking, increases the capacity of the mills, and permits better circulation within the kilns. In dry kilns of modern design the circulation of the heated air is produced mechanically by fans, and the relative humidity and temperature are held at predetermined points with the aid of automatic controlling and recording instruments.

Use of Electric Drives Removes Old Restrictions in Mill Design

A few years ago, when all saw-mills were driven by mechanically distributed power, the saw-mill designer was so burdened and harassed by mechanical details that mill-operating efficiency was often sacrificed to make possible some particular drive. To-day, these restrictions have largely disappeared, due to advances that have been made in electrical engineering. All the larger mills are electrically driven, and complicated shafting and counter-shafting, huge bevel-gears, "muley drives", and other power-stealing equipment have been relegated to the scrap heap.

To-day, the proper order of design is first a detailed consideration of the floor plan of the mill; second, the building; and, finally, the drives. The first electrical installations made use of the so-called "unit drive" system, by which power from more or less centrally located motors was distributed to various parts of the mill by belting and shafting. Now, however, the mill designer can choose between a number of types of highly efficient self-contained speed reducers, which can be coupled directly to the motors, and, therefore, most of the belting and shafting in the saw-mill have disappeared.

High-grade, steel roller chain has greatly decreased the loss due to break-downs. When the crew of a saw-mill must stand idle for a few minutes, the loss to the mill owners quickly amounts to an astounding figure.

Timber-Frame Mill Buildings Offer Advantages

Saw-mill buildings are invariably of Douglas fir. One steel and concrete mill has been erected, but the superiority of Douglas fir as a building material when maximum stiffness and strength at minimum cost is required, is apparent to all saw-mill owners who have inspected this building. Buildings must be planned to conform to the proper sawing-floor requirements. Large roof trusses can easily be built from Douglas fir. Some idea of the type of timbers that can be cut from fir trees is illustrated by the huge timber at the Forestry Museum of the University of Washington. This timber is free from wane and big knots, yet it is 18 by 18 in. in section by 156½ ft. long.

In planning the sawing floor, attention must be paid to the waste conveyors, for débris must be conveyed from the mill to the burner as rapidly and efficiently as possible. The proper design of a burner that will not throw cinders is an engineering problem that has not yet been solved.

Summary

It should be emphasized that the design of saw-mills in the Douglas fir region calls for the highest kind of engineering skill. Huge power plants must be built, the mill must handle enormous logs in an efficient manner, as well as small logs, for the trees taper, and small logs from the upper part of the stem constitute a fair proportion of the daily cut. Hemlock and cedar mills differ markedly from Douglas fir mills, because in such mills shorter logs—although they may be large in diameter—must be cut.

Every log that comes into the mill is a new problem—no two are exactly alike. A new engineering problem arises every minute, and the ingenuity of the expert mill designer is often sorely taxed—yet nowhere in the world are saw-mills as relatively efficient as in the Douglas fir region.

ELECTRIFICATION OF LOGGING AND MILL EQUIPMENT

By L. D. Beach,* Esq.

The writer has endeavored to confine this paper to a brief yet comprehensive description, of the electrical installation in general and the equipment operated by The Long-Bell Lumber Company at Ryderwood, Wash. Space does not permit mention and description of a great number of details applying to both the transmission system and the various units of electric logging equipment.

The application of electricity for driving lumber mills is not new. A number of mills were wholly, or in part, electrically driven prior to the application of electric power to logging machines. Manufacturers of electrical equipment and others have quite thoroughly covered the subject on the application of electric drive in lumber mills; however, the writer believes that it would be of interest to outline briefly several important features in electric mill drives that have not heretofore been general in their application. Comparatively recent developments in the design of motors indicates that in selecting equipment for new mills, or for mills undergoing extensive changes from steam to electric drive, serious consideration should be given the motor installations.

Power Plant and Transmission Features

Power for the operations at Ryderwood comes from a power plant located on the Company's mill site at Longview, Wash. Wood refuse and hogged fuel from milling operations is used exclusively at the power plant. The present power plant has a capacity of 18 000 kw. and consists of three 6 000-kw. turbo-generators and eight sterling water-tube boilers of 1 200 h.p. each.

Current is generated at 13 200 volts and is transmitted over three-conductor underground cables to a sub-station at the mill site, approximately 1 mile from the power plant. This sub-station serves the City of Longview, Wash., and supplies energy at its southern terminus to the high-voltage transmission line to Ryderwood.

At the sub-station the current is stepped up to a transmission line pressure of 66 000 volts, through a delta-connected outdoor bank of three 2 000-kv-a., single-phase transformers, these being connected to the transmission line through an automatic, oil circuit breaker.

The total length of the transmission line from the sub-station at Longview to the sub-station in the woods (approximately 2 miles beyond Ryderwood) is 32 miles. This line is of No. 2/0, seven-strand, bare copper cable, strung on 50-ft. cedar poles, with pin insulators on the straightaway, corners and curves being made on suspension disk insulators.

* Chf. Elec. Engr., The Long-Bell Lumber Co., Longview, Wash.

The sub-station at Ryderwood is of the outdoor type and contains a bank of three delta-connected, 1 500-kv-a., single-phase transformers, which reduce the potential from 66 000 volts to 13 200 volts.

The secondary bus is arranged with five positions for the outgoing 13 200-volt feeders, each of these feeder positions being controlled by automatic oil circuit breakers of the three-tank type and the necessary disconnecting switches, choke coil, lightning arresters, etc. The feeder lines leaving the Ryderwood Sub-Station radiate through the woods to portable sub-stations, where the line potential is stepped down to the motor-operating voltage of 600. Instead of building the lines in the woods parallel to the main line and spurs of the railroad, they are on lines dividing the yarding areas. This practice of routing the overhead lines saves from 25 to 35% of that which would obtain if the overhead lines were constructed parallel to the main logging railroad and spurs.

No poles for line construction are set in the woods, at corners, and in open spaces, the lines being carried on single disk suspension insulators fastened to the trees by short lengths of steel chain or steel cable, which are fastened in turn by bolts or cable clips.

A large portion of the woods lines are temporary, and the fastening of the lines and insulators close to the tree trunk requires only the occasional use of cross-arms. When a portable sub-station is moved to a new spar-tree location, the line feeding it is extended or moved as the case requires.

There are twelve portable sub-stations, each consisting of a 600-kv-a., 3-phase, low-reactance transformer, which steps down the potential of the woods lines from 13 200 to 600 volts. These portable sub-stations are mounted on a pair of log skids, approximately 14 ft. long, with six heavy timber cross-members connecting the two skids (Fig. 28), the entire structure being held together by heavy bolts.

The upper frame of the transformer sled is composed of 6 by 6-in. timbers, this framing also carrying the necessary auxiliary apparatus, such as the circuit breaker for the incoming line, choke coils, lightning arresters, etc.

The secondary leads from each of the portable sub-station transformers run into a steel enclosing cabinet containing copper connecting bars, arranged so that one, or if required, two, of the portable three-conductor, 600-volt, wire-armored cables can be taken from each sub-station for connection with the electric logging units. The steel cabinet also contains fuses, meters, and other equipment for metering the energy consumed and switching to one, or possibly two, logging machines which it may be supplying.

In the portable sub-stations, consideration was given to the necessity of moving them each time a unit of logging equipment was moved from one spar-tree location to another. The sub-stations are moved on railroad flat-cars, the loading and unloading being accomplished by the use of a railroad steam crane. Their construction is, therefore, unusually rugged so as to withstand rough handling.

The cable which connects the logging machines electrically to the portable sub-stations consists of three rubber-covered conductors, each of 300 000 cir.

FIG. 28.—SKID-MOUNTED, 600 KV-A., PORTABLE TRANSFORMER SUB-STATION.

FIG. 29.—COMBINATION YARDER AND LOADER.

mils, laid with tarred jute fillers, and wrapped with four layers of varnished cambric tape and one layer of half-lapped rubber-filled tape. The whole is enclosed in a galvanized steel wire armor wound with a 5-in. pitch. The short pitch in the armor winding and the fact that the cable is devoid of a lead sheath, make it very flexible and easy to handle as compared with standard cable.

In service, the cables are laid on the ground frequently through pools of water, and they are called on to withstand the rough treatment characteristic of such locations and service. The cables are made up in lengths of 500 and 250 ft. each. It is intended that the maximum transmission distance between the portable transformer sub-station and the logging machine should be 1 000 ft. However, the average distance does not exceed 500 ft.

In the woods, no provision is made for handling or moving the cable on reels. When a cable is to be moved from one location to another, it is lifted on to flat cars and laid in long loops.

Electrical Logging Equipment

At present (1926), the electric logging equipment operated at Ryderwood consists of ten units, comprising six car-mounted combination yarders and loaders one of which is shown in Fig. 29, two car-mounted interlocking skidders and loaders as shown on Fig. 30, and two single yarders mounted on sleds. This equipment was manufactured and furnished equally by the Washington Iron Works, Seattle, Wash., and the Willamette Iron and Steel Works, Portland, Ore., each of these companies supplying three combination yarders and loaders, one combination skidder and loader, and one single sled-mounted yarder. The essential difference between the two makes of machines is that the Willamette units use gearing which is controlled and shifted by compressed air to obtain high and low speeds on the main yarding line, whereas the Washington Iron Works units use a single two-speed motor to obtain the desired yard-line speeds. Fig. 31 shows a combination skidder and loader, and the spar-tree rigging.

The three Willamette yarders which are in combination with loaders and car-mounted, and one yarder which is sled-mounted, are equipped with 300-h.p., 550-volt, 450 rev. per min., variable speed type motors. The average speeds of the main yarding line are 775 ft. per min. in high and 375 ft. per min. in low gear. The average speeds of the haulback are 1 900 ft. per min. in high and 900 ft. per min. in low gear.

To eliminate mechanical shock in changing gears while under load, the gear change mechanism is such that the high-speed engagement slightly anticipates the low-speed release, the high-speed friction band dragging on its drum for a fraction of a second before the low-speed band releases. The result is an over-lapping of the two speeds which affectually prevents any surge on the yarding line during the gear (and consequent speed) change.

The Willamette loaders are equipped with 200-h.p., 550-volt, 600 rev. per min., variable speed hoisting motors and 35-h.p., 600 rev. per min., variable speed boom-swinging motors. The hoisting lines travel at an average rate of 675 ft. per min., and the boom-swinging lines at a speed of 390 ft. per min.

The Willamette interlocking skidder has a 450-h.p., 600 rev. per min., variable speed motor which operates the main line at an average speed of 750 ft. per min. in high gear and 360 ft. per min. in low. The haulback line travels at an average of 2 100 ft. per min. in high speed, and 960 ft. in low.

The three combination yarders and loaders are mounted on cars 46 ft. 9 in. long equipped with two four-wheel trucks. The weight of each of these units, devoid of any cable, is approximately 175 000 lb. The interlocking skidder and loader is mounted on a 60-ft. car with truck equipment similar to the others. The weight of this unit, without any cable, is 247 000 lb. All car-mounted units are equipped with hydraulic jacks to raise the car body, thereby relieving the truck springs of weight. Compressed air at 100 lb. pressure is used for the operation of the frictions and signals.

The Washington Iron Works yarder and skidder motors are of the two-speed type, each developing 300 h.p., and 200 h.p., respectively, on low and high speeds. The speed change is accomplished electrically by re-grouping the stator winding of the motor to obtain either 24 or 12 poles; the loader motors are 250-h.p., variable speed type and the boom-swinging motors are 50-h.p. of the same type.

In addition to the essential difference in effecting speed changes on the main lines, a further difference between the two makes of machines obtains in the motor controls. The Washington Iron Works units are supplied with electro-pneumatic operated equipment for control of the motors. The contractors are, therefore, directly operated by compressed air, instead of magnetic control. The pilot valves controlling the air cylinder are, in turn, operated by a direct-current control circuit, energy for which is furnished by a single, 1-kw., 35-volt, motor-generator set. As these units require compressed air for the operation of frictions, signals, and also control equipment, each is equipped with two 52-cu. ft. per min., Westinghouse air-cooled compressors.

The electrically operated logging machines described in the foregoing do not comprise the greatest number of units for the ultimate woods operations. The transmission lines, sub-stations, and equipment are of a design and size to supply power to at least ten additional units, each of a size not less than those now in operation.

The equipment at Ryderwood is to date the largest single installation in existence—the present and ultimate requirements were known well in advance, and the entire project was planned and built accordingly. In no instance has there developed a failure of the electric distribution system or any of the machine units to perform the maximum duty expected. In fact, every phase of the logging development has more than fully met the expectations of its designers and the company operating it. The total number of motors involved is 42, and the total aggregate horse-power, 5 750.

Table 1 shows the consumption of electricity, at point of use, for all the equipment operated at Ryderwood, with the output, in log-feet, for a 9-month period. Table 2 covers the performance data applying to each machine unit. The electric energy consumed by each unit is also included. These data cover

Fig. 30.—Combination Skidder and Loader.

Fig. 31.—Combination Skidder and Loader, Showing Spar-Tree Rigging.

two periods of operation, one of nine months from April to December, inclusive, 1925; and one period of five months from January to May, inclusive, 1926.

TABLE 1.

Month, 1925.	Equipment Consisting of Six Combination Yarders and Loaders, Two Interlocking Skidders Equipped with Loaders, and Two Sled-Mounted Yarders Which Always Work in Conjunction with Either a Combination Yarder and Loader, or an Interlocking Skidder Equipped with Loader.		
	Kilowatt-hours.	Net commercial scale, in log-feet.	Average log-foot per kilowatt-hour.
April	122 300	14 141 514	115.6
May	150 700	17 549 712	116.4
June	153 100	20 827 225	136.0
July	138 600	19 128 742	138·0
August	179 500	22 609 813	125.9
September	181 300	22 416 499	123.6
October	178 600	23 952 439	134.1
November	167 900	21 414 356	127.5
December	128 000	16 877 645	131.8
Total	1 400 000	178 917 945	127.9

Summary:	Electric Energy.
Total kilowatt-hours	1 400 000
Total log-feet (commercial scale)	178 917 945
General average, 9-month period	7.8 kw-hr. per 1 000 log-ft.

The net electric energy consumption of 7.8 kw-hr. per 1 000 log-ft. is based on actual meter readings, these meters being installed on the secondary side of each 600-kv-a., 600-volt logging transformer.

The total gross electric energy consumption as measured by the meter in the power plant includes transmission line losses, transformer losses at each end of the transmission line, also losses which obtain in the 13 200-volt woods branch lines and the 600-kv-a. woods logging transformers. These losses, it is conservatively estimated, are such that the gross consumption (as measured by the meter in the power plant) is 9.15 kw-hr. per 1 000 log-ft.

Motors and Control Equipment for Saw-Mills

It is to be noted by those familiar with the details in design of saw-mill equipment, that without exception, both electric and steam-driven mills include in their equipment a number of one-way rotation, also reversing power transmitting, devices commonly referred to as "spur friction drives", a number of which are used in the drive to live rolls.

These transmissions are inefficient, their performance is not positive, and their operation is expensive for maintenance and renewals. It is possibly the belief of some mill engineers and operators that such drives are essential, therefore a necessary evil. However, certain types of electric motors are available which, with their proper application, together with suitable reduction gears, would successfully replace any drive heretofore transmitted by one of the spur-friction type.

These motors with push-button operated, one-way rotation, or reversing, control equipment, as the case may require, together with suitable reduction gears, are capable of performing fully as many starts, stops, and reversals per minute as have ever been required through the medium of spur-friction drives. It is, therefore, possible, and in every respect practical, to equip an electrically driven mill eliminating all such drives.

TABLE 2.

NINE-MONTH PERIOD, APRIL TO DECEMBER, INCLUSIVE, 1925.

Machine.	Total log-feet for each machine.	Average hourly operation (log-feet per hour.)	Maximum recorded daily output of 8 hours, per single unit, in log-feet.
A	13 116 810	11 278	153 106
B	21 122 468	14 796	243 418
C	21 042 311	13 739	259 486
D	22 060 574	14 667	259 365
E	25 245 879	16 713	267 611
F	24 506 732	16 497	*344 945
G	27 235 955	19 384	271 008
H	24 587 216	16 085	240 250
Total	178 917 945		....

General Average (per Single Unit):
(Based on total output and total net hours in service), 9-month period, in log-feet per hour 15 381

FIVE-MONTH PERIOD, JANUARY TO MAY, INCLUSIVE, 1926.

Machine.	Number of logs.	Log-feet. (commercial scale).
A	8 809	9 804 835
B	13 030	12 428 282
C	13 456	10 787 578
D	12 284	10 490 658
E	9 895	15 755 568
F	9 984	15 236 927
G	12 098	18 097 727
H	6 797	9 701 341
Total	86 353	102 302 916

* Machine F, 344 945 log-ft. maximum for year 1925. This machine logged 443 552 log-ft., or 36 cars on March 31, 1926, which constitutes an average date, and is the highest output for one day attained by a single unit.

In the design of electrically driven mills, regardless of their size, the engineer in selecting induction motors for driving various units of equipment, has always been confronted with the problem of providing motors of adequate size to meet any reasonable operating condition.

Furthermore, occasional operating conditions would arise in which the maximum load on the motor would be in excess of what it could be expected to perform for any great length of time, and this resulted in decreased production.

If the engineer provided motors of adequate size to insure meeting occasional maximum loads, the result was that the motor operated underloaded about 85% of the time, this underloading being conducive to a low power factor.

Electrical manufacturers have made great improvements in synchronous motors and control equipment and their cost has been materially reduced. Both have been simplified and there is now available push-button operated control for them. They therefore do not require skilled attendance for their operation, and might be classified as general purpose synchronous motors, inasmuch as their starting torque is fully as great as that of the squirrel-cage motor, their starting current corresponding to full load starting torque does not exceed 450% rated full load current, and their pull out, or maximum running torque, under normal voltage and frequency, is not less than 175% of the rated full load torque.

In the design of new mills, or in making extensive alterations in existing mills, consideration should be given to the application of synchronous motors for driving fans, compressors, positive pressure blowers, trimmers, slashers, and, under certain conditions, edgers. The correct application and use of such motors would permit, where required, and remedy the evil attendant on, the use of induction motors of comparatively large size to meet maximum load conditions. The results would be higher efficiency and increased production.

ECONOMIC ASPECTS OF REFORESTATION

E. T. ALLEN,* ESQ.

The viewpoint of the lumberman, the forester, and the public on reforestation differs widely, or reforestation problems would be nearer solution.

In addition to being as interested as any citizens in the general welfare, lumbermen want to perpetuate their industry and land values. Probably they are no more nor less individually selfish. Their first concern is to stay solvent, furnishing every one lumber at a price that all can afford to pay. They have no inclination or ability to grow future forests at a loss for a public apparently unwilling to share the cost or even to provide encouraging fire and tax conditions. Experience makes them skeptical of public co-operation; tradition confined to conversion and marketing, not production, gives them no independent assurance. The broad advice they receive from foresters is so consistently optimistic that they doubt its reliability, knowing that no business enterprise is automatically secure under the conditions involved. They find it equally inconsistent in matters of important detail for, on these, foresters disagree notoriously; but as never before, lumbermen now face the last virgin supply, consequently the reforestation problem also, and they know it. They are endeavoring to solve it as a business problem. To them its economic aspects mean success or failure.

The typical viewpoint of the forester, with exceptions, is that of a professional man exalted almost into a creed by traditions of his teaching. He feels ethically constrained to seek the ideal in forest-growing, as an engineer wants to achieve it in his designing, and mostly he believes this an end in itself, bound somehow to be justifiable. Forest land not doing its best, like avoidable timber shortage, seems to him an economic crime that must be unprofitable for any one concerned. He would compel the owner to save himself such economic loss, even if he does not go so far, as many do, as to advocate the regulation of lumbering by police power in order to save the community from it. His creed is production to the capacity of the land. Seldom does this creed consider profit and loss, or who shall pay the bills, as other than secondary details that will straighten out somehow through some economic justice that he takes on faith and does not feel it his responsibility to guarantee. He sees the same obstacles the lumberman sees, and often advocates the same public remedies, but they do not assume to him the same economic aspect. He is neither the short-sighted lumberman nor the short-sighted public. He owns no lands, pays no costs, takes no risks, buys or sells no lumber. He is too often a doctor prescribing something analogous to the long rest or the trip to Europe. If the patient cannot take it, the doctor's economic aspect remains the same as ever.

* Forester in Chg., Western Forestry and Conservation Assoc., Portland, Ore.

Viewpoints Must Be Compromised

The essential differences between these viewpoints, creating misunderstandings and mutual suspicion, have done much to retard forestry in America. Perhaps each side has been equally narrow in the past. At present, when lumbermen as a class are at least interested, seeking to learn how far they can go, and how, many actually trying, the writer thinks they are showing more progressiveness of thought than the foresters as a class, who incline more to stand uncompromisingly on the ground they first occupied. When the lumberman can be induced to go as far as he sees the way clear, the forester's duty is to get out of the cloudland of an ideal future and down to the ground of to-day, so they may begin together with combined and common vision, together taking step by step forward to make forestry a self-sustaining but intelligent business that can be conducted, as well as dreamed of, for the public good.

Therefore, in this paper, to be read by professional men, and aware that it may make him an apostate in the eyes of many fellow foresters, the writer is going to express for the first time publicly a conviction that has been growing during his twenty-seven years in the work and is now positive as a result of analyzing the present situation. That is, that very great harm is done by this tradition that forestry is necessarily a profession with professional creeds and ideals never to be compromised.

Medicine quite clearly is, probably law. Engineering may be, although perhaps it sometimes involves the point the writer wishes to make. However, whether or not forestry is a profession, forestry itself as private enterprise—commercially growing and using trees anywhere but in words, or publicly subsidized forests—is a business. It is intelligent lumbering or else lumbering is practical forestry. It is not advising, but doing; with all responsibility for using the best judgment at command under existing conditions and exigencies; always a compromise, always shifting, always seeking to learn and to improve conditions, but not ignoring those confronted. Ideals and ethics, yes; but those of business may be, and usually are, as high and prideworthy as those of a profession. The real measure of each is actual resultant good.

When foresters see this, and become as proud of making the business of forestry both honorable and successful as they are of making the profession of forestry honorable if unsuccessful, and when enough lumbermen see they mean it, the three viewpoints will be reduced to two—their own and that of the public.

Public Often Inconsistent

The viewpoint of the public is simple; it merely wants the primeval forest undisturbed for sentimental reasons, considers the destroyer of a tree a social criminal, and at the same time wants lumber produced by wasteful methods if these make it cheaper. If production is so cheap that the producer goes broke, this is assumed to be a public gain. It wants reforestation, and, also, to set 60 000 fires a year to destroy it, and if this fails, to tax the crop so it cannot be held to maturity, thus ignoring not only the immorality of demanding such contribution to government while confiscating the only chance of reimbursement—crop profit—but also its evident futility. It believes in State and National forestry, but not in appropriations to conduct it. Of nearly 470 000 acres of true forest land in the United States, one-fifth is publicly owned. This belongs to the public to do with as it pleases. One-third is owned by farmers. They have a hard time anyway, so the public will not bother them. This leaves 47% owned by lumbermen, who are assumed to be more unreasonable than the others. Something ought to be done about this! There really ought to be a law compelling them to grow all the trees needed! If they owned the mines, too, they might be made to produce enough gold to make all rich. This is not a fanciful statement of composite public viewpoint, but the writer is unable to picture any economic aspect it surveys with consistency.

The economic aspect of reforestation to those who have the job to do is largely determined by the prospect of reconciling all these views. In most cases starting the crop is simple. It is doing very well starting itself. On the Pacific Coast, where natural restocking is usually swift and certain if given any chance, this is the least of the problems, certainly not the one that deters lumbermen. A large proportion of their cut-over land bears varying aged second-growth timber and little that shows no recovery needs much artificial help except better fire prevention. The problem is mainly of carrying the land, tax, and protection investment for the long term involved, with the risk of destruction before harvest. Bear in mind that private reforestation requires not only reasonable assurance that these obstacles can be overcome, but also that there will be the continuing revenue with which to do it. Since the promise to unrelated capital seeking investment is small, this means a going, profitable lumber operation for the period. In New England, successive crops since original exploitation meet this need for many companies, especially paper companies. On the Pacific Coast the reserves of uncut timber may meet the needs for many companies, but by no means for all. The problem is regionally hardest in the Central States, with little virgin timber or re-established forest. In any region, however, the owner without supply to bridge the gap until he can cut again, can seldom see his way through.

It further becomes an individual problem through the different financing methods of companies; the demands of their stockholders for early or late liquidation or for dividends re-investable in better paying lines, their plant construction, or other ability to use or sell the different products of the new crop; their transportation problems; the size and location of their holdings; the policy of their neighbors; and other things. Again, there is the fundamental question of land quality for growing new crops, or its accidental condition through fire or past error; with other factors bearing on competition with other owners or other regions, or perhaps with Government or State forest competing without interest, taxes, or even the necessity of meeting costs.

Lumbermen Are Attacking Problems

Very conspicuously, long-life operators in the two great producing regions of the country—the South and the Pacific Coast—are passing out of the indifferent drifting stage that always belongs with early exploitation and are setting themselves to the solving of these problems. That it is a joint private and public responsibility has also been expressed as National policy by the Clarke-McNary Law for the building up of Federal, State, and private cooperation to deal with fire first, so other steps may be warranted, and then with taxation, at the same time creating incident spirit and machinery for solving other problems in the same joint way. This law also recognizes, as National forest policy, that the most urgent need is not to govern the cutting of forests still uncut, affecting a comparatively small area in the near future and certain to improve in method, but to foster and protect reforestation on the vast already cut areas, on which the public will first depend, which object is exactly the one that is becoming of keen business interest to the accumulator of cut-over land.

On the Pacific Coast there are more than 9 000 000 acres of privately owned cut-over and burned forest land, the majority in some stage of natural restocking. Its area is increasing rapidly. A large proportion is capable, with small effort except protection, of producing another crop in 40 to 60 years. Some areas are well along with this crop. The question with the owner is not whether he shall engage in reforestation. He is engaged in it. He has the land and cannot dispose of it. In all Pacific Coast States except Montana there are compulsory patrol laws requiring him to protect it. Fire prevention has reached its highest development here. The organizations the writer represents spend from $1 000 000 to $2 000 000 per year on it. Therefore, the owner has the land, a crop started, or fairly assured in most cases, a heavy fire bill, and a heavy increasing tax burden. Without much forethought he has been caught in the current and is swimming. He is now calculating how long he can last. Although this is a fair way of describing an industrial situation, no two individuals have the same problem. They vary tremendously as to their own strength, the strength of the current against them, and the distance from shore. Reforestation is no more an abstract calculation than farming, fishing, or horse-racing.

About thirty large companies on the Pacific Coast have gone into the question, perhaps ten of them being committed to continuous production on their lands, and the remainder still investigating. The Research Department of the Western Forestry and Conservation Association has eighteen such clients to date, including some of the largest owners. Great variation is found in economic possibilities, even on similar cost and return estimates, due to differing productivity and condition of lands. Roughly, it sums up that well-along second-growth, if it survives, seems able to stand quite heavy charges because the carry is short; but that much land now being cut, or recently burned, so that it must be carried fifty years or more, will not pay fire and tax charges as now seen. In either case, there is the risk of still higher taxation and of fire destruction, and some companies have not the operating life to bridge the gap until another harvest.

On the other hand, there is a different way of looking at it; not the traditional forester's way, nor yet the traditional lumberman's way, but a straight business way. Modern business tries to reduce loss and waste to the minimum. Although it is often difficult to show probable profit in private reforestation as an enterprise, it is equally often easy to show certain loss without reforestation as a part of operation. In other words, if there is to be a loss in this land, it pays to reduce it. If as a by-product it has no value to be redeemed for the stockholders, except its forest-producing value, it cannot possibly be left around outdoors, a charge and a fire hazard; without any policy of management, use, or disposal; without gathering needless costs and bringing needless losses. If charges against it are inevitable, they should not be increased but the redeeming earnings should.

Responsibility Must Be Shared

This is exactly where the lumberman is arriving, by combining technical forestry appraisal of possibilities with his own technical operating administration, to make reforestation a business equation. No one knows the ultimate distribution of forest-land ownership. The industry will hold more than it now thinks, but history shows it rarely keeps one-half in any country, the less profitable majority being feasibly carried only by the public. Therefore, it will be here, the ownership and responsibility shifting for many years, under economic pressures, toward a distribution based on what the industry can hold profitably with the remainder going to State and Government either in good condition through purchase or in bad condition through enforced neglect and abandonment. The public burden of the poorest land will increase with the difficulties it imposes on private enterprise and *vice versa*.

However, whether retention or disposal is the ultimate course of any lumberman with all or part of his land, it is obviously his gain to sustain values realizable either by use or by disposal, in order to repay costs meanwhile, to the extent this can be done without too great further expense. This is becoming the policy of the progressive lumberman of the Pacific Coast. He does not know yet to what extent it may be frustrated by the public through fire, taxation, and other lack of reciprocity. He does not know whether the harvest will pay; or whether he, another, or the public will reap it. Meanwhile, however, if possible, it must be better to preserve than to destroy the productivity that is the only, if an uncertain, asset. Toward this end he is studying harder, working harder, spending more money, than any of the other eventual beneficiaries. He is succeeding very well as it is. A little more reciprocity and it will be a go.

REFORESTATION

J. B. Woods,* Esq.

During the past ten years (1916-26), many American lumber manufacturers have investigated the possibility of practising forestry and year after year increasing numbers of progressive operators are taking up these various activities, termed reforestation.

All are agreed that the future welfare of the country demands the working out of some general forest policy whereby private owners and the public may find profit in the perpetuation of productive forests on forest lands. This problem is one of land use—the production of timber trees on lands best suited to such growth.

In the final working out of permanent forestry it may be expected that timber will be produced near the various centers of consumption so that long freight hauls may be reduced to a few miles instead of thousands of miles. It is expected also that the present large areas of stump land will be restored to the beauty and productivity of the early days before the saw and axe.

Leaving aside the esthetic considerations—and they are worthy of serious thought—the commercial and industrial future of this country demands a rapid development of forestry practice. It is also fair to state that social solidity rests on a foundation of accessible and relatively cheap building materials. In other words, plentiful forest materials are essential to the small structure which shelters the typical American family or business. To maintain the supply of cheap but good building materials the forests must be perpetuated by wise use.

Problems and Hazards of Forestry

There are problems, however, before the lumberman who would practise forestry. Taxation is a serious and well-nigh universal problem. The revenue requirements of States and counties are increasing with correspondingly heavier levies year by year on cut-over lands as well as timber and physical properties. Heavy property taxes on standing timber have been instrumental in forcing a rapid depletion of the forests. Similarly, in some sections, excessive taxation of denuded lands has caused many owners to allow them to revert to the State. If forestry is to be undertaken by private capital, taxes must be kept at reasonable levels, and private owners must be able to budget this yearly item of capital expenditure over long periods. To-day, in most States, the tax laws do not recognize that timber is a crop; land taxes are excessive, and there is no way of forecasting the future tax outlay over a period of years to come. Whether timber is in the South or in the Pacific Northwest its worst enemy is fire, and the great American public is chiefly responsible for the increasing yearly toll of loss by forest fires. In the Southern States fire which runs over the ground does not kill the large pines,

* Forester, Long-Bell Lumber Co., Longview, Wash.

as a rule, but it does kill the millions of seedlings which Nature plants to replenish the forest, and repeated fires impoverish the soil so that scarcely anything will grow. In the Western pine country the effect of fire is similar to that in the South, whereas in the regions where Douglas fir predominates there is danger of crown fires which may destroy virgin timber. Fortunately, the hazard in the Northwest is restricted to the summer months.

Throughout this country the public is foolishly complacent regarding forest fires. Year by year the State and Federal forestry agencies, groups of timber owners, and individuals spend money in protective work and strive to awaken the public to a fire-consciousness, but progress is disappointing, the fire damage increases, and the land owner who would grow a new forest must face the necessity of providing fire protection over a long period of years, largely through his own efforts and with his own money.

Investigation discloses other enemies of growing forests. Hogs at large, insects, fungus diseases, windstorms, floods, and droughts are a few of these. Even coon hunters and timber thieves must be reckoned with and guarded against by efficient patrol for second growth stands containing a sprinkling of timber large enough to make into ties and round products.

One of the mainstays of forest management in Europe is selective logging, whereby tree cutting is carried on according to a pre-determined plan and results in the removal of only the largest trees leaving the smaller ones to grow; or it may be applied to improve the stand by taking poorer trees; and, of course, there are combinations of these selections.

For several years American foresters have endeavored to convince lumbermen that they should adopt selective logging methods, at least to the extent of cutting only the larger trees and leaving the smaller ones to grow. There are serious operating objections to selective logging in Southern timber and on the West Coast, and, unfortunately, neither foresters nor lumbermen in America have developed facts showing the relative advantages and disadvantages. Similarly, reliable and specific information is lacking about many other phases of forest management. For example, there are insufficient tree growth data in many localities of the South and West, and little is known of the economics of thinning young stands of sapling poles.

Virgin Timber Is Merchandising Standard

One very important fact often has been overlooked by those who urge the lumber industry to practice forestry. In the fiercely competitive business of manufacturing forest products, high quality timber is essential. In the past the buying public has demanded the best lumber obtainable, even if cheaper material might have been more suitable for certain purposes, and so long as high grade timber is available the lumberman must meet competition based on the manufacture of such timber. There are purposes for which second-growth timber and even thinnings from young stands are suitable. These uses will increase, but here, again, competition enters—the damaging competition of careless and often irresponsible marginal operators who are in business to-day and gone to-morrow. The established lumber manufacturer may place some material of this quality which he may develop, in markets where its use will be most satisfactory, but as a rule he must hold and protect this second growth until it reaches commercial maturity.

Meanwhile, in order to maintain the standards of his forest products, the lumberman must secure reserves of high-grade virgin timber to last as long as the supplies of his competitors. He can begin now to prepare for a future wherein man-grown trees will replace virgin forests by applying forestry principles to certain phases of his operation, but he knows that virgin timber will dominate the lumber markets of America for many years to come. It is evident that the application of forestry science to the business of manufacturing lumber is complicated by many economic considerations.

However, progress is being made and certain activities now being carried on by the writer's company will indicate what can be done. Taxation is a serious and almost universal problem. On the Pacific Coast some progress has been made in formulating legislation to encourage timber growing by lightening taxes. A proposed amendment to the Constitution of the State of Washington, if ratified by public vote, will form a basis on which to frame constructive tax legislation for the future.* Meanwhile, a program of reforestation has been formulated at Longview and Ryderwood, based on the proposition that the voters will give constructive tax legislation which will permit the growing of trees over a long period of years.

Longview Reforestation Plan

The underlying idea of this plan is to re-seed the cut-over land at a rate equal to the progress of denudation. This probably will range from 2 000 to 3 000 acres per year. If one could be sure that Nature would re-seed the cut-over lands, it would be very simple for the forester. He would merely protect the lands from fire and wait for the trees to start, but natural restocking is a tedious process often occupying several years. As interest on land investments, taxes, and other carrying charges must be taken into account, it is evident that the forester must take steps to get his new forests started if he expects the trees to reach merchantable age and return any income to the owner. Compound interest is his enemy.

The idea at Ryderwood is to wait two years for Nature to begin her own process of re-seeding, then it will be possible to tell where natural seeding can be expected to develop favorably. Where Nature does not appear to be able to start anything, nursery grown stock will be planted. An area cut over in the winter of 1926 would be planted in the early spring of 1928 after having been slash-burned either in the spring or fall. A word should be said about slash-burning. There is a statute of the State of Washington requiring owners or operators of logging enterprises to abate the nuisances left by them in the form of logging dèbris. The law does not stipulate that this shall be burned, but there is no other way that it can be removed and abated to-day at reasonable cost; therefore, it is necessary to burn all cut-over lands after

* This proposed amendment was defeated at the general election in November, 1926, see p. 538.

logging and before reforestation can proceed. The question of advisability of such burning may be open to argument but slash-burning is carried on regularly and with all possible precautions to prevent undue damage, outside the slash-covered area.

It is sincerely hoped that the next few years will bring about developments in wood utilization which will make possible the abatement of slashing nuisances through pulping or wood distillation and without the use of fire on the land.

Forest Nursery Maintained.—Although it is hoped that natural seeding will account for two-thirds of the cut-over area, nursery facilities are provided for growing enough plants to re-stock two-thirds each year. The nursery maintained at Ryderwood has a capacity for the continuous production of 2 000 000 seedlings per year. A tentative growth period for this new forest has been set at 50 years. On soil such as this forest will occupy, it is expected the growth in 50 years will amount to 20 000 b. m. per acre on the poorest sites and probably 40 000 b. m. per acre on the best. Probably after 25 years it will be desirable to enter these stands and remove enough poles and small trees to thin and improve the growing conditions. One of the many places that engineers can help conserve timber and encourage reforestation is in the adoption of creosoted or treated-wood products specifications of "construction materials". In the South where the writer's company maintains several creosoting plants it is possible to thin growing stands of pine at profit because this raw material is made into fence posts, telephone and telegraph poles, piling, and ties and the Company is willing to pay a satisfactory stumpage rate for it. By treating such materials the period of useful life is extended five to tenfold. Twenty years ago such a development was rarely found in the Southern States. Therefore, it is likely that the next twenty years will witness a growth of the wood-treatment business in the West and that when stands of growing Douglas fir are thinned a market will be found for these products in the construction field.

Improvement of Species.—While working out the program of starting new forests for Longview, it is felt that every reasonable effort should be made to improve the quality and variety of materials for the future cut; therefore, experiments with redwood, white pine, and Port Orford cedar are being made to supplement Douglas fir. Douglas fir is the most valuable wood for all-around use, but there are sites on which other species will do better than the fir and on these it is expected to grow redwood and Port Orford cedar and possibly some white pine. If this plan can be carried out, a balanced future forest will be obtained with Douglas fir as the principal species and certain other well-known trees for special purpose woods.

In addition to these species, it is expected that the new forest will contain large quantities of hardwood, chiefly alder, which attains large size on the Coast. Alder seedlings are planted along abandoned rail spurs to form fire screens for the protection of the stands of young conifers. The plantations are thus subdivided into compartments and the fire hazard is correspondingly diminished.

Naturally, fire protection is the prime requisite of reforestation. In addition to timberland patrol with its 100 miles of trail and telephone line, its lookout and patrol stations scattered throughout the woods, there is the camp patrol maintained by the Logging Department, and a special patrol for the new plantations of Douglas fir, redwood, and Port Orford cedar. All this is at the Ryderwood operation. In other parts of the country the writer's company maintains eleven more fire-protective organizations watching virgin timber reserves, logging operations, and young forests.

Other Forestry Activities

Forestry activities are not confined to the State of Washington. In Southern Oregon about $200 000 has been expended by a group of private owners in co-operation with Governmental authorities to arrest and control the ravages of certain pine-tree killing beetles. Despite disappointments as a result of repeated years of adverse climatic conditions which have favored the beetles by retarding tree growth, progress is being made.

In Arkansas, Louisiana, and Texas, the Company has set aside more than 200 000 acres of forest reserves where young timber is growing under the best care and fire protection that can be given. In Western Louisiana another forest nursery has been started to provide planting stock for a large program of re-stocking cut-over lands with longleaf and slash pine. It is hoped that in time the Company shall have there a naval stores enterprise similar to the hand-grown forests of Southern France, and, meanwhile the production of posts, poles, and ties will be continued for the treating plants.

Experiments in selective logging are under way in California. This involves replacement of steam skidding equipment with caterpillar tractors and two-wheeled carts, in order to save the young timber and the seedlings, but to be worth while such experiments must be made on a large scale and over a considerable period.

In common with other large operators the Long-Bell Company is attacking these reforestation problems aggressively, but with caution. Lumbermen must have help to work out such solutions as will benefit the public as well as themselves; they must have constructive tax legislation in all timber-producing regions and the helpful fire consciousness of an awakened public; and they must have a better realization of the merits of wood as a material for construction and for fabrication into other products, and through this channel a larger measure of wood utilization and less waste. The manufacturer of forest products who cannot do business profitably and who must leave much of his raw materials to rot on the ground for lack of a market will be too deeply harassed by present difficulties to devote much time to thinking about growing trees for future generations.

DISCUSSION

Roland H. Stock,* M. Am. Soc. C. E.—The great variety of physical conditions and of timber in the Northwest make logging operations considerably different from those elsewhere, so that the work of the engineer is extremely varied. In the old days most of the logging was done at tide-water and along the banks of navigable streams. The equipment was simple and the engineering was even simpler. About the only engineering structures built were log dams from 10 to 50 ft. in height, used to store water which, when released, assisted in floating logs to market. Now, the timber stands are away from streams mostly in the extremely rugged territory of the Cascades and Olympics, so that the larger operators have come to see the necessity of more thorough engineering advice.

Formerly, in starting a new district, it was customary to locate railroads on a 5% grade, to keep the curvature as low as possible, and to proceed as far as convenient. Even a few years ago, the logging superintendent would decide where the line was to go, and then hire a surveyor to help lay out the location. Soon they would be halted by a box canyon and have to start a switchback. In one instance when they got to the top of the divide, they found they were too high, so they had to put in a grade adverse to the loads. Latterly, the advice of competent engineers has demonstrated the possibility of attacking this particular problem in an entirely different way, which would have saved its cost in construction on the first mile of road. Furthermore, the correct location would have made available 200 000 000 ft. of timber that cannot be reached with the present location.

Progress, particularly in the line of new machinery, has reached a point where radical improvement is not likely. The field of the engineer lies more in the economical use of that machinery in connection with logging railroads. To the best of the speaker's knowledge little progress has been made to this end. As an illustration of the economies possible, one logging engineer was able to raise the efficiency from 1 200 to 1 800 ft. per man per day. This, however, required six months' work on the management before he could convince it of the feasibility of the plan.

The first requisite in the development of a tract is a complete and reasonably accurate estimate of the timber on the area, both as to types and amounts. Then comes a proper topographical survey, reasonably accurate, depending on the roughness of the topography.

In some of the rough Northwest country there is a field for the air map showing a mosaic of a tract. Since logging is conducted largely by non-technical men, a relief map of the entire tract also has a distinct value in evolving a plan of logging, as it gives a visual representation of the tract itself to a numerical scale.

Flumes are valuable for transportation in the so-called "short-log" country east of the Cascades, but have no value in the "big-log" country. However, as more second growth is logged this method may become of value.

* Cons. Civ. and Hydr. Engr., Aberdeen, Wash.

The speaker agrees with Mr. Donovan that reforestation is largely a matter of controlling fires. At least 75% of the logged-off lands will reforest themselves if given a chance. The first growth is generally hemlock, and, later, fir. With the heavy rainfall, the moderate climate, and a topography unfit for agriculture, the Pacific Northwest should always be the lumber center of the United States.

Hugo Winkenwerder,* Esq.—The papers comprising this Symposium are splendid. The various subjects discussed are, however, so specialized that it would be impossible for any one person to discuss all of them intelligently. The speaker, therefore, will confine his remarks to the papers of Mr. Allen and Mr. Woods.

These papers give much food for thought. It is true, as Mr. Allen stated, that people generally are not familiar with what is going on along the lines of reforestation. It is of course to be expected that the persons engaged in the lumber industry, the professional foresters, and the public, will view this problem from different angles. There is, however, a growing tendency for these groups to understand the other's viewpoint, and they are well on the road toward a common understanding. The more progressive lumbermen have come a long way toward the forester's viewpoint on reforestation as a business. While it was difficult for the forester to give up what he considered his idea and "come down to earth", every forester recognizes that the first principle of his profession is that forestry is a business. It is true that many foresters have been more or less in the clouds, but it must be recognized that they, too, have come a long way toward understanding the more practical business viewpoint of the lumbermen.

With reference to the general public, sentiment toward the practice of forestry was never better than at present. This is evidenced by the provisions of the Clark-McNary Act, by the interest displayed by the public in forest fire prevention, and by the reforestation legislation passed in recent years by the various States. These various groups, therefore, are fast approaching a common ground. The difficulty in the way of more thorough co-operation in the past has been a lack of understanding of each other's problems. What the public needs is a little more good sound business education on this problem—something to show how vital the problem is to the public generally, for it is certainly as vital to them as it is to the forester and the lumberman. Just a little better understanding by each group of the other one's special problems should result in the best spirit of co-operation.

Mr. Woods has shown, in his paper, the rapid strides being made by the Long-Bell Company in the extension of its policy of reforestation. This is most illuminating, particularly at a time when so few lumbermen on the Pacific Coast have taken any definite steps toward putting their logged-off lands under permanent forest production.

He referred to the problem of forest taxation. The present system of taxing growing forests amounts to practically the same thing as taxing the farmer on his wheat crop once a month, or even every week, until it is har-

* Dean, Coll. of Forestry, Univ. of Washington, Seattle, Wash.

vested. The young growing crop of timber is not taxed according to its present worth. The general property tax, as applied to growing forests, is fundamentally wrong in principle, and it is this system of forest taxation that is doing more to hinder the owners of timberland from adopting a policy of continuous forest production than anything else. The Federal Government is now making a special study of this problem. Certain States have enacted rather satisfactory laws based on the principle of the yield tax, outstanding examples being the States of Michigan and Louisiana. Many other States are studying the problem, and in the State of Washington considerable progress is being made.

In Washington the problem is one of extreme importance. Timber has, from the beginning, been the most important natural resource. The early industrial development of the State has hinged more largely on its magnificent virgin forests than on all other resources combined. People were attracted in the early days because the forests offered most excellent opportunities for labor, for the investment of capital, and for the development of industry. Even to this day, 65% of the industrial payroll of the State comes from the lumber industry. It is often argued that even if the timber in time will be exhausted other industries are taking the place of the lumber industry so rapidly that its failure will not materially affect industry. Even such an industry as transportation is largely dependent, in the State of Washington, on forest products; 65% of the freight shipped out of the State, over the four large transcontinental railroads, and 80% of the boat tonnage of Puget Sound are composed of forest products. This is only one illustration of the far-reaching influences of the timber resources in their relation to all industries. Again, probably only 50% of the land area of the State of Washington is suitable for agricultural development, 15% is absolutely waste land, and 35% will be valuable only if kept under timber production. This shows how intimately the forestry problem is involved with the entire land problem.

Although Washington has been used as an illustration, the same principles may be applied to every section of the country where timber is the chief resource. The real solution to the problem is to be sought in a further education of the public, which will lead to proper legislation. The Washington State Legislature has passed an amendment to the Constitution which will pave the way for proper reforestation legislation, but before it can become a law it must be approved by popular vote. This may be done at the general election in November.*

The people of the Pacific Coast region, however, are beginning to realize the necessity for action, and it may be expected that such legislation as is needed will soon be on the statute books. The problem is too big for the State and Federal Government to handle alone. It is generally believed that it will be solved only if each of the three large groups of timberland owners, namely, the Federal Government, the State, and the private owner, all do their share.

* The Constitutional Amendment was defeated at the general election in November, 1926. Similar legislation was also defeated in Oregon, but was successfully passed in California.

Timber growth becomes spontaneous (that is, the forest is naturally regenerated) provided the fire situation is handled properly. Much depends on this. There is a diversity of opinion as to whether or not the slashings should be burned after logging. The burning is a matter of future protection against fires. If the slashings are burned during the first year after logging, quite satisfactory reforestation can be expected, and the fire hazard to the new growth has been eliminated.

Douglas fir seed retains its vitality for seven years. There is quite an accumulation in the ground when the old forest is cut off, and if it is not destroyed completely in the burning there will be spontaneous growth. Mr. Allen has mentioned the subject of wind-blown seed. This method of regeneration is slower than, but as effective as, natural reforestation, and is very successful.

The utilization of the slashing material is another matter that has great possibilities. It is one of the great problems in forest conservation. Logging methods will also change in the future, and a great deal more of the small material will be utilized. The wood material will also be used in somewhat different form. Many pulp and paper companies use slashings and small-sized trees, and there are extensive possibilities for their further use.

Research work along these lines of utilization of timber waste is most urgent. More is known on this subject concerning Eastern than Western species. Products are manufactured that will yield from 50 to 400% more value than raw lumber. Through extended research, factories could eventually be established to utilize this large amount of waste and manufacture it into products that would be of great commercial value.

C. S. Chapman,* Esq. (by letter).—Mr. Woods very properly places strong emphasis on the need for tax reform and better fire protection. These are to-day the two great stumbling blocks to forest practice in the Northwest. It must be recognized that a crop requiring a century to mature should receive every consideration from a taxation standpoint. Especially is this so since the per unit yearly increment of a forest is a very small amount and the land used for forest growing is largely of a sort that cannot be utilized for any other purpose. Instead, however, of encouraging reforestation through enactment of tax legislation to meet a peculiar situation, forest crops are singled out for taxation and the timber is taxed over and over again, whereas most annual crops escape any taxation whatever. Most States are attempting, in one way or another, to remedy this situation, and it is hoped the day is not far off when the forest land owner can definitely compute his annual tax charges, paying on his crop (when cut) a proper proportion of its then value. The public cannot lose by such an equitable arrangement, which will go far toward making forest growing an attractive enterprise.

In the matter of fire prevention, Mr. Woods refers to fires in cut-over and burned-over areas where re-stocking is taking place. Losses of this kind, while at present not computable, or at least practically so, are far too general, and more co-operative effort is required to reduce the damage to a minimum.

* Forester, Weyerhaeuser Timber Co., Tacoma, Wash.

There is often, however, a mistaken idea as to the loss of mature timber through fires in the Pacific Northwest. In the past ten years since 1917, or since patrol and protective effort has become well organized, losses of this nature have been small compared with the value of the resource. In Western Washington, for example, since 1916 the computable monetary loss to logging equipment and logs has been more than three times that of standing timber.

In reality, merchantable timber should not be regarded as a resource seriously threatened by fire as long as efficient protection systems are in effect. The need for public co-operation and increasing expenditure by all agencies to keep abreast of the fire hazard is, however, apparent. Fires in the Douglas fir belt are not of a character that in any way interferes with tourist travel. In fact, fires are seldom seen along the main traveled highways.

The Northwest is quite proud of the record established by its protection organizations. It has gone a long way, although far from all the way, toward the solution of its fire problem, and it is going to pursue the forest taxation question until some rational solution is put into effect.

Wesley Vandercook,* Esq.—As pointed out by Mr. Donovan, each year lumbering is extending farther back from the river slopes. The pioneers went as far with their horse teams and wagons as they could. When modern logging equipment came—donkey engines and rails—the industry went farther, until now the remaining timber requires expensive railroad construction. Naturally, there must be large tracts to warrant such construction, there must be larger logging operations, and there must be more careful planning and engineering.

While the Northwest is very rough, its timber stand is wonderful; this makes it possible to manufacture profitably—although the margin is small. The Douglas fir of the Northwest is the greatest and best stand of timber in the United States to-day. As to its structural qualifications, engineers well know its value. The stand per acre in the Northwest is so much greater than elsewhere, that the cost per 1 000-log scale is not excessive, even if expensive equipment is required. Furthermore, the opportunities for marketing are excellent, with wonderful deep-water harbors, giving access by shipping to three-fourths of the people in the world who live in countries bordering on the Pacific Ocean.

* Chf. Engr., Long-Bell Lumber Co., Longview, Wash.

AMERICAN SOCIETY OF CIVIL ENGINEERS

INSTITUTED 1852

TRANSACTIONS

This Society is not responsible for any statement made or opinion expressed in its publications.

Paper No. 1666

SOME PHASES OF IRRIGATION FINANCE*

By D. C. Henny,† M. Am. Soc. C. E.

With Discussion by Messrs. M. C. Hinderlider, C. E. Grunsky, Joseph Jacobs, H. F. Dunham, F. H. Newell, J. C. Stevens, R. P. Teele, J. L. Burkholder, Morrough P. O'Brien, and D. C. Henny.

The arid portion of the United States is to a very great extent dependent for its development on irrigation. It must grow the bulk of its own food requirements in order to permit industries to enlarge and its resources to be developed. In the earlier years of Far Western settlement, mining was the principal industry and afforded sufficient excess profit to stand the burden of high food prices resulting from expensive transportation. With the exhaustion of exceptionally rich mining fields and the advent of other industries, growth has progressively become more dependent on local food supplies.

The part of the United States most directly affected by irrigation is comprised of the States of Wyoming, Colorado, and New Mexico, and those lying farther West. The importance of this region to the nation is due not solely to its own development, but especially to the far-reaching influence which a populous West will have on the future of the United States and the degree of pressure it will be able to exert in the solution of international problems surrounding the Pacific Ocean.

The population of the West has been growing faster than that of the country as a whole. The area under irrigation has shown even a relatively greater growth prior to 1910 than the population, as is indicated by Table 1, derived from United States Census reports.

The number of irrigated acres per inhabitant was small during the early mining years. By 1890 it had increased to 1.14 and since that time it has

* Presented at the meeting of the Irrigation Division, Seattle, Wash., July 15, 1926.

† Cons. Engr., Portland, Ore.

continued to grow, so that in 1920 it had become 1.94. From 1910 to 1920 there was no increase in this relation, which appears for the time being to have become stabilized at about 2 acres per inhabitant.

TABLE 1.*

Year.	Population.		Irrigated Area, in Acres.	
	Total.	Percentage of United States.	Total.	Per capita.
1890..............	3 102 000	4.8	3 555 000	1.14
1900..............	4 101 000	5.4	7 253 000	1.76
1910..............	6 826 000	7.4	13 202 000	1.94
1920..............	8 903 000	8.4	17 401 000	1.94

* In this, as in the following tables, large figures are expressed to the nearest thousand.

The tier of States reaching from North Dakota to Texas was excluded intentionally from these statistics. Along the western and southern borders of this area irrigation is of great importance. The eastern border, however, penetrates the humid zone and figures for all the States include preponderating population and farming areas not dependent on irrigation.

It is well known that a considerable portion of irrigation enterprises remains uncultivated for a long time after they are opened to settlement. The late R. P. Teele presented* the figures in Table 2, which are based on U. S. Census reports, relative to this statement.

TABLE 2.—Extent to Which Estimated Full Capacity of Irrigation Enterprises Is Utilized at Various Periods After Commencement of Construction.

Years.	Percentage.	Years.	Percentage.
5	36	25	60
10	45	30	62
15	52	35	63
20	56	40	65

At first sight the condition revealed by Table 2 will be regarded as exceedingly unsatisfactory and as showing serious irrigation over-development. It should be noted, however, that the term, "Estimated Capacity of Irrigation Enterprises", has a rather uncertain meaning. Mr. Teele pointed out that it represents the hopes of owners rather than actual irrigation possibilities.

If tardy settlement and over-development are under consideration, the area irrigated may best be compared with the area which could have been served with an irrigation supply. This has been done in Table 3, the figures covering all States west of a line drawn from Galveston, Tex., to Grand Forks, N. Dak., thus including all States grouped by the U. S. Census Bureau in its irrigation statistics, except Arkansas and Louisiana.

* *Bulletin No. 1257,* U. S. Dept. of Agriculture, 1924.

Table 3 tends to show that in 1920 about 6 800 000 acres were lying idle to which existing works were capable of supplying water, an area more than one-third of that actually irrigated. Although this showing is not as bad as that implied by Table 2, it would indicate nevertheless a serious condition of over-development. It is believed that these figures, however, are also strongly colored by optimism. The reports for Oregon, for instance, give an area of 350 000 acres to which water could have been served but which was not irrigated. The writer's familiarity with the State inclines him to the belief that this figure is grossly in error.

TABLE 3.

Year.	Area enterprises were capable of irrigating, in acres.	Area irrigated, in acres.	Percentage of area irrigated.
1890	Not reported.	3 631 000	.....
1900............	" "	7 519 000	.....
1910............	19 685 000	14 025 000	71
1920............	25 112 000	18 593 000	74

The reports of the United States Bureau of Reclamation are undoubtedly more accurate than the general average. These reports give for 1920 a corresponding 75% irrigation. The average age of settlement on Government projects is far less than that on the entire irrigated area of the West and for the same age a considerably higher percentage is likely to be found as compared with 74% for the whole, as given in Table 3. There may be, however, some difference in favor of Government projects as offering superior inducements.

Before drawing conclusions in a matter of this importance it may be well to consider that the partial settlement of irrigation enterprises, were it correctly known, is not in its entirety a measure of excess development. The first settlers generally select the best soil and the remnant available to new settlers leaves lesser possibilities of profitable farming. The water supply may have proved unsatisfactory for the full area reported as irrigable, some land may have, or threatens to, become water-logged and even in the most intensively farmed areas some land is always found unused due to change of ownership, failure, and other causes.

If from these considerations, 85 to 90% may be judged as the normal maximum it may be reasonably estimated that from 1 500 000 to 2 000 000 acres to which water could have been furnished, remained uncultivated in 1920. To what extent this area may consist of land which because of roughness of topography or character of soil remains unused is very doubtful. Some of this land cannot place a new settler on a competitive parity with other settlers on land in the same locality until a sufficient price difference has developed and as this, in turn, depends on crop prices, margin of profit, and availability of better land elsewhere, a large part of this land may have to be considered as not available at the present time.

A considerable slack has probably always existed and cannot in itself be regarded as evidence of over-development. In any expanding industry there is usually provided a margin ahead of pressing demands. The question of over-development of irrigation has only been generally raised during periods of agricultural depression, which affect the East and West alike. The severity of the present (1926) agricultural depression may be judged from the changes in the area of improved farm land in successive decades, as reported by the U. S. Census Bureau (Table 4).

It is of the utmost importance in connection with all irrigation finance to understand as fully as may be the causes which have contributed to this depression in order to have some judgment of its probable duration. This is especially true when dealing with reclamation projects on such scale as is now becoming unavoidable, requiring many years in the process of mere building and possibly decades in the course of their normal development.

Low crop prices are the direct cause of agricultural depression and are due mostly to over-production resulting either from lack of purchasing power on the part of the consuming public or to over-development. It cannot be said that there is any lack of purchasing power at present in the domestic market; on the contrary this is probably higher than it has ever been, all industries other than agriculture being in a reasonably prosperous state. On the other hand, the foreign market is in an unsatisfactory condition as regards absorbing any normal surplus which is usually exported. This is well illustrated by the fact that of the 31 000 000 acres decrease in improved farm land area from 1920 to 1925, wheat land accounts for 22 000 000 acres, this being about 30% of the total area devoted to wheat raising in 1920. During the same period, however, the area in cotton, prehaps the next most important article of export, has increased more than 5 000 000 acres, or about 15%, which in part accounts for the relative prosperity of far Southern agriculture until the recent slump in the price of cotton.

TABLE 4.

Year.	Land in improved farms, in acres.	Increase, in acres.
1890	623 000 000	....
1900	839 000 000	116 000 000
1910	879 000 000	40 000 000
1920	956 000 000	77 000 000
1925	925 000 000	-31 000 000

On the whole, it is probable that over-production in relation to available markets is the outstanding cause of the present depression. As far as over-production is local, it may in part be mended for those products which can stand long-distance transportation cost, by reaching out for more distant domestic markets, as has been successfully done in the case of citrus fruits and, later, of deciduous fruits.

Farm production is as yet entirely uncontrolled and unrestricted. Good prices at once cause increased production, the tendency being always toward over-production in the industrial, as well as the agricultural, field. In the former, production is in fewer hands and intelligent forecasts have their beneficial effect on output control. If large steel corporations should rapidly increase the output of certain steel products, simply because the margin of profit was high during the previous year and without reference to the absorbing capacity of the market, they would soon be in no better financial condition than the farmers.

Restriction of output to correspond with probable demand is as necessary to maintain the agricultural industry in a satisfactory condition as it is for other lines of industry, but is far more difficult of realization. Uncontrolled output results in violent fluctuation of prices with the ever-recurring succession of periods of inflation and deflation. These, in turn, produce a similar effect on land values with the aggravating subsequent combination of heavy investment and low crop returns. The writer visited Europe a few years ago and found that, in Holland, shrinkage in exports had resulted in over-production, causing a serious agricultural crisis. On the other hand, farmers in France and Germany were relatively prosperous, the effects of the World War having caused under-production.

If economic laws are not interfered with by legislation, an agricultural setback has at least this beneficial feature—that it causes marginal lands to go rapidly out of cultivation. In the meantime the growth of population maintains a rising curve in the domestic demand and it is merely a question of time when it will cross the falling curve of output. When this happens crop prices will rise, the farmer's prosperity will return, and the demand for farming land will revive. Artificial revival can be brought about by legislation. Legislative interference with economic laws is believed to be justified only under exceptional conditions and for distinctly temporary purposes. Price maintenance is extremely costly to the nation as a whole, because it aggravates the original cause by encouraging production at a time when the demand for price maintenance is created by over-production.

The importance of stabilizing crop prices when once they have reached a point yielding profits in proportion to other industries cannot be exaggerated provided it can be done without violating economic laws. It is possible that some healthy progress may be made in that direction by the distribution of reliable statistical information and by the forming of farmers' organizations leading to output restriction, in all of which Governmental action may be helpful. Upon recurrence of profitable crop prices there will develop, as far as irrigated agriculture is concerned, an immediate tendency to take up the slack by occupation of the best farming sections of the 1 500 000 or 2 000 000 acres for which water is reported to be ready. This can be done without starting new irrigation projects. If about one-half this area is destined to come into early use and if the eleven Western States should continue to increase in population as they did in the last decade at the rate of 240 000 per year, requiring an increase in irrigated area of possibly 460 000 acres, it is evident that the available excess may be absorbed with surprising rapidity.

Most irrigation projects require two years and more for construction, and some of the larger ones need in excess of four years. Ordinary human foresight, therefore, would indicate that the desirability of energetically resuming irrigation construction may become apparent before long. The present time, therefore, is not inopportune for inquiring into the various means by which expansion is most likely to be brought about and into the manner in which it will probably be financed. The agencies through which irrigation has been accomplished in the past may be judged from Table 5.

Irrigation effected by individuals, partnerships, and corporations, accounts for by far the bulk of accomplishment to the present time. It is probable that through these agencies, in numerous localities where improved transportation removes previous obstacles, small areas will continue to be developed, which, in their aggregate, will continue for a time to be an important factor of irrigation expansion. Since 1910, however, irrigation fostered by legislative action or carried on directly by Governmental agencies has been gaining rapidly in relative importance. The acreage percentage thus reclaimed more than doubled during the decade, 1910-20, while the gain in area was 2 500 000 acres as against 2 250 000 by other agencies.

TABLE 5.

Agency.	1910.		1920.	
	Acres.	Percentage of total.	Acres.	Percentage of total.
Reclamation Bureau........	396 000	2.7	1 255 000	6.5
Indian Service.............	173 000	1.2	285 000	1.5
Total, Federal...........	569 000	3.9	1 540 000	8.0
State......................	Not reported		6 000	0.003
Governmental.............	569 000	3.9	1 546 000	8.0
Carey Act..................	289 000	2.0	524 000	2.7
Irrigation districts.........	529 000	3.7	1 823 000	9.6
Sub-total..................	1 387 000	9.6	3 893 000	20.3
Other agencies..............	13 046 000	90.4	15 299 000	79.7
Total......................	14 433 000	100.00	19 192 000	100.0

The largest proportionate increase was that produced by the U. S. Reclamation Bureau, its percentage in 1920 being 2.4 times that in 1910. The largest acreage increase due to any single agency was brought about by irrigation districts, amounting to 1 300 000 acres during the decade. The Carey Act, passed in 1894, which at first held out great promise, has thus far accounted for less than 3% of the total irrigated area. It grants to each of the arid States 1 000 000 acres of desert land subject to provision for reclamation by the States. This has been done by State contracts with construction companies which provide the money for and build the works, these companies being authorized to sell water rights to parties buying the land from the States.

The Carey Act contains a sound financial principle in that it permits invested capital to earn, besides interest, a profit which may be commensurate with the risk involved. The unsatisfactory feature in its application was that companies willing to undertake the work were poorly financed and depended on advance water-right sales and the proceeds of bond issues not secured by the land, for a large part of their construction funds. The States of Idaho and Wyoming are the only ones that have largely availed themselves of this method. A few well-selected projects were reasonably successful. Others failed through insufficient water supply or from tardy settlement, causing the financial plan of interest and bond repayment to be upset, with the general result that this method of irrigation expansion is at present dormant. There is, however, no fundamental reason, except possibly inavailability of suitable public land projects, for discarding its use in the future especially if State legislation can be changed so as to permit the land itself to become security for bond issues. It is safe to say that investors will not avail themselves of this Act until a large margin of profit can be calculated, and this cannot be hoped for until crop returns and land values show a considerable advance over present conditions.

The irrigation district method of developing and handling irrigation deserves the most serious attention. From the standpoint of total acreage and recent increase of acreage, it exceeds in importance all direct financing by Governmental agencies. From the social standpoint, its comparative independence of Governmental aid and control is strongly in its favor. Dependence on commercial financing through the sale of bonds has, in addition, the advantage that selection of locality is not influenced by political considerations and that over-development is to some extent automatically checked. In considering this subject, distinction should be made between the various enterprises which now operate under the district plan. These divide into two general groups: (1) "A" Districts with land values greater, and (2) "B" Districts with land values smaller, than the face value of the proposed bond issue.

It is apparent that where the immediately existing land values, independent of any speculative element, leave a large margin over the amount of the bond issue, and other conditions are favorable, the security is good. This is generally the case with districts which have developed prosperously under some other plan and which are organized and issue bonds for taking over existing and proved works and for improving them; also, with many districts on Government projects. It is equally apparent that where the aggregate land values are far below the bond issue the case is essentially different, the security is uncertain and becomes dependent on the numerous factors which may lead to relative success or failure. There are many risks arising from possible under-estimated cost, insufficient water supply, faulty engineering, and over-estimated rapidity of subdivision and settlement.

The bond-buying public has no means of determining for itself the risks involved and, in purchasing bonds, depends on the standing of bond houses and on their representations. On the whole, bond houses have responded conscientiously to the call thus made on them by a thorough investigation on their part and by refusal to handle bonds involving excessive risks. Risk in greatly varying degree is, however, always present in the absence of an ample margin of security independent of future development. There have been many cases, of course, where bond dealers of the highest standing have misjudged the risk and also where less conservative dealers have handled doubtful issues.

This subject was ably and exhaustively discussed by Mr. Teele in *Bulletin No. 1257* of the U. S. Department of Agriculture, already referred to, which for unbiased and comprehensive information deserves more publicity and distribution than it appears to have received. In this *Bulletin* a division between districts is made along somewhat the same lines as that suggested. It distinguishes between Class I Districts organized for taking over projects developed by other agencies and Class II Districts organized for developing new projects. Class II Districts may thus be regarded as largely identical with the writer's Class B Districts, except that the former excludes, and the latter includes, districts which, although partly developed, show an unsatisfactory relation between existing land value and face value of bonds. On the basis of his division, Mr. Teele reported the results given in Table 6, after eliminating all districts which did not pass beyond the preliminary stage.

TABLE 6.

Districts.	Number.	Gone Out of Business.	
		Number.	Percentage.
Class I	246	48	19.5
Class II	156	110	70.5
Total	402	158	39.3

The showing made by Class II Districts is extremely bad and if doubtful security districts in Class I had been included in districts in Class II, so as to make it identical with Class B, it would be still worse. On the other hand, the results for Class I Districts if so amended and made the same as those for Class A, would be very good as the percentage of failures would have dropped probably below ten and possibly might be close to zero. This might be so even if the percentage of failures had included districts which have not gone out of business, but which have defaulted on their obligations.

There are exceptional cases in Class II Districts where the risk in bond investment may be sufficiently paid for by the rate of interest which these bonds carry and by the price at which they are sold, as, for instance, small districts with choice opportunities and with relative cheap irrigation supply. Again, there are instances where the risk in bond investment is deliberately incurred by parties likely to benefit in other ways by land development. On the whole, however, it must be concluded that the district bonding method is not well adapted to the reclamation of unimproved or only slightly improved land. It is mainly for this reason that efforts have been made to throw Governmental safeguards around district bond investment.

These efforts have consisted of public investigation of feasibility, requirement that bonded debt does not exceed 50% of the value of land and works, provision for certification of bonds by State Commissions, and limitation of price at which bonds may be sold. In addition, some States authorize the inclusion in the bond issue of interest for the first few years, and Oregon permits a guaranty of interest for a maximum of five years. Measures of this kind are helpful only if sound judgment is used in their application, which unfortunately has not always been the case. Pronouncing a project feasible although its success is quite uncertain and the security it offers as a bonding proposition is very unsatisfactory, is an action likely to be taken by a sympathetic State board. To certify the face value of the bonds to be no more than 50% of the value of lands and works when this can be true only, as in the case of desert land, on the basis of speculative or potential land value, is far more questionable. These things have all been done. The Oregon State interest guaranty has been granted with more genuine care but, nevertheless, at times with prospects of loss to the State, and bond buyers have probably attached too great significance to this feature as well as to State certification often prominently displayed on the face of each bond and likely to imply a far-reaching but non-existent State obligation.

All these attempts are for the purpose of helping out a situation which in the case of Class B bonds is unsound, while in the case of Class A bonds they are largely unnecessary for the purpose of financing although they may be beneficial. If reasonable excess security is lacking at the time the bonds are issued, bond buyers run a risk for which the permissible rate of interest and of selling price does not ordinarily offer just compensation, a fact which cannot be changed by law in any way except by flatly placing the credit of the State or Nation behind the district.

The belief that the lien which a district holds on the land, permitting its forced sale when taxes remain unpaid, is of special value to holders of Class B district bonds has often been rudely shaken in practice. When relatively large areas are in default the reason is not a personal but an economic one which cannot be helped by change of ownership. The general obligation clause is also of little avail in such cases because it leads to undue concentration of assessments on lands remaining in cultivation, which is sure to add to the area in default and to result in further decrease of cultivation and of bond security.

In the matter of Class A Districts the district laws have operated with gratifying results. The success attained would be still greater if Class A Districts could be removed from the cloud which the failure of Class B Districts has raised as to district bond investment generally. Class A bonds are in their nature improvement and not development bonds and if this distinction can be brought fully home to the investing public, it should be possible to sell such bonds at a better price or with a lower rate of interest. To some extent this has been successfully done in California and Idaho.

There now remains to be considered irrigation through direct Governmental financing, accounting in 1920 for 8% of the total development. Irrigation has been accomplished to a small extent by the three Pacific Coast States. The experience to date (1926) has not been up to expectation. In Washington, one small project was started with funds provided by the State Reclamation Service. Heavy reservoir seepage has compelled a severe cutting down of the project area, and the State stands to suffer a heavy loss. In Oregon, a project started with money appropriated by the Legislature for the purpose has met with a similar although somewhat less disastrous fate, also by reason of reservoir leakage. It has recently been supplied by the State with additional water and there is a probability of reasonably good results being secured, the State, however, writing off a heavy loss unless the reservoir can be made tight at no excessive expense. In California, two State projects have been built both with State aid in partial financing of settlers. The Durham Project may be regarded as wholly successful. As to the Delhi Project there appears to be great difference of opinion, it being uncertain to what extent heavy arrears in payments to the State should be fairly attributed to adverse agricultural conditions.

Federal irrigation has been developed in two directions, both controlled by the Interior Department. The Indian Service is doing very important work, which, however, is apart from commercial irrigation as it is intended primarily for the benefit of the Indians and is to be only indirectly judged by financial results. The writer has been unable to ascertain the full facts from which the benefit to the Indians and to the Nation can be judged. Within the limited scope of his own observation it is found that the Indians themselves do not take readily to intensive irrigation farming and in some reservations a large part of the land under ditches lies uncultivated. Where the lands are attractive to white settlers and can be leased by them, the results are comparable with those obtained by tenants on U. S. Reclamation Bureau projects, the Indians merely benefiting as landlords.

The work of the Bureau of Reclamation has been repeatedly the subject of public investigation. Reports have been made by committees of Congress, by an Army board, and also by the so-called Fact Finding Commission. These reports enter into great detail and have received considerable publicity for which reason the writer proposes to deal only with a few general features.

In judging the working of a law like the Reclamation Act, applied under a remarkable variety of climate, crops, transportation facilities, and cost of farm help, certain broad facts should be borne in mind, some of which affect agriculture in general, whereas others pertain solely to Western agriculture and, again, others are of a political and psychological nature.

Much has been heard of the inability of farmers on Government projects to earn a living, of the hardships and misery suffered by them, and of projects being abandoned. It may be presumed that through all the published reports and through direct observation the Western public and its

Congressional representatives are fairly well informed as to the general results achieved. In the face of the severe criticism which has been leveled at the Reclamation Bureau, it is a most significant fact that from all the Western States there is a persistent clamor for more Government projects and that this clamor is ably and vigorously supported by their Congressmen. The demand, moreover, is for new projects on an increasing scale of magnitude and is so general and unanimous that it cannot logically be ascribed to motives reminiscent of "pork barrel" appropriations. If sufficiently informed the public is not readily carried away by partisan commendation or condemnation. As regards the alleged severe suffering of Government project settlers, the desire for more from each locality where the facts should be most fully known, carries rather complete refutation.

The reports made so far are unanimous in approving and commending the technical side of Federal irrigation. Criticism has been made of the cost of the work having been under-estimated. There have been of course many cases of erroneous judgment, much of the work being of a novel nature and in partly inaccessible localities. The excess cost complained of, however, has been largely due to a persistent and unforeseeable rise in prices of labor and material and to the addition of numerous construction features not originally contemplated. To that extent criticism on this score is believed to have been unjust.

It is undeniable, however, that the financial results of the Reclamation Act from the direct Government investment angle are not what had been originally expected. The Act as first passed required the repayment of the estimated construction cost without interest in ten equal annual payments. Payment of 10% of construction cost per year, in addition to operation and maintenance charges to be paid by settlers on raw desert land, is indeed a task which, as is now fully understood, only a few could perform.

British Indian irrigation is often and with justice pointed to as an example of efficiency and financial success. There are enormous differences between British India and the United States as to economic and climatic conditions, density and character of population, and need of additional land. A direct comparison is, therefore, not practicable. Nevertheless, it is instructive to note where the Public Works Department of British India draws the line between financial success and failure. The criterion is whether within ten years of the completion of construction a project produces sufficient revenue to cover its working expenses and 5% on its capital cost. Although the aggregate results have been very satisfactory there were, out of 64 productive projects, 15 which failed to meet this test.

Irrigation district, Carey Act, and corporate experience in the United States is conclusive to the effect that the repayment requirements of the original Reclamation Act were too severe and that as a test of success or failure the inability of most farmers on Government projects to make such payments has no value. The inevitable result of these requirements was a search for the easiest way out. This was found in the discretionary power of the Secretary of the Interior to defer the time when payments should commence. That this means of escape was badly stressed even after other remedies were provided, is evident from the fact that on some of the most successful projects more than ten years elapsed after water was first turned on before construction repayments began. The next result was that by successive changes in the law, annual payments were reduced to 5% or, under certain conditions, to a graduated scale beginning with 2 per cent. This has since been further changed to 5% of the gross crop returns.

The comparative ease with which these and other relief measures were secured from Congress, the fact that not in a single case, even after the passage of the newer Acts, has the Government enforced collection by foreclosure under lien, and the ready encouragement of farmers' demands by Congressmen, have had an unfortunate effect on the psychological condition on some of the Government projects and on financial returns to the Reclamation Fund. It is to the great credit of the officers of some of the Water Users' Associations and Districts that payments have been made without demur and with a small percentage of arrears. Under these conditions it is also deemed rather creditable that out of $28 000 000 due under the new Act for construction charges nearly $23 000 000 has been paid. About the same proportion of maintenance and operation charges, namely, $14 500 000 out of $18 000 000, were collected, all as of June 30, 1925.

The economic features of Reclamation projects have lately been called to the attention of the public with entire propriety. This appears, however, to have created to some extent at least the erroneous impression that the essential elements leading to success or failure were neglected or entirely disregarded in previous planning of irrigation development. To that extent injustice has been done to earlier workers in this irrigation field. It was as well known twenty years ago as it is now that irrigation cannot be successful unless it brings suitable financial rewards and that such rewards are possible only where reasonable crop prices combine with good soil, a sufficient water supply, proper drainage, and individual industry, experience, business ability, and adequate financial resources. It was realized that requirements are high, but that they are in most essentials not different from those demanded in agriculture generally and in other gainful pursuits. An average percentage of failures, therefore, could be reasonably expected on Government projects. The number of failures has never been determined and it is, therefore, an open question whether their number is greater or smaller than in other occupations, in other irrigation enterprises, and in other gainful pursuits. It is by such determination only that results can be fairly appraised.

Since the beginning of irrigation, suitable soil and sufficient water supply have been recognized as essential factors. Soil examination by agricultural experts, as far as the writer is aware, has always preceded approval of Government projects. The knowledge of soils is advancing rapidly and much has been learned from past mistakes so that the chance of erroneous judgment is constantly lessening. As to the desired qualifications of settlers, it has been regarded as good policy for many years, especially by private irrigation managers, to select the proper kind of men. It has been found exceedingly difficult, however, to carry this policy into full effect. It has indeed been a rare occasion when any irrigation settlement scheme was confronted with a plethora of settlers from whom to select, even if an abundance of speculative investors has at times been in evidence. On the contrary the case has generally been quite the reverse, land waiting for settlers and irrigation companies making expensive efforts to sell and colonize. Under such conditions the turning away of prospective settlers no matter how poorly equipped has been frowned upon both by the community itself and by the interests in control.

On projects fostered by State or National Government the financial stress is not so immediate, but in many private irrigation enterprises the need of money has been often so great that immediate income from any settler who offers to buy, must be accepted. The exaction on Government projects of certain qualifications which a settler has to meet is based on sound economics, but in this case, too, a policy of careful selection may be found extremely difficult to enforce. A common argument for securing public funds for irrigation has been that it furnishes homes for the poor. It was only a few years ago that the late Secretary Ballinger was severely and widely criticized for stating at an Irrigation Congress that a poor man had small chance to succeed on a Government project.

If an applicant for land is in earnest but is turned away, the person responsible therefor will probably have to make repeated explanations to Congressman, Senator, or Land Board of his ruling against a worthy Republican or Democrat, as the case may be. The result, of course, should be a strict adherence to the approved policy but, unfortunately, it is likely to be an easing off or even a practical suspension of restrictions unless public opinion can be fully awakened in its support.

Lack of settlement control produces undesirable results. Yet the economic law of the survival of the fittest tends to provide a slow cure. The settler who cannot succeed for reasons inherent in himself will fail, and the sooner he engages in some other pursuit and releases his land the better for all. If a settler of that type is coddled by easy Government credit or continued release from obligations the economic law referred to, ceases to operate and both physical and psychological conditions of the community are adversely affected. To this cause is due in large part the lack of complete success of Federal irrigation. It does not result from the attitude of any man in control but from conditions beyond any one's control where business and politics cannot be kept strictly apart. This is the most valid argument which has been advanced against Federal irrigation and might be conclusive if a continued healthy expansion could be brought about by private enterprise, unless some remedy can be found which will keep politics out of Government irrigation.

This may not be altogether an irridescent dream. There may be ways in which progress is possible. For instance, a very valuable suggestion was made in that direction by Mr. R. E. Shepherd,* who advanced the proposition that Federal irrigation be placed in the hands of a corporation created by

* *Transactions*, Am. Soc. C. E., Vol. 90 (1927), p. 716.

the Government, connected with, but not controlled by, the Departments of the Interior and Agriculture. It is unbelievable that when the absolute need is apparent careful thought and discussion should fail to find some satisfactory solution.

The Reclamation Act has been frequently alleged as constituting a subsidy. The Teele *Bulletin*, previously referred to, states: "There is no justification for a National subsidy to land reclamation. If local interests justify the subsidizing of land reclamation the subsidy should be local." The writer cannot fully concur in this conclusion because he believes it is too sweeping. The great National interest in rapid development of the West has induced railroad subsidies on an enormous scale. Cities on deep water have received subsidies in the shape of funds for harbor development. Import tariffs are in the nature of subsidy to certain industries. The extensive and valuable work of the U. S. Department of Agriculture in establishing experimental farms, giving free agriculture and even engineering advice, and distributing seeds, is essentially a subsidy to agriculture. It cannot be denied that some, if not most, of this subsidial assistance has been of great benefit to the Nation. Subsidy as such is not necessarily unjust or harmful although it readily becomes so if extended unwisely or too freely.

Material expansion of irrigation involves ever-increasing expenditure per acre, as it can depend only on residual stream flow necessitating relatively greater outlay for storage and because it usually requires longer average distance of water carriage. In a broad way the rising cost is confirmed by Table 7 based on U. S. Census reports.

TABLE 7.

Year.	COST PER ACRE.	
	Construction.	Annual maintenance and operation.
1890	$ 7.96	......
1900	9.04	......
1910	15.85	$1.07
1920	26.81	2.43

As is well known, the average construction cost as reported by the U. S. Census Bureau gives no fair conception of the cost of projects being contemplated and executed, which vary from $75 to $175 and more per acre. The averages reported are low because they include the construction of a great number of early simple systems free from the necessity of storage, that were often built in the cheapest and most temporary manner and with the land close to the source of supply.

Table 7 might be revised to bring out somewhat more clearly the growing cost of irrigation. This is done in Table 8.

No accuracy can be claimed for the figures given in Table 8. The acreage is that which enterprises reported as capable of irrigation and, for reasons previously stated, this may have been seriously over-estimated, while for the practical irrigation of some of it, heavy additional outlay may be required. The figures, however, are of undoubted value as showing the rising trend.

The limitations of desert land reclamation by private finance under such conditions have been discussed. The question of helping out by local subsidy was raised by Mr. Teele who presumably referred to State subsidy. So far, the work done directly by States is very small, but it is possible that this method of financing irrigation may be utilized in the future to a greater extent, especially if in this case also the baneful effect of mixing business and politics can be avoided.

TABLE 8.

Year.	Area covered by projects, in acres.	Total cost.	Increases of area, in acres.	Increase of total cost.	Cost per acre of increased area.
1890..........	3 710 000	$ 29 534 000	3 710 000	$ 29 534 000	$ 8.15
1900..........	7 744 000	70 010 000	4 034 000	40 476 000	10.40
1910..........	20 285 000	321 454 000	12 541 000	251 444 000	20.10
1920..........	26 020 000	697 657 000	5 735 000	376 203 000	65.60

It should be remembered that most Western States are highly taxed not only because the standard of life is high, but also because a large portion of the land, in some States well exceeding 50%, continues in public ownership and pays no taxes. Much of this land is in forest reserve and in Indian reservations and has great value. It should be apparent, therefore, that although some States have made courageous efforts, no great results can be hoped for in that direction, and it is evident that Western irrigation and, consequently, population will advance slowly unless Federal aid on an increasing scale can be extended. If the belief should prevail that continued rapid growth of the West is for the good of the Nation, whether for international reasons, or because it contributes heavily to Eastern industrial prosperity and to the well-being of the transcontinental railroad system, or because it adds to the value of Government land, or for any other sound reason, a certain help from the National Government even if termed subsidy may be fully justified.

If it be conceded that National aid to Western irrigation is wise and should be extended in proportion to the need as it may develop, then it is important that any commitment which the Government may undertake, be known in advance as far as practicable, so that it may be fairly compared with the expected benefit. All tendency to minimize deliberately or carelessly such commitment should be definitely discountenanced.

In the past, construction cost estimates of U. S. Reclamation Bureau work have been as fair as engineering ability and integrity could make them. In the course of experience, however, there have come to the front elements of cost which had previously been rarely considered. One of these elements is drainage. There are some projects where surface conditions were not deceptive and natural under-drainage has fulfilled all requirements. In some, it is now apparent that artificial drainage should have been provided from the beginning, and there are others where apparently very favorable underdrainage was found blocked by dikes or other obstructions. This experience has led to the recent practice of making provision for drainage cost in all estimates.

Another and far more serious item of cost is the help which, under a new policy of the U. S. Bureau of Reclamation, is to be extended to settlers. When the Reclamation Act was first passed a general storage reservoir in aid of private irrigation, sometimes with and sometimes without a main canal covering a definite area of land, was deemed to constitute all the Federal aid wanted. Subsequently, Federal construction of main and sub-laterals together with drainage was added, and the new policy contemplates the construction of laterals on the farm itself and the preparation of the land for irrigation, with the possible further help of financing house, barn, and fence construction, farm implement purchase, and stocking of farms. Additional individual financing is to be done subject to a small rate of interest.

The writer deems the discussion of this subject beyond the scope of this paper. It is merely desired to point out that financial help thus extended from whatever source may require an expenditure of $50 to more than $100 per acre in addition to construction cost and that any financing beyond the conservative extent to which Federal Land Banks have carried such loans, no matter how beneficially it may work out in some cases, is quite certain to involve the Government if it grants such assistance, in direct financial losses which are essentially a part of the general commitment and which in some manner should be appraised and included in the estimated cost.

There is still another item of cost which has been ignored, sometimes intentionally, in making propaganda for desired projects. Reference is had to the equivalent of what in public utilities is called "early losses."

It has been found that the rate of land settlement in any one locality has a distinct limitation. It depends on the available supply of willing and well-equipped settlers attracted by the local climatic and other conditions. With the rising standard of living much has to be created in the way of roads, schools, banking facilities, domestic water supply, and numerous other things, many of which were only a short time ago regarded as luxuries by the pioneer farmer. Time and money are required to create these things and during their absence settlement is slow and discouraging. Moreover, with the high-priced projects of the future the speculative attraction of a rapid rise in land values, which has been one of the strongest motives where a rapid influx of population took place, will be largely absent. Thus, it will happen that irrigation projects comprising hundreds of thousands of acres which are not capable of being developed in small units, will be faced with an annual operation and maintenance charge far beyond the ability of the earlier settlers to pay.

This condition has existed to a serious extent on some large projects which have been faced with heavy operation and maintenance loss after ten years or more of operation. Yet these projects are small in comparison with some developments now (1926) being considered. The practice in Federal irrigation in the past has been to add these losses to construction charges on land yet awaiting settlement and to give this land longer time to pay, always without any addition for interest. Later, some of these charges have been entirely written off as loss. These losses fall of necessity for the time being on the National Treasury, while the loss of interest in any case is a permanent loss to the Nation.

This subject is not argued as a reason for non-development, but because whatever is done should be based on the fullest possible information of the real total cost likely to be involved. One specific case in hand is the Columbia Basin Project comprising the enormous area of 1 750 000 acres, all dependent on one long main canal with a number of intervening reservoirs and tunnels. Part of the division canals as well as the main canal will have a capacity far in excess of the requirements during early years of development. How long it may be before the farmers on the project will be able to pay the operation and maintenance cost on such an extensive and only partly used system no man is wise enough to foretell definitely because the experiment is quite unprecedented; but that for a long series of years heavy losses are unavoidable is entirely certain. This cost and the means of meeting it should be studied and approximated in some manner, so that authorities who may ultimately approve the construction of this and other large enterprises, will not be deceived as to the total subsidy which may be involved.

To summarize the following conclusions are believed to be justified:

(*a*) Increase of irrigated area will and should be slow when and where crop prices do not render farming profitable.

(*b*) Private enterprise will continue to bring about healthy irrigation expansion on a small scale in many localities as soon as crop prices become generally profitable.

(*c*) Irrigation districts will continue to play a large part in the financing of improvements of existing projects and, to some extent, in the construction of small new projects under especially favored conditions.

(*d*) The irrigation district method is not well adapted to the reclamation of large areas of desert land.

(*e*) Continued growth of the West will require the construction of large irrigation projects for the reclamation of desert land.

(*f*) In general, the construction of large projects involving the reclamation of desert land carries under present conditions risk out of proportion to expectation of profits and will not be undertaken by unaided private enterprises for a long time.

(*g*) Stagnation of irrigation development and the consequent slowing down of Western growth may prove of serious detriment to the Nation.

(*h*) State and National subsidy to irrigation is justifiable and desirable, provided it is restricted to the needs of the immediate future and be conditioned on the finding of a reasonable relation of anticipated benefits to total cost, including all items of present and future expenditure.

(*i*) It is important that efforts be made to sever politics from business in the administration of Governmental subsidy.

DISCUSSION

M. C. HINDERLIDER,* M. AM. SOC. C. E.—This paper is an excellent presentation and analysis of this intricate and all-important subject. Doubtless the greatest problem of America to-day is that of the farmer.

While the tribulations of the agriculturist in the humid region have been such as to bring about the abandonment of hundreds of thousands of acres of what formerly had been either fairly profitable investments, or means of complete support to himself and family, the plight in which the farmer in the arid West has been placed for several years past is even worse, due to the relatively greater cost of production, more unfavorable location with respect to markets, and less favorable facilities for financing his needs. It is true that these handicaps have been compensated to some extent by greater crop returns per acre from the more productive soils, coupled with cheaper production of live stock through the use of the great ranges of the West; but such marginal differences in favor of the farmer in the arid region are of minor importance, particularly as regards settlers on partly developed lands not under stabilized production.

In most of the conclusions reached by the author, the speaker is in accord. The first of these is, that "increase of irrigated area will and should be slow when and where crop prices do not render farming profitable". This is largely true as regards great developments financed by private enterprise; but as to developments of lesser magnitude, the conclusiveness of this statement is largely dependent on what constitutes profitable farming. If this consists entirely in the accumulation of money, then the author's conclusion is logical; if, however, the reclamation of useless lands as an abode for the rearing of a family in any particular community and under climatic and social conditions which in his judgment are most conducive to their welfare, is the principal incentive, then the continued reclamation of lands in any particular community without regard to how profitable such reclamation may be from the standpoint of monetary returns, is justified.

In many localities in which extensive reclamation has taken place through corporate and Government effort, the climatic and social conditions do not appeal to many a capable farmer who would gladly purchase a farm under a newly constructed project in a community in which he has other interests or prefers to remain. Such reclamation development is an important factor in the gradual building up of isolated districts into homogeneous communities which make for stability in commercial and transportation lines and in the diversified pursuits needful for the well-being of a prosperous and contented people.

The speaker is unable to agree wholly with Mr. Henny's conclusion to the effect that "the irrigation district method is not well adapted to the reclamation of large areas of desert land". Many of the largest and most successful developments in Colorado have been effected under the original Irrigation District Act and amendments thereto. These projects embrace a great many

* State Engr. of Colorado, Denver, Colo.

thousand acres of some of the choicest lands in the State, and numerous large storage reservoirs, with capacities running into hundreds of thousands of acre-feet. As illustrative of the success of this method of financing and administering irrigation development, one single individual through such means was instrumental in having placed under irrigation almost as great an area of land as had been served to that time by the U. S. Reclamation projects.

As a means of administration during the colonization and development period, the irrigation district system is generally regarded by irrigationists as the most practicable method. Many large Colorado projects embodied in irrigation districts have either wholly or almost completely retired their outstanding obligations, are administering their affairs in an efficient and economical manner, and have established a credit which enables them to borrow money, when the occasion arises, on a parity with municipalities. It is true that, as experience indicates, it will be necessary to amend the irrigation district acts as now adopted in most of the Western States to meet more effectively the problems of financing and administration as necessity seems to require.

The speaker is heartily in accord with the author's view, that "stagnation of irrigation development and the consequent slowing down of Western growth may prove of serious detriment to the Nation", and this being true it naturally follows that Mr. Henny's succeeding conclusion is sound, namely, that "State and National subsidy to irrigation is justifiable".

Much has been heard in regard to the over-development of irrigated regions, especially with reference to Federal reclamation and the Government's attitude toward future reclamation in the West. It seems that in all these discussions the major purpose and objective of Western land reclamation has been insufficiently stressed. All those familiar with the progress of irrigation development recognize that it has not been accomplished without financial losses and a wastage of no little effort, which, however, has been relatively no greater than the mortality to railways, banking institutions, and mining and manufacturing industries. Yet no sane person would favor for a moment curtailment of development among these other activities.

Whether the reclamation of the arid lands of the Western States, in adding hundreds of thousands of acres of virgin soil, practically inexhaustible in its fertility, will result in a greater financial return on the necessary investment; or whether it were better to attempt to bring back to a proper degree of productiveness the worn out and abandoned lands of the Eastern States, as has recently been suggested; or, again, whether such attempts in either case would result in some financial loss to the funds appropriated for such purpose, is aside from the question.

The question is, whether or not it is needful to the country's welfare, both internally and externally, for this nation to develop along consistent lines which will eliminate radical demarcations between sections of the country, and, if so, whether such necessity may be determined by the same reasonings and units of measure commonly applied to business undertakings.

Next to the air he breathes, man's greatest necessities are food and drink, and his stomach has ever been his most relentless taskmaster. The greatest problem with which man has had to contend, has been that of food supplies. This shadow from time immemorial has laid as a pall on all nations, except possibly America. No other people has escaped the ravages of famine, that dread scourge of nations. With the passing of time, is America to be less fortunate? Future generations only can answer this question.

For two generations this Nation has prided itself on the theory that it is the melting pot in which the peoples of the earth would be blended into a superior race of individuals. It has recently awakened to the fact that in this melting pot an over-burden of slag and an excess of dregs are being accumulated. To-day, the population of many great cities largely consists of peoples who have little or no conception of the ideals on which the Government is founded, with the result that these spots have become the breeding ground for all the destructive elements of society and free government.

Was it not Marcus Cato who, fifty years before Christ, said,

"It is from the tillers of the soil that spring the best citizens and the staunchest soldiers; theirs are the enduring rewards which are most grateful and least envied. Such as devote themselves to that pursuit are least of all men given to evil counsels".

These words are as much a truism to-day as in the time of that old Roman philosopher.

There are those whose conception of National wealth is measured in dollars and cents. They demand that the Nation shall cease spending its own money in turning desert areas into oases until the Government shall have recovered the money expended in the work already accomplished, forgetting that the Nation's wealth and strength are not in its accumulated hordes of gold and credits, but rather in a united and contented people; that its safety is in their ability to look ahead with that freedom of hope born of greater opportunities made possible through the vision of their leaders.

Federal or State reclamation should not be in the nature of a gratuity. The speaker does believe, however, that the Government is justified in a continuing policy of reclamation development of all worthy projects, the cost of which is beyond the ability of the State or corporations to finance, and that the difference between the legitimate cost of such development and the price at which the farmer can pay for the lands so developed should be absorbed by the Nation at large. There is no valid reason why the Government should cease to provide opportunity for the building of homes in these desert wastes, when practically every other industry of the country is subsidized through high protective tariffs.

Very properly Mr. Henny has stated that any plan for adjusting economic conditions through price fixing or other artificial means is unsound and will eventually bring about its attendant string of evils. That inexorable economic law of supply and demand is no respecter of persons or pursuits, neither can it be evaded without penalty; the law of the survival of the fittest applies to the farmer the same as to any other individual or business. If the individual farmer has it in his make-up to succeed, success will be his; if not, very likely he will fail. Much may be said in favor of the suggested plan for financing practically all the needs of the farmer under the Federal reclamation projects. On the other hand it is urged that such plan is leading directly to a condition fraught with more danger to the country than the incidental loss of a few million dollars invested in reclamation development could be. This refers to the destruction of that self-reliance and freedom of action which has been a characteristic pre-eminent in the builders of the Nation, and especially of the West, and the substitution therefor of a system of paternalism with all its attendant evils.

It is a most needful and sound policy for the Federal Government to build these necessary works, but when this has been done, let them be turned over to the management of irrigation districts, sponsored by the States, and free from Congressional influence, and at a price the land owner can pay. Charge him a graduated scale of payments and a low rate of interest on deferred payments, and require him to meet such payments just as the farmers in the East are required to meet their notes when due.

In a message to Congress, President Coolidge has stated that,

> "Efficiency of Federal operations is impaired as their scope of operations is unduly enlarged. Efficiency of State Governments is impaired as they relinquish and turn over to the Federal Government responsibilities which are rightfully theirs."

Farming in the arid regions is one of the most highly specialized industries. Success requires a rare combination of attributes, the chief of which are an inherent love for agricultural pursuits, industry, and thrift. Without these, no farmer can be a success; with these, he will succeed no matter what his environment. The degree of his success, of course, will largely depend on his other qualifications and limitations. Too many people try their hand at farming after having made a failure at other pursuits; very naturally they fail at farming too. Many then run for Congress.

With a more equitable adjustment of the discrepancy between the cost of production and the gross return for his products, the farmer who is capable will work out his own salvation, with a consequent increase in his purchasing power, followed by a rapid demand for the few hundred thousand acres of irrigated lands now unclaimed. This, in return, will provide the opportunity to finance legitimate reclamation with certainty of a proper return on such investments.

C. E. GRUNSKY,* PAST-PRESIDENT, AM. SOC. C. E.—The Engineering Profession is to be congratulated on the tendency of its members to pay more and more attention to the economic aspects of projects. This is well brought out in this paper. It takes a long time to bring most irrigation projects to the point at which income will fully cover all expenses of operation. Some good projects in California have taken thirty years to reach this point.

State aid to any project is nothing less than a subsidy or bonus. When the United States entered upon its reclamation policy, and permitted deferred

* Cons. Engr. (C. E. Grunsky Co.), San Francisco, Calif.

payments without interest, even on the assumption of payments made as contemplated, the bonus to the land owner was equivalent to about one-half the cost of the project.

The question arises, who benefits by the subsidy? The point to be made is that the subsidy given the land owner, as in the case of every such subsidy to farmers, as Mr. Henny has well stated, gives only temporary aid. The bonus cannot be passed on to the land owner's successor. Give the farmer assurance that his output will find a market at good prices, and up goes the value of the land; and the next owner gets no benefit from the improved market. He will soon be confronted by the same difficulties that disturbed the original owner before he obtained a subsidy.

It appears fundamental that, if a subsidy is granted, be it by State or by the Federal Government, it should be for the purpose of extending the area that is available for cultivation—extending the opportunity for home building. This is certainly a worthy object. However, when a subsidy is granted, as Mr. Henny shows, it should be granted with a full consciousness of what it amounts to and on assurance that it is worth while.

Joseph Jacobs,* M. Am. Soc. C. E.—The author apparently favors Governmental subsidy as a probable necessity. He has indicated the basis on which such subsidy might be granted. The matter of subsidy, however, should be hedged about with the greatest possible care, else its privileges will surely be abused. If a subsidy be granted at all, it should be within clearly defined limits and founded on absolute economic need.

There is an easily discernible and growing public sentiment against subsidies, both inside and outside legislative halls, as a result of which it will be increasingly difficult to secure them for irrigation development. Apparently, there is a definite future prospect of the Federal Government demanding, in so far as Federal reclamation is concerned, that all reclamation projects hereafter constructed repay in full to the Government both the principal and the interest on the construction cost. The speaker further believes that on a long-time payment basis, say, 40 years, and on an interest rate basis that the Government can afford to grant, say, 3½ to 4%, most of the projects that can be justified at all, can work themselves out to economic safety without the aid of any subsidy. Such a policy would incline the Government more favorably toward land reclamation and would probably result in a more rational and more rapid irrigation development than would otherwise be possible.

A legitimate exception to this is the desirability that the Government absorb the interest charges attaching to the unsettled lands. This would be justified on the grounds that if settlement be long delayed such accumulating interest charges would become an unbearable burden on the land and the settler; and the Government could afford to pay this relatively small subsidy for the direct economic and military benefits it derives from such agricultural development. In the guaranteeing of such a subsidy the Federal and State Governments might well co-operate.

* Cons. Engr. (Jacobs and Ober), Seattle, Wash.

H. F. DUNHAM,* M. AM. SOC. C. E. (by letter).—This excellent paper will long be noted for its thoroughness and sound views.

An individual or a corporation investing many millions usually conducts his first studies or investigations rather quietly and without special proclamation of future activity and success. It is true the Federal Government is under certain obligations to its citizens, yet it has a Secret Service of reasonable proportions and thus an opportunity to accomplish many things quietly.

A few years ago the country was startled by reports that disabled veterans were to be taken to the vicinity of Lake Okeechobee by the Federal Government and there cared for in a wonderful climate and given the best of opportunities to recover. Experienced engineers from Western projects were sent to make reports and numerous encouraging accounts appeared in the press. In no way was this district suited for the purpose, least of all from a patriotic viewpoint. Lake Okeechobee and its worst surroundings occupy less than one-tenth of the area of the State of Florida. Practically all the remaining nine-tenths could be made available for agriculture at less cost per acre than would be required to secure equally good financial results in the Okeechobee District.

Recently a great boom came upon Florida and many people were led into extravagance and at least temporary losses. Many wrong statements and unsupported conclusions exerted a great influence on people in other States. There has been a general disappointment, in large part temporary, and in some part due to Government methods, which encouraged ideas varying little from those of the early Spanish explorers—ideas of a Paradise without the trouble of making one.

F. H. NEWELL,† M. AM. SOC. C. E. (by letter).—This paper, issued to the public on practically the twenty-fifth anniversary of the passage of the Federal or Newlands Reclamation Act, marks an epoch in Federal relations to internal development. During the quarter of a century that has elapsed there has been a notable change, almost a reversal of attitude, toward reclamation ideals. A broader interest is being shown on the subject of Federal financing of reclamation enterprises. Inquiries are being made as to the propriety of spending the taxpayers' money for such purposes.

The paper throws a ray of light upon what has been an exceedingly sensitive, not to say a sore, spot; one which politicians and promoters have tried to conceal or from which they have endeavored to distract public attention. In one sense it has been forbidden ground. Engineers of ability have not been continued in Government service because they have been too outspoken or, in the words of the politician, have "not been practical"; meaning that the so-called practical needs of a party group has not outweighed their loyalty to the best interests of the whole country. Their mistakes were in not quietly acquiescing in unwarrantable expenditures. They were prone to paraphrase a classic, saying, "Reclamation, how many economic crimes are committed in thy name!"

---

* Civ. and Hydr. Engr., New York, N. Y.

† Pres., The Research Service, Inc., Washington, D. C.

The crucial point is summed up in the statement, with certain qualifications, that State and National subsidy to irrigation is necessary; that it is justifiable and desirable; and that large reclamation works "will not be undertaken by unaided private enterprises." To put it another way, large-scale irrigation or reclamation of waste lands does not pay under existing conditions. In a similar sense it has rarely paid. Comparing the actual cost of reclamation with the productive value of the land reclaimed, making fair allowance for interest, depreciation, and overhead, the facts stand out that these great enterprises, with few exceptions, always have been and always will be financial failures. This point has been avoided or obscured by interested parties and a review of twenty-five years of experiment and research is just bringing it out. It is an anathema to the "practical" politician seeking larger appropriations of Federal funds. It is the rock on which otherwise brilliant engineering reputations have been wrecked and where the "powers that be" have erected a warning to "keep off; discussion of real costs may be followed by dismissal. The door is always open for your departure."

Facts have an unpleasant way of asserting themselves. The author has made a plain analysis of the situation and has brought forward again the statements presented in 1924 by the late R. P. Teele, notably those in *Bulletin No. 1257*. Until the present time, this *Bulletin* has not been given the appreciation it deserves.

Twelve years ago (1915), the writer tentatively presented a discussion of this matter under the title of "Economic Advisability of Irrigation",* but the time was not ripe. Striking examples were not available without violating official courtesies. It has been necessary for the "disease to run its course" so as to establish beyond dispute, facts now available to all who care to go into the broad subject of reclamation finances.

In order that what follows may be clearly understood, emphasis is placed on the fact that there is no apparent reason for disagreeing with Mr. Henny's qualified statement that "State and National subsidy to irrigation is justifiable and desirable".

The one fact in this connection that should be made clear, on which the spotlight should be continually kept, is that there should be no secrecy nor camouflage with respect to the amount and character of this subsidy. It is of interest to the taxpayers. The public in general should not be kept in ignorance nor misled as to the extent to which the taxes are increased, directly or indirectly. The subsidy is not wrong in itself; it may be a good thing; but it should not be concealed.

No culpability can be attached to the payment of necessary subsidies to irrigation or to other forms of reclamation, provided the public in general knows how the money is being used. No excuse should be tolerated for the activities of those interested in obscuring the facts; more particularly as in so doing, attacks are made on the ability of the engineers who have planned and executed the works of reclamation.

* *Transactions,* Inter. Eng. Cong., San Francisco, Calif., 1915. Waterways and Irrigation, Paper No. 35, pp. 371–397.

A condition has existed that has gradually aroused the indignation of engineers and lovers of fair play. This has come about from the fact that, in order to justify or secure the necessary subsidy of reclamation works and to bring about a partial repudiation of the monies advanced for them, the easiest course of procedure has been to attack the engineers under whose immediate direction the money was expended. The story (a reflection on local political ethics) is simple, the details are familiar to those who have followed the history of Federal reclamation development.

The first chapter is that of eager importunity on the part of local land owners and their representatives for the expenditure of Federal funds. This is accompanied by a statement that no matter what reclamation costs the lands will be worth it and the owners will cheerfully repay it.

The second chapter is of popular enthusiasm, praise of the engineers and their operation, accompanied by urgent appeals to Washington that the works under construction be built in the most permanent manner regardless of cost; that the reservoir dams be raised; the capacity increased; the canals made larger; and ditches built to every farm.

The third chapter opens with the practical completion of the works, the turning of the water to the fields and the beginning of the time of repayment. Then comes the condition predicted by the late Speaker Cannon and other experienced politicians who fought the Reclamation Act. Their opposition was based frankly on the belief that when the time came to make payment to the Government the land owners would repudiate the claims. This opinion was based on a practical knowledge of human nature. These men were sure that the Federal Government could not collect from its citizens payments deferred over any considerable length of time. They had learned by experience that the only way for the Government to enforce payments is to have the cash in advance. The Post Office wisely demands payment before the mail is delivered; the Land Office, in contrast, shows a long list of unpaid claims, many of which have been subsequently cancelled by Congress.

While these statesmen (that is, politicians who have departed this life) clearly foresaw the ultimate conclusion, they did not point out, and, in fact, nobody appreciated, just how this amelioration of debts (not to use the harsh term "repudiation") might take place. Least of all did the engineers look forward to the treatment that was to be handed to them in the efforts to make them the scapegoats. No sooner were the terms of payment announced, however, than the same men, (the local land owners, bankers, and politicians, who had been urging that the engineers be instructed to do more work and make larger expenditures) reversed their position. Then began the long and heartbreaking campaign of attack which resulted in driving from the public service many able and conscientious engineers, technical assistants, men and women.

This is not the time nor the place to discuss matters of human and ethical relations, but they have peculiar interest to engineers in public employ, illustrating the fact that the moods of the public must be taken into account and studied with the same degree of care and impersonal attention as problems of fair and stormy weather, or drought and floods, which may destroy engineering works. Equal or greater destruction can come to the engineer and his organization through changes of public sentiment.

The doubts, censure, and personal abuse heaped on the engineers following the attempt to secure repayment from the land owners was naturally accompanied by investigations. No one has attempted to keep an accurate record of them, but the Fact Finding Commission has referred to several hundred, big and little. Some were notably expensive, not merely in the time and money involved in digging into every detail, but in distracting the attention of men in executive charge during times of the greatest stress, when every effort should have been concentrated on efficient work. It is literally true that men in direct charge of Federal reclamation projects, as well as their principal assistants, have worked night after night through long periods, assembling and re-assembling data called for. Under the strain of continued attack many a good engineer has broken, or has lost his temper at what to him has appeared the most ridiculous of accusations and demands. For example, one prominent Western Senator (now deceased) called on the Department for a list of all foremen employed on the works. No explanation was given; nor was the term "foremen" defined. At that time there were several thousand names on the payrolls, some designated as foremen mechanics, foremen carpenters, and every kind of similar designation currently used by contractors. The assembling of pay rolls and the careful scrutiny to distinguish between men who might be considered as foremen, required notable labor at a time when every effort should have been concentrated on keeping ahead of the floods and the demands for water. It is doubtful whether the Senator who asked for it even looked at the list.

This incident merely illustrates the conditions under which the Governmental forces have been compelled to work since the time the land owners were required to begin to make payment. It also illustrates the author's point that it is important to sever politics from business in the administration of this Governmental subsidy.

The question at issue is not as to whether a subsidy, as such, is a good or bad thing, but as to the misunderstanding which surrounds it and the importance of clearly bringing out, at all times, the amount and character of it. There is need here for unqualified clearness of statement; it is where the politician is most solicitous and most clever in concealing the facts. He is able to confuse the issue by a somewhat clever juggling of words. He uses the word "farmer" on all possible occasions, stressing the hardships and sufferings of the pioneer, and then the public is generally willing to expend its money freely.

Bear in mind the fact that the Government, in carrying out its reclamation policies, is dealing not with farmers as such, but with land owners. These land owners may or may not be farmers in the true sense of the word. The fact that they claim to own a piece of land which may be farmed, does not make them farmers. Possibly 40% of these land owners are non-resident. The hearings before the House Committee on Irrigation have shown that on the Government projects—to a greater extent than on private projects—the claimants to land ownership range down the alphabet from actors, bankers, and carpenters to undertakers, veterinarians, watchmen, and zoologists. Every occupation is represented; unfortunately, there is not a preponderating percentage of men who would qualify under a strict test as real "honest-to-goodness" dirt farmers. Such men are usually too wise to undertake this kind of pioneering. They prefer to wait until the hardship and the uncertainties of the life of a pioneer have past, knowing full well that, when true land values are established, they can buy a good farm, carefully selected with reference to climate, crops, and market, practically at less than real cost.

The men who seek to enter on public lands that may be reclaimed, are necessarily adventurous and certainly optimistic and imaginative. They are not held back by the dictates of experience and, as a rule, have little anticipation of remaining long in the new country. They are usually attracted by the hope of getting something for nothing and of realizing the pioneer profits. This is no reflection on them. In fact, they are what are called "typical Americans", willing to take a chance, risking comfort and even the health of their families and themselves, looking forward to something better; each doing his part according to his ability.

The turnover in ownership is large. It is popularly stated that there are at least three successive owners before a relatively permanent home is established. This means in the aggregate large individual losses with occasional gains. Each successive owner has usually contributed something in the way of buildings and labor, more or less intelligently applied, adding to the real or productive values thereby. Sometimes, however, by careless handling of the water, the land itself has deteriorated, or become impregnated with salt or alkali; about 20% of the land has thus been injured.

The popular remedy proposed is that which occurs at first to every one, namely, that the ordinary run of citizens should not be permitted to exercise their individual discretion, but should be required to pass careful scrutiny before being permitted to enter on public land reclaimed or reclaimable by Federal funds. This is fine. As a practical thing, however, there are not enough applicants or purchasers to permit this kind of selection. It has been tried at various times and under various conditions without notable success. In fact, it comes down to this: That any man who has the faith and courage to enter on such an undertaking is more than welcome, and his shortcomings are excused. Moreover, experience with thousands of families shows that sometimes success has been made by the most unpromising specimens and, on the other hand, deplorable failures have been made by men who have come on the project with plenty of money and all the qualifications specified in an approved rule of procedure. It is the intangible, the mental attitude, a thing which cannot be measured by ordinary standards, that has resulted in success or failure.

While these changes in land ownership are taking place, on a Government project as contrasted with a private enterprise, there is a steadily increasing pressure for relief. Every one is heavily in debt, the bankers, to a certain extent, are desperate over the outlook; the local politicians advertise in speeches and in broadsides that if elected they will work for relief to the land owner. They are elected on this platform. As a result Congress, year after year, has granted substantial relief. It is true that this is not the kind of repudiation predicted by former Speaker Cannon and others, but the effect is similar in that the whole amount of money advanced by the Government is not repaid. It becomes in effect what Mr. Henny describes as a subsidy and one that is partly necessary. It is not a matter to be grieved about, nor ignored; but fairness to the taxpayers of the country demands that the extent of it should not be concealed; nor should it be forgotten that private enterprise, which has reclaimed ten times the area of Federal enterprises, has had no such relief.

At present, it is peculiarly important that the public be taken into full confidence on this matter. The time is arriving when large claims on the public purse will be made for further engineering works in connection with reclamation. The Colorado River interests are demanding not millions but tens of millions of dollars. The land owners in the Columbia Basin are well organized in their demand for hundreds of millions. In fact, it is now the fashion to speak in terms of hundreds of millions when dealing with the subject of water control and development.

The cost per acre has caused several great reclamation projects to be rejected again and again; but they are still coming forward with ingenious schemes for repayment of costs (otherwise prohibitive) on the basis of a small percentage continued through several generations. Incidentally, of course, few seriously believe that Congress will ultimately insist on these large repayments, but will follow the well-established precedent of passing annual relief bills.

On top of these demands from the West, for the construction of large irrigation works with which to reclaim desert land, there comes the still greater and more urgent demand for the entire Mississippi Valley for immediate expenditure of hundreds of millions, not to extend the agricultural area, but to save that which has already become highly developed. Then, too, added to the demands of the people upon Congress, is the unsolved problem of the St. Lawrence River; the coastal or Atlantic inland waterways; the future of the Rio Grande; and the great host of flood protection, hydro-electric developments, such as Muscle Shoals, Great Falls on the Potomac, and other schemes stimulated in every part of the country. The advocates of all these are earnest, enthusiastic, and effective. The lobbies in Washington have never been so well organized and well financed. Lobbying, as such, is recognized as a necessity; even "an essential industry", in that it is impossible for the great body of Congress to understand the problems involved.

Engineers now have an opportunity to turn their attention, for a time at least, to these financial matters (pointed out by Mr. Henny) so that they will not be uninformed or swept off their feet and that the economists may be able to perform a larger notable public service by weighing the costs and benefits of the many great enterprises presented for public approval.

J. C. STEVENS,* M. AM. SOC. C. E. (by letter).—This paper presents, in condensed form and in a very sane and rational manner, the present status of irrigation institutions in the United States. It is a sort of "looking backward" on the past 50 or more years of irrigation successes and failures.

One outstanding fact about the work of the U. S. Bureau of Reclamation deserves emphasis. To June 30, 1925, twenty-three years after the passage of the Reclamation Act, more than 82% of all monies due for construction charges and nearly 81% of all maintenance and operation charges had been paid into the United States Treasury by the settlers on the various Government projects.

When one considers that much of this work was pioneering in nature, often handicapped by lack of physical data, and hindered by political maneuvers, he must concede to Government reclamation a measure of success, equal if not superior to most corporate and private enterprises.

Another feature the author could well have included in his summary is that sound financing demands that all elements of cost be studied in advance. If drainage is essential, and it frequently is, it must be included. If settlers are to be furnished with land that has been leveled, ditched, and fenced; upon which houses have been built and implements and stock supplied; if expenditures are contemplated for colonizing; if the project must be "carried" until it is sufficiently settled to pay operation costs; these items must be included in the budget of the developing organization.

If the settlers are known in advance to be unable to meet all the items of cost, then their probable payments must be fairly estimated and the balance considered in the nature of a subsidy or carried over into an account to be amortized at some future time when the project shall have become a well ordered going concern. Many of the failures may be traced to an unwillingness on the part of the developing agency to reckon with or even inquire into these extraneous elements of cost.

The term, subsidy, is too often taken to mean cash payments, whereas it really means any aid to an enterprise for public convenience. All Federal Reclamation projects are subsidized to the extent that no interest is charged on deferred payments for construction costs. In general, such subsidies are more than repaid by the general increase in taxable values resulting from conversion of raw to productive lands.

The author's Conclusion (*d*) that "the irrigation district method is not well adapted to the reclamation of large areas of desert land", must be considered in the light of the text of the paper regarding Class B lands the initial value of which is less than the funds that must be provided for reclamation.

While it is true that in the aggregate large areas of raw land distributed over a multitude of projects, have been successfully reclaimed by the irrigation district method, it is doubtful whether this method would have been successful had all these projects been thrown into one.

Settlers have diverse individual tastes and desires, and no one project or one locality will suit all. It is practically certain, therefore, that the coloni-

* Cons. Hydr. Engr. (Stevens & Koon), Portland, Ore.

zation of a multitude of smaller projects, scattered throughout the West, has generally proceeded much more rapidly than if these areas were concentrated.

The success of any enterprise for the reclamation of raw lands hinges finally on the ability to colonize it to a point where interest and operating charges may be met. Failing this the "carrying costs" will wreck almost any private or district organization. They could only be met by Federal funds the use of which would thus constitute a form of subsidy.

The writer thinks the author could well modify his Conclusion (*d*), previously mentioned, to read: "The irrigation district method is not well adapted to the reclamation of large projects of desert land".

R. P. Teele,* Esq. (by letter).—This paper agrees so completely with the writer's views† that there is little occasion to add anything to the author's discussion. It is needless to take the space to re-state points of agreement, but it would be well to discuss a few other points.

In his opening paragraph, Mr. Henny states that the West is dependent on irrigation for its development and, that "it must grow the bulk of its own food requirements to permit industries to enlarge and its resources to be developed." The implication is that the West needs more irrigation to provide its own food requirements. Yet, in the arid region, there is not one section that contains a large irrigated area that does not have to go outside to market its principal crops. In traveling over several of the larger projects, it will be found that a conspicuous feature of the local news everywhere is the number of cars of products that have "rolled" to outside markets. The point is that the bulk of the land now irrigated, is not used to produce a local food supply, nor will the bulk of the land reclaimed in the future be used for that purpose.

Mr. Henny argues, as do many others, that additional reclamation should not wait on higher prices and an actual demand for products, because it takes several years to develop a large irrigation project. In referring to the Census figures for 1920 and 1925, he gives an effective rebuttal of his own argument. He gives Census figures showing a decrease of 31 000 000 acres in "improved land" during the period 1920 to 1925. That land went out of use because of low prices. Most of it, and much other land, can and will come into use with higher prices. That 31 000 000 acres will act as a shock absorber and give ample time to build a few new projects before the shortage of tillable land becomes acute, even if the projects are not started until the pressure is felt.

It is difficult, if not impossible to follow Mr. Henny's reasoning in his discussion of the insistent demand for further reclamation in the West, when he states that:

"The demand, moreover, is for new projects on an increasing scale of magnitude and is so general and unanimous that it cannot logically be ascribed to motives reminiscent of 'pork barrel' appropriations."

* Agricultural Economist, Bureau of Agricultural Economics, U. S. Dept. of Agriculture, Washington, D. C. Mr. Teele died on August 31, 1927.

† *Bulletin No. 1257,* U. S. Dept. of Agriculture, 1924.

It will be recalled that Congress recently provided for writing off about $27 000 000 of construction costs on Government projects and extended the period of repayment of construction charges from 20 to 40 years without interest, and that a committee was appointed to hear arguments for revising existing contracts on the ground that farmers cannot meet their payments.

Mr. Henny supplies the explanation of the "general and unanimous" demand for new projects and the refutation of his own statement:

"The comparative ease with which these and other relief measures were secured from Congress, the fact that not in a single case, even after the passage of the newer Acts, has the Government enforced collection by foreclosure under lien, and the ready encouragement of farmers' demands by Congressmen, have had an unfortunate effect on the psychological condition * * *."

He takes issue with the writer's arguments against a National subsidy to land reclamation, quoting: "There is no justification for a National subsidy to land reclamation. If local interests justify the subsidizing of land reclamation the subsidy should be local;" and states that he believes it is "too sweeping." This belief is justified and the statement should be modified by limiting it to the present time. This matter has been discussed more fully in a book by the writer.* There, it is suggested that the cost be spread in proportion to the benefits. After discussing the lack of correlation between demand for additional reclamation and the need for the products to be grown, the writer states:

"The real problem for the future of reclamation is the devising of a policy that will so strengthen that relation that it will control the rate of expansion. The most effective means of accomplishing this will be to attach financial liability to demand. That is, let those who demand the undertaking of a reclamation project assume an effective liability for the cost. This can be accomplished through the district system already utilized to a considerable extent in irrigation and almost exclusively in drainage reclamation by providing for including in districts not only the land to be actually irrigated or drained, but also the territory to be benefitted indirectly, including cities and towns in the vicinity. The extent of each district should be determined by conditions in its particular case, and, in theory, cost should be apportioned in proportion to benefits, although this is an extremely difficult task in practice.

"The apportionment of cost in proportion to benefits should be a fundamental part of our reclamation policy of the future, if there is to be any public participation in reclamation. This policy can be put into effect * * * by having districts formed under public supervision and including within them all the property that will be benefitted, not overlooking the towns and cities whose chambers of commerce are so active in demanding the undertaking of new enterprises; and requiring the approval of the districts by the counties and States if there are to be county and State contributions; and by Congress if there is to be a Federal contribution.

"Certainly, if reclamation is to be undertaken because of public benefits, the reclaimed land should not be expected to repay the whole cost.

"Such a scheme is susceptible of universal application. If it appears that there will not be such a general benefit as to justify the inclusion of

* "The Economics of Land Reclamation," by R. P. Teele, The A. W. Shaw Co., Chicago, Ill., 1927.

any land outside of that to be reclaimed, the boundaries can be fixed on that basis, and the reclaimed land alone will be liable for the cost; if only lands in the immediate vicinity will be benefitted, the boundaries can be fixed on that basis; if the benefit is county-wide, counties may undertake reclamation; if it is State-wide, the States may undertake it; and if the benefit is interstate, interstate districts may be created."

This shows what the writer meant by local subsidy. Mr. Henny compares land reclamation subsidies to railroad subsidies, rivers and harbors subsidies, and the protective tariff. There is one very important difference that he and others usually overlook. The railroads are public service corporations and furnish service to all who may have occasion to use them; the rivers and harbors and highways are open to all who may pass that way; and the tariff affords protection (if it does) to any one who may produce the protected article; while an irrigation system supplies water to designated lands and to no other lands. The immediate benefit is to those lands, and the owners of those lands have exclusive use of the water supplied. The public has no right whatever to its use.

J. L. BURKHOLDER,* M. AM. SOC. C. E. (by letter).—This paper is of timely interest to every one having the welfare and development of the Western United States at heart. Under present conditions, and under irrigation district methods, it is almost impossible to finance large irrigation developments. There is an apparent lack of demand for new farms, and it is doubtful if projects, requiring settlement of people on the land, should be recommended for construction at this time. This fact, and the recent criticism of the Federal Reclamation Bureau and the apparent inability of some of its projects to meet construction payments, certainly indicates that irrigation problems should be given thorough study.

The paper has listed the various agencies heretofore utilized for accomplishing irrigation work as follows: (1) Federal; (2) State; (3) Carey Act; and (4) irrigation districts. The last of these agencies is divided into two general groups; (A) districts with land values greater, and (B) districts with land values smaller, than the face value of the proposed bond issues. The first-mentioned districts have been generally successful.

It may be of interest to note that New Mexico has recently organized a large district, under the Conservancy Act of the State of New Mexico, which closely follows the Conservancy Acts of the States of Ohio and Colorado. Ohio and Colorado used the conservancy form of law to accomplish flood-control work. The Conservancy Act of New Mexico has been adapted to the purpose of accomplishing flood control, irrigation, and drainage. This experiment with a fifth agency has heretofore not been tried.

The project extends along the Rio Grande from the Elephant Butte Reservoir on the south, to White Rock Canyon on the north, a distance of about 150 miles. The district is known as the Middle Rio Grande Conservancy District. This District would fall into the general group of "A" Districts, considered by Mr. Henny, because the land values are greater than the face value of the proposed bond issues. The organizers of the District had

* Chf. Engr., Middle Rio Grande Conservancy District, Albuquerque, N. Mex.

in mind that the conservancy form of law was better adapted to the local problems than the irrigation district methods, for the following principal reasons:

(1) It provides for the "benefit method" of assessments, which insures that the municipalities and corporations, affected by the proposed work, will be required to pay a fair share of the cost thereof. The flexibility of this method of assessing costs is also well suited to take care of the great variation in local soil and irrigation conditions;

(2) The law grants wide powers to the district, including the police powers of the State;

(3) The preparation of an official plan is required prior to the authorization of the work by the District Court. This Court, sitting as a Conservancy Court, either approves or disapproves the plan, after holding hearings thereon. If the Court approves the plan, it then holds hearings on the appraisals, and when these are confirmed, the District may proceed to issue and sell bonds.

The work of the Middle Rio Grande Conservancy District has not proceeded far enough to offer proof of the superiority of this form of law for accomplishing reclamation problems, but the writer believes that many advantages are gained under such a law, especially where the contemplated work includes a variety of features.

Perhaps, one of the difficulties that have surrounded irrigation development, under all the agencies utilized to date, has been the limitation of the powers of that agency. Some degree of flood control and river protection is a common need in many of the irrigated valleys. Drainage is now known to be necessary for protecting practically all irrigation developments.

Drainage and flood-control works may directly benefit municipalities and corporations as well as lands, and the problems involved are properly a part of the general reclamation scheme, including irrigation. As a rule, these features are so connected and inter-related that they can only be solved in the most effective and economical way by considering them as a single problem. The Conservancy District agency seems to offer many outstanding advantages for accomplishing reclamation work, involving irrigation, flood control, and drainage features. One of these is that all property that is benefited is taxed, not only the agricultural lands.

The success or failure of some irrigation developments to repay construction costs is judged entirely by an artificial financial status, which in no way represents the actual wealth created by the project. The time element of the repayment period has been an entirely arbitrary one, yet projects are classed as failures unless repayment is made within the period set. For these reasons, it may be pertinent to examine the question further before pronouncing sentence as to success or failure. Perhaps, if proper standards are set up, there will be more successful projects and fewer failures. Undoubtedly, some projects that are now pronounced as failures, will be adjudged successful after the early losses are absorbed.

Many of the private companies effecting irrigation work in the South Platte Valley, near Denver, Colo., became bankrupt in the early stages of the development. This District is quite successful at the present time, and the

City of Denver, and many prosperous smaller towns depend quite largely on the wealth created by the irrigation of about 1 500 000 acres in this vicinity.

Furthermore, it seems evident to the writer that the recent depression in irrigated farm values is largely the result of the general slump in value of farm products. This slump has affected land values in all parts of the country; in humid areas as well as in irrigated sections.

The Federal Reclamation Acts provide that the total cost of the projects shall be repaid by the benefited agricultural lands. Many cities and towns have developed and prospered along with the irrigated farms as the direct result of Government irrigation. Among the largest of these are El Paso, Tex.; Phœnix, Ariz.; Yakima, Wash.; and Boise, Idaho. The taxable wealth in these cities, and the many smaller communities on reclamation projects, is in no way a resource of the project and, yet, irrigation is responsible for the major part of the wealth represented by them.

Another case of wealth, created by irrigation, is the profit taken by individual land holders who sell before repaying their construction charges. Large and even excessive profits have been taken in this way from practically all large irrigation developments. The purchasers may now be having difficulty in meeting repayment costs and interest on the high price paid for the land, but the seller is enjoying the full profit. It is the rule, on all Federal projects, that the lands are commonly bought and sold without any account being taken of the unpaid construction charges.

On the Rio Grande Project, New Mexico and Texas, certain flood-control work is now being done by the City and County of El Paso. It is doubtful whether the Government could have accomplished this work under existing laws, but it is a normal phase of the Government's work. The Elephant Butte Dam is affording protection against floods in the City of El Paso; yet, no charge could be made against the municipality.

The original Reclamation Act contemplates only the development of large desert land areas owned, in part at least, by the Government. If irrigation development under Federal direction is confined to such areas, subsidies from the State or National Government are justifiable as offsets against the taxable wealth created by the development, which cannot be directly assessed for work accomplished. Federal development of desert land areas should be continued as fast as additional farms are in demand.

Federal reclamation has not been restricted to such developments, however, and, in some instances, the result of this has been an unequal distribution of the assessed cost of construction. If the Federal Government is to continue a program of reclamation that is suited to all the reclamation problems of the Western United States, the existing laws should be changed to permit greater flexibility and a wider scope of accomplishment. This should include drainage and flood-control work. The necessity of increasing the scope of Federal Reclamation may be open to question because many drainage and flood-control projects have land values greater than the cost of the proposed improvement. When this is the case, it is usually possible to finance work at favorable terms, and progress may thus be made through district organizations without help from the National Government.

MORROUGH P. O'BRIEN,* JUN. AM. SOC. C. E. (by letter).—While Mr. Henny presents the immediate problems of irrigation finance in an admirable manner, it seems that some of the more fundamental aspects of the situation are well worth consideration.

Although the development of the western part of the United States will undoubtedly strengthen its position in the Pacific Ocean, it will hasten the time when the population will be pressing against the limits of the available food supply. Mr. Raymond Pearl has predicted† that within a hundred years, the United States will have reached a point in the expenditure of its natural resources and food supply comparable to the present conditions in Europe. The time will come when it will be necessary to develop the sections of the arid States that are suitable for irrigation, but any premature development means economic waste, because the present available wealth would be used in an unprofitable venture. By a "premature development" is meant any improvement completed before the price of the products yielded by that improvement is sufficient to pay all the cost plus the compounded interest.

Contrary to the usual belief, an increase in the food supply per capita with a consequent reduction in prices is not a permanent benefit because, as Malthus has shown quite conclusively, the population immediately responds to this stimulus and in a few years the average condition is about the same as before the change. Previous to the introduction of mechanical industries into Germany, the population was very close to the maximum that the country could support as long as the inhabitants remained predominantly agrarian; but with the advent of machinery and the development of foreign markets for their goods, the population entered upon another cycle and is now approaching a second peak. Such fundamental changes will undoubtedly occur in the future, but it seems to be rather bad policy to depend on them to maintain a high standard of living. If the great areas of the West are developed only when they are necessary (and the evidence of such necessity should be their ability to pay for themselves) the period of general prosperity will be prolonged. Predictions as to the maximum population that a country can sustain are somewhat futile, but it can be stated, with a considerable degree of certainty, that at some future date the population will have reached a point where a considerable portion of it is barely able to sustain life. Such a condition has always led to wars of colonial conquest—for a "place in the sun"—and although the American national conscience has been against the acquisition and permanent retention of foreign colonies, a change is indicated by the attitude of the United States in dealing with the Philippines and Nicaragua. This country will probably, at some not very distant date, enter the competition for the sparsely inhabited regions of Asia, Africa, and South America.

That the irrigation of a few hundred thousand acres of arid lands is immediately going to involve the country in wars and misery is, of course,

* Toledo, Ohio.

† "The Biology of Population Growth."

ridiculous and it is not the purpose of this discussion to advance any such proposition. However, before deciding to construct projects of such magnitude as those proposed for the Columbia and Colorado Rivers, the question should first be decided as to whether they are really desirable at present or might better be held as a latent supply of wealth for the future.

When irrigation projects, of such magnitude that a single State or group of States cannot finance them, are found to be economically sound, Federal aid should be given, but only under conditions that safeguard the interests of the remaining States. It seems that the only equitable basis for such aid is that the States benefited, guarantee the full cost of the project plus the interest until the debt is paid. Although the principle of interest has been attacked from the ethical viewpoint by some writers, the fact remains that the Government pays interest on nearly all money expended, and this interest represents an important item of the total cost. A sum of money compounded at 4% will be doubled in about 17 years. If an irrigation project does not begin to pay off the original cost in that length of time, the cost to the Government is just double the original outlay. There seems to be no more reason for neglecting the interest charge than the original cost, although most writers on the subject regard the two very differently.

When it is remembered that most of the Federal irrigation projects have not paid their original cost and, in many cases, not even a substantial part of it, the demand for more projects hardly indicates their success, but shows a desire for more gifts from a benevolent and paternal Government. Naturally, the owner of arid land is anxious to have irrigation if all the increase in value will accrue to himself and the entire expense will be borne by the Federal Government. From a rather close observation of one large project, it would seem that for the most part the settlers were guilty of bad faith. When the project was completed, land values had increased to a point where an additional charge per acre for the cost of the project would have made a profit impossible and yet the land changed hands at this price. If this condition is not explained by sheer ignorance on the part of the buyers, it must have been due to a generally accepted belief that enough political pressure could be brought to bear to prevent the collection of the assessments.

In general, governmental expenditures for internal improvements should be put on a more equitable basis. It is sometimes argued that the prosperity of one section of the country reflects upon the prosperity of the whole. To say the least, this contention is difficult to prove, and it is certainly not true of competing regions such as California and Florida. It is extremely unfortunate that the "Sugar Bowl" region of Louisiana has been inundated, but it will be a little unjust if through sympathy a part of the cost of rehabilitation is placed on the sugar-beet growers of Ohio and Michigan, and this will be the result if the Government erects flood-protection works on the Mississippi without a guaranty that the States benefited will ultimately assume the indebtedness. Governmental aid to one of several competing districts without the definite obligation of repayment is doubly unjust, because it gives the one region an immediate advantage and, in addition, the cost of the improvement must be assumed in part by the competing regions.

D. C. Henny,* M. Am. Soc. C. E. (by letter).—The writer is under great obligation to the many distinguished authorities on the subject of irrigation for their discussions. He is gratified to find that the presentation of a paper, rather economic than technical in its nature, is commended; that it is not, for that reason, criticized; and that, on the whole, there appears to be fair agreement on the conclusions reached.

The reasons stated in the discussion for approval and resulting from greatly diversified experience and from viewing the subject from various angles, add great weight to the conclusions.

Mr. Hinderlider raises the question as to what is profitable farming. The writer believes that ability of the average industrious and intelligent farmer to raise a family according to reasonable modern standards and to keep out of debt, private or public, may be regarded as complete success even without accumulation of money. It is in this sense that the term, profitable farming, was used in the writer's Conclusion, (*a*) that "increase of irrigated area will and should be slow when and where crop prices do not render farming profitable". The Government, whether State or Federal, should not encourage, by subsidy, or otherwise, any increase of opportunities which would force a lowering of the standard of living for the average man.

Mr. Hinderlider questions the writer's conclusion that "the irrigation district method is not well adapted to the reclamation of large areas of desert land". In support of his criticism, he quotes developments in Colorado. He is far more familiar with Colorado conditions than the writer who cannot directly question the statement advanced that "many of the largest and most successful developments in Colorado have been effected under the original Irrigation District Act and amendments thereto".

The writer has some familiarity with conditions as they existed in Colorado thirty and forty years ago. At that time irrigation, after making great strides in the vicinity of Denver and Pueblo and on the Upper Rio Grande, all under private financing, received a severe setback through financial losses, partly resulting from the panic of 1893. Mr. Burkholder happens to refer to this subject where he states that, "many of the private companies effecting irrigation work in the South Platte Valley, near Denver, Colo., became bankrupt in the early stages of the development". The foundation thus laid was subsequently built upon by District organizations, which is quite another matter than starting reclamation from the virgin desert stage by District financing. Mr. Hinderlider does not state definitely to what extent the latter method by itself has proved successful in Colorado. The point which the writer tried to make is not refuted by the success which may at times have been achieved. The risk of failure is present in most cases to a high degree, as was well shown by the statistics compiled by the late R. P. Teele, and published and referred to in his discussion. It was also fully confirmed by other discussors of the writer's paper and also by the contemporaneous paper† of R. K. Tiffany, M. Am. Soc. C. E., and the discussions thereof.

* Cons. Engr., Portland, Ore.

† "State Reclamation in Washington," see p. 582, *et seq.*

The point is that the security at the time of bonding is practically all potential and that District bonds cannot be sold at reasonable figures unless the prospective buyer is kept in ignorance of the risk. The apparent necessity for concealment as well as the large percentage of failures which have resulted in such cases appear to the writer to furnish ample justification for his conclusion.

Mr. Hinderlider's argument in favor of turning over, at the earliest practicable moment, the operation and management of subsidized irrigation enterprises to District organizations, is fully concurred in and has for years been the process of the U. S. Reclamation Bureau in spite of frequent local opposition.

Mr. Grunsky argues that a Government subsidy consisting of any reduction from the full cost of irrigation, together with interest, is promptly absorbed by the land owner in the price he obtains for his land when he sells. This has been true for many years, but does not hold true for the last five years because of inability to sell at acceptable prices. It may also be stated that earnest endeavors are being made to counteract such absorption. One plan is to require of original land owners, before project work is commenced, an agreement that in case of sale the true selling price must be stated in the deed, in order to make a transfer legal and that at the time of sale, part payment must be made of water charges otherwise not yet due, in case the selling price exceeds a given base.

Other plans intended to hinder land speculation have been introduced by District organizations. The desirability of giving the ultimate farmer the benefit of the subsidy is fully appreciated and will probably in some manner and degree be realized in the future.

The writer is especially gratified in finding full support from Mr. Grunsky, Mr. Newell, and others of his contention that in case of subsidy the total extent of the commitment should, so far as practicable, be determined and made known. The difficulty of accomplishing this was forcibly pointed out by Mr. Newell in his statement referring to past policies as to Government officers, that "discussion of real costs may be followed by dismissal". The writer also is under popular disapproval in certain sections in the West for his insistence on this important requirement without which all subsidy becomes illegitimate and baneful.

Mr. Jacobs would prefer subsidy to be confined to the loan of funds for a long period and at a low rate of interest, $3\frac{1}{2}$ or 4 per cent. He believes that "most of the projects that can be justified at all, can work themselves out to economic safety without the aid of any subsidy". Where this is true any subsidy, whether consisting of a low rate of interest, or no interest at all, is undesirable provided the time element is not seriously affected. The truth of Mr. Jacob's contention is, however, difficult to ascertain. It is certain that future expansion of irrigation will be greatly retarded if interest payments are insisted on and economic feasibility is determined by disinterested and well qualified men. It is an open question, however, to what particular extent subsidy should be granted at any particular time and place, and it is admitted that any type of subsidy is liable to serious abuse.

Mr. Dunham comments on publicity which unavoidably advertises contemplated Government activities. The effect of resultant land speculation is, of course, harmful and has been combatted so far as possible by withdrawal of public lands and by exacting contracts from present owners. Quiet accomplishment under methods flavoring of Secret Service is, however, believed to be impracticable as well as undesirable.

Mr. Newell reviews the history of the Reclamation Bureau from an angle which, even where it goes far beyond the original scope of the paper, makes his discussion a most valuable addition. His extensive experience leads him to approve the writer's conclusion that it is important to sever politics from business in the administration of a Government subsidy.

Mr. Stevens points out that if Government subsidies consist of the loan of money free of interest "such subsidies are more than repaid by the general increase in taxable values resulting from conversion of raw to productive lands". This is an incidental benefit of unquestioned value, but cannot in itself be an argument in favor of subsidy if it is unwise in other respects.

Mr. Stevens holds that the writer's summary should have included the necessity for studying all elements of cost in advance. Conclusion (*h*) ends with the words "total cost, including all items of present and future expenditure". This expression is believed to be sufficiently comprehensive.

He also suggests a change in Conclusion (*d*) to the effect that the ill adaptation of the irrigation district method to the reclamation of large areas of desert land should refer to large areas in single projects. This was intended to be the meaning and was so understood by others discussing this point.

Mr. Teele stated that irrigation in the West is not solely for the purpose of providing for local food production, and that a far smaller area than is at present irrigated could satisfy this requirement. This is quite true, but whether exported fruit or local food be considered the by-product, it is unquestionable that either is of benefit to the other and will permit profit at lower selling prices than if production is confined, in spite of suitability of land, to one or the other alone. The writer knows of no extended irrigated area devoted solely to production for export.

Mr. Teele in his interesting discussion further argued that 31 000 000 acres, which went out of cultivation during the period from 1920 to 1925, will act as a "shock absorber" when need for more agricultural products should become evident. This is believed to be the case to a far less extent than the acreage figure would indicate, as the greater part of this area is probably land, marginal because of being situated in the semi-arid belt and, therefore, without irrigation being capable of producing a limited character of crops, mostly cereals. When shortage of food shall first become seriously felt in the United States it will probably not be because of shortage of such products. It seems rather probable that, coincident with the gradual re-use of this area and in part preceding it, additional irrigation will be necessary to preserve a desirable balance.

Mr. Teele found the general Western demand for new projects was explained by the easing off in the enforcement of financial obligations accepted by the farmers. This may be one reason, but it is by no means the predominant one. The demand generally results from the desire to realize on local assets supposed to be valuable, but now lying idle. It is probably made partly with the knowledge that past policies in this respect are changing for the better and mostly in ignorance of the exact showing made in regard to collections.

Mr. Teele further explained what he meant by local subsidy in his *Bulletin No. 1257,* U. S. Department of Agriculture, 1924, to the effect that this term did not refer to local government subsidy, but to a different method of taxation, including not only the land directly affected, but also interests indirectly benefited. In his book, "The Economics of Land Reclamation", it is recommended that cost be spread in proportion to benefits.

It is questionable whether the term "subsidy" is correct in such a case. A taxpayer does not ordinarily consider himself as a contributor to subsidy when he pays his improvement tax. However, the method of taxation on the basis of benefit has decided advantages whether in the case of irrigation alone or in connection with flood control and drainage, as was ably argued by Mr. Burkholder.

This method would make possible reclamation under the District bonding method where otherwise it would be of questionable legitimacy. It contains the elements of inherent justice. To the extent that its use is practicable and a fair division of benefits can be worked out agreeable to all interests it will reduce the need of Governmental aid. Mr. Burkholder correctly points out that this aid is inadvisable where it is not necessary. This method is likely to be on trial, as explained by Mr. Burkholder, on the Middle Rio Grande, and there is good reason for believing that it will work out successfully and that in many cases in this manner Class "B" Districts may be raised to the "A" class.

Mr. O'Brien enters into the wider field of the Malthusian theory. He argues that development in any section ahead of actual need of the whole country is premature and should not be countenanced, even if admitting that development of the West will strengthen America's position in the Pacific Ocean. If this theory had been applied during the earlier Colonial days, the United States would probably not extend beyond the Alleghanies. There would have been no free land grants on the part of the United States and no general encouragement of Western expansion. Subsequently, there would also have been no need of railroad land grants, food products having been relatively abundant ever since the first successful settlements west of the Atlantic. He believes that the United States should hold a large portion of the West as a reserve for future use. The writer holds that, ethically, the Nation cannot maintain a claim to any large portion of this continent against claims of other nations who may need it now, if held merely for future use. Many, especially in the West, may be misled by the urge of further early development, but they believe it to be founded on sound principles which dictate that the only right they have to the land they claim comes from occupation and beneficial use.

Mr. O'Brien considers that high living standards may become a peril in the future and, by implication, that they should be held lower to train Americans for effective competition in the future when population will press against the limits of food supply. Others, however, live in hope that science and experience may yet teach people how to ward off the fatal pressure against food limits otherwise logically predicted and to maintain and even raise living standards for all.

Mr. O'Brien advocates guaranty by States benefiting from irrigation development. If this benefit radiates from its center like waves in a pond, who shall say that it extends merely to an artificial delimitation of the pond and not to the shore line. Independent of this view it should be repeated that, comparatively speaking, Western States, in the money sense, are poor and that in the aggregate they contain an enormous area of Government land which receives benefits from all improvements, but pays no taxes. State aid, where extended, will probably have to be confined to help of worthy Districts in financial difficulties, origination of small new projects and assistance in colonizing large Federal projects.

In this matter of subsidy there is moreover apt to be an adjustment. The argument used by Mr. O'Brien would be even more effective if applied to the case of Government expenditures for the Harbor of New York, which surely benefits that wealthy city and State to a far greater extent than it does the West; also, to the case of tariffs which protect and benefit one industry more than another and all industries more than farming. The West is rather an inopportune section of the United States upon which to visit a strict limitation of Government aid, not applied elsewhere.

In various discussions, attention is called to the different nature of subsidy for the reclamation of private lands and subsidies, such as railroad grants, tariffs, and harbor improvement. This same point may be raised in connection with Mississippi River flood control. No one subsidy can be exactly like another, and the only question involved before it is granted is whether it is, on the whole, for the good of the Nation.

AMERICAN SOCIETY OF CIVIL ENGINEERS
INSTITUTED 1852

TRANSACTIONS

Paper No. 1667

STATE RECLAMATION IN WASHINGTON*

By R. K. Tiffany,† M. Am. Soc. C. E.

With Discussion by Messrs. James Rhea Luper, W. G. Swendsen, J. C. Stevens, O. L. Waller, Joseph Jacobs, F. H. Newell, and R. K. Tiffany.

That for many years the State of Washington has recognized the interest of the public in reclamation development is evidenced by many laws designed to aid and promote such development, and more particularly during recent years by the Reclamation and Land Settlement Acts of 1919, the Reclamation Bond Certification Act of 1923, and by the activity of the State in investigating and promoting the development of the great Columbia Basin irrigation project.

Reclamation, as the term is generally used, includes development for agricultural use of swamp, overflow, cut-over, and arid lands. Because irrigation is, and perhaps will continue to be, the predominant phase, this discussion will have chiefly to do with irrigation.

In irrigation development, Washington has passed through the various stages of evolution common to the Western States. First, the little private ditch, the partnership and community ditch, in both of which the development cost was low and the maintenance cost generally negligible. Later, came the stock companies taking up more ambitious enterprises, but the cost under these was generally not more than $10 to $20 per acre and the maintenance cost correspondingly low.

Thus far, all development was by the land owners themselves and without expectation of profit from the irrigation plan, as such. In the Nineties came

* Presented at the meeting of the Irrigation Division, Seattle, Wash., July 15, 1926.

† Superv. of Hydraulics, Olympia, Wash.

the promoters, financed by Eastern capital, attracted by a paper-showing of tremendous profits on the investment in irrigation works.

Following these projects came the first serious disappointments. The panic of 1893 checked the stream of westward immigration, thousands of acres of land under ditch lay idle, and operating costs on the small areas under cultivation, together with interest on the large investments in land and canal systems, soon brought financial ruin to practically all these enterprises. In later years, most of them were re-financed and have become rich and prosperous districts, but the initial investments were largely lost.

The topography of the irrigable lands and the river valleys of Washington differs from that of most of the Western States. The streams flow in deep, narrow valleys so that the building of the larger irrigation systems involves expensive construction in the way of tunnels, bench flumes, and pressure pipes. The large bodies of land irrigated and irrigable, with the single exception of the Yakima Indian Reservation, lie on benches at considerable elevations above the river valleys and are generally rolling and steep as compared with the plains of Idaho or the gentle slopes of the Salt River and Sacramento Valleys, and most of the other larger irrigated areas of the West. To overcome this combination of physical difficulties means necessarily high cost for the irrigation works. Of the remaining projects in the State of Washington on which careful estimates have been made the construction cost, exclusive of storage, will range from $100 to $150 per acre.

It was the experience of private corporations in the early development and the high cost of all remaining projects which brought the realization that there is little chance of additional irrigation development in Washington by private capital; and at the close of the World War, with good prices generally prevailing for farm products, with the good lands under existing ditches practically all producing, and with apparently a steady increase in demand for irrigated land, Washington, in 1919, enacted a State Reclamation Law. The object of the Act is declared to be,

"To provide for the reclamation and development of such of the arid, swamp, overflow, and logged-off lands in the State of Washington as shall be determined to be suitable and economically available for reclamation and development as agricultural lands, and the State of Washington in the exercise of its sovereign and police powers declares the reclamation of such lands to be a State purpose and necessary to the public health, safety, and welfare of its people."

A State Reclamation Board was created consisting of the State Commissioner of Public Lands, the State Treasurer, the State Hydraulic Engineer, the State Commissioner of Agriculture, and the President of the State College. This Board was afterward replaced under the new administrative code by the State Department of Conservation and Development. A State Reclamation Service was authorized and a Reclamation Revolving Fund was created by the levy of a tax of 0.5 mill on all taxable property in the State.

The plan of operation provided that the engineer of the State Reclamation Service should investigate projects brought to its attention and that, if found feasible, the Reclamation Fund should be used to purchase the bonds of properly organized irrigation districts, the construction of the works to be under the supervision of the Department, the bonds to be resold whenever they should become salable in the general market.

In the six years following the passage of the law the State Reclamation Service was extremely active, first, investigating new projects, and, later, when it appeared that there were very few projects that could safely assume the burden of repayment of the estimated cost, the activities were largely transferred to investigation and aid of old projects which were in need of additional funds for rehabilitation or extension work.

All told, about forty irrigation, drainage, and diking projects have been investigated. The State has purchased the bonds of sixteen projects to the amount of approximately $1 462 000. Of this amount the bonds of ten districts, aggregating $516 000, have been resold, practically at cost, no addition being made to cover administrative expense. Bonds of eleven districts to the amount of $946 000 are still owned by the State. Of these, $425 500 in value are considered as probably good, $316 500 as doubtful, and about $204 000 as almost certainly a total loss.

In addition to the actual purchase of bonds, advances have been made by the State to various districts for investigation and construction expense which, up to September 30, 1925, amounted to $840 000. These advances, for the most part, were made under contracts with the districts for repayment in bonds. The two principal items of these advances are $73 160 for investigation of the Methow-Okanogan Reclamation District, the repayment of which is doubtful on account of the high estimated cost; and $741 000 for the investigation and construction of the Whitestone Reclamation District, of which at least $500 000 must be charged off on account of insufficient water supply. The total loss during the first six years' operation of the State Reclamation Service on account of investigations and construction is likely to be between $777 000 and $1 093 500—this from a total investment of $2 200 000, or at the rate of 35 to 49 per cent.

Of the twenty-two projects which were fully investigated and partly or wholly financed by the State Reclamation Fund, five were aided in investigation only. Of the remaining seventeen projects, five only were new projects, the other twelve involving rehabilitation or extension of old privately owned systems. It is obvious that some of these projects were approved rather from a sympathetic motive to settlers on the ground than from any consideration of merit. Some of the heaviest losses may be traced to this cause.

The heaviest single loss is on a project which had been developed privately to serve about 800 acres and which was projected to irrigate more than 8 000 acres at a total estimated cost, including two years' interest, of $900 000. On this project, reports of competent engineers calling attention to the inadequacy of the water supply, were completely ignored, and the project was laid out and about 90% completed on the basis of serving about 8 300 acres. In September, 1925, after a comprehensive study of water supply and of storage possibilities, a board of engineers recommended the reduction of the project to 2 500 acres located in certain definite divisions, and after classification of the lands in these divisions, the District Board of Directors, with the unanimous consent of resident land owners, took action to reduce the area to 2 207 acres of irrigable land.

Two other projects of about 1 000 and 3 000 acres, respectively, are placed in the doubtful class because, although intrinsically good, they are remote from markets and were apparently built in advance of demand for the land. Efforts are now being made by land owners, bond-holders, and various local interests to secure settlers for these projects. If these efforts are reasonably successful within the next year or two, these projects may be placed on a paying basis.

Results of operation under the State Reclamation Law to date (1926), have brought a sharp difference of opinion as to the wisdom of the State continuing in the business of reclamation. Those in favor of continuing point to the beneficial results of the State's assistance to many projects at times when it was practically impossible for them to secure funds for essential reconstruction or additional water supply through the usual banking channels. In passing, it should be said that this aid to "lame ducks", although no doubt beneficial, was not within the intent of the original Act and should not be the controlling factor in determining future State reclamation policy.

Opponents of the idea of State reclamation point out that it is unfair to tax present farmers to provide additional market competition for their products, prices for which in recent years have not been even fairly remunerative. They also point to the heavy losses to the State by reason of its venture in reclamation.

A Special Committee of the State Legislature was appointed at the Special Session in 1926 with instructions to study results of State reclamation to date and to report on or before October 1, 1926, with recommendation as to a future State reclamation policy and program.

The recommendations made by the Committee are as follows:

"1. That the laws with respect to reclamation and land settlement be retained in the statutes of the State of Washington. That the organization of the department be continued for the purposes of study of resources of the State, possibilities of successful reclamation, and for co-operation with the Federal Reclamation Department in the proper development of projects which have been undertaken by the Federal Government within the State. That depository interest and bond interest on moneys in the reclamation fund be conserved within the said fund to replace losses which have accrued and to defray the administration expenses of the department.

"2. That the State department do not undertake the financing of construction on large new projects or projects which have failed in attempted development by private capital.

"3. That the department consider the possibilities of assisting in the internal improvement of proven and successful reclamation projects by investment in the bonds of such districts, and assistance in marketing same at as low a rate of interest as is possible.

"4. That the reclamation fund levy be suspended for a period of two years, as was done at the last session.

"5. That the State co-operate with the Federal Government in affording such assistance as is required by the Federal Government and is within the power of the State to render in and about the construction and development of those reclamation projects definitely approved by the Federal Reclamation Department."

It is of the greatest importance that this problem be considered carefully and without prejudice, having in mind not only the results of past operations under the law, but the probable future needs of the community for reclamation development, and possible alternative means of meeting such need through State, Federal, or private agencies.

It will be conceded by friend and foe alike of State reclamation that the State of Washington eventually will need all possible development of her agricultural area. Her rapid industrial and commercial development during the past few years, with promise of still more rapid growth in the future, based on her native resources in raw materials, her abundant and cheap water power, and her accessibility through maritime commerce to the raw materials and markets of all the countries bordering the Pacific, is sure to demand reasonably steady development of her agricultural possibilities.

Past experience and the magnitude and high cost of the undeveloped reclamation projects in the State will make it difficult, if not impossible, to interest private capital in these enterprises. Under any plan thus far put forth, the interest charges plus the operation and maintenance deficit during the development period will constitute a burden greater than can possibly be borne by the producing area during the earlier years. Investment bankers have learned from bitter experience that this means default in interest payments, hence the impossibility of interesting private capital in this type of development.

It appears that some public agency must assume the responsibility for carrying the larger irrigation projects through their development period. The United States Reclamation Service has been thus carrying projects ever since its inception. The State of Oregon has carried some projects through loans or direct appropriations for payment of bond interest. Is there any means other than State or Federal subsidy of building the remaining large projects?

One plan that has been suggested is that the county or counties that would benefit most directly from the development of a reclamation project should be organized into a district somewhat along the lines of the Miami Conservancy District, which would carry the burden of interest and of operation and maintenance deficit until the project becomes self-supporting.

An underwriting agency of this character might undertake complete development, or it might become responsible for a definite part only, as, for example, the necessary storage works. In some cases benefits other than for irrigation, such as flood control or power, might largely or entirely cover the cost of storage development. Such a plan, although theoretically workable and, in some cases, justifiable by reason of indirect benefits to the underwriting territory, would contain elements of difficulty and danger. If otherwise practicable it should be supported by provisions that would give to the underwriting district complete control of land development in the project so that this development should come in progressive blocks rather than in scattered units throughout the project, based on individual ownership.

This calls for a consideration of some of the fundamental weaknesses of the present irrigation district law as a means of developing large irrigation projects. Like the district laws of most Western States, the Washington law is based on the old "Wright" Act of California, which was undoubtedly framed to meet the needs for financing groups of actual farmers and settlers who were, as a rule, occupying and farming the lands for which irrigation was sought. Under such conditions most of the land would become productive within a short time and might reasonably be expected to bring returns sufficient to meet both interest and other irrigation charges.

In the attempt to apply this law to larger projects, however, difficulties and reverses have developed. Lacking actual settlers ready to make use of the land and water, there has often been a scattering and haphazard development requiring years to bring the project to a position in which operating charges and interest could be met from returns from the land. Scattering, partial development means not only excessive operation and maintenance costs and heavy interest burden on the producing area, but also excessive costs for roads, schools, telephones, and the necessary commercial and marketing agencies. For all these items, whether public or private, are a part of the service requirements of any new community, and the cost of establishing and maintaining them must be borne ultimately by the producing land. If the productive land is scattered, a higher cost must be paid, not only in higher tax levies for public institutions, but also in higher interest rates at the bank and longer profits to "the butcher, the baker, the candlestick maker".

The Yakima Project in the State of Washington has been widely advertised as one of the most successful instances of irrigation development in the West. There are three outstanding reasons for the success of this project: First, its productive soil and favorable climate; second, its ample water supply; and, third, the fact that it has been developed in small and rather compact units so that its growth has been approximately commensurate with the demand for its land and products.

It must be recognized that the large projects remaining in Washington and other States are composed for the most part of strictly arid lands, with few or no *bona fide* settlers. The problem of building the works is simple compared with that of settling the project and bringing it into production. To do this the land must be pooled, by some means, so as to be handled with the water and irrigation works under a single competent, aggressive, and economical management. The present individual ownership must be merged for the common good, with compensation to present owners based on dry land value only. Whether the financing is done through private or public channels, the agency furnishing the funds must have the controlling hand in the operation and management of the district until it is safely established on a paying basis.

Modifications of irrigation district laws along the lines just suggested are desirable, not only to insure the success of new projects, but for the protection of existing development. The unplanned and haphazard settlement and development of an irrigation project of 100 000 to perhaps more than 1 000 000 acres is not only difficult and dangerous to the new project in itself, but may prove seriously detrimental to established agricultural interests by unsettling their markets. For example, the effect of the great irrigation development in Southern Idaho during the decade from 1905 to 1915, may be recalled, when for a time alfalfa, the easiest crop for new settlers, was produced in quantity far above the capacity of available markets. The market was wrecked, and it required years of patient and energetic effort to build up the dairy and live-stock industries and to develop new markets to re-establish the economic balance.

Consider some of the obvious defects of the Washington State Reclamation Law. If State aid for reclamation becomes desirable and necessary at some future time, it should be on a basis that will offer to the project real help and not impossible burdens. Any one familiar with the undeveloped projects in the State of Washington will recognize that few, if any, of them can honestly undertake to meet the requirements of the law as it now stands. It contains at least two basic defects. First, it does not require specifically, and in its administration little attention has been paid to, any showing of economic need for a project. Direct State aid to reclamation can be justified only on the ground that there is a real need for the particular development proposed, and that there will be a market, present or prospective, for its products. Second, the interest rate is too high. To make the law workable and of benefit to the settlers, interest should be made very low or waived entirely during the development period. After development of the project is well along, the rate should be high enough so that the district bonds could be sold in the open market at or near par value.

Should conditions in the future warrant direct State aid in reclamation development, it might be advisable to re-establish a Reclamation Board somewhat along the lines provided in the original Act, its functions, however, to be largely advisory on matters of policy and on approval of projects, and not administrative. On such an advisory board, representation should be given to the State College, the State Land Commission, the State Departments of Agriculture and of Conservation and Development, the State Treasurer, and, possibly, the State organization of investment bankers. Most of the bonds handled by the State would probably be sold through the membership of this latter organization and its advice, being expert and non-political, should be of great value.

State Land Settlement Law.—The Washington State Land Settlement Law was enacted in 1919 to meet the anticipated passage of a National land settlement law which was at that time under consideration by Congress on recommendation of the then Secretary of the Interior, the late Franklin K. Lane, the measure having been prepared by Elwood Mead, M. Am. Soc. C. E.

The National legislation failed of passage, but in 1921 the State organigation of the American Legion urged and secured a State appropriation for soldier settlement, independent of National aid. The project selected was in the south central part of the State in the vicinity of White Bluffs and Hanford, on the Columbia River. It was doomed to failure from the beginning for several reasons, among which may be mentioned:

1.—The land was mostly very sandy and difficult to place in production. Only irrigation farmers of long experience under similar conditions could expect to achieve success.

2.—Settlement was at first limited to *ex*-service men which meant, generally, young men inexperienced in handling soils of this type.

3.—The water supply from wells was unreliable and in many cases insufficient, and the cost of electric pumping was very high, especially for the development period.

4.—The tracts were scattered, making community life and organization difficult. Community organization and co-operation is one of the essential features of Mr. Mead's plan on which the State law was founded.

5.—The land selected was remote from markets and from towns or cities offering the cultural and recreational facilities to which most of the settlers were accustomed.

The State purchased approximately 2 000 acres of land which was divided into 105 tracts of about 20 acres each. Sixty-six of these tracts were improved with small houses, barns, wells for irrigation, and pumping equipment, and were sold. Thirty-nine other tracts were partly improved and offered for settlement with no takers.

For two to five years the settlers struggled valiantly to establish themselves on the land. Some, with the better tracts of land, with some experience and ample water supply, were able to make a very good showing. Others, due to lack of experience, poor land, or insufficient water, accomplished very little. Nearly all were discouraged and unable to see any possibility of paying out. They appealed to the Legislature for relief, which was authorized. Of the 66 tracts sold, settlements were made with 64 owners at a total net loss to the State of $360 000. The remaining 39 tracts, appraised at $34 000, were sold at public auction on June 1, 1926, with all improvements, except motors and pumps which had been removed, for $50 650.

It cannot be said that this was a fair test of State-aided land settlement. The land was poorly selected, remote from markets, very difficult to reclaim, and the limitation to *ex*-service men developed a certain class feeling and political situation that would be a serious handicap for any project. The results of the experiment however, have brought out several fundamental difficulties in the way of State-aided land settlement, and it is not likely that the State of Washington will be willing to undertake another project of this kind for several years to come.

Reclamation Bond Certification Law.—Following the example of Oregon and California in an effort to improve the marketability of the bonds of sound irrigation districts, the Washington State Legislature in 1923 enacted the so-called "Certification Law". The law requires an investigation by the Director of the Department of Conservation and Development and the filing of a report with the Secretary of State, embracing conclusions on the following points:

(*a*) The supply of water available for the project and the right of the district to so much water as may be needed.

(*b*) The nature of the soil as to its fertility and susceptibility to irrigation, the probable quantity of water needed for its irrigation, and the probable need of drainage.

(*c*) The feasibility of the district's irrigation system and of the specific unit for which the bonds under consideration are desired, whether such system and unit be constructed, projected, or partly completed; and the sufficiency of the amount of the proposed bond issue to complete the improvement contemplated.

(*d*) The reasonable market value of the water, water rights, canals, reservoirs, reservoir sites, and irrigation works owned by such district or to be acquired or constructed by it with the proceeds of any such bonds.

(*e*) The reasonable market value of the lands included within the district.

(*f*) The plan of operation and maintenance used or contemplated by the district.

(*g*) The method of accounting used or proposed to be used by the district.

(*h*) Any other matter material to the investigation.

Attached to the report of the Director shall be the following:

(*a*) A certificate signed by the Supervisor of Hydraulics certifying to the amount and sufficiency of water rights available for the project.

(*b*) A certificate signed by a soil expert of the Washington State College, certifying as to the character of the soil and the classification of the lands in the district.

(*c*) A certificate signed by the Supervisor of Reclamation approving the general feasibility of the system of irrigation.

(*d*) A certificate signed by the Attorney General of the State of Washington approving the legality of the organization and establishment of the district and the legality of the bond issue offered for certification.

On satisfactory showing as provided, the Secretary of State signs a certificate in the following form which is attached to all bonds issued by the district:

"Olympia, Washington, ... (insert date) ....

"I, ..., Secretary of the State of Washington, do hereby certify that the above named district has been investigated and its project approved by the Department of Conservation and Development of the State of Washington; that the legality of the bond issue of which this bond is one has been approved by the Attorney General of the State of Washington, and that the carrying out of the purposes for which this bond was issued is under the supervision of said department, as provided by law.

"(Seal) ....

"Secretary of State."

Owing presumably to the slump in irrigation securities there have been but few requests for certification under this Act, and the bonds of five districts only have been certified. Of these, three were to cover the cost of reconstruction for old districts and two were for construction of new district works. Since the enactment of the Certification Law, investment bankers have rather insisted on certification, and the few bonds sold without it have suffered heavy discounts.

Columbia Basin Project.—The State of Washington, not content with extending aid of a general character to reclamation enterprise through the medium of the legislation referred to, has seen fit to adopt, as a State project, and by appropriation of State funds to investigate and promote plans for the development of an irrigation project equal in extent, in estimated cost, and potential production to all the irrigation projects completed during the first quarter century under the Federal Reclamation Law, namely, the Columbia Basin Project.

This project embraces approximately 1 883 000 acres of irrigable land lying in Eastern Washington in the "Big Bend" of the Columbia River from which it takes its name. The land lies between 350 ft. and 1 700 ft. above sea level. In soil and climate it closely resembles the Yakima and Wenatchee Valleys which join it on the west.

Two principal sources of water supply have been considered: First, from Clark's Fork of the Columbia River by a gravity diversion at Albany Falls near the Washington-Idaho boundary, with storage supplied by Pend Oreille Lake, or by this lake supplemented by Priest Lake, also in Idaho; and, second, by pumping from the Columbia River, using power developed by a dam in that stream to lift the main water supply into Grand Coulee, from the lower end of which it would be delivered into the main canals.

These two alternative projects lend themselves to numerous variations through the use of other sources of water supply for various parts of the main project, as follows:

Wenatchee River and Lake for Quincy unit	332 000	acres
Snake River for Five-Mile Rapids pumping unit	100 000	"
Touchet River and Wynette Reservoir for part of Eureka Flat	50 000	"
Columbia River, Priest Rapids pumping unit	113 000	"
Spokane River and Lake Coeur d'Alene, southeastern part of gravity project, about	400 000	"

This project, first investigated by the U. S. Reclamation Service in 1903, was then abandoned as being too large for present consideration. In 1919, the Legislature of the State of Washington appropriated $100 000 for its investigation and created a Columbia Basin Commission which, later, became a Division of the Department of Conservation and Development. This was followed by other State and Federal appropriations under which extensive preliminary surveys and studies have been made. The latest and presumably the most authoritative report was made in 1925 by the following Board of Engineers appointed by the Secretary of the Interior: Messrs. Louis C. Hill, Joseph Jacobs, Charles H. Locher, Richard R. Lyman, Arthur J. Turner, and O. L. Waller, all of whom are members of the Society.

This Board finds that the project is structurally and economically feasible and includes these rather striking recommendations as to State and National policy in connection with the proposed development:

"That the State should assume its proper share of the responsibility for collecting payments from the settlers, and should also bear its proper share of the losses, if any, incident to the development of the project."

* * * * * * * *

"That the Government should clear and level the land and provide a reasonable financial credit for necessary farm improvements. Also, as a guaranty against land speculation, and to insure that the settler secures the land at its fair value, that the Government acquire title to all the irrigable land within the project."

The estimated construction cost of the project as a whole, or of its constituent units, is approximately $160 per acre. If the suggestions of the Board of Engineers relative to land ownership can be successfully carried out, the combined cost of land and water to the settler might be approximately $175 per acre, which is considerably less than that on the later developed units of the Yakima Project and some of the other more successful private and Government projects of recent years.

It is recognized that because of its magnitude this development can be undertaken only by the Federal Government. The State at present is only laying the foundation for future construction by negotiating a water compact with other States interested and with the Federal Government by making an economic survey as to the need and possible market outlet for its products, and a further study of potential power in connection with, or which might be affected by, the irrigation project. The economic survey will include a study of the rate of industrial and commercial growth of the western part of the United States; domestic and foreign markets for agricultural products; past and present production of irrigated and other crops in the Pacific Northwest; and possible new products and new markets which might become available through the opening of new arteries of commerce or reduced tariffs over existing lines.

The conclusions, therefore, as to the proper functions of the State with reference to reclamation, which are briefly summarized, are as follows:

1.—Present agricultural production in this and neighboring States is equal to, if not greater than, the demand in markets that can be economically reached through available channels. The State, therefore, is not justified in expending funds raised by a tax on all property, including agricultural land and products, to increase the agricultural area by reclamation. Having in mind that the rapid industrial and commercial development of the Pacific Coast may, in a relatively short period, radically change the economic situation, the State should anticipate future needs for reclamation development by adopting a sound, basic reclamation policy. The program, as far as it can be outlined, should include:

(*a*) A comprehensive study of the possibilities and needs of the State for increased agricultural production by means of reclamation.

The water supply required for approved projects should be protected by administrative or legislative withdrawal against appropriation for less essential uses.

(*b*) A continued effort to improve State laws relating to reclamation to the end that they may encourage and foster sound and necessary projects and prevent the launching of those which are not.

2.—The State should support a National reclamation policy and program based on sound, economic principles. Selection of projects on merit only; emphasis on local responsibility, especially in operation of the projects; and a strictly business corporation for collection of charges, are some of the factors that would seem to be clearly indicated by past experience as essential to future success. During periods, such as the past few years, when agriculture is in distress and there is little or no demand for land, storage construction should be stressed rather than the building of additional canals, in order to provide for and expedite the development of new areas when needed.

3.—A study of existing projects that are now in trouble and the working out of salvage plans where practicable might be justified, particularly on those projects in which the State already has some investment or has been responsible in some measure for existing conditions.

DISCUSSION

JAMES RHEA LUPER,* ASSOC. M. AM. SOC. C. E.—The author has shown the definite policy adopted by the State of Washington in extending State aid to reclamation development.

In other words, Washington has been "attending the school of experience", and the experience seems to have covered the full range of State aid policies with the exception of Oregon's guaranty of interest on irrigation and drainage district bonds. Washington evidently has passed through the experimental stage and the experiment has been expensive. Now the danger is, that instead of profiting by the experience, the people may reverse the policy and drop all development work of this nature for this generation.

It is true that all the low-cost, easily constructed, projects have been built. The development of the remaining projects will present difficulties that require the most thorough planning by experienced men if they are to be successful.

The author asks, "Is there any means other than State or Federal subsidy of building the remaining large projects?"

It seems obvious that there is not a prospective profit in further irrigation development that will attract private capital. The real profit is to the public in the permanent wealth created and in the increased business in all channels that will inevitably follow after the project has been successfully completed. State and Federal aid can only be justified on this sound theory. Further large developments of this nature must depend on such aid.

The problems in irrigation development are many. Ample water supply, adequate drainage, good markets, good engineering design, sound financing, capable administration, the elimination of land speculation, a sound settlement program, and confidence, all are essential to success. When any one of these is lacking to any large extent complete success is impossible.

Mr. Tiffany suggests the advisability of re-establishing the Reclamation Board, a non-political organization. This seems to be essential for under the present form of government it is better for the head of the Reclamation Bureau to have some protection against political pressure, and against a misguided public sentiment that may otherwise force the adoption of an undesirable project, or his resignation.

This Board should be clothed with sufficient power to control the administrative officers of the project in which the State has invested its funds until such time as the State has been reimbursed, or until the operation of the project has been turned over to the settlers.

It must not be comprised of politicians, as the word is generally used, for it must maintain continuity of policy through different political administrations. The Board should have authority to issue State bonds to a limited extent in lieu of the direct tax heretofore imposed. The beneficial effect of the development work cannot be felt for many years. This direct tax will fall on many who will receive no benefit, while the bonds may be paid as, or after, benefits are felt.

* State Engr., Salem, Ore.

In his reference to economic need for a project, the author points out an important matter that seems to have been overlooked by many others in the recent irrigation development in the West. The development of irrigated farms ahead of the economic need not only cannot be justified, but the colonization of such projects will be an uphill struggle, if not impossible.

Conditions will change, however; in fact, they are changing now. Food consumption is overtaking food production and improvement may be felt within a year. In five years a very marked change should be experienced. In the development of large projects many years may elapse before the farms will be fully developed. It is difficult to say that substantial production on such projects will come before there is need of the crops produced.

Irrigation Districts.—Under all forms of development, whether through private financing, Federal reclamation projects, or projects financed by State funds, the organization of the water users under the Irrigation District law seems essential. The irrigation district's code as adopted in Washington, Oregon, California, Idaho, and other Western States in effect provides a means whereby an independent branch of government—a municipality—can be formed. The district has power to levy taxes and assume obligations, which are guaranteed by all the property within its boundaries. The indebtedness represents a general obligation of the district, and is paid by taxes levied either on a basis of irrigated area, or as an *ad valorem* tax.

The law presents an excellent method of collecting funds and provides administrative machinery for the operation and maintenance of constructed projects. It is good for financing to a limited extent, but when the indebtedness reaches a substantial percentage of the total value of the property in the district, a dangerous situation is created, and loss of confidence may be caused with the resulting loss of credit to all settlers regardless of the value of the individual's property.

Oregon has a system of assessing the costs of furnishing water rights in proportion to the benefits received. Many of the projects include lands that had almost full water rights before the project was created. Such land may be assessed only a nominal part of the construction cost for the additional water right to be supplied. Yet when such a district gets into financial difficulties, the failure on the part of some to pay pyramids the assessments on those able to pay until all land values in the district are entirely destroyed. By providing a means for fixing the exact amount that the water user will be required to pay for a water right, his credit will be re-established and much progress will have been made toward making the district function as it should.

Oregon has an example of financing local improvements which can be well applied in reclamation development. This is, the Bancroft Bonding Act. Under its terms, a city sells its general obligation bonds in an amount necessary to finance the improvement, and is, in turn, secured by a lien on each parcel of land benefited. The lien is for a definite fixed sum, and the land owner benefited knows exactly the amount of his obligation. It can be paid in yearly installments, or more rapidly, if desired.

Why is it not practical for a State to follow the same plan in reclamation developments by the issuance of a State bond secured by the land benefited? If thorough preliminary surveys are made—and in this must be included adequate soil surveys—the possibility of including lands that cannot bear the charge levied against them is eliminated, and the district will be free from the "kick-back" of the general obligation that occurs when the indebtedness becomes too high.

By foreclosure of its liens, the State could take the land and re-sell it just as cities have done with many vacant lots. The property will continue to have a value as long as the lien does not exceed the value of irrigated land with a water right in that vicinity.

American farmers have not yet learned co-operative development. Co-operative marketing has been successful only in certain commodities, but, on the whole, the farmers are trained in independent thought and action, and do not enter readily into situations in which their success is dependent on the success of others in the same community.

Mr. Tiffany has quoted from the Washington State Law providing for the certification of irrigation district bonds, but has refrained from criticizing that method of financing irrigation work.

It is to be noted that the law provides for an examination of the project by the State Director of the Department of Conservation and Development, whose report is filed with the Secretary of State; also, that attached to the report are certificates of various State officers to the effect that the project is feasible, that the bonds have been legally issued, that the water right is good, and that all the soils are of certain character. The certificate on the bond is signed by the Secretary of State and the seal of the State is attached.

This law has two purposes: First, to protect the investing public against the purchase of unsound securities; and, second, to promote development by making good irrigation securities salable. The State disclaims any legal responsibility for payment of the bond, but when the project defaults in either principal or interest it is difficult to convince a holder of certified bonds that the State is not morally responsible for his loss.

The State should not mar its good financial name by allowing its seal to be placed on any bond that is not essentially sound. It is not morally right, and may result in direct financial loss because of the increased interest rate that may be demanded on other financing within the State.

It is to be hoped that Washington will not go out of the reclamation business entirely, but will profit by her experiences and amend her laws so that these projects may be re-organized and that further reclamation developments may proceed on a sound basis.

W. G. Swendsen,* Assoc. M. Am. Soc. C. E. (by letter).—The history of reclamation by irrigation in the State of Washington, so well outlined by Mr. Tiffany, is repeated in Idaho and practically in all the arid States.

Much has been said about the failure of irrigation enterprises. Viewed purely from the standpoint of a return on invested capital, a large percentage of the business might well be classed as failure; if viewed, however, in its

* State Engr., Boise, Idaho.

broader aspects of developing a new country, producing the necessities of life, and increasing the taxable wealth, quite a different story is revealed.

The financial structure on which an irrigation enterprise must rest is based almost wholly on the efforts of the farmers in the area. Unfortunately, a solution of their problems is not found in any concrete formula, but is abstract in the extreme. In weighing the economic feasibility of most irrigation projects, conclusions have, therefore, necessarily been based largely on expectancy. The equation reflecting farm success is filled with many unknowns, not the least important of which is the psychology of the farmer himself, and his fitness and willingness to engage in the activity at hand. It is not surprising, under these conditions and especially in view of the fact that the art is a new one, that forecasts as to the financial outcome of irrigation projects should be found in error.

It has been a common practice on the part of the promoters in the beginning of these enterprises to absolve the engineer from responsibility in the matter of financial return; but, ultimately, and almost universally, where a financial loss has existed, the responsibility for it has been placed with the engineer. In addition to the engineer's direct personal interest, the problem of how and when the natural resources of land and water in the arid States shall be developed, is of sufficient public, State, and National importance to warrant consideration by the highest engineering and business talent.

It is true, as Mr. Tiffany states, that most of the remaining undeveloped reclamation projects are not, under existing conditions, attractive to private capital and that if they are to be constructed soon, governmental aid of some sort is necessary. Unless it is established with very reasonable certainty that additional agricultural products are necessary to the State or Nation, or to the happiness and well-being of the people, there seems to be no justification in equipping this industry with a public subsidy. The use of State or Government funds at interest rates below those prevailing in other business, or with no interest at all, can be nothing but subsidy.

Where a group of citizens are suffering hardships on farms because of insufficient irrigation water or of unoperating irrigation works, there may be some justification in using public funds for their relief, even if this term, "relief", has come within the last few years to be invoked with almost constant regularity.

Whether wisely or not, the writer has urged a policy in Idaho of directing public assistance and attention only to projects already occupied, where distressed conditions exist, considering new and undeveloped areas only to the end that their resources may be available later and unimpaired for orderly development and use when economic conditions warrant.

The engineering and structural problems in reclamation by irrigation may be definitely understood, analyzed, and solved; settling the land and bringing it to a state of profitable production is the difficult and uncertain problem. If the so-called existing "lame ducks" can be so improved that substantially all irrigated areas present successful farming conditions, much will be accomplished in stimulating the settlement of new areas. The matter of investing public funds in such enterprises must be approached with great care so as to provide financial success to the State or Government and to guard against relieving settlers of individual responsibilities they must assume if good citizenship is to endure.

The writer entertains grave doubts as to the advisability of attempting, especially at public expense or under any form of subsidy, to reclaim by irrigation any unoccupied areas until existing projects are settled and the "lame ducks" improved, especially in advance of a greater demand than now exists for increased agricultural production.

These are to be regarded as an expression of personal views and not in any sense as reflecting public sentiment in Idaho, where, as in Washington, a difference of opinion exists.

J. C. STEVENS,* M. AM. SOC. C. E.—The author believes that no more projects should be built until existing ones are entirely occupied. This policy is entirely wrong. People have particular inclinations and diversity of desires, and they will not all go on any one project. One might as well say that no more houses should be built in Seattle, Wash., until all those in Portland, Ore., are occupied.

That same principle will apply to irrigation projects. There is undoubtedly a demand for irrigation lands locally, that can only be supplied by building the smaller projects.

O. L. WALLER,† M. AM. SOC. C. E.—In administering the irrigation loan, the State of Washington has made some mistakes, but they are not serious. After the World War, some banking and business houses in the State found themselves over-extended and had to charge off some bad accounts, but they did not go out of business. Neither should the State go out of the irrigation business as long as it has lands that may be developed by irrigation. It would seem that a State should be interested in the development of its resources, particularly where the necessary expenditure is beyond the reach of private individuals and of private capital.

The time is not far distant when the United States will need more food to supply a growing population, and not only each State, but the United States, should make a study of all possible land developments that may be made, looking forward to the time when this need will be imperative. It is not important whether agriculture is developed through irrigation or by other methods; but it is to the advantage of any State to look forward to the development of all its natural resources just as much as it is to the advantage of an individual to develop his resources.

As compared to other States, Washington has small acreage now under irrigation. However, it has a large area yet susceptible of such development, and its water supply is abundant. That being the case, it should be the policy of the State to render every assistance possible in developing the lands pending the time when the growing National population will demand additional food.

* Cons. Hydr. Engr. (Stevens & Koon), Portland, Ore.

† Vice-Pres., State Coll. of Washington, and Head, Dept. of Civ. Eng., Pullman, Wash.

JOSEPH JACOBS,* M. AM. SOC. C. E. (by letter).—Are the financial losses and other difficulties which the State of Washington experienced in its reclamation work, as recited by Mr. Tiffany, attributable to defects in the law; to the method of administration; or to other causes? Are they necessary, ineradicable concomitants of State activity in this type of enterprise; or are the evils correctable by a modification of the laws and by a wiser administration of them such as would result from a policy of ignoring politics as a primary consideration in the selection of the administrators? The writer entertains the latter view and believes that the chief difficulties have been political rather than technical, economic, or fatal deficiencies in the law itself.

No accidental or obscure, mysterious causes were responsible for the financial losses mentioned in the paper. The dangers were easily discernible. Practically all the physical and economic difficulties were known in advance and, for the most part, properly weighed and reported by responsible engineers. It is creditable to engineers that they, more than any others, pointed the safe line of attack and sounded warnings. If, however, it is to be the policy of the appointing power of the State to put in control, over the engineer, men selected from the field of politics, with practically no previous experience, and whose acts and decisions may too often be colored by political considerations—then but little improvement can be expected, no matter how good the laws. Graft and willful dishonesty are not here an issue, because no such delinquencies are involved, but only the questionable policy of appointing to responsible administrative control of essentially technical or scientific departments of government men who have had no real training for such specialized work.

In this situation the Engineering Profession should make its influence felt more effectively. It should seek to have more clearly defined, by statute or otherwise, the required technical qualifications for heads of departments. It should also seek to overcome the mistaken notion, rather widely entertained, that the engineer is necessarily a narrow technician with little qualification for supreme, administrative control of a department of government, even if that department's interests are chiefly scientific and technical. It is true that the engineer is often only a technician, but it is also true that as high an average of capable, business administrators are found in the Engineering Profession as in other business callings—probably more, and certainly more than in the purely political profession. If it were necessary to admit, which fortunately it is not, that there is no hope of improving the quality of American politics, then the State Government ought to be taken entirely out of reclamation activities.

The State's remaining major projects cannot, on account of their magnitude, be built except as public enterprises. If their development is deemed necessary, the primary determination of policy should relate to whether the State or the Federal Government shall undertake them, or whether these agencies, in co-operation, shall do so. Another alternative is the creation of a large improvement district to issue its own bonds and prosecute the work. Such a

* Cons. Engr. (Jacobs & Ober), Seattle, Wash.

district would require special legislation for its creation and successful operation and, to be financially practicable, it would need to include already developed towns and other rich, taxable property to give increased security and marketability to the bonds. Such inclusion would be seriously opposed and this alternative, therefore, can be regarded as only a remote possibility.

That the State's interests in these developments—and this applies to all the irrigation States—is more intimate and immediate than those of the Federal Government cannot be gainsaid; but the Federal Government, too, has a vital interest in Western agricultural development, not only as a means of promoting National prosperity, but also in respect to military factors. Almost every consideration of the problem seems to suggest State and Federal co-operation. Because of State constitutional limitations, as well as for other substantial reasons, it would seem desirable that the actual construction of these major reclamation projects should be in charge of the Federal Government, but it is to be hoped that some satisfactory form of co-operation can be evolved that will provide for the States meeting their just obligation in the premises, particularly as relates to the colonization of the projects.

Under these auspices, and provided the Government grants long terms and low interest rates for repayment of the construction costs, it may be anticipated that these developments will be entirely successful. Under the present Federal Reclamation Act no interest is charged, but for large developments of the future it has been suggested from many sources that such interest should be charged except possibly during the period of construction and of that normally chargeable to the unsettled lands. Even these partial waivers of interest have been objected to by some as being a subsidy; but if, as a result, new values are created that redound to the advantage of the grantor as well as the grantee of the subsidy, it cannot be regarded as a charity. Purely on the basis of paternalistic charity a subsidy is not warranted, but these are not of that class. Should the Government demand interest on deferred construction cost payments, excepting only the waivers already suggested, the Western States, in the writer's judgment, should neither be surprised, nor should they complain, provided only that the time allowance is long and the interest rate low. On the contrary, they should accept such a dispensation as a sound economic basis for future irrigation development and should modify and shape their State laws to that consummation.

F. H. NEWELL,* M. AM. SOC. C. E. (by letter).—This paper has peculiar value at the present time, particularly when read in connection with the paper by D. C. Henny, M. Am. Soc. C. E., on "Some Phases of Irrigation Finance".† The whole subject of the duties and opportunities of the National and State Governments in connection with water control, development, and protection of agricultural lands is forced upon public attention as never before by the great flood in the Mississippi Valley, which, although not necessarily the greatest that may occur, surpassed in destruction all previous floods.

Members of the next Congress (1927-28) are being urged, not only to control the Mississippi floods, but also to provide funds for building a storage

* Pres., The Research Service, Inc., Washington, D. C.

† See p. 541.

reservoir to hold Colorado River floods. This is for furnishing electrical energy with which to pump water over a 1 300-ft. divide for Los Angeles, Calif., and neighboring cities. Claims are also being pushed for: Deep-water navigation in Northern New York; gigantic hydro-electric development on the St. Lawrence River; continued activity on the Atlantic deeper waterways; development of the international control of waters of the Rio Grande; the Columbia Basin Project; and innumerable local flood-protection, irrigation, and drainage operations. The ten years' discussion of Muscle Shoals and of power development on the Potomac River near Washington, D. C., will continue to be the subject of active controversies on the floors of Congress.

There never was a time when water resources, water power, and regulation assumed such great public importance or involved expenditure of such huge sums from the unexpended balance in the Federal Treasury.

In this connection let it be recalled that the Federal Government itself, or at least the Constitution under it, which has operated for nearly a century and a half, originated through a similar set of demands arising from the necessity of protecting commerce between the States. At that time commerce was largely dependent on waterways. The Constitutional Convention was called partly because of the controversies between the States over the control of the rivers and the obvious necessity of creating one central government strong enough to adjust the conflicting interests.

There is a demand for the development of a sound policy on the relation of the States to each other and to the Nation. The relative duties of each concerning water and the distribution of power across State boundaries are involved in this question.

The engineer is at the center of the picture. While the politician necessarily strives to attract attention to the wishes of his constituents, he realizes that he must have dependable facts. He may denounce engineers but he displays an almost childlike faith in the facts and figures issued by them. It is, therefore, peculiarly important at the present time for the engineers of the United States to present, as clearly as possible, the fundamental facts on which proposed appropriations and accompanying legislation must be based. These appropriations are no longer discussed in terms of millions of dollars; but, with the boldness, not to say recklessness, of expenditure growing out of the World War, the talk is in terms of hundreds of millions of dollars; amounts so large that even the wealthy States must call upon the Federal Treasury for aid.

Back of all these questions of reclamation and other developments comes the inquiry, more and more insistently made, "Will it pay?" A quarter of a century ago, when the Reclamation Act of June 17, 1902, was passed, this question was not asked. The enterprises then proposed were relatively cheap. There were a score of applicants for every farm that might be irrigated or drained.

In the quarter of a century that has passed there has been a reversal. All the relatively cheap projects have been undertaken or have passed under private control. There are no longer hordes of eager land seekers. On the contrary, thousands of people are leaving the farms each year; millions of acres of land, previously cultivated, are now left untilled. While it is popularly deplored, this condition is perfectly logical.

For years, the Federal and State Departments of Agriculture have employed the best experts obtainable. They have spent millions of dollars trying to find how to produce larger and better crops on less area and with less outlay of human energy. They have succeeded in their aims. Thousands of laborers have been released for work at more profitable wages in industry. The scientists have brought about the introduction of better methods of farming, better judgment of soils, and have encouraged, indirectly at least, the concentration of efforts by good farmers, on good soil, near good markets. The resulting suffering of poorer farmers on poorer lands and without markets is deplorable, but is the inevitable outcome of conditions that have been deliberately planned.

In the face of the rapid and, in some cases desirable, decrease of area cultivated, is it wise for the tax-payers of the Nation or of a particular State to be called upon to reclaim additional areas, even if the soil may be brought to a high degree of productiveness by large expenditures? After that comes the question as to who is to pay the cost of strenuous efforts to secure good farmers and good markets?

The various efforts of the State of Washington, made in good faith, to develop lands and to secure settlers are described by Mr. Tiffany. He shows that the early individual or co-operative efforts at irrigation were successful. The pioneers, counting the cost of their labor as nothing, succeeded in making homes and, in some cases, developed lands of high productivity. Then having "skimmed the cream", they began to fail in further efforts. Later, the State endeavored to aid or stimulate new projects. Many were investigated; considerable sums of money were spent and lost. Now the State has apparently settled down to an effort, which may be characterized as the salvage of enterprises that offer hope of rehabilitation or extension.

Through or behind these efforts runs the fundamental thought, unquestioned up to the present, namely, that eventually the State of Washington (and, indeed, each and every State) "will need all possible development of her agricultural area". Accepting this as a fact, broadly applicable to all industries and human undertakings, the real question then resolves itself into what shall be included as possible.

By offering suitable inducements, it is possible to put people on the reclaimed land who will agree to cultivate it; but is it worth while? The experience of the State of Washington, as described by the author, appears to be in the negative. It has not paid, and it is only by the exercise of supreme faith and optimism that the expenditure of hundreds of millions of dollars additional may be justified.

This does not mean that extension, enlargement, and improvement of existing systems is unprofitable or unwise. Much can and will be done, especially by local interests receiving an indirect benefit. Many land owners, who now have a "toe-hold" on the soil, and disregard the value of their own labor (which otherwise might be dissipated), can, and will, join with their neighbors and bring about gradual expansion of irrigated area. This expansion is taking place throughout the arid region, often by the formation of self-taxing reclamation districts. These districts are not held strictly as to questions of profit and loss. They are justified in levying taxes on the basis of the general benefit that came, directly or indirectly, to all industries or to commercial enterprises in the neighborhood.

These relatively small neighborhood undertakings will take care of themselves without other supervision than that generally given to school districts. However, there are the great enterprises like the Columbia Basin Project, involving enormous expenditures, with potential losses in interest and capital, before any lands are reclaimed; investments too great for even a wealthy State to make.

In these great undertakings the engineering features, the methods, and costs are, of course, fundamental. In addition, there is the less easily definable question as to how the improved land may be utilized so as to return a considerable part of the total cost. Theoretically, it is possible for the State and Federal Governments to join hands in securing settlers; but in view of the fact that all such undertakings in the past have been at least doubtful, it is now urged that the Federal Government buy up or acquire all the land that may be reclaimed.

As the owner of the reclaimed lands, the Government may be able to dictate to its tenants or purchasers the conditions under which the lands may be acquired. It can enforce needful conditions of cultivation to a degree comparable to that of the owner of a manufacturing establishment. Recital of these conditions cause strong doubts as to their feasibility. The successful farmer is a man who is called on to use his judgment hour by hour, his activities are constantly being modified by changes in weather, or by other conditions known only to himself. Judgment is essential, and if he surrenders his judgment to some one else, he loses those qualities that make him a real farmer.

It seems little short of a huge joke to imagine any bureau officer, selected in accord with Civil Service rules and made an expert farmer by virtue of a commission, undertaking to direct the activities of a body of real farmers. The earnings of any farmer should be larger than the salary usually paid to subordinate Federal employees. Imagine the responsibility assumed in directing a group of farmers; what crops to plant and when to harvest. Perhaps the potatoes might be successful, but if not sold at a profit who is responsible? In the opinion of the farmer the Government should at least make good for any such loss.

If, as is intimated, the Federal Government should come to the assistance of the State of Washington, in building the Columbia Basin Project, what about the other States? Each and all of them from Maine to Florida in the East, to California and Washington in the West, has a comparable problem, of water control, water power, drainage, or irrigation. Each and all argue that the agricultural possibilities should be maintained and water controlled or developed for power or other uses. Each State pleads that although the wealth per capita is great it cannot afford to go into these great enterprises; each is equally insistent that if the Federal Government assists one State it should also consider the needs of the other.

It has already been proposed with some seriousness, that if money is spent on the arid soils of the West, similar funds should be used in clearing the rocks and stumps from the otherwise productive farms in the East. It is pointed out that with such Federal aid and with the existence of the best markets in the world, the Italians, Portuguese, and other prolific immigrants in New England can, and will, develop an agriculture comparable to that on the irrigated lands of the West. As engineering enterprises, and as economic investments, both proposals are claimed to be equally justifiable and altogether as valuable to local industries.

All engineers and economists can agree on the program outlined by the author, namely, that a comprehensive study be made of the possibilities and need of the State for increased agricultural production; that continued effort be made to improve State laws relating to reclamation; and that the State support a National reclamation policy and program based on sound economic principles.

It is in the development of such sound economic principles that there has been and still remains the greatest need. In a certain sense, this country has been limping along under assumptions that were true a quarter of a century ago and do not apply to present conditions. The needs and opportunities of the West then were unquestioned. It was assumed that it was the duty of the Federal Government to give priority to everything demanded by the West as the child or ward of the Nation. The West, however, has advanced, and a broad review of conditions shows that in many respects it has outstripped the remainder of the country, particularly the South.

Southern statesmen, under the leadership of the late Francis G. Newlands, Senator from Nevada (but a native of Mississippi), have consistently supported the claims of the West. Since the death of Senator Newlands they have begun to adopt a more questioning attitude. In fact, several of them have definitely stated to their constituents, and particularly to the engineers and economists of the South, that if Federal aid is to be given anywhere, the South, with its pressing needs for flood protection, must have preference. Southern interests are studying the methods so successfully developed by the West. They have been in contact with the competent men sent from the State of Washington to urge appropriations for Yakima Valley and Columbia Basin. They are awaking to the fact that their own States have enterprises of equal or greater importance. It is quite possible that in succeeding sessions of Congress the engineers representing these enterprises in the South will be fully as effective and energetic as those from the West.

The discussion of methods and of Federal and State responsibilities in water control is thus coming down to hard engineering facts. The relative costs and values and the real responsibilities are being seriously studied. The taxpayers are slowly realizing the fact that these subsidies, which they are called on to pay for the benefit of land owners in distant States, do not always produce the desired results. The emotional attitude, which has been so successful in securing contributions or appropriations for relief, is giving way to questions that can be answered only by engineers who will discuss the costs and benefits impartially and clearly.

R. K. TIFFANY,* M. AM. SOC. C. E. (by letter).—The discussion of State reclamation following the writer's paper has been interesting, although it has all tended more or less toward the conclusion that State reclamation, as such, is decidedly a questionable undertaking for the present time. Mr. Luper's suggestion that the State might aid reclamation by the issuance of State bonds with a limited liability, is worthy of consideration, if and when the situation becomes such that the State, in order to secure agricultural development, is justified in loaning its credit. The writer did not criticize the Washington State Law providing for certification of irrigation district bonds, simply for the reason that it has not been sufficiently used to give basis for judgment as to its value.

Mr. Swendsen questions the advisability of reclaiming any unoccupied areas until existing projects are settled, and Mr. Stevens credits the writer with a like opinion. The writer agrees with Mr. Stevens rather than with Mr. Swendsen on this point to this extent, that he believes there are certain localities and certain conditions under which new, or extensions of existing, projects, should be made, even at the present time. Washington, in the opinion of Professor Waller, presents, or will in the future present, such opportunities for profitable development, owing to the relatively small area of irrigated land in the State and to the rapid growth (past and prospective) of her industry and commerce.

The points brought out by Messrs. Jacobs and Newell have to do largely with the broader National aspects of reclamation, rather than the question of State reclamation. With Mr. Jacobs the writer will agree to the extent that State reclamation should not be condemned and abandoned by reason of the errors and losses that have occurred in Washington. The experience in these first efforts at State reclamation may be useful to Washington and to other States when the time comes that there is need for the States to take up actively the problem of increasing their agricultural production.

As to the National reclamation policy, Mr. Newell from his broad experience points out many errors in the past and need for a more sound and conservative policy in future development. In the writer's opinion there is still much to be said in support of the doctrine that the Federal Government should continue to aid in development of the arid West.

* Superv. of Hydraulics, Olympia, Wash.

AMERICAN SOCIETY OF CIVIL ENGINEERS

INSTITUTED 1852

TRANSACTIONS

Paper No. 1668

TIDES AND THEIR ENGINEERING ASPECTS*

By G. T. Rude,† M. Am. Soc. C. E.

With Discussion by Messrs. Lewis M. Haupt, H. de B. Parsons, R. L. Faris, Earl I. Brown, Edward Godfrey, William Barclay Parsons, T. Kennard Thomson, H. F. Dunham, Ralph Bennett, Victor Gelineau, W. M. Black, Francisco J. Gaston, F. W. Scheidenhelm, Charles H. Lee and Harold F. Gray, C. R. F. Coutlee, and G. T. Rude.

Synopsis

In the formulation and support of many of his theories and conclusions the scientist generally is compelled to use evidence of a qualitative nature, which later may be open to dispute when further qualitative evidence of contrary indications becomes available. The engineer, however, requires quantitative data of indisputable character and seeks continually for the accumulation of data and material of a quantitative nature, on which to base his conclusions and specifications for future operations. These data may be the result of innumerable tests of material, of structural weaknesses, etc., from which finally mean values of almost unerring certainty are obtained; or they may result from the accumulation of records of natural phenomena of periodic or seasonal character. In consequence of this continual quest, for example, long series of observations of tides and currents have been made throughout the world.

While the primary object of these observations has been to furnish data for advance predictions of the tides and currents at any future date for the use of the mariner, within recent years the needs of the engineer have been given consideration. As a result comprehensive current and tide surveys are now being made by the United States Government of all its important harbors.

* Presented at the meeting of September 7, 1927.

† Commander, U. S. Coast and Geodetic Survey, Washington, D. C.

The data from these surveys should prove of considerable value to the engineer engaged on harbor and river development and in marine construction of all kinds. These systematic surveys were begun in New York Harbor in 1922, followed by others in San Francisco in 1923, in Delaware Bay in 1924, and in Boston and Portsmouth in 1926.

To the engineer an accurate record of the rise and fall of the tide over a considerable period is not only of advantage but generally necessary to a proper understanding of the conditions under which operations will be carried on, or of the physical conditions which will result from an engineering project. As an example of the latter the reconstruction of the Chesapeake and Delaware Canal may be cited. This canal is being lowered to sea level by the Corps of Engineers, U. S. Army. The series of continuous tidal observations made at Delaware City, Del., the present eastern terminus of the canal, and at Chesapeake City, Md., the present western end, will permit the engineer to determine very closely the expected velocity of the current through the canal and will also furnish the data necessary for the tidal mathematician to predict in advance the times of slack-water.

This paper gives a brief, non-mathematical explanation of the tides and currents from the viewpoint of the engineer, and an outline of the more important phases for those who require data only incidental to operations in connection with development projects. The paper will be confined to the procedure and methods used by the United States Coast and Geodetic Survey in its comprehensive current and tide surveys of harbors, its tidal work for the control of hydrographic surveys, and in connection with its work in the preparation of advance predictions of tides and currents. A brief description of the instruments used on this work will also be given.

The tidal work of the U. S. Coast and Geodetic Survey had its origin in the need for correcting the soundings taken in hydrographic surveys for tidal fluctuation; that is, for reducing to a common level or datum plane soundings made at varying stages of the tide. The further needs of the mariner and the engineer since the early days of the Survey have resulted in the development and extension of the work until it covers the following fields: Determination of datum planes for surveying and other engineering purposes; prediction of tides and currents and the preparation of annual tide and current tables; study of the mean sea level and its relation to probable crustal movements; study of methods of observing tides and currents and reducing tidal and current observations; development of instruments for observing and predicting tides; and the study of tidal phenomena in general.

While the tidal and current data obtained by the Survey in the past were primarily for the use of the mariner, the "by-products" have proven of considerable value to the engineer and to the scientist—to the engineer particularly (1) in the establishment of datum planes based on tidal definition; (2) in the defining of mean and extreme ranges of the tide at various places, a knowledge of which is necessary in marine construction; (3) in furnishing a knowledge of the current flow throughout harbors in connection with sewerage and under-harbor tunnels; (4) in rivers in connection with the economical maintenance of channels to follow natural flow; and (5) in coast erosion studies in which tides and currents, in addition to wave forms and wave impact, play a large part.*

At the beginning of tidal work investigators were most familiar with the tides of the North Atlantic, and on them the earlier tidal theories were based. When observations were extended to other parts of the world, in the development of ports and the extension of maritime commerce, it was found that tides in general were not so orderly as was indicated by these comparatively simple tides of the Atlantic, the tides of the Pacific being quite different from those of the Atlantic, and the tides of the Gulf still different from those of the two oceans. This led to a study of the various types and forms of tides.

This study has also a directly practical application in the predictions of tides and the preparation of annual tide tables. Since it is physically impracticable to predict and publish the state of the tide for all ports of the world, a knowledge of the different types makes it possible to predict the times and heights of each successive high and low water for relatively few harbors as standard ports, and to refer subsidiary ports to those standard ports having tides of a similar type. In many cases it is not necessary that the secondary port be near the standard port of reference; for example, a port in the North Sea may be used as a port of reference for Nelson, B. C., Canada, a railway terminal on Hudson Bay; likewise, a constant difference exists between the time of low water at Miramichi Bay, New Brunswick, and high water in the Strait of Georgia, British Columbia, on the other side of the Continent, the two places having a similar type of tide, except that the tide curves are inverted.†

NOMENCLATURE

As an aid in understanding the paper the nomenclature of tides and currents will be reviewed briefly:

Progressive Tidal Wave.—A wave the crest of which advances, so that the times of high and low water progress from one end of a body of water to the other.

Stationary Tidal Wave.—A wave that oscillates about an axis, high water occurring on one side of the axis at the same time that low water occurs on the other side.

Tidal Day.—Like the lunar day, the tidal day has an average length of 24 hours and 50 min.

"Moon's Meridian Passage."—Refers to the instant when the moon is directly above the meridian, and also the instant when the moon is directly below the meridian, or 180° distant in longitude. They are known as the upper and lower transits.

* "Problems Involved in Coast Erosion," R. S. Patton, M. Am. Soc. C. E., *The Military Engineer*, Vol. XVI, No. 90, November–December, 1924.

† "The Tides and Tidal Streams with Illustrative Examples from Canadian Waters," by W. Bell Dawson, Ottawa, 1920, p. 26.

High Water Lunitidal Interval.—The interval between the moon's meridian passage (upper or lower) and the following high water (abbreviated H. W. I.).

Low Water Lunitidal Interval.—The interval between the moon's meridian passage and the following low water (abbreviated L. W. I.).

Tidal Current.—The horizontal backward and forward movement of the water—the current floods and ebbs.

Tide.—The vertical movement of the water—the tide rises and falls.

High Water.—The maximum height reached by each rising tide (abbreviated H. W.).

Low Water.—The minimum height reached by each falling tide (abbreviated L. W.).

Range of Tide.—The difference in height between a high water and a preceding or following low water.

Mean Range.—The average difference in the heights of high and low water at any given place.

Semi-Diurnal Force.—The tide-producing force having a period of approximately one-half day. The semi-diurnal forces are the principal tide-producing forces.

Diurnal Force.—The tide-producing force having a period of approximately one day.

Long Period Forces.—The tide-producing forces having a period of one-half month, or more.

Spring Tides.—The tides occurring at the times of new moon and full moon.

Spring Range.—The range of tides at the time of spring tides.

Neap Tides.—The tides occurring at the times of the first and third quarters of the moon.

Neap Range.—The range of the tides at the time of neap tides.

Age of Phase Inequality, or Phase Age.—The phase age, generally ascribed to the effects of friction, is the lag in the response of the tide to the corresponding phases of the moon. It usually amounts to a day or two.

Perigee.—The position of the moon closest to the earth in its elliptical orbit around the earth.

Perigean Tides.—The tides with increased range occurring when the moon is in perigee.

Perigean Range.—The range of tide at the time of perigean tides.

Apogee.—The position of the moon farthest from the earth in its elliptical orbit around the earth.

Apogean Tides.—The decreased range tide occurring at the time the moon is in apogee.

Apogean Range.—The range of tide at the time of apogean tides.

Perihelion.—The position of the earth closest to the sun in its elliptical orbit around the sun.

Aphelion.—The position of the earth farthest from the sun in its elliptical orbit around the sun.

Age of Parallax Inequality or Parallax Age.—The lag in the response of the tide to the changing distance of the moon from the earth.

Declination of the Moon.—Its changing angular distance north or south of the plane of the earth's equator, as it passes through an angle of approximately 23½°, either side of the equator.

Age of Diurnal Inequality, or Diurnal Age.—The lag of the tides in response to the changing declination of the moon.

Equatorial Tides.—The tides occurring when the moon is on, or close to, the plane of the earth's equator (zero declination).

Tropic Tides.—The tides occurring when the moon in its changing declination is at its maximum semi-monthly declination and is near one of the tropics.

Synodical Month.—The month of the moon's phases, approximately 29½ days in length.

Anomalistic Month.—The month of the moon's distance, approximately 27½ days in length.

Tropic Month.—The month of the moon's declination, approximately 27⅓ days in length.

Diurnal Inequality.—The difference between morning and afternoon tides, due principally to the declination of the moon.

Higher High Water.—The higher of the two high waters of a day.

Lower High Water.—The lower of the two high waters of a day.

Lower Low Water.—The lower of the two low waters of a day.

Higher Low Water.—The higher of the two low waters of a day.

Semi-Diurnal, or Semi-Daily Type of Tide.—A tide in which two high and two low waters occur each day, but with little diurnal inequality.

Diurnal, or Daily Type Tide.—A tide in which only one high and one low water occur in a day.

Mixed Type Tide.—A tide in which two high and two low waters occur in a day, exhibiting marked diurnal inequality in the two highs or in the two lows.

Component Tide, or Component.—Each of the simple tides into which the tide of Nature is resolved.

Amplitude of the Tide, or of a Component.—The semi-range of that tide or component.

The Epoch.—The phase or time of occurrence of high water reckoned from a fixed time origin.

Harmonic Analysis.—The mathematical process by which epochs and amplitudes of component tides are disentangled from actual tidal observations.

*Principal Lunar Component.**—The lunar component (M_2) which gives two high and two low waters in a tidal day of 24 hours and 50 min.

*Principal Solar Component.**—The solar component (S_2) which gives two high and two low waters in a solar day of 24 hours.

*Component N_2.**—The tidal component which takes account of the moon's perigean movement.

*Components K and O.**—The tidal components which take account of the moon's changing declination. The periods of the two components are such

* These five components are the principal ones. Between twenty and thirty components are used in accurate predictions of tides.

that at maximum declination the components are at a maximum and when the moon is on the equator they neutralize each other.

Mean Sea Level.—The plane about which the tide oscillates.

Mean Tide Level.—The plane half way between mean low water and mean high water.

Plane of Mean Low Water.—The average of all low waters of a series of tide observations.

Plane of Mean Lower Low Water.—The average of all lower low waters where the tide is of the mixed type.

Plane of Mean High Water.—The average of all high waters of a series of tide observations.

Plane of Mean Higher High Water.—The average of all higher high waters.

Tidal Current.—A current brought about by tidal forces.

Non-Tidal Current.—A current brought about by causes independent of the tides, such as winds, fresh-water run-off, and differences in density and temperature.

Rectilinear Tidal Current.—The current characteristic of inland bodies of water, with slack-water and reversing direction, running flood for a period of about 6 hours, and ebb in the opposite direction for a period of about 6 hours.

Rotary Tidal Current.—The type of current in the ocean's offshore. These currents do not slack and reverse, but change direction continually, passing through all points of the compass in a tidal cyle of 12 hours and 25 min.

Flood Current.—The current that sets inland or up stream.

Ebb Current.—The current that sets seaward or down stream.

Types and Forms of Tides

The tides in the various parts of the world assume a number of different types and forms, yet they may be conveniently classed as three distinct types, with their different forms. The general classification may be made as (1) semi-daily; (2) daily; and (3) mixed types of tides. Fig. 1 shows automatic tide-gauge records, illustrating these simplest types—the semi-daily at Portland, Me., the daily at Manila, Philippine Islands, and the mixed at San Francisco, Calif. In the simple form of the semi-daily type two high and two low waters occur each day, the morning and afternoon tides being very similar. The simple form of the daily type has only one high water and one low water during a day; while the third, the mixed type, is caused by a combination of the daily and semi-daily types. It is characteristic of this type that two high and two low waters occur each day, but the two differ both as to form and height.

Even these simplest types vary with the moon's changing declination, as illustrated in Fig. 2, reproducing tidal records at Portland and Manila. The upper graph for Portland is known as an equatorial form, which occurs when the moon is near the equator in its changing declination. The lower graph for Portland is known as the declinational form, occurring when the moon's declination is large. This variation in the height of the two high waters, or of the two low waters, during a day, is known as the diurnal inequality in the tides, and is directly related to the declination of the moon, being least when the moon is on the equator, and greatest when it is farthest north or south from the equator, causing "tropic tides". At certain times the semi-daily tide as represented by Portland approaches somewhat the mixed type, although to a minor degree in comparison with a truly mixed type.

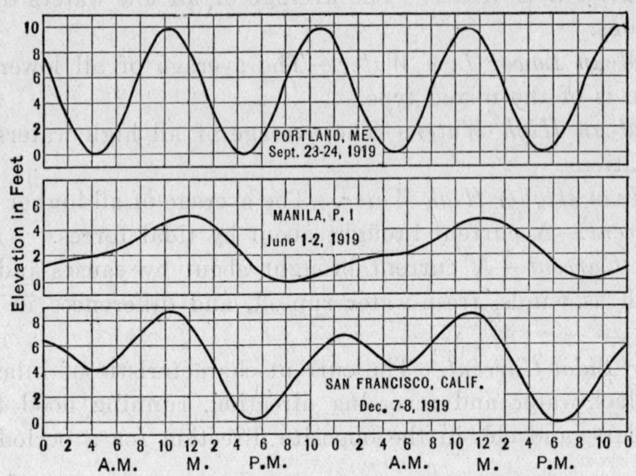

FIG. 1.—THREE TYPES OF TIDE—SEMI-DAILY, DAILY, AND MIXED.

The diagram for Manila (June 1 and 2, 1919), illustrates a tide which ordinarily is of the daily type, but which for a few days during a lunar month at the time when the moon is nearing the equator, and, therefore, when the

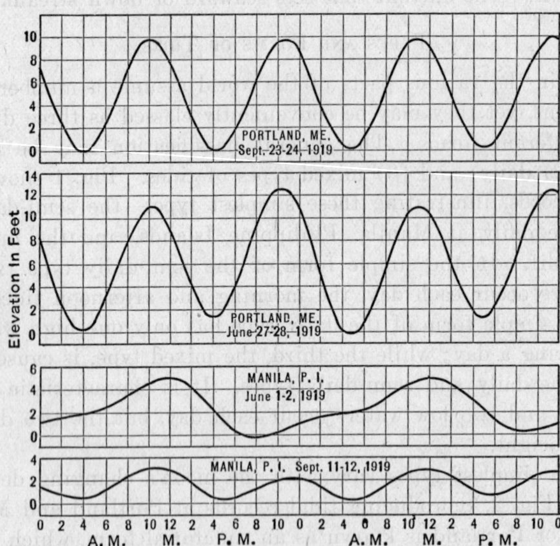

FIG. 2.—VARIATION OF TIDE CURVES DUE TO CHANGING DECLINATION OF THE MOON, EXEMPLIFIED IN TIDES AT PORTLAND, ME., AND MANILA, PHILIPPINE ISLANDS.

semi-daily forces are exerting the dominant influence, has a semi-daily variation. The remaining graph of Fig. 2 for Manila (September 11 and 12, 1919), represents the ordinary daily tide. Likewise, the tide of a port which ordinarily has a mixed type changes for a few days during the month to a semi-daily form when the moon is near the equator.

In addition to these variations two distinct forms of the mixed type occur in some localities, as illustrated by the tides at Seattle, Wash., and Honolulu, Hawaii (Fig. 3). At Seattle there is little variation in the high waters but considerable variation in the low waters, while at Honolulu the tide shows very little difference in the height of the low waters, but a marked difference in the height of the high waters. This difference in form is due, briefly, to different combinations of the diurnal and semi-diurnal waves—they may have the same phases and different amplitudes, different phases and the same amplitudes, or both different phases and different amplitudes. It is evident, therefore, that they may combine in various ways, giving rise to many other different forms.

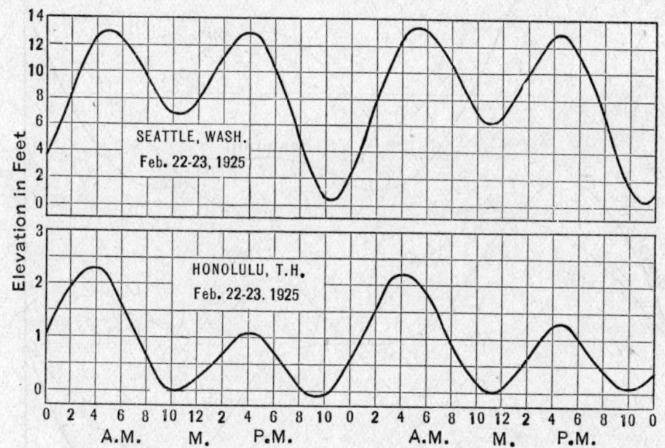

Fig. 3.—Different Forms of Mixed Type of Tide Exemplified by Tides at Seattle, Wash., and Honolulu, Hawaii.

Some of the various combinations of the diurnal and semi-diurnal waves which give rise to these many different forms of mixed types of tide are shown in Fig. 4. In the upper curve the phases and amplitudes of the diurnal and semi-diurnal waves are such that their combination results in a mixed type of tide (heavy line) in which both the high and low waters of a day differ. In the middle graph the combination of the diurnal and semi-diurnal waves results in a mixed type of tide with a marked difference in the high waters of the day and with no difference in the low waters. In the lower graph the diurnal and semi-diurnal waves have phases and amplitudes the resultant of which is the "vanishing tide"; in this type the water of the falling tide remains for several hours at a fixed height at about mean sea level, then falls to the ordinary low water.

The tide in a river draining a considerable area illustrates another type of tide. The fresh-water run-off affects the tidal wave of the river to a considerable extent, causing the graph to be steep and of a comparatively short period for the flood tide and more inclined and of a longer period for the ebb tide. This is known as the "river type tide" and is illustrated by the tide at Philadelphia, Pa., and Albany, N. Y. (Fig. 5). In the upper graph the tide was rising at Philadelphia from 3:20 A. M. to 9:00 A. M. (5 hours and 40 min.), and falling from 9:00 A. M. to 4:20 P. M. (7 hours and 20 min.); in the lower graph the tide was rising at Albany from 4:10 A. M. to 8:40 A. M. (4 hours and 30 min.), and falling from 8:40 A. M. to 4:40 P. M. (8 hours).

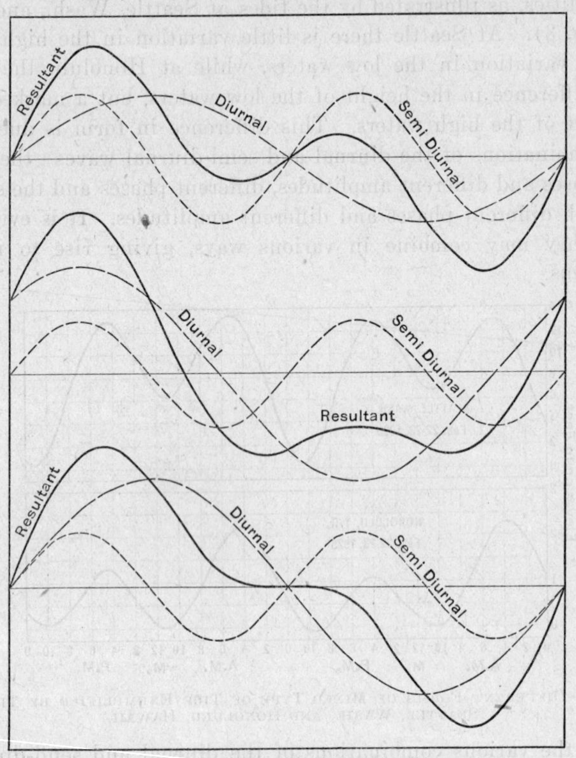

FIG. 4.—IDEALIZED TIDE CURVES ILLUSTRATING VARIOUS COMBINATIONS OF DIURNAL AND SEMI-DIURNAL WAVES WHICH GIVE RISE TO MANY DIFFERENT FORMS OF MIXED TYPES OF TIDES.

This type is very pronounced in a number of shallow rivers and estuaries which have considerable range of tide, and broad flats, bare or almost bare at low water. The extreme case is represented by the "bore"—the tide rises so rapidly that the meeting of the incoming tide wave with the natural fresh-water run-off of the river, coupled with the friction of the lower layers of water with the bottom, causes the incoming wave to assume the form of a wall of water at times several feet high, which rushes up the river or estuary. Probably the most famous bore occurs in the Tsien-tang Kiang,* in China, although smaller ones are found in Turnagain Arm, Alaska, on the Severn and Wye, in England, on the Seine, in France, on the Hoogly, in India, and on the Petitcodiac, in Canada.†

* For description see, G. H. Darwin, "Tides and Kindred Phenomena in the Solar System," p. 63.

† Observations of the bore on the Petitcodiac River have been made at Moncton, N. B., Canada, by Dr. W. Bell Dawson, formerly Superintendent of the Tidal and Current Survey, of Canada, see "Survey of Tides and Currents in Canadian Waters," Ottawa, Ont., Canada, p. 23.

As evidenced from the possible combinations illustrated in the idealized tide curves (Fig. 4), there are of course many other variations of forms of tides. The types described, however, are the principal ones. The type and form of the tides are considerably modified at times by the changing declination of the moon; that is, its position relative to the equator, as well as by terrestrial causes. There are also periodic variations in the range of the tide; that is, the heights to which the tide rises at high water and to which it falls at low water. These variations in range are brought about by astronomical causes.

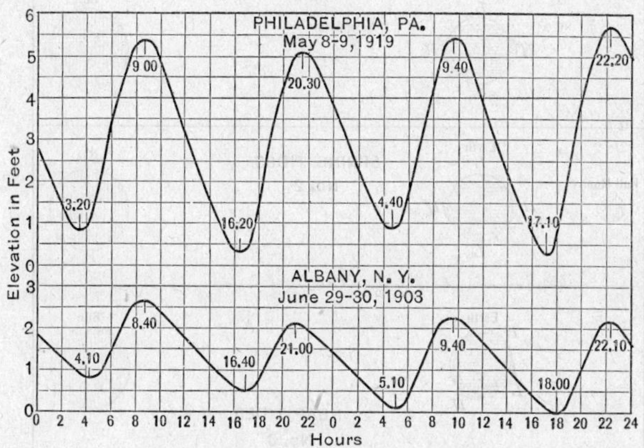

FIG. 5.—TIDE CURVES FROM RECORDS AT PHILADELPHIA, PA., AND ALBANY, N. Y., ILLUSTRATING THE "RIVER TYPE TIDE."

CAUSES OF VARIATION IN RANGE

History does not disclose just when the true relation of the moon to the tides was first recognized; but it is known that as early as the Third Century, before the beginning of the Christian era, Pytheas of Massilia, who had sailed beyond the Mediterranean Sea as far north as the British Isles, and probably to the Arctic Circle, noted this relationship. Pliny, the Elder, four centuries later, definitely ascribed the moon and sun as makers of the tide. The probable reason why history is vague as to the tidal phenomenon is because the people of antiquity who have left a history of their times lived near the Mediterranean Sea where the tidal range is small and its regular fluctuations are frequently modified and at times completely masked by meteorological conditions.

In the sixteen centuries following Pliny, the Elder, no progress was made toward a solution of the problem of the tides. The discovery of the law of gravitation by Newton (toward the end of the Seventeenth Century) furnished a rational explanation of the forces exerted by sun and moon. Newton showed that the tide was a natural consequence of the law of gravitation; having proved this he did not carry his investigations further, but left the development of the different theories to the scientists following him.

It is now well known, of course, that the tides are caused by the attraction of sun and moon on the rotating earth, the moon being the principal agent, since it is closer to the earth and since the tidal forces exerted by a foreign body vary directly as its mass and inversely as the cube of its distance from the earth. It is evident, therefore, that any variations in the distance from the earth of these two tide-producing bodies, or any variations in their relative positions with reference to the earth, will bring about corresponding variations in the tidal forces exerted and thus a periodic variation in the range of tide.

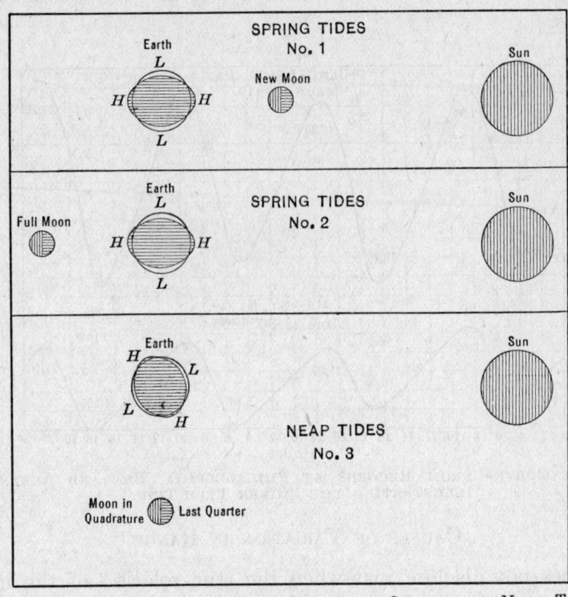

FIG. 6.—DIAGRAMMATIC REPRESENTATION OF CAUSES OF SPRING AND NEAP TIDES AND THEIR DIFFERENCES.

A non-mathematical illustration of these varying astronomical conditions is furnished by Fig. 6 which assumes the earth to be covered with water to a uniform depth. When the moon is over any point its attraction for the water under it is greater than its attraction for the solid earth; the tendency is, therefore, to pull the water away from the earth and thus cause high water. Likewise, the moon's attraction for the solid earth is greater than its attraction for the water on the opposite side of the earth from the moon; its tendency then is to draw the earth away from the water and make high water on the opposite side. The moon, therefore, as it travels around the earth causes in general two high waters each day at a place, one at the upper, and one at the lower, transit, with two low waters in between. While these conditions are not exactly true in Nature, Fig. 6 will serve to illustrate diagrammatically the causes of the so-called "spring" and "neap" tide and their differences. This diagram is untrue to Nature in that high water does not actually follow directly under the moon but has a lag, due to viscosity of water, to friction, and to land masses; and, in addition, in that the tidal forces exerted by the moon and sun are tangential and not vertical, that is, the direct lifting power of the moon and sun is slight, and the water rather is drawn together from the two sides of the earth under these bodies.

In Diagrams No. 1 (Fig. 6), the moon and sun are in line relative to the earth, and their tidal forces acting through gravity on the earth and oceans are in concert and bring about the large tides which have been designated "spring" tides. In Diagrams No. 2, although the moon is on the opposite side of the earth from the sun, the tidal forces of both bodies are again in unison and produce the spring tides which occurred a fortnight before at the time of new moon, since the moon's two high waters, one on each side of the earth, combine with the two high waters brought about by the tidal forces of the sun. In Diagrams No. 3, the moon is in quadrature. Under this condition the tidal forces exerted by the sun are at right angles to those exerted by the moon, and, therefore, working against one another, each force tending to minimize the force of the other body. This counter-attraction naturally gives rise to small range tides which have been designated "neap" tides. These neap tides occur again in about two weeks when the moon has come to its first quarter on the opposite side of the earth relative to the sun.

The path of the moon in its orbit describes an ellipse, its distance from the earth varying during the course of the lunar month, causing variations in the range of tide. When the moon is in a position closest to the earth (in "perigee"), its tidal forces are strongest; and, conversely, for its position farthest from the earth (in "apogee").

Variations in the range of tide are likewise brought about by the varying distance of the earth from the sun due to its elliptical orbit. At the time the earth is closest to the sun it is said to be in "perihelion"; when it is farthest away it is said to be in "aphelion".

When the spring tides happen to occur at the same time that the moon is in perigee, the range of the tide at some places is increased as much as 40 per cent. Likewise, when the neap tides occur at the same time that the moon is in apogee, the range is less than the mean by about 40 per cent.

An example from Fort Hamilton, New York Harbor, will serve to illustrate these differences.* There the spring, neap, apogean, perigean, and mean ranges are as follows:

Mean .... 4.7 ft.
Spring .... 5.6 ft., or 20% greater than the mean range.
Neap .... 3.8 ft., or 20% less than the mean range.
Perigean ...... 5.8 ft., or 23% greater than the mean range.
Apogean ...... 3.8 ft., or 20% less than the mean range.

The moon was full and also in perigee on July 15, 1916. On July 16, a day later, the tide record from Fort Hamilton shows a range of 6.5 ft., or 39% greater than the average range. This lag of one day in the response of the tide to the tide-producing forces is known as the "age of the tide" and is generally ascribed to the effects of friction.

The moon was in its third quarter and also in apogee on October 16, 1916 The following day the range at Fort Hamilton was 3.2 ft., or 32% less than the mean range.

* "Flood and Ebb in New York Harbor," by H. A. Marmer, *Geographic Review*, Vol. XIII, July, 1923, p. 420.

This subject of types, forms, variations in tidal range, and many other problems have required study and solution by tidal mathematicians before tide predictions could be presented to the engineer and to the mariner in their present accurate state. A study of the different types of tides and the behavior of the tide in different parts of the world played a large part in the conception and in the development of the latest tidal theory—the stationary wave theory of R. A. Harris, a mathematician of the U. S. Coast and Geodetic Survey.

Tidal Theories

Several tidal theories, based on the law of gravitation and Newton's theory, have been advanced since his time,* each looking toward a finally accepted solution of the tidal problem, among them Bernouilli's Equilibrium, or Static, Theory; Airy's Canal Theory; Whewell's Progressive Wave, or Southern Ocean Theory; and, finally, the latest—the Stationary Wave Theory of Harris. .Harris' theory is opposed to the older ones. For the idea advanced by previous theories, namely, a single world phenomenon, it substitutes regional oscillatory areas as the origin of the dominant tides of the various oceans, these oscillations being set up and maintained by the periodic tidal forces of the moon and sun.

Clearly, a wave in continuous motion does not imply that the water is moving in the same direction—it is only the forward motion of a shape as evidenced by the kind of wave traveling in from the ocean toward the land. A somewhat similar motion occurs in a rope held in the hand and violently agitated, or a wave in a pond caused by the dropping of a pebble in the water. In the case of the rope a wave will travel its length, the rope itself remaining fixed in so far as progression in direction of travel of the waves. Such a wave is known as a progressive wave (illustrated by the lower diagram, Fig. 7); the older tidal theories depended on the progressive wave as an explanation of the origin of the dominant tides of the ocean. An altogether different kind of wave may travel through a body of water. The upper diagram in Fig. 7 represents a vessel partly filled with water. If one end is raised and immediately lowered, a wave will be started throughout the vessel, and the water put into oscillation, causing a greater depth at one end than at the other, that is, high water at H' and low water at L', with a nodal line, or no change of level, at N. As the oscillation is continued, high water occurs at H and low water at L, and again a nodal line at N. High water will occur at one end when it is low water at the other, and high or low water will occur simultaneously throughout each half of the vessel. This kind of wave is known as the stationary wave.

The period of this wave or oscillation depends on the length of the vessel and the depth of the water. To cause this oscillation to keep on it is only necessary to continue the disturbing force. If this force be applied at regular intervals coinciding with the period of the vessel, the maximum effect

* For general description of the different theories see *Scientific Monthly,* Vol. XIV, No. 3, March, 1922, H. A. Marmer, pp. 209–218; for detailed explanation, see "Manual of Tides," by Harris, Pt. 1, pp. 386–465.

is obtained. Similar oscillations occur in most lakes in which the whole body of water swings back and forth with a period of from 10 min. to 1 hour and with a range of several inches. These oscillations, known as "seiches", are caused by sudden changes in atmospheric pressure or by winds over the lakes. Studies of seiches have been made for a number of lakes and given in detail in various publications.*

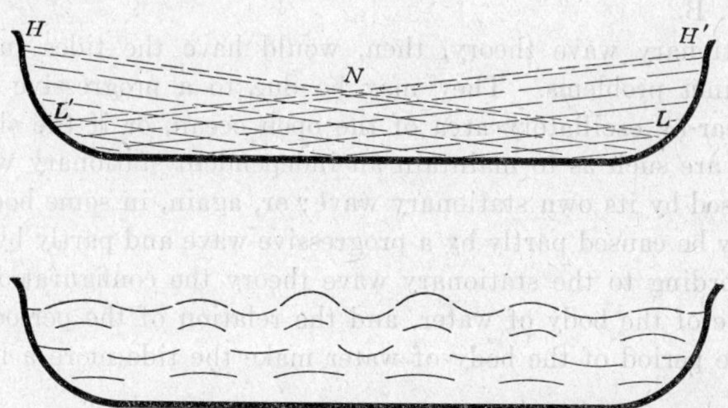

FIG. 7.—GRAPHIC ILLUSTRATION OF STATIONARY AND PROGRESSIVE TIDE WAVES. UPPER DIAGRAM IS BASIS OF A STATIONARY THEORY OF TIDES.

In brief, therefore, such a system of waves forms the basis of Harris' stationary wave theory—that the dominant tides of the world are the results of stationary waves, these oscillations being set up and maintained in the various parts of the oceans by the periodic tidal forces of moon and sun.

In most bodies of inland water connected with the ocean the tidal wave is a progressive wave thrown out by a near-by oscillatory wave in the ocean. The rate of advance of such a progressive wave up an inland body of water, such as Chesapeake Bay, is expressed approximately by the formula, $r = \sqrt{g\,h}$, in which, r is the rate of advance; g, the acceleration due to gravity which is about 32.2 ft. per sec.; and h, the average depth of the water.

If the size and depth of a body of water are such as to maintain an independent stationary wave, its tides may be caused by its own stationary wave; or again in some bodies of water the tide may be caused partly by a progressive wave and partly by a stationary wave, as, for example, in Long Island Sound and in the Bay of Fundy. The period of a body of water having a stationary wave is expressed in the formula, $T = \dfrac{4\,L}{\sqrt{g\,h}}$, in which, L is the length of the body in the direction of oscillation. In such a body high (and also low) water occurs almost simultaneously throughout its length and the range of the tide increases toward and is greatest at the head; in a body with a progressive wave high and low water advance at a rate dependent on the depth, and the range of tide generally decreases toward the head. The tides in the Bay of Fundy are the best example of the wave of the stationary type.

* "The Tides and Kindred Phenomena in the Solar System," by G. H. Darwin, p. 21, and "Effects of Winds and Barometric Pressures on the Great Lakes," by the late John F. Hayford, M. Am. Soc. C. E., Carnegie Inst. of Washington, 1922.

The Bay of Fundy may be considered as a part of the vessel of water shown in the upper diagram, Fig. 7, the tide occurring almost simultaneously throughout the length of the Bay, the range at the mouth being from 6 to 10 ft., and increasing up the Bay to about 20 ft., and, finally, at the head of the Bay to more than 40 ft. At Nantucket, off the coast of Massachusetts, the range of tide is 3.3 ft., at Monomoy Point, Mass., 3.7 ft., at Nauset, Mass., 6.0 ft., increasing gradually to 20.9 ft. at St. Johns, N. B., and to 41.2 ft. at Moncton, N. B.

The stationary wave theory, then, would have the tides in the various oceans distinct problems. They may be due to a progressive wave thrown out by a near-by oscillatory area of the open ocean, or if the size and depth of the body are such as to maintain an independent stationary wave, its tides may be caused by its own stationary wave; or, again, in some bodies of water, the tide may be caused partly by a progressive wave and partly by a stationary wave. According to the stationary wave theory the configuration of the bottom, the size of the body of water, and the relation of the period of the tidal forces to the period of the body of water make the tide more a local phenomenon.

While from astronomical considerations a mathematical expression for the tide-producing forces may be derived, from which a theoretical tide may be obtained, the actual tides of Nature are so modified by land masses that they have little or no resemblance to these theoretical tides. For the prediction of tides at any place, therefore, it is necessary first to make actual observations, extending over a period of a month to a year or more. From these observations constants are derived which may be introduced into the theoretical expressions for predicting tides as they actually occur in Nature.

Prediction of Tides

In the days of shallow-draft vessels advance knowledge of the state of the tides was of little importance, but as the draft of vessels approached the depth of water over bars and in harbors, such knowledge became of importance to the navigator. It has also become of value to the engineer in the placing of bridge spans, and in a number of similar engineering operations; to watering places for the convenience of the bather; to the fisherman in planning his fishing trips; and to a number of diverse interests too numerous to mention. Figs. 8 and 9, showing high and low tides at Anchorage, Alaska, forcibly impress the need of tide predictions in places having a considerable range of tide and comparatively shallow water at the time of low tide.

The first tide table of record is in the Library of the British Museum. It is a manuscript written in the Thirteenth Century, and gives the time of the tide at London Bridge relative to the age of the moon and not for calendar days. Each of the leading maritime nations publishes tide tables, and since the Coast and Geodetic Survey is the Bureau of the United States Government charged with the furnishing of information to the mariner, the important function of predicting and issuing tide tables naturally devolves on this Service. Tide tables were first published by the Survey in 1853. For the first fourteen years they consisted of a somewhat elaborated means for enabling the mariner to make his own predictions as occasion arose. In 1867 tables were issued for a few ports on each coast of the United States. They have since been considerably increased in size and scope until now they cover the entire maritime world.

While approximate predictions of the time of high water for a particular day can be made by adding 50 min. for each day since the full and change of the moon to the lunitidal interval (known as the Establishment of the Port), so many factors are involved in the prediction of tides that for accurate results a tide-predicting machine is necessary.

Prior to 1885 the predictions of the tides were computed by means of empirical tables and graphs. Beginning with that year the predictions were made by use of an ingenious machine* devised by Mr. William Ferrel, of the U. S. Coast and Geodetic Survey. This machine differed somewhat from that of Lord Kelvin, who conceived the idea of such a machine and who devised the first one in 1872. When predictions were extended, however, by the Survey to cover the world, it was found that the Ferrel machine was not well adapted to the prediction of certain types of tides, and since 1910 the predictions have been made on a new machine, also designed and constructed in the office of the Survey. This machine is shown in Fig. 10.† By its use a tide table for any single port can be made in about 10 hours, giving the time and height of every high and low water for every day of the year.

For the purpose of predictions the tide is assumed to be composed of a number of elementary constituent tides, each due to the motions of the sun and of the moon and to their relative positions during the year; and, since the tides are local phenomena, the first step in the making of a tide table for any port is to obtain continuous tidal observations at that port. These observations are then subjected to the harmonic analysis which resolves the tide into its constituent simple harmonic waves, or harmonic constants, the periods of which have astronomical definitions, while the amplitudes and phases are derived from actual observations of the tide.

Before beginning the predictions for any port the amplitudes (semi-ranges), and the phases (times of occurrence of high water reckoned from a fixed origin), as obtained from this analysis for each constant, are set on the proper cranks and dials of the machine. These cranks and dials are arranged so that when the machine is put in motion by a handle and gears, it will sum up the effects of all these elementary waves into a single wave representing the tide of Nature. Further, the machine is so constructed that this summation is indicated on a large dial (Fig. 10) as high and low water, and also the time of occurrence is given in standard civil time. The U. S. Coast and Geodetic Survey machine will take account of thirty-seven of these elementary tides.

It is obviously impracticable to predict the tides for all ports. To obtain the state of the tide at a place where no full predictions are made, it is referred to some other port having a similar type of tide for which predictions have been made as a standard port. The Survey makes full predictions for eighty-

* Appendix No. 10, U. S. Coast and Geodetic Survey Report, 1883, p. 253.

† "Description of the United States Coast and Geodetic Survey Tide Predicting Machine No. 2," pub. by the U. S. Coast and Geodetic Survey.

three standard ports, and furnishes a table of data from which predictions may be obtained expeditiously for about 3 500 subsidiary ports, covering the entire maritime world.

Accuracy of Tide Tables

In the prediction of tides (also for mean ranges and lunitidal intervals) for any port, the data used are based on the longest series obtainable at that place, except that, in general, due to the labor involved in the summing of hourly ordinates of the tide and in the harmonic analysis, one year's observations are considered sufficient for all practical purposes. The average of these observations will give the times and heights of the astronomical tide under average or normal conditions. Exact agreement, however, cannot be expected between predictions and actual times of occurrence, since the times and heights of the tide will be modified by the prevailing meteorological conditions which may not be normal. This is particularly true of upper reaches in rivers subject to freshet conditions, and also of comparatively shallow bays with a small range of tide.

In some bodies of water in which the range of tide is small and the depth comparatively shallow, the water will be banked up or blown out by a strong wind, causing considerable differences between predictions and actual tides, and in extreme cases completely masking the normal tide. In Chesapeake Bay, for example, a stiff northwest wind blowing for a few days will cause the tides to be later and the heights lower than those predicted. Then, again, a heavy northeast storm piles up the water in the Bay causing tides higher than predicted.

The necessity for long series of observations to obtain final values in tidal data in a river subject to freshets is brought out by the tidal curves in Fig. 11, from actual observations at Albany, N. Y. The periodic tidal fluctuation in the lower graph (May 27) is only slightly modified by fresh-water run-off, low water reading about 2½ ft. on the staff and the range being 3 ft. The tidal fluctuations on the upper graph, although regular on March 27 and 28, are decreased in range and the whole mean river level raised on the tide staff, until on March 29 the tidal fluctuation has been completely masked by the freshet, and the level of the river has risen to 11 ft. on the staff. A similar condition is illustrated on the middle graph (April 11) when there was a slight periodic tidal fluctuation with the river level raised to 11 ft. on the staff. This fluctuation is completely masked by 8:00 P. M., April 12, with the river level up to 18 ft. on the staff. These conditions, however, are extreme. Most tide predictions are made for bodies of water that are not so greatly influenced by existing meteorological conditions, either because of large tidal range or of considerable depth of water.

As an illustration of the close agreement of these predictions with the tides as they actually occur at stations not influenced to such a marked degree, observations and predictions at San Diego, Calif., and Fernandina, Fla., have been compared for the months of March and August, 1923. At San Diego, the tide is of the mixed type and has a range varying from 2 to 6 ft.; at Fernandina, the tide is of the semi-daily type and has a range of 4 to 9 ft.

FIG. 8.—HIGH WATER AT TIDE STATION, ANCHORAGE, ALASKA, READING 41.3 FEET.

FIG. 9.—LOW WATER AT TIDE STATION, ANCHORAGE, ALASKA, READING 7.5 FEET.

FIG. 10.—FRONT VIEW OF TIDE-PREDICTING MACHINE OF THE U. S. COAST AND GEODETIC SURVEY.

At San Diego for the whole month of March, 1923, 60% of the predicted times differed by not more than 0.1 hour from the observed, and 87% by not more than 0.2 hour. For August, at this station, 48% of the predicted times differed from the observed by not more than 0.1 hour, and 75% by not more than 0.2 hour. The greatest difference in each month between the predicted and observed times of tides was 0.8 hour, or about 50 min.

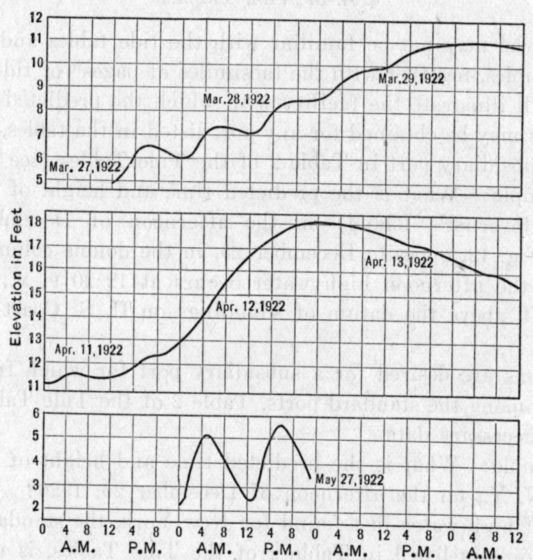

FIG. 11.—TIDE CURVES FROM RECORD AT ALBANY, N. Y., ILLUSTRATING RIVER TYPE TIDE AND EFFECTS OF FRESHETS IN UPPER REACHES OF RIVER.

At Fernandina for the whole of the month of March the percentages are as follows: 36% of the predicted times differed by not more than 0.1 hour from the observed tide; 59% by not more than 0.2 hour; and 76% by not more than 0.3 hour. During the month of August, 39% differed by not more than 0.1 hour from the observed; 55% by not more than 0.2 hour; and 79% by not more than 0.3 hour. During the month of March the greatest difference was 0.7 hour, or about 40 min., and for August the greatest difference was 0.6 hour, or about 35 min. It should be borne in mind, however, that no corrections were applied to the predicted times of tide for meteorological conditions; and, further, that near the times of high and low water the height of the tide is changing slowly and, therefore, it is not practical to determine the time of the observed high or low water with a precision greater than 0.1 hour.

It is quite evident, therefore, why a continuous record at different places of the rise and fall of the water, brought about by the tides, early became of importance to modern life. Not only were these data necessary for commerce in the advance predictions of the future state of the tides in harbors and for the reductions of soundings in hydrographic surveys, but they were of importance to the theoretical study of the tides in general. These records are also of considerable value to the engineer for defining datum planes; to the geodesist in connection with his level nets and the reduction of his large-scheme triangulation systems to mean sea level; and to the geologist for testing the stability of coast lines by reference to accurately determined mean sea level.

Use of Tide Tables

For those who may not be familiar with the tide tables and their use the following examples, together with the facsimiles of pages* of tide tables (Figs. 12 and 13), will illustrate the facility with which the predicted times of high and low waters may be obtained for any port listed in the tables, as a standard port, or as a subsidiary port in Table 2 of the Tide Tables (see Fig. 13).

As an example: What is the predicted time and height of high water at New York (Governor's Island) on the afternoon of December 25, 1926? Referring to Fig. 12, opposite December 25, in the double column, "High", it is found that the afternoon high water occurs at 12:20 P. M., and that the height is 3.5 ft. above the datum of soundings on U. S. Coast and Geodetic Survey charts.

If predictions are desired for a subsidiary port for which full predictions are not listed among the standard ports, Table 2 of the Tide Tables (Fig. 13), furnishes the necessary data.

As an example: What is the predicted time and height of high water at West Point, N. Y., on the afternoon of December 25, 1926?

The time of high water just found for New York, the standard port under which West Point is listed in Table 2 of the Tide Tables, is used to obtain that for West Point as follows (Fig. 13):

	Time.	Height.
High water at New York.............	12:20 P. M.	3.5 ft.
Tidal difference	+3:25 P. M.	—1.8 ft.
High water at West Point...........	15:45, or 3:45 P. M.	1.7 ft.

It might be well to explain briefly the remainder of the columns in Table 2 of the Tide Tables (Fig. 13). It is evident that the first and second narrow columns are the latitudes and longitudes of the ports, and the third and fourth narrow columns, the time and height differences to be applied to the standard port predictions to obtain those for minor ports. In Fig. 13, the column, "Ratio of Ranges" gives the ratio of the rise and fall of the tides at the standard and at the secondary ports. For example, the mean rise and fall of the tide at West Point is 0.6 of that at New York. The column headed "High Water Interval", gives for West Point 11 hours and 30 min., which means that high water occurs there on an average 11 hours and 30 min. after the moon crosses the meridian of West Point. The last two columns refer to the ranges, the "mean range" being the mean of all the ranges of the tide, and the "spring range", the mean range of the spring tides.

* From "Atlantic Coast Tide Tables" for 1926.

NEW YORK (Governors Island), NEW YORK, 1926.

Tide Tables.

	OCTOBER.					NOVEMBER.					DECEMBER.			
Day.	High.		Low.		Day.	High.		Low.		Day.	High.		Low.	
	Time.	Ht.	Time.	Ht.		Time.	Ht.	Time.	Ht.		Time.	Ht.	Time.	Ht.
	h. m.	ft.	h. m.	ft.		h. m.	ft.	h. m.	ft.		h. m.	ft.	h. m.	ft.
1	4 17	3.8	10 24	0.7	1	5 17	4.2	11 31	0.4	1	5 15	4.1	11 43	0.1
	4 34	4.4	10 58	0.4		5 28	4.1	11 49	0.0		5 25	3.7	11 48	−0.2
2	5 07	4.0	11 14	0.6	2	5 55	4.4	. . .	. . .	2	5 52	4.4	. . .	. . .
	5 21	4.4	11 44	0.3		6 05	4.2	12 13	0.2		6 05	3.7	12 26	−0.2
3	5 50	4.2	11 59	0.5	3	6 30	4.6	0 27	0.0	3	6 26	4.6	0 26	−0.3
	6 03	4.5	. . .	. . .		6 40	4.2	12 54	0.1		6 43	3.8	1 06	−0.3
4	6 30	4.3	0 25	0.1	4	7 01	4.7	1 03	−0.1	4	7 01	4.8	1 02	−0.3
	6 41	4.5	12 43	0.3		7 14	4.2	1 33	−0.1		7 21	3.8	1 47	−0.5
5	7 06	4.5	1 05	0.1	5	7 31	4.9	1 37	−0.1	5	7 36	4.9	1 39	−0.4
	7 16	4.6	1 23	0.2		7 47	4.2	2 11	−0.1		8 00	3.8	2 27	−0.6
6	7 38	4.7	1 41	0.0	6	8 02	5.0	2 09	−0.1	6	8 14	4.9	2 17	−0.3
	7 48	4.6	2 01	0.2		8 20	4.1	2 49	−0.2		8 41	3.8	3 10	−0.6
7	8 08	4.8	2 15	0.0	7	8 36	5.0	2 42	0.0	7	8 55	4.9	2 59	−0.3
	8 18	4.5	2 39	0.1		8 56	4.0	3 28	−0.1		9 28	3.8	3 55	−0.6
8	8 36	4.9	2 47	0.1	8	9 11	5.0	3 16	0.1	8	9 40	4.8	3 45	−0.2
	8 48	4.4	3 15	0.1		9 37	3.9	4 11	−0.1		10 19	3.7	4 44	−0.6
9	9 04	4.9	3 18	0.2	9	9 53	4.9	3 56	0.2	9	10 31	4.6	4 38	−0.1
	9 20	4.3	3 53	0.2		10 25	3.8	4 58	0.0		11 17	3.7	5 39	−0.5
10	9 37	4.9	3 49	0.3	10	10 42	4.7	4 44	0.4	10	11 28	4.4	5 40	0.1
	9 58	4.2	4 31	0.3		11 20	3.7	5 53	0.1		. . .	. . .	6 36	−0.5
11	10 16	4.8	4 22	0.4	11	11 37	4.6	5 45	0.5	11	0 24	3.7	6 51	0.1
	10 41	4.0	5 15	0.4		. . .	. . .	6 55	0.1		12 32	4.2	7 37	−0.5
12	11 02	4.8	5 03	0.5	12	0 27	3.7	7 00	0.5	12	1 35	3.8	8 03	0.1
	11 31	3.9	6 07	0.5		12 43	4.4	7 59	0.0		1 45	4.0	8 38	−0.6
13	11 55	4.7	6 00	0.7	13	1 45	3.8	8 17	0.5	13	2 46	4.0	9 13	−0.1
	. . .	. . .	7 10	0.5		1 59	4.4	9 01	−0.2		2 58	4.0	9 36	−0.7
14	0 32	3.8	7 06	0.7	14	2 59	4.1	9 26	0.2	14	3 48	4.3	10 14	−0.3
	12 58	4.6	8 18	0.4		3 13	4.4	9 59	−0.4		4 05	3.9	10 30	−0.8
15	1 46	3.8	8 26	0.7	15	4 04	4.4	10 29	−0.1	15	4 45	4.6	11 12	−0.6
	2 12	4.6	9 23	0.2		4 20	4.5	10 53	−0.6		5 05	4.0	11 23	−0.9
16	3 07	4.1	9 38	0.5	16	5 02	4.8	11 27	−0.4	16	5 37	4.9	. . .	. . .
	3 29	4.7	10 22	−0.1		5 20	4.6	11 45	−0.8		6 01	4.0	12 06	−0.8
17	4 18	4.4	10 42	0.1	17	5 55	5.2	. . .	. . .	17	6 28	5.0	0 14	−1.0
	4 38	4.9	11 17	−0.4		6 16	4.7	12 21	−0.7		6 53	4.0	12 57	−1.0
18	5 18	4.8	11 42	−0.2	18	6 45	5.4	0 35	−0.9	18	7 16	5.1	1 03	−0.9
	5 39	5.1	. . .	. . .		7 09	4.7	1 13	−0.9		7 43	4.0	1 46	−1.1
19	6 13	5.2	0 10	−0.7	19	7 34	5.5	1 23	−0.9	19	8 02	5.0	1 50	−0.9
	6 34	5.2	12 37	−0.5		7 59	4.6	2 03	−1.0		8 31	3.9	2 34	−1.1
20	7 05	5.5	0 59	−0.8	20	8 21	5.5	2 11	−0.8	20	8 45	4.9	2 37	−0.7
	7 27	5.2	1 30	−0.7		8 49	4.4	2 53	−0.9		9 16	3.8	3 20	−1.0
21	7 55	5.7	1 48	−0.9	21	9 07	5.3	2 59	−0.6	21	9 28	4.7	3 24	−0.5
	8 18	5.1	2 21	−0.8		9 39	4.2	3 43	−0.8		10 04	3.6	4 07	−0.8
22	8 43	5.7	2 36	−0.8	22	9 55	5.0	3 49	−0.4	22	10 10	4.4	4 12	−0.3
	9 09	4.9	3 14	−0.8		10 30	3.9	4 34	−0.6		10 50	3.5	4 53	−0.6
23	9 32	5.5	3 25	−0.6	23	10 43	4.6	4 40	0.0	23	10 53	4.1	5 00	0.0
	10 01	4.6	4 05	−0.6		11 24	3.7	5 25	−0.4		11 38	3.3	5 41	−0.5
24	10 22	5.3	4 16	−0.3	24	11 33	4.3	5 34	0.3	24	11 36	3.8	5 51	0.2
	10 55	4.3	4 58	−0.4		. . .	. . .	6 17	−0.2		. . .	. . .	6 29	−0.3
25	11 15	4.9	5 08	0.0	25	0 19	3.5	6 30	0.5	25	0 28	3.3	6 45	0.4
	11 52	4.0	5 53	−0.1		12 26	4.0	7 11	0.0		12 20	3.5	7 18	−0.1
26	. . .	. . .	6 04	0.4	26	1 17	3.4	7 28	0.7	26	1 19	3.2	7 42	0.5
	12 10	4.6	6 49	0.1		1 21	3.8	8 05	0.1		1 09	3.3	8 07	−0.1
27	0 52	3.8	7 04	0.6	27	2 13	3.4	8 26	0.7	27	2 11	3.3	8 38	0.5
	1 08	4.3	7 47	0.3		2 17	3.6	8 55	0.1		2 03	3.2	8 55	0.0
28	1 54	3.7	8 02	0.8	28	3 06	3.5	9 21	0.6	28	3 01	3.4	9 32	0.4
	2 09	4.1	8 42	0.4		3 09	3.6	9 43	0.1		2 58	3.1	9 41	−0.1
29	2 53	3.7	9 01	0.8	29	3 54	3.7	10 12	0.5	29	3 49	3.6	10 23	0.2
	3 05	4.0	9 35	0.3		3 58	3.6	10 28	0.0		3 53	3.1	10 27	−0.1
30	3 47	3.8	9 56	0.7	30	4 37	3.9	10 59	0.3	30	4 32	3.9	11 11	0.0
	3 57	4.0	10 23	0.3		4 43	3.6	11 08	−0.1		4 44	3.2	11 11	−0.2
31	4 35	4.0	10 45	0.6						31	5 14	4.1	11 57	−0.3
	4 44	4.1	11 08	0.1							5 31	3.3	11 52	−0.4

Time meridian, 75° W. Heavy-faced type indicates p. m. tides. Heights are reckoned from mean low water, the datum of soundings on Coast and Geodetic Survey charts.

Fig. 12.—Reproduction of Part of Table 1, Showing Data Included in Tide Tables for the Port of New York.

TABLE 2.—UNITED STATES, Atlantic Coast.

New York to New Jersey.	Latitude.	Longitude.	Tidal difference. Time of tide.	Tidal difference. Height of H. W.	Ratio of ranges.	High water interval.	Mean range of tide.	Spring range of tide.
	° ′ North.	° ′ West.	h. m.	feet.		h. m.	feet.	feet.
New York, *Staten Island*—Continued.	Standard port, **New York**, page 46.					*Time meridian, 75° W.*		
Port Richmond, Kill van Kull	40 38	74 09	+0 20	+0.1	1.0	8 11	4.5	5.4
New Brighton, Kill van Kull	40 39	74 06	−0 15	+0.1	1.0	7 56	4.5	5.4
St. George	40 39	74 04	−0 15	0.0	1.0	7 53	4.4	5.3
Fort Wadsworth Light, The Narrows	40 36	74 03	−0 25	+0.2	1.0	7 40	4.6	5.6
New York, *New York Harbor*.								
Bath, Gravesend Bay	40 36	74 00	−0 30	+0.4	1.1	7 35	4.8	5.7
Fort Hamilton, The Narrows	40 37	74 02	−0 25	+0.3	1.1	7 40	4.7	5.7
Bay Ridge	40 38	74 02	−0 15	+0.1	1.0	7 49	4.5	5.4
Gowanus Bay	40 40	74 01	−0 10	0.0	1.0	7 56	4.4	5.3
New York, Governors Island	40 42	74 01	0 00	0.0	1.0	8 04	4.4	5.4
Hudson River, New York and New Jersey.								
New York, The Battery	40 42	74 01	0 00	0.0	1.0	8 06	4.4	5.3
Jersey City, Penn. R. R. Ferry, N. J.	40 43	74 02	+0 05	−0.1	1.0	8 09	4.3	5.3
New York, Desbrosses Street	40 43	74 01	+0 05	−0.1	1.0	8 10	4.3	5.2
Hoboken, 14th Street, N. J.	40 45	74 02	+0 10	−0.2	1.0	8 16	4.2	5.2
Weehawken, Day Point, N. J.	40 46	74 01	+0 20	−0.2	1.0	8 23	4.2	5.1
New York, W. 72d Street	40 47	73 59	+0 30	−0.3	0.9	8 35	4.1	5.0
General Grant's Tomb, 122d Street	40 49	73 58	+0 40	−0.4	0.9	8 45	4.0	4.9
Manhattan Iron Works, 143d Street	40 50	73 57	+0 50	−0.5	0.9	8 52	3.9	4.8
Fort Washington Point	40 51	73 57	+0 55	−0.6	0.9	8 59	3.8	4.6
Spuyten Duyvil, W. of R. R. Bridge	40 53	73 55	+1 10	−0.8	0.8	9 13	3.6	4.4
Yonkers	40 56	73 54	+1 20	−0.8	0.8	9 25	3.6	4.4
Dobbs Ferry	41 01	73 53	+1 35	−1.0	0.8	9 40	3.4	4.1
Tarrytown	41 05	73 52	+1 50	−1.2	0.7	9 53	3.2	3.9
Ossining	41 10	73 52	+2 05	−1.4	0.7	10 08	3.0	3.7
Haverstraw	41 12	73 58	+2 15	−1.5	0.7	10 20	2.9	3.5
Peekskill	41 17	73 56	+2 45	−1.7	0.6	10 48	2.7	3.3
West Point	41 24	73 57	+3 25	−1.8	0.6	11 30	2.6	3.2
Newburgh	41 30	74 00	+4 00	−1.7	0.6	12 03	2.7	3.3
New Hamburg	41 35	73 57	+4 20	−1.6	0.6	0 01	2.8	3.4
Poughkeepsie	41 42	73 56	+4 45	−1.4	0.7	0 26	3.0	3.7

Fig. 13.—Reproduction of Part of Table 2 of Tide Tables, Showing How Secondary Ports Are Referenced to Data Shown in Fig. 12.

Instruments for the Observation of Tides

As a means toward labor-saving and time-saving, automatic or self-registering devices give continuous observations of natural phenomena over long periods for use in planning engineering works. Thus, as the importance of series of tidal observations became apparent, the plain tide staff was replaced by automatic gauges.

The earliest automatic tide-gauge* was devised by an English civil engineer, Henry R. Palmer, to obtain a continuous record of fluctuations in the River Thames for getting the effect on the tidal regimen of the river by the removal of London Bridge, "free", as expressed by Mr. Palmer, "from the inaccuracies and doubts which the frequent and long-continued observations of individuals through nights and days must be liable."

* A paper descriptive of this gauge appears in *Philosophical Transactions*, Royal Soc., 1831.

The fundamental principles embodied in this first automatic gauge are still used and although there are many forms of these gauges, the principle is a simple one.* A float is connected by a fine bronze wire or tape with a self-recording pencil or pen, which moves at a reduced scale backward and forward across a paper record which is wound on a cylinder, either vertical or horizontal. This paper revolves by means of a clock movement, thus causing the pencil to trace a curve that accurately represents the tide for that locality.

The U. S. Coast and Geodetic Survey at its primary tide stations makes use of the automatic tide-gauge shown in Fig. 14.† Its principal features are the motor clock which drives the main cylinder regulating the motion of the paper—a roll, 13 in. wide and 66 ft. long, sufficient for a month's record; the time-clock, similar to an ordinary striking clock, trips the recording pencil, making a mark on the tide graph or curve every hour; a system of pulleys and wires connects the mechanism with a tide-float which rises and falls in a well having a small opening for the entrance of the water. Usually the well is made of 2 by 12-in. planks, but at outside ocean stations it is composed of ordinary 12-in. water pipe. The opening in the well is about 1 in. to 1¼ in. in diameter for a float-well, 10 in. square, or 12 in. in diameter. The wave action is thus damped, but the hole is large enough to obviate any lag in the rise and fall as compared with the water outside the well.

To fill the need for a more portable gauge for field use, the Survey has recently developed a new automatic tide-gauge (Fig. 15). This can be used to advantage by hydrographic and tidal parties in the field at stations where it is necessary to obtain tidal observations extending over only a few days, or weeks, for the reduction of soundings taken during the survey, or for comparative purposes. In designing this instrument, the main objects were ease of installation and minimum size, commensurate with the desired accuracy.

The essential features of the gauge are its small size, its single drum on which the paper record is fastened by a spring clip, a single clock movement installed within the drum, a cast base fitting on top of a float-tube of stock iron pipe. This pipe, in addition to serving as a float-well, acts as a support for the instrument, thus obviating the necessity of providing an elaborate platform and a cumbersome float-well. This feature alone renders the gauge adaptable for use by field parties, particularly in remote localities where wharves and docks are not available. Another departure from the usual design of automatic gauge is the use of a spring instead of weights as a counterpoise for taking up the slack of the float wire on a rising tide.

The instrument is 10 in. square on the base and, with its weather-proof metal cover in place, is 11 in. high. This cover is held by a padlock, so that the mechanism cannot be tampered with when the gauge is installed in exposed places.‡

* Special types of pressure gauges have been designed for special purposes, such as the Fave "Maregraphe Plongeur," described in *Annales Hydrographiques,* 1908–10, pp. 383–437, and 1921, pp. 193–237. Various other types of automatic gauges have been described by R. A. Harris, in his "Manual of Tides," Pt. II, p. 480.

† This gauge is described in detail in *Special Publication No. 26,* "General Instructions for the Field Work of the U. S. Coast and Geodetic Survey," p. 113.

‡ This gauge is described in detail in *Special Publication No. 113,* U. S. Coast and Geodetic Survey, "A Portable Automatic Tide Gauge."

For comparison of the marigraph curve with the height of the actual tide it is necessary that a fixed zero of staff be maintained over long periods. For this purpose a standard staff and staff support has been devised, which is firmly secured in a vertical position to a wharf or pile, and carries metal guides into which the graduated staff is inserted for the readings. For accurate observations the wave action is damped by a glass tube ½ in. in diameter, in which floats a thin cork disk. This glass tube, attached to the face of the staff by spring clips, is partly closed at the lower end. A brass stop is securely fastened to the back of the staff at an exact foot mark, and a brass plate is set into the top of the staff support, the stop on the staff resting firmly on this plate as the observation is made. The staff support is covered with sheet copper in waters infested with teredos.

Mean Sea Level*

One of the important phases of the tidal work of the U. S. Coast and Geodetic Survey is the determination and establishment of datum planes based on tidal definition. Surveyors and engineers find necessity for these planes as rational datums for vertical control of their operations just as they have need for geographic positions for their horizontal control. Formerly, they used arbitrary or local datum planes which frequently made it impossible to compare the results of recent with previous surveys, and the practice led to confusion in the junction of contiguous surveys.

Formerly, the matter of rational datums was given little or no consideration, but since the extension of highways and railroads, the mapping of whole countries, and, in fact, the joining of surveys of one State or country with those of its neighbor, considerable confusion has been brought about by the use of various datums, both vertical and horizontal. To obviate the confusion resulting from such practice the Survey has been establishing and furnishing to engineers vertical datum planes, based on tidal definition, along the entire coast line of the United States. As an example, all the datum planes shown in Fig. 16, except mean sea level, are arbitrary. In order to make these arbitrary datums permanent throughout the country, the Survey is connecting by precise level nets all those used in the past by organizations, States, and municipalities. Thus, any of these various planes may be reproduced years hence through their connection with mean sea level, even if all bench-marks are destroyed.

For example, the datum plane at the Boston Station determined from a long series of observations, was lost some years ago through destruction of all bench-marks. This plane has since been accurately reproduced by a later series of observations. By a comparison with near-by long series, the second plane was reproduced by a much shorter local series of observations than was necessary for the first, as illustrated by Fig. 17, showing sea level by yearly means over the period, 1912 to 1923, for four primary tidal stations along the Atlantic Coast.

* For a more detailed discussion, see "Mean Sea Level and Its Variations," by H. A. Marmer, *Annals*, Assoc. of American Geographers, September, 1925.

FIG. 14.—FRONT VIEW OF STANDARD U. S. COAST AND GEODETIC SURVEY MODEL AUTOMATIC TIDE-GAUGE FOR USE AT PRIMARY TIDE STATIONS.

FIG. 15.—VIEW OF U. S. COAST AND GEODETIC SURVEY PORTABLE AUTOMATIC TIDE-GAUGE (WITHOUT COVER).

This graph brings out the interesting fact that the causes for a yearly variation from a mean sea level are not local; but extend, for example, along the entire Atlantic seaboard. For 1919 (the year of largest variation), the

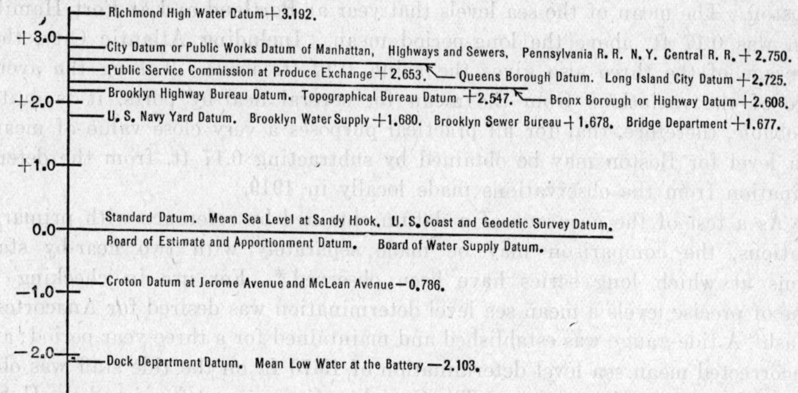

FIG. 16.—COMPARISON OF VARIOUS ARBITRARY DATUM PLANES FOR NEW YORK, N. Y., WITH MEAN SEA LEVEL. PREPARED BY SPECIAL COMMITTEE ON DATUM PLANES OF THE MUNICIPAL ENGINEERS OF THE CITY OF NEW YORK (SEE ITS *Proceedings*, 1915).

sea-level determination at Portland was 0.13 ft. above the long-period mean sea level; 0.22 ft. above at Fort Hamilton; 0.17 ft. above at Atlantic City, N. J.; and so on down the entire coast to Fernandina, Fla.

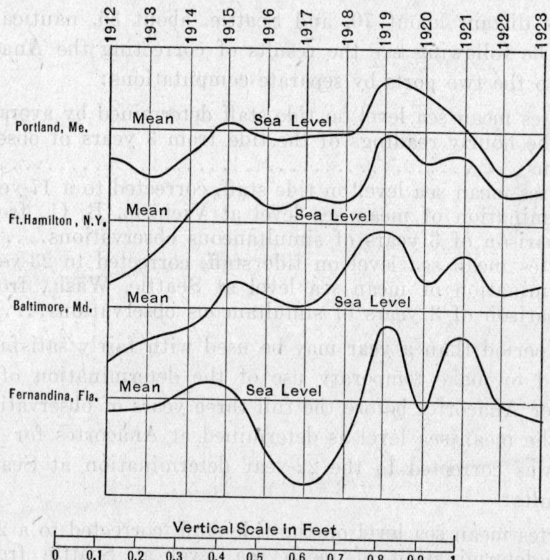

FIG. 17.—GRAPH OF SEA LEVEL DETERMINED FROM YEARLY MEANS (1912–23) AT PRIMARY TIDE STATIONS, COMPARED WITH LONG PERIOD MEAN SEA LEVEL.

The uniformity of these variations over a large area is used for practical purposes in the accurate determination of mean sea level from a short series by comparison with long series at near-by stations. For example, the nearest value to a mean sea level at Boston may be desired from local tidal observations during 1919.

Since it is clearly evident from Fig. 17 that sea level along the entire Atlantic Coast of the United States was above the long-period mean sea level during that year, this may safely be assumed to have been true also at Boston. The mean of the sea levels that year at Portland and at Fort Hamilton was 0.17 ft. above the long-period mean. Including Atlantic City, the average of the three also gives the value, 0.17 ft. above. Taking the average of the variations from the mean for several near-by ports, it is quite probable, therefore, that for all practical purposes a very close value of mean sea level for Boston may be obtained by subtracting 0.17 ft. from the determination from the observations made locally in 1919.

As a test of the accuracy of a datum obtained by reference with primary stations, the comparison may be made separately with two near-by stations at which long series have been observed.* For use in checking a line of precise levels a mean sea level determination was desired for Anacortes, Wash. A tide-gauge was established and maintained for a three-year period; an uncorrected mean sea level determination of 19.73 ft. on the tide staff was obtained from these observations. The Canadian Government furnished the U. S. Coast and Geodetic Survey the hourly readings for Victoria, B. C., for the same three-year period. These data from Victoria, with similar data from the United States Tide Station at Seattle, were used for correcting the three-year determination at Anacortes to the mean sea level datum determined from long series at the other two stations by comparison of simultaneous observations.

Victoria is distant about 70, and Seattle, about 35, nautical miles from Anacortes. The following are the results of correcting the Anacortes datum by reference to the two ports by separate computations:

Anacortes mean sea level on tide staff determined by averaging the hourly readings of the tide from 3 years of observations	19.73 ft.
Anacortes mean sea level on tide staff, corrected to a 17-year determination of mean sea level at Victoria, B. C., from comparison of 3 years of simultaneous observations......	19.81 ft.
Anacortes mean sea level on tide staff, corrected to 23-year determination of mean sea level at Seattle, Wash., from comparison of 3 years of simultaneous observations......	19.82 ft.

A shorter period than a year may be used with fairly satisfactory results. It was desired to make temporary use of the determination of a mean sea level datum for Anacortes before the full three years of observations had been obtained, so the mean sea level as determined at Anacortes for 19 months of observations was corrected to the 22-year determination at Seattle with the following results:

Anacortes mean sea level on the tide staff, corrected to a 22-year determination of mean sea level at Seattle from comparison of 19 months of simultaneous observations....	19.84 ft.

From these examples it is evident that primary tidal stations with long series along a coast line are of prime importance to tidal control of regions of which they are representative.

Therefore, primary determinations of mean sea level at various places along the coasts are important for comparison with short series of tide observa-

* *American Journal of Science*, April, 1926.

tions at near-by stations to reduce the results of the short series to mean values. These primary observations should continue over long periods, to bring out all the variations in mean sea level and to obtain mean values for all tidal constants. A period of 19 years is considered a full tidal cycle and results over such an interval are regarded as constituting mean values. Therefore, sea level derived from 19 years of observations has been generally taken as constituting a primary determination of mean sea level. Unfortunately, observations have not been continued long enough at any station to determine the difference in sea level as found from two or more full 19-year periods.

Thirty years of observations are available for the primary tide station at Fort Hamilton, N. Y. For the two overlapping 19-year periods—1893 to 1911 and 1904 to 1922—a value for sea level of 5.96 ft. on the staff is derived for the first period and 6.02 ft. for the second period.* The mean value for the entire period of 30 years is 6.00 ft. on the tide staff.

For practical purposes, however, it is hardly possible to obtain 19 years of observations at a station. Moreover, it has been found that the principal variations in sea level from year to year are cyclic in character, the level rising for a period of several years and falling for a period of years. Observations are not available for a sufficient number of years, however, to determine accurately the periods of the cycles, but there appears to be one with a period of 4 to 5 years and also one with a period of 8 to 9 years.† The variation with the period of about 9 years is quite prominent and for practical purposes, therefore, sea level determined from 9 years of tide observations may be considered as a primary determination of mean sea level.

Through the work of the Geodetic Division of the U. S. Coast and Geodetic Survey a network of precise level lines has been carried to many parts of the interior of the United States (Fig. 18). These lines have as their initial and "tie-in" points a mean sea level plane determined at the primary stations along the seaboard. Eventually every locality will be within 50 miles of a bench-mark on this net. On the Atlantic Coast long series of observations are being obtained at Portland, Boston, New York, Philadelphia, Atlantic City, Baltimore, Charleston, S. C., and Daytona, Fla.; on the Gulf Coast, at Key West and Pensacola, Fla., and Galveston, Tex.; and on the Pacific Coast, at La Jolla, Calif., San Francisco, Seattle, Ketchikan, Seward, and Valdez, Alaska. All the observations at these stations are connected with permanent bench-marks for the use of engineers locally, or for connection with precise level nets.‡

* U. S. Coast and Geodetic Survey *Special Publication No. 111,* "Tides and Currents in New York Harbor," p. 32.

† U. S. Coast and Geodetic Survey *Special Publication No. 135,* "Tidal Datum Planes," by H. A. Marmer. (See this publication for full discussion of determination of mean sea level and other tidal datum planes.)

‡ In this connection the Coast and Geodetic Survey has recently issued a publication containing the descriptions and elevations of about 1 800 tidal bench-marks in New York State, and also one of the District of Columbia containing about 85 descriptions and elevations of tidal bench-marks in the City of Washington. These publications will be followed by similar ones for other sections of the coasts and should prove of considerable value to engineers engaged on the construction of docks, bridges, harbor and river improvements, and other marine work.

Datum Planes

The simplicity of its definition, as well as the certainty with which it may be reproduced at some future time, gives value to the tidal datum as a plane of reference. In general, the most satisfactory plane is that of mean sea level, since the other tidal planes may be derived from it by knowing the range of the tide and its diurnal inequality.

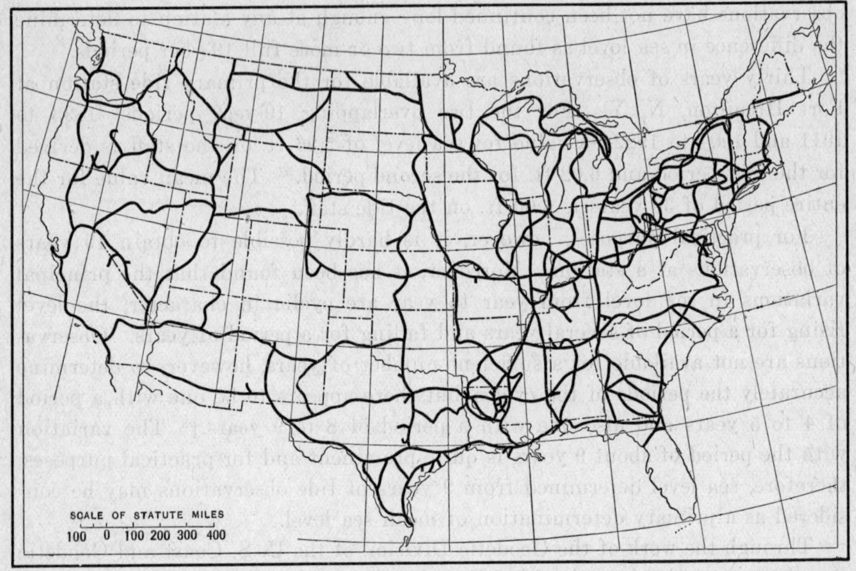

Fig. 18.—Precise Level Net of the United States. This Level Net Is Based on Mean Sea Level Datums Established at Primary Tide Stations.

Mean sea level may be defined as that level about which the tides oscillate. Since no fixed plane exists in Nature, it is necessary to devise some means for determining and for giving concrete value to this plane, above and below which the tide oscillates. The only means for making this determination is by observations of the rise and fall of the tide. It is impracticable to make use of the entire tidal curve, so that, instead of integrating the full curve, recourse is had to averaging the hourly heights of the tide. These hourly heights, tabulated from the record of the observations, are averaged over the entire period. The result is known as mean sea level, and the final accuracy of its determination is defined by the length of the series of observations. The series must be of sufficient length to have passed through varied meteorological conditions and atmospheric pressures, or must be corrected by comparison with other stations having periods of observation of sufficient length to have passed through these varied conditions.

For navigation a low-water plane is the most satisfactory because by its use the soundings on a chart will show the least depth to be expected, regardless of the state of the tide at the time the soundings were made in the hydrographic survey. A plane of mean low water, therefore, has been adopted for the whole of the Atlantic Coast; on the Pacific Coast, because of the diurnal inequality in the tides, the plane of mean lower low water is used; that is, all soundings shown on charts of the U. S. Coast and Geodetic Survey have been reduced, no matter what the stage of the tide at the time the survey was made, to the plane of mean low water on the Atlantic Coast, and, in general, to mean lower low water on the Pacific Coast and Alaska.

For other engineering purposes planes determined by high waters, higher high waters, or extreme high waters, are adopted at times. All these other tidal planes, however, are local, since they depend on the range of the tide at a given place; that is, when extended from place to place along the coast, these planes would, if visualized, be a wavy or rolling surface, while mean sea level may be considered as an equi-potential surface, forming for practical purposes a continuous smooth plane.

The purpose for which it is to be used governs the length of the series, and, therefore, the accuracy, for the determination of any tidal plane. For practical purposes a tidal plane obtained from a month of observations may be considered as being fairly well determined. Planes determined at different times, however, may differ considerably because of long period tides or seasonal changes and differences of atmospheric pressure from month to month or year to year.

These conditions make it necessary to have long-continued observations at primary stations for general tidal control. Fig. 19 shows that the determination of mean sea level is not an altogether simple matter, nor can it be obtained by a short series of observations. It will be seen that the variations from month to month are as much as 1½ ft. The seasonal variation, too, is quite evident, being much higher in summer than in winter for each year throughout this period.

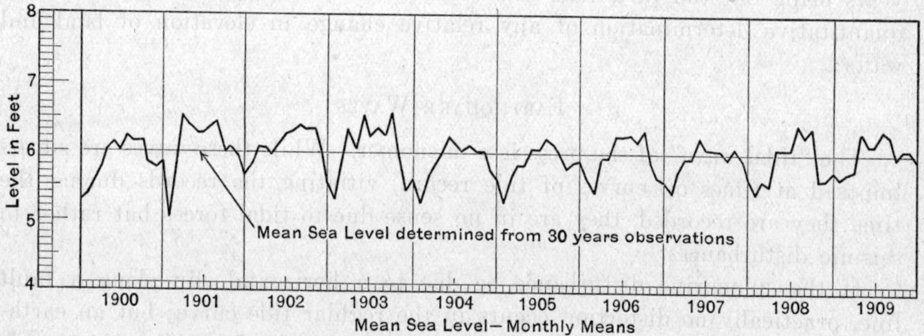

FIG. 19.—DIAGRAMMATIC REPRESENTATION OF THE PLANE OF MEAN SEA LEVEL PLOTTED FROM MONTHLY MEANS, 1900 TO 1909, AT FORT HAMILTON, N. Y.

Sea level as determined by a series of observations extending over only a month may differ as much as 1 ft. or more from that determined for another month. Even the level as determined by observations extending over a year may differ as much as ¼ ft. from a level determined during another year, so that for geodetic and other scientific work, even a year is not sufficient.

There is a distinction between the terms, "mean sea level", "mean tide level", and "mean river level". Mean sea level is obtained by integrating the tide curve, at least to the extent of taking the average height of the curve at frequent intervals; mean tide level is the plane exactly half way between the high and low waters and is obtained by taking the half sum of all high and low waters; and mean river level is the mean height of the river surface as influenced by the tide, freshets, and bottom slope, and obtained in the same manner as mean sea level.

If the tide curve were a simple sine curve the plane of mean sea level and mean tide level would coincide; actually the larger part of the curve may be above or below the mean level of the water. The difference between the two, however, is small, and if the series of observations is short the two planes may be considered for practical purposes as coincident. On the Atlantic Coast the plane of mean sea level lies above the plane of mean tide level—at Portland, 0.03 ft.; at New York, 0.05 ft.; at Atlantic City, 0.03 ft.; and at Fernandina, 0.10 ft. On the Pacific Coast, mean sea level is the lower of the two—at Seattle, 0.01 ft.; at San Francisco, 0.06.; and at San Diego, 0.05 ft. below. The planes of mean sea level and mean river level coincide at the mouth of a river, but gradually separate toward the head.

A very accurate determination of this natural standard, mean sea level, is also of considerable value to the scientist in furnishing the only means for a quantitative measure of a possible emergence or subsidence of land areas. When the determination of mean sea level has been extended over centuries quantitative evidence will be available as to the stability of coast lines of continents by reference to permanent bench-marks connected with this mean sea level datum. The primary tide stations of the U. S. Coast and Geodetic Survey are placed so as to be representative of certain regions and to furnish tidal control for these regions for practical purposes. In addition to serving these purposes, however, the continuous observations covering a long period of years bring out the variations in mean sea level, thus furnishing data for a quantitative determination of any relative change in elevation of land and water.

Earthquake Waves

The "tidal wave" of the press is a misnomer. While these waves are superimposed at times on curves of tide record, vitiating the records during the time they are recorded, they are in no sense due to tidal forces but rather to seismic disturbances.

If the submarine disturbance be due to a horizontal slip along a fault line, practically no distortion occurs in the regular tide curve; but an earthquake caused by vertical displacement produces waves of considerable magnitude. The San Francisco earthquake of 1906 was caused by a horizontal slip along an old fault line, and the tide record at Fort Point in the Golden Gate showed very little disturbance. In Japan after the disastrous earthquake of September, 1923, a resurvey of Sagami Bay indicated that a considerable vertical displacement had taken place and a wave more than 40 ft. high was reported in a part of that Bay.

Waves 80 ft. in height have been reported in some places near the origin of seismic disturbances. These waves are propagated for considerable distances over the oceans, at times reaching the shores of other continents, although with constantly diminishing amplitudes. Very destructive seismic sea waves have occurred in regions subject to earthquake disturbances throughout historical times; among others, the destruction of Helike, Greece, in 373 B. C.; at Callao, Peru, in 1724 and 1746; at Lisbon, Portugal, in 1755; Arica, Chile, in 1868; Iquique, Chile, in 1877; and on the Japanese Coast in 1896 and again in 1923.

The sea waves caused by the earthquake which occurred on November 11, 1922, off the coast of Chile were recorded on the tide records at the Survey's primary tide stations at Honolulu, San Diego, San Francisco, and at Zamboanga, Philippine Islands. The marigrams from these stations are shown in Fig. 20, all reduced to Greenwich civil time, November 11-12, 1922. It will be noted that the curve at the beginning of the tidal graph for each station has only minor fluctuations caused by wind wave effects; the remainder of the graphs, however, have distinct fluctuations of considerable amplitude.

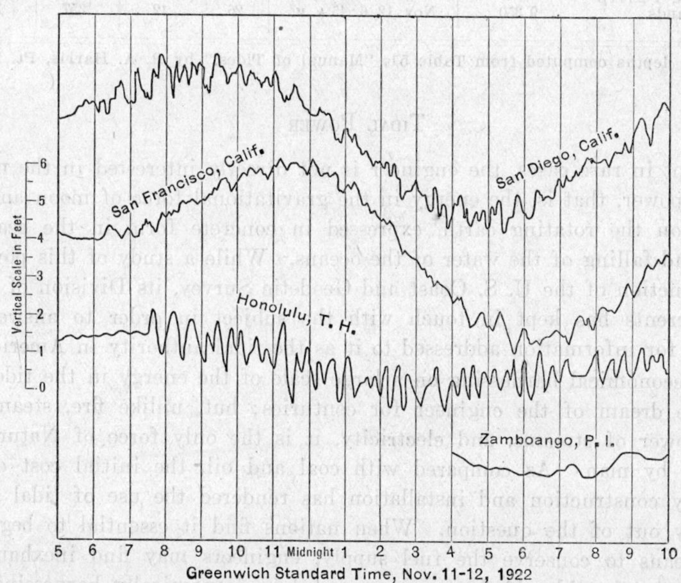

FIG. 20.—RECORDS ON THE MARIGRAMS OF TIDE STATIONS AT SAN DIEGO, SAN FRANCISCO, HONOLULU AND ZAMBOANGA, OF THE SEISMIC SEA WAVES FROM THE EARTHQUAKE WHICH OCCURRED OFF THE COAST OF CHILE, NOVEMBER 11, 1922.

The records from the seismograph stations at Honolulu, Sitka, Tucson, Cheltenham, and Vieques, indicate that the earthquake occurred on November 11 at 4:33 A. M. (Greenwich civil time), and that it originated off the coast of South America in the vicinity of Carrizal, Chile, at about 28° South Latitude. The first fluctuation on the record at San Diego (Fig. 20), began on November 11, at 5:30 P. M. (Greenwich civil time). A maximum amplitude was reached about 2 hours and 20 min. later, with a range of 1.2 ft. and with a period of from 30 to 40 min. Assuming that the propagation of the wave began at the origin of the earthquake simultaneously with the first earth tremor, its time of transmission from Carrizal to San Diego (4 480 miles) is 12 hours and 57 min., or at the rate of 346 miles per hour for an average derived depth of water of 1 750 fathoms. Table 1 gives similar comparative data for four stations.

TABLE 1.—SEA WAVE FROM EARTHQUAKE OF NOVEMBER 11, 1922, OFF THE COAST OF CHILE.

Station.	Distance from Carrizal, in nautical miles.	Arrival of wave (Greenwich civil time).	Time of Transmission of Wave.		Nautical miles per hour.	Derived depth of ocean,* in fathoms.
			Hours.	Minutes.		
Honolulu, Hawaii.....	5 850	Nov. 11, 7:30 P. M.	14	57	390	2 250
San Diego, Calif......	4 480	Nov. 11, 5:30 P. M.	12	57	346	1 750
San Francisco, Calif..	4 890	Nov. 11, 6:20 P. M.	13	47	356	1 880
Zamboanga, Philippine Islands.......	9 350	Nov. 12, 6:45 A. M.	26	12	357	1 890

* Mean depths computed from Table 51, "Manual of Tides," by R. A. Harris, Pt. III.

TIDAL POWER

Except in rare cases, the engineer is not directly interested in the matter of tidal power, that is, the energy in the gravitational force of moon and sun exerted on the rotating earth, expressed in concrete form in the ceaseless rising and falling of the water of the oceans. While a study of this power is not a function of the U. S. Coast and Geodetic Survey, its Division of Tides and Currents has kept in touch with the subject in order to answer the requests for information addressed to it as the tidal authority in America.

The economical harnessing on a large scale of the energy in the tides has been the dream of the engineer for centuries; but, unlike fire, steam, the water power of streams, and electricity, it is the only force of Nature not enslaved by man. As compared with coal and oil, the initial cost of the necessary construction and installation has rendered the use of tidal power generally out of the question. When nations find it essential to begin by some means to conserve the fuel supply, engineers may find inexhaustible resources in the tides if they are successful in economically harnessing this power. The future may then see projects, introduced by countries or States, situated favorably from a standpoint of wide range of tide. By that time, however, the engineering difficulties will have been completely overcome and the necessary machinery developed to a high state of efficiency.

Plans for the utilization of power from the tides have been rejected by many engineers as involving too great initial cost in the construction of reservoirs in proportion to the power obtained. It must be borne in mind, too, that in practice it is not possible to obtain the full theoretical power, nor to utilize the vast power of all the oceans, but only that small fraction of tidal power available near the coast where natural facilities permit empounding small parts of the sea and constructing power plants.

The Civil Engineering Department of the British Ministry of Transport has prepared plans* for the utilization of tidal power in the estuary of the River Severn, where the range of tide is from 20 to 30 ft. The English propose building a dam for impounding the waters of the Severn, using it also as a bridge for railway and vehicular traffic, connecting South Wales with the remainder of the country. The combining of the two projects will partly lower, of course, the initial cost chargeable to the tidal project; and this initial cost has previously been considered the vital objection.

The utilization of tidal power has also received attention from French engineers, who have proposed a number of plans. The northwest coast of France lends itself to such schemes. The mean ranges along the coast bordering the Bay of Biscay vary from 12.7 ft. at the mouth of the Gironde River to 14.3. ft. at Ushant Island; and along the coast on the English Channel, from 16.6 ft. at Ile de Bas to 26.8 ft. at St. Malo, decreasing to the northward to 16.2 ft. at Cape Griznez, Strait of Dover. A more recent project has been proposed in America in the plan to utilize the large range of tide in Passamaquoddy Bay, New Brunswick, and Cobscook Bay, Maine.

Heretofore, the harnessing of the tides for power purposes has been approached on a much smaller scale than these modern proposals. Tide mills of small power for grinding corn have been in existence in Spain, on the Thames in the Isle of Wight, and on the Bay of Fundy, but having an efficiency of only about 10 per cent. In all these cases the range of the tide is considerable, a necessary factor for the success of any tidal power plan. Means for furnishing power during the time the tide is rising or at a stand is another important factor in tidal power development. In addition, the variations in range during a lunar month add complexities to the problem.

Should engineers be successful in economically harnessing the tides, their use on the Atlantic Coast of the United States would be limited to Northern New England, because of comparatively small ranges of tide elsewhere. At Calais, St. Croix River, Maine, the mean range is 20.0 ft., decreasing gradually southward along the coast to 10.5 ft. at Bar Harbor, Mount Desert Island. In Penobscot Bay, the mean range varies from 9.1 ft. at Head Harbor, Isle au Haut, to 13.1 ft. at Bangor, Penobscot River. South of Penobscot Bay the mean range is less than 10 ft. along the entire Atlantic Coast, with the exception of Wellfleet, Cape Cod, where it is 10.7 ft.

Estuary Tides

Practically all research work on estuary tides has been done by the tidal mathematicians for the purpose of increasing the accuracy of predictions of tides for tide tables. A fertile field remains open for the engineer in a study of the changes in the tidal regimen in an estuary or in a river resulting from changes in topography and depth in harbor and river improvements, in order that dependable quantitative predictions may be made for proposed projects.†

* "One Million Horsepower from Tidal Energy," *Scientific American*, January 22, 1921.

† L. Bonnet's "Contribution a l'Etude Théorique des Fleuves a Marée et Application aux Rivières a Marée du Bassin de l'Escaut Maritime," goes into the theories of estuary tides and their application to the River Scheldt and tributaries.

Apparently the factors entering into the problem differ so widely for each body of water that each case requires individual treatment.

In New York Harbor, for example, where long series of observations are available covering the period during which extensive dredging operations have been carried on, the indications are that little change has occurred in the tidal regimen. The mean ranges, as derived from two overlapping 19-year series, from 1893 to 1922, in 10-year groups,* indicate an increase of 0.1 ft. in a decade, due to the improvement to Ambrose Channel between 1901 and 1914. This increase in range can be ascribed to the widening and deepening of this channel, thus allowing freer access of the tidal wave to New York Harbor.

On the other hand the dredging and development of Delaware Bay and River have made a considerable change in the tidal régime, but of a different effect; instead of an increase the tides of the Delaware have been decreased in range 0.7 ft. in some places,† and the time of the tide retarded by more than ¼ hour. This decrease has been accompanied by the raising of the mean low-water plane, the high-water plane remaining practically constant.

In Fig. 21 are shown the tidal ranges in the entire Delaware Waterway from observations prior to 1890, and from 1900 to 1924. It will be noted that no change occurred in the range from the mouth of Delaware Bay to Woodland Beach. In Delaware River, however, where extensive improvements were made during the period, 1890 to 1900, the curves diverge as much as 0.7 ft. Just below Trenton, N. J., the curves intersect again, and the range at Trenton is now 1 ft. greater than formerly.

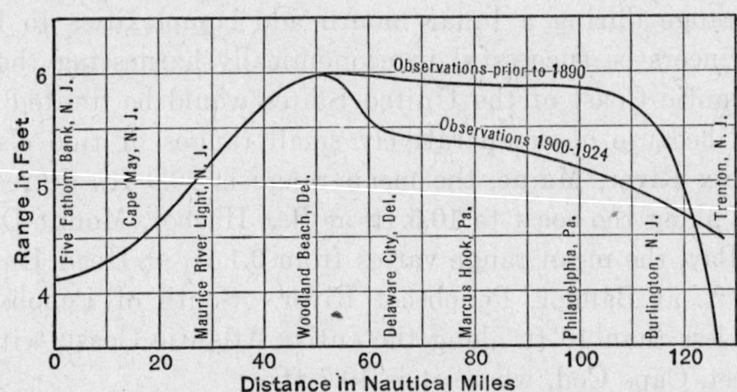

FIG. 21.—RANGE OF TIDE, DELAWARE BAY AND RIVER FOR PERIOD PRIOR TO 1890, COMPARED WITH RANGES FOR PERIOD 1900 TO 1924, AFTER EXTENSIVE HARBOR IMPROVEMENTS.

The physical reasons for this change may be ascribed to the fact that the dredging was not confined to a deepening of the channel, but involved a considerable widening of the waterway by the removal of shoal areas, allowing for a much greater cross-section to accommodate the original tidal prism entering the lower bay where no extensive developments have been made, and also tending to decrease friction in the channel.

* See U. S. Coast and Geodetic Survey *Special Publication No. 111,* "Tides and Currents in New York Harbor," pp. 45–46.

† See U. S. Coast and Geodetic Survey *Special Publication No. 123,* "Tides and Currents in Delaware Bay and River," by L. M. Zeskind and E. A. Le Lacheur.

The increase of the range at Trenton may be ascribed to the same causes that contributed to the increase of the tidal range in New York Harbor. The deepening and widening of the lower channels has given freer access of the tide to the upper reaches of the river and, therefore, increased the range. This accommodation of the upper reaches of the river to a greater part of the total tidal prism entering the whole waterway is another factor, too, in the decrease of the range in the intermediate part of the waterway.

Thus far all interpretations of data from current and tide surveys have been necessarily of a qualitative nature since sufficient data are not yet available for quantitative studies. It may be concluded, then, that in general the deepening and widening of the channels leading from the ocean into an estuary will result in a slight increase in the tidal range of the estuary; that similar operations in upper channels with no increase of the entrance cross-section will result in a decided decrease in range in the improved area, but a decided increase in range in the upper reaches of the river.

In the practical study of the tidal regimen of an estuary or river not broken by abrupt falls, and in the interpretation of the tidal data from scattered observations, a graph similar to Fig. 22 is of considerable value. This diagram has been prepared for purposes of illustration and assumes the slope of the Hudson River to be uniform (which undoubtedly is not strictly correct). Spirit-level connections between the line of precise levels that has been run from New York to Troy and various tide observations made over long periods, would undoubtedly indicate that the river profile is not strictly a straight line. Because of freshets evidently the accurate variations from a straight line can be brought out only by long series of tide observations. However, a graph from observations at relatively few controlling points, furnishes a sufficiently exact approximation of the tidal regimen for the whole river.

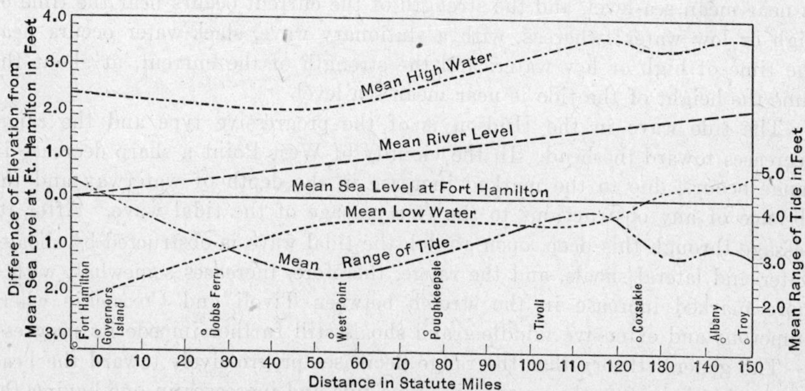

FIG. 22.—DIAGRAMMATIC REPRESENTATION OF TIDAL REGIMEN OF THE HUDSON RIVER.

The values of the tidal data, such as mean high water, mean low water, and mean ranges for various places along the river, may be plotted to scale, and smooth curves drawn through the points. In this manner a fair approximation of the tidal regimen is obtained for the whole length of the river from observations at relatively few controlling points. For example, from Fig. 22 the mean river level at West Point is 0.75 ft. above the plane of mean sea level; 1.01 ft. at Poughkeepsie; 2.06 ft. at Troy, etc.

The velocity, V, of a progressive tidal wave, such as occurs in the Hudson River and Chesapeake Bay, will be:

$$V = \sqrt{g\,h} = 5.67\ \sqrt{h}\ \text{ft. per sec.}$$

in which, $g = 32.17$ ft. per sec. (acceleration due to gravity), and $h =$ depth of water for the average cross-section, in feet.

In order to convert feet per second into nautical miles per hour, multiply by 0.592, and,

$$V = 3.36\ \sqrt{h}\ \text{nautical miles per hour}$$

The time required for the wave is,

$$t = \frac{17.87}{\sqrt{h}}\ \text{min. per nautical mile}$$

$$t = \frac{15.51}{\sqrt{h}}\ \text{min. per statute mile}$$

The character of the wave in a body of water, whether progressive or stationary, can be determined by computing the rate of advance of the tide by this formula and comparing this computed rate with tide observations along the waterway. If the actual rate is considerably in excess of the computed rate and if, in addition, the range as shown from the observations increases toward the head, it may be concluded that the body has a stationary wave tide.

The character of the tide wave may also be determined from the occurrence of the times of the slack and strength of the currents. In a body having a progressive tidal wave the time of slack water occurs about the time the tide is near mean sea level, and the strength of the current occurs near the time of high or low water; whereas, with a stationary wave, slack-water occurs near the time of high or low water, and the strength of the current, at about the time the height of the tide is near mean sea level.

The tide wave in the Hudson is of the progressive type and the range decreases toward the head. In the vicinity of West Point a sharp decrease in range occurs, due to the marked increase in the depth of waterway and the absence of any obstructions to the free passage of the tidal wave. After its passage through this deep, open stretch the tidal wave is obstructed by shoaler water and lateral shoals, and the range, therefore, increases somewhat, with a more marked increase in the stretch between Tivoli and Coxsackie where numerous and extensive middle-grand shoals still further impede its progress.

The general theory that the range decreases progressively toward the head in an estuary having the progressive type tide and increases in one having the stationary wave type, presupposes a body of uniform width and depth. The reason for any departure from this theory will generally be found in the physical characteristics of the body, as seen in the case of the Hudson.

As another example, the tide in Chesapeake Bay is of the progressive type. From the tide tables the mean ranges of the tide at points directly opposite on the western and eastern shores from the Capes to the mouth of the Patapsco River, are given in Table 2.

TABLE 2.—MEAN RANGES OF TIDE IN CHESAPEAKE BAY.

Western shore.	Range, in feet.	Eastern shore.	Range, in feet.
Cape Henry	2.8	Cape Charles	3.0
Near Point Comfort	2.2	Cherry Stone Light	2.3
Stingray Point	1.4	Mouth, Occohannock Creek	1.8
Smith Point Light	1.2	Tangier Light	1.6
Point Lookout	1.3	Holland Island Light	1.6
Cedar Point	1.2	Barren Island	1.5
Chesapeake Beach	0.9	Sharp's Island	1.3
Herring Bay	0.9	Poplar Island	1.2
Sandy Point	0.8	Love Point	1.1
Seven Foot Knoll	0.9	Tolchester Beach	1.3
Average mean range	1.36	Average mean range	1.67

The range decrease progressively up the Bay to Seven Foot Knoll on the western shore and Tolchester Beach on the eastern shore where there is a slight increase. This increase here is to be expected, since the tide wave is retarded just below these places by the constriction of the channel and by the obstruction to the progress of the wave afforded by the shoal areas off the mouth of the Patapsco River. The differences in the ranges on the two shores of the Bay will be explained hereafter.

Still another example is the Potomac River. As shown in Table 3, this river may be divided into sections as to increase or decrease in range toward the head.

TABLE 3.—CHANGES IN TIDAL RANGE IN ASCENDING POTOMAC RIVER.

FIRST SECTION—INCREASE IN RANGE.	
Point Lookout	1.3 ft.
Piney Point	1.6 "
Ragged Point	1.8 "
Blackiston Island	1.9 "
SECOND SECTION—DECREASE IN RANGE.	
Colonial Beach	1.6 ft.
Lower Cedar Point	1.4 "
Mathias Point	1.2 "
Maryland Point	1.1 "
THIRD SECTION—INCREASE IN RANGE.	
Brents Point	1.2 ft.
Quantico Creek Entrance	1.4 "
Indian Head	1.7 "
Marshall Hall, Md	2.1 "
Alexandria, Va	2.8 "
Washington, D. C	2.9 "

A chart of the Potomac will show that the first section is just below Kettle Bottom Shoals, which furnishes a considerable obstacle to the advance of the wave. It is to be expected that the ranges would increase below this point.

The second section comprises a comparatively deep, free channel and the tidal ranges, therefore, decrease as might be expected.

In the third or upper section the river is practically filled with extensive shoal areas and the channel reduced to a mere thread (relatively). The ranges increase, therefore, toward the head due to the retardation of the tidal wave.

The Bay of Fundy, already mentioned, furnishes a good example of the increase in range toward the head in a body having a stationary wave tide. Table 4 shows the ranges directly opposite on both shores of the Bay from its mouth to its head (taking as the mouth a line between Belfast and Jebogue Point).

TABLE 4.—MEAN RANGES IN TIDE IN BAY OF FUNDY.

Western shore.	Range, in feet.	Eastern shore.	Range, in feet.
Belfast, Me.	9.7	Jebogue Point, N. S.	14.0
Eastport, N. B.	18.2	Annapolis, N. S.	25.1
St. Johns, N. B.	20.9	Port George, N. S.	27.8
Moncton, N. B.	41.2	Minas Basin, N. S.	44.2
Average mean range	22.5	Average mean range	27.8

The average mean range on the eastern (right) shore in the Bay of Fundy is greater by 5.3 ft. than on the western (left) shore, as found for Chesapeake Bay.

Fig. 23 shows the ranges on both shores of the Bay of Fundy. The upper curve is drawn directly through the plottings of the mean ranges at several ports on the Nova Scotia shore as taken from the tide tables; the lower curve is for the Maine-New Brunswick shore. These two curves of ranges differ at the mouth of the Bay by about 4 ft., increasing to about 6 ft. half-way up and decreasing to about 3 ft. at the head where a narrowing of the Bay takes place. The greater range is on the right shore.

Fig. 24 illustrates the same feature in Delaware Bay. Beginning at Five Fathom Bank Light Vessel, just outside the entrance to the Bay, the two curves representing the values of the mean ranges on the two shores separate, the greatest difference of 0.8 ft. occurring about half-way up the Bay. Toward the head the two curves again approach each other. Here, too, the greater range is on the New Jersey side, the right shore facing up the Bay.

This interesting phenomenon of the difference in range on the two shores of an estuary is due to the deflecting force of the earth's rotation, acting to the right (and so causing a greater range on the right shore) in the Northern Hemisphere and to the left in the Southern Hemisphere.* The theoretical

* For formula, see *Special Publication No. 111*, U. S. Coast and Geodetic Survey, "Tides and Currents in New York Harbor," by H. A. Marmer, p. 68, Govt. Printing Office, 1925.

value, in feet, by which the ranges on the two shores of a tidal stream differ, is represented approximately by the formula, $\frac{3\,v\,d\,\sin\phi}{g}$, in which, v is the velocity of the water, in knots; d, is the width of the body, in nautical miles; ϕ is the latitude; and g is the acceleration of gravity, in feet per second (approximately 32.2).

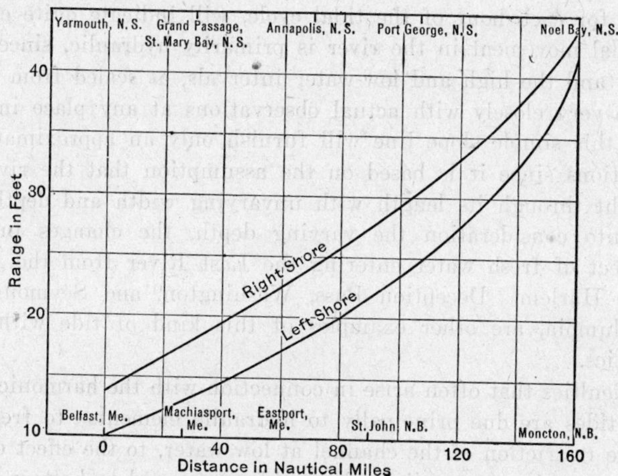

FIG. 23.—COMPARISON OF THE RANGES OF TIDE ON THE TWO SHORES OF THE BAY OF FUNDY.

Another character of tide occurs in short straits connecting two independently tided bodies of water. The movement of the water is largely hydraulic in character. The East River furnishes a good example of this type.* It will be taken up here briefly. Here the tide is derived from the tide in New York Bay, which is due to a progressive wave, and from that in Long Island Sound which is largely due to a stationary wave. These tides differ 3 hours in time and about 3 ft. in range.

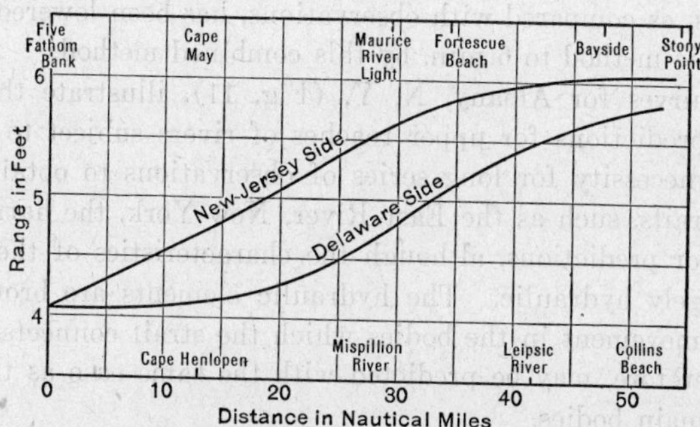

FIG. 24.—COMPARISON OF RANGES OF TIDE ON TWO SHORES OF DELAWARE.

At times the peculiar condition resulting has been ascribed to the interference of two tide waves—one from New York Bay and one from Long

* The tide in the East River is covered in detail in U. S. Coast and Geodetic Survey *Special Publication No. 111.*

Island Sound—whereas it is merely a changing height of water brought about by the changing levels in the two bodies of water which it connects. The stage in the East River at any time is conditioned on the relative heights of the water in the Upper Bay and Long Island Sound—part of the time the water in the Upper Bay is higher than in the Sound and part of the time it is lower. A simple system of slope* lines, found by plotting to suitable scale the simultaneous heights of the water levels above mean sea level at the two ends of East River for each hour of the tidal cycle, will indicate quite conclusively that the tidal movement in the river is primarily hydraulic, since the range of the tide, and the high and low-water intervals, as scaled from these slope lines, agree very closely with actual observations at any place in the river. Of course, this simple slope line will furnish only an approximation to the tidal conditions since it is based on the assumption that the river channel runs straight through its length with unvarying width and depth and does not take into consideration the varying depth, the changes in direction, nor the effect of fresh water entering the East River from the Hudson by way of the Harlem. Deception Pass, Washington, and Seymour Narrows, British Columbia, are other examples of this kind of tide with hydraulic characteristics.

The difficulties that often arise in connection with the harmonic prediction of estuary tides are due principally to hydraulic elements—to freshet conditions, to the restriction of the channel at low water, to the effect of the nontidal current on the propagation of the tide wave, and to bottom and lateral friction. The Canadians have overcome the difficulty to a considerable extent in the St. Lawrence Estuary. Correct tide tables are unusually important for Quebec, because the tides at up-river points are derived from them. The tides are predicted by the harmonic analysis for Father Point, which is near the ocean and which, therefore, has a tide answering well to the harmonic treatment; for the predictions at Quebec variable empirical corrections are applied to these Father Point predictions, varying for the synodic, the anomalistic, and the declinational months. By this method the average error in the predictions, as compared with observations, has been lowered from 26 min. by the harmonic method to 6 min. by this combined method.

The tide curves for Albany, N. Y. (Fig. 11), illustrate the difficulty in making tidal predictions for upper reaches of rivers subject to freshet conditions and the necessity for long series of observations to obtain final values.

In short straits, such as the East River, New York, the harmonic analysis answers well for predictions, although the characteristics of the tides in such bodies are largely hydraulic. The hydraulic elements are brought about by periodic tidal movement in the bodies which the strait connects, and the tidal conditions, therefore, may be predicted with the same ease as the tidal movements in the main bodies.

Tide Reductions

The methods used in reducing tidal observations may be grouped under two heads: Harmonic and non-harmonic. The harmonic method's principal

* U. S. Coast and Geodetic Survey, *Special Publication No. 111,* p. 77.

use is for tidal predictions; by this method the tide wave is decomposed analytically into a number of constituent simple harmonic waves, the periods of which have astronomical definitions, while the amplitudes and phases are derived from observation. The non-harmonic is essentially a statistical method, by which the tides are tabulated for any desired argument. These reductions are made in order that the data may be in convenient form for practical use in chart-making, surveying, and general engineering work; for the prediction of tides they also include the determination of the harmonic and non-harmonic constants.

After tabulation, the high and low waters and the hourly heights are treated in a separate manner for reduction, that for the hourly heights being known as the harmonic, and that of the high and low waters as the non-harmonic. The harmonic method of reduction employing the highly refined mathematical process of the harmonic analysis, is used principally for the determination of harmonic constants for the prediction of tides for the tide tables. It is of little use in practical engineering.

At any place the times of high and low waters have approximately fixed relations to the time of transit of the moon. The relation for high waters is called the high-water lunitidal interval, or the establishment of the port, and that for low water, the low water lunitidal interval. The intervals for each place are determined by comparison of the times of the tabulated high and low waters with the times of the corresponding moon's transits.

The datums, mean high and mean low waters, are also obtained by averaging all the tabulated heights of high and low waters. The difference gives the mean range of tide at the station, and the half-sum, the half-tide level. For stations on the Pacific Coast, because of the large diurnal inequality in the heights of the high and low waters, the average of the higher high and lower low waters are also obtained, the results being the datum plane of higher high water and lower low water.

In like manner all other planes and data may be determined, such as spring range, neap range, perigean range, apogean range, mean duration of rise, mean rise interval, mean high water diurnal inequality, mean low water diurnal inequality, mean great diurnal range, etc.*

Currents in General

To the engineer, particularly the military engineer detailed to harbor and river development, the subject of currents is of equal or greater importance than that of tides. In general, currents are caused directly by tidal action, so that a clear understanding of such action is essential to a knowledge of tidal flow. They are intimately related phenomena, or may be considered as different phases of the same phenomenon, since, accompanying the vertical movement of the water caused by the tidal forces of moon and sun, a horizontal movement also takes place, giving rise to currents.

In addition to those currents due to astronomical forces working through the tides, others are brought about by meteorological conditions and physical

* The reduction of tidal data and explanations of the forms used are given in detail in U. S. Coast and Geodetic Survey *Special Publication No. 26*, "General Instructions for the Field Work of the U. S. Coast and Geodetic Survey," pp. 128–150.

differences in sea water in different parts of the oceans. These astronomical forces, combined with topographical features, as in the case of the tides, give rise to five types of currents:

(1) The rectilinear or reversing type, illustrated by the current in most inland bodies of water, such as the Hudson River, Chesapeake Bay, Delaware Bay, etc.;

(2) The so-called hydraulic type, illustrated by the currents in straits connecting two independently tided bodies of water; for example, the East River, New York, Deception Pass, Washington, and Seymour Narrows, British Columbia;

(3) The rotary type, illustrated by the currents in the open ocean and along the sea coast;

(4) The wind-driven currents of a temporary nature, produced by the friction of local winds on the surface of the water; and

(5) The permanent currents comprising the main oceanic circulation, illustrated by the Gulf Stream of the Atlantic and the Kuro Siwo of the Pacific.

The first three types are of tidal origin and are, therefore, periodic, while the last two are non-periodic and are due to meteorological conditions, dominant winds, variations in barometric pressures over the oceans, and differences in temperatures and densities of the sea water in different parts of the oceans.

Rectilinear or Reversing Type Currents

The progression or rate of advance of a tidal wave and the velocity of the current should not be confused. The velocity of the current is the actual speed of a moving particle. On the other hand the progression or rate of advance of a tidal wave is the forward motion of a shape or wave motion. Usually this is many times greater than the velocity of the current.

Except possibly in shoal channels of varying widths the rate of advance, r, of the tide wave of the progressive type is, approximately, $r = \sqrt{g\,h}$, in which h is the depth of the body of water. The velocity of the current, however, or the actual speed with which the particles of water are moving, depends on the volume that must pass a given point and the cross-section of the channel at that point.

In a rectilinear current the distance traveled by the water particles or by a free float during a full tidal cycle may be found approximately by the following equation:

(Velocity of current at strength, in knots) × (0.6366) × (duration of period of cycle, in hours and tenths) = distance, in nautical miles, floating object will be carried.*

The form of current known as the rectilinear or reversing type occurs in all inland bodies of water connected with the ocean. These currents come to a slack and reverse, the direction being designated "flood" when referring to the horizontal movement of the water in the ocean toward the land (or "up

* For greater detail, see U. S. Coast and Geodetic Survey *Special Publication No. 111*, p. 18.

stream" in inland waters), and "ebb" when referring to the movement in the ocean away from the land (or "down stream" in inland waters).

This current is intimately related to the tidal regimen of the body of water. In a body in which the tides are due to a progressive wave the time of the reversal of the current (slack-water) occurs at about half-tide, and the strength of flood and ebb at about the time of high and low water, respectively; in a body with a stationary tidal wave, slack-water occurs at about the time of high and low water, and the greatest current velocity at about the time of half-tide.

This time relation for a current station in the Hudson River, which has a progressive tidal wave, is illustrated in Fig. 25. The upper diagram is a graph of current observations on July 24, 1922, at a station in the entrance to the Hudson River. The lower diagram shows the tidal curve at the Fort Hamilton Tide Station for the same date. In rectilinear currents it is evident that any shifting up or down of the zero current line, resulting from a steady non-tidal current, would affect the periods of duration of the flood and ebb, and make them of unequal length. Such a shift would also change the times of slack-water, but would leave unchanged the times of flood and ebb strength.*

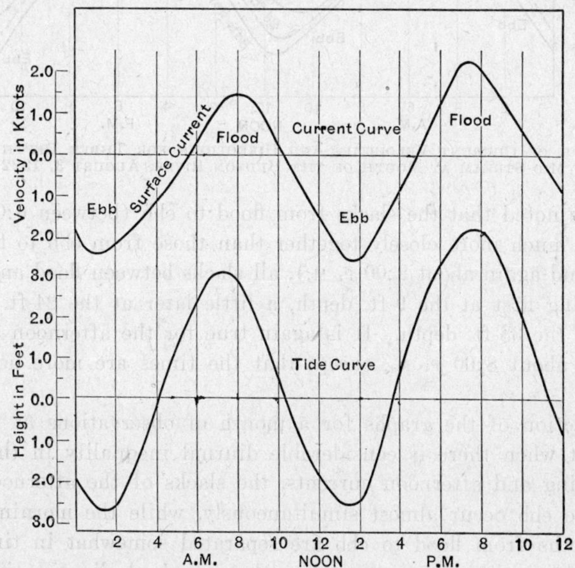

FIG. 25.—COMPARISON OF TIDE AND CURRENT CURVES, NEW YORK HARBOR.

An added advantage of such a graph for the interpretation of current data is the facility with which the duration of slack-water may be determined graphically; that is, the period during which the current velocity is less than 0.1 knot, which is becoming to mean "slack-water", although theoretically the time of slack-water is only an instant.

* For more detail, see U. S. Coast and Geodetic Survey *Special Publication No. 111*, p. 17.

The parallelism of the two curves in Fig. 25 indicates the intimate time relation between the tides at Fort Hamilton and the currents at the entrance to the Hudson; for example, the times of slack-water (upper diagram, Fig. 25), occurring at about 5:40 A. M., at 10:15 A. M., at 5:00 P. M., and at 10:45 P. M., agree very closely with the times of half-tide of the lower diagram, half-tide occurring at 4:15 A. M., 10:20 A. M., 3:40 P. M., and 11:15 P. M. This occurrence of slack-water at the time of half-tide is one of the indications that the tides of the Hudson are due to a progressive wave and not to a stationary wave.

A graph of this character has the advantage of furnishing the relation (which may be instantly detected) of the velocities of the currents at different depths. Fig. 26 is a graph of the current velocities obtained from observations at three depths, 9, 24, and 38 ft., on August 3, 1922, at a station in mid-stream, at the entrance to the Hudson.

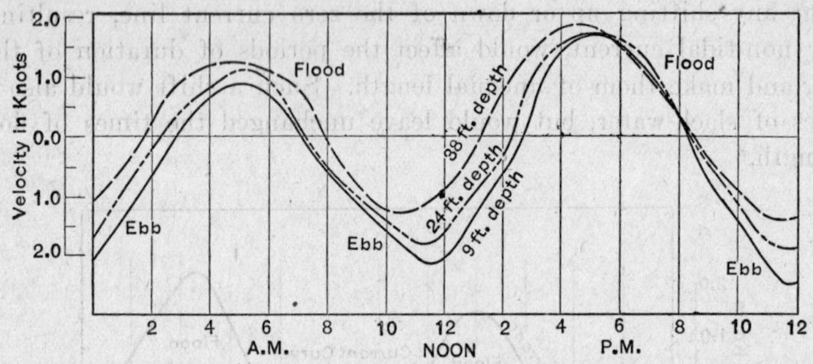

FIG. 26.—GRAPH OF CURRENT VELOCITIES AND DIRECTIONS FOR THREE DEPTHS AT STATION IN MID-STREAM AT MOUTH OF THE HUDSON RIVER, AUGUST 3, 1922.

It will be noted that the slacks from flood to ebb (between 6:00 and 8:00 A. M.) occur much more closely together than those from ebb to flood (about 2:00 A. M., and again about 2:00 P. M.), all slacks between flood and ebb, however, occurring first at the 9-ft. depth, a little later at the 24-ft. depth, and still later at the 38-ft. depth. It is again true for the afternoon slacks from flood to ebb about 8:00 P. M., except that the times are more nearly simultaneous.

An inspection of the graphs for a month of observations at this station indicate that when there is considerable diurnal inequality in the velocities of the morning and afternoon currents, the slacks of the afternoon currents from flood to ebb occur almost simultaneously, while the morning slacks at different depths from flood to ebb are separated somewhat in time; and as the diurnal inequality disappears when the moon's declination is nearing a minimum, the difference in the times of slack-water at different depths from flood to ebb become very nearly equal. The average interval between the surface and bottom slacks from flood to ebb at this station has been found from a long series to be about 12 min.

From ebb to flood, however, the times of slacks at different depths have a wider range and occur first near the bottom (1:40 A. M.), next at mid-depth (2:30 A. M.), and last near the surface (3:00 A. M.). These relations again hold for the afternoon slack from ebb to flood—occurring first at the 38-ft. depth (1:15 P. M.), next at the 24-ft. depth (2:20 P. M.), and last at the 9-ft. depth (2:50 P. M.). Thus, the time between slack-water near the bottom and that on the surface differs by about 1½ hours. This interval has been found to average 1½ hours at this station from long series of observations.

To sum up for this station when there is diurnal inequality evident in the velocities of the current the slack-water following the weaker flood occurs first on the surface, a few minutes later at mid-depth, and last at the bottom; the slack-water following the stronger flood occurs almost simultaneously at all depths. At the time of the month when there is little diurnal inequality in the flood velocities, the slack-water following both floods occurs almost simultaneously at the three depths. The slack-water following an ebb shows very little diurnal inequality in the times of slack at all depths, occurring first at the bottom, next at mid-depth, and last on the surface. The average difference between slacks at the three different depths from flood to ebb is found to be 12 min., and the average difference in slacks at the three depths from ebb to flood is found to have an average interval between of 1½ hours.

This difference of intervals for slacks at different depths following a flood current from that following an ebb, is due to the fact that on the flood the dense ocean water is flowing into the harbor against the lighter fresh-water run-off of the river, and is thus causing a commingling of the water. This action, having a tendency to bring about a uniform density of the water from top to bottom, causes the change in direction to occur practically simultaneously at all depths. On the other hand, during an ebb current, with no force to cause a mixing of the water, the dense salt water seeks the bottom and the lighter fresh water seeks the surface. When the flood water first begins running into the harbor from the ocean the dense ocean water hugs the bottom and under-runs the fresh surface water coming down on the ebb. This lower layer of heavy flood water, therefore, retards and brings to a slack, first, the lower layer of ebb current, gradually gaining sufficient momentum finally to offset the inertia of the over-running, less dense surface water.

Hydraulic Type Currents

The so-called hydraulic type currents are those occurring in straits and canals, connecting two independently tided bodies of water. They are reversing currents, although they are due primarily, not to tidal action of the purely stationary or progressive type, but rather to a temporary difference in head between the two bodies brought about by tidal action. The currents in the East River, New York, and in Cape Cod Canal, are examples of this form, and a brief description of those of the East River will serve to illustrate the type in general. Although these currents are due primarily to the hydraulic gradient, the indications are that some tidal propagation is evident; but, in general, its effects may be neglected. For purposes of predicting, for example, the time of slack-water and the velocity of the currents in such straits and canals for current tables, satisfactory results are obtained by considering only the hydraulic gradient.

The East River connects Long Island Sound with New York Bay, and the tides in these two bodies of water are decidedly different, the tides in Long Island Sound being due to a stationary wave, and those in New York Bay to a progressive wave. The tides in Long Island Sound, therefore, increase in range from the mouth toward the head, from 2.0 ft. at Montauk Point (east end) to 7.2 ft. at Willets Point, at the west end of the Sound; the tide in New York Bay, however, decreases in range from 4.7 ft. at Sandy Hook to 4.4 ft. at Governors Island. This difference in range of tide at the two ends of the East River is sufficient in itself to produce a hydraulic gradient; but, in addition, the time of the tide at Willets Point at the north entrance to the East River is 3 hours or more later than the time of the tide at Governors Island. This difference in time is the larger factor in producing the temporary difference in hydraulic head to which the considerable velocity of current in the East River is due.

As examples, high water occurs at Willets Point when the tide is about at mean sea level at Governors Island, and, therefore, the current at this time sets to the southward through the East River; and at the time of high water at Governors Island the tide at Willets Point is about mean sea level and the current then sets toward Long Island Sound. This difference of tidal conditions in Long Island Sound and New York Bay, at times causing a hydraulic gradient of 4 ft. in the distance of 17 miles from Willets Point to Governors Island, gives rise in Hell Gate to currents which attain a mean velocity, at strength, of about 5 knots; and occasionally currents have a velocity of 8 knots.

While it is a comparatively simple matter to predict the time that the heads at the two ends will be equalized and that slack-water should occur, account must be taken, with conditions such as these, of the momentum of this mass of water and of the time of the continuance of the flow after equalization of head. This information can be obtained only from observations, and to obtain mean conditions these observations should be continued over a considerable period, since the range of the tide between springs and neaps varies more than 20%, and, therefore, the current velocity at the different phases of the moon varies proportionately.

If a long series of tidal observations at a suitable place near-by are available, short series of current observations may be reduced to mean values by comparison with these tide observations, since the currents are intimately associated with the tidal regimen of the bodies of water and vary during the tidal month proportionately with the range of tide. The procedure is explained hereafter under "Current Reductions".

The hydrodynamic problems that arise in a canal connecting two large bodies of tidal waters are of so involved a nature that even where solutions have been found they necessitate a great deal of complicated numerical work. Since, however, the engineer is interested chiefly in the maximum velocities, or those that occur at times of strength of the current, simpler formulas that will give approximate results are used.

Ocean Currents

The along-shore currents of the coast have considerable importance in coast erosion and accretion studies, and since these are intimately associated with the general ocean circulation, engineers should have a general knowledge of this circulation.

Little of a quantitative nature has been done in the study of oceanic circulation by direct observations of currents. The set and drift of ocean currents have been mapped in a general way; but the principal information on which these results are based is of a qualitative nature obtained from a record of the drift of bottles and of wrecks, and from a difference between the true and the dead reckoning positions of vessels, the determination of which does not permit of a high degree of accuracy. All these, however, furnish qualitative data and quantitative data can come only from systematic observations either directly of the current or of densities and temperatures, all of which may be considered an international, rather than a national, problem.

Three reasons may be assigned for this near neglect of a phenomenon so closely associated with the subject of tides: Obviously, tidal observations may be made more economically than current observations, for which expensive vessels with full complement of officers and crew are necessary. Secondly, associated with periodic tidal currents are non-tidal currents which, in general, are produced by the wind and by differences in temperatures and densities of sea water. Data for predictions of tidal currents, since they are periodic, may be obtained from observations extending over a comparatively short time, while for non-periodic non-tidal currents a much longer series of observations is required to furnish average conditions and to permit of predictions of any degree of accuracy. Another reason is that the oceans may be considered the highways of commerce for all nations, and, therefore, the study of its problems an international rather than a national undertaking.

The subject of ocean currents is now receiving the attention of physical oceanographers, particularly in the North European countries in their fisheries conservation studies—Bjerknes, Helland-Hansen, Nansen, and Pettersson, in Europe, and McEwen, of the Scripps Institution of Oceanography, in America.

Dynamic oceanography provides a method for mapping currents over extensive ocean surfaces, and it is by these methods, rather than by direct current observations, that the present meager knowledge of ocean currents will undoubtedly be supplemented. Given the temperature and salinity observations from several known depths at stations systematically located over an ocean area, then the direction and velocity of the current are readily predicted and mapped by the physical oceanographer. Studies made at Bergen, Norway, covering density and temperature observations obtained by the International Ice Patrol, indicate the probability that, from a sufficient number of observations of density and temperature over an area, current charts can be prepared to show the probable direction and velocity of the relatively deep-seated ocean currents several weeks in advance.

The principal maritime nations have made current observations, however, on their inland waters and along their coasts. Within the last few years the U. S. Coast and Geodetic Survey has given attention to the study of coastal currents, both tidal and wind-driven. Recently, current tables have been issued containing data of importance on this subject which are vital to the safeguarding of life and property in coastwise shipping. This is particularly true on the Pacific Coast in that its currents, like its tides are more complex than those on the Atlantic; and, in addition, in that its coast harbors are many miles apart, the sailing courses long, and the periods of foggy and stormy weather of comparatively frequent occurrence.

Although the total coastal current is made up of a combination of two components, the periodic, or tidal, current and the non-periodic, or wind-driven, current, analysis of a long series of current observations made at any station serves to separate the two, so that the proper correlation can be made between each component and its causes. That is, the velocity and direction of the tidal current may be referred to the predictions at some standard port, and the velocity and direction of the wind-driven current correlated with the force and direction of the local wind prevailing at the time. These two coastal currents, although combined, are of distinct characters and will be taken up separately.

Coastal Tidal Currents.—The current observations, on which these studies of coastal tidal currents have been made, have been obtained on the light vessels along the coasts, through the co-operation of the Lighthouse Service. While the data obtained relate chiefly to the vicinities of these vessels, general laws of the action of these currents can be deduced, which, usually, will apply to other sections of the coast.

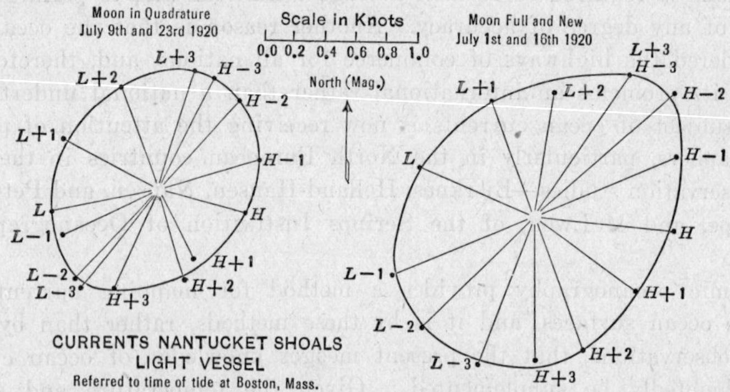

Fig. 27.—Graph of Rotary Tidal Currents, Nantucket Shoals Light Vessel, Atlantic Coast, at Times of Different Phases of the Moon.

On the open coast the tidal current is not of the rectilinear or reversing type with its period of slack-water; nor is the current ever slack—its direction changes constantly in a rotary movement. The varying velocities throughout a tidal cycle when plotted to scale on polar-co-ordinate paper approximate an elliptical shape illustrated by Fig. 27. This shows velocities and directions of current at Nantucket Shoals Light Vessel referred to the time of tide at Boston. For example, from the left diagram at $H-2$, that is, 2 hours before high water at Boston, the current sets about south by east with a velocity of 0.6 knots.

It should be noted that the current is constantly changing direction clockwise at the rate of about 15° per hour from H (high water) through each hour to L (low water) and so on to H again; and that the velocities are such that a curve through the extremities of ordinates approximates an ellipse. The velocity of the tidal current along the Atlantic Coast varies with the times of neap and spring tides (compare the right and left diagrams of Fig. 27). The direction of the set of the current, however, is in general the same at any time of the month for the same tidal hour at a standard port; for example, in both diagrams, H is in the same general direction from the origin; at L-3 (3 hours before low water at Boston), the direction is the same for both diagrams, and likewise for each tidal hour.

A graph of the tidal current at Five Fathom Bank Light Vessel (Fig. 28) illustrates that toward the coast tidal currents assume more nearly the character of the rectilinear or reversing type, the ellipse becoming more elongated than those for Nantucket Shoals Light Vessel, which is about 40 miles offshore.

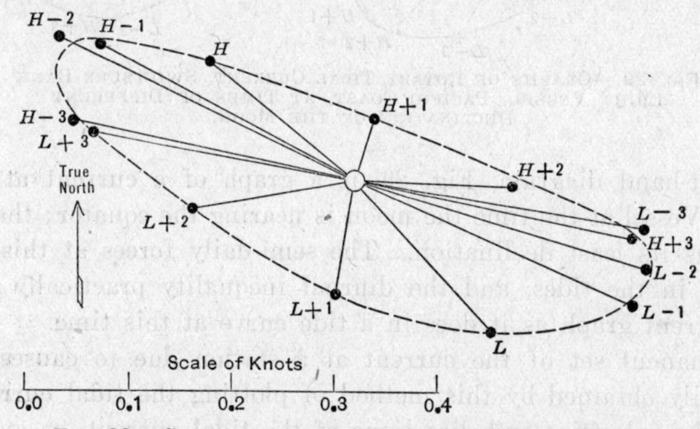

FIG. 28.—GRAPH OF ROTARY TIDAL CURRENT AT FIVE FATHOM BANKS LIGHT VESSEL, ATLANTIC COAST.

The coastal tidal currents on the Pacific Coast are also rotary, but, like its tides, they have considerable diurnal inequality. The current velocities on the Atlantic Coast vary principally with the changing phases of the moon (Fig. 28), while on the Pacific Coast the variations are principally due to diurnal inequality brought about by the declination of the moon.

The current graphs from the observations for 1919 at Swiftsure Bank Light Vessel at the entrance to the Strait of Juan de Fuca (Fig. 29), are representative of the type of coastal tidal current on the Pacific. They are referred to the times of the tide at Astoria, Ore., H representing the time of lower high water, L the time of higher low water, $H\ H$ the time of higher high water, and $L\ L$ the time of lower low water.

The left-hand diagram (Fig. 29) is made from observations at the time the moon was farthest north and farthest south of the equator, illustrating the variation in velocity due to diurnal inequality; that is, at the time the daily tidal forces are at a maximum, when the moon is at its greatest declination. It will be seen that on the Pacific the velocity of the coastal tidal current, like the range of the tide, is greater during one tidal cycle than during the next. For example, one hour after lower high water at Astoria the current at Swiftsure Bank Light Vessel has a velocity of about 1 knot; whereas one hour after higher high water the current has a velocity of only about $\frac{1}{4}$ knot. On the Atlantic Coast the two ellipses of a tidal day are practically the same, whereas the ellipse through one tidal cycle on the Pacific Coast is considerably different from that of the next tidal cycle.

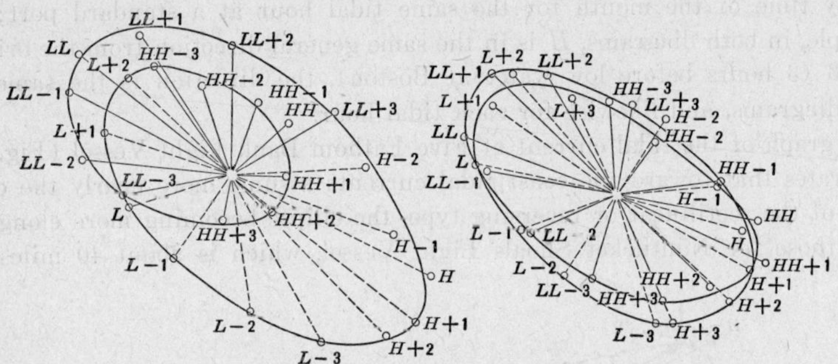

FIG. 29.—GRAPHS OF ROTARY TIDAL CURRENT, SWIFTSURE BANK LIGHT VESSEL, PACIFIC COAST, AT TIMES OF DIFFERENT DECLINATION OF THE MOON.

The right-hand diagram, Fig. 29, is a graph of a current at Swiftsure Bank Light Vessel at the time the moon is nearing the equator; that is, when the moon has its least declination. The semi-daily forces at this time predominate as in the tides, and the diurnal inequality practically disappears from the current graph as it does in a tide curve at this time.

The permanent set of the current at a station due to causes not tidal may be readily obtained by this method of plotting the tidal current graph. In Fig. 30 the velocities and directions of the tidal current, as averaged for the particular period desired, are plotted from a common origin (focus of the rays) and the true center of the ellipse, *C*, is then determined. The direction and distance to scale of *C* from the origin represent the permanent set of the current; that is, superimposed on the tidal currents there was a constant set during the month of August, 1919, passing Swiftsure Light Vessel at a rate of almost $\frac{1}{2}$ knot in a direction N. 40° W. This permanent set may be ascribed to the fresh-water run-off from the Strait of Juan de Fuca, the light vessel being stationed just off the entrance to the Strait; it may be due to several causes, among which are prevailing winds, fresh-water discharge from a strait or river, and permanent sets like the Gulf Stream.

Since the rotary tidal currents along the open coast are so closely related to tidal action, it is evident that those components due to tidal action alone may be readily and accurately predicted as to their velocities and directions by comparison with the times of high or low water at some standard port.

The problem, however, is not so easily solved, for this tidal current is only one of the components of the total coastal current. The other, due to local winds, is not only non-periodic, defying accurate predictions a long time in advance, but, in general, is of greater velocity than the tidal currents, and, therefore, proportionately of greater importance.

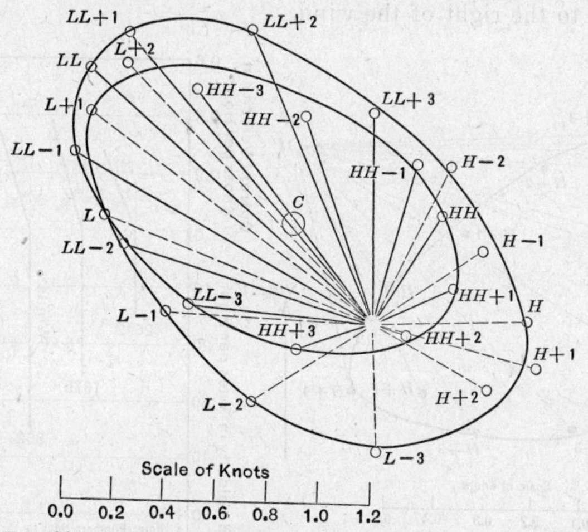

FIG. 30.—GRAPH OF ROTARY TIDAL CURRENT AT SWIFTSURE BANK LIGHT VESSEL, PACIFIC COAST.

Coastal Wind Currents.—It has been brought out that the rotary tidal-current ellipse may be displaced from its origin by a permanent set due to fresh-water run-off; at times, the current produced by heavy winds, however, retards the regular tidal current to such an extent that the origin is displaced considerably outside the ellipse. At Frying Pan Shoals Light Vessel from observations made during a northeast storm from January 29 to February 2, 1920 (Fig. 31), the wind velocity varied during the five days from 15 to 60 miles per hour, averaging 34.6 miles; the wind direction varied from north-northeast to northeast.

The origin of the graph is at P. The direction of the current varied throughout the tidal cycle from south to west and back to south; that is, from $H + 1$ to $L + 3$ by way of $L - 2$, and then from $L + 3$ to $H + 1$ again by way of $H - 1$. The velocities also varied because of the tidal forces throughout a tidal cycle and the curve through the extremities of the velocity ordinates approximates an ellipse; that is, the current, although setting to the southwestward during the entire duration of the storm varied in velocity by the amount of the acceleration and retardation due to the tidal component.

In an ocean of infinite depth it may be shown* from theoretical considerations that a current produced by winds should be deflected on the surface 45° to the right of the wind in the Northern Hemisphere and 45° to the left in the Southern Hemisphere, due to the deflecting forces of the earth's rotation.

* "On the Influence of the Earth's Rotation on Ocean Currents," *Arkiv for Mathematik, Astronomie, och Fysik,* Vol. 2, No. 11, 1905.

Near the coast it is to be expected that this deflection should be considerably modified by the configuration of the shore. Recent investigations from the comparatively long series of continuous current observations obtained during the past few years at different light vessels have verified this theory and brought out the important fact that, contrary to the belief of the mariner, a local wind creates a current setting not in its own direction, but in a direction about 20° to the right of the wind.

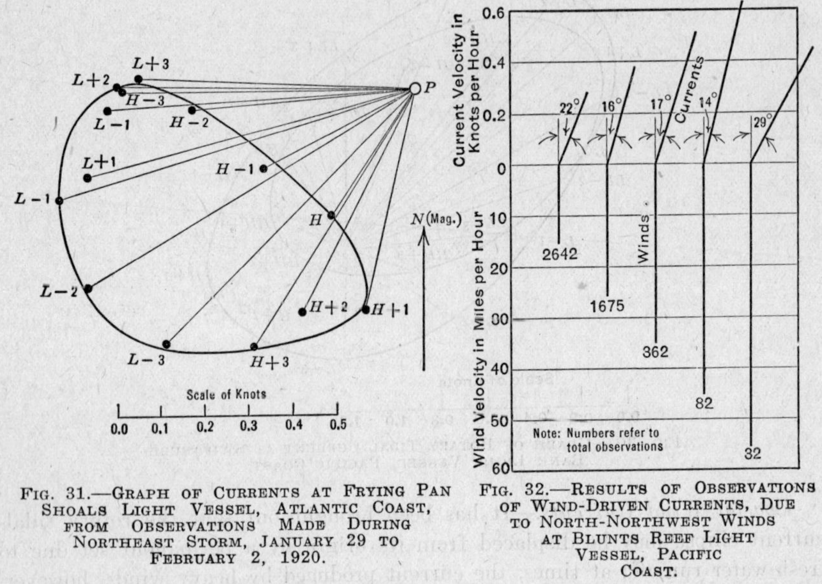

Fig. 31.—Graph of Currents at Frying Pan Shoals Light Vessel, Atlantic Coast, from Observations Made During Northeast Storm, January 29 to February 2, 1920.

Fig. 32.—Results of Observations of Wind-Driven Currents, Due to North-Northwest Winds at Blunts Reef Light Vessel, Pacific Coast.

Since a large number of observations of this character are necessary for averages of any degree of accuracy, and also for the elimination of tidal current in the resulting data, it is evident that observations of wind-driven currents have to be made over a considerable time in order to get a number of winds of 10 miles per hour, 20 miles per hour, etc., blowing from various directions. In Fig. 32 are represented diagrammatically the results from a number of observations over a period of two years (1919-20) for a north-northwest wind at Blunts Reef Light Vessel, Pacific Coast, for velocities from 10 to 60 miles per hour. The deflections of the slanting lines from the vertical indicate the deflections of the resulting currents to the right of the wind direction.

While the general law applies to the average current produced by any given wind velocity, observations are necessary at intervals along the coast, particularly well inshore, to determine the actual velocities for that particular locality. For coastwise navigation, however, the general law will hold with sufficient accuracy for practical results within 5 to 20 miles offshore; it has been found that the velocity varies fairly proportionately with the wind velocity and is about 2% in knots of the wind velocity in miles per hour on the Pacific Coast and 1½% on the Atlantic Coast.

In practice, it is necessary to take into consideration the combination of this wind-driven current with the periodic tidal current, the tidal current being obtained from predictions and the wind-driven current estimated from the local wind at the time. In actual practice the resultant current may be readily obtained from a diagram drawn to suitable scale showing the velocity and direction of each component, tidal and wind-driven, the resultant direction and velocity being scaled from this graph.

At times, however, wind-driven currents of considerable velocity appear to precede the wind to which they are due. The writer during two winters, 1915-16 and 1916-17, took current observations from the Carolinas well down the Florida Coast and from the shore out to the Gulf Stream. A number of times these showed a strong set from the southwestward during moderate weather, displacing considerably the regular tidal current ellipse from the origin of the current graphs. In every case this condition was indicative of a heavy southwest blow which followed within a few hours. At times, of course, a long swell, preceding the wind, may accompany this strong current, but sometimes even this warning of treacherous currents is absent.

While the main oceanic circulation involves a study of currents which, in general, are produced by predominant winds, such as the trades, and by differences in barometric pressures, densities, and temperatures over the oceans, little of a quantitative nature has been done toward a systematic study of these phenomena. In fact, what has been done may be considered as reconnaissance work only and volumes may be devoted later to obtaining the quantitative data necessary to such a study.

Reduction of Currents

Mean Values.—Since the tidal currents in bays and estuaries are so intimately connected with the tidal regimen in these bodies, a short series of current observations may be reduced to mean values by means of tidal data.

In the non-harmonic analysis of current observations the times of slack-water and greatest velocity are referred to the times of high and low water of the tide at some suitable place near-by. In this method the time of current is reduced to approximately mean values, since the changes in the time of current approximate the changes in the time of the tide. It is necessary, however, to reduce the velocities to mean values.

The velocities of a short series of ordinary current observations of the rectilinear or reversing type, caused by a progressive or stationary wave, may be reduced to mean values by multiplying by a factor equal to the reciprocal of the range of the tide for the same period of time during which the current observations were made, divided by the mean range of the tide for the place. The velocities of hydraulic currents, however, vary as the square root of the head (that is, of the difference in the height of water at the two ends of the strait); and to reduce the velocities of a short series of hydraulic type currents to mean values, it is necessary to multiply by a factor which is the square root of that used for ordinary tidal currents referred to heretofore.

Before multiplying the velocities of currents of both types by the suitable factors to reduce them to mean values, the non-tidal current, due to fresh-water run-off, must be eliminated. This may be done by taking as the tidal current the half sum of the observed flood and ebb strengths, and this half sum is multiplied by the correction factor in each case.

The relations as to time existing between currents and tide apply as to the moon's changing phases and also as to the moon's changing distance from the earth; but as to the moon's changing declination, the current and tide do not respond alike, the diurnal variation in the tide at a place usually being greater than the diurnal variation in the current. In regions where the tide has considerable diurnal inequality, as on the Pacific Coast of the United States, the time relations between tide and current are subject to variations. In such cases, however, it is possible to refer the current at any place to the tide at some other place that has a comparable diurnal inequality.

Instruments for Current Observations

The instruments made in the United States for the observation of currents have been devised principally for shallow depths and for use in rivers. Little attention has been given, therefore, to attachments for furnishing the direction of the current.

There are a number of types of meters, described in the catalogues of American instrument manufacturers; practically all, however, are made on a principle somewhat similar to the anemometer used by the meteorologist—several metal cups on a carriage revolving in the current and making an electric contact at each revolution of the carriage. This contact, making an audible "tick", is transmitted through an insulated cable and telephone receiver to an observer on a vessel.

The Price current meter (Fig. 33) illustrates this type. The meter is suspended on station by a triple-strand insulated cable, 0.133 in. in diameter, made up of three enameled wires, one of which is piano wire, 0.0335 in. in diameter, for carrying the weight of the meter, and the other two, copper wires, No. 20 B. and S. gauge, for the electric circuit to the telephone receivers on board the observing unit.

To hold the meter from a davit of the observing vessel vertically on station in strong currents, a spherical 200-lb. cast-iron weight is suspended near the bottom on a ½-in. steel wire cable, and the meter lowered and raised along this cable by means of its own suspending cable and two small shackles (Fig. 33). The meter is rated before and after a survey lasting several months, so that the revolutions may be reduced to exact velocity.

Since the meters furnished by manufacturers in this country do not have a means for determining the direction of sub-surface currents—an important matter in current surveys for local peculiarities of currents in large ports off piers and slips—the U. S. Coast and Geodetic Survey has developed a device for this purpose. It is known as a "Bifilar Suspension Current Direction Indicator", and appears to have solved in a simple and inexpensive manner the problem of the determination of the direction of these currents in the smooth waters of a harbor. The determinations, however, are vitiated in rough water, where the rolling of the vessel causes the comparatively heavy device to swing.

Fig. 33.—Details of Installation on the Current Survey Vessel of the Price Current Meter.

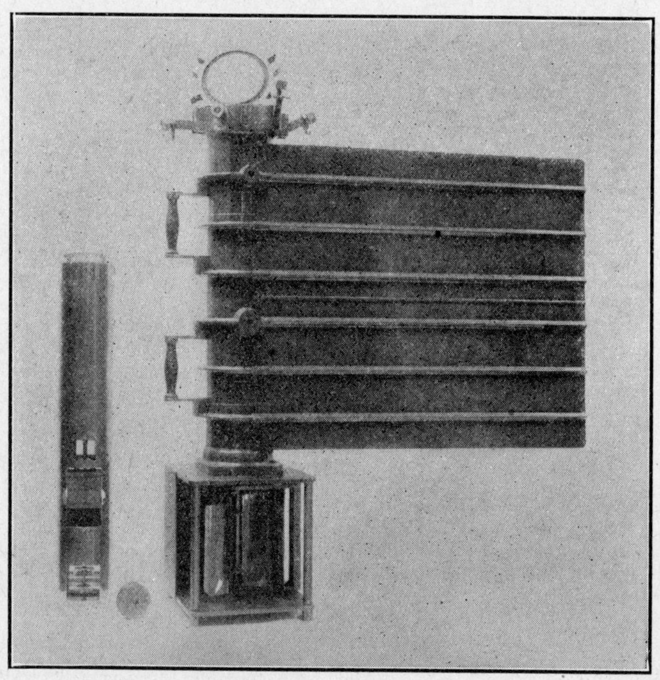

Fig. 34.—View of the Pettersson Self-Recording Current Meter.

Briefly, the device consists of a pipe, with rudder attached, free to turn in azimuth by virtue of a ball-bearing joint at its connection with an outrigger or davit on a vessel. The pipe is lowered to any moderate depth desired. A graduated pelorus at the davit indicates by a pointer the direction the bar is forced to take by virtue of the rudder acting through the taut aircraft wires.

A later development of the device (Fig. 35) permits not only of simultaneous observations at three depths, but also lessens the labor of operation by obviating the necessity of continually lowering and raising a single rudder for observations at various depths.

Foreign instrument makers have given consideration to attachments within the instrument for the determination of direction. Among others are the Ekman meter* and the Pettersson meter.† The former accomplishes the purpose by allowing metal balls, the size of ordinary shot, to drop into different compartments, one for each of the principal points of the compass, as the meter swings in azimuth; the latter by photographing on a narrow, sensitized film the graduated periphery of a glass disk, which is held in azimuth by a magnetized steel bar.

The Pettersson type (Figs. 34 and 36) is a self-recording meter and makes a photographic record each half hour of the total current passing the meter during the preceding half hour, and, in addition, of the magnetic direction of the current. The metal cartridge (left, Fig. 34), containing the recording device, is inserted into the heavy brass cylinder (right, Fig. 34), and the cap screwed down in place on top of the cylinder by heavy lug screws. A rubber gasket in the face of this cap prevents any water entering even at pressures of considerable depth.

The whole apparatus is supported on a ball-bearing shackle, permitting of a free movement in azimuth. The vane or rudder to the right (Fig. 34) forces the meter to head into the current.

The details of its operation are shown in Fig. 36. There is no mechanical connection between the current vanes, *W W,* which are wholly outside the cylinder, and the recording device on the inside of the cylinder. The vanes, *W W,* through a train of gears, turns a permanent magnet, M_1. This magnet in turn causes Magnet M_2, on the inside of the cylinder, to rotate in synchronism; Magnet M_2, through a train of gears and vertical shaft, causes the glass disk, D_1, to revolve. This glass disk is graduated on its periphery and the number of graduations past a given point in an half hour gives the number of revolutions made by the vanes, *W W,* and thus the current velocity, during that half hour. The glass disk, D_2, graduated on its periphery to every 10°, carries on its surface a magnetized needle, which holds it in azimuth.

The clock-work causes a sensitized photographic film to move at a uniform rate past an opening just above the two glass disks, D_1 and D_2. The clock-work also causes a light, L_1, to flash each half hour, thus making a record on the film of the graduations on both disks opposite the initial line, across the opening, at that instant. B_1 and B_2 are two ordinary dry cells and J is of

* "A Text Book of Oceanography," by T. T. Jenkins, p. 133, E. P. Dutton, N. Y.

† "A Recording Current Meter for Deep Sea Work," by Dr. Hans Pettersson, *Quarterly Journal,* Royal Meteorological Soc., Vol. XLI, No. 173, January, 1915.

Swedish soft iron, breaking the magnetic field between the magnets and the magnetized needle on Disk D_2. The meter is suspended from the ball-bearing shackle, *S*.

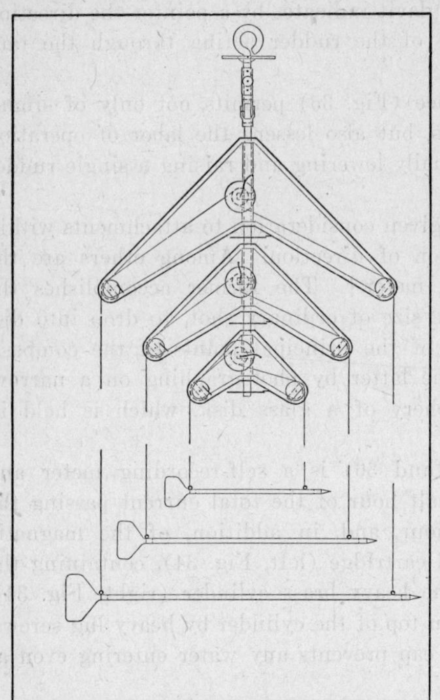

FIG. 35—BIFILAR SUSPENSION CURRENT DIRECTION INDICATOR, GIVING RECORDS AT THREE DEPTHS.

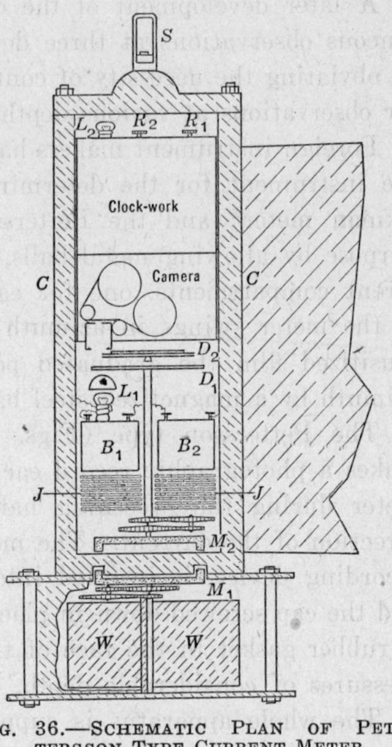

FIG. 36.—SCHEMATIC PLAN OF PETTERSSON TYPE CURRENT METER.

The meter can be lowered to any reasonable depth and left on station, suspended from a buoy, or raft, requiring no attention until the film has run out and the clock run down. The clock will run for 2 weeks and the film will accommodate 700 observations, sufficient for the corresponding record. This meter was tested by the U. S. Coast and Geodetic Survey on the current survey of Southeastern Alaska during the summer of 1925. It gave excellent satisfaction.

The U. S. Coast and Geodetic Survey has obtained good results in the observations of surface current velocities on the light vessels along the coast by the use of the current line. This consists of the ordinary log-line used in the days of the sailing ship for estimating the speed of the vessel, except that it is graduated to a 60-sec. interval for use with a stop-watch instead of a shorter interval as used with the old sand-glass. The sailing ship chip-log is replaced by a pole 3 in. in diameter and 15 ft. long, weighted with lead at the lower end to float upright, with about 1 ft. out of water. The line is graduated for the 60-sec. interval from the proportion, 3 600 sec. : 60 sec. = 6 080 ft.: X, or 101 ft. 4 in. representing 1 knot. The knot is subdivided into tenths by silk fish-line tabs.

The current line and the pole furnish a more reliable record of current velocities obtained from a vessel in rough water on the open coast than the current meter, because of the acceleration of the meter due to the rolling and pitching of the vessel.

Current and Tide Survey of Harbors

Prior to 1922 the current data available for the harbors of the United States consisted of short series of scattered observations made at various times. Thus it was impossible to reach conclusive results of the circulation throughout the harbors. Congress made additional funds available for current work in 1922 and the comprehensive current and tide surveys of the harbors of the country are being taken up in the order of their military and commercial importance. Such a survey was made in 1922 of the Harbor of New York, jointly by the U. S. Coast and Geodetic Survey and the U. S. Army Engineers, First District; in 1923 the Survey made a similar survey of San Francisco Harbor; in 1924, of Delaware Bay and its tributaries; in 1925 of Southeastern Alaska; and in 1926 of Boston and Portsmouth Harbors.

A thorough knowledge of tides and currents is necessary to a proper understanding of conditions under which harbors and rivers may be developed, in connection with sewerage problems, and in marine constructions of all kinds. Since the Harbor of New York is one of the most complicated from a standpoint of its tide and current conditions, a brief résumé of this survey will show its scope and the results obtainable. An interpretation and discussion of the tide and current observations made during this survey, together with scattered observations made by various organizations at intervals since the early Fifties, has been published.*

The Harbor of New York (Figs. 37 and 38) is made up of an outer bay, a narrows (at Fort Hamilton), an inner bay, a tidal river, a sound, and two straits, connecting independently tided bodies of water. Since the tidal and current conditions in all sections of the harbor are so intimately and vitally connected, continuous simultaneous observations throughout the entire harbor, of course, would make for an ideal survey. Unquestionably, it was uneconomical and impracticable even to approach this ideal and the problem was met by dividing the harbor for the purpose of the survey into different major sections and linking together the observations at one or two principal stations of one section while observations were in progress in the contiguous section. The actual observations continued day and night for about three months.

The dense traffic in the harbor, particularly in the East River and in the Lower Hudson, presented a rather troublesome question. The constant danger of collision to the observing units of the Survey, particularly at night and during thick weather, made it advisable in the parts of the harbor where the traffic was most dense, to utilize large flat-bottomed barges instead of the light 60-ft. launches generally used on this class of work.

The times of slack-water are of importance to shipping in a harbor in which the current velocity is considerable and the vessels entering the harbor,

* U. S. Coast and Geodetic Survey *Special Publication No. 111,* "Tides and Currents in New York Harbor."

of large tonnage. This is likewise true of exact information on local peculiarities of the currents in the vicinities of piers and slips in connection with the berthing of large vessels. The engineer engaged on marine work in the harbor, while not so vitally interested as the mariner in the predictions of the times of slack-water, must have a complete and accurate knowledge of the conditions of the current at various depths in order to plan intelligently. For example, this survey was not fully completed when a request was received from an engineer for information on the current velocities at various depths in connection with the proposed tube from Brooklyn to Staten Island.

Since the periods of slack-water in New York Harbor are short, particularly in those parts where the currents attain the greatest velocity, the predicted times of these slacks, to be of value, must be accurate. These predictions are made several years in advance and observations as furnished by this current survey are necessary to the preparation of accurate tables of current predictions. Likewise, in Admiralty Courts the time of slack-water and the velocity of the current at different times play important rôles in the settlement of cases involving collisions and suits for damages. Without accurate data on which to base computations and conclusions no authoritative statements are possible. This recent survey covers a large part of the harbor with current series of sufficient length to warrant authoritative statements for the majority of cases that will arise.

The results are also important in the studies of sewage disposal for New York City, and in the improvements to the waterways, particularly the East River, Harlem River, and Little Hell Gate. Engineers and commissions have been studying for many years these problems of sewage disposal. At the time of the creation of the New York Pollution Commission in 1903, the duties of which were continued by the Metropolitan Sewerage Commission in 1906, the question was serious and has become more so each year. Extensive float tests have been carried on from time to time to determine the final resting places of objects set adrift in the harbor. While these tests demonstrated that at times some of the floats would finally reach the ocean and others strand on the shores of the Bay, they did not furnish quantitative data on the circulation of the harbor as a whole. This recent survey, although made in five sections, has been so linked together as to make possible the study of simultaneous conditions of flow. Figs. 37 and 38 show the tidal movement in New York Harbor at the time of high water, and also at the time of low water, at Fort Hamilton.*

In general, floats are of little use for obtaining quantitative current data, except to show the different current threads in some classes of studies, such as oyster culture. For an interpretation of the entire circulation in a harbor, definite stations, with simultaneous observations, scattered over the harbor at selected points, are necessary.

In view of the purpose of the survey, it was considered of advantage to divide the current work into two parts: (*a*) Observations for determining

* U. S. Coast and Geodetic Survey *Special Publication No. 111,* in which the data from this survey are discussed, contains thirteen such diagrams of the harbor as a whole, showing the generalized tidal movement throughout the harbor each hour of the tidal cycle.

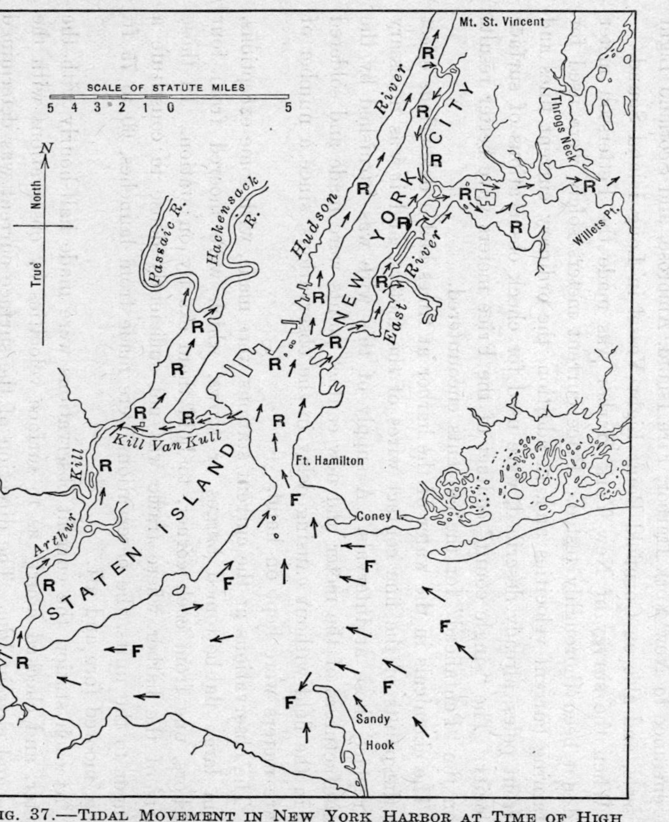

Fig. 37.—Tidal Movement in New York Harbor at Time of High Water at Fort Hamilton, N. Y. R Indicates Rising Tide.

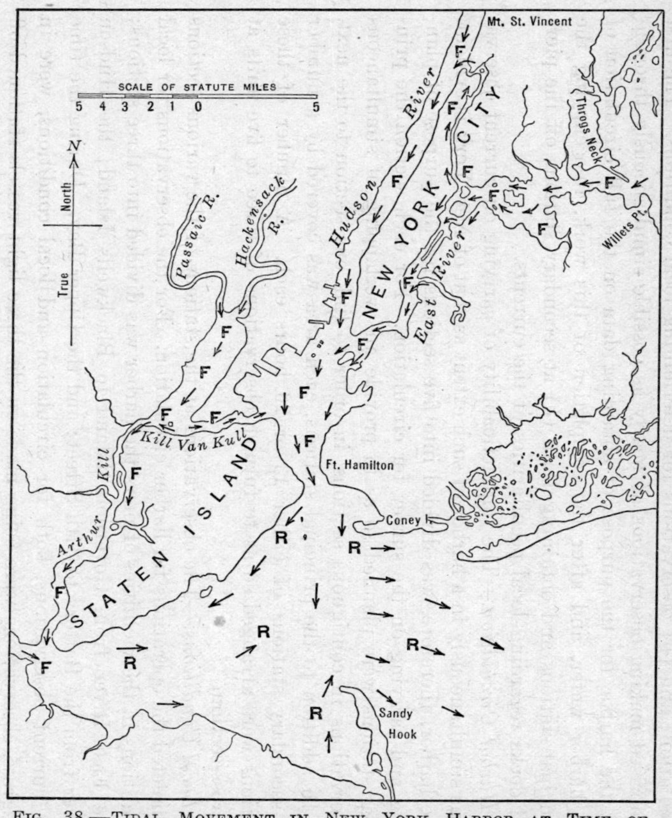

Fig. 38.—Tidal Movement in New York Harbor at Time of Low Water at Fort Hamilton, N. Y. F Indicates Falling Tide.

circulation; and (*b*) observations for determining local conditions. The first comprised making observations as nearly as possible simultaneously throughout the harbor for the purpose of obtaining data on the full circulation of the harbor water, and after the completion of this work, re-occupying the principal stations and obtaining Data (*b*) at secondary stations off the piers and docks regarding local peculiarities of the currents.

Harbor Circulation.—The impracticability of carrying on current observations simultaneously in a harbor of such extent as that of New York is evident. The harbor, therefore, was divided into five sections for the purpose of planning and carrying on the survey for circulation. For each section the principal stations were planned so as to provide an overlapping of simultaneous observations in contiguous sections, in order to link one section to the next.

In addition to the principal stations, each area was covered by a number of secondary stations of either 13 or 26 hours each. A number of these stations were arranged so as to furnish observations of three to five units at a cross-section.

Local Conditions.—The observations at the stations of the various sections completed the operations for harbor circulation. For the observations for local conditions in the vicinities of piers the harbor was divided into three sections: The East River from Governors Island to Blackwells Island; the Hudson River from the Battery to 37th Street; and the Upper Bay. During the time the current observations, both for circulation and local conditions, were in progress, observations were being made on the three light vessels stationed off the entrance to New York Harbor, Fire Island, Ambrose, and Scotland Light Vessels, and also on Cornfield Point Light Vessel in Long Island Sound.

When the survey of New York Harbor was made the Pettersson meter had not been thoroughly tested. Price current meters solely were used for obtaining current velocities and, in addition, the ordinary current lines and current poles, already described, were used for check observations of surface velocity. The "single count" contact of the Price meters gave better results than the "Pentahead" for the currents encountered.

The chemicals in the water of the harbor at times had a deleterious effect on the points of the fine contact wires of the meters, and it was necessary to replace these at intervals. A supply of this wire was furnished by the manufacturers of the meter and new contact points were made and soldered on in the field without causing delay in the observations, since a number of spare meters were kept on hand.

The observations at the current stations were made, with some exceptions, from large flat-bottomed barges or scows, which were moored from four anchors, one from each corner, to hold them exactly on station. In those parts of the harbor where traffic was not sufficiently dense to constitute a danger to the units, the observations were made from launches, 60 to 75 ft. long, moored fore and aft.

At each station the current observations were made half-hourly with the meter, and checked hourly as to surface velocities by observations with the pole and current line. The direction of the surface current was determined by laying the current line, attached to the current pole, across a graduated brass plate secured to the taffrail of the launches, or to the deck of the barges, and referred to a compass; the direction of the sub-surface current was determined by the Bifilar suspension current indicator.

Velocities were determined with the meters by observations near the surface, at mid-depth, and near the bottom. In general, readings were taken at two-tenths, five-tenths, and eight-tenths of the depth at each station, beginning with the one near the surface, followed by the mid-depth and near-the-bottom observations. Then the order was reversed and, before the meter was drawn up, the observation near the bottom was repeated; then the mid-depth; and, finally, the one near the surface.

Special weights of 60 lb. each and special hangers were provided for the Price meters because of the strong currents. This weight, however, was not sufficient to keep the meters in a vertical position below the vessel. In an attempt to overcome this difficulty a small winch was installed on the deck of each of the observing units for carrying a ½-in. wire cable holding a 250-lb. concrete block, which was hung just clear of the bottom. The meter was lowered and raised along this cable by a small shackle secured to its hanger. Subsequent experience, however, on later surveys has demonstrated that a 200-lb. spherical cast-iron weight, with its smaller surface (Fig. 33), is the more satisfactory.

In Hell Gate the velocity of the current and the traffic prohibited the anchoring of launches or barges. To obtain observations in this important waterway one of the concrete blocks was lowered from the Hell Gate Railroad Bridge by a ¾-in. cable and the meter run up and down this cable. After a series of 6 hours' observations, a tow ran into the cable and carried away the whole apparatus. The observations were then continued for a period of 13 hours from a drillboat of the Army Engineers moored off Hallets Point. The drillboat was run down a few hours later.*

Conclusion

The foregoing furnishes a brief outline only of the subject of tides and currents. Extensive further references are available.†

The finished products of the tide and current work of the U. S. Coast and Geodetic Survey for the use of the engineer and mariner appear in several forms: In tide tables and current tables which foretell the state of the tide and current for future years; in publications on tidal bench-marks, which definitely fix for the engineer the various datum planes over all the coasts of the United States; and in special publications devoted to a detailed interpretation of the tide and current phenomena of the various ports of the country.

* For more detailed discussions of the data from comprehensive tide and current surveys and of the methods and procedure used on these surveys, refer to the following publications of the U. S. Coast and Geodetic Survey: *Special Publication No. 111,* "Tides and Currents in New York Harbor"; *Special Publication No. 115,* "Tides and Currents in San Francisco Harbor"; *Special Publication No. 123,* "Tides and Currents in Delaware Bay and River"; *Special Publication No. 127,* "Tides and Currents in Southeastern Alaska"; and *Special Publication No. 124,* "Instructions for Tidal Current Surveys."

† For a more detailed, non-mathematical treatment of the phenomenon in all phases the student is referred to "The Tide," by H. A. Marmer, 1926; D. Appleton & Co., N. Y., and "Tides and Kindred Phenomena in the Solar System," by G. H. Darwin, Lond., 1911. For a mathematical treatment of the subject he should consult "Manual of Tides," by R. A. Harris, 1894–1907, Govt. Printing Office, Washington, D. C. These publications carry additional references to published material on the subject.

DISCUSSION

Lewis M. Haupt,* M. Am. Soc. C. E. (by letter).—This comprehensive paper, by Commander Rude, describes one of the most important factors in the interchange of the world's products. His statement of the complex nature of this problem, created by agencies which are constantly modifying the operation of tidal elements, is prefaced by sixty-four definitions of its many phases. Celestial and terrestrial gravitation, temperature, light and darkness, hills and valleys, continents and islands, winds, waves, and currents, are all factors which affect tidal fluctuations.

"All the rivers run into the sea; yet the sea is not full; unto the place from whence the rivers come, thither they return again". This is due to celestial and terrestrial gravitation (formulated by Newton), yet it is the returning streams that deposit the bars at the mouths of the rivers, thus affecting transportation, limiting the interchange of products, and increasing its cost. It is, therefore, a vital factor in the general welfare of humanity.

It is also worthy of note that, although on some coasts the tides are very feeble and diurnal, in others they are of great amplitude and semi-diurnal while, as the author shows, they are ever varying and are affected by other terrestrial agencies such as winds, waves, and currents.

Another factor in navigation is the form of the channel and the velocity and sectional area of the vessel, causing displacement in canals or aqueducts and creating a crest in advance with suction in the rear, which seriously affect the banks of narrow channels. These, however, are not "tides", strictly speaking.

As the tides are important factors in the erosion, transportation, and deposition of the sandy barriers which enclose the coasts and imperil navigation, it is important that they be carefully analyzed and utilized as remedial measures, as has been done by the U. S. Coast and Geodetic Survey and many foreign authorities. It has been demonstrated by maritime engineers the world over that tides may be utilized so as to create ample channels across ocean bars for the largest vessels, but in many instances these channels are being maintained by dredging to remove the drift carried in by the tides from adjacent coasts.

As an instance of vital moment, attention is called to the re-entrant angle in the coast between Long Island and New Jersey, where the inlets on both flanks have been moving toward the bar covering the 7-mile gap between Sandy Hook and Coney Island. Its greatest navigable depth at Gedney's Channel was 21 ft. until the Ambrose Channel was dredged to meet the imperative demands of commerce, but no permanent works have been constructed to check this littoral drift from Long Island. The Jamaica Bay Bar has now crossed the 50-ft. basin and is encroaching on the existing channel. It is believed that the exhaustive report made by the Coast Survey under Professor Henry Mitchell in 1858-59 has not been published, but it is an important document looking to the creation of a permanent entrance

* Cons. Engr., Physical Hydrography, Cynwyd, Pa.

to the City of New York. The problem has been under consideration for many years, and is quite feasible, but as yet has received no permanent solution, reliance being placed on dredging.

In this connection, and as a matter of record, it seems pertinent to cite a demonstration of the utility of tidal action in the creation and maintenance of an automatic channel which was inaugurated by Mr. Brewster Cameron* in 1899. He succeeded in persuading Congress to undertake the establishment of a navigable channel by constructing an offshore barrier to check the littoral drift and admit the 14-in. diurnal tides. All previous efforts had failed and the inlet has been abandoned, with the remains of the previous Government work lying across the bar at a depth of 3 to 8 ft. In 1906, after many delays, the detached offshore, curved or "reaction jetty", was reported to Congress to have been completed at a cost of only $389 203 and the Superintendent of the U. S. Coast and Geodetic Survey stated that the predicted automatic channel was in evidence, without dredging or bar advance. In January, 1910, it was desired to secure a depth of 25 ft., and it was proposed that a second jetty should be built and the offshore breakwater connected with the island. The cost was estimated at $2 028 125, with $60 000 additional to be used for annual dredging, which was not permitted under the former work, the automatic channel having been created by the 14-in. diurnal tides. A second jetty was constructed, however, and it reduced the depth immediately to 13.3 ft. at the outer end, where it was more than 25 ft., and diminished the tidal influx passing through this 2-mile entrance, thus reducing its efficiency.

Again, in 1912, another project was submitted to secure greater depths by the extension of both jetties and by dredging. The estimate submitted† was "for $2 325 000 to be completed in three years", but the diurnal tides continued to deepen along the concave reaction jetty so that this sum was entirely saved.

This example indicates the relative efficiency of purely tidal scour, due to a curvalinear directrix so well presented by H. C. Ripley, M. Am. Soc. C. E., in his paper,‡ "Relation of Depth to Curvature of Channels", in which reference is made to this reaction breakwater, which he built under authority of Congress and which is believed to be the only one in existence.

The Mediterranean Sea is regarded as tideless, yet in certain bays there are tides equal to those of the Gulf of Mexico. The Bay of Rio de Janeiro, Brazil, is notorious for the "resacas" which rise to more than 100 ft. at times, depending on the winds.

These are only a few of the main factors imposed by the tides as they affect the problems of the engineer in the creation of channels or the reclamation of beaches so vital to the welfare of the Nation.

H. de B. Parsons,§ M. Am. Soc. C. E. (by letter).— The work being done by the U. S. Coast and Geodetic Survey, as described by the author, is most

* Mr. Cameron lost his life at Niagara Falls.

† H. R. Doc. No. 1125, 62d Cong., 3d Session, December 11, 1912.

‡ *Transactions*, Am. Soc. C. E., Vol. 90 (June, 1927), p. 207.

§ Cons. Engr.; Prof. Emeritus, Rensselaer Polytechnic Inst., New York, N. Y.

useful to the profession. Some years ago, the writer undertook a study of the tidal phenomena of the Harbor of New York,* and appreciated the help that he received from the Survey.

There are only a few engineers who comprehend tidal phenomena and the regimen of the rise and fall of tidal waters. Structures are frequently erected in the beds of tidal waters and streams, and, when they are, a comprehensive knowledge of tidal ranges and of current velocities is most essential. Many engineers are prone to consider the tidal rise and fall as being approximately harmonic, and do not make proper allowance for hydraulic conditions that affect the range and the irregularities of recurring high and low waters.

It is unfortunate that engineers and surveyors use so many different datums as reference planes for engineering works. The result has been confusing because it has made it difficult to co-ordinate surveys based on different datums. In many instances, the datum used is an arbitrary assumption, and then co-ordination is impossible. The establishment of precise mean sea-level datum bench-marks throughout the United States is a development of the work of the Coast and Geodetic Survey that engineers and surveyors in civil practice should utilize, as it will eliminate confusion and make it possible to co-ordinate surveys made at various times and under different conditions. The universal use of a standard datum would be especially beneficial for hydraulic developments, railroads, highways, water supplies, sewage disposals, river regulations, and flood protection works. These are often interstate problems, and the advantage of a standard reference datum, correlating all adjacent surveys, must be evident. It frequently happens that questions relating to elevations arise in cases under litigation. Such cases would be clarified if a standard elevation had been used for the different surveys that are the bases of the questions under dispute.

The U. S. Geological Survey uses mean sea level as the datum for its topographical maps of the United States, as also does the U. S. Lake Survey for its studies of the waters of the Great Lakes. Perhaps, in the course of time, the U. S. Coast and Geodetic Survey will state the land heights on its charts as feet above mean sea level, instead of in feet above high water, or will print the correction on the charts. These charts and topographical maps are used extensively for preliminary studies of important engineering works.

In contributing this discussion, the writer has in mind the hope that engineers and surveyors will use mean sea level as determined by the U. S. Coast and Geodetic Survey when selecting their datums. When an arbitrary datum is in local use and cannot be readily changed, a note should be placed on drawings giving the correction required in order to refer the datum to mean sea level.

The writer was pleased to find that the engineers of the Board of Transportation of the City of New York had placed a note on a recent drawing, referring the arbitrary datum representing mean high water at New York, to mean sea level as established by the U. S. Coast and Geodetic Survey at Sandy Hook.

* *Transactions,* Am. Soc. C. E., Vol. LXXVI (1913), p. 1979.

Engineers interested in erosion of beaches and in harbor improvement will find the records of coastal currents extremely enlightening. This work is being carried forward by the Coast and Geodetic Survey and data (supplemented by the records of the U. S. Weather Bureau) are being accumulated that will give good pictures of normal and abnormal conditions along the shores of the United States.

The public, as well as the profession, is indebted to the engineers of the U. S. Coast and Geodetic Survey for the careful and painstaking work that is being done and published for general use.

R. L. Faris,* M. Am. Soc. C. E. (by letter).—The paper brings out well the various aspects of tides and currents as they concern the engineer. As yet the engineer has not contributed to this subject as much as might be desired, notwithstanding the fact that as regards certain phases, for example the changes in tidal régime brought about by river and harbor improvement, he is in a position to make contributions of a fundamental character.

If any one branch of the subject may be regarded as of basic importance to the engineer, it is undoubtedly that having to do with datum planes, for they are a matter strictly within his domain. It is not so many years ago that it was customary for the engineer to start with some arbitrary bench-mark as "datum" and refer all elevations within a given locality to this datum. If the bench-mark originally defining this datum were lost, or its elevation accidentally changed, no means were at hand for re-establishing it accurately at its original elevation. Furthermore, with the growth of urban communities, characteristic of the past decades when lines of levels based on such arbitrary datums met, confusion was inevitable. Datum planes based on tides represent a step in the direction of standardization.

With the adoption of datums based on the tides the engineer is in a position to recover such reference planes even if all bench-marks are lost. Furthermore, these tidal datums furnish natural, instead of arbitrary, bases which are related to physical phenomena with the concept familiar not only to the engineer but to the intelligent public.

It is to be observed that while tidal datum planes possess the advantages of simplicity of definition, accuracy of determination, and certainty of recovery, their determination is not a simple matter. The laws governing the rise and fall of the tides are such that, together with the effect of wind and weather, any phase of the tide chosen as a datum plane, as, for example, mean sea level, mean high water, lower low water, etc., changes from day to day, from month to month, and from year to year.

Despite these variations, however, as is brought out by the author, methods have been developed to reduce to mean values the results of short series of observations. By the use of these methods, in general a datum plane may be derived from a month of tide observations correct to within 0.1 ft. and from a year of observations correct to within 0.05 ft.

Even limiting the matter to that which may be of concern to the engineer, the subject is one of wide extent. Necessarily, therefore, the author has been

* Asst. Director, U. S. Coast and Geodetic Survey, Washington, D. C.

obliged to deal with the various phases of the subject in a brief manner. The full references, however, add to the value of the paper. With the improvements of tidal waterways which the growing water-borne commence will make necessary, the engineer will be called upon to solve problems that demand a knowledge of tides and currents. Such knowledge this paper gives.

EARL I. BROWN,* M. AM. SOC. C. E. (by letter).—This paper is an excellent statement of present-day scientific knowledge of tides, and of the practical uses made of such knowledge. In reading it one cannot fail to be struck most forcibly by the thought that tidal phenomena are too much neglected in textbooks on hydraulics. Papers like this go a long way toward supplying the deficiency. As the author points out, a practical working knowledge of the theory and application of tidal hydraulics is a necessity for any engineer engaged in the maintenance or improvement of channels in tidal waters. A lack of understanding of tidal mechanics has been responsible for many of the mistakes and failures made by engineers in planning and executing maritime works.

In practice, the engineer is not ordinarily concerned with the tides or currents in the open sea, far off the coast. He is interested in those adjacent to the coast, and in the inland waters, and it is these that will be understood in what follows.

There is not much in the paper to which the writer would take exception. It might be well to point out that the author's classification of waves into progressive and stationary waves is a purely arbitrary one, as there is no basic difference between them. All waves are fundamentally progressive, but when a progressive wave is reflected back upon itself at points one-half or one full wave length (or multiples thereof) from the origin, a stationary wave results from the interference of the components. The resultant wave derived from such a reflection will show characteristics more closely approaching those given as defining each class of wave, depending on how closely the point of reflection coincides with the half-wave length or its exact multiple in distance from the origin.

As the author shows, the propagation of the tide from the sea into inland waters gives rise to so many apparently confused and conflicting manifestations of heights of water, and directions and velocity of currents that to bring order out of the chaos and to deduce general laws seems to be impossible. Nevertheless, it has now been found possible to account for almost all these phenomena by considering the tidal wave entering inland waters, as a progressive wave of translation, acted upon and modified by friction of the bed, depth and width of the channel, and combined with entire or partial reflections at those points where a change of energy of the wave is effected by the bed.

The author has classified the currents flowing through a narrow strait connecting two larger tidal bodies of water as being hydraulic currents, meaning by this term a current flowing under the influence of a surface slope.

The writer has had experience on many canals connecting such bodies of water along the coast, at points ranging from Delaware to Texas. He has also

* Col., Corps of Engrs., U. S. A.; Engr., Eighth Corps Area, Fort Sam Houston, Tex.

observed many inlets connecting the sea with large inland bays, in which the connecting channel was of varying lengths from a few hundred feet to several miles. He has always found the flow through such channels, when of considerable length, to be far from hydraulic. The surface slope is not uniform, nor are the current velocity and rate of discharge uniform for the whole length of the canal. All these phenomena vary from point to point, and the current may be strongest where there is no slope or even an opposed slope. As the connecting channel or canal becomes shorter, these manifestations of true tidal propagation are less evident, but still persist, and it is only when the canal is very short indeed that true hydraulic flow may be said to prevail. The author is correct, however, in stating that the simpler hydraulic solution of problems arising in some cases may suffice for all practical needs. The engineer must bear in mind, however, that such a solution is a mere approximation, and it should be used only for very short canals or straits.

EDWARD GODFREY,* M. AM. SOC. C. E. (by letter).—The writer agrees with Commander Rude that the subject of the tides is one that ought to be discussed by engineers, particularly that phase that deals with their cause. Some scientists deal chiefly with speculation. They are not concerned with producing results; nor are they concerned with rigid proofs that certain results will be produced by certain causes. A motor, or engine, or turbine must deliver the power for which it is designed. Hence, the engineer must know definitely, what certain elements, when brought together under certain conditions, will do.

The foregoing remarks are a preliminary to a challenge of the universally accepted theory of tides, which omits mechanical principles that govern the movement of bodies, and glides over adverse facts that nullify the theory completely. Forces of gigantic magnitude are ignored, and secondary forces are given the leading, in fact, exclusive, consideration.

The theory of tides, as expounded by George Howard Darwin,† at greater length perhaps than by any other writer, is that they are the result of the gravitational pull of the moon on the water of the oceans. This is explained by the author, except that it is the centrifugal force of the earth's rotation, combined with the moon's lessened pull, that causes the tidal rise on the opposite side of the earth from that where the moon is on the meridian.

Writers on tides, including Commander Rude, show the bulges representing the high tide, directly under the moon and on the opposite side of the earth. They also state, as Commander Rude has said, that in Nature it is different, diametrically different, so to speak. The tides are perpetually low on the sides of the earth where the moon is pulling for high tide, and *vice versa*. The only explanation of this astounding nullification of the theory is that the tide lags or is retarded, presumably by the wave trying to catch up with the force which produces it. It is here that a study of engineering mechanics would be a good thing for the scientist. It would be interesting to have him answer the following questions:

* Structural Engr., Pittsburgh, Pa.

† "The Tides and Kindred Phenomena in the Solar System," by George Howard Darwin.

(1) Is the force of gravitation itself so sluggish that it takes 6 or 8 hours for it to be felt across the distance from the moon to the earth?

(2) Does not the tidal wave traverse the circumference of the earth in about 25 hours?

(3) Why does this wave not synchronize itself with the force that produces it?

(4) If gravitation is instantaneous, or nearly so, when and how is a tidal wave initiated and what keeps it going, since the force is admittedly always in an entirely different direction from that in which, mechanically, it would have to be to raise the water?

(5) Is there any action in a tidal wave analogous to flywheel action?

(6) Would a wave continue to travel around the earth from east to west, the crest and trough being 6 000 miles apart, if the moon's force were suddenly to cease?

(7) Would not that wave divide and seek a level by traveling both east and west?

A large pendulum can be made to move in wide amplitude by impulses applied by pulling at intervals on a small rubber band, if the timing of the impulses agrees with the swinging of the pendulum, in the same direction as the impulse. However, the pendulum cannot store up impulses applied contrary to its motion to be used later when it is swinging that way. Therefore, it is inconceivable that the ocean could store up, for 6 or 8 hours, a wave-raising force received from the moon and then respond to that force.

If the earth were absolutely rigid, there would be tides due to the moon's gravitational pull, but high tide and low tide would be just about exactly reversed.

The earth is not rigid and does not behave as a rigid body, in spite of the opinion of scientists. If it were a solid steel ball, of the hardest steel known, the gigantic force of the moon would of necessity elongate its diameter in the direction of a line to the moon. The moon's gravitational pull on the near hemisphere of the earth is greater than that on the far hemisphere by about 600 000 000 000 000 tons, a force that would snap a piano wire 30 miles in diameter. Is this a trifling force that can be ignored because some scientist states that in his opinion the earth acts as a rigid body in the face of the moon's tidal pull?

This force distributed uniformly over the entire cross-section of the earth considered as a solid steel bar, 4 000 miles long, would stretch it out 4 or 5 ft. Other metals and rocks do not approach this rigidity. This is not conjecture. There has never been a piece of material found in the earth that is not subject to this law and would not be elongated by this amount or a greater amount under a force of this intensity.

Furthermore, having been elongated by this force, applied in a constantly changing direction, the elongation would not cease when force and elasticity were equal. Inertia would carry the earth several feet more. A high wave, therefore, in the body of the earth itself is carried around by the moon and what is the result? Of course, a wave of water follows in the trough of the earth wave. This is the ocean tide as it is known, not a wave of water raised by the moon, but a wave of water following and remaining in the trough of the solid earth created by the gigantic differential gravitational pull of the moon.

The tidal pull, rightly understood, accounts for countless phenomena, not otherwise explained in any rational manner. Some of these phenomena are the following:

(*a*).—*Earthquakes.*—The continual kneading of the earth by its satellite accounts for the thousands of earth tremors observed yearly.

(*b*).—*Volcanoes.*—Extra movement with attendant friction below the surface of the earth creates heated spots, where peculiar rock formations exist that are conducive to movement.

(*c*).—*Hot Springs.*—The same process that produces the volcano, working on a small scale produces the hot spring.

(*d*).—*Internal Heat of the Earth.*—The heat of friction due to the continual kneading of the body of the earth by the pull of the moon and the earth's rotation accounts for the internal and absolutely constant heat of the earth. It seems strange to state that the moon and not the sun is responsible for the unfailing supply of heat in the earth, making the planet livable, particularly at night, when radiation of atmospheric heat would leave the air excessively cold.

(*e*).—*Trade Winds.*—The tidal pull of the moon on the earth's atmosphere, apart from land or ocean tides, accounts for prevailing winds, trade winds, etc.

(*f*).—*Ocean Currents.*—Instead of ocean currents being caused as claimed by trade winds, they are doubtless due to the continual travel of a wave of water forced around the equatorial region and deflected by the continents in the manner exhibited by ocean current paths.

The earth's density is several times that of rock. It is, in fact, nearly as great as steel. The interior, therefore, must be metallic. No doubt, it is largely composed of iron or steel.

This great elastic ball, subject to the enormous gravitational pull of the moon, would exhibit inertia in its tidal wave in a manner not possible in a water wave assumed to be actuated by the moon's tide-raising force. Accelerated impulses, such as those of the combined pull of the sun and moon as they approach conjunction or opposition, cause higher and higher tides, and the highest tide, on account of the inertia, would be a little later than the maximum impulse. This accounts for the fact, as pointed out by Commander Rude, that the highest tide occurs a day later than the actual time of new or full moon.

The frictional heat of the earth, due to tides, is generated comparatively near the surface, probably largely where the interior elastic metallic ball joins the exterior rock crust. The temperature at the center is probably not very great; not much if any greater than the temperature a few miles from the surface. Hence, the metallic core is elastic and not fluid.

Volcanoes are the result of heated spots where extra motion and friction are manifest; they are not an indication of the earth's general internal condition.

The moon's excessive low temperature is due to the fact that it does not rotate as does the earth; therefore, it can have no tide. Its atmosphere and water vapor have turned into snow.

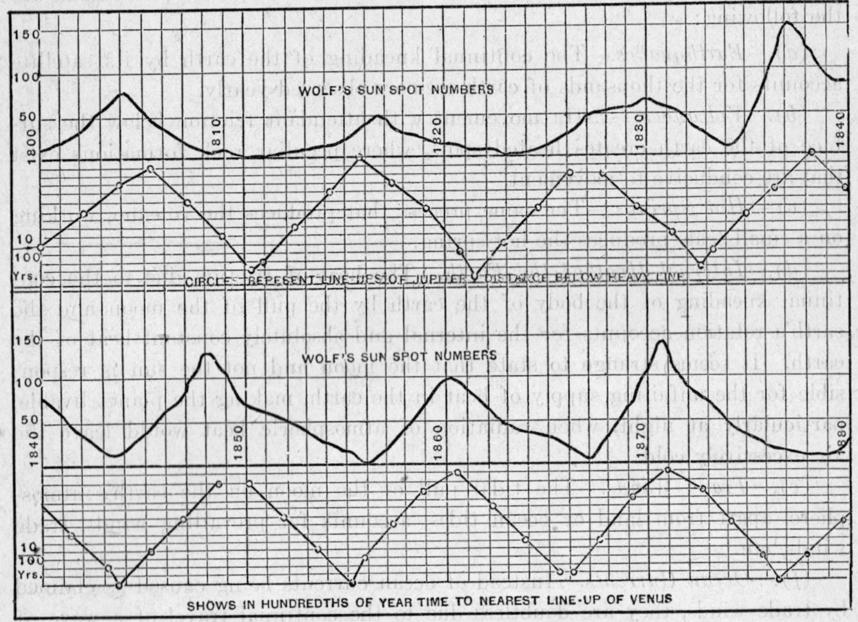

Fig. 39.—Graph of Sun-Spot Intensities.

The sun is subject to tides of gigantic force. Any one of the four planets, Mercury, Venus, the Earth, and Jupiter, exerts a tidal pull on the sun many times the tidal pull of the moon on the earth. The kneading of its great mass creates heat that is incalculable. It is this that sustains the heat of the sun. A very striking proof of this is exhibited in sun-spot counts for a period of 300 years. Sun spots are volcanoes in the sun caused by excessively heated spots, due, as in the earth, to sub-surface friction.

Astronomers have recognized that there is some general influence, over a long period of years, that intensifies sun spots in a regular period of 11.2 years and some influence that introduces an irregularity, so that the several periods are more or less than 11.2 years. The writer has discovered that there are exactly such influences at work and that the period of high sun-spot intensities agrees remarkably with those influences.

Every 11.2 years Jupiter and Venus and the Earth are almost exactly in line, thus adding their tidal pulls on the sun and intensifying its heat. Fig. 39 shows the agreement between these alignments and the high sun-spot periods. The influence that makes for irregularity is Mercury, which aligns itself with one or two of these planets in short periods.

Forty-one of Jupiter's half synodic periods is 22.387 years and twenty-eight of those of Venus is 22.381 years. Thus, every 22.38 years these planets and the Earth are within 2 days of being exactly in line. In the intermediate period these planets are twice within 7 days of being in line, as will be seen by comparing their synodic periods.

The argument that will be used against this theory is, "What about the law of the conservation of energy?" That "law" was broken down when radium was discovered. Now, however, to cover the face of the law, scientists assert that all matter has potential energy of almost incalculable amount residing in it, although they do not hesitate to calculate how long a pound of metal would run a horse-power engine, in millions of years. Let them turn engineers for a while and try to lift a fly 1 ft. by a ton of this metal in any period without using some regular old-fashioned coal, wood, or other fuel that is said to have potential energy stored in it, or by using sun radiations.

Energy is inexhaustible and is all derived from the moving, impinging, vibrating ether, traveling at the speed of light and penetrating matter without hindrance. On the earth there are limited means of converting this energy into useful work. Nature's great tidal engines must be depended upon to supply and store up the useful energy needed.

It may seem strange to set up a theory that the heat of the earth is derived chiefly from the moon and that the earth contributes immeasurably more heat to the sun than it receives from the sun; but let any one who is skeptical determine the known forces, from the law of gravitation; one that would snap a piano wire 30 miles in diameter and the other that would snap a similar wire about 150 miles in diameter, each exerted on bodies of enormous size in a different direction every hour. Calculate the horse power needed to accomplish this and the heat that would result, and some of the greatest puzzles of science will be at least partly solved. These puzzles are the undiminished supply of heat from the sun, the constant temperature of the earth, the cause and reason for the periodicity of sun spots, the cause of earthquakes and volcanoes, and, in fact, directly or indirectly, all the mechanical manifestations on the earth or sun, as well as the utter absence of them on the tideless moon.

William Barclay Parsons,* Hon. M. Am. Soc. C. E. (by letter).—This paper is an admirable exposition of a very complicated natural movement, on some of the aspects of which scientific men are not in agreement. Engineers, however, are not directly concerned with these differences in opinion in the planning and execution of their work. From the standpoint of science they may be interested in what is supposed to take place in the great tidal movements and oscillations in the deep open oceans, but in practice all they need know is what will occur under various conditions in harbors, estuaries, or other places along a coast exposed to tidal effect.

The most important factor for the engineer thoroughly to understand is that he cannot generalize with safety in respect to what will take place in tidal action in any one locality. He may know, with nice exactness, the effects

* Cons. Engr., New York, N. Y.

and movements at two places, one each side of where he is working, but he must not assume that the result at his site will be a mean of the other two. Local conditions have a tremendous, and frequently surprising, influence. There may be two progressive tidal waves each acting freely and with normal ranges and times, at the other places, but which, meeting and interfering, will give an apparently wholly unrelated result at an intermediate station. Tidal actions are also seriously affected by ocean currents as well as river flow and particularly by the depth and shape of bays and estuaries.

The writer recalls one experience where mean sea level had been previously determined for two places only eight miles distant, one from the other, by measuring high and low-water elevations at both places, taking the mean, and connecting such means with a chain of levels. Being on opposite sides of a peninsula, the places were affected by two tidal waves of different characteristics. Although the levels showed a considerable difference in elevation between the reputed mean sea levels, the elevations had been accepted as accurate. The error was not discovered until the writer had established tide stations, when it became apparent that whereas mean tide at one station was the same as mean sea level, such was not the case at the other. At the latter station there was a large body of comparatively shallow water so that, when the ebb tide was half gone, sufficient frictional resistance began to be developed to retard the flow, and, consequently, the ebbing tide never was able to reach the true low-water level. In this case mean tide and mean sea level were far from being the same.

The engineer should never accept any tidal statements as true unless they are based on accurate observations with self-recording gauges conducted through at least one lunar cycle, properly analyzed and interpreted; and even then he must be on his guard against exceptional tides and prolonged wind effects.

The author refers to the currents in channels joining two bodies of water in which there are tides with different characteristics, and cites as examples the East River, New York, and the Cape Cod Canal. The former, although highly interesting and important, is not a good example from which to draw conclusions, on account of its variable cross-section and sharp turns. The latter on the other hand is almost perfect for study, with its uniform cross-section and only two curves with long radii, well protected from wind influence. Some of the results, as deduced by the writer, were given in his paper entitled "The Cape Cod Canal".* Among other interesting data were (*a*) the curved and not straight line of low-water elevations with an upward central versed sine of about 1 ft., a factor of economic importance; and (*b*) the evident momentum of the moving body of water which causes an actual flow of water up a gradient of measurable slope. This momentum accounts, in part, for the fact that the current in tidal waters does not change direction at the same time as the tide turns.

When the Board of Advisory Engineers, of which the writer was a member, was considering the type of canal for Panama, it refused to discuss or attempt

* *Transactions*, Am. Soc. C. E., Vol. LXXXII (December, 1918), p. 1.

to determine the rate of current that would exist if a canal were built there at sea level without locks, being satisfied with a general statement that the current would not be strong enough to interfere with traffic. So far as the writer is aware no analysis of this question has ever been published.

T. KENNARD THOMSON,* M. AM. SOC. C. E.—It is fortunate for New York that the State of New Jersey did not have the benefit of Commander Rude's professional services generations ago, when New Jersey claimed Staten Island, because, it was stated, a ship could not sail around it in one day without running aground.

Unfortunately for New Jersey, New York had a captain who knew the tides and channels, and who by starting at the right place, at the right time, was able to get around without landing on a sand-bar.

Fig. 40 shows that the St. Lawrence River, Bay of Fundy, and Long Island Sound are practically parallel, although in opposite directions, and have enormously greater tidal ranges than Chesapeake Bay, Delaware Bay, and the Hudson River, which are also parallel to each other, but approximately at right angles to the first three.

The Bay of Fundy, with no outlet at its upper reach, has the greatest tide, about 47 ft., with an average, as Commander Rude has indicated, of 5 ft. higher tide on the Nova Scotia side, than on the New Brunswick side.

At Quebec, Que., Canada, the St. Lawrence River has a maximum tide of about 20 ft. and the influence of the tide is slightly felt at Montreal, where the surface of the river is about 24 ft. above mean tide level. The St. Lawrence, above Montreal, receives an enormous fresh-water flow of about 300 000 cu. ft. per sec. from the Great Lakes. This is a comparatively uniform flow.

On the other hand, Long Island Sound has two outlets, the East River and the Harlem River, with a maximum average tide of $7\frac{1}{2}$ ft., only about 3 ft. more than the average tide at Governors Island.

It would be interesting to know whether a new East River from Flushing to Jamaica Bay and a new Harlem River from Hell Gate to the Hudson, 2.50 miles long instead of 6.75 miles, would reduce the difference between the tide levels at Governors Island and Hell Gate, if each of the new rivers were, say, 50 ft. deep, and of ample width.

Fortunately for the Cities of New York, Philadelphia, Pa., and Baltimore, Md., they are not troubled with such excessive tides, and it would also be interesting to know whether this good fortune is due to the fact that they are at right angles to the direction of Long Island Sound, Bay of Fundy and the St. Lawrence; and also whether, if all these rivers, bays, and sounds were running parallel to the equator, the tidal ranges would be greatly increased.

Chesapeake Bay has a tide of only 1.2 ft. at Baltimore; Delaware Bay has a tide of about 5.2 ft. at Philadelphia; and the Hudson River, a tide of 4.5 ft. at Governors Island, with an ordinary high tide of 2 ft. at Albany, N. Y. The Hudson River, however, is subject to greater fresh-water flood variations than the others. For instance, the speaker has seen a low-water flow of only

* Cons. Engr., New York, N. Y.

600 cu. ft. per sec. in the Mohawk River near its entrance to the Hudson River, and, at the same place, he has seen a flood flow of 100 000 cu. ft. per sec. At The Narrows, where the normal flow is 76 000 cu. ft. per sec., an exceptional flood flow has amounted to between 300 000 and 400 000 cu. ft. per sec. While the flood-flow elevation is not proportionately great at Governors Island, it amounts to 18 ft. at Albany.

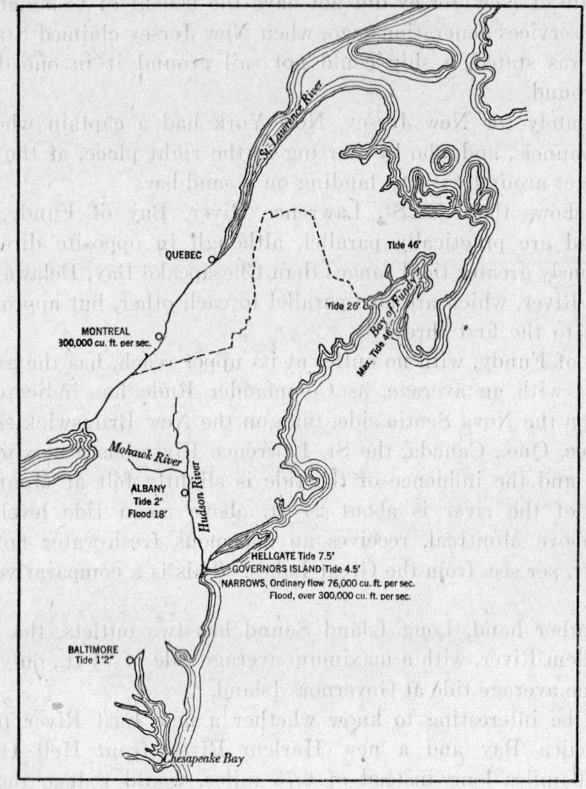

FIG. 40.—GRAPH SHOWING PARALLELISM OF ST. LAWRENCE RIVER, BAY OF FUNDY, AND LONG ISLAND SOUND.

This paper is of great personal interest on account of the plan the speaker has been advocating since about 1910, for a "Really Greater New York". When he first suggested extending Manhattan down the Bay (where it is hoped to reclaim 9 sq. miles), nearly every one thought that the one insuperable objection would be the "tidal prism theory", and it looked as if it might be necessary to construct a model, including New York, New Jersey, Connecticut, and all the fresh and salt-water flows that affect New York Harbor. Such a model, of course, would cost many thousands of dollars, but when a (then) U. S. Chief of Engineers stated that he had no use for the "tidal prism theory" in this respect, the speaker cheerfully discarded the idea of the model.

While in 1911 many laughed at this project for a "Really Greater New York", which included reclaiming a section of the East River, a number of people have recently proposed it as an original idea of their own. One went so far as to say that he had the approval of the War Department, which, of course, was absurd, because he had omitted the first essential feature of the original plan, that of providing an outlet for Long Island Sound to the Hudson River and Jamaica Bay before attempting to close the East River. He did not even pay any attention to Newtown Creek.

In addition to avoiding the danger of turning Long Island Sound into a Bay of Fundy, it is equally important to provide new docks, etc., for the people before closing off 5 miles or more of the East River.

It may be interesting to record the fact that some of the biggest financial men of the country declared that they would not be interested if the East River section of the plan was omitted. This was due (in 1913) to the fact that they realized that New York can never get enough bridges and tunnels to connect Long Island with Manhattan, and also to the relief which this plan will afford the north and south traffic.

Commander Rude has referred to the hydro-electric features of the Bay of Fundy. Two projects have recently appeared in the daily papers. One plan is for Passamaquoddy Bay between Maine and New Brunswick, of which more than three-quarters would be in Canada, with a maximum tide of 27 ft.; and the other plan is for the upper end of the Bay of Fundy, all in Canada, with a maximum tide of 47 ft.

It is claimed that the latter project would only cost one-half as much per horse power developed as the first plan, but the first promises to develop power at a cost of about four times as high as the speaker's estimates per horse power developed for a "Niagara Falls Junior". There is no immediate prospect, therefore, of the Bay of Fundy developments. However, sooner or later, engineers will have to learn how to utilize these tides economically, storage batteries not being economical; for when all the rivers are fully developed there will still be more coal used than at present, and before that time there is hope of having a new city of 9 sq. miles built in the very heart of New York City, between the Battery and Staten Island, where people will never use a pound of coal, nor any oil or gas.

H. F. Dunham,* M. Am. Soc. C. E.—The author's well organized and excellent paper will be widely read and appreciated. The "Nomenclature" is a fortunate introduction. The definitions offer a slight difficulty to one unaccustomed to these terms, namely, "perigee" and "apogee", termed positions of the moon "in its elliptical orbit around the earth". "Elliptical" as frequently used implies a return to the point or position first occupied by a moving body. In Fig. 41 the lines represent the orbits of the earth and moon on a scale of 2 000 000 miles to 1 in. Is there an elliptical orbit for the moon around the earth in addition to its elliptical orbit around the sun, similar to that of the earth around the sun?

Low-tide elevations alongshore where construction work is going forward are complicated with ground-water heights and do not require extreme accuracy. The limit for timber submergence is rather a matter of good judgment. If sub-drains or subways are to follow, the call is for better judgment.

* Civ. and Hydr. Engr., New York, N. Y.

In 1922, the Carnegie Institution of Washington published "Effects of Winds and Barometric Pressure on the Great Lakes". Tidal influences were not recognized; instead, from many observed gauge readings at various points, the 13-hour rise and fall was attributed wholly to wind and barometric pressures.*

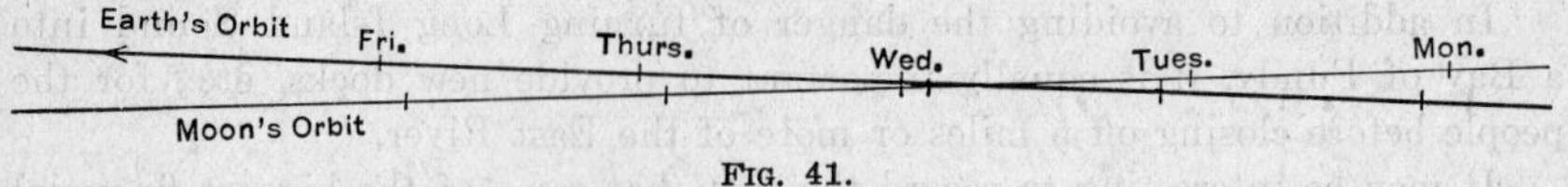

FIG. 41.

In 1903 a tide-gauge was established near the mouth of the Menominee River, on Green Bay, Wisconsin,† where conditions for accurate records were extremely favorable. An unused water intake of metal about 6 ft. in diameter,

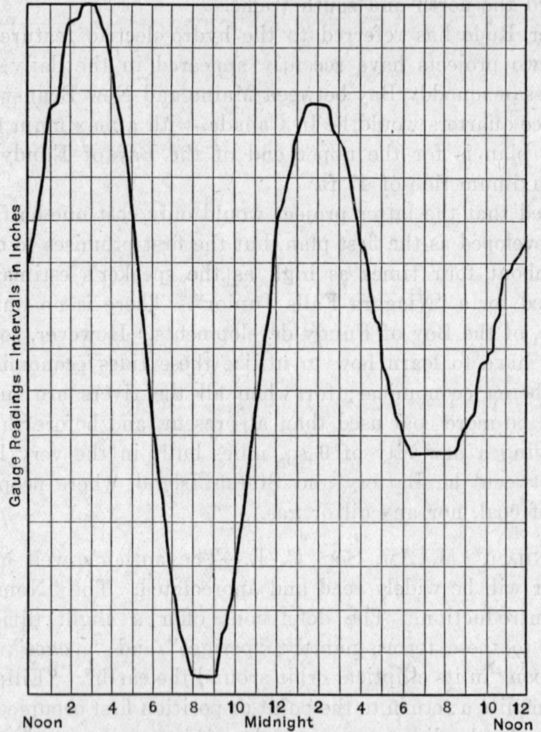

FIG. 42.—VARIATION IN WATER ELEVATION, GREEN BAY, WISCONSIN, DECEMBER 29 AND 30, 1903.

perforated with ten thousand $\frac{3}{8}$-in. holes and placed in 20 ft. of water, was connected by a 12-in. pipe line, 800 ft. long, to a vertical 16-in. pipe well having a float carrying a rod and pencil, which traced a line on a vertical clock

* "The Manual of Tides," by R. A. Harris, U. S. Coast and Geodetic Survey Report for 1907, was cited as authority.

† This gauge was set by the speaker. Records from it, faithfully kept for many months by the late J. J. Campbell, have been deposited with the U. S. Coast and Geodetic Survey, at Washington, D. C.

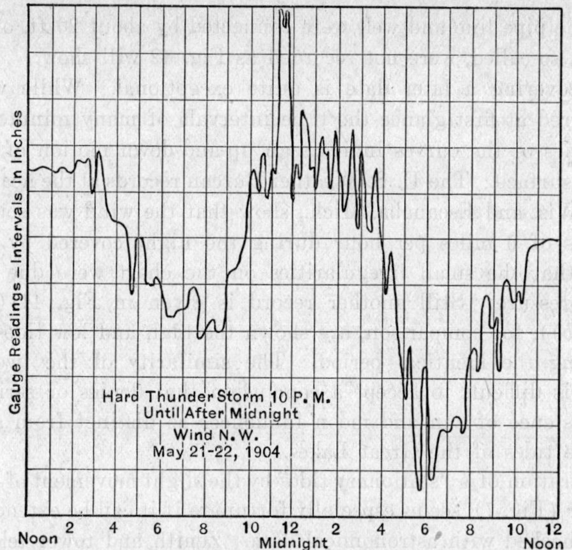

FIG. 43.—VARIATION IN WATER ELEVATION, GREEN BAY, WISCONSIN, MAY 21 AND 22, 1904.

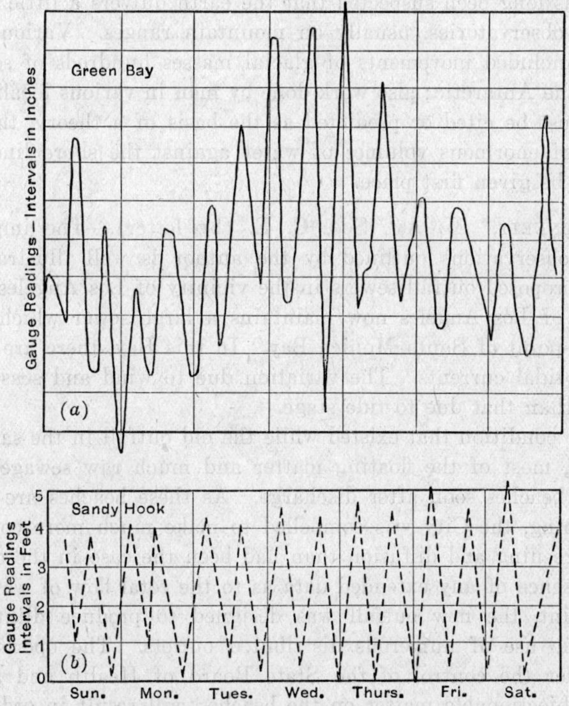

FIG. 44.—COMPARISON OF WATER ELEVATION AT GREEN BAY, WISCONSIN, AND SANDY HOOK, NEW YORK, FOR SIMULTANEOUS PERIODS, MAY 8 TO 15, 1904.

cylinder. The pipe line and well were connected by about 20 ft. of 1-in. pipe. Wave effects, so-called, were not recorded as Fig. 42 will show.

Fig. 43 covering a later date is quite exceptional. While wave action may be inferred at first glance the time intervals of many minutes shown by the inequalities of the curves indicate an up-and-down motion of large areas of the water surface. The U. S. Weather Bureau records at the nearest station, Green Bay, Wis. and Escanaba, Mich., show that the wind was southwest and not in excess of 6 miles per hour during the night covered by the record. This shows that the small irregularities on the chart were due to variable barometric pressure. Still another record is given in Fig. 44 (*a*). Below it (Fig. 44 (*b*)), for comparison, are shown the high and low tides for Sandy Hook covering the identical period. The similarity of the two graphs is marked. It is difficult to accept a conclusion that denies or seriously questions the existence of sun and moon influences as distinct from atmospheric effects on the tides of the Great Lakes.

The illustration of a "stationary tide" by the slight movement of a basin containing water (Fig. 7), seems especially fortunate if it can be extended to ocean basins and checked with astronomical data. Zenith and tower telescopes disclose a failure to fix position on the earth's surface (the latitude, for instance), closer than a fraction of a second of arc, or less than a horizontal distance of 100 ft. It has long been suspected that the earth quivers a little even at the best sites of observatories, usually on mountain ranges. Various suggested causes have included movements of glacial masses hundreds of square miles in extent in the Antarctic; also work done by man in various localities; but if something must be cited or predicted as the basis of a theory, the rhythmic tidal thrust of enormous volumes of water against the shore lines of ocean basins might be given first place.

Ralph Bennett,* M. Am. Soc. C. E. (by letter).—The importance of the current observations outlined by the author is well illustrated by the present and proposed outfall sewers in the vicinity of Los Angeles, Calif.

The City of Los Angeles now maintains a large sewer which discharges near the mid-point of Santa Monica Bay. In this Bay, there are very feeble and variable tidal currents. The variation due to wind and season is seemingly larger than that due to tide stage.

Under the condition that existed while the old outfall in the same location was operated, most of the floating matter and much raw sewage drifted on the adjacent beaches soon after discharge. As these beaches are extensively used for bathing, the City was compelled to make much more complete provision for screening and diffusion than had been the case in the old sewer.

In the absence of any extended data as to the total flow of water past the discharge point, the new outfall was designed to produce dilution of the sewage by the use of numerous distributed outlets. The operation of the sewer is under the control of the State Board of Health and any serious increase in objectionable matter on the beaches will result in orders to treat the discharge fully and to release only clear, sterile, and odorless effluent.

* Cons. Engr., Los Angeles, Calif.

The adjacent areas in Los Angeles County are quite largely sewered by the County Sanitation Districts which propose to discharge in a somewhat similar way into San Pedro Channel.

At the point of proposed discharge there is a more definite tidal flow than in Santa Monica Bay, but here, again, reliance will be placed largely on deeply submerged outlets in multiple. This location has been bitterly fought and only because of necessity has the State Board of Health permitted the construction. The sewer may ultimately be equipped for full treatment.

If, in either case, a continuous record of the direction and velocity of the ocean currents at the discharge points could be obtained, a great increase in accuracy of design might be made.

This is very noticeable in the outfall sewer of the Sanitation Districts which has been located without scientific aid. If records of the channel currents were available, it is entirely possible that a point of high velocity and seaward discharge could be found, at which a better and yet less expensive outlet could be located.

A fully continuous record is required, however, in such quiet waters as those of Santa Monica Bay. The device should be capable of producing an automatic record of both direction and velocity for a long time without attention.

A similar degree of performance has been attained in the modern curve-tracing gauges. Long-distance wind direction and velocity recorders are in use. A similar long-distance equipment, actuating a shore-located recorder from an anchored vane, deflected by the velocity of the current and swinging with the direction, can certainly be developed if the market demands it. The need is obvious. Cannot the demand be met?

VICTOR GELINEAU,* M. AM. SOC. C. E.—This paper is a valuable and illuminating treatise on a difficult but very real and practical subject. It contains a vast amount of information for engineers whose work extends to tidal waters and who are frequently required to determine the elevations of high or low water. The evaluation of tidal ranges and elevations is a vital requirement in land drainage or reclamation works and in the construction of marine works of every kind, such as navigation canals or channels, basins, wharves, sea-walls and jetties.

The author has treated a subject that has assumed great importance in the State of New Jersey; and one that has taken an advanced position in the administration of its waterways and ocean frontage. Among the activities to which this statement applies are: (*a*) The sale and lease of lands flowed by tide water, the proceeds from which, amounting to many millions of dollars, are by constitutional provision dedicated to the support of free public schools; (*b*) the construction of coast-protection structures on which the State has expended large sums; (*c*) the dredging, wherever necessary, in the improvement of an inland waterway route, approximately 120 miles in length, through the coastal lagoon system from Cape May to the Manasquan River; and, (*d*) the opening or closing of ocean inlets.

* Director and Chf. Engr., New Jersey Board of Commerce and Nav., Jersey City, N. J.

In the sale or lease of riparian lands flowed by tide water, one of the first requirements is the location of the mean high-water line (low-water line in some States) that forms the boundary between State-owned and privately-owned property. Since the right to accretion depends on riparian ownership, that is, adjacency to the limiting line of tide water recognized by the laws of the particular State, property rights of the utmost importance depend on an accurate determination of the shore line; that is, the mean high-water line or other tidal plane recognized by the law. The tide line then is a natural boundary, the position of which determines valuable property rights.

In the design and construction of wharves, bulkheads, jetties, or other water-front structures, the determination of low and high-water elevation constitutes one of the first requirements of design. In works of this nature it is the practice to place wales or stringers and other braces at or near low-water level. Serious disputes may arise over the determination of the low-water plane, especially because the contractor has only a short period during low-water slack tide in which to perform the operations at or near the low-water mark.

In the improvement or extension of waterway channels and the construction of navigation canals, the determination of the plane of reference is the first duty of the engineer. It is the object of improvements of waterways for navigation to provide a minimum depth of water at a given stage of tide, usually local mean low water, to be available when the project is completed.

The elevation of local mean low tide that is established before dredging a channel of relatively large cross-section through a tidal lagoon region, will differ in greater or less degree from the elevation of the mean low-water plane determined after dredging. The engineer must estimate in advance of dredging just how much this disparity will amount to because the enabling legislation or other regulation prescribes the minimum depth to be obtained in the channel after dredging.

This shifting of the low-water and high-water planes, which follows and is a result of the dredging operations, depends on various hydraulic factors. The disparity between the old and the new planes amounts, in some places, to a considerable proportion of the entire mean tidal range. If the dredged channel cuts through reaches of congestion, such as shoals and tortuous minor channels, relatively extensive changes in the tidal regimen of the inland waterway are to be expected.

The establishment of mean low water or other tidal datum planes is effected usually by one of several different methods, as:

(*a*) A relatively short series of comparative readings of tidal swings at the unknown station simultaneous with readings at an established primary tide-gauge station. This method, which disregards any correction factor, requires for applicability a close similarity of tidal regimen at the two stations of comparison.

(*b*) Simultaneous comparisons during a relatively short period of time at the new or unknown station and at the primary or reference station, utilizing an adjustment factor to correct for dissimilarity in the tidal regimen at the two stations of comparison; this is virtually an adaption of Method (*a*).

(*c*) Continuous independent readings of the tidal oscillations for a sufficiently long period of time.

The choice of methods will depend on many conditions, such as the degree of accuracy to be obtained and the time and equipment available. The chief defect of the method of comparative readings is the fact that the effects of strong winds which modify the tidal swings may not be felt with equal force at the two stations of comparison.

All these methods have been used in the surveys by the New Jersey Board of Commerce and Navigation. The experience gained in these operations has convinced the speaker that whenever practicable the third method, namely, that of independent establishment of tidal planes, should be resorted to frequently and should be applied for each section of waterway that differs appreciably in tidal range from the adjacent station.

Experience in New Jersey has demonstrated that continuous readings of the tidal range for one lunar month may be, and usually are, utterly inadequate for the independent establishment of the mean high or low-water plane at any station. The error in the result will probably exceed the limits permissible in projects to dredge inland waterway channels.

W. M. Black,* M. Am. Soc. C. E. (by letter).—This subject is one of great importance to all engineers engaged in any work affected by tidal action. The paper is opportune and valuable. As stated by the author, the tides of the seas have been the subject of investigation for centuries, and their action is now well known. Tidal action in estuaries and in tidal rivers is not so well understood. The best discussion of tidal action in estuaries, known to the writer, is that of L. Bonnet.†

Due to Commander Rude's well-known reputation as an expert in tidal movements, and his position in the U. S. Coast and Geodetic Survey, his paper must be considered authoritative. However, it contains a few statements which the writer, from the standpoint of an engineer who has had to deal practically with tidal action in estuaries and tidal rivers, deems likely to be misleading.

The theory followed by Commander Rude divides tidal waves into two classes, namely, progressive waves and stationary waves. This classification is not universally accepted. The classification of waves in fluid bodies as given by Bonnet seems to lend itself better to the solution of the problems of tidal action in confined tidal waterways, than that of Harris.‡

According to Bonnet, wave movements may be divided into two great classes: Waves of oscillation and waves of translation. Waves of oscillation are produced when a vertical force, such as the attractions of the heavenly bodies, or the fall of a heavy body, acts on a body of water, producing a

* Maj.-Gen., U. S. A. (*Retired*); Engr. (Black, McKenney & Stewart), Washington, D. C.

† "Contribution à l'Etude Théorique des fleuves à Marée et Application aux Rivières à Marée du Bassin de l'Escaut Maritime."

‡ "Manual of Tides."

momentary elevation or depression of the surface over a limited area. These waves have the characteristics of the progressive tidal waves described by the author.

Waves of oscillation may be periodic or ordinary. Periodic waves follow each other as ordinary waves, but the periodicity of movement follows periodicity of action, each action causing the formation of a wave. Ordinary waves are those produced by a force which acts once, or at irregular intervals.

The tidal wave of the ocean is a periodic wave of oscillation. Waves formed by a stone falling into water are ordinary waves of oscillation. These waves may be divided into two other classes: Those which seem to travel along the surface of the water, named in French, "ondes houlouses", which may be translated into English as "swells"; and those which seem to remain in one place, "ondes clapoteuses", for which the word "chops" seems the best English equivalent. The "chop" is formed in liquid masses confined by walls. Under such conditions a "swell" is reflected from the walls, with the angle of incidence approximately equal to the angle of departure and with the direction of propagation reversed. It superposes itself on the direct wave. The "swell" is the natural movement in open and deep seas when perturbing influences are negligible in amount, while the "chop" is formed in confined waters, such as rivers and small lakes.

If a force acts horizontally on a liquid mass, a wave of translation is formed. This is propagated above or below the original water surface. In the first case, it is termed positive; in the second, negative.

Positive waves of translation were first investigated by Scott Russell.* They are formed in a channel by a rapid elevation of the water surface, as manifested down stream by the opening of a movable dam, or in advance of a moving canal-boat. The forward movement of a flood crest in the Mississippi, in advance of the waters causing the flood, is another example. Negative waves are produced by the rapid creation of a depression in a liquid mass, as in the upper pool of a canalized river by opening a movable dam.

The distinction between waves of oscillation and waves of translation is of importance to engineers. In the former class, slack-water, which marks the change of current direction, occurs nearly midway between high and low water; in the latter class, it occurs at or close to high and low water. The tidal waves of estuaries and tidal rivers of the United States at the entrance are generally waves of oscillation which gradually change into waves of translation in their course toward the limit of tidal action. If it is desired to control only an ebb current at any point, and this current is produced at that point by a wave of oscillation, it is evident that the training wall need only be built to about the level of mid-tide, while if the tidal wave at that point is a wave of translation, the work must be built to high-water level.

A wave is formed through the expenditure of energy from some source, and once formed, it must continue until its energy is exhausted. The energy

* "Wave Action in Relation to Engineering Structures," Gaillard, p. 23.

of a wave is measured by the work it can do in coming to rest. The total energy comprises the potential energy due to height and the kinetic energy, or half the living force, due to the velocities of its fluid molecules. The energy of a wave of oscillation in deep water has been shown to be approximately equal to the product of the liquid mass contained in the orbit of the surface molecules by the square of the velocity of propagation of the wave.

In open and deep waters, when resistances due to friction and obstructions may be disregarded, the theoretical velocity of wave propagation approaches closely to the true velocity. This theoretical velocity is given by the formula, $v = \sqrt{g h}$, in which, v equals the velocity of propagation ; g is the acceleration due to gravity (32.17 ft. per sec.); and h is the depth, in feet. In shallow and crooked channels this formula does not give results sufficiently accurate to be of great value to an engineer.

When a wave of oscillation approaches a coast obliquely from the open sea, the end of the wave nearest the shore is retarded by the shoaling waters, while the other end continues to advance with its original velocity. Waves thus seem to swing toward the coast line. When such a wave is propagated through a broad channel, deep in the middle, and with shoal areas along the sides, the same phenomenon is observed.

When a wave enters a widely opened mouth of a bay normally, the two extremities nearest the shores, where the water is shoal, advance more slowly than the central portion. The wave then extends into a fan-shape which becomes more marked as it progresses into the bay. In a funnel-shaped bay, with its mouth seaward and with decreasing depths landward, waves entering are shortened and become higher and higher. On the contrary, when waves enter a broad, shoal bay through a narrow channel, they become longer and diminish in height.

In estuaries and tidal rivers, the tidal wave is due to the ocean tidal wave at the mouth. After entrance, the wave is acted on by the forces which produced the ocean wave, very slightly, if at all. The energy of an estuary, or river, tidal wave at the entrance is that of the incoming ocean wave. After entrance the energy gradually is exhausted by the work of friction on the bottom, and by the resistances caused by bends or obstructions in the channel. Since this tidal energy is the source of the currents by which the navigable channels are maintained, it is the task of an engineer engaged in the formation and maintenance of such channels to see that the works constructed by him are such as will conserve this tidal energy as much as possible, for the benefit of the parts of the waterway lying beyond; and, further, to see that he does not make undue demands on the energy available by forming channels with dimensions too great for it to maintain, or by obstructing, unduly, the free passage of the wave.

Commander Rude mentions the increase of the range (and, therefore, of the energy) of the tidal wave of New York Harbor due to the opening of the Ambrose Channel across the outer bar. He shows also the effect on the Delaware River tidal wave of the work done in the channel of the Delaware River below Philadelphia, Pa., but above the entrance channels to the river, as contrasted with the effect at Trenton, N. J. A similar change in the tidal range of the Hudson at Troy, N. Y., resulted from the enlargement of the channel between Troy and Hudson, N. Y. In 1876, the tidal range at Troy was 0.8 ft., with the mean low-water plane 3.43 ft. above the Barge Canal datum. In 1910, the range was 2.06 ft. with the mean low-water plane 2.2 ft. above the same datum.

The writer is in hearty agreement with the statement that,

"A fertile field remains open for the engineer in a study of the changes in the tidal regimen in an estuary or in a river resulting from changes in topography and depth in harbor and river improvements, in order that dependable quantitative predictions may be made for proposed projects."

Commander Rude's paper, as well as other papers by officials of the U. S. Coast and Geodetic Survey, give clear statements of current action in estuaries under the physical conditions which existed when the investigations were made, and when data are available, of tidal changes following changes in channel dimensions; but they do not attempt to state what changes would occur in the velocity of wave propagation, in the tidal range, and in the currents produced by the tidal wave action if extensive changes should be made in the physical conditions of the channel by works of river and harbor improvement. It is of maximum interest to engineers engaged in such works to know what such changes would be. In so far as is known to the writer, M. Bonnet is the only engineer who has gone into this subject extensively. He has been able to deduce formulas by which can be predicted the effect of physical changes in channel dimensions of the Scheldt River on the tidal action in that river.

In restricted tidal waterways, the tidal wave is always propagated at a velocity which is greater than the velocity of the currents produced by the wave. In such waterways the character of the wave frequently changes in its course from the entrance to the upper limit of tidal action. In the Hudson River, for example, the tidal wave when passing the Battery, in New York City, has the characteristics of a wave of oscillation, with the ebb slack-water occurring about midway between low and high water. As the wave progresses up the Hudson, the times of slack-water approach more and more closely to the times of high and low water, until above the City of Hudson, the times of slack-water coincide with the times of high and low water, a flood current beginning at low water. The wave there has the characteristics of the progressive type (Bonnet's nomenclature). The same is true in the East River where the wave of oscillation entering at the Battery becomes transformed into a progressive wave between the Brooklyn Bridge and Blackwells Island.

Bonnet states with truth that it is not easy to define, offhand, the exact nature of a river tidal wave, "for it is one of the most complex of the phenomena of river hydraulics." He gives the following theory to account for the formation of river tidal currents.*

* "Fleuves à Marées," Bonnet, Pt. II, Chapter II.

At the instant of low water at the mouth the portion of the wave in advance which is in the river, or the entire wave in advance as is the case in the Amazon and St. Lawrence, has a certain discharge toward the sea which is a function of the resistances of the watercourse and of the volume of flow from above.

The ebb current thus formed is increased, as the tide rises, by the volume of water left behind by the portion of the new wave advancing in the river; at the same time, this new wave itself tends to produce an up-stream current, which tendency is continuously augmented and finally neutralizes the counter down-stream current completely. At this instant, low-water slack occurs. When the manner in which this slack is produced is considered, it is seen that it must always take place when the tide is rising, even when there is no discharge from up stream. The length of the period which elapses between the time of low water and the time of ebb slack will depend on the resistances offered by the river channel and on the volume of the fresh-water discharge. After the time of ebb (low-water) slack, the counter (down-stream) current is less powerful than the current of the tidal wave, so that the resulting velocity is a flood (up-stream) velocity.

This phase of the tidal action persists until the volume of water left behind by the tidal wave in a unit of time, added to the fresh-water discharge, becomes again equal to the up-stream flow produced by the tidal wave. At this instant there is produced a new slack-water, known as flood (high-water) slack. The position of this slack with respect to high water, is no more definitely fixed than is that of low-water slack with respect to low water; but observations made on the Scheldt and its tidal tributaries show that high-water slack is always found after high water, except in the upper reaches of the tidal rivers, where, under the influence of the fresh-water discharge, the flood slack precedes high water. Close to the limit of tidal action a reach is found where the flood slack coincides with the ebb slack. Above this point, nothing but an ebb current is found, and the rise of tide is caused entirely by water from up stream.

These conclusions are the same as those reached by Van Brabant in his note on the changes of current in the river tidal wave.* After flood slack, the sections of the tidal wave growing smaller and smaller, the flow of the counter current is greater than that of the tidal wave; so that an ebb current prevails in the river. This phase of the tide persists until the subsequent ebb slack, after which a new cycle begins. The existence of a counter current explains the abnormal reduction of the velocity of propagation of the river wave and the rising of the mean level of the river in an up-stream direction.

To summarize, it can be stated that the river tide is a resultant of the combined action of a tidal wave, which goes up the course of the river, and of a return current, which is formed as the effect of the work of the river-channel resistances and of the fresh-water discharge.

* "Fleuves à Marées," Bonnet, Pt. III, Chapter II.

M. Bonnet makes a mathematical analysis of the effects of the frictional resistances encountered on the energy of a unit length of a tidal wave advancing up the river, and deduces formulas by which the tidal action in the Scheldt can be found. These formulas contain certain constants, the values of which vary for different streams, being dependent on the physical features of the river beds, which values must be determined by observation for each tidal stream.

It is to be hoped that future investigation will show the relation between these constants and the physical conditions of the tidal channel clearly enough to enable formulas to be deduced which will have a general application.

With reference to the practical application of the formulas to the problems of the improvement of any tidal stream, the writer agrees with M. Bonnet that:*

"When a project for the improvement of a tidal river is being prepared, the first task to be accomplished is the study of a mean tide of the river by means of direct observations and the computation of volumes. This preliminary study will give accurate data on the high tide cross-sections, the mean depths at mid-tide, the tidal ranges, the volumes of the flood currents, the fresh-water discharge, the mean level of the river, the velocities of the propagation of the tidal wave, the velocities of the flood and ebb currents, the periods of tidal rise and fall and of ebb and flood flow; in a word, on all of the important elements which make up the regimen of the river.

"When this preliminary study shall have been made, a possible longitudinal profile of mean depths at low tide can be determined. This profile should be selected so that there may be assured a good tidal propagation, the extinction of the river wave at the limit of tidal action in the river, the safe discharge of freshets, and the navigable capacity desired. Generally, the selection of the series of proper mid-tide mean depths will be a simple matter, since the river in its natural state gives sufficiently exact indications in its good and bad reaches of the depths to be preserved or to be modified."

From the foregoing, one of the river tide phenomena, which for a long time puzzled the writer, can be understood readily; that is, how the changes of direction of the tidal currents occur. In the Hudson, the tidal wave is more than 100 miles long, and the waves follow each other at intervals of about 12 hours, but the ebb and flood currents have a movement of only 10 to 15 miles before they change. The description of tidal wave action previously given shows that the ebb and flood slack waters, which mark the times of the changes in current direction, occur at definite periods after low and high water. As the wave progresses up a river, the slack-water phases arrive successively from point to point, so that an ebb or a flood current starts at successive points. The slack-water phases succeed each other at intervals of from 4 to 7 hours, the periods of ebb flow being the longer. At the end of each period, at each point along the river, the current direction is reversed. Since the current velocities are usually less than 2.5 miles per hour, the total distance through which a float will be moved by the current is from 10 to 15 miles. Such a float, started near the head of tidal action, will pass down the

* "Fleuves à Marées," Bonnet, Pt. IV, Chapter I.

river with the first ebb; will return to within a few miles of its starting point with the following flood; will then again start down the river; and thus gradually, after many tides, will reach the sea.

While, in a tidal waterway, for long reaches the longitudinal profile of mid-tide levels is approximately a straight line, the longitudinal profiles of the local mean high and mean low-water levels are irregular curves, as indicated in Fig. 22. This shows the necessity for establishing tide gauges as reference points at comparatively short intervals along a waterway, for the reduction of soundings in hydrographic surveying. Otherwise, true mean low-water depths cannot be found. Another phenomenon frequently found in such waterways is that at certain points, during certain phases of the tide, the surface slope of the water is up, measured in the direction of current flow; or, in other words, the water seems to flow up hill.

Referring again to Fig. 22, in his study of the Hudson River, the writer found that the longitudinal profile of mid-tide levels was formed approximately by three straight lines. Starting from the Battery, at New York, the profile had but a slight inclination upward until above Spuyten Duyvil, where a break occurred and the inclination from the horizontal became slightly greater. Thence, to a point above Hudson, the profile was a straight line. Another break occurred at this point, and thence to Albany, the inclination up from the horizontal was markedly increased. In the writer's judgment, the break above Hudson marks the change from estuary to tidal river conditions.

In the course of his duties the writer has had occasion to study the data available on the tidal action and the resulting currents in the Cape Cod Canal and to make a careful survey and study of the complicated tidal conditions at Hell Gate in the East River, New York. An analysis of conditions in the Cape Cod Canal as they existed shortly after the Canal had been opened, has been published.* The surveying methods used at Hell Gate, and the conclusions of the writer have also been published.†

The writer's experience with respect to currents formed in a narrow strait which connects two larger bodies of tidal water, is in agreement with that of Colonel Brown, as given in his discussion. Commander Rude's statement that, "The movement of the water is largely hydraulic in character," is incorrect if it means that the laws governing the ordinary flow of water in open channels are applicable in making predictions as to the effect of changes which will result in the currents of a channel connecting two bodies of tidal water, when the length, curvature, and dimensions of that channel are changed. From the standpoint of an engineer, the term used by Commander Rude is so broad as to be misleading. The hydraulic character of the movement through Hell Gate is the effect of tidal actions. To be able to modify this movement in the interest of navigation, an engineer must seek the cause.

* "The Cape Cod Canal," by William Barclay Parsons, Hon. M. Am. Soc. C. E., *Transactions*, Am. Soc. C. E., Vol. LXXXII (1918), p. 1.

† H. R. Doc. 188, 63d Cong., 1st Sess., "Survey of East River and Little Hell Gate, New York, and Resurvey of Hell Gate"; also, *The Military Engineer*, Vol. XVIII, July–Aug., 1926, p. 266, "Needed Harbor Improvement."

The writer is convinced that the conditions at Hell Gate are the result of the combined action there of two tidal waves, one reaching that point through Long Island Sound and one through Lower and Upper New York Bays and the East River. The rates of propagation and the progress of each wave can be traced clearly from the Tide Tables of the U. S. Coast and Geodetic Survey as far as Hunt's Point on the north and the north end of Blackwells Island on the south. Between these two points the evidence given in the Tide Tables is not so clear. From these as well as from the Current Tables published by the U. S. Coast and Geodetic Survey, it is seen that the rates of propagation of the tidal waves are greater than the velocities of the tidal currents produced by the waves, until Hell Gate is attained. The onward movements of the waves do not cease when these points are reached, since the tidal curves show that their energies had not then become exhausted. Tidal curves taken between Hunt's Point and the north end of Blackwells Island show clearly the superposition of the waves, and that they do meet in, and north of, Hell Gate. Other evidences of this action could be named.*

This question is of more than passing importance to an engineer. If the currents in Hell Gate are purely hydraulic in character, it would follow that an increase in the dimensions of the cross-sections of the connecting channels in Hell Gate would reduce friction and cause increased velocities. If, on the other hand, wave action does exist between the limits named, such action would cause, first of all, a change of "head" between the two points, by permitting a freer propagation of the waves, with a corresponding effect on the velocity of the currents.

An analysis of the tidal wave movements in the East River, more detailed than has yet been made, will be necessary before it is possible to predict with even approximate accuracy how, and to what extent, an increase in the dimensions and curvatures of the three channels at Hell Gate, and of the two channels to the south will change the rate and amount of tidal wave propagation, the surface slopes, and the currents in that vicinity.

Bonnet's theory of the action of a river tidal wave, and his method of analysis of tidal conditions, if followed, would throw great light on the problem of the reduction of the rapid currents in Hell Gate, a problem of primary importance for New York and the nation. A similar necessity exists for the further study of the tidal action in the other tidal waterways of the United States.

Francisco J. Gaston,† M. Am. Soc. C. E. (by letter).—This paper is most interesting and valuable. The whole world is indebted to the U. S. Coast and Geodetic Survey for its authoritative information about tides and currents.

The problem of determining the mean sea level, or mean low tide, is one that often confronts engineers, and they are not always fortunate enough, in many countries, to be able to obtain ready-made information from a reliable authority, such as the U. S. Coast and Geodetic Survey.

* See *Special Publication III*, U. S. Coast and Geodetic Survey, "Tides and Currents in New York Harbor," by H. A. Marmer, p. 77.

† Engr., River and Harbor Impvts., Dept. of Public Works, Havana, Cuba.

In preparing for an extensive final sounding, preliminary to an important dredging project in Isabela de Sagua Harbor on the northern coast of Cuba, the writer was confronted with the task of determining, in the shortest possible time, the plane of mean low tide. The datum, once selected, was to be accepted as final, for all sounding, for contract work, and for final measurements.

As no local information worth having was obtainable, mean low water during a month was found, and a correction introduced for that particular month. This was the zero or datum finally accepted for the work, and it proved to be (by a fortunate coincidence) the almost exact mean low tide for a series of years.

This matter of taking into account the monthly or seasonal variation of the level of the sea to obtain a mean of the whole year, received considerable attention. A record of tides and other meteorological information was started by the writer in 1911 and was continued under his supervision until the end of 1918. The record showed, since its beginning, the relative importance of monthly variation, on Cuban coasts, as compared with the mean range of tides. The mean low tide in January, 1912, was 0.33 m. (1.1 ft.) lower than the mean low tide in September of the same year. The mean range in Isabela de Sagua is 0.48 m. (1.6 ft.), so that the relative importance of the monthly variation is patent.

There is reason to believe that the same monthly variation occurs in Havana Harbor, where the mean range is only 0.28 m. (0.9 ft.). It is possible, therefore, that two independent observers, one in January and the other in September or October, may obtain results for the same tidal plane, which differ by 1 ft., or more; or that one observer may obtain, in a month, a mean high tide lower than the other observer has obtained in another month for a mean low tide. The year 1912 was extreme in that respect, the average of the eight years of observation giving 0.08 m. (0.26 ft.) below the mean of the year, in January, and 0.09 m. (0.30 ft.) above the mean of the year, in September and October.

The information obtained gave rise to a rule for determining the mean sea level, or mean low tide, which was to determine the average during a whole month and to apply to that value a correction, positive or negative, equal to the variation from the zero obtained in the same month at the Port of Havana, or the Port of Isabela de Sagua. If no observations were obtained from those standard ports (as is now unfortunately the case), a correction was to be applied, according to the month in which the observations were taken.

The Department of Public Works, at present (1927) building the Central Highway of the Island, a modern road 700 miles long, has announced that it will establish bench-marks, referred to mean sea level, on each kilometer post.

In the paper by Commander Rude, reference is made to this monthly or seasonal variation and the diagram (Fig. 19), giving the monthly means at Fort Hamilton, N. Y., from 1900 to 1909, inclusive, shows it plainly. The author states: "Sea level as determined by a series of observations extending over only a month may differ as much as 1 ft. or more from that determined by another month". This covers very well the experience obtained at Isabela de Sagua.

The further statement that: "For practical purposes a tidal plane obtained from a month of observations may be considered as fairly well determined", is not in contradiction with the other because it all depends on what is considered sufficient for practical purposes; but if taken separately, it may be misleading. Engineers basing their work on that authoritative source will continue to determine mean sea level or mean low tide from a month of observations and will believe they are "practical", leaving any further observations or corrections to the "theoretical" man.

The conclusion seems to be offered from the text that those monthly variations, although not always unimportant, cannot be determined on account of being due to differences of atmospheric pressure. The atmospheric pressure was determined with sufficient accuracy at Isabela de Sagua, and the diagram showing its mean monthly variation resembles, although in the opposite sense, that of the tidal planes. The highest pressure in January corresponds to the lowest level of the sea in that month and the lowest pressure in September and October corresponds to the highest level of the sea in those months. Further studies could not be made because exceptional months in the mean sea level could not be related to exceptional months in the atmospheric pressure, and thus no correction could be established for the mean sea level depending on the mean barometric pressure during the time of observations.

However, if the mean monthly variation of the sea level, depends on the difference of atmospheric pressure, this, in its turn, on account of its known regularity, must depend on some astronomical cause; and as such it is within the scope of the scientist. It is no doubt included in some of the elementary constituent tides, of yearly and semi-yearly periods, which are summed up in the wonderful tide-predicting machine of the U. S. Coast and Geodetic Survey.

Wind observations were made at the same time, in Isabela de Sagua, and were given considerable attention, both as to intensity and direction. Diagrams were thus obtained showing the average prevailing winds in each month.

This information about the wind is considered very interesting in harbor work. It may even show, in what month or season of the year, in a partly exposed location, it is advisable to proceed or to stop dredging or other harbor work. It also gives information about the best time of the year for soundings, with results that are sometimes contrary to popular belief.

Observations on atmospheric pressure, rain, and temperature were also made simultaneously.* These are subjects which also have their engineering aspects.

F. W. Scheidenhelm,† M. Am. Soc. C. E.—The respect which the speaker has had for the work of the U. S. Coast and Geodetic Survey has not been diminished in the least by this paper. Indeed it has been broadened to include

* The tabulated values and a general graphic of all the information referred to, have been published under the title, "Observaciones Mareográficas y Meteorologicas en el Puerto de Isabela de Sagua" ("Mareographical and Meteorological Observations at the Port of Isabela de Sagua"), in *Revista* de la Sociedad Cubana de Ingenieros, Sección de Obras Públicas, Vol. XI, (1919), September, October, November, and December. An article by the writer, with explanations and comments on the same, entitled "El Estudio de las Mareas y los Vientos en relación con las Obras de Puertos" ("The Study of Tides and Winds in Connection with Harbor Work") was published in *Revista* de la Sociedad Cubana de Ingenieros, Vol. XVII (1925), March–April.

† Cons. Engr. (Mead & Scheidenhelm), New York, N. Y.

the well-nigh human tide-predicting machine devised and designed by the engineers of the Survey.

The speaker is especially interested in the engineering aspects of tides as they affect water-power development. Much has been said and written about the proposed development of tidal power in the Bay of Fundy, and in regard thereto the speaker joins in marveling at the courage, and likewise the optimism, of those who seek to curb and utilize those tides for the generation of hydro-electric power on a mammoth scale. He has in mind, not the generation of power by means of tides, but rather the effect of tides on the more usual type of water-power development along streams.

At St. John, the principal city and seaport of the Province of New Brunswick, Canada, located on the Bay of Fundy, the outstanding natural attraction is the so-called "Reversible Falls" at the mouth of the St. John River. That river drains about 26 000 sq. miles and hence under ordinary circumstances would afford an attractive opportunity for the development of water power at the Falls. However, the foot of the Falls is practically at low tide, and, despite the fact that at times a fall of perhaps 12 ft. is apparent, the tides of the Bay of Fundy of about 20 ft. completely submerge the Falls at high tide. Indeed, the flow is then actually up stream, sometimes to a depth of about 12 ft. over the crest of the falls. For a period of less than an hour, at high slack tide, ships can pass from St. John Harbor over the falls up into the river.

This condition makes it apparent why the Falls by themselves are not suitable for the development of hydro-electric power. However, inasmuch as the development of tidal power in the ordinary sense involves shifting the means of development according to the ebb or flow of the tide, it may not involve too great a flight of the imagination to conceive that at some future time the Reversible Falls at St. John may be called upon to function in the generation of power for a part of each 24-hour period, with corresponding reliance placed upon some other source of power generation during periods of partial and complete submersion of the Falls.

In passing, it may be noted that the tidal fluctuations of the Bay of Fundy take place to the full extent in the Harbor of St. John and give rise to problems affecting harbor construction, the use of docks, and the handling of shipping. These problems have many interesting and difficult phases. The situation may be the better understood if one will visualize the fact that at high tide a vessel alongside a dock rides about 20 ft. higher than at low tide.

The speaker has had occasion to investigate the Provincial development (by the New Brunswick Electric Power Commission) of the power of the Musquash River, which empties into the Bay of Fundy about 15 miles west of the City of St. John. Inasmuch as the power station is located close to sea level, the great tides of the Bay play an important part. They affect the power-station tail-water for about 15 hours of each day. The power project really consists of twin developments, in each of which an intake reservoir is connected by a wood-stave pressure pipe to the power station. The twin developments operate under average effective heads of about 100 ft. and 120 ft., respectively, and the sources of water supply are not interchangeable.

In the usual type of water-power development the head is at a minimum during flood periods. In the case of the Musquash, however, the heads, so far as tail-water is concerned, are at a minimum at high tide. Naturally, it is the spring tides, as described by the author, that are the most serious in this respect. At times, the spring tide at St. John attains at least 28 ft., or about 8 ft. in excess of the relatively high normal tides.

When a spring tide coincides with a depleted condition of an intake reservoir, it follows that there will be reduction of head both at the head-water and at the tail-water. In order to maintain the turbine output at approximately normal capacity, it would be necessary to utilize greater water supply with correspondingly greater velocity of flow through the pipe line. This, in turn, causes greater friction loss and, consequently, further loss in energy.

So far as the reduction due to tides is concerned, conditions may be further aggravated if the wind should happen to be in the proper direction to heap up the tide still more. Indeed, it is not impossible that the combination of the several tidal components may result in increasing all tides, spring as well as normal, in their travel up the Musquash Estuary at the head of which the power station is located. As concerns the Musquash water-power development, it seems fortunate that it is the east and not the west side of the Bay of Fundy that has the 5-ft. higher tides. Another interesting phase of the Musquash situation is that, during the period of tidal records to which the speaker had access, there appeared to be no instance of an extreme spring tide occurring between 4:00 and 6:00 P. M. These are the hours of coincidence of industrial demand for power with the needs of power for early evening lighting during the autumn and winter, and thus they constitute the period of maximum demand on the power station. It may be, therefore, that, during that critical period of the day, the power station may be spared the reduction of its head due to the full extent of the maximum spring tides. As to whether or why maximum spring tides never occur during that period of the day, the speaker has no knowledge, nor did his inquiries meet with any satisfactory answer.

CHARLES H. LEE,* AND HAROLD F. GRAY,† MEMBERS, AM. SOC. C. E. (by letter).—The writers have been especially interested in the flow of tidal currents in estuaries and bays. In connection with the question of sewage pollution they have had to determine the rates of discharge and volumetric renewal of water in the tidal canal known as the Oakland Estuary lying between the Cities of Oakland and Alameda, Calif.

Description of Conditions.—Referring to Fig. 45, the estuary is seen to extend as a dredged channel from San Francisco Bay at its northwestern end, between the Southern Pacific (Alameda) and the Western Pacific Railway moles, to San Leandro Bay at its southeastern end. San Leandro Bay is a shallow body of salt water, much of its area being mud flats at low tide. It has a southerly opening into San Francisco Bay between Alameda and Bay Farm Island.

* Cons. Hydr. Engr., San Francisco, Calif.
† San. and Hydr. Engr., Berkeley, Calif.

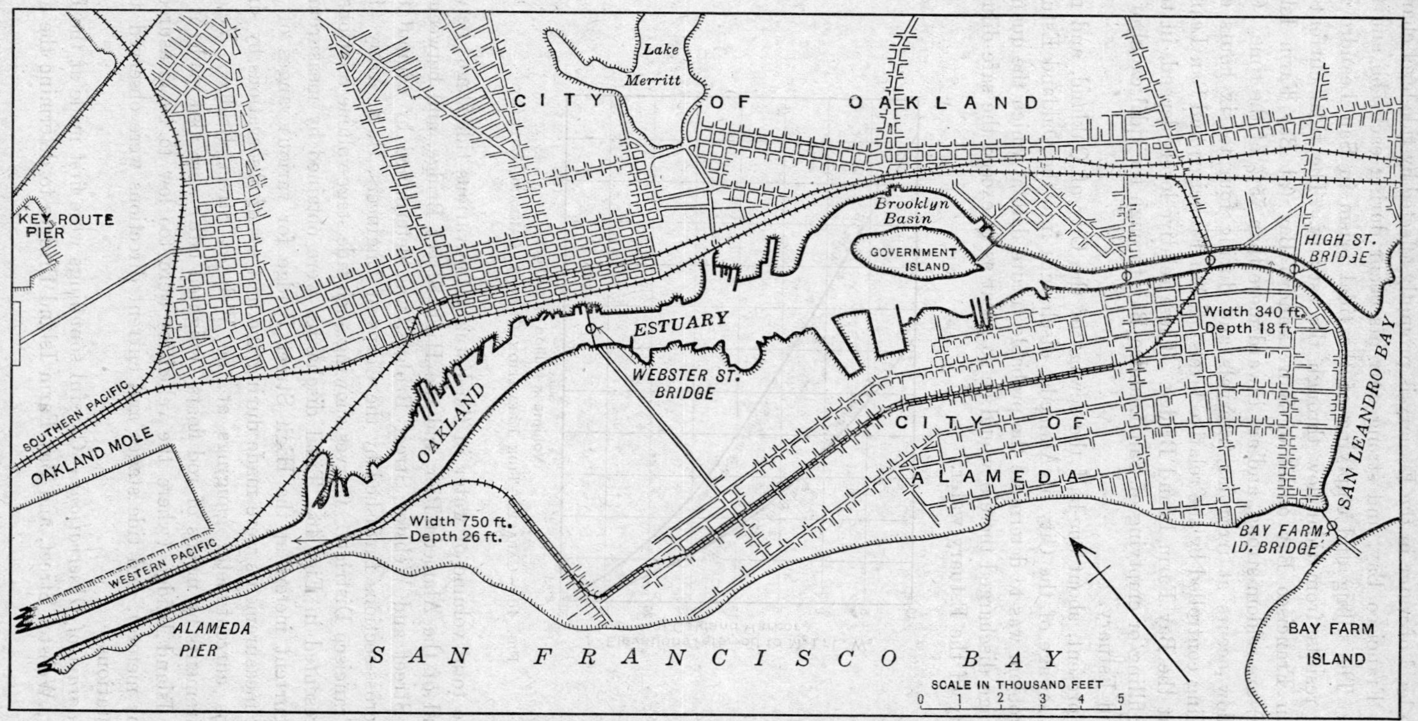

FIG. 45.—OAKLAND ESTUARY, OAKLAND, CALIF.

The level of water in the Estuary is promptly affected by tide-level changes in San Francisco Bay, and strong currents occur during each ebb and flow period. The filling and emptying of the tidal prism in San Leandro Bay largely results from tidal flow through the estuary. The tidal currents at the San Francisco Bay outlet of San Leandro Bay (at Bay Farm Island Bridge) are seldom strong, and are inward more than 75% of the time. Outward flow occurs at irregular intervals and during four to six hours each day, being controlled by the relative levels of San Francisco and San Leandro Bays at the Bay Farm Island Bridge. These relative levels depend, in turn, on the filling or emptying of San Leandro Bay through the tidal canal of the Oakland Estuary.

At present, about one-half the sewage of the City of Oakland, and most of the sewage of the City of Alameda, discharges into the Oakland Estuary. The problem was to determine the probable future date at which the quantity of sewage discharged therein would be so great as to exceed the safe dilution capacity of the Estuary water.

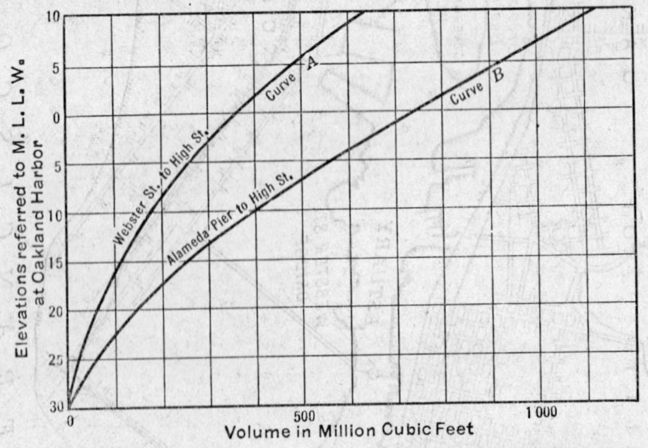

FIG. 46.—CAPACITY-TIDE ELEVATION CURVES, OAKLAND ESTUARY.

The total volume of water in the Estuary for various tide stages between the end of the Alameda Pier and the High Street Bridge, and between the High Street and Webster Street Bridges, was determined by computations from cross-sections furnished by the Corps of Engineers, U. S. Army (First San Francisco District). Curves showing such tide stage volume relationships are presented in Fig. 46. Tidal discharges were obtained by measurements with current meters at the High Street Bridge for various ranges of tide. Check measurements were made during the first set of observations by simultaneous current-meter gaugings at the Webster Street Bridge. Velocity measurements by means of rod floats (weighted lath) were also made at Bay Farm Island Bridge (where the velocities were too low to be measured by current meters), and tide stages and current directions were observed at all four stations.

Program of Observations.—Careful soundings were first made at the High Street, Webster Street, and Bay Farm Island Bridges to determine the cross-sections and to designate the current-meter stations for both incoming and outgoing tides. Staff gauges were set at these bridges and illuminated so as to be easily read at night. An automatic water-stage recorder was set at the end of the Alameda Pier.

Preliminary to the actual gaugings, the tide gauges were observed for several days to determine whether there were any marked peculiarities of flow to be considered. Current directions under the bridges were observed by suspending the meter in the water and measuring the angle between the bridge rail and the tail of the meter. At the High Street Bridge the direction of flow was at a marked angle, and this had to be taken into account in the computations.

The results of the first set of measurements indicated that discharge measurements at the High Street Bridge would give all necessary information, and check measurements at the other bridges, therefore, were not made at the times of subsequent observations.

The first set of discharge measurements was made on August 12 and 13, 1927, when a large tidal range was anticipated. The following schedule was observed:

1.—An observer was stationed at Alameda Pier to note the times of change of current direction.
2.—An hydrographer and assistant were stationed at the Webster Street Bridge, with a current meter.
3.—An hydrographer and assistant were stationed at the High Street Bridge, with a current meter.
4.—An observer with two assistants was stationed at the Bay Farm Island Bridge, to measure velocities by means of rod floats (weighted lath).

Continuous tide-gauge observations were made, and discharge measurements were repeated as frequently as possible during the tidal runs. There were numerous interruptions due to openings of the draw-spans at the Webster Street and High Street Bridges. The observations covered a tidal range of 5.0 ft. on the incoming tide from high low water to high high water on the afternoon and evening of August 12, and a tidal range of 8.4 ft. on the outgoing tide from high high water on the evening of August 12 to low low water on the morning of August 13. The results of these discharge measurements were plotted against time, and the total discharge for each tidal run was determined graphically (see Fig. 47(*a*)).

The total discharges as thus measured and computed at the Webster Street and High Street Bridges were then compared with the results computed from the formula,

$$Q_1 = (V_1 - V_2) + Q_2 \qquad (1)$$

in which,

Q_1 = volume passing Webster Street Bridge, or Alameda Pier, according to purpose of calculation;

Q_2 = volume passing High Street Bridge;

V_1 = volume in Estuary between bridges at higher tide stage; and

V_2 = volume in Estuary between bridges at lower tide stage.

For the incoming tide on August 12,

$$Q_2 = 121\,000\,000 \text{ cu. ft. (measured)}$$
$$V_1 - V_2 = 106\,565\,000 \text{ " "}$$

$$Q_1 = 227\,565\,000 \text{ " " (computed)}$$
$$Q_1 = 228\,000\,000 \text{ " " (measured)}$$

For the outgoing tide on August 12-13,

$$Q_2 = 197\,800\,000 \text{ cu. ft. (measured)}$$
$$V_1 - V_2 = 173\,152\,000 \text{ " "}$$

$$Q_1 = 370\,952\,000 \text{ " " (computed)}$$
$$Q_1 = 368\,000\,000 \text{ " " (measured)}$$

As the agreement between the measurements and the computed values at the Webster Street and High Street Bridges were thus reasonably close, subsequent measurements of flow were made at the High Street Bridge only.

The discharge curves for subsequent observations made on September 6 and October 4, 1927, are shown in Fig. 47 (*b*). The tide range on August 12 and 13 was large; that on September 6 was intermediate; and that on October 4 was small.

The total discharges for these tide runs of varying range as obtained from Fig. 47 are shown on Fig. 48. The plotted points indicate a direct relation between tidal range and discharge, as shown by the straight line. At low ranges the tidal flow west at High Street Bridge for the same tidal range is somewhat erratic. This is probably due to hydraulic conditions in San Leandro Bay, which has a flow out into San Francisco Bay only at short and irregular intervals. It is probable that this condition assumes importance only at small tide ranges. In view of its irregular occurrence it has been neglected in this investigation.

The inflow through the Alameda Pier entrance was the only one considered to be of immediate concern, for the reason that dissolved oxygen tests on the ebb flow from San Leandro Bay into the Estuary showed a depletion of about 50% below saturation. The water coming from San Leandro Bay and flowing down the Estuary on the ebb tide is, therefore, so depleted in oxygen that for practical purposes it cannot be considered as "new" water available for sewage dilution. For the calculation of replacement percentages, only the incoming water from San Francisco Bay at the Alameda Pier entrance, which is constantly at or close to oxygen saturation, should be considered.

Having determined the tide stage-discharge relationship for the High Street Bridge, as shown on Fig. 48, and having the tide stage-volume relationship as shown on Fig. 46, it is possible to determine the total tidal flow in the Estuary for any tidal run by means of Equation (1).

The critical period with respect to sewage dilution will occur when the tidal flow is the least, and during that period when the sewage has the greatest total oxygen demand. The latter condition occurs annually in September when the canneries are in operation and the temperatures are generally the highest. The former condition occurs approximately once a month. For the purpose of this discussion only the condition of minimum tidal flow will be considered.

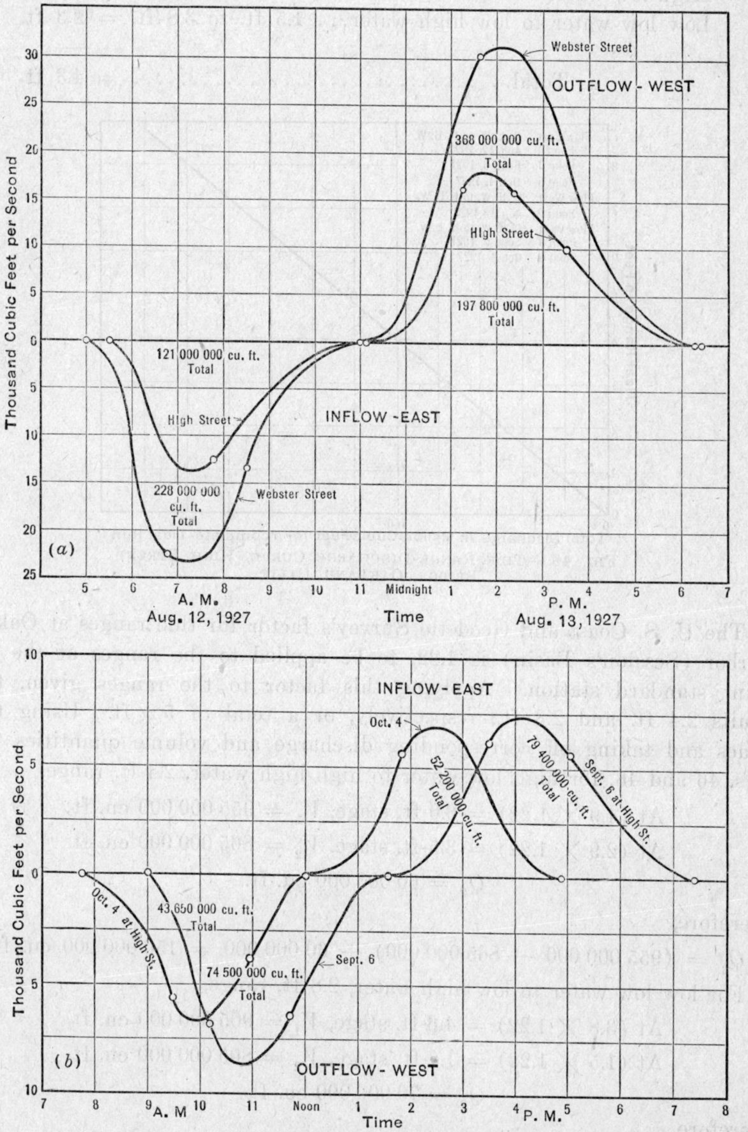

FIG. 47.—TIDAL FLOWS AT HIGH STREET AND WEBSTER STREET BRIDGES, OAKLAND, CALIF.

Excluding from consideration the ebb flow, it is apparent that the minimum inflow into the Estuary will occur when the sum of the ranges of the two incoming tides each day is the least. An examination of the tide tables shows such a minimum range on September 2 and 3, 1927, as an example. These ranges at the Fort Point standard station for San Francisco Bay are as follows:

High low water to high high water.. 2.9 ft. to 4.9 ft. = 2.0 ft.
Low low water to low high water... 1.5 ft. to 3.8 ft. = 2.3 ft.

Total.................................. = 4.3 ft.

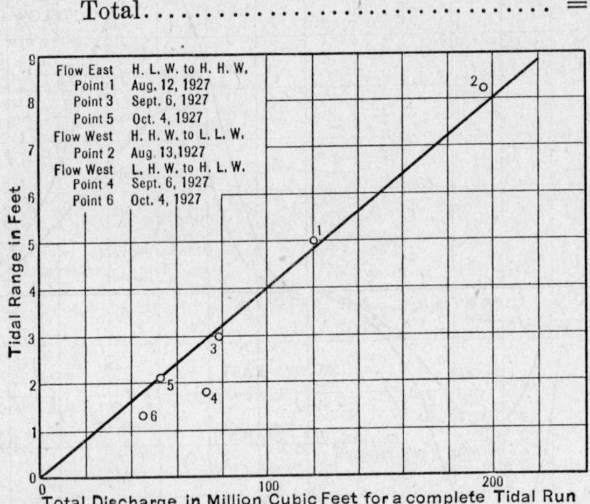

FIG. 48.—TIDE RANGE-DISCHARGE CURVE, HIGH STREET BRIDGE, OAKLAND, CALIF.

The U. S. Coast and Geodetic Survey's factor for tide ranges at Oakland Harbor (Session's Basin) is 1.22, to be applied to the ranges at the Fort Point standard station. Applying this factor to the ranges given, there results 2.4 ft. and 2.8 ft., respectively, or a total of 5.2 ft. Using these values and taking off corresponding discharge and volume quantities from Figs. 46 and 48, for high low water to high high water, 2.4-ft. range,

$$\text{At } (4.9 \times 1.22) = 6.0\text{-ft. stage, } V_1 = 955\,000\,000 \text{ cu. ft.}$$
$$\text{At } (2.9 \times 1.22) = 3.5\text{-ft. stage, } V_2 = 865\,000\,000 \text{ cu. ft.}$$
$$Q_2 = 60\,000\,000 \text{ cu. ft.}$$

Therefore,

$$Q_1 = (955\,000\,000 - 865\,000\,000) + 60\,000\,000 = 150\,000\,000 \text{ cu. ft.}$$

For low low water to low high water, 2.8 ft. range,

$$\text{At } (3.8 \times 1.22) = 4.6\text{-ft. stage, } V_1 = 905\,000\,000 \text{ cu. ft.}$$
$$\text{At } (1.5 \times 1.22) = 1.8\text{-ft. stage, } V_2 = 805\,000\,000 \text{ cu. ft.}$$
$$Q_2 = 70\,000\,000 \text{ cu. ft.}$$

Therefore,

$$Q_1 = (905\,000\,000 - 805\,000\,000) + 70\,000\,000 = 170\,000\,000 \text{ cu. ft.}$$

The total inflow at Alameda Pier will then be the sum of the two values of Q_1, or,

$$150\,000\,000 + 170\,000\,000 = 320\,000\,000 \text{ cu. ft.}$$

The volume of water in the Estuary between Alameda Pier and High Street Bridge at mean sea level is 863 000 000 cu. ft. Therefore, the approximate percentage of new water entering at Alameda Pier is,

$$\frac{320\ 000\ 000}{863\ 000\ 000} = 37$$

If, instead of calculating the percentage on the basis of the average tide stage (mean sea level), it is calculated on the basis of the volume of water in the Estuary at the beginning of each inflow, the percentages would have been 17 and 21, respectively, or a total of 38 of new water. On this basis one would expect a complete change of water in the Estuary every 2½ to 3 days (except at dead ends and in pockets alongshore) under the worst probable conditions.

As all field work was done according to standard practice and under reasonably good working conditions, the actual measurements of discharges and volumes are believed to be within reasonable limits of accuracy (possibly ± 5 per cent). In drawing the graphs of the tidal flows (see Fig. 47), it was necessary to exercise more or less judgment in order to draw curves which would represent the actual flows satisfactorily. However, a reasonable estimate of the volume of tidal flow available for sewage dilution has been obtained. This estimate, combined with information as to the present and probable future total oxygen demand of the sewage coming into the Estuary and San Leandro Bay, the amount of surface re-aeration, and other significant factors, should serve as a fair basis for the estimation of future conditions in this Estuary.

This investigation was a part of the studies being made by the Engineering Commission on Sanitation and Drainage of the City of Oakland, of which Charles D. Marx, Hon. M. Am. Soc. C. E., and the writers are members.

C. R. F. Coutlee,* M. Am. Soc. C. E. (by letter).—A subject related to tides is the founding and connecting of a concrete structure to rock bottom along the sea coast. The tide rises and wets the concrete which was perhaps, poured only an hour before.

It is suggested that the concrete be placed in canvas and deposited at a temperature of 70° Fahr. If the canvas is placed in a bottom dumping box, which is then filled at the mixer and the top of the canvas gathered and tied with wire, there will be little loss of time. This insures a good setting heat protected from rapid loss by the canvas.

Between high and low tide canvas may become an eyesore, but the inside of the form may be sheeted with it and the heat preserved. In cold weather the zone between tides had better be concreted in one operation. It should be poured hot and should contain a 2% solution of calcium chloride as well.

In the north, the tide belt is bared twice daily, and the soaked face is exposed to severe frost. Only 3 000 lb. concrete can withstand this influence and no less strength should be used.

Tidal range is destructive to timber structures because of buoyancy tending to draw the piling, especially when ice is attached. The attack of

* Ottawa, Ont., Canada.

teredo and *limnoria* occurs largely at the tide zone and can only be met with creosote treatment.

It is necessary, in localities with high tides, to design vessel beds in front of wharves so that a boat may rest on an even keel when the tide is out. Often steel vessels of considerable size lie on the soft mud without injury.

G. T. RUDE,* M. AM. SOC. C. E. (by letter).—The writer is indebted to the Society for publishing this paper, and to the members of the Society who have contributed useful information and criticism in the discussions. In submitting the paper the writer had in mind a brief, general outline of the fundamentals of the subject of tides and currents for those engineers who have neither the time from their own particular sphere of work, nor the inclination, to digest mathematical treatises on the subject.

Mr. Haupt in his discussion refers to the "resacas" of the Bay of Rio de Janeiro and by letter has very kindly furnished the writer a reference to the subject.† The "resacas" are not a part of the tidal phenomenon, but are storm waves, due to local winds or to distant storms, which enter the Bay. They do not have a vertical rise and fall of "100 ft." in the meaning of the rise and fall of the tide; but these wind-produced waves, on striking against the vertical protective walls along the cities' fronts, are at times thrown 100 ft. into the air. It is quite probable that their force is increased by the topography of the Bay and perhaps, too, by the fact that the period of oscillation in the Bay, depending upon its dimensions, may coincide very closely with the periods of the waves.

Captain Faris and Mr. H. de B. Parsons have emphasized the importance to the engineer of rational datum planes. The writer is in hearty accord that this matter is one of basic importance in the subject of tides and their relation to the engineer. There can be no argument against Mr. Parsons' recommendation in regard to mean sea level as a datum for elevations on topographic maps. This is recognized by the U. S. Coast and Geodetic Survey, as evidenced in the system of levels which that Bureau is spreading over the country for the use of the engineer and for datums for the topographic mapping of the country. For this whole system mean sea level is used as a datum.

The use of high water as the datum for elevations on a nautical chart undoubtedly had its origin in the fact that the high-water line represents the demarcation between land and sea as visible to the mariner at practically all times, being usually marked by débris, or by other objects along the shore, and by discoloration of rocks, etc. As to the land depicted on the chart, the mariner is interested in the outline of the harbor or shore as it appears to the eye, and high water more nearly fills this requirement, for in low, flat country the grass or tree line usually ends very close to the high-water line; in hilly, rolling country, eroded bluff lines coincide very closely with the high-water line for the purposes of the mariner; in rocky country, such as in New England and Alaska, cliff lines are practically the shore line shown on the chart. The mariner, therefore, quite often is able to locate his vessel by

* Commander, U. S. Coast and Geodetic Survey, Washington, D. C.

† *The Engineer*, April 11, 1924, pp. 380–388.

bearings on the visible shore line, tangents to well-defined points, islands, etc., plotting the bearings to the charted high-water line.

For these reasons the high-water line was taken as the shore line and the zero contour from which to reckon elevations on the land bordering the sea and harbors. In general, the mariner has little interest in mean sea level, but is more inclined to estimate the elevations of shore objects in their relation to the visible high-water line.

The writer is glad to have Colonel Brown's discussion, particularly regarding currents in canals. It happens that the straits and canals connecting two differently tided bodies of water, for which the U. S. Coast and Geodetic Survey has had occasion to make predictions, have been of a length and depth in which the hydraulic feature has predominated to the extent that thoroughly satisfactory results have been obtained by considering only the hydraulic gradient, with a constant for the inertia of the mass of water. It is quite probable, as pointed out by Colonel Brown, that, when occasion arises for predicting slacks and velocities for points in a long, shallow canal, this method will not suffice, and an analysis of actual current observations will have to be made.

Colonel Brown had charge of the lowering of the Chesapeake and Delaware Canal to sea level, and any studies he has made of wave propagation in the Canal will be awaited with interest by the profession. Several years ago he furnished the U. S. Coast and Geodetic Survey with records of eighteen months of continuous tide observations at Chesapeake City, Md., the western terminus of the Canal, and at Delaware City, Del., the eastern terminus. Using these data for determining the hydraulic gradient, predictions of the times of slack water were made for Chesapeake City. These times were in very close agreement with the times of observed slack waters obtained over a short period of actual current observations at Chesapeake City during the summer of 1927.

From information received from the office of the U. S. Engineers in Wilmington, Del., it appears that the times of slack waters vary considerably in different parts of the Canal, indicating that these predictions are satisfactory only for the western end of the Canal.

Mr. Godfrey's discussion is, as he states, "a challenge of the universally accepted theory of the tides."

The basic theory of the tides, pertaining to the astronomical forces involved, which has been universally accepted by scientists in the past, has been found to afford a solid foundation for practical work in this subject; and tidal predictions for all parts of the world, made not only by the United States Government, but also by other maritime nations, have agreed remarkably well with actual observations. It is to be understood, of course, that these predictions are based upon both theory and observations.

The manifestations of the astronomical tide-producing forces are complicated by terrestrial conditions which give rise to various secondary theories upon which scientists have not been in entire agreement. The stationary-wave theory of Harris, discussed briefly by the writer, seems to be in accord with most of the tidal phenomena as observed.

Gen. William Barclay Parsons has referred to an interesting and economically important characteristic of the tide in a short strait connecting two independently tided bodies of water, deduced from his studies of the Cape Cod Canal—the curved instead of straight line of low-water elevations through the canal. These deductions for the Cape Cod Canal likewise hold good in the case of the East River, New York, the same characteristic in the low-water plane existing also in that strait.*

Mr. Thomson refers to the probable results which would be brought about in the tidal régime of Long Island Sound by a new East River from Flushing to Jamaica Bay and a new Harlem River from Hell Gate to the Hudson, 2½ miles long instead of 6¾ miles, if each of the new rivers were 50 ft. deep and of ample width. Since there is no comparable project available, the matter is debatable, and, too, the results would depend somewhat on the conception of "ample width". Two such rivers, 50 ft. deep and of a width comparable with the present rivers, would probably not reduce the difference in the tide levels appreciably at Governors Island and Hell Gate.

Mr. Thomson also brings up the question whether the Cities of New York, Philadelphia, Pa., and Baltimore, Md., have a comparatively small range of tide due to the fact that the bodies of water on which they are located are "at right angles to the direction of Long Island Sound, Bay of Fundy, and the St. Lawrence, and also whether, if all these rivers, bay, and sounds were running parallel to the equator, the tidal ranges would be greatly increased." It is doubtful whether the azimuth of these bodies of water affects to any extent their ranges of tide.

The tidal graphs from observations by Mr. Dunham are very interesting, showing oscillations in Green Bay, Wisconsin, with a range as great as a foot at times and with a distinct tidal period. It is generally assumed that the fluctuations in the levels of the Great Lakes are due to wind and barometric pressure, with a periodic tidal oscillation of possibly a few inches at most, largely masked by meteorological conditions.

Mr. Bennett brings out the need for self-recording current meters for observations in waters such as Santa Monica Bay, California. To be fair to instrument designers and manufacturers it should be borne in mind that, while a degree of performance similar to that required has been attained in the modern curve-tracing tide gauges, the work required of the tide gauge and also its installation are much simpler than that required of the current meter. In fact, the difficulties of holding the current meter on station without considerable cost is a much more troublesome matter than the development of the meter itself, particularly in water of considerable depth on an open coast, such as the Pacific Coast of the United States.

Self-recording current meters have been developed. One of these, which makes a photographic record of both the velocity and the direction of the cur-

* *Special Publication No. 111,* U. S. Coast and Geodetic Survey, "Tides and Currents in New York Harbor," pp. 73-74.

rent, is described by the writer.* Another self-recording current meter, which records, electrically, the velocity and the direction of the current,† was developed on the *Maud* while that ship was drifting in the Arctic.

The photographic-recording meter (Pettersson's) is already on the market,‡ and it is understood that the electrically-recording meter (Sverdrup) is being further developed.

Mr. Gelineau calls attention to the requirement of location of the high-water line forming the boundary between State-owned and privately-owned property in the sale or lease of riparian lands flowed by tide water. In this connection the engineer can be of considerable assistance to legislative bodies in the wording of proposed laws covering such cases; that is, to have the law state definitely the high water or other tidal plane in the meaning of the law, so that a proper interpretation can be made, which will be recognized by the Courts in deciding cases of litigation. As an example, the writer recalls a case in which the term, "ordinary high water", was used. That might be taken as meaning "mean high water". This interpretation, if accepted by the Courts, might apply to the Atlantic Coast of the United States, but again that definition would not hold good on the Pacific Coast. Due to the diurnal inequality in the tides on that coast the law should be even more specific as to whether "mean high water" or "mean higher high water" is meant, since these are two comparatively widely separated tidal planes. Mean high water is the mean of all the high waters, and mean higher high water, the mean of all higher high waters.

General Black refers to the use of the terms, "progressive" and "stationary", in connection with the classification of tidal waves. The writer agrees with him that non-uniformity in the nomenclature of a particular subject is likely to be misleading. It was for this reason that the writer was careful to employ the nomenclature used by the majority of tidal students and writers on the subject of tides, both in the United States and abroad.

General Black has made a strong point in favor of a study by engineers as to what changes would ensue in the tidal régime of a body of water from certain engineering projects as, for example, in the deepening and widening of the East River. Such studies, however, would have to be predicated on the nature and extent of the proposed projects. In the case of the East River it is doubtful whether any engineering project within reason, except locks, would have any considerable effect on the velocity of the currents. The removal of rocky shoals in Hell Gate and of jutting points in the immediate vicinity would probably have the effect of eliminating, to some extent, the swirls and eddies in the currents which constitute a much greater menace to navigation than an equally high current velocity in a straight channel.

General Black is of the opinion that the characteristics of the tidal movement in the East River, New York, are due to the interference of two tide

* See pp. 662–667. Also, "A Recording Current Meter for Deep Sea Work," by Dr. Hans Pettersson, *Quarterly Journal,* Royal Meteorological Soc., Vol. XLI, No. 173, January, 1915.

† "Two Oceanographic Recorders Designed and Used on the *Maud* Expedition," by H. U. Sverdrup and H. Dahl, *Journal,* Optical Soc. of America, Vol. XII, May, 1926, pp. 537-545.

‡ Those purchased by the U. S. Coast and Geodetic Survey were obtained from Stockholm, Sweden.

waves, one entering from New York Bay and the other from Long Island Sound, and he refers to data for the East River in the U. S. Coast and Geodetic Survey Tide and Current Tables as evidence in support of this opinion. The predictions of slack waters in the East River contained in the Current Tables, however, furnish the strongest evidence that the movement of the water in that strait is without question primarily hydraulic. The predictions, made two years in advance, are based entirely on hydraulic movement, and thoroughly satisfactory results are obtained. The velocities of the current, also predicted in a similar manner, have been compared with observed velocities with like results. Beginning with the Current Tables for the calendar year 1930, the predicted velocities of the currents in the East River, based on hydraulic movement, will be published, in addition to the times of slack-water.

In further support of the idea of the combined action of two tidal waves in the East River, General Black makes the statement (page 698): "Other evidences of this action could be named", with a footnote reference to *Special Publication No. 111,* U. S. Coast and Geodetic Survey, "Tides and Currents in New York Harbor", by H. A. Marmer, page 77. The writer is unable to find any evidences in the reference (page 77) of combined action of two tidal waves in the East River. On the other hand, the text (pages 77-78) of the publication to which reference is made and the diagram of slope line both specifically bring out evidences of hydraulic movement, as follows:

"It is obvious that in the East River the tidal movement is conditioned by the fact that it is open to the tides of Upper Bay and also to the tides of Long Island Sound. It has therefore been customary to ascribe the peculiar characteristics of the tidal movement in East River to the interference of two tide waves—the one entering from Upper Bay and the other from Long Island Sound.

"However, the mechanism of the tidal movement in East River can best be understood by regarding the phenomena from the hydraulic point of view; that is, we may regard the changing height of the water in East River as brought about by the fact that part of the time the level of the water in Upper Bay is higher than in Long Island Sound, and part of the time it is lower. In other words, we may regard East River as a channel through which the water flows from the body having temporarily the higher level to the one having the lower level. The height of the water at any point in East River is therefore due to the relative elevations of the water at the two ends.

"If we plot the simultaneous heights of the level of the water at the two ends of East River, the lines joining these simultaneous heights will represent the slope of the water surface in the river and thus the height of the water at those times. These slope lines will then permit the time and range of the tide throughout the river to be determined, since the time and height of the water at any place will be represented by the highest point in the slope lines passing that place, while the time and height of the low water will be indicated by the lowest points in the slope lines."

Then follows a page of comparisons (page 78), showing that actual observations of the tides in the East River agree very closely with times and heights as read from the slope line diagram, and ending with the following paragraph:

"It is obvious that the simple hydraulic considerations upon which Fig. 25 [*Special Publication No. 111*] is based can give only a first approximation to the tidal conditions existing in the East River. The slope lines are drawn as if the channel from Governors Island to Willets Point ran straight for the stretch of 14 miles with unvarying width and depth. No account has been taken of the varying depths in the waterway, of the differences in width, changes in direction, nor of the effect of the water coming through Harlem River. These factors must obviously bring about modifications; but, notwithstanding this, it is seen that the principal tidal phenomena are easily derived by considering the movement of the water in East River as hydraulic. In the chapter [*Special Publication No. 111*] devoted to the currents in the East River it will be seen that the characteristics of the current give further proof of the correctness of the view that the tidal movement in the East River is primarily hydraulic in character."

In ordinary tidal rivers, such as the Hudson River, the observed current velocities may be corrected to mean values by a factor, which is the ratio of the mean range of tide divided by the range for the period of observations.* In the case of the East River, however, and in similar straits connecting two differently tided bodies of water, such as Seymour Narrows, British Columbia, and Deception Pass, Washington, this reduction factor to mean values is not the ratio of the mean range of tide divided by the range at the time of observations, but the square root of this ratio. This fact furnishes further evidence of primarily hydraulic motion in the East River, since in hydraulic motion the velocity varies as the square root of the head.

General Black refers to *Special Publication No. 111,* U. S. Coast and Geodetic Survey, "Tides and Currents in New York Harbor". Attention should perhaps be called to the others of a series of such publications, one of which the Coast and Geodetic Survey is issuing each year, covering the tides and currents in the principal waterways of the country.† Besides those already issued, the publication covering Boston Harbor is now (1927) in press and the manuscript of a publication covering Portsmouth Harbor is being prepared. Each of these publications is being issued following a comprehensive current and tide survey of the harbor in addition to the observations made in past years. As an example, the publication for New York Harbor discusses the data from 149 tide stations, of which 63 are in the East River; and 322 current stations, of which 93 are in the East River. This publication discusses in considerable detail the tide and current conditions as they exist in that harbor at present. The data can be used for predicting the results on the tidal regime by engineers interested in a specific project of harbor improvement. Any analysis, discussions, or predictions of results on the tides and currents in a harbor based on one or more probable projects of harbor improvement is beyond the purpose and scope of such publications. The data are furnished for tide and current conditions as they are at present; and the field is open to engineers interested in any specific project for further analysis based on that particular project.

---

* *Special Publication No. 111,* U. S. Coast and Geodetic Survey, "Tides and Currents in New York Harbor," by H. A. Marmer, p. 141.

† *Special Publication No. 116,* "Tides and Currents, San Francisco Bay"; *Special Publication No. 123,* "Tides and Currents, Delaware Bay and River"; and *Special Publication No. 127,* "Tides and Currents, Southeastern Alaska".

Mr. Gaston states:

"The conclusion seems to be offered from the text that those monthly variations [in tidal planes], although not always unimportant, cannot be determined on account of being due to differences of atmospheric pressure."

The writer did not intentionally mean to convey the idea that these variations are limited to differences in atmospheric pressures only. They may be due, in addition, to other meteorological conditions, such as fresh-water run-off, prevailing winds, etc. It is possible, too, that variations in atmospheric pressures over wider areas than those shown by local pressure observations may play a part in bringing about these variations in the tidal planes.

The writer is glad to have the references of the mareographical and meteorological observations at the Port of Isabela de Sagua furnished by Mr. Gaston. These data will be extremely valuable in any studies of the variation in mean sea level.

Mr. Scheidenhelm refers to the fact that, during the period covered by the tidal records to which he had access in connection with the Musquash water-power development, there was no occurrence of an extreme spring tide between 4:00 and 6:00 P. M. This is due to the fact that in the vicinity of the Musquash River the high-water lunitidal interval, that is, the time elapsing between the moon's passage across the local meridian and the occurrence of local high water, happens to be about 11 hours. Spring tides occur at the times of new and full moon, at which times the moon crosses the meridian at noon and midnight. Therefore, since the high-water lunitidal interval for this vicinity is about 11 hours, high water occurs at that place at about 11:00 A. M. and 11:00 P. M., during the time of spring tides. In fact, during this time, low water occurs in the vicinity of Musquash Bay between 4:00 and 6:00 P. M.

Messrs. Lee and Gray have submitted an interesting discussion on their work in determining the rates of discharge and volumetric renewal of water in the Oakland Estuary, California, in connection with the question of sewage pollution in that tidal canal. The U. S. Coast and Geodetic Survey is now obtaining a series of current observations in this estuary, the data from which will be incorporated in the Current Tables issued by this Bureau for the use of the mariner.

AMERICAN SOCIETY OF CIVIL ENGINEERS
INSTITUTED 1852

TRANSACTIONS

Paper No. 1669

PREPARING THE GROUNDWORK FOR A CITY: THE REGRADING OF SEATTLE, WASHINGTON*

By Arthur H. Dimock,† M. Am. Soc. C. E.

With Discussion by Charles Evan Fowler, M. Am. Soc. C. E.

Historical

In the fall of 1851 a little band of pioneers landed on a point of land between Elliott Bay and Puget Sound. With the optimism of the adventurer they promptly christened their new settlement "New York". They spent the winter crowded into one small log cabin and having for neighbors nearly a thousand Indians. Their time was chiefly occupied in exploration. Before determining their future course, and not being in possession of the charts made by Captain Wilkes in 1841, they made a hydrographic survey of Elliott Bay, their instruments consisting of a clothes-line and two horse-shoes. When the shoes failed to reach the bottom, they knew they had ample depth for ships. In the spring of 1852, the majority of these pioneers removed to the east side of Elliott Bay. One of the reasons impelling their removal was that the steeper slope of the shores on that side made possible much shorter wharves than the long flat slopes of "New York". One of their number, Carson D. Boren, built the first cabin in Seattle near the intersection of Second Avenue and Cherry Street, where the Hoge Building now stands. By 1853 they had constructed a saw-mill near the foot of Yesler Way and laid out and platted the new town site.

There were other pioneers on Puget Sound in those days and these used to wag sapient heads and remark "Alki New York", "Alki" being Chinook for "by and by", or "a long time ahead". Finally, "New York" was dropped, and to this day the place retains the name of Alki. For several years, however, "New York" and Seattle were rival towns.

* Presented at the meeting of the City Planning Division, Seattle, Wash., July 15, 1926.
† Cons. Engr., Seattle, Wash.

In 1855 Governor Isaac I. Stevens, who had charge of the explorations for a Northern Pacific railroad which were being made by Captain George B. McClellan, and others, for the United States War Department, of which Jefferson Davis was then Secretary, recommended the selection of Seattle as the Western terminus because of its "unequalled harbor". This report gave a great impetus to the new settlement and raised the expectations of the pioneers to the highest pitch.

Topography

The general topography of the new city and vicinity is shown on Fig. 1. Taking First Avenue and Yesler Way as the center in those early days, there lay to the south about 1 500 acres of tide flats, bounded on the east and west by steep slopes and intersected by the Duwamish River. (See Fig. 1.) The flat low-lying valley of this river, about 1 mile in width, extends southeasterly for about 8 miles, where it opens into far wider valley lands reaching to Tacoma, Wash. North of the central point are steep slopes coming directly down to the water-front, flattening in the vicinity of Pike Street to form a considerable level area about 100 ft. above high tide. Immediately north of Pike Street, and a little to the westward, lay Denny Hill, with a maximum elevation of about 240. To the east of Denny Hill was a valley extending to Lake Union, also bounded on the east by steep slopes.

About 1 mile from Pike Street and less than 2 miles from Yesler Way is the south end of Lake Union, a body of water of about 800 acres, 1 mile in length due north and south, and ½ mile in width, lying 8 ft. above high tide. It is bounded on the east and west by steep hills, but has level land at its southern end. It possessed an outlet to Puget Sound through Salmon Bay and was separated from Lake Washington by a narrow ridge. From the earliest times the pioneers dreamed of connecting these lakes with the Sound by a ship canal, which has since been accomplished. Between Elliott Bay and Lake Washington, about 20 miles long and 2 to 3 miles wide, was a series of hills and valleys. North of Lake Union was an extensive, rolling plateau.

Such, in brief, was the general character of the site selected by these pioneers for the city of their dreams. It possessed many elements corresponding to their vision. First, was the sheltered harbor with ample depth of water, which had caught the eye of McClellan, and the bays and lakes, which, when connected, were to form an internal system of water communication. Then, there were the tide lands which, when filled, were to form a manufacturing district with easy access to rail and water. The level lands in the neighborhood of Pike and Pine Streets, when extended by proper grading operations, were to become the retail business section and between the manufacturing and retail areas, on the slopes of the hillside, was ample room for the buildings of the office and financial districts. On the hills, surrounded by sea and lake and encircling snow-clad mountains, were home sites of rare beauty. The instincts of the pioneer led them aright. Although not without its difficulties, the situation of Seattle is unique among the cities of the world.

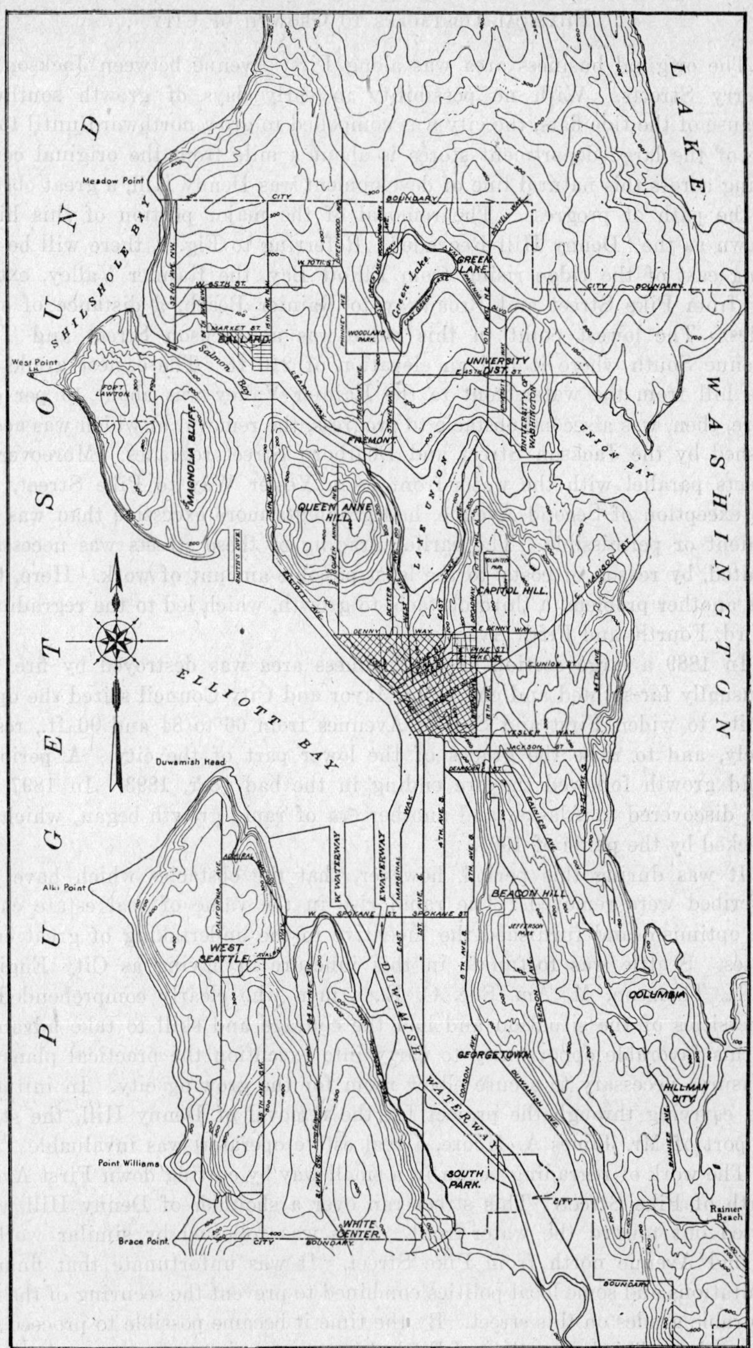

FIG. 1.—TOPOGRAPHIC MAP OF SEATTLE, WASH.

Physical Obstacles to Growth of City

The original business area was along First Avenue between Jackson and Cherry Streets. With no possibility in early days of growth southward because of the tide flats, the city was compelled to grow northward until to-day one of the large department stores is about a mile from the original center. Lying across this natural line of development was Denny Hill, a great obstacle in the path of progress. The removal of the major portion of this hill is known as the "Denny Hill Regrade". Referring to Fig. 1, there will be seen lying east of the ridge rising from Elliott Bay, the Rainier Valley, extending from Pike Street and Broadway to Rainier Beach, a distance of seven miles. The lowest point in this ridge was at Jackson Street and Tenth Avenue South where it had an elevation of 210 ft. The easiest grade over this hill from the water-front to the Rainier Valley was about 15 per cent. Here, then, was a second obstacle to progress, the removal of which was accomplished by the Jackson Street and Dearborn Street regrades. Moreover the streets parallel with the water-front from Yesler Way to Pike Street, with the exception of Second Avenue, had gradients more excessive than was convenient or permissible. The earlier grading of these streets was necessarily limited, by reason of costs, to the least possible amount of work. Here, then, was another problem, a third obstacle to growth, which led to the regrading of Third, Fourth, and Fifth Avenues.

In 1889 a large section of the business area was destroyed by fire. An unusually far-sighted and energetic Mayor and City Council seized the opportunity to widen First and Second Avenues from 66 to 84 and 90 ft., respectively, and to raise the grades of the lower part of the city. A period of rapid growth followed the fire ending in the bad year, 1893. In 1897 gold was discovered in Alaska, and another era of rapid growth began, which was checked by the panic of 1907.

It was during this period, however, that the obstacles which have been described were removed. The rapid rise in the value of real estate caused the optimism and furnished the incentive to the undertaking of great enterprises. Seattle was fortunate in this juncture in having as City Engineer R. H. Thomson, M. Am. Soc. C. E., a man who clearly comprehended the necessities of the situation and had the courage and skill to take advantage of this favorable opportunity to carry into execution the practical plans and measures necessary to secure elbow room for the growing city. In initiating and carrying through the project for the removal of Denny Hill, the strong support of Mr. James A. Moore, a real estate operator, was invaluable.

The work of regrading began in a small way by cutting down First Avenue north of Pike Street. This street ran over a shoulder of Denny Hill which jutted out toward the water-front. This was followed by similar work on Second Avenue north from Pike Street. It was unfortunate that financial limitations and some local politics combined to prevent the securing of the most desirable grades on this street. By the time it became possible to proceed with the work on Third, Fourth, and Fifth Avenues, commonly known as the Denny Hill regrade, a considerable number of new buildings had been erected along

Second Avenue. This made it practically necessary to conform the grades of the new work to that of Second Avenue and led to the creation of a hump at Second Avenue and Virginia Street, which subsequent efforts have failed to remove.

Street Grades.—Under modern conditions, however, the necessity for easy gradients has diminished. These gradients were determined formerly by considering the load a team of horses could pull, and those pavements were selected which afforded the best footing. The motor vehicle has made old theories seem very ancient indeed. It is still true that easy grades are better than steep ones, but the limits have been greatly widened. There is one street in Seattle which was paved with asphalt on a maximum grade of 12%, on the theory that it would never be used anyway; but it has become the main access to the First Hill District. It requires a sprinkling of sand under certain weather conditions, but the capitalized cost of this expense would go a very small way toward paying the cost of securing a better gradient. The ease and comfort of the lowly pedestrian is a more potent factor than motor traffic in limiting the growth of a business district and in determining limiting gradients. Traffic now will avoid detours and seek the steep short-cut whereever possible. In order to obtain a 5% gradient on one of the parkways, a series of hair-pin turns, reminiscent of stage coach days on mountain roads, was used. To-day, these turns are a source of inconvenience and even danger. A more direct route with a 12% gradient would be preferable.

The writer has recommended the use of escalators on the steep cross streets of the business district of Seattle. The practical effect of these escalators would be equivalent to the flattening out of these grades to pedestrians. Some day, owners of the property on these steep streets will awaken to the value of this mechanical means of overcoming the disadvantages of their situation. When the first street is properly equipped with this means of easy access, owners on the remaining streets will hasten to follow the lead.

The rates of grade on the different regrade projects are shown on Figs. 2, 3, and 4. The maximum grade in the Denny Hill District is 5% on the north and south streets and 6.7% on the east and west streets. In the Jackson Street District the grade on Jackson Street itself is 5%, with somewhat steeper grades on the less important streets. Dearborn Street possesses a 3% maximum, but no advantage seems to accrue to it because of this better rate. On the streets in the office district the maximum rates are as follows: First Avenue, 7%; Second Avenue, 5%; Third Avenue 3.7%; Fourth Avenue, 4.7%; and Fifth Avenue, 6 per cent.

The maximum depth of cuts on the Denny Hill project was 110 ft., on the Jackson Street project, 84 ft., and on Dearborn Street, 108 ft. The quantities of earth removed were, respectively, 5 400 000 cu. yd., 3 400 000 cu. yd., and 1 600 000 cu. yd.

Material Encountered.—Fortunately, these hills were composed of sand, gravel, clay, and hardpan. They were the product of glaciers which, in the Pleistocene Age, covered the site of Seattle to a depth of several thousand feet. Geologists state that there were two such ice sheets, each originating in the

Cordilleran center and coming down from the north. They were separated in time by a considerable inter-glacial period. Little of the deposits of the first sheet are exposed, but the handiwork of the second constitutes the foreground of much of the scenery of Puget Sound. The glacier extended to a point about 70 miles south of Seattle. It dammed the natural outlet of the Sound through the Straits of Juan de Fuca. When it began to recede and melt, the water, denied its normal outlet through the Straits, formed a lake or lakes into which flowed many of the rivers of the Sound Basin. The outlet for this water was over a low divide to the south and down the Chehalis River to the Pacific Ocean.

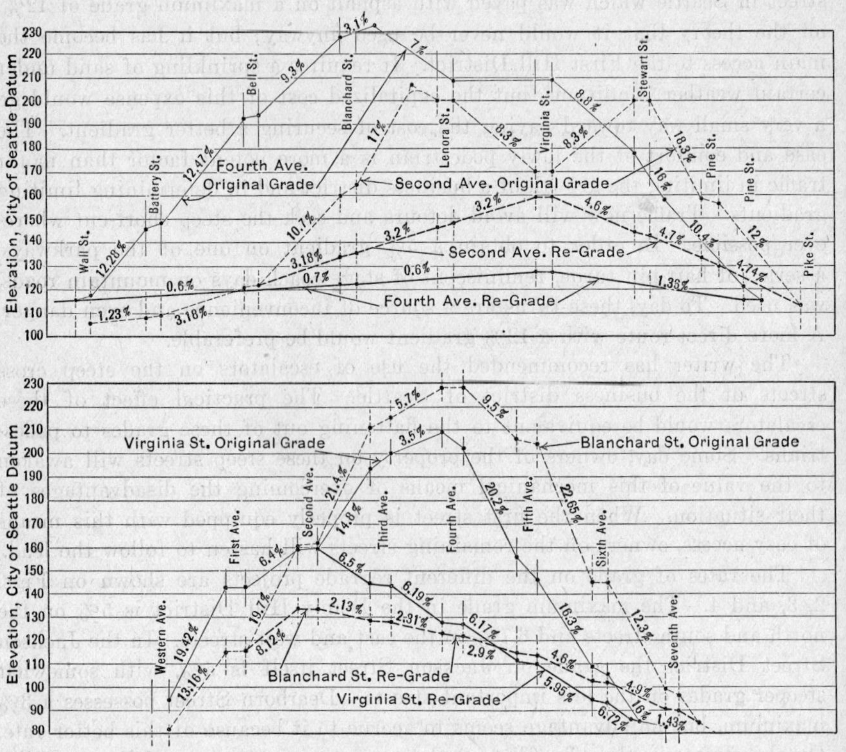

FIG. 2.—PROFILES OF DENNY HILL REGRADE.

The outwash from the glacier formed extensive gravel plains south of Tacoma which now yield a large part of the sand and gravel required for building and engineering construction in Seattle, Tacoma, and other Puget Sound cities. As only the very best and hardest of the rocks survived the action of the glacial mill, the quality of this material is exceptionally high. The retreating glacier also deposited a layer of material called Vashon Till by geologists and commonly known as hardpan. Its thickness varies from 2 or 3 to 20 ft., or more. Beneath are sand and gravel and extensive deposits of a hard blue clay, laid down in the glacial lakes from materials accumulated by the first glacier. It constitutes the foundation of much of the construction work. Rock occurs only in a very few places in the city and not at all in the business district. This, then, was the material to be moved, and as the cost of handling the large volume of excavation by orthodox methods would have been prohibitive, a new and cheaper method had to be discovered.

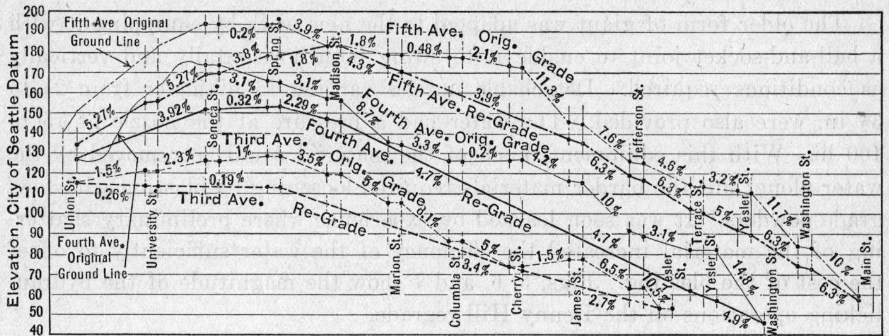

FIG. 3.—PROFILES OF THIRD, FOURTH, AND FIFTH AVENUE REGRADES.

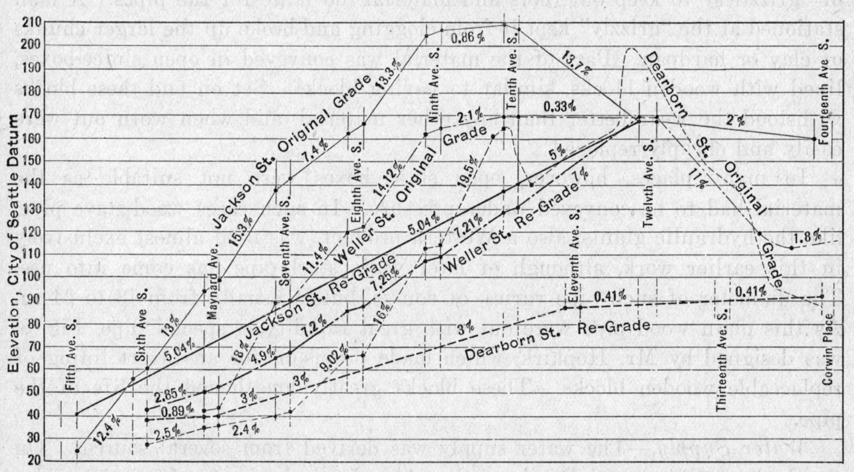

FIG. 4.—PROFILES OF JACKSON AND DEARBORN STREET REGRADES.

Application of Hydraulicking.—Mr. William H. Lewis, a lawyer more interested in engineering and constructive work than in law, possessed property interests in the Rainier Valley. This property, although close in, was separated from the business section by the ridge on Jackson Street previously described. The removal of this ridge at a cost within the ability of the property owners to pay became to him a topic of absorbing interest. His attention was called by W. C. Morse, M. Am. Soc. C. E., and by Mr. James Hopkirk, to the successful use of the method of hydraulic sluicing in extensive gold-mining operations at various points on the Pacific Coast. The method, however, had never been applied to the problem of moving large volumes of clay and hardpan on a city grading job. Many said it could not be done. Bankers refused their support, but Mr. Lewis, by his energy and enthusiasm, overcame all difficulties, worked out the problem, secured the approval of the property owners and of the City Council, and finally organized a company which obtained the contract and successfully completed the Jackson Street and Dearborn Street projects.

The older form of giant was adapted to the new work by equipping it with a ball-and-socket joint to enable it to swing both horizontally and vertically as conditions required. Detachable nozzles varying in diameter from 2½ to 3½ in. were also provided. The water had a pressure at the nozzle of 75 to 100 lb. With this equipment much of the material could be removed by the water alone; but the harder materials required loosening by blasting with low-grade powders. It was soon learned by experience where preliminary shattering of the material increased the efficiency of the water sufficiently to offset the cost of the blasting. Figs. 5, 6, and 7 show the magnitude of the hydraulicking operations on the Denny Hill regrade.

The material when broken by jet and powder was washed down to sluice-boxes provided with fan-shaped approaches and openings screened by bars or "grizzlies" to keep out roots and material too large for the pipes. A man stationed at the "grizzly" kept it from clogging and broke up the larger chunks of clay or hardpan. Part of the material was conveyed in open sluice-boxes, lined with wooden blocks, similar to paving blocks. Set on end these blocks withstood the wear better than any other material, and when worn out were easily and cheaply replaced.

In many places, however, open sluice-boxes were not suitable as the material had to be conveyed under pressure. In such cases wood-stave pipe, like the hydraulic giants, also a Western product, was used almost exclusively in this earlier work, although of later years steel pipe has come into use. The diameter of such pipe varies, of course, but is usually from 18 to 24 in. As this plain wood pipe wore out with great rapidity, a special pipe, Fig. 8, was designed by Mr. Hopkirk, which made provision for an invert lining of replaceable wooden blocks. These blocks greatly lengthened the life of the pipe.

Water Supply.—The water supply was derived from several sources. On the Jackson Street and Dearborn Street work surplus water from the Cedar River water supply system of the city was turned into an abandoned reservoir with a capacity of about 4 000 000 gal., situated about 1 mile from the work. From the reservoir this water was fed to the giants through steel and wood stave pipe. From 6 000 000 to 10 000 000 gal. per day were thus supplied at a charge of $15 per 1 000 000 gal. This, however, was not sufficient. A pumping plant was constructed on Elliott Bay, with a capacity of 12 000 000 gal. per day, consisting of four 10-in., 5-stage pumps direct-connected to two 650-h.p. motors. As the tide has a range of 16 ft., the pumps were set somewhat below extreme high tide, and provision was made for a water-tight floor and wall. The discharge was made through 24-in. wood stave pipe having staves 1⅝ in. thick and bound with No. 1 wire spaced $\frac{7}{16}$ in.

Fig. 5.—View of Old Denny Hotel, Seattle, Wash., and Vicinity.

Fig. 6.—Denny Hotel Partly Demolished. New Building on Completed Part of Regrade.

Fig. 7.—View of Regrading Operations on Denny Hill.

Fig. 8.—Section of New Spoil Pipe, Regrading Operations, Seattle, Wash.

Fig. 9.—Jackson Street Regrade, Seattle, Wash., Showing Four Giants Operating in Clay Overlaid by Hardpan or Glacial Till.

On the Denny Hill work, city water was not available. The supply was from two sources. On the water-front a 4-stage pump with a 850-h.p. motor delivered 5 000 000 gal. per day. A second plant of three units was constructed on Lake Union about 1 mile from the work. Two units consisted of two 10-in., 4-stage turbines each, with a 650-h.p. motor. The other unit was a 15-in., 4-stage pump, with a 650-h.p. motor. The total capacity was 12 000 000 gal. per day. Here, also, wood stave pipe conveyed the water to the giants.

The quantity of spoil carried by the water varied within wide limits, depending on the gradients of the discharge pipes and the character of the material. On Jackson Street the average was 6.75% of the volume of water. With a water supply of 20 000 000 gal. per day, this would mean 10 000 cu. yd. of material moved. A large allowance, however, on such work must be made for changing pipe lines, moving giants, clogging of discharge pipes, and all the innumerable petty delays incident to such work. On Jackson Street the quantity moved averaged about 4 000 cu. yd. per calendar day.

Disposal of Spoil.—In the Jackson Street regrade all the material was used to fill in the adjacent tide lands. The grades of some of this area were raised about 40 ft. In this, as in the Denny Hill project, provision was made in the specifiations for the removal of earth from private property at the same price as that paid by the City, the contractor being required to accept a lien on the property payable in ten annual installments, as in the case of the assessment for the street work. This provision applied also to the fills. The result was a substantially unanimous acceptance of this provision by the property owners, there being, however, a few exceptions.

In the Denny Hill District a large part of the spoil was wasted in the deep water of Elliott Bay about ½ mile from the work. A part, however, was used to fill in the valley lying east of Denny Hill. Grades in this valley were raised as much as 25 ft., resulting not only in a fine area for growth of business which is now coming into its own, but also in providing access by easy grades to the Broadway-Pike Street area, which has since developed into the principal motor-vehicle district. This by-product of the removal of the Denny Hill is proving to be even more valuable as affording scope for growth than the original project itself, as the largest development of Seattle is in a general northeastward direction and this valley lies almost directly along the axis of this movement. Another reason is that the Denny Hill District has been hampered in attaining the most complete benefit from its heroic work because the streets were originally laid out parallel with the salt-water front. This was perfectly natural for the pioneers to do, as they could not, at that time, visualize a removal of this hill, and they failed to grasp the northeastward trend which business later would take. Consequently, they extended this platting as determined by the direction of the salt-water shore-line up and over Denny Hill and even across a part of the valley. The result was that these streets diverge about 45° from their proper direction. A few streets paralleling the shore line and the remainder paralleling the section lines would have been almost ideal in its conformity to present necessities, for the valley lies almost due north and south. This failure to perceive the future development, therefore, has given rise to several perplexing and difficult street rectification problems which are vexing the City Planning Commission and the City Council.

A part of the excavation was carried on by steam shovel and dump cars. Much material was conveyed in this way to sluice-boxes, whence it was washed down to the Bay. Other parts were used to fill in the valley streets as outlined. In the Jackson Street District the low ground was brought up to basement level by hydraulicking (Fig. 9), and the street fills brought up to grade by the shear-board method, shown on Fig. 10, the slopes being on private property. This method, which was specially devised to meet the conditions of this work, consisted of driving stakes against which were placed a couple of 1-in. boards. These stakes were braced to the step below. The steps were, say, 1½ ft. high and 2 ft. wide. The earth was then sluiced in nearly to the top of the boards when another step was made, and so on to the top. The steps varied somewhat in height and width, depending on conditions. Much of the lumber used in these steps could be used over again, and it proved to be a cheap and efficient method of building up the fills. In a few cases wooden pile bulkheads were constructed.

On Third, Fourth, and Fifth Avenues, between Yesler Way and Pike Street, in the central business district, all excavation was carried on by steam shovel and cars. This area, because of the character of the adjoining buildings, did not permit the use of the sluicing method. Crossing this district were two cable street-car lines, affording access to important residence districts. When the excavation of adjoining areas had proceeded sufficiently, these cable roads were blocked up on timber cribwork. After the excavations had been completed, they were lowered by degrees during the night. In this way traffic was maintained almost continuously. Electric street-car traffic on the north and south streets was shifted from one street to another and handled by various other expedients. The carrying on of this work in these streets greatly inconvenienced the stores and business houses. Although every possible aid was extended to the owners by the City authorities, nevertheless, there must have been considerable loss in many cases. This was a part of the price paid for the reshaping of these streets. In the Denny Hill and Jackson Street Districts, however, the cuts were so great that the buildings were wrecked, thus leaving the area entirely free for the sluicing operations. The most conspicuous example of this razing of buildings was the Denny Hotel, a brick structure of six or seven stories.

The total quantity of earth removed on this regrading work was approximately 14 000 000 cu. yd. A part of Denny Hill was not included in the original work, but provision is now (1926) being made for the full completion of this project. A great deal of such work has been done since by the hydraulic method, but it has not possessed the magnitude and spectacular features in depth of cut and volume of material moved, of the Denny Hill, Jackson Street, and Dearborn Street projects.

FIG. 10.—VIEW SHOWING SHEAR-BOARD METHOD OF CONSTRUCTING EMBANKMENTS.

FIG. 11.—VIEW SHOWING COMPACTED GRAVEL USED IN PORTLAND, ORE., FOR CONSTRUCTION OF HIGH EMBANKMENTS BY HYDRAULIC PROCESS.

Building Embankments by Hydraulic Process

An interesting development of the art of hydraulic sluicing is the construction of embankments which are entirely free from subsequent settlement. Fills have been made in Portland, Ore., 40 to 50 ft. deep, on which houses were built shortly after the fills were finished. These houses showed no more effects from settlement than those built on original ground. The University of Washington Stadium was built by the same method. The construction of the concrete work followed immediately on the completion of the fill, and no cracking due to settlement has occurred.

For the successful use of this method, suitable material must be available. Earth containing a large percentage of clay cannot be used successfully. The process reverses the theory of hydraulic construction of dams which retains the fines in a central pool, and allows these fines to run off. The water must be kept moving at the correct velocity to prevent deposition of the fines while it drops the coarser material. Fig. 11 is a view of compacted gravel banks, used in Portland, Ore., for the construction of high embankments. Such embankments drain very rapidly and form extremely compact and solid fills. The process is somewhat similar to the construction of the slopes of the hydraulic-fill dam.

It will be noted that the dreams of the original pioneer settlers for a great city, which they visualized, perhaps, somewhat hazily and indistinctly, required for their initial realization the development of pioneer engineering methods. Hydraulic sluicing, the hydraulic giant, wood-stave water pipe, wood-stave pipe lined with blocks for carrying spoil, and the shear-board method of building up embankments, are all the product of Western conditions.

DISCUSSION

Charles Evan Fowler,* M. Am. Soc. C. E. (by letter).—The regrading of Seattle, as carried out largely under R. H. Thomson, M. Am. Soc. C. E., and the author, approached in magnitude of the material to be handled, the digging of the Panama Canal, and in some respects the difficulties were much greater. The first extensive regrading was done by steam shovels on Denny Hill near the old Washington Hotel, the material being hauled in dump cars, down the principal business streets, to the tide flats for making fill. The writer operated two steam shovels in this general district, one at the Washington Hotel, and one on the old University grounds on Fourth Avenue. The material was sold to the Great Northern Railway for tide-flat filling.

The steam shovels were served by horse-drawn, $2\frac{1}{2}$-yd. dump wagons, from 24 to 30 for each shovel, and the dirt was hauled about $\frac{1}{2}$ mile to the north end of the Great Northern Railway Tunnel, where it was chuted into railway dump cars about 30 ft. below, and hauled in trains to the final place of deposit, south of the Great Northern Station. The selling price was 7 cents per cu. yd., which, added to the excavation price, made the total receipts about 20 cents per cu. yd., or a very profitable figure for the pre-war period.

The dumping grounds were just south of the territory and comprised several hundred of the 1 200 acres of the Seattle tide flats, which were brought to grade at 2 ft. above extreme high tide. This filling was done by the writer with two 20-in. hydraulic dredges, and the 12 000 000 cu. yd. so placed, formed an essential part of the regrade work of Seattle, making usable the land from the foot of Queen Anne Hill to the southern end of Elliott Bay. The portion of the tide flats near the Jackson Street regrade was filled with the dirt sluiced down in doing this work. This, together with the material removed from the Denny Hill regrade, constitutes the greatest sluicing operation ever carried out, and it redounds to the credit of those who did the work, as well as to the City of Seattle, the possibilities of which were dependent on the great works described.

Not less notable in the making of the city that had the courage to regrade its hills, fill in its tide flats, and build its port, was the creation of the Park System. This work was planned and begun while the writer was a member and, part of the time, President of the Park Board. Parkways, now about 60 miles in length, connect the city parks proper and represent a form of regrading of the hills of the city so as to make the beautiful drives which wind about these hills and through much of the primeval forest preserved for the pleasure of future generations. This system is certainly a wonderful creation of man and is the result of allowing full play to the imagination and creative energy of the engineer. Hundreds of thousands will thank the imagination and tireless energy of Mr. Thomson who for more than a score of years was City Engineer and the creator of the future of the city.

* Cons. Engr., New York, N. Y.

AMERICAN SOCIETY OF CIVIL ENGINEERS

INSTITUTED 1852

TRANSACTIONS

This Society is not responsible for any statement made or opinion expressed in its publications.

Paper No. 1670

RE-ARRANGEMENT OF A BUSINESS DISTRICT: CHANGES IN RECENT YEARS IN PITTSBURGH, PENNSYLVANIA*

By Nathan Schein,† M. Am. Soc. C. E.

With Discussion by Messrs. Edwin K. Morse and Francis J. Mulvihill.

Incorporated as a city since 1816, and situated at the confluence of the Allegheny and Monongahela Rivers, uniting to form the Ohio, Pittsburgh, Pa., is one of the greatest industrial, financial, and distributing centers. The city proper, which has an area of 46.93 sq. miles, is divided by the rivers into three principal sections. The largest and most populous section known as "Peninsular Pittsburgh", or the "Old" City, occupies the territory between the Monongahela and Allegheny Rivers, and includes the down-town or business district. The territory south of the Ohio and Monongahela Rivers is known as the South Side, and that north of the Ohio and Allegheny Rivers, formerly the City of Allegheny, as the North Side.

The city ranks eighth in population, but the area included within a 10-mile radius and including that known as the Pittsburgh District, ranks fifth among the metropolitan districts of the United States. The down-town, or the business, section is substantially that part of the city known as the Point District, and is bounded by the two rivers and by Grant Street on the east.

The street plan in this district consists of a low-level section in which three main streets, Duquesne Way, Penn Avenue, and Liberty Avenue, are laid out parallel to the Allegheny River, with intersecting streets at right angles. To the east of Liberty Avenue, the streets and avenues are parallel to the Monongahela River, with Market, Wood, Smithfield, and Grant Streets intersecting at right angles.

The basic problem in this section is that of means of transportation, especially the problem of the street plan. Prior to 1904, this district consisted

* Presented at the meeting of the City Planning Division, Seattle, Wash., July 15, 1926.

† Div. Engr., Dept. of Public Works, Pittsburgh, Pa.

of narrow streets and ways or alleys. There was no street or avenue wider than 60 ft. except Liberty Avenue of 80 ft. (referred to subsequently), and most of them were 40 ft. wide; all the alleys or ways were 20 ft. wide.

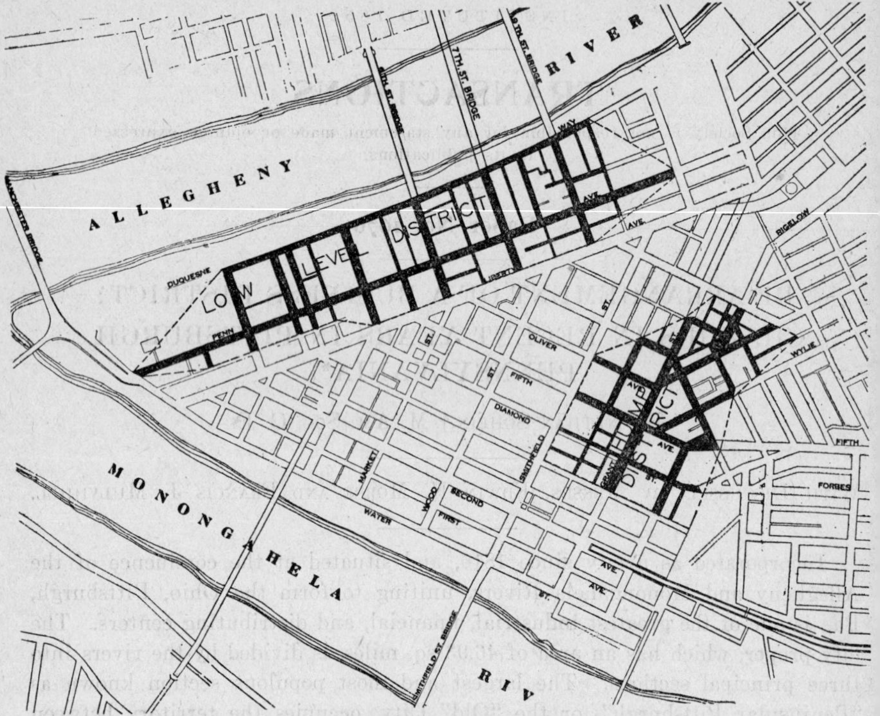

FIG. 1.—LOW-LEVEL DISTRICT, PITTSBURGH, PA., ALONG THE ALLEGHENY RIVER, WHICH WAS RAISED ABOVE FLOOD LEVEL. HUMP DISTRICT, ABOVE SMITHFIELD STREET, WHICH WAS REDUCED IN GRADE.

In 1904, the City realized the need of more street area in the down-town section and widened Diamond Street to 50 ft. from Smithfield Street to East Diamond Street, and, at the same time, Oliver Avenue was widened to 44 ft. from Smithfield Street to Liberty Avenue. In 1905, the Pennsylvania Railroad Company removed its tracks from Liberty Avenue which then became the first street of this city with a free roadway of 48 ft. between curbs. These were the only improvements that had been made in the re-arrangement of the streets in this district and the problem of transportation began to be seriously felt.

The various civic and trade organizations as well as the Department of Public Works began to study this problem. In 1910, Mr. Frederick Law Olmsted, in a report entitled "Pittsburgh, Main Thoroughfares and Down-Town District", made recommendations for the general improvement of the city, and called attention to the importance of proper and adequate city planning. This study resulted in the creation of the City Planning Department in 1911, which gives the City the power to bring about proper planning and provided a body for its administration.

In 1911, a broad and comprehensive program of street improvements was started. These projects included the improvement of main thoroughfares, particularly those leading from the business district to outlying sections; opening of new highways; elimination of grade crossings; raising of low-level areas; reduction of grades; and widening of business thoroughfares. The two methods of city planning carried out were the reduction of grade in the "Hump" District and the raising of the low-level districts above flood stage. The location of these districts is shown in Fig. 1.

Reduction of Grade in the Hump District

The improvement of streets in what is known as the "Hump" District, completed in 1913, involved the lowering of grades in an area of about 40 acres in the down-town business district, the opening of a new thoroughfare, and the widening of a number of streets. The necessity for this work arose from the fact that the grades of Fifth, Oliver, and Sixth Avenues, over which the greater part of the east-going traffic passes, were very steep. The traffic congestion on Fifth and Sixth Avenues, and the necessity for providing an outlet for Grant (now Bigelow) Boulevard, demanded the opening of an additional parallel route which was accomplished by widening Oliver Avenue. Other street widenings for the accommodation of through traffic and to meet local requirements were also made.

Twice before the grade of Fifth Avenue had been reduced, and as the last improvement had been long agitated and discussed, it was necessary to dispose of the question for all time, so as to permit property owners to develop the district with assurance of permanence of conditions.

The greater part of the area in question lies between Sixth and Fourth Avenues, and between Smithfield and Ross Streets, including Sixth, Oliver, and Fifth Avenues, and Diamond Street running east and west, and Cherry Way, Smithfield, Grant, and Ross Streets running north and south. The improvement was carried eastward as far as the intersection of Sixth and Fifth Avenues, and northward so as to afford a connection with Grant Boulevard, involving in this district Webster and Wylie Avenues, Strawberry Way, and the extension of Grant Boulevard. Oliver Avenue, Cherry Way, Diamond Street, and Fifth Avenue between Grant Street and Sixth Avenue were widened. The maximum cut of 16 ft. was at the intersection of Fifth and Wylie Avenues. The cut at Fifth Avenue and Grant Street was 14 ft., and this improvement is sometimes referred to as the 14-ft. "Hump Cut". As a result of the improvement, the grade of Fifth Avenue was reduced from 7.6 to 4.87% between Grant and Smithfield Streets, and the grades of the other streets in the district were reduced in proportion. Fig. 2 shows the new and old grades of Fifth Avenue between Smithfield and Grant Streets.

The city bore the physical cost of the work, including the grading, reconstructing the entire sewerage system, relaying of water lines, constructing new pavements and sidewalks, tearing down buildings where the street lines had been changed, and similar work. Public service corporations at their own expense relaid street railway tracks, electric conduits, and gas lines. At the same time these companies generally enlarged their facilities. The property owners attended to the shoring, underpinning, and protection of their buildings, and all the resulting reconstruction, alteration, and demolition work. Many of the older buildings were torn down, but a considerable number were lowered or additional stories provided below the former ground floor.

The city secured waivers of damage from nearly 80% of the property owners affected in so far as these related to the reduction of grade. The property owners, therefore, to a great extent defrayed the cost of the alteration and adjustment of their properties. The city, however, recompensed property owners for the net damages incurred due to widening of streets, this amount being materially reduced owing to the benefits accruing.

The total cost of the improvement amounted to $2 364 673, itemized as follows:

Cost of physical work—grading, regrading, paving, repaving, etc., Fifth Avenue, Diamond Street, and adjacent streets...	$732 019	
Cost of physical work—lowering water lines.	30 981	
Cost of alterations in Fire and Police Wiring System	13 771	
Cost of alterations to Public Safety Building	1 421	
Cost of repaving Sixth Avenue..........	2 772	$780 964
Damage awards on account of above improvements		499 059
Damage awards on account of widening:		
Fifth Avenue	$259 830	
Cherry Way	202 157	
Oliver Avenue	308 253	
Strawberry Way	130 403	
Grant Boulevard	315 404	1 216 047
Engineering and incidental expense...............		34 533
Total cost		$2 530 603
Benefits assessed by viewers:		
Widening Fifth Avenue...........	$595	
" Cherry Way	48 460	
" Oliver Avenue	92 875	
" Strawberry Way	14 000	
" Grant Boulevard	10 000	165 930
Net cost to City....................................		$2 364 673

In addition, the expense borne by the Public Service Corporations and by property owners undoubtedly reached a very high figure.

The principal items of work and the unit prices were as follows:

Excavation, 153 900 cu. yd..............................	@ $3.00
Block stone pavement, 13 800 sq. yd..................	@ 3.75
Creosoted wood block pavement, 11 000 sq. yd.........	@ 4.00
Vitrified brick pavement, 4 100 sq. yd................	@ 3.00
Protected concrete curb, 17 200 lin. ft................	@ 1.00
Concrete sidewalks, 149 700 sq. ft.......................	@ 0.20
Lumber in temporary structures 27.3 M. ft. B. M......	@ 80.00

FIG. 2.—HUMP DISTRICT, PITTSBURGH, PA., VIEW OF FIFTH AVENUE, SHOWING NEW AND OLD GRADES.

FIG. 3.—HUMP DISTRICT, PITTSBURGH, PA., FIFTH AVENUE FROM SMITHFIELD STREET TO GRANT STREET.

FIG. 4.—VIEW SHOWING FLOOD OF MARCH 28, 1913, PITTSBURGH, PA., AT 30.4-FOOT STAGE, DUQUESNE WAY AND SEVENTH STREET, WEST.

FIG. 5.—PITTSBURGH, PA., VIEW OF SECOND AVENUE WEST FROM GRANT STREET.

Work was begun April 5, 1912, and finished in November, 1913. The work was arranged so as to permit of the maintenance of traffic; work on Fifth, Oliver, and Webster Avenues was first completed, through traffic being carried on Sixth Avenue and Diamond Street. Pedestrian traffic was maintained by the erection of temporary boardwalks supported on trestles, and the public utilities were supplied by lines laid generally on the surface of the ground, as shown on Fig. 3.

Since the completion of the improvement, many costly structures have been erected within this area, among which are the William Penn Hotel, City-County Building, Union Arcade, Bell Telephone Company, Philadelphia Company, Harry Davis Theater, *Gazette-Times* Building, and others. The taxable valuation of properties in this district has greatly increased due in large measure to the erection of buildings on sites formerly vacant, or occupied by small structures. The increase in the taxation receipts for the district, assignable in a large measure to this improvement, has covered the cost and expenses borne by the City. In 1914, the Second Ward in which this district lies had an assessed valuation, for taxable purposes, of $183 398 440 and, in 1924, it was $221 804 410, a gain of about 21 per cent.

Raising of Flood District

One of the problems with which the City of Pittsburgh has had to contend, and which has been remedied to a great extent, has been the periodic flooding of the low-level business, residential, and industrial territory along the rivers, causing serious and extensive damage to property, unsanitary conditions, and the suspension of business and traffic. River control and flood prevention have been extensively studied and reported on by the Flood Commission of Pittsburgh. This Commission, in ascertaining the extent of flood damages to the city, in a careful examination of three floods which occurred within a year, from March 15, 1907, to March 30, 1908, found direct losses within the city to be as follows:

Damage to buildings, equipment, and machinery...	$782 400
Damage to materials..........................	1 698 900
Loss to employers by supension of business.......	1 974 200
Loss to employees due to shutdown.............	1 308 300
Expense of cleaning up.......................	547 400
Charities dispensed and funds for prevention of disease	27 800
Fires uncontrolled through inaccessibility or lack of water pressure.................................	175 000
Total	$6 514 000

It was found that the loss ranges as follows:

For the flood of 27.3 ft..........................	$414 700
" " " " 30.7 "........................	839 800
" " " " 35.5 "........................	5 259 500

The general condition of streets in the down-town, low-level district in 1913, during a flood stage of 30.4 ft., is shown on Fig. 4; and the enormous damage to property for floods of greater height can be easily surmised.

Since 1908, there have been fifteen floods recorded over the 25-ft. stage, and twenty-six times the Ohio River has passed the danger line of 22 ft.

The lower part of the down-town business section comprising an area of 60 acres, was raised to an elevation of 35 ft. and more, in order to avert this periodic flooding of streets. This re-grading of the low-level business district was started on April 28, and completed on December 1, 1915. The cost of the work, exclusive of the cost to the various utility corporations, was $162 000. The net damage to property owners along the improvement amounted to $165 000. The work was arranged to permit the maintenance of traffic and business. The property owners attended to the alteration and raising of their buildings to the new grades.

Having attended to the regrading of its business area, immediately following the World War, the City began again to pay attention to the congestion of traffic in the down-town section. On July 8, 1919, a $20 000 000 bond issue was approved, and, as a result, the down-town section was materially re-arranged and the city in general improved. New avenues of traffic were provided; dangerous grade intersections eliminated; the waterworks systems extended and improved; new highway bridges were constructed and some present bridges reconstructed; and provisions made for the improvement of parks and recreation facilities; extensions to the drainage system; and improvements for public health, welfare, safety, and charity services. Last, but not least, a sum of $6 000 000 was favorably voted for a start of subway construction in the down-town section.

The streets in the down-town section were materially re-arranged. Second Avenue from Grant Street to Liberty Avenue, was widened from 40 ft. to 80 ft., with a roadway width of 56 ft., sufficient for six lines of traffic, as shown on Fig. 5. Ferry Street from Water Street to Liberty Avenue, was widened from 40 to 70 ft. Diamond Street from Smithfield Street to Grant Street was widened from 25 to 54.5 ft., and Diamond Street from Ferry Street to Market Place was widened from 50 to 70 ft.

The widenings in the down-town section were very costly. The physical work in widening Second Avenue cost $177 733, and the net damages assessed against the City amounted to $1 851 460, making a net total cost to the City of $2 029 193.

The cost of the physical work on Ferry Street was $62 997, and the net damages assessed against the City were $666 480, making a total cost to the City of $729 479. The cost of the physical work on Diamond Street between Smithfield Street and Grant Street, only one block long, was $14 517, and the net damages assessed against the City were $391 795, making a total cost to the City of $406 312. On account of the valuation of property in the congested business section, it is quite evident that the cost of future widenings of streets therein will be prohibitive.

The cost in 1920 per square foot of net assessment against the City for widening Second Avenue was $45, for Ferry Street, $30, and for Diamond Street, $82 per sq. ft. The more important widenings of streets in the down-town business section are shown on Fig. 6. Diamond Street, from Liberty Avenue to Ross Street, was widened in sections at three different times, and, as a result, there is now a zigzag alignment of street.

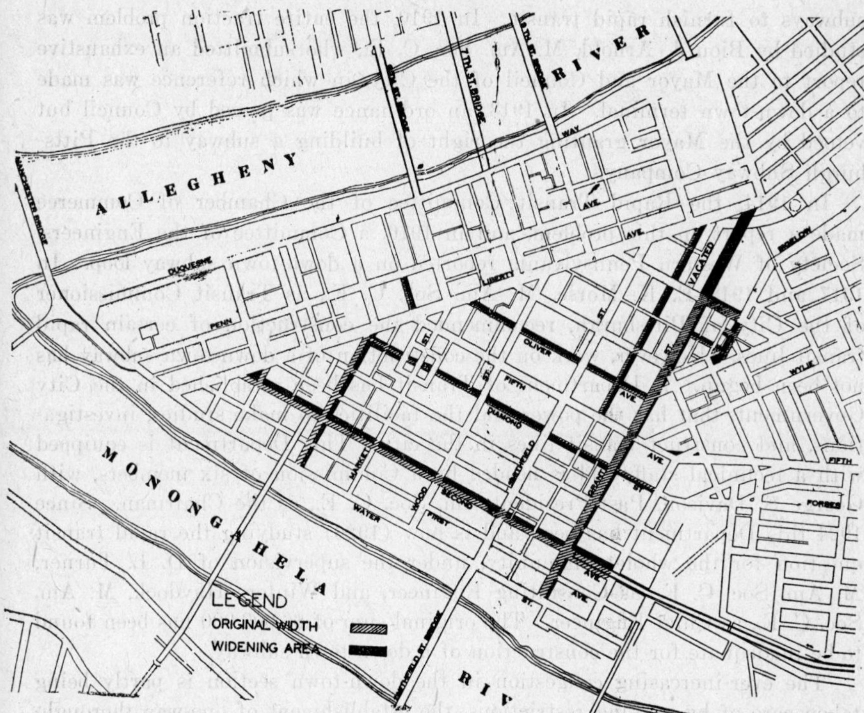

FIG. 6.—MAIN STREETS WHICH WERE WIDENED IN DOWN-TOWN BUSINESS SECTION OF PITTSBURGH, PA. DIAMOND STREET WHICH WAS WIDENED AT THREE DIFFERENT TIMES, IS NOW A ZIGZAG THOROUGHFARE AS TO ALIGNMENT.

More than any other single improvement, the new Boulevard of the Allies, caused the greatest re-arrangement of the street plan in this district. The Boulevard starts at Grant Street and Second Avenue, and extends eastward along the hillside to Bluff Street, by an elevated structure of easy grade. This Boulevard is a main thoroughfare to the down-town section from the east. It is one of the through routes of the city and has been chosen as a part of the Lincoln Highway. Its location high on the hillside overlooking the Monongahela River, as shown on Fig. 7, furnishes a picturesque driveway of a character distinctive of the rugged topography of the city. This thoroughfare which cost \$2 600 000, was named Boulevard of the Allies as a memorial to the World War, and bronze tablets on columns at the entrance, as shown on Fig. 8, serve in commemoration of that event.

The item of a down-town subway at an estimated cost of \$6 000 000 was the largest and the most important improvement proposed affecting the welfare and development of practically the entire community, especially as it opened up again the entire question of transit facilities for the City of Pittsburgh. The proposition itself was not even then new, and had been considered by both the City and by private interests. As early as 1906, the subway project was under consideration by the City Council, when the Pittsburgh Subway Company was seeking a franchise for the building of subways to furnish rapid transit. In 1910, the entire traction problem was studied by Bion J. Arnold, M. Am. Soc. C. E., who submitted an exhaustive report to the Mayor and Council of the City, in which reference was made to a down-town terminal. In 1913, an ordinance was passed by Council but vetoed by the Mayor granting the right of building a subway to the Pittsburgh Subway Company.

In 1914, the Rapid Transit Committee of the Chamber of Commerce made a report on this problem, and in 1916, a Committee of the Engineers' Society of Western Pennsylvania reported on a down-town subway loop. In 1917 and 1918 E. K. Morse, M. Am. Soc. C. E., as Transit Commissioner of the City of Pittsburgh, recommended the construction of certain rapid transit lines. However, work on the construction of a down-town subway has not been begun. A Department of Transit has been established in the City Government, that has the power and the facilities to make studies, investigations, and construct transit lines in the city. This Department is equipped with a technical staff, and is headed by a Commission of six members, with George S. Davison, Past-President Am. Soc. C. E., as the Chairman. Since 1924 this Department has been and is now (1926) studying the rapid transit question for the whole community, under the supervision of D. L. Turner, M. Am. Soc. C. E., as Consulting Engineer, and Winters Haydock, M. Am. Soc. C. E., as Chief Engineer. The original sum of $6 000 000 has been found to be inadequate for the construction of a down-town subway.

The ever-increasing congestion in the down-town section is partly being taken care of by parking restrictions, the establishment of one-way thoroughfares, and the re-routing of street cars. Most of the streets in this district are one-way thoroughfares, and the street cars are making use of short loops in the business district.

The City of Pittsburgh will again resume improvements to its public works, for in May, 1926, the people voted favorably for a bond issue of $19 902 000 to be expended for improvements to the various facilities and activities of the city. A summary of the proposed improvements is as follows:

For maintenance of service of existing facilities of water supply, bridges, sewerage, and streets........	$7 950 000
For equipment and buildings for Fire and Police Departments to provide adequate protection.........	600 000
For the care of the City's poor, insane, and sick......	2 750 000
For adding to the inadequate facilities of playgrounds.	750 000
For street improvements in widening and improvement of existing main thoroughfares to remedy traffic congestion and provide necessary arterial streets....	7 852 000
Total	$19 902 000

Fig. 7.—Boulevard of the Allies, Pittsburgh, Pa., Viaduct No. 1, View East of East End from Roe Building.

Fig. 8.—Boulevard of the Allies, West Entrance, View East, Pittsburgh, Pa.

Under this new bond issue Grant Street from Water Street to Seventh Avenue, will be widened 20 ft. on the easterly side, making an 80-ft. street. The total estimated cost of this improvement is $1 620 000, of which the physical work will cost about $90 000.

The damage estimated to be assessed against the City for this 20-ft. strip of property is $1 530 000, or $100 per sq. ft. of ground taken. Grant Street may be said to be the key street to the down-town section of the city.

The problem of transportation in the down-town section has brought forth the study of the development of the wharves of the city. A sum of $50 000 has been appropriated by Council for the payment of:

"Costs and expenses of making surveys, investigations, estimates, and plans for the improvement for public uses and purposes of the river-fronts of the Allegheny, Monongahela, and Ohio Rivers within the City of Pittsburgh, for providing adequate and improved facilities and terminals for all forms of river traffic and for such changes and improvements in the street, sewerage and drainage systems of the City, and of properties affected thereby, as may be necessary to carry out the foregoing improvements and for such other changes, improvements, and measures as may be deemed necessary therefor or desirable in connection therewith."

This study is under way in both the Department of Public Works and the Department of City Planning, and it is expected that, as a result, the City will be again asked to vote on the bond issue to make possible the improvement of the wharves in the down-town section.

Citizens Committee on City Planning

In 1918, the Citizens Committee on City Plan, an unofficial body of private citizens, was organized with the object of producing a "Pittsburgh Plan". This Committee has no political connection and no partisan purposes. It planned to give to the city, an orderly, scientific, and comprehensive program of city building. It contributed an exhaustive report in six parts: Part 1, published in 1920, dealt with the study of Pittsburgh playgrounds; Part 2, published in 1921, dealt with the Major Street Plan of Pittsburgh; Part 3, published in 1923, dealt with the transit question; Part 4, published in 1923, dealt with the Pittsburgh parks; Part 5, published in October, 1923, dealt with the railroads of the Pittsburgh District; and Part 6, published also in October, 1923, dealt with the problem of water transportation.

The City Planning Commission, with Morris Knowles, M. Am. Soc. C. E., as its Chairman, supplemented the report of the Major Street Plan as proposed by the Citizens Committee on City Plan, with a report on the Inter-District Traffic Circuit, issued in March, 1926. This report deals with the planning and estimate of the cost of the re-arrangement of the business district, and includes those thoroughfares, bridges, and other improvements that are, individually, integral parts of a so-called "Triangle By-Pass System", improvements of parts of tributary major radial streets, and modifications of minor streets immediately related to and affected by the changes proposed. The aggregate cost of these improvements will be more than $50 000 000.

In conclusion, it may be stated that the re-arrangement of a business district, such as that of the "Golden Triangle in Pittsburgh", is a basic problem of means of transportation, especially of the street plan.

The street plan requires careful consideration not only by the municipal authorities, but also by the various civic and trade organizations, citizens committees, and planning bodies, and includes problems of river and rail transportation, flooding of rivers, terminals, rapid transit, adjustment of grades, regulation of traffic, and zoning laws.

DISCUSSION

EDWIN K. MORSE,* M. AM. SOC. C. E. (by letter).—When it is realized that the area of the central business district of Pittsburgh is only 218 acres; that Chicago contains 600 acres within "the Loop"; Philadelphia, 1 400 acres; Boston, 1 900 acres; and New York City, to 42d Street, 4 000 acres, the comparison impresses one with the intensity of the Pittsburgh business man's activity, because in no equal area in the civilized world is the same volume of business so successfully transacted. The Flood Commission of Pittsburgh has presented comprehensive plans for wharf and river improvements as prepared by its Board of Engineers in April, 1925, which, if approved by the U. S. Army Engineers and carried out by the City, will add more toward maintaining Pittsburgh's supremacy than any other local construction.

By deepening the channels of the Allegheny and Monongahela Rivers to a uniform depth of 16 ft., and straightening their shore lines, it will reclaim about 57 acres of what is now a sloping wharf of little value to a small shipping interest, costing practically nothing to the City.

The plans contemplate modern slips for river and rail transportation. They specify walls around the city and along the North Side to a level above the highest known flood. The surface and basements of more than 40% of the 218 acres in the central business district were damaged during the disastrous flood of March 15, 1907.

The contemplated construction would bring about the rebuilding of all the flooded districts in the city, and in ten years would completely repay the City by increased taxation of the section benefited. The 57 acres would be turned over to the Planning Commission of the City of Pittsburgh for comprehensive study. A boulevard, 80 to 100 ft. wide and more than 2 miles long, with no streets crossing it, could then be built along the banks of the Allegheny and Monongahela Rivers. Parking space for thousands of automobiles would be provided in a location convenient to the business sections, and when the time comes, a free right of way for a double-deck street, involving no consequential damages, would be awaiting posterity.

The average yearly loss to Pittsburgh, caused by floods, is estimated at $2 000 000. This money loss could be greatly reduced if the Flood Commission's plans were adopted. If that Commission's plans for the improvement of the Allegheny, Monongahela, and Ohio Rivers, within the city limits, had been fulfilled as recommended, the level of the disastrous flood of March 15, 1907, would have been reduced at least 10 ft. and, instead of nearly $6 000 000, the City would have lost less than the present annual cost of $2 000 000. With provision for intercepting sewers, back-fill, re-grading of streets, and paving complete, the engineers of the Flood Commission estimate the cost of building the walls around the city and along the North Side at $6 000 000.

The Mayor and Council of Pittsburgh have authorized the Department of Public Works to report on the plans submitted by the Commission and submit plans for river terminals. In connection with this study, the City has just

* Pittsburgh, Pa.

completed soundings in the Allegheny and Monongahela Rivers within municipal limits.

The U. S. Government expects to complete the locks and dams on the Ohio River from Pittsburgh to Cairo, Ill., a distance of 967 miles. That will provide an all-year river transportation. Pittsburgh, strategically located for river and rail transportation, has no river terminals. The City's study contemplates making Pittsburgh the greatest inland river terminal in the United States except New Orleans, La., which is ocean and river combined. The City will have to condemn whole sections of improved property along the riverfront so as to provide adequate terminals for slips handling river tonnage and rail and river shipments. In addition to the moderately equipped docks and slips, locations are being considered for large basins in which to store floating crafts and arrange transshipment of barges between down-river and up-river ports.

The mills, factories, mines, railroads, etc., that direct traffic to the rivers, have been modernized to the limit. Nothing has been done by the City to modernize the rivers and provide river terminals. Within recent years, the big steel industries have built river steamboats and steel barges that are now sending thousands of tons of structural steel and steel products down the Ohio and the Mississippi Rivers as far as New Orleans. The Inland Waterways Corporation is operating successfully on the Mississippi and Warriors Rivers. It is hoped and believed that Pittsburgh will build modern river terminals, thereby profiting by the great tonnage received and dispatched.

Francis J. Mulvihill,* Assoc. M. Am. Soc. C. E. (by letter).—The paper by Mr. Schein is an important and direct contribution to the literature of city planning accomplishment. Because there are so few histories and progress reports of this art, the recorded experience at Pittsburgh, Pa., may suggest and stimulate additional response from "about five hundred cities and town"† in the United States engaged in city planning. The whole movement needs such accounts of accomplishment. The theory is fairly well established, but, in addition to knowing "how to do", "doing it" is important; so that practical demonstration lends impetus and acceleration to wise planning. Demonstration, too, will prove and serve to answer the question, "City planning is of what use?" The experience recorded by the author concerning the basic problem of transportation and circulation dependent on (*a*) the street plan of the Pittsburgh Business District; (*b*) the engineering data of costs and materials; and (*c*) the overcoming of physical obstacles by demonstration of engineering skill, all suggest some consideration or comment. That which follows is not critical, but is offered for the purpose of emphasis and expansion. The paper suggests relevant considerations: First, city planning procedure and accomplishment in Pittsburgh; and, second, the business district of Pittsburgh in the future.

City Planning Procedure and Accomplishment.—In general, the procedure followed and the accomplishment acquired are good. There are perhaps a

* Landscape Archt.; Town and City Planner, Germantown, Philadelphia, Pa.

† "Annual Survey of City and Regional Planning in the United States, 1926," by Theodore Kimball Hubbard, Annual Survey Number, *City Planning* (quarterly), April, 1927.

half dozen municipalities in the United States where substantial progress is being made, both in preliminary studies and actual accomplishment. Mistakes and inadequate planning cause great financial loss, entailing millions; but the annual budget of approximately $100 000 for the Department of City Planning of Pittsburgh is ungrudgingly provided by an appropriation ordinance of the City Council. No other city grants as much. In a sense it is just an insurance premium to prevent great loss. What is done now in public works is better done than it was a few years ago, and the budget amount is likely to increase. An historic background is a requisite for determining the rate of progress. Pittsburgh, like other cities, grew haphazardly and by chance from an unhappy aggregate of accidents in a series. Problems developed, consequently, and when they became serious, it was expedient to solve them. Prior to 1904 there was no comprehensive planning in Pittsburgh. Mr. Olmsted's report entitled "Pittsburgh, Main Thoroughfares and Down-Town District", in 1910, was among the first on city planning as it is understood to-day. It was only the year before, in Washington, D. C., that a meeting, the forerunner of the existing National Conference on City Planning, was held. The comprehensive Olmsted report stressed the importance of proper and adequate city planning. In 1911, the Pennsylvania Legislature passed the Enabling Act and the Department of City Planning of the City of Pittsburgh was created. The subsequent street improvements incorporated, almost in detail, the general Olmsted recommendations and the Department of City Planning established "follow-up". General studies were made by the City Planning Department for the relief of traffic congestion. In 1918, Diamond and Ferry Streets and Second Avenue were widened, and the Boulevard of the Allies was constructed. The Department of Public Works has much to do with projects of the character stated, because it is responsible for the engineering design and construction.

The supporting interest of the Citizens Committee on the City Plan is of so much value to the entire movement in Pittsburgh, that to treat its work and labors adequately would require the space devoted to the paper and more. Its report and study on playgrounds is indeed a classic of this element of city planning.

Since the paper was prepared, Grant Street has been widened from 60 ft. to 80 ft. With this widening completed, buildings of a height and architectural type new to Pittsburgh are being constructed and projected.

The Business District of Pittsburgh in the Future.—The distress of cities may be caused by difficulty in: First, making its life fit the mould of yesterday; and, second, trying to visualize to-morrow in the light of to-day's conditions. It is dangerous to attempt prophecy without the gift of vision. The Enabling Act of 1911, already mentioned, does not elaborate the functions of the Department of City Planning as does the recent Pennsylvania Act (1927). Until the present Act there was no authority at law that permitted the adoption of a thorough, studied, comprehensive, development, general design, or master city plan for the present and future guidance of Pittsburgh. The Department of City Planning is, therefore, at work on the master thoroughfare and general design plans.

The author has mentioned changes that were accomplished a few years ago, and possibly there will be changes in the future. About the beginning of 1928 the Allegheny County projects of the Liberty Tunnels and Liberty Bridge will be open to traffic. These are a part of the Inter-District Traffic Circuit. The Department of City Planning has completed the preliminary design study of another link in the Circuit, the Crosstown Thoroughfare. This study has been approved by the City Planning Commission. The widening of Grant Street has permitted a re-routing of trolley cars in a loop system. Every day, judging from congestion, the down-town streets look like Saturday afternoon, and the time is coming when they will look like the week before Christmas. Two-way streets will become one-way streets. Merchants are overcoming the fear of loss and the notion that all trolleys must pass their doors. Unlimited parking of automobiles has been replaced with limited parking or with none at all.

Streets cannot continue to be widened because of the cost. The people are realizing that the area in down-town streets is ample, but the best use of them is not practiced at present. The cost of delays to the owners of trucks, buses, taxicabs and automobiles, conservatively estimated, now is $25 000 daily. These owners will avoid the delays and effect the saving. A railroad will abandon or salvage its equipment along Duquesne Way and in "the Point"; sell its land in these locations; acquire a site and provide better modern facilities elsewhere, without any financial loss, from the proceeds of the old plant. The Point, now backward, will have a new life and business will expand into that area. The flood will be controlled and the rivers' fronts improved. The down-town traffic circuit will be operating, gyratory, one-way, along Duquesne Way, Water, Grant, and Eleventh Streets. Within the circuit there will be no vehicles, unless in an emergency, during the day. Trolleys will be in a subway loop and off the street surface. Buses and cruising taxicabs will have stations and terminals off the streets. Streets for deliveries, collection, and merchandising services will then be used at night. Vehicles will be absent from the streets down town, not because they cannot get there or are prohibited, but because of the economic loss to the owners if they attempt it. The streets will again be free to the people when every day is Christmas in Pittsburgh.

AMERICAN SOCIETY OF CIVIL ENGINEERS
INSTITUTED 1852

TRANSACTIONS
This Society is not responsible for any statement made or opinion expressed in its publications.

Paper No. 1671

THE PLANNING OF THE INDUSTRIAL CITY OF LONGVIEW, WASHINGTON*

By S. Herbert Hare,† Esq.

With Discussion by Messrs. B. L. Lambuth, Brookes Baker, and S. Herbert Hare.

"City Planning", a term applied to the orderly physical development of a community, would in most cases be more properly classed as "City Re-Planning".

The opportunity of planning a complete new city of any great extent on undeveloped land seldom presents itself. The planning of Longview, Wash., was perhaps the largest project of this kind since the planning of the National Capitol by L'Enfant under President Washington, and involved some pioneering in the field of city planning.

History of the Development

A very brief historical account of the project is as follows: The Long-Bell Lumber Company, in looking forward to a continuation of its operations after its Southern timber supply was exhausted, purchased a large tract of timber land in Lewis and Cowlitz Counties, Washington, about 15 miles north of the Columbia River. In looking about for a mill site for the manufacture of this timber, a location on the Columbia River at the mouth of the Cowlitz was finally decided upon, and options were taken on land to cover the mill site and other lands in the valley. As the operations of the Company were to be very extensive and the number of people to be employed necessitated a great increase in the population of the district, the development of a town site adjoining the mills was discussed early in 1922. The purpose was not so much to secure the profits which might result from increased land values produced by the Company's operations, as to prevent exploitation of the land in the district and a haphazard growth of unrelated development in the vicinity of

* Presented at the meeting of the City Planning Division, Seattle, Wash., July 15, 1926.
† Landscape Archt. and City Planner (Hare & Hare), Kansas City, Mo.

the mills. It was decided, therefore, that an industrial city should be built which would serve not only the Long-Bell interests but other industries as well. It was not to be a "company town" or a "one-industry town", and it was to be sold as there was demand.

In February, 1922, officials of the Company visited the site and sought advice on the feasibility of developing a town. This visit was followed later in 1922 by conferences, after which various industrial cities were investigated for information about developments similar to the one proposed, including land values, store counts, rail and transportation facilities, and many other subjects. In the meantime, a topographical survey of the lands involved was being made under the direction of Wesley Vandercook, Chief Engineer of the Long-Bell Lumber Company.

In June, 1922, after a thorough inspection of the property, the Company exercised options on approximately 14 000 acres of land, the area which has since been included in the plan for the city. At this time the writer made studies for both a skeleton plan of the entire area and for the detailed development of the interior section. In connection with these studies he had the general advice of the late George E. Kessler, Landscape Architect, and B. L. Lambuth, Realtor.

Upon arriving at a general scheme further studies were developed. These plans were made at different scales; the general plan at a scale of 1 000 ft. to 1 in.; plans for sections of the city at a scale of 400 ft. to 1 in.; and detail plans, each covering an area of 1 500 by 2 000 ft., at a scale of 40 ft. to 1 in. The detail plans, which showed lot lines, curbs, walks, easements, building and outbuilding lines, and other features, with controlling dimensions, were sent to Mr. Vandercook, in whose department calculations were made, streets and lots staked out, construction work supervised, and utilities planned.

After the initial planning was completed, special advice on commercial water-front treatment and railway problems was secured. As the building of the city progressed scores of detail plans were prepared for park areas, school sites, hospital property, and other public and semi-public developments. The first lot in Longview was sold in February, 1923, and the city was incorporated in February, 1924.

The Topography of the Site

The town site is principally a rich, flat valley bounded on the north by hills, on the south and southwest by the Columbia River, and on the east by the Cowlitz River. It includes more than 7 miles of deep-water frontage on the Columbia River, available for ocean-going vessels, and about 5 miles of frontage on the Cowlitz River suitable for barge service. On the north, the land included in the town site reaches into the hills at some points for a distance of about 1 mile and rises to an elevation of about 400 ft. The valley ranges from a little above tide level at the western end to Elevation 20 or higher at the point chosen for the center of the city. The land in the valley was included in seven separate diking districts which were merged into one large district, the intermediate dikes were removed, and a new and higher dike was built along the river-front.

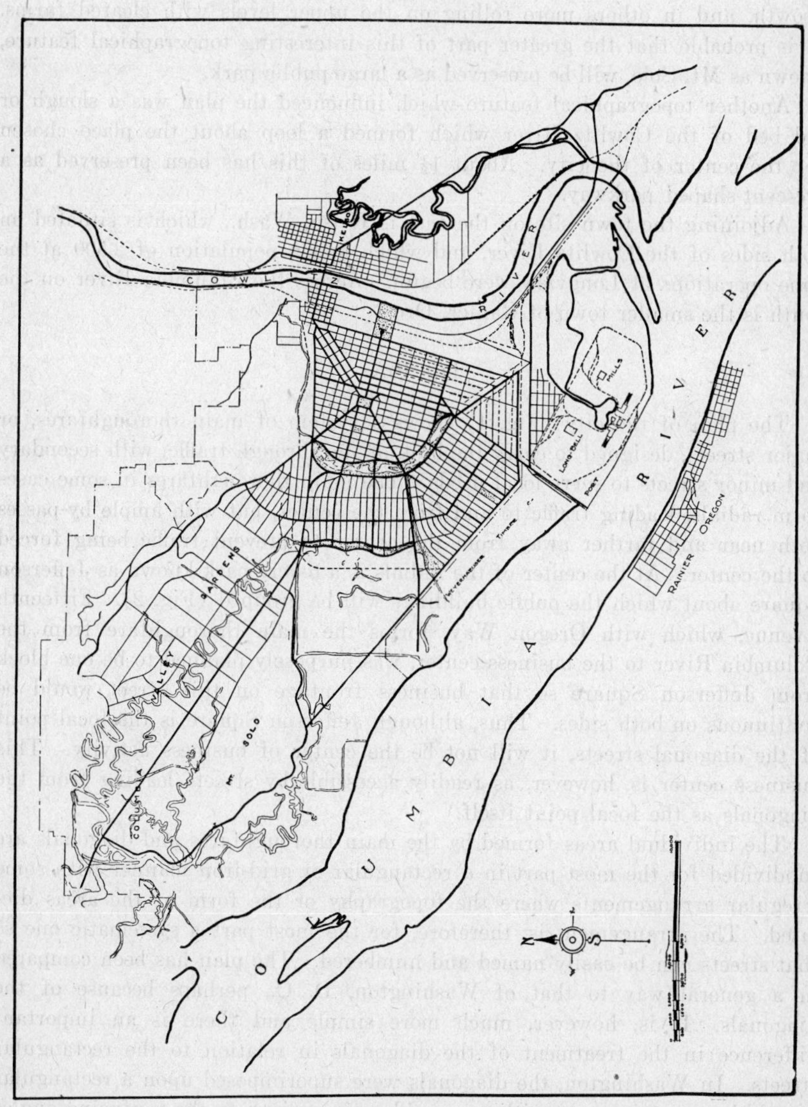

FIG. 1.—Skeleton Map of Street System, Longview, Washington.

The outstanding topographical feature of the valley is a small mountain rising from the valley floor near the western end. This mountain is more than 2 miles long and nearly 1 mile wide, reaching an elevation of 560 ft. at its peak. In some places it is very precipitous, covered with heavy tree growth, and in others more rolling on the upper levels with cleared farms. It is probable that the greater part of this interesting topographical feature, known as Mt. Solo, will be preserved as a large public park.

Another topographical feature which influenced the plan was a slough or old bed of the Cowlitz River which formed a loop about the place chosen for the center of the city. About 1½ miles of this has been preserved as a crescent-shaped parkway.

Adjoining the town site on the east is Kelso, Wash., which is situated on both sides of the Cowlitz River, and which had a population of 2 500 at the time operations at Longview were begun. Across the Columbia River on the south is the smaller town of Ranier, Ore.

The Plan

The plan of the city (Fig. 1) shows a system of main thoroughfares, or major streets, designed to carry the bulk of the through traffic, with secondary and minor streets to serve local needs. The main thoroughfares in some cases form radials, leading traffic to and from the center, but with ample by-passes both near and farther away from the center to prevent traffic being forced to the center. At the center of the radials is a 6-acre park known as Jefferson Square about which the public buildings will be grouped (Fig. 2). Fifteenth Avenue, which with Oregon Way, forms the main thoroughfare from the Columbia River to the business center, was purposely planned to be one block from Jefferson Square so that business frontage on this street would be continuous on both sides. Thus, although Jefferson Square is the focal point of the diagonal streets, it will not be the center of business activity. This business center is, however, as readily accessible by streets leading from the diagonals as the focal point itself.

The individual areas formed by the main thoroughfares and diagonals are subdivided for the most part in a rectangular or grid-iron manner with some irregular arrangements where the topography or the form of the areas dictated. The arrangement is, therefore, for the most part a systematic one so that streets can be easily named and numbered. The plan has been compared in a general way to that of Washington, D. C., perhaps because of the diagonals. It is, however, much more simple and there is an important difference in the treatment of the diagonals in relation to the rectangular streets. In Washington, the diagonals were superimposed upon a rectangular or grid-iron arrangement with no considerations given to the confusing angles which the intersections produced. At Longview, the rectangular arrangement is in a series of separate units, with connecting streets articulated across the diagonals, usually at right angles.

In order to clear the wholesale or light industrial district to the southeast of the business center from the confusion which would be caused by a

Fig. 2.—View of Longview, Wash., East from Monticello Hotel.

Fig. 3.—View During Dredging Operations on Lake Sacajawea Parkway, Longview, Wash. Smaller House District in Foreground.

diagonal, the diagonal in this direction was offset along the line of Fifteenth Avenue to a point where it could be used for an approach from the Pacific Highway across the Cowlitz River from the southeast. The location of this diagonal also offered an unusual opportunity for convenient railroad leads into the industrial districts, with only one track across the thoroughfare and with obtuse angles on the curves in the industrial tracts. The city is served directly by the Longview, Portland, and Northern Railroad, a common carrier, 30 miles long, which connects with the transcontinental lines just across the Cowlitz River.

After careful consideration a lot depth of 120 ft. was adopted as the standard for the regular portions of the city, as this depth was considered most suitable for the various uses. Alleys were provided quite generally, even in the residence districts, partly owing to a local custom in the use of slab wood for fuel. These alleys will probably not be provided in future high-class residence districts, and the districts which are being developed in the hills are irregular and carefully adjusted to the topography. A width of 20 ft. was adopted for the alleys, providing for two lines of traffic and pole lines.

In the street system, the main thoroughfares are 100 and 120 ft. wide, secondary thoroughfares and main business streets, 80 ft. wide, and other streets, 50 to 60 ft. wide. Roadways on the streets vary from 24 to 25 ft. on the minor streets to 60 ft. on the major streets. In some cases esplanades are used which may be removed when traffic demands. Block lengths are from 300 to 500 ft. in the business district and 600 to 1 100 ft. in the residence districts, the longer blocks being usually in the direction of traffic.

The distribution of schools has been given careful study and 5 acres or more have been reserved for grade school sites, with an area of 30 acres for a Junior and Senior High School, the latter to have an athletic field. Church sites, a golf club, cemetery site, and other community needs have been provided for as the complete plan developed.

In addition to the 6-acre park at the civic center, other local parks and playgrounds have been reserved at convenient intervals. It is contemplated to retain some of the more precipitous slopes in the north hills for park lands, as well as the land on Mt. Solo previously mentioned, and some of the frontage on the Cowlitz River.

The development of a part of the slough surrounding the central section of the city (Fig. 3) promises to be one of the most interesting parkways in the country. The area reserved, containing 100 acres, is from 500 to 800 ft. in width, bordered by boulevards, and is 1½ miles long. To secure material for filling in the vicinity nearly 2 000 000 cu. yd. of sand was pumped by hydraulic dredge from this parkway, forming a series of connected lakes carefully designed to simulate natural bodies of water. Four thoroughfares will cross these lakes on bridges. Complete detailed grading plans were prepared for this development, not only showing the grading by sections, but accurately indicating by contours of finished grades the naturalistic rolling ground forms desired. This parkway has been named Lake Sacajawea, after the woman Indian guide of the Lewis and Clark Expedition.

Zoning

Zoning was one of the interesting problems of the planning of the city. The uses to which various properties were to be put was necessarily determined in the planning of the street system, and this street arrangement will tend to stabilize those uses and prevent shifting values. Early in the planning, a zoning map was prepared showing areas to be used for residences, apartments, business, and light and heavy industries. As there was no municipal corporation at that time to enact a zoning ordinance and no State enabling act to authorize such an ordinance, the zoning regulations were put into effect by private restrictions. These restrictions are partly in the deeds, but are mostly filed with the plat. They follow the most modern practice and are self-perpetuating, thorough, and complete, but in no way drastic, protecting the investment of the small home owner as well as that of the more wealthy one.

One of the difficult problems in connection with zoning was the necessity of starting development in a series of more or less disconnected centers rather than in one center. This at first produced a scattered appearance and extra cost of paving and utilities, but the wisdom of the procedure is already apparent as the population is growing, and the scattered centers are gradually being joined into a homogeneous whole without conversion of property from one use to another. The plan provides for a population of 50 000 and by converting suburban acreage into city lots a much larger population could be housed on the town site. The installation of utilities and the problems of diking and drainage have been intricate.

Throughout the planning it was constantly kept in mind that this city was to be a thoroughly practical, general industrial city, one in which convenience and economy, although of primary importance, were to be combined with the highest type of beauty—that beauty which is designed into a development as an organic part rather than added to it as an ornament. The people of Longview will work amid pleasant and convenient surroundings and will enjoy some of the amenities of life.

DISCUSSION

B. L. LAMBUTH,* ESQ.—Virtually all outstanding real estate development is a product of the joint effort of skilled men drawn from many professions. The modern tendency is for the realtor, the town planner, and the civil engineer to work together toward a desired end. One of the greatest sources of interest and pleasure in connection with the Longview development was the harmonious relations between a considerable group of specialized experts, including, in addition to those mentioned, architects, lawyers, transportation men, title experts, advertising men, and others.

An interesting feature of the operations at Longview to those interested in this type of development is the fact that in theory at least it has been possible to avoid a tremendous aggregate annual loss and wastage arising as a result of the necessary reconstruction at the center of American cities which accompanies growth by a process of accretion at the circumference. The founders of the city had adopted what has been designated by Mr. J. C. Nichols, of Kansas City, Mo., as a "skeletal" plan of development, whereby the entire city site is completely planned and zoned and the actual development of each district is started in a small way in its proper relationship to a finished whole. By this means it is expected that large economies will be effected. Although on the one hand some extra cost is necessarily involved in tying the various districts of the city together by suitable street improvements and public utilities, yet, on the other hand, the great bulk of the property is carried until required for development as vacant agricultural acreage with correspondingly low overhead carrying charges, such as interest and taxes. Furthermore, the plan adopted offers the advantage of permitting one of the several districts of a city to be prepared for development in relatively small parcels as actually needed for immediate use from time to time; but the principal advantage of the "skeletal" plan is that business, housing, institutional, and, in fact, all building development, is in its proper relationship to a finished whole. Therefore, the usual necessity of tearing down and reconstructing building—improvements which ordinarily accompany growth of a city from nothing to 40 000 or 50 000 population—is quite largely obviated.

Another interesting feature of the Longview plan is the association of suburban agricultural and garden tracts with the other districts of the city, and as a part of the general scheme. This is on the principle that one of the very important and very substantial elements of urban population is the family seeking a small tract of land as a means of providing over-time employment and a home that is partly self-sustaining.

A large number of people visit Longview each year. Apparently, the first three outstanding impressions of the more thoughtful and better trained of these visitors are, first, that they are viewing a city in the making; second, that the city was planned before construction was begun; and, third, that beauty and spaciousness of design and execution have been attained.

* Mgr., Real Estate Dept., The Longview Co., Longview, Wash.

Brookes Baker,* Esq. (by letter).—The plans for Longview, Wash., appear to cover the requirements for a well-balanced community so completely that little remains to be said. As the designer states, the planning of an entire new community, with an assured future, occurs so infrequently that there are no precedents by which to judge. Most engineers who have been connected with matters pertaining to land developments have at times staked out new town sites in unsettled territory, this work being generally the mere execution, on the ground, of the promoter's desire to secure the greatest possible number of lots out of a given number of acres, without any regard for the future welfare of the purchasers of the lots. All who have done this will join in congratulating the designers of Longview on the happy solution of their problem.

The placing of the central park one block removed from the business district is a most excellent solution of the need for a park which is of the business district, but not in it. The diagonal streets are indeed convenient; the plan of adjusting the cross-streets to right angular intersections retains the most convenient rectangular spacing on the main streets, where values are greatest, and puts the angular and point lots in the less desirable locations.

The long parkway, occupying the old slough bed, with its many pools set in their banks of green, some shaded by magnificent trees, some spanned by attractive bridges, and all skirted by pleasant drives, affords an excellent example of the adaptation of an offensive waste into an object of beauty, which will contribute throughout the years to the pleasure, comfort, and refinement of the growing community.

S. Herbert Hare,† Esq. (by letter).—In the discussion by Mr. Lambuth, the important point of co-operation is again emphasized; not only the co-operation of the engineer, the city planner, the landscape architect, the architect, and others, but that of the realtor, who can render a valuable service in connection with the development of such a plan as was produced for Longview, Wash. The real estate operator who is to have the responsibility for marketing the land, if he has a broad understanding of the problem and of the aims of the city planner, should very properly have a voice in the physical arrangement and development of this land.

Mr. Lambuth has referred to the building of Longview in various nuclei as a "skeletal" plan of development and has pointed out the saving which results from such a program. The success of such a plan, of course, depends somewhat on the prophetic vision of the planner, engineer, and real estate operator in judging the market and rate of growth, and weighing the somewhat greater initial expense involved in such a procedure against the immense losses which result from converting the uses of property early in the life of constructions. The results at Longview have undoubtedly justified the decision.

The provision for suburban garden tracts to which Mr. Lambuth refers was, of course, a part of the carefully considered general plan for the city,

* Civ. Engr., Fort Worth, Tex.

† Landscape Archt. and City Planner (Hare & Hare), Kansas City, Mo.

it is trapezoidal, as shown in Fig. 2. It is the purpose of this paper to show that it is not safe to neglect the curvature and that this may lead to, and has led to, dams with tension in the up-stream face. Such a dam is not in fact a gravity dam, since it will not stand by gravity, but requires tension in the up-stream face.

Let B be the base width (Figs. 1 and 2) and H the height of a triangular section with a vertical up-stream face and let w be the weight of a cubic foot of concrete; then if uplift is assumed as negligible and if the water level stands even with the crest of the dam, the section determined by,*

$$B = H\sqrt{\frac{62.5}{w}} \qquad (2)$$

will have zero stress at the heel when the reservoir is full, provided the dam is straight. If the dam is arched there will be tension in the up-stream face, on the assumption that the cantilever carries the entire load and, in general, this assumption will be the correct one and always on the safe side.

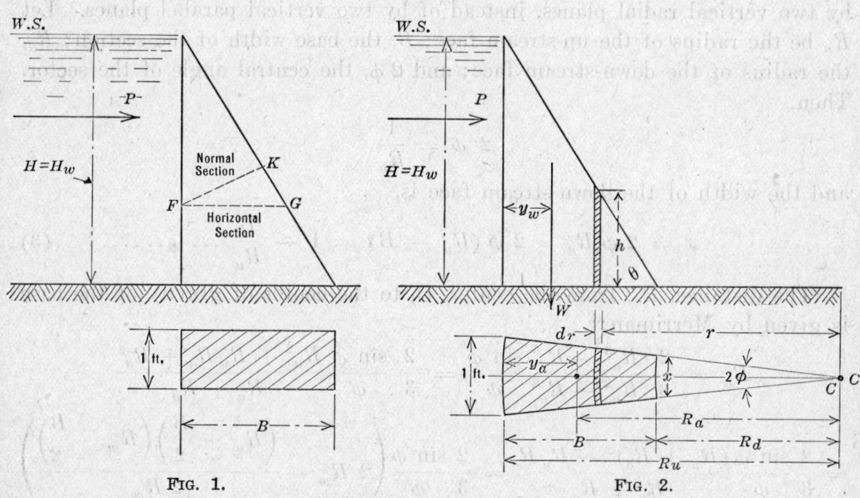

FIG. 1. FIG. 2.

In deriving the ordinary bending formulas, it is assumed that normal sections remain plane when the shear deformations are neglected; but a horizontal section, such as $F\,G$ in Fig. 1, is not a normal section, as is $F\,K$. The writer has dealt elsewhere† with this question and the approximation introduced by substituting an oblique section for a normal section, but in order to avoid mathematical complications, the assumption that horizontal sections remain plane will be maintained. It is very essential, however, that the designing engineer bears in mind that the theory is not exact; then he will not be tempted to reduce the section to the theoretical minimum.

* See, for example, the writer's discussion in *Transactions*, Am. Soc. C. E., Vol. LXXXIV (1921), p. 93.

† "Stresses in Multiple-Arch Dams," *Transactions*, Am. Soc. C. E., Vol. LXXXVII (1924), p. 289; see, also, Professor Cain's discussion on p. 316. Also, Professor Résal's paper, "Formes et dimensions des grands barrages en maçonnerie," *Annales des Ponts et Chaussées*, II, 1919.

In this paper a triangular vertical section with a vertical up-stream face will be considered. It is customary to give the up-stream face a slight batter in order that there may be no tension in the down-stream face when the reservoir is empty. There can be no objection to such a batter. On the other hand, it is much more important to make sure that tension does not exist in the up-stream face when the reservoir is full, because if this results in a horizontal crack, the tension is thereby increased. Conversely, if there is tension in the down-stream face with reservoir empty, and a crack results, the tension is thereby reduced; the crack in the down-stream face is, therefore, self-limiting and is not likely to be more than a mere surface crack, while a crack produced by tension in the up-stream face is dangerous. Two fairly large dams have failed from tension in the up-stream face several years after they were built.*

Formulas for Stresses

Consider in Fig. 2 a volume 1 ft. wide at the up-stream face and limited by two vertical radial planes, instead of by two vertical parallel planes. Let R_u be the radius of the up-stream face; B, the base width of the section; R_d, the radius of the down-stream face; and $2\,\phi$, the central angle of the sector. Then,

$$2\,\phi = \frac{1}{R_u}$$

and the width of the down-stream face is,

$$x = 2\,\phi\,R_d = 2\,\phi\,(R_u - B) = 1 - \frac{B}{R_u} \qquad (3)$$

The distance, R_a, from the center, C, to the center of gravity of the base is given by Merriman:†

$$R_a = \frac{2}{3}\,\frac{R_u^3 - R_d^3}{R_u^2 - R_d^2}\,\frac{\sin\phi}{\phi} = \frac{2}{3}\,\frac{\sin\phi}{\phi}\,\frac{R_u^2 + R_u R_d + R_d^2}{R_u + R_d}$$

$$= \frac{2}{3}\,\frac{\sin\phi}{\phi}\,\frac{(R_u + R_d)^2 - R_u R_d}{R_u + R_d} = \frac{2}{3}\,\frac{\sin\phi}{\phi}\left(2\,R_m - \frac{\left(R_m + \frac{B}{2}\right)\left(R_m - \frac{B}{2}\right)}{2\,R_m}\right)$$

$$= \left(R_m + \frac{B^2}{12\,R_m}\right)\frac{\sin\phi}{\phi}$$

in which, $R_m = R_u - \dfrac{B}{2}$, is the mean radius.

The distance from the up-stream face to the center of gravity of the base is then,

$$y_a = R_u - \left(R_m + \frac{B^2}{12\,R_m}\right)\frac{\sin\phi}{\phi} = \left(\frac{B}{2} - \frac{B^2}{12\,R_m}\right)\frac{\sin\phi}{\phi} + R_u\left(1 - \frac{\sin\phi}{\phi}\right)$$

The last term is always very small, because ϕ is small; for R_u = 100 ft., it becomes 0.0004 ft.; for R_u = 500 ft., it is 0.0000835 ft. Since y_a is approxi-

* *Minutes of Proceedings*, Inst. C. E., Vol. CLXXII, Session 1907–08, Part II, p. 73. The two dams are the Habra Dam in Algiers and the Bouzey Dam in France.

† American Civil Engineers Handbook, Fourth Edition, 1920, Section 12, Article 23, p. 1471.

mately equal to $\frac{B}{2}$, the last term is negligible and $\frac{\sin \phi}{\phi}$ is always practically equal to 1, so that, very nearly,

$$y_a = \left(\frac{B}{2} - \frac{B^2}{12\,R_m}\right) \quad \text{......} (4)$$

For a straight dam, $\frac{B^2}{12\,R_m}$ vanishes, so that $y_a = \frac{B}{2}$ as it should.

The volume of the dam sector limited by the two vertical radial planes (Fig. 2) is found by multiplying the area of the triangle, or 0.5 $B\,H$, by the length of the path described by the center of gravity of the triangle, as it revolves about the center, C. The length of this path is,

$$2\,\phi\left(R_u - \frac{B}{3}\right) = 1 - \frac{B}{3\,R_u} \quad \text{......} (5)$$

If w is the weight per cubic foot of concrete and all dimensions are in feet, the weight of the dam sector is,

$$W = \frac{w}{2}\,B\,H\left(1 - \frac{B}{3\,R_u}\right) \text{lb} \quad \text{......} (6)$$

For a straight dam, $\frac{B}{R_u}$ vanishes and Equation (6) remains correct.

The position of the center of gravity of the volume is found by determining the moment of the volume about C and then dividing by W. The moment about C of the part of a cylindrical surface indicated in Fig. 2, is,

$$\text{Moment} = w\,h\,dr \times 2\,r\,\phi \times r\,\frac{\sin \phi}{\phi}$$

since the center of gravity of this thin cylindrical surface is given by $r\,\frac{\sin \phi}{\phi}$. The moment about C of the whole volume is, then,

$$M_c = \int_{R_u - B}^{R_u} 2\,r\,w\,\phi\,h\,dr\,r\,\frac{\sin \phi}{\phi} \quad \text{......} (7)$$

From Fig. 2,

$$\frac{h}{H} = \frac{r - R_d}{R_u - R_d}$$

or,

$$r = \frac{B}{H}\,h + R_d$$

Introducing this into Equation (7),

$$M_c = 2\,w \sin \phi \int_0^H \left(\frac{B}{H}\,h + R_d\right)^2 \frac{B}{H}\,h\,dh$$

$$= w\,H\,B \sin \phi \left(R_d{}^2 + \frac{4}{3}\,B\,R_d + \frac{B^2}{2}\right)$$

The length of the path of the center of gravity of the triangle in Fig. 2, is, from Equation (5),

$$2\,\phi\left(R_u - \frac{B}{3}\right) = 2\,\phi\left(R_d + \frac{2}{3}\,B\right)$$

so that the weight of the volume of the dam is,

$$W = w\,\phi\,B\,H\left(R_a + \frac{2}{3}B\right)$$

and since,

$$\left(R_a + \frac{2}{3}B\right)^2 = R_a^2 + \frac{4}{3}B\,R_a + \frac{4}{9}B^2$$

the distance from C to the center of gravity of the volume of dam, is,

$$r_w = \frac{M_c}{W} = \left(R_a + \frac{2}{3}B + \frac{B^2}{18\left(R_a + \frac{2}{3}B\right)}\right)\frac{\sin\phi}{\phi} \quad\ldots\ldots(8)$$

Designate by y_w the distance from the up-stream face to the center of gravity of the volume, then, $y_w = R_u - r_w$, and since $\frac{\sin\phi}{\phi}$ is practically unity,

$$y_w = \frac{B}{3} - \frac{B^2}{18\,R_u\left(1 - \frac{B}{3\,R_u}\right)} \quad\ldots\ldots(9)$$

The moment of inertia of the trapezoidal base in Fig. 2 with reference to its own center of gravity is,*

$$I = \frac{B^3}{36}\left(\frac{x^2 + 4\,x + 1}{x + 1}\right) \quad\ldots\ldots(10)$$

in which, x is given by Equation (3), as,

$$x = 1 - \frac{B}{R_u}$$

By direct integration is found,

$$I = \frac{\phi}{4}\left(R_u^4 - R_a^4\right) - \frac{\phi}{2}\left(R_u^2 - R_a^2\right)R_a^2$$

The expression given in Equation (10) is much more convenient. If the water level is H_w ft. above the base, the horizontal water pressure is $31.25\,H_w^2$ and the moment about the base is,

$$M_P = -\frac{62.5}{6}H_w^3 \quad\ldots\ldots(11)$$

The weight acting in the center of gravity of the volume may be considered as producing a vertical downward thrust equal to W and applied in the center of gravity of the base, and a moment,

$$M_w = W\,(y_a - y_w)$$

This moment acts in a direction opposite to the M_P produced by the water pressure; the resulting moment is, therefore,

$$M = -\frac{62.5}{6}H_w^3 + W\,(y_a - y_w) \quad\ldots\ldots(12)$$

From Equations (4) and (9),

$$y_a - y_w = \frac{B}{6} - \frac{B^2}{36\,R_m\left(1 - \frac{B}{3\,R_u}\right)} \quad\ldots\ldots(13)$$

* See, Goodman, "Mechanics Applied to Engineering" (1912), p. 86.

The vertical stresses at the up-stream and down-stream faces, respectively, are then,

$$\left.\begin{aligned} s_u &= \frac{W}{A} + \frac{M}{I}\, y_a \\ s_a &= \frac{W}{A} - \frac{M}{I}\,(B - y_a) \end{aligned}\right\} \qquad (14)$$

in which, A, the area of the base, is,

$$A = B\left(1 - \frac{B}{2\,R_u}\right) = B\,\frac{1 + x}{2} \qquad (15)$$

In Equation (14) compression is positive and *vice versa.* The maximum compression, $s_{max.}$, occurs at the down-stream face and is parallel to that face*:

$$\left.\begin{aligned} s_{max.} &= \frac{s_a}{\sin^2\theta} \\ \text{in which,} \quad \tan\theta &= \frac{H}{B} \end{aligned}\right\} \qquad (16)$$

Influence of Uplift

Assume that uplift is a maximum at the heel, decreasing linearly to zero at the toe. If the maximum uplift pressure is $62.5\;k\;H$ lb. per sq. ft., the coefficient, k, measures the percentage, so that for $k = 1$† the maximum possible uplift is considered and for $k = 0$, there will be no uplift. The total uplift acting on the trapezoidal base is, by Equation (6),

$$U = \frac{62.5}{2}\;k\;B\;H\left(1 - \frac{B}{3\,R_u}\right)\ \text{lb} \qquad (17)$$

Its point of application is given by Equation (9), since the uplift may be considered as due to a triangular mass of water acting on the base. It follows that provision for uplift may be made by substituting, in Equations (12) and (13), $W - U$ for W, or simpler still, by reducing w accordingly. If, for example, $w = 150$ lb. per cu. ft. and full uplift is to be assumed, the new value is,

$$w' = 150 - 62.5 = 87.5 \text{ lb. per cu. ft.}$$

If w' is substituted in Equation (2) for w, this equation gives B direct. If, for example, $w = 150$, Equation (2) gives $B = 0.645\;H$; if $w' = 87.5$, that is, full triangular uplift, then $B = 0.845\;H$. Equation (2) is correct only for a straight triangular dam having water level with the crest.

The foregoing formulas are correct for any radius of curvature and, therefore, also for a straight dam for which the radius of curvature is infinitely great.

* "Stresses in Masonry Dams," by William Cain, M. Am. Soc. C. E., *Transactions*, Am. Soc. C. E., Vol. LXIV (1909), p. 208.

† $k = 1$ is a limiting condition, which may be approached but cannot be reached, since the weight of the concrete exceeds the uplift and, therefore, some part of the base must have contact with the foundation.

EXAMPLE

When the radius of curvature has a finite value, the relation between the height and the required base width cannot be reduced to a simple formula, such as Equation (2), which applies only to a straight dam. In order to ascertain the influence of curvature it is more convenient to consider an actual case—to compute the stresses on the assumption that the dam is straight and then to re-compute them for an arched dam having the same section. Consider, therefore, a horizontal section of the Exchequer Dam of the Merced Irrigation District, Merced, Calif.* At Elevation 437.5, the dimensions are, $H = H_w = 272.5$ ft.; $B = 171.4$ ft.; $R_u = 674.7$ ft.; and $R_m = 589$ ft. The actual section is not triangular with a vertical up-stream face, but has a definite top width, and the up-stream face is battered, so that at the elevation considered it lies 1.97 ft. up stream from the crest. The dimension, B, used in the calculations is the actual total base width; it has merely been shifted 1.97 ft. down stream. The approximation involved in substituting the ideal triangular section for the actual section is a very close one.

If the dam were straight the value of w, giving zero stress at the heel with the reservoir full, may be obtained from Equation (2), since the dimensions are known. This gives $w = 160$ lb. per cu. ft.—an unusually high value for designing a gravity dam; but if w is assumed as less, a straight dam of the section given would show tension in the up-stream face. Assuming, now, $w = 160$, $y_a = 81.54$ ft.; $W = 3\,418\,000$ lb.; $y_w = 54.49$ ft.; $I = 364\,000$ ft.^{4}; $x = 0.746$ ft.; and from Equation (12),

$$M = -\,210\,800\,000 + 578\,000\,w = -\,118\,400\,000 \text{ ft-lb.}$$

The area of the base is $A = 149.5$ sq. ft., and the vertical stresses at the heel and toe, respectively, are, $s_u = -\,25.9$ lb. per sq. in. (tension) and $s_d = 362.0$ lb. per sq. in., and the maximum stress is $\frac{362}{0.847^2} = 504$ lb. per sq. in. If the dam had been straight, the stresses would have been $s_u = 0$, and $s_d = 303$ lb. per sq. in. If $w = 152.0$ is assumed, the actual section ($R_u = 674.7$ ft.) gives $s_u = -\,40.5$ lb. per sq. in (tension).

Consider that there is 50% uplift at the heel and none at the toe, and a linear decrease; also, assume $w = 152$, so that,

$$w' = 152 - 31.25 = 120.75 \text{ lb. per cu. ft.}$$

Then, for $H = H_w = 272.5$ and a straight dam, from Equation (2), $B = 196$ ft. If, as before, $R_u = 674.7$ ft., $H = 272.5$ ft., but $B = 196$ ft., so that $R_m = 576.7$ ft., then the values will be $x = 0.7095$ ft.; $W = 2\,912\,400$ lb. (this is actually the weight less the uplift, since w' and not w was used); $M = -\,121\,607\,000$, since $y_a - y_w = 30.618$ ft.; the area, $A = 167.53$ sq. ft.; $y_a = 92.45$ ft.; $I = 531\,160$; and the stress in the up-stream face with reservoir full is, $s_u = -\,26.3$ lb. per sq. in. (tension).

* A section of this dam is given in *Western Construction News*, January 25, 1926, p. 25.

General Remarks

From this example evidently it is never safe to neglect the curvature; the higher the dam and the smaller the radius, the larger is the error committed when the dam is computed as straight.

It is also evident that an arched gravity dam will receive some support from the arch and, in most cases, probably sufficient support to prevent actual failure. As gravity dams are usually constructed, however, the arch cannot act until the cantilever has been broken, and in that case uplift would be present. The writer has discussed this phase in his paper entitled "Stresses in Thick Arches of Dams",* and also made mention of the shrinkage cracks in the Mulholland Dam, which proves that the dam is not acting as an arch dam. In a properly designed gravity dam the shrinkage cracks are of little consequence; but when tension is present in the up-stream face the dam should be computed as an arch dam, since it does not appear safe to rely on tension in the concrete, especially across construction joints.

In the writer's opinion the most important condition to impose on a gravity design is that there must be no tension in the up-stream face when the water surface is at the maximum height; it is also well to bear in mind that the assumption of no uplift is the least conservative that can be made, and while no doubt occasionally it is safe, especially when proper drainage is provided, there is always the possibility, not to say certainty, that the drainage will fail at least partly. For reservoir full, the stress at the toe is of importance only for very high dams, but the stress at the heel is by far the most important.

The writer is fully aware of the uncertainties involved in determining the stresses near the foundation of a gravity dam. This uncertainty arises partly from the unknown distribution of the shear near the base.† This phase of the subject has been purposely excluded, because it was desired to show the influence of curvature when the ordinary assumptions were maintained. As Professor Résal points out, a straight gravity dam may also act as an arch dam, since, in general, secondary horizontal arches may be found for any straight gravity dam. The extent of arch action will depend on the width of the site and on the method of construction; whether the dam was pressure grouted after the concrete had cured and the chemical heat had been dissipated; whether it was closed as late as possible; or, finally, whether no attempt at all was made to secure arch action in case the uplift for any reason should prove to be in excess of the assumption.

* *Transactions*, Am. Soc. C. E., Vol. 90 (1927), p. 475.

† Professor Cain calls attention to this uncertainty in the opening sentence of his paper previously referred to and Professor Résal in the paper referred to deals at some length with this subject.

DISCUSSION

George R. Rich,* Assoc. M. Am. Soc. C. E. (by letter).—Curving a gravity dam up stream does not add to the stability of the structure unless the vertical contraction joints between sections are pressure-grouted to insure contact after the heat due to chemical action has been dissipated and the resulting shrinkage has occurred. The writer believes that the volume changes of the entire mass caused by seasonal variations in temperature are of small magnitude compared to those produced by the heat liberated during the chemical process of setting. Temperature measurements on sections of the Wilson Dam show that several months may be required for the dissipation of the chemical heat.†

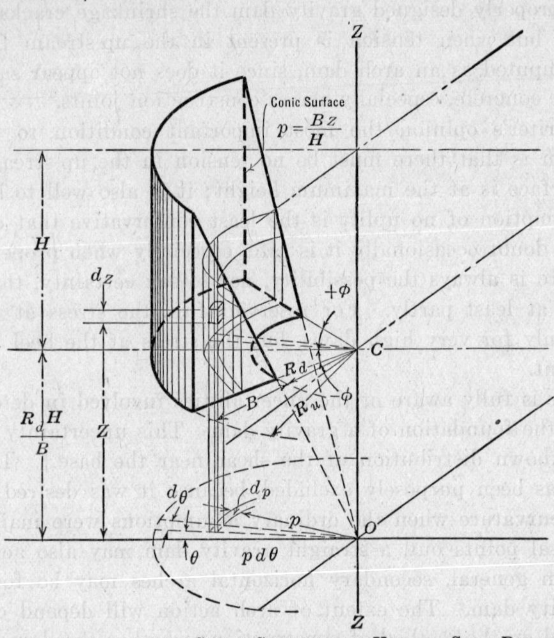

Fig. 3.—Deriving Formula for Conic Surface by Use of Semi-Polar Cylindrical Co-Ordinates.

Gravity dams of any appreciable length are ordinarily constructed in sections, with vertical contraction joints having shear keys and sealing strips, but without recourse to pressure grouting of the vertical joints. After the aforementioned initial shrinkage has occurred, there will be an opening between adjacent sections and before there could be sufficient deflection to give the contact prerequisite to action of the horizontal arch elements, the vertical cantilever elements would have to fail in tension near the heel of the dam. From this point action toward ultimate damage is progressive, owing to the effect of uplift pressure entering the tension cracks.

* Hydr. Designer, Stone & Webster, Inc., Boston, Mass.

† "Control of Mixture and Testing of Wilson Dam Concrete," by John W. Hall, *Proceedings*, Am. Concrete Inst., Vol. XXII, 1926.

The author demonstrates conclusively that the conventional method of calculating curved gravity sections does not furnish an accurate indication of the existence of heel tension with reservoir full. This analysis, excluding the uncertainty of shear distribution at the foundation as a defense of the usual method of calculation, is a step toward more rational determination of stresses in hydraulic structures.

His derivation of the fundamental formulas has the advantages of clearness and simplicity. The writer's independent check of Equations (7) and (8) by direct successive integration, using semi-polar cylindrical co-ordinates instead of the usual three-dimensional system, may be of some academic interest.

Let p = the radius vector, θ = the variable angle, and z, the height axis. (See Fig. 3.) Taking the origin of co-ordinates at the apex of the conic surface that includes the down-stream face of the dam, the equation of the conic surface is,

$$p = \frac{B\,z}{H}$$

from which the moment of the concrete about C (Equation (7)):

$$M_c = \int_{R_d}^{R_u} \int_{-\phi}^{\phi} \int_{\frac{R_d H}{B}}^{p\frac{H}{B}} w\,p^2 \cos\theta\, d\,p\, d\,\theta\, d\,z$$

$$= \frac{w \sin\phi\, H}{2\,B}\,(R_u^4 - R_d^4) - \frac{2\,w \sin\phi\, H\, R_d}{3\,B}\,(R_u^3 - R_d^3)$$

Simplifying and substituting $R_u = B + R_d$, there results:

$$M_c = w \sin\phi\, H\, B \left(R_d^2 + \frac{4\,B\,R_d}{3} + \frac{B^2}{2}\right)$$

The weight of the concrete,

$$W = \int_{R_d}^{R_u} \int_{-\phi}^{\phi} \int_{\frac{R_d H}{B}}^{p\frac{H}{B}} w\,p\, d\,p\, d\,\theta\, d\,z$$

$$= \frac{2\,\phi\,H\,w}{3\,B}\,(R_u^3 - R_d^3) - \frac{\phi\,H\,R\,d\,w}{B}\,(R_u^2 - R_d^2)$$

Simplifying and substituting $R_u = B + R_d$,

$$W = w\,\phi\,B\,H\left(R_d + \frac{2\,B}{3}\right)$$

A. Floris,* Esq. (by letter).—The author has derived formulas for the calculation of the trapezoidal stresses in curved gravity dams of a triangular profile.

The influence of the curvature on the shape of the horizontal sections is commonly considered by careful designers. The Italian professors, G. Ganassini and A. Danusso,† in checking the design of the gravity base of the Gleno

* Los Angeles, Calif.

† "Relazione peritale sopra la cause che hanno determinato la rovina della diga de pian di Gleno in Val di Scaive, crollata la mattina del 1° dicembre, 1923," *Annali* dei Lavori Publici, Anno LXII, Fasc. 5, Maggio, 1924, pp. 427–428.

Dam, after its failure, used similar expressions for the calculation of the trapezoidal stresses. The derivation of these formulas is given here in some detail.

Making (see Fig. 4):

$$d = a\,\lambda \text{ and } b = a + \mu\, d = a\,(1 + \mu\,\lambda)$$

the area of the section will be,

$$A = \frac{d}{2}\,(a + b) = \frac{a\,d}{2}\,(2 + \mu\,\lambda) \ldots\ldots\ldots\ldots\ldots\ldots (18)$$

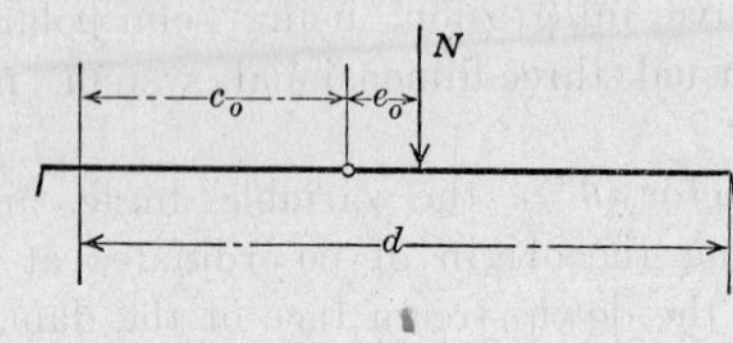

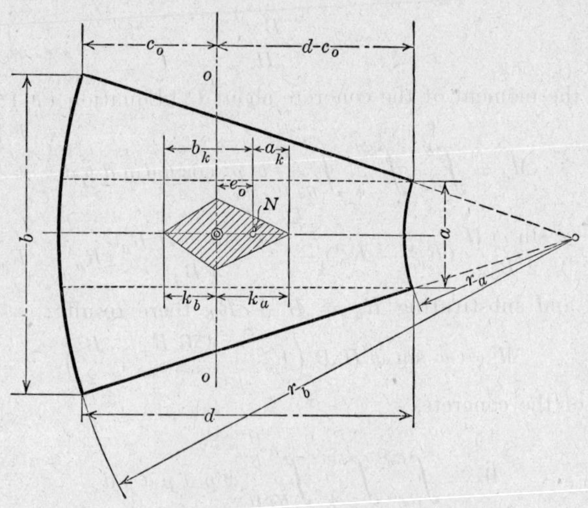

FIG. 4.—CALCULATION OF TRAPEZOIDAL STRESSES.

The distance of the center of gravity of this area from the up-stream face is,

$$c_0 = \frac{d}{3}\,\frac{2\,a + b}{a + b} = \frac{d}{3}\,\frac{3 + \mu\,\lambda}{2 + \mu\,\lambda}$$

and the moment of inertia of the section with respect to the axis, o - o, has the value,

$$I = \frac{a\,d^3}{36}\left[3 + \mu\,\lambda + \frac{(1 + \mu\,\lambda)^2 - 1}{(2 + \mu\,\lambda)^2}\right] \ldots\ldots\ldots\ldots\ldots (19)$$

which is derived as follows: Using the well-known formula:

$$I_c = I_0 + A\,c^2 \ldots\ldots\ldots\ldots\ldots\ldots\ldots\ldots (20)$$

there is obtained for the two triangles and the rectangle, respectively, into which the total area, A, may be divided, the values,

$$I_t = \frac{a\,d^3}{36}\,\mu\,\lambda$$

and,

$$I_r = \frac{a\,d^3}{12}$$

and for their sum the value,

$$I_0 = \frac{a\,d^3}{36}\,(3 + \mu\,\lambda) \ldots\ldots\ldots\ldots\ldots\ldots\ldots (21)$$

The distances of the centers of gravity of the partial areas from the center of gravity of the total area are given by,

$$c_t = \frac{d}{3}\,\frac{3 + \mu\,\lambda}{2 + \mu\,\lambda} - \frac{d}{3} = \frac{d}{3}\,\frac{1}{2 + \mu\,\lambda}$$

and,

$$c_r = \frac{d}{2} - \frac{d}{3}\,\frac{3 + \mu\,\lambda}{2 + \mu\,\lambda} = -\frac{d}{6}\,\frac{\mu\,\lambda}{2 + \mu\,\lambda}$$

while their corresponding areas are,

$$A_t = \frac{a\,d}{2}\,\mu\,\lambda \text{ and } A_r = a\,d \ldots\ldots\ldots\ldots\ldots\ldots (22)$$

so that there is,

$$A_c^{\,2} = \frac{a\,d^3}{36}\left[\frac{2\,\mu\,\lambda}{(2 + \mu\,\lambda)^2} + \frac{\mu^2\,\lambda^2}{(2 + \mu\,\lambda)^2}\right] = \frac{a\,d^3}{36}\,\frac{(1 + \mu\,\lambda)^2 - 1}{(2 + \mu\,\lambda)^2} \ldots (23)$$

The sum of the values of Equations (22) gives Equation (18), while the addition of Equations (21) and (23), according to Equation (20), results in Equation (19).

The stresses at the down-stream and up-stream faces are given, respectively, by,

$$\left.\begin{aligned} \sigma_a &= \frac{N}{A} + \frac{N\,e_0}{I}\,(d - c_0) \\ \sigma_b &= \frac{N}{A} - \frac{N\,e_0}{I}\,c_0 \end{aligned}\right\} \ldots\ldots\ldots\ldots\ldots\ldots (24)$$

Because, as the author correctly states, the middle-third theorem does not hold for curved dams, it may be appropriate to introduce the core theory (German, "kern") in the stress analysis of such structures. This gives a simple means of knowing whether or not tension does occur, because by excluding tension the resultant of all the forces must fall within the core.

The two points of the core on the line of symmetry of the section are given by the core radii:*

$$k_b = \frac{I}{A\,(d - c_0)} \text{ and } k_a = \frac{I}{A\,c_0} \ldots\ldots\ldots\ldots\ldots\ldots (25)$$

Solving for I and putting these values into Equation (24),

$$\left.\begin{aligned} \sigma_a &= \frac{N}{A}\,\frac{k_b + e_0}{k_b} = +\frac{N}{A}\,\frac{b_k}{k_b} = +\sigma_0\,\frac{b_k}{k_b} \\ \sigma_b &= \frac{N}{A}\,\frac{k_a - e_0}{k_a} = \pm\frac{N}{A}\,\frac{a_k}{k_a} = \pm\sigma_0\,\frac{a_k}{k_a} \end{aligned}\right\} \ldots\ldots\ldots\ldots (26)$$

If $e_0 = k_a$, then $\sigma_b = 0$, while when $e_0 > k_a$, there is tension at the up-stream face and σ_b is negative.

* "Die graphische Statik der Baukonstruktionen," H. Mueller-Breslau, Erster Band, 4 Auflage, 1905, p. 78; see, also, "Strength of Materials," by George F. Swain, Past-President, Am. Soc. C. E., N. Y., 1924, pp. 168-175.

Equations (25) and (26) are general expressions and valid for any section, provided the proper values for A and I are introduced.

In case the dam is straight in alignment, the horizontal section is a rectangle, and $b = a$. Consequently,

$$A = b\, d$$

$$I = \frac{b\, d^3}{12}$$

and,

$$c_0 = d - c_0 = \frac{d}{2}$$

and Equations (25) become,

$$k_b = k_a = \frac{d}{6} \ldots\ldots\ldots\ldots\ldots\ldots\ldots\ldots\ldots (27)$$

It will be seen, therefore, that the middle-third theorem is merely a special case of the more general core theorem. With the values of Equation (27), Equations (26) take the form,

$$\sigma_a = + 6\, \sigma_0 \frac{b_k}{d} \text{ and } \sigma_b = \pm\, 6\, \sigma_0 \frac{a_k}{d}$$

in which, if $e_0 > \frac{d}{6}$, σ_b becomes negative.

As far as uplift in gravity dams is concerned the following statements are perhaps of interest.*

Under the assumption of an uplift pressure distributed linearly over the entire base or a joint it can be shown† that the pressure diagram is identical with its stress diagram. From this follows as a corollary‡ that in a triangular, rectangular, or trapezoidal distribution of the uplift, the stresses at the heel are equal in all three cases, provided the intensity of the uplift at this point is assumed to be equal.

It can be concluded therefrom also that the stresses due to uplift are of no importance at any point except at the heel and that in a triangular distribution of the uplift the stress at the toe is independent of this pressure.

The author's Equation (2) for rectangular sections was given by many writers, years ago.§

The question whether inclined or horizontal sections should be considered in the calculation of the trapezoidal stresses has been the subject of much discussion in recent years. Professor J. Résal,‖ using elementary methods, devotes nine pages in order to show the necessity of investigating inclined

* "Uplift Pressure in Gravity Dams", by A. Floris, *Western Construction News,* January 25, 1928.

† "Die Staumauern", von N. Kelen, Berlin, 1926, p. 126.

‡ "Die Bestimmung der Querschnitte von Staumauern und Wehren aus dreieckigen Grundformen", von E. Link, Berlin, 1910.

§ "Ueber den Querschnitt der Staumauern," by Dr. Ing. F. Platzman, Leipzig, 1908, p. 24; "Die Bestimmung der Querschnitte von Staumauern und Wehren aus dreieckigen Grandformen," E. Link, Berlin, 1910; see, also, "Taschenbuch für Bauingenieure, M. Foerster, Berlin, 1923, p. 1231; and "Der Talsperrenbau," p. Ziegler, Berlin, 1911, p. 171.

‖ "Formes et dimensions des grands barrages en maçonnerie," *Annales des Ponts et Chaussées,* 1919, II, Mars-Avril, pp. 165–221.

sections. His main reason was that the horizontal sections are not perpendicular to the bisectrix of the angle, formed by the up-stream and down-stream faces at the crest of the dam. Professor Résal concludes therefrom that the usual bending formulas for prismatic bars are no more valid for beams of triangular shape. In order to correct this discrepancy, he suggested the assumption of the bisectrix as the neutral axis, taking the sections under consideration normal to it.

Dr. Gebauer* also recommends the investigation of these normal sections because, as he claims, tension may occur at the up-stream face of the dam, while stress investigations for horizontal sections fail to detect this. He states, further, that the stresses, thus computed, for gravity dams might be 35% higher than those found by considering horizontal sections.

The use of inclined sections can only be justified, if the dam is analyzed according to the old theory, in which the determination of the trapezoidal stresses alone was considered to be sufficient. However, if the principal stresses are calculated, the use of inclined sections is not necessary. Assuming "plane strain" and the validity of the law of the trapezoid, Dr. Kelen† has shown that for triangular profiles the same principal stresses are obtained regardless of whether horizontal or inclined sections are used. Inasmuch as the stress computations are much simpler for horizontal sections, most designers will prefer this method of procedure.

Lars R. Jorgensen,‡ M. Am. Soc. C. E. (by letter).—This is not the first time that the author has called attention to the fallacy of arching a gravity dam in plan expecting an increase in stability of the structure therefrom at all seasons. Mr. Jakobsen has shown that a gravity dam should be straight in plan for maximum safety, with a minimum expenditure of material.

If a gravity dam possess a factor of safety of two under the worst conditions of uplift, ice pressure, etc., it has been regarded as a sufficiently stable structure, and probably the future will not change anything in this respect.

Fig. 5 which was prepared for comparing the cross-sections of the highest gravity dams, shows that there is a wide difference in the various profiles. The Kensico Dam, constructed by the Board of Water Supply of New York, N. Y., apparently is the most conservative, and the Exchequer Dam, built by the Merced Irrigation District, California, the least conservative, of all high gravity dams thus far constructed. Between these two extremes is the O'Shaughnessy Dam at Hetch Hetchy, Calif., and the Camarassa Dam, in Spain. These two dams are actually a little more conservative than their relative location on the diagram would indicate, because ice pressure is negligible for both. The two sections nearly coincide and could well be termed standard gravity sections as they represent the middle between the most and the least conservative in high dams. The safety of gravity dams having sections similar to or greater than the two named cannot be questioned, but not all projects can stand the expense of such heavy sections and, consequently,

* *Beton und Eisen,* 1924, Heft 19.

† "Die Spannungsverhaeltnisse in Staumauern," Dr. Ing. N. Kelen, *Beton und Eisen,* 1925, Heft 18, pp. 287–290; also, "Die Staumauern," by the same author, Berlin, 1926, pp. 97–101.

‡ Cons. Engr., Constant Angle Arch Dam Co., San Francisco, Calif.

the safety is reduced somewhat to suit the purse of less fortunate projects. It is a fact that in many places where slim gravity sections have been built much safer arch dams could have been substituted for less money.

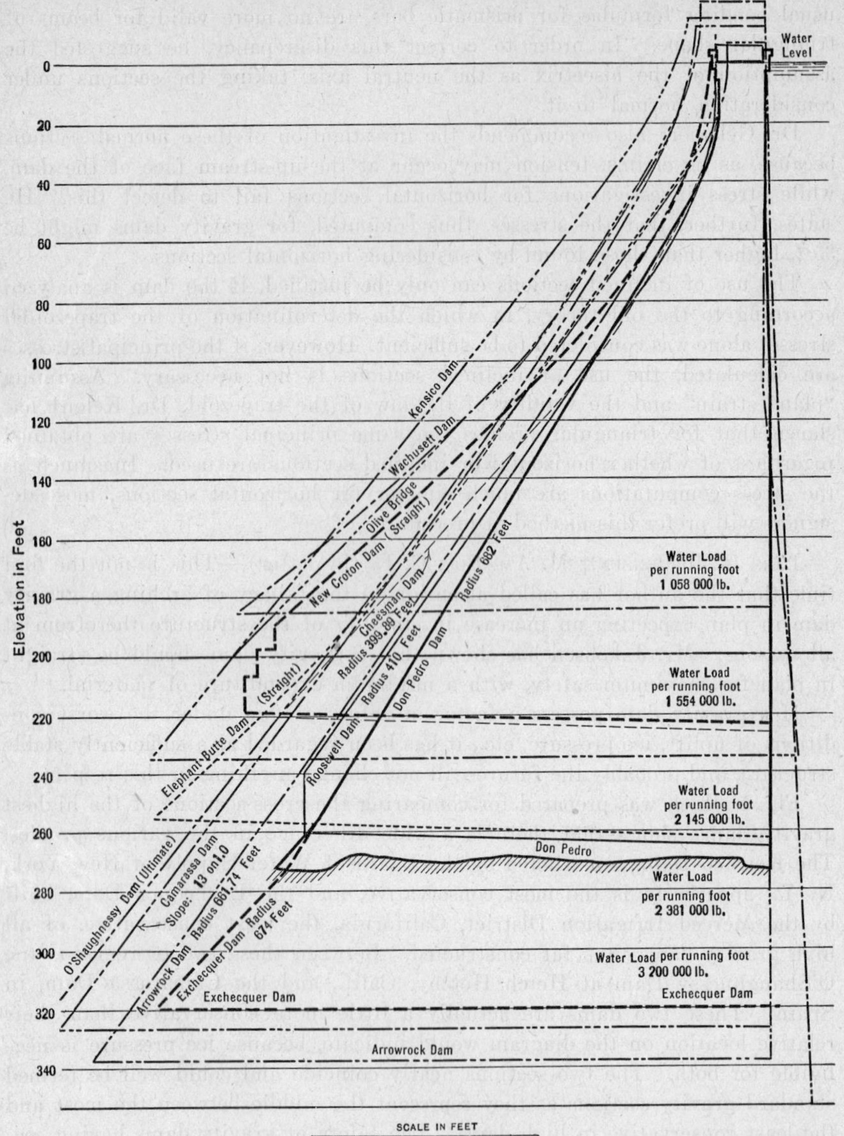

FIG. 5.—MAXIMUM CROSS-SECTIONS OF VARIOUS GRAVITY DAMS SUPERIMPOSED FOR COMPARISON.

In the past the Engineering Profession has been very much divided as to the relative merits of gravity and arch dams; this is still true although to a much less extent. At times, this controversy has resembled a political issue.

The general tendency of the profession to-day is a more favorable attitude toward the arch type in places where arch dams will fit. The problem is now better understood. The merits of strength and economy inherent in an arch dam cannot be overlooked any longer by even the most enthusiastic of gravity dam supporters.

The author's reference to the Exchequer Dam is of interest to the writer who, at one time, was connected with that project and, therefore, is well acquainted with it. An arch dam on this site would have been cheaper and safer than the one built. At that time, the State (California) authorities' distrust in arch dams prevented the construction of the one shown in Fig. 6. This design was made by A. C. Hoff, Chief Designing Engineer of the Constant Angle Arch Dam Company, and the structure was nearly 20 ft. high when the so-called gravity arch dam, described by the author, was substituted. The arch dam (Fig. 6) required 310 000 cu. yd. of concrete as compared with 370 000 cu. yd. for the gravity dam, calculated to the same estimated rock contours. The excavation proved to be more than the estimated amount, but that would not have greatly disturbed the ratio of saving in material. Therefore, a more expensive dam was substituted for a cheaper one.

The design (Fig. 6) was made so that the stresses in the arch dam, using the Cain method of calculation and assuming the entire load to be carried by the arch down to and including Elevation 500, were about 500 lb. per sq. in., compression, and less than 100 lb., tension, which is considered conservative. At and below Elevation 475 the arch does not carry all the load. Shear and various other actions take the principal part on account of the arch being short and thick, and close to the bottom. If, for instance, all the load on the dam below Elevation 475 was transmitted to the foundation through shear action along the rock contact, the average shear would be 45 lb. per sq. in. As the punching shear cannot be transmitted without calling into play arch and cantilever action, a division of load takes place. Although it is hopeless to attempt to calculate the exact distribution, it is easily seen that the part of the load falling on the arch is only small and, therefore, will not cause dangerous tension anywhere in the faces. Horizontal tension along any of the faces of an arch is not dangerous if paired with a compression of moderate value along the opposite face, and is never as dangerous as horizontal tension in the up-stream face of a gravity dam. Furthermore, any apparent tension along the up-stream face will always be greatly relieved or entirely compensated by the swelling effect of the water on the concrete.

The arch at, and below, Elevation 475 will carry the full water load, but apparent tension of more than 100 lb. per sq. in. would develop, and, at present, this tension is regarded as the upper limit. Using the simple cylinder formula as a check, the average stress at Elevation 475 would be 235 lb. per sq. in., assuming all the load to be carried by the arch. Although the stresses are not uniformly distributed for normal load, they are practically thus distributed at the point of failure, which point, therefore, evidently will not be reached until the load has been increased more than ten times the normal at Elevation 475.

Vertical cantilever action in the ordinary sense has not been counted on to support any load inasmuch as under the most unfavorable condition of water-soaking effect (a maximum water-soaking along the up-stream face decreasing gradually to nothing along the down-stream face), the cantilever bends in a down-stream direction without developing any resistance against the water pressure, and, therefore, it cannot carry any load. It is hardly possible to conceive that the water-soaking effect stops at the up-stream face, the remainder of the dam body being dry. Capillary action is always present to some extent.

Allowing for some faulty filling of the contraction joints, and for any conceivable disadvantageous action of the load, this dam can be relied on to possess a minimum factor of safety of five, and this is as much as is economically desirable.

The gravity dam which was actually built has a cross-section, as shown in Fig. 5, and is arched in plan. The arching of a gravity dam may look good, but otherwise it is a detriment to the stability of the cantilever as shown by the author. Unless the up-stream radius is much shorter than 674.7 ft., or the contraction joints are grouted properly, there will be no arch action to aid the cantilever with reservoir full during, and right after, cold weather. During this time the contraction joints have opened at the rate of approximately ¼ in. per 50 ft. length of crest and the voussoirs, therefore, have no contact.

One must not forget that, in arching a dam, the area on which the load acts becomes larger than that for a straight dam having the same amount of material and, at the same time, the center of gravity of the whole mass moves in a down-stream direction, both these items being detrimental to the stability of a dam acting by gravity.

A straight gravity dam of the same total mass as a curved one would have a greater cross-section; the distance between the center of gravity and the down-stream toe would also be greater. As the safety factor is in direct proportion to the product of weight and distance from the turning point, it is plain that it is uneconomical to arch a gravity dam in plan without having the contraction joints properly closed in order to obtain arch action.

Before arch action can take place with the voussoirs separated by a contraction crack, the middle of the dam must first slide bodily in a down-stream direction, but after such a slide it would be very difficult to make the structure water-tight. The Exchequer Dam, at the middle, should deflect slightly more than 1 in. down stream when fully loaded at the crest. This corresponds to a shortening of 0.852 in. at the crest of the dam.

Ordinarily, at the end of a cold period, the length of a dam decreases ¼ in. in 50 ft. The contraction joints open ¼ in., if spaced 50 ft. apart, cracks appear, or else tension is set up. During March and April, the crest of the Exchequer Dam, therefore, would have spaces between the voussoirs of approximately 4 in. with reservoir empty (the crest is more than 800 ft. long).

The cantilever deflection due to full load only shortened the crest 0.852 in., and there is, therefore, a space of approximately 3 in. to be closed with

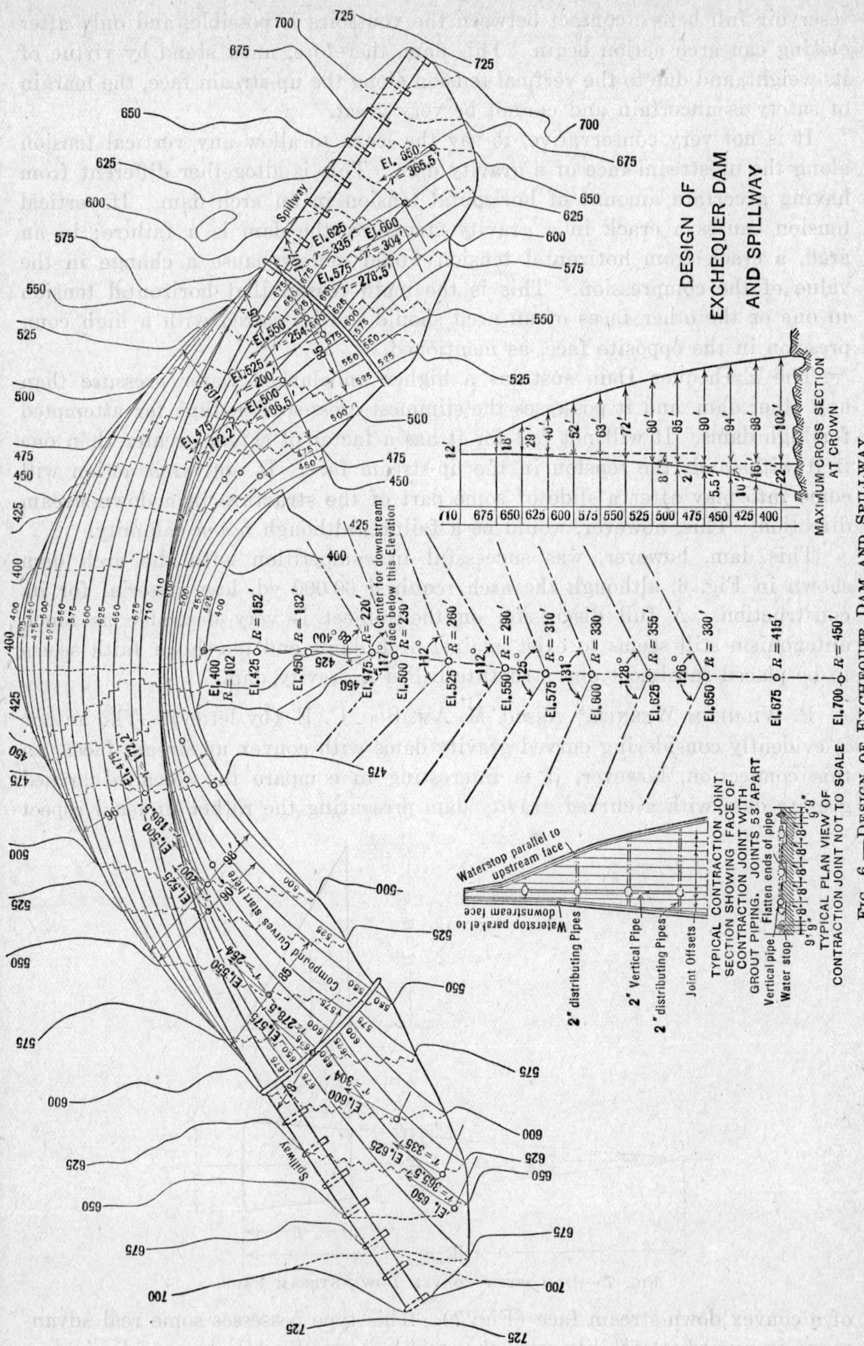

FIG. 6.—DESIGN OF EXCHEQUER DAM AND SPILLWAY.

reservoir full before contact between the voussoirs is possible, and only after closing can arch action begin. This dam, therefore, must stand by virtue of its weight, and due to the vertical tension along the up-stream face, the margin of safety is uncertain and cannot be very great.

It is not very conservative, to say the least, to allow any vertical tension along the up-stream face of a gravity dam. This is altogether different from having a certain amount of horizontal tension in an arch dam. If vertical tension causes a crack in a gravity structure, the dam is a failure; in an arch, a crack from horizontal tension would merely cause a change in the value of the compression. This is the main reason that horizontal tension in one or the other faces of an arch should not be paired with a high compression in the opposite face, as mentioned.

The Exchequer Dam sustains a higher unbalanced water pressure than any other dam, and it possesses the slimmest cross-section thus far attempted for high dams. It will not fail for it has a factor of safety greater than one if it withstands the tension in the up-stream face. If not, arch action will come into play after a slide of some part of the structure in a down-stream direction. This, however, would be a failure, although not a calamity.

This dam, however, was successful in competition with the arch dam shown in Fig. 6, although the arch required 60 000 yd. less material for its construction. A full discussion on the subject is very desirable as much antagonism still seems to exist against arch dams and too much faith seems to be placed in almost any structure called a gravity dam.

P. Wilhelm Werner,* Assoc. M. Am. Soc. C. E. (by letter).—The author is evidently considering curved gravity dams with convex up-stream face. In this connection, however, it is interesting to compare the so-called arched gravity dam with a curved gravity dam presenting the rather unusual aspect

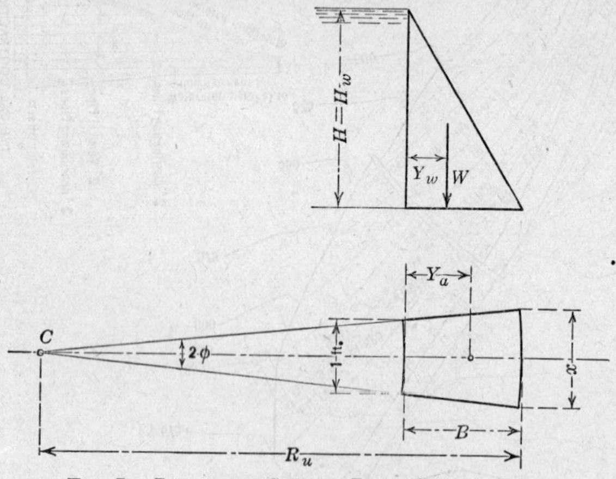

Fig. 7.—Dam with Convex Down-Stream Face.

of a convex down-stream face (Fig. 7). This type possesses some real advantages, in regard to stability, etc., that makes it worth while to consider in any actual case.

* Designing Engr., Stockholm, Sweden.

Using, as far as applicable, the same nomenclature and the same approximations for the computations as the author, the following set of formulas is developed:

$$y_a = \frac{B}{2} \frac{R_u - \frac{B}{3}}{R_u - \frac{B}{2}}$$

$$y_w = \frac{B}{3} \frac{R_u - \frac{B}{2}}{R_u - \frac{2}{3} B}$$

$$x = \frac{R_u}{R_u - B}$$

$$I = \frac{B^3}{36} \frac{1 + 4x + x^2}{1 + x}$$

$$A = \frac{B}{2} (1 + x)$$

$$W = \frac{B}{2} \frac{R_u - \frac{2}{3} B}{R_u - B} H w$$

$$M = -\frac{62.5}{6} H_w{}^3 + W (y_a - y_w)$$

Assume that the Exchequer Dam was designed with convex down-stream face, but of equal volume; so that, $H = H_w = 272.5$ ft.; $B = 171.4$ ft.; $R_u = 731.84$ ft.; $w = 160$ lb. per cu. ft.; with no uplift. This gives, $y_a = 89.5$ ft.; $y_w = 59.8$ ft.; $x = 1.305$ ft.; $I = 482\,000$ ft.[4]; $A = 197.3$ sq. ft.; $W = 4\,120\,000$ lb.; and $M = -88\,800\,000$ ft-lb. Thus, from the author's Equation (14), the vertical stresses at the heel and toe, respectively, are 30.6 and 250 lb. per sq. in., both compression.

It is especially interesting to investigate the extent to which the base width of this dam can be reduced in order to obtain zero stress at the heel with reservoir full. If $B = 164$ ft., and the other dimensions are as given previously, the values are: $y_a = 85.5$ ft.; $y_w = 57.0$ ft.; $x = 1.29$ ft.; $I = 418\,000$ ft.[4]; $A = 187.5$ sq. ft.; $W = 3\,920\,000$ lb.; and $M = -99\,100\,000$ ft-lb. Thus, from Equation (14), the vertical stress at the heel is 4.1 lb. per sq. in., compression; that is, practically zero.

Assuming that this section applies between two points, say, 200 ft. apart, the actual length of the dam would be about 201 ft. The volume then equals,

$$0.5 \times 272.5 \times 164 \times 201 = 4\,500\,000 \text{ cu. ft.}$$

The volume of a straight dam (base width = 171.4 ft.) between the same points would be,

$$0.5 \times 272.5 \times 171.4 \times 200 = 4\,670\,000 \text{ cu. ft.}$$

It is seen that the curved dam with the convex down-stream face proves to be nearly 4% cheaper than a straight dam designed according to the same governing rule. It should be noted that the assumed curvature may, or may not, be the most favorable one. It seems certain, however, that this involves a mathematical problem of finding the least cost in each actual case.

The layout of a dam in plan is, of course, to a great extent, governed by other influencing factors than stability. The geological formation at the dam site, the desirability of increasing the discharging length of the crest, and making the flood water converge better into the natural river channel below, are such factors. Aside from these points, however, under certain conditions, some economy may evidently result in giving the dam a slightly convex downstream face. The writer believes that the preference generally given to the arched gravity dam, is largely due to the additional support which the dam is assumed to receive from the arch. As arched gravity dams are usually constructed, however, this conception seems to be more or less illusory, although the arch action may prevent actual failure, if and when the cantilever has been broken. The writer is of the opinion that if it can be ascertained beyond doubt that the dam receives some support from the arch under working conditions, this should be taken into consideration in the design in order to obtain an economic structure. In case arch action cannot be absolutely ascertained, however, it seems more consistent with a proper economic design to impose upon the dam some other condition that is more easily and clearly realized.

Paul Bauman,* M. Am. Soc. C. E. (by letter).—Valuable equations have been derived by the author, which in a large measure supply the need for simple and yet accurate formulas for the determination of cantilever stresses in arch dams. Certain general conclusions have been advanced, however, which involve more or less error. A measure of the advantage or disadvantage of building a gravity dam, curved in plan, can only be determined after careful study of the topographic conditions.

A gravity dam is necessarily a very massive structure, and, due to the manner in which it is invariably built, the analysis of a thin vertical slice is insufficient. Consideration must be given to the effect of arch action and even of wedge action where the dam is built in narrow canyons. In principle, one might say that the wider the valley the less advantage there would be in a curved dam, assuming always equal foundation conditions along either a straight or curved location.

The possibilities of design of any massive dam lie between the limiting conditions of a straight cantilever dam of infinite length and a true arch dam. Under these ideal, limiting conditions there is either cantilever action or arch action only. In all practical cases, however, there will always be secondary cantilever action or secondary arch action, the amount in each case depending mainly on the ratio between the height and length, and the thickness and curvature, respectively.

It is the writer's opinion that there is insufficient justification for ignoring the effect of arch action in the case of a curved gravity dam, such as the

* Designing Engr., Quinton, Code & Hill, Los Angeles, Calif.

Exchequer Dam. Without question the actual arch action will not be in strict accordance with the computed arch action, but much less error will be involved in considering arch action than in eliminating it from consideration.

The author probably makes the assumption that, because of shrinkage in the concrete, contraction joints open and thus prevent any arch action. Compensating this shrinkage are other factors, such as plasticity and the swelling of the concrete due to absorption of moisture. Concrete has been known to flow even several years after the dam has been completed. Furthermore, contraction joints are not mathematic surfaces, and, as long as sufficient area is in contact to permit transmission of arch thrust without crushing, such arch action will be developed.

The writer has made an analysis of the stresses which, in his opinion, must closely approximate the actual stresses in the Exchequer Dam. The results of this analysis show the effect of arch support, and the conclusion is that no tensile stresses exist at the up-stream face, as claimed by the author, and that appreciable compressive stresses do occur instead, especially in the lower portions of the dam.

The radial cross-section of the dam was taken from *Western Construction News* of January 25, 1926, and the length of the up-stream face from Sheet No. 9 of the Merced Irrigation District, dated June, 1924. The water surface was assumed to be at the top of the dam at Elevation 710.0, and the up-stream radius, or R_u, constant at 675.0 ft. The notation used in this analysis is the same as that used by the author with the following additions:

t = radial thickness of dam.

h = head of water above horizontal sections.

L_u = length of extrados.

S = horizontal shear.

S'_A = deflection of arch slice $= C \dfrac{p\, r^2}{E\, t}$ (due to full load).*

δ_A = deflection of arch slice due to partial load.

δ'_B, δ'_S = deflection of cantilever due to bending and shear, respectively, due to full load.

δ_B, δ_S = deflection of cantilever due to bending and shear, respectively, due to partial load.

S_u = section modulus of up-stream face.

S_d = section modulus of down-stream face.

K_u = distance from center of gravity of horizontal section to down-stream limit of "kern".†

K_d = distance from center of gravity of horizontal section to up-stream limit of "kern".†

H_0 = polar distance of force polygons.

E = modulus of elasticity of concrete = 2 500 000 lb. per sq. in.

* "The Circular Arch Under Normal Loads," by William Cain, M. Am. Soc. C. E., *Transactions*, Am. Soc. C. E., Vol. LXXXV (1922), p. 233.

† The "kern" of a section lies within the line as described by the point of application the neutral axis of which is a tangent on the section.

For the determination of δ'_B and δ_B, Mohr's method was used,* whereas for the determination of δ'_S, the least work method was used, as follows:

$$\delta'_S = \int_0^H \frac{S' S}{G A} d x$$

in which, $G = \frac{5}{13} E$ and $S' = - P = - 1$ (Fig. 8). Therefore,

$$\delta'_S = - \frac{1}{G} \int_0^H \frac{S d x}{A} \qquad (28)$$

$$S = \frac{62.5 (H - x)^2}{2}; A = \frac{B}{H} (H - x)$$

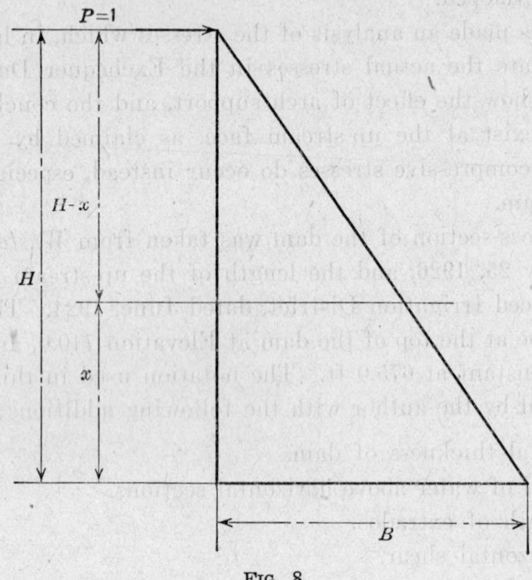

FIG. 8.

Introducing these values in Equation (28),

$$\delta'_S = - \frac{31.25 H}{G B} \int_0^H (H - x) d x = - \frac{31.25 H}{G B} \left[H x - \frac{x^2}{2} \right]_0^H + c (= 0) \qquad (29)$$

For the determination of δ_S (partial load) the $\frac{S}{A}$-area, Fig. 9 (*e*) was graphically integrated and multiplied by $\frac{1}{G}$; that is, Equation (28) was used in its form:

$$\delta_S = - \frac{1}{G} \sum_0^H \frac{S}{A}$$

In Table 1 various quantities, determined by the author's formulas, are shown. The vertical weights, W (based on a triangular section), their lever arms, $(y_a - Y_w)$, the distance, Y_a, from the up-stream face to the center of

* "Gravity and Arch Action in Curved Dams," by F. A. Noetzli, M. Am. Soc. C. E., *Transactions*, Am. Soc. C. E., Vol. LXXXIV (1921), p. 1.

TABLE 1.—ANALYSIS OF EXCHEQUER DAM.

Elevation, in feet.	h, in feet.	t, in feet.	L_u, in feet.	2ϕ, in degrees and minutes.	W, at 160 lb. per cu. ft.	$y_a - y_w$, in feet.	y_a, in feet.	y_w, in feet.	M_p, in foot-pounds.	M_w, in foot-pounds.	$M = -M_p + M_w$.	A, in square feet.	I, in feet[4].
	(1)	(2)	(3)	(4)	(5)	(6)	(7)	(8)	(9)	(10)	(11)	(12)	(13)
									−	+	−		
710	....	12.00	...	.....	....	.....	.....	.....	....	....	....	11.89	143
685	25	16.00	900	76–22	31 750	2.66	7.97	5.31	0.163 by 10^6	0.084 by 10^6	0.079 by 10^6	15.83	339
660	50	29.78	780	66–20	117 500	4.93	14.77	9.84	1.303 by 10^6	0.579 by 10^6	0.724 by 10^6	29.05	2 146
610	100	62.71	620	52–35	482 500	10.27	30.84	20.57	10.420 by 10^6	4.955 by 10^6	5.465 by 10^6	59.79	19 578
560	150	95.20	480	40–47	1 090 000	15.44	46.40	30.96	35.168 by 10^6	16.829 by 10^6	18.339 by 10^6	88.48	66 647
510	200	125.69	330	28–00	1 890 000	20.19	60.70	40.51	83.360 by 10^6	38.159 by 10^6	45.201 by 10^6	113.98	149 515
460	250	157.18	190	16–10	2 900 000	24.95	75.14	50.19	162.813 by 10^6	72.355 by 10^6	90.458 by 10^6	138.87	284 232
437.5	272.5	171.35	150	12–50	3 418 000	27.02	81.53	54.51	210.847 by 10^6	92.354 by 10^6	118.493 by 10^6	149.59	363 407

Elevation, in feet.	S_u, in feet[3].	S_d in feet[3].	K_u, in feet.	K_d, in feet.	$\frac{W}{A}$.	$\frac{M}{S_u}$.	$\frac{M}{S_d}$.	f_u, in pounds per square foot.	f_d, in pounds per square foot.	f_u, in pounds per square inch.	f_d, in pounds per square inch.	R_m, in feet.	$\frac{t}{R_m}$.
	(14)	(15)	(16)	(17)	(18)	(19)	(20)	(21)	(22)	(23)	(24)	(25)	(26)
						−	+	−	+	−	+		
710	....	....	.....	.....	... ..	......	......	.....	......	......	......	669.0	.....
685	....	....	.....	.....	... ..	......	......	.....	......	......	......	667.0	0.024
660	145.30	142.98	5.00	4.92	4 044	4 977	5 058	933	9 102	6.50	63.20	660.11	0.045
610	634.83	614.31	10.62	10.27	8 070	8 608	8 896	538	16 966	3.74	111.80	642.65	0.098
560	1 436.36	1 365.72	16.23	15.44	12 319	12 767	13 427	448	25 746	3.11	178.70	627.40	0.152
510	2 463.18	2 300.58	21.61	20.18	16 582	18 352	19 648	1 770	36 230	12.30	252.00	612.15	0.205
460	3 782.70	3 464.56	27.24	24.95	20 883	23 913	26 109	3 030	46 992	21.10	326.50	596.41	0.263
437.5	4 457.34	4 045.95	29.80	27.05	22 849	26 584	29 287	3 735	52 136	26.00	362.00	589.32	0.291

TABLE 1.—(*Continued.*)

Elevation, in feet.	C.	P', in pounds.	$\frac{R_u}{R_m}$.	P, in pounds.	$\delta_{A'} = C \times \frac{P R_m^2}{E t}$.	$\delta_{A'}$, in inches.	$\frac{M}{I}$.	$\Sigma \frac{M}{I}$.	$\delta_{B'}$, in inches.	x.	$H \times x$.	$\frac{x^2}{2}$.	$\delta_{S'}$, in inches.
	(27)	(28)	(29)	(30)	(31)	(32)	(33)	(34)	(35)	(36)	(37)	(38)	(39)
710	.....	......	.....	......	....	......	......	72 236	0.410	272.50	74 256	37 128	0.159
685	1.852	1 563	1.01	1 578	0.2260	2.710	233.20	......	0.345	......	......	......	.....
660	1.740	3 125	1.021	3 192	0.2255	2.710	337.20	65 060	0.273	222.50	60 631	24 753	0.155
610	1.025	6 250	1.050	6 565	0.1232	1.478	279.12	51 160	0.177	172.50	47 006	14 878	0.138
560	0.305	9 375	1.076	10 100	0.0354	0.424	275.15	37 290	0.100	122.50	33 381	7 503	0.112
510	0.110	12 500	1.103	13 800	0.0126	0.151	302.32	22 860	0.053	72.50	19 756	2 628	0.074
460	.....	15 625	1.132	......	0.000075*	0.0009	320.51	7 270	0.010	22.50	6 131	253	0.053
437.5	.....	17 030	1.146	......	....	......	326.06	......	.....	......	......	......	.....

Elevation, in feet.	$\delta_{B'} + \delta_{S'}$ in inches.	P, in pounds.	S, in pounds.	$\frac{S}{A}$.	$M_{P'}$, in foot-pounds.	$M' = -M_{P'} + M_w$.	$\frac{M'}{I}$.	$\Sigma \frac{M'}{I}$.	δ_B, in inches.	δ_S, in inches.	$\delta_C = \delta_B + \delta_S$, in inches.	P_C, in pounds.	P_A, in pounds.
	(40)	(41)	(42)	(43)	(44)	(45)	(46)	(47)	(48)	(49)	(50)	(51)	(52)
710	0.569	+ 2 630	....	......	....	....	....	37 500	0.2750	0.1346	0.4096	......	.....
685	0.502	− 13 800	− 11 170	706	± 0.00 by 10^6	0.0844 by 10^6	+249.00	40 500	0.2300	0.1333	0.3633	1 370	193
660	0.428	− 58 900	− 70 070	2 410	− 1.00 by 10^6	− 0.4208 by 10^6	−195.60	43 500	0.1900	0.1273	0.3173	2 750	375
610	0.315	−196 300	− 266 370	4 460	− 9.00 by 10^6	− 4.045 by 10^6	−207.00	31 220	0.1200	0.1130	0.2330	5 100	1 150
560	0.212	−293 000	− 559 370	6 320	− 29.00 by 10^6	−12.171 by 10^6	−182.50	21 485	0.0600	0.0898	0.1498	6 600	2 775
510	0.127	−353 000	− 912 370	8 010	− 65.00 by 10^6	−26.841 by 10^6	−179.50	12 435	0.0250	0.0585	0.0835	7 500	5 000
460	0.068	−430 000	−1 342 370	9 640	−120.00 by 10^6	−47.645 by 10^6	−167.60	3 760	0.0050	0.0201	0.0251	10 400	5 225
437.5	.....	−281 200	−1 623 570	10 860	−153.00 by 10^6	−60.646 by 10^6	−167.00	......	......	......	......	17 030	.....

* Arch deflection similar to beam deflection.

TABLE 1.—(*Continued.*)

Elevation, in feet.	$P' = P_C + P_A'$, in pounds.	$K = \frac{P_A}{P'}$.	$\delta_A = K \times \delta_A'$.	$\frac{W}{A}$.	$\frac{M'}{S_u}$.	$\frac{M'}{S_d}$.	f_u, in pounds per square foot.	f_d, in pounds per square foot.	f_u, in pounds per square inch.	f_d, in pounds per square inch.	Average arch thrust, in pounds.	Average arch stress, in pounds per square foot.	f_A, in pounds per square inch.
	(53)	(54)	(55)	(56)	(57)	(58)	(59)	(60)	(61)	(62)	(63)	(64)	(65)
							+	+	+	+			
710	......	......	0.4096	......	....	......	......	......	.....	......	....	......	......
685	1 563	0.124	0.3360										
660	3 125	0.120	0.3250	4 044	— 2 892	2 940	1 152	6 984	7.99	48.60	240 000	8 060	56.00
610	6 250	0.134	0.2720	3 070	— 6 950	7 180	1 120	15 250	7.77	105.70	450 000	7 180	49.80
560	9 375	0.421	0.1785	12 319	— 8 480	8 910	3 839	21 229	26.66	147.50	450 000	4 727	32.80
510	12 500	0.400	0.0610	16 582	—10 900	11 660	5 682	28 242	39.48	196.30	450 000*	3 580	24.90
460	15 625	0.335	0.0300	20 883	—12 580	13 730	8 303	34 613	57.70	240.50	400 000*	2 550	17.70
437.5	17 030	......	......	22 849	—13 600	14 980	9 249	37 829	64.20	262.80	....	......	......

Elevation, in feet.	A_A, in square feet.	ΔA_A, in square feet.	Percentage of A_A required.	$M_0 = \frac{S_u \times W}{A}$.	$M_P' = -M_0 - M_w$	h^2.	x, in feet.	$(h - x)$, in feet.	Z†, in pounds.	$M_P' = \frac{143}{160} \times M_P'$	x, in feet.	$(h - x)$, in feet.	Z‡, in pounds.
	(66)	(67)	(68)	(69)	(70)	(71)	(72)	(73)	(74)	(75)	(76)	(77)	(78)
710	12.00	....	....	....	....	......	......	.....	......	....	......	......	......
660	29.78	1.12	3.76	587 702	— 1 166 977	2 500	44.72	5.28	330	1 040 000	39.90	10.10	630
610	2.71	2.10	3.35	5 123 021	— 10 078 296	10 000	96.55	3.45	216	9 050 000	86.60	13.40	836
560	95.20	2.10	2.21	17 694 763	— 34 524 363	22 500	147.00	3.00	188	30 820 000	131.50	19.50	1 220
510	125.69	2.10	1.67	40 844 105	— 79 003 205	40 000	189.21	10.79	738	70 440 000	168.80	31.20	1 950
460	157.18	1.86	1.19	78 995 189	—151 350 189	62 500	231.99	18.01	1 125	135 400 000	207.80	42.20	2 630
437.5	171.35	....	....	101 846 297	—194 200 657	74 256	250.54	21.96	1 373	173 850 000	224.20	48.30	3 020

* Beam action is greater than arch action.

† Water load for $w = 160$.

‡ Water load for $w = 143$.

gravity, and the effective moments, M, are listed in Columns (5), (6), (7), and (11).

In Columns (12) to (24), Table 1, the areas, A, moments of inertia, I, section moduli, S_u and S_d, kern distance, K_u and K_d (Fig. 9(b)), and stresses, f_u and f_d (up-stream and down-stream face), are shown. In Columns (32), (35), and (39), the arch deflection, δ'_A, and the cantilever deflections, δ'_B and δ'_S, for full load (water surface at Elevation 710) are as shown in Fig. 9(a). The cantilever deflections, $\delta_C = \delta_B + \delta_S$, for partial load and the arch deflections, δ_A, for partial load are shown in Columns (50) and (55) to coincide closely enough to confirm the load distribution as shown in Fig. 9(e). A further adjustment of these deflections would change the respective loads very little. The stresses f_A, f_u, and f_d, due to partial arch and cantilever loads, respectively (Fig. 9(e)), are given in Columns (65), (59), (60), (61), and (62).

In determining the average arch thrust, the influence of elastic deformations has been included, and the result as shown in Columns (56) to (68), Table 1, indicates that, in the lower part of the dam, arch action is gradually being replaced by beam action until a condition is reached at the bottom of the dam where bending becomes negligible as compared with radial shear; that is, where the respective part of the dam acts as a wedge. Assuming the crushing strength of the concrete to be 1 500 lb. per sq. in., or 216 000 lb. per sq. ft., the area required to transmit this thrust is shown under δA_A, Column (67), and the maximum percentage of the existing area is shown in Column (68). Inasmuch as the behavior of an arch, as well as that of a beam of such dimensions as in the lower part of the dam, is of considerable uncertainty, it may be stated that the respective values for the percentage of A_A required, are meant to be indicative rather than exact.

In Columns (69) to (78), Table 1, the load limit lines are determined as shown in Fig. 9(e). They were calculated for W = 160 lb. per cu. ft. and W = 143 lb. per cu. ft., respectively. They represent the water load that may be brought against the dam so as to produce a stress, $f_u = \pm 0$, at the up-stream face.

The conditional equation, therefore, is:

$$f_u = \pm 0 = \frac{W}{A} - \frac{M_0}{S_u} \qquad (30)$$

$$M_0 = \frac{W \times S_u}{A} \qquad (31)$$

and as the sum of the moments must be equal to zero,

$$-M_{P'} + M_W + M_0 = 0$$

and,

$$-M_{P'} = -M_W - M_0$$

From Fig. 10:

$$M_{P'} = \frac{62.5\ h^2}{6} \times x$$

and,

$$x = \frac{6\ M_{P'}}{62.5\ h^2} = \frac{M_{P'}}{10.42\ h^2} \qquad (32)$$

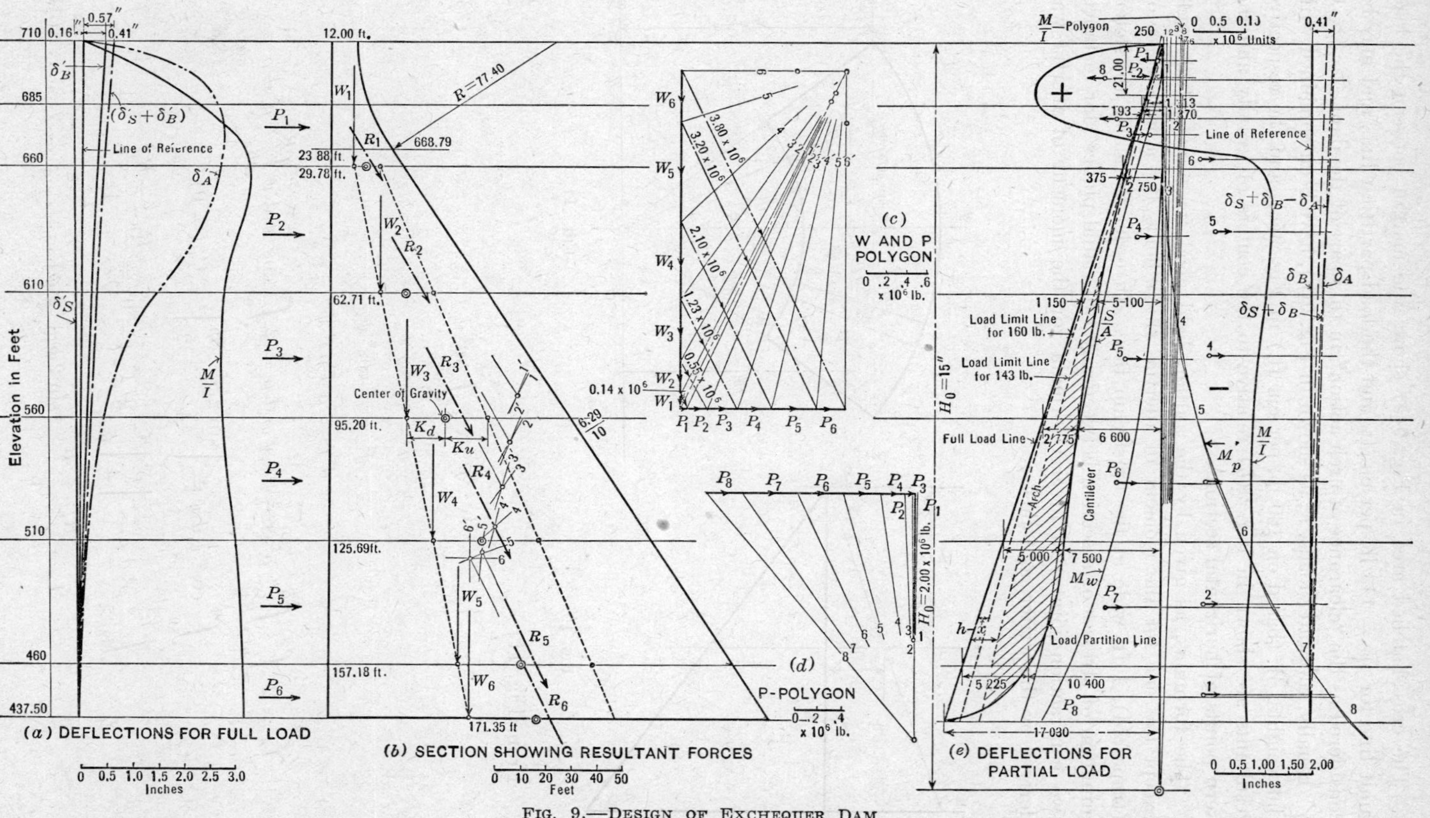

FIG. 9.—DESIGN OF EXCHEQUER DAM.

The cross-hatched area in Fig. 9(*e*) shows the margin between the load limit line for $W = 143$ lb. per cu. ft. and the load partition line, and may be considered as the "clearance of arch action" in this part of the dam.

Finally, the water loads, P, as shown in Fig. 9(*e*), have been combined with the weights, W (based on 160 lb. per cu. ft.) in Fig. 9(*c*), and the respective resultants are shown in Fig. 9(*b*) relative to the centers of gravity and the kern points of horizontal sections.

The formulas, as given by the author, hold good for any central angle except the one for the moment of inertia which holds for a hollow sector (trapezoid), 1 ft. wide at the up-stream face. In order to enable the determination of stresses of a section between any two radial planes (for instance, two contraction joints), a precise formula for the moment of inertia was derived by the writer, as follows:

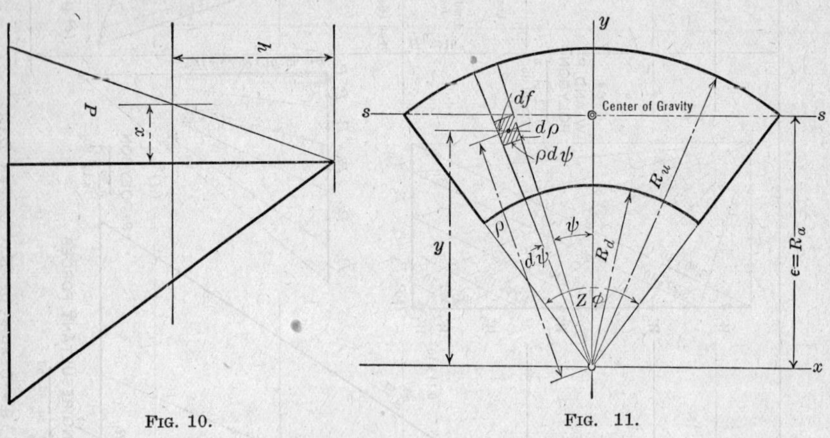

FIG. 10. FIG. 11.

From Fig. 11:

$$I_x = 2 \int_0^{\phi} y^2 \, d\, f \ldots\ldots\ldots\ldots\ldots\ldots\ldots\ldots (33)$$

$$y = \rho \cos \psi$$

$$y^2 = \rho^2 \cos^2 \psi$$

$$d\, f = \rho \, d\, \rho \, d\, \psi$$

$$I_x = 2 \int_0^{\phi} \int_{R_d}^{R_u} \rho^2 \cos^2 \psi \, d\, \psi \, \rho \, d\, \rho = 2 \int_0^{\phi} \cos^2 \psi \, d\, \psi \int_{R_d}^{R_u} \rho^3 \, d\, \rho$$

$$\int_0^{\phi} \cos^2 \psi \, d\, \psi = \left[\frac{\sin 2\phi}{4} + \frac{\phi}{2}\right] + C_1 \, (= 0)$$

$$\int_{R_d}^{R_u} \rho^3 \, d\, \rho = \left[\frac{\rho^4}{4}\right]_{R_d}^{R_u} + C_2 \, (= 0) = \frac{R_u^{\,4} - R_d^{\,4}}{4}$$

$$I_x = \frac{R_u^{\,4} - R_d^{\,4}}{8} \, [\sin 2\phi + 2\, \phi] \ldots\ldots\ldots\ldots\ldots\ldots\ldots (34)$$

$$R_u^4 - R_d^4 = (R_u^2 - R_d^2)(R_u^2 + R_d^2) = (R_u - R_d)(R_u + R_d)$$
$$[(R_u + R_d)^2 - 2\, R_u\, R_d]$$
$$R_u - R_d = t$$
$$R_u + R_d = 2\, R_m$$
$$R_u^4 - R_d^4 = 2\, t\, R_m\, [4\, R_m^2 - 2\, R_u\, R_d]$$
$$I_x = \frac{t\, R_m}{4}[4\, R_m^2 - 2\, R_u\, R_d]\,[\sin 2\phi + 2\phi]$$
$$= t\, R_m \left[R_m^2 - \frac{R_u\, R_d}{2}\right][\sin 2\phi + 2\phi] \quad \ldots\ldots\ldots\ldots\ldots (35)$$

which is the equation for the moment of inertia about the x-axis. For the moment of inertia about the center of gravity of the section:

$$I_S = I_x - F\, \varepsilon^2 \quad \ldots\ldots\ldots\ldots\ldots (36)$$

in which,

$$F = 2 \int_0^\phi d\, f = 2 \int_0^\phi \int_{R_d}^{R_u} d\, \psi\, \rho\, d\, \rho = 2\, \phi \left[\frac{\rho^2}{2}\right]_{R_d}^{R_u}$$
$$= \phi\, [R_u^2 - R_d^2] = 2\, \phi\, t\, R_m \quad \ldots\ldots\ldots\ldots\ldots (37)$$
$$\varepsilon = R_a{}^* = \left(R_m + \frac{t^2}{12\, R_m}\right)\frac{\sin \phi}{\phi}$$
$$\varepsilon^2 = \left(R_m + \frac{t^2}{12\, R_m}\right)^2 \frac{\sin^2 \phi}{\phi^2}$$
$$\left(F \times \varepsilon^2\right) = 2\left(R_m + \frac{t^2}{12\, R_m}\right)^2 \frac{\sin^2 \phi}{\phi} \times t \times R_m$$
$$2\left(R_m + \frac{t^2}{12\, R_m}\right) = \frac{1}{72\, R_m^2}\left(12\, R_m^2 + t^2\right)$$
$$(12\, R_m^2 + t^2) = 3\, R_u^2 + 6\, R_u\, R_d + 3\, R_d^2 + R_u^2 - 2\, R_u\, R_d + R_d^2$$
$$= 4\,[R_u^2 + R_u\, R_d + R_d^2] = 4\,[(R_u + R_d)^2 - R_u\, R_d] = 4\,[4\, R_m^2 - R_u\, R_d]$$

Introducing this value:

$$\left(F \times \varepsilon^2\right) = \frac{16\, t}{72\, R_m}\left[4\, R_m^2 - R_u\, R_d\right]^2 \frac{\sin^2 \phi}{\phi}$$
$$= \frac{32 \times t}{9 \times R_m}\left[R_m^2 - \frac{R_u\, R_d}{4}\right]^2 \frac{\sin^2 \phi}{\phi} \quad \ldots\ldots\ldots\ldots\ldots (38)$$

Equation (36) now becomes:

$$I_S = t\, R_m \left[R_m^2 - \frac{R_u\, R_d}{2}\right]\left[\sin 2\,\phi + 2\phi\right]$$
$$- \frac{32 \times t}{9 \times R_m}\left[R_m^2 - \frac{R_u\, R_d}{4}\right]^2 \frac{\sin^2 \phi}{\phi} \quad \ldots\ldots\ldots\ldots\ldots (39)$$

WILLIAM CAIN,† M. AM. SOC. C. E. (by letter).—The writer has been much interested in this excellent paper. For the assumptions, all the derived formulas are exact. A volume 1 ft. wide at the up-stream face is considered.

* As derived by the author.

† Prof. Emeritus, Univ. of North Carolina, Chapel Hill, N. C.

If this width had been taken as $d\,s$ in place of 1, then, at once, 1 could replace $\frac{\sin \phi}{\phi}$, and Equation (4) could be more easily derived.

Curved gravity dams are ordinarily constructed with radial, vertical contraction joints. If these are not provided, the dam is likely to develop vertical cracks. Assuming such joints or cracks to extend from top to bottom, the author's theory applies to portions of the dam between cracks when the distance between them is not too large. If, however, by reinforcement or grouting, it is possible to realize a monolithic dam, then the theory presented does not apply and recourse must be had to the theory for the dam treated as a whole, as outlined by Fred A. Noetzli, M. Am. Soc. C. E.,* or an equivalent method may be used. However, if such dams are made by simply grouting the joints or cracks after full shrinkage has taken place, it is doubtful if the dam can be maintained as a monolith under extreme changes of temperature.

The author has treated completely the arched gravity dam of triangular cross-section with a vertical water face and has applied the results to a dam of such cross-section that, if the dam is first regarded as straight, with reservoir full, and uplift neglected, the stress at the heel is zero. Afterward, the dam of this same cross-section is considered curved with an up-stream radius of 674.7 ft.; the stress at the heel is again computed and found to be tension and, in amount, 25.9 lb. per sq. in.

The conclusion is inescapable that it is dangerous to neglect curvature in a curved gravity dam, and it is plain that the error increases as the radius diminishes. The error has been computed on the usual assumptions. There are likewise "uncertainties involved in determining the stresses near the foundation of a gravity dam", as the author notes. It would seem, then, that the base of the dam should always be thicker than the usual middle-third theorem prescribes.

The author gives a complete solution for the arched gravity dam of a triangular cross-section with the up-stream face vertical. It may be of interest to indicate the solution for the usual cross-sections, as given in Fig. 12, where the lines, $F\,G$ and $G\,B$, are tangent to the curved down-stream profile, not drawn.

The value of M_c, the moment about C of the solid the cross-section of which is $A\,O\,B$ ($A\,O$ being vertical), is given directly by the author (page 769). For the remaining sections, Equation (7),

$$M_c = 2\,w \sin \phi \int r^2\,h\,d\,r$$

applies on substituting proper limits and values of r in terms of h.

Let the dotted lines in the sections, $E\,A\,O$, $O\,D\,F\,I$, and $I\,F\,G$, represent the variable ordinate, h, and let r be the radius, with center at C, corresponding to h, or the horizontal distance from C to the point where the dotted lines produced meet the base, $E\,B$. Also, let the horizontal radii from C to Points E, A, and the points on $E\,B$ vertically under F and G, be designated by the symbols, r_e, r_a, r_f, and r_g, respectively. Then, from similar triangles,

* *Transactions*, Am. Soc. C. E., Vol. LXXXIV (1921), p. 44.

Section $E\,A\,O$,

$$\frac{h}{O\,A} = \frac{r_e - r}{E\,A}$$

Section $O\,D\,F\,I$,

$$h = O\,D + (r_a - r)\tan\alpha$$

Section $I\,F\,G$,

$$\frac{h}{I\,F} = \frac{r - r_g}{r_f - r_g}$$

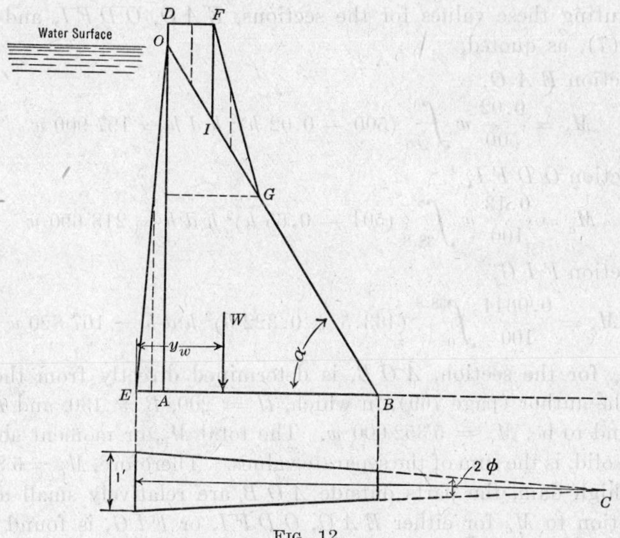

FIG. 12.

For a numerical illustration, the cross-section of the straight dam so thoroughly analyzed by the writer* will be adopted, and the dam will be regarded as curved, with an up-stream radius of 500 ft. The dimensions, in feet, will be given in reference to Fig. 12. The height to the water surface, $A\,O = 200$, $E\,A = 4$, and $A\,B = 130$, so that the base, $E\,B = 134$ ft. Also, $O\,D = 8$, $D\,F = 20$, and $I\,F = 38.8$; and, $\tan\alpha = \frac{200}{130} = \frac{100}{65}$. The radii are as follows:

$$r_e = 500;\ r_a = 496;\ r_f = 476;\ r_g = 463.5;\ r_b = 366$$

The radius to the vertical through the center of gravity of the section, $E\,O\,D\,F\,G\,B$, is 455.3 ft., and its area, 14 112 sq. ft.; so that the volume of the part of the curved dam having the central angle, $2\,\phi$, is,

$$14\,112 \times 2\,\phi \times 455.3 = 14\,112 \times \frac{1}{500} \times 455.3 = 12\,851 \text{ cu. ft.}$$

and its weight,

$$W = 12\,851\ w$$

* "Stresses in Masonry Dams," *Transactions*, Am. Soc. C. E., Vol. LXIV (1909), p. 208. This paper is likewise given in the writer's "Retaining Walls" (Van Nostrand's Science Series No. 3, 7th Edition).

Substituting the numerical values in the formulas just given, involving h and r, and solving for r:

For Section $E\ A\ O$,

$$r = 500 - 0.02\,h;\ dr = -0.02\,dh$$

For Section $O\ D\ F\ I$,

$$r = 501 - 0.65\ h;\ dr = -0.65\ dh$$

For Section $F\ I\ G$,

$$r = 463.5 + 0.322\,h;\ dr = 0.322\,dh$$

Substituting these values for the sections, $E\ A\ O$, $O\ D\ F\ I$, and $F\ I\ G$, in Equation (7), as quoted,

For Section $E\ A\ O$,

$$M_c = \frac{0.02}{500}\,w \int_{200}^{0} (500 - 0.02\ h)^2\ h\ d\ h = 197\ 900\ w$$

For Section $O\ D\ F\ I$,

$$M_c = \frac{0.13}{100}\,w \int_{38.8}^{8} (501 - 0.65\ h)^2\ h\ d\ h = 218\ 690\ w$$

For Section $F\ I\ G$,

$$M_c = \frac{0.0644}{100} \int_{0}^{38.8} (463.5 + 0.322\ h)^2\ h\ d\ h = 107\ 820\ w$$

The M_c for the section, $A\ O\ B$, is determined directly from the formula given by the author (page 769), in which, $H = 200$, $B = 130$, and $R_d = 366$, and is found to be, $M_c = 5\ 352\ 000\ w$. The total M_c, or moment about C for the entire solid, is the sum of the separate values. Therefore, $M_c = 5\ 876\ 410\ w$.

For a high dam, the parts outside $A\ O\ B$ are relatively small and a fair approximation to M_c for either $E\ A\ O$, $O\ D\ F\ I$, or $F\ I\ G$, is found by multiplying its area by the radius to the vertical through its center of gravity. This assumes a rectangular in place of a trapezoidal base for such parts. For this dam, the approximation was sufficiently close.

Having found M_c and W for the entire solid of the angle, 2ϕ, the radius to its center of gravity is,

$$\frac{M_c}{W} = \frac{5\ 876\ 410}{12\ 851} = 457.27 \text{ ft.}$$

whence, the horizontal distance from this center of gravity to E is,

$$y_w = 500 - 457.27 = 42.73 \text{ ft.}$$

y_a, the distance from E to the center of gravity of the trapezoidal base, is given by Equation (4). Thus, $y_a = 63.55$ ft. and $y_a - y_w = 20.82$ ft.

The remainder of the solution is effected by the author's Equations (10), (12), and (14).

$$x = 0.732;\ A = 116;\ I = 172\ 400;\ M = -41\ 266\ 000$$

$$w \text{ (assumed)} = \frac{5}{2}\,(62.5) \therefore W = 2\ 008\ 000 \text{ lb.}$$

$$s_u = \frac{W}{A} + \frac{M}{I}\,y_a = 17\ 300 - 15\ 240 = 2\ 060 \text{ lb. per sq. ft. stress at } E$$

or 14.3 lb. per sq. in. compression at the up-stream edge under full water load. For the straight dam, the unit compression at E was 32.24 lb. per sq. in. This ignores uplift. Where that is to be considered, Equation (17) directly applies.

The change in the vertical component of the stress at E from 32.24 lb. per sq. in. compression for the straight dam to 14.3 lb. per sq. in. for the curved dam, indicates that if the straight dam had been designed for such a value of w as to give zero stress at E, then the curved dam would be in tension at the heel, E. This result is exactly in line with the author's conclusion, and indicates that, for a curved gravity dam, the curvature should be considered in the analysis.

F. W. HANNA,* M. AM. SOC. C. E. (by letter).—The writer has been greatly interested in the author's discussion of arched gravity dams and believes that he has done the Engineering Profession a distinct service in presenting this subject in a comprehensive manner at this time. The author states that it is the purpose of his paper to show that it is not safe to neglect the curvature in calculating the stresses in an arched gravity dam and that this may lead to, and has led to, dams having tension in the up-stream face. He also states that the Habra Dam, in Algiers, and the Bouzey Dam, in France, failed from tension in the up-stream face several years after they were built. It appears to the writer that these claims are too broad and possibly may be misleading.

In regard to the Habra Dam, Wegmann states† that the main dam was straight in plan (not curved), that the failure of the dam cannot be attributed to any defect in design, but was caused, in all probability, by faults in the execution of the work, and that the dam failed on account of a defective foundation. It appears, moreover, from a discussion of the dam by M. Leon Ponchet that the foundation was unsatisfactory; that defective stone may have been used in the masonry; that the sand used was not good; that clayey red earth was used instead of sand for the inner part of the dam; that the hydraulic lime used was not very good; and that a combination of these circumstances caused the destruction of the dam. It appears, therefore, that this dam was not curved in plan and that its immediate failure was caused by defective foundation, possibly augmented by low-grade masonry in the body of the dam.

Wegmann also states that the Bouzey Dam was built straight in plan (not curved); that it was founded on red sandstone which was fissured and quite permeable; that considerable difficulty was experienced in the foundation trench from springs; that when the water reached a level of 33 ft. below the top of the dam springs of about 2 cu. ft. per sec. appeared on the lower side of the wall; that when the water reached a level 10.5 ft. below the top of the dam a portion of the dam, 444 ft. long, was shoved forward so as to form a curve convex down stream, causing additional fissures and increasing the flow of the springs to about 8 cu. ft. per sec.; that the failure of the dam is supposed to have been due to a greater tension at the up-stream face than

* Hydr. Engr., East Bay Municipal Utility Dist., Oakland, Calif.

† "The Design and Construction of Dams."

the masonry could resist; and that this tension was probably increased by an upward water pressure under the dam. It appears from this statement that the initial failure of the Bouzey Dam was caused by sliding on the foundation, and that the final failure was probably caused by combined hydrostatic pressure, sliding, and shearing within the body of the dam due to poor masonry, and possibly injury to the dam through the initial failure. Here, as in the case of the Habra Dam, there was no curvature in plan, and neglect of the radial plane stress theory had nothing to do with the failure of the dam.

In order to prove the contention that it is never safe to neglect the curvature of a gravity dam in calculating the stresses, the author selects for analysis a radial-sided slice with a chord thickness of 1 ft. at the up-stream face of an arched gravity dam. The selection of this narrow slice is evidently a remnant of the custom of considering vertical slices of this thickness in calculating the stresses in straight gravity dams. The selection of a slice 1 ft. thick ignores the fact that in straight dams the analysis of a slice of this thickness will show the same stability and stress as a slice of any other thickness and that in curved dams the analysis of a radial slice of up-stream chord thickness of 1 ft. will show results materially different from those obtained by taking a radial slice of a greater thickness. Inasmuch as a 1-ft. radial slice cannot conceivably shear out from the surrounding material, an analysis for curved dams based on this assumption cannot yield reliable results. In view of this fact it would appear that stress computations in a curved gravity dam should be considered from other viewpoints.

In the usual dam site the radial plane analysis of arched gravity dams does not give consideration to the weight of all the material in the dam. In this connection, let Fig. 13 represent the plan and crown section of a symmetrical arched gravity dam placed in a box-shaped canyon. Let the dam be divided by vertical planes parallel to the axis of the canyon as shown in the diagram. The water pressure on each of these slices is made up of a transverse component equal to the water pressure times the slice thickness times the tangent of the angle of curvature of the dam from the center line of the canyon and a down-stream component equal to the slice thickness times the water pressure per unit width of the canyon. It is evident that the transverse components on the two sides of the canyon will balance one another and will have no effect on the overturning moment in a down-stream direction. It is also evident that the down-stream components are adequately resisted at the crown section and are still more adequately resisted for the oblique sections near the sides of the canyon, if the section of the dam is safe for a dam that is straight in plan. The parallel-sided sections can be made actual sections by placing all the contraction and construction joints parallel to the axis of the canyon. By referring to Fig. 13, it will be noted that the radial plane theory entirely neglects the resistance of the triangles, *abc* and *def*, and that this material may be omitted from the dam since no arching action is to be relied on in this theory.

In an arched gravity dam with properly spaced, constructed, and grouted contraction joints, the dam can generally be relied on to act as a unit. This fact is entirely ignored in the radial plane analysis theory. It brings arch action and increased moment resistance into play. Let Fig. 14 show the plan and section of a triangular dam; and, in order to simplify the mathematical treatment, let like parabolic curves bound the up-stream and down-stream faces of the base. It will be possible to substitute such parabolic

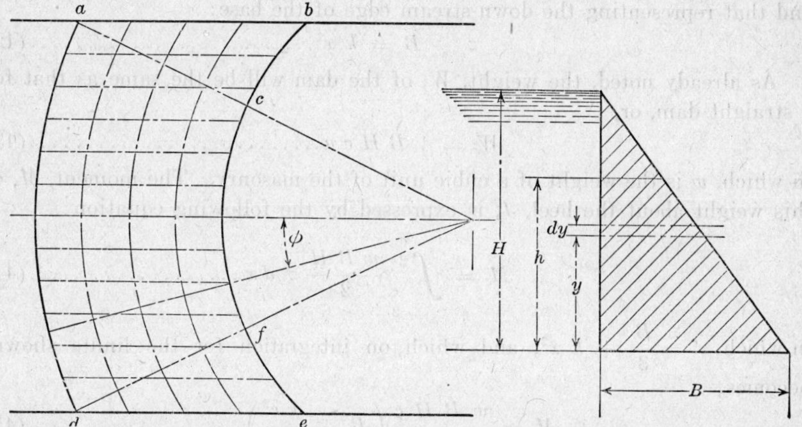

FIG. 13.—SYMMETRICAL ARCHED GRAVITY DAM.

curves for the usual arcs without material error. All vertical sections taken parallel to the crown will be equal, and the total weight of material in the dam will be the same as that in a straight dam of the same section. The basis of comparison will be very slightly unfair to the curved dam of uniform radial

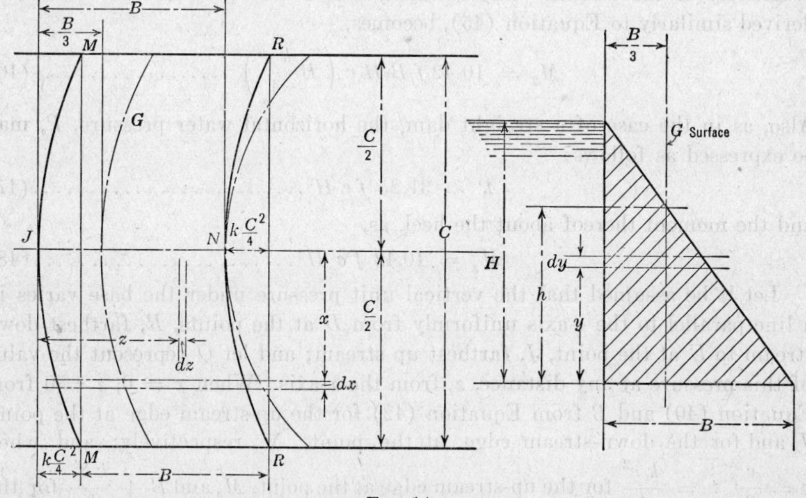

FIG. 14.

section. Let the co-ordinate axes be taken as coincident with the axis of the canyon and a line perpendicular thereto at the up-stream edge, J. Using the notation shown in Fig. 14, let the equation of the parabola representing the up-stream edge of the base be:

$$z = k\,x^2 \quad\ldots\ldots\ldots\ldots\ldots\ldots\ldots\ldots\ldots\ldots\ldots\ldots\ldots(40)$$

that representing the line, G, at one-third the distance between the heel and toe on a line parallel to the z-axis be:

$$z - \frac{B}{3} = k\,x^2 \ldots\ldots\ldots\ldots\ldots\ldots\ldots\ldots\ldots (41)$$

and that representing the down-stream edge of the base:

$$z - B = k\,x^2 \ldots\ldots\ldots\ldots\ldots\ldots\ldots\ldots\ldots (42)$$

As already noted, the weight, W, of the dam will be the same as that for a straight dam, or,

$$W = \tfrac{1}{2}\,B\,H\,c\,w \ldots\ldots\ldots\ldots\ldots\ldots\ldots\ldots\ldots (43)$$

in which, w is the weight of a cubic unit of the masonry. The moment, M, of this weight about the heel, J, is expressed by the following equation:

$$M = \int_{-\frac{c}{2}}^{\frac{c}{2}} \frac{w\,B\,H}{2}\,z'\,d\,x \ldots\ldots\ldots\ldots\ldots\ldots (44)$$

in which, $z' = \frac{B}{3} + k\,x^2$, and which, on integration for the limits shown, becomes,

$$M = \frac{w\,B\,H\,c}{6}\left(B + \frac{k\,c^2}{4}\right) \ldots\ldots\ldots\ldots\ldots\ldots (45)$$

Let the intensity of the hydrostatic uplift on the base be 62.5 $f\,H$ at the heel and zero at the toe, varying linearly between these points. The total uplift will then be 31.25 $f\,B\,H\,c$ as for a straight dam. For every slice of the dam the center of gravity of uplift may be taken vertical below the center of gravity of the weight. The moment, M_2 of the uplift about the heel, J, derived similarly to Equation (45), becomes,

$$M_2 = 10.42\,f\,B\,H\,c\left(B\,\frac{k\,c^2}{4}\right) \ldots\ldots\ldots\ldots\ldots\ldots (46)$$

Also, as in the case of a straight dam, the horizontal water pressure, P, may be expressed as follows:

$$P = 31.25\,f\,c\,H^2 \ldots\ldots\ldots\ldots\ldots\ldots\ldots\ldots\ldots (47)$$

and the moment thereof about the heel, as,

$$M_3 = 10.42\,f\,c\,H^3 \ldots\ldots\ldots\ldots\ldots\ldots\ldots\ldots\ldots (48)$$

Let it be assumed that the vertical unit pressure under the base varies in a line parallel to the z-axis uniformly from D at the points, R, farthest down stream to U at the point, J, farthest up stream; and let Q represent the value of this pressure at any distance, z, from the x-axis. When $x = 0$, $z = 0$ from Equation (40) and B from Equation (42) for the up-stream edge at the point, J, and for the down-stream edge, at the point, N, respectively; and when $x = \frac{c}{2}$, $z = \frac{k\,c^2}{4}$ for the up-stream edge at the point, M, and $B + \frac{k\,c^2}{4}$ for the down-stream edge of the base at the points, R. For any intermediate point at the distance, z, from the x-axis,

$$Q = U + \left(\frac{z}{B + \frac{k\,c^2}{4}}\right)(D - U) \ldots\ldots\ldots\ldots\ldots (49)$$

The total base pressure, P, is that on the area, $M\,J\,M\,R\,N\,R$, which may be expressed as follows:

$$P = 2\int_0^{\frac{c}{2}} \int_{k x^2}^{(B + k x^2)} \left[U + \left(\frac{z}{B + \frac{k c^2}{4}} \right) (D - U) \right] dz\, dx \ldots. (50)$$

which, on integration, equals,

$$P = B\,U\,c + \frac{\left(\frac{B^2 c}{2} + \frac{B k c^3}{12} \right) (D - U)}{\left(B + \frac{k c^2}{4} \right)} \ldots\ldots\ldots\ldots (51)$$

In a similar manner the moment, M_4, of the base pressure about the heel at J is,

$$M_4 = \int_0^{\frac{c}{2}} \int_{k x^2}^{(B + k x^2)} \left[U + \left(\frac{D - U}{B + \frac{k c^2}{4}} \right) z \right] z\, dz\, dx \ldots\ldots (52)$$

which, on integration, equals,

$$M_4 = c\,B \left[\left(\frac{B}{2} + \frac{k c^2}{12} \right) U + \left(\frac{D - U}{B + \frac{k c^2}{4}} \right) \left(\frac{B^2}{3} + \frac{B k c^2}{12} + \frac{k^2 c^4}{80} \right) \right] .. (53)$$

Let consideration now be given to results obtained from applying Equations (51) and (53), involving the parabolically curved dam with stresses calculated on a parallel-sided vertical slice, 100 ft. wide, as compared to a vertical slice, 100 ft. wide, of a straight gravity dam of the same section. Take a horizontal section of the Exchequer Dam at Elevation 427.5 as cited by the author (page 772), in which, $H = 272.5$ ft. and $B = 171.4$ ft., and let $w = 160$ lb. per cu. ft. For a straight dam of this section and masonry weight, the stress at the heel is zero. For a parabolically curved dam, a solution of Equations (51) and (53) gives U equal to 2.6 lb. per sq. in. compression at the heel, which is negligibly different from the zero stress obtained for the straight dam. This shows that, if stresses in an arched gravity dam are calculated on parallel-sided sections of reasonable width, the results do not differ materially from those obtained from calculating on the basis of the usual methods for straight gravity dams.

In the matter of arch action coming into play to relieve the overturning moment from water pressure in an arched gravity dam, let the Exchequer Dam again be considered, using the triangular vertical up-stream face section assumed by the author; and let the water elevation be assumed to be at the crest of the triangle section. When any gravity dam is subjected to water pressure, as here assumed, the down-stream fibers of the dam are compressed by bending moment much more than the up-stream fibers, which causes the dam to be deflected down stream considerably. Shearing action also tends to increase this down-stream deflection. Computations of these combined deflections for the Exchequer Dam show the total deflection at 50 ft. below the crest of the dam on the axis thereof to be about 0.74 in.; at 100 ft. below the top of the dam, 0.51 in.; and at 150 ft. below the top of the dam, 0.32 in. Assuming the water load to be carried entirely by the arch and computing the crown deflections at the same three elevations, the corresponding deflections are found to be 3.18 in., 2.28 in., and 0.81 in., respectively. These figures indicate that the cantilever deflections from the water load in the gravity section at various levels are a very considerable proportion of those of the arch sections, indicating that an appreciable proportion of the water pressure will be taken by arch action in this dam, much more, in fact, than any deficiency of computed stress resulting from applying parallel-sided instead of radial-sided slices of the dam.

The arch deflections given in the preceding paragraph are computed with Cain's formula for fixed-ended thin circular arches under normal loads. The deflections of the gravity section are computed by means of the law of displacements of the internal work theory, the fundamental formula for which is as follows:

$$\Delta_h = \int_0^h \frac{M\,m}{E\,I}\,d\,y + 3\int_0^h \frac{V\,v}{E\,A}\,d\,y \ldots\ldots\ldots\ldots\ldots (54)$$

in which, M and V are the moment and shear due to the water load acting in producing stress on the elementary strip, $d\,y$, while m and v are the respective moment and shear on dy for a unit load of 1 lb. applied at the point of deflection, h, all as shown in Fig. 13. By assigning proper values to the various quantities involved in the fundamental formula and integrating, Δ_h, for any point, h, is found to be,

$$\Delta_h = \frac{62.5\,H^3\,h^2}{E\,B^3} + \frac{46.875\,H}{E\,B}\,(2\,H\,h - h^2) \ldots\ldots\ldots\ldots (55)$$

There are, however, cases where it may be desirable to compute the stresses in arched gravity dams on the basis of radial-sided slices, such as in a canyon converging down stream, with abutments not suitable for taking arch thrust, and such as may give better foundation conditions for a curved structure than for a straight structure combined with earth abutments or abutments otherwise not suited to taking the arch thrust. In such cases, it is desirable to compute the stresses on the theory of radial-sided slices. Formulas for considering stresses on this theory are not at all out of place, but they should not be allowed to displace the customary and reliable method of computing stresses in arched gravity dams by the parallel-sided slice theory. In view of this statement the writer is submitting herein general formulas for this purpose, developed by means of the principles of calculus which check and supplement the formulas presented by the author.

Development of Formulas for Effect of Curvature on Stresses.—Assume a vertical slice of an arched gravity dam between radial planes thereof; let this vertical slice be divided into convenient segments by horizontal planes; and let Fig. 15 represent the plan and sectional elevation of one of these segments. Also, let the symbols shown on the diagram represent the quantities there indicated. Assume each segment to be acted upon only by water pressure and gravity, and take moments about a horizontal line perpendicular to the radial plane bisecting the segment and passing through the center of curvature called the center axis in the plane of the base of the segment. Consider an elementary volume and an elementary surface of the segment of the dam as shown in Fig. 15, and extend these considerations to the entire segment thereof by integration of the differential quantities between proper limits. Let all units be expressed in pounds and feet.

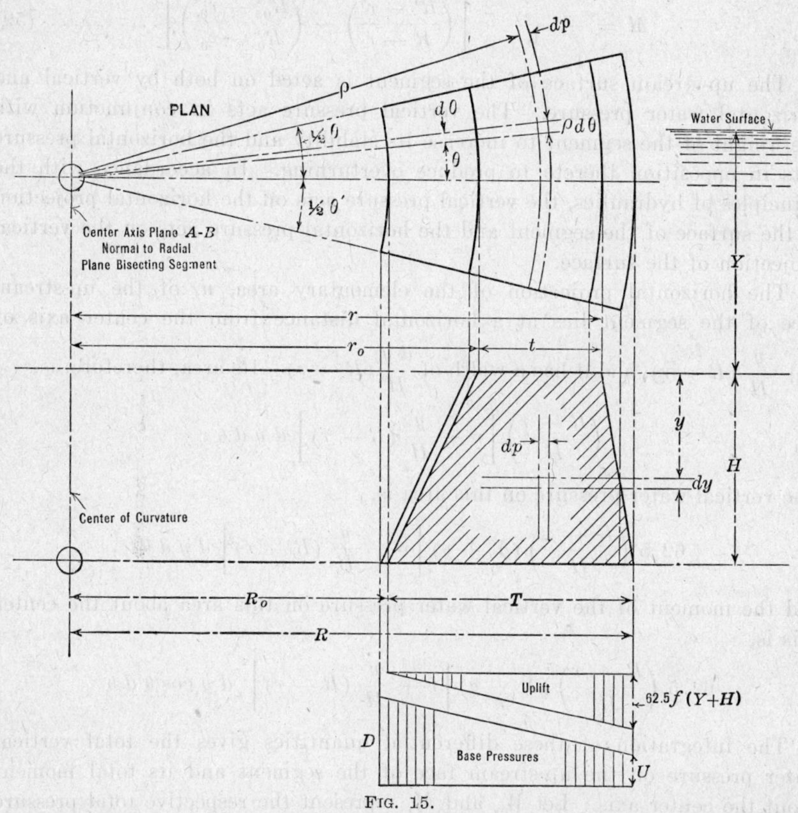

FIG. 15.

If w represents the weight per cubic foot of material in the segment, then the weight of the elementary volume, m, is $w\ dy\ d\rho\ \rho\ d\theta$, and the moment of m about the center axis, $A\ B$, is $w\ dy\ d\rho\ \rho\ d\theta\ \rho \cos\theta$. The total weight of the segment and the total moment thereof about the center axis are readily found by integrating these differential quantities between the proper limits as follows:

$$W = w \int_{y=0}^{y=H} \int_{\rho = r_0 + \frac{y}{H}(R_0 - r_0)}^{\rho = r + \frac{y}{H}(R - r)} \int_{\theta = -\frac{\theta'}{2}}^{\theta = \frac{\theta'}{2}} d\,y\,d\,\rho\,\rho\,d\,\theta \ldots\ldots (56)$$

whence,

$$W = \frac{w\,H\,\theta'}{6}\left[\left(\frac{R^3 - r^3}{R - r}\right) - \left(\frac{R_0{}^3 - R_0{}^3}{R_0 - r_0}\right)\right] \ldots\ldots\ldots\ldots (57)$$

and,

$$M = w \int_{y=0}^{y=H} \int_{\rho = r_0 + \frac{y}{H}(R_0 - r_0)}^{\rho = r + \frac{y}{H}(R - r)} \int_{\theta = -\frac{\theta'}{2}}^{\theta = \frac{\theta'}{2}} d\,y\,d\,\rho\,\rho\,d\,\theta\,\rho\cos\theta \ldots. (58)$$

whence,

$$M = \frac{w\,H\sin\frac{\theta}{2}}{6}\left[\left(\frac{R^4 - r^4}{R - r}\right) - \left(\frac{R_0^{\,4} - r_0^{\,4}}{R_0 - r_0}\right)\right] \ldots\ldots\ldots. (59)$$

The up-stream surface of the segment is acted on both by vertical and horizontal water pressure. The vertical pressure acts in conjunction with the weight of the segment to increase its stability and the horizontal pressure acts in opposition thereto to produce overturning. In accordance with the principles of hydraulics, the vertical pressure acts on the horizontal projection of the surface of the segment and the horizontal pressure acts on the vertical projection of the surface.

The horizontal projection of the elementary area, *n*, of the up-stream face of the segment lies at a horizontal distance from the center axis of $r + \frac{y}{H}(R - r)$, and it has a width of $\frac{d\,y}{H}(R - r)$. Its area, therefore, is,

$$\left(\frac{R - r}{H}\right)\left[r + \frac{y}{H}(R - r)\right] d\,y\,d\,\theta$$

The vertical water pressure on this area is,

$$62.5\left(\frac{R - r}{H}\right)(Y + y)\left[r + \frac{y}{H}(R - r)\right] d\,y\,d\,\theta$$

and the moment of the vertical water pressure on this area about the center axis is,

$$62.5\left(\frac{R - r}{H}\right)(Y + y)\left[r + \frac{y}{H}(R - r)\right]^2 d\,y\cos\theta\,d\,\theta$$

The integration of these differential quantities gives the total vertical water pressure on the up-stream face of the segment and its total moment about the center axis. Let W_1 and M_1 represent the respective total pressure and moment; then,

$$W_1 = 62.5\left(\frac{R - r}{H}\right)\int_{y=0}^{y=H}\int_{\theta=-\frac{\theta'}{2}}^{\theta=\frac{\theta'}{2}} (Y + y)\left[r + \frac{y}{H}(R - r)\right] d\,y\,d\,\theta. (60)$$

whence,

$$W_1 = 10.42\,\theta'(R - r)\left[3\,Y(R + r) + H(2\,R + r)\right] \ldots\ldots. (61)$$

and,

$$M_1 = 62.5\left(\frac{R - r}{H}\right)\int_{y=0}^{y=H}\int_{\theta=-\frac{\theta'}{2}}^{\theta=\frac{\theta'}{2}} (Y + y)\left[r + \frac{y}{H}(R - r)\right]^2 d\,y\cos\theta\,d\,\theta \ldots\ldots\ldots\ldots\ldots\ldots\ldots\ldots. (62)$$

whence,

$$M_1 = 41.66 \sin \frac{\theta'}{2} (R - r) \left[Y \left(\frac{R^3 - r^3}{R - r} \right) + \frac{1}{4} H (3 R^2 + 2 R r + r^2) \right] . (63)$$

In determining the horizontal water pressure acting on the up-stream face of the segment, the vertical projection of an elementary areal strip, *q*, across the up-stream face of the segment is used. The vertical projection of this area is,

$$2 \left[r + \frac{y}{H} (R - r) \right] \sin \frac{\theta'}{2} d y$$

the horizontal water pressure on it is,

$$125 \sin \frac{\theta'}{2} (Y + y) \left[r + \frac{y}{H} (R - r) \right] d y$$

and the moment of this pressure about the center axis is,

$$125 \sin \frac{\theta'}{2} (Y + y) \left[r + \frac{y}{H} (R - r) \right] (H - y) d y$$

By integrating these differential quantities and denoting W_2 and M_2, as the total pressure and moment, respectively, the following values are found:

$$W_2 = 125 \sin \frac{\theta'}{2} \int_{y=0}^{y=H} \left[r + \frac{y}{H} (R - r) \right] (Y + y) d y \ldots\ldots (64)$$

whence,

$$W_2 = 125 H \sin \frac{\theta'}{2} \left[\frac{Y}{2} (R + r) + \frac{H}{3} \left(R + \frac{1}{2} r \right) \right] \ldots\ldots (65)$$

and,

$$M_2 = 125 \sin \frac{\theta'}{2} \int_{y=0}^{y=H} \left[r + \frac{y}{H} (R - r) \right] (Y + y) (H - y) d y .. (66)$$

whence,

$$M_2 = 10.42 H^2 \sin \frac{\theta'}{2} \left[2 Y (R + 2 r) + H (R + r) \right] \ldots\ldots (67)$$

The uplift pressure on the base of the dam varies with the permeability of its foundation, but it is believed to be a fair assumption for the case here under consideration to assume: (1) That the intensity of pressure at the heel of the dam is equal to some specified factor times the intensity of water pressure at that point; (2) that this intensity of pressure is zero at the toe of the dam; and (3) that the intensity of pressure varies as a straight line between the heel and toe. If P designates the entire uplift on the base of the dam, f the coefficient of intensity of water pressure at the heel, and M_3 the moment of the uplift, P, on the base of the dam about the center axis, then,

$$P = \int_{\rho = R_0}^{\rho = R} \int_{\theta = -\frac{\theta'}{2}}^{\theta = \frac{\theta'}{2}} d \rho \, \rho \, d \theta \, 62.5 (Y + H) f \left(\frac{\rho - R_0}{R - R_0} \right) \ldots\ldots (68)$$

whence,

$$P = f \left(\frac{62.5 (Y + H) \theta'}{(R - R_0)} \right) \left[\frac{1}{3} (R^3 - R_0^3) - \frac{R_0}{2} (R^2 - R_0^2) \right] \ldots (69)$$

and,

$$M_3 = \int_{\rho = R_0}^{\rho = R} \int_{\theta = -\frac{\theta'}{2}}^{\theta = \frac{\theta'}{2}} d\,\rho\,\rho\,d\,\theta\, 62.5\,(Y + H)\, f\left(\frac{\rho - R_0}{R - R_0}\right) \rho \cos \theta \quad ..(70)$$

whence,

$$M_3 = 125\, f \sin \frac{\theta'}{2}\,(Y + H)\left[\frac{1}{4}\left(\frac{R^4 - R_0^{\,4}}{R - R_0}\right) - \frac{R_0}{3}\left(\frac{R^3 - R_0^{\,3}}{R - R_0}\right)\right] \quad ..(71)$$

The downward pressure on the foundation of the base of the dam is due to the weight of the superimposed masonry plus the vertical water pressure on the up-stream face thereof due to batter. The downward pressure at any intermediate point on an elementary area, $d\rho\ \rho d\theta$, is,

$$D - \frac{\left(\rho \cos \theta - R_0 \cos \frac{\theta'}{2}\right)}{R - R_0 \cos \frac{\theta'}{2}}\,(D - U)$$

in which, D is the intensity of pressure at the toe and U is the intensity of this pressure at the heel. Now, if P_1 equals the entire downward pressure on the foundation, and M_4 the moment thereof about the center axis,

$$P_1 = \int_{\rho = R_0}^{\rho = R} \int_{\theta = -\frac{\theta'}{2}}^{\theta = \frac{\theta'}{2}} d\,\rho\,\rho\,d\,\theta \left[D - \frac{\rho \cos \theta - R_0 \cos \frac{\theta'}{2}}{R - R_0 \cos \frac{\theta'}{2}}\,(D - U)\right] .(72)$$

whence,

$$P_1 = D\,\theta' \left(\frac{R^2 - R_0^{\,2}}{2}\right) - (D - U)$$

$$\left[\frac{2 \sin \frac{\theta'}{2}\left(\frac{R^3 - R_0^{\,3}}{3}\right) - \theta' R_0 \cos \frac{\theta'}{2}\left(\frac{R^2 - R_0^{\,2}}{2}\right)}{R - R_0 \cos \frac{\theta'}{2}}\right] \quad ....(73)$$

and,

$$M_4 = \int_{\rho = R_0}^{\rho = R} \int_{\theta = -\frac{\theta'}{2}}^{\theta = \frac{\theta'}{2}} d\,\rho\,\rho\,d\,\theta\,\rho \cos \theta$$

$$\left[D - \left(\frac{\rho \cos \theta - R_0 \cos \frac{\theta'}{2}}{R - R_0 \cos \frac{\theta'}{2}}\right)(D - U)\right] \quad ....(74)$$

whence,

$$M_4 = D\,\frac{2}{3} \sin \frac{\theta}{2}\,(R^3 - R_0^{\,3}) - (D - U)$$

$$\left[\frac{\frac{1}{8}(\theta' + \sin \theta')(R^4 - R_0^{\,4}) - \frac{1}{3} R_0 (\sin \theta')(R^3 - R_0^{\,3})}{R - R_0 \cos \frac{\theta'}{2}}\right] \quad .....(75)$$

The pressure intensities, D and U, can now be found from a combination of Equations (73) and (75), the total base pressure having been previously found from Equations (57) and (65), and the moments thereof from Equations (59), (63), and (67). Where hydrostatic uplift is assumed to act on the base of the dam, Equations (69) and (71) must be used to determine the modifications of stresses resulting therefrom.

Acknowledgment is made to T. L. E. Haug, M. Am. Soc. C. E., for valuable assistance in developing and checking the methods of analysis and formulas herein presented.

E. W. KRAMER,* M. AM. SOC. C. E. (by letter).—This able paper is very timely in calling attention to the danger of allowing tension in the heel of any dam that depends entirely on gravity action for its stability, and also in emphasizing the importance of considering a slice between two vertical radial planes in analyzing the stresses in a gravity dam arched in plan. The timeliness is due to the number of gravity dams exceeding 300 ft. in height, either proposed or under construction.

Among the important questions arising in connection with the planning of these structures, on which there seems to be some difference of opinion, are the following:

1.—Should a gravity dam be arched in plan where topographical conditions permit?

2.—If arched in plan, is a smaller safety factor with respect to maximum compression at the toe, tension at the heel, and uplift assumption permissible?

3.—What is the amount of uplift for which provision should be made?

4.—Should a section between radial or parallel vertical planes be considered in determining stresses?

5.—What should the allowable working stresses be?

These problems are, of course, not new. However, knowledge on the questions involved is continually being increased by observing dams actually constructed, as these subjects of observation are continually increasing in height and varying in form. Great advancement in the mathematical treatment of stresses and strains in structures has been made in recent years as well as an increase in knowledge as to the strength of the materials of which these structures are built. Therefore, it is hoped that the following discussion, in which an attempt is made to enlarge on some of the points made by Mr. Jakobsen, will be at least of passing interest.

The answer to the first question depends to a great extent upon the answers to the other questions, and more particularly to the second question. There are, however, some points that can be considered independently.

As a general rule a larger concrete yardage will be required at a greater cost per yard for the gravity dam arched in plan than for the straight dam, regardless of the stand taken by the designer on the other questions. Therefore, the arched dam will cost more. An exception to this rule might occur in a case where the arching throws the center of the dam up stream on better and higher foundations.

* Hydr. Engr., U. S. Forest Service, San Francisco, Calif.

Having decided that the arched plan will cost more, it is then necessary to justify this extra cost. The usual answer is that an additional safety factor is provided. It is the writer's opinion, however, that the arching affords only a secondary or delayed support in the case of dams arched on a greater radius than about 800 ft. This support may not come into play under certain very reasonable assumptions until after partial failure has occurred.

For instance, observations of the temperature of large concrete dams show that in the interior it rises rapidly as high as 110° Fahr. The gradual cooling will open the contraction joints. As this cooling covers a long period, there is no assurance that these contraction joints can be grouted before the load comes on the dam. In fact, it is not a general practice to grout the contraction joints of gravity dams. Some of the engineers most prominent in the design of high dams hold that it is inadvisable to do so. Observations show that these cracks are sometimes as large as 0.1 in. For a dam of long radius, computations and observations indicate that the cantilever will not deflect sufficiently to close the cracks, which is essential to bring the arch into play.

An incipient failure caused by the dam sliding on its base a matter of some hundredths of a foot would bring the arch into play. It would also greatly increase the uplift. The support given by the arch might prevent a complete and rapid failure and a serious disaster involving loss of life and property, while it might not preserve the usefulness of the dam. This additional safety factor, no doubt, has at least psychological value.

On the other hand, the science of engineering has advanced in regard to methods of exploring foundations, grouting and draining foundations, knowledge of designing and placing concrete, designing cross-section, etc., to such a point that the question arises, "is not the additional safety provided by arching a gravity dam on a long radius in most cases superfluous?" Before the designer will answer this question, it is likely that he will first determine what the arching will cost. To do this it will be necessary for him to make decision in regard to the other questions.

Confining the answer to gravity dams with radii of more than 700 or 800 ft., the writer's answer to the second question would be that it is not advisable to use a smaller safety factor with respect to compression at the toe, tension at the heel, or uplift assumption, than is customary in a straight dam For radii of less than, say, 700 ft., the answer is not so evident.

To support this answer take the case of the Exchequer Dam of the Merced Irrigation District, Merced, Calif., referred to by Mr. Jakobsen. The cross-section of this dam, as published,* is shown on Fig. 16. The radius of the up-stream face at the crest is 674 feet. The section is very nearly triangular. In order to simplify the deflection computations, assume the triangular cross-section that would be obtained by extending the principal batter of the down-stream face (10 on 6.29) to the crest and foundations. For a height of 320 ft. the bottom width will be 202 ft. and the top width, zero (very nearly).

The assumption is made that the cantilever carries the entire load and gives as great a deflection as can occur, unless cracks develop in the up-stream face.

* *Western Construction News*, January 25, 1926.

Therefore, for the present purpose, this assumption is allowable. The following equation* will be used for obtaining the cantilever deflection at the crest, neglecting shear and yielding of foundations, and assuming that the cantilever takes the entire load:

$$Y_c = \frac{62.5\ H^3}{E\ t_b^3} X^2$$

in which,

Y_c = deflection, neglecting shear;
H = height of dam;
t_b = thickness of base; and
X = height of point above base for which deflection is to be determined.

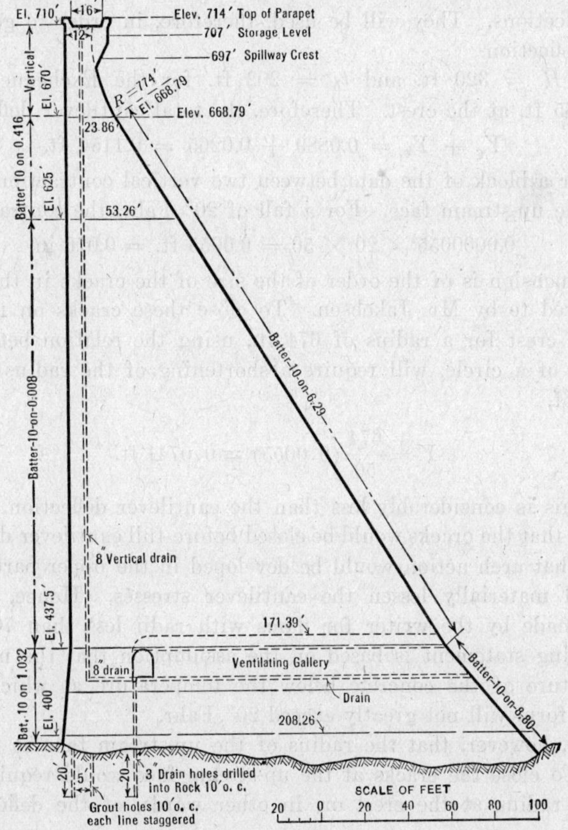

FIG. 16.—MAXIMUM CROSS-SECTION OF EXCHEQUER DAM.

For the Exchequer Dam, remembering that $t_b = 0.63\ H$,

$$Y_c = \frac{62.5\ H^3}{E\ (0.63\ H)^3}\ X^2 = 0.000000868\ X^2$$

Therefore, Y_c for the crest, when $X = 320$, is 0.0889 ft.

* Derived by F. A. Noetzli, M. Am. Soc. C. E., *Transactions*, Am. Soc. C. E., Vol. LXXXIV (1921), p. 6.

In his discussion of Mr. Noetzli's paper, to which reference has been made, Mr. Jakobsen shows that the deflection due to shear is very considerable in a case of this kind, and that it should be added to the computed cantilever deflection with shear neglected.

Mr. Jakobsen developed the equivalent of the following formula* for the determination of the cantilever deflection due to shear alone at the crest of the dam where $X = H$,

$$Y_s = \frac{1.2 \times 31.3 \times H^3}{144 \times G \times t_b}$$

Values of $E = 2\,000\,000$ and $G = \frac{2}{5} E$ are low and will give a high value for the deflections. They will be used, therefore, in order to get the largest probable deflection.

Taking $H = 320$ ft. and $t_b = 202$ ft. for the Exchequer Dam gives $Y_s = 0.0265$ ft. at the crest. Therefore, the total cantilever deflection,

$$Y_c + Y_s = 0.0889 + 0.0265 = 0.1154 \text{ ft.}$$

Consider a block of the dam between two vertical contraction joints 50 ft. apart on the up-stream face. For a fall of 20° Fahr. the contraction will be,

$$0.0000055 \times 20 \times 50 = 0.0055 \text{ ft.} = 0.076 \text{ in.}$$

This dimension is of the order of the size of the cracks in the Mulholland Dam referred to by Mr. Jakobsen. To close these cracks on the up-stream face at the crest for a radius of 674 ft., using the relation between the arc and radius of a circle, will require a shortening of the radius and hence a deflection of,

$$Y = \frac{674}{50}\,(0.0055) = 0.0741 \text{ ft.}$$

Since this is considerably less than the cantilever deflection, 0.1154 ft., it would seem that the cracks would be closed before full cantilever deflection took place and that arch action would be developed in the upper part of the dam. This would materially lessen the cantilever stresses. Hence, the doubtful exception made by the writer for dams with radii less than 700 or 800 ft. The foregoing statement is based on the assumption that the maximum fall in temperature of the concrete below the temperature at which it took its permanent form will not greatly exceed 20° Fahr.

Suppose, however, that the radius of the up-stream face at the crest was 1 200 ft. To close the cracks at the up-stream face would require a shortening of the radius at the crest or, in other words, of the deflection at the crest of,

$$Y = \frac{1\,200}{50}\,(0.0055) = 0.132 \text{ ft.}$$

which is considerably greater than the cantilever deflection at the top of the dam where it would be greatest until the arch action came into play. Remember, also, that a most liberal estimate was made of the cantilever deflection

* *Transactions*, Am. Soc. C. E., Vol LXXXIV (1921), p. 100.

and that shrinkage of the concrete, due to setting, was neglected in computing the width of the contraction crack.

The selection of a fall in temperature of 20° Fahr. may be open to criticism as being too small when compared with the high temperature that the concrete may reach while it is setting. On the other hand these high temperatures are not all closing temperatures. The practice of pouring the dam in alternate blocks allows some time factor between the peaks in the block temperatures. One alternate set of blocks may have passed their maximum temperature before the intermediate blocks were poured.

It is admitted that a greater drop of mean temperature below that at which the concrete took its permanent form in the case of the Exchequer Dam might be justified. On the other hand, it is believed that a drop of at least 20° occurred.

If any unreasonable assumptions appear in this argument, they were adverse to the argument in so far as the dam with a 1 200-ft. radius is concerned (with the one exception of making no allowance for yielding foundations). It is believed, therefore, that the statement that no reduction in the usual safety requirements should be made on account of a gravity dam being arched in plan on a radius greater than, say, about 800 ft., has been substantiated.

Some further reference to the Mulholland Dam will be made to prove that the contraction of concrete in a dam is real and not theoretical.

The writer saw the dam on March 10, 1926. It was completed in 1925. The maximum height is 200 ft. It is a concrete gravity dam arched in plan on a radius of 542 ft. The elevation of the crest is 750 ft. and that of the spillway, 746 ft. The water stood at Elevation 716 ft. or within 36 ft. of the spillway crest. No contraction joints were placed in the structure.

Numerous cracks extending from the foundations to the crest and from the front to the back face, in so far as the front face could be observed, had opened up and were still open, although the dam was under about four-fifths of its full head. While these cracks did not interfere with the usefulness of the structure, it was evident that no benefit was being derived from the arch at that time.

This condition might not be true of a higher dam arched on the same radius since the cantilever deflection at the top, say, for a 300-ft. dam, would have been sufficient to have closed the cracks theoretically at least, thereby developing arch action. Arch action in the upper part of the structure would greatly relieve cantilever stresses in the lower part.

To illustrate the probability of this latter point, some preliminary data in regard to the deflection of the Don Pedro Dam of the Turlock and Modesto Irrigation Districts of California, will be given (see Table 2). This experiment is not as yet complete, but in so far as it goes, it is believed to be accurate. It was made under the direction of R. V. Meikle, Chief Engineer of the Turlock Irrigation District.

The dam is a concrete gravity dam arched in plan on a 676-ft. radius. The maximum height is 284 ft. The section and plan are very similar to that of the Exchequer Dam, of which it appears to have been the model.

The deflections were measured on July 24, and August 1, 1923 (Table 2). Most of the concrete had been placed prior to October 1, 1922, although a gap had been left at the crest, about 90 ft. high and 32.5 ft. wide, which was closed prior to March, 1923.

TABLE 2.—DEFLECTION MEASUREMENTS, DON PEDRO DAM.

Date.	Elevation of water, in feet.	TEMPERATURE.		DEFLECTIONS.		
		Air.	Water.	Point No. 1, Elevation 1172.	Point No. 2, Elevation 1099.	Point No. 3, Elevation 1049.
July 24, 1923	1 158.45	......	......	0.022 ft.	0.029 ft.	0.0075 ft.
August 1, 1923	1 157.95	70° Fahr.	16° cent.	0.019 ft.	0.028 ft.	0.018 ft.

Three plumb-bobs were embedded in the down-stream face with their points projecting vertically at Elevations 1172, 1099, and 1049, respectively (assumed datum). The first elevation, 1 172 ft., is on top of the concrete wall on the lower side of the roadway crossing on top of the dam, the roadway and top of the dam being at an elevation of 1 168 ft.

Three points were located in the rock on the opposite side of the stream from the transit point, one in each vertical plane passing through the transit point and the plumb-bob points. This was done as carefully as possible while the reservoir was empty.

It will be noted from Table 2 that the deflection at the top under approximately full load is less (by 0.009 ft., or 0.108 in.) than the deflection at a point 73 ft. lower in this dam in the second case and almost this in the first case. This is a material difference well above the limits of error of the observation. Since the dam under cantilever stresses alone could not deflect less at the end of the cantilever than at some point below the end, this is conclusive proof that arch action was being developed at that time.

The question might well be raised in this case as to whether or not the dam had cooled off in the interior. It is planned to make further observations with empty and full reservoir, which will be of great value in settling this phase of the question.

In regard to the third question, it is believed that an allowance should be made for uplift; but that, with grouting the foundations and with proper drainage in the dam and foundations, it is hard to understand how this uplift can exceed the equivalent of 25% of the full hydrostatic pressure at the heel, diminishing uniformly to zero at the toe, except in cases where the foundations are unusually poor.

Modern concrete dams of considerable height are now provided with a drainage channel extending under the full length of the dam immediately down stream from the cut-off wall. An inspection gallery extending the length of the dam, usually at a distance of about 30 ft. from the up-stream face and above tail-water elevation, provides a free outlet for water collected from vertical drain pipes. The pipes should be about 12 ft. apart and should

Fig. 17.—Exchequer Dam with Full Reservoir.

extend from 12 to 20 ft. into the foundations. Also, good practice requires vertical drain holes on about 12-ft. centers, extending upward from the inspection gallery to the top of the dam. Since water seeks the path of least resistance, these drains collect a very large percentage of the water getting through on construction joints or reaching the bottom of the dam under the cut-off wall.

They do not get all the water, however, as is shown by the leaks appearing on the down-stream face of the horizontal construction joints. An example of this leakage is shown (Fig. 17) of the down-stream face of Exchequer Dam after first filling. The usual care was exercised in cleaning the construction joints and flushing them with mortar before pouring new concrete. This leakage decreased very materially after the reservoir had been filled only a short time. The writer has seen similar leakage in other high dams.

An allowance for uplift, varying from at least 10% to at most 25%, should be made except for foundations of a very unreliable nature. The higher figure has the writer's recommendation, even in cases of the best foundations.

As stated by Mr. Jakobsen, it is impossible for full uplift to occur under the entire dam since the concrete is heavier than the water. If sufficient allowance is made in the design to take care of the initial uplift without tension developing at the heel, there will not be, in any horizontal plane in a block of the dam between any two vertical contraction joints, more than 30 or 40% of the area which does not have contact even with careless handling of construction joints. The drainage system should safely reduce this to the equivalent of less than 25% uplift at the heel, diminishing to zero at the toe, except, possibly, in cases of very porous foundations.

On the other hand, if sufficient allowance was not made in the original design to care for the initial uplift, and tension sufficient to open cracks does develop at the heel, the uplift will increase to full hydrostatic pressure over the surface of the crack, and cause the depth of the crack to increase. Hence, it is important to provide for the initial uplift in the design.

In regard to the section that should be considered in making an analysis of the stresses in a gravity dam arched in plan, Mr. Jakobsen has shown that the method of selecting a section between radial planes will give results much more closely approaching the actual condition than those obtained by means of the parallel-plane method.

The radial-plane method was used by the engineers of the Los Angeles County Flood Control District in the design of the San Gabriel Dam to be constructed at the Fork's site. Very good reasons for its use are given in a paper by S. M. Fisher, M. Am. Soc. C. E., Chief Designing Engineer of the District.* The action in this case is very important, since this is the highest gravity dam now planned for early construction, and a very material addition to the concrete yardage was involved in adopting this method.

Taking a section between parallel planes does not account for water pressure on the up-stream face on the sections immediately adjoining the one selected. This pressure will have a component that would have to be partly absorbed or resisted by it. In other words, the down-stream end of a section

* *Western Construction News,* July 10, 1927.

between parallel planes 1 ft. apart would be subjected to the pressure from a section of the up-stream face greater in width than 1 ft.

The writer believes that considering sections between radial planes is the most correct method that has been advanced. It does not, however, in itself, provide any additional factor of safety. If it shows tension at the heel, good engineering practice requires that a change in the design be made to overcome this fault.

On the other hand, as confidence increases in the mathematical analysis applied to structures due to study, discussion, and experiment, it is the writer's opinion that higher unit stresses can be allowed, for instance, in compression in the concrete at the toe.

Concrete developing a strength in compression in laboratory tests on 6-in. or 8-in. cylinders of 1 500 lb. per sq. in. at the end of 28 days, should allow working stresses in a gravity dam of 700 lb. per sq. in., or its equivalent of 50 tons per sq. ft., since at 6 months the strength will be greatly increased. While as strong a concrete is not likely to be obtained in the dam from the same mix as in the laboratory, this is more than offset by the fact that it seems safe to assume that a large mass of concrete will safely stand a much greater unit stress than a small cylinder.

The controlling specification for gravity dams up to about 400 ft. in height is the uplift assumption and its effect on the tension at the heel and not the strength of the concrete. Mr. Jakobsen shows the maximum stress in the Exchequer Dam at Elevation 437.5 (which is 272.5 ft. below the crest) to be 504 lb. per sq. in., which the writer believes to be a very moderate stress. He finds the objectionable condition in this case to be tension at the heel even with zero uplift, unless, of course, some of the load is taken by the arch before the cantilever deflects sufficiently to allow the tension to develop. That the uplift assumption governs, is true of all gravity designs of about this height. Any reasonable section that provides for some uplift without tension at the heel will not show compressive stresses of more than 600 lb. per sq. in.

For dams of much greater height, the stress at the toe becomes one of the governing factors. For sections much more than 400 ft. in height it is necessary to place more material in the upper part of the dam than is required to keep the resultant within the middle third in the upper section, in order to steepen the batter of the down-stream face near the bottom. This is due to the Cain theory, now rather generally accepted, which states that the maximum stress at the toe is a function of the angle that the down-stream face makes with the vertical. The well-known formula being:

$$\text{Maximum stress} = \text{maximum stress in horizontal plane} \times \sec^2 \theta$$

in which, θ is the angle that the down-stream face makes with the vertical. The steeper the batter the less the secant will be, and, therefore, the less the maximum stress, other things being equal.

To show the great increase in cost due to curving a high gravity dam, two gravity designs, made by the writer, are submitted (Fig. 18). They were made for a project requiring a dam 595 ft. high above the foundations and 495 ft. high above the stream bed.

The designs were intended for the purpose of a preliminary consideration of the possibilities of constructing a high dam at the Granite Dike site on the San Gabriel River, California. Exploration of one abutment by tunneling and other factors at a later date caused the elimination of the site from further consideration. The estimated stresses are listed in Table 3. The specifications governing the design were not fixed by the writer. They were, as follows: Maximum allowable compression, 40 tons per sq. ft.; uplift assumption, 50% of the hydrostatic pressure at the heel decreasing uniformly to zero at the toe; maximum sliding factor, 0.75; maximum stresses in the downstream face to be calculated by the Cain formula; and stresses in the curved dam to be calculated by the radial slice method.

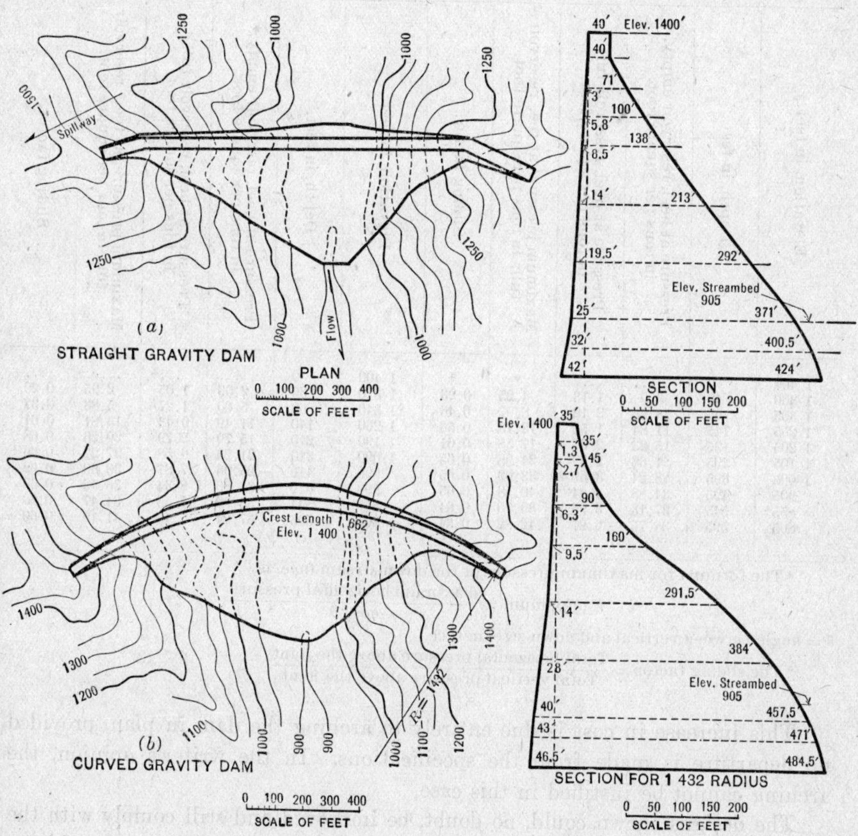

FIG. 18.—GRANITE DIKE SITE, SAN GABRIEL RIVER, CALIFORNIA.

The writer approves of all these specifications except those for maximum stresses and for uplift assumption. In the case of the uplift, it is thought that 25% instead of 50% would have been sufficient. It is believed that 50 tons per sq. ft. would not be too high for maximum stresses.

Fig. 18 (*a*) is a straight dam and Fig. 18 (*b*) is a dam arched with a radius of 1 432 ft. for the up-stream face at the crest. Unless some reliance is placed on the arch, the stresses, uplift provision, and sliding factor are about the same for both structures. The concrete yardage for the straight dam is estimated as 2 720 000 and for the curved dam 3 100 000, an increase of 380 000, or approximately 14 per cent. The yardage estimate is based on the assumption of excavating 50 ft. into the right bank, 20 ft. into the left bank, and 100 ft. below the stream bed in both cases.

TABLE 3.—Estimated Stresses in Proposed Dam on San Gabriel River, California.

Straight Gravity Dam.						Curved Gravity Dam.					
Elevation, in feet.	Depth, in feet.	Pressure at heel, reservoir empty, in tons per square foot.	Pressure at heel, reservoir full, in tons per square foot.	Maximum pressure at toe, reservoir full, in tons per square foot.	Sliding factor.	Elevation, in feet.	Depth, in feet.	Pressure at heel, reservoir empty,* in tons per square foot.	Pressure at heel, reservoir full,* in tons per square foot.	Maximum pressure, at toe,* reservoir full, in tons per square foot.	Sliding factor.†
				*	†						
1 400	0	.....	....			1 400	0	.....	....	.....	....
1 360	40	3.0	1.13	4.25	0.23	1 370	30	2.09	1.05	2.95	0.20
1 305	95	8.26	2.12	8.07	0.46	1 340	60	5.00	1.27	5.83	0.37
1 255	145	11.84	1.55	12.73	0.56	1 260	140	11.49	0.43	13.81	0.61
1 205	195	15.23	2 07	17.58	0.61	1 190	210	15.79	2.79	20.26	0.68
1 105	295	21.68	2.59	24.98	0.65	1 090	310	21.23	6.58	27.27	0.66
1 005	395	28.24	3.69	33.09	0.65	990	410	25.96	7.87	30.60	0.62
905	495	34.88	4.84	40.58	0.65	890	510	31.80	8.34	38.52	0.60
855	545	37.13	3.95	39.70	0 64	856	544	33.92	7.55	34.47	0.60
805	595	38.75	2.27	42.82	0.64	805	595	37.24	5.45	41.10	0.60

* The formula for maximum pressure at the down-stream face, is,

$$F \text{ maximum} = \frac{\text{maximum horizontal pressure}}{\cos^2 \theta}$$

θ = angle between vertical and down-stream face.

$$\dagger \text{ The sliding factor} = \frac{\text{Total horizontal pressure above the joint}}{\text{Total vertical pressure above the joint}}.$$

This increase in cost is due entirely to arching the dam in plan, provided no departure is made from the specifications. In the writer's opinion, the arching cannot be justified in this case.

The designs shown could, no doubt, be improved and still comply with the specifications. A design showing zero stress at the heel and exactly 40 tons per sq. ft. compression at the toe would reduce the yardage slightly in both cases.

Some reduction could have been made by changing the entire section for about every 50 ft. difference in height since, for heights of more than about 400 ft., material has to be added to the upper part of the section to reduce the stresses at the base. However, this method might have introduced very great arch stresses near the abutments in the curved dam for an increase in temperature much above the closing temperature. It was therefore rejected.

The writer's conclusion is that, what additional safety may be obtained in arching a gravity dam on a radius greater than about 800 ft., is, in most cases, superfluous and not worth the additional cost, except where the foundation is questionable.

All dams curved in plan should be calculated as such and no reduction should be made in the usual safety factor, unless curved on radii so short that it can be shown that arch action will be developed under any reasonable assumption, the burden of the proof being on the designer.

Maximum stresses as high as 700 lb. per sq. in. should be allowed in gravity dams for the usual concrete placed in such structures.

A. J. Wiley,* M. Am. Soc. C. E. (by letter).—So far as the writer knows, none of the arched gravity dams built to date has had its section increased over a straight gravity section and it has been considered that such dams were much safer than if they had been given the same section and had been made straight in plan. Mr. Jakobsen's paper is very well timed because at least two important arched gravity dams, recently designed, have had their sections increased beyond that required under the same assumptions for a straight gravity dam.

Of course, it has always been known and admitted that the section of an arched gravity dam between converging radii would not be free from tension in the up-stream face unless there was arch action in the dam transmitting some load horizontally to the abutments. In fact, it has been assumed that there could not be a down-stream deflection of the vertical cantilever without a corresponding deflection of the horizontal arches and a division of the load between the cantilever and the arches.

The author claims that "as gravity dams are usually constructed, however, the arch cannot act until the cantilever has been broken. * * *" This condition, he claims, is due to the shortening of the arches by setting shrinkage and temperature contractions.

The writer thinks it can be shown that an arched gravity dam is made stronger and not weaker by reason of the arch. To show this, it must be proved that the deflection of the vertical cantilevers with no tension in their up-stream face is more than the deflection of the arch when carrying enough of the water load to avoid tension in the vertical cantilever.

After developing equations for the stresses at the up-stream and the down-stream faces of a section of a dam, between converging radii, in terms of the moment of the water pressure, the weight of the section, and the area and the moment of inertia of a horizontal section, the author applies the equations to a horizontal section at Elevation 437.5 of the Exchequer Dam, where the thickness is stated to be 171.4 ft. In this discussion the writer is using the author's figures, except that he is assuming the height of the arch ring above the base as 52.5 ft. and is using 158 lb. per cu. ft. for concrete because this

* Cons. Hydr. Engr., Boise, Idaho.

was the weight of the concrete used in the designs and is also the weight given by the author's Equation (1) when correctly computed.

It is assumed that the interior of the dam, beyond approximately 20 ft. inside the faces, is practically unaffected either by seasonal temperature changes or by setting shrinkage. Proof of the first assumption is found in the paper by Charles H. Paul, M. Am. Soc. C. E., and the late A. B. Mayhew, Assoc. M. Am. Soc. C. E., entitled "Temperature Changes in Mass Concrete",* in which it is shown that beyond about 20 ft., the temperature of the concrete is not sensibly affected by seasonal changes, but gradually approaches the mean annual temperature.

The action of the concrete in the arch due to expansion by the setting heat is somewhat obscure, but it seems reasonable to assume that it is divided between the elastic compression of the concrete and of the abutments and results in up-stream deflection of the arch ring. As the concrete cools, this compression and deflection are relieved, but there seems to be no reason for assuming that it results in tension or in contraction cracks, as would be the case if the concrete could be assumed not to act elastically until it had reached a higher temperature than that of the initial set. In this, reference is made to the concrete in the interior of a large mass and not to the part near the surface where it is affected both by drying and by seasonal temperature changes.

In his discussion of the paper by Fred A. Noetzli, M. Am. Soc. C. E., entitled, "Gravity and Arch Action in Curved Dams", Mr. Jakobsen states† that,

"* * * in the lower part of high curved dams, the temperature variation is small, especially at the up-stream face, and the effect of lateral deformation due to the weight of the overlying concrete will, in most cases, more than balance any temperature shrinkage likely to take place."

The vertical compression due to cantilever action on the horizontal arch at Elevation 437.5 varies from zero at the heel to 362 lb. per sq. in. at the toe. With a lateral deformation coefficient of one-fifth the resulting compression in the arch is 72 lb. at the toe and zero at the heel, which is equivalent to a temperature change of zero at the heel and 6.5° at the toe. This seems to provide for a much greater range of temperature than exists in the body of the dam.

In the up-stream and down-stream faces of the arch, within a distance of about 20 ft. of the faces, the concrete is affected both by temperature and by setting shrinkage. In the case of two 4 by 5 by 48-in. bars, quoted by Mr. Jakobsen in his discussion‡ of the paper by Mr. Noetzli previously referred to, one beam, which was exposed to air, shrank 0.0005 in. per in. and swelled 0.00028 in. per in. on being placed in water. The other beam, which set in water, did not shrink at all.

The concrete in the face of a large dam has one face exposed to the air and the other is a part of the interior of the dam. The excess water of the

* *Transactions*, Am. Soc. C. E., Vol. LXIX (1915), p. 1225.

† *Loc. cit.*, Vol. LXXXIV (1921), p. 104.

‡ *Loc. cit.*, p. 103.

interior forms a source of moisture for the outside part, the rate of setting shrinkage for which should, therefore, be much less than that of small laboratory specimens.

The movements at the contraction joints of the Arrowrock Dam, given in the paper by Messrs. Paul and Mayhew previously referred to, show a combined average setting and temperature contraction of 0.0708 in. in 50 ft., at the face, 0.044 in. at 16 ft., and 0.0324 in. at 22 ft. from the face. This corresponds to a unit shrinkage of 0.00012 at the surface, 0.00007 at 16 ft., and 0.000054 at 22 ft. from the surface; but the last two measurements were taken on exposed surfaces of concrete, subject to local shrinkage and temperature changes in excess of the true shrinkage and temperature variations in the concrete at their respective depths from the surface. It should be noted, however, that when these measurements were made, there was still some setting temperature in the dam.

As the unit of expansion of the arch ring, due to lateral deformation from vertical compression at 20 ft. in from the down-stream face, is $\frac{151.4 \times 72}{171.4 \times E}$ = 0.000032 ft., it is thought that by neglecting 21.4 ft. of the down-stream part of the arch, the effects of temperature and setting shrinkage will be eliminated and that the intrados of the remaining part of the arch will be under compression from the lateral component of the vertical pressure.

At the up-stream face of the arch ring there is no compression from lateral expansion, but the setting shrinkage and temperature contraction are partly offset by the swelling from wetting.

The shrinkage at Arrowrock was, at a unit rate of 0.00012, and a unit rate of 0.0002 should be an ample allowance for setting shrinkage at the up-stream face.

For the swelling due to wetting, the same unit rate will be used for the up-stream face so that these two will cancel. The temperature drop in the concrete at the up-stream face may vary from the temperature of the concrete at the time of placing to the minimum temperature of water, or perhaps through a range of 50° at the surface, corresponding to a unit contraction of 0.000275. From the Arrowrock tests the temperature drop, 10 ft. from the surface, would be 8° and at 20 ft. it would be negligible.

Contraction joints at 50-ft. intervals might open 0.165 in. at the surface and 0.026 in. at 10 ft. from the surface, which, it may be noted, is more than twice that observed at Arrowrock. These contractions are confined to the outside 20 ft. of the concrete and do not affect the body of the arch ring.

There is a depth of 272.5 ft. at the arch ring so that the water pressure in the contraction joints, or in any intermediate vertical cracks, would be 118 lb. per sq. in. and the unit pressure in the arch ring would be the same. As this pressure on the arch ring would be confined to the up-stream 20 ft., considered as affected by temperature, it would not cause an up-stream deflection of the arch and can only be considered as effective in converting the up-stream part of the arch (which is affected by temperature), from a state of tension to one of compression while being deflected by water pressure.

Using the author's equations and dimensions, but with a unit weight of 158 lb. for concrete and with no arch action, there would be a tension of 29 lb. per sq. in. in the vertical cantilever at the arch ring.

If it is assumed that the unit weight of water carried by gravity action is reduced to an amount that would give zero tension on the vertical face at the arch ring 272.5 ft. below the surface, this unit weight on the cantilever will be 56.95 lb. per cu. ft. If it is assumed that the remaining weight will be carried by arch action, the unit pressure will be 5.55 × 272.5 = 1 512 lb. per sq. ft.

Using the ordinary formula for cantilever deflection, $y = \frac{p\,H^3\,x^2}{E\,t^3}$, the deflection at the arch ring is 0.0022 ft.

The author has also called attention to the increase in cantilever deflection due to foundation deformation, and to a further increase due to the fact that the plane of the horizontal section assumed in the usual cantilever deflection formula is not normal to the neutral axis and that the resulting deflection is too small.

There seems to be no doubt that the cantilever deflection would be increased by both these conditions, but the arch deflection would also be increased by foundation deformation, although probably in a less degree, and consideration has been given only to the cantilever deflection.

Using Cain's equations with shear included, and $t = 150$, $r = 600$, $Z = 14°$, and $E = 288\,000\,000$ lb. per sq. ft., the deflection at the crown of the arch ring is found to be 0.000318 ft. as compared with the cantilever deflection of 0.0022 ft. for the same conditions.

The stresses in the arch ring are as follows: At the extrados, 3.6 lb. per sq. in. compression at the crown and 4.5 lb. per sq. in. tension at the abutments; and at the intrados, 2.0 lb. per sq. in. tension at the crown and 6.7 lb. per sq. in. compression at the abutments.

For equal deflections in cantilever and arch ring the unit weight of water carried by the cantilever would be 37.5 lb. per cu. ft. and by the arch 25 lb. per cu. ft. The deflection of the cantilever from bending alone would be 0.00143 ft. and the arch deflection at the crown with shear included would be the same.

The stresses in the arch ring are as follows: At the extrados, 14.5 lb. per sq. in. compression at the crown and 17.5 lb. per sq. in. tension at the abutments; and at the intrados, 8.0 lb. per sq. in. tension at the crown and 27.5 lb. per sq. in. compression at the abutments.

The stress on the vertical face of the cantilever at the arch ring with the load divided between the cantilever and the arch to give equal deflections in each would be 14 688 lb. per sq. ft., or 102 lb. per sq. in.

The author claims that open shrinkage cracks at the down-stream face of an arched gravity dam prove that it is not acting as an arch. The writer thinks that this discussion has shown that the shrinkage or contraction cracks in an arched gravity dam extend only about 20 ft. beyond the surface. As further evidence of this it is very seldom that seepage is visible in the open contraction cracks at the down-stream face from full reservoir pressure. Even if they should show seepage, however, this is no evidence that they are not under heavy pressure. There may be uplift under the undrained base of a dam in spite of the fact that it is exerting a greater unit pressure on the foundation than is required in the arches of an arched gravity dam.

It may be claimed that there is temperature shrinkage in the whole body of a dam due to the difference in temperature between that of the concrete at the time of initial set and that of the mean annual temperature of the locality, which the interior temperature of the dam gradually approaches. Considering the quantity of water used in the concrete and its high specific heat compared with that of the other constituents, and considering the constant use of water on the concrete after placing, it does not seem probable that the average temperature at the time of initial set is above the mean annual temperature.

The temperature of the rings, or layers, placed in winter, however, will be considerably less than that of rings placed in summer, while there will be alternate rings placed in the spring and fall that will be of about mean annual temperature. The tendency, therefore, will be to have constant initial tension in some horizontal zones of the dam and constant initial compression in others, alternating with zones of no initial stress.

These stresses are independent of seasonal changes and after the setting temperatures have been dissipated, they will be constant at all times. The zones of initial compression will tend, when the dam is loaded, to carry more than their proportional share of the arch load; but there will be a tendency to equalize the load by shear between the arch rings.

This unequal initial stress condition might be equalized by pressure grouting, but it would be useless to attempt this until after the setting temperature had been dissipated. As it may require about five years to effect this, the dam will be exposed during this period to these possible concentrated arch stresses. As the arch stresses in an arched gravity dam are very low, the concentrated stresses can be safely carried permanently if desired.

The writer has not analyzed the arch stresses near the top of the dam, but thinks it would improve the design in a gravity type, whether arched or straight, to make the top thicker than customary practice and to compare the cantilever and arch ring deflections and stresses at all heights, using the author's method of computing the cantilever stresses.

W. P. Creager,* M. Am. Soc. C. E. (by letter).—The writer has checked carefully the equations and calculations contained in the author's interesting paper and can find no chance for disagreement except, perhaps, in regard to his conclusions. In order to determine whether or not a gravity dam actually has been made weaker by curving it in plan, it is necessary to investigate the fundamental reasons for providing a factor of safety against failure.

The necessary factor of safety against failure has no fixed value, but, within certain limits, usually is based on the designer's judgment guided by the probable seriousness of the calamity resulting from failure. The cost of a

* Vice-Pres. and Chf. Engr., Northern New York Utilities, Inc., and The Power Corporation of New York, Watertown, N. Y.

structure increases with the factor of safety adopted. It seems quite evident that a designer would not be warranted in requiring as great an expenditure to insure against unsightly cracks or small leakage as he would to insure against complete failure with resulting enormous financial loss and sacrifice of life.

The author states that "an arched gravity dam will receive some support from the arch and, in most cases, probably sufficient support to prevent actual failure." It is the writer's opinion, based on considerable study, that any properly designed gravity dam having a curvature sufficient to affect its strength as a gravity section materially, would undoubtedly hold as an arch dam in conjunction with its remaining strength as a gravity section, particularly if the joints were properly grouted under pressure.

Calculations by the writer indicate that the Exchequer Dam would probably hold as an arched structure irrespective of its strength as a gravity dam; although even if it were pressure-grouted, unsightly cracks and some leakage might occur before it deflected sufficiently to act as an arch.

Is it logical to assume that the Exchequer Dam, even with its slightly reduced strength caused by the curvature, still has an ample factor of safety against cracking and leakage, in consideration of the fact that the element of curvature has provided an increased factor of safety against complete failure? The writer is inclined to believe that it has.

The author states that "the smaller the radius, the larger is the error". However, the smaller the radius, the greater the ability to act as an arch, and the latter has the greater influence as affecting complete failure.

Edward Godfrey,* M. Am. Soc. C. E. (by letter).—It is encouraging to note that the author frankly recognizes under pressure as a factor in the design of a dam. His statement that even drainage is sure to be at least a partial failure should give pause to designers who recommend that under pressure be ignored or even to those who would guard against it by installing a system of drainage.

The author deduces the fact that a triangular-section gravity dam will be completely stable against up-stream pressure only if the base is about 0.65 of the height; and against both up-stream pressure and full under pressure if the base is about 0.85 of the height. It is significant to apply a triangle on the comparison of the large dams in existence (Fig. 5). The ratio, 0.85, will be found to fit all but those that are marked curved in plan. The significant thing is that the straight gravity dams that have withstood water pressure are wide enough at the base for complete stability against both up-stream pressure and full under pressure. The New Croton Dam is included among these, and this dam has several times been publicly held up as an example of a dam the designer of which did not consider under pressure.†

In Fig. 5 the dams that are curved in plan do not all come in the 0.85 class. They are nearer the 0.65 class. The author maintains that a dam convex toward the water has less stability than a straight dam of the same

* Structural Engr., Pittsburgh, Pa.

† Wegmann in *Engineering and Contracting*, December, 1922, p. 126, and *Waterworks*, June, 1923, p. 1302.

cross-section. However, in his theoretical demonstration he neglects significant forces which, in fact, should reverse the conclusion.

By analogous processes it can be apparently shown that a dam curved away from the water has greater stability than a straight dam and (as the author has done) that one curved toward the water has less stability. The actual relative stabilities, however, are just the reverse. This is because both these apparent demonstrations neglect forces of vital importance, acting on the element of the dams considered. In the case of the dam that is curved away from the water, there is a circular tension that in any ordinary dam would rupture the concrete and lift it from its abutments. In the dam curved toward the water, the author finds reduced stability. However, he neglects the forces tangent to the curve of the dam. In other words, there is arch action which aids very materially in supplying stability. This aid may, in fact, mean the difference between stability and failure.

In the writer's judgment it is the curved plan of some dams, which do not show full stability on the basis of straight gravity dams, that is responsible for their continued existence as dams. Not that this is a proper method of design, but it is the accident of design that has saved some structures. Reliance on it has wrecked more than one.

It cannot be denied that a trapezoidal element of a curved dam must exert pressure on the adjacent trapezoidal elements. The several elements are not free to rotate, and an arc of the dam tends to rotate on the ends of that arc, thus with an increased lever arm. This, however, means increased and unusual pressure against the soil at the ends of the arc which is one of the reasons to be urged against reliance on a mere curved plan.

Any dam must diminish in height toward the ends. If it is founded on rock near the ends, this rock may be utilized as abutment, and then the curved plan (convex toward the water) has undoubted and very real advantages. Arch action can be utilized under such conditions.

However, if the foundation is not rock, attempts to make long thin arch dams may result in disaster. Two dams of this type recently failed.* One of these two similar dams was 236 ft. long and 62 ft. high at the highest point. The whole dam weighed about 6 000 000 lb. while the thrust of the arch at the mid-section was 18 000 000 lb. Much of this would travel to the ends and to the small abutments. The estimated pressure on this dam in the direction of the axis of the stream was 9 000 000 lb. It is not to be expected that a dam of these proportions would stand; but if it had been built of a cross-section approaching that required for a gravity dam, the curved section might have been the salvation of it.

Real stability in a gravity dam is attained when the width of the base is made about 0.85 of the height. Failure and freezing of drainage systems can then be forgotten. No dam of these proportions has ever failed.

C. A. P. Turner,† M. Am. Soc. C. E. (by letter).—Published measurements on the experimental arch dam at Stevenson Creek, California, having

* *Engineering News-Record,* October 14, 1926, p. 616.

† Cons. Engr., Minneapolis, Minn.

a vertical up-stream face, should furnish an opportunity for testing Mr. Jakobsen's formulas and the accuracy of the assumptions involved.

The tensile fiber stress on the up-stream face when the dam was full, may be roughly computed according to his formulas at from 6 000 to 10 000 lb. per sq. in. Yet the concrete held together and the dam carried the pressure without injury and was later over-topped in a flood. The computed downstream deflection under this stress in the central part of the dam is from fifteen to fifty times greater than that measured when the dam was full. The quarter-point presented no down-stream deflection whatever, while between the quarter-point and the end of the dam the crest deflection was up stream against pressure, instead of down stream as computed by Mr. Jakobsen's notes.

This divergence of computed and measured results indicates that the predominant resistance of an arched dam, having the relative height and length of the test dam, is wholly different from that of the straight one, as assumed in the derivation of the formulas under discussion.

Consider, for example, a dam, straight in outline, that is, two or three times as long as it is high, placed in a rectangular opening in rock. Under the water pressure, the center of the dam will deflect down stream. The base, being held rigidly by the rock bottom, will not move and the ends of the dam, likewise being held rigidly by the rock sides, do not deflect. Consequently, the dam is both bent and warped or twisted. In such warping and twisting horizontal shears in vertical planes are developed, transferring a portion of the applied pressure toward the ends instead of vertically downward to the base.

In an arched dam, down-stream deflection of the crown or center of the arch cannot take place without twisting the structure. Such twisting shears transfer the reaction of the horizontal forces away from the center toward the ends of the dam and the reaction of the vertical forces shifts in like manner. The down-stream deflection of the top at the center of the dam would tend to twist the crest between the quarter-point and the end of the dam in the opposite direction. Torsion becomes the predominant resistance as opposed to the cantilever gravity action of a straight dam and the middle-third rule cannot be applied rationally to such a structure. Moreover, the curvature of the arch tends to reduce the over-turning moment on each individual element, because the axis of the moment of pressure on the individual elements makes an angle with its neighbor and with adjacent elements so that interference of moments is developed, which accentuate twist and reduce the effectiveness of the applied moment. A component of the pressure on the up-stream face produces a small amount of axial compression, or arch thrust.

If the opening is a V-formation the shift of the reaction laterally places it at a higher elevation than the base at the center or deepest part, thereby reducing the lever arm of the over-turning forces. Thus, an arched dam presents elements of resistance that the straight dam lacks. It permits an economy of material that cannot be secured when constructing a straight dam.

Rankine, in his "Applied Mechanics", states the premise on which the commonly accepted theory of flexure is founded; to wit, that the beam be subjected to transverse forces only and that the length be fifteen or more times greater than the depth. Then, shear strain may be disregarded as negligible from the practical standpoint only in determining the elastic deflection and maximum tensile and compressive fiber stresses.

In a triangular gravity section, such as that considered by Mr. Jakobsen, the ratio of base to height of strip exceeds the limits under which shear strain may be ignored. Again, because the weight of the strip constitutes a longitudinal force greater than the transverse force, the condition of transverse force normal to the axis only, under which Rankine demonstrates the ordinary theory to be approximate, is lacking.

The assumption on which the ordinary theory of flexure is based, differs widely from the elastic theory. The shearing modulus of the material, *F,* is assumed to be infinite, an imaginary value, in place of its true value of approximately three-eighths of the modulus of tension or compression. The utility of the ordinary theory is confined to the determination of the maximum fiber bending stress, at a section where rhombic shear strain passes through zero. It is not adapted to the determination of the elastic behavior or elastic stress in a beam subjected to longitudinal thrust.

For example, a wood strut, supporting concrete work, is more rigid laterally when loaded reasonably than when it is carrying little or no weight. If its deflection is to be computed correctly the moment of inertia to be applied differs from that permissible under the condition of transverse force only without axial strain, and the idea* that the center of gravity of the section constitutes the axis of internal rotational resistance must be discarded. Every attempt to solve the problem of elastic resistance by assuming perfect elasticity of material under tension and compression and no elasticity at all under shear stress invariably leads to inconsistency and error.

Arch action in an arched dam is computed by some on the assumption that no shear may be transmitted by the concrete longitudinally along horizontal planes; but if the concrete can transmit no shear longitudinally (since the material has the same resistance to shear transversely in the same plane), cantilever resistance would be an anomaly unrelieved by an additional assumption that the concrete cannot resist horizontal shear in vertical planes on which, in turn, twisting resistance depends. Thus, all assumptions, differing unreasonably from a complete acceptance of the natural characteristics of the material dealt with, lead to theoretical uncertainty and confusion.

To determine the predominant resistance of an arched dam it is necessary to consider the fact that the base of the dam on a rock formation is fixed. It does not slide down stream and it cannot be deformed† lengthwise along the rock bottom. This eliminates the idea of the predominant action as an arch, provided the height is a fraction of the length. Any strip above the base which is shortened by down-stream deflection would involve, of necessity, longitudinal horizontal shears in horizontal planes represented by twisting couples about horizontal axis normal to the face of the dam. The shift of the

---

* This erroneous idea apparently constitutes a premise in the derivation of Mr. Jakobsen's formulas.

† The section of the rock base being far greater than the dam, its elastic compression becomes relatively negligible.

reaction along the arch results in twisting couples on a normal section about the longitudinal axis of the structure and, in turn, horizontal shears in vertical planes involve a twisting couple about a vertical axis. A three-dimensional twisting strain is the result.

Computing torsional resistance involves the polar moment of inertia of the cross-section. In the case of the Stevenson Creek Dam, the polar moment of inertia resisting torsion is enormously greater than the transverse moment of inertia resisting cantilever action. Torsion accounts for the precise kind and character of deflections measured, which may not be accounted for by either arch action or cantilever strip action.

As previously noted, the stress approximately computed on the cantilever principle for the test dam would be thirty to fifty times as great as the ultimate resistance of the material; and yet it does not appear from the reports to have been cracked where the greatest tensions from torsional stress would naturally occur; that is, nearest the axis of rotation. It is to be borne in mind that the shearing resistance of concrete is far greater than the tensile resistance and one does not have to assume an imaginary tensile resistance to accompany an imaginary infinite value of the shearing modulus in order to make the computed and experimental results reasonably consistent. The fact that the experimental dam was relatively thinner than many existing arched dams would in no wise alter the character of resistance involved, because the increase in polar moment of inertia increases with the transverse moment of inertia.

Relative thinness accentuates the deflections and permits a rational deduction therefrom, which would be more difficult to make were the experimental dam thicker and the deflections too small for accurate measurement and relative comparison. In considering the torsional resistance of an arched dam structure, the engineer may well investigate the form of cross-section which will produce the minimum stress in the material. He will avoid the expensive warped surfaces embodied in certain types of design and revert to a cross-section more readily built and more nearly approaching the rectangular or trapezoidal section.

The reverse curvature of the crest deflection of the experimental dam has been attributed by some to a buckling tendency due to axial compression, but it is impossible to harmonize such a tendency with the condition of uniform hydrostatic pressure normal to the arch. Again, the exact theory of elasticity negatives such an explanation because where shear strain exists, as it must in a section of this kind fixed at the end, there is a definite limit to the number of changes of curvature and points of inflection which approximate theory fails to indicate and which are exceeded in the reported results.

A thin steel spring under compression fixed at its ends will buckle with two points of contraflexure only. To deflect, as the crown of the experimental dam was observed to deflect, would require four points of inflection because the end of the arch where the height is small was fixed in position.

Toward the conclusion of his paper, uncertainty regarding the distribution of shear at the base of the dam is noted by Mr. Jakobsen and he explains that he has purposely excluded this from his discussion, desiring only to show the influence of curvature when his assumptions were maintained. This is unfortunate because the magnitude of the resisting moment and the overturning moment depends on the relative location, position, and elevation of the reaction which determines the lever arm of the external forces.

The principle that an applied force is transferred to its support in a linear direction by the internal stresses of shear, twisting, and bending, and by the shortest path that the cross-section and rigidity of the material permit, may perhaps be utilized in mathematical form to locate the distribution of the reaction with reasonable precision, as has already been accomplished in the exact theory of plate action.

The Stevenson Creek model dam was undoubtedly selected by the engineers designing it as an average type of structure. The relative proportion of length to height and the slope of the base at the sides determine predominant action. With an angle of less than 45° to the vertical, with a height from the base to the crown two or more times the chord, the arch would modify the resistance such that the twisting of the plate would transfer a major portion of the applied force to the sides rather than to the bottom. Then, the relative moment of twisting resistance, as compared to arch resistance, would decrease so greatly for median or upper layers, that the dam with some propriety might be treated as if the predominant resistance were that of arch strips.

As engineers become more convinced of the economy of combining metal and concrete, making the concrete able to resist tension and withstand temperature stress without disintegration, and the ease with which the base of a reinforced concrete dam may be anchored into a rock foundation, construction of gravity dams will become less frequent and the monolithic reinforced structure will replace the concrete gravity dam.

The objections commonly raised to such a design may be summarized, as follows:

First.—That the steel is likely to rust and the expansion of the rust will crack the concrete and cause it to disintegrate even if the embedment is relatively deep.

Second.—That the concrete may be disintegrated by frost and, therefore, plain mass concrete is less objectionable from this standpoint. The writer's observation has been that while reinforced concrete disintegrates by the expansion of scale rust on bars that have been exposed and have not been properly cleaned before embedment, there are no well authenticated examples of such disintegration where proper care and precautions have been taken. Along the coast, where the salt air tends to increase the formation of rust, the labor involved in properly cleaning the steel is much greater than the cost of giving it a protective coating before shipment from the mill such that no rust may be formed upon it during the time it is exposed to the weather before embedment. As such coating of the proper kind increases rather than decreases the bond between the concrete and metal, it may be regarded as advantageous and economical.

A dam 3 000 ft. long, well reinforced, without expansion joints, subjected to a range of temperature from 50° below zero to 100° Fahr., above, has remained tight after a number of years, so that the objection to monolithic action on the ground that temperature changes would prevent such action, seems to be without foundation.

The engineer desires a precise mechanical theory for the computation of the elastic behavior and for the resistance of the structure he designs whether it be a frame or a concrete dam; but the computed elastic behavior depends on the values assigned to the elastic coefficients of the material.

The assumption that a plane normal cross-section of the unit strips treated by Mr. Jakobsen remains plane after flexure without rotation from the normal, requires an infinite value of the shear modulus, F.

Because deflection of the crest at the center of the dam is greater than that at the quarter-point, or toward the end, shear distortion is involved and the value of the modulus of shear which would permit distortion in the assumed absence of stress on the vertical normal plane between unit strips is zero. Hence, Mr. Jakobsen's premise consists in treating the shearing modulus, F, as varying in the same identical concrete from zero in a vertical plane to infinity in a horizontal plane. The inconsistency thus involved renders the theory without foundation or value as an elastic analysis.

While arch action and bending are affected by cracking of the concrete, torsional resistance may be transmitted by keying adjacent sections together as is customarily done by those who are prejudiced in favor of expansion joints.

B. F. Jakobsen,* M. Am. Soc. C. E. (by letter).—Mr. Rich has checked Equation (7) by a more elegant derivation and agrees that curvature should not be disregarded unless the dam is properly grouted under pressure.

Mr. Floris presents a somewhat different method of arriving at the same result.

Mr. Jorgensen's discussion will be studied with considerable interest especially his Figs. 5 and 6.

Mr. Werner develops formulas for the interesting condition of a dam curved up stream instead of down stream.

Mr. Bauman insists that gravity dams are monolithic structures, homogeneous and isotropic, and that arch action, therefore, must take place and may be determined in the usual manner. If shrinkage did not occur, there would be no reason for providing contraction joints and there would be no explanation for the large cracks which have appeared in the Mulholland Dam. This dam was not provided with contraction joints, but an effort was made to produce a monolithic structure. Unless the writer knows definitely that arch action must be present, he prefers to neglect it, because this is the safe assumption—and a safe assumption regarding arch action is particularly requisite for gravity dams, such as the Exchequer Dam. Uplift was neglected at this dam, although it may exist in spite of the drainage pipes provided.

* Cons. Engr. (LaRue & Jakobsen), Los Angeles, Calif.

Commenting on this subject, Alfred D. Flinn,* M. Am. Soc. C. E., Director of Engineering Foundation, writes,

"Some reduction of uplift may be gained also, but drainage passages cannot be depended on permanently because the leaching and depositing of salts from the masonry tend to seal the designed and accidental passages."

Likewise, in arch dam design the writer prefers to ignore the effect of the cantilevers,† and assume that the arches carry the entire load.

Mr. Bauman considers the deflection of only one cantilever, that at the crown, which is hardly sufficient,‡ and he appears to have applied Professor Cain's deflection formula for arches to the primary or original arches instead of to the secondary arches, which procedure may be equivalent to assuming that tension can be transmitted across contraction joints.§ In this manner Mr. Bauman estimates the arch action as much greater than it actually is.

Professor Cain shows that when the up-stream face is sloped, as is customary, the effect of curving the dam is to decrease the compression, and this checks what the writer found for a vertical up-stream face. Professor Cain concurs in the writer's conclusion, that it is dangerous to neglect curvature in a curved gravity dam.

Mr. Hanna quotes Wegmann to the effect that the Habra and Bouzey Dams were not arched in plan and that poor foundation was the main reason for their failure. The writer did not state that they were arched in plan, but that they failed from tension in the up-stream face and, as he knew nothing about the matter from personal observation, he referred to the source from which he quoted.‖

Dr. Unwin has stated that both dams were built of somewhat inferior material and that in each the line of the resultant fell considerably outside the middle third, so that, on the ordinary theory, there was considerable tension in the up-stream face. Both dams, he has stated, failed about half way up the dam, along a line such as AB in Fig. 19, and he was agreed with the French engineers that in both dams the initial fracture was a tension fracture which occurred at the point where the tension was greatest, according to the law of the middle third.

Mr. Hanna takes the writer to task for using a radial-sided slice, 1 ft. wide, at the up-stream face and contends that this method cannot yield reliable results. He states further:

"* * * they should not be allowed to displace the customary and reliable method of computing stresses in arched gravity dams by the parallel-sided slice theory."

A dam designed by the radial-sided slice method is safe when tested by the parallel-sided slice theory, but the reverse is not true. The writer showed this for a vertical up-stream face, and Professor Cain has shown that it

* *Transactions*, Am. Soc. C. E., Vol. 91 (1927), p. 249.

† *Loc. cit.*, Vol. 90 (1927), p. 520.

‡ "Etude sur les barrages arqués," Extrait du *Bulletin de la Suisse Romande* (1922), by Alfred Stucky.

§ See the writer's discussion of the paper by Frederick Hall Fowler, M. Am. Soc. C. E., in this volume of *Transactions*.

‖ American Civil Engineers' Handbook, Fourth Edition (1920), Section 7, Article 8, p. 686.

remains true when the up-stream face is sloped. Therefore, in the absence of some conclusive proof that the parallel-sided slice theory is correct, the writer prefers the radial-sided slice theory, because it is the safer of the two assumptions.

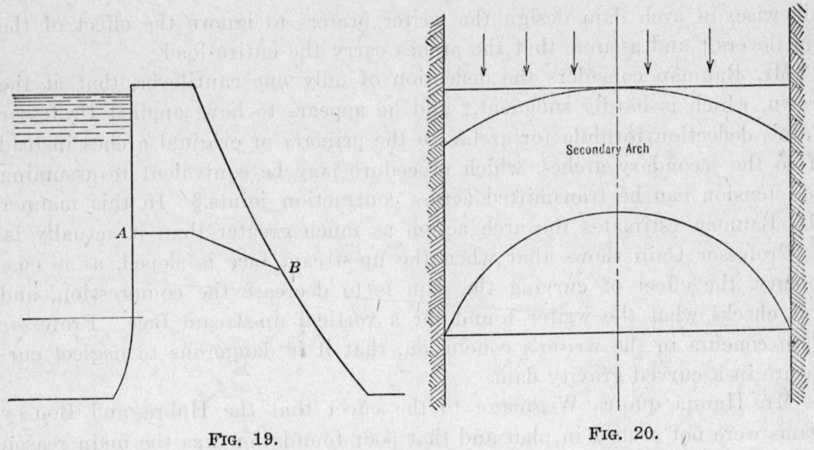

FIG. 19. FIG. 20.

Mr. Hanna assumes a monolithic structure, that is, he denies that shrinkage occurs, and then reasons that a radial-sided slice cannot deflect without encountering arch resistance. That is absolutely correct, but he overlooks the essential fact that it is equally correct for a parallel-sided slice; that is, for a straight gravity dam, provided it is monolithic. A parallel-sided slice of a straight gravity dam is not independent of the remainder of the structure for two reasons:

1.—A set of secondary horizontal arches, free from tension, exist and will resist displacements of the cantilevers in a radial direction; and,

2.—The adjoining cantilevers are not generally of the same length or height as the one under consideration, and, therefore, the deflections at the same level of these three cantilevers are different, so that one re-acts on the others.

As an illustration, take a straight gravity dam, 200 ft. high, with 50 ft. between the vertical abutments.* Such a dam would act mainly as an arch dam, notwithstanding its straight up-stream face (see Fig. 20), provided it is monolithic, as assumed by Mr. Hanna.

Equation 55 gives the deflection of a cantilever due to bending and shear. Assume that the adjoining cantilever is longer by $d\,x$, so that, for this cantilever, $H + d\,x$ and $h + d\,x$ should be substituted for H and h in the equation in order to obtain its deflection at the same elevation, $H - h$ ft. from the crest (see Fig. 14). The difference between the deflections may be obtained most conveniently by differentiating Equation (55), bearing in

* Résal, "Formes et Dimensions des grands barrages en maçonnerie," *Annales des Ponts et Chaussées*, II, 1919, p. 26.

mind that the ratio, $\frac{H}{B}$, remains constant. This gives the additional deflection, $d\,\Delta_h$, due to the additional length, $d\,x$,

$$d\,\Delta_h = \left(\frac{62.5\,H^3}{E\,B^3}\,2\,h + \frac{46.9}{E\,B}\,2\,H\right)d\,x \qquad (76)$$

This means, even if arch action is not present, that when the abutment is steep, so that in a short horizontal distance a considerable change in height occurs, the longer cantilever tends to deflect more than the shorter one. Under this condition an overloading of the shorter cantilever may occur, which may result in uplift under the shorter cantilever. For this reason, also, it is well to insist, as does Professor Cain, that the base should always be thicker than the middle-third theorem prescribes.

Mr. Hanna develops formulas for the effect of curvature on stresses (Fig. 15), for a slice of any width instead of one having a width of only 1 ft. as was considered by the writer. In order to integrate his equations, however, Mr. Hanna assumes that H is constant, and his formulas, therefore, have a very limited application. When H is variable, shear stresses are present in the vertical radial planes, because Δ_h also varies and the calculations become quite complicated, even when arch action is ignored. Of course, this holds also for a straight gravity dam, provided it is monolithic.

Mr. Wiley's discussion is of particular interest, because the Exchequer Dam was accepted by him as Consulting Engineer for the Merced Irrigation District. The gravity design was given preference over an arch dam, which required 60 000 cu. yd. less material. With reference to his Fig. 5, Mr. Jorgensen stated:

"The Exchequer Dam sustains a higher unbalanced water pressure than any other dam, and it possesses the slimmest cross-section thus far attempted for high dams."

When this gravity dam is properly analyzed, it is found to have considerable tension in the up-stream face. The writer was informed by the engineer in charge that the concrete weighed 152 lb. per cu. ft., which checks well with his own experience for this locality. The value of 158 lb. per cu. ft. used in the design, according to Mr. Wiley, seems too high and has the appearance of being an assumption on the side of danger.

The expansion of the arch ring due to lateral deformation, is, according to Mr. Wiley, 0.000032 ft., while the least contraction in a 50-ft. joint, measured 22 ft. from the surface, is, 0.0324 in., or a unit shrinkage of 0.000054, which is nearly 70% greater than the lateral deformation, as computed by Mr. Wiley. In addition, he states that there was still some setting temperature in the dam, when these measurements were taken.

In determining the lateral deformation, Mr. Wiley assumes Poisson's ratio as $\frac{1}{5}$ and that the modulus of elasticity is 2 000 000 lb. per sq. in. The writer believes that both these values are much too favorable. Turneaure and Maurer* give for Poisson's ratio, for 1:2:4 concrete, 60 days old, $\frac{1}{6.25}$ to $\frac{1}{10}$,

* "Concrete Construction," p. 25.

and for 1:3:6 concrete, 60 days old, $\frac{1}{12.5}$; and this last value would probably be more nearly correct for the very lean concrete in the Exchequer Dam. A value of $\frac{1}{8}$ for Poisson's ratio and 4 000 000 lb. per sq. in. for the modulus of elasticity is more nearly correct and at any rate more conservative, for a concrete having a compressive strength of 2 000 lb. per sq. in., or probably more* and with these assumptions the lateral deformation near the toe of the base is 0.000010, or one-fifth of that required to annul the smallest measured shrinkage. For points at this elevation, but farther away from the toe, the lateral deformation becomes smaller, because the vertical compression is smaller, and for higher elevations the lateral deformation also becomes smaller. For these higher elevations the shrinkage is possibly greater, because the section is thinner and not so well protected against drying out and cooling, and it is the arch action in the upper parts of the dam and not at the base, that is of importance.

Mr. Wiley's figures show that the contractions decrease with increasing distance from the face, and he concludes that a little farther inside the dam, it may be assumed that no contraction takes place. There is another explanation which seems more reasonable, or at any rate more conservative, that is, that the contraction inside the dam is delayed due to the fact that the setting temperature remains longer in the interior. Mr. Wiley admits that when the measurements were taken, there was still some setting temperature in the dam. All authorities seem to agree that Poisson's ratio is exceedingly difficult to measure for concrete and, therefore, if it is to be seriously considered, a very conservative value should be used. Moreover, for the upper part of the dam, where arch action might be of considerable importance, the lateral deformation is at any rate quite negligible compared to the shrinkage.

Mr. Wiley thinks that because very little leakage appears through shrinkage and contraction cracks, that shrinkage does not penetrate more than about 20 ft. below the surface. Where water-stops are provided in the up-stream face, leakage cannot very well take place, but when the writer last visited the Mulholland Dam (which was not provided with contraction joints), there was some leakage through the vertical-radial cracks and the foreman stated that an attempt was being made to stop the leakage by introducing sawdust. It is quite true that two surfaces may be in contact and transmitting heavy stresses, as Mr. Wiley contends, and still there may be some leakage. However, it is equally true that two surfaces, as at a shrinkage crack, may not be in contact and yet very little leakage may be in evidence. This latter is the safe and conservative assumption. Why accept the unsafe assumption merely because it may sometimes happen to be correct? The writer has made some calculations to determine what the leakage would be through a shrinkage crack $\frac{1}{16}$ in. wide under such heads and length of paths as would occur in the Mulholland Dam and finds that the discharge

* Stanton Walker, Assoc. M. Am. Soc C. E. "Modulus of Elasticity of Concrete," *Bulletin No. 5*, Structural Materials Research Laboratory, Lewis Inst., Chicago, Ill.

would be exceedingly small. If account is taken of the fact that the channel formed through a shrinkage crack is not uniform, being obstructed by small particles, etc., and that the crack is not a plane, the computed leakage is practically negligible. Therefore, the fact that there is only a very small leakage does not justify the conclusion that there must be arch action in the dam.

In summing up, the writer feels that Mr. Wiley has failed to show that there probably will be arch action in the Exchequer Dam, after the setting temperature is gone; and much less has he proved that it must be present, as would be required before any claims can be made for arch action. It is undoubtedly true that arch action might prevent a complete failure, but as the writer sees it, this cannot be relied upon until after the cantilever has failed and uplift must then also be admitted.

Mr. Kramer's discussion is very able and most fair. He admits that shrinkage will take place and then proceeds to show that the cantilever may possibly deflect sufficiently to bring about arch action, when certain reasonably advantageous assumptions are made. Mr. Kramer considers a block 50 ft. wide and assumes that the shrinkage is that corresponding to a temperature drop of 20° Fahr. This corresponds to a unit shrinkage of 0.000110 which should cover both temperature and setting shrinkage and the writer believes this may not be quite enough.* Mr. Kramer assumes the modulus of elasticity to be 2 000 000 lb. per sq. in., and states that this is a rather low value, which will give high values for the deflections. Stanton Walker, Assoc. M. Am. Soc. C. E., gives the following formula† for the relation between the initial tangent modulus of elasticity, E_i, and the compressive strength, S:

$$E_i = 40\,000\, S^{0.6} \qquad (77)$$

Equation (77) gives the following values:

Compressive strength, in pounds per square inch.	Modulus of elasticity, in pounds per square inch.
1 000	2 520 000
2 000	3 820 000
3 000	4 800 000
4 000	5 900 000

These values represent the grand average of a great many tests. At Exchequer Dam there was no control over the quantity of water used in mixing, but an effort was made to secure the proper mix, and by the time the dam was ready for loading, it is fair to assume that the average strength was probably 2 000 lb. per sq. in., or more, considering that most of the concrete would be at least one year old. This would give a modulus of elasticity of about 4 000 000 lb. per sq. in., or twice that assumed by Mr. Kramer, which would reduce the deflections of the cantilever proportionately.

* See, Mr. Wiley's discussion, pp. 822–823, bearing in mind that the measured contractions cannot be considered as final. See, also, "Stresses in Multiple-Arch Dams," *Transactions*, Am. Soc. C. E., Vol. LXXXVII (1924), p. 310.

† *Bulletin No. 5*, Structural Materials Research Laboratory, Lewis Inst., Chicago, Ill., p. 65.

The writer will elaborate on Mr. Kramer's analysis and carry the calculations a step farther. When the cantilever is bent, it is able to compensate for shrinkage and the amount of this is given by the difference in length between $A B$ and $A' B'$ in Fig. 21, in which, $A B$ is the length of a short element of the crest before the deflection, y, takes place. That difference is,

$$2 \phi R_u - (R_u - y) 2 \phi = 2 \phi y$$

If $A B$ is 1 ft., $2 \phi = \frac{1}{R_u}$, and,

$$e = \frac{y}{R_u} \qquad (78)$$

in which, e is the unit shrinkage that a deflection, y, can compensate for, when the up-stream radius is R_u. The compensation, therefore, depends directly on the deflection. Mr. Kramer determines the crest deflection at the crown, $y_{max.} = 0.1154$ ft.; and with $R_u = 674.7$ ft., he obtains $e_{max.} = 0.000171$, which is 1.55 times greater than the assumed shrinkage.

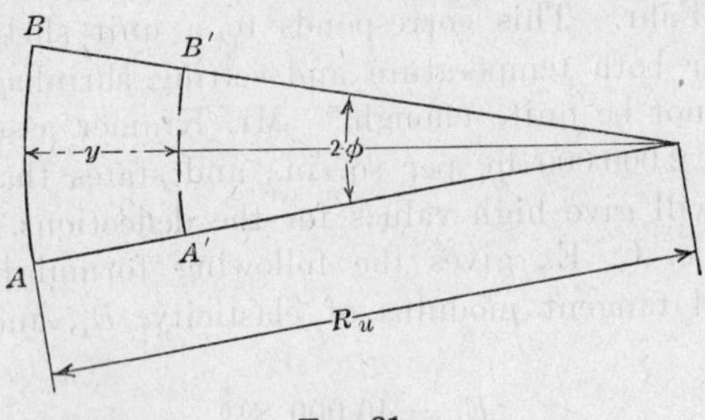

FIG. 21.

However, the maximum deflection is applicable to only one single point in the structure and is not a fair measure of the structure's ability to compensate for shrinkage. The writer calculated the bending and shear deflections for a gravity dam 200 ft. high, of triangular section and with the water standing level with the crest,* and found the deflection line to be approximately straight. Half way up the dam, therefore, the deflection is only one-half of what it is at the crest (in reality, it is somewhat less than that), while the shrinkage is not materially less, although it may take a longer time for the thicker sections to reach their final shrinkage. At the lower elevations, especially near the toe, some compensation will be derived from the lateral deformation.

Even at the crest the maximum deflection is not a fair measure, since the crest deflection at the abutment is zero. The crest deflection due to bending and shear, as developed for the 200-ft. dam previously referred to, is,

$$y = \frac{0.434}{E} (a^3 + 0.72\, a)\, h^2 \text{ ft.} \qquad (79)$$

in which, E = modulus of elasticity, in pounds per square inch, h = the height

* *Transactions*, Am. Soc. C. E., Vol. LXXXIV (1921), p. 101, Fig. 32.

of the cantilever, and $a = \frac{\text{height}}{\text{thickness}} = 1.59$ for the Exchequer Dam. Assuming $E = 2\,000\,000$ as does Mr. Kramer, the crest deflection is,

$$y = 1.12 \times 10^{-6} \times h^2 \text{ ft} \quad \text{.......... (80)}$$

This checks Mr. Hanna's Equation (55). For $h = 320$ ft., Equation (80) gives $y_{\text{max.}} = 0.1146$ ft., which checks Mr. Kramer's value of 0.1154 ft.

In order to have definite ideas, assume that the developed profile of the site, taken along the center line of the crest, is a straight line and let h be the height corresponding to an angle, θ, measured from the crown, so that,

$$h = c\,(\theta_1 - \theta) \text{ ft.} \quad \text{.......... (81)}$$

in which, θ_1 is one-half the central angle. At the crown, $\theta = 0$ and $h_{\text{max.}} = c\,\theta_1$, which determines the constant, c. If $h = h_{\text{max.}}$ throughout (then, of course, Equation (81) would not apply), $y_{\text{max.}}$ would be the average deflection. Since, however, h is variable in accordance with Equation (81), the average deflection for the crest is,

$$y_{\text{ave.}} = \frac{1}{\theta_1}\int_0^{\theta_1} y\,d\,\theta = \frac{1.12 \times 10^{-6}}{\theta_1}\int_0^{\theta_1} c^2\,(\theta_1 - \theta)^2\,d\,\theta$$

or,

$$y_{\text{ave.}} = 1.12 \times 10^{-6}\,\frac{c^2\,\theta_1^{\,2}}{3} = \frac{1}{3}\,y_{\text{max.}} \quad \text{.......... (82)}$$

Equation (81) represents an unusual profile. One that is more nearly representative is shown in Fig. 22 and is determined by:

$$h = c\left[1 + \cos\left(\pi\,\frac{\theta}{\theta_1}\right)\right] \quad \text{.......... (83)}$$

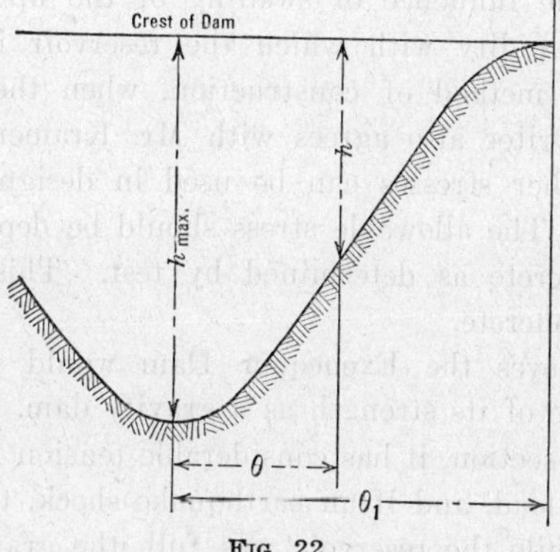

FIG. 22.

For the crown section, $\theta = 0$ and $h_{\text{max.}} = 2c$. Proceeding exactly as before, the deflection at any point is given by Equation (80) when the value of h from Equation (83) is substituted, and the average deflection, which determines, at least approximately, the average unit shrinkage that the deflections can compensate for, is,

$$y_{\text{ave.}} = 0.375\;y_{\text{max.}} \quad \text{.......... (84)}$$

In other words, instead of using the maximum crest deflection, $y_{max.}$, only about 0.333 $y_{max.}$ should be used and that will compensate for a shrinkage of,

$$e = \frac{0.333 \times 0.1154}{674.7} = 0.00006$$

The shrinkage assumed by Mr. Kramer is 0.00011. The conclusion is, that even with Mr. Kramer's rather favorable values for shrinkage and modulus of elasticity, the deflection at the crest is sufficient to compensate for only about one-half the assumed shrinkage. At elevations below the crest, the deficiency is even greater.

From these considerations may be concluded that an arched gravity dam not provided with contraction joints is less likely to crack near the crown and more likely to crack nearer the abutments. This checks well with the location of the cracks in the Mulholland Dam. Likewise, dams provided with contraction joints would be expected to show larger openings toward the abutments than near the crown.

The writer agrees with Mr. Kramer that no allowance should be made for arch action, unless it be shown that it must be present under the most unfavorable conditions which may be reasonably expected, and that the burden of proof should be on the designer.

As has been shown it appears questionable whether the Exchequer Dam, after it has cooled, can develop arch action before the cantilevers fail and introduce uplift; so many indeterminate factors enter into the calculations as to make these uncertain. To the factors already mentioned, may be added the deflections due to the yielding of the foundation, which are by no means negligible* and which will influence both the arch and the cantilever deflections, the influence of swelling of the up-stream face† due to water-soaking, the rapidity with which the reservoir is filled, temperature during construction, method of construction, when the dam was pressure-grouted, etc. The writer also agrees with Mr. Kramer that when properly calculated much higher stresses can be used in design than has been customary in the past. The allowable stress should be dependent on the actual strength of the concrete as determined by test. This will encourage the production of good concrete.

Mr. Creager believes the Exchequer Dam would probably hold as an arch dam irrespective of its strength as a gravity dam. This is to be hoped, because as a gravity section, it has considerable tension in the up-stream face with only the water load, and if an earthquake shock, traveling up the river bed, should occur while the reservoir was full, the gravity action could not be depended upon for any material assistance. If, in the last analysis, the Exchequer Dam derives its stability, or its factor of safety, from arch action or mainly from arch action, would it not have been wiser to have taken account of this in the design? Mr. Bauman gives the central angles for

* "Stresses in Thick Arches of Dams," *Transactions*, Am. Soc. C. E., Vol. 90 (1927), p. 520, and Dr. Vogt's discussion, p. 554.

† *Loc. cit.*, p. 517, and Fig. 26.

the Exchequer Dam* and Mr. Jorgensen gives the central angles for the proposed arch dam (Fig. 6). A comparison shows that the central angles are much larger and the radii much smaller for the arch design than for the gravity design, and the conclusion is inescapable that from the point of view of arch action, the Exchequer Dam is hopelessly inferior in spite of its much greater cost.

Referring to Dr. Unwin's statement, it seems to the writer quite likely that the Bouzey and Habra Dams carried a portion of the load on the secondary arches during the first years of their existence. As shrinkage and cooling became effective, the arch action was greatly reduced, tension made its appearance in the up-stream face and eventually led to failure (see pages 813-814).

The writer agrees with Mr. Godfrey and Mr. Kramer that uplift merits serious consideration and that drainage systems are not always dependable.

Mr. Turner's discussion takes him somewhat far afield. The writer stated expressly in his paper that he was aware of the limitations involved and gave his reasons for accepting the usual assumptions. He had no intention of formulating an elastic theory. Mr. Turner seems to be under the impression that there is a principal distinction to be made between straight and curved gravity dams. This question has already been discussed herein. The twisting stresses to which Mr. Turner refers, have been discussed by others, but as far as the writer knows, consideration of them has not gone beyond the conversational stage, and what engineers need are figures by which to design, based on conservative assumptions. A complete solution of the stresses in a gravity dam, straight or arched, is so complicated that it may not be attempted for some time to come. A good and conservative approximation, however, will satisfy most engineers. As study and experiments go on, knowledge of the stress distribution will be perfected.

General Remarks.—There is one factor, which has not been brought into the discussion, but which cannot be ignored, when calculating deflections that occur under prolonged loading. This is the so-called time effect. The modulus of elasticity is defined as the ratio between stress and strain, when both are measured immediately after the load is applied. Tests show that when the stress is maintained for some time, the deformation continues to increase and that it approaches its maximum value asymptotically. This continued yielding under constant stress is known as the time effect. Due to this characteristic of concrete, the stress multiplied by the modulus of elasticity, as ordinarily measured, gives only the deformation, which occurs at once, when the load is applied and this deformation is much smaller than the actual deformation due to the load acting over a considerable period of time.

F. R. McMillan, M. Am. Soc. C. E., has tested† a reinforced concrete beam in bending over a considerable period of time. The concrete was of good quality and was 6 weeks old when the test was started. Immediately

* See p. 789, Table 1, Column (4); for the crest, the central angle is about 80 degrees.

† "Shrinkage and Time Effect in Reinforced Concrete," Univ. of Minnesota, Studies in Engineering, No. 3, March, 1915, Fig. 8.

after the load had been applied, the deformation of the concrete was 0.0021 in. on an 8-in. gauge length. This was measured in the center of the span and on the compression face of the beam. After nearly 60 days under the same load, the deformation was 0.0039 in., an increase of nearly 100 per cent. At this time an additional load was applied, increasing the deformation to 0.0047 in.; 60 days later this had increased to 0.0063 in. and after an additional 60 days to 0.0072 in. Expressing the last three figures as percentages, they are 100, 134, and 153. Another beam* had a deformation of 0.0027 in. in an 8-in. gauge length, immediately after the load had been applied; 20 days later, it was 0.0064 in., and after another 20 days, it was 0.0069 in. About a year after the test was started the deformation was 0.0101 in. and this is 3.74 times the deformation which took place at once and from which the modulus of elasticity would be derived. In all these tests the shrinkage was measured separately and allowed for, so that the change in deformation given, is that due to time effect only.

Mr. Charles M. Montgomery reports† a compression test on an 8 by 16-in. concrete cylinder, which was about 4 years old at the time of test. It had been stored in damp sand for more than 3 years and the remainder of the time it had been exposed to air. The mix was approximately 1:2:4 and the crushing strength was 3 550 lb. per sq. in. A load equivalent to a stress of 300 lb. per sq. in. was applied on March 22 and the deformation was 0.0014 in., measured immediately after the load was applied. After 24 hours the load was removed and immediately replaced and the deformation was 0.0024 in. After another 24 hours, it was 0.0028 in. The results of the test are shown in Fig. 23. After about 12 to 14 days, the concrete seems to have taken its final deformation and this is about three times as great as the one first measured. The concrete appears to have been of a good grade and the stress was less than 10% of the ultimate strength. No allowance was made for shrinkage in this case, but it seems very unlikely that this could have affected the deformations more than a few per cent.

A. H. Fuller and C. C. More, Members, Am. Soc. C. E., loaded three cylinders‡ cut from the floor of a building. The cylinders were from 101 to 137 days old. With a stress of 650 lb. per sq. in., the deformation of one of the cylinders, 14 days after load had been applied, was 15 dial units, and 54 days later it was 42, or 2.8 times the first measurement. The deformation was still increasing, but at a slower rate. Another of the cylinders was tested under a stress of 1 150 lb. per sq. in.; 14 days after test started, the deformation was 33 dial units and 54 days later, it was 78, or 2.36 times the first measurement. The first reading taken on this cylinder was about a week after applying the load, when a deformation of 22 dial units was found; 250 days after starting the test, the deformation was 120, or nearly six times as large as the reading after one week of test.

* "Shrinkage and Time Effect in Reinforced Concrete," Univ. of Minnesota, Studies in Engineering, No. 3, March, 1915, p. 26, Fig. 11-*a*.

† *Transactions*, Am. Soc. C. E., Vol. LXXX (1916), p. 1712.

‡ "Time Tests of Concrete," *Proceedings*, Am. Concrete Inst., v. 12, p. 302, 1916; quoted from *Bulletin No. 24*, by W. K. Hatt, M. Am. Soc. C. E., Purdue Eng. Station, November, 1925, p. 41.

These tests will suffice to show the very great influence of the time factor; it appears that part of the deformation is plastic and part elastic and that time is also a factor in the recovery. The rapidity of filling of the reservoir will determine to what extent the time effect may be counted on to compensate for shrinkage.

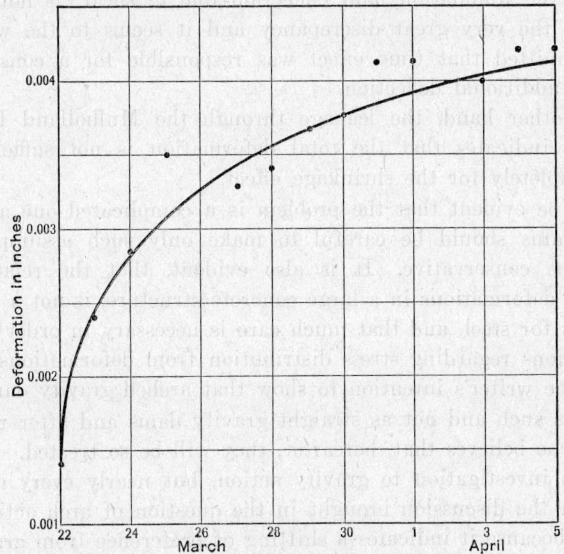

FIG. 23.—INCREASE IN DEFORMATION DUE TO TIME EFFECT.

These tests on small samples bring up the question as to whether concrete in mass will obey the same law. In discussing the Lake Spaulding Dam, F. A. Noetzli, M. Am. Soc. C. E., computed the deflection at crest* as 0.36 in., based on a modulus of elasticity of 2 000 000 lb. per sq. in. and he states that the measured deflection is 3.44 in. and, further, that: "This * * * shows, that the cantilever deflected, as measured, about ten times as much as the laws of elasticity really would permit."

Mr. Noetzli did not take account of the swelling of the up-stream face, the yielding of the foundation, and the shear deflection, but these omissions are not sufficient to account for the very great discrepancy, although they may more than double the calculated deflection. If, in addition, the time effect is sufficient to increase the deformation from three to four times, then there is a very fair agreement between calculated and measured deflections. The tests previously referred to indicate that such an increase is quite possible.

Mr. Noetzli concluded that the cantilever must have cracked at the base, since otherwise he could not account for the fact that the measured deflection was ten times larger than his computed deflection. Mr. Jorgensen, however, stated † that if the cantilever was cracked to any depth, leakage should

* *Transactions*, Am. Soc. C. E., Vol. LXXXIV (1921), p. 54.

† *Loc. cit.*, p. 70.

occur through the 6-in. drain pipes placed in the up-stream third of the dam, but that virtually no leakage had occurred. He also stated that the zero point for deflection was probably located before the chemical heat had been dissipated and while the cantilever was bent up stream by the swelling of the arches due to heat; but this effect, combined with the effect of swelling, yielding of the foundation, and deflection due to shear, is not sufficient to account for the very great discrepancy and it seems to the writer that it must be admitted that time effect was responsible for a considerable portion of the additional deflection.

On the other hand, the leakage through the Mulholland Dam, already referred to, indicates that the total deformation is not sufficient to compensate completely for the shrinkage effect.

It must be evident that the problem is a complicated one and engineers designing dams should be careful to make only such assumptions as are known to be conservative. It is also evident, that the relation between stresses and deformations in a large concrete structure, is not a simple linear one, as it is for steel, and that much care is necessary in order to draw correct conclusions regarding stress distribution from deformations in concrete.

It was the writer's intention to show that arched gravity dams should be calculated as such and not as straight gravity dams and after reviewing the discussions, he believes that, hereafter, they will be so treated. He intended to limit the investigation to gravity action, but nearly every engineer who took part in the discussion brought in the question of arch action. That is interesting, because it indicates a shifting of preference from gravity to arch dams. If arch action must be depended upon to provide the real factor of safety, this should be given due consideration in the design and that will mean large central angles and small radii; that is, arch dams. Gravity action must exist in any dam to some extent; yet engineers designing arch dams do not have to bring in gravity action to show the existence of a factor of safety, while, as this discussion has shown, the reverse is not true.

The writer feels amply rewarded for the time he has devoted to this subject by the interest shown by other engineers and in closing he wishes to thank those who have participated in the discussion.

AMERICAN SOCIETY OF CIVIL ENGINEERS
INSTITUTED 1852

TRANSACTIONS

This Society is not responsible for any statement made or opinion expressed in its publications.

Paper No. 1673

MODERN CRUSHED STONE AND GRAVEL SURFACING*

By J. W. Hoover,† Esq.

With Discussion by Messrs. Roy A. Klein, C. H. Purcell, and O. E. Stanley.

In his address at the Washington Convention of the National Sand and Gravel Association, on January 25, 1923, E. W. James, Chief of the Division of Design of the United States Bureau of Public Roads, stated that, of the roads constructed with the assistance of Federal Aid funds, 40.4% of the mileage was gravel surfaced and that such roads had absorbed approximately one-fourth of the Federal Aid funds expended to that date. States, counties, and townships construct independently, or without Federal assistance, several times the road mileage built with Federal aid. The subject, therefore, is of considerable importance to the Nation and to each individual community.

Much might be said of the economic value of stone and gravel surfacing; of the volume of traffic that will justify the change from a dirt road to a gravel or crushed rock surface and from such surfaces to more expensive and satisfactory pavement. The time at which each change becomes advisable must be determined for each road. To state as a general proposition that a traffic of 300 or 400 cars per day, or so many tons per day, justifies a change of type of surfacing, is to err. The cost of maintenance of the existing surface and the expense of the construction and maintenance of a higher type of surface differ for each locality. The value for a highway in the State of Washington would not serve in another State except as a coincidence; the principle involved is the same, however, and should be based on the various costs as affected by sub-grade, traffic, and climate.

The most important consideration is service to the public. Just how good a road is the public entitled to have? As a general rule, the automobile owner is supplying the funds; it is his money and his road; how good should it be?

A number of engineers state that the paving of a highway is warranted when the traffic has reached 400 to 500 cars per day, or approximately the

* Presented at the meeting of the Highway Division, Seattle, Wash., July 15, 1926.
† State Highway Engr., Olympia, Wash.

same number of tons per day based on certain average conditions in certain localities. None has attempted to fix the volume of traffic that would be considered sufficient to justify gravel surfacing; the general idea seems to be that if a road is worth building at all, a gravel surface is justified. The writer doubts if many paved roads are carrying less than 1 000 cars per day, and thousands of miles of gravel roads are carrying more than 1 500 cars per day.

After all, the question of the time to change the type of surface is dependent on the funds available and seldom on the real economics of the situation for the reason that improvements are far behind the requirements of traffic. A great majority of the highways are now carrying more traffic than the width and type of surface justify, considering the economic value and the service to which the public feels entitled. The question of which road shall be improved first may be answered on the basis of traffic, although often the decision is made by the legislative body making the appropriations, disregarding the merits of the respective roads.

The sub-grade on which the surfacing materials are to be placed should provide a well-drained stable foundation. The soil, as well as practical drainage, and the climate should be considered before the surfacing materials are selected and before the width and thickness of surface are determined.

After the sub-grade has been studied and the present and probable future traffic has been determined, the metal—either gravel, crushed gravel, or crushed rock—may be selected. The criterion for such selection should be that the material selected furnish the service required at the least cost. Hand in hand with the selection of the metal is the design of the cross-section.

A surface 12 ft. wide and 6 in. thick may be all that is necessary for light traffic. However, there is, and no doubt will be for some time, a large mileage of unpaved highway that is subjected to traffic sufficient to justify paving. The writer would recommend a width of not less than 18 ft., a thickness at the edges of 9 to 10 in., and a center thickness of 7 to 8 in. If the sub-grade is unstable, additional thickness should be provided. A design similar to that described is of more importance where water-bound macadam and dust-prevention methods through oiling or other surface treatments are contemplated or probable in the near future.

At first, the maximum size of gravel or crushed rock was rather large, often as much as 3 in. With more improved and extensive maintenance methods, the size was reduced until 1½ in. for the base course and ¾ in. for the top course became common, with occasional specifications limiting the base rock to a maximum of 1 in. and the top course to ¾ in.

Practically all these roads were maintained by frequent dragging, and the ideal was expressed as a smooth compact base covered with ½ in. to 1 in. of loose material to be worked back and forth across the road by the drag or grader. Highway surface construction passed through the coarse rock stage and there is now a large mileage of fine rock surfacing that may be treated to give a surface free from dust.

A tendency is now developing to change to coarser rock or gravel in surface treatments in order to secure a smooth, compact road free from loose material where the travel is heavy and where dust prevention is desirable.

The selection of gravel, crushed gravel, or crushed rock as a surfacing has been based largely on the cost of the material on the road. This has resulted in natural gravel surfaces or crushed gravel surfaces in the glaciated areas and crushed rock surfaces in unglaciated areas. In general, crushed rock has given the best service, with crushed gravel and pit-run, screened gravel in the order named. Deposits of natural fine gravel, however, sometimes give as good results as the best crushed rock.

The question of hardness of gravel or rock for surfacing has been studied a great deal and, in general, the limits set forth in the specifications of the various States produce good results. It is not practical to use the same specifications in all the States on account of differences in the materials available, the soil, traffic, and climate. Very often, the material available would not pass the specified tests, nevertheless, it makes the best of road surfacing under the circumstances. The policy of the State of Washington is to test the materials before the contract is advertised. Through the specifications the bidders are then advised of the requirements for each grade of material. In this way the contractor is fully advised before making his bid as to the sources of gravel or rock, uncertainty is greatly reduced, and the State receives a better bid for the work.

The following is a brief review of gravel or crushed-rock surfacing specifications for a roadway that is to be maintained by dragging loose material back and forth:

(1) The sub-grade shall be smooth and true to the required cross-section and all large rock removed. The surfacing material shall be uniformly distributed on the sub-grade.

If the inspector should be lax in this requirement the surfacing will not be smooth and traffic will work depressions where the material is not uniform and considerable time may be required before the maintenance forces can furnish a first-class riding surface. The usual specifications also require that the contractor, as far as practical, shall do his hauling over the surfacing as it is placed.

(2) The surfacing material shall be dragged as much as necessary to keep it smooth. Where the surfacing is to be in two courses, the contractor is required to construct as much of the base course as possible from any one setting of bunkers before beginning the top course. If the entire product of the crusher is to be placed in the base course, the entire base course shall be constructed before starting the top course. If the product of the crusher is separated into two sizes only, the base course is constructed until the section of the bunkers for the finer material is filled, at which time the top course may be started.

In this way the hauling equipment is used to secure as much compacting of the two courses as practical. By dragging the surfacing and keeping it smooth the trucks do not follow the same tracks, and the traffic is distributed over a wider area. Few specifications give sufficient attention to the binding material for the surfacing. The average specification permits the use of side-of-the-road material, or any other material that is easily available, that has binding qualities. The binding material should be a water-resistant clay which will harden when mixed with the surfacing material. The State of Oregon has given this part of the work a great deal of attention during the past few years and has secured good results.

Too much emphasis cannot be placed on the necessity for keeping the sub-grade and each course of surfacing smooth during the entire construction of the road and afterward by the maintenance organization. The best results are obtained in this type of surfacing by constructing it in at least two courses, the base course containing rock of a maximum size of 1½ in. and the top course composed of rock which will pass a ¾-in. ring. The two courses should be of equal thickness, and each not less than 3 in. The thickness of the surfacing depends on the character of the sub-grade, the traffic, and the climatic conditions. In some places, such as the arid regions of Washington where the annual rainfall is only 6 to 10 in., light surfacing wears very well. In other parts of the State a very heavy surface course is necessary as the annual rainfall may be more than 100 in. per year and the sub-grade very soft when wet. The best results in the heavy rainfall area are obtained by using the product of the crusher in the base course as this forms a crust with comparatively little binder due to the interlocking effect of the crushed material. In the arid regions the product of the crusher may be separated into the two sizes, the base course being bound with clay after which the top course is placed and bound with clay. A great variety of specifications for the size of material in each course is possible, dependent on the materials that are available.

The available materials should be thoroughly studied for each project. In some localities there is no choice. Surfacing in more than two courses is often advisable on account of a soft sub-grade that cannot be drained or raised without excessive cost. In some instances a base course of large rock is advisable and economical.

Gravel or crushed rock surfaces are maintained by dragging with a grader or drag having a comparatively long wheel-base. Some roads must be dragged more often than others, depending on the stability of the sub-grade, the character of the surface, the kind and volume of traffic, and the climatic conditions. Additional material must be added as the original material is ground up and blown away or pounded into the sub-grade. The surface must be kept smooth, for if it once becomes rough a considerable cost is entailed in scarifying, re-shaping, and compacting.

Surface treatment with oils gives promise of eliminating the dust nuisance. In some States oil treatment will be costly, as the type of surfacing in use is not adapted to such treatment and is less expensive than surfacing on which oil works best.

There is no final answer—no one final specification for a modern crushed stone or gravel road; possibly there are but few fundamentals that will apply under all circumstances. Soil, climate, traffic, materials of construction, and funds fix the limits to which construction may be carried. Surfacing of the type discussed is being studied and will be improved. Highway engineering has made wonderful strides in the last ten years and gives promise of producing a road surface that will serve adequately in many places until higher types of pavement are warranted.

DISCUSSION

Roy A. Klein,* Assoc. M. Am. Soc. C. E. (by letter).—The writer agrees that crushed stone and gravel surfacing will continue for some time to be the dominant type of surfacing for the vast mileage of rural highways of the nation.

As to the selection of the most serviceable types of road surface, the saving in operation effected by the construction of higher types does not accrue to the agency that performs the work, but rather to the people who operate motor vehicles. Therefore, since the agencies that build the highways do not operate them, it is obviously impossible to plan highway improvements based on any theory of pure economics. However, since the highway engineer represents the public in the last analysis, he should plan to build and maintain carefully the best type of surface that the funds secured by taxation will provide.

It is difficult to determine the exact amount of motor-vehicle traffic or tonnage at which it is feasible or desirable to change to a higher type of surfacing, because there are a number of different factors that affect local conditions. Stage construction, that is, building standard graded earth road first, crushed rock or gravel surface next, and then pavement, as the demands of traffic increase, is a logical and economical program. When the crushed rock or gravel surface is worn out, the road-bed will have become well stabilized and the remainder of the surfacing material will form a good base for the pavement. On the other hand, if the demands of travel do not justify pavement, a re-surface can be added at a fraction of the original cost; thus, in either case, the annual cost for the use of the road surface is a relatively small amount.

The importance of foundations has been stressed by the author, and that is a point well taken. When there is any question as to the strength of the sub-grade, the best insurance is to provide a sub-surface course of large stone, crusher run, of 4 in. maximum size, in a layer ranging from 4 to 12 in., depending on conditions. The use of large base stone on sections where the soil shows excessive capillary action has been quite successful in Oregon, the larger voids between the rocks breaking up the capillarity. On sections where these foundation courses have been used, the maintenance cost of the surfacing has been considerably less than on other sections constructed under similar conditions, because the surface does not break through in the spring.

The construction of the thickened edge and the thinner center for macadams as well as pavements appears logical and is quite simple. The edge has always been the point of weakness of the "feather-edge" macadams; particularly under softened sub-grade conditions. The thickened edge will make it possible to maintain the full designed roadway width without loss by wearing away on the sides. The Oregon State Highway Department has several thickened-edge macadams completed and the results are very satisfactory.

On main traveled roads, the surfacing should not be less than 18 ft. wide and preferably 20 ft. The greater width, of course, permits and encourages

* State Highway Engr., Salem, Ore.

the traffic to spread over the entire road rather than confine itself to a single rut, thus reducing maintenance cost.

In reference to the selection of materials and the desirability of hardness of materials or resistance to wear, it may be said that the general practice is to classify materials by the standard abrasion tests. It should be remembered, however, that all abrasion tests are made on dry materials, while material in the road is subject to the greatest wear in wet seasons. In a recent test, made in the Oregon State Highway Department Laboratory wet material showed an abrasion four times as great as dry material.

A few years ago, it was standard practice to provide a thick layer of fine materials in the top course under the principle of providing a loose mulch which could be constantly kept in shape by blade graders. Intensive maintenance was necessary under these conditions to prevent corrugations from forming. This intensive maintenance, while it rendered the road smooth, resulted in a dusty condition that was very disagreeable and actually hazardous when the road carried much traffic. Many experiments were made to set up the top surfacing with clay and produce a hard, compact surface. These tests were quite successful and, in turn, led to the use of an oil covering on the clay-bound surface.

At first glance the value of fine material would appear to be minimized by the use of oil since it would no longer be moved about by the blade machine. It would then seem that the old specification of water-bound macadam, using the larger stones, might well be adopted. However, there are several important reasons for not using larger stone: First, there would be little economy, because the improvement in crushing equipment produces the smaller sizes at practically the same cost; second, experience indicates that it is necessary to scarify an oil-treated road at intervals and if the larger stones are used, the scarifying is more expensive and the cost of resetting the materials greater; and third, it is difficult to obtain a smooth, even surface, true to grade, crown, and cross-section, with coarse materials. For these reasons there should not be less than 2 in. of compacted materials, ranging from ¾ in. to dust, in the top course. The base course material should range in size from 1½ in. to ¾ in., both courses being well graded between limiting sizes.

The practice in Oregon is to mix all courses with clay thoroughly with the blade machine, using the ridge method, the quantity of clay varying between 20 and 40%, depending on the quality. Care should be taken to secure a slow-slaking clay with a high tensile strength. In some instances, in order to secure the best clay, it has been found necessary to haul it a greater distance than the crushed rock. However, many pits and quarries contain a good natural binder by which it is possible to procure a compact surface without the use of clay. Surfacing, bound up with clay, will not be ready to receive an oil treatment until after it has gone through a winter season.

Mr. Hoover has stressed the necessity of having a smooth sub-grade before beginning construction. Generally, a rough surface is caused by a rough sub-grade, and it is very expensive to take out the irregularities on the last course of surfacing by using fine broken stone. The necessity for proper maintenance during construction is also very apparent. The Oregon specifications state the kind and minimum amount of equipment that the contractor must furnish for the construction of a crushed rock or gravel surfacing project.

No mention has been made of the desirability of crushed gravel as compared with screened materials, but the advantage is so obvious as to preclude discussion. It should be the constant aim of all highway engineers to try to discover, by trial and experimentation, better methods of building these crushed rock and gravel road surfaces, commonly called macadams. The field is large and the opportunity great.

C. H. PURCELL,* ASSOC. M. AM. SOC. C. E. (by letter).—Attention has been called by Mr. Hoover to the large amount of Federal Aid money that has been expended on crushed stone or gravel construction. The fine-rock road is the contribution that engineers have made to the solution of automobile transportation problems. It might be well to emphasize further the important place that this type of road occupies in the development of a connected system of highways.

The financing of these highway projects has compelled engineers to make thorough studies of the crushed-rock road as a means of providing a large mileage as quickly as possible. Mr. Hoover is one who is faced with this problem and his paper brings the facts out clearly.

The great distances between towns, the necessity for roads that will carry traffic at high speed every day in the year, and the limited finances available to meet the increasing demand for mileage, have resulted in this pioneer type of road. It occupies a more important position in the West than in the wealthier and more densely populated sections of the country. There it has revolutionized travel and taken care of the great increase in motor transportation.

The fine-crushed rock road is peculiarly adapted to the region between the Rocky Mountains and the Pacific Ocean. It can be laid at low costs because of the quantity production of crushed rock and gravel. Suitable road material of various kinds is available practically throughout the entire section.

The engineer's problem has been to develop a type of surfacing that could be cheaply and rapidly built, and that could be easily maintained during the dry summer period when traffic reaches its peak. The success of this type in developing traffic has brought its own problems. Dust prevention is one of the most important construction questions confronting highway engineers in the West, for dust means a loss of road metal, discomfort, and perhaps danger to the motorist.

The suggestion made by Mr. Hoover that a section following pavement design more closely, and providing an increased thickness at the edge, is one step farther toward designing this fine-crushed rock road so that it can serve in the future as one stage of a higher type of road. If properly constructed and maintained, solving the loss of metal, it will serve as a base.

* Chf. of Div. and State Highway Engr., Div. of Highways, Sacramento, Calif.

For a future 18-ft. surface it would be better if the base were extended out at least 1 ft. on each side beyond the proposed top surface. The tendency (under maintenance) to increase the crown of fine-crushed roads has produced an unsatisfactory base for future surface. When preparations are made to put on a top surface the necessary scarifying to reduce the crown often destroys the bond between the rock at the center, and sometimes a thin base is the result.

The early fine-crushed rock roads in some of the Western States were designed with a feather-edge section. All recent construction is built in a trench section, thus securing a thicker edge. This change was brought about by the desire to have sufficient thickness at the edge to support the concentrated traffic. Experience with surface treatment has shown the importance of the thickened edge. For example, many of the roads in Oregon that have been surface-treated were originally constructed with feather edges. The relatively high cost of maintenance at the edges as compared to other portions of the surface has led to the change. Mr. Hoover's suggestion for a thicker edge is worth considering. In the West where long distances were surfaced with fine rock, many of the roads were built only 12 ft. wide and the road widened out, under maintenance, into a two-way road. It became necessary to re-shape these roads and add more rock before the surface could be treated.

In New England, where surfacing of the penetration type has been developed over a long period of years, old bases of water-bound macadam have been available. The fine-crushed rock roads in the West, built of sufficient width and maintained at a proper thickness for a base (9 in. loose) will carry a penetration surface under the moderate traffic encountered. In fact, such roads, correctly built, can be designed to serve as the first step in the evolution of several better types. If they have a carefully processed top with a moderate amount of sand-clay binder, they can be given the oil treatment. Later, when the need requires it, they can be finished with an asphaltic penetration surface; and, finally, as the traffic becomes heavier, this may be followed by even higher types of surfacing.

Many of the fine-crushed rock roads have been constructed with either a 4-in. or a 5-in. bottom course and a 4-in. top course. The State of Oregon has been a pioneer in oil treatment of fine-crushed rock roads. Since the development of asphalt surface treatment, it has been building a thicker base course and a thinner top course. This change has only been made, of course, in cases where it was reasonably certain that some plan of surface treatment was to be applied as soon as the surface had become sufficiently compacted under maintenance.

The author has pointed out one of the very essential items that enter into a successful fine-crushed rock road, namely, the matter of uniform distribution of material. No matter how well the present modern field crushing plants are designed, there seems to be a lack of uniformity of grading between the different truck loads as they are deposited on the road. It is also difficult to distribute the filler or binder evenly over the surfacing material without adopting some means of mixing them after they are spread. The excellent results of surface treatment noted by the author in the section east of the Cascade Range, were due in no small measure to the attention given to this detail of construction. Great care was taken to insure a uniform mixture of material. Wherever water was available, the material was thoroughly soaked while being spread and processed on the road. If the surface is not wet down a large percentage of the binder is fanned out by the traffic and lost before the top has a chance to set up. As in the higher types of road, the most successful results can only be obtained by strict attention to the details of design and construction.

Too much stress cannot be placed upon the fact that actual service to the public is the determining factor. It is the duty of the highway engineer to emphasize continually the need of providing funds sufficient to furnish the public the highest possible type of service. The traffic volume is so large on many roads that the maximum expenditure will be warranted on the basis of service value to the traffic, and the saving in operation costs.

Many State and Government agencies have investigated the saving of cost of tire and gasoline consumption on the various types of pavement. The writer does not know of any investigation of the depreciation on automobile engine, body, and other mechanism, due to the jolting on a rough, unimproved, earth road. It may be learned that the saving in rubber and gasoline is a small sum compared with this other greater loss to the automobile owner. If this is the case, the fine-crushed rock road of the West, which has been extended so rapidly at the moderate cost of from $3 500 to $6 000 per mile, shows a remarkable saving. This accomplishment of the engineer, although not receiving as much attention as the paving, is far greater.

O. E. Stanley,* M. Am. Soc. C. E.—In Portland, Ore., there are about 200 miles of old macadam streets, built 10 to 20 years ago.

These streets are maintained by reshaping, when necessary, with a steam roller, and giving them a coat of oil. After the road is shaped to the proper cross-section (which the foreman gets with his eye, using the curbs as guides), it is sprinkled and rolled until the fine material, or "soup", is brought to the surface. The road is then left open to the traffic for probably two weeks until the fine material dries and blows away.

There are a great many complaints about dust, but as soon as the dust has worn off and the surface of the rock is exposed, oil is applied with very good results; these roads remain in good condition from 1 to 3 years. When little holes wear in the surface, after about this length of time, they are patched with a mixture of asphalt and crushed rock. Sometimes only two or three holes occur in a block.

With this oil treatment, results are obtained that make some of the contractors wish the process had not been discovered.

* Chf., Bureau of Maintenance, City of Portland, Portland, Ore.

AMERICAN SOCIETY OF CIVIL ENGINEERS

INSTITUTED 1852

TRANSACTIONS

Paper No. 1674

RELATION OF ROAD TYPE TO TIRE WEAR*

By O. L. Waller† and H. E. Phelps,‡ Members, Am. Soc. C. E.

With Discussion by Messrs. Troy Carmichael, and O. L. Waller and H. E. Phelps.

Synopsis

The study of the wear of automobile tires has been made to determine the destructive effect of different types of road surfaces on the tread rubber in order that, as far as possible, surfaces may be so improved as to make the cost of building and maintaining road surfaces and of operating the traffic over them a minimum. The cost of tires is one element of the cost of operating motor vehicles and may well be studied.

The University of Kansas, co-operating with the United States Bureau of Public Roads, and the State College of Washington, have conducted a series of tests in an effort to determine the loss of tread rubber caused by several types of road surfaces. The surfaces studied have been concrete, brick, and bitulithic pavements, penetration macadam, and several types of gravel and broken stone. The results of these tests are given in this paper. The factors influencing tire wear are discussed, and an effort is made to evaluate some of these factors. The following tentative conclusions have been drawn from the few data now available:

1.—Tire wear increases with the speed. Sufficient data are not available to indicate the rate of increase.

2.—Tire wear increases with the temperature. Road tests indicate this relationship, but are not consistent and yield no information on the rate of increase. Laboratory tests by Professor W. C. McNown, at the University of Kansas, are likewise not conclusive,

* Presented at the meeting of the Highway Division, Seattle, Wash., July 15, 1926.

† Vice-Pres., State Coll. of Washington, and Head, Dept. of Civ. Eng., Pullman, Wash.

‡ Prof., Highway Eng., State Coll. of Washington, Pullman, Wash.

but indicate a moderate rate of increase in tire wear with increase of temperature. High temperatures are very destructive to tires.

3.—The wear of rear tires is greater than that of front tires, the relative wear of rear tires being 200% on smooth pavements and as little as 118% on gravel surfaces, probably averaging 150% of the wear on front tires.

4.—Tire wear per ton of car is probably constant for any given road surface, when size of tire, load, and inflation pressure are determined by a single standard.

5.—A few records of bus companies show actual tire-mileage life on different road surfaces in approximate agreement with tire wear tests on similar surfaces.

6.—Relative tire wear index numbers, based on average concrete pavement as 1.0, are approximately 2.0 for good gravel and macadam, 4.0 to 5.0 for average Western macadam or uncrushed chert gravels, and may be as high as 10 or 11 for unusually unfavorable surfaces. Based on tire wear alone, average sized cord tires should show a life of 20 000 to 24 000 miles on pavements, 10 000 to 12 000 miles on good gravel or macadam, and as little as 2 000 to 4 000 miles on unfavorable surfaces. The corresponding costs per vehicle-mile are about 0.5 cent for pavements, 1.0 cent for average gravel or best macadam, 2.3 cents for average macadam, and perhaps as much as 5 cents per vehicle-mile on road surfaces of loose, sharp-edged stones.

Introduction

The making and operating of automobiles and the building of roads on which they are run are major American industries. In 1925 automobile owners paid $260 619 621 for registration fees, licenses, fines, etc., and, in addition, a gasoline tax, effective in all but four States, totaling $146 028 940, or a total payment by automobile owners and operators of $406 648 561 almost all of which was expended for highway purposes.

The total funds expended in the construction and maintenance of roads and streets is about $1 000 000 000 annually. About 10 000 miles of Federal Aid roads were completed in 1925 and perhaps 20 000 miles of surfaced roads were built by States and counties without aid from the National Government.

Such an enormous investment in motor vehicles and highways makes the problem of securing the most economic surface for highway transport of the utmost importance. This problem will be solved when, for any particular highway, the road surface as well as the vehicles using the road are such as to produce minimum transportation costs.

In making economic comparisons between different road surfaces, costs which arise from the operation of the vehicle and those which arise from the highway itself must be considered in order that the total cost of highway transportation may be a minimum. The condition is rapidly being reached in which the automobile owner pays both the cost of operating his car and a large part of the cost of building and maintaining the roadways upon which it operates. He should be interested, therefore, in the effect of various roadway surfaces on motor-vehicle operating costs as well as in the cost of building and maintaining such surfaces.

Road money cannot all be spent on a few miles of exceptionally fine arterial highway. Such a plan would favor some and leave the less fortunate travelers to use unimproved dirt and mud roads.

If all roads could be paved, a great saving in operating expenses would be made, but this is not possible. Only roads carrying heavy traffic can be paved. On those carrying lighter traffic, gravel and broken stone surfaces must be used. The other millions of miles of plain dirt roads are usually not well graded nor well drained; but traffic which uses these poor roads must pay not only its share for constructing the paved roads, but also must then use the unimproved roads with the added expense per car-mile. The vehicle-mile should be made the measure of road expenditures. This is a measure of the traffic service rendered.

The cost of operating a motor vehicle is the sum of the costs of gasoline, oil, tires, maintenance, depreciation, interest, insurance, garage, and license, the first five being items influenced by the roadway surface on which the vehicle is generally operated.

The gasoline requirements of motor vehicles on various roadway surfaces has been investigated by T. R. Agg, M. Am. Soc. C. E., and others, and their findings are generally known and frequently quoted. It is generally believed that the maintenance and depreciation costs are likewise influenced by the character of the road surface over which the motor vehicle is most frequently operated, but no determination of the magnitude of this influence has yet been made to the knowledge of the writers. Tire wear tests have been made at the University of Kansas and the State College of Washington. These tests are brought together in Table 1, and summarized in Tables 2 and 3. The results summarized in Table 3 are given in two units, as tire wear in pounds per 1 000 miles and as wear on various surfaces relative to the wear on concrete pavements taken as a standard.

In making tests to determine the wear on tread rubber a considerable number of elements enter into the problem, some of which are as follows:

Factors Affecting Tire Wear.—

I.—Those pertaining to the road surface:
- (*a*) The kind of surface.
- (*b*) Its condition.

II.—Those pertaining to the car:
- (*a*) Weight of car:
  - (1) Sprung.
  - (2) Unsprung.
- (*b*) Number of engine cylinders.
- (*c*) Character of springs.
- (*d*) Alignment of wheels.

III.—Those pertaining to the driver:
- (*a*) The speed used and wind resistance.
- (*b*) The method of operating brakes.
- (*c*) Number of emergency stops.
- (*d*) Skids, acceleration, and deceleration.
- (*e*) General care and skill displayed in driving.

TABLE 1.—Results of Tests.

No. of test.	Average loss, in grammes per 500 miles.	Loss, in pounds per 1 000 miles.	Kind of road surface.	Remarks.
R- 1........	47.25	0.2083	Concrete	Aggregate, ⅘ soft limestone; ⅕ Joplin flint; surface rough.
R- 3........	20.50	0.0904	"	Aggregate, medium limestone; surface very good.
R- 8........	37.25	0.1642	"	Aggregate, medium limestone; surface very good.
R-13........	48.50	0.2128	"	Aggregate, medium limestone; surface very good.
R-16........	83.25	0.3571	"	Surface fair; balloon tires.
R- 5........	61.00	0.2690	Brick-monolithic	Surface good.
R- 9........	48.25	0.2117	Brick-bituminous filled	Air, 92°.
R-10........	29.00	0.1279	" " "	Air, 92°.
R-14........	53.50	0.2359	" " "	Balloon tires; air, 64°.
R-15........	11.00	0.0485	" " "	Air. 90°.
R- 4........	68.00	0.2998	Bituminous macadam	Left-hand wheels.
R- 4........	282.00	1.2334	" "	Right-hand wheels.
R-11........	283.25	1.2389	" "	....
R-12........	301.50	1.3294	" "	....
R- 2........	148.00	0.6526	Gravel	Gravel from uncrushed chert.
R- 7........	60.50	0.2668	"	Typical of good gravel; loose surface, unplaned.
36........	......	0.0325	Concrete	Surface good, but not excellent, Car 1.
38........	......	0.0629	"	" " " " " " 1.
37........	......	0.0760	"	" " " " " " 2.
39........	......	0.0360	"	Surface good, but not excellent (1 tire only), Car 2.
42........	......	0.1136	"	Surface generally good, Car 3.
48........	......	0.0960	"	" " " " 3.
43........	......	0.2080	"	" " " " 4.
49........	......	0.0570	"	" " " " 4.
44........	......	0.1020	Bitulithic	Car 3.
46........	......	0.1890	"	" 3.
45........	......	0.1170	"	" 4.
47........	......	0.0910	"	" 4.
50........	......	0.723	Gravel	Water-worn, Car 3.
52........	......	0.527	"	" " 3.
1........	......	0.542	Macadam	Pullman to Palouse, Car 1.
5........	......	0.271	"	" " " " 1.
7........	......	0.360	"	" " " " 1.
19........	......	0.1418	"	" " " " 1.
21........	......	0.443	"	" " " " 1.
23........	......	0.275	"	" " " " 1.
25........	......	0.343	"	" " " " 1.
34........	......	0.290	"	Dishman south, " 1.
40........	......	0.244	"	" " " 1.
8........	......	0.590	"	Pullman to Spokane, " 2.
35........	......	0.618	"	Dishman south, " 2.
41........	......	0.777	"	" " " 2.
11........	......	1.122	....	Pullman south, " 2.
17........	......	1.045	....	" " " 2.
27........	......	1.456	....	" " " 2.
33........	......	0.435	....	" " " 2.
1........	......	0.911	....	Pullman to Palouse, " 3.
4........	......	0.271	....	" " " " 3.
6........	......	0.573	....	" " " " 3.
18........	......	0.965	....	" " " " 3.
20........	......	0.528	....	" " " " 3.
22........	......	0.697	....	" " " " 3.
24........	......	0.453	....	" " " " 3.
9........	......	0.308	....	Pullman to Spokane, " 3.

IV.—Climatic conditions:

(*a*) Air temperatures.
(*b*) Amount and distribution of rainfall.
(*c*) Amount of sunshine.

V.—Those inherent in the tire:

(*a*) Kind of tire.
(*b*) Quality of the tire.
(*c*) Character of the tread.
(*d*) Inflation pressure.
(*e*) Temperature of the tire.
(*f*) Age of the tire.

In order to study the effect of any one factor on the wear of tires all other factors should be kept constant during a single series of tests. This may be accomplished by using the same equipment and by making the tests over the same piece of road in the same condition of maintenance and under corresponding temperature conditions at the same speed, with tires of the same type and age and with the same degree of inflation, with the same driver and with the chassis in the same state of maintenance. In this way a considerable number of the unknown factors may be eliminated. There will still remain the type of road, the condition of the surface, both as to roughness, sharpness of material, compactness, and the quantity of uncompacted loose material floating over the surface.

The relationship between tire wear and gasoline consumption might profitably be studied. If such a relationship can be determined then every one will have a reasonably good gauge by which to measure the destructive effect of different types of road surfaces on tires and car upkeep. To do this, the gasoline should be metered by a recording device to show graphically the gasoline consumption as a continuous record.

The relationship between surface roughness and gasoline consumption and tire wear would supply much needed information on road surface types and on the best methods of maintaining earth and gravel roads. A continuous autographic record of the gas metered to the carburetor should be kept and made to synchronize with a graph showing vertical uneveness.

Preliminary to the tests at the State College of Washington, the tires and rims were removed from the wheels and were thoroughly cleaned with a brush and bellows. The valve cores were then removed and the deflated tires with the rims were accurately weighed. The valve cores were then replaced and the tires inflated to the proper pressure and replaced on the wheels. The car was then driven at uniform speed over the selected road, and at the conclusion of the test the tires were again removed, cleaned, and weighed.

The roads used for test purposes were of brick, concrete, bitulithic, penetration macadam, gravel, and Western type broken stone macadam. All the tests on brick roads were made in Kansas by Professor McNown, who likewise conducted tests on concrete pavements, penetration macadam, and gravel roads made of several different materials. The State College of Washington tests were made on bitulithic and concrete pavements, water-worn gravel, and Western type broken stone macadam.

Crushed Stone Roads in Washington

The crushed stone highways of Washington, owing to lack of water in many localities, are not water-bound. Water has been available for only a few roads. The general practice is to use finer material than is common in water-bound macadam, both in the bottom and the top courses. After construction, the roads are left for the traffic to roll. The crushed stone used is generally basalt of good quality as to hardness, toughness, and resistance to abrasion. It is usually screened into two bins, one receiving the material from ⅝ in. to 1½ or 2 in. in size, and the other bin receiving the finer material.

TABLE 2.—Summary of Tests.

	Loss, in pounds per 1 000 miles.
Best results on concrete, Washington	0.0325
" " " , Kansas	0.0904
Average of all tests, Washington concrete	0.0852
" " " " , Kansas concrete	0.1689
Poorest results on Washington concrete	0.2080
" " " Kansas concrete, cord tires	0.2128
" " " Kansas concrete, balloon tires	0.3571
Monolithic brick, a single run	0.2690
Bituminous-filled brick, average	0.1560
Bitulithic, average	0.1247
Bituminous macadam, best	0.2998
Bituminous macadam, poorest, average	1.2672
Gravel, typical good, Iowa	0.2668
Gravel, uncrushed chert	0.6526
Gravel, Washington, water-worn, average	0.6250
Macadam, Washington type, best	0.2440
" " " , average	0.5800
" " " , poorest	1.4560

The stone is spread in two courses, each approximately one-half the total thickness. A layer of clay or sandy loam is spread over the base course for a binder. The traffic and trucks hauling stone do the rolling, and a blade grader is frequently run over it to keep the ruts filled. Over this a finer top course is spread, but no binder is used. The surface of the road is left with a layer of sharp, fine, loose material, which adds considerable resistance to the movement of the car and to the wear on the tires.

TABLE 3.—Relative Tire Wear on Various Road Surfaces.

Character of surface.	Wear, in pounds per 1 000 miles.	Index number.
Bitulithic, average of all tests	0.1247	0.945
Concrete, average of all tests	0.1319	1.00
Brick, average of all tests	0.1786	1.36
Bituminous macadam, best	0.2998	2.28
" " , poorest	1.2672	9.60
Gravel, typical, Iowa	0.2668	2.02
Macadam, Washington type, best	0.2440	1.85
" " " , average	0.5800	4.40
Gravel, uncrushed, best	0.6526	4.95
Macadam, Washington type, poor	1.4560	11.05
Concrete, average of seven best	0.0657	0.49

Maintenance

The broken stone and gravel roads of Washington are in all stages of maintenance. The surfaces of new roads are loose, just as they are left by the contractor after the top course had been trued up with the blade grader. Under such conditions, automobile tires push the loose gravel or broken stone out to the sides of the road and form ruts, a process destructive to tread rubber and one that forces the car continually to ascend a constant incline.

The same conditions, only in a lesser degree, obtain on roads compacted through use, that have been recently bladed to fill pot-holes and to plane off corrugations. This kind of maintenance leaves a thinner layer of loose material for the traffic to work over and through. Where maintenance is not frequent and regular, the roads soon develop pot-holes and corrugations which greatly reduce riding comfort, shorten the life of the car, and increase the destruction of tread rubber.

For the broken rock and gravel roads here enumerated, it is difficult to describe the condition of the particular road surface under test, and certainly no standard surface conditions can be secured. The surface of any piece of test road will be subject to wide variations. Even on the same road two runs might give a wide variation in gasoline consumed and rubber worn away, depending on whether the car was driven over the well beaten track or on the loose, floating material.

It should be kept in mind that at normal speed and where the road surface is rough, full of pot-holes, or corrugated, tires are not in contact with the surface at all times, or at least the pressure on the road is not constant. When the rear wheels return to the road, the impact kick of the wheels tends further to destroy the road surface and abrade the tread. The tests of the U. S. Bureau of Public Roads have shown that the impact force in some instances has been equivalent to several times the static load. Under such conditions, the tread rubber, being always under tension, in transmitting such added power to the road, is under an additional stress, which adds to the destruction of the tread rubber.

There is generally little uniformity in these broken rock surfaces. Under wear, they range from hard smooth surfaces to loose gravel, corrugations, and pot-holes, and all these conditions may be found on any stretch of sample road.

Corrugations on the broken rock roads examined were about 26 to 27 in. from crest to crest. Consequently, the automobile wheels jump from the crest of one corrugation to the trough of the next, roll up the incline to the succeeding crown, and jump to the next trough. This continuous jumping and back-kicking of the rear wheels, wears down the tread rubber on the tires very much more rapidly than it is worn over pavement, well bound broken rock surface, or graveled road.

In all tests, the comparative roughness of the surface of the road tested and the approximate size of the aggregate material should be considered. As measured by roughness, there are many kinds of broken rock surfaces and many kinds of rocks used in such surfaces. Some kinds of broken rock present sharp edges not found on water-worn gravel.

Some gravel and broken stone roads present well compacted and hard surfaces; on others, the gravel is loose, either from having been recently placed and therefore not well bonded, or from having been recently bladed and left with a floating surface of loose material. The grade of material used, and the degree of "wash-boarding" or corrugation should be noted. Some standard of thickness of the loose floating material on the surface, and of the grade and sharpness of material, should be taken as a criterion, and all roads used in tests should be referred to this standard.

Some samples taken from a broken basalt road a year after the road was built showed the sharp edges practically gone and the fine material very much rounded. It would seem that the crushing and grinding effect of the wheels soon wears away sharp angles, rounds up the stone, and makes an old broken rock surface, when in good order, less destructive to tires than a new one.

Gas Consumption

Professor Agg states* that fuel consumption is not a direct measure of the power developed by a gasoline motor, but it is believed that the results thus obtained are comparative and sufficiently accurate for the purposes of this investigation. If the same car were used with the same carburetor setting, the same kind of gas, and operated by the same driver, the gas consumption curve would likely closely parallel the one for tire wear. Professor Agg states that "until more conclusive information pertaining to the variation of mileage costs other than gasoline is available, it is necessary to assume that all mileage costs vary with the resistance of the road surface in the same manner as does the gasoline cost." The investigations of the U. S. Bureau of Mines show that carburetor adjustments and the use or non-use of the air heater make a marked difference in mileage secured; consequently, if gas consumption is to be a reasonable measure of tire wear, all conditions relative to the car must be made uniform.

Yielding surfaces, due either to moisture or heat, require a greater consumption of fuel; more power is transmitted through the tires to the road, thereby causing a more rapid destruction of the tires.

Spring Action

It has long been known that spring action is a leading factor in the upkeep of a car. It is an important factor in the life of the car and as well as the life of the tires. Efficient springs damp the blows and thereby minimize the work done by the carcass of the tires and by the tread rubber.

Road Material

Theoretically, it would be expected that water-worn gravel would abrade a tire less than crushed rock, as crushed rock offers sharp edges to the tire. This seems to have been proved by the tests in the State of Washington on broken basalt roads and in Kansas, as shown by the tire wear, on crushed chert. The abrading effect of road materials should be studied further so that flinty material breaking with sharp cutting edges might be avoided. With

* *Bulletin 65*, Eng. Experiment Station, Iowa State Coll., Ames, Iowa.

such material, the more it is ground up by use, the more abrading angles it presents to rubber tires.

Tire Wear and Speed

It seems evident that tire wear should be influenced by the speed at which a car is operated. More power is required to drive a car at high speed than at low speed, and the bounding and spinning of wheels due to ruts should be more destructive of tread rubber at the higher speeds.

The few tests of tire wear made thus far at different speeds reveal no consistent relationship between these factors. The tests at different speeds made at the State College of Washington were on broken stone covered with a mulch of finely divided broken stone and under constant maintenance with blade graders. The differences in wear on the several tires of a car were considerable, and the various runs with the same car did not show closely similar tire wear. Plotting tire wear against speed for the cars operated on a single stretch of road produces a wide distribution of points, indicating roughly that tire wear increases with speed.

It seems obvious that high speeds should be very destructive of tires. It is well known that the life of a tire on a racing car is relatively short, although the destruction of such tires may not be due to the factor of tire wear. Of two similar tires, the one used on a car driven at moderate speed should travel many more miles than one on the same car driven at high speed.

Some light on this relation of tire wear and speed may be had from other investigations of closely related factors. The subject of power loss in automobile tires seems to have been first thoroughly investigated in the United States by Professor E. H. Lockwood, and has been continued by Messrs. W. L. Holt and P. L. Wormeley at the U. S. Bureau of Standards.

In a report on "Research on Rubber Tires" to the Advisory Board on Highway Research, Mr. Holt draws the conclusion, that,

"The power loss [in automobile tires] is very nearly directly proportional to the speed, that is, at 40 miles per hour the loss is approximately twice that at 20 miles per hour. This means that the resistance which a tire offers to rolling, or what will be referred to as the rolling resistance, is very nearly constant and is independent of the speed".

The same result was reached much earlier by Professor Lockwood who reported that "one surprising result of all measurements of rolling resistance at speeds from 20 to 40 miles per hour has been the slight increase of resistance at the higher speed. With some cars the increase of resistance is less than the observation errors. In other cases the increases amount to from 5 to 10 per cent". Considering all tests, Professor Lockwood concluded that the internal rolling resistance of an automobile is practically constant at all speeds up to 40 miles per hour; and from other tests that the tires are responsible for nearly two-thirds of the power loss in the car itself.

Both these tests were made on electrical absorption dynamometers, the essential feature of which is a smooth, flat-faced metal drum on which the tires revolve. Although tests on such apparatus show that the rolling resistance of tires is constant at all speeds, as Professor Lockwood reports, "the rolling resistance on rough, uneven and soft roads will doubtless increase materially with the speed".

In all tests made on absorption dynamometers the wind resistance is automatically eliminated. This resistance must be overcome by the power of the engine transmitted to the surface of the road through the tires. This wind resistance has been shown by L. E. Conrad, M. Am. Soc. C. E., to be given by the formula, $R — 0.0025\ A\ V^2$, in which, A is the projected area of the car and V is the relative velocity, in miles per hour, of air and car. Since wind resistance causes an increased tractive force to be exerted it seems logical to conclude that tire wear will likewise increase with the speed.

Tire Wear and Temperature

In addition to increased wind resistance, higher speeds increase tire temperatures that may result in increased tire wear through the softening of the rubber, and lessen the mileage life of tires. The generation of heat and the resultant rise of temperature of tires are the result of the work done in overcoming the rolling resistance. This increase of temperature has been computed by Professor Lockwood, and checked almost exactly by a suitably conducted test.

A few tests have been made to determine the effect on tire wear of variations in air temperature, but as yet have not yielded consistent results. The road tests made in 1924 showed that tire wear increases with an increase of air temperature, the other variables of speed—road surface, car, and driver—being kept constant.

The tire wear tests of 1925 show no consistent relationship between tire wear and temperature, probably because the tests on any one road extended over such a limited temperature range.

Laboratory tests by Professor McNown, at the University of Kansas, show that tire wear is increased at higher temperatures. The increased wear at 130° Fahr., as compared to the wear at 70° Fahr., amounted to 13% in one set of tests, and to 81% in another, the results not being entirely conclusive.

It is a popular impression that tires wear out more rapidly at high than at low temperatures. A dealer furnishing tires for a Washington bus line that descends a vertical distance of 2 000 ft. on an average 4.2% grade, ascribes the comparative low mileage (12 000) of the tires used on this run to the heat generated by the brakes on this grade. Tourists across the deserts of Southern Nevada and California describe the landscape as littered with abandoned tires, and believe the heat causes their rapid deterioration.

Considerable trouble is being experienced by auto-bus companies with tires being damaged through heat. A heavy bus traveling on a fast schedule requires frequent application of the brakes, and the heat thereby generated produces destructive temperatures, particularly on the inside tire of a dual mounting. Experience and tests have both demonstrated that brake-drum temperatures of 550° to 600° Fahr. are common. Ordinary operation over heated pavements will produce temperatures of 150° to 160° Fahr. Casings and tubes will withstand these temperatures without trouble, but they will not withstand the much higher temperatures produced by a near-by brake-drum.

Bus companies are in a position to force the dealers to supply tires on a mileage guaranty, and the experience of many dealers has not been a pleasant or profitable one. Notwithstanding the short life of many tires damaged by heat, there is little information showing the exact relationship between the wear of a tire and its temperature.

A leading bus company operating in the State of Washington, has kept tire cost records by months. On one set of buses operated by this company, forty tires were used; on the other line, seventy-four. The buses make the same trip each day; the same number of trips each month; consequently, most of the unknown factors are eliminated. The plotted curve shows a very rapid increase as the season advances to midsummer, and a similar rapid decrease as fall approaches. On one bus line the average cost for November, December, January, and February, was about one-third that for July and August. The distance traveled was 148 104 miles per year. On the other line, the July-August average was more than six times the November-December-January-February average. The distance run was 105 690 miles per year.

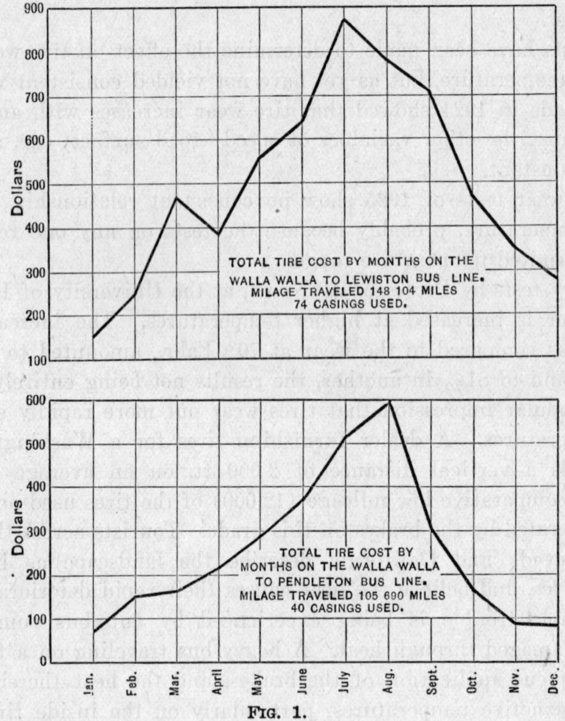

FIG. 1.

The loads may have been heavier and the roads somewhat rougher in the dry summer months than in the winter. This may account in part for the wide variation in tire costs between the summer and winter months. Fig. 1 shows these tire costs by the month.

Relative Tire Wear on Front and Rear Wheels

It is generally believed that tires wear more rapidly on rear than on front wheels. Tests show very erratic results, but averages support the general belief. The tests made at the State College of Washington show average rear tire wear of 140% on macadam, 158% on gravel, and 200% on pavement, as compared to front tire wear. The Kansas tests show smaller differences, the averages being 118% for gravel and 138% for concrete. Professor McNown states that normal front tire wear is 50% that of rear tire wear, but this may not be correct for all road surfaces.

TABLE 4.—Relative Wear, Front and Rear Wheels.

Test No.	Average Wear, in Grammes.		Miles per test.	Average Wear, in Grammes per 100 Miles.		Percentage of wear on rear tire in terms of wear on front tire.	Surface.
	Front.	Rear.		Front.	Rear.		
State College of Washington Tests.							
2	11.3	17.3	61.1	18.5	28.4	154	Macadam
5	7.9	6.8	60.0	13.2	11.3	86	"
7	7.1	12.4	60.0	11.8	20.7	175	"
19	9.1	12.9	59.6	15.3	21.7	142	"
21	8.6	13.6	60.0	14.3	22.7	159	"
23	6.7	9.8	61.3	10.9	16.0	147	"
25	7.9	10.1	60.4	13.1	15.7	128	"
34	6.3	14.9	80.4	7.8	18.6	238	"
40	5.2	12.7	80.9	6.4	15.7	246	"
8	53.0	70.3	169.0	31.4	41.6	133	"
11	9.6	8.5	23.3	41.2	36.5	89	"
17	11.3	9.9	23.6	48.0	41.9	87	"
27	14.9	15.6	23.5	63.4	66.4	105	"
33	6.1	2.8	24.9	24.5	11.3	46	"
35	23.4	21.7	80.4	29.2	27.0	92	"
1	21.1	27.1	61.1	34.6	44.4	128	"
4	21.6	14.7	60.0	36.0	24.6	68	"
6	18.9	11.7	61.1	31.0	19.2	62	"
18	25.4	25.5	59.6	42.6	42.8	101	"
20	12.0	15.8	60.0	20.0	26.3	132	"
24	4.5	19.3	59.6	7.6	34.4	427	"
Average	....	....	.....	....	....	140	Macadam
36	0.7	3.9	157.0	0.4	2.5	625	Concrete
37	13.8	4.4	170.3	8.1	2.6	32	"
42	4.4	7.9	120.0	3.7	6.7	181	"
48	5.2	5.1	117.8	4.4	4.3	98	"
43	15.2	7.8	122.0	12.5	6.4	51	"
49	2.1	5.0	119.0	1.8	4.2	233	"
Average	....	....	.....	....	....	203	Concrete
44	3.4	7.4	117.0	2.9	6.3	217	Bitulithic
46	5.6	9.2	114.1	4.9	8.0	163	"
	6.3	6.5	120.4	5.2	5.4	104	"
	2.3	7.1	114.9	2.0	6.2	310	"
Average	....	....	.....	....	....	198	Bitulithic
52	9.2	14.5	58.7	....	....	158	Gravel
Average	....	....	.....	....	....	158	Gravel

TABLE 4.—(*Continued*).

KANSAS RESULTS

Test No.	Average Tire Wear, in Grammes per 500 Miles.		Percentage of wear on rear tires in terms of wear on front tires.	Surface.
	Front.	Rear.		
R- 1	32½	62	191	Concrete.
R- 3	11½	29½	256	"
R- 8	53½	21	39	" Same as R-3.
R-13	59	38	64	" " " "
R-16	81½	85	104	" Surface fair.
Average....	....	....	131	Concrete.
R- 5	94	28	30	Brick—Monolithic.
R- 9	64½	32	50	" —Bituminous filled.
R-10	40	19	47	" " "
R-14	59	48	81	" " "
R-15	15	9	60	" " "
Average....	....	....	54	Brick.
R-11	289	278	93	Bituminous macadam.
R-12	290	314	108	" "
Average....	....	....	100	Bituminous macadam.
R- 7	60	61	102	Gravel, typical Iowa.
R- 2	136	160	118	Gravel, uncrushed chert.

Professor McNown also states that,

"It is to be expected that rear tire indices would be higher for the rough surfaces due to the bounding and spinning of rear wheels. There is abundant evidence in the above data, however, to indicate that for rough surfaces under the condition of this test the front and rear tire wear is more nearly the same than for well conditioned surfaces".

The tests at the State College of Washington (Table 4) abundantly bear out this statement.

These tests were made on Western type broken stone macadam, which, when well maintained, is covered by a thin mulch of finely broken rock, and when newly constructed or in poor condition, by a considerably thicker layer of ¾-in. rock. On such surfaces the front wheels are being pushed through a layer of loose material, spreading it out and preparing a path for the rear wheels, with the result that tire wear is more nearly equal on front and rear wheels operated over such surfaces. On smooth pavements the front wheels merely roll over the surface, the rear wheels propelling the car. The result should be that on pavements the relative wear of rear tires would be greater than on macadam.

Front tire wear is frequently greatly increased by worn bushing or other parts that throw the front wheels out of alignment. The writer knows of one case where two front tires were entirely ruined by less than 1 000 miles of travel on account of misalignment of the front wheels. In all the tests quoted, attention was given to front wheel alignment. The extremely erratic nature of the results indicate that many additional data must be secured before dependable conclusions may be reached.

Effect of Weight of Car

Owing to a lack of sufficient data an analysis of tire wear as influenced by the weight of the car is not entirely conclusive. The results (Table 5) seem to show that tire wear per ton of vehicle is either independent of the weight of the vehicle, or increases slightly with an increase in the weight of the vehicle. Averaging all results on concrete pavements, the tire wear per 1 000 miles per ton of car was 9.8% greater on the heaviest car than on the lightest, the increase of weight of car being 153 per cent. Although all four cars were not tested on the same pavement, tire wear increased with increased weight of car for the two pavements tested, and for all four cars tested.

TABLE 5.—Summary of Tire Wear Tests. Effect of Weight of Car.

Car No.	Weight, in pounds.	Average wear, in pounds per 1 000 miles.	Average wear, in pounds per 1 000 miles per ton of car.	Kind of road surface.
1	1 740	0.0477	0.0549	Concrete, Spokane to Coeur d'Alene.
2	2 750	0.0760	0.0552	" " " "
3	3 560	0.1048	0.0589	" Olympia to Vancouver.
4	4 400	0.1335	0.0603	" " "
1	1 740	0.349	0.401	Macadam, Pullman to Palouse.
3	3 560	0.628	0.353	" " "
1	1 740	0.353	0.407	" average of all runs.
2	2 750	0.863	0.628	" " " " "
3	3 560	0.588	0.330	" " " " "
1	.....	.....	0.407	" " " " "
2 and 3	.....	.....	0.479	" " " " "

On broken stone macadam the results are not consistent. Of the two cars tested on the same road between Pullman and Palouse, Wash., the light car had more wear per ton than the heavier. The average of all tests on macadam is erratic, inasmuch as the medium weight car shows the greatest tire wear per ton. This may possibly be accounted for by the fact that this model of car is notoriously known to be very rough riding and hard on tires. The average tire wear on the two heavier vehicles is 18% greater per ton of car than on the lighter one, the increase of weight being 81 per cent.

It is probable, therefore, that tire wear is independent of the weight of car, at least for those cars supplied with the correct size of tire and designed by the same engineering standards. There is some evidence to show that the wear on an overloaded tire is greater than on one carrying a more reasonable load.

Effect of Road Surface on Life of Tires

Although such tests as have been reported yield valuable information on the effect of various road surfaces on tire wear, the real factor desired is the effect of road surfaces on the mileage life of tires. This can be determined only by a long-time test, starting with new tires and operating the car continuously over the same road surface until the tires are destroyed. Many such tests would be necessary in order to secure dependable averages, and the cost of such testing would be considerable. The mileage of tires is sometimes greatly reduced by such factors as tread cuts, blisters, stone and rail bruises, shimmying, under-inflation, punctures, corrugations, ice, ruts, pot-holes, etc.

Probably the most reliable method of determining the mileage life of tires on various road surfaces, would be to secure the life history of tires from the owners of cars operated exclusively on certain road surfaces. This is difficult, as few owners keep accurate records of their tire mileage and fewer still operate their cars exclusively on one kind of surface. Cars operating exclusively on surfaces with similar wear characteristics are probably mostly owned by taxicab companies and automobile bus lines. A few records from Western bus lines and other sources are given in Table 6. These records were kept as a part of the cost data and presumably are fairly accurate.

In general, these scattered records are in agreement with the tire wear tests, inasmuch as tires operated over pavements have a mileage life at least twice as great as those driven over gravel or macadam.

In addition to a greater tire mileage on pavement, bus companies report other items of expense materially greater when operating on gravel or macadam surfaces. One company reports that there is much more tire trouble on earth, gravel, or macadam surfaces. Tacks and nails are more easily picked up and are more frequently the cause of punctures. Cuts in casings fill quickly with dirt, which soon causes blisters and tread separation.

The life of a tire is generally not determined by external but by internal wear. An interesting confirmation of this fact was obtained from Mr. Lewis A. Corbett, of Walla Walla, Wash., who stated that on the bus line to Lewiston, Idaho, tires were seldom discarded from excessive wear of tread rubber, but generally as a result of internal defects, whereas on the line to Pendleton, Ore., tires frequently lasted 30 000 to 40 000 miles. Mr. W. L. Holt, Mechanical Engineer of the U. S. Bureau of Standards, has stated that:

"Contrary to what seems to be the popular idea, the problem in tire building is not to make a tread which will wear, but to make a tire in which the component parts—the plies, the breaker, the tread, etc.—will stay together, and at the same time distribute the various strains so that the strain will not be excessive at any point. As soon as any of the parts separate, chafing immediately sets in, blisters begin to appear at various places, and the life of the tire is about gone".

Professor McNown, however, has stated that "tire manufacturers are of the opinion that at present the carcass is developed ahead of the tread and that the normal failure of a tire is by tread wear and not by carcass failure". Probably this is true for present-day tires running over improved surfaces, but it may not be true for unimproved surfaces where stresses on the carcass are very much greater.

Tire Operating Costs

Tests of tire wear on various road surfaces will be of value both to the automobile owner and to public officials who build and maintain the highways.

TABLE 6.—Tire Operating Data from Bus Companies.

Owner, or authority.	State.	From:	To:	Kind of bus.	Size of tire, in inches.	Length of run, in miles.	Reported mileage.	Surface.
Red Ball Transportation Company...	Iowa	Mason City	Algona	Fageols Macks	....	....	28 000 to 30 000	Concrete.
Red Ball Transportation Company...	Iowa	Mason City	Various places	Fageols Macks	....	....	20 000	Earth and gravel.
Hawley..................	Washington	Spokane	Coeur d' Alene	....	36 by 6	33	30 000	Concrete.
Hawley..................	Washington	Spokane	Almira	....	36 by 6	....	16 000	58 miles of macadam. 24 miles of concrete.
Hawley..................	Washington	Spokane	Almira	....	....	....	Summer, 12 000	58 miles of macadam. 24 miles of concrete.
Spokane-Lewiston Stage Line	Washington	Spokane	Lewiston, Idaho	....	34 by 7	115	12 000	102 miles of macadam. 13 miles of concrete.
S. C. Hadden..................	Indiana	Indianapolis	Richmond	2½-Ton. G. M. C.	....	....	28 000	Concrete.
Mrs. W. I. Coldiron..................	....	Indianapolis	Bloomington	Studebaker	....	....	12 000	Gravel.
J. C. Corbett..................	Washington	Walla Walla	Lewiston	White, two-ton trucks	....	100	11 800	Macadam.
J. C. Corbett..................	Oregon	Walla Walla	Pendleton	White, two-ton trucks	....	42	16 000	Bitulithic.

The automobile owner is chiefly interested in his tire cost per mile and for the year, whereas the highway engineer is interested in determining the amount he can afford to spend in providing road surfaces that reduce tire wear.

TABLE 7.

Road surface.	Index No.	Computed tire mileage.	Annual tire cost per car for 6000 miles per year.	Cost of tires per vehicle-mile.	Annual cost per mile of road per 100 cars per day.	Tire operating cost, capitalized at 5 per cent.
Concrete, average	1.0	22 750	$31.65	$0.00533	$190	$3 800
Bitulithic	0.95	24 000	30.10	0.00502	180	3 600
Brick, average of all	1.4	16 250	44.30	0.00738	266	5 300
Macadam, best	1.9	12 000	60.10	0.01002	361	7 200
Gravel, typical Iowa	2	11 375	63.30	0.01055	380	7 600
Bituminous macadam, best	2.3	10 000	72.80	0.01213	437	8 700
Macadam, average	4.4	5 175	139.40	0.02323	835	16 700
Gravel, uncrushed chert	5.0	4 550	158.25	0.02637	950	19 000
Bituminous macadam, poor	9.6	2 375	302.00	0.05033	1 728	34 600
Macadam, loose	11.0	2 050	316.00	0.05267	2 090	41 800

The following analysis of tire operating costs is based upon the tire wear indexes of Table 3, which are tentative only and subject to change as more data became available. A standard 32 by 4-cord tire will be assumed, with 3 lb. of rubber available for abrasion during its life. The cost of such a tire will be taken as $30, with interest at 5 per cent. Based on these assumptions, Table 7 has been computed.

TABLE 8.—PASSENGER AUTOMOBILE COSTS.*

Composite car.	Cents per mile.
Gasoline	1.61
Oil	0.31
Tires	0.98
Maintenance	1.24
Depreciation	5.13
Interest	1.24
Insurance	0.31
Garage	0.83
License	0.59
Total	12.24

* *Bulletin 69,* Eng. Experiment Station, Iowa State Coll., Ames, Iowa.

As a check on the cost of tires per vehicle-mile, Table 8 is presented. This table shows the cost per mile of various items of expense for a composite passenger automobile. The tire expense for this composite car is given as 0.98 cents per mile. This compares with the tire costs of practically 0.01 cent per vehicle-mile of Table 3 for typical Iowa gravel or the best Western type macadam.

for tire wear than was obtained. Such discrepancies, although they seem trivial, gain importance from the fact that they have been abused by materials companies. Wide propaganda based on these very data has been issued.

These are just a few of the more glaring instances where the authors' methods have allowed their experiment station to become an advertising medium for private interests. Numerous others could be pointed out.

The other main question concerns the design of a test to eliminate all variable factors. A tire-wear test of a few hundred miles here and there with different climatic conditions, types of car, and other "variables" and "personal equations", too numerous to mention, is of no scientific value. Apparently, Professor Waller has arrived at that conclusion. In addition to the doubts in the "Introduction" and concluding pages, practically every section opens with such frank statements as:

"The few tests of tire wear so far made at different speeds reveal no concurrent relationship between these factors."

* * * * * *

"Various runs with the same car did not show closely similar tire wear."

* * * * * *

"Many additional data must be secured before dependable conclusions may be reached."

These statements would seem to indicate that the results obtained from these tests have no real scientific value, and yet the authors have hit on a subject that is of considerable monetary importance to automobile users. The annual tire bill in the United States amounts to approximately $800 000 000, and the difference between the two highest types tested (concrete and asphalt), amounts to $50 000 000 or $60 000 000 per year in favor of asphalt.

Therefore, it appears that this test is important, and that a relative tire-wear index number for the various types of roadways prevalent in this country would be of value to the profession, and certainly very interesting. It would seem that a very reliable figure could be obtained under the following conditions:

(*a*) Testing to destruction instead of by trips of a few hundred miles.
(*b*) Using parallel or adjoining roads as long as available under practically the same climatic, grade, and age conditions.
(*c*) Selecting road surfaces as nearly perfect as possible and five years old or more.
(*d*) Keeping uniform speed as near as possible to 30 miles per hour and 300 miles per calendar day.
(*e*) Making tests simultaneously, so that weather, heat, and moisture conditions are absolutely identical.
(*f*) Starting tests with the same make of new tires and practically new cars of the same make and model.

As Professor Waller suggests, nothing short of such a test will give "accurately, final relative results".

O. L. Waller* and H. E. Phelps,† Members, Am. Soc. C. E. (by letter).—Considerable study has been made by different investigators on the wear of

* Vice-Pres., State Coll. of Washington and Head, Dept. of Civ. Eng., Pullman, Wash.
† Prof., Highway Eng., State Coll. of Washington, Pullman, Wash.

automobile tires due to different types of roads. It was the writers' aim to bring this material together, and to discuss some features of it, but there was no thought of laying down working rules. The writers were not unfair in their use of data, but simply presented the data gathered by others and drew general conclusions therefrom that are believed to be valid although necessarily approximate.

The writers had little to do with the selection of any of the pavements that were tested, but believe that at least the tests made by the State College of Washington were run over pavements fairly representative of the several road surfaces. The lack of sufficient money to make a more extended series of tests does not discredit those that were made. The fact that some types of pavements were not tested at all, is not unfair to those types, nor is it unfair to fail to find a perfect bitulithic pavement. In the Pacific Northwest it is very difficult to find any considerable length of asphaltic pavement in good condition since very little has been constructed on State highways in recent years. The writers are glad to note Mr. Carmichael's statement that the bitulithic pavement tested was in good condition and they believe the index number for average bitulithic, given in Table 3, confirms that fact. This index number is very favorable to bitulithic, and not the reverse, as Mr. Carmichael seems to have found it.

The ideal conditions under which tire wear tests should be conducted were pointed out by the writers, and these conditions are substantially re-stated by Mr. Carmichael, but without any suggestion as to how or where the ideal can be found. It would be interesting to know the location of two parallel or adjoining roads under practically the same climatic, grade, and age conditions, one paved with concrete and one with bitulithic, and both surfaces nearly perfect and at least five years old. The State of Washington has used concrete exclusively for pavement for more than eight years and there are no ideal bituminous pavements in the State highway system, nor is there any long stretch of ideal macadam or broken rock surface road.

Of course, a test in which the tires are run to destruction is better than a short-time test. The experiment should be extensive enough to eliminate the effect of variations in the quality of individual tires. An average of the extreme variations in the condition of each type of road surface should be determined in such a way that the resulting index number would accurately reflect the tire-wearing quality of that surface and the resistance of any particular type of tires manufactured. Such a test would be very expensive. It is believed that the data already secured have been thoroughly studied by careful investigators and that the results secured are reliable.

AMERICAN SOCIETY OF CIVIL ENGINEERS
INSTITUTED 1852

TRANSACTIONS

This Society is not responsible for any statement made or opinion expressed in its publications.

Paper No. 1675

AERIAL TRAMWAYS*

By F. C. Carstarphen,† M. Am. Soc. C. E.

With Discussion by Messrs. Robert C. Strachan, George Paaswell, Casper D. Meals, and F. C. Carstarphen.

Synopsis

The great industrial expansion which has occurred in the United States during the past decade has placed a premium upon the efficiency of machines and labor.

When properly designed and selected, aerial ropeways are very economical and trustworthy machines. The English bibliography is meager. This paper aims at an outline classification, together with such comments and formulas, that may be of service to engineers in determining the elements of an aerial ropeway for their needs.

These formulas have been derived, checked, and used by the writer, and are believed to be in a correct and convenient form.

It is not the object of this paper to discuss the several structures, or equipment, in detail, but as the loading may be determined by the formulas, the design may be developed in the usual way.

Aerial Tramways

Classification.—The terminology used in describing systems of transportation by means of wire rope is loose and indefinite. The following classification of aerial tramways as distinguished from mine haulages, incline planes, or other forms of surface ropeways, will be found in accordance with the views of the most prominent tramway engineers. Abroad, the tendency is to call the system "aerial ropeways", because of the general application of the word,

* Presented at the meeting of November 2, 1927.

† Cons. Engr., Denver, Colo.

"tramway", to surface-haulage installations. Wire-rope aerial transportation systems may be listed as follows:

A.—Single rope tramways (mono-cables):

(*a*) Grip attached to carriers.
(*b*) Clip attached to carriers.

B.—Stationary cable tramways:

I.—Cableways (cable cranes):

(*a*) Radial cableways.
(*b*) Cable hoist conveyors.
(*c*) Dock hoists.
(*d*) Drag-line conveyors.
(*e*) Cable excavators and conveyors.
(*f*) Movable tower cableways.
(*g*) Balanced tower cableways.

II.—Dumping cradleways:

(*a*) Single-span.
(*b*) Multiple-span.

III. Single-cable reversible tramways:

(*a*) Aerial dump.
(*b*) Terminal discharge.

IV.—Double-cable reversible tramways:

(*a*) Aerial dump.
(*b*) Terminal discharge.

V.—Double-cable tramways with continuous traction rope:

(*a*) Carriers attached by friction grips.
(*b*) Carriers rigidly attached by clips.

VI.—Automatic tramways.

VII.—Bleichert tramways.

VIII.—Bleichert stacking tramways.

IX.—Storage tramways:

(*a*) Circuitous tramways.

X.—Selective turnout tramways.

Rope Tramways

The development of aerial tramways has been rapid and substantial. To Charles Hodgson is given the credit for promoting both the single-rope and double-rope tramways. His original patent was dated 1868. However, the "Hodgson System" is understood to refer to the single-rope type of tramway. This also applies to the "Hallidie System". Tramway lines constructed of this type are rare in North America, but are being installed abroad. They are favored for the transportation of comparatively light materials, such as coffee, tea, tobacco, charcoal, bananas, copra, cotton, etc. However, by means of careful design, they have been used with success in transporting exceptional tonnages (say, 100 tons per hour) of ore and timber. The economical capacities of such lines are 50 tons per hour, or less. The speed is generally less than 450 ft. per min. As the name implies, this type of tramway has a single rope for the simultaneous support and propulsion of the carriers.

Rope.—The rope must be designed to meet two conditions: (*a*) The wires must be sufficiently large to withstand the wear and abrasion occasioned in passing over the towers and around the driving sheaves; and (*b*) they must be small enough to be flexible and thus reduce the stresses due to bending. Ropes of six strands and seven wire construction and of crucible grade are satisfactory. Nevertheless, the rapid wear of the ropes constitutes the largest item of the maintenance expenses.

Supports.—Cable supports are either of timber or steel construction, built to 6 or 8-ft. gauge of any reasonable height, and are designed to sustain a cap which carries the sheaves supporting the rope. These towers usually consist of a substructure, which is most economically framed with perpendicular posts (Fig. 1), although some manufacturers still favor the batter posts. The tower head is usually standard for any line and can be used interchangeably on any tower. It is desirable that the towers rest on concrete or masonry foundations. However, mudsills or posts set in the ground have been used with success.

Tower Sheaves.—The number of sheaves on either side of the tower may be one, two, three, four, six, or eight, depending on the weight of the load, the radius of curvature desired, and the length of the spans adjoining the tower. When more than one sheave is used, it is customary to carry them in balance by suitable rocker arms. The sheaves are usually 16 to 20 in. in diameter, have shallow rims, rib spokes, and are set-screwed to the shaft, which is carried in babbitted cap bearings.

Carriers.—The load supported by the carriers usually varies from 100 to 1 500 lb., depending on the hourly tonnage to be transported. Loads of 800 lb., or less, are preferable to those of greater weight. If the carrier is equipped with a bucket, the usual volumes are 2 to 10 cu. ft. The bucket is mounted on trunnions supported by swivel castings bolted to U-shaped bails. The trunnions are mounted so that the center of revolution is to one side of the center of gravity. When the bucket latch is tripped, the bucket dumps automatically.

Clips.—A distinguishing feature of single-rope tramways as supplied by different manufacturers is in the method of attaching the hangers to the rope by clips and by friction grips. The Hodgson System provided a saddle fitted with India rubber or wooden friction blocks which came in contact with the rope. The friction developed by the weight of the load was sufficient to transport the carriers up moderate grades. Hallidie inserted a clip in the rope. It consisted of a rod with corrugations that were made to conform with the pitch of the rope and the size of the strands. The bucket hanger was forged into a head, which was drilled to receive a pin, so as to permit oscillation in a direction parallel to the travel of the line. The clip was hinged to provide side sway. This method of attaching the carriers to the rope was positive and was successful on lines having steep gradients.

Other types of clips were developed, which depended on placing a thin sheet of metal around and squeezing the rope by means of bolts. Adolf Bleichert and Company developed a friction grip which seizes the rope automatically when it leaves the loading terminal and is detached the same way at the discharge terminal. This grip is actuated by the weight of the load and is successful on gradients of more than 30 degrees. Manufacturers of that type of tramway on which the carriers are arranged for detaching from the rope, equip the carriages with two wheels so that the carrier may be moved through the terminals when supported on suspended rails.

Automatic Loaders.—Carriers rigidly attached to the rope must be loaded and unloaded while in motion. This arrangement led to the development of automatic loading devices. The loading terminal is arranged to provide a bin for storing the material to be transported. The bin is equipped with a suitable gate so that a container of the same volume as the bucket may be loaded by the operators at will. This, in turn, is discharged into a traveling hopper which is mounted on wheels and runs on a track parallel with the ropeway. The traveling hopper engages the bucket and travels with it a distance sufficient to dump its contents automatically into the bucket. After this is accomplished, it disengages itself and returns to its former position beneath the stationary hopper. This action trips the gate of the stationary hopper and the loader is again filled, thereby completing the cycle. Various aids, such as sprocket wheels, air cylinders, etc., have been used to assist the loader in keeping pace with the bucket without disturbing the latter's equilibrium. When the bucket reaches the discharge terminal, it is automatically tripped and discharged. Carriers equipped with grips do not need automatic loaders or unloaders. They pass to the point most convenient for loading or discharging because of their greater freedom in the terminals.

Angle Stations.—Angle stations may be installed on single-rope tramways to accommodate any change in their alignment. The deflection is accomplished by horizontal sheaves mounted on supporting structures fitted with guides. The slow speed of the tramway permits the carriers to pass around the sheaves either supported directly by the clips or on curved rails, depending on the type of equipment used.

Drive.—The line is driven by either plain, wood-filled, or grip sheaves. The sheaves are fitted with brake rims and friction brakes so that the motion may be properly controlled.

Approximate Cost.—The equipment for a single-rope tramway of 6-ft. gauge, 6-ton hourly capacity, 1 mile in length, provided with an automatic loader, terminal machinery, gears, automatic dumper, supporting sheaves, stands, guides, woodwork bolts and washers, buckets, hangers, clips, crucible steel wire rope, and splicing tools, would weigh approximately 30 000 lb., and would require 28 000 ft. b.m. of timber, including a 20-ton storage bin.

The total cost for such a line installed would be about $18 000. It costs approximately $2 850 per year to operate for 300 days, and would transport 18 000 tons at a net cost of 15.5 cents per ton.

Stationary Cable Tramways

This is the name given to all systems of aerial transportation that sustain the carrier on a stationary cable as a track and propel it by means of

Fig. 1.—Steel Tower.

Fig. 2.—Dumping Cradleways for Fills.

an independent traction rope. There seems to be a further differentiation among stationary cable tramways, depending on the weight of the unit load handled and the distance through which it is moved. To illustrate, cableways are presumed to handle individual loads weighing from 5 to 10 tons, the translation being usually less than 2 000 ft. On the other hand, double-cable tramways with continuous traction ropes transport loads of 1½ tons, or less, to any distance required. All the other classes are intermediate between these extremes.

Cableways (*Cable Cranes*).—The cableway is defined as a stationary cable tramway which uses a suspended cable for a track and a carriage that is adapted to both hoisting and conveying, in sequence, or simultaneously. The carriage of a cableway is actuated by a reversing engine, either steam or motor-driven, fitted with an elliptic grooved sheave to accommodate the endless rope which is permanently attached to each end of the carriage and is used in moving it to and fro. The engine has a drum for the hoisting rope. If the span exceeds 300 ft., it becomes necessary to support the hoisting rope; otherwise, the weight of the unsupported rope is sufficient to counterbalance the empty fall-block, and the latter cannot be lowered. To overcome this difficulty, devices called fall-rope carriers have been developed. The difference in the design of these parts is the distinguishing feature of the cableways furnished by different companies. Many patents have been issued for fall-rope carriers and several systems have been proposed to eliminate their use. The method now in general use is to support them on a horn of the carriage so arranged as to hold them in place. A stationary rope is fitted with different sized buttons. As the carriage moves, the buttons engage the fall-rope carriers and they are thus automatically spaced along the track cables. When the direction of travel is reversed, the carriage picks them up. To avoid the hammering of the buttons and the wear of the button rope, the differential fall-rope carriers were designed. This design provides that the individual carriers shall move at different speeds, obtained by a change in the ratio of the diameter of the sheaves in contact with the main cable and the hoisting rope. This difference in the rapidity of travel of the differential fall-rope carriers automatically spaces them along the track cable.

When the difference in the terminal elevations exceeds one-third of the span, and when a three-part fall-block is used, the endless haulage rope may be omitted, for the load can be hoisted until the fall-block reaches the carriage before translation will begin. The carriage is returned to position by gravity and is stopped by a block clamped to the track cable. As soon as the motion of the carriage is arrested, the fall-block is lowered to the ground.

Radial cableways are those in which the tail tower is mounted on a circular track. The movement of this tower is usually confined to a sector of 40° about the head tower as a center. When the carrier moves through the head tower to a boom overhanging a boat, the installation is called a "dock hoist". If the fall-block supports a self-filling bucket, such as drag, slip, orange-peel, or clam-shell, the installation is called a "cable excavator and conveyor"; also, a "drag-line excavator and conveyor". Generally speaking, cableways are not adaptable to sites requiring multiple spans, owing to the inability of the usual carriage to pass intermediate supports. Cableways are built with both towers mounted on rails, and, therefore, can be moved laterally, thus commanding a larger area than is possible with the anchored cable. Cableways for storing coal may also be equipped with terminal masts, which swing in a plane at right angles to the cable. As the mast may function as a radius of a circle, the length of back-stays to anchorage is constant for all mast positions. Cableways have been fitted with steel towers resembling a trestle bent which may oscillate about the base. These towers are controlled by weights, which tend to maintain a constant tension in the rope. Cableways are frequently used for the operation of quarries, placer deposits, tailing dumps, etc.

Dumping Cradleways.—When deep fills are made or excessive dumps are to be accumulated at a rate faster than is obtainable by handling single cars, the dumping cradleway provides a method which eliminates trestles, promotes the speed of handling the train, and insures complete salvage of the equipment when the work is finished. Dumping cradleways (Fig. 2) consist of two stationary cables supported by towers located at the end of the span or spans. Suspended from these cables is a cradle which supports a track. The train is pushed to the edge of the fill and the cars are dumped consecutively, the empty cars passing forward on to the deck of the cradleway. The grade of the fill is controlled by a movable tower which is advanced with the cradle as the fill progresses. The elevation of the supporting cables is thereby kept constant irrespective of the position of the cradle on the span. Hold-down tackle keeps the unloaded cradle in position when the cars are drawn from it.

The Cedar Rapids Manufacturing and Power Company, at Cedars, Que., Canada, successfully used a two-span dumping cradleway to build a 2 000-ft. wing-dam of more than 125 000 cu. yd., across a channel of the St. Lawrence River. The cables were 2½-in., 6 × 37, plow steel. The cradle was 14 ft. wide and 130 ft. long, and had a maximum capacity of ten 6-cu. ft. contractors' cars. The height of the movable tower was 40 ft. The cost of the fill was reported to be less than $1.25 per cu. yd. The depth exceeded 30 ft., the velocity of current about 10 miles per hour, and a limestone bottom made cribbing and piling methods prohibitive and impracticable.

Single-Cable Reversible Tramways.—This type of equipment differs from cableways in that the hoisting feature is eliminated. Accordingly, the endless traction rope is all that is required. These lines are generally short and of small capacity. The direction of travel of the traction rope is reversed at the completion of each trip of the carrier. Such lines are usually equipped with self-dumping buckets, which may be tripped automatically while moving along the cable, or in stations. The speed of such lines is usually 600 ft. per min., but on clear spans they may be operated as fast as 1 000 ft. per min. The capacity, therefore, is directly proportional to the load and velocity, but inversely proportional to the span. The hourly capacity rarely exceeds 20 tons.

Table 1 gives the capacities, in pounds per hour, of single-cable, reversible tramways operating at a speed of 600 ft. per min. The time interval to complete the trip is given in seconds.

TABLE 1.—Capacity, in Pounds per Hour, of Single-Cable Tramway.

Length, in feet.	Time, in seconds.	Bucket Capacity.						
		400.	600.	800.	1 200.	1 500.	2 000.	2 500.
2 000	450	3 200	4 800	6 400	9 600	12 000	16 000	20 000
1 500	343	4 200	6 300	8 400	12 600	15 750	21 000	26 250
1 000	240	6 000	9 000	12 000	18 000	22 500	30 000	37 500
500	144	10 000	15 000	20 000	30 000	37 500	50 000	62 500

Double-Cable Reversible Tramways.—For efficiency it is desirable to operate reversible tramways in balance, in so far as the moving equipment is concerned. Most engineers prefer to use two track cables, thus bringing two single reversible tramways side by side, spaced 6, 8, or 10-ft. gauge, depending on the size of the bucket. Both buckets are moved by the same traction rope, which passes around a sheave at the terminal. Tail ropes are required on lines where power is necessary for their operation. Tramways of this type are operated by gravity when there is sufficient fall between the terminal stations. Like single reversibles, they may be equipped with trippers for aerial dumping of the buckets; otherwise, the bucket dumps automatically over the bins in the discharge terminal. This type of tramway is usually arranged so that all its functions are automatic, except the loading and control of the driving mechanism. One operator is sufficient for either single- or double-cable reversible tramways. The track cables are usually anchored without weight-boxes, and multiple spans are used when necessary. The proper determination of the tension of an empty track cable permits the designer to control the ultimate tension of the cable when carrying a maximum load.

Table 2 gives the capacities, in pounds per hour, of double-cable reversible tramways of different lengths, based on a speed of 600 ft. per min.

TABLE 2.—Capacity, in Pounds per Hour, of Double-Cable Tramways.

Length, in feet.	Time, in seconds.	Bucket Capacity.						
		400.	600.	800.	1 200.	1 500.	2 000.	2 500.
2 000	240	6 000	9 000	12 000	18 000	22 500	30 000	37 500
1 500	192	7 500	11 250	15 000	22 500	28 125	37 500	46 875
1 000	144	10 000	15 000	20 000	30 000	37 500	50 000	62 500
500	90	16 000	24 000	32 000	48 000	60 000	80 000	100 000

The Consolidation Coal Company has used this type of tramway for handling mine waste. At Mine 206, a three-span, double-cable, reversible tramway is installed. It is equipped with 27-cu. ft., bottom-dump buckets which hold approximately 2 000 lb. of slate, and which dump automatically into bins supplying a larry system of distribution. The difference in elevation between the loading and discharge terminals is 427 ft., and the horizontal length is 789 ft. The tramway is operated by a reversing slip-ring motor fitted with a drum controller and resistance grids capable of 50% speed regulation.

Double-Cable Tramways with Continuous Traction Ropes.—Although Messrs. Hodgson and Carrington first considered the arrangement used in double-cable tramways, it remained for Messrs. Adolf Bleichert, J. Pohlig, and T. Otto, of Germany, Cerretti and Tanfini, of Italy, and the Trenton Iron Company, Leschen and Sons, Roebling, The American Steel and Wire Company, Broderick and Bascomb, Riblett, and others, in America to demonstrate the practicability and perfection of this type of aerial tramway. Two-track cables are used to support the carriers. The usual practice is to increase the diameter of the cable carrying the loaded buckets over that used on the empty side. The traction rope is of the well-known Lang lay construction, is spliced endless, and is controlled by suitable terminal mechanism. The positive attachment of the carrier to the traction rope promotes the development of the highest efficiency possible in any system of transportation.

Tramways built on favorable gradients of 2 to 3% eliminate, owing to gravity, the friction developed by tower rollers, terminal sheaves, carriages, and other moving parts. The power developed or required in the operation of double-cable tramways is then an exact function of the load transported. This is not true for any self-propelled vehicle depending on wheel friction for tractive effort. There is no permanent ratio between the horse power of the prime mover and the load moved. On grades of 12%, the locomotive fails as a tractor under its own weight. Not so with aerial tramways which use, in a modified way, the most efficient system known of transmitting power, for example, by wire rope.

Transportation Costs.—Transportation costs are usually expressed in terms of the ton-mile. This factor is reasonable enough when the haul is of sufficient length for the grades to compensate, thereby presenting costs equivalent to hauling the loads on the level projection of the track. However, with aerial tramways of moderate length—5 miles or less—there is no material increase in operating charges over those experienced on short lines. In other words, the cost of transporting material by aerial tramways is not proportional to the length. The greater part of the expense of operation is for labor in the terminals, so that on equal tonnage lines, one being ½ mile long and the other 2 miles long, the former will show about 400% greater cost per ton-mile than the latter.

Aerial tramways of equal hourly capacity transport the same weight of material per unit of time and the capacity is independent of the length. Hence, generally speaking, the distance of the haul has no effect on aerial tramway transportation costs, as is the case in surface-haulage systems. It is noted that an aerial tramway on a level gradient, and having a capacity of 50 tons per hour, can successfully compete with surface railways less than 17 miles in length. If the topography of the site is rough and broken, double-cable tramways with continuous traction ropes are supreme. They are especially adapted to the transportation of any substance that can be readily loaded into buckets, 40 cu. ft., or less, in volume, and that produces a net weight of load of 3 500 lb., or less.

Automatic Tramways.—Double-cable tramways with continuous traction ropes, like single-rope tramways, have been developed so that one system attaches the carriers to the traction rope by means of buttons or clips—the so-called automatic system—whereas the other plan is to attach the carriers automatically to the moving traction rope by means of friction grips. The latter type is known as the Bleichert System. The Leschen Special Automatic System is probably the best known type of the button-attached buckets, whereas in the Lawson System, the carriers are attached by clips to the traction rope. This tends to localize the bending stresses in the traction rope, thereby greatly shortening its life, as compared with lines using friction grips. This latter method is favorable because it is not probable that successive grips will seize continuously the rope at exactly the same points.

The filling of the buckets is accomplished with the aid of an automatic loader, which consists of a hopper having approximately the same volume as the bucket. This hopper is mounted on rails and is movable. It is filled when the operator manipulates the gates of the storage bin. The loader engages a lug on the hanger of the carrier and moves forward in unison with it until the contents have passed to the bucket. The loader then returns to its initial position and, when refilled, completes the cycle of operation. Air pistons, chains, counterweights, and other accessories are used to control the motion of this device. Self-dumping buckets are used, so that when the latch is tripped the bucket revolves on its trunnions, thus discharging its contents. All these operations take place while the carrier is in motion.

In the Lawson or Interstate System parallel track cables are used, which support the carriers, the axes of which are approximately in the horizontal plane. These carriers are dumped when passing over a tail-drum, which reverses their direction of motion, and they return on twin track cables supported on the same structures, but below the cables carrying the loaded buckets. The track cables of both the empty and loaded sizes are sometimes arranged in the same plane, rather than one above the other.

The Leschen System uses carriers hanging in the vertical plane. As a typical automatic double-cable tramway, may be mentioned the "International Line" across the Rio Grande River, which was designed by Leschen and Sons for the Del Carmen Mining Company, of San Antonio, Tex. Its length was 31 500 ft.; its maximum capacity was 10 tons per hour, with a speed of 300 ft. per min. It was equipped with buckets holding 600 lb., which ran on 1-in. and $\frac{3}{4}$-in. track cables of flattened strand construction, cast-steel grade. The traction rope was driven by a 45-h.p. gas engine, which operated a 10-ft. grip sheave. Water carriers used on the line were equipped with hand-attached friction grips, so that they could be removed from the line at will.

Bleichert Tramways.—The Bleichert System and similar systems have carriers equipped with friction grips, which are automatically attached and detached to and from the moving traction rope. The freedom of motion attained by the carriers in the stations is of prime importance. It permits increasing the speed of these lines to 600 ft. per min. The detaching of the carriers allows their ready control in stations where, of necessity, the rail curves must have short radii. The high speed permits the development of lines of great capacity, such as 275 tons per hour. They have, however, an economical equipment of carriers and track cables. Table 3 gives the elements of Bleichert tramways, in tons per hour; also, the average number of men required on lines of 3 miles, or less. The speed of the line is assumed at 500 ft. per min.

A Bleichert tramway of very large hourly capacity was in service for several years at the mines of the Spring Canyon Coal Company, at Storrs, Utah. It was 3 050 ft. long, with a difference in elevation between the loading and discharge terminals of 330 ft. The capacity was 285 tons per hour. It was equipped with 40-cu. ft. buckets, designed to be transferred from the trucks of the mine haulage system to the hangers of the tramway carriers by a special device called a "tilting table". The empty buckets were placed on the trucks and again entered the mine, thus completing the circuit. The speed of the tramway was 520 ft. per min. Locked-coil steel track cables, in sizes of $1\frac{5}{8}$ in. and $1\frac{1}{4}$ in., were used. The traction rope was of $\frac{7}{8}$-in., Lang lay, crucible cast steel. The towers were equipped with compensating saddles on the loaded side, reducing the bending stresses in the cable. The line was under the continuous control of a sentinel brake. A speed-indicating alarm sounded a warning if the velocity of the line increased 5% above normal. The traction rope passed around an 8-ft. grip sheave equipped with differential, hand-operated brakes. When in operation the line developed 65 h.p. A 75-h.p., 3-phase induction motor could be connected to the drive by means of a friction clutch. The motor was not used except when the line was being stripped of its carriers.

Bleichert Stacking Tramways.—The Bleichert stacking tramways consist of a trussed framework, having bents securely cross-braced and designed so as to be capable of extension by the addition of one or more bents. The tip consists of an independent structure telescoped into the trussed framework. It is mounted on rollers and may be moved outward by screws or hydraulic-jacks. This tip carries a terminal sheave of ample diameter, so that the carriers which ascend the supporting double-headed tramway rail of the framework, pass around it, and are automatically dumped. As the pile grows, the tip is pushed outward. When sufficient space has accumulated, another bent is added to the structure. Piles 250 to 300 ft. in height are not unusual. When the pile has reached a sufficient height, the alignment of the framework is changed to the horizontal plane, and the pile may be extended indefinitely. A sufficient length of travel is provided for the traction-rope tension mechanism so that it is not necessary to splice in additional pieces of traction rope for every extension of the line.

Tramways of this design have been installed at the Brakepan Mines, Limited, of Johannesburg, South Africa, the Boulder Proprietary Gold Mines, Limited, of Kalgoorlie, West Australia, and elsewhere. These installations move as much as 200 tons of waste per hour.

TABLE 3.—Bleichert Tramways, Standard Equipment.

Capacity, in tons per hour.	Size of loaded cable, in inches.	Size of empty cable, in inches.	Size of traction rope, in inches.	Couplings per mile.	Capacity of carriers, in cubic feet.	Spacing of carriers, in feet.	Time interval, in seconds.	Number of carriers per mile.	Number of supports.	Weight, in pounds per 100 ft.*	Cost per 100 ft.*	Weight, in pounds per mile.*	Cost per mile.*	Horse-power required or developed.	Number of chutes.	Terminals, weight, in pounds.†	Terminals, cost.†	Tension station, weight, in pounds.‡	Tension station, cost.‡	Gauge, in feet.	Number of men.
5	1	⅞	½	4	5	1 500	180	9	20	857	$102.13	45 250	$ 5 392	0 to 7	1	26 400	$2 894	7 300	$ 733	6	2
10	1	⅞	½	4	5	750	90	16	20	897	112.49	47 360	5 940	0 to 7	1	26 400	2 894	7 300	733	6	2
15	1	⅞	½	4	5	500	60	23	20	937	122.85	49 460	6 487	0 to 7	1	26 400	2 894	7 300	733	6	3
20	1	⅞	½	4	5	375	45	30	20	977	133.21	51 570	7 034	0 to 7	1	26 400	2 894	7 300	733	6	3
25	1	⅞	½	4	5	300	36	37	20	1 017	143.57	53 680	7 581	0 to 7	1	26 400	2 894	7 300	733	6	3
25	1⅛	⅞	½	4	6	360	43.2	31	22	1 091	146.41	57 610	7 730	7 to 15	2	32 700	3 540	7 800	766	8	3
30	1⅛	⅞	½	4	6	300	36	37	22	1 127	155.53	59 480	8 212	7 to 15	2	32 700	3 540	7 800	766	8	3
40	1⅛	⅞	½	4	6	225	27	48	22	1 191	172.25	62 910	9 095	7 to 15	2	32 700	3 540	7 800	766	8	4
50	1⅛	⅞	½	4	6	180	21.6	59	22	1 256	188.97	66 330	9 978	7 to 15	2	32 700	3 540	7 800	766	8	4
50	1¼	⅞	⅝	5	12	360	43.2	32	22	1 384	183.56	73 070	9 692	15 to 30	3	38 900	4 154	9 100	900	8	4
100	1¼	⅞	⅝	5	12	180	21.6	60	22	1 625	243.48	85 780	12 856	15 to 30	3	38 900	4 154	9 100	900	8	7
100	1⅜	⅞	⅝	6	15	225	27	49	22	1 703	240.27	89 900	12 686	30 to 55	4	59 000	6 087	10 100	1 005	8	7
150	1⅜	⅞	⅝	6	15	150	18	71	22	1 923	292.19	101 520	15 428	30 to 55	4	59 000	6 087	10 100	1 005	8	8
150	1½	1	¾	6	20	200	24	55	24	2 057	290.33	108 590	15 330	55 to 85	5	64 100	6 655	10 400	1 060	8	8
200	1½	1	¾	6	20	150	18	72	24	2 247	333.51	118 640	17 610	55 to 85	5	64 100	6 655	10 400	1 060	8	9
200	1⅝	1	⅞	7	25	187½	22½	59	26	2 390	340.85	126 210	17 997	85 to 110	6	76 300	8 073	12 200	1 250	8	9
250	1⅝	1	⅞	7	25	150	18	72	26	2 554	378.03	134 860	19 960	85 to 110	6	76 300	8 073	12 200	1 250	8	10

Notes.—Weight of ore taken as 100 lb. per cu. ft.; neutral line; lines requiring power, add for automatic reversing prevention ratchet, 455 lb., $176; lines developing power, add for speed-indicating alarm, 130 lb., $120; power-operated instead of hand-operated chutes, add for each, 2 550 lb., $275; sentinel brake and control mechanism, add 6 200 lb., $850. The data given in the table do not include costs of structures or installation expenses.

* Locked-coil track cables: Lang lay, crucible cast-steel traction rope, standard carriers, equipped with grips, tower saddles, rollers and bolts, telephones and line equipment; that is, all parts affected by change in length.

† Terminal equipment: Sheaves, shafts, pulleys, clutch, tension mechanism, rails, hoods, attachers, detachers, chutes, spacing gong, and tools; that is, all parts not affected by change in length.

‡ Tension station mechanism: Rail, sheaves, rollers, chain, bolts, hoods, etc. Add one station for every mile of line.

Storage Tramways.—These are double-cable, continuous, traction-rope lines equipped with trippers attached to the track cables to trip the latches of the self-dumping buckets. The discharged material accumulates in a pile beneath the tripper. When the pile has reached a height sufficient to interfere with the dumping of the buckets, the tripper is moved farther along the cable. This permits of the accumulation of a pile of relatively narrow width, but of considerable length, in a direction parallel to the tramway. Since the natural slope of such piles is rarely greater than 34°, it is found desirable to increase the gauge of the tramway so as to cover square or circular plots rather than rectangular spaces of great length. This demand has resulted in the development of the circuitous type of storage tramway. Installations of this kind may be provided with overhead grip carriages, or underhung grips, which are capable of passing around curves of 6-ft. radius without being detached from the traction rope. When 12-ft. guide sheaves are used, the speed of the tramway should not exceed 350 ft. per min.; with sheaves, 20 ft. in diameter, 450 ft. per min. The angular throw of the bucket due to centrifugal force can be readily controlled by curved guides when the velocity is within the limits mentioned. Tramways of this type, therefore, consist of towers supporting single-track cables and the traction rope as well as angle stations, equipped with guide sheaves of large diameter. The line follows the perimeter of figures which approach the square or rhomboid in shape. The carriers are always equipped with self-dumping buckets, and it is preferable to use those having the self-righting feature as well.

Bucket trippers may be small pendant clamps, attached to the track cables, or they may be mounted in tripping frames. Tripping frames are of two classes; those that are positively attached to the cable, and, like the clips, can only be moved by sending a member of the tramway crew out on the span to loosen the frame's attachment to the cable. This procedure is more or less dangerous, and, in addition, causes considerable delay in shifting the tripper. The ambulating tripping frame consists of a hood supported on the track cables by rollers. The frame is held in position by four ground lines fitted with proper tackle. The selective ambulating tripping frame carries a toothed bar so that it may be adjusted at will by a line reaching to the ground. The buckets used on tramways equipped with selective ambulating tripping frames are provided with adjustable latch-bars which can be set in the loading terminal according to the material in the bucket. This arrangement permits the handling of various ores simultaneously and storing them in their separate piles or combining them in any proportion desired.

The Tacoma Smelting and Refining Company, of Tacoma, Wash., had such a storage tramway. This line handled zinc and copper ore, or other classes as received, and stored them simultaneously in separate or in bed piles, as the metallurgists decided. The capacity of the line was 100 tons per hour and its length, 3 000 ft. The traction rope was $\frac{5}{8}$-in. Lang lay. The track cables were $1\frac{5}{8}$-in. special locked-coil. The line was equipped with 16-cu. ft. buckets, selective ambulating tripping frames, and pneumatic power chutes. A 25-h.p. vertical motor equipped with drum controller and resistance grids for 50% speed regulation, was used.

Selective Turnout Tramways.—This tramway is used where the material transported is to be delivered at several different points, and for the sake of economy the labor required to throw the switches and detachers is eliminated by the substitution of automatic machinery. The carriers are fitted with a shoe attached to a selector bar which has as many notches as there are turnout stations. The buckets are filled at the loading terminal in the usual way, and the operator sets the selector bar in the notch representing the desired turnout station.

When the carrier arrives at this point, the shoe engages the throttle of an air-valve, which actuates the pistons of two cylinders controlling the swinging detacher and the turnout switch. The carrier automatically releases the traction rope, enters the siding, and coasts to the proper point under its own momentum. As it leaves the station, the shoe encounters a release valve, which restores the mechanism to its original position. Any carrier with the selector bar set for another station passes by this switch, because the shoe on its carriage does not engage the air mechanism.

Economic Design.—The structures of an aerial tramway are grouped into the terminal stations, which are usually independent of the length of the line and, for a given tonnage, represent a fixed cost. Tension and other intermediate structures are required only occasionally along the tramway and may be also regarded as additional cost factors. Towers for any given line will be of standard design, and, therefore, the criterion to apply in choosing the capacity of the carriers and the size of cable for economy of design is to select them so that the cost per foot of cable multiplied by the bucket spacing plus the cost of a carrier shall be a minimum, or as near thereto as the time interval will permit.

Track Cables.—The track cables are an essential part of all systems of aerial tramways. Four styles of cable have been used for this purpose. They are locked-wire, locked-coil, smooth-coil track strand, and patent flattened strand. The first three are shown in Fig. 3.

Locked-wire cable is so named from the fact that the outer wires have a Z-shape so that they interlock one with the other and thus present a smooth surface on the exterior, resulting in a uniform distribution of wear of the wires, which cannot be attained by the use of any other cable. Experience has shown that no other track cable gives as great a tonnage life as locked-wire and locked-coil cable. Table 4 gives the properties of locked-wire cables.

Locked-coil track cable is very similar to locked-wire cable, except that the core and key wires are of larger cross-section, so that the cost of manufacture is reduced and likewise the price to the trade. Fig. 4 shows a test specimen of this cable. (Note the holding power of the zinc sockets.) It is satisfactory for use as a track cable for aerial tramways carrying net loads of 5 000 lb., or less, whereas locked-wire cable is greatly favored for use on cableways where the weight of the moving load is approximately 8 to 10 tons. Table 5 gives the characteristics of locked-coil cable.

TABLE 4.—PROPERTIES OF LOCKED-WIRE CABLE.

Diameter, in inches.	Area, in square inches.	Approximate weight per foot, in pounds.	Approximate breaking stress, in tons.
2¼	3.410	12.50	190
2	2.725	10.00	160
1¾	2.080	7.65	120
1⅝	1.800	6.60	103
1½	1.550	5.70	89
1⅜	1.290	4.75	75
1¼	0.040	3.80	62
1⅛	0.858	3.15	50
1	0.680	2.50	40

When a cheaper track cable is desired, smooth-coil track strand is used. This cable is composed of a number of comparatively large round wires laid about a core wire. The number of wires and their size vary according to the size of the cable, 19, 37, and 55 being the usual construction for cables of the size used on most tramways. Should a wire break, it uncoils rapidly to the points of support of the span. With locked-coil cable, it is necessary for two or more adjacent wires to break before the wires can run. Smooth-coil track strand is superior to all other track cables except the locked-wire and locked-coil types. The use of cables, such as patent flattened strand, or of the ordinary type of wire ropes, on permanent installations, is not good practice, for the life of such cables is frequently extremely short, due to the breakage of the small wires which must be used in their construction. Table 6 gives the characteristics of smooth-coil track strand.

TABLE 5.—LOCKED-COIL CABLE.

Diameter, in inches.	Area, in square inches.	Approximate weight per foot, in pounds.	Approximate breaking stress, in tons.
2	2.60	9.4	160
1⅞	2.30	8.2	140
1¾	2.05	7.30	120
1⅝	1.80	6.30	103
1½	1.55	5.30	89
1⅜	1.35	4.40	75
1¼	1.10	3.70	62
1⅛	0.85	3.00	50
1	0.70	2.35	40
⅞	0.50	1.80	30

The modulus of elasticity of track cables in both bending and direct tension varies with the stress imposed. When a load, such as a moving carrier, passes along the track cable, bending stresses are developed in the cable. The relationship between the weight of the loaded carrier and the size of the track cable is based on the criterion that the combined bending and direct stresses in the outermost wires must be a minimum. The weight of a carrier that may be safely sustained by a track cable varies with the tension between limits of 300 to 700 times the weight per foot of the cable.

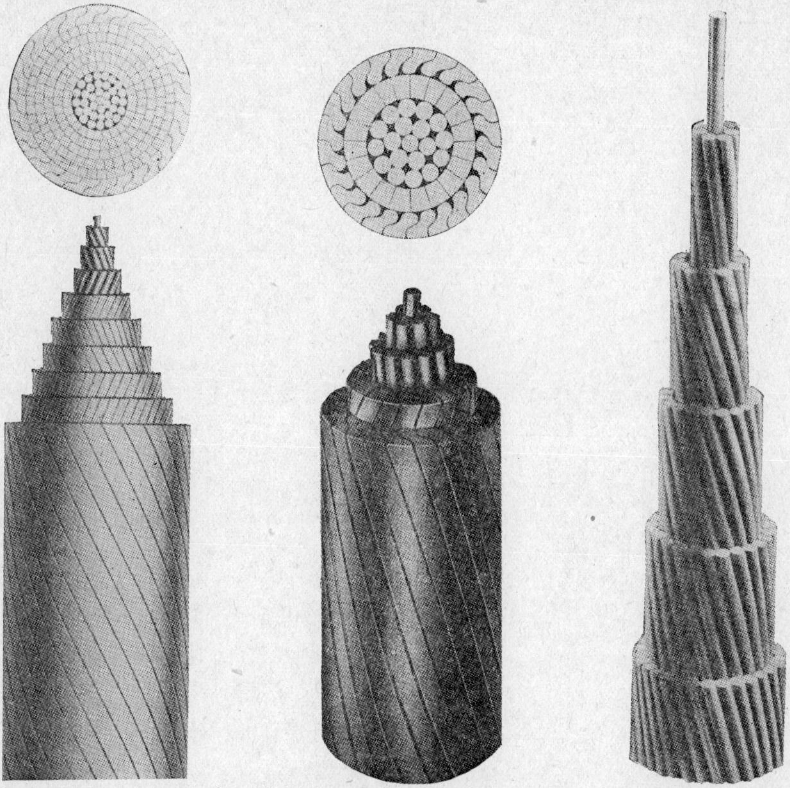

(a) (b) (c)

FIG. 3.—TRACK CABLE DETAILS.

FIG. 4.—TEST PIECE OF LOCK-COIL CABLE.

TABLE 6.—SMOOTH-COIL TRACK STRAND.

Dia meter, in inches.	Number of wires in strand.	Area, in square inches.	Weight per foot, in pounds.	Breaking Stress, in Tons.	
				Crucible steel.	Plow steel.
2	61	2.24	8.40	185.00	218.00
1⅞	61	1.97	7.28	161.00	189.00
1¾	61	1.72	6.59	145.80	171.00
1⅝	61	1.49	5.63	124.00	146.00
1½	37	1.27	4.88	108.40	127.50
1⅜	37	1.06	4.01	88.80	105.00
1¼	37	0.86	3.23	71.80	84.60
1⅛	37	0.72	2.70	60.00	70.70
1	19	0.56	2.20	49.20	58.00
⅞	19	0.44	1.69	37.60	44.40
¾	19	0.32	1.24	27.60	32.50

Tramway track cables show, when properly tested, several interesting phenomena which explain their behavior in service. The elongation of a specimen of locked-coil cable is not the same for equal values of progressive and retrogressive loading. If elongations are plotted as ordinates and the loads as abscissas, a frictional hysteresis graph is developed, and is capable of being interpreted in the same manner as the well-known engine indicator diagrams. The area bounded represents work. As the rate of application of the loading is very slow, the heat generated is small. Hence, the work shown is a measure of the internal friction developed among the wires. This force is comparable with the effect of cohesion in homogeneous bodies. As the internal friction is a function of the tension, so is the modulus of elasticity. The cable specimen does not follow Hooke's law until the tension is well advanced. Because of these properties the tonnage life of track cables is profoundly influenced by the manner of their support, the weight of the moving carrier, the amount and the method of applying the tension, and the lubrication and care received.

Radius of Saddle.—In aerial tramway designing, the ratio of load to tension should be taken as less than 0.05. As the wheel base of the carriage is known, the radius of curvature of the cable between the carriage wheels can be approximated. This value, or a greater one, should be used for the radius of the track cable saddles, so that the bending stresses in the cable at the supports will be of the same order as those developed under the carriage. If the wheel base of the carriage is 1.2 ft., the radius of curvature of the cable should be about 25 ft. Fig. 5 shows a rocking saddle.

Anchored Spans.—As track cables under high tension show properties similar to homogeneous bars, it is well to bear in mind that heavy boxes promote the development of great internal friction; in other words, there is no relief to the constituent wires from the stresses imposed by the passing carriers. These stresses are not reduced by stopping the tramway. This continuous loading results in reduced tonnage service and engineers have given their attention to the merits possessed by anchored spans.

If a loaded carrier traverses a cable span, the ends of which are firmly anchored, and the cable is assumed to be non-elastic, the only stress effect observed is an increase in the tension as the carrier moves from the support toward the center; when passed, the tension declines to that of the empty span as the carrier passes the support. As the erection tension of the empty cable is less than that required to develop an internal friction sufficient for the cable to show an elongation proportional to the stress, it follows that the continual change in the tension due to the passing carrier results in a mutual adjustment of the wires with regard to the applied stresses. The result is that broken wires are less frequent, and the usefulness of the cable is enhanced. The objection of tramway designers to the use of anchored spans is due to the difficulty of computing the erection tension of the cable so as not to exceed, when loaded, a pre-determined amount. By the use of formulas developed from the principles of the elastic theory, this objection has been overcome.

Lubrication.—In order to keep the internal friction at a minimum and protect cables from the elements, the aerial tramway track cables and traction ropes should be thoroughly lubricated with a non-acid oil. Tramway manufacturers can supply track-cable oilers which are equipped with tanks and oil pumps (some are operated by compressed air) belted to the carriage wheels and, when they are in motion, the pumps deliver a constant stream of oil to the cable. Traction-rope oilers are maintained in the terminals, and consist of tank, sheave, and wiping brushes. The sheave runs in oil and thus lubricates the rope. To insure uniform wear on the exterior surface of a track cable, experience has shown that it may be turned so as to present a different surface to the carriage wheels. If cables are turned, the operation must be done methodically. It will not do to operate a cable for a long time in one position and thereby allow the wires to assume a permanent set, due to the development of large internal adhesive forces, and then turn it, for the cable will then show broken wires very quickly. If a tramway has a capacity of 50 tons per hour and the cables are given a one-quarter turn for every 12 000 tons transported, and the other conditions of support, tension, and lubrication are favorable, the tonnage life will be increased. It has been recorded that more than 2 000 000 tons traversed a 1¼-in. locked-coil cable before complete replacement. Large sized track cables have not as yet developed a tonnage life equal to that secured from small cables, but by using the proper principles of design, the tonnage life is being greatly augmented.

Couplings.—Locked-coil and smooth-coil track cables cannot be spliced in the usual acceptance of the term. They are joined by a special device called a coupling, which consists of three pieces: Two sockets of nickel steel which are joined by a central plug having right and left-hand threads, the unscrewing of the several parts being prevented by dowel pins. The ends of the cable are introduced into the tapered sockets and are flared by thimbles driven between the several layers of core, key, and lock wires. The wires are gathered into groups by means of wedges driven lightly between them. Fig. 6 shows three lock-coil cable couplings that proved to be 92%, 80%, and 60%, respectively, as strong as the cable. The photograph also shows the nature of the failures resulting from improper driving of the thimbles.

FIG. 5.—ROCKING SADDLES.

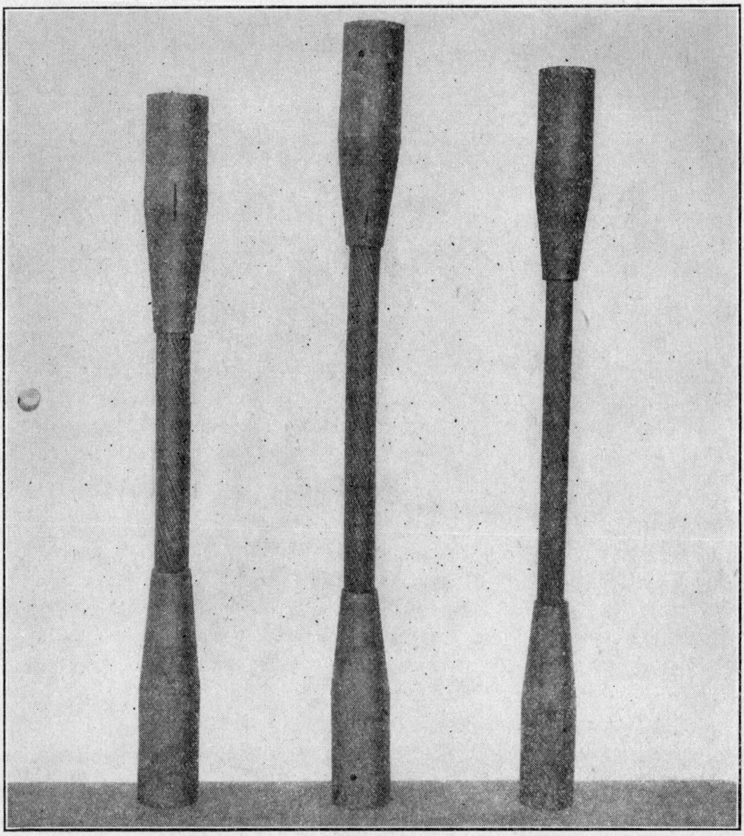

FIG. 6.—LOCK-COIL CABLE COUPLINGS.

This system of joining cables is very satisfactory, as the coupling frequently develops 90% of the ultimate strength of the cable. The sockets are made from nickel steel, and should be specially heat-treated so as best to stand the bursting pressure imposed on the tapered shell. Track cables do not fail simultaneously at all points along the line. Broken wires appear and are either welded by the oxy-acetylene blow-pipe torch, or a section of the cable is removed and a new piece coupled in, which is a very simple operation.

Traction Rope.—Practically all double-cable tramways are equipped with traction ropes made of six strands of seven wires coiled about a hemp center in a manner known as Lang lay. Steel of a grade higher than extra strong crucible is seldom used because of the hardness of the wires and the consequent tendency to rupture. Lang lay rope has the wires approximately

TABLE 7.—CRUCIBLE STEEL TRAMWAY TRACTION ROPE, LANG LAY.

Diameter, in inches.	Area, in square inches.	Approximate weight per foot, in pounds.	Approximate strength, in tons.	Proper working load, in tons.
1 ⅛	0.4606	2.	37.	7.4
1	0.3822	1.58	31.	6.2
⅞	0.2884	1.20	24.	5.3
¾	0.2129	0.89	18.6	4.7
11/16	0.1760	0.75	15.4	3.8
⅝	0.1565	0.62	13.	3.1
9/16	0.1217	0.50	10.	2.4
½	0.0954	0.39	7.7	2.

parallel in adjoining strands, which increases the flexibility and gives a greater surface of wear. Traction ropes should be lubricated regularly if satisfactory service is to be obtained. Table 7 gives the properties of Lang lay traction ropes.

Carriers.—The ordinary carrier in general use consists of a carriage that traverses the track cable. The carriage supports a trussed hanger by means of a hanger pin, which slips into a suitable receptacle in the carriage and thus permits the oscillation required by various grades on the line. The hanger holds the bucket by its trunnions and a latch. It is also provided with the necessary parts to sustain a friction grip, which may be one of several types. The carriage, hanger, and grip should be designed in accordance with the weight of the load. Table 8 gives the weight of standard empty

TABLE 8.—SIZE AND WEIGHT OF STANDARD EMPTY CARRIERS.

Size of bucket, in cubic feet.	Weight of carrier, in pounds.	Size of bucket, in cubic feet.	Weight of carrier, in pounds.
5	315	20	560
6	330	25	640
8	370	30	700
10	435	35	775
12	455	40	830
15	480		

carriers of different volume. Self-dumping buckets and odd designs weigh more. These data are of great importance in calculating deflections, horsepower, and traction-rope tensions.

Grips.—Friction grips are divided into two classes: (1) Constant closure grips, arranged so that the movement of the jaw is fixed, as long as the adjustments remain constant; and (2) compensating grips, in which the movement of the jaw is dependent on the diameter of the rope.

Grips are further sub-divided as to style, into side-opening, top-opening, and bottom-opening, depending on whether the traction rope enters the grip from the side, top, or from below.

Constant closure grips are satisfactory because the position of the closing lever is under perfect control. They are of great utility on lines having only one section of traction rope. The compensating grips, on the other hand, should be used on multi-section lines, because traction ropes, irrespective of equal stress, do not wear so as to maintain equal diameters. The Webber grip is an example of the constant closure side-opening type, the closure of the jaws being self-locking under a positive pressure, the amount depending on the position of the adjusting screws. This is classed as an underhung grip, meaning that it is mounted on the hanger below the track cable. In traversing long spans, under conditions where the traction rope has a severe tension, underhung grips show a tendency to lift from the cable. The Bleichert grip may be either overhead or underhung and is one of the best known top-opening grips. It depends on the weight of the load acting through proper leverage on the grip jaw for its holding power. It will easily handle ropes of $\frac{3}{16}$-in. difference in diameter. The Pohlig grip is of simple design and has a bolt carrying a coarse and fine thread. The coarse thread insures rapid movement of the jaws for a limited throw of the closing lever. The finer thread acts as a differential, imposing great pressure on the rope for the final movement of the closing lever. The position of the lever, when the grip is closed, is not constant, but varies with the wear of the parts and the traction rope. It, therefore, requires constant adjustment to prevent serious accident due to the closing lever under-running the detacher. The "Wico" compensating grip is regarded by many as the best friction grip yet developed. All styles of grips for satisfactory service should develop a resistance to slipping of 1 500 lb., or more, when properly closed on the traction rope.

Buckets.—Manufacturers of tramways will supply any style of bucket desired, such as self-dumping, self-dumping and self-righting, bottom dump, etc. When buckets are not required, special receptacles are used, depending on the nature of the material to be transported.

Supports.—These may be of wood or steel and cover three classes of structures, namely, towers, rail structures, and bent supports. Towers are of two general types (*a*) those in which the track cables may be mounted without threading them through the tower; and (*b*) those with closed heads. Towers of the first type are very satisfactory for loads up to 1 500 lb. Those of the second class are battered on a slope of 10 on 1 in a direction at right angles to the center line of the tramway. Tramways are usually designed with 6, 8, or 10-ft. gauges, depending on the size of the receptacles, transition being made between 6 and 8-cu. ft. buckets for the 6-ft. gauge, and 30 to 35-cu. ft. buckets for the 8 and 10-ft. gauges, respectively. Table 9 gives the quantities of timber in both types of supports of various heights for both 6 and 8-ft. gauges.

TABLE 9.—APPROXIMATE TIMBER CONTENT OF TOWERS, IN BOARD FEET.

Type.	Height, in Feet.								
	10	12	15	18	20	22	25	30	35
Closed type, 6-ft. gauge....	685	850	970	1 080	1 190	1 280	1 370	1 640	1 790
Open type, 6-ft. gauge......	455	455	780	860	918	996	1 073	1 338	1 502
	Height, in Feet.								
	40	45	50	55	60	65	70	75	80
Closed type, 6-ft. gauge....	1 950	2 265	2 440	3 100	3 275	3 780	3 930	4 350	....
Open type, 6-ft. gauge......	1 887	2 087	2 410	2 568	2 883	3 041	3 325	3 678	3 887
	Height, in Feet.								
	10	12	15	18	20	22	25	30	35
Closed type, 8-ft. gauge....	916	1 180	1 340	1 770	1 940	2 241	2 385	3 021	3 254
Open type, 8-ft. gauge......	....	....	886	906	974	1 047	1 119	1 423	1 547
	Height, in Feet.								
	40	45	50	55	60	65	70	75	80
Closed type, 8-ft. gauge....	4 016	4 244	4 980	5 470	6 000	7 180	8 360	9 180	10 000
Open type, 8-ft. gauge......	1 967	2 098	2 458	2 572	3 002	3 143	3 410	3 765	3 989

Table 10 gives the approximate weight of steel supports, depending on the height and gauge.

TABLE 10.—MINIMUM WEIGHT OF STEEL TOWERS.*

Height, in feet.	6-ft. gauge, in pounds.	8-ft. gauge, in pounds.	Height, in feet.	6-ft. gauge, in pounds.	8-ft. gauge, in pounds.
10	1 720	2 140	35	4 850	5 140
12	1 860	2 310	40	5 400	6 030
15	2 240	2 880	45	5 900	6 620
18	2 650	3 130	50	6 600	7 860
20	3 100	3 500	55	.....	8 000
22	3 280	3 680	60	.....	9 100
25	3 550	3 900	65	.....	9 910
30	4 180	4 690	70	.....	10 400

* For permanent construction, increase these weights 50 per cent.

When the tramway survey crosses a crest or summit of such height that a vertical curve of small radius is developed, tramway engineers specify rail structures composed of successive bents that support the carriers on tramway rails overhanging the cables, and thus accommodate the required curvature. These structures relieve the track cables of the severe stresses due to bending.

When the rate of change of the vertical curve for a chord length (determined by the spacing of the bents) is sufficiently moderate so that the cable can be used for the support of the carriers, the structure is called a bent-support. It is seldom that these structures have more than four bents, and they are not as desirable as rail structures when the slight difference in cost is neglected.

Tension Structures.—On tramway lines exceeding 1 mile in length, it is frequently necessary to use tension structures for the purpose of supporting weight-boxes which are connected to the track cables. This obviates the necessity of attempting to maintain a uniform tension in a cable passing over a great number of tower saddles. Tension structures are equipped with tramway rails so that the carriers pass from one section of cable to the next without difficulty. The traction rope is continuous and is supported by rollers. If the cables of one section are anchored and the other section is controlled by weights, the structure is known as an anchorage and tension structure. There are also double anchorage and double tension structures, depending on whether the four cables are anchored or weighted.

Guard Nets and Bridges.—In crossing public highways or railroads, it is sometimes necessary to provide protection against the premature discharge of the bucket, or its derailment. Such guards may be steel structures or suspended nets. Accidents, however, are of very rare occurrence, and unless the traffic is considerable, guard nets are installed for safety. Most railroads require an overhead clearance to the under side of the guard screens of more than 22 ft. Fig. 7 illustrates the use of guard screens.

Terminals.—This is the name given to the stations at the ends of the tramway. They are designed and equipped so as to make the operation of the tramway as nearly automatic as possible. On lines of ordinary length, the loading and discharge terminals only are required. In the former, the buckets are loaded (see Fig. 8), and, in the latter, they are discharged. Hence, the names, loading and discharge terminals.

Lines of considerable length, and especially those having a great difference in elevation between the loading and discharge terminals, must be divided into sections so as to relieve the stress in the traction rope. This requires the use of intermediate control stations. Also, if angles are desired, they may be installed at intermediate control stations or by the use of angle towers. The judicious utilization of angle towers frees the designer of aerial tramways from the limitation that they must be built in straight lines between stations.

The terminals are equipped with rails so that the carriers may run freely to the loading and discharging points. In these stations are located the

Fig. 7.—T-Rails Used for Guard-Screen Floor.

Fig. 8.—Loading Terminal for Mine Waste at Tipple.

attachers and detachers, which automatically close and release the levers of the carrier grips.

When the velocity of the traction rope is 500 ft. per min., or more, angle stations are not desirable. However, when the velocity of the line is 400 ft. per min., or less, angle stations with continuous traction ropes may be used, and the direction of the carrier is changed by passing it around guide sheaves of large diameter. In this case, the carriers are frequently equipped with grips of the overhead type, designed so that the jaws will pass freely between the traction rope and the sheave, irrespective of the direction of travel of the carriers. In properly designed angle stations underhung grips may be used and the large diameter deflecting sheaves omitted.

Bins.—As usually installed, aerial tramways load from, and discharge into, bins. Storage facilities at the loading and discharge terminals permit freedom in operation, for production delays do not immediately stop the tramway; and, similarly, the tramway delays do not stop the operation of the plant. As bins of large capacity are built of a number of cells, Table 11 will be found of service in estimating the dimensions of square cross-section bins with bottoms sloping 45 degrees. These dimensions are computed so as to give a maximum volume with a minimum surface for the style of bin shown. The volume is stated in cubic feet and also in tons for material weighing 100 lb. per cu. ft. The dimensions apply to the inside of the bin and the framing should be arranged accordingly.

TABLE 11.

Volume, in cubic feet.	Capacity, in tons at 100 lb. per cu. ft.	Sides of square cross-section, in feet.	Center depth, in feet.	Depth of front face of bin, in feet.	Depth of back face of bin, in feet.
100	5	5.21	3.67	6.28	1.06
200	10	6.57	4.63	7.92	1.34
300	15	7.51	5.29	9.04	1.54
400	20	8.29	5.84	9.99	1.69
500	25	8.92	6.27	10.73	1.81
600	30	9.49	6.67	11.42	1.92
800	40	10.41	7.34	12.55	2.13
1 000	50	11.24	7.92	13.54	2.30
1 500	75	12.86	9.07	15.50	2.64
2 000	100	14.16	9.97	17.05	2.89

Controllers.—Tramways having considerable difference in elevation between the loading and discharge terminals, operate by gravity, and, if not controlled, tend to accelerate until the line is wrecked by "running away". Such installations are equipped with efficient differential hand-brakes and with sentinel brakes. The sentinel brake consists of revolving cone-shaped vanes attached to hinged arms so that the radius of the path of travel changes, and hence the power absorbed varies with the cube of the speed. The sentinel brake is easily adapted to absorbing from 10 to 100 h.p. Properly selected multi-vane fans may be used, also, for tramway control.

It was formerly the custom to use hydraulic controllers, which were designed on the principle of the cycloidal pump. A valve was provided, which controlled the discharge pressure of the fluid and thus varied the resistance of the regulator. Owing to the excessive wear of the moving parts of this device, the high fluid pressure, and the danger of freezing in cold weather, it has been generally abandoned.

Tramways have been designed wherein the buckets served both as bodies of mine cars and receptacles for the aerial tramway, the transfer being effected in the loading terminal by suitable mechanism. This arrangement is not altogether desirable, for the reason that aerial tramways and mine haulages are decidedly different in principles of operation, and the class of equipment which is ideally adapted for use as mine cars is not completely satisfactory for tramway buckets.

Tramways are often equipped with elevators for raising and lowering either the empty or loaded carriers from one level to another. This usually happens when the returning carriers are loaded with back freight, which is discharged on the upper floor commanding a warehouse, and the buckets are then dropped to the lower floor, which is convenient to the loading bin.

Scales should be located in a section of the tramway rail, so that the weight of every carrier can be ascertained. These scales are equipped with type-registering beams or plain beams as required. Counters may also be installed so that the exact number of carriers passing a given point can be ascertained at any time.

Speed-indicating alarms show the velocity of the tramway at any instant. Should it exceed the predetermined speed by 5%, an electric gong sounds, which calls the operator's attention to this dangerous condition, and he may apply the brakes before disaster occurs. Special gongs are used to sound a signal for dispatching the carriers, thus insuring their uniform spacing. Electrical dispatching and loading control systems that are available reduce the toil of terminal labor to a minimum.

Reverse preventers, installed on the driving machinery of tramways, would reverse their direction due to the action of gravity on the loaded buckets. This condition always exists when the discharge terminal is at a higher elevation than the loading terminal.

Solenoid brakes have been proposed for use on aerial tramways that are motor-controlled. Alternating current is usually available, especially in the mining district. Induction motors, therefore, are used to drive or brake the tramway. Such motors "run away" when the power circuit is interrupted. The solenoid brakes operate when the circuit is broken. However, care must be utilized in choosing the size of brake so as to prevent wrecking the line due to its sudden stoppage. The speed of tramways having electrical drives is most conveniently varied by the use of drum controllers, resistance grids, and slip-ring type of motors; 50% speed regulation is easily obtained by this method.

Chutes.—A great variety of gates are used to control the flow of material from the loading bins to the tramway buckets.

Tramway Profile.—The tramway profile should be made by a competent surveyor and should have an accuracy of at least 1 to 1 500. The profile should show the topography 25 ft. each side of the center line joining the loading and discharge terminals, and the plan should show all the control points at the loading and discharge terminals. Particular detail should be given of railroad tracks, intervening structures, the shaft, or adit, as the case may be. The topography on 2-ft. contours should be given of the sites of the loading and discharge terminals, as well as of the intermediate structures. The slope of the ground surface at right angles to the line should be indicated in degrees. It is always understood that the initial station of a tramway survey is located at the loading terminal. Accordingly, slopes may be indicated to the right or left of the line without confusion.

In crossing summits the elevations should be carefully noted, for the reason that the tramway will probably require a rail structure at such points. In crossing valleys where the depth is greater than one-tenth the span, it is not necessary to carry the line to the bottom, but it should be carried well down the slopes. This is particularly true for the ends of spans which have different elevations. If the length of the line is in excess of 5 000 ft., it should be plotted 100 ft. to the inch, the horizontal distances and elevations being drawn to the same scale. On shorter lines, a scale of 40 ft. to the inch is preferable. However, profiles when analyzed mathematically may be drawn to convenient scales, as 1 in. = 500 ft. horizontally, with 1 in = 200 ft. vertically.

Stadia surveys, carefully made, are satisfactory, but the accuracy of the work is put to the final test when the track cables are stretched from terminal to terminal like a giant tape measure. Errors in elevations appear when the cable fails to rest properly on the saddles of the supports. The position of track cables when empty and loaded can be computed with such accuracy that it is not necessary to raise or lower the towers except when errors exist in the survey. The tramway designer sometimes adds to the purchaser's expense the cost of shifting supports, because of negligence or unwillingness to analyze accurately the characteristics of the cables at the point of support and thus determine the proper elevation of the saddles so as to develop proper cable pressures.

The profile should also state the horizontal length of the proposed line; the difference in elevation of the terminal points; the capacity of the tramway, in tons per hour; the weight of the material per cubic foot when broken to the size that will be delivered to the buckets; and the nature and location of the power; also, all railroad crossings, power lines, roads, buildings, snow, grazing or cultivation clearances, or other obstacles, which the tramway must cross. The minimum clearance between the ridge of a building and the track cable is 10 ft. Most railroad companies specify a minimum clearance of 22 ft. between the bottom of the tramway bucket and the top of rail.

These points should be well considered by the engineer who makes the survey. If the work is carefully done, it is not necessary to supply the tramway manufacturer with field notes other than the data shown on the profile. The elevations and station numbers should be carefully noted.

Tables 12 and 13 are given as aids in approximating the size and timber content of the several structures used on tramways. They show the name of the station, its volume, in cubic feet, the number of feet board measure, the ratio of board feet per unit volume, and the length, width, height, and capacity.

TABLE 12.—TIMBER CONTENTS OF TRAMWAY STRUCTURES.

Name.	Volume, in cubic feet.	Feet board measure.	Feet board measure, volume.	Length, in feet.	Width, in feet,	Height, in feet.	Tons per hour.	Average of
Loading terminal.....	18 260	15 000	0.85	67	22	15	37.5	24
Discharge terminal ...	50 500	25 500	0.61	62	24	35	40	24
Anchorage and tension structure.......	13 900	13 500	1.00	40	14	26	21	11
Anchorage, tension and curve rail.......	23 400	19 400	0.83	75	14	24	20	5
Curve rail structure..	15 250	12 075	0.96	53	14	20	22	19
Rail structure.........	13 450	10 830	0.92	20	14	45	20	6
5-bent structures......	9 785	6 210	0.63	35	14	20	52	2
4-bent structures......	5 975	3 695	0.64	30	14	14	103	5
Double-tension structure................	23 500	19 850	0.86	51	16	28	135	2
SINGLE AND DOUBLE REVERSIBLES.								
Loading terminal.....	3 670	10 350	6.15	17	11	14.7	15	4
Tail tower............	8 790	7 450	1.01	18	16	34	15	5

Cost of Erection.—Most tramway manufacturers supply the metal parts of the tramway in accordance with the usual terms of a material contract. The customer undertakes the erection and operation of the line, and he, therefore, finds it convenient to estimate the cost of erecting and installing the tramway. Tables 14 and 15 will be of service in this regard. It will be noted that the timber required is about 20% of the cost of the installation. Tables 9 and 12 indicate the timber contents of towers and stations, from which data the cost of the installation can be approximated.

TABLE 13.—AVERAGE WEIGHTS OF STEEL TRAMWAY STRUCTURES.

Name.	Volume, in cubic feet.	Length, in feet.	Width, in feet.	Height, in feet.	Weight, in pounds.	Weight, in cubic feet per pound.
Loading terminal............	18 260	67	22	15	37 000	2
2-bent structures............	10 860	16	16	40	17 000	1.6
Double anchorage and curve rail..........................	25 900	68	16	26	67 000	2.5
Anchor and tension...........	19 650	45	16	25	63 000	3.2
Curve rail....................	20 000	40	16	34	57 000	2.8
3-bent support	13 300	32	16	26	25 000	1.9
Double anchorage..............	12 200	35	16	22	37 000	3.0
Discharge terminal	50 500	62	24	35	111 000	2.0
Control station...............	51 000	113	25	18	162 000	3.2

TABLE 14.—Cost Data, Erection of Tramways.*

(Based on 30-ton line; 10 400 ft. long, with $\frac{7}{8}$-in. and $1\frac{1}{4}$-in. cables, and timber supports.)

Item.	Percentage.
Right of way	3.28
Trails, roads, and bridges	0.88
Excavations	3.31
Making forms	0.67
Setting forms, including engineering charges	5.44
Concreting	12.30
Back-filling	0.67
Distributing materials	11.10
Housing and roofing	8.10
Placing and assembling rolling stock	0.60
Stringing traction rope	1.88
" track cable	2.32
Placing cables in saddles	0.30
" " under tension	1.02
Framing towers	5.36
Erecting towers	5.43
Placing iron on towers	2.23
Framing loading terminal	1.68
Erecting loading terminal	1.90
Iron on loading terminal	1.95
Framing anchorage tower	1.61
Erecting anchorage tower	1.92
Iron on anchorage tower	0.71
Framing discharge terminal	1.96
Erecting discharge terminal	3.05
Iron on discharge terminal	1.15
Timber	19.70

* Installation charge equals 90% of cost of metal parts.

TABLE 15.—Labor and Cost of Operating Bleichert Tramways per Ton.

Capacity, in tons per hour.	Load terminal.	Discharge terminal.	Line rider and other help.	Total number of men.	Hourly wages @ \$2.50 per day and 1 man @ \$5.00, for 10 hours.	Cost of labor per ton	Cost of supplies and renewals.	Cost of repairs.	Miscellaneous costs.	Total cost per ton.
10	1	1	..	2	\$1.30	\$0.13	\$0.0235	\$0.0447	\$0.0200	\$0.2182
25	1	1	1	3	1.80	0.072	0.0140	0.0260	0.0100	0.1220
40	2	1	1	4	2.30	0.0575	0.0120	0.0200	0.0080	0.0975
60	2	2	1	5	2.80	0.0467	0.0080	0.0160	0.0060	0.0767
75	3	2	1	6	3.30	0.0440	0.0075	0.0140	0.0058	0.0713
100	3	3	1	7	3.80	0.0380	0.0072	0.0134	0.0052	0.0638
150	4	3	1	8	4.30	0.0287	0.0054	0.0098	0.0040	0.0479
200	5	3	1	9	4.80	0.0240	0.0042	0.0078	0.0032	0.0392
250	5	4	1	10	5.30	0.0212	0.0040	0.0072	0.0028	0.0352

Formulas Used in Designing Cable Structures

Notation.—The following list of symbols has been used by the writer:

a = carrier spacing.

A = area of cross-section of cable.

$$b = \frac{n(n-1)}{2}$$

B = distance between points of tangency of carriage wheels on cable.

$c = \frac{p\,(p-1)}{2}$

d = ratio of distance from support to first carrier to span $= \frac{m}{s} = d$.

e = base of natural system of logarithms.
E = modulus of elasticity.
f = coefficient of friction.
F = amount of friction in terminals.
g = weight of empty carrier.
G = weight of empty carrier plus load plus weight of traction rope of length, a.
h = difference in height of span supports.

J = change in length of cable for a unit load $= \frac{L}{A\,E}$.

l = length of cable in empty span.
L = length of cable in loaded span.
m = distance from support to first carrier.
n = total number of loads on span.
P = net load of the carrier.
p = number of loads to left of Point $x\ y$.
Q = capacity of tramway, in tons per hour.

q = ratio of carrier spacing to span $= \frac{a}{s} = q$.

R = radius of curvature.

r = ratio of distance to Point $x\ y$ to span $= \frac{x}{s} = r$.

s = horizontal length of span.
t = horizontal component of cable tension (empty spans).
T = horizontal component of cable tension (loaded spans).
tr = Traction rope tension, empty bucket side.
Tr = Traction rope tension, loaded bucket side.
v = velocity of traction rope, in units per minute.
w = weight of cable per unit of length.
W = weight of weight-box.
x = horizontal distance from Y-axis to point under investigation.
y = distance from X-axis to point under investigation.
α = angle of slope from horizontal of chord joining supports of span.
β = angle of tangent from horizontal to curve at any point.

λ = elongation for cable for length and load $= \lambda = \frac{T\,L}{A\,E}$.

δ = time-spacing of carriers.
Δ = angle formed by intersecting tangents.
θ = angle of slope of tramway sections.
ϕ = angular change from end to end of catenary corresponds to Δ of parabolic formulas.

Using this notation, a number of formulas will be given, which will be found most useful in designing cable structures.

Empty Horizontal Span.—For a catenary with the origin at the left support (Fig. 9):

$$y = \frac{t}{w}\left[\sinh\frac{w\,x}{t}\sinh\frac{w\,s}{2\,t} - \cosh\frac{w\,s}{2\,t}\left(\cosh\frac{w\,x}{t} - 1\right)\right] \ldots\ldots (1)$$

For deflection at center of span:

$$y = \frac{t}{w}\left(\cosh \frac{w\,s}{2\,t} - 1\right) \ldots\ldots\ldots\ldots\ldots\ldots\ldots (2)$$

Example.—Let $s = 1\,000$ ft.; $t = 10\,000$ lb.; $w = 3.6$ ft-lb.; and $x = 500$ ft.; $y = ?$

$$\frac{t}{w} = 2\,777.7778;\ \cosh \frac{w\,s}{2\,t} = 1.0162$$

$$y = 2\,777.7778 \times 1.0162 = 2\,822.7778 - 2\,777.7778 = 45.0 \text{ ft.}$$

Inclined Span.—Use plus (+) for down, and minus (—) for up, slopes:

$$y = \frac{t}{w}\left[\sinh \frac{w\,x}{t} \sinh \frac{w\,s}{2\,t} - \cosh \frac{w\,s}{2\,t}\left(\cosh \frac{w\,x}{t} - 1\right)\right] \sec \alpha \pm x \tan \alpha. (3)$$

Example.—As in Equation (2), with $\tan \alpha = 0.1$; $\sec \alpha = 1.005$:

$$y = 45 \times 1.005 = 45.225$$
$$500 \times 0.1 = 50.000$$
$$95.225 \text{ ft.}$$

Tangent.—

$$\frac{d\,y}{d\,x} = \left(\cosh \frac{w\,x}{t} \sinh \frac{w\,s}{2\,t} - \cosh \frac{w\,s}{2\,t} \sinh \frac{w\,x}{t}\right) \sec \alpha \pm \tan \alpha \ldots (4)$$

Example.—$\tan \beta = ?$ in Equation (3).

At left support:

$$\tan \beta = \left(\sinh \frac{w\,s}{2\,t}\right) \sec \alpha \pm \tan \alpha \ldots\ldots\ldots\ldots\ldots\ldots (5)$$

$$\sinh \frac{3.6 \times 1\,000}{20\,000} \sinh 0.18 = 0.1810$$

$$0.181 \sec \alpha = 0.181 \times 1.005 = 0.1819$$

$$0.1819 + \tan \alpha = 0.2819 = 15° \, 44' \text{ below horizontal.}$$

At right support:

$$0.1819 - 0.1 = 0.0819 = 4° \, 41' \text{ below horizontal.}$$

Length of Span.—

$$l = \frac{t}{w} \tan \phi \ldots\ldots\ldots\ldots\ldots\ldots\ldots\ldots (6)$$

in which, $\tan \phi$ = angular change, end to end of span.

Example.—In Equation (6), $\tan \phi = 0.2819 + 0.0819$, or 2×0.1819:

$$l = 2\,777.78 \times 0.3638 = 1\,010.556 \text{ ft.}$$

If

$$l = \frac{t}{w} \tan \phi = \frac{2\,t}{w}\left(\sinh \frac{w\,s}{2\,t}\right)$$

$\sec \alpha$ is written with the expansion of $\sinh \frac{w\,s}{2\,t}$, then,

$$l = s + \frac{w^2\,s^3}{24\,t^2} \sec \alpha \ldots\ldots\ldots\ldots\ldots\ldots\ldots (7)$$

$$l = 1\,000.00 + (5.40 \times 1.005) = 1\,010.427 \text{ ft.}$$

This compares with the parabolic formula,

$$l = s + \frac{w^2 s^3}{24 t^2} + \frac{h^2}{2 s} \quad \ldots\ldots\ldots\ldots\ldots\ldots\ldots\ldots (8)$$

$$\begin{aligned} s \quad + &= 1\,000.00 \\ \frac{w^2 s^3}{24 t^2} + &= \quad 5.40 \\ \frac{h^2}{2 s} \quad &= \quad 5.00 \\ l \quad &= 1\,010.40 \text{ ft.} \end{aligned}$$

Simple Spans (Parabola).—Caution: If $\alpha >$ than 6°, multiply the right-hand side of the equation by sec α.

The deflection at any point of a simple inclined span (see Fig. 9):

$$y = \frac{w\,x}{2\,t}(s - x) \pm x \tan \alpha \quad \ldots\ldots\ldots\ldots\ldots\ldots\ldots\ldots (9)$$

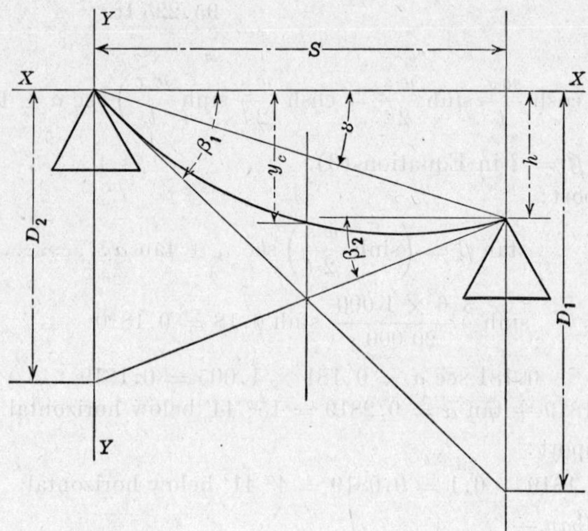

FIG. 9.—DEFLECTION OF ANY POINT OF A SINGLE INCLINED SPAN.

With the origin at either support, plus (+) indicates down slopes and minus (—), up slopes.

Example.—Let s = 1 000 ft.; w = 3.6 lb.; t = 10 000 lb.; h = 100 ft.; and x = 500 ft.

$$y = \frac{3.6 \times 500}{20\,000}(1\,000 - 500) + 500 \times \frac{100}{1\,000} = 45 + 50 = 95 \text{ ft.}$$

below the left-hand support.

Level Spans.—If the span is level, h = 0, and,

$$y = \frac{w\,x}{2\,t}(s - x) \quad \ldots\ldots\ldots\ldots\ldots\ldots\ldots\ldots (10)$$

or 45 ft. in the previous example.

Note that with a center deflection of $\frac{1}{22.2}$ of the span, the catenary (Equation (2)) and parabola equations still give equal values.

Center of Span.—If $x = \frac{s}{2}$, then,

$$y = \frac{w\ s^2}{8\ t} \pm \frac{h}{2}$$

Note that $\frac{w\ s^2}{8\ t}$ is the vertical distance below the chord, and $\frac{h}{2}$ is the distance between the chord and the x-axis through the support.

If w equals the weight of a foot of cable, 1 sq. in. in cross-section, t equals pounds per square inch, and s equals hundreds of feet, then these simple equations for center deflection of empty spans result. (See Table 16.)

TABLE 16.—CENTER DEFLECTION OF EMPTY SPANS.

t, in pounds per square inch.	Deflection at center of span.	Example. 1 000-ft. span with 100-ft. difference in terminal elevation.
10 000	$y = 0.45s^2 + \frac{h}{2}$	$y\ c = 0.45 \times 10^2 + 50 = 95$ ft.
20 000	$y = 0.225s^2 + \frac{h}{2}$	$y\ c = 0.225 \times 10^2 + 50 = 72.5$ ft.
30 000	$y = 0.15s^2 + \frac{h}{2}$	$y\ c = 0.15 \times 10^2 + 50 = 65.0$ ft.
40 000	$y = 0.1125s^2 + \frac{h}{2}$	$y\ c = 0.1125 \times 10^2 + 50 = 61.25$ ft.
50 000	$y = 0.09s^2 + \frac{h}{2}$	$y\ c = 0.09 \times 10^2 + 50 = 59.0$ ft.

Deflection Formulas for Plotting Curve of Empty Cable.—If $y = \frac{w\ x}{2\ t}(s - x) + x \tan\alpha$ be stated as,

$$y - \frac{w\ s^2}{2\ t}\ r\ (l - r) + r\ h \ldots\ldots\ldots\ldots\ldots\ldots\ldots (11)$$

formulas of the type of Equation (11) may be written for different points along the span, as in Table 17.

Any other tension in pounds per square inch can be used by (inverse) proportion.

Example.—If $t = 10\,000$ lb. per sq. in.; $s = 1\,000$; $x = 300$; $y = ?$ In Table 17, at $x = 0.30$,

$$y = 9.45 + r\ h$$

The inverse ratio of tensions $= \frac{40\ 000}{10\ 000} = 4$; therefore, at 10 000,

$$y = 4 \times 9.45 = 37.80 + r\ h$$

Tangent of Simple Spans.—(See Fig. 9):

$$\tan\beta = \frac{d\ y}{d\ x} = \frac{w}{t}\left(\frac{s}{2} - x\right) \pm \tan\alpha$$

TABLE 17.—CURVE OF EMPTY CABLE.

(Deflections with $t = 40\,000$ lb. per sq. in.; $y = 0.45s^2r\ (l - r)$; s given in hundreds of feet.)

$\frac{x}{s} = r.$	y at $t = 40\,000$ lb. per sq. in.	$\frac{x}{s} = r.$	y at $t = 40\,000$ lb. per sq. in.
0.02, or 0.98	0.00882 $s^2 + r\,h$	0.26, or 0.74	0.08658 $s^2 + r\,h$
0.04, or 0.96	0.01728 $s^2 + r\,h$	0.28, or 0.72	0.09072 $s^2 + r\,h$
0.05, or 0.95	0.021375 $s^2 + r\,h$	0.30, or 0.70	0.09450 $s^2 + r\,h$
0.06, or 0.94	0.02538 $s^2 + r\,h$	0.32, or 0.68	0.09792 $s^2 + r\,h$
0.08, or 0.92	0.03312 $s^2 + r\,h$	0.34, or 0.66	0.10098 $s^2 + r\,h$
0.10, or 0.90	0.0405 $s^2 + r\,h$	0.35, or 0.65	0.102375 $s^2 + r\,h$
0.12, or 0.88	0.04752 $s^2 + r\,h$	0.36, or 0.64	0.10368 $s^2 + r\,h$
0.14, or 0.86	0.05418 $s^2 + r\,h$	0.38, or 0.62	0.10602 $s^2 + r\,h$
0.15, or 0.85	0.057375 $s^2 + r\,h$	0.40, or 0.60	0.10800 $s^2 + r\,h$
0.16, or 0.84	0.06048 $s^2 + r\,h$	0.42, or 0.58	0.10962 $s^2 + r\,h$
0.18, or 0.82	0.06642 $s^2 + r\,h$	0.44, or 0.56	0.11088 $s^2 + r\,h$
0.20, or 0.80	0.07200 $s^2 + r\,h$	0.45, or 0.55	0.111375 $s^2 + r\,h$
0.22, or 0.78	0.07722 $s^2 + r\,h$	0.46, or 0.54	0.11178 $s^2 + r\,h$
0.24, or 0.76	0.08208 $s^2 + r\,h$	0.48, or 0.52	0.11232 $s^2 + r\,h$
0.25, or 0.75	0.084375 $s^2 + r\,h$	0.50, or 0.50	0.11250 $s^2 + r\,h$

Example.—If $s = 1\,000$ ft.; $t = 40\,000$ lb.; $w = 3.6$ lb.; $\tan\alpha = 0.1$; $x = 300$ ft.; $\tan\beta = ?$

$\tan\beta = 0.00009 \times 200 + 0.1 = 0.1180$; $\beta = 6°\ 44'$ below horizontal axis

Tangent at Supports.—Left, $x = 0$; right, $x = s$:

Left:

$$\tan\beta_1 = \frac{w\,s}{2\,t} \pm \tan\alpha\ (+ \text{ when } \alpha \text{ is below horizontal axis})$$

Example.—If $s = 1\,000$; $t = 40\,000$ lb.; $w = 3.6$ lb.; $\tan\alpha = 0.1$:

$\tan\beta_1 = 0.00009 \times 500 + 0.1 = 0.1450$; $\beta_1 = 8°\ 15'$ below horizontal axis

Right:

$$\tan\beta_2 = \frac{w\,s}{2\,t} \pm \tan\alpha\ (+ \text{ when } \alpha \text{ is above horizontal axis})$$

Example.—As before:

$\tan\beta_2 = -\ 0.00009 \times 500 + 0.1 = 0.055 = 3°\ 09'$ above horizontal axis

The tangent formula is of a type that is easily adapted to any span; thus, if $t = 40\,000$ lb. per sq. in., $w = 3.6$ lb., and s is in feet, there results:

$$\frac{w\,s}{2\,t} \pm \tan\alpha = 0.000045\ s \pm \tan\alpha$$

TABLE 18.—VALUES OF 0.000045 s FOR TENS OF FEET.

Span, in feet.	10	20	30	40	50	60	70	80	90
$\frac{w\,s}{2\,t}$	0.00045	0.00090	0.00135	0.0018	0.00225	0.0027	0.00315	0.0036	0.00405

A table, such as Table 18, may be used, by addition, for finding the tangent at the support of any simple span. Thus, let s = 545 ft.; t = 40 000 lb. per sq. in.; and $\tan \alpha = 0.1$:

$\tan \beta_1 = 0.0225$

0.0018 = 0.0245 + 0.1 = 0.1245; $\beta_1 = 7° 06'$ below the horizontal axis

0.0002

If t was 20 000 lb. per sq. in., then,

$$\beta_1 = \frac{40\ 000}{20\ 000} \times 0.0245 + 0.1 = 0.149;\ \beta_1 = 8° 29'$$

Maximum Span for Limiting Value of $\tan \beta_1$.—As it is often found advisable to limit the angle over the supports of a span, the length of such a span may be found by a reverse process. Thus, let $\tan \beta = 0.25$ and t = 40 000 lb. per sq. in. Taking from Table 18, the successive spans corresponding to the nearest smaller values of $\frac{w\,s}{2\,t}$, the total horizontal span may be found as follows:

For $\frac{w\,s}{2\,t} = 0.225$, span = 5 000 ft.

For $\frac{w\,s}{2\,t} = 0.0225$, span = 500 ft.

For $\frac{w\,s}{2\,t} = 0.00225$, span = 50 ft.

For $\frac{w\,s}{2\,t} = 0.000225$, span = 5 ft.

For $\frac{w\,s}{2\,t} = 0.249975$, span = 5 555 ft.

By the formula, for the horizontal axis,

$$s = \tan \beta_1 \times \frac{2\,t}{w} \quad \text{(12)}$$

$$= 0.25 \times 22\ 222.22 = 5\ 555.5 \text{ ft.}$$

By the formula, for the inclined axis,

$$s = \frac{t}{w} \tan \beta_1 \pm \frac{1}{w} \sqrt{t^2 \tan^2 \beta_1 - 2\,w\,h\,t} \quad \text{(13)}$$

Example.—In these data, let h = 100 ft.; then,

$$s = 0.25 \times 11\ 111.11 + 0.2778 \sqrt{100\ 000\ 000 - 28\ 800\ 000}$$

$$= 2\ 778 + 2\ 344 = 5\ 122 \text{ ft.}$$

This may be proven by correcting the value of $\tan \beta_1$ by $\tan \alpha_1$ and solving as a horizontal span. Thus, as before,

$$\tan \alpha = \frac{100}{5\ 122} = 0.0195$$

$$\tan \beta_1 = 0.25 - 0.0195 = 0.2305$$

$$s = 0.2305 \times 22\,222.22 = 5\,122$$

Lowest Point of a Simple Span.—(See Fig. 9):

If $\tan \beta = 0$,

$$x = \frac{s}{2} + \frac{t}{w} \tan \alpha \qquad (14)$$

If $\tan \beta = \tan \alpha$,

$$x = \frac{s}{2} \qquad (15)$$

Example.—If $s = 1\,000$; $w = 3.6$; $t = 40\,000$ lb.; and $\tan \alpha = 0.0100$; how far from the left support is the lowest point of the cable?

$$x = 500 + 111.11 = 611.11 \text{ ft.}$$

If the ground surface is level, the minimum clearance will be found at this point. If x is greater than the span, the right-hand support is the lowest point.

Rate of Curvature.—

$$\frac{d^2 y}{d x^2} = -\frac{w}{t} \qquad (16)$$

If, $w = 3.6$ lb. and $t = 40\,000$ lb.,

$$\frac{w}{t} = 0.00009 = \text{tan of angle per foot of span}$$

For 100 ft., $0.009 = 0° \, 31'$ as the total angular change for a 100-ft. span. If horizontal, this angle is equally divided between β_1 and β_2; that is, the slope of the tangent at the left support is altered 15.5′ for every 100 ft. of span for a cable, $w = 3.6$ lb. and $t = 40\,000$ lb. This permits computing the value of β_1 by direct multiplication. Thus, a 1 000-ft. span $= 10 \times 15.5' = 2° \, 35' = \beta_1$, if $t = 40\,000$ lb., or $10 \times 20.7' = 3° \, 27' = \beta_1$, if $t = 30\,000$ lb.

The Tangent Intercept.—Simple Spans.—(See Fig. 9):

$$D_1 = s \times \tan \beta_1 = \frac{w s^2}{2 t} + h \qquad (17)$$

But, $\frac{w s^2}{2 t} = 4 \times$ the deflection of the center of a horizontal span.

Example.—If $s = 1\,000$ ft.; $t = 40\,000$ lb. per sq. ft.; $h = 100$ ft.; $D_1 = ?$ From Table 16 (deflections at 40 000 lb. per sq. ft.),

$$yc = (11.25 \times 4) + 100 = D_1$$

$$D_2 = h + s \tan \beta_2 = h + s \left(\frac{w s}{2 t} - \tan \alpha \right) = \frac{w s^2}{2 t} \qquad (18)$$

Point of Intersection.—The equations of Line (1) and Line (2) (Fig. 9) may be written:

$$y = x \left(\frac{w s}{2 t} + \tan \alpha \right) \qquad (19)$$

$$y = + \frac{w s^2}{2 t} - x \left(\frac{w s}{2 t} - \tan \alpha \right) \qquad (20)$$

Subtracting Equation (20) from Equation (19),

$$0 = \frac{w\,s\,x}{2\,t} + x \tan \alpha - \frac{w\,s^2}{2\,t} + \frac{w\,s\,x}{2\,t} - x \tan \alpha \qquad (21)$$

or,

$$\frac{2\,w\,s\,x}{2\,t} = \frac{w\,s^2}{2\,t};\; x = \frac{s}{2} \qquad (22)$$

Therefore, the tangent rays always intersect $x = \frac{s}{2}$.

The distance below the left support is,

$$\frac{s}{2} \tan \beta_1 = \frac{s}{2}\left(\frac{w\,s}{2\,t} + \tan \alpha\right) = \frac{w\,s^2}{4\,t} + \frac{h}{2} \qquad (23)$$

Note that $\frac{w\,s^2}{4\,t}$ equals twice the center deflection of a horizontal span. Since the point of intersection and the tangent intercepts are so readily determined, the tangents to the curve at its supports are easily drawn or computed.

Radius of Curvature.—The well-known formula for radius of curvature is,

$$R = \frac{\left[1 + \left(\frac{d\,y}{d\,x}\right)^2\right]^{\frac{3}{2}}}{\frac{d^2\,y}{d\,x^2}} \qquad (24)$$

For a horizontal span, with $x = \frac{s}{2}$ and $\frac{d\,y}{d\,x} = 0$,

$$R = \frac{1}{-\frac{w}{t}} = -\frac{t}{w} \qquad (25)$$

This permits the use of circular arcs to represent cable curves. Thus, let the profile be plotted on a scale of 1 in. = 100 ft., what radius curve should be used for a cable, w = 3.6 lb. and t = 40 000 lb.?

$$R = -\frac{t}{w} = 11\,111.11 \text{ ft.}$$

But 1 in. = 100 ft. Therefore, the proper curve is R = 111.1 in., if t = 30 000 lb.; $\frac{t}{w}$ = 8 333.3 ft.; and R = 83.33 in.

Length of Simple Spans.—(See Fig. 9):

$$l = s + \frac{w^2\,s^3}{24\,t^2} + \frac{h^2}{2\,s} \qquad (26)$$

Example.—If s = 1 000 ft.; w = 3.6 lb.; h = 100 ft.; and t = 40 000 lb.; l = ?

$$s = 1\,000 \text{ ft.}$$

$$\frac{w^2\,s^3}{24\,t^2} = 0.338$$

$$\frac{h^2}{2\,s} = 5.00$$

Then,

$$l = 1\,005.338$$

Carrier Spacing, in Feet.—

Given P = the net load of a carrier.

Q = capacity, in tons.

V = velocity, in feet per minute.

$$a = \frac{0.03\ P\ V}{Q} \qquad (27)$$

Carrier Spacing, in Seconds.—

$$\phi = \frac{a}{V}\ 60 = \frac{1.8\ P}{Q} \qquad (28)$$

Example.—$P = 1\ 000$ lb.; $Q = 20$ tons per hour; and $V = 500$ ft. per min.:

$$a = \frac{15 \times 1\ 000}{20} = 750 \text{ ft.}$$

$$\phi = \frac{1.8 \times 1\ 000}{20} = 90 \text{ sec.}$$

Cable Spans Supporting Carriers.—Span Carrying a Single Load.—Note that a cable supporting loads does not present a continuous curve, but rather $(n + 1)$ parabolas which intersect with an angle, $\Delta = \tan^{-1} \frac{G}{t}$, beneath each load. (See Fig. 10.) The curve of the path of any load is continuous and may be treated accordingly.

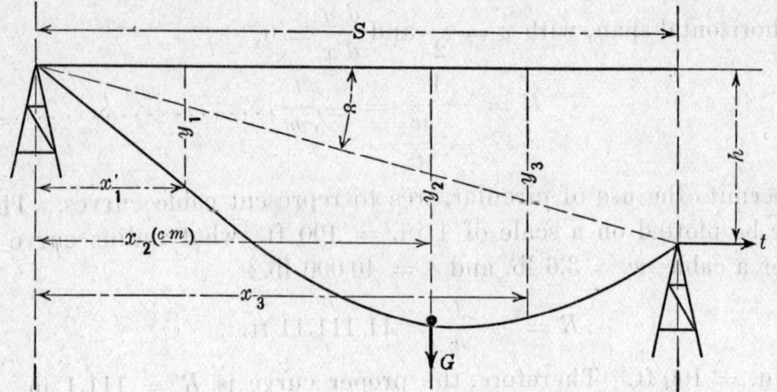

FIG. 10.—SPAN CARRYING A SINGLE LOAD.

Case I.—$m > x < s$ = equation of parabola adjoining left support:

$$y_1 = \frac{G\ (s - m)\ x_1}{s\ t} + \frac{w\ x_1}{2\ t}\ (s - x_1) + x_1 \tan \alpha \qquad (29)$$

Case II.—$m = x < s$ = equation for path of load:

$$y_2 = \frac{G\ x_2\ (s - x_2)}{s\ t} + \frac{w\ x_2\ (s - x_2)}{2\ t} + x_2 \tan \alpha \qquad (30)$$

Case III.—$m < x < s$ = equation of parabola adjoining right support:

$$y_3 = \frac{G\ m\ (s - x_3)}{s\ t} + \frac{w\ x_3\ (s - x_3)}{2\ t} + x_3 \tan \alpha \qquad (31)$$

When $x = m = \frac{s}{2}$, Equations (29), (30), and (31) become,

$$y = \frac{G\ s}{4\ t} + \frac{w\ s^2}{8\ t} + \frac{h}{2} \qquad (32)$$

Example.—Let $s = 1\,000$ ft.; $m = 500$ ft.; $x_1 = 200$ ft.; $x_2 = 500$ ft.; $x_3 = 800$ ft.; $t = 75\,000$ lb.; $w = 10$ lb. per ft.; $h = 100$ ft.; and $G = 10\,000$ lb.; y_1, y_2, and $y_3 = ?$

$$y_1 = \frac{10\,000 \times 500 \times 200}{1\,000 \times 75\,000} + \frac{10 \times 200 \times 800}{150\,000} + 200 \times \frac{100}{1\,000} =$$
$$13.33 + 10.67 + 20 = 44 \text{ ft. below left support.}$$

$$y_2 = \frac{10\,000 \times 500 \times 500}{1\,000 \times 75\,000} + \frac{10 \times 500 \times 500}{150\,000} + \frac{500 \times 100}{1\,000} =$$
$$33.333 + 16.667 + 50 = 100 \text{ ft. below left support.}$$

$$y_3 = \frac{10\,000 \times 500 \times 200}{1\,000 \times 75\,000} + \frac{10 \times 800 \times 200}{150\,000} + \frac{800 \times 100}{1\,000} =$$
$$13.33 + 10.67 + 80 = 104 \text{ ft. below left support.}$$

Tangents to Span Supporting One Load.—(See Fig. 10):

Case I.—

$$\tan \beta = \frac{d\,y}{d\,x} = \frac{w\,s}{2\,t} - \frac{w\,x}{t} + \frac{G}{s\,t}(s - m) + \tan \alpha \quad \text{(33)}$$

If $x_1 = 0$, $m = 0$,

$$\tan \beta_1 = \frac{w\,s}{2\,t} + \frac{G}{t} + \tan \alpha = \text{tangent with load at left support} \quad \text{(34)}$$

Case II.—

$$\tan \beta = \frac{w\,s}{2\,t} - \frac{w\,x_2}{t} + \frac{G}{t} - \frac{2\,G\,x_2}{s\,t} \pm \tan \alpha \quad \text{(35)}$$

If $x_2 = 0$, $m = 0$,

$$\tan \beta_1 = \frac{w\,s}{2\,t} + \frac{G}{t} \pm \tan \alpha \quad \text{(36)}$$

If $x_2 = s$, $m = s$,

$$\tan \beta_2 = \frac{w\,s}{2\,t} + \frac{G}{t} \mp \tan \alpha \quad \text{(37)}$$

Case III.—

$$\tan \beta = \frac{w\,s}{2\,t} - \frac{w\,x_3}{t} - \frac{G\,m}{s\,t} \mp \tan \alpha \quad \text{(38)}$$

If $x_3 = s$, $m = s$,

$$\tan \beta_2 = -\frac{w\,s}{2\,t} - \frac{G}{t} \mp \tan \alpha = \frac{w\,s}{2\,t} + \frac{G}{t} \mp \tan \alpha \quad \text{(39)}$$

Example.—If $s = 1\,000$ ft.; $m = 500$ ft.; $x_1 = 200$ ft.; $x_2 = 500$ ft.; $x_3 = 800$ ft.; $t = 75\,000$ lb.; $w = 10$ lb. per ft.; $h = 100$ ft.; and $G = 10\,000$ lb.; $\tan \beta = ?$

$$\tan \beta_1 = \frac{10 \times 1\,000}{2 \times 75\,000} - \frac{10 \times 200}{75\,000} + \frac{10\,000}{1\,000 \times 75\,000}(500) + 0.1$$
$$= 0.0667 - 0.0267 + 0.0667 + 0.1 = 0.2067$$

Therefore, the tangent to the cable 200 ft. from the left support makes an angle of 11° 41′ with the horizontal.

$$\tan \beta_1 \text{ at support} = 0.0667 + 0.1333 + 0.1 = 0.3000 = 16° \ 42'$$

$$\tan \beta_2 = -0.0667 - 0.0667 + 0.1333 + 0.1 = 0.1000 = 5° \ 43'$$

$$\tan \beta_3 = 0.0667 - 0.1067 - 0.1066 + 0.1 = -0.0466 = -2° \ 40'$$

It is understood that when using Equations (33) to (39) the minus signs indicate below horizontal, and the plus signs, above horizontal.

Spans Supporting More Than One Load.—(See Fig. 11 and Table 19):

$$y = \frac{G}{t} \left\{ x\,(n - p) - m \left[\frac{x\,n}{s} - p \right] - a \left[\frac{b\,x}{s} - c \right] \right\} + \frac{w\,x}{2\,t}\,(s - x) \pm x \tan \alpha \quad \text{.......... (40)}$$

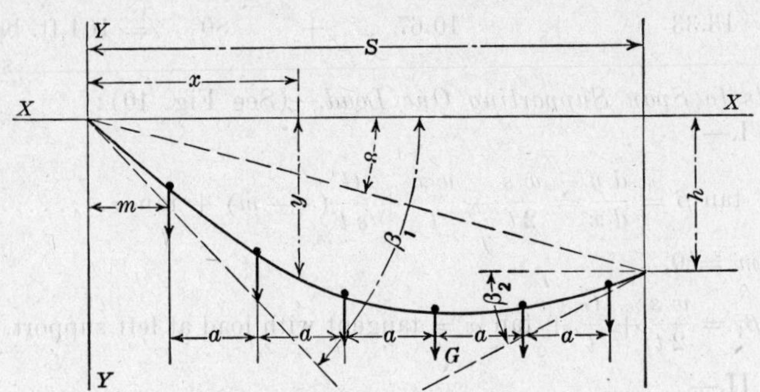

FIG. 11.—SPAN SUPPORTING MORE THAN ONE LOAD.

This may be written in the form,

$$y = \frac{G\,s}{l} \left\{ (n - p)\,r - d\,(n\,r - p) - q\,(r\,b - c) \right\} + \frac{w\,s^2}{2\,t}\,(l - r)\,r \pm r\,h \quad \text{.......... (41)}$$

Example.—Let $s = 1\,000$ ft.; $h = 100$ ft.; $G = 1\,000$ lb.; $w = 3.6$ lb.; $t = 40\,000$ lb.; $n = 4$; $a = 300$ ft.; $m = 50$ ft.; and $x = 500$ ft.; $y = ?$

$$r = \frac{500}{1\,000} = 0.5;\ d = \frac{50}{1\,000} = 0.05;\ q = \frac{300}{1\,000} = 0.3$$

$$y = 25 \left\{ 2 \times 0.5 - 0.05\,(4 \times 0.5 - 2) - 0.3\,(0.5 \times 6 - 1) \right\} + \frac{3.6 \times 1\,000^2}{80\,000}\,0.5 \times 0.5 + 0.5 \times 100$$

$$y = 10 + 11.25 + 50 = 71.25 \text{ ft. below left support}$$

Tangent to Span Supporting Multiple Loads.—(See Fig. 11):

$$\tan \beta = \frac{d\,y}{d\,x} = \frac{G}{t} \left\{ (n - p) - \frac{n\,m + b\,a}{s} \right\} + \frac{w}{t} \left(\frac{s}{2} - x \right) \pm \tan \alpha$$

which may be written,

$$\tan \beta = \frac{G}{t} \left[(n - p) - d\,n - q\,b \right] + \frac{w\,s}{t} \left(\frac{1}{2} - r \right) \pm \tan \alpha \quad \text{.... (42)}$$

Example.—Data as in previous example.

At the left support:

$$\tan \beta_1 = 0.025\,[4 - 0.20 - 1.8] + 0.027 + 0.1$$
$$= 0.050 + 0.027 + 0.1 = 0.177 = 10^\circ\ 02'$$

At the center:

$$\tan \beta_3 = 0.025\,[2 - 0.20 - 1.8] + 0 + 0.1 = 0.1 = 5^\circ\ 43'$$

At the right support:

$$\tan \beta_2 = 0.025\,[0 - 0.2 - 1.8] - 0.027 + 0.1 = 0.023$$
$$= 1^\circ\ 19' \text{ below horizontal axis.}$$

TABLE 19.—DEFLECTION AT CENTER OF SPANS SUPPORTING MULTIPLE LOADS, SYMMETRICALLY PLACED.

No. of loads.	Deflection of loads.	+ of cable.	$+\frac{h}{2}$
1	$\frac{G\,s}{4\,t}$	$\frac{w\,s^2}{8\,t}$	$+\frac{h}{2}$
2	$\frac{G\,s}{4\,t}(2 - 2\,q)$	$\frac{w\,s^2}{8\,t}$	$+\frac{h}{2}$
3	$\frac{G\,s}{4\,t}(3 - 4\,q)$	$\frac{w\,s^2}{8\,t}$	$+\frac{h}{2}$
4	$\frac{G\,s}{4\,t}(4 - 8\,q)$	$\frac{w\,s^2}{8\,t}$	$+\frac{h}{2}$
5	$\frac{G\,s}{4\,t}(5 - 12\,q)$	$\frac{w\,s^2}{8\,t}$	$+\frac{h}{2}$
6	$\frac{G\,s}{4\,t}(6 - 18\,q)$	$\frac{w\,s^2}{8\,t}$	$+\frac{h}{2}$
7	$\frac{G\,s}{4\,t}(7 - 24\,q)$	$\frac{w\,s^2}{8\,t}$	$+\frac{h}{2}$
8	$\frac{G\,s}{4\,t}(8 - 32\,q)$	$\frac{w\,s^2}{8\,t}$	$+\frac{h}{2}$
9	$\frac{G\,s}{4\,t}(9 - 40\,q)$	$\frac{w\,s^2}{8\,t}$	$+\frac{h}{2}$
10	$\frac{G\,s}{4\,t}(10 - 50\,q)$	$\frac{w\,s^2}{8\,t}$	$+\frac{h}{2}$

With an even number of loads, the deflection under load to right of center is,

$$\frac{G\,s}{4\,t}\left[N - \frac{N^2}{2}\,q\right] + \frac{w\,s^2}{8\,t}\,(1 - q^2) \pm r\,h \ldots\ldots\ldots\ldots (43)$$

With an odd number of loads, the deflection under the center load is,

$$\frac{G\,s}{4\,t}\left[N - \frac{N^2 - 1}{2}\,q\right] + \frac{w\,s^2}{8\,t} \pm \frac{h}{2} \ldots\ldots\ldots\ldots (44)$$

Example.—Let s = 1 000 ft.; h = 100 ft.; G = 1 000 lb.; w = 3.6 lb.; $n = 4$; t = 40 000 lb.; and a = 300 ft.; y at center = ?

$$q = \frac{300}{1\,000} = 0.3\,;\; m = 50 \text{ ft.}$$

$$y = \frac{1\,000 \times 1\,000}{4 \times 40\,000}\,[4 - 8 \times 0.3] + \frac{3.6 \times 1\,000^2}{8 \times 40\,000} + 50$$
$$= 6.25 \times 1.6 + 11.25 + 50 = 71.25 \text{ ft.}$$

below left support.

Note that with n equal to an odd number, the middle load is at the center of the span.

Tangents Due to Loads Only on Saddle of Adjoining Multiple-Loaded Spans.—In Fig. 12 let the loads be arranged so that one is at the support, B. Also, $q = \frac{a}{s}$, q_1 = Span A B, and q_2 = Span B C (Table 20).

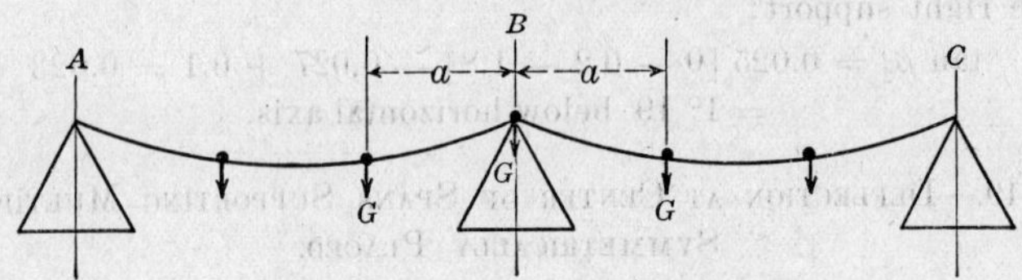

FIG. 12.—MULTIPLE-LOADED SPANS.

TABLE 20.

Span A B.	No. of loads.	Span B C.
$\frac{G}{t}(1 - q_1)$	1	$\frac{G}{t}(1)$
$\frac{2\ G}{t}(1 - \frac{3}{2}\ q_1)$	2	$\frac{2\ G}{t}(1 - 0.5\ q_2)$
$\frac{3\ G}{t}(1 - 2\ q_1)$	3	$\frac{3\ G}{t}(1 - q_2)$
$\frac{4\ G}{t}(1 - 2.5\ q_1)$	4	$\frac{4\ G}{t}(1 - 1.5\ q_2)$
$\frac{5\ G}{t}(1 - 3\ q_1)$	5	$\frac{5\ G}{t}(1 - 2\ q_2)$
$\frac{6\ G}{t}(1 - 3.5\ q_1)$	6	$\frac{6\ G}{t}(1 - 2.5\ q_2)$
$\frac{7\ G}{t}(1 - 4\ q_1)$	7	$\frac{7\ G}{t}(1 - 3\ q_2)$
$\frac{8\ G}{t}(1 - 4.5\ q_1)$	8	$\frac{8\ G}{t}(1 - 3.5\ q_2)$
$\frac{9\ G}{t}(1 - 5\ q_1)$	9	$\frac{9\ G}{t}(1 - 4\ q_2)$
$\frac{10\ G}{t}(1 - 5.5\ q_1)$	10	$\frac{10\ G}{t}(1 - 4.5\ q_2)$

Example.—If Span A B = 900 ft. and Span B C = 1 000 ft., a = 300 ft.; G = 1 000 lb.; and t = 40 000 lb., the maximum angle over Support B due to loads only, can be found, as follows:

Span A B = 3 loads = 3 × 0.025 (1 — 0.667) = 0.025 = 1° 26′
Span B C = 4 loads = 4 × 0.025 (1 — 0.45) = 0.055 = 3° 09′

Maximum angle over Support B = 4° 35′

Catenary.—The deflection of a loaded cable when treated as a catenary is:

$$y = \frac{G\ s}{t}\left[(n - p)\ r - d\ (n\ r - p) - q\ (b\ r - c)\right] + \frac{t}{w}\left[\sinh\frac{w\ x}{t}\sinh\frac{w\ s}{2\ t} - \cosh\frac{w\ s}{2\ t}\left(\cosh\frac{w\ x}{t} - 1\right)\right]\sec\alpha \pm r\ h \ldots\ldots\ldots\ldots (45)$$

At the center of span:

$$y = \frac{G\,s}{4\,t}\left[n - \frac{n^2 - 1}{2}\,q\right] + \frac{t}{w}\left[\cosh\frac{w\,s}{2\,t} - 1\right]\sec\alpha \pm \frac{h}{2} \quad \text{....(46)}$$

At the tangent:

$$\frac{d\,y}{d\,x} = \tan\beta = \frac{G}{t}\,[(n - p) - d\,n - q\,b] + \left(\cosh\frac{w\,x}{t}\sinh\frac{w\,s}{2\,t}\right.$$

$$\left. - \cosh\frac{w\,s}{2\,t}\sinh\frac{w\,x}{t}\right)\sec\alpha \pm \tan\alpha \quad \text{...............(47)}$$

The deflections of a cable span, when loaded symmetrically, can be computed rapidly, by the method of differences.* Use is made of the fact that all the second differences of the deflections are equal to $-\frac{a}{t}\,(G + w\,a)$. Further, if the number of loads on the span is odd, the first differences are numerically equal to one-half the second. If the number is even, then the first differences are equal to the second. The slope correction is constant, and is to be added or subtracted from the first differences as indicated by the direction of the slope of the chord. In using this method it is necessary only to compute one deflection (which may be for any load, but preferably a center one), because of the simplicity of the calculation, and find the others by addition, thus: Let s = 1 000 ft.; h = 100 ft.; G = 1 000 lb.; w = 3.6 lb.; t = 40 000 lb.; a = 300 ft.; and m = 50 ft.; y = ?

Compute the deflection of load nearest the left support:

$$y = \frac{G\,s\,r}{t}\left[n\,(1 - d) - q\,b\right] + \frac{w\,s^2\,r}{2\,t}\,(1 - r) \pm r\,h \quad \text{.......(48)}$$

$$\frac{1\,000 \times 1\,000 \times 0.05}{40\,000}\left[4\,(1 - 0.05) - \frac{0.3 \times 4 \times 3}{2}\right]$$

$$+ \frac{3.6 \times 1\,000^2 \times 0.05 \times 0.95}{80\,000} + 0.05 \times 100 = 2.50 + 2.14 + 5 = 9.64 \text{ ft.}$$

The second difference is:

$$-\frac{300}{40\,000} \times (1\,000 + 1\,080) = -15.6 \text{ ft.}$$

The first difference is:

$$15.6 + 0.3 \times 100 = 45.6 \text{ ft.}$$

Construct Table 21, writing the deflection found for Load 1; then add the first difference to it for the next load; then correct the first difference by subtracting the second difference and the new first difference is obtained; which, added to the deflection of the second load gives the third, etc.

TABLE 21.

Load No.	1		2		3		4
Deflection	9.64		55.24		85.24		99.64
First difference		45.6		30		14.40	
Second difference			−15.6		−15.6		

* *Transactions*, Am. Soc. C. E., Vol. LXXXIII (1919–20), p. 1383.

The deflections of loaded spans may also be quickly ascertained by the use of Figs. 13, 14, and 15 for: (1) the slope factor; (2) the deflection of empty cable; and (3) the deflection due to load. Their use may be illustrated by the following example: Let, $s = 1\,000$ ft.; $h = 200$ ft.; $g = 2\,800$ lb.; $t = 60\,000$ lb.; $w = 5.5$ lb.; $X = 100$ ft.; and $M = 300$ ft.; find y.

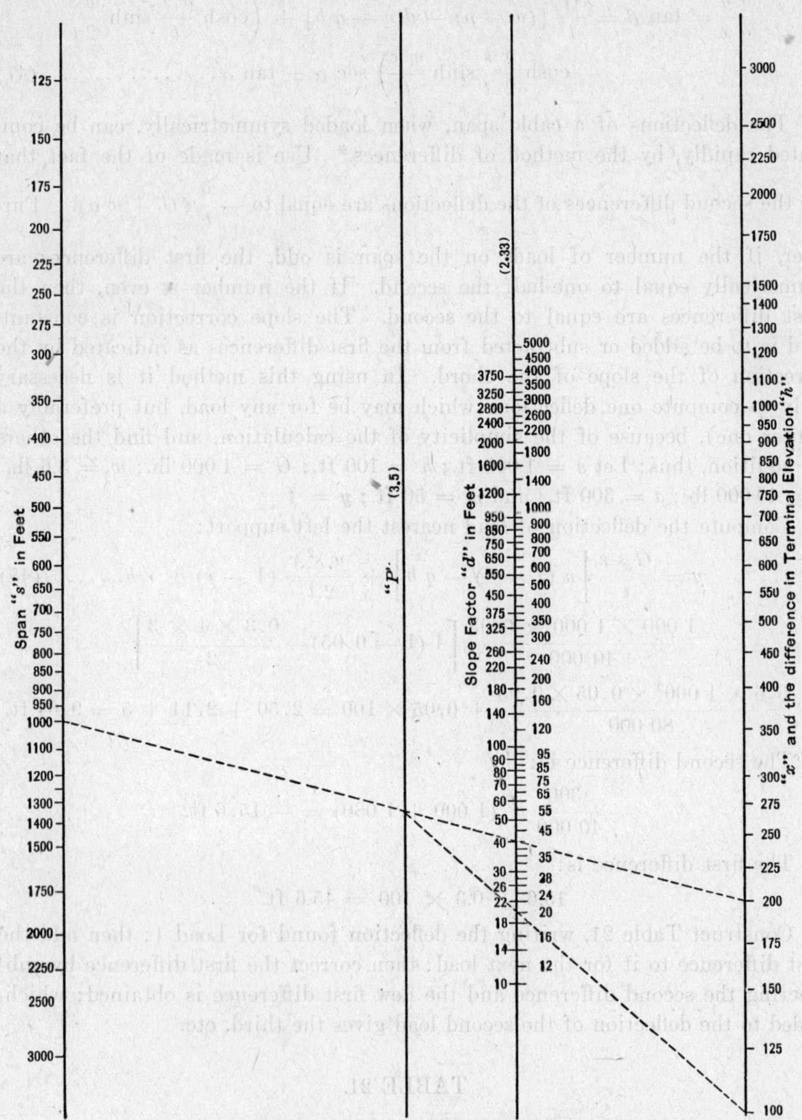

FIG. 13.—TO FIND SLOPE FACTOR, d, IN EQUATION (49).

(a) Refer to Fig. 13 and solve for the slope factor:

$$d = \frac{x}{s} h \quad \text{.......................} (49)$$

First, place the straight-edge from s to h and mark P. Then place the straight-edge from P to x and read the intercept, d.

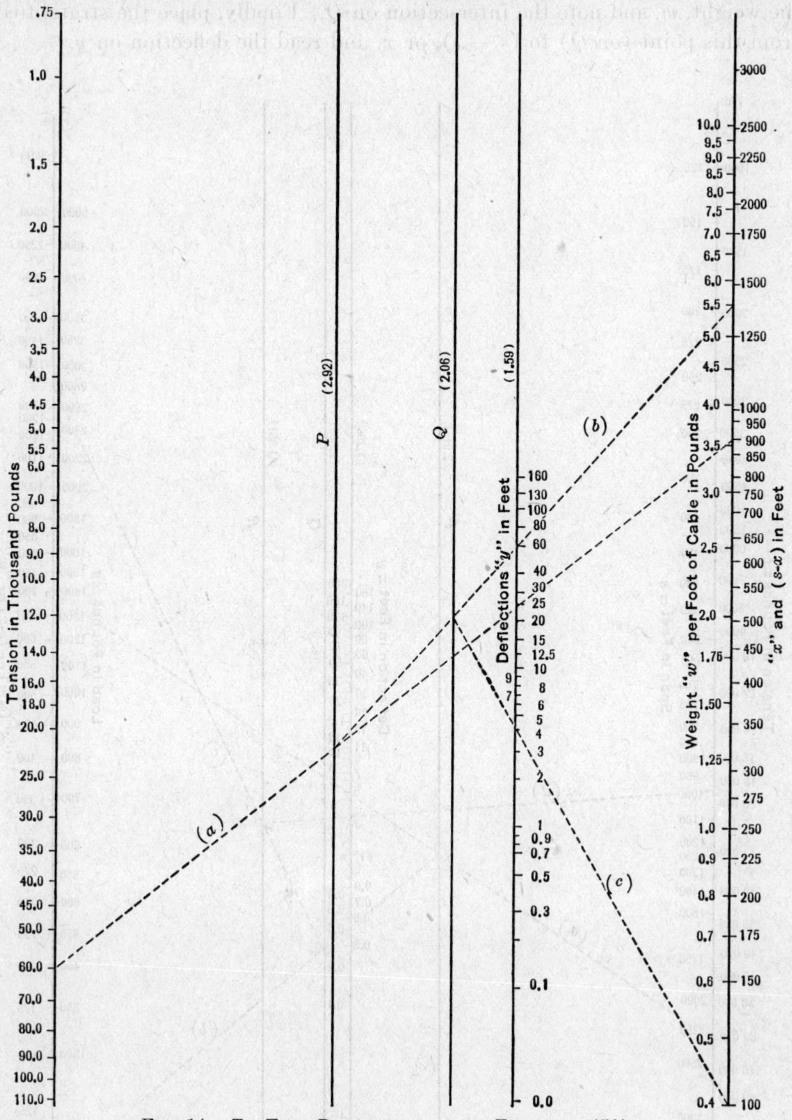

FIG. 14.—TO FIND DEFLECTION, y, IN EQUATION (50).

Thus,

$$d = \frac{100 \times 200}{1\,000} = 20 \text{ ft.}$$

(*b*) Refer to Fig. 14 and solve for,

$$y = \frac{w\,x\,(s - x)}{2\,t} \quad \ldots\ldots\ldots\ldots\ldots\ldots (50)$$

First, place the straight-edge on the given tension and on x, or $(5\,x)$ and note the intersection on P. Next, place the straight-edge from this point to the weight, w, and note the intersection on Q. Finally, place the straight-edge from this point (on Q) to $(s - x)$, or x, and read the deflection on y.

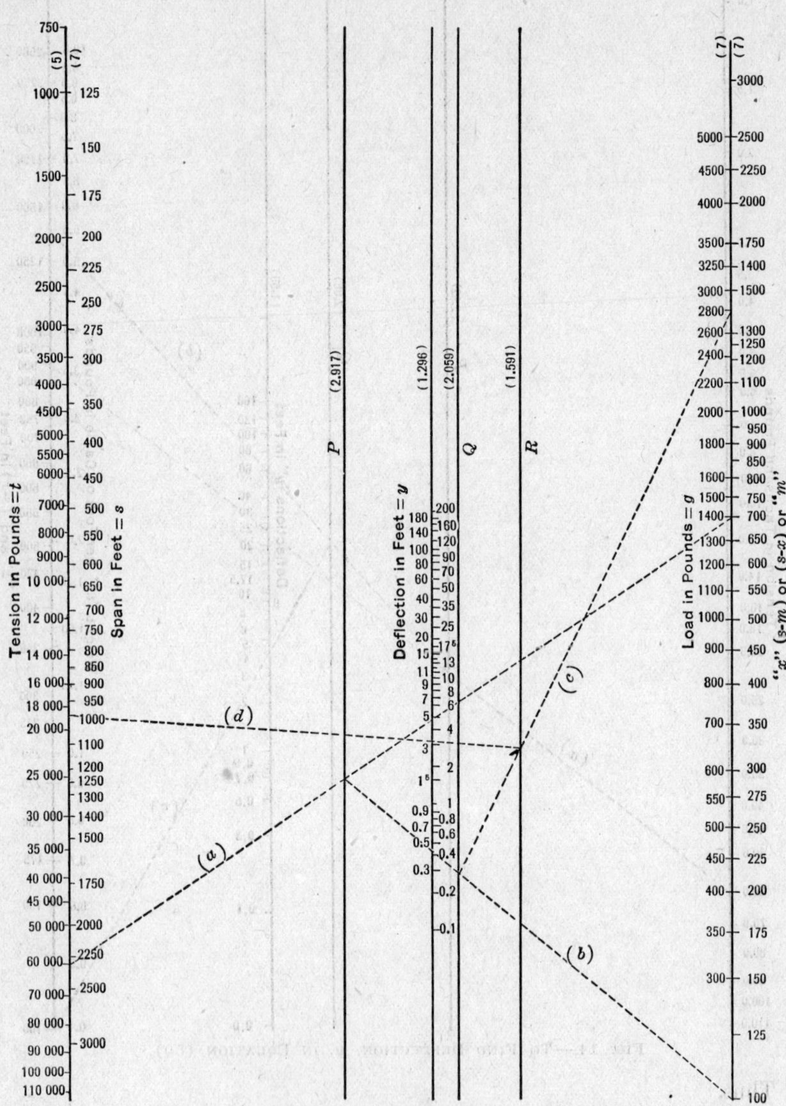

Fig. 15.—To Find the Deflection, y, for Load.

Thus,

$$y = \frac{5.5 \times 100 \times 900}{2 \times 60\,000} = 4.1 \text{ ft.}$$

The load part of Equations (29), (30), and (31) becomes:

$$y = \frac{g\,x\,(s - m)}{s\,t} \quad \text{.......................(51)}$$

when the point, xy, is between the left support and g,

$$y = \frac{g\,x\,(s - x)}{s\,t} \quad \text{.......................(52)}$$

when the point, xy, is under the load, g; and

$$y = \frac{g\,m\,(s - x)}{s\,t} \quad \text{.......................(53)}$$

when the point, xy, is between g and the right support. These may be solved by the use of Fig. 15.

First, place the straight-edge on the tension scale and $(s—m)$ and mark the intercept on P.

Next, place the straight-edge from P to x and mark Q. Then, place the straight-edge from Q to g and mark R. Finally, placing the straight-edge from R to s, read the answer on y.

Thus,

$$y = \frac{2\,800 \times 100 \times 700}{1\,000 \times 60\,000} = 3.30 \text{ ft.}$$

The total deflection below the left-hand support is:

$$20 + 4.1 + 3.3 = 27.4 \text{ ft.}$$

The diagrams may also be used to find the deflection at a point, $x\,y$, for multi-loaded spans, thus (Fig. 16); let $w = 3.5$ lb.; $t = 30\,000$ lb.; $g = 1\,800$ lb.; $a = 450$ ft.; and $m = 150$ ft.

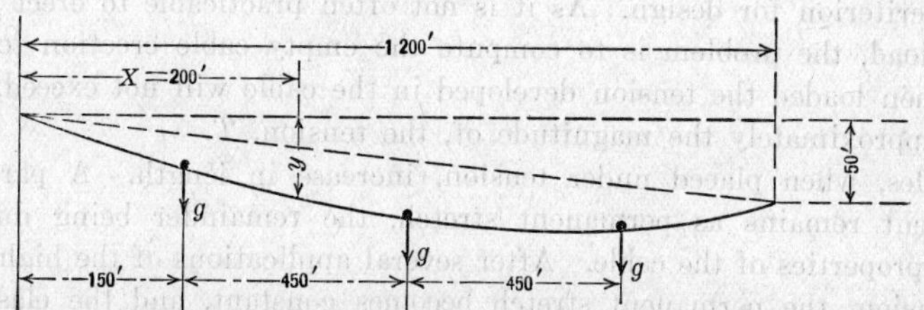

FIG. 16.—DEFLECTION AT ANY POINT ON A MULTI-LOADED SPAN.

(a) The slope factor is found from Fig. 13:

$$d = \frac{200 \times 50}{1\,200} = 8.3$$

Note since 50 does not appear on Fig. 13, use 500, but point off one place in the answer.

(b) The deflection of the cable is (Fig. 14):

$$y = \frac{3.5 \times 200 \times 1\,000}{2 \times 30\,000} = 11.7 \text{ ft.}$$

(c) To find the deflections for loads treat each one as if it were separate. As the first load is to the left of xy, the following equations result (Fig. 15):

By Equation (53):

$$y_1 = \frac{1\,800 \times 150 \times 1\,000}{1\,200 \times 30\,000} = 7.5$$

by Equation (52):

$$y_2 = \frac{1\,800 \times 200 \times 600}{1\,200 \times 30\,000} = 6.0; m = 150 + 450 = 600$$

by Equation (51):

$$y_3 = \frac{1\,800 \times 200 \times 150}{1\,200 \times 30\,000} = 1.5 ; m = 150 + 450 + 450 = 1\,050$$

$$y_1 + y_2 + y_3 = 15.0$$

The diagrams may be used to find any of the unknown factors if the others are given. Thus, let s = 1 200 ft.; w = 3.5 lb.; and y = 12.5 ft. at $x = \frac{s}{2}$; what is t (Fig. 14)?

Place the straight-edge on y = 12.5 to x = 600, and mark Q; place it on Q to w = 3.5, and mark P; and place it on P to $s - x$ = 600, and read t = 50 500 lb.

Anchored Spans.—A suspended cable hangs as a moment curve. The moment is the product of the deflection and tension. When weight-boxes are used the tension factor is made constant, and the deflection varies with the loading. It is often desirable to keep deflections within limits and have the tension vary with the loading. Such cases arise in the design of suspension bridges, cableways, and the long spans of aerial tramways. The ends of the cables of such spans are fastened to immovable anchorages; hence the term, anchored spans. To avoid injuring the cable, the loaded tension, T, is taken as the criterion for design. As it is not often practicable to erect the cable under load, the problem is to compute the empty cable erection tension, so that when loaded the tension developed in the cable will not exceed, but will be of approximately the magnitude of, the tension, T.

Cables, when placed under tension, increase in length. A part of this increment remains as permanent stretch, the remainder being due to the elastic properties of the cable. After several applications of the highest working tension, the permanent stretch becomes constant, and the elastic properties of the cable are not masked by it within this limit of tension. Therefore, anchored spans are calculated on the assumption that the cables will be erected and brought to a tension somewhat higher than the full working tension and then slackened to the empty tension.

For a span supporting a single load, such as a cableway, for instance, the loaded length, L, is given for every position of the load, by the formula,

$$L = s + \frac{G\,m}{2\,s\,T^2}(G + w\,s)(s - m) + \frac{w^2\,s^3}{24\,T^2} + \frac{h^2}{2\,s} \quad \text{.........(54)}$$

The maximum tension occurs when the load is at the middle of the span. The length of the empty span is,

$$l = s + \frac{w^2\,s^3}{24\,t^2} + \frac{h^2}{2\,s} \quad \text{.........................(55)}$$

The change in tension, $T - t$, however, causes a shortening of the cable (ΔL). Then,

$$\Delta L = \frac{(T - t)\, L}{A\, E} = (T - t)\, J \ldots\ldots\ldots\ldots\ldots\ldots (56)$$

Therefore,

$$L - \Delta L = l, \text{ or } L = (T - t)\, J + s + \frac{w^2\, s^3}{24\, t^2} + \frac{h^2}{2\, s} \ldots\ldots\ldots\ldots (57)$$

$$J\, t + L - \left(T\, J + s + \frac{h^2}{2\, s}\right) = \frac{w^2\, s^3}{24\, t^2} \ldots\ldots\ldots\ldots (58)$$

a cubic equation having one real root.

Example.—Let $s = 1\,000$ ft.; $G = 2\,000$ lb.; $w = 4$ lb.; $T_{\text{max.}} = 40\,000$ lb.; $h = 100$ ft.; $E = 20\,000\,000$ lb.; and $A = 1.1$ sq. in.; $t = ?$

$$L = 1\,000 + \frac{2\,000 \times 1\,000}{8 \times 40\,000^2}\,(2\,000 + 4\,000) + \frac{4^2 \times 1\,000^3}{24 \times 40\,000^2}$$

$$+ \frac{100^2}{2 \times 1\,000} = 1\,000 + 0.9375 + 0.4167 + 5 = 1\,006.354 \text{ ft.}$$

$$\frac{L}{A\, E} = \frac{1\,006.354}{1.1 \times 2 \times 10^7} = 0.0000457 = J$$

$$T\, J = 40\,000 \times 0.0000457 = 1.828$$

$$L - \left(T\, J + s + \frac{h^2}{2\, s}\right) = 1\,006.354 - (1.828 + 1\,000 + 5) - 0.474$$

$$\frac{w^2\, s^3}{24} = \frac{4^2 \times 1\,000^3}{24} = 666\,666\,667$$

Then,

$$0.0000457\, t - 0.474 = \frac{666\,666\,667}{t^2}$$

Table 22 results from slide-rule computations, showing a succession of assumed values of t until the equation is satisfied (the values in the last two columns are equal).

TABLE 22.—COMPUTATIONS TO FIND VALUE OF t.

Values of t.	$0.0000457\, t$.	-0.474	$\frac{666\,666\,667}{t^2}$
30 000 lb.	1.371	0.897	0.741
29 000 "	1.325	0.851	0.794
28 000 "	1.280	0.806	0.852
28 400 "	1.308	0.834	0.830

The erection tension is, therefore, 28 400 lb. The center deflections of this span are:

Loaded = 75 ft. below left support.
Empty = 67.6 " " " "

Difference = 7.4 ft.

If the cables were non-elastic, this difference in deflection would be very much smaller than indicated.

Conversely: To find T if a load, G, is placed on the mid-point of an empty span:

$$l - \left(J\,t + s + \frac{h^2}{2\,s}\right) = \frac{G\,s\,(G + w\,s)}{8\,T^2} + \frac{w^2\,s^3}{24\,T^2} - J\,T \ldots\ldots (59)$$

Example.— $s = 1\,000$ ft.; $G = 2\,000$ lb.; $w = 4$ lb.; $t = 28\,400$ lb.; $h = 100$ ft.; $E = 2 \times 10^7$; and $A = 1.10$ sq. in.; $T = ?$

$$l = 1\,000 + 0.827 + 5 = 1\,005.827 \text{ ft.}$$

$$J = 0.0000457$$

$$J\,t = 1.298$$

$$l - \left(J\,t + s + \frac{h^2}{2\,s}\right) = 1\,005.827 - 1\,006.298 = -0.471$$

$$\frac{G\,s\,(G + w\,s)}{8} = \frac{2\,000 \times 1\,000 \times 6\,000}{8} = 1\,500\,000\,000$$

$$\frac{w^2\,s^3}{24} = \frac{4^2 \times 1\,000^3}{24} = \frac{666\,670\,000}{2\,166\,700\,000}$$

$$0.0000457\,T - 0.471 = \frac{2\,166\,700\,000}{T^2}$$

TABLE 23.—Computations to Find Values of T.

Values of T.	$0.0000457\,T$	-0.471	$\frac{2\,166\,700\,000}{T^2}$
40 000	1.830	1.359	1.355

Therefore, the loaded tension will be 40 000 lb.

Aerial Dumping.—Cableways and aerial tramways are often used to accumulate stock or waste piles, in which case aerial dumping is required. To prevent the carrier leaving the cable, the weight of the load dumped should not exceed twice the weight of the empty carrier plus the weight of the cable of the span. In practice, it is best to make these weights equal, if unwelcome oscillations of the span are to be avoided.

If the load is not released instantly, then the minimum time interval for dumping it should exceed, in seconds, one-fourth the square root of the difference in deflection of the span before and after discharging the load. Thus, if the difference in deflection of the span when supporting the loaded and empty carrier is 4.82 ft., the time of dumping must exceed $\frac{1}{4}\sqrt{4.82}$, or 0.55 sec.

To protect roads, railways, or other points of danger, guard screens (see Fig. 17), suspended from anchored cables, are often installed. In order to design the structure properly, it becomes necessary to compute the instantaneous deflection of the screen due to the falling carrier.

The following solution of the problem is presented for the case of single spans with weighted or anchored cables.

THEORY OF GUARD SCREENS.

Let the normal position of the guard screen be as shown in Fig. 17. The notation used in computing the formulas for guard screens is, as follows:

s = horizontal length of span.
h = difference in terminal elevation.
W = virtual weight of the span per foot. W is to be increased by sec α when $\alpha > 10°$.
y_0 = normal deflection below the chord.
y_1 = normal deflection increased 1 ft.
y = deflection at any instant.
x = increase in normal deflection at any instant.
t_0 = tension for normal deflection.
t_1 = tension for y_1 deflection.
T = tension for y deflection.
P_0 = resistance of screen to 1 ft. deflection.
P = resistance of screen to any deflection.
L_0 = length of cable (normal).
H = fall of carrier.
$G_0 = \dfrac{\text{weight of loaded carrier}}{\text{number of cables}}$.
G_1 = hypothetical load on screen for 1 ft. deflection.
G = hypothetical load on screen for any deflection.
$d\,t_1 = t_1 - t_0$.
$d\,t = T - t_0$.

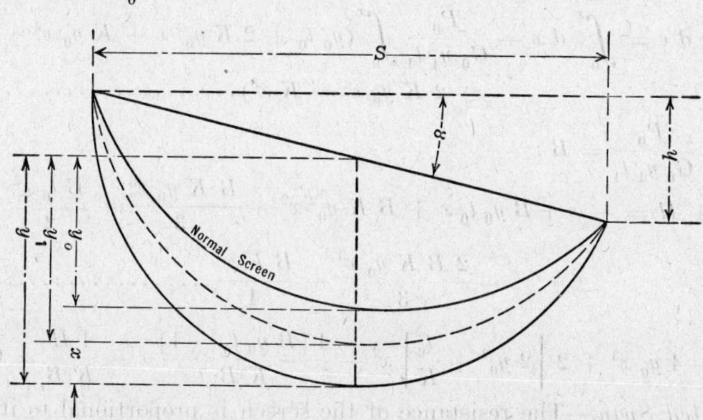

FIG. 17.—DESIGN OF A SINGLE-SPAN GUARD SCREEN.

$$y_0 = \frac{W\,s^2}{8\,t_0} \qquad (60)$$

$$y_1 = \frac{W\,s^2 + 2\,G_1\,s}{8\,(t_0 + d\,t_1)} = \frac{P_0\,s}{8\,t_1} \qquad (61)$$

$$y = \frac{W\,s^2 + 2\,G\,s}{8\,T} = \frac{P\,s}{8\,(t_0 + d\,t)}. \qquad (62)$$

$$y : y_1 = \frac{P\,s}{8\,(t_0 + d\,t)} : \frac{P_0\,s}{8\,(t_0 + d\,t_1)} \qquad (63)$$

But, $y = y_0 + x$:

$$P = \frac{P_0\, y\,(t_0 + d\,t)}{y_1\,(t_0 + d\,t_1)} = \frac{P_0\,(y_0 + x)(t_0 + d\,t)}{y_1\,(t_0 + d\,t_1)} = \frac{P_0\,(y_0\,t_0 + y_0\,d\,t + t_0\,x + x\,d\,t}{y_1\,(t_0 + d\,t_1)} \quad (64)$$

$$L_0 = s + \frac{8\,y_0^{\,2}}{3\,s},\; L = s + \frac{8\,y^2}{3\,s} \quad (65)$$

$$\lambda = L - L_0 = \frac{8\,(y^2 - y_0^{\,2})}{3\,s} \quad (66)$$

$$d\,t = \frac{\lambda\,A\,E}{L_0} = \frac{8\,(2\,y_0\,x + x^2)\,A\,E}{3\,s\,L_0} = K\,(2\,y_0\,x + x^2) \quad (67)$$

Substitute in Equation (64):

$$P = \frac{P_0\,(y_0\,t_0 + 2\,K\,y_0^{\,2}\,x + K\,y_0\,x^2 + t_0\,x + 2\,K\,y_0\,x^2 + K\,x^3)}{y_1\,(t_0 + d\,t_1)} \quad (68)$$

$$v\,d\,v = p\,d\,x \quad (69)$$

Since the carrier falls a distance, H, it has a velocity C ft. per sec. when it strikes the screen. This velocity is brought to zero in the distance, x. To state acceleration, p,

$$p = (G_0 - P)\,\frac{g}{G_0} \quad (70)$$

$$\frac{1}{g}\,v\,d\,v = d\,x - \frac{P}{G_0}\,d\,x$$

Considering the downward direction as positive and integrating:

$$\frac{1}{g}\int_c^0 v\,d\,v = \int_0^x d\,x - \frac{P_0}{G_0\,y_1\,t_1}\int_0^x (y_0\,t_0 + 2\,K\,y_0^{\,2}\,x + K\,y_0\,x^2 + t_0\,x + 2\,K\,y_0\,x^2 + K\,x^3) \quad (71)$$

Let $\frac{P_0}{G_0\,y_1\,t_1} = B$:

$$+ H = - x + B\,y_0\,t_0\,x + B\,K\,y_0^{\,2}\,x^2 + \frac{B\,K\,y_0\,x^3}{3} + \frac{B\,t_0\,x^2}{2} + \frac{2\,B\,K\,y_0\,x^3}{3} + \frac{B\,K\,x^4}{4} \quad (72)$$

$$x^4 + 4\,y_0\,x^3 + 2\left[2\,y_0^{\,2} + \frac{t_0}{K}\right]x^2 - \frac{4\,[B\,y_0\,t_0 - 1]}{K\,B}\,x - \frac{4\,H}{K\,B} = 0 \quad (73)$$

Weighted Span.—The resistance of the screen is proportional to its deflection. Tension is constant. (See Fig. 18.)

$$y_0 = \frac{W\,s^2}{8\,t} \quad (74)$$

$$y_1 = \frac{W\,s^2 + 2\,G_1\,s}{8\,t} = \frac{P_0\,s}{8\,t} \quad (75)$$

$$y = \frac{W\,s^2 + 2\,G\,s}{8\,t} = \frac{P\,s}{8\,t} \quad (76)$$

$$y : y_1 = \frac{P\,s}{8\,t} : \frac{P_0\,s}{8\,t}$$

But $y = y_0 + x$:

$$P = \frac{P_0\, y}{y_1}\ ;\ d\,t = 0$$

Substitute in $v\,d\,v = p\,d\,x$:

$$v\,d\,v = \frac{(G - p)\,g}{G}\,d\,x \qquad (77)$$

or,

$$\frac{v\,d\,v}{g} = d\,x - \frac{P}{G}\,d\,x$$

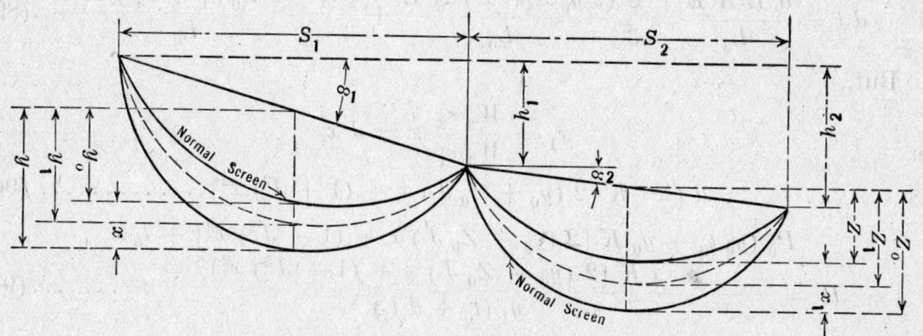

Fig. 18.—Design of Guard Screens on Adjoining Spans.

Integrating,

$$\frac{1}{g}\int_c^0 v\,d\,v = \int_0^x d\,x - \frac{P_0}{G\,y_0}\int x\,d\,x \qquad (78)$$

$$\frac{1}{g}\left[0 - \frac{C^2}{2}\right] = (x - 0) - \frac{P_0}{G\,y_0}\left[\frac{x^2}{2} - 0\right] \qquad (79)$$

$$-H = x - \frac{P_0}{G\,y_0}\,\frac{x^2}{2} \qquad (80)$$

$$x = \frac{G\,y_0}{P_0} \pm \frac{1}{2}\sqrt{\left(\frac{2\,G\,y_0}{P_0}\right)^2 + \frac{8\,H\,G\,y_0}{P_0}} \qquad (81)$$

Adjoining Spans.—(See Fig. 18):

$$y_0 = \frac{W_1\,{s_1}^2}{8\,t_0},\ Z_0 = \frac{W_2\,{s_2}^2}{8\,t_0}\ ;\ y_1 - y_0 = 1 \text{ ft.} \qquad (82)$$

$$y_1 = \frac{W_1\,{s_1}^2 + 2\,G_1\,s_1}{8\,(t_0 + d\,t_1)}\ ;\ Z_1 = \frac{W_2\,{s_2}^2}{8\,(t_0 + d\,t)} \qquad (83)$$

$$L_{y_1} = \frac{8\,{y_1}^2}{3\,s_1}\ ;\ L_{Z_1} = \frac{8\,{Z_1}^2}{3\,s_2} \qquad (84)$$

Let b = length of back-stays. Then, the normal length is $L_{y0} + L_{Z_0} + b = L_0$. $L_0\,\lambda = B$.

$$L_{y_1} + L_{Z_1} + b = L_{y_0} + L_{Z_0} + b + d\,L_1 \qquad (85)$$

$$(L_{y_1} - L_{y_0}) = C\ ;\ (L_{Z_1} - L_{Z_0}) = d = \frac{{W_2}^2\,{s_2}^3}{24\,(t^2 - {t_0}^2)} \qquad (86)$$

therefore,

$$C + d - d\,L_1 = 0\,;\quad d\,L_1 = \lambda\,(L_{y_0} + L_{Z_0} + b)\,(t - t_0)$$

$$C + \frac{W_2^{\,2}\,s_2^{\,3}}{24\,(t^2 - t_0^{\,2})} - B\,(t - t_0) = 0 \qquad (87)$$

This gives the solution for t, from which G_1 and P_0 can be computed.

$$d\,L = L - L_0 = \frac{8}{3\,s_1}\,(y^2 - y_0^{\,2}) + \frac{8}{3\,s_2}\,(Z^2 - Z_0^{\,2}) \qquad (88)$$

But,

$$y = y_0 + x;\; Z = Z_0 - x_1$$

$$d\,t = \frac{d\,L\,A\,E}{L_0} = \frac{8}{3}\,\frac{(2\,y_0\,x + x^2)\,A\,E}{L_0} + \frac{8}{3}\,\frac{(-\,2\,Z_0\,x_1 + x_1^{\,2})\,A\,E}{L_0} \qquad (89)$$

But,

$$x_1 = \frac{W_2\,s_2}{W_1\,s_1}\,x = J\,x$$

$$d\,t = K\,[2\,(y_0 + Z_0\,J)\,x + (1 + J^2)\,x^2] \qquad (90)$$

$$P = \frac{P_0\,(y_0\,t_0 + y_0\,K\,[2\,(y_0 + Z_0\,J)\,x + (1 + J^2)\,x^2] + t_0\,x + x\,K\,[2\,(y_0 + Z_0\,J)\,x + (1 + J^2)\,x^2]}{y_1\,(t_0 + d\,t_1)} \qquad (91)$$

$$v\,d\,v = p\,d\,x$$

Since the velocity of the falling carrier is brought to zero in the distance, x, to state acceleration, p,

$$p = (G_0 - P)\,\frac{g}{G_0} \qquad (92)$$

$$\frac{1}{g}\,v\,d\,v = d\,x - \frac{P}{G_0}\,d\,x$$

Considering the downward direction as positive and integrating,

$$\frac{1}{g}\int_c^0 v\,d\,v = \int_0^t d\,x - \frac{P_0}{G_0\,y_1\,t_1}\int_0^x \{y_0\,t_0 + y_0\,K\,[2\,(y_0 + Z_0\,J)\,x + (1 + J^2)\,x^2\,] + t_0\,x + x\,K\,[2\,(y_0 + Z_0\,J)\,x + (1 + J^2)\,x^2]\} \qquad (93)$$

Let $\dfrac{P_0}{G_0\,y_1\,t_1} = B$,

$$+\,H = -\,x + B\,y_0\,t_0\,x + B\left[\frac{t_0}{2} + y_0\,K\,(y_0 + Z_0\,J)\right]x^2 + \frac{B\,K\,[y_0 + y_0\,J^2 + 2_{y_0} + 2\,Z_0\,J]\,x^3}{3} + \frac{B\,K\,[1 + J^2]\,x^4}{4} \qquad (94)$$

$$x^4 + \frac{4\,y_0\,[3 + J^2 - 2\,Z_0\,J]}{3\,[1 + J^2]}\,x^3 + \frac{4\left[\dfrac{t_0}{2} + y_0\,K\,(y_0 + Z_0\,J)\right]}{K\,[1 + J^2]}\,x^2 + \frac{4\,[B\,y_0\,t_0 - 1]}{B\,K\,[1 + J^2]}\,x - \frac{4\,H}{B\,K\,[1 + J^2]} = 0 \qquad (95)$$

Anchored Cables.—

Example.—Let $W = 10$ lb. per ft.; $t_0 = 5\,000$ lb.; $y_0 = 10$ ft.; $G_0 = 1\,000$ lb.; $H = 12$ ft.; $s = 200$ ft.; $A = 1.1$ sq. in.; and $E = 20 \times 10^6$. Then:

$$L_0 = 200 + \frac{8 \times 10^2}{3 \times 200} = 201.33 \text{ ft.}; \quad L_1 = 200 + \frac{8 \times 11^2}{3 \times 200} = 201.61 \text{ ft.}$$

$$\lambda = 201.61 - 201.33 = 0.28 \text{ ft.}$$

$$d\,t_1 = \frac{0.28 \times 1.1 \times 20 \times 10^6}{201.33} = 30\,600 \text{ lb.}$$

$$t_1 = 30\,600 + 5\,000 = 35\,600 \text{ lb.}$$

$$K = \frac{8 \times 1.1 \times 20 \times 10^6}{3 \times 200 \times 201.33} = 1\,460$$

$$P_0 = \frac{11 \times 8 \times 35\,600}{200} = 15\,700 \text{ lb.}$$

$$B = \frac{15\,700}{1\,000 \times 11 \times 35\,600} = 0.00004$$

$$x^4 + 40\,x^3 + 406.86\,x^2 - 68.4\,x - 825 = 0$$

$$x = 1.41 \text{ ft.}; \ \lambda = 0.41 \text{ ft.}; \ T = 49\,675 \text{ lb.}$$

Weighted Cables.—

$$t = \frac{10 \times 200^2}{8 \times 10} = 5\,000 \text{ lb.}$$

$$P_0 = \frac{40\,000 \times 11}{200} = 2\,200 \text{ lb.}$$

$$x = \frac{1\,000 \times 10}{2\,200} + \frac{1}{2}\sqrt{\left(\frac{2 \times 1\,000 \times 10}{2\,200}\right)^2 + \frac{8 \times 12 \times 1\,000 \times 10}{2\,200}}$$

$$= \quad 4.53 \quad + \quad 11.39 \quad = 15.92 \text{ ft.}$$

Friction.—The coefficient of friction, k, of tramway carriages moving at speeds less than 700 ft. per min. were determined to be as shown in Table 24.

TABLE 24.—Coefficient of Friction of Tramway Carriages.

Load, in pounds.	Wheel-base, in inches.	Journals.*	Coefficient of friction, k.
5 525	21.5	Ball-bearings	0.0045
1 535	21.5	" "	0.0031
2 525	13.75	Cast-steel wheels on bronze pins	0.0192
2 500	13.75	Babbitt bushings on steel pins	0.0158
2 500	13.75	Bronze bushings on steel pins	0.0163
535	13.75	Bronze bushings on steel pins	0.0122
1 240	11.875	Cast-steel wheels on bronze pins	0.0160
1 245	11.875	Ball-bearing	0.0108
255	11.875	Cast-steel wheels on bronze pins	0.0073
260	11.875	Ball-bearing	0.0083

* For roller bearings, multiply values for ball bearings by 1.5.

Coasting Distance.—It is often necessary to determine the coasting distance of a detached carrier.

Let,

$\frac{G}{32.2}$ = mass of tramway carrier; G = weight, in pounds.

p = acceleration, plus or minus.

F = friction.

$\frac{F}{G} = k$ = coefficient of friction.

S = distance traveled.

V = velocity.

H = velocity head.

T = time, in seconds.

Then,

$$F = \frac{G}{32.3} p;\ p = 32.2\,k;\ S = \frac{V_1^2 - V_0^2}{2\,p} = \frac{0.0155\,(V_1^2 - V_0^2)}{k} \quad \text{.... (96)}$$

To coast to rest,

$$S = \frac{0.0155\,V^2}{k}, \text{ or } S = \frac{H}{k}.$$

Example.—If a carrier, running free upon a level rail, has an initial velocity of 8.33 ft. per sec. ($k = 0.0155$), how far will it coast?

$$S = \frac{0.0155 \times 8.33^2}{0.0155} = 69 \text{ ft.}$$

If the rail is not level, but has a slope equal to $\tan\theta$:

$$S = \frac{0.0155\,V^2}{k \pm \tan\theta} \quad \text{.......................... (97)}$$

Thus, in the previous example, if the rail grade is 1% upward:

$$S = \frac{0.0155 \times 8.33^2}{0.0155 + 0.01} = 41.9 \text{ ft.}$$

Example.—What upward grade should a rail have to stop a free running carrier moving 8.33 ft. per sec. ($k = 0.0155$), in a distance of 10 ft.?

$$\tan\theta = \frac{0.0155\,V}{S} - k = \frac{0.0155 \times 8.33^2}{10} - 0.0155 = 9.2\%$$

and the difference in elevation of the points on the rail 10 ft. apart is 0.92 ft. Should the time required to bring the carrier to rest be desired:

$$T = 0.25\sqrt{\frac{S}{k \pm \tan\theta}} \quad \text{...................... (98)}$$

$$= 0.25\sqrt{\frac{10}{0.0155 + 0.092}} = 2.41 \text{ sec.}$$

Tension in Traction Rope.—Let *A, B,* and *C,* Fig. 19, be loading, discharge, and curve rail stations, respectively, of an aerial tramway. It is desired to determine the traction rope tensions at Stations *A* and *C,* friction included. Motion is impending from Station *A* to Station *B,* loaded side. Let $T\,r$ = tension loaded side and $t\,r$ = tension empty side. The tensions at Station C for loaded and empty sides are, as follows:

$$T\,r = N_2\,G\,(\sin\theta_2 - k) + \frac{W}{2} \qquad (99)$$

$$t\,r = N_2\,g\,(\sin\theta_2 + k) + \frac{W}{2} \qquad (100)$$

in which, W is the weight of the traction rope weight-box, and k is the coefficient of friction.

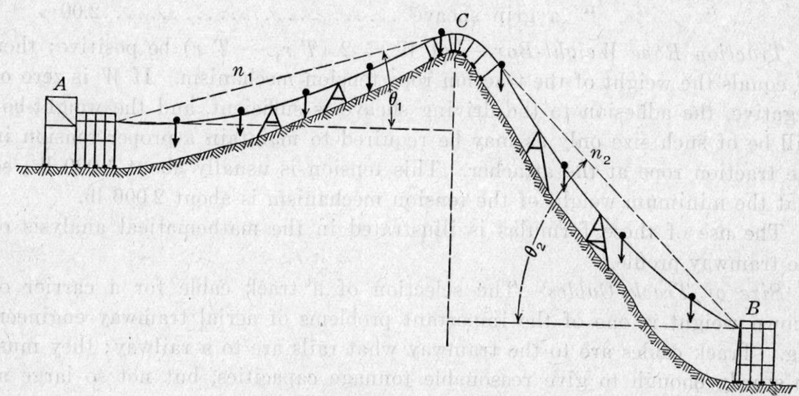

FIG. 19.—TENSION IN TRACTION ROPE.

The tension at Station A will be that at Station C increased or reduced by the loading of the Section A-C, depending on the elevation of Station A as compared with that of Station C. If Station A is lower than Station C, then,

$$T\,r = G\,[N_2\,(\sin\theta_2 - k) - N_1\,(\sin\theta_1 + k)] + \frac{W}{2} \qquad (101)$$

$$t\,r = g\,[N_2\,(\sin\theta_2 + k) - N_1\,(\sin\theta_1 - k)] + \frac{W}{2} \qquad (102)$$

$$\pm\,(T\,r - t\,r) = (G - g)\,(N_2 \sin\theta_2 - N_1 \sin\theta_1)$$
$$-\,(G + g)\,(N_2\,k + N_1\,k) \qquad (103)$$

As the relative values of $T\,r$ and $t\,r$ are not known, their difference may be plus or minus. Let this difference equal $\pm\,D$, then the horse power, $H\,P$, of the tramway may be estimated:

$$H\,P = \frac{\pm\,D\,V}{33\,000} - 2 \qquad (104)$$

When the sign is plus, power is developed; when it is minus, power is required. The number, 2, represents the terminal friction reduced to horse power, and will be found sufficient for all stations of usual design.

To prevent the traction rope from slipping, $T\,r$ must have a proper value, $2\,T\,r_1$, which is,

$$2\,T\,r_1 = D\,(1 + K)$$

in which,

$$K = \frac{e^{f \pi n} + 1}{e^{f \pi n} - 1}$$

in which, f is the coefficient of friction of the rope on the sheave, and n is the number of half laps of the rope on the sheave.

For $n = 1$, K has the following values:

Greasy rope on an iron sheave............................9.13
" " " a wood-filled sheave......................4.62
" " " a rubber and leather-filled sheave.........3.21
" " " a grip sheave..........................2.00

Traction Rope Weight-Box.—Let $W = 2\ (T\ r_1 - T\ r)$ be positive; then W equals the weight of the traction rope tension mechanism. If W is zero or negative, the adhesion to the driving sheave is sufficient, and the weight-box will be of such size only as may be required to maintain a proper tension in the traction rope at the attacher. This tension is usually about 1 000 lb., so that the minimum weight of the tension mechanism is about 2 000 lb.

The use of these formulas is illustrated in the mathematical analysis of the tramway profile.

Size of Track Cables.—The selection of a track cable for a carrier of known weight is one of the important problems of aerial tramway engineering. Track cables are to the tramway what rails are to a railway; they must be sturdy enough to give reasonable tonnage capacities, but not so large as to involve excessive first cost. The choice of track cables may be left to the results of experience, or immersed in the fog of theoretical speculation which surrounds the question of the bending stress in wire ropes. It is presumed that the determination of the bending stress in the wires of a rope has for its purpose the discovery of the reduction in strength of a wire rope due to bending. Those who have had occasion to make practical use of wire ropes by bending them around the small sheaves of wire-rope blocks, know that the loss in strength is an insignificant part of the amount it should be according to published tables based on bending stress. For instance, a 6 × 19 ¾-in. plow steel rope is reduced about 8% in strength when bent around a sheave 6 in. in diameter.

The velocity of the rope in passing around sheaves has a profound influence on its life and, for the same rope, sheaves of different diameters are required for equal service at different speeds. As aerial tramway velocities are usually less than 600 ft. per min., velocity factors may be eliminated from this discussion.

If the validity of the theory of flexure when applied to wire ropes is granted, it is easy to derive an expression for the curve of a track cable between the points of contact of the carriage wheels:

$$y = \frac{G}{t}\left[x - \frac{\sinh \sqrt{\frac{t}{E\ I}}\ x}{\sqrt{\frac{t}{E\ I}}\ \cosh \sqrt{\frac{t}{E\ I}}\ L}\right] \qquad (105)$$

and,

$$\frac{dy}{dx} = \frac{G}{2t}\left[1 - \frac{\cosh \sqrt{\frac{t}{EI}}\, x}{\cosh \sqrt{\frac{t}{EI}}\, L}\right] \quad \ldots\ldots\ldots\ldots\ldots\ldots (106)$$

Where the origin is at the point of wheel contact and L is one-half the distance between wheel contacts, I is the moment of inertia of the rope. Therefore, the curve of cable bending is a function of the load, tension, wheel base, wheels, and the construction, as well as the metal of the cable. It is noted, from an examination of the data of lock-coil cable tests, that the modulus of elasticity is a function of the tension, which influences the amount of internal friction, and thus determines the behavior of the cable when loaded. Fig. 20 illustrates three complete cycles of progressive and retrogressive loading of a 1-in. lock-coil cable. It is apparent that the stress-strain curve of restitution does not coincide with the curve of deformation. After the permanent stretch has been eliminated, a closed foot-pound diagram results, from which the magnitude of the internal friction can be estimated in a manner similar to the mean effective pressure from an engine indicator card. Table 25 gives the internal friction of several lock-coil cables under sufficient tension to follow Hooke's law.

TABLE 25.—INTERNAL FRICTION OF LOCK-COIL CABLES.

Diameter, in inches.	Internal friction, in pounds.
⅞	4 900
1	7 700
1⅛	8 800
1¼	9 700
1½	13 100
1⅝	14 800

Since the internal friction is due to the pressure exerted by the helical windings, and varies with the tension, it is clear that the cable resistance to bending increases with the tension until it takes on the semblance of a homogeneous bar, although it is noted that the modulus of elasticity does not reach the values of bars. Table 26 gives the value of the modulus of elasticity of various ropes under tensions equal to one-fourth the ultimate strength.

TABLE 26.—MODULUS OF ELASTICITY OF VARIOUS ROPES.

Kind.	Size, in inches.	Values of E, in pounds.
Lock-coil, lock-wire, and smooth coil	1¼ and smaller	23 000 000
Lock-coil, lock-wire, and smooth coil, larger than	1¼	20 000 000
6 × 7 crucible	¾	12 000 000
6 × 19 "	"	10 000 000
6 × 37 "	"	10 000 000
8 × 19 "	"	6 000 000
6 × 37 plow	2¼	15 000 000

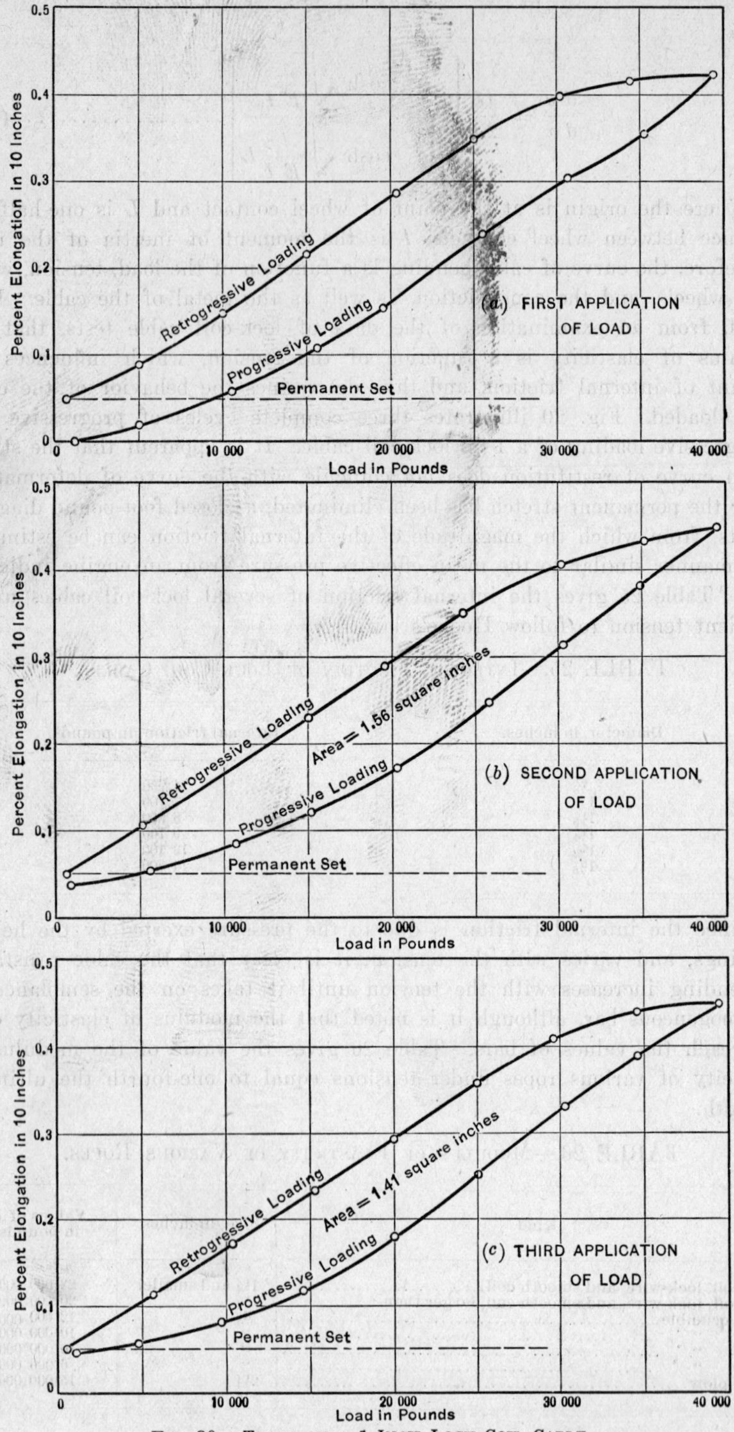

FIG. 20.—TESTS ON A 1-INCH LOCK-COIL CABLE.

For tensions less than one-quarter the ultimate, the following values of E (Table 27) are given for a 1-in. lock-coil cable.

TABLE 27.—MODULUS OF ELASTICITY FOR LOCK-COIL CABLE.

Tension, in pounds.	Values of E, in pounds.
0	1 500 000
5 000	2 400 000
7 500	3 400 000
10 000	5 000 000
12 500	7 750 000
15 000	9 250 000
17 500	12 000 000
20 000	15 300 000
25 000	23 000 000

Having ascertained the value of the modulus of elasticity with regard to tension, the value of the stress set up in the outermost wire of the cable due to bending, may be computed approximately. It can be shown that the curve of the bent track cable does not differ greatly from a circular arc, and if the intersection angle of the tangents is Δ, the radius of curvature, R'' will be,

$$R'' = \frac{W}{2 \times \sin \frac{\Delta}{2}} \qquad (107)$$

Table 28 gives the value of R for various chords and intersection angles for a 1-in. lock-coil cable.

TABLE 28.—VALUES OF R FOR VARIOUS CHORDS AND INTERSECTION ANGLES.

Δ, in degrees.	$\frac{G}{t}$.	Chord, in inches.	Radius, in feet.	Remarks.
1	0.0175	11.96	57	
2	0.0349	12.04	28.7	
3	0.0524	12.12	19.2	
4	0.0700	12.20	14.50	Wheel base, $W = 11.875$ in.
5	0.0875	12.28	11.7	Diameter of wheel = 8.25 in.
6	0.1051	12.36	9.9	
7	0.1228	12.44	8.5	
8	0.1405	12.52	7.5	

Having the radius, the bending stress, B, may be computed from the formula,

$$B = \frac{E\,d}{2\,R} \qquad (108)$$

in which, d is the diameter of the rope or cable, and R is the radius of the cable curve, in inches.

Tables 29 to 37 give the computed bending and direct stresses for several different sizes of lock-coil track cables. It will be noted that the sum of these stresses changes rapidly with the tension. This leads to the conclusion that their sum is a minimum for a given load and a variable

TABLE 29.—STRESSES IN $\frac{7}{8}$-INCH LOCK-COIL CABLE, OX CARRIAGE.*

$\left(p\right.$ = stress, in pounds per square inch, due to bending; E = bending modulus of elasticity for given tension; d = diameter of rope; R = radius of curvature of rope; $W = 11\frac{7}{8}$ in.; $r = 4\frac{1}{8}$ in.; $p = \frac{E\,d}{2\,R}$; area = 491 sq. in.$\left.\right)$

Total tension in cable, in pounds	0.0	2 500	5 000	7 500	10 000	12 500	15 000	17 500	20 000	22 500	25 000
Tension in cable, in pounds per square inch	.....	5 100	10 200	15 300	20 400	25 500	30 600	35 600	40 700	45 800	50 900
E, in millions of pounds	1.0	1.6	3.4	6.8	10.5	16.0	22.5	22.5	22.5	22.5	22.5
Angle under load on O X carriage, in degrees.	STRESS IN OUTER WIRES DUE TO BENDING, IN POUNDS PER SQUARE INCH.										
	640	1 025	2 175	4 350	6 725	10 250	14 400	14 400	14 400	14 400	14 400
1		**6 125**	**12 375**	**19 650**	**27 125**	**35 750**	**45 000**	**50 000**	**55 100**	**60 200**	**65 300**
	1 270	2 035	4 320	8 650	13 350	20 350	28 600	28 600	28 600	28 600	28 600
2		**7 135**	**14 520**	**23 950**	**33 750**	**45 850**	**59 200**	**64 200**	**69 300**	**74 400**	**79 500**
	1 890	3 020	6 425	12 850	19 800	30 200	42 600	42 600	42 600	42 600	42 600
3		**8 120**	**16 625**	**28 150**	**40 200**	**55 700**	**73 200**	**78 200**	**83 300**	**88 400**	**93 500**
	2 500	4 000	8 500	17 000	26 250	40 000	56 250	56 250	56 250	56 250	56 250
4		**9 100**	**18 700**	**32 300**	**46 650**	**65 500**	**86 850**	**91 850**	**96 950**	**102 050**	**107 150**
	3 100	4 960	10 540	21 100	32 600	49 600	69 750	69 750	69 750	69 750	69 750
5		**10 060**	**20 740**	**36 400**	**53 000**	**75 100**	**100 350**	**105 350**	**110 450**	**114 550**	**120 650**
	3 700	5 920	12 600	25 200	38 800	59 200	82 300	82 300	82 300	....	....
6		**11 020**	**22 800**	**40 700**	**59 200**	**84 700**	**112 900**	**117 900**	**123 000**	....	....
	4 280	6 850	14 550	29 100	45 000	68 500	96 300				
7		**11 950**	**24 750**	**44 400**	**65 400**	**94 000**	**126 900**				
	4 860	7 800	16 525	34 050	51 100	78 000	....				
8		**12 800**	**26 725**	**49 350**	**71 500**	**103 500**	....				
	6 000	9 600	20 400	40 800	63 000	96 000	....				
10		**14 700**	**30 600**	**56 100**	**83 400**	**121 500**	....				
	7 110	11 380	24 200	48 400	74 700	....	....				
12		**16 480**	**34 400**	**63 700**	**95 100**	....	....				
	8 200	15 100	27 850	55 700	86 200	....	....				
14		**20 200**	**38 050**	**71 000**	**100 600**	....	....				
Breaking radius, in inches, 115 000 lb. per sq. in. ultimate.	3.8	6.1	12.9	25.8	40	61	86				

*Light and heavy figures indicate bending and total stresses, respectively; values below heavy line exceed 115 000 lb. per sq. in.

TABLE 30.—STRESSES IN 1-INCH LOCK-COIL CABLE, OX CARRIAGE.*

(p = stress, in pounds per square inch, due to bending; E = bending modulus of elasticity for given tension; d = diameter of rope; R = radius of curvature of rope; $p = \frac{E\,d}{2\,R}$; area = 662 sq. in.)

Total tension in cable, in pounds	0.0	5 000	7 500	10 000	12 500	15 000	17 500	20 000	25 000	30 000	35 000
Tension in cable, in pounds per square inch		7 550	11 300	15 100	18 900	22 600	26 400	30 200	37 800	45 300	52 800
E, in millions of pounds	1.5	2.4	3.4	5	7.75	9.25	12	15.3	23	23	23
Angle under load on O X carriage, in degrees.	Stress in Outer Wires Due to Bending, in Pounds per Square Inch.										
1	1 095	1 750	2 480	3 650	5 660	6 750	8 750	11 150	16 800	16 800	16 800
		9 300	**13 780**	**18 750**	**24 560**	**29 350**	**35 150**	**41 350**	**54 600**	**62 100**	**69 600**
2	2 175	3 480	4 930	7 250	11 300	13 400	17 400	22 200	33 400	33 400	33 400
		11 030	**16 230**	**22 350**	**30 200**	**36 000**	**43 800**	**52 400**	**71 200**	**78 700**	**86 200**
3	3 240	5 190	7 350	10 800	16 750	19 900	25 900	33 000	49 700	49 700	49 700
		12 740	**18 650**	**25 900**	**35 650**	**42 500**	**52 300**	**63 200**	**87 500**	**95 000**	**102 500**
4	4 290	6 870	9 750	14 300	22 200	26 400	34 400	43 800	65 800	65 800	65 800
		14 420	**21 050**	**29 400**	**41 100**	**49 000**	**60 800**	**74 000**	**101 100**	**111 100**	**118 600**
5	5 330	8 540	12 100	17 800	27 600	32 800	42 700	54 400	81 800	81 800	......
		16 090	**23 400**	**32 900**	**46 500**	**55 400**	**69 100**	**84 600**	**119 600**	**127 100**	......
6	6 350	10 200	14 400	21 200	32 800	39 100	50 800	64 800	97 500	......	......
		17 750	**25 700**	**36 300**	**51 700**	**61 700**	**77 200**	**95 000**	**135 300**	......	......
7	7 360	11 800	16 650	24 600	38 000	45 400	58 900	75 100	......	......	......
		19 350	**27 950**	**39 700**	**56 900**	**68 000**	**85 300**	**105 300**	......	......	......
8	8 350	13 400	18 900	27 800	43 200	51 500	66 800	85 100	......	......	......
		20 950	**30 200**	**42 900**	**62 100**	**74 100**	**93 200**	**115 300**	......	......	......
10	10 300	16 500	23 100	34 300	53 200	63 500	82 500				
		24 050	**34 400**	**49 400**	**72 100**	**86 100**	**108 900**				
12	12 200	19 500	27 600	40 700	63 000	75 100	97 600				
		27 050	**38 900**	**55 800**	**81 900**	**97 700**	**124 000**				
14	14 060	22 500	31 800	47 000	72 600	86 700	......				
		30 050	**43 100**	**62 100**	**91 500**	**109 300**	......				
Breaking radius, in inches, 115,000 lb. per sq. in. ultimate	6.53	10.43	14.75	21.75	33.75	40	52				

* Light and heavy figures indicate bending and total stresses, respectively; values below heavy line exceed 115 000 lb. per sq. in.

TABLE 31.—STRESSES IN $1\frac{1}{8}$-INCH LOCK-COIL CABLE, OX CARRIAGE.*

(p = stress, in pounds per square inch, due to bending; E = bending modulus of elasticity for given tension; d = diameter of rope; R = radius of curvature of rope; $p = \frac{E\,d}{2\,R}$; area = 842 sq. in.)

Total tension in cable, in pounds	0.0	2 500	5 000	7 500	10 000	12 500	15 000	17 500	20 000	25 000	30 000	35 000
Tension in cable, in pounds per square inch	.....	2 970	5 940	8 900	11 900	14 850	17 800	20 800	23 800	29 700	35 600	40 500
E, in millions of pounds	1.7	2.8	6.3	10.8	20.0	20.0	20.0	20.0	20.0	20.0	20.0	20.0
Angle under load O X carriage, in degrees.	Stress in Outer Wires Due to Bending, in Pounds per Square Inch.											
	1 400	2 300	5 200	8 900	16 350	16 350	16 350	16 350	16 350	16 350	16 350	16 350
1		**5 270**	**11 140**	**17 800**	**28 250**	**31 200**	**34 150**	**37 100**	**40 100**	**46 000**	**51 900**	**56 850**
	2 770	4 670	10 250	17 600	32 600	32 600	32 600	32 600	32 600	32 600	32 600	32 600
2		**7 640**	**16 190**	**26 500**	**44 500**	**47 450**	**50 400**	**53 400**	**56 400**	**62 300**	**68 200**	**73 100**
	4 130	6 800	15 300	26 200	48 600	48 600	48 600	48 600	48 600	48 600	48 600	48 600
3		**9 770**	**21 240**	**35 100**	**60 500**	**63 450**	**66 400**	**69 400**	**72 400**	**78 300**	**84 200**	**89 100**
	5 465	9 000	20 600	34 700	64 300	64 300	64 300	64 300	64 300	64 300	64 300	64 300
4		**11 970**	**26 540**	**43 600**	**76 200**	**79 150**	**82 100**	**85 100**	**88 100**	**94 000**	**99 900**	**104 800**
	6 780	11 150	25 100	43 100	79 800	79 800	79 800	79 800	79 800	79 800	79 800	79 800
5		**14 120**	**31 040**	**52 000**	**91 700**	**94 650**	**97 600**	**100 600**	**103 600**	**109 500**	**115 400**	**120 300**
	8 100	13 300	30 000	51 500	95 400	95 400	95 400	95 400	95 400	95 400	....	....
6		**16 270**	**35 940**	**60 400**	**107 300**	**110 250**	**113 200**	**116 200**	**119 200**	**125 100**	....	....
	9 400	15 460	34 800	59 700	110 600	....	....					
7		**18 430**	**40 740**	**68 600**	**122 500**	....	....					
	10 600	17 450	39 300	67 300	....	....	....					
8		**20 420**	**45 240**	**76 200**	....	....	....					
	13 100	21 600	48 500	83 200	....	....	....					
10		**24 570**	**54 440**	**92 100**	....	....	....					
	15 550	25 600	57 600	98 700	....	....	....					
12		**28 570**	**63 540**	**107 600**	....	....	....					
	18 000	29 600	66 700	104 300	....	....	....					
14		**32 570**	**72 640**	**113 200**	....	....	....					
Breaking radius, in inches, 115 000 lb. per sq. in., ultimate	8.33	13.7	30.8	53.0	98.0	....	....					

* Light and heavy figures indicate bending and total stresses, respectively; values below heavy line exceed 115 000 lb. per sq. in.

TABLE 32.—STRESSES IN $1\frac{1}{8}$-INCH LOCK-COIL CABLE, OXX CARRIAGE.*

(p = stress, in pounds per square inch, due to bending; E = bending modulus of elasticity for given tension; d = diameter of rope; R = radius of curvature of rope; $p = \frac{E\,d}{2\,R}$; area = 842 sq. in.)

Total tension in cable, in pounds	0.0	2 500	5 000	7 500	10 000	12 500	15 000	17 500	20 000	25 000	30 000	35 000
Tension in cable, in pounds per square inch	....	2 970	5 940	8 900	11 900	14 850	17 800	20 800	23 800	29 700	35 600	40 500
E, in millions of pounds	1.7	2.8	6.3	10.8	20.0	20.0	20.0	20.0	20.0	20.0	20.0	20.0
Angle under load on OXX carriage, in degrees	STRESS IN OUTER WIRES DUE TO BENDING, IN POUNDS PER SQUARE INCH.											
	1 210	1 975	4 500	7 680	14 250	14 250	14 250	14 250	14 250	14 250	14 250	14 250
1		**4 945**	**10 440**	**16 580**	**26 150**	**29 100**	**32 050**	**35 050**	**38 050**	**43 950**	**49 850**	**54 750**
	2 420	3 985	8 970	15 350	28 500	28 500	28 500	28 500	28 500	28 500	28 500	28 500
2		**6 955**	**14 910**	**24 250**	**40 400**	**43 350**	**46 300**	**49 300**	**52 300**	**58 200**	**64 100**	**69 000**
	3 640	6 000	13 500	22 150	41 700	41 700	41 700	41 700	41 700	41 700	41 700	41 700
3		**8 970**	**19 440**	**31 050**	**53 600**	**56 550**	**59 500**	**62 500**	**65 500**	**71 400**	**77 300**	**82 200**
	4 840	7 980	17 900	30 800	57 000	57 000	57 000	57 000	57 000	57 000	57 000	57 000
4		**10 950**	**23 840**	**39 700**	**68 900**	**71 850**	**74 800**	**77 800**	**80 800**	**86 800**	**92 600**	**97 500**
	6 050	9 960	22 400	38 400	71 200	71 200	71 200	71 200	71 200	71 200	71 200	71 200
5		**12 930**	**28 340**	**47 300**	**83 100**	**86 050**	**89 000**	**92 000**	**95 000**	**100 900**	**106 800**	**111 700**
	7 250	11 920	26 900	46 000	85 300	85 300	85 300	85 300	85 300	85 300	85 300	......
6		**14 890**	**32 840**	**54 900**	**97 200**	**100 150**	**103 100**	**106 100**	**109 100**	**115 000**	**120 900**	......
	8 430	13 850	31 300	53 500	99 300	99 300	99 300					
7		**16 820**	**37 240**	**62 400**	**111 200**	**114 150**	**117 100**					
	9 660	15 900	35 800	61 400	113 500	......	......					
8		**18 870**	**41 740**	**70 300**	**124 400**	......	......					
	12 030	19 850	44 750	76 500	......	......	......					
10		**22 820**	**50 690**	**85 400**	......	......	......					
	14 380	23 700	53 300	91 400	......	......	......					
12		**26 670**	**59 240**	**100 300**	......	......	......					
	16 300	26 800	60 400	103 600	......	......	......					
14		**29 770**	**66 340**	**112 500**	......	......	......					
Breaking radius, in inches. 115 000 lb. per sq. in., ultimate	8.33	13.7	30.8	53.0	98.0	......	......					

* Light and heavy figures indicate bending and total stresses, respectively; values below heavy line exceed 115 000 lb. per sq. in.

TABLE 33.—STRESSES IN $1\frac{1}{4}$-INCH LOCK-COIL CABLE, OX CARRIAGE.*

(p = stress, in pounds per square inch, due to bending; E = bending modulus of elasticity for given tension; d = diameter of rope; R = radius of curvature of rope; $p = \frac{E\,d}{2\,R}$; area = 1.07 sq. in.)

Total tension in cable, in pounds	**0.0**	**5 000**	**10 000**	**15 000**	**20 000**	**25 000**	**30 000**	**35 000**	**40 000**
Tension in cable, in pounds per square inch	....	**4 670**	**9 340**	**14 000**	**18 700**	**23 300**	**28 000**	**32 700**	**37 300**
E, in millions of pounds	**1.9**	**2.7**	**5.3**	**9.5**	**15.3**	**23.0**	**23.0**	**23.0**	**23.0**
Angle under load on OX carriage, in degrees.	Stress in Outer Wires Due to Bending, in Pounds per Square Inch.								
	1 735	2 470	4 850	8 650	14 000	21 000	21 000	21 000	21 000
1		**7 140**	**13 190**	**22 650**	**32 700**	**44 300**	**49 000**	**53 700**	**58 300**
	3 450	4 900	9 625	17 250	27 800	41 800	41 800	41 800	41 800
2		**9 570**	**18 965**	**31 250**	**46 500**	**65 100**	**69 800**	**74 500**	**79 100**
	5 130	7 300	14 300	25 600	41 400	62 200	62 200	62 200	62 200
		11 970	**23 640**	**39 600**	**60 100**	**85 500**	**90 200**	**94 900**	**99 500**
	6 790	9 650	18 900	33 900	54 700	82 200	82 200	82 200	82 200
4		**14 320**	**28 240**	**47 900**	**73 400**	**105 500**	**110 200**	**114 900**	**119 500**
	8 420	12 000	23 500	42 200	67 800	102 000	....	....	....
5		**16 670**	**32 840**	**56 200**	**86 500**	**125 300**	....	....	....
	10 060	14 300	28 000	50 000	81 000	....	....	....	....
6		**18 970**	**37 340**	**64 000**	**99 700**	....	....	....	....
	11 650	16 550	32 500	58 300	94 000	....	....		
7		**21 220**	**41 840**	**72 400**	**112 700**	....	....		
	13 230	18 800	37 000	66 800	106 600	....	....		
8		**23 470**	**46 340**	**80 800**	**125 300**	....	....		
	16 320	23 200	45 600	81 600	....	....	....		
10		**27 870**	**54 940**	**95 600**	....	....	....		
	19 330	27 500	54 000	96 500	....	....	....		
12		**32 170**	**63 340**	**110 500**	....	....	....		
	22 250	31 600	62 800	112 500	....	....	....		
14		**36 270**	**72 140**	**126 500**	....	....	....		
Breaking radius, in inches, 115 000 lb. per sq. in. ultimate	**10.33**	**14.625**	**28.75**	**50.0**	**84.0**	**125.0**	....		

* Light and heavy figures indicate bending and total stresses, respectively; values below heavy line exceed 115 000 lb. per sq. in.

TABLE 34.—STRESSES IN $1\frac{1}{4}$-INCH LOCK-COIL CABLE, OXX CARRIAGE.*

(p = stress, in pounds per square inch, due to bending ; E = bending modulus of elasticity for given tension ; d = diameter of rope ; R = radius of curvature of rope ; $p = \frac{E\,d}{2\,R}$; area = 1.07 sq. in.)

Total tension in cable, in pounds	**0.0**	**5 000**	**10 000**	**15 000**	**20 000**	**25 000**	**30 000**	**35 000**	**40 000**	**45 000**
Tension in cable, in pounds per square inch		**4 670**	**9 340**	**14 000**	**18 700**	**23 300**	**28 000**	**32 700**	**37 300**	**42 000**
E, in millions of pounds	**1.9**	**2.7**	**5.3**	**9.5**	**15.3**	**23.0**	**23.0**	**23.0**	**23.0**	**23.0**
Angle under load on OXX carriage, in degrees.	Stress in Outer Wires Due to Bending, in Pounds per Square Inch.									
1	1 500	2 130	4 180	7 500	12 100	18 200	18 200	18 200	18 200	18 200
		6 800	**13 520**	**21 500**	**30 800**	**41 500**	**46 200**	**50 900**	**55 500**	**60 200**
2	3 000	4 270	8 370	15 000	24 200	36 400	36 400	36 400	36 400	36 400
		8 940	**17 710**	**29 000**	**42 900**	**59 700**	**64 400**	**69 100**	**73 700**	**76 400**
3	4 500	6 400	12 550	22 500	36 200	54 500	54 500	54 500	54 500	54 500
		11 070	**21 890**	**36 500**	**54 900**	**77 800**	**82 500**	**87 200**	**91 800**	**96 500**
4	6 000	8 530	16 700	30 000	48 300	72 700	72 200	72 200	72 200	72 200
		13 200	**26 040**	**44 000**	**67 000**	**96 000**	**100 700**	**105 400**	**110 000**	**114 700**
5	7 500	10 650	20 900	37 500	60 400	91 000	91 000	91 000	....	....
		15 320	**30 240**	**51 500**	**79 100**	**113 300**	**119 000**	**123 700**	....	....
6	9 000	12 780	25 100	45 000	72 500	109 000	....	....	....	....
		17 450	**34 440**	**59 000**	**91 200**	**132 300**	....	....	....	....
7	10 500	14 900	29 300	52 500	84 500	....	....			
		19 540	**38 640**	**66 500**	**103 200**	....	....			
8	11 950	17 000	33 400	59 750	95 800	....	....			
		21 670	**42 740**	**73 750**	**114 500**	....	....			
10	15 000	21 300	41 800	75 000	121 000	....	....			
		25 970	**51 140**	**89 000**	**139 700**	....	....			
12	17 900	25 400	50 000	89 500	....	....	....			
		30 070	**59 340**	**103 500**	....	....	....			
14	20 800	29 600	58 000	104 000	....	....	....			
		34 270	**67 240**	**118 000**	....	....	....			
Breaking radius, in inches, 115 000 lb. per sq. in. ultimate	**10.33**	**14.625**	**28.75**	**50.0**	**84.0**	**125.0**	....			

* Light and heavy figures indicate bending and total stresses, respectively.

TABLE 35.—Stresses in $1\frac{3}{8}$-Inch Lock-Coil Cable, OXX Carriage.*

(p = stress, in pounds, per square inch, due to bending; E = bending modulus of elasticity for given tension; d = diameter of rope; R = radius of curvature of rope; $p = \frac{E}{2}\frac{d}{R}$, area = 1.266 sq. in.)

Total tension in cable, in pounds	0.0	5 000	10 000	15 000	20 000	25 000	27 500	30 000	35 000	40 000	45 000	50 000
Tension in cable, in pounds per square inch		3 950	7 900	11 850	15 800	19 750	21 700	23 700	27 600	31 600	35 500	39 500
E, in millions of pounds	2.2	2.8	4.6	7.6	11.8	17.2	20.0	20.0	20.0	20.0	20.0	20.0
Angle under load OXX carriage, in degrees.	**Stress in Outer Wires Due to Bending, in Pounds per Square Inch.**											
1	1 920	2 440 **6 390**	4 020 **11 920**	6 630 **18 480**	10 300 **26 100**	15 000 **34 750**	17 500 **39 200**	17 500 **41 200**	17 500 **45 100**	17 500 **49 100**	17 500 **53 000**	17 500 **57 000**
2	3 840	4 900 **8 850**	8 030 **15 930**	13 250 **25 100**	20 600 **36 400**	30 000 **49 750**	35 000 **56 700**	35 000 **58 700**	35 000 **62 600**	35 000 **66 600**	35 000 **70 500**	35 000 **74 500**
3	5 750	7 320 **11 270**	12 000 **19 900**	19 800 **31 650**	30 800 **46 600**	45 000 **64 750**	52 400 **74 100**	52 400 **76 100**	52 400 **80 000**	52 400 **84 000**	52 400 **89 900**	52 400 **91 900**
4	7 650	9 750 **13 700**	16 000 **23 900**	26 400 **38 250**	41 000 **56 800**	60 000 **79 750**	69 600 **91 300**	69 600 **93 300**	69 600 **97 200**	69 600 **101 200**	69 600 **105 100**	69 600 **109 100**
5	9 550	12 200 **16 150**	20 000 **27 900**	33 000 **44 850**	51 200 **67 000**	74 800 **94 550**	88 000 **109 700**	88 000 **111 700**	88 000 **115 600**	88 000 **119 600**	....	....
6	11 450	14 650 **18 600**	23 900 **31 800**	39 800 **51 650**	61 500 **77 300**	89 500 **109 250**	104 000 **124 700**	....	....			
7	13 350	17 000 **20 950**	27 900 **35 800**	46 200 **58 050**	71 700 **87 600**	104 500 **124 250**	....					
8	15 250	19 400 **23 350**	31 900 **39 800**	52 700 **64 550**	81 800 **97 600**	....	....					
10	19 000	24 200 **28 150**	39 700 **47 600**	65 700 **77 550**	102 000 **117 800**	....	....					
12	22 600	28 800 **32 750**	47 250 **55 150**	78 000 **89 850**	....	....	....					
14	26 400	34 900 **38 850**	55 200 **63 100**	91 000 **102 850**	....	....	....					
Breaking radius, in inches, 115 000 lb. per sq. in., ultimate	13.125	16.75	27.5	45.5	71.0	102.5	120.0					

* Light and heavy figures indicate bending and total stresses, respectively; values below heavy line exceed 115 000 lb. per sq. in.

TABLE 36.—STRESSES IN $1\frac{1}{2}$-INCH LOCK-COIL CABLE, OXX CARRIAGE.*

(p = stress, in pounds per square inch, due to bending; E = bending modulus of elasticity for given tension; d = diameter of rope; R = radius of curvature of rope; $p = \frac{E\,d}{2\,R}$; area = 1.464 sq. in.)

Total tension in cable, in pounds	0.0	5 000	10 000	15 000	20 000	25 000	30 000	35 000	40 000	45 000	50 000	55 000	60 000
Tension in cable, in pounds per square inch	....	3 420	6 830	10 250	13 650	17 000	20 500	23 900	27 300	30 700	34 100	37 500	41 000
E, in millions of pounds	2.5	3.0	4.5	6.9	10.3	14.6	20.0	20.0	20.0	20.0	20.0	20.0	20.0
Angle under load OXX carriage, in degrees.	Stress in Outer Wires Due to Bending, in Pounds per Square Inch.												
1	2 380	2 860	4 280	6 560	9 820	13 900	19 000	19 000	19 000	19 000	19 000	19 000	19 000
		6 280	**11 110**	**16 810**	**23 470**	**30 900**	**39 500**	**42 900**	**46 300**	**49 700**	**53 100**	**56 500**	**60 000**
2	4 750	5 700	8 550	13 100	19 550	27 750	38 000	38 000	38 000	38 000	38 000	38 000	38 000
		9 120	**15 380**	**23 350**	**33 200**	**44 750**	**58 500**	**61 900**	**65 300**	**68 700**	**72 100**	**75 500**	**79 000**
3	7 150	8 570	12 900	19 700	29 450	41 750	57 200	57 200	57 200	57 200	57 200	57 200	57 200
		11 990	**19 730**	**29 950**	**43 100**	**58 750**	**77 700**	**81 100**	**84 400**	**87 900**	**91 300**	**94 700**	**98 200**
4	9 500	11 400	17 100	26 200	39 150	55 500	76 000	76 000	76 000	76 000	76 000	76 000	76 000
		14 820	**23 930**	**36 450**	**52 800**	**72 500**	**96 500**	**99 900**	**103 300**	**106 700**	**110 100**	**113 500**	**117 000**
5	11 850	14 200	21 300	32 700	48 800	69 300	95 000	95 000	95 000	....			
		17 620	**28 130**	**42 950**	**62 450**	**86 300**	**115 500**	**118 900**	**122 300**				
6	14 200	17 000	25 600	39 200	58 500	83 000	....	....	....	....			
		20 420	**32 430**	**49 450**	**72 450**	**100 000**	....	....		....			
7	16 500	19 800	29 700	45 500	68 000	96 500	....						
		23 220	**36 530**	**55 750**	**81 650**	**113 500**	....						
8	18 900	22 850	34 000	52 200	78 000	....	....						
		26 270	**40 830**	**62 450**	**91 650**	....	....						
10	23 600	28 300	42 500	65 000	97 300	....	....						
		31 720	**49 330**	**75 250**	**110 950**	....	....						
12	28 200	33 800	50 800	77 800	....	....	....						
		37 220	**57 630**	**88 050**	....	....	....						
14	33 000	39 600	59 500	91 000	....	....	....						
		43 020	**66 330**	**101 250**	....	....	....						
Breaking radius, in inches. 115 000 lb. per sq. in., ultimate	16.3	19.5	29.37	45.0	67.25	95.5	130.0						

* Light and heavy figures indicate bending and total stresses, respectively; values below heavy line exceed 115 000 lb. per sq. in.

TABLE 37.—Stresses in $1\frac{5}{8}$-Inch Lock-Coil Cable, OXX Carriage.*

(p = stress, in pounds per square inch, due to bending; E = bending modulus of elasticity for given tension; d = diameter of rope; R = radius of curvature of rope; $W = 13\frac{3}{4}$ in.; $r = 5$ in.; $p = \frac{E\,d}{2\,R}$; area = 1.779 sq. in.)

Total tension in cable, in pounds.	0.0	5 000	10 000	15 000	20 000	25 000	30 000	35 000	40 000	45 000	50 000	55 000	60 000	65 000	70 000
Tension in cable, in pounds per square inch	....	2 800	5 620	9 400	11 240	14 000	16 850	19 700	22 500	25 300	28 000	30 900	33 700	36 500	39 300
E, in millions of pounds	2.9	3.2	4.0	5.3	7.2	9.6	12.5	15.9	20.0	20.0	20.0	20.0	20.0	20.0	20.0
Angle under load OXX carriage, in degrees.	**Stress in Outer Wires Due to Bending, in Pounds per Square Inch.**														
1	2 990	3 300	4 120	5 460	7 425	9 860	12 900	16 400	20 600	20 600	20 600	20 600	20 600	20 600	20 600
		6 100	**9 740**	**14 860**	**18 665**	**23 860**	**29 750**	**36 100**	**43 100**	**45 900**	**48 600**	**51 500**	**54 300**	**57 100**	**59 900**
2	5 970	6 600	8 250	10 900	14 800	19 800	25 750	34 750	41 200	41 200	41 200	41 200	41 200	41 200	41 200
		9 400	**13 870**	**20 300**	**26 040**	**33 800**	**42 600**	**54 450**	**63 700**	**66 500**	**69 200**	**72 100**	**75 900**	**77 700**	**80 500**
3	8 950	9 450	12 200	16 200	22 200	29 600	38 600	49 000	61 800	61 800	61 800	61 800	61 800	61 800	61 800
		12 250	**17 820**	**25 600**	**33 440**	**43 600**	**55 400**	**68 700**	**84 300**	**87 100**	**89 800**	**92 700**	**95 500**	**98 300**	**101 100**
4	11 930	13 200	16 500	21 800	29 600	39 500	51 200	65 500	81 500	81 500	81 500	81 500	81 500	81 500	81 500
		16 000	**22 120**	**31 200**	**40 840**	**53 500**	**68 050**	**85 200**	**104 000**	**106 800**	**109 500**	**112 400**	**115 200**	**118 000**	**120 800**
5	14 900	16 450	20 600	27 200	37 000	49 300	64 200	81 800	102 800	102 800	......	......	......	......	......
		19 250	**26 220**	**36 600**	**48 240**	**63 300**	**81 050**	**101 500**	**124 300**	**128 100**	......	......	......	......	......
6	17 850	19 700	24 600	32 600	44 300	59 100	76 900	98 000	123 200	......	......	......	......	......	......
		22 500	**30 220**	**42 000**	**55 540**	**73 100**	**93 750**	**117 700**	**145 700**	......	......	......	......	......	......
7	20 800	23 000	28 700	38 000	51 700	68 800	89 600	......	......						
		25 800	**34 320**	**47 400**	**62 940**	**82 600**	**106 450**	......	......						
8	23 800	26 300	32 800	43 500	59 100	78 800	102 700	......	......						
		29 106	**38 420**	**52 900**	**70 340**	**92 800**	**119 550**	......	......						
10	29 600	32 700	40 800	54 100	73 500	98 000	......	......	......						
		35 500	**46 420**	**63 400**	**84 740**	**112 000**	......	......	......						
12	35 500	39 200	49 000	65 000	88 250	......	......	......	......						
		42 000	**54 620**	**74 400**	**99 490**	......	......	......	......						
14	41 500	45 800	57 200	76 000	103 000	......	......	......	......						
	......	**48 600**	**62 820**	**85 400**	**114 200**	......	......	......	......						
Breaking radius, in inches, 115 000 lb. per sq. in., ultimate	20.5	23.0	28.25	37.0	51.0	67.0	86.5	112.5	141.5						

* Light and heavy figures indicate bending and total stresses, respectively; values below heavy line exceed 120 000 lb. per sq. in.

tension, or *vice versa*. Below this point the cable fails by bending; above it, by the direct tension.

Fig. 21 shows the load and tension for a stress of 115 000 lb. per sq. in. in the outermost wire. The ultimate strength of the wire is 140 000 lb. per sq. in. On the left-hand edge of each curve the upper number shows the total tension and the lower number the tension per square inch of cable.

TABLE 38.—LOADS FOR LOCK-COIL CABLE.

Size, in inches.	Weight per foot, in pounds.	Area, in square inches.	Tension at 30 000 lb. per sq. in.	Maximum load, in pounds.
7/8	1.8	0.50	15 000	900
1	2.5	0.70	21 000	1 250
1 1/8	3.1	0.85	25 500	1 550
1 1/4	4.0	1.10	33 000	2 000
1 3/8	4.75	1.35	40 500	2 350
1 1/2	5.50	1.55	46 500	2 750
1 5/8	6.4	1.80	54 000	3 200
1 3/4	7.3	2.05	61 500	3 650
1 7/8	8.20	2.30	69 000	4 100
2	9.4	2.60	78 000	4 700

For cableways, and similar designs, in which the carrier does not pass the supports, moderate tensions may be used to advantage. For aerial tramways in which the cable angles over the tower saddles are small, the higher cable tensions are preferable. Considering these results in the light of experience, Table 38, of loads for lock-coil cable, is presented.

Profiles.—The calculation of aerial tramway profiles is as follows: Let Table 39 be a record of the survey of the center line, the initial station at the proposed loading terminal, topography being omitted.

TABLE 39.—RECORD OF SURVEY OF CENTER LINE FOR AERIAL TRAMWAYS.

Station.	Elevation.	Station.	Elevation.
0	6 130	15	5 660
1	6 118	Deep gorge	
2	6 077	29	5 525
3	6 058	30	5 570
4	6 062	31	5 605
5	6 015	32	5 630
6	5 948	33	5 590
7	5 920	34	5 538
8	5 898	35	5 460
9	5 868	36	5 380
10	5 855	37	5 325
11	5 835	38	5 278
12	5 807	39	5 245
13	5 752	40	5 225
14	5 715	41	5 215
15	.....	42	5 210
..	.....	43	5 200

The stations have been plotted, and are shown in Fig. 22. By using a horizontal scale of 1 in. = 500 ft. and a vertical scale of 1 in. = 200 ft., the diagram becomes of a size convenient for analysis.

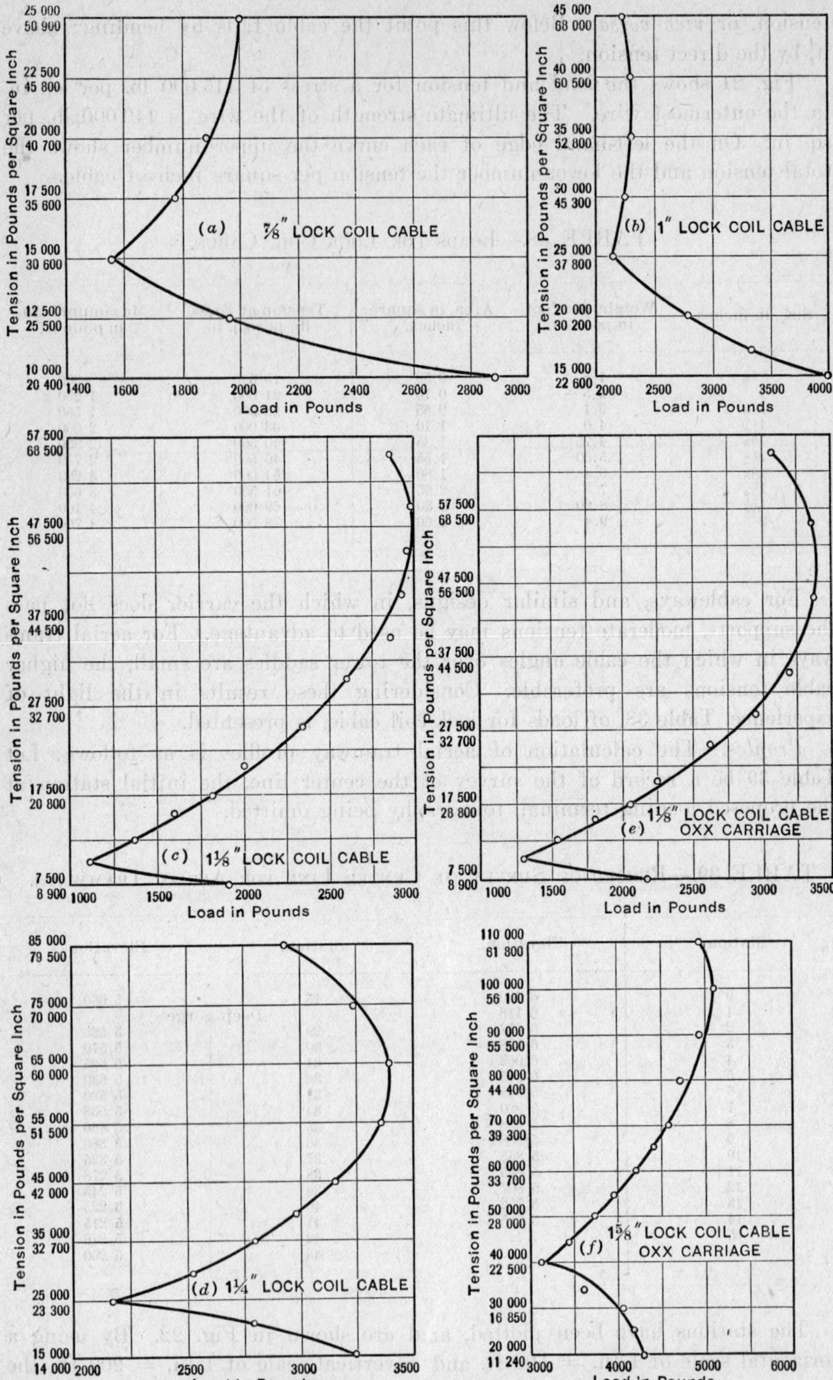

FIG. 21.—LOAD CAPACITY OF LOCK-COIL CABLES FOR DIFFERENT TENSIONS, STRESS IN OUTERMOST WIRE, 115 000 POUNDS PER SQUARE INCH.

The capacity of the tramway is 72 tons per hour of ore weighing (in buckets) 100 lb. per cu. ft., with a velocity 500 ft. per min. The bucket spacing is best determined by the criterion that the cost of the carrier is equal to the cost of the track cable between carriers. Thus, if the cost of a 12-cu. ft.

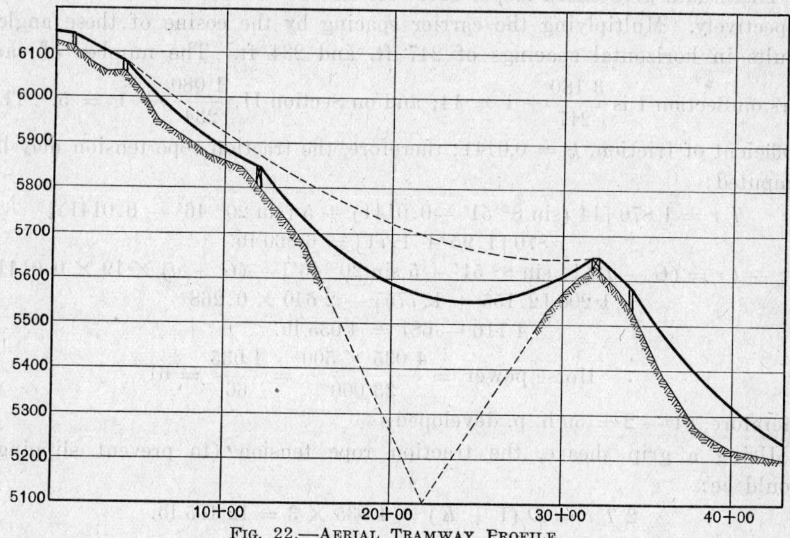

FIG. 22.—AERIAL TRAMWAY PROFILE.

carrier is \$150.00 and 1¼-in. locked-coil cable costs \$0.60 per ft., the spacing should be about 250 ft. As the carriers hold 1 200 lb., the spacing is calculated as follows:

$$\frac{0.03 \times 1\,200 \times 500}{72} = 250 \text{ ft.}$$

Therefore, the spacing of carriers based on velocity and tonnage agrees with the cost criterion. A study of the bending stress of lock-coil cables under tension and of their frictional hysteresis, and personal experience, lead to the following conclusion: The weight of the loaded carrier plus the weight of a traction rope of a length equal to the spacing should not exceed 500 w or 525 w (w = weight per foot of cable) for track cables under tensions of 30 000 lb., or 40 000 lb., per sq. in., respectively.

The weight of an empty 12-cu. ft. carrier may be taken as 450 lb., that of ore as 1 200 lb., and 250 ft. of traction rope as 220 lb., a total of 1 870 lb. This sum, divided by 500, indicates a track cable weighing 3.8 lb. per ft., or 1¼ in. in diameter, when under 30 000 lb. per sq. in.

Assuming a snow clearance of 10 ft. for structures along the line, this profile may be divided in two sections as follows:

Section I:

Loading terminal....	Station	0	....Elev.	6 145
Curve rail..........	"	31 + 80	.... "	5 650
		3 180 ft.		495 ft.

Section II:

Curve rail	Station 32 + 20	Elev.	5 645
Discharge terminal	" 43 + 00	"	5 235
	1 080 ft.		410 ft.

These data give chord slopes of 8° 51′ and 20° 46′ for Sections I and II, respectively. Multiplying the carrier spacing by the cosine of these angles results in horizontal spacings of 247 ft. and 234 ft. The number of carriers on Section I is $\frac{3\,180}{247} + 1 = 14$; and on Section II, $\frac{1\,080}{234} + 1 = 5$. The coefficient of friction, $k = 0.0141$; therefore, the traction rope tension may be computed:

$$T\,r = 1\,870\,[14\,(\sin 8°\,51' - 0.0141) + 5\,(\sin 20°\,46' - 0.0141)]$$
$$1\,870\,[1.95 + 1.71] = 6\,860 \text{ lb.}$$
$$T\,r - t\,r = (G - g)\,[14 \sin 8°\,51' + 5 \sin 20°\,46'] - (G + g) \times 19 \times 0.0141)$$
$$1\,200\,[2.155 + 1.775] - 2\,540 \times 0.268$$
$$4\,716 - 681 = 4\,035 \text{ lb.}$$
$$\text{Horse power} = \frac{4\,035 \times 500}{33\,000} = \frac{4\,035}{66} = 61$$

Therefore, 61 — 2 = 59 h. p. developed.

Using a grip sheave, the traction rope tension (to prevent slipping) should be:

$$2\,T\,r = D\,(1 + K) = 4\,035 \times 3 = 12\,105 \text{ lb.}$$

in which, $T\,r = 6\,055$ lb. This, compared with the load tension of 6 860 lb., indicates that a nominal weight for the tension mechanism may be chosen, say, 3 000 lb.

The total tension in the traction rope is then 6 860 + 1 500 = 8 360 lb. Since the stress due to bending a traction rope around a grip sheave 8 ft. in diameter is inconsequential, the size of traction rope may be tested by multiplying 8 360 lb. by a factor of safety of 4 = 33 440 lb. A 6 × 19, ¾-in. crucible steel, Lang lay traction rope has a listed strength of 17.5 tons; therefore, the traction rope weight used in these calculations is correct.

In order to locate, approximately, the position of the important structures on the profile, the empty and loaded cable curves should be drawn. If templates are not available they may be easily prepared. Referring to the table of coefficients (Table 17) of deflections at points located at multiples of 2% of the span under 40 000 lb. tension, the corresponding coefficients for 30 000 lb. may be found by multiplying the tabular values by $\frac{4}{3}$, and a curve plotted for the empty cable, say, on a span of 5 000 ft. The loaded curve is prepared on the assumption that the weight of the carrier may be distributed along the track cable for a distance equal to the carrier spacing. In this case:

1 200 + 450 = 1 650 lb. ÷ 250 ft.	=	6.60 lb per ft.
Track cable	=	4.00 " " "
Traction rope	=	0.90 " " "
Total	=	11.50 lb. per ft.

Since a track cable with a cross-section of 1 sq. in. weighs 3.6 lb. per ft., the cable will hang as if the tension were $\frac{3.6}{11.50 \times 30\,000 \text{ lb.}}$, or 9 425 lb. In other words, the deflections are $\frac{11.50}{3.6} = 3.19$ greater than those of the empty cable. From these data the two curves are plotted and templates are prepared for the scales used on the diagram. If the diagram had been plotted with the same scale for vertical and horizontal measurements, say, 1 in. = 100 ft., the radius of circular arcs could be determined from the $\frac{t}{w}$-relationship. The radius for the empty cable is $\frac{30\,000}{3.6} = 8\,333$ ft. Divide by the scale chosen and the radius of the circular arc is 83.33 in. The loaded curve is approximated in a similar manner, namely, $\frac{30\,000}{11.50} = \frac{2\,609}{100}$ results in a radius of 26.1 in.

The curves enable the computer to locate quickly the critical points of the profile. By referring to Fig. 14, it will be noted that the empty cable has an approximate center deflection of 60 ft. and 191 ft. when loaded, or a change of more than 130 ft. If weights are to be used to maintain a constant tension, space must be provided in the station for a travel of,

$$\frac{8}{3 \times 2\,000}(191^2 - 60^2) = 44 \text{ ft.}$$

resulting in a lofty and expensive structure. The change in the cable slopes at the ends of the span are as follows:

$$\tan \beta = 0.0006 \times 2\,000, \text{ or } 6° \; 50' \text{ empty cable.}$$
$$3.19 \times 6° \; 50' \quad , \text{ `` } 21° \; 00 \text{ loaded ``}$$

or a difference, say, of 14 degrees.

The station hoods for transferring carriers from cable to rail cannot accommodate so great a change in slope, not to mention the many other difficulties of design and operation that will be encountered if the change in cable slopes is not limited to reasonable values. This may be done by anchoring both ends of the track cables.

When the line is in operation, the tension of the traction rope of the long span exceeds 3 200 lb., an amount sufficiently great to carry a part of the carrier weight; that is, the equivalent weight per foot of track cable is reduced from 11.50 lb. to 11.00 lb. per ft. Therefore, care must be used in stripping the line to remove alternate carriers and avoid fouling of the track cable and traction rope. Also, the track cable supporting the empty carriers must be placed under such a tension that winds will not blow it into the loaded side.

By the proper use of the templates and the deflection charts (Figs. 13, 14, and 15), structures have been located and elevations adopted for checking by calculation. It is desirable to record these data in a simple manner and to arrange them so that the calculations follow in sequence. Such a form is shown in Table 40. For convenience the elements of design have been recapitulated.

TABLE 40.—Calculations of Profile.

(Data as follows: Capacity, 72 tons per hour; weight of material in buckets, 100 lb. per cu. ft.; velocity, 500 ft. per min.; spacing, 250 ft.; weight of loaded carrier on the line, 1 870 lb., and of empty carrier, 670 lb.; traction rope, $\frac{3}{4}$-in. crucible steel at 0.89 lb. per ft.; track cables, $1\frac{1}{4}$-in. and $\frac{7}{8}$-in. lock coil for loaded and light sides, respectively; cross-sectional areas, 1.1 and 0.5 sq. in.; at 30 000 lb. per sq. in., the tensions are 33 000 lb., and 15 000 lb. in the horizontal components of the track cables; $\frac{G}{t} = 0.0567$, or 3° 15′; the slope angle at support for empty cable is 20.7′ of arc per 100 ft.)

Type of structure.	Station.	Elevation.	tan α.	α.	Δ.	Empty cable.	Total.	Loads.	Total.	Saddle.	Radius, in feet.
(1)	(2)	(3)	(4)	(5)	(6)	(7)	(8)	(9)	(10)	(11)	(12)
Loading terminal..........	0 + 00	6 142.00									
	90	1.80	0.0200	1°09′		0°18′		3°15′			......
	0 + 90	6 140.20			3°25′		3°45′		3°15′	7° 0′	......
	10	.80	0.0799	4°34′		0° 2′		0′			
Three-bent support......	1 + 00	6 139.40			3°41′		3°45′		3°15′	7° 0′	......
	10	1.45	0.1450	8°15′		0° 2′		3°15′			
	1 +100	6 137.95			2°32′		3°34′		3°31′	7°05′	......
	280	53.34	0.1905	10°47′		1° 0′		3°31′			
	3 + 90	6 084.61					— 9°47′			— 9°47′	......
Curve rail.......	24	7.07	0.2946	16°25′							
	4 + 14	6 077.54			17°02′		19°41′		6°54′	26°35′	70.82
	768	235.25	0.3063	17°02′		2°39′		6°54′			
	11 + 82	5 842.29			17°02′		14°23′		7°29′	7°29′	
Curve rail.......	36	11.00	0.3055	16°59′							......
Double anchorage..........	12 + 18	5 831.29					12°07′		14°10′	26°17′	114.03
	1958	184.00	0.0940	5°22′		6°45′		14°10′			
	31 + 76	5 647.29			5°22′		1°13′		14°10′	15°23′	......
Curve rail.......	48	2.56	0.0533	3°03′							78.65
Double anchorage..........	32 + 24	5 644.73			17°56′		18°00′		3°15′	21°15′	......
	76	24.60	0.3237	17°56′		0°14′		3°15′			
Tower...........	33 + 00	5 620.13			1°23′		1°57′		3°15′	5°12′	......
	95	33.30	0.3505	19°19′		0°20′		3°15′			
	33 + 95	5 586.83			4°32′		4°54′		3°15′	8°09′	......
Two-bent structure..........	10	4.42	0.4421	23°51′		0° 2′		0′			
	34 + 05	5 582.41			— 2°38′		0°29′		7°40′	8°09′	......
	895	347.41	0.3881	21°13′		3°05′		7°40′			
Discharge tunnel	43 + 00	5 235.00					18°08′		7°40′	10°28′	......

Explanation of Table 40.—Column (1) indicates the type of structure, such as loading terminal, two-bent support, curve rail, and double-anchorage structure, tower, discharge terminal, etc. Column (2) indicates the survey station and the horizontal distance between. Column (3) gives the elevations of the saddles and the differences in height between them. Column (4) gives the tangents, and Column (5), the slope angles of the chords. Column (6) records the intersection angle of the chords. Plus (+) indicates downward pressure; minus (—), uplift. This angle may be changed at will by shifting the elevations of the adjoining saddles. Column (7) has the slope angle of the tangent to the empty cable at the saddle. This angle is easily computed from the fact that cables of constant cross-section have a definite curvature per foot; for instance, a track cable weighing 3.6 lb. per ft., under a tension of 30 000 lb., curves 41.4′ of arc per 100 ft. of span, hence the slope of the tangent is 20.7′ per 100 ft. The angle of the empty cable on the saddle is the algebraic sum of the intersection and cable angles, as shown in Column (8). The former may be negative; the latter is always positive. Column (9) gives the angular increase due to the loads. These are quickly determined from the table for load tangents (Table 20). Column (10) gives the sum of the load angles at the support. Column (11) gives the result of the calculation, namely, the total angle of the loaded cable over the saddle. It is the usual aim of profile designers to impose equal cable angles on adjacent saddles. When the slope angles of cables entering or leaving structures are known, the loads imposed, and the radius of rail curvature, can be readily computed. Column (12) gives the radius of the curve tangent to the cable slopes. Experience indicates that the curvature of track cables of small diameter over saddles should be less than 9°; and less than 6° for cables $1\frac{3}{8}$ in., or larger.

To determine the position of the empty cable on the long span, the erection tension must be computed. The simplicity of the calculation, by the method of second differences, is shown in Table 41.

Anchored Span.—The data used in computing the anchored span are as follows: Locked-coil cable, $1\frac{1}{4}$ in. in diameter, weighing 4 lb. per ft.; maximum horizontal tension, 33 000 lb.; horizontal span, 1 958 ft.; difference in terminal elevations, 184.0 ft.; weight of loaded carrier, 1 870 lb.; spacing of loads, 250 ft.; slope of chord, 5° 22′; horizontal spacing, 250 cos 5° 22′=248.91 ft.; number of loads, 8; distance from support to first load, 107.83 ft.; and deflection of fourth load from left support:

$$y = \frac{1\,870 \times 1\,958}{4 \times 33\,000}\left[8 - \frac{64 \times 248.91}{2 \times 1\,958}\right] + \frac{4 \times 1\,958^2}{8 \times 33\,000}\left[1 - \left(\frac{248.91}{1\,958}\right)^2\right]$$

$$+ \frac{854.55}{1\,958} \times 184.0$$

$$= 109.062 + 57.143 + 80.305 = 246.51 \text{ ft.}$$

In this case the first and second differences are equal:

$$-\frac{248.91}{33\,000}[1\,870 + 4 \times 248.91] = 21.607 \text{ ft.}$$

$$\text{Slope factor} = \frac{248.91}{1\,958} \times 184 \qquad = \underline{23.386}$$

$$\text{Total} \qquad = 44.993 \text{ ft.}$$

TABLE 41.—DEFLECTIONS OF ANCHORED SPAN BY FIRST AND SECOND DIFFERENCES.

Load No.	0.	1.	2.	3.	4.	5.	6.	7.	8.	9.
Deflection..........	5 831.29	5 784.58	5 696.37	5 629.77	5 584.78	5 561.39	5 559.62	5 579.44	5 620.88	5 647.29
First difference....	46.71	88.207	66.60	44.993	23.386	1.779	19.828	41.435	26.41	
Second difference..		21 607	21.607	21.607	21.607	21.607	21.607	21.607	21.607	

To check Table 41, compute the deflection of the load nearest the support:

$$y = \frac{1\,870 \times 1\,958 \times 0.05507}{33\,000}[8\,(1 - 0.05507) - 0.1271 \times 28]$$

$$+ \frac{4 \times 1\,958 \times 0.05933 \times 0.05507 \times 0.94593}{2} + 0.05507 \times 184.0$$

$$= 24.460 + 12.114 + 10.133 = 46.707 \text{ ft.}$$

Therefore, the deflections given in Table 41 are correct.

The length of the loaded span is:

$$1\,958 + \frac{46.71^2 \times 26.41^2}{2 \times 107.83}$$

$$+ \frac{88.207^2 + 66.60^2 + 44.993^2 + 23.386^2 + 1.779^2 + 19.828^2 + 41.435^2}{497.82}$$

$$= 1\,958 + 13.35 + 33.95 = 2\,005.30 \text{ ft.}$$

The length of the empty span, when loaded, is increased to 2 005.30 ft., that is,

$$2\,005.30 = 1\,958 + \frac{4^2 \times 1\,958^3}{24\,t^2} + \frac{184^2}{3\,916} + \frac{0.000041 \times 1\,954}{1000}(33\,000 - t)$$

or,

$$t + \frac{5\,005\,000\,000}{t^2} = 36.01 + 0.00008\,t$$

Solving by slide-rule for $t = 11\,650$,

$$\frac{5\,005\,000\,000}{t^2} = 37.00$$

Similarly,

$$36.01 + 0.00008\,t = 36.95$$

Therefore, erect at a tension of 11 650 lb.

Conclusion

In conclusion, it may be stated that the foregoing remarks only hint at the magnitude and scope of aerial tramway systems of transportation. It should be emphasized that the highest degree of engineering skill and advanced mathematical analysis are required to design properly and erect a successful and economical aerial tramway. It is recalled that multi-loaded spans are not continuous functions, but a series of arcs which intersect under each carrier with an angle the tangent of which is equal to the weight of the load divided by the horizontal component of the tension. Because of this, the determinations of deflections, tangent slopes, and other properties of the cable spans have developed a system of mathematical analysis, which is as distinctive as that used in railroad location, or any other engineering specialty. In other words, aerial tramways are best designed by those who are fitted by experience and training to undertake this type of construction.

The advance in freight rates in this country makes it imperative to supply a system of transportation for industrial plants, mines, and quarries, which is safe, free from meteoric conditions, and economical, and aerial tramways meet these specifications in a most practical and satisfactory manner.

DISCUSSION

ROBERT C. STRACHAN,* M. AM. SOC. C. E. (by letter).—Without questioning the correctness of the author's formulas relating to unloaded spans, it appears that the inherent complexity of the equations, when the origin is taken at one support, might well be avoided; more especially since the operations in problems of the catenary, even under the most favorable assumptions, are as a rule not simple.

Let the origin for the curve shown in Fig. 9 be taken at the lower extremity of the parameter as indicated in Fig. 23.

Use the author's notation and, in addition, let z = parameter $= \frac{t}{w}$; $\frac{S_1}{z} = u_1$; and $\frac{S_2}{z} = u_2$.

Therefore,

$$\frac{S}{z} = u_1 + u_2 \qquad (109)$$

The equation of the curve then takes its simplest form,

$$y = \frac{t}{w}\left(\cosh \frac{x\,w}{t}\right) \qquad (110)$$

or,

$$y = z \cosh \frac{x}{z} \qquad (111)$$

For any point of the catenary distant x to the left or right of the Y-axis, the vertical distance below L or R is,

$$v_L = z\left(\cosh u_1 - \cosh \frac{x}{z}\right) \qquad (112)$$

$$v_R = z\left(\cosh u_2 - \cosh \frac{x}{z}\right) \qquad (113)$$

The derivation of u_1, u_2, and other required elements, is as follows: It may be shown that,

$$\frac{\frac{1}{2}(u_1 + u_2)}{\sinh \frac{1}{2}(u_1 + u_2)} = \frac{S}{\sqrt{l^2 - h^2}} \qquad (114)$$

and,

$$\tanh \frac{1}{2}(u_1 - u_2) = \frac{h}{l} \qquad (115)$$

From the author's assumed data,

$$\frac{t}{w} = z = 2\,777.7778 \text{ ft.}$$

$$\frac{S}{2\,z} = \frac{1}{2}(u_1 + u_2) = 0.18000 \text{ hyps}\dagger$$

* With The Port of New York Authority, New York, N. Y.

† Hyperbolic radians, or sectorial ratio.

therefore,

$$\sinh \frac{1}{2}(u_1 + u_2) = 0.18098$$

and from Equation (114),

$$l^2 = \frac{(0.18098)^2 S^2}{(0.18)^2} + h^2 \quad \ldots\ldots\ldots\ldots\ldots\ldots\ldots\ldots (116)$$

Therefore,

$$l = 1\,010.405 \text{ ft.}$$

From Equation (115),

$$\tanh \frac{1}{2}(u_1 - u_2) = \frac{100}{1\,010.405} = 0.09897$$

therefore,

$$\frac{1}{2}(u_1 - u_2) = 0.09929 \text{ hyps.}$$

$$u_1 = 0.18000 + 0.09929 = 0.27929 \text{ hyps.}$$

$$u_2 = 0.18000 - 0.09929 = 0.08071 \text{ hyps.}$$

$$\beta_1 = \text{gd. } u_1{}^* = 15° \ 47.9'$$

$$\beta_2 = \text{gd. } u_2 = 4° \ 37.2'$$

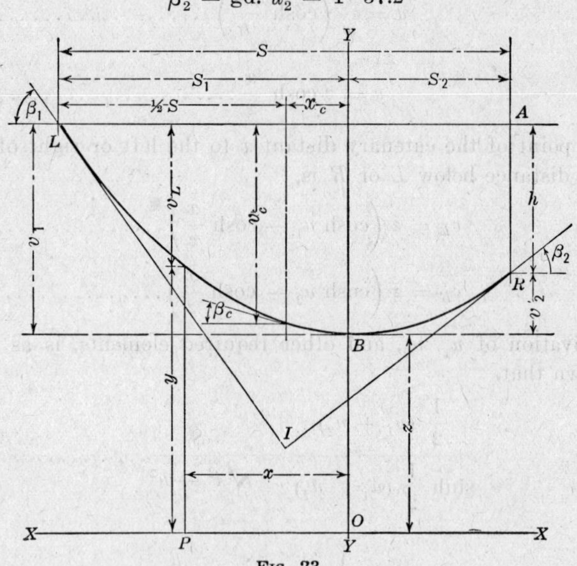

FIG. 23.

No calculation other than interpolation in the hyperbolic tables, is necessary to obtain β_1 and β_2.

$$S_1 = z\,u_1 = 775.806 \text{ ft.}$$

$$S_2 = S - S_1 = z\,u_2 = 224.194 \text{ ft.}$$

$$v_1 = z\,(\cosh u_1 - 1) = 2\,777.778 \times 0.03926 = 109.055 \text{ ft.}$$

$$v_2 = v_1 - h = z\,(\cosh u_2 - 1) = 2\,777.778 \times 0.00326 = 9.055 \text{ ft.}$$

* This equation states that the angle, β_1, is the "Gudermannian angle" corresponding to the hyperbolic sectorial ratio, u_1.

If l_1 and l_2, the arcs, respectively, under S_1 and S_2 are required,

$$l_1 = z \sinh u_1 \ldots\ldots\ldots\ldots\ldots\ldots\ldots\ldots (117)$$

$$l_2 = l - l_1 = z \sinh u_2 \ldots\ldots\ldots\ldots\ldots\ldots\ldots (118)$$

Let x_c = distance from Y-axis to the center of Span $S = \frac{1}{2}(S_1 - S_2)$, and, let $u_c = \frac{x_c}{z}$. Then,

$$u_c = \frac{1}{2}(u_1 - u_2) \ldots\ldots\ldots\ldots\ldots\ldots\ldots\ldots (119)$$

Let v_c = vertical distance from center of span, S, to the curve, then,

$$v_c = z\,(\cosh u_1 - \cosh u_c) \ldots\ldots\ldots\ldots\ldots\ldots (120)$$

and β_c = the inclination of the tangent = gd. u_c

$$x_c = S_1 - \frac{1}{2} S = 275.806 \text{ ft.}$$

$$u_c = \frac{1}{2}(u_1 - u_2) = 0.09929 \text{ hyps.}$$

therefore,

$$\cosh u_c = 1.00493$$

and, by interpolating as before,

$$\beta_c = \text{gd. } u_c = 5^\circ\ 40.8'$$

From Equation (120),

$$v_c = z\,(1.03926 - 1.00493) = 95.361 \text{ ft.}$$

v_c is designated y_c in Fig. 9 and the result of the calculation is given as 95.225 ft.

The introduction of the author's nomographic charts, Figs. 13, 14, and 15, draws attention anew to the saving in time and labor made possible by this means, with no sacrifice of needful precision. This is an advantage to which reference was made by the writer in his paper* on the designing of such charts.

GEORGE PAASWELL,† M. AM. SOC. C. E. (by letter).—While the entire paper is so interesting and unusual, both in its topic and in its lucid manner of presentation that the writer would like to discuss every feature of it, he is confining these notes to a treatment of two minor points, the hyperbolic functions and the cubic equation. The former may be computed to any degree of exactness from the trigonometric functions and tables and the latter may be solved directly. Few engineers seem to be aware of this latter fact.

The hyperbolic functions bear a direct relation to the circular function of a characteristic angle the geometric significance of which need not be discussed herein. The relations may be given as follows: $\sinh u = \tan v$; $\cosh u = \sec v$; $\tanh u = \sin v$; $\coth u = \csc v$; $\text{sech } u = \cos v$; and $\text{csch } u = \cot v$. The relation between u and v is given by the formula,

$$u = 2.3025851 \log \tan\left(45^\circ + \frac{v}{2}\right)$$

* "Nomographic Solutions for Formulas of Various Types," *Transactions*, Am. Soc. C. E., Vol. LXXVIII (1915), p. 1359.

† Engr., Corson Constr. Corporation, Brooklyn, N. Y.

The method of computation will be seen in the solution of the cubic equation. Given a cubic equation in its most general form,

$$x^3 + a\,x^2 + b\,x + c = 0$$

it is reduced to a form,

$$y^3 - 3\,p\,y - 2\,q = 0$$

by substituting $x = y - \frac{a}{3}$.

The roots of the cubic equation in y are then found from the following, depending upon the signs of p and q:

(1) If both p and q are plus and q^2 is greater than p^3, use the substitution,

$$\cosh u = \frac{q}{\sqrt{p^3}}$$

The three roots are then,

$$y_1 = 2\sqrt{p}\cosh\frac{u}{3}$$

$$y_2 = -\frac{y_1}{2} + i\sqrt{3\,p}\sinh\frac{u}{3}$$

and,

$$y_3 = -\frac{y_1}{2} - i\sqrt{3\,p}\sinh\frac{u}{3}$$

(2) If p is positive, q, negative, and q^2 is greater than p^3, use the substitution,

$$\cosh u = \frac{-q}{\sqrt{p^3}}$$

and the three roots are,

$$y_1 = -2\sqrt{p}\cosh\frac{u}{3}$$

$$y_2 \text{ and } y_3 = -\frac{y_1}{2} \pm i\sqrt{3\,p}\sinh\frac{u}{3}$$

(3) If p is negative,

$$\sinh u = \frac{q}{\sqrt{-p^3}}$$

and the three roots are,

$$y_1 = 2\sqrt{-p}\sinh\frac{u}{3}$$

$$y_2 \text{ and } y_3 = -\frac{y_1}{2} \pm i\sqrt{3\,p}\cosh\frac{u}{3}.$$

(4) If p is positive and q^2 is less than p^3, substitute,

$$\cos u = \frac{q}{\sqrt{p^3}}$$

and the three roots are,

$$y_1 = 2\sqrt{p}\cos\frac{u}{3}$$

$$y_2 \text{ and } y_3 = -\frac{y_1}{2} \pm \sqrt{3\,p}\sin\frac{u}{3}$$

Refer to the cubic equation,

$$0.0000457\,t - 0.474 = \frac{666\,666\,667}{t^2}$$

and, to reduce the size of the coefficients, take the unit load as 100 000 lb. The equation then reads,

$$4.57\,t^3 - 0.474\,t^2 - \frac{1}{15} = 0$$

or,

$$t^3 - 0.1037\,t^2 - 0.01459 = 0$$

reducing to the standard form by placing

$$t = x + \frac{0.1037}{3}$$

$$x^3 - 0.003585\,x - 0.0145 = 0 \ldots\ldots\ldots\ldots\ldots(121)$$

In Equation (121) $p = 0.001195$ and $q = 0.00725$. This form of the cubic equation comes under Case (1),

$$\cosh u = 175.6$$

Then, from the circular relations already given,

$$\log \cosh u = \log \sec v = 2.2445245$$

$$v = 89°\ 40'\ 24''$$

From the relation between u and v,

$$u = 2.302585 \log \tan 89°\ 50'\ 12''$$

$$u = 5.8602$$

$$\frac{u}{3} = 1.9534$$

To obtain v,

$$1.9534 = 2.3026 \log \tan \left(45° + \frac{v}{2}\right) \log \tan \left(45° + \frac{v}{2}\right) = 0.84835$$

and,

$$v = 73°\ 51'\ 40''$$

$$\cosh \frac{u}{3} = \sec 73°\ 51'\ 40'' = 3.5975$$

The real root of Equation (121) is, therefore,

$$x = 3.5975 \sqrt{(0.001195)} = 0.24873$$

$$t = x + \frac{0.1037}{3} = 0.28363$$

or, reducing to pounds, the real root is 28 363 lb.

These processes illustrate the comparative simplicity of both the computation of hyperbolic functions from trigonometric tables and the direct solution of the cubic equation.

CASPER D. MEALS,* ASSOC. M. AM. SOC. C. E. (by letter).—This comprehensive paper fills a big gap; the wealth of practical, usable data therein bespeaks the concluding thoughts, namely, that aerial tramways are best designed by those who are fitted by experience and training to do so.

Dumping Cradleways, or Contractors' Suspension Bridges.—When calculating the size of the cables to be used, the live load moving on to the platform is to be taken as the empty car weights only, the material being dumped off the cars as they pass on to the platform. For a 9-car trip, 8 empty cars and 1 loaded car will be on the platform, but part of the reaction of the latter is carried on the bank end, so that to consider the moving load as 9 empty cars will be sufficiently accurate.

The platforms are usually 14 ft. wide, 75 to 130 ft. long, and weigh from 170 to 250 lb. per lin. ft. and the suspender rope spacings are from 10 to 18 ft. on centers, the average being 12 ft. The empty cars weigh from 5 000 to 9 000 lb., the average being 6 000 lb. The suspenders are generally made up of ½ or ⅝-in., 6 × 19, plow steel rope, and two double sheave tackle blocks; 10-in. blocks for the ½-in. rope, and 14-in. blocks for the ⅝-in. rope.

TABLE 42.—CABLE FOR DUMPING CRADLEWAYS.

Diameter of rope, in inches.	Construction.	Pounds per foot.	Metallic area, in square inches.	APPROXIMATE BREAKING STRENGTHS, IN TONS.	
				Catalog.	Actual.
1½	7 × 7	3.70	1.057	90	98
1⅝	7 × 19	4.34	1.257	106	115
1¾	7 × 19	5.10	1.460	124	140
1⅞	7 × 19	5.90	1.630	144	158
2	7 × 19	6.73	1.816	164	175
2⅛	7 × 19	7.60	2.230	185	195
2¼	7 × 19	8.52	2.436	208	220
2⅜	7 × 19	9.5	2.722	232	250
2½	7 × 19	10.5	3.106	256	275
2⅝	7 × 19	11.6	3.522	283	300
2¾	7 × 19	12.7	3.774	310	330
3	7 × 37	15.5	4.243	360	385

The hold-down tackle at the end of the platform is usually of ¾-in., 6 × 19, plow steel rope, reeved on 16-in. double sheave blocks. The deflection of the main cables is usually taken at 6 to 7% of the length of the span and the size of the cables may be based on a factor of safety of 3 as a minimum on the actual breaking strengths of the cables. For the one installation of a dumping cradleway noted by Mr. Carstarphen (page 882), the main cables are given as 2½-in., 6 × 37, plow steel rope. A 2¼-in., 7 × 19, galvanized plow steel, bridge cable of approximately the same breaking strength would have been more economical.

The actual breaking strengths of galvanized plow steel bridge cables are in excess of the manufacturers' standard lists, and data pertaining to suitable size of bridge cables for these dumping cradleways are given in Table 42.

* Chf. Engr., Am. Cable Co., Inc., New York, N. Y.

The modulus of elasticity of these cables may be taken at 17 000 000 lb. per sq. in. for new cable, and 20 000 000 lb. per sq. in., for cable that has been repeatedly stressed.

The maximum stress in the main cable span may be determined from:

$$T_{\max.} = \left\{ \frac{w\,S^2 + 4\,\rho\,k\,(S - k)}{8\,d} \right\} \sec \beta \qquad (122)$$

The unloaded cable deflection (see Fig. 24) at which it must be erected before any dead or live loads are applied, may be determined from,

$$d_1 = d - \frac{15\,\Delta L}{16\,(5\,b - 24\,b^3)} \qquad (123)$$

in which,

$$\Delta L = \frac{H_1\,S}{A\,E}\left(1 + \frac{16\,b^3}{3}\right)$$

$$H_1 = \frac{4\,\rho\,k\,(S - k)}{8\,d}$$

$$b = \frac{d}{S}$$

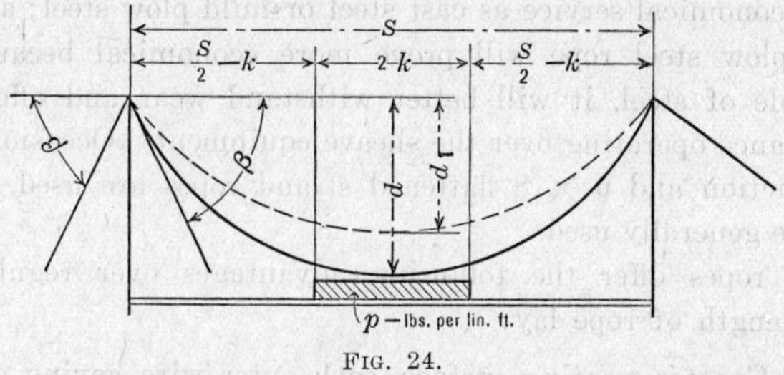

FIG. 24.

Track Cables.—The breaking of a wire in a smooth-coil track strand does give trouble by uncoiling to the nearest tower support or coupling. However, there has been developed for this service a pre-formed, smooth-coil, track strand in which this objection has been eliminated, the wires being pre-shaped to their position in the cable and, therefore, being unrestrained in their place in the strand. The outer wires will stay in place and also will wear to a much thinner section before breaking, thus prolonging the life of the strand.

The physical properties of this type of strand (known as the Tru-Lay Brand), correspond to values given in Table 6. The E-values may be taken at 20 000 000 lb. per sq. in. for a 19-wire strand, and 18 000 000 lb. per sq. in. for the 37-wire strand. For a greater number of wires it will be even less, as there is relatively greater looseness in the strand construction of a 61-wire strand than in that of a 19-wire strand and, consequently, the E-value of the former must be lower.

The deflections of the main cables are usually limited from 2 to 2½% of the span length, S, so as to eliminate steep grades at the towers which would require a larger traction rope and greater engine duty.

The frictional hysteresis loops noted by Mr. Carstarphen (page 893), for progressive and retrogressive loadings of the strands, have been noted also by the writer in tests made of both strands and wire ropes.

The "rocking saddle", shown in Fig. 5, should have the merit of reducing the wear and abuse on the track strand or cable at the saddle by pivoting, and thereby reducing the angle that the cable will make when the carriage is approaching or going off the saddle. If this point is attained, then the rocking saddle would eliminate the use of protection hoods over the track cables at the saddles.

Couplings for Joining Sections of the Track Cables.—The writer was not aware that couplings to smooth-coil track strands were ordinarily attached in the same manner as the locked-coil and wire strands by means of wedges. Certainly, a zinc socket attachment should be more effective, considerably cheaper, and should eliminate the possibility of loose wires in the strand, because, unless extreme care is exercised in driving the wedges in that particular type of connection, some wires will be disturbed and loosened in the strand.

Traction Ropes.—It has been the writer's experience that plow steel ropes will give as economical service as cast steel or mild plow steel; and for severe service, the plow steel rope will prove more economical because, being of a higher grade of steel, it will better withstand wear and offer as great a fatigue resistance operating over the sheave equipment. Occasionally, 6 × 19 Seale construction and 6 × 8 flattened strand ropes are used, although the 6 × 7 is more generally used.

Lang lay ropes offer the following advantages over regular lay ropes of the same length of rope lay:

(*a*) Greater wearing surface, each outer wire having approximately three times the length exposed for wear, leading to lower bearing values.

(*b*) Greater flexibility, because the outer wires of the strand are parallel to the axis of the rope against the manila core and set up less frictional resistance in bending.

(*c*) Lower bending stresses, the bending stress in a Lang lay rope being approximately 80% of that in a regular lay rope of the same construction.

The bending stress in a wire is greater the farther away it is from the axis of the rope and the nearer it runs parallel to the axis. In a regular lay rope, this combination of unfavorable conditions is found. In a Lang lay rope it is not found, because where the wires do lie parallel to the axis of the rope, they are nearest to the axis and are embedded in the manila core of the rope.

A Lang lay rope is inherently "cranky," due to the fact that the wires in the strands, and the strands in the rope, are laid up in the same direction. A Lang lay rope of the Tru-Lay type, fabricated with pre-formed wires and strands, will eliminate entirely the "crankiness" so typical with Lang lay ropes and will also wear longer and withstand bending better because the individual wires and strands of the rope are in an unrestrained position.

Carriers.—Carriages are usually made up with two sheaves of 10 to 14-in. treads in a pivoting frame attached to the bucket bale as described by Mr. Carstarphen. The writer would like to know whether the weights given in Table 8 include the weight of the carriage with sheave and the grip? The carriage, with sheaves, weighs approximately 100 to 150 lb., and the grips from 35 to 75 lb., depending on the type and the loads.

Data pertaining to minimum steel tower weights for 8-ft. gauge cables, for towers, 65 to 100 ft. high, are as follows:

Height, in feet.	Weight, in pounds.
65	10 000
70	11 000
80	13 000
85	14 500
100	17 000

Bolts and washers for timber towers of the closed type, including the anchor-bolts and washers, will be approximately as follows:

Height, in feet.	Weight, in pounds.
10	400
20	425
30	500
40	650
50	800
60	1 100
70	1 300
80	1 800

Tension in Traction Ropes.—The coefficient values as given for K include that of a greasy rope on a rubber-lined and leather-lined sheave. Is it implied from this that such driving sheaves are used? Unless the unit radial bearing pressure of the rope on the rubber and leather lining is kept within a value of 65 to 75 lb., the lining will soon be cut out.

The radial pressure of a rope in a sheave groove is a function of the rope tension and the sheave diameter. It should not be confused with the resultant of the tensions in the rope with regard to the angle the ropes make with each other. The unit radial pressure is determined from:

$$u = \frac{P}{r\,d} \qquad (124)$$

d being the rope diameter; r, the radius of the tread of the sheave, in inches; and P, the load, in pounds.

Size of Track Cables.—If the choice is guided by experience, it will pertain to the construction rather than the size; for, after all, the stress requirements, which are calculable, are the governing consideration in the size and quality. The bending stresses need not be considered because the deflections are relatively so shallow and the traveling loads so light, that the bending of the track cables by the carriage wheels or at the tower saddles is not of prime importance. Bending stresses and the reduction or loss in strength of a wire rope bent around a sheave are not analogous.

Bending stresses are applicable only to moving ropes operating over sheaves and have to do with their "efficiency" in service and not to their reduction in breaking strength. There must be a limit to the smallness of the sheaves for operating ropes in relation to the rope diameter of various constructions. By this is meant that there is a "critical" sheave diameter, smaller than which the strands of the rope cannot slide past each other to adjust themselves to the bend and, consequently, constructional restrictions are set up within the rope. This condition sets up excessive internal stresses absolutely beyond the scope of mathematical treatment, although the writer is convinced that bending stresses in wire ropes are not susceptible to precise mathematical investigation as there are too many variables involved, such as, relation of wire sizes, core condition and size, strand and rope lays, strand constructions, lubrication, etc.

The critical tread diameters of sheaves for various constructions of ropes are given in Table 43.

TABLE 43.—Critical Sheave Diameter Ratios for Operating Ropes.

Construction	6 × 7.	6 × 19 Seale.	6 × 19 Warrington.	6 × 25 Spacer Seale.	6 × 37.	8 × 19 Warrington.	8 × 19 Seale.
Critical ratio, $\frac{D}{d}$	28	20	16	16	14	14	16

For sheave sizes less than those given in Table 43, bending stresses are of little value in any calculations.

The reduction or loss in strength of ropes bent around sheaves (this applies only to non-operating ropes) has been reported* quite fully. It is shown that for 6 × 19 ropes the efficiencies are as given in Table 44, in which, D is the tread diameter of the sheave, and d, the rope diameter. Because of these values the writer believes that the loss in strength of a $\frac{3}{4}$-in., 6 × 19, plow steel rope bent around a 6-in. sheave is 24% instead of 8% as noted by Mr. Carstarphen (page 936).

TABLE 44.—Efficiencies of 6 × 19 Ropes Bent Around Sheaves Under Static Load.

Ratio, $\frac{D}{d}$	8	10	12	14	16	18	20	22	24	30
Efficiency, percentage	76	79	81	86	88	92	93	95	95	95

The moduli of elasticity of various ropes, given by Mr. Carstarphen in Table 26 are at a variance with values secured by the writer in numerous

* "Some Tests of Steel Wire Rope on Sheaves," *Paper No. 229*, U. S. Bureau of Standards.

tests. However, some of this may have been due to a difference in the strand and rope lays and also in the construction of the strand. Tests made by the writer gave the following values of E, in pounds per square inch:

19 wire strand......	20 000 000	6 × 19 rope with independent wire rope center	16 000 000
37 wire strand......	18 000 000	7 × 7 and 7 × 19 bridge cables	17 000 000
6 × 7 rope.........	14 000 000		
6 × 19 rope........	13 000 000		
6 × 37 rope........	12 000 000		
8 × 19 rope........	10 000 000		

These values are for new steel ropes, ½ in. in diameter, and larger. For old ropes that have been in service, the E-values will be approximately 20% in excess of the values given in the tabulation.

To indicate the strand construction variable in the E-values for wire rope: The 2¼-in., 6 × 37, suspender ropes on the Delaware River Bridge between Philadelphia, Pa., and Camden, N. J., were made up of a three operation strand, all wires being laid in the same direction, and the rope had a 7 × 7, Independent wire rope center of Lang lay. The E-value was only approximately 12 000 000 lb. per sq. in., and for the first run or initial loading it was only approximately 8 000 000 lb.* Incidentally, the monograph from which these values were taken, verifies Mr. Carstarphen's data that the E-values increase with an increment in the load on the rope.

F. C. Carstarphen,† M. Am. Soc. C. E. (by letter).—This paper has brought forth a greater discussion, both private and public, than was anticipated by the writer. It appears that the question of stresses in wire ropes, when supporting moving loads, should have been treated with greater detail. This remark may also apply to the derivation and the form of several of the equations presented.

Mr. Strachan finds the equations of the catenary with origin at the support to be inherently complex. He submits a solution of the problem which is a masterful presentation of the power and beauty of the hyperbolic functions in finding the elements of the catenary; and, yet, it seems that the technic was not simplified by shifting the origin from the support to an undetermined position of the parameter.

The possible inference to be drawn from the comment that "without questioning the correctness of the author's formulas relating to unloaded spans", makes it necessary to compare the results obtained by the several formulas when entered by the same argument. The writer believes that all those who make calculations of this nature will find it to be simpler to compute the deflection of an inclined span by Equation (3) than by Mr. Strachan's method. Except for purposes of checking calculations it does not appear that any useful purpose is served by selecting an origin the co-ordinates of which are unknown at the outset of the investigation. For this reason all the cable formulas have been derived, deliberately, with a known position of the origin—

* These values are given in the recent monograph published as a Final Report of the Board of Engineers to the Delaware River Bridge Joint Commission of Pennsylvania and New Jersey, p. 120.

† Cons. Engr., Denver, Colo.

one of the supports—so that the computation of the element desired could be undertaken directly. In this manner one of the great barriers to rapid numerical calculation is swept away.

Accuracy cannot be sacrificed for convenience, unless so stipulated, and it is advisable to weigh the differences between the answers obtained by the several methods of computation.

It will be noted that the writer used four-place tables for values of the hyperbolic functions in solving the problems given on page 909. If cosh $\frac{w\,s}{2\,t} = 1.01624$, the deflection is 95.336 ft. compared with 95.361 ft. derived from Equation (120). Using sinh $\frac{w\,s}{2\,t} = 0.18097$,* Equation (6) gives a length of 1 010.358 ft. compared with 1 010.405 ft. by Equation (116). If sinh $0.18 = 0.18098$, the length is 1 010.444 ft. These several values are in close agreement, but there is a difference of about 3′ of arc in the direction of slope of the terminal tangents. This is due to the use of sec α as an operator to swing the horizontal span formula to a moderately inclined position. For those who would avoid this device and yet prefer the origin at a support, the hypothetical horizontal span for a cable passing through the other support may be used as follows.

In Equation (1) let:

$$\sinh \frac{w\,x}{t} = A = \sinh \frac{3.6 \times 1\,000}{10\,000} = 0.36783;\ A^2 = 0.13530$$

$$\frac{w\,s}{2\,t} = u$$

$$\left(\cosh \frac{w\,x}{t} - 1\right) = B = \cosh 0.36 - 1 = 0.06550;\ B^2 = 0.00429$$

$$\frac{w\,y}{t} = C = \frac{3.6 \times 100}{10\,000} = 0.036;\ C^2 = 0.001296$$

Then, Equation (1) may be written:

$$A \sinh u - B \cosh u - C = 0$$

$$A \sinh u - B \sqrt{1 + \sinh^2 u} - C = 0$$

$$\sinh^2 u + \frac{2\,A\,C}{B^2 - A^2} \sinh u + \frac{B^2 - C^2}{B^2 - A^2} = 0$$

$$\sinh u = \frac{-A\,C}{B^2 - A^2} \pm \frac{B}{B^2 - A^2} \sqrt{A^2 + C^2 - B^2} \ldots\ldots\ldots (125)$$

Substituting the given values of A, B, and C, and their squares, $\sinh u = 0.28292$, $u = 0.279277$, and $\cosh u = 1.03926$.

Equation (1) may now be written for the deflection, y, when $x = 500$ ft.:

$$y = 2\,777.7778 \left[\sinh \frac{3.6 \times 500}{10\,000} \sinh u - \cosh u \left(\cosh \frac{3.6 \times 500}{10\,000} - 1\right)\right]$$

$$= 2\,777.7778 \times 0.03432 = 95.333 \text{ ft.}$$

* Smithsonian Tables for sinh 0.18.

The value of the theoretical span is not required, but it may be easily found:

$$s = \frac{2\,t}{w}\,u = \frac{20\,000}{3.6}\,0.279277 = 1\,551.539 \text{ ft.}$$

Hence the value of x for the parameter is 775.77 ft.

The tangent at the left support is,

$$\beta_1 = \text{gd. } u = \tan^{-1} 0.28292 = 15° \; 47.8'$$

By Equation (4), but without sec α or $\pm$ tan α:

$$\tan \beta_2 = (1.0655 \times 0.28292 - 1.03926 \times 0.36783)$$
$$= 0.38227 - 0.30145 = 0.08082$$
$$= \tan^{-1} 0.08082 = 4° \; 37.2'$$

The length of cable between supports is given by Equation (6) as,

$$(0.28292 + 0.08082)\; 2\,777.7778 = 1\,010.389 \text{ ft.}$$

A comparison of the results of the three calculations shows them to be in agreement and establishes the use of the operator, sec α, as indicated for rapid calculating.

The writer wishes to thank Mr. Paaswell for his interest in solving the cubic equation of the tension by means of the hyperbolic functions. Here, again, is an illustration of their power in mathematical analysis. This method may be used to advantage when unusual accuracy is desired. For all practical solutions of these particular cubic equations the slide-rule may be used with "neatness and dispatch."

Mr. Paaswell calls to mind the relation between the function and its Gudermannian; that is, gd. u = an angle, v, in the equation,

$$u = \log_e \tan\left(\frac{\pi}{4} + \frac{v}{2}\right)$$

or,

$$u = 2.3025851 \tan\left(45° + \frac{v}{2}\right)$$

The proper value for the sinh 0.18 may be ascertained:

$$\frac{0.18}{2.3025851} = \tan\left(45° + \frac{v}{2}\right)$$
$$v = 10° \; 15' \; 30''$$
$$\sinh u = \tan v = 0.1809797$$

thereby showing 0.18098 to be a better value than 0.18097 as given in the Smithsonian Tables previously quoted.

It is a pleasure to note the comments, and to thank Mr. Meals for his favorable expressions concerning the subject-matter of the paper. It may be of interest to state that the writer does not limit the design of dumping cradleways to the light decks and loads mentioned by Mr. Meals. On the contrary, 12-cu. yd. air-dump cars may be used, weighing 25 000 lb. empty, and cradleway decks weighing 350 lb. per ft., exclusive of rails and supported by suspender tackle on 30-ft. centers. In so far as the deck is always close to the movable tower, if for no other reason than to keep the fill up to grade, Equations (122) and (123) would give doubtful values for the maximum tension and the proper center deflection of the empty cable. The former would be unreasonably large and the latter too small. However, let this be as it may, contractors are not alert, who fail to inform themselves concerning this handy and economical method of building fills and waste piles.

It has been stated, often, that good ropes require good wire. Good wire can be made only from high quality steel. The transformation of high quality steel billets into No. 5 rods takes place in a rod mill, and the rods are coiled hot on 30-in. spools. Therefore, the rods are formed to a curve having a radius of about 15 in. Later, these rods are taken to a wire bench and are pulled cold, through the die-plate, and wound under high tension on wire blocks 22 in. in diameter or smaller. In fact, the entire wire-making process from billets to ropes is only the winding and unwinding of "process" wire on spools of small diameter, with a few intermediate treatments. Accordingly, when rope wire of ordinary manufacture is assembled, as shown in Fig. 25, it must be kept under tension, for its inherent tendency, when free of restraint, is to assume the position shown in Fig. 26. This is true of wire ropes as well as wires.

That is, under conditions of minimum stress, a wire or rope naturally takes the form of a helix and, by permitting rotation about the axis of the helix, the assembly may be passed over sheaves having a radius of curvature equal to the loops, without imposing on the wires, stresses due to bending in passing the sheaves.

Accordingly, it may be stated that the act of passing a wire rope around a sheave is not, in itself, conclusive evidence that additional stresses have been developed in the component wires. It merely leaves a doubt, to be settled by experiment, as to whether a certain type of rope will find operating conditions favorable, or otherwise, for satisfactory service, and whether its performance will be excellent or poor. Rope manufacturers, therefore, have been forced to develop a great variety of wire ropes, both as to quality and construction, because it has been noted that, if one type of rope fails to discharge a given duty, a different kind may attain success. The maximum number of varieties of construction in wire ropes has practically been reached and, therefore, attention has again turned to wire treatments before rope-laying.

One such treatment attempts to eliminate the "set" of wire manufacture by an additional "permanent set", that is, by pre-forming the wire and strands to assume a definite curvature called "Tru-Lay." While such treatments result in ropes that are more or less "dead"—that is, they do not assume the helical form if free from tension—the same behavior has been found by other methods. The merit of the "Tru-Lay" construction remains to be determined by experience. Already, it is credited with excellent results, and some poor ones, so that it remains to be seen whether the average performance of pre-formed wire ropes will exceed that of equal grades of ropes of usual manufacture. The history of wire rope is filled with cases that are conspicuous by their success, and failure, and so it may be well to temper Mr. Meals' enthusiastic endorsement of "Tru-Lay" construction for ropes that "will wear

FIG. 25.—ROPE WIRE UNDER TENSION.

FIG. 26.—POSITION ASSUMED BY SOME WIRE AND ROPES NOT UNDER TENSION.

longer and withstand bending better because the individual wires and strands of the ropes are in an unrestrained position". As it is difficult to see how a pre-formed wire can be free from strain (destructive ones perhaps), it is desirable that performance records of "Tru-Lay" ropes be made available soon to the Engineering Profession.

In closing, the writer expresses his appreciation of the courtesy of those who have read the paper, for in so doing they have helped in establishing aerial tramways to be the product of engineering skill, worthy of confidence as an instrument devised for economical transportation of materials, rather than a contraption offered by the manufacturers of wire rope to provide a remunerative outlet for their products.

AMERICAN SOCIETY OF CIVIL ENGINEERS

INSTITUTED 1852

TRANSACTIONS

This Society is not responsible for any statement made or opinion expressed in its publications.

Paper No. 1676

STREAM POLLUTION IN THE PACIFIC NORTHWEST*

By William F. Allison,† M. Am. Soc. C. E.

With Discussion by Messrs. William J. Roberts, Augustus Smith, A. H. Dimock, and Kenneth Allen.

The problems presented by the pollution of streams and lakes in the States bordering on the North Pacific Ocean are different from those in older communities only in degree and acuteness. Much of the difficulty that has arisen is due to a feeling that streams and lakes flowing into the Pacific Ocean, and its arms, are unlimited in their capacity to absorb pollution, and that, therefore, population and industry need not seriously concern themselves in disposing of wastes which have little, if any, commercial value.

In the early days the chief form of pollution was caused by the miners who stirred the muck and gravel from the bottom of the streams, and after removing the gold, sluiced the tailings out on the arable land below as the easiest method of disposing of it. Usually, these arable lands were still in the hands of the Federal Government, but this was slight bar to the easiest disposal of waste as placer miners saw fit. The miner will still contend that prior use of stream and land gives him a permanent right to use them for his purposes, regardless of the interest of later comers. Much of the land covered by this waste had agricultural possibilities and was eventually acquired by private parties who, to secure their rights, carried the contest into the Courts. These lawsuits are particularly notable in California, where they have invariably been decided in favor of the farmer. The placer miner, when he stakes a claim, makes the possibility of disposal of tailings one of his chief considerations.

* Presented at the meeting of the Sanitary Engineering Division, Seattle, Wash., July 15, 1926.

† Prof., Municipal and Highway Eng., Univ. of Washington, Seattle, Wash. Prof. Allison died on July 6, 1927.

Agriculture and mining again come in conflict when the lode miner, after running his ore through a stamp mill, seeks a means of disposing of the tailings of the mills. This waste is usually pulverized quartz which, when carried down to irrigation ditches and finally deposited on an alfalfa field, is highly injurious to the growing crops, acting not at all like the silt deposited in the Valley of the Nile during a period of flood.

The farmer, who must use the water of these streams to irrigate his land, must find some method of disposing of this finely pulverized quartz before it reaches that land. Ordinarily, this is done by impounding the water in a reservoir where the suspended particles are allowed to settle. It is periodically removed from the reservoir or settling basin at a cost of a great deal of hard labor and much time.

This sedimentation does not remove the solids in solution which may have a deleterious effect on this water for domestic purposes, and to some extent, for irrigation. Some of the streams of Colorado have an appreciable quantity of sulfuric acid which sedimentation and screening through gravel does not remove. The taste of the water is much impaired and its use in the making of tea and coffee is quite unsatisfactory, inasmuch as the tea takes on the color of ink.

The heavy deposits of pulverized quartz are being cared for nowadays by compelling the mining and milling companies to dispose properly of the wastes due to their operations. However, this is done with some reluctance, as increased cost may result in suspension of work in a basic industry and a consequent unemployment of labor. The problem is similar to that, but not precisely the same as, in the mining regions of the East.

Lumbering is another basic industry in the Pacific Northwest that has a waste problem to solve. This problem is practically the same as that faced by the lumberman of the East. Sawdust and refuse from saw-mills are more easily disposed of by depositing them in a stream than in any other manner. There they rot and in a short time become exceedingly foul, to the destruction of fish, and thus they tend to destroy another basic industry. Quite generally this is overcome by compelling the saw-mill operators to burn their waste, which perhaps causes some danger to plant and surrounding timber. The much heralded danger from forest fires must be considered when plans for burning waste are considered.

A third growing industry that seriously pollutes the water of streams and lakes is the manufacture of wood pulp and paper. The sulfite liquor used in pulp making is harmful to fish life, and it is found that small fibers in the waste become entangled in the gills of fish and cause their death. An economical and satisfactory method of caring for this waste has not yet been found. The problem is an old one and any efforts to solve it should be made along lines which will not injure the pulp and paper business. Competition with European pulp is keen and any irksome restrictions may drive American manufacturers out of business.

The Federal Government is spending much money in the promotion of fisheries on the Pacific Coast. It cannot look with approval on pulp manufacture on the coast of Alaska, where there is said to be much suitable pulp wood, if pulp making destroys young fish which have been so carefully reared and protected.

The protection of fish is one of the chief objects of Fish and Game Commissions of the States of this region. Over-fishing and out-of-season fishing are prohibited, but, in any contest with other industries, the fish are likely to be sacrificed to the economic demands of other desirable lines of endeavor.

The effect of sewage pollution has a considerable bearing on the fishing industry of the Pacific Coast, as is common on the Atlantic seaboard. The shellfish industry of Puget Sound has been only partly developed, but already the presence of *B. coli* in the oysters has been observed. It is believed that oyster culture can be greatly increased if steps are taken to prevent raw sewage from flowing into Puget Sound. A proper educational program will be necessary to overcome prevailing ideas in this respect. The sale of oysters grown in certain localities on the Atlantic Coast is generally forbidden by Boards of Health and the same regulations may be anticipated regarding the oysters of the Pacific Coast if steps are not taken to prevent pollution of areas that may be used as oyster beds.

There is a considerable business in the marketing of clams, but inasmuch as clams are almost always cooked before eating, it is felt that there is no great danger from contamination, although clams obtained from sludge deposits would be in little demand from the public and probably would not have the approval of the health authorities.

Sewage seems to be very destructive to fish life that has a high commercial value. A few years ago, near one of the salmon hatcheries in the southern part of the State of Washington, it was observed that young salmon on being turned into a stream near the mouth of a sewer, died very quickly. A considerable portion of the sewage flowing into the stream was traced to a hospital, and it was believed that there was enough poison in the sewage to kill the fish. Probably storm sewage containing oil and gasoline from the streets would have the same effect.

The two most conspicuous examples of sewage pollution of fresh water in this State are the disposal of the sewage of the City of Spokane in the Spokane River, and the pollution of Lake Washington at the eastern edge of the City of Seattle by the sewage of urban and suburban districts bordering on that lake. Spokane permits its sewage to go into the Spokane River, below the city, which, in turn, flows into the Columbia River.

It is contended that the Spokane River, in flowing over a series of falls and rapids and through ponds which act as settling basins, causes the sewage to oxidize to such an extent that it becomes practically harmless when it reaches the Columbia. It is by no means certain that this is true. Typhoid is more or less endemic all along the eastern slope of the Cascade Mountains and is sometimes a menace to the surrounding country. Water used for irrigation is often rather heavily polluted, and workers in the fields and on the fruit ranches are careless about drinking water from the irrigation ditches, being thus exposed to the fever. The occasional cases that are found in the cities of the Puget Sound region are contracted in this manner, and make it difficult to stamp out typhoid on the Pacific Coast. Regulations and rules of Departments of Health are frequently violated and, for several years, the Board of Health of Washington has carried on a campaign of education in matters relating to the pollution of streams and of the proper disposal of sewage. It has seemed that education of this kind must face the decided opposition of political and commercial interests.

For several years, the before-mentioned pollution of Lake Washington has been a subject of controversy. The lake is a natural receptacle for the drainage of a considerable area. This area lies partly within the city limits of Seattle and includes the rapidly growing district east of the lake. Until a few years ago the lake was the source of water supply for the city. With the growth of the city and the towns surrounding the lake, it became increasingly more difficult to prevent sewage from draining into the lake. Private sewers became a constant source of trouble. After Seattle began to obtain its water from Cedar Lake, forty miles southeast of the city, it was believed by people living near the lake that the difficulty was settled for all time. The best and most accessible fresh-water bathing beaches, however, are here available, and there is much sentiment against their destruction.

The construction of the ship canal and locks prevents for all time the use of lake water for domestic purposes, as the operation of the locks admits an appreciable quantity of salt water into the lake. It has been contended by some that a fresh-water harbor would not compensate the city for the loss of fresh water which, in the future, might be needed for a city supply. However, it seems probable that sufficient water may be obtained from mountain streams for all purposes, although it will probably have to be filtered and sterilized before using. Be this as it may, the flow of sewage into the lake has materially detracted from its value for bathing purposes, and the problem now presented is to treat the sewage in such a manner that bathing may be safe and satisfactory. Bonds have been voted to build intercepting sewers to carry the sewage of this district into Puget Sound, which is an expedient that will improve the water in the lake, but will tend to increase the trouble with the Sound waters. The writer can see no solution of the problem except to treat all sewage flowing into the Sound and to sterilize it to the satisfaction of the State Board of Health.

The City of Seattle has had some trouble because of the location of and opposition to small sewage treatment plants. A careful survey of surrounding property, together with the proper design and operation of such plants, perhaps might tend to reduce the opposition. Certainly, the benefit that may be derived from them should be much greater than the damage caused.

Water obtained from mountain streams is not always free from sewage, although the sources of such streams are springs and glaciers. The City of Wenatchee, Wash., proposed a few years ago to obtain its water from a glacial stream called the Icicle, hoping thus to eliminate the typhoid prevailing in and about that city. Upon examination of water from the Icicle, it was found that a considerable number of *B. coli* was present, and the water could not be approved by the Board of Health unless satisfactorily treated. This, together with the heavy cost of obtaining the water from the Icicle, eliminated this as a source of supply. A filtered supply from the Columbia River, being cheaper and meeting the requirements of the State Board of Health, was adopted instead.

The Columbia River is the great natural drain for large parts of Washington, Oregon, and Idaho, and whenever it becomes necessary to use this water for a city supply, it must be put through a course of purification. The waters of many of the streams of this region have considerable colloidal clay in suspension, which should be considered in designing any filtration system. Mountain streams, although appearing to be clear, will almost always carry considerable silt. It is well known that rock-fill and earthen or timber dams gradually silt up and become tight with age.

In the main, information and experience gained in building and operating purification plants in the East will apply on the Pacific Coast, and with the information that is available, the engineer in the Northwest must familiarize himself with local conditions and then work out his own salvation.

The engineer will have some difficulty in convincing the people of the need for improvement and of the efficiency of his proposal. Many of them are "from Missouri" and have been hectored by men with something to sell. In 1913 the City of Centralia experienced a serious epidemic of typhoid which was traced to the water supply that came from wells along the river. It was shown that seepage from the river was getting into the wells and was the source of the epidemic. Dr. Eugene Kelley, who at that time was Commissioner of Health of Washington, was asked by the city officials why he did not warn them of the danger impending. Dr. Kelley turned to the files of the local newspapers. In one of the glaring headlines it announced that Dr. Kelley had visited the city and, as a result of his investigations, was maligning Centralia by finding fault with the water supply and insisted that the dangers foreseen were purely imaginary. Had his warning been heeded, this otherwise prosperous community would have escaped the sacrifice of the health of its people and an expenditure of a large amount of money. Needless to say, the City of Centralia now has a good water supply.

DISCUSSION

William J. Roberts,* M. Am. Soc. C. E.—The author upholds high ideals, and many of them are worthy of heartiest support. It has, however, been demonstrated beyond question that there are places on Puget Sound where it is neither necessary nor expedient to follow the author's advice "to treat all sewage flowing into the Sound and to sterilize it to the satisfaction of the State Board of Health."

An outstanding example is furnished by Camp Lewis, American Lake Cantonment. As Consulting Engineer, collaborating with the Constructing Quartermaster, the speaker found that the water supply and the proper disposal of sewage for 50 000 troops presented many intricate problems. The demand for healthful conditions was no more imperative than the demand for speed in construction; and always the question: "Is it sanitary?" was followed by the remorseless demand: "Can the work be completed on time?"

Fortunately, "Sequalichew Springs" about 1.5 miles from Camp Headquarters, proved adequate in quantity, yielding, when developed, more than 6 000 gal. per min. The quality of this water was pronounced, after frequent tests, to be "as pure as distilled water." Thus, the problem of obtaining an adequate and pure water supply was solved.

The logical disposal of the sewage was into Puget Sound 3.5 miles from Headquarters, without treatment. After a thorough investigation, and careful consideration of all possible objections, the point of discharge was selected at mean sea level, 3.5 miles from the nearest barracks; more than a mile from the nearest dwelling, but only a short distance from a double-track railroad carrying a heavy passenger traffic. The tidal range of the Sound at this point is about 12 ft. At the outlet the channel is about 1.5 miles wide and several hundred feet deep. Thus, the shores of the Sound are thoroughly cleansed twice a day by the large volumes of flowing tides. So thoroughly is this cleansing process carried on that a passenger on the train can not discover, by sight or odor, the outlet of the sewer. No inconvenience or harmful effects of this plan of disposal touched the lives or even the comfort of the soldiers at Camp Lewis nor its environment. If ever there was a place where disposal by dilution and dispersion is permissible, because rational, then this is that place. The demand for perfect sanitation and great speed in construction was satisfactorily met; 40 miles of water mains and 30 miles of sewers were actually laid in 78 days.

It is estimated that the tortuous channels of Puget Sound with all its inlets and islands within the State of Washington amount to 3 600 miles of shore lines. The volume of ocean water pouring into Puget Sound through the Strait of Juan de Fuca, 16 miles wide, with a maximum channel depth in excess of 1 000 ft., assures a satisfactory dilution and dispersion of any sewage discharged into the Sound.

The Sanitary Field Officers at Camp Lewis, remembering the troubles occasioned in some of the camps during the Spanish-American War, were

* Cons. Engr., Tacoma, Wash.

alert to avoid anything unsanitary. Hence it was a pleasure to learn from the best information obtainable that not a single case of typhoid fever could be traced to impure water at the Camp or to bad sewerage during the entire training period from August, 1917, to November, 1918.

As has been well stated:*

"Skimping funds may often lead to danger to the public health, and the enforcement of requirements for an unnecessarily high degree of purification of sewage to useless waste of money."

Augustus Smith,† M. Am. Soc. C. E.—It may be of interest to consider what is being done in New Jersey relative to stream pollution. The State has been handling the matter of stream pollution through the State Department of Health. It has also a Fish and Game Commission, which has been very active. Frequently, this Commission has come into contact with the other State Departments because it could not get all the support it wanted in its work of preventing the pollution of streams.

In 1924, the State created the Sanitary and Economic Water Commission, of which the speaker is a member. The idea behind that legislation was to create "a permanent jury", so to speak, to give judgments as to the "economic" policy on the pollution of any stream or water in the State. The new Commission was formed by the Governor appointing one member from the State Department of Health, one from the Fish and Game Commission, one from the Shell Fishery Commission, one from the State Board of Conservation and Development (which has charge of all State lands), and one from the Board of Commerce and Navigation (which deals with problems concerning navigable waters), and the Attorney General of the State.

The Commission has been functioning only since 1925, but one of its first acts was to adopt the method of classifying streams recommended by W. L. Stevenson, M. Am. Soc. C. E. It divides streams into three classes:

(*a*) Those streams, or portions of streams, used or reserved for potable purposes.

(*b*) Those streams clean enough for recreation, for enhancing the value of real estate, and for fishing.

(*c*) Those streams passing through communities where the industrial needs are paramount.

It has seemed to this Commission, that the first step in trying to recover or preserve the purity of the streams, is to arrive at a general consensus of public opinion as to the best use of a stream from an economic standpoint.

A. H. Dimock,‡ M. Am. Soc. C. E.—After discussing various ways by which the waters of Puget Sound are polluted, the author comes to the general conclusion that all such polluting matter should be treated and sterilized before discharge. While the speaker is heartily in favor of keeping all waters in the best possible condition, and especially all fresh waters, nevertheless this conclusion seems somewhat sweeping.

* Preface to "American Sewerage Practice," Vol. III, "Disposal of Sewage," by the late Leonard Metcalf, M. Am. Soc. C. E., and Harrison P. Eddy, M. Am. Soc. C. E.

† Pres., Bergen Point Iron Works, Bayonne, N. J.

‡ Cons. Engr., Seattle, Wash.

Puget Sound, including Admiralty Inlet, is a body of water about 60 miles long from the Straits of Juan de Fuca to Tacoma, Wash., and from 3 to 6 miles wide. South of Tacoma it narrows to less than a mile and then widens and breaks up into an intricate maze of channels and bays. In this southern portion are situated a number of oyster beds. The bays are shallow, the flat areas extensive, and the movement of water is more or less restricted. The treatment of sewage entering this portion becomes, in general, more desirable. Each particular problem, however, must be decided in the light of its own local conditions.

In the larger part of Puget Sound, north from Tacoma, however, the channel is very deep, varying as much as 120 fathoms. The tides have a range of 16 ft., and there is necessarily a considerable movement of the water. The volume and character of these movements are not definitely known. Oyster beds are few. There is none along the main channel, and the shores, generally, have good slopes. It would seem, therefore, that the oxidizing capacity of this part of Puget Sound is an asset of considerable importance to the towns and cities on its banks, and may be utilized without detriment to health, the public welfare, or private business.

When the speaker was designing the main sewerage system for the larger part of Seattle, Wash., about 1905, extensive observations of currents were made by floats. This survey revealed many beaches which were highly undesirable as points of discharge for sewage, for the reason that the currents set chiefly toward the shore. Some places were found, however, where the currents for 80% of the time were offshore. The outfall of a main sewer 12 ft. in diameter was located at such a place and extended to a point where the water was 40 ft. deep. The only trouble that has been experienced at this point, has been at outfalls where discharge was permitted on the surface or at shallow depths. The remedy is obvious. It would certainly be a "counsel of perfection", under such conditions, to spend large sums for artificial treatment plants, when Nature has provided one far more efficient, the use of which is free of operating charges and involves no menace to health.

The case of Lake Washington, in Seattle, is different. This lake is 20 miles long by 2 to 4 miles wide and lies parallel to the salt-water front at a distance of 2 to 7 miles. Its shore, within the city limits, is used almost exclusively for residential purposes, with the exception of a few ferry landings, one sawmill, and other minor business. The lake is subject to navigation, but this use is small. The sewage from as much of the drainage area as was possible has been intercepted and carried to the salt-water outfalls; but there remained about 4 500 acres, the sewage from which has been discharged into the lake. The growth of population and the largely increased use of bathing beaches created the necessity for some action. It was proposed to build a series of Imhoff tanks and to chlorinate the effluent. The speaker investigated the problem on behalf of the City and came to the general conclusion that Lake Washington was an asset of great value to the city both because of the desirability of the residential sites along its shores, with their entrancing views of lake and forests and snow-crowned mountains, and because of its recreational possibilities; a use which will be more and more essential to the public welfare as the population increases. For these reasons it was held desirable to exclude from its shores everything that was even suggestive of unpleasant things, and that sewage treatment plants, which would necessarily be more or less visible, and from which odors might emanate, should not be permitted if some other means could be found within a reasonable cost limit.

The speaker sought to determine a standard of purity for the waters of Lake Washington. It is not used as a source of water supply except in the sparsely settled section on the east shore, several miles from the Seattle side. Its main use is recreational. In 1925, 365 000 people used the bathing beaches, which are far more popular than the salt-water beaches due to the higher temperature of the water and the more convenient access. A considerable diversity of opinion as to a proper standard was found to exist among the experts, ranging from not more than 10 *B. coli* per cu. cm. in swimming pools in New York and in salt-water beaches in California to a drinking-water standard insisted on by some authorities. Just how the latter standard can be maintained either at an open bathing beach or in a closed swimming pool is difficult to understand. The chief danger is from infection arising from promiscuous bathing at the same time of diseased and healthy persons. No practicable excess of chlorine can prevent, although it may reduce, this danger. The remedy would seem to lie in proper inspection and regulation and not in the futile endeavor to maintain a drinking-water standard. It was the speaker's conclusion, that, if the water of Lake Washington was negative as to *B. coli* in 1-cu. cm. samples, it would be safe anywhere for individual bathing, and that such a standard might be attained by diverting all sewage. At the bathing beaches, because of the pollution contributed by the bathers themselves, it was thought that regulation of use and chlorination would be essential, even if the water in the lake could be brought to the drinking-water standard.

The means recommended to accomplish the desired results were the diversion from the lake of all sewage plus rain water to a total amount of 0.033 sec-ft. per acre, by the construction in one case of a tunnel and in others of suitable automatic pumping stations discharging into existing intercepting sewers. These stations are to be provided with storm-water overflows discharging in about 30 ft. of water. It is thought that, under the conditions that obtain, no further treatment of storm water will be necessary. The average annual rainfall in Seattle is 33 in. The intensity is remarkably low. The number of storms equal to or exceeding the rates shown during a period of 30 years are, as follows:

0.80 in. per hour........	0	0.40 in. per hour........	12
0.70 " " "	1	0.36 " " "	14
0.60 " " "	2	0.30 " " "	30
0.50 " " "	8	0.25 " " "	55

Using a capacity of 0.033 sec-ft. per acre as stated, and assuming a population of 25 per acre and a run-off factor of 0.25, it was found that all rains of less than 0.12 in. per hour would be diverted from the lake and that there would be only 28 hours per year when that rate would be exceeded; an average of 1 hour of rain every 13 days.

KENNETH ALLEN,* M. AM. SOC. C. E. (by letter).—With higher standards of living and an increasing demand for eliminating pollution from rivers and harbors, the danger of going further in this direction than can be properly justified, should be kept in view by State and municipal officials. Public funds available for sanitation should be applied in the most effective manner, and it is quite conceivable that the public may be better served by allocating the entire sum to better water supplies, hospitals, and playgrounds, than to a refined treatment of sewage. Without personal familiarity with Puget Sound, the writer's views on this point are in sympathy with those expressed by Mr. Roberts.

Each case should be considered on its individual merits, and, in approaching the subject, the standard of purity should be considered of prime consideration. If the result of the discharge of crude or screened sewage will not offend the senses or endanger health—as is frequently the case on the seaboard—the additional cost of tanks, filters, or chlorination, had better be applied to other purposes.

This is the policy being followed by the City of New York in its program for sewage disposal, where every variety of condition is met as to dilution, salinity, depth, current, and pollution. Where fine screening will answer, nothing more is planned; but where conditions call for the greatest possible improvement, treatment by the relatively expensive activated sludge process, or its equivalent, will without question be used.

---

* San. Engr., Office of Chf. Engr., Board of Estimate and Apportionment, New York, N. Y.

AMERICAN SOCIETY OF CIVIL ENGINEERS

INSTITUTED 1852

TRANSACTIONS

This Society is not responsible for any statement made or opinion expressed in its publications.

Paper No. 1677

THE SEWAGE DISPOSAL PROBLEM OF LOS ANGELES, CALIFORNIA*

By Willis T. Knowlton,† M. Am. Soc. C. E.

With Discussion by Messrs. A. M. Rawn and Willis T. Knowlton.

Synopsis

The continued and rapid growth of Los Angeles, Calif., has required constant attention to the matter of sewage disposal, and especially since 1920 when the population took such an upward trend that plans were required for a Metropolitan System. Studies were then made for the collection and disposal of sewage from all the area to the north and west of the city.

This paper describes how the outfall sewers required for this area have been planned to serve the Metropolitan Districts, regardless of political boundaries. Considerable data on the basis of design are given. The problem of ocean disposal of the effluent from the screening plants and the final disposal of the sewage screenings will require continued attention as the sewered population increases. In addition to sanitary sewage, the disposal of industrial waste is a problem to which reference is also made.

Early History

The City of Los Angeles commenced the construction of public sewers in 1873, when the population was about 7 000, although there are records of sewers as early as 1863. In 1887 the first comprehensive plan for a sewerage system was made by Frederick Eaton, M. Am. Soc. C. E., then City Surveyor. His plan, designed for sewage only, provided for intercepting sewers which

* Presented at the meeting of the Sanitary Engineering Division, Seattle, Wash., July 15, 1926.

† San. Engr., City of Los Angeles, Los Angeles, Calif.

were to discharge into an outfall sewer having a capacity for a total population of 200 000. This plan before its adoption was submitted to the late Rudolph Hering, M. Am. Soc. C. E., for his examination and approval. In 1900, the area of the city had increased 50% over its size in 1887, the total population was 102 479, and the system contained 160 miles of sewers.

The outfall sewer, as planned by Mr. Eaton, had a capacity of 30 sec-ft. As originally built, it contained two inverted siphons and its ocean end at Hyperion consisted of 24-in. cast-iron pipe laid into the ocean for a distance of 600 ft. This pipe was superseded in 1904 by a 30-in., steel pipe outfall which was laid on a pier to a distance of 940 ft. from shore. This steel pipe sewer was superseded in 1908 by a 34-in. wooden stave pipe, which had a capacity of 116 sec-ft., and provided for a population of 750 000. The wooden stave-pipe sewer discharged into a vertical pipe which carried the flow of sewage to a depth of about 6 ft. below mean sea level, where the water was about 16 ft. deep.

Growth of City

Owing to the continued growth of the city in all directions, the quantity of discharge into the main outfall sewer increased from an average daily flow of 15 000 000 gal. in 1910 to 23 000 000 gal. in 1915. This increase indicated that, to remedy complaints arising from this disposal, the sewage should be treated before discharge into the ocean at Hyperion. Accordingly, a bond issue for a sewage treatment plant at Hyperion was submitted to the voters in 1916, but was defeated. A similar proposition was submitted in 1917, but without success. On account of the World War, nothing was done until 1920, when the increasing volume of raw sewage discharged at this location made it necessary to plan for a new outfall as well as for the treatment of the sewage before disposal into the ocean.

In January, 1920, the population of Los Angeles was 576 673; in 1922, it was about 800 000, and a recent estimate (June, 1926) places it at 1 250 000. All estimates of future population must be considered as speculative, but a conservative estimate of the population of Los Angeles in 1950 would be not less than 4 000 000.

The sewage flow in the outfall during the past six years has increased in practically the same way as the population. In 1920, the sewage discharged at Hyperion averaged 33 000 000 gal. per day. In July, 1922, this flow had increased to 50 000 000 gal. per day, and, at present (1926), the flow from all parts of the city, except the Harbor District, averages 78 000 000 gal. per day.

North Outfall Sewer Planned

Preliminary plans were made in 1920 for a new outfall sewer to supplement the existing one, and also for the treatment of the sewage. These plans provided not only for the conditions at that time, but also for a period of about thirty years thereafter. The plans contemplated the collection of sewage from all areas tributary either to the existing outfall or proposed new outfall, regardless of political boundary lines. The new outfall has been designated as the "North Outfall Sewer" and the existing outfall as the "Central Outfall Sewer".

After making plans for the North Outfall Sewer an educational compaign was required to acquaint the voters with the needs. Civic bodies and local engineers approved the plans and recommended that bonds be voted for the work. Owing, however, to opposition from those who considered land disposal preferable to ocean disposal and who thought that there should be a reclamation of sewage for fertilizing values, a Special Sewage Disposal Commission was appointed to investigate the entire problem and submit a report. This Commission, consisting of George W. Fuller, the late George C. Whipple, and William Mulholland, Members, Am. Soc. C. E., confirmed the plans and recommended that the North Outfall be built for a capacity of at least 210 000 000 gal. per day and that the sewage be discharged into the ocean after passing through a fine screening plant. Opposition to the work proved, however, to be too great and the proposal was defeated in June, 1921.

Plans for another election were immediately commenced as the sanitary conditions in certain parts of the city were becoming intolerable. To obtain all necessary data, for acquainting the voters of the true situation, an examination of conditions in other cities was made by the City Engineer and the writer. The report of this examination, together with that of the Special Sewage Disposal Commission, was published in August, 1921, following which an educational campaign was conducted. As a result of these combined efforts, the election in August, 1922, approved the issue of sewer bonds.

Temporary Outfall Sewer

In 1922 a temporary relief sewer to carry the overflow from the Central Outfall was built as far as Ballona Creek, about 3½ miles below the point where the Central Outfall was intercepted by this relief sewer. Owing to complaints against the pollution of this creek, the City was ordered to take measures to prevent the discharge of raw sewage into the creek or provide for its treatment if the overflow was to continue. A coarse screening plant was built to remove all floating material before the flow in the Temporary Outfall was discharged into the creek. To prevent further pollution, the effluent from the plant was treated with liquid chlorine.

The upper end of the Temporary Outfall had a capacity of about 40 sec-ft., but owing to the increase of flow from new connections being constantly made to the system, the capacity of the lower end was increased to about 30 000 000 gal. per day. Records of the flow in this sewer from September, 1923, to May, 1924, gave an average of 28.2 lb. of chlorine and 13.4 cu. ft. of screenings per 1 000 000 gal. of sewage. The screens consisted of a double set of vertical units of ½-in. mesh arranged so that one set was in place while the other was being cleaned. The bottom of the channel of Ballona Creek was graded to assist in preventing a nuisance. However, the continued discharge of this treated sewage caused a second suit to be filed against the City by the City of Venice for conditions in the lower part of Ballona Creek where it empties into the ocean near Playa del Rey.

It thus became necessary to continue the construction of the Temporary Outfall to the ocean and to abandon the plans for the settling tanks and sprinkling filters to treat the flow in this outfall. A site of thirty-eight acres had been purchased for this treatment plant, but opposition from property owners compelled the City to continue the Temporary Outfall to the ocean. This sewer having a length of 10 miles was used for disposal of the overflow from the Central Outfall into the ocean from April to December, 1924. The outlet end of the Temporary Outfall which was laid on the bottom of the ocean for a distance of 600 ft. from shore, where the depth was 12 ft., consisted of 44-in. riveted steel pipe. The pipe was assembled on the beach, made air-tight, and bulkheaded. It was then tugged into the water, floated into position, and sunk under a trestle that had previously been prepared for its protection. When the North Outfall was completed so that the Temporary Outfall could be abandoned, the material used for the latter was salvaged.

North Outfall Sewer Drainage Area

Immediately after the successful election held in August, 1922, contract plans were made for the construction of the North Outfall. It was decided at that time that this sewer should be divided into fourteen sections so that the work could proceed simultaneously at various points. Tunnel routes to Hyperion and along the brow of the del Rey Hills were studied. Although longer, it was found that the del Rey route would be cheaper, and accordingly it was adopted for the lower part of the North Outfall. The total length of this sewer, which was completed in November, 1924, is 17.6 miles. The discharge capacity at its lower end is 340 000 000 gal. per day.

When the outfall was proposed in 1920, it was planned to provide for the disposal of sewage from a large Metropolitan District, comprising all the area north of Manchester Avenue, then the southerly border of the city proper, and all the area west of the easterly boundary of the city. This district included a large area in Los Angeles County south of Fernando Pass.

As it was necessary that that portion of Los Angeles County east of the city and south of Manchester Avenue should also plan for the disposal of its sewage, a tentative arrangement was outlined in November, 1924, whereby all areas tributary to the North and Central Outfall Sewers should be planned so to discharge their sewage. Similarly, those areas tributary to an outfall sewer, proposed to discharge into the ocean on the south coast of the County, would be accordingly planned. The dividing line between these two Metropolitan Areas was established by joint action of the engineers of the City and those representing the County Sanitation Districts. The area of the North Metropolitan District, which is tributary to the North Outfall Sewer, is about 513 sq. miles, and that of the South Metropolitan District about 605 sq. miles. On account of the size and continued growth of the city, there are sections which must have their sewage discharged into the so-called South Outfall Sewer which, when built, will be the main outlet for the South Metropolitan District.

In accord with the foregoing, the North Outfall was designed to carry the sanitary sewage from all parts of the city north of Manchester Avenue and include therewith the entire San Fernando Valley. The major part of the Valley added by annexation about 170 sq. miles to the area of the city in 1915, and since then eight other annexations in the Valley have added about 24 sq. miles. There are, however, other cities and county areas in the North Metropolitan District which were considered in the design of the North Outfall. These cities include Glendale, Burbank, San Fernando, Beverly Hills, Culver City, Santa Monica, and El Segundo, which have a combined population of more than 140 000. In view of the rapid growth of this Metropolitan District and the demand for sanitary improvements, considerable study was required for future conditions.

Basic Data for Sewer Design

In the main part of the city it was thought that the business growth would cover the entire congested area extending from Figueroa Street to San Pedro Street and from Sunset Boulevard southerly to Washington Street.

Careful records were made of the water consumption in the different parts of the business district and a maximum allowance of 0.15 sec-ft. per acre and 0.02 sec-ft. per acre of floor area was provided. In the industrial districts a factor of 0.2 sec-ft. per acre was measured. Owing to the rapid increase in the number of laundries, creameries, canneries, and other plants discharging much waste water into the sewers, the use of zones created for such plants has proved to be of much benefit. In the Hollywood District it was found that water used for washing the films in the laboratories of the moving picture plants would add about 0.5 sec-ft. per plant. For an average of the industrial district it is believed that the waste water amounts at least to 10 gal. per capita per day.

Records of sewage flow in the residential districts show a variation of 30 to 80 gal. per capita per day. From gauging in several parts of the city it is believed that 60 gal. per capita represents the average flow, and the records of adjoining cities where sewer gauging has been made, give 50 to 70 gal. per capita for a similar flow. At a point on the Central Outfall Sewer, records of the sewage flow have been kept since 1906. These records show an increase in the average flow per capita during the period, 1922-26, of 72 to 82 gal., which is due to industrial growth with possibly some infiltration.

The problem of designing for the proper density for large areas in the Metropolitan Districts, which at this time are but partly developed, has received much study. The present population varies from 34 per acre in the center of the city to 10 per acre 5 miles from the center. For the entire municipal area the density is 4.2 persons per acre. In the San Fernando Valley an allowance of 1 person per acre was made in 1920, but in a recent study this factor has been increased to 3. It should be noted, however, that in the different centers of population in the San Fernando Valley, such as Van Nuys, Lankershim, and Owensmouth, the density to be planned for will vary from 15 to 30 persons per acre.

In connection with the study of the future population a check has been made of the present population by applying a factor to the number of registered voters, the school census, the number of water, gas, and electric meters in use, and the directory. For the registered voters the factor used has been 3.37; for the school census, 3.54; for water meters, 5.5; for gas meters, 4.0; for telephone service, 4.5; and for the directory census, 2.25. At present (July, 1926), the population of the City of Los Angeles is estimated at 1 250 000.

Hyperion Screening Plant

The construction of a screening plant at Hyperion was included as a part of the work of building the North Outfall Sewer. This plant is divided into two parts. In order to clarify the sewage from the Central Outfall at the earliest possible date and to prevent any further pollution of the adjoining beaches, the southerly plant was built and placed in service in 1924. The North Plant began operation in March, 1925. The combined capacity of the two plants is now (July, 1926), 230 000 000 gal. per day, with space for additional units that will make a total capacity of 420 000 000 gal. per day.

These plants use drum-type revolving screens and include pits, elevators, and pneumatic sludge ejectors with complete electrical equipment. At the South Plant there are eight 8 by 8-ft. screens, each with a capacity of 10 000 000 gal. per day. Each screen is driven by a 5-h.p. motor and has a separate enclosed bucket elevator driven by a 1-h.p. motor to raise the screenings into metal hoppers from which they are ejected by compressed air. The sewage entering the plant passes through inclined bar screens. At the North Plant only one-half the screens, or one row of five screens, is now in use. These screens are 14 ft. in diameter and 12 ft. long, each with a capacity of 30 000 000 gal. per day. Each screen is driven by a 40-h.p. motor and equipped with a screening elevator driven by a 2-h.p. motor. The screenings are discharged into metal hoppers 3 ft. in diameter and 10 ft. deep, from which they are ejected by air pressure. This plant is operated by six men in the day shift and two in each of the two night shifts. After leaving the drum screens, the effluent from each plant is measured by a Venturi recording meter.

Table 1 shows the volume of sewage flow that has passed through the Hyperion Plant, together with the quantity of screenings removed from the flow for an 18-month period.

The average cost of the maintenance and operation of the plant during 1925 was $105 per day, or $1.26 per 1 000 000 gal. At present, these screenings are buried in the sandhills adjacent to the plant, but studies are in progress to determine the feasibility of using screenings for fertilizing purposes after a sufficient reduction of the *B. coli* and moisture content.

Ocean Disposal

The screened effluent from the Hyperion Plant is discharged through the 7-ft. reinforced concrete pipe sewer laid below the bottom of the ocean for a distance of 5 093 ft. from shore, where the depth is 54 ft. below mean sea level. The outer end of this ocean section is divided into two 5-ft. branches which have an average length of 210 ft. from their junction with the 7-ft. sewer.

TABLE 1.—SEWAGE AND SCREENINGS AT HYPERION TREATMENT PLANT, JANUARY 1, 1925, TO JUNE 30, 1926.

Date.	Total.		Average.		
	Sewage, in million gallons.	Screenings, in cubic feet.	Sewage per day, in million gallons.	Screenings, in cubic feet. Per day.	Screenings, in cubic feet. Per million gallons.
1925:					
January	2 320	32 000	75	1 032	14
February	2 010	32 000	72	1 142	16
March	2 360	22 300	76	760	10
April	2 300	32 000	77	1 070	14
May	2 560	39 000	83	1 260	15
June	2 520	40 000	84	840	16
July	2 600	53 200	84	1 716	20
August	2 419	55 440	78	1 788	23
September	2 900	47 700	97	970	16
October	2 750	51 000	89	887	19
November	2 740	43 600	91	1 450	16
December	2 780	39 930	90	1 288	14
Total	30 259	488 170	83*	1 339*	16.1*
1926:					
January	2 412	49 880	78	1 609	21
February	2 402	43 300	86	1 544	18
March	2 450	49 130	78	1 585	20
April	2 569	50 710	86	1 690	20
May	2 514	53 030	81	1 705	21
June	2 302	50 190	85	1 726	20
Total	14 649	296 240	81*	1 643*	20*

* Average.

Biological surveys have been made since 1925 of the surf waters along the beach adjacent to the Hyperion Plant, to determine the number of *B. coli* present. These surveys made at semi-monthly intervals indicate that, except for the mile directly in front of the plant and adjacent to the outfall, there has been no count of more than 10 *B. coli* per cu. cm., which condition has been considered by the California State Board of Health as safe. In the outer ocean and on each side of the outfall, surveys were made in January, May, and October, 1925, and in January, 1926, to determine the area affected by the discharge of sewage. In all four surveys the sewage field containing 10 or more *B. coli* per cu. cm., has been outlined, and the results obtained are as given in Table 2.

On account of the discharge of raw sewage and the fact that there were some leaks in the outfall, the results obtained are not considered final and further surveys are being planned. However, it is considered that the discharge from the Hyperion Outfall receives sufficient dilution to prevent pollution of the adjacent beaches. After the repair of the leaks in the outfall, the effect of the diffusion and dilution should be much more in evidence than has previously been noted. The absence of any sewage odor, even over the point of discharge of the outfall, has been one direct result of the construction of the Hyperion Plant and Outfall Sewer.

In addition to the surveys for *B. coli,* the quantity of dissolved oxygen in the ocean waters adjacent to the end of the outfall has been determined at irregular times. These records indicate an average value of about 90% saturation within ½ mile radius of the sewer outlet, and at no point is it less than 84 per cent.

TABLE 2.—SURVEYS OF SEWAGE FIELD, LOS ANGELES, CALIF., FOR *B. coli* CONTENT.

Date.	Sewage field, in acres, containing 10 or more *B. coli* per cu. cm.	Approximate maximum sewage flow, in million gallons per day.	Acres per million gallons per day.	Acres per 1 000 population.
1925:				
January 21	700	115	6.1	0.70
May 11	305	115	2.6	0.30
October 1	360	120	3.0	0.36
1926:				
January 25	613	105	5.8	0.61

Disposal of Industrial Wastes

Surveys are in progress to determine whether waste liquids and solids are being discharged into the sewerage system, that should not be permitted to enter. Especial attention is given to the disposal of refuse from fruit and vegetable canneries. Such waste not only overtaxes and clogs the system, but causes additional cost for treatment at the ocean disposal plant. Gasoline and oil are not permitted to be discharged in the sewers, but such disposal is in evidence at times. Some consideration has been given in some cities to a special charge for the disposal of such industrial waste, but should not the remedy be made at the plant of the industry?

In this connection it may be added that in the disposal of sewage from other cities and county sanitation districts into the City System, a clause in the contract with the City of Los Angeles states that all requirements imposed by the City shall likewise apply to such outside areas, thus establishing a standard for the Metropolitan District. The City has made contracts for sewage disposal with seven outside cities and four county sanitation districts. The total sewage from these outside areas is estimated eventually to be 59 000 000 gal. per day. The total length of public sewers in the city on July 1, 1926, was 1 457 miles.

DISCUSSION

A. M. Rawn,* M. Am. Soc. C. E. (by letter).—From Mr. Knowlton's paper, covering the history of the development of the Los Angeles City Metropolitan Sewer System, the writer abstracts two facts of outstanding importance that bear directly on the design and progress of similar works in other parts of California and elsewhere.

It is apparent that there is room for much study regarding the action of sewage when discharged into salt water; especially with reference to the direction and depth of discharge below the water surface and the amount of diffusion into the sea water. The selection of material used in the construction of the ocean section of the outfall plays an important part in determining whether the capacity life will be reached prior to elemental destruction.

The outfall sewer, designed for the City of Los Angeles in 1887, according to Mr. Knowlton, with the ocean end constructed of cast iron and extending 600 ft. into the ocean, provided for a capacity of 19 000 000 gal. per day, which should have provided for disposal into the ocean until about 1910. Nevertheless, it is found to have been superseded twice during its capacity life; once in 1904, with a steel pipe outfall extending 340 ft. farther seaward and, again, in 1908, with a wood stave pipe outfall of a length equal to the steel pipe, but with a different method of discharge into the water at the ocean end.

The wood stave outfall was designed with a capacity of 75 000 000 gal. per day and should have sufficed the needs of the city as an outfall sewer until about 1923. It has been superseded twice since construction; once, in 1918, with a wood stave line extending 2 000 ft. seaward and, again, in 1925, with the present outfall which extends about 1 mile seaward, discharging under 60 ft. of water. Thus, eight years prior to reaching capacity, the outfall constructed in 1908 was abandoned for a larger one (which is still (1927) in existence); and the latter, in turn, was abandoned for a still longer and larger one.

It would appear from this, which is an outstanding example, and which finds its parallel in many ocean outfalls constructed elsewhere, that sufficient experimental work and study should be conducted to enable the engineer to predetermine, with a fair degree of accuracy, the length of the outfall and other requirements of discharge that will enable him to construct the ocean end of the system with the same degree of permanency as the part on shore.

The second outstanding feature is the policy of the City of Los Angeles in building its sanitary sewer structure for the use of many communities not a part of its municipality and not bonded for its construction and then selling the allocated capacity to such communities, instead of attempting the organization of a large sanitary sewer district in the first place and attempting to persuade the communities for which sewerage facilities were to be provided, to participate in the original cost of construction.

* Asst. Chf. Engr., Los Angeles County Sanitation Dists., Los Angeles, Calif.

A well constructed outfall sewer is always a merchantable commodity in a growing district if it can be reached by a community which otherwise needs to resort to expensive local treatment, and this is clearly shown by the avidity with which the cities surrounding Los Angeles, and for which capacity has been provided in the North Outfall, are seizing the opportunity to discharge sewage into the North Outfall Sewer System under conditions dictated by the City of Los Angeles.

The writer is an advocate of the sedimentation process, as compared with fine screening, as a means of clearing up the effluent prior to disposal by dilution. Such treatment tends to reduce the dilution necessary, with consequent reduction of ocean-section costs; and, furthermore, the settled material resulting from sedimentation is much more responsive to reduction treatment than it is to screening.

WILLIS T. KNOWLTON,* M. AM. SOC. C. E. (by letter).—The writer has read with much interest the discussion by Mr. Rawn, and considers that the depth of the sewer outlet below the surface is an important factor in disposal into salt water. The distance from shore must also be taken into account. The Los Angeles Outfall of 1887 was of sufficient capacity for more than twenty years, but its proximity to the surf and the action of the waves caused its destruction.

Although the steel pipe outfall of 1904 had a capacity that was ample for many years, the action of the salt water and moisture caused the material to disintegrate, and this sewer was replaced four years later by a wooden stave pipe. The abandonment of the outfall of 1908 ten years later was probably due to different causes. First, the condition of the pier, which had been in use for fourteen years, was not satisfactory. Winter storms and floating material dashed against it at such times had weakened its construction. Similar damage also occurred to other piers in the vicinity, and in one case it was necessary to abandon more than 1 000 ft. of one not far from the sewer pier. Second, the metal bands around the wooden stave pipe became rusty and, consequently, leaks were found at various points along the line of the outfall. These conditions were not uncommon at that time in other outfalls of that type, especially where they were exposed to the elements.

In 1918 the City of Los Angeles built an outfall sewer into the ocean for a distance of about 2 000 ft. from shore. This sewer consisted of a 52-in. wooden stave pipe laid below the floor of a pier. This floor and pipe were practically level, having a fall of only 1 ft. in the entire length. At the outer end of the pier, the average depth of the ocean was about 30 ft. and sewage was discharged at this end through five outlets, each extending 18 ft. below mean sea level.

When this 1918 outfall was built, it was not considered that the sewage could be discharged into the ocean without treatment. As stated by the writer, unsuccessful bond issues for a treatment plant at Hyperion were submitted in both 1916 and 1917.

---

* San. Engr., City of Los Angeles, Los Angeles, Calif.

It was realized in 1918 that the disposal of sewage would require more attention than would be afforded by the 2 000-ft. outfall, which, in itself, had capacity for twenty years or more. Plans for Imhoff tanks and sludge beds at Hyperion had been prepared, but no funds for such construction were available. Consequently, the plans made in 1920 for a new outfall and treatment of sewage resulted in the construction, in 1924, of a 7-ft. reinforced concrete pipe sewer laid below the bottom of the ocean for a distance of 5 093 ft. from shore, where the depth is about 60 ft.

Considerable experimental work and study can and should be made in advance of the construction of outfall sewers, so that the engineers may predetermine the proper length and capacity of ocean sections, but the writer does not think that the same degree of efficiency can be obtained for the ocean end as is obtained for the land sections. The use of metal in the earlier Los Angeles outfalls was not advised in the outfalls of 1918 and 1924, and it is believed that the durability of the 1924 outfall is sufficient for many years. There are, however, some construction details in an ocean outfall which may not permit the sewer to be water-tight and which will permit leaks. If these leaks should occur at sufficient distance from shore, their effect may be negligible.

AMERICAN SOCIETY OF CIVIL ENGINEERS
INSTITUTED 1852

TRANSACTIONS

Paper No. 1678

THE WORK OF THE LOS ANGELES COUNTY (CALIFORNIA) SANITATION DISTRICTS*

By Albert K. Warren,† Assoc. M. Am. Soc. C. E.

In May, 1923, the Governor of California approved an enactment known as the "County Sanitation District Act of 1923", providing for the creation, government, and maintenance of County Sanitation Districts. The governing body of these Districts is empowered to employ engineers and other persons; to acquire real or personal property and rights of way; to issue bonds of the district; and to levy and collect assessments on real property.

For several years the south coast cities of Los Angeles County—Manhattan Beach, Hermosa Beach, and Redondo Beach—had attempted to provide a satisfactory method of sewage disposal. Immediately after the Act became effective those cities united in what is known as the South Bay Cities Sanitation District.

Even before the Act became effective citizens of Watts, Compton, and the vicinity, took steps toward the formation of a district to include six incorporated municipalities and some contiguous unincorporated area. It was first believed that this area, known as County Sanitation District No. 1, was the only one having urgent need of sewage disposal facilities. It was contemplated that this District could resort to local disposal until other areas might desire to join in the construction of a more comprehensive system. To the contrary, however, other areas in the Metropolitan Area of Los Angeles County took action almost immediately, with the result that six districts had been formed by July, 1923, and since that time three additional districts have been organized.

There are now (1926) nine County Sanitation Districts in Los Angeles County, covering approximately 432 sq. miles and including 35 incorporated cities, 35 unincorporated communities, and a rather large rural area, with a total population of about 521 400, as shown in Table 1.

---

* Presented at the meeting of the Sanitary Engineering Division, Seattle, Wash., July 15, 1926.

† Chf. Engr., Los Angeles County Sanitation Dists., Los Angeles, Calif.

TABLE 1.—SANITATION DISTRICTS IN LOS ANGELES COUNTY, CALIFORNIA.

District.	Area, in square miles.	Present (1926) population.	Incorporated cities included within districts.
South Bay Cities....	11.89	20 000	Hermosa Beach, Redondo Beach and Manhattan Beach.
District No. 1........	38.4	99 000	Huntington Park, Maywood, South Gate, Lynwood, Compton, parts of Vernon, Long Beach, and Los Angeles.
District No. 2........	59.8	64 000	Montebello, and a part of Los Angeles.
District No. 3........	51.7	121 000	Long Beach and Signal Hill.
District No. 4........	2.2	12 000	Part of Los Angeles.
District No. 5........	72.3	55 000	Inglewood, Hawthorne, Torrance, and a part of Los Angeles.
District No. 6........	74.26	27 400	Whittier, and a part of Long Beach.
District No. 7........	90	120 000	San Marino, South Pasadena, Alhambra, San Gabriel, Monterey Park, Sierra Madre, Monrovia, Arcadia, El Monte, Azusa, Glendora, Covina, and West Covina.
District No. 8........	31.8	3 000	A part of Long Beach.

It was possible, therefore, to disregard any temporary expedient and to work for a final solution of the problem.

There is a well-defined drainage divide along the southern and eastern boundaries of Los Angeles. All the territory north and west of this divide drains naturally into the Los Angeles City Sewerage System which has already been constructed, and that south and east of the divide drains to the south, and with this the Los Angeles County Sanitation District plan is particularly concerned.

The Los Angeles City Sewerage System discharges through the recently constructed North Outfall Sewer. The South Bay Cities Sanitation District and County Sanitation District No. 4 lie within the area which drains to this system, and contracts have been made with the City of Los Angeles whereby the sewage from the two Districts will be discharged into the City System and disposed of through the North Outfall Sewer. Both these Districts have voted bonds to provide the necessary funds. Construction work in the South Bay Cities Sanitation District and County Sanitation District No. 4 is completed. County Sanitation Districts Nos. 1, 2, and 5 voted $9 120 000 in bonds in February, 1925, for the construction of the Los Angeles County Sanitation Districts Metropolitan Sewerage System.

In the plan of the Metropolitan Sewerage System there were five steps of procedure:

First.—The determination of a satisfactory plan for sewage disposal on which to base an estimate prior to a bond election.

Second.—The conduct of a bond election in each Sanitation District.

Third.—If the bond election is successful, to adapt the preliminary plan to one modified by conditions subsequent to the bond issue.

Fourth.—The construction of the project.

Fifth.—Its operation and maintenance.

County Sanitation Districts Nos. 1, 2, and 5, at present (1926), are in the fourth stage. Districts Nos. 3, 6, 7, and 8, directly concerned in the joint undertaking, are prepared with a plan and are in a position to call elections to determine whether they will provide the necessary funds. Fig. 1 gives the outlines, physical characteristics, and plan of the Los Angeles County Sanitation Districts as organized.

In this paper, the writer will discuss the problems in bringing the formation and plan of the County Sanitation Districts to its present stage of completion, with particular reference to the engineering organization in determining a satisfactory means for sewage disposal prior to a bond election, and to the activities of the engineering organization in conducting the bond elections.

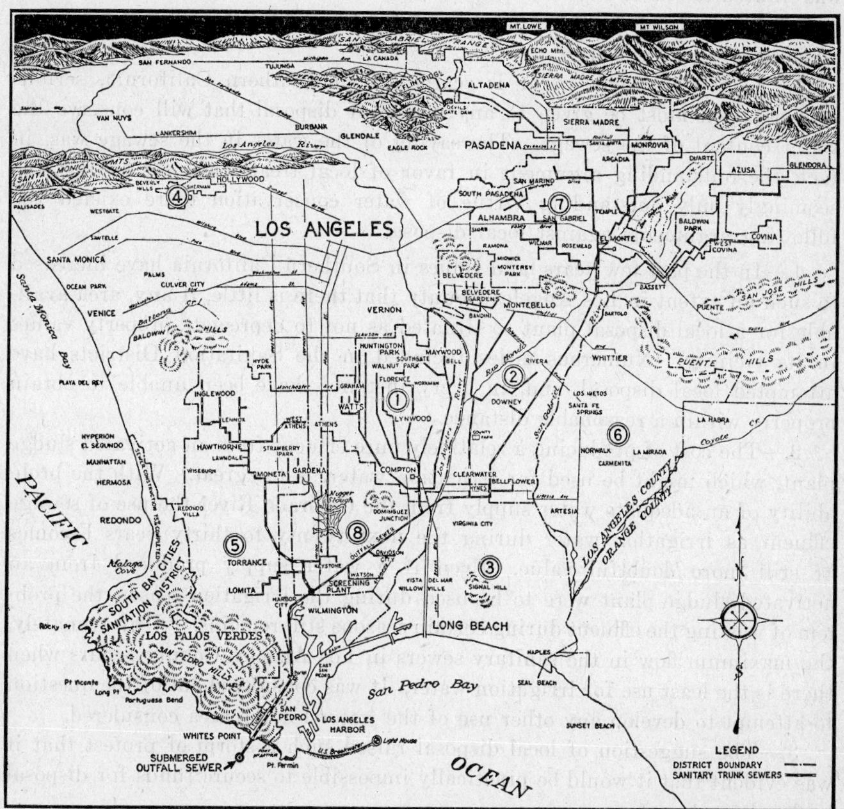

Fig. 1.—General Map of Metropolitan Sewerage System in Los Angeles County Sanitation Districts.

At the time the comprehensive sanitary sewerage system was planned for Los Angeles County, the North Outfall Sewer System of the City of Los Angeles, previously mentioned, was under construction. The North Outfall drained a well-defined area so that the problem was confined to an area lying south and east of Los Angeles and draining normally south to the ocean.

For such an area the natural process of accumulation would be through lines running in a general north and south direction accumulating sewage at, or near, the southerly ends of any districts formed. The final design for the Sanitation Districts finds trunk sewers extending north and south through the Districts, converging with other trunk lines to the south and concentrating at the southerly boundaries of the several districts.

The Districts have steep slopes in the northerly extremities where the sewage flows are light, and relatively flat slopes in the southerly reaches where sufficient sewage will be concentrated to assure good velocities on relatively flat grades.

The design for a system for central accumulation was, therefore, comparatively easy, the principal problem being the means of disposal. The choice was limited to one of two means, namely, that of disposal by refined treatment, such as the activated sludge process; or by disposal in the ocean, sufficiently offshore to avoid nuisance.

In a district where water is scarce, as in Southern California, serious consideration must be given to any means of disposal that will conserve the water content of the sewage. The saving of the water in the sewage was, in fact, the outstanding argument in favor of local treatment. As against the seemingly only outstanding virtue of water conservation there existed the following arguments against local disposal:

1.—In the past few years land values in Southern California have increased to such an extent in Los Angeles County that there is little, if any, area available for a local disposal plant so situated as not to depreciate property values in its vicinity. Numerous cities included in the Sanitation Districts have attempted local disposal, and, in every instance, have been unable to obtain property within a reasonable distance.

2.—The cost of producing a relatively pure effluent from an activated sludge plant, which might be used for irrigation water, is too great. With the probability of an adequate water supply from the Colorado River the use of sewage effluent as irrigation water during the next twenty to thirty years becomes of still more doubtful value. Even if a water supply produced from an activated sludge plant were to be used during the irrigation season the problem of wasting the effluent during certain seasons still remains. Unfortunately, the maximum flow in the sanitary sewers in Los Angeles County occurs when there is the least use for irrigation water. It was considered out of the question to attempt to develop any other use of the water for the area considered.

3.—The suggestion of local disposal raised such a storm of protest that it was evident that it would be practically impossible to secure funds for disposal by local treatment.

4.—The activated sludge process cannot be considered as a permanent means of disposal. It is undergoing many changes in the method of application of air to sewage and the treatment and disposal of the sludge. Although many theories have been advanced for its solution, the method of sludge disposal still remains unsolved and, at best, presents a problem involving a tremendous expense in operation and construction.

5.—It was early determined that the cost of an activated sludge treatment plant was approximately the same as that of a joint outfall sewer to the ocean, if a site could be selected where such disposal would not create a nuisance.

As opposed to the activated sludge process, the Sanitation Districts had recourse to a plan for disposal in the ocean, provided a suitable point of disposal could be determined.

Economy of construction and of operation and maintenance, permanency, established practice and custom, and deference to public opinion, all indicated that a jointly constructed outfall to the ocean would be the most adaptable solution.

The foregoing outlines briefly the problem presented to the County Sanitation Districts prior to bond election. The plan, as finally prepared, proposed a jointly constructed outfall to the ocean, and, based on this plan, the three Districts then concerned successfully carried bond elections by large majorities.

One of the most difficult problems was the control and regulation of a campaign prior to bond elections in the Districts. It was recognized that in a community with as many cities and communities involved, misinformation might spread rapidly, and that it would be much more difficult to correct a misapprehension than to register the correct information in the first place. For this reason it was decided that at every public meeting held in the interest of bond elections a representative from the Chief Engineer's office should attend to present facts. The Chief Engineer or his Principal Assistant, therefore, attended every public meeting where sewer bonds or sewage disposal was under discussion. The results were very gratifying. In each of the three Districts where bond elections were attempted under the plan as first proposed, the issues carried by overwhelming majorities.

There is only one other feature in the preparation of the plan for sewage disposal of the County Sanitation Districts that is of especial interest, namely, that of determining a future population on which to base the capacity life of the sewer system to be constructed. There is no well-established criterion for indicating a future population for districts in Los Angeles County. Few, if any, communities have ever made such forward strides in population as this area, and, therefore, predicted populations for Los Angeles County appear exceedingly optimistic if compared with past population increases for most counties of similar size in the United States.

In predicting future population, it was recognized that the population in certain areas would increase much faster than in others, and that no method of proportioning the increase directly over the entire district would be successful. The growth of each community, therefore, was studied separately, its future population predicted from year to year, and the future population curve of the district as a whole determined as a summation of the predictions for individual communities. Based on such a method the curves of growth for the districts are believed to be reasonably correct.

Prior to the design of the trunks sewers, a population density and concentration map was prepared, which served as a guide in predicting the quantity of sewage to be cared for at the expiration of a definite period of years. It was necessary to outline areas that would probably become industrial centers. It is impossible to predict the location and type of future industries, but presuming a fair average of manufactured products, the quantity of waste from industrial areas has been determined with some degree of accuracy. No attempt was made to lump industrial wastes, but the total quantity to be cared for is a summation of the quantities resulting from predicted development of industries, based on predicted population growth.

In a project of this size, proposing to discharge a relatively large volume of sewage into the ocean, it is inevitable that the property owners near the outfall should feel uneasy regarding the outcome. For this reason the State Board of Health has deferred final action on a permit for the location of the ocean end of the outfall until a detailed investigation of the entire plan can be made. In the meantime, construction work is in progress on the interior trunks of the several Districts.

AMERICAN SOCIETY OF CIVIL ENGINEERS

INSTITUTED 1852

TRANSACTIONS

This Society is not responsible for any statement made or opinion expressed in its publications.

Paper No. 1679

THE LAKE WASHINGTON SHIP CANAL, WASHINGTON*

By W. J. Barden† and A. W. Sargent,‡ Members, Am. Soc. C. E.

With Discussion by Messrs. Ernest B. Hussey, Charles Evan Fowler, Joseph M. Clapp, L. C. Sabin, and W. J. Barden and A. W. Sargent.

Synopsis

The Lake Washington Ship Canal, lying wholly within the limits of the City of Seattle, connects Puget Sound with a large fresh-water harbor comprising Salmon Bay, Lakes Union and Washington, and connecting waters, with a total area of about 25 000 acres. A dam and two locks, one large and one small, near the canal entrance hold the waters of the lakes 25 ft. above extreme low water of the Sound. This paper gives a general description of the locality, the original condition, a brief history of the improvement, and a description of the locks, dam, and appurtenances, and of the construction methods. The traffic developed is given, together with a summary of the beneficial results of the work. Under the headings, "Maintenance and Operation" and "Salinity", are given some of the results of the ten years' experience of operation and observation, with suggestions as to changes that might be desirable in future work of a similar character.

General Description

Seattle, the largest city of the State of Washington, is situated on Elliott Bay, an arm of Puget Sound, 47 miles south of the Strait of Juan de Fuca and 147 miles from the Pacific Ocean. Elliott Bay, 2 miles wide and 4 miles long, is protected from all severe storms and is accessible to the largest vessels afloat at all times. Deep water extends close to the shore except at Smith's Cove at the northern end and at the tide flats of the Duwamish River at the southern end. In these flats two waterways, each 750 ft. wide, 34 ft. deep, and 1 mile or more in length, have been excavated and the lower part

* Presented at the meeting of the Waterways Division, Seattle, Wash., July 15, 1926.

† Col., Corps of Engrs., U. S. A., Headquarters, 2d Corps Area, New York, N. Y.

‡ Civ. Engr., U. S. Engr. Office, Govt. Locks, Seattle, Wash.

of the Duwamish has also been straightened and dredged to form a waterway suitable for commercial purposes with authorized depths of 15 to 30 ft.

To this commodious salt-water harbor the construction of the Lake Washington Ship Canal has added a fresh-water harbor of approximately 25 000 acres, comprising Salmon Bay, Lake Union, and Lake Washington, and connecting waters. (Fig. 1.) This improvement lies entirely within the city and extends from Puget Sound through Shilshole Bay, Salmon Bay, Lake Union, Portage Bay, and Union Bay, to deep water in Lake Washington. The distance by channel from deep water in Puget Sound to deep water in Lake Washington is approximately 8 miles. The tidal reach extends to the locks, approximately 1¼ miles. The extreme tidal range is 19 ft. The range between mean lower low water and mean higher high water is 11.3 ft. and between mean lower low water and extreme low water, 4 ft.

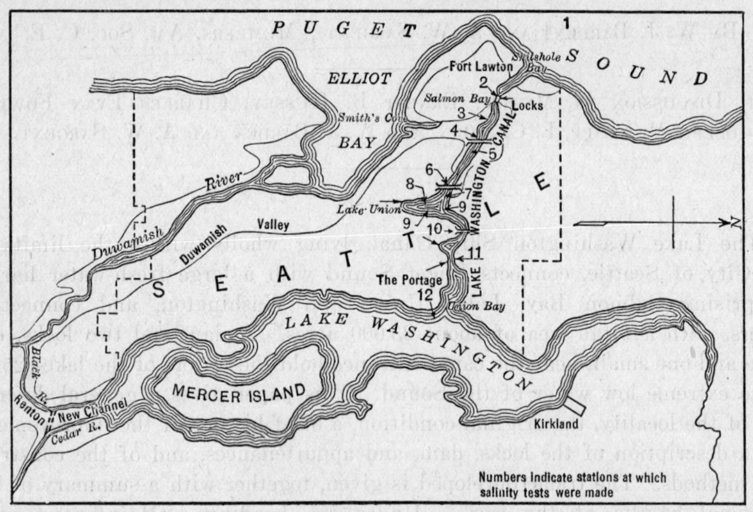

FIG. 1.—OUTLINE OF SEATTLE HARBOR AND LAKE WASHINGTON SHIP CANAL.

The double lock and fixed dam with movable crest are at the Narrows, at the westerly end of Salmon Bay, and hold the waters of Salmon Bay and the lakes 25 ft. above extreme low water in Puget Sound, with an allowable variation of 1 ft. above and 1 ft. below this plane.

The dredged channel below the rocks is 300 ft. wide at the bottom and 34 ft. deep at mean lower low water, with a passing basin and log basin in the turn below the Great Northern Railway Bridge which is just below the locks and dam. (See Figs. 2 and 3.) From the locks to Lake Union the channel is 100 ft. wide on the bottom and 36 ft. deep. From the easterly end of Lake Union to deep water in Lake Washington the channel is 75 ft. wide at the bottom and 25 ft. deep. These dimensions will be increased to meet the needs of commerce. The main body of Lake Union required no dredging.

The large lock is 80 ft. wide and will accommodate vessels with a maximum length of 760 ft. and a draft of 36 ft. The small lock is 150 ft. long and 30 ft. wide, with a depth of 16 ft. over the sill.

Fig. 2.—Lake Washington Ship Canal: Lock and Dam, Looking East from Great Northern Railway Bridge.

Fig. 3.—View of Upper End of Large Lock, Lake Washington Ship Canal, Showing Recesses in Which Foundations for Emergency Dam Were Constructed.

Original Condition

Originally, there was no connection between Lake Union and Lake Washington, and Lake Union had no navigable connection with Salmon Bay. Lake Washington, through the Black and Duwamish Rivers, had a navigable connection with Puget Sound with sufficient capacity for the transportation of logs.

Lake Union, the smaller of the two lakes, situated in the heart of Seattle, has an area of nearly 1 000 acres, of which 500 acres has a depth exceeding 40 ft. The general elevation of Lake Union was originally 25.5 ft. above extreme low tide in Puget Sound. Between Lake Union and Puget Sound is a high ridge, cut by a low valley at the extreme western end of the lake. Through this valley the natural drainage of the lake found its outlet to Salmon Bay.

Salmon Bay extends in a westerly direction to Shilshole Bay, an arm of Puget Sound. Salmon Bay and Shilshole Bay were originally navigable at high tide, but both were practically dry at extreme low tide. At mean lower low water a narrow, crooked channel, approximately 2½ miles long and 3 ft. deep, extended from Puget Sound to near the head of Salmon Bay.

South of this valley and of Salmon Bay are two high hills between which is a low narrow valley connecting the head of Salmon Bay with Smith's Cove, an indentation in the north end of Elliott Bay.

Lake Washington forms the easterly boundary of the City of Seattle. It is 19 miles long, with an average width of 2 miles. The elevation of the lake originally fluctuated between 33 and 37 ft. above extreme low tide in Puget Sound. It is separated from Lake Union and from Elliott Bay by a high ridge, extending along its western side. In this ridge is a low depression at a point where the shores of Lake Union and Lake Washington approach each other to within 2 000 ft. At this point, known as "The Portage", a narrow channel had been cut by private enterprise about 1888, for the passage of logs. The natural outlet of the lake was at the southern end through Black and Duwamish Rivers to the waters of Puget Sound at the southern end of Elliott Bay. Cedar River, which entered the Black River about ½ mile below the outlet of Lake Washington, is subject to annual floods, due to the melting of snow in the head-waters of the river in the Cascade Mountains. During the height of these floods the direction of the current in Black River between Lake Washington and the mouth of Cedar River was reversed, and a large quantity of water emptied into the lake, which acted as a storage reservoir preventing excessive flooding of the Duwamish Valley.

When the canal was constructed, Salmon Bay was raised and Lake Washington lowered to the level of Lake Union. Cedar River was diverted from the Black River into Lake Washington and the outlet through Black and Duwamish Rivers no longer exists.

History

The idea of a canal to connect Puget Sound with Lake Union and Lake Washington is practically as old as the City of Seattle, and the subject received Federal recognition as early as December 9, 1867, in a report of a Board of Engineers for the Pacific Coast, which recommended the lakes as a site for a Naval Station on Puget Sound. From then until 1890 it was frequently referred to in official reports, but more from a naval than from a commercial point of view.

The River and Harbor Act of 1890 authorized the appointment of a board of three officers "to select and survey the most feasible location and estimate the expense of construction of a ship canal * * *". The Board's report, dated December 15, 1891, considered five possible routes. The present general route, being less expensive and having a better alignment, was considered preferable.

Several later investigations and reports were made, but the existing project, adopted by the River and Harbor Act of June 25, 1910, is based on the report of December 2, 1907, of the late H. M. Chittenden, M. Am. Soc. C. E. The terms of local co-operation required that, in addition to furnishing all rights of way, the County of King, or other local agency, should do the excavation in the waterway above the lock, and hold the United States free from any claim for damages on account of lowering the level of Lake Washington, raising the level of Salmon Bay, or any other alterations of the levels of any other part of the waterway.

In September, 1911, construction work was actually begun under the direction of the late Col. James B. Cavanaugh, Corps of Engineers, U. S. A., the District Engineer, who was in charge of the entire project, both as to Federal and County expenditures, until the completion of the main part of the work.

The total amount expended by the Federal Government has been approximately \$3 500 000; King County has expended about \$750 000, and the State of Washington about \$250 000, in addition to the cost for right of way.

The cost of maintenance and operation, which is borne by the permanent indefinite appropriation for operation and care of canals, is about \$80 000 per year.

Spillway Dam

The spillway dam (Fig. 4), extends from the small lock to the south shore of Salmon Bay. It is 240 ft. long, with six spillway openings, each 32 ft. long. A fish ladder for the passage of salmon to the spawning grounds above the locks, and an opening for discharging salt water from the upper pool, are provided through the dam. There are two walks extending the entire length of the dam, one at the elevation of the lock-wall, for pedestrians, and one at a higher elevation, from which the gates are raised and lowered. These are carried on arches spanning the piers which separate the spillway openings.

The fixed part of the dam is of ogee section with a vertical up-stream face and a toe 4 ft. long extending up stream. The total width of the base is 46 ft. A concrete apron, with its top 10 ft. below extreme low tide, extends 114 ft. below the dam. The total height of the dam, not including cut-off walls, from the foundation to the spillway crest, is 37.75 ft. The latter is

17.75 ft. above extreme low tide. The six spillway openings are closed by Taintor gates. The gates are arranged to rotate around the trunnions until they rest on the lower footwalk of the dam, when necessary for painting or repairs. The gates are raised and lowered by two chains which are attached when desired to cross-heads on an electrically driven machine which can be moved from gate to gate on the upper walk of the dam. The cross-heads are moved back and forth by means of revolving screws, and a gate can be raised wide open in one operation.

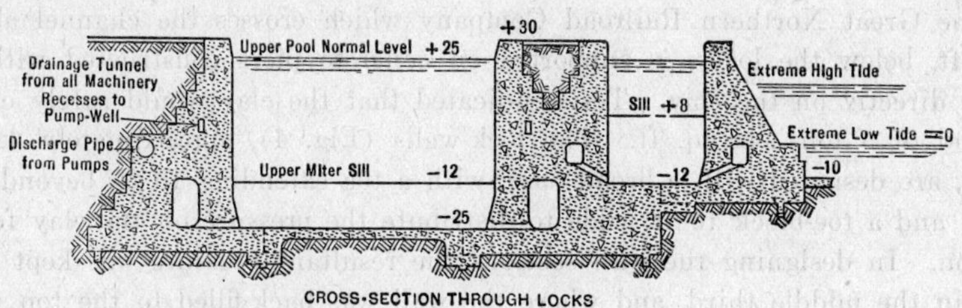

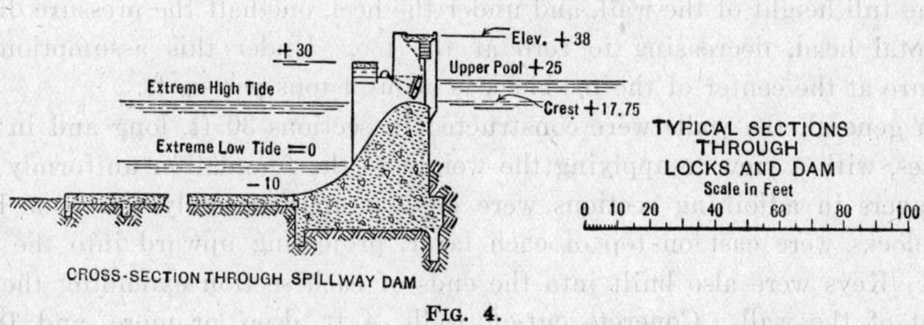

FIG. 4.

The capacity of each spillway opening is 2 350 sec-ft. at normal upper pool level, and with all the gates open no trouble with scour has been experienced beyond the lower edge of the apron. The dam was constructed in sections, 36 ft. long, each section consisting of three horizontal layers well keyed together. After two horizontal layers had been placed the piers were constructed, then the spillway sections, after which the footwalks were built.

Locks

Table 1 gives the principal features of the locks.

TABLE 1.—PRINCIPAL FEATURES OF THE LOCKS, LAKE WASHINGTON SHIP CANAL.

Item.	Large lock.	Small lock.
Clear width of chamber, in feet	80	30
Maximum available length, in feet	760	123
Maximum lift, in feet	26	26
Depth on upper miter-sill at low water in upper pool, in feet	36	16
Depth on intermediate miter-sill at mean lower low water, in feet	29	....
Depth on lower miter-sill at mean lower low water, in feet	29	16

The large lock is 825 ft. long and is divided into two chambers by an intermediate gate, the lower and the upper chambers being 375 ft. and 450 ft. long, respectively. The small lock, alongside and south of the large lock, is designed to accommodate with the minimum of delay the large number of launches, tugboats, and small craft continually passing in and out of the canal.

The locks are constructed on a bed of hard impervious clay. At the upper end this clay bed slopes off rapidly, but below the locks the hard formation extends almost to Puget Sound. The double-track bascule railway bridge of the Great Northern Railroad Company which crosses the channel about 700 ft. below the locks, is supported on concrete piers constructed without piles directly on the clay. Tests indicated that the clay would safely carry a load of 5 tons per sq. ft. The lock-walls (Fig. 4), approximately 62 ft. high, are designed with a broad base, with a toe extending 10 ft. beyond the face, and a toe-block 10 ft. wide to distribute the pressure on the clay foundation. In designing the wall sections the resultant pressure was kept well within the middle third, and where the wall was back-filled to the top with earth it was assumed that there would be hydrostatic pressure along the back, for the full height of the wall, and under the heel, one-half the pressure due to the total head, decreasing to zero at the toe. Under this assumption the pressure at the center of the toe-block is about 4 tons per sq. ft.

In general, the walls were constructed in sections 30 ft. long and in 5-ft. courses, with a view to applying the weight to the foundation uniformly; the top layers in adjoining sections were kept at approximately the same level. Key-blocks were cast on top of each layer, projecting upward into the next layer. Keys were also built into the ends of each section extending the full height of the wall. Concrete cut-off walls, 4 ft. deep, or more, and 18 in. thick, were built under the heels of the walls, under the miter-sills, and under the entire length of the dam to the south bank. Below the floor level, lead stop-waters were placed between all wall sections, down the cut-off walls, between floor sections, and between the toe of the wall and the floor; also, between the sections of the dam. At the upper end of the large lock beyond the guard-gate, where the foundations were not as satisfactory as over the remainder of the area, cellular walls were built.

The floor of the large lock, which is only 3 ft. thick, was designed merely as a pavement to prevent scour in the lock. No relief valves were provided against hydrostatic pressure, reliance being placed on the cut-off walls to prevent excessive leakage. No difficulty has been experienced from this source when the lock is unwatered; in fact, holes drilled through the floor a few years ago to ascertain if there was any pressure, showed that, although a small quantity of water had accumulated under the floor, no pressure had developed due to the 50-ft. head along the outside of the lock, showing that the precautions taken as to cut-off walls and lead stop-waters had been successful.

Gates.—The gates of both locks are of the mitering type. In the large lock there are five gates, the upper and lower guard-gates, and the upper, intermediate, and lower service gates.

The lower guard-gate, which is used only when the lock is unwatered for purposes of repair and inspection, is designed to withstand a head of 43 ft. It is 46 ft. high and each leaf weighs 207 tons. The lower service and intermediate gates are each 56 ft. high and designed to withstand a head of 26 ft. Each leaf weighs 237 tons. The upper service and guard-gates are smaller, being only 43 ft. high, but are subjected to a head of 38 ft. when the lock is unwatered. Each leaf weighs 180 tons.

All gates of the large lock are constructed with horizontal girders spaced equi-distant on 3½-ft. centers, and five transverse vertical frames built in between the girders extending from the bottom to the top of the leaf. The skin-plates extend the full height of both up and down-stream sides of the gate. The lower part of the gate forms an air chamber to lighten the weight on the pintle and anchors, while water is allowed to run freely in and out of the upper part, through openings in the up-stream skin just above the air chamber and through the girders and vertical frames.

Provision is made for blowing out by compressed air any water that may enter the air chamber. A 2½-in. pipe extends down to and is attached to the top of the chamber. Through this pipe a 1¼-in. pipe extends almost to the bottom of the gate, the air entering through the large pipe and the water being forced out through the smaller one.

Access is provided to all parts of the interior of the gates through openings in the girders and vertical frames and through the manhole which extends from the top of the gate, through the water chamber, into the air chamber.

The wall reaction bearing consists of a structural steel, built-up member embedded in the concrete, to which are bolted steel castings which have a slightly concave surface, with which the convex reaction casting on the gate comes in contact when closed. The miter edge of the gate has adjustable steel bearing pieces extending the full height, behind which Babbitt metal was poured to bring it into proper alignment.

The forged steel pintle is supported on a steel casting embedded in the concrete. The top surface is hemi-spherical in shape, and the bushings on which the gates rotate are of vanadium steel held in place in a steel casting on the heel of the gate. The pintle is free to move on its foundation whenever the gate is forced out by obstructions on the sill.

The gate anchors are heavy steel trusses embedded in the concrete and connected with the gate by forged steel eye-bars and pins. The eye-bars are bronze-bushed and are connected by sleeve nuts with a square thread, 1-in. pitch in the one half and ¾-in. pitch in the other half, both right-hand threads, so that when the coarse thread is being taken up the finer thread is being unscrewed, and *vice versa*.

At the lower edge of the down-stream side of the gate greenheart timbers were fastened into a structural steel channel. When the gate is closed, the timber comes in contact with a similar timber fastened in a steel chair on the miter-sill. After four years of service it was found that the timbers on the lower guard-gate of the large lock had been honeycombed by marine borers and that it would be necessary to replace them with other material. Iron bark was tried, but in two years it was found that this also had been destroyed by marine borers and that the timbers attached to the miter-sill were partly destroyed. Considerable study was then given to determine the best method of overcoming the difficulty. It was thought impracticable to replace the timbers on the miter-sill by diver. A coffer-dam could only be constructed at considerable cost and would also necessitate the closing of the lock for a considerable period. The plan finally adopted was to remove the timber on the sill with the assistance of the diver. The gate was then removed and docked, and steel castings were made and attached to it. These castings (Fig. 5) extend out so as to come in approximate contact with a steel chair which formerly held the timbers on the miter-sill, and take the pressure in case of failure of the leaves to miter properly. A lip extending downward from the castings carries a heavy piece of rubber belting which forms the water-seal between the gate and the concrete sill. This arrangement proved to be satisfactory and a similar device has been placed on the lower guard-gate of the small lock. No such trouble has been experienced with any of the other gates, probably because the service gates are regularly used and the water at the upper guard-gates is mainly fresh.

The gates of the small lock (four in number, two service and two guard) are composed of horizontal I-beams with skin-plates on one side only. Mitering devices, consisting of a jaw at the top of one leaf, which engages a post on the other leaf as they swing together, are provided on all gates.

Culverts and Valves.—The culverts in both locks are in the side walls, with laterals extending into the chambers at the floor level (Fig. 4). The ends of the culverts are between the service gates and the guard-gates, and all gates and valves are accessible when the lock is unwatered, except the exterior surfaces of the guard-gates.

The culverts of the large lock are 8½ ft. wide and 14 ft. high, with corners rounded to a radius of 3.5 ft. The intake end is increased in size to 16 ft. in width and 14 ft. in height, and the discharge ends are 10 ft. wide and 16 ft. high. Both ends turn at an angle of 90° horizontally into the lock. The bottoms of the culverts are at the floor level except at the discharge end where they are raised 5 ft. with a view to overcoming difficulties attendant on the difference in density of the water above and below the gates. The laterals are 4 ft. wide and 2 ft. high. There are twenty-four entering the upper chamber and twenty-eight for the lower chamber.

The valves of the large lock are of the Stoney gate type, raised and lowered by means of two vertical screws revolving in fixed nuts in the cross-head which is attached to the valve stem. The valve stem passes through a stuffing-box in a water-tight bulkhead which closes the bottom of the machinery recess. The latter is about 22 ft. below high-water level in the lock. The valves are equipped with roller trains which are raised and lowered with the valves, but at half speed, by pulleys over which a chain is taken. One end of the chain is fastened to the cross-head on the valve stem and the other passes through a stuffing-box in the water-tight bulkhead over the valve. The valves of the small lock are of the cylindrical type.

Signal lights installed in the controllers in the operating houses indicate whether the valves are in the open or closed position. Limit switches are provided for controlling the travel of the valves.

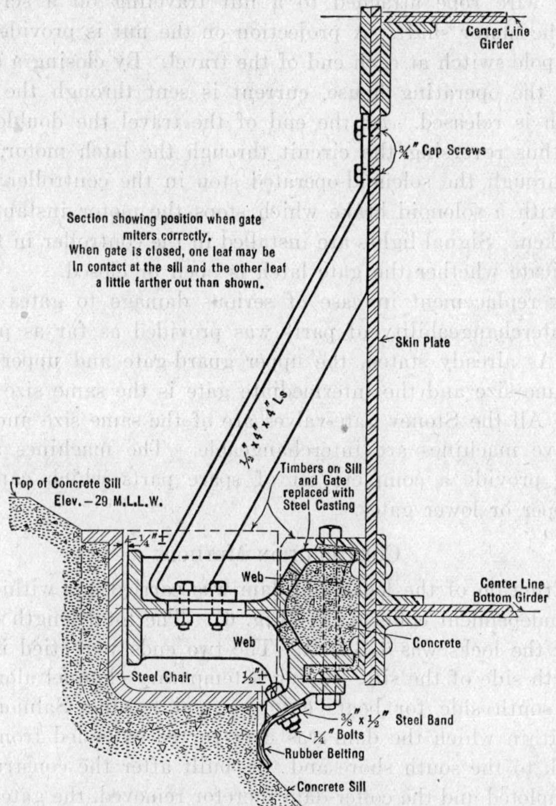

FIG. 5.—LAKE WASHINGTON SHIP CANAL, WATER SEAL, LOWER GUARD GATE—LARGE LOCK.

OPERATING MACHINERY

The gates are operated by electrically driven winding drums acting through cables attached to the gates near the outer end of each leaf. The cables pass from the drum over rollers and round sheaves, through passages in the lock-walls to the two sides of each gate leaf, the operation of each leaf being entirely independent of the other. The opening cable is 1 in. in diameter and the closing cable ⅞-in., 6/19 plow steel rope. The drums are spirally grooved, driven in the large lock by 20-h.p. motors through worm and spur gears. The drums are connected with the spur gears through adjustable slip friction clutches arranged so that in case of an excess load the clutch will slip. The radii of the drum spirals are proportioned so that there will be no excess slack in the cable as the gate swings through its arc of revolution. The ends of the cable are attached to the drums through adjustable screw fastenings, in order that the slack due to the stretch of the cables can be taken up.

Gate latches are provided for each leaf of the service gates of the large lock to hold them securely in the open position. A movable latch bolted to the lock-wall engages a catch on the gate leaf. The latch is operated by a flexible wire rope attached to a nut traveling on a screw which is attached to the motor shaft. A projection on the nut is provided for reversing a double pole switch at each end of the travel. By closing a switch in the controller in the operating house, current is sent through the latch motor and the catch is released. At the end of the travel the double pole switch is reversed, thus reversing the circuit through the latch motor, and closing the circuit through the solenoid-operated stop in the controller. The motor is provided with a solenoid brake which stops the motor instantly when the circuit is broken. Signal lights are installed in the controller in the operating house to indicate whether the gate latch is open or closed.

For quick replacement in case of serious damage to gates or operating machinery interchangeability of parts was provided as far as practicable in the design. As already stated, the upper guard-gate and upper service gate are of the same size and the intermediate gate is the same size as the lower service gate. All the Stoney gate-valves are of the same size and all parts of gate and valve machines are interchangeable. The machines at the intermediate gate provide a complete set of spare parts which can be used at either the upper or lower gates.

Construction Methods

The construction of the locks and dam was carried out within the protection of two independent coffer-dams (Fig. 6). The total length of the coffer-dam wall for the locks was 1 320 ft. The two ends were tied into the bank along the north side of the site, leaving a temporary channel along the coffer-dam on the south side for boats entering and leaving Salmon Bay. The coffer-dam within which the dam was constructed extended from the wall of the small lock to the south shore and was built after the construction of the locks was completed and the coffer-dam therefor removed, the gates of the large lock being left open for navigation.

The coffer-dam walls, which were 20 ft. apart, were constructed of round piles, wales, and Wakefield sheet piling, and were tied together by iron rods. The sheet-piles were driven a short distance into the underlying hard material, not quite to refusal. It was found that if they were driven too hard it was difficult to hold them up close together, and they had a tendency to move off line away from the wales. A better job was obtained by not driving them to refusal. The material for filling and banking was supplied from excavation in the lock-pit. This material was excavated by dipper dredges before the coffer-dam was completed, and the foundation was cleaned to grade by pick and shovel. The surplus material was removed by crane and skip to the bank just inside the coffer-dam. Although at high tide the deepest part of the excavation was 58 ft. below water level, there was practically no seepage through the coffer-dam or through the clay foundation into the lock-pit, and two or three 2-in. centrifugal pumps, at different points within the enclosure, were more than ample to handle all seepage and rain water.

All concrete work in the locks and dam, the construction of permanent buildings, and the work on the grounds were done by hired labor and Government plant. Separate contracts were let for the excavation and coffer-dam, gates, machinery, permanent pumping plant, and the removal of the coffer-dams, as well as a number of smaller contracts for minor parts of the work.

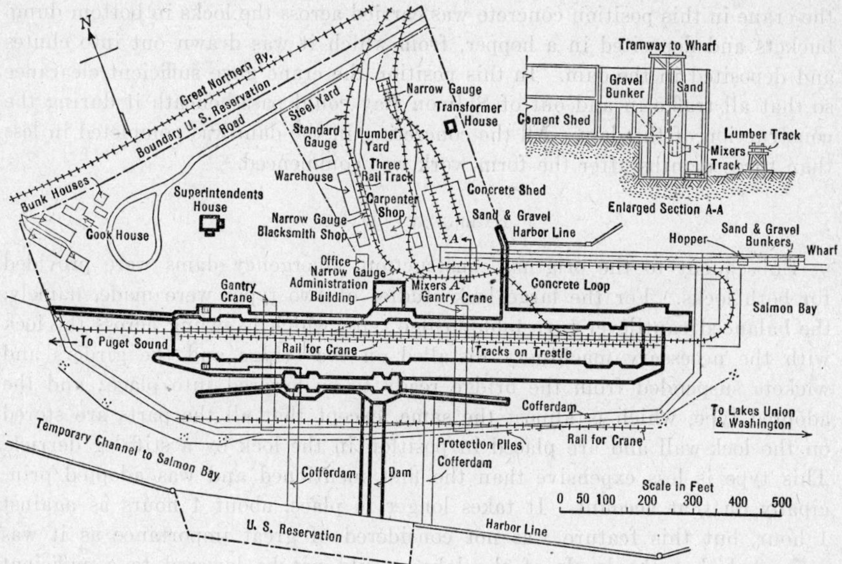

FIG. 6.—GENERAL LAYOUT, WASHINGTON SHIP CANAL, PERMANENT LOCKS AND DAM (HEAVY) AND CONSTRUCTION PLANT (LIGHT).

All concrete in the locks was handled by two gantry cantilever cranes which were constructed across the lock-pit, one rail being along the axis of the lock just above the floor level and the other partly on top of the coffer-dam and partly on pile trestle. Each crane was equipped with two 30-h. p. electric hoists which operated two trolleys, each capable of lifting 5 tons. The concrete was delivered from the mixing plant, consisting of three $1\frac{1}{2}$-cu. yd. mixers, into bottom dump buckets, which were carried on cars by steam locomotive to the cranes, where they were picked up, two at a time. Six buckets were placed on the cars in each train so that two could be filled simultaneously at the mixers, and two picked up at the same time by the crane. As much as 1 140 cu. yd. was placed in an 8-hour day, and the highest monthly average was 24 000 cu. yd. Approximately, 150 000 cu. yd. was placed in 9 months (from May, 1913, to January, 1914). The bulk of the concrete in the locks was placed at a cost of $4.00 per cu. yd., and the average cost of all concrete in the locks, dam, and permanent buildings was approximately $5.50 per cu. yd.

The forms were mainly of the cantilever type, fastened to the wall with $\frac{7}{8}$-in. bolts, 2 ft. long, with threads on both ends. The outer end was made square so that it could be easily turned by a wrench while the concrete was setting. On the inner end a nut and a washer 3 in. square were used, which were left in the concrete. The bolts were removed when the forms were taken off and were used again repeatedly. Each form was used five or six times and then knocked down, the lumber being utilized for building rough forms.

After the completion of the locks one of the gantry cranes was lifted up and supported on top of the lock-wall, and on a tower near the dam. With the crane in this position concrete was carried across the locks in bottom dump buckets and deposited in a hopper, from which it was drawn out into chutes and deposited in the dam. In this position the crane gave sufficient clearance so that all traffic in and out of Salmon Bay could pass beneath it during the construction of the dam. All the concreting in the dam was completed in less than three months after the form work was commenced.

Emergency Dams

Subsequent to the original construction, emergency dams were provided for both locks. For the large lock studies of two types were made, namely, the balanced cantilever turn-table bridge type, which is swung across the lock with the necessary machinery installed on the bridge and the girders and wickets suspended from the bridge ready to be lowered into place; and the adopted type, which is almost the same, except that all the parts are stored on the lock-wall and are placed in position in the lock by a stiff-leg derrick. This type is less expensive than the first mentioned and was adopted principally on that account. It takes longer to place, about 4 hours as against 1 hour, but this feature was not considered of great importance as it was estimated that the levels of the lakes would not be lowered to a sufficient degree during the time required for placing it to cause serious damage.

Figs. 7 and 8 show the dam in storage position on the lock-wall and a down-stream view when in position. Fig. 9 shows a cross-sectional view. The dam consists of two removable bridges which span the lock when in use, six wicket girders which form the framework, twenty-four wickets which complete the closure, a stiff-leg derrick, and the necessary operating machinery for handling the various parts. Needles are also provided for closing the clearance between the vertical rows of wickets.

The wicket girder bridge consists of a horizontal truss which supports the upper edge of the dam and two vertical trusses which support the dead load. It is placed by the derrick in recesses provided in the lock-walls. Its weight is approximately 72 tons.

The operating bridge is placed about 35 ft. up stream from the girder bridge and carries the machinery for lowering the wicket girders against the sill in the lock floor which supports the lower edge of the dam. The machinery consists of a two-speed electric hoist with six drum units operated through a line shaft, each unit consisting of two drums which are geared to the line shaft and are engaged or disengaged by means of jaw clutches. Each drum unit operates the hoisting tackle which is provided for lowering a wicket girder.

The six wicket girders, the skeleton of the dam, are delivered one at a time by the derrick in a horizontal position. They are then lowered until the

Fig. 7.—Lake Washington Ship Canal: Emergency Dam in Storage Position on Lock Wall.

Fig. 8.—View of Placing Next to Last Wicket, Looking Up Stream, Emergency Dam, Lake Washington Ship Canal.

upper end is hooked over pins provided on the up-stream face of the girder bridge, the hoisting tackle on the operating bridge is attached to the lower end and, after the derrick tackle has been disconnected, the girder is lowered to a bearing against the sill.

The wickets are twenty-four in number and consist of steel frame and buckle-plates. They are on roller-bearing wheels and are guided into place over a track on the up-stream flanges of the wicket girders by the derrick. They are placed across the channel in four horizontal rows, six wickets in each row. There is sufficient cable attached to each wicket to fasten the upper end over hooks on the girder bridge after it has been disconnected from the derrick hook, so that the wickets can be readily removed after use.

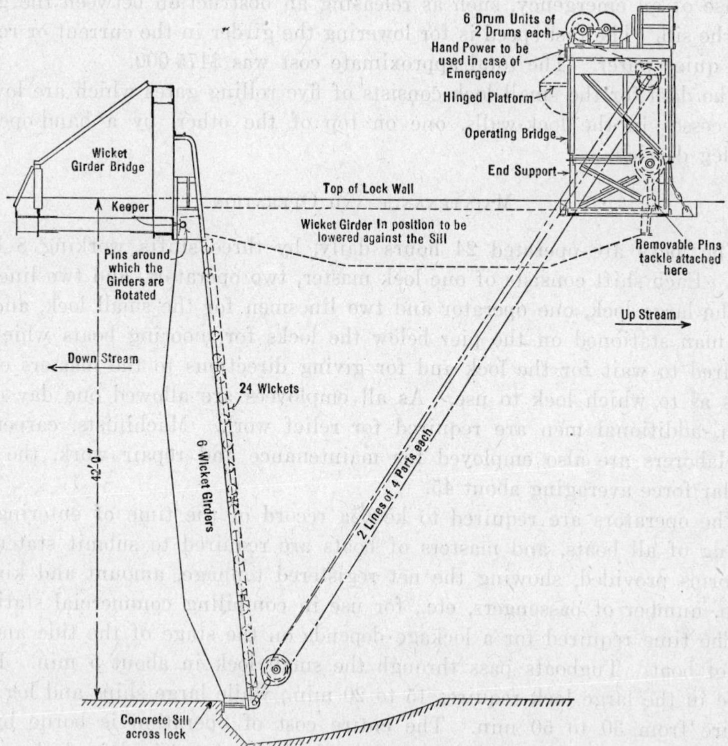

FIG. 9.—LAKE WASHINGTON SHIP CANAL EMERGENCY DAM: CROSS-SECTION OF DAM IN THE LOCK.

The capacity of the derrick is 75 tons at 60-ft. radius. The mast is 45 ft. high and the boom 102 ft. long. The main hoist tackle has twelve parts and is used only for handling the wicket girder bridge and the operating bridge. Farther out on the boom is an auxiliary tackle designed for the rapid handling of the wicket girders and the wickets. The wickets are hoisted on a single line at 125 ft. per min., and the girders are handled at half this speed by hooking the end of the line to the boom and hanging a snatch-block in the bight. The boom tackle is designed for a load of 309 000 lb. and has seventeen parts. The maximum vertical uplift on the stiff legs is 300 000 lb.; the speed of the boom fall is 93.7 ft. per min.; and that of the main hoist and auxiliary hoist falls is 125 ft., per min. The speed of the swinger cable is 31 ft. per min.

The derrick is operated by an electric hoist with three drums, each drum being connected through worm gearing to its own 100-h.p. motor. The swinger hoist is of standard design operated by a 40-h.p. motor. The hoist on the operating bridge for lowering the wicket girders in the current is operated through a worm by a 40-h.p. motor. It has two speeds, 8 and 32 ft. per min., respectively. The slow speed is for raising the wicket girders in the current in case of an emergency, such as releasing an obstruction between the girder and the sill. The fast speed is for lowering the girder in the current or raising it in quiet water. The total approximate cost was $175 000.

The dam for the small lock consists of five rolling gates which are lowered in recesses in the lock-walls, one on top of the other, by a hand-operated stiff-leg derrick.

Maintenance and Operation

The locks are operated 24 hours daily, by three shifts working 8 hours each. Each shift consists of one lock master, two operators, and two linesmen for the large lock, one operator and two linesmen for the small lock, and one pier man stationed on the pier below the locks for mooring boats which are required to wait for the lock and for giving directions to the masters of the boats as to which lock to use. As all employees are allowed one day off in seven, additional men are required for relief work. Machinists, carpenters, and laborers are also employed for maintenance and repair work, the total regular force averaging about 45.

The operators are required to keep a record of the time of entering and leaving of all boats, and masters of boats are required to submit statements on forms provided, showing the net registered tonnage, amount and kind of cargo, number of passengers, etc., for use in compiling commercial statistics.

The time required for a lockage depends on the stage of the tide and the size of boat. Tugboats pass through the small lock in about 5 min. Barge traffic in the large lock requires 15 to 20 min., while large ships and log rafts require from 30 to 50 min. The entire cost of operation is borne by the Federal Government, there being no fees of any kind required for lockage.

As was to be expected, some difficulties have been experienced with the opening of the gates and in navigation through the locks due to the difference in density of the fresh water above and the salt water below. In theory, this difference would cause the flow through the culverts in filling or emptying the lock to cease when equal pressures were reached there, which would be before the level above the gate had fallen to that below, and there would remain a positive pressure against the lock-gates making it difficult to open them. In practice, this is so in different degrees dependent on the stage of the tide, the admixture of salt and fresh water, the somewhat different conditions at the upper, intermediate, and lower service gates, and the methods of lockage.*

At the upper gate of the locks, which is generally used as such, and with either the intermediate or lower gate used as a lower gate, this difference in pressure is quite marked. The difference in head is usually 3 or 4 in., but sometimes it is as much as 6 in. There is some over-travel of the water through the culverts with temporary corresponding rise of the water in the lock, as explained subsequently, and advantage is taken of the resulting diminution of the pressure against the gates to open them before the condition of equilibrium has been reached. When the difference in head is more than 4 in., it is preferable in order to reduce the strain on the cables and operating machinery to freshen the water in the lock by lowering and refilling before the gate is opened.

When the lower chamber is used and the intermediate gate becomes the upper gate there is a marked over-travel of the water in the culverts before the filling ceases and at the same time the forebay is temporarily lowered so that the water in the lock rises slightly higher than the level above the gates which thus become subjected to a reverse head tending to open them. This condition lasts only momentarily, and equilibrium is soon reached, with the level of the water above the gates higher than that below, due to the difference in density. As an illustration the following example is given: With the upper pool at Elevation 25 ft. 7 in. and the tidal elevation at 8 ft., the lower gate was opened and time allowed for the water in the lock to reach full salinity. The intermediate gate was then closed, the upper chamber filled, the upper gate opened, and time allowed for the water to become quiet. The lower gate was then closed, the valves of the intermediate gate opened, and the lower chamber filled. The water in the forebay, that is, the upper lock chamber, was lowered somewhat when the valves were first opened and surged up and down for a few minutes. The lower chamber filled to Elevation 25 ft. 7 in. The miter broke and actually pushed the gate away from the sill until held by the cables. No attempt was made to open the gate and in less than a minute it moved back against the sill. The water in the lower chamber lowered quite rapidly 7 in. to Elevation 25 ft., while above the gate the water became quiet at Elevation 25 ft. 7 in., or the upper pool level. The pools then remained with this difference of elevation of 7 in. against which it was impracticable to open the gate. To do this it was necessary to lower the water in the chamber and re-fill. Under substantially similar conditions the difference in head after equilibrium has been established, when the upper gate is used, is about 5 in. The over-travel of the water and the surge in the pool elevations is also less, probably partly due to the shorter length of the column of water in motion through the culverts. Due to these more unfavorable conditions at the intermediate gate the lower chamber is seldom used, the smaller boats being always taken into the upper chamber when only part of the lock is required.

---

* Quite a complete mathematical discussion of this matter will be found on pp. 85–99 of the Annual Report of the Isthmian Canal Commission for 1911, together with measures proposed to obviate the anticipated difficulties that would arise therefrom.

Not much difficulty is experienced in the opening of the lower gate or of the intermediate gate when used as a lower gate. The miter frequently breaks, probably due to the over-travel of the water through the culverts and the momentary surge in elevation above and below the gate. After equilibrium is reached there is some difference in elevation and some head on the gate, but generally it can be opened easily. There does not appear to be much difference in the conditions at the two gates.

Immediately after opening the lower gate a strong surface current sets up, which lasts for several minutes, running out of the lock with the corresponding under-current running in. This is troublesome to the smaller vessels entering and leaving the lock, and they are often held in the lock for several minutes until the current subsides. Vessels with tows are also delayed several minutes when leaving the lock at the upper end due to the strong surface current flowing into the lock when the upper gate is opened and the salt water in the lock chamber flows up stream.

The locks are unwatered at least once each year for painting the service gates and for general repairs to machinery, valves, etc. The lower guard-gate of the large lock, which is in salt water, is removed and painted at least once every 4 years and the upper guard-gate once in about 6 or 7 years. This is accomplished with the assistance of the snagboat *Swinomish*. The openings for admitting water into the water chambers are closed at low tide and the water remaining in the chamber is pumped out; at the same time fresh water in sufficient quantities to preserve its equilibrium, is pumped into the bottom of the leaf. Then, at a little before high tide, when the resultant weight of the leaf is only a little greater than its buoyancy, the outer edge of the leaf is raised by the boat's tackle until there is no weight on the hinges. The hinge-pins are then removed, the leaf is lifted and towed out of the way of traffic, and the air chamber is unwatered by compressed air. The leaf, now floating on its straight side, which is the heavier, has heretofore been beached for cleaning and painting, but a small dry dock is now being constructed for this purpose. It is then towed back to the lock, and the air chamber is partly filled with water until the leaf stands almost upright. The boat then lifts it back on to the pintle and the anchors are attached. The operation of removing and replacing the hinge-pins must be done very quickly at the lower gate, as a slight fall in the tide will often change the buoyancy of the leaf so that the lift will be too great for the boat to handle safely. To provide for this emergency a pump is kept at hand for removing the water from the leaf as the tide recedes. The removal of the upper gate in water of constant elevation is a much simpler undertaking.

The guard-gates of the small lock are hoisted by an A-frame and tackle on to the lock-wall, where they are cleaned and painted and then lowered back into place.

A pumping plant consisting of two 30-in. pumps with a capacity of about 50 000 gal. per min., one 10-in pump, with a capacity of about 2 000 gal. per min., and a 3-in. sump pump, all electrically operated, has been provided for unwatering the locks. The pumps are located in a well under the administration building, the intake being through the lock-wall from a sump just above the intermediate gate. The discharge is carried in a concrete pipe supported on the back of the lock-wall and emptying just below the guard-gate. The pumps are installed near the bottom of the well at about the elevation of the lock floor and have vertical shafts. The large pumps are driven by 300-h.p. motors and the 10-in. pump by a 75-h.p. motor, all located over the well on the basement floor. The pump-well is never allowed to fill with water, the seepage being pumped out by the sump pump which operates automatically. The drainage from all the machinery recesses in the lock-walls is carried through tunnels to the pump-well whence it is removed by the sump pump. It usually requires about eight hours to unwater the large lock, and the painting and repairs are usually accomplished in a week.

The lowering of Lake Washington made it necessary to carry all the water from the Lake Washington and Cedar River water-sheds (580 sq. miles) through the canal to the sea. The maximum known run-off from the water-shed is 12 000 sec-ft. for a period of 24 hours; 6 000 sec-ft. for a period of 10 days; and 3 600 sec-ft. for a period of 90 days. In the low-water season the run-off from the land area is at times so small that it does not equal the evaporation from the lake surface. These periods, however, are of brief duration and occur only when extreme drought and high temperature reduce the run-off and correspondingly increase evaporation from the water areas. Owing to the large capacity of the reservoir formed by the lakes and Salmon Bay the control of this variable run-off can be easily taken care of with an allowable fluctuation of 2 ft. by raising the lake levels to about the high-water elevation before the commencement of the dry season and by lowering the level during the winter months to take care of sudden floods. The discharge over the spillway dam is regulated so as not to cause excessive currents below the locks, and the current through the canal above the locks is never troublesome to vessels.

Electric power for the operation of the locks is delivered at the transformer station at the locks at 13 200 volts and is transformed at the lock site to 2 300 volts, 220 volts, and 110 volts, for operating motors and for lighting the grounds and buildings. The lock-gates and valves are controlled from operating stations on the lock-walls. Three stations are provided for the large lock and one for the small lock. All operating machinery is placed in covered recesses in the top of the lock-walls. For replacing broken cables and doing necessary under-water work, a complete diving equipment is provided, and a diver who is ordinarily employed as an operator on the lock force is sent down to make the necessary repairs.

The delay due to broken cables, which almost invariably affects one or more vessels, has been considerable, probably 2 to 4 hours for each break. Although the gate-operating method is otherwise satisfactory the difficulties arising from this feature suggest that if another lock were to be constructed in the future it might be advisable to try the spar and bull-wheel method similar to that used at Panama, which has all the operating mechanism above water.

As noted previously a small dry dock for docking one leaf of the guard-gates at a time for painting and repairs is being constructed back of the north wall of the large lock, a little below the upper service gate. The lock-wall forms one side of the dock and the quay wall one end. The other side is constructed of two rows of round piles and sheet-piles tied together with iron rods, and filled and banked with clay. The other end will be closed by a timber gate-sill and the gate, which consists of a horizontal girder and needles.

The time required for filling the large lock is about 8 min. at medium low tide. If the culverts were somewhat larger, this time would be decreased. It may be questioned, however, whether this decrease in time would be commensurate with the necessary increase in cost of the original construction of larger valves and operating mechanism.

As constructed, the number of laterals in the lower half of the lock is greater than in the upper half. The idea was that this would result in a more nearly uniform filling of the lock. In practice, it appears that the filling takes place faster in the lower end, resulting in a slight up-stream current in the lock. This has not been particularly troublesome, but in a new design the number of laterals in the lower half should probably be made the same as, or even less than, in the upper half.

Also, in a new design, a larger salt-water sump and outlet would undoubtedly be provided as suggested under the discussion on "Salinity", and if part of the water now passing over the spillway were carried through the dam at as low an elevation as practicable some additional salt would be carried off.

The concrete work of the locks and dam has now been subjected to the action of both fresh and sea water for more than ten years and does not show any appreciable deterioration, except that the face of the lock-walls has been worn off to a limited extent by the rubbing of vessels and other craft. It is true that it is not subjected to extreme changes of temperature, nor to the action of ice, but its general excellence is such as to make it interesting to record in more detail its composition and method of placing.

The mixture used was practically 1:3:6. The sand and gravel were obtained by washing the material from a bank with sea water, using screens of the desired mesh. The sand was well graded, but the gravel had an excess of fine material and generally in mixing 2½ parts of sand to 6½ parts of gravel were used. The proportions, 1:2:6, would give nearly the maximum density for the materials used. The cement was manufactured by the Superior Portland Cement Company and tested in accordance with specifications of the U. S. Bureau of Standards, except that 85% instead of 75% by weight was required to pass the 200-mesh sieve. The concrete was mixed in 1½-cu. yd., Smith, tilting dump mixers, 2 min. being required for each batch. Each batch was dumped into bottom dump buckets which were carried on flat cars about 1 000 ft. to the site. The buckets were picked up by crane and lowered so as to leave just enough clearance for the doors to open before the batch was emptied. All concrete was spread out in layers and carefully spaded, especially next to the form. No tamping was required. The consistency of the mixture was such that a man would sink about half way to his knees. No parts of the work were subjected to the action of sea water until the concrete was thoroughly cured.

Salinity

The up-stream under current of salt water and the down-stream surface current of fresh water during lockages due to the difference of density have been referred to previously. The flow of salt water into the upper pool would eventually turn the lakes into a salt-water reservoir if some means were not provided to return the salt to the lower pool. To meet this difficulty a salt-water basin about 2 000 ft. long and 200 ft. wide, with its bottom 4 to 8 ft. below the elevation of the upper miter-sill was dredged immediately above the lock. From the lower end of the basin a pipe 30 sq. ft. in cross-section extends to the spillway dam. Its outlet is 4 ft. below high tide, which gives a maximum head of 11 ft. and thus forces the salt water from the bottom of the basin through the drain into the lower pool. The flow is continuous and at the rate of 100 to 200 cu. ft. per sec. This discharge of salt water from the upper pool is increased by opening the valves in the culverts at times when the lock is not busy and when water can be spared for that purpose. These measures are ordinarily effective, but when there are a number of consecutive lockages during the dry season the salt-water basin becomes filled with sea water faster than the drain carries it off and it then overflows and some salt water flows up the canal into the bottom of Lake Union. The lake acts as another settling basin, preventing the flow of salt water into Lake Washington. It has been found that the sea water that enters Lake Union tends to distribute itself throughout the waters of the lake, owing to natural diffusion, disturbances caused by currents, changes in temperature, and the passage of boats. However, it is believed that the greater quantity of the sea water will remain below the 40-ft. level.

To determine accurately the extent of this infiltration into the lakes, the services of Professor E. Victor Smith, of the Department of Chemistry, of the University of Washington, were engaged to conduct a continuous set of observations at different points in the canal and lakes and these have been carried on since the canal was opened in 1917. Professor Smith and his colleague, Professor Thomas G. Thompson, were much interested in this work and presented a paper* before the American Chemical Society giving the results of their studies. What follows is extracted from that paper.

The device generally used for sampling the waters for analysis is a reversing water bottle of the Eckman type, with attached reversing thermometers. For determining the quantity of chlorine present in the water, various methods were studied. Attention was given to conductivity and specific gravity methods, but results of considerable variation were obtained, owing to difference of temperature and contamination from industrial plants along the waterway. The Mohr method gave the most concordant results. Parts per

* "The Control of Sea Water Flowing into the Lake Washington Ship Canal," *Industrial and Engineering Chemistry,* Vol. 17, No. 10, October, 1925, p. 1084.

million of chlorine were determined, which was considered to give a relative measure of the concentration of sea water. These results were checked by running, on several occasions, complete analyses of the water from Lake Union and comparing the data with those secured from sea water, calculating for the dilution of the water from the lake. Samples were also occasionally checked in the laboratory by the Volhard method.

As from one hundred to two hundred analyses were necessary for each study it was almost impossible to collect samples and transport them to the laboratory. Accordingly, an improvised laboratory was set up on the U. S. Motor Boat *Orcas,* and as fast as the samples were brought aboard they were analyzed by pipetting off 100 milli-litres and titrating. Two standard solutions of silver nitrate of different concentrations were used, one for water of low salinity and the other for water of high salinity. Possible discrepancies due to temperature changes were within the ordinary experimental error, there seldom being a variation greater than 7° cent. in the temperature of the water throughout the entire year.

The chlorine content of the waters at various depths in and near the locks is shown in Table 2. All the samples from which the data were secured were collected the same forenoon. Series 1 shows, in parts per million, the chlorine obtained from the water taken at various depths in Puget Sound about 1 mile from the entrance to the locks. The effect of drainage water from the land into the sea is distinctly indicated in this series of analyses, as the concentration of chlorine on the surface is decidedly lower than that secured at greater depths.

TABLE 2.—PARTS PER MILLION OF CHLORINE AT VARIOUS DEPTHS AT STATIONS 1 AND 2.

(Puget Sound and in the Locks.)

Depth, in feet.	Series 1.		Series 2.		Series 3.		Series 4.	
	Temperature, in degrees centigrade.	Parts per million, chlorine.	Temperature, in degrees centigrade.	Parts per million, chlorine.	Temperature, in degrees centigrade.	Parts per million, chlorine.	Temperature, in degrees centigrade.	Parts per million, chlorine.
Surface...	13.3	14 450	14.2	144	....	68	14.5	66
10	....	......	12.2	8 681	13.9	64	14.2	117
20	....	......	11.0	13 760	13.6	106	14.0	244
30	....	......	10.8	14 340	13.3	663	13.0	573
40	....	......	10.7	14 520	12.4	5 355	12.4	7 180
50	10.4	15 900	....	......	....	......	....	......
100	9.5	16 590	....	......	....	......	....	......
200	8.9	16 600	....	......	....	......	....	......
300	8.9	16 640	....	......	....	......	....	......
400	8.9	16 640	....	......	....	......	....	......
500	8.8	16 730	....	......	....	......	....	......

The collection of samples under Series 2 was started 10 min. after the lock was opened to the sea and during an ebbing tide. The samples were taken at a point midway between the two lock-gates. The data indicate how completely the sea water replaces the fresh water in the locks when they are opened to the sea.

Immediately after securing the samples of Series 2, those of Series 3 were obtained on the fresh-water side of the upper lock-gate. On the completion of this operation the lower gate was closed to the sea, the water in the lock raised to the level of the upper pool, and the upper gate opened. As soon as the currents in the lock had ceased, samples were taken from the same position as that from which those of Series 2 had been secured. The results, given under Series 4, demonstrate that the sea water had largely disappeared by flowing into the basin above the lock. The sample taken from the bottom of the lock below the elevation of the upper miter-sill was the only one showing a high degree of salinity.

It is impracticable to show all the data secured during the eight years that this investigation has been under way. From those presented in Table 2 it is obvious that the waters of the canal near the locks undergo constant change. However, as the distance from the lock increases, the analyses of the water indicate fairly constant conditions. For example, in Lake Union the change is relatively slow, so that remarkably constant results may be obtained from month to month, especially at the greater depths. Samples were taken at the different stations, indicated in Fig. 1, at every 10 ft. Table 3 gives the relative distances of the respective stations from the locks.

TABLE 3.

Between Stations.	Distances between the various stations, in feet.	Distance from locks (Station 2), in feet.
1 and 2	......	......
2 and 3	1 500	1 500
3 and 4	3 650	5 150
4 and 5	2 500	7 650
5 and 6	5 400	13 050
6 and 7	1 650	14 700
7 and 9	3 000	17 700
9 and 10	5 000	22 700
10 and 11	4 500	27 200
11 and 12	10 500	37 000

In Table 4 are given analyses obtained on February 21, 1920, October 8, 1921, and June 10, 1922, at various depths and at the different stations. The results of February, 1920, are illustrative of minimum conditions of salinity, although, in March, 1921, the entire system was cleared of sea-water contaminations. The worst conditions of the eight years were encountered in October, 1921, after a very dry summer, and were due in part also to the clogging of the salt-water drain for a time by a sunken log. This shows very well the ease with which the waters of the canal and lakes might have become contaminated if proper control had not been provided. The data for June, 1922, indicate the effect of drainage resulting from winter rains and spring freshets. In Fig. 10 the logarithms of the parts per million of chlorine for the maximum and average conditions are plotted for the various depths at the different stations along the waterway.

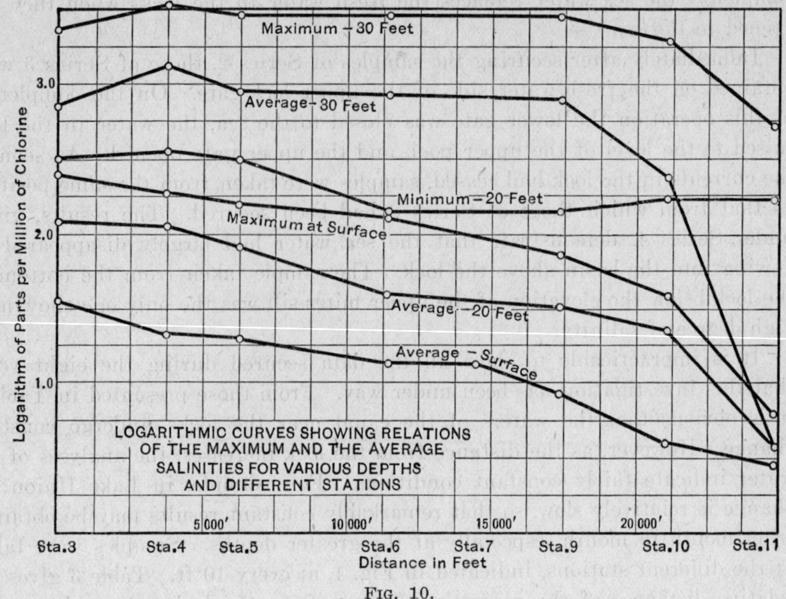

FIG. 10.

Rather peculiar results for maximum conditions at depths of 20 ft. and 30 ft. and for average conditions at 30 ft. are indicated by the curves in Fig. 10 at Stations 3 and 4. The former, being nearer the locks, should show a

TABLE 4.—PARTS PER MILLION OF CHLORINE, SHOWING MAXIMUM AND MINIMUM CONDITIONS OBTAINED AT VARIOUS DEPTHS AND DIFFERENT STATIONS.

Station.	Date tested.	DEPTH, IN FEET.							
		0.	10.	20.	30.	32.	40.	45.	50.
3	Feb. 21, 1920	......	......	......	......	......	......	......	......
	Oct. 8, 1921	244	237	310	2 315	......	7 800	9 075	......
	June 10, 1922	10	9	33	325	......	......	......	......
4	Feb. 21, 1920	16	16	26	55	130	......	......	......
	Oct. 8, 1921	193	198	360	3 555	......	......	......	......
	June 10, 1922	6	8	13	600	......	......	......	......
5	Feb. 21, 1920	16	15	16	14	......	......	......	......
	Oct. 8, 1921	169	171	315	2 920	......	......	......	......
	June 10, 1922	3	4	7	75	......	......	......	......
6	Feb. 21, 1920	9	12	15	14	......	......	......	......
	Oct. 8, 1921	128	137	135	2 940	3 125	......	......	......
	June 10, 1922	3	3	4	20	28	......	......	......
9	Feb. 21, 1920	7	9	9	9	......	4 149	5 040	......
	Oct. 8, 1921	70	111	145	2 875	......	4 710	5 830	......
	June 10, 1922	4	3	5	10	......	420	3 995	......
10	Feb. 21, 1920	3	3	3	3	......	3	......	......
	Oct. 8, 1921	36	37	178	1 985	......	2 507	......	......
	June 10, 1922	3	3	3	4	......	4	......	......
11	Feb. 21, 1920	3	3	3	3	......	......	......	......
	Oct. 8, 1921	6	14	173	505	......	......	......	......
	June 10, 1922	3	3	3	3	......	......	......	......
12	Feb. 21, 1920	3	......	......	......	......	......	......	3
	Oct. 8, 1921	3	......	......	......	......	......	......	3
	June 10, 1922	3	......	......	......	......	......	......	3

greater degree of salinity, but much of the data collected show that Station 4 generally gave higher concentrations. This is probably the result of countercurrents.

The following conclusions were reached:

(1) That the concentration of sea water in the Lake Washington Ship Canal is dependent on the amount of rainfall, the number of lockages, the proper functioning of the salt-water drain, and the methods of disposal of surplus water.

(2) That if the surplus waters are conducted as much as possible through the lock culverts, the degree of salinity can be maintained at a minimum far lower than if the surplus is permitted to run wholly over the spillways.

(3) That greater efficiency could undoubtedly be obtained if the salt-water basin were enlarged in length and width, or depth.

(4) That Lake Union serves as a secondary salt-water basin and prevents the contamination of the waters of Lake Washington.

(5) That storage of surplus water of the winter and spring months is used as far as practicable for drainage through the lock-culvert valves through the dry season which aids materially in decreasing the salinity of the canal system.

The discharge through the spillway gates of the dam is very small between February and October, and from July to October there is usually no discharge, except that for lockages, passing through the salt-water pipe and over the fishway. The large lock is usually filled from 200 to 400 times per month and the small lock from 500 to 1 000 times.

TRAFFIC

The canal has been in operation since August, 1916, and there has been a substantial increase in traffic and in the value of commodities from year to year. The commerce for 1917 was 872 359 tons of freight, valued at $4 254 202 and, in 1920, 1 368 898 tons, valued at $15 567 829. In 1925, it amounted to 2 418 613 tons valued at $14 712 520, and consisted of 1 192 540 tons of floated and barged timbers, valued at $6 372 380; 898 892 tons of sand and gravel, valued at $898 892; 174 677 tons of lumber products valued at $2 649 020; 54 634 tons of fuel oil, with a value of $524 486; 23 350 tons of refined oil, valued at $1 097 800; 23 433 tons of coal and coke, valued at $187 764; 19 950 tons of hogged fuel, with a value of $11 970; and 31 137 tons of miscellaneous, valued at $2 970 208. The number of passengers carried was 49 792. In addition, there were carried by general ferries 269 031 tons and 1 401 037 passengers in 1925.

The bulk of the traffic passing through the locks is between points on Puget Sound, Salmon Bay, Lake Union, and Lake Washington, but lumber is shipped through the canal to points on the Pacific and Atlantic Coasts, and to foreign countries, and there are considerable imports of logs, coal, etc., from Canada.

Vessels using the canal are increasing in size as well as in numbers. During 1917, 22 392 vessels with a net registered tonnage of 591 310 passed through the locks; in 1920, there were 27 377 vessels, with a net registered tonnage of 1 120 591; and, in 1925, this had increased to 35 433 vessels, with a net registered tonnage of 2 279 131. The largest number of vessels passing through the large lock in a single day has been 104, which included small boats, as the small lock was closed. The greatest number of vessels passing through the small lock in a single day has been 157.

Practically all freight passes through the large lock and about one-half of the total consists of logs, floated loosely between boom sticks in rafts. At times, there has been some congestion of traffic, and an examination has been authorized by Congress with a view to determining the necessity for an additional lock. It does not appear, however, that the capacity of the lock has been fully reached. Delays to boat traffic could be largely reduced by restricting the passage of log rafts to the night time when other traffic is normally at a minimum. If this were done a mooring ground, safe from storms, should be provided in Shilshole Bay near the entrance from Puget Sound.

Greater efficiency of operation could be obtained if the logs were made up in sections of deeper draft or transported in barges. During 1924 there was some traffic in logs transported in barges from British Columbia, 400 000 to 800 000 ft. B. M. being carried in each barge. Logs transported in this way are not subject to delay on account of stormy weather and for long hauls transportation by barge is found quite economical. From Puget Sound ports, however, where the haul is relatively short, the additional expense for loading, upkeep of barge, etc., would more than offset the expense saved in towing and loss by storms, and if a restrictive regulation of this kind were put into effect it would tend to increase the price of logs entering the canal from all Sound ports.

On account of the current previously referred to caused by the meeting of fresh and salt water in and near the locks, and the current from the spillway dam when the gates are open, a material saving in time would be accomplished if the use of only powerful tugs were permitted for bringing heavy tows into the locks.

The small lock, which is 30 by 150 ft., was designed primarily to accommodate small craft, such as tugs without tows, pleasure boats, etc., and the dimensions for this class of traffic are sufficient. The increase in traffic, however, shows the need of a lock of greater width, capable of handling barge traffic when the large lock is unwatered for annual repairs, as well as relieving the latter from some of this traffic at other times. A lock, 34 to 38 ft. wide and 160 to 170 ft. long, would handle the present traffic more efficiently than the lock as built.

Results

The beneficial results of the construction of the canal may be generally summarized, as follows:

(*a*) It has opened to commercial and industrial use a fresh-water harbor, lying in and adjacent to the City of Seattle, with an area of 25 000 acres and a shore line of 100 miles. This harbor consists of three distinct bodies of water, Salmon Bay, Lake Union, and Lake Washington, all standing at the same level and connected by free and unobstructed channels. This harbor is perfectly protected from storms and free from tidal fluctuations and currents, and, with the salt-water harbor on Elliott Bay, affords harbor facilities which are possibly unsurpassed in the United States.

(*b*) A large and important commerce has already been developed, and Lake Union, located less than a mile from the business center of Seattle and accessible to both rail and deep-water shipping, with depths ranging from 40 to 50 ft., and an area of 905 acres, seems logically destined to become a great distributing center and warehouse district.

(*c*) In the fresh water of these lakes untreated pile and timber structures may be maintained free from destruction by marine wood borers, the marine growth on ships' bottoms is killed by contact with fresh water, and ships may be more economically loaded and unloaded on account of having a fixed water level.

(*d*) The lowering of Lake Washington and the diversion of Cedar River from the Black and Duwamish Rivers into the lake has practically ended the annual floods which formerly visited the Renton, Duwamish, and Sammanish River Districts, and former swamps have been converted into favorable sites for industries, the principal of these tracts being in the Renton District at the south end of the lake, easily accessible to all the railroads entering Seattle, and in the Bothell District at the north end of the lake.

DISCUSSION

ERNEST B. HUSSEY,* M. AM. SOC. C. E. (by letter).—The treatment of the subject of selecting one of five possible routes for the location of a ship canal to connect Lake Washington with tide-water is a valuable digest of the varied and interesting events that finally culminated in the adoption of the route chosen. With this phase the writer was identified in a consulting capacity and had occasion to go into the subject somewhat exhaustively. The final selection by the Government and the subsequent operation of the canal leaves no doubt but that the right location was adopted and that future generations will sustain that judgment.

The lowering of the surface of Lake Washington to that of Lake Union, thereby eliminating a lock between the two lakes, was unquestionably a sound plan; not especially from the point of economy in construction, but more particularly from that of efficiency in transportation. Further, Lakes Union and Washington become a prospective great fresh-water harbor for the commerce of Seattle and its hinterland.

While cut-off walls were placed 4 ft. deep under the heels of the walls of the locks and under the miter-sills, no valves or other devices were provided to relieve possible hydrostatic pressure. The fact that holes drilled through the 3-ft. floor of the large lock showed a very small quantity of accumulated water indicates how well the work of installation of the cut-off walls was accomplished. However, it is the writer's opinion that measures should be adopted in such construction to relieve automatically any hydrostatic pressure that may develop. The use of drains from the areas protected by the cut-off walls, freely discharging into sumps readily accessible for observation, is a measure of precaution well worth its cost in works of such importance, particularly as the heavy floor might be subjected to 53 ft. of hydrostatic head when the lock is unwatered. Much reliance may be placed on the hard impervious clay substrata; but such a foundation is the safer, and the imposed works are the more surely preserved, if ample automatic tell-tale drainage is provided.

The inclusion of greenheart timbers on the bottom of the gates as contacts between similar timbers on the miter-sills appears to be good design. Probably these timbers would not have been affected by marine borers if the gates and miter-sills had been protected by a flow of fresh water. This could have been accomplished by using small conduits in the side-walls of the locks, conveying fresh water from the upper pool and discharging it continuously along the lower guard-gate and its miter-sill.

The method of replacing the timbers is especially commendable under the existing circumstances, necessitating the practical re-design and installation of contact members between the bottom of these particular gates and their respective miter-sills. It is a question, whether the remedy can be considered better than the original installation of greenheart timbers, provided the timbers had been protected against the activities of marine borers. To have

* Cons. Civ. Engr., Seattle, Wash.

installed the re-designed contact members without placing the lock out of commission, is a notable feat. It illustrates impressively the ingenuity of man when put to the test.

The emergency dams installed subsequent to the original construction were wise provisions against accident. Some such device was undoubtedly in contemplation at the time of the original design of the locks. The use of wickets and girders stored on the lock-walls, to be placed in position in the lock by a stiff-leg derrick in an emergency, effects a considerable saving over other forms of emergency dams, but, in view of the importance of these works, the writer believes that the comparatively quicker and more positive balanced cantilever turn-table type, having wickets ready to be lowered into place, would have been preferable. The value of the varied commercial structures damaged by undue delay would justify the additional installation cost and carrying charges. In an emergency, moments of time conceivably may cause hundreds of thousands of dollars of property damage. The best and most rapid type of emergency dam is then none too good or too expensive. It is at such times that the difference in cost is entirely lost to sight and the engineer is hardly thanked for any saving.

Possibly by enlarging the design described practically all the sea water entering Salmon Bay through the locks might be trapped and conveyed back to tide-water. The creation of a salt-water basin above the locks to the greatest reasonable depth would probably be much more effective in trapping the salt water than would result if the basin was only increased in width.

The authors' praise of this fresh-water harbor of 25 000 acres is well justified. It is a signally remarkable harbor. The writer is of the opinion that these works afford harbor facilities that are unsurpassed in the world. The authors are certainly justified in their summarization of the beneficial results to commerce by virtue of the construction of these waterways.

Charles Evan Fowler,* M. Am. Soc. C. E. (by letter).—The writer became interested in the Harbor of Seattle on his arrival there in 1900, when the city had a population of only 85 000, and the harbor facilities consisted of a limited number of pile and timber wharves located on the immediate deep-water front on Elliott Bay. Contracts were soon entered into, by the Company of which the writer was President and Chief Engineer, for the excavation of the East and West Waterways at the head of Elliott Bay and the filling of the eastern portion of the tide flats, which comprised about 1 200 acres. Only 75 acres of this fill had been completed in the five years prior to 1900.

The Waterways were dredged to a width of 1 000 ft. with pier-head lines 500 ft. apart, and a depth of 38 ft. at low tide. The permanent bulkheads were of fir brush, from 12 to 24 ft. in length, laid up to a 45° slope, with the butts outward as the filling progressed. The temporary bulkheads were of piles and plank, of the stepped type, and were used for bringing sections to the grade of 2 ft. above high tide, so that certificates could be issued by the State of Washington for completed work. These certificates drew 8%

* Cons. Engr., New York, N. Y.

interest and were a first lien on the land so created. The cost allowed by the State was 16 cents per cu. yd., with an added general profit of 15%, or a total of 18.4 cents per cu. yd. The first contracts up to 1905 were for a total of about 12 000 000 cu. yd., which was excavated and pumped to a distance as great as 5 300 ft. by two 20-in. hydraulic dredges.

As a Trustee of the Seattle Chamber of Commerce and a member of its Harbor Committee, the writer became interested in the promotion of the Lake Washington Canal, and, later, in the formation of the Port of Seattle. One of the first efforts was to convince the War Department and Congress of the necessity, or at least the desirability, of the canal, and that in place of a $7 000 000 two-lock canal, a one-lock canal was all that was required. It is interesting to note that the cost estimate made at that time by the writer, was $3 800 000, and this type of project was finally adopted. Construction was begun by dredging the entrance from deep water in Puget Sound to a place near the present lock site in Salmon Bay. This contract was secured by the writer's Company at 26.7 cents per cu. yd., and much of the material was of the hardest type of blue clay hardpan. The dredge built for the work was of the dipper type, with machinery for a 7-yd. dipper, but, owing to the hard material to be dug, a 3½-yd. dipper was used.

The second contract entered into was for the test borings over about 2 miles of the canal route, up to the Ballard Bridge. This was carried out by using a floating pile-driver rig, on the gins of which was placed a square drill shaft turned by a pulley at the deck level, through which the drill bar passed loosely in a square hole. The drills were 2 to 2½-in. augers. The cost of the work under this contract was about 50 cents per vertical ft. The third contract, for additional excavation through Salmon Bay, was carried out by the use of the dipper dredge at a cost of about 43 cents per cu. yd.

The construction of the lock was carried out in a manner that calls for the highest praise of the late Colonel Cavanaugh and the authors, and also reflects the greatest of credit upon the U. S. Corps of Engineers. The extremely low unit cost of the concrete was due to some extent to the low price obtained on cement at that time, and to the fact that the finest kind of sand and gravel was purchased at 25 cents per cu. yd. on the Government scows at the Point Defiance gravel pits, and towed a distance of about 30 miles to the lock site by the Government tug, *Gen. J. M. Wilson*. Notwithstanding all this, a record was probably set for all time in the matter of cost for such a great piece of work.

The writer also had charge of the final dredging of the canal through Salmon Bay, Lake Union, and Union Bay in Lake Washington. This work was undertaken at a very low price, less than 9 cents per cu. yd., so that the only way possible of reaching profitable figures was to sell the dirt for filling low lands along the line of the canal. All that excavated in Salmon Bay was so used, although much of it came out of the 22-in. pipe so soupy as to cause a great deal of it to be lost. The material in Lake Union was sold for a large fill, but much of this was so soft as to make it impossible to bring all the fill to grade. The excavation in Union Bay was in soft silt and peat, which was pumped on to Park property, a distance of 4 000 ft., with an output of as high as 47 000 cu. yd. per day. The digging of the old logging canal to full size, between Lake Union and Union Bay, required the excavation of a large quantity of very tough material (hardpan and cemented gravel), which was as hard as soft concrete. This digging was done by using a rock cutter on the 22-in. electric hydraulic dredge, and pumping the material a distance of about 2 000 ft.

The whole work was most difficult in many respects, yet it was well worth while as one feature of the opening of the last frontier, and was a great step in the building of the Metropolis of the Northwest.*

JOSEPH M. CLAPP,† M. AM. SOC. C. E. (by letter).—The writer had the Lake Washington Ship Canal as his home work, under the direction of the District Engineers, for the ten years from 1901 to 1911; gathered much of the physical data used in solving the problems in relation to the project; is familiar with the locality and its geological characteristics; and takes pleasure in adding a few details relating to this great project.

Something has been said of the late Colonel Cavanaugh's connection with this project and the manner in which he directed it. It is only fair that greater stress should be laid to the fact that much pertaining to the details of design and the actual work of construction was done by Mr. Sargent, the very efficient Engineer Assistant. It was his untiring efforts that made possible the economical design of the system and of the plant and its operation during construction; all of which resulted in the very low cost of the locks and dam as a whole.

It has been stated that the lowering of Lake Washington and the outflow of the Cedar River, *via* Ballard and the locks, has lessened the flood problems in the Duwamish Valley. While this is so, it is not as great a factor as the divorcement of the waters of the White River from the Valley of the Duwamish to its new channel *via* the Puyallup Valley to the Sound. The run-off from the White River shed during flood seasons is several times greater than that from Lake Washington and its tributaries.

A hard clay formation is the bed-rock of the country and, once it is well defined, is considered sufficient to support the structures that are built in this section. To use piles under the walls where this clay formation is met, if the weight is less than 5 tons per sq. ft., is superfluous and may result in poor construction for the reason that, to drive wooden piles to any penetration into the clay means to upset the fiber, cause the pile to telescope, and thus destroy its bearing value for heavier weights. Steel or reinforced concrete piles would have to be used if greater weights were to be supported.

In the early days of this work it was the writer's duty to direct the excavation of a ditch so as to bring the outlet of Lake Union through a channel located wholly on the canal right of way and under the control of the War Department. The Northern Pacific Railway crossed the right of way at a

* Many of the details have been omitted, as they can be found in the writer's book entitled "Sub-Aqueous Foundations."

† Cons. and Contr. Engr., Seattle, Wash.

point north and west of Fremont, Wash. The Railway Company constructed its trestle crossing in the dry and before excavation in its vicinity was begun. On working the excavation under the trestle many of the piles were exposed, and it was found that they had telescoped and were of no real value. The crossing had to be rebuilt, and sills and posts were substituted for the piles.

At the portage separating Lake Union from Lake Washington, where the narrow channel was provided for the passage of logs in 1888, it might be mentioned that at first a lock was actually provided, 50 ft. long, 18 ft. wide, and 4 ft. deep, for the passage of small steamers. Several lockages of steamers were made, but there was no profitable business. Eventually, the locks were allowed to decay and a raceway for the passage of logs was constructed and operated on a toll basis by the Lake Union Mill Company.

In determining the location for the canal, the routes through Salmon Bay were canvassed and the present route determined by a Board of Engineers, all prior to 1896, when the writer first became familiar with the project and the District Office was established at Seattle. Later, about 1906, another route was canvassed to enter Lake Washington by way of the Duwamish Valley, with a canal to be dug through Beacon Hill and the territory intervening between the Duwamish Valley and Lake Washington, about on line with Spokane Avenue.

The plan contemplated the excavation of a canal between Lake Washington and Lake Union and either the raising of the waters of Lake Union to the level of Lake Washington; lowering Lake Washington to the level of Lake Union; or lowering one and raising the other to some intermediate point. This plan was advocated by a company interested in the reclamation of the tide-flats at the mouth of the Duwamish River, known as the Lake Washington Canal Company.

The cross-country canal involved excavation through a hill about 130 ft. high and the moving of a great many million cubic yards of material. It was the writer's duty to make comparative estimates for the information of the Board of Engineers that judged this work. After careful consideration the Board discarded this route, for obvious reasons, in favor of the present very logical route, which had been previously determined upon by other Boards of Engineers.

Some consideration was also given to a possible canal by way of the Black River and the Duwamish River to Puget Sound. Thus, it will be noted that careful consideration was given the matter of routing this canal.

L. C. Sabin,* M. Am. Soc. C. E. (by letter).—This comprehensive and interesting paper has one serious defect. The entire installation worked so well that nothing is left for adverse criticism. Possible exceptions to this general statement are the complications arising from the fact that the upper pool is fresh, while the lower pool is sea water, and the suggestions of the authors that the laterals from the main culverts should have been distributed in a different manner.

* Vice-Pres., Lake Carriers' Assoc., Cleveland, Ohio.

The former condition has been carefully studied and practically corrected. The latter seems not to have received corresponding attention, and it is to this feature that this discussion is addressed. In lock design there are several considerations that render it impracticable to predetermine accurately by theory the action of a certain proposed arrangement of culverts, valves, and ports or laterals. For the emptying culverts, where the flow is from a restricted chamber to the open canal, the arrangement seems to be comparatively unimportant as to its effect on surge in the chamber; but in filling, considerable and variable differences in level may occur at the two ends of the lock with consequent objectionable currents within the chamber.

According to the data given in the paper there are two culverts in the 900-ft. lock, each having an area of 108.5 sq. ft. The ports or laterals are generally 4 ft. wide and 2 ft. high but eight of the laterals are 6 ft. high to afford easy access to the culverts for inspection and repairs to valves. Four of the larger ports and twenty of the smaller ones enter the upper chamber, 450 ft. long, while four of the larger and twenty-four of the smaller ports enter the lower chamber, 375 ft. in length.

Considering the lock as a whole the ratio of port area to horizontal cross-section of the chamber is approximately:

$$\frac{(2 \times 6 \times 4) + (4 \times 2 \times 20)}{450 \times 80} = 0.0058$$

for the upper portion, and

$$\frac{(2 \times 6 \times 4) + (4 \times 2 \times 24)}{375 \times 80} = 0.0080$$

for the lower portion. The authors state that,

"The idea was that this would result in a more nearly uniform filling of the lock. In practice, it appears that the filling takes place faster in the lower end, resulting in a slight up-stream current in the lock. This has not been particularly troublesome, but in a new design the number of laterals in the lower half should probably be made the same as, or even less than, in the upper half."

In the Pedro Miguel Lock of the Panama Canal the main culverts discharge into small laterals under the floor which, in turn, communicate with the chamber through ports through the floor. Disregarding the area between service and guard-gates and considering the chamber as a whole, there are in the upper half, six laterals from the side culverts and four laterals from the center culvert, each having an area of 41 sq. ft. (although apparently restricted by openings from the culvert having an area of but 33.2 sq. ft.), giving a total area of laterals of 410 sq. ft. In each lateral there are five ports having an area of 12.24 sq. ft. each, or a total area of ports of 612 sq. ft.

In the lower half there are five laterals from the side culvert and six from the center culvert, giving a total of 451 and 673 sq. ft. for laterals and ports, respectively. The ratio of lateral area to horizontal cross-section of lock is thus, approximately:

$$\frac{410}{110 \times 500} = 0.0074$$

for the upper half, and,

$$\frac{451}{110 \times 500} = 0.0082$$

for the lower half. The ratio of port area to horizontal cross-section of lock chamber is approximately 0.0111 for the upper half and 0.0122 for the lower half. There is nearly equal distribution of ports throughout the lock, but with more ample provision of port areas than in the Lake Washington Lock.

In the latest locks at St. Marys Falls Canal there are six culverts under the floor in each lock. The outer culverts have forty ports each and extend only about half way down the lock. The other four culverts extend the entire length of the lock and each is provided with fifty-nine ports spaced 30 ft. apart at the upper end, this spacing being gradually reduced to 15-ft. centers at the lower end. Each culvert has a net cross-sectional area of 88.07 sq. ft. and the ports are each 1 by 3 ft. In the upper half of the 1 350-ft. lock chamber there are about 178 ports fed by six culverts and in the lower half about 138 ports fed mainly by the four central culverts. The design contemplated that in actual operation the valves of the central culverts would be opened first and those in the outside culverts only when filling had progressed so far that ample opening under the reduced head would not result in surge.

The fact that the several culverts communicate with each other near the upper end to relieve side pressure on the culvert walls complicates any analysis of flow conditions when only part of the valves are opened, but when all the valves are open, the ratio of port area to horizontal cross-section of lock chamber is:

$$\frac{178 \times 3}{80 \times 675} = 0.0100$$

for the upper half, and,

$$\frac{138 \times 3}{80 \times 675} = 0.0077$$

for the lower half.

For these three locks the ratios of port area to horizontal area of lock chamber are given in Table 5.

TABLE 5.—Ratio of Port Area to Horizontal Area.

Lock.	Upper half of chamber.	Lower half of chamber.
Lake Washington	0.0058	0.0080
Pedro Miguel	0.0111	0.0122
Sault Ste. Marie	0.0100	0.0077

In the Lake Washington Lock, with the area of ports in the lower half of the chamber 138% of that in upper half, the authors state: "It appears that the filling takes place faster in the lower end, resulting in a slight upstream current in the lock."

In his paper on the action of the water in the Panama locks* H. F. Hodges, Maj.-Gen., U. S. A. (*Retired*), M. Am. Soc. C. E., states:

"When any one of the locks is filled, using the side wall culvert only, the discharge is noticeably greatest at the opening in the floor farthest from the culvert, and nearest the middle wall. The velocity of flow in the laterals evidently carries the water past the first two or three openings without giving them their full share of the discharge. Were the laterals lengthened, doubtless this effect would become less and less marked; and, finally, the maximum discharge would be found at some opening nearer the source of supply. With the proportions which they have, however, there is no doubt that the openings nearest the middle wall discharge a larger volume of water than those nearer the side wall, when the side culvert only is used. The result is a slight slope of the water's surface, which draws vessels away from the middle wall toward the side wall. This effect is not serious and disappears when both culverts are used.

"The side culvert occupies much the same relation to the laterals which draw from it as does each lateral to the openings through which it discharges. The side culvert is, however, made longer, and it is not plain to the eye which one of the laterals gets the largest share of the water at any instant. The ones farthest up stream discharge first, the boils from these beginning to show in about one minute after the first motion of the valves. The flow becomes apparent to the eye progressively down through the length of the lock, the lateral at the lower end—that is, the one farthest from the filling valve—showing flow last of all."

At the Sault locks,† where the area of ports in the lower half is only 77% of that in the upper half, it appears that when filling with either four or six valves the boils begin to show first at the upper end and the water at this end momentarily rises faster, but the water in the chamber is nearly level for the first minute, and the down-stream end is then higher for about a minute, the maximum difference being nearly 2 ft. Thereafter, the level fluctuates back and forth, the water being first higher at one end and then at the other, with a maximum difference of about 1 ft. and gradually reducing.

In view of these several observations it appears that immediately after opening the valves the ports at the upper end of the locks will begin to discharge first, but as soon as the inertia of the water has been overcome the level will be higher near the down-stream ends of the culverts for a short time. This seems to hold true whether the ratio of port area to chamber area at the lower end is 40% greater or 23% less than the same ratio for the upper end. Accordingly, it appears to be impracticable to correct the situation by variation in this ratio in the design of the culverts.

Unless this fluctuation is extreme the effect ordinarily is not great, but it has been entirely overcome at the Sault by the method of operation. At first, the plan adopted was to open the central pair of valves first, the intermediate pair after 3 min., and the outside pair 3 min. later. This confined the rate of rise in the chamber to a maximum of 4 ft. per min. Later, it was found that still smoother operation could be secured by opening each pair of valves very slowly, consuming about 1½ or 2 min. in opening each pair. By this method

* "Action of Water in Locks of the Panama Canal," *Professional Memoirs*, Corps of Engrs., U. S. A., Vol. VII, No. 31, p. 18.

† "Filling and Emptying the Third Lock at St. Marys Falls Canal," *Professional Memoirs*, Corps of Engrs., U. S. A., Vol. IX, No. 44.

the tendency to surge is eliminated and only very moderate stress on the mooring lines is required. While the lock can be filled in about 6 min. by opening all valves simultaneously, about 10 min. are consumed in ordinary operation.

TABLE 6.—COMPARISON OF CULVERT AND PORT DESIGNS.

Subject.	Lake Washington Canal.	St. Marys Falls Canal.	Pedro Miguel Lock.
Horizontal dimensions, in feet	80 by 825	80 by 1 350	110 by 1 000
Horizontal area, in square feet	66 000	108 000	110 000
Net Area:			
Main culverts, in square feet	217.0	528.4	510.0
Area ports, in square feet	448	948	1 285
Ratio, culverts to chamber	0.0033	0.0049	0.0046
Ratio, ports to culverts	2.06	1.79	2.52
Ratio, ports to chamber	0.0068	0.0088	0.0117
Approximate time, in minutes, to fill from 18-ft. head to zero	7⅓	6	5

Although the data at hand are not entirely sufficient, a comparison of the culvert and port design and the approximate time of filling the three locks referred to may be of interest. The data as far as available are given in Table 6.

The Sault installation gives a value for the coefficient of flow in culverts of 0.75 for six valves; the value for the Panama locks is given as 0.78. From such data as are given in the paper, it is inferred that the coefficient for Lake Washington is about 0.70.

The more rapid filling of the Pedro Miguel Lock seems to be due to the ample port area, since the culvert area has about the same relation to the chamber as in the Sault lock. On the other hand, the flow into the Lake Washington Lock appears to be throttled by the culvert area since the relation of ports to culverts is somewhat greater than at the Sault although less than at Pedro Miguel. This does not indicate, however, that the culverts should have been larger, as the rate of filling would seem to be entirely satisfactory for the traffic concerned.

W. J. BARDEN* AND A. W. SARGENT,† MEMBERS, AM. SOC. C. E. (by letter).—The authors are appreciative of the information given and comments made in the discussions of their paper.

Mr. Hussey thinks that more direct and positive provision should have been made for the relief of possible hydrostatic pressure under the lock floor, and suggests the use of valves or a system of drains. Both these methods have been used in some instances, but have not always been found entirely satisfactory. The present practice, where the floors are not designed to resist full upward pressure, appears to be to use a paving of concrete blocks with weep-holes. In the Seattle Lock, having in mind the more or less impervious character of the foundation, the cut-off walls provided, and the clay back-fill

* Col., Corps of Engrs., U. S. A., Headquarters, 2d Corps Area, New York, N. Y.

† Civ. Engr., U. S. Engr. Office, Govt. Locks, Seattle, Wash.

which was carried to a depth of 20 to 30 ft. over the steps on the back of the walls, the designers evidently considered that hydrostatic pressure sufficient to endanger the lock floor was unlikely to develop and the results have apparently justified their conclusion. It may be added that should failure occur in the future, repairs would not be difficult, and sufficient provision against subsequent trouble could probably be made by drilling a system of weep-holes.

The suggestion that a flow of fresh water conducted along the timbers of the guard-gate and miter-sill would have protected them from marine borers is of much interest. It is possible that such a procedure might be effective in keeping the steel gates free from barnacles which adhere to and destroy the paint, necessitating extensive cleaning and repainting every year.

Approval has been secured to deepen and widen the present salt-water basin and to lower the intake of the salt-water drains 7 ft. It is believed that this will materially reduce the quantity of salt water passing into the lakes. The latest salinity tests, taken at the end of the dry season, show a little less salt than usual at such times, due probably to an unusually cool summer with resultant smaller evaporation, thus allowing more water to be wasted through the locks.

Mr. Fowler gives interesting additional historical data and details on canal construction. The following costs may be of interest: The cost of cement f. o. b. cars at the lock site was $1.49 per bbl.; unloading, 2 to 4 cents per bbl.; testing, 5 cents per bbl.; sand and gravel f. o. b. barge at pit, 23.8 cents per cu. yd.; towing, 12 to 18 cents per cu. yd.; and unloading and delivering to bunkers at mixer plant, 5 to 8 cents per cu. yd. These costs do not include plant costs or overhead.

Mr. Clapp also gives some interesting historical data and a description of previous studies leading to the adoption of the present plan. Limitation of space prevented the authors from giving more details concerning these features. The statement that the diversion of the waters of the White River to the Puyallup has a greater beneficial effect in the prevention of floods in the Duwamish Valley than the construction of the canal, is correct. It was intended to list this feature merely as a collateral benefit.

The authors agree with Mr. Sabin's comment that,

"In lock design there are several considerations that render it impracticable to predetermine accurately by theory the action of a certain proposed arrangement of culverts, valves, and ports or laterals".

His analysis of the designs of the Pedro Miguel Lock of the Panama Canal, the latest locks at St. Marys Falls Canal, and the Lake Washington Lock, so far as these features are concerned, is of great interest, but his statement as to the experience in operating the locks at the two former places would seem to indicate that no materially better results were secured by the designs adopted there than at the Lake Washington Locks. At the St. Marys Falls Canal Locks, where the culverts are under the lock floor with a system of ports distributed over the floor area, it appears that fluctuations of level from one end of the lock chamber to the other occur with a maximum difference of about 1 ft. While the lock can be filled in about 6 min. by opening all valves simultaneously, in order to reduce this surge, about 10 min. are consumed in ordinary operation. At the Lake Washington Lock, culverts and laterals were designed to fill the lock in 8 min., but the actual time is only about 7⅓ min. There are no noticeable cross-currents and the up-stream current is not perceptible until the chamber is practically filled and it is then insufficient to affect ships. The latter are always moored to the north wall and the opening of the north valve is started a few seconds before that of the south valve, so as to avoid the possibility of any cross-currents that would tend to pull the ship away from the wall.

At the Pedro Miguel Lock, where the main culverts discharge into small laterals under the floor, the water apparently passes the first two or three ports in the laterals. The discharge is greater near the wall opposite the culverts, and this results in approximately the same distribution as with the laterals or ports in the side walls discharging directly into the chamber. In general, it would appear that whatever the design may be, the most satisfactory results in operation can only be secured as the result of experience and the exercise of good judgment on the part of the operating force.

AMERICAN SOCIETY OF CIVIL ENGINEERS

INSTITUTED 1852

TRANSACTIONS

Paper No. 1680

THE WORK OF THE PORT OF SEATTLE, WASHINGTON*

By George F. Cotterill,† Esq.

With Discussion by Messrs. D. W. McMorris, Joseph M. Clapp, and Charles Evan Fowler.

The "Port of Seattle" must be considered in a dual sense: First, in its broadest meaning as the great harbor of the North Pacific, with a continent for a hinterland and an outlook on the ocean highways, strategically located by Nature and equipped by development to serve the needs of world commerce; and, second, in its lesser scope as the official designation of a municipal corporation charged with certain powers and duties in the development and service of commerce in the Harbor of Seattle.

Strategic Location of Seattle

In geographical terms, the Port of Seattle may be described as situated on Elliott Bay, on the eastern and continental side of Puget Sound approximately 125 miles from the open Pacific Ocean, passage being made through the Strait of Juan de Fuca, Admiralty Inlet, and Puget Sound. The Strait is about 15 miles wide at the Pacific entrance between Cape Flattery and Carmanah Lights, and extends eastward, with an average width of more than 10 miles, between the State of Washington on the south and Vancouver Island on the north, for about 50 miles to Race Rocks, on the Canadian side, there expanding to the northeast and continuing eastward, with an average width of 18 miles, for 30 miles, connecting northward through Georgia Strait into the Canadian waters east of Vancouver Island, thence back to the North Pacific and inside passages of Southeastern Alaska, also connecting southerly through Admiralty Inlet into Puget Sound extending for 75 miles into the

* Presented at the meeting of the Waterways Division, Seattle, Wash., July 15, 1926.

† Civ. Engr. and Port Commr., Seattle, Wash.

heart of Western Washington. The Strait of Juan de Fuca extends eastward from Cape Flattery to Point Wilson, about 85 miles, there connecting southward into Admiralty Inlet and Puget Sound, which have a width from 3 to 5 miles, continuing for 40 miles to the Port of Seattle and 30 miles farther south to the Port of Tacoma. Both Strait and Sound are of ample depth, varying from 150 fathoms at Cape Flattery to 25 fathoms minimum at the Admiralty Inlet entrance to Puget Sound, which has similar variations of depth from 150 to 25 fathoms minimum at the opening into Elliott Bay—the Port of Seattle. Here is a natural harbor, with 9.7 miles of shore line, including 3 800 acres of surface area, very deep and free from natural obstructions or dangers throughout its entire extent—a land-locked bay indenting the continent from an inland sea, the open hand of a mighty arm of the ocean extended 125 miles inward for the largest service of commerce with utmost safety and convenience.

Viewed from the continental hinterland the Port of Seattle demonstrates the most strategic location, nearest to central for seven, and the focal Pacific port of concentration for three, transcontinental railway systems. Two northern routes traverse Canada from the Atlantic to the Pacific, finding a Pacific outlet at the Port of Vancouver, but with rail and water connections to the Port of Seattle, 150 miles to southward. Likewise, two routes from the Middle West and the Pacific Northwest find their way down the Columbia River to the Ports of Portland and Astoria in Oregon and to the new Ports of Vancouver and Longview in Washington, but these railway systems have also joint ownership and common-user operating rights over the 150 miles of almost water-grade railway northward from the Columbia River to Puget Sound and the Port of Seattle. Midway between these four connecting routes of Canada and the Columbia River are the three great American northern transcontinental systems, covering the great Northwestern Empire from the Great Lakes and the Upper Mississippi Valley to the Pacific slope—these converge at the Port of Seattle.

The Climax of a World Quest

There is a historical background worthy of note before turning from the geographic picture of the Port of Seattle and passing to detail consideration of its development and progress. Columbus, seeking the westward route "to India and Cathay", found it blocked by two continents linked by an isthmus barrier. Diaz and De Gama demonstrated the southeast passage *via* the Cape of Good Hope to India and the East Indies; to which Magellan soon added his momentous contribution of the southwest route by the Straits which bear his name, to the Indies and the first circumnavigation of the globe. Balboa meanwhile crossed the Isthmus of Panama and discovered the "South Sea", along which Spain soon extended her conquests southward to Peru and northward to the Gulf of California. Then began the search for a "Northwest Passage" to China around the supposed north coast of, or through, North America. It was first pressed by England, then by France in the North Atlantic. Meanwhile, Spain was extending her knowledge of the North Pacific. Two Philippine ships in 1584 and 1595 made a dim record;

in 1602, Viscanio from Spanish Mexico went north to the Bays of San Diego and Monterey, and on to 42° latitude—the northern boundary of California. In 1603, Martin Aguilar reached 43°, named Cape Blanco and claimed to have discovered the mouth of a large river. Globes and maps of this period began to indicate an indefinite "Strait of Anian", probably the expression of a hope of an opening eastward, somewhere north of known discoveries and fading away into the unknown.

Discovery lagged after the first third of the Sixteenth Century, while the nations of Europe turned to exploration, development, and extension of their domains and claims on the continent that barred the way to the Orient. On the Pacific side, Spain coasted north from Mexico, Cabrillo in 1542-43 exploring the southern coast of California and Ferrelo in 1543 as far north as the Oregon coast. The name, California, is first found in a Spanish romance of 1510, described as being "on the right hand of the Indies, very near the terrestrial paradise", hence it was applied by Cabrillo to the coast he explored in 1542. Lower California was considered an island and so mapped up to 1721.

The war between Spain and England in the Elizabethan era was carried to all the seven seas, over which Spain held sway as the mistress of world commerce. Bent on a mission of war destruction, Sir Francis Drake left England in December, 1577, went down the east coast of South America, through the Straits of Magellan (September, 1578), plundered Spanish possessions in Chili and Peru, seized ships, and demoralized Spanish Pacific commerce all the way up the coast to Mexico and California, particularly intercepting their treasure ships from the Philippines and East Indies en route to Panama and the Atlantic. Laden with rich prizes of war—after landing and refitting at Drake Bay, near San Francisco—Drake sought a shorter route to England by way of the supposed "Northwest Passage". He proceeded north, up the California and Oregon and perhaps the Washington coast, seeking an opening or trend of the coast to the eastward. Whether he stopped at 43° North Latitude or continued to 48°, just south of the great strait opening into Puget Sound, accounts differ. It was late summer of 1579, and Drake feared that even if he continued north and found an eastward passage it would only lure him into the frozen regions of the North Atlantic. Hence, he turned westward across the Pacific, doubtless making the first trans-Pacific voyage by the northern route, and continued by way of the Indian Ocean and the Cape of Good Hope to England in 1580.

At this stage there was published by an English author the purported memorandum of Michael Lok of a conversation at Venice in 1596 with an old Greek pilot, Juan de Fuca. By this third-hand authority there came the story which pointed the finger to an unknown Puget Sound as the Pacific portal of the Northwest Passage—the American exit of the trade route to the Orient. Juan de Fuca was reported as giving the story of a voyage in 1592, sent out by the Viceroy of Nova Spania (that is, Western Mexico).

For a century and a half the search for the Northwest Passage and the trade route to the Orient languished. Before the middle of the Eighteenth

Century came the awakening. In 1728, the Danish explorer, Bering, in the service of Russia, demonstrated that Asia and North America were two continents, with a sea and strait between, connecting from the Pacific to the ice-bound Arctic. Also, in 1741, Bering coasted North America down to 54° 40′. The fur trade of the North Pacific developed and the merchants of all nations sought to enter it. England, meanwhile, had taken over the Portuguese possessions in India and Southeast Asia and was securing trade footholds in South China. On the American Continent her Hudson's Bay Company was stretching westward up great rivers toward the mountains and the Pacific that lay beyond. The only available market for the North Pacific furs were the Ports of South China and India. England reopened the book of discovery after nearly two centuries, at the page turned down by the Juan de Fuca story of 1592, and offered a $100 000 reward for the demonstration of the "Northwest Passage". With this incentive, Captain James Cook—just 200 years after Drake's vain effort of 1579—sought the prize. It was the third and last voyage of this greatest of British navigators. Sailing on March 7, 1778, from the Sandwich Islands—which he had discovered and named on a previous Pacific voyage—he sighted the coast at the North California or Spanish boundary and followed it northward to Nootka Sound on the west coast of Vancouver Island, observing neither the Columbia River or other opening in the Coast line, having been driven to the open ocean by a gale.

Fourteen years after Cook failed where Drake fell short two centuries before, the lot fell on Captain George Vancouver to solve the problem and dissolve the mystery of three centuries. The British Admiralty having accepted the conclusion recorded by Cook, the fur trade developed from the Nootka base, with the South China and East India market, participated in by British and American merchantmen after the treaties of 1783 closing the Revolutionary War. Suddenly, in 1790, the news was brought to London by Captain John Meares, of the Spanish seizure of his two British merchantmen at Nootka, with their cargoes of furs. The menace of war was aroused, but soon there was an Anglo-Spanish treaty, including apologies and reparation. More important than his news of seizures and demand for reparation, however, Meares had brought to London the news of new discoveries in the North Pacific, and particularly that "John de Fuca's Strait" really existed, despite Cook's 1778 record of non-existence. Meares confronted the 1790 London world of geography with a map entitled "A Chart of the Interior Part of North America; Demonstrating the Very Great Probability of an Inland Navigation from Hudson's Bay to the West Coast". The map showed "John de Fuca's Straits" entering from the ocean eastward to an undefined open end; a dotted line around to the northward and back into the Pacific Ocean north of Nootka, marked "Sketch of the Track of the American Sloop *Washington* in 1789"; an indication of "The Sea" to the eastward; a short section of the "Oregon River" in the interior, with dotted lines indicating probable connection to the inland sea and straits; also an intricate system of lakes and rivers covering the Continent to the north and eastward. By this Meares map and information, all the doubts and hopes of a Northwest Passage as the great trade route from Occident to Orient were renewed. The British Admiralty acted promptly, deciding to combine with the Naval Expedition to adjust the Spanish seizures at Nootka, a final and thoroughly equipped scientific solution or dissolution of the North Pacific mystery. Hence, the Vancouver Expedition of 1791-93.

Captain Vancouver faithfully discharged his mission, entered the Straits of Fuca, spent the season of 1792 in a survey and charting of the right-hand coast line of the Continent, testing out every inlet of the intricate ramifications of the inland sea, east and south and north and northwest, until at last he came out into the Pacific north of Vancouver's Island. The high point of this great voyage of discovery was reached May 26, 1792, when Vancouver rounded the point into Commencement Bay, the Harbor of Tacoma. The record reads:

"Towards noon we landed on a point on the eastern shore * * * round which we flattered ourselves we should find the inlet take an extensive easterly course. This conjecture was supported by the appearance of a very abrupt division in the snowy range of mountains immediately south of Mt. Rainier, which was very conspicuous from the ship, and the main arm of the inlet appearing to stretch in that direction from the point we were then upon.

"We here dined, and although our repast was soon concluded, the delay was irksome, as we were excessively anxious to ascertain the truth, of which we were not long held in suspense. For having passed round the point, we found the inlet to terminate here in an extensive, circular, compact bay, whose waters washed the base of Mount Rainier".

Thus ended the search for the "Northwest Passage". The dream was dissolved into the reality of a North Pacific "Mediterranean", with sheltered harbors destined for great ports, ready to serve the continents through the giant gateway of the spacious straits to the world highway of the greatest ocean.

The age of steam and steel, dawning a half-century after Vancouver, made possible the realization of the Northwest Passage and the world's greatest trade route by the steamship and the railway. On Vancouver's Puget Sound of 1792, the story of the Port of Seattle was started sixty years later. It is the realization of a vision, the fulfillment of destiny.

Development of the Port of Seattle

The Port of Seattle, in its limited official scope, is a municipal corporation, covering the territory of Seattle and its surrounding County of King, organized and operated under authority of Washington State Law in 1911.

Prior to this public port organization, Seattle had developed, during the preceding forty years:

(1) A large "mosquito fleet" commerce covering the intricate ramifications of Puget Sound and tributary inland waters, serving the suburban vicinity and the industrial and agricultural communities of the Puget Sound region, which always included more than one-half the population of Washington;

(2) A coast-wise, inland waters, and deep-sea commerce with British Columbia and Alaska, and with the California port; and,

(3) A trans-Pacific commerce initiated by the Great Northern Railway in connection with a Japanese steamship company in 1896, and, later, with its own great American cargo steamer, the *Minnesota*. There was occasional service by British companies in the Oriental trade; also,

(4) An industrial commerce in lumber to South American, Australian, and other Pacific markets, and some small share of the grain shipments from the Inland Empire to the United Kingdom and Europe.

The port facilities for the handling of this growing volume of commerce prior to 1911, had developed from the original Yesler Mill Wharf of 1853, around which the city was founded, to a considerable magnitude by 1889, when an $8 000 000 conflagration destroyed the central business section, including the entire water-front, with perhaps $1 000 000 of wharves and warehouses. All were rebuilt on larger scale in 1889-90 and expanded to meet the growing needs of commerce. Before 1911 and public port organization, there had been developed about thirty wharves and piers, owned by railroad and steamship companies, industrial concerns, and a few commercial dock companies, all privately owned and operated, under slight degree of regulative State authority in some cases.

The extent and growth of these port facilities prior to 1911, may be gathered from the statistics of 1910 as compared with those of 1890 as given in Table 1.

TABLE 1.

	1890.	1910.
Seattle population	42 837	233 194
Water-borne tonnage	430 260	860 000
Value of shipments	$48 000 000	$96 091 040

During this 20-year period, while the population increased fivefold, the volume of port commerce only doubled. It was evident to all studious observers for several years prior to 1910 that commercial development was not keeping pace with the rapid growth of the city. It became apparent that the port facilities and equipment were inadequate to attract and hold increasing commerce. The Panama Canal was approaching completion, and it was plain that it would mean a re-adjustment of routes of commerce. Looking north and south, Seattle saw every Pacific port from Vancouver to San Diego, planning great port improvements, backed by the public credit of their communities. With freight rates from the interior on a practical parity to all Pacific ports, and trans-Pacific ocean rates identical from all to Oriental ports, with a likelihood of similar parity in intercoastal traffic with the oncoming Panama régime—it was clear that those ports which offered commerce the most adequate facilities and efficient service at the lowest cost would hold their own and go forward in the new era of world commerce which impended with the opening of the Panama Canal; and, *contra,* that any port which failed to prepare for the new era would find itself left in the race.

Seattle girded herself to prepare for this new era. It was obvious that private investment could not be induced or attracted to meet the situation.

With tariff rates, necessarily fixed by competition with other Pacific ports, all backed and supported by public credit and taxations, as required, there could be no profit in constructing port facilities in advance of their need, sufficient to invite investment of private capital in common-user water-front terminals. It was absolutely necessary that there be authority for public port organizations in the State of Washington, if it was to hold its own with the public ports of British Columbia, Oregon, and California.

Civic committees besieged three State Legislatures, in 1907, 1909, and 1911, before gaining the required general law of port authorization. Briefly, the law enables any harbor district, including part or all of a county, to organize by vote of the people, as a port municipal corporation, endowed with the public credit up to 3% of the assessed total of taxable resources of the district, with taxing power for debt charges and up to 2 mills per year for any port purpose. The port is managed by a commission of three, one elected annually for a 3-year term. Port development must proceed on a comprehensive plan, with specific units of improvement, adopted by majority vote of the electors of the district, and bonds for indebtedness by a 60% vote.

The Port of Seattle was the first to avail itself of this authority and was organized in September, 1911. Tacoma, Bellingham, Everett, Gray's Harbor, Olympia, Port Angeles, Port Townsend, Longview, Vancouver, and several smaller harbor cities of Washington have applied the same general law.

Progress of Port of Seattle

Space forbids the detail description of the accomplishments of the Port of Seattle in its fifteen years of history. Seven port terminals and equipment affording service for the varied needs of commerce have been provided at cost of about $9 000 000, with an eighth terminal site purchased for $600 000, and an area of State land valued at $600 000, dedicated free for port industrial sites. Most of the construction was done before World War prices prevailed, and even with full allowance for depreciation, the present (1926) value of port properties and improvements is at least $12 000 000. These terminals include:

(1) Salmon Bay Terminal; headquarters for fishing fleet; industrial sites, etc.; present value.................. $600 000

(2) Smith's Cove Terminal; two great ocean piers, 40 and 41; largest in world; special equipment for heavy lifts, facilities for oils, molasses, etc.; industrial area adjoining; present value 3 400 000

(3) Bell Street Terminal; central water-front wharf; four-story concrete warehouse and office buildings; six-story, 80 by 104-ft. cold storage annex; present value. . 960 000

(4) Marion Street Ferry; single slip landing; two-story business and office frontage; present value............. 110 000

(5) Stacy-Lander Terminal; double wharf, with transit sheds and two-story warehouse frontage; four-story concrete warehouse, 78 by 318 ft.; present value...... 1 050 000

(6) Hanford Street Terminal; 1 000 000-bushel grain elevator, conveyors, and water-side loading facilities; wharf and two-story transit shed; present value..... 1 100 000

(7) Spokane Street Terminal; wharf and two-story transit shed, 90 by 882 ft.; two-story salmon warehouse, 147 by 514 ft.; fish-freezing and storage facilities, 121 by 172 ft., and 101 by 109 ft.; ice storage, 5 000 tons; cold storage building, seven stories, 147 by 195 ft.; compressor, refrigerating, and ice plant; present value $1 300 000

(8) Unit No. 15; central water-front site, 26 acres; cost, $600 000; present value.......... 1 800 000

(9) Canal waterway (vacated); industrial sites.......... 600 000

Since these public port facilities have been added to the service of commerce the development during fifteen years may be summarized as in Table 2.

TABLE 2.

	1910.	1925.
Seattle population..........	237 174	400 000*
Water borne tonnage..........	860 000	7 995 083
Value of shipments..........	$96 091 040	$730 668 972

* Estimated.

Since the organization of the Port of Seattle, the population has almost doubled, while the volume of water-borne commerce has increased eightfold. Manifestly, this remarkable commercial progress did not result entirely through the efforts and operations of the Public Port Corporation, but it is capable of utmost demonstration that the organized Port of Seattle, sustained by the public credit, made possible the provision of modern port facilities, attracting new and varied forms of commerce, presenting a community front to the whole world of trade, and stimulating the older forms of private initiative to expansion and larger activities. It has been the policy of the Public Port Corporation not to supplant but to supplement existing facilities; to plan and build in advance of need, and especially to develop new lines of commerce to swell the community total.

All the public port facilities, except the second and larger Pier 41 of the Smith's Cove Terminal, were planned, constructed, and ready for service by 1914, the year of the completion of the Panama Canal. The Port of Seattle was prepared and equipped to meet the new era of re-adjustment of world routes of commerce; but the clouds of war suddenly impended and four years of world conflict absorbed all energies. Normal commerce was destroyed or brushed aside, but an abnormal war commerce, meeting emergency war needs, sprang into existence. Shipping from the Orient, the East Indies, and India, driven from its normal Suez route to Europe by the torpedo menace in the Mediterranean Sea and South Atlantic Ocean, turned eastward to the Pacific ports of America and the protected routes eastward under neutral auspices. When the United States entered the war in 1917-18, the volume of war supply commerce was vastly augmented. The Port of Seattle, with its strategic location, new port facilities, and adequate equipment, seemed as if providentially prepared for the service of this abnormal period. Its commerce suddenly swelled to a volume of foreign trade second only to that of the premier American port, New York. Without suggestion of profiteering, the Port handled this tremendous volume of war-period commerce, with financial return sufficient to carry the entire public investment without need of supporting tax levy, creating also a surplus of almost $1 000 000 which was available and applied to additional port improvements without need of bonds and debt.

Re-Adjustment and Revival

After the war came the slump and re-adjustment period. The war commerce faded away like a dream, and the awakening of America and the world to a commerce rebuilt from the bottom was a slow process. The Port of Seattle was prepared for this new era and progress has been steadily upward. The upward turn came in 1922, since which time the record of water-borne commerce, foreign and domestic, shows as follows:

1922	5 888 044 tons
1923	6 662 889 "
1924	7 886 137 "
1925	7 995 083 "

During this post-war period the public terminals of the Port of Seattle have been maintained and operated with the financial showing noted in Table 3.

TABLE 3.

Port of Seattle.	1921.	1922.	1923.	1924.	1925.
Earnings	$877 521	$920 591	$964 983	$1 059 374	$1 054 201
Expenses	657 493	712 284	737 742	772 298	716 451
Operating gain	$220 058	$208 307	$227 341	$287 076	$337 750
Interest and depreciation	$469 872	$511 864	$467 308	$463 718	$468 055
Net loss	$249 814	$303 557	$240 067	$176 642	$130 315

It may be noted from Table 3 that the sum total of these annually decreasing net investment losses for the five years, 1921-25, approximately equal and offset the net investment surplus accumulated during the preceding five years of abnormal war commerce. Considering, therefore, the entire period from the initiation of operations following the construction period of 1912-13, up to and including 1925, the Port of Seattle has been self-sustaining, carrying the full investment of the public credit, without tax support for any of its operations. The Port is now fully established as a going concern, on a sound financial basis, facing a future of continued expansion to meet the largest demands of commerce with ample resources and credit.

It will be interesting to note the sources and destinations of the 7 995 083 tons of commodities water-borne to and from the Port of Seattle in 1925, as follows:

Domestic (U. S.) Commerce:	Tons.
Puget Sound and local	3 408 239
Pacific coastwise	2 223 233
Atlantic ports	594 639
Alaska	395 503
Gulf ports	54 636
Total domestic tonnage	6 676 250
Foreign Commerce (also, Hawaii and The Philippines):	
Orient, Japan, China	404 685
British Columbia	260 327
United Kingdom and Europe	135 663
Hawaii	97 602
Philippines and East Indies	85 262
South and Central America, Mexico, West Indies	42 034
Australia and New Zealand	36 624
Canada, Africa, and all others	264 318
Total foreign tonnage	1 318 833
Port of Seattle, 1925 tonnage	7 995 083

Exports and Imports

Illustrative of the service of the Port of Seattle to the producers and industries of its vicinity and tributary hinterland, the following are some of the commodities exported in foreign trade:

914 683	boxes of apples.
5 622	tons of automobiles.
8 282	tons of canned goods (except fish).
22 692	tons of coal and coke.
13 040	tons of raw cotton.
42 984	tons of fish, canned, pickled, etc.
62 406	tons of flour.
13 361	tons of fodders and feed.
1 339 734	bushels of grain.
12 210	tons of hardware, iron and steel manufactures.
140 325	million ft., B.M., lumber, logs, piling, etc.
4 903	tons of machinery.
9 114	tons of canned milk.
13 932	tons of crude oil and products.
14 746	tons of paper.
3 340	tons of potatoes.
7 767	tons of tobacco.
4 214	tons of wood manufactures (except furniture).
6 795	tons of chemicals.

These are the leading items in a total of 649 581 tons exported (foreign) from Seattle. More than twice this total of these and other commodities are exported (domestic) over Seattle wharves—1 333 082 tons of domestic exports.

Foreign imports through the Port of Seattle in 1925 totaled 669 252 tons, of which some of the leading items were:

11 200 tons of burlap and bagging.
26 954 tons of cement.
91 270 tons of coal and coke.
19 834 tons of coal-tar and products.
2 634 tons of coffee.
3 553 tons of cotton, raw and waste.
4 626 tons of fodders and feed.
1 239 tons of glass.
71 514 bushels of grain (except rice).
5 396 tons of hemp and jute.
12 455 tons of iron and steel.
6 675 tons of lime and plaster.
6 399 tons of minerals.
42 899 tons of oils (bean, cocoanut, peanut, wood, etc.).
30 278 tons of paper.
9 720 tons of peanuts (and other nuts).
9 432 tons of porcelain and pottery.
3 534 tons of seeds and bulbs.
7 736 tons of shingles.
14 597 tons of silk, raw and waste.
2 809 tons of sugar.
13 468 tons of syrup and molasses.
4 613 tons of tea.
4 919 tons of wood, pulp and paper stock.
6 446 tons of carpets and rugs.
1 849 tons of prepared eggs.
$444 089 value of furs and manufactures.

The domestic imports to and through the Port of Seattle reached a 1925 total of 5 343 167 tons, eight times the foreign volume.

Seattle Realizing Its Destiny

As an evidence that Puget Sound and the Port of Seattle are winning the commerce of the great trade route between the Occident and the Orient, the 1925 record shows that Oriental commerce with American Pacific ports, compared on a tonnage basis, is distributed, as follows: 39.7% through Washington ports; 32.0% through Oregon ports; and 28.3% through California ports.

When the comparison is based on valuation rather than tonnage, the northern route to Puget Sound—shorter by 281 miles than the northern route from San Francisco to Yokohama, and by 1 230 miles as compared to the southern route from San Francisco *via* Honolulu—the strategic location of the Port of Seattle is emphasized by the fact that the silks of the Orient, at the rate of $229 000 000 in 1925, were drawn across the short North Pacific route, whereas less than one-quarter of that volume used the longer route *via* the Golden Gate.

Witness, then, the dream of centuries realized in the actuality of to-day, and the vision of a greater to-morrow. American railway systems converging on Puget Sound and the Port of Seattle serve the old European Occident and the New World of Columbus in trade relations over the shortest Pacific path to the hundreds of millions of the Orient. The fabled "Straits of Anian" of the Sixteenth Century and the demonstration of Puget Sound in the closing Eighteenth Century, have, in the dawning of the Twentieth Century, revealed a "Northwest Passage" beyond the hopes of Drake, the dream of de Fuca, and the achievements of Vancouver and Gray. And the Port of Seattle stands at the gateway to serve world commerce.

DISCUSSION

D. W. McMorris,* M. Am. Soc. C. E.—There was a very interesting incident in connection with the development of the Port of Seattle, that Mr. Cotterill has not touched upon; the so-called "Bush Terminal Plan of Improvement", that was developed by a number of persons who desired to obtain control of practically all port facilities.

There was a strong sentiment among the more progressive and aggressive members of the community to provide such ample and convenient facilities for trans-oceanic shipments of freight and merchandise as to care for not only all business that would probably reach the port, but also to offer special inducements to new business seeking a Western shipping terminal.

Much was said about the type of development that had been in successful operation at Brooklyn, N. Y., by the Bush Terminal Dock and Warehouse Company.

The report on the "Plan of Seattle" had been recently made by the late Virgil G. Bogue, M. Am. Soc. C. E., with whom the speaker had been associated, laying out a similar plan of development on Harbor Island. "The Harbor Island Terminal Company" was formed and a tentative agreement prepared setting forth with considerable detail the plan of development and the terms of a proposed lease of all the Port's property on Harbor Island.

The effect of the proposed agreement was to have the Port provide the funds necessary to carry on an elaborate construction program and then lease the entire Harbor Island project to the Terminal Company. The sentiment in favor of the project was so strong that it was seriously proposed by some that the Commissioners' regular program give way to the Company's plan which would have made the Port merely a means of financing the promoter's project.

Finally, the alluring possibilities of the Harbor Island plan were set aside and the Port development proceeded on more conservative lines. The speaker has always felt disappointed, however, that some way was not found to modify the proposed agreement with the Harbor Island Terminal Company so as to have justified the Port Commission in having had the development completed, as it is certainly an ideal location for such an improvement.

Joseph M. Clapp,† M. Am. Soc. C. E.—In his interesting and valuable paper Mr. Cotterill may have left the impression that the Port of Seattle owned all the water-front area and had developed part of it at a cost of about \$10 000 000 which, together with certain areas deeded the Port from the State, made the value of the Port property about \$12 000 000. The citizens of the District were not unanimously favorable to the development as at present accomplished.

Seattle Port is one of the land-locked harbors of Puget Sound on which a large commercial city is located. There are five such harbors or ports, all located on the mainland and at the mouths of rivers draining into Puget

* Asst. City Engr., Seattle, Wash.

† Cons. and Contr. Engr., Seattle, Wash.

Sound. Puget Sound has a coast line of approximately 2 000 miles composed of a ribbon of sand, flanked on one side by high bluffs and on the other by deep water. Six important rivers empty into the Sound and drain important valleys which constitute the gateways from the back country. Here are found extensive flat areas on which the cities are built.

The City of Bellingham is located near the mouth of the Nooksack River; Everett, at the mouth of the Snohomish River; Seattle, at the mouth of the Duwamish River; Tacoma at the mouth of the Puyallup River; and Olympia, at the mouth of the Deschutes River. No city is built at the mouth of the Nisqually River.

At the mouth of the Duwamish River the flatlands of Seattle were reclaimed, and a large industrial area was created with harbor and waterway frontage provided, all at the south end of the harbor, perfectly landlocked from prevailing storm winds, except an occasional "Northwester". It is here that many of the citizens thought the development of the Port should have been concentrated and ocean piers constructed.

These piers would naturally have followed very closely in design the piers built at Smith's Cove and at the East Waterway. The adjacent areas were available for small and large factories, and this arrangement would have lessened the congestion of freight shipments, now experienced.

Building the piers in this flat area would have lessened the overhead maintenance and left the immediate city water-front for the mosquito fleet and coasting vessels. Many other factors of economy would have resulted. Three of the four transcontinental lines enter Seattle from the south and one from the north. Thus, the location of the piers in the south end of the harbor would have resulted in a single line of railway to handle freight at this point, instead of the three lines now obliged to handle a large part of their ocean freight to the north and less protected area. The movement of freight along the water-front from south to north, as at present, creates considerable confusion which is intensified when ocean vessels dock at the central front.

While the Port owns and operates the twelve various developments they are not operated at a profit, but at a loss. All this loss is borne by taxing the property lying within the district. The taxpayer derives some benefit, of course, because of the increased shipping with modern and adequate facilities for handling it. This district also comprises water-front property, privately owned, which is taxed to support a competitor.

Charles Evan Fowler,* M. Am. Soc. C. E. (by letter).—The very considerable part played by the writer in the formation of the Port of Seattle, causes him to read with much interest of the complete success of this municipal undertaking. As a member of the Harbor Committee of the Seattle Chamber of Commerce, the suggestion was made in 1911 of forming an unofficial Seattle Harbor Commission. About fourteen organizations appointed members, and these with the Mayor, the City Engineer, and the Corporation Counsel composed the body which planned the Port of Seattle, and secured the passage of the State law authorizing such legal municipal bodies for

* Cons. Engr., New York, N. Y.

any of the ports of the State, comprising either the entire county in which the port was located, or such portion of the county as might be set apart for the district which was to be subjected to taxation for creating the port properties.

The Committee that drew the law, consisted of Corporation Counsel Scott Calhoun, the late A. O. Powell, M. Am. Soc. C. E., and the writer, who believed the district should be greater than the city and less in size than the county, in order to keep it out of local politics. When the Port was organized, it was as the entire County of King, and notwithstanding this, it is pleasant to record that most of the members during the past fifteen years have been free from political influence. The writer, as Acting Chairman of the Engineering Committee of the unofficial Commission, during most of the formative period, gathered information from all over the world, and made trips to Portland, Ore., San Francisco and Los Angeles, Calif., Chicago, Ill., New York, N. Y., Baltimore, Md., and Washington, D. C., in search of data as to methods of organization and construction in use in the various ports.

This Committee also made plans and estimates of cost of sea walls, piers, warehouses, and all the appurtenances of a port, and it was upon these data that the first \$6 500 000 was fixed for the initial units. The Committee favored one large concentrated terminal, preferably at Harbor Island in Elliott Bay. The first official Commission of the Port of Seattle was very fortunate in having as a member the late H. M. Chittenden, Brig.-Gen., U. S. A. (*Retired*), M. Am. Soc. C. E., and he as first Chairman was also in favor of a concentrated terminal. However, local politics did have a say and, as a result, part of the port improvements are on the East Waterway, part on the old water-front of the city at Bell Street, and part on Salmon Bay, or on the Lake Washington Canal. Later, the great concentrated terminal at Smith's Cove was begun, and the full development of this has dwarfed the smaller scattered units, which now only add to the cost of administration.

The smaller units, however, serve the separate districts well in providing space for the vessels in the Puget Sound, coastwise, and Alaskan trade, and the fishing fleet. While the business of the port proper is not a great factor in the growth of a port city, it is likely that these small units are more effective in increasing local business, than is the large terminal at Smith's Cove, where exchange is made from the ocean ships to the rail lines. The City of Seattle should be able to answer much better than the older ports, just how much the meeting of ship and rail lines has to do with the making of a metropolis, but in so doing full value must be given to the lumber and Alaskan trade, and to the business carried by the great fleet of smaller vessels plying the waters of Puget Sound.

This is work for the statistician and the port engineer that will be of great value in the future development of coast cities, and in the furtherance of the commerce which passes through them. Certain it is that the great ocean commerce of the future will be found on the Pacific, and this will add in untold measure to the land commerce west of the Mississippi River.

AMERICAN SOCIETY OF CIVIL ENGINEERS
INSTITUTED 1852

TRANSACTIONS

This Society is not responsible for any statement made or opinion expressed in its publications.

Paper No. 1681

BASIC INFORMATION NEEDED FOR A REGIONAL PLAN*

BY HAROLD M. LEWIS,† M. AM. SOC. C. E.

WITH DISCUSSION BY MESSRS. RUSSELL V. BLACK, GEORGE F. UNGER, ARTHUR A. SHURTLEFF, HALE J. WALKER, JOSEPH W. SHIRLEY, GUY WILFRID HAYLER, WILLIAM BOWIE, HOWARD STRONG, CHARLES W. ELIOT, 2D, U. N. ARTHUR, CHARLES WELLFORD LEAVITT, HARLAND BARTHOLOMEW, DONALD M. BAKER, HARRY J. MARCH AND HAROLD M. LEWIS.

As the concentration in cities has increased and the size and complexity of the individual city have grown beyond anything that could have been foreseen a few years ago, it is only natural that the scope of planning has also increased. Starting with a concentration on the civic center, planners enlarged their activities to the comprehensive city plan; then they studied the environs and grouped together two or more closely related communities in the regional plan. The State of New York has made studies for a State-wide plan and articles have been written in regard to a National plan. The writer has been asked to describe the type of material that should be assembled as a basis for determining the elements of a regional plan.

Most of the published information on city and regional planning gives the conclusions and details after the plan has been completed, or describes methods of co-operation or publicity necessary to carry out such projects. A description of the basic data required and the form of presentation is likely to be considered a matter of routine work which is probably standardized and almost surely uninteresting. When a large regional planning project is undertaken, however, the collection of this material becomes so huge a problem that it is well worth while to have it carefully planned and organized. A paper of this kind can only attempt to point out the "high spots" of the subject, it being understood that a large amount of subsidiary information

* Presented at the Joint Meeting of the City Planning Division with the American City Planning Inst., Philadelphia, Pa., October 7, 1926.

† Executive Engr., Regional Plan of New York and Its Environs, New York, N. Y.

must also be gathered. It is based primarily on an analysis of what has been accomplished toward developing a regional plan for New York and its environs. Although some of the steps described may seem to be unimportant details, most of them represent the result of careful experiment and, as such, should be of some value to the professional regional planner.

It seems desirable first to give some attention to the definition of a "regional plan". By a "region" is meant a group of separate communities which form a single metropolitan district with common interests. This, as a rule, will center about a large port or manufacturing headquarters. Obviously, the "plan" should comprise only those details which have some importance in the development or welfare of the entire region, or in the promotion of the orderly and efficient development of one of its integral parts.

Mr. Edward M. Bassett has defined the city or regional plan as "the determination of land areas stamped with definite characters by law", and points out that the community or region establishes its own plan through its legislative body or bodies. This is true of the legally adopted plan which will have positive control over future growth, but that must be preceded by planning studies which should be defined in greater detail. The late Nelson P. Lewis, M. Am. Soc. C. E., in a paper* entitled "Regional Planning" has stated that when he used this term he had in mind the following type of studies:

"Larger areas must be studied and instead of beginning with present centers and providing for expansion outward, absorbing one after another of outlying towns and villages, it is time to begin at the outer edges of a great metropolitan district, to study existing communities and strive to encourage the development of their centers, to create new social, commercial, and industrial centers, and strive to protect what is worth saving from being drawn into the vortex at the big center and absorbed bodily by it, with no line of demarcation and with no barrier to the steady outward movement of population."

The writer would suggest the following definition:

"A regional plan is one for the co-ordinated physical growth of a group of communities forming a single metropolitan district, based on the most desirable and efficient development of the whole region."

A summary of the type of data required is necessarily largely a list of headings, but is important to those who are organizing a regional plan. The following classifications are essential: (1) Physical; (2) economic; (3) social; (4) legal; and, (5) financial.

A combination of graphic, statistical, and descriptive presentation is required. The physical survey is the largest and most complicated undertaking, as it includes the preparation of those maps on which the planner must base the details of the regional plan. It might be called a survey of existing conditions, both visible and officially mapped. What is included under this heading and the form in which it should be presented will be described in considerable detail. The material required under the other four headings will only be very briefly outlined. This does not mean that they are unimportant, but they are largely supplemental. Each type of investigation

* *Transactions*, Am. Soc. C. E., Vol. LXXXVI (1923), p. 1326.

can be expanded into many sub-headings, some of which may lead the investigator far afield. Each should be tested by the following questions:

1.—Should this appear in a final report?

2.—Is it essential in order to arrive at conclusions that must be incorporated in the final report?

3.—Will the expense of obtaining it be practicable and justified?

The Regional Plan of New York and Its Environs is a pioneer project in its immensity. Started in 1921, it did not reach until 1925 a stage where it was felt that surveys and the gathering of data should be subordinated to planning studies. Much information has probably been obtained that will remain buried in the files. As there was no past experience of a comparable project to serve as a guide, this was unavoidable. Other communities can save time and expense by profiting from the experience in New York. Smaller and less complicated communities will probably not require as many types of information as have proved most useful in studying this particular problem. The Committee on a Regional Plan of New York and Its Environs was organized by the Russell Sage Foundation, which is a National organization with National interests. It was justified, therefore, in doing considerable research work along such lines as:

(*a*) Highway capacities under different conditions.
(*b*) Recreation space requirement standards.
(*c*) Length of haul of motor vehicles and transit lines.
(*d*) Standards of population and housing density.
(*e*) Variation in riding habit on transit lines.
(*f*) Model plans for a neighborhood unit.

It is hoped that some of this information may be of value to other communities. It must always be used, however, with due allowance for a difference in living conditions, habits, etc.

The main sub-headings under each of the five types of studies referred to are as follows:

Physical Survey.—

1.—Topography, boundaries, and other such basic physical features as influence the plan.

2.—Population—distribution, density, and rates of growth.

3.—Communication facilities:

(*a*) Highways;
(*b*) Transit—rapid transit, trolleys, and motor buses;
(*c*) Transportation system—somewhat arbitrarily defined as including the railroad, waterway, and airway systems.

4.—Parks, parkways, and other open spaces.

5.—Sanitation—water supply, sewerage, and refuse disposal.

6.—Port and industrial development (will overlap with communication facilities).

7.—Miscellaneous, including such as:

(*a*) Zoning (land uses established by existing zoning ordinances);
(*b*) Land values;
(*c*) Location of public buildings;
(*d*) Power supply facilities.

Economic Survey.—A study of the history of the principal industries within the region should determine:

1.—Trends in location.
2.—Probable space demand in the future city.
3.—Probable future relative importance.

Social Survey.—

1.—Housing.
2.—Recreation.*
3.—Schools.
4.—Public health and sanitation.*
5.—Correctional institutions.

Legal Survey.—

1.—Ascertainment of city planning powers of the various political units.
2.—Study of new legislation needed to carry out the regional plan.

Financial Survey.—

1.—Cost of public improvements and methods of assessment.
2.—Distribution of funds available.

The first item to be determined is the area to be studied. This may vary greatly for different regions. It should be large enough to include all those communities, the business and recreational life of which are linked with the principal business center. It should include any of those suburbs from which an appreciable number of commuters travel daily to the business center. It should extend far enough to take in all industrial plants which are directly served by, and linked with, a common port. It should also contain those larger recreational spaces which are within easy reach by rail or automobile of the city or suburban dweller. The area studied in the New York Region corresponds roughly to that within a 50-mile radius of New York City Hall. On the north it extended approximately 60 miles, on the south, about 40 miles, and on the east all of Long Island was included, although it extends about 110 miles from the center of New York City. As a general rule, the area of a regional plan may vary between that within a 10 or 50-mile radius from the metropolitan center.

Maps of the entire region should probably be prepared on at least three different scales. These maps might be defined as follows:

1.—Regional table maps, by which is meant such maps as can readily be prepared and studied on an ordinary drafting table. On a scale of 1 in. = 2 to 3 miles.
2.—Regional wall maps. On a scale of 1 in. = 1 mile for a very large region, and perhaps on the scale of 1 in. = ½ mile for smaller regions.
3.—Detail sectional maps. On a scale of 1 in. = 2 000 ft. for large regions, or about 1 in. = 1 000 ft. for smaller ones.

Where particularly difficult problems require a local study, larger maps must be prepared of the areas concerned, on scales of 1 in. = 100 to 1 000 ft.

Each of these classes of maps should contain different types of data presented in different forms.

The so-called table maps should be merely outlines on which a single type of information should be shown. On such maps should be presented popula-

* Items 2 and 4 will necessarily overlap with the "Physical Survey."

tion statistics, existing railroad, rapid transit, and waterway systems, parks and parkways, and all the material necessary to study the regional aspects of all the items covered by the headings listed under "Physical Survey."

The regional wall maps will serve primarily for group discussions of the main elements of the regional plan and for exhibition purposes. They should contain the principal topographic features (in the New York District, which has elevations from sea level to more than 1 600 ft., 100-ft. contours were sufficient), the principal communication and recreation facilities, and one main feature which should be strongly emphasized. In the New York study, these maps were about 10 ft. square, and it was found desirable to have one of them to emphasize each of the following features:

1.—Highways.
2.—Railroads, including the main rapid transit systems.
3.—Parks and parkways.
4.—Sanitation, including water-sheds used for water supply and the location of sewage disposal plants.
5.—Land uses.

An excellent method of using these maps for planning studies is to have them covered with a transparent celluloid coating after all the existing features have been added. This coating can be worked upon in water or oil colors, crayons, or a soft pencil, and proposed facilities can be tentatively added in this way. Such information can be wiped off with a wet or oily rag and revised at will without any damage to the map beneath. The coating also acts as a protecting covering.

The detail sectional maps might be called the base maps of the regional plan. They should show in considerable detail the topography, street system, streams and waterway systems, transportation systems, parks and parkways, political boundaries, pier-head and bulkhead lines, and principal existing land uses. It is upon such maps that details would be worked out after their importance was determined from study of the regional wall maps. From them final sectional maps might be reproduced at smaller scale for publication. It has been found that these maps are not very suitable for discussion at conferences, as such discussion is likely to be sidetracked on detail locations which would not be apparent on maps of smaller scale. The regional importance of any proposal cannot be readily grasped unless it is on a map all parts of which can be readily seen at one instant. The 2 000-ft. scale maps prepared of the New York Region formed a map about 18 by 20 ft. in size when assembled. Such a map is effective in an exhibition, but is too large to use as a basis for serious discussion.

It was made up of enlargements from twenty-three of the standard Government topographic sheets. They were prepared at cost for the Regional Plan Committee by the U. S. Geological Survey and corrections in the shore lines, railroads, main highways, and larger park areas were incorporated. They were printed in three colors, with a few copies without the contours, some of the latter being printed in non-photographic blue. All but the outer edges of the region were covered, and as the Government sheets, 1 mile = 1 in., were the only ones available at uniform scale for a large part of the territory outside New York City, there has been considerable local demand by official bodies and individuals for copies of the sheets. Part of their cost, therefore, has been recovered by the sale of some of the copies.

Three complete maps are being prepared on copies of this base map. Each map includes six sections made up from four (in one case, three) of the 2 000-ft. scale sheets. These maps are about 6 by 7½ ft., which is about as large as can be readily used. Joining these maps with additional sections for title and legend, respectively, the 18 by 20-ft. rectangular map already referred to, was obtained.

The first of these maps showed existing land uses classified as follows:

Industrial areas.
Principal business areas (in communities of more than 25 000 population).
Close residence development.
Parks and parkways of more than 25 acres and forest and water supply reservations.

Golf and country clubs. Cemeteries of more than 25 acres. Large public institutional properties. Aviation fields.	Shown by same color with different symbols superimposed.

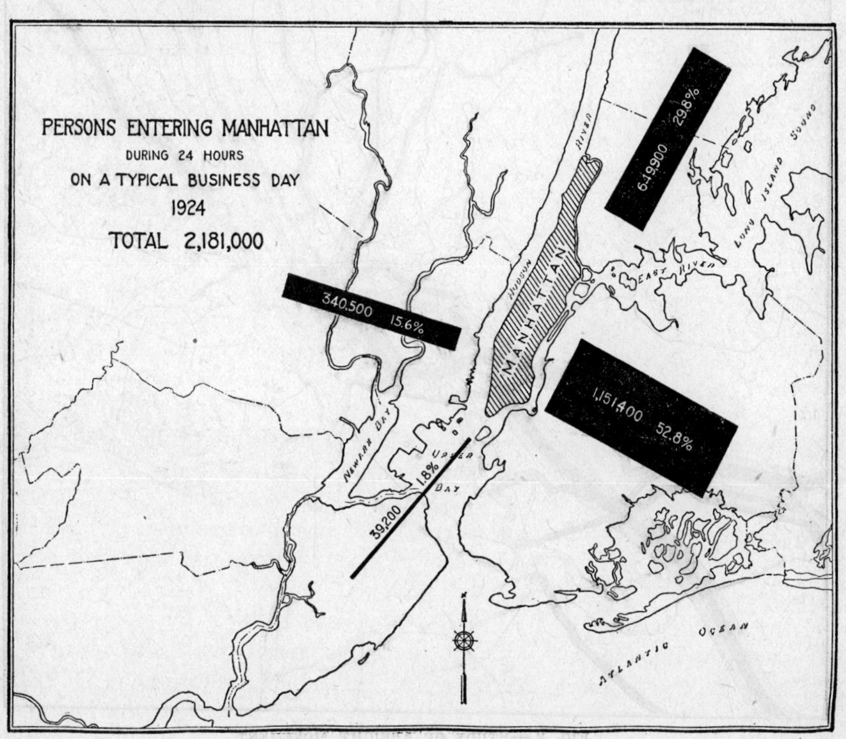

FIG. 1.—STUDY OF PASSENGER MOVEMENT.

The classification of the first three groups was largely a matter of judgment and was intended to show the type of use which predominated in any particular area. Airplane maps and oblique views were found to be very useful in the preparation of this map, and it was constantly revised as more complete information was obtained. It was necessary, therefore, to use colors that could readily be changed, and flat tints, obtained by rubbing in powdered school chalk with a piece of chamois, were found to be very satisfactory. They can be readily removed with an ordinary soft eraser.

The second map was a composite of all proposals for communication facilities of regional importance (as shown, for example, in Figs. 1 and 2) which seemed worthy of serious consideration, including those put forward by other bodies and individuals and developed by the Regional Plan Staff. This was found invaluable as a basis of discussion of the relative merits of highway, railroad, transit, and waterway projects.

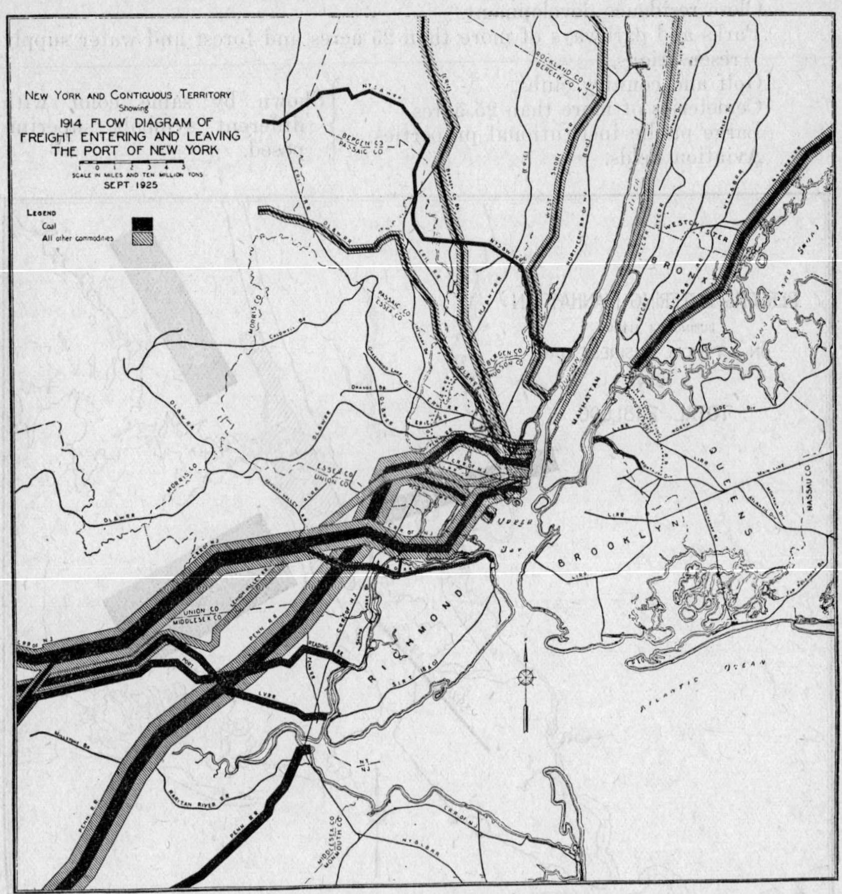

FIG. 2.—STUDY OF FREIGHT MOVEMENT.

The third map has been called the draft regional plan and is a first attempt at co-ordinating all proposals for land uses, communication facilities, waterfront and port development, sanitation, etc. It is necessarily complicated, but it has been found essential to present all such proposals on the same map so that they can be properly co-ordinated and their interdependence understood. It can be considered as the final major step in the accumulation and presentation of basic information. Conferences and discussions will surely lead to many changes in such a map, but if the work to this point has been carefully and thoroughly done the main elements of the regional plan should need only minor changes.

An important consideration in collecting the large amount of material required for a regional plan is the form in which it will be prepared for office use. It is easy to lose a large number of valuable data through filing. It has been very helpful to prepare photostat copies of uniform size of all important maps and bind them in logical sequence. When a particular study is nearing completion, folders have been prepared in letter-size form, which include copies of maps and diagrams relating to a specific subject and descriptive text in typewritten form. From this shape the material can readily be prepared for publication in monographs or bulletins. For the studies other than the physical survey, the material should be prepared in the same letter-size form, but in these cases it will be mainly descriptive, although maps and graphs should be freely used.

Even if the regional planning organization is an official one, a large degree of co-operation between different municipalities is essential for its success. When the organization is an unofficial one, its success depends entirely on such co-operation. It is important, therefore, that a large amount of the basic information be published early in a form readily understandable to both the laymen and the local city planners. For an unofficial body, definite suggestions may well be omitted from the first publications. If the survey material is forcibly presented, the different communities will be assisted in arriving at proper details of a regional plan. Preliminary publications may include the following:

(1) Monographs setting forward the material collected under the main headings of each of the different surveys. These should be largely pictorial, with maps and graphs that can be readily understood by the layman. (In city planning projects such reports may also contain the details of that part of the final plan which bears on the particular phase of the problem to which the monograph is devoted. Excellent examples of this are the reports published by Pittsburgh, Pa., and Toledo, Ohio).
(2) Bulletins on specific problems urgent in importance.
(3) Progress reports designed to keep the various communities informed as to the scope of the work being carried on.
(4) A periodical publication, such as has been published in Pittsburgh and Los Angeles, Calif., may be useful in keeping contact with a large number of individuals.

This general description of the kind of basic information required indicates that a regional plan is complicated. In addition to all such information as can be put down in written or map form, there is also required an intimate personal knowledge of the region, specialized technical ability along various lines, and a wide general knowledge of city and regional planning principles.

These qualifications can seldom be combined in a single individual and regional planning is, therefore, essentially a group project. The eventual plan must be the evolution of a staff working in close co-operation and aided by the best expert advice available. It is necessarily a compromise between conflicting proposals and ambitions of the various communities affected. Although in its final form it may not seem best for an individual community, it probably will prove to be so, as only a well-rounded and balanced plan is practicable.

DISCUSSION

RUSSELL V. BLACK,* ASSOC. M. AM. SOC. C. E.—In formulating a survey program for the Philadelphia Tri-State District regional study many diverse points of view have been expressed. One man of professional prominence advises, "Stop gathering information. Make plans." Another, of equal prominence in his field, remarks on the superficial character of the survey program of the New York Regional Plan, which has spent nearly five years and approximately $750 000, largely in gathering data and getting acquainted with its region.

The Philadelphia District is operating on very limited funds. In the light of planning experience and personal judgment, its members cannot proceed to plan without first learning a great deal more than is now known about their region. On the other hand, they can afford neither time nor money for the collection of unnecessary data, and depending, as they do, on public support, they must show some planning progress comparatively early in the work.

Mr. Lewis has given much helpful guidance as to the extent of material to be obtained and as to survey and study procedure; but the speaker is disappointed in not receiving more specific suggestions as to basic information indispensable to the preparation of a workable regional plan. It may be that the field of regional planning is still too little explored and the problems of the many districts too diverse to offer any very definite general suggestions of scientific approach. However, it would seem that, compelled as they have been to blaze absolutely new trails of survey and research, the several regional planning projects which have made noteworthy progress, must have made some recognizable errors; must have gone up some "blind alleys"; and that, were they to do the work over again, they would go about it somewhat differently. It is this experience which the Philadelphia District would find so valuable and which it has hoped might, in some way, be made available.

From brief experience, two or three conclusions in this matter of survey making have become evident. In the natural development of regional planning from city planning, it is questionable, as Mr. Lewis has described it, if the tendency to "follow the leader" has not led many planners to collect a great deal of thoroughly useless information. In the early and quite experimental age of city planning, men, new to the field, groped about for a formula and some sort of foundation with, and upon, which to erect their future cities. They conceived that certain groups of information might be valuable, and formulated a survey program accordingly. There is some evidence that present methods have not advanced far beyond those first efforts, and that surveys still hold a little of the old chaff that could well be discarded.

The regional plan should not concern itself with matters of purely local character. Local administrations are naturally somewhat jealous of their prerogatives and can usually handle their affairs to better advantage than any outside body. The plan should be limited in its application to those problems and development projects which involve two or more political jurisdic-

* Chf. Planning Engr., Regional Planning Federation of Philadelphia Tri-State Dist., Philadelphia, Pa.

tions, and for the solution and conduct of which no other machinery exists. A Regional Planning Federation, as an agency for the promotion of sound planning, might encourage the proper provision and distribution of neighborhood playgrounds and school grounds; but matters of such local moment should not be made a part of the regional plan. Likewise, it might be a function of a Federation, in furthering the general welfare of the region, to encourage a proper alignment of minor streets, a good width of lot, or the proper distribution of neighborhood store groups; but, again, these things are not a part of a regional plan. Such a plan involves determining the broad uses of land, the completion of a system of connecting and trunk highways, regional and intercommunity parks, regional water supply, the purification of streams, the conservation of natural resources, the broader phases of transportation, co-operative sewage and drainage, and other matters demanding the joint effort of two or more political sub-divisions. It follows that physical data, collected to serve as basis for a regional plan, should be in scale with its purpose, and that, by keeping this scale constantly in mind, a great deal of useless material can be eliminated.

In the field of economic and social survey it is more difficult to know where to stop searching. Too much cannot be known about the laws that govern the conduct of the human race nor of the foundation and controlling forces of an ever-changing economic system. At this moment, every one is pitifully ignorant of the degree to which the modern great city is inherently fundamental to the nature and progress of mankind and the degree to which it is simply a diseased overgrowth. Until more is known certainly of what this phenomenon of city growth is, decentralization of population cannot be adjudged as even desirable; much less can it be attained through present feeble efforts. This is the sort of knowledge needed in order to direct the destinies of great metropolitan areas; but it is the kind of knowledge that requires much more painstaking research than present-day planning organizations can afford in time or money. Fortunately, the knowledge gained in these directions in one part of the country, and to some extent, the world, is almost equally applicable in every other part. Supplemented by a familiarity with the local social and political structure, the general background to be obtained from present-day observation would probably provide as good a sociological basis for regional planning procedure as can be found.

In developing a program, local regional planning has been divided, somewhat roughly, into two steps: Step (1), preliminary, getting acquainted with the region, making tentative suggestions as need may demand, and feeling out and developing public opinion; and Step (2), laying down the master plan, piece by piece, and as based on an exact knowledge of existing conditions and present and probable future needs.

Step (1) is usually attended by small funds and large public skepticism. It must be conducted, not only with the idea of making sound progress, but equally with the object of gaining public attention and approval. A great deal of information, of little purpose other than to awaken public interest, must be collected and appealingly presented. This period is largely educational, with first efforts bent toward pointing out general existing conditions;

the sorry situation resulting from lack of earlier planning and the possibilities of planning for the future. The material collected for Step (1), while necessarily insufficient as a basis for definite planning proposals, should, nevertheless, be such as to serve as a foundation for the more detailed information to follow.

This refers, largely, to physical surveys which might include the topography of land, as given by the U. S. Geological Survey; the distribution and relative density of population, defined by minor civil divisions for several preceding census periods; the larger existing parks and playgrounds, cemeteries, and other potential open places; principal waterways; steam railways, and electric interurban lines; aviation fields; general sewage disposal facilities and character of water supply; extent of public service—gas, electricity, and telephones; other similar classes of data; and, perhaps most important, the broad use of land, including indication of the forest areas, farm lands, open suburban development, sub-divisions not built upon, principal business and industrial areas, large parks, private recreation areas, and large institution grounds.

This should provide sufficient basis for a fairly comprehensive understanding and statement of the condition and needs of the region. Coupled with a reasonable familiarity with the social and economic status of the region and with an appreciation of the bearing of existing legislation, this much of a survey should permit of tentative planning proposals and the first roughing out of the plan. What the schedule of procedure in making these tentative proposals might be, and whether or not the preliminary survey, as outlined, is to be completed before any of the planning studies are undertaken, depends on local necessity. It would seem, however, that at least this much of a picture of the region should be finished before very much planning is done.

Step (2) would involve more specific recommendations and the laying down of a workable skeleton plan with a considerable degree of exactitude. The gaining of public support is no less important at this stage of the work because, without the sympathy and co-operation of public officials and the sanction of the taxpayers, nothing can be accomplished; but the engineering and planning factors must be given more thorough consideration. There should be available at this phase of the study an aero-photographic map of the entire region at a scale not smaller than 2 000 ft. to the inch. There should be an accurate topographic map, in a scale ranging from 1 000 ft. to 200 ft. to the inch, depending on the nature and probable intensity of development of the locality. Each factor of the plan, such as sewage disposal and drainage; water supply; rail, water, and air transportation; highways and bridges; and parks and other recreational areas, would require its special consideration, although closely co-ordinated, detailed, and studied. Perhaps this phase of regional planning should ultimately be directed into the hands of a permanent official or semi-official body, functioning to execute the plan and to keep it adjusted to changing needs.

Such a program (especially Step (2)) is costly, but regional planning is an important undertaking which, if effective, must guide billions of dollars worth of public and private development projects. It holds the possibility of saving many times any possible engineering or planning costs. Done wisely, no other single instrument offers as great an opportunity for the advancement of the general welfare. Ill-considered and superficially done regional planning holds almost equal opportunity for injury. It deserves, and must ultimately have, all needed public funds and the best engineering, economic, and sociologic thought of the time.

GEORGE F. UNGER,* ASSOC. M. AM. SOC. C. E. (by letter).—It is of great interest and value to have a paper presented on basic information needed for a regional plan. Many cities are growing so rapidly that they are over-reaching their present boundaries, thereby creating a decided influence on the adjacent territory and extending activities to various political sub-divisions, all of which have a common interest. This necessarily involves a treatment of the larger area in the broad sense of regional planning, and when presented to the planners of a metropolitan district, it immediately suggests the formulation of some definite outline of procedure.

The Niagara Frontier Planning Board is significant in that it was created in a way differing somewhat from other regional planning bodies. Legislation was obtained, giving it an official status and providing for a method of financing with public funds, the District included being the political sub-divisions of Erie and Niagara Counties. This seemed to be the territory containing communities whose interests are common and whose commercial and recreational life is closely allied with the principal business centers. Subsequent to this legislation, funds were appropriated by the respective Boards of Supervisors, for carrying on the work. The Board consists of twelve *ex officio* members, designated by law, including the Mayors of the six cities of Erie and Niagara Counties and three members of the Boards of Supervisors of each county. The thirteenth member is chosen by the Board and acts as its Chairman.

The area which constitutes this District is about 1 556 sq. miles, extending from Lake Ontario on the north, to Cattaraugus Creek on the south, the Niagara River and Lake Erie on the west, and the county lines on the east, covering a distance of 60 miles north and south and 25 miles east and west, and containing 6 cities, 22 villages, and 37 townships.

Several commercial and industrial centers are located within this District, Buffalo being the largest, with Niagara Falls next, at a distance of 18 miles northwest. Tonawanda and North Tonawanda lie midway between, with Lockport in the northeastern section and Lackawanna bordering on the southern boundary of Buffalo. A portion of Canada contiguous to the Niagara River and lying to the west is also considered in close relationship to this area and planning is being developed to connect it with proposed structures crossing the Niagara River.

The District is divided, by the topography of the land, into four distinct natural sub-divisions: First, the table-land at the north, bordering on Lake Ontario, and extending with a gradual rise in elevation to the Lewiston Escarpment. This section is known as the "Niagara Fruit Belt," being devoted

* Chf. Engr., Niagara Frontier Planning Board, Tonawanda, N. Y.

largely to fruit growing, but with extensive general farming. At the escarpment, the elevation rises rather abruptly from an average of 400 ft. above sea level on the lower table-land to another elevation of 600 ft., running gradually to the south over a considerable area about 800 ft. In this second section are the six thriving cities and a network of railroads, highways, and navigable waters, and within which the tremendous development of the region is largely confined. The third division comprises rolling uplands with elevations from 800 to 1 200 ft., devoted to the dairy industry and general farming; while the fourth division, the extreme southern portion of the District, is fairly mountainous in character, rising to an elevation of 1 900 ft. above sea level. Although some portions of this hilly country are not easily accessible, it contributes liberally to the food supply of the District and also affords recreational facilities, forest preserves, and natural scenery.

While the outline made for obtaining data in this District does not conform exactly with that presented by Mr. Lewis, it carries the same general provisions. It is essential, also, to determine how the information that is collected is to be used in preparing a regional plan.

An accurate base map was first prepared on a scale of 1 in. to the mile, made from the U. S. Geological Survey Sheets, showing highways, railroads, waterways, parks, boundaries of political sub-divisions, and contours at 100-ft. intervals. The size of this map is 42 by 72 in. Base maps of the District were also prepared on a scale of 1 in. equals 2 miles and 1 in. equals 4 miles. Both these scales were used for mapping statistical data in relation to population, valuations, highways, transportation, and traffic. Maps of the cities and villages were prepared on a scale of 1 in. equals 600 ft. and of townships on a scale of 1 in. equals 2 000 ft., these being used for the purpose of more detailed studies in regard to the various communities.

The function of this Planning Board is not only to study the District as a whole, but to devote considerable attention to community planning as well, organizing local planning bodies to carry out the work of their own political sub-division. Due to the fact that this District has only been organized for about a year, most of the time has been spent on the physical survey, mapping the data in regard to topography, boundaries, population, highways, transportation facilities, parks and parkways, water supply, and sewage disposal. This information has been assembled in such a manner and extent as to enable some definite recommendations to be made on problems that have already been developed and require immediate consideration. Detailed plans have been prepared for the purpose of making some of the necessary developments.

Because of the National and International reputation of this District, visited by more than 1 000 000 tourists every year, great importance is placed on the scenic wonders as well as the other available natural resources which include water power and waterway transportation.

One of the most noteworthy projects recently planned, is that of a Regional Parkway System, which will ultimately be developed along the Niagara River. There is located in the Niagara River an island of 28 sq. miles, called Grand Island, lying adjacent to the most rapidly developing section of the District. A straight line drawn from the center of Buffalo to the center of Niagara

Falls, passes through the middle of this large undeveloped area. It seems very desirable to connect this area with the mainland. The construction of two bridges and a highway, crossing diagonally across Grand Island, will shorten the distance between Buffalo and Niagara Falls about 4 miles. It will then be possible to develop a parkway, about 6 miles long, on the western side of the island along the Niagara River. This parkway can be made to connect with the New York State Reservation at Niagara, and the parkway system laid out in and adjacent to Buffalo, thereby forming not only a link in the State Parkway System, but affording a beautiful driveway between the two largest communities. It will ultimately be extended northward along the Niagara River from Niagara Falls to Lake Ontario and southward through Erie County, passing to the east of Buffalo and connecting with Allegany and Letchworth State Parks.

Another project of regional importance recently completed is a highway bridge known as the "Peace Bridge," across the Niagara River at Buffalo to Fort Erie, Ont., Canada. The American terminus of this bridge is in one of the large city water-front parks, which is connected by parkways with the Buffalo Park System, while the Canadian terminus joins a parkway about 25 miles in length, extending northward along the shore of Niagara River to Niagara Falls and Queenstown, where bridges now cross to the American side. The New York State Parkway previously mentioned, is planned so as to make a river drive from Lewiston to Buffalo, comparable with the improvement so admirably carried out by the Park Commission in Canada.

It is impossible in this brief discussion, to elaborate on the work done either in preparing for planning this Region, or the inestimable value of the data already obtained. As the work of gathering the necessary information proceeds, it will be found that the paper presented by Mr. Lewis, will be a guide in obtaining results more efficiently than heretofore, and that other regions will profit greatly by the experience of the planners for New York and Its Environs.

ARTHUR A. SHURTLEFF,* ESQ. (by letter).—This paper is sufficiently complete to be considered a good example of the kind of data which the engineer of to-day should collect for a great metropolitan area. Some data which at present are considered novel, will become, in later years, a matter of routine. Water supply and sewage disposal were novelties seventy-five years ago. Electric service was a novelty recently, and good motor traffic accommodation is a novelty now.

The writer hazards an opinion regarding one of the new problems that city planners will be forced to consider during the next two or three decades. By that time, it is to be hoped, the accommodation of vehicular transportation will have become fairly commonplace. Architectural excellence undoubtedly will be more general then; and better living and working conditions may be expected. Standardization of these more perfect things, however, will tend to create uniformity, which, on a vast scale, will become objectionable in itself.

* Landscape Archt., Boston, Mass.

Objectionable uniformity is something more than that which merely bores. It is a uniformity which becomes actively oppressive when repeated endlessly, mile after mile, no matter how complete or how attractive the objects may be in themselves. Beginnings of depressing uniformity of excellent things are to be seen in the central portion of the City of New York, and of less excellent things in the Everett-Chelsea-Somerville Districts of Boston, Mass. These depressing uniformities hurt the pleasantness of cities and, to that extent, threaten the continued earning power of the vast sums of money invested in great metropolitan regions, and they hurt the spirit of men.

The era is passing when a great city can hold out unique attractions of a compelling kind to the dweller in country districts. There was a time when great cities were maintained, in spite of heavy death rates, by the influx of families and workers from villages and farms seeking the city on account of its novelties, shelter, culture, entertainments, and its opportunities for social intercourse and employment. To-day, that situation is slowly tending to reverse. The urge from the great cities toward the suburbs and toward the villages is becoming stronger with the development of cheap transportation, with the growth of large isolated industrial plants, with the general provision of schools and hospitals, and with the facilities for ready construction of homes equipped with "modern improvements" of extraordinary completeness. Opportunities for recreation in natural surroundings are also acting as a strong urge toward the towns.

Parks have been built in cities to provide an opportunity to enjoy recreation in rural surroundings. However, parks in great metropolitan cities are gradually assuming a new and exceedingly valuable rôle quite aside from recreation spaces. The mere existence of areas of open ground covered with trees and grass is becoming an enormous asset in breaking up the monotony of great city areas. In most metropolitan cities, strips of vacant private land still remain between the smaller integral cities and towns and give these centers sufficient local separation to save their individuality from complete eclipse in the great fabric of buildings and streets. When town after town becomes closely knitted to its neighbor, as, for example, the Dorchester-Roxbury District, of Boston, and the Brooklyn region, of Greater New York, the entity of villages and towns becomes lost. The resulting monotonous repetition of street upon street and building upon building appals the human spirit and cannot be ameliorated by perfection of transportation, excellence of architecture, street trees, or perfect housing and attractive employment, because each of these good things tends toward its own endless repetitions.

The time is fast approaching when metropolitan regions must include in their budgets monies for the maintenance of large areas of open ground distributed in long strips or winding bands throughout the built-up area to relieve monotony of this kind, quite aside from the recreational value which the ground or the landscapes, contained in such strips, may possess. Vast appropriations for metropolitan thoroughfares are common. Expenditures as great, or greater, for the acquisition of open spaces required to safeguard metropolitan areas from depreciation in value, through an intolerable increase in monotony resulting from too continuous up-building, are destined to become as common.

In coming years engineers will devote much time to the mapping and classification of vacant lands on the outskirts of cities and towns which are being absorbed in metropolitan districts. Much study will be needed to decide what land shall be saved for permanent strips or bands of open ground; its extent; its relation to the topography of hills and stream courses and lowlands; its contact with adjacent boundary streets and transportation routes; and the most favorable time for its acquisition. Evidently, these strips must be wider, or closer together, in cities which lack varied topography than in those the sites of which are naturally diversified.

The purpose of these costly public acquisitions will be the same as that for which even greater sums are being spent in private enterprises for the mere embellishment of office buildings, stores, factories, and residences; namely, to secure attractive appearance. In these times, not to secure attractive appearance in great private undertakings, means the risk of jeopardizing all the money invested. Mere structural strength, convenience, and comfort are not enough to meet the approval of the public.

The same approval must be reckoned with in great metropolitan areas. Mere convenience of transportation, beauty of buildings, excellence of light and air conditions, absence of confusion in building heights and uses, opportunities for amusement, recreation, and employment, will not be enough to satisfy the man who is enmeshed too completely by walls and streets. He will demand freedom from depressing monotony, or he will go where he can find it, readily and cheaply, in the small city or town the call of which is becoming clearer and stronger each decade.

Metropolitan areas need the most intelligent study and watchfulness which men can apply to them to prevent this call from becoming destructive in its consequences, either to the great treasure of money and culture which is contained in them or to the human beings, counted by millions, who depend on the city as the environment of body and spirit.

Hale J. Walker,* Esq.—In looking over this paper one is impressed by the scope of the outline. Every kind of necessary survey information would certainly find its place somewhere in the various and broad sub-heads.

A definition of "open spaces" would probably be as follows: All types of land, public, semi-public, and private, for the most part not built up in the third dimension, which gives to the region permanent breathing spaces. They have been described by some city planners as the "lungs of the city". Under "open spaces", information should be gathered, giving the location of all public lands, such as parks, parkways, and recreational areas, institutions (Government, State, County and City), town forests, airplane landings, waterways (rivers, lakes, ponds, creeks, swamps, reservoirs, and their catchment areas), and the location of public utilities requiring open space.

In gathering survey material the tendency has been to collect information on all public open spaces and to neglect semi-public and private open spaces.

* Town and City Planner, Cambridge, Mass.

Included under this heading then, will be information giving the location of semi-public and private open spaces that promise permanence, such as private schools and colleges, hospitals, sanitariums, cemeteries, churches, institutions, golf courses and country clubs, boat clubs, airplane landings, fair grounds, historic monuments and sites, commercial amusement parks, professional baseball fields, and swimming pools. There should also be noted that region of large country estates which could be made an effective open space by zoning. Some of the larger industries also furnish this type of open space. A large acreage is often required by gasoline and oil storage companies, furnishing an open space of sorts, but still a factor in the calculation of population density and in determining the character of future built-up areas. Information collected under the other sub-heads may also furnish material for open spaces—existing or proposed.

The topographical plan shows the basic physical features, such as mountains, lakes, forests, and other areas with strong topographical characteristics difficult of changing by the hand of man and particularly adaptable for park use. The mapping of population distribution also bears a direct relation to this subject. There might be added under this heading a collection of data on soil conditions and the mapping of existing agricultural lands. Agricultural belts and wedges have been recommended by city planners as breathing spaces for a large city or metropolitan region. Perhaps since, at present, city planners have no power to zone land to agricultural use, this type of open space may not seem very permanent. Nevertheless, the planner, in some cases, should consider land particularly adaptable for agricultural purposes as an open space, and design his region so as to discourage sub-division and to encourage truck gardening and agricultural pursuits. In designing agricultural land for this purpose, perhaps more intensive development of the area can be held off until it can be legally adopted for agricultural use.

The question of control of private open spaces makes the use of this information a somewhat hazardous problem in the design of a region. Of the list of private open spaces, colleges and cemeteries seem to be the most permanent. The first might fall under Mr. Lewis' heading, "Recreation." The latter holds a doubtful position. It might be considered as a park, but properly it falls under the heading of sanitation. There are instances in California where cemeteries have been re-designed for park purposes. A new type of cemetery is also being designed with park drives, gravestones and monuments being prohibited, so that the finished product is essentially a park. It is not uncommon to find park systems in Eastern cities linked up with cemetery drives.

Scope of Planning Proposals.—The collection of survey material for a certain region will be influenced and guided by the aims and purposes of the designer or designers. Preliminary investigations will bring out the needs of the region and, to a certain degree, the extent of the planning proposals. The scope of planning proposals covering the general topics which are normally included in a regional planning program will guide the collector of survey data so that there will be less chance of gathering data "which will remain buried in the files".

The following outline was prepared for a county regional plan:

SCOPE OF PLANNING PROPOSAL.*

I.—Planning Services.—

(*a*) Preliminary Investigation:

A field investigation or local survey, by the planner and his associates, of the physical features, economic factors, social conditions, customs, and public opinion of the county, county seat, other towns and cities, and adjoining region.

(*b*) County Planning:

(1) Circulation: Lines of communication.

(*a*) Highways:

Comprehensive Highway System: Main highways (State and County); secondary roads; minor or local roads; special drives and boulevards; bridges.

Transportation: Buses; bus stations; trucking; trucking terminals.

Suggested Road Improvements: Widenings, extensions; new roads.

Highways and Road Sections: Roadway widths; planting spaces.

Highway and Road Intersections: Study of important highway and road intersections.

Study of Special Problems in Relation to Highway Traffic.

Development of Highway Views.

Highway and Road Decoration: Lighting equipment; trees and shrubs; paving of roadways; removal of unsightly poles, wires, and signs.

(*b*) Railroads: The Place of the Railroads: Tracks, main lines, local lines, belt lines; stations—passenger, freight; grade crossings and grade eliminations; relation to present and future agricultural, horticultural, and industrial output.

(*c*) Water: Harbor and waterway terminals.

(*d*) Air Terminals: Selection of sites; requirements.

(2) Allocation of Areas for Appropriate Uses:

(*a*) Industry: Type of industrial development to best interest of the county; most appropriate areas.

(*b*) Areas for Colored Population: Present locations; probable future needs.

(*c*) Development of Water-Front (Ocean, River, Creeks, Ponds, or Lakes): Public and private use of shore land; residence; recreation; industry; commerce.

(*d*) Regulation of Land Sub-Division: Methods of securing proper development; acceptance of plats.

(3) Open Spaces:

(*a*) Parks and Parkways: Development of Parks and Parkways: Water-front parks; bird and game sanctuaries; neighborhood, or community parks;

* Covering the general topics which are normally included in a regional planning program. The scope of the proposal, of course, would have to be modified to some extent to meet local conditions.

(3) Open Spaces (*Continued*):

large parks, incorporating natural features as woodland of the region; connecting parkways and boulevards; promenades; park connections; small open spaces.

Linking up Parkways with City Systems.

Correlation of Open Spaces.

The Effect of Parks on Land Values.

(4) Schools:

(*a*) Standard Requirements for School Sites: Grade schools; junior high schools; senior high schools; agricultural schools; special schools and colleges.

(5) Recreation:

(*a*) Requirements of Permanent Population: Possibilities in Recreation: Playgrounds; county golf courses; athletic fields; swimming pools; beaches; piers; sailing and motor boating.

(6) County Building Sites:

Location of Buildings Important to the County.

Advantages of Grouping of County Buildings.

Possible Sites for Administration and Resort Buildings, such as county court house; county auditorium; agricultural hall; county library; branch libraries; county fair grounds; county agricultural experimental stations; county institutions, alms, etc.; county fish hatcheries; aquariums; county jail; county dock; county railroad shipping centers; citrus exchange; municipal cultural centers for farmers.

II.—Zoning Services within the Area of Jurisdiction.—

(*a*) Preliminary Investigation:

Field investigation by the planner and his associates of the present use of land, density of population, height of structures, and public opinion of the county.

(*b*) Zone Plan:

Use Districts: Business; industry; residential built areas; agriculture.

Height Districts.

Area Districts.

(*c*) Zone Ordinance.

III.—Report.—

Typewritten report, with illustrations, setting forth the recommendations and supplementing the studies and plans. Overseeing printing of report for distribution.

IV.—Schedule of Plans.—

(*a*) Existing Conditions Map:

Showing the following: Highways; roads; parks; parkways; schools; playgrounds; public property; railroad facilities; industrial areas.

(A record of existing conditions at commencement of work and basic map for planning studies.)

(*b*) General Planning Study:
Outlines in a broad way the planning proposals.

(*c*) Preliminary Zone Study:
Preliminary districting for various uses of land, height of buildings, and area to be built upon.

(*d*) Study of Major Roads and Highways.

(*e*) Highway and Road Sections:
Suggesting appropriate widths of roadways, walks, and planting strips for the various types of streets.

(*f*) Zone Plan:
Showing proposals for use of land.

(*g*) Major Roads and Highways Plan.

(*h*) Parks and Recreation Areas Plan:
Showing all parks, parkways, boulevards, playgrounds, and park connections.

(*i*) Comprehensive Regional Plan:
Master plan of all proposals. Guide to all future developments.

(*j*) Sketches of Details:
Selected sketches necessary to supplement the general plans.

JOSEPH W. SHIRLEY,* ESQ.—It is evident that the author has given the subject of the requirements for a regional plan much real study, and has completely covered all the essential points. This is highly desirable.

Most cities are not so fortunate as the City of New York in having an organization such as the Russell Sage Foundation, which has been planned to conduct this and other similar investigations. In the majority of cities one great difficulty is to arouse public interest in a study of this kind and to secure funds, either by private subscription or from the public treasury, with which to conduct the investigations.

In the preparation of such a report, great care should be exercised that it be made in a practical, common-sense way, readily understandable to the layman who is not familiar with technicalities. It should not be filled with scientific matter. Furthermore, when the whole problem is presented, its immensity should not be such as to stagger the public and make it hesitate to carry out the recommendations. Another feature not to be overlooked is the item of time. Every one will admit the danger of continuing investigations over such a long period that when the time comes to act much of the information collected has already become out of date.

The data needed, as specified by Mr. Lewis, are highly desirable, but it does seem that each community must modify this information to serve its own needs, bearing in mind not only the appropriations required for the preparation of the report, but also whether the community can stand the expense in carrying out some of the ideals that engineers believe cities should have. After all, is not the public concerned with what is actually to be accomplished as a result of these exhaustive reports? So many cities have been "fed up" with elaborate reports on city planning, traffic, and other features that the

* Engr. of Plans and Surveys, Dept. of Public Works, Baltimore, Md.

inevitable outcome has been to shelve them after large amounts of money have been paid in their preparation. To put it plainly, it means to fit the plan to the pocketbook of the city.

It has only been within comparatively few years that the American public has been interested in city planning. Regional planning is justified by the results which have been obtained, even in these very few years, by proper city planning. However, almost as much missionary work will be needed to convince the community that it should not confine its plans within its present limits, as was necessary to interest it in a study of the area for its own immediate use.

For the collection of general basic data, it is fortunate for the people of this country that such an organization as the Russell Sage Foundation has been established. Much of the information gained by its exhaustive studies, a single community could not afford to collect for itself. The information concerning:

"(*a*) Highway capacities under different conditions
"(*b*) Recreation space requirement standards
"(*c*) Length of haul of motor vehicles and transit lines
"(*d*) Standards of population and housing density
"(*e*) Variation in riding habit on transit lines
"(*f*) Model plans for a neighborhood unit"

outlined by Mr. Lewis, could be accepted by every municipality making a regional study if this information is available to those who desire it.

One of the essential things which should be done by any city contemplating city or regional planning is to supply itself with a thoroughly reliable and complete topographic map. If the regional area is large, a map on the scale of 1 mile to the inch would serve very well. If that area is small, a larger scale map would be more desirable. The making of the proper kind of topographic map is expensive, but this is an expense which cannot be avoided. If there are no U. S. Geological Survey maps, or State maps, available the general map of the smaller scale can often be obtained at a relatively low cost from an aerial survey. These aerial maps can be enlarged and topography added in various neighborhoods as needed. In studies in Baltimore, Md., it has been found, where detail is necessary, that a topographic map on the scale of 200 ft. to the inch works out very well. This scale is small enough to place the situation on a workable size sheet, at the same time covering a large area. From this scale map, work can be carefully planned and many calculations made.

For information concerning population and future distribution of population the zoning maps of the city are very useful. In some cities, public service companies have compiled much valuable data. Many railroads have perfected plans for their future development which are kept under cover for obvious reasons. An effort should be made to secure the confidence of these companies by those conducting the investigation so as to gain this valuable information.

Let engineers bear in mind that results are wanted and that care must be exercised not to spend too much time in making preliminary studies and elaborate reports.

GUY WILFRID HAYLER,* ASSOC. M. AM. SOC. C. E. (by letter).—This interesting paper opens up a wide vista of the scope and methods necessary for the successful completion of regional planning work. Regional planning is, as Mr. Lewis states, "a complicated piece of work", and the methods of one locality can not, and should not, be necessarily applied to another locality. Every city and every region is entitled to a personality of its own, and it would be deplorable to standardize cities so that they would be more dull and uninviting than they frequently are. While regional planning may be said to be physical in its groundwork and economic in its approach, there is also an underlying factor to be taken into consideration, that is, the recognition of the "soul of the city". This alone can give any plan "the punch" necessary to make it sufficiently appealing to the taxpayers who have to pay the bill.

The basic information needed for regional planning is necessarily limited by the amount of money that can be expended on research and the personnel of those engaged in the studies. Then, again, the treatment of the subject by an unofficial organization will be different from that of an official authority. From the point of view of research it might be doubted if an unofficial body could do as well as an official body, but there would most certainly be an advantage offered by the former in that it could explore into many unknown fields, initiate new methods, and display greater originality. From this point of view the methods of the New York Regional Plan seem likely to establish many definite features which any regional plans of the future will be obliged to consider. It is very fortunate that the New York plan is being undertaken by such an important body as the Russell Sage Foundation which is National in scope and has considerable funds to prosecute its work. This should stand out as a significant fact to other localities proposing to do regional planning work and proclaim to them that a large sum of money is really necessary and the most highly trained experts are required, if studies and recommendations for regional development worthy of the name, are to result. The greatest failure of city planning in America has been due to the large number of communities that have started on the work with insufficient funds and negligible personnel, resulting in apathy in a very short time and no appreciable record of progress. Unless energetic city planning bodies are operating throughout a region, an all-inclusive planning body for that region is faced with a herculean task. If cities do meet the regional planning body half way, it is surely possible to eliminate many municipal problems and devote the time and money to the better purpose of establishing the wider co-ordination. It is necessary to think of regional planning from this angle if any foundation is to be established for the basic information. Of course, it is assumed that such regional planning is proposed in regions that are fairly well settled and comprise at least one large town or city as a center and scattered towns or suburbs in its sphere of influence. Assuming then, that a reasonable amount of money can be guaranteed over a period of years, and that a number of qualified men are available to undertake research and planning work, the general basic principles can be formulated.

* Planning Engr., Regional Plan Assoc., Inc., for San Francisco Bay Counties, San Francisco, Calif.

The Regional Plan Association of San Francisco Bay Counties has been in existence since 1924 and operates in a district composed of towns and cities of a strong individual character with a surprisingly small civic outlook as the city planner sees it. It has, therefore, been a matter largely of pioneering, where the education of the people comes first, and with it, the grouping of those anxious to undertake the formulation of a wide comprehensive plan. Under these circumstances progress is necessarily slow, and internal city problems which should be outside the general scope of regional planning are first in consideration, owing to the fact that there are no local organizations offering the technical help required. This may be an inevitable situation and it requires some ingenuity to prevent the wider vision from being obscured.

Coming to the matter of finance which is a limitation to research and to anything else, the San Francisco Bay Regional Plan Association has been fortunate in securing the active co-operation of Mr. Fred Dohrmann, Jr., a well-known Pacific Coast merchant, who has undertaken to carry the financial burden until the work has been established. This period is now (1926) drawing to a close as the organization is establishing itself in the nine counties surrounding the Bay. This splendid piece of civic patriotism has enabled the technical groundwork to be laid, together with a commencement on base maps, survey reports, and the promotion of several features of a regional plan.

The work has been built up by establishing the sectional elements of the research required. These are: (1) statistical; (2) streets and highways and traffic; (3) transportation; (4) harbor and water-front; (5) industries; (6) housing; (7) public utilities; (8) public health and safety; (9) education; (10) parks and recreation; and (11) agricultural resources.

While in the main this is understood to be a physical survey, the economic and social sides will be covered in the detailed "working out" of the elements of each particular section, together with the legal and financial aspects. A regional plan may be said to be in essence the ideal plan, and it must be practicable, legally and financially as well as physically, to complete it satisfactorily. Laws, however, can be changed and will be changed if the authorities and the people see that it is to their advantage to change them and, in that sense, the legal side may be said to be of an ephemeral character. Finance, as it is involved in the cost of public improvements and methods of assessment, is also largely a matter of legal enactment once the reasonableness of the cost of improvements is recognized.

In the San Francisco Bay District the sub-divisions of research before mentioned are probably the minimum in extent and yet cover the area of regional development with the least waste of time and money in collecting, verifying, and putting into form the data and suggested improvements. There is no object gained in spending valuable time and money over facts and statistics that are not necessary to prove points at issue, because such facts and statistics are generally obtainable from their original sources by any one who may wish to use them. The writer considers charts embracing the main points of research to be studied as one of the most useful elements in developing planning data and would advocate the wide use of colored pencils on maps used in the field. In the hands of qualified men this will insure a cer-

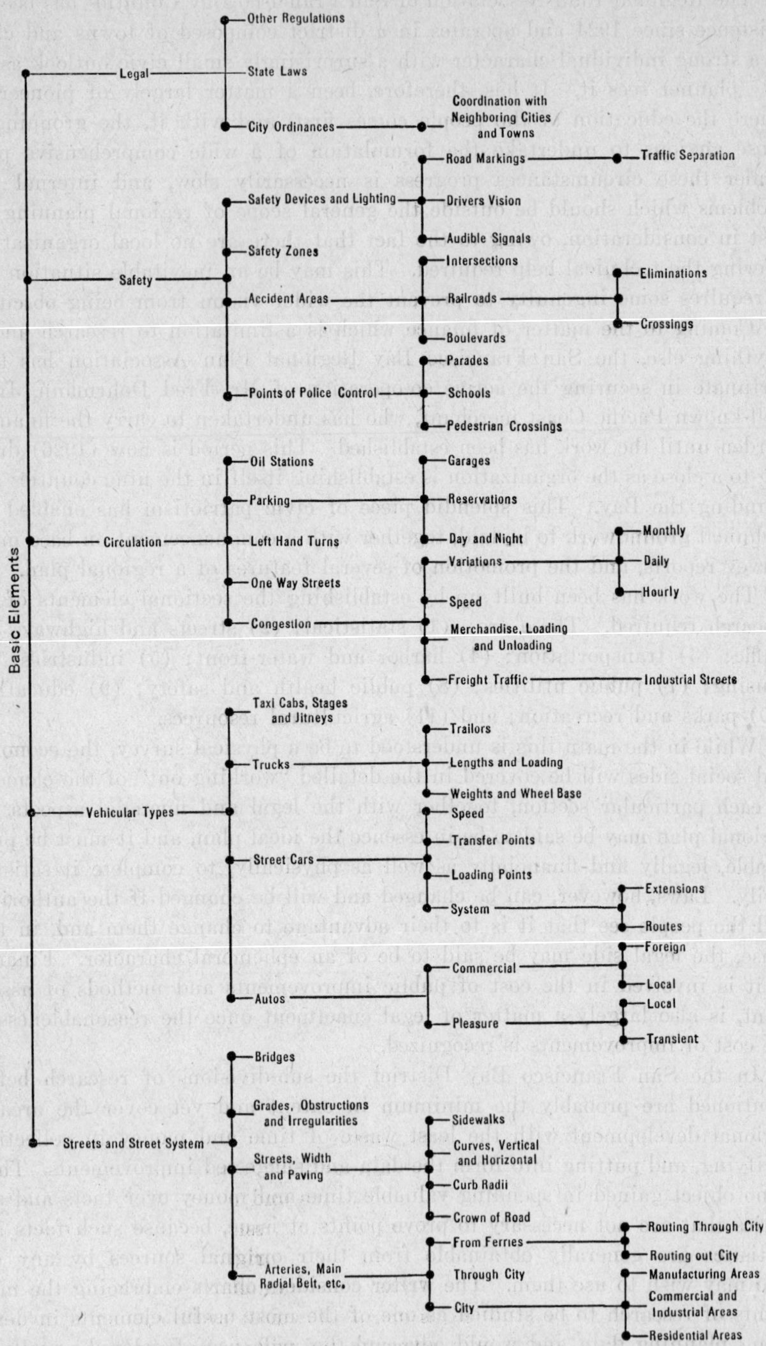

FIG. 3.—OUTLINE OF A CITY TRAFFIC SURVEY.

tain standardized method of gathering the data. When the latter reach the central office, they can then be readily transferred to base maps, office files, and special scrapbooks covering the various subjects.

The regional planner will probably be faced with the possibility of altering many existing maps so as to secure a uniform scale and he is then concerned with the best size of map to use. It is obviously impossible to lay down any particular size for this purpose, but the San Francisco Association has found it convenient to use a map measuring 4 ft. 3 in. by 3 ft. 4 in., covering the area within a 50-mile radius and drawn to a scale of 2 miles to 1 in. All smaller maps will bear some relationship in size to these foregoing maps. The technical details of map preparation have been so thoroughly devised by the organization responsible for the Regional Plan of New York that very little can be said to amplify them. However, as the information obtained will necessarily receive the attention of persons largely unversed in technical details, it is imperative that this fact should be kept in mind. This qualification also applies to the form in which charts of statistics are prepared, and it is desirable that these should be designed on as graphic a basis as possible. The foregoing might be said to apply to an unofficial organization preparing a regional plan, even more than an official body. A danger which must not be overlooked, however, is the stressing of a pictorial method without due attention to its accuracy; this should be avoided. Many misleading charts have been prepared from time to time, attempting to portray trends of development that have been little else than elaborate cartoons, rather than scientific explanations.

It is desirable that the basic information, as it is gathered, should be grouped in the political sub-divisions of the region where the least difference in boundaries has taken place over a wide period of years. This will prevent the overlapping of information and confusion of statistics. The best way to begin gathering this information is to prepare as large a number of maps as possible that will show the political sub-divisions of counties, towns, cities, and other administrative districts, and the variation of boundaries with time. Once this fundamental is established, an unassailable basis is made for statistics and contemporary conditions. As an example of a definite outline for attacking a problem, the writer has prepared what he considers are the fundamental considerations for a city traffic survey which will need little further elaboration to cover a region (see Fig. 3). Such an outline of requirements should be prepared for the study of each problem and in drawing them, a wide local knowledge on the part of some one is required to lay down, tentatively, the main points.

In conclusion, the writer would like to emphasize the element of time in all that appertains to city and regional planning. While there need be no undue haste, it is obvious that statistics and information, once they are gathered, rapidly become old and are affected by other elements that may develop from time to time. If they are to be of any use, and if the plan is to show itself as a live, wide-awake, aggressive piece of public work, time should be considered in every stage of the proceedings. If this is done the heavy labor of research will be felt to have achieved some reward and indeed the final success of improvements recommended will be much nearer fulfillment.

WILLIAM BOWIE,* M. AM. SOC. C. E.—The function of the surveyor is to make his computed positions, his maps, and his plans useful to other engineers. His province is to supply exact knowledge of the terrain, in place of approximations and guesswork.

They are facing a heavy responsibility who are studying the physical needs of modern cities and who are directing the enunciation of the principles which bear directly on a city's growth and on the activities of its citizens. Exact knowledge is no handicap to a city planner, even when he is dealing with such general questions as street and park layouts and suburban communications. The laws of urban growth and development are imperfectly understood, and it is possible that a close study of detailed topographic conditions will reveal influences to which much consideration must be given.

The fiscal ally of the city planner, the tax assessor, can be easily persuaded of the value of an accurate cadastral survey which will show, in convenient form, all taxable real estate and the improvements thereon. Many instances are known where the increase in the taxable real property, disclosed by an accurate and complete city survey, has paid for the survey and left a considerable margin. The city planner and the city engineer need not show, in dollars and cents, the value of an accurate survey to their own particular activities.

The problem then, for the surveyor, is to furnish a survey with its resultant maps, plans, elevations, and positions which will serve the purposes of the city planner, the city engineer, the tax assessor, and all the general engineering interests of the modern city.

HOWARD STRONG,† ESQ.—In the discussion of this paper, two extremes, perhaps, have been presented—one represented in a degree by the New York position; the other possibly by the Chicago method. The one would subordinate or even entirely disregard the various specific projects that may be before the region and would devote its entire attention to the studies preliminary to the making of a definite plan. The other seems to subordinate the surveys and studies in preparation for the plan and to emphasize the promotion of specific projects. There is a possible danger in either one of these extremes, even if, as in the case of the New York Regional Plan, finances are ample to go ahead with the making of studies and plans without regard to the attitude of the region.

If too much time is given to the making of the plan, and the actual planning accomplishment is entirely neglected for a number of years, it seems likely that the interest, enthusiasm, and support of the people in the region, upon whom, after all, depends the adoption of the plan, is likely to be lost. On the other hand, if too much emphasis is put on the project method, the picture is likely to get out of perspective, and the projects, themselves, will not be properly articulated in the general scheme.

It is certainly necessary to retain public support and, for that reason, some attention must be given to programs in which the people have an

* Chf., Div. of Geodesy, U. S. Coast and Geodetic Survey, Washington, D. C.

† Secy. Director, Regional Planning Federation, Philadelphia, Pa.

immediate interest. At the same time, the plan itself, which, after all, is the principal business in hand, must not be neglected. The only solution that will develop an adequate plan and, at the same time, will retain the interest of the people who must ultimately accept the plan, is a nice balance between the two extremes.

Charles W. Eliot, 2d,* Esq.—In Washington, D. C., the National Capital Park and Planning Commission is generally following the program laid down by Mr. Lewis in his most interesting paper; but there are two exceptions.

In the first place, he suggests that the first step in regional planning work should be the definition of a boundary. The Commission has carefully avoided setting any limits, and is going to avoid it as long as possible because it feels that the extent of the influence of the Capital City is a very indeterminate factor and something that will bear a great deal of study before any such limit is set.

In the second place, it has departed from the suggestions in regard to "open spaces". In Washington, a different set of indications are used from those suggested by Mr. Lewis. The idea has been to indicate areas withdrawn from urban occupation. That includes both private and public areas in very much the same way that Mr. Walker has outlined, but it is, perhaps, a little more accurate definition of "open spaces" than just those two words.

The City of Washington was very fortunate in the equipment that was available at the start for planning work. The U. S. Geological Survey, the U. S. Coast and Geodetic Survey, and the Air Service have made a great many studies and many maps of the Washington region. The basic maps, drawn to a scale of ½ mile to the inch are found to be entirely satisfactory. For more detailed studies, there are remarkably accurate maps of the District of Columbia at 400-ft. scale and general street maps at 1 600-ft. and 1 000-ft. scales.

In most regional planning work the studies are entirely separate from the city planning studies; but, in Washington, that is impossible, because the National Capital Park and Planning Commission has particular executive functions in the District of Columbia. It has the power and money to purchase land for parks and it has the guardianship of the "Highway Plan", which controls the platting of sub-divisions. Congress has seen fit to give it power to make regional studies, but it is forced constantly to meet immediate problems of design and planning within the District of Columbia. Although the attempt is made to keep the regional planning studies in a fluid state while data are being collected, the Commission is constantly having to make decisions in the District of Columbia that affect the regional plan. That is another reason why it is trying to keep the boundaries of its region somewhat indefinite because there is no knowing how far immediate decisions are going to influence the regional plan. Admitted that this method of going at the work is unfortunate—to have to be controlled by immediate decisions—that is the state of affairs.

Regional planners in Washington are grateful for the work that has been done in New York and particularly for Mr. Lewis' helpful suggestions; and

* City Planner, National Capital Park and Planning Comm., Washington, D. C.

hope, if they can get the co-operation of engineers, landscape architects, and all others interested in city planning, to be able to produce a plan, for the National Capital and the region around Washington, that will be a serviceable guide for the growth of that community and an inspiration for the remainder of the country.

U. N. Arthur,* Esq.—Among the various outstanding problems confronting the great centers of population probably none is of greater moment than the development of a comprehensive plan. Regional planning, being still in its infancy, will measure its accomplishments by the basic principles governing the method of attack. Therefore, it is fortunate, indeed, to have the subject outlined as clearly and concisely as in this paper.

A finer opportunity is afforded for the planning of the large area of a region or district than that of city areas. This follows from the fact that, before any attempt had been made at scientific city planning, the area within the incorporated city limits was often largely platted and sufficiently developed to make impracticable any radical change in the system of major thoroughfares, parks, playgrounds, etc., while, for regional work, large areas are often open and susceptible of being properly planned to care for the various factors essential to the growth of the community.

While there can be no question as to the wisdom of supplying the various types of data suggested by Mr. Lewis, it might be well to emphasize the necessity of securing the basic physical, or land, facts of the area before any concentrated effort is made to produce a regional plan.

The three fundamental factors with which a community of any size has to deal, are: (*a*) The land it occupies; (*b*) the people that dwell in the land; and, (*c*) the social and industrial development. The other factors influencing the study and development of the plan are: First, general information; second, provision for making changes easily; and, third, means for accomplishing the final object—the plan.

The willingness with which planners often accept general information as sufficient for planning purposes has been a principal source of criticism. Often the weak points in a finally submitted plan are exposed to the attack of critics who claim that all planners are dreamers and that money expended on the study and development of a city or regional plan is money wasted. The exigencies of the case often require that the broader the extent and scope of the planning operation, the more generalized is the information secured. Such information, spread too thin, means vague information, which is frequently deceptive and leads to the development of plans that are impractical and expensive and often cast doubt on the honest intent and purpose of the planner.

It is a truism that, in most cases, the sites of cities and present centers of population were not selected because the physical surroundings were adaptable to easy development, but because of the existence of important crossroads; or because of the transportation facilities afforded by navigable rivers; or because of natural harbor and port facilities. Such situations often have

* Chf. Engr., Pittsburgh Planning Comm., Pittsburgh, Pa.

immediate surrounding topography of the most rugged nature. It seems, therefore, that, in the first analysis, basic information is the securing of physical facts relating to the land—geodetic, geologic, and topographic. It is true that at the initial conception of most planning undertakings, ample funds have not been available for securing the engineering data so essential to the proper and economic completion of the work. However, if those data were properly evaluated and their importance recognized, in most cases, provision would be made for assembling them as a part of the planning program and as the logical first step toward real planning progress. The first fundamental consideration with which any community has to deal, is the land it occupies. It is not only the first, but it is perpetual. Bridges and viaducts may be built across rivers and valleys; hills may be tunneled; extensive grading operations may be carried out; but regardless of the magnitude of these engi-

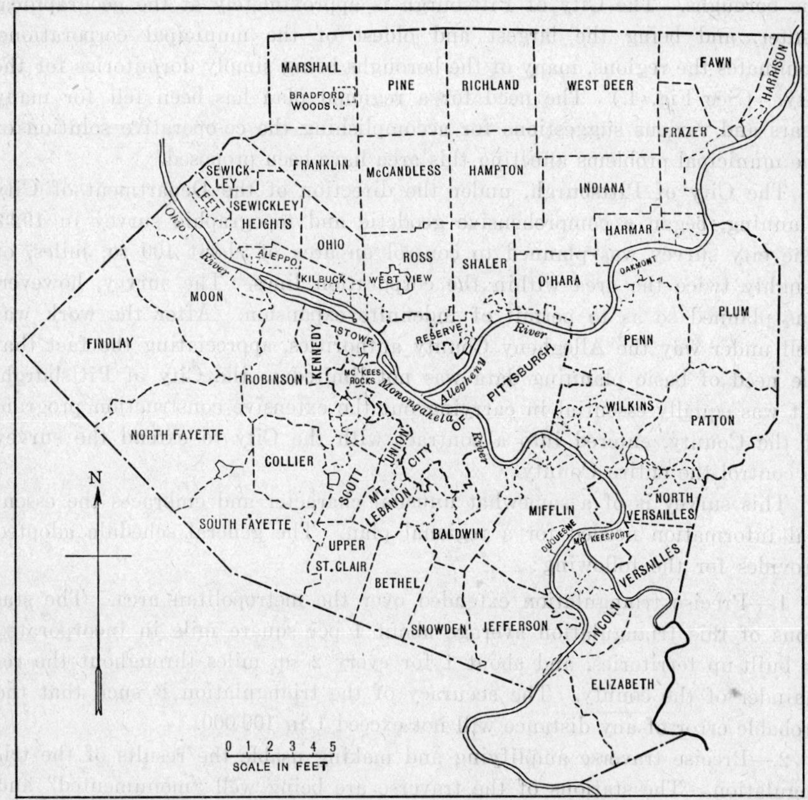

FIG. 4.—MAP OF ALLEGHENY COUNTY, PENNSYLVANIA.

neering feats, the terrain is altered only to an insignificant degree. Whatever be the location of the site, that it remains. The social, economic, and industrial development of the location and the chances for the existence and happiness of the population depend exclusively on the logical and scientific development of the site.

The basic physical, or land, facts are, and always will be, unavoidable. If they are ignored during the planning stage of any undertaking, they will be encountered during the construction stage. Disregarding these facts results in experimental building, and the structure (street, bridge, viaduct, tunnel, public building, sewer, etc.) that does not satisfactorily meet the physical conditions is inevitably replaced by one that does. Frequently, the cost of relieving one situation that has become insupportable is more than sufficient to have paid for securing basic data to serve the whole region.

As a specific example, illustrating both the necessity for, and economy to be gained by, a regional plan, the speaker believes no better case can be cited than is afforded by Allegheny County, Pennsylvania. This County has an area of 732 sq. miles. Within its boundaries are 4 cities, 70 boroughs, and 51 townships, many of the latter having legislative functions similar to those of the boroughs. The City of Pittsburgh is approximately at the geographical center, and being the largest and oldest of the municipal corporations, dominates the regions, many of the boroughs being simply dormitories for the city. (See Fig. 4.) The need for a regional plan has been felt for many years and various suggestions for accomplishing the co-operative solution of the municipal problems affecting this area have been proposed.

The City of Pittsburgh, under the direction of the Department of City Planning, began a comprehensive geodetic and topographic survey in 1923. The city survey was planned to control an area of about 100 sq. miles, or roughly twice the area within the corporation lines. The survey, however, was planned so as to permit of indefinite expansion. After the work was well under way the Allegheny County authorities, appreciating the fact that the need of basic planning data was not limited to the City of Pittsburgh, but was equally essential in carrying out the extensive construction program of the County, entered into a contract with the City to extend the survey to control the entire County.

This survey is of a somewhat unusual character and embraces the essential information needed for a regional plan. The general schedule adopted provides for the following:

1.—Precise triangulation extended over the metropolitan area. The stations of this triangulation average about 1 per square mile in incorporated or built-up territories, and about 1 for every 2 sq. miles throughout the remainder of the county. The accuracy of the triangulation is such that the probable error of any distance will not exceed 1 in 100 000.

2.—Precise traverse amplifying and making usable the results of the triangulation. The stations of the traverse are being well "monumented" and referenced. They coincide, as far as practicable, with existing property monuments. The traverse will have an accuracy represented by a limiting closing error of 1 in 20 000.

3.—Precise levels with bench-marks established on permanent structures along the routes and on traverse and triangulation monuments.

4.—Topographic sheets of the city area on a scale of 1 in. equals 200 ft.

5.—A property map of the city area on a scale of 1 in. equals 50 ft. This is to be the base map for all departmental information where dimensions are required.

6.—A wall or desk map on a scale of 1 in. equals 1 000 ft., compiled from the data shown on the large-scale topographic maps.

Topographic Survey.—Description.—The topographic map, which is being made of the Pittsburgh Area, is a definite and valuable result of the survey. On it are shown to exact scale and position all streets, roadways, curbs, retaining walls, steam and electric railroads and bridges; public, semi-public, and industrially important buildings; as well as streams, lakes, etc. The conformation and elevation of the surface of the ground are shown by contour lines. From the topographic map grades may be accurately computed, drainage areas may be scaled within a fraction of an acre, and excavation quantities computed. The Pittsburgh map sheets are published on a scale of 1 in. equals 200 ft., with a 2.5 and a 5-ft. contour interval. The datum plane for contour elevations is mean sea level, thus placing the maps on the ultimate datum plane and agreeing with Federal, State, and other maps.

The publication scale of 1 in. equals 200 ft. was adopted as best fitting the conditions imposed, which are:

1.—The map scale must be large enough to indicate clearly and accurately all the information desired.

2.—The scale should bear a definite relation to the accuracy of field measurements, and, since the majority of the positions are located by stadia, and stadia distances are dependable only within 1 ft., the scale should be such that distances may be plotted and scaled to the nearest foot.

3.—The scale of the map must be small enough so that the area covered by any one map sheet would be of such size that ordinary district improvement projects may be covered and studied upon it, without the necessity of assembling and matching the various adjoining sheets.

4.—From an economic standpoint it is desirable to keep the scale as small as possible, in order to decrease the cost of the field work and of reproduction.

While the scale of publication is 200 ft., the field scale, on which the maps are sketched in the field, is 165 ft. The purpose of this is the possible increase in accuracy of scale by the reduction, which is a part of the photographic process of publication, and the sharpening of lettering and other cartographic details and consequent improvement in appearance of the final published copies. It is of further advantage to make the field scale as large as is consistent with stadia methods for the purpose of making enlargements. For instance, it is possible to make a better photographic enlargement to a scale of 100 ft. by using an original copy on a scale of 165 ft., than would be the case if the original were on a 200-ft. scale.

Map Projection.—In deciding on the system of projection to be used on the map sheets, there were four conditions to be considered:

1.—The projection must be such that the maps will always be in correct orientation; that is, the boundaries of each sheet should always be true north and south, east and west, in order that the true azimuth or bearings of any line may be quickly scaled from the map.

2.—The projection should permit of practically indefinite expansion.

3.—In order to be joined correctly and easily to other maps, such as those published by the Federal Government, State, Interstate Commerce Commission, etc., the boundaries of each map sheet should be some even value of latitude and longitude, these values being co-ordinates based on the North American datum.

4.—For ease and simplicity of ordinary distance, bearing, and position computations, the maps should have superimposed upon them a rectangular system of co-ordinates.

Reproduction.—After completion, the field sheet is reproduced in four colors. Cadastral information is shown in black, contours in brown, drainage in blue, and public property in green. The reproductions are to exact scale within the limits of paper expansion, and registration is correct at all points, the allowable registration error being 0.01 in. Two hundred copies on light-weight paper of these four color reproductions are printed on the initial order. In addition, ten copies are printed on "lenora" cloth for use in binding in atlas form. It is also expected that several copies will be secured showing the cadastral information only.

Estimates.—The estimated unit costs for the completed survey are, as follows:

Triangulation:

City area.........$350 per sq. mile, including monuments and computations.

County area.......$300 per sq. mile, including monuments and computations.

Precise Levels:

City area.........$70 per lin. mile, including the setting of benchmarks and computations.

County area.......$60 per lin. mile, including the setting of benchmarks and computations.

Precise Traverse:

City area.........$100 per lin. mile, including monuments and computations.

County area.......$90 per lin. mile, including monuments and computations.

Topography:

City area.........$1 800 per sq. mile, including reproduction.

County area.......$1 500 per sq. mile, including reproduction.

Charles Wellford Leavitt,* M. Am. Soc. C. E. (by letter).—Any one not familiar with the difficulties that have attended the gigantic undertaking of "planning New York and its environs" will find it almost impossible to compare this project with anything in regional planning taken up elsewhere, as there is no gauge that can be used to compare New York with any other city. Mr. Lewis has endeavored to stress this point with which he is perfectly

* Civ. and Landscape Engr. (Charles Wellford Leavitt & Son), New York, N. Y. Mr. Leavitt died on April 22, 1928.

York work. If one were to single out a specific subject for discussion, it might be the question of a base map. The inadequacy of existing maps of particular regions is complete. They just do not exist. In Washington, D. C., as in New York, for instance, it was found necessary to resort to the sheets of the U. S. Geological Survey and with the co-operation of the latter to bring existing information up to date and at a workable scale. The 2 000-ft. scale map used in the New York studies is very desirable and will undoubtedly become more or less standard. The U. S. Geological Survey has just completed a new survey of the Los Angeles, Calif., region at this (2 000-ft.) scale, which is exceptionally good. Where the Geological Survey sheets are not available, or are not up to date, there is an initial and well-nigh insuperable handicap on the work of starting a regional plan. There is even an astounding lack of good topographic maps in cities. One of the by-products of regional planning, as of city planning, will be more and improved topographic maps.

The scope of this subject is inexhaustible. Mr. Lewis includes in his "Physical Survey," "Population—distribution, density and rates of growth", and also mentions that special inquiry has been made of "Standards of Population and Housing Density". This information is of particular importance and should be augmented considerably. To what extent it has been considered in the New York study Mr. Lewis does not indicate, but this will doubtless be found in present or future reports of the Committee. Here, the economic and social surveys overlap the physical. Ultimately, regional planners are going to find out how widely they can disperse a given population (or congest it for that matter) and produce a condition that is both socially desirable and economically sound. This is "basic information" of the greatest importance.

Donald M. Baker,* Assoc. M. Am. Soc. C. E. (by letter).—The author has classified the various types of information necessary for the development of a regional plan as: Physical, economic, social, legal, and financial. He has also outlined an excellent program of securing this information. Emphasis has been placed, however, on the physical data necessary and detailed descriptions are given of the methods of collecting and filing it.

Engineers who are connected with planning work are often apt to place too great emphasis on the physical aspects of planning and not enough on other aspects, particularly the legal and financial. Too many plans and planning reports consist, almost in their entirety, of a physical plan with no discussion of the legal and financial methods of attaining the plan.

Use of property within the planned area can be governed by proper zoning, proper streets and traffic arteries through undeveloped territory may be secured by sub-division control, and housing can be regulated, but the necessary public agencies must be set up with adequate powers to carry out this administrative work. Improvements, such as new or wider streets and parkways, park areas, rapid transit and other transportation lines, can be made, but proper proceedings must be initiated for these improvements, rights of way and easements

* Cons. Engr.; Member, Board of City Planning Commrs., Los Angeles, Calif.

acquired, money must be raised for the payment of costs, and the costs must be prorated on an equitable basis.

Much regional planning work is now done in an advisory way through associations supported by private contribution or the assistance of municipal bodies, but ultimately planning work must be done in each locality by a body with legal authority to enforce adherence to the adopted plan. All States have more or less different laws granting authority to administrative agencies relative to planning work, and Court decisions in each State differ, as do local conditions. Any physical plan outlined for a locality must take these into account, and must also include suggestions for new statutes or necessary changes in existing statutes in order that the proper planning body may be created with adequate authority. Courts are rapidly awakening to the urgent need of planning and are adopting a sympathetic attitude toward the exercise of the police power in connection with it. State legislatures as well as city and county governing bodies are realizing more and more the imperative necessity of proper planning and of agencies to administer the work, and it is now much less difficult to obtain satisfactory legislation and sympathetic Court decisions than it was a decade ago.

Planning includes not only the laying out of developed areas and the providing of facilities for future population, but also the correction of existing mistakes and conditions resulting from uncontrolled settlement and development. The latter phase often results in the necessity of acquiring property, rights of way, or easements through condemnation, as well as the need of construction work.

Laws in many States, by means of which public improvements must be authorized, are relics of the "horse-and-buggy" days, when the several years required to complete a right-of-way condemnation proceeding was of no moment, and when the costs of improvements and their allocation were simple and not burdensome. The type of improvement was left to the judgment of a few property owners who paid the bill, and who were not in a position to determine whether such type fitted in with a well co-ordinated plan or with the use to which the improvement was to be put. It is just as important that improvements, once they are decided upon as necessary, should be expeditiously carried out and not wait years for Court awards in condemnation as it is that they should be of a type that fits in with a proper plan or that they satisfy the use to be made of them.

Any plan, city or regional, should include a thorough study of improvement laws and should suggest amendments or new laws which will satisfy present-day conditions, and this work should be done at the same time that other investigations are being made and physical data collected, because it sometimes takes a few years to obtain new legislation and have it tested in the Courts.

The entire theory behind the American system of taxation is that payment is made in proportion to the benefits received, and in paying for public improvements resulting from planning, the benefits may be divided into two classes: Those applying to the property directly affected by the improvement, thereby tending to enhance its value from an income standpoint, and personal benefits reflecting on residents who might use the improvement, but whose property is so far removed from it as not to have its value appreciably affected. In short, benefits are specific and general, with no sharp line of division.

It is sometimes hard to classify, in a city or regional plan, those improvements that are "nice" and those that are "necessary". There is, however, always such a thing as inability to pay for an improvement. When the cost of improvements becomes an excessive burden on property owners, it may result in evils to them and to the community greater than the existing ones that made the improvement necessary.

In the "horse-and-buggy" days it was a simple matter to assess the benefits resulting from any public improvement. In general, they were either borne by the entire community, or by property immediately contiguous to the improvement. Nowadays, principally on account of the advent of the automobile and other improved forms of transportation, much study and investigation is necessary to assess equitably the costs and benefits resulting from any improvement.

The creation of a park in a neighborhood enhances, very greatly, the value of the immediately surrounding property for residences or apartment houses, but the man living 5 miles away and possessing an automobile is only 15 min. ride from it and probably uses it in a physical sense as much as the man living across the street. The opening or widening of a major traffic artery may be a positive detriment to property owners living upon it, from the standpoint of noise and dirt, and still be a benefit to them and to owners over a large area due to the convenience it affords them in reaching places of work, recreation, or pleasure.

Any improvement, such as a direct traffic artery or a rapid transit line, which brings a place of residence from 15 to 20 min. nearer a place of work, may add several hundred or even several thousand dollars to the value of a single piece of property, and all property so benefited should contribute toward the cost of the improvement. However, the method of payment should be adjusted so that it can be handled by the property owner and still allow him to reap some substantial benefit after he has paid the bill.

This discussion is given not in criticism of the very excellent outline of physical data to be obtained in formulating a plan, but in an effort to emphasize the fact that there are other types of data and other lines of research just as necessary in preparing a regional plan. Since planning work seems to be offering a considerable field to the Engineering Profession it is important to call attention to the importance of other than the physical aspects. Every engineer who has had any contact with public improvement work is more or less familiar with the legal and financial aspects of it, and it is usually far easier for him to understand them than it would be for a lawyer or financier to comprehend the physical and engineering aspect of planning, and therein lies the engineer's opportunity of correlating the three.

Harry J. March,* M. Am. Soc. C. E. (by letter).—The author deserves great commendation for the comparatively exhaustive and highly clarified presentation of a seriously complicated subject.

* Chairman, Executive, and Engr., City Planning Committee; Chairman, Board of Appeals, Buffalo, N. Y.

Regional planning has to do with the physical harmonizing and co-ordinating of all the various utilities and resources in the affected area. At the same time, because of its very nature, it causes naturally more or less conflict of persons, ideas, and plans. This is particularly so where glory or money is being dispensed. The various major and minor civil divisions composing the region have their respective officials who are more or less jealous of their prerogatives, not to speak of duties. The regional plan must not unduly trespass upon the respcctive plans of the units, but must correlate and coordinate them. Therefore, basic data must be obtained and impressively presented, so that it will be compelling in interest and objective.

While in this modern age it is recognized that communities are dependent, one upon the other, even if some of them are remotely separated, the insatiable craving of humanity for something different, whether it be in season or out of season and whether its immediate environment be favorable or unfavorable, has caused illimitable unrest and untold strife. The regional planner should first ascertain the existing and potential resources of the several communities within its scope, irrespective of the resultant glory of one community as compared with another, or the profits and benefits accruing therefrom. There must be community team work for effective success.

The life of the several communities must be systematically controlled. Any resources found lacking for the reasonable life of any community should be supplied, if not too prohibitive in cost. In other words, the life of the community should be as well-rounded as that of the individual. There should be varied housing, varied business, varied industry, varied educational and cultural pursuits and varied recreations and diversions.

Large intervening open spaces, which afford the breath of life, as it were, to the adjoining communities, might well form the division area between communities whose specific interests are different, but whose general interests are common.

Planners should know thoroughly the products which may best be developed on the lands within the region, as well as the potential resources of the waters in terms of commercial transportation, power, or recreational phase. For instance, in the portion of the Niagara Frontier Region north of the Lewistown Escarpment, there exists a fertile soil readily adaptable for the larger fruits, peaches, apples, etc.; the middle area, or that to the south of this area, has soil conditions that are favorable for sheep farming and dairying; the southern area is valuable for the smaller fruits, grapes, etc. These several areas partly encircle the large ones of varied industries at Niagara Falls, the Tonawandas, and Buffalo, which are respectively supplied by intervening housing and business areas. The writer desires to stress at this point the great advantage of resources available for the development of the communities, because, with the flagging of one industry, there may be an increase or acceleration of another that is entirely different.

All these conditions constitute the make-up of the self-contained community and produce an enviable economical result that cannot be surpassed by a region lacking varied resources and facilities. The regional plan must be so comprehensive in its scope and compelling in its benefits that the individualized communities will subordinate their selfish interests to those of the comprehensive and economic interests of the whole region.

In the development of regional planning, the basic information to be procured should be that incident to landscape engineering, supplemented by landscape architectural considerations.

In the procurement of data, there perhaps is no better medium than that of a regional planning association for publicity purposes and that of a regional planning board for the technical work involved. The Niagara Frontier Planning Association and the Niagara Frontier Planning Board are typical examples of the effectiveness of such bodies. These organizations have developed an inter-community spirit worthy of emulation, and their members are looking forward to the attainment of some big objectives which perhaps could be obtained in no other way.

Harold M. Lewis,* M. Am. Soc. C. E. (by letter).—The discussion on this paper indicates that regional planners are subject to two rather opposite faults—on the one hand to gather much more information than will prove useful, and on the other hand to obtain too little data in regard to existing topographic conditions. Somewhere between these two tendencies there must be a mean which will combine thoroughness with efficiency. Mr. Black has expressed a disappointment that more information was not given concerning the types of basic information that will not prove essential for future regional planning surveys. The writer would not recommend that other regional plan organizations should spend as much time as was spent in New York on special research work in general and somewhat theoretical problems. He believes that the Committee on Regional Plan of New York and Its Environs was justified, for two reasons, for spending as much time and effort as it did. In the first place, while the Committee was working on a single region, it was financed by a foundation with National interests, the primary work of which is research; and, secondly, at the time when the studies were started, there was little published material available on such subjects. To-day, the condition is quite different. A large amount of information on the various standards of highway capacities, recreation use, population and housing densities, and community developments have been published within recent years. Much of it appears in the *Transactions* of the Society.

Mr. Leavitt referred to the "menace" of "the amassing of information that cannot be classified". It has been attempted to provide against this in the New York studies by publishing ten regional survey volumes which will be a classified reference library of basic information relating to the New York Region. Based on this material there will be published two additional volumes dealing with the conclusions and proposals as they relate to the Regional Plan.

Several of the discussors have stressed the need for early official co-operation and for speed in arriving at specific conclusions. The writer believes that such procedure is highly advantageous and can be followed more and

* Executive Engr., Regional Plan of New York and Its Environs, New York, N. Y.

more in later regional plan activities. In the New York studies, which were started in 1921, it was necessary to "sell" the idea of regional planning in a district where State and municipal boundaries and rivalries made it exceedingly difficult. It would probably have been impossible to establish any degree of official co-operation at the start within a region which contained parts of three States and was subdivided into about 425 different political units. It was essential to get together a large amount of material before any attempt at such co-operation could be made.

To-day (1928), the need and justification of regional planning is fairly well recognized, and other regions can undertake similar activities with a considerable advantage over New York. This does not mean that they will not have to collect information under the various survey headings suggested, but that they should be able to make much better progress in compiling and making available such material.

It is important that basic survey information, particularly when gathered by a non-official organization, should be prepared for publication at the earliest possible date. In New York, this was done in the hope that when placed in the hands of local communities and planning bodies it would guide them indirectly toward a correct solution of their own problems. By deferring the publication of a comprehensive plan, it developed that many of the proposals which had been studied by the Regional Plan Staff were taken up by and received the local backing of different political units within the New York Region. It is believed that many excellent projects have been advanced toward consummation in this way, that might have been opposed if presented at an earlier date under Regional Plan auspices.

Basic information, such as collected for a regional plan, should prove useful for both regional and local purposes. It is impossible to draw any distinct line between information that is only essential for one scope of planning. The development of general principles of local application can be considered as regional planning. Their specific application would generally be local planning, although an example might well be given in a regional plan report to demonstrate their use. It is important, as Mr. Black has stated, that the regional plan "should not concern itself with matters of purely local character".

Mr. Shurtleff's plea for the reservation of open spaces adjacent to built-up areas is very timely. The writer believes that they are needed not only to "relieve monotony" and to prevent "depreciation in value", but also because intensive building cannot be carried out over large areas without causing an impossible traffic burden on street systems already fixed by existing developments, and creating excessive costs for the necessary systems of rail transportation. Buildings of large bulk, therefore, must be balanced against extremely low buildings or open spaces.

Mr. Eliot has urged that the boundaries of a region be kept flexible. When the writer stated that the "first item to be determined is the area to be studied", he did not mean to imply that its boundary should be inflexible, but only to state that before making a map of a region one must decide where he is to stop his map. The boundaries should be placed far enough out at the beginning to include all areas for which basic information will be required. As the work progresses more detail studies can probably be restricted to a smaller area.

The importance of the legal and financial surveys has been emphasized by Mr. Baker. The Legal Division has been a very important part of the New York Regional Plan Staff, but most of its investigations come under the head of special studies and planning details, rather than basic information. The financial problem in a regional plan is more a matter of guiding expenditures along efficient lines than of finding new sources of revenue. It should be studied primarily with the aim of preventing the waste of public funds rather than of finding methods of increasing the normal capital expenditures.

AMERICAN SOCIETY OF CIVIL ENGINEERS
INSTITUTED 1852

TRANSACTIONS

Paper No. 1682

HOUSING AND THE REGIONAL PLAN*

BY JOHN IHLDER,† ESQ.

WITH DISCUSSION BY MESSRS. JAMES FORD, BENJAMIN H. RITTER, BERNARD J. NEWMAN, BLEECKER MARQUETTE, W. C. RICE, E. M. BASSETT, FRANK B. WILLIAMS, U. S. GRANT, 3D, AND JOHN IHLDER.

The great American novel, the coming of which we used to discuss with such animation, has not been written and probably never will be, for a novel must have location and must picture, with fidelity to detail, individual characters as well as groups of characters. This necessary detail inevitably makes it sectional, provincial, differentiates its people and its atmosphere from the people and the atmosphere pictured in another novel equally good, equally true, the scene of which is laid in another part of the country, or which deals with a different group of people. These differences will cause Americans of other sections to disclaim both books as representative of America as they know it, although to foreigners, both books may seem typically American. We, close at hand, see most clearly the differences of detail, accept subconsciously the likenesses; they, farther away, miss the detail and see only the broad likenesses.

Thus, it must be with regional planning and the housing that is to develop as regional planning becomes accepted practice. The broad likeness that will be characteristic of regional plans and the housing for which they provide, will lie in acceptance of the proposition that they shall provide adequately, even generously, in terms of open spaces, of sanitary equipment, of "modern" conveniences; that they shall be based on the well-known but, fortunately, never clearly defined "American standard of living"; fortunately, because

* Presented at the Joint Meeting of the City Planning Division with the American City Planning Inst., Philadelphia, Pa., October 7, 1926.

† Mgr., Civic Development Dept., Chamber of Commerce of the United States, Washington, D. C.

this standard is ever changing, ever rising. Other nations may accept present standards, seeking merely to modify them so that they may be tolerable; other nations may calculate closely on economies which they believe the hard conditions of their life force upon them—definitely discard, for example, water-borne sewage and a sewerage system, not only because of cost of installation and operation, but also because of loss of fertilizing content which they believe they must have for their farms. Americans, however, who are coming to reckon farm productivity in terms of bushels per man, while other nations reckon it in terms of bushels per acre, will base their plans on the health, efficiency, and more abundant living of the population rather than on the amount of money not spent for a sewerage system or an imported or manufactured fertilizer. Water carriage of sewage may go into the discard, but not until a better method of safeguarding human well-being has been found.

Inside such broad American characterization, however, regional plans will doubtless take on many differentiating characteristics due to sectional habits, traditions, resources, and climate. Consequently, in a paper like this, dealing with the subject for the whole Nation, one must paint in broad strokes, describe objectives in general terms that are subject to infinite modification in their detailed application, and give approximations rather than exact measurements.

To engineers this may seem an indication of loose thinking, but knowledge of the fact that a 7½-ft. ceiling height may be adequate in Maine, whereas a 14-ft. ceiling height may be good economy in Southern Florida, gives the writer courage to persist.

A house is not a commodity of uniform sizes and character. Its variations are infinite, although they all fall into fairly clearly defined classifications. The use of each of these classifications will be affected by the regional plan if that plan proves effective in guiding metropolitan or regional development. Consequently, an outline of a regional plan from the housing point of view is necessary, if subsequently housing is to be fitted into it understandably.

Regional Plan Outline

The metropolitan region may roughly be defined as the area within commuting distance of the central or mother city. It may be an area about one or two cities of small or medium size, as well as that about a large city. At present, it may contain only one or two units of really urban character, the remainder of the region being residential suburban. If it does not have other urban units now, it will acquire them later as the population increases and neighborhood business districts develop. Moreover, in this day, when every chamber of commerce is seeking factories, and when factory managements are thinking in terms of industrial distribution, it is almost inevitable that the metropolitan region outside the mother city will develop industrial districts. Consequently, provision must be made in the regional plan for both industrial areas and commercial areas, in addition to residential areas. These, normally, will grow into separate towns, and, unless preventive measures are taken, they ultimately will merge into one great city, as Philadelphia, Pa., and its satellites have done.

Philadelphia has developed much as the regional planner would have a city develop, except that adequate provision was not made for traffic and that the separate communities were not kept separate by adequate intervening open spaces. The original City of Philadelphia with its mill satellites, Kensington and Manayunk; its factory satellites, Nicetown and Tacony; its residential satellites, Germantown and Chestnut Hill, each separated from the others by open areas, the brook valleys preserved instead of being filled to make uncertain sites for the foundations of buildings, would have been a more pleasing city than it is, with its interminable streets filled with monotonous rows of houses. By the same token, the Philadelphia of to-day is a more pleasing city, with such access as it has to the open country, than it will be if its present streets stretch out and out until they join those of Chester and the other satellites that have succeeded to the opportunities once offered to Kensington and Germantown.

How Urban Units Are to Be Separated

The metropolitan region of the future, therefore, will be planned to contain a number of distinct urban communities which will be enabled to preserve their individuality by surrounding open areas. In part, these will consist of parks, some formal, such as Fairmount Park which to-day separates Philadelphia from the main-line towns, and some natural parks or forest reserves, such as those now being acquired by Boston, Mass., Chicago, Ill., and other cities. Park land alone, however, will not be enough. So much open space is required for the proper ventilation of cities that a considerable part of it must be devoted to productive uses that will pay its way. Cities like New York, N. Y., and its New Jersey neighbors, and the great congeries of cities that are growing up about San Francisco Bay have been blessed, largely against their wills, by open water spaces that seem to some persons far larger than are required—just as in the past with some cities, it was thought that certain streets were too wide, only to find to-day that they are not wide enough. It would be difficult to over-estimate the economic value of the breezes from the water that blow through the streets of New York and the Bay cities.

Awakening to the advantages which Nature forced on some fortunate cities, we shall provide adequately for the new kind of harbor that is coming with the airplane. We doubtless shall, under stress of necessity, calculate carefully how small an air field may be, how high the surrounding buildings may be permitted to rise, in order to bring the air harbor as far in town as possible so as to minimize change in existing values. As the railroad induced river towns to turn their backs on the levees so the airplane may induce them to face in a new direction, and those towns which make the most adequate provision are likely to reap a benefit.

Air harbors like water harbors, however, will prove inadequate to the purpose, and other uses, such as truck gardening and farming, will be found for these open areas.

How Urban Units Are to Be Connected

Isolation, however, is not an objective in the regional plan. Each of the urban units in the region must be readily accessible from the others, more accessible than the upper east side of New York from Riverside Drive. Water routes, rail routes, air routes, and main or arterial highways will be carefully planned so that each center in the region may be easily and quickly reached from every other center. Remembering that by far the greatest daily travel of an urban population is between home and place of employment and that in such cities as New York or Chicago, with their overgrown central business districts, where vocations that have no direct connection are jumbled together, the working population must pass twice daily thousands of buildings that have no possible part in their lives, the waste of time, effort, and money becomes obvious. Although like businesses instinctively tend to group themselves, and thus simplify the transport problem of the workers after arrival for the day's work, these employees still waste much time every morning and evening in passing the buildings of other groups and the dwellings that house the employees of these other groups. The regional plan will reduce this waste by segregating vocational groups more effectively and will bring the homes and workshops of each group closer together. The need of occasional intercourse between representatives of different groups will be met by express routes, rail and highway—perhaps in the near future, air—between the urban centers in the region.

The better segregation of vocations, which can be secured by intelligent regional planning and zoning instead of depending on the blind instinct that has guided in the past, will bring the home and the work closer together and in smaller urban units. As a result not only will time of travel—to-day worse than wasted because of crowded cars that sap the rider's strength and vitality—be reduced, but the character of the dwelling may be improved because more space will be available.

Transit Routes as District Boundaries

The transit routes that tie the urban centers of the region together will largely form the boundaries of residential districts. Along parts of these routes, especially at the intersections of arterial highways, will be minor or neighborhood business districts, containing neighborhood stores, banks, moving picture theatres, etc. Within the space they bound will be a residential area large enough to support one or more schools, playgrounds, small neighborhood parks, a branch library, a community center, churches, so that children at least will have small occasion to cross the busy main traffic streets.

These main traffic streets or arterial highways are one of the most interesting of the problems that confront regional planners. Their primary function is to carry traffic from center to center within the region or to more distant destinations. How they should be designed, what width should be secured for rights of way to provide against future needs, whether they should contain facilities for rail as well as for road vehicles, are questions outside the scope of this paper. It is necessary, however, to point out that they will carry not only a heavy volumn of traffic, in some cases a constant stream of traffic by day and a considerable and increasing amount of traffic by night, but that they will carry heavy vehicles. The increasing weight of trucks and buses has become a matter of public concern. Admitting, what seems to be the fact, that while the large truck and bus make for economy of operation for their owners, they at present cause great expense to the community as a whole and to property owners along many of their routes where they are permitted to range at will. Street paving that would carry passenger cars for years goes to pieces quickly under their pounding which also cracks the walls of dwelling houses, and which, together with their noise, seriously depreciates the value of whole residence districts. The main arterial highways apparently must be designed and built to carry vehicles that will some day be excluded from residential streets.

The old theory that every street-car street was potentially a business street, was a poor one and was based on inadequate experience. Inadequate as the basis always was, it is becoming every day less adequate. Not only are merchants realizing that the string business district can not compare with the compact district; not only are buses that operate on parallel streets applying the same argument to those parallel streets, but the public is learning that business can never occupy all the frontage on street-car streets. Recent studies have indicated that, outside the principal down-town shopping district, not more than 5% of an area will be occupied by business.

If this is borne out by further studies, it seems that the frontage on the main arterial highways of the region must in large part be devoted to other than business uses. Attempts to develop such frontages to residential use are not proving permanently successful, even for multi-family houses. The inhabitants of multi-family houses object less to noise and movement than those of one-family houses, but even they are beginning to find that noise and movement can be increased to such a degree as to become intolerable. Thus, although the non-business frontage of these arteries may be zoned for multi-family house occupancy, even such dwellings will have to be given protection if they are not to be blighted. The suggestion the writer would offer is that in addition to the ample right of way for traffic purposes, the community shall take possession of strips on either side of the traffic artery. These strips should be parked, and on each side of them should be a minor street serving the dwellings. The dwellings should then be set back, to provide for two screens of planting between them and the traffic highway. The park strip might be so wide that when business expansion can utilize it in part it will provide suitable sites.

This may seem extravagant but it will prove less costly than the slow and spotty development of property abutting directly upon a main traffic highway and the inevitable depreciation of such dwellings as may be there erected.

City Facilities and Neighborhood Facilities

Housing cannot be considered adequately apart from facilities offered by the city or community and their accessibility. To the wage earner distance from place of employment translated into terms of money for means of transit and time or effort is of greater importance than to those whose means are greater and hours of work shorter. To every one, however, the waste involved in needless daily travel is an economic loss of moment unless it can be transformed into a strength-giving, or health-giving, or inspiration-giving factor. The well-to-do man who drives from a pleasant home to an office near a parkway, may well find this interval an asset, but one who must travel morning and evening in a closely packed subway train is almost sure to find it a distinct liability.

The best means of transit yet invented is that one, reminiscent of days before the horseless carriage, known as "shank's mare." For the normal man a half hour's walk, especially if it can be along a pleasant route, is a good prelude to a day of sedentary or indoor labor. Next, perhaps, comes the bicycle, for this too involves exercise. Then, come vehicles that give their occupants the benefit of sun and air, and last comes underground transit. As the old-fashioned, outside, iron fire escape, now happily disappearing, was a confession of failure to construct buildings properly, so the subway is a confession of failure to construct cities properly. There is room enough in the United States for all to live above ground except the miners. Such failures, forcing people to patronize crowded or sub-surface vehicles, have a direct effect on housing by compelling a choice of two evils—these means of transit, or an inferior type of dwelling nearer the place of employment.

Although access to place of employment is usually the chief consideration, access to schools and to places of recreation, are of some importance. These merge into facilities offered by the neighborhood which is the area that, ideally, lies between main traffic streets and all parts of which are within easy walking distance of home even when home is part of a district of widely spaced, garden-surrounded one-family houses. Here will be the grade schools and the playgrounds for small children, perhaps a High School, or at least a Junior "High," for the older children, a library, or a community center, and a neighborhood playground for adults, and churches—set in grounds large enough to permit their expansion without violating the area provisions of the zoning code. Most congregations seem to be pessimistic of their future, yet instances are known of churches having had occasion to expand and their officers had no hesitation in asking that a rule made for the benefit of the community and the protection of their neighbors should be suspended in order that they might escape the penalty of lack of foresight or lack of faith.

Within the region and its units, thus broadly outlined, the problem is to fit housing so as to give the people of urban America the greatest possible facilities for living abundantly.

A Few Assumptions

In order to summarize the subject, several assumptions will be given, as follows:

1.—It is desirable to decrease the speculative elements in housing and to increase the investment element until the first has been reduced approximately to the vanishing point and the latter has become controlling. This means that values should be stabilized. Stabilization of house values is dependent on stabilizing the character of the neighborhood and in this stabilization regional planning, supplemented by zoning, is essential.

Conceding the great part that speculation has played in producing the dwellings of America, it must also be admitted that it has played as great a part in destroying them, in blighting whole sections of cities, in promoting rapid transition that lowers housing values so quickly that the investor has withdrawn from a large part of the market, leaving it to the "home owner" whose controlling motive is sentiment, in deteriorating construction until the buildings erected to-day have a much shorter expectation of life and a far higher expectation of repair and maintenance costs than those of our fathers and grandfathers, and, most important, in leading to the acceptance of dwellings inferior in type. From the one-family house it has led to the multi-family house and has gradually squeezed and cramped this lower form of dwelling until a large and increasing part of the urban population lives in one, two, and three-room apartments. These multi-family dwellings are popularly supposed to have investment value, but experience is showing that the rapid obsolescence of a multi-family house often prevents its being rated as a high-class investment. From the social point of view its destructive effect on family life is a matter of concern.

2.—The preservation of the family—meaning parents and children—is essential. The population of voting age may be everything that candidates for public office tell its members they are, but its life and its work would lose significance if there were no children to carry on. With the children lies the whole future. Consequently, children are of first importance. As the house is the shell in which the family functions, as it exerts a constant influence in moulding and shaping the family, even in determining whether or not there shall be children, the question of housing should be approached from the point of view of the well-being of children.

3.—The one-family house with generous open spaces about it is the best house for a child. Consequently, every effort should be made to promote the erection, to protect the continued existence of such houses.

4.—While the one-family house is the most important type of dwelling, there is a legitimate demand for other types, ranging from the two-family house through the so-called multi-family house and the apartment hotel to the hotel. This demand must be met, but because these socially inferior types of dwellings with their possibilities of land overcrowding and cramped living quarters can under-live the one-family house and drive it out, just as Oriental labor can under-live and drive out white labor, it must be restricted to certain specified sections of the community and must be strictly regulated so that it will provide the essentials of wholesome living—light, air, room space, sanitation—for its inhabitants.

Classification of Urban Population

In urban communities there are several easily recognized groups for each of which housing provision should be made. First and much the most important, because with them lies the future, are the families with children or expectation of children. They call for first consideration. They themselves may be divided into two classes. First are those who are fairly permanently located in the community, whose interests and fortunes have been and will be bound up with those of their neighbors and fellow citizens. They are the most valuable element for they have developed or can develop a lively sense of community responsibility. Less valuable, but more in need of assistance, is the second class, composed of families which, because of the nature of the bread winner's work or because of the temperament of father or mother, frequently move from city to city. They range from high salaried officials of large corporations, army and navy officers, professional men and women—civil engineers, social workers—to the automobile tramps who have become an interesting and puzzling phenomenon of modern life, whose younger children have never known a more stable home than the "flivver" and whose importunities are increasing the burden carried by charity organizations. Even those among this second class who are best placed economically have a difficult problem in providing homes for their children in these days when the choice lies between buying a proper house or renting an apartment.

In the first group it will be noted that families with "expectation of children" have been included as well as those with children. There is a great deal of talk about giving the young married couple a shelter that will just fit their present needs, assuming that when the expected happens they will move from their furnished two-room flat to that idyllic vine-covered cottage where love traditionally abides. Considered as a matter of pure economics, there is much to be said for all this, but while sound economics should be the foundation of living, pure economics is a sterile soil which will not produce an adequate crop of babies. Marriage, the family, is an adventure. Reason it out too coldly, balance economic items too carefully, and the young couple will grow to middle age, still living in their apartment, still thinking first of their own safety, their own comforts. Then the Nation may well ask why it was taxed to provide for their schooling, to protect their health, when they have been unwilling to pass on the heritage they received. The first home of the young couple should be at least a promise of its future home, should have in it the room, the play-yard that every day ask when the expected is to arrive. This may be economic waste, but the greater part of the joy of living consists of what cannot be strictly justified on the score of pure economics; it may be beyond the means of many young married couples, but it is an objective to be approximated as closely as we—and they—can.

Next to be considered, because they have not shirked but have rendered their service to society, is the group composed of those who have reared their children and sent them out into the world. The home that sheltered them when all the family were together may now be too large, too much of a burden. Many will continue to maintain it because of sentiment, but others will desire and should have a more convenient shelter. Their problem is not met by old folks' homes, however those may be disguised by luxury. Perhaps the nearest approach to a solution is the occasional multi-family dwelling where through some happy circumstance of management, tenant leadership, or a common dining room, the inhabitants mingle for a time in the evening, and the older people have opportunity to maintain some daily contact with younger people.

Then come the unattached individuals who form the tragedy of civilization, often not recognized by its victims until they reach middle age. Their variety is so great, class merges into class so imperceptibly that it is difficult to classify them definitely. They range all the way from the well-to-do bachelor who lives at his club and thus has the casual social intercourse with his fellows that fills so many of the odd moments of contented living, the lack of which reduces living to periods of conscious effort interspersed with periods of loneliness; from the two spinsters who have joined forces to fight off loneliness and who live together in a little apartment, through those forlorn ones who inhabit boarding houses—a form of housing now apparently on the decrease—hotels and rooming houses—a form of housing now apparently on the increase. This great army is recruited from the youth of the land who venture forth in search of fortune. Its veterans are those who fail to make a family harbor. The problem of the unattached, whether it be the well-known "homeless man" who patronizes municipal lodging houses, or the wage-earning woman, whether it be the raw recruit or the veteran left-over, is one that has not yet begun to be solved in spite of the voluminous literature dealing with fragments of it—perhaps because this literature does deal with fragments only instead of with the problem as a whole.

Classification of Houses

For the population that is to be housed in a carefully planned region there is choice among the following types of dwellings:

- One-family houses (one family occupying the whole house from cellar to roof.): Detached; semi-detached; group; or, row.
- Two-family houses (one family above the other) subdivided as previously described.
- Multi-family houses (ranging from the building in which every apartment is equipped for housekeeping, through that where a common dining room supplements or supersedes the housewife's efforts, to the hotel where cooking in an apartment is strictly forbidden.) Detached; group; or row.

Somewhat apart from any of those mentioned are the boarding house and the lodging or rooming house. These are not a distinct type of housing, but are merely the result of opportunist attempts to utilize the waste resultant from lack of city planning and a housing policy in the past. When the day comes that there are no more blighted districts, no more cast-off dwellings, the boarding house and rooming house, as they are known to-day, will disappear, their places being taken by houses designed for the purpose. Instead of a shame-faced dilapidation, recalling better days, they will evidence the self-respect of those who accomplish what they intend to do.

With this classification of houses; with a clear understanding of the function of each class; with a regional plan, zoning regulation, and an intelligent distribution of centers of employment so that there will be ready access from home to shop; with a stabilization of the character of neighborhoods and, consequently, of house values, and, not least important, a clearer recognition of the value of space, both inside and outside the house, but part of the same domain so that alterations and improvements may be made, it will be comparatively easy to develop a housing policy designed to serve adequately the needs of the population.

Each individual has conflicting desires among which he must choose. Each might prefer to live in the White House, not because of an ambition to be President, but because the house has the desirable characteristics of a family dwelling; it is spacious and set in a very pleasant yard large enough for children's play and even contains a tennis court, and, in addition, it is most accessible from its tenant's office which is easily reached by his chief business associates, and, to add excellence to excellence, to satisfy the other head of the family, it is cheek by jowl with the principal shopping district, within a block or so of two theatres, and within easy reach of the others. In short, it would seem to be ideal. Certainly, as Lincoln is reported to have observed, most of its tenants desire to renew their leases.

Although this combination is provided for Presidents, most families have to make choices. If convenience of access of department stores is more important than home or children, an apartment near the center of one of the larger urban units or along one of the arterial highways is selected. If we no longer have children or expectation of them, a similar choice may be made, although some recent sub-divisions give reason to hope that it will be possible to find a small house of five or six rooms, attractively designed and located in a pleasant neighborhood, thus doing away with the present hard choice between an eight to ten-room house and a five-room apartment. If there are growing children a one-family dwelling will be chosen, a little less accessible from the centers of work and amusement, but compensating for this by giving neighbors who have the same chief interest and who have a greater tendency to "stay put" long enough for the development of family acquaintance, parents with neighbors' children, as well as the horizontal acquaintance of apartment-house populations which tends to follow the line of age groups.

The greater stabilization of the character of neighborhoods will encourage investment in rental housing by increasing the life expectancy of the individual house. It will lead to the wider use in one-family house districts of services now characteristic of multi-family houses. Stabilization which reduces the speculative factor in real estate, which turns attention to permanent investment values, should result in creating again the estate or company that owns or manages a considerable number of one-family houses, for these depreciate, become obsolescent less rapidly, cost less to maintain and, provided they have open space about them, are more readily kept in step with "modern improvement," than are multi-family dwellings. Some of the finest dwellings are one-family houses built 50 or 100 years ago. Some of the old one-family house districts after a period of decadence have come back strongly. Few multi-family dwellings have maintained the standing of their youth until reaching their majority, and none, so far as the writer knows, has ever come back after it once lost prestige.

Probably this has been due chiefly to misplacing. They have themselves spoiled many neighborhoods and, in time, have suffered from the deterioration they caused; or they have been injured by the invasion of business. In a planned and zoned region these causes should be removed. There will obviously be space enough so that the temptation to land-overcrowding will be reduced. There will be system and order so that each type of dwelling will have that place best fitted to its purpose. Zoning does not imply a series of girdles about an urban center, but it does imply an arrangement in relation to traffic and traffic facilities. The regional plan will guide the development of traffic facilities, types of dwellings will be placed in accordance with their need of these facilities, and zoning regulations will prevent the placing of an inferior type in a district where it does not belong.

DISCUSSION

James Ford,* Esq. (by letter).—This paper is the ablest discussion of the civic and social aspects of housing in its relation to the regional plan that has come to the writer's attention. It shows clearly the paramount importance of making the regional plan contribute to human welfare and civic progress. The author outlines specific ways of escape from the present deplorable tendency to let selfish interest dominate public interest.

In America, ugliness and unsightliness in industrial and residential districts, and noise and inconvenience in traffic arrangements, have become so common that they are taken as matters of course. There is no reason why access to the amenities of life should be the exclusive right of the well-to-do. If the highly trained minds of the Engineering Profession can be applied with equal force and skill and practical judgment to the problem of providing better homes and better neighborhoods and better community life for wage earners, America will make over its industrial districts so radically that they will be a source of justifiable pride.

Mr. Ihlder points out effectively that the next generation should be the object of chief concern. Progress and America's contribution to world civilization rest with them. They are largely the creatures of their environment and cannot far transcend it. The drab, monotonous, unkempt, crowded, treeless, industrial quarters of American cities can hardly produce enthusiasm for public service or good judgment as to what constitutes civic interest. Housing conditions that make for wholesomeness in home life and respect for government are, therefore, necessary and the regional plan is clearly the first point of attack.

Sunless, unventilated, crowded homes produce irritability and low vitality, if not actual ill health. The detached dwelling, placed with careful consideration of orientation, makes it possible to have sunlight and cross ventilation in each room and provides for adequate privacy and control of the factors of home life. It also makes possible the home garden and the safe home playground. It can provide relative freedom from the dust, noise, and accident danger, which characterize crowded residential districts. It unquestionably provides larger opportunities for self-development on the part of parents and children. The home ownership, which it makes possible and which, for the majority of the population, is advisable, contributes to civic interest, for the home owner ceases to be a nomad, puts down roots in his neighborhood, recognizes community and civic interests, and bends his energies to the improvement of his neighborhood and of his city.

Carefully considered regional planning, as outlined by Mr. Ihlder, will, in time, make these values accessible to all. There are few civic measures more significant than this.

Benjamin H. Ritter,† Esq.—The author has outlined the basic principles of regional planning, which must be observed in any metropolitan district if housing is to be developed and maintained on a sound basis.

* Executive Director, Better Homes in America, Washington, D. C.

† Executive Secy., Pennsylvania Housing and Town Planning Assoc., Philadelphia, Pa.

Surely all will agree that adequate open spaces surrounding accessible individual homes with sanitary equipment and modern conveniences, are the primary requisites of good housing. As indicated, this requires the proper distribution of population over a given area. Therefore, the outstanding need of any region, from the housing standpoint, is the adoption of a practical plan that will facilitate the conveniences of the home and prevent congestion and overcrowding of the land.

In the absence of plans, regulations, and possibly some of the necessary equipment in the past, many centers of population have been allowed to become overcrowded to the extent of 100 to 700 persons per acre. These conditions are not limited to Manhattan Island, or to any large city. They are found even in the small mining towns of Pennsylvania. Such practices have resulted in what has been termed, very fittingly, "the American blight." Unquestionably, the time has come when the authority vested in municipal governments must be exercised to check and control this injurious form of city growth.

The problem does not seem so complex when it is realized that in the United States there are 50 metropolitan centers, each with a population of 150 000 and more, scattered over 3 000 000 miles of land, most of which is habitable. These centers with their surrounding territories represent the country's metropolitan reservoirs. Knowing where the reservoirs of people are and the topography of the land surrounding them, it should be more or less easy to determine the flow of population and properly to provide for it.

The machinery for handling this job is in the making. No one ventures to say that it is perfect, but the various experiments made with it, and the many new parts patented during the past ten years, convince one that it will be effective. Its successful operation will depend on the willingness of individual urban communities to co-operate as a unit under the guidance of some form of a regional organization.

To make it effective and carry the proper weight, it seems that membership in this regional organization should be by election or administrative appointment from the various municipalities concerned. A nominal fee for attending meetings might not be out of order. This board with its complete data and maps, showing the general layout of the region, elevation of territory, incorporated villages, transportation lines, present use of land, the location of industry, commerce, and residential districts, open spaces, population density, and curves of population growth, will be in a position to direct the proper development of the region, preserve the individuality of the small towns, and yet enable them to carry on their various public activities as one large unit.

A properly laid out street and road system will serve as a reliable guide for future sub-divisions and platting of land. Parks, playgrounds, club houses, shops, stores, and all the complex equipment of a modern city can be located with a definite economical relation to each community center as well as to the district as a whole. This will encourage regional light, power, gas, water, and sewage systems, in addition to many other community enterprises, both public and private. It will tend to reduce the cost of supplying necessary conveniences to suburban districts. With the coming of the automobile, motor-bus line, and adequate suburban streets and transportation lines, isolation will give way to united communities with all the advantages found in any city plus a more delightful home environment. This will give rise to incentives that bring about the proper decentralization of people and will make it economically possible for families to live in homes of better selection.

Even now, the doors of the suburban districts are opening to thousands of middle-class families even if the bread-winners must continue to work in the city. It remains the duty of each incorporated unit in metropolitan regions to safeguard this movement by protecting all residential districts with proper zoning regulations. Likewise, it is the obligation of government to see that sufficient space for industries is reserved in some of the resident districts, so that employment may be provided for those who may wish to work near home. Here, again, a guiding hand for the metropolitan region is of greatest importance, for it may be just as necessary to advise a municipal unit what not to do, as it is to advise it what to do.

It must be realized that industrial plants and even a variation of housing accommodations are just as necessary as individual homes. One cannot survive without the other. A properly regulated factory or an office building may be just as essential to one locality as a hotel or an apartment house is to another. The complexity of modern life will not permit any of these factors to be overlooked. The manner in which they are correlated will determine the future housing in metropolitan regions.

Bernard J. Newman,* Esq.—The author, looking out over an expanse of slum waste in American cities presents a vision by which, if consistently held, home life may be changed so that it will produce the man power needed to maintain the supremacy of the nation. Large areas in American cities are a waste to-day. There is no justification for herding tens of thousands of families in congested centers. The inhumanity of it is apparent. The social loss is measurable. In Philadelphia, Pa., for example, more than $28 000 000 are spent annually to care for defectives, dependents, and delinquents. That is not a foundation, but an annual expenditure of public and private charity for the care of the waste product of urban living. Under the right program, of which planning is a part, much of it can be salvaged for capital expenditures.

The paper assumes that the fundamental note of all city or regional planning is human welfare. Through highways are recommended; parks, parkways, and recreational centers are suggested; the unification of sewer systems is proposed; and common sources for regional water supplies are advocated, not as technical engineering problems, but as adjuncts to serve man in the various aspects of living.

The author has implied that the regional planner is more than a technician with an engineering problem before him. His technique, based on the fundamental principles of his profession, is essential to the solution of his problem, but it is secondary to its object, namely, the layout of the area for constructive

* Managing Director, Philadelphia Housing Assoc., Philadelphia, Pa.

communal service. If this is accepted, the logical deduction is that any regional plan proposed is defective if it is not evolved from a concept wherein the human side of communal life is of more concern than the mechanical aids toward its expression. Such mechanical aids are not thereby minimized in importance, but are properly subordinated to their place as aids. In other words, the physical city as it is to-day is of no value except as it is a place in which man may live, work, or play. The hollow echoes of abandoned mining towns stir only historic interest. Their street plans, business areas, and housing are of merely academic significance. Man has forsaken them. Cities are concerned with physical expression, solely because of suitability or non-suitability to meet the every-day needs of those who there live, work, or play. Manifestly, in their planning or re-planning, the object of prime importance is that they may serve man in each of his major interests with the least restraint or injury. If they do not so serve him, then the logical and the practical thing to do is to control all future urban development or re-development so as to avoid past mistakes.

In determining the significance of all that comprises an urban area and in planning for its utilitarian as well as its artistic expression, the fact must not be lost sight of, that the preservation of family life, which the sociologist declares is the unit of all social life, is of fundamental and primary importance. In short, highways, transportation facilities, parks and civic centers, are not entities in themselves, but are correlated units, obtaining their real value from the service they render to their community. To the extent that their construction or placement is unsuitable, or produces a problem in any other phase of communal life, they are subject to remedial action; to the extent that their planning or promotion fails to take into account this interrelationship, they are faulty. There is an interdependence between the physical expression of the city, in its provisions for industrial and commercial needs, and those other aspects of such physical expression manifest in residential areas and the social needs accessory thereto.

This fact has not received adequate consideration in city growth. If it had, there would be little need for legally expressed regulation for zoning; multiple housing would not have gained headway; there would be no such widespread areas of slums; cities would not be so concerned with population "bigness"; and there would not be such concentration of land values with all the attendant increases in the cost of production and government. In like manner there would not be so many sectional plans concerned with getting a business population into or out of a business center. Things as they are would not be considered fixed, with attention given to alleviatory plans which, as in the subway in New York, or the loop hazard in Chicago, often serve to accentuate the problem.

This thought must be kept in the foreground of all proposals for city development advanced by the city and regional planner. Has it been so kept? The speaker does not think so. It has been subconsciously accepted, but there is little evidence available in proposed plans to justify the belief that it has been an ever-conscious companion of the planner's thoughts. For this reason, therefore, it is very pertinent to analyze the place of housing in the regional plan.

Mr. Ihlder has very properly pointed out the illogical development of cities to-day with land loads, in building and people, that have placed heavy burdens on family life, with a slum virus that has not only menaced communal health, but destroyed the industrial efficiency and commercial resources of hundreds of thousands of workers and their families. He has challenged the practicality of congested business districts and concentrated industrial areas. He has emphasized the necessity for decentralization, pointed out its feasibility, and outlined means whereby the present trend may be expedited through satellite communities, interrelated with, but separated, geographically and physically, from the parent city. As a natural corollary, he has indicated the compelling necessity for suitably planned and adequately supplied housing accommodations.

Cities are not fixed entities, but units, breaking down in spots by natural processes through the withdrawal of industries to more suitable sites and the migratory practices encouraged by business concerns chasing each other to more strategic centers of trade. A constant process of wedging in and drawing out is written in the records of the decadence, alteration, or demolition of buildings in all older areas. A financial district may remain static in a city like New York and the insurance district change, or the insurance district may have sent its roots down and the financial district changed, as in Philadelphia, but there is constantly going on, in all American cities, that illusive maneuvering for the "best" locations, which is conclusive evidence of faulty planning. The greatest loss is to the home life of the people, which is ruthlessly encroached upon. The dwelling, in which such home life is centered, loses some of its desirability. Its occupants, in order to preserve those attributes of home life most prized, are forced to move to other areas farther away from centers in which they trade or labor. Regional planning, therefore, offers the opportunity to reverse this mistaken policy, especially in new areas. In the almost virgin territory outside large cities it can plan for those satellite communities which are practically complete entities in themselves, but are so connected with the parent city by highways and transit facilities that the ultra-cultural advantages offered by the latter may be available to the former. In such satellite cities, interrelated and co-operating with each other for the economic operation of service needs, will be found the antidote to the lure that over-populates urban centers while depopulating rural areas. There, adequate housing can be established and protected without loss to or encroachment on industrial or commercial life.

Mr. Ihlder has outlined the essential elements, industrial and commercial, cultural and recreational, that are needed in such smaller communities, and has emphasized the feasibility of providing satisfactory home environment with space in and about the dwelling to serve family needs. Decentralization is the keynote. Its popularity cannot be questioned in the face of the present higher rate of growth of suburban towns as compared with the cities to which they are adjuncts. The trend is that way, but it needs wise directing in order to obtain for the future citizen the best results. The practical difficulty, under present land-development practices, of maintaining the necessary isolation from the parent city is remedial. The suggestion is made that intercommunity parks separate geographical boundaries and that, by low land cost, agricultural belts be established which, because dedicated to agricultural use, cannot rise to the prohibitory land values accompanying other forms of development. The speaker doubts whether there can be any insurmountable legal disqualification to the establishment of such community safeguards. The processes involved to secure them are: By voluntary gift of civic-minded property owners, or landlords and others interested, of land for park purposes, specially designated for all time for such uses; by municipal purchase, especially of areas where land costs are lower; by excess condemnation when boulevards or transit lines tap undeveloped districts; by zoning; by prior designation of use, as practiced in small park and street platting in Philadelphia, prior to the actual taking title thereto by the municipality, so as to forestall the erection of private structures with an attending higher condemnation cost to the local government; by preferential tax rates and assessments of land according to city, suburban, or farm use; and similar methods which have been adopted where public control over land has been exercised by towns and cities.

The author has discussed many phases of the part that housing plays in the regional plan. The major contribution he has made is his emphasis on the need to expedite a movement already under way and to guide it so as not to create a flock of evils in new centers similar to those so costly in the old. He clearly sees that the promotion of housing betterment in urban centers must always labor under the handicaps of faulty planning, or lack of planning, of the past and although relief can be secured, nevertheless compact construction dooms family life to be satisfied with less than the normal advantages essential to wholesome living.

BLEECKER MARQUETTE,* ESQ. (by letter).—This scholarly paper goes to the root of the housing problem. There can be no question in the mind of any one who has had experience in this line, that there are no arbitrary city boundaries that can confine within their limits the housing problem of a city.

The importance of the proper allocation of industry and homes for workers is quite properly stressed. It is desirable to eliminate, at least to some extent, the severe strain on the vitality of workmen in the long period of unnecessary travel to and from work. Few people have any real conception of the ill effect of the terrific hustle and bustle of modern city life. The fact that mental disease is found to be uniformly more common in cities than in rural areas is enough to justify careful study of ways and means of decreasing the strain of modern city life.

The writer is not discouraged with the possibilities of regional planning, but it will take a great deal of effort and much education before the attainment of real progress toward Mr. Ihlder's ideal of locating industry and housing so that the amount of unnecessary time spent in travel will be cut to the minimum. Perhaps, some day, leaders of industries will see that they have much

* Executive Secy., Cincinnati Better Housing League, Cincinnati, Ohio.

to lose by locating in large cities, and will seek smaller communities where their workmen will have an opportunity to enjoy the amenities of living. At the moment it must be admitted the trend seems altogether in the opposite direction.

Mr. Ihlder presents a unique point of view when he discusses the difficulty of finding logical use for land adjoining main highways in cities. This is a great problem and will become a greater one. Certainly, business will never occupy all the properties along these highways. Zoning laws usually locate apartment districts adjoining them. Tenants of such apartment buildings are already beginning to recognize the disadvantages of the noise, dust, and commotion, and architects and builders are reflecting their objections. They are demanding that sites be provided for apartment houses away from main highways. The suggestion, made by Mr. Ihlder, that minor streets be laid out parallel with thoroughfares, separated from them by parked strips, and that apartment houses be constructed along these minor streets, seems worthy of consideration.

The housing of a city cannot be safeguarded without regional planning. That was learned early in the game, before anything was known about regional planning. Builders soon find that limitations are placed on the shack type of house in the larger cities, but that they can step outside the city limits and build just about as they please. The better the housing regulations in the city, the more temptation for "jerry builders" to carry on "beyond the pale". Nothing is more distressing than this to the person active in housing improvement in a community. Just as he has begun to bring about a reasonably satisfactory situation in the city, he finds himself confronted with a serious housing problem in the outlying district. This is exactly what has happened in Cincinnati, Ohio. The city has a reasonably good building code, and the housing regulations are now in the process of complete revision. It has perhaps as intelligent and conscientious enforcement of the regulations as could be asked for by any city. It has a good zoning law and a comprehensive city plan. In the meantime, while attention has been directed toward problems within the confines of the city, little slums have been growing up in the county. Some method of controlling the development of these areas is becoming absolutely imperative, and the regional plan is undoubtedly the way to meet the problem.

Cincinnati has eight distinctive satellites, several of which are nearly surrounded by the city. They are practically a part of the city life, participating in its benefits and materially affecting its welfare. Most of their inhabitants earn their living in the city, use the city's streets, and profit by practically all the safeguards of city government. They do not want annexation. A regional plan would help to make it possible to fit these satellite communities into the whole and to bring about a situation in which they will play a proper part in the city's life and in the maintenance of its government. A State law is already in effect which provides for the establishment of a county and regional planning commission. Forward-looking citizens interested in the proper development of Cincinnati regard regional planning as the next big forward step.

W. C. Rice,* Esq.—As Mr. Ihlder points out each regional plan will have to meet the conditions of its local setting. The speaker desires to indicate some trends affecting the Pittsburgh, Pa., Industrial District.

General Features.—The Pittsburgh District owes its general layout to its topographical features, which determined its location on account of water transportation. The railroads follow the waterways, giving the District its present formation in which the lowlands have been taken over by industry and the highlands by residential districts. Future development will continue along these lines, with the unoccupied lowlands being taken up by industries. The railroad connections available are now generally supplemented by an improved system of highways. Therefore, the main river valleys and the valleys of the larger creeks, in which railroads now exist, will form the industrial sections of the future Pittsburgh Metropolitan District. The highlands between these valleys form the logical location for residences and the sections that lie closest to the valleys should be considered as the best location for the homes of the operatives of the adjoining industries. The more remote highlands should be preserved for the more expensive residential developments and for parks and other public recreational features.

Facts Influencing Location of Residences.—This is influenced, however, by the demand for housing accommodations of those who are not directly concerned with the operation of the industries, but who serve the industrial population as a whole in the various commercial enterprises. It is also affected by those who, on account of an improvement in their economic condition and the diversity of occupations in the family group, are not located in close proximity to the mills where they work. The changing conditions in employment and the improvement in living conditions have been the great influences that have changed neighborhoods.

Proper Basis for Area Requirements.—The present practice of zoning on the basis of the family unit is not as logical as zoning on the basis of the individual. The classification suggested by Mr. Ihlder is not comprehensive or elastic enough to form a proper basis for a housing-control program. There are certain minimum requirements of area and volume per individual that govern, and if a reasonable limitation is made as to area per individual, the multiple house will lose the greater part of its objections. Ample area and street frontage would then be available, and the light and air space of the adjoining property owners would not be injuriously affected.

In neighborhood commercial districts, where the ground floors are used for business and the upper floors for residences, in addition to the minimum area per capita requirement, the lot should be of sufficient area to allow twice that occupied by business. For land located in the lowlands and which is obviously a future industrial site, the minimum requirements per capita should be considerably increased for the reason that these locations are generally not as healthful because of the prevalence of fog, smoke, and dust.

With these basic considerations determined, the early sub-dividers should be given wide latitude in laying out their property. Further development of

* Pittsburgh, Pa.

the property by houses would then be easily controlled by proper building code and fire protection restrictions.

Multiple versus Single-Family Houses.—The single-family house may not be the ideal one for a large industrial population. It is more expensive than the multiple house. If the speculative builder is eliminated and the cost of building construction continues at its present level, the opportunity of the individual to secure a single-family house ample for his needs will decrease. Then, if the accommodations are not furnished by the industries, doubling up of families and greater congestion than that which now exists, are bound to occur under the pressure of economic necessity. On the other hand, if the speculative builder is encouraged and controlled by proper building regulations and zoning restrictions, he will use proper materials in his buildings.

The housing of the Pittsburgh Regional District must depend more and more on the speculative investment builder and on the industries themselves. The growth of financial knowledge, the increasing mobility of people, and the changing ideal in the family will cause them to view with concern any tendency toward establishing themselves by a considerable investment in one definite place. This would tend to restrict their ability to take advantage of opportunities in other parts of the District or other sections of the country.

Some of the tendencies along this line, which must be recognized, are the greater investments being made in automobiles, radios, and similar facilities for enjoying life. Stocks, bonds, and similar investments, which do not require so much oversight on the part of the owner, are also gaining in popular favor. The prosperity enjoyed by the inhabitants of the industrial sections of this country—increased pay, shorter hours, restriction of emigration, and aversion to manual labor by the younger generation—are also dominant factors.

E. M. Bassett,* Esq.—City plan maps must be precise because they mark the different characters of parcels of land. The boundary of a park must be definite—a definite line; the boundary of a street must be a definite line; the boundary of a zoning district must be a definite line; so with the school site, a fire-house site, the site of a court house; and, also, with pierhead and bulkhead lines. It is the determination of those lines that constitutes city planning.

Open spaces between communities—how shall they be obtained? Mr. Ihlder has properly stated that they cannot be parks, because parks are an expense to a community and yield nothing by taxation. These open development spaces must be put to use, as flying fields, fair grounds, race tracks, country estates, golf courses, etc. They probably cannot be obtained through adjustment of taxation. A low tax rate will cause increased value, because the land is favored by taxation. With any low taxation there must be regulation of the percentage of land to be covered by buildings. Probably a 3% limit of cover cannot be attained through the police power because the Courts would decide that it was a "taking" and not a police power regulation. Perhaps these open development spaces can be taken by the State imposing an

* Counsel, Zoning Committee, New York, N. Y.

easement that will prevent structures occupying more than 3% of the lot. Such an easement could be taken by eminent domain. Owners of country estates dread the incoming of developments of 30 by 50-ft. lots. Some of these estate owners would not make claims for damages if the State imposed an easement of 3% cover on the land.

This country is the only one where the acts of legislative bodies can be set aside by Courts, and, therefore, citizens can only do by legislation those things that can be brought under the police power. If it is not possible to accomplish the result under that power, it must be accomplished by eminent domain, and eminent domain is expensive.

FRANK B. WILLIAMS,* ESQ.—This paper has inspired a quickened sense of the importance of the proper regulation of the region as a whole and has strengthened the belief that by itself regional planning, in the sense usually attached to that term, is insufficient for that regulation.

There are many reasons why regional control is becoming rapidly and increasingly necessary:

First.—With the growth of cities, urban population is more and more seeking the remoter suburbs. Population is thus increasing not only in the centers, but in the entire region.

Second.—Throughout the region, and not in cities alone as formerly, people are demanding urban facilities, and local officials are finding the problem of satisfying these demands, and reconciling them with those of other localities, more and more difficult of solution. Urban problems, now region wide, are almost impossible of solution by local effort alone.

Third.—Urban facilities in rural and semi-rural localities are bringing with them poles, billboards, filling stations, "hot dog" stands, and other nuisances, prevalent in cities, to escape which city people have gone to the remoter suburbs. There is a deepening feeling that, to-day, these conveniences can be furnished in the country without giving the offense which is often regarded as necessarily incident to them. This, however, can be done only by restrictions covering broad areas.

Evidently the planning of a region or any other area is not enough. The plan, to be effective, must be enforced. The growing importance and difficulty of regional planning is bringing to the forefront, as never before, this problem of the administration of regional planning, which in this country still awaits solution. In so far as such administration has been attempted it has been of two kinds:

(1) The jurisdiction of the city has been extended a certain distance over the adjacent outlying territory. This has proved to be both too much and too little. It is undemocratic to govern one community by the vote of another, and this practice will not be continued. Indeed, in the more developed parts of the country where regional administration is especially important, it is not feasible. Thus, Nassau and Westchester Counties, New York, will not tolerate any control over them by New York City. Because it is undemocratic, it seems

* Attorney-at-Law, New York, N. Y.

impossible, anywhere, to give the central city the planning powers over the outside land, which are necessary for a sufficient measure of control. For instance, no central city is allowed to zone outside areas in spite of the great need of harmony in the zoning of the entire region.

(2) Regional control is attempted by extending the boundaries of the central city. This extension, often greatly delayed by local interests, is never wide enough to give the regional control necessary, and if it were sufficiently extensive for that purpose, would unduly destroy local government, so necessary for efficiency and happiness; for, with all its faults, home rule, in large measure, is more advantageous than centralized control of local affairs.

There seems to be no immediate prospect of the attainment of effective regional planning administration in this country. Abroad such administration exists, and is obtained by State supervision of local planning, harmonizing local conflicts, and furnishing the incentive to local governments in their work. It is along this line, it would seem, that real regional planning must come in America. To some it seems contrary to the principle of home rule; but, in fact, it preserves home rule by giving just the proper amount of regional control without further interference with local government. Other systems fail by reason of ineffectiveness or excess; State supervision succeeds by keeping to the golden mean. Successful abroad, it will surely come in this country.

U. S. Grant, 3d,* Assoc. M. Am. Soc. C. E.—The speaker, whose practical work with city planning has only covered a few years, has been engaged in some regional planning which includes the National Capital, and some rather peculiar problems that have arisen there.

In the first place, it appears that city planners are likely to be too intent upon the problems of the moment, especially traffic and business problems; and that the urgency of a solution to these problems is very apt to lead any planning commission from the more general, and to the speaker's mind, more important, problem of planning for the future. Work on the two must go on simultaneously, and one cannot be neglected in order to take care of the other. Moreover, the more immediate problems demand attention and, therefore, are sure to be solved in the natural course of events, so that the really serious problem, which the city planning profession alone can appreciate and handle, is that of preventing too great a concentration of population, and the evils that come therefrom; that is, the problem of preserving the open spaces. Parks alone, and the high cost of securing them, even by exercising the right of eminent domain, will hardly save the situation for the present; although this may take care of it in the future, if some other way can be found to increase the available amount of open spaces to meet present needs.

A partial lien on open spaces used for other purposes certainly does indicate a legal method of preserving all the open space that is still left. However, there is another legal method of carrying out the combined operation of different authorities, as in the State of California, where a plan of flood control,

* Lt.-Col., Corps of Engrs., U. S. A.; Director, Public Bldgs. and Parks of the National Capital, Washington, D. C.

extending over nearly all the northern part of the Valley of California has been adopted jointly by the Federal Government and the State. Each has set up a board with authority to modify the approved plan to some extent, and each has passed laws by which plans inconsistent with the adopted project cannot be carried out. In the case of interference of this plan, with irrigation and other local projects, the proponents of the latter can, of course, have recourse to the Courts and show a damage which is covered by appropriation or assessment; but thus far this method of prevention has worked very well, and the Supreme Court of California has sustained the legality of the legislation. It offers a compromise measure which is immediately possible where planners have to deal, as they do in the region of which Washington is the center, with municipalities or States and the United States; and even in other cases, where separate States mutually agree upon some general plan for the preservation of certain open spaces, each contributing toward its cost an amount proportioned to the features in which each individual State is particularly interested. Each State would constitute its own board to carry out its part of the plan; and both boards, meeting together, could arrive at a mutual decision as to general changes in the plan, which were found in the interest of both sides. Within the limits of its own jurisdiction each State Board would then prevent any development inconsistent with the project during the period necessary to complete it, and increases in taxation of open spaces remaining in private ownership could be prevented, wholly or in part, as long as their open character beneficial to the public is maintained.

The question of the cost of parks is one that deserves more study than it usually gets. Those who come into city planning from the Engineering Profession are especially inclined to look upon parks as a luxury that is expensive and, therefore, something that should be dispensed with as much as possible. In many cases, especially where they are laid out after careful study, parks may actually result in an economy to the city in which they are placed. One park project, over which urban development would have been very much more expensive than park treatment, has been before the City of Washington for about twelve years, and is now (1926) nearing completion. The only possible loss to the city because of the park is the reduction in taxation due to losing the assessments that might have been raised on the property located within the park limits; but no such loss will actually occur because the increase in taxable values of the land adjacent to the park may be expected to equal the former value of the land taken, not to mention the benefits in traffic and other facilities which it offers. There is an actual gain of about $4 000 000 to the city in the cost of the park as compared with what it would have cost to make the usual street developments.

The open spaces must include, not merely playgrounds and small city square parks, but larger areas. The necessity for them is very much greater than it was, because the public has a much greater amount of leisure time to spend out of doors, for which provision has to be made. Twenty-five years ago the laboring man worked 10 to 12 hours per day, and his children began to work quite early in life. Nowadays, those children are still going to school at the age of 14 and 15 during part of the year only, and then just a few hours of the day, and the working man himself has a considerable amount of leisure time during the day and in the evening. They cannot find a safe or satisfactory place for exercise on the streets, because of the crowded condition, and the parks are their only safe and sane recourse.

JOHN IHLDER,* ESQ. (by letter).—The writer has been fortunate—or unfortunate—depending upon one's viewpoint, in the discussors of this paper. With a single exception, each party to the discussion sees practically "eye to eye," so they leave nothing further to be said except by way of expressing appreciation for the greater emphasis and clarity they have given to points made in the paper, and for additional data, which the writer has found instructive and helpful.

The writer takes issue with Mr. Rice on two points—which really are one. Believing, as he does, that the family is the essential unit of society (the paper recognizes the fact that there are individuals who must be provided for), the writer cannot agree that the requirements of the individual form a proper basis for a housing program. Consequently, also, he cannot agree that "if a reasonable limitation is made as to area per individual, the multiple house will lose the greater part of its objections." To quote from the paper,

"The preservation of the family—meaning parents and children—is essential. * * * The one-family house with generous open spaces about it is the best house for a child."

Mr. Rice apparently believes that proper housing is fully provided if the house is sanitary and has adequate light and ventilation. The writer believes that this is not enough, that the predominant type of house must also be a home which makes adequate provision for children. Therefore, he disagrees with the statement of Mr. Rice that "the single-family house may not be the ideal one for a large industrial population." An industrial population has children.

It may be that under existing conditions in many American cities the wage-earners must live in two or three-room apartments, but that does not make these apartments ideal. Mr. Rice's supporting argument is that the single-family house "is more expensive than the multiple house." In that statement he raises a question which he does not answer, one which cannot be answered briefly because it involves many factors. One can say, however, that before the World War, when housing conditions were more nearly normal than they have been since, the rent of a six-room one-family brick house in Philadelphia was lower than that of a rear five-room unheated, walk-up tenement in New York, or that of an apartment in a wooden "three-decker" in Boston.

* Mgr., Civic Development Dept., Chamber of Commerce of the United States, Washington, D. C.

AMERICAN SOCIETY OF CIVIL ENGINEERS

INSTITUTED 1852

TRANSACTIONS

This Society is not responsible for any statement made or opinion expressed in its publications.

Paper No. 1683

CULTURAL OPPORTUNITIES IN REGIONAL PLANNING*

By Andrew Wright Crawford,† Esq.

With Discussion by Messrs. Henry V. Hubbard, James Sturgis Pray, Noulan Cauchon, E. M. Bassett, Jacob L. Crane, Jr., Charles Wellford Leavitt, Morris Knowles, Harold M. Lewis, R. H. Randall, C. H. Howell, Charles W. Eliot, 2d, Winters Haydock, Gilmore D. Clarke, Harry J. March, John Ihlder, and Joseph Barnett.

On his return from a tour through the Southern and Western States, Otis Skinner related that he had done numerous one or two-night stands in typical "Main Street" towns, with all the stale, flat dullness that one associates with that description. In nearly every case, however, some one asked him to play on the golf course, which he generally did; and he always found the delightful, charming loveliness, with all the beauty and abiding cheerfulness of Nature, which the well-kept swards and the long green vistas, required by the game, produce at every turn.

The introduction of golf has brought a cultural opportunity to the dullest, drabbest town that boasts a course. Golf courses are the anti-toxin of "Main Street". Doctors state that golf is prolonging the lives of many men, but, important as that service is, it seems surpassed by this observation of Mr. Skinner. Many individuals will echo an agreement, and give parallel citations of their own experiences. "Bangor" used to bring the recollection of terrible meals in a wretched station in a hopeless town; but now the name conjures the vivid picture of a river vista bordered by the tapis vert of the golf course, dotted with glorious New England elms.

Culture is assisted much by education, much by travel, much by reading, but it depends in large measure upon physical adjuncts. It is possible to

* Presented at the Joint Meeting of the City Planning Division with the American City Planning Inst., Philadelphia, Pa., October 8, 1926.

† Attorney-at-law; Secy., Philadelphia Municipal Art. Comm., Philadelphia, Pa.

conceive of a cultured man living in a town with no schools, no libraries, no playgrounds, no parks, no golf courses. But while one individual, like a "sport" in horticulture, might arrive and stay in such a place, it is not reasonably possible to conceive of such a town becoming a community of cultured men and women. The opportunity has to be present. Schools for the children, with the play space where they learn so much, libraries, churches, and community centers must be provided. Consider the charm of an ancient street of a New England town with great elms arching over it in cathedral forms. The mere thought suggests refinement. Cut every tree down and the suggestion is obliterated.

If the regional plan gives adequate locations for libraries, for common and high schools, for colleges, for universities—all on the educational side; if locations are plotted for playgrounds—preferably to be recreational playgrounds —although in crowded centers they must be largely pedagogical playgrounds; if the opportunity to get back to Nature for city people is provided through country parks in sufficient number to make it a frequent experience; if the regional plan gives sufficient examples of the plotting of street trees with as much care and particularity as the plotting of street conduits (be it noted that in some foreign countries the engineering plan always shows the locations of trees); if these things are done, then the regional plan will be of distinct service in helping to create the physical surroundings which are an important aid in the production of a cultivated community.

This is not all. If public structures, or structures extending over public property, like bridges of all types, signs, lighting fixtures, etc., are well designed, they will be at least as cheap as ugly structures. They will add to or detract from values of the neighborhood in exact proportion to their beauty. An ugly bridge seldom lasts out its life. The community gets rid of it before its expectation of life is run. An engineer who does not point that out to his client, when the latter wants him to design an ugly bridge (but which he calls "merely utilitarian"), fails in his duty to that client.

An investment in ugliness is as extravagant an investment as the directors of a corporation, the council of a city, or any group may make. If Washington, Paris, and Pasadena, show the money-making power of municipal attractiveness, how completely do Hoboken, Weehawken, and Manayunk demonstrate the sheer cost of ugliness. Effective regional planners, therefore, will see to it that over each and every region into which the regional plan reaches, some authority is recommended to be set up, like the State Art Commissioners or Art Juries—of which there are now about thirty in the United States—which will consist of men who will have the backbone to say to politicians seeking favors for important voters, that no ugly thing will be permitted to depreciate the values, financial and cultural, of their city, suburb, or country. An ugly bridge decreases all values around it, especially in suburban sections, and an attractive one increases that value.

In Philadelphia, the tradition of attractiveness in suburban development has become so strong that its suburbs have become world famous. Nevertheless, much could be done in this region to improve the architecture of the smaller houses. In one or two foreign countries, "Bureaus of Building Advice" have been created, the function of which parallels for private owners (who purpose to build on private property) those of the public art commissions as to public buildings. Plans are submitted to the "Bureau of Building Advice" and it advises the owners as to the effect of the appearance of their buildings on the values and worth of the community. The owners do not have to accept the advice; but they do not care to have the advertisement that their buildings have been condemned by the "Bureau of Building Advice" and, consequently, they do accept the advice in many cases. It would be well, therefore, for the regional planning central group to recommend and then to secure the creation of such "Bureaus of Building Advice" in its community.

Fifty years ago individual parks were regarded as luxuries. Thirty years ago they were accepted as necessities, but parkways to link them into an organic whole were regarded as luxuries. To-day, parkways are regarded as necessities, and some automobilists would have us create super-parkways to give them super-opportunities for killing others as well as themselves.

It is assumed that the creation of an adequate park system, including the reservation of creek valleys, the preservation of places of natural beauty or historic interest, the acquisition of certain high plateaus in the region for public use and public enjoyment, will be accepted for what they are, as fundamental portions of the regional plan.

It is important, however, to refer to two points—one of which is obvious and more or less becoming the practice, but the other of which, curiously, has been lost to sight. Parkways should be regarded as traffic thoroughfares. Opportunities for the operators of motor trucks, as well as of pleasure vehicles, to drive, in the course of their daily employment, or on their way to or from work, through attractive thoroughfares, is one which is somewhat recognized, but not as completely as it should be. The idea that a park or parkway is somewhat the old-fashioned parlor—only to be used on Sunday when the parson comes for dinner after church—is one that should be completely discarded—the idea, not the parson. Motor-truck routes and motor touring-car routes should be devised for their every-day attractiveness and for every hour of the day. This means occasionally a slightly additional expense for width. It means hardly anything in the way of the development expense of the property; perhaps it really means a reduction of cost, instead of an increase, because property fronting on a parkway is more valuable than one that does not.

The second point that it is desired to emphasize in this respect is the one that has been forgotten. A practice has grown that is in direct contrast with the theory with which modern city planning in America was begun about twenty years ago. It was the basic argument for city planning then that one improvement to a city frequently was plotted, or designed, or conceived solely with reference to that improvement and without reference to the program of the city as a whole and the proposed order for other adjacent improvements. City planners insisted that this was wrong and that the entire problem should be considered together. Then zoning came along and many city planners lost sight of their argument for comprehensiveness. Zoning systems, plotted without regard to park systems, are numerous. Zoners think that if they zone property in a certain way because it fronts on a park, that they have sufficiently recognized the park system.

One has yet to see a zoning plan in which zoning for use is made complete. If property is to be used for residences, business, or manufacturing, the zoning plan shows it; but if the property should be used for parks the zoning plan by itself does not show that use. Obviously, a zoning plan should suggest areas for public use in the form of parks or playgrounds, just as it should zone areas for private use in the form of single-family and multiple-family houses, commerce, or industry. Zoners have failed adequately to see the opportunity for living up to the principle for which the city planners began twenty years ago—of preparing the plan in its entirety.

In addition, however, an opportunity for parks in connection with zoning, has certainly not been emphasized. There is no reason why zoners should not frankly divide a commercial or a transportation industry from a residential district by the interposition of a public park. True, it may not be so acquired, but it should be submitted as a recommendation. In Philadelphia, there is such a natural division. The Midvale Steel Works lies in a valley and a suburban section of Southern Germantown lies just over the crest of the hill. The hill and the slope are occupied by Fernhill Park—53 acres in extent. Why should not this principle be frequently applied in zoning?

The opportunity is especially available in connection with regional planning. When a region is planned the opportunity for placing elongated, wide, or narrow parks as a boundary, with residences on one side and heavy or light industry or business on the other, is so obvious and the opportunity is so great that this paper will be considered worth while if it conveys this thought, plus Otis Skinner's observation of the cultural power of golf courses.

Sixty to seventy-five years ago, when American cities first began to acquire such parks as Fairmount Park, Central Park, Franklin Park, and Druid Hill Park—in Philadelphia, New York, Boston, and Baltimore, respectively—it was thought that just one big park was all that was necessary. When the writer became Secretary of the City Parks Association, in 1900, there was put into his hands a pamphlet by President Elliot, of Harvard University, on the question of how to get the people to the parks. It has been answered by taking the parks to the people in the form of small parks and the park system, by establishing, as it were, a central park and branch parks.

The same psychological change has occurred in connection with libraries. The great Public Library in Boston—great because of its beauty, not because of its size—was just in course of completion a little more than a third of a century ago. In that short space of time the need for taking the library to the people has been recognized, and every large city has built many branch libraries. Numerous American cities (Philadelphia among them) have recently completed or are completing great central art museums. They are absolutely important to the cultural development of the city; but equally important will be branch art museums throughout the region. The recognition of this psychology is just at the beginning. We had to take parks to the people. We had to take libraries to the people. We equally have to take art museums to the people. Only within the last year has New York City opened its first Branch Museum, at 196th Street. The regional plan must, of necessity, if it is to be adequate to its cultural opportunities, plot the locations of a sufficient number of branch art museums to take pictures to the people as effectively as the branch libraries have taken books to the people.

It is suggested that the next generation will create branch universities. Imagine the University of Pennsylvania with eight or ten branches in the region within 30 or 40 miles of Philadelphia. It is not such a great advance over what has already been done, educationally, as it appears. In 1890, there was just one High School in Philadelphia. To-day, there are eleven High Schools and twelve Junior High Schools. In other words, the Central High School—a City College—is supplemented by branch high schools, some of the teachers of which think their own branches are higher than the High School. In some respects their thought is true. It would be interesting, or at least advantageous, to have locations for branches of institutions of higher learning in outer regions suggested by the regional plan. The first regional plan that does so will be regarded in the future as prophetic.

What is the opportunity of civil engineers in presenting on paper plans directed to the securing of locations in the region for the creation of cultural opportunities in all these different and diverse ways? What are the qualifications of civil engineers for the job? Well, it may be stated, in the first place, they understand construction; but only a few of them understand that construction is not design. Here is an illustration. If a plumber attaches three pipes to a main so that the water spouts from the other ends, he has not designed a fountain—he has constructed it; he has done the plumbing part. If an engineer builds a bridge merely sufficient to stand the traffic, he has not designed the bridge; he has only constructed it; he is only a plumber. If an engineer takes the trunk of a tree and makes kitchen chairs sufficiently strong to stand the weight of the cook, he has constructed the chair, but he has not designed it. An artist, taking another portion of that same tree trunk, will, by adding design to construction, produce a Chippendale chair worth $40 compared to the engineer's chair with a value of $4. Only those engineers who know design as distinct from construction should have anything to do with the regional plan. If that cuts out 95%, they can overcome the difficulty by studying design as distinct from construction. Again, such constructors can prevent other engineers from lacking what they lack by insisting that institutes of technology shall teach design to engineers, as well as how to calculate strength of materials, stresses, and strains.

Some civil engineers have felt justified in complaining of the injection of architects and landscape designers into city planning, because it seemed especially the field of civil engineers; but the civil engineers had the field entirely to themselves for the whole of the Nineteenth Century, and they have only themselves to blame that the public, weary at last of the drab, stupid, stale rectangularity of the checker-board cities which were all the civil engineers of a century produced, relegated them to the subordinate position of drawing the working plans for designs conceived by others. "By their fruits, ye shall know them." And the public has judged of civil engineers as city planners by the Nineteenth Century gridiron. The end is not yet. A graduate of civil engineering asked the writer whether, as the result of fifteen years direct contact with the supervision of plans for bridges, he thought architects would supersede engineers as designers of bridges. The answer was that it depends on whether engineers learn to design—present trends indicate they would not—and that, with the astonishing advance in the determination of American cities to use Art as their daily servitor, the architects in another decade will have pushed the engineers down to the subordinate position of calculating stresses and strains for the plans of bridges designed by their architect-employers.

One had only to go to the Sesqui-Centennial in Philadelphia to see how Art has come into its own. If the Sesqui Art Museum and all it contained had been entirely removed, the whole exhibition would have remained a great art exhibit. Consider how the steel industry was most conspicuously represented. Jones and Laughlin, steel manufacturers, showed what? They showed what was essentially a notable work in sculpture. It could have been with advantage less literal; but the whole conception was fundamentally sculptural. That was the method of appeal to the public; that was the advertisement chosen by a great steel concern. In the housing of individual exhibits, every form of Grecian, Roman, and Byzantine architecture was used.

The mere engineer will become only a skilled workman unless he looks to design. What should those engineers, qualified by a knowledge of design, as well as of construction, for the job of regional planning—what should they study, what facts should they ascertain in order to be able to plan for the cultural development of an entire region? Chief traffic routes must be studied. Such mistakes, as that in New York, where Central Park blocks two vitally needed north and south routes, must be avoided. Opportunities along the traffic routes for the preservation of places of natural beauty and historic interest should be determined.

Obviously, the topography must be studied. A poor topography may require a somewhat larger area for a park system than a favorable one. The City of Philadelphia is fortunate. Such a deep narrow valley as the Wissahickon requires less area for the preservation of extraordinarily great natural charm, than a level terrain would have required. The percentage of the total area which should be taken for the park system necessarily will vary with the topography, with the character of the community so far as it can be predetermined by zoning, and with other elements. Ten per cent. is a principle which has stood the test of many years. Probably a good regional park system will approximate that. Larger playfields, covering 10 to 20 acres, should be plotted about 1 mile from each other, and the smaller playgrounds within 5 min. of each child's home. This, again, will vary in accordance with the expected intensity of residential development as forecast by the zoning system.

In connection with playgrounds, and harking back to Otis Skinner, the writer would emphasize the importance of pay-as-you-play golf courses, and, in addition, a method for making privately owned golf courses permanent in their locations. Golf courses are open spaces. If completely permanent they would be open air parks, by which is meant parks which would be enjoyed by the public even if it could not walk over them. How can they be made as nearly permanent as possible?

It is submitted that if the golf club is willing to throw its course open to any member of the public who behaves himself and who pays the greens' fee, which averages from $1 to $3, that would be a sufficient justification, either for entirely exempting the golf club from taxes or for making the rate, say, about one-half the ordinary tax rate. In the City of Philadelphia there are three tax rates—the "city" rate, the "suburban" rate, and the "rural" rate. The suggestion is that taxes on golf courses, which are open to those who pay the greens' fee, should be either the rural rate or else that the taxes should be waived altogether. This would require legislation, but it would be a cheap means of increasing the permanent open spaces of a region. Within a journey of ½ or ¾ hour of Philadelphia there are more than sixty golf courses—which means there are sixty open spaces, averaging about 100 acres. If all these spaces could be made permanent by a stroke of the pen, it would be a blessing. Freedom from taxation would be a great incentive to a club to remain where it is. Otherwise, increases in values may not only make it desirable to move, but may make it imperative.

There is one other thought in this respect. If any golf club intends to sell its property, it ought to give some public authority about six months' opportunity to purchase it at a price equal to the highest price offered.

Zoning will also help to predetermine the natural location for school houses and libraries. If zoning, in its logical development, is finally sustained by the Courts, the needs of the region and of each section of the region in respect to thoroughfares, all sorts of public conveniences will be able to be forecasted, for fifteen or twenty years, with much greater accuracy than at present. Nevertheless, forecasts must be attempted through the familiar methods of studying the growth of communities by maps and otherwise.

In answer to the query as to the kind of investigation that should be made, in order to plan effectively for the cultural development of a community, so far as physical accomplishments can help toward that development, the items of calculation and of investigation are pretty much the same as in regard to the other elements of the regional plan. Growth of population, directions of that growth, topography, natural and artificial barriers, locations of railroad, rapid transit lines, traffic arteries, and secondary streets, all are to be included. It would be easy to take the ordinary list of divisions and sub-divisions of a schedule, and repeat, but to engineers it is unnecessary. Indeed, when one takes up one of the published summaries and sub-divisions presented for an ideal investigation, the effect is appalling. The investigator is apt to think that each particular head and sub-head must be investigated with equal meticulousness before he dare make a decision.

If to-day one could present a perfect plan for Metropolitan Philadelphia, twelve months later it would be not more than 97½% perfect. In four years, it might not be more than 90% perfect. Most big plans take at least ten years to realize, and a regional plan will take thirty or forty years. A perfect plan to-day may not be more than 60% of perfection by the end of thirty years. Every city plan and every regional plan that is under way to-day can be convicted of too much meticulousness in the information sought. The time spent in investigating and getting minute details is so great and the value of those details is so negligible that a great deal of impatience with regional planning is justified.

It is necessary, therefore, to determine when all the really worth while investigation has been made, and all the information that is important has been obtained, but use much good sense as well as "horse" sense in determining that which is important. Hasty decisions are not advocated, but delayed decisions are strongly deprecated. These lists and tables of matters to be investigated have written over them on each page, in enormous letters so big that they are never seen, the words "Excuses for Delays". Refuse to emphasize the various points that might be investigated. The engineer can readily find such schedules, but when he finds them he should spend no more time than is absolutely necessary in answering each of them and should see whether genuine efficiency, not the meticulous kind so much preached and regrettably also practiced, does not dictate that many of them go uninvestigated. If a physician made every possible investigation that he might make in the case of each patient, his patient would probably die before he were a quarter finished.

It is important, too, to recollect that some of the modern gods may not prove immortal. Especially is this true of the god, Speed. To-day, speed automobilists have the public by the throat. All they have to do is to present an appeal against some kind of obstruction to infinite speed in order to have that obstruction wiped away. If a circular park at an intersection can be shown to delay automobilists 2 or 3 sec., weak-kneed city officials remove the circle. At the time of the Philadelphia Sesqui-Centennial, a Philadelphian took an educated Chinaman from the Exposition to a charming suburban home, ten miles out, going by a beautiful route. On returning, he told his guest that they would come back by the less interesting Lincoln Highway, because it would save 10 min., whereupon the Chinaman said, "And what will you do with it?" The automobilist, abashed, was unable to reply. Propaganda for speed is in sad need of "debunking".

A cultivated community may come accidentally, but it will come far more adequately and far more certainly if it is consciously planned. The ideals of one generation become the accepted realities of the next—sometimes sooner. In 1906 an intimate friend—the city editor of a great Philadelphia daily—referring to a project at which many were hammering away, said: "The Fairmount Parkway is a dream". In coming to the Convention of the Society in 1926 many used the dream of 1906.

Engineers are practical men and because of that fact the writer wants to emphasize this thought—that dreams are the most practical forces in the world. Engineers can be mere technicians or they can be much more. Remember that mere dreamers have accomplished far more than mere engineers. Why not be both engineer and dreamer?

DISCUSSION

HENRY V. HUBBARD,* ESQ.—The author emphasizes the idea of bringing the parks to the people. Every one agrees, but the process has its limits. Books can be brought to people because the book is the same whether one reads it in a great public library, in the branch library, or at home; but the essence of a big park is its bigness, and that cannot be brought to the people by distributing the same recreation area among their homes in small fragments. The playground and the little park can be brought to the people. The people must be taken to the big park.

Mr. Crawford speaks very truly of the desirability of zoning the region with due regard to the park areas. This principle should be applied also to the uses permitted in parks and parkways after they have been acquired by the public; that is, subsidiary uses destructive of their main purpose should not be allowed to invade the park areas. Landscape charm, reasonable quiet, and safety are essential attributes in parks and parkways. The cultural value of the parkways to the motor-truck drivers, whose welfare Mr. Crawford so feelingly bespeaks, would not be sufficient to compensate for the destruction which the noisy dangerous passage of the trucks would work in those qualities of the parkway which fit it for its main and essential recreational use.

As to the engineer's contribution to city planning, it should be remembered that the engineers of the early Nineteenth Century were fighting alone in the front line of the battle. There were at that time no art juries, no city planners, and no lawyers trained to give counsel to engineers and to help them in their difficulties; but even so they were not without their triumphs in the field of esthetics and of broad plan conception. Major L'Enfant, for instance, was an engineer.

As to the future of engineers in regional planning, it is plain that whoever lays out the broad conception of future community development, his work will be bad unless it is based on engineering knowledge; and, in any case, most of it will be built by engineers.

The main lesson of this discussion is obvious. For the fuller development of all the cultural opportunities of the city and the region, there should be fuller co-operation among all the professions involved; each profession knowing that it is only one wheel of the city-planning cart. The cart would not run well without that one wheel, but it would run still worse supported on one wheel alone. Many examples of effective common sense co-operation between professions in regional planning may be seen, and it will not be long before it will be a matter of course.

JAMES STURGIS PRAY,† ESQ. (by letter).—This topic opens up an enormous field. Mr. Crawford brings out effectively and suggestively many of these cultural opportunities. Culture may mean very different things to different

* Editor, *City Planning Magazine* and of *Landscape Architecture,* Cambridge, Mass.

† Charles Eliot Professor of Landscape Architecture, and Chairman, School of Landscape Architecture, Harvard Univ., Cambridge, Mass.

people—in short, anything from *Kultur* to refinement of taste. If the development or strengthening of the mental powers is meant; or improving or refining of the mind, the morals, the taste;* and not merely the culture and refinement of the few, but rather the advancement and uplift of the many; then, surely comprehensive, competent, and far-seeing regional planning not only offers unlimited opportunities for culture, but is essential to the most widespread culture. It is known that culture, proverbially, has bulked larger in cities, but cities have no monopoly of it. Some of the most truly cultivated minds are possessed by individuals who have spent their whole lives in the country, and some by those who have lived a large part of their lives in the wilderness, for example, John Muir. The region, the term as now commonly used for a great metropolitan area with a city center and extensive outlying suburban and rural districts, embraces both city and country. The whole strong aim and tendency of regional planning to-day is, not only to extend into the country as many as possible of the advantages long accruing almost exclusively to city dwellers but, also, to bring into the city all possible of the advantages of life in the country. This is far more important. All the opportunities for culture offered by the physical and human environment may then be provided by regional planning, for it is not necessary to except wholly even such as may be had only in the wilderness, since areas in a wilderness can be conserved by planning for their use; as, say, in the region of Geneva, Switzerland.

Any region will, of course, even without what is called regional planning, offer many of these opportunities. That is, it will offer these opportunities in ways limited either to certain classes of the population or to all classes in certain respects only, and within certain none-too-broad limits. However, great metropolitan areas to-day, without regional planning, offer also much, and in some ways more and more, that works powerfully against culture. Crowding without planning, and the speeding up of life of which large populations tend to become victims, operate against health; the lack of planning adequately for ease of circulation leads to colossal inefficiency and waste; and the thoughtless piling up of ugliness in many parts of these great areas certainly dulls the popular sensitiveness to beauty and deadens even the aspirations for beauty in environment. Culture may exist in a slum or in a deadly monotonous suburb or in the most repulsive industrial area, but certainly these conditions in themselves do not make for culture; yet normal humans, the uneducated as well as the educated, the simpler minded as well as the more sophisticated, are responsive naturally to beauty in their environment and particularly to beauty in its universal and its highest forms. Given sufficiently widespread understanding and will to co-operate in bringing about a better set of conditions in the city or region, there is every reason why not only living areas and recreation areas to which much attention to beauty is already given, but all working areas as well, should supply a vastly more beautiful environment than they do at present.

The control by regional planning of these matters, when it includes regional zoning, will increase these opportunities for culture in the following principal ways. True culture comes both from hard work and from times of

* Standard Dictionary.

relaxation and is, perhaps, like genius, one-third inspiration and two-thirds perspiration. Sound regional planning will go far to promote and assure public health and the general physical well-being of the people living, working, and playing within a region. It will bring increased alertness, sensitiveness, and greater sanity, and will give to the workers at once more power to draw culture from their hours of labor and more energy to devote their spare time to things that make for culture over and beyond what their regular pursuits may bring them. Therefore, sound regional planning spells greater community efficiency, and from this greater efficiency, result important economies of time and money, thus affording both more money and more leisure.

Assuredly, there is no occasion to emphasize here the tremendous gains in efficiency of life in a metropolitan community, which accrue from a comprehensive, well-organized plan for the whole area and in which the component districts are set apart for their respective dominant functions of residence, business, industry, and recreation; each such district is not just conventionally but really functionally planned with respect to sizes and shapes of blocks, as well as the continuity and cross-section of local streets. The whole is tied together by a comprehensive system of main thoroughfares—radial, diagonal, and circumferential. Nor is it necessary to dwell on the colossal economy from such efficient, comprehensive, functional planning. Nevertheless, it is important to note that, from these gains in efficiency and economy, there must come to the great masses of the people greatly increased opportunities for culture. For although, of course, neither increase of wealth nor added leisure necessarily leads to increase of culture, both greatly enlarge the opportunities for some of its highest, most precious forms. Nor is there need to urge that comprehensive, functional planning in itself produces the highest order of functional or organic beauty, the sort of beauty that results inevitably from the perfect adaptation of the form of an object to the use for which it is designed. All are familiar with the classic example of this: The clipper ship which, in the old days, was built for speed and the profit accruing from quick passages to foreign ports rather than for beauty, but which offers one of the most beautiful forms ever created by man.

Indeed, one does not have to go back to that time. The modern world is full of examples, such as the electric locomotive, the functional highway, the modern factory building, and the airplane.

Beyond this sort of beauty, there is still needed, through all planning and zoning, a conscious seeking for outward visual beauty of form, color, texture, and composition, such as can be supplied only by those specially trained to create it. While the mass of the people cannot be expected to unite readily in securing this beauty, it can be brought about through the leadership of the competent. When through competent far-reaching regional planning, beauty in regional environment shall widely prevail, will not the people who grow up and work and play amid these beautiful surroundings, be far more intolerant of all that is ugly than people are to-day? Will they be satisfied any longer with what is merely poor, mediocre, indifferent, uninteresting? Does not beauty beget beauty?

Is it not true, for instance, that, if or when Philadelphia, or New York, or Boston, or Chicago, shall realize a wide, comprehensive dream of beauty, the influence over the country and over the world for beauty will be beyond one's utmost power to imagine?

The more perfectly organized the physical plan of the area of a community for health, efficiency, and economy, the more the members of that community can accomplish within it in a given time by the same expenditure of effort or money, and so the more time they will have over for cultural pursuits—pursuits which both further culture in themselves and also indirectly increase cultural opportunities.

This, however, is not enough, because a regional plan is not truly efficient that does not assure the absence of ugliness and the presence of the maximum of possible beauty throughout its whole three-dimensional extent, from dignified uplifting building groups to the artistic design of street name plates and mail boxes. No such dream as this can be realized that is not based on comprehensive, systematic, unified planning of the region. Then, out of this realized efficient and beautiful regional environment can come, and will come, more freely than ever before and far more widely, opportunities for culture.

NOULAN CAUCHON,* ESQ. (by letter).—Engineers should have as an indispensable part of their education, a serious grounding in the principles of design in art. Without it, it is not safe to allow them at large. Look at the resultant atrocities of the merely utilitarian which some of them have perpetrated on the unsuspecting democracy. Henry Fairfield Osborn makes clear in his recent trenchant restatement of the truth of evolution† that the physical evolution of man is the least distinctively human part of him. In his intellectual and spiritual side lies the great advance beyond the brute. The brute has all the adaptabilities for fitness to purpose in a given environment. Are people to be restricted to thinking in merely the three quantitative dimensions of which the so-called "practical" man (and the brute) is cognizant, or should they not soar in a fourth qualitative dimension of the intellect and the spirit and insist on events and intervals being acceptable on the more human basis—something better than brute bluntness to impressions of hunger and shelter?

As Mr. Crawford so well puts it, things beautiful cost no more than ugly expressions of buildings, bridges, and landscape. Let planners express Nature, which is Truth, in its myriad forms, in such a way that all, from childhood to maturity, may get close to it in school, playground, and park, in home, workshop, and council chamber, to draw strength and cheer and guidance on the path of progress, individual and collective—National. Also, civilization has advanced to the point where amenity has become a negotiable value to the most dense. An art jury is desirable for all communities as a source of helpful, constructive criticism and restraining influence on private and public aberrations.

A further thought which Mr. Crawford advances for consideration is that public amenities, parks and parkways, should come into the daily life of the

* Ottawa, Ont., Canada.

† "Science and Religion in Education."

people, be used to and from, between their homes and work, and that they be planned to create this condition. Some years ago, it was the writer's privilege to suggest that in a mountain park development the pedestrian pathways, in threading their way through the park, should be kept as far as possible away from the highways. Need one argue with trained minds on the cultural opportunities that lie within regional planning and of the necessity that it be comprehensive planning?

It is the civil power which is always "skinning" the engineer's estimates, generally leaving very little with which to develop things of beauty.

Mr. Crawford, in attacking the gridiron plan, has, in the writer, a staunch supporter. The gridiron is vestigial of prehistoric limitation to two-dimensional thinking; it has an inherent property of congestion. On the other hand, hexagonal planning, in a four-dimensional state of mind, has an inherent property of diffusing traffic. The plan, by analogy, must fulfill the principles of organic evolution, that is, be adaptable to circumstance, that its continuity must be nourished by fitness for purpose—the high purpose of good living conditions and the fulfillment of human life.

E. M. Bassett,* Esq.—Houses will back upon parkways unless there is an intervening street. A parkway has no street front because the owner of the parkway (city or State) can build a high wall or put up an iron fence along its edge. The reason is that a parkway is a park. The abutting owners along a parkway have no easement of access or of light and air over a parkway. It is well to keep that distinction in mind between a highway and a parkway. Parks should be zoned by municipalities for height and bulk. They can not be zoned for use, because all parks are devoted to recreational use, and only those buildings can be erected that are connected with recreation. If a school board begins to put up a school on a park area, any taxpayer can enjoin the board because it would not be a building intended for park use. In New York City, parks are zoned for height and bulk, but not for use. The zoning of a lot for a park would be wiped out by the Courts as soon as the property owner brought it to their attention.

Art juries can pass on beautiful designs for public buildings, and for buildings in streets and parks, but not for those on private property; at least in the United States. The reason seems to be that their's is the realm of æsthetics, and police power does not extend to æsthetics. Probably this is because the Courts conceive that they would have to depend on opinion evidence as to what was and what was not beautiful, and opinion evidence would vary so much that there would be no criterion. One expert might say that in a certain place a certain color was right and another would be equally sure that it was not right. In other words, the Courts in this country conceive that they cannot decide disputes regarding taste, and they look on æsthetics as a matter of taste.

However, it is proper and lawful to bring in the principle of design in city planning. For instance, the pyramidal buildings in Greater New York, that many architects like, are often considered beautiful. Part of their

* Counsel, Zoning Committee, New York, N. Y.

creation was city planning, and part was something else. They are mostly in the "two times" district on the zoning map; that is, the building can go up two times the width of the street on the property line, and then it must set back at the rate of one to four. The city planning part is to stamp on the land the zoning height district of two times. When the land is so stamped, it is for the architect to produce the building. If he would produce it in exact accordance with the set-back plans, it would probably not be a thing of beauty. It is the architect's ability to make a good design within the requirements stamped on the land that produces the beautiful building.

JACOB L. CRANE, JR.,* M. AM. SOC. C. E. (by letter).—Writing from the viewpoint of the professional town planner and referring to the statement in Mr. Crawford's interesting paper that the civil engineers had the city planning field entirely to themselves for the whole of the Nineteenth Century, it is true that the planning of streets and sub-divisions was carried out during that period largely by engineers and surveyors. However, the writer feels that "the stale, flat dullness" of "Main Street" towns and the "drab, stupid rectangularity of the checker-board cities" must be charged equally against the architects and builders who were responsible for the design and placing of the principal visual features, namely, the structures, and still more to the uncritical taste and frequently greedy haste of the American public.

The placing of the blame is not important except to realize that it is not only the engineers who need to be roused out of the easy habit of commonplace, hurried design. Further, the writer wishes to take exception to the reference to the "money-making power of municipal attractiveness". He believes that there is good reason for not continuously harping on the slogan that "beauty pays" in the campaign for a more satisfactory visual environment. As Mr. Crawford points out, the ugly ground plans and buildings are more rapidly replaced, while the beautiful objects continue to satisfy and are preserved. On the other hand, for the individual commercial enterprise, the ugly ground plan or building sometimes is actually most profitable to the individual concerned. In the second place, whether "beauty pays" is not the question. A visual environment, satisfying because of its loveliness, must be considered a justification in itself aside from its purely incidental dollars and cents value. Finally, the writer believes that planners can afford to be careful in their conception of what beauty really is. It has been easy for the zealous landscape architect to destroy the native picturesque beauty of a piece of marsh land, or a finely modeled hillside, or even an old abandoned gravel pit, by imposing upon them the neat and sophisticated design of the professional; and for the architect to spoil the structural feeling and silhouette of a building by too much ornamentation and, particularly, by too great ostentatiousness.

The writer finds that some steel bridges, industrial plants, grain elevators, and machines are among the most beautiful things created in modern life. And they are all the work of the engineer.

* Municipal Development Engr., Chicago, Ill.

Referring to Mr. Crawford's suggestion for "Bureaus of Building Advice", it should be pointed out that such bureaus are, in effect, established in a number of towns and cities in the Middle West. They are constituted as special citizens' or architects' committees. They operate largely by persuasion, but with a marked effectiveness.

Replying to Mr. Crawford's criticism that zoning plans do not indicate sites for parks, a legal zoning map cannot designate property for public use in advance of its having been taken for that use; and it is necessary to designate the zoning of all private property, even if some of it is recommended for park purposes on the general development plans, where such recommendations should properly be indicated.

The writer doubts the effectiveness of the suggestion that golf courses may be made permanent open spaces by remitting the taxes on daily fee courses. Such courses are ordinarily privately owned by an individual or a small syndicate as a purely commercial enterprise; and, while the remission of taxes would undoubtedly be appreciated by such a syndicate, they could not be expected to hold the land for semi-public use when the opportunity arrives to profit by a large increase in land value.

There is a cultural opportunity in regional planning which may be worth mentioning, namely, the extension of the citizen's imagination to include in his civic ideal, not only the territory within the legal limits of his city, but the entire interrelated and interdependent region. It is not easy to define a cultural opportunity, but in all city planning and regional planning work one of the greatest cultural effects seems to the writer to be the stimulation of the imagination and the broadening of the interests of the average citizen.

Mr. Crawford very well points out that the dreamers are entitled to the credit for most of the advancement, and one of the primary purposes of regional planning should be to make a dreamer, not only of the engineer, but of all members of the community. Great city and regional plans will eventually be the crystallization of the dreams of many men and women.

Charles Wellford Leavitt,* M. Am. Soc. C. E.—The author has said much with which all can agree without hesitation, such as the dignity of elms bordering streets in a New England village engendering culture. In one such village where the elms were cut down to provide greater width for a street instead of building a parallel relief street, the people will regret it for the next 200 years at least, if not longer. The dignity and beauty of the town are gone, and it is now ordinary, sordid, and like many other ugly towns throughout the United States.

Art commissions and juries are important, with Bureaus of Building Advice on the side; the value of parks, parkways, playgrounds, and auto-parking places are admitted without argument. Zoning is good and should include zoning for parks. Putting a park between the industries and the home is fine. Central and branch parks with connecting parkways undoubtedly is a great thought. Art museums are certainly cultural with or without

* Civ. and Landscape Engr. (Charles Wellford Leavitt & Son), New York, N. Y. Mr. Leavitt died on April 22, 1928.

the central structure and branch attachments; and a central university with little universities all around sounds like the acme of cultural phenomena.

The Philadelphia Sesqui-Centennial with all the art removed would still be the best advertised exhibition in the world—by a prize fight. It was wonderful, if not cultural.

What is meant by a "poor topography" is a question. Topography is topography. Engineers have to take it as they find it and do their best with it.

Golf courses are certainly a God-send in providing some light and air. A good meal is pleasant to remember, but not to be compared with a vista, or a tapis vert—if one is not hungry. Throwing private golf courses open to the public by the payment of a green's fee might cultivate the masses; but would it be cultural for the club members? It is doubtful. Yet the speaker would like to see all golf courses maintained as open spaces in the future. Should golf courses be exempt from taxes? In case the course be sold for profit or sub-divided, the total accumulated taxes with interest should be paid at the time of transfer.

Traffic study is cultural, for without this cultural activity people would soon be dead, not cultivated.

A city or regional plan is apt to be held up if an attempt is made to carry on as a whole, or in a full and comprehensive way. The speaker is heartily in accord with the idea of knowing what has to be done, but of not advertising the whole plan at once, simply one of the items to be accomplished, and when this has been secured to take up others until the whole city has been re-made, no matter how long this may take. A complete comprehensive plan is very apt to scare the taxpayers, the would-be developers of cities.

The city planner must be prepared to change the plan and keep it up to the best interests of the city, as ideas change frequently and very often for broader and better living conditions.

Does Mr. Crawford suggest that the decision be whether to speed or not to speed? If so, it will undoubtedly be "speed"; but speed made safe by, and with, culture. Probably the American will use the moments saved to go to a cultural movie.

The Fairmount Parkway was a dream. Through the persistent efforts of Mr. Crawford and others in Philadelphia, it was brought to a reality—a great achievement. The process of endeavor and achievement meant much culture. The parkway may still further cultivate if the city is governed by cultured officials. If not, the reverse may obtain, and this "culture" will be spelled with a "K".

No one has a greater respect for the designing talent of the architect than the speaker. It is regrettable that more engineers have not had greater training in the art of design and the sense of proportion which are so carefully studied by the architect. Some civil engineers, like some architects, landscape architects, city planners, lawyers, doctors, and plumbers, are not fitted for the job of designing a bridge, or a chair. However, the speaker must beg to differ as to the engineer being entirely lacking in the power to design. There have been many statements such as this. Consider the Brooklyn Bridge, and other bridges in United States parks, in Spain, and in Italy, the Washington Monument, the Sixty Wall Street Building, New York, the engineering part of the Delaware River Bridge; and then, by comparison, notice some of the later East River bridges and their approaches in which the architects have had a hand. The public buildings in Philadelphia, the New York Post Office, and the Capitol Building in Albany, N. Y., are products of architects—it does not require more than amateurs to judge that, in these instances, the palm will fall to the credit of the engineer.

It matters not whether he calls himself an engineer, a landscape architect, a city planner, or an architect, if he but have the power of design and sense of proportion. An artist versed in the sense of proportion and design can easily be recognized by his work. It is deplored that many who write titles after their names, meaning designers, fall far short of being true artists.

If its leaders are cultured, America may fairly compete with, or surpass, in the development of its coming race, the best examples in Europe of cultured citizens and resplendent cities. If we are not able to recognize true artistic leaders, we will be following false prophets and the development of our peoples and the appearance of our cities will fall far short of those ancient Greeks and Egyptians of whose achievements young students love to cant. We should follow the artist, whether he be a Brooklyn Bridge engineer, a Major L'Enfant, or the architect of New York's beautiful City Hall—John McComb; and we should avoid the designer or planner who, though he may call himself what he will—architect, engineer, or otherwise—cannot produce anything better than some of the existing public structures which do not please the best sense of proportion.

By being critical and judging these objects for himself, whether he is professional or amateur, and by his efforts of seeing, observing, and careful analysis and criticism, an engineer will surely develop culture spelled with a "C".

Morris Knowles,* M. Am. Soc. C. E.—An apt illustration of culture in engineering is the Philadelphia-Camden Bridge. It is certain that there never could have been any controversy between the architect and the engineer on that bridge, else the result would not have been so successful as it is a great tribute to the profession and a notable example of the application of simplicity of engineering design. It is a production with which every one is satisfied.

After all there really is no need of a controversy. There are engineers who are good designers and also those who are poor designers, and there are architects in both classes. It is not a question of profession, it is one of personality; the criterion is whether the man himself has the ability to see beyond and through the things he is trying to do. It is not a question of whether he is an engineer or an architect, any more than it is a question of whether a lawyer can be a successful business man. Many engineers make successful business managers and many others cannot successfully handle their own affairs. Engineers do poorly to discuss this question from the pro-

* Pres. and Chf. Engr., Morris Knowles, Inc., Pittsburgh, Pa.

fessional angle. What they should do is to try and cultivate and stimulate culture in every one, be he an engineer or an architect.

Harold M. Lewis,* M. Am. Soc. C. E.—Perhaps the reason both engineers and architects have fallen down, to a certain extent, in trying to arrive at the best solution of a modern city plan, is the great increase in the complexity of such plans. Mr. Harvey W. Corbett, a well-known New York architect, who has also had an engineering training, has said that the engineer deals in "facts" and the architect in "fancies", and that both are essential for the successful completion of a large modern building. The speaker believes this should be supplemented by stating that they both deal in design, based primarily on different points of view.

A combination of fact and fancy is still more essential in the development of a practical and adequate city or regional plan. The great size of large metropolitan centers has been made possible by improved methods of transportation, sanitation, and building construction. This has brought many new problems, with which the engineer is specially trained to deal. Carefully prepared and analyzed facts are necessary as the basis for any plan, but the successful regional planner must have broad vision and must be somewhat of an idealist. Engineers would do well to develop such qualities to a greater extent.

The future should not be merely an extension of past trends, but should bring opportunities for improved culture of the kinds referred to by Mr. Crawford. As the execution of a regional plan is based on a co-operation between local planning authorities, so should its preparation be based on the best that both engineers and architects can give. If such co-operation is successfully accomplished there is plenty of room for credit for both, where credit is due.

R. H. Randall,† M. Am. Soc. C. E.—It may appear at first that Mr. Crawford is just a trifle hard on the engineer, and that the outlook is dark, or even black. Somewhere, perhaps in the explanatory text on the back of the U. S. Geological Survey standard maps, there is a phrase to the effect that "culture, or the works of man, is shown in black". While it is good map practice to show the works of man (which are naturally and usually the product of the engineer) in black, the terms, "culture" and "black", are not synonymous, even by inference and as they are chargeable to the engineer.

Both engineers and architects have produced structures so ugly as to be actually limited in their usefulness. However, there is noticeable a present and increasing betterment in this respect. Mr. Crawford's paper should serve as a valuable incentive toward continued improvement in both engineering and architectural design; a reminder of what now and always needs to be done, rather than an arraignment for past shortcomings.

C. H. Howell,‡ M. Am. Soc. C. E. (by letter).—The author states that, "if an engineer builds a bridge merely sufficient to stand the traffic, he has not designed the bridge; he has only constructed it; he is only a plumber".

* Executive Engr., Regional Plan of New York and Its Environs, New York, N. Y.

† Pres. and Chf. Engr., R. H. Randall & Co., Toledo, Ohio.

‡ Designing Engr., The J. G. White Eng. Corporation, City of Mexico, Mexico.

However close to the plumber the construction engineer may be in Mr. Crawford's opinion, it is certain that some one designed the bridge. Presumably, it was a bridge engineer.

Webster's Dictionary defines the word, "design", as follows: "To produce a scheme or plan for the making of anything". Anything that is planned is designed, according to this definition, and Mr. Crawford is, seemingly, at variance with Webster.

The writer also submits, that the one outstanding example of non-rectangular city planning of this country, Washington, D. C., was the design of an engineer, L'Enfant.

Not all the "drab, stupid, stale rectangularity of the checker-board cities" should be charged against civil engineers. Some of the drabness, stupidness, and other terrors of the older parts of old cities are the results of, shall it be said, designs by architects? The writer believes the best engineering talent of the Nineteenth Century produced work comparable to that of the best architects and that the common or garden variety of engineering work was quite superior to the common run of architectural efforts.

The graduate, to whom Mr. Crawford referred, need have no fears about architects supplanting civil engineers as designers of bridges. Bridge design is a highly specialized science. No mere architect can afford the time to master it. If he does master it, he becomes an engineer. "The end is not yet"—except in dreams.

Charles W. Eliot, 2d,* Esq.—There is a great need for agreed definitions among planners and generally among the public as to what is a park or parkway and as to the proper functions of a park. Confusion concerning these terms has apparently upset Mr. Crawford. A parkway is not a boulevard; neither is it a traffic thoroughfare. The use of the Bronx Parkway in New York by large numbers of automobiles, traveling at high speed, does not make the parkway into a traffic thoroughfare. Perhaps Mr. Crawford only means that more thoroughfares should be wider and more attractive. That would be a great advantage, but it would not make them parkways. Is it not possible for the Society, or a similar organization, to put before the public in a forcible way, the differentiation between the purposes of different kinds of parks, and particularly the difference between a park and a semi-public, or other kind of open space?

Winters Haydock,† M. Am. Soc. C. E.—An interesting relationship may be discovered between the subject of Mr. Crawford's paper and an announcement in the public press, an announcement which undoubtedly is of great significance on account of its economic, sociological, and cultural implications.

The head of a large industry employing an enormous number of workers has announced that he intends to adopt a 5-day week. That announcement immediately raised a storm of protest on the part of industrial leaders throughout the country, a protest which was the greater on account of the prestige which the author of the announcement, Mr. Henry Ford, enjoys

* City Planner, National Capital Park and Planning Comm., Washington, D. C.

† Directing Engr., Dept. of City Transit, Pittsburgh, Pa.

as a successful pioneer in new fields. The plan was immediately denounced as being economically unsound.

For many reasons it is very improbable that any general change in the working week is an immediate prospect. However, would it not be very rash of any one to declare to-day that it is improbable that the 5-day week will be in the accepted order of things a quarter of a century hence? Suppose that it does become the order of the day? What will that mean? The problem is then immediately thrust on the city planner in a much graver aspect. Does not his responsibility then become as great as that of the leaders in education and in other cultural fields whose well-recognized responsibility it is to determine and make provision for the cultural requirements of the people? If this is true, is not one of the most important functions of the city planner and the regional planner the insuring for the future of facilities for the advantageous utilization of this growing leisure of the masses?

GILMORE D. CLARKE,* ESQ. (by letter).—This paper justifies the wide circulation it has received. Not only is it valuable for engineers, but for the fine arts as well. To-day, these professions have been brought face to face with tremendous problems in connection with the planning of regions, cities, and counties, and of all their component parts.

The problems cannot be solved by members of any one profession. The multiplicity of detail which enters into regional planning are such that no single profession can ever master it. Mr. Crawford brings the Engineering Profession to task for its accomplishments in connection with city planning in the Nineteenth Century. He states that,

"* * * they [engineers] have only themselves to blame, that the public, weary at last of the drab, stupid, stale rectangularity of the checker-board cities, which were all the civil engineers of a century produced, relegated them to the subordinate position of drawing the working plans for designs conceived by others".

This is true, but there are many engineers who now realize the necessity for collaboration with the professions of the arts, in order to effect results in the planning of areas and in the design of structures which will be more satisfying to others as well as to themselves.

A concrete example of collaborative work on the part of members of the professions of engineering, landscape architecture, and architecture, is the following: A Commission was organized in 1922 to prepare a park and parkway plan for Westchester County, New York, which lies just north of New York City between the Hudson River and Long Island Sound. The area of the county is about 500 sq. miles, the richest suburban area in the country. The working organization is made up of a Chief Executive Officer, whose title is "Chief Engineer", a Deputy Chief Engineer, whose duties have to do with engineering design and construction, and a Landscape Architect charged with the planning and design of park and parkway areas and the design of park structures. Architects are called upon to design all buildings which do not come under the category of "minor structures". In addition, there are

* Landscape Archt., Westchester County Park Comm., Bronxville, N. Y.

other departments, such as legal, land purchase, maintenance, and secretarial and accounting departments.

There has been no disposition on the part of the efficient engineers in this organization to complain of the injection of the landscape architect and the architect into this regional planning problem. As a matter of fact, they have welcomed these representatives from the arts, and the results of this co-operation are noteworthy.

In the matter of bridge design, the writer has had an interesting experience in working out more difficult problems with the Commission's structural engineer. There has never been any disposition on the part of this engineer to accomplish work in design that normally is in the field of architecture. The writer believes that, because the bridges designed for the Westchester County Park Commission are the result of collaborative effort, they represent the best there is in modern bridge design in the world.

Mr. Crawford holds out some hope that the engineer may some day become competent to design artistically—to be a "dreamer". The writer doubts it. The mind of the average engineer is trained to precision, to the definite practical working out of problems, to things concrete. Such a mind does not easily re-act to the artist's business of dreaming and imagining. What must be accomplished is to bring these minds together, for one individual to realize the shortcomings of the other, to the end that, when working together on a single problem, it will represent joint efforts and will produce the finest results.

Engineers are practical men, and it is hoped, for the sake of engineering, that they may remain so. Dreaming must be left to other souls; and then the dreamer and the practical man, by getting together and collaborating, will accomplish more than if the attributes of both were centered in one individual.

Harry J. March,* M. Am. Soc. C. E. (by letter).—Mr. Crawford has evidently not yet sensed the relative importance, first, of economic design, and, second, of pictorial design; or, in other words, first the work of the engineer and then that of the architect. There must be first a substantial structure that will serve the highest utility purposes and then let it be painted. The writer is not unmindful of the character of utility in the artistic design, but it is not an absolute necessity. To illustrate, he has in mind a landscape architect's dream of a development which, while beautiful in its effect, utterly disregarded economic traffic conditions. The architect had to be shown by the engineer the relative value of the traffic and the artistic phase, and he finally subordinated the latter to the former. There is a need to stress the importance of co-ordinating the work of the architect and the engineer. The architect should be more of an engineer and the engineer should be more of an architect. Co-ordination is the keynote of the whole development of regional planning as well as of municipal planning. Would that "the powers that be", controlling as they do the extent and intent of public improvements, could realize the value of such development!

* Chairman, Executive, and Engr., City Planning Committee; Chairman, Board of Appeals, Buffalo, N. Y.

This phase of the inter-relationship of the architect and engineer is an important one in the development of regional planning, particularly where bridges are to be erected and county parks or forest preserves established. Every one is quite familiar with the terms, "City Engineer", "City Architect", and "County Engineer", but one seldom hears of a "County Architect". The regional area in its development should bear the impress of the architect to the same proportional extent as the municipal area bears the impress of the City Architect. The idea could be best comprehended, perhaps, under the term, "landscape engineering", rather than "landscape architecture".

JOHN IHLDER,* ESQ.—It seems that in the case of boulevard, parkway, etc., the author and the speaker are talking or thinking of two or three different things, because they do not always supply the same definition to a word.

The increase of heavy truck traffic in American cities has become a matter of serious concern. It not only results in breaking up light pavements, but it is injuring neighboring property. In Washington, D. C., the walls of houses are being cracked, and there are also instances of window panes being cracked by the vibrations of heavy trucks. Something has to be done to regulate that kind of traffic.

Heretofore, apparently, city planners have considered it only from the point of view of facilitating traffic movement, in the case of parkways, by forbidding trucks. In Washington, trucks are now forbidden on the main arterial roads, such as 16th Street and Massachusetts Avenue, etc., the idea being that they delay the movement of lighter automobiles.

This, however, is only one phase of the problem. It must also be considered from the point of view of the character of neighborhood. The present prohibition in Washington is causing trucks to use the minor residential streets to the great detriment of the neighborhood. Should not city planners begin to consider the creation of a system of heavy traffic streets that will adequately serve trucking needs in the cities, and not simply prohibit and divert it from one street or road to another?

JOSEPH BARNETT,† ASSOC. M. AM. SOC. C. E. (by letter).—This is the day of specialists and in the nature of things, specialization will increase as time goes on. The sum total of human knowledge increases steadily, and it is becoming more and more difficult for the individual, in one life time, to learn, appreciate, and develop the ability to use even a small percentage of the information on any one subject. Therefore, whether the subject for discussion is regional planning as a whole, such as the laying out of a city, or a great park system, or whether consideration is being given to one of the details, say, the adaptability of a certain type of structure, it seems advisable to get different viewpoints on the subject. If each specialist has a proper appreciation and respect for the outlook of the others, pleasing as well as economical results will be obtained. Mr. Crawford uses the word, "designer," as if a dress or piece of furniture is under discussion. In regional planning the

* Mgr., Civic Development Dept., Chamber of Commerce of the United States, Washington, D. C.

† Chf. Draftsman, Westchester County Park Comm., Bronxville, N. Y.

functions of design must be divided. The designing engineer, landscape architect, and other specialists all have proper functions to perform.

The Bronx River Parkway, which is a part of the Westchester County, New York, Park System, is an excellent example of the results which can be obtained by co-operation. The bridges are an important feature of this development. To state that they could have been designed by architects alone would be just as untrue as to state that they could have been as successfully designed by the engineer alone. The fundamental structural designs for these bridges were made by the Designing Engineer. Not just the "plumbing" as Mr. Crawford calls it, the computation of stresses and strains, but the conceptions of proportions which made these bridges possible; the development of the solid section rigid frame with variable moment of inertia. Incidentally, on almost every bridge except one, the architect's name appears alone.

To blame all ugly structures of the past on the engineer is a refusal to recognize the fact that such structures were the products of the times. The people more or less controlled the funds for public improvement and any expense over and above the bare requirements formerly met with considerable opposition. Monuments, art museums, and city halls were generally excepted, but to place cut stone facing on a highway bridge of twenty years ago would have been considered the height of extravagance. The modern trend, however, is toward a greater appreciation of the esthetic value of those things with which people come in daily contact and this fact makes Mr. Crawford's paper timely indeed, because designers should keep just a little ahead of the tastes of the times. It would be an excellent thing if all civil engineers, especially those engaged in design, would read, carefully, Mr. Crawford's paper; but regional planning would derive just as much benefit from a similar paper illustrating the necessity of architects acquiring an appreciation of things engineering.

Engineers need not fear having architects called in to lend advice on the esthetics of structures on account of the cost because pleasing structures can be built at very little extra expense, provided the architect has a proper appreciation of the engineering aspects of the problem. Likewise, architects should not assume that engineers have no esthetic taste and that they persist in violating esthetic rules when insistence on extreme economy is not pressed on them. At times, engineers can improve the appearance of a structure very materially. The writer has in mind a case in which outlines for a number of bridges were laid out having intrados curves resembling ellipses. The architects properly recognized that multiple-centered curves would not be smooth, but when the designing engineer suggested curves following fixed mathematical laws instead of the free-hand curves at first laid out, the suggestions were rejected although fundamental clearances and heights were retained. After the first bridges were built they were found to have the appearance of sagging at the crown. On later bridges, mathematical curves were used with perfect effect. One of the structures was a two-span bridge with different span lengths and by applying the same formula to both intrados curves, matched curves resulted. Incidentally, the formula used was,

$$\frac{x^{2.2}}{a^{2.2}} + \frac{y^{2.2}}{b^{2.2}} = 1$$

The slight variation from the true ellipse provided greater clearances at the haunches. This bridge is now finished and the intrados curves are probably the most graceful in this set of bridges.

Therefore, to obtain the best results in regional planning, or any allied project, it is not necessary to have the engineer learn architecture, or *vice versa,* but to teach each an appreciation of the other and the public an appreciation of both.

AMERICAN SOCIETY OF CIVIL ENGINEERS

INSTITUTED 1852

TRANSACTIONS

Paper No. 1684

FORECAST: THE REGIONAL COMMUNITY OF THE FUTURE*

By Thomas Adams,† Esq.

With Discussion by Messrs. Robert Kingery, Howard Strong, William J. Wilgus, Frederic H. Fay, William T. Lyle, Charles Wellford Leavitt, Morris Knowles, and Thomas Adams.

Introduction

The modern city is a product of science—applied to manufacture, to transportation, and to modes of living. It reveals in its conditions of growth that science may deflect the path of society and still do little or nothing to arrest the weaknesses that accompany the changes or movements inherent in human action. Yet the science that has brought about so much progress in the arts of industry and transportation, apparently could, if applied collectively on a wide community basis, make for better cities. It must be admitted, however, that whatever social progress may be attained, or expected, in this direction, by means of physical improvements, can only lessen and not remove defects in living and working conditions.

The complex dynamic forces that enter into the composition of the city may lead in the future along one of a thousand different avenues of growth. Who can calculate all the forces that might enter into one of these possibilities? Who can predict the periods and degrees of advancement and recoil, of action and re-action, of growth and decay, and, therefore, calculate their effect? Who can visualize how changes and innovations in individual and collective practice will operate to bring about new trends in growth; or in what measure and over what periods the government of the future will

* Presented at the Joint Meeting of the City Planning Division with the American City Planning Inst., Philadelphia, Pa., October 8, 1926.

† Gen. Director of Plans and Surveys, Regional Plan of New York and Its Environs, New York, N. Y.

be influenced by principle or expediency? These questions indicate how rash it is to try to picture what the future regional community will be like. Yet, it is worth while to weigh and investigate future possibilities and opportunities in the light of knowledge of facts and tendencies of community growth; it is worth while to attempt to create some practical ideal and try to guide communities toward its achievement.

William James has stated, "If shown a certain way, a community may take it; if not, it will never find it."

The function of the city planner is to show the community the way that leads toward the healthiest and most efficient pattern of town development. To do so he must first have developed in his mind an ideal pattern which he conceives to be within practical reach; and, second, have worked out the ways along which it is possible and best for the community to travel toward its achievement. Lack of this ideal for the community, or of an intelligent means of reaching it, and not technical imperfections, lies at the foundation of many failures in city planning and zoning.

It is the writer's purpose to give a general conception of the regional community of the future, based on the belief that the growth of the science and art of city planning, aided by the play of economic forces, will influence the direction and form of urban growth toward a higher and more ideal civic pattern and more rational forms of development. Before presenting this general conception, some of the conditions and problems of the modern city will be discussed.

Some Conditions and Problems of Modern Cities

The modern city does not differ from cities of previous times in regard to the underlying character and causes of its defects; changes have rid it of some evils and brought others to take their place. The large city has always suffered, in different forms, from congestion of building and traffic, from poverty and bad housing, and from the inherent selfishness of man in dealing with private property. Since these are the results of human tendencies, that do not change with time and circumstance, they will always be present. The conditions and problems of New York, N. Y., and Philadelphia, Pa., differ in character and to some extent in degree from those of thirty or forty years ago. The automobile has not made congestion, but has created new forms of congestion; and it is still possible to move about the congested centers of the great cities with more expedition and more agreeably than in the days of horse-drawn vehicles. The high building has brought new kinds of evils, but is not so unhealthy in some respects as the unsanitary building facing the narrow streets of medieval cities. Science has relieved poverty by providing man with more abundance of food and clothing, but in the great city the poorer classes still suffer from low standards of housing accommodations and bad environment. The control of private property is effected by laws that lag far behind changes in growth. In spite of all the lessons of the past, man is too slow in adjusting himself to changes of conditions. This is what is meant by lack of foresight in dealing with the problems of the city.

The conditions and problems of the modern great city that are exceptional, are the results of the unprecedented size and rapidity of growth of urban aggregations. For instance:

(1) Evils of congestion that were bearable in small areas, where development proceeded slowly, have created almost intolerable conditions when extended over large rapidly growing urban areas.

(2) Separation of the home from the place of occupation of the worker, desirable in some respects in the smaller cities, has intensified congestion and caused serious economic waste in the large cities of to-day.

(3) Lack of space for movement, light, air, and recreation in the crowded central areas of cities was not a serious problem when the country fields lay within walking distance; but in the big city that spreads its buildings over 1 000 sq. miles, or more, it is found to be the chief defect in its growth.

(4) Co-ordination of municipal action in matters of public improvements and utilities was hardly necessary when cities were small, of comparatively slow growth, and widely scattered; to-day, every metropolitan region is suffering serious injury from lack of co-ordination between its constituent communities.

It is evident, therefore, that the demand for regional study and treatment of large cities is in large measure the result of peculiarities of modern urban growth. In approaching the study of regional problems, the unknown factors are so many and knowledge of past growth is so illusive as a basis for planning for the future that scientific investigation will be of only limited value. The investigations have to be reinforced in a special degree by reason and common sense, and the price of developing a new experience and a new science will have to be paid.

Important Trends in City Development

Tendencies in connection with transportation by rail and highway within regional areas are all toward facilitating quicker movement and more efficient distribution. These tendencies will continue to promote concentration of large populations in urban regions. This concentration has of course a great economic value, and as long as it is not permitted to lead to congestion, it need not be injurious to health, safety, or general welfare. The causes of congestion, as distinct from an efficient degree of concentration, lie in the lack of proper control of land development; the support that is given by law to abuses of property rights; the lack of proper standards of density and height of buildings as a basis for zoning; and the lack of harmony between physical planning and zoning regulations. The greatest menace to the modern city is that it will persist in avoiding the removal of these causes and simultaneously develop its facilities for transportation and promote new sources of energy. These facilities and forces will produce good or ill in proportion as the concentration they cause will be well or badly regulated by law and planning.

Perhaps the most hopeful fact in the metropolitan regions of America is the extent to which land is being acquired for parks. It may be many years before zoning of private property can be based on standards that will give cities ample space for freedom of movement and for light and air in buildings, and before it can be given a permanence that will make it really effective in preventing congestion; it may be still longer before areas of land in these regions can be zoned for agriculture and horticulture and made integral parts of the open areas of cities; but the movement toward acquiring large areas of land for permanent open spaces for parks and parkways has gained an impetus that is full of promise as a means of giving future areas of urban expansion a large degree of lung space permanently dedicated to public use and ever present as a stimulus to better balanced development.

In the future, the architect, the engineer, and the social investigator will take a broader view of city problems. Zoning has already given a lead to a new architectural conception of city building, and as a force in town development it is still in its infancy. Scientific developments in relation to electric power, production of metals, improvement of machinery, and transportation; needs of great urban regions in regard to comprehensive systems of drainage, water supply, and adequate open spaces; these and other things will bring the engineer and the landscape architect face to face with great concrete problems of regional development, and make them more expert in the art of regulating city growth.

If nothing else forces action of governments and communities to plan comprehensively, compulsion will come from economic necessity. Great cities to-day are within sight of the end of the financial resources available to meet their needs, a condition that has been brought about by the wastes and inefficiencies incidental to economically unsound methods of development which permit unhealthy and unsafe conditions both of over-crowding in the central areas and of under-crowding in suburban and rural areas.

New York's Problems and Future Growth

Data regarding present and future conditions and problems in the New York Region will be referred to briefly.

The area of the City of New York is 298 sq. miles, but the area regarded as appropriate for regional planning around the Port of New York comprises 5 528 sq. miles. This area is in three States and has more than four hundred separate units of administration. This indicates a geographical extent and a complexity of physical and social conditions that sufficiently proves how extraordinarily different the modern city is from anything in the past.

In 1900 the population of the New York Region was 5 384 734; to-day, it is more than 9 000 000 and, in 1965, it is likely to be at least twice the latter figure.* About 58 000 dwellings are required annually to house the increasing population and between now and 1965 more than 2 000 000 dwellings are likely to be required. Whether or not much by way of reform of conditions affecting more than 2 000 000 buildings already erected, can be achieved, much can and should be achieved in influencing the proper development of an equal number in the next forty years.

* Estimates based on past growth give 21 000 000 as the population in 1965.

The number of manufacturing plants in the New York Region grew from 19 416 in 1900 to 57 753 in 1920, or 197.5%; but the plants have become smaller on the average as the increase of employees is only about 100% in the same period. Railroad lines serving those industries have a mileage of 1 884. Terminal facilities are inadequate for the existing need, and transit lines are ten years or more behind what is required for efficient handling of passengers and freight.

No prospective development of the water-front is likely to absorb more than a small percentage of its mileage for commercial purposes. At present (1926), only 125 miles of 1 800 are so used, yet hundreds of miles are not being put to the best economic use because of false expectations regarding the potentialities of industrial growth.

The average density of population is 160 per acre in Manhattan, 30 per acre in the whole of New York City, including Manhattan, and 1 per acre in the remainder of the Region. In the city there is the comparatively ideal average of 7 houses to the acre, but in parts of Manhattan the density is as high as 150 families per acre. It is extraordinary how little variation there is in the average density of large cities and how congestion always seems to have its complement of vacant or sparsely developed land. To show that there need be no congestion with proper regulation of growth, 26 000 000 people can be provided for, at an average of between 20 and 30 to the acre, within a 30-mile radius of the center of the city. More even development must be secured if the decay that comes from the complementary processes of over and under crowding of city areas is to be prevented.

More than 2 800 000 people travel into and out of down-town Manhattan daily, but the crowding of this multitude into one small area will become less necessary as natural obstructions to horizontal growth are removed by improved transportation facilities. There is a growing tendency toward development of new neighborhood centers of manufacture and business. More belt-line communication is needed to give impetus to this movement. There is no true economic basis for the congestion of great cities like New York, and if it is continued the effect will be to strangle the pulse center of the community. A city has to avoid being stultified by its own wealth. Hilaire Belloc states that history proves that when cities reach their highest point of wealth they become congested, refuse to accept a remedy, and pass on to decay. He adds that:

"The main motive is a blunder in the science of economics. It is the idea that the destruction of a number of imaginary economic values is an expenditure of real wealth. So far is this not being the case that there is no example in all history of a congested street system being reformed without the wealth of the city increasing after the change."

If, in future years, cities can be made to realize that great public improvements, if properly conceived, are good investments, the future can be viewed with optimism. In the Park Avenue District in New York the gain caused by the improvements within and around the Grand Central Terminal was 255% in land value and 932% in values of improvements in 20 years. The total gain was from $60 750 000 to $311 500 000, or 410 per cent.

Increases in land values are greatest in the centers and outlying suburbs. Great areas lie between, where values are more or less stationary, and many areas are blighted. If people cannot live near their work they prefer to get as near the open country as possible. Tendencies toward decentralization are strong enough to overcome the difficulties inherent in making changes of location. The number of factories has decreased in Manhattan and increased in Brooklyn and Queens. Suburban increases of garages and theatres indicate the trend of outward movement. The rapid shifting of the population is doubling the number of children in suburban schools.

Heights of buildings even in New York have not reached the point of increasing average heights over older cities like Berlin, Paris, and central parts of London. The average height of buildings in Manhattan is only 4.8 stories, although there were 1 019 buildings between 10 and 19 stories in height in 1924 and 100 buildings of 20 stories and more, below 65th Street. Until more high buildings raise the average the effect of such buildings on traffic and business cannot be foretold.

High buildings have been the product of high land values and, in turn, high land values are causing high buildings. However, real estate owners and leading financial corporations now claim that the best business investments are low buildings, even in valuable locations. The following statements confirm the writer's views. Mr. W. Burke Harmon, of the National Real Estate Corporation, writes:

"All floors above the second floor can be largely eliminated as contributors toward the income of the building over a long period of years. The cost of upkeep of the upper stories and the interest on the investment represented thereby, plus taxes, would barely be met by the revenue derived from this space in normal times."

Mr. Richard M. Hurd, President of the Lawyers Mortgage Company, and an eminent authority on land values, writes:

"Low buildings in valuable locations pay a much higher percentage of income than high buildings. This is in line with my comments on office buildings, on which, as I told you, we never lend money, chiefly because such buildings are normally overbuilt.

"The term, 'taxpayer', is a misnomer and obviously a one-story building in a good store location approaches nearer in its earnings to pure ground rent than any other type of improvement."

These statements indicate how false are the economic standards on which much crowded development takes place. What justification can there be for crowding high buildings together, with all the evils of congestion incidental to this crowding, if they do not pay? As they become more crowded, they will become less profitable, owing to diminished light, air, and over-supply of space in central areas, and to the increased taxes necessary to meet expenses incidental to congestion.

Individual high buildings have their place and purpose and as long as they are made to conform to proper regulations regarding the amount of space surrounding them, they may be desirable elements in the growth of great cities. What is wrong with skyscrapers are the conditions which do not give them a proper chance to perform their functions, owing to lack of space surrounding them. The greatest enemies of concentration are those who confuse it with congestion; and the greatest enemies of high buildings are those who deny that all buildings require adequate space surrounding them for movement and other social needs, and that the amount of space should be increased in proportion as bulk and height of building increase.

At present, in New York the assessments and taxes are higher than at any other time in the history of the city. The real estate assessment amounted to approximately $13 000 000 000 for 1926.

More than 95% of the tax permitted by law is levied. The budget for 1926 amounted to $437 000 000. The tax rate has increased in 20 years from an average 1.50 to an estimated 2.79 for 1926. The percentages of the total budget proposed to be spent include 30% for debt services and tax deficiencies, 19.9% for education, 14.7% for protection of life and property, and 1.5% for recreation, science, and art, which includes parks. The greatest increases in expenditures are for subways, policing, street cleaning, and fire prevention—all incidental to congested growth. As has been stated:* "More important than immediate economies will it be to make far-visioning plans for the future."

Financial plans will not be enough. The physical planning of the city must be made to follow lines that will lessen waste and reduce public contributions to private services. It is significant that the Planning Commission appointed by the Mayor of New York has as one of its duties that of discovering new sources of revenue.

Proposals to relieve this congested growth by construction of more subways, wider streets, bridges, tunnels, etc., put forward by responsible authorities would involve an estimated expenditure of about $2 000 000 000.

Congestion of streets is reaching the saturation point in some places. Forms of relief, such as traffic regulations, parking prohibition, narrowing of sidewalks, and street widening, are all more or less palliative. The point must soon be reached when nothing further can be done in these directions.

These and many other problems of the great city confront the regional and city planner. There are economic forces at work and scientific developments taking place that will aid in the task of influencing city development in the right directions. What then may be forecast as a reasonable prospect for the urban region of the future?

The Future Urban Region

On the whole the writer agrees with J. B. S. Haldane that science and human tendency are becoming less materialistic. It may also be assumed that the center of industrial gravity will shift to some extent as a result of the development of new sources of energy. Transportation has been the chief motive force in concentration in the past century, but it will be linked with electric energy in promoting new and more evenly distributed areas of con-

* *New York World*, September 11, 1926.

centration in the future. Great urban aggregations will continue to grow; and the hope lies not in restricting the quantity, but in improving the quality, of development.

The writer can visualize two forms of great city regions that will exist on this continent when the youths of to-day have entered the final laps of their race with life. Great centers like New York and Philadelphia will still be striving to maintain their supremacy, but a new kind of urban region will have sprung up to influence them and compete with them.

Just as the manufacturer has discovered the value of discarding old machinery in favor of new, the city will learn that old dilapidated buildings are a liability and that the making of great physical improvements is a sound investment. In the future old cities will be reshaping and rebuilding their blighted areas as a matter of self-preservation.

Developers of real estate will not be permitted to speculate in land, as a necessity of life. Those who sub-divide land for building will be required to make it fit for building by constructing roadways, sewers, and other local improvements in advance of the sale of the land. Playground space will have to be provided as an essential feature in any new sub-division just as street areas are at present. Building codes will require more durable forms of construction, and the cost of fire prevention will be greatly decreased. Great transportation and park corridors will radiate out from and surround the cities, giving rapid means of communication through open areas devoted to park and spacious residential areas. At strategic points along these corridors satellite cities will have grown up, connected by railroad and highway with the metropolitan center and amply provided with space for expansion of industry and healthy living conditions.

Several classes of highway will exist. There will be speedways from 120 to 150 ft. in width paralleling railroads and serving the lighter industry, business, and apartment-house areas. Interchange of freight and passengers between railroad and highway will be a common practice. The use of streets for loading and unloading of merchandise will be gradually disappearing. Owners of property will be required to carry on their business on their own premises, and streets will be more and more confined to public purposes. Buses and other highway vehicles will have properly equipped terminals as the best railroads have to-day. Parkways from 150 to 500 ft. in width, with driveways through them for rapid automobile traffic, will penetrate through areas largely used for residential purposes. In central areas elevated railroads will have largely disappeared. Air rights over many railroads will be used for elevated highways. The tendency in the centers will be to place railroads with their electric equipment underground, and to have raised sidewalks for pedestrians fronting on or arcaded into buildings. This will not add to congestion, but merely remove some of the effects of congestion created at the beginning of the Twentieth Century.

Zoning will have become more constructive and more stable. It will be based on adequate and sound standards of health and safety. Physical planning and zoning will be linked together so that, as the requirements of the law in regard to height and area of occupancy are strengthened, less necessity will arise for restricting the character of use. Factories and apartment houses will have more spacious surroundings and will fit in agreeably with adjacent residences. The owner of the factory will have learned the lesson of the Fifth Avenue merchant that ugly ancillary features and disorderly surroundings are an injury to his business.

Interspersed between the closely developed areas along railroads and highways there will be areas zoned and permanently reserved for agricultural purposes. Regional co-operation will have ended the pollution of drinking waters and developed comprehensive systems of sewage disposal. The social needs of the community will be largely met without great loss of time in traveling, because it will be realized that there is enough land in the country to provide all facilities necessary for healthy living conditions within easy reach of every inhabitant.

The "hot dog" stand and the gasoline station will be things of the past. Just as the old English inn was a picturesque feature along the highway, so there will grow up a new kind of hostel, with pleasant surroundings where all the needs of the highway traveler can be provided.

Special ways will be set apart for pedestrians, so that walking will have become a restored art. Speedways will have bridges and subways provided for pedestrians, and separation of grades for important intersecting roads.

Motor cars will pay a proper share of the cost of highways and thereby keep up the balance between increase of vehicles and provision of highway facilities for motor travel. Rapid transit will not only pay for itself, but will yield a profit to the city for purchase of parks and playgrounds. More facilities for recreation, the results of education, and more stringent application of justice will have reduced crime.

High buildings will still be erected, but under proper regulations as to area of occupancy, so that they will have become less crowded and more in the nature of isolated monumental features of the city.

There will be a reaction against the crowding of high office buildings together and also against the apartment dwelling as a residence. A compromise will have been reached between the apartment building and the cottage which will give to a new type of home the advantages of each of the others.

Provision will have been made for numerous landing fields for airplanes —used for long-distance transportation and mail service. Commuting, not having increased on the whole, will be more than amply served by transit lines and improved highways. Trolleys will still operate on special rights of way, but bus services will have taken the place of many trolley lines now in use and will have become the most popular form of transit for short distances.

The more even and more open form of development, and the prevention of land speculation by irresponsible developers, will produce more stable land values. In the aggregate, land values will be no lower, but they will be more evenly distributed. Assessment of land and taxation will be more carefully adjusted to the best productive uses of land. For instance, taxes for urban improvements based on potential building values will not be levied on land permanently zoned for cultivation, or for recreation areas, such as golf courses, thereby making possible the reservation of open areas on private land.

Forty years hence New York may have its 16 000 000 or even 20 000 000 of people with less overcrowding than its present 9 000 000. Manhattan will still be the center of distribution, of exchange, of banking, and of certain industries that can be economically carried on where land is relatively expensive in the hub of the region. There will be a few more bridges and tunnels between Manhattan, Long Island, and New Jersey, but they will be planned as part of a comprehensive system that will have spread industry and population over wide areas and lessened the areas of congestion, the areas of deterioration, and the areas of waste vacant land. Many high buildings, as they have deteriorated and become out of date, will have been replaced with lower buildings, as being more profitable. Belt-line railroads, boulevards, and speedways will link together the radial system of communications. Large open areas in private ownership will be used for cultivation and recreation in the suburbs. The blighted areas along the water-front of Manhattan, Brooklyn, and The Bronx will be replaced with modern buildings giving efficient service to the port and fronting on wide streets and squares, fittingly adorned to make a dignified entrance to the city and region. The East River water-front and the Harlem River Valley will have been developed on two levels, the lower for commercial uses and the upper for monumental business and residence structures. The Hackensack Meadows will have been reclaimed and divided in use between industry, residence, and recreation. Large areas in New York City, now held out of economic use for ambitious projects that can never be realized, will have been developed, with consequent relief to formerly congested areas.

Great new railroad terminals in The Bronx, Queens, and New Jersey will have been developed, and new business centers will have grown up in their neighborhood. Long Island, The Bronx, and New Jersey will be so linked together that great volumes of traffic now passing through Manhattan will be by-passed around it. A wide parkway will extend from New York to Philadelphia. It will be intersected by a speedway for passenger cars and be paralleled by a railroad, a rapid transit line, and a speedway for mixed motor vehicles. Numerous satellite communities will be spread along this park and transportation corridor.

Great central power plants will have been developed, and power will be distributed over wide areas, serving widely scattered industrial areas.

New Regional Communities

The writer has stated that the older cities will not be the only centers of the urban regions of the future. Great new centers will arise and be developed with the aid of knowledge of the past and in keeping with new opportunities. These new communities will be so developed as to cause the older communities to mend their ways.

The transmission system of the Shawinigan Water and Power Company of Quebec, Que., Canada, may be cited as an illustration. This Company, the fourth largest in the world, distributes 580 000 h.p. over an area of 15 000 sq. miles. It had a total output of 2 000 000 000 kw-hr. in 1925. The area served is intersected by an international waterway. Within it are three large and numerous small cities—connected by an elaborate system of railroads and highways.

The defect of this area is that the great waterway of the St. Lawrence is closed for navigation for several months of the year, but it illustrates the type of area that will provide scope and opportunity for great regional communities of the future. These areas will be so large and the places suitable for efficient concentration within them will be so numerous that there will be no necessity for congestion. Large sections of land suitable for cultivation will lie between the transportation and power corridors and focal points and maintain an efficient and economical balance of development. The older city regions will gain much of their impetus to improvement from competition with these new communities.

Thus, the growth of science, the pressure of economic forces, and perhaps the growth of average intelligence, will bring into being new communities and re-shape the old in accordance with sane, practical ideals of what a great regional community should be. All that city planners can do is to help in pointing the way toward the realization of these ideals and develop their science and art so that they will be ready to make their contribution to the demands of the future.

DISCUSSION

Robert Kingery,* Esq. (by letter).—In Mr. Adams' splendid forecast of the regional community of the future, the writer finds the expression that is the foundation of the entire activities of the Chicago Regional Planning Association, namely, "regional co-operation will have ended the pollution of drinking waters and developed comprehensive systems of sewage disposal". In the region surrounding Chicago, city planning has had its "ups and downs" just as in many other parts of the country. A large number of city and village plans have been prepared, splendid reports have been written, and nothing has been done about them. Many of the local and public officials scoff at city planning and call it the impractical dreams of the "uplifters".

The reason for this is not difficult to find. In most cases city and village plans have been prepared with a minimum of co-operation and aid from the local city engineer and official who, under the law, is charged with the responsibility for spending the money which would be used for carrying out the project proposed in the plan. The second reason is that the apparent objective of the plan commissions is a plan and a report, and not so much attention is given to perfecting organizations that will put the plan into the construction stage.

The City of Chicago is the notable exception. A great body of citizens has been appointed on a permanent plan commission and has insisted upon maintaining a staff of engineers for the purpose of carrying out the Chicago Plan.

Regional planning is far more difficult than city planning because of the greater number of local governing officials, each of whom has a specific duty under the laws of his State, and under the powers granted his particular office. To proceed with regional planning in such a way that each of these public officials of highway commissions, drainage districts, sanitary districts, park districts, the private utility organizations, such as telephone, electric light, rapid rail transit, and others, has a share in the preparation of plans is to develop a plan or series of plans which, in advance, holds the confidence of the public or private officials who are going forward with their public works whether or not there is a regional plan.

In the Chicago Region, the Planning Association has thus far been moderately successful by combining, into a general highway scheme, the different programs of the many highway building agencies, simply by arranging that they meet over a common general map, study how their own programs fit, or do not fit, with those across the imaginary, invisible boundary lines. In practically every case these officials have agreed on such modifications of their programs as were necessary to produce a system of connecting highways.

The fact that six county boards, with a combined area of 3 150 sq. miles of unincorporated land, have adopted and are administering sub-division

* Secretary, Regional Planning Assoc., Chicago, Ill.

regulations which require the real estate men to meet certain high standards in the platting of land, indicates that the method used in drafting these regulations was sound. Members of the Sub-Dividers Division of the Real Estate Boards, plat officers of counties and cities, the surveyors' organizations, and the city planning engineers combined in developing and agreeing on these regulations. They are in ordinance form also, and are rapidly being adopted in the cities and villages of the Region. If a little group had retired to the privacy of their offices to develop such a regulation and then had sought to put it into effect, without having had the benefit of all the views that went into its determination, it is doubtful whether it would have been in effect in any of the cities and villages to-day.

If the Regional Planning Association of Chicago can make one suggestion to regional and city planners, it is that regional and city planning is not alone a gift of a few men who have had certain training and have done certain reading on the subject. Some of the most obscure city, county, sanitary district, and park officials and some of the public utility engineers can do, and are doing, by co-operation in the Region of Chicago, some very successful regional planning.

Howard Strong,* Esq.—The author has given a masterly presentation of some of the evils that have resulted from modern concentration of population; of certain economic and social fallacies that have controlled the development of the modern city; and has presented an enheartening picture of what may be hoped for the future of New York and, by implication, of other large cities.

However, as he states, who can calculate the forces that will mould the city of the future? Who can predict the scientific discoveries, the overturning in social and economic thought that may revolutionize human action? A pattern for the future growth of the city may be moulded and complete, when some simple invention may upset the entire calculation.

In 1890, or thereabouts, an ordinance was passed in Cleveland, Ohio, requiring that every self-propelled vehicle on the city streets be preceded 100 ft. in advance by a man carrying, by day, a red flag and, at night, a red lantern. It may be assumed that the development of the horseless carriage to its present stage of efficiency, has rendered somewhat impracticable this particular application of the accepted principle of the responsibility of the community for the safety of its citizens. The provision of Bear Mountain Park, thirty-five miles from New York City, would have been preposterous twenty-five years ago, but the present widespread use of automobiles has made such a regional park the greatest of boons. The proposal of a large neighborhood theatre in every community of consequence, in those days, would have led its proposer to a court of inquiry, but the moving picture has made such provision an accepted necessity of village life. The complex dynamic forces which operate and the infinite potentiality of scientific discovery and of changing thought, may lead along any one of a thousand different avenues.

What possibility, then, is there for foreseeing and preparing for the future? Does not the greatest hope lie in the direction of discovering the underlying

* Secy.-Director, Regional Planning Federation, Philadelphia, Pa.

The first of these obstacles is serious because a multitude of varying interests, too often antagonistic or indifferent, have not found a common ground on which to approach the law-making bodies for needed legislation. The remedy would seem to lie in the voluntary co-operation of all interests in the regional community—political, corporate, and individual—by an organized method that would fairly recognize the weight that should be given to the voice of each member. Such a body, working through a small executive committee of high-minded, able, and public-spirited citizens, and guided by the advice of experts of note, should be successful in formulating plans and legislation acceptable to enlightened local sentiment and, therefore, compelling upon the legislatures and upon Congress. From a movement of this kind should come forth a compact organization having the will, the capacity, and the power to accomplish things for the general good.

The second of the obstacles would fade away if the idea could be dispelled that funds for public works necessarily must be provided through taxation. That is a bugbear that paralyzes the community and kills progress. The average citizen looks on taxes with aversion because he sees no tangible direct return for his expenditure. As a rule he does not object to paying for that which brings an obvious immediate reward that caters to his pleasure, convenience, or necessity, or by reason of which he may make or save money. A case in point is the Holland Vehicular Tunnel, beneath the North River, which has been financed by the States of New York and New Jersey on the promise of toll collections from those who will use the tunnel in preference to ferries. In this respect, the beneficiaries who pay the bill would have been even better served if real estate bordering the entrances and exits had been compelled to contribute toward the cost a fair share of the increase in value which it is reaping because of the changed conditions. Another instance is that of the Grand Central Terminal development, to which the writer ventures to refer with some diffidence because of his responsibility for its inception. There, departure from precedent and the utilization of dormant "air rights" have brought a golden reward from by-products much more than sufficient to carry the enterprise without placing an additional burden on the traveler or the public at large. In a word, lack of capital, as an obstacle to adequate planning and building for the future, will disappear if Man will have the ingenuity to utilize, to the last degree, all revenue-producing by-products that can be made to flow from the new conditions, and also the courage to allocate the remaining net costs among the beneficiaries, namely, the users and reapers of benefits.

Engineers, then, owe their fellow citizens, not only dream pictures of what should be done for their own and their children's welfare, but also forceful reminders of what they must do to realize them. These may be attained by organizing effectively for the adoption and fruition of sound plans, and by financing new projects in part through the utilization of by-products and in part through the allocation of the remaining costs among the beneficiaries rather than exclusively through taxation foisted on the public at large. Stated differently, as the writer sees it, effective organization and self-support to the fullest possible extent, are the keynotes of success in the timely fulfillment of major plans for the future of regional communities.

FREDERIC H. FAY,* M. AM. SOC. C. E. (by letter).—This excellent paper brings strikingly to mind the rapidly widening field of city planning and the need of ever-broadening vision on the part of those who have to deal with the future development of urban communities. It is only a little more than thirty years since the World's Columbian Exposition at Chicago, Ill., awakened an interest in the question of the development of cities. In the popular mind, city planning in this country dates from the Middle Nineties, and at first dealt essentially with small units within the cities and with matters of appearance, such as the placing of public buildings, the development of civic centers and open areas, etc. City planning was then synonymous with the "City Beautiful". A few years later consideration came to be given to the orderly planning of the development of cities as a whole, and while attractiveness was still an important element, emphasis was laid more especially on the welfare of the people and the conditions under which they live and work. It is only a few years since, for the larger cities, that planning has been carried systematically beyond the boundaries of the municipality and that consideration has been given to the needs and the development of the larger territory, which will be a part of, or within the zone of influence of, the larger city of the future. With the increase in area within the scope of city planning comes also increase in the number and diversity of problems falling within the scope of the planner's consideration. Before many years, properly constituted agencies, systematically studying and planning for the development of States and of the Nation as a whole, will be common. When that time comes some broader term than city planning must be adopted to indicate the field of the planner's activity.

New York presents problems in regional planning that are doubtless as large, diverse, and complex as those of any great city of the world. Other cities of lesser size, however, present problems in regional planning on scales smaller than New York, but often with diversified features. In fact, each large urban region has planning problems purely its own, although many problems are fundamental and common to all.

The Boston Metropolitan District is an urban area in which regional planning along certain lines has been carried on for many years through force of necessity. In fact, the Boston Metropolitan District is probably the earliest example, in this country, of official action in regional planning. The District to-day comprises, in addition to the City of Boston itself, thirty-nine other municipalities.

Table 1 is a comparison of the areas and populations of the City of Boston, the Boston Metropolitan District, and the City of New York. It is interesting to note that in 1925 population density per square mile within the city limits of Boston was 16 306, as compared with the corresponding figure of 18 79[illegible] within the city limits of New York, Boston thus having a density about seven eighths that of New York City.

* Cons. Engr. (Fay, Spofford & Thorndike), Boston, Mass.

What is the story of regional planning in the Boston Metropolitan District? Massachusetts was the first State in the Union to establish (in 1868) a State Board of Health. About that time the City of Boston and other near-by municipalities took steps to improve sanitary conditions along streams draining into Boston Harbor, by the construction, independently of each other, of certain sewerage and drainage works. The territory was so closely built upon, however, that it was soon realized that independent action by the several communities must prove ineffectual. The State Board of Health took a hand, and the result was the establishment, by legislative enactment in 1889, of the Boston Metropolitan Sewerage District and the creation of the Metropolitan Sewerage Commission to handle the sewage and drainage problems of the district as a whole, irrespective of municipal boundary lines. This is believed to be the first official step taken by any State in regional planning. In 1893, the State Legislature created the Metropolitan Parks District under the charge of the Metropolitan Park Commission, which in the succeeding years, has admirably supplemented the nucleus of the great park system previously established by the City of Boston, such that now the park areas of the Boston Metropolitan District are widely and favorably known throughout the country. In 1895 the necessity for co-operation between Boston and the surrounding cities and towns in the matter of water supply led to the creation of the Metropolitan Water Board and Water District, also by State legislation. More recently, the maintenance and operation of the Metropolitan Parks, Water Supply, and Sewerage Systems has been under a single commission, the Metropolitan District Commission. However, in 1926, the necessity having arisen for a large addition to the Metropolitan Water Supply System, a special commission was created by legislative enactment to develop a system of additional water supply.

TABLE 1.—Areas and Populations of City and Metropolitan District of Boston, Mass., Compared with New York, N. Y.

Districts.	Area, in square miles.	Population in 1925.	Density, in 1925, per square mile.
City of Boston	47.8	779 620	16 306
Boston Metropolitan District	409.3	1 808 845	4 419
City of New York	299.0	5 620 048	18 796

The regional planning of the Boston Metropolitan District thus sketchily outlined, has been that relating to certain specific problems in which the mutual interests of the cities and towns of the District forced co-operative action. In each case this regional planning and the constructions resulting therefrom have been carried out by an official State Commission.

More recently, in the Metropolitan Boston Region, a strong sentiment has developed regarding the need of regional planning on broad lines; planning that is not limited to a few immediate and specific problems, but looks ahead over a long period to the general development of the city of the future. Largely through the initiative of the Boston Chamber of Commerce, there was created by legislative enactment in 1923 the Division of Metropolitan Planning within the Metropolitan District Commission. The Metropolitan Planning Board consists of seven members, four of whom are State or City officials representing separate departments, and three, including the Chairman, are appointed by the Governor from among the citizens of the District. The Metropolitan Planning Division was created primarily to study the question of transportation in its broadest sense in the whole metropolitan area, transportation by rail, water, highway, and air. The problem of transportation, however, is necessarily linked with and dependent on other problems of metropolitan development such that the field of activity of the Metropolitan Planning Division becomes a broad one. The Division is given a reasonable appropriation for its work, and it has a permanent engineering and technical staff. Therefore, while in New York the great problem of regional planning is being carried out by private agency, in Massachusetts many of the broad problems of regional planning for the Boston Metropolitan District have been and are being studied and solved through official action by the State.

The question may arise, "Why the need of regional planning?" In the case of Greater Boston, for example, where the cities and towns of the Metropolitan District having common interests are solely within the limits of a single State, why not annex these cities and towns to Boston itself and thus establish as a single municipal entity the real city of Boston as a single municipal unit? Then all problems of regional planning could be dealt with directly by the government of the larger city. This has been often suggested and as often rejected. It brings up an interesting point of city and regional planning, that is, the psychological feature. In the case of many of the smaller cities and towns surrounding Boston, local pride, historical tradition, and differences in racial and political complexion, all weigh against outright annexation. The communities are jealous of their existence as separate entities, although willing to join with others in matters of mutual concern. It seems unlikely that "Real Boston", as many people call it, will result from the annexation of approximately forty municipalities of the Metropolitan District, the interests of which are to large extent identical with those of Boston. On the other hand, these various communities are gradually being knit closer together through common bonds of interest, and the best development of the real Boston of the future can take place only through wise regional planning which takes account, not only of the physical, but also of the psychological problems involved.

What the Boston regional community of the future will be is largely a matter of speculation, although its development along certain lines may fairly be forecasted through economic necessity. As Mr. Adams well states, "There is no true economic basis for the congestion of great cities like New York, and if it is continued the effect will be to strangle the pulse center of the community." The work now under way in planning for the transportation needs of the future with the increased use of the automobile, will do much toward dispersing population and the development of suburban areas. The growth in population, therefore, of Greater Boston is likely to be almost entirely in the territory outside the present city limits. The Boston Metropolitan District offers a broad and inviting field for regional planning which, if well done, may be of inestimable benefit to those who are to live in Greater Boston in the next and succeeding generations.

WILLIAM T. LYLE,* M. AM. SOC. C. E. (by letter).—The remarkable progress made during the last few years, and even during the last few months, in city and regional planning is attracting wide attention. This progress is not so much in the art itself as in the confidence of the public of its possibilities, a confidence promoted by an expanding conception in the minds of city and regional planners of the scope and dignity of their art. City and regional planning is assuming an aggressiveness not characteristic of recognized conservative engineering.

This paper is suggestive and stimulating. In city and regional planning the writer would call attention to the folly and even futility of incomprehensive work. The art must operate not only in its physical, but also in its human applications. The older planning was concerned with maps, layouts, and architectural developments; the new planning is considering human beings in their business, domestic, recreational, cultural, and even moral requirements.

City and regional planning needs both vision and courage. Its determinations are not always made on the basis of well buttressed predictions. It is doubtful if they can be, with the determining factors of transportation and power development in a state of uncertainty and change. City and regional planning constitutes a new field of engineering—broad, comprehensive, dignified —reaching out into the realms of economics and human relationships.

The new planning calls for promptness in execution. When a recognized need is experienced there should be a corresponding response in construction. In public works, however, a lag almost always occurs between the need and the fulfillment. Of course, exceptions may be cited to the rule. Some communities are more far-sighted, courageous, and energetic than others. In projecting and constructing its new water supply the City of New York furnishes a good example. The new work was carried through before the dreaded succession of dry years became an actuality. So, also, in its response to the challenge, "Shall we save New York?", it passed the zoning ordinance of 1916, which has wrought such a benefit in the stabilization of real estate values.

Regional planning to-day is applying the principles of harmonious relationships so important in business. Since their establishment, American cities have grown without regulation. They are notorious examples of discord, where selfish interests in private promotion schemes were permitted to operate without check and were even supported by law.

The unregulated liberation and production of power in modern civilization may constitute the gravest menace. Only when properly directed and utilized can it become a blessing. Prosperity will result in the even balance between a healthy need and an adequate and well-directed supply.

The author considers that "perhaps the most hopeful fact in the metropolitan regions of America is the extent to which land is being acquired for

* Prof., Civ. Eng., Washington and Lee Univ., Lexington, Va.

parks". Proofs of this are easily established, not only on hygienic, cultural, and moral grounds, but for economic reasons as well. The assessed valuation, in 1856, of the three wards adjoining Central Park, New York, was $20 500 000. By 1873, it had risen to $236 000 000. The natural increase as obtained by averaging the gain in the other wards was found to be $53 000 000, making the earning capacity of the park during seventeen years for the three adjoining wards, $162 500 000.

City planning heretofore has emphasized too much the visible to the neglect of the invisible. It has concerned itself with streets, parks, railroads, and civic centers, and has neglected drainage and water supply on the assumption that they are properly and exclusively in the province of the city engineer. This should not be so, for drainage and water supply powerfully influence the selection and improvement of parks and parkways, and, in turn, are equally influenced by them. The foul drainage channel by reason of its location and the architectural asset of trees and sloping banks is the ideal location for a parkway; and the great forest preserve or reservation the ideal location for a reservoir.

Much has been written on the subject of overcrowding and congestion. The companion idea of undercrowding deserves more thorough consideration. The fundamental law is the fullest and best use of each unit of area, depending on its location and other characteristics. Less need be said than formerly on the debated question of concentration *versus* decentralization. The future regional community will derive its character from the spreading of metropolitan populations.

In the new regional planning, governmental barriers that have restricted progress will be broken down. For example, a great river, the Delaware, the upper reaches of which have never been extensively utilized for public benefit, will be harnessed for power, and will be drawn from as an important metropolitan water supply. This discussion does not contemplate the consideration of political questions, although the writer is convinced that political doctrines that continually challenge human progress will eventually give way.

Mr. Adams speaks of great centers like New York and Philadelphia, striving to maintain supremacy in competition with the surrounding urban regions of the future. This may be the case, although it is to be hoped that wiser counsels will prevail in the development and perfecting of controlling doctrines of city and regional planning, namely, co-ordination and co-operation. The surrounding regions need the centers and the centers need them. Neither can fully prosper in adverse rivalry with the other. Subsequently, however, he speaks of the regional co-operation needed to end the pollution of drinking waters and promote the development of comprehensive systems of sewerage. It is this co-operation that is so necessary and that is so replete with rich reward. An example of the benefits of co-operation is to be found at Boston, Mass., where several municipalities, each guarding its local autonomy, have wisely united to obtain the benefits of a water supply, sewerage system, and parks which would be beyond the reach of each municipality operating independently. A great metropolitan region will come into its own as fast as it learns, practically, the important lessons of harmonious co-operation.

CHARLES WELLFORD LEAVITT,* M. AM. SOC. C. E. (by letter).—Throughout this paper one senses the fact that the author has built up his forecast largely upon the work done on the "Plan of New York and Its Environs". Therefore, in reading it, one should realize that there is little, if any, comparison between New York and any other city; that the forces acting in the creation of New York will, in all probability, act differently upon other metropolitan areas; and that the regional communities of the future will be unlike the regional community of New York.

"Regulation of city growth" is not always possible. The forces making for city growth are human, and while they are amenable to certain laws and regulations by the police for the general health and welfare of the community, they are not always willing to follow, for instance, the directions laid down by a regional plan. The success which the city builders are after may depend on their originality, backed by their energy; and those drawing up a regional plan should make it sufficiently flexible to take care of these city builders and not block them in their ventures, except when their acts might endanger the lives, health, and general welfare of the country.

For instance, if a plan of New York had been prepared some years ago it would undoubtedly have provided for large manufacturing plants, whereas, in the past twenty years, the author states that plants have been growing smaller although more numerous.

Guiding or regulating the location of people's homes into the so-called blighted districts where there is now perhaps only 1% density of population, in order to avoid the congestion of certain other popular sections, may be a very laudable, though difficult task. Forces other than general direction or regulation must be called upon, and here is one of the great problems of the city planner, to study the psychology of the builders and provide what may be necessary to attract them into the blighted districts.

The quotation from Hilaire Belloc is pertinent, and should be taken to heart. It should be possible, with all the enlightenment of past ages and present rapid growths, to develop plans that would stabilize city realty values and avoid what has recently become so prevalent, namely, the moving of commerce, manufacturing, business, shopping, and residential districts so rapidly from one section of the city to another that good buildings have not time to wear out, but must be sacrificed to the movement of one district into the fashions calling for another; and quite frequently the abandonment of the building suitable for one purpose, to the wretchedness of an area which has been blighted by this movement.

The cities of the old world are far more stable in character than American towns, built and occupied by a cosmopolitan race whose great objective is to speed up and arrive somewhere "where they aint", with a pot of gold in hand.

Such motives do not encourage stable real estate investments, which must come about from a population more satisfied and slower to move; although on the other hand, without movement, there results stagnation which may be even worse than constant movement. The ideal would be one of reasonable

* Civ. and Landscape Engr. (Charles Wellford Leavitt & Son), New York, N. Y. Mr. Leavitt died on April 22, 1928.

activity with a general tendency toward better conditions in both residences and business.

Water-front development is again peculiar to seaboard, lake, gulf, and coast towns and does not apply to some of the inland metropolitan regions, which also have a future.

Can any other section of the world compare with the Park Avenue District in New York? However, "we do find in such cities as Atlanta and Kansas City problems of growth just as puzzling"; but what has helped in studies of New York does not aid in these cities but rather tends to lead astray.

Again, in the quotation from Mr. Richard M. Hurd in regard to the returns on low *versus* high buildings, is found an argument most upsetting to smaller towns where a big price will be paid for the sky-scraper; and it is nearly impossible to convince any one that a sky-scraper is harmful to a town; for, while the writer feels with Mr. Adams and Mr. Hurd, that the building of tall structures is apt to hurt, yet in many instances towns have remained asleep until the tall building came to wake them into activity; but it did not become epidemic as in New York, Chicago, and Detroit. A hard and fast rule may not work for the smaller metropolitan regions.

Anything that may tend to re-establish a demand for land in these blighted areas is bound to be of great assistance, not only in that immediate neighborhood, but throughout the entire region. These blighted districts are usually equipped with sewers, water, electricity, and, frequently, paved streets, in which the city has a large investment without any chance to recapture it except by activity and building. Otherwise, this city money lies without return in adequate taxes, just as a sub-divider, who has equipped his land with all street improvements, is eaten up with interest if he does not sell his lots promptly.

Leaving vehicular traffic on the surface and putting wheeled transportation beneath and pedestrians above, may help a little for a time, but will not the section, so treated, soon again be overcrowded with no form for relief and thus in the end "confusion worse confounded" reign? Has all this not proved that the best way to produce reasonable living conditions, as well as areas in which to work, is by decentralization with careful thought given to building code and zoning?

Into the rural communities, along the main arteries of travel, is now pushed a ribbon-like development, making the roads between large cities such as New York, Boston, and Philadelphia, almost a continuous row of citified houses, and one wonders if the predictions of the author of "Road Town", published about twenty years ago, is not to be realized. In England, this ribbon development is giving the lovers of rural attractions considerable concern, because such rural drives as were enjoyed in the past, have ceased to exist in many cases and one drives from city to city through an apparent city.

Will the regional plan of the future correct these blighted districts, congested areas, and sky-scrapers, and relieve the owners of single-family houses from looking directly into the windows of their neighbors? Will some of the country outside the city remain rural? These are points over which the intelligent citizen must pause, and if such regional plans as have been drawn give promise of relief, then the citizens of seaboard, lake, gulf, and coast towns as well as cities inland, will demand that they too be included in the comprehensive plan for the future.

MORRIS KNOWLES,* M. AM. SOC. C. E. (by letter).—The regional community is an interesting subject, and the author's forecast of future urban regions may well arouse enthusiasm and stimulate discussion. Comparison with present-day development serves only to magnify the problems; those of construction as well as those of administration. However, there is ample experience now, from the results of not anticipating and planning for the future in the building of American cities, to provide a background of helpful consideration. The measure of success in the future will depend upon how well this experience is to be utilized in planning and in effecting governmental and administrative control. The two are inseparable. If improvement is to be realized, first it must be conceived, then designed, that is, planned; and then comes the necessity of practical administration to convert the plans into actual accomplishments. A look into the future, as to the probable type of new governmental agencies, necessary to secure results is the burden of this discussion.

Aside from the inherent social instinct, concentrated community life has come about naturally because of the advantages that accrue from the pooling of human endeavors. Different forms of government have been evolved and machinery has been set up for the construction of public facilities and the administration of public affairs. Through these agencies, the needs of the community have been supplied; water and sewerage systems have been planned and built; streets have been laid out and paved; police and fire protection methods have been developed; and all the other conveniences and comforts of modern life.

In accomplishing these results, some extravagance and waste have been inevitable; more often than not the needs of the future have been under-estimated in the construction of public works; mistakes have been made which have proved costly or impossible to correct; streets have been laid out with insufficient width; there has been too much crowding of the land in building operations; water and sewerage systems, as constructed, have proved inadequate, and many other deficiencies have been found to exist.

Early Development of Comprehensive Planning.—Out of this has come the modern conception of comprehensive city planning, designed to correct some of the mistakes of present city activities and to create an ideal toward which to build in the future. The subject is quite new, its development as a definite, conscious ideal having been within the past ten or twelve years. However, it was soon realized that many of the problems of such planning would be of a regional character and necessarily must include the suburban, satellite, and semi-rural districts surrounding the city and, in many instances, neighboring communities.

Regional planning as a basis for community activities and the problems involved in such study were presented by Mr. Adams—then Housing and

* Pres. and Chf. Engr., Morris Knowles, Inc., Pittsburgh, Pa.

Town Planning Adviser of the Canadian Government—at the meeting of the National Conference on City Planning at Niagara Falls and Buffalo, N. Y., in 1919. Since then, much study has been given to the subject and to practical methods of adapting well-intentioned theories to actual practice. Various methods and agencies have been suggested, some of which have been tried and found to be partly successful; but there is still a realization that, while much educative effort has been developed, the correct solution has not yet been presented. The process of evolution in the consideration of the problem has been somewhat as follows:

(1) The need of a regional conception of utility development has been apparent.
(2) Realization that single unit utilities, however well planned and executed, sometimes fail to co-ordinate with each other, has brought about a recognition of the necessity of comprehensive planning.
(3) Failure to find ready means to carry well-intentioned plans into execution, has shown a need of an adequate agency to finance and execute these comprehensive plans.
(4) Thus has come about a recognition that a new governmental attitude is necessary.

It is the writer's purpose to amplify and explain some of this development of thought in this discussion and suggest a type of government for the regional community.

Utilities—A Basis for Regional Planning.—Probably the first recognition of regional planning originated through the need of co-operation in the development of public utilities, where the service was common among municipal units arbitrarily separated by political lines. The city, in addition to its legislative, taxation, educational, and police power functions, is an industrial plant and its government an organization for carrying on the affairs of municipal management. It is apparent, therefore, that public works and utilities are of first importance in considering co-operative action.

Where municipalities lie so closely together as to be practically continuous, many municipal functions can be most efficiently performed under a single management. Such services as water supply, drainage, sewerage, main thoroughfares, general park developments, and regional planning are obviously accomplished best under unified control. Only in this way can haphazard development and duplication be avoided. These problems cannot be correctly solved within man-made political boundaries, but must be treated as watershed and area problems for a district having similar conditions. Finally, it is generally true that economy, both in construction and operation, is obtained by collective action.

Entirely apart from these engineering and economic considerations, however, there are sound reasons of political morality for the co-operative solution of such problems. No one "liveth to himself" and urbans and ruralists are all "members one of another". The suburbanite, working and buying in the city, is as dependent on the city's service as the city dweller who trades and visits in the environs, is on the facilities of the outdoor area. Mutual dependence involves mutual obligations and there is mutual advantage in sharing alike the common benefits in costs.

The earliest method devised to bring about concerted action among neighboring communities has been through organization of metropolitan districts for specific purposes. However, co-operative community development involves consideration of a much broader field of activity.

Problems of Regional Planning.—Because of the influence and effect of one group upon another in such matters as fire and police protection, water supply, sewage disposal, and prevention of the spread of disease, it is necessary to think in terms of the region, rather than of the separate units which enter into the combination. For example, one community may have an improved and sanitary water system, while a neighboring city may furnish an unwholesome supply. Similarly, the discharge of waste from one community may pollute the stream from which another draws its water; or, in the control of the milk supply, unified action is necessary if it is to be effective in accomplishing the desired results. These illustrations, while they refer only in a meager way to the many problems to be considered, include examples both of control and of planning.

Area Affected.—The region, with which such planning is concerned, might be defined as an area which, on account of the interdependence of the various communities therein, may be considered as a unit in physical and cultural development. Such an area might include several important cities, perhaps approximately of the same size, all having common interests and mutually dependent one upon another; or it might comprise a metropolis and its neighboring suburbs and satellite towns.

The latter type illustrates a most interesting fact about the modern growth of great cities; that is, the tendency to spill their populations out over a large area rather than to develop progressively outward from the center as was formerly the case. Thus, separate communities spring up all along the transit lines and at other favored spots, adjacent to the city, but outside its corporate limits. Mercantile establishments frequently find it profitable to move farther from the heart of the city; and high-class shopping districts, including theatres and hotels, are springing up in the outlying communities. Industries also find it to their advantage to choose sites farther from the center, where land values are lower and where there is room for new and modern housing developments which will be attractive to workmen.

Importance of Common Problems.—The planning and development of the region, therefore, including all the various towns and communities tributary to the parent city, offer far greater opportunities than in the case of the old-time progressive expansion of the city from the center outward; but, at the same time, new problems are introduced which were not present when one political boundary line enclosed the entire urban community, and growth beyond it was in concentric rings. Consequently, as the satellite communities grow, regional problems become grievous and separate municipalities find it difficult to arrive at any solution unless one helps the other, or joins with the other, and all agree on a common plan.

Advantages of Co-Operation.—Even superficial thought on the subject will convince one, therefore, that resulting benefits may be expected if a large number of political units—separated only by imaginary political boundary lines, but forming as a whole one unit as to economic, industrial, commercial, and social life—are united by some plan that makes concerted action possible in the conduct of public affairs. Some of the results of practical co-operation to be expected, are conservation of resources, economy in the development and construction of public facilities, and greater efficiency in governmental administration.

However, reference to some actual accomplishments of consolidation may be of interest and will afford convincing argument as to the advantages. The following is quoted from a paper* by Professor Chester B. Maxey, of the Western Reserve University, referring to the formation of Greater Philadelphia, during the Mid-Nineteenth Century:

"The immediate results of the Consolidation and Annexation were unquestionably beneficial. For many years Philadelphia and her environs had been disgraced by civil turbulence almost impossible to prevent or control. * * * These disturbances and disorders quickly disappeared when unified local government went into operation. * * * Other beneficial results of consolidation were the development of a comprehensive system of water supply and sewage disposal to replace the separate systems of the former independent municipalities; the establishment of a metropolitan park system; and a marked increase in the assessed valuation of property throughout the metropolitan area."

Similar illustrations could be given, but there is no need of repetition.

Regional Planning Commissions.—Naturally, in order to accomplish effective results in regional planning, there must be some form of centralized control over the major functions of the separate communities, in matters of common concern. Various methods of accomplishing such control have been considered and some have been tested, with more or less success. The Standard City Planning Enabling Act, as prepared by the Advisory Committee on City Planning and Zoning of the U. S. Department of Commerce, and published in preliminary form in February, 1927, makes provision for the establishment of regions and for the creation of regional planning commissions.

One method of creating the regions is that of having the Governor determine the boundaries and appoint the members of the regional planning commission. This would be done on request of the planning commission of any municipality, the county commissioners of any county, or upon petition of a certain number of citizens. An alternative method also is described, which contemplates the creation of the regional planning commissions on the initiative of one or more local planning commissions and the county commissioners of the counties involved. In the latter instance these agencies, by mutual agreement, would decide on the boundaries of the region and would determine the relative share of the cost of the work to be borne by the respective municipalities and counties and the size and method of selection of the regional planning commission.

* "Political Integration of Metropolitan Communities," *National Municipal Review,* August, 1922.

The organization of the commission and the powers and duties as proposed, would be similar to those of a city planning commission. Provision also has been made in the Act for certification of the regional plan to the various interested agencies within the region; for the adoption of the plan by municipalities; and for the legal status of the regional plan after its adoption.

This, so far as it goes, is a beginning, but an equally if not more important consideration is the creation of centralized administrative and executive control. In the city, after the planning commission has developed a general city plan, the existing departments of the municipal government are available for the handling of the detailed designs and for the construction of improvements; but in regional planning there is no form of centralized government available to bring about concerted action in matters of common interest, nor to initiate, execute, and administer the regional projects that have been conceived. Commissions or boards may be appointed of course to carry out some detail of the general plan, but the co-ordination of such specific features with other improvements proposed by the regional planning commission may be forgotten. Moreover, such efforts refer more particularly to construction problems and do not take into consideration the consolidation of the community in other important matters of public welfare. The real solution lies in the development of some form of definite governmental authority which will secure the benefit of combining the resources of the separate political units in matters of regional character; but which will guarantee to such separate units local control in affairs of purely local concern.

Methods of Organization.—While the details of organization and administration may differ, as proposed in any particular instance, the various plans tried, or proposed throughout the country, may be grouped under one of three headings, as far as general principles are concerned. Stated briefly, these are as follows:

1.—Annexation of Adjoining Territory.

2.—Metropolitan Districts for Specific Purposes.

3.—A Federated City Plan of Government.

Annexation.—This is the oldest method of consolidation and the one that has been resorted to in the growth of practically every city. It includes the actual incorporation of adjacent territory into the city, and complete centralization of authority with respect to public works, public safety, legislation, taxation, and all other municipal functions. The result may be brought about by mutual agreement between the city and the annexed suburbs; or, under some forms of legislation, by the sovereign power of the State, or by a majority of all the voters in the territory affected, regardless of the wishes of the voters of the suburbs to be annexed.

Voluntary annexation of neighboring suburban towns in the larger cities often may be difficult to accomplish. This is not difficult to understand, for the people of smaller communities are vastly more homogeneous in regard to their concerted actions than people of the wards of the city. They feel more at home and more friendly with each other, because the people in city communities are changing so rapidly that permanency of abode does not exist to a sufficient degree to promote acquaintance and friendliness. Pride in one's own small community is natural and to be encouraged, and it is not to be expected that residents in such places will voluntarily delegate to a larger municipal authority, more or less removed, powers which have to do with purely local affairs and which now are thought to be capably managed by officials whom they know and who, perhaps, are neighbors.

However, if the need be sufficiently urgent, annexation may be carried out and has been, in several important instances, sometimes voluntarily and sometimes forcefully or involuntarily. The difficulty lies, not in any consitutional limitations in most States in applying the latter method, for the municipality, of course, is simply a creature of the State and subject to whatever laws the Legislature may formulate; nor is the only objection the fact that the principle of home rule would be discarded entirely.

The fact is that annexation, whether voluntary or otherwise, does not solve the problem. There is destroyed that very desirable quality of people wishing to do things for themselves; pride in small local affairs is lessened; the older, well-developed portions of the city are burdened with the cost of improvements in outlying sections; and the tendency is again toward centralization and congestion. Thus, the problems of municipal government become increasingly complex and difficult, leading too often to misgovernment and mismanagement.

Metropolitan Districts.—This method approaches the solving of regional problems through metropolitan commissions, each charged with some particular type of public works or activity, and functioning within a region known as a metropolitan district. This plan has had its greatest development in London, England, through the activities of the London County Council, and has been copied, to some extent, in this country. For example, around Boston, Mass., there have been various metropolitan commissions since about 1890, and some of the best examples in the United States: First, a Sewerage Commission, covering Boston and 15 towns within a radius of 15 miles or more of the State House; then, in 1895-96, the development of the Metropolitan Water Commission; and, about the same time, the Metropolitan Park Commission. Some time later, the Metropolitan Police was organized.

These various commissions have cared wonderfully well for certain types of public improvements, and for their proper design and efficient operation. It should be remembered, however, that the operation of these Boston commissions is entirely in the hands of the State through commissions appointed by the Governor. This paternalistic authority of the State over the communities is really more exacting and detailed than a municipality would be likely to have exercised. The local communities have nothing to say; they do not vote for appropriations or commissioners; they do not get together; the State does it all and then charges the cost to each.

Recently, having in mind that these things were not operating as well as if they were more unified, the authorities resolved to join the three commissions having to do with water supply, sewerage, and parks, into one Metropolitan Commission. This has helped, because it means that, when water-works are planned, there will be some consideration given to drainage and sewerage and parks, and *vice versa.* It readily can be seen, however, that many other features of the metropolitan area also are affected. There is still a lack of co-ordination of the various governmental affairs within the region, which must be considered. Conflicting action rather than harmony is produced. Only recently a retrogression has occurred in the creation of a board for the development of a new, distant source of water supply.

There are many other metropolitan commissions functioning in American cities, most of them having to do with only one particular kind of public works. The Sanitary District of Chicago, for instance, comprises all of Cook County and some territory outside. Its Commissioners are elected by the people. Another example is the Miami Conservancy District. This is probably the largest area of its kind in the United States and is a somewhat special case. The District embraces all or parts of nine counties and includes the Cities of Dayton, Middletown, and Hamilton, Ohio. It was organized for the purpose of constructing and maintaining flood-prevention works, and its government rests with a Board of three, appointed by a Court, consisting of one Common Pleas Judge in each of the counties affected.

Another example is the Essex Border Utilities Commission, constituted by Special Act of the Ontario Parliament, in April, 1916. Its object has been the solution of problems affecting the whole of the border municipalities, as distinguished from those to be dealt with by any one of them in particular. These problems include sewerage, water supply system, health, parks, planning, etc. The Commission consists of nineteen members, eleven of whom are elected and eight are *ex officio,* all serving without remuneration.

While the metropolitan district plan is frequently adapted to the development of certain specific public improvements, there are certain faults and disadvantages to be considered. Sufficient co-ordination between the various types of improvements is lacking; control is remote from the people directly affected; and there is a possibility of much confusion and wasted effort from the overlapping jurisdictions of a great number of such commissions if many activities are undertaken.

Federated City Plan of Government.—This is the type of organization that has been adopted by the Pennsylvania Commission for the Study of Consolidation of Municipalities, after several years' study of the various methods, and this type is proposed for Greater Pittsburgh.

The plan proposed is somewhat analogous to that of New York City, but there are important differences. While New York comprises five Boroughs—each one a large city in itself, and some of which even have regional characteristics—the Pittsburgh Plan will include 124 municipalities, most of them already distinct and separate communities, which will be preserved within the consolidated city.

While the plan that has been proposed was formulated to meet particular local conditions within Allegheny County, in Western Pennsylvania, its general principles may be considered applicable to the majority of similar situations; and an explanation of its more important features may be of general interest.

The Greater Pittsburgh Plan.—The area included in the Pittsburgh Plan coincides with that of Allegheny County. Within this area, in addition to the City of Pittsburgh, there are three cities of the third class, sixty-six boroughs, and fifty-four townships. The population included will approximate 1 500 000. One of the basic principles adopted by the Commission in its preliminary consideration of the problem, as set forth in its report to the Governor, was:

"That such a plan, to be made satisfactory, should give to the constituent and smaller municipalities, proper and reasonable control of their local affairs * * *. No government must become too remote from the people. The greater things should be handled in a greater way; the smaller and more intimate things in a smaller way, a local way—home rule by home people. Local officials should and must be close to the citizens for whom they function, giving service as desired, never remote from or unmindful of the constituents, or out of constant touch with them."

An amendment to the Constitution of the State was found necessary in order to enable the adoption of such a plan. It was passed first at the special session of the Legislature in 1926 and again at the regular session in 1927. It will be placed before the people of the State in the form of a referendum in November, 1929.

While the constitutional amendment is largely of an enabling nature, the general features to be observed in the plan have been incorporated in it. This was done to insure certainty of rights to the smaller communities. They include provisions for the general functions and powers of the consolidated city; a statement that local powers are to be reserved to constituent municipalities; and an outline of the method of framing and adopting the new charter.

The charter, under which the consolidated city will operate, will be authorized by the General Assembly and will provide for,

"* * * the consolidation of the county, poor districts, cities, boroughs and townships of the County of Allegheny and the offices thereof, into a consolidated city and county, with the constitutional and legal capacity of a municipal corporation, to be known as the City of Pittsburgh and * * * provide for a charter for its government".

This provision will give to the consolidated city, authority to deal with problems affecting any two or more municipalities, or the whole district. Among such problems may be mentioned water supply, including the planning of a general system, where found advisable; sewerage systems, particularly the consideration of main trunk lines and of disposal; transit lines, including the beginning of a rapid transit system to serve adequately the greater city; main thoroughfares, through highways, tunnels, subways, and bridges; and other public works of a regional character which should be accomplished by, or under, the direction of the consolidated city government.

Another of the provisions relating to powers conferred on the new government refers to zoning, making such procedure constitutional beyond any possible doubt within the Greater City. Another grants authority to the Commissioners of the Central Government to create special improvement districts for the financing and construction of certain works, such as drainage, sewage disposal, or garbage collection and disposal.

Certain debts of the constituent units, incurred for the construction of public works which would be transferred to the Greater City, will be assumed by the Central Government. In addition, the charter may provide,

"For the assessment of property for taxation, the levying and collection of taxes and the payment of the costs of any public improvement, either in whole or in part, by special assessment upon abutting and non-abutting property materially benefitted thereby, and for this purpose real estate so charged shall be classified as urban, suburban, and rural, and adjustment made in accordance with such classification".

This obviously is the proper method of assessment for improvements rather than that which places the burden of the entire cost on abutting properties by general taxation through bond issues.

A guaranty against forcible annexation is given to the separate communities in case the charter is adopted, but there is nothing to prevent two or more of the separate municipalities joining together voluntarily whenever they desire.

The local powers to be kept by the several cities, boroughs, and townships are definitely stated in the proposed amendment, and include the following:

1.—The constitutional and legal capacity of municipal corporations, except as limited in the charter.

2.—The power to levy and collect taxes for any lawful power of the separate municipalities.

3.—The power to acquire, own, construct, maintain, and operate public property, works, improvements, utilities or services dealing with only local needs.

4.—The power to maintain a local police and fire department. In some cases this may be supplemental to the department of the consolidated city.

5.—All other powers not specifically granted by the charter to the consolidated city.

Provision is made for the voluntary surrender of any of these powers to the consolidated city, by vote of the electors in one of the separate municipal divisions, and by acceptance in each instance of such delegation of power and responsibility by the Board of Commissioners of the consolidated city.

Those who have given most thought to the situation, feel that the Pittsburgh Plan will provide a practical solution for regional problems of planning and for construction and operation of regional public works. Much will depend on the type and details of the charter yet to be drawn. However, even if all the results as to governmental operation may be as anticipated, the working out of the details and the thorough and practical planning of the region will be essential to effective accomplishment.

Wisdom of Regional Planning.—Community planning is based on the principle of co-ordination. Public facilities always have been planned to some extent but usually as independent and separate projects, so that there was a lack of harmony in fitting them into the general community plan. This has been the deficiency that brought about a realization of the need of something different and that has been responsible for the development of the present-day art of community planning. The important difference lies in the co-ordinating of all improvement plans and fitting them together into an harmonious and unified scheme of general design whether it be for a village, a city, or a region.

Consequently, the planning of a regional utility, such as a water supply or a sewerage system, by a regional or metropolitan board may be contrasted with the separate planning of a similar utility for one of the constituent communities, by the city engineer or by a municipal commission. Efforts like the latter cannot be described as regional planning activities; real value can come only from a comprehensive consideration of all the problems that are of a regional character. Otherwise, the same difficulties that have become so manifest with the growth of urban communities will eventually be experienced as the larger regional area becomes more compactly developed.

The difficulties, at the present time, lie in the lack of governmental machinery for developing the regional plan, and after having developed it, in making the plan effective in its administration. Whatever the method may be, the three steps to be considered in the development of a regional community are: (*a*) The conception and creation of the form of consolidation; (*b*) the establishment of the boundaries of the region; and (*c*) the adequate planning of public facilities and services for this area.

The whole subject is so new that there are only a few precedents or experiments as illustrations of what to do or of what to avoid; but in all private and public endeavors, planning should precede execution. Therefore, whether the start be made through the creation of a regional planning commission, with the subsequent details of the regional municipal organization to be developed later; or whether the general plan of governmental consolidation be first conceived, and the planning done thereunder, perhaps is immaterial. In either event both are essential to complete success.

Finally, community planning, whether it be that which is concerned with a single municipality or whether it be sufficiently enlarged in scope to include many diverse political entities, should be conceived to accomplish more than the economical construction of public utilities, or the development of more efficient forms of public control. The psychological result should be to create a public consciousness and appreciation of community problems, and this, in turn, should be used to advantage in promoting enthusiasm for a large and intelligent program for the whole community. The modern development of American cities, and the advent of the automobile, which has made possible the scattering of populations over large areas at no sacrifice of time in transportation, have re-acted to a lack of participating interest in the larger civic affairs by those who make their homes in the suburbs or in the neighboring countryside. The larger community interests, because of their remoteness, have become secondary to those of the immediate local neighborhoods; but regional endeavors should be a means of bringing about a closer bond of sympathy and helpfulness in the solution of the many problems that confront the larger urban developments of the present day. The Pittsburgh Plan of Municipal Consolidation is offered as an advanced idea in the hope that it will merit public discussion and point the way to making regional plans effective through the development of a widespread civic consciousness in governmental affairs over large areas having common problems.

Thomas Adams,* Esq. (by letter).—From certain points of view, the writer agrees with Mr. Kingery that regional planning presents greater difficulties than city planning, but this should not be taken to mean that the technical preparation of a regional plan involves more labor and difficulty than the preparation of a city plan. The former covers a larger area than the latter, but it is not so hampered by the necessity of complying with legal requirements or of compromising with existing conditions. Subject to being based on sound principles and to being comprehensive in its treatment of problems, it may be said that the more elastic and the broader in outline the regional plan is, the better it will be.

Mr. Strong shows by his emphasis on principles that he has the right conception of what is most needed. The regional plan is confined so much to problems of the future that planners need not be greatly influenced by political expediency or by pressure of vested interests in existing bad conditions. Therefore, they have no excuse for developing a plan that is not sound in principle, from the point of view of what is best for the community. As Mr. Fay states, regional planning should be based on the policy of looking ahead over a long period of years, and in the development of its main features it should consider sociological as well as physical and economic problems.

It goes without saying that co-operation is the keynote of a regional plan. In fact, there can be no regional planning without much co-operation. The fact and extent of this co-operation between authorities of adjacent regions, which Mr. Kingery and Professor Lyle emphasize, are more important than the need of effecting governmental and administrative control as referred to by Mr. Knowles. The writer predicts the operation of governmental control through the city organization rather than through the unorganized region. Nevertheless, Mr. Knowles has raised a most interesting point which will have greater significance in the future, namely, the desirability of new types of government for great urban regions. On this subject Professor Munro, of Harvard University, has recently written in support of those who advocate a regional form of government.†

Mr. Kingery's claim that some of the most obscure local officials are doing some very successful regional planning does not carry conviction. The work and projects of these officials are no doubt being developed in co-operation with his association and thereby are given a regional emphasis. It is most dangerous, however, to assume that the piecing together of different local projects is regional planning, even if this is done with co-operation. A regional plan should develop from considerations of the region as a whole down to the local considerations rather than take the form of a collection and composite of local projects.

There does not appear to be much ground for concern about lack of centralized organization or lack of capital, in spite of the truth of Colonel Wilgus' statement that these represent two formidable obstacles to be over-

* Gen. Director of Plans and Surveys, Regional Plan of New York and Its Environs, New York, N. Y.

† *The Forum,* January, 1928, p. 108.

come. They do present such obstacles in relation to all major engineering projects which are proposed within or without a regional plan, but they are no greater than have to be overcome in connection with all forms of planning and government. Since they have to be fought in any event, it is better that planners should have to fight them for some purpose that is really worth while. The writer's fear, in getting the dream of a better city brought into reality, is not for the lack of organization or capital, but for the lack of well-informed public opinion regarding what is true and false in the building of the city.

The differences between New York and other regional communities of the future, referred to by Mr. Leavitt, only relate to certain physical aspects. The New York Region contains the same social and economic elements and reflects the same tendencies of growth as other great urban aggregations.

No regional plan will correct blighted districts, congested areas, and the evils of skyscrapers. All it can accomplish is to show what is likely to happen from certain conditions and tendencies and to stimulate the operation of social and economic forces in those directions that will bring greater convenience, health, safety, and public well-being than is possible to be obtained with the present haphazard and disorganized growth within meaningless political boundaries.

The distinguished authorities who have discussed this presentation of a difficult subject, involving an attempt to make shrewd guesses into the future, have given the writer a greater confidence in the general predictions that he ventured to put forward with great temerity. If some of the things hoped for cannot be attained, there still remains the satisfaction of having hoped.

AMERICAN SOCIETY OF CIVIL ENGINEERS

INSTITUTED 1852

TRANSACTIONS

This Society is not responsible for any statement made or opinion expressed in its publications.

Paper No. 1685

THE HISTORY AND DEVELOPMENT OF ROAD BUILDING IN THE UNITED STATES*

BY THOMAS H. MACDONALD,† ESQ.

Between this Sesqui-Centennial Year (1926) and the founding of the first Colonial settlement at Jamestown, Va., the great event of 1776 stands almost at the mid-point of time. The men who gathered in Philadelphia to affix their signatures to the Declaration of Independence looked back upon a period of American history a little longer than that which has since unfolded. At the end of their sesqui-centennium the journeys they made from their several homes were only slightly less arduous and time-consuming than they would have been at its beginning. To-day—150 years later—the same journeys are made in hours instead of days, and days instead of weeks.

The signers insisted that they acted for thirteen independent States. To-day, it is difficult to conceive of the States as separate Commonwealths possessing original authority and yielding only to a restricted power which they, themselves, have conferred on the Federal Government. In the popular mind they have become no more than the political subdivisions of the Republic.

To what extent was the form of government, as originally established, the product of inadequate facilities of communication between the Colonies; and what relation is there between the gradual transfer of authority to the Federal Government and the development of the railroads, the telegraph and telephone, the radio, the motor vehicle, and the modern improved highways? The writer is convinced that it would be wiser if, in the teaching of American history in the schools, more time were given to the study of such fundamental economic questions, and less to the lives and ambitions of political leaders and the wars in which America has been involved by their blundering.

It is an absorbing pursuit in reading history to speculate on the effect of transportation in shaping America's destiny as a nation. To what extent

* Presented at the meeting of the Highway Division, Philadelphia, Pa., October 6, 1926.

† Chf., U. S. Bureau of Public Roads, Washington, D. C.

was the general improvement of roads that followed immediately after the Revolution owing to the preservation and gradual strengthening of the bond which precariously united the Thirteen Colonies?

What seeds of disunion are to be found in the fact that the later movements of the people and the building of roads, canals, and railroads were mainly westward both from the South and the North; and that between the Hudson and the Mississippi not a single major waterway runs north and south?

What would now be the western boundary of the United States if exploration and travel over the Oregon Trail had been delayed by as much as a decade?

What conception of the true rôle of the railways was held by those who built the early roads? The writer is convinced that they thought of them as merely a new form of highway, to replace entirely the common roads. No other conception and no less profound ignorance of the economics of railway transportation can explain the hundreds of thousands of short lines built without connection or possibility of adequate revenue; and no other conception will account for the complete abandonment of the common roads.

What importance as an underlying cause of the Civil War attaches to the fact that, in 1850, there were less than 10 000 miles of such inadequately located railways in the entire country and, in 1860, but slightly more than 30 000 miles? And what, in view of the general agreement that the South was starved into submission, was the effect of the fact that, in 1864, there were less than 6 000 miles of railway under Confederate control, all in utter disrepair?

These are interesting historical speculations. In the forces with which they are concerned is found a truer cause of the course and progress of the Nation than many of those of a purely political nature to which such importance has been attached by historians.

Amusement as well as intellectual profit may be derived from this study of the history of transportation. Whenever opposition is expressed to the granting of franchises for the use of the public highways by common carrier motor trucks, the writer is reminded of the completeness with which the Governor of New Jersey disposed of a similar complaint by the Assembly in 1707. Of the result of this so-called monopoly he stated:

"At present everybody is sure, once a fortnight, to have an opportunity of sending any quantity of goods, great or small, at reasonable rates, without being in danger of imposition; and the sending of this wagon is so far from being a grievance or monopoly, that by this means and no other, a trade has been carried on between Philadelphia, Burlington, Amboy, and New York, which was never known before, and in all probability never would have been."

Let the legal retainers of the public service commissions strive as they may, there is no more adequate reply to the numerous complaints, which it is their duty to answer, than that.

When one hears the fear expressed, as frequently happens, that the improvement of roads and their use by motor vehicles will destroy the business of the railroads, the writer is again reminded of the instance cited by a citizen of Pennsylvania in an essay he prepared in 1891 in the hope of winning a prize offered by the University of Pennsylvania. He was informed, so he states:

"By a gentleman in the business of furnishing road material, that a prominent official of a great railroad refused to deliver material for him at a point on their road where it would have been a great convenience to have had it, and gave as a reason that they did not wish to accommodate the turnpike company that wanted the material, as their road was too good already, and was competing with the railroad to the injury of their business."

If, in 1891, before ever the honk of a motor horn had disturbed the quiet somnolence of the peaceful Pennsylvania countryside, a "prominent official of a great railroad" could scent danger in highway improvement, it is not surprising in this day of greatest railroad prosperity, that other "prominent officials" betray similar fears, but it is problematical whether they still hope to halt the proper development of highway transportation.

These are merely random historical allusions by way of preface to the specific subject of this paper, which is confined to a review of the development of highway construction and maintenance.

Colonial Road Building

With the exception of the primitive streets of Jamestown no roads were built in the Colony of Virginia by the first settlers. The settlements were close to the river banks and fear of Indian attack kept the colonists from wandering far inland. The first road law of the Colony, which was also the first American law with respect to highways, was passed by the General Assembly in 1632. It provided for the laying out of the simple ways required by the small settlement in the following terms:

"Highways shall be layd out in such convenient places as are requisite accordings as the Governor and Counsell or the Commissioners for the monthlie corts shall appoynt, or accordings as the parishioners of every parish shall agree."

Brief and elementary as were its terms, this law was doubtless entirely adequate for a community in which, according to the inventory of goods and chattels made in 1625, there was but one horse, and that in the possession of the Governor.

The first New England law of record, and the second to be passed in all America, was enacted in Massachusetts in 1639. Although somewhat longer than the Virginia Act, its terms were similar in their general effect. It is notable from the point of view of the engineer, however, as the first law in which there is any specification as to the manner in which the roads were to be constructed. After providing for the laying out of the roads by two or three men chosen from every town, and after carefully protecting the rights of property owners from encroachment by the road builders, it lays upon the locators this single injunction, that, "in common grounds, or where the soil is wet or miry, they shall lay out the ways the wider, as six, or eight, or ten rods, or more in common grounds."

In this law is found the first provision, loose and flexible as it was, governing the width of the highways. As yet there was no definition of the manner in which the ways were to be made; and it was not until 1664 that, in the regulations established by the Government of New York, the first definite prescription of this nature was given. That part of the regulation was, as follows:

"The highways to be cleared as followeth, *viz.*, the way to be made clear of standing and lying trees, at least ten feet broad; all stumps and shrubs to be cut close by the ground. The trees marked yearly on both sides—sufficient bridges to be made and kept over all marshy, swampy, and difficult dirty places, and whatever else shall be thought more necessary about the highways aforesaid."

Although this was the first legal definition of a method to be followed, it is probable that the regulation merely embodied the common practice of the day and that methods and practices very similar were followed in all the Colonies.

That but little advance had been made by the opening of the Eighteenth Century is indicated by the Maryland Law of 1704, which contains much the same provisions with respect to clearing and grubbing, and merely increases the width to 20 ft. This law, however, is of interest mainly because of its Fifth Section which constitutes what is perhaps the first definite regulation for marking of roads in America, and, incidentally, indicates how easy it must have been to lose one's way on the rude tracks which served for roads. This curious provision was as follows:

"V. And that all the roads that lead to any Ferries, Court-house of any County, or to any church, or leading through any county to the port of Annapolis, should be marked on both sides the Road with Two Notches; if the Road lead to Annapolis, the Road that leads there, at the leaving the other Road, shall be marked on the face of the tree, in a smooth Place cut for that purpose, with the letters A A set on with a Pair of Marking-Irons and coloured; and so with Two Notches all along the Road; and where at any Place it leaves any other Road shall be again distinguished with the Mark aforesaid, on the Face of the Tree, with a Pair of Marking-Irons, and coloured as aforesaid. And any road on the Eastern Shore in Talbot County, that leads to the port of William-Stadt at the entering of the same, and in parting with or dividing from any other Road, shall be marked on the face of a tree, in a smooth place cut for that purpose, with the letter, W, and so with two notches all along the road. And the Roads that lead to any County Court-house, shall have two Notches on the Trees on both sides of the Road as aforesaid, and another Notch a Distance above the other. And any Road that leads to a Church, shall be marked at the entrance into the same, and at the leaving any other Road, with a Slip cut down the Face of the Tree, near the ground. And any road leading to a Ferry, and dividing from other public roads, shall be marked with Three Notches of equal distance at the Entrance into the same. And these Rules and Methods the Several Justices of the County Courts, shall, from Time to Time, give in charge to the overseers of the Highways, by them to be appointed for that purpose; who are likewise enjoined carefully and strictly to observe and perform the same, under the Penalty aforesaid."

Along at least one of these ancient roads in Southern Maryland, still known as the "Three Notch Road", notches, some of a remote date, may still be discerned in the bark of many of the oldest oaks.

The law in which this odd provision was made constituted, with minor amendments, the sole road legislation of the Province of Maryland for nearly three generations, and Maryland was not more backward than the other Colonies. Indeed it must be said that from the point of view of the road builder the progress made during the entire Colonial period was practically negligible, as may be seen from the following passages taken from the work of the Maryland historian, Thomas Scharf:

"* * * where water routes were not available, the means of locomotion, though various, were all primitive. Long journeys were made on horseback. People of consequence rode in their coaches, with four horses attached, the leaders mounted by liveried postilions. So Washington came from New York to Annapolis, to attend the ball given there in his honor after the peace. He left New York, December 4, and arrived at Annapolis, December 17, thirteen days to a ride which may now be made inside of eight hours. So Washington went to Philadelphia from Mount Vernon to attend the Constitutional Convention, having to lie over at Havre-de-Grace all night because it was too stormy to cross the Susquehanna. The stage-coach was just coming into use in this country at the time of which we write, and the importance of regular communication between one point and another was beginning to be seen. There were a few, but not many post-routes, and those chiefly maintained by private enterprise.

"The carrier's cart plied between Alexandria and Philadelphia, by way of Baltimore; the Conestoga wagon was the means of communication between Baltimore and Harrisburg, Frederick, Hagerstown, etc., while these outlying places in their turn were brought into intercourse with the backwoods and the wilderness by means of strings of pack-horses. * * * Roads were all bad and ill-kept, narrow, obstructed by gates and seldom permitting two vehicles to pass one another. * * *

"The good roads—comparatively good, we mean—and the best post-routes were due to private enterprise. The Kent Island post-route was owned by a Tilghman, and Henry Callister threatened an opposition unless it was better managed. * * * It took a day of almost twenty-four hours, to ride from Elkridge Landing to Annapolis (about 30 miles)—yet the thrifty Germans of Frederick County traded with Georgia by way of the Valley of Virginia, sending their manufactures of wool, flax and leather on the backs of pack-horses."

Pioneer Roads to the West

If such was the state of the roads in the settlements during the Revolution it may be assumed that the few roads which previously had been pushed westward across the mountains were even more primitive. The first of these was laid out in 1743 by the Ohio Company, a party of Virginia gentlemen who had been granted 200 000 acres on the Ohio River between the Monongahela and the Kanawha on condition that 100 families should be settled on it in two years.

According to Hulbert:

"The road was probably nothing more than a blazed trail with possibly some alteration of route at certain points; it may be that in low ground which could not be avoided the road was 'corduroyed', but this is quite doubtful."

It was over this road that Washington traveled, in 1753, at the behest of the Virginia Governor to inquire of the French their rights to build forts on the Allegheny River. Again, in 1754, when war with the French seemed inevitable, he made the same trip over the same road, this time taking with him 300 men and possibly 10 swivel guns, to move which it was necessary to widen and straighten the road. Finally, in the following year (1755), it was over this same road that Braddock advanced from Fort Cumberland with 2 200 men and 600 pioneers, leading the way, to widen and corduroy the trail for the Army. This time the road was evidently made with some care, for Washington complained that the movement of the army was being delayed because the road-makers were stopping to level "every mole-hill".

This, the first road across the mountains, was the only one until 1758, when Gen. John Forbes, sent against Fort Duquesne to redeem the failure of Braddock, built or rather opened a new one by way of Bedford and Ligonier, in Pennsylvania; and this road with its predecessor remained as the only routes of white-man travel across the mountains until 1775.

In that year the Transylvania Company was organized, and Daniel Boone was sent to mark out the Wilderness Road through the Cumberland Gap to Kentucky. Although made later than the roads of Braddock and Forbes, the Wilderness Road quickly became the most important of the three as a thoroughfare and for a time actually outrivaled the Ohio River as a pioneer route. Of this road a Kentucky historian says:

"The road marked out was at best but a trace. No vehicle of any sort passed over it before it was made a wagon road by action of the State legislature in 1795. The location of the road, however, is a monument to the skill of Boone as a practical engineer and surveyor. It required a mind of far more than ordinary caliber to locate through more than two hundred miles of mountain wilderness a way of travel which, for a hundred years, has remained practically unchanged, and upon which the State has stamped its approval by the expenditure of vast sums of money."

Although the State did undoubtedly approve and profit greatly from the work of the intrepid Boone, its approval apparently did not express itself in any substantial way, for in 1796, he wrote as follows to Governor Shelby:

"Sir, after my best Respts to your Excellency and famyly, I wish to inform you that I have sum intention of undertaking this New Rode that is to be cut through the Wilderness, and I think my Self intitled to the ofer of the Bisness as I first Marked out that Rode in March 1775 and Never rec'd anything for my trubel and Sepose I am no Statesman I am a Woodsman and think my Self as Capable of Marking and Cutting that Rode as any other man. Sir if you think with Me I would thank you to wright me a line by the post the first oportuneaty and he Will Lodge it at Mr. John Milers on hinkston fork as I wish to know Where and when it is to be Laat [let] so that I may atend at the time I am Deer Sir your very omble sarvent.

"DANIEL BOONE."

But, alas, the contract was given to others, to Boone's great disappointment. Such was the experience of the first American "engineer" who took it into his head to "go into contracting." How many have been the similar experiences of his successors the record does not state.

The mountains crossed, progress of exploration westward was rapid after the Revolution. The pioneers opened the trails and the Army followed close behind, establishing forts for the protection of travelers and settlers against Indian attack. The "road building" that was an incident of the advance of those brave and adventurous spirits, however, was invariably of the sort already described; that is, a mere breaking and blazing of trails in the difficult places, and, in the open country, only the choosing of a path which by continued use was worn into a well-marked route.

For the opening of certain of these routes, Congress, which under the Constitution was given the right to govern the territories, was urged to contribute money, and did actually contribute to a few, among them the famous Natchez Trace which ran from Nashville, Tenn., to Natchez, Miss., and Zane's Trace in Ohio. The character of the work done on the former is indicated by the fact that the appropriation was $6 000.

Of similar character were the great trails of the West, on which exploration began early in the Nineteenth Century. In all the annals of America there are no more thrilling passages than the records of the travels and the path-finding of the pioneers who, following the Santa Fé, the Overland, and the Oregon Trails, settled and held for the United States the great dominions of the West. The highways they marked out were so truly remarkable that they are still, in the main, the principal routes of travel in the territories they traverse. One of them—the Oregon Trail—has been described as:

"The most remarkable road known to history * * *. Considering the fact that it originated with the spontaneous use of travelers; that no transit ever located a foot of it; that no level established its grades; that no engineer sought out the fords or built any bridges or surveyed the mountain passes, that there was no grading to speak of, nor any attempt at metalling the road bed; and the general good quality of these two thousand miles of highway will seem most extraordinary."

Early Turnpike Ventures

It will not be possible, however, in this paper to follow the development of the routes of exploration westward. The principal object being the study of the development of road construction methods, the writer must return to the Eastern States, where, immediately after the close of the Revolution, the first great movement for the betterment of American roads was at its inception—the establishment of the turnpikes.

The first American turnpikes of which there is record were established in Virginia, Connecticut, and Maryland. From the interesting book by Frederic J. Wood entitled "The Turnpikes of New England", it is learned that Virginia led the way by the erection of gates on the roads leading into Alexandria from Snigger's and Vesta's Gaps. The travel on these roads had become so heavy that extensive repairs were imperative and, the resources of the territory traversed being inadequate, it was proposed to set up toll-gates as a means of collecting the necessary revenues, an idea suggested, no doubt, by the English experience with turnpike trusts which had been in operation for at least twenty years previously. The Act of the

Legislature providing for the erection of the turnpikes was passed in 1785, and, as an existing road was taken over and the only construction necessary was the erection of the gates, it is safe to say that they were in operation by 1786.

A heavy travel passed over this road for several years, and the tolls imposed by the Legislature were insufficient to maintain its surface. Accordingly, in 1795, representations were made to the Legislature that "an artificial bed of pounded or broken stone" was necessary, and that the expense of this, being too great to be financed by the usual methods, it should only be assumed by private enterprise. This is the first reference the writer has been able to find to any form of construction resembling what is now classed, very loosely, as a macadam surface. It is probable that stone and gravel surfaces had been laid in England for some years previously, and there may have been some more or less unsystematic use of stone in America also at an earlier date; but it is reasonably certain that this Virginia road was at least one of the earliest to be deliberately planned as a stone-surfaced highway. As a result of the representations made, the "Fairfax and Loudon turnpike-road company" was incorporated on December 26, 1795, and given the privilege of reconstructing the old turnpike from "Little River, where the present turnpike crosses it, to Alexandria." The first company finding the task too great, nothing was accomplished under its charter, and, in 1802, a new charter was granted to the "President, Directors, and Company of the Little River Turnpike Company." Under this charter, with the help of the State of Virginia, which appropriated the "muster fines" in 1805 to the purchase of 100 shares of stock, the old road was rebuilt and operated as a toll road for more than ninety years.

The second and third turnpikes were in Connecticut where, in 1792, the Mohegan Road, between New London and Norwich, and the Old Post Road, in Greenwich, were made subject to toll. A year later, in 1793, a gate was set up on the Reisterstown Road, in Maryland and, later, other gates were established on the York and Frederick Roads near Baltimore. These Maryland cases were followed, in 1801, by the establishment of a gate on the old road through Cumberland Gap, in Tennessee; and, in 1804, North Carolina provided for the construction of a 14-mile road through the Cherokee lands by granting to the builder the privilege of collecting tolls for fifteen years. All these were Government enterprises, and they are the only exceptions to the practice, which was shortly to become general, of allowing the turnpikes to be built by private capital. Later, these, too, were transferred to private companies, but the first road to be built in this manner was the famous Lancaster Turnpike, in Pennsylvania, which was built by the Philadelphia and Lancaster Turnpike Company, incorporated by the Governor on April 9, 1792. This road which was more than 62 miles in length, was built at a cost of $7 450 per mile and was finally completed in 1796.

Following this example similar corporations were created in rapid succession in all the States, and in his report to Congress, in 1808, Albert Gallatin, the Secretary of the Treasury, was able to report definitely that 770 miles were completed in Connecticut, more than 3 000 miles were under construction or completed in New York, and hundreds of miles in other States.

The Character of Early Turnpikes

This same report of Gallatin's gives the first detailed description of the character of the "artificial roads" built by the early turnpike companies.

Referring to the road from Trenton to Brunswick, in New Jersey, he reports that:

"The distance is twenty-five miles; the greatest angle of ascent, three degrees; and the road is nearly in a straight line, the only considerable obstruction being the 'sand hills', through which it was necessary to dig at the depth of thirty feet, in order not to exceed the angle of ascent. The road is thirty-six feet wide, fifteen feet of which are covered with about six inches of gravel. A few wooden bridges, with stone abutments, and piers have been erected across the intervening streams. The whole expense is stated at $2 500 a mile."

On the road in Pennsylvania from Philadelphia to Perkiomen, which had two branches to Willow Grove and Chestnut Hill, he wrote:

"The distance * * * is twenty-five miles and a quarter; the two branches extend one ten miles, and the other seven miles and a half; making together near forty-three miles. The angle of ascent is four degrees; the breadth of the road fifty feet, of which twenty-eight feet, having a convexity of fifteen inches, are covered with a stratum either of gravel eighteen inches thick, or of pounded stones twelve inches thick. One-half of the stones forming the lower part of the stratum are broken into pieces not more than five inches in diameter; the other half or upper stratum consists of stones broken into pieces not more than two inches and a half in diameter, and this difference in the size of the stones is represented as a considerable defect. Side or summer roads extend on each side of the gravel or stone road. The five miles next to Philadelphia have cost at the rate of $14 517 a mile; the other twenty miles and a half at the rate of $10 490 a mile. Yet there were no natural impediments, and only small bridges or culverts were necessary. The capital expended on these twenty-five miles and a half is $285 000; the tolls amount to $19 000; the annual repairs and expenses to $10 000; the net income to about $9 000, or a little more than three per cent. on the capital expended."

Among Maryland roads he notes the Reisterstown Turnpike, 24 ft. wide and surfaced with 12 in. of pounded stone not more than 3 in. in diameter; the Frederick Road, 22 ft. wide and surfaced with 10 in. of pounded stone not more than 3 in. in diameter, over which were spread 2 in. of gravel or coarse sand, the entire surface having a crown or convexity of 9 in.

South of the Potomac Gallatin reports that few "artificial roads" had been undertaken. One, which he briefly describes—the road from Manchester to the coal mines of Falling Creek, in Virginia—was 36 ft. wide and graveled and the cost of 12 miles he gave as $50 000. This construction, he reports, was sufficiently substantial to admit wagons carrying 4 tons.

"The greater progress made in the improvement of roads in the northern parts of the Union," he ascribes, "to a more compact population, which renders those improvements more necessary, and at the same time supplies with greater facility the means of effecting them. The same difference is perceptible in the number of bridges erected in the several States."

In this famous report is direct evidence of the construction, prior to 1808, of roads surfaced with both gravel and broken stone. The Philadelphia-Perkiomen Road was constructed of a stone surface in two courses in a manner similar, except for the large size of the stone and the heavy crown and the absence of rolling and sprinkling, to the methods used in building modern macadam roads. Wherein lay the "defect" of using two courses, as mentioned in the report, is not made clear.

MacAdam's Principles

It is not to be assumed, however, that these roads embodied in their construction the principles of MacAdam; nor can it truthfully be stated that present roads do. They were probably patterned after the roads then being constructed in England, and the great road builder, whose name is now associated with any form of stone surface, had not yet demonstrated the particular methods which properly should be attributed to him. He was still engaged in the preparatory studies which led to the development of the methods he first applied when he became the Surveyor of Roads in Bristol in 1816.

According to MacAdam's view, the function of the stone surface was not to support the weight of vehicles, but to form a covering or roof over the natural soil on which, in its dry condition, he relied entirely to support the load.

He, therefore, regarded a heavy course of metal as unnecessary, and large stone as positively objectionable in that a road so formed would be likely to be more pervious than one made of small stone. His idea was that, "every piece of stone put into a road, which exceeds an inch in any of its dimensions, is mischievous"; and he based this conclusion not only on the thought that the use of larger stone would increase permeability, but, also, and perhaps mainly, on the greater tendency for the larger stones to be dislodged by the wheels of vehicles. He was also opposed to the use of heavy crowns on the ground that they were unnecessary for drainage purposes and that they tended to concentrate traffic at the center and, thereby, actually defeat the ends of drainage by causing the formation of ruts.

His methods, explained in his own words, were as follows:

"As no artificial road can ever be made so good, and so useful as the natural soil in a *dry state,* it is only necessary to procure and preserve this dry state of so much ground as is intended to be occupied by a road.

"The first operation in making a road should be the reverse of digging a trench. The road should not be sunk below, but rather raised above, the ordinary level of the adjacent ground; care should at any rate be taken that there be a sufficient fall to take off the water, so that it should always be some inches below the level of the ground upon which the road is intended to be placed: this must be done, either by making the drains to lower ground, or if that be not practicable, from the nature of the country, then the soil upon which the road is proposed to be laid, must be raised by addition, so as to be some inches above the level of the water.

"Having secured the soil from *under* water, the road-maker is next to secure it from rain water, by a solid road, made of clean, dry stone, or flint, so selected, prepared, and laid, as to be perfectly impervious to water; and this cannot be effected, unless the greatest care be taken, that no earth, clay, chalk, or other matter, that will hold or conduct water, be mixed with the broken stone; which must be so prepared and laid, as to unite by its own angles into a firm, compact, impenetrable body.

"The thickness of such a road is immaterial, as to its strength for carrying weight; this object is already obtained by providing a dry surface, over which the road is to be placed as a covering, or roof, to preserve it in that state: experience having shewn, that if water passes through a road, and fills the native soil, the road, whatever may be its thickness, loses its support, and goes to pieces."

It must be borne in mind that MacAdam applied his art more often to the repair of existing surfaces than to the construction of new ones, and in making such repairs he particularly recommended and used the process which he called "lifting the road" which consisted in loosening the upper portion of the surface and breaking all old stones of more than about 6 oz. in weight before applying the new stone. As he did not have a roller he advocated applying the new stones in thin courses, allowing time between successive applications for the metal to be compacted by traffic. He suggested a three-time application as desirable and particularly insisted on the necessity of keeping the road well shaped during the intervals when it was being compacted.

He surprised the members of the Parliamentary Committee appointed to inquire into methods of improving the turnpikes and highways by informing them that he would prefer to construct his surface on a soft foundation rather than a hard one, because "when a road is placed upon a hard substance, such as a rock, the road wears much sooner than when placed on a soft substance".

This statement elicited from his amazed interlocutor the exclamation: "You don't mean you would prefer a bog?" to which the calm reply was; "If it was not such a bog as would not allow a man to walk over, I should prefer it."

With these views, so remarkably in accord with the most modern ideas, there is scarcely a fault to be found, yet the fact remains that they have been honored more in the breach than in the observance in American practice, at least.

As MacAdam did not begin to practice his art until 1816 and as his methods were essentially different from those common at the time in England, it is not possible that the stone surfaces constructed on the fast multiplying American turnpike roads prior to that date were macadam roads in the strict application of the term, although, from the descriptions available, it is probable that they were not unlike many of the roads to which the name is now applied.

When, in 1832, it became necessary to repair the surface which had been constructed on the Cumberland Road east of the Ohio River, the orders of General Gratiot, then Chief of Engineers, were that the macadam system was to be followed, and this system he defined exactly as MacAdam had described it in his "Remarks on the Present System of Road Making", published in 1820. It is not improbable that this was the first application of the true method in America, and it may have been the last.

The National Pike

The story of the National Pike has been told too many times to need more than a brief reference herein. The earliest Act of Congress relating to it was passed in 1802 and simply provided that 5% of the revenue received from the sale of Ohio lands should be set aside for public road improvement and that two-fifths of this amount should be devoted to constructing a road from the Potomac River westward to the Ohio River.

In 1805, the building of the road from Cumberland, Md., to the Ohio River was authorized, and the Act further provided that the proposed road was to have a right of way of 4 rods, a roadway of 20 ft., a maximum grade of $8\frac{3}{4}$%, and a surface of stone, earth, gravel, or sand, or a combination of these. Later, in Ohio, the width of right of way was increased to 80 ft.

The first contract for construction was let on April 11, 1811, and the road was completed from Cumberland to Wheeling, W. Va., about ten years later. The total length of this section is 131 miles and the total cost of construction was $1 706 845, or an average of $13 029 per mile. The entire section east of Wheeling was surfaced with broken stone put down in two courses. The specifications provided that the stone for the bottom course should pass a 7-in. ring, and that for the top course, a 3-in. ring. The top course was 6 in., and the bottom, 12 in., before compacting, and as the traffic was depended upon to effect the compacting, there is little doubt that travel over the road in springless wagons was not unduly comfortable, especially as it is said that the engineers in charge of the work had a way of erecting barriers which were frequently shifted in order to prevent honest travelers from using any part of the surface after it had become compact.

The first appropriation for continuing the "National Road" west of the Ohio River was made in 1825, and the final appropriation for completing it in Ohio and continuing it in Indiana and Illinois was made in 1838. The section in Indiana was constructed east and west from Indianapolis, and was practically completed before the Government discontinued its appropriations, but in Illinois no surfacing was laid. Congress provided that only grading should be done on this section, in order that the Government might later put down a steam railroad on the grade if it so desired.

Turnpike Companies the First Public Service Corporations

The turnpike-road companies, by which the majority of the early artificial roads were built, were the first public service corporations. They operated under charters granted by the State Legislatures, authorizing them either to build and maintain an entirely new road or to take over from the public the maintenance of an existing road.

What now seem to be very severe restrictions were imposed upon them. They were limited strictly to the building and maintaining of a road, and were not allowed to do anything else. Rates of toll were fixed in the charter, and the number of gates to be erected was also specified. The location of the road was not entrusted to the judgment of those who were investing their money, but was delegated to a committee appointed either by the Legislature or by the Judge of the County Court.

In spite of these restrictions the stock of the companies at first was very attractive to investors; but it was not long before it was discovered that the roads could not be expected to pay a large return. Few of the companies were able to show, even at first, net earnings of more than 2 or 3%, and as time went on and the cost of maintenance increased, and as, finally, the railroad came to take away a large part of the traffic, even these small profits vanished, and the turnpikes became, generally, very unprofitable investments. Most of the hundreds of companies that were organized had failed and the roads had reverted to public control by 1850; but a few remained in operation, after a fashion, until very recent years, their roads anathema to all who were compelled to use them.

The word "turnpike" has come to be associated with a stone surface, mainly because the surviving "pikes" were all, or practically all, of that character. In the early days, however, many of the companies, perhaps the majority, built only a graded road. On many roads the surface was of gravel, in others, shell, and in some, in order to make the roads passable, the companies resorted to corduroy. Quite a large number, as will be noted later, were incorporated for the special purpose of building plank roads.

The railroads sounded the knell of the turnpike companies. One by one they came on financial difficulties so great as to cause them to give up their charters, until, by 1850, few were left in existence. With their passing the roads reverted to public control—which meant county control—and so out of the picture until the late Eighties, except for the rather curious vogue of the plank road.

The Plank Road Epidemic

The first plank road on the continent, and probably in the world, was laid at Toronto, Ont., Canada, in 1835-36. The originator is believed to have been Dr. Darcy Boulton. About ten years later, a road was built, in all respects like the Toronto example, at Syracuse, N. Y. This was probably the first road of its kind in the United States. Within four years more than 2 000 miles had been constructed in New York State alone, at an average cost of $1 833 per mile. Several were built, also, in New Jersey, and a number in Vermont and Connecticut. At least one was built in Massachusetts. These, so far as the record goes, were the only Eastern developments; but the idea spread to the interior States and there the planked surfaces may still be found occasionally.

Of the construction of the plank roads, Mr. Frederic Wood,* writes as follows:

"They were in nearly all cases of single track, laid on the right side of the road as one faced the large town to which it led. In the prairie regions the planking lay on the original surface of the ground, but in some places a small amount of grading was needed to avoid short, steep ascents. The sub-

* See also "The History, Structure, and Statistics of Plank Roads," published in 1850, by W. Kingsford.

grade once established, longitudinal trenches were dug in which sills consisting of 3-inch plank four and eight inches wide were placed, and on them were laid the planks, three inches thick and eight feet long, at right angles to the direction of the road. The sills were set slightly below the surface of the ground, and the planks were pounded down to rest upon them by means of a large mallet known as a 'commander'. No nails or pins were then needed to hold the planks down, and it is reported that it was hard work to take one of them up. After the planks were laid the earth was packed against their ends and soundly tamped into place. The portion of the highway not occupied by the plank road was usually maintained as a common dirt road and was locally known as the 'turn-off', because light loads had to leave the planks and follow it when passing a team proceeding the other way. In order that a wagon might regain the planked surface without its wheels sliding along the edges, the planks were staggered, that is, one-half of them had their ends in a straight line with each other, while the other half were alternately advanced to a line six inches farther out, producing a border effect like the battlements of a castle. Ordinarily, two stringers were used but occasionally three. Over the completed planking a layer of sand was spread and maintained, which preserved the road by reducing the cutting by the calks of the horseshoes. It was claimed for this coating that a saving of forty to fifty per cent was secured in the wear of the road. Very few double-track roads were ever laid, and in the few cases it was preferred to lay two single tracks, apart from each other and supposedly on opposite sides of the 'turn-out'.

"Yellow pine was preferred for the planking in Central New York, on account of its durability and freedom from knots, but hemlock and white pine were extensively used while beech, maple, and elm were employed in some places. * * * Of course the planks would rapidly decay, and it was considered necessary to figure that a road would have to be rebuilt at the end of every seven years."

The Development of Modern Types of Pavement

Passing immediately to the later Eighties no development of any importance will be missed so far as the highways are concerned, except the inventions of the stone crusher by Blake in 1858 and of the steam road roller by Lemoine in 1859. The former, at least, was apparently not received with enthusiasm, because the author of a prize-winning essay wrote in 1890 that:

"Hand-broken stone is much superior to that crushed by a machine, which is generally of irregular shape and seldom cubical, so that it does not readily bind together, which is the essential qualification of macadam."

Some time during this period, probably after 1876, the third, or binder, course was added to the macadam process. In his book entitled "A Practical Treatise on Roads, Streets, and Pavements", published in 1876, the late Q. A. Gillmore, M. Am. Soc. C. E., makes no reference to it, except as a top dressing of gravel or earth spread on after the rolling of the last application of stone. This is the method practiced even in MacAdam's day of which he strongly disapproved. The consolidation of the road with stone chips flushed and rolled into the surface was apparently unknown to Gillmore when the first edition of his book was printed; but some time between 1876 and 1890 it became the common practice.

It was during the latter part of this same period (1850-90) that the first brick and sheet asphalt surfaces were laid; the brick in Charleston, W. Va., in 1872, and the first extensive sheet asphalt surface on Pennsylvania Avenue, in Washington, D. C., in 1879. Prior to 1879 the first rock asphalt surface had been laid opposite the City Hall in Newark, N. J. This was in 1870; and there are conflicting claims to priority in the construction of short experimental sections of sheet asphalt, one being that the first section was laid in New York in 1873 and the other that it was in Washington Square, Newark, in 1877. For many years, however, construction of both the brick and asphalt surfaces was confined to cities. Until 1890, at least, the only materials generally considered as practical for surfaces of rural highways were broken stone, gravel, and—where the materials were available—shell and slag. The latter were laid in the same manner as gravel and stone. The plank surface was already condemned. Surfaces of "burnt clay"* had been suggested, but were still untried.

The organization of the League of American Wheelmen in 1880 may probably be considered as the turning point marking the beginning of the modern period of highway improvement, and the League itself as the first of the influences which have led to so great a change in the public attitude. One of the principal objects of the organization was to secure better roads, and it worked energetically to attain its purpose; but it was not until eleven years later that the first tangible result of its efforts was accomplished in the passage of the first State Aid Law in New Jersey. Writing in 1889, Jeremiah W. Jenks† pictures the condition existing at that time when he states that:

"A very large proportion of our people, too, have never seen a really good road for hauling purposes, and have, in consequence, no clear idea of the gain that would come from good roads."

The Renewal of State and Federal Participation

The passage of the New Jersey State aid legislation in 1891 was the first practical step taken, anywhere in the United States, to remedy the situation. With one exception, it was also the first instance in which any State had undertaken to participate directly in the construction of roads. The exception is Kentucky, which had a State Highway Department and a well-defined State road policy from 1821 to 1837, and during that period completed upward of 340 miles of roads.

The next fruit of the League's efforts is found in the establishment of the United States Office of Road Inquiry in accordance with an Act of Congress approved March 3, 1893. The purpose of this Office, as defined in the statute, was to make inquiries in regard to systems of road management throughout the United States; to make investigations in regard to the best methods of road making; to prepare publications, and to assist agricultural colleges and experiment stations in disseminating information, on the subject. The appropriation made for this purpose was $10 000.

It will thus be seen that the renewed participation of the Federal Government after a lapse of fifty-five years was limited to activities of an educa-

* "Road Making and Maintenance," by Charles Punchard, published with other essays in "A Move for Better Roads," Univ. of Pennsylvania Press, 1891.

† "Road Legislation for the American State," by Jeremiah W. Jenks.

tional character, but these it must be said were carried on with excellent judgment and the utmost vigor possible with the meager appropriation provided.

The actual construction of the roads being still under the control of county and township authorities, the Federal Office carried its message directly to these local officials and by actual demonstration on short sections of object-lesson roads in every State, taught them the methods of road construction which, from its studies, it found to be best. The general public it reached through the medium of bulletins, lectures, and good roads trains, and there is no doubt that its urging was responsible for the creation of more than one of the early State highway departments.

Following the New Jersey precedent, laws providing for the establishment of such departments and the granting of State aid were passed in Massachusetts in 1892, in California and Connecticut in 1895, and in Maryland, New York, and Vermont in 1898. Thus, by the end of the Nineties there were seven States—all but one on the Atlantic seaboard—that had taken the initial step toward the solution of the road problem; and as the century opened they were followed by many others. The dates of passage of the first laws in the several States are shown in Table 1.

TABLE 1.—DATES OF PASSAGE OF STATE-AID HIGHWAY LAWS.

State.	Year in which first State-aid law was passed.	State.	Year in which first State-aid law was passed.
Alabama	1911	Nevada	1911
Arizona	1909	New Hampshire	1903
Arkansas	1913	New Jersey	1891
California	1895	New Mexico	1909
Colorado	1909	New York	1898
Connecticut	1895	North Carolina	1901
Delaware	1903	North Dakota	1909
Florida	1915	Ohio	1904
Georgia	1908	Oklahoma	1911
Idaho	1905	Oregon	1913
Illinois	1905	Pennsylvania	1903
Indiana	1917	Rhode Island	1902
Iowa	1904	South Carolina	1917
Kansas	1911	South Dakota	1911
Kentucky	1912	Tennessee	1915
Louisiana	1910	Texas	1917
Maine	1901	Utah	1909
Maryland	1898	Vermont	1898
Massachusetts	1892	Virginia	1906
Michigan	1905	Washington	1905
Minnesota	1905	West Virginia	1909
Mississippi	1915	Wisconsin	1911
Missouri	1907	Wyoming	1911
Montana	1913		....
Nebraska	1911		....

The State-aid policy as adopted by the various States took a number of forms. In some States the aid offered consisted only of advice which might be accepted or rejected by the local authorities who retained absolute control over all the roads. In such States no financial aid was extended. In those States which provided for financial aid its acceptance generally implied an agreement on the part of the county to accept the supervision of the State authorities until the work of construction was completed, after which the road reverted to full county control. In still other States the joint participation of the State and county in the construction of certain classes of roads, generally the most important ones, was made mandatory; and there were still other variations which differentiated the systems adopted by the various States.

Road Conditions in 1904

While the pioneer States were making this radical departure from long established methods of highway administration, certain seemingly unimportant and unrelated events were occurring in various parts of the country. Three men—whose names were Duryea, Haynes, and Ford—had made themselves horseless carriages; and in Bellefontaine, Ohio, a road had been built entirely of concrete. Concrete had been used as a base for block and sheet asphalt pavements for many years; but the short section built in 1893 in the Ohio city was the first to be built with concrete as the wearing surface. As with brick and asphalt surfaces, it was several years, however, before use of the new type was extended to the rural highways; and the same may be said of the automobiles. Although their numbers increased remarkably in the cities, it was several years before they became a problem to the rural highway builder.

In 1904, the U. S. Office of Public Roads, lineal descendant of the U. S. Office of Road Inquiry, took the first census of American roads. It found that there were then, in the United States, 2 151 570 miles of rural highways, of which 153 662 miles had been surfaced with various materials. Of these surfaced roads, 38 622 miles were improved with water-bound macadam; 114 899 miles with gravel, sand-clay, shell, plank, and other low-type surfaces (the great majority being gravel); and 141 miles with surfaces better than macadam. The last included 123 miles paved with brick, of which 104 miles were in the two States of Ohio and West Virginia, and 18 miles of bituminous roads, of which 2 miles were in Massachusetts and the other 16 in Ohio. Except for the oiled earth roads, of which more than 2 500 miles (included with the gravel and other low-type improvements in the previous classification) had been built in California by the so-called petrolithic process, these 18 miles were the only representatives, in 1904, of a type which was destined shortly to become exceedingly important. Sheet and rock asphalt surfaces had been laid in the cities since the Seventies, and both bituminous macadam and bituminous concrete surfaces had been built in England before 1890, but the only bituminous surfaces to be found anywhere in the United States in 1904 were 2 miles of tarred road in the Town of Tisbury, Mass., and 13 miles of bituminous macadam and 3 miles of asphalt in Ohio.

Modern Progress in Its First Decade

This year—1904—marks the end of a period. To that time there had been no important change in the methods of road construction that had been used for a century or more. Either of the major types of surfacing—gravel and macadam—was known to give entire satisfaction under the traffic normal to the country roads of the time. The other types that had been developed and used in small mileage, such as the shell roads of the Tidewater States and the sand-clay roads of the South, were suggested by the availability of the materials rather than by any difference in the demands of the traffic that used them.

Viewed broadly the few types of surface constructed up to this time may all be considered as of one class. In the construction of all, the same principles governed; in all, a fragmental mass was bound together more or less firmly by a natural cement in the manner made familiar by a century of practice; and all alike depended for their efficiency on the conic principle of pressure transmission by which they spread the vehicular loads and thus reduced the intensity of pressure borne by the sub-grade.

That need was felt for no other kind of construction was due, of course, to the fact that the traffic on all roads was much the same. Even in the more populous States the greater part of the traffic using the roads consisted of relatively light, horse-drawn, steel-tired vehicles, to which were added near the cities a bicycle traffic which, although it might attain considerable volume, was never more than a negligible factor in determining the type of surface. This was the normal traffic condition which existed practically up to 1904. What makes that year a turning point in highway history is the fact that about that time there began the great outpouring of motor vehicles from the cities, which quickly set the inter-city roads apart from others as a class requiring different treatment.

The peculiar effect of the automobile on water-bound macadam roads is so well known as to require no description, and the manner in which the road builders met the challenge by substituting tars and asphalts for the weaker mineral binders has been an oft-told tale. First as dust layers, then as protective surface coatings, then as binders, introduced into roads of the macadam type by penetration, and, finally, as hot admixtures according to the bituminous concrete principle, these materials, borrowed from the stock in trade of the city street builder, solved the automobile problem in a manner that was apparently entirely satisfactory.

The effect of this development in the road-building art is shown by comparison of the statistics of 1904 and 1914, the dates which, to all intents and purposes, mark the beginning and crest of the wave of bituminous construction. In 1904, according to the records, there were in the entire country only 18 miles of bituminous rural roads, all in the two States of Massachusetts and Ohio. By 1914 there were 10 500 miles, a mileage which was nearly three-quarters of the aggregate length of all roads of higher type than macadam. This was the high-water mark of the lower forms of the bituminous types. That it by no means marked the end of their usefulness is indicated by the fact that 3 367 miles of the surface-treated and penetration types were built in 1924. The recession of the tide is indicated, however, by the fact that the mileage of the two types existing in 1924 was less than 50% of the mileage of all types better than water-bound macadam in comparison with the 75% level reached in 1914.

It is generally recognized that these two types, which came into use with the development of passenger automobile traffic, are especially adapted to that class of traffic. The relative decline in their use began when motor trucks in considerable numbers began to appear on the rural highways; and coincidentally an increasing swing toward the rigid pavements of concrete and brick and bituminous concrete on a concrete base is noted. The turning point was reached in 1914, or perhaps a year or two earlier.

Although the first concrete road had been built in 1893, there were no more than 5 miles of that type on rural highways in the entire country in 1909. In that year approximately 4 miles were built; in 1910, about 20 miles were added; the following year, 40 miles; and then the first big increase occurred in 1912, when more than 250 miles of rural highways were paved, to be followed in 1913 with 500 miles and in 1914 with more than 1 500 miles. At the close of 1914 there were 2 348 miles in the entire country; and 10 years later the mileage had increased to 31 146 and construction was proceeding at the rate of more than 6 000 miles per year, a rate approached by no other type better than gravel.

The more extensive use of brick, and of bituminous pavements of the mixed type on concrete base, began also at about the same time and was due to the same cause—the increased use of motor trucks. In 1914 there were approximately 1 600 miles of brick pavement; in 1924, there were 4 319 miles. In 1914 the mileage of rural highways paved with bituminous concrete or sheet asphalt was still negligible; in 1924, there were more than 9 700 miles of these types.

Trunk Lines versus Farm-to-Market Roads

The decade following 1904 was marked not only by the development of new types of road, but also by two other changes of even greater significance. The first of these was a general increase in the radius of travel by highway occasioned by the use of the automobile; and the second—the natural result of the first—was a change in the character of the public demand for highway improvement.

In 1904, the automobile had still to prove its ability for sustained performance. Its ownership was still limited to a small and wealthy class. The popular demand for improved roads was, therefore, still predicated on the use of the bicycle and the horse-drawn vehicle. The farmers, always conservative, were still, for the most part, either actively hostile to road improvement or lukewarm in support of it. In general, their demand was for the improvement of the roads connecting their farms with the railroad shipping points or near-by towns. More positive influence was exerted by city and town merchants who sought by road improvement to extend the trading radius and business of their towns, and by the limited but influential class of motorists who longed for smoother, mud-and-dust-free roads on which to operate their vehicles. All these influences combined at first to produce a demand for short stretches of improved roads radiating from the towns and rail shipping points. Later, as the automobile was perfected and its users became more numerous, the latter created a demand for longer, unbroken stretches of improved roads, forming a network connecting the larger towns, a claim that was resisted by the farmers who continued to favor the so-called farm-to-market type of movement.

In the smaller Eastern States the conflict never became acute, largely because the distance between towns and market points was so short that the farm-to-market plan of improvement, when carried to its ultimate development, became practically identical with the inter-town or trunk-line plan. Thus, the issue was satisfactorily settled in Rhode Island as early as 1902 by the adoption of a definite system of State highways for construction by the State Board of Public Roads. A similar proposal by the Highway Commissioner of Connecticut, made originally in 1906, was enacted into law by the State Legislature in 1913; and, in the meantime, Maryland had settled the question definitely by the adoption of an inter-county seat, trunk-line system to be improved and maintained in its entirety with State funds under the State Roads Commission. Maryland's system was designated in 1908, and was the first to be placed completely under State control for both construction and maintenance.

That the controversy was not so quickly settled in many of the other States was due mainly to two reasons: First, the important lines of travel in a number of the States were not sharply defined. In some this resulted from sparsity of settlement, and in others from the contrary condition of close settlement with numerous centers of more or less uniform size and importance. States, such as Texas and Wyoming, were typical of the first group. In them, the long distances between centers and the condition of the roads delayed the development of highway traffic between the towns and promoted a use of the highways largely as feeders to the rail lines; and the same remoteness of the towns one from another prevented the early harmonizing of the two plans of development as in the smaller Eastern States by the evolution of one into the other. Of the second class there were such States as Iowa, Kansas, and Wisconsin, in which the very number and uniform size of the town centers caused a diffusion of traffic over many roads and delayed the recognition of routes of outstanding importance. In these States, also, the towns are essentially agricultural centers, and this fact contributed further strength to the demand for farm-to-market roads as opposed to trunk lines.

The Federal Aid Road Act

The instances mentioned furnish examples of one of the reasons for the prolongation of the controversy which raged over the question of farm-to-market *versus* trunk-line development. The second reason was simply that many of the States as yet had no State agency for the administration of a highway plan of State-wide scope, and the development of the trunk-line plan naturally presupposes the existence of such an agency.

The second of these reasons was promptly removed after the passage of the Federal Aid Road Act in 1916 by the provision of that Act requiring the creation of adequate highway departments in all States as a condition precedent to participation in the benefits of the Federal aid.

The Act of 1916 appropriated \$75 000 000 to be expended in five years under the direction of the Secretary of Agriculture in co-operation with the State highway departments, for the improvement of post roads. It provided for the apportionment of the appropriation among the several States in proportion to their area, population, and mileage of post roads; and it permitted the expenditure of Federal funds for improvement in any amount up to 50% of the cost, but not exceeding \$10 000 per mile. This latter limit was later raised to \$20 000 and then reduced to \$15 000 as at present.

Since 1916, amendments have been made to the Federal Aid Road Act appropriating, or authorizing the appropriation of, additional funds to a total, including the fiscal year, 1927, of \$690 000 000; and the mileage of road improved under the co-operative plan up to June 30, 1926, amounted to nearly 56 000.

A first step toward the ultimate settlement of the trunk-line question in all States was made when the U. S. Bureau of Public Roads, acting for the Secretary of Agriculture, as one of its first administrative acts requested of all States the submission of a 5-year program map showing the system of roads on which the State highway departments would request Federal aid during the period covered by the appropriations provided by the first Act of Congress. Although the systems designated in response to this request were understood to be merely tentative, the request of the Bureau had the effect of directing attention—in many States for the first time—to the desirability of establishing a definite program for the improvement of a system of highways as distinguished from the more or less casual improvement of unrelated sections of roads.

Load Limitation a Consequence of the World War

The Federal aid work had scarcely begun, however, when the World War intervened and practically put a stop to all operations; and the war did a number of other things to the existing improved roads which, however disastrous they may have appeared at the time, have turned out to be blessings in disguise. At the outset the construction and maintenance of highways were declared to constitute a non-essential industry. As a consequence new construction, except as required for the immediate service of the Army, was greatly curtailed. Maintenance also was greatly hampered by the difficulty of obtaining the necessary materials and the scarcity and high wages of labor. At the same time there was released upon roads generally inadequate to stand it an unprecedented traffic of heavy motor trucks. To this experience and the heavy damage which followed, the public owes the development of most of the sound principles and policies which now govern the improvement of highways.

The first result was a strong reaction against the use of heavy motor trucks. There were large numbers of people who, forgetting that a road is of service only in so far as it accommodates the need for economical transportation, demanded that the manufacture and operation of vehicles too heavy for the existing roads be prohibited. As few of the roads were designed to carry motor-truck traffic, to have taken this course would have amounted to the throttling of a new development in transportation before it had a chance to demonstrate its utility, and it was rightly opposed with great energy by the manufacturers of motor vehicles. The latter, on the other hand, took a position at the opposite extreme from which they demanded the right to manufacture and sell vehicles of large capacity and heavy weight, without regard to the strength of the roads, on the theory that the greater the capacity of the vehicle the smaller would be the cost of operation per unit of capacity. Their slogan was, "build the roads to carry loads", and this was met by the opposite party with the equally dogmatic demand that the loads should be limited to the capacity of the existing roads.

The issue thus joined, the principals to the controversy—highway officials on the one side and the manufacturers on the other—wisely agreed to submit their differences to the test of mutual discussion; and out of the series of conferences that ensued there came an agreement on certain fundamental facts and principles, which has served as the basis for a harmonious co-operation of the two groups, and which now constitutes the foundations of highway improvement policy in all States.

It was agreed at the outset that, for the first time in history, the weight of vehicles had become a critical factor in rural highway design. Hitherto, the minimum practical thickness of road metal had been sufficient to carry the maximum vehicular load. The development of the motor truck had altered this situation. It called for stronger surfaces that would spread its heavier load over a wider area of the sub-grade in order to reduce the intensity of the pressure to an amount that the soil could support.

It was clear also that whereas deterioration of the highways had previously resulted mainly from the attrition of the surface, a new form of deterioration approaching rapid destruction would result unless the roads on which the heavier motor trucks were being operated were strengthened so as to enable them to carry the increased weights; and whereas, the amount of the deterioration had formerly been a function of the volume of the traffic and of time, the new destruction by excessive weight might be caused by a few vehicles in a very short time.

It was agreed, therefore, that the highway officials must have definite knowledge of the maximum weight to be supported as a first condition of design; and this knowledge was supplied, in a measure, by the voluntary decision of the manufacturers to limit to 7½ tons capacity the future production of vehicles. Engineers were thus assured that if, in the reconstruction of the thoroughfares on which heavy trucking had developed, they would design to accommodate a vehicle of 7½ tons capacity they would not see their handiwork quickly destroyed by vehicles of much greater size and weight.

Differences Between Main Highways and Local Roads Accentuated

This alone, however, was not a sufficient basis for the design of all roads. The building of roads of sufficient strength to carry 7½-ton trucks required a heavy investment of public funds, which could be justified only if the economies inherent in the transportation of goods in vehicles of large capacity were sufficient to outweigh the increased cost of the roads. It was recognized clearly for the first time that the cost of highway transportation is made up of the cost of the highways and the cost of operating the vehicles over the highways, and it was agreed that the common purpose of the public highway officials, vehicle manufacturers, and operators should be to reduce the total cost of transportation rather than one or the other of the elemental costs.

It could be proved that the number of trucks of large capacity already using some of the highways—principally those radiating from and connecting the larger cities—had already grown to the point where the combined savings in operating cost would more than balance the greater cost of providing highway service for them. As to these highways there could be little doubt of the wisdom and economy of building a type of surface adequate for the heavy truck traffic. Other roads, similarly located with respect to cities, had not yet developed a sufficient amount of the heavy traffic to repay the additional cost of the stronger construction, but it was not difficult to foresee that such a condition would develop in the future. On the majority of the roads, however, the development of traffic of sufficient weight to justify the higher types of construction was very remote; and it was apparent that the one-time prevailing condition of uniformity of traffic on all roads had been definitely broken down. Instead, a new and much different condition had arisen under which the main inter-city roads were found to be carrying traffic far in excess of the much greater mileage of local roads.

Under the new condition the economic justification for the improvement of the main roads lay to a far greater extent than formerly in the reduction of transportation costs and to a lesser degree in the effect on the value of property. The main roads had become through traffic arteries, as distinguished from the more numerous local roads, which continued to be of value primarily through the service they rendered in giving access to the land.

As to the main roads, which carried a wide-ranging traffic, it was now clearly apparent that the character of their improvement must be commensurate with the density of their traffic; that continuity of improvement was of the highest importance; and that the traffic was already so great that the loss in operation of vehicles in the absence of road improvement would exceed the cost of improvement. These roads also were distinguished in one other respect, namely, that their traffic tended to increase far more rapidly than that to be found on the local roads, the condition of which remained much as it had been. Where the main roads carried long-distance traffic, the local roads served the traffic of a neighborhood; where the main roads were collectors of traffic, the local roads were feeders and distributors; where the traffic of the main roads tended to grow in direct proportion to the growing use of motor vehicles and the growing resort of industry and the entire people to highway transportation, the local roads served the much lighter, and, from the standpoint of growth, the far more stable traffic produced by a single agricultural community.

It became apparent, therefore, that the economic justification of local road improvement would continue to rest largely in the value and importance of the land; that, in the main, the traffic would demand only a low type of improvement; and that continuity of the improvement was not so essential as in the case of the main, through roads.

The need of continuity in the improvement of the main roads was the first of the new conditions to be met with appropriate action. From 1915, all States in rapid succession designated systems of State roads, including generally the main inter-city roads, to be improved under the more or less direct supervision of the State highway departments; and the several State systems were substantially welded into a National network by the designation, in accordance with the Federal Highway Act of 1921, of the Federal aid highway system on which it is now required that all Federal appropriations shall be expended.

Economic Principles Enunciated

Continuity of improvement of the main roads thus being assured, it remained for a Joint Committee representing the American Association of State Highway Officials and the National Automobile Chamber of Commerce to enunciate a policy with respect to the rate and manner of the improvement, which could win general support and adoption.

Briefly, that policy may be stated as follows: It is accepted as a truism that the volume of traffic on the main roads is so great that the economies in transportation effected by road improvement clearly outweigh the cost of the improvement. This being true, the improvement should proceed as rapidly as available supplies of labor and material will permit and without other limit. All roads should be improved to the degree justified by the operating savings that may be expected to accrue to the traffic, and no road should be improved to any greater degree. Where the mileage of road to be improved is so great that the type of improvement indicated by the traffic can not be completed on the whole mileage within a short period the most important sections should be raised immediately to ultimate type, and the remainder of the mileage should be advanced through the initial stages of grading, draining, and low-type surfacing, in order to spread as much of the benefit of improvement as quickly as possible over the entire road system, further improvement to await the completion of the first stage over the whole system. This is known as stage construction, and it is the only feasible practice in the numerous States in which a large mileage of main roads remains to be improved in the face of a traffic already highly developed. It is also the logical plan of development for the main roads of the States in which traffic has not yet grown to the proportions justifying high type surfacing.

In any case the stage-construction plan takes account of the rapid growth of traffic, which is a characteristic especially of the main roads, by providing fully in the initial stage for the subsequent construction. Grades and alignments are designed to meet ultimate requirements; drainage structures are built of durable materials; rights of way of ample width for the future are obtained; and the initial surfacing becomes the sub-base of the second-stage surfacing. Obviously the soundness of the plan is contingent on the complete and continuous maintenance of each stage of the construction, a kind of maintenance which—thanks to the war experience and the standard established by the Federal Highway Act—practically all States are now prepared to give.

The accepted policy contemplates the improvement of the main roads, to which these methods are applicable, as a responsibility of the States to be assumed through the agency of the State highway departments, and financed, in large measure, by the revenues derived from the taxation of vehicles and motor fuel. The local roads are viewed as the responsibility of the counties and lesser subdivisions. With a few important exceptions, as in the vicinity of large cities, the degree of improvement required does not rise above the lower types of surfacing, the expense of which may be met, as it should be, by taxation of the local land and property.

These, then, are the outstanding developments in highway improvement of the post-war period: The classification of highways according to traffic density; the designation of State highway systems in all States, the systems including the heavy traffic highways of State-wide importance; the interconnection of the State systems by means of the Federal Aid System; the improvement of roads in accordance with traffic demands to the limit set by probable operating savings; the stage-construction plan of progressive improvement of the entire system; and the development of adequate maintenance provisions. In the main, all are outgrowths of the war experience fostered by Federal aid.

Highway Research

One other great advance has characterized this period—the application of scientific research to the problem of developing types of construction and methods of administration and finance adequate to meet the demands of the fast-growing traffic. In this, also, the initial impulse came from the Federal Government, and, in co-operation with State highway departments and universities, it is continuing to support numerous studies in several fields, as a result of which there is being built up gradually the structure of a new science—the science of highway engineering.

The investigations include studies of the characteristics of materials—sand, stone, gravel, bituminous materials, cement, concrete, and brick; determination of the forces applied to road surfaces by standing and moving vehicles; of stresses developed in the structure of roads and bridges by live loads, by temperature, and by other natural causes; analyses of sub-grade soils and tests of methods designed for their improvement; and studies of the flow of water through drainage structures, of the run-off from drainage areas, of the effect of moisture on soils, and many others of fundamental importance and value.

Popular interest has centered on the large scale tests, such as those of the Bates Road, for which entire credit is due the Illinois Highway Department; the Pittsburg, Calif., experiments; the impact tests at Arlington, Va.; and the intensive studies of highway traffic conducted by the U. S. Bureau of Public Roads in co-operation with the authorities of Connecticut, Maine, Pennsylvania, Ohio, California, Tennessee, and Cook County, Illinois.

Much that is of immediate practical benefit has already been derived from these investigations; but, for the most part, they are dedicated to the future. It is not to be expected that their fullest benefits shall be realized immediately. The building of a science is a laborious, a painstaking process, and at present (1926) the groundwork is not much further advanced than were the foundations of the modern science of medicine and surgery fifty years ago. If fifty years hence the science of highway engineering has been built up to the point now attained by the physicians and surgeons, this effort now being put forth will be abundantly repaid, and not too late. For the improvement of highways in the United States is a process that must be continued indefinitely.

Highway Conditions at the Close of the Second Decade

At the end of 1924, according to reports received by the U. S. Bureau of Public Roads, there was a total of 3 004 311 miles of highways in the United States, of which 707 138 miles had been improved in some degree, 235 471 miles by grading and draining, and 471 667 miles by surfacing. Of the roads surfaced, 64 086 miles were improved with sand clay, 246 357 miles with gravel, 60 467 miles with water-bound macadam, 45 172 miles with bituminous macadam, 9 691 miles with bituminous concrete, 31 188 miles with Portland cement concrete, 4 710 miles with brick and other block pavements, and 9 996 miles with various unclassified types of surface.

It is idle to talk of completion when less than one-fourth of the 3 000 000 miles of highways has been graded, only one-sixth has been surfaced, and one-sixtieth paved; when little more than one-half the mileage of the main State roads has been improved with any kind of surfacing, and there remain on these important arteries thousands of unsubstantial one-way bridges and dangerous railroad grade crossings; when the number of motor vehicles registered is doubling every fifth year and the traffic with them; when the size of cities, the magnitude of industries, and the amount of material wealth are increasing at an almost unprecedented rate. As long as these conditions continue it will be necessary to continue to build, maintain, and rebuild the roads.

At the present rate approximately 40 000 miles per year is being surfaced and the annual expenditure approximates $1 000 000 000. There is no indication of an early reduction in these rates of construction or expenditure, dwarfed as they are by the annual production of a 1 000-mile procession of motor vehicles and an annual expenditure for operation approaching $10 000 000 000. The nation has set its hand to the economic improvement of means of highway transportation. It is not a task to be accomplished in a day. It is, and must be, a continuous process. There is only one limit which may reasonably be set. It is this: No road should be improved by expenditures of public funds in excess of its earning capacity. The return to the public in the form of economic transportation is the sole measure and justification of the degree of highway improvement.

AMERICAN SOCIETY OF CIVIL ENGINEERS
INSTITUTED 1852

TRANSACTIONS

This Society is not responsible for any statement made or opinion expressed in its publications.

Paper No. 1686

HISTORIC REVIEW OF THE DEVELOPMENT OF SANITARY ENGINEERING IN THE UNITED STATES DURING THE PAST ONE HUNDRED AND FIFTY YEARS

A SYMPOSIUM*

With Discussion by Messrs. James W. Armstrong, J. W. Ellms, Caleb Mills Saville, M. M. O'Shaughnessy, Morris Knowles, George H. Fenkell, Harry G. Payrow, W. Kiersted, John H. Gregory, Karl Imhoff, Kenneth Allen, George S. Webster, L. L. Tribus, N. T. Veatch, Jr., Arthur E. Morgan, Arthur M. Shaw, W. B. Gregory, R. A. Hart, L. L. Hidinger, Roy N. Towl, E. R. Jones, H. F. Gray, James E. Brooks, W. G. Stromquist, Thornton Lewis, Samuel R. Lewis, Leonard Greenburg, George W. Fuller, Harrison P. Eddy, S. H. McCrory, J. A. LePrince, and George Truman Palmer.

---

* Presented at the meeting of the Sanitary Engineering Division, Philadelphia, Pa., October 6, 1926.

HISTORIC REVIEW OF THE DEVELOPMENT OF SANITARY ENGINEERING IN THE UNITED STATES DURING THE PAST ONE HUNDRED AND FIFTY YEARS

INTRODUCTION

By HARRISON P. EDDY,* M. AM. SOC. C. E.

One hundred and fifty years ago the inhabited part of the United States consisted principally of the area east of the Allegheny Mountains and between the St. Lawrence River and the Spanish Province of Florida. The first census (1790) of the new Republic showed a population slightly less than 4 000 000.

Westward migration began during the Revolution and has continued with the extension of boundaries. Naturally, the course of migration was along the river valleys where ease of traveling was obtainable. Towns sprang up around border trading posts and forts, such as Pittsburgh, Cincinnati, Detroit, St. Louis, and Chicago.

The living conditions of the great mass of the people were extremely simple. Houses were of logs or of loose unpainted clapboards. Cooking was before open fires or in brick ovens. Lighting by night was by tallow candles, the sperm-oil lamp, or by the open wood fire. The friction match had not been invented, and flints and steel and tinder were the means for procuring fire. Clothing was chiefly homespun manufactured in the household with spinning wheels and hand looms. Few public water supplies and no public sewerage systems existed. Plumbing was practically unknown. Primitive methods for the removal and disposal of household waste and excretal matters prevailed.

At the time of the first census, only four municipalities had populations in excess of 10 000—New York, N. Y., 33 131; Philadelphia, Pa., 28 522; Boston, Mass., 18 320; and Baltimore, Md., 13 503. The remaining population was living under rural or semi-rural conditions.

The development of water supply and water purification, of sewerage systems and sewage treatment, and of refuse collection and disposal, has been coincident with the growth of cities. Land drainage has followed westward migration and the establishment of farms in the level areas of the western river valleys. Until the end of the Nineteenth Century the part played by the mosquito in the transmission of malaria and yellow fever was unknown, but, in the last two or three decades, an extraordinarily successful campaign has been waged against the mosquitoes conveying these diseases. In the early days the problem of ventilation was non-existent but, to-day, with large gatherings of individuals in halls, schools, and theatres, the problem has become acute.

During the 150-year period there has been an unprecedented utilization of science and engineering for the amelioration and control of man's environment. The papers which follow, outline the progress in those branches of engineering which have done so much to promote human health and comfort.

* Cons. Engr. (Metcalf & Eddy), Boston, Mass.

WATER-WORKS

By George W. Fuller,* M. Am. Soc. C. E.

Prior to 1870 the history of water-works in the United States presents a picture of isolated and spasmodic community efforts to obtain supplies, then, for about a generation, increased activity due largely to the enterprise of business men making water-works equipment, and then a continuous and fairly active growth caused by the rapid increase in urban population, culminating in the general recognition—since 1900—that the design and operation of modern water-works offer opportunities for research, engineering, and administrative skill of the highest grade.

The few water-works of the Colonies were crude affairs, frequently consisting of a bored log pipe line leading from a masonry walled hillside spring to a trough in the center of the town, as exemplified by the plant built at Schaefferstown, Pa., in 1730. As a rule, however, these early community works were large wells, from which the householders carried water, as is done in little European hamlets to-day. According to Mr. M. N. Baker, there were seventeen water-works in the United States at the close of 1800, all but one privately owned. It seems probable that public wells used by communities would increase this number, but the now unknown instances of such works can be discovered only as a by-product of more important historical research, through old newspapers and local records, in diaries, and in books of travel.

The early Seventies was the period of the great fires in Chicago, Ill., and Boston, Mass., and there has been a tendency to attribute the increased rate of water-works construction during this decade, from 243 plants in 1870 to 598 in 1880, to a better appreciation of the importance of public water-works as a fire-protection resource and an increased standard of living that demanded running water in homes. The facts, however, seem to be that the most important influences were furnished by promoters working for manufacturers of water-works equipment. The late J. James R. Croes, Past-President, Am. Soc. C. E., explained† the situation as follows:

"The rapid increase in the number of water works constructed within the last sixteen years is mainly due to the competition of enterprising business men. About the year 1870 Mr. Birdsill Holly, of Lockport, N. Y., a builder of pumping engines, began an active canvass of the towns which had no water supply, with the view of furnishing a type of engine and pump manufactured by him by which the pressure was pumped directly into the mains without the use of a reservoir, and at any desired pressure variable at will of the engineer, thus enabling the whole pipe system to be used as a fire engine if necessary. By organizing a private corporation to build works and asking from the public only a certain fixed annual subsidy based on the number of fire hydrants furnished and guaranteed to deliver on demand a fire stream under 100 pounds pressure, the Holly Company were able to induce many towns to allow water-works to be built.

* Cons. Engr. (Fuller & McClintock), New York, N. Y.

† In the preface to the Third (1887) Edition of his "Statistical Tables of American Water Works."

"The practicability of the scheme being proved, and the financial success of several such enterprises having been demonstrated, other pump builders followed the example of the pioneer, and with such success that competition has compelled all parties to build better pumping machinery than ever before and to increase their guaranties of efficiency, durability and economy of operation."

Table 1 shows the available data on growth and ownership of water-works used for public supply in the United States. These data are taken from the "Manual on American Water Works Practice," published in 1925, by the American Water Works Association. When it is realized that more than five years' work, with the help of more than 300 collaborators, resulted in a volume of more than 800 printed pages to tell what is good water-works practice, it will be appreciated how meager must be the historic outline which can be set forth in the limited space here available.

TABLE 1.—Growth of Water-Works in the United States, and Changes in Character of Their Ownership.

Year.	Total. plants.	Public plants.	Private plants.	Ownership unknown.	Percentage of Total.		
					Public.	Private.	Unknown.
1800	16*	1	15*	....	6.3*	93.7*	....
1810	26	5	21	....	19.2	80.8	....
1820	30	5	25	....	16.6	83.4	....
1830	44	9	35	....	20.5	79.5	....
1840	64	23	41	....	35.9	64.1	....
1850	83	33	50	....	39.7	60.3	....
1860	136	57	79	....	41.9	58.1	....
1870	243	116	127	....	47.7	52.3	....
1880	598	293	305	....	49.0	51.0	....
1890	1 878	806	1 072	....	42.9	57.1	....
1896	3 196	1 690	1 489	17	52.9	46.6	0.5
1924†	9 850†	6 900†	2 950†	....	70.0	30.0	....

* Since this table was compiled, another private water-works, built prior to 1800, has been discovered.

† Estimated.

Two supplementary comments are needed, to indicate:

First.—That although the proportion of privately-owned water companies is less than previously, the hit-or-miss type of franchise, or contract both as to quality of service and rates of charges, has largely disappeared. In its place have come State regulatory commissions which, under the provisions of the police powers of the State, now supervise rates of charges and in many States the quality of service, with or without the co-operation of State health commissions.

Second.—That the water-works industry is more extensive than is indicated by the number of plants used wholly or in part in supplying water to the public. The water-works for the exclusive use of many of the large industrial plants are both extensive and important. Water for condensing purposes is highly important, although the subject is clearly outside the scope of this paper.

Distributing Systems

There is little positive information about the distributing systems leading from the primitive collecting works in American communities. In Great Britain, where it was customary to supply water to each consumer for only a short time during each day, cisterns were constructed in the attics of buildings and connected by lead pipes to the street mains. A man (called a "turncock") went around every day, turned a cock on the service pipe and filled the cistern. If it did not hold enough water to meet the requirements for the next 24 hours, the occupants either did without water or procured some from outside the building.

The scheme of intermittent supply never gained a foothold in the United States, but house cisterns were used, on account of low street pressures They served a useful purpose, during periods of scanty supply, by making available, during the day hours of heavy draft and consequent low pressure, water which slowly filled them during the night.

The early pipes were practically all bored logs, sometimes with a ring of iron shrunk on each end to prevent splitting. Such pipes had long been used in Europe, and were not a makeshift adopted on account of the exigencies of construction in a new country, as is sometimes stated. As a matter of fact, bored wood pipe are still made and used to a considerable extent, chiefly for mine drainage in the East and for water-works on the Pacific Coast. The manufacture of such pipe, and of banded stave pipe was greatly improved about 1850 by Wyckoff, of Elmira, N. Y. The banded type was the forerunner of the large banded wood-stave aqueduct pipes used to-day in the West for irrigation, hydro-electric plants, and water-works.

About 1800 cast-iron pipe began to supplant wood pipe in England. Such pipe, with flanged joints, had been tried by the Chelsea Water Company, of London, about 1746, but without much success on account of difficulty with the joints. After studying the causes of the trouble, Thomas Simpson, the Company's engineer, about 1785, designed the first successful bell and spigot pipe with a lead joint. It was quickly adopted, but the facilities for manufacture restricted its introduction for some time. Such pipe, imported from Great Britain in 1807 and laid in Philadelphia, inaugurated the use of cast-iron water mains in the United States.

It was soon found, however, that, in some cities, the interior of uncoated pipe carrying water became tuberculated, and that the carrying capacity was much inferior to that of new pipe. The problem of preventing tuberculation was solved by Dr. Angus Smith, who in 1848 produced the coating that has since borne his name. Although this tar product, which rapidly came into general use, did not prevent tuberculation entirely, it was an excellent and inexpensive deterrent when made of the materials and prepared and applied as he recommended. After the success of this coating was proved, cast-iron pipe had no serious rival for water-works, except in localities where transportation charges made it preferable to use materials which were less expensive although they might not be so durable.

Quite recently a desire for a still better coating for cast-iron pipe, has developed, and the subject is again one of the live topics of discussion in water-works circles.

As the demand for cast-iron pipe began to increase, there was a corresponding increase in the range of thicknesses adopted for pipe walls, and in the shapes of the bells, spigots, and special castings. This complexity at last became intolerable, and in 1902 a standard set of specifications for pipe and specials was adopted by the New England Water Works Association. In 1908 the specifications of the American Water Works Association were adopted, and have since been the standard in America. Although they may need revision to-day (1926), as to coatings and quality of material, and perhaps in other respects, they have been invaluable alike to pipe purchasers and makers.

Wrought-iron pipe appeared in the Forties as a material for distribution mains and service pipes. The pipe was used as a shell, being lined with cement mortar and coated on the outside with some form of preservative. These cement-lined pipes had a decided vogue, particularly in New England, for about twenty-five years, but finally were adjudged less economical than cast-iron pipe in the long run. Owing to recent changes in commercial conditions, they are again back on the market.

In the Fifties, when hydraulic mining in California was becoming a notable industry, large quantities of water had to be dealt with. Although open flumes served as conduits in most places, there were occasional dips below the hydraulic grade where pipe of some sort had to be provided. Cast iron was out of the question on account of cost and transportation difficulties; wrought iron had to be used. When the late Hermann F. A. Schussler, M. Am. Soc. C. E., began the construction of the San Francisco Water-Works, in the Sixties, his knowledge of the satisfactory service of wrought-iron pipe in mining led him to use it for the larger mains of those works As a consequence of the early satisfactory experience in, San Francisco, wrought-iron and steel water pipe gained a foothold on the Pacific Coast from which they have never been dislodged.

The first important riveted wrought-iron pipe in the East was laid in Rochester, N. Y., in 1873-75, but it was not until after steel had replaced wrought iron to a great extent that the construction of riveted pipe was considered seriously in this part of the country. Exterior protective coating and the lining of riveted and similar plate pipes have recently received much attention, and some of these methods are so encouraging that, even in the East, steel has become a strong competitor of cast iron in the larger sizes. Both materials, however, are relying, more than ever before, on coatings and linings to preserve their inherent advantages.

In this commercial struggle, active competition has arisen from reinforced concrete pipe, for places where the pressure is not too great. It has been used for aqueducts and other pressure lines for little more than a decade, but in this brief period has shown encouraging results as to low first cost, freedom from leakage, and maintenance of discharging capacity.

Not until about 1875 or 1885 was any general attention paid to what might be called distribution economics. The early distribution systems, after a time, did not deliver the theoretical quantity of water they should, at different parts of a city. This seems to have been one of the reasons for the attention paid to service reservoirs and stand-pipes long before any serious study was made of the hydraulics of distribution systems as a whole.

In some cities attempts were made to improve the distribution of water by partly closing the gates of mains that fed districts where the pressure was highest. When serious fires made an ample supply necessary in a section fed by one of these throttled mains, it was found that the practice was a hazardous makeshift. Engineers finally undertook a careful study of the subject, and an early result was a paper, presented in 1892 to the New England Water Works Association by John R. Freeman, Past-President, Am. Soc. C. E., which attracted wide-spread atttention.

Many years prior to this, one cause of low street pressures was known to be the leakage of water through defective plumbing fixtures, services, and street mains. The leakage inside buildings was attacked by metering the services, but progress was very slow for years, except in some of the thrifty New England cities. Where metering was impracticable, attempts were made to inspect the plumbing, but this also met with violent objection in many cities. To-day, it is difficult for anybody unfamiliar with the facts to realize the bitterness of the opposition to metering as late as the Eighties, and it is fitting in this general discussion to mention the long and forceful campaign for metering conducted a generation ago by Henry C. Meyer, F. Am. Soc. C. E., in his paper* and in other ways.

The opposition to metering service pipes on dwellings was so strong that the method of detecting waste, by dividing a city into districts and then searching for all instances of leakage in one district after another, was developed. In its most elaborate form, due to Mr. G. F. Deacon, of the Liverpool Water-Works, the water delivered to each district was measured by a continuously recording meter. By inspection of plumbing and by using early forms of what is now called the aquaphone, most of the serious leaks and cases of waste in a district were detected and remedied. After that, the district meter register indicated any material increase in waste. The system was tried in only one city of the United States—Boston. It was successful technically, but was so expensive that it was finally abandoned.

When Clemens Herschel, Past-President, Am. Soc. C. E., invented the Venturi meter, in the Eighties, he furnished the first reliable device for measuring large quantities of water supplied through pipes from reservoirs and pumping stations; for the actual discharge of pumps in those days was affected to such an extent by the unknown slip in the pump valves that the only sure thing about the discharge was that it was much less than the reading of the pump counters. Then, in the late Nineties, E. S. Cole, M. Am. Soc. C. E., developed the pitometer, by which the discharge of any pipe can

* *The Sanitary Engineer.*

be determined. With these devices, everything formerly accomplished by the Deacon district system can be done at much less cost.

Obtaining Water Supplies—Sources

With the early water-works there was rarely any difficulty in finding near at hand ample supplies which seemed to be of satisfactory quality. In Philadelphia, for example, after the early wells were deemed inadequate, an unlimited supply could be obtained by pumping from the Schuylkill River.

In New York, the case was unusual. Public water-works began with public wells, the first dug by the Dutch in 1658. Many others were dug later, and those in each ward were placed in charge of its alderman and councilmen. The wells in the heart of the town became so polluted and the water so offensive that it was little used. Just before the Revolution, a private company, under the direction of Christopher Colles, sunk a large well near the present site of the Tombs Prison, from which a less objectionable supply was pumped, by a Newcomen engine, to a small reservoir and then delivered by gravity through log pipes. The enterprise was soon abandoned on account of the war.

Next came Aaron Burr's water-works, built by the Manhattan Company in 1799, under an Act of the Legislature. The works consisted of a large well, two pumps, and the reservoir built by Colles. The Company made hardly more than a nominal attempt to furnish water, as its real object was to conduct a bank, permitted by an innocent looking clause, in its perpetual charter, regarding the investment of its surplus funds. In 1823, it had 23 miles of pipe, nearly all wood, two small steam pumps, and a masonry reservoir holding 550 000 gal. This plant and many wells furnishing water of very inferior quality supplied the city until 1830, when a well, 16 ft. in diameter and 112 ft. deep, was sunk at 13th Street and Broadway, most of it in rock. The water was too hard for domestic purposes, and was used chiefly for fire protection. A small steam pump raised the water to a large cast-iron tank, and the supply was delivered through about 9 miles of cast-iron pipe, from 6 to 12 in. in diameter. This was the first municipal plant in New York.

By 1832 the supply furnished in the city by the Manhattan Company and by the public and private wells was so offensive that all who could afford to do so purchased water brought in hogsheads from unpolluted wells in the northern part of the island. About 600 hogsheads were furnished daily in this way at $1.25 per hogshead. A very bad outbreak of cholera during that year was followed by an increase in the already strong demand for an adequate public supply. It was at first thought that water could be obtained from the Bronx River, but later it was shown that the nearest available supply was from the Croton water-shed. In 1835 the Croton project was approved by the citizens at a special election, bids for construction were opened in 1837, and Croton water, practically the first fit to drink after the days of Dutch control, was delivered in 1842, when the city had attained a population of more than 300 000.

Intakes.—The construction of intakes, by which water was drawn from rivers and ponds, developed so slowly and by such small advances that it is hardly possible at this time to give credit for significant improvements in design, except in one respect. The first public water supply in Chicago was established in 1831; it was merely a public well. The municipal water-works were begun in 1851. After the sewerage system of the city was built and the sewage was carried out into Lake Michigan by the Chicago River, apprehension was felt that the water about the intake in the lake would become dangerously polluted. The extension of the intake pipe farther out into the lake, beyond the area of pollution, was the remedy most favored. The City Engineer, the late E. S. Chesbrough, Past-President, Am. Soc. C. E., opposed this vigorously and insisted that only a supply drawn through a tunnel in the lake bed would be free from serious danger of interruption of service. Such a subaqueous tunnel was then an engineering feat of the first order, but it was at last built in 1867, establishing a practice followed in many cities, not only on the Great Lakes, but also on some of the larger rivers.

Dams and Reservoirs.—Turning to those works for which a supply is obtained by impounding surface waters, one naturally recalls first the dams which form the reservoirs. The development of the details of gravity dams has been slow but continuous. The outstanding novelties have been of a different nature, and of rather limited availability. First there is the hydraulic-fill dam, a form of construction first used by the late James D. Schuyler, M. Am. Soc. C. E., in making railway embankments in Western Canada; then the rock-fill dam, with an impervious covering on the back; and the arched dam, particularly suited for high, narrow gorges. Somewhat later the hollow dam was introduced, for the purpose of saving part of the cost of gravity dams. It has developed into two types, both having transverse parallel buttresses supporting the up-stream back. In one type the back, of reinforced concrete slabs, slopes gently upward to the crest, and the weight of the water on it contributes to its stability. In the other type, nearly vertical arches between the buttresses form the back. Although only bare mention can be made of these types, the general interest in them has resulted in a large volume of printed information regarding their relative merits.

Hydrology.—One of those features of the development of water-works practice that has had a profound influence is inextricably tied up with the gradual increase in the knowledge of hydraulics and hydrology. For a long time so much water was available that there was no shortage except what was due to lack of ordinary common sense in procuring a supply. Little by little, however, there were shortages that could not be explained by the engineering knowledge of those times, and so water-works engineers began to search for their causes. Later, the necessities of irrigation and hydraulic power development increased the interest in this group of subjects, culminating in the interesting utilization of the mathematics of probability, under the leadership of Allen Hazen, M. Am. Soc. C. E.

So far as the co-ordination and direct utilization of this kind of knowledge is concerned, it should be mentioned that in the Nineties the late F. P. Stearns,

Past-President, Am. Soc. C. E., in investigations for the Massachusetts State Board of Health, and C. C. Vermeule, M. Am. Soc. C. E., in studies of the water supplies of New Jersey, for the Geological Survey of that State, developed general methods of adjusting reservoir capacities to the run-off from a water-shed. Just before that time there had been in the West, a few cases of expensive irrigation reservoirs, which could not be filled. The economical maximum capacity of reservoirs to utilize the run-off of a water-shed was, therefore, manifestly more than an academic topic.

Underground Water.—Underground water supplies are more numerous than surface supplies, although their total yield is not so great. It is unfortunate, therefore, that nobody has yet undertaken to gather and digest all the existing definite information regarding the engineering aspects of underground supplies, as has been done with surface supplies.

Pumping Water

The Keystone State not only holds the record for the first public water supply, but also for the first public supply furnished by pumping. In 1754 Hans Cristopher Christiansen, a Danish millwright, began the construction of the first water-works of Bethlehem after the general method already in use in several places in Europe. His pump, constructed of lignum-vitæ and driven by an over-shot water-wheel, raised water from a spring to tanks on the hillside above the village.

The first steam pumps in America were used for draining New Jersey mines. They were built in England, of the Newcomen type as improved by Smeaton. The first Newcomen pump used for town supply was erected in New York just before the Revolutionary War by a short-lived private company.

The first steam pumping plant in Pennsylvania was put in operation in 1801, in Philadelphia, where a low-lift pump, on the Schuylkill River at the foot of Chestnut Street, raised the water to an open basin, from which it flowed by gravity through a conduit in Chestnut Street to Centre Square, now the site of the City Hall. There, at another station, the water was elevated about 50 ft. to wooden tanks, of about 17 000 gal. capacity, on top of the building.

The boilers at both plants were wooden boxes, 9 ft. high, 9 ft. wide, and 15 ft. long, of 5-in. white pine plank thoroughly bolted and braced. The fire-box, constructed of wrought-iron plates with vertical cast-iron flues, was inside. The engines were the Watt vertical, double-acting type attached to a Cornish pump. The pump of each was of wood lined with copper. The steam cylinder was of cast iron.

It had been recognized, from the days of Savery and Newcomen, that the load on pumps is pre-eminently adapted for being carried by a steam engine. It is steady and always accompanied by enough water for condensing purposes. As a consequence, the early history of the development of the steam engine is largely that of the development of pumping engines. The condition is just the opposite, however, with boilers which furnish the steam to the pumps. The early pumping stations had boilers carrying very low pressure, and, when more pumping capacity was added, the low pressure was retained in order that the old boilers could still be used. This condition kept station efficiency low, in spite of efficient pumping engines. As a matter of record of an important feature of pumping station development, the following statement, prepared by the late Charles A. Hague, M. Am. Soc. C. E., shows the maximum steam pressures in such stations:

Year	1800	1830	1850	1875	1900	1906
Steam pressure, in pounds.	5	20	50	75	125	175

There was a period of quiescence in the field of pumping machinery, down to the Sixties, due chiefly to patent conditions. Small pumps were usually direct-acting, and the larger pumps were improvements on the Bull-Cornish or Watt-Cornish types. In the Sixties the late Henry R. Worthington, M. Am. Soc. C. E., brought out the duplex, direct-acting pump, and other inventors followed soon with other devices for utilizing the duplex principle. At about the same time the Holly quadruplex crank-and-flywheel pump was introduced, and thus began a business competition between the two types of pumping engines that resulted in great improvements in each and a substantial reduction in their cost.

In England another type of pumping engine was developing, the Simpson compound engine, first used there in 1848, and in the United States in Philadelphia in 1872. Others were erected in a number of cities of the United States, the largest plant being that of the West Side Pumping Station in Chicago.

A few pumping engines used in the United States at that time were designed by consulting engineers, among whom the late E. D. Leavitt, M. Am. Soc. C. E., was prominent, but nearly all were designed by the builders. Competition was severe. It was necessary, not only to meet constantly rising guaranties, but also to reduce manufacturing costs, and naturally the improvements were in details rather than in general types. Finally, the experience with the Simpson type seemed so certain to establish it as the single standard for handling large volumes of water that the Worthington high-duty attachment, for the duplex engine, was brought out, and the Holly-Gaskill crank-and-flywheel engine was designed to improve the economy of the Holly quadruplex, crank-and-flywheel type.

In the Eighties, the Reynolds triple-expansion pump was designed, the first being built at Milwaukee in 1886; this soon became the standard high-duty, large-capacity, American pumping engine.

By 1900, earlier experience and commercial competition had rather definitely established certain types of pumping engines for the different kinds of service, and those interested in the subject will find them described by Irving H. Reynolds, M. Am. Soc. C. E.*

About 1900 the centrifugal pump became a really strong candidate for favor for water-works use. It was largely the development of reliable steam turbines and reduction gears that established such pumps in the favor they now hold in water-works practice. Originally, such pumps were used only

* *Transactions*, Am. Soc. C. E., Vol. LIV (1905), Part D, p. 513.

for low-lift service, but the field has gradually widened as the methods of design have been improved, and electrically driven centrifugal pumps are now operated against very high heads. This development has brought about one interesting change in pumping-station practice.

In the early plants these turbo-centrifugal units were generally placed in an old pumping station, where it was desired to handle the largest possible quantity of water with pumps occupying a definite space. The steam pressure was low, and other conditions were unfavorable for economy, but when turbo-centrifugal pumps were put in service under better conditions, using superheated steam at pressures most suitable for turbines, their economy rose very favorably, just as it did in the early days of turbines in industrial power plants and central stations. It became very evident then that station economy, rather than prime-mover economy, was the real measure of the success of the design.

Electrically operated centrifugal pumps, when the motors and pumps are suitably designed for the loads carried, are now standardized equipment. The chief drawback to their use is the possible unreliability of the current supply from outside sources. This is a serious matter where only a small quantity of water is stored in tanks or reservoirs.

The danger of interruption of current supply for motor-operated pumps, both centrifugal and reciprocating, has been met in many small pumping stations by adding a high-speed gasoline engine to help out in emergencies. Although the gasoline engine is cheap, its fuel is much more expensive than the oil used in Diesel engines. These were introduced about 1895, and have been improved steadily ever since, until to-day they are capable of satisfactory operation for a considerable range of speed, although, like all internal combustion engines, they must not be given overloads. Two considerations seem to be chiefly influential in determining their use. The first is the present and probable future price of fuel oil and its availability at any place; the second is the length of satisfactory service of these engines. Concerning the second point, there is difference of opinion which probably cannot be reconciled until after longer experience with them.

The reciprocating well pump has been slowly improved, but, usually, it is not economical. The shocks and vibrations attending its operation and its relatively complicated construction make its maintenance high in comparison with the quantity of water it delivers. Attempts to avoid these drawbacks have taken two forms, both successful and widely used: The air-lift and the centrifugal well pump, which deserve more than this brief mention.

Quality of Supplies

Presumably, this branch of the topic is the most important to develop in historic outline at present. Its consideration relates to the development of the modern germ theory of disease, particularly regarding the transmission of water-borne disease. In a strict technical sense, modern views as to the relation between the quality of a water and the health of the communities using such water date from the early or middle Eighties. Such matters, however, were then under discussion for the most part by highly trained scientists in a few of the larger cities, and the general mass of water consumers, even including those well informed on educational topics in general, did not give much recognition to the significance of water-borne diseases until after the terrific outbreak of Asiatic cholera in Hamburg, Germany, in 1892-93.

The best index of the successful fight waged against water-borne disease in America is the decrease in the typhoid fever death rate, shown by Table 2. Although the pasteurization of milk, fly suppression, and the education of the public in the rules of sanitation and hygiene have contributed to this decrease, the improvement in the quality of water supplies has been the chief cause.

Prior to the development of modern views as to transmission of disease, there was a well-recognized belief that a public water supply should not be obtained from a filthy source. This theory, originating in England, had much to do in explaining the progressive changes made by numerous cities and towns in efforts to get water from clean sources. Most of the rivers of Western and Central Europe are only of moderate turbidity, and can be clarified suitably on sand beds such as were first constructed at London in 1829. The idea of these sand beds spread quite rapidly to various places in England and on the Continent.

Kirkwood's Report.—In 1866-68, the late James G. Kirkwood, Past-President, Am. Soc. C. E., then Chief Engineer of the St. Louis, Mo., Water-Works, made a thorough-going study of the methods used in filtering European supplies. It was a most admirable report, and its merit was well recognized by its translation into German and its becoming a standard work of reference in several European countries. On account of the unusually heavy turbidity or muddiness of the local rivers at St. Louis, Mr. Kirkwood did not recommend sand beds for the local supply, and this report was followed by no activities in the adoption of European filtration practice other than the two small sand filter beds which he built for Poughkeepsie and Hudson, N. Y., in the early Seventies.

Conditions in the Early Nineties.—It is difficult for the younger engineers to realize the extent to which the United States suffered from the scourge of sewage-polluted waters, which caused severe epidemics and in many places continuous or endemic conditions as to typhoid fever. The explanation is simple enough when one considers the close proximity of sewer outlets and water-works intakes. No wonder typhoid fever records were frequently from ten to twenty times higher than ordinarily found at present. The scourge was particularly severe in the manufacturing cities of Massachusetts and in the steel districts of Western Pennsylvania, where many of the population paid little or no attention to warning notices against drinking public water supplies. One of the sad features of the Columbian Exposition at Chicago in 1893 was the number of visiting engineers who contracted typhoid fever while there.

TABLE 2.—Annual Typhoid Fever Death Rates per 100 000 Population for Some American Cities.

Year.	Philadelphia, Pa.	Chicago, Ill.	Milwaukee, Wis.	Detroit, Mich.	Cleveland, Ohio.	Buffalo, N. Y.	Boston, Mass.	New York, N. Y.	Manhattan and The Bronx New York, N. Y.	Jersey City, N. J.	Baltimore, Md.	Washington, D. C.	Pittsburgh, Pa.	Cincinnati, Ohio.	Louisville, Ky.	New Orleans, La.	Minneapolis, Minn.	St. Louis, Mo.	Kansas City, Mo.	San Francisco, Calif.
1880	58	34	37	....	44	....	42	25	....	24	59	54	135	70	....	24	......	40	......	34
1881	74	105	47	....	99	67	56	38	....	63	58	46	151	71	....	30	......	53	......	37
1882	73	82	32	....	68	69	57	32	....	121	47	66	158	55	....	33	......	45	......	61
1883	64	62	25	....	65	34	52	32	....	49	35	62	107	51	....	23	......	41	......	64
1884	71	56	31	....	60	42	56	29	....	84	42	76	70	56	....	25	......	42	......	58
1885	64	75	28	....	34	23	40	27	....	71	42	65	76	42	....	17	......	31	......	44
1886	64	69	30	39	56	28	34	26	....	60	39	71	68	54	....	13	......	30	......	49
1887	63	50	31	65	52	34	44	26	....	54	41	78	128	142	....	15	......	28	......	23
1888	78	47	42	46	47	29	40	23	....	74	42	87	87	70	....	19	......	31	......	33
1889	71	48	28	31	74	30	43	24	....	83	47	94	95	49	....	17	......	33	......	55
1890	64	92	41	19	69	40	35	22	23	98	59	112	132	69	....	21	41	31	52	44
1891	64	174	33	34	50	51	34	23	25	100	35	82	101	62	....	24	55	29	42	42
1892	40	124	30	94	59	34	29	22	25	72	44	89	100	40	....	20	44	93	33	32
1893	41	54§	35	42	52	37	31	21	23	66	49	86	111	44	....	15	76	44	39	32
1894	33	38	25	28	29	59	29	17	19	53	47	91	56	55	....	29	56	34	26	37
1895	40	38	26	24	35	26	33	17	18	95	36	86	78	39	....	44	48	21	27	34
1896	34	53	18	23	43	20	31	16	16	84	38	58	62	52	....	33	32	20	23	26
1897	33	29	12	15	23	20	33	16	16	20	37	48	64	32	....	52	78	23	28	19
1898	46	41	17	22	34	27	34	21	20	40	36	71	73	33	....	66	44	17	37	41
1899	75	27	17	13	32	24	30	16	15	19	29	73	111	37	....	55	36	23	36	22
1900	35	20‡	17	27	54	26	26	21	18	21	35	78	144	39	64	40	39	29	40	13
1901	34	29	22	21	36	27	25	20	19	16	27	60	125	55	46	48	59	34	44	22
1902	44¶	45	15	24	33	33	24	21	18	20	42	78	134	62	61	45	27	37	36	27
1903	70	32	17	20	114	35	20	17	16	15	36	48	134	42	61	39	42	47	74	24
1904	53	20	14	20	48	23	23	17	13	19	37	47	142	79	63	36	42	36	39	27
1905	48	17	23	21	15§	23	20	16	13	19	36	48	99	40	51	32	25	20‖	53	24

TABLE 2—(*Continued.*)

Year.	Philadelphia, Pa.	Chicago, Ill.	Milwaukee, Wis.	Detroit, Mich.	Cleveland, Ohio.	Buffalo, N. Y.	Boston, Mass.	New York, N. Y.	Manhattan and The Bronx, New York, N. Y.	Jersey City, N. J.	Baltimore, Md.	Washington, D. C.	Pittsburgh, Pa.	Cincinnati, Ohio.	Louisville, Ky.	New Orleans, La.	Minneapolis, Minn.	St. Louis, Mo.	Kansas City, Mo.	San Francisco, Calif.
1906	74	19	31	24	20	23	20	15	15	20	35	50*	130	70	71	30	34	17	32	58
1907	61	18	26	35	19	28	10	17	16	14	41	35	125	45	71	55	27	15	33	30
1908	35**	16	17	22	13	20	25	12	11	9§§	33	37	45	18*	47	33	19	14	29	19
1909	22††	13	23	23	13	23	14	12	12	9	25	33	23*	13	45	29*	21‖	16	30	14
1910	17†	14	45	20	19	20	12	12	11†	7	42†	23	28†	6†	32*	32	....	13	....	....
1911	14‡‡	11	20	15	14	25§	9	11	10	8	27§§	22	26	12	24	31	12	16	30§§	15
1912	13*	7	26	15	7†	12	8	10	7	8	24	22	13	8	22	14	12	11	12	14
1913	16§§ ‖‖	10†	12§§	25§§	14	15	9	7‡‡	7	11	22	16	20§§	7	24	17	12*	17§§	22	16
1914	8	7	8	11	8	16	9	7	6	8	21	11	15	7	27§§	22	13	12	16	13
1915	7	5	5	10	8	10§§	6	6	5	6	19	11	11	8	14	21	8	7*	10	9
1916	8	5	16	11	5	11	4	4	4	8	16*	12	9	3	14	23	6	10	12	3
1917	6	2§§	6	13	7	10	3	4	4	4	13	12	12	4	16	24	7	8	12	5
1918	5	2	6	8	5	7	3	4	4	5	10	11	10	5	15	20	9	8	15	4
1919	5	1	4	5	3	7	2	2	....	2	9	4†	4	3§§	6	13	3	6	11	3
1920	3.4	1.1	2.2	5.1	3.3	5.1	1.5	2.4	2.1	3.7	4.7	6.6	2.7	2.7	5.5	7.0	2	2.7	7.4	3.1
1921	2.2	1.1	1.9	5.8	3.5	3.5	3.2	2.4	2.1	3.7	5.5	6.4	3.2	3.7	4.7	9.3	1.3	3.8	11.5	4.0
1922	2.8	1.1	2.5	5.3	2.2	3.6	1.4	2.2	1.9	1.6	3.9	5.1	3.3	3.0	7.2	5.7	1.8	4.4	4 6	4.3
1923	1.5	1.9	0.8	4.0*	1.9	4.1	1.3	2.4	2.5	1.6	4.1	6.0	2.1	3.0	4.1	4.0	1.5	4.2	4.8	2.6†
1924	2.2	1.6	1.0	3.0	1.2	2.8	2.1	3.1§§	....	2.6	2.8	4.3	3.9	2.5	1.9	10.0	2.1	3.7	3.6	2.6
1925	2.3	1.5	1.4	2.7	1.5	4.5	3.5	3.3	....	4.1	3.6	5.0	3.2	4.2	5.8	19.8	3.3	3.9	1.9	2.2

* Filtration effective for city.
† Sterilization of water supply begun.
‡ Drainage canal in service.
§ New intake.
‖ Coagulation introduced.
¶ One per cent. of water supply filtered.
** Fifty per cent. of water supply filtered.
†† Ninety per cent. of water supply filtered.
‡‡ Sterilization of 66% of water supply.
§§ Sterilization of entire water supply.
‖‖ Coagulant applied during periods of high turbidity.

Lawrence Filter.—When the Massachusetts State Board of Health was re-organized in 1886, one of its most important steps was the establishment of the Experiment Station at Lawrence where, since that date, a vast fund of information has been developed on the subject of purifying water and sewage. One of the outstanding characteristics of these investigations, under the direction of the late Hiram F. Mills, Hon. M. Am. Soc. C. E., was that it embodied data of an engineering, chemical, and biological nature. Such thorough-going and unusually well co-ordinated data have had much to do with the development of sanitary engineering during the past forty years. In 1891-92, one of the most important pieces of work at Lawrence was an investigation of the ability of ordinary sand filters to remove typhoid fever germs, a matter of more than usual importance in the Merrimac Valley, where the Lawrence water-supply intake is only eight miles below the Lowell sewers.

In the late summer of 1892 Asiatic cholera appeared on vessels quarantined in New York Harbor, and, under these circumstances, it was not difficult for Mr. Mills to obtain from the City Council of Lawrence, authorization for the construction of the Lawrence filter. This filter was completed in September, 1893, and embodied in its design the application of many of the data derived under Mr. Mills' direction at the State Experiment Station. The success of this filter, in reducing typhoid fever in that city, was so notable that it became a landmark in the train of developments which characterized the improvements in the quality of water supplies in America.

Louisville Investigations.—What the Lawrence experiments were to the development of slow sand filters, the results of the investigations at Louisville, Ky., were in respect to rapid or mechanical filters. The late Charles Hermany, Past-President, Am. Soc. C. E., found, as did Mr. Kirkwood at St. Louis, that the muddy Ohio River water was not susceptible to filtration in a practical way through sand beds, as used in Europe and later adopted with some modifications at Lawrence. In 1895 he began investigations, continuing for nearly two years, on various ways of coagulating and filtering muddy Ohio River water, the writer being in immediate charge of the work. Prior to that period mechanical filters had been in use at a few mills, for removing coarse material, but had obtained practically no standing for municipal supplies. They had been studied shortly before by the late E. B. Weston, M. Am. Soc. C. E., at Providence, R. I., and extensive investigations immediately followed those at Louisville, one set being conducted at Cincinnati, Ohio, by the writer and the other at Pittsburgh, Pa., by Mr. Hazen. In those days mechanical filters were contained within wooden tubs or metal cylinders, and it happened that their status became largely enhanced through the development of reinforced concrete for the filter units such as first adopted at Little Falls, N. J., in 1901. Since that date there have been marked developments in mechanical equipment for the efficient control of various filter arrangements.

Filtration Practice.—At present (1926) there are approximately 635 filter plants, having capacities in excess of 1 000 000 gal., serving about 23 750 000 people, and having a total daily rated capacity of 5 000 000 000 gal. There are 47 slow sand filters and 588 mechanical filters, having a rated daily aggregate capacity of 915 000 000 and 4 085 000 000 gal., respectively.

Algæcides.—One aspect of the quality of water has been the tastes and odors associated with the growth and decay of various forms of microscopic life. The late George W. Rafter, M. Am. Soc. C. E., began a painstaking study of this matter, at Rochester, N. Y., and, later, at Boston, Mass., with the aid of the late George C. Whipple, M. Am. Soc. C. E., who for about fifteen years conducted thorough-going investigations into the various factors related to tastes and odors in surface water supplies at Boston and New York. To the engineer, perhaps, it may be of most interest to indicate that by the use of copper sulfate or other algæcides much can be done toward controlling these tastes and odors by killing the organisms producing them.

Aeration.—Stored waters frequently stagnate, with the result that water in the lower parts of deep reservoirs becomes offensive to sight and smell. Aeration will restore the depletion of atmospheric oxygen, lessen the free carbonic acid, and offset the products of decomposition found in the deep parts of large reservoirs. Advantageous use of aeration is to be found in the works of the Catskill project for New York City.

Chlorination.—One of the results of the cholera epidemic at Hamburg was the development of the fact that bleaching powder was an efficient sterilizing agent, although in Europe the idea was to apply it in cases of emergency only. Beginning in 1908, with the Boonton Reservoir supply of Jersey City, N. J., the regular use of chlorine was adopted for the purpose of destroying objectionable bacteria. This practice has become general in America, and it is estimated that there are in service now more than 3 200 chlorinating plants, capable of supplying about 4 000 000 000 gal. of water daily.

Iodizing.—Beginning in 1922 at Rochester, N. Y., there recently has been added to public water supplies intermittent small doses of sodium iodide, for the purpose of supplying the deficiency of iodine. This deficiency in some water supplies is believed to be an important factor in the causation of common goiter.

Methods of Analysis.—The quality and composition of waters in various parts of the United States vary greatly, and the methods of analysis suitable in Western Europe and in New England are quite inadequate for many of the waters of the Southern and Western States. It is of importance to record an unusual amount of good team work in America in improving and unifying methods of analysis. The first edition of "Standard Methods of Water Analysis" appeared in 1905, under the auspices of the American Public Health Association, and, in 1925, its sixth edition appeared under the joint auspices of that Association and the American Water Works Association. It is of interest to note that the standard methods in use in America are to be translated into French and German, under the sponsorship of the Health Section of the League of Nations. It is to be hoped that the co-operative work, carried on in America for thirty years, may assume a wider scope under the guidance of an international committee.

Iron Removal Plants.—Many ground-water supplies contain objectionable quantities of iron and manganese, so that, on exposure to the air, objectionable deposits and discolorations are formed. It is thoroughly practicable to remove these objectionable constituents by aeration and filtration. Chemicals are sometimes used—and in a few instances iron settling basins—for the removal of the deposit, rather than filters.

Removal of Carbonic Acid.—Some water supplies, particularly those derived from deep underground sources, contain large quantities of free carbonic acid, and this is of much significance in connection with the correction of corrosion of metals. It is thoroughly feasible, by aeration and filtration, and, if need be, with the aid of quicklime, to reduce the carbonic acid content to practical limits for safe use. A plant for removing such corrosive properties has been established for the new deep well supply at Memphis, Tenn.

Water Softening.—There are a few well-known water-softening plants in America. The most comprehensive data have come from Columbus, Ohio, in a paper by John H. Gregory, M. Am. Soc. C. E.* Some supplies of hard water undoubtedly should be softened, but views have not been well crystallized as to where to draw the line separating a hard water justifying softening from one where it is not worth while to pay the cost of such softening. This view, however, for public supplies, does not relate to the opinions held by those in charge of the water supplies of many industrial and power plants. What is said of softening also applies to the removal of carbonic acid and other corrosive properties.

Filter Loading.—Engineers are faced to-day with one problem that very soon must receive more attention than has been accorded to it hitherto. Sources of water supply are being contaminated by industrial wastes to a serious degree in some sections, and the pollution due to the discharge of sewage into such waters after little or no treatment is causing apprehension in well-informed circles. The time is fast approaching when the loads thrown on some water purification plants will be unreasonably heavy, and engineers should consider carefully the advisability of abandoning the old attitude that, except in unusual instances, it is a matter of indifference as to purification of sewage so long as public water supplies derived from a polluted source are purified. In twenty-five years cities have grown rapidly, and the industries discharging objectionable wastes have grown even more rapidly. Rivers and lakes have about the same volume of water now as they had a century ago. What was good practice in 1900 is no longer such in many cities, because of the changes that have taken place. This view is adopted in the treaty between the United States and Great Britain, ratified in 1909, in which it is stated that boundary waters between the United States and Canada should not be polluted on one side of the river so as to be injurious to those living on the other side. These matters were interpreted to deal with filter loading, after the International Joint Commission, to which these matters were referred, had conducted extensive investigations and inquiries.

* *Transactions*, Am. Soc. C. E., Vol. LXVII (1910), pp. 235 *et seq.*

SEWERAGE AND DRAINAGE OF TOWNS

By Harrison P. Eddy,* M. Am. Soc. C. E.

Historical

Early American Conditions.—At the founding of the United States, the living conditions of the great mass of the people were extremely simple. Plumbing was practically unknown. Few public water supplies and no public sewerage systems existed, and primitive methods for the removal and disposal of household wastes and excretal matters prevailed.

Sewerage and Growth of Cities Coincident.—The development of sewerage systems and methods of sewage disposal has been coincident with the growth of cities. At the time of the first census, in 1790, only four municipalities had populations in excess of 10 000—New York, N. Y., 33 131; Philadelphia, Pa., 28 522; Boston, Mass., 18 320; and Baltimore, Md., 13 503. The remaining population was living under rural or semi-rural conditions. Individual water supplies, in the form of wells, and wastes disposal systems, in the form of privies and cesspools, existed on the same premises, too often in close proximity.

Effect of Introduction of Public Water Supplies.—With the introduction of public water supplies into growing towns, and the gradual increase of houses provided with plumbing, the need for prompt and inoffensive removal of liquid wastes became acute. The pail system, for the collection and removal of excretal wastes, as adopted to a considerable extent in Europe, never became popular in America. Leaching cesspools took care of liquid wastes where soil conditions were suitable, but in many instances offensive wastes were discharged on the ground or into surface gutters. Drains built by individuals or by groups of persons, for the removal of surface waters, were often utilized to carry the liquid wastes to the nearest watercourse.

In Boston it was not until 1823 that the city took over the maintenance of existing drains and the building of new ones. Fecal matters were excluded by law until 1833. Even then, only liquid wastes were allowed, the admission of solid matters being prohibited.

These early drains and sewers were built without regard to the needs of the community as a whole, and did not follow any technical basis of design. The materials of which they were constructed were stone, brick, and wood. Sections were circular, semi-circular, rectangular, and of various odd shapes. In many cases slopes were inadequate, and sometimes actually pitched the wrong way.

Introduction of Water-Carriage System.—Due to the poor design and construction of the early drains there was a marked prejudice against the discharge of excretal matters into them, it being claimed that this would cause offensive odors and be detrimental to health, and it was not until about 1850 that the water-carriage system for liquid wastes, including excretal

* Cons. Engr. (Metcalf & Eddy), Boston, Mass.

matters, began to come into general use. In Baltimore, the prohibition relating to the direct discharge of such matters into sewers continued until 1911, at which time the new and comprehensive system of sewers and the sewage treatment plant were put into operation.

Yellow Fever and Cholera.—In the early days of the Republic many epidemics of yellow fever and cholera occurred. In New York there were epidemics of the former in 1791, 1795, 1798, 1799, 1805, 1819, and 1822. That of 1798, when the population was only about 80 000, resulted in more than 2 000 deaths.

In Southern cities yellow fever persisted almost until the Twentieth Century. Even before the discovery of the part played by the mosquito in the transmission of the disease, the introduction of sewerage and the drainage of cities resulted in a marked diminution of this malady, due to the reduction of breeding places for mosquitoes.

Cholera, another disease now unknown in America, was prevalent from time to time in the past. Serious epidemics occurred in 1832, 1834, 1849, 1854, 1866, and 1873, thousands of deaths resulting from it in New York alone. A relation between this disease and improper drainage and filthy methods of disposal of household wastes appears to have been recognized to some degree at an early date. This recognition undoubtedly was a stimulus to the establishment of drainage and sewerage systems in the larger towns.

Sewerage Systems

Early Systems.—The first complete systematic sewerage system in the world appears to have been that of Hamburg, Germany, begun in 1843 after the plans of the elder Lindley, a distinguished English engineer. In the United States the first application of engineering skill to the design of sewers was in 1857 when the late Julius W. Adams, Past-President, Am. Soc. C. E., was appointed to prepare plans for the sewerage of Brooklyn, N. Y. For many years thereafter these sewers served as models. In the following year the late E. S. Chesbrough, Past-President, Am. Soc. C. E., submitted his first report on a comprehensive sewerage system for Chicago, Ill. In 1874 the late J. Herbert Shedd, M. Am. Soc. C. E., established the basic principles for the design of a sewerage system at Providence, R. I. Two years later, a committee, consisting of Messrs. E. S. Chesbrough, the late Moses Lane, M. Am. Soc. C. E., and Dr. C. F. Folsom, reported on the sewerage of Boston, Mass., advocating the general plan of main drainage now in effect. In 1880, the late Col. Waring at Memphis, Tenn., and Benezette Williams at Pullman, Ill., constructed the first systems of separate sewers in America. The separate sewerage and drainage systems of New Orleans, La., followed in the early part of the present century, and, in 1911, one of the largest separate systems of sewers in the country went into service at Baltimore. At present (1926) no large municipality is without its sewerage system.

Storm-Water Drains, Separate Sewers, and Combined Sewers.—Following the advocacy of separate sewers by Col. Waring, and with the increasing need for sewage treatment, American practice tended toward the separation of storm drainage and domestic sewage. Of recent years, however, experience with American municipal administration has shown that it is practically hopeless to secure complete elimination of storm-water from separate sewers and of sewage from storm drains, particularly in the larger cities, and the tendency has been to build combined systems, using intercepting sewers with storm-water overflows when necessary to carry the dry-weather flow a long distance for treatment or disposal.

Pumping.—Although steam-driven pumping machinery had been developed for water-works and for mine drainage prior to the beginning of the Nineteenth Century, there was at that time no comprehensive sewerage system in America, and, consequently, no demand for sewage pumping. Such sewers as were built at an early date discharged by gravity. One of the earliest sewage pumping stations is that of the Boston main drainage works, put into service in 1884. This was followed in the succeeding year by the station in Milwaukee, Wis. In recent years notable pumping plants have been established at Washington, D. C., Baltimore, Chicago, and New Orleans.

The earlier stations were equipped with steam-driven plunger pumps; later, steam-driven centrifugal pumps were used with success, and, more recently, electric motor-driven pumps have predominated. For lifts of only a few feet, screw pumps have been used for many years in connection with flushing tunnels at Milwaukee and Chicago where lake water is pumped to provide additional dilution in sewage-laden streams. At New Orleans very large screw pumps are used for handling drainage or storm run-off. Now that pumping equipment has become more dependable and efficient, and electric current is almost everywhere available at reasonable cost, engineers do not hesitate, as they once did, to resort to pumping. On both small and relatively large projects, automatically operated equipment is commonly used, thus avoiding the necessity of constant attendance by an operating staff.

Design.—There is little evidence to indicate that prior to about 1850 engineering skill entered into the design of sewers. Following this date empirical formulas for determining their requisite size came into use. Among the best known of these were those of Hawksley (London, 1857); Bürkli-Ziegler (Zürich, 1880); Adams (Brooklyn, 1880); McMath (St. Louis, 1887); and Hering (New York diagrams, 1889). These formulas have given place quite generally to adaptations of the "rational method" for estimating quantities of storm-water run-off. This method, which takes into consideration the fact that the rate of run-off at any point is dependent on the rate of rainfall and the time required for the water to reach the drain, was advocated by the late Emil Kuichling, M. Am. Soc. C. E., in 1889. However, it should be noted that in the modern city the covering of streets and sidewalks with smooth, water-proof pavements and the utilization of a large part of the remaining areas for building purposes, is bringing about a larger proportion of impervious area. These changes cause rates of run-off more nearly equal to rates of precipitation than formerly, resulting in the need for more liberal sewer and drain capacities.

Materials.—The early sewers, built after 1850, were generally vitrified clay or cement mortar pipes for small sizes, and brick for the large sections. In the older part of New York a great deal of wood-stave sewer was used. In 1885, at Washington, David E. McComb, M. Am. Soc. C. E., was the first American engineer to build large sewers of concrete. Since then, concrete for large and medium-sized sewers has come into wide use, those at St. Louis, Kansas City, Mo., Detroit, Mich., and Philadelphia being particularly large. In some cases, also, segmental vitrified clay tile has found favor.

Construction Methods.—With increasing activity in the establishment of sewerage systems and in general building construction, and also as a result of advancing wages, there followed improved methods of construction. Excavations for the early sewers were made by hand, stagings being used in deep trenches. This method was then modified by the use of bucket machines, such as those devised by Howard A. Carson, Hon. M. Am. Soc. C. E., during the construction of the Boston main drainage works. Later, on large work, the steam shovel was used; still later, the drag-line excavator; and, on smaller work, the trench excavating machine has come into quite general favor.

For rock excavation, except on small jobs, hand drilling has been replaced by power drills, first of the tripod type and later of the hammer type; and improved explosives have displaced black powder.

Advance has also been made in the methods of handling water encountered in trenching. The old hand-operated diaphragm pump is now driven by a direct-connected gasoline engine, and has been replaced on large work by power-driven pumps of several other types.

Marked progress has been made in the construction of concrete sewers, the hand-turning of concrete having been superseded largely by machine mixing, and collapsible steel forms in many instances having replaced the old wooden ones.

Maintenance.—The early sewers and drains apparently did not receive any attention until stoppages or other troubles occurred, and this is practically true at present in many cities. With the organization of sewer departments in the better managed cities, however, regular maintenance has become more general, and has been facilitated by the development in the past fifty years of improved equipment, such as devices for flushing and for removing obstructions.

Plumbing.—Coincident with the development of public water supplies and the introduction of the water-carriage system for sewage there occurred an evolution in the art of household plumbing. The flush water-closet was invented about 1809, but practically all really sanitary types have been developed within the past forty years.

About 1855 attention began to be given to possible dangers to health from the escape of sewer air or sewer gas. Subsequently, strenuous efforts were made to prevent even the most minute escape of sewer air into houses, and there ensued an era of complicated plumbing layouts fostered by elaborate plumbing codes.

The first important plumbing legislation in Massachusetts was in 1882 when the City of Boston was authorized by the Legislature, to regulate plumbing by ordinance. In 1924, the late George C. Whipple, M. Am. Soc. C. E., as chairman of a sub-committee, reported to the Department of Commerce on minimum requirements for plumbing. This report described the situation relative to plumbing codes as chaotic, and disclosed an utter lack of uniformity in legal procedure governing such matters. The findings of this committee marked an important step toward increased standardization and simplification of plumbing practice.

Sewage Disposal

Stream Pollution.—In the early days filthy privy vaults and overflowing cesspools in populous districts led to the construction of common sewers, which discharged generally into the nearest stream or other body of water. By this practice the nuisance at the individual premises was transferred to the point of discharge of the sewer, resulting in an extension of the offensive conditions to the stream or along the water-front. The construction of intercepting sewers with a single outlet, in turn, served to concentrate the polluting material, and with increasing volumes of sewage the intensity of pollution in many instances became intolerable.

In 1872 the State Board of Health of Massachusetts was authorized to investigate the problem of stream pollution, and in the following year William R. Nichols, Professor of Chemistry of the Massachusetts Institute of Technology, submitted to the Board a comprehensive report on sewerage, sewage disposal, and stream pollution. In the same year the late Phinehas Ball was engaged in a study of the Worcester sewage problem, and in 1875 the late J. P. Kirkwood, Past-President, Am. Soc. C. E., made an investigation and report on stream-pollution conditions in Massachusetts. Since that time numerous investigations and reports have been made by other investigators and also by State and Federal departments.

Legislation and Administrative Control.—Nearly all the States have passed legislative measures intended to restrict and control stream pollution. Some of these laws and regulations have been so drastic as to be impossible of strict enforcement. Recently, however, a tendency toward a more rational regulation of the use of streams has developed, as illustrated by the formation of the Sanitary Water Board of Pennsylvania and its classification of streams in three groups, with restrictions for the disposal of sewage and industrial wastes applicable to the needs of each group.

In general, the control of stream pollution has been vested in the respective State departments or boards of health. In the case of interstate streams, only the Supreme Court of the United States has jurisdiction. There have been, however, a few agreements between the departments of health of several States. The first of such agreements was that in 1922 between the Health Departments of Pennsylvania and New Jersey, with respect to the Delaware River. Since then the Health Departments of Pennsylvania, Ohio, West Virginia, Kentucky, and New York have executed general agreements relating to the streams passing through these States. In this manner it may be possible, by exercising their respective local authority, for the several States jointly to accomplish control of pollution of interstate waters without recourse to Federal authorities.

Scientific Research.—In 1880 the discovery of the bacillus of typhoid fever, by Eberth in Germany, marked the beginning of a new era in sanitation. Previously, the relation of pollution to disease had been but faintly understood, such sanitary works as were built being due to a desire for cleanliness and a sentiment of common decency. Although such motives remain in force to-day, and in fact in many instances govern, the most vital consideration now is "prevention of disease."

Fifty years ago the science of bacteriology was in its infancy, and its application to matters of stream pollution and sewage disposal had not been grasped. In 1877 Shloesing and Muntz, in France, and, in 1882, Robert Warington, in England, proved conclusively that the oxidation of ammonia and organic matter was effected by the agency of living organisms, and Warington proceeded to devise practical methods whereby living organisms could be utilized for the nitrification of the organic matters in sewage.

In 1887 the Lawrence Experiment Station of the Massachusetts State Board of Health was established, under the direction of the late Hiram F. Mills, Hon. M. Am. Soc. C. E. Through its studies the fundamental biological conditions underlying the oxidation processes of sewage treatment became established. These researches have been continued to the present day (1926), constituting an unparalleled contribution, from a single source, to the art of sewage treatment.

Dilution.—Although sewage disposal by dilution was the earliest method adopted by municipalities, it was not until about 1887 that investigation of the factors entering into it was made by the late Rudolph Hering, M. Am. Soc. C. E., in connection with the problem of sewage disposal at Chicago. His studies resulted in the construction of the Main Drainage Canal of the Sanitary District of Chicago, completed in 1900. In Massachusetts studies undertaken at about the same time established the limiting dilution ratios which served as a basis of general practice for many years. More recently much information bearing on the disposal of sewage by dilution has been accumulated. Particularly noteworthy have been the studies made by the United States Public Health Service in connection with the Ohio and Illinois Rivers.

Although seacoast municipalities have seldom adopted methods other than that of dilution, it has often proved necessary, even with them, to take precautions with respect to the location of outlets, so that pollution of shores and bathing beaches should be prevented. In the case of the Boston main drainage works, for instance, special attention was paid to the location of outlets, the sewage being temporarily stored, and released only at ebb tide. In the case of certain seacoast towns where it is desirable to protect shellfish areas from contamination, treatment of the sewage has been adopted, with the addition of disinfection.

Broad Irrigation.—The treatment of sewage to render it inoffensive was undertaken even before the principles involved began to be understood. The earliest method was that of broad irrigation, or the application of the sewage to relatively level areas of land, where it could become absorbed and purified by the soil. To operate satisfactorily, large areas of porous and easily drained soil were required, and, to avoid annoyance from flies and odors, it was necessary that the "sewage farms", as such tracts were called, be well isolated. Usually an effort was made to utilize the manurial value of the sewage by growing crops on the irrigated fields. Among the first attempts of this sort in the United States may be mentioned the farm established at Lenox, Mass., in 1876, where both subsurface irrigation and broad irrigation were used; the broad irrigation areas at the State Insane Asylum in Worcester, in 1876; at Amherst, Mass., and at Pullman, Wash., in 1881; and at South Framingham, Mass., in 1889. Due to the large tracts of land required, however, and also for esthetic reasons, this method of treatment never was adopted widely in the United States, and, with a few minor exceptions, is no longer in use.

Intermittent Filtration.—As a result of the Lawrence Experiment Station studies there was developed in New England a modified form of broad irrigation, known as "intermittent filtration," by which crude, or settled, sewage is applied evenly to the surface of prepared areas of sand or other fine material a few feet in depth, underdrained by lines of tile with open joints. During its passage through the bed the sewage is purified as a result of the removal, and changing, of the organic matter into more stable substances, by physical and biological agencies in conjunction with atmospheric oxygen present in the interstices of the sand. The process derives its name in part from the necessity of intermittent application of the sewage in order that the air required for the oxidation of the organic matters may enter the voids of the sand. In New England, where soil conditions are favorable, this method was promptly adopted by many towns. The area required is much less than for broad irrigation, but greater than for later types of filters. Owing to the large area required, and the cost of operation, this method is adopted now only for small towns where conditions are favorable.

Chemical Precipitation.—Another early method of sewage treatment is that of "chemical precipitation", involving the addition of lime, lime and sulfate of iron, or other coagulants, to form an inorganic floc, which absorbs and on settling carries down with it particles of suspended solids, leaving a relatively clear liquid. The sludge produced is large in volume and somewhat offensive in character.

The earliest plants of this type were those at Coney Island, New York, put in operation about 1887; at East Orange, N. J., in 1888 or 1889, and at Worcester, in 1890. Later, other plants of this type were built at various places, the most recent large one being that at Providence, built in 1902. Due to the incomplete purification secured, the high cost of operation, and the large volume of sludge produced, chemical precipitation as a means for treating sewage, has gone out of favor, although it is still recognized as of value in the treatment of some industrial wastes. Recently, the City of Worcester abandoned this method of treatment and, in 1925, put into operation a large Imhoff tank—trickling filter plant.

Septic Tanks.—The sedimentation of sewage in tanks, without the use of chemicals, has been practiced for many years. The combination of the sedimentation of solids and their digestion by bacterial action has been utilized in the septic tank, the Travis tank, and the Imhoff tank.

The septic tank is a sedimentation tank, designed and operated so as to foster the decomposition of the settled solids in the absence of oxygen. It was originally believed that nearly complete liquefaction of the suspended solids could be obtained in this manner. Experience has shown, however, that the proportion thus liquefied is much less than was formerly thought. Such tanks, unless covered, frequently are offensive smelling, the treated sewage is black and foul, and difficulties in operation result from the accumulation of the solids in the form of a floating mass of scum on the surface of the sewage.

Similar tanks were first used in America at the State Insane Asylum at Worcester in 1876, and later were adopted at other places. An installation at Saratoga Springs, N. Y., in 1903, led to a lawsuit brought by the owners of certain septic tank patents, which resulted in judgment for the plaintiffs. From the beginning of septic tank patent litigation the consensus of opinion among American sanitary engineers has been that the patents covered principles and practices which had long been known and publicly used. Consequently, under these patents, which long since have expired, the payments were few and small.

Imhoff Tanks.—The favor in which septic tanks were once held later turned largely to the two-story tank in which the processes taking place in the septic tank are separated, sedimentation occurring in an upper compartment, and digestion of the solids going on in a chamber below, separated from the one above by a sloping partition containing narrow slots through which the solids pass into the lower compartment.

This tank was developed for the Emscher District, in Germany, and was introduced into this country largely through the efforts of Mr. Hering.

The earliest plant in America was that at Madison-Chatham, N. J., in 1911, and the first large tanks were constructed at Atlanta, Ga., in 1912. Since then there have been many important installations, among them those at Rochester, N. Y., Fitchburg, Mass., Cleveland, Ohio, and Philadelphia. This tank is a material improvement on the older septic process in that the treated sewage is less offensive and the solids may be digested to such a degree that the resulting sludge is practically free from odor and can readily be dewatered on porous beds. In some places, however, difficulties have been experienced due to unfavorable sludge digestion, which has resulted in foaming or in excessive scum formation. Recent work, at the New Jersey Sewage Experiment Station, and at other places, indicates that by controlling the reaction (pH) of the sludge and scum, proper digestion can be secured.

Separate Sludge Digestion.—It has been held by some engineers that the processes carried out in the two-story tanks can be accomplished better in two separate tanks, the solids being settled out in one and drawn or pumped from it into the digestion tank. In some cases the sedimentation tanks have been equipped with mechanical devices for the continuous removal of the settled solids.

The earliest attempt at separate sludge digestion on a large scale in America was at Baltimore in 1912, where open tanks were introduced for the storage during digestion of solids removed from preliminary settling tanks. On the whole, the Baltimore experience, although not yet fully satisfactory, has demonstrated that sludge may be digested in separate tanks and that this process may prove of advantage in some cases, if conditions favorable to the requisite biological action can be provided and maintained.

Separate sludge digestion generally has resulted in acid fermentation accompanied by offensive odors and the production of a foul-smelling sludge. Research at the New Jersey Sewage Experiment Station and at Harvard University has shown the importance of controlling the reaction of the sludge and the advantage which can be secured by maintaining a favorable temperature. At Plainfield, N. J., experiments relating to this subject have been carried out on a large scale, and at Boonton, N. J., a plant has been constructed in which provision has been made for collecting and burning the gases from sludge digestion and for utilizing the heat therefrom for heating the glass-housed sludge beds and the contents of the separate sludge digestion tanks.

Contact Beds.—Because of the large areas required, and the unavailability of suitable soil for broad irrigation or for intermittent filtration, coarse-grained sewage filters, in the form of contact beds, originated in England in the early Nineties and were adopted somewhat later in America. Contact beds consist essentially of tanks, filled with broken stone, coke, or other coarse medium, which are alternately filled with settled sewage and emptied, periods of several hours being allowed for standing full and remaining empty.

Oxidation and nitrification are brought about by the film of micro-organisms growing on the surface of the medium, the supply of oxygen being obtained from the air entering the voids of the material during the draining period. Comparatively few contact beds have been built in America, and several of those have now been replaced by other forms of treatment. This was due to the almost coincident development of trickling filters, which are superior to contact beds in some respects, chief among them being the much larger volume of sewage which can be treated on a unit area of trickling filter.

Trickling Filters.—Trickling filters, also adopted in England on a large scale prior to their use in America, differ from contact beds in that the sewage is distributed more or less uniformly and continuously over the surface of beds of coarse material. A trickling filter is primarily a bed of broken stone several feet deep, laid on a concrete floor covered with a system of underdrains. Settled sewage is applied intermittently, at short intervals, to the surface of the filter in the form of fine drops, by using symmetrically spaced spray nozzles or other devices, comparatively few mechanical distributors, such as are commonly used in England, having been built in America. As the sewage is sprayed through the air and passes through the porous bed, atmospheric oxygen is absorbed and is utilized in the biological oxidation and mineralization of the organic matter. The effluent is usually settled in order to remove humus-like solids which, from time to time, escape from the filter and thus prevent it from becoming clogged.

The first municipal filter of this type to be put in service was that at Reading, Pa., in 1908. At present, trickling filters preceded by Imhoff tanks, probably constitute the type of treatment most generally in use in America. The largest installation of such filters is that at Baltimore, where about 30 acres are in use.

One unsatisfactory feature of the trickling filter is the occurrence at times of large numbers of the small gray fly, *psychoda*. Control of these flies has been accomplished by flooding the filters for brief periods at regular intervals, during the breeding season, although this has interfered somewhat with the efficiency of the filters. At Schenectady, N. Y., during the last two years, considerable success has attended an effort to control this fly by treating the settled sewage, just prior to its application to the filters, with either bleaching powder or liquid chlorine. The control of odors around the Imhoff tanks and the trickling filters, by the treatment of the sewage with liquid chlorine, is also being investigated, and gives promise of beneficial results under some conditions.

Activated Sludge.—During the past ten years the activated sludge process has been adopted in a number of places in the United States, Canada, and abroad. The process is the outcome of experiments on the aeration of sewage, by numerous American workers, particularly the investigations at the Lawrence Experiment Station in 1912, which led to the work, in England, of Fowler and Mumford in 1913 and of Arden and Lockett in 1914. This treatment consists essentially of aerating sewage with a mixture of aerated or activated sludge and subsequently allowing the mixture to settle. The development of the process as a practical means of treating sewage has resulted largely from investigations made at Milwaukee, Chicago, Indianapolis, Ind., and several other places.

Beginning in 1914, the City of Milwaukee conducted what is undoubtedly the most extensive large-scale experimental investigation ever carried out in the field of sewage treatment. Based on the results of these experiments, a plant, the largest in the world at present (1926), has been constructed at Milwaukee, which was put into operation in 1925. At present, there are comparatively few activated sludge plants in America, that at San Marcos, Tex., built in 1916, having been the first. Large plants have since been constructed at Houston, Tex., Indianapolis, and Chicago. In the latter city a plant for the treatment of the sewage from a population of 800 000 is now under construction.

Racks, Grit Chambers, and Screens.—In order to protect pumps and other mechanical equipment from clogging and injury, and to simplify and improve the efficiency of various processes of treatment, it has become general practice to provide preliminary treatment for the removal of trash, mineral matter, and the coarser suspended organic substances. In a few cases provision has also been made for the removal of floating oil and grease.

Cage racks for the interception of trash were constructed at the main drainage pumping station in Boston and first operated in 1884. Grit chambers for the removal of the heavier mineral solids were built at Worcester in 1904. Stationary bar screens, manually and mechanically raked, have been in use for a long time, but only during the past 15 or 20 years has there been a marked development in fine, moving screens cleaned by brushing or flushing. The first of these in America was the Weand screen built at Reading, in 1908. This was followed by the Riensch-Wurl screen at Rochester in 1916 and later by others, such as the Dorrco and Link Belt screens, at various places. During the last few years such screens have been used for treating sewage preparatory to more complete treatment by other processes, and for removing the larger and more easily visible floating and suspended matter where more complete treatment is not necessary.

Sludge Disposal.—One of the troublesome features of sewage treatment has been the disposal of the solid particles removed by screening or by sedimentation. In general, screenings have been used for filling, or have been plowed under in an effort to utilize their fertilizing properties. To a limited extent, also, screenings have been incinerated. Sludge from septic and single-story settling tanks is generally offensive and difficult to dry satisfactorily on beds of sand or similar material. Properly functioning two-story tanks produce sludge which is easily dried and inoffensive. As rains and freezing weather interfere with drying in the open air, beds have been built with covers, like greenhouse structures, notably at Marion and Alliance, Ohio. At Houston and Indianapolis activated sludge has been lagooned.

During the early years of the treatment of sewage, attempts were made to utilize its manurial value by growing crops on the areas used for broad irrigation. Later, there was considerable effort to utilize the fertilizing ingredients in the sludge resulting from chemical precipitation. In some cases such sludge was dewatered by the common filter press, notable plants being at Worcester and Providence.

Recently, air-dried digested sludge has been sold to farmers at Baltimore, Rochester, and Schenectady. The value of such material is small, because of its high water content and the low proportion of fertilizing ingredients contained in it. In some localities it appears to have been profitable for farmers to haul and utilize such sludge, even if a nominal price had to be paid for it.

In the case of activated sludge, the proportion of fertilizing ingredients, particularly nitrogenous compounds, is materially greater than in sludges from other processes, and, therefore, the opportunity for its profitable utilization as a fertilizer has proved somewhat attractive.

By far the greatest progress in this direction has been made at Milwaukee, where a large plant has been built for dewatering and drying activated sludge, thus converting it into a marketable fertilizer which is being sold under the name of "Milorganite." At Chicago, also, for several years, activated sludge has been dewatered, dried, and converted into fertilizer.

Disinfection.—Where treated sewage is tributary to public water supplies or where effluents are discharged into tidal waters used for oyster culture, it has become customary to provide for disinfection with chlorine. The first plant for this purpose was at Brewster, N. Y., on the Croton water-shed, where an electrolytic plant for the production of chlorine from salt solution was built in 1892. In 1909 the efficiency of hypochlorite of lime for the disinfection of sewage, was demonstrated, and, at present, Providence is using this agent to disinfect the effluent from its chemical precipitation plant. Liquid chlorine, however, is used more generally. Chlorination plants have been installed at Cleveland and at a number of other places where raw or treated sewage is discharged into waters used for bathing.

Industrial Wastes.—England, due to her smaller streams, was compelled to devote attention to the treatment of industrial wastes, as well as of sewage, long before it became urgent to do so in America. Rafter and Baker, in their book, "Sewage Disposal in the United States," published in 1894, state as follows:

"Thus far in this country manufacturers have not, except in a few instances, been compelled to purify their own polluted wastes, and inasmuch as few have undertaken the purification, of their own volition, very little experience under American conditions has thus far been gained."

Even to-day the foregoing statement holds true in considerable degree, although that part dealing with the lack of experience under American conditions should be modified. In New England and elsewhere numerous plants have been built for the treatment of industrial wastes. Furthermore, manufacturers are less wasteful than in previous days, and the quantities of polluting matters discharged in the waste waters are in some cases somewhat less. In general, the processes used in treating industrial wastes include sedimentation, chemical precipitation, intermittent filtration, oxidation in trickling filters, or, in short, processes or combinations of processes which have been found applicable to the treatment of sewage.

Increase in Sewage Treatment.—In 1875 not one of the sixty-seven cities having a population of 100 000 or more by the 1920 Census, used any method for the treatment of its sewage. By 1900 only two of these cities—Worcester and Reading—had built treatment plants, their aggregate population then being approximately 197 000. At present (1926) about twenty of these cities, with a total population of approximately 6 500 000 by the 1920 Census, have treatment plants. Of these plants those receiving the sewage from a population of about 3 700 000 consist of tanks only, or of tanks preceded by screens; the remaining plants, receiving sewage from about 2 800 000, provide for tank treatment combined with some oxidation process, such as activated sludge or trickling filters.

The change in the art of sewage treatment chiefly by biological processes is illustrated by a comparison of the space required by different types of plant for the treatment of a unit volume of sewage—for example, that from a city of 100 000 population. The early method of intermittent filtration, including settling tanks, sludge beds, and sand filters, would need a total of not less than 130 acres and 23 000 000 cu. ft.; the more modern Imhoff tank—

trickling filter plant, with sludge beds and appurtenances—would require about 10 acres and 3 000 000 cu. ft.; and a plant for the most recent activated sludge process would require about 2 acres and 1 000 000 cu. ft.

Operation of Treatment Plants for Sewage and Industrial Wastes.—Although much progress has been made in the art of sewage treatment, and many sewage treatment plants have been built, there remains considerable lack of realization, on the part of the public and of municipal officials, of the necessity for continuous, careful, and intelligent operation of such plants. Prior to 1900 only about two sewage treatment plants in the United States were under the control of resident technical operators, these plants being at Brockton, Mass., and Worcester. By 1910 several other treatment plants were under technical supervision, notably at Columbus, Ohio, Plainfield, and Reading. Since that time many new plants have been constructed, of which the larger have been provided almost invariably with technical operators. The smaller plants, however, in far too many instances, are operated without proper supervision.

Technical supervision of plants for the treatment of industrial wastes is even less common, largely because such plants are a source of outgo rather than of income, and, consequently, do not enlist the interest of the proprietors. On the other hand, some progressive manufacturers have provided for the expert technical supervision of intelligent non-technical operators, with excellent results.

SUMMARY

Reviewing the history of the last 150 years, it is seen that the advance in the development and application of the art of sewerage and drainage of towns, although slow at first, has attained such an acceleration that there is a wide gap between the conditions as of the beginning and the ending of the sesqui-centennial period.

In the early years the privy, the cesspool, and the drain to the nearest watercourse prevailed. Cities were without water supplies and without sewers. The well and the cesspool or privy existed side by side. Visitations of cholera and yellow fever occurred from time to time, and typhoid and malarial fevers were prevalent. The relation to disease, of parasites conveyed by food and drink, or by insect hosts, was unknown. The general death rate was abnormally high, viewed in the light of present conditions, and little attention was given to the sanitation of such towns and cities as existed.

During the latter part of this period, discoveries in the science of bacteriology, relative to the causation of disease and the various methods of its transmittal, have resulted in rapid strides in the sanitation of the environment. The prevention of pollution of water supplies, their purification in case of contamination, and the proper removal and disposition of the waste products of human activities, have made remarkable progress. Resulting in large measure from the application of scientific knowledge, coupled with engineering skill in the control of man's environment, cholera and yellow fever have disappeared, typhoid fever and other water-borne diseases have almost been eradicated, and the general death rate has been diminished materially.

Progress in the field of sewage disposal has been more spectacular than in those of sewerage and drainage, using these terms in a restricted sense. Even fifty years ago, the principles of sewage purification, either solely by natural means or by artificial processes utilizing natural agencies, were not known. To-day, many of these principles are known, and processes are available by which municipal sewage can be purified practically to any degree desired.

The fundamental reason for progress has been the ever-broadening development of science and its application to the art of sanitary engineering. Such application of knowledge has been greatly stimulated by the ever-increasing growth in population and the aggregation of this population into communities of restricted area.

The Future

If it were possible to project a curve of the accumulation of knowledge, it would be less hazardous to prophesy future developments.

In the field of sewerage and drainage there does not seem to be any reason to anticipate radical departure from the principles now established. Data useful as a basis of design, however, will become more complete, and the application of engineering skill will result in better design and construction as time goes on.

Household plumbing will be somewhat simplified, but there will be a still further increase in plumbing conveniences and a greater volume of household sewage. This increase, however, will be offset in some degree by general metering of water supplies and by greater economy in the use of water in the industries.

With continued increase in density of population there will be greater demand for the proper regulation of stream pollution. It is probable, however, that the comparatively recent tendency in some places to attempt a complete cleaning up of streams, will give way to a policy of reasonable use, subject, however, to far better control than is exercised in most localities at present.

With an increasing number of workers in the field, it is certain that better methods of sewage treatment will be devised and developed. The progress of the last fifty years has been confined primarily to the utilization of biological forces, the means of accomplishing which will be greatly improved in the future. The most promising opportunity for the development of new and better methods now appears to lie in the field of physical chemistry, research in which may show a way by which organic colloids can be removed from sewage without the aid of biological agencies. Such a development may lead to simpler methods, less susceptible to temporary derangement. Although it seems improbable that a net income will be derived from the recovery of the fertilizing ingredients of sewage, it is probable that sewage sludge will be utilized as fertilizer in an increasing degree.

The serious handicaps under which most sewage plants are operated to-day, due to lack of adequate funds and proper management, will be overcome in the course of time. The most promising means of accomplishing this is State legislation, of which the Ohio Act of April 5, 1923, is a forerunner. This provides for sewer rentals to cover the cost of operation and maintenance of sewerage works.

The work accomplished during the past 150 years in the field of sewerage and drainage of towns has been the result of the effort of relatively few individuals. Looking backward, the achievements appear to have been great, notwithstanding the difficulties resulting from lack of knowledge. The future increase in population and the raising of the standards of sanitation will afford large opportunities. Looking forward, it appears that the number of workers in the field is destined to increase, and that the accumulation of knowledge in science and in the arts may well enable the engineers of the future to accomplish results even more remarkable and beneficial than those of the past.

STREET CLEANING AND THE COLLECTION AND DISPOSAL OF REFUSE

By Samuel A. Greeley,* M. Am. Soc. C. E.

General Statement

The cleansing of cities involves the removal and disposal of the solid wastes resulting from the activities of the inhabitants. These wastes collect in various ways on the surfaces of streets, yards, vacant areas, and roofs. Such solid wastes, commonly termed refuse, include all the products of community life except sewage. Refuse materials comprise garbage, ashes, rubbish, street dirt, manure, trade refuse, dust, etc. By manual labor and by the use of wagons, trucks, and other special equipment, refuse materials are collected and disposed of.

In the absence of regular and frequent removal, such materials accumulate principally on streets and in alleys, and to a less extent on vacant areas and in yards. There has been, and still is, a marked tendency on the part of individuals to throw their refuse into the streets. In the early days, the hog was the common scavenger, and roamed about and partly cleaned the city. The following was written in the early Fifties:†

"Our streets and alleys should be cleaned everywhere, especially in and around the neighborhood of the square. The brick bats, trash, old hats, old boots and shoes, rags, bones, manure and many other things which grace our streets, should be hauled off, and hog holes filled up."

The need for final disposal was not yet clearly recognized. People in Quincy, Ill., considered geese better scavengers than hogs, and so let them roam the town.

The rapid growth of cities has made for a constantly changing problem in connection with city cleaning, and it has been difficult from the average point of view to keep pace with the necessary demands.

Gradually, people began to understand that the accumulation of refuse is unhealthy. Dr. Frank M. Wells, Health Officer of Cleveland, Ohio, in 1876, wrote:

"It is a sanitary necessity that cities should be kept clean and their refuse, which is organic matter in a state of decomposition, should be promptly removed. This can be accomplished with greater facility when streets are paved, and therefore the paving of streets demands the attention of sanitary bodies. * * * The importance of a constant and thorough cleaning of the streets can not be over-estimated. * * * Of more importance, perhaps, than the condition of the streets, is that of the yards connected with the dwellings, since they are in such close relation with the house that the effect of filth deposited in them is more readily felt."

Refuse left without removal promotes the breeding and growth of vermin, mosquitoes, flies, and rats, all of which tend to spread diseases among human

---

* (Pearse, Greeley & Hansen), Chicago, Ill.

† In *The Journal*, Springfield, Ill.

beings. During certain seasons, the refuse dries, and is pulverized to dust, which fills the atmosphere, to the annoyance of the people and often to the great damage of merchandise. Such influences are directly proportional to the quantity of refuse and the density of population. The quantity of refuse per unit or area in a community increases with the density of the population, and the effect of such accumulations on public health and comfort is greater in crowded, heavily populated districts than in open rural communities. Thus, the development of sanitary engineering in the field of city cleaning during the past 150 years follows closely the development of cities and the sharp increase in urban population.

Growth of Cities

The first considerable growth of cities in the United States began during the twenty years preceding the Civil War. The winning of the Mississippi Valley, the building of railroads, sundry improvements in farm machinery, and successful inventions earned an era of prosperity and stimulated industry. Cities grew. Following the Civil War and the development of the West, factories were built and people flocked to the cities. The increasing density of population in several large cities is shown by Table 3, the data for which are taken from the U. S. Census.

TABLE 3.—Density of Population in a Few American Cities.

City	Population per Acre.	
	1900	1924
New York, N. Y.	18.6	31.5
Philadelphia, Pa.	15.5	24.2
Boston, Mass.	21.4±	28.3
Chicago, Ill.	13.9±	24.1
St. Louis, Mo.	14.7	21.0
New Orleans, La.	2.3	3.6
Average	14.4	22.1

This concentration of population forced the adoption of special measures for city cleaning. In some notes on street cleaning in the Common Council Manual of New York City (1862), it is stated:

"In May, 1701, the assistant aldermen of the different wards were instructed to call on the several inhabitants in their respective wards and ascertain what they are willing to pay towards cleaning the streets and carrying away the dirt; but this method not meeting with a proper response on the part of the inhabitants, an order was made in the same month that the inhabitants of the city, on every Friday, sweep the dirt in heaps before their respective premises * * * for removal by the city cartmen."

In 1887, the Ladies Health Protective Association addressed a memorial to the Mayor of New York, stating that "Modern science has fully exposed the imminent dangers that beset health and life in a malodorous and dust covered town" and, after reviewing methods of city cleaning, urged that "the street cleaning system of New York be wholly reorganized, or that a far different spirit of energy and efficiency should be infused into it."

Thus, if the need for city cleaning has grown with the cities, the effectiveness of city cleaning has developed more or less consistently with progress in municipal government and the enlightenment of public opinion. The contrast between the cleanliness of New York City under the administration of the late Colonel Waring and during the next four years under Tammany as described by a sanitary engineer, William F. Morse, of New York, may be cited as follows:

"Beginning in 1898, with the inheritance of a well-organized and thoroughly equipped service, with labor and money-saving devices and apparatus in running order, with plans and purposes well-defined for carrying on a practical and successful line of work in an honest and economical way; now at the end of four years, as the result of incompetent management and complete surrender to the machine politicians, the department is in a position of absolute contempt."

Progress has been secured in growing cities, despite periods of stagnation caused by incompetent management. The sharp reduction of the general death rate from around 25 per 1 000 about 50 years ago to less than 15 at present (1926), has been caused by improved city cleaning as well as by advances in water supply, sewerage, and public health administration.

Elements of Progress

Broadly speaking, progress in city cleaning depends on the degree of excellence of municipal government, and on the methods and equipment developed by sanitary engineers for use by city officials. It may be said, then, that two of the major elements of progress in this field are (*a*) the intelligence and character of public opinion, as it determines the character of the municipal government; and (*b*) the zeal and skill of outstanding individuals leading the way beyond their contemporaries. The latter provides the facilities for improved methods of city cleaning and the former marks the extent of efficiency in operation and results.

The excellence of municipal government is, of course, largely an outgrowth of public opinion. The more intelligent, experienced, and outspoken the public opinion, the better, in the long run, will be the municipal government. This, in turn, stimulates the science and practice of city cleaning. Outstanding events which picture clearly to the average person important factors of public health mark forward steps. The picturesque descriptions of the work of Pasteur among cattle and silk worms are typical. Perhaps in America the great losses from typhoid fever spread by flies from privies during the Spanish-American War stirred public opinion toward better standards of municipal cleanliness more than any other single event. The conquest of yellow fever by Gorgas resulted from improved cleaning of cities as well as through drainage, and demonstrated to the public the gain in public health through public hygiene. During the quarter century following the Spanish-

American War, progress in city cleaning was more marked by far than at any other time.

Among the names of those active in city cleaning work within memory are Wells, Waring, Landreth, Parsons, Goodnough, Whinery, Morse, and Hering. Such men conducted scientific investigations, studied experience here and abroad, and applied their knowledge to actual operation. One of the first comprehensive investigations of the subject was begun in 1887 by the Garbage Committee of the American Public Health Association, of which the late Rudolph Hering, M. Am. Soc. C. E., was Chairman. One of the best early efforts in this direction was by Dr. Frank M. Wells, Health Officer of Cleveland, in 1876. In a notable report to the Board of Police Commissioners entitled "Filth and Its Relation to Disease", Dr. Wells states the fundamental aspects of city cleaning. After limiting his subject matter to sewers and scavenging, he disposes of the then conflicting theories of disease—one holding that diseases spring spontaneously from filth, and the other that filth furnishes a favorable atmosphere for the multiplication of the organisms of disease—by the following statement:

"Practically these two theories are identical since there is but little difference, whether filth directly causes disease, or is an essential factor in the development of the organisms which produce disease.

"That unsanitary conditions bear a certain relation to a particular class of infections, is now the opinion of the majority of the medical profession."

Early Practice

The beginnings of city cleaning were undoubtedly in street cleaning. Residents deposited their refuse in piles in the street whence it was removed, by a public scavenger, to a public dump beyond occupied districts. Roaming hogs disposed of the garbage they could eat. Thus, hog feeding of garbage and land fill had their beginnings. Practice in Cleveland in 1876 is thus described by Dr. Wells:

"The refuse, which is usually deposited in the yards, consists of ashes, swill, and garbage, which, under the present ordinances governing these articles, form, I believe, a very prolific source of filth. These ordinances provide that no ashes shall be mingled with the swill and garbage (the very means which would render them inoffensive), and that they shall be removed by the Contractor not less than two times a week during the months of May, June, July, August, September, and October, and as many times oftener as may be necessary to prevent the swill deposited from becoming offensive; and not less than once a week during the rest of the year, upon notice from the householder being sent to him. By another section, every householder is obliged to provide water-tight receptacles for the swill and garbage which may accumulate during 48 hours."

Practice, prior to 1887, and its trend for the future, is outlined in the Memorial of the Ladies Health Protective Association as follows:

"Our third point is, that neither ashes nor garbage should ever be placed on the pavement, but that, like the mail carriers, the collectors of house refuse should have a whistle to warn of their coming, and that when they ring, the cans should at once be taken out of the house, emptied into the cart, and returned at once into the house. We think that refuse carts should have high sides and a sloping cover with a hopper in the center, and that every householder should be required to own a galvanized iron receptacle fitted with a cover and with a sliding bottom, so that when placed over the hopper and the slide pulled out, the contents will be received into the closed cart, and the now intolerable blowing of ashes and dust about the streets from the carts be thus avoided. We are agreed that, to get rid of the house ashes and garbage, and of the street sweepings, crematories should be built, similar to the so-called 'Destructors' and 'Carbonizers' in use in England, and that the house ashes and garbage should be burned in the Destructors and the street sweepings in the Carbonizers, and the residuum used for making mortar in one case and fertilizers in the other, as is now so successfully done in Leeds and other English cities. The system at least pays for itself, and if adopted here, the wasteful, pernicious, and disgusting practice of dumping city refuse either inside or outside of the magnificent bay of New York, might be wholly discontinued."

Dr. Henry I. Bowditch, of Boston, Mass., gathered statistics for the Centennial Exposition in 1876 from about seventy cities in the United States, and summarized them as follows: In about twenty-five of the seventy cities, the house offal is moved in carts. The remaining forty-five places report a variety of methods, such as: (1) Thrown into cesspools; (2) fed to hogs; (3) thrown into river; (4) dumped in valley; and (5) used as fertilizer. Thus, less than one-half the cities reporting appeared to have a regular collection service.

The collection and disposal began with dumping refuse on the streets, whence it was gradually removed by hogs, scavengers, and the disintegration of traffic. Then came removal and dumping by the municipality, the householders being required to provide cans. Special methods of disposal began in the decade, 1880 to 1890. In 1873 a report to the American Public Health Association by Dr. C. A. Leas, of Baltimore, Md., states as follows:

"* * * Again, in other localities, the scavenging service is wholly or partly intrusted to Contractors, who mainly regard their own pecuniary interests rather than the public health. The municipal authorities of some towns and cities employ scavenging forces, but without fixed regulations. * * * In some cities the collection of kitchen offal and house ashes is made separately by two sets of carts, with a view to the utilization of the ashes for the filling of sunken lots, and the vegetable and animal offal for the feeding of swine. * * * Whilst in others it is collected together. * * *."

The report then describes a complicated system of composting the garbage with sifted ashes, a tank treatment of night-soil, with a decanting of the liquids to the compost pits, and the final preparation of a fertilizing material. This process appears to have been tried at Baltimore at about this time, but evidently was not continued.

General Development Since 1876

The condition of the streets and the collection of refuse are closely related to the habits and actions of the residents and housekeepers. Their co-operation is important. The general development of city cleaning has depended a great deal on the increased understanding of the public. Much educational work has been accomplished by street-cleaning departments and those charged with the collection and disposal of refuse. The growing familiarity of foreign sections of the population of American cities with city cleaning rules and regulations and the efforts of the cleansing departments have facilitated and improved the work. Great numbers of kitchen cards, based on ordinances regulating the house treatment of refuse, have been distributed. The separation of refuse materials at the house, where ordered, is much better secured. Although not so readily landmarked, better co-operation by the public has contributed largely to the progress of city cleaning in the last half century.

Street cleaning and collection equipment has been developed with the advance in manufacturing and the development of motor vehicles. Perhaps even more important is the better understanding gained by experience in operation, of the fundamental principles involved. Frequent time studies of the work of collection units have been made, and careful consideration of the relations between the size of the wagon, its loading height, the location of the receptacles, the speed of loading, the length of haul, and means for secondary transportation have secured better economy and efficiency. Small single-horse carts have given way to larger wagons, the tractor-trailer system, and motor trucks. Long hauls have been handled better by secondary methods of transportation, such as trains of tractor-drawn vehicles, railroad cars of special design, barges, and large trucks. Street flushers, snow loaders, sweeping machines, and similar equipment have become available. The displacement of horses by automobiles has lessened the work of street cleaning, and the extension of pavements has made the work done more effective. Thus, a sounder balance between hand and machine work has been secured.

Development in Reduction Plants

The reduction of garbage into grease and fertilizer was first practiced on a working scale in Buffalo, N. Y., in 1887. The Merz process was used, in which the refuse was first dumped into a large hopper from which the free water was allowed to drain. It was then spread out, and cans, bottles, rags, metals, bones, etc., were picked out. The remaining garbage was then passed through hot-air dryers and the partly dried material treated with a solvent for the extraction of grease and the recovery of the solids as tankage or fertilizer base. This process, with some modifications, is still used in Chicago, Ill., Detroit, Mich. (in part), and elsewhere. Other processes for the recovery of grease and fertilizer were invented and plants built. In them the problem of odors and nuisance was difficult to solve.

A notable development in garbage reduction is known as the Cobwell process (1912). The garbage is first placed in a reducer, which is a round, flat-bottomed, covered, steam-jacketed tank, with a diameter of at least twice its height. In this, the garbage is flooded with naphtha and then cooked by admitting steam to the jacket under a pressure of 85 lb. per sq. in. Agitation arms in the reducer keep the contents in motion. The temperature of the garbage and naphtha is held at less than 200° Fahr., under which conditions the original moisture content is carried off with the vaporized solvent. Thus, the garbage is dried. When the water is gone, the temperature in the reducer rises, and the dried garbage is washed several times with naphtha (gasoline) to extract the grease. Finally, the residual material or tankage is dried in the reducer with live steam. Thus, the entire process is conducted in a single tank without exposure, and odor control is better secured. Recently, economies in operation have been made by a partial preliminary drying in hot-air dryers, but with an increased odor hazard.

The greater unit value of the dried product (tankage) as a stock food instead of a fertilizer has led to further developments. At Indianapolis, Ind., Dayton, Ohio, and Michigan City, Ind., so-called "Morrison" plants have been built. In this process the garbage is first placed in vertical digesters or cookers, holding 4 or 5 tons, where it is cooked with live steam for several hours. It is then pressed in the tank under live steam, grease and water being drawn off to a settling tank where the grease is recovered. The tank or digester is then closed tightly and the residue dried further under a partial vacuum by admitting steam to the jacket. After drying, a door near the bottom of the digester is opened, and the dried material is discharged on a conveyor. The dried material or tankage is then separated, screened, and ground for the market. Some grease is recovered by skimming the liquid drained from the digester, but it is understood that a part of it remains in the residual tankage.

At present (1926), following operations at Toledo, Ohio, a so-called "Pan-American" process plant is being installed at Kansas City, Mo. This process involves a separation of foreign materials, such as metals and glass, from the garbage, with a drying operation. The dried material is then prepared for sale as a stock food.

Except as just stated, developments in garbage reduction plants have been chiefly in better equipment and machinery. Experience gained in operation with dryers, digesters, piping, and other apparatus has resulted in better and more durable design and construction. Materials better able to withstand the corrosive action of the hot liquids and gases are used. Thus, improvements have come in design and construction, rather than in the invention of new processes.

Incineration

Incineration of garbage in the United States was first practiced in 1885 when a plant to burn garbage with coal was designed by Lieut. H. J. Reilly, U. S. A., for the Federal Government, and built on Governors Island, New York. Designs by Engle, Dixon, Decarie, Lewis, Morse, and others, for burning chiefly garbage with an additional fuel followed, and plants were built by several cities. In the meantime, in England and on the Continent, many incinerators or so-called destructors were built for burning a mixture of garbage, ashes, and rubbish, and this was burned generally without additional fuel.

In 1908, J. T. Fetherston, M. Am. Soc. C. E., introduced mixed refuse incineration into America and built plants on Staten Island. Other plants of this type were built in Seattle, Wash., Milwaukee, Wis., Paterson, N. J., Memphis, Tenn., Atlanta and Savannah, Ga., and elsewhere, generally prior to 1915. In these plants a mixture of garbage, ashes, and rubbish was burned under boilers, and some power was developed. Such works were generally situated nearer the centers of the cities than was the case with reduction plants, as the odor hazard was less.

Recently, there has been an adaptation of incinerators of this type to the burning of garbage and rubbish only. Experience indicated that ashes added more to the cost of incineration than was justified by their fuel value, and, as they could be dumped satisfactorily, it was more expedient in many cases not to burn them. Adjustments in the design included a wider drying hearth, deeper grates, the use of occasional small quantities of additional fuel, and proper flue areas. Such furnaces operate generally with a forced draft of pre-heated air. Incinerators for this service have been built in New York, Brooklyn, N. Y., Philadelphia, Pa., Asheville, N. C., Muskegon, Mich., Charleston, W. Va., and elsewhere.

Perhaps the chief addition to English experience contributed by American designers has been the development of mechanical charging devices and ash-removal apparatus. Many plants are equipped with charging hoppers that are controlled by sliding doors operated by hydraulic pistons and worked by the fireman. The hoppers are filled from above by grab-buckets or by hand from storage hoppers. This arrangement permits 24-hour operation and the use of refuse of such quantity and quality as to maintain the best rate of combustion. A few plants have mechanical clinkering or ash-removal, but, with the omission of ashes from the mixture burned, there has been less need for this device.

Meanwhile, designs have been developed from the older garbage furnaces for burning rubbish with the garbage with a reduced quantity of additional fuel. Such furnaces are of larger internal capacity than the destructor type, and much of the material is discharged directly into them from the collection wagons. Such plants have been built in many Southern cities and in smaller and medium-sized cities of the North. Table 4 contains data indicating the furnace capacities of various types.

TABLE 4.—DATA ON INCINERATOR FURNACES.

(Approximate capacity, 100 tons.)

Type of plant.	Area, in Square Feet.		Inside volume of furnace, in cubic feet.	Combustion chamber volume, in cubic feet.	Outside storage hopper, in cubic yards.
	Burning grate.	Drying hearth.			
A............	433	192	4 000	1 410	0
B............	120	360	3 992	......	0
C............	100	62	976	1 006	290
D............	120	80	1 110	924	152
E............	181	142	2 296	1 464	150
F............	120	....	1 280	2 110	218

Incinerators are still generally purchased by municipalities under general specifications requiring the fulfillment of stated guaranties covering capacities, temperatures of combustion, and operating costs. This practice opens the bidding to a variety of designers, and the selection of a contractor may be decided by a comparison of the total annual costs and the likelihood of satisfactory operation, as judged by records of routine service elsewhere. There is, at present, a tendency toward more detailed specifications and general plans.

Other Methods of Disposal

Perhaps feeding to hogs has changed from early practice more than any other method, although a wide range in operating still prevails. Hogs used to be allowed to roam over dumps (in Louisville as late as 1917) and even streets searching for garbage. Now, better house treatment is practiced, and cleaner, fresher material is hauled to the hogs at one or more farms. It is spread on concrete platforms, and the unconsumed parts and hog manure are gathered and disposed of generally by burial. Shelters and running yards are provided, and the animals are inoculated against cholera, which items have much improved this method of disposal.

Dumps continue to be a chief method for disposing of street sweepings, ashes, trade refuse, some rubbish, and some garbage, and great areas of low and submerged lands near cities have been reclaimed. Parts of Chicago, Boston, and other cities have been converted from low marsh land to drainable upland by filling with refuse. In Seattle, Portland, Ore., and other Pacific Coast cities, garbage has been dumped successfully with a proper cover of street sweepings, waste building materials, and other relatively inert substances. In the smaller cities some garbage is buried. Dumps are better regulated, with less miscellaneous scavenging, better control of fires, and more cover with inert materials. The use of other methods of garbage disposal has influenced the making of better dumps.

Odor Control

The growth of cities and the increased quantity of refuse has emphasized the dangers and discomforts caused by atmospheric pollution. Not only have odors been produced by the special methods of garbage disposal developed, but those from dumps and hog farms have become a nuisance to more people, and hence have demanded attention. Probably no other branch of sanitary engineering causes such frequent recourse to the Courts for the abatement of nuisance. Consequently, measures for odor control and elimination are a mark of progress in this field. Some of the steps which have been taken in America are:

a.—The separation of garbage from other refuse to be disposed of on dumps, so that dumps are more sanitary.

b.—The separation of rubbish from other refuse to prevent fires, smoke, and odors from dumps.

c.—The use of water-tight collection wagons, washed and painted more frequently.

d.—The careful covering of organic matter on dumps with soil or other relatively inert material.

e.—The use of concrete feeding platforms at hog farms, and the better disposal of residues.

f.—Not only the use of incinerators, but improved design and construction, including better facilities for receiving and handling refuse at the plant, and more ample combustion chambers.

g.—Chlorination, scrubbing, and other improved methods of treating dryer and digester gases from reduction plants.

h.—Better floors and buildings, and an appreciation of the advantages of general plant cleanliness.

i.—Careful selection of disposal plant locations, with reference to the cost of delivering refuse and the character of plant.

Summary

The cleansing of cities, including street cleaning and the collection and disposal of refuse, has thus progressed during the past 150 years with their growth and the development of sanitary science. During the first half of the period, there were few large cities, and the problem was not acute. Following the middle of the Nineteenth Century, cities enlarged rapidly and required cleansing. A full realization of the dangers of incomplete city cleansing, with means for its better accomplishment, did not appear, however, until after the Centennial year. Since that time the dangers and discomforts to the public from filth and dirt have been recognized, and sanitary engineering has made use of available appliances and has developed methods for the cleaning of streets, the collection of refuse, and its final disposal. The operation of these appliances and methods has called for skilled management and the employment and organization by public officials of a considerable number of men. Consequently, the efficiency with which appliances have been used and the excellence of the work done has depended very largely on the quality of the public administration. The cleansing of cities is thus interwoven so clearly with their management that efficiency of operation and progress in the future will depend in large measure on the character and training of municipal governments.

HISTORICAL NOTES ON LAND DRAINAGE IN THE UNITED STATES

By S. H. McCrory,* M. Am. Soc. C. E.

Land drainage in the past 150 years has had an important part in the development of American agriculture and in the improvement of the public health. Complete statistics of drainage have not been compiled, but 50 000 000 acres added to the cultivable land area in the United States and an equal amount made more productive and profitable doubtless would be a conservative estimate of the benefit to agriculture. The benefits to health would be exceedingly difficult to measure, but it is known from early records that malaria was generally prevalent in Illinois, Indiana, Michigan, and Ohio, where drainage is most complete, and that it is much less common in those States to-day. The experience in the South, also, has been that after drainage the extent and seriousness of malaria have generally diminished.

Early Drainage in America

Drainage of farm lands undoubtedly began in each of the Colonies soon after the first settlement was made. Early practices followed those in use in England at that time. Open ditches probably were most used, but blind drains made by digging a trench and filling the lower part with poles, brush, or stones, were used to some extent. In 1767, Elkington, of England, discovered his method of intercepting drainage; this was described in a treatise by John Johnston in 1797, and laid the foundation for modern under-drainage. It was reprinted in England several times, and in 1838 was first published in the United States at Petersburg, Va.† In 1804, drain tile was laid in England; perhaps James Graham was the first user, and tile laid by him were still giving good service in 1887. Deep, or "thorough", drainage was introduced in England by James Smith, of Devonston, Sterlingshire, Scotland; his views came under general notice about 1832, and had great influence on drainage work in England.

In America, under-drainage started in 1835 when John Johnston, of Seneca County, New York, brought over from Scotland patterns from which clay tiles were moulded by hand and laid on his farm near Geneva. By 1838, hand-made tiles were manufactured at Waterford, N. Y., and sold for $24 per 1 000 pieces. In 1851, Mr. Johnston reported that he had laid 16 miles of tile drains on his farm; and in the meantime a number of other farmers, chiefly in New York State, had followed his example and reported success. Among these American pioneers in the art of draining was John Delafield, a neighbor of Johnston's, who in 1848 imported what was believed to be the first tile-making machine used in America. This operated on the same principle as

* Chf., Div. of Agricultural Eng., Bureau of Public Roads, U. S. Dept. of Agriculture, Washington, D. C.

† Supplement to the *Farmers' Register*.

the modern machines for making clay tile, and the work it could do has been described,* as follows:

"This improved tile machine produces drain tiles in the form of a horseshoe, rising 2½ and 4 inches; it makes pipes also for draining, from 1 inch bore up to 6 inches diameter, each size varying about half an inch. Soles or flat tiles are made on which to lay the tiles when desired. Semi-cylinders are made of 8 and 11 inches diameter. It also produces with equal readiness, pan tiles for roofing and ridge tiles."

The horseshoe-shaped tiles, 12 to 15 in. long and usually laid on the flat sole tiles, were the common kind in the beginning. The cylindrical tiles do not seem to have come much into use for drainage until about 1858.

The principles underlying successful under-drainage apparently were well understood by Johnston and his contemporary progressive farmers, for one finds, in the discussions and papers of that day, the current arguments advanced for under-drainage, such as soil aeration and warming, improvement of soil texture, and removal of injurious salts. Moreover, stress is laid on the necessity for "thorough" drainage, as contrasted with shallow drainage. As early as 1848 John Delafield stressed the value of drainage for much land that was already sufficiently dry to be producing cultivated crops.

Development of Tile Drainage

Stone and pole drains were still much in vogue after the middle of the Nineteenth Century, but perhaps no one since has better stated the present view as to the superiority of tile over these materials than did Henry D. French when he said:† "No system of drainage can be made sufficiently cheap and efficient for general adoption, with other materials than drain-tiles."

Modern drainage began in the United States when Johnston laid the first tile drains, in 1835. The Ohio and Mississippi Valleys were then just being settled. Much of this land, although very fertile, could not be cultivated until it was drained and malaria was prevalent throughout large sections. Following the importation of the first tile-making machine, in 1848, the use of tile for drainage spread rapidly. In 1853, Samuel Lillie, of Allen County, made the first tile in Indiana, and, in 1859, James Stewart started the first horse-power tile factory in that State. The number of tile factories established in the United States were as follows: from 1850 to 1859 inclusive, 66; from 1860 to 1869, 234; and from 1870 to 1879, 840.

On January 1, 1880, there were 1 140 factories in operation, as follows: Indiana, 486; Illinois, 320; Ohio, 230; Michigan, 63; Iowa, 18; Wisconsin, 13; New York, 8; and Pennsylvania, 2. Thus, at that date, the center of tile manufacture had already moved from the East to the Middle West. To May 1, 1882, there had been laid in Indiana, 9 798 256 rods (30 619.55 miles) of tile, with one county not included in the statistics.

The sizes manufactured increased steadily, and in the early Eighties some plants were able to make 24-in. tile. Machines for manufacturing concrete tile were placed on the market in the Eighties, and the use of this material

* *Transactions,* New York State Agricultural Soc., 1848.

† In his book "Farm Drainage," 1859.

increased gradually, especially for tile 18 in. in diameter or larger. The sizes used in farm drainage have increased gradually; very little tile smaller than 4 in. is now (1926) used, and in large sections of the Middle West, 5-in. tile is considered the minimum size. In Iowa and Minnesota, 36-in. tile outlet drains are now common and drains from 42 to 54 in. in diameter are constructed occasionally.

The hand tools used in constructing drains underwent much improvement during the period from 1840 to 1880. About 1873, Manley Miles invented a drain scoop which could be either pushed or pulled, and made grading the trench much more rapid and easy than it had been. The skeleton spade was also invented during this period.

As the sizes of tiles and the depth of drains increased, there came a demand for a machine that would dig trenches. Among the early types were the Blickenderfer ditching machine, the Hickok, the Rennie elevator ditcher (patented in 1869), and the Johnson tile ditcher, all operated by horses. In 1880, seven kinds of ditching machines were reported* in use, or as having been tested, but with unsatisfactory results. In 1883, the Plumb ditching machine was demonstrated. It was the first one operated by steam, and seems to have been fairly successful. Soon after this several other steam-operated machines came on the market, and from these the modern trenching machines were developed.

The problem of computing the carrying capacity of drain tile received serious consideration by the early drainage engineers. Poncelet's formulas were generally used. In 1916 and 1917, Yarnell conducted extensive experiments and developed formulas for the flow in drain tile.

Investigations of the run-off from drained areas and the relation of depth and spacing of tile to drainage, have been or are in progress in Alabama, Iowa, Illinois, North Carolina, and Minnesota. The problem is intricate and much additional work will be necessary before reaching a full understanding of the laws that control the movements of water to drains.

Construction of Open Ditches

It early became apparent that, if under-drains were to be successful, large outlet drains must be provided. These were mostly open ditches, constructed either by hand, or with teams and scrapers. Usually they were not more than 5 ft. deep, the bottom width only occasionally exceeding 4 ft. In Ohio, Indiana, and Michigan, and in the Upper Mississippi Valley States, the construction of such outlet drains increased rapidly as the States were settled. In January, 1884, the Drainage Committee of the Ohio Society of Engineers and Surveyors reported that, in Ohio, 20 000 miles of county and township ditches had been constructed, benefiting 11 000 000 acres of land. The report placed much emphasis on the benefit these drains had been to the health of the State. Most of these ditches were found to be too small, however, for providing the degree of drainage that was desired. There was need for an economical means of constructing large open ditches.

* *The Drainage Journal*, 1880.

In 1882 the Mason and Tazewell Special Drainage District was organized in Mason and Tazewell Counties, Illinois. The drainage plan of this district comprised a main ditch 14½ miles long, 10 ft. deep, varying in top width from 30 to 60 ft., with side slopes of 1 to 1; approximately 37 miles of lateral ditches, 10 feet deep; and 30 miles of spade and scraper ditches. About 7 miles of laterals were added later. Construction was started in 1883 and completed in 1886. The cost of the improvement was approximately $300 000. On this work five dipper dredges were used by the contractor, W. A. McGillis and Company. The dredges were constructed by the Bucyrus Foundry and Machinery Company, of Bucyrus, Ohio, and probably were patterned after dredges used in digging navigation canals. This was the first drainage district on which dredges were used, and the main ditch when constructed was the longest in the United States. Mr. Herbert Hamilton, of Petersburg, Ill., was the Engineer for the District. The *Engineering News,* in commenting on the work, stated: "This was the first work done with a dredge, and has been so satisfactory that it may be said to have worked a revolution in such matters."

Since this work was done the development of dredges has been rapid. The vertical spud was replaced by the bank spud, which permitted the use of a narrower hull, thus enabling the machine to dig smaller ditches. On the other hand, the design of larger and larger ditches led to the design of larger dredges, until at present (1926) floating dredges range in size from the small ½-yd. machine, with a 25- or 30-ft. boom, to the 5-yd. machine with a 100- to 125-ft. boom. The success of floating dredges led to the development of the dry-land dipper excavator for use where sufficient water was not obtainable for the floating type.

Soon after the first dipper-dredges were put in operation, dredges equipped with grab-buckets were used, their principal advantage being that they could be equipped with a longer boom. Machines of this type have been highly developed in California, where they are used for ditches and levees in peat lands.

In 1903 Page and Schnable built the first drag-scraper excavator, and this was used on the Hennepin Canal. It was first used on ditches in 1906, and was originally considered a dry-land excavator, but it has gradually supplanted the floating dipper-dredge for constructing drainage ditches. It is built in a wide variety of sizes, and various methods are used for moving it. The great advantage of the drag-line excavator over other types is its flexibility. There are well-defined limits to the size of ditches that can be constructed by floating dipper-dredges of a given size, but such limits do not apply so closely to the drag-line. It has the added advantage that on large ditches it is possible to provide a wider and cleaner berm than is possible with dipper excavators. Experience has shown that the securing of an ample berm is of much importance when large deep ditches are to be dug.

The early dredges were operated by steam engines fired with either wood or coal. Internal combustion engines began to be used on drag-line excavators soon after their introduction. Electric current, where readily available, now affords a convenient source of power.

Pumping for Drainage

The use of low-lift pumps to drain lands was early practiced along the coast. Drainage wheels were first used, and were operated probably by animal power or by windmills. About 1850 centrifugal pumps began to be used. In the late Sixties the Ivens pump was invented, and special designs for low-lift pumping were developed and used extensively. In 1880 the Menge pump was introduced. It could be easily and cheaply erected, and was used widely for drainage pumping.

As projects became larger, and centrifugal pumps were improved in efficiency, they gradually supplanted other types. Recently, screw pumps, giving still higher efficiency on low lifts, have been introduced. About 1900 drainage by pumping began to be practiced along the Upper Mississippi and Illinois Rivers. At present (1926), practically all the bottom-land along the Illinois River has been reclaimed in this way.

Drainage of Irrigated Land

Soon after irrigation was started in the West, some of the land began to be damaged by seepage and the accumulation of alkalies. As early as 1884, Mr. George C. Roeding, a nurseryman of Fresno, Calif., began drainage experiments to relieve this condition. He laid tile drains in 1893 which were said to be still working in 1909. As this trouble was becoming widespread, the Bureau of Soils, U. S. Department of Agriculture, built several experimental drainage systems in 1902. These experimental systems followed Eastern drainage practices as to depth and opening, but were not as effective as had been expected. In 1902 the position of Drainage Expert was created in the U. S. Department of Agriculture, and the late C. G. Elliott, M. Am. Soc. C. E., a prominent drainage engineer, was appointed. He gave much attention to the drainage of irrigated lands; and a small group of engineers was assembled to work on this problem It was found that shallow drains were ineffective, but that a deep drain, properly located, frequently would drain an entire field. From the work thus started has developed a method of drainage which has reclaimed or protected much irrigated land.

Lands containing calcium carbonate—commonly, called black alkali—have always been exceedingly difficult to reclaim by drainage. Chemists as well as engineers have devoted considerable study to this problem, but it has not yet been solved. Seepage and the accumulation of alkalies must be prevented if irrigation agriculture is to be made permanent. The engineers of the United States have developed and perfected methods of draining irrigated land to a greater extent than ever before.

Drainage District Laws

Even in small drainage undertakings several land owners frequently are interested, and it is often difficult to secure voluntary co-operation. When many land owners are concerned, it is practically impossible to secure unanimous action. This difficulty brought about the passage of laws which provide means of constructing necessary drains and forcing all land owners to pay their just share of the cost.

Almost every State now has a general law which permits the organization of drainage districts, provides the necessary means of securing co-operation among a number of land owners to construct the improvement, and specifies the manner of distributing the costs among the affected lands and of securing the privileges of long-time payments. These laws are based on early English laws for drainage and sewerage, which provide that a citizen shall consent to pay his proportional part of the cost of a public, local improvement in the same way that he consents to share in other expenses of government. The authority to enact such laws is exercised by the State Legislatures, and is subject to the limitations placed on legislation by State and Federal Constitutions. The history of drainage legislation in each State is a story of repeated attempts to enact laws which should conform to these constitutional requirements, and meet the changing needs of the owners of wet or overflowed lands.

The first drainage law in the United States of which there is authentic record was enacted by the Colony of New Jersey, on September 26, 1772, and it was re-enacted by the State when it adopted its Constitution, on July 2, 1776. This was an act drawn for the purpose of clearing obstructions in the free course of the waters of the Passaic River, near Little Falls.

The act provided for co-operation among a number of land owners to secure field protection, for a division of the costs, and for a method of collecting the costs; it established the public interest in such work by reason of the improvement of the public highways. It did not, however, provide for the inclusion and assessment of a minority of land owners who did not desire to co-operate in the project, nor did it provide for spreading the payments over a period of years.

One of the earliest general drainage acts was passed on April 9, 1804, in New York State. This act was declared unconstitutional, on the ground that it provided for the taking of private property for a private, rather than a public, use.

Another early general drainage law is found in the Revised Statutes of Massachusetts, 1836, Chapter 115. This act provided for the improvement of low lands by removing obstructions from streams and by ditching. It provided for a petition to be signed by a majority of land owners setting forth the proposed improvement, for notice to land owners who did not sign the petition; for a judicial hearing, for a board of commissioners to be appointed by the Court to construct the improvements, for an assessment of the expenses to be made on all proprietors according to the benefit each should receive from it, for damages to be paid to injured parties, and for appeals to high Courts. Thus, it is clear that this law was a marked advance over earlier ones in that it provided for the forced participation of non-petitioning land owners and for legal safeguards to prevent abuses of this power.

Under the earlier drainage acts the work to be done was small, and in many cases was performed by the land owners themselves, but, as the projects grew in size, and expensive machinery was required for economical construction, it was necessary to engage contractors, and these contractors had to be paid on the completion of the work. As it was impossible for the land owners to raise the large sums thus required, drainage development, for a time, awaited legislation which would allow adequate and proper financing. In 1879, Illinois passed its Levee and Farm Drainage Acts, which permitted the district to issue bonds to be sold for cash to pay for the construction. These bonds were first liens on all assessed lands within the district, and arrangements were made whereby the land owners had a long time in which to pay the costs assessed against them and thus redeem the bonds.

Except for minor improvements and adjustments further to protect the interests of the bond buyers, this was the final step in the development of general drainage laws as now known. In almost every State laws have been developed, and approved by the Courts, by which drainage and flood protection districts can be established and financed under the supervision of the Courts, having the following characteristics:

1.—By law they are made a continuing form of corporation, and act through a board of officers.

2.—They can borrow money and issue bonds in the name of the district.

3.—They are financially responsible, and may sue and be sued in the district's name.

4.—They possess machinery for making an equitable distribution of costs in proportion to benefits conferred.

5.—They are authorized to levy taxes against each piece of land, to the extent of benefits conferred, and to use State machinery for collecting such taxes.

6.—They have the power of eminent domain, which gives them the right to condemn property needed for carrying out the purposes of the district.

7.—They possess the power to construct such improvements as are necessary to accomplish the reclamation of the lands in the district.

8.—They may hold and convey property.

Extent and Cost of Drainage

Statistics as to the growth of drainage by private individuals, firms, or corporations, have not been collected, but, in 1920, the Fourteenth Decennial Census gathered data as to the status of drainage on farms. These figures show that about 53 000 000 acres were drained by ditches or tile. This is equivalent to 10.5% of the improved lands in farms. Illinois has drained more than 8 000 000; Iowa and Ohio more than 7 000 000 acres. Farm lands still needing drainage were reported as 39 000 000 acres.

During the Census of 1920 statistics concerning land drained by drainage districts were also collected. In 1920, the area benefited and assessed for the cost of the drainage thus provided was more than 65 500 000 acres. These figures do not include statistics for levee districts which had not constructed drains. In addition, 3 900 000 acres were in organized drainage districts which had not begun construction. The area is probably not less than 75 000 000 acres in 1926, estimating conservatively from nearly complete data secured in 1923. There has been much overlapping of enterprises, particularly in Ohio, Michigan, and Indiana, chiefly because in some States the enlargement or clearing of an old drain required the establishment of a new drainage district.

According to the Census, the drainage works of the districts completed or under construction prior to 1920 comprised 111 770 miles of open ditch, 45 174 miles of tile drains, and 4 330 miles of levees, or a total of 161 274 miles. All but 7 974 miles had been completed on the Census date. The cost of this drainage cannot be determined accurately as records of the early work are incomplete in States where the most has been done by allotment to the land owner instead of by contract. The Census shows $183 000 as the cost of all enterprises prior to 1860; $10 000 000 to 1880; $60 800 000 to 1900; and $434 600 000 to 1920, including the cost of the completion of work under construction. The cost of drainage done by farmers is difficult to estimate. From fragmentary data available it is conservatively estimated that at least $600 000 000 has been spent for such improvements, and, if more complete information were available, it is possible that the figure might reach $1 000 000 000. Drainage work by districts and individuals had cost, to 1920, from $1 150 000 000 to $1 500 000 000.

What have these works accomplished? First, they have generally greatly improved the health of the communities in which they were constructed; second, they have made available to the farmers about 65 000 000 acres of the best land in the United States—land that, in its original condition, could not be cultivated profitably; third, they have increased yields, and made crops more certain on the lands drained; fourth, they have reduced the losses of crops due to floods and inadequate drainage; and, fifth, they have removed surplus water and thus made easier the construction and maintenance of roads and railroads.

Future Developments in Drainage

In the future benefits accruing to agriculture and health will cause much land to be underdrained that at present is not thought to need it. Within the next two decades the Middle, South Atlantic, and Gulf States will be practicing under-drainage on the same scale as that now followed in Iowa, Illinois, and Indiana.

As the density of population increases and more intensive farming is practiced, much land now drained will need more thorough drainage. This will require deeper and larger outlet ditches, with flatter side slopes than has been customary in the past; and detention reservoirs, to prevent damage by floods, will become practicable in many places where they are not now economically feasible.

Excavators capable of digging, without rehandling, ditches with a cross-sectional area of 6 000 sq. ft. and upward, to any desired section, with berms of any width desired, and capable of distributing the excavated material in such manner that the weight will not be unduly concentrated, will be developed.

Tidal marshes will be reclaimed. This will involve construction of embankments and pumping plants of a magnitude not yet attempted, particularly along the Gulf Coast, where, in addition to securing drainage, it will be necessary to provide protection from storm tides caused by tropical hurricanes.

The size of drainage districts will increase, and eventually districts will be organized co-extensive with the water-sheds on streams, such as the Saginaw in Michigan, or the Yazoo in Mississippi, with permanent staffs who will handle all problems involving water, such as drainage, flood control, water power, navigation, and control of erosion.

Drainage laws will be further simplified and made more effective. Simpler and less costly methods of organizing small districts will be developed. It is to be hoped that the administration of districts will eventually be entirely removed from the judiciary and assigned to men qualified by training and experience for such work.

HISTORICAL REVIEW OF DEVELOPMENT OF CONTROL OF DISEASE-BEARING MOSQUITOES

By J. A. LePrince,* Esq.

Disease-bearing mosquitoes have played an important part in the early settlement and development of all countries in the temperate and tropical zones of the Western Hemisphere. The second expedition of Columbus was nearly wrecked by them at Santo Domingo, and, later, Prescott wrote of mosquito-borne disease as follows: "The moment a town is founded, or a commercial center created, it is certain to cause the explosion of the latent malignity of poison in the air." In early days the Colonies suffered severely from both yellow fever and malaria. Quinine was scarce and costly, and other remedies used for malaria had little value.

Mosquito-Borne Disease a Menace of Importance

One is apt to consider yellow fever as a semi-tropical, or tropical, sea coast disease, but it has not always been so. It was intermittently present in the Southern States from Colonial days to 1905, and not entirely absent in the Northern States. In eight States north of Virginia, from 1693 to 1870, eighty yellow fever outbreaks are recorded.

In the records of New York, N. Y., yellow fever appeared during seventeen summers, and at Philadelphia, Pa., during fifteen summers. Reports show 2 086 deaths from yellow fever in New York in 1798, and 3 506 in Philadelphia in the same season. In the Philadelphia epidemic of 1793, in a population of about 40 000, more than 4 000 deaths were recorded, and reporting was not as complete then as it is to-day. Longfellow's "Evangeline" contains a description of one of these Philadelphia outbreaks.

The Colonists were painfully aware that malaria played a decidedly important part in retarding development. Jamestown, Va., was situated on low land close to a large wet depression. No attempt was made at drainage, and it is easy, to-day, to understand why this Colony was a failure. It is recorded that the original colony at Charleston, S. C., was first situated on the mainland near swampy areas like those around Jamestown, and two years later, due to sickness among the colonists, was moved to its present location, at the end of a peninsula, where health conditions were more satisfactory. In the early days at Savannah, Ga., malignant malaria fever was common, and the situation became so serious that the town authorities passed a law to forbid the maintenance of "wet culture," as rice was then called, and reimbursed land owners for loss of potential crops. This was probably the first serious early attempt at malaria reduction by an American city.

Following the Declaration of Independence, with the settling of new territory westward from the Atlantic Coastal Plain, malaria prevalence was common, even as far north as New England, Illinois, and Michigan. In fact, it

* Senior San. Engr., U. S. Public Health Service, Memphis, Tenn.

was widely distributed in the Northern States as late as the Eighties, and then began to decrease with the extension of intensive farm drainage, improved living conditions, the reduction in the cost of quinine and its more general use, and the provision of metallic screens for the protecton of homes.

During the Civil War one-fourth of all hospital admissions were due to malaria fever, and in military camps in the Southern States in the Spanish-American War period so many soldiers were infected by malaria before leaving for Cuba that only a small part of some regiments was fit for service.

The First Mosquito Campaign

During the Nineteenth Century the number of deaths from malaria among the native population of Havana, Cuba, in some years was greater than that of the total deaths caused by yellow fever. The first effective campaign against mosquito-borne disease was begun by Americans at Havana in 1901. At that time yellow fever had become so prevalent in that city as to affect seriously the military occupation of the Island. The cause of the transmission of the disease was then discovered; the mosquito that conveyed it was reduced below the danger point, and yellow fever was eliminated.

During the first yellow fever battle the campaigners felt so certain of the final outcome that they instituted an anti-malaria campaign, and reduced malaria prevalence about 80% before the first period of American occupation terminated. A few years later, due to the absence of yellow fever and the rarity of malaria, the city became a tourist resort, although previous to anti-mosquito measures, it was known as the cradle of yellow fever and malaria.

It is of interest to know that, during this historic campaign, an American sanitary engineer kept a chart, in connection with yellow fever control measures, and estimated the date when yellow fever would be eradicated. As he happened to be directing the field control measures, he became too enthusiastic over obtaining results, and yellow fever was eradicated 60 days earlier than his first estimate. His friends having told him that an engineer's estimate should be more accurate, he replied that it would be made so as soon as they could show him how to determine the existence and location of walking cases of yellow fever.

Although it was thus definitely proved in 1901 that both yellow fever and malaria could be eliminated at a reasonable cost, no serious and thorough effort was made to control disease-bearing mosquitoes in the United States until the outbreak of yellow fever in New Orleans, La., in 1905 and then only in that city until yellow fever had been eliminated.

The Panama Canal Zone was occupied by Americans in 1904; yellow fever was eliminated by 1905, and an extensive anti-malaria campaign was initiated and has since been continued.

English Suggestions and American Inventions

The mode of transmission of malaria was discovered by Sir Ronald Ross, who, during his visit to Panama in 1905, stated:

"What is most necessary for *Anopheles* control is for us to find a cheap powder to act as a larvacide that we can toss to the right or left, and also we should devise a trap we can bait to catch disease-bearing mosquitoes."

These two suggestions were developed later by American sanitarians. One of the most prolific sources of malaria mosquitoes known is on the Potomac River, and is now being treated by the application of dust clouds of Paris green from airplanes; and the mosquito trap has been perfected so that one trap, less than 2 cu. ft. in volume, has caught more than 1 100 malaria mosquitoes in a single night. The inventor used for bait the odor of the canal construction laborers whom these mosquitoes desired to bite.

The Public and a New Idea

It is surprising that no attempt was made to control disease-bearing mosquitoes in the United States until 1913, when malaria surveys were first made in Virginia and North Carolina by Dr. H. R. Carter, of the United States Public Health Service, on his return from Panama. Dr. Carter was a graduate civil engineer as well as a physician of international reputation, and, because of his education and experience as a public health officer in the control of yellow fever and malaria, was peculiarly fitted to define the malaria problem of the United States and outline a program for its solution. At that time it was estimated that the annual economic loss caused by malaria alone in this country was $100 000 000. The ravages of yellow fever in Southern ports had also caused many deaths, much suffering, and enormous financial losses. Even as late as 1922, when a dengue epidemic swept over the country from Florida to Texas, its rapid rate of travel indicated clearly the extensive prevalence of the yellow fever mosquito in towns and villages. This mosquito spreads both yellow fever and dengue, and breeds only in man-made water containers in or near occupied homes.

Malaria Control in Military Camps

In 1914, a Federal appropriation of $16 000 was made for malaria studies and investigations by the U. S. Public Health Service, and in conducting these investigational studies 22 surveys and 3 malaria control demonstrations were made in 7 States during that year. This appropriation and the investigational study were continued until the United States entered the World War, when the small personnel employed were assigned to control measures connected with war activities. At that time zones of health protection were established at all cantonment towns and in areas a mile wide surrounding each military cantonment and near-by town in all sections where malaria was prevalent.

If the same malaria sick rate and death rate that took place in Southern military camps during the Spanish-American War had prevailed during the World War, there would probably have been a loss of 5 000 men by deaths from malaria. By rapid training of engineers in malaria-control measures, and quick, hard work, the total deaths from malaria in Southern military camps throughout the war was held down to 36. This enormous reduction is worthy of consideration, yet more important is the fact that enlisted men were not sent to France saturated with malaria to unfit for duty a large part of the military forces, as was the case in the Spanish-American War before the method of malaria transmission and control measures were known. During the World War, 193 men were constantly incapacitated by malaria, but with the same rate as obtained in the Civil and Spanish-American Wars, 38 000 would have been incapacitated each day of the war from April, 1917, to December, 1919.

At the termination of the World War, the U. S. Public Health Service co-operated with the International Health Board and the State Health Departments of Southern States, and succeeded in starting malaria-control activities in fourteen of such States. As soon as the State Health Departments were able to supervise their local control projects, Federal supervision was withdrawn, and, to-day, the State Health Departments are assisting counties and communities in mosquito-control activities.

Previous to 1914 probably less than six communities had undertaken malaria-control measures, and the results of such limited effort were unsatisfactory. Up to that time, not a single State health department was taking any action toward malaria elimination, although in many counties malaria was the most important health problem. No State or county had made any appropriation for malaria reduction. In 1916, the physicians of one State alone reported to the State Health Department 158 779 cases of malaria.

Public Demand for Mosquito Elimination

As an illustration of the change in the public attitude toward malaria control and mosquito elimination that has taken place since 1914, the U. S. Public Health Service has co-operated with State Health Departments in malaria-control measures in 343 communities in 216 counties in 17 States, and in activities connected with mosquito surveys, control measures, and investigations, in 667 communities in 376 counties in 24 States.

In addition, many communities have undertaken control measures that are not included in the recorded data, and the State Health Departments of Alabama, Georgia, and Texas, report that they are now overwhelmed with requests for advisory supervision from communities desiring to undertake mosquito-control activities.

It was the writer's good fortune to be present when the campaign against disease-bearing mosquitoes in the Western Hemisphere was inaugurated at Havana, Cuba, in 1901, to take part in the sanitation of that city, and then go with General Gorgas and Dr. Carter to the Canal Zone, where the fight against disease-bearing mosquitoes was inaugurated under even greater difficulties, but with equal success. In 1914, the writer returned to the United States, and since that time has followed the trail of the *Anopheles* all over the South.

As soon as the way was found, it was comparatively easy to control *Stegomyia* mosquitoes and eradicate yellow fever. The control of *Anopheles* and malaria is a much more complicated matter, but it can be done. Yellow fever has not been of any sanitary importance to any city in the United States since 1905, and within that time malaria has been greatly reduced. Who can say what the next 25 years will bring forth! Every indication points to a continued reduction in malaria throughout the United States at an equal or possibly even more rapid rate than has been attained in the past 25 years. Should this prove true, it needs no prophet to foretell the outcome.

CHANGING CONCEPTIONS OF VENTILATION SINCE THE EIGHTEENTH CENTURY

By George Truman Palmer, Esq.*

The history of ventilation is a chronicle of the effort to analyze accurately the causes of a harmful effect. The effect has been human discomfort, lowered efficiency, and, not infrequently, injury to health.

In general terms, the cause has been bad ventilation. For years, however, there has been difficulty in picking out the specific features that make for badness, and this has handicapped the engineer in designing proper corrective measures.

At the birth of the American Republic there was a consciousness that the air of an enclosure occupied by human beings had some real though intangible relation to health. It was the growing concentration of population, however, which really brought ventilation to the fore. Increasing numbers of children in school, the substitution of the factory system for isolated home manufacturing, the advent of many-storied dwellings and office buildings, the construction of commodious theatres and other meeting places, all these conditions have accentuated the necessity of lessening the discomfort inevitable from indoor crowding.

Vast changes have taken place, both in understanding the basic principles of ventilation and in methods of adapting indoor air to healthful uses.

A century and a half ago it took the most persuasive arguments of Benjamin Franklin to secure the opening of a sleeping-room window when he and John Adams had occasion to be bedfellows in an hostelry in New Brunswick, N. J. To-day, the open bedroom window is general practice.

The grate and the stove warmed habitations prior to 1800. To-day, a steam pipe serves this purpose, even if one's office may be on the fiftieth floor of a skyscraper.

In 1834 ventilation of the British House of Parliament was served by a tower on the roof, 110 ft. high, with a fire at the base for the purpose of creating a draft; and this pulled air into the room through thousands of small holes in the floor.

To-day, not only public buildings, but factories, theatres, eating places, and other inclosures are served by smoothly running direct-connected, electrically-driven, multi-vane blowers controlled by an insignificant looking switch.

The Unfolding of Ventilation Principles

Ventilation has had a more difficult course to pursue than bridge building. In addition to the laws of gravity, stresses, and strains, ventilation has had to satisfy the shifting theories of the hygienist and, worst of all, the discordant demands of human comfort.

* Director, Div. of Research, American Child Health Assoc., formerly Chf. of Investigating Staff, New York State Comm. on Ventilation, New York, N. Y.

Several things happen to the air in a crowded room: The temperature rises; humidity increases; oxygen diminishes; carbon dioxide increases; volatile organic matter and unpleasant odors are added; more dust is afloat and, largely in consequence, more floating bacteria can be detected.

Are all these changes identified with discomfort? If not, which are important and which are not? The job of the ventilating engineer is to restore comfort. Against what shall he direct his attack? It has taken a century and a half to tag these elements, and even to-day it can hardly be said that complete satisfaction has been attained.

The study of these ventilation factors began in the chemical laboratory. Prior to 1880, three main theories prevailed as to the causes of discomfort in a crowded room: First, that it was due to a diminution in oxygen; second, that it was caused by the poisoning effect of the accumulating carbon dioxide; and, third, that it was due to the toxic effect of organic matter given off in the breath.

The early suspicion against oxygen depletion arose from the then recent discovery (1774) of the existence and significance of oxygen in respiration. It was assumed that the amount of depletion was serious. It is now known that, owing to the multiple opportunities for leakage through walls and crevices, the oxygen content is actually lowered only an insignificant amount. In fact, the worst ventilated room has far more oxygen than a mountain health resort where the partial pressure of oxygen is greatly reduced by the high elevation.

It was Lavoisier who shifted the suspicion from oxygen to carbon dioxide. There was very little basis for this view, but, once enunciated, it has persisted even to this day. Brown, in 1870, refers to carbon dioxide as a "fatal gas". Even in 1913 the engineers, Hoffman and Raber, in their Handbook, class carbon dioxide with the other "impurities", and regret that some way has not been found for dissociating it from the remainder of the atmosphere.

Pettenkofer, in 1863, made it clear that carbon dioxide was not in itself poisonous, but that it served as a useful index of other harmful substances in respired air which he believed were instrumental in lowering resistance to disease. This suggestion gave birth to the carbon-dioxide standard of ventilation, and this, in turn, led to the most common air-flow standard of 30 cu. ft. per min. per person.

The worst ventilated room rarely reaches 50 parts of carbon dioxide in 10 000. Before unfavorable symptoms can be produced, under laboratory conditions, it is necessary for the carbon dioxide to be increased to 300 or 400 parts. The school child actually breathes more carbon dioxide when curled up on his sleeping porch than when sitting in the school room.

The organic-poison theory was sponsored by Brown-Sequard and d'Arsonval. Their viewpoint is represented by Russell in the "Smithsonian Miscellaneous Collections", who wrote as late as 1896, that organic matter in respired air "is a dangerous and pernicious element in all aggregations and, combined with carbon dioxide, produces, when in moderate quantity, depression, headache, sickness, and other ailments." The great majority of workers have been quite unable to produce the slightest evidence of the existence of an organic poison in respired air.

The relative unimportance of the chemical factors in the air as a cause of discomfort and the primary significance of the thermal factors—temperature, moisture, and air motion—was first brought out clearly by Hermans in 1883. In 1896, Billings, Mitchell, and Bergy in America reviewed and repeated much of the experimental work previously reported. They voiced the conclusion that it is "very improbable that the minute quantity of organic matter contained in the air expired from human beings has any deleterious influence on men who inhale it in ordinary rooms, and, hence, it is probably unnecessary to take this factor into account in providing for the ventilation of such rooms". In their eyes, the two great causes of discomfort, although not the only ones, in crowded, ill-ventilated rooms, were excessive temperature and odors.

This viewpoint has been confirmed in substance again and again by Flügge and his associates in Germany, by Haldane, Pembrey, Leonard Hill, and others in England, and by Benedict, Crowder, the New York State Commission on Ventilation, and others in America.

Present-Day Conceptions of Ventilation

The present-day attitude with respect to the different elements in ventilation may be summed up as follows:

Elevated indoor temperature in the winter, even up to 75°, produces discomfort, lowers working efficiency, forces the heart to extra effort, and measurably elevates the body temperature. As far as possible, the air of an inclosure should be cool and fluctuating in temperature within narrow limits, rather than constant or unvarying.

Likewise, air motion should be variable or fitful, rather than of uniform velocity. Variability or pulsation in air motion stimulates the pleasant feeling of an outdoor breeze, cooling, but not sufficiently prolonged to be chilling.

Humidity may vary within rather wide limits and still be comfortable. In fact, there is little to justify humidities above 40% in the ordinary room in winter at temperatures around 70 degrees. Nor is there evidence that humidities as low as 20% are harmful or uncomfortable. There is a difference between dryness and "dryingness". A low humidity without marked air velocity may be dry, but not drying.

The present air-flow standard is undoubtedly excessive. This may be decreased by one-half in such places as school rooms without discomfort or harm to the occupants.

Except with very dirty clothing and people, there will not be volatilization of odors in cool rooms. One objection to higher humidities is that it accentuates odor.

Ordinarily, the bacterial content of indoor air is of no practical importance. The likelihood of disease being spread by bacteria that float about in the air is so remote as not to warrant serious consideration. In the ordinary room the dust content of the atmosphere is inconsequential to health.

Organic matter and carbon dioxide need not enter into the calculation, although measurements of the latter are useful as an indirect determination of the amount of air flow.

It is recognized, of course, that in special situations factors ordinarily unimportant loom large. In the submarine, oxygen depletion and excessive carbon dioxide are factors to be reckoned with. In certain industrial processes dust or fume removal is of the highest importance; and some situations require high humidity, as in the textile industry.

Changing Practices in Ventilation

Although theories relating to ventilation have shifted from time to time, their influence on practice has not been felt until recently. This is because no deliberate effort was made a century ago to ventilate the ordinarily occupied room. Efforts, to be sure, were made in special fields, such as the rotary fan for deep mines, used in Savoy and Bohemia, as far back as 1553, and the use of bellows for extracting air from the holds of ships, devised by Triewald, the Swedish architect, in 1741. Also, there is the application of bellows for hospitals and mines, described by Stephen Hales, an English clergyman, in 1758. Prior to 1850, however, the most commonly used method for securing air propulsion was the chimney draft. Tall towers with fire grates at the bottom were built specifically for the purpose of creating a circulation of air. A later development was the placing of hot water or steam pipes in the chimney or duct, to accelerate the draft.

Ventilation has always been closely associated with heating. Hot water, and particularly steam heating, paved the way for the development of indirect or hot-blast heating, which is so common to-day.

At the birth of the American Republic, rooms were warmed with grates and stoves. The heating and ventilating equipment of Independence Hall in 1776 consisted of two open stoves (which cost about $135) and wooden shutters or ventilators. Hot-water heating was being tried out for chicken incubators in France and England. James Watt was warming his study with an iron box connected to a boiler in the room below. The difficulties of this period had to do with the control of heating.

By 1850 steam had begun to find extensive use, and this opened the way for the rapid heating of air in quantity, in other words, indirect heating. This method, also known as the plenum, or the hot-blast, system grew in favor and, in 1867, Chicago installed its first mechanical plant with indirect heating, for a school building. From a main duct in the basement two tin ducts were carried up through the wardrobes, terminating in openings in the classroom about 12 in. above the floor. Deflectors over the openings directed the incoming air down toward the floor. Needless to say, there was considerable complaint of drafts.

Between 1850 and 1900 mechanical ventilation found greatly extended use, but there were no radical changes in methods or principles. In fact, in looking back over the history of the subject, it is rather striking that no particular method characterizes a particular period. In 1870 discussion waged over the relative merits of the hot blast and the split system. The same discussion is rife to-day. The Tobin tube and the Sherringham valve, of the early Nineteenth Century, were methods of introducing air directly through the wall of a room. This method is exemplified to-day in the window deflector and the unit ventilator, to which the fan has been added.

The problem of ventilation has been how to warm an inclosure in cold weather, or cool it in warm weather, and at the same time circulate air in such a manner as to remove odor, conserve heat or cold, and not cause unpleasant drafts. The matters at issue have been whether to heat directly or indirectly, whether to admit air at the top of the room or the bottom, whether there should be a single air inlet to the room or many, whether air should be forced through an inclosure or exhausted, or both.

The improvements that have taken place, in addition to artisanship, are largely refinements in control and increases in capacity, which have been made possible through developments in the use of steam and electricity.

Air Conditioning

Since 1900 the most notable changes have been in the field of air conditioning, humidification, and dehumidification. A form of humidification was practiced in 1838 when the air supplied to the British House of Commons was made to pass through a sheet of water dropping from perforated pipes. The development of humidification, however, took place mainly in the textile industries, where high moisture content was necessary to prevent the breaking of threads. Humidification by the release of steam from a jet gave way to the use of a pan of water heated by steam pipes, and known as an evaporating pan. This, in turn, was followed by the combined air washer and humidifier, consisting of spray nozzles, the water being circulated by a rotary pump. The degree of humidification was controlled by a thermostat in the washwater or by a humidostat in the air duct.

Effect of Changing Theories on Recent Practices

In the last twenty-five years changing theories of ventilation have left their mark on progress. So long as respired air was supposed to be poisonous, there could be no let up in the amount of air change. This viewpoint led to unnecessary restrictions, and actually retarded progress. An illustration is the English weaving sheds where an upper carbon dioxide limit of 6 parts per 10 000 was specified. This did not bring comfort, for the places reeked with steam and were unbearably hot. After a thorough study of the situation —and even at the suggestion of the operatives—the air flow was cut down, the CO_2 limit was raised to 11 parts and, what was most important to comfort, an upper limit was placed on the wet bulb temperature.

Another instance is in mines, where an unnecessarily high standard of oxygen was specified. Later, it was learned that lower concentrations of oxygen were preferable as this reduced the danger of mine explosions.

For years a controversy has waged over the ventilation of school buildings, fresh-air enthusiasts speaking of mechanical ventilation as "canned air". Engineer extremists, on the other hand, would not even apply the term ventilation unless propulsion of air was by mechanical means. Once having recognized the non-poisonous character of respired air, there should not be the slightest objection to window ventilation and gravity exhaust, although this method will not insure a continuous air flow equivalent to the 30-cu. ft. standard. For this reason, laws which require mechanical ventilation in school buildings, indirectly through the provision calling for 30 cu. ft. of air per min. per person, are unnecessarily severe, and should be amended.

A clearer understanding of the ventilation elements made possible also the practice of recirculating air, thus saving fuel cost. This would have been deemed impossible at a time when a different attitude prevailed with reference to carbon dioxide and organic matter. The Young Men's Christian Association Training School at Springfield, Mass., found this procedure entirely practical and economical, during the course of experiments in 1913. The method has now found application in theatres and factories, and to some extent in schools. The use of ozone to cut down odors has been tried in conjunction with recirculation, and has met with favor, particularly in the schools of St. Louis, Mo.

The unit ventilator, or combined blower, humidifier, and heater for individual rooms, has been a recent development. The apparatus is more costly, but it permits individual room control. This saves in the operation of a central plant when only one or two rooms need to be ventilated.

Ventilation Laws

Compulsory ventilating laws for public buildings and factories have been enacted largely since 1900. Regulations are to be found at an earlier period; Detroit, Mich., for instance, prescribed ventilation appliances for places of employment in 1881. State-wide acts were passed in New Jersey in 1903, and in Ohio and New York in 1905. In approximately twenty-four States there are now (1926) laws or regulations prescribing ventilation in schools and other places. For the most part, these laws require forced ventilation, with an allowance of 30 cu. ft. per min. per person. They also specify floor space and cubic space standards per occupant. To a lesser degree, temperature standards are also laid down.

Contributions of Ventilating Practice to Human Welfare

To-day ventilating engineering represents a distinct profession. Evidence of this is seen on all sides. Habitations are much more comfortable as a result, and the hazards of indoor life are unquestionably reduced thereby. The dust which used to becloud the worker in the polishing room is now removed locally. Steam vapors from vats, which formerly rendered their attendants invisible a few feet distant, may now be carried away through exhaust hoods. Basement and sub-basement space, which formerly had limited use, is utilized by cafeterias which, through the aid of electric lights, ventilating ducts, and a dehumidifying system, are made attractive and comfortable for thousands of people daily.

Ventilation, an ephemeral thing at the dawn of the century, now invades the theatre bill posters, where glaring letters give almost as much prominence to the cooled, washed air, as to the names of the play and the comments of the critic.

The American Society of Heating and Ventilating Engineers, organized in 1895, has grown to large proportions, and now conducts a research laboratory, where the problems confronting the profession are being studied.

In spite of the advances made and the numerous illustrations of good ventilation, there is room for a much wider use of good equipment in such places as theatres and meeting halls. It is the rule and not the exception to leave a theatre after a 2 or 3-hour performance, hot, sticky, and thoroughly uncomfortable. Engineers have yet to learn how to counteract the heat production of a hall full of people so that temperatures at the close will be nearer 70 than 80 degrees.

Outlooks for Ventilation Progress

The changes in ventilation perceived in the immediate future are likely to include:

(*a*) Refinements in the control of temperature;
(*b*) The introduction of cyclic or variable air motion, as opposed to unvarying and monotonous air flow;
(*c*) The development of methods of cooling during warm weather;
(*d*) A more economical use of fuel through the medium of recirculation;
(*e*) Rewriting and modernizing legislative requirements; and
(*f*) More intensive study of plant operation.

From the wealth of evidence available, overheating is more threatening to human comfort, health, and efficiency than any other single ventilation element. There is need for continued improvement in thermostatic control and regulating instruments.

The oscillating wall fan is an improvement over the stationary type. It cools but does not chill. Intermittent air propulsion by blowers will soon be accomplished. One of the most justifiable criticisms against mechanical ventilation is its deadly uniformity. This is not an idle criticism. Outdoors one is used to the intermittent play of air on the skin. This is missing indoors, unless the windows are open. This is one of the attractive features of window ventilation, and is one of the reasons for the insistence on open windows. There is no reason why this condition cannot be quite successfully imitated mechanically. It is not the alternate starting and stopping that is wanted, but the actual reproduction of the irregular outdoor velocity cycle.

When this comes it will be possible to introduce air at lower temperatures, which will be more stimulating and fairer to the nose and throat. The intermittency of the action will produce the sensation of a breeze, but not that of a draft. It is this refreshing, draftless breeze which is more needed than anything to vitalize mechanical ventilation.

People are accustomed to think of ventilation as a winter problem, but are beginning to see its uses as a protection against the debilitating heat of summer. The circulating fan is growing in popularity. The cooled and dehumidified theatre is here. Who knows but what the gas compressor and expansion coils may cool the living and work rooms as well as the ice box?

The re-circulation of air will find wider and wider application, for this means fuel economy. Large spaces with relatively slight crowding are particularly suitable for this practice.

There are numerous examples of well-intentioned, but illy worded and unwarranted legislation bearing on ventilation. This distracts attention from the really important questions, provides a ground for controversy, and hinders progress. This situation is bound to be remedied.

The literature of the subject contains many more accounts of projected works than of impartial critical tests of operating results. In order to learn the most from experience, there must be careful observations of equipment in use. This is necessary in order to verify or disprove the practical success of engineering ideas which are constantly being introduced. It is to be hoped that the research staff of the American Society of Heating and Ventilating Engineers may find opportunity to enter this field and bring forth scientific data.

Most to be desired is air that is cool rather than warm, dry rather than damp, diverse in temperature in different parts and at different times rather than uniform and monotonous, moving rather than still, and, finally, free from annoying odors and floating matter. This is fresh air. It is the object of ventilation to reproduce this condition indoors as faithfully as possible.

DISCUSSION

James W. Armstrong,* M. Am. Soc. C. E.—Touching as it does almost every phase of the water-works problem this is an interesting paper. Mr. Fuller has shown very clearly the value, to humanity, of a pure water.

One or two points have recently come under the speaker's observation that might be of some interest in connection with pipe coating. He recently had occasion to inspect the inside of a 7-ft. steel water main that had been in service about eleven years. It is laid under 25th Street in Baltimore, Md., and is protected on the outside by a concrete casing and on the inside by a coating of bitumastic enamel.

A walk of about ½ mile and return through this line showed it to be entirely free from tuberculation. The only defects discovered, were around the rivet heads in the bottom of the pipe. The evidence is that workmen, in passing through the pipe line, had knocked the protective coating from some of the rivets and corrosion had set in at such places.

If bituminous enamels are properly put on they make an excellent waterproof coating for both steel and concrete, but as they have to be put on hot, it is necessary to have the surface to which they are applied clean and perfectly dry. Failure of bitumastic coatings can generally be traced to neglect on the part of workmen to comply with these precautions.

A piece of casting taken from a broken water main in New Orleans, La., revealed the fact that the interior was nearly free from corrosion and that a thin smooth coating of lime had been deposited, which formed a natural and effective protection. This would indicate that cities using lime for softening purposes have little to fear from tuberculation of cast-iron pipe.

In Baltimore, where the water is naturally corrosive, sufficient lime is added after filtration to maintain a pH value of about 8.2 for all water entering the city mains. The alkalinity is thus maintained at a point sufficiently high to reduce its corrosive qualities very greatly. Cities annoyed with the corrosion of pipes might avoid much of their trouble by raising the alkalinity of the water delivered to the city mains.

In tracing the history of the water-works pump, Mr. Fuller has shown that the electrically operated centrifugal pump has, after a long struggle, come into its own. There are three great advantages in pumps of this kind: (1) Low first cost; (2) very little repair work; and (3) an absolute minimum of labor for operation. At Montebello, the low-lift pumping station contains five electrically driven centrifugal pumps, having an aggregate capacity of about 250 000 000 gal. per day. For more than eleven years, practically all Baltimore's water supply has passed through this pumping station, and there is no other power available, should the electricity fail. For several years, after first placing the station in service, power was supplied over a single underground cable. On one occasion a blow-out in this cable caused considerable uneasiness, but it was repaired before the storage in the 15 000 000-gal. reservoir ran out. A second cable was afterward installed, and since then

* Filtration Engr., Baltimore City Water Dept., Baltimore, Md.

there have been only momentary interruptions in the power supply. During the entire time this station has been in operation, only one man has been employed on each shift of eight hours, except for repair work.

The cost of pumping water, neglecting fixed charges and overhead, from 1916 to 1919, against an average head of about 40 ft., was $1.62 per 1 000 000 gal. During the entire life of the plant, more than eleven years, the cost averaged about $2.10 per 1 000 000 gal. for pumping against heads ranging from 30 to 43 ft. The high price of coal during the World War was the principal cause of the increased total cost.

The plant at Little Falls, N. J., should be considered the prototype of all modern filter plants, as it was the first to be entirely constructed of reinforced concrete. The use of reinforced concrete for such purposes spread very rapidly. The great variety of forms and shapes into which it could be moulded, led many engineers to believe that its use was the solution of most of their structural problems and has made them a bit slow about recognizing its limitations. Lately, many have learned that concrete, passing as excellent when fully protected from the elements, may fail utterly when exposed to the weather for a few years.

It has also been learned that concrete through which water is leaching, is doomed; that the passage of water through concrete will, in turn, dissolve both the calcium and aluminum compounds; and that the dissolving of these compounds robs the concrete of its strength and leaves it an easy prey to the action of frost and the elements. To secure imperviousness for all water-bearing or exposed concrete is of the utmost importance.

If field operations could be carried on with the precision of laboratory work, it might be possible to secure satisfactory concrete, but the difficulty of controlling the human factor may make futile the most painstaking and careful work in securing a proper quality, grading, and mixing of materials. Unless some method of securing denser concrete can be obtained, engineers of the future may come to rely more on some outer coating to render concrete impervious.

In the ordinary distribution system valves are not operated often, and an old superintendent might, after years of service, not have had experience enough to judge rightly the merits of a particular valve. With the advent of large mechanical filter plants where valves are opened and closed every day, certain weaknesses have developed that had not been realized. Special efforts should be made to improve the details of valves designed to operate in a horizontal position.

J. W. Ellms,* M. Am. Soc. C. E. (by letter).—The survey by Mr. Fuller of the progress made in the past half century in the water-works field, is both interesting and instructive. To the older members of the Society, whose professional activities have run parallel with the development of the art, this record may seem commonplace. However, does it not naturally raise the question of how such improvements have been made possible, and to what specific cause the advance may be attributed?

* Engr., Water Purification and Sewage Disposal Dept., Public Utilities; Cons. San. Engr., Cleveland, Ohio.

The general increase in scientific knowledge is doubtless a partial answer to the question; but is it not more specifically answered by the vast amount of research work which has been carried on in this field during the past fifty years by professional men? The labor of individuals and of associated groups for the solution of specific problems has furnished the real basis for these improvements. The large sums of money expended in research work have not always been appreciated; but without these funds the present status of the art could not possibly have been reached. State, municipal, and private funds have enabled scientists to cope with the problems arising in this field of applied science. The benefits that have been derived from systematic research in the past is a sufficient guaranty of what may be accomplished in the future. Co-operative research during the World War certainly proved what can be done under the stress of necessity.

While the writer realizes that much is now being done by National engineering societies in furthering research work, he believes that more may be accomplished and greater advances in the art secured by more active and properly directed group action. The field is broad and the rewards ample for all those who have a genuine interest in the progress of applied science in water-works engineering. The problems to be solved involve the fundamental branches of science, such as physics, chemistry, and biology; and in applied science, the arts of civil, mechanical, and electrical engineering. Where among human activities could one find a more fascinating or varied field for labor? To the younger members of the profession, it should offer a life work of usefulness.

Caleb Mills Saville,* M. Am. Soc. C. E. (by letter).—Mr. Fuller has performed a notable service to engineers and others specializing in water supply work in bringing together in such a concise but comprehensive manner this critique of water-works practice during the past century and a half.

While probably the great fires in Chicago, Ill., and Boston, Mass., in the early Seventies furnished an impetus to water-works construction, it is notable that many of the works in Northern cities were started about ten to fifteen years earlier. For some reason, the late Fifties and early Sixties seems to have been a time of considerable water supply work in this section, possibly because of growth in population and increase in value of property.

Apparently, the largest increase in public water supply works came after 1880. Of the 9 850 plants estimated as in service in 1924 and given in Mr. Fuller's Table 1, 6.1% were installed prior to 1880; 32.5% prior to 1896; and 67.5% since that date. That is, about two-thirds of the total number of water supply systems in the United States, as estimated in the "Manual of American Water Works", were installed between 1896 and 1924.

The use of house cisterns or tanks connected with the public supply was a very common mode of supply for individual buildings, because they could be filled at night when the city draft decreased. This reserve helped during the day when the city supply, due to inadequacy of trunk lines, was unsatisfactory on the higher elevations. Previous to this, and in the transition period from

* Mgr. and Chf. Engr., Hartford Water-Works, Hartford, Conn.

dug wells to public supply, many private houses had water-tight cisterns in their cellars, in which rain water from the roof was stored and pumped by hand-operated force pumps to tanks in the upper part of the house. Often these cisterns were supplied with charcoal filters through which the water was passed before being used. In many towns and cities, about a century ago, large public cisterns were located in various parts of the municipality, in which water was stored for fire protection purposes. Such cisterns were existent in Malden, Mass., and Hartford, Conn., up to within a few years, although abandoned many years ago, probably with the introduction of aqueduct water. The locations of these cisterns were often forgotten and only recalled when they were accidentally uncovered or broken through by heavy loading.

Wooden pipes of bored logs were used in many localities. They were in service for some years in Boston and elsewhere. In Hartford, such pipes were used as early as 1803 in at least two supply systems bringing water to the center of the city from springs several miles away. On Fig. 1 is shown a photograph of one of these wooden pipes removed in 1926 in the center of the city during the construction of a large building. On Fig. 2 is shown a 42-in. cast-iron pipe for purposes of comparison.

The use of cement-lined pipes seems to deserve somewhat more attention than Mr. Fuller was able to accord it. As he states, this pipe had considerable vogue, particularly in New England, and its value then and now seems not to have been fully appreciated. The best treatise on the subject of cement-lined water pipes known to the writer, is found in a paper* entitled "Wrought-Iron Cement-Lined Water Pipe" by the late Leonard Metcalf, M. Am. Soc. C. E. A perusal of this paper indicates the widest variation in experience, from good to bad.

As an example of satisfactory use, it is of interest to note the 30-in. cement-lined main of the old Charlestown, Mass., Water-Works, laid from the reservoir on Walnut Hill through Broadway, Somerville, Mass., for a distance of several miles. Installed in July, 1871, it is still in service as an integral part of the present Metropolitan (Boston) Water Supply System. Possibly, in systems where so much trouble was experienced with this kind of pipe, the makers and not the material were most to blame.

The reliance on linings and coatings to protect both cast-iron and steel pipes is mentioned very briefly by Mr. Fuller. The absolute dependence on the integrity of a covering to protect cast-iron pipes from rust tubercles that reduce flow and form corrosion that soon destroys steel pipe when exposed to "aggressive" waters is, however, worthy of more than a passing comment. The importance of the work of the committees of the several water-works associations now considering this matter of pipe covering, is realized when one recalls the steel pipes that have completely failed within a few years after being laid in adverse conditions of soil or exposed on the interior to corrosive water. Steel pipes undoubtedly have a large place in water-works construction, but that place must be suitable for their use.

* *Journal,* New England Water Works Assoc., March, 1909, p. 1.

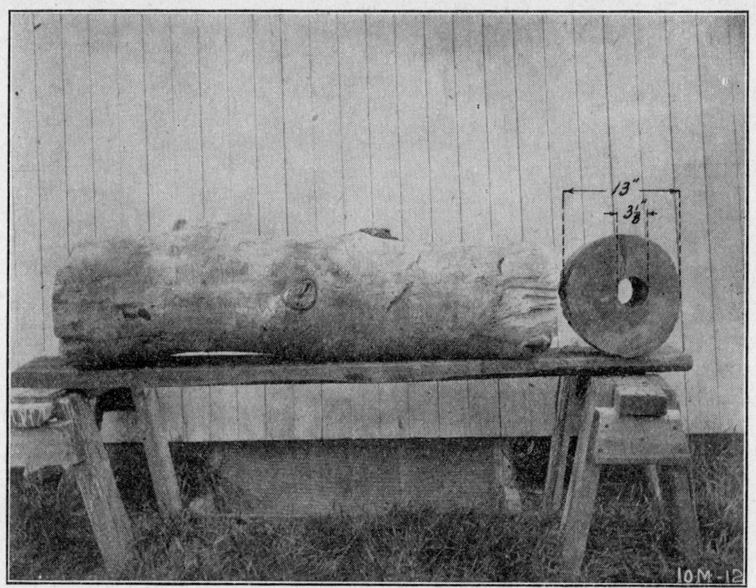

Fig. 1.—Wood Pipe, Original Water Supply Line, Hartford, Conn.

Fig. 2.—Cast-Iron Pipe, Present Water Supply Line, Hartford, Conn.

In the matter of "distribution economics," it seems desirable to record the vast improvement that has resulted from the intensive work of the National Board of Fire Underwriters, under the able leadership of George W. Booth, M. Am. Soc. C. E., Chief Engineer, in developing such adequacy of supply and delivery systems that it has been possible to reduce rates for insurance considerably; which is only another way of stating that the fire hazard has been greatly diminished by the advancement in water supply work. Present conditions in a large Western city indicate that if one is searching for information concerning the "bitterness of the opposition to metering" it is unnecessary to revert to the Eighties.

The methods used in Philadelphia, Pa., and New York, N. Y., in securing a source of water supply were similar to those in Boston, when the first water supply was brought in through the "ancient conduit" installed by a company of citizens under authority of an Act of the May Session of the General Court of the Massachusetts Colony in 1652, or six years previous to the dug wells of the Dutch in 1658 and 141 years prior to the Manhattan Company of Aaron Burr, chartered by the New York Legislature in 1799. Two years earlier than that date, 1797, the Hartford Aqueduct Company was given a charter by the General Assembly of Connecticut. In February, 1795, the General Court of Massachusetts gave a charter to the "Jamaica Pond Aqueduct Corporation" to bring water from "any part of the Town of Roxbury into the Town of Boston."

In skimming the history of the development of pumping engines, the performance of the E. D. Leavitt triple expansion engine, installed at the Chestnut Hill Pumping Station of the Boston Water-Works in 1895, should not be overlooked. This pumping engine, on the authority of the late Desmond FitzGerald, Past-President, Am. Soc. C. E., is said to be "one of the most remarkable in existence in respect to duty and workmanship." Its three cylinders are 13.7 in., 24.375 in., and 39 in. in diameter, respectively. High speed was made possible by use of Riedler valve construction. The normal speed of the engine is 50 rev. per min., at which the pump capacity is 20 000 000 U. S. gal. per 24 hours. The duty of this engine was 145 000 000 ft-lb. per 1 000 000 B. t. u. It is stated that this engine has been run at a speed of 70 rev. per min., or 40% in excess of the contract, with smooth and economical operation.

The epoch-making Louisville, Ky., investigations and their result in directing future work in water purification, was due almost entirely to the minute attention to detail, the untiring enthusiasm and good judgment of Mr. Fuller.

It would seem desirable to call more attention to the two types of filtration works on which dependence is placed for safe-guarding public health and supplying attractive water; and especially to the advance made since 1895 in the art of clarifying the turbid waters of the South and West; due, first to the hit-or-miss methods of commercial exploitation and, finally, placed on a sound scientific basis by the technical work of the late E. B. Weston, M. Am. Soc. C. E., Mr. Fuller, and Robert Spurr Weston, M. Am. Soc. C. E.

The failure of the slow sand filter, in many cases, was due not to the type of filter, but to its limited application and inadaptability to meet some conditions imposed. To overcome these difficulties, modern art has developed a much more efficient machine than the slow sand filter. The largest slow sand plants in this country are those at Pittsburgh, Pa., Philadelphia, and Washington, D. C. Slow sand plants giving most satisfactory results as to quality of effluent and cost of production are in operation at Springfield, Mass., and at Hartford. In these places, as in many others in the north and east portions of the United States, where the natural waters carry little turbidity and only a moderate amount of color, the slow sand filter is particularly well adapted. Where this type can be used, the resulting effluent generally is much more satisfactory. After-sterilization is usually unnecessary and the operation of the plant is more "fool proof" than the rapid sand type. The latest of the larger filter plants of the rapid sand type is the installation at Providence, R. I., designed and constructed under the advice of Allen Hazen, M. Am. Soc. C. E.

The rise in regulation of public utility works in the past two decades seems well worth comment and has demonstrated the wisdom of this method of control of water supply as well as other utility business. This regulation has injected into utility operation business methods which have been almost as efficacious in producing satisfactory working conditions as the improvement in technique has advanced the quality of the water supplied. In fact, these two are interdependent, for without economical financial control, the improvements in supply and purification would have been much less available for public use.

In a statement of this kind covering as it does a period of many years, it seems desirable to give brief note of some of the leaders in this branch of engineering who have now passed on. Among these may be mentioned James B. Francis, J. James R. Croes, Alphonse Fteley, Frederic P. Stearns, and Desmond FitzGerald, Past-Presidents, Am. Soc. C. E.; Hiram F. Mills, Hon. M. Am. Soc. C. E.; and Joseph P. Davis, Dexter Brackett, and George C. Whipple, Members, Am. Soc. C. E.

It is of interest to note also that most, if not all these names, as well as those of many others eminent in water supply work, were associated at times either with the Boston Water-Works, or that institute of public health work administered so efficiently by Dr. Thomas M. Drown, William T. Sedgwick, and Dr. Henry P. Walcott, the Massachusetts State Board of Health.

M. M. O'Shaughnessy,* M. Am. Soc. C. E. (by letter).—Mr. Fuller is to be complimented on the exhaustive handling of the subject of water-works, included in his brief summary. The most valuable tabulation is the great increase in number of publicly owned water systems *versus* privately owned (Table 1). The United States is to be congratulated on making the greatest advance in the science of water distribution and measurement as indicated by the Venturi meter developed by Clemens Herschel, Past-President, Am. Soc. C. E.

* City Engr., San Francisco, Calif.

In describing hydraulic-fill dams Mr. Fuller ignored the credit that belongs to the late Julius M. Howells, M. Am. Soc. C. E. He successfully constructed the first two hydraulic-fill dams in the United States; the first in Texas and the second at La Mesa, San Diego, about 70 ft. high. The latter has since been submerged by a higher buttressed arch concrete dam immediately below it. The late James D. Schuyler, M. Am. Soc. C. E., had the discretion to pick up Mr. Howells' ideas and methods and, with a broader practice, develop the subject of hydraulic-fill dams more exhaustively.

Mr. Fuller ignores the importance of the rock-fill dam, devoting less than one sentence to it. It is entitled to more consideration, as the largest dam east of the Mississippi River is the rock-fill dam, more than 280 ft. high, across the Dix River in Kentucky, which was completed in 1925 as a restraining reservoir for power uses. The water-tight curtain is properly on the water face of the dam where it belongs, and not on the back.

He contributes a very valuable section toward the history of pumping water, including a description of the Worthington pumps. Modern electrically operated centrifugal pumps have displaced all the heavy, cumbersome machinery and equipment in vogue thirty years ago.

The Medical and Engineering Professions are to be complimented on the improved sanitary condition of water supplies for drinking purposes, as indicated by the lowering typhoid fever death rates in American cities. Table 2 shows at once that there is at present only one-twentieth of the deaths from this disease that there were 20 years ago. This shows progress.

The City of San Francisco has taken elaborate precautions for the preservation and purification of its water supply by extensive land ownership around reservoirs. This is a wise precaution. It is a foolish idea for water companies and cities to encourage pleasure-seeking people to enjoy the fishing or boating on domestic water supplies, and the only safe rule for public health is exclusion. In this regulation the San Francisco engineers are supported by the public health authorities.

Morris Knowles,* M. Am. Soc. C. E. (by letter).—In discussing Mr. Fuller's paper, there is little fundamental information that can be added. The author covers the subject completely and concisely, and any addition must necessarily be an expansion of some item already mentioned.

The trends of the demand of people, as regards quality of water, is one factor which is seldom mentioned, but which has played an important part in the history of public water supply systems. As in everything else, the people are demanding an improved quality of water for their use. The time when it was necessary that a water be safe for drinking purposes only, has passed. Even during the past 10 to 20 years, the demand of the people as regards quality of water has grown. The people of New England dislike mud and hardness, but will put up with color. Western people have put up with turbidity and hardness, but dislike color. The time is not far distant when a water that has turbidity, color, or hardness will not be tolerated anywhere.

* Pres. and Chf. Engr., Morris Knowles, Inc., Pittsburgh, Pa.

In other words, water must not only be safe for drinking purposes, but must be pleasing in appearance and pleasant and easy to use.

It has been known for a long time that one of the prime requisites of an industrial community is soft water. This is being more and more realized and, consequently, the demand for such water is increasing. The importance of this factor is well shown by the number of softening plants that are being installed. In the State of Pennsylvania, there are twelve such plants, four of which supply a population of more than 50 000.

Another quality of water that is becoming important is its temperature. This is indicated by the fact that many plants equipped with condensers of the water-works type have had to discontinue their use, due to the fact that the few degrees rise in temperature of the water that results has been the cause of many complaints.

The demand for improved quality of water has been almost in direct ratio with the education of the people on the subject of water supply. As soon as they know that they can get a good quality of water, they will demand it. Although the people are better informed on the question of water supply than they have been in the past, there is still room for more education. In every line of endeavor, be it industry, art, or other activity, it is necessary that education of the people proceed with the progress that is made, or the progress will soon cease.

A great number of people, knowing nothing about water, revolt against drinking purified water that has come originally from a known rather polluted stream. In order to overcome that difficulty, either the pollution will have to be removed, or the people will have to be educated to the idea that the water is satisfactory in spite of its antecedents. In almost any city in the country where good water may be obtained by turning a tap, there is also a company engaged in the business of selling so-called "spring", well or distilled water for drinking purposes. This may be an indication that the public water supply is not what it should be, but more often it is simply lack of education on the part of the people relative to the subject of water supply and safety of the water from public systems, as compared to the doubtful quality of other water.

The water-works engineer now has many problems dealing with the art and details of public water supply and the education of the people. He will probably always have these, but he has, and will have, assistance that will tend to make the solution of the problems less difficult. This aid is, and will be, given through the agencies of supervision, co-operation, and consolidation.

The developments during recent years in the fields of governmental supervision and inspection of drainage areas, of interstate agreements, and of consolidation of public water supplies, are of particular interest to, and should be welcomed by, the water-works engineer. It is in this direction that people must look for the solution of problems that have to do with the increasing pollution of streams by such material as industrial wastes and mine drainage that cannot be dealt with by present water purification methods. In order to solve these problems, engineers must either correct conditions at the source of the pollution, or go to one of the few remaining unpolluted streams for water.

Since about 1890, there has been a gradual change in the United States in conditions as regards sources of public water supply. Previous to that time, practically all American streams were relatively unpolluted, and the problem of locating a surface source for public water supply purposes consisted of locating a convenient stream having the necessary flow. With the greater stream pollution of the present day and the greater demand for sources of public water supply, the problem has become more complicated. In order to find a source of supply, a city, in many cases, must go outside its own jurisdiction and must look to State and even Federal administrative bodies for assistance.

State assistance and supervision of public water supply has become available through Sanitary Divisions of State Health Departments. In 1890, Massachusetts had about the only effective State Health Department in this respect in the country. Since that time practically all States have provided for Sanitary Bureaus and in more than one-half the States it is necessary to obtain the approval of these agencies on water supply and sewerage projects. People must look largely to these governmental agencies for the preservation of present sources of public water supply.

In the cases of large sources of water supply, Sanitary Divisions of State Health Departments are not capable of handling the question, as most large streams flow from one State to another. In such instances they must look to interstate agreements and sometimes Federal supervision, such as the U. S. Public Health Service. Interstate agreements are usually the result of meetings in which the interested State Governments, manufacturers, and others concerned are represented. The Interstate Stream Conservation Agreement concerning the Ohio River, in which Pennsylvania, Ohio, West Virginia, Maryland, New York, Indiana, Illinois, Kentucky, and Tennessee are represented, is one example of the effectiveness of such procedure. The success of this co-operative group will probably lead to the development of other similar agencies and agreements, in an effort to solve other similar problems.

In solving the question of mine drainage pollution in Pennsylvania, the ultimate answer will probably be the preservation of certain drainage areas against such pollution for use as sources of public water supply. This is about the only satisfactory solution in sight and the Court decision in the Indian Creek case would indicate that this procedure is feasible. Such solution will involve not only activity and increased power on the part of the State Government, but also the probable formation of regional and other combined water supply districts, inasmuch as it would be impossible for the smaller cities to have their own protected drainage areas.

The development of the art and of the details of public water supply has been extensive and should continue, but one of the more important developments as regards public water supply will probably be in the field of co-operation and consolidation.

George H. Fenkell,* M. Am. Soc. C. E. (by letter).—Mr. Fuller has made a very complete and interesting résumé of the advance in water supply prac-

* Supt. and Gen. Mgr., Dept. of Water Supply, Detroit, Mich.

tice during practically the full life of water supply systems in the United States. To the student, historian, and others, who may wish to pursue the subject in further detail this paper will serve as an authoritative reference and starting point.

The author's quotation from a paper by the late J. James R. Croes, Past-President, Am. Soc. C. E., regarding the development of a method of pumping water direct to a distribution system and of controlling pressures at the point of pumping, is very interesting, as this method is still in common use in many cities and towns, particularly in the Middle West. The development of the motor-driven fire-pump has eliminated, to a great extent, the necessity for excess ranges of pressure on the distribution system, which pressures were apt to have a bad effect on the plumbing systems of the buildings served with water. The increasing use of elevated storage tanks, and the gradually increased capacity of those being built, also tend to smooth out some of the pressure variations which always accompany the use of this system of distribution.

For the purpose of completing the record it is to be regretted that Mr. Fuller did not extend the data on maximum steam pressures used for pumping water beyond the year 1906, and, at the same time, add information relative to pump efficiency and duty. For completeness, some recent performance of steam turbine and electric motor-driven centrifugal pumps would have been interesting, as these are fast coming into more general use.

The development of intakes for lakes and rivers having small variations in level has probably been more marked on the Great Lakes and in tributary waters than elsewhere. This has been due to the great extent of this region and the large population making use of these waters. Throughout this district, winter weather is generally severe, and serious trouble from ice may be expected even in the southernmost part. Frazil, or needle ice, and the grounding or piling up of surface ice are usually most troublesome, and dangers arising from the heavy lake traffic must also be considered. These factors materially affect the design and maintenance of intakes on the Great Lakes.

The simplest intakes consist only of a pipe line laid on the lake bottom, and may terminate in an upturned elbow, or tee, covered with a screen or straining device of some kind. The elbow may have no support, or rip-rap may be piled around it. In some cases the pipe terminates in two or three elbows. A more elaborate design of the inlet end of the pipe (and this type was used by the City of Detroit, Mich., in 1858) consists of a boiler-plate cylinder having a dome top perforated with a great number of ½-in. holes. Another variation has a cast-iron or steel hood or cage placed over the inlet elbow or toe of the pipe line, which is pierced with holes ½ in. or more in diameter. Designs which included no protecting crib were probably in more extensive use formerly than now.

At Toronto, Ont., Canada, the inlet is carried above a protecting crib and, for the older intake, is protected by a cone consisting essentially of twenty-eight 1¼-in. round bars, spaced equally around the circumference, and for the new intake by a steel plate supported 30 in. above the lip by 1¼-in. round rods, spaced 8⅛ in. on centers.

For the larger intake pipes it is customary to protect the inlet end by a submerged crib. There is considerable variation in the construction of these cribs. The larger ones have usually taken the form of a square or octagonal timber crib having a solid floor. They are divided into compartments by the cross-timbering. The conduit is carried through the cribbing above or below the floor to the central compartment or well, terminating in an elbow. In some cases, to provide for future extension, the conduit is carried across the entire crib, the end being closed with a blank flange outside the crib and a tee provided at the central well. The crib is towed out to its final position and sunk, and as many compartments as are necessary to hold it down are filled with broken stone or concrete, or both. The usual practice is to cover the central well, and often the four compartments adjoining the sides of the well, with a grating of plank placed on edge and spaced about 2 in. in the clear. In some cases, as at Toronto, the pipe is carried above the crib and the inlet protected.

The submerged type of intake structure is usually built in connection with a pipe conduit, but at Gary, Ind., Crib No. 5 at Cleveland, Ohio, and the new intake at Milwaukee, Wis., the conduit is a tunnel. Practically all exposed intake structures have been built in connection with tunnels, but that at Montreal appears to be the exception. These structures are usually limited to depths of 40 ft., or less. Crib No. 3 at Cleveland is in the deepest water, about 49 ft.

An exposed crib consists essentially of a central well enclosed by massive walls of sufficient thickness to give strength and stability to resist the forces of wind, wave, and ice action. The intake shaft of the tunnel draws the water from this well, and ports in the crib walls admit the water to the well. These cribs are built on shore, launched, towed to position, and sunk on a bottom which had been previously leveled off by dredging.

There has been considerable change in the design of exposed intake cribs. The City of Chicago, Ill., with its large population and heavy shore pollution requiring the location of its intakes at increasing distances from shore, has taken the lead in developing exposed intake structures. Two-Mile Crib, completed in 1867, was the first. It was built entirely of timber, pentagonal in shape, with 58-ft. sides, and a height of 40 ft. The central well was of similar shape, and the seven compartments of the wall space were filled with rubble during sinking. The Hyde Park or 68th Street Crib is of similar construction, but hexagonal in plan. These two intakes are peculiar in that they are enclosed by a heavy breakwater. Crib No. 4, the first exposed crib at Cleveland, built prior to 1890, was pentagonal and was constructed entirely of timber. The Four-Mile Crib, built during 1890-94, the Lake View Crib, completed in 1896, and the Carter M. Harrison Crib, built about the same time, at Chicago, mark a change in construction. They are all circular or polygonic in plan and have a base of heavy timber grillage through which the ports pass. On this base are two concentric steel shells with radial bulkheads forming compartments which, in the case of the Four-Mile Crib, were filled with concrete. Crib No. 3, at Cleveland, built about 1898, is very similar in construction.

The Detroit intake crib, built during 1905-06, was constructed entirely of timber and the compartments were filled with concrete. Its shape is an elongated octagon. The City of Buffalo, N. Y., completed a crib in 1910 having two concentric steel shells with no bottom. It was divided radially into compartments, a number of which were closed at the bottom with timber for buoyancy when towing the crib to position. The crib was landed on a concrete foundation ring resting on rock, and then filled with concrete.

The Wilson Avenue Crib, at Chicago, completed about 1918, presents another variant. There were two concentric steel shells with radial compartments, but no floor. The bottom of each shell had a cutting edge. For buoyancy, the ports were bulkheaded, and buoyancy tanks were built between the shells. When sunk, the steel shoes entered the clay and sealed the bottom. Concrete was used for filling.

Exposed cribs are usually provided with a more or less elaborate superstructure with quarters for attendants. Except for the Wilson Avenue Intake, Chicago, the Linwood Avenue Intake, Milwaukee, and the Buffalo Intake, the tunnels have been driven through clay.

Ice is a source of much anxiety and trouble for many who maintain intakes on the Great Lakes, because it may greatly reduce, and, at times, cut off the flow. Sheet ice and frazil ice are usually the source of trouble, sheet ice chiefly after breaking up, for it is then carried by wind and current and may form ice jams obstructing the flow to the conduit. Frazil ice, by adhering to the sides of inlet openings and ports, gradually builds up and becomes a serious obstruction, often cutting off the flow entirely.

Various remedial measures have been used to overcome ice troubles, particularly from frazil ice, but none has been uniformly successful. Experience has shown that the depth of the port opening below the surface has a marked effect. The depth depends on local conditions, but 35 to 40 ft. will usually give freedom from trouble with frazil ice. The velocity of flow through the ports has also been reduced on various intakes in an effort to minimize the tendency of frazil ice being drawn into the ports. Velocities of less than 0.5 ft. per sec. have been used, but there are no available data as to the maximum velocity which will not overcome the buoyancy of this ice.

Back pressure on the intake ports of submerged cribs has been used more or less effectively to remove adhering frazil ice. Steam and compressed air have also been used, and dependence, in some cases, is placed on sufficient storage to tide over the demand until natural causes assist in removing the obstructing ice. On exposed intakes, particularly at Chicago, a crew of men is stationed on the crib to combat the ice. Pike poles, steam, and small charges of dynamite are used for this purpose.

In shore wells where ice frequently clogged the screens, traveling screens replacing the former stationary screens, have eliminated trouble in many cases.

The steam-operated power plants on the Great Lakes also use large quantities of water for condensing. The maximum consumption per plant of the Detroit Edison Company ranges from 184 000 to 500 000 gal. per min. The average is more than 2 gal. per min. per kw. The intake arrangements of the power plants are quite different from those of the water supply plants. The water usually comes through a short canal, or a forebay, which may or may not have a boom across the entrance to deflect floating débris and ice. At the Avon Plant of the Cleveland Electrical Illuminating Company, and at a plant in Milwaukee, a lagoon has been built on the lake shore using heavy rip-rap for the enclosing dikes.

Traveling screens are usually installed at power plants to remove débris and ice. These plants are also arranged so that the heated cooling water can be discharged into the forebay and thus prevent trouble from ice.

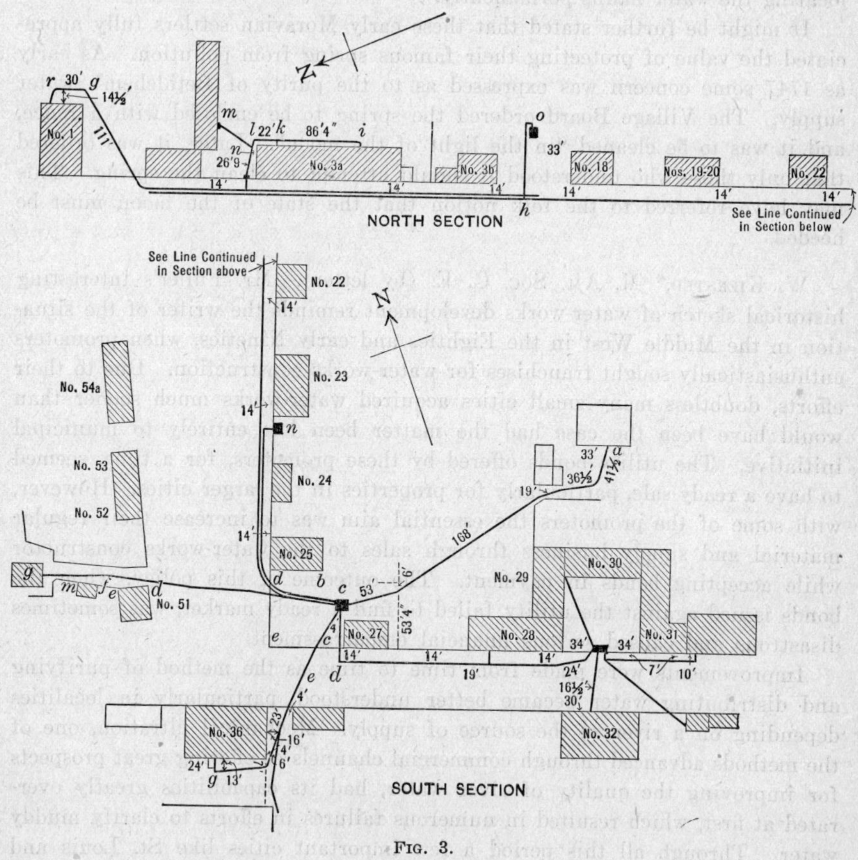

FIG. 3.

HARRY G. PAYROW,* M. AM. SOC. C. E. (by letter).—As a resident of Bethlehem, Pa., the writer was interested in Mr. Fuller's reference to the first water-works pumping plant in the United States, which was operated

* Asst. Prof., Civ. Eng. Dept., Lehigh Univ., Bethlehem, Pa.

there. A few years ago he saw the original plans of both the pumping station and a layout of the distributing system. Both plans were well executed, the lettering being in German script. Fig. 3 is a traced copy of the distributing system that may be of some interest, at least as to its comprehensiveness.

The lignum-vitæ pump first successfully forced water from a spring up to a wooden tank on May 27, 1755, and on June 27 of that year, the regular operation of the Bethlehem Water-Works was commenced (see Fig. 4). The pump lift was about 45 ft. The pipes were generally bored logs of hemlock, although some that were recently excavated, were gum and walnut. Fig. 5 shows a bored hemlock water pipe, laid about 1754, which was excavated in 1927. Apparently, a considerable length of lead pipe was used for connections to cisterns and buildings. As the pipe was laid, offsets were taken, chiefly to buildings, thus showing considerable foresight on the part of the builders in locating the water mains permanently.

It might be further stated that these early Moravian settlers fully appreciated the value of protecting their famous spring from pollution. As early as 1747 some concern was expressed as to the purity of Bethlehem's water supply. The Village Board ordered the spring to be enclosed with a fence, and it was to be cleaned "in the light of the moon". Later, it was ordered that only those who understood it should attempt to clean the spring. This may have referred to the folk notion that the state of the moon must be heeded.

W. Kiersted,* M. Am. Soc. C. E. (by letter).—Mr. Fuller's interesting historical sketch of water-works development reminds the writer of the situation in the Middle West in the Eighties and early Nineties, when promoters enthusiastically sought franchises for water-works construction. Due to their efforts, doubtless many small cities acquired water-works much sooner than would have been the case had the matter been left entirely to municipal initiative. The utility bonds offered by these promoters, for a time, seemed to have a ready sale, particularly for properties in the larger cities. However, with some of the promoters the essential aim was to increase their regular material and supply business through sales to the water-works constructor while accepting bonds in payment. The outcome of this policy, when the bonds issued against the utility failed to find a ready market, was sometimes disastrous and caused serious financial embarrassment.

Improvements were made from time to time as the method of purifying and distributing water became better understood, particularly in localities depending on a river as the source of supply. Mechanical filtration, one of the methods advanced through commercial channels as offering great prospects for improving the quality of river water, had its capabilities greatly overrated at first, which resulted in numerous failures in efforts to clarify muddy water. Through all this period a few important cities like St. Louis and Kansas City, Mo., and Omaha, Nebr., located on the Missouri River, continued to rely on sedimentation as a means of water clarification; and of these three cities, Kansas City was the last to construct what are termed modern purifica-

* Cons. Engr., Kansas City, Mo.

First Water Works in United States

Fig. 4.—Pump-House as It Looks To-Day.

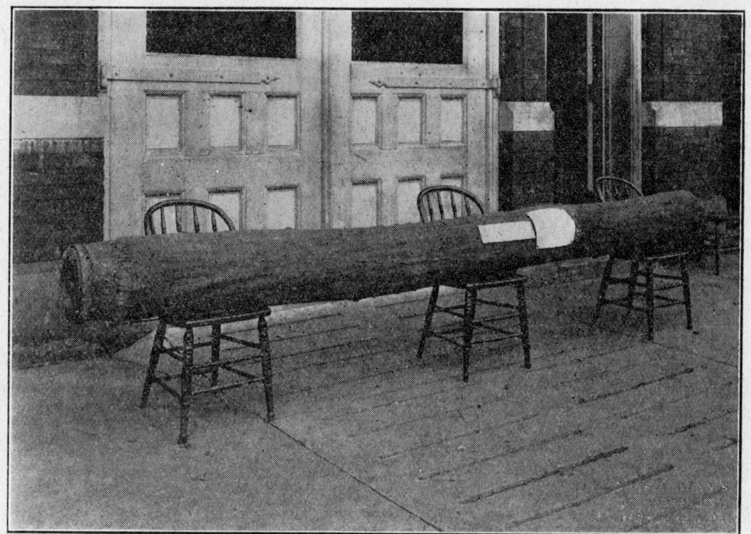

Fig. 5.—Bored Hemlock Water Pipe, Laid About 1754.

tion works. Mr. Fuller could have consistently added a paragraph with regard to the evolution of the sedimentation process, particularly as it is the main dependence of successful filtration. The experience of Kansas City is a good illustration of what can be accomplished in clarifying water by sedimentation and of rendering a water safe and potable through the aid of chlorination. It is worth while to give the experience of this city during the fiscal years, 1921 to 1926. These general results are given in Table 5.

TABLE 5.—PHYSICAL CHARACTERISTICS OF KANSAS CITY, MO., WATER SUPPLY.

Fiscal year.	Average turbidity of water distributed, in parts per million.	Percentage of turbidity removed.	Typhoid deaths per 100 000.
1921	23	96.68	11.5
1922	23	98.28	4.6
1923	29	97.7	4.8
1924	16	95.5	3.6
1925	11	99.54	1.9
1926	8	99.68	3.46

In a large measure these highly gratifying results are due to the efficient effort of Dr. George F. Gilkison, although he was compelled to use settling basins not altogether scientifically designed. The results of sedimentation considered in connection with the low typhoid death rate seem to be conclusive evidence that the mechanical filter is, in fact, of secondary importance in clarifying and purifying the river waters of the Central West. Future development of the art of water purification should see more attention given to the design of the settling basin and to methods of breaking up the colloidal condition of sediment in the preparation of water for the filter. Further development of the filter itself should be directed toward simplifying and cheapening its construction. The topic of sedimentation is too important to be obscured by the prominence of an associated topic of less real importance, namely, that of mechanical filtration. The latter process must rely on the settling basin to prepare the water for filtration and on chlorination to sterilize the filtrate.

Mr. Fuller's suggestion that the collection and digestion of available information relating to the engineering aspects of underground supplies, is a valuable one because this source of supply is greatly under-rated in localities where underground water supplies are abundant. Lack of an appreciation of the value of the underground source of water supply is perhaps the reason for advising cities, in a few instances, to abandon an available and abundant underground water supply for one from a polluted and muddy river. Propaganda relating to the mechanical filter may be responsible indirectly in no small measure for the obscurity surrounding the underground water supply in that it has engrossed, so completely, the minds of engineers.

It is worthy of note, however, that late developments show that a large quantity of water can be pumped from a single well sunk in fine water-bearing sand. This is certainly an achievement, particularly in the method by which wells in such material can be successfully constructed, operated, and maintained. Success in this particular direction has greatly broadened the range of development of underground water and has added a new stimulus to further effort along similar lines.

Referring to Mr. Eddy's paper the developing stage through which the disposal of sewage is now passing is quite likely to leave in its wake many abandoned or transformed structures formerly erected in compliance with some theory or principle which, at the time, appeared promising. The septic tank is now of the past for community use. The Imhoff tank, although still a recognized device for treating sewage, will likewise become a thing of the past, except for small towns, because experience has shown the insurmountable difficulties of attempting to combine, successfully, the purely mechanical process of sedimentation with the biological process of sludge digestion. A sacrifice of essential principles of one or the other of the processes is likely to follow attempts to co-ordinate them in a single structure.

Preliminary sedimentation is an essential factor for consideration in any method of sewage purification, and its importance is so great as to entitle it to an independent structure wherein the governing principles of sedimentation can be applied without interference with those of an entirely different process. This treatment cannot accomplish all that is desired, however, because it does not remove the colloids and, therefore, does not reduce the sewage to a condition suitable for application to either land or sprinkling filter. The desirable intermediate treatment is one that will break up the colloidal condition of the remaining sediment and reduce the sewage to a state susceptible of further improvement in a secondary settling basin. The writer regards this intermediate treatment of sewage as the most important phase. It invites the closest attention of the chemist and the engineer in arriving at the best and most economical process by which a maximum percentage of suspended matter can be removed from sewage, before attempting to purify it still further by any natural process. When this end is accomplished the final disposal of sewage by irrigation in the arid and semi-arid sections of the United States, or by intermittent filtration in other sections of the country more generously watered by Nature, will receive well merited consideration. Neither method of land disposal should be considered obsolete as long as a natural process of sewage purification remains acceptable.

The sprinkling filter, notwithstanding its many merits, must disgorge itself of organic accumulations periodically or become clogged. The usual offensiveness of the disgorging process can be alleviated in a great measure through the previously mentioned intermediate treatment. Then the danger of overburdening the natural activities will be decreased; there will be less occasion for the use of after-sedimentation; and the area of the filter, always expensive to construct, can be materially reduced.

The method of sludge disposal, which is of secondary importance, should be adapted, of course, to local surroundings. Although they are accompanied with some odor, reservoirs cheaply constructed of earth offer a satisfactory solution in isolated places. In other localities, open or closed separate digestion tanks may be required, wherein some kind of treatment will probably be needed.

In short, it is the writer's belief that future development should be directed toward a larger removal of suspended matter before sewage is applied to land or sprinkling filters.

John H. Gregory,* M. Am. Soc. C. E.—Mr. Eddy has presented an exceedingly interesting paper on the history of the sewerage and drainage of towns. There are many phases of the subject that might be discussed at length, but the speaker will confine his discussion to one phase only; that is, the question of the separate or combined system of sewers for cities. There is much to be said for both systems. The speaker holds no brief for either type, but there are some phases of the subject that should be considered rather carefully. Take, for example, the question of storm overflows from a combined system. When a large city is located on a stream which has a large volume of flow, the question of storm overflows may not be of much importance; whereas, if the city is located on a stream the flow of which during dry weather may be almost nothing, storm overflows become of great importance.

With reference to maintenance and operation, both systems present certain difficulties. With the combined system there are catch-basins and, with the separate system, surreptitious connections of rain-water leaders to the sanitary sewers, sometimes causing flooding of cellars, and also surreptitious connections whereby sewage is discharged into storm-water drains.

However, it seems that there is very much to be said for the separate system in the case of a large city located on a stream that has a very low stream flow in summer, especially if the stream runs through the heart of the city. The speaker has in mind one city having a population of about 300 000 which is sewered mainly on the combined system. The city happens to be located on a stream having a water-shed of 1 500 sq. miles and a dry-weather flow in the stream of less than 10 cu. ft. per sec.; which is almost nothing. Under such conditions storm-water overflows are of great importance, and the volume of overflow must be kept at a minimum if nuisance in the stream is to be avoided. If the city was sewered on the separate system, the problem of keeping the stream clean would be much simpler.

The tendency in the country is for cleaner streams, and if streams are to be kept clean it is a question whether the advantages do not lie with the separate system, rather than with the combined system, if the sewage is to be treated.

Karl Imhoff,† M. Am. Soc. C. E.—The scientific conditions of the digestion of sewage sludge in separate tanks (separated from the flowing sewage) were first studied by Mr. H. W. Clark, in Boston, Mass., in 1899. Since 1906 sludge digestion has been successfully carried out in the lower chamber of two-story settling and sludge-digesting tanks. Later, sanitary engineers learned also to digest sludge successfully in entirely separate tanks by the same alka-

* Cons. Engr.; Prof. of Civ. and San. Eng., The Johns Hopkins Univ., Baltimore, Md.
† Chf. Engr., "Ruhr-Verband," Ruhrverband, Essen, Germany.

line methane fermentation that is observed in the lower chamber of good two-story tanks.

The digestion depends only on two factors: Mixing and temperature. The fresh sludge is mixed with ripe alkaline sludge in order to avoid acid fermentation in the former. The pH value of ripe sludge is 7.3 to 7.6.

The temperature should be between 6° and 25° cent., the higher the better. In the Southern States the natural temperature of separate tanks may be sufficient. In the Northern States, two-story tanks are better because the sludge tank is kept warm by the flowing sewage of the upper chamber. Artificial heating is easier in separate tanks.

Liming (against acid fermentation) was first tried in 1913 by W. L. Stevenson, M. Am. Soc. C. E., and K. Thumm, in Berlin. It is also recommended by Dr. W. Rudolfs. It may have value in ripening time, or for special acid trade waste; but, ordinarily, it is not necessary.

KENNETH ALLEN,* M. AM. SOC. C. E. (by letter).—Mr. Eddy has presented an adequate and comprehensive review of progress made in salient features of sewerage and sewage disposal practice in a few pages of print to which little of importance can be added. Nevertheless, the following notes may be of enough interest to be mentioned.

The separate system of sewers was advocated by Edwin Chadwick in England in 1842 and by John Phillips in 1847, more than thirty years before its introduction in the United States by the late Col. George E. Waring. The City of Paris built its first modern sewer in the rue de Rivoli in 1851. The practice of flushing to remove deposits in the crudely designed sewers of the period by damming and then releasing the flow had been used to a considerable extent in London, England, and in Germany; but with the advent of the separate system, in which deposits were liable to occur because of the small diameters used and the intermittent flows of sewage near the upper ends of laterals, the Rogers-Field automatic flush tank came into use as a more practicable device. These tanks were deemed an essential accessory to such systems by Waring, who introduced them at Memphis, Tenn., and, with later modifications, they were largely adopted in the design of separate systems during the latter part of the Nineteenth Century, until it became apparent that their effect was more limited and their use of water more costly than at first supposed. They still find a legitimate field of usefulness under restricted conditions.

Concerning the introduction of sewerage in New York, it may be remarked that the first "Public Necessity House", or comfort station, was built in 1691, while the first public sewer is said to have been laid in Broad Street, as a result of a petition to the Town Council, in 1696; but it probably was not until 1805-07 that an important sewer, still incorporated in the existing system, was built in Canal Street. In 1860 egg-shaped sewers were introduced and, in 1864, vitrified pipe.

The first sewer in Chicago, Ill., is said to have been laid in 1835, but it was not until 1856 that construction under a systematic plan was put into effect.

* San. Engr., Office of Chf. Engr., Board of Estimate and Apportionment, New York, N. Y.

It is said that water-closets existed in Herculaneum in 400 B. C., but in spite of the precedent it was not until 1776 that a patent was issued for this device. In 1846, plumbing was introduced in America as a special luxury. Siphon traps were suggested for water-closets by the Metropolitan Sanitary Commission in England in 1847 and by 1852 they were being introduced in that country. A quarter of a century intervened, however, before the use of water-closets became common in the United States.

The question of sewer ventilation has received more attention in England and on the Continent than in this country, where reliance has been usually placed on holes in the manhole covers. These were introduced in New York in 1875. Where the sewers are designed or operated so that they keep clean, this seems to meet the sanitary demands of the case. It was just before this (1873) that Baldwin Latham published his "Sanitary Engineering", which is probably the first comprehensive treatise on the subject of sewerage in the English language.

Mr. Eddy has referred to the screw pumps at Milwaukee, Wis., Chicago, Ill., and New Orleans, La. A similar pump was installed about fifteen years ago at the head of Gowanus Canal, Brooklyn, N. Y., to flush the waters of that stream by pumping, either from it into a 12-ft. tunnel, 6 270 ft. long, leading to Buttermilk Channel, or *vice versa.* The capacity of the pump is 14 000 000 gal. per hour.

The practice of discharging sewage or sewage effluents from submerged outlets has met with increasing favor since the construction of this type at Hamburg, Germany, Boston, Mass., and Washington, D. C., about 1900. The advantage is very apparent where the depth is more than 30 ft. and where, as in more recent construction at Cleveland, Ohio, Deer Island (Boston), and in the case of the Passaic Valley sewage, discharge is distributed by means of multiple outlets.

In 1647, an Act to Prevent Pollution of Boston Harbor was passed, but for more than two and a half centuries nothing of importance was done to preserve the purity of American rivers, lakes, and harbors.

In 1876, the Massachusetts State Board of Health issued a special report dealing with the "Pollution of Rivers", the "Water Supply, Drainage, and Sewerage of the State", and on the "Disposal of Sewage", calling attention to methods used abroad and to the necessity of adopting similar measures in the interests of sanitation. This, and a report the following year, on "Pollution of Streams", were notable in rendering the results of foreign experience available to American sanitarians and engineers.

The first comprehensive report on methods of disposal, presenting definite recommendations for construction, was submitted by the late Samuel M. Gray, M. Am. Soc. C. E., to the City Council of Providence, R. I., in 1884, although a few attempts at disposal on a small scale had already been made. The first attempt, involving irrigation, had been made at an insane asylum at Augusta, Me., in 1876, and at Cheyenne, Wyo., in 1883.

The water-closet was by that time being introduced and the condition of watercourses in the more densely populated districts was becoming more serious. Land disposal was in vogue as a method, and chemical precipitation was coming into favor. The plant recommended by Mr. Gray was built at Providence and was followed by others elsewhere, as mentioned by Mr. Eddy. Among the smaller plants was that utilizing the Dortmund type of tank designed by Allen Hazen, M. Am. Soc. C. E., and operated at the World's Columbian Exposition in Chicago, in 1893.

During the two decades following 1880, irrigation or intermittent filtration was introduced at Pullman, Ill., South Framingham, and Brockton, Mass., Plainfield, N. J., Pawtucket, R. I., Canton, Ohio, and elsewhere. The experiments on filtration, conducted by the Massachusetts State Board of Health, at Lawrence, during and subsequent to the late Nineties, under the direction of the late Hiram F. Mills, Hon. M. Am. Soc. C. E., added emphasis to the important part played by air, and were followed by the development of the contact bed and trickling filter. At Reading, Pa., a double-deck filter was constructed above ground, where screened sewage was first strained through a bed of coke and delivered to a filter of sand resting on cinders. After percolating through this bed the sewage fell about 10 ft., in the form of rain, to a second filter consisting of sand resting on slag. The process provided a good effluent, but proved expensive and, later, was abandoned.

In 1909, aerators, leading the air caught by cowls to the bottom of trickling filters, were introduced by the late Rudolph Hering, M. Am. Soc. C. E., at Atlanta, Ga.

Among the more recent applications of air to filtration should be mentioned that of Strogonoff, at Moscow, where oxidation is hastened by introducing air in the bottom of an enclosed filter of fine material about 11 ft. deep. In this way it is claimed that ten times the volume of sewage can be treated per acre as by the ordinary trickling filter.

Meanwhile, the septic tank came into favor for sedimentation, followed by the Imhoff tank, of which type the Calumet Plant at Chicago deserves mention, while methods of artificial aeration were being attempted in a small way.

The important rôle played by the free contact with air in the treatment of sewage was recognized in England by Angus Smith as early as 1882. In 1891, Col. Waring began experiments at Newport, R. I., by forcing air into a bed of gravel or broken stone, which process he patented and introduced at small plants in Brooklyn, N. Y., Philadelphia, and Wayne, Pa., and elsewhere. In 1892, Lowcock came out with a somewhat similar process in England. In 1910, Black and Phelps conducted experiments in forcing air through colloider tanks at the 26th Ward Plant, Brooklyn, and, in 1913-14, the activated sludge process was developed by Fowler and his associates at Manchester, England. It was patented in America in 1915 by Mr. Leslie C. Frank.

A recent development along the lines of activated sludge has been made by Karl Imhoff, M. Am. Soc. C. E., in what is called an "Emscher" filter, or "contact aerator", introduced at Kettwig, Germany, in 1925. In this a certain degree of activation is brought about through the artificial aeration of the biological growth on filter media submerged in the upper compartment of an Imhoff tank, resulting in the elimination of separate aeration tanks.

Disinfection of sewage by calcium hypochlorite was tried out in 1884 in London by Dibdin and was investigated in Germany by Proskauer, Elsner, and Dunbar, and in the United States by Phelps, who, in 1907, applied it on a practical scale at Red Bank, N. J. More recently liquid chlorine has largely supplanted hypochlorite, and its use has extended rapidly for the protection of shellfish and bathing beaches. It has also been advocated to defer the oxygen demand of effluents.

Reviewing the development of sewerage and sewage treatment in America, experience, first in England and, later, in Germany, has been freely utilized; but it has been modified to the different climatic demands and in accord with independent research, of which the outstanding example was the early work of the Massachusetts State Board of Health. Irrigation, intermittent filtration, chemical precipitation, the contact filter, and the septic tank, have all seen their day; while fine screening, the Imhoff tank, sedimentation tanks with mechanical sludge removal, the activated sludge process, and chlorination, hold their own as standard and reliable methods of treatment.

George S. Webster,* Past-President, Am. Soc. C. E.—Relative to Mr. Eddy's paper, the speaker has been asked to discuss briefly the growth of the sewerage system in Philadelphia, Pa. Philadelphia was one of the first of the large cities in the United States to be laid out on a systematic plan. This was done in 1682 by Thomas Holme, Surveyor to William Penn, the first proprietor of the Commonwealth of Pennsylvania. In the development of these early plans, provision was made for drainage systems.

The first of these drainage channels was built about 100 years ago. They were built of bricks laid with dry inverts, that is, without mortar joints; were generally 7 or 8 ft. deep and were intended to carry off both surface and ground-water. No buildings were connected with them at that time. Later, many of these drainage channels became part of the combined system of sewers of the city. The first effort to determine the size of sewers for run-off was made by the Board of Aldermen and not by the City Engineer. The Aldermen decreed that all branch sewers should be 3 ft. in diameter.

In 1875, the speaker was in charge of a Field Corps of Engineers at the Centennial Exposition Grounds in Philadelphia and, under direction of those in authority, gave lines and grades, and supervised the construction of sanitary sewers discharging directly into the Schuylkill River above the dam and into the pool from which a part of the City's water supply was taken and furnished without treatment to the citizens. This resulted in typhoid fever in October and November, 1876—a serious epidemic in Philadelphia.

This instance indicates the state of the science of Sanitary Engineering at that date and emphasizes the great advancement that has been made in the last 50 years.

At the time of the Centennial Exposition in 1876, the late Rudolph Hering, M. Am. Soc. C. E., obtained from the Swiss Exhibit, a diagram showing the Ganguillet and Kutter curves for the flow of water in channels and the speaker made a tracing of it for the use of the City Engineering Department and for the Engineering Profession in general.

* Cons. Engr., Philadelphia, Pa.

The first empirical formula of which the speaker has any knowledge, that was used for determining run-off when designing sewers in Philadelphia, was "one cubic foot per acre per second", which is equivalent to 1 in. of rainfall per hour, all reaching the sewer. This is not a bad rule for an engineer to use as a rough check on his assistants in calculating run-off for large sewers.

In 1880, the American Public Health Association sent Mr. Hering to Europe to investigate sewerage practice, and his report thereon marks one of the turning points in sewer design in this country as it placed such design on a scientific basis rather than by rule-of-thumb. He brought back with him the Burkli-Ziegler formula. This was thought to be the last word in determining the run-off for storm-water sewers. It was soon found, however, that in a city like Philadelphia, with street grades varying from 1 ft. in 1 000 ft. in the flat sections to 10%, or more, in high suburbs, this formula did not give acceptable results in all cases.

The McMath or St. Louis formula, a modification of the Burkli-Ziegler, was tried for a time. It gave better results, but did not prove satisfactory. The City then established 6 pluviometer stations for recording intensity, duration, and the amount of rainfall in the city limits and also installed automatic recording flow gauges in a number of sewers; and from the information thus collected, a new formula known as the "Philadelphia formula" was evolved. It was in reality an extension or modification of the Burkli-Ziegler and McMath formulas. This was an advance over previous methods of determining run-off, but did not give correct results under all conditions.

All these investigations led to the adoption of what is called "the rational method of designing sewers" which is based on data collected in Philadelphia and on facts evolved by the late Emil Kuichling, M. Am. Soc. C. E., in his work at Rochester, N. Y.

Finding that the streams into which sewers discharged were becoming very heavily polluted and that the maintenance of public health demanded that some corrective steps should be taken, the City of Philadelphia has adopted a comprehensive plan and has entered on the treatment of its sewage on a large scale. There is in operation a treatment plant on the Delaware River near the Torresdale intake to the City's water supply. At this plant, Imhoff tanks, sprinkling filters, chlorination, and sedimentation are successfully used. In the northeast section of the city, a series of Imhoff tanks have been installed and are in operation, while in the southwestern section, preparations are under way for the erection of a large plant for sewage treatment.

L. L. Tribus,* M. Am. Soc. C. E.—Mr. Greeley's paper relating 150 years of municipal history, has naturally included many items of interest, but of necessity has had to omit enlargement where it sometimes would have proved very interesting.

No one can remember conditions farther back than perhaps one-third of the period, but the important phases of municipal housekeeping that comprise the cleaning of streets, gathering of waste products, and disposing of them, have all been developed in the past 50 years.

* Cons. Engr. (Tribus & Massa), New York, N. Y.

The perfection of pavement cleanliness now demanded, was impossible (even if wanted), prior to the advent of hard and smooth pavements. Macadam could not be machine-swept without risk of injury to the surface coat, unless maintained with greater care and at larger cost than cities would sanction. Cobble-stones, which covered so many miles of some city streets, afforded ideal gathering places for innumerable filth germs.

So far as the speaker recalls, the only place on earth where cobble pavements had any real excuse for existence is at Funchal, in the Madeira Islands, where transportation is by ox teams drawing sleds with well-greased wooden runners.

As people advance in desires, their demand is for larger municipal operations; and *vice versa,* larger operations re-act on the people. The speaker well remembers certain experiments of about 20 years ago. He selected three ill-paved, ill-kept, slum streets in different parts of a city. The buildings were largely devoid of paint; windows were rarely fully glazed; shutters hung by one hinge; house refuse was thrown in the gutters; children abounded and, equally with their parents, were a slovenly lot.

The curbing was then straightened; good curb-to-curb pavements were laid; a street sweeper in white uniform was assigned to each street; and notices were served asking house occupants to put refuse in sound receptacles, for regular daily collection by the city. What happened? Within six months windows were glazed; shutters hung; painting had begun; sidewalks were being repaired or renewed; garbage and wastes were almost completely placed in metal containers; some plate-glass store fronts appeared; children were less tattered and more frequently actually washed; and the parents began to be self-respecting. In one year the transformation was complete, and has been lasting.

Mr. Greeley has called attention to the basic fact in municipal house-cleaning problems, that only when those at the head take a real interest in their jobs, does efficiency show in the work itself. An enthusiastic head, honest and capable, will secure, out of even poor raw material, results that will bring credit and community praise.

The inter-relationship of pavements and street cleanliness is so vital that only with the former in first-class shape can the latter obtain. Street cleanliness usually re-acts on the maintenance of properties, but not always.

Municipalizing garbage and refuse collection and treatment systems is rather the last great step, aside from transportation, in city life. Water-works, sewage systems, and various other utilities reach approximate perfection, but private ash collection continues, with its greater per capita cost, until places for dumping refuse or for feeding garbage to hogs, and for reduction processes, cannot be readily obtained. Then municipal relief is demanded.

The Oriental and near-Oriental sensibility to smell and sight does not seem as keen as that of the conglomerate and amalgamated American with its Anglo-Saxon predominance; so the dog and vulture scavengers that comprise the street-cleaning personnel of many populous cities are even yet tolerated.

The speaker is glad that he visited Constantinople before the thousands of street dogs were destroyed, and saw the groups of mangy curs, large and small, appropriating the sidewalks, while pedestrians walked in the streets. These groups knew their own districts, perhaps by virtue of dog vote and determination, for it was immediate destruction for any dog to step outside his own territory. Not a scrap of any edible refuse could long be found in the streets of that wonderful cosmopolitan city. The unpaid, non-uniformed, four-footed corps did the trick, until finally banished to a neighboring island. They are said to have disappeared through the process of killing and eating each other. Lack of general sanitation, however, produces a terrible death toll when epidemic breaks out in Oriental cities.

Mr. Greeley has outlined the types of treatment plants with some of their respective merits, but on the economic side has not had time to emphasize sufficiently two points: (*a*) The relationship of costs of collection and haul, to the locations, sizes, and types of disposal systems; and (*b*) the possible market, if any, and means of reaching it, for recoveries of by-products and residues.

As a general principle, a large community must consider the whole services as one of net expense, with perhaps opportunity for some returns by the way.

For historical accuracy as to the introduction of the English furnace into this country, the speaker desires to give large credit to Mr. George Cromwell, who as President of the Borough of Richmond, City of New York, by his broad-gauged intelligent co-operation and authorizations permitted the completion of a long course of experiments. These were conducted by the writer, with Mr. Richard T. Fox (later of Chicago, Ill.), and John T. Fetherston, M. Am. Soc. C. E. (later, Commissioner of Street Cleaning of the three larger boroughs of New York), as chief assistants.

The findings were confirmed by Mr. Fetherston in a visit to Great Britain and the English type of high-temperature incinerator was subsequently adopted to serve the needs of Staten Island.

The speaker's special contribution to the change from the original English type of furnace, was the joint cooling of the clinker and heating of the forced-draft air, by driving it through the hot clinker while held on a lower grate. Mr. Fetherston's very valuable and useful patent was the making of a ridged grate, which formed breakage lines in the clinker, rendering its removal simple. The hydraulic charging pan was first perfected in the West New Brighton, Staten Island, N. Y., station.

Concurrently, with the Staten Island experiments and independently therefrom, the City Engineer of Seattle, Wash., reached the same conclusion, namely, that high-temperature incineration was the best form where utilization was not expedient and where the early destruction of organic matters was essential.

Staten Island seems to have been, not only the early nursery of scientific garbage treatment, following its first two Dixon furnaces, but the site of a very large Cobwell reduction plant that furnished cause for much litigation, throughout the course of which the speaker was consultant to those in opposition, led by the District Attorney and committees of the people. Briefly, the proven excessive nuisance from odors caused the final closing of the plant, not condemning the Cobwell system *per se,* but rather the operation of that particular installation.

Smooth, hard pavements, rubber tires, and horseless vehicles have lessened street noise and pavement wear, making street cleaning much simpler, more efficient, and cheaper than formerly. Municipal garbage and refuse collection, with treatment in high-temperature furnaces, has made for betterment.

Snow removal is a factor in large city housekeeping in the temperate zones. "Old Sol" looks after the situation in the southern range of cities where snow occasionally falls. "Jack Frost" largely holds the snow in place in the northern communities, until spring thawing attends to the matter; sidewalks are cleared, adding to the depth of snow in the roadways where sleigh and sled traffic soon packs it down.

More of the largely populated places come within the first series, and the problems have been many. Gathering by scrapers, and hand-shoveling, with carting to water-front dumps, have been most generally adopted; but probably the most efficient method, where sewers are large enough, is gathering and dumping into sewer manholes, aided, if the weather be not too cold, with urge of water from fire hose lines. A light fall may even be wholly flushed by hose into corner basins. The total of annual expense runs into many millions of dollars.

What the next 150 years may bring forth is hard to predict. Perhaps boneless synthetic foods will be prepared that will entirely eliminate garbage wastes, and only the containers will require disposal! The imagination might well run riot, as to the future, in view of past achievements—so well reviewed by Mr. Greeley. In general, however, engineers had better report upon accomplishment, rather than prophesy.

N. T. Veatch, Jr.,* M. Am. Soc. C. E. (by letter).—The subject of street cleaning and the disposal of refuse, discussed by Mr. Greeley, is one which, in a way, may be termed an "orphan child" of the Engineering Profession. Few engineers have had the desire, or perhaps the nerve, to make any effort to study the subject from its engineering or scientific angles, and, as a consequence, the profession does not have the wealth of engineering data and background of precedents in this particular field that it enjoys in many others. An engineering writer who is usually well informed on the subject once offered, in substance, the following statement, as one of the reasons for its present status from an engineering standpoint: "The question of collection and disposal of refuse has been made a 'political football' so to speak, and there is an almost universal lack of realization on the part of city officials that the subject is really an engineering matter."

This assertion is undoubtedly true, as is evidenced by the fact that, generally speaking, this particular division of municipal service is handled by branches of the city government not connected with the engineering department, and with comparatively few exceptions it is given no engineering advice or supervision. As a result, there are numerous examples of failures in practically every method of handling the problem, and practically every city official, in whose department the refuse collection and disposal is controlled, feels that he has started his duties as a public official with a veritable "stone hung around his neck".

* Cons. Engr. (Black and Veatch), Kansas City, Mo.

The lack of proper methods in street cleaning and the collection and disposal of refuse has been, and still is, responsible for the loss of many lives among the urban populations of this and other countries. This is true to a degree sufficient to challenge the interest and effort of every one interested in sanitary science. The fact that, at best, the refuse problem is a difficult and unpleasant one, due to its very nature and its political entanglements, is perhaps one of the causes for its not receiving the attention it should from the Engineering Profession in general. However, the difficulties that the problem seems to carry with it are causes only, and should not be made into excuses. In spite of difficulties, an immense amount of scientific engineering thought and study has been given to the problem, and there are numerous examples of outstanding service on the part of conscientious city officials and members of the Medical and Engineering Professions. There are also numerous examples of cities having efficient and successful handling of their street cleaning and refuse problems, and it is pleasing to note that most of them have had scientific and technical advice, and that they have followed it.

Much valuable data have been accumulated both in this country and abroad, valuable service has been rendered, and valuable results have been obtained by a rather small coterie of the Engineering Profession. Mr. Greeley is one of that number, and the profession is indebted to him as well as many other contributors. He is undoubtedly correct when he states that, "efficiency of operation and progress in the future will depend in large measure on the character and training of municipal governments."

In Kansas City, Mo., the question of garbage collection and disposal was for years a "thorn in the side" of the city officials. The service has been, and still is, obtained through private contract. For a long period, the contractor was paid a lump sum per year, the amount being increased from time to time as the city increased in population. This plan did not give the best results, as the house service was unsatisfactory. The contractor fed the collected garbage to hogs, and in consequence a considerable amount of material that goes into the usual house garbage was rejected by the collectors, and numerous complaints of non-collection were made. Such results, perhaps, could be expected where the contractor's co-operation depended in no way on the amount of garbage collected.

In an attempt to solve the problem, the city officials found themselves confronted, not only with the question of proper collection, but also with one of disposal, because the location of the hog-feeding pens was unsatisfactory. Due, somewhat, to lack of proper engineering guidance, the city at one time tried to enter into contract with a private disposal company on the basis of building, at the city's expense, a plant to dispose of the garbage by a patented process, which to that time had not demonstrated its feasibility. This action was stopped by injunction. Later, the city had engineering specifications prepared, and called for bids including those for both collection and disposal. The contractor was to select his own method in the latter. The successful bidder turned the matter of mechanical garbage disposal over to a sub-contractor and agreed to assume all expense of installation and responsibility for the operation of the plant.

As soon as the contractor had his work under way, and his routes organized in a preliminary manner, the city had an engineering survey made, and a report prepared covering the services included in the contract. This report included a careful study of the city, its population distribution and concentration, character, and quantities of garbage from different sections of the city, manner of house treatment, operation and routing of collection units, together with all other features entering into the problem. As a result of this engineering study, and a rather unusual effort in co-operation on the part of the contractor, marked improvement in the collection service was soon noted.

The contract calls for payment by the city on the basis of tons of garbage collected, and carries with it a definite penalty clause covering complaints for lack of service. This plan has resulted in continued good service.

The patented process used for garbage disposal is known as the "Pan-American process", mentioned by Mr. Greeley. While the plant has not been in operation long enough to prove its practicability definitely, the process, if successful, will be a decided benefit, and its feasibility is looked forward to with a great deal of interest.

Although there may be considerable question as to whether the best service can be given under municipal operation or private contract, there is no question but what Kansas City benefited materially from the scientific manner in which its garbage disposal problem was handled.

ARTHUR E. MORGAN,* M. AM. SOC. C. E.—In every phase of the development outlined by Mr. McCrory is seen the same characteristic of gradual growth from crude and simple origins to great and complicated operations. The author describes the beginning of tile drainage in New York State 50 years ago with the use of 1, 2, and 3-in. tiles, and the beginning of open drainage with small farm ditches. From these have developed the extensive systems of underground drains in the Middle West, laid with great tile 2 or 3 ft. in diameter, and the open channels, sometimes 100 ft., or more, in width, in systems draining hundreds of square miles. In the development of excavating machinery there has been the same gradual growth, from the time when all work was done by hand, to the present day of dipper-dredges, drag-lines, cableway excavators, and suction dredges.

In the associated legal developments can be seen the same trend from the old primitive laws, enabling a few farmers to co-operate, each digging his share of the neighborhood ditch, to some of the modern codes, under which as many as 50 000 tracts of land have been assessed to pay the cost of a single improvement.

In most of that legal development it has been characteristic that lawmakers have seen but a little way ahead. The speaker has been interested in following the history of drainage law. As a rule each statute that has been passed, has been in the interest of some single project or type of project, and reflects the particular experiences of those who drafted it. Each law generally accepts the code that has gone before, and makes modifications of particular features. The process has been a step-by-step development, each

* Pres., Antioch Coll.; Pres., Dayton Morgan Eng. Co., Dayton, Ohio.

new code carrying along the vestiges and appendages of obsolete legal and administrative procedure. Land drainage engineers are only beginning to devise and create codes that are new in their general structure, based on comprehensive study of needs and of legal and administrative procedure.

The progress of drainage has depended, not upon the improvement of any single factor, but upon the co-ordinate development of all factors, technical, mechanical, legal, and administrative, that enter into such a development. If a single factor falls behind, the whole development must suffer.

Some years ago the speaker saw a drainage canal recently excavated by a dipper-dredge to drain part of the Dismal Swamp in Virginia. The work was done from plans made by George Washington. In his early days he had dreamed of draining the Dismal Swamp, but his plans waited 150 years because no equipment was available for their execution. The speaker first worked with Mr. McCrory in 1907, in Colorado. There they made plans for reclaiming "alkali" lands which, if executed, would reclaim a large waste area; but because of inadequate legislation 15 years passed before any substantial progress was made.

The process of reclamation does not depend on engineering design or on excavating equipment alone, but on the co-ordinate development of every factor that is involved. In his proper function the engineer is the person who co-ordinates and synchronizes all these factors. Anything that affects the ultimate success of the project is a proper part of his work. Sometimes, the engineer sees himself as concerned only with technical design. Until he can rise above that concept, and can see his work to include all factors necessary for the proper development and co-ordination of all elements, he will not come into his own.

When the speaker first planned extensive drainage work in Minnesota before 1905, the drainage laws were very inadequate. He spent a year in revising the Drainage Code and in getting his revision approved by engineers and lawyers, and passed by the Legislature. There was no suitable power equipment in the State and there were no experienced contractors to operate the equipment; so he searched the entire country for both. In his opinion, these efforts were normal and proper elements of engineering.

In the subsequent 20 years of practice this conviction has been strengthened. Is it not true that the factor most lacking to-day in the control of water is a larger concept of his functions by the engineer? There are great projects in this country that never can be fully realized until the engineer has a picture of the possibilities, and until he possesses the co-ordinating mind that brings together all necessary factors.

The engineer must see himself as the center of these developments. He must be enough of a lawyer to appraise the legal factors; enough of an engineer to plan the destinies of streams rather than the expediency of particular cases; enough of a business man to co-ordinate and define policies; enough of a developer to bring about the necessary adaptation of mechanical equipment; and enough of an administrator to bring all these factors together to effect his purposes.

The time is coming when the co-ordinating work of the drainage and reclamation engineer must extend beyond State lines. On the Colorado River there is a deadlock because of the lack of interstate machinery. There are great projects in Missouri and Arkansas similarly waiting for the technique of interstate co-operation. The compact now being worked out between New York, Pennsylvania, and New Jersey to give unified control to the Delaware River is a step in the right direction.

The control of water should not be exercised with reference to any one interest, but all probable uses and effects of water must be considered in engineering programs. About 1915 the speaker endeavored to outline, for the Water Supply Division of the State of Pennsylvania, a statement of policy for the use of its waters for all purposes.* An effort was made to consider the water supply of the State as one of its major resources, to be administered for all its uses by a department of the State Government, that should pass upon conflicts of interest.

Water is one of the prime essentials of civilization, and must be controlled and used with recognition of all the interests involved, and not of one alone. Sanitation, agriculture, power development, navigation, fisheries, or water supply must not be considered alone, but each one in relation to all the others. Organization and design must replace the present anarchy.

A striking example is the control and use of the waters of the Great Lakes. Navigation interests assume that they are all-important; power interests endeavor to direct events to further their own ends; the City of Chicago thinks chiefly of the Great Lakes as furnishing water for waste disposal; and public sentiment inclines to the attitude that the flow from the Lakes should first of all be conserved to maintain scenic effects at Niagara. The Great Lakes present a single problem in the control and use of water. To realize that, a single co-ordinated system of control, with all interests and uses taken into account, must replace the present conflict of interests.

To bring about such changes as this, the development of engineering statesmanship is needed. The engineer, more than any one else, is able to see the whole problem, and to bring the comprehensive control of waters to a level with the best phases of present civilization. Just as efforts for the control of water have grown in importance from the farmer's ditch to the control of the Great Lakes, so the work of the hydraulic engineer must lead from the country drain surveyor to the engineering statesman who devises and administers the control and use of great water resources.

ARTHUR M. SHAW,† M. AM. SOC. C. E. (by letter).—Mr. McCrory presents, in an interesting manner, the evolution of the modern system of drainage, especially sub-drainage, as an adjunct to agricultural development. Few people who live in cities realize the vital importance of controlling soil moisture by drainage. Irrigation, being frequently more spectacular, appeals to the imagination although infinitely more agricultural products come from lands that have been drained artificially (to a greater or less extent) than are produced by irrigated lands.

* Report of 1916.

† Cons. Engr., New Orleans, La.

The various steps in drainage became synchronized with the growth of the country, although it is doubtful whether artificial drainage ever was practiced to any great extent by the early New England colonists. With important exceptions, the practice of sub-drainage, originating in England, jumped the more rugged lands of New England and came to its greatest early development in Western New York. From there, the idea was taken into the "Western Reserve" and, later, into Indiana, Illinois, Iowa, and farther west and north.

By the time that these newer areas were brought under cultivation, it had been found that clay drain tile were so superior to the pioneer "blind drain", made of stones or brush, that few of the latter were used; but some temporary substitute was found necessary to serve the sections where tile could not be secured or where the farmers were not able to bear the initial expense. Such substitutes were the "Mole" and the "Bull Ditcher."

The original "mole" was a crude but heavily constructed sled with a steel plate extending down from the bottom of the sled to a depth of about 30 in. The plate was placed in such a position that, in pulling the sled along, a slit was cut in the ground by the edge of the plate, the lower end being given a sufficient "lead" to insure its remaining in the ground to its full depth. At the rear edge of the plate, near its bottom, was attached a short piece of chain, at the other end of which was a 4-in. forged iron ball; or, if available, an old cannon ball. The "machine" required about twenty yoke of oxen to pull it, although it frequently was pulled by one team of horses operating a home-made windlass.

The "bull ditcher" resembled a giant, double mold-board plow and was used in digging open ditches. In its later form, it could dig a ditch of 3 ft., or more, in depth. To avoid excessive draft, it usually was designed to construct a V-shaped ditch with side slopes of 2 on 1, or flatter. This equipment was used in the drainage of thousands of acres of prairie and marsh lands, principally in Northern Iowa and in Minnesota. The writer used an adaptation of the idea a few years ago in the preliminary ditching of a 1 500-acre tract of Louisiana "trembling prairie". A huge cypress log was sharpened at one end and provided with a stiff coulter and a pair of heavy plank wings for spreading the dirt. This crude appliance was pulled through the soft muck by a cable running to a donkey engine which was mounted on a barge. Canals had been dug at ¼-mile intervals and these served for transferring the power equipment.

Except under very favorable soil conditions, the useful life of the "mole" drain did not extend over a period of more than two or three years, but the "bull ditcher" proved to be a real success for its time. In digging comparatively shallow, flat slope ditches in suitable soil, free from rocks or stumps, it is doubtful if any modern machine could compete with it in its low cost of operation and upkeep.

A history of land drainage in the United States would not be complete without reference to the thousands of miles of open ditches still used in the drainage of the sugar plantations of Louisiana. Until recently they were dug and maintained by hand labor and this method is still utilized on the majority of the plantations, although machine ditchers of the wheel, or the endless chain and bucket type, are coming into use. Many experiments have been made in the sugar belt with tile sub-drains, but they have not been as successful as in other sections.

W. B. Gregory,* M. Am. Soc. C. E. (by letter).—The paper by Mr. McCrory presents the main points in the history of modern drainage and, of necessity, the author has omitted many points of local interest.

To the inhabitants of the State of Louisiana the problem of drainage will always claim a lively interest. This State ranks second in area of swamp lands, the State of Florida alone having a greater area. The City of New Orleans, the metropolis of the South, is built on alluvial land, a portion of which is below mean Gulf level. Except for narrow strips along the Mississippi River, the lands of Southeast Louisiana are at or near the level of the waters of the Gulf.

Under these conditions the problem of drainage by pumps becomes of considerable importance. The sugar plantations, with high lands near the river, were first drained by means of open ditches. Later, the amount of cultivable land was extended by building levees around the rear of the plantations and pumping out the drainage water. The pumps first used (as noted on page 1254), were drainage wheels, modeled after scoop wheels, used hundreds of years ago in Spain and other parts of Europe. In its later development these wheels were 28 to 30 ft. in diameter, with widths of from 6 to 8 ft. They were used to pump large volumes of water through small lifts, usually not more than one-fourth the diameter of the wheel.

One difficulty encountered with the scoop wheel was in the foundations, which were expensive and difficult to maintain. With the development of centrifugal pumps, the Ivens or the Menge pump was used because of the lower cost of installation, but not because of more efficient operation.

In turn, the centrifugal pump has found a competitor in the screw pump. The City of New Orleans is an example of the change in methods of pumping. The first pumps were of the scoop type, then the centrifugal, and now screw pumps are largely used.

Practically the same changes have taken place in the pumping of drainage water from agricultural lands, for while a few drainage wheels are still to be found on plantations, there are many more centrifugal pumps and some modern installations use screw pumps.

A notable example of drainage of swamp lands is to be found in the Fourth Jefferson Drainage District, comprising about 30 000 acres of Jefferson Parish, just west of the Parish of Orleans—the City of New Orleans. A large part of the area is swamp land, but the run-off from the high lands along the river is also to be pumped by four large pumping plants, each having two units of screw pumps, each of which is capable of removing approximately 120 000 gal. per min., at low lifts, the capacity falling off slightly at higher lifts. Each pump is driven by a 330-h.p., 4-cycle, Diesel engine. The net capacity of the pumps is sufficient to remove a run-off of 1.5 in. in 24 hours.

* Cons. Engr.; Irrig. Engr., U. S. Dept. of Agriculture; Prof. of Experimental Eng., Tulane Univ. of Louisiana, New Orleans, La.

The drainage of swamp lands is highly desirable in Southern Louisiana for many reasons, among which may be mentioned the elimination of mosquito-breeding areas and the additional area of very fertile lands to be used as homes. There was an ambitious beginning of this work in the first decade of the Twentieth Century, but the work was halted by the World War and its attending economic conditions. With vast areas of uplands in this section, that may be drained by gravity and yet are uncultivated (although not as fertile as alluvial lands), there is little incentive at present to drain swamp lands unless they are near enough to a city to promise returns that are not of a purely agricultural nature. However, some economists are discussing the approach of an era when the production of food for a vastly increasing population will be one of the gigantic problems. When the time comes that an agricultural return will justify the outlay for swamp-land reclamation, this State and many other sections of the South will come into its own and will drain these wet lands which are among the most fertile and productive to be found in the world.

R. A. Hart,* M. Am. Soc. C. E. (by letter).—The paper by Mr. McCrory leaves little to be desired. It is not made exactly clear that the work of the late Charles G. Elliott, M. Am. Soc. C. E., as Chief of Drainage Investigations, extended throughout the United States, and that his staff was concerned with the drainage problems of the humid as well as the arid regions.

With characteristic modesty, the author has refrained from mentioning his own contribution to the history of land drainage in the United States, but it is a well-known fact that he and his staff have played a dominant part in establishing land drainage on a scientific basis and have been directly instrumental in forwarding large drainage developments.

With respect to drainage of irrigated lands, one additional thought is worthy of consideration. Such drainage has to do with colonized, improved lands, in which large investments have been made, and which represents redemption of lands formerly highly productive, or the protection of lands now highly productive, rather than the reclamation of lands of relatively low market value and productiveness, as is the case with humid lands susceptible of drainage. The redemption or protection of irrigated lands by drainage often is the sole method of saving the original investment.

L. L. Hidinger,† M. Am. Soc. C. E. (by letter).—Mr. McCrory has assembled interesting and fairly complete data on the most important phases of the subject. However, it occurs to the writer that the section, "Construction of Open Ditches" might have covered a somewhat wider field.

Mr. McCrory refers to the fact that floating dipper-dredges have been largely replaced by drag-line excavators. This change has made the construction of more stable side slopes possible. Prior to 1920 practically all the dredging for open drainage channels was accomplished by floating dipper dredges. This type of dredge is a very unwieldy machine. It is impracticable to dig side slopes flatter than 1 on 1 with this type of equipment and,

---

* Secy.-Mgr., Western Clay Products Assoc., Salt Lake City, Utah.

† Pres., Morgan Eng. Cos., Memphis, Tenn.

as a rule, the slopes are left considerably steeper. Some of the first work was laid out with side slopes of 1 on ½, because it is not economically practicable to dig flatter slopes with a floating dipper-dredge. This was done with the expectation that the banks would weather down to a flatter slope and still leave sufficient capacity in the drainage channel. The floating dredge was almost invariably too large to dig short laterals to a properly designed cross-section, so that deterioration from the side slopes was not considered a serious defect, provided they were laid out deep enough to allow some sedimentation in the bottom without impairing the drainage of adjacent lands.

The substitution of drag-line excavating equipment for floating dredges has made possible the construction of drainage channels with any side slope that may be considered stable. Since the common use of this type of equipment, side slopes have been changed from 1 on ½ to 1 on 1½, or flatter, as may be deemed necessary. The present tendency is to dredge open drainage channels with 1 on 2 side slopes where they are located in ordinary alluvial soils, and flatter where the material is unstable.

Another important change in the construction of open drainage channels that has come about through the use of drag-line equipment, is a better balanced drainage system. When floating equipment was in common use it was cheaper to excavate small laterals with the dredge than by other means. This resulted in over-sized laterals that left an unbalanced drainage system. It is a recognized fact, among well informed reclamation engineers, that it is not economically feasible to construct channels for land drainage purposes large enough to carry off rainfall as fast as it is precipitated, and that part of it must be stored temporarily. Such being the case, it is imperative that a drainage system be balanced as carefully as possible so that lateral drains will not have excess capacity and thus overload the outlet channels. The drag-line has made possible the construction of drainage channels in accordance with the design, so that a better balanced drainage system can be installed and the flooding of lower lying lands can be largely prevented.

TABLE 6.—Capacity of Drainage Systems.

Location.	Year.	Cubic feet per second per square mile.
Southeast Missouri	1910	7.4
Northeast Arkansas	1912	8.8
Southeast Arkansas	1913	13.5
Southeast Missouri	1924	15.4
Northeast Arkansas	1925	17.4
Southwest Arkansas	1925	20.0

There has been a steady increase in the designed capacity of drainage channels. The first run-off curves provided only about one-third the capacity that is now used. Table 6 shows the increase in capacity of drainage systems located in the Lower Mississippi River Valley within the last 18 years. It is based on an area of 300 sq. miles.

Roy N. Towl,* M. Am. Soc. C. E. (by letter).—It has been the writer's privilege during recent years to study silting problems affecting the maintenance of drainage ditches in the Missouri River Valley from Yankton, S. Dak. to St. Louis, Mo. The average fall of the river is about 0.8 ft. per mile. The banks are several feet higher than the sag of the valley between the river and the bluffs, which latter rise to an elevation of 200 to 300 ft. The natural drainage of the valley is generally parallel with the river for a distance of 10 to 20 miles before finding a natural outlet or making an artificial ditch outlet. Hence, it is necessary to receive small tributaries directly into the drainage system and, consequently, many drainage systems have been destroyed with silt deposits, or seriously burdened, requiring frequent and expensive clean-out operations.

About 1905, W. E. Pratt, County Surveyor at Tekamah, Nebr., protested to the County Board against allowing Silver Creek, with a water-shed of 25 sq. miles, consisting of loess bluff formation, to enter the main drainage system without first spreading over its delta and partly de-silting its flood waters. Also, in the same water-shed, York Creek having a like drainage area, filled the main drainage ditch with silt to about 65% of its carrying capacity in one flood. In both these cases, the silt-laden flood waters have been diverted from the drainage system and carried directly to the Missouri River across the natural line of drainage. The drainage ditches are carried through undersluice-ways at crossing points. The floodway for the silt-laden stream must have a silt-transporting velocity. It is also found desirable to provide a spillway at or near the point of diversion to relieve the floodway of excess waters which may be clarified in a relatively small area before reaching the drainage system. Such diversion ditches and settling basins, separately or combined, have been used by a number of drainage districts in Iowa, Nebraska, and Missouri since 1915, with very satisfactory results.

In most cases artificial delta formation is limited to a small area for a period of 6 to 10 years and then transferred to another limited area, etc. It is desirable to de-silt flood waters on a natural or artificial flood-plain. This may be readily accomplished by removing levee embankments on one or both sides of the offending tributary stream and permitting the overflow to be distributed at a shallow depth for a considerable distance, and flooding the adjoining land, as in irrigation, and then providing for drainage of clarified waters into the main system. In certain cases of this kind, corn has been successfully raised without any loss from flooding and with a gradual deposit of rich soil on a well-drained slope on account of the inundation. This result may be expected if standing water is removed in a reasonable length of time.

Undoubtedly, this is the oldest chapter in drainage and flood regulation found in the book of Nature. The writer anticipates that it may be adapted successfully as a part of the program even for streams of the magnitude of the Colorado River. In support of this proposition he would suggest a study of the stabilized channel below Yuma, Ariz., which existed for possibly fifty years prior to attempted regulation.

* Civ. Engr. (Towl, Nelson and Schwartz), Omaha, Nebr.

Desirable channel conditions, especially with respect to maintaining drainage ditches, have been and always will be subjects for careful consideration. In this connection the writer has observed many natural and artificial drainage outlets subject to submergence and back-water from the Missouri River, which apparently were adverse; but actually the hydraulic flood grade line indicated better flowage characteristics than would seem possible. In fact, submerged silt deposits are carried out in flood time and the coefficient of roughness is very much less than that found in upper portions of the same channel not subject to back-water, but which are invaded with growth of vegetation.

Increased low-water flow in the Illinois River at Beardstown, Ill., which maintains a wider and smoother channel than would otherwise be possible, has a beneficial effect. The increased discharge at low stages has been approximately equivalent to the increased flowage from Lake Michigan during the past 20 years without any increase in stage for said increment of inflow. Thus, it may be expected that, in connection with detention and storage reservoirs, better channels will result on account of improved low-water cross-sections. The writer is also studying the problem of slack low-water flow in its relation to maintaining wider and better cross-sections in drainage channels. In this case he has found many natural examples of channels with irregular bottom profiles and fairly good, uniform flood profiles.

In conclusion, the writer must admit that his best lessons are exemplified in natural streams and more forcibly in artificial construction that refuses to become stabilized in conformity with the adopted plans and specifications for the project.

E. R. Jones,* Esq. (by letter).—The drainage policy throughout the United States has changed since 1920 from one of extensive to one of intensive drainage. By the former method is meant the practice of constructing large outlet drains for great undeveloped areas for the purpose of creating more farms. Intensive drainage means the drainage, usually by means of drain tile, of the wet spots within or at the edges of existing farms and fields.

Prior to 1920 both types of drainage were making steady progress. The agricultural depression beginning then made extensive drainage unprofitable. The demand for land, particularly new land, became less, the price of land fell, and new reclamation practically ceased.

This was not true of intensive drainage. In the face of high labor costs, and low prices for agricultural products, the farmer had to look around for means of reducing the cost of production in order to keep up his profits. He found that he had to keep two hired men during the cultivating season to give adequate cultivation to a 40-acre cornfield if it was mutilated with wet spots and swales. The fields were too wet so much of the time that he had to have a double crew ready to work fast when these spots did dry up.

Then he got tired of feeding and paying the extra hired man. He began to tile-drain the wet swales in those fields for the chief purpose of reducing the cost of cultivation. Increasing the yield was a mere incident. He found

* State Drainage Engr., Madison, Wis.

that there were commonly twice as many hours during June when a well-drained cornfield could be cultivated than were available in a field mutilated by wet swales. This meant that one man could cultivate as much corn in a well-drained field as two in a poorly drained one. That is why farmers are draining the wet spots in their fields.

One of those farmers is a resident of Reedsburg, Wis. He can use a tractor on his farm after draining the wet spots in his fields. He has paid for the tractor with the money he saved by discharging the extra hired man and with the increased yield of corn. The drain tile is his remedy for the high cost of farming. Fifty-eight carloads of tile were laid in his township in 1926.

Fortunately, intensive drainage does not cost as much as extensive drainage. With the latter, 200 rods of 5-in. tile, laid in trenches 3 ft. deep, discharging into a ready creek, at a total cost of $2 per rod, will commonly dry up all the wet swales in a 40-acre field. This $400 expenditure reflects a value on the entire field, because the wet swales made the slopes between them inaccessible in stormy weather. On extensive areas of wet land, not only do outlet ditches have to be dredged, but lines of tile 4 rods apart on the whole area may be necessary, at a total cost of $100 per acre instead of $10. That does throw the dredge or big-tile outlets into the discard. They are still necessary, however, in many old communities where a sluggish creek now forms an inadequate outlet for the lines of tile on the wet swales in the cultivated fields. Likewise, the three-cornered fields west of Brodhead, Wis., can be made rectangular and economical only by improving the channel of Juda Creek for 4 miles. This project is now under way. Because of the flashy run-off from the surrounding hills, a big ditch is better in that case than a big tile.

H. F. GRAY,* M. AM. SOC. C. E. (by letter).—At the beginning of his paragraph on "The Public and a New Idea", Mr. LePrince states that no attempt was made to control disease-bearing mosquitoes in the United States until 1913.

Pioneer work was done in California as early as 1910, and has continued since that time.† The initiative was taken by William B. Herms, now Professor of Parasitology, College of Agriculture, University of California. Under his direction, what was probably the first campaign in the United States for malaria control through the prevention of mosquito breeding was undertaken at Penryn, Calif., beginning early in March, 1910. Late in the same month, another campaign for the same purpose was begun at Oroville, Calif. In August, 1910, Bakersfield, Calif., began an anti-mosquito campaign. The first malaria-control campaign on an irrigation district was carried on at Los Molinos, Calif., in 1912, as related‡ by Thomas H. Means, M. Am. Soc. C. E.

Although these early campaigns were intended primarily as practical demonstrations of the possibility of malaria control through mosquito reduc-

* Cons. San. and Hydr. Engr., Berkeley, Calif.

† *Am. Journal of Public Health*, Vol. 2, No. 6, pp. 452–455.

‡ *Transactions*, Am. Soc. C. E., Vol. LXXVI (1913), p. 778.

tion, were handicapped by inadequate funds, and lacked official recognition through statute authority, they were so successful that the work was continued under various auspices, and extended to many other communities in the State. Finally, in 1915, the California Legislature passed a bill* authorizing the formation of mosquito-abatement districts, and providing for funds through taxation of the lands benefited. At present (1927), there are approximately twenty organized mosquito-abatement districts in the State, of which six or seven are primarily concerned with the control of salt-marsh mosquitoes; the remainder are concerned primarily with malaria control.

James E. Brooks,† Esq.—The human mind is generally so burdened with the things of the present that it forgets the things of the past; especially so if the things of the past have not been personal experiences. People think very little about the terrors and horrors of smallpox and yellow fever epidemics. In this part of the world they are things of the past, and few communities have experienced them. However, the victory over yellow fever came so much later than that over smallpox that some of those who took part in the victory over yellow fever at Havana are still living.

Mr. LePrince, who is a civil engineer, was with the late General Gorgas at Havana, and, subsequently, at Panama. He is a pioneer in the fight against disease-carrying mosquitoes, and he is still carrying on the fight.

Mr. LePrince has not painted the picture of yellow fever black enough. Of the epidemic of 1878, Gorgas says: "In this epidemic over 13 000 people in the Mississippi valley alone lost their lives, and the loss of wealth is estimated at considerably more than a hundred million dollars." Yellow fever has been epidemic as far north as Quebec, Canada, and Swansea, in Wales.

In the fight against disease-carrying mosquitoes the physician, the biologist, and the engineer should work together, hand in hand. The late Dr. Henry R. Carter was not only a physician, but a graduate civil engineer. In 1898, while he was a surgeon in the U. S. Marine Hospital Service, Dr. Carter wrote a paper on his observations upon the extrinsic incubation of yellow fever, made at Orwood and Taylor, Miss. It has been said that,

"Measured by the results produced, this was one of the most important papers ever written. * * * It was one of the great steps in establishing the true method of the transmission of yellow fever."

The life habits of the different species of mosquitoes vary greatly. While in the larva and pupa stage they all live in water, but some develop in salt water and some in fresh water; some require clean water, while others will thrive in water so polluted that fish die in it within a few minutes. Some pass the winter in the adult or winged stage, some as eggs, and a few in the larval form.

It is fortunate that warfare against mosquitoes began with a species that is readily brought under control. The successful fight against the yellow fever carrying mosquito at Havana and Panama encouraged people to fight other species without a realization of the greater difficulties to be encountered.

* Chapter 584, Statutes of 1915.

† Cons. Engr., Essex County Mosquito Extermination Comm., Newark, N. J.

The mosquito which carries yellow fever is called *Stegomyia fasciata* by some and *Aëdes œgypti* by others. Malaria is carried from person to person by mosquitoes of the genus *Anopheles*.

Mr. LePrince speaks of the rapidity with which yellow fever was brought under control, but he makes no such statement about malaria. The war against *Anopheles* will be long and expensive, but the victory will be worth the price.

In New Jersey the fight began at South Orange in 1901, and it has been going on with increasing intensity ever since. It was started to get rid of an intolerable nuisance, and was directed against mosquitoes in general without regard to species.

To-day (1928) the nine counties along the eastern border, from Bergen to Cape May, and Passaic County, have mosquito commissions acting under a law passed in 1912, and their total annual appropriations amount to more than $300 000. In only one or two of these ten counties does the control work cover the entire county. Essex County, with an area of about 125 sq. miles, and 500 000 population, spends $75 000 per year for mosquito control. This is approximately 15 cents per person. There are still eleven counties without mosquito commissions, and of all the salt marsh in the State a little more than one-half has been drained. The work is being advanced each year. Most of the undrained salt marsh is in the southern part of the State.

Methods of Mosquito Control.—All mosquitoes, in their larval stage, live in water. At present, the attack is directed against the larva; and obviously, the elimination of standing water is the most effective method. This may be accomplished either by drainage or filling.

On the salt marsh, filling is expensive and is proceeding slowly, while drainage has been accomplished rapidly. Three methods are used: Open ditches connected with tide-water; dikes with automatic tide-gates; and pumping.

On the upland, the practice of draining and filling is followed wherever it is feasible. Where water cannot be removed it may be stocked with some top-feeding fish, or treated with some chemical called a larvæcide, or the surface of the water may be covered with a film of oil. In warm weather the larvæcide or oil film must be renewed at intervals of from 8 to 10 days. As an example of routine work, in Essex County about 10 500 sewer catch-basins are treated with oil once every 10 days from the middle of June to the end of September. A cheap, safe, effective, and lasting larvæcide has not been discovered.

Results.—The relief obtained through mosquito control work in New Jersey has been very great, and has more than justified the expenditures made, both from the standpoint of increased personal health and comfort, and the increase in taxable ratables.

Failures.—A female mosquito of the genus *Aëdes* will fly about laying eggs, one at a time, on the surface of the ground where some day they may be covered with water. This may be near a pool of water or in a depression in some field or woods. Months, or even years, may pass, when a heavy

the health and comfort of all human beings. Dr. Palmer's paper is a real contribution to the literature of this subject. It is sane and well balanced. Unfortunately, only a few of the men who have attempted to discuss this subject in recent years, have had such a broad and comprehensive view of ventilation.

As a matter of fact there is a controversy raging at present between what might be called the open-window theorists and the mechanical ventilation advocates. It is not really for engineering bodies to decide this question. The Medical Profession should determine what is proper for man's health so far as air conditions are concerned. Then, the duty of the engineer is to provide these conditions. Technically speaking, the engineer should not take part in the determination of what is necessary for public health and the medical man should not concern himself with the method by which these conditions are obtained by the engineer. Unfortunately, neither of these professions has entirely done its duty in this respect.

The ventilating engineers, however, have established a research laboratory at Pittsburgh, Pa., which is operated in co-operation with the U. S. Bureau of Mines for the determination of basic facts relating to ventilation and heating. This work has been proceeding since 1919 and some very valuable results have been obtained, but the end is not yet in sight.

In this work the engineers have been ably assisted by the U. S. Public Health Service, which has made the physiological determinations, and one of the results of this very fine co-operative work has been the comfort chart. This chart shows what temperature and percentage of relative humidity gives the greatest degree of comfort. This has been termed "effective temperature". Scientists and those interested in heating and ventilating from commercial standpoints have been awaiting this chart for years. This is only the beginning, however, and with further co-operation from the Medical Profession still more light can be thrown on the troublesome question of ventilation.

Dr. Palmer mentions the common standard of 30 cu. ft. of air per min. per person, which has been written into most of the State laws governing the ventilation of school buildings. He states that this provision is unnecessarily severe, and should be amended. Perhaps he is right. Let it not be forgotten, however, that it has taken years to secure any standard of ventilation in school buildings of the various States and before efforts are made to destroy the standards that have been set up, let the correct standard first be determined.

The proponents of open-window ventilation also state that the 30-cu. ft. standard is too large, but they do not indicate the correct amount. They fail to recognize that with the method they offer, there will be times when no ventilation will be secured, for the wind does not always blow. If there is a school building with rooms on the four sides, the wind can blow on only one or two sides, at most, at the same time. The open-window ventilation is not positive ventilation.

One prominent engineer, and an authority on the subject of ventilation, has compared open-window ventilation to the old sailing ships, which were governed purely by the whim of the wind, and mechanical ventilation to the steam-driven modern palace of the sea. Certainly, there is some analogy in this comparison.

No engineer in the country to-day, who is familiar with the question of ventilation, would oppose a change in existing laws to lower the amount of air per person introduced into schools or other buildings where human beings are assembled, provided the change was made to some standard that had a scientific basis.

Most ventilating engineers feel very much as the Civil Engineering Profession would feel if a physician came along and said that the factors of safety used for steel structures were wasteful and that, instead of 10, some other factor of safety, lower than this, was all that was needed. If he did not accompany this statement with any definite scientific information as to what the lower factor should be, the engineer would feel that it was better to adhere to the higher one which was known to be safe, and which certainly could not produce harm, than to allow some law to be passed that would reduce it below that where the safety of the public was assured. That is the position of most ventilating engineers to-day. They welcome any scientific information on this subject, but they will oppose the tearing down of the progressive standards already built up until those standards can be replaced with new ones based on facts and not on theories.

The speaker is forced to disagree with Dr. Palmer when he states: "Engineers have yet to learn how to counteract the heat production of a hall full of people so that temperatures at the close will be nearer 70 than 80 degrees." The absorption of this heat production has already been solved, not only in theory, but in practice, and is being used in a great many theatres and other buildings to-day. The reason it is not more generally used is that such a system is not only costly to install, but also expensive to operate. The theatre owner, however, who is largely interested in the box-office receipts, has found that in summer it will pay to use this costly system to give comfort. The further use of this system is limited only by its commercial value and not by the ability of the ventilating or air-conditioning engineer to produce these results. In the manufacture of many products, such as capsules, photographic films, artificial silk, etc., it has been found that air conditioning, even if expensive, is profitable and, therefore, it is being used. When the general public considers its own health and comfort equal in value to a manufactured article, it will be able to secure the proper air-conditioning equipment to produce the desired result.

The speaker does not mean to suggest by this latter statement that he disagrees with Dr. Palmer in his forecast of the progress to be made in ventilation; for certainly there will come tremendous improvements in this art as well as in others. However, a more intelligent public opinion is needed on the subject of ventilation and public health and a great deal more interest on the part of medical men than in the past. It is very encouraging to see the Society considering a paper of this character. It is also encouraging to observe several co-operative efforts being made by members of the medical fraternity, public health associations, and the ventilating engineers. It is only through such movements that an early solution of this very complex question can be reached.

In the last 100 years there have been radical changes. Formerly, people lived out-of-doors most of their lives, but now they have become an indoor people. Even transportation systems, such as subways and closed automobiles, do not allow them to be outdoors as much as they need to be. It is, therefore, necessary, as Dr. Palmer points out, to furnish fresh air for indoor conditions. The ventilating engineer needs the assistance of the physician and the chemist to tell him what quality there is in the outdoor air that makes it "fresh". He can undoubtedly provide "fresh air" if he knows what it is.

Samuel R. Lewis,* Esq. (by letter).—The writer agrees in general with Dr. Palmer, except in his statement that:

"The present air-flow standard is undoubtedly excessive. This may be decreased by one-half in such places as school rooms without discomfort or harm to the occupants".

It is hardly fair or in keeping with the temperate statements of the remainder of the paper, to imply that these sentences express the consensus of present-day opinion in regard to ventilation.

In many cases, the present air-flow standard may be excessive. The air volume required is believed now to be governed by requirements of temperature and odor control, rather than by chemical or organic substances in the air.

There is evidence to support the belief, now held by many students of the subject, that an increase in health and comfort in school rooms may be gained by a supply of air per pupil per minute considerably less than the usual 30 cu. ft.

Leonard Greenburg,† Esq. (by letter).—The steps by which progress has been measured in the field of heating and ventilating during the last one hundred and fifty years are clearly described by Dr. Palmer.

It seemed certain in the earlier days that the discomfort one felt when placed in a poorly ventilated room was due to the vitiation of the atmosphere, brought about either by the production of subtle exhaled toxins, or by the accumulation of carbon dioxide. It has since been proved that these theories are incorrect and to-day most people are convinced that the discomfort is due primarily to overheating.

Every one must eat food in order to obtain the energy necessary for bodily activity. This energy is obtained from the oxidation of an amount of foodstuff capable of yielding approximately 1 to 3 000, or more, calories per day. The heat of this oxidation is liberated within the human body and in the body tissues. Some of it is needed to keep the body warm (98.6°), but a large portion must be wasted. This is done by the usual means (conduction, convection, radiation, and evaporation) from the lungs and the surfaces of the body.

* Chairman, Comm. on Research, Am. Soc. Heating and Ventilating Engrs., Chicago, Ill.

† Associate San. Engr., U. S. Public Health Service, and Lecturer in Public Health, Yale Medical School, New Haven, Conn.

If the environment is too warm, the body will have a difficult or almost impossible task in dissipating its excess heat, the heat-regulating and vascular systems of the body will be overtaxed, and discomfort will ensue. The problem of ventilation, in the light of present knowledge, resolves itself chiefly into the task of warming rooms without overheating them. To be sure, the problem of air supply is still of importance, for it is by this means that the heat is removed from large spaces, such as auditoria or theatres. To be specific the room must be comfortable when people enter it, and must remain so, in spite of the continuous contribution of heat from the people, as well as that from the heating sources which are in use. It is the regulation of these heating sources and, if necessary, the removal of body heat which must be accomplished if the environment is to be kept at the proper temperature. All this must be accomplished, as Dr. Palmer states, without the production of unpleasant drafts of cool air.

The engineer has been accustomed to deal with physical structures and materials which he can measure and weigh. To him the problem of ventilation presents one peculiar aspect, for the test of ventilation in the room is the production of a condition which shall feel comfortable to the majority of the occupants. Feeling is something new to the engineer; it is a yardstick that is more familiar to the physician. Fortunately, it is possible to translate feeling into temperature for it has been found that healthy sedentary people usually feel uncomfortable indoors in the winter when the air temperature is more than 70 degrees.

In addition to the importance of the subjective sense of comfort as a criterion of ventilation there appears to be one other aspect of the problem to which the ventilating engineer attaches insufficient importance, namely, the necessity for variability in the atmospheric conditions to which the body is exposed. The human body is peculiar, in that conditions which are continuously uniform are monotonous and distasteful to it. For this reason, the window method of ventilation with its intermittent breezes of cool and warm air, is much more pleasant than the method of closing windows and ventilating by means of the fan in the basement.

One of the real stumbling blocks in the progress of ventilation has been the indifference of the ventilating engineer to the advances which have been made in the field of physiological research. In spite of established facts there are still many ventilating engineers who demand an air change of 30 cu. ft. per person per min. It is important to note that if this change is supplied at a higher temperature than 70°, it may serve to overheat the room and produce discomfort, whereas if it is too cold, it will chill the occupants of the room. The temperature of the air is the important consideration which many still overlook.

Ventilation laws prescribe the supply of 30 cu. ft. per person per min. Few of them definitely state the temperature at which the environment should be maintained. It is obvious that they overlook the all important part of the problem. In addition, they actually impose a financial burden on the owners of the buildings and, in return, yield atmospheric conditions which, according to the studies of the New York State Commission on Ventilation, are responsible for many respiratory diseases.

Dr. Palmer's tabulation of the changes in ventilation likely to take place in the immediate future, is excellent. The writer suggests a slight change in the order of importance of these developments. To a very great degree engineers lack an understanding of what ventilating systems, once installed, will accomplish. In order to design new systems which will work with the utmost efficiency it is necessary to know the working characteristics of those now in use. On a basis of such studies, engineers will be enabled to alter designs and take into account some factors which, perhaps, are now overlooked and, what is still more important, they will learn how to operate existing plants. It will be possible to instruct those in charge of operation just what to do, when atmospheric conditions arrive at the optimum, in order to maintain these conditions. A ventilation plant should not be compared with a bridge or a building designed by an engineer because these structures usually require little or no operation, but it should be compared with the water purification or sewage treatment plant; these require expert operation and receive it as a matter of course.

It is to be hoped that, in the future, the ventilating system will be given more expert supervision and operation. If this is lacking one naturally turns his attention to the use of automatic temperature control apparatus and, without question, the improvements to be expected in this field should do much to increase operating efficiency. At first glance the problem may appear to be a simple one, but more careful study and reflection will prove it to be complicated. It must be borne in mind that direct sources of heat, such as radiators, are large heat reservoirs, and when the steam is cut off they still continue to give off heat to the room atmosphere. This suggests, at once, that radiators should be turned off somewhat below the upper limit of the comfort temperature. The satisfactory operation of thermostatic control devices depends in a large measure on adjustment and maintenance, which again emphasizes the need of trained personnel.

The field of industry presents the most interesting and important tasks for the ventilating engineer. The ventilating problems of industry are manifold, and they continue to grow in number each year. Plants for the removal of heat, for refrigeration by means of cold air, and for the removal of noxious gases, dusts, and poisons, require the services of the ablest workers. Exact knowledge of the necessary elements in designs of this type are in the hands of relatively few, and new data are essential as newer problems arise. Furthermore, these problems are complicated by industrial conditions and plant processes. They are important both from the health and economic standpoint, and should receive increased attention from the Engineering Profession.

Problems of cooling in the warm months of the year and re-circulation during the heating season depend in a large measure for their solution on the economics involved. It appears to the writer that the ventilating engineer can cool the ordinary auditorium very satisfactorily, provided the rather large expense involved is no handicap. Re-circulation can well be practiced if the economic return is justified by the design required. That improvements in this latter type of system are required there is no doubt, but these are largely of the nature of thermostatic temperature control discussed previously. The odor problem, which is of importance in this connection, may be solved partly by the careful control of temperature and humidity (odors are more pronounced at higher temperatures and humidities) and, in some measure, by the admission of outdoor air.

The chemical and not the physical viewpoint of the problem of ventilation may be regarded as the one single important obstacle in the way of ventilation progress. When this is completely eradicated progress in this field will be more rapid than it has been in the past.

George W. Fuller,* M. Am. Soc. C. E. (by letter).—The writer is appreciative of the several discussions amplifying the paper, which at best could only be brief and fragmentary on a subject with so many ramifications. As Mr. Fenkell indicates, it is to be regretted that recent performances of steam turbines and electric motor-driven centrifugal pumps, as well as data on maximum steam pressures used, were not included in the paper. However, it is probably best now to deal with them by reference rather than to include them in this discussion. These and a number of statistical and other data of interest will be found in the Manual of Water Works Practice issued by the American Water Works Association in 1925.

Harrison P. Eddy,† M. Am. Soc. C. E. (by letter).—It is always difficult to be sure of the accuracy and completeness of historical data. In presenting his paper, the writer felt that, while the information given therein was based on good authority, much other material of interest was preserved in local records or in the memories of a few. For this reason, it is gratifying that Mr. Allen and Mr. Webster have added interesting data relative to the early history of sewerage in this country, particularly as regards New York, N. Y., and Philadelphia, Pa.

The writer is inclined to believe that Mr. Kiersted has put it a little too strongly when he refers to "the insurmountable difficulties of attempting to combine, successfully, the purely mechanical process of sedimentation with the biological process of sludge digestion" in the Imhoff tank. The successful operation of Imhoff tank installations indicates that the difficulties are not insurmountable, and it is likely that Imhoff tanks will continue to occupy an important place among the devices for the treatment of sewage. The writer agrees with Mr. Kiersted in the matter of adequate preliminary sedimentation with the view of removing as large a proportion of suspended solids as possible, prior to subsequent treatment. The trickling filter functions excellently with well clarified tank effluent, although the removal of colloidal solids will materially increase its capacity, particularly with strong sewage. The periodic unloading of trickling filters is an established phenomenon, but the material unloaded by no means consists of the solids applied. Much of it is composed of

* Cons. Engr. (Fuller & McClintock), New York, N. Y.

† Cons. Engr. (Metcalf & Eddy), Boston, Mass.

organisms having their origin in the filter and would occur irrespective of the degree of removal of colloids. Sludge disposal is still a problem of importance and is often difficult to accomplish satisfactorily. As Mr. Kiersted notes, lagooning of sludge at isolated sites is often both economical and satisfactory; in other cases, however, the problem cannot be solved so easily.

Professor Gregory's emphasis of the advantages of the separate system of sewers will appeal to many engineers. Under certain conditions separate sewers are advisable and frequently decision between the two systems is difficult and is dictated by local conditions rather than by general principles. In the case of large streams, storm-water overflows may not cause serious pollution; but, as Professor Gregory indicates, such overflows may cause decidedly objectionable conditions in small streams. The common misuse of separate sewers and storm-water drains is a reflection on American municipal conditions.

Dr. Imhoff's references to sludge digestion are of interest, although data from the Imhoff tanks at Schenectady, N. Y., indicate slightly higher temperatures in the sludge compartments than in the sedimentation compartments. This fact suggests thermolytic action as a result of the digestion processes. Confirmatory evidence from other installations is desirable in this connection.

The several discussions emphasize two points: First, the great advance made in sewerage and drainage since the middle of the Nineteenth Century; and, second, the fact that much remains to be established in the scientific principles underlying proper sewage treatment and disposal.

S. H. McCrory,* M. Am. Soc. C. E. (by letter).—The writer is grateful to those who have taken part in the discussion. The development of drainage laws has been a slow process. Frequently, as Mr. Morgan suggests, laws have been passed to meet the immediate purpose. At times, emphasis perhaps has been placed on legal and engineering technicalities, and the agricultural side of the problem has been neglected. The tendency in recent laws has been to make the organization of the districts easier. It is probable that such laws have been too liberal in this respect, and that in future laws the organization of districts will be made more difficult. In considering new drainage projects there is an increasing appreciation of the importance of examining all possible uses to which the land can be put, and selecting the use for which it is best adapted.

Under-drainage is needed over a large area in the United States. Its advantages are well described by Mr. Jones. The mole drain described by Mr. Shaw had been almost abandoned when changed economic conditions made it necessary to find a cheaper method of under-drainage than the use of tile, and the mole drain came into use again. By substituting the tractor for the capstan and thus speeding up the work it is possible to construct drains 2 rods apart at the rate of 30 acres per day, at an approximate cost of about $2 per acre. Where the soil is of such texture that these drains can be used, they afford fairly adequate drainage at low cost.

Mr. Hidinger emphasizes the importance of proper balance in designing drainage systems with modern excavating machinery. Drains can be cut to

* Chf., Div. of Agricultural Eng., Bureau of Public Roads, U. S. Dept. of Agriculture, Washington, D. C.

specified size, and slopes can be adjusted to the materials through which the drains pass. The control of silt brought down by small hill streams by settling basins, as suggested by Mr. Towl, can be used to advantage on many streams. Studies now in progress under the writer's direction indicate that such basins should usually be proportioned so as to have, within the basin, from 1% to 2% of the area of the water-sheds.

The permanence of irrigated agriculture depends to a large extent on the establishment and maintenance of satisfactory drainage. As Mr. Hart states, these drains must often be constructed to prevent the loss of large areas of productive land which, under irrigation, are becoming water-logged and alkaline.

J. A. LePrince,* Esq. (by letter).—The California State Board of Health has issued a *Bulletin*† of value to those who are interested in prevalence or elimination of malaria. To a considerable extent this prevalence of malaria is due to irrigation, mining, and other operations of an engineering nature. Irrigation with inadequate drainage, seepage waters, and irrigation canals overgrown with vegetation demand attention and treatment by engineers. In the engineering schools of South Carolina, the students are taught to appreciate the importance of this phase of their work.

With regard to the mosquito control activities of New Jersey, all "mosquitoölogists" agree that it would be financially advantageous for all States with mosquito problems of economic importance to follow the lead and methods taken by New Jersey. Within the past year (1927) some unjustifiable criticism relative to anti-mosquito work in New Jersey and on Cape Cod, Massachusetts, was published in a prominent American engineering journal. The writer investigated the situation on Cape Cod and found that the total appropriation made for mosquito control was $1 000. Yet some one expected mosquito freedom over all the Cape Cod territory for that sum and stated that the enormous sums spent, had been wasted. Such news items in engineering journals are at least misleading.

Mr. Brooks states that the annual appropriations now made by the counties of New Jersey exceed $300 000 and it is probable that less than $500 000 are being appropriated by the counties of all other States taken together for mosquito control.

If such a sum were available for a few years exclusively for the control of malaria, this disease would soon disappear from the country, assuming that the elimination work was directed by competent specialists applying the newer control methods that have been devised and are being developed by the U. S. Public Health Service. These new methods are now being used in a number of countries of both hemispheres.

In connection with the elimination of pestiferous mosquitoes, the time will soon come when the public will expect the Engineering Profession to avoid building mosquito-breeding places in thickly settled communities. It means that storm-water catch-basins must be designed so that they will be dry except at time of rain.

* Senior San. Engr., U. S. Public Health Service, Memphis, Tenn.

† *Bulletin No. 44*, State Board of Health, Sacramento, Calif.

Mr. Brooks has shown unusual foresight in the general plan of ditching of the meadows of New Jersey. To have used additional smaller ditches to care for the unusually rainy seasons would have increased first costs as well as maintenance costs and, since emergency control measures are now being investigated, it is probable that sanitary engineers will be able to use the new and satisfactory supplementary measures in the years when the rains are spaced so as to be particularly favorable to mosquito life.

In regard to the statement that it is fortunate that warfare against mosquitoes began with a species (*Aedes aegypti*) that can be readily brought under control, it should be remembered that when the first campaign started it was not known that such was the case, and the public press of Havana claimed the efforts of the sanitary engineers were useless because all mosquitoes destroyed would be replaced by "others carried in from the yellow fever districts by favorable winds."

This pioneer work done in Cuba in 1901 had little effect on the reduction of the yellow fever mosquito in the Southern States, as is evidenced by the rapid spread of dengue fever in 1922. In that year there were more cases of dengue than have ever existed at any time in American history.

The relation of impounded water to malaria prevalence is now being studied by malariologists of other countries and they are sending to America for information, because the State health regulations in regard to the subject in this country have been published, and are based on scientific investigations conducted by the U. S. Public Health Service.

George Truman Palmer, Esq.* (by letter).—In closing the discussion on ventilation, the writer would like to call attention to certain mitigating circumstances which have tended to retard ventilation progress.

People can exercise choice in what they drink, what they eat, and what they wear; but, in the matter of air, they are forced to be communistic. At least, the occupants of the same enclosure are forced to share the same air environment. Within the same room, one person cannot have low temperature and another a higher temperature at the same time. So long as "some like it hot and some like it cold" there will continue to be differences of opinion on air comfort, and, in consequence, a certain amount of dissatisfaction. In the effort to eliminate the objectionable and the unhealthful in ventilation, sanitary experts can never hope to surmount entirely this question of personal preference and individual idiosyncracies.

The writer's criticism of certain existing legal requirements as to ventilation are made on the ground that they hinder progress. The 30-cu. ft. requirement obstructs the development of new methods. Window ventilation with gravity exhaust has its application. There is scientific evidence and practical experience to support this method. Many State laws, however, prohibit this practice. It is fully believed that there is less evidence to justify these laws than there is to sustain them.

If the laws were altered to permit real competitive development of ventilation methods, the better methods would eventually reveal themselves by their

* Director, Div. of Research, American Child Health Assoc., New York, N. Y.

survival. The substitution of the 15-cu. ft. requirement in place of 30 cu. ft., would make this competition possible and the experimental evidence is surely sufficient to provide assurance that health would not suffer by the change.

Mr. Samuel Lewis is quite right in criticizing the writer's statement about the desirability of reducing air-flow requirements as not representing the consensus of opinion. This should have been stated more carefully. The writer feels, however, that even if a majority of ventilating engineers may not agree with this attitude, nevertheless such a change is warranted by the experimental evidence available and by practical experience.

AMERICAN SOCIETY OF CIVIL ENGINEERS

INSTITUTED 1852

TRANSACTIONS

Paper No. 1687

INDUSTRIAL WASTE DISPOSAL

A SYMPOSIUM*

With Discussion by Messrs. Edmund B. Besselievre, George W. Fuller, Almon L. Fales, Robert Spurr Weston, and G. K. Spence.

* Presented at the meeting of the Sanitary Engineering Division, Philadelphia, Pa., October 7, 1926.

INDUSTRIAL WASTE DISPOSAL

INTRODUCTION

By W. L. Stevenson,* M. Am. Soc. C. E.

The conservation of water resources is of importance to the health and prosperity of the people of the United States. Life in modern cities is impossible without adequate public water supplies, and the protection and promotion of the public health demand that such water be pure and palatable.

Industry must have water for use in processes of manufacture, and for many industries such water must be clean. In agricultural areas clean streams are needed for watering stock, and the trend toward outdoor recreation is increasing the need for clean streams for that purpose in suitable localities.

Streams, however, are the natural drainage channels of the land and of necessity must receive the rain water which falls upon their catchment areas, carrying with it substances eroded from the surface of the earth and dissolved by the ground-water from beneath the surface.

Similarly, but artificially, the streams must also receive back again the water which having been used as public supplies in towns becomes sewage, and having been used in manufacturing becomes industrial waste, and being pumped or flowing by gravity from mines, oil wells, etc., carries substances from sub-surface strata. All these are hereinafter called waste waters.

The rule of law that each riparian owner is entitled to receive water from up-stream owners "unimpaired in quality" was undoubtedly just at the time it was declared and was practicable everywhere in this country when it was first settled. It may still be applied in the undeveloped and sparsely settled parts of the country, but elsewhere modern civilization, with sewered cities, industries, and the development of underground resources, has completely changed the primitive conditions which existed in the days of the pioneer.

Therefore, if real conservation of water resources is to be attained in order to make adequate provision for all the manifold and diverse uses of streams in the developed parts of the country, it will be necessary to adopt and carry out, on a nation-wide scale, a broad comprehensive plan for the sanitary conservation and the prudent utilization of the water resources.

Such a plan should be based on the fundamental principle that conservation is primarily intended to render the water resources increasingly useful for the well-being of the Nation, but it is not intended to return them to a state of pristine purity nor arbitrarily to estop the discharge of all unpurified waste waters to them.

Such a comprehensive plan, therefore, should include:

(*a*) An order of precedent of use of water, in which the first and highest use generally will be for sources of public water supplies for domestic and municipal purposes.

(*b*) An allocation of the use of river systems, streams, or even parts thereof, for whatever purpose best serves the general public interests and is not directly incompatible with the local interests.

* Chf. Engr., Pennsylvania Dept. of Health, Harrisburg, Pa.

(*c*) A recognition of the natural capacity of rivers to assimilate inoffensively and purify ultimately limited quantities of certain kinds of waste waters.

(*d*) An equitable and just assignment of this natural assimilating capacity among those parties who properly discharge waste waters to the rivers and also an equitable and just assignment of responsibility for purifying before use the water of the streams among other parties who divert the water for various proper purposes.

(*e*) An economical and practicable procedure to determine the assimilating capacity of streams for various kinds of industrial wastes and to find reasonable and practicable ways and means of treating industrial wastes to produce effluents capable of inoffensive assimilation.

In some States discretionary power is vested in the executive officer, board, or commission, which administers the statutes relative to sewerage, and the discharge of sewage and industrial wastes. This makes possible the adoption of a comprehensive plan such as that described. In the statutes of other States there are inflexible and positive prohibitions against any discharge of enumerated substances to streams, or against groups or classes of wastes deemed detrimental to certain uses of streams, and in such cases worth while results cannot be obtained where the prohibition is impracticable or merely idealistic. Also, anti-stream pollution statutes are generally of State-wide application and do not differentiate between the widely varying characteristics and needs of the different sections of the State.

The folly of this principle is being corrected in the matter of municipal development through the zoning of cities, whereby the variation of requirements for residential and industrial uses is recognized and defined. The principle of zoning is applicable to a comprehensive plan for the conservation of water resources.

As this is an introduction to an industrial waste symposium, only that part of the proposed comprehensive plan concerning the assimilating capacity and methods of treatment of waste waters will be considered herein.

Many scientific investigations have been made of the conditions of streams receiving sewage, so that definite knowledge is now available as to the amount of sewage which streams can inoffensively assimilate. Also, processes have been developed and established whereby sewage can be treated to any required degree. As regards sewage, therefore, the needed data are now at hand, and the problem is largely one of determining the required degree of treatment of the sewage, if any, the designing of structures, providing funds, constructing works, and then efficiently operating them.

Such, however, is not the case with industrial wastes. For many years, both technical and lay investigations have been made concerning the treatment of various industrial wastes. All over the country industrial waste treatment works have been installed—some entirely satisfactory and efficient, others, regardless of the expenditure of considerable funds, failures or gravely inefficient.

Ofttimes only the engineer who designed the works and the company that operates them know any of the details of either the successes or the failures. Such data are not generally available to the Engineering Profession, nor to industry as a whole.

It is certainly uneconomical for any one company engaged in a certain industry to expend its own funds in research and experimental installation in order to find out how to treat an industrial waste which is or may be a common problem to many other companies engaged in the same industry, except in special cases or for the profitable recovery of by-products.

For the solution of such problems in any State a more practicable and economical procedure is for the State agency which administers the statutes having to do with discharge of industrial wastes to enter into co-operative agreements with the various groups of industries, whereby funds are provided to be expended by a committee of competent technical experts in investigations to determine:

(1) The polluting strength and characteristics of the ingredients of the industrial waste.

(2) The assimilating capacity of streams for the industrial waste, untreated and treated to various degrees.

(3) Reasonable and practicable processes of treatment to provide a progressively increasing quality of effluent so as to meet the varying requirements of different streams.

(4) Cost data of construction and operation.

There are technical problems which are common to several industries and questions to be answered of common interest to different industries, such as the basic principles underlying standards of cleanliness of streams used for various purposes. To solve these technical problems and answer these questions there should be co-operation between the industrial waste committees of the various States.

Certain industries operate in many States and in such cases economy of funds and enlargement of scope of work may be attained by providing for co-ordinating or even unifying investigations of industrial waste disposal through a National committee made up of representatives of the State officials, the technical experts, and the executives of the industry in those States where such co-operative agreements may be put into effect. Such a project is not a theory. It has been inaugurated.

In Pennsylvania, technical committees have been created and are at work on the unsolved problems of disposal of tannery wastes and on pulp and paper mill wastes.

In Ohio, committees have been created for the study of the waste disposal problems confronting the canning, dairy, acid, iron, and paper industries.

In Wisconsin, pea-canning and pulp and paper committees are in existence and, in Michigan, a tannery committee has been organized.

The American Paper and Pulp Association has created the "National Stream Purification Committee for the Pulp and Paper Industry", consisting of representatives of the industry and of five State officials.

Therefore, it appears possible to build on the existing foundations a superstructure which will be a sane, practical, comprehensive plan for the sanitary conservation and prudent utilization of the water resources of the United States.

TREATMENT OF WASTES FROM OIL REFINERIES

By Robert Spurr Weston,* M. Am. Soc. C. E.

The treatment of wastes from oil refineries is different from that of most industrial waste liquids. This is because oil-refining processes differ so greatly from those the wastes of which the engineer is usually called upon to treat.

An outline of typical refinery practice has been presented† by the writer and will not be repeated here. It is sufficient to state that in an ordinary refinery much water is used for cooling; various petroleum products are treated with chemicals and washed with water; and, at times, there are leakages from condensers and from the multitude of tanks and pipes containing the oil and oily products. All these waste liquids reach the refinery sewer, together with many results of bad or experimental processes and many operators' mistakes.

So much for the waste liquids. There are also waste semi-solids and solids. Refinery practice varies widely. In some refineries the crude oil is only "topped", that is, the gasoline is distilled, the residue being used for fuel. In others, the whole range of products from petroleum ether to coke, is made. The heavier products, petroleum residues, waxes, and coke, are sometimes denser than water.

As time goes on, one may expect that the waste liquids from oil refineries will become more and more complex, because the petroleum industry is still in its infancy. Thus far, oil refining has existed largely for the separation and sale of the various groups of elements in crude oil. In the future, it is certain that, in addition, as many products will be made from petroleum as are now made from coal-tar. When this day comes, one may expect more complications in the treatment of refinery wastes.

Refinery sewers are usually on the combined system, and the sewer inlets from refinery yards (seldom paved) carry much dirty storm water in addition to the usual leakage of ground-water and the refinery wastes themselves.

Most refineries have a separator into which the refinery sewer discharges. Usually this is a simple basin with skimming-boards and swinging, floating arms by which the oil is decanted from the surface of the separator and pumped back to the refinery to be passed through the process again. In many refineries the basin is divided into several compartments to facilitate the skimming of oil.

From one point of view, separators for liquid wastes alone may be considered as subsiding basins upside down. They receive oil and water and separate them by gravity. Unfortunately, the operation is not so simple as this conception. In many of the processes, and in tanks and pumps, emulsions are formed which are difficult to destroy. Also, treatment with various

* Cons. Engr. (Weston & Sampson), Boston, Mass.

† *Transactions*, Am. Soc. C. E., Vol. 89 (1926), p. 383.

chemicals causes the formation of oily products with densities about the same as that of water, or greater. In many refineries, only the easily recoverable oils are skimmed off, the remainder being wasted. All these add to the difficulty of separation. After a time the oil discharged with the waste water inevitably separates, usually as a film on the surface of the body of water into which it is discharged.

The coke and heavier residues present a more difficult problem than the oils. Many of these residues are hot and fluid when discharged, but become plastic solids when mixed with the cooler wastes in sewer and separator, where they subside as pasty masses difficult to remove.

The design of the separator is usually simple, shallow basins with either vertical or sloping sides being customary. In the best practice, the wastes are passed through fore-basins where the larger part of the oil is readily skimmed off and the mass of settleable solids collected. These fore-basins greatly reduce the volume of water accidently skimmed off with the oil and minimize the labor of removing the heavier solid matter from the system of basins.

Probably because refineries have been located on large bodies of water where the discharge of waste therefrom has not been particularly objectionable, few have done more than to build simple separators. This has been done more to save oil than to protect the water receiving the effluent. A few other refineries have been compelled to go further.

In the manufacture of lubricating oils, wastes which are emulsions of oil and water are quite prevalent. As is well known, the permanence of oily emulsions is more or less dependent on chemical reaction, and although it is probably possible to separate and treat these preliminary wastes by adjusting the reaction and separating the oil by centrifugal machines, the practice is not general.

The coke residues are removed from separators either by hand or by hand and bucket hoist. There seems to be much opportunity for improvement in this regard, and apparently there is no reason why automatically cleaned tanks of the type used so successfully for sewage should not be adapted to oil refinery wastes.

Thus far, the chief factors in the purification of refinery wastes are gravity and time, and regarding the latter, there is no standardized practice. There are large refineries with small separators and *vice versa,* and it is rarely ever known what periods of detention are necessary or desirable.

The separator of one refinery was observed by the writer's firm for a year. The brackish water (30 to 50% sea water) used for condensing was returned through the sewer and separator, with its content of oily matter. The separator had a capacity of about 4 hours' flow, and the effluent from the basin generally contained from 5 to 19 parts per million of oily matter (ether soluble). There were, however, two days on which the content of oil rose to 42 and 78 parts per million, respectively. The variations are shown on Fig. 1. The average quantity of oil found was 12 parts per million. The body of water into which this effluent discharged had an average oil content of 3.1 parts per million. This refinery was in a large city, and the presence of oil in the water receiving the effluent was due only in part to the discharges from the refinery and in part to the discharges from ships and from the sewers of the city, where much oil was used for fuel.

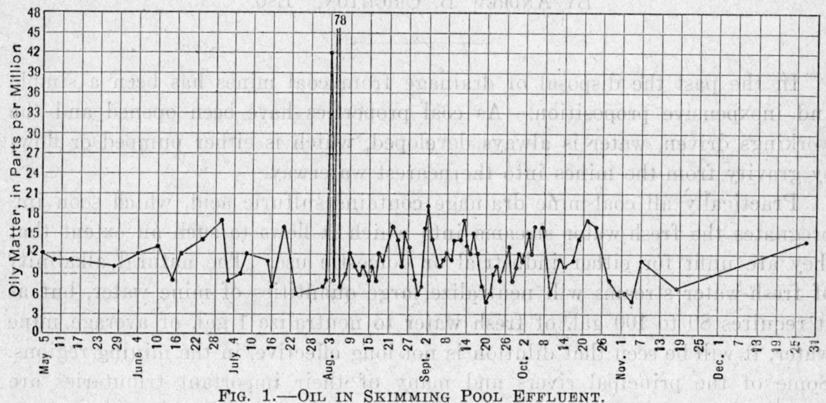

FIG. 1.—OIL IN SKIMMING POOL EFFLUENT.

Two other separators that were tested, produced effluents having the characteristics given in Table 1.

TABLE 1.

	Parts per Million.	
	Separator *A*.	Separator *B*.
Total solids	17 540	17 200
Loss on ignition	3 850	3 815
Turbidity	95	300
Oils (ether soluble)	40	40
Acidity, as H_2SO_4	....	421
Alkalinity, as $CaCO_3$	110	.....

The conclusion from Table 1 is that at present the art of treating oil-refinery waste is rather rudimentary, and although methods are effective to a certain degree there are many improvements which suggest themselves.

A satisfactory treatment works should discharge an effluent practically free from settleable solids and one containing less than 20 parts per million of oily matters (ether soluble).

DISPOSAL OF DRAINAGE FROM COAL MINES

By Andrew B. Crichton,* Esq.

In the past the disposal of drainage from coal mines has been a simple and inexpensive proposition. As coal properties have been opened and the workings driven, water is always developed, which is either pumped or flows by gravity from the mines into the nearest waterway.

Practically all coal-mine drainage contains sulfuric acid, which soon impregnates the fresh-water streams into which it flows to such an extent that they are unfit for either industrial or domestic use. The natural alkalinity of fresh-water streams will neutralize large quantities of mine water, but as it requires 80 to 100 gal. of fresh water to neutralize 1 gal. of average mine water, it will be seen that dilution is not long effective, in the mining regions. Some of the principal rivers and many of their important tributaries are acid for long distances during their flow through the coal regions.

The stream-pollution problem from mine drainage is by no means new, and in the mining regions has long been the cause of great inconvenience and expense both to the mining companies and the public. Until quite recently it has been strictly a mining community problem. As the mining companies usually controlled the communities, if a water supply were destroyed by mine drainage no attempt to treat the water was made if other unpolluted supplies could be found. In many instances large sums have been spent in building treatment plants, which because of unsatisfactory results have later been abandoned and unpolluted water brought long distances at great expense.

The largest industries and public utilities have suffered most from stream pollution from mine drainage, because of their large and growing needs for pure water. Nearly one hundred water companies in Pennsylvania have similar problems, which are daily becoming more serious.

For years the mining industry has been considered paramount, but one is forced to admit that although coal is necessary, water is necessary for human existence; that one is dependent on the other, and that both are vital to the welfare and prosperity of the Nation. The development of the coal industry has gradually progressed during most of the past century, but has not nearly reached its maximum. Whatever ills have come with it have likewise been long in developing, so that good judgment and patient investigation, rather than drastic legislation, should govern in handling this problem.

Importance of the Coal Industry

The Nation could not long survive without the coal industry. It is the principal source of power and serves mankind in so many and varied capacities that one can hardly recount its blessings. The value of its gas and chemical products to civilization has never been properly appraised or appreciated. With the decline of oil resources the country will become even more dependent

* Min. Engr., Johnstown, Pa.

on the coal industry, and nothing should be done that will needlessly add to the cost of producing coal, or that will in any way affect its usefulness to mankind.

Coal is produced in twenty-eight States and is fairly well distributed. The capacity of the developed mines is said to be 750 000 000 tons annually. The United States produces about one-half the world's supply of coal and the value of this annual product is more than $1 500 000 000 at the mines. Including freight charges and other transportation costs, the ultimate cost to the consumers would be more than $4 500 000 000. Proposed National legislation prohibiting the discharge of acid mine drainage into the streams might easily add $200 000 000 to the annual coal bill, with doubtful results or without materially improving the fresh-water supplies.

Additional Legislation not Advisable

Until some satisfactory method has been found to treat or take care of mine drainage no additional legislation is needed. It has been said by many that this is a National issue, that any legislation requiring the disposal or treatment of mine drainage that will add to the cost of producing coal, should bear equally upon the whole industry. The operators of one State or district should not have any advantage over another as a result of legislation, but National legislation will not bear equally upon all districts, because the problem is not the same everywhere.

The problem is most acute in Western Pennsylvania, Northern West Virginia, and Ohio, and under any plan the cost of disposal will be greater in those districts than elsewhere. Mine drainage from Northern West Virginia flows through Pennsylvania, so that Pennsylvania legislation without any control of West Virginia mine drainage would be ineffective and would add an additional burden to the coal operators of Pennsylvania. Any apparent disregard of the rights of others or the protection of water supplies by the mining industry may in a measure be attributed to the principle laid down by the Pennsylvania Supreme Court in the now famous Sanderson case.

Court Decisions Affecting Mining

In 1886 Sanderson bought a property in the City of Scranton through which flowed Meadow Brook, a pure, unpolluted stream. He built a dam and developed a water supply for his own use. About the same time the Pennsylvania Coal Company opened a coal mine which soon produced acid mine drainage, destroying the use of the brook water. Sanderson brought suit for damages resulting from loss of the stream. The case was twice tried in the Courts of Lackawanna County, Pennsylvania, and was twice before the Supreme Court of Pennsylvania. The first Supreme Court decision affirmed the lower Court's award of damages to Sanderson; Justice Paxson filed a strong dissenting opinion, which was sustained in the second Supreme Court decision.

The Court took the position that if Sanderson could collect damages, every riparian owner thus affected could do likewise, and if they could collect damages they could also enjoin the pollution of streams by mine drainage, which would practically stop all mining operations, except by consent of the lower riparian owners; that trifling inconvenience to particular persons must sometimes give way to the necessities of a great community, especially where the leading industrial interest of the State is involved. The Court further stated in its opinion that the Coal Company was making the natural and ordinary use of its property, and that Sanderson, with others, was then securing an abundant supply of pure water from other sources, but that it would not say that a case "may not arise in which a stream, from such pollution, may not become a nuisance, and that the public interests as involved in the general health and well being of the community may not require the abatement of that nuisance".

Pollution a Problem of Long Standing

Since about 1885 one water supply after another has been abandoned in Pennsylvania, due to mine drainage pollution, until there are few available supplies not polluted or subject to pollution. The protection of water supplies, to meet the constantly increasing demands for domestic and industrial needs, is, therefore, imperative.

In 1905 and shortly prior thereto the Pennsylvania Railroad Company was put to considerable trouble and expense by a water shortage. Old sources of supply had become polluted, and attempted treatment was unsatisfactory, resulting in engine failures and serious delays in operation. Millions of dollars were appropriated to secure an adequate supply for the Company's present and future needs. It was then not possible to secure supplies reasonably convenient to points of consumption which were not being polluted nor subject to pollution from mine drainage.

Development of Indian Creek Supply

The Mountain Water Supply Company was organized in 1905 and appropriated the waters of Indian Creek to supply the Pennsylvania Railroad System in Southwestern Pennsylvania, as far west as Pittsburgh. A large storage dam was built about 4 miles from the mouth of Indian Creek. The drainage area above this point is 110 sq. miles, of which 55 sq. miles are underlaid with the lower productive coal measures. At the time there were numerous small "country bank" openings for local supply for the farmers in the valley, but no commercial development of the coal lands. Several years later the Indian Creek Valley Railroad Company constructed a standard gauge track from Indian Creek, a point on the Baltimore and Ohio Railroad, up the valley to its headquarters, following which development of the lumber and coal resources was begun, but there was no material development until about 1917.

In addition to supplying the Railroad Company, the Water Company furnished water to several municipalities in Western Pennsylvania, supplying about 75 000 people. Active coal development began on a large scale, and it was apparent that this important water supply would be quickly destroyed for the purpose intended, unless something were done to keep the acid mine drainage out of the stream above the dam. During this time both the coal and water interests conducted studies and experiments in an effort to find some satisfactory method of treating acid mine drainage that would permit the mining of the coal without the destruction of the water supply, but without success. The Water Company finally appealed to the Courts for an injunction to restrain the coal companies from discharging acid mine drainage into Indian Creek above the dam.

Indian Creek Pollution Suit

This case is known as the "Indian Creek Pollution Suit". The Fayette County Court decided there was no public use of the water and that preventing the mining companies from discharging water into Indian Creek would deprive them of the use of their property. The Court refused to grant an injunction restraining the mining companies from discharging mine water into this stream. The Pennsylvania Supreme Court reversed the lower Court, declaring that it was not a question of property rights, but that it was a nuisance to pollute the stream, and that the mining companies should not, after a certain period, discharge the mine water into Indian Creek or its tributaries above the dam of the Water Company. This opinion, which was concurred in by the United States Supreme Court, states:

"It is controlled by one fact and a single equitable principle: the fact that the stream has been polluted, and the principle that this creates an enjoinable nuisance, if the public uses the water".

The difference between the Sanderson and the Indian Creek decisions is that Sanderson, an individual who had access to another good supply of water, was not permitted to stand in the way of Pennsylvania's greatest industry, whereas in the Indian Creek case the public, also represented by the Commonwealth, is fighting to preserve one of the last available pure water supplies of the State, and the present decision merely carries out one of the principles enunciated in the Sanderson decision. As a result, there has been considerable discussion as to what constitutes mine drainage, or mine water. The water companies sought an injunction to restrain the mining companies from discharging acid mine waters into Indian Creek. It was admitted by both sides that eventually this mine drainage would destroy this water supply for the purpose for which it was then and is now being used. Some of the leading chemists, and water-works and mining experts of the United States were witnesses in the case, and there was no disagreement as to the fact that continued pollution by mine drainage would eventually utterly destroy this stream and render it unfit for any use.

There was much testimony introduced regarding the treatment or disposal of mine water, without material disagreement regarding it. Nearly every one in discussing "treatment" refers to neutralization by the introduction of lime. A prominent chemist, in a paper prepared especially for the purpose of fixing accurate and understandable definitions, repeatedly mentions "purifying" mine water by introducing lime. There is much confusion as to what is meant by treatment. The Conservation League wants a water that will not kill fish or vegetation; the Army engineers apparently want an alkaline water that will not affect the metal parts on the locks and dams, or interfere with shipping; the water companies, for the domestic and industrial user, want a water fit for human consumption and industrial use; and every one would like the iron oxide kept out of the stream beds.

Treatment of Mine Water

The neutralization of acid mine water by the introduction of lime does not make the water fit for either domestic or industrial use. This matter was clearly before the Court, and was undoubtedly the reason for the decree that the mine waters must be kept out of the stream. The meaning of that decree is surely that the water supply is to be preserved in condition for use, and the only safe way to do that is to eliminate the mine water.

Of the total rainfall, it is estimated that only 25% penetrates into the ground, and only a small proportion of these percolating waters reach great depth. The sandstones and shales overlying the coal seams become great reservoirs, storing vast quantities of water. Immediately under the coal seam is usually found a stratum of impervious fire-clay through which these percolating waters do not penetrate. It is at these levels that surface springs are found, and through which the ground-waters find their way back into the streams. In the coal regions, the surface springs are an important guide in prospecting for coal. Prior to coal mining, these percolating waters, although penetrating the coal seams and carrying varying amounts of dissolved solids, do not become acid.

It requires the combined action of air and water to dissolve the iron pyrites, found in the coal seams, to form sulfuric acid. This acid combines with other elements in the water, usually calcium, magnesium, and iron, and forms sulfates, so that waters not showing free acid, but containing magnesium and calcium sulfates, are often highly corrosive and are hard and unfit for either domestic or industrial use. There is quite general agreement that when a water supply contains 4 grains of sulfates per U. S. gallon, it requires softening. When the pollution exceeds 12 grains, treatment is no longer effective because the large quantity of soda ash required so heavily charges the waters with solids as to cause foaming in boilers and renders it undesirable for domestic use. It will be seen, therefore, that if the waters require treatment with the small percentage of coal mined, with continued mining it will be only a comparatively short time until treatment by any known method is no longer effective.

On exposure to air the iron constituents become less soluble and are precipitated, causing the yellow deposit in the beds of the streams so familiar to every one in the mining regions. After the rocks are coated with this iron deposit, the acid in the stream has no further access to whatever neutralizing elements the rocks may contain, and the only further change in the acid content of the stream waters is from the natural alkalinity of fresh-water tributaries, the process of dilution.

In the course of mining, as the coal is removed, the inferior coal, carbonaceous shale, iron pyrites, and other refuse material, as far as possible, is stored in the mine. As mining proceeds, water is developed from the coal and the overlying strata and flows promiscuously through the mines, coming in contact with this refuse material containing the acid-forming elements, and reaches the surface as acid mine drainage. In upward of 300 mines examined, only 4 or 5 have been found in which the drainage was not acid. In one mine it was due to dilution from surface waters encountered in shaft-sinking, and, in others, to the percolating waters coming in contact with limestone. Large quantities of this refuse material are also hauled from the mines and stored in great piles around the mine openings, and there is less chance of control of the acid from these dumps than that from the mines. Any contemplated plans for disposal or the treatment of mine drainage seem to have overlooked this prolific source of pollution.

Quantity of Mine Drainage

To determine the quantity of mine water to be expected from the mining of coal, 250 to 300 mines have been examined. It was realized that probably no two mines in any region are operating under exactly similar conditions, but average conditions could be expected in entire fields of about the same size operating the same measures. It was realized that the daily or annual production of coal has slight, if any, relation to the quantity of water to be expected, although that method has been so often referred to in the anthracite region, and in recent Government reports. The area of coal exhausted was considered to be the most reliable basis for an estimate, although it, too, has many factors affecting the results. Some of these factors are the thickness and nature of the overlying strata; the thickness of the seams and methods of mining, particularly regarding the drawing of pillars—whether pillars are drawn near the crop or in extremely shallow cover; the protection given to streams; and the pitch of the measures.

An acre of coal exhausted in the bottom of a coal basin might affect a large surface-drainage area. This accounts for unusually high yields per acre in some small mines. In fairly deep mining, say, 250 ft. or more, the maximum yield of mine drainage should not be expected to exceed 25% of the rainfall, the estimated penetration. However, with the drawing of pillars, serious surface breaks occur where the coal has as much as 600 ft. of cover. In such cases undoubtedly a much larger percentage of the rainfall reaches the mines, reducing proportionally the surface run-off. This increased quantity of mine drainage during wet-weather periods does not reduce the acid content of mine waters, but the waters reaching higher levels in the mine come in contact with new sources of pollution and usually contain more acid.

Effect of Mine Development on Yield of Drainage Area

In the mines examined, the area of coal exhausted and the mine-drainage flows were measured, showing in one extreme a yield of 10 000 gal. of mine water per acre per day, although the average of all mines was about 1 100 gal. per acre per day. Average mining conditions show yields of 2 000 to 2 500 gal. per acre per day where less than 100 acres are exhausted. With increased mining the rate per acre naturally declines, until an average of about 1 000 gal. per acre per day is reached.

Under average conditions the flow of mine drainage is relatively constant, and does not vary directly with rainfall. In a coal field in Central Pennsylvania where 4 300 acres of coal were exhausted, and where the cover on the coal averaged 250 to 300 ft., records of rainfall and mine drainage were kept over a period of a year. The average rainfall was 3 300 gal. per acre per day, whereas the average mine drainage was about 900 gal. per acre per day, or 27% of precipitation. The surface drainage area was much larger than the worked-out coal area, but the coal area was compact, and these figures fairly represent the percentage of percolation. The difference between the average and the minimum mine flows was only 17 per cent. Another coal operation in Pennsylvania (average cover on coal about 300 ft.; area exhausted, 2 200 acres; over 60% of which pillars have been drawn) the average rainfall was 3 000 gal. per acre per day and the mine drainage was 1 300 gal. per acre per day, showing a percolation of 43 per cent. This field is on the east side of a coal basin where additional territory than that actually mined is drained. The difference between the average and minimum monthly flow was about 14 per cent.

A drainage area of 36 sq. miles practically all underlaid with coal, of which one-half is mined, on a certain day in October, 1920, yielded 23 600 000 gal. of water, of which 10 800 000 gal., or 46%, was mine drainage. The yield of the drainage area was 1 025 gal., and of the mines, 937 gal. per acre per day. A drainage area of 62 sq. miles, 52 sq. miles containing coal, of which 12 sq. miles are exhausted, yields 41 200 000 gal., of which 7 600 000 gal. are mine drainage. This shows a yield of 1 039 gal. per acre in the total drainage area, whereas in that part of the territory developed by mining, the mine drainage yield was 989 gal. per acre exhausted per day.

If the exhaustion of less than 10% of the total coal reserves has already produced mine drainage sufficient to destroy such a large part of the water supply resources, it is apparent that continued coal mining will soon destroy the few remaining fresh-water supplies. During the summer of 1926, in the Pittsburgh District, the railroad companies were compelled to haul water for their own use and for the use of coal operations on their lines.

Quality of Mine Water

The quality of mine drainage is quite as important as the quantity. Table 2 gives typical analyses of mine waters, in grains per U. S. gallon, by Mr. E. C. Trax.

Some Pittsburgh seam mines in the Greensburg District of Pennsylvania show total apparent acidity, in grains per gallon, as follows:

Mine.	Grains per gallon.
Keystone Shaft	98.42
Sewickley	61.74
Greensburg Nos. 2 and 3	121.68
Seaboard Shaft	137.68
Claridge	169.40
Salem	91.20
Crow's Nest	123.96

TABLE 2.—TYPICAL ANALYSES OF MINE WATERS, IN GRAINS PER U. S. GALLON.

	Miller Shaft.	Puritan Shaft.	Sonman Shaft.	Berwind No. 35.	Yellow Run Shaft.	Morrellville.	Argyle.	Blair.	Howard.	Rogers.	Oneida.
Total solids	266.01	330.18	276.50	146.42	135.33	608.82	135.88	266.17	218.54	175.53	329.48
Probable incrustants	190.15	247.59	200.67	96.26	75.84	368.13	70.59	85.85	......	......	......
Suspended matter	7.29	9.92	3.21	10.50	8.75	1.20	4.14	......	......	......	......
Iron oxide	21.56	40.10	29.37	9.22	10.10	128.11	10.27	......	27.32	28.88	55.19
Aluminum oxide	12.90	6.73	9.14	3.38	4.38	38.21	3.73	......	5.43	11.45	8.72
Calcium oxide	30.55	27.17	20.90	16.47	9.60	20.76	13.13	7.14	29.47	11.40	27.62
Magnesium oxide	9.05	16.25	12.01	9.77	5.66	15.63	4.79	5.57	12.73	5.49	15.33
Sulfuric anhydride (SO_3)	129.40	157.52	130.84	72.74	57.50	295.64	70.93	141.89	85.79	55.17	111.95
Sulfuric anhydride (acid sulfate)	20.82	37.33	37.68	10.04	11.67	87.06	21.88	16.47	......	......	......
Free sulfuric acid (H_2SO_4)	34.42	61.25	45.50	23.62	28.00	247.06	26.47	115.00	25.04	41.53	50.31
Chlorine	0.70	0.82	0.58	0.47	0.76	2.27	2.70	0.29	......	......	......

The average total acidity at sixty mines of the H. C. Frick Coke Company was 100 grains per U. S. gal. Analyses of the waters of some of the polluted streams in Pennsylvania, at much above minimum flows, are given in Table 3.

TABLE 3.—ANALYSES OF WATERS OF POLLUTED STREAMS IN PENNSYLVANIA.

Name of stream.	Grains per Gallon.		
	Sulfuric anhydride, SO_3.	Sulfuric anhydride acid sulfate.	Free sulfuric acid, H_2SO_4.
West Branch, Susquehanna River, at Moss Creek	44.40	5.90	10.60
Quemahoning River, at dam	4.20	0.40	0.50
Conemaugh River, at Portage	35.23	6.80	12.40
Conemaugh River, at South Fork	24.25	5.40	9.70
Shade Creek, at mouth	4.72	1.00	1.40
Paint Creek, at mouth	37.70	7.40	14.10
Red Stone Creek, at mouth	32.89	6.77	9.33
Jacobs Creek, at mouth	19.49	3.83	8.03
Sewickley Creek, at Hunker, Pa.	40.27	9.80	16.33
Turtle Creek, at Wilmerding, Pa.	48.40	16.33	8.75

NEUTRALIZATION

In treating acid mine water the custom is to neutralize it with lime, converting it into hard water, and then to add soda ash to soften it. Most waters that have been treated with any degree of success have contained a very low percentage of sulfates, as compared with mine drainage. The writer does not know of any successful attempt to treat mine drainage of the quality encountered in the Pennsylvania coal fields. After the decree of the Court in the Indian Creek case was made effective, three of the mining companies built plants to neutralize the mine water by the introduction of hydrated lime, as a compliance with the decree, but this attempted method is very expensive and is not satisfactory.

In Table 4 is given the analyses of mine water before and after treatment with hydrated lime at the plant of the Melcroft Coal Company, made for that Company by Mr. J. O. Handy, Chemist.

TABLE 4.—ANALYSES OF MINE WATER BEFORE AND AFTER TREATMENT WITH HYDRATED LIME.

(Acidity and Alkalinity Expressed in Parts per Million as $CaCO_3$.)

	Raw.	Treated.
Total acidity	940	....
Alkalinity	.....	5
Sulfate (SO_4)	1 600	1 500
Iron (Fe)	250	2
Aluminum	5	1
Calcium	200	630
Magnesium	78	43
Silica	40	8

From Table 4 it will be apparent that there is little change in the total sulfates before and after treatment, and that the water is still unfit for use. Besides, the Melcroft water is not what would be considered a bad mine water, or nearly as high in acidity as the average mine drainage of Western Pennsylvania. The companies are now building a tunnel to carry the mine drainage to a point below the dam before discharging it into the stream. This may be a compliance with the Court's decree in the Indian Creek case, but it does not solve the problem—the disposal of mine drainage.

The cost of neutralizing mine water has been variously estimated by different chemists at 15 to 25 cents per 1 000 gal. This depends on the cost of lime, the cost of gathering the water to one central plant, the capacity of the plant, the labor, and the handling of the sludge which alone is an exceedingly difficult and expensive, if not impossible, proposition. The cost of constructing a plant for lime treatment would be about $100 per 1 000 gal. daily capacity, thus making a 1 000 000-gal. plant cost $100 000.

QUANTITY OF DRAINAGE AND COST

A recent estimate of the acreage worked out in the bituminous mines of Pennsylvania, based on the total tonnage exhausted, would indicate a total production of mine drainage of 750 000 000 gal. daily. The cost of lime treatment plants for this enormous quantity of water would be $75 000 000. The annual cost of treatment, at 15 cents per 1 000 gal., would be $41 062 500, and at 25 cents per 1 000 gal., $68 437 500. It is estimated that the mine drainage reaching the streams from anthracite mines is 700 000 000 gal., daily, so that these estimates for the entire State of Pennsylvania would be about doubled.

It must be understood that the cost mentioned is for neutralization only, and that even after this treatment, which is the one most often referred to, the water is still unfit for either domestic or industrial use. To soften the water would cost more than double the estimate for neutralization, and even with that the value of the product, or the final result, would be doubtful. It will be seen that, with an average annual production of 160 000 000 tons in the bituminous fields of Pennsylvania, the cost will be from 26 to 43 cents per ton for neutralization, and from 50 to 90 cents per ton for softening.

Difficulty of Handling Sludge

In the bituminous fields of Pennsylvania alone there would be more than 4 000 tons daily, or 1 460 000 tons yearly, of sludge to handle. Even if dried and piled outside, it would be likely to reach the stream beds with every rain storm, and would eventually fill them. This iron oxide may be used for purifying gas and in the manufacture of paint, but it has a very limited market, and with such quantities as would then be available it would be without value. To mining men it would be nothing but slimy yellow mud, too thick to pump and too thin to shovel. In the writer's opinion, the disposal of this sludge presents almost as expensive and difficult a problem as mine drainage itself.

There have been other methods of treatment suggested, but none has proved to be satisfactory, from one cause or another. By the use of barium salts it has been found that calcium sulfates can be removed from water, but the cost is prohibitive, and as barium is poisonous the Department of Health would not permit its use. The electrolytic process has been suggested as a possible solution for the removal of sulfuric acid and its compounds from water, but the cost would be excessive, and the handling of sludge would still present its difficulties.

Satisfactory Treatment Yet to Be Found

As far as known, there is no satisfactory method of treatment of acid mine water in quantities such as are now being produced by the mines of the United States. Acid wastes are being treated in small quantities by lime, and as a result extravagant claims are being made as to what could be done with coal mine drainage. It is apparent that these claimants do not realize either the bad quality or the enormous quantities of mine drainage that would have to be handled. Increasing the alkalinity of the stream by the introduction of lime in the mine water would greatly increase the assimilating power of the stream, but in most cases there is so much mine water that dilution would not be effective, even after the high cost of lime treatment. With these tremendous costs in Pennsylvania alone, the cost of treatment for the coal industry throughout the Nation would be staggering, and never could be justified.

In addition to the acid drainage from coal refuse dumps, there are millions of gallons flowing daily from old abandoned mines, most of which would have to be handled in some satisfactory manner before treatment of the remainder would render results worth while. In many places the sealing of abandoned mines would be helpful, by preventing the flow of mine water; perhaps shutting off the air would prevent the formation of sulfuric acid, and thus more nearly restore original conditions, but this likewise would be difficult and expensive, and the question arises as to who is now responsible?

Legislation has been introduced in Congress which, if passed, would make it unlawful within the limits prescribed by the Secretary of War to discharge any free acid into navigable waters or their tributaries. It places in the hands of the Chief of Engineers, U. S. Army, the power to require neutralization of acid water or wastes, and provides a fine for each offense, of $500 to $2 500, or imprisonment of not less than thirty days, or more than one year.

The State and individuals have spent thousands of dollars in attempts to solve this problem, but without success, so that the time has surely come for wise Governmental action—not the hasty passage of drastic laws as now proposed, that would so greatly embarrass the mining and manufacturing industries, but a sane public policy that will tend to preserve the water supplies at as little cost to the community as possible.

One thing seems certain, that is, that coal cannot be mined without destroying the water in the mining regions. Therefore, the only sure and practical method of conserving the water supply is to stop mining coal in the few little developed areas yet remaining. This cannot well be done as between individuals, and the Government or the State is justified in purchasing, if necessary, under some plan to be devised, coal lands necessary to the protection of the few remaining water supplies in Western Pennsylvania and elsewhere. That the State of Pennsylvania recognizes the importance of this problem is evidenced by its participation with the water companies in the Indian Creek case.

The leaders in the coal industry are beginning to realize the seriousness of this situation, and that the water supplies must be preserved. There would be no objection to spending a few cents per ton of output if, in doing so, the problem could be satisfactorily solved. Some coal operators of Western Pennsylvania are suggesting that a supply of water be obtained from Lake Erie when mine drainage pollution becomes excessive. Further drains on Lake Erie would not likely be permitted, even if such a plan were feasible. However, this scheme is no further afield, and would not cost as much as the proposal that all mine drainage be treated. Any solution must be economically sound, and the writer is certain that it would cost less in Pennsylvania and elsewhere to preserve the present unpolluted streams and to stop mining in some little developed areas, in order to protect the water supplies for the present and future.

The policy of the Pennsylvania Department of Health, to protect all unpolluted streams; to stop further pollution of all streams that can be restored; and to use those now destroyed for carrying sewage, industrial wastes, and mine drainage, is the first real step toward a solution of this problem. It is commendable, and undoubtedly will result in much good at the least possible cost to the community.

PULP AND PAPER MILL WASTES

By G. K. Spence,* Esq.

The first paper mill in America was established in 1690 at Germantown, near Philadelphia, Pa., by William Rittenhouse. Since then the manufacture of pulp and paper has expanded until at present (1926) it constitutes one of the major industries of the United States.

Paper in various forms has come into use for so many purposes that it is now an essential necessity of domestic and industrial life, and it was so considered during the World War.

There are 844 paper mills and 310 pulp mills in the United States, located in 34 of the 48 States. New York State leads with 244 pulp and paper mills; Wisconsin is next with 115; followed by Massachusetts with 112; Pennsylvania with 87; Maine with 75; Michigan with 71; Ohio with 58; New Jersey with 44; Connecticut with 43; New Hampshire with 41; Illinois and Indiana each with 31; and so on down to four States with one mill each.

More than 8 000 000 tons of pulp, paper, and paper-board are annually made in this country, which output is valued at more than $900 000 000. The prosperity of the United States is, therefore, directly affected by the stability of the industry.

Paper is made from different pulps in various proportions, selected according to the grade of paper desired. Of the paper manufactured in the United States 90% is made from wood pulp, the remainder being made from rag, straw, jute, hemp, and other fiber-producing materials.

Rag Pulp

The rags are first sorted by hand, cut and dusted by machinery, and then passed to the cooking boilers where they are cooked under pressure with either a solution of caustic soda or caustic lime. After cooking, the liquor containing the soluble substances is washed from the pulp, requiring about 65 000 gal. of wash water per ton of rags treated. The washed pulp is then bleached with a solution of calcium hypochlorite and again washed in order to remove the last trace of bleach preparatory to using the pulp for the manufacture of paper.

Wood Pulp

There are two classes of wood pulp, namely, mechanical wood pulp and chemical wood pulp.

Mechanical Wood Pulp.—This pulp contains all the intercellular substance, the wood being ground to a pulpy mass by being pressed against a revolving stone in contact with water. This is the cheapest grade of wood pulp made, and, as the intercellular matter has not been removed, it deteriorates very

* Chf. Chemist, Castanea Paper Co., Clarion Mills, Johnsonburg, Pa.

rapidly. It is for this reason that newspapers, which are made mostly from mechanical wood pulp, cannot be preserved for any length of time.

The pulp from the grinders is run into a vat, taken up by a wire-covered revolving cylinder, and transferred to an endless felt, which, in turn, transfers it to a wooden roll on which it accumulates until the desired thickness is reached. It is then cut off and folded into laps for shipment or use in the beaters.

Chemical Wood Pulp.—There are three processes used for the manufacture of chemical wood pulp, namely, sulfite, soda, and sulfate.

The wood is prepared in practically the same manner for treatment by any one of the processes. It comes to the preparing room in 4 or 5-ft. lengths and from 6 to 10 in. in diameter. If the bark has not been removed, the wood is passed through revolving cylindrical drum barkers. By tumbling around in these drums in contact with water, the sticks by rubbing against each other are stripped of the bark which is washed through slots in the side of the drum. Some drum barkers are of the batch type; others are continuous, that is, the wood is fed in at one end and the barked sticks removed at the other. Sticks too large for the chipper are split to the desired size.

From the preparing room the sticks are passed to the chipper, which is a revolving cast-iron disk with projecting steel knives set so that the size of the chip can be regulated. The wood is fed through a slanting trough and moves forward by its own weight until it comes in contact with the projecting knives on the revolving disk. The size of chips in soda pulp mills varies from $\frac{3}{8}$ to $\frac{3}{4}$ in, whereas those in sulfite and sulfate pulp mills are from $\frac{3}{4}$ in. to $1\frac{1}{4}$ in. In chipping the wood, fine pieces, or sawdust, is produced, which is screened from the chips of the desired size.

The Sulfite Process

This process has reference to the method of manufacturing pulp through the isolation of the intercellular matter by means of bi-sulfite liquor. This liquor is made by burning sulfur and absorbing the sulfurous acid gas either in milk of lime or in towers filled with limestone over which water is sprayed. The resultant cooking liquor is calcium bi-sulfite when high calcium lime is used, or bi-sulfite of calcium and magnesium when Dolomitic lime is used, an excess of sulfurous acid being produced in each case. The intercellular matter is removed by cooking the chips in this liquor, under pressure, in large vessels termed digesters. The cooking liquor forms soluble calcium salts of ligno-sulfonic acid, and the lignin and other intercellular matter is removed from the fiber by washing and bleaching.

The Soda Process

The soda process has reference to the method of manufacturing pulp through isolation of intercellular matter by means of a solution of caustic soda. The caustic soda solution is prepared by causticizing sodium carbonate with caustic lime. The intercellular matter is removed by cooking the chips in this liquor, under pressure, in digesters similar to the sulfite digester, except that they are not lined, the lining being necessary in sulfite digesters due to the acid action. In the soda process the cooking liquor forms soluble salts of the organic acids present in the wood, such as sodium acetate, sodium formate, sodium resinate, etc., and thus the intercellular matter is removed from the fiber by washing and bleaching.

The Sulfate Process

This process is very similar to the soda process in action, the cooking liquor being made up of a mixture of caustic soda and sodium sulfide. The sodium sulfide is prepared by smelting sodium sulfate in contact with carbonaceous matter which reduces the sulfate to sulfide. The caustic soda is prepared by causticizing sodium carbonate with caustic lime as in the soda process. The cooking takes place under pressure in digesters similar to those used in the soda process. The chemical action, although practically the same as in the soda process, is not as severe, due to the fact that there is a smaller excess of caustic soda present, and, as the cooking takes place in a reducing atmosphere, there is less tendency to over-cook or form oxycellulose. When cooking for strength, as is necessary in Kraft stock, the sulfate process is used.

In soda and sulfate pulp mills there are elaborate systems for the recovery of the soda used in cooking the wood. In both processes the stock from the digesters is washed with as little water as possible. The liquor from the stock is concentrated by passing it through multiple-effect evaporators after which the concentrated liquor is passed to rotary incinerators.

In the soda process the liquor is burned in the incinerators to a black ash containing 80% sodium carbonate and 20% carbon, which ash is later leached free from soda. The carbonate liquor is passed from the leachers to the alkali room, where it is re-causticized with fresh lime to be re-used in cooking more wood, 90% of the original soda used being recovered.

In the sulfate process the liquor is not burned as completely in the rotary, being discharged as a sticky mass into the smelters where fresh sodium sulfate is added to make up for loss in recovery. The carbonaceous matter present reduces the sulfate to sulfide, the mass being discharged from the smelter in the molten state, the excess carbon having been completely consumed in the operation.

Straw, hemp, jute, etc., are cooked in somewhat the same manner as rag stock, either caustic soda or caustic lime being used. As considerably less chemicals are used in cooking, it has not been considered economical to recover them.

Reclaimed Paper Stock

More than 2 000 000 tons of old papers and magazines are reclaimed annually. They are cut, soaked in a solution of sodium carbonate in order to free the ink, defibered, washed, and bleached. This reclaimed paper stock is mixed with other pulps in making certain grades of paper.

Paper is made by mixing the different pulps, according to the quality desired, in vessels termed beaters. At this point, china clay, talc, or some other form of filler is added to load the sheet and improve its finish; sizing material is added to make it more water- and ink-resistant; and the proper coloring matter is added either to tint the sheet or to dye it to the desired color.

After preparation in the beater the paper stock is passed through the Jordans or refining engines where the fibers are cut to the proper size for the desired formation, and thence to the paper machine.

The paper machine consists of a moving endless wire with a lateral shake, on which the suspended stock flows, and forms into a sheet, the excess water passing through the wire. The sheet is then carried through the press rolls by means of a felt and thence over the cylindrical steam-heated dryers, where the remainder of the moisture is removed. At the end of the paper machine, the sheet is passed through highly polished steel rolls termed calanders, where the desired finish is imparted, after which it is either cut into sheets, or slit and wound on reels into rolls, of the desired size.

Pulp and paper mill wastes could, if not properly handled, enter the stream from the following sources.

1.—Bark from the wood-preparing room. This varies from 12 to 24% of the weight of the wood, depending on the kind used.

2.—Sawdust from the chipper room where the wood is reduced to the proper size for cooking. This does not amount to more than 1% of the weight of the wood chipped.

3.—Dust from preparation of the rag stock, which represents about 3% of the weight of the rags treated.

4.—Washings from the cooked stock in rag, straw, jute, and hemp pulp mills, as well as soda and sulfite wood pulp mills. These washings contain the soluble salts of the intercellular substances removed from the fibers. As the yield from rag stock is about 85% of the weight of the prepared rags, that from hemp and jute, 60%, and that from straw, soda, sulfite, and sulfate pulp processes, 40%, the washings will contain, respectively, 15%, 40%, and 60% of the weight of the raw materials treated, in addition to the excess chemicals used, and entrained short fibers representing about 1% of the total fiber production.

5.—Wash water from the brown stock thickeners in mechanical wood, sulfite, soda, and sulfate pulp mills, the water containing finely divided unbleached fibers. The loss of fiber at this point is from 4 to 5% of the total production in mechanical wood pulp mills, and from 2 to 3% in chemical wood pulp mills.

6.—Wash water from the white stock thickeners of rag, soda, and sulfite pulp mills, which contains finely divided bleached fiber. The loss of fiber at this point is from 2 to 3 per cent.

7.—Occasional small quantities of entrained spent liquor from the evaporator in soda and sulfate pulp mills. From a stream-pollution standpoint this waste is negligible.

8.—Black carbon residue left after leaching sodium carbonate from the black ash in soda pulp mills. This amounts to about 15% of the weight of the total pulp production.

9.—Lime sludge (calcium carbonate) containing a small percentage of calcium and sodium hydrates from the alkali room of soda and sulfate pulp mills. The weight of this sludge amounts to about 50% of the total pulp production of the mill.

10.—Lime sludge containing a small percentage of calcium hypochlorite, discharged from the bleach-dissolving department of rag, sulfite, and soda pulp mills. This discharge is proportionately small and can be considered negligible.

11.—Wash water, containing finely divided fibers from the beaters, where the stock is washed and prepared for the paper machines. The loss of fiber at this point is about 1% of the total production.

12.—Excess white water from the paper machines which contains finely divided fibers, clay, and colored water from the pigments and dyes used to color the paper, about 45% of the clay used and 5% of the fiber produced passes away with this white water.

13.—Wash water from the reclaimed paper stock, containing finely divided fiber, clay, and carbon from the removed ink. The waste materials in this water amounts to about 25% of the weight of the old papers treated.

Effects Upon the Receiving Body of Water

Finely divided particles of bark and sawdust from the wood-preparing room and chipper, as well as black ash residue from the soda pulp mills and entrained fibers from the various steps in the manufacture of pulp and paper, will not have any deleterious effect on the sanitary conditions of the stream. However, they will have a tendency to increase the turbidity, and render the stream less pleasing to the sight. In addition, there is a possibility of these materials affecting aquatic life by entering the gills of fish and, through settling on the bed of the stream, affecting the spawning. On the other hand, fish have been known to thrive at the mouth of small streams copiously charged with such effluent.

Spent liquor from sulfite mills, on account of its dark color, will have a tendency to impart a brown coloration to the stream. In addition, the liquor is charged with sulfur dioxide which, being a de-oxidizing agent, will reduce the dissolved oxygen content of the stream.

Spent liquor from soda and sulfate pulp mills will slightly increase the alkalinity content of the stream, but has no deleterious effect, either from the standpoint of sanitation or aquatic life. It will, however, impart a brown coloration and frothy appearance to the stream, making it appear more harmful than it really is.

Lime sludge when discharged into the stream will increase the turbidity. Being composed of lime salts, the hardness of the water will be increased, decreasing its fitness for boiler purposes. It will not affect aquatic life, and will improve the sanitary condition of the water. This discharge has been known to improve greatly the waters in some localities where they are subjected to acid discharges from manufacturing plants.

Clay discharges will increase the turbidity of the stream, but otherwise are entirely inactive. After a rain storm many times the quantity of clay that could possibly be discharged from paper mills is naturally washed into the streams by the surface water. This waste material, therefore, should not be considered from a stream-polluting standpoint.

The lime sludge from the bleach-dissolving department which contains a small percentage of calcium hypochlorite will increase the turbidity, but has no deleterious effect. However, the presence of free chlorine will improve the sanitary condition of the water.

Assimilating Power of Streams

Although, to the writer's knowledge, no concrete study has been made relative to the amount of pulp and paper mill effluent a stream of a given flow can inoffensively assimilate, it is known from observations that the streams are very effective in this capacity.

When reviewing the points at which waste materials might enter the stream from pulp and paper mills, the worst possible conditions were cited, that is, a mill operating entirely for production without any reference to economy of operation or removal of waste materials from the effluent, as was true before the days of industrial research chemistry.

The pulp and paper companies of the United States, through their research departments, have spent millions in developing uses for, and devising means of, disposal of waste materials from the mills. In addition, the Technical Association of the Pulp and Paper Industry has done considerable work toward eliminating stream pollution, and, at the same time, curtailing waste in the industry.

There are three phases to be considered in discussing waste in pulp and paper mill effluent: First, the improvement of the condition of the stream; second, the re-use of the materials removed; and, third, clarifying the waste waters to such a degree that they can be re-used in the mill and thus conserve the use of fresh water. This last phase is very important for mills dependent on small streams for water supply, which streams are very low during the summer.

Owing to the extensive investigations made by the pulp and paper manufacturers, many of the problems relative to waste in the industry have been solved, and the others are rapidly approaching a satisfactory solution.

Known Methods for Elimination of Waste and Improvement of Streams

Bark from the wood-preparing room is pressed to remove excess moisture and burned in Dutch ovens for its fuel value.

Sawdust from the chipper room is burned either in Dutch ovens or rotary incinerators for its fuel value.

Dust from the rag department has found a market with manufacturers of roofing paper and other similar products.

Improvements have been made in the methods of washing brown stock in soda pulp mills, so that at present the quantity of colored water entering the stream from this source has been reduced to the minimum. If the cycle washing system or continuous filters are used, no washings enter the stream, the drain line being locked.

Waste water from brown and white stock thickeners in rag, mechanical wood, sulfite, soda, and sulfate pulp mills is being passed to efficient save-alls where as much as 98% of the suspended fiber is being removed before passing the water to the stream, or re-using it in the system.

At present, lime sludge from soda and sulfate pulp mills is passed to filters, where the excess water is removed, and thence to rotary dryers, or incinerators, where the lime is either dried, prepared and marketed as agricultural lime and whiting, or re-burned and used again to causticize more soda.

Wash water from the beaters and excess white water from the paper machines is at present being passed to efficient save-alls where as much as 98% of the suspended fibers and 92% of the suspended clay is removed before passing the water to the stream or re-using it in the system.

Unsolved Problems—Waste Sulfite Liquor

Although more money has been spent and more research work conducted to find methods for the disposal of waste sulfite liquor than on any other pulp or paper mill waste, it is still considered one of the unsolved problems. Considerable progress has been made toward reaching a practical solution. Some companies have been able to dispose of some of the waste sulfite liquor for core binder, road binder, tan extract, linoleum cement, and a few other uses, which only consume a very limited quantity of the supply to be had, should all the sulfite pulp companies re-claim this liquor.

It has been contended that the liquor can be evaporated and burned in boiler plants for its fuel value, and this has been tried in several mills; but as the heat value of the organic solids is about 8 000 B.t.u. per lb., and it costs about $5.50 per ton to evaporate it to the point at which it can be burned, this outlet does not appear to be very promising. Some coal companies have found it profitable to briquette hard coal dust by means of waste sulfite liquor and are using the liquor from two mills. When all coal companies reach this same conclusion, they will be in a position to use all the waste liquor at present entering the streams from sulfite pulp mills. This appears to be the not far distant solution to this problem of waste sulfite liquor disposal.

Spent Liquor from Soda and Sulfate Pulp Mill Evaporators

There are times when a small quantity of spent liquor will pass the vacuum pump of the evaporators in soda and sulfate pulp mills. Evaporator manufacturers have improved their product to such an extent that the liquor entering the stream from this point has been reduced to the minimum; when it does occur it only imparts a frothy appearance to the surface of the stream without any deleterious effect.

Carbon Residue from Soda Pulp Mills

At present, some of the black ash residue from soda pulp mills is being prepared and marketed under the names of Filchar, Nuchar, "Superchar", and other trade names, some of it being activated and used as a decolorizing agent. A limited quantity is used as an adulterant for lamp black, and some has been used for the case-hardening of steel.

The outlet for these various purposes is limited, and the disposal of the greater bulk of this waste is still an unsolved problem. However, a furnace has recently been designed and experiments are being conducted for completely burning the carbon in reclaiming the sodium carbonate, thus utilizing its fuel value in the steam boiler plant. If successful, this will be the future method for the recovery of sodium carbonate in soda pulp mills, and will eliminate waste carbon from the mill effluent.

Lime Sludge from Bleach-Dissolving Plants

There has been no satisfactory means for the disposal of lime sludge from bleach-dissolving plants; but as most mills have resorted to the use of liquid chlorine, this discharge is very small, and as it contains a small quantity of calcium hypochlorite, it will act as a germicide.

Pigments and Dyes in Paper Machine Waste Water

There is no known practical method by which the color can be removed from waste water from paper machines when dyes or pigments have been used to produce a high colored sheet. The quantity of such water, however, is small and has no deleterious effect on the stream.

Wash Water from Reclaimed Paper Stock

Numerous experiments have been conducted and considerable money has been expended in endeavoring to dispose of the waste materials washed from de-inked paper stock. It is very difficult to handle this waste material with any form of filter, and as it has so little value, due to the ink carbon content, when reclaimed, the problem of economically handling it is as yet unsolved; but paper manufacturers are optimistic regarding a satisfactory solution in the near future.

Pulp and paper manufacturers are doing everything consistent with operating conditions to improve the waters of the streams. Committees have been formed in some of the States, consisting of State engineers and technical representatives of the various pulp and paper companies, so that they can cooperate in reaching an early solution of the problems. In addition, the President of the American Paper and Pulp Makers' Association has appointed a National committee to deal with these problems.

STUDIES ON TANNERY WASTE DISPOSAL

By Wilhelm Howalt,* M. Am. Soc. C. E., and Edwin S. Cavett,† Esq.

Synopsis

This paper presents the results obtained in a two-year investigation of the disposal of tannery wastes, conducted by the Tannery Waste Disposal Committee of Pennsylvania, which is presided over by the Chief Engineer of the Department of Health of Pennsylvania, and is composed of representative engineers and chemists from the tanning interests of that State. The writers served as Resident Engineer and Assistant Resident Engineer, respectively, of the Committee.

The wastes used throughout the investigation were produced by a medium-sized sole leather tannery at which the vegetable tanning process was used. The study is presented in this paper in four main parts, as follows:

Part I.—Laboratory study of the individual wastes, including chemical analysis of each.

Part II.—Laboratory study of the wastes to find methods of treating by mixing in various combinations, by chemical treatment, etc., to produce reduction of color, of suspended solids, of oxygen demand, etc. From the results obtained a number of treatments were developed and selected for full-scale experimentation.

Part III.—Experimental plant: The experimental plant located at Instanter, Pa., was equipped to operate at full scale. The selected treatments were experimented with in this plant, studies being made by analysis of the various effluents and sludges. All operating data, such as volumes of wastes, effluents and sludges produced, chemical consumption, etc., were collected.

Part IV.—The manner in which the various full-scale treatments affected the receiving body of water was determined by analyzing the river water at certain places for a distance of 12 miles below the tannery. The results are presented in tabular form.

Conclusions are drawn concerning the facts presented and their relation to the general problem of tannery waste disposal.

Introduction

The pollution of streams by industrial wastes has been recognized for many years as an impending problem to the use of water supplies for domestic and municipal purposes. Many industries produce putrescible and deleterious wastes. Some of the more important producers of such wastes are: Coal mines, oil refineries, gas-works, water-gas and coal-gas, chemical works, coke ovens, creameries, tanneries, distilleries and breweries, canneries, municipal sewage, pulp and paper mills, and tin-plate, tubing, and galvanizing works. Many of these industries lately have appreciated the fact that the treatment of industrial wastes, regardless of whether marketable or useful products can

* Asst. Chf. Engr., Elk Tanning Co., Ridgway, Pa.

† Chemical Engr., A. C. Lawrence Leather Co., Peabody, Mass.

be recovered from them, is a just charge against their processes. This more reasonable attitude has resulted both from economic conditions and from increasing power given the State and municipal authorities regarding stream pollution.

The importance of stream pollution is emphasized by the fact that almost every State has such a problem and that legislative and constructive measures for its prevention have been steadily increasing.* Practically every State and many municipalities have some law dealing with the pollution of the waters within their jurisdictions.†

In Pennsylvania this subject comes within the jurisdiction of the Health Department and the Sanitary Water Board. In general, this State forbids the discharge into streams of wastes deleterious or detrimental to public health.† Discharge of sewage is forbidden except under permit. Discharge of wastes detrimental to fish is prohibited unless all practicable means are used to prevent pollution. The tanneries are included in these rulings, compliance with which means either the withholding of the wastes or effecting some treatment thereof. Obviously, treatment is the only way open to the tanneries because it would be practically impossible for them to withhold the wastes entirely.

The importance is further emphasized by the magnitude of the tanning industry. The value of all leather tanned in the United States is, roughly, $500 000 000 per year. Probably 50 000 men are employed in the tanneries as wage earners. The hides and skins from the following animals are tanned annually into leather in this country:

Cattle	25 000 000
Calves	15 000 000
Goats	40 000 000
Sheep	33 000 000
Other animals	7 000 000

The Census of Manufacturers of 1921 ranks leather and its finished products—boots, shoes, etc.—as fifth in importance, and the relative position of States producing leather, according to the value of the product, is as follows:

(1) Pennsylvania.
(2) Massachusetts.
(3) New York.
(4) Wisconsin.
(5) New Jersey.
(6) Illinois.
(7) Michigan.
(8) Delaware.
(9) Ohio.
(10) Virginia.
(11) North Carolina.
(12) West Virginia.
(13) California.
(14) Tennessee.

Just what position, on the list of industrial wastes, tannery waste would occupy is a matter of conjecture, although the general public usually considers it the source of obnoxious odors and unsightly, colored, and poisonous liquids, and, being governed thereby, would probably rate it among the worst.

* U. S. Public Health Report, January 15, 1926.

† 69th Cong., H. R., Doc. No. 417.

The problem of tannery waste disposal has never been adequately solved to the satisfaction of interested parties, although the literature contains many references to tannery waste disposal.* Most of them, however, are descriptions of specific treatments and disposal plants and do not contain many data.† No account has been found of an investigation which would presume to set forth any general principles governing the treatment of these wastes.

Realizing the importance of studying the problem from the viewpoint of the industry as a whole, rather than from that of the individual tannery, a committee was formed of engineers and chemists representing the tanning interests of Pennsylvania and having for its Chairman the Chief Engineer of the Department of Health of that State. This Committee, known as the Tannery Waste Disposal Committee of Pennsylvania, has functioned uninterruptedly since 1924. The work was financed by the tanning interests of the State and by the State of Pennsylvania, the money to be expended for laboratory studies, construction, and operation of a full-scale treatment plant, and for river studies. It is the final intention of this Committee to publish a report covering various progressive steps of treatment in order that there may be available an answer for every tannery working under its particular conditions both as to size, process, surroundings, and size and nature of the receiving body of water. It is the object of this paper to describe the results to date.

The investigation was conducted in the following sequence:

1.—A study was made of the characteristics of the individual wastes.
2.—Experiments were performed to find methods of treatment for the wastes.
3.—Full-scale operations were carried out on selected methods of treatment.
4.—Effect of these treatments was determined on the receiving body of water.

The individual wastes were studied by means of chemical analysis. Information of this kind served several purposes. It provided a means of classifying the wastes as alkaline, or acid, as to color, and as to process, such as beam house, tan yard, and scrub house. It also provided a means of establishing an order of degree of putrescibility. In practically all cases, these classifications had a direct bearing on the planning and the undertaking of the laboratory investigations for methods of treatment. For these laboratory investigations the wastes were mixed in a carefully planned sequence of combinations and studied as to rates of settling, color reduction, solids reduction, etc. This particular end of the investigation has not been thoroughly and exhaustively completed as yet, but for the type of full-scale operation available and for the degree of treatment desired at this time, a sufficient number of methods have been developed.

Several selected treatments, which, from the laboratory viewpoint, seemed promising, were chosen by the Committee as worthy of trial on full scale. These treatments were carefully studied in all respects from the practical and

* Bibliography of Tannery Waste Treatment, by P. A. Esten, *Journal*, Am. Leather Chemists Assoc., October, 1911.

† *Public Health Bulletin No. 100*, November, 1919.

economical standpoint as well as from the degree of success and efficiency obtained. Finally, the effect of the effluents on the stream, after treatment and after they had been discharged to the stream, were studied by analyses of the receiving body of water, sampled at five carefully selected stations along the 12 miles of stream immediately below the point of discharge.

The laboratory investigation and the routine analyses of the river water, and treatment plant samples were made in the main laboratory of the Elk Tanning Company, Ridgway, Pa. The treatment plant was at the Instanter Tannery of the same Company, at Instanter, Pa., and the river water samples were taken over a course of 12 miles on the East Branch of the Clarion River, between the Towns of Instanter and Johnsonburg, Pa. There were several excellent reasons for selecting this tannery and this location:

First.—The Instanter Tannery is a typical example of a sole leather tannery working an average number of hides and producing an average volume of wastes. These facts were confirmed by a survey of all the tanneries practicable. A questionnaire was sent to all the tanneries in Pennsylvania. The authorities of Ohio and West Virginia, having signified their intention of co-operating with the Tannery Committee in Pennsylvania, were also supplied with questionnaires for distribution in their respective States. These questionnaires asked for specific information regarding the pounds of hides worked and the volumes of waste produced per day from the various operations of the tanning process. Fifty-one tanneries, in ten States, returned answers. Tanneries in other States sent replies by reason of the fact that several members of the Committee represented companies having tanneries in these States which were likewise supplied with the questionnaires. The 51 tanneries were distributed as follows: 24 in Pennsylvania; 10 in West Virginia; 8 in Ohio; 2 in New York; 2 in Wisconsin; 1 in Maryland; 1 in Michigan; 1 in Kentucky; 1 in Tennessee; and 1 in Virginia. Of the 51 reported, 45 manufacture sole and belting leather. There was great variation in the amount of waste produced, which, based on 100 lb. of hide, ranged from 230 to 1 790 gal. per day, due to scarcity or abundance of water supply. The Instanter Tannery, with 617 gal. per day per 100 lb. of hide, is a good average.

Second.—The tannery is situated just at the confluence of two small streams, neither of which receives any pollution from sewage or industrial waste. Likewise, below this point of confluence, and for 12 miles down stream, there is no incoming sewage or industrial waste, the tannery being the only user of the river within this distance.

Third.—It was allowable for the tannery to pollute the river at will within the 12-mile distance in order to experiment with the various degrees of treatment.

Fourth.—The convenience and almost necessity of having the laboratory so near the whole field of action made the location at Instanter unusually favorable to the investigation.

Thus, an ideal situation obtains for making a direct study of the receiving body of water to determine the effect of dilution, temperature, aeration, and the various other factors influencing the wastes in their course down the river.

Origin and Description of Individual Wastes

Instanter Tannery is a sole leather tannery, and uses the vegetable process, which is the most common of all in use at present for tanning heavy leather. The finishing processes for such leathers are somewhat different in various tanneries, but, as a rule, the wastes produced are few and are negligible as compared with the whole volume of the other wastes. At Instanter the bulk of the wastes studied were produced from three departments of the tannery, namely, the beam house, the tan yard, and the scrub house. The individual wastes produced from these three places and their volumes per day are, as follows:

Wastes from:		Gallons per day.
Beam House:		
Soaks	9 600	
Limes	2 900	
Hot water	2 900	
Unhairing machine	3 100	
Wash wheel	25 800	
Fleshing machine	7 200	
Float box	4 700	
Green stock pools	43 600	
Brown hair wash	14 300	
White hair wash	1 200	
Total		115 300
Tan Yard:		
Spent tan liquor	7 800	
Total		7 800
Scrub House:		
Acid bleach	1 700	
Soda bleach	1 700	
Acid water	1 700	
Total		5 100
Floor Wash:		
Floor wash from all departments		1 800
Grand total		130 000

The wastes as produced from the three departments can be classified as continuous, or those discharging continuously during the day, and as intermittent, or those released at a certain time once each day.

The three principal departments of the average tannery of this kind are the beam house, the tan yard, and the finishing department, of which the scrub house is a part. The beam-house operations prepare the hide for tanning; the hides are tanned in the tan yard; and the leather is finished in the finishing department. The description of the tanning process at Instanter, therefore, naturally starts with the beam-house operations.

Beam House

Soaking.—Heavy, green, salted cow and steer hides are first placed in vats containing water which is discharged twice a week. They hang in these vats for one day, after which they are moved forward into another vat. The water is discharged once a week. The hides are moved in this manner every day during the 3 to 5 days comprising the soaking period. As the hides move forward from vat to vat, they become cleaner and softer, so that generally the last soak waters can be used longer than the first. This accounts for the fact that the first soak is renewed twice a week and the others only once a week. A stream of clean water runs into the vats day and night. Thus, the waste soak waters will contain the dirt, dung, blood, and considerable quantities of hair and sodium chloride as major impurities, and are usually a dark, dirty, olive green color. They will vary in strength from day to day, making it possible to discharge four different strengths. During the normal operations, three vats are discharged daily, amounting approximately to 9 600 gal. per day.

Liming.—The hides, having been thoroughly cleaned and softened in the soak vats, are reeled into vats containing a super-saturated solution of calcium hydroxide, to which a small percentage of sodium sulfide has been added. In the lime solution the hair is loosened by the dissolution of the outside layer of the hide—the epidermis—and the cementing substances in the hair follicles. The process requires usually from 4 to 6 days, depending on the kind of hides. The lime solutions are used from 1 to 3 weeks, being strengthened daily with fresh lime. When the lime solution has been in use so long that it will no longer give the proper action, it is discharged as a waste liquor. At Instanter, the supernatant lime liquor is discharged to the sewer, and the lime sludge, which accumulates in the bottom of the vats, is shoveled out and hauled away. It is not washed into the discharge sewers. The principal impurities of the lime liquors are dirt, hair, and dissolved organic matter of a putrescible nature. It has a typical milk-of-lime appearance with a slight bluish color and contains much lime in suspension. There are six different kinds, or strengths, of limes resulting from the fact that the hides dirty the first limes more than the later ones and for other reasons having no bearing on the problem at hand. This waste amounts to about 2 900 gal. per day.

Hot Water.—The last lime solution, called the hot-water solution, differs from those preceding it in that it is not strengthened after it is once made up and that it is maintained at a temperature of about 90° Fahr. This solution is never used longer than three days, when it is discharged and made up new. It has the general appearance of the lime wastes and is discharged in the same manner. It amounts to about 2 900 gal. per day.

Unhairing Machine, Brown Hair Wash, White Hair Wash.—When the hides are removed from the hot water, the hair has been loosened and can easily be removed. This operation is performed on the unhairing machine by a heavy, revolving, roller knife sweeping down over the hide and brushing the hair off. A small quantity of water trickles over the knife during the time it is in operation and washes the hair into a trough below, down which it floats into a vat where it is automatically removed. This hair is the brown hair, which is then collected and washed in a stream of clean, running water, the overflow from which unites with that from the aforementioned vat to form the combined unhairing machine and brown hair wash wastes. The white hair, having been removed by hand previous to the unhairing operation, is washed separately, and furnishes the white hair waste. The unhairing machine, brown hair wash, and white hair wash produce daily wastes amounting to 3 100, 14 300, and 1 200 gal., respectively. The appearance of all three wastes is much the same, having a slight turbidity due to lime and containing some fine hair which has escaped the screens.

Wash Wheel.—The hides having been unhaired and fleshed still contain much lime. To remove this lime the hides are placed in large wheel drums and drummed while a stream of clean water is flushed on them. The pounding and tumbling in the wheel works the lime out and the water carries it away. The wash-wheel waste is quite large in volume, amounting to about 25 800 gal., and contains mainly lime and small pieces of flesh. It is slightly turbid and has the appearance of milky water.

Fleshing Machine.—After the hides have been unhaired and drummed, the flesh, more or less of which is always present on the back of the hide, is removed by a machine similar to that used for unhairing. The fleshings drop down behind the machine and are floated in water into a vat from which the water passes to the sewer. This wash water carries with it small pieces of flesh and a considerable amount of fine particles of fleshings and fat in suspension. This is highly putrescible waste, has a cream-colored appearance, and averages about 7 200 gal. per day.

Float Box.—The float box is nothing more than a long vat with a stream of clear water running in at one end and overflowing at the other. Its purpose is to keep the unhaired, fleshed, and washed hides in a water-soaked condition from the time they leave the fleshing machine until they are ready to be trimmed and hung in the clear-water pools. The float-box water contains very little lime and a small amount of suspended matter composed principally of small pieces of hide substance. It has the appearance of clear water with light-colored particles suspended in it, and amounts to about 4 700 gal. per day.

Green Stock Pools.—Into green stock, or clear-water, pools the now thoroughly washed and cleaned hides are placed to await the tanning process. Clean water is run into these vats continuously, and the waste water contains very few impurities and shows practically no discoloration or suspended matter. It has a slight turbidity and amounts to about 43 600 gal. per day, or one-third the total daily waste from the tannery.

This process concludes the beam-house operations, which furnish the bulk of the daily wastes from the tannery.

Tan Yard

Rockers.—The hides are taken from the green stock pools and placed in the oldest and weakest tanning liquor in the system. The tanning liquors are composed chiefly of infusions of chestnut wood, quebracho wood, and hemlock bark. This liquor, containing only about 0.5% of tannin, is known as the "tail rocker". The name, "rocker", is attributed to the fact that the

TABLE 5.—Chemical Analyses of Individual Wastes.

No.	Wastes.	Gallons per day.	Specific gravity, 20° cent.	Total Solids. Parts per million.	Total Solids. Pounds per day.	Suspended Solids. Parts per million.	Suspended Solids. Pounds per day.	Fixed Residue. Parts per million.	Fixed Residue. Pounds per day.	Volatile Solids. Parts per million.	Volatile Solids. Pounds per day.	Total Alkalinity, CaO. Parts per million.	Total Alkalinity, CaO. Pounds per day.
	Soaks, first		1.0173	23 820	1 940	1 888	154	21 233	1 729	2 587	211	689	56
	Soaks, second		1.0022	3 101	249	383	31	910	73	2 191	176	140	11
			1.0022	3 030	243	262	21	1 556	125	1 474	118	392	31
1*	Soaks, third	9 600	1.0028	4 400	353	1 002	80	1 803	145	2 597	209	168	13
			1.0040	7 522	605	630	51	3 044	245	4 478	360	279	22
	Soaks, fourth		1.0097	14 250	1 152	701	57	13 240	1 070	1 010	82	416	34
			1.0100	18 456	451	8 193	200	14 662	358	3 794	93	13 186	322
	Limes, first (6 days)		1.0100	18 780	458	10 254	251	14 491	354	4 289	101	7 030	172
			1.0090	11 949	292	1 951	48	8 504	208	3 445	84	2 514	61
			1.0156	25 270	621	13 305	327	24 896	612	374	9	24 434	600
2*	Limes, second (2 weeks)	2 900	1.0145	14 987	368	4 800	118	†	†	†	†	14 844	364
	Limes, third (2 weeks		1.0150	23 432	575	7 605	187	18 463	453	4 969	122	6 331	155
	Limes, fourth (3 weeks)		1.0128	28 764	705	17 003	417	27 834	682	920	23	28 766	705
	Limes, fifth (3 weeks)		1.0140	23 026	565	6 134	150	16 446	403	6 580	161	5 730	141
	Limes, sixth (2 to 3 weeks)		1.0122	19 332	473	8 352	204	13 251	324	6 081	149	16 403	402
			1.0045	8 235	200	2 477	60	6 292	153	1 943	47	6 364	155
3*	Hot water	2 900	1.0096	8 653	211	3 312	81	4 857	119	3 796	93	3 444	84
			1.0075	9 965	243	3 481	85	†	†	†	†	3 836	93
4	Unhairing machine	3 100	1.0000	1 906	49	1 102	28	908	23	998	26	751	19
5	Wash wheel	25 800	1.0000	1 620	349	448	96	524	113	1 096	236	224	48
6	Fleshing machine	7 200	1.0000	3 557	214	2 571	154	†	†	†	†	112	7
7	Float box	4 700	1.0000	276	11	146	6	†	†	†	†	28	1
8	Green stock pools	43 600	1.0000	385	140	94	34	135	49	250	91	112	41
9	Brown hair wash	14 300	1.0035	2 434	291	984	118	876	105	1 558	187	112	13
10	White hair wash	1 200	1.0016	2 212	22	909	9	1 308	13	904	9	420	4
11*	Spent tan liquor	7 800	1.0152	34 255	2 262	817	54	5 079	335	29 176	1 927	......	......
12*	Soda bleach	1 700	1.0171	30 105	434	2 565	37	7 103	102	23 002	332	4 021	58
			1.0190	33 720	477	2 983	43	8 169	118	25 551	359	3 720	37
13*	Acid bleach	1 700	1.0233	36 349	527	20	...	5 992	87	30 357	440	......	......
			1.0256	41 158	599	643	9	6 728	98	34 434	501	......	......
14*	Acid water	1 700	1.0110	17 242	247	19	...	2 813	40	14 429	207	......	......
			1.0140	21 361	307	147	2	3 629	52	17 732	255	......	......
		128 200	......	......	6 342	......	921	......	2 261	......	3 868	......	669

* Nos. 1, 2, 3, 11, 12, 13 and 14 are intermittent wastes. † No analysis made. ‡ Composite sample.

TABLE 5.—(*Continued*).

	Wastes.	Gallons per day.	Specific gravity, 20° cent.	Sulfuric Acid.		Sodium Chloride.		Total Nitrogen.		Hide Substance.		Five-Day Oxygen Demand, 20° Cent.	
				Parts per million.	Pounds per day.	Parts per million.	Pounds per day.	Parts per million.	Pounds per day.	Parts per million.	Pounds per day.	Parts per million.	Pounds per day.
1*	Soaks, first	9 600	1.0173	......	......	19 901	1 621	303	24.7	1 701	139	190‡	15‡
						2 263	182					558‡	45‡
	Soaks, second		1.0022	......	......	3 118	250	49	3.9	275	22		
			1.0022	......	......	1 962	157	43	3.5	243	20		
	Soaks, third		1.0028	......	......	2 792	224	86	8.9	483	39		
			1.0040	......	......	6 215	499	382	30.7	2 145	172		
						10 677	858						
	Soaks, fourth		1.0097	......	......	12 111	979	159	12.9	893	72		
						3 212	260						
2*	Limes, first (6 days)	2 900	1.0100	......	......	......	......	271	6.6	1 524	37	3 300‡	80‡
			1.0100	......	......	......	......	286	7.0	1 608	39	1 510‡	37‡
			1.0090	......	......	......	......	135	3.3	758	19		
	Limes, second (2 weeks)		1.0156	......	......	......	......	410	10.1	2 300	57		
	Limes, third (2 weeks)		1.0145	......	......	......	......	516	12.7	2 900	71		
	Limes, fourth (3 weeks)		1.0150	......	......	......	......	754	18.5	4 234	104		
	Limes, fifth (3 weeks)		1.0128	......	......	......	......	604	14.8	3 395	83		
	Limes, sixth (2 to 3 weeks)		1.0140	......	......	......	......	1 135	27.8	6 380	156		
			1.0122	......	......	......	......	696	17.0	3 908	96		
3*	Hot water	2 900	1.0045	......	......	......	......	361	8.8	2 030	49	526‡	13‡
			1.0096	......	......	......	......	122	3.0	686	17	2 255‡	55‡
			1.0075	......	......	......	......	538	13.1	3 029	74		
4	Unhairing machine	3 100	1.0000	......	......	......	......	80	2.1	448	12	140	3.6
												136	3.5
5	Wash wheel	25 800	1.0000	......	......	......	......	105	22.6	590	127	502	108
												462	95
6	Fleshing machine	7 200	1.0000	......	......	......	......	105	6.3	590	35	828	50
												310	19
7	Float box	4 700	1.0000	......	......	......	......	†	†	†	†	44	1.7
												6	0.3
8	Green stock pools	43 600	1.0000	......	......	......	......	17	6.8	97	35	3	1.2
9	Brown hair wash	14 300	1.0035	......	......	......	......	79	9.5	444	53	138	16
												328	39
10	White hair wash	1 200	1.0016	......	......	......	......	71	0.7	399	4	431	4
												82	0.8
11*	Spent tan liquor	7 800	1.0152	1 206	80	......	......	89	5.9	500	33	5 725	373
												4 340	283
12*	Soda bleach	1 700	1.0171	......	......	......	......	34	0.5	192	3	3 144	47
			1.0190	......	......	......	......	23	0.3	127	2	2 715	38.5
13*	Acid bleach	1 700	1.0233	17 597	255	......	......	52	0.8	292	4	1 700	24
			1.0256	18 633	271	......	......	58	0.8	326	5	1 655	23
14*	Acid water	1 700	1.0110	5 186	74	......	......	34	0.8	191	3	1 500	21
			1.0140	5 866	84	......	......	41	0.6	228	3	1 025	15
		128 200	......	......	422	......	743	......	94.8	......	531	......	706.4

* Nos. 1, 2, 3, 11, 12, 13 and 14 are intermittent wastes. † No analysis made. ‡ Composite sample.

frames upon which the hides are suspended in the vats are rocked slowly up and down. After remaining in the tail rocker one day, the tail-rocker liquor is drained off, as waste or spent tan liquor, and is run to the sewer. This waste is highly colored and represents the worst single waste from the tannery as to color, solids, oxygen demand, etc. It amounts to about 7 800 gal. per day, has a reddish, chocolate brown color, and is slightly acid in character. The hides are then passed from the rockers to vats called "layers", containing heavy tanning liquor in which the tanning is completed. No liquor from the layers finds its way to the waste. The only waste produced in the tan yard is that from the tail rocker.

Finishing

Scrub House.—In this department the leather from the layers is bleached and impregnated with oils, concentrated tanning liquor, sugar, salts, etc., depending on the character of leather desired. Except for the bleach, none of the other operations furnishes waste. The bleach liquors are made up daily and discharged to the sewer at the end of the working day. The bleaching proper takes place in a solution of sodium carbonate, after which the leather is given a dip in a weak sulfuric-acid solution to neutralize the excess sodium carbonate, and, finally, a dip in water. The three wastes are designated soda bleach, acid bleach, and acid-water bleach, each furnishing 1 700 gal. per day.

Part I.—Chemical Analysis of Individual Wastes

The object of carefully analyzing the individual wastes was to bring out the differences existing between them so that they might be classified physically and chemically according to their several attributes. It was found that the volumes of the wastes varied somewhat from day to day, due mainly to the use of different quantities of water in the processes, but that the actual constituent parts of the wastes remained fairly constant. In some instances, therefore, more than one analysis was made of a given waste to note this effect. A study of these analyses threw considerable light on the subject of treating the wastes, and on the accurate planning of the preliminary laboratory work. These analyses are shown in Table 5.

The hide substance was calculated from the total nitrogen, assuming that the nitrogenous matter represented that of hide matter and that it equalled 17.8% thereof. Only three of the wastes were acid, namely, the spent tan liquor, the acid bleach, and the acid-water bleach. Combined, these three weak acid wastes amounted to only approximately 11 000 gal., which was 8.5% of the whole volume of waste and would have little influence toward neutralizing the combined volume of the other wastes, due to their high alkalinity. The remainder of the wastes, except the soda bleach, originated in the beam house and were alkaline, due to the lime used there; that is, all the wastes discharging from the beam house following the limes were contaminated, so to speak, with the lime carried over by the hides from the lime vats. Approximately 50% of the alkalinity of the soaks, however, was due to free ammonia, whereas the alkalinity of the soda bleach was due to sodium carbonate.

Referring to Table 5, the wastes listed as intermittent represent by far the worst. They are all vat wastes, or those which result when the solutions in the vats, having been used over and over, no longer function properly and are discharged. In general, the characteristics of the intermittent wastes were that they contained the most total solids, suspended solids, and color, had the greatest oxygen demand, and were responsible for most of the variation in volume from day to day.

All the continuous wastes were alkaline; and as they originated from a washing operation were neither as putrid nor as concentrated as the intermittent wastes. This fact is interesting, because it means that at some tanneries on large streams these wastes can be disposed of without treatment. On the other hand, where it is necessary to treat all the wastes, these would serve well for dilution purposes. In this investigation, however, all the wastes were used in the experimentation, as obviously no such investigation would be complete unless all were included in the study.

TABLE 6.

	First Set.						Second Set.					
	Oxygen demand, in parts per million.	Order.	Percentage quantity units, in pounds of oxygen.	Quantity units, in pounds of oxygen.	Order.	People = $\frac{Q.U.}{0.167}$	Oxygen demand, in parts per million.	Order.	Percentage quantity units, in pounds of oxygen.	Quantity units, in pounds of oxygen.	Order.	People = $\frac{Q.U.}{0.167}$
*Spent tan...........	5 725	1	49.3	373.0	1	2 230	4 340	1	43.2	283.0	1	1 695
*Limes.............	3 300	2	10.6	80.0	3	478	1 510	5	5.7	37.0	7	221
*Soda bleach.........	3 144	3	6.2	47.0	5	282	2 715	2	5.8	38.5	6	231
*Acid bleach.........	1 700	4	3.2	24.0	6	144	1 655	4	3.4	23.0	8	138
*Acid water bleach..	1 500	5	2.8	21.0	7	126	1 025	6	2.3	15.0	10	90
Fleshing machine..	828	6	6.6	50.0	4	299	310	10	2.8	19.0	9	114
*Hot water..........	526	7	1.7	13.0	10	79	2 255	3	8.3	55.0	3	319
Wash wheel.........	502	8	14.3	108.0	2	648	462	8	14.5	95.0	2	570
White hair wash....	431	9	0.5	4.0	11	24	82	12	0.1	0.8	12	5
*Soaks..............	190	10	2.0	15.0	9	90	558	7	6.9	45.0	4	269
Unhairing machine.	140	11	0.48	3.6	12	22	136	11	0.54	3.5	11	21
Brown hair..........	138	12	2.10	16.0	8	96	328	9	6.0	39.0	5	234
Float box...........	44	13	0.22	1.7	13	10	6	13	0.46	0.3	13	2
Total...........	.....	..	100.00	756.3	..	4 528	.....	..	100.00	653.1	..	3 909

*Intermittent wastes.

Referring to the determination of 5-day bio-chemical oxygen demand given in the last column of Table 5, an interesting arrangement of the wastes is obtained when using this determination for the standard. This arrangement is shown in Table 6.

Two sets of samples of the wastes, shown in Table 6, were collected on two different days. In the first column of each set is given the 5-day oxygen demand at 20° cent., in parts per million. The number in the column, "Order", refers to the order of intensity, No. 1 having the highest oxygen demand, No. 2 the next highest, etc. The figures in the column, "Quantity Units, in Pounds of Oxygen", are obtained by reducing the parts per million results to a pound basis. These figures represent the pounds of oxygen required in five days by each waste for stabilization. If they are divided by 0.167 in each instance, the pounds are converted into people; that is, the average person produces enough waste material in a day of 24 hours to create a 5-day oxygen demand of 0.167 lb. at 20° cent.* These figures are given under the column, "People". The other column gives the "Percentage Quantity Units".

It is interesting to note that the spent tan liquor, although only representing 6% of the entire waste by volume, accounted for almost 50% of the total oxygen demand; also, that the combined wastes per day represented the sewage from a town of about 4 200 people; that is, for a tannery of 300 hides per day, 1 hide produces waste with an oxygen demand equivalent to that of the sewage of 14 people.

Another point of interest is the wash-wheel waste. It has a relatively low oxygen demand, eighth in order of intensity, but when converted to quantity units assumes a position second only to the spent tan liquor, representing about 14% of the total oxygen demand of the wastes. This is by reason of its relatively large volume of 14 300 gal., or 11% of the total daily wastes from the tannery.

The statement made previously that the intermittent wastes were by far the worst is very strikingly brought out by the figures of Table 6. In both sets of samples the intermittent wastes represent slightly more than 75% of the total oxygen demand, whereas their combined volume is less than 30% of the total daily waste from the tannery.

The principal points of importance learned from the preliminary investigation of the wastes are:

(1) The majority of the wastes were found to be alkaline; only the acid bleach, acid-water bleach, and the spent tan liquor proved to be acid.

(2) In many cases the continuous wastes probably could be disposed of without treatment, or could be used as a diluent in treating the other wastes.

(3) With the exception of the soda bleach, all the alkalinity found was due to lime.

(4) The spent tan liquor and the three bleach liquors contained most of the coloring matter of the wastes.

(5) The intermittent wastes constituted about 75% of the total oxygen demand of the wastes.

(6) The continuous wastes representing more than two-thirds of the total volume of all the wastes accounted for only 25% of the total oxygen demand.

(7) Based on quantity units, the spent tan liquor required about 45% of the total oxygen demand.

Part II.—Laboratory Studies

The object of the laboratory tests was to develop methods of treatment by making a thorough study of all the possible mixtures of the various wastes. In order to make such an investigation it is first necessary to learn the proper-

* "Treatment of Packing-House, Tannery, and Corn Products Wastes," *Industrial and Engineering Chemistry*, October, 1926.

ties of the individual wastes and then to study systematically their behavior when mixed each with the other, then each with two others, etc., until all possible combinations have been tried. The sterilizing, deodorizing, stabilizing, decolorizing, etc., of tannery waste is not a difficult problem as such, but to do all this by merely mixing the wastes in combinations which produce chemical reactions, precipitation, sedimentation, etc., at low cost, throws an entirely different light on the problem. To date more than one hundred such combinations have been investigated.

A limitation defining the proportion of each constituent in the mixtures made it necessary to consider in these laboratory investigations the importance of always mixing the wastes in the same proportions in which they are discharged. Not only a change in the proportion of one or more constituents in a mixture, but also in practice, the time of day of discharge of a given waste, or its variation in amount, strength, and character from day to day, might influence the success of a treatment.

In the preliminary study of the various mixtures, practically the only objectives were rapidity and adequateness of sedimentation, solids removed, and color removed. Whenever an outstanding mixture, with regard to these qualities was obtained, it was studied in greater detail. In other words, unless a mixture proved to be above the average, it was listed as a matter of record as negative information.

The equipment used in the laboratory for the study of sedimentation, color, and general physical characteristics were either 1 000 or 500-cu. cm., graduated glass cylinders. They were of uniform bore and colorless, and a practice was made from the start to use cylinders of the same size throughout a given experiment; that is, the contents in a 500-cu. cm. cylinder were never compared with the contents of a 1 000-cu. cm. cylinder.

Sampling

Throughout these experiments the wastes were always sampled in the same manner, and only fresh samples were used. The soaks, limes, and hot waters were sampled by plunging up the vats just prior to their discharge to the sewer. The unhairing-machine wastes were sampled by taking a quantity from the trough and removing the excess hair. The wash-wheel waste was sampled by placing a bucket beneath the wheel so as to catch a small quantity of the wash water during the whole time the wheel was running, care being taken to prevent the bucket from overflowing. The fleshing-machine waste was sampled in the same manner as the unhairing-machine waste, but large pieces of flesh were removed. The float-box waste was sampled by merely dipping out a pailful. The green stock pools were sampled in the same manner as the float box. The brown hair wash was sampled by placing a bucket near the overflow so as to catch a small portion of the waste over a period of several hours, care being taken not to overflow the bucket. The white hair wash sample was taken from the wash water contained in the white hair washing vat, first plunging up the water and withdrawing a quantity. The soda, acid, and acid-water bleaches were sampled by plunging up the vats just prior to their discharge, and a sample taken from each. The spent tan liquor was sampled by making a composite sample of the six rocker vats discharged each day. It was not practicable to obtain a sample of the various floor washes which varied so much in quantity and character, and because of their relatively small volume they were neglected.

Treatment of Intermittent Wastes

It has already been stated that the intermittent wastes represent by far the worst group from the tannery. Considerable time, therefore, was spent in experimenting with these seven wastes in whole, in part, and with chemical treatment. The particular result looked for in these treatments was rapidity of settling the settleable solids, and the reduction of color, oxygen demand, and suspended solids.

Experiment No. 14 (Fig. 2) was performed several times in order to note the main reactions between the individual wastes. Unless there was a tendency to settle or a decided change in the two constituents, the mixture was termed "no reaction". Experiments Nos. 2 and 3 (Fig. 3), 4 and 5 (Fig. 4), 7 and 8 (Fig. 5), 11 (Fig. 6), and 12 (Fig. 7), are examples of many such experiments using several combinations of wastes, permitting them to settle, and then combining the resulting supernatants. The object of these experiments was to find ways and means, without chemical treatment, to effect good settlement and to produce light-colored and clear effluents. Experiment No. 1 (Fig. 8), shows the general characteristics of the whole mixture of intermittent wastes.

After a considerable number of experiments had been performed similar to those described, it became evident that to produce a really worth-while effluent and not to complicate a treatment with too many refinements, the number of separate treatments of any of the wastes or combinations thereof should be kept as low as possible. Treatment of a large number of small units materially introduces operating difficulties which are hard to overcome. Also, the cost attending the handling of any treatment consisting of a group of small units usually is prohibitive. From a practical standpoint a mixture of all the wastes in one batch would offer the simplest means for treatment in most cases, and even if additional agents, such as acids, alkalis, coagulants, etc., were required, the ease and simplicity of operation would probably be a deciding factor in its favor.

One of the most difficult problems was to produce a mixture which would settle readily. Several plans were developed which gave encouraging results, but the disadvantage was that several separate units had to be treated individually in order to produce the desired effect. As stated, it became apparent that a paramount requisite was simplicity; that mixing all these wastes together seemed the most promising method for further study. As such, however, as was shown by Experiment No. 1 (Fig. 8), and reproduced many times thereafter, the mixture of the intermittent wastes was alkaline, and there was little or no tendency toward sedimentation. A number of experiments having to do with the treatment of all the intermittent wastes mixed together, therefore, were carried out, using the chemical agents, lime, sulfuric acid, sulfur dioxide, aluminum sulfate, ferrous sulfate, etc. Three typical examples of this study are shown by Experiments Nos. 9 (Fig. 9), 26(*a*) (Fig. 10), and 42 (Fig. 11).

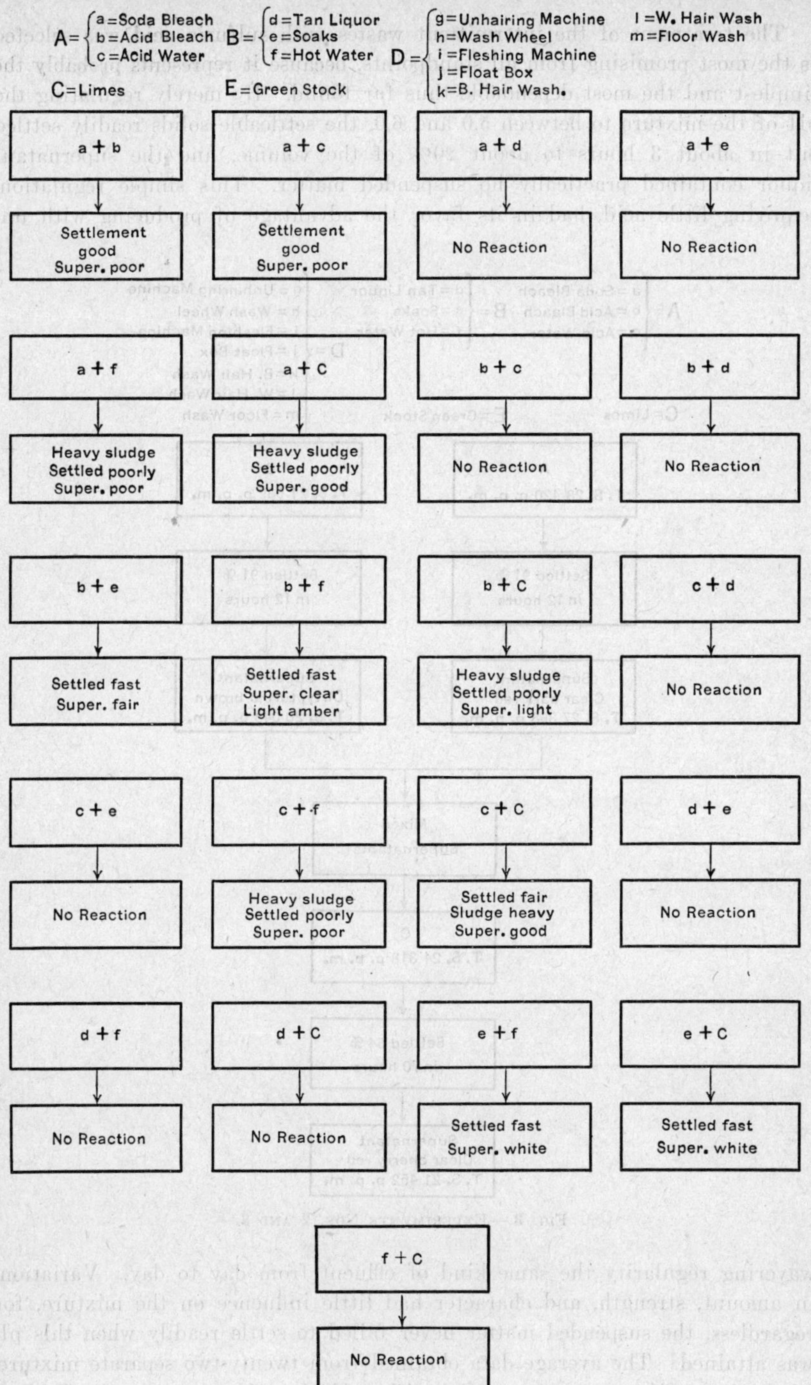

FIG. 2.—EXPERIMENT NO. 14 TO NOTE MAIN REACTIONS BETWEEN INDIVIDUAL WASTES.

The treatment of the intermittent wastes with sulfuric acid was selected as the most promising from all standpoints, because it represents probably the simplest and the most dependable thus far found. By merely regulating the pH of the mixture to between 5.0 and 6.0, the settleable solids readily settled out in about 3 hours to about 20% of the volume, and the supernatant liquor contained practically no suspended matter. This simple regulation, requiring little acid, had in its favor the advantage of producing with un-

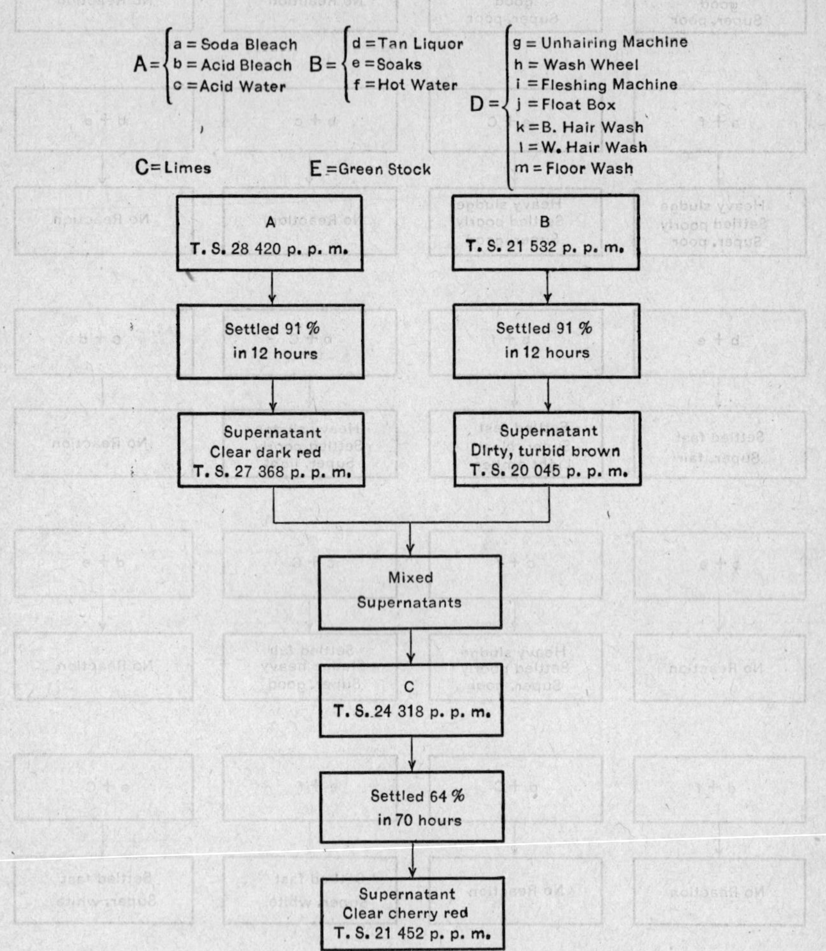

FIG. 3.—EXPERIMENTS NOS. 2 AND 3.

wavering regularity the same kind of effluent from day to day. Variations in amount, strength, and character had little influence on the mixture, for, regardless, the suspended matter never failed to settle readily when this pH was attained. The average data obtained from twenty-two separate mixtures of the intermittent wastes, treated with sulfuric acid, are given in Table 7.

TABLE 7.—ANALYSIS OF INTERMITTENT WASTES BEFORE AND AFTER TREATMENT WITH SULFURIC ACID.

	Total solids, in parts per million.	Hide substance,* in parts per million.	Organic matter, in parts per million.	5-day oxygen demand, in parts per million.	Color.
Whole mixture	27 090	1 235	15 116	3 302	8 500
Supernatant	24 213	362	12 511	1 274	3 000
Percentage reduced	10.62	70.70	17.23	61.40	64.75

* Average of three samples.

There are probably many cases where this kind of treatment of the most foul wastes would suffice. In such, it would be assumed that the continuous wastes were of such a nature, or the receiving body of such magnitude, that they could be disposed of without treatment.

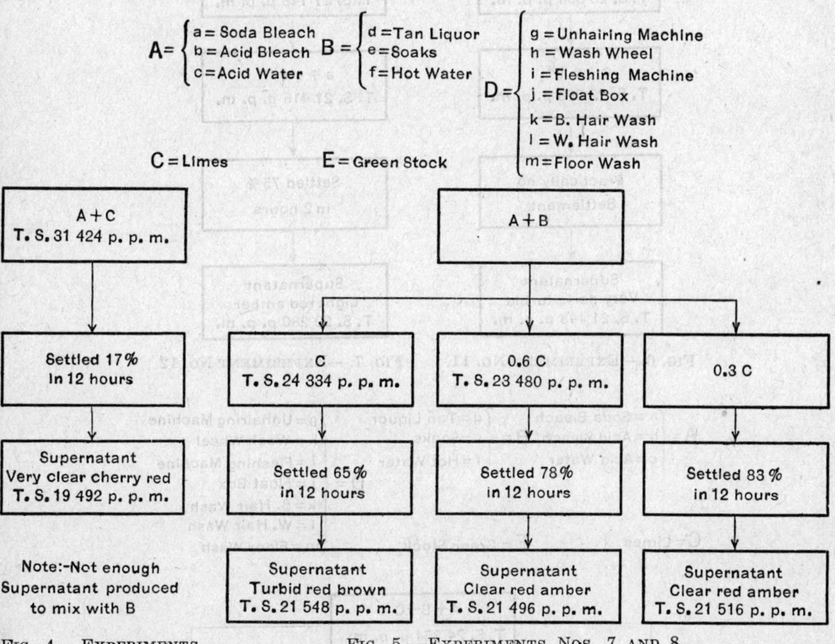

FIG. 4.—EXPERIMENTS NOS. 4 AND 5.

FIG. 5.—EXPERIMENTS NOS. 7 AND 8.

Treatment of Intermittent and Continuous Wastes

In this section of the paper the writers consider not only the intermittent wastes, but, in addition, the continuous wastes, except the green stock. Many experiments were carried out with these wastes in much the same manner as that followed in the preceding section. They were studied first, by mixing them in small units, permitting sedimentation, and eventually combining the supernatants until the final effluents represented all the wastes; then, less complicated methods were tried; and, finally, the number of separate mixtures

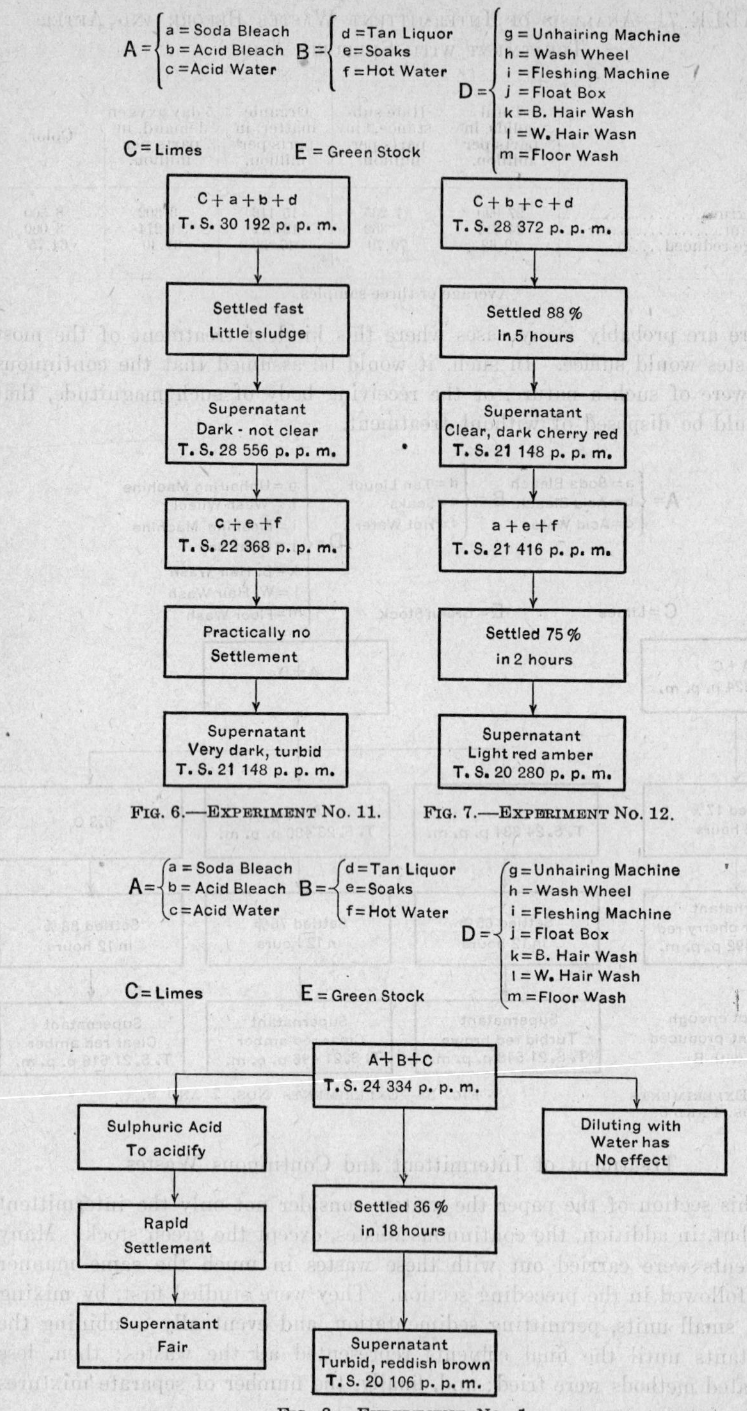
A = a = Soda Bleach, b = Acid Bleach, c = Acid Water
B = d = Tan Liquor, e = Soaks, f = Hot Water
D = g = Unhairing Machine, h = Wash Wheel, i = Fleshing Machine, j = Float Box, k = B. Hair Wash, l = W. Hair Wash, m = Floor Wash
C = Limes
E = Green Stock
C + a + b + d
T. S. 30 192 p. p. m.
Settled fast
Little sludge
Supernatant
Dark - not clear
T. S. 28 556 p. p. m.
c + e + f
T. S. 22 368 p. p. m.
Practically no
Settlement
Supernatant
Very dark, turbid
T. S. 21 148 p. p. m.
C + b + c + d
T. S. 28 372 p. p. m.
Settled 88 %
in 5 hours
Supernatant
Clear, dark cherry red
T. S. 21 148 p. p. m.
a + e + f
T. S. 21 416 p. p. m.
Settled 75 %
in 2 hours
Supernatant
Light red amber
T. S. 20 280 p. p. m.
A + B + C
T. S. 24 334 p. p. m.
Sulphuric Acid
To acidify
Rapid
Settlement
Supernatant
Fair
Settled 36 %
in 18 hours
Supernatant
Turbid, reddish brown
T. S. 20 106 p. p. m.
Diluting with
Water has
No effect

FIG. 6.—EXPERIMENT NO. 11. FIG. 7.—EXPERIMENT NO. 12.

FIG. 8.—EXPERIMENT NO. 1.

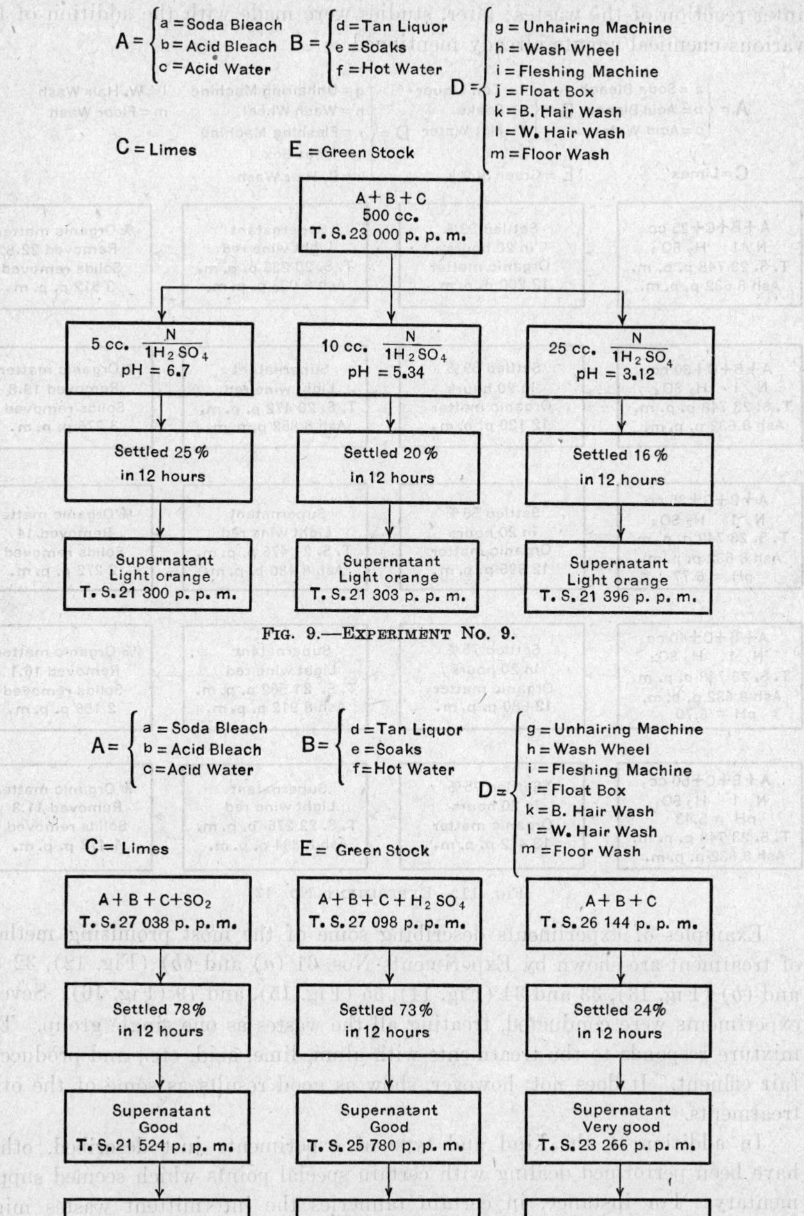

Fig. 9.—Experiment No. 9.

Fig. 10.—Experiment No. 26 (*a*).

was reduced to one. At first, it was attempted to produce results by natural inter-reaction of the wastes; later, studies were made with the addition of the various chemical agents already mentioned.

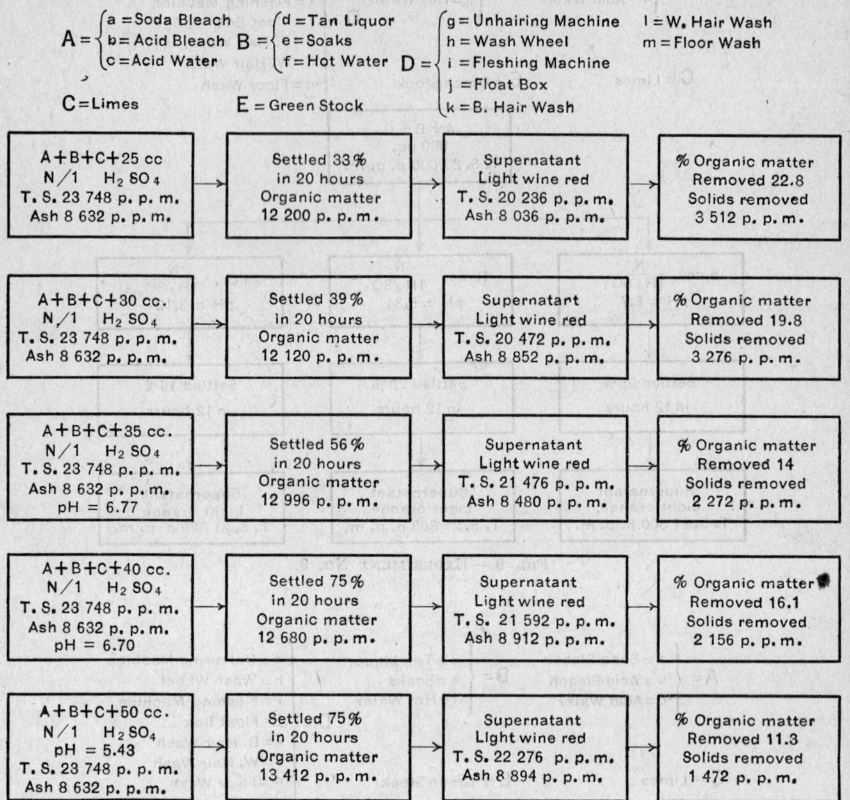

FIG. 11.—EXPERIMENT NO. 42.

Examples of experiments describing some of the most promising methods of treatment are shown by Experiments Nos. 31 (*a*) and (*b*) (Fig. 12), 32 (*a*) and (*b*) (Fig. 13), 33 and 34 (Fig. 14), 55 (Fig. 15), and 79 (Fig. 16). Several experiments were conducted, treating all the wastes as one single group. This mixture responds to the treatments with alum, lime, acid, etc., and produces a fair effluent. It does not, however, show as good results as some of the other treatments.

In addition to the kind and type of experiments just described, others have been performed dealing with certain special points which seemed supplementary. For instance, in certain tanneries the intermittent wastes might not form as alkaline a conglomerate as at Instanter. In such an event the omission of the soda bleach in the first treatment would lessen the alkalinity and, in some cases, to such an extent as not to require an acid treatment. Again, several experiments were based on the theory that a reaction of the tannin on lime would remove a large amount of solids in the form of an insoluble calcium tannate. This proved to be the case, but was only practicable when the lime and spent tan were diluted at least once with fairly clean waste, such as the green stock. Treated in this manner the settlement was good and the effluent was fairly clear. A still better procedure included the soda bleach with the lime and tan liquor. When the supernatant from this mixture was added to the remaining wastes, together with alum and sulfuric acid, a very good effluent was produced.

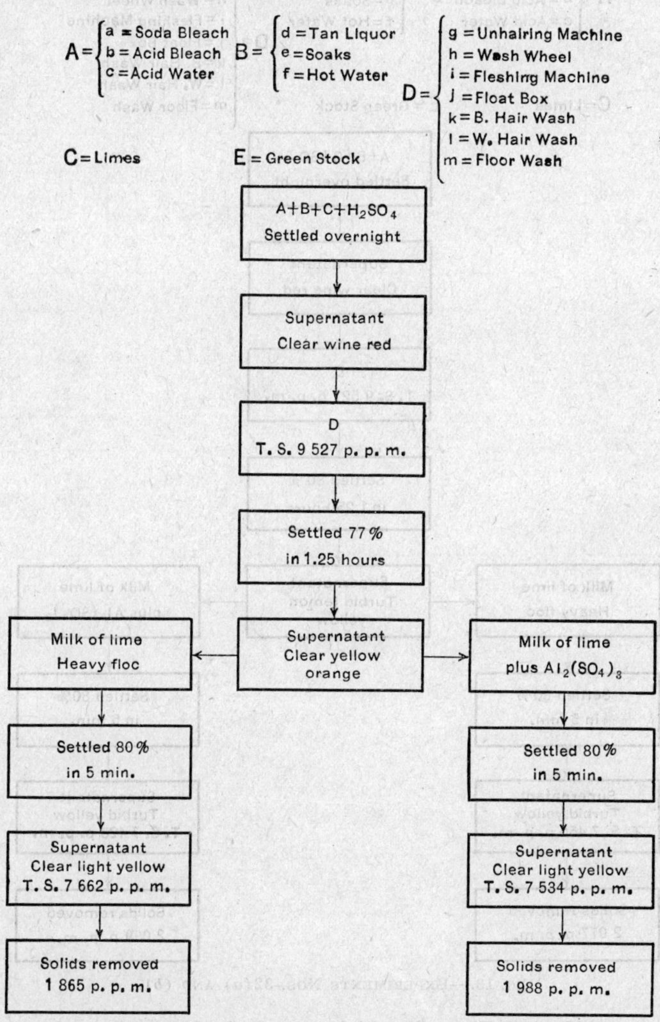

FIG. 12.—EXPERIMENTS NOS. 31(*a*) AND (*b*).

Several experiments involving the use of lime sludge as a precipitant did not show favorable results.

An experiment permitting the lime and tan liquor to re-act several hours before mixing with the other intermittent waste, did not show favorable results; that is, there was nothing in the way of improvement to sanction the separate treatment of the tan liquor.

Separate treatment of the bleaches, separate settling of a mixture of the lime and spent tan liquor, and the resulting supernatants mixed with the other wastes, gave very good results.

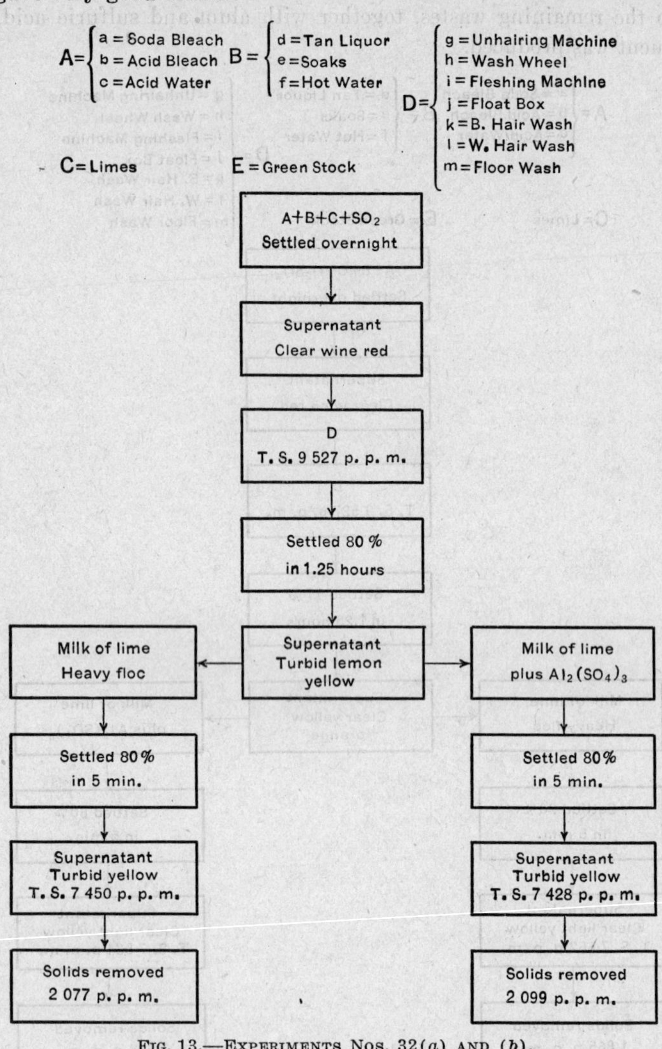

FIG. 13.—EXPERIMENTS NOS. 32(*a*) AND (*b*).

Experiment No. 55 (Fig. 15), which is typical of a number of such experiments performed, describes a very good and dependable method of treatment. In this type of treatment the intermittent wastes were mixed together, and the pH of the mixture regulated to about 5.5 by the addition of sulfuric acid. This mixture was then permitted to settle quietly over night as would have been done in actual operation. The next day the supernatant liquid was added to

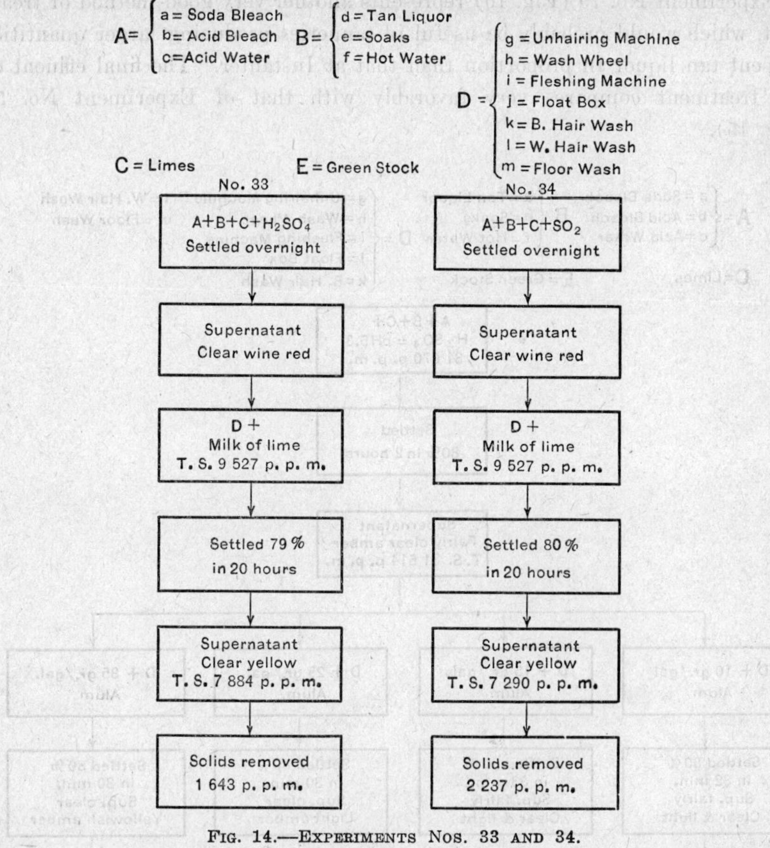

FIG. 14.—EXPERIMENTS NOS. 33 AND 34.

the continuous wastes, except the green stock, together with 20 grains per gal. of aluminum sulfate, and the whole mixed thoroughly. The mixture was then permitted to settle quietly. This particular treatment has been repeated in the laboratory with about twenty-five different samples of the wastes and has been found to give very uniform results. In Table 8 are shown the important determinations made on the final supernatant, which represents the effluent that would be discharged from the tannery after treatment.

TABLE 8.—AVERAGE ANALYSIS OF FINAL SUPERNATANTS, EXPERIMENT NO. 55 (FIG. 15).

	Total solids, in parts per million.	Suspended solids, in parts per million.	5-day oxygen demand, 20° cent., in parts per million.	Color.
Final supernatant......	9 335	176	854	1 203
Percentage reduction..	31.1	93.6	57.1	60

Experiment No. 79 (Fig. 16) represents another very good method of treatment, which would probably be useful in tanneries producing larger quantities of spent tan liquor in proportion than that at Instanter. The final effluent of this treatment compares very favorably with that of Experiment No. 55 (Fig. 15).

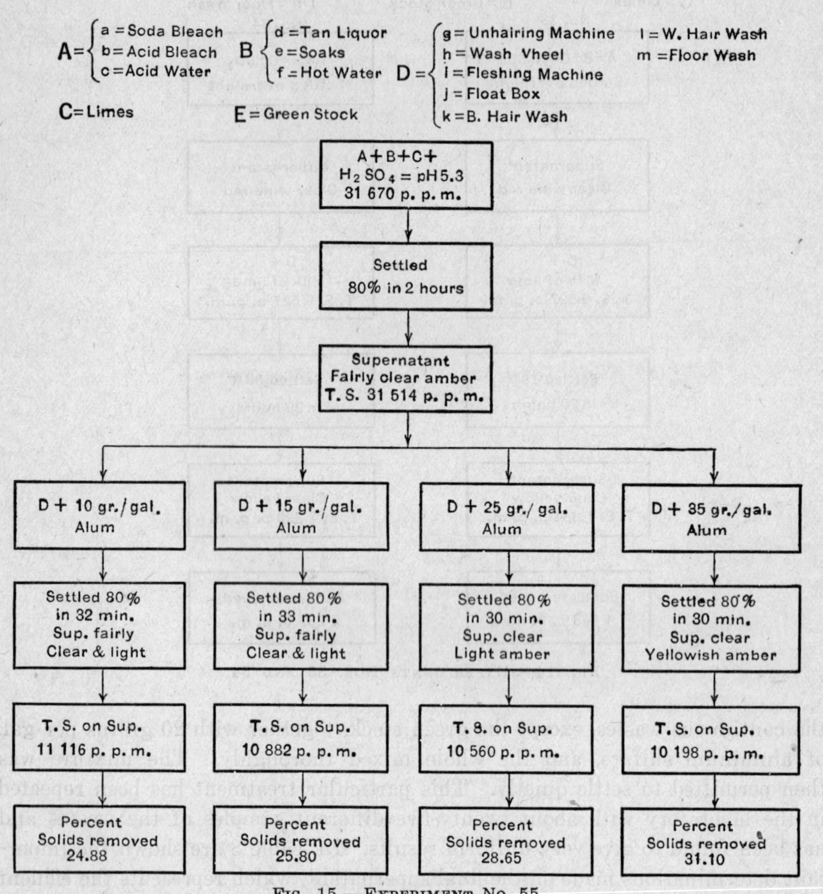

FIG. 15.—EXPERIMENT NO. 55.

It is important to note that in treating all the wastes there was strong evidence in favor of the "two-treatment" process. By two treatments is meant separate treatment of the foulest wastes, and then the effluent from this treatment mixed with and treated together with the remaining wastes. Many modifications of the treatments could be arranged, but the basic facts underlying them would be materially the same. The two-treatment process requires a little more equipment, but this is more than offset by the increased efficiency obtained. It is continuous, does not require skilled labor to operate it, and is reliable and inexpensive.

To summarize briefly the laboratory investigations on both the intermittent wastes alone, and then on the intermittent wastes plus the continuous wastes, the following points were noted:

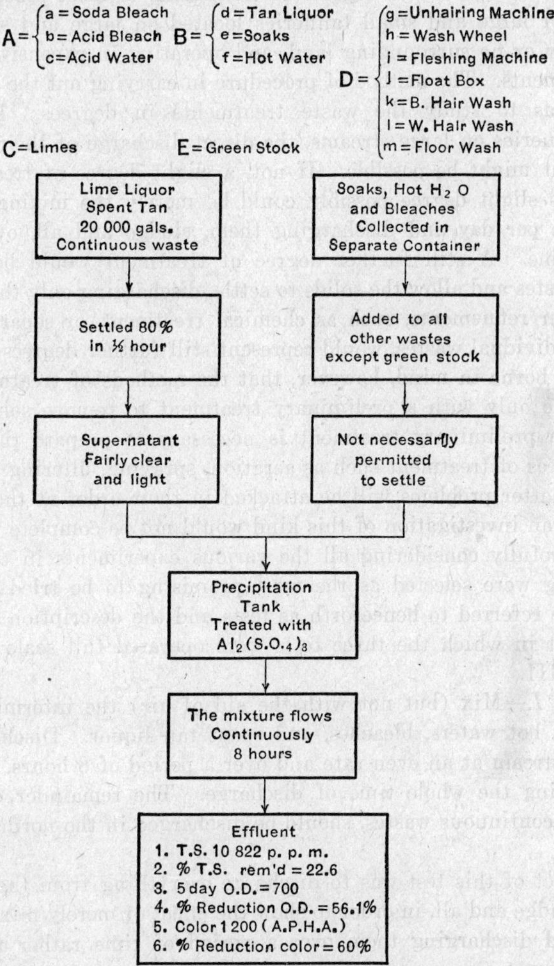

FIG. 16.—EXPERIMENT NO. 79.

(1) Several mixtures were obtained which gave good results and which did not require chemical treatment.

(2) Chemical treatment, or regulation of the pH of the mixture of intermittent wastes, produced the best improvement.

(3) In treating all the wastes from the tannery it appeared that two treatments were necessary to insure good and uniform results.

Selected Treatments

The most promising of the foregoing experiments were selected for full-scale experimentation and will be described in more detail later. Each of the treatments selected represents, in the writers' opinions, the best method developed for that particular degree of treatment, based on the laboratory results. The object of the investigation was to solve eventually the problem in enough ways and by enough degrees of treatments to meet practically all the conditions for large and small tanneries located on large and small streams, having plenty or no surrounding land, and operating in expensive or inexpensive environments. The method of procedure in carrying out the investigation, therefore, was to study the waste treatments in degrees. For instance, for some tanneries on large streams, the direct discharge of their wastes without treatment might be possible. If not, a slight degree of treatment might suffice. This slight degree possibly could be merely the mixing of the combined wastes per day and discharging them, sludge and all, over a selected period of time. A still further degree of treatment would be to mix the combined wastes and allow the solids to settle, discharging only the supernatant liquid. Other refinements, such as chemical treatment, or separate treatment of certain individual wastes, would represent still further degrees of treatment. It should be borne in mind, however, that the methods of treatments referred to have to do only with a preliminary treatment to remove solids and color, etc. Such a preliminary treatment is necessary to prepare the effluent for further degrees of treatment such as aeration, spraying, filtering through sand, etc. These latter problems will be attacked in their order at the proper time, as naturally an investigation of this kind would not be complete without them.

After carefully considering all the various experiments in the laboratory, the following were selected as the most promising to be tried on full scale. They will be referred to henceforth as tests and the description of the experimental plant in which the three tests were operated full scale will be given under Part III.

Test No. I.—Mix (but not with the aid of air) the intermittent waste—limes, soaks, hot waters, bleaches, and spent tan liquor. Discharge the mixture to the stream at an even rate and over a period of 8 hours. Agitate (not by air) during the whole time of discharge. The remainder of the wastes, namely, the continuous wastes, should be discharged in the normal and regular manner.

The object of this test was to discharge everything from the tannery into the river, sludge and all, in order to show the effect of merely mixing the wastes together and discharging them over a period of time rather than releasing them vat by vat.

Test No. IV.—Thoroughly mix the intermittent wastes—limes, soaks, hot waters, bleaches, and spent tan liquor—by plunging up with compressed air. Regulate the pH to about 5.5 by the addition of sulfuric acid. Allow to settle over night. Draw off the supernatant liquid at an even rate and over a period of 8 hours, and discharge directly to the stream; all other wastes to be discharged without treatment. Deposit sludge on sludge beds.

Test No. VII.—Same as Test No. IV up to the point of discharge. Draw off the supernatant liquid and flow by gravity into a precipitation or sedimentation tank at an even rate and over a period of 8 hours. At the same time pump the continuous wastes into the sedimentation tank at an even rate and

following day this mixture, while being agitated in the reaction tanks, was withdrawn and discharged at an even rate and over a period of 8 hours.

In the 1925 test an average of 32 000 gal. of the intermittent waste mixture were handled per day and in the 1926 test, 39 856 gal. were produced. The analyses of the mixtures used in the two tests are shown in Table 9.

TABLE 9.—AVERAGE ANALYSIS OF MIXTURES OF INTERMITTENT WASTES.

	November, 1925.*		July, 1926.†
	Start of run-off, in parts per million.	End of run-off, in parts per million.	Composite taken over period of discharge, in parts per million.
Specific gravity, 20° cent.	......	......	1.0166
Total solids	22 244	22 186	20 552
Soluble solids	19 518	18 612	16 666
Suspended solids	2 726	3 574	3 885
Volatile solids	11 773	9 896	10 461
Fixed solids	10 471	12 290	10 091
Color	8 400	8 600	9 800
pH	6.65	6.70	5.62
5-day oxygen demand, 20° cent.	3 315	1 551	3 876
Alkalinity, CaO	......	......	3 388

* Air used for agitation.
† No air used for agitation.

Each analysis in Table 9 is the average of five analyses. The important facts brought out by the analyses of the 1925 test, which were later confirmed by laboratory experimentation, were the decrease of 50% in the 5-day oxygen demand and the increase in color and in suspended solids in the wastes at the end of the run-off period. These differences were due to the aeration effect while agitating the mixture with air.

Test No. IV

Operation.—Test No. IV, as previously described, was conducted during June, July, August, and part of September, 1926. The intermittent wastes were held daily, mixed in the 32-ft. sump, and delivered to the reaction tanks in the same manner as in Test No. I. Here, they were treated with concentrated sulfuric acid until a pH of about 5.5 was reached. The pH was determined colorimetrically. The acid was added by hand from carboys. Usually the correct pH was obtained on the second trial, the whole acid-adding operation requiring less than 30 min. After the acid treatment a sample of the contents of the tanks was preserved in liter-graduated cylinders and permitted to stand quietly over night. In this manner the sludge content could be gauged very precisely the next morning and the quantity of supernatant liquid to be discharged that day could easily be determined. The mixture in the tank was permitted to settle quietly over night. The next morning the supernatant was started discharging at an even rate and for 8 hours thereafter. Composite samples for analysis were taken of the mixture before the acid treatment and of the effluent during the discharge. Whenever the sludge accumulated to the extent that it interfered with the efficiency of the tanks, it was drawn off, a proportionate part being placed on the sludge beds. The continuous wastes were discharged directly to the creek without treatment in the normal and regular manner.

The average quantity of the daily intermittent waste mixture, based on 16 days' operation, was 37 937 gal., having an average specific gravity of 1.0135 at 20° cent. The average effluent produced per day from this mixture was 27 546 gal., having a specific gravity of 1.0141 at 20° cent. The difference, or 10 391 gal. per day, was retained as sludge, having an average moisture content of 96.78 per cent. In other words, 27.40% by volume of the total daily intermittent waste mixture was retained as sludge. The average sulfuric acid, 66° Baumé, used per day was 206 lb. Table 10 shows the average results of the sixteen analyses of this mixture before treatment and of the effluent as discharged.

TABLE 10.—AVERAGE ANALYSIS OF INTERMITTENT WASTE MIXTURE, BEFORE ACID TREATMENT, AND OF EFFLUENT.

	Before Acid Treatment.		Effluent Discharged to Creek.		Percentage retained as sludge.	Percentage of reduction.
	Parts per million.	Pounds per day.	Parts per million.	Pounds per day.		
Specific gravity, 20° cent.	1.0135	......	1.0141	......	.....	.....
Total solids	21 632	6 807	20 581	4 799	30.88	4.86
Soluble solids	19 137	6 140	19 484	4 538	26.10	—1.78*
Suspended solids	2 494	800	1 097	261	67.40	56.10
Volatile solids	9 836	3 177	8 765	2 147	32.48	10.90
Fixed solids	11 729	3 763	11 373	2 652	29.48	3.04
Color	12 132	......	5 715	......	.....	52.30
pH	5.81	......	5.04	......	.....	.....
5-day oxygen demand, 20° cent.	3 773	1 210	3 425	799	33.92	9.22
Total alkalinity, CaO	2 373	762	1 836	428	43.80	24.10

* Increase.

Test No. VII

Just as Test No. VII, as described, was to be started, circumstances over which the Committee had no control caused the Instanter Tannery to cease operations. On September 8, 1926, the Committee was officially notified that hides would cease to be worked in at that tannery on September 11. Efforts were immediately concentrated on Test No. VII, although it was realized that it would probably be impossible to make a thorough study of this test in so short a time. It was possible, however, to obtain a complete and normal daily waste discharge for 9 days, which has indicated, in a general way at least, the character of this test.

Operation.—Test No. VII included the treatment of all the wastes except the green stock. The intermittent wastes were treated in the same manner as in Test No. IV. The effluent from the intermittent wastes contained in the reaction tanks was discharged into the main trough leading to the sedimentation tank. The continuous wastes were also pumped into this trough. This mixture was discharged into the sedimentation tank at the rate of about

12 000 gal. per hour. Before the mixture entered the sedimentation tank, however, it was passed through a small mixing box at which point a solution of aluminum sulfate was added. The nominal retention period in the sedimentation tank averaged about 2 hours. The effluent was discharged to the creek at the same rate the wastes entered the tank, namely, about 12 000 gal. per hour. The average length of discharge was 8 hours during the working period of the tannery. The contents of the sedimentation tank were permitted to stand quietly during the night. It was found necessary to remove the sludge accumulated in this tank twice during the 14 days it was in operation. The averages of the data collected during 9 days are given in Table 11.

TABLE 11.

Total wastes handled per day.	Quantity.
Continuous and intermittent:	
1. Total, in gallons per day	102 193
Intermittent wastes:	
1. Total in gallons per day	40 406
2. Effluent, in gallons per day	32 700
3. Sludge, " " "	7 706
4. Acid added, in pounds per day	218
Continuous wastes:	
1. Total, in gallons per day	61 787
Combined continuous wastes and effluent from intermittent waste:	
1. Total, in gallons per day	94 487
2. Effluent, in gallons per day	94 487
3. Sludge, " " "	2 980
4. Aluminum sulfate, in pounds per day	250
5. Aluminum sulfate, in grains per gallon	18
Sludge produced:	
1. Sludge from intermittent wastes, in gallons per day	7 706
2. Sludge from sedimentation tank, in gallons per day	2 980
3. Total sludge produced, in gallons per day	10 686

The amount of sludge produced daily in the sedimentation tank was 3.15% by volume based on the daily volume treated in this tank. The moisture content was 97.42 per cent. Considering the total daily volume of wastes, except the green stock, there was an average of 10 686 gal. of sludge produced per day, or 10.45% by volume.

The average results of the nine sets of samples taken during the operation of Test No. VII are presented in Table 12.

In Table 12 the column, "Combined Mixture—No Treatment", is the analysis of the mixture, as produced, of all the intermittent and continuous wastes except the green stock; the column, "Before Alum Treatment", is the analysis of the mixture consisting of the effluent from the intermittent wastes after the acid treatment and the continuous wastes; and the column, "Effluent Discharged to Creek", is the analysis of the effluent from the sedimentation tank. This effluent is produced by treating with aluminum sulfate the mixture, the analysis of which is given in the column, "Before Alum Treatment", and, subsequently, permitting sedimentation to take place in the tank.

The usual preliminary adjustment and regulation of the functioning of the sedimentation tank could not be accomplished before starting this test, owing to the limited time available. Consequently, several alterations, glaringly in need, could not be made. A more efficient method of removing the sludge would have provided a somewhat longer retention period. Lack of sufficient ground space on which to store the sludge forced the sedimentation tank to operate beyond its point of efficiency, due to sludge piling up inside. This fact partly explains the relatively large amount of suspended solids noted in the effluent. There is no doubt that this tank can be operated much more efficiently when it is properly adjusted.

TABLE 12.—AVERAGE ANALYSIS OF WASTE MIXTURES.

	Combined Mixture.* No Treatment.		Before Alum Treatment.		Effluent Discharged to Creek.		Total amount retained as sludge, percentage.	Amount retained as sludge from sedimentation tank, percentage.	Reduction, percentage.
	Parts per million.	Pounds per day.	Parts per million.	Pounds per day.	Parts per million.	Pounds per day.			
Specific gravity, 20° cent.	1.0071	......	1.0068	.....	1.0040	.....	.....	.....	.....
Total solids	13 557	11 640	11 687	9 240	6 465	5 100	56.15	44.80	52.25
Soluble solids	10 732	9 224	9 816	7 772	5 614	4 428	52.05	43.00	47.65
Suspended solids	2 825	2 416	1 871	1 468	851	672	72.25	54.20	69.95
Volatile solids	....	......	5 928	4 710	3 090	2 440	.....	61.70	.....
Fixed solids	....	......	5 759	4 530	3 375	2 660	.....	43.70	.....
Color	3 000	......	2 747	.....	850	.....	.....	.....	71.70
pH	7.0	......	5.38	.....	5.69	.....	.....	.....	.....
5-day oxygen demand, 20° cent.	2 000	1 719	1 769	1 399	1 026	808	53.00	42.20	48.60
Alkalinity, CaO	....	......	2 290	1 811	1 717	1 364	.....	25.20	.....

* Laboratory mixture.

The point of draw-off, being only 10 in. wide, caused the effluent to be accelerated in that region, resulting in considerable stirring up of the sludge. This trouble can be eliminated by simply making the draw-off trough the width of the channel of the tank. These, and other mechanical features, can easily be adjusted. Color and suspended matter showed 72% and 70% reduction, respectively. The 48.60% reduction in 5-day oxygen demand is also notable because it must be remembered that no special treatment for oxidation, such as aeration, biological filtration, and the like, was made. This reduction in oxygen demand is due primarily to the removal of solids in suspension and in solution. Attention is called to the fact that of the 56.15% removal of solids, 45% was accomplished in the sedimentation tank. This, of course, was by reason of the relatively much larger volume treated in this tank and does not minimize in the least the efficiency of the acid treatment of the intermittent wastes because the efficacy of both treatments has already been ably demonstrated by these tests. The removal of approximately five-sevenths of the total suspended matter and two-thirds of the total oxygen demand was accomplished in the sedimentation tank.

The success of this test is evident from the actual facts noted. The production of a suitable effluent has consumed practically the entire attention of the investigation to date (1926). A detailed study of the sludge problem will be taken up as soon as the experimental plant has been transferred to another tannery. Although the abandonment of Instanter Tannery cut short further experiments, the information derived from the tests is valuable.

Summary of Full-Scale Operations

1.—Test No. I, which amounts to mixing certain wastes, and prolonging their discharge, undoubtedly could be used to advantage by some tanneries.

2.—The use of air for mixing produced a 50% reduction in the oxygen demand of the untreated intermittent wastes.

3.—Test No. IV proved to be a dependable method of producing sedimentation of the intermittent waste mixture at little cost and little labor.

4.—Test No. VII, although not operated long enough to prove its ultimate efficiency, clearly indicated an effective treatment.

Part IV.—River Studies

River studies were made to determine the effect of the various treatments described in the preceding section, on the East Branch of the Clarion River, immediately below the point of discharge of the wastes, and for a distance down stream of about 12 miles. The river studies were carried on only during the summers of 1925 and 1926. Most of the river work of the summer of 1925 consisted in determining its condition during the regular and normal daily operations of the tannery. The river investigation during the summer of 1926 consisted only of the study of Tests Nos. I, IV, and VII.

The samples of the river water obtained for analysis were taken from carefully selected stations located at definite points along the river over the 12-mile stretch.

Station 1 was immediately below the point of discharge of the tannery waste, but far enough down stream to insure thorough mixing of the water and waste.

Station 2 was 1½ miles below Station 1, and just above the junction of Straight Creek with the Clarion.

Station 3 was 3 miles below Station 1 and 1½ miles below Station 2, just above the junction of Swamp Creek with the Clarion.

Station 4 was 5.6 miles below Station 1 and 2.6 miles below Station 3, about ½ mile above the junction of Crooked Creek with the Clarion.

Station 5 was about 12 miles below Station 1 and 6 miles below Station 4.

The river was accurately gauged at each station so that the discharge, area, and velocity could be determined whenever desired. The time of flow between stations was also determined a number of times.

During the sampling of the river no sludge or other extraneous matter likely to mask the effect of the treated wastes was permitted to discharge into it. Samples of the river water were collected at each station during 24-hour periods—one sample taken each hour during the period. The dissolved oxygen, temperature, pH, and turbidity were determined in the field, and the total solids, soluble solids, suspended solids, color, oxygen demand, etc., in the laboratory, all results being calculated to standard discharge conditions. The standard drought flow discharges for the sampling stations are as follows:

Station 1..................	5.0 sec-ft.
" 2..................	5.0 " "
" 3..................	7.9 " "
" 4..................	10.2 " "
" 5..................	13.9 " "

Although figures are submitted in this paper, the writers feel that final conclusions cannot be given at this time (1926). It is known that a number of foreign factors have upset, to some extent, the results, and before these factors and their influence have been fully analyzed, definite statements cannot be made.

Preliminary Stream Study, Summer, 1925

In the normal and regular daily operation of the tannery the wastes are discharged, sludge and all. The practice is to remove the plug in the vats and permit the wastes to discharge directly to the creek. Most of the heavy lime sludge deposited in the bottom of the lime vats is shoveled out in a pile, but does not find its way to the stream. The continuous wastes are pumped to the stream directly. The only waste from the Instanter Tannery which does not regularly discharge into the creek is the spent tan liquor. This waste is pumped up into earthen lagoons, situated above the tannery, in which the liquor is permitted to settle and otherwise to trickle over and filter through the sides, and down the hill. In this manner considerable oxidation occurs before the waste finally reaches the river.

The average analysis of the 24-hourly samples by stations is given in Table 13. The column, "1", is the analysis of the water at Station 1, and is comparable in all respects with the analyses of the other stations given in the table, except that in this case the spent tan liquor was discharged directly to the creek, whereas in the others it was pumped into the lagoons at the tannery. Only one station was sampled with the tan liquor discharged direct, because the officials of a large paper plant at Johnsonburg, 12 miles below, seriously objected to its presence in the water.

TABLE 13.—Analysis by Stations. Tannery Producing Normal and Regular Daily Wastes.

	Station.					
	1.*	1.	2.	3.	4.	5.
Total solids, in parts per million..........	448	417.5	339	427.5	893.0	131
Dissolved oxygen, in parts per million...	2.44	†	4.2	5.4	6.9	8.21
Dissolved oxygen, percentage saturated.	33.13	†	48.4	58.9	75.0	88.0
5-day oxygen demand, 20° cent...........	40.50	28.1	6.4	11.5	3.3	0.89
Color..................	1 368	219.5	144	394.5	245.5	17.4
Turbidity..................	453	65.9	14.4	54.3	21.8	5.70
pH..................	6.10	6.6	6.8	6.9	6.9	6.95
Temperature, in degrees, centigrade.....	18.21	16.7	21.	16.8	17.4	17.91
NaCl, in parts per million..............	....	62.3	112	69.3	55.6	19.6

* Spent tan liquor discharged direct.

† No samples.

Test No. I, November, 1925, and July, 1926

In this test each station except Station 3 was sampled twice, once in November and once in July. The average analysis for each station is given in Table 14.

TABLE 14.—AVERAGE ANALYSIS BY STATIONS, TEST NO. I.

	Stations.						
	1.	2.	4.	5.	Instanter Creek.	Seven-Mile Run.	Straight Creek.
Total solids, in parts per million....	483	1 071	792	600	66.0	69.0	50.0
Soluble solids, in parts per million..	371	851	584	482	....	....	....
Suspended solids, in parts per million.	112	220	208	198	....	....	....
Dissolved oxygen, in parts per million..........................	4.99	7.59	6.86	8.85	8.4	7.7	7.4
Percentage of saturation, dissolved oxygen........................	45.78	60.32	61.57	80.66	91.3	84.4	86.2
5-day oxygen demand, 20° cent......	47.69	71.33	31.95	12.97	0.17	0.33	0.73
Color..............................	654	457	340	195	12.5	18.8	10.0
Turbidity..........................	116	155.4	111	26	0	0	0
pH.................................	6.5	6.44	6.67	6.8	6.0	5.4	6.8
Temperature, in degrees centigrade.	10.06	11.24	13.43	12.35	17.3	17.3	20.3

The analyses of Instanter Creek, Seven-Mile Run, and Straight Creek are given in Table 14 to show the character of the water of these tributaries. Instanter Creek and Seven-Mile Run are the two little creeks which come together just below the tannery, to form the East Branch of the Clarion River. Station 1, as stated, was just below the junction of these two creeks. The samples obtained for analysis from these creeks were taken immediately above the tannery on Seven-Mile Run, and just above the junction point on Instanter Creek. Straight Creek flows into the Clarion at Straight, Pa., 1½ miles below Station 1. A practice was made throughout the investigation of analyzing the waters of these creeks frequently in order to detect outside sources of pollution.

As in this test everything produced as waste at the tannery is discharged to the river, except the lime sludge, it should constitute the worst condition. Consequently, the removal of any suspended matter from the river should lessen the load on the stream to a noticeable degree. In Test No. IV, in which the intermittent wastes were treated with sulfuric acid, permitted to settle, and only the supernatant liquid permitted to flow to the creek, the retention of the settled material should be noticeable by a general improvement in the condition of the river.

Test No. IV, Summer, 1926

The stations were sampled once each in June, July, and August, during the operation of Test No. IV. The average analysis for each station, of the three times sampled, is given in Table 15.

There is an improvement noted in these analyses over those made for Test No. I. The condition noted farther down stream, however, is not as good as was expected. It is difficult to ascertain at present just how much influence the wood distillation plant, situated on Straight Creek, several hundred feet from its mouth, had on the results below Station 2. All the samples below this point contained a strong odor of wood creosote, and Straight Creek showed a much higher oxygen demand than was noted before. The wood distillates are composed of a large proportion of unsaturated compounds and have a very high oxygen consumed value. The slight yellow color imparted to the water from the wood oils and tars seems to predominate for great distances, only dilution tending to diminish it.

TABLE 15.—AVERAGE ANALYSIS BY STATIONS, TEST NO. IV.

	Stations.				
	1.	2.	3.	4.	5.
Total solids, in parts per million	378	448	259	242	561
Soluble solids, in parts per million	331	414	220	206	527
Suspended solids, in parts per million	47	34	39	36.1	34
Dissolved oxygen, in parts per million	4.71	4.74	5.44	5.91	7.26
Percentage of saturation, dissolved oxygen	48.42	50.66	56.93	65.91	77.94
5-day oxygen demand, 20° cent	33.07	17.30	18.22	7.65	5.60
Color	269	262	247	277	198
Turbidity	43.7	52.6	24.4	18.05	26.2
pH	6.06	6.59	6.76	6.77	6.73
Temperature, in degrees centigrade	17.08	18.23	17.18	18.85	17.03

The dissolved oxygen and the percentage saturation of dissolved oxygen increased steadily with distance from the tannery. The turbidity, color, and oxygen demand decreased steadily. Most of the improvement seemed to have been accomplished in the first three miles below the tannery. From that point the change was very gradual.

The analysis was not the only means of detecting the improvement in the river condition. The removal of the sludge, of course, disposed of considerable suspended solids, the effect of which was very marked at Station 1. Throughout this test the water was clear enough to see the bottom plainly. At no time during the summer of 1925 and during the operation of Test No. I in July, 1926, was this possible. The quantity of small fish in evidence near Station 1 during this test was considerably greater than before, and the jet black appearance of the river bed seemed to have been washed to a more natural color. Thus, not only by analysis, but also by observation, was an improvement noticed at Station 1.

Test No. VII, September, 1926

The effluent from the tannery during this test hardly discolored the water at Station 1. The color at this station at the time of sampling was 33, barely noticeable in an ordinary household tumbler. This represented more than a 50% reduction in the color at this station.

The average analyses of the stations made during Test No. VII are given in Table 16.

TABLE 16.—AVERAGE ANALYSIS BY STATIONS, TEST NO. VII

	Stations.							
	1.	2.	3.	4.	5.	Instanter Creek.	Seven-Mile Run.	Straight Creek.
Total solids, in parts per million	662.01	521.85	523.6	461.98	244.4	44	53	34
Soluble solids, in parts per million	587.61	464.13	465.1	361.48	227.6	42.4	51.8	29.2
Supended solids, in parts per million	74.4	57.72	58.5	100.5	16.8	1.6	1.2	4.8
Dissolved oxygen, in parts per million	8.83	7.90	7.84	8.44	8.09	9.76	9.94	9.24
Percentage of saturation, dissolved oxygen	86.21	78.95	79.09	84.19	84.13	98.57	97.81	90.67
5-day oxygen demand, 20° cent	19.05	9.20	32.19	17.54	1.79	0.38	0.05	1.21
Color	293	245	385	224	188	30	45	45
Turbidity	43.87	31.12	43.89	32.30	20.2	4	4.5	
pH	6	6.3	6.1	6.3	6.3	5.6	5.7	6.3
Temperature, in degrees centigrade	12.8	14.09	14.24	13.89	15.6	14.15	12.5	12.9

Conclusions

In order to compare broadly the results obtained from the river during the various tests, Table 17 is presented.

TABLE 17.

Station.	Test.	Saturation dissolved oxygen, percentage.	5-day oxygen demand. 20° cent., parts per million.	Color.	Turbidity.
1	No. I	45.78	47.69	654	116
	" IV	48.42	33.07	269	44
	" VII	86.21	19.05	293†	44
2	" I	60.32	*71.33	457	*155
	" IV	50.66†	17.30	262	* 53
	" VII	*78.95	9.20	245	31
3	" I	......	......	......	......
	" IV	56.93	*18.22	247	24.4
	" VII	*79.09	*32.19	*385†	* 44†
4	" I	61.57	31.95	340	111
	" IV	65.91	7.65	*277	18
	" VII	*84.19	*17.54	224	* 32
5	" I	80.66	12.97	195	26
	" IV	77.94†	5.60	198	* 26
	" VII	*84.13	1.79	188	20.2

* These figures are out of line when comparing the test results by stations.
† These figures are out of line when comparing the results of tests at each station.

In Table 17, Tests Nos. IV and VII show a decided reduction at each station in oxygen demand, assuming that Test No. I represents the worst condition. Paralleling this reduction throughout is the increase in the percentage saturation of dissolved oxygen. The color likewise shows improvement. It may be, however, that the colors noted in the lower stations are normal, that is, that the colors in the upper stations are not very persistent and are easily and quickly diffused or lost. The average color of the waters at Station 4 and at Station 5 at the time of sampling was about 25 and 12, respectively.

It is practically impossible to make conclusive statements about the river work. The importance, however, of the river studies cannot be over-estimated. The results thus far obtained demonstrate that it was possible to observe and show by analyses that Test No. IV was an improvement on Test No. I, and that Test No. VII was an improvement on Test No. IV. The fact that it was possible to bring out these differences in the water is a most important feature. It is hoped by future work to be able to calculate, or to forecast, the effect of any concentration and volume of tannery waste on any river.

General Summary

1.—Chemical analysis of the individual wastes revealed the fact that the intermittent wastes contributed about 75% of the total putrescence. Their volume was only 28% by volume of the total daily wastes.

2.—The laboratory experiments indicated that chemical treatment was necessary for dependable results.

3.—Several different types of treatment were developed in the laboratory.

4.—Two full-scale tests accomplished satisfactory removal of suspended matter in the wastes treated, one treating the intermittent wastes only, and the other treating all the wastes, except the green stock.

5.—The river studies proved to be important. The analyses of the river water showed that about 50% of the improvement is accomplished in the first 3 miles of the 12-mile stretch immediately below the tannery.

DISCUSSION

EDMUND B. BESSELIEVRE,* M. AM. SOC. C. E. (by letter).—Broad-minded and far-sighted ideals have been the background of the Department of Health of the State of Pennsylvania for a long time. The Keystone State, perhaps the first, and by far the foremost, State of the Union to recognize and accept the doctrine of co-operation between State and industry, has progressed far in regard to the allocation of streams to their most economic uses, the recognition of the basic rights of industry, and the discrimination between selfish interests and those necessary to the State's welfare. As have other States, Pennsylvania has some citizens who believe that their pleasure or convenience is paramount to any other consideration. It makes a good argument to claim that fish are killed because of stream pollution. However, is it right to stifle or penalize an industry which produces millions of dollars of revenue and employs thousands of people, for the sake of providing a few fishermen the right to pursue a sporting proclivity? No! The State of Pennsylvania (and here much of the credit is due to W. L. Stevenson, M. Am. Soc. C. E.) has been wise enough to form a Board to have jurisdiction over its intra-state waters. This Board, in turn, has promulgated wise rules that fully weigh the inherent rights of the individual as to industry and health.

Co-operation with industry, in assisting industrial groups to solve problems of pollution peculiar to that industry, has been another feature of Pennsylvania foresightedness which has been followed elsewhere. It is a basic fact, known to those who are closely identified with stream pollution, that industry is prone to balk at stringent requirements arbitrarily made and enforced. Waste treatment at its best is an expense, and an industrial plant owner cannot be blamed for holding off the fatal day as long as possible. Therefore, an inclination to assist by working with the industry and devising a sensible program of experiment is bound to be received with satisfaction. The only fault the writer can see in this policy is that it may lead to procrastination; that is, an industry, if faced with an expensive treatment, could continue its experimental work indefinitely and thus stall eventual compliance with the law. That is not true in the co-operative measures thus far undertaken, because the larger industrial groups have sensed the inherent justice of discontinuing pollution, and are genuinely ready to find a reasonable way of compliance. Much good can be accomplished by this industrial group work, as the financial burden entailed on any one member is small, and at the same time sufficient funds can be obtained to enable really worth-while work to be carried on. It should be encouraged, provided satisfactory and economical methods of treatment for the waste in question are not already known.

The third, and by no means the least important, co-operative measure developed in Pennsylvania has been the fostering of joint action with adjoining States over interstate waters. Obviously, no relief can be obtained on a stream which divides two States, without concerted action by both States involved. The co-operative arrangements among the States of Pennsylvania,

* San. Engr. and Mgr., Eastern Territory, San. Eng. Div., The Dorr Company, Inc., New York, N. Y.

Ohio, West Virginia, and New Jersey, and the work that has been done on the rivers which separate these States, is the best answer to the value of this phase of clear-sighted public health work. It is hoped that nothing will be allowed to interrupt or halt this good work so essential to the welfare of all.

Setting a standard of treatment or degree of purification is one of the best ways to get action, provided the standard is logical and practicable. Oil refinery wastes, as discussed by Mr. Weston, have not been given the extensive study that other wastes have received, and the efforts have been to extract as much of the oil and tar as possible by gravitational means. This simple treatment has sufficed in many cases, mainly because the volume of the diluting water receiving the wastes has been great. There are cases, however, where greater results must be produced, and sufficient work has been done on wastes from large refineries to show that Nature can be assisted at moderate cost.

Precipitation of tars and coagulation and flotation of lighter oils may be accomplished chemically, electrically, and mechanically. With proper sedimentation basins provided with mechanical skimming devices and means for collecting the deposited sludge, this process can be made continuous and will occupy little space. Assumptions, however, are dangerous in industrial waste practice, and tests should be made in each case to determine the best and most economical method to adopt.

Mr. Crichton is correct in his premise that treating coal mine wastes with lime or other chemicals is simply shifting the burden from the shoulders of the mine operator to the shoulders of the public through its water filtration plant. The question arises as to the relative economy of neutralizing acidity at one place, and reducing the increased hardness at another place, as against carrying out all the treatment at one place. The cost of treatment or neutralization mentioned, 15 to 25 cents per 1 000, is not excessive as compared to the cost of treatment of other wastes; but, although a few cents per 1 000 gal. may seem small, when multiplied by thousands of thousands the bills pile up swiftly.

At this point, it is proper to call attention to the fallacy of considering industrial waste treatment problems on the basis of cost of treatment of a small volume tested without ascertaining the true cost of the total volume to be handled in a given case. It does not seem expensive to throw a little chemical, perhaps a few grains, into a beaker of waste to achieve a result; but multiply those few grains by the number of gallons required to be treated, and the small pinch of chemical becomes a carload or a ton of the material. Investigations should be carried out with this clearly in mind, because frequently different methods may be required if one proves to be impracticable from a cost standpoint. Also, at this point, the relative initial cost of the plant, as compared to operating expense from the viewpoint of the chemical bill, must be visualized. If ground area is available, and experiment shows that a larger plant will require less chemical, and the interest charge on the investment for the larger plant is less than the cost of chemical for the smaller one, then the larger plant is the most economical.

Referring to the Melcroft problem, the writer was consulted on this, and the investigations showed that the wastes could be neutralized at about 16 cents per 1 000 gal., but that the hardness of the water was increased. This fact was reported to the Melcroft Company as was duly proper.

Paper mill wastes, discussed by Mr. Spence, are one of the few industrial wastes that offer a hope for economical recovery of usable material. To attack industrial waste problems in general from the standpoint of showing a profitable recovery of some ingredient is wrong in principle and is misleading. Very few wastes are entirely free from potentially valuable constituents, but the cost of reclaiming these substances is very often "a delusion and a snare", and new raw material may frequently be purchased at less than the cost of reclamation. Expensive plants have been built to recover waste materials and after operating for short periods at great cost close down. Industrial waste treatment should be attacked from the viewpoint of producing the desired result and of letting any recovered product be used as a partial stand-off of the cost of treatment. Do not spend the savings before they are made, but be happily surprised if a slight return comes from the operation.

A great deal of work has been done in the treatment of paper mill wastes, and it has been demonstrated to the satisfaction of some very large companies that sufficient pulp can be recovered not only to warrant the original expense of the plant, but to amortize the entire cost in a period of from one to three years. Recoveries of 95% and more of the wasted pulp are common, and even in cases where the pulp is valued at 1 cent per lb., it has been found to be a paying investment. In those cases of high-grade papers where pulp is worth 6 to 7 cents per lb., or more, the writing off of the initial investment is a matter of months. Carefully designed and constructed save-alls are in operation in many mills and that the results are satisfactory to the owners is attested by the purchase of duplicate plants for other mills. Sometimes, it is necessary to add alum to produce efficient results, but as in some high-grade papers, alum is used in the normal process of manufacture, this does not destroy the value of the recovered pulp.

In deciding between two competitive devices, one of which produces a much higher recovery by using alum or some other coagulant and the other of which achieves a lesser recovery without the use of alum, there are two factors to weigh: First, if the higher recovery is necessary to satisfy health authorities, then the unit producing the lesser recovery is out of the question, despite its possible lower cost; and, second, if one unit is cheaper in first cost than another, but requires the use of alum to procure a high recovery, which cost must be capitalized and added to the first one, and the other unit does not, the relative recoveries must be considered and evaluated. If a unit does not produce the required result it is bound to be an unsatisfactory investment despite the apparent saving of a few dollars a year. Guaranteed results are what count, and statements of expected results that are not based on test, should be looked at askance.

Relative to the paper by Messrs. Howalt and Cavett, the treatment of tannery wastes may be properly subdivided into two classes rated according to the difficulty of achievement of the object, namely, (1) partial treatment; and (2) complete treatment. It has been the writer's experience that the second of these objects is the one least often sought for, at all events, this is true at present. It may be that, owing to the size and the nature of the streams in Pennsylvania and the location of the tanneries, the necessity for complete treatment in that State exceeds any other demand, but elsewhere this is not so.

Tannery wastes are relatively easy to treat from a standpoint of eliminating or reducing the elements of nuisance—solids, hair, sludge banks, scum, and odor. At present, a large number of installations in various parts of the country are satisfactorily achieving the purpose for which the plants were installed.

It is a recognized fact that a great deal of the hair, fleshings, and small leather scraps, may be most economically and satisfactorily removed by mechanical fine screens. This feature has been adopted at some of the largest and leading tanneries in the United States. Removal of the coarser solids and the hair, by mechanical fine screens, eliminates not only several of the elements of unsightliness and trouble where tannery wastes are conveyed in sewers or streams, but also lightens, materially, the load on subsequent units of treatment, where required. Screenings are mechanically handled and placed in convenient receptacles for final removal.

Tannery wastes contain (as Messrs. Howalt and Cavett show) large quantities of solids. These are mostly organic and, therefore, highly putrescible, and their reduction is desired at the least cost. Sedimentation alone (3 to 4 hours' detention period) will usually remove 75% of these solids. The addition of chemicals will add to this percentage, so that, if necessary, a clear effluent may be procured.

Clarity, however, costs money and all phases of a problem should be investigated before it is declared necessary to produce a clear effluent. Color is frequently hard to remove, at least to the point of invisibility in the effluent. After all, why remove it to that extent if the dilution factor of a stream is so high as to dissipate color when the effluent is mixed with it? Nature provides a decolorizing agent in the stream and it should be used.

Sedimentation basins have been developed, which eliminate the difficulties of older types. Manual handling of sludge, dewatering to remove it, duplicate basins, and deterioration of effluent by accumulating sludge, all have been eliminated by the use of the modern, mechanically cleaned, sedimentation basins, which have been successfully used at a number of tannery waste treatment plants.

Sedimentation alone will not remove color or bacteria. If their removal is required, other methods of treatment will be necessary. The work being done by the Joint Committee of Tanners and State Health Officials will undoubtedly add much to the literature of this subject and will provide an answer to the particular problem to be solved in Pennsylvania. As to its application elsewhere, the use of whatever remedy is finally decided upon as a result of these tests should be tempered with good judgment and careful study in order to make sure that that which is best for the client is recommended. The best for the client means the most economical form of treatment from a standpoint of first cost and operation cost, that will meet the requirements of the compelling authority. More than this is unequitable; less is prejudicial to health. Let the good work of experiment continue, but let engineers apply the results with good judgment.

George W. Fuller,* M. Am. Soc. C. E.—Mr. Crichton's paper deals with an important and many sided problem. He has presented well its several phases which involve conflicting interests of unusual magnitude and numerous technical details. The Sanderson case dealt with the matter individually, while in the Indian Creek case the decision is founded on the interests of the public. The Sanderson case, which has meant so much for forty years in Pennsylvania, was never accepted by the Courts of last resort in any other State, except Indiana, the decisions in other States being less favorable to nuisances created by basic industries.

Mr. Crichton has stated that the coal mining companies are now building a tunnel to discharge their mine drainage into Indian Creek below the impounding dam from which the Indian Creek water supply of the Pennsylvania Railroad and subsidiary companies is obtained. This means that the pollution problem will simply be transferred to the lower reaches of the stream. This is an expedient that has been followed before in the case of some of the reservoirs of Allegheny County, at Johnstown, and in the Altoona District. Such diversions, aside from postponing the ultimate solution of the pollution problem, introduce another problem as to the capacity of existing reservoirs. More waters must be stored to compensate for the diversion. The speaker has too great an appreciation of the difficulties involved in connection with mine drainage to believe that a simple permanent solution may be found along the line of legislation alone. They must be dealt with in a practical way along the line of a comprehensive program that will be fair to conflicting interests. Such a program is contemplated in the creation of the Sanitary Board, which has set up a classification of the different kinds of water-sheds in Pennsylvania.

In this connection the speaker recalls the handling of some large projects in Great Britain, particularly the development of a large water supply in the midland country in England north of the City of Sheffield, involving cities like Nottingham, Leicester, and others. In Great Britain the rights of lower riparian owners are satisfied by compensation in kind, which ordinarily is taken to mean the release of water at times of dry weather roughly equal to the ordinary dry-weather flow of the stream. In the Sheffield instance, it is said that little or no impounded water was released at times of extreme drought as a supply of water can be taken from the lower reaches of the river and softened, filtered, and delivered to the vicinity of the impounding reservoir for use of riparian owners below. The speaker does not suggest, of course, this particular arrangement for the project under discussion, but merely cites it as an example of the way in which, from the standpoint of public policy, attempts have been made to balance equities and conveniences elsewhere. Surely there will come some way by which sizable communities may procure satisfactory water supplies and yet let industries flourish.

* Cons. Engr. (Fuller & McClintock), New York, N. Y.

ALMON L. FALES,* M. AM. SOC. C. E. (by letter).—This paper shows that very valuable studies on tannery wastes disposal were made, under the direction of Messrs. Howalt and Cavett, for the Tannery Waste Disposal Committee of Pennsylvania. As the authors have pointed out, their investigations thus far have been confined to the so-called partial or preliminary treatments. They have studied the effects of discharging the continuous-flow wastes without treatment, and mixing together the more objectionable intermittent wastes followed by uniform discharge into the stream during eight hours without sedimentation, after sedimentation alone, and after sedimentation followed by chemical precipitation, the continuous-flow wastes being included in the last-named treatment. Investigations remain to be made of the sludge disposal problem and of methods for the complete treatment of the wastes.

In considering the effects of the discharge into a stream, of untreated wastes or of mixed wastes, including sludge produced by the interaction of different wastes, it must be borne in mind that organic solids, deposited in the bed of the stream, tend to rob the overlying water of the dissolved oxygen required to maintain the stream in an inoffensive condition. Organic matter deposited in a stream in cold weather, when there is little or no bacterial activity, unless flushed out by high stream flows, will undergo decomposition during the following summer, thus adding to the current oxygen demand load on the stream. The effects of such deposits may have influenced the results of the studies during the second summer when the settleable solids were being removed from the wastes.

A period of 8 hours each day for uniform discharge of wastes or effluents was presumably selected because the bulk of the wastes are produced during this period, and the operation could be confined to one shift. From the point of view of the condition of the stream, it is desirable to discharge the wastes uniformly with respect to the stream flow. If the stream flow is substantially the same during the 24 hours, it is desirable to distribute the load as uniformly as practicable throughout the day and night.

It is stated that the tannery selected for the studies is representative of the sole-leather tanneries operating with the vegetable tanning process in general use. Variations were found in the composition and strength of various wastes at different times during the day and on different days. Still greater differences may occur between the wastes from different tanneries. In view of the differences in the quality and quantity of wastes, variations in the character and volume of stream flow available for dilution, and other varying local conditions, an investigation should be made at each tannery to determine the extent and kind of treatment required to satisfy the local conditions. Studies such as those made by the authors are of great advantage in solving these problems.

It may be helpful to describe briefly some of the tannery wastes treatment investigations and experience of the writer and of the firm of which he is a member.

* Cons. Engr. (Metcalf & Eddy), Boston, Mass.

The writer was first introduced to tannery wastes about 1900 at Worcester, Mass., where the wastes from a large sole-leather and belting tannery are discharged into the city sewer system. The tannery wastes in combination with the acid-iron wastes from the wire mills and foundries caused the sewage to be colored black, blue, or brown, much of the time, and the color was not always entirely removed by the method of chemical precipitation with lime, then in use. In this connection, it should be emphasized that if sulfate of iron, or copperas, and lime are used for chemical precipitation of tannery wastes, it is important to maintain an excess of lime in the wastes to prevent the formation of tannate of iron, which is an ink. It is reported that in recent years the quantity of lime in the wastes discharged by the tannery at Worcester has increased, causing precipitation of large quantities of hydroxide of iron in the new Imhoff tanks, and greatly increasing the quantity of sludge.

At Gloversville, N. Y., the tannery wastes constitute such a large proportion of the sewage of the city, that for studying the sewage disposal problem, a testing station was run for about a year in 1908 and 1909 to determine how the tannery wastes would affect the different methods of sewage treatment. It was found that these wastes more than doubled the strength of the sewage, but did not render the methods of sewage treatment inapplicable. A very good effluent was produced by preliminary sedimentation, trickling filter treatment, secondary sedimentation, and intermittent sand filtration, and a treatment plant was built embodying these features. This plant has functioned well, but difficulties have been experienced in handling the sludge because of excessive quantities of lime, hair, and fleshings in the tannery wastes, which were expected to be removed by tanks at the tanneries prior to discharge into the sewers.

About 1900, a question arose as to whether the wastes from a tannery at Ballston Spa, N. Y., would be susceptible of treatment by bacterial methods. It was found that although certain individual wastes from the tannery were sterile, the combined wastes contained considerable numbers of bacteria which increased on incubation.

At the C. S. Harriman Tannery, in North Wilmington, Mass., where heavy leathers are manufactured, studies made in 1913 indicated that the combined wastes could be treated satisfactorily by sedimentation and intermittent sand filtration, and a plant built for such treatment has proved very satisfactory. The effluent is discharged into a small brook. The sludge formed in the sedimentation tanks is removed periodically and de-watered on small sand beds. The de-watered sludge is reported to be excellent material for application to grass land. The sludge, when pumped to the sludge beds, created a strong hydrogen sulfide odor which was very objectionable for several days. This trouble has been overcome by applying creolin or crude coal-tar disinfectant to the sedimentation tank the night before cleaning, after the tank has been put out of service.

The wastes from the tannery of the White-Son Company, in Walpole, Mass., manufacturers of fancy leathers, are quite different from the wastes produced by the heavy leather tannery in North Wilmington. Nevertheless, similar treatment by sedimentation and intermittent sand filtration has been satisfactory. The effluent is discharged into a small mill pond. The sludge is drawn about once a month to one of the sand filter beds and the de-watered sludge is used for filling low land near-by. This sludge, which is largely spent ground sumac, has no value, but is unobjectionable in character.

At the tannery of the J. G. Curtis Leather Company, in Ludlow, Pa., a detailed investigation of the wastes disposal problem in 1916 and 1917 indicated that the most practical method of treatment was to bring the different wastes together for interaction and sedimentation, and a plant for this treatment was recommended, including pumping station, sedimentation tanks, and sludge beds, with provision for the construction of works for more complete treatment if and when such treatment should become necessary.

At the Buckman Tanning Company Factory, in Woburn, Mass., where heavy leathers are made and subsequently split for the manufacture of patent leather, earth basins were originally provided for the wastes, but without adequate means of sludge removal. The effluent from this plant seriously polluted the brook into which it was discharged and the plant itself created a serious odor nuisance. The hydrogen-sulfide gas given off turned all the white houses in the neighborhood black, due to the formation of lead sulfide. The sedimentation basins were rebuilt and provision was made for removal of the sludge, thus greatly reducing the odors. It was found that by treatment of the wastes with sulfate of alumina solution, using sulfuric acid for the control of the hydrogen-ion concentration, or pH value, a well clarified effluent could be obtained; and this treatment, although not entirely satisfactory, is being used pending the construction of a sewer which will connect the tannery with the Metropolitan Sewer System. One difficulty experienced in this treatment is that the reduction in alkalinity causes hydrogen sulfide to be released to a greater extent on agitation of the wastes, but the odor from this source is much less than that formerly produced by the earth basins.

At the tannery of Winslow Brothers and Smith Company, in Norwood, Mass., where sheep, goat, and calf skins are tanned, and wool is scoured, it was found advisable to separate the wastes into three classes: Rinse waters from the wool department; wool scouring wastes; and combined wastes from the tannery and wool scouring wastes degreasing plant. The effluents are discharged into a small brook emptying into the Neponset River, which is already polluted by paper mill wastes.

The rinse waters from the rinsing of wool after scouring, contain bits of wool, but comparatively little other organic matter. They are passed through plate screens having $\frac{3}{32}$-in. perforations and then discharged directly into the stream. The wool removed by the screens is returned to the wool department.

The wool scouring wastes are exceedingly turbid and strongly alkaline. They contain much suspended and dissolved organic matter including considerable grease—sometimes as much as 2 or 3 per cent. These wastes are discharged into tanks for sedimentation and cooling, the resulting sludge being pumped from time to time to the sludge beds. The settled wastes are pumped to "acid-cracking" tanks where they are acidified with sulfuric acid to precipitate the grease. The grease separates partly as sludge at the bottom and partly as scum at the top, and the clarified "middle liquor" is drawn off to the channel carrying the wastes from the tannery. The grease sludge is drawn off to "magma" beds of sand, and, after draining and drying, is wrapped up in pieces of burlap to form "puddings" which are placed on metal plates in the steam boxes of hydraulic presses where the grease is melted and pressed out, leaving a fairly dry, thin cake which has been used to some extent for fertilizer by farmers in the vicinity. The expressed oil is separated from the water by flotation in tanks and refined by boiling with sulfuric acid, forming "acid wool degras" which is put on the market.

The combined wastes from the tannery and degreasing plant are pumped to sedimentation tanks. The resulting sludge is drawn to sludge beds every 2 to 4 weeks in warm weather and every 3 to 6 weeks in cold weather. The de-watered sludge is used in part for fertilizer by farmers in the vicinty and the remainder is hauled to waste land.

During periods of cold weather and high stream flow, the sedimentation tank effluent is discharged into the stream without further treatment. Sedimentation accomplishes the removal of about 50% of the suspended solids, but the effluent is still colored and extremely turbid, and contains much finely divided suspended and colloidal organic matter.

During periods of warm weather and low stream flow, the settled wastes are treated by chemical precipitation with sulfate of alumina, the hydrogen-ion concentration, or pH value, of the wastes being controlled by the addition of sulfuric acid to give the most efficient and most economical treatment. The wastes are usually very strongly alkaline. Whenever there is a deficiency in alkalinity, milk-of-lime is added to the wastes. The combined wastes vary greatly in strength and composition during the day, and it is necessary to equalize the quality of the wastes, as by passage through the sedimentation tanks, prior to chemical precipitation. The chemically treated wastes are passed through tanks and the resulting sludge is discharged periodically on to the sludge beds.

The chemical effluent is well clarified, but contains considerable dissolved organic matter and is quite putrescible. This effluent is further treated by intermittent filtration to the capacity of the available area of sand filter beds, and the remainder is treated by dilution in the brook with water drawn from a reservoir owned by the Company. During periods of extremely low flow, practically all the tank effluent is filtered. The filter-bed effluent is practically clear and colorless and non-putrescible.

Experimental investigations of the treatment of the settled wastes by the trickling filter and activated sludge processes were carried out on a working scale, and it was found that a satisfactory effluent could be produced by either process, if all the wool scouring wastes were degreased prior to discharge into the tannery wastes channel. It was found that the activated sludge process would entail a considerably smaller capital expenditure, but much larger annual expense for operation and maintenance. An experimental sand filter bed was operated in conjunction with the experimental trickling filter, and it was found that the trickling filter effluent could be applied to the sand bed at a high rate and produce a highly purified effluent. By following the method of treatment previously described, it has not been necessary to build either trickling filters or an activated sludge plant.

It has been pointed out that local conditions will govern the extent of treatment required at different places. It is also true that the extent of treatment required at a given place will vary with varying conditions of temperature and stream flow at different seasons of the year. This fact is well illustrated by the regulation of the treatment of the wastes from the Winslow Brothers and Smith Company tannery according to the requirements of the stream.

To recapitulate, during the winter, when there is little or no bacterial activity in the stream, and, in the spring, when the stream flow is relatively high, only the strongest of the wool scouring wastes are degreased and the other wastes are treated only by mixing and sedimentation. As summer approaches and the stream flow decreases, all the wool scouring wastes are conducted to the degreasing plant and water is drawn from the water supply reservoir for dilution of the sedimentation tank effluent. If the water-shed and reservoir were large enough, no further treatment, of course, would be required; but it is necessary to conserve the water and provide a more complete treatment of the wastes. The next step is the starting of chemical precipitation of the sedimentation tank effluent and regulation of flow of reservoir water drawn for dilution. Subsequently, the filter beds are put in operation.

By such regulation of the treatment, it is possible with a minimum expenditure, to produce an effluent at all times, which will meet the stream requirements.

Robert Spurr Weston,* M. Am. Soc. C. E. (by letter).—Since preparing his paper, the writer's attention has been called to an interesting treatment of oil wastes.†

At the El Segundo Refinery of the Standard Oil Company of California, where 20 000 000 gal. of salt water are taken from the ocean daily and used for cooling and other purposes, good results are obtained by means of a series of tanks baffled in such a way that the mixture of water and oil is kept moving toward the surface of the tank, rather than toward the bottom, as is the practice in tanks designed for separating heavy suspended matter from water.

This plan apparently accelerates the movement of the oil to the surface. Mr. Geiger states that all traces of the oil are removed from the surface of the water. The analytical methods used, are not given.

G. K. Spence,‡ Esq. (by letter).—In discussing the paper, Mr. Besselievre states that paper mill wastes are among the few industrial wastes offering hope for economical recovery of usable materials. He also cites that in other

* Cons. Engr. (Weston & Sampson), Boston, Mass.

† Methods Used by Oil Company to Stop Pollution of Streams," by Charles W. Geiger, *Water Works Engineering*, Vol. 81, p. 90.

‡ Chf. Chemist, Castanea Paper Co., Clarion Mills, Johnsonburg, Pa.

industries recovery plants have been constructed at great costs and, after operating for a short time, have been compelled to shut down.

This same thing is true of the paper and pulp industry. The writer knows of a paper company in Pennsylvania that built a waste sulfite liquor recovery plant several years ago at a cost of $300 000, which was only operated for two months when it was compelled to shut down, the plant being a total loss. Other paper companies have expended enormous sums of money on this same problem, as well as on the utilization of the waste carbon from soda pulp mills and many other wastes which have brought no returns. However, as Mr. Besselievre states, there have been some wastes from the mills which have been reclaimed at a profit.

To the present, if all the money expended on solving these problems were compared with the profits made, the pulp and paper manufacturers would be very much on the wrong side of the ledger. The writer is, however, optimistic as to the future in regard to all wastes from pulp and paper mills being reclaimed at a profit, or at least a "break-even" proposition, but until such a time the manufacturers will continue to expend large sums of money on research and experimental installations necessary in solving these problems.

AMERICAN SOCIETY OF CIVIL ENGINEERS

INSTITUTED 1852

TRANSACTIONS

Paper No. 1688

PROBLEMS IN CONCRETE DAM CONSTRUCTION ON THE PACIFIC COAST*

By Arthur S. Bent,† Affiliate, Am. Soc. C. E.

With Discussion by Messrs. Arthur P. Davis, M. M. O'Shaughnessy, R. A. Hill, and Fred A. Noetzli.

The first thought that arises out of a long experience in the building of dams is that no two of them are exactly alike and no one plan of operation is the optimum for more than a single location. This is true in spite of the obvious fact that different contractors might have different plans for the same work. Thus, it is evident that the success of an operation is measured by the correctness of what might be called its diagnosis. In the case of one notable California dam, the plan of an unsuccessful bidder for handling the work was so radically different from the one actually used, as to indicate definitely that they were not equally good and could not possibly produce anything like the same results in costs or speed.

It follows, therefore, that the first step in estimating, and by far the most important, is a painstaking, thorough study of the site and all its conditions, and this is where the contractor's skill and vision are tested. If he is inexperienced in the building of dams he will probably learn much on his first job, but even with long experience he will be impressed with the truth of the opening statement that no two projects are alike. While remembering all the things that did not operate well on previous work and all the unexpected conditions that arose, he must not be bound by precedent. He must have the ability to discard every type of plant and method of attack he ever used if they do not seem to fit, and to devise those that will. Standing on the untouched site

* Presented at the meeting of the Construction Division, Seattle, Wash., July 15, 1926.

† Pres., Bent Bros., Inc., Los Angeles, Calif.

with the plans before him, he must have the vision to follow through step by step the processes ahead and see clearly and in detail the methods, organization, and equipment required for each one.

After a lifetime spent in construction work of various kinds the writer believes this is more difficult with a Western dam than with any other structure. Compared with a Class "A" building, for instance, a dam seems very simple—just a block of concrete between two walls; but it is a significant fact that many fortunes have been sunk on single dams, while on others very low bidders have made good profits.

This paper is an attempt to suggest, from a long experience, the fundamental elements that must be carefully and intelligently considered in advance to make a success of a concrete dam, and to outline some of the methods of meeting specific problems.

Estimates

In the preliminary estimate the first thing to consider is the owners with which one has to deal. Are they responsible and fair-minded? are their financial plans sound? are they likely to use up in other developments the funds that should go into the dam before it is completed? What are the character, reputation, and experience of the engineers? An unfair, hard, or inexperienced engineer can make any job a misfortune to the contractor and take all the joy out of it without adding to the safety or usefulness of the structure. If a contractor has reason to believe that he will be in the hands of such a man, he should not bid—it does not pay.

The site should be visited many times and a long and thorough study made of it. The writer's method is to have independent studies and plans of operation made by different members of his organization, these being later reconciled in the office, so that the plan finally adopted represents the consensus of its best judgment.

These site studies must include accurate knowledge of the topography, water run-off, high-water period, weather history, water supply for entire year, length of working season, and possible methods of river diversion. Thought must be given to the effect on the plant and work of the inevitable floods and the work so scheduled as to reduce this misfortune to a minimum. Here, again, the co-operation or otherwise of the engineer is important. On one project the engineer needlessly delayed the placing of the concrete in the foundation with the result that an unexpected flood filled the excavation and cost the contractor a loss of $20 000. The remoteness and inaccessibility of most dams is an important matter. None of the ordinary facilities for securing skilled labor, supplies, repairs, and spare parts is at hand. The job must be constantly supplied with all these facilities and must be completely self-contained at all times.

Excavation

The estimate must take into careful consideration the character and proportions of soil and rock and their disposal after excavation. This seems too obvious to be worthy of mention, but it is probably on this item that errors of judgment are most common. Certainly, there is greater difference in methods and plant for handling the excavating than for the concreting. On one of the writer's jobs it was believed that bed-rock was nowhere more than 14 ft. below the stream bed, but in one section it was found at a depth of 52 ft. through large boulders and much water. This required a complete and costly re-adjustment of the entire excavating plant.

As a rule the estimated cost of excavating and wasting proves inadequate. The excavating constantly suffers all the disadvantages of the work. For instance, it is the reservoir for the poorest of the labor. Untried men are put in the excavating crew. If they prove extra good they are transferred to something else. Again, shooting of rock cannot be done in the most advantageous way because of the two dangers of injuring the plant and shaking the foundation. Also, other work is usually going on simultaneously and has the precedence, from which it happens that excavating frequently must be done at night, or in very restricted areas, each of which increases the cost.

Cleaning the bed-rock (which should be computed by the square foot) is slow and costly and, although computed only once, frequently must be done several times. Here, again, the engineer is an uncertain element. It must be done to his satisfaction, and this may mean removing loose stuff and hosing off, or it may mean much hand-picking and scrubbing with wire brushes, and jetting with compressed air and water.

Wasting should be definitely planned and carefully computed. It is a frequent cause of loss. The quantity may far exceed that anticipated and thus bring in an entirely new problem of disposal, which possibility should be clearly provided for in advance.

Altogether the excavation on dams generally costs much more than other excavation jobs that appear to be similar, and has proved to be abnormally difficult to estimate with accuracy.

Plant and Method

On these depend in the main the success of the work and final decision in regard to them is determined by many considerations. The time limit and transportation facilities affect the selection of plant almost as importantly as the type of dam and the topography. If there is no railroad, and the job is large and the time short, it will pay to build one. A railroad also should be provided usually if work is to be carried on through the winter. On a recent job, during which 400 000 cu. yd. of concrete were placed in 16 months, no trucks were used either at the dam or at the gravel pit which was 20 miles away. Where aggregates can be had near the work it sometimes proves economical to haul and store cement and equipment during the dry season. This would apply particularly to small dams in remote locations. The distances and quantities to be hauled should be accurately ascertained. On one of the writer's contracts a difference of $0.01 per ton on aggregates alone meant a saving of $10 000.

On high dams a hillside plant is desirable. This set-up takes full advantage of gravity, and reduces the flood hazard and the danger from falling rocks. However, when roads cannot reasonably be built to the top and there is room for both concrete and excavation plants in the stream bed, a tower is better. In all cases the concrete delivery point should be well above the dam crest and chutes should be amply large.

Low long dams frequently are best handled by trestle plants with the mixers at one end.

In general, although it is easy to "over-plant" a small job, it is highly important that the equipment should be fully adequate, always bearing in mind that rate of progress cannot be determined by dividing daily capacity into the total time allowed by the contract. The plant will produce its maximum output only in the middle of the construction. This further suggests that costs are increased by the fact that the same plant must be maintained throughout, while at the start and finish the output is small because of limited working space.

On a fair-sized job it pays well to make a solid and thorough set-up, using plenty of concrete for foundations of derricks, mixers, compressors, etc. The extra cost is more than compensated by regularity and certainty of operation.

The plant which is to produce the aggregate should be of ample capacity. Delays for materials are disastrous not only to costs but to morale, and in spite of seemingly careful preparation this very often happens. The writer's practice is to provide for an output fully 50% beyond the needs and on rush jobs to double the estimated demand, yet he has never overdone it.

If the rock is to be quarried near the work the usual estimating cost of $1.50 per yd. should be about doubled, and the manufacture of sand should be avoided at almost any cost of haul.

The supply of compressed air, power, and light should be ample and reliable, and the last two should be electric wherever possible because of greater flexibility. A complete machine shop and a saw-mill are essentials.

Finally, the equipment should be not only adequate, but first-class throughout, and the supply of rails, pumps, tanks, pipe, cables, nails, clips, fittings, rope, wire, and small tools should always be kept well ahead of the needs.

Camp

Too much emphasis cannot be laid on the importance of this unit because the character of labor attracted to the work and its contentment and efficiency are largely the result of the living environment of the men. Quarters must be adequate, well lighted, heated, and ventilated. Sanitary regulations must be perfect, drinking water pure and palatable, the dining-room fly-proof, and the food first-class in quality and variety. There should be an ice plant, refrigerator, bakery, store for families, plenty of hot and cold showers, hospital with doctor and nurse in constant attendance, police and fire protection, post-office, telephone, schools, amusement hall, and recreation features. Different quarters should be provided for the different shifts as well as separate meal hours. As many as eighteen different meal hours may be required on rush jobs.

On one of the writer's projects the boarding-house plant cost $15 000. Incidentally, it was completely destroyed by fire early in the job. Notwithstanding the fact that the camp was on a side-line railway, with no road for automobiles, on the third day after the fire it was again in complete running order. Only two meals were served in the open and the construction work was never halted.

It is of prime importance that no reasonable detail be overlooked that will add to the comfort and well-being of the men.

A contented little city on his job is a matter of pride and satisfaction to a right-minded contractor. He should regard it not merely as a matter of enlightened self-interest, but as a fortunate opportunity to make life as good as possible for the group of men who, for a little while, come closely within his range of influence. He may never have that privilege again.

Organization

The superintendent must be selected with the utmost care and with particular reference to the work in hand. Splendid building superintendents can fail utterly on a dam. A rare combination of resourcefulness, speed, economy, executive ability, tact, good judgment, energy, and poise is required. He should also have technical training sufficient for the clear understanding of complicated plans, a first-hand intimate knowledge of all his equipment and machinery, and actual experience in rigging. He should of course neither drink nor gamble on the job, and his loyalty to his employer should outrun every personal consideration. An absolute desideratum, however, is the ability to plan every detail of the operation long in advance, without oversight or errors. He must never be caught unprepared by any detail of the work or by any emergency. His task is very similar to that of a military commander and his blunders may be as serious. Under the superintendent are carefully chosen heads of departments as follows: (1) Accounting and purchase; (2) commissary; (3) transportation; (4) excavation; (5) aggregates; (6) carpentering; (7) rigging; (8) mechanics; (9) electricity; (10) steel; (11) concrete; and (12) engineering.

Transportation

This has already been touched upon, but may be elaborated briefly as it is of great importance. A wrong guess on this feature at the outset may paralyze the work later. Provision must be made for handling materials rapidly and certainly and single pieces of equipment weighing as much as 75 tons. Motor trucks may be relied upon, but must be furnished with a first-class roadbed constantly maintained or they cannot give adequate and uninterrupted service. Almost any amount of money is well spent in securing reliable transportation.

Conditions must determine the best plan and these are never twice alike. On one of the writer's projects, everything had to be transported through a 5 by 7-ft. tunnel, 4 miles long. This compelled the cutting and re-welding of large mixer-drums and similar heavy units. Where the yardage is comparatively small and the country extremely rugged tramways can be used to advantage. On major projects such as the Exchequer and Hetch Hetchy Dams, standard gauge railways are indicated, and they should be operated as systematically as main-line roads.

Diversion of Water

In the diversion of water the constructor of dams faces one of his most serious problems. A mistake of judgment may cost him not only great damage to his plant and work, but the loss of a whole season's work. On one project it was stipulated in the contract that such a delay would damage the owner $500 000. Nobody prayed for rain on that job.

The problems involved in handling the water are many, for the bottom may be solid rock, or it may be quite pervious and the run-off may vary during the life of the job from a few to tens of thousands second-feet. Diversion is accomplished by tunnel, flume, wing-dams, or an open section through the dam, controlled by gates. Pumping must be expected and its cost is nearly always under-estimated. If the rock is fissured, pumping may become a heavy expense. When coffer-dams are used they should be placed far enough from the site to be safe from injury by blasting.

Demolition

Demolition is a trying part of the work and unless exceptional vigilance is exercised, and the morale of the crew carefully maintained, it will show loss and waste. The writer's system is to sell at once as much of the plant as possible, and on major projects a yard with railroad facilities is rented for the temporary storing and handling of equipment. All equipment, whether to be sold or retained, should be put in first-class order and painted without delay, and all loose parts should be marked to prevent confusion and loss.

The energetic handling of this feature may determine the entire outcome, as it is not uncommon to find on a heavily "planted" job that its profits must come out of salvage. This may be regarded as one of the results of unintelligent competition.

Dam building is at once one of the most interesting and precarious types of construction. In spite of experience and care there is constant hazard from conditions beyond control. On the great majority of the writer's jobs floods have repeatedly submerged the work. Temperatures range from snow to 115° Fahr. on single projects. In one case a mountain side above the dam slid down dumping 25 000 cu. yd. of rock on the concrete. In two days the contractor's steam shovel and narrow-gauge railway working double shift cleared it away, and this equipment had to be taken 200 ft. up the vertical face of the mountain. These things suggest the necessity for a liberal contingency item in the estimate for unforeseen and uncontrollable emergencies.

The interest in dam building lies in the fact that conditions are never the same and the ever-changing vicissitudes of the work call forth almost daily the utmost resources of the constructor. More than in any other type of structure, the final outcome depends on his foresight, energy, and courage. A big dam is always a splendid adventure in construction.

DISCUSSION

Arthur P. Davis,* Past-President, Am. Soc. C. E.—The speaker agrees with the stated undesirability of manufacturing sand where it can be avoided. At the site of the Roosevelt Dam, for instance, no suitable sand was available in Nature and had to be manufactured from existing materials. The first attempt was with a pure hard limestone which was being used in the manufacture of the cement. In crushing this rock for sand it had a tendency to chip into long thin flakes and was deficient in fine particles. After some experiments with that, an attempt was made to mix it with other rock, and, finally, a mixture of half limestone and half sandstone was adopted, both of which were conveniently at hand and made an excellent combination which tested high and was satisfactory throughout the job.

Another experience was that of the contractor in the construction of the Shoshone Dam, Wyoming, where conditions were especially difficult on account of limited working space, a narrow gulch with high cliffs on each side forcing such operations some distance up stream where more space was available. No suitable sand was available in sufficient quantities, and the little that was at hand required washing and was very fine. The contractor tried to crush granite rock which was very hard, and this hardness made the operation extremely difficult. One machine after another was worn out and cut to pieces in use. It was almost impossible with that granite to get a sufficient proportion of fine material without discarding a great deal of coarse. Finally, by washing the fine sand and using this, to the extent available, with the granite, it was possible to make a passable sand still lacking somewhat in gradation.

Another experience was in the Klamath Valley, Oregon, where no rock was available except lava flows. After a great deal of experimenting, it was discarded and sand was shipped from Marysville, Calif. After these and other trials, the speaker is certainly in accord with the motto of the author, "don't do it".

M. M. O'Shaughnessy,† M. Am. Soc. C. E. (by letter).—Having been identified with the construction of about twenty dams, the writer is sincerely interested in some of the viewpoints advanced by Mr. Bent.

All first-class engineering plans should include information about topography, water run-off, high-water period, weather history, water supply for the entire year, length of working season, and possible methods of river diversion. It should not be necessary for the contractor to waste any time in worrying over those subjects, as any one who is going to build a large dam must have employed engineers of sufficient standing and experience to procure precise information on all of them.

In the matter of excavation for foundations, careful consideration of surface examination may disclose, when the digging is done, that the bottom will

* Chf. Engr., East Bay Municipal Utility Dist., Oakland, Calif.

† City Engr., San Francisco, Calif.

be quite different from that anticipated, and it is well always to provide a liberal estimate for such contingencies, which are bound to occur.

Experienced rock men can blast a foundation without serious damage to machinery, if the latter is properly placed. Except in the core trench and scab rock on the surface, the shooting should not be serious. Cleaning the bed-rock is an important element. A successful expedient in the foundation of the dam at Hetch Hetchy was the use of a sand blast to clean off the old scum from submerged granite rock, which was buried under 100 ft. of loose rock and gravel.

Mr. Bent is correct in stressing the necessity of a railway. A standard gauge railway, 68 miles long, was built to the dam at Hetch Hetchy. Six locomotives were found to be inadequate at the peak period of construction, and a seventh had to be rented to haul cement, over 4% grades, up to the dam.

The author's statement that hillside plants are desirable, does not always hold. It was found desirable for the dam at Hetch Hetchy to provide a mixing and hoisting plant near the foundation, up-stream portion of the dam, and there build a tower, 350 ft. in height, to handle all materials. The reason for this was that any amount of excellent broken fragmentary rock from the granite bluffs was found around the basin within 1 mile of the dam site. It was crushed ½ mile away from the dam, assembled in heaps, and hauled by a separate narrow-gauge railway down to the mixing plant. At first, it was thought that the contractors had made a mistake, and that a high-head plant with a quarry would have been more economical; but the high cost of powder from 1919 to 1923, and the high cost of labor, demonstrated that the contractor's plans, with a crushing plant in the valley and a mixing plant near the dam, were the most economical.

An interesting feature in connection with the dam was that the most attractive and accessible sand in the river bed near the dam and mixing plant was physically undesirable, because for thousands of years a grove of oak trees grew over it. The leaves and drippings from the oaks saturated the sand with tannic acid, which proved fatal to its setting qualities in concrete, and sand was brought from an excellent uncontaminated bed that contained more than 200 000 cu. yd., about 3 miles up stream from the dam.

Mr. Bent's camps are always orderly, sanitary, and well conducted, and all experienced contractors and engineers are now educated to the necessity and desirability of having first-class comfortable camps for the men.

Building contractors will surely fail in dam construction, because it is a business about which they know nothing. The writer knows two instances of builders attempting this kind of construction, with a consequent loss, in one case of more than $100 000 and in the other of more than $200 000. Builders are not trained for successful dam construction.

The most important suggestion Mr. Bent has made is in regard to the handling of water and saving the construction plant from destruction by floods. It was the writer's duty to compel a contractor to raise a proposed diversion dam more than 5 ft. higher than his contemplated plans in order to deflect a stream of 8 000 sec-ft. during flood periods into a diversion tunnel.

Raising the dam was the only thing that saved his plant from destruction and his pocket from a damage loss.

On the whole the author, as well as the Society, deserves credit for bringing the practical man's point of view into the construction of dams, thereby causing engineers to think over many of the problems the contractor has to study before successfully building them.

R. A. Hill,* M. Am. Soc. C. E. (by letter).—The author very aptly calls attention to the fact that no two dams are identical, and that they all usually require radical differences in construction methods. He emphasizes justly the necessity of a painstaking, thorough study of the site and all its conditions, and the further need for the contractor to be able to discard all precedent in his visualization of the processes involved from the excavation of the foundation to the final cleaning up of the work.

With rare exceptions, engineers responsible for the design of dams, spend a great deal of time in the compilation of data regarding the conditions which will affect the cost of construction. Generally there is furnished to bidders all available knowledge, such as the frequency and time of occurrence of floods. In some instances, such information is not available, and it is regrettable that in others the engineer does not realize his responsibility and gives extremely limited information to bidders. Yet, how many contractors make a careful study of the information which is furnished them?

Unfortunately, the basis of estimation set forth by the author is not followed by a large proportion of contractors. Not long ago bids were asked on one of the most unusual and difficult pieces of dam construction yet to be attempted. It was the boast of one entirely responsible contractor that he arrived at the site of the work at 10:00 A. M., investigated the possible sources of aggregate, and returned to a near-by town in time for lunch. Another contractor bidding on the same work assumed that his plant would cost a fixed sum per cubic yard, and at the time he submitted his bid he did not even know where he would locate his construction plant if he was awarded the contract. This contractor did not start to estimate his costs (which ran into millions of dollars) until two weeks before the opening date of the bids.

A short time ago a number of bids ranging from less than $10 000 000 to more than $15 000 000, were submitted on a tremendously large dam. It is generally known that a few of the bidders followed the ideal practice, set forth by the author, and spent several months analyzing all the factors affecting the cost of such a tremendous project. On the other hand, there were certain bidders who practically ignored some of the very important considerations. For example, one contractor expressed the opinion that transportation was the only item which required special study, and that the plant and methods of pouring several million cubic yards of concrete were of relatively slight importance. In his opinion, this was purely a manufacturing process and entirely straightforward, although a variation in cost of only 10 cents per cu. yd. would make a difference of $400 000 in his profits or losses.

These instances, unfortunately, are typical of the procedure followed by many who are deemed responsible contractors. Under press of other work,

* Cons. Engr. (Quinton, Code & Hill), Los Angeles, Calif.

contractors are prone to postpone the preparation of estimates, so that the limitation of time usually requires that detailed studies be omitted. Yet, it is common to hold engineers' estimates in scorn and to view contractors' bids with reverence. The writer does not wish to imply that he is a proponent of force account work, as it is his opinion, that, in so far as practicable, all construction of this character can be best handled by contract. He does wish to stress, however, the fact that the procedure outlined by the author is an ideal one and is not customarily followed, except by a minority of contractors.

In most cases, however, it would be advisable to segregate the hazardous and uncertain items of construction from those subject to no especial contingencies, rather than include all the work in a lump-sum contract by which the owner must pay for all contingencies which the contractor thinks might arise. This is particularly applicable in the case of foundation excavations within the limits of the stream channel, which, as it involves river control, is one of the major uncertainties. The amount and character of wet excavation are almost indeterminable in advance, in spite of the number of borings which may be made, except in a few cases where bed-rock is exposed for practically the entire width of the river channel. The borings can do little more than determine the depth to rock, and only by actual excavation is it possible to fix on the exact amount of excavation into rock that is desirable.

There is one important step in the preparation of bids, and in the execution of the work, which the author has not stressed. The time available for the construction of a dam is usually fixed by the contract, and, consequently, the entire work must be scheduled so as to be finished within the allotted period. To be sure, extensions are granted, but these are in themselves an expense to the contractor, due to the ever-present item of overhead.

A careful study of the climatic conditions, and the occurrence of floods in the river, immediately brings out the necessity of beginning certain operations at specific times. In the western part of the United States, it is generally possible to determine with reasonable accuracy the number of days during which work must be stopped due to adverse climatic conditions. It is also possible to determine the time at which floods may be expected and the probable magnitude and duration of such floods. The writer has recommended to contractors of his acquaintance the advisability of preparing a chart covering the entire period of operation, upon which should be shown a typical occurrence of storms and a typical number and grouping of floods in the river. Obviously, the actual conditions will not correspond with this typical weather chart and river hydrograph, but the total number of off days and their general occurrence will correspond quite closely to the actual conditions. With such a chart available, it is then possible to analyze each operation, such as river diversion, excavation in the river channel, cleaning of foundations, pouring of concrete up to river level, re-diverting the river, and closing temporary outlets. The time required for any of these operations is subject to considerable variation. The number of men and amount of equipment necessary to complete each operation in the time available are then matters of calculation, which, while not absolute, at least materially reduce the element of uncertainty.

The author discusses the necessity of a superintendent who can foresee such contingencies and who can plan his work a long time in advance. It would seem that this procedure results in shifting the responsibility for the plan of execution from the contractor to his superintendent. A very careful scheduling of operations, from the inception to the completion of the work, might better be prepared by the contractor in conjunction with the superintendent. Such a schedule, covering the entire job, and prepared as the result of the co-ordination of the best thought of the contractor's organization, certainly is to be preferred to the limited foresight of one man directly engaged on the work.

The advisability of constructing a railroad to the dam site is a matter to be determined in each specific case. Some contractors so much prefer the use of railroads that they are inclined to disregard the possibility of truck transportation. Other contractors, particularly those whose early experience has been on highway work, or on work in the close vicinity of a city, are disposed to overlook the saving which can be effected by railroad operation. The reliability of motor-truck transportation is steadily increasing, as are the number of suitable highways, so that the construction of a railroad is becoming of less importance than heretofore.

The concrete plant should be regarded as a step in the flow of material from the source of supply to the completed work. Usually there are certain conflicting considerations. If a plant is placed so that it is easy of access it usually is difficult to distribute the materials from this plant. On the other hand, if the plant is so located that the delivery of mixed concrete is easiest, it becomes extremely complicated to get material to the plant. On account of the fact that there is a single product sent out from the plant, it is generally simpler to provide this single line of outflow than several lines of approach for materials which go to make up the product.

The writer agrees that for the construction of a dam in a narrow canyon it is generally advisable to bring in materials to a point above the crest of the dam, and then let them flow downward to the plant and from the mixer downward into the dam. If such a procedure can only be accomplished by hoisting all materials to a point well above the crest of the dam before they enter the plant, the advantage of this location immediately disappears.

The author favors distribution by a trestle for a long low dam, with the plant located at one end. A typical layout of this character was analyzed some time ago, and it was found that if the concrete plant were located at one end there was an average haul of 1 400 ft., with a maximum haul of almost 2 000 ft. By locating the plant on the bank of the river down stream from the dam, and by hoisting directly from the plant to the trestle, the average haul was reduced to less than 500 ft. and the maximum haul was reduced to about 1 200 ft. In either case, the material had to be lifted to the same height.

No hard and fast rule can be followed, and as much consideration must be given to the ease of access to the plant as to that of distribution of the mixed concrete after it leaves the plant. Irrespective of the position in the line of flow of materials, the same tonnage must be handled. In other words, the shortest and easiest route from the source of supply to the finished structure should be followed, and the concrete plant should be placed along the line of flow wherever it will produce the smoothest operation.

A great many dams which have been built, or which are proposed for construction, are located in relatively inaccessible places, so that each job must be a self-contained unit. As the author states, the success of the work depends on maintaining a high morale, thereby reducing the labor turnover to a minimum. Not only is turnover expensive in itself, but the desired smoothness of operation can only come from the work of men familiar with their tasks. In order to create and maintain this desirable "elan", the environment in which the men live must be maintained at a high standard. For a great number of years, construction camps were, to say the least, undesirable places. Far-sighted contractors have brought about a change in this condition, and it is safe to say that the future will see even better and more complete facilities provided for the men. It is noteworthy that the camps on force account work are frequently of a lower standard than those provided by contractors.

Summarizing, the writer is of the opinion that far less study than should be, is given to the conditions surrounding the construction of a dam by any one risking his capital or his reputation. This, of course, does not apply to all contractors, but, unfortunately, it does apply to a great number of contractors, and likewise to a great number of engineers responsible for the execution of work of the magnitude of a dam. Most of the uncertainty and contingencies, which contractors provide for by arbitrarily adding 10, 15, or 20% to their cost estimates, could be eliminated by a detailed analysis of all conditions, and by careful scheduling of operations and co-ordination of the different steps involved in the construction of any large concrete dam.

Fred A. Noetzli,* M. Am. Soc. C. E. (by letter).—The problems encountered in dam construction are many and varied. No two dams are exactly alike, each site or type of dam involving new problems in one way or another. Usually, it is hard-earned experience that points the way for the proper planning and efficient execution of the work. Lack of experience in dam construction often leads contractors to under-estimate rather than over-estimate the difficulties and, therefore, the cost.

In some recent cases the estimate of the highest bidder was almost double that of the lowest bidder, which is hard to explain for relatively simple structures like concrete dams, especially when the contract is to be let on the basis of unit prices. Perhaps the low and "successful" bidder has the right explanation for this discrepancy after he is through with the job.

The author's organization has built more dams than probably any other construction firm on the Pacific Coast. His paper deserves most careful consideration by engineers as well as by contractors.

In dam construction, probably more than in any other type of building, a close co-operation between the constructors and the supervising engi-

* Cons. Hydr. Engr., Los Angeles, Calif.

neers is essential to the economic and structural success of the work. The engineering plans and specifications should be as complete as possible. Besides structural features, they should also include as much information as practicable on the peculiarities of the rock formation, especially as to what extent blasting will be permitted; and on the stream flow and methods of river diversion, size of temporary flood openings in the dam, and the methods and anticipated time of closing these openings.

On the other hand the contractor should not fail to make due allowance in his bid for many items which, in estimating, are often overlooked or simply included in the bid prices per cubic yard of rock excavation or concrete. The proper cleaning of the surface of the bed-rock and the joints between successive layers of concrete are especially important items. Many dams suffer from unsightly leaks, usually in some joints. Lack of adequate engineering supervision and inspection is not always to be blamed entirely for this evil.

The author cites some instances in which the sound bed-rock was found at a much greater depth below the stream bed than was anticipated. Such conditions may call for a practically complete re-design of the dam, especially in case of an arch dam of variable radius. For instance, during the construction of several dams of this type with which the writer is familiar, the excavation was carried somewhat farther into the side abutments than had been assumed in the preparation of the original designs. It became necessary, therefore, to change the arch radii at practically all elevations of the dam. Prompt co-operation between the designers and the contractors was necessary to take care of these and other incidental changes, in order not unduly to delay the construction program of the contractors.

Mr. Bent stresses the desirability of a railroad for major projects. Where the concrete aggregate is to be brought from the outside over considerable distances, a railroad is no doubt advisable. However, where cement, steel, and contractor's equipment are the main items involving transportation, the use of trucks has been found to be more economical. For the Coolidge Dam, now under construction on the Gila River, in Arizona, the contractors have installed an aerial tramway between the gravel-pits in the river bed below the dam site and the mixing plant on the side hill above the dam. All other materials are hauled by truck. The nearest railroad station is San Carlos, located less than 10 miles from the dam site. This job is completely motorized, and is conspicuous by the absence of horses and mules.

The writer has been identified with the design and construction of about twelve dams that have been built since 1918, or are now (1928) in course of construction. In more than one instance he has seen contractors lose large sums of money, quite unnecessarily, on account of the violation of one or the other of the fundamental principles that are so ably presented by the author.

AMERICAN SOCIETY OF CIVIL ENGINEERS
INSTITUTED 1852

TRANSACTIONS

Paper No. 1689

EARTH WORK BY THE HYDRAULIC METHOD*

By Roy E. Miller,† M. Am. Soc. C. E.

With Discussion by Messrs. DeWitt D. Barlow, and William Gerig.

This subject will be discussed from the standpoint of the contracting engineer, with particular reference to the aid that can be derived in making estimates of the cost of earth work from a series of laboratory tests of samples of the earth to be moved.

When a project is under consideration, one of the vital factors to be given attention by all concerned is, "What will the work cost?" The point of view of each interested party depends on his personal interest in the work. When the project has progressed to the stage where it comes to the attention of the contracting engineer, the estimate of the cost is the all-absorbing factor. The contracting engineer goes a step farther than the project engineer in that he is obliged to make good his idea of cost by personal performance and financial guaranties. This means that every assistance that he can call on makes for security in his business, and helps to stabilize engineering and construction.

The character of the soil is the controlling factor in the cost of the work where material is to be excavated and placed by hydraulic dredging or by sluicing. Throughout this paper when reference is made to an hydraulic dredge, it should be understood to mean a pipe-line dredge of the radial type, that is, one swinging from a "spud" anchorage, and with a cutter for an agitator, which machine has come to be practically a standard tool for contractors' use in the United States. Sluicing, likewise, is meant to cover excavation by giants or monitors, and delivery through flumes by gravity or by booster pumps through pipes to the place of deposit.

The character of the material determines the difficulty or ease of digging or excavating, of pumping, and of retaining within the fill area. The writer's

* Presented at the meeting of the Construction Division, Seattle, Wash., July 15, 1926.

† Vice Pres. and Gen. Mgr., Puget Sound Bridge & Dredging Co., Seattle, Wash.

experience includes fills behind bulkheads to reclaim tide lands and marsh lands, to grade streets, platted city property, and mill and factory sites, to build dams for storage and river diversion for irrigation projects and city water supply, to replace railway trestles and bridges, and to permit the construction of harbor works, piers, docks, elevators, and warehouses.

The methods of estimating the cost of such work have been unsatisfactory on account of the many unknown and incomputable elements as compared with the degree of accuracy in estimating other engineering projects involving dry earth work, concrete, steel, etc.

In December, 1921, the Puget Sound Bridge and Dredging Company took a contract for building a storage dam on the Big Wichita River, about 50 miles from Wichita Falls, Tex. This dam was to be an hydraulic fill, 100 ft. high, with a reservoir capacity of approximately 550 000 acre-ft. In determining whether to take this work the Company was faced immediately with two important problems. The first was whether the borrow field contained the proper materials for making a satisfactory hydraulic fill and dam, should a large hydraulic dredge be used as was intended. Samples of the material were obtained, and Mr. I. F. Laucks, a chemist and assayer of Seattle, Wash., was called in to assist in analyzing the materials in order to arrive at an answer to this problem. The second—the cost of the work—could only be determined by rough comparison with results achieved elsewhere and of necessity was based wholly on personal knowledge and experience of the probable monthly output of the dredge. This, in turn, largely determined the unit cost of material handled, as the cost of operating the dredge was comparatively easy to estimate.

Dams have been built by sluicing methods for many years, and it was the experience gained therein that gave the Company the added confidence necessary to undertake to build the first dam with a dredge. Believing that a new field was being entered, wherein hydraulic dredging would find a place in the construction of earth dams, and knowing the difficulty of estimating work of this kind, and, further, finding so much aid from Mr. Lauck's laboratory work, the next logical step was to define some method of examining samples of earth taken from a proposed borrow field, which would assist in estimating the cost of work, particularly the probable output of a given dredge and the action of that material in a dam or fill.

Accordingly, it was decided to learn whether it would be possible to formulate a set of standard tests to be used as a basis for comparing specimens, as has been done with cement, steel, and other materials. It was hoped that a basis of comparison of earth samples could be established which would furnish a more or less correct idea of the probable action of the earth and of the performance of the machinery to be placed on the work.

It was recognized that any basis of predicting the behavior of a new earth or soil for dredging work would have to be comparative. There were no methods of testing soil to determine the cost of dredging. However, by determining the properties of various kinds of earths of which the characteristics and cost factors were known, and comparing them with the physical properties of a new earth it was believed that such comparisons could be used as the basis for predicting the cost of working the new earth.

After considerable preliminary work had been done, it appeared that the most important element in a soil, as affecting its ease or difficulty of working, was the clay content and the special properties of the clay. Clay is the binding element which makes soils stiff, hard to dig, hard to disintegrate, sticky, etc. There are, of course, certain earths which might be cemented by calcareous or siliceous binder, but these are not nearly so common as clay binders. Looking at this problem in another way, a pure sand or gravel, or even a pure silt, presents no particular difficulties as far as digging is concerned. It is only when the sand or silt is held together by some binding agent that difficulty begins, and the most common binding agent is clay.

Clay is merely an empirical term for particles of a certain range in size and does not signify any pure substance with certain specific properties. In other words, clays will vary among themselves very greatly, depending principally on their fineness.

In this paper all particles are considered as clay which, when suspended under proper conditions in a considerable volume of water, refuse to settle in 24 hours, through a depth of 15 cm. This gives particles of a maximum size of 0.001 mm. Some authorities have defined clay as all particles less than 0.001 mm. in size; others include as clay all material less than 0.01 mm. Taking the definition of clay and considering the maximum size as 0.001 mm., it will be noted that there are all sizes from this upper size down to particles infinitely fine; that there is as much variation between the smallest and largest clay particles as there is between a fine silt and a large cobblestone. It is generally agreed that the special properties of a clay, as, for instance, its plasticity, stickiness, binding properties, etc., depend on the fact that it is a finely subdivided material, and, moreover, that these properties vary with the fineness, and shape. The surface area of the clay particle, or rather the ratio of the surface area to the mass, seems to be the important factor, and this ratio increases enormously with the fineness, and varies with the shape, of particles.

The tests which are proposed for each sample of earth, are not meant to be necessarily final, as it may be found that certain tests are not of much value and may be dropped, or that others are needed. However, it is believed that the following tests will be fairly comprehensive:

1.—The Percentage of Water Required to Bring the Earth to the Plastic Stage.—Instead of leaving this determination to the judgment of the laboratory operator, it is proposed to measure the penetration of a weighted needle into the mass of clay, which is fairly definite and can be checked quite closely. In experimental work the ordinary asphalt penetrameter is used. A penetration of 80° in 15 sec., the needle having no additional weights added, was adopted as standard.

2.—The Percentage of Water in the Earth in Its Natural Condition.—The test is to find plasticity of the earth in its natural condition as determined by the distance to which the needle will penetrate under the same conditions as in Test 1.

Tests 1 and 2, therefore, will indicate the stage of the earth in its natural condition as compared with the plastic stage. For example, if an earth in its natural state has a penetration of the needle of 20°, it is certain that it will require much more effort to dig than it would if it were at the plastic state. So another earth having a penetration of 40° would be easier to dig than one with a penetration of 20 degrees. If an earth required 20% of water to bring it to the plastic stage, that is, with a penetration of 80°, it would be found that the earth in its natural state, with a penetration of 20°, would contain perhaps 10% of water. If, on the other hand, a natural earth had a penetration of 140°, one would expect it to be easier to dig, as far as the power requirements are concerned, but it would be very sticky and might cause trouble by adhering to the cutter, etc.

3.—Determination of the Percentage of Clay, Silt, and Sand.—Clay is considered to be all those particles that fail to settle through 15 cm. of water in 24 hours. This gives the maximum size of 0.001 mm.

Silt is considered to be all particles which settle through 15 cm., in less than 24 hours, but fail to settle in 1 min. This gives a range of particles from 0.001 mm. as the finest to about 0.01 mm. as the maximum.

Sand is all particles coarser than the silt, subject, of course, to the distinction between sand and gravel.

Wherever the sand content of an earth is considerable, a screen test should be made on the sand. In the preliminary work a number of samples were graded into six fractions finer than sand. All the fractions were obtained by water settling through various periods and were then examined under the microscope and measured, but it was not considered necessary to do this in routine testing.

4.—Absorption of Water Vapor and a Dye.—This test is designed to distinguish clays of varying degrees of fineness by taking advantage of their ability to obsorb either water vapor or a dye. The dye used has been methyline blue. The finer the clay, the more of either is absorbed. It has been found that silt and sand absorb very little, so that the main absorption is due to the clay portion. This test is made on a dry earth.

5.—Rise of Water by Capillarity.—This test is made by filling a glass tube to a depth of 20 cm. with a dry earth packed by tamping until no further subsidence occurs. The lower end is closed with loose cloth and immersed in water. The rise of the water through the earth in the tube is measured from time to time; the time required for the water to rise 20 cm. is taken as the unit. Curves of time and height of rise for various earths showed a marked difference. This is largely a comparative test, but it is believed that further experiments with it will enable it to be made of considerable value in classifying an unknown earth.

6.—Percentage of Waters Absorbed by Capillary Action.—This is determined by pushing out the wet column of earth in Test 5 after the water has risen to the top and determining the percentage of water content. This is a comparative test, and is very important in determining certain actions of the material.

7.—Percentage of Water When Saturated.—This is determined by allowing some of the dry earth to absorb all the water that it will. The percentage of water is then determined.

Tests 5, 6, and 7 would also have an immediate practical bearing where the bank of dry earth to be dug will be submerged by the dredging pond. In such case, it is important to know how this bank of dry earth will absorb water by capillary action and how it will act after the water has been absorbed.

8.—Shrinkage in Volume Between the Saturated Condition and the Dry Condition.—This is determined by drying the saturated earth of Test 7 and measuring the contraction in volume.

9.—Slaking or Disintegrating Tendency of Natural Earth.—A piece of natural earth is immersed in water and the time required for the earth to fall to pieces is measured. Great differences have been found in samples tested. This is intended as a comparative test, and also as of immediate practical importance in considering earths that are to be passed through pipe lines.

10.—Water Absorbed by an Earth in Its Natural State and the Change in Plasticity Due to Such Absorption.—A piece of the natural earth is immersed in water, the quantity of water absorbed at different periods of time being measured. The penetration of the needle is also found. This is a comparative test, but also has immediate practical interest in regard to the change of the state of an earth when immersed by a dredging pond.

11.—Presence of Organic Matters.—This is merely a qualitative test to detect considerable quantities of organic matter.

12.—Rate of Settling of a Suspension of an Earth in Water.—This is designed to detect soluble salts or alkalies which may be present in an earth and which will affect the properties of the clay portion. For example, it is known that certain salts, such as gypsum, calcium bi-carbonate, iron salts, and others affect the properties of a clay by what is known as flocculation. These soluble matters cause the minute particles of clay to adhere to each other, to "flock together" to form an aggregate particle many times the size of the component particles. A clay thus flocculated tends to act more like sand or silt because the peculiar properties of clay depend on the fineness of the particles. On the other hand, substances such as sodium carbonate tend to deflocculate a clay. Whether a clay is flocculated or deflocculated is easily seen by its rate of settling in distilled water. This test would also have practical bearing with reference to the rate of settling in a fill.

Tests 13, 14, and 15, relative to percentages of voids in a natural earth, the ratio of the volume of water to the volume of voids in a natural earth, and the specific gravity of the particles, respectively, are comparative tests. It is also likely that Tests 13 and 14 will be found to be quite important as far as the working properties of an earth are concerned.

Proposed Method of Applying Data Secured

It is assumed that cost of work depends very largely on the daily output of the dredge and that all other cost factors are subordinate. On this assumption the following method of procedure is suggested: For example, select a fairly uniform bed of earth sufficient for the dredge, say for one week, or for whatever time is considered sufficiently long to determine accurately its daily capacity in the material. Sample the earth in several places so as to be representative of material to be removed. The capacity of the dredge for this week would then be determined in the field, together with any special conditions encountered or properties of the earth which affect the ease or difficulty of working. In other words, the capacity of the dredge for the week and the ideas of the man in charge as to why the dredge had that particular capacity would be recorded. The samples would then be sent to the laboratory for testing.

This procedure would be followed as often as possible, the number of samples depending largely on conditions. That is, if the dredge had to dig in a strata of sand and clay during the week, the capacity would be influenced both by the sand and the clay, and there would be no object in taking samples of the mixture as the results would not be dependable, because it would not be known how long the dredge would be in the sand or the clay.

This procedure would give two sets of data, one from the field and the other from the laboratory. After a considerable number of samples had been thus tested and correlated with the field figures, it is believed it would be safe to begin predicting on samples taken from projected work. The procedure on projected work would be to sample the various kinds of earth and determine the properties of each. After these properties were determined, the results would be compared with those from samples on which work had already been done and on which the cost of digging had been ascertained.

It is probable that the properties will not match exactly, but curves can be established so that the values for new samples can be plotted and thus compared with old ones.

It will not be advisable to make predictions on new samples until a considerable number have been tested, as it is only by correlating the tests with known results of cost in the field that a foundation can be laid for foretelling the action of new samples.

Sampling of Earths

The samples should represent a body of earth of fair uniformity, should be taken from the earth in place, and should be put in tight containers so that no change will take place before the sample is tested. Samples for testing should not be taken to represent too large a body of earth because considerable variations may occur over large areas.

About 5 lb. of earth will be required to make the test outlined, and a 2-qt. tin can with a full width friction top, or some other tight-fitting top, will be satisfactory for carrying samples.

In more than three years since this plan of testing was begun, the writer's Company has had occasion to make estimates on earth work, particularly for hydraulic-fill dams, at widely separated points in North America, and has found the laboratory work to be of great help. Considerable success has also been had in analyzing materials to determine their suitability for fill purposes.

The most important factor determining the estimated cost of earth work by the hydraulic method is the probable output of the contractor's plant. In sluicing work the ability of the giants to excavate the material very often determines the output. In dredging, more often than not, the ability of the dredge to excavate the material determines the output, rather than its pumping capacity. This is particularly true of hydraulic-fill dams as they generally have good foundations which means either rock, hard-pan, or clay, and it is hardly to be expected that such material as soft harbor mud, or loose, water-bearing sand, will be found in such locations. Wherever the output is dependent on the ability of the dredge to excavate the material, the study of earth samples as suggested is meant to apply.

Sufficient time has not elapsed to give a complementary set of records in the field and in the laboratory which will enable the Company to depend largely on the laboratory reports. It is too much to expect that laboratory reports may take the place of practical knowledge and experience, particularly as so many other factors have a bearing on the cost of work. It is expected, however, that in a few years the laboratory work will have been perfected, records will have been accumulated as to performance, and knowledge increased so that the laboratory will be a valuable adjunct to the earth-moving business.

If work is limited to a comparatively small field, particularly on tide-water, there may be no justification for a study such as suggested. However, the average dredging job is no longer a simple problem of excavating harbor and mud and pumping it a short distance, wasting the material, or, at best, making a simple fill with it. Broader knowledge is required by those responsible for hydraulic operations, and this, in turn, requires more dependence on laboratory research work.

DISCUSSION

DeWitt D. Barlow,* Assoc. M. Am. Soc. C. E. (by letter).—The author has described a method for classifying field data with the view to building up a store of information that will enable dredging engineers to estimate their work with less uncertainty. The proposed method is to record the hourly "capacities" of hydraulic dredges wherever they work in uniform beds of material, and simultaneously to record certain physical characteristics of the material as the same may be revealed by laboratory tests for absorption, flocculence, etc. The method seems obvious enough, especially to one not acquainted with the physics of the problem. It assumes that the output of the dredge varies with the previously mentioned characteristics of the material dredged, and with nothing else. Both assumptions are false.

In the writer's opinion the procedure described under the heading "Proposed Method of Applying Data Secured", will not produce results of any value. The capacity of the dredge is a variable quantity of great complexity, contingent on many things other than the material dredged.

The output of a hydraulic dredge (per engine-hour) is governed by two main factors, both of them complex; that is, the amount the dredge can dig, and the amount it can pump ashore. Either quantity may control. It cannot pump more than it can dig, and it cannot continue to dig more than it can pump, so that the first thing the experimenter must do, is to classify the material as to its digging and its pumping qualities.

The digging must be canvassed, not on the basis of what the dredge can do, but on the type of cutter used, the horse power and torque applied to the cutter shaft, and the tension and horse power on the swinging wires. When these data are assembled, they should be examined in connection with the physical characteristics of the material with which they vary.

The author's statement that "more often than not the ability of the dredge to excavate the material determines the output, rather than its pumping capacity", is only another way of stating that the dredges that have come within his observation were under-powered on the cutter or over-powered on the pump. It is incorrect.

The best way to classify material with respect to cutting is to measure its resistance to cutting. For this purpose the writer prefers an auger to any amount of litmus solution. Entirely satisfactory estimates are made in this manner. The hazards in hydraulic dredging estimates do not reside there. They are to be found in the extreme sensitiveness of the pumping operation to differences in the coarseness of particles to be pumped and to variations in the material excavated from the samples on which the estimates were based.

Consider the question of pumping, assuming that the cutting power is adequate. The operation of hydraulic dredging consists in maintaining a flow of water through a pipe line and of introducing into the stream, solid material which is carried in suspension and along the bottom of the pipe. The cutting

* Pres. and Director, Atlantic, Gulf & Pacific Co., New York, N. Y.

or digging, referred to, is the introducing process. The stream is kept in motion by a centrifugal pump; the solid material is introduced on the suction side. In the conduct of the operation it is possible to run more solids into the stream than the stream will carry off. That is what is meant by the statement that the pumping controls. Under that condition some of the solids settle out and lie in the bottom of the pipe, the cross-section is throttled, the output is diminished, and a limit is found to the pumping capacity. This limit is controlled by many factors; among others, the available torque on the pump, the maximum speed of the pump, its efficiency (which varies from zero through 70% and back to zero for different speeds and heads), the horse power of the prime mover, its power characteristics, the length of pipe line, its size and character (pontoon lines ordinarily consume, in power per unit of length, from 150 to 200% of that consumed by the shore line), the elevation of the end of the hydraulic grade, and the material.

In order to discover the effect of variation in material on the rate of pumping, it is necessary to eliminate or standardize the other factors. The way to do that is to ascertain, not what the dredge will do in a given material, but to determine the horse power (hydraulic) consumed per unit length of a standard pipe, per cubic yard of that material carried in suspension at the saturation point. That figure is important and is the one that dredging engineers want. It varies with several factors, more especially specific gravity and coarseness. Most sands, clays, and muds are of a silica base, so that the specific gravity is usually constant. There is, of course, the widest range in the size of particles, and a corresponding wide range in the "dredging power factor", if the writer may be allowed to coin a term. In fact, the "dredging power factor" is so sensitive to the size of particle that hardly anything else counts. As between fine beach sand and sand of the consistency of granulated sugar, there is a range of 300% or more. If one goes as far up the scale as gravel of, say, the size of lima beans, the range will be more than 1 000 per cent. The larger the particle, the more power required to move it.

The way to determine the coarseness of material is to sift it. When that is done and its specific gravity is known, one can classify it as to its power factor, but the error, due to the character of the experimental data, will be a quantity of far greater magnitude than the whole field affected by capillarity and the experiments mentioned by the author.

These remarks should not be taken in disparagement of research. It is badly needed in dredging. The writer is enthusiastic for research and wants to direct it where it will be effective. The author's method is far too empirical. It assumes a simple relation where there is a complex one, and the aspect of that relation which it investigates is negligible. It is completely masked by the major phases of the problem, which he ignores.

WILLIAM GERIG,* M. AM. SOC. C. E. (by letter).—The author proposes laboratory experiments to determine the cost of work done by hydraulic methods. In view of the many unknown quantities that go to make up the cost of hydraulic work, even if the character of the material is known, the writer

* Senior Engr., Office of Chf. of Engrs., U. S. Army, Washington, D. C.

does not see how such data will be of much value. Some of these unknown factors are, capacity of the dredge, capacity and power of the cutter, design of the sand pump and cutter, efficiency of the plant as a whole and of the crews, etc. Therefore, even with the laboratory data at hand, one must also know the capacity of each piece of plant in the material under consideration.

Laymen and even some engineers appear to believe that the only requisites for hydraulic suction dredging are a pump, an engine, and the necessary suction and discharge pipes, while the cost of excavation is assumed to be about 10 cents per cu. yd. The fact is that economic hydraulic dredging by suction dredges costs from 3 to 90 cents per cu. yd., a wide range which no doubt will be questioned by many readers of this discussion, but which can be proved to be true.

While laboratory experiments are useful to the profession and the writer does not wish to discourage them, he does not feel that they are entirely dependable. Judgment and experience are the prime factors in determining the cost of hydraulic work, and no laboratory rule or method alone will enable the inexperienced engineer or layman to estimate such cost with any degree of precision.

An interesting case illustrating these statements is that of the deep-water channel for Tampa, Fla., entailing the removal of about 2 500 000 cu. yd. Borings and probings showed about one-half the material to be coral rock and the remainder, or overlying material, to be sand. The types of plant considered by the engineers to be best adapted to this work were suction and dipper dredges. Specifications were prepared and bids invited. Two bids were received, one, $5.20, and the other, $4.63, per cu. yd. These bids, being considerably in excess of the estimate, were rejected and the work was done by a Government-owned cutter pipe-line dredge.

The rock and the sand were both removed at a total cost of 90 cents per cu. yd., including interest, depreciation, insurance, etc. This cost would have considerably exceeded 90 cents, however, had any other type of plant been used. Many millions of dollars were saved by using this type of dredge.

In this case the character of the material was known and yet, due to the type and efficiency of hydraulic plants considered for the work, there was a wide difference of opinion as to the estimated costs, and the actual costs were considerably less than the estimate.

AMERICAN SOCIETY OF CIVIL ENGINEERS

INSTITUTED 1852

TRANSACTIONS

Paper No. 1690

THE HYDRAULIC DESIGN OF FLUME AND SIPHON TRANSITIONS*

By Julian Hinds,† M. Am. Soc. C. E.

With Discussion by Messrs. H. B. Muckleston, F. Theodore Mavis, W. H. R. Nimmo, Carl Rohwer, and Julian Hinds.

Synopsis

Considerable attention has been given by the United States Bureau of Reclamation to the hydraulic design of transitions for flumes and siphons, and rules have been established for the proportioning of important structures. A summary of these rules and of the experiences leading up to them is herewith presented. No attempt is made to furnish a complete treatise on transition structures, and only points on which definite experience has been gained, or opinions have been formed, are introduced.

Although the discussion is generally confined to inlets and outlets to and from inverted siphons and flumes, the principles established may be applied to any structure designed to change the shape or cross-sectional area of an open stream of water.

In this paper the following principal facts are shown:

1.—Unimportant transitions, where velocities are low, may be designed arbitrarily, by adaptation from successful structures operating under similar conditions.

Note.—The Special Committee on Irrigation Hydraulics selected the subject of "Losses in Canal Conversions" as one of ten for study and research. This paper was submitted to the Committee by the author, and the Committee recommended its publication. (See Progress Report of the Committee, *Proceedings*, Am. Soc. C. E., March, 1927, Society Affairs, p. 121).

* Published in October, 1927, *Proceedings*.

† Res. Engr., The J. G. White Eng. Corporation, Pabellón, Aguascalientes, Mexico.

2.—For important structures, especially those involving velocities in excess of 6 to 8 ft. per sec., careful detailed computations must be made. Extremely slender, and carefully constructed, transitions, if not proportioned in exact accordance with the hydraulic requirements, may prove seriously defective. Examples of such cases are shown, and a proposed method of computation is outlined.

3.—Experimental data collected by the U. S. Bureau of Reclamation are summarized, showing the efficiencies that may be expected with various types of construction, the effects of conduit curvature on outlet efficiency, and the influence of critical flow and the hydraulic jump on the action of inlets and outlets.

Division of Subject

The subject is discussed under four main headings, as follows:

1.—Unimportant, or low-velocity structures, not involving the hydraulic jump or flow at the critical depth.

2.—Important, or high-velocity structures, not involving the hydraulic jump or flow at the critical depth.

3.—Structures involving the hydraulic jump or flow at the critical depth.

4.—Experimental data.

Notations and Abbreviations.—The notations and abbreviations used are listed for convenient reference, as follows:

A = area of water prism.
Q = discharge.
V = velocity.
$W\,S$ = water surface.
$\Delta\, W\,S$ = change in water surface.
h_v = velocity head.
$\Delta\, h_v$ = change in velocity head.
B = bottom width of channel.
T = width of channel at water surface.
d = depth of water.
H = height of lining or wall.
s_f = friction slope.
h_f = head lost in friction.
W = width of channel at top of lining or wall.

1.—The Design of Secondary Structures not Affected by Critical Flow

All structures for changing the shape or cross-sectional area of a water conduit cause disturbances in flow, which may be objectionable in themselves or in the resulting losses in head. In designing an inlet, it is necessary to provide for a drop in the water surface, sufficient to produce the required increase in velocity head and to overcome friction and entrance losses. At an outlet the water surface will rise theoretically a vertical distance equal to the reduction in velocity head. The actual rise, usually referred to as recovery of head, is less than the theoretical, because of frictional and outlet losses.

No satisfactory theory for computing the transition losses for a given structure has been proposed. The magnitude of these losses can only be determined experimentally at present. The simple considerations outlined herein are often taken as sufficient for the design of a transition, the form and details being determined from precedent.

The U. S. Bureau of Reclamation, over a period of more than twenty years, has accumulated a large variety of detailed designs for transition structures of secondary importance. The preparation of a new design for a structure of this class is usually accomplished by changing the details of a previous structure, known to be satisfactory, to suit the new conditions. A collection of possible types of simple transitions, sketched from some of these designs, is shown on Figs. 1, 2, 3, and 4. These structures differ widely in degree of perfection, and in the losses which they may be expected to produce.

The simplest forms of pipe inlets or outlets are illustrated by Types (1), (2) and (3), Fig. 1. These types are used for culverts, and are satisfactory for small pipes. It is probably reasonable to assume entrance and outlet losses equal to 0.5 and 1.0, respectively, of the velocity head in the pipe for these structures. Types (4), (5) and (6), Fig. 1, are somewhat more complicated structurally, and are perhaps slightly better hydraulically. Type (7), Fig. 1, which is sometimes used for carrying small irrigation canals under roads and railroads in cuts, is poor hydraulically, and is subject to stoppage by silt and weeds. Types (8) and (11), Fig. 1, are slightly better, but more expensive to construct. Types (9) and (10), Fig. 1, are fairly efficient, involving entrance and outlet losses, respectively, of perhaps 0.25 and 0.50 of the velocity head. Types (12) to (17), inclusive, Fig. 2, illustrate trash rack, weir, and control-gate arrangements for pipe inlets.

It is considered advantageous to affect velocity changes under pressure, where convenient, and Types (18) and (19), Fig. 2, are perhaps more efficient than the somewhat similar Types (9) and (10), Fig. 1. However, it is doubtful whether their increased cost is justified. Type (20), Fig. 2, shows a device sometimes used to check high velocities at the outlet of a pipe or culvert. Types (21) and (22), Fig. 2, show pipe ends which may be constructed without the use of forms, provided the bank around the pipe can be trimmed to the required dimensions. An inside form is required for the bellmouth in Type (21). Type (23), Fig. 3, utilizes a precast bellmouth, and requires no forming. Types (24) to (28), inclusive, Fig. 3, represent the best practice in transition structures constructed without accurately computed proportions. It is doubtful whether an outlet as elaborate as those shown on Types (27) or (28) should ever be constructed without having the proportions carefully calculated throughout. Fig. 4 shows a number of flume transitions varying from a simple head-wall, Type (30), to a carefully warped structure, Type (40).

A type of structure suited to a given set of conditions may be selected from the examples in Figs. 1 to 4, the probable loss of head estimated by comparison with some structure for which the losses have been measured, and a reasonably good design prepared. The observed data given on Fig. 17 will be found helpful for estimating the losses.

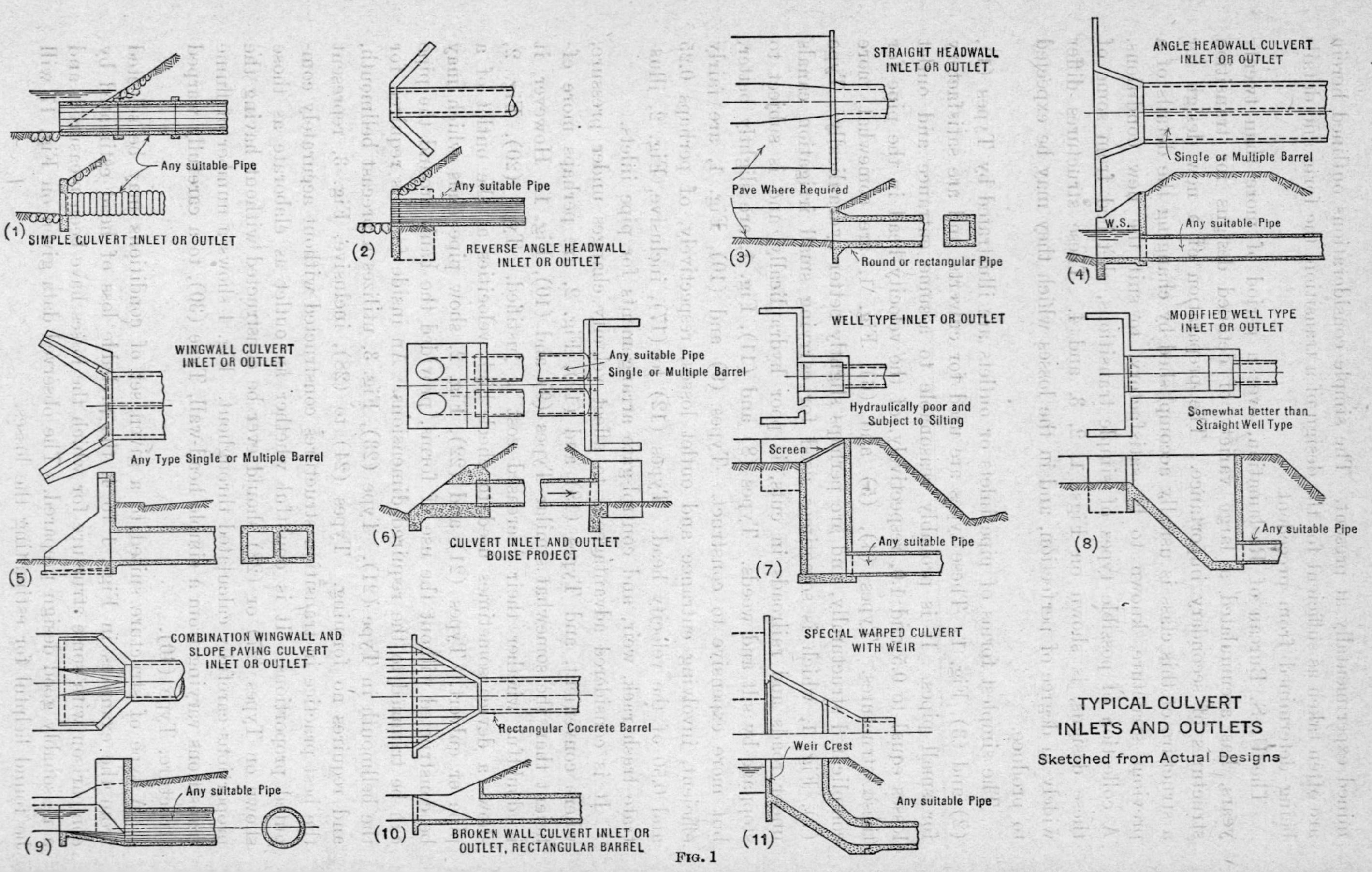
(1) SIMPLE CULVERT INLET OR OUTLET
Any suitable Pipe
(2) REVERSE ANGLE HEADWALL INLET OR OUTLET
Any suitable Pipe
(3) STRAIGHT HEADWALL INLET OR OUTLET
Pave Where Required
Round or rectangular Pipe
(4) ANGLE HEADWALL CULVERT INLET OR OUTLET
Single or Multiple Barrel
Any suitable Pipe
W.S.
(5) WINGWALL CULVERT INLET OR OUTLET
Any Type Single or Multiple Barrel
(6) CULVERT INLET AND OUTLET BOISE PROJECT
Any suitable Pipe Single or Multiple Barrel
(7) WELL TYPE INLET OR OUTLET
Hydraulically poor and Subject to Silting
Any suitable Pipe
Screen
(8) MODIFIED WELL TYPE INLET OR OUTLET
Somewhat better than Straight Well Type
Any suitable Pipe
(9) COMBINATION WINGWALL AND SLOPE PAVING CULVERT INLET OR OUTLET
Any suitable Pipe
(10) BROKEN WALL CULVERT INLET OR OUTLET, RECTANGULAR BARREL
Rectangular Concrete Barrel
(11) SPECIAL WARPED CULVERT WITH WEIR
Weir Crest
Any suitable Pipe
TYPICAL CULVERT INLETS AND OUTLETS
Sketched from Actual Designs

FIG. 1

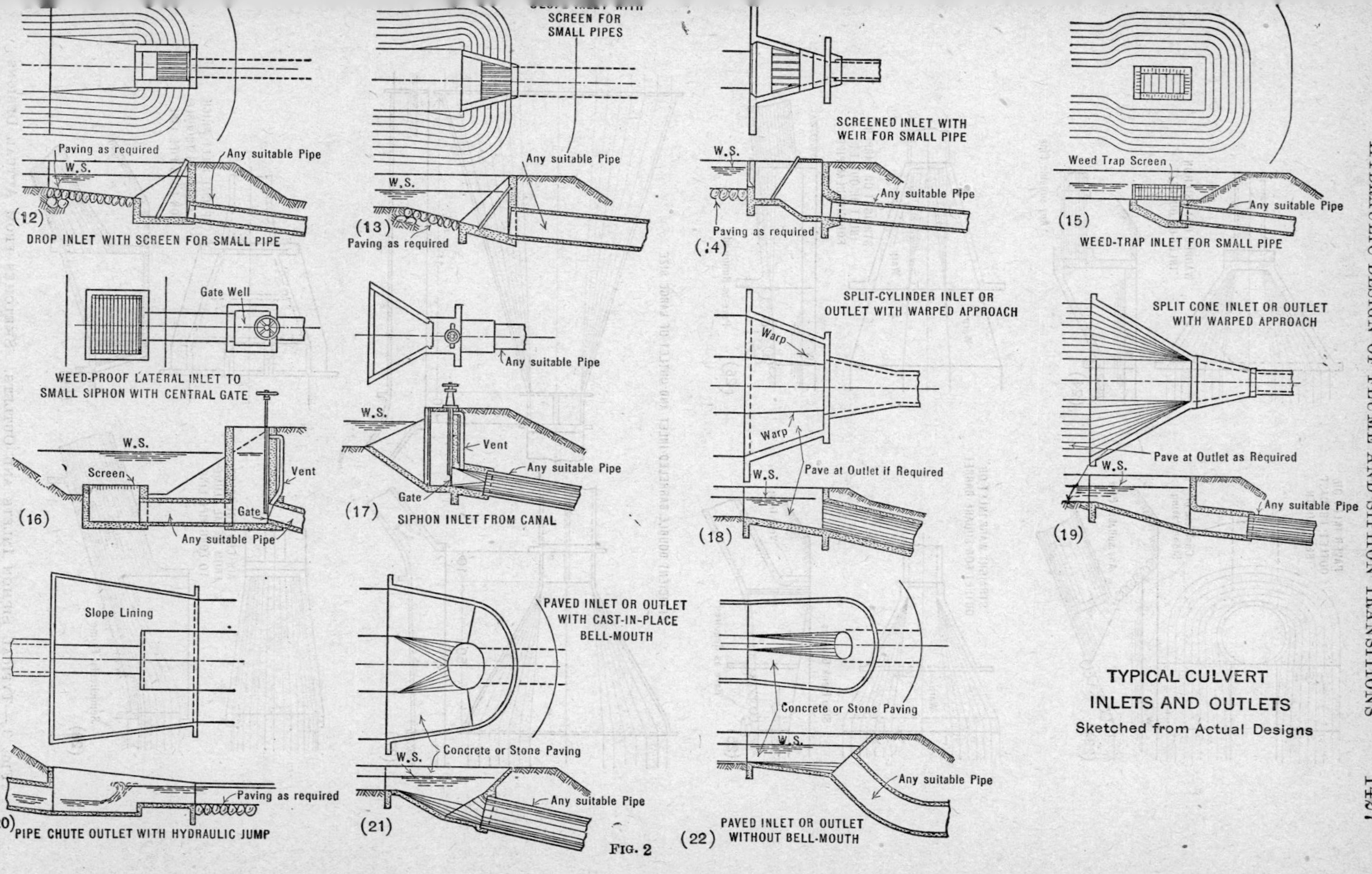
SCREEN FOR
SMALL PIPES
Paving as required
W.S.
Any suitable Pipe
(12)
DROP INLET WITH SCREEN FOR SMALL PIPE
Any suitable Pipe
W.S.
(13)
Paving as required
SCREENED INLET WITH
WEIR FOR SMALL PIPE
W.S.
Any suitable Pipe
Paving as required
(14)
Weed Trap Screen
Any suitable Pipe
(15)
WEED-TRAP INLET FOR SMALL PIPE
Gate Well
WEED-PROOF LATERAL INLET TO
SMALL SIPHON WITH CENTRAL GATE
W.S.
Screen
Vent
Gate
Any suitable Pipe
(16)
Any suitable Pipe
W.S.
Vent
Any suitable Pipe
Gate
(17)
SIPHON INLET FROM CANAL
SPLIT-CYLINDER INLET OR
OUTLET WITH WARPED APPROACH
Warp
Warp
W.S.
Pave at Outlet if Required
(18)
SPLIT CONE INLET OR OUTLET
WITH WARPED APPROACH
Pave at Outlet as Required
W.S.
Any suitable Pipe
(19)
Slope Lining
Paving as required
20)
PIPE CHUTE OUTLET WITH HYDRAULIC JUMP
PAVED INLET OR OUTLET
WITH CAST-IN-PLACE
BELL-MOUTH
Concrete or Stone Paving
W.S.
Any suitable Pipe
(21)
Concrete or Stone Paving
W.S.
Any suitable Pipe
(22)
PAVED INLET OR OUTLET
WITHOUT BELL-MOUTH
TYPICAL CULVERT
INLETS AND OUTLETS
Sketched from Actual Designs

Fig. 2

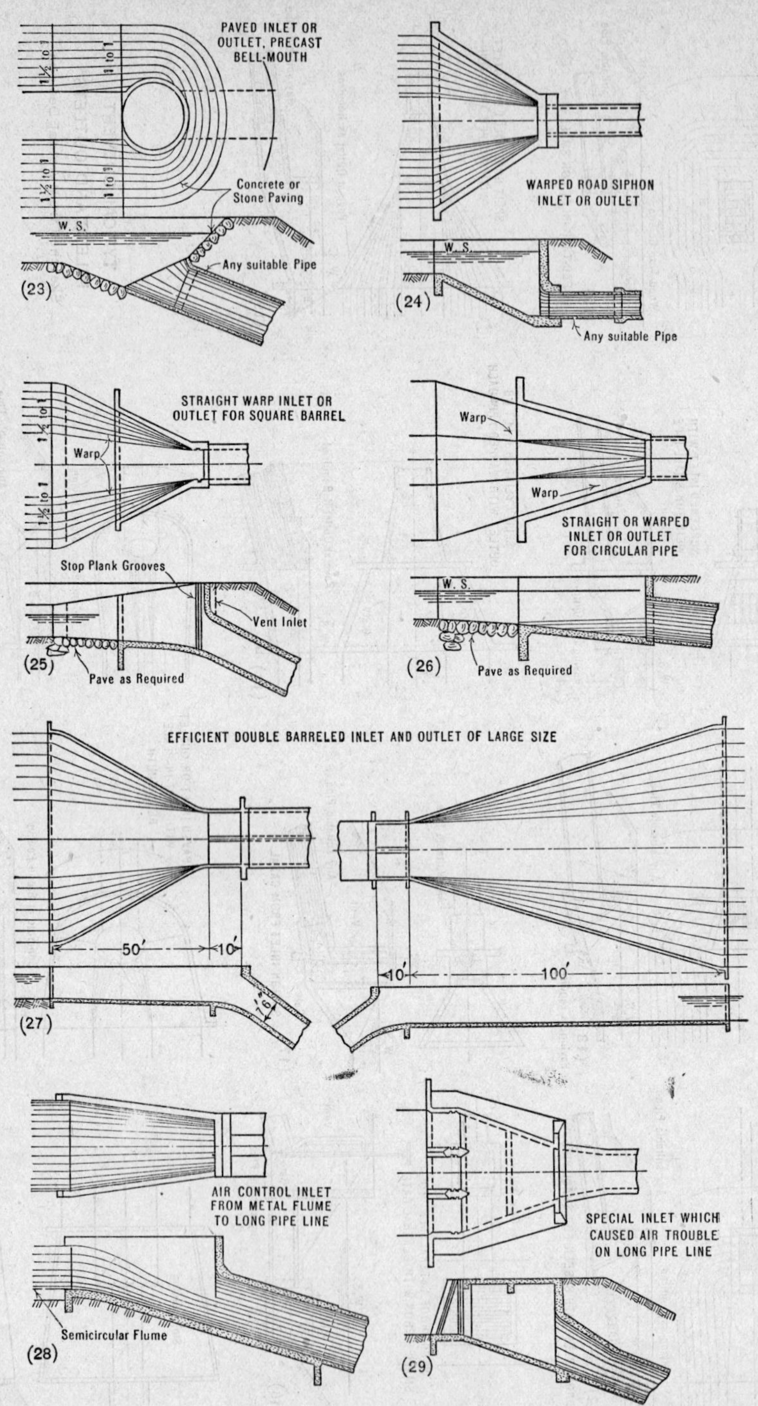

FIG. 3.—TYPICAL SIPHON INLETS AND OUTLETS. SKETCHES FROM ACTUAL DESIGNS.

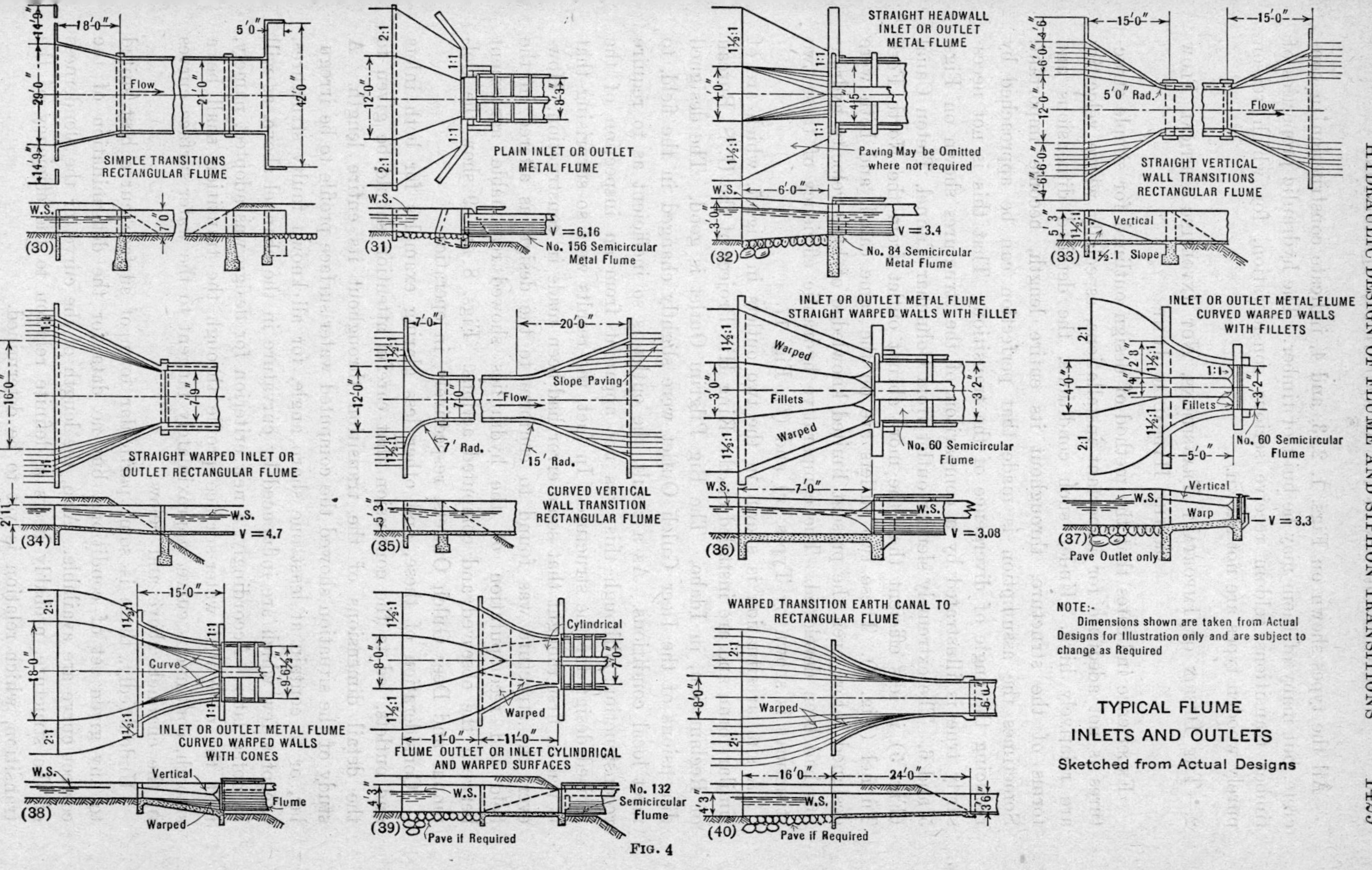
SIMPLE TRANSITIONS
RECTANGULAR FLUME
(30)
PLAIN INLET OR OUTLET
METAL FLUME
V = 6.16
No. 156 Semicircular
Metal Flume
(31)
STRAIGHT HEADWALL
INLET OR OUTLET
METAL FLUME
Paving May be Omitted
where not required
V = 3.4
No. 84 Semicircular
Metal Flume
(32)
STRAIGHT VERTICAL
WALL TRANSITIONS
RECTANGULAR FLUME
Vertical
1½:1 Slope
(33)
STRAIGHT WARPED INLET OR
OUTLET RECTANGULAR FLUME
V = 4.7
(34)
CURVED VERTICAL
WALL TRANSITION
RECTANGULAR FLUME
Slope Paving
Flow
7' Rad.
15' Rad.
(35)
INLET OR OUTLET METAL FLUME
STRAIGHT WARPED WALLS WITH FILLET
Warped
Fillets
No. 60 Semicircular
Flume
V = 3.08
(36)
INLET OR OUTLET METAL FLUME
CURVED WARPED WALLS
WITH FILLETS
Fillets
No. 60 Semicircular
Flume
Vertical
Warp
V = 3.3
(37)
Pave Outlet only
INLET OR OUTLET METAL FLUME
CURVED WARPED WALLS
WITH CONES
Curve
Vertical
Flume
Warped
(38)
FLUME OUTLET OR INLET CYLINDRICAL
AND WARPED SURFACES
Cylindrical
Warped
No. 132
Semicircular
Flume
(39)
Pave if Required
WARPED TRANSITION EARTH CANAL TO
RECTANGULAR FLUME
Warped
(40)
Pave if Required
NOTE:-
Dimensions shown are taken from Actual
Designs for Illustration only and are subject to
change as Required
TYPICAL FLUME
INLETS AND OUTLETS
Sketched from Actual Designs

FIG. 4

All the types shown on Figs. 1, 2, 3, and 4, indicate construction in concrete, but many of them may be built of timber. The hydraulic properties of timber transitions seldom receive serious consideration, for which reason purely wooden types are not shown.

2.—The Design of Important Transitions, Not Involving Critical Flow or the Hydraulic Jump

Experience indicates that the method of design outlined for simple structures is not adequate for important installations, especially where velocities are relatively high. Under such conditions, the detailed dimensions and forms of the structure, throughout its entire length, become important. Sometimes the assumption is made that perfection can be approached by reducing the angle of divergence of the transition. That this is not necessarily true is illustrated by a comparison of the structures shown on Figs. 5 and 6. The extremely slender outlet from Columnar Tunnel, Tieton Canal (Fig. 5) is less efficient than the more abrupt outlet from the North Fork Tunnel (Fig. 6). These two outlets are on the same canal, and both were designed before even the present limited knowledge of high velocity hydraulics had been developed. The comparative hydraulic efficiency of these two structures is shown by Types (*r*) and (*t*), Fig. 17.

A similar situation is shown in the two outlets in Fig. 7, which are of similar form, and are installed on the King Hill Project of the U. S. Bureau of Reclamation, in Idaho. The Big Pilgrim Outlet is good. The designed dimensions of the Deer Gulch Outlet were slightly changed in the field, to meet local conditions. As a result, the outlet is so inefficient as to require reconstruction, although this was not apparent from an inspection of the revised design for the structure. In fact, the results were so surprising that it was at first thought that some error had been made in construction. However, the structure was found to conform to the design as altered in the field and recomputation of the hydraulics showed reasonable agreement between the observed and computed actions. Figs. 8 and 9 show the Columnar and Deer Gulch Outlets, respectively, in operation.

Consideration of these, and other less glaring examples for both inlets and outlets, led to the conclusion that careful attention should be given to the detail dimensions of the transition throughout its entire length. A study of the situation showed the computed water-surface profile to be irregular, or to contain at least one sharp angle, for all known faulty structures, except a few which are influenced by curvature in the channel above, as will be noted later. Accordingly, a new criterion for design was adopted, namely, that the computed water-surface profile through the transition shall be a smooth, continuous curve, approximately tangent to the water-surface curves in the channels above and below.

Undoubtedly, there is some particular form of surface curve best suited to any given set of conditions, but no data for the determination of the correct curve are available. Also, the length of the curve, or the slenderness of the structure, probably bears a definite relation to the efficiency of the transition, which relation is yet to be determined.

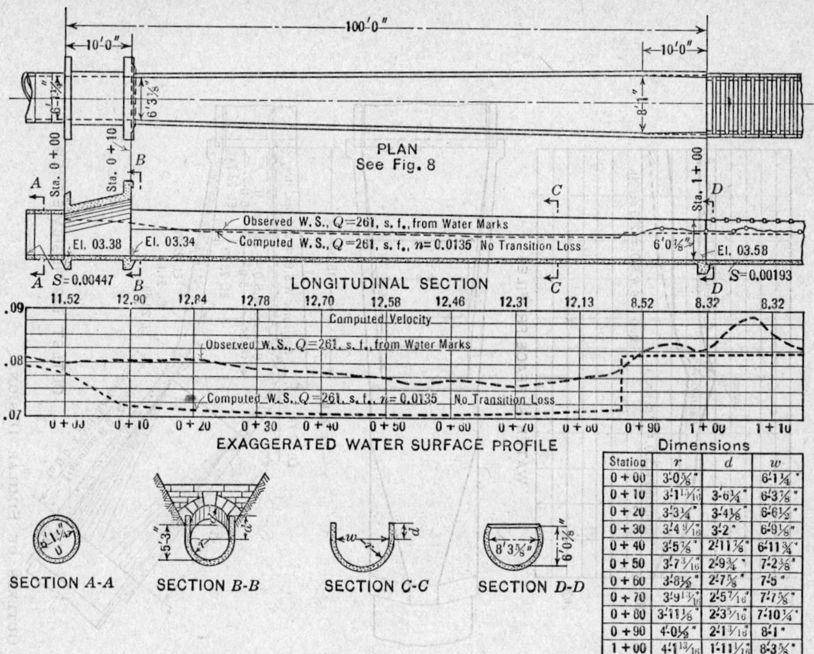

Dimensions

Station	r	d	w
0 + 00	3'-0⅝"		6'-1¼"
0 + 10	3'-1 15/16"	3'-6¼"	6'-3⅞"
0 + 20	3'-3¼"	3'-4⅛"	6'-6½"
0 + 30	3'-4 9/16"	3'-2"	6'-9⅛"
0 + 40	3'-5⅞"	2'-11⅞"	6'-11¾"
0 + 50	3'-7 3/16"	2'-9¾"	7'-2⅜"
0 + 60	3'-8½"	2'-7⅝"	7'-5"
0 + 70	3'-9 13/16"	2'-5 7/16"	7'-7⅝"
0 + 80	3'-11⅛"	2'-3 5/16"	7'-10¼"
0 + 90	4'-0½"	2'-1 3/16"	8'-1"
1 + 00	4'-1 13/16	1'-11 1/16"	8'-3⅝"

FIG. 5.—PLAN AND CROSS-SECTIONS OF OUTLET, COLUMNAR TUNNEL, TIETON CANAL.

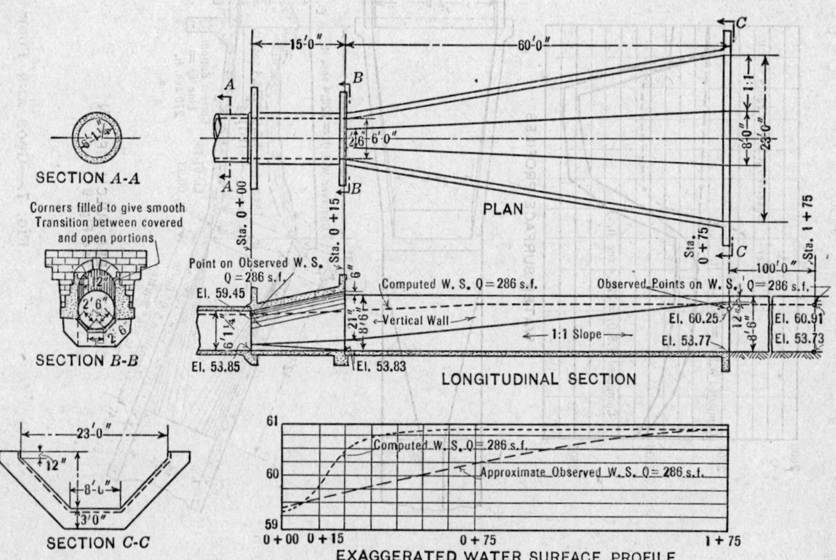

FIG. 6.—PLAN AND CROSS-SECTIONS OF OUTLET, NORTH FORK TUNNEL, TIETON CANAL.

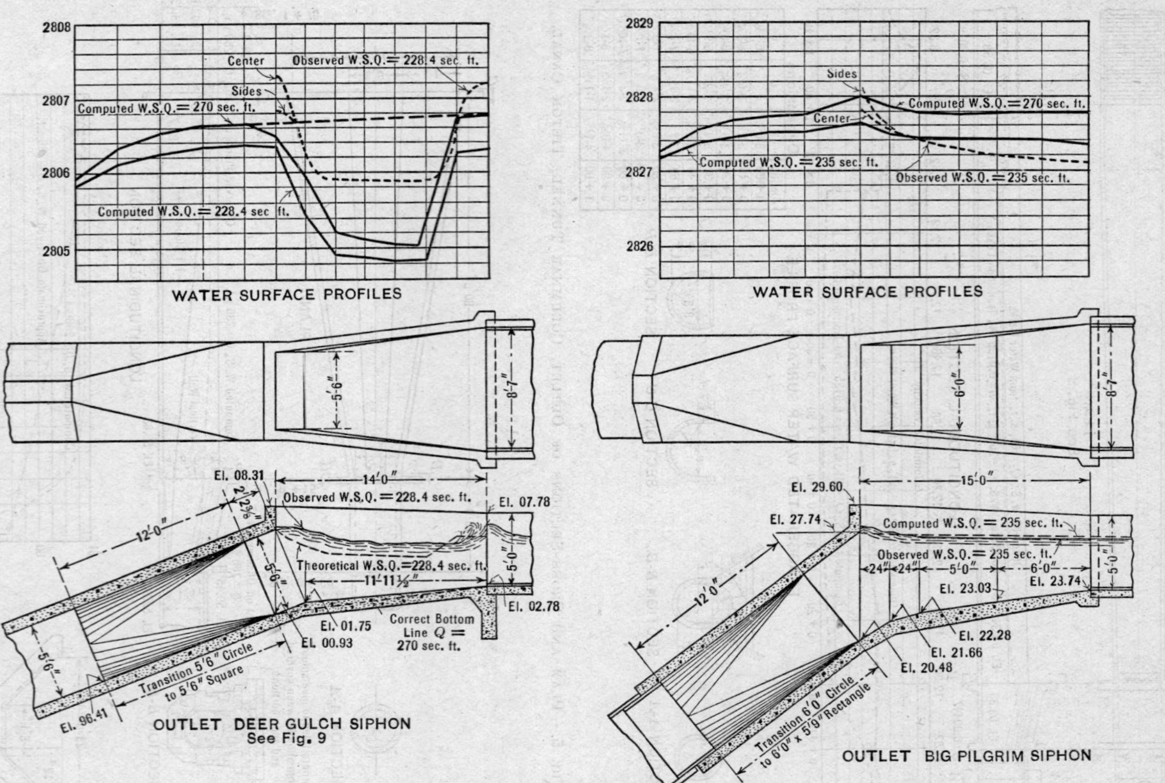

Fig. 7.—Good and Poor Siphon Outlets of Similar Design.

FIG. 8.—VIEW OF OUTLET, COLUMNAR TUNNEL.

FIG. 9.—VIEW OF OUTLET, DEER GULCH SIPHON.

The application of the rule just given is illustrated by the two simple structures shown in Figs. 10 and 11. Before computing the hydraulics, the inlet shown in Fig. 10 might be considered good. However, if the hydraulics are computed at short intervals throughout the structure, the surface curve will be found to contain a sharp angle at the junction with the narrow channel, and marked disturbances in flow may be expected. By properly curving the walls of the inlet, as shown in Fig. 11, this condition can be avoided, the rate of change in acceleration being changed in such a way that the water-surface profile becomes a smooth, continuous curve.

A plan based on the principles illustrated in Fig. 11 is used by the U. S. Bureau of Reclamation for all important transitions. If desired, the dimensions of the structure may be assumed and the surface curve computed from Bernoulli's theorem, the dimensions being subsequently changed and the curve recalculated until satisfactory results are secured. A more direct solution is obtained if the water-surface curve is first determined and the dimensions of the structure are computed to conform. The procedure recommended will be illustrated by examples of actual designs. Before attempting to prepare designs similar to these examples the discussion of experimental data should be reviewed, especially that part which relates to the effect of curvature in flumes and siphons on the action of their outlet structures.

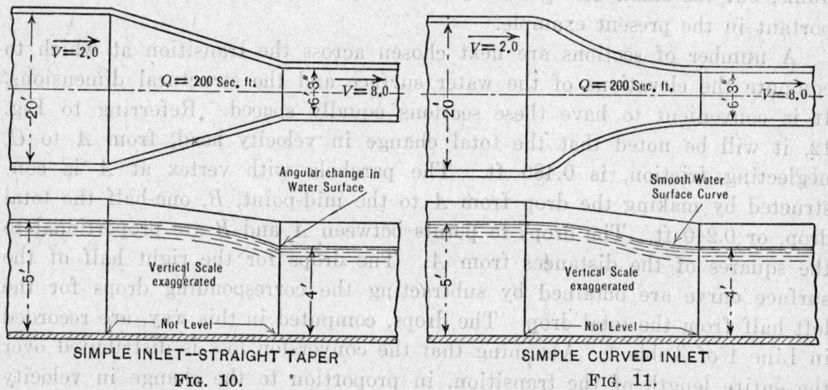

FIG. 10. FIG. 11.

Example of a Flume Inlet.—Referring to Fig. 12, let it be required to design an inlet from an earth canal with a bottom width of 18 ft., side slopes of 2 : 1, to a rectangular concrete flume, 12 ft. 6 in. wide. The hydraulic properties of the canal and the flume may be assumed to be known, as shown on the diagram.

It is desirable first to determine approximately the length that will be required for the transition. In the absence of specific knowledge this must be done arbitrarily. For structures of the type under consideration the U. S. Bureau of Reclamation has adopted the rule of making the length such that a straight line joining the flow line at the two ends of the transition, as *D-E*, Fig. 12, will make an angle of about 12½° with the axis of the structure. In the example shown the resulting length is 50 ft.

From information given in the discussion of experimental data, it appears that, for a structure of the type contemplated, the entrance loss may be safely assumed as 0.1 the change in velocity head, making 1.10 Δh_v, the total drop to be provided, plus the drop necessary to overcome friction. If the water-surface elevation in the canal at the upper end of the inlet is known, and if friction is temporarily neglected, the water-surface elevation in the flume at the lower end of the transition can be found, and the two end points, A and C, of the water-surface profile, A B C, Fig. 12, determined. Between A and C the water surface theoretically may be made to follow any desired profile, within reasonable limits, the profile being controlled by the shape and size of the transition structure.

If the flow is to be smooth and the structure efficient, the theoretical water surface must be free from angles or sharp curves. The particular curve that fits the given conditions better than any other not being known, any smooth curve tangent to the normal water surface in the canal, at A, and in the flume, at C, may be used. It may be drawn arbitrarily or computed. In Fig. 12, the water surface, neglecting friction, is taken as two equal parabolas, horizontal, respectively, at A and C, and tangent at B. Strictly, the parabolas should be tangent to the water-surface slopes in the canal and the flume, but the small divergence of these slopes from the horizontal is unimportant in the present example.

A number of sections are next chosen across the transition at which to compute the elevations of the water surface and the structural dimensions. It is convenient to have these sections equally spaced. Referring to Fig. 12, it will be noted that the total change in velocity head, from A to C, neglecting friction, is 0.480 ft. The parabola with vertex at A is constructed by making the drop from A to the mid-point, B, one-half the total drop, or 0.240 ft. The drops to points between A and B are proportional to the squares of the distances from A. The drops for the right half of the surface curve are obtained by subtracting the corresponding drops for the left half from the total drop. The drops, computed in this way, are recorded in Line 1 of Table 1. Assuming that the conversion loss is distributed over the entire length of the transition, in proportion to the change in velocity head, values of Δh_v are obtained by dividing the computed values of $\Delta W S$ by 1.10. The velocity head is obtained by adding Δh_v to the velocity head at A. The velocities corresponding to the assumed water-surface curve are then determined, as recorded in Line 4, Table 1, and the required area of cross-section is computed as shown in Line 5. Except that no allowance has been made for friction, this completes the hydraulic design, the area of the section at each point of sub-division being known. It remains, however, to choose shapes for the various sections, such that they will fit with each other to produce a structure of pleasing appearance, free from angles and sharp curves. The work from this point depends largely on the skill and experience of the designer. Sections may be either arbitrarily chosen and platted until satisfactory results are obtained, or the problem may be attacked systematically.

TABLE 1.—COMPUTATIONS FOR FLUME INLET.

In flume, $V = 5.98$ $h_v = 0.553$ Elevation of water surface at $0 + 00 = 57.41$
In canal, $V = 2.75$ $h_v = 0.117$ Entrance loss $= 0.1\ \Delta h_v$

$\Delta h_v = 0.436$ Water surface, reversed parabola.

Line.	Item.	Station.										
		0 + 00.	0 + 05.	0 + 10.	0 + 15.	0 + 20.	0 + 25.	0 + 30.	0 + 35.	0 + 40.	0 + 45.	0 + 50.
1	$\Delta W S$ = Drop in $W S$*	....	0.010	0.038	0.086	0.154	0.240	0.326	0.394	0.442	0.470	0.480
2	$\Delta h_v = \Delta W S \div 1.1$	....	0.009	0.035	0.079	0.140	0.218	0.296	0.357	0.401	0.427	0.436
3	$h_v = 0.117 + \Delta h_v$	....	0.126	0.152	0.196	0.257	0.335	0.413	0.474	0.518	0.544	0.553
4	V	2.75	2.85	3.13	3.55	4.07	4.64	5.15	5.52	5.77	5.91	5.97
5	Area = $Q \div V$	114.40	110.50	100.60	88.75	77.40	67.88	61.20	57.10	54.60	53.30	52.70
6	$0.5\ T$ = Half width at $W S$.	17.600	17.000	15.427	13.460	11.228	9.139	7.717	6.847	6.458	6.315	6.25
7	$0.5\ B$ = Half bottom width.	9.000	8.625	7.917	7.250	6.958	6.771	6.667	6.563	6.458	6.315	6.25
8	$0.5\ T + 0.5\ B$ = Average width	26.600	25.625	23.344	20.710	18.186	15.910	14.384	13.410	12.916	12.630	12.500
9	d = Area ÷ Ave. width	4.30	4.309	4.310	4.280	4.260	4.264	4.252	4.253	4.225	4.220	4.220
10	s_f = Friction slope	0.00015	0.00017	0.00020	0.00026	0.00034	0.00046	0.00061	0.00076	0.00083	0.00087	0.00090
11	$h_f = 5\ s_f$ (use ave. s_f)	....	0.00080	0.00090	0.00115	0.00150	0.00200	0.00270	0.00345	0.00400	0.00425	0.00445
12	Σh_f	....	0.00080	0.00170	0.00285	0.00435	0.00635	0.00905	0.01250	0.01650	0.02075	0.02520
13	$W S$ Elev. = 57.41 − $\Delta W S - \Sigma h_f$.	57.410	57.399	57.370	57.321	57.252	57.164	57.075	57.003	56.951	56.919	56.905
14	Grade = $W S$ Elev. − d	53.110	53.090	53.060	53.041	52.992	52.900	52.823	52.750	52.726	52.699	52.685
15	$0.5\ T - 0.5\ B$	8.600	8.375	7.510	6.210	4.270	2.368	1.050	0.284	....	....	....
16	Side slopes	2.000	1.945	1.744	1.447	1.000	0.554	0.247	0.067	....	....	....
17	H = Height of lining	5.330	5.295	5.270	5.234	5.228	5.265	5.287	5.305	5.274	5.236	5.205
18	$0.5\ W - 0.5\ B$ = Side slope × H.	10.660	10.310	9.210	7.575	5.228	2.920	1.305	0.354	....	....	....
19	$0.5\ W$ = 0.5 top width	19.660	18.935	17.127	14.825	12.186	9.691	7.972	6.917	6.458	6.315	6.250
20	$0.5\ W$ to nearest ½ in.	19 ft. 8 in.	18 ft. 11 in.	17 ft. 1½ in.	14 ft. 10 in.	12 ft. 2 in.	9 ft. 8½ in.	7 ft. 11½ in.	6 ft. 11 in.	6 ft. 5½ in.	6 ft. 4 in.	6 ft. 3 in.

* Neglecting friction temporarily.

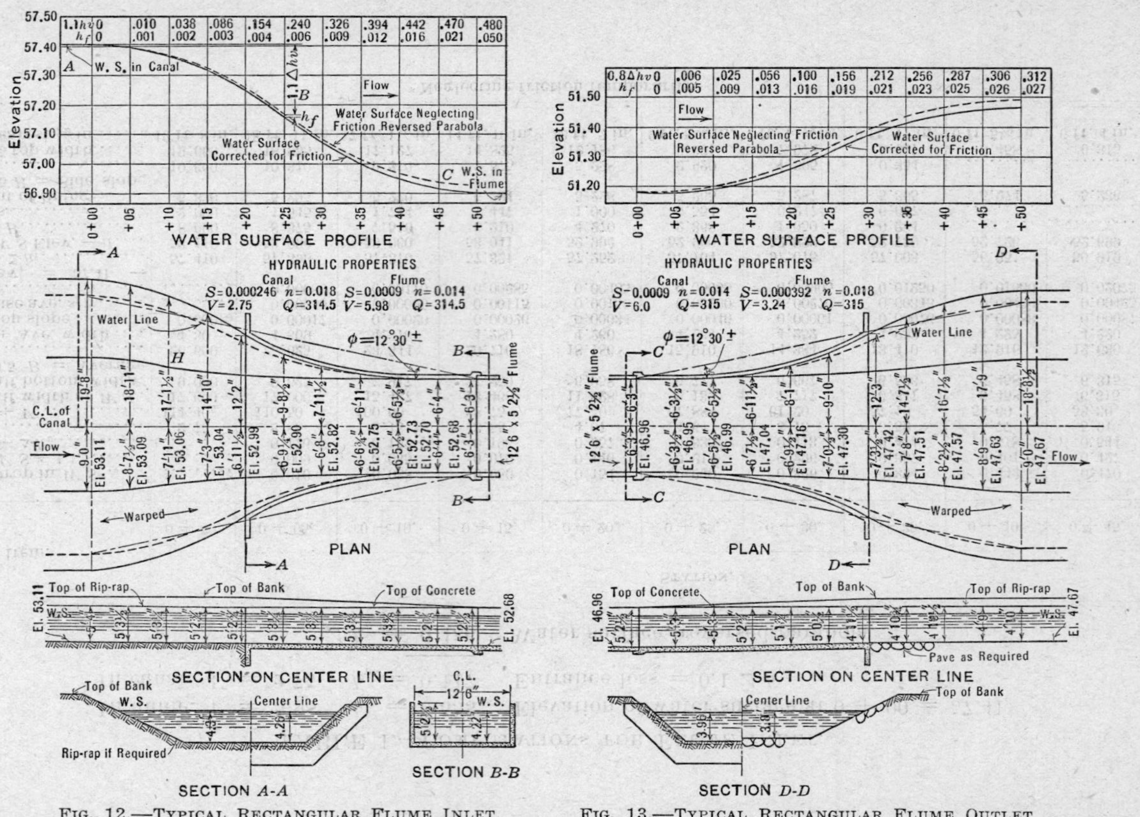

FIG. 12.—TYPICAL RECTANGULAR FLUME INLET.

FIG. 13.—TYPICAL RECTANGULAR FLUME OUTLET.

A convenient start may be made from arbitrarily sketched plans of the water line, shown dashed in Fig. 12, and of the intersection of the side slope and the bottom. The proper trial shape of these plans is a matter of judgment. The maximum angle of divergence between the water line and the axis of the structure should not be too great. A limit of 25° is recommended. These two plans having been drawn, the half top widths and half bottom widths are scaled, as recorded in Lines 6 and 7, Table 1. The sum of these half widths gives the average width from which the depth of water may be computed.

Having determined the velocity, and the shape and depth of the channel, the friction slope, s_f, and the accumulated friction head, h_f, for each point may be computed. The water-surface profile may then be corrected for friction, and the profile of the bottom of the channel computed and platted. This latter profile should be free from objectionable irregularities. Otherwise, the assumed plan may be changed as required, to increase or decrease the depth at points of irregularity. If it is not possible to secure regularity in both the plan and the bottom profile, the assumed water-surface profile may be altered. A slight change in the elevation of the water surface at a given point usually makes an appreciable change in the dimensions of the structure.

It is advisable to plat a preliminary bottom profile before computing the friction slope. The friction makes very little change in the form of the bottom profile, and labor is saved by leaving it until the profile is otherwise satisfactory. In fact, the frictional losses may often be entirely ignored without serious error.

The last six lines of Table 1 relate to the structural dimensions of the transition, and are self-explanatory. Figures for these lines need be inserted only for the design finally adopted.

Example of a Flume Outlet.—An outlet transition from a flume is designed in the same way as an inlet, the only essential difference being that the conversion loss is subtracted from Δh_v to obtain $\Delta W S$. A typical design for an outlet from a rectangular flume to an earth canal is shown in Fig. 13. The computations are shown in Table 2.

In the example shown, the length of the outlet structure is determined on the same basis as the length of the inlet structure. It is now generally conceded that for equal efficiency an inlet may be made shorter than an outlet, for the same velocity change, and it is hoped that the discussion of the subject will bring out definite rules for determining the proper length of each type of structure. The experience of the U. S. Bureau of Reclamation indicates that for properly designed outlets of the type shown in Fig. 13, a length as determined by making $\phi = 12\frac{1}{2}°$ is sufficient for ordinary purposes. Inlets are generally made the same length because: (*a*) Sharper warps are difficult to construct; (*b*) short transitions do not afford secure anchorage to the canal; (*c*) using the same length makes the forms interchangeable; and (*d*) an average divergence of $12\frac{1}{2}°$ yields a structure of pleasing appearance and reasonable cost.

Table 2 is similar to Table 1. It will be noted that an allowance of 0.2 Δh_v is made for outlet losses, which is somewhat more than might be expected from existing experimental data. Any excess in possible recovery of head over the computed recovery affords a small margin of safety against a reduction of free-board due to fouling of the canal below the flume. If there is any doubt as to the maintenance of a clean channel below the flume a greater allowance for outlet loss should be made. In extreme cases it may be desirable to assume no recovery at flume outlets, even for structures of careful design. The full actual recovering capacity of the outlet is thus made available for raising the canal water surface above normal without encroaching on the computed free-board in the flume.

Where an allowance is made for a greater outlet loss than is actually necessary, the destruction of the excess energy must be considered. If the flume velocity is relatively low, the depth being greater than the critical depth, a recovery will actually occur at the outlet, whether provided for or not. The velocity in the flume will be increased because of the excess head, and the depth decreased, making recovery necessary. If flow in the flume is at or below the critical depth no draw-down above the outlet is possible, and the excess energy must be dissipated in waves and eddies, or by a hydraulic jump, in the canal or in the outlet. The resulting eddies may cause the canal to erode.

Example of a Siphon Inlet.—The design of a transition from an earth canal with a 12-ft. bottom width to a siphon 7 ft. in diameter is illustrated in Fig. 14 and Table 3. The procedure shown differs from that recommended for flume inlets in two particulars. Part of the change in velocity is made under cover, in the transition from square to circular conduit. Any attempt to control minutely the form of this part of the transition results in construction difficulties. The transition, therefore, is usually computed only up to the head-wall. Since the velocity is still increasing at the head-wall, it is not desirable to use two equal tangent parabolas for the surface profile through the inlet. The part of the surface curve to the right of the point, J, on the water-surface profile, Fig. 14, is fixed. The curve from I to J should be drawn approximately tangent to it. However, certain other necessary irregularities at J make exact tangency unimportant, and the practice has been established of assuming a single parabola, with a vertex at I, passing through the computed water surface at J. The parabola is chosen for convenience, and not because of any supposed superiority over other forms of curves. The drop from I to J is taken as 1.1 Δh_v, the velocity at J being computed from the area of the square covered conduit.

It is considered desirable to have the top of the siphon barrel at the head-wall of the transition slightly submerged at full flow. This is thought to minimize reduction in capacity due to the introduction of air into the siphon. It is the practice of the U. S. Bureau of Reclamation to place the theoretical corner at the intersection of the head-wall and the top of the siphon barrel 1.5 Δh_v below the water level at the up-stream end of the inlet, with a minimum of 18 in. This practice makes it impracticable to construct the

TABLE 2.—COMPUTATIONS FOR FLUME OUTLET.

In flume, $V = 5.98$ $h_v = 0.553$ Elevation of water surface at 0 + 00 = 51.18

In canal, $V = 3.24$ $h_v = 0.163$ Outlet loss $= 0.2\ \Delta h_v$

$\Delta h_v = 0.390$ Water surface, reversed parabola.

Line.	Item.	STATION. 0 + 00	0 + 05	0 + 10	0 + 15	0 + 20	0 + 25	0 + 30	0 + 35	0 + 40	0 + 45	0 + 50
1	ΔWS = Rise in WS*	....	0.006	0.025	0.056	0.100	0.156	0.212	0.256	0.287	0.306	0.312
2	$\Delta h_v = \Delta WS \div 0.80$	....	0.008	0.031	0.070	0.125	0.195	0.265	0.320	0.359	0.382	0.390
3	$h_v = 0.553 - \Delta h_v$	0.553	0.545	0.522	0.483	0.428	0.358	0.228	0.233	0.194	0.171	0.163
4	V	5.97	5.92	5.80	5.57	5.25	4.80	4.30	3.87	3.53	3.32	3.24
5	Area $= Q \div V$	52.78	53.25	54.30	56.55	60.00	65.62	73.30	81.40	89.20	94.90	97.22
6	$0.5\ T$ = Half width at WS	6.250	6.292	6.458	6.890	7.824	9.300	11.232	13.210	14.800	16.010	16.600
7	$0.5\ B$ = Half bottom width	6.250	6.292	6.458	6.628	6.792	7.042	7.292	7.667	8.208	8.750	9.000
8	$0.5\ T + 0.5\ B$ = Average width	12.500	12.584	12.916	13.515	14.616	16.342	18.524	20.877	23.008	24.760	25.600
9	d = Area ÷ Ave. width	4.220	4.232	4.202	4.182	4.104	4.018	3.955	3.900	3.876	3.835	3.800
10	s_f = Friction slope	0.00090	0.00088	0.00085	0.00075	0.00063	0.00051	0.00041	0.00033	0.00027	0.00024	0.00023
11	$h_f = 5\ s_f$ (using ave. s_f)	....	0.005	0.004	0.004	0.003	0.003	0.002	0.002	0.002	0.001	0.001
12	Σh_f	....	0.005	0.009	0.013	0.016	0.019	0.021	0.023	0.025	0.026	0.027
13	WS Elev. $= 51.18 + \Delta WS - \Sigma h_f$	51.180	51.181	51.196	51.223	51.264	51.317	51.371	51.413	51.442	51.460	51.465
14	Grade = WS Elev. $- d$	46.960	46.949	46.994	47.041	47.160	47.299	47.416	47.513	47.566	47.625	47.665
15	$0.5\ T - 0.5\ B$	....	....	....	0.262	1.032	2.258	3.940	5.543	6.692	7.260	7.600
16	Side slopes	....	....	....	0.0625	0.247	0.553	0.997	1.422	1.727	1.892	2.000
17	H = Height of lining	5.210	5.255	5.244	5.231	5.146	5.041	4.958	4.895	4.876	4.751	4.845
18	$0.5\ W - 0.5\ B$ = Side slope $\times H$	....	....	....	0.326	1.270	2.790	4.940	6.960	8.420	9.000	9.690
19	$0.5\ W$ = 0.5 top width	6.250	6.292	6.458	6.955	8.062	9.832	12.232	14.627	16.628	17.750	18.690
20	$0.5\ W$ to nearest ½ in.	6 ft. 3 in.	6 ft. 3½ in.	6 ft. 5½ in.	6 ft. 11½ in.	8 ft. 1 in.	9 ft. 10 in.	12 ft. 3 in.	14 ft. 7½ in.	16 ft. 7½ in.	17 ft. 9 in.	18 ft. 8½ in.

* Neglecting friction temporarily.

TABLE 3.—COMPUTATIONS FOR SIPHON INLET.

In siphon, $V = 4.25$ $h_v = 0.280$ Elevation at water surface at $0 + 00 = 95.82$.
In canal, $V = 2.31$ $h_v = 0.083$ Entrance loss $= 0.1\,\Delta\,h_v$.

$\Delta\,h_v = 0.197$ Water surface, single parabola.

Line.	Item.	Station.									
		0 + 00	0 + 05	0 + 10	0 + 15	0 + 20	0 + 25	0 + 30	0 + 35	0 + 40†	0 + 45†
1	$\Delta\,W\,S$ = Drop in $W\,S$*	......	0.003	0.011	0.024	0.043	0.067	0.096	0.131	0.172	0.217
2	$\Delta\,h_v = W\,S \div 1.1$	......	0.002	0.010	0.022	0.039	0.061	0.088	0.119	0.156	0.197
3	$h_v = 0.083 + \Delta\,h_r$	0.083	0.085	0.093	0.105	0.122	0.143	0.171	0.202	0.239	0.280
4	V	2.310	2.34	2.44	2.60	2.80	3.03	3.32	3.60	3.92	4.24
5	Area = $Q \div V$	91.52	89.00	85.10	80.10	74.20	68.60	62.80	57.70	53.00	49.00
6	0.5 T = Half width at $W\,S$	14.800	14.200	13.050	11.600	9.800	7.650	5.950	4.550	3.800	3.500
7	0.5 B = Half bottom width	6.000	5.950	5.750	5.400	4.900	4.350	4.000	3.600	3.500	3.500
8	0.5 T + 0.5 B = Ave. width	20.800	20.150	18.800	17.000	14.700	12.100	9.950	8.120	7.300	7.000
9	d = Area ÷ Ave. width	4.400	4.415	4.545	4.710	5.045	5.670	6.310	7.080	7.260	7.000
10	s_f = Friction slope.	0.00011	0.00012	0.00013	0.00014	0.00016	0.00018	0.00022	0.00030	0.00045	0.00074
11	$h_f = 5\,s_f$ (using ave. s_f)	....	0.001	0.001	0.001	0.001	0.001	0.001	0.001	0.002	0.003
12	$\Sigma\,h_f$	....	0.001	0.002	0.003	0.004	0.005	0.006	0.007	0.009	0.012
13	$W\,S$ Elev. = 95.82 − $\Delta\,W\,S - \Sigma\,h_f$	95.820	95.815	95.807	95.793	95.773	95.748	95.717	95.682	95.639	95.591
14	Grade = $W\,S$ Elev. − d	91.420	91.400	91.262	91.083	90.728	90.078	89.407	88.602	88.379	88.591
15	0.5 T − 0.5 B	8.800	8.250	7.300	6.200	4.900	3.300	1.950	0.950	0.300	....
16	Side slopes	2.000	1.870	1.600	1.316	0.970	0.582	0.309	0.134	0.038	....
17	H = Height of lining	5.790	5.800	5.950	6.130	6.480	7.370	8.280	9.320	10.560	11.800
18	0.5 W − 0.5 B = Side slope × H	11.580	10.850	9.520	8.060	6.280	4.280	2.560	1.250	0.402	....
19	0.5 W = 0.5 top width	17.580	16.800	15.270	13.460	11.180	8.630	6.560	4.850	3.900	3.500
20	0.5 W to nearest ½ in.	17 ft. 7 in.	16 ft. 10 in.	15 ft. 3½ in.	13 ft. 5½ in.	11 ft. 2 in.	8 ft. 7½ in.	6 ft. 6½ in.	4 ft. 10 in.	3 ft. 11 in.	3 ft. 6 in.

* Neglecting friction temporarily.

† Grade elevations at Stations 0 + 40 and 0 + 45 are arbitrarily changed to 87.60 and 86.60 to obtain a smooth grade curve.

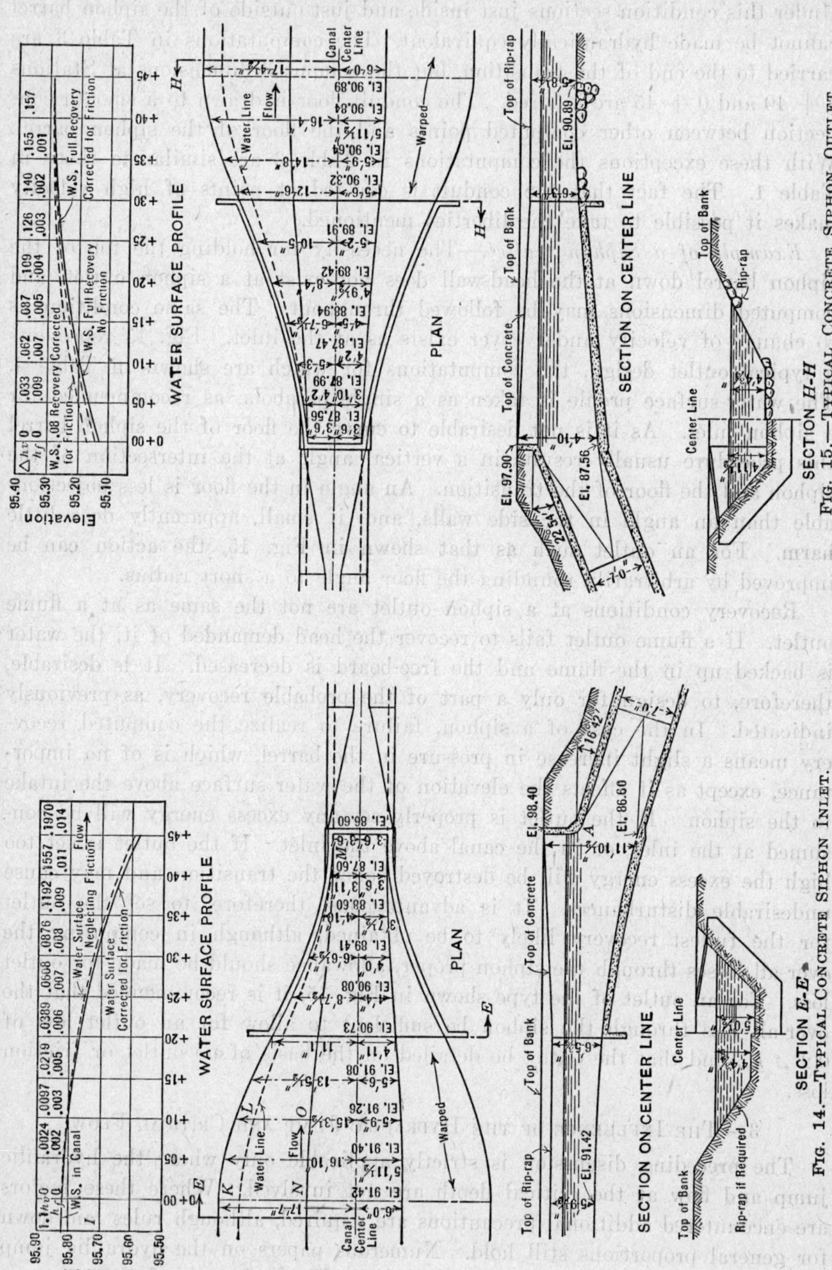

Fig. 14.—Typical Concrete Siphon Inlet.

Fig. 15.—Typical Concrete Siphon Outlet.

lower end of the transition strictly in accordance with the computations. Under this condition sections just inside and just outside of the siphon barrel cannot be made hydraulically equivalent. The computations in Table 3 are carried to the end of the transition, but the computed dimensions at Stations 0 + 40 and 0 + 45 are ignored. The conduit floor is drawn to a smooth connection between other computed points and the floor of the siphon barrel. With these exceptions the computations in Table 3 are similar to those in Table 1. The fact that the conduit is covered at points of high velocity makes it possible to take the liberties mentioned.

Example of a Siphon Outlet.—The necessity for holding the top of the siphon barrel down at the head-wall does not exist at a siphon outlet, and computed dimensions may be followed throughout. The same condition as to change of velocity under cover exists as at the inlet. Fig. 15 represents a typical outlet design, the computations for which are shown in Table 4. The water-surface profile is taken as a single parabola, as recommended for a siphon inlet. As it is not desirable to curve the floor of the siphon barrel this procedure usually results in a vertical angle at the intersection of the siphon and the floor of the transition. An angle in the floor is less objectionable than an angle in the side walls, and, if small, apparently does little harm. For an outlet such as that shown in Fig. 15, the action can be improved by arbitrarily rounding the floor angle to a short radius.

Recovery conditions at a siphon outlet are not the same as at a flume outlet. If a flume outlet fails to recover the head demanded of it, the water is backed up in the flume and the free-board is decreased. It is desirable, therefore, to design for only a part of the probable recovery, as previously indicated. In the case of a siphon, failure to realize the computed recovery means a slight increase in pressure in the barrel, which is of no imporance, except as it affects the elevation of the water surface above the intake to the siphon. If the outlet is properly set any excess energy will be consumed at the inlet, or in the canal above the inlet. If the outlet is set too high the excess energy will be destroyed below the transition and may cause undesirable disturbances. It is advantageous, therefore, to set the outlet for the fullest recovery likely to be obtained, although in computing the over-all losses through the siphon proper, allowance should be made for outlet loss. For an outlet of the type shown in Fig. 15, it is recommended that the over-all loss through the siphon be sufficient to allow for an outlet loss of $0.2\ \Delta\ h_v$, and that the outlet be detailed on the basis of no outlet or friction loss.

3.—The Influence of the Hydraulic Jump and Critical Flow

The preceding discussion is strictly applicable only where the hydraulic jump and flow at the critical depth are not involved. Where these factors are encountered additional precautions are required, although rules laid down for general proportions still hold. Numerous papers on the hydraulic jump have been published in the last few years. The influence of these factors on the design of transitions was discussed by the writer in 1920.* No im-

* "The Hydraulic Jump and Critical Depth in the Design of Hydraulic Structures," *Engineering News-Record,* November 25, 1920, p. 1034.

TABLE 4.—COMPUTATIONS FOR SIPHON OUTLET.

In siphon, $V = 3.93$ $h_v = 0.240$ Elevation, water surface, Station 0 + 45 = 95.29.

In canal, $V = 2.31$ $h_v = 0.083$ Outlet loss neglected.

$\Delta h_v = 0.157$ Water surface, single parabola.

Line.	Item.	STATION.									
		0 + 00	0 + 05	0 + 10	0 + 15	0 + 20	0 + 25	0 + 30	0 + 35	0 + 40	0 + 45
1	$\Delta h_v = \Delta W S$ = Rise in $W S$*	......	0.033	0.062	0.087	0.109	0.126	0.140	0.149	0.155	0.157
2	$h_v = 0.240 - \Delta h_v$	0.240	0.207	0.178	0.153	0.131	0.114	0.100	0.091	0.085	......
3	V	3.93	3.65	3.38	3.14	2.90	2.71	2.54	2.42	2.34	......
4	Area = $Q \div V$	52.95	57.00	61.42	66.30	71.60	77.05	82.00	86.00	89.00	91.52
5	$0.5\,T$ = Half width at $W S$	3.500	4.100	4.970	6.110	7.500	9.250	11.050	12.730	14.030	14.800
6	$0.5\,B$ = Half bottom width	3.500	3.850	4.150	4.450	4.800	5.150	5.500	5.800	5.950	6.000
7	$0.5\,T + 0.5\,B$ = Ave. width	7.000	7.950	9.120	10.560	12.300	14.400	16.550	18.530	19.980	20.800
8	d = Area ÷ Ave. width	7.570	7.180	6.730	6.280	5.820	5.360	4.950	4.640	4.450	4.400
9	$W S$ Elev. = 95.133 + $\Delta W S$	95.133	95.166	95.195	95.220	95.242	95.259	95.273	95.282	95.288	95.290
10	Grade = $W S$ Elev. − d	87.563	87.986	88.465	88.940	89.422	89.909	90.323	90.642	90.838	90.890
11	$0.5\,T - 0.5\,B$	......	0.250	0.820	1.660	2.700	4.100	5.550	6.930	8.080	8.800
12	Side slopes	......	0.348	0.122	0.264	0.463	0.766	1.122	1.493	1.815	2.000
13	H = Height of lining	10.337	9.694	8.995	8.300	7.598	6.891	6.257	5.938	5.742	5.690
14	$0.5\,W - 0.5\,B$ = Side slope × H	......	0.337	1.098	2.190	3.520	5.280	7.025	8.880	10.430	11.380
15	$0.5\,W$ = 0.5 top width	3.500	4.187	5.248	6.640	8.320	10.430	12.525	14.680	16.380	17.380
16	$0.5\,W$ to nearest ½ in.	3 ft. 6 in.	4 ft. 2 in.	5 ft. 3 in.	6 ft. 7½ in.	8 ft. 4 in.	10 ft. 5 in.	12 ft. 6 in.	14 ft. 8 in.	16 ft. 4 in.	17 ft. 4½ in.

* Friction and outlet loss ignored in detailing outlet structure. In computing total drop through siphon allow for outlet loss = $0.2\,\Delta h_v + \Sigma h_f$.

portant new data on this subject have been developed by the U. S. Bureau of Reclamation.

It may be well to emphasize again the fact that the unexpected and unnecessary introduction of critical flow conditions is a frequent source of trouble in transitions. This condition is illustrated in the outlet shown in Fig. 5. Although the total length of this structure is 100 ft., the velocity actually increases to a point near the lower end, where it suddenly "jumps" to approximately canal velocity. The normal depth in both the tunnel and the canal is above critical, and, if proper attention had been given to the detailed dimensions, the jump would have been avoided and the efficiency of the outlet increased. In addition, heavy wave action in the canal would have been avoided.

A situation of this kind is not likely to escape notice with the plan of computation recommended in this paper. However, it is essential that any approach to the critical depth be carefully noted. Before attempting to plan an important transition the designer should be thoroughly familiar with the phenomenon of critical flow.

Impact Troubles in Long Siphons.—As previously mentioned, the excess energy in a pipe line is consumed in the canal above the inlet, in the inlet, or in the upper end of the pipe. If the excess fall is small it is usually absorbed in a moderate increase in velocity in the canal, which does little harm. With greater fall, racing in the canal may become serious, and a check may be required at or near the intake to the siphon. The destruction of energy is thus transferred to the inlet.

In irrigation conduits, pipe lines are seldom controlled by gates or valves, the fall provided being only that required to maintain flow at maximum capacity. In the interest of conservatism the allowance for losses is usually greater than the actual requirement. If the pipe line is long the excess fall may be too great to be entirely absorbed in the inlet, and the water will race down the pipe for a distance at part depth, to be checked suddenly where it meets the back-water from the outlet. In large siphons of considerable length, operating at part capacity, this condition often results in serious vibrations. Because of certain manifestations this phenomenon is frequently referred to as "air trouble," and many unsuccessful attempts have been made to relieve the vibrations by the installations of vents, or by revision of the inlet structure. This is not a transition problem and is treated here only because it is often considered to be related to the inlet structure.

An example of a pipe line operating in this way is shown in Fig. 16. This siphon, which is on the King Hill Project, in Idaho, was constructed by a predecessor of the U. S. Bureau of Reclamation at a time when the project was expected to embrace a larger area than that ultimately developed. The capacity is considerably in excess of the actual requirements. The conditions shown in Fig. 16 were observed in July, 1925, with a flow of 120 sec-ft. With this discharge a heavy rumbling and a very noticeable vibration were noted some distance down the pipe from the inlet.

The disturbance appeared to lie wholly below the hydraulic gradient computed from the outlet structure as a control. This is in accordance with

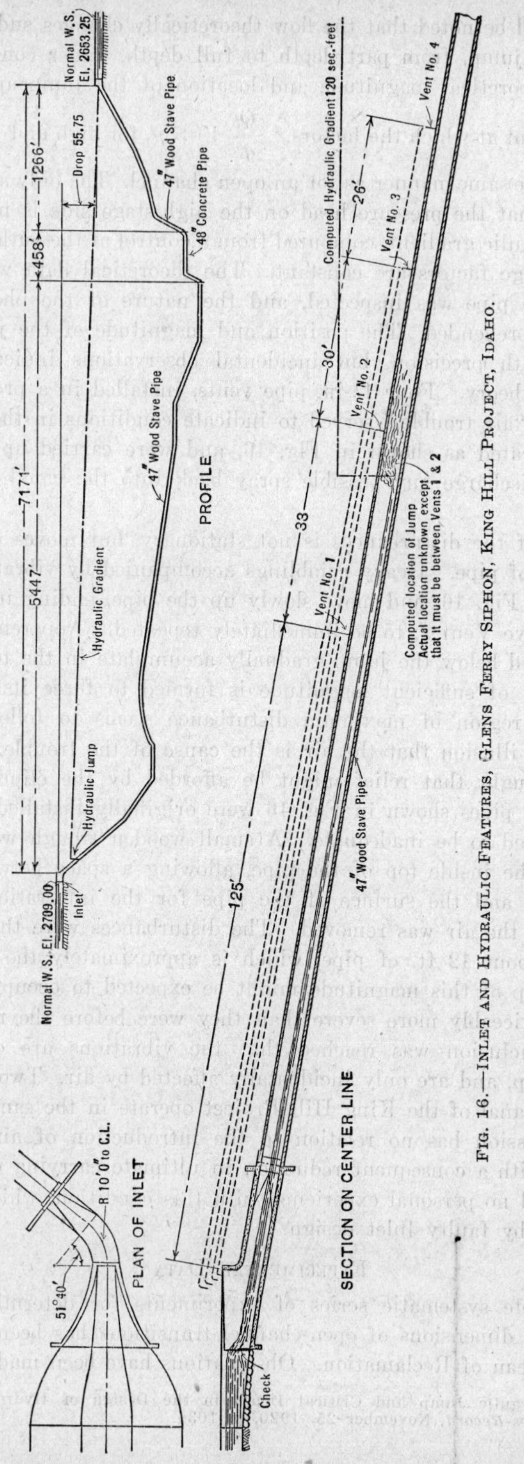

FIG. 16.—INLET AND HYDRAULIC FEATURES, GLENS FERRY SIPHON, KING HILL PROJECT, IDAHO.

theory. It will be noted that the flow theoretically changes suddenly through the hydraulic jump, from part depth to full depth, under considerable pressure. The theoretical magnitude and location of the jump are obtained by finding the point at which the factors,* $\frac{Q}{g} V + p$, for high and low-stage flow, are equal, in the same manner as for an open channel. The only special features in a pipe is that the pressure head on the high-stage side is measured down from the hydraulic gradient, computed from a control at the outlet, and that all other high stage factors are constant. The theoretical data were not available when the pipe was inspected, and the nature of the phenomenon was not fully comprehended. The position and magnitude of the jump were not determined with precision, but incidental observations indicate close conformity with theory. Four 1½-in. pipe vents, installed in a previous attempt to relieve the "air trouble," served to indicate conditions in the pipe. These vents were located as shown in Fig. 16, and were carried up the pipe and arranged to discharge any possible spray back into the canal over the inlet head-wall.

The seat of the disturbances is not stationary, but moves over a considerable length of pipe. Heavy rumblings accompanied by vibrations originate below Vent 3, Fig. 16, and move slowly up the pipe, ending in an explosion at a point above Vent 2, to be immediately repeated. Apparently, small air-bubbles released below the jump gradually accumulate in the top of the pipe until a pocket of sufficient magnitude is formed to force its way back up stream. The region of maximum disturbance seems to follow the bubble, producing the illusion that the air is the cause of the trouble.

It was thought that relief might be afforded by the elimination of the air. The vent pipes shown in Fig. 16 were originally installed for this purpose, but proved to be inadequate. A small wooden trough was temporarily bolted along the inside top of the pipe, allowing a space between the edges of the trough and the surface of the pipe for the infiltration of air, and apparently all the air was removed. The disturbances were then confined to a length of about 12 ft. of pipe, which is approximately the length that a hydraulic jump of this magnitude might be expected to occupy. The vibrations were noticeably more severe than they were before the removal of the air. The conclusion was reached that the vibrations are caused by the hydraulic jump, and are only incidentally affected by air. Two other siphons on the main canal of the King Hill Project operate in the same way.

This discussion has no relation to the introduction of air into siphons at full flow with a consequent reduction in ultimate carrying capacity. The writer has had no personal experience with this condition, which is supposed to be caused by faulty inlet design.

Experimental Data

No complete systematic series of experiments for determining the correct form and dimensions of open-channel transitions has been attempted by the U. S. Bureau of Reclamation. Observations have been made on a limited

* See "Hydraulic Jump and Critical Depth in the Design of Hydraulic Structures," *Engineering News-Record*, November 25, 1920, p. 1034.

number of existing structures, some of which have been mentioned previously. The results of others are shown on Fig. 17. These tests consist principally of measurements of outlet and entrance losses.

Methods and Precision.—The approximate nature and inconsistency of some of the data are readily apparent. For example, the abrupt inlet, (*a*), Fig. 17, shows practically no entrance loss, whereas the comparatively slender inlet, (*b*), shows a loss of 46% of the change in velocity head. Practically all the head losses shown on Fig. 17 were obtained from level readings with the end of a level rod held on the water surface. There is always sufficient oscillation to destroy the precision of readings taken in this way, especially where the fall to be measured is small. Even with comparatively smooth flow, maximum fluctuations of as much as an inch may occur. An error of ½ in. would materially affect many of the coefficients shown on Fig. 17.

Heads within the closed conduits were obtained by drilling through the siphon barrels and inserting ⅛-in pipe nipples to which a ¼-in. air-hose was connected. In concrete pipes the holes were first closed with wooden plugs which were afterward drilled for the nipples. The water pressure was determined by holding the free end of the hose at such a level that it was on the point of overflowing. Although this method is not extremely accurate the results obtained were definite. Water was allowed to run freely from the hose, except when the elevation was actually being determined, to eliminate temperature and air effects. All taps were inserted with the pipes flowing full, and the inside ends of the holes could not be inspected.

The dimensions were taken from the plans from which the conduits and structures were built, and were not in all cases checked in the field. Although it is believed that the errors resulting from this procedure are practically unimportant, they undoubtedly detract from the scientific value of the data.

It is believed that the data obtained are sufficiently reliable to be valuable for the purpose for which they were taken. Where the elevation of the water surface is uncertain, due to fluctuation, there is little practical purpose in finding the mean of the fluctuations with precision, however desirable such a procedure may be from a scientific point of view. It is believed that the assembled data show a general trend that is worthy of study.

Flume Inlet Losses.—It will be noted that of the twenty-nine sets of observations in Fig. 17, shown for ten flume inlets, only three observations show a loss greater than 0.1 Δh_v, and only one greater than 0.14 Δh_v. In a number of cases there appeared to be no loss, and the average loss is about 0.04 Δh_v. In several cases the observed loss actually appeared to be negative, probably due to error or inaccuracy in measurements. All such losses are marked "None" on Fig. 17. If the negative values are included, the average observed loss is approximately zero.

Siphon Inlet Losses.—Of the five tests recorded for four siphon inlets, three show inlet losses of zero. One of the remaining two observations shows a loss of 0.33 Δh_v, and one of 0.15 Δh_v, making the average for all five approximately 0.1 Δh_v. As previously explained, all the excess head in a siphon is concentrated at the inlet. This makes it difficult to secure a rating

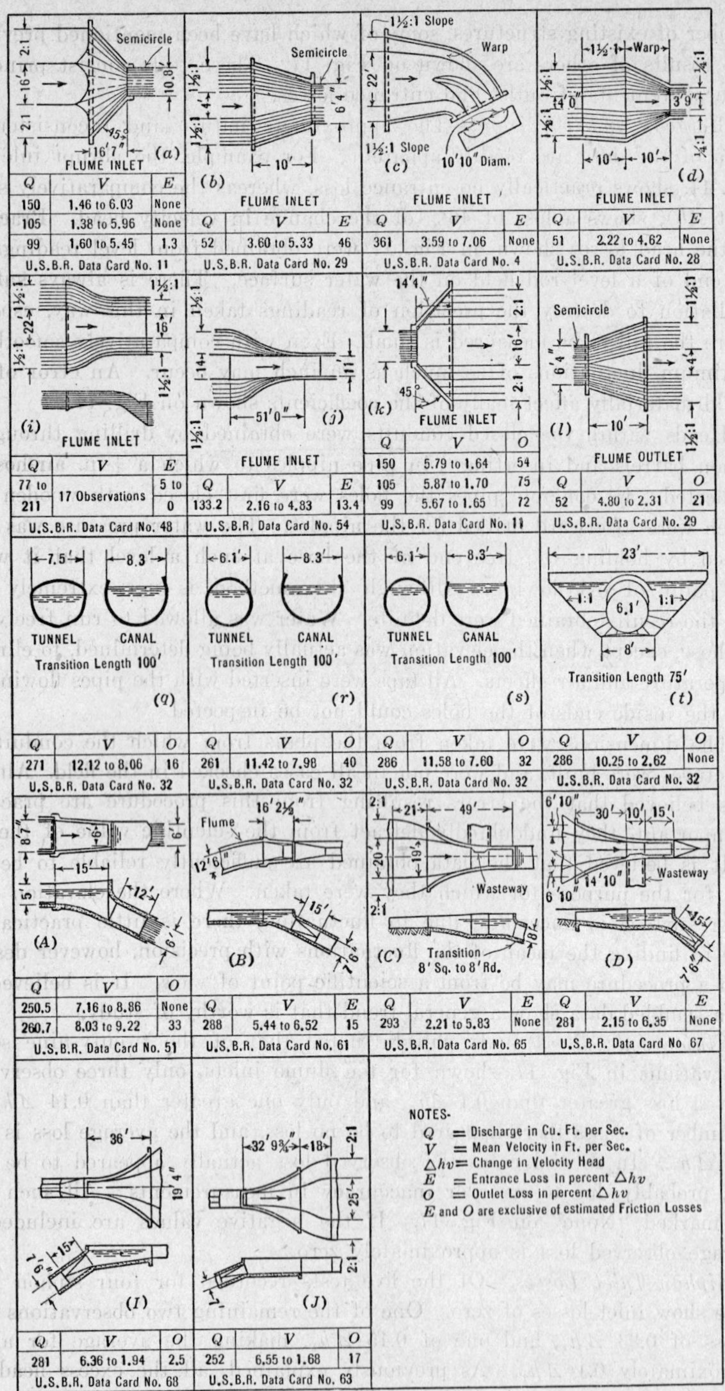

FIG. 17.—TABULATED DATA ON TRANSITION

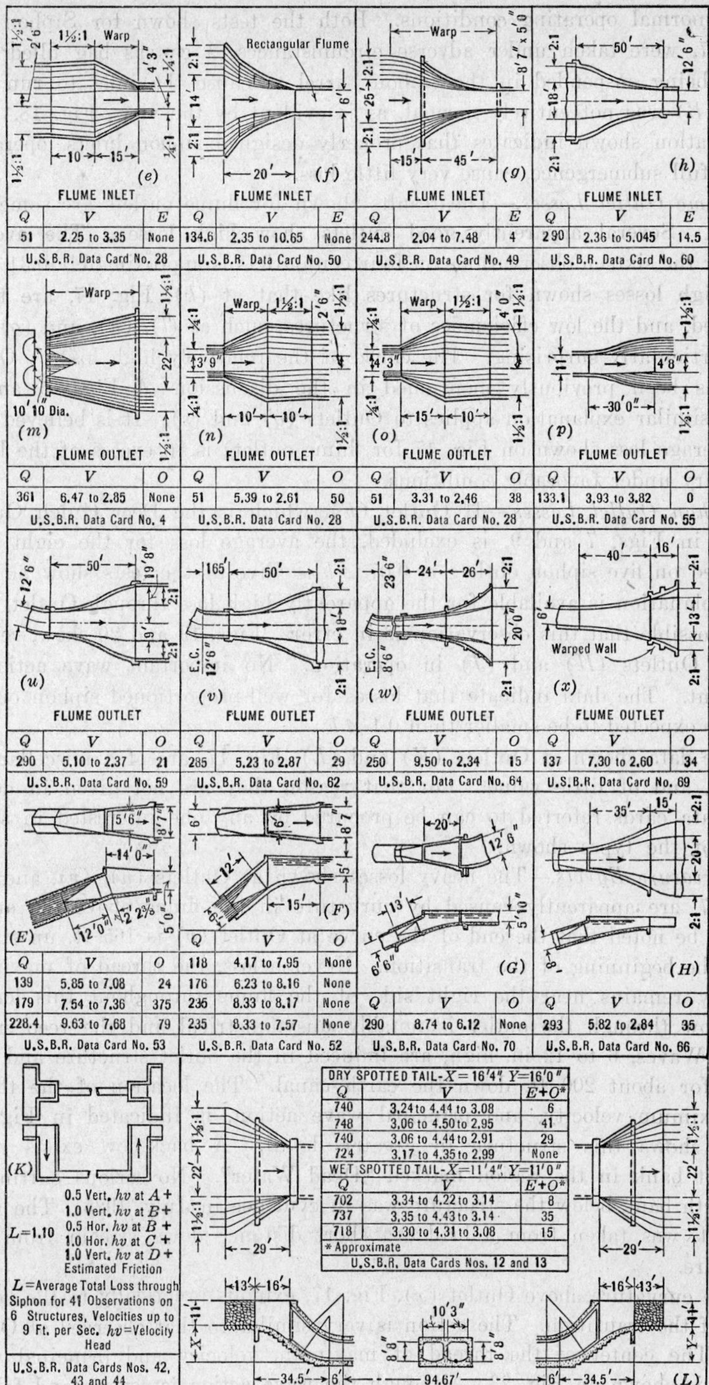

(e) FLUME INLET
Q V E
51 2.25 to 3.35 None
U.S.B.R. Data Card No. 28
(f) FLUME INLET
Rectangular Flume
Q V E
134.6 2.35 to 10.65 None
U.S.B.R. Data Card No. 50
(g) FLUME INLET
Q V E
244.8 2.04 to 7.48 4
U.S.B.R. Data Card No. 49
(h) FLUME INLET
Q V E
290 2.36 to 5.045 14.5
U.S.B.R. Data Card No. 60
(m) FLUME OUTLET
10′10″ Dia.
Q V O
361 6.47 to 2.85 None
U.S.B.R. Data Card No. 4
(n) FLUME OUTLET
Q V O
51 5.39 to 2.61 50
U.S.B.R. Data Card No. 28
(o) FLUME OUTLET
Q V O
51 3.31 to 2.46 38
U.S.B.R. Data Card No. 28
(p) FLUME OUTLET
Q V O
133.1 3.93 to 3.82 0
U.S.B.R. Data Card No. 55
(u) FLUME OUTLET
Q V O
290 5.10 to 2.37 21
U.S.B.R. Data Card No. 59
(v) FLUME OUTLET
Q V O
285 5.23 to 2.87 29
U.S.B.R. Data Card No. 62
(w) FLUME OUTLET
Q V O
250 9.50 to 2.34 15
U.S.B.R. Data Card No. 64
(x) FLUME OUTLET
Warped Wall
Q V O
137 7.30 to 2.60 34
U.S.B.R. Data Card No. 69
(E)
Q V O
139 5.85 to 7.08 24
179 7.54 to 7.36 375
228.4 9.63 to 7.68 79
U.S.B.R. Data Card No. 53
(F)
Q V O
118 4.17 to 7.95 None
176 6.23 to 8.16 None
236 8.33 to 8.17 None
235 8.33 to 7.57 None
U.S.B.R. Data Card No. 52
(G)
Q V O
290 8.74 to 6.12 None
U.S.B.R. Data Card No. 70
(H)
Q V O
293 5.82 to 2.84 35
U.S.B.R. Data Card No. 66
(K)
0.5 Vert. hv at A +
1.0 Vert. hv at B +
0.5 Hor. hv at B +
L=1.10 1.0 Hor. hv at C +
1.0 Vert. hv at D +
Estimated Friction
L=Average Total Loss through Siphon for 41 Observations on 6 Structures, Velocities up to 9 Ft. per Sec. hv=Velocity Head
U.S.B.R. Data Cards Nos. 42, 43 and 44
DRY SPOTTED TAIL-X=16′4″ Y=16′0″
Q V E+O*
740 3.24 to 4.44 to 3.08 6
748 3.06 to 4.50 to 2.95 41
740 3.06 to 4.44 to 2.91 29
724 3.17 to 4.35 to 2.99 None
WET SPOTTED TAIL-X=11′4″ Y=11′0″
Q V E+O*
702 3.34 to 4.22 to 3.14 8
737 3.35 to 4.43 to 3.14 35
718 3.30 to 4.31 to 3.08 15
* Approximate
U.S.B.R. Data Cards Nos. 12 and 13
(L)

Losses, U. S. Bureau of Reclamation.

under normal operating conditions. Both the tests shown for Siphon (*A*) Fig. 17, were taken under adverse circumstances, a canvas bag filled with water being suspended in the siphon barrel to cause the inlet to run full. Inlet (*B*) was not entirely normal, as is evident by the view, Fig. 18. The information shown indicates that properly designed siphon inlets, operating under full submergence, cause very little loss.

Flume Outlet Losses.—The results shown for flume outlets are somewhat erratic. Several apparently good outlets show high losses. The average loss for the sixteen observations on fourteen outlets is approximately 0.31 Δh_v. The high losses shown for structures like that at (*k*), Fig. 17, are to be expected, and the low efficiencies of structures, such as (*l*), (*n*), and (*o*), are not particularly surprising. The cause of the relatively high loss at Outlet (*r*) has been previously mentioned in the discussion of Figs. 5 and 8, and a similar explanation applies to Outlets (*q*) and (*s*). It is believed that the average loss shown on Fig. 17 for flume outlets is in excess of the losses necessary under favorable conditions.

Siphon Outlet Losses.—If Outlet (*E*), which is the Deer Gulch Outlet, shown in Figs. 7 and 9, is excluded, the average loss for the eight tests recorded on five siphon outlets is 0.07 Δh_v. Five of the tests show no loss. No explanation is available for the apparently high loss through Outlet (*H*). It is possible that this observation is in error. Figs. 19 and 20 show, respectively, Outlets (*H*) and (*J*) in operation. No important wave action is apparent. The data indicate that losses for well-proportioned siphon outlets may be expected to be smaller than 0.1 Δh_v.

The data shown at Outlets (*K*) and (*L*), Fig. 17, are of a miscellaneous nature, and of little value. For that reason they are not given in detail. The data cards referred to can be procured by any one interested in structures of the types shown.

Curvature Effects.—The heavy losses shown at Outlets (*u*), (*v*), and (*x*), Fig. 17, are apparently caused by curvature in the flume above the outlet. It will be noted that the end of the curve at Outlet (*v*) is 165 ft. up stream from the beginning of the transition. Nevertheless, the thread of maximum velocity remains near the right side of the flume throughout this length. The flow through the outlet is notably unsymmetrical and the recovery is poor. Waves, 6 to 12 in. high, are induced in the outlet structure and continue for about 200 ft. down the earth canal. The location of the thread of maximum velocity, and principal wave action, is indicated in Fig. 22, which shows this structure in greater detail. A back-flow exists along the left bank in the region marked "Dead Water". No serious cutting of the earth bank below the structure was in evidence in July, 1925. The view, Fig. 21, was taken from a bridge a short distance down stream from this structure.

The curvature above Outlet (*x*), Fig. 17, extends practically to the beginning of the transition. The action is very similar to that observed at Outlet (*v*). The center of the thread of maximum velocity and principal wave action is shown on Fig. 23. Although the wave action is severe, and follows

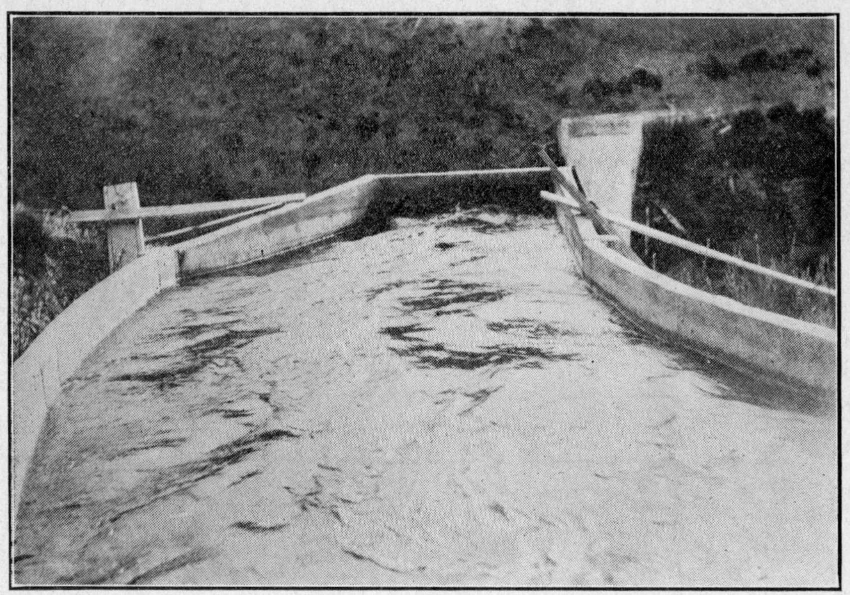

Fig. 18.—Inlet, Little Concrete Siphon, King Hill Project.

Fig. 19.—View of Outlet, Toana Siphon, King Hill Project, $Q = 293$ Second-Feet.

FIG. 20.—VIEW OF OUTLET, LITTLE PILGRIM SIPHON, KING HILL PROJECT, $Q = 252$ SECOND-FEET.

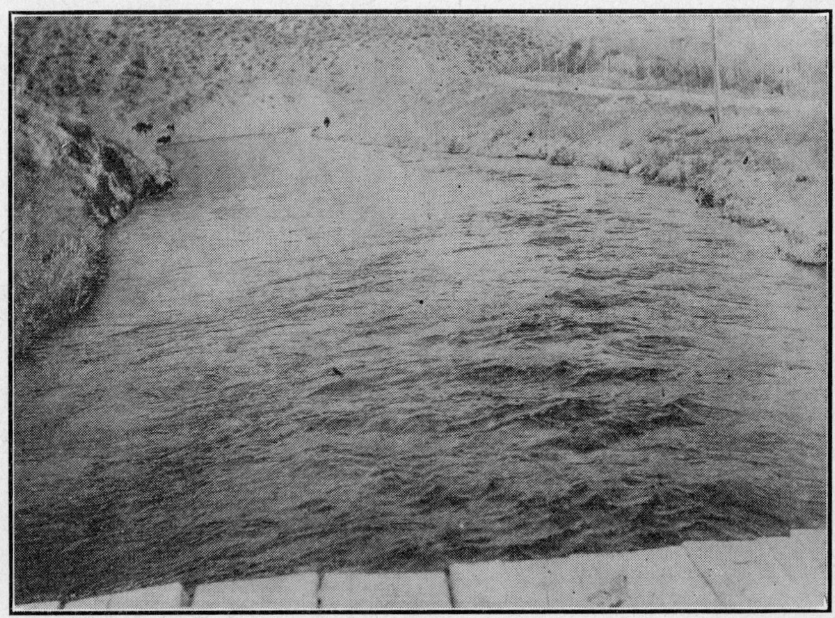

FIG. 21.—OUTLET, ONE-MILE FLUME, KING HILL PROJECT, SHOWING WAVE ACTION DUE TO CURVATURE IN FLUME ABOVE OUTLET.

the right bank of the earth canal closely, this structure operated several seasons with no apparent tendency to cut. Then cutting began suddenly and a 4-ft. thickness of material was eroded from the first 100 ft. of bank in a day. The eroded bank was temporarily protected, and later lined with concrete.

Similar conditions exist at Outlet (u), Fig. 17, but the disturbances, for some reason, are less severe. It is possible that the disturbing effect is partly offset by a reversal of curvature.

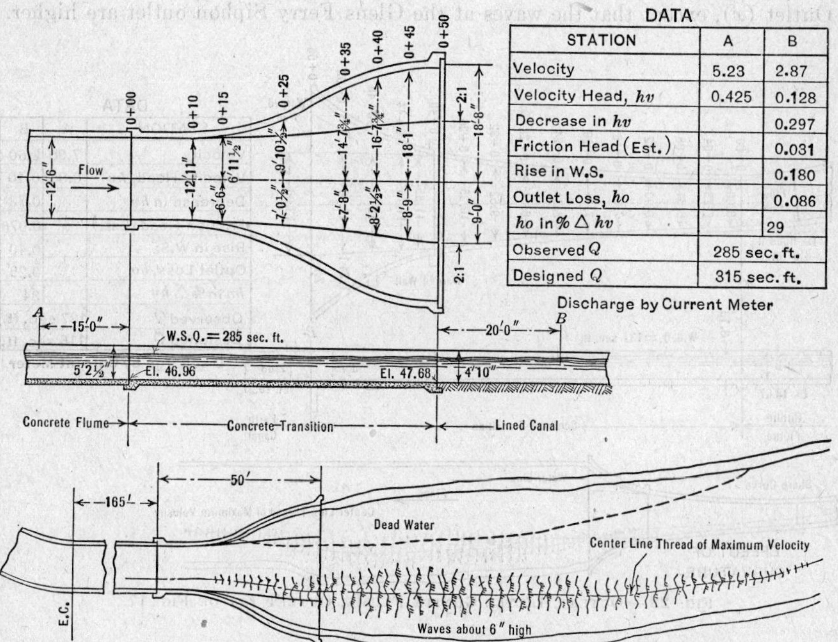

Fig. 22.—Outlet, One-Mile Flume, Outlet (v) of Fig. 17.

The flume above Outlet (w) is also curved, and the velocities are materially higher than for Outlets (u), (v), and (x). Nevertheless, the wave action is not particularly severe and the recovery is fairly good, the reason for which is not apparent. The data at hand are not sufficient to permit the determination of the cause of curvature effects. In fact, it is not definitely known that the unsatisfactory action of these outlets is entirely due to curvature. It is understood that other observers have noticed a tendency for the line of high velocity to be deflected to one side or the other at outlets from straight channels, the direction of deflection being apparently accidental.

Few comparable observations on outlets from flumes with and without curvature are available. The flume above Outlet (p), Fig. 17, is straight, but the velocities are low. Outlets (k), (l), (m), (n), and (o) are of such different forms as to render comparisons useless. Outlets (q), (r), and (s), as previously mentioned, involve the hydraulic jump. Outlet (t) appears to substantiate the assumption that the current deflection is due to curvature.

The tunnel above this structure is straight, and the transition appears to work efficiently, with moderately high velocities.

The action of the siphon outlets shown on Fig. 17 tends to disprove the theory of instability of outlet flow. All the pipes leading up to these outlets are straight in plan, and in no case was there evidence of unsymmetrical flow. However, the Glens Ferry Siphon, a profile of which is shown on Fig. 16, has a horizontal curve a short distance from its down-stream end, and the action at the outlet is very similar to that observed at Flume Outlet (x), except that the waves at the Glens Ferry Siphon outlet are higher.

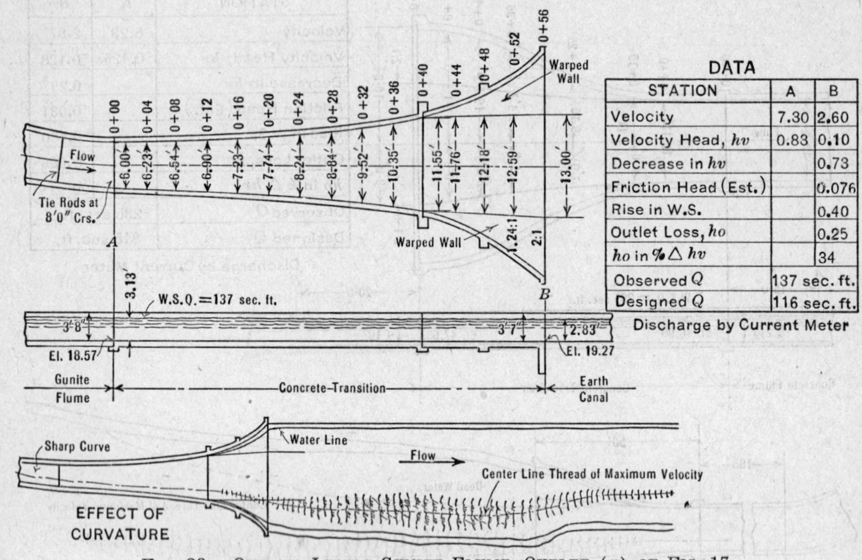

DATA

STATION	A	B
Velocity	7.30	2.60
Velocity Head, hv	0.83	0.10
Decrease in hv		0.73
Friction Head (Est.)		0.076
Rise in W.S.		0.40
Outlet Loss, ho		0.25
ho in % $\triangle hv$		34
Observed Q	137 sec. ft.	
Designed Q	116 sec. ft.	

Discharge by Current Meter

FIG. 23.—OUTLET, LITTLE GUNITE FLUME, OUTLET (x) OF FIG. 17.

SUMMARY

The present state of the art of designing transition structures, as practiced by the U. S. Bureau of Reclamation, may be summarized, as follows:

1.—Sufficient fall must be allowed at all inlet structures to accelerate the flow and to overcome frictional and entrance losses.

2.—The theoretical recovery at an outlet structure is reduced by frictional and outlet losses.

3.—At open channel outlets a small factor of safety may be obtained by setting the transition for less than its maximum recovering capacity, but erosion below the structure may be slightly increased.

4.—At siphon outlets a small factor of safety may be obtained and erosion avoided by setting the transition for more than its assumed recovering capacity.

5.—Simple designs may be prepared by adapting the details of previous designs, known to be satisfactory, if proper allowance is made for loss of head.

6.—Important structures, where velocities are high, must be carefully designed to conform to a smooth theoretical water surface. Sharp angles must be avoided.

7.—Horizontal curvature in the conduit above an outlet appears to reduce its efficiency, and to produce objectionable cutting velocities in the canal below.

8.—The transition loss through an inlet of the type shown in Fig. 12 or Fig. 14, is likely to be less than 0.05 Δh_v. An allowance of 0.1 Δh_v is safe for use in designing.

9.—The outlet loss at a properly designed transition of the type shown in Figs. 13 and 15, may be expected to be less than 0.1 Δh_v, unless the conduit above the structure is curved. An allowance of 0.2 Δh_v is safe for use in designing.

10.—No definite data as to the best form of water-surface profile, best form of structure, or most efficient length of transition, are available.

11.—Special care is required where the critical depth is approached or where the hydraulic jump is involved.

12.—The disturbances often observed in long, uncontrolled siphons, at part capacity, are not caused by entrained air, but by the hydraulic jump in the pipe.

DISCUSSION

H. B. Muckleston,* M. Am. Soc. C. E. (by letter).—The flow of water in an open channel of variable section is such a complicated phenomenon that a really exact analysis by mathematical methods is more an ideal than a possibility. By making various assumptions of more than doubtful validity, it is quite possible to arrive at a result, seemingly correct to any number of decimal places, but which is not in fact any more accurate than the assumptions on which it is founded. Present knowledge of hydraulic phenomena is entirely empirical and the resulting formulas bristle with coefficients intended to account for the many factors that are either unknown in their action or else not susceptible of measurement. Such important factors as roughness of perimeter and shape of cross-section cannot be defined in any physical unit of measurement; their influence can only be expressed by some numerical factor, chosen in the light of individual or collective experience. In view of this condition, a paper such as this, based as it is on the observation of an organization with a long and diverse experience, cannot help but be a valuable addition to engineering knowledge.

Surface Curve.—If the flow through a transition is certain to be always well above the critical depth, or, in case of an accelerating transition, whether it is or not, it is the writer's experience that time and labor are saved, with no sacrifice beyond the appearance of accuracy, if the energy gradient be assumed outright as a beginning. The hydraulic dimensions of the flume or siphon and of the canal are supposed to be known; and, therefore, the elevation of the energy gradient above the bottom of the channel is known at two points and the assumption of the total loss fixes, at once, the elevation of the bottom at the end of the transition.

The total loss of energy in the transition is usually divided, as in the paper, into friction losses, so-called, and conversion losses. In both cases they are really the losses due to the formation of eddies and whorls in the water, and the real cause of most of these is to be found in the irregularities of the surface, whether minute as in the friction loss or relatively large as in the conversion loss. In analysis it may be convenient to separate these two forms of the same thing, but the writer does not believe that this can be done in experimental determinations. For a reasonably uniform cross-section, the friction loss in a given channel can be predicted with some approach to certainty; but little is known about the law governing friction loss in channels of varying cross-section, even when the variation follows some simple mathematical rule, and still less when it follows no ascertainable rule whatever.

Very little is known about conversion losses even in circular channels. Whatever the law may be, experience with closed channels seems to show that it is not the same for converging and diverging channels; but whether these laws, if they were known, would hold for open channels is doubtful. Probably they would not, as the conditions are radically different. For this

* Cons. Engr., Vancouver, B. C., Canada.

reason, complicated analysis of friction and conversion losses does not seem a justifiable labor. The losses can only be calculated by a cut-and-try process, and the final result depends so much on assumptions that it is quite as logical to assume the losses in the first place if one has a little experience to guide him. When something like finality has been reached, there may be more logic in detailed calculation, but it is doubtful.

With the energy gradient fixed, the water-surface profile follows and the remainder of the process is a matter of adjustment by cut-and-try to obtain smooth curves for the sides and bottom. The first selection of a surface profile may result in unsuitable shapes and dimensions, in which case a new profile must be assumed and the process repeated. If a raised floor is necessary, as mentioned later, this will fix the elevation of one point on the floor and more or less determine the profile; or if a hydraulic notch is required, it will fix the cross-section at one point and influence those throughout the transition.

Velocity Head.—The apparent velocity head is somewhat less than the real velocity head. From a few gaugings, in which the distribution of velocity over the cross-section had been observed, the writer has estimated that the difference may amount to from 1 to 6%, with a mean value of about 4 per cent. The law of the increase is not known, but as the shapes of the section and the mean velocity at various points is the last thing known, the exact law is not of importance. The writer suggests that a mean increase of about 4% would be close enough. It is unimportant in the lower velocities but more so in the higher. For a velocity of 8 ft. per sec., it is 0.04 ft., which is more than the total friction loss in the whole transition.

Accelerating Transitions.—A well-designed transition should prevent the occurrence of harmful velocities up stream in the canal at all stages. If a transition is designed with only the conditions at full supply in mind, the surface drop is the difference in the velocity heads plus whatever is allowed for loss, and this fixes the elevation of the bottom at the end of the transition. If, now, conditions at less than full supply, say, at half depth, are investigated, and a back-water curve is calculated, beginning at water level in the flume, for that stage, it may happen that the water level thus found for the entrance to the transition is far below the theoretical water level for that stage in the canal. The result is that acceleration begins a long way up stream and scouring velocity may be attained before the water enters the transition. To avoid this condition, it is necessary to constrict the entrance of the water in such a way that acceleration does not begin until the transition is reached for all stages of supply. To do this absolutely for all stages would involve expensive form work for the sides and bottom, which would not be justified by the accuracy of the calculations. A notch can be designed with straight sides and walls that, in theory, will be correct for any two stages and, in practice, sufficiently correct for all stages. If the end velocity in the transition is above the critical velocity for all stages of supply, it is not very material which stages are chosen as the bases for designing the notch; the result is a true, or very nearly true, hydraulic notch, and the bottom will be at the same level as the bottom of the canal.

If the end velocity is below the critical for all stages, the two stages should be full supply and about half depth (not half supply). The resulting notch will have its bottom raised above the level of the canal bottom. Direct calculation is not practicable, and a cut-and-try process brings results more quickly.

If the end velocity is above the critical at full supply stage and below it at lower stages, the two stages chosen should be: For the higher, that stage at which the end velocity passes the critical; and, for the lower, about half that depth. There may be some acceleration in the canal at full supply, but probably not sufficient to be dangerous. If the discharge at which the end velocity passes the critical is less than about half supply, the transition may be designed as a hydraulic notch. In this case, a jump will develop in the flume at the lower discharges, but that will be of no great importance.

When the end velocity is below the critical at full supply and above the critical at lower stages (a condition common in siphon transitions), the upper design stage should be chosen as full supply and the lower at that stage where the end velocity passes through the critical. In extreme cases the notch may be quite narrow and its bottom may be depressed below the level of the canal. When this occurs, uncomfortable acceleration may be expected at very low stages and some rip-rap may be needed as a cure.

Decelerating Transitions.—If the flow in the high velocity channel is at less than critical velocity, the process of design is much the same as for accelerating transitions. The length should be much greater than is necessary for accelerating transitions. In fact, experience indicates that converging channels may be quite obtuse without great loss in efficiency; but if even moderately obtuse angles are used for diffusing channels, the water shows a tendency to stick to the center for a long distance down stream.

Decelerating transitions should be investigated for conditions at partial supply. It is quite possible for a transition that acts with satisfaction at full supply to give strong evidence of scour at lower stages. The reason is that all the deceleration does not take place in the designed length, and there is still an excess of velocity remaining when the water leaves the transition.

If the flow in the high velocity channel is below the critical depth, it is almost impossible to design a transition that will surely effect a smooth deceleration through the critical region. A jump is almost certain to occur; and as it involves a loss of head it is better to design for the loss. Otherwise, the result may be an overflowing flume.

Siphon Transitions.—At siphon inlets the design follows the same general principles as for flumes. Outlets may be designed on the same principles as flume outlets if the velocity is not greater than the critical velocity for the same quantity in the canal. If it is greater, the deceleration should be accomplished under pressure until the critical region is comfortably passed.

The length of the diffusing section may be shortened without sacrifice of efficiency if the flow through the diffuser is forced to take place along spiral lines. As shown by Mr. F. zur Nedden,* the efficiency of a polished cone

* "Induced Currents of Fluids," *Transactions*, Am. Soc. C. E., Vol. LXXX (1916), p. 844.

with an angle of 8° 20′ was raised from 88.3 to 98.9% by so doing, and it is probable that a similar result would follow in a cone of much larger angle. If this is true, the same efficiency might be expected from a relatively obtuse cone with spiral flow as from an acute cone with straight flow.

F. THEODORE MAVIS,* ASSOC. M. AM. SOC. C. E. (by letter).—The flow of water through the more common types of transition sections can be calculated quite accurately by the methods which the author has discussed. Occasionally, one sees an unusual type of transition section which cannot be investigated by the analytical methods available at present, and the studies must be carried on almost entirely in the hydraulic laboratory. It may be desirable to rely, in part at least, on experimental methods if the transition sections are of unusual shape or if the velocities exceed the critical velocity.

One of the most unique examples of tunnel inlet transitions which has come to the writer's attention is that for the proposed flood diversion tunnel at Nürnberg, Germany. This tunnel is designed to divert 12 400 cu. ft. per sec. from the Pegnitz River in times of extreme floods in order to protect the "Alstadt", which is one of the oldest and most picturesque towns in Germany. Just above the tunnel inlet, 2 800 cu. ft. per sec. is to be diverted into power canals and into the old river channel through the city.

Under the direction of Professor Theodore Rehbock, extensive tests for this project were made in the Hydraulic Laboratory of the Technische Hochschule in Karlsruhe on eleven models of inlet transitions, two models of outlet transitions, and three combined models of inlet and outlet connected by a short piece of tunnel. Figs. 24, 25, and 26 show sketches and views of nine of the proposed inlet structures which were studied in the laboratory. All linear dimensions are in meters and all velocities, in meters per second in the full-sized structures as indicated by tests of the models. Most of the models were made to a scale of 1:100.

The inlet transition which was proposed in the original plans is essentially a sector of a right circular cone with side slopes of 1 on 9 and a central angle of about 70° between retaining walls. Fig. 24 (*a*) shows a plan of this inlet and Fig. 24 (*b*) a longitudinal section with the water surface in the prototype determined from the model experiments. The flow through this inlet section was marked with high waves which lapped the roof of the tunnel. Under these conditions of flow there is grave danger of air trouble which has already been discussed by the author. The changes in the velocity of flow through the section were not smooth and gradual; there were abrupt changes near the entrance to the tunnel and below the sill or weir crest where the flow passed the critical stage. The velocity changed from 1.03 m. per sec. in the approach channel to 2.92 m. per sec. at the weir crest. A hydraulic jump occurred below the weir. The velocity changes to 5.24 m. per sec. in the tunnel, with a minimum of 1.17 m. per sec. in transition. The slope of the water surface changes from 1 on 10 in transition to 1 on 700 in the tunnel. These velocity changes are shown in Fig. 24 (*c*).

* Urbana, Ill.

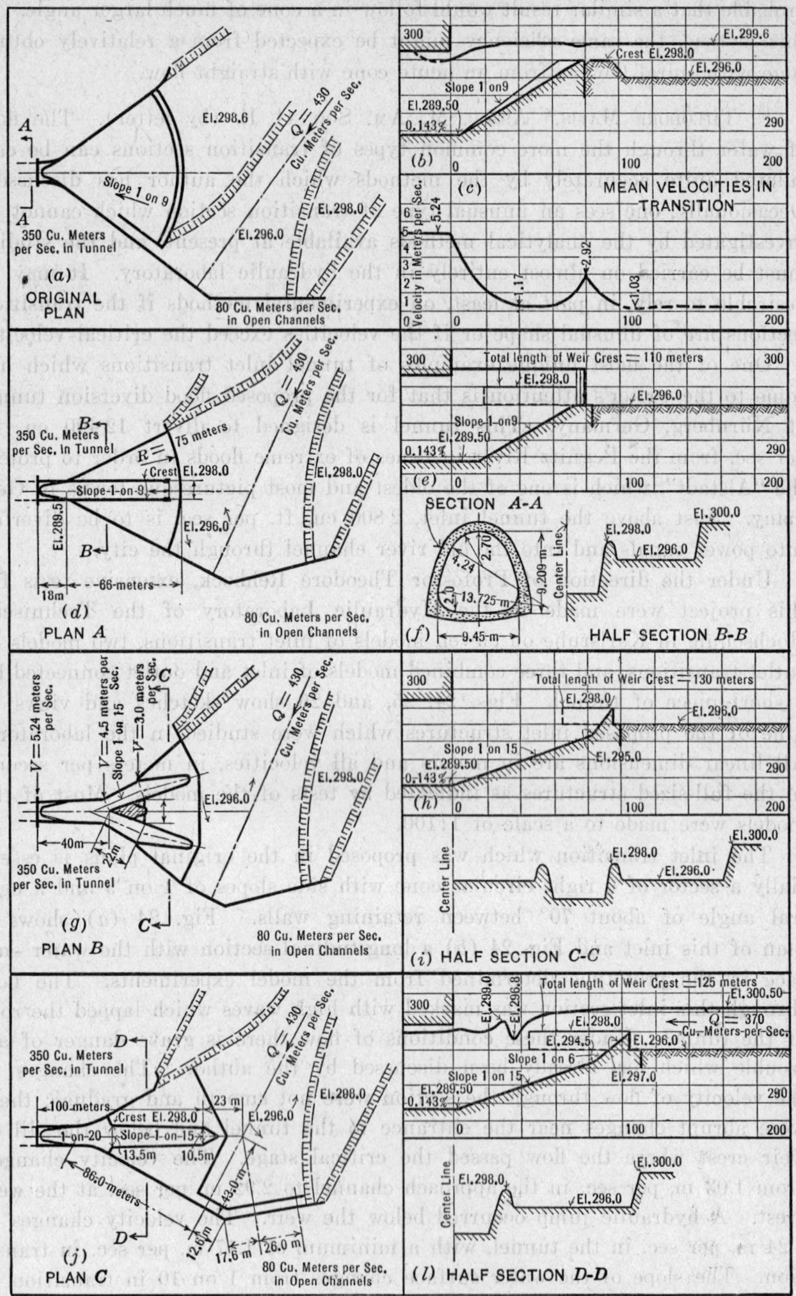

FIG. 24.—PLANS FOR DIVERSION OF PEGNITZ RIVER FLOODS AT NÜRNBERG, GERMANY.

FIG. 25.—VIEW OF FLOW THROUGH MODEL FOR PLAN *A*.

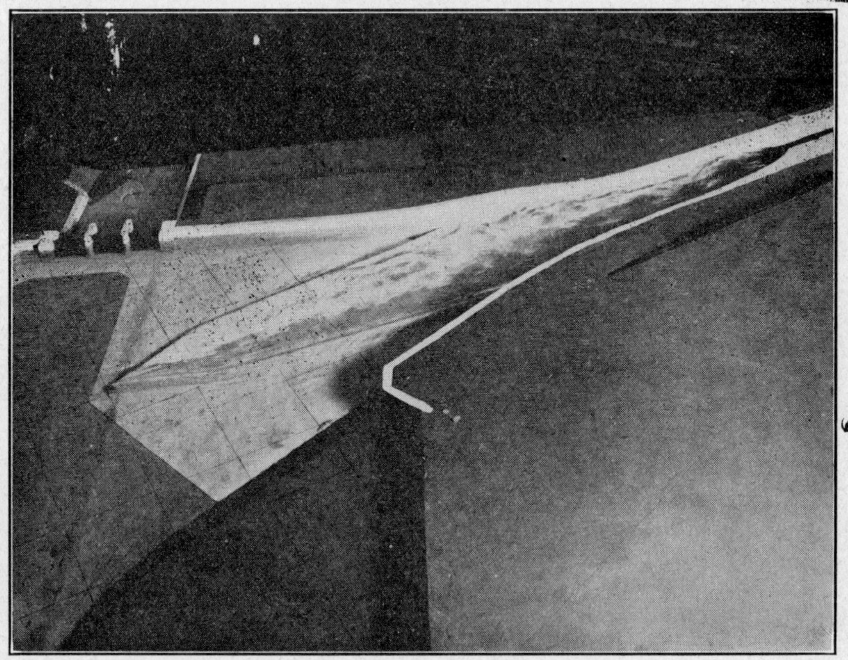

FIG. 26.—VIEW OF FLOW THROUGH MODEL FOR PLAN *E*.

The subsequent plans provided that the bottom of the river channel was to be extended to the full width of the inlet transition section. Plan *A*, Fig. 24 (*d*), (*e*), and (*f*), provided for a collecting trough 35 ft. wide and 180 ft. long, with sides or sills 6.6 ft. above the bottom of the approach channel. The bottom of this trough was sloped upward (1 on 9) from the bottom of the tunnel to the level of the river bed, but the bottom of the transition section outside the trough walls was level and at the elevation of the river bottom (Elevation 296.0). The flood water spilled over the sides of this trough and was then directed into the tunnel.

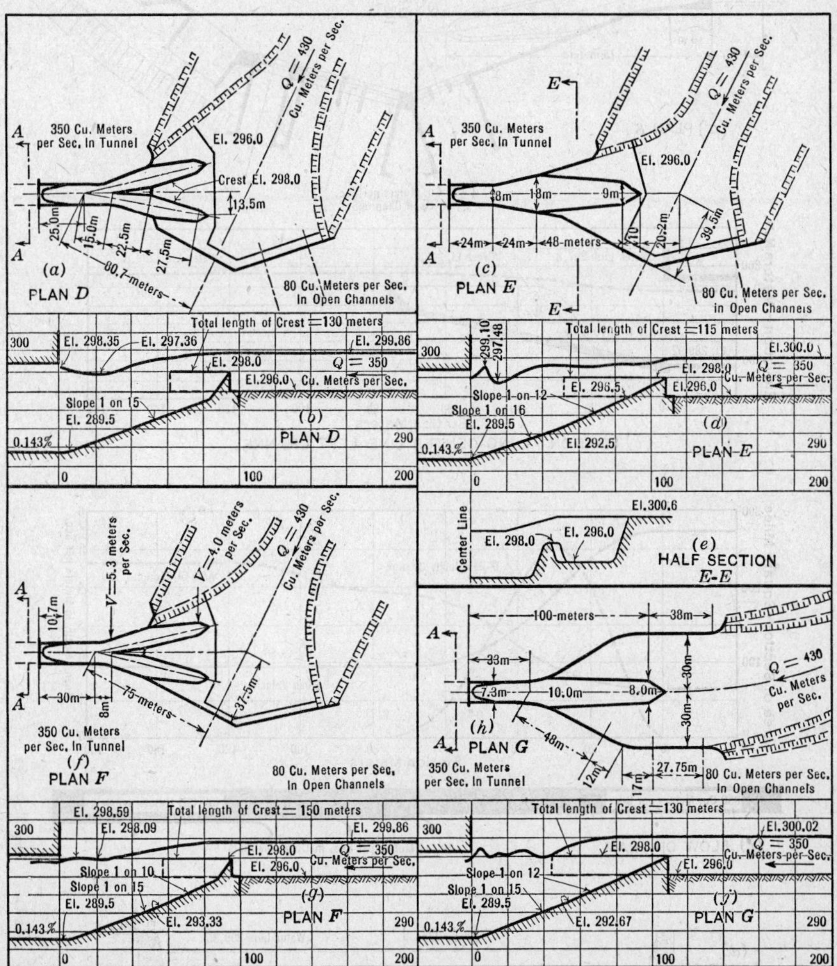

Fig. 27.—Plans for Diversion of Pegnitz River Floods at Nürnberg, Germany.

The flow through the inlet of Model *A* was not satisfactory because, although there was a smooth flow in the approach channel, strong eddies were formed near the point where the sills of the trough joined the side walls

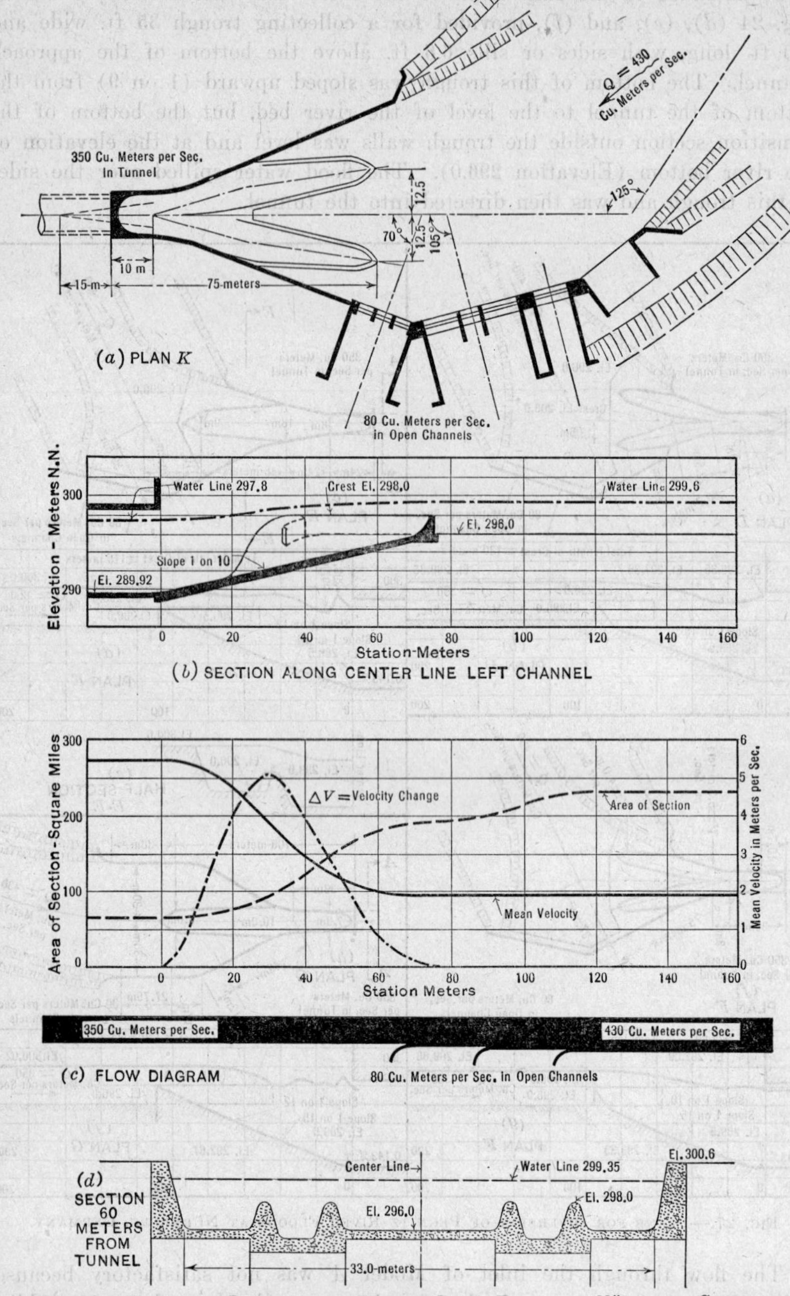

FIG. 28.—PLANS FOR DIVERSION OF PEGNITZ RIVER FLOODS AT NÜRNBERG, GERMANY.

Fig. 29.—View of Flow Through Model *H*.

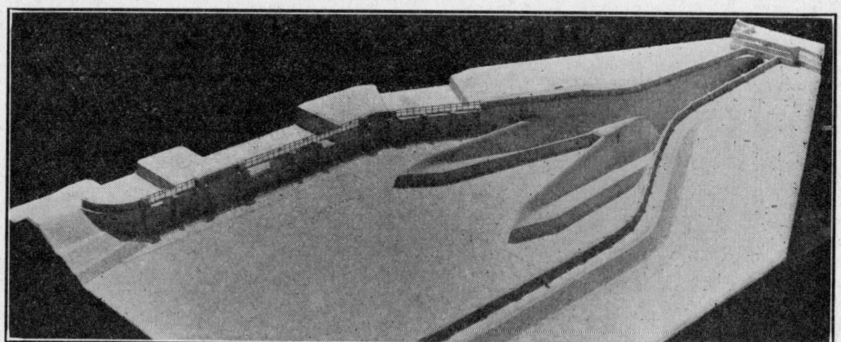

Fig. 30.—View of Most Satisfactory Model.

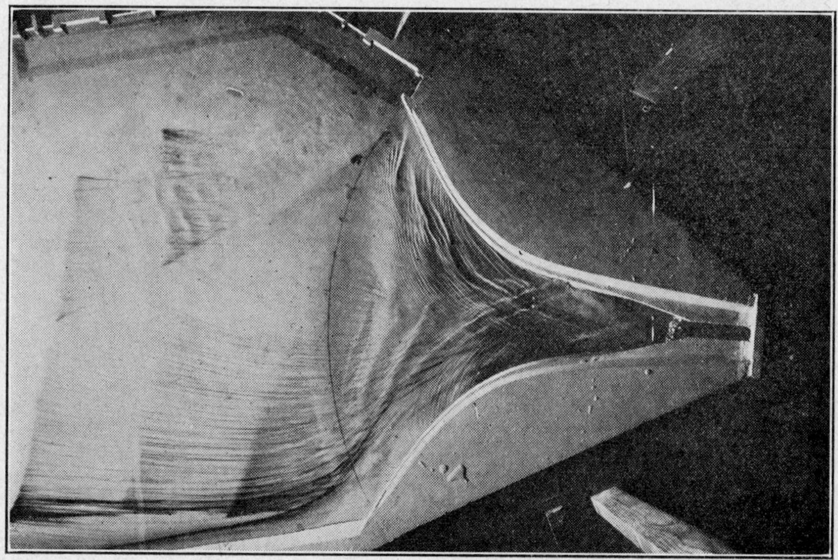

Fig. 31.—View of Flow Through Model *J*.

of the transition section. These eddies restricted the effective discharge area near the tunnel mouth and caused a high wave just above the tunnel entrance. Fig. 25 shows the flow through the model during a test run. The eddies and the wave in the approach to the tunnel are clearly visible.

Plan *B* (Fig. 24 (*g*), (*h*), and (*i*)), shows a double trough section in which each trough is tapered toward the up-stream end. The flow through this transition was much smoother than that through the one originally proposed or through the transition of Model *A*. The waves that form at the up-stream end of the "ships" can be eliminated by pointing the "prows".

Plan *C* (Fig. 24 (*j*), (*k*), and (*l*)), Plan *E* (Fig. 27 (*c*), (*d*), and (*e*)), and Plan *G* (Fig. 27 (*h*) and (*i*)), are single-trough transitions which have the same general shape but different sized troughs. The flow in the model for Plan *E* was much smoother than in that for Plan *C*, but was not considered satisfactory. In Plan *G* the flow was smoother than in Plans *C* or *E*, with strong eddies near the junction of the weirs and side walls. Fig. 26 shows the flow through the inlet of Model *E* during a test run. It will be noted that, although the flow is smoother than that shown in Fig. 25, it is not wholly free from eddies and that a wave is formed in the transition section just above the entrance to the tunnel.

Plan *D* (Fig. 27 (*a*) and (*b*)), Plan *F* (Fig. 27 (*f*) and (*g*)), Plan *K* (Fig. 28), and Plan *H* (Fig. 29) provide for double-trough transitions similar to Plan *B*. In the model for Plan *D* there was observed a smooth flow and no large waves. The troughs of Plan *K* are 50 ft. shorter than those of Plan *H* (Fig. 29) and the direction of flow into the transition is more nearly axial in the latter than in the former plan. The flow through Model *H* (Fig. 29) was very smooth and there were no appreciable waves or eddies in the transition section for the maximum rate of discharge corresponding to 12 400 cu. ft. per sec. Fig. 30 shows a model of the inlet, which was finally recommended as the most satisfactory one of those studied in the laboratory.

Fig. 28 (*c*) shows the cross-sectional areas, mean velocities, and velocity changes in the transition of Plan *K* and Fig. 28 (*b*) shows the water surface determined from the tests. It is interesting to compare these with Fig. 24 (*b*) and (*c*), which show the water surface and mean velocities in the transition section originally proposed. Remembering that sudden changes in velocity are accompanied by energy transformations and shock losses, it is not surprising to find that the flow in the model of the inlet shown in the original plan was not as smooth as that in the model of the inlet shown in Plan *K*.

Fig. 31 shows the flow in the model of Plan *J*, which is a modification of Model *A*. Crystals of potassium permanganate were scattered in the channel to show the direction of flow of the bottom water filaments and produced the streaks which are shown in the photograph. The flow just above the mouth of the tunnel is near the critical velocity and there is an abrupt drop in the water surface just above the portal. The maximum in the transition section of Model *J* represented a velocity of 31 ft. per sec. in the prototype, while the maximum velocity in the transition section of Plan *H* (Fig. 29) represented a velocity of 19 ft. per sec.

It is said that although the single-trough sections were more satisfactory than the transition proposed in the original plan, the heads required to produce a maximum discharge of 12 400 cu. ft. per sec. were greater than those required to produce the same discharge in the double-trough sections. The waves were smaller and the eddies were weaker in the double-trough models than in the single-trough models.

The transition which was recommended below the tunnel outlet is 450 ft. long, 200 ft. wide at the lower end, and slopes upward from the bottom of the tunnel to the canal, which is at a grade 24.6 ft. above the bottom of the tunnel.* The tests conducted for a discharge corresponding to 12 400 cu. ft. per sec. indicated that there was practically a complete recovery of head although the velocity was reduced from 17.4 to 6.9 ft. per sec. The observed water surface in the model showed a very satisfactory agreement with that calculated by methods similar to those discussed by the author.

The writer is indebted to Professor Rehbock, of the Technische Hochschule, in Karlsruhe, for permission to present this abstract of reports† and test data in his personal files and for the photographs presented herewith.

W. H. R. Nimmo,‡ Assoc. M. Am. Soc. C. E. (by letter).—The valuable paper presented by the author is of special interest to the writer who, during 1919, was in charge of the construction of a diversion project of 450 sec-ft. capacity, involving a decelerating transition from a concrete flume to a canal excavated in earth. The properties of the flume were: Grade of floor, 0.00303%; width, 9 ft.; sides, vertical; normal depth of water at full capacity, 5 ft.; average velocity, 10 ft. per sec.; velocity head, 1.56 ft.; and Kutter's $n = 0.015$. The corresponding properties for the canal were: Grade, 0.000757%; bottom width, 24 ft.; slope of sides, 1 on 1.25; normal depth, 4.32 ft.; average velocity, 3.5 ft. per sec.; velocity head, 0.19 ft.; and Kutter's $n = 0.026$.

The excavation was in firm clayey soil which would permit of the building of warped side slopes in concrete without back forms. In order to avoid turbulence, the writer proposed to construct a warped transition, 132 ft. in length, allowing for a loss of head of 0.17 ft., or 13% of the total change in velocity head from flume to canal. This length of transition would have been more than double the minimum length allowed by the author's rule (page 1435), but the whole distance need not have been in concrete. The allowance for regain of head was perhaps rather liberal, but it was intended also to have slightly increased the free-board on the flume for a short distance in case the full amount of regain was not realized. It was also proposed that the area of the cross-section occupied by water should vary proportionally to the change in kinetic energy. In view of the evidence presented by the author, it seems that the proposed transition would have operated satisfactorily.

* See "Die Wasserbaulaboratorien Europas", V. D. I. Verlag, Berlin, 1926, p. 108.

† Th. Rehbock, "Gutachten Über den Entwurf für die Regulierung der Pegnitz zur Beseitigung der Ueberschwemmungen in Nürnberg," May, 1914; "Nachtrag-Gutachten, etc.," December 20, 1914, with supplementary reports of June 21, 1915, and February 16, 1916.

‡ Chf. Draftsman, Main Roads Comm., Brisbane, Queensland, Australia.

FIG. 32.—VIEW OF TRANSITION WITHOUT FLOW.

FIG. 33.—VIEW OF TRANSITION IN OPERATION.

The Department responsible for the design of the transition, however, held the view that it would not be possible to regain any head and, therefore, a transition—or rather a stilling-pool—was built in accordance with a design supplied to the writer. The transition as actually constructed is shown in plan, and longitudinal section in Fig. 34 and is shown empty and full in Figs. 32 and 33. To satisfy riparian rights provision was made for delivering water to the river, when necessary, by means of pipes leading from the bottom of two outlet pits built in the floor of the transition, the horizontal dimensions of each pit being 5 ft. 9 in. by 3 ft. 0 in. The sections in Fig. 34 illustrate the theoretical conditions for flows of 450 cu. ft. per sec. and 200 cu. ft. per sec., respectively. In these sections, d denotes depth; E, energy line (depth plus velocity head); and the suffixes, n, c, and a, refer, respectively, to the normal, critical, and actual depth.

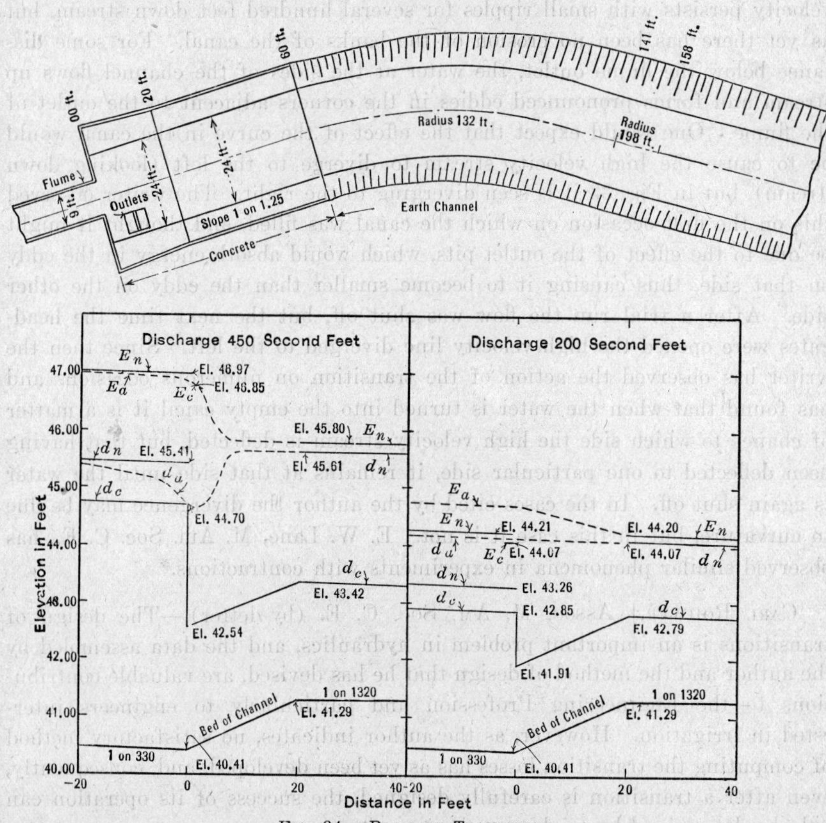

Fig. 34.—Plan of Transition.

For a flow of 450 sec-ft., it is seen that a considerable drop in the energy line must take place in passing through the transition, but since at the entrance to the transition E_c is below E_n, the actual water surface will follow the line, d_a, passing through the critical depth and then jumping to the normal depth for the canal. In Fig. 33, which shows a flow of approximately 450 sec-ft., the drawing down of the water surface in the flume and the turbulence due to the ensuing jump are clearly seen. The transition is, therefore, not an efficient stilling device when flowing full, since it actually increases the velocity in the flume from 10 to 11.75 ft. per sec. before the jump takes place.

For a flow of 200 sec-ft., E_c at the entrance is below E_n at the outlet and, consequently, the water surface cannot drop to the critical depth. In this case there is no jump and the actual water surface backs up in the flume on some back-water curve, such as d_a, which accounts for the observed fact that the transition operates without great turbulence at the lower rates of flow.

The flume is straight for a considerable distance up stream from the transition, and the canal curves to the right (looking down stream) at a point 40 ft. beyond the down-stream end of the transition. The stream of high velocity persists with small ripples for several hundred feet down stream, but as yet there has been no erosion of the banks of the canal. For some distance below the flume outlet, the water at the sides of the channel flows up stream and forms pronounced eddies in the corners adjacent to the outlet of the flume. One would expect that the effect of the curve in the canal would be to cause the high velocity stream to diverge to the left (looking down stream), but in Fig. 33 it is seen diverging to the right. The writer observed this on the first occasion on which the canal was filled, and thought it might be due to the effect of the outlet pits, which would absorb energy in the eddy on that side, thus causing it to become smaller than the eddy on the other side. After a trial run the flow was shut off, but the next time the headgates were opened the high velocity line diverged to the left. Since then the writer has observed the action of the transition on numerous occasions and has found that when the water is turned into the empty canal it is a matter of chance to which side the high velocity stream is deflected, but that having been deflected to one particular side, it remains at that side until the water is again shut off. In the cases cited by the author the divergence may be due to curvature, but in this case it is not. E. W. Lane, M. Am. Soc. C. E., has observed similar phenomena in experiments with contractions.*

Carl Rohwer,† Assoc. M. Am. Soc. C. E. (by letter).—The design of transitions is an important problem in hydraulics, and the data assembled by the author and the method of design that he has devised, are valuable contributions to the Engineering Profession and particularly to engineers interested in irrigation. However, as the author indicates, no satisfactory method of computing the transition losses has as yet been developed, and, consequently, even after a transition is carefully designed, the success of its operation can only be determined by trial.

A study of the experimental data submitted by the author shows that very little loss of head actually occurs in transitions when the velocity is increased,

---

* "Experiments on the Flow of Water Through Contractions in an Open Channel," *Transactions*, Am. Soc. C. E., Vol. LXXXIII (1919–20), p. 1207.

† Associate Irrig. Engr., Div. of Agricultural Eng., U. S. Dept. of Agriculture, Fort Collins, Colo.

and, apparently, there is no correlation between the suddenness of the transition and the loss in head. The question naturally arises whether the complicated inlets shown by the author are justified when the simpler structures seem equally efficient. Much greater losses arise through structures where the velocity is decreased and the loss increases with the abruptness of the transition; but very little, if any advantage is shown by the bell-shaped outlets, which are certainly more difficult to construct.

In calibrating the improved Venturi flume,* which consists of inlet and outlet sections connected by a short throat section (see Fig. 35(*a*) and (*b*)), observations were made on the loss in head through the structure in order to find the net sacrifice of head necessary for the successful operation of the device. The gauges for determining the heads were not placed so as to make it possible to segregate the inlet and outlet losses, but it was possible to determine the inlet loss between the points, *M* and *N*, and the outlet loss between the points, *P* and *R*. The losses are based on staff-gauge readings at *M* and *R* (Fig. 35), and hook-gauge readings at *N* and *P* for the flumes with a throat width of from 1 to 8 ft. For the 10-ft. flume, the losses are based on readings with an engineer's level and rod on the water surface. The hook-gauge readings are reliable, but errors are possible in the staff-gauge and level readings which might affect the results materially. Representative results of these observations are shown in Table 5,† which is based on tests made to

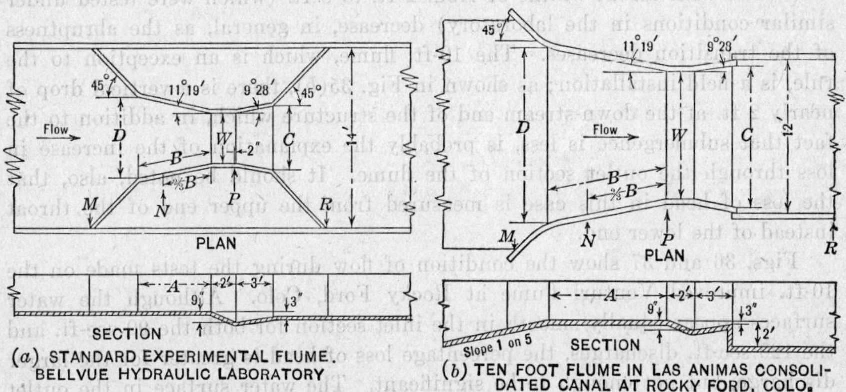

(*a*) STANDARD EXPERIMENTAL FLUME. BELLVUE HYDRAULIC LABORATORY

(*b*) TEN FOOT FLUME IN LAS ANIMAS CONSOLIDATED CANAL AT ROCKY FORD, COLO.

FIG. 35.—SECTION OF IMPROVED VENTURI FLUME.

determine the free-flow discharge. In Tables 5 and 6 the author's terminology is used, as follows:

Q = discharge, in cubic feet per second.

V = mean velocity, in feet per second.

Δh_v = change in velocity head.

* "The Improved Venturi Flume," by R. L. Parshall, Assoc. M. Am. Soc. C. E., *Transactions*, Am. Soc. C. E., Vol. 89 (1926), p. 841.

† Prepared from data of Irrigation Investigations of the Div. of Agricultural Eng., Bureau of Public Roads, U. S. Dept. of Agriculture, co-operating with the Colorado Agricultural Experiment Station.

E = entrance loss, in percentage of Δh_v, measured between Points M and N.

O = outlet loss, in percentage of Δh_v, measured between Points P and R.

E and O include friction losses.

The results of these observations indicate that, although there is an abrupt transition at the inlet end of the flume, very little loss occurs in this section and there is no relation between the suddenness of the transition and the loss in head. The losses are, however, somewhat greater than those reported by Mr. Hinds.

Outlet losses are, to a great extent, determined by the elevation of the water surface at the lower end of the transition, and, consequently, a wide variation in the percentage recovery is possible, regardless of the correctness of the design of the structure. In calibrating the Venturi flume under free-flow conditions, it was necessary to keep the down-stream depth low enough so that it would not back the water into the throat of the flume and raise the head above the condition of maximum flow. At this point the down-stream depth may vary considerably without materially affecting the condition of maximum flow; consequently, some of the tests chosen (see Table 5) do not show as great a recovery in head as would have been possible if the down-stream depth had been increased. However, the outlet losses of the flumes with throat widths of from 1 ft. to 8 ft. (which were tested under similar conditions in the laboratory) decrease, in general, as the abruptness of the transition decreases. The 10-ft. flume, which is an exception to the rule, is a field installation; as shown in Fig. 35(*b*), there is a vertical drop of nearly 2 ft. at the down-stream end of the structure which, in addition to the fact that submergence is less, is probably the explanation of the increase in loss through the outlet section of the flume. It should be noted, also, that the loss of head in this case is measured from the upper end of the throat instead of the lower end.

Figs. 36 and 37 show the condition of flow during the tests made on the 10-ft. improved Venturi flume at Rocky Ford, Colo. Although the water surfaces appear equally smooth in the inlet section for both the 90 sec-ft. and the 120 sec-ft. discharges, the percentage loss of head is greater for the larger discharge, but not enough to be significant. The water surface in the outlet is much smoother for the 90 sec-ft. discharge than for the 120 sec-ft. discharge, but the percentage loss of head is greater. This is due to the fact that, as is shown in Table 5, the submergence is less in the case of the smaller discharge.

The loss of head through the improved Venturi flume, when the down-stream depth has been increased until it backs the water into the throat section and causes submerged flow, is shown in Table 6,* which is based on the submerged flow calibration data of the Venturi flume. These tests were made on the same flumes that were used in the free-flow tests and on similar discharges, and any change in the loss in head is due to the increase of the rela-

* Prepared from data of Irrigation Investigations of the Div. of Agricultural Eng., Bureau of Public Roads, U. S. Dept. of Agriculture, co-operating with the Colorado Agricultural Experiment Station.

TABLE 5.—ENTRANCE AND OUTLET LOSSES THROUGH IMPROVED VENTURI FLUMES OF VARIOUS SIZES FOR DIFFERENT FREE-FLOW DISCHARGES.

Test No.	STANDARD DIMENSIONS, IN FEET. (SEE FIG. 35(*a*).)						FLOW CHARACTERISTICS.					
	W.	*A.*	⅔ *A.*	*B.*	*C.*	*D.*	*Q.*	Submergence.*	*V* (canal to flume).	*E.*	*V* (flume to canal).	*O.*
6 481	1	4.50	3.0	4.41	2	2.77	15.13	65.3	0.423 to 2.82	16.5	6.67 to 0.429	135
6 491							10.00	62.5	0.363 to 2.43	22.2	5.40 to 0.384	91
6 488							7.48	76.9	0.325 to 2.16	14.1	3.95 to 0.317	121
6 434	2	5.00	3.33	4.89	3	3.96	33.0	71.1	0.85 to 3.88	13.4	6.65 to 0.87	203
6 438							25.03	65.3	0.78 to 3.55	16.0	6.09 to 0.82	305
6 445							14.93	71.3	0.64 to 2.93	0.0	4.19 to 0.66	67
6 386	4	6.00	4.00	5.88	5	6.35	55.90	69.8	1.57 to 4.40	19.0	6.25 to 1.69	172
6 372							35.66	65.1	1.36 to 3.79	20.5	5.07 to 1.52	27.5
6 399							15.13	78.0	0.96 to 2.62	21.5	2.55 to 1.05	0
6 339	6	7.00	4.67	6.86	7	8.75	49.50	71.7	1.97 to 3.88	34.5	4.56 to 2.18	28.0
6 353							30.06	70.3	1.64 to 3.21	42.0	3.35 to 1.86	0
6 359							20.12	75.3	1.42 to 2.77	22.7	2.43 to 1.44	0
6 336	8	8.00	5.33	7.84	9	11.06	57.96	64.1	2.62 to 3.95	0	4.48 to 3.08	24.4
6 513							35.08	72.7	2.16 to 3.24	11.1	2.99 to 2.32	0
							REFER TO FIG. 35(*b*).					
†	10	9.00	6.00	8.82	11	13.53	126.12	67.5	2.20 to 4.92	6.7	7.65 to 2.38	93
†							90.73	51.3	1.89 to 4.50	0	6.34 to 2.01	137

* Submergence based on the ratios of the upper and lower heads.

† Special tests.

TABLE 6.—ENTRANCE AND OUTLET LOSSES THROUGH IMPROVED VENTURI FLUMES OF VARIOUS SIZES OF DIFFERENT SUBMERGED-FLOW DISCHARGES.

Test No.	Standard Dimensions, in Feet. (See Fig. 35(*a*).)						Flow Characteristics.					
	W.	*A*.	⅔ *A*.	*B*.	*C*.	*D*.	*Q*.	Submergence.*	*V* (canal to flume).	*E*	*V* (flume to canal).	*O*.
6 490	1	4.50	3.00	4.40	2	2.77	7.48	92.3	0.246 to 1.60	0	2.82 to 0.230	27.4
6 447	2	5.00	3.33	4.89	3	3.96	14.67	94.2	0.471 to 2.04	0	2.68 to 0.437	27.5
6 384	4	6.00	4.00	5.88	5	6.35	43.42	90.5	1.27 to 3.40	0	3.93 to 1.23	0
6 341	6	7.00	4.67	6.86	7	8.75	50.96	88.2	1.86 to 3.59	20.5	3.78 to 1.84	0
6 298	8	8.00	5.33	7.84	9	11.14	55.57	91.0	2.30 to 3.41	0	3.22 to 2.20	0

* Submergence is based on the ratio of the upper and the lower heads.

Fig. 36.—Discharge, 120 Cubic Feet per Second, Improved Venturi Flume, Las Animas Consolidated Canal.

Fig. 37.—Discharge, 90 Cubic Feet per Second, Improved Venturi Flume, Las Animas Consolidated Canal.

tive depth of water in the outlet end of the flume. The results show that both the inlet and outlet losses are materially less than the free-flow losses and also less than the losses observed by the author. They indicate that, for low velocities at least, it is possible to obtain high efficiencies by proper control of the down-stream depth of water, even if the transitions are abrupt.

JULIAN HINDS,* M. AM. SOC. C. E. (by letter).—Many of the problems of the important subject of flume and siphon transition design remain unsolved, and an attempt was made in the paper to develop a definite method of procedure, based upon the partial data available, which might be used until something better is proposed. Many helpful suggestions and criticisms have been contributed in the discussions. The subject has, of course, barely been opened up, and it is hoped that much new and valuable data will be forthcoming at an early date.

The discussion presented by Mr. Muckleston brings up a number of interesting and important points. His first observation is to the effect that the computations for a transition can be made with greater facility if the energy gradient, rather than the surface curve, is assumed. This is a matter of opinion, and is not essentially at variance with the procedure outlined by the writer. In fact, some designers prefer to assume a structure and check its hydraulics, or to use other special devices. Often in making final adjustment several methods of attack may be combined to advantage. Failure to call attention to the various possible procedures was an over-sight. The water surface varies more rapidly than the energy gradient, making it a somewhat more stable factor for assumption.

Attention is called to the generally recognized fact that the mean velocity head is greater than the head corresponding to the mean velocity. An allowance for this difference may be necessary with high velocities, but it should be remembered that this allowance is included in the experimental losses shown in the paper.

The possibility of utilizing inlet structures as checks, or automatic controls, was purposely omitted, because of the special nature of this problem. Mr. Muckleston's discussion of this point might lead the casual reader to believe that all inlet transitions need to be designed to act as controls. Automatic checking is seldom necessary at the inlet to a short siphon or flume. For long siphons involving appreciable excess head for partial flows some form of check at the inlet is often essential.

The discussion of the relation of the end velocity in the transition to the critical velocity might also confuse those who have not given special attention to critical flow. For an inlet to control the flow above it the critical velocity must be attained or exceeded at some point within its length. If the velocity at the down-stream end of the transition is below critical, the transition does not control it. Instructions given for end velocities below critical for all flows are meaningless, because control is not possible without the elimination of this condition. The statement that when the end velocity is above critical for all stages the problem is simple, and that the floor of the notch comes at

* Res. Engr., The J. G. White Eng. Corporation, Pabellon, Aguascalientes, Mexico.

the level of the canal bottom is not thought to be entirely correct. At the least it is not complete. For a practical notch the form and bottom elevation are inter-related, the relation involving many factors. Usually, the floor of the notch can be made level with the bottom of the canal, if desirable, by making a slight sacrifice in point of theoretically correct control. As a matter of fact exact, or even approximately exact, theoretical control is seldom essential. It is only necessary that scouring velocities be avoided. It should be remembered that "normal" canal velocities are lower for partial flows than for full flows, and that some "racing" for low discharges is permissible. An occasion demanding a deep narrow notch, with "uncomfortable acceleration" for very low flows has never been encountered by the writer.

The general subject of critical flow has received a great deal of attention in the last decade. The writer has previously discussed, in published form, the principles involved in the present problem.*

The examples of Nürnberg Tunnel inlet experiments presented by Mr. Mavis are extremely interesting. Mr. Mavis does not state whether the various plans tested were obtained mathematically, or by simple trial. A theoretical analysis of the flow through the double trough would be interesting, and might lead to a better understanding of the general laws of flow through transition structures.

The variable position of the "thread of maximum velocity" below the flume outlet described by Mr. Nimmo illustrates the state of instability which exists in many outlet structures. It is difficult to "push" water up hill. Wherever a large recovery is to be made it is important that conditions be such that each water particle can rise to its new level by its own momentum, with the smallest possible manifestation of impact. The conditions noted by Mr. Nimmo were also observed in some of the outlets cited in the paper.

The data presented by Mr. Rohwer have no important bearing on the subject of transition losses or design. The "improved Venturi flume" as illustrated in Fig. 35, is not perfect from the point of view of smooth hydraulic flow. This fact need not detract from its usefulness as a meter. It should be noted that the inlet to the improved Venturi flume is not particularly abrupt, the angle of inclination of the sides to the axis being about 11°, or less than the average divergence recommended by the writer.

If the statement, in regard to inlets, that "there is no relation between the suddenness of the transition and the loss in head", is intended to apply specifically to the data shown in Tables 5 and 6, it may be considered correct, there being no variation in the suddenness of the transitions. The statement has no general application, however, being known to be untrue. Mr. Rohwer's idea that the recommended lengths can be materially shortened without detriment to the practical hydraulic performance is believed to be well founded, but it is not substantiated by the examples presented.

In discussing outlet losses the statement is made that these losses are rendered uncertain by the accidental relation of the water level in the receiv-

* "The Hydraulic Jump and Critical Depth in the Design of Hydraulic Structures," *Engineering News-Record*, November 25, 1920, p. 1034; "Venturi Flume Data Throws Light upon Control Weir," *Engineering News-Record*, December 23, 1920; and discussion on "The Improved Venturi Flume," by Ralph L. Parshall, Assoc. M. Am. Soc. C. E., *Transactions*, Am. Soc. C. E., Vol. 89 (1926), p. 859.

ing canal to the elevation of the bottom of the flume. Each velocity-reducing transition has a definite recovering capacity, and its performance can be computed for one depth of tail-water as well as for another. The depth of the tail-water is one of a number of factors affecting the performance of the outlet, and the efficiency may vary with this, as with other conditions. The view taken of this factor is probably responsible for the impossible outlet losses shown in Table 5. For six outlets the losses exceed 100%, one running as high as 305 per cent. Such apparent losses indicate that the throat velocities recorded were not the maximum velocities in the structure. To secure rational results it is necessary that the recovery be computed from the point at which the reduction in velocity begins. If this is done the depth of tail-water has no arbitrary effect on the coefficient of recovery. The efficiency of the structure is, of course, affected by the velocity of flow, and particularly by the velocity change. Almost any transition is good enough for a small change at low velocity. For large reductions from high velocities great care may be required.

The question of the expensiveness of the well-designed transition has been mentioned. It is evident that a straight head-wall can be built more cheaply than the more or less intricate warped surfaces recommended in the paper for important structures with high velocities. However, after allowing for increased free-board, larger losses of head, and additional bank protection required with the poorer design, the apparent economy will in many cases disappear.

Usually, a certain length of transition is required to connect the flume or siphon properly with the earth canal. If the transition is shortened the main structure must be lengthened. This is one factor that has led to the use of relatively long inlet structures by the U. S. Bureau of Reclamation. The main structure, especially in the case of a flume, may be less costly than the transition structure, in which case some saving can be effected by a shorter inlet or outlet.

In conclusion, it is believed well to state with emphasis again that not all transitions need be proportioned in accordance with the rules given for important structures. The rules, which are only tentative, are given only for use where needed.

AMERICAN SOCIETY OF CIVIL ENGINEERS

INSTITUTED 1852

TRANSACTIONS .

Paper No. 1691

SURVEYING AND MAPPING IN THE UNITED STATES*

By C. H. Birdseye,† M. Am. Soc. C. E.

With Discussion by Messrs. T. P. Pendleton, C. L. Hall, John C. H. Lee, and C. H. Birdseye.

The history of surveying and mapping is the history of civilization. A complete collection of maps would be the best kind of a record of man's activities on earth, but it would be a bulky volume. Just as all early industrial efforts were crude, so were early maps—some of them mere sketches that would not be a credit to a modern school boy. As civilization progressed, however, methods and instruments were improved and the art of surveying and mapping was developed to keep pace with man's need for more accurate records.

At least as far back as 3000 B. C., man discovered that some sort of graphic representation of the earth's surface was a far more reliable record than written or oral description. The first surveys were guesses as to distance and direction. The first maps were of small areas and were pictorial in form, representing features by means of drawings. These maps had little geographic value, but, as the need for more accurate data developed, maps of larger areas were made and features were represented in more nearly correct geographic position. During this period the world was continually engaged in warfare and success in wars of conquest was based largely on knowledge of the fields of operation. Consequently, from the very beginning, maps were made mostly for military and naval activities. In fact, the history of mapping can be divided into two major periods, the first for military purposes, and the second for economic or engineering uses.

Prior to the Seventeenth Century little effort was made to show relief, and map data were confined to representation of the natural and artificial features.

* Presented at the meeting of the Surveying and Mapping Division, Philadelphia, Pa., October 6, 1926.

† Chf. Topographic Engr., U. S. Geological Survey, Washington, D. C.

In 1674 a map of Paris and vicinity was made on which relief was represented by hachures. The first use of contour lines is recorded in 1728, and rapid development in the portrayal of comparative relief followed in response to a need for more accurate military data.

Early in European history fragmentary surveys around fortified places were connected by other surveys, and a systematic plan was adopted to survey and map the entire country, so that, to-day, most of the European nations have maps of their territory adequate for most military and civil needs. It is surprising that the United States did not profit by the experience of Europe and start a systematic program of surveying and mapping immediately after the Revolution. To be sure, one of the first problems was to dispose of the public land, and as early as 1796 Congress authorized the appointment of a Surveyor General, under whose direction public land surveys were started in what is now the State of Ohio. Soon after this work was begun Congress directed the Surveyor General to "cause a fair plat to be made of the townships and fractional parts of townships contained in the lands, describing the subdivisions thereof and the marks of the corners." This direction has resulted in the preparation of plats of all the surveyed public lands, but these plats are not much more than graphic records of the surveyed lines. If those responsible for the early planning of public land surveys had used a little more foresight, adequate topographic maps of most of the original public land in the United States would now be completed.

The two periods in the history of American mapping can be divided roughly at the time of the Civil War. Before that the surveys were largely for military purposes, but afterward the exploratory surveys were inaugurated purely for scientific and economic study.

The need for topographic maps was recognized during the Revolutionary War, and on July 22, 1777, Congress authorized the appointment of a "geographer and surveyor of the roads, to take sketches of the country and the seat of war." On March 3, 1813, Congress authorized the appointment of eight topographic engineers and eight assistant topographic engineers under the direction of the General Staff of the Army. These officers formed the nucleus of the first Army Corps of Topographic Engineers. The Corps continued to function as an independent unit until the Civil War, but early in 1863 it was absorbed by the Corps of Engineers.

Before the Civil War many expeditions under the direction of officers of the Army explored the vast territory lying west of the Mississippi River. At first, the instruments and methods used were rather crude, but later improvements gradually resulted in better maps. However, practically none of the results secured prior to the Civil War could be incorporated in the standard map of the United States. During that period several systematic surveys were started by the Federal Government and by some of the Eastern States. The most far-reaching move was the creation of the United States Coast and Geodetic Survey in 1816. This organization made an accurate hydrographic and topographic survey of a narrow strip along the Atlantic Coast line, and in this connection established the first accurate system of triangulation in the

United States. Its surveys included the topographic mapping of the principal rivers entering the Atlantic Ocean. Relief was shown by hachures. Not until 1846, when it mapped an area around the Harbor of Boston, did the Coast Survey use contour lines for representation of vertical heights. This, however, was not the first contour map made in the United States, for in 1835 the Geological Survey of Maryland issued a contour map of a small area that is believed to be the first American map of this kind.

At the outbreak of the Civil War all surveys, except those needed for military purposes, ceased; but after the war the territory west of the Mississippi River again became the center of mapping activity, and many exploratory surveys were carried on by the Federal Government and by universities, railroad companies, etc. The most important of the Government surveys were as follows:

1.—The U. S. Geological and Geographical Survey of the Territories, directed by Professor F. V. Hayden, from 1867 to 1879, under the Interior Department.

2.—The geographical surveys west of the 100th meridian, directed by Capt. George M. Wheeler, from 1868 to 1879, under the War Department.

3.—The U. S. Geographical and Geological Survey of the Rocky Mountain Region, directed by Maj. J. W. Powell, from 1869 to 1879, under the Smithsonian Institution.

4.—The U. S. Geological Exploration of the Fortieth Parallel, directed by Clarence King, from 1871 to 1879, under the War Department.

These four surveys were alike in character—all were exploratory, but they covered large areas completely and resulted in the first really comprehensive topographic maps made in America. Astronomic observations were made, base lines were measured, and an accurate system of triangulation was extended over the areas mapped. Differences of elevation were determined by vertical angles and by barometers. The representation of physiographic forms was somewhat crude as compared with present-day practice, but it was such an improvement over previous work that in the period from 1867 to 1879 more progress was made in geographic research than any other period of similar length in American history. The Hayden, Wheeler, Powell, and King Surveys ceased in 1879 when Congress created the U. S. Geological Survey.

Four Federal organizations, the Coast and Geodetic Survey, the General Land Office, the Corps of Engineers, and the Geological Survey, have continued to the present day as the principal surveying and mapping agencies.

The survey of the coasts of the United States was authorized by Congress on February 10, 1807, but no field work was undertaken until 1816. The Coast Survey was a bureau of the Treasury Department until 1903, except for a brief period under the Navy. It was then transferred to the newly organized Department of Commerce and Labor; and, in 1913, was placed under the jurisdiction of the Department of Commerce.

For half a century its work was confined to surveys along the coasts and navigable rivers of the United States, but in 1871 Congress appropriated funds for connecting the surveys along the Atlantic Ocean with those along the Pacific Ocean by a system of triangulation. As a logical result of this action the name of the organization was changed in 1878 to the Coast and Geodetic Survey.

Practically all the coast lines of the United States, Porto Rico, Hawaii, and the Philippine Islands have been surveyed, and hydrographic charts made of the adjacent waters. Similar surveys and charts have been made for a considerable part of the Alaskan Coast. Because of the rapidly changing channels formed by sand-bars and shoals, resurveys are required from time to time; consequently, this work will never be completed.

The Coast and Geodetic Survey performs a work absolutely essential to the Geological Survey and other map-making organizations of the United States, for, in addition to preparing the charts of the coasts, it furnishes the main control points for all other local surveys. Its elevations and geodetic positions are surpassed in accuracy by no other organization. It computes and publishes tidal constants for the principal ports of the United States. It determines magnetic declinations, its mathematicians have devised and developed new methods for computing geodetic constants relating to the size and shape of the earth, and its investigations in isostasy are known all over the world. Its publications are numerous and invaluable to navigators and students in all lines of geodetic work.

The sub-division of the public domain into townships and sections was authorized by Congress in 1785. The first public land surveys were made in 1796 in the area north of the Ohio River and west of the Pennsylvania State line.

In 1812 the General Land Office was organized as a bureau of the Treasury Department. In 1849 it was transferred to the Department of the Interior, where it has remained until the present time. The General Land Office has jurisdiction over the survey and sale of the public lands of the United States, including Alaska.

Previous to 1910 all field surveys were made by contract surveyors, a procedure which resulted in much work of doubtful accuracy. Since 1910 the surveys have been made by regular employees of the Land Office, with resulting decrease in costs and great increase in accuracy.

The sub-division and sale of the public land require cadastral surveys only. Such topographic features as are shown on the plats are incidental to the regular cadastral work. The shores of lakes and large rivers are meandered, but, in general, the accurate location of streams, roads, trails, and other natural and artificial features are determined only at the crossings of the public land lines, and the intermediate data are sketched on the plats. Relief is shown generally by hachure lines, but in a few special surveys contour lines based on accurate elevations have been used. The horizontal control is furnished by a system of base lines, principal meridians, standard parallels, and guide meridians, but only recently has an effort been made to tie these control lines to the standard triangulation scheme of the United States.

Public land surveys have been carried on in all States except the thirteen original States and Tennessee, Kentucky, and Texas. Seventeen of the older States have been completely surveyed, but as some of the early surveys were inaccurate or insufficiently marked, parts of these States are being resurveyed at the rate of about 1 000 000 acres per year. Original surveys are being extended annually over about 2 000 000 acres.

The Corps of Engineers of the Army was amalgamated with the Corps of Topographic Engineers of the Army in 1863, and in the early days engineer officers were the surveying pioneers in the West. Since that date the Corps has executed or supervised practically all the mapping operations of the Army. Prior to the entry of the United States into the World War the mapping operations of the Corps of Engineers were usually reconnaissance in nature, except on river and harbor and fortification projects, and in the Philippines, Hawaii, and Panama. However, experience in the World War demonstrated the importance of accurate topographic maps for all kinds of military operations (a fact always known to military engineers) and a new impetus was given to military mapping. The Corps of Engineers has trained a Topographic Battalion, and its men are engaged on accurate topographic mapping within, as well as without, the United States. Modern methods of topographic mapping form an important part of the training of all engineer troops. Especial stress is laid on full use of airplane photographs. The best camera for mapping purposes was developed by an engineer officer, who received his mapping training in the Geological Survey.

Close co-operation exists between the Corps of Engineers and the Geological Survey so that the mapping efforts of the Army are confined to surveys of strategic importance, to resurveys which have been inadequately mapped, and to surveys which the Geological Survey for any reason has been unable to map. Each year, a substantial part of the Army appropriation for military surveys and maps is made available to the Geological Survey for special work urgently needed by the Army.

The organic act of the Geological Survey provided that the Director "shall have the direction of the Geological Survey and the classification of the public lands and examination of the geologic structure, mineral resources, and products of the National Domain." Clarence King was the first Director. From his experience on the King Survey he realized that no adequate classification of lands and no geologic examination could be made without topographic base maps; hence in the earlier years topographic maps were made a part of the general work of the Geological Survey, and allotments of funds for this purpose were made from the general appropriation. The first specific appropriation for topographic surveys was made in the Sundry Civil Act of October 2, 1888, and amounted to $199 000. Appropriations for topographic mapping have been continued each year. The amounts have fluctuated somewhat, but reached $300 000 in 1903. During the next twenty years the appropriations remained between $300 000 and $350 000. In 1924 the appropriation was raised to $500 000 and has continued to this year (1926) at approximately that figure. Including funds allotted in the early years from the general appropriation of the Survey, approximately $13 200 000 has been expended for topographic mapping. The Geological Survey has also received special appropriations (amounts approximate) for surveying National forests, $2 200 000; for military surveys and maps, $1 400 000; and allotments by co-operating States, $5 100 000; so that the total expenditures for topographic mapping, including those for the present fiscal year (1926), amount to approximately $21 900 000. The current Federal appropriation for topographic mapping by the Geological Survey is $451 700; the allotment for military maps is $12 500; and State allotments amount to $380 000, so that the total amount available for topographic mapping during the current fiscal year is about $844 200.

The area of the Continental United States, exclusive of Alaska, is more than 3 000 000 sq. miles. In the 47 years of the Survey's existence about 43% of this area has been surveyed and the results are published in nearly 3 400 different topographic maps. Some of the early maps were made by methods so crude that the area must be resurveyed. Consequently, only about 30% of the area of the country is covered by maps that are adequate for present-day uses. Some of the States are already completely surveyed. Notable among these are Ohio, West Virginia, and Maryland, which are covered by modern maps resulting from an early adopted and well co-ordinated plan of co-operation. Other States, such as Massachusetts, Rhode Island, Connecticut, New York, New Jersey, and Delaware, are also completely surveyed, but some of the maps are old and out of date and need revision or resurvey. New York has just started a program of revision, and other States have indicated a desire to follow.

During the current year (1926), co-operation is being maintained in 24 States and Hawaii. Exclusive of the States that are completely surveyed, co-operative mapping is being carried on in all but 17, and work of purely Federal interest has been undertaken in 3 of these, so that surveys are in progress in 27 States and 1 Territory. At the past rate of progress it would take nearly 100 years to complete the mapping of the United States. That is too long a period, and American engineers have united in demanding more rapid progress, so that this generation may reap a larger benefit. After carefully considering the problem the Geological Survey proposed a 20-year program. This was approved by Congress in what is known as the Temple Act. The Act authorizes the completion of the mapping in 20 years and contemplates appropriations gradually increasing for a number of years and then decreasing toward the end, both for geodetic and topographic work. As the Act only authorizes the first year's appropriation and does not actually appropriate any money, further legislative action is required.

The Geological Survey long ago adopted a policy of State co-operation by which those States that desired could pay one-half the cost of the work in order to expedite the mapping of the areas within their borders. The Temple Act recognizes this co-operation and contemplates the continuation of the policy. In areas in which the Federal interest is supreme, such as the National Forests, National Parks, and Indian Reservations, the Federal Government should pay the entire expense, but in other areas the States will be expected to bear one-half the cost of the surveys.

The estimated cost of completing the mapping of the United States is $49 200 000. Of this amount, $4 200 000 will be spent for precise surveys—

triangulation, traverse, and spirit leveling—to obtain horizontal and vertical control. This work is done by the Coast and Geodetic Survey and must be executed a year or more in advance of the mapping operations. It is estimated that the several States, or their sub-divisions, will contribute about $12 000 000, so that the Federal cost of the mapping will be about $33 000 000. Spread over a period of 20 years this is not a large investment—not much more than the cost of a single battleship—and the investment will be more than returned to the taxpayer by direct savings made in the construction of public works, etc.

The President, by Executive order of December 30, 1919, created a Federal Board of Surveys and Maps, composed of representatives from each of the Government organizations engaged in surveying and mapping. This Board has made great progress in the co-ordination of mapping operations and in standardization of results. Little serious duplication of effort was found to exist. Most of the lack of co-ordination has been corrected—not by orders or regulation, for the Board has only advisory powers—but by bringing together into close contact the men responsible for the immediate supervision of the mapping efforts of the Federal Government. These men are brought in closer touch with the map-using public through an Advisory Council. This close personal contact is the secret of real co-ordination.

The Advisory Council is made up of representatives of non-Federal agencies interested in mapping. The mapping needs of the United States have been presented and plans have been made to meet them. The existence of much valuable survey data from non-Federal sources has been discovered, and these data have been made available to the Federal mapping agencies, so that now a Government project is rarely undertaken without examining all available data and using all that have merit.

The Executive order creating the Board of Surveys and Maps also directed the establishment of a central Map Information Office to classify, index, and distribute to the map-using public information regarding survey and map data. This Office has proved to be of great assistance to the Federal organizations interested in mapping as well as to individuals seeking map data. The Office is not a distributing agency, but it has recorded most of the Federal map data and much non-Federal map material. Use of this Office is recommended to all who do not know whether the data they desire are in existence or where to find them if they are.

Among some of the noteworthy results of the work of the Board may be mentioned the following:

Standard specifications for control surveys.
Standard map symbols.
Adoption of standard projections for different types of maps.
Selection of a standard series of base maps.
Standard instructions for executing control surveys and topographic surveys.
Research in problems of aerial photography.
Establishment of an efficient Map Information Office.

No discussion of mapping is complete without reference to aerial photography. Much misleading information has been given to the public. Claims have been made in the public press that the entire area of the United States will be mapped immediately by use of aerial photographs and at a cost much lower than by ground methods. The Federal mapping agencies wish that these claims were correct, but the truth is that aerial photography will never replace ground surveys entirely, although it will aid them, expedite them, and lessen the final cost.

Under certain conditions the use of aerial photography will eliminate most of the ground survey work. It is especially useful in flat areas that are open or not too densely timbered, such as the marsh lands in the deltas of some of the Southern rivers, where there are no roads, trails, or houses, and where a single determination of elevation may be sufficient for contouring a large region. In mapping large cities the use of aerial photography is of tremendous value. In the revision of old surveys, made necessary by changes in the works of man, aerial photographs may make it possible to publish an up-to-date map without the necessity of any resurvey by ground methods.

However, the whole of the United States will not be photographed for many years—probably never, at least for use in mapping. In certain areas the photographs would be of so little help to the map maker that the expense of making them would not be warranted for the purpose of map making alone. Any densely timbered area presents an example of conditions that are most unfavorable to photographic surveying, either from the air or from ground stations. The meanders of the streams would of course be indicated on the pictures, but the topographer must traverse these streams to determine their fall, measuring accurately differences of elevation, particularly where possibilities of power development exist. He must locate every trail and house and must tie his surveys to the section and township corners of the public-land survey. The pictures can not show these features in such an area, and new processes must be perfected before aerial surveys will be of much help to topographic mapping in dense forests.

In areas of considerable relief the use of aerial photographs is of doubtful value for small-scale topographic mapping. For example, in the high Rocky Mountains the scale usually employed by the Geological Survey is 2 miles to the inch, and surveys by ground methods cost about $20 per sq. mile. An aerial photograph is only a perspective view from the lens of the camera, and every plane of elevation in a single picture will of course have a different scale. These differences in scale can be co-ordinated, but the process is laborious and expensive, and with present developments the cost of taking the pictures and rectifying the photographic data may exceed the cost of a ground survey. Moreover, the use of photographs of such a region requires an abundance of control points accurately located by triangulation, an operation performed by the topographer in the course of his ground survey. The topographer has to climb all over the region in any event, not only to make the control surveys, but to make the connections with the public land lines.

No practicable method has been devised for determining elevations and portraying contour lines on small-scale maps of large areas by the use of aerial photographs. Some who are familiar with developments in mapping from photographs may challenge this statement, but the writer knows of only one firm in the United States that has successfully solved the problem of the accurate portrayal of contour lines from aerial photographs, and this only in surveys on a very large scale.

Aerial photography is welcomed as a supplement to ground surveys, but it does not promise to replace them to any large extent, particularly in the Western Mountain States. In 1925 the Navy Department and the Geological Survey spent considerable money in making aerial photographs of an area adjacent to the naval oil-shale reserve near Grand Valley, Colorado. The field surveys were completed before the pictures were available, and about the only use it was possible to make of them was in inspecting and checking the field mapping. In Texas, on the other hand, hardly a square mile has been mapped during the last two years without the aid of aerial photographs, thus saving about 30% of the ordinary cost.

Aerial photography has passed the experimental stage, and future improvements in apparatus and economies of procedure promise a much larger use than is now possible. It will pay to use this new method when and where the map data can be gathered by it cheaper than by surveys on the ground. It will not pay when and where the expense of taking the photographs and of reducing the data is greater than the cost of collecting the information from ground surveys. The Geological Survey will use aerial photography where it pays and will not use it when the evidence indicates that it will not save time and money.

It has been the experience of the Geological Survey that as fast as improvements are devised in methods and instruments, which might be expected to cheapen the product, a demand has arisen for more detailed maps, and the increased cost of meeting this demand has offset the saving made by the new methods. Therefore, the topographic surveys now in progress in the United States may be expected to yield better maps rather than cheaper ones, because of this new aid to the topographic engineer.

DISCUSSION

T. P. PENDLETON,* ASSOC. M. AM. SOC. C. E. (by letter).—This interesting paper presents very concisely the history of surveying and mapping in the United States, in so far as it relates to National surveys. It shows that the first crude surveys of large areas were made in the West and were largely of an exploratory nature. It is interesting to learn that the first contour map in the United States was made in 1835, although it was not until after the Civil War that the method was extensively adopted. It was only natural that many methods were tried and discarded in the search for that which presented the most advantages. A description of the various methods that were used in the days of the Hayden, Wheeler, Powell and King surveys would make interesting reading, as would no doubt the personal experiences of these pioneers in the art.

Maps that are classified as small scale would have been called large scale by these early surveyors, and the accuracy that is now obtained would probably seem to them sufficient for many years to come. However, the need of the country continually calls for better and better maps, and that this need is recognized by the Geological Survey is clearly shown by a casual inspection of maps made at 10-year intervals since the first appropriation for topographic surveys was made in 1888.

The United States not only needs better maps, but more of them. This need can be met by existing organizations and bureaus on short notice whenever Congress realizes that ample appropriations for this purpose are an investment that will make big returns to the country. It is necessary to look into the future in mapping, for it is for future needs that maps are made. The safest policy is to supply maps as good as can be made at the moment, for there is little doubt that unless this is done they will be found inadequate in the not distant future. A well-made map should be constructed on a framework consisting of accurate triangulation or traverse to assure reliable map positions. The contours and elevations should be dependent on near-by precise level lines; all other level lines should be so carefully run that it will not be necessary to make adjustments for any but very small circuit closures; and, finally, the contour lines should be located so well that any check that can be applied to them will indicate that they are not incorrectly located more than a short distance. This last requirement is admittedly difficult when surveys of brushy or timbered areas are made by methods now commonly in use, but recent tests of maps made by aerial photography prove that such terrain is no longer impossible to map with accuracy.

A strict observance of the conditions mentioned will assure a map that can be revised from time to time at small cost and kept as up to date as are mariners' charts. The map then becomes a living thing, as it were, that is constantly changing as the country grows. Unfortunately, such revision cannot be made unless the map, as first constructed, is sufficiently accurate to serve as a base to which new cultural features can be added. To revise a

* Topographic Engr., Brock & Weymouth, Inc., Philadelphia, Pa.

map successfully, it should only be necessary to add the new features and delete those that have disappeared, but not to change other details. It is impossible to use an inaccurate map as a base for revision if satisfactory results are expected, as the changes that occur due to expansion of industry and growth of population have a perverse habit of manifesting themselves in weak spots of old maps. That re-survey and not revision is needed in the case of many Government maps is appreciated when their method of construction and the cost of the original surveys are investigated. Fine maps, like most other things, cannot be obtained for "a song", and unless they are well made in the first place they will be a continual source of expense for maintenance, and of loss to industry due to their inherent errors.

The author shows that this country might have had adequate topographic maps of the public lands, had it not been for a lack of foresight in the days when this work was inaugurated. The loss due to the inaccurate early public land surveys was immeasurably increased by the fact that this splendid opportunity to secure topographic maps of all the public domain was entirely overlooked. The country is still paying the cost of that mistake.

About 57% of the Continental United States, exclusive of Alaska, has never been mapped even in the roughest manner. What the percentage may be that is mapped accurately enough to justify revision, it is difficult to state, although it can be said without hesitation that it is small. For these reasons it is to be hoped that the Temple Act providing for the completion of the topographic map of the United States will soon be put into effective operation, and that the maps produced under this Act will be of such a high standard of accuracy that they will serve satisfactorily for many years. The entire cost of all maps made by the U. S. Geological Survey has undoubtedly been returned to the country many times, but this usefulness and the corresponding savings would surely have been greatly increased had their accuracy been greater. Who can say how many times their cost would have been repaid had accurate maps of the Mississippi Valley been in existence during 1927? What would they now be worth for the study of river control?

Observations by the writer indicate that the general purpose map, on the scale 1 to 62 500, is widely used for general studies and for studies of many special problems of relatively small areas by engineers in the business world. In order to use these maps in such studies, it is necessary for the engineer to enlarge the map so that the proposed structure will be of appreciable size and can be properly visualized in relation to other features. This introduces a grave difficulty, as the enlargement is always much greater than the field scale used by the topographer in the original survey. Consequently, his map suffers by comparison with even a crude map made on a larger scale. It seems that by increasing the original map scale it would be possible greatly to extend the usefulness of these small scale maps without changing the publication scale or greatly increasing the cost. This increase in accuracy is worthy of consideration, for not only would the value of the maps be enhanced for present needs, but it would assure their satisfactory revision when this is needed.

The author fully appreciates the possibility that future mapping will be done by aerial photographic methods to a large degree. As he states, such methods will probably never entirely replace ground surveys; nor is this desirable, as place names, political and property boundary lines, and a certain amount of fundamental control will always have to be obtained on the ground. In certain areas it may even be necessary to gather other essential data, although it should be possible to arrange the field work so that this may be obtained when other necessary information is secured.

The accuracy and ease with which contours may now be drawn by stereoscopic methods in timbered country is a never-ending cause of surprise, and to attempt to state what will eventually be done by this method in such areas is impossible.

In his comments on the use of aerial photography, the author undoubtedly had in mind the method now used by the U. S. Geological Survey, in which planimetric detail only is taken from the photographs and the contours are added in the field. Otherwise, it is difficult to account for his statement that streams must be traversed to determine their fall when photographic methods are used. It can confidently be said that any method of applying aerial photographs in mapping, that fails to make use of image displacements caused by ground relief, omits the most valuable aid that such photographs can render the topographer. This partly accounts for the unsatisfactory results that were obtained in 1925 near Grand Valley, Colorado, for there is no reason to believe this area would have offered any difficulty had it been photographed for mapping by stereoscopic methods.

The writer quite agrees that there is little chance for small scale maps to be produced at lower cost in the future, as the demand for increased accuracy will offset any new economy in operation. For this reason, aerial mapping methods that can promise greater accuracy without a great increase in cost should be judged by comparing their cost per square mile with those of ground surveys of equal accuracy, and not by a direct comparison of costs per unit of area.

C. L. Hall,* M. Am. Soc. C. E. (by letter).—There seems to be but one assertion made by the author, on which critical comment is in order.

Colonel Birdseye divides the history of mapping into two major periods: One in which mapping was performed "for military purposes", and the other in which it was performed "for economic or engineering uses". These periods are not, however, as the author seems to indicate, epochs in world history, nor even in National history, since they are of radically different duration in different parts of the world. A considerable portion of the mapping now going on in the world, including some being paid for by the United States, is intended primarily for military purposes. In France and Great Britain, while the economic importance of maps may now exceed their military importance, surveys are still conducted under military control and largely by military personnel. On the other hand, in pre-war Germany, as one example, intensive surveys were often conducted by civil personnel under civil control, primarily

* Maj., Corps of Engrs., U. S. A., U. S. Engr. Office, Rock Island, Ill.

for military purposes. It is believed that the military value of a map of an area exceeds its economic value if there is a good chance of a war occurring in that area before the map becomes hopelessly out of date. The major periods of the mapping history of the United States named by the author are, in reality, based on the good fortune of this country in keeping its territory—outside of a few Indian areas—clear of the horrors of war since 1865.

Colonel Birdseye's excellent review of the present status of the art of aerial surveying should be of special interest. Particular attention should be drawn to his statement that in the revision of old surveys, made necessary by changes in the works of Man, aerial photographs would make it possible to publish an up-to-date map without the necessity of re-surveying by ground methods. This use of the airplane in surveying points the way to the possibility of keeping topographical maps up to date with reasonable economy. If any constant demand could be stimulated among the general public for up-to-date topographical maps, the political authorities of the nation would doubtless provide the comparatively small sums necessary for the annual revision of maps of the more quickly changing areas. The road map maker has to revise his maps annually; the commercial atlas publisher has to revise his atlas annually; and the Post Office Department has to revise its maps at frequent intervals. The U. S. Geological Survey should not be the only mapping agency in the world required to print re-editions with culture so out of date that often the map is of interest only to local historians.

Colonel Birdseye properly calls the attention of the profession to the backwardness of the United States in mapping activities. This situation, while probably known to most engineers, does not seem to have appealed to them as a matter requiring urgent representations to the political authorities, National and State. This National ignorance of topography has recently become a matter of some interest to the general public.* The basic law which should ensure the mapping of the country has been passed.† All that is needed is popular demand produced by educated leadership which is also enthusiastic. This leadership should be supplied by the Engineering Profession.

JOHN C. H. LEE,‡ ASSOC. M. AM. SOC. C. E. (by letter).—This interesting and instructive paper accurately describes the harmonious relation and efficient co-operation which have been developed between the U. S. Geological Survey and what Army engineers like to consider its old parent organization, the Corps of Engineers. The same general specifications and standard requirements of accuracy are recognized, so that the economically important topographical maps of the Geological Survey are becoming, in all essential respects, satisfactory tactical maps for the military forces. Also, the accurate military surveys are being accepted as standard topographic sheets.

The author gives an interesting résumé of the widely needed project for completing the general topographic map of the United States. How important the completion of this survey project is to National defense, can perhaps be appreciated with the realization that among the 60% of uncompleted sheets,

* Editorial, *Saturday Evening Post,* October 15, 1927.

† Act of February 27, 1925, Chapter 360, 68th Cong., 2d Sess.

‡ Maj., Corps of Engrs., U. S. A.; Dist. Engr., Vicksburg, Miss.

there are many vitally important strategic areas. Modern military doctrine recognizes the importance and almost the necessity of correct topographical maps as military plans for large troop concentrations and for successful field operations. Divisions and larger units cannot be rapidly and reliably moved or supplied without good maps. American military forces are all trained under this principle. The use of maps becomes second nature to them. Without maps their operations would be greatly hindered and their success jeopardized. Nevertheless, the fact remains that along wide stretches of this country, including areas of vital strategic value, there are still no maps worthy of the name. From a military standpoint, therefore, the program authorized under the Temple Act should be carried to completion, especially along the borders of the United States.

From the Army engineer's standpoint, moreover, the project should be completed within the borders as well. Studies of flood control and waterway improvement not only can be materially facilitated through good topographic maps, but, as was the case recently in the Mississippi Valley, can be seriously hampered without them. This need was brought into bold relief during the high-water fight of 1927. There were no reliable maps available for much of the back-water country over which extremely important relief operations were being conducted.

The Army engineer recognizes also the value and importance of good topographic maps in planning railway and highway communications with which he is charged in time of war within the period of operations. Whereas no one now sees the eventuality which would bring warfare within the borders of this country, it may be recalled that five or ten years prior to the World War, practically no one ever thought that American troops would fight in Europe.

Since this problem confronts the Army—the problem of no maps for important strategic areas—the task of making emergency maps during actual operations must be faced. The solution of this difficulty is being sought through experiments in aerial photographic surveying and map reproduction in the field. The problem of rapid field triangulation that can be carried on without molestation of the enemy; the rapid and reliable means of obtaining the necessary over-lapping photography; and, finally, a swift and certain method of reproducing the completed map in quantity under field conditions, becomes a task worthy of high engineering talent. This work is all under the direction of the Chief of Engineers. It is of the highest importance in a military sense and not without its peace-time economic value.

As stated by Colonel Birdseye, aerial photographic surveying has become an important adjunct to the general project, the total cost of which would seem to justify the expenditure of sufficient funds to develop the new art in a thoroughly practical sense.

C. H. Birdseye,* M. Am. Soc. C. E. (by letter).—This paper was presented at the first meeting of the Surveying and Mapping Division with the idea of giving the members a brief résumé of the history of surveying and

* Chf. Topographic Engr., U. S. Geological Survey, Washington, D. C.

mapping. The writer did not intend it to be a comprehensive presentation of the subject, and he is not surprised that the discussion uncovered several incomplete and immature statements.

Major Hall questions the writer's division of the history of mapping into two major periods, "the first for military purposes and the second for economic or engineering uses." One would need to be well equipped to debate this subject with Major Hall, who is one of the most profound students of military engineering in the United States Army, and the writer is quite willing to admit that the division of mapping activities into these two periods is inadequate.

Mr. Pendleton is correct in his assumption that the writer had in mind the use of aerial photography as practised by the Federal mapping agencies at the time the paper was written (1926). It should be noted, however, that he specifically referred to densely timbered areas in connection with the statement, "but the topographer must traverse these streams to determine their fall * * *." At the time the paper was prepared the writer was only vaguely familiar with the stereoscopic methods used by the firm of engineers with which Mr. Pendleton is associated. Later, opportunity to investigate these methods carefully has convinced him that the stereoscopic use of arerial photographs will provide elevations along rivers even in timbered country, well within the allowable error of small scale mapping. However, the writer has been unable to find any solution, by aerial photography, of the problem of locating section corners in the timbered areas of the Western Public Land States.

The U. S. Forest Service is a large user of topographic maps, and one of the principal requirements of that organization is the correct location of section lines and corners with relation to streams and other physical features. The principal point which the writer tried to bring out is that aerial photography cannot be expected to replace ground surveys entirely, and in densely timbered areas of the Western Public Land States it does not promise any great reduction in the cost of small scale mapping. The writer is still convinced of the soundness of this view, but does wish to emphasize his statement that, in most cases, the use of aerial photography will yield better maps.

Major Lee stresses the value of the standard topographic map for military purposes, and emphasizes the importance, from the standpoint of National defense, of completing the mapping program authorized by the Temple Act.

The writer is exceedingly interested in Major Lee's testimony that studies of flood control in the Mississippi River Valley have been seriously handicapped by the lack of adequate topographic maps, particularly in view of recent statements of some members of the Corps of Engineers that such maps are not essential to the solution of the flood problems. The area of the alluvial valley of the Mississippi River is about 30 000 sq. miles, of which about 20 000 sq. miles was flooded in 1927. Only 1 400 sq. miles, or about 7% of the alluvial valley, is topographically mapped, and it is inconceivable that any engineer engaged on flood control or flood relief problems does not need all the knowledge he can secure of the topography of the area subject to floods.

AMERICAN SOCIETY OF CIVIL ENGINEERS

INSTITUTED 1852

TRANSACTIONS

Paper No. 1692

SURVEYS ON THE COAST OF NEW JERSEY*

By Victor Gelineau,† M. Am. Soc. C. E.

With Discussion by C. V. Hodgson, M. Am. Soc. C. E.

All surveys of a coastal region should be based on the fact that shore lines shift their positions, thereby changing land ownership. This applies with particular force to New Jersey, for it is almost surrounded by water. The shore line is a property boundary and its variations, within historic times, are most interesting to the physiographer, the surveyor, and the civil engineer. Probably these changes are not in fact more extensive than have occurred in other ocean-front States, but the relatively high degree of development of the New Jersey Coast has compelled the study of shore-line variations and of measures to preclude radical change of contour. The only means of measuring the changes in shore line is by executing repeated surveys referred to a common datum.

Shifting of Shore Lines

Whenever water waves beat on a shore they tend, in general, to level down land forms. The result of tidal and wave forces is to carry beach material in one dominant direction. Thus, in New Jersey, Barnegat Inlet is approximately the division point of the shore drift. From Barnegat Inlet northward to Sandy Hook, the beach material generally tends to drift northward, while south of Barnegat the direction of the alongshore drift is southward. This is not always true, for certain storms will cause a quick reversal of drift and there are sections where local movements are almost always opposite in direction to the general movement.

* Presented at meeting of the Surveying and Mapping Division, Philadelphia, Pa., October 6, 1926.

† Director and Chf. Engr., New Jersey Board of Commerce and Nav., Jersey City, N. J.

The travel of this material along the beach is the primary cause of (*a*) the alteration in direction and position of the inlet gorges; and (*b*) the tendency of certain inlets to close, particularly those the lagoon areas of which are relatively small.

Examples of Shifting Inlets

The shifting and the closing of inlets and their subsequent re-opening by natural or artificial agencies and the formation of new inlets have served to complicate the location of property lines and have in fact obliterated large land holdings. A series of inlets existing on the New Jersey Coast within recent times were of virtually no value from the standpoint of navigation, but were always a menace from the standpoint of coast erosion, and could be rather confidently expected to close up every year or two. The inlets leading into Deal Lake, Sunset Pond, Wesley Lake, Goose Pond, Duck Pond, Silver Lake Inlet, and Sea Girt Inlet were examples in point. To-day, these inlets are all permanently closed, except for flumes or gates that permit drainage of the pond or basin.

Shark Inlet and Manasquan Inlet, the lagoon areas of which are relatively restricted, are two interesting examples of the tendency of inlets to shift and, occasionally, to close. Their behavior prior to the improvement of Shark Inlet was almost parallel. The normal position of the inlet gorge would be approximately at right angles to the general line of the beach, making a most favorable condition for the ebb and flood flows. The gorge would remain in this position for a more or less indeterminate period, but the actively moving alongshore drift of sand would gradually shift the inlet gorge to the northward so that its channel would flow that way nearly parallel to the beach for several hundred feet before swinging eastward into the ocean. Ultimately, a position would be reached, owing to the great length of the gorge, where the velocity of the tidal current would be insufficient to scour the sand out and the inlet would close. An abnormal difference in the water levels between the lagoon and the ocean, accompanied by storm conditions, might result in the inlet's gorge re-establishing itself in the normal position; or the opening might be made by dredging a ditch or a small canal across the sand-bar. Then the cycle would repeat itself.

Shark Inlet was fixed in position after 1911 when the State enacted legislation and made the necessary appropriations. Manasquan Inlet was closed from April, 1926, to January, 1927. At the time of the U. S. War Department Survey in 1878 it was fully 1 100 ft. north of its normal position. A number of other inlets, referred to in old works and records, have been closed for perhaps 100 years or more. Their location must now be guessed by such evidence as the meadow islands and soundings will furnish. Cranberry Inlet comes within this description. There is some evidence that it was used during the War of the Revolution. Its former existence furnishes an explanation for giving the name of Island Beach to the beach that extends northward from Barnegat Inlet. Attempts were made by Michael Ortley, in 1821, and Anthony Ivins, Jr., in 1847, to re-open an inlet in this vicinity, but without success.

Triangulation Control

The foregoing demonstrates conclusively how vital it is, in surveying on the ocean front, especially wherever a yielding, mobile shore material is impinged upon by swift currents or large waves, to fix all stations accurately from reference points of reasonable permanence. Monuments should be placed well back from the high-water line and all important points should be referenced and located by triangulation or by an adaptation of the three-point method. Three points, however, may not be enough; partly because they may be poorly located and, therefore, fail to give a good intersection, but primarily because of the probability that some of them may be destroyed within a relatively few years. In 1912, for instance, the traverse points of a survey were referenced by the three-point method to a lighthouse and two water towers, all very substantial structures. The towers were removed when the pumping plants were enlarged and, in a re-survey of 1925, the traverse monuments had to be recovered by other methods.

The writer urges an application of the triangulation system. It is almost invariably superior to traverses for surveying in the vicinity of waterways other than the ocean front. The inter-visibility of the stations, the ease with which adjustments can be made, the facility with which stations can be recovered, and the impracticability of chaining across large bodies of water, are strong arguments for its use.

Authority for Making Surveys

There is no unit of the State Government of New Jersey that applies itself primarily to the making of surveys and maps. Each State Department the operations of which require surveys (and there are several) has its own individual surveying organization to execute the surveys and plans required by that Department. The first "system" of surveys established in New Jersey includes the necessarily scattered locations of tracts granted by the ancient Proprietors of West Jersey or East Jersey. It seems advisable to explain the source of land proprietorship or title in New Jersey.

Land Titles

New Jersey was originally a Dutch Colony, settled under the auspices of the Dutch West India Company. Many years after the Dutch settlement, the activities of the Dutch marking them as dangerous enemies to Sweden, Gustavus Adolphus of Sweden, in 1638, sent out an expedition which settled on both sides of the Delaware. Prosperous for a time, the Swedish settlements weakened and, in 1655, the Dutch conquered New Sweden. From this year until 1664, New Jersey was absolutely a Dutch Colony.

On March 12, 1664, Charles the II, of England, granted to his brother, James, Duke of York, all of what is now New Jersey, as well as Long Island and other territory to the north and east. During that year the British Naval

Power compelled the surrender of the Dutch claims. In the meantime (June 23-24, 1664), the Duke of York, by indenture of lease and release, conveyed to John, Lord Berkeley, and Sir George Carteret, lands which include what is now New Jersey. These are described* as follows:

"All that tract of land adjacent to New England, and lying and being to the westward of Long Island, and Manhitas Island, and bounded on the east part by the main sea, and part by Hudson's river, and hath upon the west Delaware bay or river, and extendeth southward to the main ocean as far as Cape May at the mouth of Delaware bay; and to the northward as far as the northermost branch of the said bay or river of Delaware, which is forty-one degrees and forty minutes of latitude, and crosseth over thence in a strait line to Hudson's river in forty-one degrees of latitude."

The famous quintipartite deed which defines the division between East and West Jersey was executed in July, 1676. This was preceded by some other conveyances which it is not necessary to consider. The southeasterly terminus of the partition, or province line, is described in this quintipartite deed as "the most southardly point of the east side of Little Egg Harbour aforesaid;" but Little Egg Harbor Inlet has shifted over several miles in location during the intervening centuries.

The Proprietors, who derived their title in the manner just outlined, sold parcels to applicants. Briefly, the procedure was to send out a deputy surveyor who located the lands applied for and then made his return to the Proprietors. Much of this survey work of the Eighteenth Century and the early part of the Nineteenth Century was very inaccurate, as might be expected in view of the very low value of the lands.

Earlier Surveys

From relatively early times, the State of New Jersey did show a commendable desire to obtain good maps and probably was pre-eminent among the States of the early Nineteenth Century in endeavoring to obtain them, but all that was accomplished still left much to be desired. The first real system of surveys, worthy of the name, was that established by the United States Coast and Geodetic Survey about 1840. To-day, this furnishes the chief reliance in defining the position of shore lines before the more detailed surveys, made necessary by the development of the coastal cities. It must be remembered here that the magnificent cities of the New Jersey Coast are institutions dating back very few years. Let this great evolution serve as an example to people of other localities, who may believe that their beaches will not develop into valuable lands in the near future.

The State Geological Survey of New Jersey made a valuable contribution in producing the surveys which form the basis for the maps now published by the Board of Conservation and Development. The topographical survey of that Department is reviewed in the report of the State Geologist of 1887, which recommended that the entire State be covered by a cadastral and economic survey. It consisted essentially, as to the coastal region, in transit and stadia surveys of the marshes and waterways, and was controlled by the U. S.

* See Leaming and Spicer, "Grants and Concessions of New Jersey," p. 8 *et seq.*

Coast and Geodetic Survey monuments and triangulation stations. Unfortunately, the Legislature did not carry out the recommendation of the report.

Modern Water-Front Surveys

The Board of Commerce and Navigation (successor to the Riparian Commission), the Department of Inland Waterways, the Harbor Commission, etc., are extending their surveys over the water-front of the State as rapidly as possible. They require surveys for such different purposes as the establishment of riparian or pierhead and bulkhead lines; the improvement of inland waterway channels; and the measuring of rate of erosion or accretion on the beaches. As far as practicable, each survey is planned to meet the needs of all Departments. It is hoped that within a very few years the Board will have accurate detailed surveys of the entire tidal water-front of the State. This information is of untold value to land owners. It will remove from future litigation, the element of uncertainty in the location of high-water mark boundaries.

Most maps of the former Riparian Commission of New Jersey are very valuable, but they necessarily cover rather limited areas because they were made merely to meet the demand for the establishment of riparian lines. The former Department of Inland Waterways which constructed the inland waterway system from Cape May to Bayhead, covered some of this area with surveys of high precision.

Lack of Accurate Surveys

The legal complexities which arise through a confusing description of a beginning point are most serious and discouraging. A most striking example is the mischief caused by uncertainty in the location of the Province Line between East and West Jersey. The line was run by George Keith, Surveyor General of East Jersey, in 1687; but it has been stated* that, "the western proprietors thought too much of their best lands were surveyed to the eastward, and were uneasy with it." In Governor Coxe's report (1687) to the Proprietors of West Jersey, he compares the excellent maps of his adversaries of East Jersey with the unsatisfactory maps of his associates of West Jersey. He states,†

> "They * * * of East Jersey have in this respect, exercised the highest prudence, knowing the whole country to a little, and thereby have both overreached you. I have seen their draughts than which nothing can be more exact;"

A map, dated 1747, shows another location of this line as run by Lawrence in 1743.

New Inlet, at the southerly end of Long Beach, opened in about 1800, during a violent storm. The position of Little Egg Harbor Inlet affects vitally the division line between properties. It entered prominently into the establishment of the county lines. In fixing the county line about 1885, it was found necessary to rely almost entirely on tradition to establish the time that New

* Smith's "History of New Jersey," p. 196.

† *Loc. cit.*, p. 546 *et seq.*

Inlet was opened because Beach Haven Inlet was not then in existence. A large number of the elderly people gave their ancestors' statements as evidence of its time of opening and its position at that time.

Comparison of Two Major Inlets

Thus, there are now two inlets: What is known as New Inlet, which opened in about 1800, and Beach Haven Inlet, farther north, which opened in 1920. A survey of Beach Haven Inlet was made in 1923 by the U. S. Coast and Geodetic Survey and the New Jersey State Board of Commerce and Navigation. Whether the two inlets will co-exist for any length of time is a question for the future. In the meantime the submerged lands have practically no value, and the isolated area known as Tucker's Beach has also very little value. The behavior of this inlet, or pair of inlets, is in some degree paralleled by the behavior of Great Egg Harbor Inlet between Longport and Ocean City, which has, at times, had two branches separated by a large sand-bar island. The Lake Survey of 1881 shows a single inlet, with Longport Point far south of its present position. Longport has since lost approximately 184 acres (see Fig. 1).

Example of Accretion

Sand beaches tend to shift oceanward or landward in the course of years. The tendency of sand dunes to move is well known and the existence of a series of lines of sand dunes indicates movement of the beach line. The late Henry S. Haines, M. Am. Soc. C. E., in fixing a survey on an undeveloped section of one New Jersey beach, drove iron pipes which extended 3 or 4 ft. above the ground level. They were set at the foot of the sand dunes on the ocean side. Some years later, when called upon to retrace this survey, he found the beginning corner almost buried and on the opposite, that is, landward, side of the sand dune. In other words, the sand dune had moved oceanward perhaps 150 ft.; yet this change was not apparent to the eye. Most beaches change slowly at points remote from the inlets; but at the inlets serious changes may be caused by one storm, if coast-protection measures have not been provided.

Survey Methods

The State has received about $12 000 000 from the sales and leases of lands under water and has expended about $2 000 000 in the improvement of its inland waters and protection of its beaches. The surveys of the New Jersey Board of Commerce and Navigation should be made for three purposes in order to be of maximum value, namely, the establishment of riparian grant lines; the possible improvement of the waterways; and, the measurement of the rate of change in the shore line. By shore line is meant the line of mean high water, for that is a property division line in New Jersey. This necessitates somewhat more detail than would be required for navigation maps and the accuracy should approximate 1 in 10 000. Traverse lines, carefully referenced to existing curb lines, board walks, and street monuments, are used in and near cities on the beach front. Frequent cross-sections of the beach are

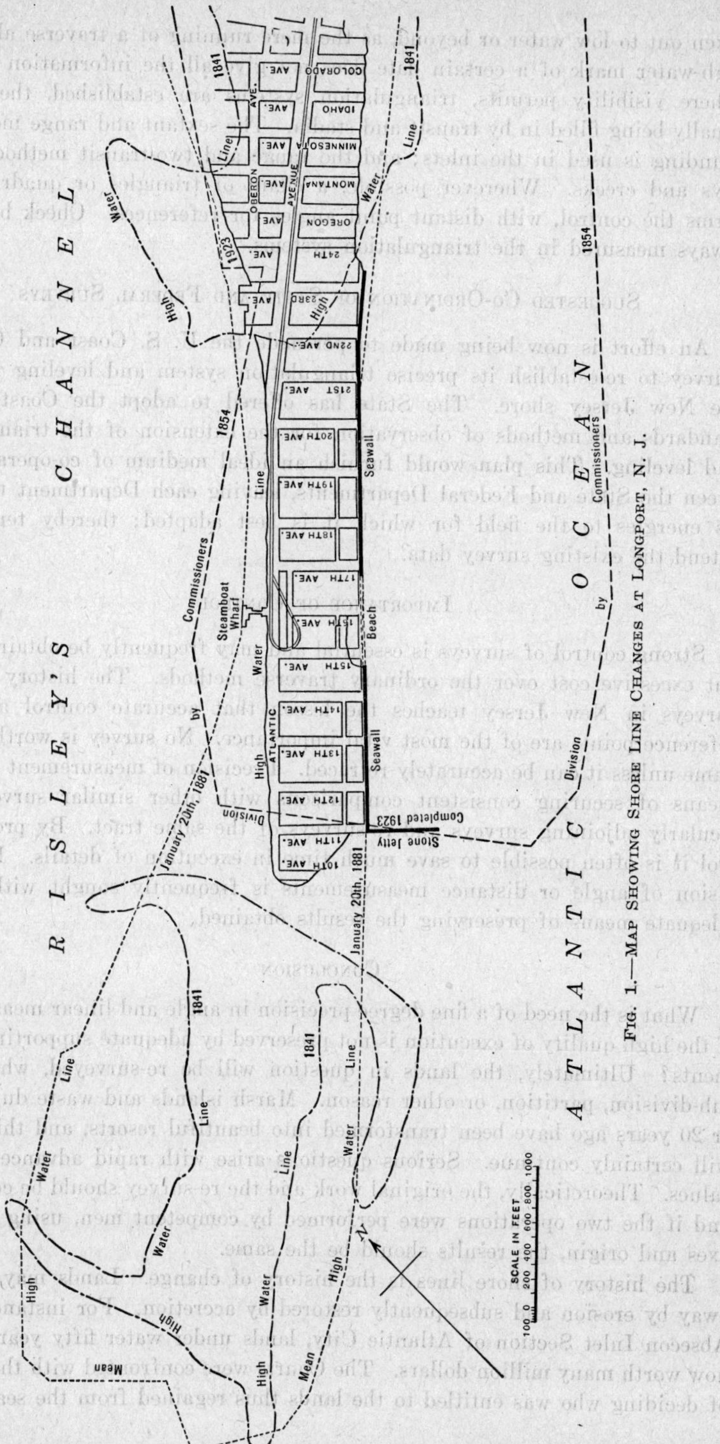

FIG. 1.—MAP SHOWING SHORE LINE CHANGES AT LONGPORT, N. J.

taken out to low water or beyond, as the mere running of a traverse along the high-water mark of a certain date does not give all the information desired. Where visibility permits, triangulation systems are established, the details usually being filled in by transit and stadia. The sextant and range method of sounding is used in the inlets; and the range and two-transit method in the bays and creeks. Wherever possible, a chain of triangles or quadrilaterals forms the control, with distant point angles for references. Check bases are always measured in the triangulation systems.

Suggested Co-Ordination of State and Federal Surveys

An effort is now being made to persuade the U. S. Coast and Geodetic Survey to re-establish its precise triangulation system and leveling net over the New Jersey shore. The State has offered to adopt the Coast Survey standards and methods of observation for the extension of the triangulation and leveling. This plan would furnish an ideal medium of co-operation between the State and Federal Departments, leaving each Department to devote its energies to the field for which it is best adapted; thereby tending to extend the existing survey data.

Importance of Control

Strong control of surveys is essential and may frequently be obtained without excessive cost over the ordinary traverse methods. The history of coast surveys in New Jersey teaches the lesson that accurate control and good reference points are of the most vital importance. No survey is worthy of the name unless it can be accurately retraced. Precision of measurement is only a means of securing consistent comparisons with other similar surveys, particularly adjoining surveys and re-surveys of the same tract. By proper control it is often possible to save much time in execution of details. Fine precision of angle or distance measurements is frequently sought without any adequate means of preserving the results obtained.

Conclusion

What is the need of a fine degree precision in angle and linear measurement if the high quality of execution is not preserved by adequate supporting monuments? Ultimately, the lands in question will be re-surveyed, whether for sub-division, partition, or other reason. Marsh islands and waste dunes of 15 or 20 years ago have been transformed into beautiful resorts, and this process will certainly continue. Serious questions arise with rapid advances in land values. Theoretically, the original work and the re-survey should be consistent, and if the two operations were performed by competent men, using the same axes and origin, the results should be the same.

The history of shore lines is the history of change. Lands may be swept away by erosion and subsequently restored by accretion. For instance, in the Absecon Inlet Section of Atlantic City, lands under water fifty years ago are now worth many million dollars. The Courts were confronted with the problem of deciding who was entitled to the lands thus regained from the sea.

How should these accretions be apportioned? The broad legal principle, perfectly simple and just, is that the accretion shall be equitably admeasured among the riparian owners. In the application of this legal principle it is often very difficult to determine who the riparian owners are, and how the regained land shall be apportioned. Important questions must first be solved. Where was the shore line at the time of a transfer of title? Did the vendor retain a strip of land adjacent to the water? The calls in the deed may or may not indicate what the vendor and vendee contemplated as to this vital point. In other words, the difficulties are due primarily to meager or contradictory evidence.

In these circumstances there is no substitute for maps plotted from good surveys. The work done by the U. S. Coast and Geodetic Survey has been invaluable in establishing the location of shore lines as they were years ago, and surveyors of coastal land would do well to profit by its experience. The shifting of inlets especially should serve as a striking warning that surveys on the seashore must be very thoroughly and accurately referenced to mainland points of reasonable permanency.

DISCUSSION

C. V. Hodgson,* M. Am. Soc. C. E. (by letter).—Three factors necessary to a satisfactory survey have been admirably stressed by Mr. Gelineau, these being adequate accuracy in angle and length measurements, permanent monumentation, and connections to the National system of triangulation surveys. All three factors are important to any survey, but the last two are especially so in regions where the boundary monuments are subject to disturbance by natural causes or by the hand of Man. A slight amplification of these three points may be warranted.

Accuracy.—Mr. Gelineau states that the three purposes which the survey of beach lands must serve, demand that the principal lines of traverse or triangulation be in error not more than 1 part in 10 000, or 1 ft. to 2 miles. This corresponds to what is known as second-order accuracy in Federal surveys. At first thought this accuracy may seem excessive until it is recalled that one object of the New Jersey survey is to define the boundaries of riparian grants, and that the beach lands have a very high value.

For years the U. S. Coast and Geodetic Survey was criticized for what was considered to be the excessive accuracy of its coastal surveys—a specified error of not to exceed 1 part in 5 000 for its main lines of third-order triangulation. It now appears that for many purposes that accuracy is not sufficient, although ample for charting and mapping. It is doubtful, however, if the surveying agencies of the Federal Government would be justified in increasing the accuracy of detailed control surveys at the present time. Greater accuracy may frequently be needed for cadastral or improvement surveys, but they usually lie outside the province of the Federal Government.

An accuracy represented by a maximum error of 1 part in 10 000 in determined distance is neither difficult nor expensive to secure if proper instruments and methods are used. Where an extensive area is involved, or where there is a strong probability that the value of the land will increase considerably in the future, the accuracy specified by Mr. Gelineau is by no means excessive.

Monumentation.—To monument a survey permanently in a region subject to erosion is a practical impossibility. It is also very difficult to establish monuments which can be easily recovered in a region where accretion or sedimentation is noticeable or where movements of sand dunes are changing the surface of the ground. Various expedients have been tried by the Coast and Geodetic Survey in regions subject to these shore-line changes, including deep sub-surface marks and cypress or cedar posts as witness marks. The present practice is not to mark the station permanently if it is in a location subject to erosion, but to reference it by two monuments placed far enough back from the shore to be secure for a number of years and yet near enough to serve in relocating the old station at any time, with an error of not more than about 1 in.

If the coastal control is by the triangulation method and a line of stations has been established inland on solid ground in locations easily visible from

* Asst. Chf., Div. of Geodesy, U. S. Coast and Geodetic Survey, Washington, D. C.

the coast, the preservation of the outer line of exposed station marks is not so important, for they can be relocated at any time from the inner line of stations. In localities where sand drifts or sediments may cover up the marks, witness posts are used in connection with fairly large concrete monuments at the station. These monuments can be readily located by prodding with an iron bar through a considerable depth of mud or sand.

Where the ground is stable it is economy to establish permanent marks. A slight increase in the cost of monumentation may double the period of years during which the survey may be retraced. Underground marks separate from the surface marks, and substantial reference marks placed in property lines, will perpetuate a survey for a long period of years at slight additional expense.

Connection to National Datum.—There are two ways in which a survey may be connected to the North American datum. By the first method one or more control stations on the National datum are tied in by traverse or triangulation to the new survey, but are used simply as reference points. By the second method the origin of a local system of plane co-ordinates is either made to coincide with a station on the National datum or is connected to it. The latter system is usually followed when detailed surveys are to cover a considerable area. Either method has the effect of making every control station in that region which is on the National datum a reference mark for the new survey, and is the surest method of perpetuating it. If the connection to the National datum stations is made part of the legal record, there is little doubt that any Court would give such evidence great weight in any retracement surveys.

AMERICAN SOCIETY OF CIVIL ENGINEERS
INSTITUTED 1852

TRANSACTIONS

Paper No. 1693

A GRAPHIC METHOD FOR DETERMINING THE STRESSES IN CIRCULAR ARCHES UNDER NORMAL LOADS BY THE CAIN FORMULAS*

By Frederick Hall Fowler,† M. Am. Soc. C. E.

With Discussion by Messrs. B. F. Jakobsen, William Cain, Walter L. Huber, Glen Edgar Edgerton, Lars R. Jorgensen, Fred A. Noetzli, and Frederick Hall Fowler.

Synopsis

This paper presents a series of curves for determining the stresses, in pounds per square inch, at the extrados and intrados of crown and abutments of circular arches under normal loads.

The curves fall in three groups based on three separate sets of formulas developed by William Cain, M. Am. Soc. C. E.:

Group I.—Arches with "fixed ends" (neglecting shear). (Figs. 3, 4, 5, and 6.)

Group II.—Arches with "hinged ends" (neglecting shear). (Figs. 7, 8, and 9.)

Group III.—Arches with "fixed ends" (including influence of shear). (Figs. 10(*a*), 10(*b*), 10(*c*), 10(*d*), 11(*a*), 11(*b*), 11(*c*), 11(*d*), 12(*a*), 12(*b*), 12(*c*), 12(*d*), 13(*a*), 13(*b*), 13(*c*), and 13(*d*).)

The curves represent the stresses due to a full water load corresponding to a 10-ft. head; but, by the methods outlined, they may be used for any head. They afford a quick and easy method of applying a very complicated and rigorous method of analysis.

The problem of determining with reasonable accuracy the stresses in arch dams has commanded an important place in engineering literature, partic-

* Published in October, 1927, *Proceedings*.

† Cons. Civ. Engr., San Francisco, Calif.

ularly during the past six years. In the *Transactions* and *Proceedings* of the Society alone, from 1919-20 to date (1927), there have been seven papers* devoted exclusively or in large part to the study of stresses in the ordinary arch dam, and three others† devoted to the special problems of the multiple arch.

These papers propose formulas that range from rough approximations to the most rigid mathematical determinations. Two valuable contributions of the group were by Professor Cain. In the first of these, "The Circular Arch Under Normal Loads", the author developed, by refined mathematical methods, formulas for computing moments and thrusts, and the resulting stresses in arches with "fixed" and "hinged" ends.

Fig. 1 taken from this paper is supposed to represent a horizontal circular arch, 1 ft. thick, perpendicular to the plane of the paper.

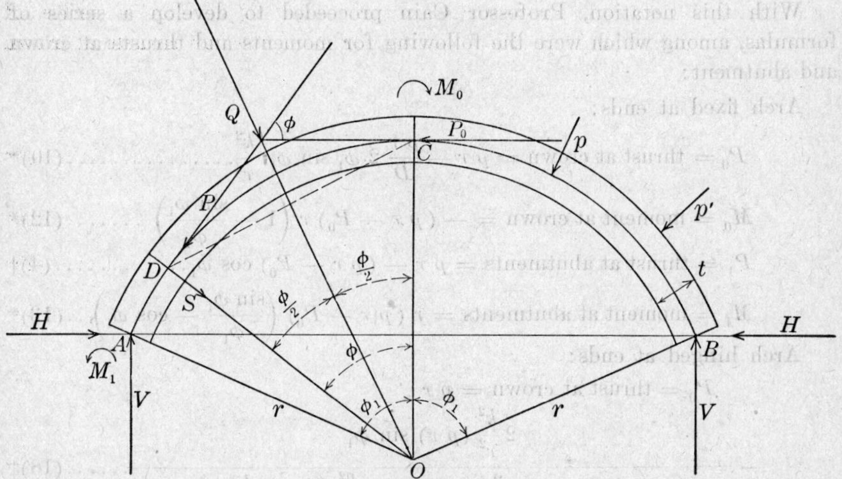

Fig. 1.—Circular Arch of Uniform Radial Thickness, Fixed at the Ends and Subjected to a Uniform Normal, Radial Pressure.

The notation used‡ (omitting symbols that did not enter into the formulas for moments and thrusts), was as follows:

Let t = uniform radial thickness of arch, in feet;

r = radius of center line of arch, in feet;

* "Improving Arch Action in Arch Dams," by L. R. Jorgensen, M. Am. Soc. C. E., *Transactions*, Am. Soc. C. E., Vol. LXXXIII (1919–20), p. 316; "Arched Dams," by B. A. Smith, M. Am. Soc. C. E., *Transactions*, Am. Soc. C. E., Vol. LXXXIII (1919–20), p. 2027; "Gravity and Arch Action in Curved Dams," by Fred A. Noetzli, M. Am. Soc. C. E., *Transactions*, Am. Soc. C. E., Vol. LXXXIV (1921), p. 1; "The Circular Arch Under Normal Loads," by William Cain, M. Am. Soc. C. E., *Transactions*, Am. Soc. C. E., Vol. LXXXV (1922), p. 233; "The Relation Between Deflections and Stresses in Arch Dams," by F. A. Noetzli, M. Am. Soc. C. E., *Transactions*, Am. Soc. C. E., Vol. LXXXV (1922), p. 284; "Stresses in Thick Arches of Dams," by B. F. Jakobsen, M. Am. Soc. C. E., *Transactions*, Am. Soc. C. E., Vol. 90 (June, 1927), p. 475, containing a discussion and solution by the principle of least work, by William Cain, M. Am. Soc. C. E., p. 522; and "Experimental Deformation of a Cylindrical Arched Dam," by B. A. Smith, M. Am. Soc. C. E., *Transactions*, Am. Soc. C. E., Vol. 91 (December, 1927), p. 705.

† "Stresses in Multiple-Arch Dams," by B. F. Jakobsen, M. Am. Soc. C. E., *Transactions*, Am. Soc. C. E., Vol. LXXXVII (1924), p. 276; "Improved Type of Multiple-Arch Dam," by Fred A. Noetzli, M. Am. Soc. C. E., *Transactions*, Am. Soc. C. E., Vol. LXXXVII (1924), p. 342; and, "Multiple-Arch Dam at Gem Lake on Rush Creek, California," by Fred O. Dolson and Walter L. Huber, Members, Am. Soc. C. E., *Transactions*, Am. Soc. C. E., Vol. 89 (1926), p. 713.

‡ *Transactions*, Am. Soc. C. E., Vol. LXXXV (1922), p. 235.

r' = radius of extrados, in feet;
p' = normal radial pressure, in pounds per square foot, on extrados;
p = normal pressure, in pounds per square foot, on center line

$$= \frac{p' \, r'}{r};$$

ϕ = angle with radius of crown for any point, D;
ϕ_1 = half central angle, $A\,O\,B$;
s = length of arc, $C\,D = r\,\phi$, $\therefore\ ds = r\,d\,\phi$;
M_0 = moment at crown, taken positive clockwise;
P_0 = thrust at crown;
M and P are, respectively, the moment and tangential component of the thrust at D (r, ϕ).

With this notation, Professor Cain proceeded to develop a series of formulas, among which were the following for moments and thrusts at crown and abutment:

Arch fixed at ends:

$$P_0 = \text{thrust at crown} = p\,r - \frac{p\,r}{D}\,2\,\phi_1 \sin\phi_1 \,\frac{k^2}{r^2} \quad \ldots\ldots\ldots\ldots\ldots (10)^*$$

$$M_0 = \text{moment at crown} = -\,(p\,r - P_0)\,r\left(1 - \frac{\sin\phi_1}{\phi_1}\right) \quad \ldots\ldots (12)^*$$

$$P_1 = \text{thrust at abutments} = p\,r - (p\,r - P_0)\cos\phi_1 \quad \ldots\ldots\ldots\ldots (4)\dagger$$

$$M_1 = \text{moment at abutments} = r\,(p\,r - P_0)\left(\frac{\sin\phi_1}{\phi_1} - \cos\phi_1\right) \quad \ldots (13)^*$$

Arch hinged at ends:

$$P_0 = \text{thrust at crown} = p\,r - \frac{2\,\frac{k^2}{r^2}\,(p\,r)\sin\phi_1}{\phi_1\,(2 + \cos 2\,\phi_1) - \frac{3}{2}\sin 2\,\phi_1 + \frac{k^2}{r^2}\left(\phi_1 + \frac{1}{2}\sin 2\,\phi_1\right)} \quad \ldots\ldots (18)\ddagger$$

$$M_0 = \text{moment at crown} = -\,(p\,r - P_0)\,r\,(1 - \cos\phi_1) \quad \ldots\ldots (3)\S$$

$$P_1 = \text{thrust at abutment} = p\,r - (p\,r - P_0)\cos\phi_1 \quad \ldots\ldots\ldots (4)\dagger$$

$$M_1 = \text{moment at abutment} = 0.$$

The stresses s, in pounds per square inch, at the extrados and intrados at the crown and the abutments were computed by substituting the values of thrust and moment in the well-known formula:

$$s = \left(\frac{P}{t} \pm \frac{6\,M}{t^2}\right) \div 144$$

It should be noted regarding these formulas for thrust and moment that (*a*) they did not include the influence of shear; (*b*) they were referred to the center line of the arch ring and not to its neutral axis; and (*c*) the water pressure, p, was at the center line of the arch ring and not at the extrados.

* *Transactions*, Am. Soc. C. E., Vol. LXXXV (1922), p. 237.
† *Loc. cit.*, p. 236.
‡ *Loc. cit.*, p. 242.
§ *Loc. cit.*, p. 236.

A separate formula for shear, S (Equation (14)* was included in the body of the paper, several valuable observations on that subject followed in the discussion, and in his closure,† Professor Cain developed a more detailed formula for the value of $(p\,r - P_0)$, including shear.

The mathematical treatment of the problem was so clear and complete that the formulas were accorded wide acceptance and were extensively used (either with or without supplementary studies for shear). Subsequently, Professor Cain‡ developed further formulas for stresses in circular arches under normal loads. The more rigorous method here adopted differed from the original in the following important particulars: (*a*) The formulas for moment and thrust included the influence of shear; (*b*) both moment and thrust were referred to the neutral axis of the arch ring; and (*c*) water pressures were referred to the extrados.

The revised notation§ adopted by Professor Cain was, as follows:

"The arch to be considered is a horizontal circular arch of constant radial thickness, t, and a vertical height of 1 ft., fixed at the ends, and subjected on the extrados to a water pressure of p_e lb. per sq. ft. Generally, this is not the full water pressure at the level of the medial plane of the arch, but the part carried by the arch, the remainder being carried by the supposed cantilever.

"In Fig. 2, representing the half arch,

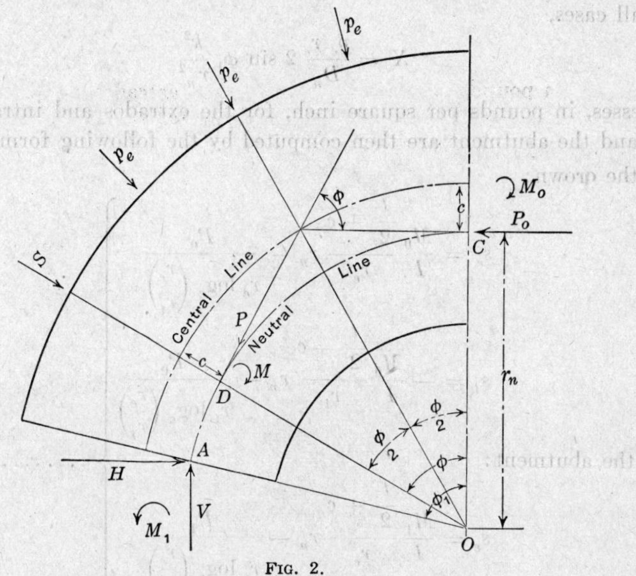

FIG. 2.

t = uniform radial thickness of arch, in feet;
r = radius of the center line, in feet;
r_n = radius of neutral line, in feet;

* *Transactions*, Am. Soc. C. E., Vol. LXXXV (1922), p. 238.

† *Loc. cit.*, p. 269.

‡ "Stresses in Thick Arches of Dams," by B. F. Jakobsen, M. Am. Soc. C. E., *Transactions*, Am. Soc. C. E., Vol. 90 (June, 1927), p. 475, containing a discussion and solution by the method of least work, by William Cain, M. Am. Soc. C. E., p. 522.

§ *Transactions*, Am. Soc. C. E., Vol. 90 (June, 1927), pp. 528-529.

r_e = radius of extrados, in feet;
r_i = radius of intrados, in feet;
p_e = normal radial pressure, in pounds per square foot, on the extrados;
ϕ = angle with radius of crown for any point, D;
ϕ_1 = one-half the central angle = $A\ O\ C$.

"The arc, $A\ D\ C$, is the neutral line, so that if s = length of the arc, the distance, $C\ D = r_n\ \phi$, $d\ s = r_n\ d\ \phi$.

P_0 = thrust at the crown, acting at C, on the neutral line;
M_0 = moment at crown, taken positive when clockwise;
M, P, and S = respectively, the moment, normal component, and shear on the section through D $(r_n\ \phi)$;
$c = r - r_n$;***"

The revised formulas for thrust and moment developed with this notation are:

$$P_0 = \text{thrust at crown} = p_e\, r_e - X \qquad (103)^*$$

$$M_0 = \text{moment at crown} = -X\, r_n \left(\frac{1 - \sin \phi_1}{\phi_1}\right) \qquad (105)^*$$

$$P_1 = \text{thrust at abutment} = p_e\, r_e - X \cos \phi_1 \qquad (99)\dagger$$

$$M_1 = \text{moment at abutment} = +X\, r_n \left(\frac{\sin \phi_1}{\phi_1} - \cos \phi_1\right) \qquad (106)^*$$

In all cases,

$$X = \frac{p_e\, r_e}{D_n}\, 2 \sin \phi_1 \frac{k^2}{{r_n}^2}$$

Stresses, in pounds per square inch, for the extrados and intrados of the crown and the abutment are then computed by the following formulas:

At the crown:

$$s_e = \frac{M_0}{I}\, \frac{\frac{t}{2} + c}{r_e}\, r_n - \frac{P_0}{r_e \log_e \left(\frac{r_e}{r_i}\right)}$$

$$s_i = -\frac{M_0}{I}\, \frac{\frac{t}{2} - c}{r_i}\, r_n - \frac{P_0}{r_i \log_e \left(\frac{r_e}{r_i}\right)}$$

At the abutment: .... (107)‡

$$s_e = \frac{M_1}{I}\, \frac{\frac{t}{2} + c}{r_e}\, r_n - \frac{P_1}{r_e \log_e \left(\frac{r_e}{r_i}\right)}$$

$$s_i = -\frac{M_1}{I}\, \frac{\frac{t}{2} - c}{r_i}\, r_n - \frac{P_1}{r_i \log_e \left(\frac{r_e}{r_i}\right)}$$

* *Transactions*, Am. Soc. C. E., Vol. 90 (June, 1927), p. 531.
† *Loc. cit.*, p. 529.
‡ *Loc. cit.*, p. 533.

The complete analysis of stresses at the crown and abutments of a dam, by any of these formulas, involves a large expenditure of time.

Even neglecting shear, the conditions are so complex that analysis by the rigorous mathematical methods results in complicated equations, the solution of which is a slow and laborious process. This fact was clearly recognized by Professor Cain, who strove to lighten the labor by including in his first paper, previously mentioned, a tabulation giving the values of the complicated variable expression, $\frac{2\,\phi_1}{D_0}$. Originally the tabulation* included values for this term corresponding to five different central angles and seven different values of $\frac{t}{r}$; in the discussion, B. F. Jakobsen, M. Am. Soc. C. E., plotted the results of the tabulation, somewhat amplified, in a chart† showing, on a semi-logarithmatic scale, curves for central angles varying from 40 to 180° by steps of 10°, and for values of $\frac{t}{r}$ ranging from 0.02 to 0.30; in his closure, Professor Cain further amplified the data by presenting them in both tabular and diagrammatic form.‡ This later table covers twenty-seven values of central angle (40 to 55° by steps of 2.5°; 55 to 130° by steps of 5°; and 130 to 180° by steps of 10°); in the diagram mentioned (Fig. 10),‡ in order to avoid complication, it was necessary to omit some of the curves, but, notwithstanding these omissions, the curves included facilitate the determination of any value of $\frac{2\,\phi_1}{D_0}$ for central angles ranging from 40 to 180°, and of $\frac{t}{r}$ from 0.02 to 0.30.

Even with these aids the computation of stresses at four points (the extrados and intrados at the crown and the abutment) in a single arch ring requires:

1.—Abstracting from tables five trigonometric functions or constants; and

2.—Performing thirty or more arithmetical computations (multiplications, divisions, additions, and subtractions), involving both positive and negative quantities and numbers varying from millions down to ten thousands.

Not only are these various computations laborious, but they offer many chances for arithmetical errors, and no opportunity for checks save by duplicate computation. The revised formulas, including the effect of shear, published in the discussion on Mr. Jakobsen's paper on "Stresses in Thick Arches of Dams",§ are even more rigorous in their treatment and, hence, more complicated.

---

* *Transactions,* Am. Soc. C. E., Vol. LXXXV (1922), Table 2, p. 246.

† *Loc. cit.,* Fig. 8, p. 257.

‡ *Loc. cit.,* Table 6, p. 266, and Fig. 10, p. 267.

§ *Loc. cit.,* Vol. 90 (June, 1927), pp. 522–601, inclusive.

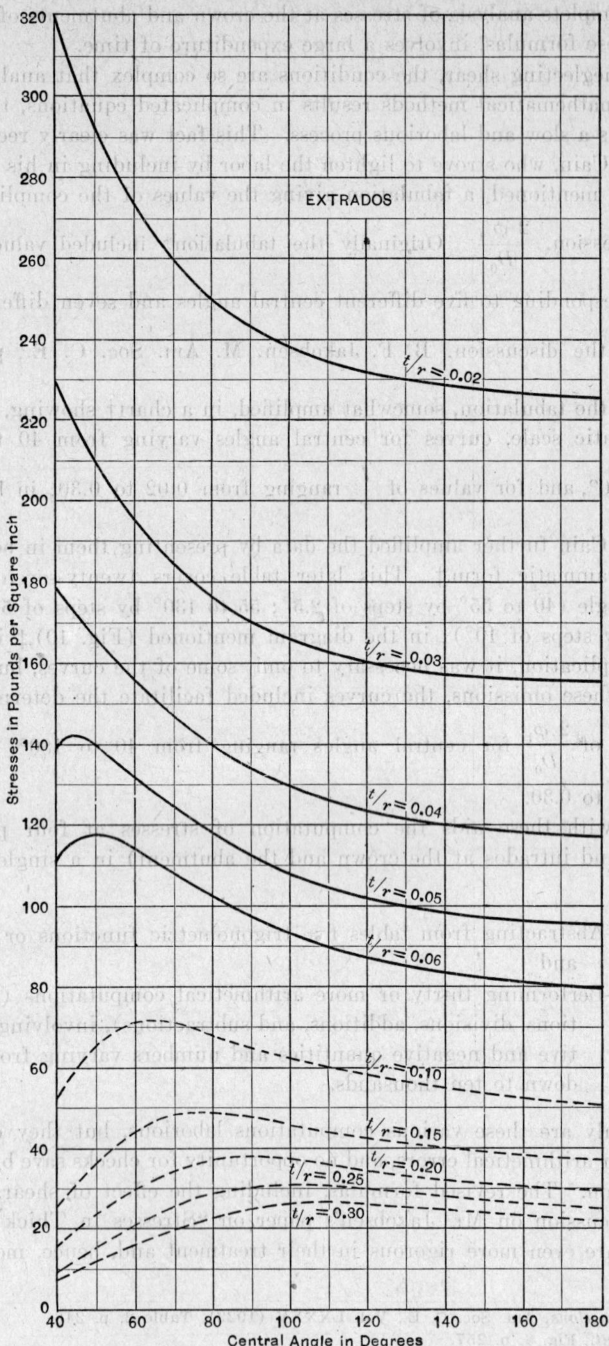

FIG. 3.—STRESSES AT CROWN—EXTRADOS. FOR 10-FOOT HEAD.

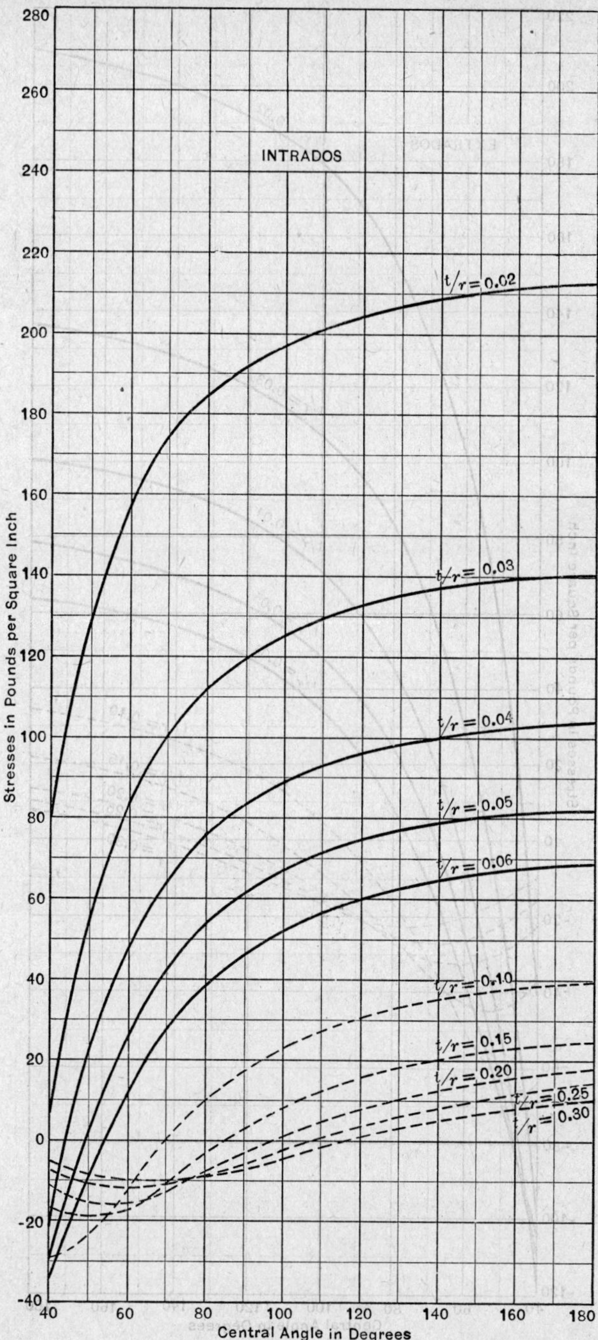

FIG. 4.—STRESSES AT CROWN—INTRADOS. FOR 10-FOOT HEAD.

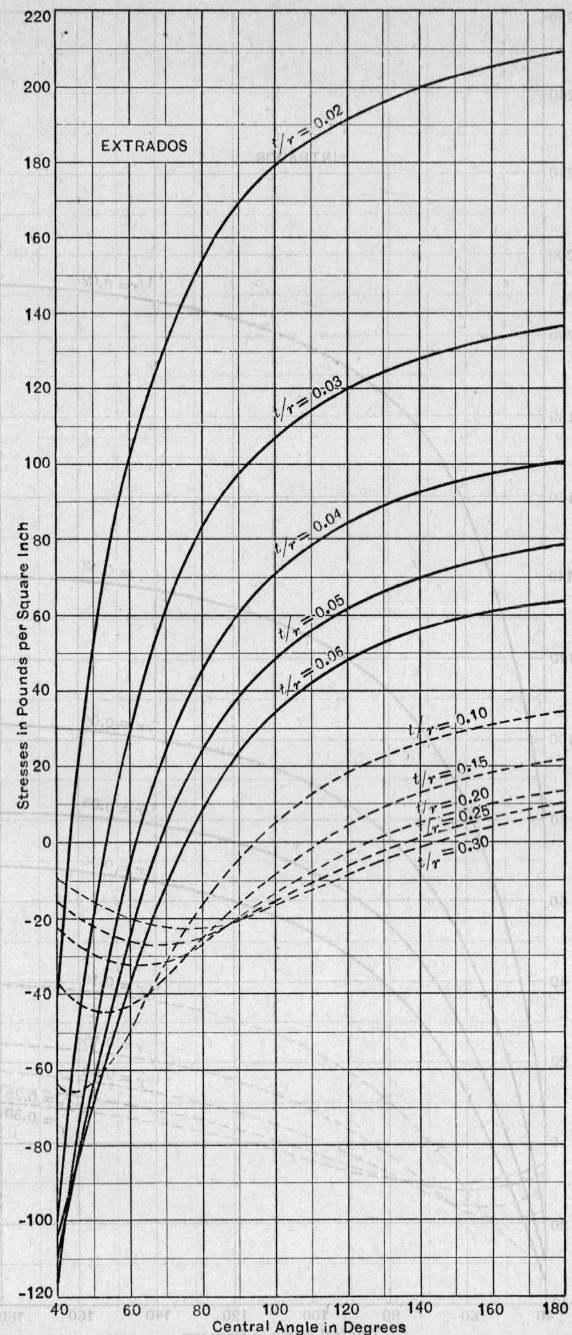

FIG. 5.—STRESSES AT ABUTMENTS—EXTRADOS. FOR 10-FOOT HEAD.

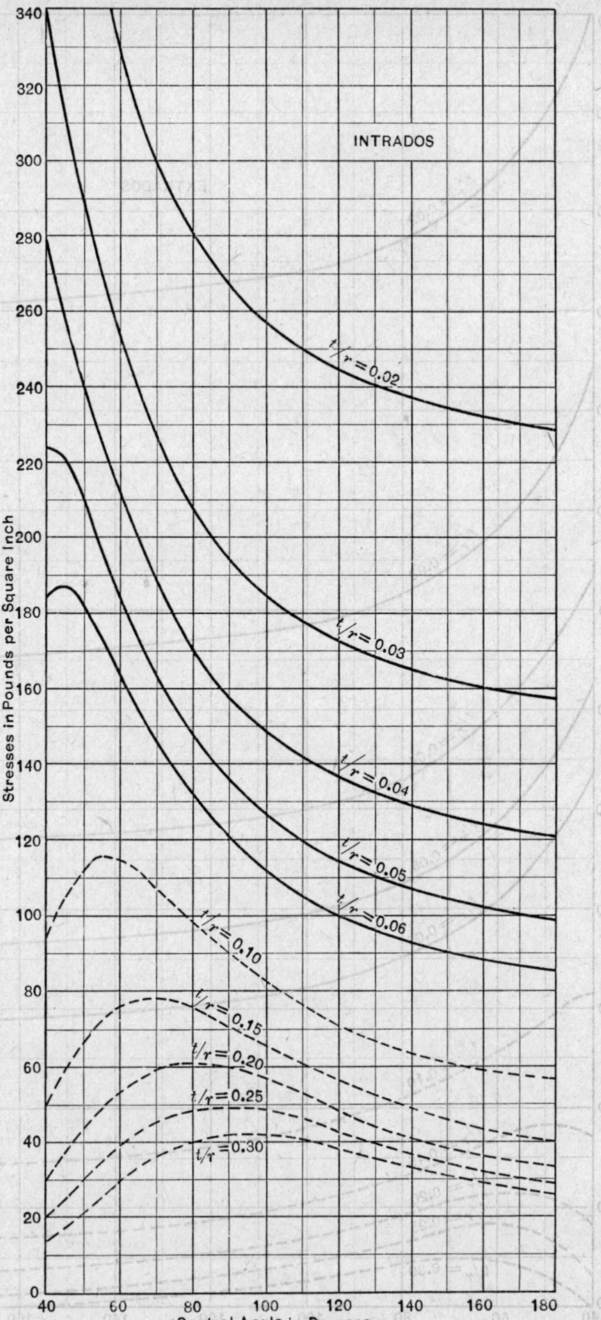

FIG. 6.—STRESSES AT ABUTMENTS—INTRADOS. FOR 10-FOOT HEAD.

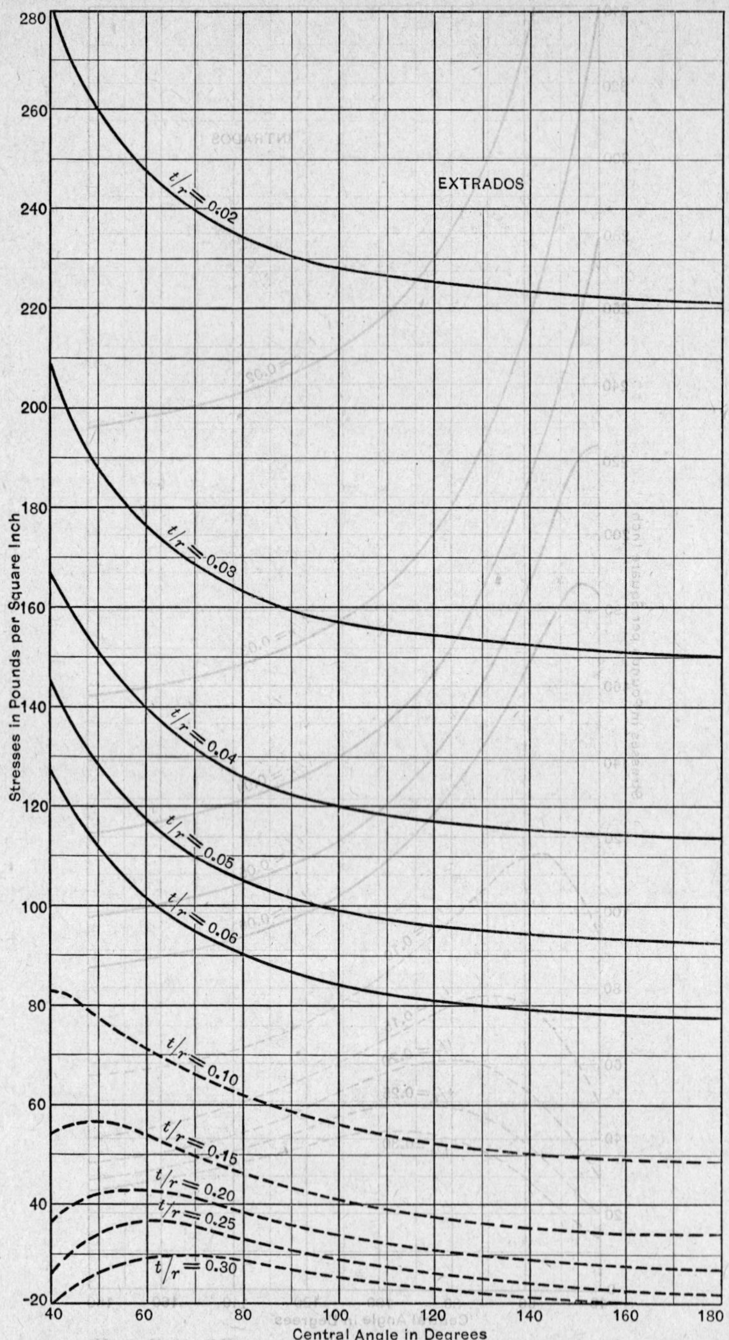

FIG. 7.—STRESSES AT CROWN, HINGED ENDS—EXTRADOS. FOR 10-FOOT HEAD.

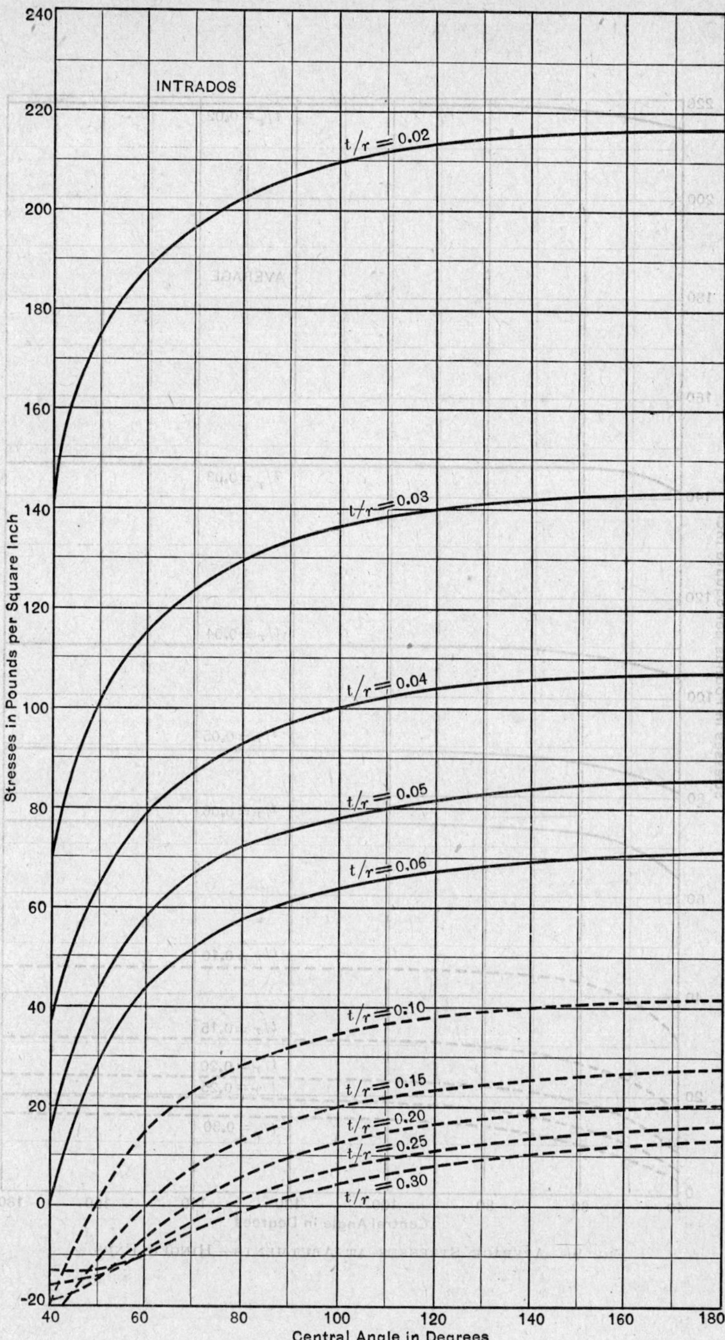

FIG. 8.—STRESSES AT CROWN, HINGED ENDS—INTRADOS. FOR 10-FOOT HEAD.

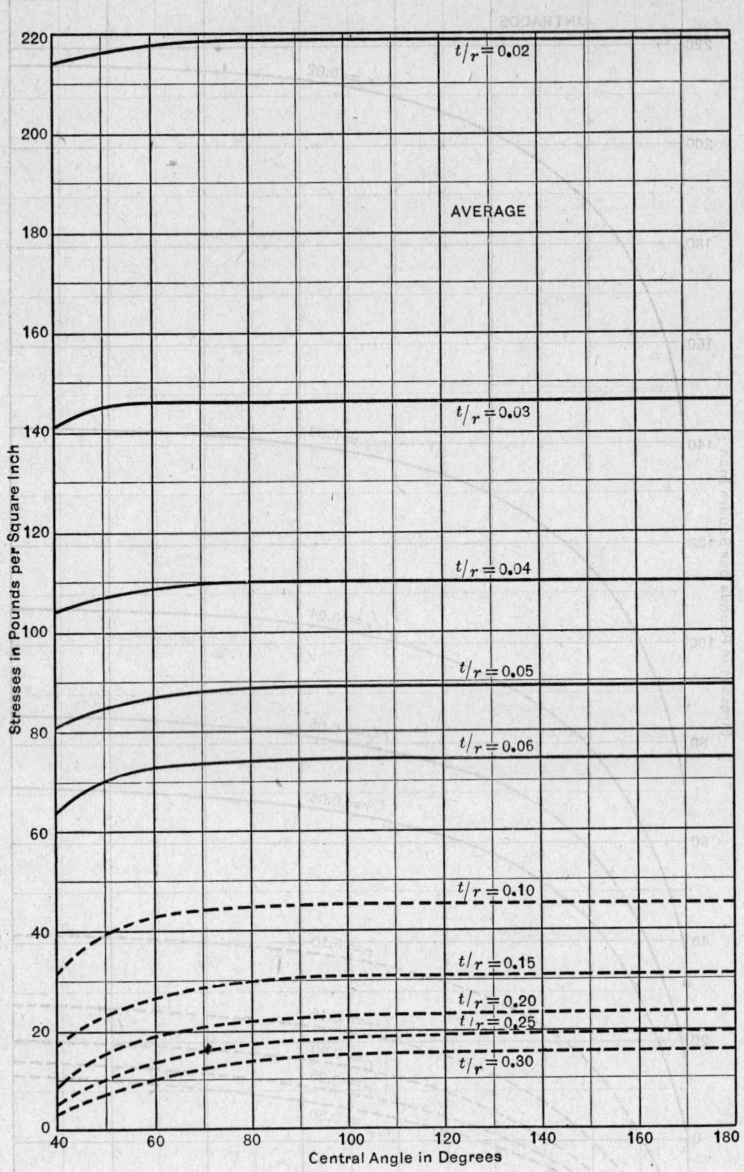

FIG. 9.—AVERAGE STRESSES AT ABUTMENTS—HINGED ENDS.

The curves presented in this paper resulted from an attempt to simplify the use of these valuable contributions to a complex engineering problem.

Due to the number of variables it would appear, at first glance, impossible to devise a simple graphic solution. For example, practically all dam sites decrease in width from top to bottom. The dam itself increases in thickness from top to bottom in order to withstand the head, which increases in like manner. The central angle of the arch may vary in practice from, say, 40 to 130°, or more. The radius varies with the width of the site at any given level and with the central angle. It is obvious, therefore, that with the different conditions encountered at various elevations in any structure there is no direct relation between the stresses at any two given levels.

If, however, an imaginary arch dam is assumed, of fixed central angle and radius and uniform thickness throughout its entire height, the stresses in the arch rings at any two levels will be in proportion to the heads, and the computed stresses for a convenient head—say, 10 ft.—when multiplied by 10, will give the stresses for the arch ring under 10 $\times$ 10, or 100-ft. head; this relation permits the use of a single set of computations as a measure for the stresses at all heads.

The value of r used in such computations is immaterial, since when the head and the central angle are equal, the stresses in any two arch rings remain equal and constant so long as the ratio, $\frac{t}{r}$, remains constant—even if the length of the radius of each ring is freely changed. It is this constant relation of stresses to values of $\frac{t}{r}$ that makes it possible to show the formulas graphically.

In preparing the curves the stresses at the extrados and intrados of the crown and abutment of an "imaginary" arch were computed for a head of 10 ft., for central angles ranging from 40 to 180°, and for varying ranges in the values of $\frac{t}{r}$ depending on the formulas.

The three groups of curves are based on the three sets of formulas developed by Professor Cain:

Group I.—Arches with "fixed ends" (neglecting shear). Formulas developed on pages 235 to 238, *Transactions,* Am. Soc. C. E., Vol. LXXXV (1922); this set of curves (Figs. 3, 4, 5, and 6) covers central angles ($2\ \phi_1$) ranging from 40 to 180°, and values of $\frac{t}{r}$ ranging from 0.02 to 0.30. The curves for values of $\frac{t}{r} = 0.10$ to 0.30, are included, however, only for comparison with curves of Group III, which are more accurate since they include the influence of shear.

Group II.—Arches with "hinged ends" (neglecting shear). Formulas developed on pages 241 to 243, *Transactions,* Am. Soc. C. E., Vol. LXXXV (1922); this set (Figs. 7, 8, and 9) covers the same range and values of $\frac{t}{r}$.

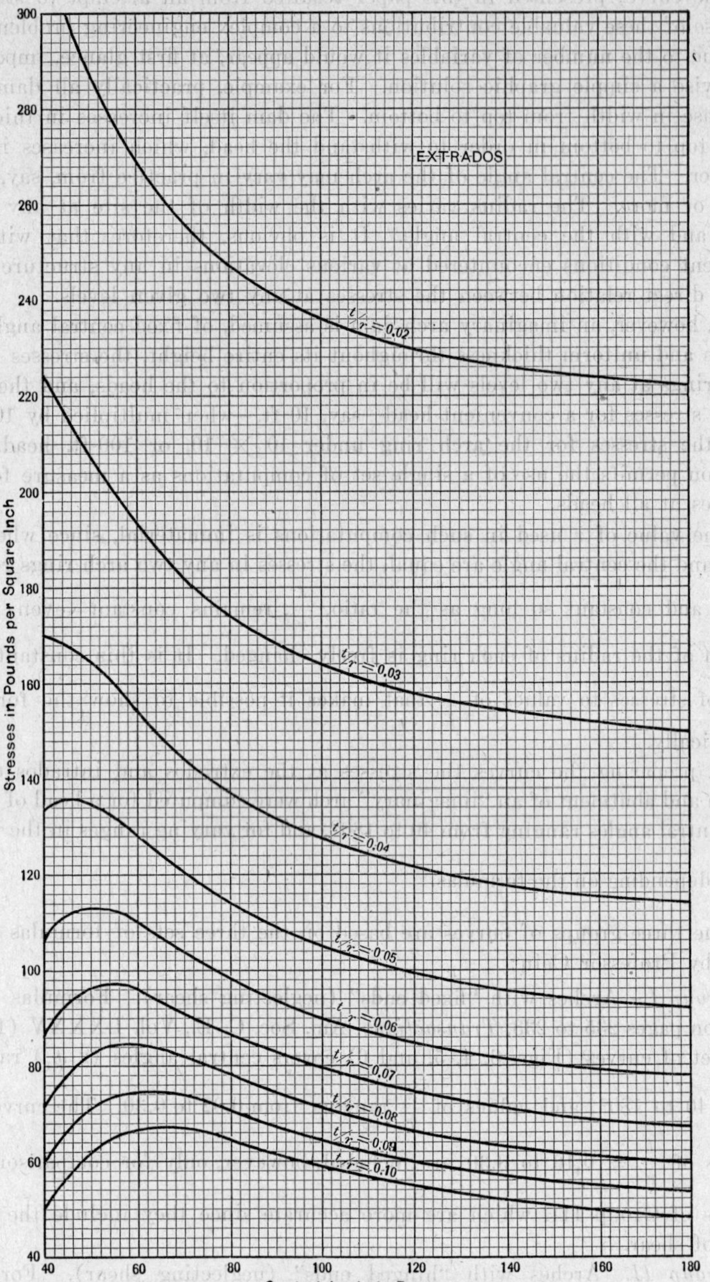

FIG. 10 (a).—STRESSES AT CROWN—EXTRADOS. FIXED ENDS, INCLUDING SHEAR. FOR 10-FOOT HEAD.

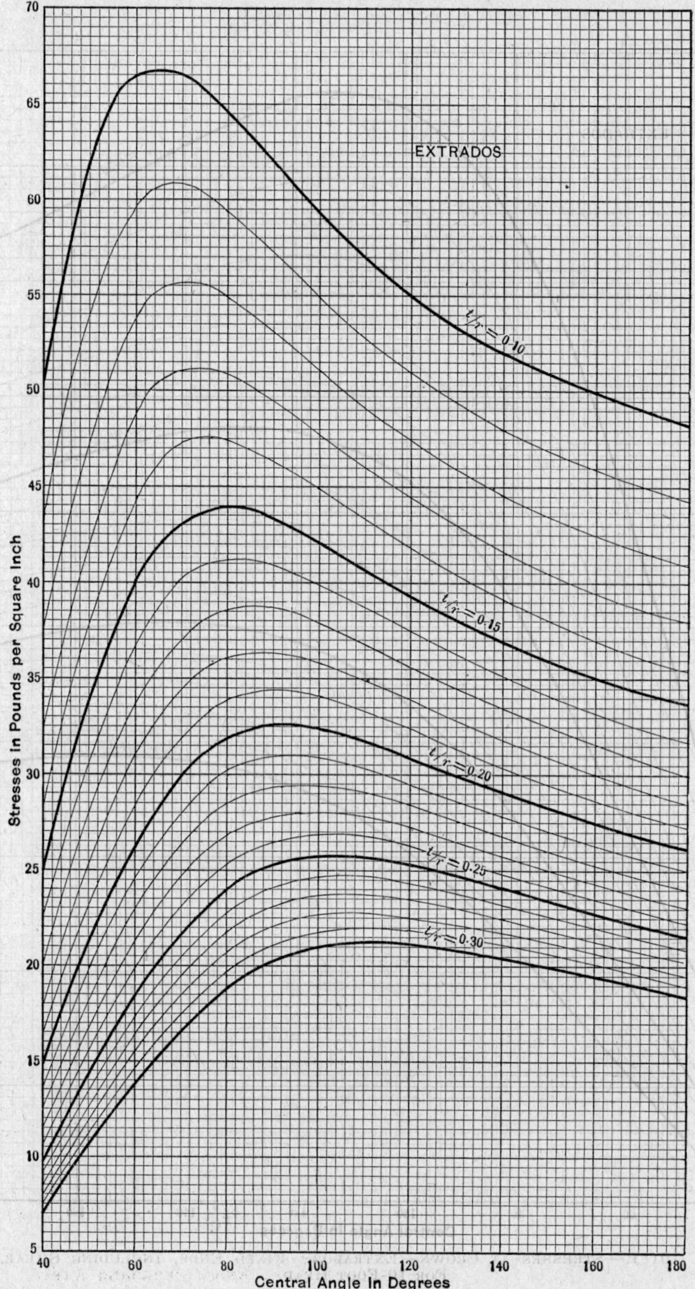

FIG. 10(*b*).—STRESSES AT CROWN—EXTRADOS. FIXED ENDS, INCLUDING SHEAR. FOR 10-FOOT HEAD.

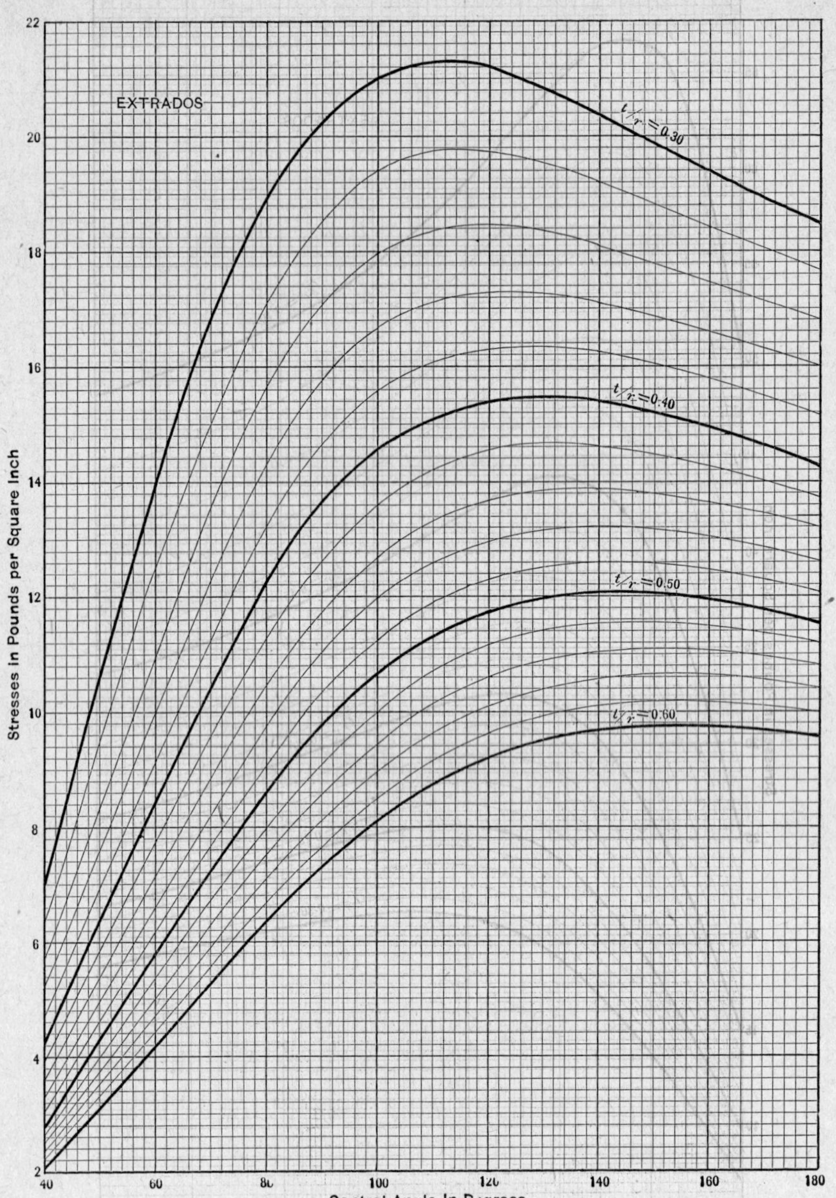

FIG. 10(*c*).—STRESSES AT CROWN—EXTRADOS. FIXED ENDS, INCLUDING SHEAR. FOR 10-FOOT HEAD.

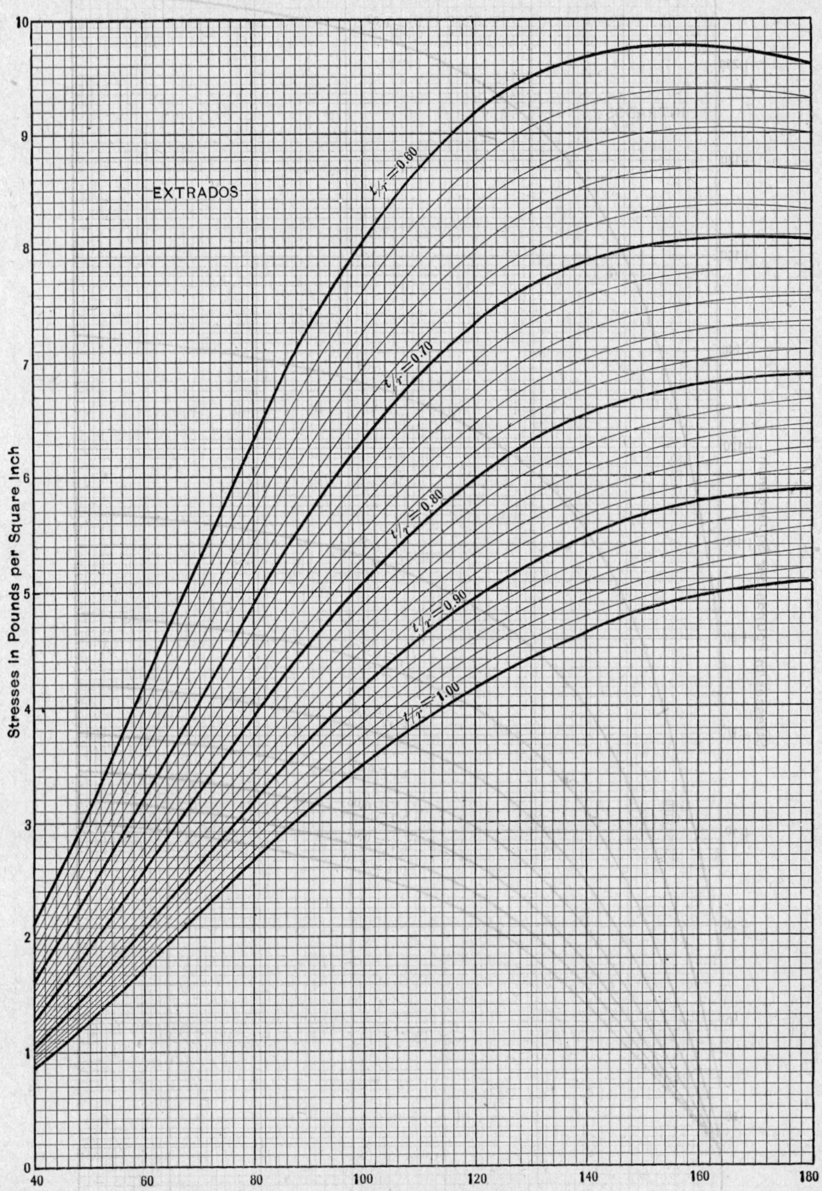

FIG. 10(*d*).—STRESSES AT CROWN—EXTRADOS. FIXED ENDS, INCLUDING SHEAR. FOR 10-FOOT HEAD.

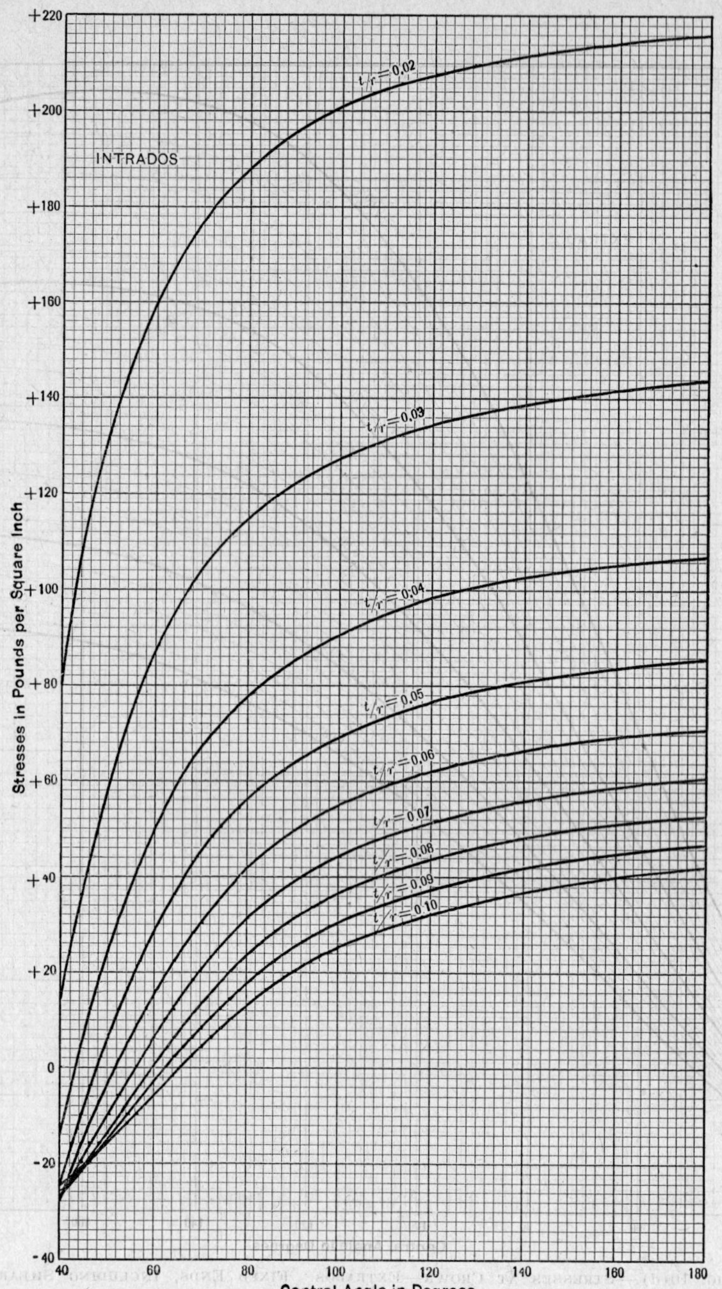

FIG. 11(*a*).—STRESSES AT CROWN—INTRADOS. FIXED ENDS, INCLUDING SHEAR. FOR 10-FOOT HEAD.

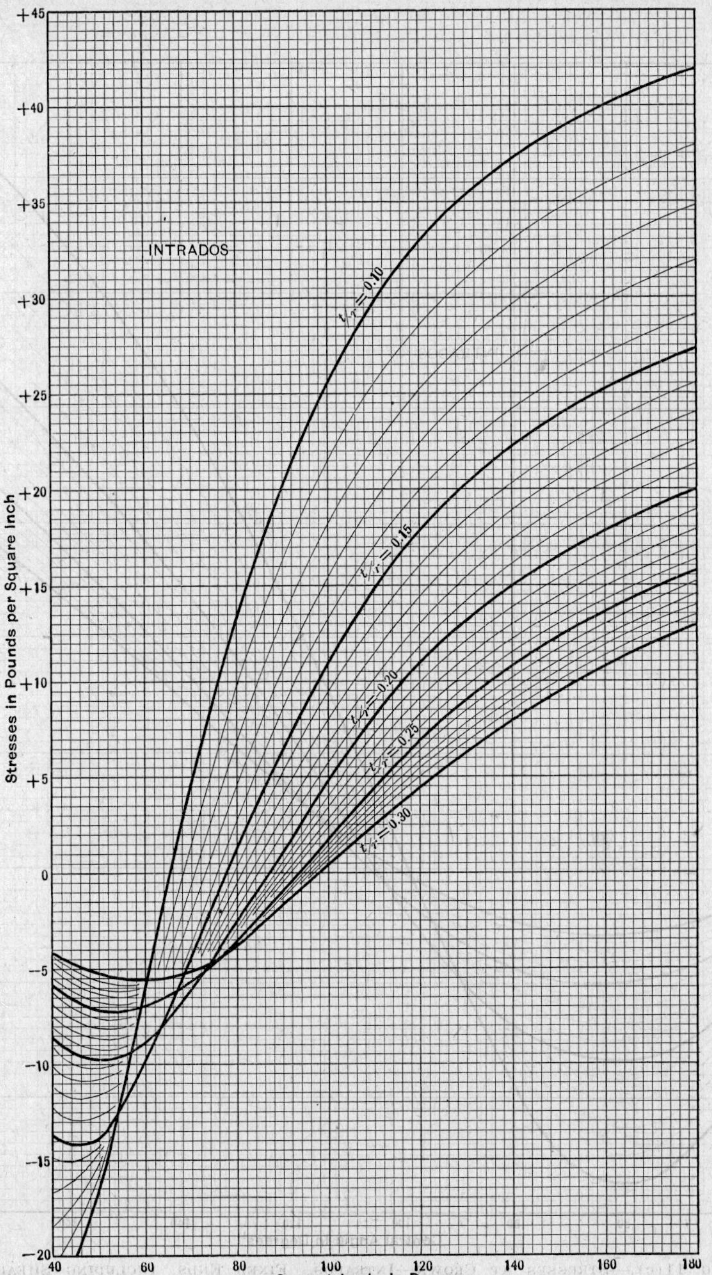

Fig. 11(*b*).—Stresses at Crown—Intrados. Fixed Ends, Including Shear. For 10-Foot Head.

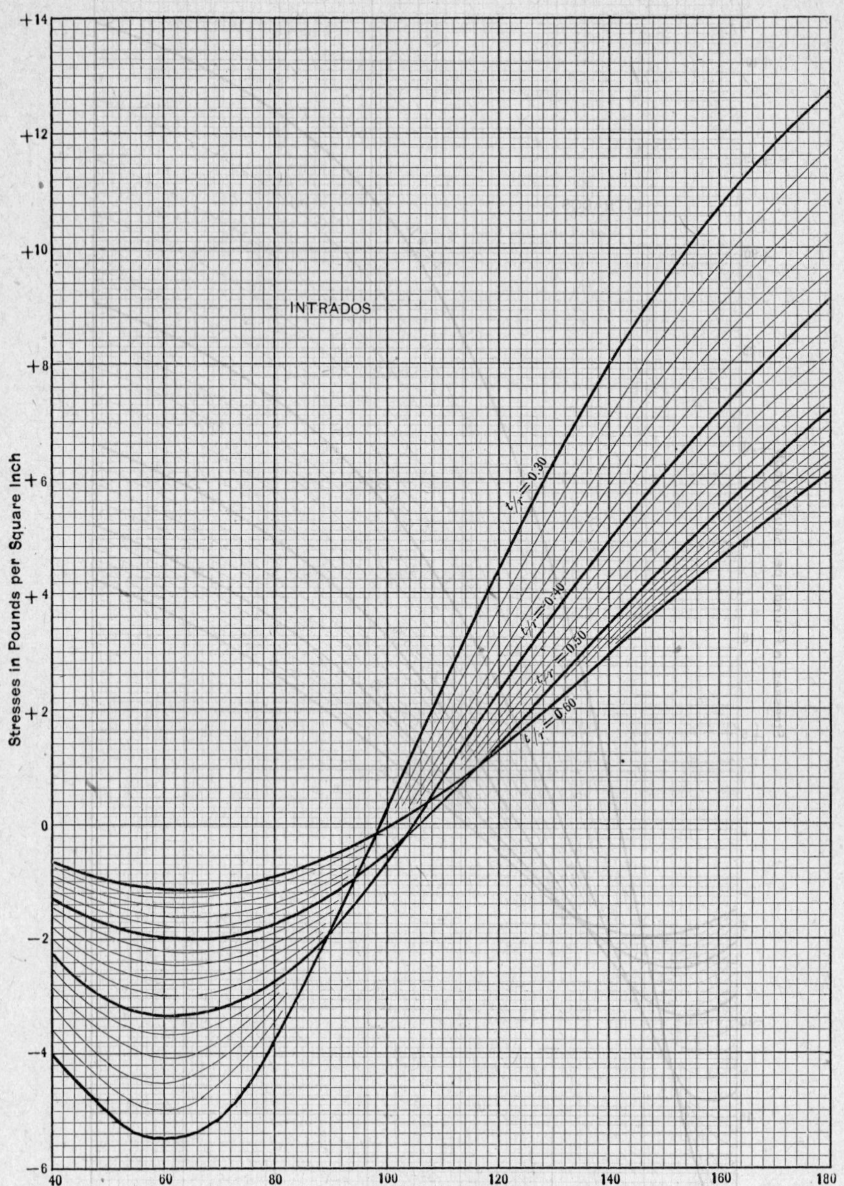

FIG. 11(*c*).—STRESSES AT CROWN—INTRADOS. FIXED ENDS, INCLUDING SHEAR. FOR 10-FOOT HEAD.

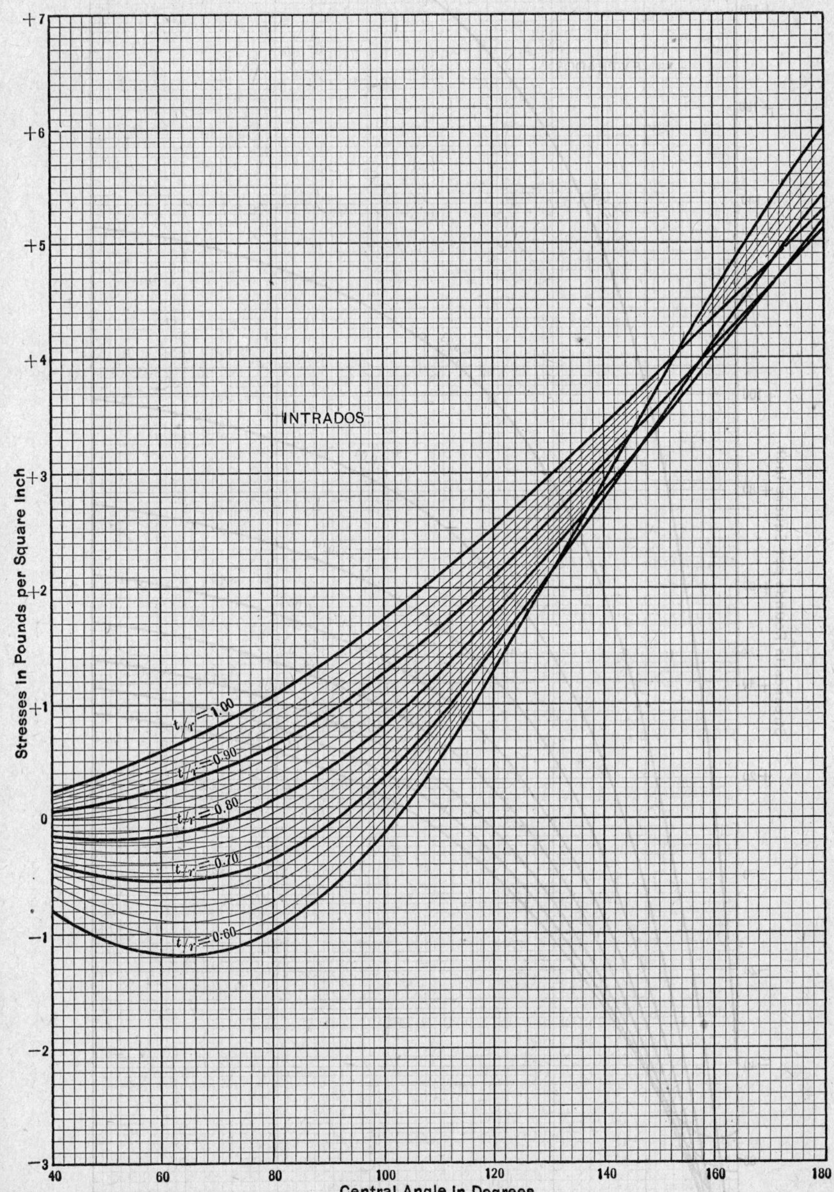

FIG. 11(*d*).—STRESSES AT CROWN—INTRADOS. FIXED ENDS, INCLUDING SHEAR. FOR 10-FOOT HEAD.

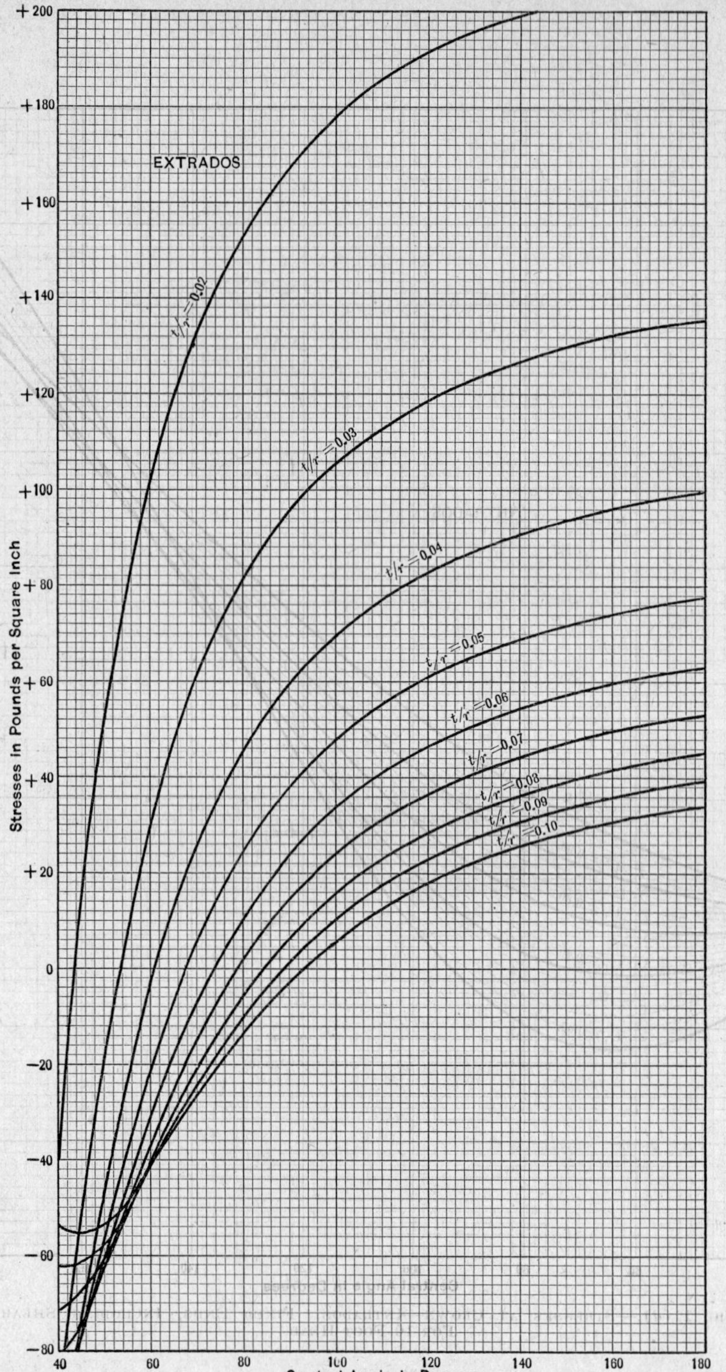

FIG. 12(*a*).—STRESSES AT ABUTMENTS—EXTRADOS. FIXED ENDS, INCLUDING SHEAR. FOR 10-FOOT HEAD.

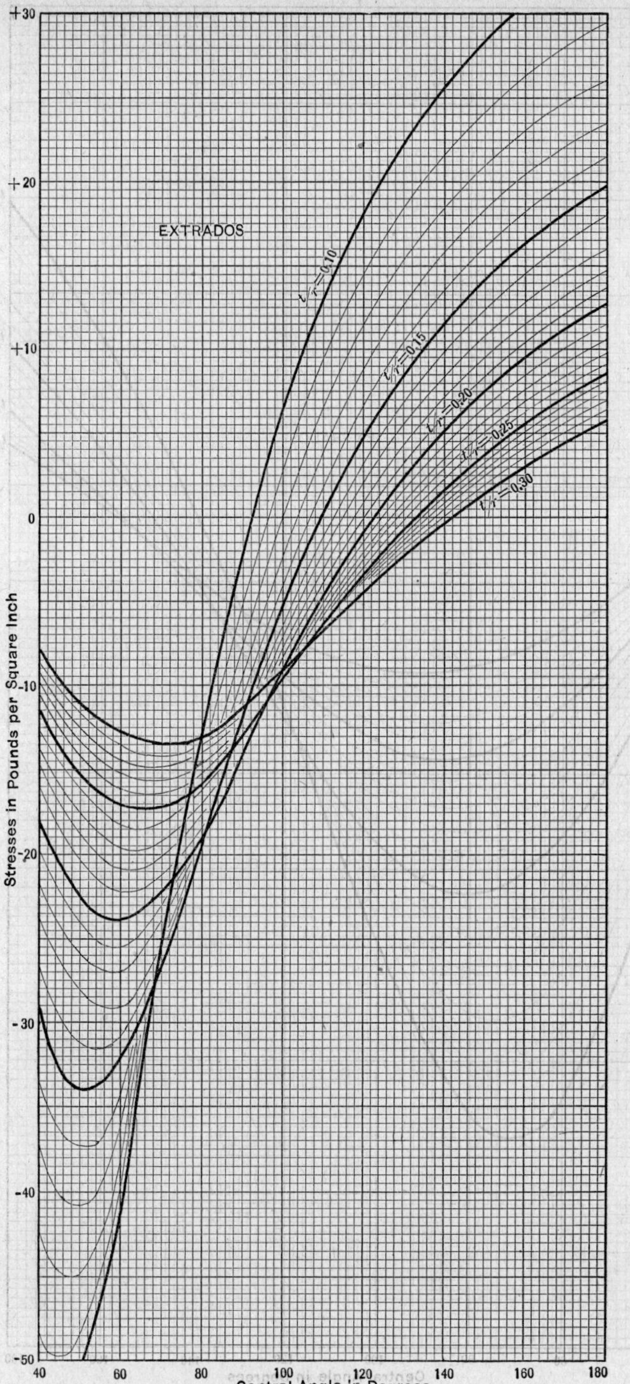

FIG. 12(b).—STRESSES AT ABUTMENTS—EXTRADOS. FIXED ENDS, INCLUDING SHEAR. FOR 10-FOOT HEAD.

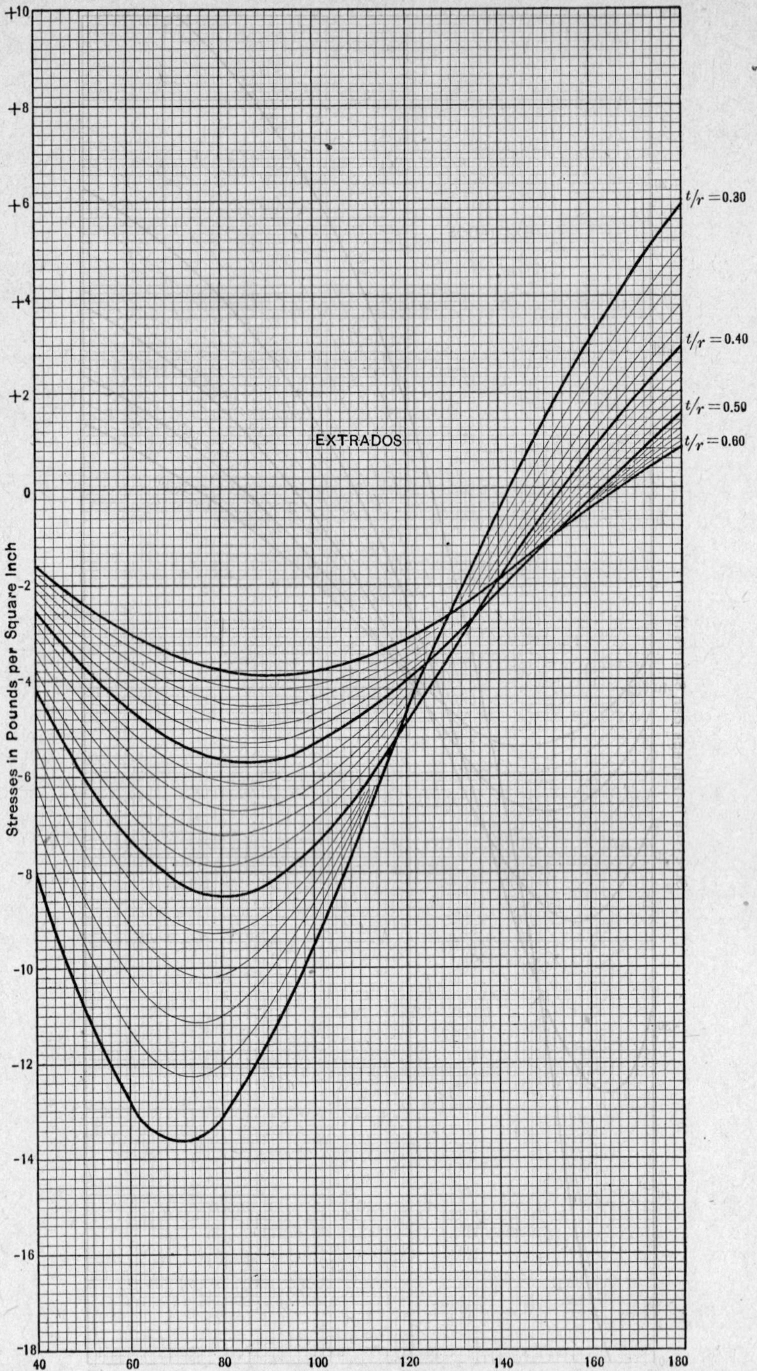

FIG. 12(c).—STRESSES AT ABUTMENTS—EXTRADOS. FIXED ENDS, INCLUDING SHEAR. FOR 10-FOOT HEAD.

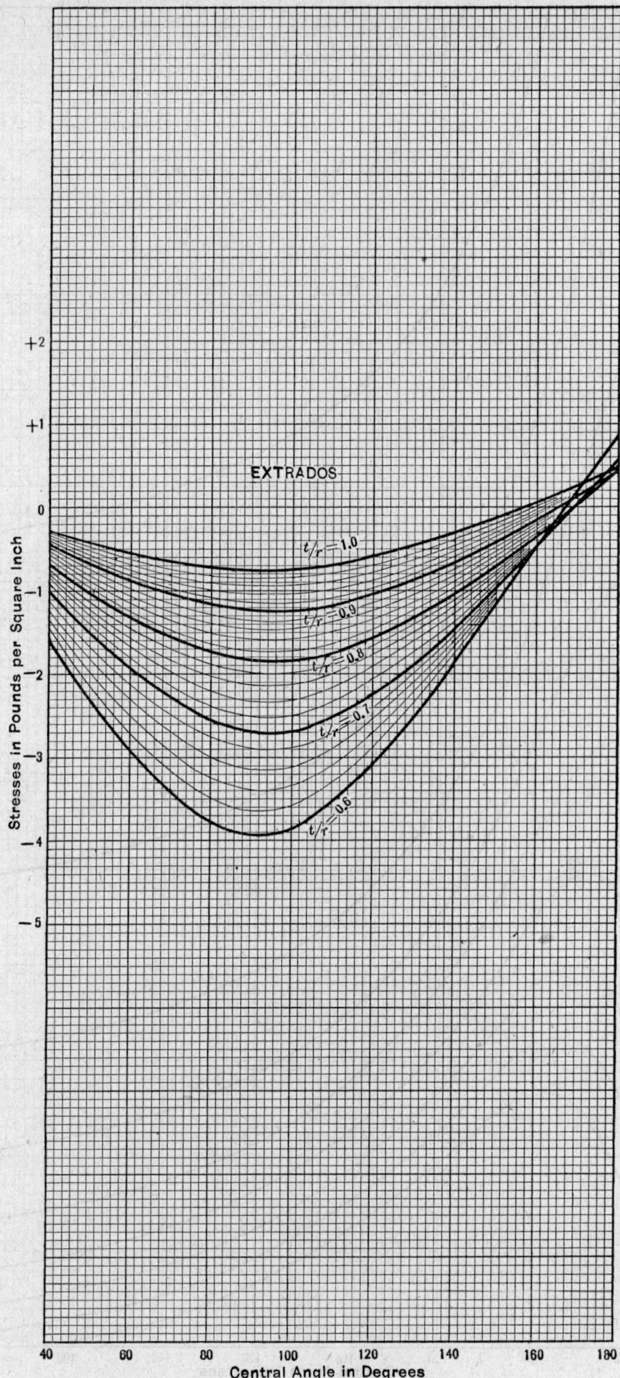

FIG. 12(*d*).—STRESSES AT ABUTMENTS—EXTRADOS. FIXED ENDS, INCLUDING SHEAR. FOR 10-FOOT HEAD.

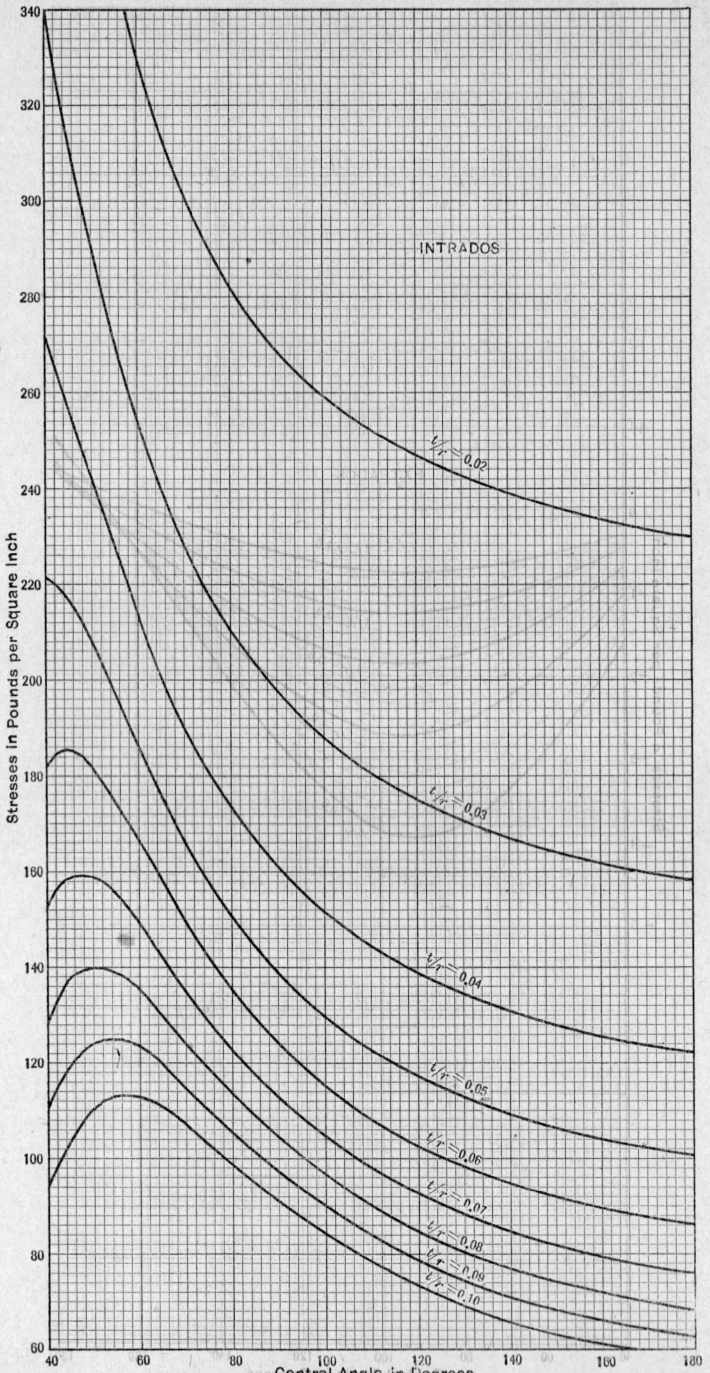

FIG. 13(*a*).—STRESSES AT ABUTMENTS—INTRADOS. FIXED ENDS, INCLUDING SHEAR. FOR 10-FOOT HEAD.

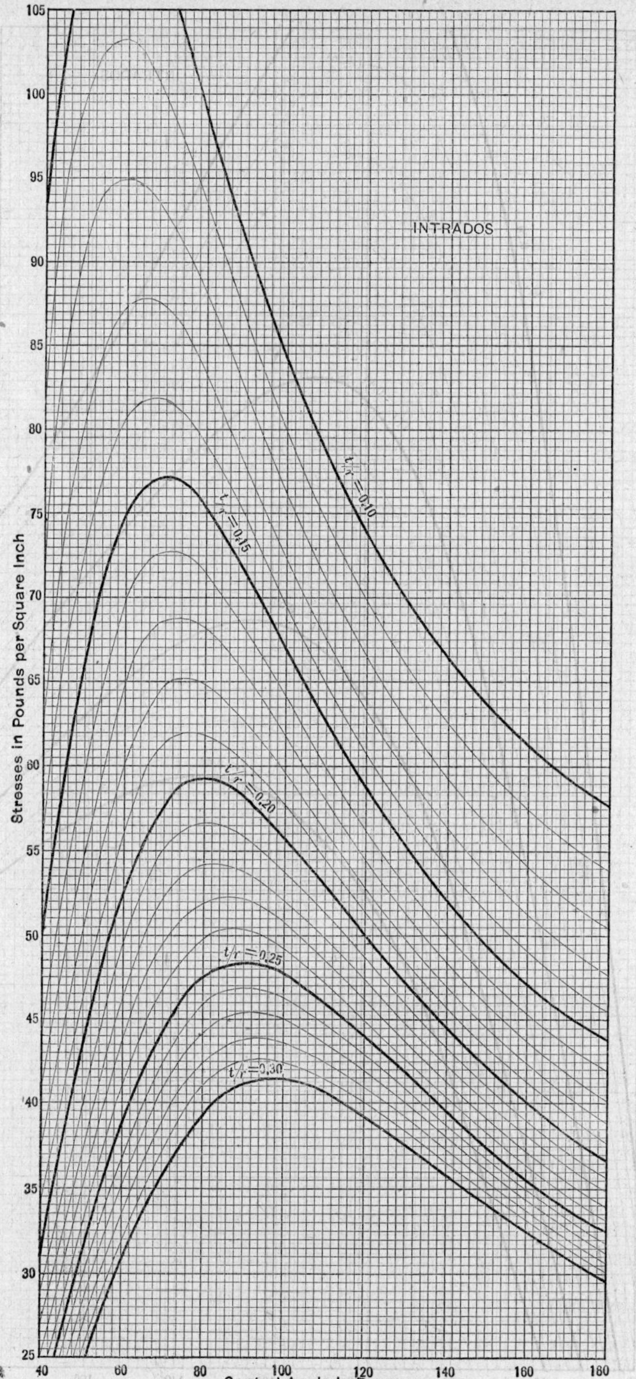

FIG. 13(b).—STRESSES AT ABUTMENTS—INTRADOS. FIXED ENDS, INCLUDING SHEAR. FOR 10-FOOT HEAD.

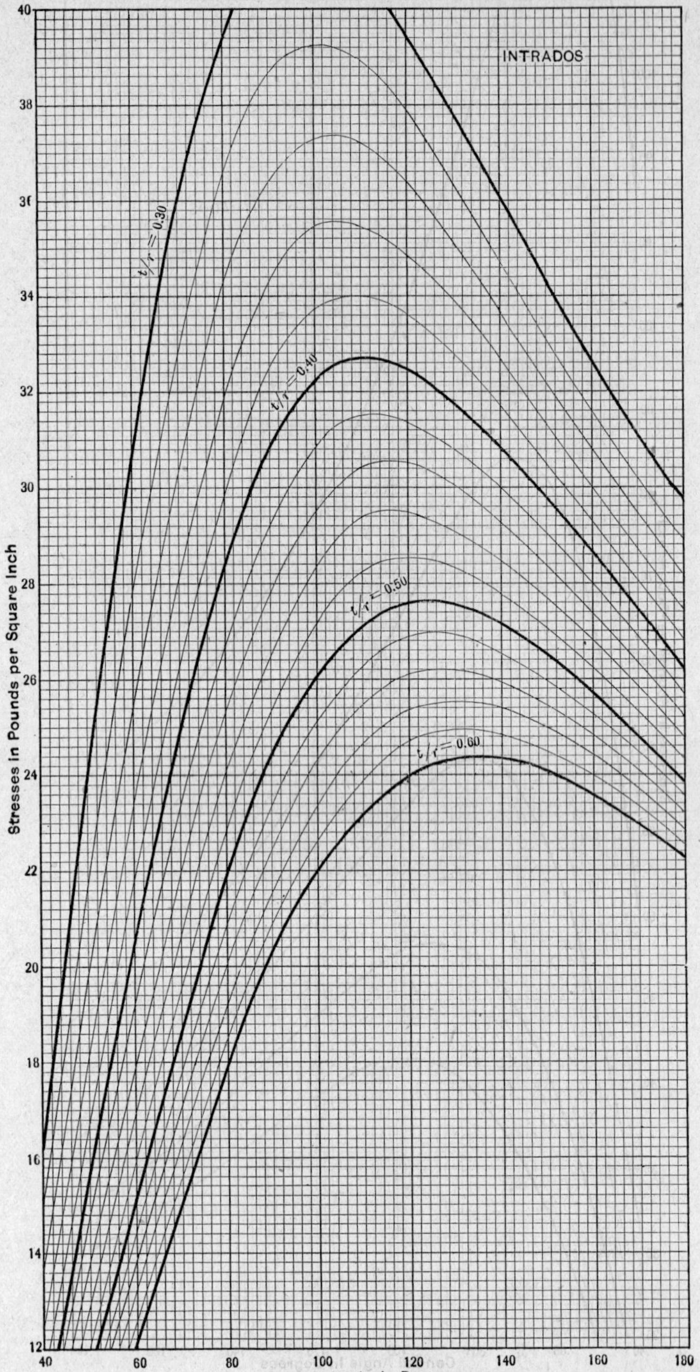

FIG. 13(*c*).—STRESSES AT ABUTMENTS—INTRADOS. FIXED ENDS, INCLUDING SHEAR. FOR 10-FOOT HEAD.

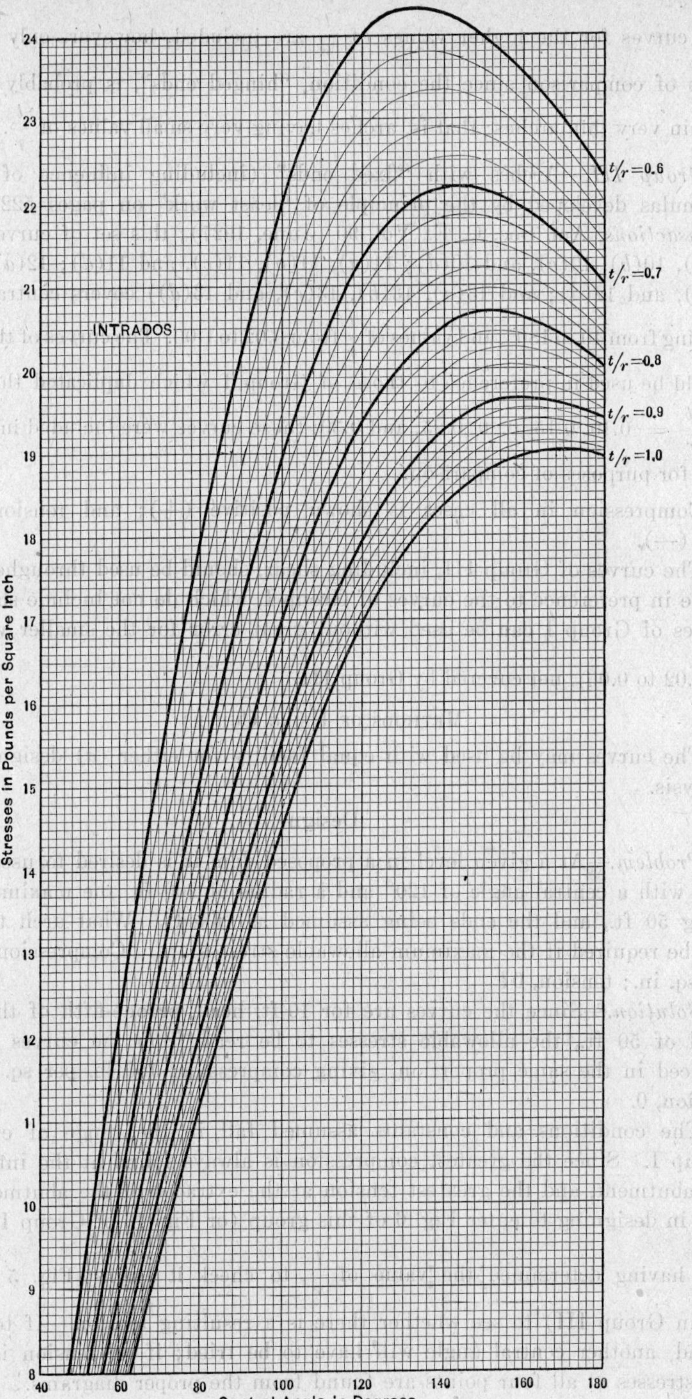

FIG. 13(*d*).—STRESSES AT ABUTMENTS—INTRADOS. FIXED ENDS, INCLUDING SHEAR. FOR 10-FOOT HEAD.

The curves for the higher values of $\frac{t}{r}$ are included, however, only for purposes of comparison since the condition, "hinged ends", is probably realized only in very thin arches; that is, arches having very small values of $\frac{t}{r}$.

Group III.—Arches with "fixed ends" (including influence of shear). Formulas developed by the principle of "least work" on pages 522 to 534, *Transactions*, Am. Soc. C. E., Vol. 90 (June, 1927); this set of curves (Figs. 10(*a*), 10(*b*), 10(*c*), and 10(*d*); 11(*a*), 11(*b*), 11(*c*), and 11(*d*); 12(*a*), 12(*b*), 12(*c*), and 12(*d*); and 13(*a*), 13(*b*), 13(*c*), and 13(*d*)) covers central angles ranging from 40 to 180°, and values of $\frac{t}{r}$ from 0.02 to 1.00. The curves of this group should be used in preference to those of Group I which duplicated the curves for $\frac{t}{r}$ = 0.10, 0.15, 0.20, 0.25, and 0.30; these curves were included in Group I only for purposes of comparison.

Compression in all cases is shown positive (+); and tension, negative (—).

The curves of Group III, including shear, should be used throughout their range in preference to the curves of Group I, which do not include shear; the curves of Group I can be used without great error for the smaller values of $\frac{t}{r}$ (0.02 to 0.06), not covered by Group III.

Methods of Using Curves

The curves may be used with equal facility for either (*a*) design, or (*b*) analysis.

Design

Problem.—At a given level in a proposed dam it is desired to use an arch ring with a central angle of 120° and a radius of 200 ft., the maximum head being 50 ft., and the ends being assumed as "fixed". What arch thickness will be required if the maximum allowable stresses are: Compression, 500 lb. per sq. in.; tension, 0?

Solution.—Since the curves are for 10-ft. head, or one-fifth of the actual head of 50 ft., the allowable stresses to be read from the curves must be reduced in the same proportion, giving compression, 100 lb. per sq. in., and tension, 0.

The conditions and constants assumed fall in the range of curves of Group I. Since the greatest compression is always found at the intrados of the abutment, and the greatest tension at the extrados of the abutment, it is best in designing to enter Fig. 6 of this group (or Fig. 13 of Group III) first, and having determined the value of $\frac{t}{r}$, to check it against Fig. 5 (or Fig. 12, in Group III) to see whether there is a resulting tension. If tension is found, another central angle will have to be tried; if no tension is shown, the stresses at all four points are found from the proper diagrams.

In the present case it is found that the curve, $\frac{t}{r} = 0.06$, passes through the intersection of the vertical line for 120° and the horizontal line for 100 lb. per sq. in.; checking by Fig. 5, the stress horizontally opposite the intersection of the vertical from 120° and the curve, $\frac{t}{r} = 0.06$, is + 48 lb. per sq. in., or 48 lb. compression, which satisfies the condition that there shall be no tension. The stresses in the actual arch are given in Table 1.

TABLE 1.—STRESSES IN PROPOSED ARCH DAM.

Point.		Stresses read from diagram, in pounds per square inch.	Multiplying factor.	Stresses in arch, in pounds per square inch.
Abutment:	**Intrados**	100	5	500
	Extrados	48	5	240
Crown:	**Intrados**	60	5	300
	Extrados	87.5	5	438

The radius on the center line of the arch ring being 200 ft. and $\frac{t}{r}$, 0.06, the thickness, t, is 12 ft. The radius of the up-stream face (extrados) is 206 ft. and that of the down-stream face (intrados) is 194 ft. Had the stress and $\frac{t}{r}$ been assumed in the problem, the required angle could have been read from the curves.

Analysis

Problem.—What are the stresses in the Kerckhoff Dam (already constructed) at Elevation 900, (*a*) neglecting shear, and (*b*) including shear?

Measurements* show that at that level the head is 95 ft., $t = 28.9$ ft., $r = 143.3$ ft., $\frac{t}{r} = 0.201$, and the central angle, $(2\,\phi_1) = 82°\ 40'$.

Solution.—

(*a*) Neglecting Shear.—The stresses read from Figs. 3 to 6, horizontally opposite the intersection of the vertical through 82° 40′, and an interpolated curve, $\frac{t}{r} = 0.201$, are given in Column (2) of Table 2, and the actual stresses in the given section of the dam $\left(\frac{95}{10} = 9.5 \text{ times as great}\right)$ in Column (3). Minus signs in all cases denote tension.

(*b*) Including Shear.—The stresses read from Figs. 10 to 13, horizontally opposite the intersection of the vertical through 82° 40′ and an interpolated curve through $\frac{t}{r} = 0.201$, are given in Column (2), and the resulting stresses under a 95-ft. head in Column (4), of Table 3.

* *Transactions*, Am. Soc. C. E., Vol. LXXXV (1922), p. 258.

The solutions represented by the curves of Group III were made on the basis of m (in Poisson's ratio) $= \alpha$; σ_x (vertical unit stress on the arch ring) $= 0$; and $I_n = I$.*

TABLE 2.—STRESSES IN KERCKHOFF DAM, NEGLECTING SHEAR.

Point. (1)		Stress read from diagram, in pounds per square inch. (2)	Multiplying factor. (3)	Stress in dam, in pounds per square inch. (4)
Crown:	Extrados...............	37	9.5	352
	Intrados...............	− 7.5	9.5	− 71+
Abutment:	Extrados...............	−26	9.5	−247
	Intrados...............	60	9.5	570

All the curves were computed on the basis of the arch ring at 10-ft. depth taking the full water load; in using them to compute the stresses in a ring at, say, 100-ft. depth, carrying the full water load, the unit stresses shown by the curves should be multiplied by 10; but if it is assumed that the ring at the 100-ft. depth carries only 0.8 of the water load (the remainder being carried by the vertical cantilever), the stresses read from the curves should be multiplied by 8 and not by 10.

TABLE 3.—STRESSES IN KERCKHOFF DAM, INCLUDING SHEAR.

Point. (1)		Stress read from diagram, in pounds per square inch. (2)	Multiplying factor. (3)	Stress in dam, in pounds per square inch. (4)
Crown:	Extrados...............	32.3	9.5	307
	Intrados...............	− 1.6	9.5	− 15
Abutment:	Extrados...............	−17.4	9.5	−165
	Intrados...............	59.0	9.5	560

It is possible that future experimental data secured from actual structures may lead to some modification of the Cain formula, but in the meantime it is hoped that the diagrams presented herewith may prove of practical assistance to those using Professor Cain's most valuable method of analysis.

* For comparison of unit stresses under different assumptions, by the Cain and by the Jakobsen formulas, see *Transactions*, Am. Soc. C. E., Vol. 90 (June, 1927), Table 10, p. 540.

DISCUSSION

B. F. Jakobsen,* M. Am. Soc. C. E. (by letter).—The real value of this paper lies in the information it affords about the relation between $x = \frac{t}{r}$, the central angle, $2\,\phi_1$, and the stresses. For stress calculations the curves and tables prepared by William Cain, M. Am. Soc. C. E.,† were quite sufficient, but the curves prepared by the author give an excellent picture of what happens when either $\frac{t}{r}$, or $2\,\phi_1$, or both, is varied, and, therefore, they should assist the designer by enabling him to see more quickly what may be accomplished in a specific case by varying the design in a certain direction. The writer has found it necessary, when designing arch dams, to plot for a limited region such curves as the author submits, but has never made a systematic investigation, such as that presented by Mr. Fowler.

In analyzing the stresses in the Kerckhoff Dam at Elevation 900, the author's solution involves a tension of 165 lb. per sq. in., which should exist between the concrete and the rock abutment. The existence of a tension of this magnitude between concrete and rock, however, is highly improbable and, at any rate, something on which a careful designer would not rely. The usefulness of the Cain formulas is due to the fact that in such cases a fairly accurate estimate of the maximum stress can be obtained by applying the theory of the secondary arch.‡

Referring to Fig. 14, *F D B N* is the original arch, which has tension at, and around, Point *D* and possibly also at, and around, Point *N*. Assuming that the arch cannot withstand any tension, the concrete will move away from the rock abutment, beginning at Point *D* and continuing to a point, *E′*, where the stress is zero. The load is now carried on the secondary arch, *F E′ B M*, and this secondary arch is determined by the fact that the stress at Point *E′* is zero, when the water is assumed to act on the arc, *F E′*. The actual load is on the arc, *F D*, but water may also be assumed to act on *D E′* and these two loads combined equal the water load on arc *F E′*.

From the curves in Figs. 5 and 12, it may be seen that for any value of $x = \frac{t}{r}$, there is a definite value of the central angle that gives zero stress at the abutment of the up-stream face. If the central angle remains the same, but $\frac{t}{r}$ is increased, tension will occur at the abutment of the up-stream face; if $\frac{t}{r}$ is decreased, compression will occur. Consequently, a curve may be plotted

---

* Cons. Engr. (La Rue & Jakobsen), Los Angeles, Calif.

† *Transactions*, Am. Soc. C. E., Vol. LXXXV (1922), p. 233; also, Vol. 90 (June, 1927), p. 522.

‡ "Stresses in Thick Arches of Dams," *Transactions*, Am. Soc. C. E., Vol. 90 (June, 1927), p. 510, where reference is made to the work of L. J. Mensch, M. Am. Soc. C. E., Prof. Cain, and Prof. Résal.

from these limiting values of $x = \frac{t}{r}$ and $2\ \phi_1$. Such a curve has been plotted in Fig. 15 by utilizing the author's diagrams. As an illustration, for $x_0 = \frac{t_0}{r_0} = 0.3$, Fig. 15 gives $2\ \phi_0 = 142°$ for the limiting central angle, and this angle was obtained from Fig. 12(*b*) for $\frac{t}{r} = 0.3$ and zero stress.

In general, it is necessary to try several secondary arches before the right one is found. By determining a constant, B, as a function of $\frac{t}{r}$ and $2\ \phi_1$ and also as a function of the limiting values, x_0 and $2\ \phi_0$, and plotting B in Fig. 15, the secondary arch can be determined directly. The following considerations lead to the curve, B, in Fig. 15.

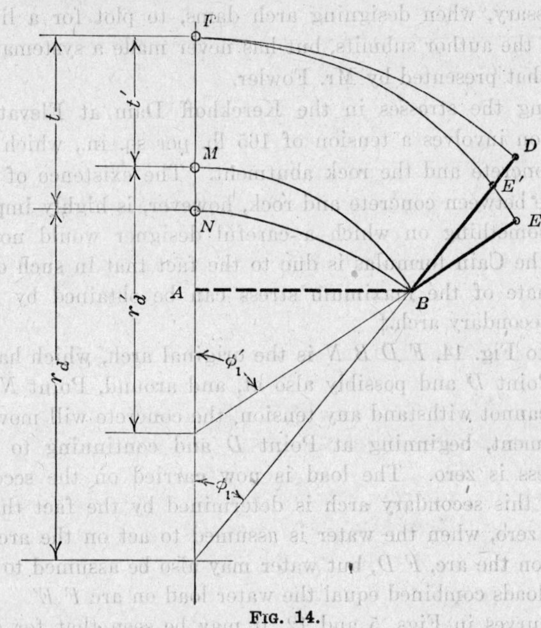

FIG. 14.

In Fig. 14, a secondary arch is shown as $F\ E'\ B\ M$; assume that the secondary arch is $F\ E\ B\ M$ instead of $F\ E'\ B\ M$. This assumption will not introduce any objectionable errors, but will facilitate the calculations. The dimensions of the original arch are t, r, r_d, and ϕ_1, as shown in Fig. 14, and the dimensions of the secondary arch are t', r', r'_d, and ϕ'_1. Then, from Fig. 14:

$$A\ B = r_d \sin \phi_1 = r'_d \sin \phi'_1$$

or,

$$r'_d = r_d \frac{\sin \phi_1}{\sin \phi'_1} \ldots\ldots\ldots\ldots\ldots\ldots\ldots\ldots (1)$$

Also, from Fig. 14:

$$F\ A = t + r_d (1 - \cos \phi_1) = A \ldots\ldots\ldots\ldots\ldots\ldots (2)$$

Let,

$$B = \frac{A}{r_d \sin \phi_1} \quad \text{.............................(3)}$$

The value of A can be determined from Equation (2) as soon as the dimensions of the original arch are known and, likewise, the value of B may be determined from Equation (3).

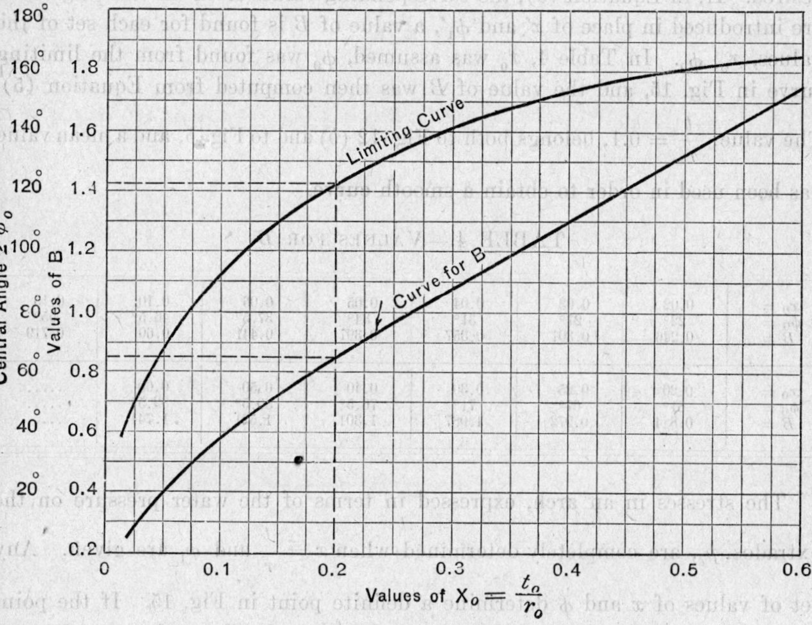

FIG. 15.—CURVES FOR DETERMINING SECONDARY ARCHES.

A and B, however, may also be expressed in terms of the dimensions of the secondary arch. From Fig. 14:

$$F A = A = t' + r_d' (1 - \cos \phi_1') \quad \text{..................(4)}$$

From Equations (3) and (1):

$$B = \frac{A}{r_d' \sin \phi_1'} = \frac{t' + r_d' (1 - \cos \phi_1')}{r_d' \sin \phi_1'}$$

$$= \frac{t'}{r' - 0.5\, t'} \operatorname{cosec} \phi_1' + \frac{1 - \cos \phi_1'}{\sin \phi_1'}$$

in which, r' is the mean radius of the secondary arch. Dividing the first term on the right-hand side of the equation sign by r', and multiplying by 2:

$$B = \frac{2\, x'}{2 - x'} \operatorname{cosec} \phi_1' + \tan \left(\frac{\phi_1'}{2}\right) \quad \text{..................(5)}$$

From what precedes, it is evident, that:

$$B = \frac{2\, x}{2 - x} \operatorname{cosec} \phi_1 + \tan \left(\frac{\phi_1}{2}\right) \quad \text{....................(6)}$$

Equation (6) shows that B is a function of the dimensions, x and ϕ_1, of the original arch and may be computed as soon as these are known. On the other hand, Equation (5) shows that B is a function of the dimensions, x' and ϕ_1', of the secondary arch. Of all the different corresponding values that it is possible to give to x' and ϕ_1' in Equation (5) while B remains constant, only those corresponding values of x' and ϕ_1' that lie on the limiting curve are desired. If, in Equation (5), the corresponding values from the limiting curve are introduced in place of x' and ϕ_1', a value of B is found for each set of the values, x_0, ϕ_0. In Table 4, x_0 was assumed, ϕ_0 was found from the limiting curve in Fig. 15, and the value of B was then computed from Equation (5). The value, $\frac{t}{r} = 0.1$, belongs both to Fig. 12 (b) and to Fig. 5, and a mean value has been used in order to obtain a smooth curve.

TABLE 4.—VALUES FOR B.

$x_0 =$	0.02	0.03	0.04	0.05	0.06	0.10	0.15
$\phi_0 =$	22°	27°	31°	34°	37.5°	46.5°	55°
$B =$	0.246	0.307	0.357	0.397	0.441	0.60	0.719
$x_0 =$	0.20	0.25	0.30	0.40	0.50	0.60	.....
$\phi_0 =$	61°	67°	71°	76.5°	80.5°	82.5°	.....
$B =$	0.8[illegible]4	0.972	1.087	1.301	1.521	1.741	.....

The stresses in an arch, expressed in terms of the water pressure on the extrados, p_e, are completely determined when $x = \frac{t}{r}$ and ϕ_1 are given. Any set of values of x and ϕ determine a definite point in Fig. 15. If the point is located above the limiting curve, as, for example, the arch, $x = 0.1$ and $2\,\phi_1 = 120°$, there is compression throughout the arch. If the point lies on the limiting curve, there is compression throughout the arch, except at the point, E, of Fig. 14 where there is zero stress. If, finally, the point lies below the limiting curve, there is tension at the extrados of the abutment and possibly, also, at the intrados at the crown. In this case the theory of the secondary arch must be utilized in order to determine the maximum stress. This is accomplished by computing the value of B from Equation (6) and then, from Fig. 15, determining the corresponding values of x_0 and $2\,\phi_0$. Then, x_0 and $2\phi_0$ determine the secondary arch for the given primary arch, and the maximum stress, which occurs at the intrados of the abutment, may be taken from the author's diagrams, bearing in mind that the stresses found in the curves are for a 10-ft. head.

For example: Suppose the original arch gives $B = 0.845$; then, from Fig. 15, using "Curve for B", it is found that $x_0 = 0.2$ and the limiting angle, which corresponds to $x_0 = 0.2$, is $2\,\phi_0 = 122$ degrees. This is the secondary arch. If the conditions at the abutments are not as shown in Fig. 14, some modifications may be necessary, but the writer has found the two curves shown to be of considerable value in actual design, even for very thick arches, although for these the yielding of the abutments must be taken into account.*

The question proposed by the author, "What are the stresses in the Kerckhoff Dam?" may now be solved with the understanding that the maximum stress found is most likely somewhat in excess of the actual existing maximum stress, but will be a good guide in design and quite reliable except perhaps for very short thick arches. At Elevation 900, the dimensions are $x = \frac{t}{r} = 0.201$ and $2\,\phi_1 = 82°\ 40'$; this gives $B = 0.7154$ from Equation (6), and from "Curve for B", in Fig. 15, is found $x_0 = 0.145$ and $2\,\phi_0 = 108$ degrees. These are the dimensions of the secondary arch (r_d' can be determined from Equation (1)) and the maximum stress may now be read from Fig. 13(*b*); this gives 66 lb. per sq. in. for a 10-ft. head and 627 lb. per sq. in. for a head of 95 ft. The stresses at the crown may be found by referring to the author's diagrams. Generally, however, the stress at the intrados of the abutment is the maximum stress occurring and if there is not tension at the extrados of the abutment, there is no tension in the arch; that is, when the stresses are determined by the Cain formulas and the yielding of the foundation is neglected.

The author, as he states, took the dimensions of the Kerckhoff Dam from the writer's discussion of Professor Cain's paper,† in which the water surface was considered as standing 10 ft. above the Taintor gates. When designing the Kerckhoff Dam, the writer took as the maximum possible head, that which might come on the dam if all the gates were closed and an extreme flood of about 100 000 sec-ft. was flowing in the river. The actual maximum operating head is only 85 ft. on the section at Elevation 900, the top of the Taintor gates being at Elevation 985;‡ therefore, the maximum stress is found to be:

$$\frac{627 \times 8.5}{9.5} = 561 \text{ lb. per sq. in.}$$

When the writer, in May, 1919, took charge as Designing Engineer for the Kerckhoff Development of the San Joaquin Light and Power Corporation, Fresno, Calif., he found a gravity arch dam design, that would have cost $1 000 000 to build. The saving of the arch dam as re-designed amounted to approximately $400 000, or 40% of the total, and the stress calculations show that the factor of safety of the arch dam is much greater than for most gravity dams.

The curves plotted by the author also give information as to how the maximum stress varies when the central angle is held constant, while the ratio, $\frac{t}{r}$, is varied. For example, for $2\,\phi_1 = 140°$, $\frac{t}{r} = 0.02$, 0.05, 0.10, and 0.20, the maximum stress being, respectively, 237, 107, 66, and 44 lb. per sq. in. for a 10-ft. head.

* See discussion by Dr. Fredrik Vogt, *Transactions*, Am. Soc. C. E., Vol. 90 (June, 1927), p. 554.

† *Transactions*, Am. Soc. C. E., Vol. LXXXV (1922), p. 258.

‡ *Loc. cit.*, Vol. LXXXIV (1921), p. 107.

In other words, when $\frac{t}{r}$ is increased 10 times, from 0.02 to 0.20, the stress is decreased only 5.4 times, or, the arch, $\frac{t}{r} = 0.02$, is nearly twice as efficient as the arch, $\frac{t}{r} = 0.20$, when the central angle is 140 degrees. This gives an indication of the great importance of utilizing a high strength concrete produced under competent inspection. The writer's experience while in charge of the construction of the Pacoima and Big Santa Anita Dams,* and the experience of other engineers, have shown that when the water-cement ratio is kept under close control, it is possible to produce a high grade and uniform concrete under actual construction conditions. The fact that the thinner arch is so much more efficient than the thick arch, is bound to have a considerable influence on concrete production.

The curves presented by Mr. Fowler are a welcome addition to the literature of stresses in arches and should be helpful in the design and study of arched dams.

William Cain,† M. Am. Soc. C. E. (by letter).—Any one who has computed the unit stresses at extrados and intrados, at crown and abutment, for even one circular arch subjected to uniform normal loads, can readily appreciate the enormous amount of labor required to construct the many diagrams given in the author's Figs. 3 to 13. Mistakes are easily made for any one example, but they are readily discovered where successive values are plotted. A smooth curve gives confidence in the results. The author's diagrams are very clear and cover every desirable central angle and many ratios, $\frac{t}{r}$, and they should prove of great value to the busy designer. The writer has only checked the values of s_e and s_i, given in Figs. 10 to 13, for $\frac{t}{r} = 0.3$, with central angles, $(2\ \phi_1)$, of 40°, 90°, and 180°, and has found all of them to be correct.

As it is not evident from the equations given for "thick arches", for a given head and central angle, that the stresses, s_e, s_i, vary only with the ratio, $\frac{t}{r}$, a proof will be given.

By reference to the writer's discussion,‡ it is seen that,

$$\frac{t}{r_n} = \log_e \left(\frac{r_e}{r_i}\right) = \frac{t}{r}\left(1 + \frac{1}{12}\left(\frac{t}{r}\right)^2 + \frac{1}{80}\left(\frac{t}{r}\right)^4 + \cdots\right)$$

Also, since $I = \frac{1}{12}\, t^3$ and $k^2 = \frac{1}{12}\, t^2$, the value of D_n§ can be written,

* *Transactions,* Am. Soc. C. E., Vol. 90 (June, 1927), p. 585.

† Prof. Emeritus, Univ. of North Carolina, Chapel Hill, N. C.

‡ *Transactions,* Am. Soc. C. E., Vol. 90 (June, 1927), p. 524, Equation (94) and footnote.

§ *Loc. cit.,* p. 531, Equation (104) and footnote.

$$D_n = \left(\phi_1 + \frac{1}{2}\sin 2\,\phi_1\right)\left(1 + \frac{1}{12}\left(\frac{t}{r_n}\right)^2\right) - \frac{1 - \cos 2\,\phi_1}{\phi_1}$$

$$+ 0.24\left(\frac{t}{r_n}\right)^2\left(\phi_1 - \frac{1}{2}\sin 2\,\phi_1\right).$$

Thus, since $\frac{t}{r_n}$ can be expressed in terms of $\frac{t}{r}$, D_n can be written as a function of $\frac{t}{r}$ and constants for a given central angle.

It will now be shown that the unit stresses, s_e and s_i, at the extrados and intrados at the abutment section, making the angle, ϕ_1, with the crown section, for a constant head and central angle, vary only with $\frac{t}{r}$. On substituting the value of

$$X = \frac{p_e\, r_e}{D_n}\,\frac{\sin\,\phi_1}{6}\left(\frac{t}{r_n}\right)^2$$

in the values for P_1 and M_1, the last two formulas of Equation (107) (page 1516), can be written (after reduction),

$$s_e = p_e\left\{\frac{2\sin\,\phi_1}{D_n}\left(\frac{\sin\,\phi_1}{\phi_1} - \cos\,\phi_1\right)\frac{\frac{t}{2}+c}{t}\left[\frac{\frac{1}{t}}{r_n} - \frac{\sin\,\phi_1}{6\,D_n}\left(\frac{t}{r_n}\right)\cos\,\phi_1\right]\right\}$$

and,

$$s_i = p_e\,\frac{r_e}{r_i}\left\{-\frac{2\sin\,\phi_1}{D_n}\left(\frac{\sin\,\phi_1}{\phi_1} - \cos\,\phi_1\right)\frac{\frac{t}{2}-c}{t}\left[\frac{\frac{1}{t}}{r_n} - \frac{\sin\,\phi_1}{6\,D_n}\left(\frac{t}{r_n}\right)\cos\,\phi_1\right]\right\}$$

The values of s_e and s_i for the crown can be similarly derived. In fact, these unit stresses may be written down from the last two formulas on replacing $\cos\,\phi_1$ by 1 and leaving the other terms unaltered.

On noting that,

$$\frac{\frac{t}{2}+c}{t} = \frac{1}{2} + \frac{r - r_n}{t} = \frac{1}{2} + \frac{\frac{1}{t}}{r} - \frac{\frac{1}{t}}{r_n}$$

$$\frac{\frac{t}{2}-c}{t} = \frac{1}{2} - \frac{r - r_n}{t} = \frac{1}{2} - \frac{\frac{1}{t}}{r} + \frac{\frac{1}{t}}{r_n}$$

and,

$$\frac{r_e}{r_i} = \frac{r + \frac{t}{2}}{r - \frac{t}{2}} = \frac{1 + \frac{t}{2\,n}}{1 - \frac{t}{2\,r}}$$

and since $\left(\frac{t}{r_n}\right)$ has been expressed in terms of $\left(\frac{t}{r}\right)$, it is seen that, for a given p_e and ϕ_1, s_e and s_i vary only with $\frac{t}{r}$. This is not true for P_0, M_0, P_1, and M_1, but it is true for s_e and s_i at either crown or abutment. It is thus seen that the same values are derived for $t = 15$ and $r = 50$, as for $t = 30$ and $r = 100$, since $\frac{t}{r} = 0.3$ in both cases.

In using Equation (107) (page 1516), any convenient values of t and r that have the assumed ratio, can be used. The values of s_e and s_i thus derived can be checked by the formulas for s_e and s_i just given. Evidently, these formulas furnish the shortest solution for the unit stresses.

In using them, for assumed values of t and r, giving the required ratio, it is best to compute c from Equation (95),*

$$c = r - r_n = r - \frac{t}{\log_e \left(\frac{r_e}{r_i}\right)}$$

and thus derive, directly,

$$\frac{\frac{t}{2} + c}{t} \text{ and } \frac{\frac{t}{2} - c}{t}$$

Also, $\frac{t}{r_n} = \log_e \frac{r_e}{r_i}$ is directly computed without the use of the infinite series.

As Mr. Fowler, in drawing his diagrams, has assumed a 10-ft. head,

$$p_e = \frac{10 \times 62.5}{144} = 4.34 \text{ lb. per sq. in.}$$

to agree with the diagrams. The stresses vary directly as p_e, or as the head.

The formulas for s_e, s_i, reduce to those for a prismatic beam on assuming, for t finite, that r increases indefinitely, so that $c = 0$, $r_n = r$, and $p_n = p$. This will be evident if, in the usual formula for the unit stresses in a straight beam,

$$\frac{P}{t} \pm \frac{6\ M}{t^2},$$

the values of P and M (page 1514) are substituted; when, on reduction, the previous values for s_e, s_i, corresponding to $c = 0$, $r_n = r$, and $p_e = p$, are derived.

In deriving the formulas for thick arches, the writer ignored the work of the radial stress, as its influence was found to be small.† Also, Poisson's ratio was assumed equal to zero. This ratio is easily included, as B. F. Jakobsen, M. Am. Soc. C. E., has shown.‡ His pioneer work on this subject, and the effect of water-soaking, are both important contributions. However, it may be remarked, that the experiments for determining Poisson's ratio have been made on very small specimens and it is very doubtful if the ratio thus found applies to arches 30 to 50 ft. thick.

In addition to this uncertainty, there are others that militate against the hope of an exact solution, such as the unknown shrinkage of concrete in drying out, the changes in E with stress and time, the effect of plasticity, water-

* *Transactions*, Am. Soc. C. E., Vol. 90 (June, 1927), p. 525.

† *Loc. cit.*, p. 538.

‡ *Loc. cit.*, p. 488; also, see "Example," p. 539.

soaking, and the elastic yielding of the foundation and abutments. Besides, there is doubt about the uniformity of the water pressure on a horizontal arch, and as to the relative proportion of the water pressure carried by the arch and the cantilever; so that the computation of stresses for the given hypotheses, which are so greatly facilitated by the author's diagrams, although a necessary step, is not the complete solution, for the engineer must consider all the influences mentioned in the design of arch dams. Mr. Jakobsen has stated* that "he had hoped to install some resistor type of cartridges for measuring deformations in both the Pacoima and the Big Santa Anita Dams, but was unable to obtain the necessary funds". This is greatly to be regretted. Experiments on thin arch dams that buckle and crack are valuable for such conditions, but they do not represent the conditions for thick dams where the device of grouting to avoid cracks has been used and where buckling is not experienced. Experiments on such dams will tend to clear a number of doubtful points, and it is to be hoped that they may be instituted in the future.

WALTER L. HUBER,† M. AM. SOC. C. E. (by letter).—The writer has made much practical use of the diagrams prepared by Mr Fowler. Before accepting them as a substitute for the more laborious methods of exact calculation he made some comparisons of the two methods. The difference is, in every case, very small, being much less than various uncertainties of assumptions governing practical designs. William Cain, M. Am. Soc. C. E., through his formulas, made a very valuable contribution to engineering literature. Mr. Fowler has made this contribution readily available to the designer of arch dams and for this service deserves the thanks of all members of the profession engaged in designing structures of this character.

GLEN EDGAR EDGERTON,‡ M. AM. SOC. C. E. (by letter).—The curves presented by Mr. Fowler should prove to be of great assistance to engineers engaged in the design or investigation of dams of the arch type. The increasing number of structures of this type that have been erected in recent years and the indisputable economies made possible by them when circumstances are favorable, indicate that more and more frequently in the future, engineers will be required to consider arch dam design, even, perhaps, in many cases in which other types may finally be adopted.

Designs for arch dams that show reasonably conservative unit stresses under analysis by the Cain formulas have been approved in several instances by the Federal Power Commission, and by State and local public officials as well. To that extent, at least, these formulas may be considered to have become established as acceptable standards in practice as well as in theory.

Without attempting to make a general check of the curves presented by Mr. Fowler, several designs previously analyzed by the Cain formulas and computation methods have been investigated by means of them. The critical stresses calculated by the two methods agree very closely. Figs. 3, 4, 5, and 6 were used. The central angles for these calculations ranged

* *Transactions*, Am. Soc. C. E., Vol. 90 (June, 1927), p. 586.

† Cons. Engr., San Francisco, Calif.

‡ Maj., Corps of Engrs., U. S. A.; Chf. Engr., Federal Power Comm., Washington, D. C.

from 84° 44′ to 134° 0′; $\frac{t}{r}$, from 0.0448 to 0.312 (the latter value requiring extrapolation); and the head, from 25 to 185 ft. The maximum difference between the unit stresses determined by the two methods amounted to 19 lb. per sq. in.

Mr. Fowler has made a valuable contribution to the engineering art in developing these time-saving charts.

LARS R. JORGENSEN,* M. AM. SOC. C. E. (by letter).—Most engineers who have had to make calculations of arch dams, have no doubt been looking for a method to simplify this tedious work. The first that suggests itself is the plotting of curves to avoid as much of the routine calculation as possible. The writer has seen at various times several sets of curves intended for the simplification of arch dam calculation. Such curves have also been used to great advantage for several years in the office of the Constant Angle Arch Dam Company; but until Mr. Fowler's diagrams appeared the writer had never seen a set where the result sought could be obtained by looking for it in just one place, on just one curve. When the writer saw the curves for the first time, he wondered where Mr. Fowler had made a mistake, since he had so easily been able to simplify arch dam calculation to the limit.

The author is to be highly commended on his work in plotting these curves because they are of very great help to any one interested in arch dam calculation. In Figs. 10 to 13, inclusive, the principal part of the information necessary for the calculation of stresses in any arch dam is available. Mr. Fowler has seized upon the clever idea of using the ratio, $\frac{t}{r}$, for plotting purposes, which is the main reason for the simplicity.

At and toward the very bottom of an arch dam, arch action is very ineffective since other actions (principally punching shear along the contact area) will resist the load with less deformation required and, consequently, will take the greater part of the load. Inasmuch as it is generally difficult to design an arch dam (using the conventional arch formulas) where the arch is short and thick, as is mostly the case at and near the bottom of a dam, the ability of the punching shear developed along the contact area to hold the dam in place should be investigated.

Whenever this punching shear stress is less than 65 lb. per sq. in., for instance, on the contact area between the rock and the concrete, the structure should be entirely safe, assuming all load to be resisted by shear.

If the bottom is calculated as an arch, carrying the full water load and using conventional formulas, such as those of Professor Cain, stresses of 800 lb. compression and as much as 200 lb. per sq. in. tension should be allowable. Such calculated stresses may generally be more conservative in this part of the dam than one-half these values would be at a point higher up where the arch has to take the load acting as an arch. The load, at the bottom especially, divides between punching shear, arch action, cantilever action, etc., with punching shear generally taking the largest share. In

* Cons. Engr., Constant Angle Arch Dam Co., San Francisco, Calif.

calculating the structure as an arch close to the bottom, it is safe to use larger unit stresses, both in compression and in tension, as it is known that the actual stresses will be considerably lower than the calculated stresses.

FRED A. NOETZLI,* M. AM. SOC. C. E. (by letter).—This paper is of much value to designers of arch and multiple-arch dams. The labor of calculating the stresses in the elementary arch slices of such structures is reduced to the very minimum by the use of the curves presented by Mr. Fowler.

In order to get an idea of the degree of accuracy that may be obtained with these curves, the stresses in one of the arch slices of the Stevenson Creek Test Dam were calculated and compared with the stresses as determined from the tests.† Table 5 gives the data for the elementary arch slice at a height of 30 ft. above the base of the dam. For this elementary arch, $\frac{t}{r} = \frac{2}{99} = 0.0202$. The central angle is $2\phi = 43°\ 30'$. The head of water for full reservoir is 30 ft., but according to the results of the tests only about 84% of the water pressure at this elevation was carried by the horizontal elementary arch, the remainder being supported by the vertical cantilever.‡ The full water pressure being 30 × 62.5 = 1 875 lb. per sq. ft., the net load on the arch element as determined from the test was, therefore, approximately, 0.84 × 1 875 = 1 570 lb. per sq. ft. Consequently, the "multiplying factor" to be used in connection with Figs. 10 to 13, inclusive, is $\frac{1\,570}{62.5 \times 10} = 2.52$, corresponding to a net head of water of 25.2 ft. The stresses in the dam as determined by means of the curves (for "fixed" arches) are given in Table 5, Column (4). The stresses as found from the tests in 1926 are given in Column (5), and by way of comparison there are shown in Column (6) the values of the stresses as determined in the design of the dam made by the writer in 1925 for the Committee on Arch Dam Investigation.

The agreement between the various values is reasonably close considering the fact that in the design of the dam the net water pressure supported by the arch at the 30-ft. elevation was found to be 1 335 lb. per sq. ft., while the tests gave the somewhat larger figure of 1 570 lb. per sq. ft. Therefore, in order to afford a comparison on the proper basis between the values of the stresses as determined by the use of the author's Figs. 10 to 13 and those computed in the design, these latter values must be multiplied by $\frac{1\,570}{1\,335} = 1.175$. The corresponding design stress would then be as listed in Table 5, Column (7). Thus, if the same water pressure as determined in the tests, is used as a basis for the computations, there is found a reasonably close agreement between the theoretical values of the stresses and those calculated from the strains measured in the dam.

* Cons. Hydr. Engr., Los Angeles, Calif.

† See *Bulletin No. 5*, Arch Dam Investigation, Engineering Foundation; also, *Engineering News-Record*, July 14, 1927, p. 66.

‡ See Fig. 5, *Bulletin No. 5*, Arch Dam Investigation, Engineering Foundation.

By the use of Figs. 7, 8, and 9 and the "multiplying factor" of 2.52, the stresses of this arch (for hinged ends) are as given in Column (8), Table 5.

A comparison of the values of the stresses found in the tests (Column (5)) with those computed from the curves for "fixed" (Column (7)) and "hinged" (Column (8)) arches, respectively, would indicate that undoubtedly there is a much better agreement between the test values and the theoretical stresses for a "fixed" arch than for "hinged" end conditions. Inasmuch as the arches of the Stevenson Creek Test Dam are probably thinner than those encountered in most service dams of the single-arch type, it may be concluded that the curves for fixed arches, including shear, are the ones that should be used in all practical cases. The thicker an arch dam the more nearly correct will probably be the assumption of "fixity" at the abutments.

TABLE 5.

Point.	Stress read from Figs. 10 to 13, inclusive, in pounds per square inch.	Multiplying factor.	Stress in Dams, in Pounds per Square Inch.				
			Fowler.	Test, 1926.	Design, 1925.	Design, 1925, adjusted for comparison (fixed ends).	Design, 1925 (hinged ends).
(1)	(2)	(3)	(4)	(5)	(6)	(7)	(8)
Crown:							
Extrados...	310	2.52	780		665	782	692
Intrados...	95	2.52	240	260†	207	243	390
Abutments:							
Extrados...	—2	2.52	—5		—11	—13	516‡
Intrados...	400*	2.52	1 008	940†	879	1 032	516‡

* Exterpolated from curves.

† From "Tests on Stevenson Creek Dam: Deflections and Stresses," *Engineering News-Record,* July 14, 1927, Fig. 5.

‡ Average values.

The stresses in the arches of the Stevenson Creek Dam as determined in the design made in 1925 prior to construction, were computed by treating rib-shortening as separate from axial arch compression.* In many cases, there is a certain advantage in this method in that it gives a clearer conception of the influence of the rib-shortening pull and of the corresponding stresses. The rib-shortening pull may be assumed as acting in the center of gravity of the arch. If the arch is not of uniform thickness from abutment to abutment, the rib-shortening pull acts in the center of gravity of the elastic weights.

The author's Figs. 10 to 13 do not permit of the determination of the temperature stresses. These stresses can be readily computed by means of the curves and formulas given by Wegmann.*

Temperature stresses in arch dams are of considerable importance as are those due to the shrinkage of the concrete. The stresses resulting from a uni-

* "The Design and Construction of Dams," by Edward Wegmann, M. Am. Soc. C. E., Eighth Edition, 1927, p. 448.

form swelling of the arches due to water-soaking may be computed in a manner similar to those due to temperature. Water-soaking tends to expand the concrete and the effect on the stresses in an arch dam is beneficial rather than harmful.

The author's Figs. 10 to 13 will diminish the labor of computing the arch stresses from water pressure to such an extent that the analysis of an arch ring, either of a single arch dam or of a multiple-arch dam, can be accomplished in a few minutes.

FREDERICK HALL FOWLER,* M. AM. SOC. C. E. (by letter).—The discussion of this paper has brought forth formulas and curves of distinct value to the profession, and some comments to which the writer desires to add a few words.

Mr. Jakobsen has further developed the theory of the secondary arch and has presented curves (Fig. 15) for the ready determination of secondary arches. These curves will be of great value to engineers who desire to apply this theory. In citing the computations for the Kerckhoff Dam as an example, however, the writer had no thought that the question of secondary arches would be brought under discussion. Reference was made to these computations merely because they had been published,† were therefore available to the profession, were the result of detailed and laborious computations, and thus served as a standard of comparison for the results that could be secured by use of the curves.

In his closing paragraphs, Mr. Jakobsen has well illustrated the value of the curves in exploring the range of arch stresses when one element of the design, such as central angle, is held constant and the others are varied.

Professor Cain, author of the original formulas that form the bases for the graphic method, has contributed a detailed proof that the stresses, s_e and s_i, vary only with the ratio, $\frac{t}{r}$. The writer is in full accord with Professor Cain's statement that the computation of arch stresses for the given hypotheses, by use of the curves, "although a necessary step, is not the complete solution", and that "the engineer must consider all the influences mentioned,‡ in the design of arch dams." A computation of arch stresses under given assumptions is, however, an unavoidable step in the design of an arch dam, and without the use of curves it is a very laborious step. It was for this reason that the curves were prepared, and not with the thought that they would be a complete solution of the many other factors that enter into the design of such structures. The curves will go no farther in that direction than the original set of formulas on which they are based, which, by the way, includes only a few of the valuable formulas developed by Professor Cain.

Mr. Noetzli's discussion is of great interest since it points out that the stresses read from the curves for "fixed ends", agree more closely with the design and test data for the very thin arch of the Stevenson Creek Dam, than do the stresses given by the curves for "hinged ends". The question

* Cons. Civ. Engr., San Francisco, Calif.

† *Transactions*, Am. Soc. C. E., Vol. LXXXV (1922), p. 258.

‡ Such as Poisson's ratio, water-soaking, shrinkage of concrete, changes in E with stress and time, effect of plasticity, yield of abutments, etc.

of the portions of the load carried by the arches and cantilevers in any given structure is still a matter of controversy. Several designers hold that in actual practice a structure should be so proportioned that the arches will be capable of carrying the entire water load without developing excessive stresses and that no dependence should be placed on cantilever action. If, however, a distribution of load between the arch and cantilever elements is assumed, the use of the curves will be limited to the determination of stresses due to the part of the load assumed to be carried by the arches; Mr. Noetzli's discussion has given in detail the method of use under such assumptions.

The writer is glad to note that Mr. Huber and Mr. Jorgensen, in their consulting practice, and Major Edgerton, as Chief Engineer of the Federal Power Commission, have found the curves of value in simplifying calculations for structures that they have had to analyze. The writer has received similar comments from other engineers to whom he has furnished sets of curves for trial use and comparison with extended computations. The consensus of opinion appears to be that curves for arches with "fixed ends, including the value of shear" (Figs. 10 to 13), are by far the most generally applicable, most nearly correct, and, therefore, the most valuable in their work. In response to many suggestions, these diagrams have been extended to include values of $\frac{t}{r}$ ranging from 0.02 to 0.10 and amplified to show interpolated curves in the ranges of $\frac{t}{r}$ from 0.10 to 1.00. The substitute curves are shown in Figs. 10 (*a*) to 13 (*d*). These were computed on the same basis as the original diagrams now superseded by them.*

Even a casual inspection of Figs. 10 to 13, will show in many instances a considerable latitude in the selection of the central angle and the value of $\frac{t}{r}$ when designing for a certain limiting stress, the particular combination finally adopted depending to a great extent on the economy in yardage. A set of diagrams similar to those given in Fig. 16 is, therefore, often found convenient in making approximate comparative computations that will give the most economic design. In Fig. 16 (*a*) are shown the quantities, in cubic yards per unit of radius squared, for an arch ring of uniform thickness, and 10-ft. vertical depth; Fig. 16 (*c*) gives similar quantities in terms of the square of the span (or width of the dam site at the given elevation), also for 10-ft. vertical depth. The central diagram, Fig. 16 (*b*), included merely for convenience, gives squares of span or radius for given values of W or r. A more accurate determination of these squares could be secured from a table.

If it is desired to find the yardage in a ring with a central angle of 100°; a radius, r, of 140 ft.; and a thickness of 42 ft. (or $\frac{t}{r} = 0.30$); entering Fig. 16 (*a*), the volume per unit of r^2 is found at the intersection of the vertical for

* In passing, it should be noted that new curves for $\frac{t}{r} = 0.10$ and 0.30 differ very slightly from the originals at certain points.

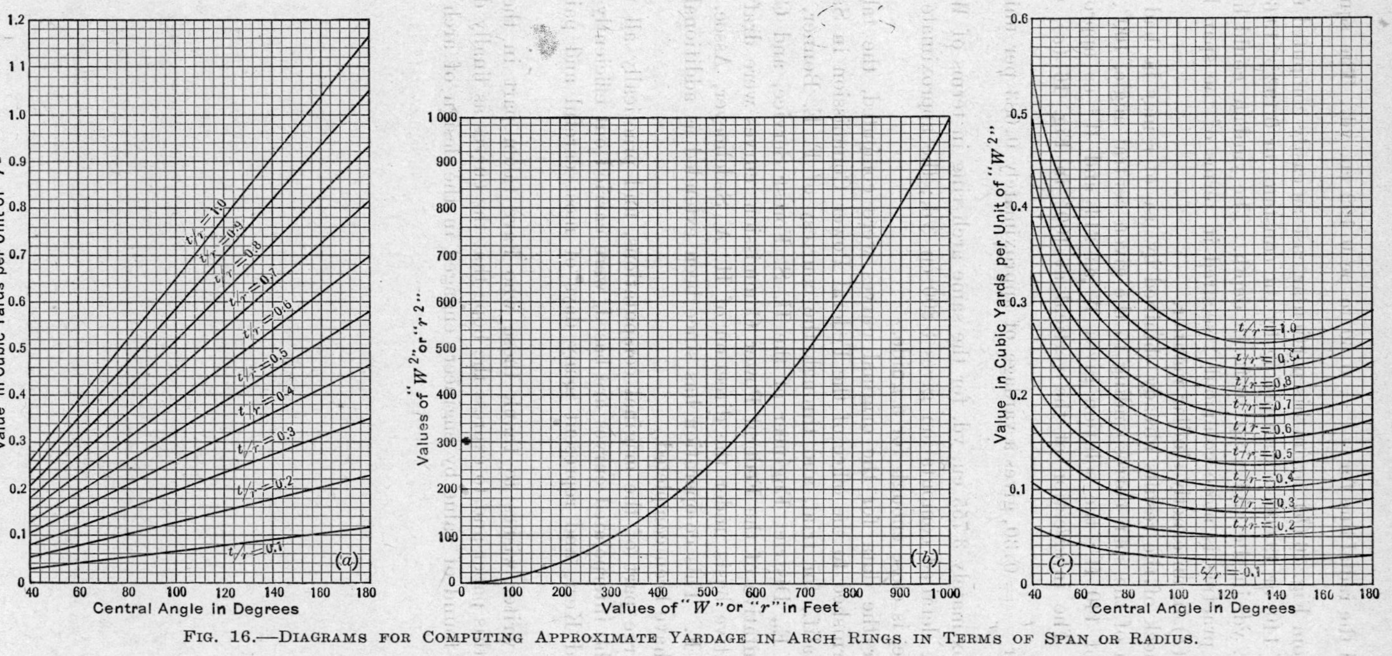

FIG. 16.—DIAGRAMS FOR COMPUTING APPROXIMATE YARDAGE IN ARCH RINGS IN TERMS OF SPAN OR RADIUS.

100° and the radial line for $\frac{t}{r} = 0.30$ to be 0.192 cu. yd. The square of r taken from Fig. 16 (b), or in this particular case as easily computed mentally, is 140×140, or 19 600. Multiplying by the constant, or $0.192 \times 19\,600$, gives 3 763 cu. yd. in the arch ring 10 ft. in depth. The yardage could have been (and in practice is more commonly) secured in terms of the span by using Fig. 16 (c) in an exactly similar manner.

A check of the results already obtained by use of r may be had by computation of the span corresponding to the given central angle, 100°, and the radius of 140 ft.; the solution gives W as 214 and W^2 as approximately 45 800. The intersection of the vertical at 100° in Fig. 16 (c), with the curve for $\frac{t}{r} = 0.30$, gives a yardage of approximately 0.083 per unit of W^2, or approximately 3 755 cu. yd. for the same arch ring in terms of W instead of r. A detailed computation gives 3 800 cu. yd.; the approximate method, therefore, is close enough for a guide.

After the data for the original curves were computed, the tabulations were furnished to the office of the Federal Power Commission in San Francisco, Calif., for trial, and through the courtesy of F. E. Bonner, M. Am. Soc. C. E., District Engineer of the U. S. Forest Service, and California Representative of the Federal Power Commission, curves were drafted on a co-operative basis under the direction of H. A. Sedelmeyer, Assoc. M. Am. Soc. C. E. This co-operation has since been extended as additional computations have been completed.

A large part of the original computations, and practically all those on which the interpolated curves are based, were carried out efficiently by Miss Winifred Kerr, and represent many days of most careful and painstaking work.

The writer wishes to thank those who have taken part in the discussion of this paper and to express the hope that the curves as finally developed may be found of value by engineers engaged in the design of arch dams.

AMERICAN SOCIETY OF CIVIL ENGINEERS
INSTITUTED 1852

TRANSACTIONS

This Society is not responsible for any statement made or opinion expressed in its publications.

Paper No. 1694

SIDE SPILLWAYS FOR REGULATING DIVERSION CANALS*

By W. H. R. Nimmo,† Assoc. M. Am. Soc. C. E.

With Discussion by Messrs. Edward S. Lindley, A. P. Flockart, George M. Bacon, and W. H. R. Nimmo.

Synopsis

In 1922, the Hydro-Electric Department of the Government of Tasmania completed a diversion channel of 450 sec-ft. capacity to convey water from the Upper Ouse River, at Liawenee, to the Great Lake storage. The intake of this channel is in a deep and narrow gorge where a low weir, only about 100 ft. long, suffices to divert the normal flow into a flume, ½ mile in length, built on a rock bench excavated along the wall of the gorge. From the outlet of the flume a canal, part of which is excavated in earth, conveys the water a farther distance of 5 miles where it is discharged into the Great Lake.

Within the catchment area are a large number of snow-fed lakes and lagoons and the stream is very flashy, the flow sometimes increasing from a few hundred to 12 000 sec-ft. within about 10 hours. The estimated maximum flood flow is 20 000 sec-ft. At present, the flow in the canal is controlled by a gate operated by a resident attendant but, as the country is inhabited only by a few shepherds in summer and is practically uninhabited in winter, it is desirable that some means of automatically regulating the flow in the canal should be devised. To be satisfactory in service any automatic arrangement must comply with the following conditions: (1) When the flow of the river does not exceed 450 sec-ft., all the flow must be allowed to pass into the concrete flume; and (2) when the total flow in the river exceeds 450 sec-ft., the flow in the concrete flume must not exceed 550 sec-ft. To meet the fore-

* Published in October, 1927, *Proceedings*.

† Chf. Draftsman, Main Roads Comm., Brisbane, Queensland, Australia.

going conditions several types of mechanically operated gates were considered, but those depending for their action on small differences of water pressures were discarded as they would fail to function during freezing weather. As the head-works are likely to become coated with ice for several weeks at a time, the forces applied to move the gate must be large, and for this reason gates operated by floats were found to be unsuitable. The writer then investigated the theory of flow in a side spilling channel with a view to devising a type of regulator without moving parts.

This paper presents the theory developed, describes the experiments carried out to test it, and the adaptation of the theory to the design of automatic head-works for the Ouse-Great Lake Canal.

Head-Works of the Ouse-Great Lake Canal

The head-works include a low concrete weir having a vertical up-stream face, a flat top, and a sloping down-stream face. At one end of the weir a converging channel, shown on Fig. 1, leads the water into the flume, this channel being bounded by the curved end of the weir on one side and by a concrete wall on the other. The crest of the weir is just high enough at all points to provide the necessary velocity head and entrance losses for the normal flow of 450 sec-ft. Down stream 184 ft. from the throat of the converging channel, is a head-gate 9 ft. wide, with vertical walls (visible in Fig. 5), which controls the entrance to the concrete flume. The outer guides of the gate are recessed so as to be flush with the walls of the flume and offer no obstruction, but the central guide consists of a 5 by 4½-in. by 18-lb., rolled steel joist.

Between the head-gate and the converging channel, there is a timber flume of trapezoidal section shown in plan, Fig. 1. Structural details of this flume are shown in Fig. 2, and Fig. 4 is a general view, looking up stream from the head-gate. Fig. 4 also shows the converging inlet and the weir, in which openings, now closed by stop-planks, have been left to carry the dry-weather flow during future alterations to the head-works. For a distance of 40 ft., up stream from the head-gate, the timber flume is on a curve of 198 ft. radius. The floor, which is flush with that of the concrete flume, has a normal width of 5 ft. 8 in. The side of the flume next to the river is intended to act as a spillway throughout the straight portion of its length, and the lip is 5 ft. above the floor, at which depth the water area is 45 sq. ft., being the same as that of the concrete flume, at its normal depth of 5 ft. The floors of both the timber and the concrete flumes are laid on a grade of 1 in 330. Along the entire side away from the river and on the curved portion of the side next the river, the wall of the flume is built 2 ft. above the lip of the spillway portion.

The throat of the converging channel has a width of 9 ft. and a depth of 5 ft., corresponding to the width and normal depth of flow in the concrete flume. At the down-stream end of the timber flume, a transition, 14 ft. long, connects the trapezoidal section to the rectangular section at the head-gate. In this transition the slope of the walls decreases uniformly and, consequently,

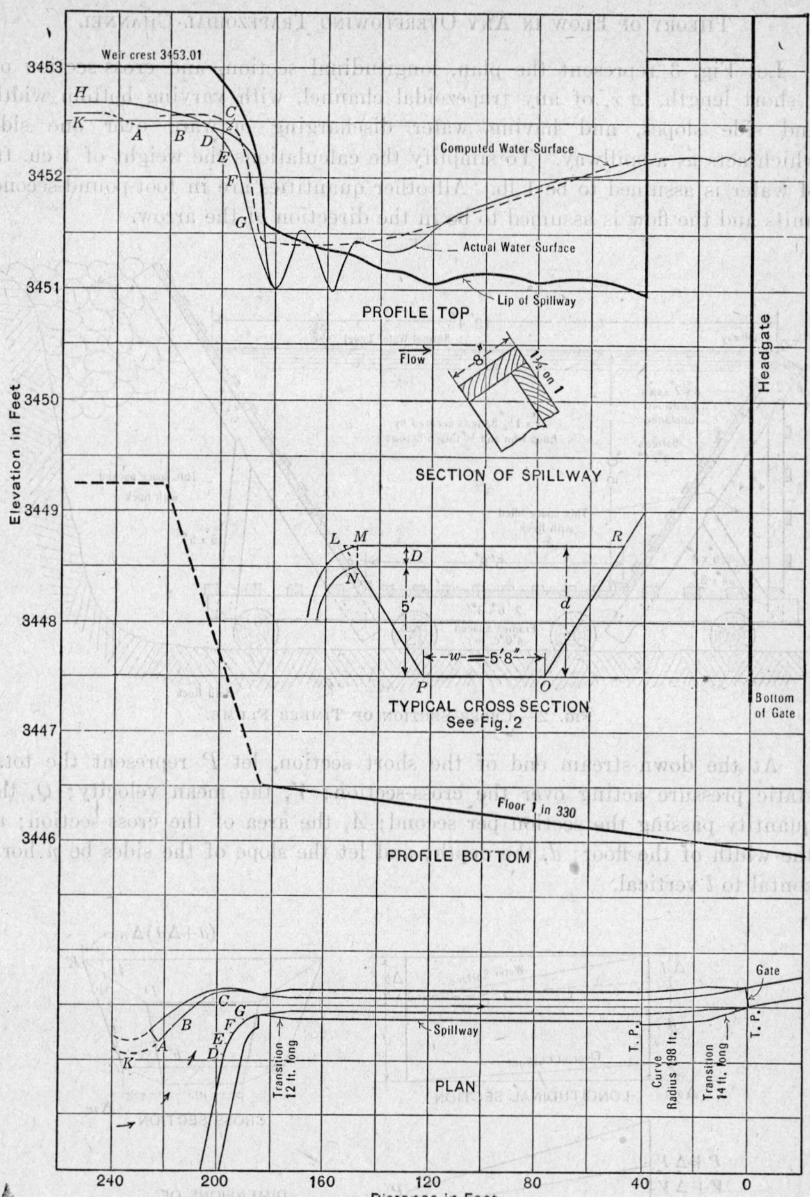

FIG. 1.—LIAWENEE FLUME EXPERIMENT NO. 19, GENERAL PLAN.

their surfaces are slightly warped. At the up-stream end of the timber flume a similar transition, 12 ft. long, connects with the throat of the converging channel. Figs. 5 and 9, which were taken when the head-gate was closed, show the whole flow of the river—approximately 400 sec-ft.—discharging over the side of the timber flume. The concrete flume is 6 ft. deep, the free-board being 1 ft. at the normal flow of 450 sec-ft.

Theory of Flow in Any Overflowing Trapezoidal Channel

Let Fig. 3 represent the plan, longitudinal section, and cross-section of a short length, Δx, of any trapezoidal channel, with varying bottom width and side slopes, and having water discharging outward over one side which acts as a spillway. To simplify the calculations the weight of 1 cu. ft. of water is assumed to be 1 lb. All other quantities are in foot-pound-second units and the flow is assumed to be in the direction of the arrow.

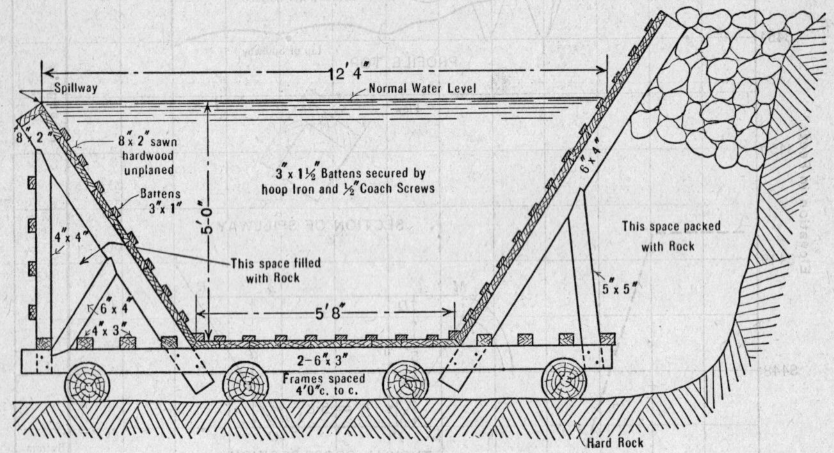

Fig. 2.—Cross-Section of Timber Flume.

At the down-stream end of the short section, let P represent the total static pressure acting over the cross-section; V, the mean velocity; Q, the quantity passing the section per second; A, the area of the cross-section; w, the width of the floor; d, the depth; and let the slope of the sides be n horizontal to l vertical.

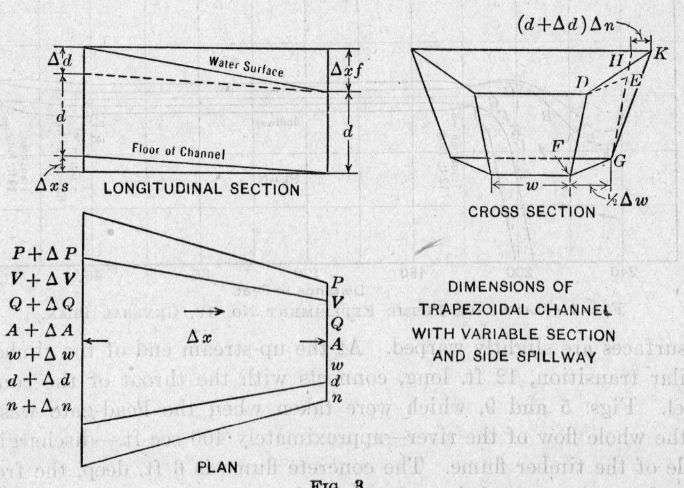

Fig. 3.

At the up-stream end of the section the corresponding quantities are to be denoted by $P + \Delta P$, $V + \Delta V$, $Q + \Delta Q$, $A + \Delta A$, $w + \Delta w$, $d + \Delta d$, and $n + \Delta n$, respectively. ΔQ, Δw, Δd, and Δn are positive, when Q, w, d, and n, respectively, are increasing up stream. Also, let f represent the loss of head per unit length due to friction and s, the slope of the floor per unit length, s being positive when the floor of the channel slopes down stream.

Then, ΔQ represents the quantity of water which is discharged over the side of the channel in the length, Δx, and, as it retains its momentum parallel to the channel, a certain amount of momentum is lost with it. The value of ΔQ is given by the usual equation

$$\Delta Q = c \, \Delta x \, D^{\frac{3}{2}} \qquad (1)$$

in which, D is the head of water over the spillway lip, and c is the constant.

From the principle of conservation of momentum, the change of momentum in the length, Δx, less the momentum lost with the overflowing water, must equal the algebraic sum of the external forces. The external forces are:

(1) The static pressures on the end areas, given by,

$$P = \left(\frac{w \, d^2}{2} + \frac{n \, d^3}{3}\right) \qquad (2)$$

and,

$$P + \Delta P = \left(\frac{(w + \Delta w)\,(d + \Delta d)^2}{2} + \frac{(n + \Delta n)\,(d + \Delta d)^3}{3}\right) \qquad (3)$$

(2) The reaction from the projected area of the side-walls: The rectangle, $D\,E\,G\,F$, and the triangle, $H\,K\,G$, may be taken as closely representing the actual area, $D\,K\,G\,F$. The reaction for both sides of the channel is given by,

$$\frac{\Delta w \, d^2}{2} + \frac{\Delta n}{3}(d + \Delta d)^3 = \frac{\Delta w \, d^2}{2} + \frac{\Delta n}{3}(d^3 + 3\,d^2\,\Delta d + 3\,d\,\Delta d^2 + \Delta d^3) \qquad (4)$$

Neglecting products and powers of Δ-quantities, Equation (4) becomes,

$$\frac{\Delta w \, d^2}{2} + \frac{\Delta n \, d^3}{3} \qquad (5)$$

(3) The retardation due to friction: This is very nearly equal to $\Delta x \, f \, (A + \frac{1}{2}\Delta A)$, but for short sections of any channels met with in practice, $\Delta x f$ will be very small, and $(A + \frac{1}{2}\Delta A)$ will be nearly equal to A. The retardation therefore, may be represented with sufficient accuracy by the term, $\Delta x \, f \, A$.

(4) The force due to gravity which may be represented by the term, $\Delta x \, s$: The momentum lost with the overflowing water is very nearly equal to,

$$\frac{\Delta Q \, (V + \frac{1}{2}\Delta V)}{g} \qquad (6)$$

in which, $V + \frac{1}{2}\Delta V$ is the average mean velocity in the length, Δx.

Equation (7) can now be written:

$$\frac{Q\,V}{g} + \frac{\Delta Q\,(V + \frac{1}{2}\Delta V)}{g} - \frac{(Q + \Delta Q)\,(V + \Delta V)}{g}$$

$$= \left\{\frac{(w + \Delta w)\,(d + \Delta d)^2}{2} + \frac{(n + \Delta n)\,(d + \Delta d)^3}{3}\right\} - \left(\frac{w\,d^2}{2} + \frac{n\,d^3}{3}\right)$$

$$- \frac{\Delta w \, d^2}{2} - \frac{\Delta n \, d^3}{3} - \Delta x\,(f - s)\,A \qquad (7)$$

Putting $V = \frac{Q}{A}$ and $V + \Delta V = \frac{Q + \Delta Q}{A + \Delta A}$ and rejecting products of Δ-quantities,

$$\frac{Q^2}{g A} + \frac{Q \Delta Q}{g A} - \frac{(Q + \Delta Q)^2}{g (A + \Delta A)} = \left\{ \frac{(w + \Delta w)(d^2 + 2 d \Delta d)}{2} + \frac{(n + \Delta n)(d^3 + 3 d^2 \Delta d)}{3} \right\} - \frac{w d^2}{2} - \frac{n d^3}{3} - \frac{\Delta w d^2}{2} - \frac{\Delta n d^3}{3} - \Delta x (f - s)(w d + n d^2) \ldots\ldots\ldots\ldots (8)$$

from which,

$$\frac{Q^2 w \Delta d + Q^2 \Delta w d + 2 Q^2 n d \Delta d + Q^2 \Delta n d^2 - Q \Delta Q w d - Q \Delta Q n d^2}{g \left\{ (w d + n d^2) + (w + 2 n d) \Delta d + \Delta w d + \Delta n d^2 \right\} (w d + n d^2)} = (w d + n d^2) \Delta d - \Delta x (f - s)(w d + n d^2)$$

rejecting Δ-terms in the denominator, this reduces to,

$$\frac{\Delta d}{\Delta x} = \frac{(f - s) - \frac{Q}{g} \times \frac{1}{(w d + n d^2)^2} \times \frac{\Delta Q}{\Delta x} + \frac{Q^2}{g} \times \frac{d}{(w d + n d^2)^3} \times \frac{\Delta w}{\Delta x} + \frac{Q^2}{g} \times \frac{d^2}{(w d + n d^2)^3} \times \frac{\Delta n}{\Delta x}}{1 - \frac{Q^2}{g} \times \frac{w + 2 n d}{(w d + n d^2)^3}} \ldots (9)$$

In Equation (9), if the channel is not acting as a spillway, then ΔQ vanishes and the second term of the numerator vanishes. If w be constant, the third term vanishes, and, if n be constant, the fourth term vanishes. The equation then reduces to:

$$\frac{\Delta d}{\Delta x} = \frac{f - s}{1 - \frac{Q^2}{g} \times \frac{w + 2 n d}{(w d + n d^2)^3}} \ldots\ldots\ldots\ldots (10)$$

For a rectangular channel, $n = 0$, and the equation further reduces to:

$$\frac{\Delta d}{\Delta x} = \frac{f - s}{1 - \frac{Q^2}{g} \times \frac{w}{w^3 d^3}} = \frac{f - s}{1 - \frac{Q^2}{g A^2 d}} = \frac{f - s}{1 - \frac{V^2}{g d}} \ldots\ldots (11)$$

Also, if the slope of the bed of the channel is just sufficient to overcome the resistance due to friction, then $f = s$, and Δd vanishes, or, in other words, the depth becomes constant which is the condition of normal flow in a uniform channel.

Again, when,

$$\frac{Q^2}{g} \frac{w + 2 n d}{(w d + n d^2)^3} = \frac{Q^2}{g A^2} \frac{w + 2 n d}{w d + n d^2} = \frac{V^2}{g} \frac{w + 2 n d}{w d + n d^2} = 1 \ldots (12)$$

that is, when,

$$\frac{w d + n d^2}{w + 2 n d} = \frac{V^2}{g} = \text{twice the velocity head} \ldots\ldots\ldots (13)$$

the denominator vanishes, and the ratio, $\frac{\Delta d}{\Delta x}$, becomes infinite in the limit, or, in other words, the water surface becomes vertical. This can only occur when passing through the critical depth. For a rectangular channel, as n is then zero, the critical depth occurs where the depth is twice the velocity head, or,

$$d = \frac{V^2}{g} \qquad (14)$$

For a channel, such as the spillway, into which water flows from the reservoir, the water enters at right angles to the axis of the channel and introduces no additional momentum corresponding to the loss of momentum which takes place when water flows outward from the channel.

The equation of flow for this condition is given by Equation (7) if the term, $\frac{\Delta Q\,(V + \frac{1}{2}\,\Delta V)}{g}$, is omitted, and a new equation corresponding to Equation (9) is then obtained:

$$\frac{\Delta d}{\Delta x} = \frac{(f - s) - \frac{2\,Q}{g}\,\frac{1}{(w\,d + n\,d^2)^2}\,\frac{\Delta Q}{\Delta x} + \frac{Q^2}{g}\,\frac{d}{(w\,d + n\,d^2)^3}\,\frac{\Delta w}{\Delta x} + \frac{Q^2}{g}\,\frac{d^2}{(w\,d + n\,d^2)^3}\,\frac{\Delta n}{\Delta x}}{1 - \frac{Q^2}{g}\,\frac{w + 2\,n\,d}{(w\,d + n\,d^2)^3}} \qquad (15)$$

By writing $y - xs$ for d, and bx for Q, and omitting the friction term, f, it can be shown that Equation (15) is another form of the equation,

$$\frac{d\,y}{d\,x} = \frac{V}{g}\,\frac{d\,V}{d\,x} + \frac{b\,V^2}{Q\,g} \qquad (16)$$

which is given by Julian Hinds, M. Am. Soc. C. E., in his paper on "Side Channel Spillways".*

Flume Experiments†

Equations (9) and (15) are only strictly correct when the average velocity is equal to the mean velocity, that is when,

$$\frac{1}{2}\,M\,V^2 = \frac{1}{2}\,\Sigma\,m\,v^2 \qquad (17)$$

in which, for any elementary stream tube, m represents the mass passing the section per second, and v the velocity. This condition is never quite satisfied in any ordinary stream owing to the irregular distribution of velocity over the cross-section. In the case of a channel discharging a large quantity of water over the side, it was thought that the disturbance set up by eddies might be

* *Transactions*, Am. Soc. C. E., Vol. 89 (1926), p. 881.

† The Liawenee experiments were carried out in November, 1922, and January, 1923. A full description of these experiments and the theory of flow in an overflowing channel are contained in an unpublished thesis presented by the writer to the University of Melbourne early in 1924.

TABLE 1.—COMPUTATION BY EQUATION (9) FOR WATER SURFACE CURVE IN LIAWENEE FLUME EXPERIMENT NO. 19, SHOWN IN FIG. 1.

Distance from gate, in feet.	Δx.	d.	w.	Δw.	n.	Δn.	Q.	D.	ΔQ.	V.	r.	f.	s.	$\Delta x\,(f-s)$.	$\frac{Q^2}{g} \cdot \frac{d}{(w\,d+n\,d^2)^3} \cdot \Delta w$.	$\frac{Q^2}{g} \cdot \frac{d^2}{(w\,d+n\,d^2)^3} \cdot \Delta n$.	$\frac{Q}{g} \cdot \frac{1}{(w\,d+n\,d^2)^2} \cdot \Delta Q$.	Sum of Columns (15), (16), (17), and (18).	$1-\frac{Q^2}{g} \cdot \frac{w+2\,n\,d}{(w\,d+n\,d^2)^3}$.	Δd, Column (19) ÷ Column (20).
(1)	(2)	(3)	(4)	(5)	(6)	(7)	(8)	(9)	(10)	(11)	(12)	(13)	(14)	(15)	(16)	(17)	(18)	(19)	(20)	(21)
30	..	6.20	5.67	.....	.667	....	125.0	....	....	2.06	2.96	0.00010	0.00303	−0.0293	......	....	......	−0.0293	0.969	−0.030
40	10	6.17	5.67	.....	.667	....	125.0	1.22	....	2.09	3.14	0.00010	0.00303	−0.0293	......	....	0.0491	−0.0784	0.971	−0.081
50	10	6.089	5.67	.....	.667	....	170.1	1.11	45.1	2.89	3.10	0.00018	0.00303	−0.0285	......	....	0.0597	0.0882	0.942	−0.094
60	10	5.995	5.67	.....	.667	....	209.1	0.99	39.0	3.63	3.05	0.00029	0.00303	−0.0274	......	....	0.0662	0.0936	0.907	−0.103
70	10	5.892	5.67	.....	.667	....	242.7	0.93	33.6	4.32	3.01	0.00042	0.00303	−0.0261	......	....	0.0732	0.0993	0.866	−0.115
80	10	5.777	5.67	.....	.667	....	273.2	0.88	30.5	4.73	2.95	0.00053	0.00303	−0.0250	......	....	0.0652	0.0902	0.836	−0.108
90	10	5.669	5.67	.....	.667	....	298.7	0.72	25.5	5.60	2.89	0.00073	0.00303	−0.0230	......	....	0.0650	0.0880	0.765	−0.115
100	10	5.554	5.67	.....	.667	....	318.5	0.63	19.8	6.13	2.81	0.00091	0.00303	−0.0212	......	....	0.0597	0.0809	0.710	−0.114
110	10	5.440	5.67	.....	.667	....	334.7	0.56	16.2	6.63	2.78	0.00110	0.00303	−0.0193	......	....	0.0598	0.0791	0.656	−0.120
120	10	5.320	5.67	.....	.667	....	349.3	0.54	14.5	7.12	2.72	0.00128	0.00303	−0.0175	......	....	0.0478	0.0653	0.594	−0.110
130	10	5.210	5.67	.....	.667	....	359.8	0.33	10.5	7.55	2.66	0.00146	0.00303	−0.0157	......	....	0.0284	0.0441	0.533	−0.083
140	10	5.127	5.67	.....	.667	....	365.5	0.26	5.7	7.85	2.61	0.00164	0.00303	−0.0139	......	....	0.0156	0.0295	0.486	−0.061
150	10	5.066	5.67	.....	.667	....	368.5	0.12	3.0	8.04	2.58	0.00172	0.00303	−0.0131	......	....	0.0057	0.0188	0.454	−0.042
	10								1.0											

TABLE 1.—(*Continued.*)

Distance from gate, in feet.	Δx.	d.	w.	Δw.	n.	Δn.	Q.	D.	ΔQ.	V.	r.	f.	s.	$\Delta x\,(f-s)$.	$\frac{Q^2}{g}\cdot\frac{d}{(w\,d+n\,d^2)^3}\cdot\Delta w$.	$\frac{Q^2}{g}\cdot\frac{d^2}{(w\,d+n\,d^2)^3}\cdot\Delta n$.	$\frac{Q}{g}\cdot\frac{1}{(w\,d+n\,d^2)^2}\cdot\Delta Q$.	Sum of Columns (15), (16), (17), and (18).	$1-\frac{Q^2}{g}\cdot\frac{w+2\,n\,d}{(w\,d+n\,d^2)^3}$.	Δd, Column (19) ÷ Column (20).
(1)	(2)	(3)	(4)	(5)	(6)	(7)	(8)	(9)	(10)	(11)	(12)	(13)	(14)	(15)	(16)	(17)	(18)	(19)	(20)	(21)
160		5.024	5.67	.....	.667	....	369.5	0.06		8.15	2.56	0.00180	0.00303	—0.0123	.....	....	0.0015	0.0138	0.434	—0.032
	10								0.3											
170		4.992	5.67	.....	.667	....	369.8	....	....	8.23	2.54	0.00200	0.00303	—0.00206	.....	....	.....	—0.00206	0.423	—0.005
	2																			
172		4.987	5.67	.....	.667		369.8	....	....	8.23	2.54	0.00200	0.00303	—0.00103	0.0652	—0.0650	.....	—0.00083	0.424	—0.002
	1			0.278		—0.0555														
173		4.985	5.948		0.611		369.8	....	....	8.24	2.54	0.00198	0.00303	—0.00210	0.0655	—0.0652	.....	—0.00075	0.431	—0.002
	1			0.278		—0.0555														
174		4.983	6.226		0.555		369.8	....	....	8.24	2.54	0.00198	0.00303	—0.00105	0.0656	—0.0652	.....	—0.00065	0.444	—0.001
	1			0.278		—0.0555														
175		4.982	6.50		0.499		369.8	....	....	8.25	2.54	0.00198	0.00303	—0.00210	0.1320	—0.1304	.....	—0.0005	0.458	—0.001
	2			0.56		—0.111														
177		4.981	7.06		0.388		369.8	....	....	8.24	2.52	0.00200	0.00303	—0.00721	0.4570	—0.4560	.....	—0.0062	0.483	—0.013
	7			1.94		—0.388														
184		4.968	9.00		0.000		369.8	....	....	8.27	2.36	0.00215	0.08000	—0.38925	0.4750	....	.....	0.0858	0.573	0.150
	5			2.00		0.000														
189		5.118	11.00		0.000		369.8	....	....	6.68	2.60	0.00125	0.08000	—0.39375	0.4290	....	.....	0.0358	0.735	0.048
	5			3.50		....														
194		5.116	14.50		0.000	....	369.8	....	....	4.93	3.02	0.00105	0.08000	—0.39475	0.1550	....	.....	—0.2397	0.855	—0.280
	5			3.00		....														
199		4.886	17.50		0.000	....	369.8	....	....	4.32	3.13	0.00077	0.08000	—0.39615	0.0501	....	.....	—0.3470	0.880	—0.394
	5			1.50		....														
204		4.492	19.00		0.000		369.8	....	....	4.32	3.05	0.00076	0.08000	—1.0885	0.2760	....	.....	—0.9120	0.870	—1.048
	15			9.00		....														
219		3.335	28.00	.....	.....	....	369.8	....	....	3.83	....	....	....	....	.....	....	.....	....	.....	

sufficient to vitiate entirely the results obtained from Equation (9) and, therefore, it was considered necessary to make a large scale experiment before applying the equation to the design of new head-works.

Fortunately, the timber flume made it possible to carry out an experiment—known as Liawenee Flume Experiment No. 19—the results of which are shown in Fig. 1 and Table 1. The lip of the spillway was slightly irregular owing to warping of the timber, and the profile of it, shown by the heavier full line in Fig. 1, was obtained by spirit leveling. The observed water surface, shown by the thinner full line in Fig. 1, was also obtained by spirit leveling, the staff being held close to the wall of the channel on the side opposite the spillway and it is, therefore, probably slightly higher than the mean level of the water surface.

Owing to the centrifugal effect in the curved converging inlet and the fact that the velocity of approach in the river above the weir slightly heaps up the water at the point marked, H, in Fig. 1, the water level on the two sides of the channel differs considerably. The points lettered on the longitudinal section correspond with those on the plan. The grade of the floor in the converging inlet had not been accurately determined and, for that reason, it is shown dotted in Fig. 1. The walls of the inlet are cement, but the floor is rough and the value of Kutter's n has been taken as 0.020. In the computations in Table 1, Kutter's n for the timber flume was taken as 0.015, although it was later found to be 0.017, but the effect of the friction term is so small that the level of the computed water surface is not appreciably affected thereby.

The flow in the flume was determined by current meter at a permanent gauging station on a uniform section of the canal a few hundred feet down stream from the outlet of the concrete flume. In this experiment, the total flow entering the timber flume was 360 sec-ft., of which quantity, 235 sec-ft. were discharged over the spillway, the remaining 125 sec-ft. passing under the head-gate, the lower edge of which was 1.37 ft. above the floor of the flume. It should be noted that spilling over the edge of the flume commenced 40 ft. up stream from the gate and ceased at 172 ft. and, therefore, was confined to a straight length of flume of normal cross-section, having a bed width of 5 ft. 8 in. and side slopes of $\frac{2}{3}$ horizontal to 1 vertical.

The water surface, shown by the dotted line in Fig. 1, was computed by Equation (9), the calculations being presented in Table 1. In order to find values of ΔQ for use in Table 1, it was necessary to determine the value of the coefficient for the spillway lip, a detailed cross-section of which is shown in Fig. 1. The mean value of the head, D, on the spillway was determined for each 4-ft. length, and the value of the coefficient, c, was found to be 3.57 from Equation (18):

$$\Sigma \Delta Q = c \Sigma (\Delta x D^{\frac{3}{2}}) = c \Sigma (4 D^{\frac{3}{2}}) = 235 \ldots\ldots\ldots\ldots (18)$$

In Equation (9), the expression, $(w d + n d^2)$, represents the complete trapezoid, $L R O P$ (see cross-section, Fig. 1), but, in the computation in Table 1, the area, $M R O P N$, was utilized as more nearly representing the actual cross-section of the water area. This procedure resulted in more labor in calculation than would have been involved if the complete trapezoidal area had been adopted and as the maximum area of the triangle, $L M N$, is only 0.006 of the area, $L R O P$, no appreciable error would have resulted if the area, $L R O P$, had been adopted instead of the area, $M R O P N$.

The actual water-surface level at a point 30 ft. up stream from the gate was adopted as a starting point from which to obtain the computed water-surface curve (dotted line, Fig. 1) which, in general, agrees closely with the actual water surface. From the head-gate to Station 40, the flume is curved and the centrifugal effect here would be to lower the actual water surface along the side of the flume opposite the spillway and this is probably the explanation of the divergence between the actual and computed water surfaces between Stations 30 and 60. The critical depth for the flume for a flow of 360 sec-ft. is 4.22 ft. and as the waves, which occur at the up-stream end of the flume, do not extend down to the critical depth, they are not hydraulic jumps. The water issues from the curved inlet at a velocity of 8.27 ft. per sec. and, as the upper portion of the walls of the timber transition flare outward from the end of the concrete inlet, the rapidly moving stream cannot immediately accommodate itself to the changed direction of the walls, and, consequently, a partial vacuum occurs against the upper portion of the walls, and is marked by a small area of turbulence which can be seen at the extreme left in Fig. 5. Equation (9) is based on the assumption that the water exerts a pressure against the walls at all points equal to the full static pressure due to the depth, and the waves are due to the fact that this condition does not hold just at the entrance to the transition. Up stream from the throat the computed water surface agrees fairly well with the mean of the observed water surfaces in the curved inlet. The computed total discharge of 370 sec-ft. (see Table 1) agrees well with the measured discharge of 360 sec-ft.

Proposed Design for New Head-Works for Ouse-Great Lake Canal

As the foregoing experiment showed that Equation (9) could be satisfactorily applied in practice on a comparatively large scale, it was decided to make a new design for the head-works of the canal based on the theory just developed. A diagrammatic longitudinal section of the proposed head-works is shown in Fig. 6. The existing curved inlet, shown in Fig. 1, from Station 184 up stream will be retained. At Station 184 a square-edged concrete baffle-wall will be constructed above the throat of the inlet and will extend across to the wall of the gorge so that water can enter the flume only by means of the orifice, 5 ft. high by 9 ft. wide, under the baffle. No gate is required at this point, but provision for stop-planks will be made. A second orifice, 5 ft. high, will be formed by a square-edged concrete head-wall in the position occupied by the existing head-gate, and a sector gate having the full width of the concrete flume will be provided for closing this orifice when it is desired to prevent water from entering the canal.

Between Stations 0 and 184, the existing timber flume will be replaced by a rectangular concrete flume, 9 ft. wide, designed to act as a spillway between

Stations 30 and 152. It will be noted that, between Stations 10 and 174, the floor of the flume is lowered about 5 ft. below the normal grade line of 1 in 330 to form a deep pool throughout the spillway portion of the flume. In the actual design the sharp changes of grade shown in Fig. 6 at Stations 10, 30, 152, and 174, will be rounded, but the hydraulic computations are simplified by considering them as being sharp and this assumption has no appreciable effect on the results.

Before investigating the behavior of the proposed head-works in detail, it is necessary to decide on suitable values for the coefficient of roughness of the concrete flume and the coefficients of discharge of the spillway and the orifice at the inlet and head-gate.

Coefficient of Roughness of Flume.—Gaugings taken in the existing concrete flume show that the value of Kutter's n varies from 0.014 in summer to 0.015 in winter, owing to the fact that a growth appears on the walls and floor during the high-water period when the flume is continuously filled. This growth dies again if the flow ceases frequently. The value of 0.015 was adopted for Kutter's n, but the shape of the water-surface curves shown in Fig. 6 would be very slightly affected by a considerable error in the value of n.

Coefficient of Discharge for Spillway.—A cross-section of the crest of the proposed spillway is shown in Fig. 6. For a triangular weir, sharp crest, up-stream face vertical, top sloping 2 horizontal to 1 vertical, the value of c in Equation (1):

$$\Delta Q = c \, \Delta x \, D^{\frac{3}{2}}$$

for a head of 1 ft. on the crest is given by King* as 3.50. Bazin's experiments on wide crested weirs showed an increase of 9% in the value of c when the up-stream edge was rounded to a radius of 4 in. Assuming the same increase for the spillway, the value of c would become 3.82. A value of 3.80 was adopted for the spillway.

Coefficient of Discharge of Orifices.—At both the inlet and head-gate orifices, the floor and the two walls of the flume are continuous so that contraction is entirely suppressed on these three sides, but the top of the orifice is sharp-edged and the velocity of approach is usually considerable. No published experiments dealing with orifices of this nature could be found and, therefore, some experiments (referred to as the "baffle experiments") were carried out in January, 1923, by placing a timber baffle in a straight portion of the existing concrete flume. The data obtained from Experiments B2-6 and the profiles of the water surface are shown in Table 2 and Fig. 7 which is self-explanatory. The bottom of the baffle in all experiments was sharp-edged and was located at Distance 0; in Experiment 3 the baffle was inclined 45° up stream. The depth, d_1, was measured 5 ft. up stream from the baffle. The floor of the flume had a grade of 1 in 330. In Experiment B-1 the water backed up and overflowed the wall of the flume, therefore, the results have been discarded. The water-surface profiles were obtained by measuring downward, with a rod graduated in inches, from points on the wall of the flume, the elevations of which had been determined with an engineer's level. As the result of these experiments, 0.58 was adopted as the value of c for the inlet and head-gate.

* "Handbook of Hydraulics."

Fig. 4.—View of Timber Flume, Looking Up Stream from the Head-Gate.

Fig. 5.—View Showing Entire Flow of Ouse River Discharging Over Side of Timber Flume.

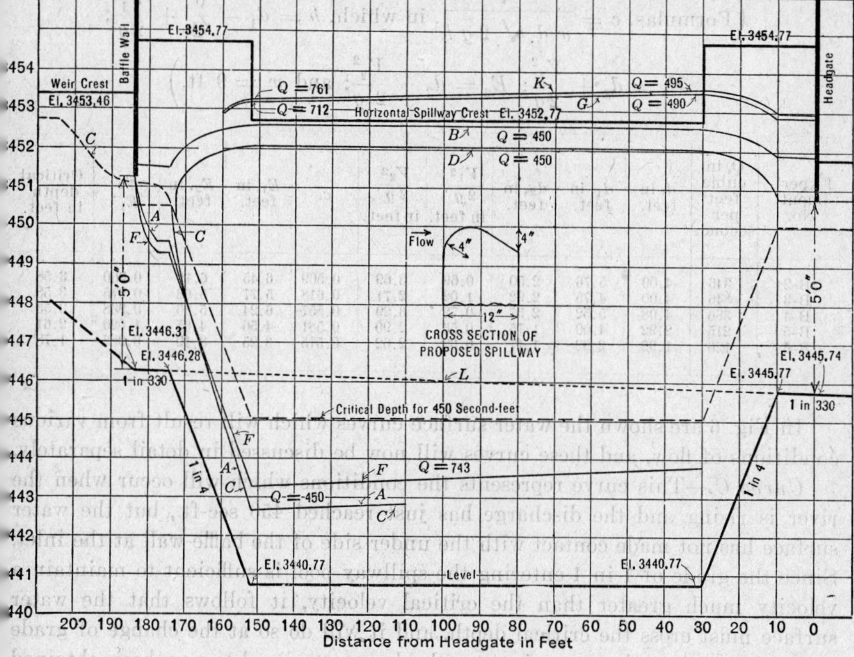

FIG. 6.—PROPOSED DESIGN FOR HEAD-WORKS. DIAGRAMMATIC SECTION ON CENTER LINE.

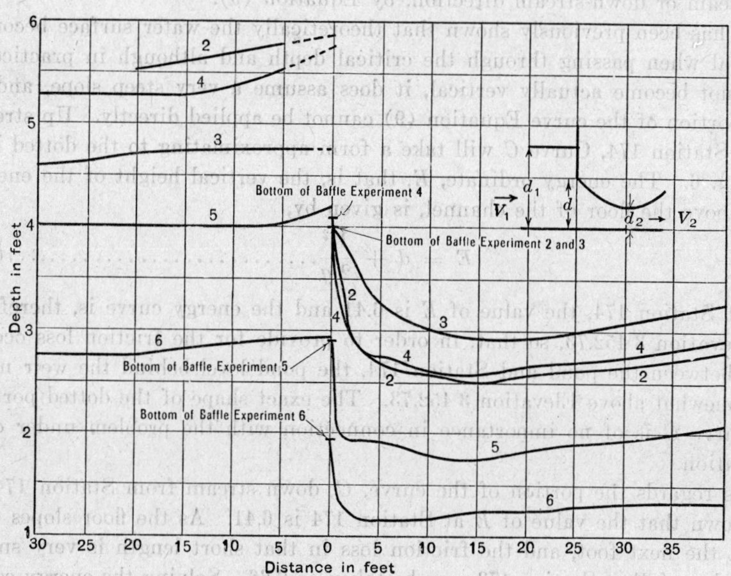

FIG. 7.—PROFILES OF WATER SURFACE, BAFFLE EXPERIMENTS.

TABLE 2.—BAFFLE EXPERIMENTS, JANUARY 8 TO 11, 1923.

$$\left(\text{Formulas, } c = \frac{Q}{w\,d.\sqrt{2\,g\,h}}, \text{ in which, } h = d_1 - \frac{d}{2} + \frac{V_1^2}{2\,g};\right.$$

$$\left. E_1 = d_1 + \frac{V_1^2}{2\,g};\ E_2 = d_2 + \frac{V_2^2}{2\,g};\ \text{and } w = 9 \text{ ft.}\right)$$

Experiment No.	Q, in cubic feet per second.	d. in feet.	d_1, in feet.	d_2, in feet.	$\frac{V_1^2}{2g}$, in feet.	$\frac{V_2^2}{2g}$, in feet.	c.	E_1, in feet.	E_2, in feet.	$\frac{E_2}{E_1}$.	Critical depth, in feet.
B-2	346	4.00	5.76	2.50	0.69	3.69	0.569	6.45	6.19	0.960	3.58
B-3	346	4.00	4.75	2.92	1.02	2.71	0.618	5.77	5.63	0.975	3.58
B-4	336	4.08	5.52	2.57	0.72	3.29	0.557	6.24	5.86	0.938	3.53
B-5	215	2.92	4.00	1.75	0.56	2.90	0.581	4.56	4.65	1.020	2.61
B-6	120	1.92	2.92	1.17	0.33	2.02	0.575	3.25	3.19	0.982	1.78

In Fig. 6 are shown the water surface curves which will result from various conditions of flow, and these curves will now be discussed in detail separately.

Curve C.—This curve represents the conditions which will occur when the river is rising and the discharge has just reached 450 sec-ft., but the water surface has not made contact with the under side of the baffle-wall at the inlet. Since the grade of 1 in 4 entering the spillway pool is sufficient to maintain a velocity much greater than the critical velocity, it follows that the water surface must cross the critical depth, and it will do so at the change of grade at Station 174. A known point on a back-water curve has now been obtained and, in most cases, the form of the curve could be computed, in either the up-stream or down-stream direction, by Equation (9).

It has been previously shown that theoretically the water surface becomes vertical when passing through the critical depth and although in practice it does not become actually vertical, it does assume a very steep slope, and to this portion of the curve Equation (9) cannot be applied directly. Up stream from Station 174, Curve C will take a form approximating to the dotted line on Fig. 6. The energy ordinate, E, that is, the vertical height of the energy line above the floor of the channel, is given by,

$$E = d + \frac{V^2}{2\,g} \qquad (19)$$

At Station 174, the value of E is 6.41 and the energy curve is, therefore at Elevation 3 452.73, so that, in order to provide for the friction loss occurring between the pond and Station 174, the pond level behind the weir must be somewhat above Elevation 3 452.73. The exact shape of the dotted portion of Curve C is of no importance in connection with the problem under consideration.

As regards the portion of the curve, C, down stream from Station 174, it is known that the value of E at Station 174 is 6.41. As the floor slopes 0.25 ft. in the next foot, and the friction loss in that short length is very small the value of E at Station 173 may be taken as 6.66. Solving the energy equation, the depth at Station 173 is found to be 3.54 ft. From Station 173 down stream, Curve C has been computed by Equation (9) in a manner exactly similar to that used in computing the water surface in Experiment No. 19 (Fig. 1), as shown in detail in Table 1, except that, for Curve C, ΔQ, ΔW, and Δn are all zero, and the calculation is thereby simplified.

Curve D.—The normal depth for 450 sec-ft. in the concrete flume being 5.0 ft., therefore, if the water surface is not touching the under side of the head-gate, a depth of 5 ft. at Station 0 may be adopted as a starting point from which Curve D can be computed up stream by Equation (9).

In applying Equation (9) to those portions of the curve between Stations 10 and 30 and Stations 152 and 172.5, where the slope of the water surface is changing rapidly, it is necessary to take extremely small steps in making the calculations, but, owing to the great depth, the energy lost in friction in each of these portions does not exceed about 0.01 ft., and, therefore, no appreciable error is introduced by considering the energy line to be at the same elevation throughout these portions of the flume. The value of d can then be determined by solving the energy equation,

$$E = d + \frac{V^2}{2\,g} = d + \frac{Q^2}{2\,g\,w^2\,d^2} \qquad (20)$$

This method of dealing with the steeper portions of the curves avoids the great amount of labor involved in applying Equation (9) and has been adopted in determining such portions of all curves shown in Fig. 6. Between Stations 30 and 152, Curve D has been computed by Equation (9).

Curves C and D.—The water entering under the baffle cannot continue to follow Curve C indefinitely as the bottom of the flume is level, and energy is being absorbed by friction. In order to pass under the head-gate, the water must change by some means from Curve C to Curve D and, as this involves crossing the critical depth, the change can only take place through an hydraulic jump. An hydraulic jump between any two curves can only take place at a point where the value of the momentum,

$$M = \frac{A\,d}{2} + \frac{Q\,V}{g} \qquad (21)$$

is the same for both curves.

The curves in Fig. 8 show the value of M at various points on the correspondingly lettered curves in Fig. 6. Referring to Curves C and D in Fig. 8, it is seen that they intersect at Station 170 and, therefore, the water surface must jump from Curve C to Curve D (Fig. 6) at that point.

Curve A.—This curve represents the conditions which will occur with a falling stage of the river when the flow is 450 sec-ft. and the water is in contact with the under side of the baffle. From the formula,

$$Q = A\,c\,\sqrt{2\,g\,h} \qquad (22)$$

it is found that the head, h, over the center of gravity of the orifice is 4.65 ft. The crest of the weir, therefore, must be 7.15 ft. above the bottom of the orifice, that is, at Elevation 3 453.46, in order that no water shall be wasted over the weir until the flume is receiving 450 sec-ft.

The value of E on the up-stream side of the baffle is 7.15 and Baffle Experiments No. B-2 to B-4 (Table 2 and Fig. 7) show that a loss of about 4% of the energy occurs in passing the baffle. Therefore, on the down-stream side of the baffle, the value of E will be about 6.86, from which it is found that the depth at about 6 ft. on the down-stream side of the baffle will be 3.33 ft. From Station 178 down stream, Curve A has been computed by Equation (9) and merges into Curve C.

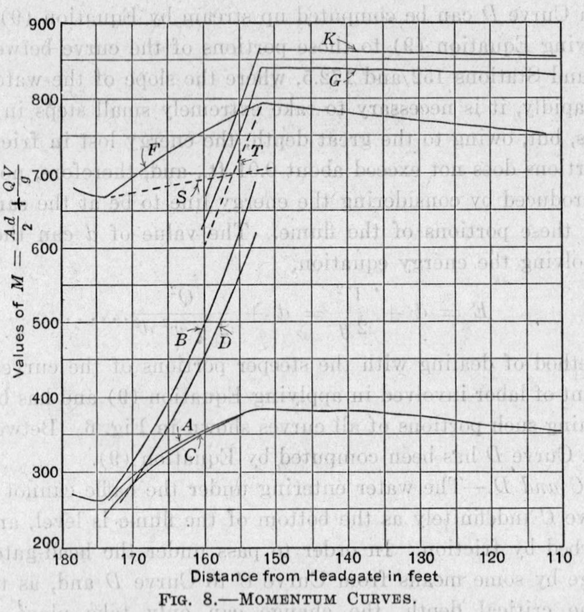

FIG. 8.—MOMENTUM CURVES.

Curve B.—This curve represents the conditions occurring with a falling stage of the river when the flow is 450 sec-ft. and the water touches the under-side of the head-gate. From the formula, $Q = A\ c\ \sqrt{2\ g\ h}$,

$$h = d + \frac{V^2}{2\ g} - 2.5 = 6.92 \text{ ft.}$$

from which, for the up-stream side of the head-gate, d, by trial, equals 8.64 ft.

Curve B is then computed from the head-gate up stream in exactly the same manner as has been described in the case of Curve D. Curve B fixes the lowest level at which the spillway can be placed without losing water when the total flow in the river does not exceed the normal canal capacity of 450 sec-ft. To provide some margin for error in the calculations, the spillway has been placed slightly above Curve B, being horizontal and exactly 12.0 ft. above the floor of the channel.

Curves A and B.—The water, entering under the baffle and flowing along Curve A, must jump to Curve B in order to pass the head-gate. Reference to Fig. 8 shows that the momentum Curves A and B intersect at Station 173.5 and at this point the jump must take place.

Curve F.—This curve represents the surface curve that will be assumed by the water passing under the baffle during the maximum flood which is estimated to rise to a height of 8 ft. above the crest of the weir, that is, to a height of 15.15 ft. above the bottom of the orifice. Therefore, $h = 12.65$ ft., and,

$$Q = A\ c\ \sqrt{2\ g\ h} = 743 \text{ sec-ft.}$$

As the velocity head at the up-stream side of the baffle is negligible, the energy ordinate, E, at this point is equal to the depth, d_1, that is, 15.15 ft. Allowing 4% loss of energy in passing the baffle the energy ordinate on the down-stream side, E_2, becomes 14.55 ft., from which, $d_2 = 3.04$ ft. is obtained by trial. This depth will occur about 6 ft. down stream from the baffle, that is, at Station 178. From Station 178 down stream, Curve F has been computed by Equation (9).

The critical depth, d_c, for 743 sec-ft. is given by,

$$d_c = \sqrt[3]{\frac{Q^2}{g\ w^2}} = 5.97 \text{ ft.} \qquad (23)$$

and it is obvious that the water cannot pass through the head-gate without first jumping across the critical depth to some curve, such as G or K, and while flowing along such a curve a large quantity of water will be discharged over the spillway, although the flow under the head-gate will also be somewhat in excess of the normal canal capacity of 450 sec-ft.

For the flow to take place along any curve, such as G or K, two conditions must be satisfied: (1) That the value of M on the given curve, at the point where the jump takes place, must be equal to the value of M for Curve F at the corresponding point; and (2) the sum of the discharges over the spillway and under the head-gate must be 743 sec-ft. The curve which will satisfy these conditions can be found by trial as explained subsequently.

Curve G.—Let it be assumed that the quantity of water passing under the head-gate is 490 sec-ft., then, in the same manner as has been explained in regard to Curve B, it is found that the depth, d_1, against the up-stream side of the gate is 7.07 ft. From Station 0 to Station 30 and from Station 152 to Station 160, Curve G has been computed by the energy equation as previously explained for Curve D. Throughout the length of the spillway, that is, between Stations 30 and 152, Curve G has been computed by Equation (9), and the computation is shown in Table 3.

Referring to the momentum curves in Fig. 8, it will be seen that Curves F and G intersect at Station 154, and, therefore, at this point the water can jump from Curve F to Curve G. On referring to Table 3, it is noted that the value of Q increases from 490 sec-ft. at the down-stream end of the spillway (Station 30) to 712 sec-ft. at the up-stream end (Station 152), but this latter value should be 743 sec-ft. in order to satisfy Condition (2) as stated. The water surface, therefore, must take up some position above Curve G.

Curve K.—Assuming that the quantity of water passing under the head-gate is 495 sec-ft., it is found that the depth, d_1, against the head-gate is 7.20 ft., and from this point Curve K is computed in exactly the same manner as Curve G. In Fig. 8, it is seen that the momentum curves, F and K, intersect

TABLE 3.—COMPUTATION OF CURVES G AND K, (FIG. 6).

	Distance from gate, in feet.	Δx.	d.	D.	Q.	ΔQ.	V.	r.	f.	s.	$\Delta x\,(f-s)$.	$\frac{Q}{g}\cdot\frac{1}{(w\,d+n\,d^2)^2}\cdot\Delta Q$.	Sum of Columns (11) and (12).	$1-\frac{Q^2}{g}\cdot\frac{w+2\,n\,d}{(w\,d+n\,d^2)^3}$.	Δd, Column (13) ÷ Column (14).
	(1)	(2)	(3)	(4)	(5)	(6)	(7)	(8)	(9)	(10)	(11)	(12)	(13)	(14)	(15)
Curve G	30		12.73	0.73	490.0		4.28	3.32	0.000371	0.000	0.0074	0.0553	—0.0479	0.9552	—0.050
	50	20	12.68	0.68	537.4	47.4	4.71	3.32	0.000435	0 000	0.0087	0.0548	—0.0461	0.9403	—0.049
	70	20	12.631	0.631	580.0	42.6	5.10	3.31	0.000527	0.009	0.0105	0.0534	—0.0429	0.9355	—0.046
	90	20	12.585	0.585	618.1	38.1	5.45	3.32	0.000588	0.000	0.0117	0.0511	—0.0394	0.9262	—0.043
	110	20	12.542	0.542	652.1	34.0	5.78	3.31	0.000667	0.000	0.0133	0.0485	—0.0352	0.9167	—0.038
	130	20	12.504	0.504	682.4	30.3	6.06	3.31	0.000715	0.000	0.0157	0.0504	—0.0347	0.9080	—0.038
	152	22	12.466	......	712.3	29.9	6.35	....	....	......	......	......	....	......	....
Curve K	30		12.84	0.84	495.0		4.28	3.33	0.000412	0.000	0.0041	0.0338	—0.0297	0.9568	—0.031
	40	10	12.809	0.809	524.2	29.2	4.54	3.33	0.000400	0.000	0.0080	0.0678	—0.0598	0.9496	—0.063
	60	20	12.746	0.746	579.4	55.2	5.06	3.32	0.000500	0.000	0.0100	0.0669	—0.0569	0.9374	—0.061
	80	20	12.685	0.685	628.3	48.9	5.50	3.32	0.000606	0.000	0.0121	0.0648	—0.0527	0.9173	—0.057
	100	20	12.628	0.628	671.4	43.1	5.91	3.32	0.000713	0.000	0.0214	0.0923	—0.0709	0.9134	—0.078
	130	30	12.550	0.550	728.1	56.7	6.45	3.31	0.000832	0.000	0.0183	0.0582	—0.0399	0.8964	—0.044
	152	22	12.506	......	760.7	32.6	6.76	....	....	......	......	......	....	......	....

FIG. 9.—VIEW OF TIMBER FLUME, UP STREAM FROM THE HEAD-GATE, SHOWING HYDRAULIC JUMP.

FIG. 10.—VIEW OF TIMBER FLUME UNDER NORMAL CONDITIONS.

at Station 155, which is the only possible position for the jump. Table 3, however, shows that the value of Q increases from 495 sec-ft. at Station 30 to 761 sec-ft. at Station 152, but, as in order to satisfy the conditions the latter value should be 743 sec-ft., it follows that the water surface must take up some position below Curve K and, therefore, it must occupy some position between Curves G and K.

It is necessary to consider to what extent the degree of regulation will be affected by errors in the adopted values for Kutter's n and the coefficients of discharge of the baffle and head-gate and of the spillway. Table 3 shows that the friction term in the numerator of Equation (9) is very small compared with the term in ΔQ and, therefore, variation in the value of n will not appreciably affect the water surface opposite the spillway. The coefficient adopted for the baffle and head-gate is based on actual experiments made under conditions exactly similar to those that will obtain at the baffle and head-gate, and it is not likely therefore to be seriously in error.

Assuming, however, that the true value of the coefficient is 5% greater than the adopted value, the discharge under the baffle would be increased by 37 sec-ft. and the discharge under the head-gate by about 24 sec-ft. The increase in the discharge of the spillway would be only about 13 sec-ft. and the level of the water surface would be very slightly changed. An increase of 5% in the value of the coefficient, therefore, would increase the excess in the canal to about 15% of the normal flow. A small decrease in the value of the coefficient, of course, will improve the regulation, but will raise the level of Curve B to some extent, for which reason the spillway crest has been placed a little higher than Curve B.

The coefficient for the spillway is the factor which is most likely to be in error, but Curves G and K (Table 3) show that a variation of 44 sec-ft., or 20% of the total discharge over the spillway, only causes a variation of 5 sec-ft. in the discharge under the head-gate, so that the value of the coefficient for the spillway may be considerably in error without appreciably affecting the regulation of the canal.

The proposed design for the head-works, therefore, will probably prevent the normal capacity of the canal being exceeded by more than 10% and will certainly prevent it being exceeded by more than 15% which is equivalent to 70 sec-ft. Since the canal is provided with spillways where it crosses natural drainage channels and can be operated for a reasonable period under an overload of 100 sec-ft., the proposed design which involves no moving parts and is, therefore, "fool-proof" and frost proof, will provide satisfactory regulation.

If the floor of the spillway portion of the channel were not lowered, but were constructed to the dotted line, L, in Fig. 6, the momentum, M_L, of the water leaving the baffle orifice at the lower stage, would exceed the momentum, M_U, for the upper stage, which would be the normal depth. If a jump is to occur, the value of M_L must be decreased until it equals the value of M_U. As friction would be the only force tending to decrease the value of M_L, the high velocity stage might persist to a point beyond the head-gate. Therefore, in order to make the spillway effective, some means must be adopted to ensure that a jump will occur at some definite point close to the baffle. Similar conditions were met in the experiments of the Miami Conservancy District* in the design of outlets from its flood-detention reservoirs. In that case the reaction of a submerged obstruction was used to decrease the value of M_L, but in order to avoid raising the water level too high in passing over the obstruction, the obstruction was placed below the normal floor of the channel and the water led to it down an incline which had the effect of first raising the value of M_L.

In the proposed head-works design shown in Fig. 6, a definite location for the jump is secured in a different manner. The function of the deep pool is to make the value of M_U greater than that of M_L. Instead of decreasing M_L, it is necessary, therefore, either to increase M_L or to decrease M_U, or to do both. The curves in Fig. 8 show clearly that the steep grade of the floor in Fig. 6 does both increase M_L and decrease M_U, causing the curves to intersect at a decided angle and thereby definitely locating the jump within the limits of the steep grade.

The view, Fig. 9, looking up stream from the head-gate during a moderate flood in the river, shows a good example of an hydraulic jump occurring at about the center of the timber flume. The jump is due to the fact that the head-gate was partly closed, thus backing up the water in the flume. In comparison, Fig. 10 shows the flume under more normal conditions.

For the particular head-works under discussion, the very narrow space available at the side of the gorge renders the method of obtaining regulation by lowering the floor very suitable. It is not the only possible method, however, and similar results could be achieved by widening the channel behind the baffle at the inlet and contracting it again at the head-gate. Thus, if the width of the floor be increased from 9 ft. at Station 174 (Fig. 6) to 40 ft. at Station 152, the dotted curve, S, in Fig. 8 shows the variation of M_L for a discharge of 743 sec-ft. The dotted curve, T, shows the approximate value of M_U, assuming a depth of 1 ft. of water over the spillway at Station 152. Although no incline is used, the intersection of Curves S and T (Fig. 8) shows that the jump will be just as definitely located in the transition in this instance as it is for the design shown in Fig. 6 and many cases might arise in practice where it is preferable to widen the channel rather than deepen it.

For the Ouse-Great Lake Canal, regulation of the flow within 15% of the normal is sufficient, but if closer regulation were desired it could be obtained by installing a second baffle, stilling pool, and spillway immediately down stream from Station 0 (Fig. 6) and moving the head-gate to the down-stream end of this second pool. If necessary, a series of stilling pools and spillways, separated by orifices, might be used.

The problem of regulating the flow in a diversion channel taking water from a river subject to rapid and considerable changes of level is one which must frequently be encountered, and where some type of automatic gate is not suitable, the principles of the design illustrated in Fig. 6 may find a practical application.

---

* Miami Conservancy District, Technical Reports, Pt. 3.

DISCUSSION

EDWARD S. LINDLEY,* M. AM. SOC. C. E. (by letter).—The author arrives at a coefficient of 3.82 for the spillway section shown on Fig. 6. This is probably about the maximum value of coefficient that it is possible to realize, as long as no negative pressures are induced at the control section; but tests made by the writer† indicate that that value is likely to be realized.

In the formulas and calculations of Table 2, the author measures the head causing velocity down to the center of the orifice. That is the text-book method for a small orifice the jet from which discharges freely into the air all round it; but a different solution applies when the height of orifice is not small relative to its submersion up stream, and when down-stream water is above its bottom. Where, as here, side and bottom contractions are completely suppressed, and the jet from the orifice is supported on the sides and bottom, Bernouilli's theorem gives a simple rational formula, so elementary that no demonstration is needed.

Following the author's notation, but splitting his coefficient of discharge into:

c_v = the coefficient of velocity;

c_c = the coefficient of top contraction; and

h_a = the head to be added to allow for velocity of approach $\left(\text{actually greater than } \frac{V^2}{2\,g}\right)$;

$$Q = c_v\, c_c\, d \sqrt{2\, g\, (d_1 + h_a - c_c\, d)}$$

The simplest case is that of a bellmouth orifice with c_c equal to unity. The writer has confirmed it in tests of a 6 by 3-in. orifice, under heads up to about 2.5 ft. Plotting the squares of discharges against the up-stream water level, the "curve" was a straight line which cut the axis of zero discharge at the level of the top of the orifice; the bellmouth used had a c_v of 0.975 over the range of heads tested.

In the sluices of the Assuan Dam‡ there is contraction, and c_c varies with the gate-opening, at any rate when the slightly belled tunnel opening comes into play with bigger openings. Discharge from the tunnels being freely into air, the head was measured to the center of the orifice, as in textbooks, and the resulting coefficient was found to vary with the head. At the writer's suggestion the rational formula was applied to the data, when the coefficient was found to be independent of the head, and the top contraction was calculated.

Where, as in the observations given by the author, the height of orifice is greater than the critical depth of flow, and probably also where it is only a little less than that depth, conditions are uncertain; they are even probably unstable, undergoing a slow pulsation.

---

* Superintending Engr., Indian Public Works Dept., Panjab Irrig. Branch, London, England.

† *Paper 97*, Panjab Eng. Congress, 1925.

‡ *Minutes of Proceedings*, Inst. C. E., Vol. CCXVI (1922-23), pp. 213 and 257.

The observations are too few for analysis; and it would seem that they are not full and certain enough to make analysis worth while. The author has measured his d_1 at the up-stream face of the gate, including banking up, and has still taken the whole velocity of approach into account. Velocities were so high that the difference between h_a and $\frac{V^2}{2g}$ would be appreciable.

A. P. FLOCKART,* ESQ. (by letter).—The structures described by Mr. Nimmo were designed and erected prior to the publication of information on hydraulic jump problems† by Julian Hinds, M. Am. Soc. C. E. It was intended that at full supply 450 cu. ft. per sec. should flow 5 ft. deep at 10 ft. per sec. through both wood and concrete flumes, no allowance being made for possible difference in hydraulic properties of the sections, nor for the obstruction caused by the gate stanchion. In operation, 410 cu. ft. per sec. ran 5 ft. deep in the wooden flume; it drew down through the transition to a depth of 3 ft. 6 in. just beyond the gate, and then gradually rose to normal depth some distance down the concrete flume. Experiments were then undertaken to determine what was causing the apparent throttling, with the result that the gate stanchion was ruled out, as also was the slight curve preceding the gate.

About 1920 the method of analysis by drawing the minimum energy line was introduced. This showed a hump at the end of the wooden flume section and also showed that the water levels down stream were not high enough to drown out this possible control, which, therefore, operated and caused a disturbance down stream. The throttling was thus caused solely by a change of shape of cross-section which has been avoided in the design for permanent works.

In Mr. Nimmo's proposed design, provision has been made for all the flow conditions that can be foreseen, and it is hoped that Equation (9) will prove to be accurate. There is a great need, however, for some simpler expression which will indicate the effect of altering the various factors without having to make a complete calculation. It would certainly be of interest to know the effect of sloping the floor of the pool from Station 150 to the outlet with the object of reducing the yardage of concrete.

The statement that the water surface becomes vertical when passing through the critical point is obviously not correct when, for instance, water passes over a broad-crested weir. An examination of Equation (11) shows that, at the critical point, not only does the value of $\frac{\Delta d}{\Delta x}$ take the values of plus and minus infinity, but that the equation itself becomes discontinuous. This would be illustrated if the equation could be integrated and a more general expression for the relation between d and x written.

It is possible, however, to integrate the expression graphically by plotting $\frac{\Delta x}{\Delta d}$ on d as abscissa, in which case the areas under the curve represent the

* Hydr. Engr., Hydro-Elec. Dept., Hobart, Tasmania.

† *Engineering News-Record*, 1920.

lengths of conduit between successive values of d, and so permit the surface curve to be drawn. This does away with the labor and uncertainty of "arithmetical integration", and permits both back-water curves and Equation (11) to be studied. The method is not applicable however, to Equation (9).

George M. Bacon,* M. Am. Soc. C. E. (by letter).—This paper should command the interest of all engineers who have to deal with problems involving the distribution of water. All such engineers are constantly on the watch for, and seeking after, devices which shall be perfectly automatic in their action. In general, the big problem is to provide for the situation when everything is not going exactly as planned.

Past observations have long ago given the writer a definite suspicion that large volumes of flowing water fail to behave in accordance with any set of formulas. It would be interesting to see what results would be obtained from analyzing this problem on the basis of a thin sheet of water the lower surface of which was that bounded by horizontal lines extending across the flume from the lip of the spillway. This thin slab would naturally have the velocity of the water immediately below its lower bounding surface and the assumptions as to one would, in a measure, apply to the other. This slab could be considered as being acted upon by two forces, one representing the momentum of the water along the direction of the flume and the other a force represented by the slope, at right angles to the flume, which the upper surface of the slab must take in discharging water over the edge of the flume.

In Equation (1), how is the momentum that has just been mentioned taken care of? Independent of this case it is easy to see that this momentum might be sufficiently great to allow very little over-flow. A factor certainly should be taken into account covering the loss of momentum as the flow in the flume loses its velocity.

It is not entirely clear just how static pressures on the end areas can be compared, with no particular reference to the velocity involved or the force of gravity keeping up or modifying the velocity.

It would be extremely interesting to have the results of the experiment which the author states is fully described in his thesis presented to the University of Melbourne. These results would be extremely valuable if they indicated some definite relation between over-flow, capacity of flume, and length of over-flow, as calculated from the formula, and that found from actual experiment. It is obvious that if no particular limit is fixed for the length of the spillway all surplus water will be ultimately lost especially if reasonable provision can be had for a considerable length of flume in which the flow of water has a chance to become quite uniform and regular.

The results of experiments of this kind might have a distinct bearing on what could be considered the reverse of the present problem, namely, that of a spillway channel of a reservoir which was fed by the ordinary over-flow on a long crest, the channel being designed so as to carry away from the edge of this over-flow the water as fast as it is fed into the channel. This problem

* State Engr., Salt Lake City, Utah.

would not occur very often in actual practice as conditions usually admit of making such a channel sufficiently deep and steep so that the water in it will not become crowded and thus build up a back-water resistance.

W. H. R. NIMMO,* ASSOC. M. AM. SOC. C. E. (by letter).—The writer is obliged to Mr. Lindley for drawing attention to the tests† which he has made and which apparently confirm the value of $c = 3.80$ for the weir shown in Fig. 6.

The equation given by Mr. Lindley is undoubtedly the rational form of expression for the discharge through an orifice of the type under consideration, but he is in error in stating that the writer measured his d_1 at the up-stream face of the gate, including banking up. The quantity, d_1, was measured 5 ft. up stream from the gate at a point where there was no visible banking up. As far as could be seen, banking up was confined to a small area of turbulence immediately against the gate. The writer did determine a coefficient from the formula,

$$Q = c_1 \, w \, d \sqrt{2 \, g \left(d_1 + \frac{V_1^2}{2 \, g} - d_2 \right)}$$

and, if $h_a = \frac{V_1^2}{2 \, g}$ and $c_c = \frac{d_2}{d_1}$, then this formula is identical with that given by Mr. Lindley and $c_1 = c_v \, c_c$. For the four experiments with a vertical baffle (Table 2), the values of c_1 are 0.605, 0.597, 0.610, and 0.602, respectively. With the approximate methods of measurement adopted, it was not possible to determine the value of d_2 with great accuracy and, since the results of the experiments were to be applied directly to another orifice of the same type and dimensions, it was thought advisable to use the coefficient, c, which does not depend on the value of d_2. The measurements were not sufficiently precise to justify splitting the coefficient, c, into coefficients of velocity and contraction.

Mr. Flockart has described and explained the phenomena which take place at the existing gate at the entrance to the concrete flume. He is also correct in stating that the water surface does not actually become vertical when crossing the critical depth. Plotting $\frac{\Delta x}{\Delta d}$, as he proposes, provides a useful method of showing the water surface curve at points close to the critical depth, for which condition Equation (11) cannot be applied in practice.

* Chf. Draftsman, Main Roads Comm., Brisbane, Queensland, Australia.

† *Paper 97*, Panjab Eng. Congress, 1925.

AMERICAN SOCIETY OF CIVIL ENGINEERS
INSTITUTED 1852

TRANSACTIONS

Paper No. 1695

EMERGENCY DAM ON INNER NAVIGATION CANAL AT NEW ORLEANS, LOUISIANA*

By Henry Goldmark,† M. Am. Soc. C. E.

With Discussion by Messrs. F. R. Harris, R. H. Whitehead, R. O. Comer, W. J. Barden, Roger D. Black, Samuel McC. Young, T. B. Mönniche, and Henry Goldmark.

Synopsis

This paper is devoted primarily to a description of the so-called "emergency dam" in the Inner Navigation Canal at New Orleans, La., an important harbor work, completed in 1922. Such "emergency dams" are designed to shut off the flow of water through a lock, such as may occur when one of the lock-gates is struck by a vessel and seriously injured.

As the dam at New Orleans differs radically in its design from those previously built and has the merit of being lower in first cost and requiring a smaller operating force, a description of the work should be of interest to engineers. The paper first enumerates certain protective devices for preventing accidents to the gates, such as special guard gates, power capstans, and electric towing locomotives for controlling vessels in transit, and chain fenders for bringing them to a stop if improperly handled. A brief reference is then made to some emergency dams previously built, especially those in the Sault Ste. Marie and Panama Canals. Finally, a full description is given of the New Orleans Dam.

This design may be called the "stop-log" type, since the flow of water is checked by a number of transverse girders spanning the lock chamber, placed one above the other, like the stop-logs in hydraulic power plants. These gir-

* Presented at the meeting of December 7, 1927.

† Cons. Engr., New York, N. Y.

ders are lowered and raised by a hoisting engine carried on a revolving crane, similar in appearance to a railroad swing bridge. The several parts of the dam are described and illustrated.

Introduction

Although the risk of serious accidents in properly built and operated ship locks is very small, there are unquestionably certain dangers inherent in their use. Such accidents as do occur arise, in most cases, from injuries to the lock-gates when they are accidentally struck by vessels. Even if the damage to the gate is small, the repairs are difficult to make and certain to result in delays to traffic. If the gate is more seriously injured it is likely to be carried away by the rush of water; other gates may then be torn loose, and a heavy flow established from the upper to the lower pool.

Various safeguards are installed in locks to prevent vessels from striking the gates. The most common of these are duplicate lock-gates, the so-called "guard gates", placed above and below the ordinary operating gates to act as barriers to protect the latter from injury.

As a further measure of safety many large locks are fitted with power capstans for controlling vessels in transit. At Panama, however, all vessels are towed through the locks by special locomotives traveling on tracks laid on the lock walls. In this way the ships are kept under full control at all times.*

As an additional protection to the gates, heavy chain fenders stretched across the lock chambers have been installed in the approaches and upper chambers of the Panama Canal, and have also been in use for many years in a number of English harbors. When struck by a vessel, the chain pays off under a heavy braking strain, gradually bringing the ship to rest. At Panama, these fenders have proved their value in actual service.† In several instances, vessels, some of them of large size and moving at a fair rate of speed, were brought to a stop by the chain without injury to the vessel, fender, or lock-gate.

Besides such safeguards intended solely to prevent vessels from striking the gates, special devices have been installed in some locks for shutting off the flow of water if, in spite of these safeguards, one or more of the gates is seriously injured. However, such "emergency dams" are necessary only in exceptional cases. They are not required, for instance, in tidal locks, since in these there is slack-water at each period of high and low tide when the guard gates at the ends of the lock can be closed without trouble.

They are also superfluous where the pool above the lock is small, or where a series of locks is separated by short stretches of canal. In these cases the water above the lock can be readily drained off, so that a special dam is unnecessary.

When, however, the body of water above the lock is a large river or lake, unquestionably it should be possible to shut off the flow in case of an acci-

* "Electrical and Mechanical Installations of the Panama Canal," by E. Schildhauer, M. Am. Soc. C. E., *Transactions*, Int. Eng. Cong., San Francisco, Calif., 1915 (The Panama Canal), Vol. II, No. 20.

† "Lock-Gates, Chain Fenders, and Lock Entrance Caisson," by Henry Goldmark, M. Am. Soc. C. E., *Transactions*, Int. Eng. Cong., San Francisco, 1915 (The Panama Canal), Vol. II, No. 17.

dent, to permit repairs to be made with reasonable promptness. In some cases it would be impracticable—in any event, very time-consuming—to improvise means for accomplishing this object after the accident had occurred.

Special "emergency" dams have been installed, therefore, in the canals at Sault Ste. Marie and Panama, and in some other waterways. The latest of such dams is that built in the Inner Navigation Canal, at New Orleans, which is the special subject of this paper. A brief reference to some of the older ones, however, may be of interest.

Early Emergency Dams

As far as is known to the writer the first "movable" or "emergency" dam installed in connection with a lock was designed by the late Alfred Noble, Past-President, Am. Soc. C. E., for the United States Canal at Sault Ste. Marie, Mich., about 1885. It was removed later when the canal was widened. Its general appearance was that of a railroad swing bridge revolving about a vertical pivot on the lock-wall. Along one of the arms a series of wicket girders was hinged by pins. After the dam had been turned across the lock, these girders were revolved in planes at right angles to the axis of the dam until their lower ends rested against a concrete sill. After the girders were thus put in place, the openings between them were successively closed by small wickets.

This gradual reduction in the cross-section of the flowing water is essential on account of the high velocity with which it moves. Such a principle is necessarily followed in all dams of whatever type.

At a later period, an emergency dam of quite similar design was built on the Canadian side of the St. Mary's River, also at Sault Ste. Marie. It is unique in having been actually tested under emergency conditions.

The accident, which occurred in June, 1909, was due to a vessel approaching the locks from below and striking the lower operating gates forcing them partly open and causing a heavy flow of water from the lock. At this time a vessel was in the lock and the upper gates were being closed. The heavy flow broke the fastenings of the upper and lower gates. Some of the leaves were torn entirely loose and others were badly damaged.

The vessel in the lock, the one in the lower approach, and a third one just above the lock were all carried away into the lower river, fortunately without loss of life. The flow of water was checked by closing the emergency dam, which was accomplished without serious difficulty. Figs. 1 to 4 show various phases of this accident.

In addition to these dams, which are all essentially of the same type, at least one other important structure of different design, but serving a similar purpose, should be mentioned. This is the "butterfly" dam on the Chicago Drainage Canal, which revolves about a vertical axis at one edge of the channel, the clear opening being 160 ft.

Panama Canal

When the plans for the Panama Canal were being matured, it was decided to adopt an emergency dam of the swing type with girders and wickets, quite similar to the dams at the "Soo". This decision followed the recommendations of a Board of Army Engineers appointed some years before to study the general question of emergency dams.

The Panama dams,* six in all, are longer and heavier than any others. Great care was taken to make them perfect in all their details, so that their operation is smooth and rapid. The swing span is revolved and the girders and wickets are lowered and raised by separate electric motors.

New Orleans Inner Navigation Canal

This canal is situated in the lower part of the City of New Orleans and connects the Mississippi River and the tidal inlet known as Lake Pontchartrain.† Its primary purpose is to furnish an "inner harbor" of approximately constant depth, but it may ultimately provide an outlet to the Gulf of Mexico shorter and in other ways more desirable than the Lower Mississippi. The canal is 5 miles long, with a lock at its upper end close to the river in order to overcome the difference in elevation between the Mississippi and Lake Pontchartrain. Both sides of the canal between the lower end of the lock and the lake are to be lined with docks or piers, while it will also be possible to utilize the shores of Lake Pontchartrain for docking purposes. The canal has a bottom width of 150 ft. The lock is 75 ft. wide, with a depth of 30 ft. on the lock-sills and a maximum lift of 19 ft. (Fig. 5).

In case of serious accident to the lock-gates, a heavy flow of water would occur between the upper and lower levels, the maximum volume being computed to be in excess of 70 000 sec-ft.—about equal to one-third the total flow over the American and Canadian Falls, at Niagara. As a large part of the city below the lock, including important railroad yards, would be flooded in case of an accident, it was vital that the dam should be reliable beyond question and rapid in operation.

The emergency dams on the Panama Canal meet these requirements, but their cost was very high and a large number of attendants is required for their operation. It was thought possible that some other form of construction might be devised, which would be as efficient as the Panama dams but lower in first cost, and require a smaller operating force.

After several types had been considered, in addition to the standard swing-bridge design, it was suggested by Mr. R. O. Comer, Designing Engineer of the New Orleans Port Commission, that it might be possible to shut off the flow of water by a series of transverse girders, sliding in grooves in the side walls, like the "stop-logs" used in power plants. It would be necessary, of course, to provide suitable structural work and machinery for placing and removing the girders when operating the dam.

A careful study showed that a dam of this kind could be built—one that would be simple and reliable and cost decidedly less than the standard form used elsewhere. It was therefore adopted for construction (Fig. 6). At that

* The Panama dams are described in detail in a paper by their designer, T. B. Mönniche, M. Am. Soc. C. E., and published in *Transactions,* Inter. Eng. Cong., San Francisco, Calif., 1915 ("The Panama Canal"), Vol. II, No. 18.

† A brief description of the entire Inner Harbor Navigation Canal, by the writer, may be found in *Proceedings,* Brooklyn Engrs. Club, Vol. XXV, Pt. I (October, 1926), pp. 36–49.

FIG. 1.—ACCIDENT TO SAULT STE. MARIE LOCK, SHOWING LOWER GATES SHORTLY AFTER THEY HAD BEEN HIT BY VESSEL.

FIG. 2.—DAMAGED SAULT STE. MARIE LOCK, LOOKING EAST FROM UPPER END OF LOCK, SHOWING RECESSES FOR UPPER GATES TORN AWAY BY FLOW.

FIG. 3.—OPERATION OF EMERGENCY DAM, LOOKING DOWN STREAM. FIRST WICKETS BEING LOWERED INTO PLACE, REMAINDER SUSPENDED IN AIR BELOW BRIDGE.

FIG. 4.—CLOSURE OF EMERGENCY DAM ALMOST COMPLETED, SHOWING LEAKAGE WHICH COULD NOT BE AVOIDED.

FIG. 5.—GENERAL VIEW, NEW ORLEANS INNER NAVIGATION CANAL LOCK, WITH EMERGENCY DAM IN FOREGROUND.

FIG. 6.—OPERATION OF EMERGENCY DAM, LOWERING STOP-LOG GIRDER FROM REVOLVING CRANE.

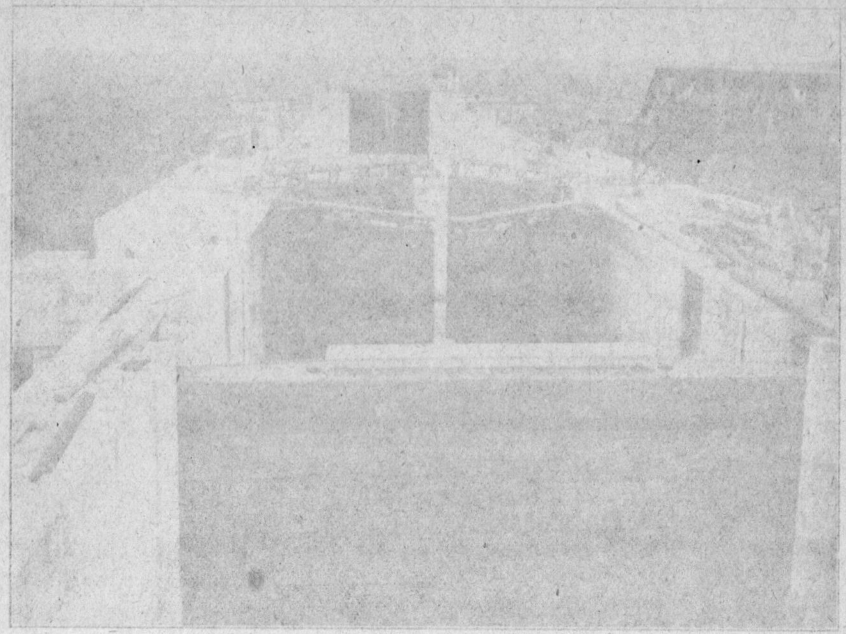

time the stop-log type of dam was believed to be entirely novel in lock construction, but it was afterward found that at least one dam of the kind had been built in Canada, on the Trent Canal, although on a much smaller scale, and with entirely different details.

General Features—New Orleans Dam

The general arrangement of the New Orleans Dam is given in Fig. 7, showing the ground plan, cross-sections, and end elevation. Various details of the structural work and mechanical parts are shown in other diagrams and photographs.

It will be seen that the stop-log girders are handled by a huge revolving crane or swing span, with its pivot on one of the lock-walls. Except when in use for closing the lock-opening, the girders rest on the top of the back-fill with their axes radial (Fig. 7). From these positions they are raised by the handling machinery, the swing span is revolved, and the girders are then placed one above the other, with their ends in the recesses in the side walls. This operation is reversed when they are being removed after they have served their purpose.

While the dam was built primarily for checking the flow of water in case of accident, the same girders are also used to form a coffer-dam at the upper or lower end of the lock when it is desired to pump it out completely and expose all the lock-gates for inspection, painting, and repair. When the girders are to be used at the lower end, they are lifted from their seats in the storage yard by the revolving crane and lowered into the water in the position indicated by the dotted outline in Fig. 7. They are then floated through the locks. Of course, it was necessary to add vertical seats for the girders at the lower end of the lock, and a simple form of hoist was also installed for raising and lowering them. These hoists are operated by two of the power capstans ordinarily used for handling vessels in transit. It will be seen that the additional expense entailed was quite moderate.

In order to give a clearer understanding of the construction and operation of the dam, it has seemed best to describe its various parts separately. They are:

I.—The Stop-Log Girders.
II.—The Swing Span, or Revolving Crane, with the Mechanism for Turning It.
III.—The Hoisting Machinery for Handling the Girders.

I.—The Stop-Log Girders

The girders are of box-form with plate-webs and side-plates (Fig. 8). There are eight girders in all. Six of them, which are used at the lower as well as the upper end of the lock, are designed so as to float when free from water. The other two are not adapted for floating. All the girders are 84 ft. long over-all, and 7 ft. 9⅛ in. wide horizontally at the center of the span. Their depth is about 6 ft. The weight of the heavy girders in the dry is

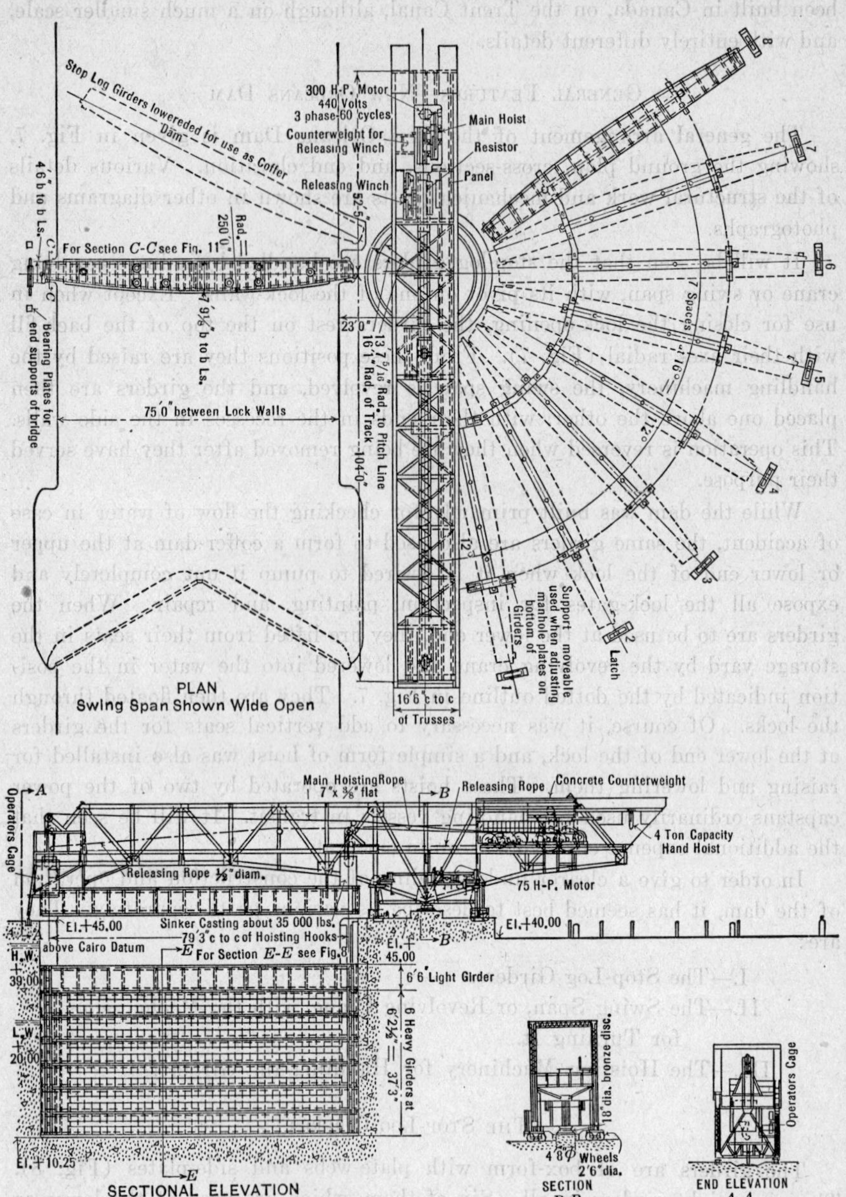

FIG. 7.—GENERAL PLAN, NEW ORLEANS EMERGENCY DAM.

174 000 lb. In these, both the web and side-plates are strengthened by closely spaced channel stiffeners.

When the lock is pumped out the girders are under maximum hydrostatic pressure, the water extending to the top on the upper face with no water on the lower side. While this maximum head will act only on the bottom girder, it was thought best to make all the "heavy" girders of identical construction to guard against errors in placing them.

When the girders are being lowered into place under emergency conditions—that is, when there is a flow of water through the lock—the horizontal pressures are a combination of the velocity head due to the flow and the static head at the various levels. The computation of the loads due to these conditions is quite involved. In this case, too, the worst possible conditions have been assumed.

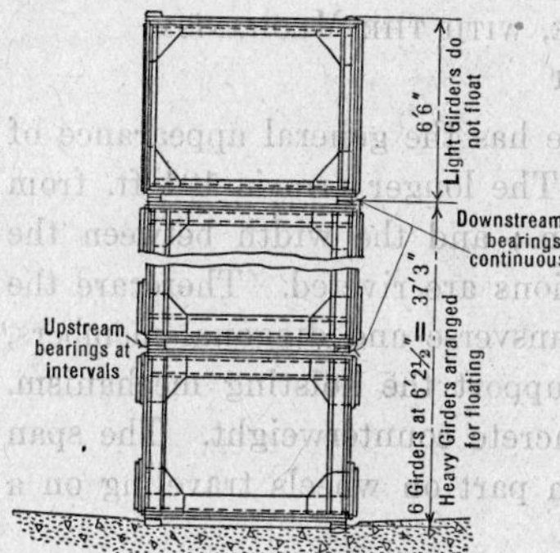

FIG. 8.—VERTICAL SECTION THROUGH STOP-LOG GIRDERS, SECTION *E-E* OF FIG. 7.

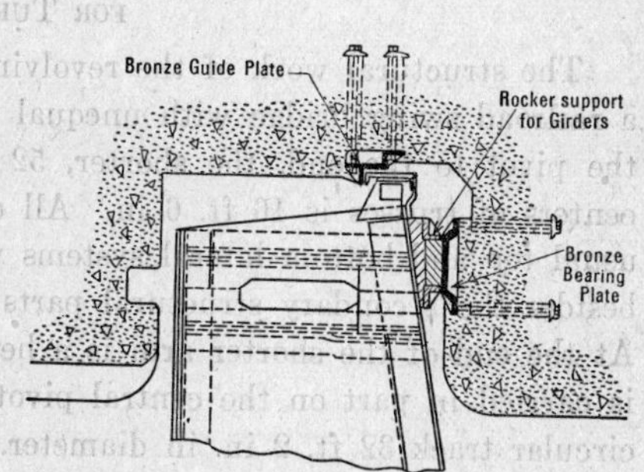

FIG. 9.—SECTION THROUGH SLOT IN WALL, SHOWING BEARING AND GUIDE-PLATES.

As noted, most of the girders are arranged for flotation, but when they are being lowered, they must be filled with water, to insure their sinking. This made it necessary to supply these girders with a sufficient number of openings fitted with adjustable covers. These openings also allow the water to flow out of the girders at a proper rate when they are being raised, thus guarding against an over-load in the hoisting machinery and excessive stresses in the stop-logs.

In operation, the heavy horizontal pressure exerted against the up-stream side of the girders produces frictional resistances between the bearings and the slots in the side walls. Much study was given to the proper design of these bearings, shown in Fig. 9. While roller bearings would have reduced the friction materially, it was thought best to avoid devices that were complicated and subject to corrosion in the brackish water of the lock. It would also have been necessary to provide separate means to insure water-tightness. The fixed bearings in the wall, therefore, were made continuous from top to bottom. They are of bronze at the upper, and of cast iron at the lower, end of the lock. The bearing plates on the several girders are of steel and are made as rockers revolving slightly about their vertical axes, to adjust themselves to inequalities from errors in workmanship or from deflections of the girders under their loads. The fitting of these bearings has proved to be excellent; there is no leakage even when the lock is pumped out and the girder is under full hydrostatic head.

Water-tightness along the horizontal joints between the several girders and also between the lowest girder and the bottom of the lock chamber is insured by continuous metallic bearings along the down-stream flanges. These joints also have proved to be tight. At their ends, the girders are fitted with vertical steel channels. Similarly, continuous bronze guide-plates are fastened to the face of the concrete.

This description covers all parts of the stop-log girders, except some mechanical attachments, which may be described more properly in connection with the hoisting machinery.

II.—Swing Span, or Revolving Crane, with the Mechanism for Turning It

The structural work of the revolving crane has the general appearance of a railroad swing bridge with unequal arms. The longer arm is 104 ft. from the pivot to the end, the shorter, 52 ft. 5 in.; and the width between the centers of trusses is 16 ft. 6 in. All connections are riveted. There are the usual top and bottom lateral systems with transverse and diagonal members, besides the secondary structural parts that support the hoisting mechanism. At the end of the shorter arm is a heavy concrete counterweight. The span is carried in part on the central pivot and in part on wheels traveling on a circular track 32 ft. 2 in. in diameter.

The details of the pivot are shown in Fig. 10 and a diagrammatic view of the device for attaching the hoisting hooks in Fig. 11. The pivot has an upper disk of phosphor bronze, 18 in. in diameter, which turns with the span; and a lower disk of the same size made of forged steel, which is secured to a steel casting resting on the concrete (Fig. 10). The wheels that travel on the circular track are eight in number. Their diameters are 2 ft. 6 in. and the width of face is 5½ in. They have cast-steel centers and rolled-steel tires. The axles are 7 in. in diameter and turn in journals on four truck bodies of cast steel bolted to the lower side of the bridge truss.

The swing span is turned about the pivot by a system of gears operated by a 75 h. p., electric motor, the type of mechanism being that commonly used in draw-bridge machinery. The principal details are shown in Fig. 12.

Stresses in Truss Members and Reactions on Pivot and Truck Wheels.— The loads carried by the truss are: (1) The dead load, which consists of the structural steel, the machinery, the concrete counterweight, and various minor parts; and (2) the live load, that is, the heaviest stop-log girder.

The calculation of the stresses and reactions presented some interesting features differing from those met in similar structures. It was thought worth while, therefore, to include in this paper, a tabular statement of the stresses and reactions which occur under various cases of loading (Table 1) and a diagram (Fig. 13), giving an outline of the truss, together with the panel loads.

In Table 1 the make-up of the various members is given in Column (10). The size of the concrete counterweight (277 000 lb.) was computed to balance the whole dead load and one-half the live load so that the reaction against the truck at Panel Point 9 (Fig. 13) when the dead load alone is being carried should be exactly the same as the reaction at Panel Point 7 when the trusses also carry the live load. In the case under Column (5), Table 1, all

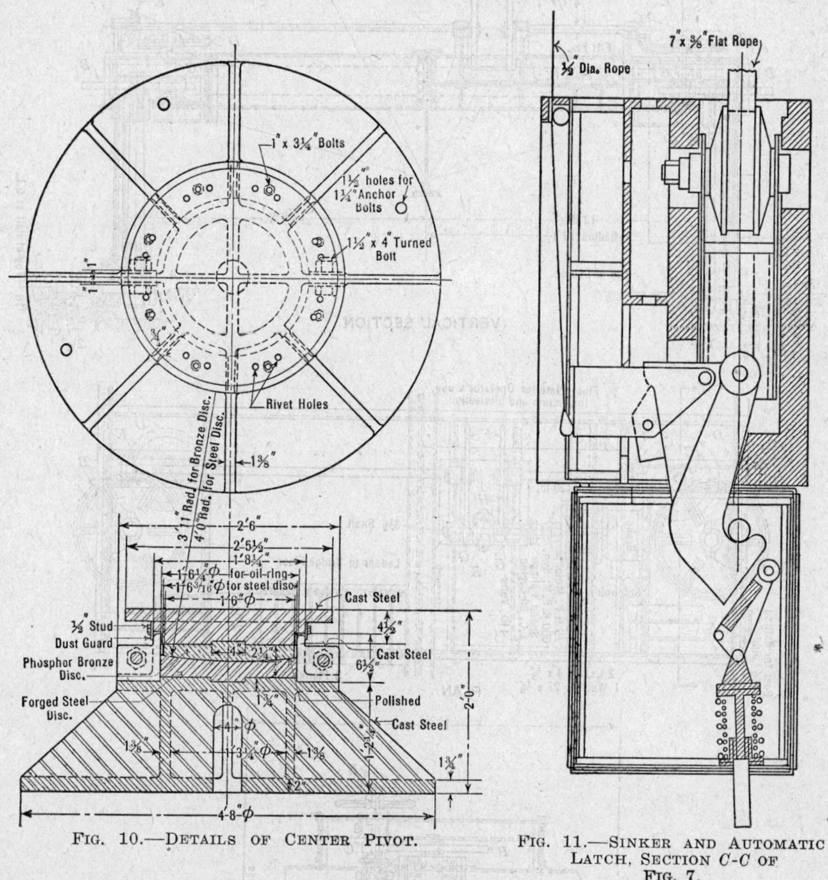

FIG. 10.—DETAILS OF CENTER PIVOT.

FIG. 11.—SINKER AND AUTOMATIC LATCH, SECTION C-C OF FIG. 7.

the load $(D + \frac{1}{2} L)$ is carried by the pivot, Panel Point 8. This condition prevails for an instant only while the girder (live load) is being picked up or set down by the hoisting machinery. The assumption in Columns (8) and (9), Table 1, corresponds to the girder containing 1.43 ft. of water, a condition that prevails for a few seconds when the girder is being drawn out of the water at a speed of 30 ft. per min. The details of the various loads carried by the trusses are given in Table 2.

In the computations, both arms of the truss were taken as cantilevers, as this condition will prevail practically at all times. It was deemed best, however, to fix the end of the long arm vertically when the truss has been swung

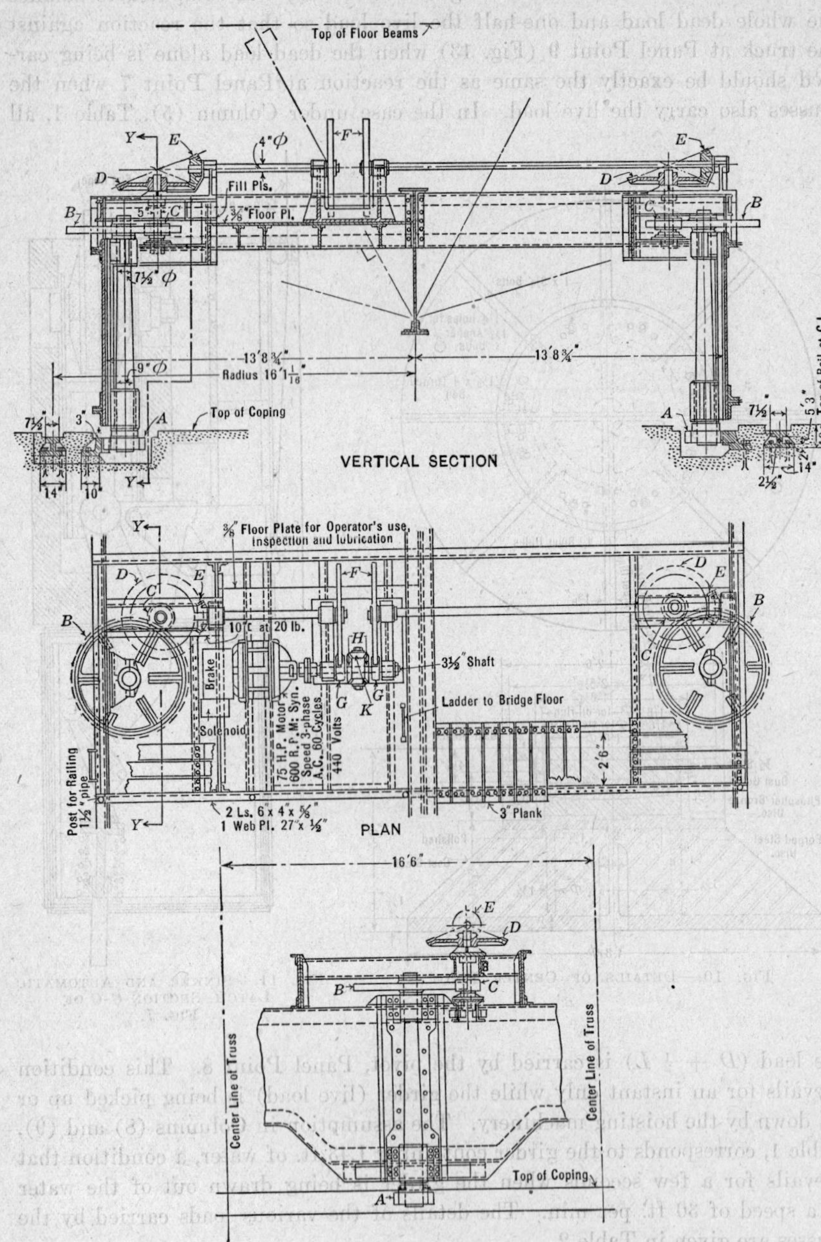

FIG. 12.—DETAILS OF MACHINERY FOR TURNING BRIDGE.

across the lock and the girders are being raised or lowered. A braced framework, therefore, was attached to the truss at Panel Point 0, so that the end of the truss can be slightly raised by a screw-jack attached to the framing. Under these conditions, a small part of the dead and live loads is supported by the side wall, but the stresses in the truss are only slightly changed (Fig. 7).

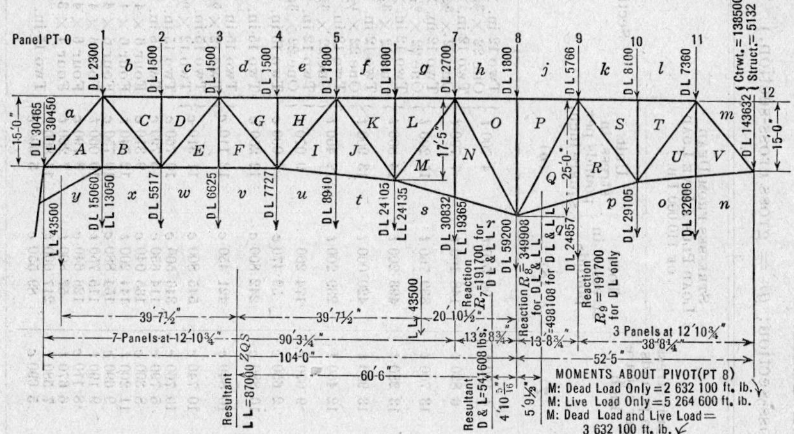

Fig. 13.—Diagram of Truss. Governing Stresses in Various Members for One Truss Are Shown in Table 1.

III.—The Hoisting Machinery for Handling the Girders

The hoisting machinery includes not only the hoisting engine proper, but also the cables with their sheaves, the so-called "sinker castings," the hooks for lifting the girders, and certain devices for detaching the hooks from the girders, after the latter have been lowered into place. These last devices are important features of the dam. Their design proved to be quite difficult.

The general arrangement of the machinery is given in Fig. 7, while Fig. 14 shows the hoisting engine on a larger scale, as well as an outline of the electric apparatus connected with it. It also shows a small hand-operated winding engine forming a part of the machinery used in detaching the hooks. The details of these two engines were developed by the contractor for the hoisting machinery.

The two main hoisting cables consist of 7-in. by $\frac{3}{8}$-in., flat, steel ropes. One end of each rope is wound about a separate drum in the hoisting engine, the two drums being connected by gearing and driven by a single 300 h. p. electric motor. The other end of the rope passes around three 30-in. sheaves, multiplying the lifting power threefold, and connects with the massive hook from which one end of the girder is suspended. The journals for two of these sheaves, at each end of the truss, are bolted firmly to the structural work, while the third sheave moves up and down as the hook is raised or lowered. A bight of the flat rope makes a half-turn about this sheave, while the end of the rope is fastened to a clevis through which the axle of the sheave passes. From the same axle a riveted structural frame is hung, to which the hook for suspending the girders is connected. (See Figs. 11 and 15.)

TABLE 1.—STRESSES IN ONE TRUSS.*

(t = tensile stress; c = compressive stress; n = net cross-section; gr = gross cross-section.)

	Member.	Cross-section, in square inches.	Stresses from dead load, in pounds.	Stresses from live load, in pounds = 87 000.	Stresses from one-half live load, in pounds = 43 500.	Total maximum stresses, in pounds.	Unit stress, in pounds per square inch.	STRESSES FROM DEAD LOAD PLUS A LIVE LOAD OF 110 000 LB. Total stresses, in pounds.	STRESSES FROM DEAD LOAD PLUS A LIVE LOAD OF 110 000 LB. Unit stress, in pounds per square inch.	Section adopted.
	(1)	(2)	(3)	(4)	(5)	(6)	(7)	(8)	(9)	(10)
End post.	*a A*	19.2 *n*	39 900 *t*	39 900 *t*	19 950 *t*	79 800 *t*	4 150 *t*	90 570 *t*	4 700 *t*	Two 12-in. × 25-lb. channels. One 22 × 3/8-in. cover plate.
Upper chord.	*b C* and *z D*	19.2 *n*	67 330 *t*	63 600 *t*	31 800 *t*	130 930 *t*	6 820 *t*	148 100 *t*	7 700 *t*	Two 12-in. × 25-lb. channels. One 22 × 3/8-in. cover plate.
Upper chord.	*d G* and *e H*	22.4 *n*	168 560 *t*	134 850 *t*	67 425 *t*	307 010 *t*	13 700 *t*	339 760 *t*	15 200 *t*	Two 12-in. × 25-lb. channels. One 22 × 9/16-in. cover plate.
Upper chord.	*f K* and *g L*	33.4 *n*	260 000 *t*	183 600 *t*	91 800 *t*	443 600 *t*	13 280 *t*	493 200 *t*	14 800 *t*	Two 12-in. × 40-lb. channels. One 22 × 3/4-in. cover plate.
Upper chord.	*h O* and *j P*	30.2 *n*	314 000 *t*	106 000 *t*	106 000 *t*	420 000 *t*	13 900 *t*	420 000 *t*	13 900 *t*	Two 12-in. × 40 lb. channels. One 22 × 1/2-in. cover plate.
Upper chord.	*k S* and *l T*	19.2 *n*	239 200 *t*	0	0	239 200 *t*	12 460 *t*	239 200 *t*	12 460 *t*	Two 12-in. × 25-lb. channels. One 22 × 3/8-in. cover plate.
End post.	*V m*	19.2 *n*	174 200 *t*	0	0	174 200 *t*	9 070 *t*	174 200	9 070 *t*	Two 12-in. × 25-lb. channels. One 22 × 3/8-in. cover plate.
Lower chord.	*A y* and *B x*	19.8 *gr*	26 200 *c*	26 180 *c*	13 090 *c*	52 380 *c*	2 650 *c*	59 470 *c*	3 000 *c*	Two 15-in. × 33-lb. channels.
Lower chord.	*E w* and *F u*	19.8 *gr*	114 500 *c*	101 000 *c*	50 500 *c*	215 500 *c*	10 880 *c*	242 800 *c*	12 250 *c*	Two 15-in. × 33-lb. channels.
Lower chord.	*I a* and *J t*	34.8 *gr*	214 150 *c*	163 200 *c*	81 600 *c*	377 350 *c*	10 840 *c*	421 450 *c*	12 110 *c*	Two 15-in. × 33-lb. channels. Two 12 × 5/8-in. plates.
Lower chord.	*M s* and *N r*	45.8 *gr*	291 700 *c*	200 100 *c*	100 050 *c*	491 750 *c*	10 740 *c*	545 800 *c*	11 910 *c*	Two 15-in. × 55-lb. channels. Two 12 × 9/16-in. plates.
Lower chord.	*Q q* and *R p*	32.2 *gr*	346 500 *c*	0	0	346 500 *c*	10 760 *c*	346 500 *c*	10 760 *c*	Two 15-in. × 55-lb. channels.
Lower chord.	*U o* and *V n*	19.8 *gr*	114 650 *c*	0	0	114 650 *c*	5 790 *c*	114 650 *c*	5 790 *c*	Two 15-in. × 33-lb. channels.
Web members.	*B C*	14.4 *gr*	62 640 *c*	56 990 *c*	28 495 *c*	119 630 *c*	8 300 *c*	135 040 *c*	9 370 *c*	Four 6 × 4 × 3/8-in. angles.
Web members.	*D E*	11.5 *n*	71 820 *t*	56 990 *t*	28 495 *t*	128 810 *t*	11 200 *t*	144 200 *t*	12 540 *t*	Four 6 × 4 × 3/8-in. angles.
Web members.	*F G*	14.4 *gr*	82 500 *c*	56 990 *c*	28 495 *c*	139 490 *c*	9 690 *c*	154 880 *c*	10 750 *c*	Four 6 × 4 × 3/8-in. angles.
Web members.	*H I*	11.5 *n*	68 550 *t*	37 170 *t*	18 585 *t*	105 720 *t*	9 190 *t*	115 750 *t*	10 060 *t*	Four 6 × 4 × 3/8 in. angles.
Web members.	*J K*	14.4 *gr*	80 580 *c*	36 260 *c*	18 130 *c*	116 840 *c*	8 110 *c*	126 640 *c*	8 790 *c*	Four 6 × 4 × 3/8-in. angles.
Web members.	*L M*	8.0 *n*	36 900 *t*	16 460 *t*	8 230 *t*	53 360 *t*	6 670 *t*	57 800 *t*	7 220 *t*	Four 4 × 3 × 3/8-in. angles.
Web members.	*N O*	14.6 *n* 17.6 *gr*	70 740 *c*	181 280 *t*	18 350 *c*	110 540 *t* 89 550 *c*	7 580 *t* 5 090 *c*	217 000 *t* 89 550 *c*	14 860 *t* 5 090 *c*	Two 15-in. × 33-lb. channels.

* When one-half the live load is being carried. Itemized loads are given in Table 2.

TABLE 1.—(*Continued.*)

	Member.	Cross-section, in square inches.	Stresses from dead load, in pounds.	Stresses from live load, in pounds = 87 000.	Stresses from one-half live load, in pounds = 48 500.	Total maximum stresses, in pounds.	Unit stress, in pounds per square inch.	Stresses from Dead Load Plus a Live Load of 110 000 Lb.		Section adopted.
								Total stresses, in pounds.	Unit stress, in pounds per square inch.	
	(1)	(2)	(3)	(4)	(5)	(6)	(7)	(8)	(9)	(10)
Web members.	*P Q*	13.6 *n* 19.8 *gr*	39 900 *t*	218 750 *c*	0	39 900 *t* 178 850 *c*	2 930 *t* 9 040 *c*	39 900 *t* 178 850 *c*	2 930 *t* 9 040 *c*	Two 15-in. × 33-lb. channels.
	R S	11.5 *n*	157 100 *t*	0	0	157 100 *t*	13 700 *t*	157 100 *t*	13 700 *t*	Four 6 × 4 × ⅜-in. angles.
	T U	21.2 *gr*	221 000 *c*	0	0	221 000 *c*	10 430 *c*	221 000 *c*	10 430 *c*	Four 6 × 4 × 9/16-in. angles.
	A B	8.0 *n*	15 060 *t*	13 050 *t*	....	28 110 *t*	3 500 *t*	31 560 *t*	3 940 *t*	Four 4 × 3 × ⅜-in. angles.
	E F	8.0 *n*	6 625 *t*	0	0	6 625 *t*	830 *t*	6 625 *t*	830 *t*	Four 4 × 3 × ⅜-in. angles.
	I J	8.0 *n*	8 910 *t*	0	0	8 910 *t*	1 110 *t*	8 910 *t*	1 110 *t*	Four 4 × 3 × ⅜-in. angles.
	M N	26.5 *gr* 20.5 *n*	30 832 *t*	172 467 *c*	9 682 *t*	141 635 *c* 40 514 *t*	5 340 *c* 1 980 *t*	239 270 *c* 40 514 *t*	9 030 *c* 1 980 *t*	Four 6 × 4 × 9/16-in. angles. One 14 × ⅜-in. plate.
	Q R	28.2 *gr* 22.0 *n*	166 840 *c* 24 857 *t**	0 0	 0	166 840 *c* 24 857 *t*	5 920 *c* 1 130 *t*	166 840 *c* 24 854 *t*	5 920 *c* 1 130 *t*	Four 6 — 4 × 9/16-in. angles. One 14 × ½-in. plate.
	U V	8.0 *n*	32 606 *t*	0	0	32 606 *t*	4 100 *t*	32 606 *t*	4 100 *t*	Four 4 × 3 × ⅜-in. angles.
	C D	9.9 *gr*	1 500 *c*	0	0	1 500 *c*	150 *c*	1 500 *c*	150 *c*	Four 4 × 3 × ⅜-in. angles.
	G H	9.9 *gr*	1 500 *c*	0	0	1 500 *c*	150 *c*	1 500 *c*	150 *c*	Four 4 × 3 × ⅜ in. angles.
	K L	9.9 *gr*	1 800 *c*	0	0	1 800 *c*	180 *c*	1 800 *c*	180 *c*	Four 4 × 3 × ⅜-in. angles.
	O P	14.4 *gr*	1 800 *c*	0	0	1 800 *c*	125 *c*	1 800 *c*	125 *c*	Four 6 × 4 × ⅜-in. angles.
	S T	9.9 *gr*	8 100 *c*	0	0	8 100 *c*	820 *c*	8 100 *c*	820 *c*	Four 4 × 3 × ⅜-in. angles.
Reactions.	Reaction R_7	....	0	191 700	0	191 700	....	293 000	....	....
	Reaction R_8	(pivot)....	262 908	87 000	235 200	†498 108 ‡349 908	....	§498 108 ‖271 600	....	....
	Reaction R_9	....	191 700	—191 700	—191 700	191 700	....	191 700	....	....

* When one-half the live load is being carried.
† Dead load + one-half live load.
‡ Dead load + live load.
§ Dead load + live load of 48 500 lb.
‖ Dead load + live load of 110 000 lb.

Sinker Castings.—The "sinker castings" are two massive blocks of cast iron (each weighing about 35 000 lb.), which are suspended from the axles of the movable sheaves just mentioned. They are shown on a small scale in Figs. 7 and 11, and in greater detail in Fig. 15. They may also be observed in the photograph, Fig. 6.

TABLE 2.—LOADS CARRIED BY TRUSSES, IN POUNDS.

Loads.		Two trusses.	One truss.
Dead load:			
Structural steel		339 174	169 587
Castings and turning machinery		58 392	29 196
Concrete and windows in machinery room		50 200	25 100
Creosoted timber in footwalks, etc.		10 919	5 460
Hoisting machinery proper	75 450		
Sheaves and brackets	12 100	173 530	86 765
Sinkers and hooks	86 000		
		632 215	316 108
Concrete counterweight		277 000	138 500
Total dead load		909 215	454 608
Live load:			
One stop-log girder in dry		174 000	87 000
Total dead and live load		1 083 215	541 608

The purpose of the "sinker castings" is to increase the weight, thus tending to overcome the frictional resistances when the girders are being lowered in their recesses. This is of special importance in an emergency, when the flow of water through the lock produces lateral forces, increasing the friction. In order to utilize their extra weight, the sinkers, of course, must rest directly on the top of the girders when the latter are being lowered. This was insured (as may be seen in Figs. 11 and 15), by giving an oblong shape to the holes in the castings, through which the axles of the "movable sheaves" pass.

It will also be seen that the structural member from which the hook is suspended passes directly through the sinker casting, and that certain mechanical details, forming a part of the mechanism for detaching the hooks, are fastened to the sinkers.

Attaching of Hooks.—The hooks for supporting the girders when they are being raised or lowered (Fig. 15) are of forged nickel steel and are suspended from pins 5 in. in diameter in a riveted frame within the sinker casting. When carrying their load these hooks engage 6½-in. pins fastened to the inside of the girders. The center lines of the upper and lower pins, when the hooks are attached, are in a vertical plane passing through the center of gravity of the girder, which therefore hangs vertically.

The hook is entered and withdrawn from the girder through a slot 7 in. wide and 2 ft. 3 in. long in the top plate of the girder. As may be seen from Fig. 16, the position of this slot and the shape of the hook are such that the latter, when lowered, will be deflected sidewise and enter the slot. On being lowered farther inside the girder, the hook swings back to a vertical position, and then, upon being raised, engages the hoisting pin.

Detaching of Hooks.—In order to detach the hooks this process is reversed. They are first lowered slightly to clear the hoisting pin, then deflected sidewise, and, finally, raised through the slot in the top plate of the girder. A separate mechanism is required to give the lateral deflection to the hook.

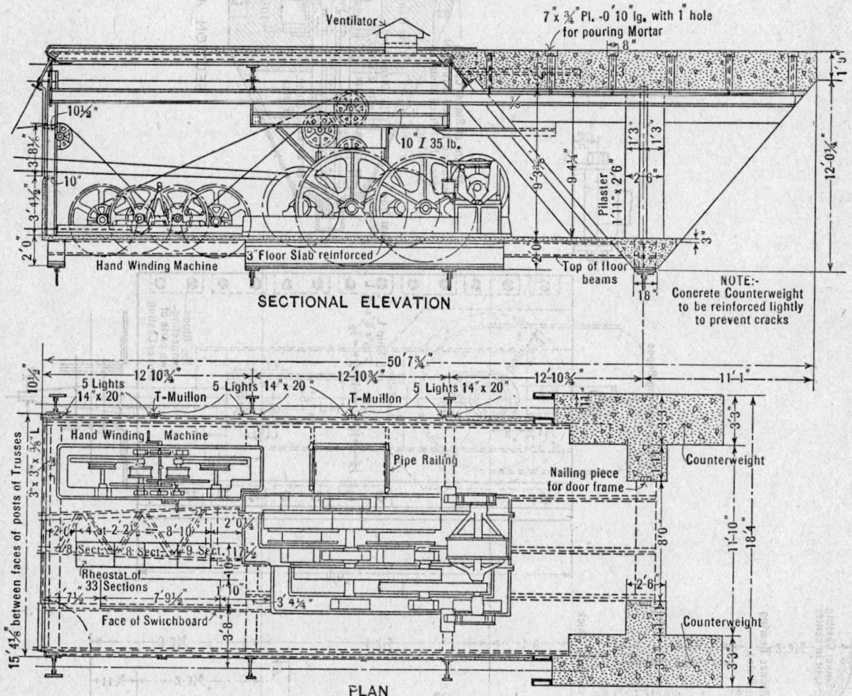

FIG. 14.—PLAN OF MACHINERY HOUSE AND COUNTERWEIGHT, EMERGENCY DAM, INNER HARBOR NAVIGATION CANAL.

Two devices are provided for this purpose. The first of these is the spring shown in detail in Fig. 16. It forms a permanent part of each girder. A stem projecting from the bottom plate near the end of the girder is forced upward when the girder becomes seated, compressing the spring, so that its thrust is transmitted through a bell-crank lever and the hook is pushed sidewise. This device, which operates automatically, comes into play after the girders have been deposited in the recesses in the side walls to shut off the flow of water through the lock or to permit its unwatering.

In this case, the ends of the girders come to a solid bearing on the floor, or on the girder next below, and the projecting stem is forced upward. The automatic spring device cannot be used when the girders are placed on their seats in the storage yard, since under these conditions the ends of the girders will project beyond the supports. Similarly, of course, it cannot be used when

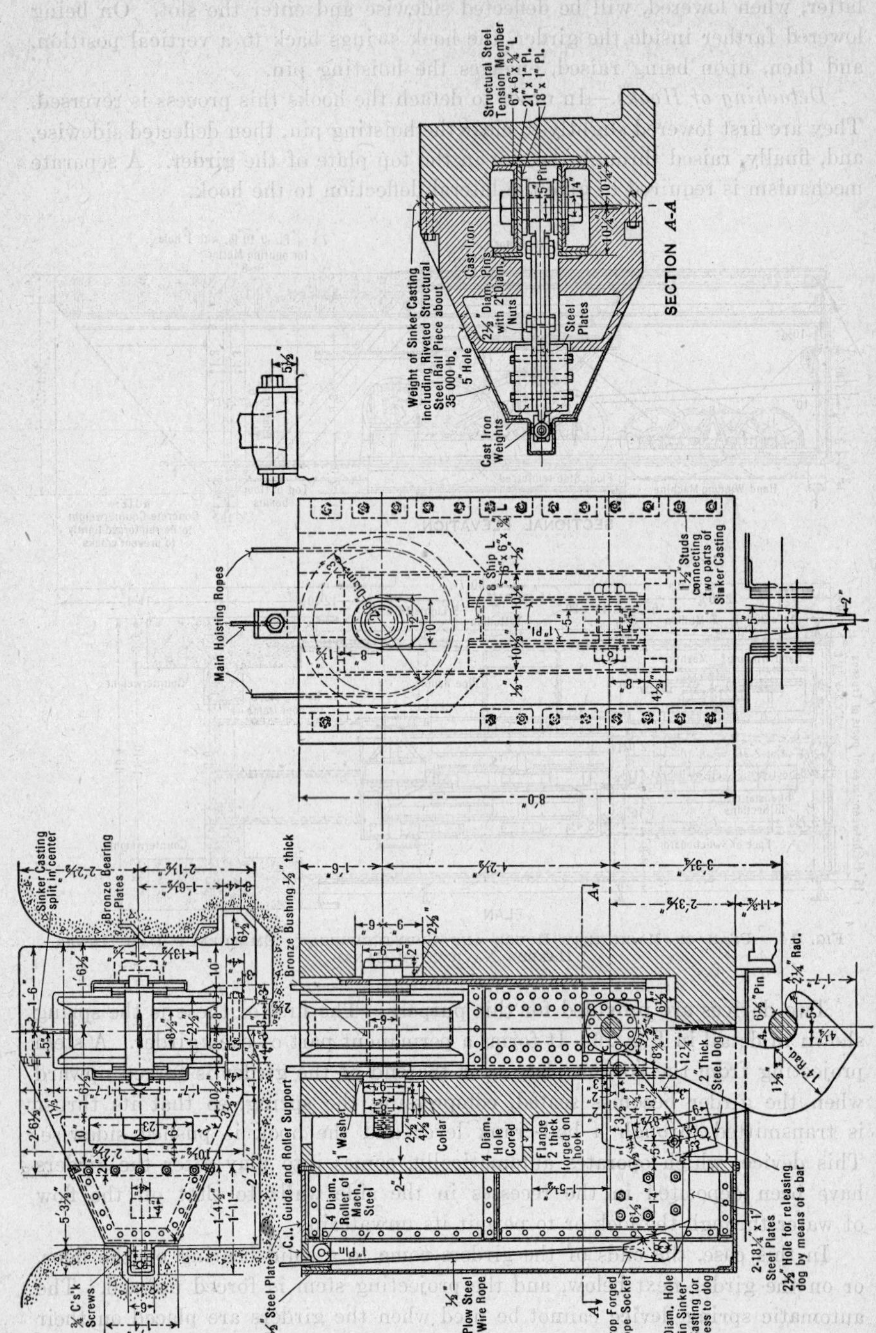

FIG. 15.—DETAILS OF SINKER CASTING, HOOK, AND RELEASING DEVICE. EMERGENCY DAM, INNER HARBOR NAVIGATION CANAL.

the girders are lowered into the water of the lock to be floated to the lower end for use as a coffer-dam. For service in the last two cases, a hand-operated mechanism has been provided. This device is shown in Figs. 11 and 15. Its essential feature is a lever hinged to the vertical flange on the hook and

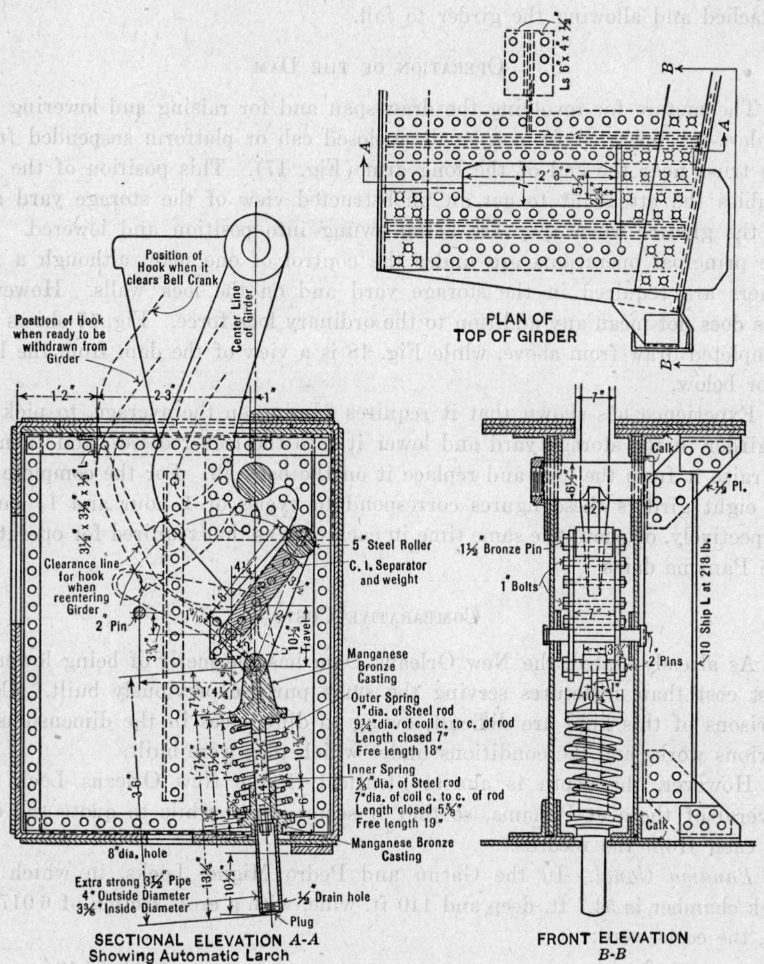

Fig. 16.—Details of Automatic Latch.

operated by a ½-in. wire rope connected to the hand-winding machine on the short end of the truss (Fig. 14). This lever deflects the hook by bearing against its horizontal ribs so that it can be hoisted through the oblong hole in the top plate.

In order to prevent interference between the two devices for giving the horizontal displacement, and to guard against accidents in lowering the girder, the second device is designed so that it will operate only when a 2-in.

block of steel, called "the dog," is in place. When the spring mechanism is relied on to deflect the hook, this dog is released before attaching the hook to the girder, making the hand-operated device inoperative. If, now, in lowering the girder one end becomes wedged in the recess and, at the same time, the ½-in. rope breaks, there will be no danger of the hook becoming detached and allowing the girder to fall.

Operation of the Dam

The motors for revolving the draw-span and for raising and lowering the girders are operated from a small enclosed cab or platform suspended from the truss near the end of the long arm (Fig. 17). This position of the cab enables the attendant to get an unobstructed view of the storage yard and of the girders when they are being swung into position and lowered. All the principal operations are under the control of one man, although a few others are required in the storage yard and on the lock walls. However, this does not mean any addition to the ordinary lock force. Fig. 17 shows the completed draw from above, while Fig. 18 is a view of the dam from the lock floor below.

Experience has shown that it requires 7 min., on the average, to pick up a girder in the storage yard and lower it into the lock recesses, and 12 min. to raise it from the lock and replace it on the back-fill. For the complete set of eight girders these figures correspond to cycles of 1 hour and 1½ hours respectively, or about the same time in each case as that required for operating the Panama dams.

Comparative Costs

As already stated, the New Orleans Dam has the merit of being lower in first cost than structures serving the same purpose previously built. Comparisons of this kind are difficult, owing to differences in the dimensions of various works and the conditions under which they were built.

However, the depth is almost identical in the New Orleans Lock and several of those at Panama, so that it seems worth while to quote the cost of each from the records.

Panama Canal.—In the Gatun and Pedro Miguel Locks, in which the lock chamber is 54.7 ft. deep and 110 ft. wide, with a cross-section of 6 017 sq. ft., the costs were:

Total	$432 475.10
Per square foot	72.00

New Orleans Canal.—In this canal, the lock-chamber is 55 ft. deep and 75 ft. wide, with a cross-section of 4 125 sq. ft., and the costs were:

Total	$353 523.68
Per square foot	85.70

The Panama work was done about 1912, at which time the cost of structural steel was unusually low, while the New Orleans Dam was built under World War conditions, the labor and material at this site being fully twice

FIG. 17.—VIEW SHOWING EMERGENCY DAM IN TRIAL OPERATION.

FIG. 18.—VIEW OF EMERGENCY DAM AND SWING SPAN FROM LOCK FLOOR BELOW.

as high as at Panama in 1912. It seems reasonable, therefore, to ascribe the small increase (about 20%) in the cost per square foot of lock opening at New Orleans, mainly to the more economical type of design.

Contractors and Personnel

The material for the emergency dam, with the exception of the concrete counterweight and some minor parts, was furnished by the following contractors:

Swing span, including turning machinery. Bethlehem Steel Bridge Corporation
Stop-log girders........................... McClintic-Marshall Company
Hoisting machinery.................... Wellman-Seaver-Morgan Company

The structural work was divided between two firms in order to expedite the work which was begun during the World War, its speedy completion being important from a military standpoint.

The Consulting Engineers for the Inner Navigation Canal were George W. Goethals and Company, the writer being retained by the Commission of the Port of New Orleans to prepare the designs for the structural, mechanical, and electrical equipment of the lock. All plans for this part of the work were made in his office. Special credit should be given to F. E. Sterns, M. Am. Soc. C. E., his Principal Assistant.

DISCUSSION

F. R. Harris,* M. Am. Soc. C. E.—This is a very interesting contribution to the very little that has been written on this subject. Such structures are not only necessary and an insurance against possible very serious damage to locks, amounting in some cases even to their entire destruction, but they are an adjunct necessary to enable periodic unwatering and inspection, together with the necessary repair and maintenance work involved.

The stop-log emergency dam and canal lock is new to the speaker. Mr. Goldmark states that at an earlier period an emergency dam was built on the Canadian side of the St. Mary's River, and that it was actually tested under emergency conditions. The views, Figs. 1 and 2, of the accident are very interesting.

However, the feature of making steel girder stop-logs capable of being floated to any location is a novel one. The speaker is not sure that he entirely understands how water is admitted to them to overcome their buoyancy when lowered into position. That is, whether this is an automatic device or a special hand preparation. It would seem that when lifting them from the water, unless the openings are very large to permit the interior water to be discharged, great care would have to be exercised so as not to strain the lifting truss or the hoisting mechanism, unless, of course, the designer had provided for this by additional strength for the additional weight of water.

The speaker would anticipate some difficulty in securing and maintaining water-tightness of the box girders. He does not know whether these have been provided with caulking edges and caulked, or whether the water-tightness is dependent on gaskets. In either case, when these stop-logs have been subjected to load and consequent deflection, it would seem that the joints would start leaking. It would be interesting to know what experience had revealed in this line.

The author's hooking and unlatching device is very ingenious and would require careful attention so that corrosion may not occur and interfere with its operation. This apparatus, which is principally for emergency use, may lie unused for long periods, and the temptation is to neglect proper inspection and upkeep. When the emergency arises the apparatus is often not in proper condition. There is no way to overcome this except to insist on periodic use and placing of the apparatus for inspection purposes, whether it is or is not actually required. Unless something of this kind is done, it is either not on hand or not in usable condition when required.

The speaker has used similar stop-log dams, although of much smaller dimensions, in the discharge culverts of dry docks. Their purpose in this case is a somewhat similar one. They are provided for use in the event of the breakage of a sluice-gate or gate-valve, in order to prevent reverse flow of the water and back-race of pump impellers, together with the incident flooding when flooding is not desired. Also, they are used as an emergency dam to permit inspection and repair of discharge culverts and chambers. As

* Rear-Admiral, U. S. N. (*Retired*); Cons. Engr., New York, N. Y.

they are much smaller, with less head and span, they are much simpler and can be improvised. The speaker has had several experiences of deciding to use them and then, after specifying them, making the discovery that they could no longer be found. The Dock Master had gotten tired of seeing them lying around so long and not being used and had sent them to the scrap heap or had broken them up and used the material for other purposes.

It would be interesting to know something about the extent of leakage in horizontal joints between abutting girders or stop-logs. The leakage in this type of emergency dam cannot, presumably, be greater than that at Panama. On the other hand, when considering this type of dam as compared to the type of emergency dam at Panama, attention must be given to the greater span of the Panama locks and the consequent greater depth of girder (horizontally), greater bending moment, and consequent greater weight.

Considering the theoretical design of an emergency dam a series of horizontal beams, such as Mr. Goldmark has evolved, will have to be computed to take the entire water pressure. In general, the steel required and the cost would bear a direct relation to the width of the opening and the depth (horizontally) of the beams. In the case of the Panama emergency lock, there is one horizontal girder at the top having a span the full width of the opening. The sum of the reactions received by it from the vertical members, or beams, will equal one-third the water pressure, the remaining two-thirds being taken by the sill. Likewise, for the vertical beams, in turn, since the maximum moment will be at a point about one-third the distance from the bottom (all other factors being equal), the steel structure, on the basis of the Panama design, will have to take care of only two-thirds of the water pressure as compared with all the water pressure for a stop-log dam. It is, of course, very probable that the details in the Panama design, as compared to the relative simplicity in the stop-log design, might more than make up this difference, although in comparing costs with the New Orleans costs—attempting to equalize the difference on account of the conditions existing at the different times of construction—the greater depth and span, in the case of Panama, should generally result in higher cost.

It is difficult to compare the costs of a design completed before the World War, with one made under existing conditions, because the cost of labor and materials is so much higher.

Going back again to the question of water-tightness for flotation purposes, it has occurred to the speaker that in the long span of 75 ft. there would necessarily be some deflection due to water pressure. What effect would this have on water-tightness, especially after continued repetition of deflections? The matter of water-tightness is of considerable importance in considering the stability of these box girders because they are at times a floating structure, and it is evident that, when so floating, the center of gravity is above the center of buoyancy, giving a type of stability dependent entirely on the righting effect, which is computable in terms of moment of inertia of the water plane of flotation. Any water in the girder, due to leakage, for example, would cause it to careen, with consequent instability and a tendency to roll over on the side. If this does occur, and it will occur with leakage, there will be some difficulty in attaching the lifting hooks. The speaker would like to inquire if anything like this happened.

The paper was also not very clear as to whether the process of flooding the gates and making them water-tight was automatic or whether it was a hand operation. At one time it is stated that they are arranged so as to freely take water in order that they can be lowered and at another time that they must be water-tight.

As an alternate suggestion to prevent leakage in horizontal joints, the speaker recommends making the meeting surfaces of a soft wood, such as white pine. The Federal Government has been very successful in using that material instead of rubber gaskets for meeting surfaces of gates.

R. H. WHITEHEAD,* Esq. (by letter).—The Panama Canal type of dam is an emergency dam, pure and simple. The stop-log type described by Mr. Goldmark has the merit of not only being ready as an emergency dam, but the girders used take the place of the very expensive floating caisson of the Panama Canal. If the latter type of emergency dam had been used in the Inner Navigation Canal at New Orleans, it would have been necessary to supplement it with a floating caisson for overhauling the lock-gates at the upper and lower ends of the locks, assuming that the operating policy was to guard the equipment against deterioration. From the standpoint of simplicity, there is no doubt that the stop-log type is simpler than the Panama type; but the writer does not regard this of very great importance, because it is the business of the operating force in charge to master any details of operation and to be ready to respond with efficiency to any emergency. However, when it comes to maintenance, the Panama Canal type requires more careful maintenance to keep it in a high state of efficiency, and this is expensive and demands close supervision.

The choice of types of dams, either the stop-log or the Panama Canal type, depends on the size of the opening to be closed. The writer does not believe that the stop-log type, while it seems to be a very good type for New Orleans, would be the correct type to use at Panama. The importance of the Panama route makes expense secondary and of minor importance, and speed of operation in an emergency of major importance.

Mr. Goldmark states that it requires 1 hour to put the Panama Canal in position. On the contrary, from the time the emergency occurs it requires, at a maximum, only ½ hour. It takes an hour to put the smaller New Orleans Dam in position, and it is evident by considering the designs that, basically, the Panama Canal type is a faster one to operate. It is true that it was originally expected that an hour would be required to put the Panama Canal Dam in position, but the operating force, by the proper indexing of the clutches required for handling the gates in storage, and by proper training, has reduced this time by half.

The Panama Canal type of dam is safer for Panama than the stop-log type, because the area is blocked off by separate independent units in a vertical plane rather than separate dependent units in a horizontal plane.

* Vice-Pres. and Gen. Mgr., The New Haven Clock Co., New Haven, Conn.

In regard to Mr. Goldmark's method of calculating the cost on a square-foot basis and comparing the two types, it would probably be a better comparison if the two dams were calculated on a tonnage basis, because after all is said and done, if the New Orleans type of dam, which is 75 ft. wide, was built to cover a width of 110 ft., such as in Panama, the cost per square foot would mount up much more rapidly than in direct proportion to the relative areas. In calculating on a pound basis, it would be found on certain sizes of openings that the Panama Canal dam, considered simply as a dam, is cheaper when the area becomes sufficiently large, than the stop-log type, and *vice versa*. As the area becomes smaller from a critical amount, the stop-log type will show more and more economy. There appears little doubt but that the stop-log type is the correct one for New Orleans and that the Panama Canal type is the best for locks of their size.

The writer wishes to pay tribute to the author. The operating force of the Panama Canal has always looked on the lock-gates that Mr. Goldmark designed and that the McClintic-Marshall Company built as the greatest single engineering achievement of the Panama Canal.

R. O. Comer,* Esq. (by letter).—The author has presented an interesting and valuable summation of the efforts that have been made to devise machinery to check the uncontrolled flow of water in locks and other large channels. Furthermore, he has given a specific and accurate description of how this has been done in a relatively cheap, simple, and effective way.

Devices of this kind are few in number and the cases are fewer still where these devices have been put to use under emergency conditions. The time is probably quite remote when any considerable amount of data will be derived from lock accidents. The designer in this problem is obliged, therefore, to visualize every possible mechanical weakness or defect and to provide against an extended chain of events in a calamity which he, in all probability, will never see.

In comparing the stop-log type of dam and the wicket-girder type, the writer's remarks are based on observations made on the Panama dams and the New Orleans Dam in each case. The stop-log type of dam is favored over the wicket type, under the conditions ordinarily met with in lock design, for the following reasons:

1.—The bridge, in the general design and in the details, is simpler. The hoisting machinery is likewise more simple. On the other hand, the wicket girder dam is a very complicated machine both structurally and mechanically.

2.—The cost, as shown by Mr. Goldmark, is less.

3.—The time necessary for planning, fabrication, and erection, is less.

4.—The maintenance should be less. There are relatively few parts in the stop-log girder type of dam to get out of order. The details are generally simple and rugged and, with few exceptions, all parts are readily accessible for painting, inspection, and repair. However, as far as accessibility is concerned, there is little choice between the two types.

5.—The number of men required for operation is less. The stop-log girder dam is a one-man operated machine in the emergency case. No great amount

* Syracuse, N. Y.

of skill is required. On the other hand, the wicket-girder dam seems to require a crew of about fourteen or fifteen well-trained men for good results.

6.—The stop-log girders can be adopted for use as a lock caisson with small extra expense.

7.—The weight of the loaded bridge under the same conditions will no doubt be less, since only a part of the dam proper is carried at one time. This was no small advantage at New Orleans because of the low bearing value of the soil and because of the fact that the dam and its foundation necessarily formed an unfavorably located concentrated load on one wall of the lock.

8.—The leakage rate is a great deal less. At the time of the test at New Orleans, full head was artificially created on the up-stream face by pumping the forebay full of water to approximately the 1922 high-water mark. The entire down-stream face was bared by pumping. Under these conditions, the leakage was so small that no one thought it worth while to go to the trouble of measuring it. It was thought at the time that between 100 and 200 gal. per min. would account for all of it. The leakage was confined almost entirely to a number of open spaces in the steel horizontal sealing strips between the upper girders. The strips of the lower girders appeared absolutely tight, very likely because of the superimposed weight of the upper girders. The vertical seals in the lock walls were likewise quite tight, not only because of good workmanship, but because of the large unit pressures on the sealing surfaces. Before the test, when the girders were piled up across the lock in the dry, the joints were inspected for tightness by noting the amount of light coming through and testing the openings with strips of thin flat steel. There were only a very few places that showed more than 0.02-in. opening. It is recalled that perhaps 50 or 60% of the length of the seals showed no light coming through at all. Under the heat of the sun, the upper girders would be bowed up so that they had a bearing only at the ends.

The steel sealing strips were made in short sections to conform with the down-stream curved outlines of the girders. The strips were fitted with adjusting or leveling screws and were backed up with Babbitt metal. Obviously, this construction made for accuracy.

It can be readily appreciated that the workmanship in lining up the sealing strips was unusually good. The records show that the leakage under a similar test at Panama was 950 cu. ft. per sec. This can be regarded as a practicable minimum for the wicket-girder type of dam. No particular effort was made at the time of the New Orleans test to treat the sealing surfaces. There was the usual coat of slush oil on them which had been applied some weeks previously. The girders for the purposes intended can be pronounced tight. It seems that the degree of tightness stated is about the best it is practicable to secure using sealing strips of steel. If in future work a greater degree of tightness is desired, the design of the seals very likely can be changed. However, some sacrifice in durability would no doubt have to be made.

9.—It is obvious that the most essential requirement of an emergency dam is certainty of action. In the wicket-girder type the multiplicity of relatively small leaves with numerous sliding surfaces offer an opportunity for jamming. The leaves at Panama jammed on some occasions during routine drills, at least in the earlier days of operation. The one instance of emergency operation, cited by Mr. Goldmark, at Sault Ste. Marie, was not an unqualified success, since it is understood that improvised wood closures had to be made, because some of the leaves had failed to go down. The degree of closure, even then, was not sufficient to admit closing a pair of gates on the leakage current without danger.

The dam at New Orleans was placed in service after remarkably few adjustments. It has been operated once each month, as a matter of routine, since 1923. There is no knowledge of any failure to function. The great weight and strength of the vital parts should be much in its favor in an emergency. The chances for sticking have been reduced to the simplest number of surfaces, namely, two. Jamming, due to "drawer action", has been eliminated by the design. The operation of the New Orleans Dam is more largely automatic than is the case at Panama. The personal factors affecting the emergency operation have been reduced by having only one operator.

The duties of the operator are simply the ordinary duties of a crane man. The principal thing to look out for is to see that, after landing the girders below water, he slacks off on the hoist far enough to allow the unlatching mechanism at both ends to function. There is a possibility that if this is not done, he may have released one end of the girder and not the other. If, under these conditions, the girder is hoisted, it may be swept out of the slots on the lock walls and defeat the purpose of the entire investment. The hoist is so powerful that an inexperienced operator, during routine operation, has some difficulty in sensing whether he has only the sinker casting or the sinker casting plus one end of the girder on a hook. The water has a high turbidity and nothing can be seen below the surface.

The New Orleans dam cannot be operated by hand. It is, therefore, exposed to the danger of an interruption in the power supply. The stop-log girders were shop-fabricated at Pottstown, Pa., and were sent completely assembled to New Orleans by rail.

W. J. Barden,* M. Am. Soc. C. E.—As stated by Mr. Goldmark, the risk of serious accidents to properly constructed and operated locks is in general small, but there is always the inherent danger of a ship striking and injuring the gates with consequent serious damage. Provisions against such accidents are all matters of insurance and, like any other insurance, cost money and are, therefore, used to such extent only as the circumstances in each case appear to justify.

Emergency dams, as Mr. Goldmark states, are not essentially protective devices, but a means by which damage done by the breakage of lock-gates and the consequent flow of water through the lock may be minimized by stopping the flow more quickly than could otherwise be done. The emergency dam designed by him and constructed at the New Orleans Inner Navigation Canal is a new application, on a much larger scale than had ever before been undertaken, of the simple stop-log method of closing water openings.

* Col., Corps of Engrs., U. S. A., New York, N. Y.

At the Lake Washington Ship Canal locks, the condition existed under which emergency dams are indicated as desirable, namely, a large body of water above the lock which would be drained were the flow not stopped in a reasonable time. There, the damage would not be done below the lock, as in the case of New Orleans, but above it. Mr. Goldmark estimates the discharge that would take place at New Orleans as 70 000 sec-ft. As a comparison that computed for the Lake Washington lock would be about 58 000.

The type of dam adopted for the latter lock was an adaptation of the balanced cantilever turn-table bridge type used at Sault St. Marie, Mich., and at Panama, and designed to decrease the cost at the expense of some speed in placing.* All parts are stored on the lock wall and placed in position by a stiff-leg derrick, first the bridge supporting the upper end of the six wicket girders, next the operating bridge placed up stream and carrying the machinery for lowering the girders after they have been attached to the main bridge, and then the gates, twenty-four in number.

This dam has been placed in slightly more than 4 hours against as much head as could be secured by opening the culvert valves to full capacity. The lowering of the lakes, the area of which is about 26 000 acres, in that or even somewhat longer time, would probably not be sufficient to cause any very material damage.

The lock is 80 ft. wide, with a draft of 36 ft. over the upper miter-sill. The cross-section of the opening is, therefore, a little more than 3 000 sq. ft., as compared with 4 125 sq. ft., for the New Orleans lock. The total cost, the work having been completed about 1924, was approximately $175 000, or somewhat less than one-half that at New Orleans.

At the small lock, which is 30 ft. wide, with about 17 ft. on the upper sill, the emergency dam consists of five rolling girders or "stop-logs" which are lowered into recesses in the lock walls by a hand-operated stiff-leg derrick.

The author states, that the time required for placing the dam at New Orleans is about the same as that at Panama, namely, 1 hour. It would be interesting to know whether this is in still water, and what experience, if any, has been had in placing it under conditions as nearly similar as practicable to those in time of emergency.

Roger D. Black,† M. Am. Soc. C. E.—Mr. Goldmark's excellent paper and the discussion which has followed it bring sharply to mind certain extremely interesting conditions surrounding the general subject. One is the paucity of actual experience in the operation of these dams under the situation of extreme emergency which they are designed to meet; another is the grave seriousness of the results in the event that one of them fails to function when the emergency occurs. A third condition is that a service test of an emergency dam must always be difficult and dangerous and is often found to be impracticable. From these three conditions it is apparent that the design must be based almost entirely upon the correct application of sound theory and

* For more detailed description of this dam, see the paper by the writer and A. W. Sargent, M. Am. Soc. C. E., entitled "The Lake Washington Ship Canal," p. 1001.

† (Leaycraft & Black, Associated), New York, N. Y.

yet must produce a structure which can be depended upon in the emergency. Obviously, the problem is one of the most serious and difficult which arises in engineering practice.

Mr. Goldmark's paper is particularly interesting in that the dam which he describes is almost unique and a radical departure from the general type which for many years might have been looked upon as almost standard for major locks in the United States—the type which was adopted for the Panama Canal locks and the great lock at Seattle described by Colonel Barden, and the only type which in a serious practical emergency is known to the speaker to have functioned successfully, namely, in the accident at the Canadian Sault Ste. Marie.

It will be recalled that the stop-log principle, as against the Panama Canal type, was adopted at New Orleans on the score of economy in first cost. As this consideration may lead to its further adoption which, in turn, would undoubtedly follow a careful re-study of all existing emergency dams, it seems manifestly proper to invite attention to another emergency dam—a dam differing materially from either of those mentioned and one which was designed after giving full consideration to the Panama and other then existing types. This is the emergency dam* protecting the lock in the concrete dam crossing the Hudson River at Troy, N. Y., which was built by the Federal Government between 1910 and 1915 to replace the old State dam at that point.

The State dam, a stone-filled timber-crib structure, was erected in the early part of the Nineteenth Century, partly for power purposes and partly to create a pool above Troy with adequate depth for the traffic of the Erie and Champlain Canals.

The Federal Government's project of 1910 for the improvement of the Upper Hudson River was undertaken with the particular purpose of providing adequate channel accommodation for the traffic to be expected from the new Barge Canals. Below the State dam at Troy the elevation of the rock underlying the channel bed and the bank conditions were such as to permit open-channel improvement by dredging, rock excavation, and regulation, but the conditions above Troy (including the elevation given the miter-sills of the lowest locks of the Barge Canals) were such that, coupled with the possibility and desirability of utilizing power, replacement of the State dam was decided upon.

The transverse dimensions of the new lock conform to Barge Canal standards, that is, a width of 45 ft. with a depth over the miter-sills at the established low water of 14 ft., to ensure under all possible changes in the regimen of the river a navigable depth of 12½ ft. To provide adequately for the combined traffic of the Champlain and the Erie Branches of the Barge Canal System, the lock (Fig. 19) was made approximately one and one-half times the length of the standard Barge Canal locks and given three sets of miter-gates, dividing it into two chambers, one equal in length to the standard of the Barge Canal, the other one-half that length. Using the smaller chamber

* Described by Frank P. Fifer, M. Am. Soc. C. E., in *Professional Memoirs*, Corps of Engrs., U. S. Army, and Engr. Dept. at Large, Vol. 10, No. 53, September-October, 1918.

alone, economy in the use of water is effected in locking the large portion of Barge Canal traffic which moves in boats less than 150 ft. in length. The longer chamber alone will obviously take any craft that the Barge Canal can pass, and with the center gates open the two chambers in combination materially increase the lockage capacity over that of a standard Barge Canal lock. In addition, the culverts and river wall were so designed as to permit the construction in the future of a duplicate lock at a minimum cost.

The head on the dam at low stages, such as 5 000 cu. ft. per sec., is approximately 14 ft., which decreases as the discharge increases until it practically disappears. For example, in the great flood of 1913, with a discharge computed in excess of 200 000 cu. ft. per sec., the slope at the dam was less than that induced by bank contraction at various points in the river below it, the depth on the dam being about 13 ft.

It is obvious that the volume of water and the conditions of flow in the pool above the lock are such as to make it highly desirable to be able to stop flowage through the lock in the event of the destruction of the miter-gates. The importance of having a simple and dependable emergency dam, however, was greatly enhanced by the position of this lock as the gateway to two great canals, and by the responsibility of the Federal Government to limit interruption of their traffic to the absolute minimum.

The Barge Canal System itself is without emergency dams in its locks for the reason that the pool levels and the flow of water to the locks are otherwise subject to control; for example, by the regulating dams along the Mohawk which apply the principle of the Panama Canal type of emergency dam, except that the supporting structures are in the form of fixed bridges instead of swing draws.

The design of the emergency dam adopted for the Troy lock was derived in part by the application of principles used in the movable dams on Western rivers. Economy in first cost and in maintenance was, of course, a consideration; but the governing consideration was dependability in operation, in turn to be derived mainly from simplicity.

The essential elements of the dam are three trestle bents, a service bridge deck, and a set of roller wickets, each wicket being made up of a steel frame about 11 by 5 ft. over all and supporting six buckle-plates. When not in use the trestles nest one on the other in the bottom of the lock chamber (Fig. 20) behind, and protected by, a heavy concrete sill; and the bridge deck and wickets are stored on shore. To erect the dam the trestle bents are revolved 90° in a direction at right angles to the current, thus placing them in a vertical position (Fig. 21); their tops are then secured to each other and to the lock-walls by the service bridge deck, and the wickets are lowered into position one by one in front of and against the trestles, thus shutting off the flow gradually until closure is completed.

The three trestle bents are spaced 11 ft. 3 in. on centers, and the center line of the easterly trestle is the same distance from the face of the land lock-wall. When nested, the upper parts of the bents revolve into a recess in the river wall (Fig. 20). The rollers on the outer ends of the outer sets of

Fig. 19.—Troy Lock, Nearing Completion, Emergency Dam Erected and in Use as Coffer-Dam.

Fig. 20.—Emergency Dam Under Construction. Trestle Bents Nested in Normal Position When Not in Use.

FIG. 21.—EMERGENCY DAM UNDER CONSTRUCTION. TRESTLE BENTS IN SERVICE POSITION AND CONNECTED BY STRINGERS OF SERVICE BRIDGE DECK.

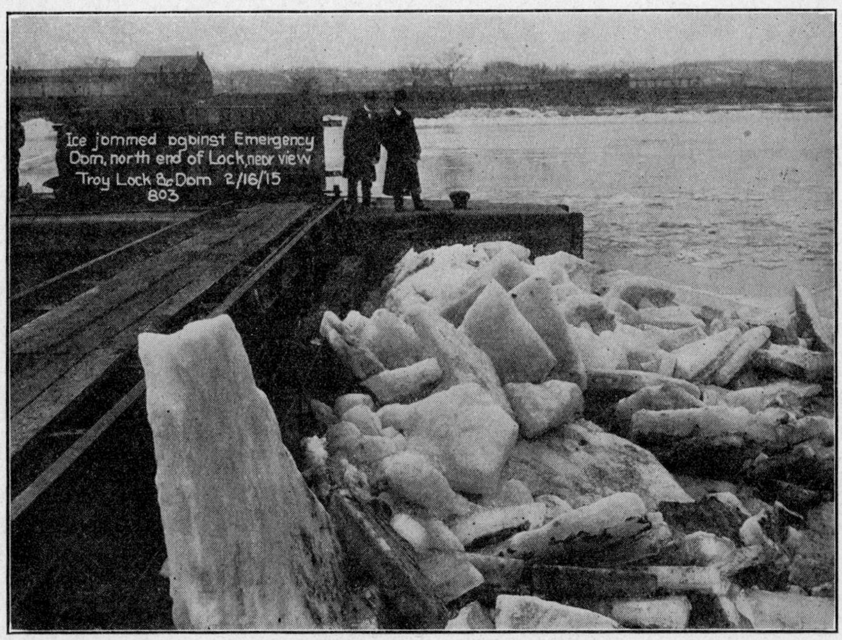

Ice jammed against Emergency
Dam, north end of Lock, near view
Troy Lock & Dam 2/16/15
803

FIG. 22.—EMERGENCY DAM IN SERVICE.

wickets bear on steel castings set in recesses in the lock-walls. All intermediate wicket rollers bear directly on the faces of the up-stream trestle legs. The bearing face of the casting in the land wall is in line with the up-stream faces of the trestles, but the similar recess in the river wall (Fig. 22) is advanced up stream sufficiently to clear the trestle recess, so that the westerly set of wickets rests at a slight angle up stream from the others.

The entire structure is designed to resist a hydrostatic head of 26 ft. plus a velocity head of 11 ft. per sec. The three trestle bents, which are identical, are designed to function in the vertical position as cantilevers, transmitting the portion of the load brought to them by the wickets, to anchorages in the lock floor (Fig. 20), through the bearings on which the trestle legs rest and about which they revolve.

Each trestle bent consists of a vertical front, or up-stream, leg, and an inclined back leg, connected by a horizontal member at the top supporting the service bridge deck, and by three inclined and one horizontal web members. There is no member connecting the feet of the trestle legs, but the web members are so arranged (Figs. 20 and 21), as to carry the entire horizontal component of the load to the down-stream bearing. There it is adequately cared for by inclined anchor-rods leading from the shoe of the bearing up stream and downward to a suitable anchorage buried in the lock floor. The up-stream bearing is likewise anchored, but only to resist the upward reaction.

Each up-stream vertical leg is divided by the web members into three panels. In the lowest panel it acts as a cantilever (extending downward) and in the upper panels as a continuous girder, thus carrying the horizontal load to the web members, and relieving the up-stream bearing of all horizontal thrust. The panel points are so spaced that, under this horizontal loading and the tension due to the vertical reactions, a uniform section is used in the front leg with practically uniform unit stresses throughout its length.

The interesting advantage gained in concentrating the entire horizontal thrust at the down-stream bearing, is that all uncertainty is removed as to its distribution between the two bearings under unequal wear or faulty setting of their surfaces, and that the anchorage can be designed accordingly with precision.

The tops of the trestle bents are connected by a heavy chain which, when they are nested, lies on them and leads across the lock to the land wall where it reaches the surface through a vertical recess. To raise the bents this chain is hauled in by a winch bringing them into a vertical position successively. As they reach the vertical position their tops are connected by light channels which hold them in place and become the stringers on which the service bridge deck is laid. From this service bridge the wickets are lowered by chains and if necessary forced down, shutting off the flow bit by bit. The lowest roller wickets in the erected position rest on the concrete sill previously mentioned. Leakage is controlled by timber stops bolted to the wickets, and can be prevented entirely by simple caulking after the dam is erected.

This emergency dam performed an important function during the construction of the lock. As soon as the up-stream sections of the lock-walls were completed, the dam was erected. This permitted the removal of the northerly end of the steel sheet-pile coffer-dam which was re-erected near the southerly end of the lock. For a period of two years the emergency dam thus acted as a coffer-dam (Fig. 19) and incidentally withstood exceptional pressure from ice and the ravaging effect of several periods of high water. It has since been erected almost annually to permit complete unwatering of the lock and inspection of itself as well as of the upper miter-gates.

In a report* submitted by the Albany Office of the United States Engineer Department on May 14, 1919, the cost of the emergency dam at Troy is given as "cost in place, 93 398 lb. @ \$0.05¾, \$5 360.53".

The width of the lock is 45 ft. and the depth on the miter-sills, 14 ft. This gives a cross-section protected by the dam of 630 sq. ft. at a cost of \$8.50 per sq. ft., a figure which it is interesting to compare with the data given by Mr. Goldmark for the Panama Canal and the lock at New Orleans.

When in charge of the construction of the lock in 1913-14 the speaker cherished a desire to give this emergency dam a service test under full head. It is believed that one of the best features of the design is the ease and comparative safety with which such a test could be made. Obviously, the dam would be erected in still water with the upper miter-gates closed. The miter-gates could then be opened and the roller wickets of the emergency dam removed one at a time until the desired flow to give a proper service test and all measurements connected therewith had been produced. During this operation precautions could be taken and tested out to make absolutely sure that the gates could be replaced under full flow. It is doubtful whether the Panama Canal type, or the stop-log type at New Orleans, is susceptible of such a practical test with so little real danger.

In considering this problem probably the most serious uncertainty has always been as to whether under service conditions the friction in the roller bearings of the wickets would be so great as to neutralize their effectiveness, but even if this were the case it is believed that little difficulty would be had in forcing these wickets down with jacks operating from the service bridge; or, if necessary, from a heavy girder placed across the top of the bridge to take the vertical thrust.

Whatever may be said of other designs, it is true that the emergency dam in the lock at Troy was designed and erected with the primary object of dependability in operation, but nevertheless the suggestion is made that its effectiveness can never be completely proved until it is tried under emergency conditions. In view of the importance of this lock and the waterways to which it is an outlet, would it not be interesting for the Society to arrange with the Federal Government for a service test?

Samuel McC. Young,† M. Am. Soc. C. E. (by letter).—In reading this interesting paper, one is impressed with the simplicity and the economy of the design. At the same time, an examination of the diagrams for the sinker

* Loaned by courtesy of Col. R. R. Ralston, Corps of Engrs., U. S. Army, Dist. Engr., 1st N. Y. Dist., U. S. Engr. Dept.

† Chf. Engr., Board of Commrs., Port of New Orleans, La.

castings (Fig. 15) and the automatic latch mechanism (Fig. 16) will reveal the results of careful thought and considerable ingenuity.

This equipment has been operated, for testing only, about once a month since its installation in 1922, and no serious difficulty has developed in this respect. However, due in part to local conditions, certain little operating kinks, here and there, have been discovered as a result of experience. For example, an accumulation of silt on the floor of the lock when the Emergency Dam is being placed may interfere with the proper operation of the spring device which should release the hooks. In that case, it becomes necessary to use the hand-operated mechanism provided for releasing the hooks when placing the girders in the storage yard.

Another detail, which may not have been thought of in the preparation of plans, but which is more or less important, is the use of tell-tale ropes or cords for determining when both hooks have become engaged or released, as the case may be. When an Emergency Dam girder is being placed in, or is being removed from, the dam, suitable weights, with ropes attached, are placed one on each end of the girder, and two men, standing on the lock-walls opposite the ends of the girder, hold these ropes with their hands, keeping them taut. Then, should only one hook be engaged when the lifting mechanism is being operated, one rope will remain taut while the other will begin to be slack. This condition will indicate that only one hook is engaged and that only one end of the girder is being raised. The lifting mechanism, which is being handled very carefully at this stage of the operation, is stopped at once, or else the girder might become jammed between the lock-walls. It is then necessary to go through the process again of engaging the loose hook or of disengaging the other, depending on what is being done with the girder. It may be more convenient, when lowering the girders into the lock chamber, to attach the tell-tale ropes directly to the girders in a manner in which they may be easily released after the hooks are disengaged.

A few minor modifications of the original design were made in the field. These had to do principally with the latching mechanism and the sinker castings. In order to detach the hooks when the girders are to be floated to the north end of the lock, it is necessary to take the weight of the sinker castings off the girder, as the girders have not sufficient buoyancy to carry the sinkers. This is accomplished by inserting in the oblong holes of the castings 2 by 2 by 6-in. steel blocks which transfer the weight of the sinker castings to the axles of the movable sheaves.

Even the weight of the hooks is sufficient to overcome the buoyancy of a floating girder, and, consequently, in order to re-engage the hooks, it is necessary to hold them back with the dogs to permit the latching mechanism to be lowered to a position where the hooks will engage. In this position, the dogs are tripped and the hooks take hold. To facilitate the proper alignment of the sinker castings and latching devices in picking up a girder, two cone-shaped steel dowels, 4½ in. in diameter by 2 in. high, have been attached to the bottom of each sinker casting, and corresponding holes were drilled in the tops of the girders. To prevent these castings from swinging about their supports, suitable guides and braces have been attached to the crane structure.

The counterweights, which were attached to the hooks, were found to be unnecessary, and their removal has facilitated the detaching of the hooks.

While this Emergency Dam has not been tested under the actual conditions for which it was designed, there is every reason to believe that it would be equal to such a test.

T. B. MÖNNICHE,* M. AM. SOC. C. E. (by letter).—This paper is of great interest to the profession. It describes a novel structure, and, as the literature on emergency dams is very meager, any addition to this subject should be of value. The problems involved in the design of an emergency dam are far more complex than one would imagine.

The author claims that the New Orleans Dam is as reliable in operation as the Panama Canal dams; that it requires a smaller operating force; and that it has the merit of being lower in cost than any emergency dam previously built. The writer is of a different opinion. He also believes that it would have been entirely infeasible to construct a dam of the "stop-log" type for the Panama Canal, whereas the type adopted there could have been used to great advantage at New Orleans.

When the writer began designing the Panama Canal dams, no emergency dam had ever been tested under actual emergency conditions, so that there were no practical results to follow. Calculations were made of the flow of water that would occur at each site of the dams in case of an emergency. The most serious condition was found to be at Gatun (see Fig. 23), where there is a double flight of three locks, each 110 ft. wide and about 1 000 ft. long. The depth of water at the upper lock-sill is 49¾ ft. and the difference in elevation of the water at the top lock and the bottom lock is 88 ft. The computed result was a discharge of 95 000 cu. ft. per sec., with a velocity of 24.1 ft. per sec. It became apparent at once that, in trying to stop a flow of such magnitude, it would be practically impossible to do so simply by enlarging upon the dams already constructed at Sault Ste. Marie. The wicket girders became so long that, in order to counterbalance their weight, the horizontal truss had to be placed on the down-stream side of the down-stream vertical truss, instead of, as at the "Soo", between the two vertical trusses; and the rolling gates could not be made (as at the "Soo") in one length, but had to be made in sections and hung up under the floor so as to clear the flow of water. This is shown in Figs. 23 and 24.

The principal point considered in the design of the wicket girders and gates was to construct them so as to make their lowering in the swift current as reliable as possible. The possibility of the wicket girders meeting obstructions at the sill was guarded against by placing large concrete pockets, 32 ft. wide and 14 ft. deep, in front of the sill. These would have to be filled before any obstruction could settle on the sill. Furthermore, the shape of the sill was made such that any obstruction which might settle would be washed away by a current of 24 ft. per sec. If some obstruction should be caught between the sill and the wicket girders just as the latter are approaching the sill, the hoisting machines have been made so powerful that these

* Boquete, Panama.

Fig. 23.—View Showing West Emergency Dam in Position Across Lock Chamber, Gatun Locks, Panama Canal.

Fig. 24.—Panama Canal Emergency Dams, Pedro Miguel Locks, View Showing Lowering of Wicket Girders.

girders may be raised against the current so as to allow the obstruction to pass. In lowering the gates in the current they are subjected to pressure caused by the static head and the kinetic energy of the water. In order to ascertain what the friction would be for each set of gates during lowering, tests were made on full-sized gates. These tests showed that the average load required to overcome the friction due to the loads produced by the current, was 3.2% of the weight of the gates.

Only a few months after the plans of the wicket girders and gates for the Panama Canal had been made, the accident at the "Soo" occurred. This was the first time an emergency dam had been brought into actual use and its successful operation proved its feasibility. The most serious mishap that occurred was that, in lowering one pair of wicket girders, they struck some obstruction, so that they did not get properly seated and were warped into a twisted mass. However, the principal framework of the dam was intact and the opening was later closed by provisional means. The gates, which were provided with wheels (but without roller bearings), failed to function, so they had to be jacked down into place. It was a satisfaction for the writer thus to obtain an actual proof of the importance of those points on which he had laid so much stress in his design.

The lock force on the Panama Canal is given a routine drill once a month in operating the emergency dams. The force which usually operates the dams at the Atlantic locks consists of ten "gold" and twenty "silver" employees, which is approximately 14% of the "gold" and 10% of the "silver" force. During the six months from August, 1927, to January, 1928, the average time for closing one dam, either day or night, was 25 min., the maximum time was 26 min., and the minimum time, 24 min. The force used in drilling during the same months at the Pacific locks consisted of eight "gold" and twelve "silver" employees. This represents, at Pedro Miguel, 16% of the "gold" and 12% of the "silver" force. The average time for closing was 29 min. for Pedro Miguel, and 24 min. for Miraflores. These forces are not the minimum required, as some of the men are oilers and stand-by men.

The lockmaster swings the dam and is in charge of the drill. As each pair of wicket girders is provided with a separate hoisting machine and limit switch, the lockmaster alone can start the lowering of each pair of wicket girders one after the other. The switches automatically cut off the current for each machine when the wicket girders reach the bottom sill. In a similar manner each horizontal set of gates may also be lowered. In lowering the gates, however, two additional men would be required to ascertain that the hooks for the gates are not interfering with the gates properly engaging the rails of the wicket girders. Thus, the dams for the Panama Canal may, if necessary, be operated with a minimum force of three or four men. The time for closing the dam in this manner would be increased to about double the present time.

The author states that the principal operations of the New Orleans Dam are under the control of one man, although a few others are required in the storage yard and on the walls, and that "this does not mean any addition to the ordinary lock force." He also states that a "large number of attendants" is required for the operating of the Panama Canal dams. As no addition to the ordinary lock force is required for operating the New Orleans Dam, and as only 14 to 16% of the lock force is ordinarily used for operating the Panama Canal dams, it seems to the writer more probable that it takes a larger force to operate the New Orleans Dam than those of the Panama Canal. It would be interesting to know the exact number of men required for operating the New Orleans Dam, and the recorded time used during the day and night, including that lost between each operation. The Panama Canal dams have to resist forces, and to check the kinetic energy of water, of about twice the magnitude of the New Orleans Dam and, according to the available figures, this is done in less than one-half the time.

The author's statement that the New Orleans Dam is as reliable as those of the Panama Canal does not seems to the writer to be quite correct. The experience gained by the accident at the "Soo" shows the importance of guarding against improper seating of girders due to meeting obstructions. Possibly this point has been given little consideration by the author in his design, one of the principal features of which is the use of releasing hooks with which large box girders spanning the width of the lock chamber are lowered into place. The releasing of these hooks depends on the proper seating of each box girder. The chances for one of these box girders meeting obstructions while being lowered in a swift current are far greater than for all the wicket girders at the "Soo" or at the Panama Canal, because these box girders are to be seated across the entire width of the lock chamber, and as there are eight of them, the chances are still further multiplied.

No provision has been made for raising the box girders to allow obstructions to pass. With this type of emergency dam it would be practically impossible to do so on account of the enormous loads to which the hoisting machine would be subjected. It might happen, therefore, that the first girder to be lowered would meet an obstruction, so that the releasing hooks would not function and thus would put the dam entirely out of commission. A catastrophe of this kind could not occur at the Panama Canal. If a pair of wicket girders should not get properly seated, so that a set of gates could not be lowered, the principal structural framework of the dam would remain intact and the small opening in the dam could be closed later by some provisional means, as was actually done at the "Soo".

Unfortunately, the author has not given the hydraulic conditions for the New Orleans Dam. He simply states that the computed volume of the flow of water will be "in excess of 70 000 sec-ft.", without giving the velocity. From this figure the writer has computed the entrance head to be about 16 ft.; and the entrance velocity, about 28 ft. per sec.

In computing the flow for the Panama Canal the surface drop at the end of the three flights of locks was not taken into consideration either, as it would only have complicated the problem and have had little effect on the final result, because this drop occurs about 88 ft. below the upper level. At New Orleans, however, the conditions are such that the surface drop at the end of the lock will greatly affect the computations. The writer, therefore, has made approximate calculations, the result of which is a discharge of 50 000 sec-ft., and a velocity of 16.5 ft. per sec. During the lowering of the stop-log girders at New Orleans the maximum static head imposed on them is estimated by the writer to be about 9 ft., whereas at the Panama Canal the maximum static head during the lowering of the gates is 24 ft.

The author ascribes the low cost per square foot of lock opening at New Orleans mainly to the more economical type of design. The writer believes it is uneconomical, because it is subjected to the full static head, whereas at the Panama Canal two-thirds of the reaction of the static head is carried by the sill and only one-third by the dam itself.

In the author's comparison of the cost of the New Orleans Dam with the Panama Canal dams, no account is taken of increased moments due to longer spans, nor to increased loads due to greater volume of flow, velocity head, and static head. This comparison is identical to estimating the weight of two bridges by simply calculating their weights in straight proportion to their respective spans without considering the different loads to which they are subjected. Evidently, in comparing costs it should be kept in mind that the moments vary in proportion to the square of the span; that the kinetic energy of the flow of water varies in proportion to the cross-section of the flow multiplied by the square of the velocity; and that the horse-power required and the weight of the machinery and its supports vary in inverse proportion to the time required for closing. In this connection it should be remembered that an emergency dam is practically nothing but one huge machine. The Panama Canal dams are subjected to:

Moment due to span.......... $= \left(\frac{110}{75}\right)^2 = 2.15$ times New Orleans Dam.

Kinetic energy of flow $= \frac{4\,000}{3\,050} \times \left(\frac{24.1}{16.5}\right)^2 = 2.8$ " " " "

Machinery and supports........... $= \frac{60}{25} = 2.4$ " " " "

If proper allowance is made for these factors, the cost of each emergency dam for the Panama Canal ($432 000) compares very favorably with the cost of the New Orleans Dam ($353 000).

The greater reliability in the operation of the Panama Canal dams should also be taken into account. The use of releasing hooks was at first considered for the Panama Canal dams. A preliminary design was published in the Annual Report of the Isthmian Canal Commission for 1908. The principal feature in the operation of this dam was identical with that of the New Orleans Dam, because the whole operation of the dam was to be performed from a central power plant and releasing hooks were to be used. This design was abandoned because releasing hooks were considered unreliable on account of the possibility that they might not release if the wicket girders or the gates should meet an obstruction at their lower ends. The design was low in cost. Its estimated weight was 1 870 000 lb., whereas the dams constructed weigh 6 700 000 lb. each. Thus, the estimated weight of each emergency dam for the Panama Canal as originally designed with releasing hooks amounted to only 28% of the weight of each of the present dams. This large increase in weight was caused not only by abandoning the use of releasing hooks and substituting separate hoisting units, but also by enlarging the size of the gates, thus reducing the time of closing; by furnishing the gates with roller bearings; and by providing the hoisting machines with sufficient power to raise the wicket girders against the current. The increased cost due to this increase in weight was of minor importance on the Panama Canal where reliability was given first consideration.

If it is desired to make a comparison between the "stop-log" type of emergency dam as used at New Orleans with the wicket-girder type as used at the Panama Canal, it should be made with the original design for the Panama Canal, using releasing hooks. The result of such a comparison, making proper allowance for the different spans, loads, and time required for closing, will show that the stop-log type as built at New Orleans is several times as expensive as the wicket-girder type with releasing hooks would have been if built in its stead. The writer believes that the New Orleans Dam, instead of having "the merit of being lower in first cost" than any emergency dam previously built, has the defects of being higher in cost and less reliable.

All the merits claimed by the author in favor of the New Orleans Dam as compared with the Panama Canal dams are lost, when it is considered that the stop-log type used at New Orleans would not be feasible for use at the Panama Canal. Following the author's design the stop-log girders, if used for the Panama Canal would have the following dimensions: Length, out to out, 120 ft.; horizontal depth at ends, 6 ft. 6 in., and at the middle section, 11 ft.; and vertical depth, 6 ft. 2 in. The horizontal area of each girder, A_h, would be 1 000 sq. ft. and the vertical area, A_v, would be 745 sq. ft. As the spans at the Panama Canal and New Orleans are 100 ft. and 75 ft., respectively, and as the static head, when the locks are empty, is practically the same at both places, the weight of the stop-log girders for the Panama Canal would be $\left(\frac{110}{75}\right)^2 = 2.15$, say, twice the weight of those for the New Orleans Dam. The sinker castings might be proportioned accordingly, and thus the weight of one stop-log girder with sinker castings for the Panama Canal would be $D = 2 \times 244\,000$ lb. $= 488\,000$ lb.

A study of the hydraulic conditions for the Panama Canal dams, during and after the lowering of each gate has been published by the writer.* In order to calculate the loads on the stop-log girders, if used for the Panama Canal, the writer has, for the sake of convenience, assumed that the upper edge of each stop-log girder will be lowered to the same depth as the upper edge of each tier of gates of the Panama Canal dams. In this manner the

* *Transactions,* Inter. Eng. Congress, San Francisco, Calif, 1915, "The Panama Canal", Vol. II, No. 18.

complicated computations made for these dams may be utilized for calculating the loads. The data thus utilized are given in Table 3, Columns (1), (4), (6), and (8). Fig. 25 illustrates the hydraulic conditions just before a stop-log girder reaches its final position, when its upper edge is at the same elevation as the upper edge of Gates No. 3 of the Panama Canal dams.

TABLE 3.

UP STREAM.

Gate No.	Horizontal pressure, p, in pounds per square foot. (1)	Horizontal load, $H = p \times A_v$, in pounds. (2)	Friction, $F = 0.2 \times H$, in pounds. (3)	Static head, H_u, in feet. (4)	Vertical load, $V = H_u \times A_h \times 62.5$, in pounds. (5)
1	1 120	835 000	±166 000	39.0	2 450 000
2	1 400	1 040 000	±208 000	32.5	2 030 000
3	1 375	1 020 000	±204 000	24.8	1 540 000
4	790	588 000	±117 000	15.5	970 000
5	190	141 000	± 28 200	4.8	0

DOWN STREAM.

Gate No.	Velocity, v, in feet per second. (6)	Velocity head, $h = \frac{v^2}{2g}$, in feet. (7)	Static head, H_d, in feet. (8)	Uplift, $U = (H_d + h) \times A_h \times 62.5$, in pounds. (9)	Lowering, $V + U + D - F$, in pounds. (10)	Raising, $V + U + D + F$, in pounds. (11)
1	22.9	8.2	—24.6	—1 020 000	1 752 000	2 084 000
2	21.4	7.1	—12.3	— 325 000	1 985 000	2 401 000
3	18.0	5.0	— 1.3	0	1 824 000	2 232 000
4	8.8	....	......	0	1 341 000	1 575 000
5	0	....	......	0	460 000	516 000

It may be seen that when the water rushes between the stop-log girders, a contraction will take place due to the sharp corners, and that a partial vacuum will be created on the under-side and down-stream side of the stop-log girders (shown at (a), Fig. 25). These girders are filled with water while being lowered; during the lowering, they will also be subjected to the load of water flowing over them. These loads are given in Table 3, Column (5). No account has been taken of the loads produced by the partial vacuum. The uplift in the girders caused by the down-stream pressure is given in Column (9). The load carried by the hoisting machinery, while lowering the stop-log girders, is equal to the loads given in Column (5), minus the loads given in Column (9), and minus the friction produced at the ends of the girders given in Column (3). While raising the girders the load carried by the hoisting machinery is equal to the loads given in Table 3, Column (5) minus the loads given in Column (9) plus the friction, Column (3). The resultant loads to be carried by the hoisting machinery when raising and lowering the girders are given in Columns (10) and (11), respectively.

It may be noted that the loads to be carried by the hoisting machinery when the stop-log girders have been lowered to the same elevation as Gate No. 2 will be, for lowering, 1 985 000 lb., and for raising, 2 401 000 lb., or in other words, more than the total estimated weight of each emergency dam for the Panama Canal as originally designed with releasing hooks. These figures should be sufficient to show the infeasibility of using the stop-log type of emergency dam for the Panama Canal.

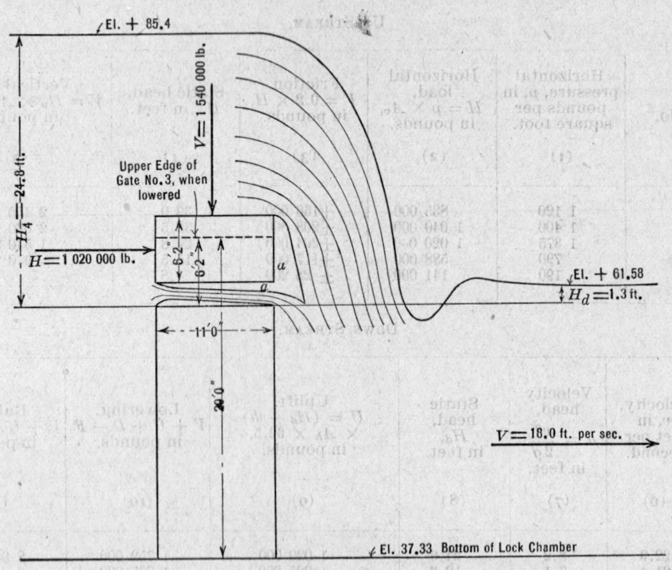

FIG. 25.—HYDRAULIC CONDITIONS FOR THE PANAMA CANAL IF STOP-LOGS WERE TO BE USED.

On the other hand, the stop-log type may be feasible for the New Orleans Dam, but it is difficult to form a definite opinion as to this because the hydraulic conditions while lowering the stop-log girders are not given. The author merely states:

"When the girders are being lowered into place under emergency conditions * * * the horizontal pressures are a combination of the velocity head due to the flow and the static head at the various levels. The computation of the loads due to these conditions is quite involved. In this case, too, the worst possible conditions have been assumed."

The author mentions nothing about the vertical loads imposed upon the girders by the flow of water. For the Panama Canal these vertical loads, as may be seen from Table 3, are about twice as large as the horizontal loads. It would be interesting to know the magnitude of the vertical loads for the New Orleans Dam under emergency conditions. It would be especially so because it is due to these loads that an emergency dam of the stop-log type is infeasible for the Panama Canal.

The author states that while lowering the girders they are filled with water, but while raising them, at a rate of 30 ft. per min., the water is allowed to flow out at the proper rate, so that the girders will contain, for a few minutes only, 1.43 ft. of water, thus guarding against an overload in the hoisting machinery and excessive stresses in the girders. It appears to the writer, that the critical condition for the hoisting machinery and the girders is not during the raising of the girders in still water, but during the lowering of them under emergency conditions, when they are filled with water and also have to carry a large volume of water flowing over them. The vertical loads thus carried by the stop-logs would be the equivalent of a head of several feet for a considerable period of time, instead of 1.43 ft. for a few minutes. The writer, therefore, fears that under emergency conditions excessive stresses may be produced in the hoisting machinery as well as in the stop-log girders of the New Orleans Dam.

HENRY GOLDMARK,* M. AM. SOC. C. E. (by letter).—The writer wishes to express his appreciation of the discussions contributed by several members. Replying to Admiral Harris' questions on the subject of water-tightness, it should be explained that this term refers to two different things: First, the tightness of the several stop-logs when empty and immersed in the canal; and, second, the leakage through the horizontal joints between the several logs when the water is pumped from the lock and through the vertical joints between the ends of the logs and the sidewalls. In both these respects an extreme degree of water-tightness was obtained, as stated by Mr. Comer.

The openings for admitting and discharging water are closed by square sliding covers operated by hand. Their size, as explained on page 1603, is large enough to be safe under the maximum load to be lifted.

Because of the extreme water-tightness of the box girders, no instability is experienced when the openings are closed and the stop-logs are floating.

Mr. Whitehead believes that perhaps the principal merit of the stop-log type of dam is that it can serve for closing the end of the lock-chamber when it is to be pumped out for inspection, thus making unnecessary an expensive caisson as used at Panama and elsewhere. His experience in operating the Pacific locks for several years after the opening of the Panama Canal makes his opinion of great value.

The greater simplicity of the stop-log design Mr. Whitehead does not consider of vast importance. While the writer cannot agree with him on this point, he is pleased that Mr. Whitehead agrees as to the merits (for that location) of the design adopted at New Orleans.

With regard to the times of operation, it should be borne in mind that at New Orleans, when the girders have been lowered into place, the dam is absolutely tight so that the uninjured mitering lock-gates below can be closed without delay.

On the other hand, in dams of the wicket type, there is considerable leakage through the vertical joints between adjacent panels. Hence, special closing pieces are necessary, and these are inserted after the wickets and gates have been lowered.

* Cons. Engr., New York, N. Y.

On the Canadian side at Sault Ste. Marie, no such closing pieces were provided. After the accident there in 1909, the flow, even after all the wickets and gates had been lowered, was very considerable. It proved very difficult to close the mitering gates. They were deformed; that is, bent out of shape by the flow of the water, and it was only because they were of wood that they escaped injury. At least, this was the view expressed to the writer by one of the principal Canadian engineers in charge, soon after the accident. This official was satisfied that steel miter gates could not have withstood the deformation caused by the flow of water and could not have been safely closed.

It appears no more than reasonable, therefore, to include the additional time required for placing the closing pieces in wicket dams, when comparing them as to speed of operation with other designs. If this is done, there will be little difference between the Panama and New Orleans dams, even if the wickets and gates in the former are placed more rapidly than in the early tests witnessed by the writer.

Mr. Comer's discussion is of special value as he was closely connected with the dam from its inception until it was completely erected, and witnessed its operation from the beginning. Mr. Comer explains nearly all points raised in other discussions, besides giving many additional facts which throw light on the design. There is no one whose opinion is of more value.

Colonel Barden's description of the dam in the Lake Washington Ship Canal is very interesting, although the conditions under which it works are different from those in most other places. Its low cost is a matter of interest. This is explained, in part, by the fact that it requires a relatively long time to operate. As stated by Colonel Barden, this slow operation is not of special importance at Lake Washington.

The emergency dam in the Hudson River near Troy, N. Y., described by Colonel Black, is another interesting structure, although it is of relatively small size. As this lock is practically a part of the Barge Canal System, its proper functioning is most important and it is interesting to note that notwithstanding its very low cost it seems to meet satisfactorily the conditions prevailing at the site.

Mr. Young's discussion is based on his experience as Chief Engineer of the New Orleans Port Commission for a term of years during which he has been in charge of the canal operation. His favorable opinion of the dam is, therefore, of much significance. Some minor modifications made by him in the method of handling the girders, etc., are very interesting.

Mr. Mönniche describes certain features of the Panama dams, designed by him, and claims for them various advantages over other designs, especially the stop-log type. It was by no means the writer's purpose to assert that the latter type is the most suitable one for all widths and depths of the lock-chamber. It is clear that the choice of type must depend on local conditions, as well as on the functions which the dam is to fulfill. The stop-log type was chosen for New Orleans largely on account of its economy because, aside from serving to stop the flow of water in case of accident, these dams can also be used as coffer-dams to close the ends of the lock-chamber when unwatering it.

Apart from its greater economy, however, the writer believes that the stop-log design is better, in this location, because the girders and the machinery are simpler than the more numerous and complex parts required in other types. The massive horizontal girders, securely guided in wall recesses, are less liable to injury, when being lowered or raised, than pairs of wicket frames hinged at the top and connected by rather light bracing. Each such pair is comparatively weak and subject to damage if the current makes an angle with the axis of the lock.

It was the belief of at least one competent observer that the difficulty in closing certain panels after the accident in the "Soo" was due to such a current, which swayed one of the structural frames so as to hold it up against the adjoining one, injuring one or both frames.* The horizontal stop-logs are also almost absolutely water-tight, when lowered into place, without additional closing pieces. The mechanism for handling the girders is also much simpler than that used in other types.

Mr. Mönniche's argument to show that the operating force at Panama is really smaller than that used at New Orleans is not convincing. As well stated by Mr. Comer, it is unquestioned that the satisfactory operation of the New Orleans Dam—including both the revolving of the swing-span, the attachment and release of the separate girders, as well as the operations of raising and lowering—is, at all times, done by a single operator stationed in a cage near the end of the swing-span.

Mr. Mönniche criticizes the value (70 000 sec-ft.) given by the writer (page 1636) as the flow of water at New Orleans when the lock-gates are carried away, the river level being + 39 and the lake level + 20. Mr. Mönniche finds that this value is only 50 000 and suggests that the writer has omitted the "surface drop" at "the end of the lock" from his calculations. Presumably he refers to the lower end of the lock. The writer used the standard method of computation employed when two bodies of water at different elevations are connected by an open conduit. A number of different values are assumed for the flow, and, for each of these values, the elevations of the water surface at various points from one end of the conduit to the other are computed, until the correct value is found. This value will be the one for which the sum of the hydraulic heads, due to the change in potential energy and to frictional resistances, is exactly equal to the difference in elevation of the two bodies of water connected by the conduit.

The conditions prevailing in the New Orleans Canal are shown in Figs. 25 and 26. Fig. 25 gives the plan of the canal and lock, with cross-sections, and Fig. 26 shows the elevations of the water surface at various points. As there is no sudden drop in the bottom of the lock and hence no weir effect on the flow, there can be no surface drop at the lower end of the lock, as claimed by Mr. Mönniche. It will be noted that the bottom of the canal below the lock is taken at Elevation — 8.25, while the lock bottom is at Elevation — 10. The canal, at some later time, will be deepened to Elevation — 10. This, of course, will make a change, although probably a slight one, in the results of the calculation.

* Letter to the writer, dated September 22, 1909, from M. J. Butler, M. Am Soc. C. E., then Deputy Minister and Chief Engineer, Department of Railways and Canals, Canada.

The writer is satisfied that the results obtained by his computations, as shown in Fig. 26, are reasonably correct, the only uncertain quantities being the coefficients of friction in the lock chamber and in the canal channel. He feels the greater confidence in their correctness since he applied the same method in the case of the accident on the Canadian side at Sault Ste. Marie in 1909. In this case, there was a quite close agreement between the calculated results and the actual measurements made by the engineers on the ground and furnished to the writer at the time.

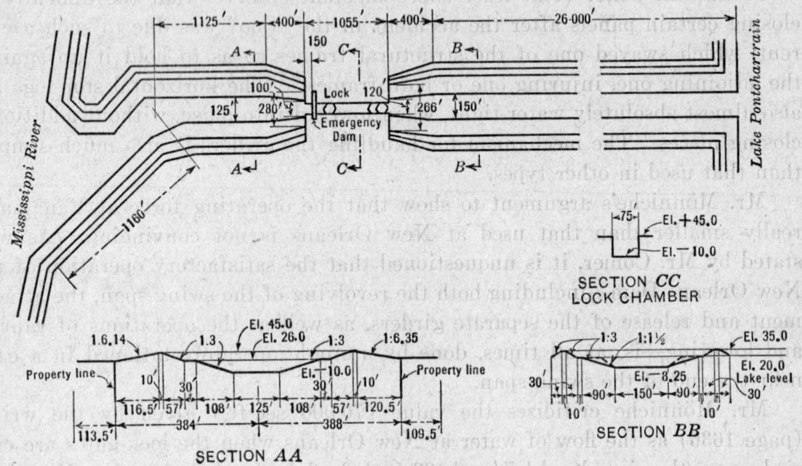

FIG. 25.—PLAN AND TYPICAL SECTIONS, INNER NAVIGATION CANAL.

In the paper the total costs of the New Orleans Dam and one of those at Panama are given and also their costs per square foot of lock section. Making allowance for the increase in the unit price of steel (about 2.4 to 1) the cost per square foot at Panama would be $180 as against $85.70 at New Orleans. The width of the Panama locks is only about one and one-half times as great as that at New Orleans, while the depth is the same. The weight of the Panama dams as built was three times as great and their cost per square foot two and one-tenth times as great. These figures seem disproportionately large as compared with the increase in the lock width.

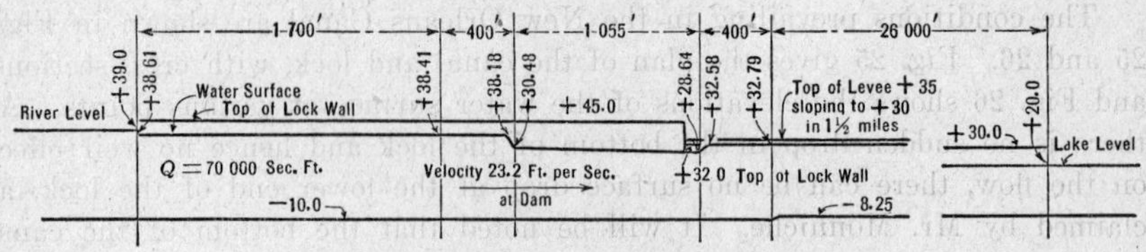

FIG. 26.—PROFILE, INNER NAVIGATION CANAL.

However, apart from any comparison with other locations, the great economy of the dam at New Orleans can be clearly shown by its double function as an emergency dam as well as a coffer-dam for shutting off the lock at either end when it is to be unwatered for periodic inspection. If the dam were not able to fulfill this last function it would have to be supplemented by a separate floating caisson at a greatly increased cost. This is the case, although in order to use the stop-logs at the lower end of the lock they were arranged so as to float, making them much heavier, while their weight was still further increased by making them all identical and strong enough to withstand the full static head at the bottom when the lock is empty. Even with this increase in weight and cost the combined function of the New Orleans dam saves a great deal of money when compared to the cost of two separate structures.

The Panama caisson, which was built about 1912, cost approximately \$350 000. It is 114 ft. long and 65 ft. high. A caisson in the New Orleans lock would be about 80 ft. long and 65 ft. high. Considering its smaller size, but also the increased present-day cost of material, the cost of a caisson may be safely estimated at from \$300 000 to \$350 000. The great economy obtained by using a stop-log dam, at a cost of \$350 000, needs no further argument.

AMERICAN SOCIETY OF CIVIL ENGINEERS

INSTITUTED 1852

TRANSACTIONS

This Society is not responsible for any statement made or opinion expressed in its publications.

Paper No. 1696

BUILDERS, DEFENDERS, AND POLITICAL DESPOILERS OF OUR COUNTRY

ADDRESS AT THE ANNUAL CONVENTION AT BUFFALO, N. Y., JULY 18, 1928

By Lincoln Bush,* President, Am. Soc. C. E.

The progress of humanity has always depended on two things: First, on the strength of the natural instinct; and, second, on those necessities which a Mother Nature has sternly although kindly imposed upon her children. These two conditions have been the great drive wheels of the human engine, while the human mind—the reasoning power—has been the potent lever which for good or for ill, depending on the skill, the courage, the power, and the inspirations of the engineer, has commanded and controlled the whole machine.

Builders of Our Country

The laws of progress are but a compilation of the unwritten statutes of the Creator. Clearly discernible among these may be noticed the motives, the inspirations, the incentives, and the impelling forces, prompting through all life and ages to beneficence and accomplishment. This is exemplified by our former member, James B. Eads, in the dedication of soul and self to the construction of the Mississippi River jetties in these words,

"I therefore undertake the work with a faith based upon the ever-constant Ordinances of God, Himself, and so certainly as He spare my life and faculties for two years more, I will give to the Mississippi through His Grace and by the application of His Laws, a deep, open, safe, and permanent outlet to the Seas."

Forty-nine years have since passed and there now remains a clear channel of 40 ft. in depth, at the South Pass Jetties, and Eads' memory is enshrined in the Hall of Fame.

* Cons. Engr., East Orange, N. J.

The learned explorations, the scientific discoveries, and the mental developments of each succeeding generation are but the outgrowth of a clearer and a fuller understanding of these laws. What a beneficent creation! With delight we pursue; with gratification, possess. There are no limitations of the materials with which to work; no end of new truths, new laws, and new relations, which intelligent thought and energy cannot develop and grasp. Have you not heard of the new one-span structure reaching from Rocky Point to Rugby, 3 200 miles across the Atlantic? Invisible and intangible, its chords and web members were assembled on the evening and the morning of the Second Day, fifty-nine centuries ago; and engineering science, invention, and research are only now sending the first message across this vibrant mystery. Diamonds at our feet and world without end!

Undaunted by the failure of France, after thirty years of effort and the expenditure of $200 000 000 to build the Panama Canal, our engineers have said to the United States Government, "This is a practicable and a feasible proposition; we can build this great waterway". And within a decade we gave to the world that of which it had dreamed for 400 years, making New York from the Philippines only 9 600 miles instead of 13 600 miles, and the Golden Gate from Liverpool only 8 000 miles instead of 13 800 miles, and we now challenge the world for the billions of commerce of the East and West and for the inter-coastal trade of the two Americas. Conquests of the Civil and Sanitary Engineers: Wallace, Stevens, Goethals, and Gorgas!

The following record of our War Department was made only a few years before the last spike was driven in our first great transcontinental railroad in 1869; a record made by men who believed they were correctly forecasting the future of our present Great West beyond the Missouri and Mississippi Rivers, which reads as follows:

"From these vast prairies will be derived one of the great advantages to the United States, namely, the restriction of her population to some central limits and thereby a continuation of the Union. They [meaning the people] will be constrained to limit themselves to the borders of the Missouri and Mississippi, while they leave the prairies beyond, incapable of cultivation, to the wandering and uncivilized Aborigines of our Country".

Across these arid plains and tables of our Great West, we see in the sands and sage-brush the stakes and footprints of the Civil Engineer; and, following in his wake, we find the storage reservoirs, the irrigating channels, the shimmering fields of golden grain, and the Great American Desert is no more.

Instead of these vast prairies, declared incapable of cultivation, we have on this same territory to-day, the largest flouring mills, the greatest stock ranges, the largest granaries, and many of the richest ore mines of the world. Instead of these wandering and uncivilized aborigines we have to the west of the Mississippi River, the homes and firesides of 36 000 000 of our most intelligent people, the backbone of your own and New England's best stock, and heirs of the blood and courage of the pioneer. Instead of the aborigine's tepee, we have, to the west of this great river, 284 universities and colleges, a wealth represented by $102 000 000 000 of tangible property, and the emigrants' trail of '49 has been buried under 127 000 miles of the most modern and well equipped railroad of our Country.

What a marvelous development in our great transportation systems, with only 23 miles of railroad in the United States in 1830 and 250 000 miles of railroad in the United States in 1925! They have stretched out over mountain and plain, up and over the great Rocky Ranges of our West and Northwest into that land of sunshine and flowers, and still on to the Yukon and Circle City, into a country with a coast line of 8 000 miles, of which the half has never been told, with 1 mile of rail for every 470 of our people against 1 mile of railroad for every 2 050 of Continental Europe, without which our great West, beyond the "Father of Waters," never could have been and the Louisiana Purchase would have been of little comparative value—a vast empire of 875 000 sq. miles, stretching west from the Mississippi to the Great Continental Divide and north from the Gulf to the Canadian Border. This acquisition barred forever the erection of a hostile or foreign State, made inevitable the annexation of Texas, New Mexico, California, and Oregon, and gave birth to a new nation of continental proportions and world influence.

Some one will say, "capital and labor have done these great and wonderful things", and they have done their part; but the inspired, scientific minds which conceived these great things and the constructive, courageous minds which executed these great things are superior to those instruments which they have employed.

What an epic of engineering and human progress has made possible our civilization and our Country with greater liberty, greater opportunity, and greater happiness to a greater number than has come anywhere at any time in the World's history.

Defenders of Our Country

Then came the World War with its years of bloodshed and sacrifice. Our civilization had been established and it must be defended. Mindful of the past and thoughtful of our future, we went forth, to protect and preserve our Country, its ideals and institutions, wrought from a wilderness after 140 years of superhuman effort by a great, a courageous, a patriotic, and a noble people, and we went forth to protect and preserve a world from chaos.

The Founder Societies, Engineering Council, National Research Council, civilian and commissioned engineers in all branches of transportation and industry, rendered indispensable service in the World War, but their activities were too diversified to be treated separately here. I shall speak of the Construction Division of the Army, which was a great human institution having only six Regular Army men in its entire organization and functioning under the single idea of emergency construction for war purposes; an assemblage of engineering and business skill of unusual and extraordinary capacities, consisting of chief engineers, consulting engineers, assistant engineers, water and sewerage experts, construction superintendents, and business men, supported by the War Industries Board with the vast resources at its command and ably led by Brigadier-Generals Littell and Marshall.

The Committee on Emergency Construction and Engineering of the War Industries Board, with only advisory powers, was formed in early May, 1917,* and its immediate problem was the housing of 1 344 000 men by September of that year. Before contracting any project, the General Staff requested and recommended it, the Emergency Construction Committee of the War Industries Board recommended it and recommended a contractor with an alternate. The Director of Purchases approved the recommendation, and the Construction Division, if it concurred, had to obtain the Secretary of War's approval of the project and the contractor and obtain his authority to proceed with the construction. Under such regulations and restrictions, the possibility of favoritism in the selection of the best, available, qualified contractor and the possibility or probability of collusion or conspiracy between five independent Departments and Bureaus, to defraud our Government in the great crisis, is too remote for an informed or a straight-thinking mind to believe and as an Officer in the Construction Division of the Army, I was in an advantageous position to know.

The Construction Division of the Army, with its 1 429 commissioned officers in charge of 30 000 clerical employees and a maximum of 427 000 laborers and mechanics, was an independent Staff Corps, without relation to the Quartermaster's Corps or to the Corps of Engineers. Prior to the World War, with three officers and thirty civilians, Colonel I. W. Littell was in charge of the construction and repair work at the Regular Army Posts, which quartered 100 000 men. Upon his retirement as Brigadier General in 1917, after having worn himself out leading his organization through the successful completion of the first cantonment program, he was superseded by Brigadier-General R. C. Marshall, Jr., M. Am. Soc. C. E.

On April 6, 1917, war was declared and on April 12, 1917, the Secretary of War declared that an emergency existed within the meaning of the "Revised Statutes and other Statutes", which exempted war emergency expenditures from the necessity of advertising for bids, and the Secretary ordered that until further instructed such contracts would be so made. The immediate problem confronting the Government was the construction of sixteen National Army Camps within a period of three months for the housing and training of 660 000 men. Before the construction of these sixteen camps was well under way, the Division was directed to construct within two months sixteen additional tent camps for the National Guard with a capacity for 684 000 men, and to be ready for the first contingent in two weeks. The civilian engineers and construction leaders of the country realized that a staggering program confronted the Nation for the housing and training of men and for the construction of innumerable other war projects on which the destinies of the overseas forces must depend.

In addition to the construction of the thirty-two National Army and National Guard Camps, this vast building program involved the construction

* This Committee consisted of William A. Starrett, M. Am. Soc. C. E., *Chairman*, M. C. Tuttle, transferred to the Emergency Fleet Corporation in 1918 and replaced by Major Clair Foster, C. W. Lundoff, Assoc. M. Am. Soc. C. E., Frederick Law Olmstead, and William Kelly, Major, Corps of Engineers, U. S. A., M. Am. Soc. C. E., later transferred overseas and replaced by John Donlin, representing the American Federation of Labor, with the late Leonard Metcalf and George W. Fuller, Members, Am. Soc. C. E., constituting the Sub-Committee on Engineering.

of hospitals with 121 000 beds; of terminal ports requiring roads, railroads, docks, wharves, and piers; of interior storage warehouses at industrial centers; of proving grounds, arsenals, and plants for the manufacture and storage of powder, high explosives, acids, and gases; of flying fields for the Signal Corps and Division of Military Aeronautics; of mechanical repair shops for assembling and repairing of automobiles and trucks in connection with the mobile artillery for the Motor Transport Corps; and of embarkation facilities for the Transport Service; with numerous other projects of lesser magnitude.

The camp and building sites for these projects had not been selected, the topography of the ground was not known, the extent of the projects had not been determined. Sewerage, drainage, and water supply had to be provided and typical buildings had to be designed that could be adapted to the sites when selected. It was at once evident to the War Industries Board that a form of contract must be devised that would expedite construction and safeguard the Government's interest; that a supervisory, administrative Governmental organization must be set up; and that a nation-wide survey of the construction industry must be made in order to obtain the most competent organizations in the construction fields, as no department of the Government had any adequate, up-to-date information on the construction industry.

Within two weeks the War Industries Board had secured reliable information on 1 500 contracting companies in the United States, based on information from engineers, architects, and the contractors themselves, and nationally known civilian engineers and experienced men were summoned by wire to fill the important posts in the Emergency Organization.

Under the emergency form of contract, the Government was enabled to proceed with its building program before details were completed, to push the work at any speed desired on any project great or small, to change the plan or scope of the work at will, and to get it done for such a reasonable fee as to be beyond the criticism of any informed individual.

After the thirty-two camps and cantonments had been completed and the advisability of concentrating construction work under a single head had been demonstrated, the Secretary of War on October 5, 1917, ordered that all construction for every Bureau and Division of the War Department within the United States, would be done by the Construction Division. This involved a total cost of $1 200 000 000 for 581 separate projects, located in every State of the Union except Arizona. It was made possible by an emergency construction program based on three considerations—the emergency form of contract that protected the Government's interest and was fair; the Construction Division organization that acted as administrators; and the competent, experienced contracting organizations that served as executors.

Under the emergency form of contract the contractor was allowed the actual cost at the site of the project with no "overhead", to which was added a sliding scale fee, depending on the magnitude of the job. On a contract estimated at $100 000, or less, the fee was based on 10% of the estimated cost, the maximum upset fee in all cases being fixed in advance by the contract. On a project estimated at $10 000 000 his fee was based on 2½% of the estimated cost, and on a project estimated at $25 000 000 (of which there were several), his fee was based on 1% of the estimated cost, with a maximum upset fee fixed in advance by the contract.

In March, 1918, the Secretary of War appointed a Committee* to report on the methods of executing emergency work being done under the Construction Division. After careful consideration of the purchase and hire method, the lump sum contract, and the agency form of contract, the Committee reported unanimously in favor of the contract known as "cost of the work plus a sliding scale percentage with a maximum up-set fee" and further recommended that existing construction organizations be used for executing the work.

The complications in the construction industry arising from war conditions cannot be better illustrated than in the unfortunate experiences of the subway contractors of New York City. In the years 1914 to 1916, inclusive, 31 subway contracts were awarded on a unit price basis totaling $125 000 000. When war was declared, there remained $40 000 000 of unfinished work on these contracts. Nine suits for increased war costs on these contracts have been sustained and settlements have been made for $5 100 000, and six other suits are now pending (July, 1928). Out of twenty of these subway contractors who became heavily involved in losses incident to the war, eight are still engaged in construction work, seven have never recovered from their financial losses, and the other five have gone out of business.

It must be evident from such a record of losses and failures on these unit price subway contracts, due to increased war costs, that either the Construction Industry would have been wrecked or the Government would have been compelled to pay prices out of all reason had unit price contracts been adopted for the war emergency construction.

Each camp was a self-contained community with every modern facility for the comfort and health of the men and Camp Grant, at Rockford, Ill., costing $11 000 000 was typical. It had 1 600 separate buildings for quartering 43 000 men and 12 000 animals, with a hospital for 1 000 beds, and was ready to receive the incoming draft forces within 2⅓ months after construction was started. As fast as these camp facilities were completed, the Utilities Section of the Construction Division took charge of the upkeep and operation of the heating and lighting plants, the sewer and water systems, and the roads. Thus, the Army entered and occupied a completed city in working order, with an adequate fire protection system.

Provisions were made for supplying each of our men with 50 gal. of water per day and the animals with 15 gal., which exceeded the British, Belgian, Canadian, French, and German supplies by 80 per cent. The greatest care and sanitary precautions were exercised in the disposal of sewage and wastes by modern methods, so that not a single case of typhoid fever or other water-borne disease was traced by the Medical Corps to impurities of the camp water

* This Committee consisted of: A. N. Talbot, *Chairman*, then President, Am. Soc. C. E.; Charles T. Main, President, Am. Soc. Mech. Engrs.; E. W. Rice, President, Am. Inst. E. E.; John Laurence Mauran, President, Am. Inst. of Archts.; R. G. Rhett, President, Chamber of Commerce of the United States; Frederick L. Cranford, President, Associated Gen. Contrs. of America, Inc.; John R. Alpine, Representative, Am. Federation of Labor; and Oscar A. Reum, Representative, Bldg. Constr. Employers Assoc.

supplies. As evidence of the efficient measures taken for proper drainage, comfortable housing, adequate hospitals, mosquito control, sewage disposal, and pure water, it is noted in the Mexican War that the deaths from disease amounted to 110 per thousand men; in our Civil War, to 65 per thousand; and in the Spanish-American War to 26 per thousand. In July and August, 1918, when the camps and cantonments were in full operation, the death rate from disease was 2.8 per thousand, which was one-fortieth that of the Mexican War, less than one-twentieth that of the Civil War, one-tenth that of the Spanish-American War, and less than one-half the death rate for men of military age in civilian life. This was a remarkable record of splendid service by our sanitary and water supply engineers in the greatest emergency this country has ever known.

Hospitals to the number of 294 were provided at a cost of $128 000 000, with accommodations for 121 000 patients, 12 000 nurses, 4 000 doctors, and 34 000 enlisted men. For the Ordnance Department, 60 projects costing $175 000 000 were constructed, consisting of arsenals, ammunition storage plants, gas plants, industrial plants, and proving grounds. At Aberdeen, Md., the proving grounds had a plant for assembling gun carriages and artillery and the largest machine shop in the United States. The reservation contained 35 000 acres, with facilities for every conceivable test for guns and munitions; a bombing field; and a field of 4 000 acres with equipment and plant for the manufacture and testing of gas shells, which was known as the Edgewood Arsenal and cost $30 000 000. There were quarters at this plant for 12 000 men, with a gas-filling plant having a capacity of 120 000 loaded shells per day and facilities for the production of caustic soda, mustard gas, phosgene, and picric acid, on an enormous scale.

Among the larger projects built by the Construction Division and representing the best types of terminal port facilities, were the seven Army Supply Bases at Boston, Mass., Brooklyn, N. Y., Port Newark, N. J., Philadelphia, Pa., Norfolk, Va., Charleston, S. C., and New Orleans, La., at which were collected the vast stores for overseas shipment. They were connected by rail to the fourteen interior warehouses at industrial centers, such as Philadelphia, Pa., Baltimore, Md., New Cumberland, Pa., Pittsburgh, Pa., Schenectady, N. Y., Columbus, Ohio, Chicago, Ill., St. Louis, Mo., and Jeffersonville, Ind.

These Army Supply Bases were combinations of railroad terminal facilities, storehouses, and piers for transhipment by ocean-going vessels. The Brooklyn Army Base, of the multiple-story type and the largest one built, has three 8-story concrete warehouses connected with one open dock and three double deck piers, which provide loading or unloading berths for twelve 8 000-ton ships at a time, with the necessary railroad tracks and yards to facilitate operations. This project was completed in fifteen months at a cost of $30 000 000, and has a total net floor area of 113 acres. These seven Terminal Ports and fourteen interior warehouses have a combined storage floor space of 631 acres with an additional open-shed area of 50 acres. The docking space at the seven Terminal Ports is sufficient to berth 65 ships of 8 000-ton capacity at one time. Eight hundred and forty-four miles of railroad tracks and 1 061 miles of concrete roads serve these 21 projects, the total cost of which was $234 000 000.

In July, 1918, the War Department appointed a "Board of Review of Construction"* to advise on the methods and procedure for carrying on the war construction program and to investigate and report on the work which had already been done by the Construction Division and by all other Bureaus of the War Department. The Board worked for more than a year with its own engineers and assistants, had free access to Government and contractors' records, and visited personally more than fifty construction projects. It reported as follows:

"The Board finds that the use of this form of contract, as finally developed, was well justified and contributed to the success of the emergency program; that by its use, speed was obtained in war construction projects; and that it is probable that such work could not have been performed in the time available without it or its equivalent.

"The Board of Review endorses and commends the action of the War Department in placing its construction work under one Bureau, entirely separated from the combatant units of the army, conducted with a minimum of military control, according to modern business methods. The Board is of the opinion that such construction so placed was done with a remarkable speed, was superior in quality, was characterized by economy of design, and was as economically performed as the requirements of speed and other war conditions permitted. The facts ascertained and given in the accompanying report indicate that such construction performance contributed materially to the success of the army operations."

How well these engineers and constructors carried out a great emergency construction program, is set forth in the following extracts from the Secretary of War's Reports of November and December, 1917 and 1918, to the President of the United States:

"The assembling of an organization and the planning and execution of the work was undertaken with a view of accomplishing all that human ingenuity, engineering and construction skill could devise in the brief time available and involved construction work which was in itself, in view of the time limitation, an almost staggering task."

* * * * * * * * *

"The preparation of places for the training of the recruits thus brought into the service, was a task of unparalleled magnitude."

* * * * * * * * *

"In spite of the stupendous difficulties involved, the entire housing enterprise was completed on schedule time, consisting of one of the most remarkable accomplishments of the war."

Despoilers of Our Country

After all this the heart of our nation was saddened and our thoughts were mingled with hatred at the excesses and the indecencies of some of our politicians, the greatest menace to our Country and the most destructive agencies of our institutions.

It became politically expedient to discredit the War Administration, so Congress appointed the Graham Committee to investigate war expenditures. Three thousand pages of *ex parte* testimony were exhibited for public consump-

* This Board consisted of Francis G. Blossom, M. Am. Soc. C. E., of Sanderson and Porter, W. Saunders Davies, President, Am. Inst. of Accountants, and Charles A. Morse, M. Am. Soc. C. E., President, Am. Ry. Eng. Assoc., and Chf. Engr., C., R. I. & P. Ry.

tion at the October Criminal Term of the Supreme Court of the District of Columbia in 1922, and the Assistant Secretary of War, with the Chairman and five members of the Committee on Emergency Construction and Engineering, were indicted for conspiracy to defraud our Country in carrying out its war construction program. To quote in part from the Jury findings:

"* * * said conspirators procured said work to be done at great expense to the United States by civilian engineers and their assistants, and consulting engineers and town planners, selected by said conspirators at large fees and great expenditure of the public funds of the United States, the aggregate amount thereof to the grand jurors unknown, but which they charge was in excess of one million dollars."

Relating to the findings of the Talbot Committee:

"* * * At Washington, D. C., in said District, in aid of inducing and procuring the continuance of the system of cost-plus contracts, awarded without competitive bidding, said Defendant, William A. Starrett, about March 12, 1918, named and procured to be appointed by Defendant Benedict Crowell, as Acting Secretary of War, a committee, of which committee, certain members were interested in such contracts and system, ostensibly to investigate and report on the merits of said plan and system, which committee assembled on March 14, 1918, and reported on March 15, 1918, by adopting substantially as their report extended written statements and arguments made to them by said Defendant William A. Starrett and one Richard C. Marshall, Jr., then at the head of the Construction Division of the Army; to which report, as though it were a report of a thorough and impartial investigation, wide publicity was given."

Relating to the report of the Board of Review of Construction:

"* * * At Washington, D. C., in said District, about June 24, 1918, regardless of the interests of the United States, and in aid of procuring the indefinite continuance of the use of the cost-plus system of contracts without competitive bidding, said Defendants William A. Starrett and Clair Foster named and procured to be appointed by Defendant Benedict Crowell, as Assistant Secretary of War, a second committee composed of persons interested in said plan and system, ostensibly to investigate and report on said plan and system, and said conspirators then procured wide publicity to be given to such committee's report, as though said report was that of a disinterested and impartial investigation."

The Defendants entered demurrers to these criminal indictments and were sustained by Justice Hoehling, of the Supreme Court of the District of Columbia, in the following ruling:

"Accordingly, the Court is of the opinion, and so orders, that the demurrers filed herein be, and the same hereby severally are, sustained."

Civil suits amounting to $55 000 000 were brought against eleven of these cantonment contractors in 1922 by the Attorney General and, later, an additional suit was instituted, all charging a waste of public funds with the result that the men who built these cantonments, were without justification virtually and publicly branded as traitors. Many technical societies and similar organizations followed the lead of our Society and passed resolutions demanding of the Attorney General that he prove his allegations.

Primed with political chicanery and lacking in bills of particulars attempting to show how public funds had been squandered, only one of these suits ever reached a jury. Within 3 min. after the Court's charges were concluded, the Jury returned a verdict for the Defendant. The Attorney General did not subpœna the former responsible officers of the Government in his attempt to prove his charges, and the following former officers appeared for the Defendant: The Secretary of War; the Chief of the Construction Division of the Army; the Chairman and Consulting Engineer of the Committee on Emergency Construction and Engineering, and the Construction Quartermaster; the Supervising Engineer and the Supervising Auditor on the job.

Yet it was ten years after the cantonments were completed and five years after these suits were instituted when the administrator of the Department of Justice finally took action to dismiss the remaining eleven suits.

The criminal indictments of the Assistant Secretary of War and of the Committee on Emergency Construction and Engineering, the clearly implied charges of conspiracy against our outstanding and nationally known engineers, and the suits instituted against twelve of our competent cantonment contractors, indispensable in turning the tide of war, were brazen exhibits of political indecency and a slander on the patriotism of our people. The toleration of such conditions is a menace to our Country.

MEMOIRS OF DECEASED MEMBERS

DESMOND FITZ GERALD, Past-President, Am. Soc. C. E.*

Died September 22, 1926.

Desmond FitzGerald was born on May 20, 1846, at Nassau, New Providence, Bahama Islands. His father, an officer in the British Army, in which he attained the rank of Captain, was born at Turlough Park, in the western or northwestern part of Ireland, of Irish gentry. Desmond FitzGerald, in 1901, went to this region, enjoyed a pleasant visit with cousins and other relatives, and was able to trace his family back through several generations. The lands which had been long in the family retained several interesting ancient landmarks.

His maternal grandfather, a native of Scotland, had been Judge of the Court of Admiralty and President of His Majesty's Council at Nassau. His mother, although born in Nassau, came of Colonial stock and through her he was a descendant in the seventh generation from Roger Williams, a prominent figure in New England history, who, when banished from Massachusetts on account of his religious and political opinions, established the City of Providence, R. I., and the First Baptist Church there. He secured to Providence Plantations full power to rule themselves, and was the first Governor of Rhode Island. As late as 1923, Desmond FitzGerald owned several lots of land in Providence, part of a tract which was granted to Roger Williams and had never been out of the family.

Mr. FitzGerald thus had an unusually fine inheritance, and it is not to be wondered at that he was able to maintain an independence of action and to secure a freedom from improper interference with his duties as Engineer or Superintendent by members of committees or commissions whose experience was political rather than technical. His success in this way was so striking that it became the subject of comment.

In 1848, after the death of his grandfather, the family moved to Providence, where they lived for many years.

Mr. FitzGerald's early education was received in the public schools of Providence. He did not receive college training either in the arts or engineering. Following his Providence schooling, he spent a year studying art in France, as at that time he desired to become a sculptor. On his return to the United States he entered Phillips Academy, at Andover, N. H., from which he was graduated in 1864. At this fine Academy he evidently improved his opportunities to learn how to study and acquired the habit of thoroughness. After a short interval, and while still under age, he became Deputy Secretary of the State of Rhode Island, and, in 1866, was Private Secretary to General Burnside, then Governor of the State. During this period he found time to engage as "student" in the engineering office of Cushing and Dewitt.

* Memoir prepared by the following Committee: George F. Swain, Past-President, Am. Soc. C. E., and C. Frank Allen, M. Am. Soc. C. E., and William E. Foss, Esq.

Here, again, he was fortunate, or wise, for the Cushing office was for many years the leading engineering office in Providence.

In 1867, he was enterprising enough to start West to seek his fortune, first as Axeman on the Indiana and Vincennes Railroad. It has been stated that the fact that his stakes were better formed and better marked than was usual brought him to the notice of his Chief. A mastery of Henck's Field Book also gained him a desirable reputation, and within a year he became Locating Engineer. He was engaged on various railroads in the Middle West as Locating, Division, or Assistant Chief Engineer, and for a time was in the Federal employ on river improvement work.

In 1871, he returned to Boston, Mass., residing in Brookline where he lived until his death. He soon became Engineer of the Boston and Albany Railroad, accepting this position, which was none too well paid, in preference to a Government position on construction in Boston Harbor; also, in preference to a partnership in an architect's office. Much important construction work was in progress on this railroad, and Mr. FitzGerald, still a young man, was fortunate in having as Consulting Engineer the late Edward S. Philbrick, M. Am. Soc. C. E., upon whom he could rely in part.

His work on this railroad brought him in contact with the late Joseph P. Davis, M. Am. Soc. C. E. This led to his appointment as Superintendent of the Western Division of the Boston Water-Works, which included the Brookline and Chestnut Hill Reservoirs, Lake Cochituate and the connecting aqueduct, embracing substantially all the sources of supply of the city. This position he held from 1873 until 1898.

While in office as Superintendent, he was the active factor in overcoming a reluctance on the part of the City authorities (other than the City Attorney, who supported him) in bringing suit to secure elimination of pollution of the water supply, partly by manufacturing wastes and partly by municipal sewage. This was the case of Pegan Brook in Natick, Mass. Upon Mr. FitzGerald fell the task of securing evidence and tracing actual cases of pollution to their source. The case, perhaps the first of its kind in the United States, after seven years of litigation, resulted in a final decision by the Supreme Court of the State in favor of the City of Boston.

Desmond FitzGerald was the pioneer in the study of color in water and methods of reducing it, resulting in the draining of swampy lands within the water-shed contributing to the water supply, and also to take advantage of the sunlight in bleaching storage waters, as well as stripping top soil and humus from reservoir beds.

He was the first to establish a biological laboratory in connection with water supply and to study especially the bacteriology of water, employing the late George C. Whipple, M. Am. Soc. C. E., then a young graduate in civil engineering, to carry on that work. This was the first and for many years the only biological laboratory operated in this country in connection with a water-works system. He made other studies and investigations in hydraulic engineering, along lines closely connected with his work. His paper on

"Evaporation"* received the Norman Medal in 1887, and has recently been closely confirmed by laboratory experiments. A later paper, "Rainfall, Flow of Streams, and Storage",† also received the Norman Medal, this time in 1893. Other worthy papers along similar lines were presented by him before this and other societies. His studious habit of mind is well attested by these papers and his investigations while in the employ of the City or the later Commission.

When the old system of supply for Boston was absorbed under the newly created Metropolitan Water Board in 1898, its Chief Engineer, the late Frederic P. Stearns, Past-President, Am. Soc. C. E., retained Mr. FitzGerald as Engineer of the Sudbury Department. During his employment with this Board it was understood and provided that he was free to act as Consulting Engineer for other municipalities, and he was actively engaged in this outside work.

During his terms of service on the water supply of Boston he had charge, as Resident Engineer, of the construction of some of the most important storage reservoirs of the System.

In 1902 he resigned from the position which in one form or another he had held since 1873. Previous to this time he had been given leave of absence for six months in 1899 to become Consulting Engineer to the Chicago Drainage Canal, at a salary reputed to be the largest paid to any civil engineer up to that time.

Mr. FitzGerald was a member of a Commission under the Secretary of War, to investigate the Lydecker Tunnel, designed by the United States Corps of Engineers, and then under construction for the water supply of the City of Washington, D. C. The City of San Francisco, Calif., also employed him in connection with its water supply in the important matter known as the Hetch Hetchy case.

He served as Consulting Engineer on the water supply and sewerage of Manila, in the Philippines, involving many questions comparatively new in character. Incidentally he was of considerable assistance in connection with an important highway project there. Later, he was called as one of the experts for the Metropolitan Sewerage Commission of New York with relation to the proper standard of purity for the waters of New York Harbor.

He acted as Consulting Engineer for a considerable number of cities and towns in other States as well as in Massachusetts. He was also retained, and appeared as expert, in a number of noted water cases.

An invitation to become a Lowell Institute Lecturer in Boston is a recognized honor, and Desmond FitzGerald delivered four lectures in a course of twelve on Engineering, his subject being "Water-Works." That his record as a civil engineer was highly distinguished cannot be questioned.

He also set a high standard of public-spirited citizenship. For the Commonwealth of Massachusetts he served for several years as Chairman of the Topographical Survey Commission under the direction of which the New

* *Transactions*, Am. Soc. C. E., Vol. XV (1886), p. 581.

† *Loc. cit.*, Vol. XXVII (1892), p. 253.

York-Massachusetts State line was re-run. This was made difficult by the fact that the important State monuments had been forcibly removed and shifted far from their proper positions. The difficulty was overcome and the line, although at first rejected, was afterward accepted by the State of New York. The re-setting of town bounds also presented problems which were successfully met. He was an active and a valuable member of the Metropolitan Improvement Commission of Massachusetts, in which capacity he not only gave much attention to railroad problems, but also made a study and a report on foreign harbors.

In the Town of Brookline, where he made his home, Mr. FitzGerald was Chairman of the Park Commission from 1897 until his health made it advisable for him to retire in 1926. He was also President of the Civic Society of Brookline and was one of the Trustees of the Public Library from 1887 to 1926. He was one of the Trustees of the Walnut Hills Cemetery, under town control from its establishment in 1875. He and the two other members first appointed served continuously together for more than fifty years until his death.

When the Town Meeting became so large that a smaller representative body was elected, he was chosen as a member, and had much influence in its meetings. He was unusually effective in securing what he felt was needed in connection with his official interests even when considerable opposition was manifested. During the World War he drilled with the local unit, lectured on patriotism, and was otherwise active for the cause.

Not altogether from self-interest, Desmond FitzGerald was a member of many societies and semi-public bodies, not all of them professional; he gave as well as received.

He was, at the time of his death, third in seniority of service on the Corporation of the Massachusetts Institute of Technology, on which he was an active and influential member; a Fellow of the American Academy of Arts and Sciences; Fellow of the Royal Meteorological Society of England; an officer in the New England Meteorological Society; member of the Council of the Society of Colonial Wars, of the Massachusetts Society of Sons of the American Revolution, and of the New England Historical Genealogical Society, to which he contributed in 1911 a booklet showing much research as to his ancestry both in Ireland and the United States. He was also a member, and at one time Councillor (on Art), of the Appalachian Mountain Club, with the interests and activities of which he had a natural sympathy. In 1925, in his eightieth year, he spent the summer months in the mountains of the Pyrenees, traveling partly on foot, partly on mule-back.

Desmond FitzGerald was a lover of art. When eleven years old he went to Paris and spent a year there in school. His cousins with whom he resided were people of wealth and influence, and this, in connection with the opportunities which Paris afforded, may have had great influence on his taste for art and his love of it. He seemed then much interested in sculpture, but finally chose engineering as a career. He could undoubtedly have been an artist of note had he chosen that field. His circumstances as well as his taste and temperament, later in life, qualified him to become a patron of art as well as a connoisseur and critic, and in these combined capacities he was a leading figure around Boston. Dodge MacKnight, a brilliant water color artist, most highly regarded in Boston, received his first substantial recognition from Mr. FitzGerald, who not only led in public encouragement of the artist, but also acquired and owned three-score of his pictures, covering various stages of his development; and, in addition, he was the author of a monograph on Dodge MacKnight, privately printed and circulated.

Desmond FitzGerald also was among the first in this country to appreciate the early impressionist, Claude Monet, and others who followed in the same school. He was on terms of personal friendship with MacKnight and Monet, and also with John Singer Sargent.

To accommodate his paintings, he built an art gallery, 27 by 61 ft., adjoining his residence, which later proved all too small for his collection. This gallery was open to the public. He was a Trustee of the Boston Museum of Fine Arts. Following his death, the Trustees adopted the minute of which a part is as follows:

"By the death of Desmond FitzGerald on the twenty-second of September the Museum lost a friend who was deeply interested in its work. In 1916 he was appointed a member of the Board of Trustees by the Institute of Technology, a position which he held up to the time of his death. From 1914 he was a member of the Visiting Committee of the Department of Paintings, and for the last seven years of his life he served as its Chairman. He was affiliated with a great variety of institutions and commissions, and was more or less associated with all the societies that had to do with art in Boston. As a member of the Copley Society he was for years the Treasurer of the committee that had charge of its many memorable loan exhibitions; and he was always generous in lending his own pictures to those exhibitions, and in lending them to other exhibitions where he thought the public would have a chance to see and enjoy them. He had great sympathy with young painters, and he bought their work and did all that he could in other ways to help and encourage them. He was an extensive traveler and traveled intelligently, for he cared for the things he saw from the point of view of an artist as well as from that of an engineer. He loved Nature and even more he loved its pictorial representations, and in his museum in Brookline he had a remarkable collection of modern landscapes and other paintings, and some fine examples of Oriental pottery. He was an optimist enamored of the fine arts, and was kindly, courteous, and cheerful, for to him art was always a joyful inspiration—an inspiration that added greatly to his gaiety and happiness throughout his long and useful life."

Mr. FitzGerald was not without ability as an amateur artist, and his crayon portraits of members of his family were to be seen on his walls. He traveled much, and his artistic taste and his skill as a photographer resulted in several interesting illustrated lectures, mainly if not altogether to his friends, personal and professional.

His professional activities were constant. He was active in the revival of the Boston Society of Civil Engineers in 1873 and 1874, and was among the earliest of the younger men to be elected President. Later, he was elected an Honorary Member. For many years he had made a liberal annual contribution to the Society's permanent fund, and remembered it in his will. He also, in 1910, established a fund for the award of a bronze medal annually to the author of the best paper of the year; a medal of bronze which could be kept in sight, rather than of gold usually placed in a safe for protection, the honor rather than the value being the essential point.

Mr. FitzGerald had been President of the New England Water Works Association, and Honorary Member of the American Water Works Association, and was also a member of the American Institute of Consulting Engineers.

As President, Honorary Member, and twice Norman Medallist of the Society, he attained a unique distinction. His standing as an engineer is secure.

Of clubs, he had membership in the Union, St. Botolph, Boston Art, Engineers', and the Country Club of Brookline. At the time of his death he was Senior Warden of St. Paul's Protestant Episcopal Church, of Brookline.

Slight in stature, he had an abundance of physical and mental energy, and accomplished much in the various lines of his activities, and his genial presence supplemented his other fine qualities. As a public citizen, few gave more for the betterment of the community. In his love for art and its encouragement, and in his church work, he qualified in the finer things of life, artistic and spiritual.

Desmond FitzGerald was married in 1870 to Elizabeth E. C. Salisbury, and is survived by two daughters and two sons.

He was much more than a mere technical engineer. He was a broadly cultivated man with many points of contact outside of engineering. He was thoroughly human, not enclosed in a rigid shell of mathematics or technical detail. Great as he was in engineering, he could have been great in other fields. He was delightful as a companion and had hosts of friends, in the hearts of whom his passing will leave a void which can never be filled.

Mr. FitzGerald was elected a Member of the American Society of Civil Engineers on September 3, 1884, and an Honorary Member on October 15, 1923. He served as Director from 1892 to 1894, as Vice-President from 1895 to 1896, and as President in 1899.

JAMES EKIN ALLISON, M. Am. Soc. C. E.*

Died September 19, 1926.

James Ekin Allison was born at Xenia, Ohio, on May 10, 1865. He was the son of Matthew Corey Allison, a manufacturer at Xenia, and of Frances (Ekin) Allison. He attended the public schools of Xenia and prepared for Harvard University, at Andover, Mass. He received the degree of Bachelor of Arts at Harvard in 1887.

Mr. Allison's first professional experience was as Manager and Engineer of the Xenia Gas, Light and Coke Company, which position he held for two years. He left this work to become Manager and Chief Engineer of the Southern Manufacturing Company, at Nashville, Tenn. This and miscellaneous enterprises occupied his attention until the Spanish-American War, when he was appointed Captain and Adjutant of John Logan's Volunteer Illinois Cavalry.

From 1898 to 1907 Mr. Allison practiced as a Consulting Engineer in St. Louis, Mo. During this period he was employed by the Louisiana Purchase Exposition and invented the gates which were used at that Exposition, to record, at a central control office, the entrance of each person passing through them. In 1907, he became Head of the Department of Boilers and Elevators and Chairman of the Board of Engineers for St. Louis. He held this latter position until 1909, when he was appointed Commissioner and Chief Engineer of the St. Louis Public Service Commission, in which capacity he served until 1913. From 1913 until his death, he maintained an engineering office in St. Louis, where, as a Consulting Engineer, he specialized in public service valuation work. In this work he became very well known and was called upon by utilities and municipalities in all sections of the United States and Canada. Many of the largest utilities in the country came to him as clients, and among the municipalities were St. Louis, San Antonio, Tex., and New Orleans, La.

Mr. Allison held the principle that "reproduction new" costs should govern in finding the value of the physical items of a plant. His belief in this principle was founded on a deep and careful study of economics. He was an early and outstanding opponent of the theory of depreciation based on the so-called straight-line method.

He wrote many treatises and articles on valuation and other economic subjects. The most noteworthy of these are "Analysis of Rate Calculations" (1910); "Ethical and Economic Elements in Public Service Valuation" (1912); "Should Public Service Utilities Be Depreciated to Obtain Fair Value in Rate or Valuation Cases" (1912); "Rate of Return" (1914); "Criticism of Theoretical Depreciation" (1915); and "Theoretical Depreciation" (1917).

He held membership in a number of social clubs and learned societies. Among his other technical affiliations the following may be mentioned: Engineer's Club of St. Louis, American Institute of Consulting Engineers, and

* Memoir prepared by the following Committee of the St. Louis Section: Messrs. Edward Flad, *Chairman*, J. H. Porter, C. E. Smith, Members, Am. Soc. C. E., and H. J. Pfeifer, Esq.

American Society of Mechanical Engineers. He also was, for several years, a member of the Faculty of Washington University, at St. Louis.

Mr. Allison had an active and keenly analytical mind which delighted in discussions of abstract theories and the effort required to ally them with everyday practical problems. In his valuation work he strove to fasten all his methods to basic economic principles. His efforts were to establish methods whereby values could be ascertained that would be true in all cases, for the future as well as for the present. His forceful and attractive personality made many sincere and enduring friendships.

On October 15, 1895, he was married to Jeanie Bass, of Nashville, Tenn. He is survived by his widow and one child, Frances Allison Porter.

Mr. Allison was elected a Member of the American Society of Civil Engineers on October 1, 1913.

CHARLES IRVING ANDERSON, M. Am. Soc. C. E.*

Died June 15, 1927.

Charles Irving Anderson was born on July 27, 1878, at Fahlun, Sweden. While still a child he came to America with his parents, who settled in Georgetown, Colo., where Mr. Anderson attended the public schools. He received his technical training at the University of Colorado, at Boulder, Colo., from which he was graduated in May, 1905, with the degree of Bachelor of Science in Civil Engineering.

Mr. Anderson's experience in engineering work, as exemplified in mining and tunneling and the use of mining tools, began prior to the time he entered the University of Colorado. As early as 1898, he was engaged in mining operations and contracted for tunneling work, which contracts he fulfilled both before entering college and during his vacation periods as a student.

Immediately after his graduation in June, 1905, he took charge of a field party in the service of the U. S. Coast and Geodetic Survey. He continued in this work until he entered the Engineering Department of the Illinois Central Railroad System in November of that year, as Masonry Inspector on concrete bridge and retaining wall construction.

In June, 1909, Mr. Anderson left the employ of the Illinois Central Railroad Company to become Superintendent of Construction for shops then being built by George B. Swift Company, at Macon, Ga., for the Central of Georgia Railway Company, and, in March, 1910, he again changed employers to act as General Foreman for the Bates and Rogers Construction Company on the building of subways, retaining walls, conduits, and signal bridges in connection with its contract on the Passenger Terminal of the Chicago and North Western Railway Company, in Chicago, Ill.

In December, 1910, Mr. Anderson returned to the Illinois Central System and was engaged in engineering work with that Company until his death, with the exception of a short period from March 11 to September 30, 1918, when he was given a leave of absence to assist in the construction of the U. S. Government Explosives Plant C, at Nitro, W. Va.

His duties with the Illinois Central Railroad Company were in connection with construction, valuation, and special work relating to ordinances and other matters, sometimes of a technical and at other times of a diplomatic nature. His judgment in matters assigned to him for handling and solution was usually approved by his superiors without question.

At Nitro, his opinions were particularly sought, especially as to foundation conditions, although he was also in charge of roads, drainage, and building construction, subject to orders from the Director.

In the winter and early spring of 1926, Mr. Anderson's health began to fail quite noticeably, and it was thought that a change of climate might be of some benefit. Accordingly, in June, 1926, he was transferred, at his own request, from the position of Assistant Engineer of Buildings in Chicago to

* Memoir prepared by W. C. Pauli, Assoc. M. Am. Soc. C. E.

that of Assistant Engineer in charge of track elevation and new passenger facilities at Clarksdale, Miss., and he was so engaged when he was stricken with the illness which culminated in his death. This work, his final assignment, was practically completed at that time.

Mr. Anderson had the happy faculty of making loyal friends, but he also gave loyalty and friendship in prodigal fashion. He seemed to see the best side of a person's character, and was always ready to defend those he knew against attacks reflecting on their ability or integrity.

His life was marked by devotion to his family. Mrs. Anderson survives him, with six children, three sons and three daughters.

He was a member of the Tau Beta Pi Fraternity; Georgetown Lodge No. 12, A. F. and A. M., Georgetown, Colo.; Western Society of Engineers; Structural Engineers Association of Illinois; and the American Railway Engineering Association.

Mr. Anderson was elected a Member of the American Society of Civil Engineers on January 13, 1919.

WARREN MARTIN ARCHIBALD, M. Am. Soc. C. E.*

Died January 16, 1928.

Warren Martin Archibald, the son of Charles D. and Martha R. Archibald, was born in Medford, Mass., on August 25, 1876. After receiving his preliminary education, Mr. Archibald was registered from 1895 to 1899 as a Special Student at the Massachusetts Institute of Technology, at Cambridge, Mass. During the summers he was employed as Rodman for the New York and New England Railroad Company, and also for the City of Medford. After leaving college, he was engaged as Rodman and Instrumentman for the Metropolitan Water-Works, in Boston, and Clinton, Mass.

In 1900, he entered the employ of Ford, Bacon and Davis, Consulting Engineers of New York, N. Y., remaining with this firm until 1908. During this time he acted as Draftsman and Designer on street railway construction, in Atlanta, Ga., later taking full charge of lines, grades, and construction for one division of track work in Birmingham, Ala. Subsequently, he went to Kansas City, Mo., where he was engaged as Chief Designer of special track construction and Resident Engineer on tunnel reconstruction, in charge of the building of three bridges across the Kaw River. From 1904 to 1908, he was in charge of track and building construction for the Nashville Railway and Lighting Company, in Nashville, Tenn. This work included the design and construction, with Company forces, of steel and concrete structures for a fireproof car barn and terminal building, power-houses, bridges, etc., valued at $2 000 000.

In May, 1908, Mr. Archibald returned to New England, where he served as Resident Engineer on the construction of a 12-mile, high-pressure pipe line and temporary dam and intake, in New Britain, Conn. In 1909, he acted as Superintendent for the contractor on dam construction, in Russellville, Ark.

During the following two years he was again with the firm of Ford, Bacon, and Davis, as Resident Engineer in Houston, Tex., on the design and construction, with Company forces, of a new underground conduit system, complete, with the necessary sewers, manholes, paving, wires, transformers, poles, etc., for operating the entire system.

In 1911, Mr. Archibald was appointed Engineer of Maintenance of Way with the Houston Electric Company, at Houston, in full charge of all track and overhead line construction. This work included paving, drainage, and public relations as well as the usual track and overhead problems. He was also engaged in a consulting capacity with the Galveston-Houston Interurban Railway Company.

From June to September, 1917, he served as Superintendent of steam railroad track construction at Camp Travis, San Antonio, Tex., after which he again entered the employ of Ford, Bacon, and Davis, as Senior Engineer in charge of field and office work in the Report and Valuation Department. His work consisted of reports on public utilities, inclusive of all the States east

* Memoir prepared from information on file at Society Headquarters.

of the Rocky Mountains and foreign countries. These reports related to financing, rate cases, etc., and demanded a complete inspection of the properties as to their condition and maintenance as well as to the general business conditions in the immediate vicinity. During 1920, he was Assistant to the Chief Engineer on the report and design for a water supply system, sewer system, and sewage disposal for the Cities of Athens and Pireaus, Greece. He also made two trips into Honduras on valuation reports and the inspection of railroads and tram tracks, together with the shops and their equipment.

In 1924, Mr. Archibald resigned his position because of ill health caused by an attack of influenza some years before. He took a year's needed rest, and in June, 1925, entered the employ of Henry A. Symonds, M. Am. Soc. C. E., as Resident Engineer at Lynnfield, Mass. In 1926, he was appointed Assistant Engineer in the City Engineer's Office at Medford, and was made Acting City Engineer in December of that year. Just previous to his death, he had been told of his appointment as City Engineer.

He was a member of the Houston, Tex., Lodge of the Benevolent and Protective Order of Elks and of the Kiwanis Club and Mount Hermon Lodge, A. F. and A. M., of Medford. His church affiliations were Unitarian.

Mr. Archibald was quiet and unassuming, of a stern integrity, and always loyal to friend or employer. A former Chief Engineer, with whom he had been associated for several years, says of him,

"We have been through many a hard campaign together and no one knew better than I his sterling qualities as a man and his remarkable ability as an engineer".

He was never married, and is survived by his sister, Jennie S. Archibald, of Medford, Mass.

Mr. Archibald was elected a Member of the American Society of Civil Engineers on January 3, 1911.

THOMAS WILLIAMS BALDWIN, M. Am. Soc. C. E.*

Died September 29, 1926.

Thomas Williams Baldwin, the son of Thomas Williams and Margaret Josephine (Bacon) Baldwin, was born on December 27, 1849, at Bangor, Me., where his parents were then residing.

He was a descendant on his mother's side of Stephen Hopkins who came to America on the *Mayflower* and on his father's side of Thomas Cushing who was a member of the Continental Congress, as well as Acting Governor of Massachusetts in 1785, and of John Avery, Secretary of State in Massachusetts for several terms in Revolutionary times.

Mr. Baldwin prepared for college at Phillips Academy, Exeter, N. H., from which he was graduated in 1869. He was graduated at Harvard College in 1873, and, in 1874, entered the Junior Class of the Massachusetts Institute of Technology, from which he was graduated in 1876 with the degree of Bachelor of Science. During vacations in his college years he served as Rodman and Transitman on surveys for the European and North American, and the Bangor and Piscataquis Railroads.

In 1878, Mr. Baldwin opened an office in Bangor, Me., for the practice of his profession, and was Acting City Engineer until March, 1879, when he was elected City Engineer, which position he held until 1883. Declining further service in that office he accepted the position of Division Engineer on the Bangor and Piscataquis Railroad extension work, but retired after a few months' service on account of illness. Upon recovery he returned to private practice in his Bangor Office.

In 1895, he removed to Boothbay Harbor, Me., to engage in business and, in 1903, became President of the Baldwin Fish Company, which position he held until he removed to Boston, Mass., in 1908.

While in Boothbay Harbor Mr. Baldwin served for ten years on the School Committee, and was a Representative for two terms in the Maine Legislature. He was also a Director of the First National Bank and a Corporator of the Savings Bank of Boothbay Harbor.

On removing to Massachusetts, he became actively interested in genealogical research and published a genealogy of William Patten, who, in 1636, settled in Cambridge, Mass.; also one of Michael Bacon who was in Natick, Mass., in 1640. In addition, he edited and published with a memoir the "Revolutionary Journal" of Col. Jeduthan Baldwin, his great-grandfather. He also compiled and published the vital records of twenty-one Massachusetts cities and towns, a lasting monument to his patient and persevering labors.

Mr. Baldwin held minor positions with the Highway and Civil Service Commissions of Massachusetts, after taking up his work of compiling vital records, but the state of his health did not permit active practice of his profession.

* Memoir prepared by John Carroll Chase, M. Am. Soc. C. E

Although of a retiring disposition he always had a keen interest in people and in public events; and was patriotic, affectionate, and loyal. His liking for historical and genealogical matters made his later occupation very congenial to his tastes. In his more active years, he had traveled extensively throughout the United States and Canada.

Mr. Baldwin was a Life Member of the American Unitarian Association and was affiliated with the Republican party. He was also a member of the New England Historic Genealogical Society, the Sons of the American Revolution, and the Society of the Cincinnati.

After a short residence in Boston he lived in Wellesley, Cambridge, and Hardwick, Mass., where the end came after several years of failing health.

On December 8, 1880, he was married to Maud, daughter of John and Emeline (Young) Patten, of Bangor, who survives him, with two daughters, Mrs. Chalmers Stevens Clapp, of Abington, Mass., and Miss Dorothy Arno Baldwin, of Hardwick. He also leaves four grandchildren.

Mr. Baldwin was elected a Member of the American Society of Civil Engineers on April 2, 1884.

THOMAS HOWARD BARNES, M. Am. Soc. C. E.*

Died November 15, 1927.

Thomas Howard Barnes was born in Waltham, Mass., on December 15, 1860, the son of Phineas H. and Elizabeth Howard (Miles) Barnes. His childhood was spent on a farm and his early education was obtained in the public schools of Waltham. In 1877, he entered the Massachusetts Institute of Technology, with the Class of 1881, but lacked sufficient means to continue after the second year.

His first professional position was as an Assistant Engineer in the office of the City Engineer at Cambridge, Mass. After five years in this position, he returned to Waltham as Inspector of Plumbing for the Board of Health. He was also engaged in private practice as a Civil Engineer.

In 1887, Mr. Barnes went to Alabama to lay out and plan the Town of New Decatur. The following year he went to New Birmingham, Tex., where for four years he was employed in similar work.

After a brief period in the City Engineer's office, in Newton, Mass., he again engaged in private practice in Waltham. While there, he was appointed Engineer of the Medford, Mass., Sewerage Commission, in charge of the design and construction of the sewers of that city. This was followed by his appointment as the first City Engineer of Medford. In 1900, he resumed private practice, this time in Boston, Mass., where for the next four years he specialized chiefly in sewerage and water-works design and construction.

In 1904, Mr. Barnes made his first trip to tropical countries, in which field he was later to become an authority. His mission included the study and design of water supply and sewage disposal systems in the Cities of San José and Puerto Limon, Costa Rica. He then went to Bocas del Toro, Panama, to undertake the filling and sanitation of that port. The site of the town was a mangrove swamp, which made it necessary for all buildings to be erected on piles; elevated plank walks served as streets, and the ebb and flow of the tides was the sole and dubious means of sewage disposal. A sea-wall was built around this town, sewer pipes were laid, and sand, which had been dredged from the harbor bottom, was pumped in. Thus, the transformation from an unlivable jungle site to a healthy town was complete. Mr. Barnes later served as Engineer on other projects of a similar nature.

While engaged in the work at Bocas del Toro, Mr. Barnes was retained by the United Fruit Company to design and construct a wharf at Almirante, Panama, which town was the outlet for the banana trade from the Company's entire Changuinola Division. This wharf, it is believed, was the first to be built of reinforced concrete, and, until its completion and a thorough demonstration of its reliability, was a source of concern to many engineers and practical construction men. Time demonstrated the soundness of the design, and to-day the wharf stands as an example of resistance to deterioration under unfavorable tropical conditions. Other wharves of a similar type were

* Memoir prepared by C. MacCallum, Esq., New York, N. Y.

designed and built in various ports of Central America, many of them by Mr. Barnes, until he came to be recognized as an authority on tropical wharf construction.

From 1908 to 1913, Mr. Barnes served both the United Fruit Company and the International Railways of Central America. His work included the design and construction of wharves, hospitals, warehouses, office buildings, water-works, sewer plants, and other projects in Guatemala, Salvador, Honduras, Panama, Colombia, and Jamaica. From 1913 to 1918, he acted as Consulting Engineer for these two companies, with headquarters in New York, N. Y., with frequent trips to Central America and the West Indies.

In 1918, he re-entered private practice as a Consultant on Tropical Engineering. During the ensuing nine years, he served such companies as the International Railways of Central America, the Demerara Bauxite Company, the Cuyamel Fruit Company, and the International Products Corporation, as well as several of the large oil companies, and various Latin-American municipalities and governments. His more important work included a $3 000 000 beef-packing plant and dock facilities at Covenas, Colombia; hospital designs for Santo Domingo, Dominican Republic, Maracaibo, Venezuela, Cartagena, Colombia, and Puerto Cortés, Honduras; railroad shops in Salvador and Guatemala; wharf construction at Puerto Barrios, Guatemala; work for the American Legation at San Salvador; and a harbor and dock improvement project of great magnitude in Callao Harbor, Peru, on which he was engaged at the time of his death.

During his twenty-three years' practice in tropical engineering, Mr. Barnes visited virtually every country and every important town in Central America and the West Indies. His grasp of the human and economic, as well as the strictly technical, aspects of tropical problems, gained for him the respect of the many important companies which he served. Time and again, it was necessary first to plan and provide sanitary measures, living quarters, water and food supply, and to import labor and the most elementary building material, before actual work on the project in hand could be started.

His consideration for the physical and mental well-being of his employees, high and low, and his unswerving fairness and loyalty to them, won for him, not only respect, but unalloyed affection. His knowledge of the Spanish language and the Spanish temperament, combined with a singular mixture of uncompromising uprightness and firmness of purpose, and his realization of the devious circumlocution necessary in negotiating with Latin-Americans, commanded for him widespread respect and prestige, and a measure of personal affection seldom accorded a "gringo".

The following tribute comes from his Class, Massachusetts Institute of Technology, '81:

"Howard was one among us who seemed to have discovered the fountain of perpetual youth. His sturdy figure and pleasant smiling countenance underwent little apparent change as the years rolled by. Youthful enthusiasm and the joyful zest for living were undiminished, and whenever he returned from the South Countries—after long or short absence—he slipped into his accustomed seat by the fireside of our friendship, quite naturally and without undue commotion.

"And so—for all his friends, men who knew him for a generation, or for some shorter period—Howard has gone back to his Far Country, but the seat by the fireside shall be his always."

On April 30, 1890, Mr. Barnes was married to Martha Middleton Simmons, of Rusk, Tex., who with a son, Harold Simmons, of Upper Montclair, N. J., and a daughter, Eleanor, of Yonkers, N. Y., survives him.

Mr. Barnes was a member of the Boston Society of Civil Engineers; the New England Water Works Association; the American Water Works Association; the American Public Health Association; and the American Association of Port Authorities. His clubs were the following: The Technology Club of New York; the Park Hill (Yonkers) Community Club; the Whitehall Club; and the Surf Club, of Cartagena, Colombia. He was a Trustee of the Church of the Divine Paternity (Universalist), New York, N. Y., and was also a Mason. On numerous occasions, he contributed technical articles, which were of genuine merit, to the various engineering societies.

Mr. Barnes was elected a Member of the American Society of Civil Engineers on October 4, 1899.

CORNELIUS CONWAY FELTON BENT, M. Am. Soc. C. E.*

Died November 11, 1926.

Cornelius Conway Felton Bent was born in Boston, Mass., on July 3, 1849. He was the son of George Elbridge and Martha Conway (Felton) Bent, both natives of Massachusetts and descendants of old New England families of English extraction.

Mr. Bent was educated in the Latin School of Boston until his family moved to Philadelphia, Pa., where he entered Chase School, a private institution, from which he was graduated at the age of seventeen. Circumstances prevented him from following his ambition of attending Harvard University, of which his uncle, Cornelius Conway Felton, had been President at one time, and, in 1866, he entered the service of the Port Deposit and Perryville Railroad Company, in Maryland, as a Chainman. He continued with this Company until 1867 when he accepted a position with the Chester Creek Railroad Company, in Pennsylvania, having been, successively, Levelman and Transitman with this Company on location and construction work.

In 1869, Mr. Bent went West to become a Transitman on Location, and Engineer in Charge of Construction of the Lake Superior and Mississippi Railroad. He remained in the service of this Company until 1870, when he was appointed Chief Engineer of Location and Construction for the Lancaster Railroad Company, in Massachusetts. In 1875, he entered the service of the Pennsylvania Railroad Company as Assistant Supervisor and was promoted to be Supervisor in 1876. He remained with this Company until 1879, when he became Assistant Engineer for the Columbus, Chicago, and Indiana Central Railway Company, continuing with that Company until June, 1881.

At this point in his railroad career, Mr. Bent transferred his activities to the field of operation, holding, successively, the following positions: From June, 1881, to October, 1882, he served as Superintendent of the Chicago Division, of the Columbus, Chicago and Indiana Central Railway Company, and from October, 1882, to January, 1884, he was Superintendent of the New York and New England Railroad Company. From April, 1884, to October, 1885, he held the position of Superintendent of the Louisville, New Albany and Chicago Railroad Company, and from December, 1885, to 1889, he was Superintendent of the Ohio and Mississippi (now the Baltimore and Ohio) Railroad Company. Mr. Bent was engaged as General Superintendent of the Ohio and Mississippi Railroad Company from 1889 to February, 1894, when he was appointed Superintendent and General Agent of the Baltimore and Ohio Railroad Company at Philadelphia, where he remained until April, 1905.

From April, 1905, to January, 1907, he was General Superintendent of the Baltimore and Ohio Railroad Company at Baltimore, Md. In January, 1907, he was appointed General Manager and transferred to Cincinnati, Ohio, where he remained until July, 1910, when he was made Vice-President of the

* Memoir prepared by H. A. Lane, M. Am. Soc. C. E.

Staten Island Railway Company and General Superintendent of the Baltimore and Ohio Railroad Company, New York Division, at New York, N. Y. Mr. Bent held this position until January, 1916. In April, 1916, he was appointed General Agent of the Baltimore and Ohio Railroad Company, at Philadelphia, which position he held at the time of his death.

About eight years before his death, Mr. Bent was compelled to undergo a serious surgical operation which weakened him physically for the remainder of his life. His death resulted from pneumonia after an illness of only four days.

He was a man of sterling integrity, well liked by his associates and superiors, and famed for his justice and fairness to his subordinates. That he was also a man of great ability, is evidenced by his rise from one of the lowest to one of the highest positions in railroad service. He belonged to several New York and Philadelphia clubs.

Mr. Bent was elected a Member of the American Society of Civil Engineers on May 1, 1889.

CHARLES WALTER BRYAN, M. Am. Soc. C. E.*

Died June 25, 1927.

Charles Walter Bryan was born in Warren County, Missouri, on May 5, 1863. He was the second son of Archibald Bryan and Mary Elizabeth Sterigere, and a lineal descendant of Daniel Boone. The Bryan family came to Missouri about 1800 and were prominently identified in the early settlement of Kentucky and Missouri.

From 1869 to 1875, he attended private schools, and from 1875 to 1880 the public schools of Washington, Mo. During the summers from 1878 to 1880, Mr. Bryan worked on his father's steamboats, which carried supplies to the Upper Missouri and Yellowstone Rivers. During these trips as an Assistant Pilot he saw many phases of frontier life. In the fall of 1880 he entered Washington University, St. Louis, Mo., and was graduated therefrom with honor as a Civil Engineer in 1884. In 1905, Washington University conferred upon him the honorary degree of Master of Arts.

From July to November, 1884, Mr. Bryan was a Draftsman with the Pond Engineering Company, St. Louis. In November, 1884, he was called to the Edge Moor Iron Company, of Wilmington, Del., as a Draftsman by George H. Pegram, Past-President, Am. Soc. C. E., Chief Engineer. From November, 1885, to June, 1886, he was a Draftsman with the noted bridge engineer, the late C. Shaler Smith, M. Am. Soc. C. E., at St. Louis, and from June, 1886, to June, 1887, he was again a Draftsman with the Edge Moor Iron Company. From June to September, 1887, he was in the Bridge Department of the Missouri Pacific Railway, and, in September, 1887, he returned to the Edge Moor Iron Company as Engineer in charge of design and construction. During 1888, the Edge Moor Bridge Works was organized and Mr. Bryan continued his work with the new Company. He was appointed Chief Engineer in February, 1896, and retained this position until the Edge Moor Bridge Works was acquired by the American Bridge Company during 1900. At Edge Moor, he designed and had charge of the construction of the Wheeling Bridge, Wheeling Bridge and Terminal Railway; the Steubenville Bridge and Cincinnati Bridge, Pennsylvania Lines West; the Kenova Bridge, Norfolk and Western Railway; the Cincinnati Bridge, Cincinnati and Covington Suspension Bridge Company, and many other important structures.

During the Edge Moor period, Mr. Bryan developed unusual ability as a salesman, in addition to his skill in purely engineering work. The American Bridge Company appointed him as Agent, in the Railway Contracting Department, at Pittsburgh, Pa., and during 1901 he became Division Contracting Manager of the American Bridge Company of New York, at New York, N. Y. During 1906, he was appointed Chief Engineer of the American Bridge Company of New York, in addition to his duties as Division Contracting Manager. Early in 1911, he was relieved of his duties as Division Contracting Manager and appointed Chief Engineer of the American Bridge Company, which posi-

* Memoir prepared by Otis E. Hovey and C. G. Emil Larsson, Members, Am. Soc. C. E., and George H. Pegram, Past-President, Am. Soc. C. E.

tion he held at the time of his death. In this position Mr. Bryan was the executive and responsible head of the engineering organization of a large corporation engaged in the construction of bridges, buildings, and other structures in the United States and in many other countries. In addition to his engineering duties, he was frequently called upon for advice in matters relating to contracting.

Mr. Bryan was joint author with the late J. B. Johnson and F. E. Turneaure, Members, Am. Soc. C. E., of the well-known treatise, "Modern Framed Structures", first published in 1893.

He was one of the founders of the Huguenot Trust Company, in New Rochelle, N. Y., of which he was a Director and served as President from 1912 to 1915, and afterward as Chairman of the Board of Directors. He had also served on the Board of Education, the Board of Public Works, and the Park Commission of New Rochelle. He was one of the organizers of St. Paul's Protestant Episcopal Church, a Vestryman, and Chairman of the Building Committee.

"If a man die shall he live again?" It is generally believed that he will, and all agree that a man of such fine character as Mr. Bryan does live in his permanent influence for good. He was a gentle, modest, and friendly man whose qualities endeared him to all his friends and associates. He was considerate of the feelings and opinions of others, but had definite ideas of his own, and when it was necessary to insist upon them, he had a way of quietly leading one to his point of view in a shrewd and effective manner which left no sting of disappointment. His mind was keen and active, and he seemed to sense a situation almost by instinct. He had unusual ability to see another man's point of view, and it often seemed as if he penetrated hidden motives by intuition. He was gifted with a quaint and sparkling humor which made even a business interview with him a pleasure to be remembered. He had a genius for friendship in both business and social relationships. His friends were friends to the end, and there are many who will sadly miss the intimate associations of years.

In his earlier experience Mr. Bryan was largely occupied in the design of bridges. He had excellent technical ability and was accurate and very rapid in his work. His designs were marked by simplicity of construction and were well adapted to their economic use. In the later period, while Chief Engineer of the American Bridge Company, his executive responsibilities largely prevented him from undertaking actual designs. His work was rather to guide those associated with him toward better design and better methods of construction in the great number and variety of structures built by the Company. He was freely consulted by members of the Engineering Staff and by customers, their engineers, and others, and in this way his influence toward better engineering was greater and more widely felt than would have been possible if he had been engaged in private practice. He always sought for the best, and kept fully abreast and often in advance of the progress of engineering practice.

With his attainments as an engineer Mr. Bryan combined good business ability, and for many years his work was of a kind in which each was of equal importance. He quickly established cordial relations with customers, and they became and continued to be his friends.

Mr. Bryan's personal qualities, his ability, and his keenness of mind were such that his influence on his associates was strong, and was particularly stimulating to younger men, in whom he was much interested. Many applied to him for advice and guidance, and he gave freely of his time and thought in their behalf.

Mr. Bryan maintained a growing interest in his Alma Mater, and did much for its advancement. He was one of the founders of the Washington University Alumni Association in New York, and frequently served as its President.

He was a good citizen and, as such, was always interested in public questions and gave liberally of his time whenever he found a way to be of service to the communities in which he lived. His public service was unselfish and for the good of all and never for his own advancement.

One cannot write the sum of the influence of the life of such a man as Mr. Bryan; but one can be sure that it is great and will continue. The members of the Engineering Profession are fortunate to have been able to count him among their number, and will remember him as another of the great men who have finished their work and left a record which will be an inspiration to those who follow.

In 1889, Mr. Bryan was married to Mary Elizabeth Shaw, daughter of David and Ann Poole Shaw, of Philadelphia Pike, near Edge Moor, Del. He is survived by his widow and by his four children, Charles W. Bryan, Jr., of New York, Philip D. Bryan, of Albany, N. Y., Mrs. William F. Washburn, of Rochester, N. Y., and Mrs. Lowell Milligan, of Worcester, Mass.

He was a member of the American Iron and Steel Institute, the American Society for Testing Materials, and the St. Louis Engineers' Club. He was also a member of the New Rochelle Yacht Club, the Wykagyl Country Club, and the Engineers' Club and the Railroad Club, in New York.

Mr. Bryan was elected a Member of the American Society of Civil Engineers on June 3, 1903.

GEORGE ANSEL CARPENTER, M. Am. Soc. C. E.*

Died December 15, 1927.

George Ansel Carpenter, the son of George Albert and Lydia Clark (Gage) Carpenter, was born on March 4, 1864, in what later became the City of Pawtucket, R. I. He was educated in the public schools, having been graduated from the High School in 1883.

On leaving High School, Mr. Carpenter entered the employ of the late D. Lawrence Wilkinson, a Civil Engineer of Pawtucket, and remained with him until August, 1888. Mr. Wilkinson became City Engineer when Pawtucket was incorporated as a City in 1886 and Mr. Carpenter became his First Assistant. From August, 1888, to February, 1891, he was Chief Engineer for the Board of Sewer Commissioners of that portion of the Town of Lincoln, R. I., which shortly afterward became the City of Central Falls.

In February, 1891, Mr. Carpenter succeeded Mr. Wilkinson as City Engineer of Pawtucket and held this position continuously until his death, during a period of nearly thirty-seven years. The City of Pawtucket increased in population severalfold during this time and his re-appointment year after year, regardless of the changes in political administration, is a striking tribute to his ability and to the universal confidence which he inspired, both among the politicians of all parties and among his fellow citizens. As City Engineer, he designed and supervised the construction of highways, sewers, water-works, bridges, and other municipal structures, and was called on and expected to advise regarding a variety of problems covering almost the entire field of municipal activities, both engineering and non-engineering.

From April, 1899, to May, 1911, Mr. Carpenter was also Chief Engineer on investigations for grade-crossing elimination in the Cities of Pawtucket and Central Falls, in which work the late Edwin P. Dawley, M. Am Soc. C. E., acted as Consulting Engineer. His plans were finally adopted, and the work was completed in 1915.

The sewer system of Pawtucket was designed and built by Mr. Carpenter, as were also the major additions to the original water-works. In recent years, routing of street traffic, street widenings, and improvements better to accommodate motor vehicles, systems of street signals, etc., occupied his attention, with a resultant marked improvement in a difficult traffic problem.

Although Mr. Carpenter devoted his entire professional life to his native city, refusing to be attracted by offers of more alluring financial rewards elsewhere, his interests were broad and his acquaintanceship large.

He was a member of the Boston Society of Civil Engineers for 33 years and of the New England Water Works Association for 17 years, and was President of the latter at the time of his death. He was also a member of the American Society for Municipal Improvements for 22 years and was active in its work. He was one of a small group who, in 1915, organized the Providence Engineering Society. This Society, which had grown to a

* Memoir prepared by Francis B. Marsh and Frank E. Winsor, Members, Am. Soc. C. E.

membership of 1 200 before he died, owes much of its marked success to his wise counsel and sustained interest. He served as its President in 1918-19.

Mr. Carpenter was a Past Master of Union Lodge No. 10, A. F. and A. M., and a member of the Holy Sepulchre Commandery, Knights Templar, of Pawtucket, and of Palestine Temple, Nobles of the Mystic Shrine, of Providence. He was a member of the High Street Universalist Society, of which he was President for about 20 years, a member of the Board of Trustees of the Pawtucket Memorial Hospital, and a member of the Pawtucket Lions Club.

He was a keen analyst, with an unusual facility of expression, carrying his points clearly and forcibly, but so kindly as to disarm opposition and to leave no sting among those at variance with him. He was extremely modest, with friendly qualities which endeared him to a multitude of lifelong friends, as well as to the younger men of the profession who were so fortunate as to be associated with him. His native city owes him a debt of gratitude which is inestimable, and his influence in the community will continue to live after him and be an inspiration to those who follow.

On January 5, 1888, Mr. Carpenter was married to Jennie Smith Shepardson, of Pawtucket, who, with two daughters, Gladys Randall (Mrs. Norman R. Earle) and Margaret Allyn (Mrs. Raymond C. Newton), both of Pawtucket, survives him.

Mr. Carpenter was elected a Member of the American Society of Civil Engineers on May 7, 1902.

REDMOND STEPHEN COLNON, M. Am. Soc. C. E.*

DIED OCTOBER 9, 1927.

Redmond Stephen Colnon, the son of John W. and Harriet (Perkins) Colnon, was born at Brownville, N. Y., on June 29, 1862. After his preliminary education, Mr. Colnon entered Cornell University, at Ithaca, N. Y., from which he was graduated in 1887, with the degree of Civil Engineer.

Soon after his graduation from college, he was engaged as Assistant Engineer in the office of the late Emil Kuichling, M. Am. Soc. C. E., at Rochester, N. Y. In 1889, he became Assistant Engineer with Charles H. Ledlie, M. Am. Soc. C. E., of St. Louis, Mo., and, in 1890, occupied a similar position with the firm of Johnson and Flad, in charge of the construction of an inclined cable, at an estimated cost of $75 000, for the Western Railway Company. From 1892 to 1895, he was employed as Engineer with the Fruin-Bambrick Construction Company, General Contractors, in charge of an inshore tunnel on the water-works plant for St. Louis. From 1895 to 1900 he was engaged in various construction work.

In 1900, Mr. Colnon entered into partnership with Mr. Jeremiah Fruin under the firm name of Fruin and Colnon, General Contractors. With this corporation, his work included the construction of a warehouse for the St. Louis Transfer Company and a water intake plant for the Anheuser-Busch Brewing Association, as well as city paving and sewers for St. Louis and East St. Louis, Ill., and the building of new settling basins for the City Water-Works at Chain of Rocks, Mo.

In 1908, the Fruin-Colnon Contracting Company was organized. This Company specialized in public works, railroad contracting, etc., and, from 1912 until his death, Mr. Colnon served as its President.

He was a member of the St. Louis School Board from 1903 to 1909. He was appointed a member of the St. Louis Terminals Commission in 1905, and was a member of the St. Louis Library Board from 1926 to his death. He was also a Director and Vice President of the Missouri Portland Cement Company, and a Director of the Merchants Laclede National Bank, of the Scullin Steel Company, and of the St. Louis Frog and Switch Company.

Mr. Colnon was a member of the following social and fraternal organizations: The Noonday Club, the Racquet Club, the Circle Club, the Engineers' Club of St. Louis, the City Club, the Bellerive Country Club, the Sunset Hill Country Club, Theta Delta Chi Fraternity, Cornell University Alumni Association, and the St. Louis Council of the Knights of Columbus.

He was married on January 9, 1895, to Katherine Fruin, of St. Louis, who survives him.

Mr. Colnon was elected an Associate Member of the American Society of Civil Engineers on July 9, 1906, and a Member on July 12, 1926.

* Memoir prepared from information on file at Society Headquarters.

CHARLES GOBRECHT DARRACH, M. Am. Soc. C. E.*

Died June 1, 1927.

Charles Gobrecht Darrach, the son of William and Christiana Elizabeth (Gobrecht) Darrach, was born in Philadelphia, Pa., on September 8, 1846, and was of distinguished Colonial ancestry.

Mr. Darrach was graduated from the Philadelphia Central High School in 1866, and began his technical career as Assistant Engineer in the office of George W. Leuffer, Chief Engineer of the Philadelphia and North Branch Railway Survey, with whom he remained until 1867.

He held successively the following positions: In 1868, he was Assistant Engineer with the Reading Railroad Company and, during 1869, with the Jersey Shore, Pine Creek, and Buffalo Railroad Company. From 1870 to 1871, he served as Principal Assistant Engineer with the New Orleans and Selma Railroad Company; and, in 1871, he was employed as Locating Engineer with the Baltimore and Ohio Railroad Company, from Tiffin, Ohio, to Chicago, Ill. During 1872 and 1873, he was Assistant to the Chief Engineer of the Elizabethtown, Lexington, and Big Sandy Railroad Company (now the Chesapeake and Ohio Railroad Company); and from 1873 to 1875, Construction Engineer for the Reading Railroad Company.

In 1875, Mr. Darrach accepted the appointment of Principal Assistant Engineer of the Water Department of the City of Philadelphia, under Dr. William H. McFadden, and remained with the Department until 1885, when he became a member of the firm of Wilson Brothers and Company, Architects and Engineers. His work in this connection consisted in the design and construction of a large number of office buildings and institutions, among which were the Drexel Institute, the Reading Terminal, the United Gas Improvement Building, and the Fidelity Building, in Philadelphia. This construction covered a period of thirteen years. In 1888, Mr. Darrach also designed and constructed the Water-Works System in the Borough of Ridley Park, Delaware County, Pennsylvania.

In 1899, he engaged in private consulting practice which he continued about five years before his death which occurred on June 1, 1927, after an illness of several months. He was identified with much important appraisal work for railway and electric traction systems; made expert examinations and reports in legal cases; and prepared many reports, papers, and discussions on railways, public utilities, water and sewage purification, the mechanical installation for office and other large buildings, and the heating and ventilation of hospitals, etc. One of his most important contributions to engineering literature was his paper on "Mechanical Installation in the Modern Office Building".†

He also made reports on proposed improvements of port facilities and the betterment of water supply and sewage disposal in Philadelphia, and planned and constructed the water-works, drainage, and sewer systems for various

* Memoir prepared by J. W. Ledoux, M. Am. Soc. C. E.

† *Transactions*, Am. Soc. C. E., Vol. XLVIII (1902), p. 1.

towns, for the State Insane Asylum, at Wernersville, Pa., etc., as well as power plants, heating and ventilating systems, electric installations, etc., for large buildings in Philadelphia and elsewhere.

Mr. Darrach was a man of sterling integrity and, as a good citizen, was greatly interested in municipal matters, particularly those involving engineering problems. He had very strong religious convictions, which he practiced throughout his life.

He was the founder and first President of the Institute of Operating Engineers, a member of the American Geographical Society, and an Honorary Member of the American Association of Hospital Superintendents. He was also a member of St. James's Protestant Episcopal Church, of Philadelphia.

He was married, in 1876, to Martha Amy Elizabeth Tearne who survives him, together with three daughters, all of whom reside in or near Philadelphia, and two sons, Charles G. Darrach, Jr., of Los Angeles, Calif., and Walter T. Darrach, of Miami, Fla. He was a most affectionate husband and father.

Mr. Darrach was elected a Member of the American Society of Civil Engineers on January 5, 1876.

ROBERT FRANCIS EASTHAM, M. Am. Soc. C. E.*

Died February 10, 1926.

Robert Francis Eastham, the son of Virginia (Fisher) and F. Dabney Eastham, was born in Flint Hill, Va., on August 24, 1882. He was educated in the public schools of Virginia and at the Virginia Military Institute, Lexington, Va., and was graduated from the latter as a Civil Engineer in 1902.

Soon after his graduation, and for a period of about three years, Mr. Eastham was engaged by the Whitebreast Fuel Company, of Illinois, in making surveys for the development of mines in Illinois and Iowa. In the fall of 1905 and in 1906, he was employed as Engineer in charge of construction of 36 miles of electric railroad in Northern Illinois.

In June, 1907, Mr. Eastham decided to engage in Railroad Engineering and started with the Baltimore and Ohio Railroad Company as Instrumentman on the construction of its double-track work west of Pittsburgh, Pa. Later, in the same year, he was engaged with the Board of Supervising Engineers on the reconstruction of the Chicago, Ill., City Railways.

During 1908, Mr. Eastham was employed by the Grand Trunk Railroad Company in charge of the construction of its shops at Battle Creek, Mich. Afterward, he became General Superintendent of the General Contracting Company, of Toronto, Ont., Canada, and was engaged principally in paving and reinforced concrete construction. In March, 1909, he was employed as Assistant Engineer on the location of the Illinois Central Railroad from Birmingham, Ala., to Jackson, Tenn., and, later, was made Resident Engineer in charge of the reconstruction of the yards of that Company at Centralia, Ill.

In 1910, Mr. Eastham returned to his home in Virginia and became interested in the improvement of highways in Rappahannock County. Through this work he became interested in Highway Engineering as a profession, and immediately associated himself with the Virginia State Highway Commission as Resident Engineer in charge of the construction of highways in several places in the State during the next four and one-half years.

In October, 1914, he resigned his position with the Virginia State Highway Commission to become Highway Engineer with the United States Bureau of Public Roads. Soon after Congress established Federal Aid in road building for the States, Mr. Eastham was selected to have immediate charge of such work in Maryland and Delaware, which position he retained until his death.

Mr. Eastham was married on February 22, 1913, to Mary B. Browning, of Flint Hill, Va., who, with four children, Robert, William J., Lucy Beale, and Frances, survives him.

He was of a most agreeable, courteous, and kindly disposition, always cheerful, with nothing delighting him more than to hear a good anecdote and to relate one. He will be greatly missed by all those who were acquainted with him.

Mr. Eastham was elected a Member of the American Society of Civil Engineers on September 10, 1923.

* Memoir prepared by Vernon M. Peirce, M. Am. Soc. C. E.

GEORGE DANA EMERSON, M. Am. Soc. C. E.*

Died August 23, 1927.

George Dana Emerson was born at Wilmington, Del., on August 20, 1876, the son of Charles and Katherine (Hill) Emerson. His early boyhood was spent in Colorado where he received his preliminary education.

After graduation from the East Denver High School, Mr. Emerson entered the University of Colorado, where he remained for a period of two years before transferring to the Massachusetts Institute of Technology, at Boston, Mass., from which he was graduated in 1899.

His first employment was with the Edison Electric Illuminating Company, at Boston, in the making of surveys and preparation of plans for underground conduit construction. For a brief period he acted as Assistant to Howard A. Carson, Hon. M. Am. Soc. C. E., Consulting Engineer, in connection with some special studies for sewer systems.

Early in 1900 Mr. Emerson accepted employment with the Massachusetts Telephone and Telegraph Company, assuming charge of the survey and plan work involved in the installation of an underground conduit system for its lines in the City of Boston. Later, he supervised the construction of the works.

During 1901 and 1902 he was engaged by the Union Iron Works at San Francisco, Calif., on designs for various electrical and mechanical appliances.

In February, 1903, Mr. Emerson entered the employ of the Boston Transit Commission as a Special Engineering Assistant. For the first few years he was engaged chiefly in connection with experimental work, drafting, and designs for structures, ventilation, pumping plants, and miscellaneous features. He retained his connection with this service until December, 1917. During this period he filled many important assignments in connection with the development of the Rapid Transit System of the City of Boston.

In 1906 he was given charge of the difficult task of underpinning the Ames Building, at Washington and Court Streets, Boston, preparatory to the construction of Section 7 of the Washington Street Tunnel. This structure, built with walls of solid granite masonry, was at that time the heaviest building in the city. The methods adopted for re-supporting its massive exterior walls in order to permit the locating of the proposed tunnel immediately adjacent to the property line, at a considerable depth below the original footings, involved engineering and construction expedients of unusual ingenuity and novelty.

On the successful completion of this work Mr. Emerson was assigned to supervise the interior finish work of several of the Washington Street Tunnel Stations, and, in addition, the construction of the ventilation system of the Tunnel.

In 1909 he conducted the preliminary studies and prepared structural designs for a tunnel under Beacon Hill, which would extend the Cambridge Subway to a connection with the Boston Subway at Park and Tremont

* Memoir prepared by Charles R. Gow, M. Am. Soc. C. E.

Streets, and, subsequently he assumed charge of this construction. Later, in 1912, when this line was extended to Andrews Square, South Boston, he was assigned to supervise the greater part of the work. The most difficult undertaking involved in this extension was the construction of a sub-aqueous section of approximately 3 000 lin. ft., under Fort Point Channel, which was completed by the pneumatic process.

In the fall of 1917, Mr. Emerson was engaged for a brief period in connection with the building of Hog Island Shipyard. Early in 1918 he was employed by the firm of Fay, Spofford, and Thorndike, Consulting Engineers, in connection with the building of the Boston Army Supply Base where he exercised supervision over all construction work amounting in the aggregate to nearly $25 000 000.

On September 28, 1918, he was commissioned Captain in the United States Army and assigned as Assistant to the Constructing Quartermaster at the Boston Army Supply Base, in which position he served until February 20, 1919.

At the conclusion of his military service, Mr. Emerson retired from the active practice of his profession and made his home at Cocoanut Grove, Fla., devoting himself to fruit-growing and other local interests. For several years he served as a member of the Cocoanut Grove City Council and participated in many activities connected with the welfare and development of that community.

He was extremely fond of outdoor life, and spent considerable time in travel, mountain climbing, horseback riding, canoeing, and other forms of open-air exercise.

He was a member of the Florida Society of Civil Engineers, the Miami City Club, the Cocoanut Grove Community Club, the Appalachian Mountain Club, the Sierra Club, the Colorado Mountain Club, and the Mountaineers, of Seattle, Wash.

Mr. Emerson possessed a lovable personality. He was by nature somewhat quiet, reserved and conservative in manner, but extremely courteous and considerate in his treatment of others. He was uniformly just, generous, and tactful in the discharge of his responsibilities toward those with whom he had occasion to deal. He was admired alike, by his subordinates and superiors. His unusual sound sense, engineering knowledge, and rare good judgment elicited the highest praise from his associates, and from those whose activities he had occasion to supervise. Few engineers of his period possessed as fine a grasp of the essential principles of construction work. He had the rare ability of obtaining the highest quality of workmanship in all the undertakings assigned to him, without appearing to be unfairly exacting in his demands. His accomplishment in this regard stands as a worthy model, deserving of wide emulation.

He was married on January 7, 1911, at Somerville, Mass., to Mildred A. Avery, who survives him. He died very suddenly at Estes Park, Colo., on August 23, 1927.

Mr. Emerson was elected an Associate Member of the American Society of Civil Engineers on June 3, 1908, and a Member on April 14, 1919.

JOHN ERNST ERICSON, M. Am. Soc. C. E.*

Died April 16, 1927.

John Ernst Ericson was born in Upland, Sweden, on October 21, 1858, the son of Anders and Sophia (Lind) Ericson. He received his early education in the common schools, and in 1872 he entered the High School and College at Upsala, Sweden, which he attended until 1876, when he entered the Royal Polytechnic Institute at Stockholm, Sweden. He was graduated from this institution with the degree of Civil Engineer in 1880.

Mr. Ericson came to the United States in 1881, his first post of importance being that of Resident Engineer with the Toledo, Cincinnati and St. Louis Railroad Company, with headquarters at Cowden, Ill. He retained this position until the summer of 1882, when he accepted that of Bridge Designer with Hopkins and Company of St. Louis, Mo. In 1883, he was appointed Assistant on Government surveys in connection with the proposed enlargement of the Illinois and Mississippi River Canal and the construction of the Hennepin Canal. He had an important part in the making of the surveys on these projects as well as some share in outlining the entire plan.

In 1884 and during a part of 1885, he was a Draftsman in the Water Department of the City of Chicago, Ill. He became Assistant City Engineer of Chicago in 1885, and retained this position until 1889, when he was selected as Assistant Chief Engineer of the City of Seattle, Wash., to aid in developing the new gravity water-works system, which was then about to be built there.

In 1890, the Sanitary District of Chicago, the corporation which has control and supervision of the great Drainage Canal System, claimed the services of Mr. Ericson. He remained with the District until 1892, when he became Assistant Engineer in the Bureau of Engineering. In 1893, he was appointed First Assistant City Engineer of Chicago, and in 1897 was elevated to the post of City Engineer, which position he held until his death.

As First Assistant City Engineer and as City Engineer he was in charge of the design and construction of all additions to the water supply system of the city, projects involving the outlay of millions of dollars to provide water for the second greatest city in the United States.

As City Engineer, Mr. Ericson was also in charge of all bridge design, construction, and operation, and was called upon to give expert opinion on a multiplicity of engineering subjects connected with the many city betterments which are taken up every year by the City of Chicago in order to care for the increased business and living facilities necessitated by the rapidly spreading metropolis. Mr. Ericson had exceptional opportunities for experiments to determine the elements of flow of water in large tunnels, and presented an extensive treatise† on this subject to the Western Society of Engineers in 1911, for which he received the Society's medal. He also published

* Memoir prepared by Loren D. Gayton, Assoc. M. Am. Soc. C. E.

† "Investigations of Flow in Brick Lined Conduits," *Journal*, Western Soc. of Engrs., Vol. XVI, No. 8 (October, 1911), p. 657.

other papers and reports on water-works, paving, harbors, subways, etc., among which may be mentioned the following: "The Water Supply System of Chicago, Its Past, Present and Future"; "Report on Transportation Subways for Chicago"; "Report on Creosote Block Pavements"; and "Report on Public Water-Works".

He was President of the Swedish Engineers' Society of Chicago, and a member of the American Society of Mechanical Engineers, Western Society of Engineers, and the American Water Works Association.

Mr. Ericson was recognized as one of the leading authorities in the United States on city betterment, and as an engineer who successfully solved many of the great obstacles that beset the larger municipalities in devising systems of caring for their giant populations. Numerous structures and edifices stand to-day as monuments to his engineering ability.

He died on April 16, 1927, at the Presbyterian Hospital, in Chicago, after undergoing an operation. He is survived by his widow, Mrs. Esther Elizabeth Ericson, and a daughter, Mrs. Ralph Haven Quinlan.

Mr. Ericson was elected a Member of the American Society of Civil Engineers on May 7, 1902.

WILLIAM HENRY FINLEY, M. Am. Soc. C. E.*

Died March 17, 1926.

William Henry Finley was born near Delaware City, in New Castle County, Del., on January 22, 1862. His father, William Francis Finley, was born in County Galway, Ireland, and his mother, Mary Mortimer McDonough, was a native of Castle Bar, County Mayo, Ireland. His parents came to the United States in 1835, and settled in New York, N. Y., but later moved to a farm in Delaware where William was born.

When the boy was 13 years of age the family moved to Wilmington, Del., where he attended High School, finishing at the age of 16. He then secured employment with the *Delaware Gazette* as a printer's "devil". He did not remain long in this capacity, however, for at the end of four years he had become a journeyman printer. By this time he had concluded that the printer's trade was not to his liking.

Mr. Finley had a natural aptitude for mathematics and drawing and while working on the *Delaware Gazette* he began studying drafting at a night school. Subsequently, he entered the employ of the Edge Moor Iron Company as a blueprint boy, doing some tracing in his spare time. He continued to study at night, most of the time without an instructor, a fact that caused his associates to become interested in him and led them to assist him in his efforts to acquire an education.

The Edge Moor Iron Company had at that time one of the largest bridge shops in the United States and many large and notable structures were fabricated by it. Mr. Finley had the opportunity of seeing these structures designed and manufactured. While he was engaged with the Company, it was building the steel structural work for the Brooklyn Bridge, and he had a part in this work.

He remained with this Company until 1887, at which time he accepted a position with the Engineering Department of the Chicago, Milwaukee and St. Paul Railway Company, where his opportunities and responsibilities were greater. He was an indefatigable worker and took full advantage of the opportunities presented to him in this position with the result that, in 1892, although only 30 years of age, he was offered the position of Engineer of Bridges of the Chicago and North Western Railway System, then aggregating about 6 000 miles of lines. He accepted this position and, in 1901, was promoted to be Principal Assistant Engineer of that road. He left the employ of the Chicago and North Western Railway Company in 1905 to become Vice-President of the Widell-Finley Company, a contracting organization. After about a year with this Company he entered consulting engineering work.

However, in 1906, Mr. Finley returned to the Chicago and North Western Railway Company as Assistant Chief Engineer and, in 1913, was promoted to be Chief Engineer, which position he held until shortly after the railways were

* Memoir prepared by a Joint Committee of the Society and the Western Society of Engineers, consisting of E. T. Howson, *Chairman,* and I. F. Stern, Members, Am. Soc. C. E., G. W. Hand, Assoc. M. Am. Soc. C. E., and Charles F. Loweth, Past-President, Am. Soc. C. E.

taken over by the Government in 1918, when he was elected President of the Chicago and North Western Railway Company. In 1922, he was also elected President of the Chicago, St. Paul, Minneapolis and Omaha Railway Company. Because of failing health he resigned from these positions in 1925 with the intention of taking a rest for a year or more. The constant demands for advice and consultation, however, prevented him from realizing his intentions, and he finally opened an office as Consulting Engineer, in Chicago, in November, 1925. He died on March 17, 1926.

Mr. Finley was a great lover of the sea and as a boy spent much of his time about the shipbuilding works in Wilmington, gaining information which was of value to him in later years. As an illustration, when Bridge Engineer of the Chicago and North Western Railway Company he was confronted with the problem of replacing a drawbridge extending across the Chicago River at the entrance to the passenger station in that city. It was necessary to develop a method of erection which would not interfere with the operation of the structure it was to replace, while the track arrangement would not permit of it being placed anywhere except on the alignment of the old bridge. Drawing on the recollections of his boyhood days, Mr. Finley conceived the idea of erecting the new structure on ways on the bank of the river some distance from the site that it was to occupy and launching it as he had seen ships launched. This idea, while then novel to bridge builders in the West and regarded with no little skepticism by them, was successful as well as economical.

His later railroad connections were at a time when the railroad companies were rapidly expanding their lines and their engineering activities were extensive. Mr. Finley was connected therefore with a number of large engineering structures, including the Des Moines River Viaduct, at Boone, Iowa; several vertical lift bridges; the controlling of the channel of the Missouri River in the vicinity of several bridge crossings; and other equally important projects. To all of these he contributed largely and efficiently. He was one of the pioneers in the development of the rocker-bearing to take care of expansion in steel structures and his efforts in connection with cylinder piers in bridge foundation work did much to bring this form of construction into more general use.

Although Mr. Finley never had the opportunity to attend a technical school or college, he was always of the opinion that they were of great value and preferred to select his assistants from among the ranks of engineers who had been graduated from college. He possessed and applied a large measure of energy and had great strength of purpose, coupled with an abundance of initiative. Throughout his life he laid great stress on the necessity for the development of initiative and originality. One of his earlier associates writes of him:

"I first met Mr. Finley when I went to Edge Moor as a Draftsman during September, 1886. He had then been in the office for some time and was probably the best Draftsman in the office as far as neat and rapid production was concerned. As he had not had the advantage of a technical education, he was not versed in the methods of stress calculation and design. For some months

I observed that he seemed to think that there was little prospect of substantial advancement for him. My roommate and I easily induced him to take up more advanced studies of immediate interest to his work and he spent many evenings in our room, studying and talking about theory and design. I believe that previous to this period he had been studying mathematics alone and with some instruction from others. I remember those evenings with great pleasure, for his personal charm won our affections, and he was unusually quick to understand things then new to him."

A man of broad human sympathies, Mr. Finley was ever interested in the activities of his fellow men. It overflowed the limits of his own professional activities, but did not stand in the way of his giving to the organized efforts of his own chosen profession a very large measure of his time and interest. He was, therefore, active and helpful in the affairs of engineering societies in which he held membership, and his contributions in that respect were notable.

Mr. Finley became a member of the Western Society of Engineers in 1894, was made Second Vice-President in 1900, First Vice-President in 1901, and President in 1902. In addition, he served on a number of its important committees, contributed several notable papers, and frequently discussed constructively papers submitted by other members. He was also an interested member of this Society, and at the time of his death was serving his second term as its representative on the Washington Award Commission. He was for many years a member of the American Railway Engineering Association and had contributed to its technical work. He became interested in the American Association of Engineers early in its formation and was its President in 1918 and 1919 when his wise and sympathetic counsel were of great benefit.

On March 8, 1883, Mr. Finley was married to Sarah H. Ferré, at Philadelphia, Pa., who, with four children, three sons and one daughter, survives him.

Mr. Finley was elected a Member of the American Society of Civil Engineers on February 4, 1903.

FRANCIS CLARKE GAMBLE, M. Am. Soc. C. E.*

Died November 13, 1926.

Francis Clarke Gamble, the son of Clarke Gamble, and Harriet Eliza (Boulton) Gamble, was born in Toronto, Ont., Canada, on October 23, 1848. As a boy he was educated in the public schools of that city, after which he attended Upper Canada College, where he received his primary education, later continuing his studies under private tuition. After four years of practice in field engineering on the Intercolonial Railway and the Great Northern Railway of Canada, Mr. Gamble entered Rensselaer Polytechnic Institute, Troy, N. Y., where for a year or more he took a special course. It was there that the writer first met him and, being fellow countrymen, a close friendship soon developed, that endured for more than half a century.

At Rensselaer, Mr. Gamble, being a special student, thus belonging to no particular class, and being several years older than most of the other students, did not become widely acquainted; but he was well liked by all who knew him intimately. In selecting his studies he chose those that were mainly of a utilitarian character, especially those that bore on his adopted specialty of railroading. That he probably made a wise selection is shown by the success he achieved in after life; for not only did he hold high positions in railroading in Canada, but he was also elected President of the Canadian Society of Civil Engineers (now the Engineering Institute of Canada).

After leaving Rensselaer, Mr. Gamble worked for a short time as Contractor's Engineer on the Prince Edward Island Railway, then returned to the Intercolonial Railway Company as Engineer in charge of ballasting. His next position was as Transitman on the Georgian Bay Branch of the Canadian Pacific Railway, and late in 1877, he served as Assistant Engineer of Construction on the Quebec, Montreal, and Ottawa Railway. He then returned to the Canadian Pacific Railway Company as First Assistant Engineer on Contracts Nos. 42 and 62.

In the spring of 1881, he entered the Department of Public Works of the Dominion Government in British Columbia; and, in 1889, he became Resident Engineer in that Department, having in charge all harbor and river improvement and the erection of public buildings. It was not long before he was placed in full charge of all public works under the Dominion Government in the Province of British Columbia.

In 1897, Mr. Gamble was engaged in private practice; and in 1898, he was appointed Public Works Engineer for the Provincial Government of British Columbia, becoming, in 1910, Chief Engineer of the Department of Railways for the Province, which position he held until 1918, when he retired from active practice. He continued to reside in Victoria until his death.

He took a great interest in the affairs of the Engineering Institute of Canada, of which he became a member in January, 1887. He was elected a

* Memoir prepared by J. A. L. Waddell, M. Am. Soc. C. E.

Member of Council in 1892 and again in 1898. In 1913 and 1914, he was Vice-President, and, in 1915, he became President. He was also a member of the Institution of Civil Engineers of Great Britain.

Within the profession and in all walks of life Mr. Gamble was held in the highest esteem by all with whom he came in contact. He was a man of the strictest integrity, and was always governed in his actions by the loftiest ethical principles and ideals. He was recognized throughout the Dominion as a high authority on the various professional works to which his energies were devoted.

He is survived by his only son, Clarke W. Gamble, of Cairo, Ill.

Mr. Gamble was elected a Member of the American Society of Civil Engineers on April 1, 1891.

HUBERT EDWARD GREEN, M. Am. Soc. C. E.*

Died September 7, 1927.

Hubert Edward Green was born at Edgbaston, Warwickshire, England, on August 17, 1859. He received his grammar school and college education in Auckland, New Zealand.

From 1874 to 1884, Mr. Green was with the Public Works Department of the New Zealand Government, on the construction of its railway system. In June, 1880, he was appointed Overseer, in charge of wharf building, and of road and bridge repairs, and in July, 1882, he was made Office and Field Assistant.

In 1884, Mr. Green came to the United States, and from February of that year until September, 1886, he served as Construction Engineer for the Sierra and Mohawk Valley Railway Company, a narrow-gauge line running west into California from a point about 30 miles north of Reno, Nev. During the following two years, he was in charge of the City Engineer's office at San Diego, Calif.

In 1888, Mr. Green entered the employ of the International Company of Mexico, with headquarters at Ensenada, Lower California, and made explorations to classify land over the Company's concession of 18 000 000 acres. He was engaged as head of the Railroad Engineering Corps and was employed on a railway survey from San Quintin to Yuma, Ariz., branching at Real del Castillo to San Diego. Considerable difficulty was experienced due to scarcity of water and transportation over the heavy sands through the Cocopo Desert and the intense heat.

Returning to the United States in 1890, he had charge of the construction of the railroad trestle across Elliott Bay, for the Seattle Terminal Railway Company. In February, 1891, he served on a location and canal survey for the Lands Department of the Northern Pacific Railway Company, between North Yakima and Prosser, Wash. He was also engaged from 1891 to 1893 on the location of railroad lines in Texas for the Atchison, Topeka and Santa Fé Railroad Company from Conroe, Tex., to the Trinity River. In July, 1893, he was placed in charge of levels, with the Imperial Valley and Colorado River Irrigation Company, under C. R. Rockwood, Chief Engineer.

From 1893 to 1896 Mr. Green was with the San Diego City and County and Coronado Beach Company, superintending the laying of the foundation of the Morena Dam, which extended 100 ft. below the stream bed. During 1897 and 1898 he was engaged in placer mining in British Columbia and in the general practice of civil engineering in San Francisco, Calif. In 1899, he was employed on the construction of electric railroads in Los Angeles, Calif., and from 1900 to 1902, he acted as Field Assistant for the United States Geological Survey.

During 1902 and 1903 Mr. Green served as Assistant to J. B. Lippincott, M. Am. Soc. C. E., in charge of surveys, estimates, and designs for pipe lines

* Memoir prepared by M. M. O'Shaughnessy, M. Am. Soc. C. E.

for the Seaside Water Company, of Long Beach, Calif. While engaged in this capacity, he made divisional surveys of the Hetch Hetchy Valley and Lake Eleanor Reservoir sites for the City of San Francisco.

On May 4, 1903, he was appointed Designing Engineer of the United States Reclamation Service, in charge of the construction of the Belle Forche Diversion Dam. He held this position until his resignation in 1907. From 1907 to 1910, he designed and built irrigation works for La Sierra Heights, at Riverside, Calif.

During 1910 and 1911 he was employed by the Mountain Power Company, of Crescent City, Calif., in making surveys and designs for the power dam on the Smith River, and from 1912 until his death, he acted as Chief Engineer for the Compañia Constructora Richardson, at Esperanza, Sonora, Mexico, where he died on September 7, 1927.

Mr. Green was a man of sterling character and ability, modest and retiring, the reason, perhaps, why he did not occupy as conspicuous a position as his abilities warranted. He will be greatly missed by his many engineering friends in California.

It was the writer's pleasure, as a young man, to work under Mr. Green on the construction of the Sierra Valley and Mohawk Railway, in Plumas County, California, in 1885. He then learned to have great respect for his keen knowledge as an engineer. Since that time, during a period of forty years, he had had many friendly experiences with him. He was possessed of great patience, but was firm in his decisions, as was illustrated by the difficulties he overcame in laying the foundation of the core of the Morena Dam, when he was representing the City of San Diego. At this time he encountered opposition from ignorant foremen who wished to use inferior concrete, which course Mr. Green, with his careful engineering training, resisted.

Mr. Green was twice married, first, to a young woman from San Francisco, who died in 1907, and, subsequently, to a New Zealand friend of his youth, who survives him.

Mr. Green was elected a Member of the American Society of Civil Engineers on December 2, 1903.

HENRY STEVENS HAINES, M. Am. Soc. C. E.*

Died November 3, 1923.

Henry Stevens Haines was a descendant of Deacon Samuel Haines who settled in New Hampshire in 1632. His father, Henry Stevens Haines, had established himself in Wilmington, N. C. His mother was a member of the old Coffin family of Nantucket Island, Mass., and it was during a visit to her mother's home there that Henry Stevens Haines was born, on November 21, 1836.

After the discovery of gold in California his father sent a cargo of building material and partly constructed houses around Cape Horn to San Francisco, Calif., but he himself went by way of the Isthmus of Panama, stopping long enough to accept and complete a contract for cross-ties for the Isthmian road, then under construction. In the California venture he was very successful and was about to return to his home in Wilmington, when he died suddenly of smallpox, leaving his widow with four young sons, of whom Henry Stevens Haines was the eldest.

The boy had a keen mind and a retentive memory. He was taught by two masters in schools, one in Massachusetts and the other in North Carolina. He never went to college, but became a student of men and affairs, a first-class mathematician and geographer, with a good working knowledge of four languages.

Mr. Haines' first connection with railway service was in 1853 or 1854 when he was employed by the Wilmington and Manchester Railroad Company of North Carolina. His next work was with the North Eastern Railroad Company in North Carolina and South Carolina, in the machine shops and as Locomotive Engineer.

When the Civil War began, he was Assistant Engineer on the construction of the Charleston and Savannah Railroad. With his three brothers, he enlisted in the Confederate Army, but soon was returned to railroad construction where he could be of more service, the railroads being most important to the Confederacy. He completed several bridges and other structures in his district and in the course of his work witnessed many battles and was under fire on various occasions. When Charleston, S. C., fell, he was in charge of the transportation of the retreating Southern forces.

After the war, in 1866, Colonel Haines was appointed General Superintendent of the Atlantic and Gulf Railroad which, in common with Southern railroads at that time, was deficient in equipment and was in a bad financial condition. This line extended from Savannah to Thomasville, Ga. From it, however, Colonel Haines developed the Savannah, Florida, and Western Railroad, which, together with the Charleston and Savannah Railroad, became one of the important systems of the South. He later extended the line through Florida to Tampa, with steamers to Key West and Cuba. With the Alabama, Midland, and Montgomery Railroad, these lines comprised the

* Memoir prepared by Charles O. Haines, Esq., Norfolk, Va.

Plant System, of which Colonel Haines was General Manager and Vice-President from 1882 to 1895.

During these years, Colonel Haines and his wife, Elizabeth Owens, of Charleston, made their home for a time in Charleston and, later, in Savannah. They had six children, of whom only two sons survive him. During his long residence in Savannah, Colonel Haines was active in both City and State affairs whether working in the midst of a yellow fever epidemic or promoting the building of the Georgia School of Technology.

During the last years of his connection with the Plant System, he moved to New York, N. Y. By this time he had long been known as an experienced railroad executive. Largely through his efforts the American Railway Association had been organized, of which he served several terms as President. Colonel Haines was one of the first members of the Southern Society in New York. He was also a member of the Engineers' Club of New York and had served as one of its Vice-Presidents. He and his associates initiated standard time and the standardization of tracks throughout the South.

In 1895, the American Railway Association sent him to England as its representative at the first International Railroad Congress, where his speeches and addresses attracted wide attention. On his return from Europe in the autumn of 1895, Colonel Haines severed his connection with the Plant System to become Commissioner of the Southern States Freight Association, with headquarters in Atlanta, Ga. His wife died in December of that year. He held this office for about two years, when he resigned to travel abroad.

After his return to this country, Colonel Haines was married to Anna Davies, of Detroit, Mich., the daughter of the Bishop of the Protestant Episcopal Diocese of Detroit, who, with their two sons, survives him. For a short time after his return, Colonel Haines was Vice-President of the Atlantic and Danville Railroad Company. While living abroad some years later, he was appointed by the American Government as its representative at the International Railroad Congress held in Berne, Switzerland.

He retired from active business, however, in 1900, and after spending several years in travel, settled with his wife's people in Springfield, Mass., with a summer home at Lenox, Mass., where he died on November 3, 1923.

Colonel Haines' theory of railroad management was based on the delegation of authority as far as possible, but with the proviso that responsibility should rest on the chief operating official. He was of an eminently judicial turn of mind and just in his relations with other men. He was fond of people, always seeking to bring out their best qualities, was never overcritical, and was anxious that all subordinates or business associates should receive every possible acknowledgment of their efficient co-operation or assistance in the successful operation of the railroads entrusted to his care.

His interest in the welfare of the railway employees led to the organization of the Employees' Mutual Relief Association, a benefit and insurance society, and of the Co-Operative Store. In the latter not only were dividends paid to the stockholders, but there was a division of profits at certain fiscal periods.

At the suggestion of a member of his family, Colonel Haines collected his various addresses and published them, with some re-arrangement, in a book entitled, "American Railway Management". It met with a sufficient demand for him to continue writing on various phases of railway problems, and he wrote continuously until his death. His other works are, "Railway Corporations as Public Servants", "Problems in Railroad Regulation", and "Efficient Railroad Operation".

His was a successful life in its truest sense; his work was well done, and those who were associated with him became his friends and remained so to the end.

Colonel Haines was elected a Member of the American Society of Civil Engineers on November 2, 1887. He served as Director of the Society from 1897 to 1899 and as Vice-President from 1901 to 1902.

EDWARD AUGUSTUS WHITE HAMMATT, M. Am. Soc. C. E.*

Died March 18, 1927.

Edward Augustus White Hammatt, the son of Samuel Parkman and Maria (White) Hammatt, was born in that part of West Cambridge, Mass., that is now Belmont, on September 30, 1854, and received his early education in the public schools of that place. Later, he entered the Massachusetts Institute of Technology at Boston, Mass., from which he was graduated in the Class of 1875.

After his graduation, Mr. Hammatt was employed as Rodman on a preliminary railroad survey, and, subsequently, as Rodman on the construction of the water-works, at Newton, Mass., until he became Assistant Engineer with the late J. P. Frizell, M. Am. Soc. C. E., in 1876. The following year he was engaged in miscellaneous work, and, in 1878, was appointed Draftsman on the water-works at Lewiston, Me., and, later, as Assistant Engineer with the New York and New England Railroad Company. During 1879 he served as Draftsman for the American Tool and Machine Company, and also for the Boston Bridge Works, and, in 1880, he became Assistant Engineer in the office of the Proprietors of Locks and Canals on the Merrimac River, at Lowell, Mass. During the following three years he was employed as Chief Assistant Engineer with the late M. M. Tidd, M. Am. Soc. C. E., on water-works construction at Marlboro, Hudson, Weymouth, Holbrook, Randolph, and Hyde Park, Mass., and at Gardiner, Me.

In 1883, Mr. Hammatt opened an office in Boston, Mass., where he engaged in private practice as a Civil Engineer. In addition to the regular work coming to such an office, of which he took charge, he designed and built several sewer systems, and did considerable topographical and hydrographical work for power development projects. In 1891, he opened a branch office in Hyde Park, where he was engaged in the engineering work of the city.

In 1906, he went with Charles T. Main, M. Am. Soc. C. E., and a party of engineers on an expedition to the Arros River, in Mexico. Their object was to investigate a hydro-electric development project for furnishing electric current to mining camps in Northern Mexico and in Arizona, and to select a site for a dam, head-house, and similar structures. Mr. Hammatt was left in charge, and remained there for about a month, doing, what he termed later, the hardest piece of work he ever attempted. He found numerous dam sites with heads varying from 70 to 285 ft. Owing, however, to lack of provisions, time, and the great expense entailed, the project was temporarily abandoned, and Mr. Hammatt returned to Hyde Park.

In 1912 he removed to Newton Center, and, in 1916, to South Orleans, Mass., where he continued his private practice as Civil and Hydraulic Engineer until his death.

He was married on October 16, 1882, to Mary Louise Fifield, who, with four children, Richard Fox, Francis Parkman, Robert Wallace, and Alice Louise, survives him.

* Memoir prepared by George Bowers and E. S. Dorr, Members, Am. Soc. C. E.

Mr. Hammatt had served as Secretary-Treasurer and Historian of the Class of 1875 of the Massachusetts Institute of Technology for forty-two years. He was a member of the Boston Society of Civil Engineers, the New England Water Works Association, and the Masonic Fraternity.

He was one of the kindest of men, a friend on whom one could always rely, unobtrusive in character, his life was one of faithful service. As an engineer he ranked high, loving his profession and serving it to the last.

Mr. Hammatt was elected a Member of the American Society of Civil Engineers on June 5, 1901.

GEORGE ALEC HARWOOD, M. Am. Soc. C. E.*

Died November 4, 1926.

George Alec Harwood was born on August 29, 1875, at Waltham, Mass., the son of Alexander Thorndike and Emma Dean (Smith) Harwood. He was graduated from the Waltham Public Schools and the English High School of Boston, Mass., and then entered Tufts College, Medford, Mass., from which he was graduated in 1898 with the degree of Bachelor of Science in Electrical and Civil Engineering. In 1901, he received the degree of Master of Science and in 1913 the degree of Doctor of Science from the same college. During his high school and college career he was able, by his high scholarship, to earn awards that made easier for him the problem of financing his educational adventure.

In 1893 Mr. Harwood entered railroad service as a Chainman on the Fitchburg Railroad, where he continued as Rodman and Assistant Engineer during his college vacations and after his graduation.

In 1900, in response to an advertisement, he became a Draftsman in the Engineering Department of the New York Central and Hudson River Railroad Company. He successively filled positions as Chief Draftsman; Assistant Engineer in charge of construction at and near Syracuse, N. Y.; Assistant Engineer with special assignments from the Chief Engineer; Engineer of Grade Crossing Elimination; Assistant Terminal Engineer; and Terminal Engineer.

In November, 1906, Mr. Harwood was appointed Chief Engineer, Electric Zone Improvements. In 1916, he became Engineering Assistant to the Vice-President of the New York Central Lines and, during Federal Control of the railroads, he served as Engineering Assistant to the Federal Manager of the New York Central Railroad, and as Corporate Chief Engineer of the various companies comprising the New York Central System Lines. In 1920, he became Assistant to the President, New York Central Lines, and in April, 1924, he was elected Vice-President, in charge of improvements and development, which position he held at the time of his death.

Mr. Harwood was a Director of the Monongahela Railway Company; the New York and Fort Lee Railroad Company; the Pittsburgh, Chartiers and Youghiogheny Railway Company; the Raquette Lake Railway Company; the Chartiers Southern Railway Company; the Kanawha and West Virginia Railroad Company; the Michigan Air Line Railroad Company; the Fulton Chain Railway Company; the Hudson River Bridge Company, of Albany, N. Y.; the Hudson River Connecting Railroad Corporation; the Evansville, Mt. Carmel and Northern Railway Company; and the New Jersey Junction Railroad Company. He was also a Director of the Scarsdale Improvement Corporation; the Scarsdale National Bank; and the Mutual Fire, Marine and Inland Insurance Company.

He was a member of the American Railway Engineering Association; the Academy of Political Science; the Sons of the Revolution; the Century

* Memoir prepared by George W. Kittredge, M. Am. Soc. C. E.

Association; the New University Club, of Boston; the Railroad Club; the Scarsdale Town Club; and the Scarsdale Golf Club. He was also a Trustee of Tufts College and a member of the Alpha Tau Omega Fraternity.

Throughout his railroad life Mr. Harwood was noted for his industry, his thoroughness, his integrity, and his honesty. He was unassuming, but, at the same time, a man of force, ability, and mature judgment. As Chief Engineer of Electric Zone Improvements he was prominent in the development of the Grand Central Terminal and the area in its vicinity. In connection therewith, he showed his broadmindedness by placing credit where credit was due in a talk given by him during the period of greatest activity, when there were employed approximately 150 men on engineering designs and plans, 100 on supervision, and 3 000 on field construction. He then stated:

"If this terminal is a success, it will be so because it is not a one-man affair, but a splendid piece of team work in which the thought and experience of the operating man, the traffic man, the business man, the lawyer, the architect, and the engineer have been combined".

The following is extracted from the Minutes of the Board of Directors of the New York Central Railroad and the other roads comprising the System Lines, at meetings held subsequent to his death:

"Mr. Harwood ranked high in his profession as a civil engineer. His knowledge of engineering, however, was but the foundation of his great ability in solving difficult problems and of his capacity to bring to successful conclusion important undertakings. He had an all-round and well-balanced mind. His breadth of vision, his grasp of affairs, his sound judgment, his industry made him a unique man. That he was such a man was demonstrated by the work which he did during the reconstruction of the Grand Central Terminal; and this was fully confirmed by his entire subsequent service."

Mr. Harwood's interest in the Village of Scarsdale, in which he lived, was always great. He freely rendered generous service in connection with the financing and installation of the sanitary sewer system; with securing property for the Athletic Field and the adjoining area for park purposes; with shaping the policy of the village as expressed by the Charter Commission; with educational matters, having served for many terms as President of the Board of Education; with problems relating to village planning; and with improvements in many directions throughout the neighborhood where the results of his wise counsel and advice may be noted. As a citizen and as a property owner, he was active in all things pertaining to its welfare.

In 1900, Mr. Harwood was married to Grace Isabelle Hawley, who, with two sons, Herbert Hawley Harwood and Robert Thorndike Harwood, survives him.

Mr. Harwood was elected an Associate Member of the American Society of Civil Engineers on February 5, 1902, and a Member on February 5, 1907. He served as a Director of the Society from 1915 to 1917.

BENJAMIN FRANKLIN HOWLAND, M. Am. Soc. C. E.*

DIED MAY 27, 1927.

Benjamin Franklin Howland, the son of Reuben R. and Martha Y. (Brightman) Howland, was born at New Bedford, Mass., on June 8, 1877. His early years were spent in his native city, where he received his primary and secondary education. He later attended the Friends' School, at Providence, R. I.

After a few years of business experience in Boston, Mass., Mr. Howland removed to Hawaii in 1899, entering the employ of a firm of civil engineers and surveyors at Hilo, and for several years was engaged in a variety of work having to do with railroad location, underground water development, and intricate surveys. In 1903, he became the Engineer for a large sugar company, and, in 1905, was employed, at Honolulu, by the Engineering Bureau of the Public Works Department for the Territory. In this position he was responsible for the design of extensions to the sewer system, roads, bridges, reservoirs, and City water-works, also acting at times as Engineer for the City and County, with its numerous and varied demands.

In 1909, he spent a number of months in Cuba, as Engineer for a large sugar corporation, and, after his return to Hawaii in 1910, was employed in several responsible capacities, until he left to take a special course at the Massachusetts Institute of Technology, where he spent most of 1912 and 1913.

For several years, following his return to Honolulu, in 1914, Mr. Howland was employed by a prominent contracting company in designing, estimating, and as Superintendent of Construction, on numerous important contracts, several of which were for buildings of the United States Government.

In 1920, he became Chief Engineer for one of the large sugar agencies, controlling thirteen important plantations, in which capacity he designed and erected sea walls, dams and reservoirs, sewer systems, water supply and power pipe lines, together with numerous buildings and residences.

At various times, he was employed by the Territorial Survey Department, as an expert in adjusting old surveys. In the later years of his life, he was a partner in an engineering organization, specializing in the design and installation of fire protective apparatus for safeguarding large concentrations of value in and about the sugar-mills and pineapple canneries of the various Islands in the group.

Mr. Howland's alert mentality, unswerving integrity, and tireless energy, combined with a long and varied experience in the multitude of engineering problems of a rapidly growing city, and in the development and operation of the hydraulic and transportation elements of large-scale sugar production, made his services and advice of inestimable worth in the community, to the welfare of which he devoted so large a share of his professional career. He was a member of the Benevolent and Protective Order of Elks.

* Memoir prepared by Sidney G. Walker, Esq., Honolulu, Hawaii.

On November 24, 1914, he was married to Rheta C. Macdonald, of Boston, Mass., and to this union were born two daughters, Rheta Russell, and Anne Bartlett Howland, all of whom survive him.

Possessing rare qualities of heart, his home life was exceptional, and his passing has bereft a large circle of friends and intimates which he had built around a useful and unselfish life.

Mr. Howland was elected a Member of the American Society of Civil Engineers on October 2, 1922.

JOSEPH WRAY HUNTER, M. Am. Soc. C. E.*

Died May 19, 1927.

Joseph Wray Hunter was born on July 23, 1853, in Haverford Township, Delaware County, Pennsylvania. His father was Thomas and his mother, Henrietta (Schwend) Hunter. His early life was spent in Lower Merion Township, Montgomery County, and Radnor Township, Delaware County, Pennsylvania, and he was educated in public and private schools, having been graduated in 1870, second in his class from the Mantua Academy, in West Philadelphia, Pa.

Mr. Hunter's first work was with the late Samuel L. Smedley, M. Am. Soc. C. E., Surveyor and Regulator of the 11th Survey District, of Philadelphia, with whom he served until 1874, when he became engaged with Mr. G. M. Hopkins on map survey work. In 1875, he moved to Jenkintown, Pa., where he resided for the remainder of his life. In 1878, he engaged in the private practice of surveying in Jenkintown, and, in the same year, entered public life by being elected Justice of the Peace in his community.

Mr. Hunter started his long experience in highway work when, in 1890, he began, as the Borough Engineer of Jenkintown and Township Engineer for Cheltenham and Abingdon Townships, the construction of roads of the macadam and Telford macadam types. From 1902 to 1904 he was a member of the State Commission appointed to determine, survey, and re-establish the boundary line between the City of Philadelphia and Delaware County, Pennsylvania. He carried out a considerable part of the field work in this connection.

In 1903, he was appointed by Governor Pennypacker as the first State Highway Commissioner of Pennsylvania. He organized this Department and served in it in various capacities until his death.

During his early life Mr. Hunter filled a number of positions to which he was elected and in which he served faithfully, as he held all such matters of public trust in the highest regard. He was elected and re-elected Justice of the Peace. He was elected County Surveyor of Montgomery County, in 1872, and in 1887 Register of Wills for the same county. These elections and the manner in which he filled the positions led to his appointment as the first State Highway Commissioner. When he appointed Mr. Hunter to this position, Governor Pennypacker expressed his high regard for him as an Engineer, and this expression was repeated by successive Governors who re-appointed him to the Department. He served under Governors Pennypacker, Stuart, Tener, Sproul, Brumbaugh, Pinchot, and Fisher.

Mr. Hunter was outstanding as an engineer, a public servant, and, most of all, as a man. He was the most widely known and most loved man in highway circles in Pennsylvania. He had a depth of understanding and sympathy that won the unswerving loyalty of hundreds of young men whom he started on careers and whose close friendship he retained to the end. He was widely

* Memoir prepared by H. A Thomson, Esq., Upper Darby, Pa.

known to thousands of Township Supervisors of Pennsylvania whose counselor he was for many years and whose State Association had conferred on him the honorary title of "Dean of the Highway Department."

By thousands of these Supervisors as well as by hundreds of engineers in the Highway Department the name of "Uncle Joe" Hunter was revered. His advice was sought and heeded by many. He was a man who knew highway construction and was ahead of his time in the early years of the State Highway Department. He had tact and judgment; he did not force his ideas on an unwilling populace. He made suggestions quietly and lived to see his plans successfully adopted.

Mr. Hunter was closely associated at all times with the men who built the roads as well as with the people who provided the funds with which they were built. In laying the foundations for the great highway system of Pennsylvania, he had to deal with what was at first an unwilling majority, but by persistently demonstrating that his ideas were correct, he succeeded in converting his opponents to his views. This he accomplished not only by the soundness of his engineering ideas, but by his sense of appreciation of the other man's viewpoint. His was not a single-track mind, nor did he ever seek publicity. He was a mild-mannered, kind-hearted gentleman.

Mr. Hunter held membership in a number of technical clubs and societies, having been active in the American Society for Testing Materials and the Atlantic Deeper Waterways Association. He was a member of the American Road Builders Association; the Engineers Club of Philadelphia; Friendship Lodge, A. F. and A. M., of Jenkintown; Lu Lu Temple, A. A. O. N. M. S., of Philadelphia, and other branches of the Masonic order.

As long as the Pennsylvania State Department of Highways exists no history can be complete without a full and grateful recognition of the services of Joseph Wray Hunter in laying the foundations for the great organization in its early days. He will be remembered particularly for his services in organizing the Township Division and in purchasing the private turnpike system of the State, but most of all for his kindly and valuable advice given to successive executives of the State Highway Department. He was indeed the type of man for whom many treasure the thought that "he was my friend."

Mr. Hunter was elected a Member of the American Society of Civil Engineers on May 3, 1910.

CHARLES DAVIS JAMESON, M. Am. Soc. C. E.*

Died February 13, 1927.

Charles Davis Jameson was born in Bangor, Me., on July 2, 1855, the eldest son of Charles Davis Jameson, who during the Civil War served as a General in the Union Army, and Julia Lambert (Smith) Jameson. He passed his boyhood chiefly in Maine, attending school in Stillwater, Bath, and Bangor, principally at Dillingham's School at the latter place. After the death of his father, he lived for some years in Memphis, Tenn., with his uncle, Judge Thomas R. Smith. Later, he attended Bowdoin College at Brunswick, Me., where he was a member of the Alpha Delta Phi Fraternity, and from which he was graduated in Civil Engineering in 1876.

Mr. Jameson's first work was on the Bangor Dam across the Penobscot River, following which he went to St. John, N. B., Canada. In 1878, he became Section Engineer on the Memphis and Charleston (now the Southern) Railroad from Memphis, Tenn., to Huntsville, Ala.

Two years later he accepted a position in Mexico as Engineer in Charge and Superintendent of Construction on the Mexican Central Railroad. He was first stationed in the City of Mexico, but, later, was transferred to the sections from Leon to Irapuato. He also built tramways in Leon and Guanajuato, and was engaged in the preliminary location from Silao to Lake Chapala and Guadalajara, and from Tepic to San Blas.

In 1883, Mr. Jameson went to the Isthmus of Panama where he was employed under Count de Lesseps, as Assistant Engineer of the American Contracting and Dredging Company, and, later, as Chief Engineer and Superintendent. Having contracted the Chagres fever, he was forced to return to the United States. In 1885, he made standard plans for wooden structures for the European and North American Railroad Company.

On June 23, 1886, he was married to Florence Miller, of New York, and Memphis, Tenn. During the winter of 1886-87 he taught Engineering at the Massachusetts Institute of Technology, Boston, Mass.; and from 1887 to 1895, served as Head of the Department of Engineering at Iowa State University, Iowa City, Iowa.

In 1895, Mr. Jameson went to North China where for the next twenty-three years he was actively engaged in his profession. He became Chief Consulting Engineer and Architect for the Imperial Chinese Government, and, as such, made many surveying trips throughout China, Manchuria, etc., penetrating to places never before reached by white men. He also built a number of Government buildings, notably the Wai-Wu Pu Foreign Offices, the best constructed Government building in China.

After the fall of the Empire, Mr. Jameson became Chief Engineer for the American Red Cross. In this connection, he drew up all the plans for river conservancy in connection with flood and famine relief in China. These elaborate plans, involving the expenditure of about $50 000 000 by the Chinese

* Memoir prepared from information on file at the Headquarters of the Society.

Government, were interrupted by the World War and subsequent conditions in China.

In 1918, he returned to the United States and made his home in Bangor. He died in Sarasota, Fla., on February 13, 1927. On January 31, 1927, Mr. Jameson was married to Margaret French, of Washington, D. C., and is survived by his widow, a son, Wylie Blount Jameson, and a grandson, Wylie Blount Miller Jameson.

He was a member of India House, the Cosmos Club, of Washington, D. C., and the Loyal Legion. He was the author of a book on the making of Portland cement, of numerous monographs in engineering journals, and of an account of his experiences during the Boxer troubles in China, which was privately printed.

Mr. Jameson was elected a Member of the American Society of Civil Engineers on March 7, 1888.

WILBER MACAULAY JUDD, M. Am. Soc. C. E.*

Died November 13, 1924.

Wilber Macaulay Judd, the son of the Rev. Frederick F. Judd and Jeanette (Wilber) Judd, was born at Parsippany, N. J., on June 20, 1862. He entered Union College, Schenectady, N. Y., for the regular civil engineering course and additional academic subjects, so that at his graduation in 1884 he received both the degrees of Civil Engineer and Bachelor of Arts. His standing was the highest in his class, entitling him by appointment of the Faculty to the highest commencement honor, that of Valedictorian.

His first engineering work was done under the direction of his college preceptor, Cady Staley, M. Am. Soc. C. E., on the construction of a sanitary sewer system for Schenectady. This employment led to his becoming associated with the firm of Staley and Pierson in sanitary and hydraulic engineering work, which connection was continued during the first fifteen years of his professional career.

Some of the important pieces of work of which Mr. Judd had charge during this period were, as follows: From 1886 to 1887, he was Assistant City Engineer of Kalamazoo, Mich., and from 1887 to 1888, he had general charge of the construction of the sewer system of Watervliet, N. Y. From 1890 to 1891 he served as Assistant City Engineer of Lincoln, Nebr., and from 1891 to 1894 he was in general charge of the construction of sanitary sewer systems for Dayton and Conneaut, Ohio. From 1895 to 1896 he held the position of Assistant City Engineer of Peoria, Ill., and in 1897 was Construction Engineer for the Merodocia Levee and Drainage District, Albany, Ill. During 1898 and 1899, he carried out all civil engineering work for the Illinois Steel Company, at Joliet, Ill.

In 1899, Mr. Judd became associated with the late Selwyn M. Taylor, M. Am. Soc. C. E., and was in charge of mine development, etc., at Luzerne, Pa. Later, he was Resident Engineer for the plants at Luzerne, Footedale, and Buffington, Pa.

In 1903, he became a member of the firm, The W. G. Wilkins Company, Engineers and Architects, of Pittsburgh, Pa., and continued in this partnership until his death. As a member of the firm Mr. Judd had general charge of drafting-room work, estimating, and designing, and more or less field supervision of all civil engineering and mining work.

As to his standing as an engineer the writer quotes from a letter written by George S. Pierson, M. Am. Soc. C. E., with whom Mr. Judd was long associated:

"Mr. Judd was exceptionally well grounded in his profession. His personality was most pleasing and his judgment excellent and of a quality of expression and fairness as between conflicting interests that was most convincing."

* Memoir prepared by Professor James H. Stoller, Dept. of Geology, Union College, Schenectady, N. Y.

Mr. Judd was married on April 9, 1917, to Marietta Fallsbush, of Pittsburgh, who survives him.

As known to his college classmates he was of a quiet and modest bearing, genial and companionable to those who sought him out, a man of clear, strong mind and fine character.

He was a member of the Engineers Society of Western Pennsylvania; the Coal Mining Institute of America; the Chamber of Commerce of Pittsburgh; and the Civic Club of Allegheny County, Pennsylvania. He was also a member of the Presbyterian Church.

Mr. Judd was elected a Member of the American Society of Civil Engineers on October 4, 1905.

CHARLES ALBERT JUDSON, M. Am. Soc. C. E.*

Died September 30, 1926.

Charles Albert Judson was born on August 11, 1856, on a farm near Florence, Ohio. His early education was obtained in the district schools of Erie County. He lived and worked on the farm until he was twenty years of age, after which he taught school for several winters. He then attended the Academy at Delaware, Ohio, for a year, and spent four years in Oberlin College, having been graduated from the latter in 1882, with the degrees of Bachelor of Arts and Master of Arts.

Immediately after his graduation, Mr. Judson took up his residence in Sandusky, Ohio, where he studied and practiced civil engineering. His instructors were Mr. George Morton, and his father, Mr. Albert W. Judson, who at that time, was the Engineer and Surveyor of Erie County. From 1882 to 1884, Mr. Judson acted as Deputy Surveyor, following which he was City Engineer of Sandusky for eight years. In all, he served the City of Sandusky, either as City Engineer or Superintendent of Water-Works, for seventeen continuous years.

In 1902, Mr. Judson was elected State Senator from the Thirtieth District of Ohio. He served in this capacity for two terms, acting on a number of important committees, including those of Geological Survey, Sanitary Laws and Regulations, Railroads and Telegraphs, Roads and Highways, and Drainage and Irrigation. From 1904 to 1913, he was Collector of Customs for the Port of Sandusky.

From the time of his graduation until his death, Mr. Judson carried on almost continuously his engineering work. His surveying and engineering activities covered consulting work for the municipalities of Port Clinton, Fremont, Norwalk, and Huron, Ohio, including plans for, and the construction of, sewers, water-works, and interurban railways.

He made preliminary surveys for what is now the branch of the Pennsylvania Railroad from Sandusky to Columbus, Ohio, and had charge of the engineering on the construction work of that road from Sandusky to Bellevue, Ohio, as well as of the construction of the Lake Shore Electric Railway between Sandusky and Lorain, and between Norwalk and Ceylon Junction, Ohio. In addition, he made preliminary surveys for other lines. His activities also included a variety of bridge work, overhead construction, and street paving. At the time of his death, he was serving as one of the City Commissioners of Sandusky.

Mr. Judson was an active member of the Sandusky Masonic Lodge, and of the First Congregational Church of that city.

He was married to Roxie E. Lowry, of Berlin Heights, Ohio, in 1883. Both he and Mrs. Judson were killed on September 30, 1926, near Belmont, N. Y., when their automobile was struck by a fast freight train of the Erie Railroad Company. They are survived by five children.

* Memoir compiled from information on file at the Headquarters of the Society.

One who was an intimate friend and co-worker of Mr. Judson, has prepared the following tribute to him:

"Mr. Judson never laid aside his intellectual interests. He could botanize, work mathematical problems with the children, on occasion read a little Greek and more Latin, and prepare papers for the Literary Club of which he was for so many years a member.

"Mr. Judson lived a successful business life. His services as a civil engineer were valued all through this part of the State.

"He took a man's part in politics. He was Customs Collector and for two terms served in the State Senate. He had the high ideals of political action that are expected of a scholar, and these ideals rooted down into a steady participation in practical politics year after year.

"He was a strong Churchman, in the choir, in the Sunday School as a teacher, giving unsparing personal attention to all the work of the church. He was an outspoken Christian man, without apology and utterly without ostentation.

"In every sphere in which he worked what he did was characterized by a restrained force and tact that enabled him to see the other man's side of the matter fully and fairly and yet not always share it—if necessary, oppose it vigorously. There are two adjectives that applied to him, 'fearless' and 'friendly'. He was afraid of no one and friendly to every one. He had a keen sense of humor that went with his fearlessness and friendliness. He understood the fine art of getting on with people, and was always ready to take hold with bare hands and do what needed to be done. He was a plain, hard-working, high-thinking, right-minded, forward-looking, public-spirited citizen, who made himself felt in the community life".

Mr. Judson was elected a Member of the American Society of Civil Engineers on January 3, 1894.

GEORGE THOMAS KEITH, M. Am. Soc. C. E.*

Died September 4, 1927.

George Thomas Keith was born on February 4, 1843, at Bridgewater, Mass. He was the only son of Thomas Mitchell and Caroline (Jones) Keith, and a lineal descendant of Captain Miles Standish, John Alden, and Priscilla Mullens.

Mr. Keith was graduated from the Bridgewater State Normal School at the age of eighteen. In the same year, 1861, he enlisted in the Third Massachusetts Volunteers, Company K, and was sent with his regiment to Newbern, S. C. Although he was actively engaged in five great battles of the Civil War, among which were Goldsboro, Kingston, and Whitehall, he suffered no wounds or illness during his entire service. At the close of the war he refused to apply for a pension, but when it was decided that pensions be granted to all Civil War veterans, he finally agreed to accept one.

Following his discharge from the Army, Mr. Keith became a student for three years in the office of the late Thomas Doane, M. Am. Soc. C. E., of Boston, Mass. During this time he was employed as Land Surveyor on the Cape Cod Railroad and the Hoosac Tunnel.

He completed his apprenticeship in 1864, when he became Assistant Engineer on the construction of the Bradford Branch of the Erie Railroad, which position he held for one year. From 1865 to 1868, he was employed, principally, as Engineer in coal mines in the United States Land Company's office, in Bradford, Pa. He then served as Engineer of the Land Department of the Erie Railroad Company, at Hornellsville (now Hornell), N. Y., from 1868 to 1873.

In 1873, Mr. Keith was made Assistant Engineer in charge of construction of the reservoir of the Lawrence Water-Works, at Lawrence, Mass. He held this position until 1876, when he engaged in private practice, with offices at Olean, N. Y., and Bradford, Pa., until 1889. During this period he constructed water-works plants at Newark, Ohio, and at Chester, Pa., and was engaged at Bradford, Pa., on surveys for pipe lines for the transportation of crude oil. He was also employed as Contractor for the water-works at Cuba, N. Y. In 1889, Mr. Keith became a member of the firm of Woltman and Keith, of New York, N. Y., and as such constructed water-works at Tallapoosa, Ga., Henderson, N. C., and elsewhere. His greatest work during this period was, perhaps, the establishment of the water-works in the seven municipalities of Montreal, Que., Canada, all of which were included in the Montreal Water System. From 1896 to 1904, he was engaged on the construction of electric railroads at Olean, N. Y., and Oil City, Pa.

Ill health then made it necessary for Mr. Keith to retire from active work for a time. When he had recovered sufficiently, he applied for a position on the New York State Barge Canal which was then under construction. The appointments of engineers on this work were made by competitive essays,

* Memoir prepared from information on file at the Headquarters of the Society.

or themes, submitted to the Barge Canal Commission. Mr. Keith received the highest award for his paper, and consequently, became the first Resident Engineer to be appointed on the Barge Canal construction in 1904. By personal request to the State Commissioner of Highways, he was transferred to the New York State Highway Department, at Olean, in 1907.

He was the author of "Keith's Railroad Tables", and "Functions of Curves", for the "Transit Note Book", published by Keuffel and Esser, which is well known, and is used as a college text.

In 1870, Mr. Keith was married to Evelyn Agnes Moore, who died in March, 1916. He is survived by an only daughter, Mrs. Mildred Evelyn Thynge.

He was a member of the Grand Army of the Republic; the National Geographic Society; and President of the Cattaraugus County Society for the Prevention of Cruelty to Animals. He was also a member of the Olean Country Club and the Olean City Club.

Mr. Keith was elected a Member of the American Society of Civil Engineers on May 4, 1881.

THOMAS JAMES McMINN, M. Am. Soc. C. E.*

Died September 21, 1927.

Thomas James McMinn was born at Port Hope, Ont., Canada, on October 8, 1854. In 1874 he began his technical work on the construction of the new water-works for Toronto, Ont., Canada, under the late P. A. Peterson, M. Am. Soc. C. E. He remained on this work and its various subsequent extensions, until 1879, when he was made Assistant Engineer to the late R. J. Brough, M. Am. Soc. C. E.

The following year he was engaged in making surveys, plans, specifications, and estimates for the construction of a 6-ft. oak conduit, to be built and extended for a considerable distance into Lake Ontario. In 1881, he was appointed Resident Engineer on this "lake extension", and served in this capacity during 1881 and 1882.

From 1882 to 1889, Mr. McMinn was employed as Assistant Engineer and Draftsman in the Water-Works Department of Toronto. During this period he made a barometric survey of the country extending to the north of Toronto, in connection with a proposed gravitation supply for the locality.

On leaving the Water-Works Department, he came to the United States and entered the employ of the late Rudolph Hering, M. Am. Soc. C. E., who was engaged in the private practice of engineering, in New York, N. Y. Mr. McMinn remained with Mr. Hering until January, 1898, when he was elected Assistant Secretary of the Society, which position he retained until his retirement in 1919. Shortly afterward he removed to Bridgeport, Conn., and then to Philadelphia, Pa., where he died on September 21, 1927. During this time he was engaged in editing several technical books for the late Mr. Hering and others.

Such, in brief, is an outline record of a useful life. To most members—and Mr. McMinn was widely known in the Society—his most valuable work was comprised within his official term as Assistant Secretary. The duties of this office were varied, especially in the early days, when the smallness of the organization demanded a wide variety of service of each officer. Always, however, Mr. McMinn gave his main efforts to publications.

At one time he handled the many phases of this work—editing, attending to engraving, proof-reading, and supervising the printing. Later, however, as the work expanded, he devoted his time mainly to the editing. In this he was, happily, successful. Endowed naturally with a clear perception of the fitness of expression, he was at once painstaking, well read, and widely versed in engineering methods. Many of the details of style he instituted are still standard practice, to the lasting credit and reputation of the publications.

Throughout his life his interest in these publications never flagged. A year before he died he went over a number of *Proceedings* in detail and submitted a long list of suggested improvements in its grammatical form—re-

* Memoir prepared from information on file at the Headquarters of the Society.

visions that none but his practiced and discerning eye would have noted. A similar trait of character was noticeable in his reading. Much of his library came to the Society; many of his books, especially the engineering volumes, showed traces of his critical taste in apt marginal notations of improvement in style.

During so many years' intimate connection with the Society journals, he gained a wide and close acquaintance among the members. Endowed with a mildness of manner and a gentlemanly bearing, his relations were always pleasant. No one could exchange ideas with him anent engineering matters, especially the details of rhetorical expression, without feeling his innate grasp of such intricacies.

His qualities of person and character endeared him to his many colleagues at Society Headquarters. He had made for himself a solid place in their esteem. Apparently, the feeling was mutual; the several years after his retirement were punctuated by frequent visits to New York, at which times he always made it a point to keep his many friendships in good repair.

Mr. McMinn was essentially a literary editor and an excellent one. But he was also an engineer; and, above all, a man. His lengthening years of Society work only served to ennoble his character, to bring into stronger relief the qualities of mind and of person that made him revered and loved. His place in the annals of the Society is secure.

Mr. McMinn was married on June 4, 1884, to Ada Jeannette Petman, of Toronto, Ont., Canada, who survives him, together with four children, George, Stanley P., Mrs. Lowell Grossman, and Mrs. W. C. Hooven. His home life was ever an inspiration to his friends, and his family indeed lived "to call him blessed".

Mr. McMinn was elected a Member of the American Society of Civil Engineers on March 5, 1890. He was also a member of the Engineering Institute of Canada.

ALEXANDER MAITLAND, JR., M. Am. Soc. C. E.*

Died December 24, 1926.

Alexander Maitland, Jr., was born on February 9, 1866, on a farm, near Richmond, Mo. He was the son of Alexander Maitland and Mary Grieves (Oliphant) Maitland and the eldest of a family of eight children, two sons and six daughters. He was of Scotch-Irish descent, his father's parents having been born in Scotland, and his mother's parents having come from Ireland. On his father's side, he was a descendant of the Scotch Earl of Lauderdale.

He attended a country school until 1886, when he entered the University of Missouri, from which he was graduated in 1889, with the degree of Civil Engineer.

After his graduation, Mr. Maitland entered the service of the King Bridge Company, of Cleveland, Ohio, as a Draftsman, and for a period of two years he was employed by this Company and the Keystone Bridge Company, of Pittsburgh, Pa., in estimating and designing various classes of steel structures. In 1892, he returned to the University of Missouri as Assistant Professor of Civil Engineering.

The following year he entered the employ of the Missouri Pacific Railroad Company, as Assistant Engineer in the Bridge and Building Department, and remained in the service of this Company until 1899. His work consisted of the design and supervision of the construction of substructures and superstructures for permanent bridges and buildings.

From 1899 to 1900 Mr. Maitland was engaged as Resident Engineer at Kansas City, Mo., for the Pittsburgh Bridge Company, of Pittsburgh. From 1900 to 1904 he was Contracting Manager for the American Bridge Company at Butte, Mont., and at Kansas City. From 1904 until his death, he was President of the Kansas City Bridge Company, of Kansas City.

During 1918 and 1919 he was Manager of the Gulf District of the United States Shipping Board, Emergency Fleet Corporation, in charge of the construction of wooden ships, with headquarters at Houston, Tex. For several years, previous to and at the time of, his death, he was, also, a member of the firm of Fuller and Maitland, Consulting Engineers, engaged in the design and supervision of construction of the new water plant at Kansas City.

Mr. Maitland was endowed with great mental and physical energy, which made him a leader in civic and social matters, as well as in his professional activities. He was a man of winning personality, who made friends easily and held them by loyalty, and a sense of fair play. He was intensely interested in his life work, and was always willing to contribute his time and engineering experience to all his business associates, especially to the younger members of the profession. His loyalty and friendship will be treasured by his large circle of friends.

* Memoir prepared by George F. Maitland, Herbert S. Crocker, and Milo S. Ketchum, Members, Am. Soc. C. E.

On January 8, 1896, Mr. Maitland was married to Desdemona Henderson, of Pacific, Mo. He is survived by his widow and six children, Alexander, 3d, Gladys, Helen, George, Ralph, and John.

Mr. Maitland was a member of the Masonic Lodge, and of the Benevolent and Protective Order of Elks. He was also a member of the Engineers Club of Kansas City and the Kansas City Club.

Mr. Maitland was elected a Member of the American Society of Civil Engineers on November 6, 1901. He served as a Director from January 1, 1925 until his death.

CONRADO EUGENIO MARTINEZ Y RENGIFO, M. Am. Soc. C. E.*

Died May 21, 1927.

Conrado Eugenio Martinez y Rengifo was born in Havana, Cuba, on April 26, 1881. He was graduated in 1896 from the High School, Santa Clara, Cuba, with the degree of Bachelor of Arts. Soon afterward, he came to the United States and entered Lehigh University, at South Bethlehem, Pa., from which he was graduated in 1901, with the degree of Civil Engineer, the first on the Roll of Honor.

After leaving college, Mr. Martinez obtained a position as Rodman with the Pennsylvania Railroad Company, which position he held until December, 1901.

He then returned to Cuba, and entered the Government Service in the Engineer Department of the City of Havana, starting in January, 1902, as Rodman and working his way up to the position of Superintendent of the Department of Streets and Parks, which position he attained in January, 1903, and held until January, 1907. He was then transferred, as Assistant Engineer, to the Direction General of Public Works. Shortly afterward, he was appointed Engineer in charge of the location and construction of the highway from Cabanas to Bahia Honda, a distance of 20 miles, on the North Coast, which position he held until August, 1907, when he was appointed Chief Engineer of Public Works for the Province of Matanzas, Cuba.

In March, 1909, Mr. Martinez was transferred to Havana as Principal Assistant Engineer of the Havana Sewer and Paving Contract, where he remained until February, 1912. During this period he frequently acted as deputy for the Chief Engineer.

From March, 1912, until August, 1914, he was engaged in important private practice in designing and construction. In August, 1913, he was appointed Engineer Member of the National Board of Health which position he filled until shortly before his death. In August, 1914, he was appointed Chief Engineer of the Havana Sewer and Paving Contract and remained on this work until August, 1915, when he was transferred to the Direction General of Public Works as Chief Engineer in charge of examination of projects and inspection of new construction work for the Department of Public Works. In November, 1916, he was appointed Chief Engineer in charge of the Sewerage and Paving Contract for the City of Cienfuegos, Cuba, and in June, 1917, he was made Engineer in charge of the construction of water-works for the City of Marianao, Cuba.

In June, 1918, Mr. Martinez engaged once more in private practice as Consulting Engineer, in partnership with his brother, Rolando A. Martinez, Assoc. M. Am. Soc. C. E. In that capacity he undertook varied and important engineering enterprises, such as bridge and wharf construction; the design and construction of water-works and sewers; extensive land sub-divisions; surveys; appraisals; design of molasses pumping plants, etc., until his death.

* Memoir prepared by Manuel D. Diaz, Esq., Havana, Cuba.

On November 22, 1924, Mr. Martinez received the degree of Doctor of Laws, from the University of Havana after having taken the full course prescribed for the degree. Subsequently, while engaged in engineering work, he found time for the successful practice of his new profession.

Although financially independent, his love for the profession originally chosen by him, made him an indefatigable and enthusiastic toiler. A lover of truth, he spoke it, and wrote it, irrespective of its bitterness. His blunt honesty with his modesty and great worth made him many friends to whom his untimely death was as severe a shock as it was to his family and to those closely associated to him socially and professionally.

Mr. Martinez is survived by his widow, and two daughters, Clara and Blanca, to whom he leaves an example of faithfulness, truth, and integrity.

He was a member of the Union Club, of the Country Club of Havana, of the Association of Members of American National Engineering Societies in Cuba, and of the Tau Beta Pi Fraternity.

Mr. Martinez was elected an Associate Member of the American Society of Civil Engineers on October 7, 1908, and a Member on September 9, 1919.

FRANK OLIN MARVIN, M. Am. Soc. C. E.*

Died February 6, 1915.

Great achievement in engineering is not always evidenced by the magnitude and importance of the buildings, great bridges, or public works that have been designed and built, nor by the economic importance of the industries that have been conceived and developed by an individual. Many engineers have done such outstanding work along these lines of design, construction, invention, and development that their fame will be lasting; and the world has come, through that work, to a full realization of the great part that engineering has had in the development of the present civilization.

Of equally great human value is the work of the man who, in the training of engineers, not only places emphasis on truth, accuracy, and thoroughness, but who by precept and example urges broadness of training and of interest, the cultivation of things that are fine and beautiful, the participation in civic and social activities, and the living of a Christian life.

When such a man comes to an administrative place in any school of engineering, his influence in character moulding, in the building of good citizens, and the implanting of high ideals of citizenship, of literature, art, music, and religion, along with a sound and thorough professional training, is of incalculable benefit to the profession. The engineering of men, the building of engineers, while not spectacular, is of lasting value to the world.

Frank Olin Marvin, Dean of Engineering of the University of Kansas, was such a man. He lived a quiet, beautiful life. He exerted a great influence in many fields of activity. His life work was as an educator and character builder. He influenced the career of several hundred engineers who will pass on to other generations the ideals of this teacher of the truth.

Frank Olin Marvin was born at Alfred, N. Y., on May 27, 1852. He was the son of the Rev. James Marvin and Armina (LeSuer) Marvin. He was graduated with science honors from Allegheny College, at Meadville, Pa., in 1871. During his years in college his chief interest was in the sciences, especially botany and geology, but he undoubtedly there laid the foundation for the appreciation of literature and the arts which developed so fully in his later years. In 1874, he received the degree of Master of Arts from Allegheny College.

In July, 1871, Mr. Marvin entered the service of the Missouri, Kansas, and Texas Railway Company as Engineer on Construction. In 1872 he became Chief Draftsman for the Company, and, later, Chief Clerk in the Chief Engineer's Office. He began teaching in 1875, so that his subsequent engineering work was done either during vacation periods or in a consulting capacity. From 1878 to 1880, he was Chief Engineer for the Great Eastern Irrigation Company and designed and located 100 miles of irrigation canals and ditches, with the dams and other essential structures. From 1889 to 1892, or 1893, he was Consulting Engineer for the City of Lawrence, Kans., on the

* Memoir prepared by Henry Earle Riggs, M. Am. Soc. C. E.

revision of sewerage plans, and on the construction of storm sewers, arch culverts, and various minor structures. In 1894, and in later years, he designed heavy retaining walls and a stone warehouse for a milling company; as Engineer for the University of Kansas, he had much to do with grading, heating tunnels, and other improvements on the campus; he made various reports on sewage disposal, street railways, and other public works in cities and for institutions in Kansas; and, with the State Geologist, he made an extended investigation of the building stones of the State.

It was as a teacher that he did his real work. In September, 1875, he began teaching in the Preparatory Department of the University of Kansas. From 1876 to 1878 he was Principal of the Lawrence High School. In September, 1878, he became Assistant Professor of Mathematics and Engineering. In 1883 he was appointed Professor of Civil Engineering, and, in 1891, Dean of the newly created School of Engineering, which position he held until 1913, when he retired on account of ill health, and became Advisory Dean.

Of Professor Marvin's forty years of teaching work, thirty-seven years were devoted to the service of the University of Kansas during the period of its growth and development. The School of Engineering was his creation, and his personality and character were impressed on the graduates in Engineering, from the beginning of their instruction in the institution. He stood firmly for thoroughness of training in the basic sciences, for careful preparation and accuracy of presentation in class work. He was mild of manner, gentle of voice, of unlimited patience, and was never unfair or unjust to the students. He did not believe in doing work for the pupils, but insisted on each one doing his own thinking and solving his own problems.

Professor Marvin was one of the active leaders in the work of learned and technical societies. He was a member of the Kansas Academy of Science, Kansas Water, Gas and Electric Light Association, Kansas Engineering Society, and American Society for Testing Materials. He was a Fellow of the American Association for the Advancement of Science and Vice-President of Section D in 1896. In 1901 he was President of the Society for the Promotion of Engineering Education, having been one of the most active workers during its early years. He was a member of Phi Beta Kappa and of Sigma Xi for which he worked very earnestly, and of which he became National President in 1909 and 1910. Some of his most intimate contacts with his students came through his active interest in the Science Club of the University, an organization which brought the students of the Eighties very close to the human side of the members of the Faculty. He always urged upon his students the need, after graduation, for such contacts with other members of the profession.

Professor Marvin was married twice, first on August 30, 1876, to Elinor G. McKean who died October 1, 1899, and afterward on December 31, 1901, to Josephine B. March, of Lawrence, who survives him, and who since his death has been living in California. During the long years that his first wife was an invalid, his constant care for her, and his consequent foregoing of many social pleasures, won for him the highest regard of his neighbors. Home life meant much to him. He built a substantial, comfortable house and found great enjoyment in his library and study in which practically all his work was done for many years.

No memoir of Professor Marvin would be complete that did not lay stress on his citizenship and on his intense interest in the fine things of life outside of the professional field.

He was a lover of music. He had a fine and well trained voice and was for a time a member of a well known quartette, but it was as an organist that he is best remembered. For twenty-six years, from 1877 to 1903, he was Organist of Plymouth Congregational Church. He wrote a number of compositions for the organ, which were usually prepared for some special occasion. He also wrote a number of Christmas and Easter carols, composing both the words and music.

He was also a lover of art. He owned a notable collection of etchings, and did excellent work in this line himself. His work was the first of the kind done in the West and his first etched plate is said to have been the earliest made in the State of Kansas.

He was a lover of literature. His library bespoke his taste for the fine things of all ages and all nations.

Professor Marvin was a good citizen, although a modest and unassertive one. His only active participation in civic affairs was to serve as a member of the City Council of Lawrence for a two-year term from 1900 to 1902, but as an adviser and councilor he assisted in straightening out many a tangle. For many years he was the unofficial consultant and adviser to the City Engineer, always regarding such unpaid services as the duty of a good citizen.

That his years of service were recognized is amply proved by the fact that the Engineering Building at Kansas University is named Marvin Hall; by the fact that the fine new organ recently dedicated in Plymouth Church was appropriately named the Marvin Memorial Organ; and by the fact that in the Engineering Library of the University, to which his books on professional subjects were given, there is a bronze portrait bust and tablet to his memory, placed by the Engineering Alumni in memory of a teacher and friend. These things show that he was known, loved, and appreciated. There is no doubt that his gentle, quiet, effective work for the University and the community endeared him to all with whom he came in contact, and commanded the respect of those who did not know him well.

The writer knew Professor Marvin, first as a teacher of ability, who never used a harsh or sarcastic word in his classes; then, as an adviser, who could always be depended upon to consider and weigh carefully every matter before passing judgment upon it; finally, as a friend of his maturer years, who seemed to find real pleasure in going over the work his "boys" were doing. He would offer a suggestion here, or a mild criticism in the form of a question there, always seeking to encourage more artistic design, or more finished construction. He was an unerring judge of the ability of his students. The writer has employed a number of them on Professor Marvin's recommendation, every one of whom made good in a large way, and every one of whom is now a successful engineer and an active worker in the Society.

Professor Marvin wrote no books. His writing was confined to papers and addresses before the various societies of which he was a member. The subjects had largely to do with pedagogical matters, but some of these subjects clearly indicate his interests, namely, "The Cultural Value of an Engineering Education"; "The Artistic Element in Engineering"; and "Why not Teach About Men?" Once, when the writer was discussing with him the subject of work for an advanced degree, Professor Marvin urged that it be along purely literary lines, because he thought every one ought to develop along lines other than those of his professional work. He continually urged that each of his "boys" cultivate some fad or hobby that would get him far from the field of his practice.

Some of his early writing was prophetic of the great change in American engineering and public works, which has recently been taking place. The finer design, the greater regard for the artistic, the abolition of the ugly things, that is so marked in present-day practice, were foretold by him more than thirty years ago.

More than twelve years have passed since Professor Marvin's death on February 6, 1915. To those of his students who knew him outside the classroom his presence is just as real to-day as it was when they sat in his classes or chummed with him in the years following their graduation, and his gentle, kindly personality and his many lovable qualities will always be a real inspiration to them. Judged by his works, the great engineering school he founded and built up, and the scores of fine and broad engineers who gained their inspiration from him, not only in accuracy and thoroughness, but in love of the fine things of life and in ideals of good citizenship, he may indeed be called a great teacher. As the writer, in recent years, has come to know more intimately the problems of the engineering schools and made contacts with the leading present-day teachers of engineering, he has been brought more fully to a realization of the true worth of Frank Olin Marvin.

Professor Marvin was elected a Member of the American Society of Civil Engineers on May 5, 1897.

THOMAS HOGGAN MATHER, M. Am. Soc. C. E.*

DIED MARCH 23, 1927.

Thomas Hoggan Mather, the son of William and Isabella Hoggan Mather, was born near Glasgow, Scotland, on May 2, 1860. His father was an engineer and encouraged his son to follow the same profession.

Mr. Mather's early engineering training was received as an articled pupil with Kyle, Dennison, and Frew, Civil Engineers of Glasgow, and as a student in special classes at Glasgow University. Upon the completion of his university study in 1879, he was appointed Surveyor of Roads, Cadder Parish, Lanarkshire, Scotland.

In 1882, Mr. Mather removed to Canada and for the ensuing nine years he was engaged in a variety of work in that country and in the United States. He served consecutively as Transitman for the Canadian Pacific Railway; Superintendent of the Las Vegas, N. Mex., Water System; Office Engineer and Chief of Location Party for the Canadian Pacific Railway; Chief of Location Party for the Quebec Central Railway and for the Témiscouata Railway; Chief Engineer on Reconnaissance for the Gaspé Short Line; District Engineer on Location and Construction for the Calgary and Edmonton Railway; and District Engineer for the Norfolk and Western Railroad.

In 1892, he removed to Syracuse, N. Y. With the exception of the four years from 1918 to 1921, he resided there continuously until his death.

A period of private practice in partnership with Henry C. Allen, M. Am. Soc. C. E., was followed by twenty years' service as Chief Engineer of construction and maintenance for high-speed electric railways. During 1915, Mr. Mather served as Commissioner of Public Works for the City of Syracuse. Two years of private practice were succeeded by more than three years of Government service as Supervising Engineer of Construction at Harrisburg, Pa., and as Superintendent of Utilities at the Quartermaster Corps Depot in the same city.

After a brief interval when he was engaged in private practice in Brooklyn, N. Y., he was appointed City Engineer for the City of Syracuse in January, 1922, which position he held for four years. At the time of his death, Mr. Mather was serving as Chief Engineer of the Syracuse Grade Crossing Commission, having been appointed to that position in January, 1926.

He is survived by his widow, Mrs. Isabella Layfield Mather, and by two daughters, Mrs. Harry H. Motheral, of Brooklyn, N. Y., and Mrs. John C. Adams, of Jersey City, N. J.

Mr. Mather was a member of the Syracuse Chamber of Commerce, Technology Club, and Citizens' Club of Syracuse. He was also affiliated with Central City Lodge, F. and A. M., of which he was a Past Master, and with Central City Commandery No. 25.

As he was endowed with good humor and possessed of a fund of good stories effectively told, he contributed enjoyment to any festivity which his

* Memoir prepared by Glenn D. Holmes, M. Am. Soc. C. E.

presence graced. For recreation, Mr. Mather sought the woods, at home and abroad, and the wild plant life—particularly the ferns—to be found there. His personal friends of whom there were many, found attraction and pleasure in his conversation and company.

The greater part of his life was spent in railroad work, the branch of the profession which he most enjoyed. Those associated with him acquired a high esteem for his professional ability and his attractive personal qualities. The Grade Crossing Commission, with which he was engaged at the time of his death, recorded a tribute to his exceptional skill, his impartial attitude to the solution of its many problems, his unlimited application to his work, and the serious and sincere devotion to his duty. The City of Syracuse has lost a very able, conscientious, and valuable public servant.

Mr. Mather was elected a Member of the American Society of Civil Engineers on October 1, 1902.

JOHN DEVEREUX O'REILLY, M. Am. Soc. C. E.*

Died November 6, 1927.

John Devereux O'Reilly was born at Denver, Colo., on May 4, 1884, the son of Anthony J. and Fredrica (Devereux) O'Reilly. His early youth was spent in Colorado, but by the time he was of college age, his family had moved to New Orleans, La., where Mr. O'Reilly attended Tulane University. In 1904 he matriculated at the Virginia Military Institute, at Lexington, Va., and was graduated from that institution in 1907, having completed the course in Civil Engineering.

Immediately after graduation, he accepted employment as Instrumentman with the Asheville and Hendersonville Interurban Railroad Company. Later, he returned to New Orleans where he was engaged on various engineering projects from 1909 to 1915.

In May, 1915, Mr. O'Reilly was appointed Chief Engineer of the Board of Commissioners of the Port of New Orleans, in which position he continued until 1919. During his connection with this Board, which, as an agency of the State of Louisiana, owns and operates the port facilities of New Orleans, a number of very important projects were undertaken. Notable among these were the Public Cotton Warehouse, the Public Grain Elevator, and the Inner-Harbor Navigation Canal, all of which were undertakings of great magnitude.

During the World War, President Wilson appointed Mr. O'Reilly as a member of the Council of National Defense, which had headquarters at Washington, D. C. As a member of this Council, his duties included the preparation of civil and military defenses against possible hostile attacks in the Harbor of New Orleans and in other United States ports.

In 1919, he severed his connection with the Board of Port Commissioners and resumed the private practice of engineering and contracting in and around New Orleans, and he was engaged in this work to the time of his last illness.

A man of pleasing personality who made friends readily, he was well known socially in New Orleans. He was a member of the Louisiana Club, the Delta Kappa Epsilon Fraternity, and of other organizations.

On June 30, 1908, Mr. O'Reilly was married to Beatrice Gilmore, who, with five children, four girls and one boy, survives him.

Mr. O'Reilly was elected a Member of the American Society of Civil Engineers on August 31, 1925.

---

* Memoir prepared by Samuel McC. Young, M. Am. Soc. C. E.

CHARLES LESTER PARMELEE, M. Am. Soc. C. E.*

Died April 4, 1927.

Charles Lester Parmelee, the son of Myron Holly and Emma (Lester) Parmelee, and a descendant of one of the founders of Guilford, Conn., was born at Syracuse, N. Y., on January 16, 1873. He spent a year studying civil engineering at the University of Michigan and, in 1890, went to the Massachusetts Institute of Technology, from which he was graduated in 1895 as Bachelor of Science in Civil and in Sanitary Engineering.

His college vacations were spent in civil engineering work. From 1895 to 1898 he served as Assistant Engineer to George W. Fuller, M. Am. Soc. C. E., on the experimental water filters at Louisville, Ky., and again on the experimental filters and preliminary designs for the Cincinnati, Ohio, Water-Works.

From 1898 to 1902, Mr. Parmelee was Chief Engineer, successively, of the Continental Filter Company and the New York Continental Jewell Filtration Company, in charge of design and construction of filtration works for many communities and industrial plants, including the works at Little Falls, N. J., the first large concrete filter plant built on the American system. For the next two years he acted as Consulting Engineer to the New York Continental Jewell Filtration Company on various enterprises, including a dry dock for the Federal Government, at Charleston, S. C., Oak Lane Reservoir, Philadelphia, Pa.; First Street Tunnel of the Pennsylvania Railroad Company, Washington, D. C.; Wantagh Infiltration Works of the Brooklyn, N. Y., Water Supply, and other work having an aggregate value of about $5 000 000.

In 1904 and 1905 he held the position of Consulting Engineer to the City of Toledo, Ohio, on water-works improvements, including a 32 000 000-gal. filter plant. In 1906 and 1907 he served as Consulting Engineer to J. G. White and Company, in connection with a dam across the Colorado River near Yuma, Ariz., preliminary studies for the Los Angeles Aqueduct, and other investigations.

From 1907 to 1912, Mr. Parmelee was Chief Engineer of the T. A. Gillespie Company, General Contractors, and the East Jersey Pipe Company, manufacturers of lock-bar and riveted steel pipe. These engagements connected him with contracts totaling approximately $15 000 000, including water purification works for Pittsburgh, Pa.; two locks and dams on the Ohio River; the Rondout Creek and Hudson River pressure tunnels of the Catskill Aqueduct, of the New York, N. Y., Water Supply; Granite Dam across the Yadkin River, at Whitney, N. C.; extension of the power plant at Massena, N. Y.; pipe lines at Brooklyn and Lockport, N. Y., Pittsburgh, Pa., and Portland, Ore.

For the next six years he held the position of Consulting Engineer to a number of contractors on large construction in hydraulic and railroad undertakings. He also made examinations of railroad, water-power, water-works,

* Memoir prepared by Alfred D. Flinn, M. Am. Soc. C. E., and John B. Stein, Assoc. M. Am. Soc. C. E.

timber, oil, gas, and coal projects. In 1917, Mr. Parmelee served as Captain in the Engineers Reserve Corps, on cantonment work, and in 1917 and 1918 as Consulting Engineer for the Oil Division, United States Fuel Administration. From 1918 until his death, he practiced as a Consulting Engineer, mainly in charge of the construction of oil refineries for the Sinclair Refining Company, aggregating $40 000 000 in value.

In 1896, Mr. Parmelee was married to Helen F. Donnelly, who died in 1920. Two daughters by this marriage, Emma Lester and Helen Donnelly, survive him. In 1923, he was married to Gertrude M. Pankan, who also survives him.

He was a member of the following technical societies and clubs: American Institute of Mining and Metallurgical Engineers; The Engineers' Club of New York; Railroad Club of New York; University Club of Chicago, Ill.; Essex County Country Club of West Orange, N. J.; Glen View Club of Illinois; and Old Colony Club of New York.

Mr. Parmelee was elected a Member of the American Society of Civil Engineers on February 4, 1913.

JOHN CURTIS PATTERSON, M. Am. Soc. C. E.*

Died January 6, 1927.

John Curtis Patterson was born in Germantown, Philadelphia, Pa., on July 12, 1857, the son of Joseph Patterson and Lavinia Horstman Patterson.

He received his early education at the Faires Classical Institute in Philadelphia and was the first student from this Institute to enter directly the Towne Scientific School of the University of Pennsylvania, as a member of the Class of 1878. He pursued his studies in Civil Engineering until December, 1877, in his Senior year, when he withdrew from college to take a position as Rodman with the Engineer Corps of the Madeira and Mamoré Railway, in Brazil, joining the ill-fated Collins Expedition sent out from Philadelphia to build this railway around the Falls of the Madeira River, a branch of the Amazon. Mr. Patterson was selected for this expedition because of his excellent physique and strong constitution, but he barely escaped the treacherous climate with his life, after suffering from the sickness which caused the abandonment of the enterprise for the time being.

On his return from South America in April, 1878, he entered the employ of the Philadelphia and Reading Railroad Company as Rodman and continued in this position until August, 1880, when he became Rodman on an Engineer Corps of the Pennsylvania Railroad Company.

In November, 1880, Mr. Patterson went to Colima, Mexico, where he served as Levelman and, later, as Division Engineer for the Mexican National Construction Company (the Manzanillo and Laredo Railway Company). Returning from Mexico in May, 1882, he was Assistant Engineer on surveys for the Gettysburg and Harrisburg Railroad, at Carlisle, Pa., until April, 1883, when he became Division Roadmaster of the Lebanon Division of the Philadelphia and Reading Railroad and continued in this position until February, 1885. He then became Secretary and Treasurer of the Philadelphia Drainage Construction Company, Limited, and, in November, 1887, he again returned to the Philadelphia and Reading Railroad Company as Assistant Engineer. He continued in this position until November, 1888, when he became Assistant Chief Engineer, and, later Chief Engineer, of the Poughkeepsie Bridge and Central New England and Western Railroad Company.

Following this Mr. Patterson was, successively, Engineer in Charge of Construction of the Quaker City Mortar Company's Plant in Philadelphia; Assistant Chief Engineer of Surveys for the Baltimore and Cumberland Railroad; Chief Engineer of the Pittsburgh and Eastern Railroad Company in Clearfield County, Pennsylvania; and Chief Engineer for the Government of Ecuador on the construction of the railway from Guayaquil to Quito, an interesting engineering achievement. After his return from Ecuador, until his death, Mr. Patterson was engaged in consulting work in Philadelphia.

He was married to Charlotte Dallas Morrell, by whom he is survived, with a sister, Mrs. Meredith Bailey, of Portland, Ore.

* Memoir prepared by Clark Dillenbeck, M. Am. Soc. C. E.

Mr. Patterson was a man of exceptionally genial and attractive personality, and a most delightful conversationalist, who will be greatly missed by his fellow engineers and his many friends. In his youth, he was a notable athlete, an excellent player of baseball and cricket, interested in the beginning of amateur baseball playing and also in that of the modern game of football.

He was a member of the Delta Psi Fraternity and of the St. Anthony's Clubs of Philadelphia and New York, and, at various times, of the Engineers' Club of Philadelphia, the Philadelphia Gun Club, the Germantown Cricket Club, the Huntington Valley Country Club, the Devon Golf Club, the Racquet Club, and the Philadelphia Country Club.

Mr. Patterson was elected a Member of the American Society of Civil Engineers on October 2, 1889.

FRANK WILLIAM PERKINS, M. Am. Soc. C. E.*

Died May 18, 1927.

Frank William Perkins was born in Chicago, Ill., on September 5, 1882. On graduating from Grammar School, he accepted a position in the Map Department of the Underwriter's Mutual Insurance Company. After leaving this Corporation, he was employed by various firms as Draftsman.

When Mr. Perkins was nineteen years old he determined to become an architect and for a series of years his evenings were devoted to study. In 1908 he was examined for his Architect's License at the University of Illinois, and passed with high honors.

From 1906 to 1908, Mr. Perkins was in charge of the design and erection of new buildings at the Morton Salt Plant, at Hutchinson, Kans. For two years thereafter, he was engaged in the private practice of Architecture and Structural Engineering in Chicago.

In August, 1911, he entered the employ of the International Packing Company, as Architect and Structural Engineer, where he remained until 1913. From 1913 to 1916 he held a similar position with the Morton Salt Company, in charge of the design and construction of building operations at Hutchinson, Kans., Port Huron and Ludington, Mich., and Grand Saline, Tex. At this time Mr. Perkins was regarded as being more experienced in the design, both structural and mechanical, of salt plants than any of his contemporaries. In 1916, he received his engineering license and for the next five years was engaged in private practice, designing domestic, public, and industrial buildings.

In May, 1921, he went to Manistee, Mich., as Designer, Engineer, and Superintendent of Construction of the Ruggles and Rademaker Salt Plant, which had a daily output capacity of 8 000 bbl., and was probably the largest and most modern salt plant in the world.

When Mr. Perkins returned to Chicago in August, 1922, his interest turned to architectural designing, and he was employed as a designer for various architectural firms. From September, 1924, until February, 1927, he was engaged in remodeling the interior of the First National Bank of Chicago, which was incorporated with the First Trust and Savings Bank. From February to May, 1927, he was Chief Designer for Graven and Mayger, Architects, during which time he designed, in part, the Wetzman Theatre in Detroit, Mich., and the Albee and Keith Theatre, in Rochester, N. Y.

It was while working on the latter theatre that Mr. Perkins became ill with spinal meningitis. He died on May 18, 1927. He was married in 1901 to Vera Ramenstein. He is survived by a son, Frank W., and a daughter, Vera.

* Memoir prepared by Isidore Cohen, M. Am. Soc. C. E.

Mr. Perkins was of a modest and sympathetic disposition, a most lovable and agreeable companion. To those who knew him, his friends and associates, his death was a severe shock. The community at large has suffered by the premature death of a man and worker who mentally combined a rare esthetic taste with not inconsiderable engineering ability.

Mr. Perkins was elected a Member of the American Society of Civil Engineers on July 11, 1921.

CHARLES JULIUS POETSCH, M. Am. Soc. C. E.*

DIED OCTOBER 7, 1926.

Charles Julius Poetsch was born in Wriezen, near Berlin, Germany, on July 17, 1850. He was educated in the public schools and the German Real Schule (a college), and came to Milwaukee, Wis., in 1871.

Mr. Poetsch began his engineering work in the United States as a Draftsman and, later, was appointed Assistant Engineer on the survey and construction of the Milwaukee and Northern Railway, having been with this Company from 1870 to 1874. In 1875, he was Assistant Engineer for the Green Bay and Western Railway Company, all this work having been done in the State of Wisconsin. He then became Resident Engineer for the Chicago, Milwaukee and St. Paul Railway Company, at Minneapolis, Minn., which position he held from 1875 to 1878.

In 1878, he returned to Milwaukee, where he was appointed a Division Engineer in the City Engineer's Office, also acting as Assistant City Engineer. This work consisted of giving lines and grades for various street construction, water mains and sewers, bridge construction, and other miscellaneous municipal improvements. He remained in this position until 1899 when he was appointed City Engineer.

In this capacity, Mr. Poetsch was also *ex officio* President of the Board of Public Works, and his guidance in the policy of local improvements enabled the City to undertake many notable projects. The construction of the Grand Avenue Bridge, the first bascule bridge erected in Milwaukee, was directed by Mr. Poetsch. Since then all other bridges erected by the City have been of this type. Two long viaducts of steel construction, spanning the lowlands of the Menominee River Valley, were also designed and constructed under his direction.

A flushing tunnel, a pumping station, and an intake from Lake Michigan, delivering water to the upper reaches of the Kinnickinnic River to prevent stagnation of the river waters during the low-flow periods of the summer, was also built by Mr. Poetsch.

The water-works of the city were also directly in his charge, as Superintendent. In that capacity he directed the purchase of pumping equipment, the first enlargement of the present North Point Pumping Station on the shore of Lake Michigan, the inland high-service pumping station, and the extensions of large feeder mains and the pumping station at West Allis, Wis., a suburb of Milwaukee. The first method for treating the water supply with chlorine, using hypochlorite dosing, was designed by Mr. Poetsch.

In all his works, he was ever thoughtful of economy in construction, and the various local improvements were made at the greatest saving to the citizens.

In 1911, Mr. Poetsch severed his connection with public work and engaged in private practice. He established the firm of Poetsch and Geiger, Con-

* Memoir prepared by C. S. Gruetzmacher, Assoc. M. Am. Soc. C. E., and H. P. Bohman, Supt., Water Dept., Milwaukee, Wis.

sulting Engineers on municipal work of all kinds. Ill health in 1916, and subsequent thereto, caused the abandonment of his private practice and forced his retirement from active engineering work. He was President of the Cummings Boulevard Land Company and a Director in the Home Savings Bank of Milwaukee, and he devoted his time to these and other business activities in which he was engaged.

During the later years of his life, Mr. Poetsch always found time to revisit the scenes of his former activities in the City Engineer's Department, lending able advice. He was a frequent visitor at the meetings of the local engineering societies and the Old Settlers' Club of which he was a member. He was also a member of the Wisconsin Lodge No. 1, Knights of Pythias. During his long services in public office, he gained a vast acquaintance by whom he will be greatly missed.

He was married in 1873 to Minnie E. Rausch. They had one daughter, now Mrs. Daisy L. Laming, of Tonganoxie, Kans., who, with her mother, survives him.

Mr. Poetsch was elected a Junior of the American Society of Civil Engineers on May 4, 1881, and a Member on May 2, 1883.

MERLE WILLIAM ROSECRANS, M. Am. Soc. C. E.*

Died October 9, 1927.

Merle William Rosecrans, the son of William E. and Florence S. (Cornwell) Rosecrans, was born at Ruthven, Iowa, on September 1, 1889. He received his Grammar School education in the schools of Bridgewater, S. Dak. and his High School training at Canton, S. Dak. He was graduated from the Iowa State College, at Ames, Iowa, in 1912, with the degree of Bachelor of Science in Civil Engineering.

During his undergraduate days, Mr. Rosecrans spent his summers with various survey parties in South Dakota and Iowa. On graduating from college he entered the general contracting business with his father, Mr. W. E. Rosecrans, and they built a number of water-works and sewer systems for various cities in Iowa. In 1913, Mr. Rosecrans went to Oregon as Assistant Engineer for C. W. Woodruff, Consulting Engineer, of Portland, but resigned in 1915 to again enter into business with his father. He was engaged in the saw-mill and logging industry until 1918, when he closed out his interests and become Assistant Professor of Civil Engineering at the Oregon State College. In 1919, he left the College and became Assistant Bridge Engineer for the Oregon State Highway Commission, which position he held until his death in the Salem General Hospital on October 9, 1927, after an illness of one month.

Mr. Rosecrans was admirably fitted for the positions of trust and responsibility which he held. Entering the Highway Department, as he did, at an early period in its organization, his keen insight into human nature and his knowledge of construction did much to smooth out the many troubles incident to a young and rapidly growing organization. His executive ability and unquestioned fairness were great factors in binding the Department together and co-ordinating its work to the high standard of efficiency in which he left it. Beyond every other trait which he possessed stands out that priceless quality of loyalty, not only to his work and to his superiors, but also to those subordinate to him. It was this quality that endeared him to all who were so fortunate as to be associated with him. During his eight years of faithful service with the Highway Department, Mr. Rosecrans handled contracts amounting, in the aggregate, to many millions of dollars, and it is a remarkable commentary on his sterling character, kindly personality, and keen appreciation of his responsibilty that he was generally regarded, not as a stern task master and uncompromising public official, but rather as a sincere friend and valued adviser by all with whom he worked.

* Memoir prepared by L. P. Campbell, and C. B. McCullough, Members, Am. Soc. C. E., and G. S. Paxson, Assoc. M. Am. Soc. C. E.

Mr. Rosecrans was prominent in fraternal circles. At the time of his death he was Master of Pacific Lodge No. 50 A. F. and A. M. He was also Secretary of the Northwestern Society of Highway Engineers, and he was a member of Tau Beta Pi.

He was married in 1922 to Margaret Hodge who, with his father, William E. Rosecrans, and his brother, Richard Rosecrans, survives him. It can be truthfully said of him that he left a place in the hearts of his relatives, friends, and business associates that can never be filled.

Mr. Rosecrans was elected an Associate Member of the American Society of Civil Engineers on October 11, 1920, and a Member on October 1, 1926.

CHARLES HENRY RUST, M. Am. Soc. C. E.*

Died September 22, 1927.

Charles Henry Rust was born at Great Waltham, Essex, England, on December 25, 1852. He was educated at Brentwood Grammar School in the same county and, in 1872, went with his family to Canada.

Soon after his arrival in Canada, Mr. Rust accepted a position on the Engineering Staff which was then engaged on a preliminary survey of the Ontario and Quebec Railway. Five years later, he entered the service of the City of Toronto, Ont., as Rodman on the Engineering Force under the late Frank Shanly, who was then City Engineer.

In 1881, Mr. Rust was appointed to the office of Assistant Engineer by the late R. J. Brough, M. Am. Soc. C. E., City Engineer and Manager of Water-Works, and, in 1883 was made Assistant Engineer in charge of sewers, which position he held until 1891. During this period he also served as Principal Assistant Engineer, and in the spring of 1892, after the resignation of Mr. Granville C. Cunningham, who had been Acting City Engineer, he was made Acting City Engineer until the appointment of the new City Engineer, the late E. H. Keating, M. Am. Soc. C. E., in July of the same year. Mr. Rust was immediately appointed as Deputy City Engineer, and held this office until February, 1898, when, on the resignation of Mr. Keating, he was appointed City Engineer and Manager of the Water-Works.

During his connection with the City of Toronto, Mr. Rust originated and carried out a complete system of main drainage and sewage disposal; a modern filtration plant; a new intake and tunnel for the water-works; numerous important bridges; and many other improvements of lasting benefit to the city. His duties also included reports on many plans, which, although they required much time and painstaking study, were never brought to fruition.

He reported at intervals on water-works and sewerage problems for neighboring municipalities and occasionally acted as an arbitrator. Although his services were frequently in demand as a consultant and expert, his routine duties occupied so much of his time that he was unable to accede to many requests for professional advice.

In 1912, Mr. Rust, having been attracted by the mild climate, and the prospect of the pending construction of a new municipal water supply, resigned the position of City Engineer of Toronto to accept a similar one in Victoria, B. C. While in Victoria he was requested by the Government to report on the Greater Vancouver Sewerage Scheme. At this time he also reported on the Second Narrows Bridge, near Vancouver, B. C.

In 1918, he returned to Toronto under an engagement with the management of the Toronto Street Railway and Toronto Electric Light Company.

* Memoir prepared by A. C. D. Blanchard, M. Am. Soc. C. E.

Later, these organizations were brought under municipal control, and thus Mr. Rust again became identified with the City of Toronto, this time as an official of the Toronto Hydro-Electric System. He retained this position until his death.

In 1887, Mr. Rust was elected as one of the first members of the Canadian Society of Civil Engineers, now the Engineering Institute of Canada. He was greatly interested in its affairs and served in various capacities until in 1911 he was elected President of the Society. In 1902, he was elected President of the American Society of Municipal Improvements. He was also a member of the Executive Committee of the American Water Works Association and, for many years, of the Royal Canadian Yacht Club as well as of the National Club of Toronto.

In 1879, Mr. Rust was married to Alice Preston, who survives him. His kindly and affectionate disposition endeared him to all those who were privileged to know him intimately. His mature judgment, unfailing courtesy, and tactful manner fitted him for the numerous high positions which he held in the Engineering Profession. He was loved and respected by his many business associates.

Mr. Rust was elected a Member of the American Society of Civil Engineers on April 5, 1899, and served as Vice-President in 1913 and 1914.

GODFREY LEWIS SMITH, M. Am. Soc. C. E.*

Died July 2, 1927.

Godfrey Lewis Smith was born in San Francisco, Calif., on July 13, 1876, the son of Charles J. J. and Julia B. (Kelley) Smith. He was graduated from the San Francisco Public Schools and High School. In September, 1894, he entered the Massachusetts Institute of Technology and remained there as a student, until February, 1899, with the exception of one year when he was ill.

As a boy, Mr. Smith spent many of his free hours in a machine shop owned by his uncle, Lewis Kelley. He was so adaptable that, at the age of fifteen, he was able to operate all the machines in the shop, including firing the boiler and running the steam engine.

On leaving college he entered the employ of the Newport News Shipbuilding and Dry Dock Company, at Newport News, Va., and from February until June, 1899, he was in charge of filing and indexing hull drawings. From June, 1899, to May, 1905, he was engaged in designing and calculating ships' lines and structure, testing materials, estimating the cost of hulls, and surveying of property.

In September of the same year, Mr. Smith was made Engineer in charge of construction, which position he held until March, 1909. During this time he was in charge of the design and construction of one of the largest dry docks then built in the United States. He was appointed Civil Engineer in March, 1909, and in that capacity had charge of all designs and construction of dry docks, piers, bulkheads, trestles, shipways, buildings, tracks, roads, foundations, and other plant work, including some mechanical equipment. He held this position until January, 1924, when he was transferred to the Sales Department of the Company where he remained until his death, at which time he was Acting Sales Manager.

Mr. Smith took a prominent part in the civic and political affairs of Newport News and at one time was President of the Chamber of Commerce and a member of the Board of Directors of that body for a number of years. He was also a member of the Chamber of Commerce of the State of Virginia.

He served several terms as a member of the City Council and during a part of this time he was Chairman of the Finance Committee. He waged an almost constant fight for sound city financing and was an authority on the subject.

For many years before the city management form of government was adopted in Newport News, Mr. Smith was an interested and active advocate of simplified municipal government, and it was largely through his efforts that

* Memoir prepared by E. G. Rogers, Esq., Newport News, Va.

this plan was accepted by the city. He was so active in behalf of the reform that he was known to many of his associates as the "Father" of the City Manager form of government and when the new method became effective, he was the only member of the old Council to be returned to office.

On June 9, 1908, Mr. Smith was married to Miriam Post who, with four children, Margaret Post, Elizabeth Lewis, Walter Post, and Godfrey Lewis, Jr., survives him.

Mr. Smith was elected a Member of the American Society of Civil Engineers on July 6, 1920.

JOHN CLARK SPENCER, M. Am. Soc. C. E.*

Died July 6, 1927.

John Clark Spencer was born in Clinton, Iowa, on August 26, 1869. He attended the State University of Iowa, from which he was graduated with the degree of Civil Engineer in 1891.

After leaving college, he entered the employ of the Chicago Bridge and Iron Company, of Chicago, Ill., holding a position in which he detailed, designed, and estimated highway bridges. This work included the Winona High Bridge over the Mississippi River, at Winona, Minn., and the Vermillion River Bridge, at Danville, Ill.

In 1893, Mr. Spencer became Engineer for the Portland Bridge and Building Company, of Portland, Ore., in which capacity he had charge of all the preliminary work for the South Eleventh Street Viaduct, Tacoma, Wash. Two years later, as Engineer for the Clinton Bridge and Iron Works, Clinton, Iowa, he was in charge of the office and shop work comprising the design and construction of the Mississippi River Bridge, at Brainard, Minn. In 1897, he completed a course in law at the Cleveland Law School, Cleveland, Ohio, and successfully passed the bar examination. He practiced law to some extent, but soon returned to engineering.

From February, 1898, to May, 1900, he was employed with the Keystone Bridge Works, at Pittsburgh, Pa., as Squad Master in charge of bridge, viaduct, and heavy mill building. At this time, he also made preliminary studies for new Bridge Shops, and after being transferred to the Designing Department in 1899, he planned the major part of Hot Metal Bridge for the Union Railroad Company, at Rankin, Pa.

In May, 1900, Mr. Spencer served in the Berlin and New York Offices of the American Bridge Company. As Designing Engineer, he made the plans for all classes of mill and factory buildings, pier sheds, coal bunkers, and similar structures. Subsequently, he was employed for one year with the Brown Hoist and Machinery Company, on the design of coal and storage plants. Three years later, in the employ of the American Bridge Company of Pittsburgh, he designed all classes of structural steel for manufacturing, office, and mercantile buildings. Among these were the Masonic Temple, at Carnegie, Pa.; the Maloney Building, at Pittsburgh (thirteen stories, not built); the Candler Building, at Atlanta, Ga.; and the high, steel frame, power house for the Central Heating Company, at Detroit, Mich.

In 1905, Mr. Spencer opened an office in Cleveland, where he practiced as a Consulting Engineer. He designed the steel work for the Rockefeller Office Building, as well as several other large buildings in Cleveland and in various other cities. His last work was the planning of the steel construction for the new, 22-story, Brotherhood of Locomotive Engineers Bank Building, at Cleveland, which was completed previous to his death.

* Memoir prepared by Charles M. Clark, Esq., Cleveland, Ohio.

Mr. Spencer was always unselfishly interested in Cleveland's civic affairs and gave much of his time to the study and investigation of contemplated city improvements. He was a close observer of men, and very active in his profession up to within a short time of his death.

He was a great lover of books, his studies covering the arts, sciences, philosophy, and law. He was very modest and unassuming, and impressed all with whom he came in contact as dependable and honorable—a gentleman in every respect. He was very approachable and had helped many young men to get a start in life, either by good advice or by financial assistance. Those with whom he was associated learned to know him as one inspired by the highest motives.

He was married, soon after his graduation from the Iowa State University, to Mary E. Huston, the daughter of J. M. Huston, County Surveyor and Engineer, of Clinton, Iowa, who survives him. They had known each other since childhood, and their home life was ideal.

Mr. Spencer was elected a Member of the American Society of Civil Engineers on December 6, 1904.

ALLEN NEWHALL SPOONER, M. Am. Soc. C. E.*

Died January 2, 1928.

Allen Newhall Spooner was born at Jersey City, N. J., on October 2, 1864. He was the son of Edward A. and Angela (Newhall) Spooner, a grand-nephew of William Howe, the inventor of the Howe truss bridge, and also, a second cousin of Elias Howe, Jr., the inventor of the sewing machine. Mr. Spooner's earlier education was obtained in the public schools of Jersey City. In 1882, he entered the School of Mines, Columbia University, New York, N. Y., from which he was graduated in 1886 with the degree of Civil Engineer. He was a member of the Psi Upsilon Fraternity, and active in behalf of his Alma Mater, both as an undergraduate and as an Alumnus.

Immediately after his graduation, Mr. Spooner entered the employ of the Pennsylvania Railroad Company as a Rodman and Draftsman, and, in 1888, he was appointed a Hydrographer in the Department of Docks of the City of New York. From 1889 to 1906 he was Assistant Engineer in charge of construction work, and built most of the granite bulkhead wall along the Manhattan shore of the East River. In 1906, he was appointed Commissioner of Docks under Mayor McClellan, and it was under his régime that the Chelsea Piers were completed, the South Brooklyn water-front developed from 24th to 39th Streets, and the Staten Island and 39th Street, South Brooklyn, Ferry Terminals put into operation. Previous to his appointment as Commissioner of Docks Mr. Spooner was retained as Consulting Engineer and expert on water-front real estate valuation by such well-known companies as James Shewan and Sons, Incorporated, the North German Lloyd and Hamburg-American Steamship Lines, the New York Dock Company, and the Standard Oil Company of New Jersey.

From 1910 to 1913, Mr. Spooner was Chief Engineer of the New York Submarine Contracting Company and successfully handled the difficult work of placing two 36-in. submarine gas mains across the Harlem River at 210th Street, and one 48-in. main at 129th Street. In 1914, he organized the contracting firm of Allen N. Spooner & Son, Incorporated, and through his indefatigable efforts, his power in handling men, and his exceptional executive ability, during the period of thirteen years prior to his death, he, as President of the Company, brought it from a position of the smallest to one of the largest and best organized water-front contracting organizations in New York Harbor.

Mr. Spooner's career was cut off when he was about to realize the rewards of a life devoted to business; at a moment when the responsibilities of a long period of both public and private service were to be laid aside for the quiet pleasures of retirement. His rare qualities of character were apparent to all who came in contact with him. He was most charitable and tolerant, profoundly sympathetic, and an accurate judge of human nature. He had unusual powers of organization and exceptional executive ability which made

* Memoir prepared by F. R. W. Cleverdon, M. Am. Soc. C. E.

it possible for him to secure the loyal co-operation of subordinates. Added to a modesty and generosity of spirit, was an inflexible integrity in behalf of the highest business and personal standards. All these qualities stand out as an inspiration to those in the profession, and a rich memory to his family and to all who had the privilege of his personal friendship.

He died at St. Luke's Hospital, in New York, after a major operation, on January 2, 1928. He is survived by his wife (*nee* Bertha Klaproth) and three children by his first wife (*nee* Emma F. Browne), Mrs. Violet Langsford Sears, John Irving Spooner, Affiliate Am. Soc. C. E., and Ray Newhall Spooner, M. Am. Soc. C. E.

Mr. Spooner was elected a Member of the American Society of Civil Engineers on December 5, 1900.

HORACE AUGUSTUS SUMNER, M. Am. Soc. C. E.*

Died December 31, 1926.

Horace Augustus Sumner, the son of Robert S. and Mary Beals Sumner, was born at Stoughton, Mass., on March 18, 1845, and received his education in the public schools.

In July, 1864, he entered the Engineering Department of the Old Colony Railroad Company and was engaged as Chainman and Rodman on location and construction in Massachusetts and Vermont. He was also employed on similar work on the Portland and Ogdensburgh Railroad.

From April, 1868, to January, 1870, Mr. Sumner served as Transitman on location of the Burlington and Missouri River Railroad in Iowa. During this time he had charge of a division and constructed thirteen miles of the road near Corning, Iowa.

In April, 1870, he became Transitman on location of the Burlington and Missouri River Railroad, in Nebraska, from Crete to Fort Kearney, and from July, 1870, to July, 1871, he was Engineer in charge of location and construction of the Burlington and Southwestern Railroad from Rulo to Humboldt, Nebr. From July, 1871, to November, 1873, he acted as Assistant Chief Engineer of the Burlington and Southwestern Railroad from Viele, Iowa, to Unionville, Mo., and from July, 1874, to May, 1875, he was Engineer of Public Works, Burlington, Iowa.

He then accepted the position of Division Engineer in charge of about ten miles of construction of the Knoxville Branch of the Chicago, Burlington, and Quincy Railroad, near Knoxville, Iowa, and carried on this work for a year.

Mr. Sumner was Chief Engineer of the Burlington and Southwestern Railroad Company, including the territory from Viele, Iowa, to Laclede, Mo., from May, 1876, to January, 1882, when he became Chief Engineer of the St. Louis, Keokuk, and Northwestern Railroad and the Chicago, Burlington, and Kansas City Railroad Companies. He held this position, until May, 1884, with headquarters at Keokuk, Iowa.

From June, 1885, to March, 1886, he was Resident Engineer on construction of thirty miles of the Chicago, Burlington, and Northern Railroad, at East Dubuque, Ill. In June, 1886, he engaged on location work in Colorado, principally in the mountains, on what is now the Moffat Railroad over the Continental Divide, and in February, 1894, he accepted the position of Chief Engineer of the Florence and Cripple Creek Railroad Company. He held this position until April, 1895, when he was appointed State Engineer of Colorado, which office he held for two years.

---

* Memoir prepared by R. S. Sumner, M. Am. Soc. C. E.

Mr. Sumner served as Chief Engineer of the Alamogordo and Sacramento Mountain Railroad Company, in New Mexico, from November, 1897, to September, 1898, when he was appointed Chief Engineer of the El Paso and Northeastern Railway Company and was engaged on construction from El Paso, Tex., to Dawson, N. Mex. He resigned in 1902 to become Chief Engineer of the Moffat Railroad, in which position he made surveys from Denver, Colo., to Salt Lake City, Utah, and was also engaged in construction work from Denver to Steamboat Springs, Colo.

From 1912 to 1914, he was Chief Engineer on location surveys in California and Oregon for a company that was absorbed by the Southern Pacific Railway Company which built the line from Medford to Marshfield, Ore. From 1914 until his death he was engaged in general consulting work in Denver, Colo.

Mr. Sumner is survived by his widow and two sons, Robert S. Sumner, M. Am. Soc. C. E., and Lewis A. Sumner.

His past record is amply covered by the following tribute:

"Mr. Sumner * * * was an engineer of National prominence; but he was also a moral engineer, for he constructed his life on the divine lines of force, of integrity and uprightness, humility and gentleness, love and magnanimity, a reasonable and sincere faith in God. He was a towering pine of the forest. His many friends join in sympathy with his wife and sons, not only because they are our friends, but because we share with them their love of this great man who has died."

Mr. Sumner was elected a Member of the American Society of Civil Engineers on October 4, 1899, and served as Director of the Society from 1909 to 1911.

ROBERT L'HOMMEDIEU TATE, M. Am. Soc. C. E.*

DIED DECEMBER 20, 1927.

Robert L'Hommedieu Tate, the son of Robert W. and Susan (L'Hommedieu) Tate, was born at Union Springs, N. Y., on September 3, 1888.

He attended the public schools of New York City, and was graduated from Morris High School in 1907. He then entered Cornell University, Ithaca, N. Y., from which he was graduated in 1912 with the degree of Civil Engineer.

Mr. Tate's preliminary professional apprenticeship was as a Surveyor and Topographer on the Costa Rica-Panama Boundary Survey in 1912. Subsequent to his return to the United States, he was engaged for a short period in the office of F. A. Molitor, M. Am. Soc. C. E., Consulting Engineer, New York City. Later, he became a Draftsman on a hydro-electric project in West Virginia.

In 1914, he was an Assistant Engineer for the Delaware, Lackawanna and Western Railway Company on Maintenance of Way and Construction, which position he retained until 1917.

During the participation by the United States in the World War, between May, 1917, and July, 1918, Mr. Tate was engaged in the military service of his country. He attended the first Officers' Training Camp, at Madison Barracks, N. Y., and on April 16, 1917, was commissioned a First Lieutenant in the Engineer Officers Reserve Corps. On May 26, 1917, he was ordered to active duty, having been assigned to the 303d Engineers, the Divisional Engineer Combat Regiment of the 78th Division. He went overseas with his regiment in May, 1918, was promoted to the rank of Captain in July, 1918, and served in the St. Mihiel and Meuse-Argonne offensives. During a portion of this period he acted as Regimental Personnel Adjutant. At the close of the war he returned to the United States, and was honorably discharged in June, 1919.

As a Junior Officer, Mr. Tate's military service was founded on the same patriotism as that which prompted so many of the younger engineers to "learn the game" at Officers' Training Camps. With many others of the same age he "did his bit" with fortitude and success, both from a military and an engineering standpoint.

Following his discharge from the Army, Mr. Tate again entered foreign service as an Assistant Engineer on the design and construction of a town and plant for the mining of bauxite in Dutch Guiana. Here, he designed and constructed a complete town site, with business and residential buildings for 4 000 people, including the installation of electric lights, as well as a sewer system and a surface mining plant. This work entailed a stadia survey, under difficult topographic conditions, through dense tropical jungles along the boundary line.

* Memoir prepared by Frederic Molitor, M. Am. Soc. C. E.

He returned from Dutch Guiana in April, 1921, and from the early part of 1922 until June, 1924, was engaged with A. B. Cohen, M. Am. Soc. C. E., Consulting Engineer, whom he assisted in the design, plans, and estimates for a reinforced concrete bridge that was to carry the Hudson Boulevard at Journal Square, Jersey City, N. J. From 1924 to the time of his death, he was engaged as a Resident Engineer on the Hudson Boulevard project, in charge of the field work incident to the construction of this bridge.

Mr. Tate's professional career was marked by a close attention to detail, thorough research studies, and a complete application to the problems assigned to him. He gave promise of a broad and distinguished future, and his many friends in the Engineering Profession expressed keen regret that such a career should have been cut short by an untimely and early death. Mr. Tate was noted for the warm friendships that he made in the profession and in the Army.

At the time of his death, he held a commission as Major in the Engineer Officers Reserve Corps. He is survived by his mother and his widow, Leonora T. (Van Derhoef) Tate.

Mr. Tate was elected a Junior of the American Society of Civil Engineers on March 4, 1913; an Associate Member on April 17, 1917; and a Member on December 14, 1925.

OSCAR HOLMES TRIPP, M. Am. Soc. C. E.*

Died August 24, 1927.

Oscar Holmes Tripp was born January 15, 1852, at Waterboro, Me., the son of the Reverend Leander and Louisa A. Tripp. His father was a Baptist clergyman and his early years are difficult to trace because of the migrations made necessary by this calling. His youth was spent in Hancock County, Maine, where he received his primary education in the public schools. He afterward attended one of the Maine academies and later studied law, being admitted to the Hancock County Bar, and subsequently practicing at Bluehill, Me. As was not uncommon in the earlier days, he carried on the practice of surveying in conjunction with the practice of law, but gradually a keener interest in the problems of engineering drew him from the legal profession and it was as an engineer that he was known.

From 1881 to 1884, Mr. Tripp was employed as Assistant Engineer on the Bangor and Katahdin Iron Works Railway, and the Bangor and Piscataquis Railroad. Both these roads are now part of the Bangor and Aroostook System. In 1885, he opened an office at Rockland, Me., for the general practice of engineering, and except for occasional short engagements in other sections of Maine, and fifteen months of the years 1898 and 1899 spent as Assistant Engineer in the Sewer Department at Arlington, Mass., he was located at Rockland. During this period, he served for several terms as City Engineer.

He was an assiduous reader, with a taste for literature and history as well as science. He was very observant and this, coupled with the fact that he made a record of his observations and the happenings of the day, gradually made his office a treasure house of accurate information on local history.

Mr. Tripp was a member of the Knox County Bar Association and, for several years, had served it most efficiently as Treasurer and Librarian. He was a member of the Congregational Church. He was a Scottish Rite and a York Rite Mason. He was also a member of the Boston Society of Civil Engineers.

He died suddenly of heart failure in the Houston-Tuttle Book Store in Rockland, while browsing, as was so often his custom, among the new books. For several years Mr. Tripp had been in ill health and none realized as well as he, how near death hovered. Nevertheless, he continued his work up to the day preceding his death. He was unmarried, and his nearest surviving relative is a niece, Mrs. Flora T. Cooper, of Portland, Ore.

Mr. Tripp was elected an Associate Member of the American Society of Civil Engineers on October 7, 1896, and a Member on September 5, 1905.

* Memoir prepared by Walter C. Groves, Assoc. M. Am. Soc. C. E.

PETRUS WAHLMAN, M. Am. Soc. C. E.*

Died March 11, 1926.

Petrus Wahlman was born at Gefle, Sweden, on March 11, 1879. He received his early education at a school in Gefle and his technical training at the Royal University of Technology in Stockholm, Sweden, from which he was graduated in May, 1902, with the degree of Civil Engineer, having specialized in highway and hydraulic subjects. During his summer vacations he was engaged on railway location and survey work.

From June, 1902, to March, 1904, Mr. Wahlman held the position of Superintendent on the construction of the water-works and sewer system for Hudiksvall, Sweden, the cost of which was $110 000, and from March to August, 1904, he conducted the work on the extension of the water-works of Oxelösund, Sweden.

In September, 1904, he investigated the stresses, through elongation tests, in two of the bridges of the State Railways of Sweden and in November, 1904, he became affiliated with the Hydraulic Engineering Company, Limited, of Stockholm, continuing in this position until May, 1907. During this period he made field studies, reports, and complete designs of water power plants in Sweden and Norway and supervised the design and construction of the water-works and sewer system for Djursholm.

In 1907, Mr. Wahlman came to the United States and in June of that year secured a position as Draftsman with the firm of Vielé, Blackwell, and Buck, of New York, N. Y., on the design of the hydraulic plant of the Great Western Power Company.

From March, 1908, to February, 1909, he was engaged in work for the New York State Water Supply Commission, at Albany, making studies and designs for water power plants, storage dams, etc., and the utilization of the water powers of New York State for electrification. From March to June, 1909, he was occupied on hydraulic computations and the design for a power plant at Boulder, Colo., which was being erected by the Central Colorado Power Company. In June, 1909, he was engaged by the Ontario Power Company, of Niagara Falls, N. Y., to make hydraulic computations and designs for the extension of the Company's plant.

During the period from 1910 to 1913, Mr. Wahlman acted as Chief Engineer of the Construction Department of the Hydro-Electric Company of Tucuman, Argentine Republic, where he had responsible charge of the design and construction of an 18 000-h.p. water power plant on the Lules River and of two railways, the cost of which was $2 500 000. His duties included the building of a water-power plant for the utilization of two falls with a combined output of 40 000 h.p. situated at the foot of the Andes Mountains, approximately 600 miles from Buenos Aires, Argentine Republic. At times, he had as many as 1 000 workmen and many engineers in his employ.

* Memoir compiled from information on file at the Headquarters of the Society.

In 1914, Mr. Wahlman made reports on engineering conditions in the South American Republics on the Pacific Coast and also visited the then more recently constructed water power plants in the United States, Canada, and Alaska. He was also interested in the development of the Speel River water-power project in Alaska.

In 1915, he became associated with Mr. R. D. Johnson, and under the firm name of Johnson and Wahlman carried on consulting work in hydraulic engineering in New York. This firm also contributed toward the development of the water-power projects on the Canadian side of Niagara Falls, where many new and valuable designs were carried out.

Late in December, 1924, he was forced to withdraw from his work and go South for his health, returning a little later to his home in Sweden. All his efforts to recover his strength were in vain, and he passed away on his birthday, March 11, 1926.

Through his engineering affiliations and his large circle of friends Mr. Wahlman quietly assisted many Swedish engineers who came to the United States in search of employment. Although he did not consider his services of great consequence, he will long be remembered by those men whose road to success was made easier by his advice.

He was very fond of sports, having participated as gymnast and swimmer in the first modern Olympic Games at Athens, Greece, in 1906. His favorite games were football and tennis and as a fancy skater he had won a championship.

His individuality was strongly marked by a most unusual self-control, evincing itself in a demeanor of faultless good breeding and gentility, kindliness and modesty of disposition, and unselfish consideration for others. His most outstanding characteristic in the opinion of all his acquaintances was that of a thorough gentleman in every sense of the word. He was a true son of the Nordic race and his many fine characteristics made him esteemed by all who knew him.

Mr. Wahlman was elected a Member of the American Society of Civil Engineers on December 6, 1915.

PHILIP ALBERT WELKER, M. Am. Soc. C. E.*

Died December 24, 1926.

Philip Albert Welker, the son of Philip and Maria (Pauly) Welker, was born at Toledo, Ohio, on June 1, 1857. He received his education in the public schools of Toledo, and was graduated from the High School in June, 1874. He then entered Cornell University from which he was graduated in June, 1878, with the degree of Civil Engineer.

After serving for a year as Assistant with the City Civil Engineer of Toledo, he was appointed in July, 1879, to a position with the United States Coast and Geodetic Survey and was engaged on the transcontinental triangulation in Missouri.

From 1880 to 1890, Mr. Welker was occupied in primary triangulation and astronomical work in British Columbia, Washington, Southern California, Utah, Nevada, and Florida. He carried out work in precise levels in the States of Arkansas, Illinois, and Tennessee, as well as special surveys for the Navy Yard Site Commission in Escambia Bay, Florida, and for the location of the trans-meridianal line at Toledo. He also made hydrographic surveys of the harbor at Baltimore, Md., San Francisco Bay and tributaries, San Pablo Bay, and Suisun Bay, California, as well as of the Atchafalaya River, in Louisiana, Pensacola Bay and tributaries, in Florida, and, also, Maumee Bay, Ohio, for the State Fish Commission. During this period he made observations for the transit of Venus over the sun at Tepusquet, Calif., and a determination of the magnetic elements at the U. S. Coast and Geodetic Survey, as well as observations of the annular eclipse of the sun at San Francisco.

From 1891 to 1910, he carried out work in hydrographic surveying in Florida, Louisiana, and along the Atlantic Coast as far north as Maine. In 1893, he represented the Government of the United States in field observations connected with the survey of the boundary between Alaska and Canada. During the two years following, he continued to carry on boundary survey work in Alaska. In 1898, he was placed in command of the U. S. Coast and Geodetic Survey Steamer, *Bache,* continuing in this capacity until 1910, during which time he made surveys of Portsmouth Harbor and its approaches in New Hampshire and Maine, and along the coasts of the Atlantic Ocean and Gulf of Mexico, and in the Caribbean Sea.

In 1910, Captain Welker again represented the Government of the United States on a Commission of Engineers created for the purpose of determining the location and ownership of the Fort Myers Military Road, Virginia. While on a furlough of six months he organized the Welker Supply Company, at Cleveland, Ohio, and was elected President of the Corporation.

On the expiration of his furlough, Captain Welker was sent to Alaska where he determined the longitude of the Cities of Fairbanks and Tanana.

* Memoir prepared from information on file at the Headquarters of the Society.

On February 26, 1911, he was given charge of the Sub-Office of the U. S. Coast and Geodetic Survey at Manila, Philippine Islands, and until February 28, 1914, served as Director of Coast Surveys in the Islands. He also served as a member and Secretary of the Philippine Committee on Geographical Names and as a member of the Harbor Lines Commission of the Philippine Islands.

On October 10, 1914, he was appointed Assistant in charge of the office of the U. S. Coast and Geodetic Survey of Washington, D. C., and served in that capacity until July 1, 1917, when the designation was changed to Hydrographic and Geodetic Engineer in charge of the office. On July 1, 1920, he was designated as Personnel Officer of the U. S. Coast and Geodetic Survey and held that position until he was retired from active duty on August 1, 1921.

During approximately fifteen years of his service with the U. S. Coast and Geodetic Survey, Captain Welker was in command of vessels. His surveys of the coasts of Porto Rico and off the Isthmus of Panama formed the basis for some of the first complete navigating charts of these waters prepared by the Federal Government. His service included all branches of activity in the Bureau, from triangulation and astronomical observations in his earlier days, through the duties of Hydrographer, to responsible administrative positions in Manila and Washington.

He died at his home in Washington, D. C., on December 24, 1926, and is survived by his widow, formerly Gertrude M. Lanahan, of Baltimore, a son, Philip Lanahan Welker, and a daughter, Mrs. Howard R. Willis, of Cleveland, Ohio.

The conspicuous services of Captain Welker deserve more than the expression of regret for the loss of an able engineer. Through his systematic operations he played an important part in the security and extension of American commerce by determining and describing the dangers in its path. His results had always in evidence a distinctive mark of originality of execution scientifically accomplished, thereby increasing the efficiency and precision of the methods and work of the U. S. Coast and Geodetic Survey and the reputation which it has always sustained.

His kind and genial disposition gained for him the regard of all his associates in the field and office work of the Survey, and all those who dealt with him could rely implicitly on his innate sense of justice. In private relations, Captain Welker was high in the esteem of a large circle of acquaintances, and he will be remembered for the steady practice of all the virtues and amenities which adorn social life.

He was a member of the Washington Society of Engineers, Beta Theta Pi, Cosmos and Federal Clubs in Washington, the University Club of Manila, and the Philippine Club of New York, N. Y. He was also a member of the St. John's Protestant Episcopal Church, a Thirty-second Degree Mason, and a Knights Templar.

Captain Welker was elected a Member of the American Society of Civil Engineers on April 25, 1921.

LEVI LOCKWOOD WHEELER, M. Am. Soc. C. E.*

Died March 13, 1927.

Levi Lockwood Wheeler was born on a farm near Jackson, Mich., on February 5, 1851, the only son of four children, of Sarah Houseman and Lorenzo Dow Wheeler. After receiving his primary education at a country school, he was graduated from the High School at Jackson, in 1870, and, subsequently, entered the University of Michigan at Ann Arbor, Mich. He completed the regular four-year course in Civil Engineering, and received the degree of Civil Engineer in June, 1874.

Mr. Wheeler entered the Civil Service of the United States on May 8, 1874, as Sub-Assistant on the United States Lake Survey at Detroit, Mich., where, with the exception of one summer, he continued until April, 1881. While on this work he ran one of two lines of precise levels for determining the elevations of the Great Lakes above sea level and, later, he reduced the data relating to this subject and prepared them for publication.† During his connection with the U. S. Lake Survey, Mr. Wheeler aided in the comparisons of standards of length, in the determination of latitudes and longitudes, and in the reduction of the notes relating thereto.

During the summer of 1881, he worked on his father's farm in Jackson County, Michigan.

In February, 1882, Mr. Wheeler was appointed an Assistant Engineer with the Mississippi River Commission at St. Louis, Mo., and remained in this position for six years. He made the topographic and hydrographic surveys of the Mississippi River and adjacent territory from Vicksburg to Natchez, Miss., and for a reach 110 miles long above Memphis, Tenn. He revised the methods which had been in use on precise level work under the Commission, pointed out the errors in methods formerly used, and prepared instructions for field work, which were subsequently followed by the Commission and used on other important surveys in the United States. Mr. Wheeler also had charge of the Computing Division for a number of years and prepared data for the use of the Commission and for publication.

In September, 1888, he was placed in charge of a Government survey for a 14-ft. waterway from Lake Michigan to the Illinois River. He made surveys covering two locations from Lake Michigan to Joliet, Ill., the report and maps of which were printed and used by the Sanitary District of Chicago, Ill., in the construction of the main canal and the Calumet-Sag Canal.

In November, 1890, Mr. Wheeler was appointed United States Assistant Engineer in charge of the location and construction of the Illinois and Mississippi Canal, extending from the Illinois River, near Hennepin, to the Mississippi River, near Rock Island, Ill. The summit level of the canal is supplied by a Feeder carrying the water from Rock River at Sterling, Ill. The main line and Feeder have a surface width of 80 ft. and a depth of 7 ft.,

* Memoir prepared by John W. Woermann, M. Am. Soc. C. E.

† *Professional Papers No. 24,* Corps of Engrs., U. S. A., Chapter XXII.

the main canal being 75 miles long and the Feeder 29 miles long. Mr. Wheeler was in immediate charge of the Western Section of the main canal which is 27 miles long, and also of the entire Feeder.

The structures on the Illinois and Mississippi Canal (better known as the Hennepin Canal) include 34 locks, 9 aqueduct bridges, 9 railway bridges, 69 highway bridges, 60 culverts, 3 dams, 51 houses, and numerous smaller structures. Construction was commenced in 1892, and the water was turned into the canal on October 24, 1907. Mr. Wheeler was subsequently in charge of the operation and maintenance of the canal until his retirement in 1921. A large number of the structures were designed as well as built under his direction and about $4 200 000 was expended on this canal under his immediate supervision.

In addition to his Government work, Mr. Wheeler was engaged in private practice, mainly in hydraulic work, and as Consulting Engineer and expert witness in connection with a number of projects. He designed and supervised the construction of water-power dams across the Rock River, at Sterling, Dixon, Oregon, and Sears, Ill., two of which were crib dams and two, concrete dams. He also designed a dam for Grand Detour, Ill., which was not built.

Mr. Wheeler was retired from the Government Service on February 5, 1921, at the age of 70 years, the retiring age prescribed by Congress for the Civil Service. On April 5, 1921, he returned home from a visit to his son in the Hawaiian Islands, and on April 15 suffered a cerebral hemorrhage, from which he never recovered. Eleven months before his death, he fell in his room, breaking a hip, as a result of which he was confined to his bed until his death on March 13, 1927. His daughter, Mrs. Clingan, states that "Never, in all the six years of his illness did he complain, but was ever thoughtful of others, and wanting others to be happy."

Mr. Wheeler was a great lover of Nature in all her aspects. He loved to fish and hunt, and was well posted on fish, birds, animals, trees, and flowers. He always enjoyed working in his garden and took pride in the beauty and variety of his fruits and flowers, especially of his tulips and irises. He was also an authority on bees and kept a number of hives in connection with his garden.

Extremely thorough, methodical and accurate in all his work, Mr. Wheeler was satisfied with nothing less from his subordinates. In connection with the construction of the Hennepin Canal he established a record for economy and efficiency which seldom has been equalled. He was gifted with a mind and physique which made it possible for him to keep in contact with all the details of his work, as well as with its larger and broader features. He seemed to be equally at home in the field, on location and construction, and in the office, in computing and designing. He was a man of fine appearance, possessed of remarkable energy and unusual capacity for hard work.

On January 7, 1880, Mr. Wheeler was married, at Detroit, to Isabella Chambers, who died on January 16, 1912. He is survived by four children, Arthur Chambers Wheeler, M. Am. Soc. C. E., of Hilo, Hawaii; Frank Dow Wheeler, Civil Engineer, of Chicago; Mabel Alice Wheeler, of Detroit; and Mrs. Grace Wheeler Clingan, of Sterling; also, one grandchild, Lee Grant Wheeler, of

Hilo, Hawaii. Mr. Wheeler was greatly devoted to his family, always keenly interested in their happiness and welfare, and never more happy than when spending his evenings at home surrounded by them.

He was a member of the Benevolent and Protective Order of Elks, at the rooms of which, he was a frequent attendant after his wife's death, and was at one time President of the Sterling Club, a social organization. For a number of years prior to his illness, he had been a Trustee of the First Presbyterian Church of Sterling, from which he was buried.

Mr. Wheeler was elected a Member of the American Society of Civil Engineers on June 4, 1884.

PHILIP AYLETT, Assoc. M. Am. Soc. C. E.*

Died November 28, 1927.

Philip Aylett was born on April 30, 1867, at "Montville", the Aylett Plantation on the Mattaponi River, in King William County, Virginia. Although of unassuming mien, he could have boasted of an ancestry scarcely equaled by any of his peers. He could have claimed, among others, Alexander Spottswood, one of the early Governors of Virginia, and Patrick Henry, one of the founders of this Nation. His father was William Roane Aylett, who as Colonel commanded the 53d Virginia Regiment of the Confederate Army, and his mother was Alice Brockenbrough Aylett, of Richmond County, Virginia.

After Mr. Aylett had received a thorough preparatory training, he was entered, in 1884, as a Cadet in the Virginia Military Institute, at Lexington, Va., from which he was graduated as a Civil Engineer in 1888. Afterward, he accepted a position as Principal and Instructor of Mathematics at Sunnyside Academy in Virginia. He held this position for one year and then commenced his life work as a Civil Engineer.

It would take more space than is permitted, to tell of the various surveys, engineering projects, etc., undertaken and accomplished by Mr. Aylett. His work carried him south as far as New Orleans, La.; west as far as St. Louis, Mo.; and north as far as Albany, N. Y. Early in his career he was engaged as Assistant Engineer in charge of tunnel work for the Baltimore and Ohio Railroad Company, at Harper's Ferry, W. Va. At another time, he was Construction Engineer on the Albermarle Sound Bridge for the Norfolk and Southern Railroad Company, and during 1894 and 1895 he was Engineer of Bridges on the Seaboard Air Line Railroad, at Portsmouth, Va. In 1906, he was appointed Principal Assistant Engineer on the Mississippi River Bridge at St. Louis. Traces of his engineering handiwork may be found in widely distributed places, among which are McKeesport, and Johnstown, Pa., Radford and Manchester, Va., and Winston, N. C., and Algiers, La.

The last years of his life were spent in and around New York, N. Y., where he was connected with the Valuation Department of the New York Central Railroad Company as well as with other similar important enterprises.

During the years between 1889 and 1927, Mr. Aylett gave unstintedly of his time in the furtherance of his chosen profession. He not only accomplished the work before him, but also found time to invent and patent a lock-joint pipe of very definite value, as well as a suspension system for constructing arch bridges without falsework. He also contributed illustrated articles on bridges, foundations, etc., to various publications, including *The Engineering News, The Cement Age,* and *Engineering and Contracting.*

* Memoir prepared by Richard T. Goodwyn, Esq., Athens, Ga.

He was the author of Part VIII of "European Bridges", in Volume III of Hool's "Concrete Bridges and Culverts", and relative to this, made a trip abroad in 1914 to inspect concrete bridges.

Mr. Aylett was a man of strong personality and of unblemished character, who took particular delight in trying to uplift the down trodden and oppressed. Although small in stature, he was of great mentality. A propensity for speaking, possibly inherited from his paternal grandfather, Patrick Henry, led him as a college student, and, later, as a mature man, to discard the usual reticence of the average engineer, thus evincing his ability as a forceful and fluent speaker. He was a member of the National Security League and during the World War, and thereafter, proved a valuable speaker on "Americanization and What It Means".

Mr. Aylett was married in 1900 to Hilma C. Fernquist, of Hartford, Conn., who, with one daughter, Elsie, survives him. While sitting at his desk with the day's work before him, he suffered a stroke of apoplexy and was called to the Great Beyond.

Mr. Aylett was elected an Associate Member of the American Society of Civil Engineers on June 3, 1896.

OSCAR ERNEST BULKELEY, Assoc. M. Am. Soc. C. E.*

Died January 4, 1927.

Oscar Ernest Bulkeley was born on April 2, 1885, at Oneida, Ill. He was the son of John A. and Emma H. (Copley) Bulkeley. His father was a native of Canton, Ill., and his mother came from Pennsylvania. John A. Bulkeley was an artist and photographer until the failure of his health necessitated the removal of himself and family in 1890 to Grand Junction, Colo., where he engaged in ranch work. Mrs. Bulkeley died in 1897 and three years later the family moved to Riverside, Calif.

Oscar Ernest Bulkeley attended the public schools and High School at Riverside and was graduated in 1902. He then entered Knox College at Galesburg, Ill., and completed the course with first honors in three years, graduating in 1905 with the degree of Bachelor of Science.

His first engagement was with the Grand Junction Electric Light Company. With a desire for practical experience in mining he entered the employ of the Amalgamated Copper Company in 1906, at Butte, Mont. He began work in the copper mines as a laborer in order to become familiar with mining methods. His ability was soon recognized and at the end of four years he had been promoted to be General Purchasing Agent.

In February, 1910, Mr. Bulkeley entered the University of Illinois to further equip himself for engineering work for he then believed he wished to be a civil engineer. He was graduated in the Civil Engineering Course in 1912 and took the position of Engineer of the Water Department of Rockford, Ill. He was soon promoted to be Assistant Superintendent and remained on that work until January, 1916. His success at Rockford resulted in his selection as Superintendent of the Water Department at Jackson, Mich., where he continued until April, 1918. At that time he was sought by the Dupont Engineering Company on the construction of the mammoth Government powder plant near Nashville, Tenn. Soon afterward he was placed in charge of its water-works plant, which position he retained until after the Armistice.

From February, 1919, to January, 1920, he was associated with the Ross P. Beckstrom Engineering Company, of Rockford, Ill. In January, 1920, Mr. Bulkeley went to Lansing, Mich., as Engineer for the Electric Light and Water Board. On May 1 of that year he was made Acting Superintendent and, on November 1, Superintendent of both the light and water activities of the City of Lansing. This position he held at the time of his death.

At the time Mr. Bulkeley went to Lansing the city was operating five water pumping stations. The Central Station was used both for pumping water and generating electricity. An old generating plant had been purchased from a private company and was not in efficient condition. This plant was changed almost entirely and converted into a municipal steam-heating station. The development of electricity was transferred to a fine new generating plant,

* Memoir prepared by Edward D. Rich, M. Am. Soc. C. E.

realized largely through Mr. Bulkeley's wise judgment and energy. This installation cost about $2 500 000 and with the extensions now projected and under way the investment will be nearly $4 000 000.

In 1924, a new pumping station, wells, and storage reservoir which furnishes a large part of the municipal water supply was completed under Mr. Bulkeley's direction, at a cost of nearly $350 000.

The Electric Light and Water Board placed great confidence in Mr. Bulkeley's advice in extending and improving the service. He was untiring in his efforts to work out a new street lighting system, in the removal of overhead wires in the business district, and in the development of an adequate water supply, all with broad vision of the future needs of the city.

He was always unselfishly interested and active in the upbuilding of his city and gave generously of his time to those civic, social, professional, and religious activities which are beneficial to mankind. He and Mrs. Bulkeley were members of and active in the work of the Plymouth Congregational Church. His unfailing courtesy and kindliness endeared him to a host of friends who mourn his departure as a keen personal loss.

Mr. Bulkeley was taken ill with influenza on December 14, 1926. Pneumonia developed and caused his death on January 4, 1927.

On December 21, 1912, he was united in marriage to Edna S. Best, at Chicago, Ill., as a culmination of a romance of their school days in California. His widow and two children, Mary Louise and William Warren, survive him.

He was a member of the Phi Gamma Delta and Tau Beta Pi Fraternities; Lansing Lodge No. 33 F. and A. M.; Lansing Rotary Club; American Water Works Association; and the Lansing Engineers' Club, of which he was President in 1924.

Mr. Bulkeley was elected an Associate Member of the American Society of Civil Engineers on October 9, 1917.

JOHN DUBUIS, Assoc. M. Am. Soc. C. E.*

Died May 11, 1927.

John Dubuis was born on October 8, 1884, in the Tyrol, Austria. His mother died soon after his birth and his father, an American artist, working and studying in Europe, died three years later while still abroad. The 3-year old son was brought back to the United States, and, as a boy, lived in Kentucky and South Carolina. He was graduated from Presbyterian College of South Carolina in 1905, and received the degree of Civil Engineer from Cornell University in 1909.

Mr. Dubuis moved to Oregon in 1909, and for the next eighteen years he was associated with many of the more important engineering developments in that State. He was engaged in the investigation of irrigation projects in Warner Valley and at Grant's Pass, and in the construction of the Hood River Hydro-Electric Plant, of the Pacific Power and Light Company, and the irrigation system of the Walker Basin Irrigation Company, near Lapine.

As Chief Engineer, he supervised the construction of the Gold Hill Irrigation District System. He was also Consulting Engineer for the North Canal Company from 1921 to 1924, and for several smaller projects. He served one and one-half years as Instructor in Hydraulics at the Oregon State Agricultural College, and for three years as Engineering Inspector for the Desert Land Board of the State of Oregon. Mr. Dubuis' most important work was no doubt the water supply system for the City of Bend, Ore., involving a 13-mile pipe line, intake dam, reservoirs, etc., recently completed. His death occurred at Spokane, Wash., as the result of infection following an operation for appendicitis.

He was married in 1913 to Marion K. Curtis, of Ithaca, N. Y. He is survived by Mrs. Dubuis and by two daughters, Marion and Jeanne.

Mr. Dubuis was very active in Masonry, having been a member of Portland Lodge No. 55, Pilgrim Commandery of Knights Templars, of Bend, Al Kader Temple of the Mystic Shrine, and Bend Chapter No. 109 of the Eastern Star. He was especially active in the Pilgrim Chapter, De Molay, having been a member of the Advisory Board, and in the Boy Scouts, having served as Scoutmaster.

He was beset with the necessity common to most civil engineers of frequent removals from place to place; nevertheless, he was able to make a host of friends all over the State of Oregon. Those who knew him best will probably agree that his outstanding personal characteristic was his never-failing cheerfulness, even in the face of discouragement and adversity.

Mr. Dubuis was elected a Junior of the American Society of Civil Engineers on October 1, 1912, and an Associate Member on January 6, 1915.

* Memoir prepared by Fred F. Henshaw, M. Am. Soc. C. E.

HENRY GARNER HARPER, Assoc. M. Am. Soc. C. E.*

Died March 24, 1927.

Henry Garner Harper was born at Ashland, Pa., on November 15, 1891, the son of Henry C. and Catherine Harper. He received his public school education in Ashland and was graduated from the High School in 1908.

From 1908 to 1911, Mr. Harper was employed as Chainman at Ashland by the Philadelphia and Reading Coal and Iron Company. In the autumn of 1911 he entered Pennsylvania State College, from which he was graduated in 1915 with the degree of Bachelor of Science in Civil Engineering, as well as Bachelor of Science in Highway Engineering.

After his graduation from college he entered the service of the Pennsylvania Department of Highways, with which he was continuously employed until the time of his death, except during the period of his military service in the World War.

Mr. Harper's first assignment in the State service was for one year as Draftsman at the Harrisburg Office. This was followed by two years as Assistant Engineer in the Bureau of Township Highways. In June, 1918, he entered the Government military service and was commissioned a First Lieutenant in the Artillery. He served until he was honorably discharged early in 1919.

In May, 1919, Mr. Harper resumed work with the Pennsylvania Department of Highways as Resident Engineer in charge of construction work in McKean County. On January 1, 1920, he was appointed as District Engineer with headquarters at Sunbury. In August, 1921, he was transferred to Bedford, where he filled assignments as District Engineer and Assistant District Engineer, respectively, until June, 1923, when he was transferred to Hollidaysburg as District Engineer in charge of highway work in Blair, Cambria, and Huntingdon Counties. The latter assignment he was filling at the time of his death.

As District Engineer, Mr. Harper had charge of both construction and maintenance work, as well as of all other departmental activities. The Pennsylvania Department of Highways carried out its largest construction program during the period that Mr. Harper served as District Engineer, and many large construction projects were completed under his direction. In the midst of these activities he was stricken with spinal meningitis, following a mastoid operation, and died at the Altoona Hospital on March 24, 1927.

In 1917, Mr. Harper was united in marriage with Pauline Sharpless who, with a son and daughter, survives him.

He had a charming personality, with a keen sense of humor and a ready smile that won him many friends. He was known among his associates as a man of sterling integrity and possessed of the highest ideals of professional ethics.

* Memoir prepared by S. W. Jackson, M. Am. Soc. C. E.

After his graduation he kept in close touch with his Alma Mater and was particularly interested in the welfare of the Sigma Pi Fraternity of which he was a member. He was also a member of the American Legion, Fort Fetter Post No. 516, Hollidaysburg, Washington Lodge No. 265, F. and A. M., the Benevolent and Protective Order of Elks, of Bloomsburg, Pa., and the Kiwanis Club, of Hollidaysburg.

Mr. Harper was elected an Associate Member of the American Society of Civil Engineers on October 11, 1920.

GUY FREDERIC HOSMER, Assoc. M. Am. Soc. C. E.*

Died January 27, 1928.

Guy Frederic Hosmer, the son of Nathaniel M. and Mary A. (Howe) Hosmer, was born in Shrewsbury, Mass., on March 14, 1877.

He was graduated from the Shrewsbury High School in 1892, at the age of fifteen. In 1894, he had his first engineering experience when he assisted Mr. Romeo E. Allen, of Shrewsbury, on the survey of the Old Post Road. The following year Mr. Hosmer became associated with the engineering office of Shedd and Sarle, of Worcester, Mass., and Providence, R. I. When this firm dissolved partnership, he remained in the office of O. Perry Sarle, M. Am. Soc. C. E., of Providence, with which he was connected for many years.

In this position, Mr. Hosmer had a varied experience, including general surveying, oyster bed surveying, triangulation, design and construction of water-works, sewer systems, wharves, dams, mill buildings, power houses, and the taking of stream-flow measurements. From 1903 to 1905, he was in charge of the preliminary surveys and construction for a system of water-works and sewers, including a pumping station, stand-pipe and sand filtration plant, for Hickory, N. C. During 1906 and 1907 he was in charge of the design and construction of brick and iron buildings, with reinforced concrete floors and columns, for the Penobscot Chemical Fibre Company at Great Works, Me., and, in 1908, Engineer in charge of extensive improvements in the water power system at the D. Goff and Sons Mill, at Pawtucket, R. I.

In 1913 and 1914, Mr. Hosmer supervised the building of a sewage disposal plant, at Central Falls, R. I., which involved the construction of an Imhoff tank and sprinkling filters. In 1914 and 1915, he was in charge of the field work for preliminary plans of a $1 000 000 water-works plant for the Town of Warwick, R. I.

Mr. Hosmer remained in Mr. Sarle's office until January 1, 1917, when he accepted a position as Engineer of the Maine Coated Paper Company, at Rumford, Me. In 1921, this Company was consolidated with the Oxford Paper Company, and Mr. Hosmer became Assistant to the General Engineer, which position he retained until his death. As such, he was in charge of the design and erection of new buildings and the alteration of old ones, as well as the laying out and installation of new equipment. He also designed and invented various improvements which were added to the machinery in the Coating Mill. While in this position, he had charge, in 1922, of the remodeling of the plant of the Nashwaak Pulp and Paper Company, at St. John, N. B., Canada.

Mr. Hosmer was very active in community affairs. He was President of the Rumford Mechanics Institute; a member of the Rumford Board of Selectmen; one of the promoters, as well as Director and Chairman of the Greens Committee of the Oakdale Country Club; Chairman of the 1927 Rumford Winter Carnival Committee; and a member of the Building Committee of the Rumford Community Hospital, and also of the Methodist Episcopal Church.

* Memoir prepared by Percy W. Sarle, Esq., Rumford, Me.

He was a member of the Association of Professional Engineers of the Province of New Brunswick, Canada, and the Bangor, Me., Lodge of the Benevolent and Protective Order of Elks.

Mr. Hosmer had a very keen and analytical mind and was ever ready to solve problems of his own and his associates. He was always greatly interested in new engineering ventures and kept himself informed as to the latest developments in the Engineering Profession.

The greatest tribute that can be paid him is that all his associates, within the organizations he served, or individuals of other organizations with whom he came in contact, are proud that they knew him.

In every position, industrial or civic, which he held, Mr. Hosmer was unsparing in his efforts, unusually efficient, and faithful to every detail. His work was always well done.

He was never married, and is survived by three brothers, William H. and Arthur C. Hosmer, of Camden, Me., and Harry P. Hosmer, of Boston, Mass.

Mr. Hosmer was elected an Associate Member of the American Society of Civil Engineers on November 6, 1907.

THOMAS WAKEFIELD MACARTNEY, Assoc. M. Am. Soc. C E.*

Died November 23, 1926.

Thomas Wakefield Macartney was born in Des Moines, Iowa, on November 20, 1883. Following his preparatory education in the public schools of Des Moines, Mr. Macartney received his technical and engineering training at Purdue University from which he was graduated with the degree of Bachelor of Science in Mechanical Engineering in 1906.

Soon after his graduation he accepted a position as Draftsman with Mr. W. S. Hook at Los Angeles, Calif. After serving a year in this position he entered the office of the City Engineer of Seattle, Wash., where he served as Computer, Draftsman, and, later, assisted in the preparation of plans for street improvements, sewers, and extensions to the water system. He was also connected for one year with the Municipal Plans Commission.

In January, 1914, Mr. Macartney left Seattle to accept a position as Assistant County Drainage Engineer in Yakima County, Washington. In this position he assisted in the location, design, and construction of many large drainage systems and acquired much valuable experience in this field of engineering.

In August, 1917, he left the service of Yakima County and entered the employ of the Boering Airplane Company, of Seattle, soon afterward becoming its Chief Inspector.

He returned to Yakima County in January, 1919, as Chief Assistant Drainage Engineer and was appointed Chief Drainage Engineer in August, 1919, which position he held until his death. During this period he had charge of the design and construction of thirty drainage improvement districts having an aggregate area of 25 000 acres. On this work 20 miles of large open drains and 60 miles of deep closed drains were built at a cost of $876 000. The construction was difficult for this type of work and much of it was done by force account under the direction of Mr. Macartney. In addition, he had charge of the design and construction of several diking improvement districts for bank protection on the Yakima River.

In the field of drainage engineering for the reclamation of irrigated land, Mr. Macartney stood very high indeed, ranking with the best. The drainage systems that were built by him are models of excellent design and good construction. They reflect the skill and ability of the builder and the Yakima Valley owes to him a debt of gratitude for his work of reclamation and protection.

Mr. Macartney accepted responsibility conscientiously and served the public with highest integrity. His fine tact, good judgment, and even temperament enabled him to work harmoniously with many different district boards and commissioners. He was constantly and steadfastly guided by the best principles of engineering and sought to do that which was for the greatest good. He was wholly without conceit or sham, and his courtesy and

* Memoir prepared by L. T. Jessup, Assoc. M. Am. Soc. C. E.

lovable disposition endeared him to all who knew him. His very sudden and untimely death caused by pneumonia was a severe shock to his many friends.

He took an active part in civic and community affairs. At the time of his death he had served eight years as Vestryman of St. Michael's Protestant Episcopal Church, at Yakima, Wash. He was a member of the Rotary Club and of the American Association of Engineers.

He was married on September 6, 1911, to Margaret Scarborough, by whom he is survived. He is also survived by a son, Thomas Wakefield, Jr., a sister, Catherine N. Macartney, of Iowa City, Iowa, and three brothers, George W. Macartney, of Helena, Mont.; Robert H. Macartney, of Cheney, Wash., and Morton Macartney, M. Am. Soc. C. E., of Orlando, Fla.

Mr. Macartney was elected an Associate Member of the American Society of Civil Engineers on January 19, 1920.

JAMES ROY MAC BEAN, Assoc. M. Am. Soc. C. E.*

Died July 8, 1927.

James Roy MacBean, the son of James Dean and Mary (Murphy) MacBean, was born in Philadelphia, Pa., on January 19, 1885. On the completion of his early education in the public schools, he entered Drexel Institute for a course in Civil Engineering.

In the spring of 1903, Mr. MacBean entered the employ of the Chicago, Rock Island, and Pacific Railway Company as Rodman and Instrumentman and remained with that Company for about three years. Subsequently, he was engaged for about six years on work with the Pennsylvania and Chicago Great Western Railroad Companies. He was employed by the Spanish-American Iron Company in charge of mining and railroad construction in Cuba during parts of 1906 and 1911.

For various periods between 1907 and 1924, Mr. MacBean was engaged for about five years as Draftsman and Chief of Party on sub-division and municipal work with private engineering firms of Philadelphia and Jenkintown, Pa. In 1918, as Assistant Superintendent for the Austin Company, he was engaged on the construction of a concrete roundhouse for the Philadelphia and Reading Railway Company. Later, he accepted a position as Erecting Engineer for the United Gas Improvement Construction Company, of Philadelphia, remaining with this Company until the summer of 1923.

From August, 1924, until his death, Mr. MacBean was employed as Resident Engineer for the New Jersey State Highway Department. As such, he was engaged on reconnaissance surveys in connection with the entrance and connecting roads for the Delaware River Bridge Extension from Camden, N. J., to the main State highway routes of Southern New Jersey. On the completion of the preliminary work he had charge of the construction of the northerly section of the connecting road. Shortly before his death, he had completed the construction of the concrete State Road between Egg Harbor and Mays Landing, in Atlantic County.

Mr. MacBean met his death as the result of an automobile accident while returning from work on the afternoon of July 8, 1927.

He was married on May 16, 1914, to Esther C. Copperfield, of New York, N. Y., who, with a son, Roy Hamilton, survives him. He was a member of the West Park Presbyterian Church, of Philadelphia.

Mr. MacBean was elected an Associate Member of the American Society of Civil Engineers on June 6, 1927.

* Memoir prepared by M. W. Grimes, M. Am. Soc. C. E., and E. H. Maier, Assoc. M. Am. Soc. C. E.

HOWARD B. MERRICK, Assoc. M. Am. Soc. C. E.*

Died December 14, 1926.

Howard B. Merrick was born at Wrightstown, Pa., on January 2, 1871, the son of George T. and Mary Ann (Short) Merrick. His father was a Pennsylvania Quaker and his mother was of Vermont stock, but not a Quaker. As a youth he attended the Friends' School at Wrightstown and also, for a time, the Newtown High School, but did not complete the High School course.

In the fall of 1893, he entered the University of Michigan by examination, but not having been prepared in all subjects necessary for entrance without conditions, he spent part of the time of the first semester in the Ann Arbor High School in order to complete his entrance requirements. He depended largely on his own earnings to pay the expenses of his University course, and each of the summers of 1894 to 1897, inclusive, he spent in surveying work, serving as Rodman for the Elkhart and Western Railway Company the first summer and for the Great Northern Railway Company the other three summers.

Mr. Merrick was graduated from the College of Engineering of the University of Michigan in 1898, having taken the degree of Bachelor of Science in Civil Engineering. One of the years intervening after his entrance into the University was spent in the College of Literature, Science, and the Arts. The summer following his graduation he was Masonry Inspector for the Great Northern Railway Company, and from October, 1898, to November, 1902, he served successively as Levelman, Transitman, Assistant Engineer, and Engineer in Charge of Location and Construction for the same Company, in Minnesota, North Dakota, and Montana. In the former State his work took him into the iron country on the Mesaba Range where he became interested in iron mining as carried on in that district, and from December, 1902, to September, 1903, he was Engineer in Charge of Drills for E. J. Longyear and Company. His work in this connection was the exploration of the territory in the vicinity of Hibbing, Minn., for the purpose of locating bodies of iron ore.

Five years after his graduation Mr. Merrick was called by his Alma Mater to serve as Instructor in Surveying, and began his teaching in the fall of 1903. He was advanced to Assistant Professor of Surveying in 1906 and to Associate Professor in 1918. In 1913, he was granted the degree of Civil Engineer, presenting as part of the requirement for that degree a thesis on "The Welfare of Railways in the United States Since the Passage of the Interstate Commerce Act". From 1922 until his death, he was Associate Professor of Geodesy and Surveying.

During his term of service at the University, Professor Merrick was engaged in some outside practice in general surveying, and undertook several special pieces of work. In June, 1913, he was with Mr. M. W. Thompson

* Memoir prepared by James B. Pollock, Professor of Botany, Univ. of Michigan, Ann Arbor, Mich.

preparing data for use in the Duluth, South Shore and Atlantic Railway rate case, and in August and September of the same year he worked on the valuation of the Lake Shore and Michigan Southern Railway for the same firm. In the employ of H. E. Riggs, M. Am. Soc. C. E., he was in charge of the computation of earthwork on the appraisal of the Pere Marquette Railway, from June to October, 1914. He also worked at appraising real estate belonging to the Eastern Michigan Edison Company, from September, 1915, to February, 1916.

Besides his teaching Professor Merrick served the College of Engineering in several other capacities. He was in charge of the Summer Camp of the Junior Civil Engineering students from 1904 to 1911, and was the first Head Mentor in the Freshmen Mentor System which was inaugurated at the Engineering College in 1913. He also had charge of the Freshmen Assemblies in the College of Engineering in 1917 and 1918. Shortly before his death, he had completed a committee assignment connected with the current study of engineering education. His professional services were not only utilized by the University of Michigan and by various railway corporations, but a foreign nation, China, availed itself of his engineering talents.

In 1918, Professor Merrick was one of three men chosen from the Department of Geodesy and Surveying of the College of Engineering to go to China under the direction of Joseph Ripley, M. Am. Soc. C. E., an eminent graduate of the same College, in the employ of the American International Corporation, to aid the Chinese Government in the improvement of the Grand Canal. From August, 1918, to November, 1919, Professor Merrick served as one of the Principal Assistant Engineers to the Grand Canal Improvement Board in China. He was also in charge of precise level work, covering a distance of 325 miles, and of the office work in the reduction and plotting of the field notes of the topographic survey parties.

At the request of the Chinese Government he was transferred in December, 1919, to the Commission for the Improvement of the River Systems of Chihli, a large province of Northeast China. He served as Engineer in Charge of Surveys, and, as such, re-organized the field and office forces and had complete supervision of the surveying and mapping of 30 000 sq. miles in the Province of Chihli. He directed a force of about 400 men, of whom 90 were engineers. A majority of the chiefs of parties were engineers who had been educated in America, England, or Japan, while many of the subordinates were graduates of Chinese engineering colleges having American teachers. Professor Merrick served the Commission for the Improvement of the River Systems of Chihli until June, 1922, having spent almost four years in China. He was then obliged to return to his duties at the University of Michigan.

That his work was done in a manner eminently satisfactory to all concerned, is attested by several facts. The Chinese Government was anxious to retain his services. Mr. Ripley, under whose direction Professor Merrick went to China, has expressed high appreciation of his accomplishments. Each of two groups of engineers under his charge in China, the staff and the sub-staff, presented him with a silver loving cup, engraved with an expression of "their high esteem and affection for him as their Chief during three years of association in the Survey Department of the Chihli River Commission." After his departure for the United States the Chinese Government awarded him a Fifth Class Chiao Hu Decoration, in recognition of his valuable services. Mr. G. G. Stroebe, a graduate of the University of Michigan, who became Chief Survey Engineer of the Yangtse River Commission about the time Professor Merrick returned to the United States, writes that "Professor Merrick's surveys are considered equal to the very best of those executed by the U. S. Coast and Geodetic Survey in this country." Mr. Stroebe also remarks, "They all say here that Mr. Merrick was a past master in dealing with delicate situations in China."

In his family life he was an ideal husband and father. He was married on December 12, 1900, to M. Grace Green, of Holly, Mich. Mrs. Merrick survives him, as do two daughters, Ruth Carolyn, a Sophomore in the College of Architecture, and Alice Mary, a Senior in the University High School. Two sisters are left also to mourn his loss.

A man's personality is perhaps best appreciated by his neighbors and intimate friends, a teacher's by his students and colleagues. Judged by them, Professor Merrick ranks very high. Dean Mortimer E. Cooley, M. Am. Soc. C. E., of the Colleges of Engineering and Architecture, said* of him:

"Since the very beginning he was closely in touch with our students and enjoyed their confidence. His equable temperament, his kindly heart and his charming manners will long be remembered. He will be a great loss to the University, particularly to the Geodesy and Surveying Department, and his place will be hard to fill."

Neighbors wrote of him, "He was one of the finest, best, kindest men I ever knew." "His consideration for others was such an outstanding characteristic." A classmate reports, "Howard was one of the most esteemed members of our class of '98 Engineers." A student of a later time says, "I gained Professor Merrick's friendship while a student in his classes, and have valued it above most of my other friends."

Although reared a Quaker Professor Merrick was not so narrow in his religious views but that he could ally himself with other religious organizations and bear his share of their responsibilities, in a community where the Quakers had no organization. In recent years he was leader of a troop of Boy Scouts and freely gave them of his time, his wisdom, and his friendship.

In his professional relations he was a member of the Association of Chinese and American Engineers, the Association of American Engineers, and the Michigan Engineering Society.

Professor Merrick was a member of the Phi Sigma Kappa Fraternity, and of the Tau Beta Pi, an honorary engineering society, the University Club, and Huron Hills Golf Club.

He was also a member of the Masonic Order, and helped to found a lodge in Tientsin, to which he transferred his membership while he was in China, and which he served in various capacities. After returning to Ann Arbor,

* *Michigan Daily*, December 15, 1926.

he joined with others in the establishment of a third local lodge and at the time of his death was holding an important office therein.

In a summary of Professor Merrick's life it may be said in all truth and without exaggeration, that he was an ideal husband and father; the finest, truest, and most lovable of friends; a man ever thoughtful and considerate of others; an excellent citizen, an inspiring teacher, an efficient executive; a painstaking and exact worker in his profession, a civil engineer of high standing; a courteous advocate, pressing his point with reason and kindness rather than with aggressive domination; gentle in manner, but adamant in his advocacy of what he conceived to be right, like his ancestors the Friends or Quakers, accepting the "inner light" as his ultimate guide and authority.

Professor Merrick was elected an Associate Member of the American Society of Civil Engineers on July 1, 1909.

ROBERT BRUCE ROBINSON, Assoc. M. Am. Soc. C. E.*

DIED FEBRUARY 1, 1927.

Robert Bruce Robinson was born at Mount Holly Springs, Pa., on March 3, 1878. He received his technical education at the University of Illinois, and entered the service of the Union Pacific Railroad Company in April, 1899, as a Rodman on the Kansas Division. In 1904 he went to the Oregon Short Line Unit of the Union Pacific System where he was engaged for several years in locating and constructing new branch lines, one of which was the North Side Branch, extending from Rupert to Bliss, Idaho.

After some time spent as a Special Engineer on investigation work, he was made Division Engineer of the Idaho Division of the Oregon Short Line, and, in 1916, accepted the position of Engineer, Maintenance of Way, for that railroad, with headquarters at Pocatello, Idaho. He served in this capacity until May, 1919, when he was promoted to be Engineer, Maintenance of Way, of the Union Pacific Railroad with headquarters at Omaha, Nebr., which position he held at the time of his death.

He died at St. Joseph's Hospital, Omaha, on February 1, 1927, from blood-poisoning resulting from the extraction of an infected abscessed tooth.

Mr. Robinson was an indefatigable worker, who gave unstintingly of his time and energy because of an intense love for the upbuilding of the great railroad system which it had been his part, as an engineer and builder, to introduce to many unsettled sections in the mountain States of the West, where prosperous communities have since sprung into existence.

He possessed that priceless executive trait of being able to get the best from his men at all times. In the strenuous work in which he was engaged, emergencies are the natural order, and he himself was always on the scene at the earliest possible moment to direct operations whenever serious floods and other troubles threatened to endanger the track. His personality was such, however, that even under the most trying conditions, when some one had failed, his kindly criticism produced more lasting results than all the harsh words that could ever be spoken, and no employee ever left a conference with Mr. Robinson with a feeling of bitterness or resentment.

It can be said with all sincerity that no general officer ever had a firmer grip on the affections of his men, and he was likewise warmly respected by the executive officers of the Company.

His widespread popularity was attested by the large attendance of friends, including many from far distant points, in addition to those of the Union Pacific family, at the funeral services held February 3, at the Scottish Rite Cathedral, in Omaha, as well as by the exceptional number of beautiful floral offerings. On account of his love for the mountains, his remains were taken to Salt Lake City, Utah, and laid at rest on February 7, 1927, in the shadow of the stately Wahsatch Mountain Range. The services at Salt Lake City

* Memoir prepared by E. W. Plotz, Chf. Clerk, Maintenance of Way Dept., Union Pacific R. R., Omaha, Nebr.

were the occasion for a large outpouring of friends in that community where much of his earlier work had centered.

Mr. Robinson was a member of the American Railroad Association, the American Railway Engineering Association, the American Railway Bridge and Building Association, and other technical societies. He was also a member of various Masonic bodies and of El Korah Temple, A. A. O. N. M. S., at Boise, Idaho.

He is survived by his widow, Mrs. Audley B. Robinson, and two children, Eleanor and Robert. His parents, Dr. and Mrs. R. E. Robinson, two sisters, Laura Robinson and Mrs. P. H. Simpson, all of Morrison, Ill., and two brothers, Arthur Robinson, of Pocatello, and Edward Robinson, of Cleveland, Ohio, also survive him.

Mr. Robinson was elected an Associate Member of the American Society of Civil Engineers on July 9, 1912.

REUBEN BENJAMIN SLEIGHT, Assoc. M. Am. Soc. C. E.*

Died November 14, 1927.

Reuben Benjamin Sleight, the son of Levi J. and Katherine C. (Buchler) Sleight, was born at Laingsburg, Mich., on June 30, 1889. He received his early education in the public schools of his native State, and in 1908 entered the University of Michigan, where he studied engineering for three years.

In June, 1911, Mr. Sleight was employed by the Racine Boat Manufacturing Company, at Muskegon, Mich., as a Draftsman in the mechanical and structural design of lightships for the Federal Government. The opportunities of the West attracted him to Denver, Colo., where he entered the office of the Field, Fellows, and Hinderlider Engineering Company, in September, 1912. His experience with this firm was in designing, drafting, and field surveys, for the Parkman Irrigation District of Wyoming and the Cherry Creek protective work, at Denver.

In January, 1913, Mr. Sleight left this work and was employed immediately as Construction Foreman and Concrete Inspector on irrigation structures and well development for the Tucson Farms Company, near Tucson, Ariz. In June he was transferred to a new line of work, a duty-of-water investigation in the Mesilla Valley, New Mexico. This study under co-operation between what is now the Division of Agricultural Engineering of the United States Department of Agriculture, the New Mexico Agricultural Experiment Station, and the farmers of Mesilla Valley, consisted in the design of gas and electric power pumping plants, their installation and testing,† and assistance in tests on submerged orifices, the results of which have been published.‡ Mr. Sleight's work in New Mexico was under the immediate direction of F. L. Bixby, M. Am. Soc. C. E.

On June 2, 1913, Mr. Sleight was appointed Assistant Irrigation Engineer in the U. S. Department of Agriculture, which position he held until he entered the Army in 1917. During the winter of 1913-14, he was assigned to the Headquarters Office of the Division of Agricultural Engineering at Washington, D. C., as an Assistant to F. C. Scobey, M. Am. Soc. C. E., on hydraulic engineering research. Subsequently, he returned to his former work in New Mexico.

In September, 1914, on leave of absence from his Government position, Mr. Sleight re-entered the University of Michigan from which he was graduated as a Bachelor in Marine Engineering in the early summer of 1915. During his Senior year at the University, he was made an Assistant in the Department of Civil Engineering. On leaving the University and resuming his Government connection, in July, 1915, he was assigned to the work of

---

* Memoir prepared by R. L. Parshall, Assoc. M. Am. Soc. C. E.

† The report of tests on turbine centrifugal pumps was published in *Journal of Agricultural Research,* Vol. XXXI, No. 3.

‡ "Research Studies on the Flow of Water in Open Channels Carrying Heavily Silted Water," *Bulletin 97,* New Mexico Agricultural Experimental Station.

establishing a research laboratory, at Denver, for the purpose of studying the evaporation from free water surfaces, soils, and river-bed materials. The results of these studies, which were started early in the season of 1916, were published under the title, "Evaporation from the Surfaces of Water and River-Bed Materials."* This discussion on a subject of great interest to the Engineering Profession was a comprehensive and authoritative scientific contribution of high value, and immediately attracted wide attention. Of the many manuscripts prepared by Mr. Sleight, it is thought his summary of the work on evaporation was the most outstanding.

Mr. Sleight's military career began in October, 1917, with his appointment as Production Engineer, Signal Corps, U. S. Army. In this capacity he directed his efforts to the compilation of production statistics until January 16, 1918, when he was commissioned as Second Lieutenant in the Signal Reserve Corps. He was promoted to First Lieutenant, Air Service, U. S. Army, on September 25, 1918, and made Tonnage Officer in charge of compiling estimates for the General Staff and the American Expeditionary Force, of tonnage of all air service material to be carried overseas. He remained in the Air Service until July, 1919, but had no foreign experience. He held the commission of Captain in the Air Service Officers' Reserve Corps until his death.

In September, 1919, Mr. Sleight accepted a position as Appraisal Engineer with H. E. Riggs, M. Am. Soc. C. E., at Ann Arbor. While with Professor Riggs, he assisted in the appraisals of the Detroit United Railways; the Kentucky and West Virginia Power Company; the Northern Ohio Light and Power Company; the Columbus Power Company; the Columbus Railroad Company; and the Gas Light Company, all of Columbus, Ga., as well as the Augusta-Aiken Railway and Electric Corporation. In this appraisal work, he was, first, a Field Inspector, then in charge of field investigations and, later, assigned to office engineering.

He severed his connection with the appraisal work at Ann Arbor in 1922 to take the position of Engineer with the Minnesota Tax Commission. An arrangement was made whereby the College of Engineering and Architecture of the University of Minnesota supervised the valuation of public utilities, and, occasionally, of other properties for the Tax Commission. The Engineering Department of the Commission was thus established, and Mr. Sleight was engaged to do the appraisal work. He placed the Department on an efficient and effective basis and was most highly thought of by all who came in contact with him during the five years he spent in Minnesota.

Because of his ambition and earnestness of purpose, he was recognized as an outstanding leader in engineering and scientific circles. His proficiency as a scholar gained for him a membership in the University of Michigan Chapter of Sigma Xi in 1915, while yet an undergraduate.

Mr. Sleight was a registered Civil Engineer of the State of Michigan, and a member of the Engineers' Club of Minneapolis. He was the author of a number of papers published in various engineering and scientific periodicals,

* *Journal of Agricultural Research*, Vol. X, No. 5, July 30, 1917.

and in 1927 wrote an important paper on Engineering Economics which, in a National contest, gained such recognition as to result in his appointment on the Engineering Staff of the Federal Department of Commerce as an Aide to the Secretary, Herbert Hoover, Hon. M. Am. Soc. C. E.

As an Assistant to Secretary Hoover, he was detailed to work out special waterways problems. At the time of his death, on November 14, 1927, he was in Vermont, having left Washington in an airplane to gather advance information for Mr. Hoover in the areas then flooded. The injuries from which he died were suffered in the landing of the plane at Montpelier, Vt.

He was married on October 30, 1913, to Doris M. Cutter, of Muskegon, Mich., who survives him.

By nature modest and retiring, Mr. Sleight's manner was tactful and most courteous. He had the power to command loyal service and form sincere friendships, and those who knew him well were continuously gratified by his successful advancement in his chosen life work.

Mr. Bixby, under whom he was engaged in New Mexico, states that Mr. Sleight's work was of the highest order, and that he possessed to a high degree the ability to combine an understanding of the technique of engineering investigations with the practical application of theory, while his pleasant personality and earnest willingness to co-operate with others in the solving of difficult engineering problems, gave promise of a successful career in scientific research. Moreover, his affability did not prevent his strict and conscientious attention to business when on duty, although his company in leisure hours was most enjoyable. Mr. Bixby feels that in the death of this young man the Engineering Profession suffers an inestimable loss.

Mr. Sleight was elected a Junior of the American Society of Civil Engineers on December 6, 1915, and an Associate Member on April 25, 1921.

RALPH JEROME SMITH, Assoc. M. Am. Soc. C. E.*

Died August 8, 1926.

Ralph Jerome Smith, the only son and youngest of five children of the late Charles Aaron and Jennie (Snow) Smith, was born at Indian Orchard, Mass., on May 12, 1889. Here he resided until he moved with his parents to Longmeadow, Mass., in 1912, which has since been the family home. He was the direct descendant of a long line of old New England families. Through his mother, he was descended from John Alden and Priscilla Mullens, also from Francis Cooke, all of whom were passengers on the historic *Mayflower*. His paternal New England ancestry, of which he was the last male member in his line, dates from 1636 when Lieut. Samuel Smith with his family removed from Hadleigh, England, to America on the ship *Elizabeth,* settling first at Watertown, Mass., later, at Wethersfield, Conn., and, finally, going with a party from that place to settle the Town of Hadley, Mass. Ralph Smith's great-great-grandfather, Ebenezer Smith, was a soldier in the Revolutionary War.

Ralph Jerome Smith received his early education at Indian Orchard, having attended the Myrtle Street Grammar School. He then entered the Springfield, Mass., High School with the idea of fitting himself for the Medical Profession. About a year and a half later his father was severely injured, and he was obliged to leave school for a time to look after his father's business. Upon the latter's recovery, the business was disposed of, and Mr. Smith then entered Williston Seminary. He found that his professional leanings had changed from medicine to engineering, so he returned to the Springfield Technical High School from which he was graduated in 1909.

After leaving High School he worked as a Draftsman on machine detailing for the Consolidated Wrapping Machine Company, of Springfield. About a year later he became a Valve Draftsman for the Chapman Valve Manufacturing Company, of Indian Orchard. He then spent about two years as Rodman and Chainman on surveys in and around Springfield, first with Durkee, White, and Towne, of Springfield, then with the General Engineering Company of the same place, and, finally, with the Boston and Albany Railroad Company.

From 1912 to 1915, Mr. Smith was employed by the General Engineering Company, of Springfield, on reservoir and hydro-electric development work, road construction, and real estate development. During this time he worked as Computer of capacities of storage reservoirs; Inspector of wash-borings and soundings for the foundation of a proposed dam; Instrumentman on levels and surveys; Draftsman on maps and proposed buildings; Chief of Party on topographic survey for hydro-electric development; and Superintendent of road construction and general real estate development. He then spent a year as Production Clerk for the Strathmore Paper Company of Woronoco, Mass.

---

* Memoir prepared by Carl C. Cooman, Assoc. M. Am. Soc. C. E., and Robert B. Jeffers, M. Am. Soc. C. E.

In 1916, he became associated with the Fred T. Ley Company, of Springfield and New York, N. Y., and for the next four and one-half years he was engaged in that connection on construction work in the eastern part of the United States. He spent a year as Local Purchasing Agent on the construction of the James Deering residence at Miami, Fla. He then became Engineer of Construction for a large group of farm buildings built by the Company for the owner of the McCallum Silk Mills, at Plainfield, Mass.

During the World War, Mr. Smith was Employment Manager for the Fred T. Ley Company, Contractors, on the construction of Camp Devens at Ayer, Mass., the Ammonium Nitrate Plant for the Atlas Powder Company at Perryville, Md., and the aerial bomb-loading plant for the Marlin-Rockwell Loading Corporation at Rockwell Park, Mount Pleasant, Del. After the signing of the Armistice, he was employed in adjusting accounts in dispute between the vendors and the Government Accounting Department on the construction of Camp Devens, and as Custodian of Property for the Contractor during the period of transfer of the buildings and materials from the Contractor to the Government. Returning to Springfield, he became Specification Writer and Personnel Manager in the Company's Engineering Department.

In 1919 he was sent to Rochester, N. Y., as Engineer and Superintendent of Construction for the Company during the construction of a factory building for Bastian Brothers Company of that place.

In October, 1920, Mr. Smith became Assistant Engineer with the Eastman Kodak Company, of Rochester, N. Y., and was employed for five years in the Engineering and Maintenance Department at the Kodak Park Works. He at first supervised building construction in the field and, later, had charge of the planning and scheduling of shop work for the Department.

His health had been poor for some time and for this reason, thinking that a change of climate would benefit him, he went to Fulford, Fla., near Miami, in the fall of 1925, on real estate development work for Mr. H. B. Graves of Rochester. The climate, however, did not agree with him, so he returned to Rochester the following spring. On June 1, 1926, he began work as City Engineer of Olean, N. Y., which position he held at the time of his death.

Mr. Smith was an active member of the Masonic Fraternity. He was a life member of Brigham Lodge, A. F. and A. M., Ludlow, Mass., of which lodge his father was a Charter Member. He was also a member of the Morning Star Chapter, Royal Arch Masons, Springfield, Mass.; Springfield Council, R. and S. M.; Cyrene Commandry No. 37, Knights Templar, Rochester; Rochester Consistory, A. A. S. R., Rochester; Damascus Temple, A. A. O. N. M. S., Rochester, and Bela Grotto, M. O. V. P. E. R., Springfield. He was also a member of Lodge No. 948, Benevolent and Protective Order of Elks, of Miami.

From early childhood Mr. Smith was very fond of music, particularly of singing, and was possessed of a beautiful tenor voice. As a lad, he sang in the children's choir in the Evangelical Church at Indian Orchard. During his High School career, he was a member of the Glee Club. He also sang in the choir of St. Peter's Protestant Episcopal Church and, later, of Trinity Methodist Episcopal Church, at Springfield. During his stay at Perryville, Md., he sang in the Methodist Episcopal Church at Havre de Grace, Md., and while in Miami, in 1916, in the White Temple as tenor soloist.

When he went to Rochester in 1920, Mr. Smith transferred his church membership to the Central Presbyterian Church, where he sang in the choir. He was also a member of the Chanters of Damascus Temple at Rochester and of a Male Octette organized among the Kodak Park employees of the Eastman Kodak Company. He often appeared at special functions as a soloist and occasionally sang over the radio after its advent as a regular medium of entertainment.

During his Grammar School days, he once won a story-writing contest given for the school children of Springfield by the *Springfield Daily News*. The prize was a fine picture which still hangs on the walls of the Myrtle Street School bearing a plate inscribed with his name and the reason for the award. He never cultivated this natural bent for writing, but was always a great reader, being interested especially in books on science, religion, philosophy, and theosophy.

Mr. Smith was a tall, rather heavily built man, deliberate of movement, and possessing a quiet, cheerful, friendly nature. He impressed all with whom he came in contact as being dependable, honorable, and unassuming. Those with whom he had any dealings found him to be all that his appearance indicated. He had a marked ability of smoothing out difficulties in a calm, unhurried manner that was usually effective and, at the same time, convincing and reassuring to all concerned, whether in personal or professional association. He was in every respect a gentleman.

On November 6, 1920, Mr. Smith was married to Mary E. Decker, of Rochester, formerly of Coudersport, Pa., who survives him. There were no children. He is also survived by his aged mother, Mrs. Jennie Snow Smith, and two sisters, Mrs. Frederick N. Fowler, and Mrs. Edson R. Dorman, both of Longmeadow, Mass.

Mr. Smith was elected an Associate Member of the American Society of Civil Engineers on October 10, 1921. During his sojourn in Rochester he was active in the Rochester Local Section. He was also a member of the Rochester Engineering Society.

HARRY BRONSON SNELL, Assoc. M. Am. Soc. C. E.*

DIED JULY 3, 1927.

Harry Bronson Snell was born in New Haven, Conn., on March 28, 1875, the son of Adolphus Gaylord and Mary Andruss Snell.

After his graduation from Sheffield Scientific School, Yale University, New Haven, Conn., he became Assistant Civil Engineer with the Hartford Street Railway Company, until August, 1903. He then accepted the position of Assistant Engineer for the Long Island Railroad Company, Atlantic Avenue Improvement, Brooklyn, N. Y.

In September, 1905, Mr. Snell was appointed Principal Assistant Engineer for the Brooklyn Grade Crossing Commission, Brighton Beach Improvement, and, in 1916, he became Superintendent of Construction for the Turner Construction Company, of New York, N. Y., and Boston, Mass., which position he held until his death.

Mr. Snell died at the Griffin Hospital, Derby, Conn., on July 3, 1927, following an operation for appendicitis and after an illness of only a week. He had just attended the re-union of his class at Yale.

On February 2, 1916, he was married to Emily M. Sturdevant, of Deposit, N. Y., and is survived by his widow and by his brother, Thomas C. B. Snell, M. Am. Soc. C. E.

Mr. Snell was elected an Associate Member of the American Society of Civil Engineers on December 5, 1906. He was also a member of the Sons of the American Revolution.

* Memoir compiled by T. C. B. Snell, M. Am. Soc. C. E.

HUNTER IMBODEN SNYDER, Assoc. M. Am. Soc. C. E.*

DIED JANUARY 28, 1928.

Hunter Imboden Snyder was born on March 29, 1884, at Elizabethton, Tenn. He attended the public schools at Covington, Va., and at Knoxville, Tenn. His technical training was received at the University of Tennessee, at Knoxville, where he was a student in Civil Engineering from October, 1901, to June, 1902, and from October, 1903, to June, 1904.

Mr. Snyder's early experience in engineering work included the following assignments: From June, 1902 to October, 1903, various positions preparatory to that of Assistant Resident Engineer with the Knoxville, La Follette, and Jellico Railway Company; from June, 1904, to July, 1906, Assistant to the Engineer in Charge, the Knoxville Terminal Buildings and Clinch Avenue Viaduct for the Louisville and Nashville Railroad Company; from July, 1906, to January, 1907, Assistant to the General Superintendent and Field Engineer for the Oliver Company on the construction of a reinforced concrete warehouse at Nashville, Tenn.; from January to November, 1907, Superintendent for the L. B. Davidson Company, of Knoxville, in charge of concrete work for the South and Western Railroad Company; from November, 1907, to May, 1908, Inspector of concrete work for the Knoxville Division of the Louisville and Nashville Railroad Company; and from May, 1908, to March, 1909, Designing Engineer in charge, the Memphis Branch of the Contractors Engineering Supply Company, of Knoxville.

In March, 1909, Mr. Snyder entered private practice as Consulting Engineer on structural work. He was continuously employed in this field until July, 1915, and his work in this connection consisted of the design and construction of many important reinforced concrete warehouses, among which were the following: A five-story cold storage warehouse at Tampa, Fla.; a five-story warehouse for the Cheek Neal Coffee Company and a ten-story warehouse for Delcher Brothers, at Jacksonville, Fla.; also a warehouse for the Dalton Flour Mills, at Dalton, Ga. Other similar work included a mill construction warehouse for the De Sota Oil Company at Memphis, Tenn. He was Consulting Engineer for the F. W. Long Company on the construction of the sub-structure for the Municipal Lighting Plant and the remodeling of a power plant into a sub-station for the City of Jacksonville. He also acted as Consulting Engineer for the Architects on a hospital building for the St. Luke's Hospital Association at Jacksonville.

From 1913 to 1915, Mr. Snyder was associated with H. G. Perring, M. Am. Soc. C. E., as Consulting Engineer on the design and construction of various projects in Florida, as follows: A double-tube tunnel under St. Johns River at Jacksonville; a paving program for the City of St. Augustine; structural work on the Duvall County Court House and the Duvall County Armory; the Barstow Jail; the Palm Beach County Court House; the Tampa City Hall; the Hillsboro Hotel, in Tampa, and private road work in Baker County.

* Memoir prepared by J. L. Savage, M. Am. Soc. C. E.

Mr. Snyder was also associated with Mr. Perring on the following bridge work: A reinforced concrete bridge over the Halifax River, at Daytona; a bridge over the San Sebastian River for the City of St. Augustine; bridges over McGirts Creek and Trout Creek and a number of other smaller bridges in Duvall County, Florida.

Mr. Snyder's engineering work during 1915 brought him in contact with various bond houses in connection with the purchase of county and district bonds and his success in this field attracted much attention. In July, 1915, he accepted an attractive offer from Dewitt, Trimball, and Company and thereafter was employed by different bond houses as follows: From July, 1915, to June, 1916, with Dewitt, Trimball, and Company, Chicago, Ill.; from July, 1916, to March, 1918, with Seasongood and Mayer Company, Cincinnati, Ohio; from March, 1918 to May, 1919, witth C. W. McNear and Company, Chicago, and from May, 1919, to February, 1920, with R. M. Grant and Company, Chicago and New York, N. Y.

In 1920 he was compelled to give up his work that he might seek a more healthful climate and from then until his death, on January 28, 1928, he spent most of his time in Colorado, in 1922 definitely establishing his home in Denver.

Mr. Snyder was a splendid type of man, having a high order of integrity, a brilliant mind, and a certain natural friendliness which gave him an unusually magnetic personality. Although practically an invalid for the last few years of his life, he never lost his cheerful disposition nor his hopeful outlook. His continued interest in the activities of the Society and in engineering activities in general, was a source of surprise and satisfaction to those of his engineering friends who knew of his long enforced separation from his work.

His life was marked by devotion to his parents and to his wife, Nancy Abell Snyder, all of whom survive him.

Mr. Snyder was elected an Associate Member of the American Society of Civil Engineers on January 7, 1913.

ROBERT TEETERS SOMERS, Assoc. M. Am. Soc. C. E.*

Died April 5, 1927.

Robert Teeters Somers was born in Angola, Ind., on September 21, 1889. He received his early education in the public schools of Auburn, and Huntington, Ind., and afterward attended Oberlin College where he received the degree of Bachelor of Arts in 1914. The same year he entered Purdue University from which he was graduated in 1916 with the degree of Bachelor of Science in Civil Engineering.

Mr. Somers began his engineering career as Draftsman in the Pittsburgh, Pa., Office of the Pittsburgh-Des Moines Steel Company. Soon after the United States entered the World War he tried to enlist in the Coast Guard Division, but was rejected because of near-sightedness. About this time the Pittsburgh-Des Moines Steel Company began fabricating eight radio towers for the Lafayette Radio Station in France. Mr. Somers continued with this firm as Production Engineer until 1920. This work involved the adjustment of steel stock to the requirements of contracts and overseeing shop schedules of contracts.

Long hours of service during the war period, followed by an attack of influenza, undermined his health, and from February, 1920, until June, 1921, he lived in the mountains of Pennsylvania.

After his recovery, he assisted Mr. E. Paul Rothrock, afterward State Geologist of South Dakota and Head of the Geology Department of the University of South Dakota, in plane-table mapping of the topography and structure in Lawrence County, Kentucky, for the Washington Oil Company, of Pittsburgh. On the basis of this survey, the Company leased considerable land.

When this work was completed Mr. Somers went temporarily with the Pittsburgh Division of the United States Bureau of Standards, his work consisting of testing the strength of certain materials and computing the strain which would bring the breaking point.

When the Bureau of Standards was moved to Washington, D. C., in September, 1922, he became Assistant Engineer of the Pittsburgh District of the Portland Cement Association. His work at this time was promotional and educational in the uses of concrete. He answered technical inquiries and expedited field work. His personal interest was in the use of concrete for bridges and roads, and he took great pleasure in inspecting new concrete bridges or stretches of road in the vicinity of Pittsburgh, although inspection was not one of his official duties.

It was with great regret that a second physical breakdown forced him to leave the Portland Cement Association early in 1924. Except for a few months of temporary work at the end of that year, Mr. Somers was never able to work again.

* Memoir prepared by Irving D. Goodwin, Assoc. M. Am. Soc. C. E.

He died of chronic myocarditis, on April 5, 1927, in San Antonio, Tex., where he and Mrs. Somers had gone in October, 1926, hoping that the milder climate would be beneficial to him.

Mr. Somers was a member of the Mt. Lebanon United Presbyterian Church, in Pittsburgh, and of the Theta Xi Fraternity.

In May, 1917, he was married to Rachael Wagner, an Oberlin College classmate, who survives him.

Mr. Somers was elected an Associate Member of the American Society of Civil Engineers on June 6, 1921.

HARRY THOMAS SPENGLER, Assoc. M. Am. Soc. C. E.*

Died April 23, 1927.

Harry Thomas Spengler was born in Bethlehem, Pa., on March 19, 1883. He attended the Bethlehem Public Schools, and when, in 1898, he removed with his parents to Easton, Pa., he enrolled as a pupil there. He prepared for college in the Easton High School and the Bethlehem Preparatory School, and entered Lafayette College in 1905 as a member of the Class of 1909. He was graduated from Lafayette with the degree of Civil Engineer, having been awarded the Bassett Prize in Civil Engineering as first in rank in his class.

Mr. Spengler's first position was with the Maintenance of Way Department of the Lehigh Valley Railroad Company at Easton. In 1911, he became Assistant Engineer in the office of the Chief Engineer, in New York, N. Y., resigning in 1912 to accept appointment to the Faculty of his Alma Mater. His last work with the Lehigh Valley Railroad Company was the supervision of the construction of the Newark Station, at Weequaic Park (Park View Station), N. J.

At Lafayette College he was Instructor in Surveying and Railroad Engineering from 1912 to 1915; from 1915 to 1918, he served as Assistant Professor of Surveying and Railroad Engineering; and from 1918 to 1921 he was Associate Professor of Civil Engineering. In 1920-21 he had charge of the Department of Civil Engineering, and in 1921, he was made a full Professor with the title of Professor of Railway Engineering, which position he held until his death.

Professor Spengler had served since 1922 as Engineer for the City of Easton Planning Commission; he was also a member of the American Association of University Professors; the Society for the Promotion of Engineering Education; and of the Engineers' Club of the Lehigh Valley.

He was a devoted member of the First Presbyterian Church of Easton and a Trustee of that congregation; a member of Dallas Lodge No. 396, F. and A. M., and of the Northampton County Historical Society, having served as its Secretary for several years. Until shortly before his death, he was a member of the Easton Rotary Club.

While in college he was a member of the Glee Club and in his Senior Year, its leader, as well as a member of the "Calumet Club", "Knights of the Round Table", and the "Sock and Buskin" dramatic organization. He was a member of the Gamma Epsilon Chapter of the Sigma Nu Fraternity, and Alumni Treasurer of the Chapter.

After his graduation from college, Professor Spengler studied music under Professor F. Bristol, of New York. For ten years he was baritone soloist in the choir of the First Presbyterian Church, at Easton, leaving this position to become Choir Director at the First Methodist Episcopal Church, and again

* Memoir prepared by F. O. Dufour, M. Am. Soc. C. E.

leaving this to become Director of the Musical Clubs and of the Chapel Choir at Lafayette College.

Professor Spengler was active in church, college, and civic affairs, and was a leader in all undertakings with which he was connected. His wide acquaintance in the community and his unfailing tact and good judgment were invaluable to the interests he served.

He was not only a friend of his colleagues on the Lafayette College Faculty, but he was respected and beloved as well by the many students who were privileged to know him as their teacher, adviser, and friend.

He was married in 1910 to Blanche E. Speer, of Easton, by whom he is survived, with two sons, Harry Thomas and Edgar Laubach Spengler, his parents, Mr. and Mrs. A. P. Spengler, a brother, Alfred L. Spengler, of Charleston, W. Va., and a sister, Mrs. John W. Magee, of Germantown, Pa.

Professor Spengler was elected an Associate Member of the American Society of Civil Engineers on January 17, 1921. He was also a member of the Lehigh Valley Section of the Society.

CLARENCE HARD THOMPSON, Assoc. M. Am. Soc. C. E.*

Died March 10, 1927.

Clarence Hard Thompson, the son of Lucella and Guy Thompson, was born at Odessa, N. Y., on December 2, 1867. After completing his studies in the public schools, he entered the Classical Course of the Cortland, N. Y., Normal High School from which he was graduated in January, 1888.

After having taught school for three years, Mr. Thompson, in 1891, entered the Engineering Department of the Groton Bridge and Manufacturing Company, of Groton, N. Y. As a result of his marked ability, he was made Chief Draftsman in 1894, which position he held until 1901 when he accepted a similar engagement with the Owego Bridge Company, of Owego, N. Y.

In 1903, Mr. Thompson entered the employ of the Solvay Process Company, of Syracuse, N. Y., as a Structural Engineer and Computer, where he remained until ill-health forced him to retire in February, 1926. During this period he was engaged in the design and supervision of plans for many buildings of structural steel framework, brick, and reinforced concrete.

He was very methodical in his business life and left a complete record of computations covering a period of twenty-three years. His keen judgment augmented by constant study, enabled him to solve many complicated problems in his line of work. Among his associates he was considered an authority on engineering projects dealing with construction work.

In disposition and manner Mr. Thompson was modest and cheerful, but firm in facing unpleasant situations, stoutly maintaining his opinion when he knew he was in the right.

He was a faithful member of the Good Will Congregational Church, of Syracuse, where he taught a large Bible Class for more than twenty years. He was married in 1896 to Mary H. Chapman, who survives him.

Mr. Thompson was elected an Associate Member of the American Society of Civil Engineers on September 7, 1904.

* Memoir prepared by Charles E. Harris, Esq., Syracuse, N. Y.

FRANK WAGNER, Assoc. M. Am. Soc. C. E.*

Died December 24, 1927.

Frank Wagner was born in Philadelphia, Pa., on December 16, 1887. He received his preparatory school training in the public schools of Philadelphia, having been graduated from the Northeast Manual Training School in 1907. The same year he entered the Civil Engineering Department of the University of Pennsylvania from which institution he was graduated in 1911 with the degree of Bachelor of Science in Civil Engineering.

While at college he worked on structural and railroad work during his summer vacations and after his graduation he was engaged with the American Bridge Company, at the Pencoyd Plant, as Structural Draftsman. With the advent of the Blankenburg Administration, he entered the employ of the City of Philadelphia, remaining from April, 1912, until June, 1918, first as Inspector and, later, as Assistant Engineer, specializing in roadway construction and the general improvement of highways.

In June, 1918, he became Inspector for the Merchant Shipbuilding Corporation, of Bristol, Pa., but only remained in that position a few months, transferring early the following year to the United States Railroad Administration, then to Cox and Stevens, and, finally, to the United States Army, where he remained until the spring of 1921. During this three-year period, he was engaged in inspecting machinery and other war materials, and also barges for service on the Mississippi River and the New York Barge Canal. About the latter part of this period, he was transferred to Cordova, Ala., to take charge of the design and construction of a large coal tipple. While at Cordova, in the spring of 1921, he suffered a nervous breakdown and was obliged to give up engineering and spend more than a year recuperating at Wernersville, Pa.

Restored to health in 1923, Mr. Wagner was for a time Town Engineer of Branford, Conn., and later, was with the Johns-Manville Company, as Estimator on building materials. In October, 1925, attracted by the Florida boom, he went South. After engaging in several projects he became, in 1926, Resident Engineer on the Matanzas Bascule Bridge, at St. Augustine, Fla., for the P. T. Cox Company, and remained on that structure until its completion in the middle of 1927.

During the spring of 1927, Mr. Wagner had an attack of influenza from which he never fully recovered. Soon after his return North in July, he suffered another nervous breakdown and went a second time to Wernersville for a complete rest. He seemed to be making progress toward recovery until about a week before Christmas when he had a relapse and was obliged to go to the hospital, where he passed away on December 24, 1927.

* Memoir prepared by William G. Grove, M. Am. Soc. C. E.

Mr. Wagner was never married. He was a member of the Lutheran Church and of the Masonic Order, and was a Licensed Engineer in the States of Florida and Pennsylvania. Perhaps his outstanding characteristic was his loyalty to his friends, particularly those with whom he grew up from childhood. His passing means a great personal loss to those who knew him best.

Mr. Wagner was elected an Associate Member of the American Society of Civil Engineers on May 19, 1924.

JESSE ALBERT CURREY, Affiliate, Am. Soc. C. E.*

Died June 23, 1927.

Jesse Albert Currey, the son of William B. and Anna Mary (Cloud) Currey, was born at Philadelphia, Pa., on August 2, 1873.

His first employment of a business nature probably moulded his career to a large degree for at the age of nineteen, he entered newspaper work in Philadelphia and continued in that field in that city and in Wilmington, Del., for ten years.

In 1902, he entered the engineering field by appointment as Superintendent of drilling operations for the Eastern Texas Oil and Mineral Company in the vicinity of Hemphill, Tex.

Mr. Currey devoted the next two years to work for the Baltimore Construction Company which had under way the construction of piers at Locust Point for the Baltimore and Ohio Railroad Company and the North German Lloyd Steamship Company, as well as improvements to docking facilities in Baltimore, Md., Harbor. During his connection with that organization, Mr. Currey held the position of Paymaster, Superintendent, and, finally, that of General Manager.

Traveling next claimed his attention and, beginning in 1904, he toured extensively throughout the United States. He finally located at Portland, Ore., where he first became engaged in the real estate business. In 1906, he was made Pacific Northwest Manager for the Truscon Steel Company, which position he held at the time of his death.

His connection with the Truscon Steel Company brought him in close contact with the major building operations in his territory, and he aided greatly in the design of large viaducts, hospitals, power stations, as well as bridges and buildings for various railroad companies. When he found his Company had no effective means of cutting metal lath, Mr. Currey invented a machine for this purpose.

He was married, in Philadelphia, on April 26, 1905, to Frances Whiteley, who survives him.

Although Mr. Currey had been affiliated with various engineering enterprises during the last twenty-five years of his life, he was perhaps better known throughout the United States and foreign countries for his activities in the culture of roses.

He was a member of the Royal Horticultural Society and the National Rose Society, of England, and, at the time of his death, a Director of the American Rose Society. His life work in the field of his avocation brought him honor and fame.

He was also a member of the Portland Rotary Club and the Portland Chamber of Commerce. His activities in both organizations were earnest and

* Memoir prepared by J. C. Stevens, M. Am. Soc. C. E.

painstaking. He was always ready to undertake any task great or small that had to do with the betterment and upbuilding of the community in which he lived.

Mr. Currey was elected an Affiliate of the American Society of Civil Engineers on February 1, 1910. He was very active in local Society matters, seldom missed a meeting of the Portland Section, and served with great credit on several important committees.

JOHN MILTON GOODELL, Affiliate, Am. Soc. C. E.*

Died June 21, 1927.

John Milton Goodell, the son of John B. Goodell, was born August 3, 1867, in Worcester, Mass. He was educated in the Public Schools and the Worcester Polytechnic Institute, from which he was graduated in 1888 with the degree of Bachelor of Science in Civil Engineering. He was also awarded the Salisbury Prize for scholarship.

After a year in Europe, studying at Zurich Polytechnic Institute and traveling, Mr. Goodell was engaged as Instructor in Mathematics at Adelphi Academy, Brooklyn, N. Y. Later, he spent a short time in the engineering office of the late Charles A. Allen, M. Am. Soc. C. E., of Worcester.

In June, 1890, he began his career as an editor of technical periodicals by joining the staff of *Engineering News,* of which later he became Associate Editor under the late Arthur M. Wellington, M. Am. Soc. C. E. In 1892, he transferred to the *Engineering Record,* of which Henry C. Meyer, F. Am. Soc. C. E., was Editor and Proprietor. His editorial work, in various connections, continued throughout a great portion of his life, although such work was interrupted by other engagements and during certain periods received but part-time attention. As an Editor, he was able, painstakingly accurate, and sound in his judgment of situations and men.

From 1895 to 1897, Mr. Goodell was Assistant Secretary of the Society and performed valuable service in the establishment of its effective office and publication methods. In 1901 and 1902, he was Resident Engineer on the staff of Joseph H. Wallace, M. Am. Soc. C. E., of New York, N. Y., on operations near Sault Ste. Marie, Mich. From 1913 to 1915, he collaborated with the late Leonard Metcalf, M. Am. Soc. C. E., and Harrison P. Eddy, M. Am. Soc. C. E., in the preparation of their three-volume work on "American Sewerage Practice." In 1915 and 1916 he devoted his energies to the re-organization of the American Concrete Institute, of which Leonard C. Wason, M. Am. Soc. C. E., was then President.

During 1916 and 1917, he did special work for Fairfax Harrison, President of the Southern Railway Company, assisted in completing the work for which the American Highway Association was organized, and was engaged in war-time organization work for several Government bureaus. For the first six months of 1918 he was Employment Manager of the Emergency Fleet Corporation, of New York, N. Y. Subsequently, he was Acting Chairman of the National Highway Council, which had charge of all materials, labor, and transportation for street and road work during the last six months of the World War. He also was Consulting Engineer of the United States Bureau of Public Roads, in connection with its re-organization.

* Memoir prepared by Alfred D. Flinn, M. Am. Soc. C. E.

The remainder of Mr. Goodell's life was devoted mainly to literary work related to engineering and to statistical investigations, the former including the *Journal* of the American Water Works Association and publicity for the Babcock and Wilcox Company. During his entire life his major interests were in the fields of water-works, highways, and sanitation. He translated Baumeister's "Cleaning and Sewerage of Cities", and was the author of "Water Works for Small Cities and Towns," as well as "Location, Construction, and Maintenance of Roads."

He was a member of the American Society of Mechanical Engineers, American Water Works Association, New England Water Works Association, and the Cosmos Club of Washington, D. C.

Mr. Goodell was elected an Affiliate of the American Society of Civil Engineers on July 29, 1891.

JOHN MICHAEL LALLY, Affiliate, Am. Soc. C. E.*

Died October 8, 1925.

John Michael Lally was born in Lockport, N. Y., on July 22, 1865. His parents, Michael and Elizabeth Lally, later moved to Detroit, Mich., where his early youth was spent.

Mr. Lally's first professional work was with his father's construction company, known as the McRae, Lally, and Sons Company. He was associated with this Company in various capacities ranging from Instrumentman to Superintendent of Construction. From 1881 to 1893, he was in charge of construction for the Michigan Central, the Pere Marquette, and other railroad companies, as well as water-works, docks, and dredging on various projects, in Michigan, Wisconsin, Pennsylvania, and New York.

From 1893 to 1894, he was Chief of Party in charge of a preliminary survey and estimates for a railroad from San Salvador to La Libertad in Central America, and from 1894 to 1898, he had charge of the construction of a dam at Sault Ste. Marie, Mich., for the Michigan Central Railroad Company, a 10-mile extension of the Chicago Stockyards, and track operation improvements in the vicinity of Detroit. During this same period, he placed 25 miles of railroad lines for the Hocking Valley Railway Company in Jackson, Mich., and an extension for the Pittsburgh, Shawmut and Northern Railroad Company, in Southern New York; also, 11 miles of double track on the New York Central Railroad, near Depew, N. Y.

From 1899 to 1906, Mr. Lally was engaged as Superintendent of Construction and Supervisor of Track on the New York Central Railroad, at Buffalo, N. Y., where he had charge of the territory from Batavia to Tonawanda, N. Y., including the Buffalo Railroad Yards. In 1906, he became General Superintendent in charge of construction of 140 miles of railroad for the J. G. White Company, General Contractors, from Raleigh to Washington and Newbern, N. C., which position he retained until 1909.

From 1909 until his death, he was in charge of construction and engineering work for the New York Central Railroad Company, and the following year he was Superintendent in Charge of Improvements on the Electric Zone. During the period of Federal Control, he was attached to the Corporate Organization of the System's various lines, inspecting and reporting on their condition. After the World War, and previous to his death, he was Assistant Engineer on the staff of the late George Alec Harwood, M. Am. Soc. C. E., at that time Vice-President in Charge of Improvements and Development of the New York Central Lines.

Mr. Lally was a man of sterling character, and exceptional ability as a Construction Engineer. All his life he had charge of large construction work with an organization of loyal men. His ability for keeping the good

* Memoir prepared by L. C. Hammond, M. Am. Soc. C. E.

will and confidence of the men who worked for him, helped him to secure excellent results in his work. Many younger men who received their experience under his direction remember him with gratitude and respect for the patient and kindly help which he was always ready to give them.

Death came suddenly from heart disease at his home, in Yonkers, N. Y. The funeral services were held in St. Denis Church, Yonkers, with the Rev. Joseph Cameron, of Rochester, N. Y., the Rev. Ignatius Cameron, of Geneva, N. Y., brothers-in-law of the deceased, and the Rev. James Doris, of Yonkers, officiating. Burial was in Detroit. He is survived by his widow, Mary C. Lally, and by three brothers and two sisters living in Detroit.

Mr. Lally was elected an Affiliate of the American Society of Civil Engineers on September 2, 1908.

FRANK PRICE, Affiliate, Am. Soc. C. E.*

Died February 5, 1927.

Frank Price was born at Dos Oris, Glen Cove, Long Island, N. Y., on May 4, 1852, the son of George James Price, a prominent New York City business man and builder, and Susan Louise (Thompson) Price. He was educated in public and private schools, and by tutors, and gained a thorough mechanical and practical training by five years' service in the structural iron works of Bailey and Debevoise. He continued his practical experience on the Pacific Coast, with vacations spent as cowboy and sheep herder, thereby building up a rugged constitution.

In 1879, Mr. Price was Superintendent of First Order United States Lighthouses at the Phœnix Iron Works, Trenton, N. J. Later, he designed and supervised the construction of the machinery and apparatus for moving Cleopatra's Needle, the Egyptian obelisk which was presented to the City of New York in 1880 and erected in Central Park in 1881. It is a granite monolith 70 ft. long, weighing nearly 400 tons. The handling and transportation of such a slender and brittle shaft under the heavy stresses developed by its own weight, as well as the necessity of moving it from a vertical to a horizontal position, presented a difficult and unprecedented problem. Mr. Price accompanied the late Henry H. Gorringe, Commander, U. S. N., Affiliate, Am. Soc. C. E. to Alexandria, Egypt, to take charge of dismounting and shipping the obelisk in a special ship to New York, thence transporting it to Central Park and erecting it.

In 1881 he superintended the making of important repairs to Princeton University Observatory, Princeton, N. J., and, until 1883, was in charge of the Structural Department of the Phœnix Iron Company, at Trenton. From 1883 to 1885, he was Assistant Superintendent, and, later, Assistant to the Receiver of the American Ship Building Company, at Philadelphia, Pa. In 1885, he was Superintendent of the reconstruction of the famous New York Stock Exchange, replacing the roof, 100 ft. high, with massive steel girders, without interrupting business.

In 1888, Mr. Price was Superintendent of the Composite Iron Works, New York, N. Y. In 1889, he founded the Price and Company Structural Iron Works, New York, of which he was chief owner, President, and Director of Designs. After disposing of this business in 1894, he was able to spend more time on the beautiful family estate, Dos Oris, where he carried out many improvements of a structural nature intended to preserve this old Colonial residence, adding modern sanitary and architectural features and enhancing the great natural beauties of the place. This was his most delightful avocation, to which he devoted more and more time, as opportunity afforded, during his entire life.

In 1889, Mr. Price was Superintendent of construction of large reinforced concrete bridges in Porto Rico and, from 1902 to 1908, he acted as Mill and

* Memoir prepared by Frank W. Skinner and James B. French, Members, Am. Soc. C. E.

Shop Inspector for the Long Island Railroad Company. In 1908, he was Chief Shop Inspector of Transmission Towers for the Electric Bond and Share Company, New York.

From 1909 to 1911 he held the position of Chief Shop Inspector for structures built for the New York State Barge Canal, and, from 1911 to 1912, he was Chief Shop Inspector, for the United States Government, of the 60 000-ton, steel lock-gates and fender chains for the Panama Canal. In 1915, Mr. Price was retained by the Federal Government as expert witness in the \$2 500 000 Panama Canal, lock-gate litigation and from 1915 to 1927, he was engaged on bridge and building work for the Long Island Railroad Company and other organizations.

Mr. Price was a competent engineer, an able designer, and a successful constructor. His skill, experience, and broad knowledge of machinery, materials, and methods, added to his high standards of workmanship and ethics, and his appreciative consideration of employers and employees, made his shop and field work unusually efficient. He was a close observer and a deep thinker, of much ingenuity and originality. He had great mechanical skill and ability in the use of tools, and found recreation in delicate construction, as demonstrated by the miniature model of Cleopatra's Needle, and the mechanical apparatus used for its transportation and re-erection in New York, which he made and presented to the Metropolitan Museum of Art, together with a concise description of the obelisk.

Mr. Price was a student of the best English and American literature, and a charming writer. He loved Nature, and was fond of outdoor occupations and sports, especially boat-building and sailing. His disposition was manly and straightforward, with a vein of quiet humor, and warm affection and loyalty for his many personal and professional friends. He never married, and always made his home in the old family residence. His death was due to a violent attack of pneumonia occurring before he had fully recovered from a similar attack a few months previous.

Mr. Price was elected an Affiliate of the American Society of Civil Engineers on February 6, 1912.

MOTT TITUS CARROLL, Jun. Am. Soc. C. E.*

Died August 5, 1927.

Mott Titus Carroll, the son of Edward T. and Virginia (Titus) Carroll, was born at El Dorado, Kans., on July 31, 1897. His father was a native of New York, N. Y., and his mother of Racine, Wis.

Mr. Carroll received his technical education at the Kansas State Agricultural College, at Manhattan, Kans., from which he was graduated in June, 1926, with the degree of Bachelor of Science in Civil Engineering. He was a brilliant scholar and was awarded the Kansas State Section Prize of Junior Membership in the Society.

During his summer vacations, while at college, he was engaged as Rodman and Draftsman with the Butler County Highway Department, at El Dorado. After his graduation, Mr. Carroll was appointed Resident Engineer with the Kansas Highway Commission, in charge of the construction of Federal Aid Project No. 333, near Sharon, Kans. After completing this work, he accepted a position as Bridge Designer and Draftsman with the Butler County Highway Department, at El Dorado. This position he held at the time of his death.

Mr. Carroll was just entering on his professional career, and his energy, perseverance, and keen mind gave promise of a successful future. His kindly personality will be greatly missed by his friends and associates.

On July 14, 1927, he underwent an operation for appendicitis, resulting in complications which caused his death on August 5. He is survived by his widow, two small children, his father, and a sister, Mrs. B. D. Sisson.

He was a member of Phi Delta Theta Fraternity and Wichita Lodge No. 99, A. F. and A. M.

Mr. Carroll was elected a Junior of the American Society of Civil Engineers on January 17, 1927.

* Memoir prepared by E. S. Elcock, Assoc. M. Am. Soc. C. E.

HOWARD AUGUSTUS SHERIDAN, Jun. Am. Soc. C. E.*

Died August 2, 1927.

Howard Augustus Sheridan was born in Elizabethport, N. J., on December 17, 1900. In 1906, his parents moved to Toronto, Ont., Canada, where he attended the Clinton Street School, until 1910, when his family changed their residence in Buffalo, N. Y. He was graduated from the public schools, and entered Lafayette High School at the age of twelve years. In his Junior year, his father moved to a fruit farm in New York State, and the boy was transferred to the Lockport, N. Y., High School, from which he was graduated at the age of sixteen years. He helped on the farm until the following summer, when he attempted to enlist at Buffalo, but was rejected because of his age.

Mr. Sheridan then enrolled in the Reserve Officers Training Corps, at Ann Arbor, Mich., and on its disbandment, returned to Buffalo, where he took a business course at the Bryant and Stratten College. In 1920, he re-entered the University of Michigan, which he left the following year in order that he might teach school at Niagara Falls, N. Y., but he returned again to Ann Arbor in 1923. During his attendance at the University, he was prominent in campus activities, having been a member of Web and Flange (Honorary Civil Engineering Society), Tau Beta Pi, and the Student Chapter of the Society, of which he was President. He was graduated in 1925, with honors and a degree in Civil Engineering.

Immediately after his graduation, Mr. Sheridan entered the employ of the F. R. Patterson Construction Company, of Detroit, Mich. A few months later, he transferred to the Gannett, Seelye, and Fleming Company, at Harrisburg, Pa., where he remained until the spring of 1926, when he returned to the F. R. Patterson Construction Company to serve as Engineer on the Fordson High School Building. From December, 1926, until the time of his death, he was Assistant General Superintendent of the Patterson Company.

He was killed on August 2, 1927, while on his way to work, when his car was struck by a train at Dearborn, Mich.

Mr. Sheridan proved himself a capable and efficient engineer, and while serving as Assistant General Superintendent for the F. R. Patterson Construction Company he showed considerable ability as a construction organizer. He was unmarried.

Mr. Sheridan was elected a Junior of the American Society of Civil Engineers on October 12, 1925.

* Memoir prepared by A. Radtke, Jr., Esq., Detroit, Mich.

TRANSACTIONS

OF THE

AMERICAN SOCIETY OF CIVIL ENGINEERS

INDEX

VOLUME 92

1928

SUBJECT INDEX, PAGE 1802

AUTHOR INDEX, PAGE 1818

Titles of papers are in quotation marks when given with the author's name.

VOLUME 92

SUBJECT INDEX

MEMOIRS OF DECEASED MEMBERS.

AUTHOR INDEX